The Law
of
Private Companies

Second Edition

In memory of my father
Tom Courtney Senior
(1929-1992)

The Law of Private Companies

Second Edition

by

THOMAS B. COURTNEY

BA, LLB, Solicitor

with contribution from

G. BRIAN HUTCHINSON

BCL, LLM, DAL, BL

Associate Dean, Faculty of Law

University College Dublin

Butterworths

A Member of the LexisNexis Group

Members of LexisNexis Group worldwide:

Ireland	Butterworth (Ireland) Ltd, 24-26 Upper Ormond Quay, DUBLIN 7
Argentina	Abeledo Perrot, Jurisprudencia Argentina and Depalma, BUENOS AIRES
Australia	Butterworths, a Division of Reed International Books Australia Pty Ltd, CHATSWOOD, New South Wales
Austria	ARD Betriebsdienst and Verlag Orac, VIENNA
Canada	Butterworths Canada Ltd, MARKHAM, Ontario
Chile	Publitecsa and Conosur Ltda, SANTIAGO DE CHILE
Czech Republic	Orac sro, PRAGUE
France	Editions du Juris-Classeur SA, PARIS
Hong Kong	Butterworths Asia (Hong Kong), HONG KONG
Hungary	Hvg Orac, BUDAPEST
India	Butterworths India, NEW DELHI
Italy	Giuffré, MILAN
Malaysia	Malayan Law Journal Sdn Bhd, KUALA LUMPUR
New Zealand	Butterworths of New Zealand, WELLINGTON
Poland	Wydawnictwa Prawnicze PWN, WARSAW
Singapore	Butterworths Asia, SINGAPORE
South Africa	Butterworths Publishers (Pty) Ltd, DURBAN
Switzerland	Stämpfli Verlag AG, BERNE
United Kingdom	Butterworths Tolley, a Division of Reed Elsevier (UK) Ltd, Halsbury House, 35 Chancery Lane, LONDON, WC2A 1EL, and 4 Hill Street, EDINBURGH EH2 3JZ
USA	LexisNexis, DAYTON, Ohio

A CIP Catalogue record for this book is available from the British Library.

First Edition 1994

ISBN 1 85475 2650

ISBN 1-85475-265-
9 781854 752659

Typeset by Marlex Editorial Services Ltd, Dublin
Printed and bound in Great Britain by Antony Rowe Ltd, Chippenahm, Wiltshire
Visit us at our website: http//www.butterworths.ie

Foreword to the First Edition

It has often been pointed out that our company law has its roots in mid-nineteenth century English legislation which is of limited relevance only to contemporary Ireland. In particular, the fact that the Victorian legislators had as their object the regulation of joint stock companies seeking funds from the public has resulted in a statutory framework which fails to reflect the reality of Irish commercial life, ie that the private company is the standard form of business organization.

Naturally, Irish textbooks, in common with their English counterparts, have sought to provide students and practitioners alike with a comprehensive guide to the complex structures of modern company law. Mr Courtney has, however, adopted a bold and imaginative new approach in confining his new study to the private company. The result is a valuable addition to the growing library of Irish commercial law.

Judges have frequently lamented the ever growing complexity of the regulatory structure they are called upon to interpret. There is a growing anxiety that legislation tends to provide elaborate machinery for the prevention of various evils, particularly the abuse of limited liability, without any accompanying effort by the executive to ensure that there are sufficient resources to ensure that breaches of the law are effectively policed.

Mr Courtney as the editor of the Commercial Law Practitioner is well aware of these problems and keeps a vigilant eye on the constant flow of judicial decisions and new laws and regulations, emerging from the courts, the Oireachtas, government departments and the Commission of the European Union. His book brings together all these divers elements as they effect the private company with great skill. His task is not made easier by the vast number of unreported judgments with which he has to cope, to say nothing of the avalanche of decisions from across the Irish sea which, while of persuasive authority only, must also form part of the Irish lawyer's armoury. Mr Courtney's remarkable industry will make the task of practitioners in particular much easier in ensuring that all relevant materials are before them as they come to advise their clients on the more abstruse aspects of law which affect private companies.

I have had experience of Mr Courtney's energy and learning for some time. He has told me of the considerable assistance he received from Mr Brian Hutchinson, of whose abilities I had also personal experience when he worked as a researcher in the Law Reform Commission. The result is this remarkable and encyclopaedic work on the law of Irish private companies which will prove of incalculable benefit to generations of practitioners and students – not the mention judges – to come.

Ronan Keane,
The High Court,
Four Courts,
Dublin 7.
23 November 1994.

Preface

The developments in Irish company law since the first edition of this book was published in December 1994 have been many and varied. Apart from three new Companies Acts, about one hundred written decisions of the Irish High Court and Supreme Court and significant decisions from other jurisdictions and myriad statutory instruments, there has been a sea change in Irish Government policy on company law compliance, enforcement and reform. A new agency – the Office of the Director of Corporate Enforcement – has been established and its Director conferred with extensive powers by the Company Law Enforcement Act, 2001. The Registrar of Companies has also been afforded new powers and has exercised his existing power to strike companies off the register for failure to file annual returns with more vigour than was anticipated in 1994. The significance of this new found intolerance by the State and its agencies of company law transgressions is paralleled by the importance now placed on structured company law reform as witnessed by the establishment on a statutory basis of the *Company Law Review Group*.

And all of this in just eight years. The most significant influence on Irish company law during the period since the publication of the first edition of this book was the *Working Group on Company Law Compliance and Enforcement*, chaired by the present Minister for Justice, Equality and Law Reform and former Attorney General, Mr Michael McDowell SC. Mr McDowell's swift identification of the deficiencies in company law and determination to execute radical reform was informed by a pragmatic vision for state of the art companies' legislation.

Although this book has increased substantially in size (from over 850 pages to over 1,600 pages of text) I have retained the essential structure of the first edition, where the law relating to private companies is considered in isolation to the law relating to public companies.

I am delighted to record my appreciation to *Brian Hutchinson* for agreeing to update and revise the chapters he contributed to the first edition and which are now chapters 4, 5, 13, 14, 15 and the parts of chapter 28 where the topics addressed in those five chapters are considered from the perspective of the public company.

There are a number of people I would like to thank. First and foremost I would like to thank my wife Aileen for her patience and her support for my writing this book over the last four years, grabbing what time I could in the evenings after work and at weekends. Also, my daughters Alison and Sophie helped lighten the time when this book was not being written. I also acknowledge with gratitude the support and encouragement given liberally and often by my mother Susan Courtney and by my friends, Hugh Garvey, Niall O'Brien, PJ Maher, William Johnston, Pat Hanley, Joe O'Reilly, Ben O'Floinn and Leonard Silke all of whose support is very much appreciated.

I am especially grateful to William Johnston, partner in Arthur Cox, who read and commented on most of my chapters, which have benefited from his insightful comments. Others who read individual chapters and to whom I am also very grateful are the State's stalwart company law expert in the Department of Enterprise, Trade and

Employment, Mr Vincent Madigan; Mr Paul Egan, partner in Mason Hayes and Curran; and Ms Nora Rice, solicitor with the Companies Registration Office.

I would also like to acknowledge the encouragement received from my colleagues in ICS Building Society and in the wider Bank of Ireland Group and from Mr Pat Nolan and all my other colleagues on the *Company Law Review Group*. I am also extremely thankful for the support given by Louise Leavy of Butterworths.

I have taken every care to state what I believe to be the law in Ireland as at 30 September 2002, however, no legal responsibility or liability is accepted, warranted or implied by the writers or publishers in respect of any errors, omissions or mis-statements. All readers are urged to carefully consider all legal decisions in the light of their own legal advice.

Thomas B Courtney
Blackrock
Co Dublin
30 September 2002

Contents Overview

Contents

Chapter 3 Private Constitutional Documentation

(TB Courtney)

Chapter 12 Company Law Compliance and Enforcement

(TB Courtney)

Chapter 13 Accounts and Auditors

(GB Hutchinson)

Chapter 15 Shares and Membership

(GB Hutchinson)

Table of Cases

A

D

E

G

H

I

J

M

O

P

Q

R

S

T

U

V

W

X

Y

Z

X

XYZ [illegible] (199[illegible]) [illegible] 530 .... 16.17

Y

Yeovil Glove Co, Re [1965] Ch 148, [1964] 3 All ER 849 (CA) .... 25.080, 25.096, [illegible]

Ya[illegible] [1991] 2 All ER 344 .... [illegible]

Y [illegible] v Hussey & Hutton Ltd [illegible] [illegible] .... [illegible]

Yorkshire Woolcombers' Association Ltd, Re [1903] 2 Ch 284, [1904] AC 355 .... 20.096, 20.090

Youngs v [illegible] [illegible] Engineers Pty [illegible]
(1984) [illegible] 283 .... 20.024

[illegible] v [illegible] and [illegible] and D[illegible]
(1858) 3 C B 731 .... [illegible]

Yorkshire Gas Co, Re [1894] [illegible] .... [illegible]

Yukong Line Ltd of Korea v Rendsburg Investments Corp of Liberia (No 2)
[1998] 4 All ER 82 .... [illegible]

Z

Zinotty Properties Ltd, Re [1984] 1 WLR 1249, [1984] 3 All ER 754 .... [illegible]

Z[illegible] Bridges & [illegible] [1985] [illegible] .... [illegible]

Table of Statutes

Ireland - post 1922

Companies Act 1963 (contd)

Companies Act 1963 (contd)

Companies Act 1963 (contd)

Companies Act 1990 (contd)

Ireland pre-1922

Constitution of Ireland

United Kingdom

European Treaties and Conventions

Other Jurisdictions

Statutory Instruments

Table of Abbreviations

Statutory abbreviations:

CA 1963	The Companies Act 1963
C(A)A 1977	The Companies (Amendment) Act 1977
C(A) A 1982	The Companies (Amendment) Act 1982
C(A)A 1983	The Companies (Amendment) Act 1983
C(A)A 1986	The Companies (Amendment) Act 1986
C(A)A 1990	The Companies (Amendment) Act 1990
CA 1990	The Companies Act 1990
C(A)A 1999	The Companies (Amendment) Act 1999
C(A)(No 2)A 1999	The Companies (Amendment) (No 2) Act 1999
CLEA 2001	The Company Law Enforcement Act 2001
BSA 1989	The Building Societies Act 1989
CUA 1997	The Credit Union Act 1997
ECA 2000	The Electronic Commerce Act 2000
PA 1890	The Partnership Act 1890
RNBA 1963	Registration of Business Names Act 1963

Other Abbreviations:

CRO	Companies Registration Office
PLC	Public Limited Company
ODCE	Office of the Director of Corporate Enforcement
The Director	The Director of Corporate Enforcement

Chapter 1

The Private Company in Context

Introduction[1]

[1.001] The private company has a place of particular prominence in Irish business. The *Companies Report 2001*[2] states that of the 146,331 companies registered with the Companies Registration Office ('CRO') in Dublin Castle at year's end 2001, 89.2% were private companies limited by shares[3]. Although no breakdown is given for the other two types of private company (the private company limited by guarantee and the private unlimited company) it can reasonably be assumed that the total percentage of private companies is in the region of 94%. A private company is one in which the membership is confined to 50 members and the public is not invited to join. It is ironic that when the Companies Acts refer to 'a company' few real distinctions are made between private companies and public companies. Indeed, as shall be considered later, the private company is defined by the Companies Act 1963, s 33 ('CA 1963') not as the norm, but as a particular manifestation of the 'company' referred to in the Companies Acts[4]. Before considering the nature of the Irish private company this chapter first overviews other legal structures available for the organisation of business in Ireland and then examines the origins of the private company's generic form, the *registered company.* Next, the history and sources of Irish company law are examined and finally we discuss the nature and attributes of the Irish private company. This chapter is structured under the following four headings:

[A] Legal forms of business organisation.

[B] An historical outline of registered companies.

[C] An overview of Irish company law.

[D] The private company and public company.

[A] Legal Forms of Business Organisation

[1.002] There are a number of legal forms of business organisation which an Irish entrepreneur can avail of in establishing himself in business. Some of the available forms of business organisation do not involve the creation of an independent legal status for the

---

1 See generally, Prime & Scanlan, *The Law of Private Limited Companies* (1996); Fox and Bowen, *The Law of Private Companies* (1991).

2 See the Department of Enterprise, Trade and Employment's *Companies Report 2001*, for the year ended 31 December 2001, p 73.

3 Of the remaining 10.8%, 0.6% are public limited companies, 2.1% are unlimited companies, 5.8% are guarantee companies, 2.3% are external companies and 0.005% are European Economic Interest Groups (EEIGs) as at 31 December 2001.

4 See para **[1.114]**.

organisation (eg sole traders, partnerships and unincorporated associations); others do involve the creation of a separate legal person (eg registered companies, industrial and provident societies, building societies and credit unions). Each particular form of business organisation has its own advantages and disadvantages. The legal forms of business organisation considered here are:

1. Sole traders.
2. Partnerships.
3. Industrial and provident societies.
4. Building societies.
5. Credit unions.
6. Unincorporated associations.
7. Unregistered companies.

Sole traders

[1.003] The most basic form of business organisation is where a person chooses to engage in business as a sole or single trader[5]. A sole trader may be defined as a natural person who is engaged in a trade, profession or business on his or her own account. Traditionally, most farmers, tradesmen, small retail outlets (eg newsagents, grocers etc) and professionals (eg solicitors, doctors, dentists, accountants, barristers etc) working on their own account conducted business as sole traders. Nowadays, where permitted by law[6], such people commonly elect to incorporate a private limited company, the spectre of unlimited liability for a failed business's debts – and possible bankruptcy – being the primary motivating force. The following issues are now considered:

(a) Restrictions on acting as a sole trader.
(b) The Registration of Business Names Act 1963.
(c) Advantages and disadvantages of being a sole trader.

(a) Restrictions on acting as a sole trader

[1.004] There are very few restrictions imposed upon persons who seek to conduct business as sole traders for we live in a society which, in principle, recognises (and occasionally vindicates) private enterprise. Of course all sole traders engaged in business for profit must comply with revenue law and register with their local inspector of taxes. Actual *restrictions* on acting as a sole trader may be categorised as either relating to the *person* or relating to the *business activity.*

Restrictions on the *person* are few and far between. Generally, anybody can become a sole trader in business for themselves, even convicted criminals and people of unsound mind. Exceptions to this general rule are aliens, ie non-Irish or non-EU citizens who may be restricted under the Aliens Act 1935, and minors. In the case of the latter, whilst there are no restrictions per se on minors acting as sole traders, the law of contract may

---

5 See generally, Forde, *Commercial Law* (2nd edn, 1997), p 10 and O'Malley, *Business Law* (1982), p 14.

6 Certain professions are not permitted to incorporate, eg, solicitors and barristers.

make it difficult if not impossible for minors to effectively conduct business due to the legal restrictions on enforcing certain contracts against minors.

Restrictions relating to engaging in particular *business activities* do exist. On grounds of public policy a person cannot establish himself in business as a solicitor, barrister, doctor, etc without first having obtained the appropriate qualifications and membership of a recognised professional body. Other business activities such as selling insurance, lending money to consumers, operating a public house or dance hall, acting as an auctioneer or taxi-driver etc are subject to regulation in the form of registration and/or licensing. The general rationale for restrictions relating to business activity is the protection of the public.

(b) The Registration of Business Names Act 1963

[1.005] The purpose of the Registration of Business Names Act 1963[7] ('RBNA 1963') is to make public the identities of individuals, partnerships and companies that carry on business under a business name which is different from his, their or its own name[8]. To that end the Registrar of Companies, who is also registrar for the purposes of CA 1963[9], keeps an index of business names registered under CA 1963[10]. Consequently, where a sole trader (or partnership[11] or body corporate[12]) carries on business under any name other than his own he is required to furnish certain particulars to the Registrar of Companies. Section 3(1)(b) of RBNA 1963 provides that subject to the provisions of that Act:

> '...every individual having a place of business in the State and carrying on business under a business name which does not consist of his true surname without any addition other than his true Christian names of the initials therefor;
>
> ...shall be registered in the manner directed by this Act.'

Moreover, the requirement to register also arises where an individual has changed his name (except in the case of a woman in consequence of marriage)[13].

[1.006] Section 4(1) of RBNA 1963 specifies the particulars which a person must furnish to the Registrar of Companies. In the case of a sole trader these are:

— the business name, including in the case of the proprietor of a newspaper, the title of the newspaper;

— the general nature of the business;

— the principal place of the business;

---

7 Commenced by the Registration of Business Names Act 1963 (Commencement) Order 1964 (SI 1964/46). See also the Business Names Regulations: SI 1964/47, SI 1976/63, SI 1980/399, SI 1983/260, SI 1987/100, SI 1993/138 and SI 1997/357, made pursuant to RBNA 1963, s 17.

8 As at 31 December 2001, 179,516 business names had been registered pursuant to RBNA 1963: *Companies Report 2001*, p 76.

9 RBNA 1963, s 15.

10 RBNA 1963, s 13.

11 See para **[1.012]**.

12 See Chapter 2, *Formation, Registration and Conversion of Private Companies*, para **[2.045]**.

13 RBNA 1963, s 3(c).

- the present Christian name and surname, any former Christian name or surname, the nationality, if not Irish, the usual residence, and the other business occupation (if any) of such individual; and
- the date of the adoption of the business name by that person.

Where a business is carried on under two or more business names each of those business names must be stated[14]. Under RBNA 1963, s 9(1), the Minister for Enterprise, Trade and Employment may require any person to furnish to the Minister within such time as the Minister may require, a statement of such particulars as may appear necessary to the Minister for the purpose of ascertaining whether or not the person should be registered under the RBNA 1963 or whether or not an alteration should be made in the registered particulars. In appropriate cases the Minister may subsequently require that the person furnishes the required particulars to the Registrar of Companies: RBNA 1963, s 9(2)[15].

[1.007] The statement required for the purpose of registration must be signed by the sole trader[16]. The particulars required to be furnished under RBNA 1963, s 4 must be furnished within one month after the adoption of the business name[17]. Details of any changes in the particulars registered must be furnished to the Registrar of Companies within one month after the change; this is referred to as a 'section 7 statement'. Section 8(1) of RBNA 1963 provides that upon receiving a statement pursuant to either ss 4 or 7 the Registrar of Companies shall issue a certificate of the registration of the business name to the person applying for registration. A certificate of registration must 'be kept exhibited in a conspicuous position at' the sole trader's principal place of business and every branch office or place where business is normally carried on; on summary conviction, default attracts a fine not exceeding €126.97[18]. Section 12(1) of RBNA 1963 obliges a person (or, if deceased, his personal representatives) who has registered a business name, but who ceases to carry on business under that name, to send a statement in the prescribed form to that effect to the Registrar of Companies within three months. The registrar is also given powers to remove a business name from the register in specified circumstances[19].

[1.008] One of the few consequences of the registration of a business name by a sole trader is that RBNA 1963, s 18(1) provides that in all business letters, circulars and catalogues on or in which the business name appears and which are sent by that person,

---

14 RBNA 1963, s 4(2).

15 A failure to furnish such a statement or particulars or of change 'without reasonable excuse in so doing' is punishable, on summary conviction, by a fine not exceeding €126.97: RBNA 1963, s 10. It is also an offence to furnish a statement which contains any matter which is false in any material particular to the knowledge of any person signing it and punishable, on summary conviction, by imprisonment for a term not exceeding six months or to a fine not exceeding €126.97 or to both: RBNA 1963, s 11. Generally, the RBNA 1963 provides that summary proceedings in relation to any offence under the Act may be brought and prosecuted by the Minister for Enterprise, Trade and Employment: RBNA 1963, s 20(1).

16 RBNA 1963, s 5(1).

17 RBNA 1963, s 6(1).

18 RBNA 1963, s 8.

19 RBNA 1963, s 12(3)–(5).

he shall state in legible characters his present Christian name or the initials thereof, and present surname, any former Christian names and surnames, and his nationality if not Irish. Default in compliance with this provision will render the sole trader liable on summary conviction for each offence to a fine not exceeding €31.74: RBNA 1963, s 18. In *Kent Adhesive Products Company t/a KAPCO v Ryan*[20] the defendant company registered a business name under the RBNA 1963 but Costello J found that it did not comply with s 18(1) because it had failed to put the name of the company on the business letters of the company. The plaintiffs sought injunctive relief for, inter alia, passing off. Costello J required, inter alia, an undertaking from the defendant to comply with the provisions of the Companies Acts and the RBNA 1963 and to refrain from using the company's present letterheads and to print further letterheads in accordance with the Acts.

[1.009] Section 14 of RBNA 1963 provides that the Minister for Enterprise, Trade and Employment may refuse to permit the registration of any name which in his opinion is undesirable; however, an appeal may be made to the High Court against such refusal. The use of a business name, the registration of which has been refused by the Minister, is an offence which is liable on summary conviction to a fine not exceeding £126.97: RBNA 1963, s 14(2). It is especially important to note that the mere registration of a business name does not make the person who uses it immune from civil action by an aggrieved third party. Section 14(3) states:

> 'The registration of a business name under this Act shall not be construed as authorising the use of that name if apart from such registration the use thereof could be prohibited.'

It is, accordingly, no defence to an action for passing off or infringement of a trademark to claim that registration of a particular business name was effected under the RBNA 1963[21]. In this respect the effect of registration of a business name under the RBNA 1963 is no different to the registration of a company name under the CA 1963[22].

(c) Advantages and disadvantages of being a sole trader

[1.010] The *advantages* of carrying on a business as a sole trader may be categorised under the headings of formation, compliance and management. The most significant advantage is the relative ease with which a person can commence business as a sole trader. For an Irish citizen, subject to registration for taxation purposes, there are minimal registration requirements for a sole trader and a minimum of legal expense. After formation, compliance for the sole trader is at a minimum; no annual return is

---

[20] *Kent Adhesive Products Company t/a KAPCO v Ryan* (5 November 1993, unreported), High Court (Costello J).

[21] In *DSG Retail Ltd v PC World Ltd* (13 January 1998, unreported), High Court (Laffoy J) the plaintiff which operated a chain of computer superstores in the UK, Northern Ireland and Ireland under the title of PC World, sought an injunction to prevent a passing off by the first defendant. In the evidence it was heard that there were a number of other parties using the name 'PC World' in Ireland and that one of those parties had registered the name as a business name under the 1963 Act. It was noted that this did not prevent the plaintiff from commencing injunction proceedings against that party also.

[22] See Chapter 2, *Formation, Registration and Conversion of Private Companies*, para **[2.045]**.

required to be filed and the business cannot be 'struck-off' any register[23]. As regards management, the advantages enjoyed by a sole trader are that he has complete control over the business and can make decisions without having regard to any other person. Furthermore, where the business makes a profit, the net profit belongs alone to the sole trader. Finally, details of a sole trader's finances and accounts can be kept confidential as there is no requirement for the public disclosure of accounts etc[24].

[1.011] The *disadvantages* to conducting business as a sole trader will, for many, be found to by far outweigh the advantages. The principal disadvantages are as follows. First, the sole trader has unlimited liability for the debts of his business, so just as profits belong alone to him, so too do its debts; where a sole trader's debts exceed his assets (personal as well as business) the sole trader may be declared a bankrupt and his assets divided amongst his creditors[25].

Secondly, it can be relatively more difficult to dispose of a sole trader's business – whether on death or inter vivos – than, say, a business owned by a private company. Apart from the possible legal uncertainty in transferring chattels and goodwill, the transfer of any real property may incur substantial stamp duty; by contrast the owner of the shares in a company which owns a business can sell the shares, and thus the business, more tax efficiently[26]. Partial disposal (where, say, a sole proprietor wishes to reward a deserving employee by giving him a share in the business) is not possible for a sole trader as the effect of creating an additional proprietary interest is to create a partnership (even if the partner's entitlements are unequal).

Thirdly, a sole trader may be restricted in obtaining finance because of the inability to create floating charges over his chattels and other property and also because of the difficulties in creating fixed charges over chattels by reason of the Bills of Sale (Ireland) Acts 1879–1883[27]. This may prove a particular problem to a sole trader where a considerable amount of his assets are in the nature of personalty and/or more amenable to being secured by a floating rather than a fixed charge eg a publican. It may be noted, however, that a sole trader who is engaged in farming will not encounter the same difficulties when creating fixed or floating charges over 'agricultural stock'.[28]

Fourthly, it is generally recognised that the circumstances in which the tax code favours the sole trader are generally less numerous than when it favours a private company.

---

23 Cf companies incorporated under the Companies Acts 1963–2001 which can be struck off the register and cease to exist as separate legal entities: see Chapter 12, *Company Law Compliance and Enforcement*, para **[12.132]** *ff*.

24 See generally, Ellis, *Irish Company Law for Business* (1998), p 37–38.

25 On bankruptcy, see generally, Sanfey & Holohan, *Bankruptcy Law and Practice in Ireland* (1991).

26 See generally, Chapter 16, *Share Transfers in Private Companies*.

27 See Chapter 21, *Corporate Borrowing: Registration of Charges*, para **[21.037]** and also Maguire, 'The Bill of Sale: The Forgotten Relation?' (1997) 4 CLP 3.

28 See Chapter 21, *Corporate Borrowing: Registration of Charges*, para **[21.109]** and also Maguire, 'Agricultural Chattel Mortgages' (1997) 4 CLP 170.

Partnerships

[1.012] It is beyond the scope and purpose of this book to consider the law of partnerships in any detail and the reader is referred to the many excellent specialised works on that topic[29]. What follows here is a short analysis, by way of comparison, which seeks to place partnerships in context vis-à-vis the private company. Partnerships are considered now under the following headings:

(a) Partnership defined and described.
(b) Partners' dealings with outsiders and inter se.
(c) Dissolution of partnerships.
(d) Limited partnerships.
(e) Advantages and disadvantages of partnerships.

(a) Partnership defined and described

[1.013] Partnership is defined by the Partnership Act 1890, s 1 as 'the relation which subsists between persons carrying on business in common with a view of profit'. Whether or not a partnership exists is a de facto question[30]. A valid partnership does not need to be registered anywhere and the intentions of the partners is generally irrelevant; all that is required is that (a) two or more persons (b) carry on a 'business'[31] (c) with a view to making profit. A partnership can be composed of natural persons, bodies corporate or a combination of both. Critical to a true understanding of the nature of a partnership is recognition of the fact that a partnership is *not* a separate legal entity and does not have an existence, independent to that of its partners.

[1.014] The law of partnership evolved as part of the common law and equity. The Partnership Act 1890 merely codified the existing common law of partnership. The legal basis for a partnership is rooted in the laws of contract and agency. In the first place the basis for every partnership is a contract, whether express or implied, between the partners. The law of agency is important as otherwise one partner could not bind his fellow partners to contracts entered into between him and outsiders; by virtue of the law of agency each partner makes his fellow partners his agents with full power to bind him. The Partnership Act 1890 will only govern the relations between partners inter se to the extent to which a partnership agreement does not otherwise provide.

[1.015] The minimum number of persons required to constitute a valid partnership is two; one person acting alone in business is a sole trader. By law the maximum number of partners which a partnership can have is 20[32]. There are, however, a number of

---

29 See Twomey, *Partnership Law* (2000); Ivamy; *Underhill's Principles of the Law of Partnership* (12th edn, 1986); and I'Anson Banks, *Lindley and Banks on the Law of Partnership* (17th edn, 1995). For a succinct overview of Irish partnership law see O'Malley, *Business Law* (1982), pp 17–26.

30 The question as to whether or not a partnership existed has been considered by the courts in a number of cases eg *Macken v Revenue Commissioners* [1962] IR 302; *Greenham v Gray* (1855) 4 ICLR 501; and *Cox v Hickman* (1860) 8 HL Cas 268 to mention but three. See also *Bass Brewers Ltd v Appleby* [1997] 2 BCLC 700.

31 Defined by Partnership Act 1890, s 45 to include 'every trade, occupation or profession'.

32 CA 1963, s 376.

exceptions: first, banking partnerships[33]; secondly, partnerships of solicitors and accountants[34]; and thirdly, partnerships formed for the purpose of carrying on the business of thoroughbred horse breeding[35].

[1.016] A partnership which adopts a firm name[36] other than the true names of the partners must register that name as a business name under the RBNA 1963. In this respect s 3(1)(a) provides:

> '...every firm having a place of business in the State and carrying on business under a business name which does not consist of the true surnames of all partners who are individuals and the corporate names of all partners which are bodies corporate without any addition other than the true Christian names of individual partners of initials of such Christian names...'

must register under the RBNA 1963. The RBNA 1963 has been considered above[37] in the context of sole traders and its provisions apply *mutatis mutandis* to partnerships.

[1.017] Property (real or personal) used by a partnership may either be owned by all of the partners collectively, in which case it is 'partnership property', or it may be owned by an individual partner personally. Any property bought with partnership money is deemed, by the Partnership Act 1890, s 20, to be prima facie 'partnership property'.

[1.018] In the absence of agreement to the contrary each and every partner is entitled to participate in the management of the partnership[38]. This general rule can, however, be varied by the agreement of the partners.

(b) Partners' dealings with outsiders and inter se

(i) Dealings with outsiders

[1.019] In the absence of an agreement to the contrary all partners are *jointly and severally* liable on the partnership's contracts and debts and for the partnership's torts[39]. Each and every partner is liable to the full extent of his personal assets for the debts of the partnership[40].

[1.020] The partners in a partnership may, by agreement, limit the actual authority of individual partners. Notwithstanding any such internal agreement, each partner will be bound by the acts of a fellow partner by reason of Partnership Act 1890, s 5 which provides:

> 'Every partner is an agent of the firm and his other partners for the purpose of the business of the partnership; and the acts of every partner who does any act for carrying on in the usual way business of the kind carried on by the firm of which he is a member bind the

33 CA 1963, s 376.

34 C(A)A 1982, s 13.

35 SI 1988/54.

36 Partnership Act 1890, s 4 provides that partners are collectively called a firm and that the name under which they carry on business is called the firm name.

37 See para **[1.005]**.

38 *Peacock v Peacock* (1809) 16 Ves Jr 49; *Rowe v Wood* (1795) 2 J & W 553.

39 Partnership Act 1890, s 9.

40 Cf the liability of limited partners considered at para **[1.024]**.

> firm and his partners, unless the partner so acting has in fact no authority to act for the firm in the particular matter, and the person with whom he is dealing either knows that he has no authority, or does not know or believe him to be a partner.'

This section makes clear the application of the doctrine of ostensible or apparent authority to partners' dealings with outsiders[41]. The leading Irish case in point is that of *Kett v Shannon & English*[42] where the Supreme Court applied the doctrine of ostensible authority as set out in the leading English decision in *Freeman & Lockyer v Buckhurst Park Properties (Mangal) Ltd*[43].

(ii) Dealings inter se

[1.021] In the absence of a contrary agreement each and every partner is entitled to participate in the management of the partnership. Section 24 of the Partnership Act 1890 provides that, in the absence of agreement to the contrary, every partner may participate in the management of the partnership; the consent of all of the partners is required to vary the partnership agreement; and every partner is entitled to share equally in the profits and obliged to share equally in the losses of the partnership.

[1.022] Partners are in a fiduciary position vis-à-vis each other[44]. Indeed, today, it may be said that the very term 'partnership' as used in the context of certain private 'quasi-partnership' companies[45] *implies* notions of mutuality, good faith and trust between the participants. Partners are each entitled to full disclosure from the other partners as to the affairs of the partnership. A partner is obliged to account to the other partners for any personal gain from the use of partnership property and, like a company director, is liable for any gain made through undisclosed competition with the partnership[46].

(c) Dissolution of partnerships

[1.023] A partnership may be dissolved after a specific date or event; it can be dissolved by a partner giving notice of his intention to dissolve the partnership; it will dissolve on the death or bankruptcy of a partner; it may be dissolved by order of the court on a petition grounded on, inter alia, insanity, incapacity, misconduct or where such is just and equitable[47].

(d) Limited partnerships

[1.024] The Limited Partnership Act 1907 facilitates the creation of a partnership in which some of the members may have limited liability for the debts of the partnership[48]. A limited partnership is not, however, a separate legal entity[49]. The 1907 Act requires, however, that there must be at least one 'general partner' whose liability is unlimited and

---

41 *Nationwide Building Society v Lewis & Williams* [1997] 3 All ER 498.

42 *Kett v Shannon & English* [1987] ILRM 364. See Chapter 7, *Corporate Contracts: Capacity and Authority*, para **[7.099]**.

43 *Freeman & Lockyer v Buckhurst Park Properties (Mangal) Ltd* [1964] 2 QB 480.

44 *Helmore v Smith* (1886) 35 Ch D 436.

45 See para **[1.128]**.

46 Partnership Act 1890, ss 28–30.

47 See Partnership Act 1890, ss 22–24.

48 See Twomey, 'The Limited Partnership Act 1907' (1996) 3 CLP 211.

49 *Re Barnard* [1932] 1 Ch 272.

there must be at least one 'limited partner' whose liability is limited to the amount of capital contributed by him to the partnership[50]. A further restriction is that the limited partner must be excluded from the management of the firm and cannot have any authority to bind the other partners. The sanction for contravention of this is that the limited partner will automatically have unlimited liability for the debts and liabilities of the firm incurred during the period when he participated in its management[51]. Moreover, every limited partnership must be registered with the Registrar of Companies; the sanction for non-compliance is that a limited partner cannot claim limited liability[52]. As at 31 December 2001 there were 440 limited partnerships registered with the Registrar of Companies[53]. It may be noted that there are proposals in the UK for the introduction of a new variant of limited liability partnership (LLP)[54].

(e) Advantages and disadvantages of partnerships

[1.025] The primary *advantages* of organising a business as a partnership include the following. First, the formation of a partnership and its on-going compliance with partnership rules involves minimal effort; there is no requirement that a partnership be registered[55] or even that there be a written contract, although it is, in practice, often advisable for the partnership agreement to be reduced to writing to avoid ambiguity. Secondly, because the law of contract is the essential basis of a partnership it is relatively easy to tailor a particular partnership to meet the needs of the partners. Thirdly, the confidentiality of the relationship between the partners inter se (and particularly of their finances) can be maintained. Fourthly, each and every partner is entitled to participate in the management of the partnership[56].

[1.026] The primary *disadvantages* of organising business as a partnership include the following. First, the general rule[57] is that each and every partner in a partnership is jointly and severally liable for all of the debts of the partnership, which can be satisfied from their personal assets up to and including making them bankrupt. The absence of limited liability is probably the greatest disadvantage. Secondly, the continuity of a partnership is affected by the death or insanity or bankruptcy of any one partner, and the consequence will be its dissolution. Thirdly, shares in a partnership cannot be as easily transferred as can the shares in a company. Fourthly, there are limits on the numbers of persons who can be partners in a partnership.

Industrial and provident societies

[1.027] Industrial and provident societies – commonly referred to as co-operatives or co-operative societies – may be registered under the Industrial and Provident Societies Acts

---

50 LPA 1907, s 4(2).
51 LPA 1907, s 6(1).
52 LPA 1907, s 5. See *McCartaigh v Daly* [1986] ILRM 116.
53 See *Companies Report 2000*, p 44.
54 See Glanville, 'Partnership Liability – All Aboard the LLP Train?' (1997) 4 CLP 226.
55 Cf a limited partnership. Note also the possible application of the RBNA 1963.
56 See generally, Ellis, *Irish Company Law for Business* (1998), p 38–39.
57 Cf a limited partnership.

1893–1978[58]. An industrial and provident society is defined by the Industrial and Provident Societies Act 1893, s 4 as:

> '...a society for carrying on any industries, businesses, or trades specified in or authorised by its rules, whether wholesale or retail and including dealings of any description with land.'

In Ireland, traditionally, the co-operative movement was particularly strong in the area of agricultural food produce. In recent times, however, a number of the larger co-operatives have converted to public limited companies (PLCs). When registered, a co-operative becomes a body corporate with limited liability. Section 21 of the Industrial and Provident Societies Act, 1983 provides:

> 'The registration of a society shall render it a body corporate by the name described in the acknowledgement of registry, by which it may sue and be sued, with perpetual succession and a common seal, and with limited liability...'

Although co-operatives have much in common with registered companies, they have a fundamentally different nature to that of certain forms of registered companies. In *Kerry Co-operative Ltd v An Bord Bainne Co-operative Ltd*[59] McCarthy J said a co-operative may be contrasted:

> '...with a company of limited liability in that its shareholders invest their efforts in the betterment of activity in co-operation with each other being persons of a like interest, rather than their seeking a return on investment capital, which is the role of the investor in a company of limited liability; the latter is indifferent to the operation of the company so long as he is assured of an adequate return on his investment.'

Whilst this is undoubtedly true when comparing a co-operative society to a public limited company ('PLC')[60], it is thought that this comparison does not hold up when comparing a co-operative society with a private company. As at the end of 1996, the *Report of the Registrar for Friendly Societies* stated that there were 942 such societies registered.

[1.028] Co-operatives are registered on the register of friendly societies. This is located within the Department of Enterprise, Trade and Employment which is responsible for the administration of the Industrial and Provident Societies Acts 1893–1978. A co-operative society must have at least seven members[61] and registration is effected by completing the appropriate form, which must be signed by the seven members and the intended secretary, and sending it, together with two copies of the rules (also signed by the eight persons), and the appropriate fee to the Registrar of Friendly Societies. Unlike

---

58 See O'Malley, *Business Law* (1982), pp 36–39; Ussher & O'Connor, *Doing Business in Ireland*, para 3.04[2]; Forde, *Commercial Law* (2nd edn, 1997), p 19 and at p 464; Schmitthoff, *Palmer's Company Law* (24th edn, 1987), p 1691.

59 *Kerry Co-operative Ltd v An Bord Bainne Co-operative Ltd* [1991] ILRM 851 at 863.

60 For PLCs, see generally Chapter 28, *The Public Company in Context*.

61 Provident Societies Act 1892, s 5(1). Note that a society consisting solely of two or more registered societies may be formed: the Industrial and Provident Societies (Amendment) Act 1913, s 1.

the members of registered companies, the members of co-operatives have just one vote each.

[1.029] All co-operative societies must have rules which are similar to a registered company's articles of association[62]. The rules of a co-operative society bind the members and the company[63]. In many respects, however, there are differences between the rules of a co-operative and those of a registered company. In the first place the rules of a co-operative must be approved by the Registrar of Friendly Societies. In the second place, the Industrial and Provident Societies Act 1893, Sch 2 specifies certain matters which *must* be covered by the rules. In the third place amendments to the rules have no validity until such time as they are actually registered under the Industrial and Provident Societies Act 1893, s 10[64].

[1.030] Industrial and provident societies are highly regulated. Under the Industrial and Provident Societies Act 1893 a special resolution is required for a change of name (s 52); to approve the amalgamation with another co-operative (s 53(1)); to transfer engagements to another co-operative (s 53(2)); and to convert into a company or amalgamate or transfer engagements to a company (s 54(1)). Section 51(a) and (b) of the Industrial and Provident Societies Act 1893 provides that a special resolution is one that is passed by a majority of not less than 75% of the co-operative's members for the time being entitled to vote under the rules and that is *subsequently confirmed* by a majority of such members at a subsequent general meeting held not less than 14 days nor more than one month after the passing of the first resolution. In the case of the amalgamation of two or more co-operatives each of which has amongst its objects and is engaged in the manufacture of butter, cream or other dairy product, the 75% requirement in Industrial and Provident Societies Act 1893, s 51(1) was changed to a simple majority by the Industrial and Provident Societies Act 1971. It may also be noted that Industrial and Provident Societies Act 1893, s 4(a) restricts the number of shares that can be held by a member (other than another co-operative) in a co-operative. This restriction varies, however, depending upon the type of co-operative and a member of an agricultural and fisheries co-operative can hold no more than €126,973.81.

Building societies

[1.031] Building societies have a long and distinguished history in facilitating the provision of houses for their members[65]. The law of building societies is found in the Building Societies Act 1989 ('BSA 1989') which introduced reforms and consolidated the then existing legislation[66]. Building societies originated in the late eighteenth century

62 As to which see generally, Chapter 3, *Private Constitutional Documents*.

63 See *Kerry Co-operative Ltd et al v An Bord Bainne Co-operative Ltd* [1990] ILRM 664 (HC) and [1991] ILRM 851 (SC).

64 *Re Londonderry Equitable Co-Operative Society* [1910] 1 IR 69.

65 See Forde, *Commercial Law* (2nd edn, 1997), p 462. For a short analysis see Murdock, *Building Society Law in Ireland* (1989), p 1–6. For analysis of the English law on building societies, see Wurtzburg & Mills, *Building Society Law.*

66 See *Irish Current Law, 1989*, p 89/17/1. The BSA 1989 has been amended by the Central Bank Act 1997, the CUA 1997, the Asset Covered Securities Act 2001, the Housing (Miscellaneous Provisions) Acts 1992 and 2002 and the Euro Changeover (Amounts) Act 2001.

as small associations of private individuals who banded together to assist each other in obtaining housing. Typically, a small number of people made contributions towards the cost of site acquisition and then the cost of building houses, one by one, for the group until all members were housed, whereupon the group was dissolved. In later years such societies began to have members who made contributions to the common pool to earn interest on their savings as opposed to building a house. Notwithstanding the conversion of two of Ireland's leading building societies – Irish Permanent Building Society and First National Building Society – into public limited companies (Irish Life and Permanent plc and First Active plc respectively) building society activity in the Irish housing market remains strong. The three remaining building societies are the EBS Building Society, Irish Nationwide Building Society and the ICS Building Society. The latter – the ICS – is peculiar in that up to the mid-1980s it had investment shares quoted on the Stock Exchange and when the entire of its investment shares were acquired by the Governor and Company of the Bank of Ireland, it became the bank's subsidiary. It is beyond the scope and purpose of this work to comprehensively treat the law relating to building societies. What follows is a brief analysis of the following issues:

(a) Formation.

(b) Powers of building societies.

(c) Central Bank supervision.

(d) Management, meetings and accounts.

(e) Conversion of buildings societies to PLCs.

(a) Formation

[1.032] Upon incorporation, a building society becomes 'a body corporate...having perpetual succession and a seal and the power to hold land'[67]. Section 10(2) of BSA 1989 provides that a building society may be formed by ten or more persons acting in the following way[68]:

— agreeing on the objects of the society and on the extent of its powers in a memorandum[69];

— agreeing in its Rules[70], for the regulation of the society[71]; and

— delivering to the Central Bank of Ireland ('Central Bank') three copies of the memorandum and rules[72], each signed by the ten persons and the society's intended secretary.

---

67 BSA 1989, s 10(6).

68 Who are not disqualified under BSA 1989, s 64.

69 The provisions of the memorandum must comply with BSA 1989, Sch 2, Part I.

70 In *Irish Civil Service Building Society v Registrar of Friendly Societies* [1985] IR 167 it was held that the building society legislation only provided a framework for making rules and that individual building societies could make such rules as they thought fit for their administration and management.

71 The provisions of the rules must comply with the BSA 1989, Sch 2, Part II.

72 When registered the memorandum and rules are binding upon the society, every member and officer thereof and all persons claiming on account of a member or under the rules and all such members, officers and persons are taken to have notice of those provisions: BSA 1989, s 11(1).

The authority to incorporate a building society rests with the Central Bank, which took over the regulation and supervision of building societies from the Registrar of Friendly Societies pursuant to the BSA 1989. The Central Bank's discretion to register a building society and issue it with a certificate of incorporation will be exercised where it is satisfied[73] that:

— its memorandum and rules are in conformity with the 1989 Act and any regulations made thereunder and that the name of the proposed society is not undesirable;

— there is no reason to believe that the society will not be authorised to raise funds in accordance with the BSA 1989, s 17; and

— registration would not be prejudicial to the orderly and proper regulation of building societies generally.

A refusal by the Central Bank to register a building society may be appealed to the High Court by all ten of the persons seeking to form the society[74]. Where registration is effected and a certificate of incorporation is issued, the certificate shall be:

> '...sufficient evidence until the contrary is shown that all the requirements of this Act in respect of registration and of matters precedent and incidental thereto have been complied with and that the society is a society duly registered and incorporated under this Act.'[75]

There have been no new building societies registered since the enactment of the BSA 1989.

(b) Powers of building societies

[1.033] The doctrine of ultra vires applies to building societies as it applies to registered companies[76], A measure of protection is afforded to outsiders by BSA 1989, s 12(1), which provides:

> 'Any act or thing done by a building society, which if the society had been empowered to do the same would have been lawfully and effectively done, shall, subject to *section 11(1)*, be effective in favour of any person relying on such act or thing who dealt with the society in good faith notwithstanding that the society had no power to do such act or thing.'

Section 12(1) of BSA 1989 is based on CA 1963, s 8 and case law on the latter section would influence, if not bind, the interpretation of BSA 1989, s 12(1)[77]. In England, it has been held that even where a building society acts outside its legislative framework, such action will not necessarily be unenforceable[78].

---

73 BSA 1989, s 10(3).

74 BSA 1989, s 10(4).

75 BSA 1989, s 10(7). A mistake made in the incorporation of a building society has been held not to render its incorporation void: *Irish Permanent Building Society v Registrar of Building Societies* [1981] ILRM 242.

76 See Chapter 7, *Corporate Contracts: Capacity and Authority*, para **[7.043]** *ff*.

77 Chapter 7, *Corporate Contracts: Capacity and Authority*, para **[7.077]** *ff*.

78 In *Nash v Halifax Building Society* [1979] Ch 584 it was held that where a building society took as security a 'second' mortgage (ie ranking after a mortgage in favour of another lending institution) that security was still enforceable although it contravened the English legislation.

[1.034] Subject to certain exceptions, a building society may not raise funds or advertise for or otherwise solicit deposits or subscriptions for shares unless there is in force an authorisation granted by the Central Bank: BSA 1989, s 17(1). A breach of this provision entitles the Central Bank to petition to have a building society wound up[79]. Building societies may have as their objects the undertaking of any of the activities permitted by or under BSA 1989 Act and shall have as one of their objects 'the raising of funds for making housing loans'[80]. Building societies have the powers conferred by BSA 1989 and any incidental powers necessary for the achievement of their objects subject to: compliance with any requirement that, for a power to be exercisable, it must be adopted by a building society; and the exercise by the Central Bank of its functions under BSA 1989 and the Currency and Central Bank Acts or regulations made thereunder[81]. Building societies have power to raise funds and borrow money subject to the restrictions contained in BSA 1989, s 18. Other powers enjoyed by building societies include: the acquisition and provision of premises; the holding and developing of land; the making of housing loans and other loans[82]; the charging of tiered interest rates; the assessment of security for loans; the sale or retention of mortgaged property; the discharge of mortgages; the investment in and support of bodies corporate; and the provision of conveyancing services, auctioneering services and other services relating to land. The exercise of powers outside the State, the hedging of interest rates and the linking of services are all regulated by BSA1989[83]. The power to provide financial services and to give bonds and sureties were, in 1989, new powers for building societies[84]. Section 36 of BSA 1989 regulates the exercise, by a building society, of its powers.

[1.035] There are some major differences between the Irish law of building societies and that pertaining in England. An example of this is a building society's ability to create a floating charge. An English building society is prohibited from creating a floating charge[85]. There is no such prohibition on Irish building societies. Moreover, the obstacle to an individual creating a floating charge – the Bills of Sale Acts[86] – does not apply to corporations[87].

(c) Central Bank supervision

[1.036] Building societies are supervised by the Central Bank which is given wide-ranging powers under the BSA 1989. Part IV of BSA 1989 specifically concerns the control and supervision of building societies. Section 37(1) of BSA 1989 imposes a duty on the Central Bank to supervise and regulate building societies with a view to the

---

79 BSA 1989, s 17(8).

80 BSA 1989, s 9(1).

81 BSA 1989, s 9(2).

82 BSA 1989, ss 20–23.

83 BSA 1989, ss 24–28 and 31–35, respectively.

84 BSA 1989, ss 29 and 30.

85 Building Societies Act 1986, s 9B(1) (UK).

86 See para **[1.011]**.

87 In *NV Slavenburg's Bank v Intercontinental Natural Resources Ltd* [1980] 1 All ER 955 at 975, Lloyd J said that 'the Bills of Sale Acts apply to individuals only and not to corporations at all'.

protection by each society of the funds of its shareholders and depositors and the maintenance of the financial stability and wellbeing of societies generally. Specifically, building societies are required to meet certain asset and liability ratios[88]. The Central Bank's powers include the power to revoke a building society's authorisation; it can also authorise inspection, require information, control advertising by building societies, apply to court to prohibit certain contraventions of BSA 1989, require the disclosure of information and appoint inspectors to a building society[89]. In all respects the supervision of building societies by the Central Bank is on a par to its supervision of banks.

(d) Management, meetings and accounts

[1.037] Every building society must have at least three directors, one of whom must be the chairman of the board of directors; the chairman may not, however, also be the chief executive (or managing director) unless the Central Bank consents to this[90]. A building society is required to have a chief executive and a secretary who again, and save with the Central Bank's consent, may not be one and the same person[91]. The appointment and retirement of directors are regulated by BSA 1989, ss 50 and 51 and Central Bank approval is required for the appointment of directors or secretaries of building societies. Many of the provisions contained in the Companies Act 1990, Part III had forerunners in BSA 1989[92]. These include: the disclosure by directors of interests in contracts; directors' contracts of employment; the inspection of directors' service contracts; substantial property transactions involving directors and connected persons; and restrictions on loans, quasi-loans, credit transactions, guarantees and the provision of security to directors[93].

[1.038] Meetings of members of building societies and resolutions at such meetings are regulated by BSA 1989, Part VI. In practice, however, a society's rules (which must be in conformity with the provisions of BSA 1989) will regulate the convening and holding of meetings and the passing of resolutions thereat.

[1.039] Accounts and audit of building societies are regulated by BSA 1989, Part VII. The failure by a building society to keep proper accounting records and to establish and maintain systems of control of their businesses would entitle the Central Bank to revoke or suspend authorisation. Section 112 of BSA 1989 makes provision for the imposition of personal liability on the officers of a building society where proper accounting records are not kept[94].

---

88 BSA 1989, s 39.

89 BSA 1989, ss 40–47.

90 BSA 1989, s 47(1), (3) and (4). Subsection (2) provides that a society shall not have a body corporate as a director.

91 BSA 1989, s 48.

92 As to CA 1990, Part III, see, generally, Chapter 11, *Statutory Regulation of Transactions Involving Directors and their Companies*.

93 BSA 1989, ss 53–59.

94 BSA 1989, s 111 also makes such officers liable to criminal sanction.

(e) Conversion of buildings societies to PLCs

[1.040] Part XI of BSA 1989 facilitates the conversion of a building society to a public limited company. Section 101(2) of BSA 1989 details the conditions which a building society must fulfil in order to convert to a PLC. This provides that a building society must: pass a conversion resolution approving of a conversion scheme; obtain the Central Bank's confirmation to the conversion scheme; and it must have itself registered as a company under the Companies Acts 1963–2001 in accordance with the provisions in Part XI and regulations made thereunder. Section 102 of BSA 1989 also contains certain protective provisions which guarantee the independence of the successor company for a period of five years following conversion.

Credit unions

[1.041] Credit unions were originally formed under and regulated by the Industrial and Provident Societies Act 1893; credit unions were simply financial co-operatives. As they grew it became apparent that separate, specialist, legislation was required and in 1966 the Credit Union Act 1966 was passed. This legislation was later supplemented by the Industrial and Provident Societies (Amendment) Act 1978, Part III. Both the 1966 Act and Part III of the 1978 Act were repealed and replaced by the current legislation, the Credit Union Act 1997 ('CUA 1997')[95]. The CUA 1997 was necessitated by the fact that many credit unions had evolved from being small, unsophisticated, local saving societies to becoming large organisations offering a wide range of financial services to their members. The supervision of credit unions continues to vest in the Registrar of Friendly Societies, whose powers of supervision have been bolstered by the CUA 1997.

[1.042] Section 6(1) of CUA 1997 facilitates the formation of a credit union. It provides that a society may be registered as a credit union if the Registrar of Friendly Societies is satisfied as to certain matters.

First, it must be formed for the objects detailed in CUA 1997, s 6(2)(a)–(c) and no other objects save those in s 6(2)(d)–(g)[96]. Those objects are:

- the promotion of thrift among its members by the accumulation of their savings;
- the creation of sources of credit for the mutual benefit of its members at a fair and reasonable rate of interest;
- the use and control of members' savings for their mutual benefit;
- the training and education of its members in the wise use of money;
- the education of its members in their economic, social and cultural wellbeing as members of the community;
- the improvement of the wellbeing and spirit of the members' community; and
- subject to s 48, the provision to its members of such additional services as are for their mutual benefit[97].

95 See generally Bird's annotations on CUA 1997 in *Irish Current Law, 1997*, 1997 No 15.

96 CUA 1997, s 6(1)(a).

97 As detailed in CUA 1997, s 6(2).

Secondly, admission to membership of the society must be restricted to persons each of whom has, in relation to all of the other members, at least one of the following common bonds[98]:

- following a particular occupation;
- residing or being employed in a particular locality;
- being employed by a particular employer or having retired from employment with a particular employer;
- being a member of a bona fide organisation or being otherwise associated with other members of a society for a purpose other than that of forming a society to be registered as a credit union;
- any other common bond approved by the Registrar of Friendly Societies[99].

Thirdly, it must have at least 15 members who are of full age[100]. Fourthly, its rules must comply with CUA 1997, s 13[101]. Fifthly, its registered office must be within the State[102]. Sixthly, if registered it must participate in a savings protection scheme approved under CUA 1997, s 46(1)[103]. Seventhly, and finally, it must have in force on registration a policy of insurance of the kind required by CUA 1997, s 47[104].

Unincorporated associations

[1.043] Unincorporated associations can refer to a wide variety of organisations eg clubs, political parties, campaign groups, residents' associations etc[105]. The meaning of 'unincorporated association' was defined by Lawton LJ in *Conservative and Unionist Central Office v Burrell*[106] in the following terms:

> '...two or more persons bound together for one or more common purposes, not being business purposes, by mutual undertakings each having mutual duties and obligations, in an organisation which has rules which identify in whom control of it and its funds rests and on what terms and which can be joined or left at will'.

An unincorporated association has no separate legal personality; such legal personality as it has is the sum of the legal personalities of its members. The legal basis of an unincorporated association is the law of contract, ie the rights and duties of the members

98 CUA 1997, s 6(1)(b).

99 As detailed in CUA 1997, s 6(3). In ascertaining whether a common bond exists between the members of a society the Registrar of Friendly Societies is required, by the CUA 1997, s 6(4), (a) to have regard to the qualifications which are stated in the rules to be required for admission to membership of the society; and (b) may, if he considers it proper in the circumstances of the case, treat the fact that admission to membership is restricted as mentioned in sub-s (1)(b) as sufficient evidence of the existence of a common bond.

100 CUA 1997, s 6(1)(c).

101 CUA 1997, s 6(1)(d).

102 CUA 1997, s 6(1)(e).

103 CUA 1997, s 6(1)(f).

104 CUA 1997, s 6(1)(g).

105 See generally, Warburton, *Unincorporated Associations* (2nd edn, 1992).

106 *Conservative and Unionist Central Office v Burrell* [1982] 1 WLR 522 at 525.

of an unincorporated association are governed exclusively by contract[107]. The formation of an unincorporated association is a de facto process: when two or more come together with a non-business common purpose with the intention of forming an unincorporated association, an unincorporated association may be said to exist. Serious unincorporated associations will make rules to govern the relations between the members inter se and will elect a committee and officers. Because of the lack of separate legal personality, any property 'owned' by a club or other unincorporated association will have to be held in the names of individuals on its behalf. It is most common for 'club' property to be held by trustees on trust for the members in accordance with the rules of the club. An unincorporated association cannot be liable in tort, again for the reason that it has no separate existence; individual members of an unincorporated association will only be liable for their personal breaches of duty and will not ordinarily be vicariously liable for the torts of other members[108]. Similarly, an unincorporated association cannot make or be sued on a contract. Where an unincorporated association purports to make a contract, the individual members who actually make it may be personally liable or, if the rules authorised them to act as agent, the principal in such agency – all of the members – will be personally liable.

Unregistered companies

[1.044] Section 377(1) of CA 1963 applies the provisions of the Companies Acts that are listed in CA 1963, Sch 9 to all bodies corporate incorporated in and having a place of business in the State, save those mentioned in CA 1963, s 377(2), 'as if they were companies registered under this Act and subject to such adaptations and modifications (if any) as may be prescribed'. The carve-out in s 377(2) is extensive. It prevents the application of the Companies Acts to the following bodies:

- any body corporate incorporated by or registered under any public general statute;
- any body corporate not formed for the purpose of carrying on business which has for its object the acquisition of gain by the body or by the individual members thereof;
- any body corporate which is prohibited by statute or otherwise from making any distribution of its income or property among its members while it is a going concern or when it is in liquidation; and
- any body corporate for the time being exempted by the Minister for Enterprise, Trade and Employment.

The combined effect of these provisions is that there would seem to be only one entity that is in practice classified as an 'unregistered company' to which the provisions listed in CA 1963, Sch 9 apply. This is the Governor and Company of the Bank of Ireland, a

107 See *Walsh v Butler* [1997] 2 ILRM 81 (Morris J) where it was said of a particular association that the 'relationship as between members must be regarded as a contractual relationship based upon the rules of the Club'. See also *Re Bucks Constabulary Widows' and Orphans' Fund Friendly Society (No 2)* [1979] 1 WLR 936.

108 *Baker v Jones* [1916] 2 AC 15. See also *Thompson v Douglas Amateur Football Club Social Club* [1999] Scot SC (27 June 1999), (Bailii).

chartered corporation, the existence of which derives from the Bank of Ireland Act of 1781–1782[109] and a Charter granted by George III in 1783. As a perusal of the Ninth Schedule will show, not all of the provisions of the Companies Acts apply to unregistered companies; however, the list of provisions can be amended by Ministerial order[110].

[B] AN HISTORICAL OUTLINE OF REGISTERED COMPANIES

Private companies, registered companies, and corporate status

[1.045] The modern Irish private company is a species of *registered* company[111], so described because the company is registered with the CRO in accordance with the requirements of the Companies Acts 1963–2001. The registered company is a legal structure which *all* persons – including so-called *fictitious*[112] persons such as the State, government ministers, and even other registered companies – may employ as a means of conducting their affairs[113]. The registered company is principally used in Ireland as a vehicle for conducting business activity, but there is no requirement in the Companies Acts that companies registered under them be formed with a view to the making of a profit[114]. Thus, for example, social clubs[115] and management committees of large shopping centres or apartment complexes are sometimes operated through the medium of the registered company.

[1.046] The registered company is a form of *corporation* or *body corporate*, and as such constitutes a legal person with a legal identity separate and distinct from that of its individual members or shareholders[116]. A distinction may be drawn at the outset between *corporations sole* and *corporations aggregate*. A corporation *sole* 'comprises one individual holding an office subject to perpetual succession'[117], the paradigm example of which is a government minister or a clerical bishop[118]. A corporation *aggregate*, on the

---

[109] 21 & 22 Geo III c 16.

[110] See, eg, Companies Act 1963 (Ninth Schedule) Regulations 1999 (SI 1999/63) and Companies Act 1963 (Section 377(1)) Order 1999 (SI 1999/64) which facilitated the application of CA 1990, Part XI (which deals with the acquisition of own shares and shares in holding company), the European Communities (Public Limited Companies Subsidiaries) Regulations 1997 etc, to unregistered companies.

[111] As, indeed, is the *public* company; see Chapter 28, *Public Companies in Context*.

[112] See generally, Chapter 4, *Incorporation and its Consequences*, para **[4.024]**.

[113] As to registered companies of which the State is a member see para **[1.055]**.

[114] By way of contrast, the Partnership Act 1890, which is the principal source of the law governing partnerships in this jurisdiction, defines a partnership as 'the relation which subsists between persons carrying *on a business in common with a view to a profit*': Partnership Act 1890, s 1(1), (italics added). Where, however, such a relation subsists between the members of a registered company it is not a partnership: Partnership Act 1890, ss (2)(a). On partnerships see para **[1.012]** *ff*, and generally, see I'Anson Banks, *Lindley and Banks on the Law of Partnership* (17th edn, 1995); and Ivamy, *Underhill's Principles of the Law of Partnership* (12th edn, 1986).

[115] See, for example, *Re Parnell GAA Club Ltd* [1984] ILRM 246.

[116] CA 1963, s 18; *Salomon v Salomon & Co* [1897] AC 22. See generally, Chapter 3, *Incorporation and its Consequences*.

[117] See Wylie, *Irish Land Law* (3rd edn, 1997), para [4.027].

[118] On the corporation sole, see, Maitland, 'The Corporation Sole' (1900) 16 LQR 335.

other hand, may be defined as an association, comprising of a number of individual members, which has a legal existence separate from its members. Until recently all registered companies were corporations aggregate. The advent of the single-member private limited company means that all registered companies cannot be accurately described as being corporations aggregate. It is thought, however, that this goes no deeper than the accuracy of the description and that the significance of there being just one member does not, in fact, cause a registered company to cease, *in law*, to be a corporation aggregate.

It is the separate legal identity, or *corporate personality*, and the consequences which stem from it, which are the principal attraction of the registered company as a means of conducting business. This is because the risk, liability, obligations and duties associated with the business will rest with the company and *not*, generally speaking, with the individual shareholders or members[119]. The registered company acquires this corporate personality through the process of *incorporation by registration*, ie through registration of the memorandum of association of the company with the Registrar of Companies in accordance with the Companies Acts 1963–2001. Section 18 of CA 1963 provides that:

> '(1) On the registration of the memorandum of a company the registrar shall certify under his hand that the company is incorporated and, in the case of a limited company, that the company is limited.
>
> (2) From the date of incorporation mentioned in the certificate of incorporation, the subscribers of the memorandum, together with such other persons as may from time to time become members of the company, shall be a body corporate with the name contained in the memorandum, capable forthwith of exercising all the functions of an incorporated company, and having perpetual succession and a common seal, but with such liability on the part of the members to contribute to the assets of the company in the event of its being wound up as is mentioned in this Act.'

Upon registration, then, a metamorphosis occurs and the signatories to a company's memorandum of association become members of a new body corporate. This process and its consequences are described in detail in later chapters[120].

[1.047] It would be inaccurate to equate the incorporation of a company by registration with the *formation* of a company. It may prove useful at this stage to observe that although nowadays we tend to think of a company as a corporation, it has been said 'the word *company* has no strictly legal meaning'[121]. In common parlance the word is used to connote an association of some kind. It is common, and quite legal, for partners, notably solicitors' firms, to carry on their business in the name of, say, 'A,B,C & Company'.[122]

---

[119] See Chapter 4, *Incorporation and its Consequences*. For exceptions to this principle see Chapter 5, *Disregarding Separate Legal Personality*.

[120] See Chapter 4, *Incorporation and its Consequences*. For exceptions to this principle see Chapter 5, *Disregarding Separate Legal Personality*.

[121] *Re Stanley* [1906] 1 Ch 131 at 134, per Buckley J. Of course when the Companies Acts refer to 'company' the term means 'company' as defined by CA 1963 s 2(1): see Chapter 2, *Formation, Registration and Conversion of Private Companies*, para **[2.054]** *ff*.

[122] However, where the trading name of a partnership does not consist of the true names of all the partners it must be registered in the Registry of Business Names, maintained by the Companies Registration Office, pursuant to the RBNA 1963.

The Companies Acts 1963–2001 impose no requirements for the formation of a company as such; instead they provide a means of registration through which a company may achieve corporate status, and lay down a number of minimum requirements for companies seeking such corporate status[123]. They also contain a number of provisions regulating the activities of companies which have been registered and have achieved corporate status.

[1.048] An examination of some of the more significant historical developments in the law of business corporations may assist in understanding the basis of the Companies Acts 1963–2001. First, brief reference will be made to a development of paramount significance to all corporations which has shaped the way corporate status may be obtained to this day, namely, the *concession theory* of corporations.

The concession theory of corporations

[1.049] The general idea of a corporation as a legal person has been identified in the Code of Hammurabbi dating back to 2,000 BC[124]; and there are indications that primitive society was regarded by its members as being made up of corporate bodies of groups of men united by the reality or the fiction of blood relationship, and that the family, clan and tribe were recognised as distinct entities of society before individuals were so regarded[125]. The importance of the *túath* ('tribe' or 'petty kingdom') and *fine* ('kin group') in early Irish law suggest that our Irish ancestors of the seventh–eighth centuries regarded society in a similar light[126]. The concept of the corporation was well known to the ancient Romans, and the writings of Savigny identify corporations of dependent towns, brotherhoods of priests, gods, temples, and brotherhoods of artisans, such as blacksmiths, bakers, and boatmen, in ancient Rome[127]. It seems that in those early days a corporation could be formed through the simple gathering together of persons with a shared interest; thus Blackstone refers to the early Roman maxim *très faciunt collegium*[128]. Corporate personality in those days was simply the legal recognition of group interests which, as a practical matter, already existed.

[1.050] All this was to change, however, with the fostering, late in the Roman Empire, of the *concession theory*[129] of corporations. The central thesis of this theory is the notion

[123] See Chapter 2, *Formation, Registration and Conversion of Private Companies*.

[124] See Henn & Alexander, *Laws of Corporations and Other Business Enterprises* (3rd edn, 1983).

[125] Sir Henry Maine, *Ancient Law: Its Connection with the Early History of Society and its Relation to Modern Ideas* (12th edn, 1930); see Williston, 'History of the Law of Business Corporations Before 1800' (1888) 2 Harv LR 105.

[126] See generally Kelly, *A Guide to Early Irish Law* (1988).

[127] Savigny, *System des Heutigen Römischen Rechts*, vol II; see generally Williston, 'History of the Law of Business Corporations Before 1800' (1888) 2 Harv LR 105.

[128] I *Commentaries* 472.

[129] There are signs of this theory in Savigny's accounts of corporations in ancient Rome: see Williston, 'History of the Law of Business Corporations Before 1800' (1888) 2 Harv LR 105 at 107, fn. 2. Its chief protagonist was Pope Innocent IV, Sinibald Fieschi, who was made Bishop of Rome in 1243. The spread of the Church's influence can have played no small part in the propagation of the concession theory in Western Europe and the British Isles. See Hessen, *In Defence of the Corporation* (1979), Chs 1 & 2; Halliss, *Corporate Personality: A Study in Jurisprudence* (1930); Henn & Alexander, *Laws of Corporations and Other Business Enterprises* (3rd edn, 1983), p 145.

that a corporation may be formed only by imperial concession or fiat. By Blackstone's time, the theory was firmly rooted in English law. He wrote: 'with us here in England the King's consent is absolutely necessary to the erection of any corporation'[130]. Although the sovereign power in Ireland is no longer vested in the Crown but in the State[131], the concession theory continues to be a feature of the Irish law of corporations, with the consequence that all corporations formed here must be created by, or in accordance with, statutes. Thus, the Constitutional right of free association[132] does not 'include the right to form bodies with corporate existence...[t]he latter is a statutory right, given by statute and controlled by statute'[133].

[1.051] Continued adherence to the concession theory of corporations requires the assent of the Sovereign or the State to the creation of a body corporate. The Sovereign or State may give this assent in any of three ways:

(a) By royal charter.

(b) By statute.

(c) By registration under the Companies Acts 1963–2001.

(a) Corporations created by royal charter

[1.052] One means of obtaining the assent of the Sovereign or State to the creation of a corporation was to obtain the grant of a royal charter. This method enjoyed some popularity in the past, and a number of corporations created by the grant of a royal charter still exist in Ireland today. The most obvious examples of these are the Law Society of Ireland – the solicitors' professional body – which was founded in 1830 and which was incorporated by royal charter in 1852[134]; the Bank of Ireland, which obtained its charter in 1783; the Royal College of Surgeons, which obtained its charter in 1785; and Trinity College, Dublin, which obtained its latest charter in 1911. The granting of a charter had the effect of creating a body corporate which was distinct from its members, enjoyed perpetual succession, could sue and be sued in its own name and had a seal[135]. The primary motivation for obtaining a charter, however, was not so much the achievement of corporate status. Rather, it was the obtaining of patronage and monopoly rights from the Crown. Thus, the procedure by which such a charter was obtained was often founded in nepotism, since it operated on the basis of representation to the Crown requesting the grant of a charter. Bartholomew Dewhigg, describing the events which led to the obtaining by the Honourable Society of King's Inns of a charter in 1792,

---

130 1 *Commentaries* p 471.

131 *Byrne v Ireland* [1972] IR 241. See Articles 28.2 and 49.1.2 of Bunreacht na hÉireann 1937.

132 See Article 40.6 of Bunreacht na hÉireann 1937.

133 *Private Motorists Provident Society Ltd v Attorney General* [1983] IR 339 at 355 (Carroll J).

134 See Hogan, *The Legal Profession in Ireland 1789–1922* (1986), the Incorporated Law Society of Ireland. Interestingly, the Honourable Society of King's Inns – the barristers' professional body – which was founded in 1539, was denied incorporation by King Henry VIII (in whose honour the society had been named) in 1542. It was finally incorporated by royal charter from King George III in 1792 – only to lose its charter in the following year; see Kenny *King's Inns and the Kingdom of Ireland* (1992) Irish Academic Press in association with the Irish Legal History Society.

135 *Sutton's Hospital case* (1612) 10 Co Rep 1.

depicted the events as 'the outcome of efforts by a minority...to extend the sphere of influence and patronage of the local governing élite in Ireland.'[136] The power of the Crown to grant a charter was subsequently curtailed by Parliament as gradually the House of Commons assumed the entire effective control of government, and the Crown's authority to grant a charter became referable to parliamentary permission[137].

[1.053] The foundation of the State in 1922 closed the avenue of incorporation by royal charter, but the prerogative to create corporations by charter was probably succeeded to by government[138]. Nevertheless, no new chartered corporations have been created in Ireland since 1922.

(b) Corporations created by statute

[1.054] A second means of obtaining the assent of the Sovereign or State to the creation of a corporation is by way of a special statute creating the corporation. A corporation may, of course, be formed by statutes other than the Companies Acts 1963–2001, and such corporations are generically referred to as statutory corporations. The principal feature of the statutory corporation is that it may be incorporated without having to observe the requirements of the Companies Acts. The statutory corporation was a popular means of conducting large-scale enterprise in the past, particularly in the realm of quasi-State services such as railways and canals[139], although it was also used as a means of enriching those who had enough influence to persuade Parliament to pass an Act. Nowadays, the requirement of special legislation for the creation of a statutory corporation renders it impractical as a means for the conduct of private business; however, it is an ideal means for the conduct of State-controlled public utilities and for bodies with special objects. Statutory corporations fall into one of two categories: State-corporations and non-State statutory corporations.

(i) State-corporations

[1.055] Many of the statutory corporations created before the foundation of the State have been dissolved and their assets and undertakings transferred to state-controlled corporations. Examples of statutory corporations established since the foundation of the State and controlled by the State[140] include the Central Bank of Ireland[141] and Radio Telefís Éireann[142]. However, corporations of this kind should be distinguished from state-controlled companies established by special statutes which authorise them to become incorporated by registration under the Companies Acts 1963-2001. Since the foundation of the State it has not been uncommon for the Oireachtas to pass enabling

---

136 Kenny, *King's Inns and the Kingdom of Ireland* (1992) Irish Academic Press in association with the Irish Legal History Society, p 240.

137 An example of the procedure involved in obtaining a charter in those days is to be found in *Re Commercial Buildings Co of Dublin* [1938] IR 477 at 480.

138 Under Articles 49.1.2 and 28.2 of Bunreacht na hÉireann 1937. See also CA 1963, s 377(4), which recognises the power of the Government to grant charters.

139 See Hessen, *In Defence of the Corporation* (1979), p 28.

140 See Goulding, 'The Juristic Basis of Irish State Enterprise' (1978) 13 Ir Jur (ns) 302.

141 Central Bank Act 1942.

142 Broadcasting Authority Act 1960.

Acts of this nature, such as the Air Navigation and Transport Act 1936, which authorised the Minister for Finance to apply for the incorporation of a registered company[143]. The result was a company (Aer Rianta Teoranta) incorporated under the Companies Acts 1908–1924, but conceived by an enabling Act of the Oireachtas. Other corporations organised in this way include the ACC Bank plc and An Post plc[144]. Although these companies are registered companies, their power to deal is often circumscribed by their establishing Acts. While these state-controlled statutory corporations share many of the features of the companies considered in this title, detailed discussion of them lies outside the scope of this work.

(ii) Non-State statutory corporations

[1.056] A second type of statutory corporation is the non-State statutory company incorporated by private persons pursuant to *special statutes* which provide a means for the incorporation of bodies having special objects such as, for example, the supply of gas[145], or the operation of a building society[146]. These special statutes bear many resemblances to the Companies Acts 1963–2001, and occasionally may even apply provisions of the Companies Acts to the corporations formed under them; however, detailed discussion of these kinds of corporations also lies outside the scope of this work.

(c) Corporations created by registration under the Companies Acts 1963–2001

[1.057] A third means of obtaining the assent of the Sovereign or State to the creation of a corporation is by way of registration in accordance with the provisions of the Companies Acts 1963–2001. This procedure, which is the means by which the private company obtains corporate status, has been referred to already[147], and is discussed in further detail later[148].

Developments in the law of business corporations since the 1700s[149]

[1.058] The facility to incorporate by registration is a convenient mechanism for the formation of corporations. It does away with the difficulties involved in the acquisition of a charter (which would probably not nowadays carry with it the incidental benefits of patronage and monopoly) or in the acquiring of a special statute. But why should the State provide such a convenient means of incorporation? Indeed, why should the State allow private enterprise to be conducted through the means of a corporation at all? To answer these questions we must consider, albeit briefly, a number of developments in the law of business corporations since the 1700s which have led to the introduction of today's system of incorporation by registration.

---

143 Air Navigation and Transport Act 1936, s 68.

144 Postal and Telecommunications Services Act 1983.

145 See the Gas Regulation Act 1982.

146 See the BSA 1989, considered at para **[1.031]**.

147 See para **[1.045]**.

148 See Chapter 2, *Formation, Registration and Conversion of Private Companies*.

149 See Gower, *Principles of Modern Company Law* (5th edn, 1992), Chs 2 and 3. For an examination of the major economic themes in the development of modern company law see Farrar, Furey and Hannigan, *Farrar's Company Law* (3rd edn, 1991), pp 7–14.

[1.059] The history of the developments in the law of companies from the 1700s to the early part of the twentieth century are sketched as follows:

(a) Joint stock companies.
(b) The Bubble Act 1720.
(c) Deed of settlement companies.
(d) The repeal of the Bubble Act 1702.
(e) The Joint Stock Companies Act 1844.
(f) The Limited Liability Act 1855.
(g) The Joint Stock Companies Act 1856.
(h) The Companies Act 1862.
(i) The Companies Act 1907.
(j) The Companies (Consolidation) Act 1908.

(a) Joint stock companies

[1.060] Although the law of business corporations can be traced back through the Middle Ages to Roman times[150], it is convenient for present purposes to skip to the decades immediately preceding 1720[151]. At that time so called *joint stock companies*, which had their roots in the medieval guilds, were flourishing in the realm of domestic trade. Unlike the medieval guilds, these companies traded on their members' behalf, each member contributing to the *joint stock* or capital of the company, and each member taking a share of the profits proportionate to the amount contributed by him. Also, by that time the members of joint stock companies, unlike the members of the medieval guilds, had, in general, long since ceased to act as traders themselves; instead, they were investors in a business enterprise. Gambling with investment in joint stock companies was endemic during the early decades of the eighteenth century.

[1.061] Where the joint stock company enjoyed corporate status (whether by obtaining a charter or through special Act of Parliament) the members of the corporation were absolutely immune from suit in respect of the company's liabilities. This was because, as a corporation, the company was a separate legal person with rights and obligations distinct from those of its members. However, the advantages of incorporation were not apparent to many members of incorporated joint stock companies. Not all of these joint stock companies enjoyed corporate status – indeed, it appears, incorporation may not even have been high on the list of priorities for many of the rash and unwary investors of that time. However, for those companies wishing to improve their reputation, and hence their marketability, the obtaining of a royal charter was perceived to be an important step in attracting investors rather than as a means of achieving immunity from suit for the company's debts. But since obtaining a royal charter was a difficult, lengthy and expensive process[152], the practice began of acquiring 'second-hand' charters from defunct companies and carrying on the new business of a joint stock company in the old

---

[150] See para **[1.049]**.

[151] For an interesting account of England's first joint-stock corporation, the Russia Company, see Griffith, 'The Russia Company – 439 Years Not Out!', (1994) 15 Co Law 105.

[152] See para **[1.052]**.

corporate name. For example, a company which proposed to lend money on the security of land in Ireland, and, later, a banking company, both in turn acquired the charter of the old Sword Blade Company which had been incorporated in 1690 to manufacture hollow or channelled sword blades[153]. Where the obtaining of a charter was impossible because of lack of finance or influence, joint stock companies carried on business as unincorporated associations in a manner not unlike the modern partnership. The many varieties of joint stock company led to confusion among investors, for they could be certain neither of whether the company had corporate status, nor, if it was incorporated, of whether it would pursue the objects set out in its charter. In this confusion, rash speculation and fraudulent deception flourished. One deception involved the invitation to the public to subscribe for shares in a 'company for carrying on an undertaking of great advantage, but nobody to know what it is'. An observer wrote:

> 'The man of genius who essayed this bold and successful inroad upon public credibility, merely stated in his prospectus that the required capital was half a million, in five thousand shares of £100 each, deposit £2 per share. Each subscriber, paying his deposit, would be entitled to £100 per annum per share. How this immense profit was to be obtained, he did not condescend to inform them at that time, but promised, that in a month full particulars should be duly announced, and a call made for the remaining £98 of the subscription. Next morning, at nine o'clock, he found that no less than one thousand shares had been subscribed for, and the deposits paid. He was thus, in five hours, the winner of £2,000. He was philosopher enough to be contended with his venture, and set off the same evening for the Continent. He was never heard of again.'[154]

(b) The Bubble Act 1720

[1.062] In 1720, a House of Commons Resolution[155] drew attention to the many joint stock companies which were falsely purporting to act as corporate bodies, and the many joint stock companies which had acquired incorporation through the acquisition of second-hand charters which were not pursuing the objects stated in the charters. The resolution described these practices as tending 'to the prejudices of the public trade and commerce of the kingdom' Parliament, responding in no half measure, promptly passed the Bubble Act 1720[156], which prohibited:

> '...all public Undertakings and Attempts tending to the common Grievance, Prejudice or Inconvenience of his Majesty's subjects, or great Numbers of them, in their Trade, Commerce, or other lawful affairs...and more particularly the acting or presuming to act as a Corporate Body or Bodies, the raising or pretending to raise transferable Stock or Stocks, the transferring or pretending to transfer or assign any Share or Shares in such Stock or Stocks, without legal Authority, either by Act of Parliament, or by Charter from the Crown...and all acting or pretending to act under any charter, formerly granted from the Crown, for particular or special Purposes therein expressed, by Persons who do or shall use or endeavour to use the same Charters, for raising a Capital Stock, or for making

---

[153] See Gower, *Principles of Modern Company Law* (5th edn, 1992), Chs 2 and 3; Pennington, *Company Law*, (6th edn, 1990), *Introduction*.

[154] MacKay, *Extraordinary Popular Delusions and the Madness of Crowds* (1841). Quotation reproduced courtesy of Litrix Reading Room (www.Litrix.com).

[155] HC Jour XIX 351.

[156] 6 Geo 1 c 18.

> Transfers or Assignments or pretended Transfers or Assignments of such Stock, not intended by such Charter to be raised or transferred...'

The result was that many existing incorporated joint stock companies were threatened with the forfeiture of their charters, and unincorporated joint stock companies could no longer pretend to be incorporated.

[1.063] One of the motivations for the passing of the Bubble Act 1720 may have been the protection of a scheme which had been put in motion by the South Sea Company (a trading company founded in 1711, with operations in South America and the Pacific) to take over most of the English National Debt, which then exceeded some £31 million[157]. The company's grandiose plan was to entice the holders of government securities to transfer them to the company in return for shares in the company. The company hoped to use these securities as a means of raising further investments to expand its trade. The Government was heavily involved with the company, and it hoped that the suppression of other joint stock companies via the Bubble Act would result in greater investment in the South Sea Company[158]. The company acquired a monopoly to conduct England's trade with Spanish colonies in the West Indies and South America and it was publicly mooted by the promoters of the company that permission to conduct such trade would be granted by Spain as part of the peace-package for ending the War of the Spanish Succession (1703–1713). Confidence in the stock was staggering and people borrowed to acquire it. Bribery and corruption were widespread. The company actively drove up the price of the stock by artificial means, blocks of stock being given by way of bribes, thereby creating an apparent demand for the stock which induced the public to buy-in heavily. Between January and June 1720 the stock rose in price from £128 to £1,050; by December 1720 it had fallen back to £128. Thousands of people were ruined, bankruptcies soared and following a public inquiry many of those whom it could be established had taken bribes were incarcerated in the Tower of London and had their estates confiscated.

The Bubble Act had a disastrous effect on investment in companies. The institution of proceedings for the forfeiture of charters against companies which were carrying on business contrary to the terms of their charters spread a wave of panic amongst investors in all companies, and the South Sea Company ultimately collapsed. The decline and collapse of the South Sea Company is but one illustration of the way in which the Bubble Act backfired. What was required was an Act which made it easier for joint stock companies to incorporate while at the same time protecting the public and the members from fraud and negligence. Instead, the Act made it more difficult for joint stock companies to assume a corporate form and contained no rules regulating the promotion and management of companies which did obtain corporate status[159]. Furthermore, what it did it did vaguely, so that the confusion which surrounded incorporated joint stock companies in the first two decades of the eighteenth century was replaced by confusion emanating from the rambling Bubble Act.

---

[157] For an interesting albeit fictional, account of the fall-out from the South Sea Company, see Robert Goddard, *Sea Change* (2000).

[158] See Pennington, *Company Law* (6th edn, 1990), 'Introduction'.

[159] Holdsworth, *History of English Law*, Vol 8, pp 219–220.

(c) Deed of settlement companies

[1.064] After the passing of the Bubble Act 1720, and until its subsequent repeal in 1825[160], it was the unincorporated joint stock company which was mainly used as a means of conducting business enterprise. The unincorporated joint stock company was a form of partnership. It was formed by a mutual covenant between the members, contained in a *deed of settlement* (which is analogous to what are now described as the *articles* in modern companies and partnerships), and consequently this species of joint stock company came to be known as the *deed of settlement company*. The more developed deed of settlement companies ingeniously employed the *trust* as a means of settling the mutual assets and undertaking of the company's members on trustees, with whom the members covenanted. The resulting company was an unincorporated association, whose management was controlled by a committee of directors, whose existence was continuous and whose property was held by trustees. The terms of the trust deed commonly provided that the trustees could sue and be sued on behalf of the company; but while the courts of equity seem to have permitted suit by the trustees[161], it was not firmly established until 1843[162] whether the courts of law would allow such action[163]. There were further doubts as to whether the shares and stock of such companies could be transferred without breaching the provisions of the Bubble Act. It was the persistence of these doubts, despite the general acceptance of the deed of settlement company (which was the favoured vehicle for the establishment of insurance companies and friendly societies), that led to the repeal of the Bubble Act 1720, 105 years after its introduction.

(d) The repeal of the Bubble Act 1720

[1.065] The repeal of the Bubble Act in 1825[164], paradoxically, did little to further the cause of the deed of settlement company. Since it was an unincorporated association[165], anyone suing it had to worry about tracking down the individual members to make them answerable, which was particularly difficult where the company had numerous members[166]. Clauses in the deed of settlement which allowed the trustees of the company to sue and be sued on behalf of the company were of doubtful effect even then because the repealing statute had provided that undertakings should be dealt with according to common law (as opposed to equity). Nevertheless, a wave of speculation and investment began again in 1834, but a great number of deed of settlement companies were formed at this time to perpetrate frauds on investors by pursuing undertakings other than those upon which investment was based. A need for regulation of joint stock companies was quickly perceived; but calls were not answered until 1844.

---

160 6 Geo 4, c 9, s 1.

161 *Metcalfe v Brian* (1810) 12 East 400.

162 *Garrard v Hardey* (1843) 5 M & G 471; *Harrison v Heathorn* (1843) 6 M & G 81.

163 Because, it seems, considerable use was made of private arbitration rather than litigation: Gower, *Principles of Modern Company Law* (5th edn, 1992), p 30.

164 6 Geo 4 c 91.

165 See para **[1.043]**.

166 See, eg, *Von Sandau v Moore* (1825) 1 Russ 441.

[1.066] Section 2 of the repealing Act did, however, contain one provision of great significance in the development of company law: it enabled the Crown to declare the extent of the members' liability upon the grant, by charter, of incorporation to a company. This provision meant that the incorporation of a company no longer rendered the members of a corporation absolutely immune from liability for the corporate debts. Indeed, it might be regarded as an early legislative instance of disregarding the separate legal identity of the company and its members. Such liability could be, at the Crown's pleasure, without limit. Limits to the liability of members for corporate debts were not to be imposed by statute for a further thirty years[167].

(e) The Joint Stock Companies Act 1844

[1.067] In 1843, William Gladstone, then president of the Board of Trade, presented the Joint Stock Companies Bill, which was to become law as the Joint Stock Companies Act 1844. The legislation was primarily introduced to provide a system whereby fraud and malpractice would be less likely to occur, and more easy to deal with if they did. Thus, it prohibited large unincorporated associations, and provided for simple incorporation by way of registration of the deed of settlement rather than by way of charter or special Act, without any form of prior authorisation from the State. Incorporation by registration under the Act was a two-stage process:

— first, the company would be registered provisionally, and would be authorised thereupon to conduct only strictly limited activities; and

— secondly, the registration would be completed upon the filing of a deed of settlement containing the provisions set out in the Act.

Companies were required to incorporate, inter alia, in order to reduce the difficulties which persons dealing with them might otherwise encounter in conducting actions against them. However, although no member of the company could be sued for company debts, each member remained personally liable to any of the company's judgment creditors who obtained leave from the courts to levy execution on the private property of the members. This Act also established the office of the Registrar of Companies, which survives to this day.

(f) The Limited Liability Act 1855

[1.068] There had been much debate[168] around the time the Joint Stock Companies Act 1844 was introduced concerning *limited liability* for the members of joint stock companies. The concept of the limited partnership or *société en commandite* had been popular on the continent for some time, and although legislation permitting such associations had been introduced in Ireland in 1781[169], they never really took off in either Ireland or England. In the 1840s it was argued that the introduction of limited liability for the members of joint stock companies would help to revitalise business. A number of companies at this time were seeking incorporation under French and American laws to achieve limited liability for their members. Among the arguments in favour of limited

---

[167] See para **[1.069]**

[168] See Gower, *Principles of Modern Company Law* (5th edn, 1992), pp 41–45 for a detailed account.

[169] Irish Anonymous Partnership Act 1871.

liability were that it would enable small capital to be turned to profitable employment and would encourage work on projects such as railways, canals, and docks; it prevented prudent men from becoming members of unincorporated companies which were still popular among the rash and reckless; and it was in keeping with the idea of free trade which was then in vogue[170]. Despite these arguments however, a Royal Commission, set up to review the prospects of limited liability, objected to its introduction in 1854[171].

[1.069] The privilege of limited liability for the members of a company incorporated under the Joint Stock Companies Act 1844 was finally granted by the Limited Liability Act 1855. Even if it had not been introduced by statute, the principle would probably have developed as a matter of contract[172]. In *Hallett v Dowdall*[173], the Court of Exchequer upheld the validity of a clause in a deed of settlement which purported to create limited liability for the members of a joint stock company, and held that the clause could be binding on third parties with express notice of it. The widespread use and acceptance of such clauses may have accounted for a change in opinion in favour of limited liability[174]. The Limited Liability Act 1855 provided that the liability of the members of a company would be limited to the amount, if any, unpaid on shares held by them. Limited liability was not lightly granted by Parliament, and certain conditions were imposed upon this legislative gift, such as the requirements that the company should have at least 25 members who between them held at least 75% of the nominal value[175] of the company, each member having paid up at least 20% of the nominal value of his shares; that the word 'limited' be included in the company's name; and that the deed of settlement itself provided that the liability of the members should be limited.

(g) The Joint Stock Companies Act 1856

[1.070] The Joint Stock Companies Act 1844 and the Limited Liability Act 1855 were both repealed and replaced by a single Act, the Joint Stock Companies Act 1856. This new Act did away with the two-stage registration process and required every company registering under the Act to simply present a memorandum and articles of association in the same form as required today. Only seven persons were required to act as signatories to a memorandum of association. Model articles of association were set out in the schedule to the Act. As Gower[176] points out, the provisions of the Act mark the heyday of *laissez faire*, allowing both incorporation and limited liability for the members of joint stock companies, without imposing the restraints contained in the Act of 1855. The only real safeguards were that the word 'limited' be used in the name of the company, and that the directors would incur personal liability if they paid a dividend knowing that the company was insolvent. The Joint Stock Companies Act 1856 is the forerunner of our

---

170 See Farrar, Furey and Hannigan, *Farrar's Company Law* (3rd edn, 1991), p 20.

171 1854 BPP Vol XXVII.

172 Maitland, *Collected Papers* (1911) Fisher (ed), Vol III, 'Trust and Corporation', p 392. See Farrar, Furey and Hannigan, *Farrar's Company Law* (3rd edn, 1991), p 21.

173 *Hallett v Dowdall* (1852) 21 LJ QB 98.

174 See Farrar, Furey and Hannigan, *Farrar's Company Law* (3rd edn, 1991), p 82.

175 The total nominal values of the shares which the company was authorised to issue by its deed of settlement.

176 Gower, *Principles of Modern Company Law* (5th edn, 1992), p 46.

modern Companies Acts, containing most of the primary concepts which have shaped our company law today.

(h) The Companies Act 1862

[1.071] Subsequent developments in the history of company law belong to modern company law, and may be dealt with more briefly. The first piece of legislation to carry the principles embodied in the Joint Stock Companies Act 1856 through to our modern companies' legislation was also the first in a long line of 'Companies Acts', namely the Companies Act 1862. This Act consolidated all previous Joint Stock Companies Acts, giving rise to the 'first great consolidation Act concerning companies [which] was a masterpiece of draughtsmanship and arrangement and, apart therefrom, introduced a number of amendments'.[177] The amendments included the introduction of companies limited by guarantee and unlimited companies, as well as detailed provisions on the winding up of registered companies.

(i) The Companies Act 1907

[1.072] The Companies Act 1907 was the first Companies Act that introduced the private company[178]. Under the heading of 'Miscellaneous', the Companies Act 1907, s 37(1) accorded a statutory definition to the private company providing:

> 'For the purposes of the Act the expression "private company" means a company which by its articles—
>
> (a) restricts the right to transfer its shares; and
>
> (b) limits the number of its members (exclusive of persons who are in the employment of the company) to fifty; and
>
> (c) prohibits any invitation to the public to subscribe for any shares or debentures of the company.'

The statutory definition of the private company has changed little over the years, the only differences being that today, ex-employees are also discounted in determining the number of members in the company, and, secondly, all private companies must have a share capital.

(j) The Companies (Consolidation) Act 1908

[1.073] The Companies (Consolidation) Act 1908 was a consolidating Act of major significance to Ireland in that it was the last major piece of company legislation which we have had in common with English law. As Keane has observed, this Act formed the bedrock of company law for Irish lawyers for over half a century. The definition afforded to private companies by s 37 of the Companies Act 1907 was reproduced by the Companies (Consolidation) Act 1908, s 121(1).

[1.074] From the foregoing analysis it may be seen that today's registered company is a response to a number of significant developments in the period 1700–1908. In particular, it is accorded corporate personality to provide, inter alia, a means by which

[177] See Schmitthoff (ed), *Palmer's Company Law*, (24th edn, 1987), para 2–09.

[178] Strongly instrumental in the introduction of private companies was Sir Francis Beaufort Palmer. See generally Ireland, *The Triumph of the Company Legal Form, 1856–1914*, in Adams (ed), *Essays for Clive Schmitthoff*, (1983).

actions against large associations of undertakings may conveniently be pursued. It was also observed that the concept of limited liability was introduced only in the last century[179], and that it is not necessarily an incident of corporate personality[180]. Furthermore, the registered company is accorded corporate status through the medium of the Companies Acts because corporate personality is a concession which may be granted only by the State[181].

It remains now to examine how the registered company has been treated in Ireland since the foundation of the State in 1922.

[C] AN OVERVIEW OF IRISH COMPANY LAW

Irish Company Law Statutes from Independence to 1963[182]

[1.075] The first step towards company law reform taken by the Irish government after independence was the establishment of a committee to investigate the law and procedure relating to bankruptcy and the winding up of companies. This committee reported in 1927 but the government of the day, and succeeding governments, took no steps to implement its recommendations. In particular, no legislation equivalent to the English 1929 and 1948 Companies Acts was passed in Ireland in this period.

[1.076] The most important committee established during this period was the Cox Committee on Company Law Reform, established in 1951[183]. This committee reported in 1958. The secretary of the committee was Mr Justice John Kenny whose judicial career and influence on Irish company law has been profound. Some of the issues considered by the Cox Committee were the following:

— *Company accounts*: It was recommended that the essential difference between the public and private company be recognised when implementing any new provisions regarding disclosure of accounts. In particular, the Committee recommended, and the CA 1963 later provided, that the exemption from filing accounts in the case of private companies should continue. Any difficulties to creditors were considered to be offset by the enormous inconvenience which would otherwise be caused to small businesses incorporated as private companies[184].

— *Winding-up provisions*: The Committee made two recommendations, neither of which was implemented by the legislature. The first concerned the creation of a new office, that of Official Receiver, a position analogous to that of the Official Assignee in Bankruptcy. The second recommendation was that debts owed to

---

179 See para **[1.069]**.

180 See generally, Chapter 4, *Incorporation and its Consequences*.

181 See paras **[1.057]–[1.058]**.

182 See Keane, *Company Law* (3rd edn, 2000), ch 2.

183 *Report of the Company Law Reform Committee*, (1958).

184 It is interesting to note that the *Task Force Report on Small Business* which reported in March of 1994 recommended (pp 133 and 134) the abolition of the requirement that certain small companies must have their accounts audited. This change was finally introduced into Irish law by the Companies (Amendment) (No 2) Act 1999.

the Revenue Commissioners ought *not* to have priority over debts owed by the company to other unsecured creditors. Again this was not accepted nor implemented by the legislature.

— *Corporate capacity*: The Committee sought to obviate the effects of the doctrine of *ultra vires*. The doctrine provides that transactions not authorised by a company's objects clause are beyond the capacity of a company and are unenforceable and void, to the obvious detriment of outsiders unaware of the lack of corporate capacity. The Committee's suggestion that the effects of the doctrine be curtailed by extending protection to *bona fide* outsiders was in fact accepted by the legislature in CA 1963[185].

The Committee also reported on many other aspects of Irish company law, and although some were not implemented immediately by the CA 1963, much of what was recommended eventually became law under the subsequent Acts.

The Companies Acts 1963–2001

[1.077] It is the Companies Acts 1963–2001 that are the concern of this work. In all there are presently ten Companies Acts. These Acts are now reviewed briefly and the main reasons for their enactment identified.

(a) The Companies Act 1963

[1.078] The CA 1963 remains the main Companies Act in Ireland today, albeit an ever increasingly tattered and piecemeal statement of the law. Since 1977, CA 1963 has continually been amended and although it contains some 399 sections, the other nine Companies Acts, together, contain some 595 sections of legislation. The need for a consolidating Act is now greater than ever in that the nine amending Acts and numerous statutory instruments have substantially changed CA 1963.

(b) The Companies (Amendment) Act 1977

[1.079] The Companies (Amendment) Act 1977 was designed to simplify certain activities connected with Stock Exchange transactions by companies. This introduced more streamlined procedures in relation to the transfer of shares in public companies.

(c) The Companies (Amendment) Act 1982

[1.080] The Companies (Amendment) Act 1982 may best be considered as a work of domestic housekeeping. This Act was concerned with a wide variety of matters: the registration of companies; striking inactive companies off the register of companies; the exception of certain professional partnerships from the numerical constraints on membership imposed by the CA 1963 on partnerships generally; and a number of other miscellaneous matters.

(d) The Companies (Amendment) Act 1983[186]

[1.081] The Companies (Amendment) Act 1983 owes its introduction not to any particularly conscientious domestic legislative concern, but rather to Ireland's membership of the European Union ('EU'). This Act gave effect to the Second EU

---

185 See generally, Chapter 7, *Corporate Contracts: Capacity and Authority*, para **[7.077]** *ff*.

186 See generally, Forde, 'The Companies (Amendment) Act 1983' (1983) 18 Ir Jur (ns) 289.

Directive on Company Law, the main concern of which was the level of capitalisation of public companies[187]. Whilst the Act has prominence in this and other texts on Irish company law many of its provisions are solely applicable to public limited companies. It is the 1983 Act which introduced the term 'public limited company' or 'PLC' and imposed certain basic restrictions on both the formation and continuance of public companies.

(e) The Companies (Amendment) Act 1986

[1.082] Again, the Companies (Amendment) Act 1986 owes its existence more to EU harmonisation than it does to national creativity. The 1986 Act gives effect to the Fourth EU Directive on Company Law which concerns annual accounts. One consequence of the 1986 Act was to eschew the philosophy of the Cox Committee which considered it too onerous that *all* companies, even small private companies, should publish accounts. This Act provides that both public and private companies must publish accounts. However, private companies were considered a special category and were broken down into three sizes: small, medium and large, each with progressive disclosure requirements. Corporate accounts are considered later in both the context of the private company[188] and the public company[189]. The Fourth EU Directive on Company Law is noted later in this chapter[190].

(f) The Companies (Amendment) Act 1990

[1.083] The Companies (Amendment) Act 1990 ('C(A)A 1990') was most definitely a domestically motivated enactment, albeit prompted by middle-eastern influences[191], passed by a legislature which feared that, were it not brought into law, dire economic consequences would befall Ireland's largest beef company, the Goodman Group. When fear turned to an immediate danger that the group might face liquidation, it was decided to hive off what had been a part of the Companies Bill 1987[192] and to enact it as C(A)A 1990.

[1.084] The essence of C(A)A 1990 is that companies which are in financial difficulties can be given a chance to have their affairs reorganised by an individual, termed an *examiner*, whose principal task is to report to the court on the company's prospects of survival. During the period of the examinership, the company is under the protection of the court and its creditors cannot enforce their claims against the company. Often the examiner's proposals will involve compromising some or all of the creditors' claims against the company. The C(A)A 1990 gives the court a discretion to confirm such proposals. The desired result is that through the reduction of creditors' claims, the company will be given an opportunity to continue to trade, hopefully back to full financial health.

---

187 See para **[1.094]** *ff.*

188 See Chapter 13, *Accounts and Auditors.*

189 See Chapter 28, *Public Companies in Context*, para **[28.071]** *ff.*

190 See para **[1.096]**.

191 See generally, McCormack, *The New Companies Legislation* (1991), p 185 *ff.* See also Chapter 23, *Examinerships.*

192 This was previously Part IX of the Companies (No 2) Bill 1990.

(g) The Companies Act 1990

[1.085] The Companies Act 1990 also owes its existence to domestic concerns that although the CA 1963 had proved to be a successful piece of legislation it needed a radical overhaul. Circumstances and business practices had so changed that it was considered necessary that the Oireachtas should take cognisance of these developments and enact a statute to address such commercial changes.

[1.086] The Companies Act 1990 has 262 sections and is comprised of 13 parts[193]. That it is a substantial piece of legislation in its own right is seen by its title, as it is the first Act since the CA 1963 not to use the label 'Amendment', and it radically amended Irish company law. The main provisions of the 1990 Act were as follows:

- Part II replaced the provisions of CA 1963 which govern the investigation of companies through the appointment of an *inspector*. These provisions have been tested by a number of *cause célèbre* cases, such as the so-called Telecom Affair, considered later[194].
- Part III imposed restrictions on corporate transactions with directors. The measures provided in Part III proved in practice to be one of the most far-reaching series of provisions contained in the Act. Of considerable importance is the application of these provisions to *shadow directors*.
- Part IV imposed requirements in respect of the disclosure of certain persons' interests in shares held in companies.
- Part V introduced into Irish company law the concept of *insider dealing*, which had been part of company law in England for many years. In brief terms, Part V criminalises and provides civil redress where certain persons make use of information which they have acquired because of their intimate connection with a public company to make a profit[195].
- Part VI amended some of the provisions of CA 1963 which concern the winding up of companies. In particular, the statutory declaration as to the solvency of a company in a members' voluntary winding up was substantially bolstered, having the effect of inevitably reducing the number of members' voluntary windings up which occur where the company is in fact *not solvent*[196].
- Part VII concerns the imposition of *restrictions* and *disqualifications* on persons acting as directors of a company, principally where a company becomes insolvent and goes into liquidation. It has been suggested that the measures are intended to counteract the so-called 'phoenix syndrome' whereby a company which is wound up is reincarnated by virtue of the involvement in a later company of persons who were directors or shadow directors of the wound-up company[197].

---

193 See generally, McCormack, *The New Companies Legislation*, (1991), p 185 *ff*.

194 See generally Chapter 14, *Investigations and Inspectors*.

195 See Chapter 28, *Public Companies in Context* at para **[28.107]**.

196 See Chapter 25, *Winding Up Companies* and Chapter 27, *Realisation and Distribution of Assets in a Winding Up*.

197 See Chapter 8, *Corporate Governance: Management by the Directors*.

- Part VIII revamped the law on *receivers* and imposed a number of restrictions on both their appointment and their powers[198].
- Part IX amended C(A)A 1990 relating to the placing of companies under the protection of the court.

(h) The Companies (Amendment) Act 1999

[1.087] The Companies (Amendment) Act 1999 is a short, mono-purpose Act of seven sections and one schedule. It was enacted to permit stabilisation activity in relation to the issue or sale of securities and was considered to be needed in the context of the floatation of what was Bord Telecom (subsequently Eircom plc).

(i) The Companies (Amendment) (No 2) Act 1999

[1.088] In 1994 the then Minister for Enterprise and Employment, Mr Ruairí Quinn, established on an ad hoc basis a company law review group with a brief of reviewing a number of specific issues. The group published its report in February 1995 but for many years its recommendations gathered dust[199]. It was not until the passing of the C(A)(No 2)A 1999 that effect was eventually given to most of the recommendations under two particular headings – those on examinership and those on an exemption from audit for small companies[200]. In addition, as a result of great political concern over the use of Irish companies by unscrupulous foreign concerns, C(A)(No 2)A 1999 also sounded the death-knell for the so-called *Irish registered non-resident company* or IRNR[201]. The C(A)(No 2)A 1999 is a substantial piece of legislation, running to 54 sections and two schedules.

(j) The Company Law Enforcement Act 2001

[1.089] The Company Law Enforcement Act 2001 ('CLEA 2001') is a very substantial piece of legislation, running to 114 sections and one schedule. The CLEA 2001 arose directly from the recommendations of the *Working Group on Company Law Compliance and Enforcement*, chaired by Michael McDowell SC (the '*McDowell Group Report*'). This working group was established in September 1998 by the Tanaiste and Minister for Enterprise, Trade and Employment, Mary Harney. Its establishment was in response to a growing concern that companies were being abused by the unscrupulous and that compliance with the requirements in the Companies Acts, particularly relating to the filing of documents, was unacceptably low[202]. One of the most significant provisions in CLEA 2001 is the creation of the Office of the Director of Corporate Enforcement. Other major changes introduced included: changes to the law relating to investigations; changes to the law relating to the restriction and disqualification of directors; and changes to the law on winding up.

---

[198] See Chapter 22, *Corporate Borrowing: Receivers*.

[199] See Courtney, *Company Law Review 1995*, (1996), p 1–13.

[200] See further Chapter 23, *Examinerships* and Chapter 13, *Accounts and Auditors*, respectively.

[201] See Chapter 2, *Formation, Registration and Conversion of Private Companies*, para **[2.052]**.

[202] See, generally, Chapter 12, *Company Law Compliance and Enforcement*.

(k) The Statutory Company Law Review Group

[1.090] One of the recommendations of the *McDowell Group Report* was the establishment on a statutory basis of a Company Law Review Group. The purpose of this was to get serious about company law reform: by establishing a statutory group to review company law and charged with the responsibility for producing a report after every two-year work programme, the State committed itself to achieving a state-of-the-art company law code for Ireland. In anticipation of CLEA 2001 the review group was established on an ad hoc basis in February 2000. Sections 67–71 of CLEA 2001 established the Company Law Review Group on a statutory basis. Its first report was delivered to the Tanaiste and Minister for Enterprise Trade and Employment on 31 December 2001, and published on 28 February 2002.

The European Community dimension to the development of Irish company law[203]

[1.091] Since Ireland's accession to the European Union in 1973, company law in Ireland has been reformed as part of the overall harmonisation of the company law of all Member States. Community law has four major sources:

- the Treaty of Rome;
- regulations of the Council of Ministers;
- directives of the Council; and
- case law of the European Court of Justice.

Harmonisation in general is addressed by Article 100 of the Treaty of Rome, and Article 54(3) is specifically concerned with the harmonisation of company law in Member States[204]. Harmonisation is achieved by *directives* passed by the European Council which must be implemented by the domestic national law of each Member State. Domestic implementation of EU directives is usually achieved by ministerial regulations, in the form of statutory instruments.

[1.092] In addition, the European Council has taken on the task of the harmonisation of company law in EU Member States, through the adoption of certain Council regulations. Council regulations have direct effect and do not need to be transcribed into domestic law. The result of these regulations and directives is the ad hoc and piecemeal reform of Irish company law[205].

(a) First Directive – disclosure, validity and nullity[206]

[1.093] The First EU Directive on Company Law, adopted on 9 March 1968, has been implemented in Ireland by the European Communities (Companies) Regulations 1973 (SI 1973/163), and is discussed in Chapter 7[207]. The underlying rationales are threefold.

---

[203] See generally, Keane, *Company Law* (3rd edn, 2000), ch 3, and McMahon & Murphy, *European Community Law in Ireland* (1987).

[204] See, generally, Looijestijn and O'Keeffe, 'Harmonisation of Company Law in an Expanding European Union' (2002) 9 CLP 9.

[205] For a comprehensive analysis of all directives and conventions of the EC affecting company law, see generally, Myles, *EEC Law Brief*, Volume 2.

[206] (68/151/EEC) OJ Special Edition 1968(1), pp 41–45.

[207] See Chapter 7, *Corporate Contracts: Capacity and Authority*.

The first is the protection of persons who deal with a company which is not properly registered and is consequently a nullity. Second is the protection of persons who deal with a company unaware that the company does not have the capacity to enter the transaction in question. Third is the protection of persons who enter into transactions with officers who do not have the requisite authority. Since by C(A)A 1983, s 5(4)[208] the certificate of incorporation of a company is conclusive evidence that the requirements of registration have been complied with, it was considered unnecessary to amend the law to address the question of nullity. Accordingly, the European Communities (Companies) Regulations 1973 only considered the questions of disclosure, capacity and authority (validity).

***(b) Second Directive – capital requirements of PLCs*[209]**

[1.094] The Second EU Directive on Company Law, adopted on 13 December 1976, has been implemented in Ireland by C(A)A 1983, which Act created the *public limited company*, or 'PLC' and provided that it must meet certain capital requirements[210].

***(c) Third Directive – national mergers of PLCs*[211]**

[1.095] The Third EU Directive on Company Law, adopted on 9 October 1978, has been implemented in Ireland by the European Community (Mergers and Divisions of Companies) Regulations 1987 (SI 1987/137). The directive is concerned with the merger of PLCs within Member States, as opposed to between Member States, a topic which is addressed by the draft Tenth Directive on intra-Member State mergers.

***(d) Fourth Directive – annual corporate accounts*[212]**

[1.096] The Fourth EU Directive on Company Law, adopted on 25 July 1978 was implemented in Ireland by the Companies (Amendment) Act 1986[213]. The directive imposes varying disclosure requirements on most companies. Now, in addition to an annual return, accounts must also be filed with the CRO. The classification of a company as being either a PLC or a large, medium or small-sized private company, dictates what is required to be delivered to the CRO. It is understood that the Fourth Directive is being revisited with a view to modernisation.

(e) Fifth Directive – employee participation

[1.097] The Fifth EU Directive on Company Law was first promulgated on 9 October 1972, but has not been implemented in Ireland. The directive, which is aimed at PLCs, provides that regulations should be introduced which oblige PLCs to have either a two-tier management structure (management and supervisory) or a one-tier management structure (administrative organ). It is intended that the result will be that employees will become more active in moulding the direction of their company, by being privy to its

[208] The conclusiveness of the certificate of incorporation was previously provided for in CA 1963, s 19. See generally, Chapter 4, *Incorporation and its Consequences*, para **[4.004]** *ff*.

[209] (77/91/EEC) 20 OJ, L 26, 31 January 1977, pp 1–13.

[210] See Chapter 28, *Public Companies in Context*, para **[28.038]**.

[211] (78/855/EEC) 21 OJ, L 295, 20 October 1978, pp 36–43.

[212] (78/660/EEC) 21 OJ L 22, 14 August 1978, pp 11–31.

[213] See Chapter 13, *Accounts and Auditors*.

management decisions. It is perhaps because such a concept is foreign to the legal and, more importantly, socio-economic structures of many Member States, that this directive has not been implemented.

***(f) Sixth Directive – division of PLCs*[214]**

[1.098] The Sixth EU Directive on Company Law, adopted on 17 December 1982, has been implemented in Ireland by the European Community (Mergers and Divisions of Companies) Regulations 1987, considered above[215].

***(g) Seventh Directive – corporate consolidated accounts*[216]**

[1.099] The Seventh EU Directive on Company Law, adopted on 13 June 1983, has been implemented by the European Communities (Companies: Group Accounts) Regulations, SI 1992/201. It is concerned with the availability of information to the public on the finances of companies and the harmonisation of national legislation on the consolidated accounts of company groups. The regulations provide that all companies which have subsidiary undertakings must prepare group accounts. In this regard, 'subsidiary undertakings' are defined. The format and content of accounts and reports are also set out in the regulations[217]. It is understood that the Seventh Directive is being revisited with a view to modernisation.

***(h) Eight Directive – corporate auditors*[218]**

[1.100] The Eighth EU Directive on Company Law deals with the professional integrity, independence and qualifications of corporate auditors. The focus is upon the harmonisation of the qualifications of auditors, so that in Member States there will be a basic minimum standard for *approved persons* who can be auditors. The substance of this directive has now been implemented into Irish law by CA 1990[219].

(i) Ninth (draft) Directive – groups with a PLC-member

[1.101] The Ninth EU Directive on Company Law is a draft directive and as such has not been implemented into Irish law. Its intention is to introduce a harmonised legal framework within which corporate groups can effectively be managed and outsiders' interests protected.

(j) Tenth (draft) Directive – intra-Member State PLC mergers

[1.102] The Tenth EU Directive on Company Law is a draft directive. Although its concern is similar to that of the third directive this draft directive is concerned with mergers between PLCs from different Member States.

---

214 (82/891/EEC) 25 OJ, L 378 31 December 1982, pp 47–54.

215 See para **[1.095]**.

216 (83/349/EEC) 26 OJ, L 193, 18 July 1983, pp 1–17.

217 See generally, Chapter 13, *Accounts and Auditors*.

218 (84/253/EEC) 27 OJ, L 126, 12 May 1984, pp 20–26.

219 See Chapter 13, *Accounts and Auditors*.

(k) Eleventh Directive – disclosure by branches[220]

[1.103] The Eleventh EU Directive on Company Law has been implemented into Irish law by the European Communities (Branch Disclosures) Regulations 1993[221]. Its objective is to facilitate the right to establishment contained in the Treaty of Rome by enabling companies to establish branches in other Member States. This directive has limited application to the vast majority of Irish companies.

(l) Twelfth Directive – single-member private companies[222]

[1.104] The Twelfth EU Directive on Company Law had perhaps the greatest potential impact on Irish company law. It was adopted on 21 December 1989 and was implemented by the European Communities (Single-Member Private Limited Companies) Regulations 1994[223]. The regulations were signed by the Minister for Enterprise, Trade and Employment on 8 September 1994 and took effect from 1 October 1994. The single-member private company is considered below[224].

(m) Thirteenth (draft) Directive – takeovers

[1.105] The Thirteenth EU Directive on Company Law (draft) was principally concerned with PLCs which become involved in takeovers. When the European Parliament rejected the draft Fifth Directive on Takeover Bids in July 2001, the European Commission established a High Level Group on Company Law Experts in Issues Related to Takeover Bids. The purpose of that Group was to provide advice on issues related to pan-European rules for takeover bids and, thereafter, on key priorities for modernising company law[225].

(n) European Economic Interest Groupings

[1.106] European Economic Interest Groupings ('EEIGs') are associations in contemplation of commerce which involve an aggregate of sole traders, partnerships or bodies corporate, at least one being from a *different* Member State to the others, with a view to pooling knowledge and resources in areas where they have a common interest[226]. This continental creature appears to have been conceived from the spirited passion of European Union. Such is evidenced by the fact that the primary intention of EEIGs is not to generate an economic profit, but rather to enhance the marketing of products and the stimulation of research and development. It should be noted that the making of profit is not prohibited. EEIGs are now capable of being formed in Ireland by virtue of the European Community (European Economic Interest Grouping) Regulations 1989[227]. As

---

220 32 OJ 1989, L 395, 30 December 1989.

221 SI 1993/395. See Chapter 13, *Accounts and Auditors* at para **[13.154]**. The Companies (Forms) Order 1994 (SI 1994/100) prescribes the forms to be used for the return of information under CA 1963, Part XI and the Branch Disclosures Regulations 1993.

222 (89/667/EEC) 32 OJ 1989, L 395/40, 30 December 1989. See generally, MacCann, 'Company Law Reform: One Man Companies' (1990) ILT 166.

223 SI 1994/275.

224 See para **[1.119]** *ff.*

225 See the *Report of the High Level Group of Company Law Experts on Issues Related to Takeover Bids*, 10 January 2002, chaired by Jaap Winter.

226 See Keane, *Company Law* (3rd edn, 2000), para 3.23.

227 SI 1989/191.

at 31 December 2001, eight EEIGs had been registered in Ireland[228]. Although similar in many respects to our own partnership, unlike a partnership, once formed it becomes a body corporate, possessing many of the usual traits of such entities. The constitution of an EEIG is quite similar to that of a registered company in that its members are bound by its constitutional documentation which takes the form of a contract between the parties who come together.

(o) The European Company Statute

[1.107] Terms for the creation of a European public limited liability company or *Societas Europaea* ('SE') were finally agreed by Member States on 8 October 2001, with the passing of the EU Council Regulation on the Statute for a European Company (SE)[229]. In relative terms, the SE is likely to be of very limited interest to the vast majority of Irish corporators. In the first place, the SE is a variant of the PLC – a type of company that, as has been noted earlier, is numerically scarce[230] even if they do generate and hold the lion's share of Ireland's wealth[231]. In the second place, the regulation is aimed at facilitating companies whose businesses are 'not limited to satisfying purely local needs.'[232] Accordingly, to form an SE two or more PLCs may merge provided that at least two of them are governed by the law of different Member States[233]; or public and private limited companies may promote the formation of an SE provided, once again, that at least of two of them are governed by the law of a different Member State[234] or, alternatively, a PLC may be transformed into an SE if for at least two years it has had a subsidiary company that has been governed by the law of another Member State. Finally, if the foregoing were not in themselves sufficient reason to make the likelihood of the participation of Irish registered companies as SEs a rarity, by virtue of a supplemental Council Directive[235], information and consultation procedures with employees at trans-national level are mandatory and if and when participation rights exist within one or more companies establishing an SE, they are preserved through their transfer to an SE. The Council Regulation on the SE is binding in its entirety, has direct effect and comes into force on 8 October 2004[236].

---

228 *Companies Report 2001*, p 73.

229 Council Regulation (EC) No 2157/2001 of 8 October 2001 on the Statute for a European Company (SE).

230 As at 31 December 2001 there were 914 PLCs registered in Ireland: *Companies Report 2001*, p 73.

231 It may be noted, however, that public and private companies (whether limited by shares or by guarantee and having a share capital) may, in certain conditions, promote the formation of a holding SE: Council Regulation (EC) No 2157/2001, art 2(2).

232 Council Regulation (EC) No 2157/2001, Recital (2).

233 Council Regulation (EC) No 2157/2001, art 2(1).

234 Council Regulation (EC) No 2157/2001, art 2(2).

235 Council Directive 2001/86/EC of 8 October 2001 supplementing the Statute for a European company with regard to the involvement of employees.

236 Council Directive 2001/86/EC, art 79.

(p) The EU Insolvency Regulations

[1.108] The draft Convention on Bankruptcy, Winding-up, Arrangements, Compositions and Similar Proceedings[237] was superseded by the EU Council Regulation on Insolvency Proceedings[238]. Being a Council Regulation this applies directly, but incidental and optional matters will be implemented into domestic law, most likely by regulation. The primary effect of this regulation is the recognition of other Member States' insolvency proceedings and liquidators across the EU. These regulations are considered further in Chapter 26[239].

[D] THE PRIVATE COMPANY AND PUBLIC COMPANY

[1.109] The socio-legal relations underlying many private companies are often vastly different from those that prevail in public companies. Notwithstanding this, it is the one body of law contained in the Companies Acts 1963–2001 that governs the legal structure of all companies[240].

[1.110] Although not all public companies will be public limited companies, it is the *public limited company* ('PLC') – and more particularly, the *listed* PLC – that provides the greatest contrast with the private company[241]. The PLC is a company that is, by definition, *public*, in that its membership is largely comprised of the investing public. PLCs are widely rooted companies, in the sense that they will generally have many members who are often unrelated to each other. The association of the members in a listed PLC will usually be the result of their subscription to a prospectus[242] or, alternatively, the result of their purchasing shares on the Stock Exchange. It usually follows that where the *members* of the company are so widely dispersed they will be divorced from the *management* of the company. So, when the members meet in *general meeting* and elect the directors the election will usually be carried on the basis of the professionalism of those put forward for such positions. The result is a genuine separation of powers between the members and the directors. The general body of members does not usually have a direct say in the day-to-day management of the company, this task being left to the directors. There are surprisingly few PLCs registered in Ireland[243].

[1.111] In stark contrast are the many thousands of *private companies* that make up the backbone of Irish commercial life. While it has a number of manifestations[244] the typical

---

[237] See Myer, Co Law – Bankruptcy Convention.

[238] Council Regulation (EC) No 1346/2000 of 29 May 2000.

[239] See para **[26.055]** *ff.*

[240] See Chapter 28, *Public Companies in Context*, where the public company and PLC are treated and the essential differences between them and the private company are considered.

[241] See para **[1.133]** to **[1.135]** and Chapter 28, *Public Companies in Context.*

[242] A 'prospectus' is a document which invites the public to subscribe for shares in a new venture so as to give the promoters sufficient capital to launch the company: see Chapter 28, *Public Companies in Context*, para **[28.016]**.

[243] See para **[1.134]**.

[244] See para **[1.116]** for the *types* of private company and **[1.118]** *ff*, for the *forms* which the private company may take.

private company found in Ireland will not have the features described above. The *members* of a private company will be frequently either the directors of the company or they will be personally acquainted with the directors. They will often have decided to join the company because of personal connections. The *separation of powers* in many private companies will be frequently blurred because of the tendency for the members and the directors to be the same persons. As we shall see later, this feature of the private company has given rise to the issue of the 'duality of roles'[245] which arises where the same people are obliged to carry out tasks in different capacities. This difference between private and public limited companies is even more stark when one considers that the single-member private limited company has, by definition, only one member.

[1.112] It is important at the outset to distinguish true private companies from those which are merely subsidiaries of public limited companies[246]. Such private companies are controlled by a PLC which will typically appoint the private company's directors. Often, these private companies are in effect, puppets, that are utilised to permit part of the PLC's operation to be the subject of a more favourable statutory regime. A common reason for PLCs to avail of private companies is to avoid full financial disclosure under the Companies (Amendment) Act 1986[247].

Concessions to the private company

[1.113] Ever since their creation by the Companies Act 1907 the legislature has made certain concessions to private companies. Today's concessions include: only one member is required to form a private company whereas seven are required in the case of public companies; private companies do not need to file a statement *in lieu* of a prospectus; a private company does not need to obtain a trading certificate before commencing business; small and medium sized private companies are not required to file full accounts with the CRO; and there is no minimum capitalisation requirement as in the case of public limited companies.

The private company defined

[1.114] Although the vast majority of companies formed and registered under the Companies Acts 1963–2001 are *private companies*, 'the company' envisaged by those Acts seems to be the *public company.* Ironically, by according the private company with a specific definition, CA 1963, s 33(1) presupposes that the mean or average company is the public company of which the private company is but a peculiar variation[248].

A company's internal affairs are governed by its articles of association. Part I of Table A of the First Schedule to CA 1963 sets out the model articles of association for public companies limited by shares. Notwithstanding that the vast majority of companies registered in Ireland are private companies, Part II of Table A *applies* Part I, with a few modifications, to private companies limited by shares[249]. Although there is little legal

---

[245] See Chapter 8, *Corporate Governance: Management by the Directors*, para **[8.001]**.

[246] See Schmitthoff, *Palmer's Company Law* (24th edn, 1987), p 4–06.

[247] See Chapter 13, *Accounts and Auditors.*

[248] Compare the position in the UK by the Companies Act 1985, s 1(3) (UK).

[249] See Chapter 3, *Private Constitutional Documentation*, para **[3.050]**.

significance attaching to this, such provisions indicate that the private company originated as a legislative afterthought.

[1.115] Section 33(1) of CA 1963 defines a private company as a company which *has a share capital* and which by its articles of association:

— restricts the right to transfer its shares; and

— limits the number of its members to fifty[250], not including persons who are in the employment of the company and persons who, having been formerly in the employment of the company, were, while in that employment, and have continued after the determination of that employment to be members of the company; and

— prohibits any invitation to the public to subscribe for any shares or debentures of the company.

CA 1963, Sch 1, Table A, Part II, model reg 2 contains these restrictions.

To be a private company, a company must have a *share capital*[251]. Accordingly, *companies limited by guarantee* which do not have a share capital are not private companies. Practitioners most frequently encounter companies without a share capital as *management companies* in large shopping centres or apartment complexes. Where the membership of a company exceeds fifty, it cannot by definition be a private company. Where circumstances require a non-trading company's membership to exceed fifty it is usual to incorporate a public company limited by guarantee without a share capital[252]. Where two or more persons hold one or more shares in a company jointly, they shall for the purposes of s 33, be treated as a 'single member'.

Where a company's articles of association include the three provisions enumerated in CA 1963, s 33(1)(a)–(c) but the company defaults in complying with any of those provisions, CA 1963, s 34 provides that it shall cease to be entitled to the privileges and exemptions conferred on private companies under CA 1963, ss 36, 128(4), 213(d) and 215(a)(i). Moreover, CA 1963, ss 36, 128, 213 and 215 shall apply as if it were not a private company. Where the failure to comply was accidental or due to inadvertence or to some other sufficient cause or where on other grounds it is just and equitable to grant relief, the court may on the application of the company or any other person interested and on such terms and conditions as seem to the court just and expedient, 'order the company be relieved from the consequences referred to in subsection (1)'.[253]

[1.116] The definition accorded a private company by CA 1963, s 33(1), permits the creation of three specific *types* of private company. These are:

— private companies limited by shares;

— private companies limited by guarantee and having a share capital; and

— private unlimited companies having a share capital[254].

---

250 CA 1963, s 33(2).

251 Contrast a private company defined by CA 1907, s 37(1), para **[1.072]**.

252 See further, Chapter 28, *Public Companies in Context*, para **[28.007]**. The limitation of 50 members in private companies was abolished in the UK by their Companies Act 1980.

253 CA 1963, s 34(2).

254 It should be noted that for the purposes of the C(A)A 1986, s 1(1) provides that except where the context otherwise requires, 'private company' does *not include an unlimited company.*

Of course the articles of association of all three types of private company must contain the restrictions set out in CA 1963, s 33(1). The crucial mark of a private company, apart from the restrictions which it must contain in its articles, is that it must have a *share capital*. Of these three types of private company, it is the private company limited by shares that is by far the most commonly incorporated type, accounting for 89.2% of all registered companies.

[1.117] The European Communities (Single-Member Private Limited Companies) Regulations 1994[255] permits *single-member* private *limited* companies. Therefore, not all three types of private company recognised by CA 1963, s 33(1) can become single-member companies. A *private unlimited company having a share capital* can neither be formed as, nor convert to being, a single-member company by reason of the fact that all single-member companies must be *limited* companies. Regulation 3(1) provides:

> 'Notwithstanding any enactment or rule of law to the contrary, a private company *limited* by shares or by guarantee may be formed by one person, and may have one member (in these regulations referred to as a single-member company), to the extent permitted by the Companies Acts and these regulations.'[256]

Accordingly, only private companies limited by shares or by guarantee may be formed as, or convert to, single-member companies.

[1.118] Having distinguished the three *types* of private company permissible by CA 1963, s 33(1), it is now proposed to distinguish a number of *forms* which the private company may take. Irish private companies may be broken down into a number of related, yet distinct forms, all having in common the basic requirements contained in CA 1963, s 33(1). Five forms of private company can be readily identified[257]:

(a) The single-member private limited company,

(b) Family owned private companies,

(c) Closely-held private companies,

(d) Quasi-partnership private companies,

(e) Private companies with unconnected membership.

Notwithstanding this fivefold classification, it ought to be realised that there will be often a cross-over between some of the various forms of private company. Although the single-member company has a clear legal significance, the significance of being one or other of the remaining forms of private company may amount to no more than a factor to be considered when the court exercises its discretion under particular sections of the Companies Acts[258].

(a) The single-member private limited company

[1.119] Until 1 October 1994, the only single-member companies in Ireland were de facto single-member companies. Although de jure single-member companies have only

255 SI 1994/275.

256 Italics added.

257 See Courtney, 'Shareholders' Agreements in Irish Private Companies' (1993) Dli – The Western Law Gazette 69.

258 Eg under CA 1963, ss 205 or 213.

been permitted since 1 October 1994, prior to this date many private companies were in reality owned by only one person. In such companies one person beneficially owned 100% of the shares in the company: that person legally holding 99% of the shares, his spouse or other nominee legally holding the remaining 1%. In this way the former requirement that a private company have two members was satisfied. By virtue of the European Communities (Single-Member Private Limited Companies) Regulations 1994[259] it is now legally possible to form a single-member private limited company and to convert an existing private company limited by shares or by guarantee to a single-member company. At the outset it is important to note that notwithstanding that the *ownership* of a private company may vest in one person, it remains the case that the *management* of a private company legally requires the involvement of two persons. This is because of CA 1963, s 174, which bluntly provides that '[e]very company shall have at least two directors', was not altered by the regulations.

[1.120] The so-called single-member company has long been recognised by the courts as being a de facto reality, the legal requirement of the second member being satisfied by a nominee. In the landmark case of *Salomon v Salomon & Co*[260] Lord MacNaghten said:

> 'It has become the fashion to call companies of this class "one-man companies." That is a taking nickname, but it does not help one much in the way of argument. If it is intended to convey the meaning that a company which is under the absolute control of one person is not a company legally incorporated, although the requirements of the Act of 1862 may have been complied with, it is inaccurate and misleading: if it merely means that there is a predominant partner possessing an overwhelming influence and entitled practically to the whole of the profits, there is nothing in that I can see contrary to the true intention of the Act of 1862, or against public policy, or detrimental to the interests of the creditors.'

Whilst the legislature decreed that a private company had to have at least two members, it did not attempt to provide that both members must hold equal shares. Moreover, even where one person is the beneficial owner of all of the shares in a company, the principle of separate legal personality will prevail and the company will not, without more, be deemed to be the beneficial owner's agent[261].

[1.121] As has been noted above[262] not all private companies can convert to single-member companies. Unlimited companies which are private companies by virtue of having a share capital and the restrictions in their articles required by CA 1963, s 33(1), *cannot* become single-member companies. Although unlimited private companies cannot achieve de jure single-member company status, they may still be de facto single-member private companies. Where the membership of an unlimited company falls below two, the corporate existence of the resulting single-member company is not automatically in question[263]. Rather, corporate life continues, although it is possible that a petition may be presented to have the company wound up under CA 1963, s 213(d),

---

[259] SI 1994/275.

[260] *Salomon v Salomon & Co* (1898) AC 22 at 53. See further, Chapter 4, *Incorporation and its Consequences*.

[261] See Chapter 5, *Disregarding Separate Legal Personality*, para **[5.020]** *ff*.

[262] See para **[1.117]**.

[263] See Fox & Bowen, *The Law of Private Companies*, (1991), p 168.

considered below[264]. The dis-application of CA 1963, s 36[265], by the European Communities (Single-Member Private Limited Companies) Regulations, reg 7(1), to private companies limited by shares or by guarantee, does not affect unlimited private companies. However s 36 has always been of negligible importance to the members of an unlimited company since their liability for corporate debts is, by definition, unlimited[266].

[1.122] The *objective* of the Twelfth EU Directive on Single-Member Companies is to provide a harmonised legal framework within which a single individual can conduct business as a private limited company. Thus, whilst the label 'single-member private company' is used, it may be equally apt to refer to the objective of this directive as allowing a sole trader to have limited liability. The *contents* of the Twelfth Directive have been succinctly described by *Myers*[267]:

> '...a company may have a sole member, either when it is formed or when all the shares come to be held by a single person (single member company). The Member States may, until such time as their laws relating to groups are co-ordinated, lay down special provisions or sanctions for cases where: (a) a natural person is the sole member of several companies or (b) a single-member company or any other legal person is the sole member of a company. Where a company becomes a single-member company because all its shares come to be held by a single person, that fact, together with the identity of the sole member, must either be recorded in the file or entered in the Register provided for in the First Directive or be entered in a register held by the company and accessible to the public. Decisions taken by the sole member in relation to the powers of the general meeting must be recorded in minutes or drawn up in writing...A Member State need not allow the formation of single-member companies where its legislation provides that an individual entrepreneur may set up an undertaking the liability of which is limited to a sum devoted to stated activity, on condition that safeguards are laid down for such undertakings which are equivalent to those imposed by the Twelfth Directive or by any other Community provisions applicable to [private companies limited by shares or by guarantee].'

It is next proposed to consider how the Twelfth Directive has been implemented in both Ireland and England and Wales.

(i) England and Wales

[1.123] The Twelfth EU Directive on Company Law was implemented in England and Wales by the Companies (Single-Member Private Limited Companies) Regulations 1992[268]. What is remarkable about these regulations is their brevity, containing a mere

---

264 European Communities (Single-Member Private Limited Companies) Regulations 1994, reg 11 only provides that CA 1963, ss 213(d), 215(a)(i) are disapplied in the case of private companies limited by shares or by guarantee, and so continue to apply to unlimited private companies. See Chapter 25, *Winding Up Companies*.

265 This provides that, in certain circumstances, where the membership of a private company falls below two members, the remaining member may be made personally liable for the company's debts: see Chapter 5, *Disregarding Separate Legal Personality*, para **[5.075]**.

266 But note that the unlimited liability of the members of an unlimited company only arises in the context of a winding up: see Chapter 4, *Incorporation and its Consequences*, para **[4.074]** *ff*.

267 Co Law – 12 at –03.

268 SI 1992/1699, which came into force on 15 July 1992.

three articles, and a schedule with eight paragraphs. Article 2(1) of the English Regulations permits the formation of, and conversion to, private limited companies with one member. This is facilitated by a general 'catch-all' measure, coupled with a number of specific measures. The *general* measure provides that:

> '...any enactment or rule of law which applies in relation to a private company limited by shares or by guarantee shall, in the absence of any express provision to the contrary, apply with such modification as may be necessary in relation to such a company which is formed by one person or which has only one person as a member as it does in relation to such a company which is formed by two or more persons or which has two or more persons as members...'

The specific measure goes on to provide that the companies legislation applicable to England and Wales shall, without prejudice to the generality of the foregoing passage, be modified by the eight paragraphs in the Schedule to the regulations. The principal amendments set out in the Schedule to the regulations concern the following matters:

— *Formation*: One person is sufficient to form a private company limited by shares or by guarantee.

— *Minimum membership*: One person is sufficient in the case of a private company limited by shares or guarantee.

— *Contracts with sole members*: In the case of single-member private companies a written memorandum of the terms of such contracts is required to be recorded in the minutes of the meeting of the directors of the company.

— *Statement that company has only one member*: Disclosure of the fact there is only one member is achieved by the requirement that where the membership of a private limited company falls to one, the company's *register of members* must contain a statement to this effect, and the date upon which this occurred.

— *Meetings*: Notwithstanding anything in a company's articles of association, one member present in person or in proxy is a quorum in a single-member private limited company.

— *Recording of decisions by the sole member*: All decisions taken by a single-member which may be taken by the company in general meeting, must be recorded in writing. However, it is provided that failure to comply shall not invalidate the decision taken.

(ii) Ireland

[1.124] The Twelfth Directive was implemented in Ireland by the European Communities (Single-Member Private Limited Companies) Regulations 1994[269] with effect from 1 October 1994. Our regulations may achieve similar results to their English counterpart but they enact the Twelfth Directive in a different manner. The enabling statutory instrument contains 14 regulations. Although each regulation is discussed in detail elsewhere in this book as it alters the existing law of private companies, it is convenient to summarise the regulations here:

---

[269] SI 1994/275.

— *Citation, commencement and construction*: Provides the proper title of the regulations, the date upon which they become operational, and the fact that they shall be construed as one with the Companies Acts. (reg 1)
— *Interpretation*: Contains a number of definitions which are necessary to construe the regulation. (reg 2)
— *The operative regulation*: This provides the authority for a single-member company notwithstanding any enactment or rule of law; provides, in much the same way as the English statutory instrument does, that any enactment or rule of law ordinarily applicable to private companies limited by shares or by guarantee shall apply to single-member companies; and applies the provisions of the Companies Acts generally to single-member companies[270]. (reg 3)
— *Formation*: This authorises the formation of single-member private companies limited by shares or by guarantee, notwithstanding CA 1963, s 5 which required at least two persons to sign the memorandum of association of a private company[271]. (reg 4)
— *Conversion*: This authorises the conversion of a private company limited by shares or by guarantee to a single-member company and prescribes the appropriate notification and creates an offence in the event of default in notification[272]. (reg 5)
— *Cesser of single-member company status*: This prescribes the conditions applicable where a single-member company becomes a two-member company again; prescribes the notification procedure and again creates an offence in the event of default in notification[273]. (reg 6)
— *Dis-application of CA 1963, s 36*: This provides that s 36 shall not apply to single-member companies but provides that the regulation is not retrospective in regard to personal liability incurred prior to 1 October 1994[274]. (reg 7)
— *Annual general meeting:* This provides, inter alia, that the sole member of a single-member company may dispense with the holding of an annual general meeting. There are other detailed provisions and safeguards which are considered below[275]. (reg 8)
— *Exercise of powers of sole members*: This provides that instead of passing resolutions, sole members of single-member companies can make a decision recorded in writing. Again, safeguards are included in this regulation[276]. (reg 9)
— *Quorum at sole member's meetings*: In a single-member company one person in present or by proxy shall be a quorum[277]. (reg 10)

---

270 See Chapter 2, *Formation, Registration and Conversion of Private Companies*, para **[2.017]**.
271 Chapter 2, *Formation, Registration and Conversion of Private Companies*, para **[2.018]**.
272 Chapter 2, *Formation, Registration and Conversion of Private Companies*, para **[2.065]**.
273 Chapter 2, *Formation, Registration and Conversion of Private Companies*, para **[2.066]**.
274 See Chapter 5, *Disregarding Separate Legal Personality*, para **[5.075]**.
275 See Chapter 9, *Corporate Governance: Meetings*, para **[9.013]**.
276 Chapter 9, *Corporate Governance: Meetings*, para **[9.074]**.
277 Chapter 9, *Corporate Governance: Meetings*, para **[9.043]**.

— *Non-application of certain provisions*: CA 1963, ss 213(d) and 215(a)(i) are expressed not to apply to single-member private companies limited by shares or by guarantee[278]. (reg 11)

— Regulation 12 has been repealed[279].

— *Contracts with sole members*: This provides that contracts entered by sole members of single-member companies with their companies must be in writing, save where entered into in the ordinary course of business; although a failure to comply with this is an offence, the validity of the contract is not affected[280]. (reg 13)

— *Offences*: The final regulation provides that a person guilty of an offence under the regulations shall be liable on summary conviction to a fine not exceeding £1,269.74 (reg 14)

Where indicated, each of these new regulations are considered in detail in subsequent chapters.

[1.125] Both of the foregoing enactments do only that which they are permitted to do by the Twelfth Directive, namely to allow the formation of single-member companies. It is noticeable that the Irish enactment fails to address the requirement that two persons are involved in the *management* of a private company[281]. In England and Wales it has been possible for some time for companies to have only one director[282]. Although it is clear that one person can *own* an Irish private limited company, *all* Irish companies must still have two directors and a secretary[283]. Even in a single-member company the 'nominee-syndrome' continues as a feature of Irish corporate life, with nominee-directors satisfying the requirement that all companies have two directors.

(b) Family–owned private companies

[1.126] Family owned private companies are not a separate statutorily recognised legal category of private company. Yet, since they can be said to be almost intrinsic to Irish business life, they deserve to be considered separately. Such companies meet the requirements of CA 1963, s 33(1) but are peculiar by virtue of the fact that they are exclusively, or predominantly, controlled by the members of the same family, whether of the nuclear or extended variety. Apart from their incestuous membership, there is

---

278 See Chapter 25, *Winding Up Companies*, para **[25.057]**.

279 Regulation 12 of SI 1994/275 which deemed a sole member to be a person connected with a director of a company for the purposes of CA 1990, s 26 was deleted by the European Communities (Single-Member Private Limited Companies) Regulations 1994 (Amendment) Regulations 2001 (SI 2001/437), reg 3. See further Chapter 11, *Statutory Regulation of Transactions Involving Directors and Companies*, **[11.010]**

280 See Chapter 7, *Corporate Contracts: Capacity and Authority*, para **[7.006]**.

281 See the 'Editorial' (1994) CLP 34.

282 Companies Act 1948, s 176 (UK).

283 Even in England and Wales two persons are required to manage a private limited company because although the Companies Act 1985, s 282 (UK) (which replaced Companies Act 1948, s 176) allows a company to have one director, s 283 provides that a sole director cannot also be the company's secretary.

nothing else especially peculiar about this form of private company. Potentially explosive in such companies is the possibility that there may be a shift in shareholdings, through death, marriage, sale or otherwise. Such a potential source of dispute may be prospectively catered for by means of strong *pre-emption* rights on the transfer or transmission of shares[284]. Pre-emption rights may be contained in either a company's articles of association or in a shareholders' agreement[285]. Frequently, family-owned private companies may also be characterised as being *quasi-partnership* companies, or closely-held companies, the two variants of private company next considered.

(c) Closely-held private companies

[1.127] A closely-held private company may be described as one where a company's membership is confined to a small number of persons who are known to each other. Descriptions of closely held companies, or corporations, (to use the terminology of the United States) have varied. One description of a closely-held company is found in *Donahue v Rodd Electrotype Co of New England, Inc*[286] where the Supreme Judicial Court of Massachusetts said:

> 'There is no single, generally accepted definition. Some commentators emphasise an "integration of ownership and management", in which the stockholders occupy most management positions. Others focus on the number of stockholders and the nature of the market for the stock. In this view, close corporations have few stockholders; there is little market for the corporate stock. The Supreme Court of Illinois adopted this latter view in *Galler v Galler* 32 Ill 2d 16, 203 NE 2d 577 (1965): "For our purposes, a close corporation is one in which the stock is held in a few hands, or in a few families, and wherein it is not at all, or only rarely, dealt in buying or selling". We accept aspects of both definitions. We deem a close corporation to be typified by: (1) a small number of stockholders; (2) no ready market for the corporate stock; and (3) substantial majority stockholder participation in the management, direction and operations of the corporation.
>
> As thus defined, the close corporation bears striking resemblance to a partnership. Commentators and courts have noted that the close corporation is often little more than an "incorporated" or "chartered" partnership. The stockholders "clothe" their partnership "with the benefits peculiar to a corporation, limited liability, perpetuity and the like"...*Surchin v Approved Business Machine Co* 286 NYS 2d 580...In essence, though, the enterprise remains one in which ownership is limited to the original parties or transferees of their stock to whom the other stockholders have agreed, in which ownership and management are in the same hands, and in which the owners are quite dependant on one another for the success of the enterprise. Many close corporations are "really partnerships, between two or three people who contribute their capital, skills, experience and labor". *Kruger v Gerth*, 16 NY 2d 802...'

Again, the concept of closely-held company is not a self-contained category and it is capable of being applied to family companies or quasi-partnership type companies. Moreover, a company may be closely-held even though there is no particular quasi-fiduciary relationship between the members of the company, and so a medium-sized private company can be described as being closely-held where its members are few in

---

[284] See Chapter 16, *Share Transfer in Private Companies*, para **[16.063]** *ff.*

[285] See Chapter 3, *Private Constitutional Documentation*, para **[3.109]**.

[286] *Donahue v Rodd Electrotype Co of New England, Inc* (1975) 367 Mass 578, 328 NE 2d 505.

number and are all intimately involved in the management of the company. There are no particular consequences in company law for a company being designated a closely held company[287]. It is only where a closely held company displays other characteristics which result in it being properly termed a quasi-partnership that there are appreciable consequences.

(d) Quasi-partnership private companies[288]

[1.128] Where a relationship of equality, mutuality, trust, and confidence[289], based on a personal relationship[290], subsists between the members of a private company[291] in which the owners (shareholders) and managers (directors) are the same persons, it may be appropriate to describe it as a quasi-partnership[292]. The closest relationship that the members of a company can have is a quasi-partnership; as a matter of law, the members of a registered company cannot be in a legal 'partnership' because the Partnership Act 1890, s 1(2)(a) explicitly provides that their relation 'is not a partnership within the meaning of this Act.' Murphy J put the matter thus in *Crindle Investments Ltd v Wymes*[293] in a passage cited with approval by Keane J in the Supreme Court:

> 'Whilst I have already indicated that I accept that duties may be imposed or accepted by parties above or beyond those derived from particular offices or status I believe that the presumption must be that parties who elect to have their relationship governed by corporate structures rather than, say, a partnership intend their duties – and where appropriate their rights and remedies – to be governed by the legal provisions relating to such structures and not otherwise. It would require, in my view, reasonably clear evidence to impose obligations on directors or shareholders above and beyond those prescribed by legislation or identified by long established principles.'[294]

---

287 There may, however, be taxation consequences: see, generally, Feeney, *The Taxation of Companies*.

288 See generally, Fox and Bowen, *The Law of Private Companies* (1991), p 178. See also, Twomey, *Partnership Law*, (2000), para [8.68] *ff.*

289 See *Re Murph's Restaurant Ltd* [1979] ILRM 141 at 151.

290 See *Re Astec (BSR) plc* [1999] BCC 59 where Jonathan Parker J found (at 86) that in order to give rise to an equitable constraint based on 'legitimate expectations' 'what is required is a personal relationship or personal dealings of some kind between the party seeking to exercise the legal right and the party seeking to restrain such exercise, such as will affect the conscience of the former'. One of the best examples of a personal relationship is seen in *Re Apollo Cleaning Services Ltd; Richards v Lundy* [1999] BCC 786 and *Re Legal Costs Negotiators Ltd* [1999] BCC 547 where pre-existing partnerships had been converted into a limited company.

291 In England it has been said that there was no room for 'legitimate expectations' in public companies: *Re Blue Arrow plc* (1987) 3 BCC 618 at 623; *Re Astec (BSR) plc* [1999] BCC 59 at 87D. Twomey, *Partnership Law*, (2000), p 177 suggests that once the entity in question is in substance a partnership, 'the court may apply partnership law principles to it'. It is thought to be a matter of evidential proof rather than high principle that gives rise to most quasi-partnership companies being private companies and not public companies.

292 In *Third v North East Ice & Cold Storage Co Ltd* [1998] BCC 242 it was held that where a company was a quasi-partnership, but circumstances changed rendering it no longer a quasi-partnership, 'legitimate expectations' would be displaced.

293 *Crindle Investments Ltd v Wymes* [1998] 4 IR 567 at 576.

294 [1998] 2 ILRM 275 at 285.

Although there is a *presumption* that those who chose to incorporate a company have chosen that the legislation governing companies should govern their relationship, that presumption can be rebutted by clear evidence. Indeed, the phenomenon of the quasi-partnership company was clearly recognised by the Supreme Court in *McGilligan v O'Grady*[295] where Keane J said:

> 'It is undoubtedly the case that, if there is a relationship between shareholders in a company indicating a degree of mutual confidence and trust, the court may order the winding up of the company on the just and equitable ground where one or more of the shareholders and/or directors exercise their powers in a manner which is inconsistent with that relationship. Specifically, this may arise where the right of the shareholders to participate in the management of the company is infringed, as for example by the removal of a director. These principles were laid down in *Ebrahimi v Westbourne Galleries* [1973] AC 360 and were adopted in this jurisdiction by Gannon J in *Re Murph's Restaurants Ltd* [1979] ILRM 141 at 144'.

[1.129] The basis for finding the relationship of quasi-partnership in a private company is that there are personalities behind the legal personality which is the separate legal status of the company[296]. In such companies there will be some sort of a relationship which involves 'equality, mutuality, trust and confidence' between the members of the company. In Ireland, Gannon J has recognised in *Re Murph's Restaurant Ltd*[297] that in some private companies the members can be:

> '...equal partners in a joint venture, and that the company was no more than a vehicle to secure a limited liability for possible losses and to provide a means of earning and distributing profits to their best advantage with minimum disclosure.'

Clearly this goes beyond the mere fact that persons have associated and subscribed for shares in a company. The relationship between the shareholders must go further and display, to some noticeable extent, characteristics similar to those that tend to prevail in a partnership and they must have acted in a way that is incompatible with the nature of a company. To be a quasi-partnership company, there must be, or have been, a *mutuality of understanding* between the members.

[1.130] It is thought that there is a greater likelihood that a quasi-partnership will be found to exist where the members hold their shares equally[298]. So in *Re Murph's Restaurant Ltd*[299], Gannon J referred to persons being 'equal partners in a joint venture'. Whether there are two, three or more members, it is thought that a court will more readily accept that they had the intention of being treated as partners, where their shares are equal. It is ironic that whilst in real partnerships, partners can and frequently do hold unequal shares, evidentially an inequality of shareholding is anathema to the mutuality that has consistently been found to be a requirement for a quasi-partnership company.

---

295 *McGilligan v O'Grady* [1999] 1 ILRM 303 at 343, 344.

296 See *Ebrahimi v Westbourne Galleries Ltd* [1972] 2 All ER 492 at 499,500.

297 *Re Murph's Restaurant Ltd* [1979] ILRM 141 at 150.

298 In *Irish Press plc v Ingersoll Irish Publications Ltd* (15 December 1993, unreported), High Court Barron J referred to 'equal shareholdings in a company'.

299 *Re Murph's Restaurant Ltd* [1979] ILRM 141 at 150.

[1.131] What then is the consequence of finding that a company properly falls to be treated as a quasi-partnership? As one writer has observed[300] the 'whole *rasion d'être* for the concept of quasi-partnerships is to apply principles of partnership law to non-partnerships'. Finding that a company is a quasi-partnership will, prima facie, entitle its quasi-partners to:

— participate in its management[301];

— expect that their fellow quasi-partners act in good faith[302];

— object to any fundamental change in the direction of the company's business activities[303].

Breach of any of the foregoing can ground reliance upon the most far-reaching consequence, namely that a petition can be brought to have the company wound up on the just and equitable ground, ie CA 1963, s 213(f)[304].

(e) Private companies with unconnected membership

[1.132] Sight must not be lost of the fact that a great many Irish private companies have an unconnected membership. Their members are not closely related by blood, marriage or friendship. In unconnected private companies, there will be no fiduciary relationship between the members, who will have no connection with each other, save the fact that they are shareholders in the same company. Furthermore, the management of such companies will typically be independent of its ownership and a true separation of powers will exist between the directors and the members. Accordingly, the 'duality of roles' seen so often in the other forms of private companies will not exist here[305]. In unconnected private companies the members will elect the company's directors in general meeting on the basis of their professional expertise to manage the company. The directors may be executive directors, or career-directors, although some of the directors may have a proprietary interest in the company by holding shares. The chief characteristics of such private companies are that their membership is typically larger than other private companies and that there is a discernible *separation of powers* between the members in general meeting and the board of directors.

Public companies

[1.133] All companies registered under the Companies Acts 1963–2001 which are not private companies (because they do not satisfy the conditions contained in CA 1963, s 33(1)) are public companies. Section 2 of C(A)A 1983 defines a *public company*, as 'a company which is not a private company', and also defines a PLC as:

---

300 Twomey, *Partnership Law* (2000), para [8.86].

301 *Re Murph's Restaurants Ltd* [1978] ILRM 141.

302 *Irish Press plc v Ingersoll Irish Publications Ltd* (15 December 1993, unreported), High Court (Barron J).

303 *Re Tivoli Freeholds Ltd* [1972] VR 445, cited by Twomey at [8.91].

304 See Chapter 25, *Winding Up Companies*, para **[25.076]**.

305 On the *duality of roles* prevalent in many private companies, see Chapter 8, *Corporate Governance: Management by the Directors*, para **[8.001]**.

'...a public company limited by shares or a public company limited by guarantee and having a share capital, being a company—

(a) the memorandum of which states that the company is to be a public limited company; and

(b) in relation to which the provisions of the Companies Acts as to the registration or re-registration of a company as a public limited company have been complied with on or after the appointed day.'

It has been noted[306] that this is the first time that the Companies Acts have defined a public company. The theory up until 1983 was that the public company was the basic form of company and that the private company was but a variant on the average company. However the new form of public company, the PLC, created as a result of EU requirements, needed to be defined.

[1.134] All public companies that are listed on the Stock Exchange are public limited companies or PLCs. Compared with private companies, public companies are few in number: of the 130,516 companies registered with the CRO, as few as 914 (or 0.6%) are public limited companies[307]. Fewer than half of these are listed on the Irish Stock Exchange; and yet the PLC is, quite rightly, regarded as being of enormous importance. The reason for this is because, despite being few in number, the vast bulk of Ireland's private property is owned by PLCs which also employ the greatest number of people, have the greatest number of shareholders and generate the lion's share of the country's wealth. This does not, however, justify the tail wagging the dog and it is inappropriate that Ireland's Companies Acts should be designed to afford premier service to the numerically few (albeit the economically important) where this is to the detriment of the private company limited by shares, which accounts for around 9 out of every 10 registered companies. There is thought to be an unanswerable case for restructuring the Companies Acts and elevating the private company to centre stage[308].

[1.135] There are, in all, six different types of public company, three that are manifestations of the PLC and three that are manifestations of the old public company, as follows:

— PLCs that are limited by shares;
— PLCs that are limited by guarantee and that have a share capital;
— PLCs that have a variable share capital;
— public companies limited by guarantee that do not have a share capital;
— public unlimited companies that have a share capital; and
— public unlimited companies that do not have a share capital.

Each of these different types of company is considered in Chapter 28, *The Public Company in Context*. There, the public company in all its manifestations is distinguished from the private company. Those areas of law treated in Chapters 2–27 in the context of private companies are considered again in Chapter 28, but only insofar as the law applicable to public companies differs from the law applicable to private companies.

---

[306] See Keane, *Company Law* (3rd edn, 2000), para [4.02].

[307] See the *Companies Report 2001*, p 73.

[308] See the recommendations in Chapter 3, *Simplification of Irish Company Law* of the Company Law Review Group, *First Report, 2000–2001*, (2002).

Chapter 2

Formation, Registration and Conversion of Private Companies

[2.001] In the previous chapter the private company was placed in its historical context. The modern private company was considered and distinctions were drawn between the various types and forms of private company that are prevalent in Ireland. It now falls to consider how a private company comes to be *formed* and *registered* and also the circumstances in which foreign companies become obliged to register under the Irish Companies Acts 1963–2001. This chapter also considers the application of the Companies Acts and concludes by considering how a company can convert or morph from one type (or sub-type) of company to another.

[A] FORMATION AND REGISTRATION OF A PRIVATE COMPANY

[2.002] In this section, the following issues in formation and registration are considered:

1. Why incorporate?
2. Incorporating an existing business.
3. Formation of private companies.
4. Methods of corporate formation.
5. The steps in forming a private company.
6. The requirement that a company carries on an 'activity' in the State.
7. Registration by the Registrar of Companies.
8. Delivery of particulars to the Revenue Commissioners.
9. Statutory obligations incidental to registration.
10. Registration of foreign companies.
11. Companies authorised to register under the Companies Acts 1963–2001.
12. Irish registered non-resident companies.
13. The application of the Companies Acts 1963–2001.
14. Investment companies.

Why incorporate?

[2.003] There is today an almost automatic tendency for entrepreneurs to incorporate before commencing business. The fact is that there are many rational and sensible reasons why an entrepreneur should incorporate his business. For the Irish entrepreneur, the following are some of the advantages to be obtained through the incorporation of a private limited company[1]:

---

1 See Chapter 4, *Incorporation and its Consequences* at para **[4.021]** *ff*.

- limited liability for the members;
- tax advantages;
- the ability to raise finance on foot of security unavailable to other business structures;
- the ability to have up to 50 members;
- the ease of transfer of an interest in the business;
- the ability to clearly define the management structure.

It is important to recognise that the protective veil which limited liability provides to the members of companies is considerably less sacrosanct than it once was, by virtue of statutory inroads, equitable considerations and the realities of commercial practice[2].

[2.004] It is perhaps the realities or exigencies of commercial practice which are today the most far reaching claw-back of the statutory advantages of incorporation. More and more frequently the separate legal personality of the private company is being disregarded *by agreement*. An example in point is that where a private company is incorporated, its separate legal personality may be disregarded by agreement between its member-directors and outsiders dealing with the company. This might occur where such a company takes, say, a 35-year lease of its business premises, or is afforded facilities by a lending institution and its controlling member-directors are required to provide personal guarantees for the company's obligations[3]. Notwithstanding this practical dilution of the advantages of incorporation, the entrepreneur behind a business who decides to incorporate still has the advantage that, in other day-to-day transactions involving the company and outsiders, he will not as a general rule personally incur either contractual or tortious liability.

[2.005] This section assumes that persons in business have decided that they wish to incorporate, and shows the various options open to them within this form of business association and explains the main steps involved in forming a private company.

Incorporating an existing business

[2.006] Sometimes, it will be the case that the proprietors of an existing business will decide to incorporate their business. They may make this decision for a variety of reasons. Where the existing proprietor is a sole trader, it may be the case that he is contemplating retirement or perhaps inviting one of his children to come into the family business. His concern may be to find a suitable way of achieving this whilst at the same time retaining control of the business and continuing to provide financially for himself and his wife. In such circumstances, it may make good sense to incorporate the existing business. Alternatively, the existing business may be owned by a partnership, whose partners wish to put the management and ownership of the business on a more solid footing and to facilitate the granting of an interest in the business to their industrious employees and worthy children.

[2.007] To understand better why an existing business might be incorporated, we shall look at an example involving the ubiquitous Mr A and Mr B. They have been in partnership together for over ten years, operating a garage business. The partnership holds a 35-year

---

2 See generally Chapter 5, *Disregarding Separate Legal Personality.*

3 Chapter 5, *Disregarding Separate Legal Personality*, para **[5.014]** *ff.*

lease to the garage premises from which they sell and repair motor vehicles. Business has been good and they estimate that their gross annual profit is in the region of €80,000. The net worth of the partnership assets is €110,000, which are roughly broken down as follows:

— their leasehold premises is worth €40,000;

— their stock-in-hand is worth €30,000;

— their cash in the bank is €15,000;

— their debtors owe €5,000;

— the goodwill of the business is estimated by the partnership's auditors to be worth €20,000.

Although the business association of the partnership has been advantageous to them, there are a number of reasons why they feel that the time is right for them to incorporate[4].

In the first place, although neither of them intends to retire for some years, they feel that they should at this stage provide for the future and the possible entry of their children into the business. Secondly, one of their longest-serving and most valued employees, Mr C, has indicated that unless he is given a share in the business he may leave their employment and set up in business by himself. Thirdly, Mr A and Mr B are considering whether or not to purchase another garage which has come on the market. To acquire and get this up and running, they will need to borrow €60,000 from a bank. However, because as partners they have unlimited liability, should the new venture fail, they could quite easily lose everything, including their family homes, through judgment being levied against them[5]. How can incorporation help Mr A and Mr B?

[2.008] The three concerns set out above can to a large extent be catered for by the incorporation of a private company limited by shares. A number of possibilities would emerge on the incorporation of a company. In the first place, if Mr A and Mr B wish, they could transfer some of their shares to their respective families and provide that such shares should have no voting rights until a future time, so as to enable Mr A and Mr B to retain control of the business. In the second place, on the incorporation of *A and B Garages Ltd*, shares in the new company could be transferred to Mr C, whether outright or – on the basis of the principle that it's best not to give away the goods too soon – staggered over a period of time based on Mr C's future performance. Thirdly, Mr A and Mr B could arrange for *A and B Garages Ltd* to take a loan in the company's name, secured by the assets which would be transferred to it on its incorporation. By doing this, the bank's security will be confined to the assets of the business[6] and the personal assets of Mr A and Mr B will not

---

4 On partnerships see Chapter 1, *The Private Company in Context*, para **[1.012]** *ff*, and, generally, see Twomey, *Partnership Law* (2000); Ivamy, *Underhill's Principles of the Law of Partnership* (12th edn, 1986); and I'Anson Banks, *Lindley and Banks on the Law of Partnership* (17th edn, 1995).

5 On bankruptcy generally, see Sanfey and Holohan, *Bankruptcy Law and Practice in Ireland* (1991). Bankruptcy should always be borne in mind when one operates business other than through a limited liability company, since for individuals, the Bankruptcy Act 1988 provides an alternative to corporate winding up under the Companies Acts 1963–2001.

6 This assumes that the lending bank does not require personal guarantees from A and B. Even where personal guarantees are required, it may be possible to have these capped at a specific amount.

be at risk because of the new venture and the vicissitudes of commercial life. Indeed, a bank will be more inclined to lend to a company, particularly as it will be able to take additional security over and above that which Mr A and Mr B as individuals could offer: *A and B Garages Ltd* can create a *floating charge* over its assets[7].

[2.009] The actual mechanics involved in incorporating a private company limited by shares are relatively straightforward, although it must be stressed that proper legal, accounting and taxation advice should be obtained to avoid any pitfalls. The steps involved can be summarised as follows:

— *A and B Garages Ltd* is incorporated with a suitable objects clause[8] having an authorised share capital of, for example, €500,000, and an issued share capital of €110,000.

— Mr A and Mr B enter into an agreement and execute all the necessary documents with *A and B Garages Ltd* whereby they exchange their business for 110,000 €1 shares in *A and B Garages Ltd*[9].

— Mr A and Mr B may (and it is submitted, should) enter into a shareholders' agreement which will govern their relations *inter se*, and address issues such as management, the powers of directors and other matters[10]. Problems anticipated and legislated for can be resolved more readily.

— Shares can be allotted to the employee, Mr C, immediately, or a share option agreement entered into whereby Mr C can acquire shares in the new company over a period of time. This may be performance related. It is prudent to provide

---

7 See Chapter 4, *Incorporation and Its Consequences*, para **[4.079]**, and generally, Chapter 20, *Corporate Borrowing: Debentures and Security*, para **[20.063]** *ff.*

8 On a company's objects clause, see Chapter 3, *Private Constitutional Documentation*, para **[3.012]** and Chapter 7, *Corporate Contracts: Capacity and Authority*, para **[7.043]** *ff.* Upon the incorporation of an existing business it is common to include in the objects clause an express object to acquire the existing business. Such an object may provide that the company has the capacity to, inter alia:

> '...acquire as a going concern the business of sale and repair of motor vehicles now being carried on by A and B currently trading under "A and B's Garage" together with all property, assets and liabilities tangible or intangible of that business and for that purpose, to enter an agreement with A and B and execute all documents required to give effect to the foregoing acquisition'.

An example of such an object is to be found in the case of *Re Westwinds Holding Company Ltd* (21 May 1974 unreported), High Court per Kenny J, where the company concerned had as its principal object the taking over and carrying on of the business of builders and public works contractors formerly carried on by its promoter.

9 Extreme caution must be exercised from a taxation perspective in carrying out this transaction, in that A and B may be liable for capital gains tax on the disposal of their business, and stamp duty and value added tax may be payable on the assignment of the lease of the business premises to A and B Garages Ltd. See Chapter 18, *The Maintenance of Capital*, para **[18.094]** on the possibility of issuing shares at a premium to avoid capital duty on the allotment of shares.

10 For shareholders' agreements generally, see Chapter 3, *Private Constitutional Documentation*, para **[3.109]** *ff.*

that if and when shares are allotted to Mr C he will also enter into a shareholders' agreement with Mr A and Mr B so as to ensure that all three are aware of their respective rights and liabilities.

— Mr A and Mr B can bequeath their respective shares to whoever they wish and achieve familial continuity of interest and ownership – if that be desired.

As a general rule, Mr A's and Mr B's personal liability is limited to the amount, if any, unpaid on the shares held by them, and so their other personal assets are not at risk.

The primary disadvantage to Mr A and Mr B is that they will open their business to public inspection and will have to comply with the myriad responsibilities and duties imposed – even upon such small enterprises – by the Companies Acts. There are costs involved in pursuing any course of action and in this case the costs may be categorised as the ceding of privacy, additional administrative bureaucracy and being open to the supervision of the Director of Corporate Enforcement.

Formation of private companies

[2.010] By far the most common type of company incorporated in Ireland today is the private company limited by shares. Four distinctive types of private company need to be distinguished and considered. Section 33 of CA 1963 recognises three types of private company: those which are limited by shares; those which are limited by guarantee and have a share capital; and those which are unlimited and have a share capital. To these the European Communities (Single-Member Private Limited Companies) Regulations 1994[11] has added a fourth, which is a variation on two of the other three types of private company. The formation of the following types of private company is now considered:

(a) Private companies limited by shares.

(b) Private companies limited by guarantee.

(c) Private unlimited companies with a share capital.

(d) Single-member private companies.

It is first proposed to outline the essential features of each type of private company.

(a) Private companies limited by shares

[2.011] The most commonly formed company in Ireland is the private company limited by shares. A private company limited by shares (or indeed, any 'limited' company) does not itself, of course, have limited liability: the company remains, at all times, fully liable for all of its (the company's) debts. Where a company is *limited by shares*, what is meant is that the liability of the company's members to contribute to the assets of the company is limited to the amount, if any, unpaid on the shares for which they have subscribed. Accordingly, if a member holds ten shares of €1 each, once he has paid €10 he will have no further liability for the company's debts. While a company's memorandum of association[12] must state the company's *authorised* share capital and the division of that capital into shares of specific values, the company is not obliged to disclose in its memorandum of association its *issued* share capital ie the number of shares which have actually been issued, thus

[11] SI 1994/275.

[12] See Chapter 3, *Private Constitutional Documentation*, para **[3.003]** *ff*.

disclosing the value of share capital in the company[13]. Accordingly, one should not be impressed by the fact that a company has an authorised share capital of €1 million – it might have issued just two €1 shares!

(b) Private companies limited by guarantee

[2.012] At the outset it must be recognised that not all companies which are limited by guarantee are private companies. Section 33(1) of CA 1963, is most specific: only companies limited by guarantee and which *have a share capital* are private companies; a company limited by guarantee which does not have a share capital is a public company. Very few companies that are limited by guarantee have a share capital, and so very few companies limited by guarantee are private companies. Of course, to be a private company, not only must a company limited by guarantee have a share capital, but, also its articles of association[14] *must contain the three restrictions* set out in CA 1963, s 33(1)[15].

[2.013] Where a company is limited by guarantee, this means that the liability of the members is limited to the amount of their guarantee to contribute to the company's assets in a winding up. Accordingly, if the members guarantee to contribute €10 to the company, their liability to the company is limited to €10. It should be noted that a company only can only look to its guarantee fund *when it is being wound up* and cannot rely on the guarantees of its members to secure a loan: *Re Irish Club Ltd*[16].

[2.014] Where a company is limited by its members' guarantees and also has a share capital, the liability of its members on a winding up is limited to pay for the shares for which they have subscribed and to pay the amount that they have guaranteed. Companies limited by guarantee and which *do not* have a share capital are public companies and are most frequently employed as management companies of buildings divided into apartments and in shopping centre developments, where it is necessary that all tenants have an interest in the company and where there may be more than 50 tenants. In such circumstances, a public company limited by guarantee must be used because CA 1963, s 33(1) restricts the number of members in a private company to 50. Whether, theoretically and rationally, this is a justifiable basis for deeming a company to be 'private' or 'public' is very debatable[17].

(c) Private unlimited companies with a share capital

[2.015] The third type of private company is a private company which has a share capital and in which the members have unlimited liability. An unlimited company is defined by CA 1963, s 5(2)(c) as being 'a company not having any limit on the liability of its members.' Unlimited companies are not generally used as trading-companies because CA 1963, s 207(1) provides that in the event of a company being wound up, past or present members[18]:

---

13 See further Chapter 18, *The Maintenance of Capital*, para **[18.004]**. It may be noted, though, that the amount of a company's issued share capital can be ascertained by carrying out a search at the CRO.

14 See Chapter 3, *Private Constitutional Documentation*, para **[3.048]** *ff*.

15 See Chapter 1, *The Private Company in Context*, para **[1.115]**.

16 *Re Irish Club Ltd* (1906) WN 127.

17 See Chapter 28, *The Public Company in Context*, para **[28.007]**.

18 Ie, contributories: see Chapter 27, *The Realisation and Distribution of Assets in a Winding Up*, para **[27.117]**.

> '...shall be liable to contribute to the assets of the company to an amount sufficient for the payment of its debts and liabilities, and the costs, charges and expenses of the winding up, and for the adjustment of the rights of the contributories among themselves...'

It is possible for an unlimited company to be registered without a share capital, but this is a rare occurrence. Where an unlimited company is incorporated, it will almost always be the case that it will have a share capital and will consequently be a private company where its articles of association comply with CA 1963, s 33(1).

[2.016] Given the potential for personal financial disaster, why should any promoter[19] cause a company to be registered with unlimited liability for its members? The incorporation of unlimited companies is largely driven by the desire to keep secret financial information concerning the company, particularly if it is a holding company. The use of an unlimited company to avoid the disclosure requirements under the Companies (Amendment) Act 1986 ('C(A)A 1986') was curtailed by the European Communities (Accounts) Regulations 1993[20] which extended the provisions of C(A)A 1986 to certain types of unlimited companies and partnerships[21]. Previously it was the case that the holding (non-trading) companies of many of the leading companies in Irish commercial life were unlimited, one of the primary reasons being to avoid the provisions of C(A)A 1986. As at 31 December 2001, the total number of unlimited companies on the register was 3,069, which represented 2.1% of the total number of companies on the register as at that date as compared with 3,666 (representing 2.5%) as at 31 December 1994[22]. It is not, therefore, apparent that the 1993 regulations have had any appreciable effect on the number of unlimited companies.

(d) Single-member private limited companies

[2.017] By virtue of the European Communities (Single-Member Private Limited Companies) Regulations 1994[23] it is now possible to form a single-member company. Regulation 3(1) provides that:

> 'Notwithstanding any enactment or rule of law to the contrary, a private company limited by shares or by guarantee may be formed by one person, and may have one member (in these regulations referred to as a single-member company), to the extent permitted by the Companies Acts and these regulations.'

Although the regulations do not explicitly state that their application is confined to private companies limited by shares and private companies limited by guarantee *and which have a share capital*, this must be the case by implication since a private company must have a share capital. It should be noted that *not all* types of private companies may convert to single-member companies. By reason of the fact that reg 3(1) specifically refers only to

19 For the definition of a promoter, see Chapter 10, *Duties of Directors and Other Officers*, para **[10.140]**.

20 SI 1993/396, considered in Chapter 13, *Accounts and Auditors*, para **[13.018]**.

21 See SI 1993/396, considered in Chapter 13, *Accounts and Auditors*, para **[13.018]**.

22 Indeed the number of unlimited companies peaked in 1998 when at year's end there were 6,171, which represented 3.5% of companies on the register: *Companies Reports* 1995, 1999 and 2000.

23 SI 1994/275.

private companies 'limited by shares or by guarantee', the regulations do not permit the formation of an unlimited single-member private company[24].

[2.018] A single-member company is formed by one person subscribing his name to the new company's memorandum of association. Accordingly, the European Communities (Single-Member Private Limited Companies) Regulations 1994, reg 4 provides:

> 'Notwithstanding s 5(1) of the 1963 Act, one person may, for any lawful purpose, by subscribing his or her name to a memorandum of association and otherwise complying with the requirements of the Companies Acts and these regulations relating to registration, form an incorporated company being a private company limited by shares or by guarantee.'

Apart from the fact that only one person will be a subscriber to the memorandum of association of a single-member private limited company, all of the other requirements relating to the registration of a private company will apply to single-member private companies[25]. As at 31 December 2001 the number of single-member private limited companies on the register was 14,719[26].

Methods of corporate formation

[2.019] There are three main ways of forming a private company.

(a) The first method is by lodging all the forms on the 'ordinary list' with the Companies Registration Office ('CRO').

(b) The second and shorter way is through membership of the Company Incorporation Scheme, and proceeding on the 'ten-day list' or '*Fé Phráinn*' method.

(c) The third way is by means of the CRODisk method, whereby incorporation can be achieved within five working days where particulars are lodged with the CRO on floppy disk.

(d) In addition, a ready-made 'shelf company', if available, may be purchased from a company formation firm. It should be noted that one effect of C(A)(No 2)A 1999, s 42, which requires that a company when formed will carry out an activity in the State, has been to make scarce the numbers of shelf companies that are available.

(a) The ordinary list

[2.020] Incorporation of a company by means of the *ordinary list* can, depending on the workload of the CRO, take over one month from the initial lodging of the application to the issuing of the Certificate of Incorporation. The documentation which must be lodged to form a company is set out below[27].

(b) The Company Incorporation Scheme

[2.021] The *Fé Phráinn* method of incorporation is referred to by the CRO as the 'Company Incorporation Scheme'[28]. The function of this method of company formation,

---

24 See further Chapter 1, *Private Companies in Context*, para **[1.121]**.

25 SI 1994/275, reg 3(2).

26 Department of Enterprise, Trade and Employment's *Companies Report 2001*, p 73.

27 At para **[2.026]**.

28 See, in this regard, and indeed on the topic of company formation generally, *Company Incorporation*, Information Leaflet No 1, March 2000 (CRO).

introduced in 1986, is to provide a scheme whereby participants are guaranteed to have companies incorporated within ten working days of all documentation being lodged in the CRO. Only private companies limited by shares or by guarantee and unlimited companies may be formed by this method. A company can only be formed using this scheme by a participating firm, which is registered with the CRO and which has submitted 'model' memoranda and articles of association. No amendments may be made to the approved text without the express prior approval of the CRO.

[2.022] The CRO has a number of requirements which must be complied with if a firm is to be registered under the Company Incorporation Scheme. These are that:

— the memorandum and articles of association should be *printed* (as opposed to typed or produced by computer) in clear black type on durable paper;

— no alterations may be made to the pre-printed model memorandum and articles save the name, main objects, liability and the share capital;

— only companies required for immediate commercial use are permitted to be registered;

— where the promoter makes an error, and an application has to be resubmitted, it will be treated as a new application;

— the CRO is the final arbitrator as to the interpretation of the Scheme's conditions.

The model memorandum and articles of association submitted to the CRO become the standard texts for the constitutional documentation of all companies registered by that participant under the scheme. The speed of the incorporation of a company incorporated under this scheme is achieved through standardisation which allows the CRO to assume safely that the vast majority of the paperwork is in order. Under the ordinary list, every provision of the individual documents submitted must be scrutinised by the staff of the CRO. The model memorandum of association submitted to the CRO under the scheme will only leave the name clause, 'main objects' clause, liability clause, and share capital clause blank. Accordingly, it is only the variations in these clauses which must be scrutinised. It should be borne in mind that this method of incorporation is only available to companies required for immediate use.

[2.023] Section 80(1) of the Company Law Enforcement Act 2001 ('CLEA 2001') is a variation on the same theme. This provision facilitates swift incorporation through the recognition of reference memoranda and articles of association by providing:

> 'The registrar of companies may accept for registration a document containing standard form text from the objects clause of a memorandum of association or articles of association and shall assign a reference number to each document so registered.'

Company formation firms may lodge reference memoranda and articles of association that do not relate to a particular company[29]. Thereafter, they may lodge memoranda and articles of association in relation to specific companies that omit the tracts of text already contained in the 'reference' documents, which are specifically incorporated, by reference, into their memoranda and articles[30]. Where text is referred to in this manner it is 'deemed

[29] CLEA 2001, s 80(2).

[30] CLEA 2001, s 80(3).

for all purposes' to be incorporated in the memoranda and articles of association of companies[31]. As at the time of writing, CLEA 2001, s 80 has not been activated by the Registrar of Companies.

(c) The CRODisk Scheme

[2.024] In 2000 the CRO introduced a new electronic company incorporation scheme whereby incorporation is guaranteed within five working days provided the terms and conditions of the scheme are fulfilled[32]. CRODisk is open to members of the Company Incorporation Scheme and is intended to facilitate presenters who require speedy company incorporation without the inconvenience of manually lodging the documents with the CRO cash office. Instead, company information is presented directly to the new companies' section on floppy disk; however, the usual paper incorporation documents continue to be required, fully completed, in addition to the disk. The CRO provides participating presenters with the software necessary to manage data entry, form production and disk creation. In addition to formation, change of principal object, change of name, change of registered office and change of directors can all be lodged using CRODisk[33].

(d) Shelf companies

[2.025] Shelf companies are companies that are formed by specialist organisations ('company formation firms') and solicitors' firms in anticipation of demand and which are later sold to persons who require a company immediately. Thus, the company formed will have as its first subscribers and directors the managers of the company formation firm, a nominal share capital and a name. Once a willing buyer is found, the managers of the formation firm will transfer the shares issued in the company to the new owners and, having appointed the new owners or their nominees as directors, they will themselves resign as directors. The share capital, the registered office and the company's name may be subsequently changed at the new owners' leisure. As alluded to above[34], C(A)(No 2)A 1999, s 42 has obstructed (but not, it appears, thwarted) the formation of shelf companies by reason of the new requirement that, on formation, all companies must carry on an activity in the State. This requirement can be mitigated, however, by incorporating companies temporarily engaged in a recognised activity (for example, holding a nominal piece of property such as a share in a company)[35]. In causing a company to hold a share in another company care must be taken not to inadvertently create a group of companies within the meaning of CA 1963, s 155[36] and thereby restrict the company's entitlement to avail of the audit exemption permitted by C(A)(No 2)A 1999, Part III[37].

---

[31] CLEA 2001, s 80(4).

[32] See, further, *Company Incorporation*, Information Leaflet No 1, March 2000 (CRO).

[33] At the time of writing, it is understood that this service is available only in respect of those companies that were incorporated using CRODisk.

[34] See para **[2.019]**.

[35] 'Activity' is very widely defined by CLEA 2001, s 47(2): see para **[2.031]**.

[36] See generally, Chapter 17, *Groups of Companies*.

[37] See Chapter 13, *Accounts and Audit*, para **[13.185]** *ff*.

The steps in forming a private company

[2.026] To incorporate a *private company limited by shares*, the following are usually lodged with the CRO:

- the memorandum of association[38];
- the articles of association[39];
- Form No A1;
- a statutory declaration that the company will carry on an activity in Ireland[40] (said declaration being incorporated within Form No A1); and
- the appropriate fees[41].

In the case of a private company limited by shares its memorandum of association should be in accordance with the form set out in Table A, or as near thereto as circumstances permit[42]. It is not essential that articles of association are lodged with an application to form a private company limited by shares. Where individual articles are not lodged with an application to form a new company, the unamended model articles set out in CA 1963, Sch 1, Table A, Part II will become the articles of the new company by default[43].

[2.027] The Form No A1 requires, inter alia, the following details to be inserted:

- the name of the company;
- the company's registered office;
- the name, address and signature of the secretary;
- the name and address of the solicitor acting;
- particulars of the directors, including their signatures and whether they are Irish residents[44];
- the signatures of two subscribers/solicitor acting;
- a Declaration of Compliance that all the requirements of the Companies Acts 1963–2001 have been complied with, signed by a solicitor engaged in the formation of the company or a person named as a director or secretary of the company, witnessed by a Commissioner for Oaths/Notary Public/Peace Commissioner[45];
- a declaration that the purpose for which the company is being formed is the carrying on by it of an activity in the State[46]; and
- completion and signature of the Capital Duty Statement[47].

---

38 See Chapter 3, *Private Constitutional Documentation*, para **[3.003]**.

39 See Chapter 3, *Private Constitutional Documentation*, para **[3.048]**.

40 As required by CA(No 2)A 1999, s 42. See para **[2.031]**.

41 The fees payable to the CRO are listed at http://www.cro.ie/.

42 CA 1963, s 16.

43 See generally, Chapter 3, *Private Constitutional Documentation*, para **[3.050]** *ff*.

44 CA(No 2)A 1999, s 43 requires a bond to be lodged if one of the directors is not resident in Ireland: see para **[2.039]** and, further, Chapter 8, *Corporate Governance: Management by the Directors*, para **[8.022]**.

45 C(A)A 1982, s 3.

46 C(A)(No 2)A 1999, s 42(4). See para **[2.031]**.

47 See *Companies Registration Office Information Manual*, p 28 for a detailed list of the information required.

Before proceeding to lodge the necessary incorporation documentation, it is advisable to check that the proposed name for the company is not similar to the name of a company which has already been incorporated by checking with the Registrar of Companies[48].

[2.028] To form a *single-member private limited company* a person must subscribe his or her name to a memorandum of association and comply with the same requirements as apply in the case of a private company limited by shares, considered above. The appropriate form is again a Form No A1. Shortly after it became possible to form a de jure single-member private limited company, there were a great many conversions from so-called 'multi-member' private companies. Where a company converts to, or for that matter ceases to be, a single-member company, the appropriate forms for use in the return of this information are prescribed by the European Communities (Single-Member Private Limited Companies) (Forms) Regulations 1994[49].

[2.029] To form a *private company limited by guarantee and having a share capital*, again, a memorandum and articles of association together with a Form No A1 must be lodged with the CRO. However, there are some differences in the particulars required. In the first place the memorandum of association will reflect the fact that the company is limited by guarantee. Secondly, unlike a company limited by shares, there *must* be registered with the memorandum of association, articles of association which are signed by the subscribers to the memorandum and which prescribe regulations for the company[50]. In this regard the appropriate form of memorandum is to be found in CA 1963, Sch 1, Table D, Part I and the appropriate articles of association are to be found in Part III of Table D. Both memorandum and articles of association should be in accordance with the forms set out in Table D, or as near thereto as circumstances admit[51]. Thirdly, the articles must state the number of members with which the company proposes to be registered[52].

[2.030] To form an *unlimited private company having a share capital* a memorandum and articles of association and Form No A1 must be lodged with the CRO. As in the case of companies limited by guarantee and having a share capital, again, articles *must* be lodged with the application to form an unlimited company[53]. The form of memorandum for an unlimited private company which has a share capital is set out in CA 1963, Sch 1, Part I ,Table E. The appropriate articles of association are to be found in Part III of Table E of the First Schedule. Both the memorandum and articles of association of unlimited companies should be in accordance with the forms set out in Table E, or as near thereto as circumstances permit[54].

---

48 This invitation is extended in the *Company Incorporation*, Information Leaflet No 1, March 2000 (CRO), p 3. See, further, Chapter 3, *Private Constitutional Documentation*, para **[3.006]**.

49 SI 1994/306. To change from a multi-member private company to a single-member private company a Form No M1 is used, to convert the other way from single-member to multi-member, a Form No M2 is used. See para **[2.065]**.

50 CA 1963, s 11.

51 CA 1963, s 16.

52 CA 1963, s 12(2). Where the numbers of members subsequently increases beyond the registered number the company must notify the CRO within 15 days after the increase was resolved: CA 1963, s 12(3).

53 CA 1963, s 11.

54 CA 1963, s 16.

The requirement that a company carries on an 'activity' in the State

[2.031] In an attempt to combat the abuses of Irish registered non-resident companies (IRNRs)[55] C(A)(No 2)A 1999, s 42(1) provides that a company 'shall not be formed and registered...unless it appears to the Registrar of Companies that the company, when registered, will carry on an activity in the State, being an activity that is mentioned in its memorandum'. 'Activity' is widely defined by s 42(7) to mean '...any activity that a company may be lawfully formed to carry on and includes the holding, acquisition or disposal of property of whatsoever kind.'

Section 42(2) of C(A)(No 2)A 1999 provides that the Registrar of Companies may accept as 'sufficient evidence that a company, when registered, will carry on an activity in the State' a *statutory declaration* in the prescribed form. This additional statutory declaration has been embodied in the Form No A1 used to incorporate all companies[56]. The declaration must include the following particulars:

(a) if it appears to the person making the declaration that the activity belongs to a division, group and class appearing in the relevant classification system—
  (i) the general nature of the activity, and
  (ii) the division, group and class in that system to which the activity belongs;

(b) if it appears to the said person that the activity does not belong to any such division, group and class, a precise description of the activity;

(c) the place or places in the State where it is proposed to carry on the activity;

(d) the place, whether in the State or not, where the central administration of the company will normally be carried on.

In classifying the particular activity which the company proposes to engage in, the appropriate NACE code classification (which is the common basis for statistical classifications of economic activities within the EU[57]) must be used. If the activity cannot be classified under the NACE code, a precise description of the activity must be given. The NACE code is available on the CRO's website at http://www.cro.ie/. Where the purpose or one or more of the purposes for which the company is being formed is the carrying on of two or more activities, the matters referred to in paragraphs (a)–(c) above shall be those that relate to what the maker of the declaration considers to be 'the 1963 Activity for which the company is being formed to carry on in the State'.[58] Those who are recognised as having the capacity to swear the statutory declaration are:

— one of the persons named as directors in the statement delivered under C(A)A 1982, s 3;

— the person or persons so named in the section 3 statement as secretary or joint-secretaries; or

— the solicitor, if any, engaged in the formation of the company[59];

---

55 See para **[2.052]**.

56 The changes to the Form No A1 were introduced by the Companies (Forms) Order 2000 (SI 2000/62) which came into operation on 18 April 2000.

57 Set out in the Annex to Council Regulation (EEC) No 3037/90 of 9 October 1990.

58 C(No 2)A 1999, s 42(3).

59 C(No 2)A 1999, s 42(4).

Registration by the Registrar of Companies

[2.032] Once the requisite documentation has been lodged, it is then for the Registrar of Companies to decide whether or not to register the company. One of the most common reasons for refusing to register a company is because of a failure on the part of the person who forms the company to complete the Form No A1 properly. A high degree of accuracy is required in completing the Form No A1.

[2.033] The Registrar of Companies, through his assistants, will scrutinise the documentation, especially the memorandum, to satisfy himself that 'all the requirements of the Companies Acts in respect of registration and of matters precedent and incidental thereto have been complied with'[60]. These requirements include the statutory declaration required by C(A)(No 2)A 1999, s 42, considered in para **[2.031]**, above. When a company is registered the memorandum and articles will be retained and registered[61] by the Registrar and a document analogous to a birth certificate for a human person, a Certificate of Incorporation, will be issued for the company.

[2.034] The effect of registration is set out in CA 1963, s 18(2), which provides that:

> 'From the date of incorporation mentioned in the certificate of incorporation, the subscribers of the memorandum, together with such other persons as may from time to time become members of the company, shall be a body corporate with the name contained in the memorandum, capable forthwith of exercising all the functions of an incorporated company, and having perpetual succession and a common seal, but with such liability on the part of the members to contribute to the assets of the company in the event of its being wound up...'.

And so corporate life begins[62].

Delivery of particulars to the Revenue Commissioners

[2.035] Section 882(1) of the Taxes Consolidation Act 1997 (as inserted by the Finance Act 1999, s 83) requires every company, incorporated in the State or which commences to carry on a trade, profession or business within the State, to deliver within 30 days of certain stated events[63], a written statement to the Revenue Commissioners[64]. This statement must state:

— the name of the company;

— the company's registered office;

— the address of its principal place of business;

— the name and address of the secretary;

---

60 Pursuant to C(A)A 1983, s 5(1).

61 CA 1963, s 17.

62 See further Chapter 4, *Incorporation and Its Consequences*, para **[4.021]** *ff*.

63 The stated events are: (a) the date it commences to carry on a trade, profession or business, wherever carried on, (b) the date at which there is a material change in information previously delivered by the company under that section; and (c) the giving of a notice to the company by an inspector requiring a statement under that section: Taxes Consolidation Act 1997, s 882(2).

64 This section applies (a) in the case of companies that are incorporated on or after 11 February 1999, as on and from that date; and (b) in the case of companies that are incorporated before 11 February 1999, as on and from 1 October 1999: Finance Act 1999, s 83(2).

- — the date of commencement of the trade, profession or business;
- — the nature of such trade, profession or business;
- — the date up to which accounts relating to such trade, profession or business will be made up; and
- — such other information as the Revenue Commissioners may consider necessary. In addition, in the cases of companies that are incorporated, but not resident in the State, and companies that are neither incorporated nor resident in the State, certain other information is required[65].

This measure, which along with the Taxes Consolidation Act 1997, s 23A (as inserted by the Finance Act 1999, s 82) was intended to combat the problem posed by non-resident Irish companies[66], is considerably strengthened by the ability to invoke C(A)A 1982, s 12A. Section 82(3) of the Finance Act 1999 provides:

> 'Where a company fails to deliver a statement which it is required to deliver under this section then, notwithstanding any obligations as to secrecy or other restriction upon disclosure of information imposed by or under any statute or otherwise, the Revenue Commissioners may give a notice in writing to the registrar of companies (within the meaning of the Companies Act 1963) stating that the company has so failed to deliver a statement under this section.'

Where the Revenue Commissioners serve such a notice the Registrar of Companies has power under C(A)A 1982, s 12A to strike the company off the register[67]. The cumulative effect of these provisions is to empower the strangulation at birth of non-compliant companies so that corporate life can end as quickly as it has begun where companies fail to deliver the statement required under the Taxes Consolidation Act 1997, s 882(1).

Statutory obligations incidental to registration

[2.036] Once registration takes place and a company is incorporated, many consequences ensue. The most important of these consequences are considered in Chapter 4, *Incorporation and its Consequences*. In addition to these legal consequences, when registered, a company becomes subject to a number of statutory *obligations*. Although the private company is the most popular legal business structure, it is entrammeled by statutory obligations. The more important statutory obligations which arise upon a company's incorporation appertain to:

(a) Registered office.

(b) Directors and secretary.

(c) Display of certain information.

(d) Publication of notices.

(e) Use of a business name.

---

65 Finance Act 1999, s 83(2)(i) and (iii).

66 See para **[2.052]**.

67 For the Registrar of Companies's power to strike-off a company, see Chapter 12, *Company Law Compliance and Enforcement*, para **[12.132]**.

It must be stressed that these statutory obligations are far from exhaustive. A comprehensive list of the statutory obligations of companies (and their directors and other officers) is detailed in Chapter 12.

(a) Registered office

[2.037] Every company must have a *registered office* within the State by virtue of CA 1963, s 113[68]. The purpose of this requirement is to ensure that every company formed and registered in Ireland has an address to which all communications and other notices may be sent. A company's registered office must be notified to the Registrar of Companies prior to its incorporation[69]. This is facilitated by the Form No A1 which is lodged with a company's memorandum and articles of association when application is made for registration and incorporation. Where a company changes the location of its registered office, it must notify the Registrar of Companies within fourteen days[70]. The company and every officer who is in default of the foregoing requirements are liable to a fine not exceeding €634.87.

[2.038] Another feature of a company's registered office is that several provisions of the Companies Acts 1963–2001 require that certain documents must be kept and retained at the registered office:

- the register of debenture holders[71];
- copies of instruments which create charges[72];
- the register of members[73];
- book of minutes of general meetings[74];
- books of account[75];
- register of directors and secretary[76]; and
- register of directors' and secretary's interests in shares[77].

It must be said that although the foregoing are legal requirements, in practice a relaxed approach is taken by some private companies and the requirements of the Companies Acts 1963–2001 are all too often an afterthought.

(b) Directors and secretary

[2.039] Sections 174 and 175 of CA 1963 require that all companies, including single-member private limited companies, have two directors, and a company secretary, who may also be a director[78]. The names of the first two directors must also be delivered to the

---

68 As amended by C(A)A 1982, s 4(1).

69 CA 1963, s 113(2).

70 CA 1963, s 113(3). Note that it is not sufficient for the company to record the change of the registered office in its Annual Return for that year.

71 CA 1963, s 91.

72 CA 1963, s 109.

73 CA 1963, s 116(5).

74 CA 1963, s 146(1).

75 CA 1963, s 147(3).

76 CA 1963, s 195(1).

77 CA 1990, s 59.

78 See Chapter 8, *Corporate Governance: Management by the Directors,* para **[8.021]** *ff.*

Registrar of Companies with the application for registration and their consent to so act, shown by their signatures on the Form No A1[79]. Any change in directors and secretary or in their particulars must be notified to the Registrar of Companies by the company within 14 days[80]. As a result of C(A)(No 2)A 1999, the general rule is that every Irish company must have at least one director who is resident in the State[81].

(c) Display of certain information

[2.040] When a company has been incorporated, and it commences trading, it will often have headed notepaper printed. Under CA 1963, s 196[82], such headed paper, or 'business letters of the company' which contain the company's name and where sent by the company to any person, must state in legible characters in relation to every director the following particulars:

- present Christian name, or initials, and surname;
- any former Christian or surnames; and
- his nationality, if not Irish.

The Minister of Enterprise, Trade and Employment may grant an exemption where he is of the opinion that an exemption from this requirement is expedient, subject to such conditions as he may think fit. Where there is default in complying with these provisions, the company and any officers who are in default, will on summary conviction be liable to a fine[83]. Proceedings under this section can only be taken by or with the consent of the Minister for Enterprise, Trade and Employment[84].

[2.041] It should be noted that the reference to a 'director' in this section applies to any person in accordance with whose instructions or directions the directors of a company are accustomed to act: CA 1963, s 196(6). Accordingly, a company should include the names of all *shadow directors*, as defined by CA 1990, s 27 on its business letters.

[2.042] Section 114 of CA 1963 makes further disclosure requirements for a company. These include:

- painting or affixing its name on the outside of every office or place in which its business is carried on, in a conspicuous position, in letters easily legible: s 114(1)(a);
- having its name engraved in legible characters on its seal: s 114(1)(b);
- having its name mentioned in legible characters in all business letters of the company and in all notices and other official publications of the company, and in

---

79 See the C(A)A 1982, s 3 as amended by C(A)A 1983, Sch 2, Part II.

80 CA 1963, s 195.

81 An alternative to having a director resident in the State is to provide a bond pursuant to s 43 or, following incorporation, a certificate pursuant to C(A)(No 2)A 1999, s 44.

82 Which, by subs (3) applies to all companies which: are registered under the Companies Acts 1963–2001; or registered under Companies (Consolidation) Act 1908 unless registered before 23 November 1916; or to foreign companies which have an established place of business within the State, unless such was established before 23 November 1916; or which are registered under the Moneylenders Act 1933 (as amended).

83 CA 1963, s 196(4), as amended by C(A)A 1982, Sch 1.

84 CA 1963, s 196(5).

all bills of exchange, promissory notes, endorsements, cheques and orders for money or goods purporting to be signed by or on behalf of the company and in all invoices, receipts and letters of credit of the company: s 114(1)(c).

Failure to comply will render the company and every officer of the company liable to a fine[85]. Furthermore, in certain circumstances, considered in Chapter 4, officers may be made personally liable where the company's name is incorrectly stated[86].

[2.043] Further disclosure and publicity is required by the European Communities (Companies) Regulations 1973[87] in respect of business letters and forms of a company. These regulations only apply to limited companies and unregistered companies: reg 3 as amended by CA 1963, s 377. Regulation 9(1) provides that every company shall have the following particulars on its letters and order forms:

— the place of registration of the company and the number with which it is registered;

— the address of the registered office;

— where a company is a limited company, but has been given a dispensation allowing it not to include the word 'limited' in its name, the fact that it is a limited company[88]; and

— in the case of a company which is being wound up, the fact that it is being wound up.

Furthermore, where there is reference to the share capital of the company, such reference must be to the *paid-up* or *issued* share capital of the company, as opposed to the authorised share capital[89].

(d) Publication of notices

[2.044] Regulation 4(1) of the European Communities (Companies) Regulations 1973[90] obliges a limited liability company, or an unregistered company with limited liability to publish in *Iris Oifigiúil* notice of the delivery to, or the issue by the Registrar of Companies, of the following documents and particulars:

— any certificate of incorporation;

— the memorandum and articles of association, or equivalent documents, or documents amending them, together with the amended documents;

— any return relating to the directors or a change in the directors;

---

85 CA 1963, s 114(2).

86 See Chapter 5, *Disregarding Separate Legal Personality*, para **[5.078]** and also see Chapter 7, *Corporate Contracts, Capacity and Authority*, para **[7.012]**.

87 SI 1973/163.

88 On dispensations from the requirement to include the word limited in a company's name, see CA 1963, s 24 (as repealed and substituted by CLEA 2001, s 88) considered in Chapter 3, *Private Constitutional Documentation*, para **[3.008]**.

89 SI 1973/163, reg 9(2).

90 SI 1973/163.

— any return relating to the persons, other than the board of directors, who are authorised to enter into transactions binding the company, or notification of a change among such persons ('registered persons');
— its annual returns;
— any notice of its registered office or of a change;
— any copy of a winding-up order;
— any order for the dissolution of the company;
— any return by a liquidator of the final meeting of the company on a winding up.

Regulation 4(2) provides that such notice shall be published within six weeks of the relevant delivery or issue. In practice, the Registrar of Companies ordinarily obliges companies by causing such notices to be published in *Iris Oifigiúil*.

(e) Use of a business name

[2.045] The Registration of Business Names Act 1963 ('RBNA 1963') has application to companies registered under the Companies Acts 1963–2001. Where a company decides to use a name other than its own corporate name, CA 1963, s 22 provides that it shall register that *business name* in the manner directed by law for the registration of business names. The general requirements of the RBNA 1963 have been considered in Chapter 1[91].

Registration of foreign companies

[2.046] Leaving Irish companies to one side, we now turn to companies that were either formed or registered abroad. Part XI of CA 1963 is expressed, by CA 1963, s 351, to apply to:

> '...all companies incorporated outside the State which, after the operative date, establish a place of business within the State, and to companies incorporated outside the State which have, before the operative date, established a place of business within the State and continue to have an established place of business within the State on the operative date.'

Section 352(1) of CA 1963, provides that:

> 'Companies incorporated outside the State, which, after the operative date, establish a place of business within the state, shall, within one month of the establishment of the place of business, deliver to the registrar of companies for registration—
>
> (a) a certified copy of the charter, statutes or memorandum and articles of the company, or other instrument constituting or defining the constitution of the company, and, if the instrument is not written in the English or Irish language, a certified translation thereof;
>
> (b) a list of the directors and secretary of the company containing the particulars mentioned in subsection (2)[92];
>
> (c) the names and addresses of some one or more persons resident in the State authorised to accept on behalf of the company service of process and any notices required to be

---

[91] See Chapter 1, *The Private Company in Context*, para **[1.005]**.

[92] CA 1963, s 352(2) provides that various particulars should be included in the list referred to in CA 1963, s 352(1)(b), eg, the names, addresses, nationalities, business occupations, and particulars of other directorships of Irish companies of the foreign company's directors, etc.

> served on the company and also the address of the company's principal place of business in the State.'

Part XI no longer applies, however, to limited companies incorporated outside the State which establish a *branch* within the State: reg 14 of the European Communities (Branch Disclosures) Regulations 1993 (SI 1993/395). The regulations require disclosure of particulars similar in many respects to those sought by Part XI, though a distinction is made between companies incorporated in EU Member States and those incorporated elsewhere.

[2.047] For a company with an established place of business within the State, the *mechanics of registration* are as follows. At least three forms must be completed, namely Forms 1E, 2E and 3E. These must be accompanied by the equivalent of the company's memorandum and articles of association. All such documentation must be *certified* by, for example, a notary public or the equivalent of the Registrar of Companies in the foreign company's country of incorporation. In addition, such documents must also be *authenticated*, a procedure usually involving the Irish embassy in the company's country of origin[93]. If necessary, documentation must be *translated*. It should be noted, however, that the law on authentication and legalisation has been changed dramatically as a result of Ireland's accession to the Hague Convention and the convention abolishing the legalisation of documents in the Member States of the EC, both of which came into force here on 9 March 1999[94]. No authentication is required in respect of documents originating in Belgium, France, Denmark and Italy, where the certification of the document is by a person entitled under the laws of the relevant jurisdiction to witness a declaration (such as a notary public)[95].

[2.048] The question of whether or not a foreign or 'overseas' company has an *established place of business* has proved to be troublesome[96]. Much of the case law in this area concerns situations where a foreign or overseas company which is not registered under the Companies Acts executes a charge over its Irish assets. While this is considered later in Chapter 21, for present purposes it is sufficient to note what was said to be the meaning of 'established place of business' by Oliver LJ in *Re Oriel Ltd*[97]:

> 'Speaking for myself, I think also that when the word "established" is used adjectivally, as it is in [s 352] it connotes not only the setting up of a place of business at a specific location, but a degree of permanence or recognisability as being a location of the company's business...The concept, as it seems to me is of some more or less permanent location, not necessarily owned or even leased by the company, but at least associated with the company and from which habitually or with some degree of regularity business is conducted.'[98]

---

93 Documents may be authenticated by Irish companies by the signature of a director, secretary or other authorised office and need not be under seal: CA 1963, s 42.

94 See the Companies (Forms) Amendment Order 1999 (SI 1999/14).

95 For documents originating in Hague convention countries, authentication is now pursuant to the Apostille system.

96 See generally, Courtney, 'Registration of Charges: Foreign Companies and the Slavenburg File in Ireland' (1992) Gazette ILSI 157 and Gill, 'Foreign Companies and Establishing 'A Place of Business' (1989) ILT 265.

97 *Re Oriel Ltd* [1985] 3 All ER 216, [1986] WLR 180.

98 *Re Oriel Ltd* [1985] 3 All ER 216 at 220.

In *Lord Advocate v Huron and Erie Loan and Savings Co*[99] it was held that to have an established place of business, a company must have a location occupied by people who are servants or officers of the company, and not merely agents[100].

Companies authorised to register under the Companies Acts 1963–2001

[2.049] Part IX of CA 1963 concerns companies which were *not* formed under the Companies Acts 1963–2001, but which are nonetheless *authorised to register* under the Acts[101]. Section 328(1) of CA 1963 provides that with certain exceptions[102] the following companies can register under the Companies Acts 1963–2001 as unlimited companies or as companies limited by shares or by guarantee:

— any company consisting of seven or more members which was in existence on 2 November 1862, including any company registered under the Joint Stock Companies Acts[103]; and,

— any company formed after 2 November 1862 under any other statute or by letters patent or being otherwise duly constituted according to law which also consists of seven or more members.

It would seem that to register in Ireland merely to avail of the provisions on winding up contained in the Companies Acts 1963–2001 will not be of itself a sufficient reason to refuse registration.

[2.050] Any company entitled to register under CA 1963, s 328 must obtain the sanction of a majority of its members in person or by proxy at an extraordinary general meeting[104]. However, where the company is unlimited, a qualified majority of not less than three-quarters of the members must vote in favour of the registration[105].

[2.051] The requirements for registration under the Companies Acts 1963–2001 by joint stock companies[106] and other companies[107] are set out in CA 1963. Other provisions concerning the registration of certain companies not formed under the Companies Acts

99 *Lord Advocate v Huron and Erie Loan and Savings Co* (1911) SC 612.

100 See Lingard, *Bank Security Documents* (3rd edn, 1993), para 3.28.

101 See CA 1963, ss 328–343.

102 CA 1963, s 328(2) excludes companies registered under the Companies Act 1862 or the Companies (Consolidation) Act 1908 or any company which has neither its registered office nor principal place of business in the State. Subsection (3) prohibits companies from registering in Ireland where their members' liability is limited by statute or letters patent, and which are not Joint Stock Companies. Furthermore, by sub-s (4) a company whose members' liability is limited by statute or letters patent may not register as an unlimited company or a company limited by guarantee. By sub-s (5) a company which is not a Joint Stock Company cannot register as a company limited by shares.

103 See Chapter 1, *The Private Company in Context*, para **[1.067]**. See also the definition of 'Joint Stock Company' contained in CA 1963, s 329.

104 CA 1963, s 328(6).

105 CA 1963, s 328(7). Where it is sought to register the company as a company limited by guarantee, sub-s (8) contains additional safeguards.

106 See CA 1963, s 330 as amended by C(A)A 1983, First Schedule, para 19.

107 See CA 1963, s 331.

1963–2001 are set out in CA 1963, ss 332–336. Ancillary provisions concern the vesting of property[108] and the effect of registration where the company concerned is involved in litigation[109]. Furthermore, by CA 1963, s 341, power is given to substitute memoranda and articles of association for the old deed of settlement where this was the governing constitutional document of the company.

Irish registered non-resident companies

[2.052] Irish registered non-resident (IRNR) companies flourished in the 1990s. Originally, they were primarily formed for tax purposes[110]. With the break-up of the Eastern Bloc countries, many nefarious individuals – including, it was reported, the Russian mafia and other organised criminals – became acquainted with the utility of IRNR companies. Ireland was one of the few countries that did not have deeming provisions whereby companies formed and registered here were deemed to be resident in the jurisdiction for tax purposes. The Department of Foreign Affairs received many complaints from foreign authorities' law and tax enforcement agencies arising from the frequency with which IRNRs were cited as entities involved in international fraud and general malpractice. The result was the taking of steps, the effect of which was to effectively outlaw the IRNR. In the first place, the Finance Act 1999, s 82(2) provides that subject to certain limited exceptions, '...a company which is incorporated in the State shall be regarded for the purposes of the Tax Acts and the Capital Gains Tax Acts as resident in the State.'

The exceptions to this are twofold. First, a company will not be deemed to be resident where it is a 'relevant company' and carries on a trade in the State or is related to a company that carries on a trade in the State: the Finance Act 1999, s 82(3)[111]. Secondly, a company that is regarded for the purposes of any arrangements as resident in a territory other than the State and not resident in the State shall be treated for the purposes of the Tax Acts and the Capital Gains Tax Acts as not resident in the State. Other steps taken include C(A)(No 2)A 1999, s 42 (the general requirement that all companies must carry on an activity in the State)[112], the requirement that all Irish companies have at least one Irish resident director[113] and the requirement that all companies formed and registered here must deliver specified particulars to the Revenue Commissioners within 30 days of commencing business[114].

---

[108] See CA 1963, s 337.

[109] See CA 1963, ss 338, 339, 342 and 343.

[110] See Kavanagh, 'Non-Resident Irish Companies' (1994) CLP 141.

[111] Relevant company is one, in effect, that is under the control of persons who are resident for tax purposes in the EU or other territory with which the State has made tax arrangements, and not under the control of a person who is not so resident: the Taxes Consolidation Act 1997, s 23A(1)(a) inserted by the Finance Act 1999, s 82(1).

[112] See para **[2.031]**.

[113] See para **[2.039]**.

[114] Taxes Consolidation Act 1997, s 882(2) as inserted by the Finance Act 1999, s 83(1); see para **[2.035]**.

[2.053] By making a company non-resident in Ireland the desired effect was to ensure that it would not be liable inter alia, for Irish corporation tax[115]. The means employed to make a company Irish registered but non-resident was to form and register it in Ireland pursuant to the Companies Acts 1963–2001 but to ensure it was prevented, by its constitutional documentation, from being *controlled* from within the State. Although it was not essential to the determination of a company's *residence* that it did not conduct business in Ireland, it was material[116] and many non-resident companies' constitutional documentation so provided. The IRNR company will be remembered as a short-lived curiosity that had the potential to cause great harm to Ireland's commercial reputation on the international stage.

The application of the Companies Acts 1963–2001

[2.054] Section 2 of CA 1963 gives the word 'company' a very specific meaning. As such, when any provision of the Companies Acts 1963–2001 uses the word 'company', only certain bodies corporate are subject to that provision. This can be of particular importance in determining the application of restrictive measures in the Companies Acts 1963–2001. The definition assigned to 'company' by s 2 is '...a company formed and registered under this Act or an existing company.'

This short, but very precise, definition of 'company' shall now be considered.

[2.055] The first aspect to the definition of '*company*' is that it includes a company which is 'formed *and* registered' under the Companies Acts 1963–2001 in so far as they are read as one Act[117]. The word 'and' must be read as a conjunction, so that in order to come within the definition in s 2, a company must be both formed *and* registered under the Companies Acts 1963–2001. A company which is registered as a foreign or external company under CA 1963, Part XI[118] is not, therefore, a 'company' within the meaning of s 2, as it merely satisfies one limb of the definition ie it is 'registered' under the Acts (see, however, CA 1963, s 325(1))[119]. It follows that unless expressly stated to the contrary, the provisions of the Companies Acts 1963–2001 do not apply to foreign companies. Instructive here is the case of *Rover International Ltd v Cannon Film Sales Ltd*[120] where a provision in the Companies Act 1985 (UK) (similar to CA 1963, s 37 concerning pre-incorporation contracts) was found to be inapplicable to foreign companies[121]. *Re Tuskar Resources plc*[122] concerned an application to appoint an examiner. In refusing to appoint an

[115] Contrast the liability to pay value added tax: *WLD Worldwide Leather Distribution Ltd v Revenue Commissioners* [1995] 1 IR 99, per Flood J, noted by Hutchinson, 'Registering For VAT – A Recent Case' (1994) CLP 239.

[116] See, eg, *Re Little Olympian Each Ways Ltd* [1994] 4 All ER 561 where Lindsay J held that an English company would not be ordinarily resident there where its central control and the management of the company actually resides and is exercised overseas.

[117] See the CA 1990, s 3.

[118] See para **[2.046]** *ff*. Note, however, the application of CA 1963, Part IV to such companies: CA 1963, s 111.

[119] See para **[2.057]**.

[120] *Rover International Ltd v Cannon Film Sales Ltd* [1987] BCLC 540.

[121] See Chapter 7, *Corporate Contracts: Capacity and Authority*, para **[7.041]**.

[122] *Re Tuskar Resources plc* [2001] 1 IR 668 (McCracken J), considered in Chapter 23, *Examinerships*, para **[23.021]**.

examiner to Tuskar Resources plc, an Irish company, McCracken J also refused to appoint an examiner to a 'related company' which happened to be a Nigerian company:

> '…in my view the definition of a related company in s 4(5) [C(A)A 1999] does not include a company registered outside this jurisdiction, as it sets out the conditions in which 'a company is related to another company', and the word 'company' as defined in the Companies Act 1963 means a company formed and registered under that Act, or an existing company. In the present case the Nigerian company is not formed or registered under the 1963 Act.'[123]

Similarly in *Harrington v JVC (UK) Ltd*[124] O'Hanlon J declined jurisdiction to make an order for security for costs against a Northern Ireland registered company[125]. The making of an order for security for costs against a company that was allegedly formed and registered in England and Wales in *Windmaster Developments Ltd v Airoglen Ltd*[126] is not an exception to the foregoing principles of jurisdiction as in that case it appears only to have been noticed after the making of the order that the company might not, in fact, have been formed and registered in Ireland and in the subsequent hearing no evidence of foreign incorporation was adduced.

[2.056] The second aspect to the definition of 'company' is that it includes an 'existing company'. Section 2 of CA 1963 provides that an 'existing company' means:

> '...a company formed and registered in a register kept in the State under the Joint Stock Companies Act, the Companies Act 1862, or the Companies (Consolidation) Act 1908.'

Although s 2 dictates the automatic application of the Companies Acts 1963–2001 to existing companies, CA 1963, Part VIII addresses in detail certain companies formed or registered under former Acts. By CA 1963, s 324(1), the Companies Acts 1963–2001 are deemed to apply to 'existing companies' whether limited or unlimited in the same manner as if they had been formed and registered under the Acts. By reg 3 of the European Communities (Single-Member Private Limited Companies) Regulations 1994 (SI 1994/275), the provisions of the Companies Acts 1963–2001 are applied to single-member companies.

[2.057] Section 325(1) of CA 1963 provides that the Companies Acts 1963–2001 apply to every company registered (in a register kept in the State) but *not* formed under the Joint Stock Companies Acts, the Companies Act 1862 or the Companies (Consolidation) Act 1908. Part VIII contains a number of other provisions in relation to other varieties of existing companies[127]. Section 377(1) of CA 1963, as amended by CA 1990, s 250 applies the provisions of the CA 1963, Ninth Schedule, as replaced by s 250, to all *unregistered companies* incorporated in and having a principal place of business in the State other than

---

[123] [2001] 1 IR 668 at 679.

[124] *Harrington v JVC (UK) Ltd* (16 March 1995, unreported), High Court (O'Hanlon J).

[125] See Chapter 6, *Corporate Civil Litigation*, para **[6.026]**.

[126] *Windmaster Developments Ltd v Airoglen Ltd* (10 July 2000, unreported), High Court (McCracken J).

[127] Therefore, CA 1963, s 326 applies the Companies Acts 1963–2001 to unlimited companies re-registered as limited companies under former Acts, and CA 1963, s 327 addresses old Joint Stock companies.

those specified in CA 1963, s 377(2). The Ninth Schedule applies many, but not all, of the provisions in the Companies 1963–2001 and various companies regulations to such unregistered companies.

[2.058] Where an old company[128] registers under Part IX, by virtue of CA 1963, s 340(2):

> 'All provisions contained in any statute or instrument constituting or regulating the company, ...shall be deemed to be conditions and regulations of the company, in the same manner and with the same incidents as if so much thereof as would, if the company had been formed under this Act, have been required to be inserted in the memorandum, were contained in a registered memorandum, and the residue thereof were contained in registered articles.'

Section 340(3) of CA 1963 further provides that all provisions of the Companies Acts 1963–2001 shall apply to the company, its members, contributories and creditors as if it was formed under those Acts, with certain exceptions.

Investment companies

[2.059] Part XIII of CA 1990 permits the formation of a new type of company, termed an investment company. Such companies can be private companies, but are a highly specialised form of company that are primarily utilised in an International Financial Services Centre (IFSC) context. *Investment company* is defined[129] as meaning a company to which CA 1990, Part XIII applies. Section 253(2) provides that Part XIII applies:

> '...to a company limited by shares (not being a company to which the UCITS Regulations[130] apply)—
>
> (a) the sole object of which is stated in its memorandum to be the collective investment of its funds in property with the aim of spreading investment risk and giving members of the company the benefit of the results of the management of its funds; and
>
> (b) the articles or memorandum of which provide -
>
> (i) that the actual value of the paid up share capital of the company shall be at all times equal to the value of the assets of any kind of the company after the deduction of its liabilities, and
>
> (ii) that the shares of the company shall, at the request of any of the holders thereof, be purchased by the company directly or indirectly out of the company's assets.'

Before an investment company is permitted to carry on business in the State it must obtain authorisation from the Central Bank under CA 1990, s 256. The essential attribute of an investment company is that it has variable capital, which has resulted in the relaxation of ordinary capital maintenance rules[131]. Accordingly, investment companies are, subject to safeguards, empowered to purchase their own shares[132].

---

128 Ie a company as defined by CA 1963, s 328(1).

129 CA 1990, s 252(1).

130 European Communities (Undertakings for Collective Investment in Transferable Securities) Regulations 1989 (SI 1989/78).

131 See generally, Chapter 18, *The Maintenance of Capital.*

132 CA 1990, s 254.

[B] CORPORATE CONVERSIONS

[2.060] When registered, a company will be of a specific type: eg limited by shares, limited by guarantee, public, private, unlimited etc. It may, however, at any time subsequent to its original registration, convert or morph to another type of company. Here, it is proposed to outline some of the conversions that are possible.

1. Converting from an unlimited to a limited company.
2. Converting from a limited to an unlimited company.
3. Converting from a PLC to a private company.
4. Converting from a private company to a PLC.
5. Converting from a multi-member private company to a single-member private company.
6. Converting from a single-member private company to multi-member private company.

Converting from an unlimited to a limited company

[2.061] An unlimited private company can be converted to a limited company in accordance with s 53 of the Companies (Amendment) Act 1983 ('C(A)A 1983')[133]. This can be effected where the members of the company pass a *special resolution* that the unlimited company should re-register as a company limited by shares or by guarantee. In addition, the special resolution should set out the necessary changes to its memorandum and articles of association[134]. The *mechanics* of re-registration involve the lodging of the following documents with the CRO:

— Form 25B, which is obtained from the Revenue Commissioners, and must be stamped by the Revenue;

— Form 86, obtainable from the CRO;

— a special resolution, referred to above; and

— any amended memorandum and articles, as are appropriate.

Upon receiving the foregoing documents properly completed, the Registrar of Companies shall issue an appropriate certificate of incorporation[135].

Converting from a limited to an unlimited company

[2.062] Conversely, a limited liability company can change its status to that of an unlimited company in accordance with C(A)A 1983, s 52. A more stringent statutory procedure applies in this instance. It is a fundamental principle of company law that the liability of a member cannot be increased without his consent[136]. Accordingly, because all of the members will on conversion assume full personal liability for the debts of the company, their *unanimous* assent to the conversion is required. The procedural requirements are as follows:

---

133 Note that CA 1963, s 20 has been repealed by C(A)A 1983, s 54.

134 C(A)A 1983, s 53(2).

135 C(A)A 1983, s 53(4).

136 CA 1963, s 27.

- Form D6, which must be signed by all of the members of the company, or where a proxy signs, the written authorisation of such members is required;
- a declaration of the directors: the directors of the company must sign a declaration that those who signed are the only members and that those who signed were empowered to sign; and
- amended memorandum and articles, as appropriate.

The new unlimited liability of the members does not extend to past members, who are only liable to contribute that which they would have had to contribute had the conversion not taken place[137].

Converting from a PLC to a private company

[2.063] PLCs may convert to private companies. In order to become re-registered as a private company, a PLC must change its memorandum and articles of association in order to comply with the requirements set out in CA 1963, s 33(1)[138]. Alterations to a PLC's constitution must be effected by special resolution. Section 14 of C(A)A 1983 provides that the PLC's memorandum of association must be changed by the deletion of the reference to the statement that the company is a PLC. Section 15 of C(A)A 1983 affords protection to dissenting minority shareholders, unhappy with the re-registration as a private company.

Converting from a private company to a PLC

[2.064] Of the relatively few public limited companies formed in Ireland many will have begun corporate life as private companies which were subsequently converted[139]. A conversion of this nature requires a private company to amend its constitutional documentation and capital structure to accord with the requirements for a public limited company ('PLC'). The capital requirements for a PLC include:

- the nominal share capital must be at least €38,092.14 (C(A)A 1983, s 19);
- the nominal share capital must be paid up in money or money's worth to at least 25% of the nominal value;
- the net assets of the company as per the balance sheet must at least equal the total of its called up share capital and undistributed reserves.

Sections 9 and 10 of C(A)A 1983 set out the basic conditions which must be satisfied. The actual mechanics of re-registration involve the lodgement of the following documents:

- Forms 71 and 72;
- a special resolution;
- amended memorandum and articles of association;
- an auditors' statement;
- the balance sheet and auditors' unqualified report; and
- a valuation sheet (if applicable).

---

137 C(A)A 1983, s 52(6).

138 See Chapter 1, *The Private Company in Context*, para **[1.115]**.

139 See Keane, *Company Law* (3rd edn, 2000), para 4.36. See also, generally, Chapter 28, *Public Companies in Context.*

It should be noted that before a public company can commence business, there exist additional statutory requirements under the Companies Acts 1963–2001[140].

Converting from a multi-member private company to a single-member private company

[2.065] The circumstances in which a private company limited by shares or by guarantee can convert to being a single-member private company are set out in the European Communities (Single-Member Private Limited Companies) Regulations 1994, reg 5(1)[141]. This provides:

> 'A private company limited by shares or by guarantee registered with two or more subscribers to its memorandum of association, in accordance with the Companies Acts, shall become a single-member company, on such date as the number of members is reduced to one and all the shares in the company are registered in the name of a sole member.'

It will be noted, immediately, that an unlimited private company may not convert to a single-member company: the regulations only apply to private companies limited by shares or by guarantee. It should also be noted that where the circumstances set out in reg 5(1) are met, the conversion of the company to a single-member company *is automatic*, occurring by operation of law. In this regard, such a conversion is the least encumbered by restrictions as it is not dependent upon the issue of a new certificate of incorporation or any action by the CRO. However the company must cause the fact of conversion, the date upon which the conversion occurred and the identity of the single member to be notified in writing, in the prescribed form, to the Registrar of Companies within 28 days from the date of conversion[142].

Converting from a single-member private company to multi-member private company

[2.066] A single-member company will be deemed to have *automatically* converted to a multi-member private company limited by shares or by guarantee where the circumstances in reg 6(1) of the European Communities (Single-Member Private Limited Companies) Regulations 1994, are satisfied. This provides:

> 'A company which is incorporated as, or becomes, a single-member company, in accordance with these regulations, shall cease to be a single-member company on such date as the number of members increases to more then one but shall continue to be a private company limited by shares or guarantee, as the case may be, while the number of members does not exceed 50.'

---

140 See Chapter 28, *Public Companies in Context*, para **[28.038]** *ff*.

141 SI 1994/275.

142 European Communities (Single-Member Private Limited Companies) Regulations 1994, reg 5(2). The prescribed form (M1) has been ordained by the European Communities (Single-Member Private Limited Companies) (Forms) Regulations 1994 (SI 1994/306), Part I. Failure to comply with reg 5(2) will mean that the company and every officer of the company, who is in default, is guilty of an offence: reg 5(3).

Here again, the company is obliged to cause the fact and date on which it ceased to be a single-member company to be notified in writing to the Registrar of Companies in the prescribed form within 28 days from the date of the conversion[143].

---

[143] European Communities (Single-Member Private Limited Companies) Regulations 1994, reg 6(2). The prescribed form (M2) has been ordained by the European Communities (Single-Member Private Limited Companies) (Forms) Regulations 1994 (SI 1994/306), Part II. Failure to comply with reg 6(2) is an offence for both the company and every officer of the company who is in default: reg 6(3).

Chapter 3

Private Constitutional Documentation

Introduction

[3.001] A company's memorandum of association sets out the basic parameters of legitimate corporate existence, finance, capacity and activity. Furthermore, the incorporation of a company is achieved through the registration of the memorandum of association. The articles of association are the internal rules or regulations of a company and govern relations between the company and its members and between the members inter se. On incorporation, both must be delivered to the Registrar of Companies for registration and retention[1]. Together, these two documents form the 'corporate constitution', in that they govern the company's relations with outsiders and insiders and define the company. However, in many private companies there also exists a 'hidden constitution', which arises through the adoption of a shareholders' agreement. Unlike true constitutional documents, shareholders' agreements are only binding on those who are parties to them.

[3.002] The provisions in a company's memorandum and articles of association are of fundamental importance. Although the memorandum of association is the dominant document and its provisions will prevail in any conflict with the articles, the particular articles of association adopted by a company are of great significance in many different company law contexts. The articles of association are the rules by which the members of a company agree to be bound. They are created by the first subscribers and accepted by all future members. As such, the articles underscore the importance of the concept of 'association' to company law. Corporations aggregate are associations, and have always had an internal constitution. Single member private companies[2] will also have articles that will regulate the relationship between the sole member and the company's directors. The fact that both the memorandum and articles are alterable, generally, by the shareholders does not detract from their importance. Unless and until they are altered, they are sacrosanct and the power to alter them must be exercised bona fide and in the interests of the company[3]. In this chapter the foregoing issues are considered in four separate sections:

[A] The memorandum of association.

[B] The articles of association.

---

1 CA 1963, s 17. This was amended by CLEA 2001, s 83 to facilitate the registration of standard memoranda and articles of association, permitted by CLEA 2001, s 80: see para **[3.005]**. On the modalities of formation and registration, see Chapter 2, *Formation, Registration and Conversion of Private Companies*, para **[2.026]**.

2 Permitted by the European Communities (Single-Member Private Limited Companies) Regulations (SI 1994/275), considered generally in Chapter 1, *The Private Company in Context*, para **[1.124]** *ff*.

3 See para **[3.075]** *ff*.

[C] The statutory contract in section 25 of the Companies Act 1963 .

[D] Shareholders' agreements

[A] The Memorandum of Association

[3.003] A company's memorandum of association is the principal document by which its registration is effected. The Companies Act 1963, s 5 ('CA 1963') facilitates corporate formation by providing:

> '...where the company to be formed will be a private company, any two or more persons, associated for any lawful purpose may, by subscribing their names to a *memorandum of association* and otherwise complying with the requirements of this Act relating to registration, form an incorporated company, with or without limited liability.'

Of course, now a single-member private company can be formed and reg 4 of the European Communities (Single-Member Private Limited Companies) Regulations 1994[4] provides that one person may sign his name to a memorandum of association. Historically, it was perceived that the memorandum contained matters so fundamental to the company that it could not be altered, in contrast with the articles which could always be altered by a special resolution of the members[5]. Today the memorandum of association *is* also alterable where the alterations comply with the provisions of the Companies Acts 1963–2001.

Compulsory clauses

[3.004] Section 16 of CA 1963 prescribes that the form of the memorandum shall be in accordance with the forms set out in CA 1963, Sch 1 Tables B, C, D and E, 'or as near thereto as circumstances admit'. Furthermore, the memorandum must be printed (in an entire format or in a form pursuant to the Company Law Enforcement Act 2001, s 80 ('CLEA 2001')[6], stamped, signed and attested[7]. The most common company formed is the private company limited by shares, the model memorandum for which is to be found in Table B. There are five compulsory clauses, namely:

(a) The name clause.

(b) The objects clause.

(c) The liability clause.

(d) The capital clause.

(e) The association or subscription clause.

It is important to note that although the foregoing are compulsory clauses, a company may have *additional* clauses in its memorandum, such as a clause providing for life directors.

[3.005] Section 80 of CLEA 2001 facilitates the registration process by allowing persons applying for the registration of a company to lodge only those elements of the

---

4 SI 1994/275.

5 See Schmithoff (ed) *Palmer's Company Law* (24th edn, 1987), para 6-02.

6 CA 1963, s 7 was amended to so provide by CLEA 2001, s 81.

7 CA 1963, s 7 as amended by the Finance Act 1996, s 112. 'Printed' is defined by CA 1963, s 2 to include 'reproduced in any legible and durable form approved by the registrar of companies'.

memorandum and articles of association that are peculiar to that company. This works in conjunction with a previously lodged 'reference' document for association with the specific elements lodged with the application. Section 80(1) of CLEA 2001 provides that the Registrar of Companies can accept for registration a document containing standard form text from the objects clause of a memorandum of association or from articles of association and that he shall assign a reference number to each document so registered for identification purposes[8]. Accordingly, a memorandum and articles of association may contain a statement that either or both are to incorporate the text of the reference document previously registered[9]. The effect on a memorandum or articles of such a reference to a previously registered reference articles or memorandum is provided for in s 80(4):

> '...it shall be deemed for all purposes to incorporate within it the text of the relevant document filed with the registrar pursuant to subsection (1), so that it shall form and be read as one entire document, and where such a memorandum or articles of association has been registered by the registrar and is inspected by any person, the registrar shall also make available for inspection the related document filed with him or her pursuant to subsection (1).'

The consequence of this change for the Companies Registration Office ('CRO') will be to reduce the numbers of memoranda and articles of association that are currently scanned and, thereby, improve the efficiency of the CRO.

(a) The name clause

[3.006] Every company must have a name, for it is this which identifies it from other companies[10]. Choosing a name can often pose a practical problem when forming a company, since delay may be caused where a company is lodged for registration with a name unacceptable to the Registrar of Companies. Persons are well advised to telephone the CRO to ascertain whether or not a proposed name has been registered already. In addition to the Registrar objecting to a name which is already on the register, a name can also be refused where it is offensive, misleading or otherwise objectionable[11]. Section 21 of CA 1963 also provides that no name shall be registered which in the opinion of the Registrar is undesirable, subject to an appeal to court. This was previously the function of the Minister for Enterprise, Trade and Employment but was transferred to the Registrar of Companies by CLEA 2001, s 86, as indeed was the responsibility for administrative decisions, generally, relating to company names.

---

8 CLEA 2001, s 80(2) provides that notwithstanding anything in the Companies Acts, a document filed pursuant to sub-s (1) 'need not relate to a particular company or contain the registered number of a company'.

9 CLEA 2001, s 80(3).

10 CA 1963, s 6(1)(a), as amended by C(A)A 1983, First Schedule.

11 Certain statutes prohibit the use of certain words in companies' names. So, the National Standards Authority Ireland Act 1996, s 26, provides that a company shall not be registered by a name containing the words 'Irish Standard'; 'I.S.' or the Irish equivalent thereof or by a name so nearly resembling such words or initials as to be likely to deceive.

[3.007] Furthermore, where a company is limited by shares or by guarantee, the word 'limited' or 'teoranta' must be the last word in the name[12]. Only a company that has limited liability may, however, use the word 'limited' or 'teoranta' in its name. Section 381(1) of CA 1963 provides:

> 'If any person or persons trade or carry on business under a name or title of which "limited" or "teoranta" or any contraction or imitation or either word, is the last word, that person or those persons shall be, unless duly incorporated with limited liability, guilty of an offence[13].'

Where persons who are committing such an offence fail to desist from its continued commission within 14 days of being served notice so to do, the Registrar of Companies or the Director of Corporate Enforcement is empowered to apply to court for a prohibitory injunction against them[14].

[3.008] Prior to the CLEA 2001, it was the case that ministerial permission could be sought by a limited company, to dispense with the use of the word 'limited' in its name[15]. The new regime is that any company that satisfies the provisions of CA 1963, s 24 (the original wording of which was repealed and substituted by CLEA 2001, s 88) will automatically be exempt from having to use the word 'limited' in its name. The new regime operates by providing that a limited company will be exempt from the provisions of the Companies Acts relating to the use of the word 'limited' as part of its name and publishing of its name but shall enjoy all the privileges and be subject to all the obligations of limited companies provided it complies with the provisions of s 24(1), namely:

> '(a) its objects are the promotion of commerce, art, science, education, religion, charity or any other prescribed object, and
>
> (b) its memorandum or articles of association—
>
> (i) require its profits (if any) or other income to be applied to the promotion of its objects,
>
> (ii) prohibit the payment of dividends to its members, and
>
> (iii) require all the assets which would otherwise be available to its members to be transferred on its winding up to another company whose objects comply with paragraph (a) and which meets the requirements of this paragraph, and
>
> (c) a director or secretary of the company (or, in the case of an association about to be formed as a limited company, one of the persons who are to be the first directors or the person who is to be the first secretary of the company) has delivered to the registrar of companies a statutory declaration in the prescribed form that the company complies or, where applicable, will comply with the requirements of paragraphs (a) and (b).'

---

12 CA 1963, s 6(1)(a), as amended by C(A)A 1983, First Schedule. An abbreviation of the words is acceptable, eg 'Ltd' or 'Teo': CA 1963, s 22(2).

13 CLEA 2001, s 98 repealed the old CA 1963, s 381 and substituted a new s 381.

14 CA 1963, s 381(2). The court may order costs against the persons against whom an order is made: sub-s (3).

15 CLEA 2001, s 88(2) saves exemptions made by ministerial direction under the 'old' CA 1963, s 24, notwithstanding its repeal by CLEA 2001, s 88(1).

The form of declaration of compliance with the requirements of CA 1963, s 24(1)(a) and (b) has been prescribed by statutory instrument[16].

[3.009] This procedure should also be followed where a company that is already incorporated wishes to omit 'limited' on a change of name application[17]. The Registrar of Companies is empowered to refuse to register a limited company without the word 'limited' in its corporate name where the declaration referred to in CA 1963, s 24(1)(c) is not forthcoming[18]. Companies that are exempt cannot subsequently change their memoranda or articles of association so as to cease to comply with s 24(1)(b)[19]. Where it appears to the Registrar of Companies that a company that has qualified for exemption has:

— carried on business in furtherance of an object other than those mentioned in CA 1963, s 24(1)(A); or

— has applied any of its profits or other income otherwise than in promoting such objects; or

— has paid a dividend to any members,

the Registrar may direct in writing the company to change its name[20] and such change shall be effected in accordance with CA 1963, s 23, considered below[21]. Providing incorrect, false or misleading information in the CA 1963, s 24(1)(c) statutory declaration, altering the articles so as not to comply with CA 1963, s 24(1)(b) and failing to comply with a direction from the Registrar are all offences[22] that can be prosecuted summarily by the Registrar[23].

[3.010] Where the directors of a company and others use the incorrect name of the company they may, in certain circumstances, incur personal liability[24]. Under CA 1963, s 114, every company is by law required to paint or affix its name on the outside of every office or place in which its business is carried on, in a conspicuous position, in letters easily legible[25], have its name on its seal[26] and use its name in legible characters on all business letters of the company and on all notices and other official publications of the company[27]. A failure in any of these respects renders the company liable to a fine[28].

---

16 See the Schedule to the Companies Act 1963 (Section 24) Regulations 2001 (SI 2001/571).

17 CA 1963, s 24(3).

18 CA 1963, s 24(2).

19 CA 1963, s 24(4).

20 CA 1963, s 24(5). Where a company receives a direction, it may not in future avail of the automatic exemption and must seek the registrar's approval: CA 1963, s 24(6).

21 See para **[3.024]**.

22 CA 1963, s 24(7).

23 CA 1963, s 24(8).

24 See CA 1963, s 114(4), which is considered later in Chapter 5, *Disregarding Separate Legal Personality*, para **[5.078]** *ff*.

25 CA 1963, s 114(1)(a).

26 CA 1963, s 114(1)(b).

27 CA 1963, s 114(1)(c).

28 CA 1963, s 114(2),(3).

[3.011] It must be stressed that although, subject to the veto of the Registrar of Companies, a company is free to chose its own name, by using a name similar to that of another company, it may be liable for the tort of passing off. This may occur where its name is so similar to that of another company as to cause a confusion in the minds of the public[29]. Where a company carries on business under a name other than its registered name or, 'corporate name', it must register such a 'business name' with the Registrar of Companies under the Registration of Business Names Act 1963: CA 1963, s 22(1)[30].

(b) The objects clause

[3.012] Section 6(1)(b) of CA 1963 provides that the memorandum of association of every company must state 'the objects of the company'. The objects clause is one of the most important of the compulsory clauses in the memorandum of association, its function being to set out the parameters of permitted corporate activity. As discussed in Chapter 7 in the context of *corporate capacity*[31], there is voluminous case law on situations where companies act beyond their capacity, or ultra vires their objects clause. For present purposes it is sufficient to say that the objects clauses of practically every company formed today fly in the face of the brevity set out in the model tables to the Companies Acts. Typically, companies are incorporated with a multitude of express objects and powers which are ancillary to the main objects.

[3.013] A company may not have an object which is contrary to the law of the land, and to the extent that it does, that object is void. In *R v Registrar of Joint Stock Companies*[32] the proposed registration of an English company whose objects included the sale of tickets in the Irish Free State Hospitals Sweepstake was objected to by the English Registrar of Companies because such lotteries were illegal in England. The promoters of the company sought a writ of mandamus to compel registration, but failed. In the words of Slesser LJ '[i]t is clear that a company cannot be formed whose proposed constitution necessarily involves an offence against the general law'.[33]

(c) The liability clause

[3.014] The next compulsory clause found in a company's memorandum of association will be the liability clause. It is usual for this to state succinctly 'The liability of the members is limited', or, in the case of an unlimited company, 'The liability of the members is unlimited'.

[3.015] The phrase 'limited liability company', is something of a misnomer in that every company will always have unlimited liability[34]. Rather, what may be limited is the liability of the members. Their liability is not non-existent, but 'limited' in the sense that

---

29 See McMahon & Binchy, *Law of Torts* (3rd edn, 2000), Ch 31.

30 As to the requirements for registration under the RBNA 1963, see Chapter 1, *The Private Company in Context*, para **[1.005]** *ff*.

31 See Chapter 7, *Corporate Contracts, Capacity and Authority*, para **[7.043]** *ff*.

32 *R v Registrar of Joint Stock Companies* [1931] 2 KB 197.

33 [1931] 2 KB 197 at 201. See also *Bowman et al v Secular Society Ltd* [1917] AC 406, and *McEllistrim v Ballymacelligott Co-operative and Dairy Society Ltd* [1919] AC 549. In the latter case, an object which constituted an unreasonable restraint of trade was held to be void.

34 See generally Chapter 4, *Incorporation and its Consequences*, para **[4.072]** *ff*.

it is limited to the amount, if any, unpaid on their shares or in the case of a company limited by guarantee, to the amount of the guarantee[35]. Typically, private companies will acquire capital in ways other than by share capital eg through borrowings. The vast majority of private companies formed are what used to be called 'two pound companies', because only two £1 shares are issued. In view of this, whether they are paid up or not is academic as regards the liability of the members who hold them.

[3.016] Previously, in all cases where the membership of a private company fell below two and the company carried on business for more than six months the remaining member who knew that it was carrying on business would have unlimited liability for the debts of the company contracted after the period of six months: CA 1963, s 36[36]. It is now the case that reg 7(1) of the European Communities (Single-Member Private Limited Companies) Regulations[37] provides that s 36 shall not apply to a private company limited by shares or by guarantee. However, it should be noted that reg 7(1) is not retrospective[38].

(d) The capital clause

[3.017] Section 6(4)(a) of CA 1963 provides that the capital clause must set out the total amount of the company's authorised share capital ie the amount of share capital with which the company proposes to be registered, and the division thereof into shares of a fixed amount[39]. The amount of the capital can be as large or as small as the company's promoters think fit. It is normal for the *authorised* share capital to be a relatively high figure eg €1 million. Normally, this will be divided into 1 million shares of €1 each. This bears little or no relation to the *issued* share capital, which will often be as little as €2.

[3.018] It is often the case that a company will have not one, but two or more classes of shares with different rights. Rather than set out what these classes are, the capital clause will usually facilitate the division of shares into classes by providing:

> 'The shares in the original or any increased capital may be divided into several classes, and there may be attached thereto respectively any preferential, referred or other special rights, privileges, conditions or restrictions as to dividend, capital, voting or otherwise.'

---

35 In the case of a private company limited by guarantee, that also has a share capital, the liability of the members is double: ie the amount if any unpaid on their shares and the amount of the guarantee. This is unusual, and while only a fraction of companies formed will be limited by guarantee, an even smaller number will be limited by guarantee having a share capital.

36 See *Nisbet v Shepherd* [1994] 1 BCLC 300. See Chapter 5, *Disregarding Separate Legal Personality*, para **[5.077]**.

37 SI 1994/275.

38 European Communities (Single-Member Private Limited Companies) Regulations (SI 1994/275), reg 7(2). See further Chapter 5, *Disregarding Separate Legal Personality*, para **[5.075]**.

39 CA 1963, s 67 provides: 'A limited company may by special resolution determine that any portion of its share capital which has not been already called up shall not be capable of being called up except in the event and for the purposes of the company being wound up, and thereupon that portion of its share capital shall not be capable of being called up except in the event and for the purposes aforesaid.'

The company is thereby expressly authorised by its memorandum of association to issue a variety of classes of shares, with different rights attaching thereto as desired. Although the different classes are commonly set out in the capital clause, the *rights* attaching to each class are usually set out in the company's articles of association[40].

[3.019] For regulatory and other reasons[41], sometimes companies will wish to be capitalised to a particular amount. One of the disadvantages of capitalising a company by paying into its share capital is that there is 1% capital duty on the issued share capital. During the 1990s, in order to mitigate the payment of this duty, whilst at the same time ensuring that regulatory and other requirements were satisfied, persons took to making 'capital contributions' which are also referred to as 'equitable contributions','equitable capital', 'contributed surplus' and 'contributed capital'. The effect is that the company receives additional capital without having to issue additional shares. The propriety of these contributions to companies' capital seems to have been accepted, albeit on an informal basis, by the Irish Revenue Commissioners. Capital contributions have also been recognised in other jurisdictions. In *Kellar v Stanley Williams (Turks and Caicos Islands)*[42] the Privy Council were asked to decide who was entitled to the proceeds of a capital contribution where the company into which it was paid went into liquidation. On the one hand it was argued that the capital contribution was like a loan, repayable to its maker; on the other hand it was contended that after the discharge of the company's debts, the contribution was divisible amongst the company's shareholders in proportion to the nominal amount of shares issued in the company. The facts there were that the applicant was the sole beneficial owner of B Ltd, a company that imported liquor into the Turks and Caicos Islands. A Ltd had been formed to provide a shipping agency that could more economically obtain shipping and trucking services for B Ltd. The respondent was manager of B Ltd and it was agreed that he would hold the majority stake in A Ltd as he was a citizen of the islands. Accordingly, he held 51% of the shares and the applicant held the balance. The applicant capitalised A Ltd through a capital contribution. The Privy Council accepted that on the facts there was no clear indication as to whether the applicant had intended the contribution to be in the nature of a loan or in the nature of a capital contribution and upheld the Court of Appeal's decision that the contribution was distributable amongst the shareholders and not repayable to the applicant. On the propriety of capital contributions, the Privy Council said:

> 'If the shareholders of a company agree to increase its capital without a formal allocation of shares that capital will become like share premium part of the owner's equity and there

---

40 In this regard CA 1963, s 66 provides that: 'A company, if so authorised by its articles, may do any one or more of the following things—(a) make arrangements on the issue of shares for a difference between the shareholders in the amounts and times of payment of calls on their shares; (b) accept from any member the whole or a part of the amount remaining unpaid on any shares held by him, although no part of that amount has been called up; (c) pay a dividend in proportion to the amount paid up on each share where a larger amount is paid up on some shares than on others.'

41 In Ireland, capitalisation other than by the issue of shares has arisen in the context of companies operating from the IFSC.

42 *Kellar v Stanley Williams (Turks and Caicos Islands)* [2000] 2 BCLC 390.

> is nothing in the company law of the Turks and Caicos Islands or in the company law of England on which that law is based to render their agreement ineffective'.[43]

In the absence of any evidence to the contrary, in such circumstances the law will lean against presuming the contribution was a loan and in favour of it being divisible amongst the shareholders in proportion to their shareholdings.

(e) The association or subscription clause

[3.020] An *association clause* is required in the memorandum of an ordinary private company. It is not a substantive clause, in that it does not exist for any purpose other than to conform to the requirement that the signatories to the memorandum must bind themselves together. In the case of an ordinary private company it typically provides as follows:

> 'We, the several persons whose names, addresses and descriptions are subscribed, wish to be formed into a company in pursuance of this memorandum of association and we agree to take the number of shares in the capital of the company set opposite our respective names.'

What follows this are the names, addresses and descriptions of the shareholder-members/subscribers and the number of shares taken by each, together with the signature of a witness.

[3.021] In a single-member private company a *subscription clause* will be appropriate whereby the single member subscribes his name to the memorandum of association[44].

Non-compulsory clauses

[3.022] The vast majority of memoranda of association registered today do not contain any more than the compulsory clauses. However, on being formed, the members may decide to copper-fasten certain matters by 'enshrining' or 'entrenching' them in the memorandum. One matter which may be enshrined is provision for a life director where the directorship of some person is perceived to be intrinsic to the company. The significance of doing this is that, unlike the obligatory clauses, such clauses can be made unalterable by virtue of CA 1963, s 9. This provides that the memorandum of association cannot be altered, save to the extent for which express provision is made by the Companies Acts 1963–2001. As is considered below, CA 1963, s 28(3) enables the memorandum itself to provide that certain clauses may be expressed to be unalterable.

Alteration of the memorandum of association

[3.023] Having reviewed the typical memorandum of association, it remains to consider the mechanics of and restrictions on, the alteration of the provisions set out in the memorandum. The alteration of each clause of the memorandum is governed by different provisions in the Companies Acts. Consequently each of the compulsory clauses of the memorandum must be considered separately in the light of the authorised means of alteration. Where an alteration is made to a company's memorandum of

---

43 [2000] 2 BCLC 390 at 395.

44 European Communities (Single-Member Private Limited Companies) Regulations 1994 (SI 1994/275), reg 4.

association, every copy of the memorandum issued by the company after its alteration must be in accordance with the alteration[45].

(a) Alteration of the name clause

[3.024] A company may change its name by virtue of CA 1963, s 23, as amended by CLEA 2001, s 87 which transferred the function of the Minister for Enterprise, Trade and Employment to the Registrar of Companies. This provides that the members of a company can change the company's name by passing a *special resolution*[46]. This does not mean that a company can vote in favour of changing its name so as to delete the word 'limited', or its Irish equivalent[47]. Where a company's members vote in favour of changing its name the consent in writing of the Registrar of Companies is required. Having obtained the Registrar's consent, the company must send the special resolution and two copies of the amended memorandum to the companies registration office together with the appropriate fee. In due course, the Registrar will issue a 'Certificate of Incorporation on Change of Name', which will supersede the original Certificate of Incorporation[48].

[3.025] A company may be obliged to change its name by order of the Registrar. Section 23(2) of CA 1963 provides:

> 'If, through inadvertence or otherwise, a company on its first registration, or on its registration by a new name, is registered by a name which, in the opinion of the registrar of companies, is too like the name by which a company in existence is already registered, the first mentioned company may change its name with the sanction of the registrar of companies and, if he so directs within 6 months of its being registered by that name, shall change it within a period of 6 weeks from the date of the direction or such longer period as the registrar may think fit to allow.'

It is important to note that the Registrar may only direct that a company change its name where the name is, in his opinion, 'too like the name by which a company in existence is already registered', and not because it is, say, offensive etc.

[3.026] Where a company validly changes its name, such will not affect any rights or obligations of the company or render defective any legal proceedings by or against the company and any legal proceedings continued or commenced against it by its former name may be continued or commenced against it by its new name[49]. Where a company is wound up within one year of changing its name, its old name as well as its existing name must appear on all notices and advertisements in relation to the winding up[50].

---

[45] CA 1963, s 30(1).

[46] In the case of a single-member private company, a written decision of the single member will suffice instead of a special resolution: European Communities (Single-Member Private Limited Companies) Regulations 1994, reg 9(1).

[47] In a limited liability company, the word 'limited' can only be deleted where consent is obtained under CA 1963, s 24. It is an offence for a private company to represent itself as a public limited company ('PLC') when it is not: C(A)A 1983, s 56.

[48] CA 1963, s 23(3).

[49] CA 1963, s 23(4).

[50] CA 1963, s 24(6).

(b) Alteration of the objects clause

[3.027] *Re Cyclists' Touring Club*[51] shows that, under former companies' legislation, the alteration of a company's objects clause would only be approved of by the court where it did not destroy the *substratum* of the company ie where the alteration would make the existing business more efficient rather than abandon the existing business in favour of another business. Today, however, the objects clause may be altered in any manner by a special resolution of the members. Section 10(1) of CA 1963, provides that:

> '...a company may, by special resolution, alter the provisions of its memorandum by abandoning, restricting or amending any existing object or by adopting a new object and any alteration so made shall be as valid as if originally contained therein, and be subject to alteration in like manner.'

While principally an enabling section, s 10 also embodies certain safeguards. Thus sub-s (2) provides that if an application is made to court, the purported alteration shall not have effect, save where it is confirmed by the court. This procedure safeguards dissident shareholders by affording them the right to apply to the court to overturn any alteration. It is incumbent upon the company to alter the objects clause bona fide and in the interests of the company as a whole: *Re Cyclists' Touring Club*[52]. To seek relief, applicants must be the holders of not less than 15% of the aggregate in nominal value of the company's issued share capital or any class thereof, or if the company is not limited by shares, by not less than 15% of the company's members, or the holders of not less than 15% of the company's debentures[53]. Those who make application to court must not themselves have voted in favour of the special resolution proposing the amendment, or have consented to the alteration[54]. Such application must be made within 21 days after the date of the special resolution[55]. Where a limited company that has been authorised to dispense with using the word 'limited' in its name proposes to alter its objects clause, the same notice as is required to be given to the holders of debentures must also be given to the Registrar of Companies[56].

[3.028] At the hearing of an application by a dissenting minority, CA 1963, s 10(6) provides that:

> '...the court may make an order cancelling the alteration or confirming the alteration either wholly or in part and on such terms and conditions as it thinks fit, and may, if it thinks fit, adjourn the proceedings in order that an arrangement may be made to the satisfaction of the court for the purchase of the interests of dissentient members, and may give such directions and make such orders as it may think expedient for facilitating or carrying into effect any such arrangement.'

It can be seen that sub-s (6) specifically provides that the court may order the purchase of dissidents' shares. Regrettably, the subsection is silent as to the factors upon which

---

51 *Re Cyclists' Touring Club* (1907) 1 Ch 269.

52 *Re Cyclists' Touring Club* (1907) 1 Ch 269.

53 CA 1963, s 10(3).

54 CA 1963, s 10(4).

55 CA 1963, s 10(5).

56 CA 1963, s 10(8), as amended by CLEA 2001, s 85.

the court should exercise its jurisdiction. However, it is clear that in order for an objection to be cognisable by the court, it must be made by the members concerned, *qua* member, ie in their capacity as members and not something else: *Re Munster and Leinster Bank*[57]. In that case seven solicitors failed to prevent the alteration of a company's objects clause which would enable the company to undertake trusteeship work, as the objections were designed to preserve the solicitors' profits and not the shareholders' interests. The Master of the Rolls said:

> 'If these seven gentlemen had even now come forward and opposed this petition, as shareholders, I should, perhaps, have given more weight to their objections, and to the arguments offered on their behalf; but the learned counsel who nominally appeared for them did not seek to deny, but rather prided himself on the fact, that he represented, not individual shareholders, but the Incorporated Law Society of Ireland and the Southern Law Society...it is apparent that [the resolutions of the Law Societies] were framed not really in the interests of shareholders but in apprehension of the injury which might result to the solicitor profession from the proposed extension of the objects of the bank.'[58]

This passage indicates that although a member's objection must be made *qua* member, the court may not reject a proffered objection merely because the member's objection serves another purpose, divorced from his membership. In *Re Jewish Colonial Trust*[59] it was said that the decisive factor for the court will be the relative 'fairness' or 'unfairness' of the alteration between the shareholders or the classes of shareholders.

[3.029] There is however another alternative open to a shareholder who is less than happy with the alteration of the objects of the company. This is to petition for the winding up of the company on 'just and equitable' grounds, for failure of substratum[60]. *Failure of substratum* can be said to occur where a company which was formed with a particular purpose in mind subsequently discontinues that purpose. This recognises that some companies are quasi-partnerships that are formed on the basis of a mutual understanding between the shareholders. Where a company is formed by individuals with a particular purpose in mind, for a majority of them subsequently to divert the aim of the company is perceived to be unfair and in breach of the implicit partnership which subsists[61]. Hence, it is open to a court to hold that an alteration which destroys the substratum justifies the winding up of the company on so-called 'just and equitable' grounds.

(c) Alteration of the liability clause

[3.030] A private company's liability clause can be changed, and the liability of the members *increased*, made *unlimited* or, in the case of a company registered as unlimited, made *limited*. In the first place, the liability of the members may be increased. This is regulated by CA 1963, s 27, which provides that notwithstanding anything either in the memorandum or articles no member shall be bound by an alteration after he becomes a

---

57 *Re Munster and Leinster Bank* [1930] 1 IR 237.

58 [1930] 1 IR 237 at 247.

59 *Re Jewish Colonial Trust* (1908) 2 Ch 287.

60 See CA 1963, s 213(f). See generally, Chapter 25, *Winding Up Companies*, para **[25.076]** *ff*.

61 See *Ebrahimi v Westbourne Galleries Ltd* [1973] AC 360, adopted in Ireland in *Re Murph's Restaurant Ltd* [1979] ILRM 141.

member that requires him to take or subscribe for more shares than the number held by him at the date on which the alteration is made, or in any way increases his liability as at that date to contribute to the share capital of, or otherwise to pay money to, the company. Clearly, any amendment that gives rise to a liability to subscribe for more shares is prohibited by this provision. As shall be considered below, it has also been held that this section will prohibit *any* forced pecuniary contribution to the company's assets beyond the amount unpaid on shares held[62]. By virtue of CA 1963, s 27(2) members can, however, waive their veto in writing.

[3.031] A limited liability company can change to an unlimited company. This change is facilitated by Companies (Amendment) Act 1983, s 52 ('C(A)A 1983'), which details the matters required to achieve such a change in status. Finally, an unlimited company may apply to be re-registered as a limited company by virtue of s 53 of C(A)A 1983.

(d) Alteration of the capital clause

[3.032] The capital clause may also be altered by a company, subject to further built-in safeguards against abuse of this power. However, here a clear distinction must be drawn between an alteration which *increases* as opposed to *decreases* the capital of the company. First, however, will be considered the question of redenomination and renominalisation of share capital in euro.

(i) Redenomination and renominalisation of share capital in euro

[3.033] The advent of the euro has had a dramatic, albeit well-managed, effect on all pre-existing legal documents that referred to the national currency of participating Member States[63]. The Economic and Monetary Union Act 1998 makes provisions for the smooth conversion (redenomination and renominalisation) of companies' share capital.

Automatic redenomination from 1 January 2002

[3.034] Automatic redenomination of Irish companies' share capital occurred by operation of law on the stroke of midnight on 31 December 2001. Article 14 of the EU Council Regulation 974/98 provides that with effect from 1 January 2002 all references in legal documents to national currency units will be read as references to the equivalent amount in euro units. In Ireland, the fixed conversion rate is IRL£1 = €1.269738 (or €1 = IRL£0.787564). Section 24(2)(a) of the Economic and Monetary Union Act 1998 provides:

> 'Where the share capital of a company or any part of such capital is redenominated into euro after the transitional period under Article 14...such redenomination shall be effected at the whole or any part of the total issued or to be issued share capital, including each class of the foregoing (where any separate classes exist).'

Moreover, by s 24(2)(b) of the 1998 Act it is provided that the redenominated nominal share par value shall be calculated by dividing the total redenominated amount

---

[62] See *Ding v Sylvania Waterways* [1999] NSWSC 58 Supreme Court of New South Wales of 15 February 1999. This case is considered in the context of the alteration of the articles of association, para **[3.071]**.

[63] See Yeowart, 'Impact of the Single European Currency on Company Share Capital', [1997] 7 JIBL 266.

determined in accordance with paragraph (a) by the total number of shares authorised, issued or to be issued, or in the relevant class, as appropriate, so that the nominal value is expressed in unrounded euro amounts.

Voluntary redenomination prior to 1 January 2002

[3.035] For some companies that had availed of the Economic and Monetary Union Act 1998, s 25, however, redenomination had already taken place prior to 31 December 2001. Section 25(2) of the 1998 Act provides:

> 'Where the whole or part of the total authorised share capital of a company, the total issued share capital or to be issued share capital of a company including any class of the foregoing (where any separate classes exist) is, in its memorandum or articles of association, expressed in Irish pounds or in the currency of another participating Member State immediately before the 1st day of January, 1999, such share capital, class or part thereof may be redenominated into the euro unit in accordance with subsection (3).'

This mechanism is now redundant, but operated during the 'transition period' from 1 January 1999 to 31 December 2001[64]. Section 25(3) of the 1998 Act provided that the shareholders of a company could pass an ordinary resolution, whether at a general meeting or (where permitted by its articles) by written resolution so as to:

> '...determine that the whole or part of the total authorised share capital of a company, the total issued share capital or to be issued share capital of a company including any class of the foregoing shall be redenominated into the euro unit at the conversion rate and converted in accordance with Article 4, and rounded in accordance with Article 5, of Council Regulation (EC) No 1103/97 of 17 June 1997 on certain provisions relating to the introduction of the euro.'

Again, the redenominated nominal share par value is to be calculated in the same manner as where there was automatic redenomination on 1 January 2002 in accordance with Article 14, referred to above[65].

[3.036] Where redenomination resulting from adherence to the foregoing procedure has the effect of causing a reduction in the nominal value of issued share capital, such 'shall be deemed not to be a reduction of share capital within the meaning of the Companies Acts'[66]. Moreover, it is expressly provided by the Economic and Monetary Union Act 1998, s 25(5) that any redenomination will not:

> '...in any way change the rights, privileges or advantages that were held by, or obligations, restrictions or limitations imposed on, shareholders prior to the passing of the resolution in relation to dividends, voting at meetings or other matters'.

Companies that redenominate are obliged to send a printed copy of any shareholders' redenomination resolution to the Registrar of Companies within 15 days of its passing[67].

---

64 Economic and Monetary Union Act 1998, s 25, other than sub-ss (6), (7) and (8) ceased to have effect from 1 January 2002: s 25(8) of the 1998 Act.

65 Economic and Monetary Union Act 1998, s 25(3)(b). See para **[3.034]**.

66 Economic and Monetary Union Act 1998, s 25(4).

67 Economic and Monetary Union Act 1998, s 25(6). Failure to comply is an offence: Economic and Monetary Union Act 1998, s 25(7).

Renominalisation of shares[68]

[3.037] Whether redenomination arose automatically or voluntarily, its effect is to cause the value of shares and the amount of share capital to be expressed in inconvenient euro amounts. The purpose of *renominalisation* is to express share capital in convenient amounts. An uneven share and share capital can be rounded, whether upwards or downwards. If it is rounded up, the effect can be to increase the nominal value of shares; if rounded down, the effect can be to decrease the nominal value of shares.

[3.038] Renominalisation is facilitated by the Economic and Monetary Union Act 1998, s 26, and can be availed of up to 30 June 2003[69]. Section 26(2) provides that following redenomination, the authorised and issued or to be issued share capital and the nominal par value of shares in a company 'may be further adjusted to achieve nominal share values considered appropriate to the then share price in the euro unit' in either of two ways, provided that 'such adjustments shall not reduce the nominal value of any share to zero'. The two ways referred to turn on whether the effect of renominalisation is to increase or decrease the company's share capital.

[3.039] The simplest procedure is where renominalisation *increases* share capital. In such cases the procedure in the Economic and Monetary Union Act 1998, s 26(3) can be followed. This provides that a company can pass an ordinary resolution, whether at a general meeting or (where permitted by its articles) by written resolution so as to alter the provisions of its memorandum and articles of association to effect renominalisation. The proviso to proceeding in this way is contained in s 26(3), which states that the foregoing is

> '...provided there is an appropriate adjustment in distributable reserves (being profits available for distribution to which s 45(2) of the Companies (Amendment) Act 1983, relates) or through the introduction of additional capital, which shall be properly accounted for, and where there is not a decrease in share capital.'

In other words, where a company wishes to renominalise a share with a value of €1.269738 to the more convenient amount of €2, it can either:

- find the additional €0.730262 from monies that would otherwise be available for distribution; or
- introduce new capital.

The latter is likely to be used only where there are insufficient distributable reserves. Such a renominalisation shall be deemed not to be a reduction of share capital within the meaning of the Companies Acts.

[3.040] On the other hand one can renominalise and have the effect of *reducing* the share capital and *decreasing* the nominal value of shares. In such an event, one must utilise the procedure in the Economic and Monetary Union Act 1998, s 26(4)(a), which

---

68 See generally the CRO's website (www.cro.ie) under 'Doing Business – The Euro' where the procedures and worked examples of renominalisation are set out in some detail.

69 Economic and Monetary Union Act 1998, s 26(11). Thereafter, any change to a company's share capital can only be made by complying with the ordinary provisions on the alteration of the capital clause, contained in s 68 (increasing share capital) and s 72 (decreasing share capital) of the 1963 Act. See paras **[3.042]** and **[3.044]**, respectively.

provides that where the result of renominalisation would be a decrease in the whole or part of the authorised and issued share capital or in a class of shares, a special resolution must be passed by the shareholders (or in the case of a class of share, by the shareholders of the class). That resolution must have the effect that there shall be transferred to a fund called the *Capital Conversion Reserve Fund*, an amount equal to the aggregate amount of the capital reduced on foot of the renominalisation and that the amount so transferred does not represent more than 10% of the reduced share capital. One effect of the 10% rule is that where a share had a nominal value of IRL£1.00 and was converted to €1.269738, renominalisation could not reduce its value to €1.00 as this would breach the 10% rule. Section 26(4)(b) states that the provisions in CA 1963 that relate to the reduction of share capital shall, except as provided in s 26 of the 1998 Act, 'apply as if the Capital Conversion Reserve Fund were paid up share capital of the company concerned'[70]. Accordingly, any reduction in the Capital Conversion Reserve Fund is a deemed decrease in share capital which would attract the application of CA 1963, s 72, considered below[71]. Although the procedure contained in s 26(4)(a) is more onerous than that applicable where the effect of renominalisation is to increase a company's share capital, it is still relatively less onerous than the procedure contained in CA 1963, s 72. After 30 June 2003, where a company wishes to renominalise and the effect is to reduce its share capital, s 72 must be complied with and the reduction will require court confirmation.

[3.041] Any renominalisation of shares under CA 1963, s 26 does not operate of itself to affect or vary the obligation of a shareholder to pay the amount, if any, unpaid on such shares[72]. As in the case or redenomination, it is expressly provided by CA 1963, s 26(7) that any renominalisation will not:

> '...in any way change the rights, privileges or advantages that were held by, or obligations, restrictions or limitations imposed on, shareholders prior to the passing of the resolution in relation to dividends, voting at meetings or other matters'.

Companies that redenominate are obliged to send a printed copy of any shareholders' redenomination resolution to the Registrar of Companies within 15 days of its passing[73].

(ii) Increasing share capital

[3.042] The euro aside, CA 1963, s 68 contains a relatively simple procedure whereby the company can *increase* its share capital[74]. Accordingly, provided that the articles of

---

70 Economic and Monetary Union Act 1998, s 26(10) provides that 'The Capital Conversion Reserve Fund may, notwithstanding any other provision of this section, be applied by the company concerned in paying up unissued shares of that company (other than redeemable shares) to be allotted to shareholders of the company as fully paid bonus shares.'

71 See para **[3.045]**.

72 Economic and Monetary Union Act 1998, s 26(6).

73 Economic and Monetary Union Act 1998, s 26(8). Failure to comply is an offence: s 26(9) of the 1998 Act.

74 The practice of informal increases in share capital through the making of a so-called 'capital contribution' has been noted earlier: see para **[3.019]**.

association of that company authorise it[75], on the passing of an ordinary resolution in general meeting, a company may:

- — increase its share capital by new shares of such amount as it thinks expedient;
- — consolidate and divide all or any of its share capital into shares of larger amounts than its existing shares;
- — convert all or any of its paid up shares into stock, and re-convert that stock into paid up shares of any denominations;
- — subdivide its shares, or any of them, into shares of a smaller amount than is fixed by the memorandum, so however, that in the subdivision, the proportion between the amount paid and the amount, if any, unpaid on each reduced share shall be the same as it was in the case of the share from which the reduced share is derived;
- — cancel shares which, at the date of the passing of the resolution in that behalf, have not been taken or agreed to be taken by any person, and diminish the amount of its share capital by the amount of the shares so cancelled[76].

Section 70 of CA 1963 provides that notice of an increase in a company's share capital must be sent to the Registrar of Companies within 15 days after the passing of the resolution. Notice of any other alteration must, by CA 1963, s 69, be given to the registrar within one month. Section 71 of CA 1963 provides that an unlimited company which re-registers as a limited company can increase its nominal share capital by increasing the nominal amount of each share, provided that the increased capital will only be capable of being called up where the company is being wound up.

Although a company cannot contractually agree not to increase its share capital, the members of a company can contractually agree, inter se, not to vote in favour of an alteration of the company's memorandum and articles of association so as to effect an increase in share capital and such a contract will be enforceable. This is the effect of the finding of the House of Lords in *Russell v Northern Bank Development Corp Ltd*[77], a decision considered in the context of shareholders' agreements[78].

(iii) Reducing share capital

[3.043] Where a company decides that it wishes to *reduce* its share capital, the requirements of the Companies Acts are more restrictive. The main reason why the law imposes such restrictions is to protect creditors, a company's share capital being perceived as a 'creditors' fund': *Trevor v Whitworth*[79]. The rationale for this is based on the fact that where a company has limited liability a creditor can look only to the assets of the company for the payment of his debts. Thus, for creditors it is important that the company's assets remain intact. Where a company reduces its share capital by making

---

75 As will be the case where model reg 44 of CA 1963, Sch 1, Table A, Part 1 is adopted.

76 This is not a reduction in share capital because this provision only relates to shares, which have never been issued.

77 *Russell v Northern Bank Development Corp Ltd* [1992] 3 All ER 161.

78 See para **[3.127]**.

79 *Trevor v Whitworth* (1887) 12 App Cas 409. See generally, Chapter 18, *The Maintenance of Capital*.

repayments to its shareholders, creditors are potentially disadvantaged. It is the same philosophy which motivates the restrictions on a company purchasing its own shares or providing financial assistance for the purchase of its own shares. Accordingly the reduction of a company's share capital is strictly controlled by CA 1963, ss 72–77.

[3.044] Section 72(1) of CA 1963 provides that as a general rule, and save as expressly provided by the Acts, it is not lawful for a private company limited by shares or a private company limited by guarantee and having a share capital, to purchase any of its shares or to reduce its share capital in any way. The purchase by a company of its own shares is dealt with elsewhere[80]. Notwithstanding this general prohibition, a company may reduce its share capital by following the procedure set out in the Companies Acts, namely that:

- the company is authorised by its articles of association to reduce its share capital; and
- it passes a special resolution approving the reduction; and
- the alteration is *confirmed by the court*.

While, the reduction of share capital may, subject to the foregoing, be made in any way, CA 1963, s 72(2) specifically mentions three methods, namely, where the company decides to:

- extinguish or reduce the liability on any of its shares in respect of share capital not paid up; or
- either with or without extinguishing or reducing liability on any of its shares, cancel any paid up share capital which is lost or unrepresented by available assets; or
- either with or without extinguishing or reducing liability on any of its shares, pay off any paid up share capital which is in excess of the wants of the company; and may, if and so far as is necessary, alter its memorandum by reducing the amount of its share capital and of its shares accordingly.

Accordingly, it is possible to alter the capital clause in the memorandum of association of a company where the effect is to reduce its share capital. It is important to note that, to be effective, the reduction of share capital must obtain court confirmation[81] and whilst CA 1963, s 73, says that a company that has passed a special resolution, reducing its share capital, '*may* apply to court for an order confirming the reduction', unless court approval is obtained the reduction is ineffective.

[3.045] The rights of creditors are paramount. Where the proposed reduction of share capital involves either diminution of liability in respect of unpaid share capital, or the payment to any shareholder of any paid up share capital, and in any other case if the court so directs, CA 1963, s 73(2) provides that the following provisions shall have effect:

> '(a) every creditor of the company who at the date fixed by the court is entitled to any debt or claim which, if that date were the commencement of the winding up of the

---

[80] Chapter 18, *The Maintenance of Capital*, para **[18.017]** *ff*.

[81] CA 1963, s 72(2).

company, would be admissible in proof against the company, shall be entitled to object to the reduction;

(b) the court shall settle a list of creditors so entitled to object, and for that purpose shall ascertain, as far as possible without requiring an application from any creditor, the names of those creditors and the nature and amount of their debts or claims, and may publish notices fixing a day or days within which creditors not entered on the list are to claim to be so entered or are to be excluded from the right of objecting to the reduction;

(c) where a creditor entered on the list whose debt or claim is not discharged or has not determined does not consent to the reduction, the court may, if it thinks fit, dispense with the consent of that creditor, on the company securing payment of his debt or claim by appropriating, as the court may direct, the following amount—

(i) if the company admits the full amount of the debt or claim, or, though not admitting it, is willing to provide for it, then the full amount of the debt or claim;

(ii) if the company does not admit and is not willing to provide for the full amount of the debt or claim, or, if the amount is contingent or not ascertained, then an amount fixed by the court after the like inquiry and adjudication as if the company were being wound up by the court.'

This is, however, subject to s 73(3), which provides that where a proposed reduction of share capital involves either the diminution of any liability in respect of unpaid share capital or the payment to any shareholder of any paid up share capital, the court may, if, having regard to any special circumstances of the case, it thinks proper so to do, direct that sub-s (2) shall not apply as regards any class or any classes of creditors.

The important point to note is that it is within the discretion of the court to confirm the reduction or not. Section 74(1) provides:

> 'The court, if satisfied in relation to every creditor of the company who, under section 73, is entitled to object to the reduction, that either his consent to the reduction has been obtained or that his debt or claim has been discharged or has determined, or has been secured, may make an order confirming the reduction on such terms and conditions as it thinks fit.'

By s 74(2) the court may, if it decides to confirm the reduction, direct that the words 'and reduced', be added to the name of the company, for as long as the court may order.

[3.046] Section 75 of CA 1963 states that the Registrar of Companies, when shown the court order, a copy thereof and a 'minute' of the changed capital, must register the order and minute. The consequences for the shareholders of a company that reduces its share capital are detailed in CA 1963, s 76. The primary consequence is that:

> '...a member of the company, past or present, shall not be liable in respect of any share to any call or contribution exceeding in amount the difference, if any, between the amount of the share as fixed by the minute and the amount paid, or the reduced amount, if any, which is to be deemed to have been paid, on the share, as the case may be.'[82]

[82] CA 1963, s 76(1).

This is, however, strictly subject to s 76(2), which continues to afford protection to creditors. This provides:

> 'If any creditor entitled in respect of any debt or claim to object to the reduction of the share capital, is, by reason of his ignorance of the proceedings for reduction, or of their nature and effect with respect to his debt or claim, not entered on the list of creditors, and, after the reduction, the company is unable within the meaning of the provisions of this Act relating to winding up by the court, to pay the amount of his debt or claim, then—
>
> (a) every person who was a member of the company at the date of the registration of the order for reduction and minute, shall be liable to contribute for the payment of that debt or claim an amount not exceeding the amount which he would have been liable to contribute if the company had commenced to be wound up on the day before the said date, and
>
> (b) if the company is wound up, the court, on the application of any such creditor and proof of his ignorance as aforesaid, may, if it thinks fit, settle accordingly a list of persons so liable to contribute, and make and enforce calls and orders on the contributories settled on the list, as if they were ordinary contributories in a winding up.'

The provisions of s 76 are, however, without prejudice to the rights of contributories between themselves[83]. It may be noted that although creditors who are ignorant of the reduction have a right to remedial relief, every officer of a company that wilfully conceals the name of any creditor entitled to object to the reduction; or wilfully misrepresents the nature or amount of the debt or claim of any creditor, is guilty of an offence[84].

Alteration of the non-compulsory clauses

[3.047] Unlike the *compulsory* clauses[85] which are contained in the memorandum, the non-compulsory clauses (if any) are capable of being rendered unalterable where the memorandum itself expressly so provides[86]. Where this is not expressly so provided the non-compulsory clauses can be altered by special resolution, by virtue of CA 1963, s 28(1). However, sub-s (4) provides that a dissenting minority of 15% can object to the alteration and may apply to the court for the alteration to be cancelled.

Why would the subscribers of a company provide that certain fundamental matters provided for in the memorandum be unalterable? The reason is intrinsically linked to the rationale behind many closely-held private companies: while in law they are companies, in reality many are tantamount to partnerships. However, because of the entrenchment of the concept of 'majority rule', the company will be governed by the majority in spite of any real or imagined 'understandings'. Where certain provisions in a company's memorandum of association are made unalterable, this is usually referred to as an 'entrenchment' of rights.

---

83 CA 1963, s 76(3).

84 CA 1963, s 77.

85 See Ussher, *Company Law in Ireland* (1986), p 59–60.

86 See CA 1963, s 28(3) which provides: 'This section shall not apply where the memorandum itself provides for or prohibits the alteration of all or any of the said provisions, and shall not authorise any variation or abrogation of the special rights of any class of members.'

[B] THE ARTICLES OF ASSOCIATION

The nature of the articles

[3.048] The articles of association are the publicly registered rules of a company which govern its internal regulation. The members of private companies sometimes also adopt a shareholders' agreement, which can be seen as supplementing the company's statutory constitutional documents. This is however, a private contract to which the company may not be party. Unlike a shareholders' agreement, the articles automatically *bind* the company with its members and are simultaneously *public documents*[87].

[3.049] In the case of a private company limited by shares there is no actual requirement that articles be registered with the CRO prior to incorporation[88]. By contrast, a private company limited by guarantee (which has a share capital[89]) must register its own articles, as must an unlimited private company[90].
Section 12(1) of CA 1963 provides that in the case of an unlimited company the articles must state the number of members and the amount of the share capital with which the company proposes to be registered. Any increase in the number of members must be notified to the Registrar within 15 days after the increase was resolved or took place[91].

Where private companies limited by shares do not voluntarily register their own articles, the model articles set out in CA 1963, Sch 1 will automatically be deemed to be the articles of association of the company as if they had been duly registered[92]. In addition, even where such a company does register its own articles, the provisions of Table A of the First Schedule will continue to apply save insofar as they have been excluded or modified[93]. Section 14 of CA 1963[94] provides that a company's articles of association must be printed (in an entire format or in a form pursuant to CLEA 2001, s 80)[95], divided into paragraphs which are numbered consecutively, bear the same stamp as if they were contained in a deed and be signed by each subscriber of the memorandum of association in the presence of one witness who must attest the signature. Furthermore, by CA 1963, s 29(1) a company shall on being so requested by a member, send him a copy of its

87 See, generally, Nicholson, *Table A Articles of Association* (1997).

88 See CA 1963, s 11, as amended by C(A)A 1982, s 2.

89 The form of memorandum and articles for a private company limited by guarantee are set out in CA 1963, Table D, Parts I and III, respectively.

90 The form of memorandum and articles for a private unlimited company are set out in CA 1963, Table E, Parts I and III, respectively.

91 CA 1963, s 12(2).

92 CA 1963, s 13(2) provides: 'In the case of a company limited by shares and registered after the operative date, if articles are not registered or, if articles are registered, in so far as the articles do not exclude or modify the regulations contained in Table A, those regulations shall, so far as applicable, be the regulations of the company in the same manner and to the same extent as if they were contained in duly registered articles.'

93 In *McNeill v McNeill's Sheepfarming Co Ltd* [1955] NZLR 15 it was held that in case of conflict between the model articles and the company's own express articles, the latter would prevail.

94 As amended by the Finance Act 1996, s 112.

95 CA 1963, s 14(1) was amended to so provide by CLEA 2001, s 82.

memorandum and articles on payment of a nominal fee: *Securities Trust Ltd v Hugh Moore & Alexander Ltd*[96].

The model articles of private companies

[3.050] In the case of a private company limited by shares, the relevant model regulations are set out in CA 1963, Sch 1, Table A, Part II ('the model regulations'). Model reg 1 of Part II provides that, with certain modifications, the regulations contained in Part I (which apply to public companies limited by shares) shall apply to private companies. The modifications are that model regs 8 (entitlements of share transferee), 24 (directors' power to decline registration of a share transfer), 51 (notice of members' meetings), 54 (quorum for members' meetings), 84 (directors' voting on contracts in which directors interested) and 86 (quorum at directors' meetings) of Part I are disapplied to private companies. In place of these Regulations, Part II applies its own variations in regs 10, 3, 4, 5, 7 and 8, respectively. In addition, regs 2, 6, 9 and 10[97] of Part II are *additional* regulations that are included in the model articles of association of private companies limited by shares. The irony that the articles of association of the most popular type of company registered should be ascertainable by those applicable to companies that are numerically few, has been noted[98]. It is also ironic that the supposedly simpler type of company should have more model articles than its supposedly more sophisticated relation.

The model articles, applicable to a private company are subdivided under the following headings:

Share capital and variation of rights. Liens on shares. Calls on shares. Transfer, transmission and forfeiture of shares. Conversion of shares into stock. Alteration of capital. General meetings. Notice of general meetings. Proceedings at general meetings. Votes of members. Bodies corporate acting by representatives at meetings. Directors. Borrowing powers.	Powers and duties of directors. Disqualification of directors. Rotation of directors. Proceedings of directors. Managing director. The secretary. The company seal. Dividends and reserves. Accounts. Capitalisation of profits. Audit. Notices.[99] Winding up. Indemnity.

96 *Securities Trust Ltd v Hugh Moore & Alexander Ltd* [1964] IR 417.

97 Inserted into Part II by C(A)A 1977, s 5(5).

98 See Chapter 1, *The Private Company in Context*, para **[1.114]**.

99 Note that in *Re Thundercrest Ltd* [1995] 1 BCLC 117 it was held that a provision in a company's articles that deemed members to have received a notice within 24 hours of its positing could be ignored where it was proved that the letter enclosing the notice had been returned undelivered.

The fact that a company must have articles does not mean that the legislature is attempting to control the operation of the company. On the contrary, the fact that a company may adopt and adapt the model articles at will indicates that the legislature was merely concerned that doubt and uncertainty should be minimised by ensuring that certain basic matters are provided for.

Usual amendments to the model articles

[3.051] It would be most unusual for any company to adopt en bloc the model articles, without modification or exclusion. Indeed, company formation firms, responsible for the incorporation of most Irish companies, invariably amend the model articles[100]. The advisability of modifying the model articles cannot be stressed enough. The model articles provided in the Companies Acts are totally unsuited to many private closely-held companies[101]. They do, however, have the advantage of certainty, in that they and their predecessors have been the subject of judicial scrutiny in many courts over the years. In an attempt to make the articles of companies accord more with the needs of their corporators, practitioners have been forced to try to adopt the articles of private closely-held companies[102].

[3.052] In the case of single-member private companies it is thought that in time the model articles of association employed in such companies will be tailored more closely to suit the needs of a company whose ownership is in the hands of one individual. Where radical changes are effected to such companies' articles all amendments should be reconsidered where a single-member subsequently converts to a multi-member private company.

[3.053] In an ordinary private company the articles typically targeted for modification and expansion include the following:

- (a) Shares.
- (b) Members' meetings.
- (c) Directors.
- (d) Voting rights.

It must be stressed that many other amendments are often effected to the model articles. The amendments set out below are simply some selected examples[103].

(a) Shares

[3.054] The first usual amendment of note is the modification of model reg 22 to provide that, in respect of a share transfer, it is sufficient for the transferor alone to

[100] Thus, some formation firms exclude in private companies CA 1963, Articles: 5, 47, 75, 79, 91, 92, 93, 94 and 95 of Table A, Part I, and reg 7 in Part II. Other variations include the deletion of regs 3, 22, 76, 77, 96, 97, 98, 100, 102, 109, and 138 of Table A, Part I, and reg 9 in Part II.

[101] See Ussher, *Company Law in Ireland* (1986), pp 62, 63 for a short but perceptive commentary on the model articles.

[102] See Young, 'Agreements Between Shareholders Relating To The Operation Of A Small Company' (1979) Society of Young Solicitors, Lecture 118.

[103] On many of the possible amendments to the model articles, see generally, Stedman & Jones, *Shareholders' Agreements*, (3rd edn, 1998), pp 7–57.

execute the instrument. This simple amendment avoids the otherwise cumbersome practice of both transferor and transferee having to execute a share transfer in order for it to be valid and effective[104].

[3.055] In private companies model reg 24 (Part I) is automatically deleted and replaced by model reg 3 (Part II). Model reg 3 provides:

> 'The directors may, in their absolute discretion and without assigning any reason therefor, decline to register any transfer of any share, whether or not it is a fully paid share.'

This will seldom be considered sufficient. Although a strong prohibition on the alienation of shares in a private company it is usual for this article to be extended further, whether in the articles of association or in a shareholders' agreement. Model reg 3 is typically bolstered by the inclusion of *pre-emption rights* in either the company's articles of association or in a shareholders' agreement[105]. Although there are many different types of pre-emption rights, the formula which is most used is one which provides that where a member desires to sell or otherwise dispose of his shares he must first offer them to the existing members of the company. The offer to the other members will usually entitle them to take up the shares on a pro rata basis to the shares which they already hold. Extreme care ought to be exercised in the drafting of such rights because case law shows that they will be strictly construed, the courts leaning in favour of free alienation of shares[106]. Whether such a policy is justified in the context of private companies in view of their often quasi-partnership nature, is doubted. A valid pre-emption clause will be upheld by the courts either by injunction[107], or by the court refusing a decree for specific performance[108] for the sale of shares. Pre-emption rights are considered further in Chapter 16.

(b) Members' meetings

[3.056] Sometimes, the requirement that general meetings are held within the State, provided for by model reg 47, is deleted. Furthermore, the notice provisions in respect of company meetings contained in reg 51 are often restricted. Usually the notice provision in CA 1963, s 141 is expressly adopted by the articles.

[3.057] It is important that CA 1963, Sch 1, Table A, Part I model reg 6 be included in the articles of association of private companies. This model article provides the internal authorisation required by CA 1963, s 141(8) if a company is to be permitted to utilise the unanimous written resolution procedure[109].

---

104 See generally, Chapter 16, *Share Transfers in Private Companies*, para **[16.006]**.

105 See Stedman & Jones, *Shareholders' Agreements* (3rd edn, 1998), p 26 *ff*. For an old judicially considered Irish example, see *Attorney General for Ireland v Jameson* [1904] 2 IR 644. See generally, Chapter 16, *Share Transfers in Private Companies*, para **[16.063]** *ff*.

106 See *Safeguard Industrial Investments Ltd v National Westminster Bank Ltd* [1982] 1 All ER 449 and *Lyle & Scott Ltd v Scott's Trustees* [1959] 2 All ER 661.

107 See *Curtis v JJ Curtis & Co Ltd* [1986] BCLC 86, Court of Appeal of New Zealand.

108 *Lee & Co (Dublin) Ltd v Egan (Wholesale) Ltd* (7 April 1978, unreported), High Court (Kenny J).

109 See, generally, Chapter 9, *Corporate Governance: Meetings*, para **[9.076]**.

[3.058] An automatic legislative amendment is effected to the articles of association of a single-member private company by reg 10 of The European Communities (Single-Member Private Limited Companies) Regulations 1994[110]. This provides:

> 'Notwithstanding any provision to the contrary in the articles of a single-member company, one member present in person or by proxy shall be a quorum.'

Meetings in the context of single-member private companies are considered in Chapter 9.

(c) Directors

[3.059] Although the directors of a private company are in law officers of the company, bearing all the responsibilities which pertain to that office, in many private companies they may also be the only members of the company. Consequently, provisions providing for the rotation of the directors (model reg 92 *ff*) are an anomaly in a company where the directors will almost always be the same. Sometimes, the articles will provide that the directors of the company will be life directors, and that model reg 99 be deleted, although it should be noted that such can be altered by the passing of a special resolution. Life directors may however be provided for in a provision in the memorandum of association, which may be expressed to be unalterable[111].

[3.060] As regards the powers of directors, model reg 79 places a fetter on the power of the directors to borrow, by limiting the maximum amount of borrowings without the authorisation of the members in general meeting to the nominal amount of share capital issued[112]. Where a company is of the 'two euro' variety, it means that the directors may only borrow up to two euro. Where the company itself does not modify this to give the directors unlimited borrowing powers, the company may be forced to do so on the first occasion it seeks to raise finance by borrowing. In such a situation a lending institution will usually require as a prerequisite to corporate borrowing the substitution for model reg 79 of powers unfettered by reference to the company's issued share capital[113].

[3.061] In most private companies it is normal for the provisions of model reg 80 to be adopted unamended, since it gives the directors wide powers as to the management of the business of the company[114]. The proceedings of directors are sometimes modified by the amendment of model reg 109 to provide that resolutions of the directors shall be valid where such resolutions are made up of two or more documents. In addition, a

---

110 SI 1994/275.

111 See para **[3.047]**.

112 See *Re Shannonside Holdings Ltd* (20 May 1993, unreported), High Court per Costello J, considered at para **[3.090]** where the company's articles of association contained an article in similar terms to model reg 79.

113 Although some companies give directors more elaborate powers to borrow, a simple alternative may provide that: 'The directors may exercise all the powers of the company to borrow money, and to mortgage or charge all or any part of its undertaking, property and uncalled capital, and to issue debentures, debenture stock and other securities whether outright or as security for any debt, liability or obligation of the company or of any third party without any limit.'

114 See Chapter 8, *Corporate Governance: Management by the Directors*, para **[8.004]** for the text of model reg 80.

recent development which goes to highlight the latitude allowed to companies as regards the individuality of their articles, is the facilitating of meetings of the board of directors over the telephone where all parties to the meeting can hear the proceedings and be heard[115]. A further amendment is the common modification of model reg 138, which indemnifies directors, the secretary and others out of the company's assets against any proceedings '...whether civil or criminal, in relation to his acts while acting in such office...'. This is often amended to provide that officers shall also be indemnified out of the company's assets against all costs and expenses incurred in or about the execution and discharge of the duties of their office.

(d) Voting rights

[3.062] Quite apart from any voting rights which specifically attach to shares of a particular class[116] the members of a company may wish to *load* the voting rights of some or all of the members, either generally, or in respect of a particular vote. This has been considered permissible since the decision of the House of Lords in *Bushell v Faith*[117] which upheld the validity of the following provision inserted in the articles of association of a company:

> 'In the event of a resolution being proposed at any general meeting of the company for the removal from office of any director, any shares held by that director shall on a poll in respect of such resolution carry the right to three votes per share.'

The facts in *Bushell v Faith* may not today seem all that unusual, but the dispute went the whole way to the House of Lords. The company in question had been incorporated by the mother of the parties to the proceedings who had transferred a block of flats to the company in return for an allotment of 300 shares, one being held by her nominee. The shares subsequently came to be held equally by her three children: the plaintiff, her sister and their defendant brother. When a dispute arose as to the defendant's conduct as director, a general meeting was held and the plaintiff and her sister voted in favour of a resolution that their defendant-brother be removed from office as a director. The defendant naturally opposed the resolution. The ensuing dispute centred upon whether the resolution was passed by 200 votes to 100 votes, or defeated by 300 votes to 200 votes. The validity of the article, quoted above, which enabled a director to remain in office was questioned in the light of s 184(1) of the Companies Act 1948 (UK) which empowered a company to remove a director by ordinary resolution *notwithstanding anything in its articles*[118].

---

[115] See *The Irish Times*, 17 April 1991, where it was reported that Woodchester Investments plc put the following new regulation to its shareholders to adopt: 'Any director or alternative director may participate in a meeting of the directors or any committee of the directors by means of a conference telephone or to other telecommunications equipment by means of which all persons participating in the meeting can hear each other and such participation in a meeting shall constitute presence in person at the meeting.'

[116] See Chapter 15, *Shares and Membership*, para **[15.094]** *ff*.

[117] *Bushell v Faith* [1970] AC 1099.

[118] See CA 1963, s 182(1).

By a four-to-one majority the House of Lords upheld the validity of the clause. Lord Upjohn began by observing that the *mischief* which the legislature sought to prevent in enacting the Companies Act 1948, s 184(1) (UK) was to make a director removable by virtue of an ordinary resolution instead of a special resolution, or making it necessary to alter the company's articles of association. After noting that model reg 2 of Part I of Table A gives companies a completely unfettered right to attach to any share special voting rights on a poll or restrict voting rights, he said:

> 'Parliament has never sought to fetter the right of the company to issue a share with such rights or restrictions as it may think fit. There is no fetter which compels the company to make the voting rights or restrictions of general application and it seems to me clear that such rights or restrictions can be attached to special circumstances and to particular types of resolution.'[119]

Lord Upjohn went on to reconcile this with the right contained in s 184 of the 1948 Act, saying:

> 'This makes no mockery of s 184; all that Parliament was seeking to do thereby was to make an ordinary resolution sufficient to remove a director. Had Parliament desired to go further and enact that every share entitled to vote should be deprived of its special rights under the articles it should have said so in plain terms by making the vote on a poll one vote one share. Then, what about shares which had no voting rights under the articles? Should not Parliament give them a vote when considering this completely artificial form of ordinary resolution? Suppose there had been some preference shares in the name of Mr Faith's wife, which under the articles had in the circumstances no vote; why in justice should her voice be excluded from consideration in this artificial vote?
>
> I only raise this purely hypothetical case to show the great difficulty of trying to do justice by legislation in a matter which has always been left to the corporators themselves to decide.'[120]

Such clauses have now come to be known as *Bushell v Faith* clauses.

[3.063] In private companies the ability to provide that certain shares have *weighted* or *loaded* voting rights has an important role to play in copperfastening the shareholders' understanding of the basis of their relationship. By ousting the right of the majority to prevail in certain votes, minority shareholder-investors are afforded a degree of comfort. Although not yet specifically considered by the Irish courts it is thought that the decision in *Bushell v Faith* should and will be followed.

[3.064] In must be appreciated that the foregoing review of usual amendments is but an attempt to 'second guess' the persons involved in company formations, be they solicitors or formation companies, and accordingly whenever one is dealing with a company, the articles of that particular company must be read in detail and their meaning understood[121].

---

119 [1970] AC 1099 at 1109E.

120 [1970] AC 1099 at 1109F–H.

121 *Northern Bank Finance Corporation Ltd v Quinn* [1979] ILRM 221, cf *Re Shannonside Holdings Ltd* (20 May 1993, unreported), High Court per Costello J which casts doubts on the application of the doctrine of constructive notice to a company's articles of association at pp 6, 7 of the transcript.

Alteration of the articles

[3.065] Every company may alter its articles of association by passing a special resolution: CA 1963, s 15. As shall be considered in Chapter 9, a special resolution is a resolution passed by at least 75% of the members of the company entitled to vote at a general meeting[122]. A single-member private limited company's articles may be altered by a decision of the single member drawn up in writing in accordance with reg 9 of the European Communities (Single-Member Private Limited Companies) Regulations 1994[123].

[3.066] In addition to a company having a *positive* right to alter its articles of association, it is also the case that a company cannot in law deprive itself of that right[124]. Accordingly, where by agreement a company purports to so deprive itself, the agreement is void to that extent[125]. Where an alteration of the articles has the effect of resulting in the breach of a contract entered into by the company, then the view of the court has been historically that this will not justify the court preventing by injunction the alteration of the company's articles. Where a person has a contract with a company, and becomes aware that the company intends to alter its articles in breach of the contract, he will not get an injunction to restrain the alteration[126]. The rationale is that the outsider affected by the breach has his usual rights in the law of contract.

[3.067] Notwithstanding the existence of the inalienable power of alteration there are certain restrictions on the members' exercise of the right to alter a company's articles of association by special resolution:

(a) Where alterations are contrary to law.

(b) Where an additional liability is imposed on members.

(c) Where the articles are altered and the members have not acted bona fide and in the interests of the company as a whole.

(a) Where alterations are contrary to law

[3.068] A company cannot alter its articles where the resulting change would be contrary to the provisions of that company's memorandum of association, the provisions of the Companies Acts 1963–2001 or the general law of the land. In *Hennessy & Others v National Agricultural and Industrial Development Association*[127] an alteration of the articles of association of the defendant company which was limited by guarantee was

---

[122] Either an Annual General Meeting ('AGM') or Extraordinary General Meeting ('EGM').

[123] SI 1994/275. See Chapter 9, *Corporate Governance: Meetings*, para **[9.074]**.

[124] *Peter's American Delicacy Co Ltd v Heath* (1938–39) 61 CLR 457; *Walker v London Tramways Company* (1879) 12 Ch D 705.

[125] *Allen v Gold Reefs of West Africa Ltd* [1900] 1 Ch 656, considered below, and *Malleson v National Insurance and Guarantee Corporation* [1894] 1 Ch 200.

[126] *Southern Foundries (1926) Ltd v Shirlaw* [1940] AC 701 at 740 and *Punt v Symons & Co Ltd* [1903] 2 Ch 506. Cf *British Murac Syndicate Ltd v Alperton Rubber Co Ltd* [1915] 2 Ch 186, where an injunction was granted to restrain the alteration of a company's articles, where such would result in the breach of a contract with an outsider.

[127] *Hennessy v National Agricultural and Industrial Development Association* [1947] IR 159.

declared null and void. This was because the company's memorandum of association provided that the consent of the Minister was required in order to validly alter the company's articles. Since this was not properly obtained, Overend J held:

> 'Now s 13, sub-s 1 of the Companies Act 1908[128] only confers on a company power to alter its articles "subject to the provisions of this Act and to the conditions contained in its memorandum of association". Clause 5 [of the Memorandum] imposes such a condition...and it is clear in my opinion that, until the Minister had given his definite and final approval, the company's power to alter its articles did not come into existence under s 13 [now CA 1963, s 15] of the Act. Any amendments purporting to have been made without such previous approval were null and void.'[129]

Another example of an invalid alteration is seen in CA 1963, s 24(4)[130] whereby it is provided that a company that is exempt from the restrictions on the use of the word 'limited' in the company name, shall not alter its articles (or memorandum) so that it ceases to comply with the requirements for exemption in s 24(1) where it does not have the word 'limited'[131] in its name.

[3.069] An alteration of class rights can be made the subject of a court application by the holders of at least 10% of the shares so affected[132]. It should also be noted that under CA 1963, s 205 a company may be compelled by the court to alter its articles or memorandum to protect the interests of an oppressed minority of members. Furthermore, once so ordered by the court under s 205, the Supreme Court held in *Re R Ltd*[133] that:

> '...subject to the provisions of the order, the company concerned shall not have power without the leave of the court to make any further alteration in or addition to the memorandum or articles inconsistent with the provisions of the order...'

Alterations made pursuant to a court order have the same effect as if duly made by resolution of the company.

(b) Where an additional liability is imposed on members

[3.070] An alteration of the articles of association cannot have the effect of increasing the liability of any member. Section 27(1) of CA 1963 provides that notwithstanding anything in a company's memorandum and articles of association:

> '...no member of the company shall be bound by an alteration made in the memorandum or articles after the date on which he becomes a member, if and so far as the alteration requires him to take or subscribe for more shares than the number held by him at the date on which the alteration is made, or in any way increases his liability as at that date to contribute to the share capital of, or otherwise to pay money to, the company.'

---

128 Now CA 1963, s 15(1).

129 [1947] IR 159 at 191.

130 As substituted by CLEA 2001, s 88(1).

131 Or 'teoranta'.

132 CA 1963, s 78, and Bourne, 'Variations on the Class Theme' (1988) Accountancy 128.

133 *Re R Ltd* [1989] ILRM 757.

It is clear that companies may not alter their articles so as to provide that existing members must subscribe for more shares or otherwise increase their liability to contribute to the company's share capital. This rule of company law is a necessary adjunct to the principle of members' limited liability, namely that a member's liability is to pay the unpaid part (if any) of the issue price of the shares, and nothing more. The injunction against any alteration in the articles or memorandum that increases a member's liability 'or otherwise to pay money to' the company can give rise to real difficulties, particularly for incorporated clubs or schemes of any kind where the members may, subsequent to incorporation, be required to increase payments to the company.

[3.071] One of the few modern cases to consider this narrow but important point of company law is the decision of the Supreme Court of New South Wales in *Ding et al v Sylvania Waterways Ltd*[134]. There, the net question was whether the articles of a company could be amended to impose on its shareholders a liability to contribute to the recurring or administrative expenses of the company. The essential facts in that case were that the plaintiffs were shareholders in the defendant-company. The plaintiffs were also residents in a housing estate that abutted a waterway. The company acquired the waterway and most of the adjoining landowners (including the plaintiffs) acquired shares in the company. Each of the plaintiffs paid a fee on joining. In June of 1995 the company in general meeting resolved in favour of altering its articles of association to provide for the payment of an annual levy for the purpose of maintaining the navigability of the waterways and to fund its ongoing expenses. The annual levy was set by ordinary resolution of the members to be $1,275 per annum for three years. The plaintiffs sought a declaration that they were not obliged to pay this by reason of *s* 140(2)(b) of the Australian Corporations Law, which was in all material respects identical to CA 1963, s 27(1)[135]. Austin J held that the use of the words 'otherwise to pay money' were sufficiently wide as to cover an amendment to oblige members to make payments in respect of recurring administrative and maintenance expenses of the company. The company's claim that those words were to be qualified by some such words as 'in the nature of share capital' was rejected by Austin J on the grounds that 'the word "otherwise" appears to me to be intended to rebut any possible construction ejusdem generis with the preceding words of sub-paragraph (b)…'.[136]

[3.072] The company claimed that an examination of the legislative history of the provision would show that all that was intended was to make clear that amendments that require payments in the nature of share capital would not be binding on dissenters but that articles could be amended to introduce fees or levies for administration and maintenance. Following a thorough review of the legislative history, and cases that

---

[134] *Ding et al v Sylvania Waterways Ltd* [1999] NSWSC 58 (15 February 1999).

[135] CA 1963, s 140(2)(b) provided: 'Unless a member of a company agrees in writing to be bound, they are not bound by a modification of the constitution made after the date on which they became a member so far as the modification…increases the member's liability to contribute to the share capital of, or otherwise to pay money to, the company.'

[136] *Ding et al v Sylvania Waterways Ltd* [1999] NSWSC 58 (15 February 1999) at para 20.

tended for (referred to as the *Lion Insurance* group of cases)[137] and against[138] the contention, Austin J rejected the company's submission. Acknowledging the tension between the two groups of authorities, Austin J said:

> 'In my opinion the true explanation for the decisions in the *Lion Insurance* group of cases is that the obligations held to be enforceable against the members, notwithstanding s 38 of the 1862 Act, were found to have been undertaken on the facts as simple contractual obligations. True it is that the obligations arose by virtue of the members becoming members of the company, and their content was defined in the constitution of the company. Nevertheless, the obligations in each of those cases acquired their binding force by virtue of an act of assent which was both assent to membership of the company and assent to the additional contractual obligations known to the assenting members and recorded in the constitution.'[139]

In other words, the only circumstances in which members of a company will be required to pay up on foot of an amendment to the company's constitution is where there is found to be a *special contract* between them and the company[140]. Where the only contract is the ssection 25 *statutory contract* the courts will not oblige members to make payments in respect of recurring administrative and maintenance expenses of the company[141]. Austin J went on to say:

> 'If, therefore, the constitution of a company contains provisions which impose special pecuniary obligations on members, and those provisions are known to the applicant for membership when the application for membership is made, and the surrounding circumstances point to an intention to make a special contract, the court may well conclude that the pecuniary obligation is enforceable by the company...In this way the law recognises the constitutional provisions of mutual or co-operative companies and clubs.

---

[137] Cases that tended to support the contention that under the Joint Stock Companies Act 1856 and the Companies Act 1862, companies could impose a pecuniary liability on members beyond the liability to contribute the amount unpaid on shares included: *Peninsular Company Ltd v Fleming* (1872) 27 LT (NS) 93; *Re Maria Anna & Steinbank Coal and Coke Company Ltd, Maxwells Case* (1874) 20 Eq 585; *Re Maria Anna & Steinbank Coal and Coke Company Ltd, McKewan's Case* (1877) 6 Ch D 447; and *The Lion Mutual Marine Insurance Association Ltd v Tucker* (1883) 12 QBD 176. In the latter case it was held that the original prohibition on increasing members' liability did not limit the contributions that could be payable by a member in his capacity of mutual insurer under the articles, and only applied to liabilities incurred by members in their capacity as such.

[138] Cases against the company's contention were: *Shalfoon v Chedar Valley Co-operative Dairy Co Ltd* [1924] NZLR 561; *Manners v St David's Gold and Copper Mines Ltd* [1904] 2 Ch 593 and *Bisgood v Henderson's Transvaal Estate Ltd* [1908] 1 Ch 743.

[139] *Ding et al v Sylvania Waterways Ltd* [1999] NSWSC 58 (15 February 1999) at para 43.

[140] As to the difference between 'special contracts' and the 'statutory contract' see para **[3.106]**.

[141] Cf *Pelzan v Boaron Diamonds Ltd* Supreme Court of Israel, December 1996, noted by Berg [1997] 11 ICCLR C-173. There is seems that the fact that the memorandum and articles of association were a statutory contract coupled with the fact that the legislation permitted them to be altered, was found to be a sufficient basis for the Israeli Supreme Court to uphold an amendment to the articles that was added after the plaintiff became a member, which imposed personal liability on members in respect of all business dealings carried out with another member of the company whose members were in the business of a diamond exchange.

For example, the obligation of members of an incorporated club to pay an annual membership fee set by its constitution is probably based on this reasoning.'[142]

Austin J went on to find that in the instant case, although there was a 'special contract', there was neither an express nor an implied term that authorised the company to introduce a new pecuniary liability in the nature of what it purported to introduce[143]. Accordingly, the plaintiffs were successful in their application for a direction that they were not obliged to pay the annual levy.

[3.073] The ratio of *Ding* is, first, that an article that imposes a pecuniary liability to pay an annual fee or levy is enforceable against members whose membership arises after the article is adopted or who otherwise assent in writing to it as contemplated by CA 1963, s 27(2). Secondly, the statutory limitation on liability does not render such an article invalid because the members expressly or implicitly assent to the obligation when they become members and thereby enter into a special contract in addition to their normal membership contract an envisaged by CA 1963, s 25. Thirdly, where, however, such an article is adopted by amendment it cannot bind existing members by reason of CA 1963, s 27(1) unless those members have agreed in writing to be bound because that section applies to a modification of the memorandum or articles that increases a member's pecuniary liability to the company in any way. Where it is envisaged that a company will seek to increase annual fees, the advice given by Austin J is instructive:

'...the only practical solution would appear to be either to draft the original article in such a way as to include within its terms a mechanism for increasing the charge (for example, by authorising the board of directors to determine the charge from time to time), or to ensure that applicants for membership sign a written application form or similar document in which they expressly agree in writing to be bound by subsequent amendments which increase the charge.'[144]

In this way, any alteration to increase members' liability will not be thwarted because either no amendment to the articles is needed as the articles delegate the power to fix an increasing charge to the directors ab initio, or any increase in charge will be in accordance with an express term of a special contract.

(c) Alterations not bona fide and not in the interests of the company as a whole

[3.074] The greatest and most nebulous prohibition on the alteration of the articles of a company is that such an alteration will be declared to be null and void where the power to alter the articles is not exercised bona fide and in the interests of the company as a whole[145]. At the outset, it should be noted that this, the traditional test for alteration of articles, as promulgated by Lindley MR in *Allen v Gold Reefs of West Africa Ltd*[146] has

[142] *Ding et al v Sylvania Waterways Ltd* [1999] NSWSC 58 (15 February 1999) at para 47.

[143] Austin J also said that where there is a special contract which contains an implied term authorising the amendment which has been made, the effect of a CA 1963, s 27 type provision was to 'override the implied term and to declare that non-assenting members are not bound by the amendment even thought they have previously entered into a special contract containing an implied term to contrary effect'.

[144] *Ding et al v Sylvania Waterways Ltd* [1999] NSWSC 58 (15 February 1999) at para 70.

[145] See *Allen v Gold Reefs of West Africa Ltd* (1900) 1 Ch 656, considered below.

been rejected as inappropriate by Australia's highest court in *Gambotto v WCP Ltd*[147]. The traditional test applied to establish the propriety of alterations of a company's articles of association is considered under the following headings:

(i) The traditional test defined.

(ii) The meaning of 'company as a whole'.

(iii) An objective or subjective test?

(iv) Divergent disputes: the traditional test applied.

(v) Alternative approaches: the traditional test discredited.

(i) The traditional test defined

[3.075] The traditional test for determining the validity of an alteration of a company's articles of association is that a resolution altering the articles must be made, *bona fide and in the interests of the company as a whole*. This has its accepted roots in the case of *Allen v Gold Reefs of West Africa Ltd*[148]. Inherent in this test is a conflict between some equally honourable principles, namely, the democratic right of a majority within a company to determine the direction of that company, and, the proprietary right of a shareholder to exercise his voting rights as selfishly as he chooses[149], versus the right of a minority of the shareholders to have the basis upon which they entered the company unchanged[150] and, in particular, the right not to have one's shares compulsorily acquired, or expropriated by the majority[151]. Indeed, it is alterations that effect an expropriation where the justice of an alteration becomes most acute.

[3.076] In *Allen v Gold Reefs of West Africa Ltd* the articles of the company provided that the company had a lien on members' shares for 'all debts, obligations, and liabilities of any member to or towards the company upon all shares (not being fully paid)'. The company purported to alter this regulation by the deletion of the words '(not being fully paid)'. The members were disposed to resolve in favour of this alteration because of the death of the late and unfortunate Zuccani, a member who died insolvent owing the company £6,072 and 10 shillings. Presumably, after the initial mourning for the loss of one of their number, the remaining members decided that it would compound the tragedy were his debt to the company to die with him. So, it was decided to alter the company's articles on the terms outlined, the result being that the company then had a lien over Zuccani's shares, although they were *fully paid*. When the matter came before the Court of Appeal, Lindley MR held in the often quoted words:

---

146 [1900] 1 Ch 656.

147 *Gambotto v WCP Ltd* (1995) 13 ACLC 342. For comment, see Moshinsky and Rosedale, 'A Victory for the Small Shareholder in Australia', [1995] 7 ICCLR 229. See para **[3.087]**.

148 *Allen v Gold Reefs of West Africa Ltd* [1900] 1 Ch 656.

149 See *PMPS Insurance Co Ltd and Moore v Attorney General* [1984] ILRM 88, and *Pender v Lushington* (1877) 6 Ch D 70.

150 See Rixon, 'Competing Interests And Conflicting Principles: An Examination Of The Power Of Alteration Of Articles Of Association' (1986) MLR 447, for a detailed and perceptive treatment of the law applicable to the alteration of a company's articles.

151 *Gambotto v WCP Ltd* (1995) 13 ACLC 342.

'The power thus conferred on companies to alter the regulations contained in their articles is limited only by the provisions contained in the statute and the conditions contained in the company's memorandum of association. Wide, however, as the language of s 50 [now CA 1963, s 15] is, the power conferred by it must, like all other powers, be subject to those general principles of law and equity which are applicable to all powers conferred on majorities and enabling them to bind minorities. It must be exercised, not only in the manner required by law, but also *bona fide for the benefit of the company as a whole*, and it must not be exceeded. These conditions are always implied, and are seldom, if ever, expressed.'[152]

Lindley MR went on to hold that the alteration in this instance was *valid*. While undoubtedly a generalisation[153], his expression of the restriction on the majority to impose its will on a dissenting minority was, until recently[154], one of the most sacred of shibboleths in company law. While the intention behind the test 'bona fide' is clear, unfortunately it is characterised by uncertainty in its application. Similarly, the meaning of '*company as a whole*' is far from clear and, as now considered, is open to two interpretations.

(ii)The meaning of 'company as a whole'

[3.077] The phrase, 'company as a whole', can mean either the company as a separate entity, *or* the corporators (members) as a general body. Many of the reported cases interpret the phrase as meaning for the benefit of the company as a separate entity. In the *Allen* case itself, the alteration was clearly in the interests of the company as a separate legal entity; it was the direct beneficiary of the alteration and obtained the lien over Zuccani's fully paid shares.

[3.078] In other cases the result is different and the beneficiaries of the alteration will be the very people who vote in favour of the change: the members themselves and the words 'company as a whole' have also been interpreted as meaning the members or corporators as a general body[155]. Thus in *Greenhalgh v Arderne Cinemas Ltd*[156] the articles of the company in question contained pre-emption rights to the effect that a member could not transfer his shares to a non-member without first offering them to the other members of the company. This pre-emption clause was altered to provide that sales to non-members were permissible where sanctioned by an ordinary resolution without the transferor having to offer them to existing members. The majority shareholder who initiated this alteration had a personal interest in that he wanted to sell his shares to a non-member. However, the plaintiff, Mr Greenhalgh, objected and sought a declaration that the alteration was invalid as not being bona fide and in the interests of the company as a whole. It was said by Evershed MR, that:

---

152 *Allen v Gold Reefs of West Africa Ltd* (1900) 1 Ch D 656 at 671 (emphasis added).

153 See Rixon, 'Competing Interests And Conflicting Principles: An Examination of the Power of Alteration of Articles of Association' (1986) MLR 446.

154 *Gambotto v WCP Ltd* (1995) 13 ACLC 342. See para **[3.087]**.

155 See *Sidebottom v Kershaw, Leese & Co* [1920] 1 Ch 154 and *Greenhalgh v Arderne Cinemas Ltd* [1950] 2 All ER 1120

156 *Greenhalgh v Arderne Cinemas Ltd* [1950] 2 All ER 1120. See also *Re Williams Group Tullamore Ltd* [1985] IR 613, where Barrington J cited in part the dictum of Evershed MR.

> '...the phrase, "company as a whole", does not (at any rate in such a case as the present) mean the company as a commercial entity as distinct form the corporators. It means the corporators as a general body. That is to say, the case may be taken of an individual hypothetical member and it may be asked whether what is proposed is, in the honest opinion of those who voted in its favour, for that person's benefit.'[157]

After distinguishing between the two meanings of 'company as a whole', Evershed MR proposed an alternative test in cases where a company's articles are altered by resolution of the members:

> 'I think the thing can, in practice, be more accurately and precisely stated by looking at the converse and by saying that a special resolution of this kind would be liable to be impeached if the effect of it were to discriminate between the majority shareholders and the minority shareholders so as to give to the former an advantage of which the latter were deprived.'[158]

In this case Evershed MR rejected the plaintiff's claim holding that 'when a man comes into a company, he is not entitled to assume that the articles will always remain in a particular form'[159]. He went on to hold that unfair discrimination did not exist and that accordingly, the resolution to alter the articles was valid.

[3.079] Albeit in another context[160] the Irish High Court, in *G & S Doherty Limited v Doherty*[161], per Henchy J held that 'for the benefit of the company as a whole' means, 'the shareholders as a whole'. It has been said[162] that in deciding which version of the test is appropriate on an alteration of the articles, it is essential to determine the *context of the alteration*. Thus, alterations which give rise to conflicts between the company and its members must be distinguished from conflicts between the members inter se. Depending upon which matter is in issue the phrase 'company as a whole' must, chameleon-like, adapt its colour.

(iii) An objective or subjective test?

[3.080] There is a principled reluctance by the courts to interfere in the internal management of a company[163]. However, the courts are the ultimate fora where dissenters can be heard, and are thus faced with the unenviable choice of having to apply a test to the actions of a majority of shareholders. On the one hand the court could apply an *objective test* by which it would look at the action of the majority, and ask could a reasonable shareholder have thought that it was in the interests of the company as a whole. On the other hand, the court could apply a *subjective test* and confine its enquiry

[157] *Greenhalgh v Arderne Cinemas Ltd* [1950] 2 All ER 1120 at 1126.

[158] *Greenhalgh v Arderne Cinemas Ltd* [1950] 2 All ER 1120.

[159] *Greenhalgh v Arderne Cinemas Ltd* [1950] 2 All ER 1120 at 1127.

[160] Namely that the exercise of the powers of the directors of a company must be exercisedn, bona fide and in the interests of the company as a whole.

[161] *G & S Doherty Limited v Doherty* (19 June 1969, unreported), High Court at p 22 per Henchy J, of the transcript. See also Henchy J's prior judgment of 4 April 1968, and the later Supreme Court judgment of the 19 December 1969, per O'Dalaigh CJ.

[162] Rixon, 'Competing Interests And Conflicting Principles: An Examination of the Power of Alteration of Articles of Association' (1986) MLR 446.

[163] See generally, Chapter 19, *Shareholders' Remedies*.

to whether or not the majority shareholders actually believed that what they were doing was in the interests of the company as a whole[164].

It is thought that the better view is that the courts should apply a subjective test, as was done in the case of *Shuttleworth v Cox Brothers & Co (Maidenhead) Ltd*[165]. In this case, the articles of the company provided that five directors should be life directors, unless disqualified by any one of six events. Mr Shuttleworth was thought to be somewhat delinquent in that he had failed to account for company money on no less that 22 occasions within the space of one year. The company reacted by altering its articles to provide that a life director could be disqualified where the other directors resolved that he should resign. The Court of Appeal held that the alteration was valid because it was *bona fide* and in the interests of the company as a whole. Atkin LJ said:

> 'The only question is whether or not the shareholders, in considering whether they shall alter the articles, honestly intend to exercise their powers for the benefit of the company. If they do then, subject to one or two reservations which have been explained, the alteration must stand. It is not a matter of law for the court whether or not a particular alteration is for the benefit of the company; nor is it the business of a judge to review the decision of every company in the country on these questions...In my view the question is solely for the shareholders acting in good faith.'[166]

Atkin LJ achieved an honourable balance between the competing tests when he said[167]:

> 'The circumstances may be such as to lead to one conclusion only, that the majority of the shareholders are acting so oppressively that they cannot be acting in good faith; or, to put it another way, it may be that their decision must be one which could be taken by persons acting in good faith with a view to the benefit of the company.'

Thus we see that the primary test is to be seen as being essentially subjective, but having an objective element from an evidential standpoint[168].

(iv) Divergent disputes: the traditional test applied

[3.081] Where a court does intervene in such a dispute, its primary task will be to establish the *motive* behind the alteration of the articles. The court will ask whether the alteration was motivated by intentions which were bona fide and in the interests of the company as a whole, which will mean either the company as a separate entity or all of the shareholders, depending upon the context of the alteration. Sometimes the motive behind the alteration will be obvious, where for example, the alteration could only affect one member, or one sector of the membership, and such may be evidence of a lack of bona fides[169]. On the other hand, the action of the shareholders in altering the articles may clearly show that they have gained nothing personally, thus inclining the court to accept that they acted bona fide[170].

---

[164] See *Dafen Tinplate Co Ltd v Llanelly Steel Co (1907) Ltd* [1920] 2 Ch 124, per Peterson J.

[165] *Shuttleworth v Cox Brothers & Co (Maidenhead) Ltd* [1927] 2 KB 9.

[166] [1927] 2 KB 9 at 26, 27.

[167] [1927] 2 KB 9 at 27.

[168] This seems to have been followed in later cases eg *Greenhalgh v Arderne Cinemas Ltd* [1951] 1 Ch 286.

[169] Eg *Sidebottom v Kershaw, Leese & Co* [1920] 1 Ch 154 at 173 *ff*, per Eve J.

[170] See *Rights & Issues Investment Trust Ltd v Stylo Shoes Ltd* [1965] 1 Ch 250 at 256D, per Pennycuick J, who could see no grounds for finding that there was any oppression.

Usually the motives behind the alteration will be unclear, and the actions of the voting shareholders open to several interpretations. In such cases, the court will have to apply some test. Although several different tests appear in the reported cases, two very different situations must be distinguished. On the one hand, the alteration may result in a conflict between *the company and some of its members*. On the other hand, it may result in a conflict between the members *inter se*.

Company versus members

[3.082] Where the alteration results in a conflict between the company and its members, it is submitted that the appropriate test is that set out in *Shuttleworth v Cox Brothers & Co (Maidenhead) Ltd*[171] where Bankes LJ said:

> 'So the test is whether the alteration of the articles was in the opinion of the shareholders for the benefit of the company. By what criterion is the court to ascertain the opinion of the shareholders upon this question? The alteration may be so oppressive as to cast suspicion on the honesty of the persons responsible for it, or so extravagant that no reasonable men could really consider it for the benefit of the company. In such cases the court is, I think, entitled to treat the conduct of shareholders as it does the verdict of a jury, and to say that the alteration of a company's articles shall not stand if it is such that no reasonable man could consider it for the benefit of the company.'

The essential point is that the test which the court is applying is that the alteration will be invalid where the majority of the shareholders *acting in the interests of the company* pass a special resolution to alter the articles, and such could not be said to be *a reasonable alteration* of the constitution from the viewpoint of the affected minority.

[3.083] In the *Shuttleworth* case, the shareholders were clearly acting reasonably and in the interests of the company in that the alteration was directed against a perceived delinquent director. A similar motive was evident in the case of *Sidebottom v Kershaw, Leese & Co*[172]. There, an alteration was made to the articles of association empowering the directors to compel the transfer of the shares (at full value) of any member who competed with the business of the company. In effect the alteration was in the nature of an expropriation of shares, but although such may be evidence of a *mala fide* intention, in this case the expropriation was not motivated by selfish desires of individual shareholders, but rather in the interests of the company. Lord Sterndale MR said:

> 'I think, looking at the alteration broadly, that it is for the benefit of the company that they should not be obliged to have amongst them as members persons who are competing with them in business, and who may get knowledge from their membership which would enable them to compete better.'[173]

---

171 *Shuttleworth v Cox Brothers & Co (Maidenhead) Ltd* [1927] 1 KB 9.

172 *Sidebottom v Kershaw, Leese & Co* [1920] 1 Ch 154.

173 [1920] 1 Ch 154 at 166. Lord Sterndale MR went on to say that the fact that it was directed at the wayward Mr Bodden did not, per se, render the alteration mala fides. That it was directed at Bodden, was, he said, nothing more than the shareholders saying: 'It was the position of Mr Bodden that made us appreciate the detriment that there might be to the company in having members competing with them in their business, and we passed this, and our intention was, if it became necessary, to use it in the case of Mr Bodden; that is what we had in our minds that Mr Bodden is not the only person who might compete, and therefore we passed this general article in order to enable us to apply it in any case where it was for the good of the company that it should be applied.'

Again, the test is whether the company's interests are being protected by the use of reasonable measures.

Member versus member

[3.084] In *Re Williams Group Tullamore Ltd*[174] Barrington J said, referring to the dilemma which must be addressed in cases where there is a conflict between members:

> 'There is no doubt that shareholders, voting at a general meeting of the company, are entitled to have regard to their own interests. The problem is the degree to which they are entitled to disregard the interests of other shareholders.'

Where the alteration of the articles leads to a conflict between the members inter se, ie where the alteration is of no tangible benefit to the company, the test should in logic be different. So, in such cases, it is submitted that the appropriate test is whether or not the majority of the shareholders who vote for the alteration better their interests at the expense of the minority. This is a variation of the test proposed by Evershed MR, and already quoted, in *Greenhalgh v Arderne Cinemas Ltd*[175] where he said that an alteration would be invalid:

> '...if the effect of it were to discriminate between the majority shareholders and the minority shareholders so as to give to the former an advantage of which the latter were deprived.'[176]

It is opined that this test should be applied where the majority shareholders try to use their voting power to unfairly impose their will on the minority and thereby adversely affect the interests of the minority. Such a situation is totally different to the situation where there is a conflict between the company and its members. There, the members exercise their voting power in the interests of the company, and only indirectly in their own interests. In the present situation, the members exercise their voting power *in their own interests*, and not those of the company.

Here there is a real conflict between the interests of the minority and the proprietary rights of the majority to exercise their vote as selfishly as they wish. It is suggested that in a member/member conflict in a private company, the proprietary rights of the majority ought not be allowed to prevail[177]. In such a company the member shareholders will have more in common than simply all having shareholdings in the same company. Rather, they will often be quasi-partners in business and their relations ought to be recognised as such. The test which the courts should apply to such a member/member conflict ought to

---

174 *Re Williams Group Tullamore Ltd* [1985] IR 613, a case concerning CA 1963, s 205, considered in Chapter 19, *Shareholders' Remedies*, para **[19.015]**.

175 *Greenhalgh v Arderne Cinemas Ltd* [1950] 2 All ER 1120.

176 See also *Peters' American Delicacy Co v Heath* [1938–9] CLR 512.

177 Here, as in so many other ways, the eternal distinction between the private and public company is evident in that in the case of a public company, the considerations will often be different and it is submitted that in public companies, in the absence of fraud, the members ought to be allowed to vote as they wish, unfettered by consideration for the minority. In a public company the shareholders are in no way related by any bonds or quasi-fiduciary relations and so ought not be bound to observe the same standards expected of the members of a closely-held private company.

reflect the sanctity of the relations between the members, and demand an honourable standard from all members in the exercise of their voting rights.

(v) Alternative approaches: the traditional test discredited

[3.085] It is suggested that the so-called traditional test in *Allen* is at best merely an attempt to postulate a general principle. Without regard to the nature of the alteration it can, at worst, be interpreted as a misleading generalisation. One alternative approach frees itself of the constraints of the traditional test and is seen in *Clemens v Clemens Brothers Ltd*[178]. There, Foster J said:

> 'I think that one thing which emerges from the cases to which I have referred is that in such a case as the present Miss Clemens is not entitled to exercise her majority vote in whatever way she pleases. The difficulty is in finding a principle, and obviously expressions such as "bona fide in the interests of the company as a whole", "fraud on a minority" and "oppressive" do not assist in formulating a principle. I have come to the conclusion that it would be unwise to try to produce a principle, since the circumstances of each case are infinitely varied. It would not, I think, assist to say more than that in my judgement Miss Clemens is not entitled as of right to exercise her votes as an ordinary shareholder in any way she pleases. To use the phrase of Lord Wilberforce[179], that right is "subject...to equitable considerations...which may make it unjust...to exercise [it] in a particular way".'

In that case the plaintiff owned 45% of the shares in the defendant company and a Miss Clemens held the remaining 55% of the shares. It was proposed to make an issue of shares which would, inter alia, have the effect of reducing the plaintiff's shareholdings in the company to under 25%. Resolutions were passed to this effect, and the plaintiff sought a declaration that they be set aside as being oppressive. Foster J granted the orders on the grounds as set out above. Although that case was not strictly concerned with the alteration of the articles, it is submitted[180] that in view of the artificialities inherent in the traditional analysis, there is some merit in the 'equitable considerations' approach set out in the *Clemens* case[181].

[3.086] Perhaps it is because of the difficulties associated with the traditional test that more and more members who feel aggrieved by an alteration of a company's articles of association will not seek to rely upon the common law, preferring instead to petition the court under CA 1963, s 205[182]. Such is now facilitated by the acceptance that the section

---

178 *Clemens v Clemens Brothers Ltd* [1976] 2 All ER 268.

179 In *Ebrahimi v Westbourne Galleries Ltd* [1972] 2 All ER 492 at 500.

180 See also *Browne v British Abrasive Wheel Co* [1919] 1 Ch 291 at 295, where Astbury J said: 'The question therefore is whether the enforcement of the proposed alteration on the minority is within the ordinary principles of justice and whether it is for the benefit of the company as a whole. I find it very difficult to follow how it can be just and equitable that a majority, by failing to purchase the shares of a minority by agreement, can take the power to do so compulsorily.' Clearly, the court took cognisance of the underlying equities of the situation.

181 Cf Keane, *Company Law* (3rd edn, 2000), para 6.08, where he doubts whether as a general principle *Clemens v Clemens Brothers Ltd* [1976] 2 All ER 268 can be supported.

182 See *Re Williams Group Tullamore Ltd* [1985] IR 613 and generally, Chapter 19, *Shareholders' Remedies*, para **[19.015]** *ff*.

has application to isolated incidents of oppression or acts of disregard for the interests of a minority.

[3.087] The Australian High Court has recently considered the vexed issue of alteration of articles of association in *Gambotto v WCP Ltd*[183] and in doing so has lent support in favour of an 'oppression' test. The essential facts in that case were that the defendant-company sought to alter its articles of association to allow any shareholder holding 90% or more of the company's issued share capital to acquire compulsorily all of the remaining shares, in circumstances where the statutory compulsory appropriation provisions were inapplicable[184]. At the relevant time, a corporate group owned 99.7% of the issued share capital in the defendant. The plaintiff minority shareholder objected to the alteration on the basis that the appropriation of his shares was oppressive. In finding for the plaintiff, the Australian High Court departed radically from the traditional test:

> 'In the context of a special resolution altering the articles and giving rise to a conflict of interests and advantages, whether or not it involves an expropriation of shares, we would reject as inappropriate the "*bona fide for the benefit of the company as a whole*" test of Lindley MR in *Allen v Gold Reefs of West Africa Ltd*. The application of the test in such a context has been criticised on grounds which, in our view, are unanswerable. It seems to us that, in such a case not involving an actual or effective expropriation of shares or of valuable proprietary rights attaching to shares, an alteration of the articles by special resolution regularly passed will be valid unless it is *ultra vires*, beyond any purpose contemplated by the articles or oppressive as that expression is understood in the law relating to corporations. Somewhat different considerations apply, however, in a case which as the present where what is involved is an alteration of the articles to allow an expropriation by the majority of the shares, or of valuable proprietary rights attaching to the shares, of a minority. In such a case, the immediate purpose of the resolution is to confer upon the majority shareholder or shareholders power to acquire compulsorily the property of the minority shareholder or shareholders. Of itself, the conferral of such a power does not lie within the "contemplated objects of the power" to amend the articles'.[185]

The distinction was thus made between alterations that involve an expropriation of shares or of valuable property rights from those that do not. Where the alteration does not involve an expropriation of shares, the court was inclined to a test akin to that contained in the Irish section 205 remedy: is the alteration oppressive? In company law, it is established that by oppression is meant 'burdensome, harsh and wrongful'[186]. In addition, the alteration must also be intra vires and not beyond the purpose contemplated by the articles.

[3.088] In relation to alterations that involve the expropriation of shares, the test promulgated in *Gambotto* was stated thus:

---

[183] *Gambotto v WCP Ltd* (1995) 13 ACLC 342. For comment, see Moshinsky and Rosedale, 'A Victory for the Small Shareholder in Australia', [1995] 7 ICCLR 229.

[184] See Chapter 16, *Share Transfer in Private Companies*, para **[16.080]** *ff*.

[185] (1995) 13 ACLC 342 at para 25 of the majority judgment.

[186] See *Re Greenore Trading Company Ltd* [1980] ILRM 94 at 100,101; *Scottish Co-operative Wholesale Society Ltd v Meyer* [1959] AC 324. See, generally, Chapter 19, *Shareholders' Remedies*, para **[19.011]** *ff*.

'The exercise of a power conferred by a company's constitution enabling the majority shareholders to expropriate the minority's shareholding for the purpose of aggrandising the majority *is valid if and only if to the extent that the relevant provisions of the company's constitution so provide*. The inclusion of such a power in a company's constitution at its incorporation is one thing. But it is another thing when a company's constitution is sought to be amended by an alteration of articles of association so as to confer upon the majority power to expropriate the shares of a minority. Such a power could not be taken or exercised simply for the purpose of aggrandising the majority...In our view, such a power can be taken only if

(i) it is exercisable for a proper purpose and

(ii) its exercise will not operate oppressively in relation to minority shareholders.

In other words, an expropriation may be justified where it is reasonably apprehended that the continued shareholding of the minority is detrimental to the company, its undertaking or the conduct of its affairs – resulting in detriment to the interests of the existing shareholders generally – and expropriation is a reasonable means of eliminating or mitigating that detriment.'[187]

Examples of justified expropriation that the court gave were:

— where a shareholder was competing with the company (as in *Sidebottom v Kershaw, Leese and Co*[188]) so long as the *terms* of the expropriation were not oppressive; or

— where necessary to remove a particular shareholder in order to comply with a regulatory requirement.

The test thus formulated by the court seems to only permit expropriation to prevent a negative consequence for the company rather than to positively advance the company's or the majority members' interests. This is further borne out by the court's general comments on alterations to effect expropriations:

'Notwithstanding that a shareholder's membership of a company is subject to alterations of the articles which may affect the rights attaching to the shareholder's shares and the value of those shares, we do not consider that, in the case of an alteration to the articles authorising the expropriation of shares, it is a sufficient justification of an expropriation that the expropriation, being fair, will advance the interests of the company as a legal and commercial entity or those of the majority, albeit the great majority, of corporators. This approach does not attach sufficient weight to the proprietary nature of a share and, to the extent that English authority might appear to support such an approach, we do not agree with it. It is only right that exceptional circumstances should be required to justify an amendment to the articles authorising the compulsory expropriation by the majority of the minority's interests in a company. To allow expropriation where it would advance the interests of the company as a legal and commercial entity or those of the general body or corporators would, in our view, be tantamount to permitting expropriation by the majority for the purpose of some personal gain and thus be made for an improper purpose[189]. It would open the way to circumventing the protection which the Corporations Law gives to

[187] (1995) 13 ACLC 342 at para 26 of the majority judgment.

[188] *Sidebottom v Kershaw, Leese and Co* [1920] 1 Ch 154. See para **[3.083]**.

[189] Citing *Brown v British Abrasive Wheel Co* (1919) 1 Ch 295, 296.

> minorities who resist compromises, amalgamations and reconstructions, schemes of arrangement and takeover offers'.[190]

Clearly, the position of the Australian High Court is that an alteration of the articles to effect an expropriation of shares will only be valid where its purpose is *defensive* ie to prevent *negative* consequences befalling the company and will never be permitted to positively improve or advance the interests of the company or the majority. In those limited circumstances when an expropriation alteration passes this first hurdle, the Australian courts will also require that it be fair. Fairness in this context was held to require the disclosure of all relevant information to the expropriated minority *and* also the payment of market value or above. It was also held that the onus of proof rests with the appropriating majority.

Informal alteration of the articles of association by shareholders' agreement

[3.089] Difficult questions of law arise where the members purport to alter a company's articles of association without formally passing the requisite special resolution referred to in CA 1963, s 15. In *Cane v Jones*[191] the articles of association of the company provided that two persons, Percy and Harold Jones, should be its life directors. It was also provided that the directors should elect a chairman of the board of the directors who should have a casting vote at both board and general meetings of the company. However, all of the shareholders entered into an oral shareholders' agreement which provided inter alia that the chairman should *not* exercise a casting vote and that if an equality of votes occurred an independent chairman would be appointed. Later, the shareholding in the company changed and a dispute arose concerning, inter alia, whether or not the prior unanimous agreement of the shareholders had the effect of altering the articles of association of the company. Michael Wheeler QC held that:

> 'In my judgment, s 10[192] of the Act is merely laying down a procedure whereby some only of the shareholders can validly alter the articles; and, if, as I believe to be the case, it is a basic principle of company law that all the corporators, acting together, can do anything which is intra vires the company, then I can see nothing in s 10 to undermine this principle.'[193]

It is thought that this decision makes good law.

[3.090] In Ireland, CA 1963, s 141(8) may undermine this principle, since it provides that where a company is so authorised by its articles a resolution in writing signed by its members is as valid as if it had been passed at a general meeting of the company[194]. The crux of the matter is that for an informal resolution to be validated by statute, it must be in writing. The question is, does s 141(8) oust the common law principle that an oral agreement by all the corporators will suffice to alter the articles? There is a recent indication that the Irish courts accept that the common law principle has not been

---

[190] (1995) 13 ACLC 342 at para 28 of the majority judgment.

[191] *Cane v Jones* [1981] 1 All ER 533.

[192] Which was similar to CA 1963, s 15.

[193] [1981] All ER 533 at 539.

[194] This is considered further in Chapter 9, *Corporate Governance: Meetings*, para **[9.076]**.

displaced by CA 1963, s 141(8). In *Re Shannonside Holdings Ltd*[195] the question before Costello J concerned the existence and validity of a debenture created by the company. After finding that the debenture did on the balance of probabilities exist, Costello J turned to consider whether it had been validly executed. As in what is now model reg 47, the company's articles of association provided that all members' meetings of the company should be held within the State. Contrary to this, the company's members held a meeting in Chicago, USA for the purpose of resolving that the company's directors could borrow in excess of the issued share capital[196]. It was subsequently claimed that the debenture was invalid because the general meeting was held in Chicago instead of within the State. This was rejected by Costello J who said:

> 'In my opinion, non-compliance with...Regulation [47] does not invalidate any resolutions passed at the meeting. It seems to me that the members of the company can mutually decide to have meetings anywhere they like, even though the articles indicate that they are to be held in the State. Should they decide to hold meetings outside the State, they are entitled to do so provided there is agreement. If there was no formal indication that such agreement was forthcoming, it would be clear that it was to be implied in the circumstances of this case.'[197]

The learned Costello J appears to have accepted as a basic principle of Irish company law that the corporators in a company may together do as they wish, and in this regard implicitly proceeded on the same basis as did Michael Wheeler QC in *Cane v Jones*. The alteration of the articles in *Shannonside* may not have been contentious, and it remains to be seen whether the High Court will follow Costello J's decision where, say, the members informally decide to vary a pre-emption clause. Notwithstanding the decision in this case, it would seem prudent, where possible, for all informal resolutions altering articles of association to be in writing, signed by all of the company's members. Informal written and non-written resolutions, generally, are considered in detail in Chapter 9[198].

[3.091] In the case of a single-member private company there exists an additional ground for believing that the common law rule has been ousted by the legislature. Regulation 9(3) of the European Communities (Single-Member Private Limited Companies) Regulations 1994[199] provides that:

> 'Subject to paragraph (2)[200], any provision of the Companies Acts which—
>
> (a) enables or requires any matter to be done or to be decided by a company in general meeting, or
>
> (b) requires any matter to be decided by a resolution of the company,

---

[195] *Re Shannonside Holdings Ltd* (20 May 1993, unreported), High Court, per Costello J.

[196] The company's articles of association contained a fetter on the directors' exercise of their borrowing powers, in terms apparently similar to model reg 79. See generally, para **[3.060]**.

[197] (20 May 1993, unreported), High Court at p 7.

[198] At para **[9.076]** *ff*.

[199] SI 1994/275.

[200] Paragraph (2) of reg 9 provides that a single-member company must comply with CA 1963, s 160(2)(b), 160(5) and 160(6) and hold a meeting before removing an auditor from office. See further Chapter 9, *Corporate Governance: Meetings*, para **[9.074]**.

> shall be deemed to be satisfied, in the case of a single-member company, by a decision of the member which is drawn up in writing and notified to the company in accordance with this regulation.'

Although reg 9(8) provides that a single member's failure to notify the company of his decision will not invalidate the decision, it is noticeably silent with regard to a failure to draw up the decision *in writing*. In that the operative part of reg 9(3) provides that the provisions in the Companies Acts, referred to at (a) and (b) above, are *deemed to be satisfied*, it is arguable that if they can be satisfied in the manner found by Costello J in *Shannonside*, an unambiguous oral resolution of a single member may also be valid to alter the company's articles.

The relationship between the memorandum and the articles

[3.092] The accepted rule is that the memorandum of association is the dominant constitutional document which will prevail in a conflict between it and the articles of association. So Carroll J said in *Roper v Ward*[201]:

> 'In construing the articles I am guided by the principle that they are subordinated to and controlled by the memorandum of association which is the dominant document. While the articles cannot alter or control the memorandum or be used to expend the objects of the company, they can be used to explain it generally or to explain an ambiguity in its terms.'

In construing a clause in a company's memorandum of association, the regulations in the articles can only have the role of resolving any anomalies[202].

The construction of the memorandum and articles of association

[3.093] Where a company's memorandum or articles of association are ambiguous, they will be construed so as to make them workable[203]. In *Roper v Ward*[204] Carroll J held that:

> 'The memorandum and articles of association of a company are commercial documents and should be construed to give them *reasonable business efficacy*.'[205]

Where there is an ambiguity which cannot be resolved on a literal interpretation the courts will imply whatever is necessary to make a company's constitutional documents workable.

[3.094] There are very definite limits to the circumstances in which the courts will imply terms into a company's articles of association. Whilst it is accepted that the documents will be construed so as to give them *reasonable business efficacy*, a distinction has been

---

201 *Roper v Ward* [1981] ILRM 408 at 409.

202 *Duncan Gilmore and Co Ltd The Company v Inman* [1952] 2 All ER 871; *Angostura Bitters (Dr JGB Siegert & Sons) Ltd v Kerr* [1933] AC 550; *Guinness v Land Corporation of Ireland* [1885] 22 Ch D 261; *Re Wedgewood Coal and Iron Company (Andersons Case)* 7 Ch D 75.

203 See *Holmes v Keyes* [1958] 2 All ER 129 at 138, where Jenkins LJ held: '...the articles of association of the company should be regarded as a business document and should be construed so as to give them reasonable business efficacy, where a construction tending to that result is admissible on the language of the articles, in preference to a result which would or might prove unworkable.'

204 [1981] ILRM 408 at 412 (emphasis added).

205 See also *Stillwell Trucks Party Ltd v Nectar Brook Investments Party Ltd* [1993] 10 ACSR 615.

made between a situation where clarification of an express provision in the articles is required, in contrast to where it is sought to imply a term into the articles from extrinsic evidence. This distinction was made by the English Court of Appeal in *Bratton Seymour Service Co Ltd v Oxborough*[206]. In this case the company was a management company, formed to hold the common areas of a property known as the Bratton House Development. The defendant purchased part of the property, sold off six flats and retained three lots for his own use. In the conveyance of the property to the defendant, he covenanted to contribute to the maintenance of what could be described as the *utility* areas of the development. Later, all of the common parts, including the utility areas, and what can be termed the *amenity areas*, were conveyed to the plaintiff management company.

The defendant was asked to contribute to the maintenance of both the utility and amenity areas of the development. He agreed that he was bound to contribute to the maintenance of the utility areas, but disputed that he was so bound in respect of the amenity areas. The plaintiff company argued that such an obligation was implicit in the company's articles of association, an argument which succeeded at first instance.

The Court of Appeal rejected that such a term could be implied into a company's articles. Steyn LJ held:

> 'Here, the company puts forward an implication to be derived not from the language of the articles of association but purely from extrinsic circumstances. That, in my judgment, is a type of implication which, as a matter of law, can never succeed in the case of articles of association. After all, if it were permitted, it would involve the position that the different implications would notionally be possible between the company and different subscribers. Just as the company or an individual member cannot seek to defeat the statutory contract by reason of special circumstances such as misrepresentation, mistake, undue influence and duress and is furthermore not permitted to seek a rectification, neither the company nor any member can seek to add to or to subtract from the terms of the articles by way of implying a term derived from extrinsic surrounding circumstances. If it were permitted in this case, it would be equally permissible over the spectrum of company law cases. The consequences would be prejudicial to third parties, namely potential shareholders who are entitled to look to and rely on the articles of association as registered.'[207]

It is clear that the court will only imply terms into a company's articles of association in exceptional cases[208].

[3.095] Some examples of permitted implications in the case of a company's articles of association are seen in the judgment of Sir Christopher Slade in *Bratton Seymour*. These include surrounding evidence to identify people, places or other subject matter referred to in the articles. The fact that the term which was sought to be implied in this case involved the imposition of a financial burden on the member may be seen as influencing the Court of Appeal's decision. As has been seen, the members of a company may, by passing a special resolution, alter the articles of association, subject to this being bona

[206] *Bratton Seymour Service Co Ltd v Oxborough* [1992] BCLC 693.

[207] [1992] BCLC 693 at 698, 699.

[208] See also *Australia Securities Commission v Multiple Sclerosis Society of Tasmania* [1993] 10 ACSR 489.

fide and in the interests of the company as a whole. However, the power to alter the articles is subject also to the proviso that where the alteration imposes an additional burden of contribution on a member, that member must agree to its imposition on him[209].

[C] THE STATUTORY CONTRACT IN SECTION 25 OF CA 1963

Section 25 creates a 'statutory contract'

[3.096] A company's memorandum and articles of association together comprise a *statutory contract* by virtue of CA 1963, s 25. In this section the nature, extent and scope of this unusual contract are examined. When the initial subscribers associate with a view to forming a company it is a prerequisite that they sign the memorandum and articles of association[210]. One of the consequences of this is that, by subscribing, the members are deemed to have entered into a *statutory contract* by CA 1963, s 25(1), which provides:

> 'Subject to the provisions of this Act, the memorandum and articles shall, when registered, bind the company and the members thereof to the same extent as if they respectively had been signed and sealed by each member, and contained covenants by each member to observe all the provisions of the memorandum and of the articles.'

Similarly, when the sole member of a single-member private company signs the memorandum and articles of association, he will enter into a statutory contract with the company[211]. The wording of s 25 can be traced back to the Joint Stock Companies Act 1844, which adopted the old method of forming a company by deed of settlement. The deed of settlement was a contract between the members who sealed it. The effect of s 25 is to bind the members of a company, and the company itself, to observe the provisions of its memorandum and articles of association[212].

[3.097] In *Clark v Workman*[213] Ross J said, in the context of a company's articles of association, that:

> 'They constitute a contract between every shareholder and all the others, and between the company itself and all the shareholders. It is a contract of the most sacred character, and it is on the faith of it that each shareholder advances his money.' [214]

---

209 CA 1963, s 27(1). See para **[3.070]** *ff.*

210 In the case of the memorandum, by virtue of CA 1963, s 5(1); in the case of the articles, by virtue of CA 1963, s 14(d) as amended by the Finance Act 1996, s 112.

211 European Communities (Single-Member Private Limited Companies) Regulations 1994 (SI 1994/275), reg 4.

212 In *Kerry Co-Operative Ltd & Others v An Bord Bainne Co-Operative Ltd* [1990] ILRM 664 it was said that: '...membership of [a registered company] constitutes a contract between the member and the corporate entity which...is to be found in its memorandum and articles of association (CA 1963, s 25).' In *Roper v Ward* [1981] ILRM 408 at 412, Carroll J said of the memorandum and articles of association, that '[t]hey are in effect a contract between the company and its members. When they are registered they bind the company and its members as if they had been sealed and signed by each member...'

213 *Clark v Workman* [1920] 1 IR 107.

214 [1920] 1 IR 107 at 112.

The parties to this contract are the members and the company itself. It is enforceable by the members inter se, by the members against the company and by the company against the members. It is however an unusual contract, and its interpretation has been the subject of much academic debate[215]. Steyn LJ described the special and distinctive nature of the section 25 contract thus in the Court of Appeal in *Bratton Seymour Service Co Ltd v Oxborough*[216]:

> 'By virtue of [the English equivalent to CA 1963, s 25] the articles of association become, upon registration, a contract between a company and members. It is, however, a statutory contract of a special nature with its own distinctive features. It derives its binding force not from a bargain struck between the parties but from the terms of the statute. It is binding only insofar as it affects the rights and obligations between the company and the members acting in their capacity as members. If it contains provisions conferring rights and obligations on outsiders, then those provisions do not bite as part of the contract between the company and the members, even if the outsider is coincidentally a member. Similarly, if the provisions are not truly referable to the rights and obligations of members as such it does not operate as a contract. Moreover, the contract can be altered by a special resolution without the consent of all the contracting parties. It is also, unlike an ordinary contract, not defeasible on the grounds of misrepresentation, common law mistake, mistake in equity, undue influence or duress. Moreover...it cannot be rectified on the grounds of mistake.'[217]

The distinctive features of the *statutory contract* spoken of by Steyn LJ, which arise by virtue of s 25, are considered next.

---

215 See Wedderburn [1957] Cam LR 194; Goldberg (1972) MLR 362; Prentice (1980) Co Law 179; Gregory (1981) MLR 526 where the English equivalent of the CA 1963, s 25 contract is examined in detail.

216 *Bratton Seymour Service Co Ltd v Oxborough* [1992] BCLC 693.

217 [1992] BCLC 693 at 698. In *Bailey v New South Wales Medical Defence Union Ltd* (1996) 18 ACSR 521, McHugh and Gummow JJ (at para 70) described the unusual features of the statutory contract thus:

> 'First the members are deemed to have contracted on the basis that, since the articles, and in general the memorandum, can be altered by special resolution of the company, the terms of the contract are variable from time to time without agreement of both parties to that variation. Secondly, there is no jurisdiction in a court of Equity to rectify the articles of association even if they do not accord with the concurrent intention of all the signatories thereof at the moment of signature; the articles may be amended only pursuant to statutory authority. Thirdly, the direct enforcement by a member of rights under such a contract against the company may have to overcome obstacles placed in its path by the rule in *Foss v Harbottle*. Fourthly, as Salmond J pointed out in *Shalfoon v Cheddar Valley Co-operative Dairy Co* (1924) NZLR 561 at 580, whilst a contract binds those who made it and their personal representatives, the articles in a company limited by shares bind the owners thereof for the time being and the obligations imposed by the deemed covenant are appurtenant to the shares and pass with ownership of them. Finally, the view has been taken, not without doubt, that, in the absence of some other statutory provision, the effect of the decision in *Houldsworth v City of Glasgow Bank* (1880) 5 App Cas 317 is to preclude a member of a company limited by shares from suing the company for damages for breach of contract whilst still a member and obtained without seeking recission of the contract whereby the shares were obtained'.

The distinctive features of the section 25 contract

[3.098] The legislature left unanswered a number of questions which arise in considering the unusual features of the section 25 contract. These are essentially threefold: are both the members and the company bound?; are the members bound to the other members?; and can members enforce the contract acting in a capacity other than as members? Over the years, the courts have enunciated the following principles in interpreting the section 25 contract:

(a) Section 25 of CA 1963 binds the members and the company.

(b) Section 25 of CA 1963 binds the members to the other members.

(c) Section 25 of CA 1963 is only enforceable by and against members acting qua member, or in their capacity as members.

The reason why such controversy exists is because of the clash between two principles: the right of a member to see that the existing rules of the company are observed versus the principle of *majority rule* embodied in *Foss v Harbottle*[218], which implies that the majority can alter the rules if they so wish.

(a) Section 25 of CA 1963 binds the members and the company

[3.099] The section 25 contract can be enforced by a member against the company and by the company against a member. The rights that can be enforced by a member are solely those *personal rights*, which he has by virtue of his membership[219]. In *Hickman v Kent or Romney Marsh Sheepbreeders' Association*[220] the defendant company was incorporated with the objects of, inter alia, encouraging the breeding of Kent or Romney Marsh sheep and the:

> '...establishment and publication of a flock book of recognised and pure-bred sires...and the annual registration of the pedigrees of such sheep as are proved to the satisfaction of the council to be eligible for entry'.[221]

In addition, reg 49 of the company's articles of association[222] provided that disputes as to the intent, construction, incidents or consequences of the articles should be referred to arbitration. Alfred J Hickman was a member of the company for just over nine years when the conduct of the company's business became disagreeable to him. Rather than resort to the arbitration provision in the articles, Hickman went to court and, *inter alia*, sought damages from the company for refusing to register his sheep, together with a declaration that he was entitled to have his sheep registered. The company was contemporaneously trying to expel Hickman as a member and sought to have his action stayed to force him to abide by the arbitration mechanism contained in the articles. Astbury J held that the company was entitled to have the action stayed, because the

---

218 *Foss v Harbottle* (1843) 2 Hare 461. On the principle of majority rule and the rule in *Foss v Harbottle* generally, see Chapter 19, *Shareholders' Remedies*, para **[19.082]**.

219 See para **[3.103]**. See generally Chapter 15, *Shares and Membership*, para **[15.083]** for a discussion of a member's personal rights and Chapter 19, *Shareholders' Remedies*, para **[19.092]** for the distinction between a member's personal rights and the rule in *Foss v Harbottle*.

220 *Hickman v Kent or Romney Marsh Sheepbreeders' Association* [1915] 1 Ch 881.

221 [1915] 1 Ch 881 at 882.

222 [1915] 1 Ch 881 at 884.

articles were binding on the members and so the reference to arbitration was binding on Hickman. In so deciding, Astbury J looked at two streams of dicta: one saying that the articles did not constitute a contract[223]; the other[224] saying that it did, and also that a company is entitled as against its members to enforce and restrain breaches of its articles of association. This latter stream also said that a member could enforce and restrain breaches of his company's regulations[225]. Astbury J eventually said:

> 'It is difficult to reconcile these two classes of decisions and the judicial opinions therein expressed, but I think this much is clear, first, that no article can constitute a contract between the company and a third person; secondly, that no right merely purporting to be given by an article to a person, whether a member or not, in a capacity other than that of a member, as, for instance, as solicitor, promoter, director, can be enforced against the company; and, thirdly, that articles regulating the rights and obligations of the members generally as such do create rights and obligations between them and the company respectively.'[226]

It is clear that the memorandum and articles are contractually binding on both the members and the company itself. By initially subscribing to a company's memorandum and articles of association, or by having shares transferred to them, members agree to be contractually bound to abide by the terms of the company's constitutional documentation.

(b) Section 25 of CA 1963 binds members to other members

[3.100] The section 25 contract is also enforceable as between the members themselves, and in addition to binding members to the company it binds members to each other[227]. So, a member can sue another member who fails to observe the provisions of the articles or memorandum. In such a case, the member is not bound by the rule in *Foss v Harbottle*[228].

[3.101] Among the cases which establish that the memorandum and articles of association are enforceable by the members *inter se*, is *Rayfield v Hands*[229]. In that case, as with many of the cases on this point, the rights which were sought to be enforced were pre-emption rights attaching to shares[230]. The articles of the company provided that:

---

223 *Prichard's case* LR 8 Ch 965; *Melhado v Porto Alegre Ry Co* LR 9 CP 503; *Eley v Positive Life Assurance Co* (1876) 1 Ex D 20, 88; *Browne v La Trinidad* (1877) 37 Ch D 1.

224 *MacDougall v Gardiner* (1875) 1 Ch D 13; *Pender v Lushington* (1877) 6 ChD 70; *Imperial Hydropathic Hotel Co, Blackpool v Hampson* 23 Ch D 1.

225 For example see, *Bradford Banking v Briggs* 12 App Cas 29 and *Welton v Saffery* [1897] AC 299.

226 *Hickman v Kent or Romney Marsh Sheepbreeders' Association* [1915] 1 Ch 881 at 900.

227 *Rayfield v Hands* [1960] 1 Ch 1, considered at para **[3.101]**.

228 *Foss v Harbottle* (1843) 2 Hare 461. See generally Chapter 19, *Shareholders' Remedies*, para **[19.082]** *ff*.

229 *Rayfield v Hands* [1960] 1 Ch 1, [1958] 2 WLR 851.

230 Pre-emption rights to shares are considered further in this chapter at para **[3.055]**. Pre-emption rights on share transfer are considered in detail in Chapter 16, *Share Transfers in Private Companies*, paras **[16.063]** *ff*; pre-emption rights on the allotment of shares are considered in Chapter 15, *Shares and Membership*, para **[15.055]** *ff*.

> 'Every member who intends to transfer shares shall inform the directors who shall take the said shares equally between them at a fair value...'[231]

The plaintiff, Rayfield, owned 725 fully paid shares of £1 each, and purported to rely on the foregoing article by serving notice on the directors of his intention to transfer his shares to them. The directors refused to buy the shares, contending that the articles did not impose an obligation on them to take shares, but was merely an option which they could exercise. This was rejected by Vaisey J who construed the words 'will take the shares' as importing an obligation and not an option. Central to that decision was the fact that the contract was enforceable by the plaintiff-member against the directors *in their capacity as fellow members*[232]. Vaisey J held that the directors (acting qua member) were obliged to buy the shares, saying:

> 'On the whole, if the proper way to construe the articles of association of a company is as a commercial or business document to which the maxim "validate if possible" applies, I think that the plaintiff in this action ought to succeed. Not one of the judges in the case to which I have already referred, *Dean v Prince*[233], showed any signs of shock or surprise in the assumption there made of a contract between directors being formed by the terms of a company's articles. I am encouraged, not I hope unreasonably, to find in this case a contract similarly formed between a member and member-directors in relation to their holdings of the company's shares in its articles. The conclusion to which I have come may not be of so general an application as to extend to the articles of every company, for it is, I think, material to remember that this private company is one of that class of companies which bears a close analogy to a partnership...'.[234]

The latter sentiment shows that in the case of private companies, the memorandum and articles of association bear a close analogy with a deed of partnership. Where this is the case, it may be seen by the courts that there is a stronger case for giving effect to the contract subsisting between the persons who associate in such circumstances. A breach of such mutually agreed provisions may ground a petition alleging *oppression* under CA 1963, s 205[235] or a petition that the company be wound up on just and equitable grounds under CA 1963, s 213(f)[236].

[3.102] The principle that the memorandum and articles of association bind the members *inter se* has been accepted in Ireland in several cases[237]. An example is *Lee &*

---

231 [1960] Ch 1 at 2.

232 So, Vaisey J said at 6: '[n]ow the question arises at the outset whether the terms of Article 11 relate to the rights of members inter se (that being the expression found in so many of the cases), or whether the relationship is between a member as such and directors as such. I may dispose of this point very briefly by saying that, in my judgment, the relationship here is between the plaintiff as a member and the defendants not as directors but as members.'

233 *Dean v Prince* [1954] Ch 409, [1954] WLR 538, [1954] 1 All ER 749.

234 [1960] Ch 1 at 9.

235 See generally, Chapter 19, *Shareholders' Remedies*, para **[19.006]** *ff.*

236 See generally, Chapter 25, *Winding Up Companies*, paras **[25.076]** *ff.*

237 See also *Attorney General for Ireland v Jameson* [1904] 2 IR 644. There too, pre-emption rights were accepted as binding. As Boyd J said at 679, '...the restrictive clauses were as much terms of his contract as his title to the shares. His title was clogged with these clauses, and he accepted the shares which were allotted to him...on the terms and conditions agreed to by him and the other shareholders'. So also Kenny J said (at 670) of the right to share in any surplus of the company's assets on a liquidation that: '[i]n acquiring these rights – that is, in becoming a member of the company – he is deemed to have simultaneously entered into a contract under seal to conform to the regulations contained in the articles of association.'

Co (Dublin) Ltd v Egan (Wholesale) Ltd[238] where the defendant company's articles contained pre-emption rights. One member contracted to sell his shares to an outsider, without offering the shares to the other members pursuant to the pre-emption rights. When, for his own reasons, he later repudiated the contract with the outsider, an order for specific performance was sought by the would-be purchaser. This action failed, and the court held that it would not succeed until such time as the other members had been given the opportunity to exercise the forgotten (or ignored) pre-emption rights.

(c) Section 25 of CA 1963 is only enforceable by and against members acting qua member

[3.103] The section 25 contract is only enforceable by and against members in their capacity as members, or 'qua member'. As has been seen in *Hickman's* case, Astbury J made it quite clear that the section 25 contract did not bind, and could not be enforced, by outsiders. Furthermore, he held the section 25 contract was only enforceable by members in their capacity as members and not, for example, in their capacity as directors or solicitors or others, even if they were incidentally shareholders[239]. Therefore, a right conferred on a member by the articles of association to information in respect of the company must be distinguished from a right in the articles of association to be, say, the company's solicitor. In *Eley v Positive Government Security Life Assurance Company Limited*[240] the articles of a company provided that Eley would be the company's solicitor for life, and that he was only removable for misconduct. Eley acted as company solicitor for some time without a written or oral contract of employment. When the company ceased to engage Eley's services, he sued for breach of contract grounded on the provision in the articles of association. The House of Lords held that the articles did not oblige the company to employ Eley in his capacity of solicitor, and that there was no contract between Eley, the solicitor, and the company. Lord Cairns LC said:

> '...the articles state the arrangement between the members. They are an arrangement *inter socios*, and in that view, if the introductory words are applied...it becomes a covenant between the parties to it that they will employ the plaintiff. Now, so far as that is concerned, it is *res inter alios acta*, the plaintiff is no party to it. No doubt he thought that by inserting it he was making his employment safe as against the company; but his relying on that view of the law does not alter the legal effect of the articles. This article is either a stipulation which would bind the members, or else a mandate to the directors. In either case it is a matter between the directors and the shareholders, and not between them and the plaintiff.'[241]

Thus the rule is that the rights conferred on members are only conferred on them *in their capacity as members* and cannot be availed of in any other capacity[242].

---

238 *Lee & Co (Dublin) Ltd v Egan (Wholesale) Ltd* (27 April 1978, unreported), High Court, per Kenny J.

239 [1915] 1 Ch 881 at 900.

240 *Eley v Positive Government Security Life Assurance Company Ltd* (1876) 1 Ex D 88.

241 (1876) 1 Ex D 88 at 90.

242 See *Browne v La Trinidad* (1877) 37 Ch D 1 where a director could not rely on the articles to secure his tenure as director.

[3.104] The corollary to this rule is that obligations imposed upon members in a capacity other than in their capacity as members are not enforceable by CA 1963, s 25. Persons who become members should not become bound to do something unrelated to their membership of a company as a consequence of a provision one would not expect to find in the constitution of the company in question. The subject matter of the statutory contract was identified by McHugh and Gummow JJ in *Bailey v New South Wales Medical Defence Union Ltd*[243]:

> '...the broad trend of authority referred to above, particularly since *Hickman*, has been to identify the subject-matter of the "statutory contract", so far as concerns the relations between the corporation and the members, not as commercial rights but as the government of the corporation and the exercise of the constitutional powers of the corporation. Such matters as inspection of the register, the right to receive a share certificate, to vote, to receive informative notice of meetings, to receive payment of duly declared and payable dividends, and the like, even where not specifically supported by statutory provision, have been treated as inherent in the relationship between the corporation and its members'.

In that case, the facts of which are considered below[244], the judges held that the provisions in the articles of association in question – concerning insurance of the company's medical practitioner-members – could not consistent with *Hickman* be described as flowing from the general regulations of the union as applicable alike to all shareholders. It has been contended, therefore, that the statutory contract does not extend to 'commercial rights' and is confined to the government and exercise of constitutional powers of a company[245].

[3.105] The rule that the section 25 contract is only enforceable *qua* member is not without controversy. The debate has focused on reconciling the apparent anomaly that s 25 of the 1963 Act cannot be relied upon to enforce the rights or obligations of members enjoyed in an outside capacity. It has been suggested[246] that the Irish courts ought not to feel fettered by the old English authorities and ought not differentiate between the member enforcing his rights as member and a member enforcing outsider-rights which he may have. It is submitted that this is the most sensible way forward, particularly in the case of private closely-held companies[247]. It seems to be self-evident that in a private company there is an unanswerable case that the section 25 contract ought to be enforceable by the parties thereto, *in whatever capacity they may act.*

---

243 *Bailey v New South Wales Medical Defence Union Ltd* (1996) 18 ACSR 521 at para 79.

244 See para **[3.106]**.

245 See Lipton & Hertzberg, *Understanding Company Law* (9th edn, 2000), p 85.

246 See Ussher, *Company Law in Ireland* (1986), p 165, who suggests that the courts in Ireland should '...eschew the artificialities introduced by Eley's case...', and where 'section 25 privity' is found, a member should be able to enforce the contract against the company and the other members.

247 Because CA 1963, s 205 has been interpreted as enabling members to petition the court for relief where they are oppressed other than qua member, it is arguable that a similar view can be taken of CA 1963, s 25.

The 'statutory contract' distinguished from 'special contracts'

[3.106] It is settled law that any rights that a member may have against the company enjoyed in another capacity, are not enforceable by virtue of CA 1963, s 25. Such rights may, however, be enforceable where a '*special contract*'[248] (as opposed to the *statutory* contract) exists between a member (acting as an individual) and the company. The position was put thus by the Australian High Court in *Bailey v New South Wales Medical Defence Union Ltd*[249]:

> 'Whilst the articles of association of a company regulate the relations of the members amongst themselves as members and with the company, they do not preclude a member from contracting individually with the company upon terms which may or may not be defined by reference to the articles. Such a contract has been called a special contract to differentiate it from the deemed covenants to which [the Australian equivalent to CA 1963, s 25] refers, which regulate the position of a member as a member and not as an individual. Even if the terms of a special contract are to be determined by reference to the articles, an alteration to those articles will not necessarily mean an alteration to the terms of the contract. It will depend upon the intention of the parties to the contract, namely, the member and the company.'[250]

In that case Mrs Bailey was the executrix of the late Dr Bailey. Dr Bailey had been sued by a patient for damages for injuries caused during the patient's treatment. The defendant, New South Wales Medical Defence Union Ltd (the Union) had initially conducted Dr Bailey's defence but, subsequent to his death, filed a notice ceasing to act for his estate. The patient obtained judgment against the estate of Dr Bailey and also against the Union. Judgment was also given in favour of Dr Bailey's estate on its cross-claim against the Union and against this the estate and the Union appealed. Both appeals were dismissed but only the Union appealed to the Australian High Court. On this appeal, the issue of relevance was whether the Union was liable to indemnify the estate and that question turned on the construction of the Union's articles of association.

[3.107] The Union's articles provided for an indemnity for members and their personal representatives against liability for damages or costs arising from any claim against a member for professional acts or omissions. The initial articles provided that where a member was expelled, the board of directors of the Union, referred to as the Council, had discretion to refuse an indemnity. The High Court noted that Dr Bailey had never been expelled. The articles of association were amended on several occasions. The most significant change was when the articles were amended to provide that the Council had sole and absolute discretion in relation to the assistance (including indemnity) to be given to members and provided that the Council could also terminate an indemnity that had already been given and cease to assist a member, also at its sole and absolute discretion, and without the need to terminate membership. After that change had been made, the Council had resolved in favour of providing assistance to Dr Bailey.

[248] The expression 'special contract' seems to have been coined by Romer LJ in *Allen v Gold Reefs of West Africa Ltd* (1900) 1 Ch 656 at 673, 674.

[249] *Bailey v New South Wales Medical Defence Union Ltd* (1996) 18 ACSR 521.

[250] (1996) 18 ACSR 521 at para 14, from the majority judgment of Brennan CJ, Deane and Dawson JJ.

Subsequent to Dr Bailey's death, the Council resolved to withdraw assistance. On the facts of the case the Australian High Court held that the relationship between the Union and Dr Bailey was not confined to the statutory contract but extended to a 'special contract'. The majority held:

> 'There can be no doubt that during each of the years in which Mr Crawford suffered injury there was a contract of insurance between the Union and Dr Bailey. Nor, in our view, can there be any real doubt that, notwithstanding that its terms were largely to be found in the company's articles, the contract was made individually with Dr Bailey as an insured and was therefore a special or actual contract which was distinct from the covenants which were deemed to arise from the articles under the relevant companies' legislation.'[251]

The High Court held that the terms of the contracts of indemnity were to be found largely, but not wholly, in the company's articles of association and that there was such a contract in place when the patient had been injured. The majority held that it 'cannot have been the intention of the parties that insurance cover already purchased upon terms contained in the articles should be diminished by a subsequent alteration to those articles'[252]. The majority concluded:

> 'Thus, the alteration[s]...to extend the discretion of the Council of the Union to refuse indemnity to a member who had ceased to be a member whether by expulsion or otherwise did not affect the terms of a contract made upon the basis of the articles before the alteration. A fortiori, the amendments...were ineffective to vary the terms of any contract previously made upon the basis of the articles in their unaltered form. Those amendments sought to give the Council sole discretion whether to grant indemnity at all and were entirely inconsistent with the terms of a contract concluded upon the basis of the articles as they stood before the amendments. It follows that the attempt by the Union to vary the terms of such a contract by means of an alteration to its articles giving its Council discretion to terminate any grant of assistance or indemnity to a member who sought assistance from the Union before [a particular date] was ineffective.'[253]

[3.108] In the concurring decision of McHugh and Gummow JJ in *Bailey v New South Wales Medical Defence Union Ltd* it was said:

> 'The present case did not involve a "statutory contract" constituted solely by the articles and unsupplemented by any external facts. The particular rights to indemnity upon which the Estate sues the Union could not, consistently with *Hickman*, be described as flowing from the general regulations of the Union as applicable alike to all shareholders.'[254]

Accordingly, where there is a 'special' or 'actual' contract that is based in whole or in part on the company's articles of association, any alteration in the articles will not automatically unilaterally vary that contract. It should be noted, however, that this is a matter of contract as opposed to legal principle and a term in the articles or side-contract might have ousted the decision in *Bailey*. Even if the Irish courts are slow to overrule *Eley* and other authorities that only allow rights enjoyed qua member to be enforced under the section 25 contract, rights extraneous to membership might be capable of

[251] (1996) 18 ACSR 52 at para 21 of the judgment.
[252] (1996) 18 ACSR 52 at para 24 of the judgment.
[253] (1996) 18 ACSR 52 at para 25 of the judgment.
[254] (1996) 18 ACSR 52 at para 81 of the judgment.

being enforced in quasi-partnership companies on the basis of a special or actual contract.

[D] SHAREHOLDERS' AGREEMENTS[255]

[3.109] Although rarely[256] referred to or discussed in the standard company law texts, shareholders' agreements are very commonly employed by the members of private companies. A shareholders' agreement may loosely be defined as an agreement between some or all of the shareholders in a company and perhaps the company itself, which is intended to govern the rights and obligations of the parties thereto, whether generally, or in particular circumstances. Frequently, shareholders' agreements will also deal with the management of the company, and in so doing may carefully displace the many inappropriate provisions for private companies which are contained in the Companies Acts 1963–2001. In this regard, a shareholders' agreement may be viewed as supplementing a company's statutory constitutional documentation. Viewed from the position of shareholders' agreements being a compromise between actual shareholder protection and the limitations of a statutory regime, one book describes shareholders' agreements as:

> '...a device designed to improve the hand dealt to shareholders and to give them more protection than reliance on that compromise would do. It is a legally binding contractual agreement between some or all the shareholders of a limited liability company to which the company may be a party. The object of the agreement is to specify the way in which the parties' relationship as shareholders will be regulated. Shareholders may lawfully bind themselves by way of an independent shareholders' agreement simply to vote in a specific way on issues regulated by the terms of the agreement or they may enter into a much more detailed and complex agreement, such as where they are parties to a joint venture or a buy-out.'[257]

Shareholders' agreements are considered here under the following headings:

1. The articles of association contrasted.
2. The uses of shareholders' agreements.
3. Types of shareholders' agreement.
4. The enforcement of shareholders' agreements.

The articles of association contrasted

[3.110] The articles of association of any company could easily accommodate most, if not all, of the usual provisions found in shareholders' agreements. Such could be done, ab initio on the formation of the company, or subsequently, after the company has been

---

255 See generally, McGovern, 'Shareholders' Agreements – Their Nature and Effect' (1995) 2 CLP 113; McGovern, 'Shareholders' Agreements – Some Drafting Considerations' (1995) 2 CLP 148; Courtney, 'Shareholders' Agreements in Irish Private Companies' (1993) Dlí 69; Reece Thomas & Ryan, *The Law and Practice of Shareholders' Agreements* (1999) and Stedman & Jones, *Shareholders' Agreements* (3rd edn, 1998).

256 See however, Farrar, Furey and Hannigan, *Farrar's Company Law* (3rd ed 1991), pp 138–145 and Hahlo & Farrar, *Hahlo's Cases and Materials on Company Law* (3rd edn, 1987), p 153.

257 Reece Thomas & Ryan, *The Law and Practice of Shareholders' Agreements* (1999), para 1.1.

formed, by amending the articles. What then is the difference between a company's articles of association and a shareholders' agreement?

First, while the articles will automatically bind the company to its members, the members to the company and the members inter se by virtue of CA 1963, s 25, a shareholders' agreement will only bind those parties who are privy to it. By definition it is an agreement between shareholders, although often the company will also be a party. This may easily be achieved where the shareholder-signatories are also directors, or where they have the power to influence the management of the company. However, the general rule is that the predominant influence upon those who are parties to a shareholders' agreement is freedom of contract.

Secondly, unlike the articles of association, shareholders' agreements are not part of a company's constitutional documentation proper. While often it will be the *hidden constitution* of the company it is not in law a true constitutional document. Consequently, even where adopted, a shareholders' agreement will not be a *public document* in the same way as will companies' memoranda and articles of association. Where a shareholders' agreement confers special authority on persons, such as directors, outsiders will not have notice of the extent of such authority because the shareholders' agreement is not a public document.

Thirdly, shareholders' agreements do not enjoy the privilege of being a recognised statutory document, in that they must each be considered on the basis of their own provisions, subject to the ordinary rules of contract law. Consequently, whilst the provisions of shareholders' agreements will no doubt in time, through greater use, become familiar to the courts, they do not enjoy the certainty of the articles of association.

[3.111] One question which arises in comparing shareholders' agreements with articles of association is when, if ever, will a shareholders' agreement be required to be registered with the CRO? One of the greatest advantages of a shareholders' agreement is that it will generally not be registered, and accordingly, its provisions remain secret. Where a shareholders' agreement provides that its provisions have precedence over the company's articles of association and where the articles of association are only capable of interpretation by reference to a shareholders' agreement, it is more likely that the shareholders' agreement should be registered. The reason why a shareholders' agreement would ever have to be registered is that it may amount to a special resolution amending a company's articles (or even memorandum) of association and all special resolutions are required to be registered in the CRO: CA 1963, s 143. In practice, perhaps comfort may be derived from the fact that the only sanction for failing to register is a fine[258].

The uses of shareholders' agreements

[3.112] There are a number of reasons why people choose to govern their relations with shareholders' agreements, notwithstanding that most of their concerns could be easily incorporated into a company's articles of association. Often the predominant reason is to ensure secrecy for those provisions which could be publicly sensitive. Frequently, such

[258] CA 1963, s 143(5) and (6).

agreements are quite explicit as to the remuneration of the directors of the company, and other financially sensitive matters which the parties would not wish to be made known to the public at large. Were such matters dealt with in the articles of association, which are public documents, their contents could easily be discovered by searching the CRO. Accordingly, shareholders' agreements are often the favoured way of regulating relations between shareholders and indeed the internal management of the company. However, there exist other reasons as to why shareholders' agreements are used[259]. These are summarised below.

[3.113] First, shareholders' agreements can be used to give rights and to impose obligations upon shareholders that could not be given or imposed by the articles. Where a shareholders' agreement is employed, a member who was a solicitor may be provided with the security of tenure denied Eley in *Eley v Positive Government Security Life Assurance Co*[260]. *In Eley's* case the company's articles could not be relied upon to enforce a member's rights as an individual, only rights *qua member*[261]. Accordingly, shareholders' agreements can constitute 'special contracts' : see para **[3.106]**.

[3.114] Secondly, shareholders' agreements can be used to bolster the rights and powers, especially of veto, of minority shareholders. Particularly in quasi-partnership type private companies where people associate in a joint venture, it is common to give minority investors comfort in the form of loaded or weighted voting rights. The effect of such rights is to oust majority rule which would otherwise prevail[262]. Specific shareholders' agreements, such as *pooling agreements*, may seek to concentrate voting between groups of members[263]. One definition of a pooling agreement is:

> '...an agreement amongst some of the shareholders in a company in which no one shareholder individually has a controlling interest. The shareholder parties to the agreement agree to act as a unit, for example, in managing the company and may agree a right of pre-emption amongst themselves giving each other an option to purchase any shares another party may be selling'.[264]

In this way a unified minority of shareholders can contractually agree to combine their interests in furtherance of mutually desirable courses of action.

[3.115] Thirdly, shareholders' agreements are often seen as a way of binding the company and/or its directors to a certain course of action. It is safer to bind both the company and the directors by making both parties to the agreement, rather than simply the directors. Because directors are fiduciaries who must act bona fide and in the best interests of the company[265] there is a potential conflict where they fetter their discretion

---

259 See Stedman & Jones, *Shareholders' Agreements* (3rd edn, 1998), p 49.

260 *Eley v Positive Government Security Life Assurance Co* (1876) 1 Ex D 88, considered at para **[3.103]**.

261 See also *Shalfoon v Chedar Valley Cooperative Dairy Co Ltd* [1924] NZLR 561 per Salmond J.

262 See generally *Bushell v Faith* [1970] AC 1099, which is considered at para **[3.062]**.

263 Kruger, 'Pooling Agreements Under English Company Law' [1978] 94 LQR 557; *Greenwell v Porter* [1902] 1 Ch 530.

264 See Reece Thomas & Ryan, *The Law and Practice of Shareholders' Agreements* (1999), pp 18–20.

265 See para **[3.126]** and generally, Chapter 10, *Duties of Directors and Other Officers*, para **[10.027]**.

as to the management of the company, and may be liable for breach of their duty to the company. By making the company a party to the agreement, this danger is lessened. However, even though the company may be joined to the agreement, in law it may be held not to be bound by certain provisions[266]. Moreover, future shareholders will not be bound by a shareholders' agreement automatically, ie they will not be bound unless they consent[267].

[3.116] Fourthly, through the employment of a shareholders' agreement, the members of a private company may mould the form of their chosen legal structure so as to make it accord more with their purposes. Many shareholders' agreements contain terms and conditions commonly found in a partnership agreement, underscoring the similarity between many Irish private companies and a partnership. It is more usual though, for a shareholders' agreement to contain a 'no partnership' clause. The purpose of this is to oust the possibility that on proper construction of s 1 of the Partnership Act 1890 the shareholders' agreement would make the parties partners. This could have the unforeseen consequence that one party could incur debts or other liabilities for which the other parties would be liable jointly and severally.

Types of shareholders' agreements

[3.117] Various categorisations of the different types of shareholders' agreements have been put forward[268]. Two broad categories of shareholders' agreements can be distinguished, although it must be stressed that they are not mutually exclusive, and very often an agreement will be a composite of both.

First, there are *formation agreements*. Such can be used by two or more *future shareholders* in a company which is not yet formed, or by existing shareholders, shortly after the incorporation of a company. These will often fall to be categorised as joint-venture type agreements. An example of such an agreement can be seen in the case of *TGM v Al Babtain*[269]. The rationale for employing a shareholders' agreement is that the parties recognise that the company about to be formed is in reality a partnership which has the advantage of limited liability, and as such the agreement entered into is tantamount to a deed of partnership. In a private closely-held company the pomp and ceremony imported into every company registered under the Companies Acts can be incongruous with the *true* relationship of the parties engaged in business. With careful legal draftsmanship the parties can achieve a relationship which at least strives for reality. Such agreements will typically detail the shareholdings in the future company

---

266 See para **[3.127]**.

267 *Russell v Northern Bank Development Corp Ltd* [1992] 3 All ER 161.

268 Farrar, Furey and Hannigan, *Farrar's Company Law* (3rd edn, 1991), p 139 distinguish between three types of shareholders' agreements: agreements between the company and the members collateral and supplementary to the articles of association; agreements between all the shareholders inter se and agreements between some of the shareholders. Reece Thomas & Ryan, *The Law and Practice of Shareholders' Agreements* (1999), p 12–20 suggest six types: joint venture agreements; quasi-partnership company agreements; minority protection agreements; informal and implied agreements; pooling agreements; and express voting trust agreements.

269 *TGM v Al Babtain* [1982] ILRM 349 at 350 *ff*. See para **[3.124]**.

and the rights attaching to such shares. Often the first general meeting of the company is planned in advance, and the parties contract that at that meeting, 'the company' will allot a certain number of shares to each member, and go on to provide for the appointment of directors and the secretary. Such agreements are characterised by a forward planning approach of the future shareholders who try to put their 'simple relationship' beyond the complex vicissitudes of the Companies Acts 1963–2001.

Secondly, there are *limited shareholders' agreements*, which may be entered into by shareholders in respect of matters such as voting at meetings[270], pre-emption rights of members to acquire shares held by members, the appointment of directors, and other miscellaneous matters connected to the management of the company.

[3.118] Shareholders' agreements embody the 'hidden constitution' of many private companies and should be recognised as being incidental to the constitutional documentation of such companies. However it must be stressed that shareholders' agreements are founded on the law of contract, and are only enforceable by the parties thereto inter se: they do not concern the separate legal entity which is the company, unless of course it is also a party to the agreement. Because the parties to a shareholders' agreement are free to contract in respect of whatever they wish, any consideration of 'typical provisions' will necessarily be limited. However, most such agreements will have a number of basic clauses.

[3.119] A typical joint-venture type shareholders' agreement will begin by reciting the parties to the agreement, and go on to define the various phrases referred to in the agreement[271]. From then on, the agreement will address the main concerns of the parties thereto. Normally, the issues to the fore of the minds of the shareholders will be the subscription for shares, defining the business of the company, agreeing contracts of employment, the structure of the company and completion of the contract thus entered into (all in the case of a company to be set-up in the immediate future), the transfer of shares, and in particular pre-emption rights attaching to such shares, the powers of the directors and their remuneration, alteration of capital and dividends payable to the members. It will be noted that there is a considerable overlap between the articles of a company and the provisions in a shareholders' agreement.

The enforcement of shareholders' agreements

[3.120] A shareholders' agreement is quite simply a contract, between the parties thereto. Although not necessarily written contracts, they are generally reduced to writing[272]. As such, ordinary principles of contract law will apply to their interpretation and enforcement[273]. When such agreements come before a court for interpretation, the

---

270 See as an example of an express voting trust agreement *Neville v Wilson* [1996] 3 All ER 171.

271 Thus terms such as 'The Board of Directors', 'Equity Share Capital', 'Financial Year', 'Subsidiary', 'Permitted Transferee', 'Shareholder', 'Accountant', and standard references to the 'masculine' including the 'feminine', etc, are defined so as to avoid the possibility of there being an equivocal interpretation of the agreement.

272 For a type of oral agreement, see *Pennell v Venida Investments Ltd* (25 July 1974, unreported), High Court (Eng) per Templeman J and Burridge (1981) 44 MLR 40.

273 Cheshire, Fifoot & Furmston's, *Law of Contract* (12th edn, 1991); see also Clark, *Contract Law in Ireland* (3rd edn, 1992).

court will first of all see if there is indeed a contract, then it will ask whether or not the clauses sought to be relied upon have been incorporated into the contract, and finally it will construe the clause in hand. Parties to a shareholders' agreement can avail of Order 83 of the Rules of the Superior Courts 1986 and state a case concerning the interpretation of an agreement to the High Court[274].

[3.121] There is a general willingness on the part of the courts to enforce and respect shareholders' agreements. A recent example is provided by the English Court of Appeal decision in *Harman v BLM Group Ltd*[275]. In that case the Court of Appeal was asked to make an order for the convening of a general meeting of a company under s 371 of the Companies Act 1985 (UK)[276]. To order such a meeting would have resulted in the breach of a shareholders' agreement. The company in question had both 'A' shareholders and 'B' shareholders and the agreement provided that a meeting would only be quorate where one 'B' shareholder was present. The petitioners under s 371 of the 1985 Act were 'A' shareholders who owned in excess of 50% of the shares in the company and were desirous of convening a meeting to dismiss certain directors. The directors whom it was intended to dismiss had the support of the 'B' shareholder who would not attend a meeting of the company's members and so had effectively thwarted the holding of a members' meeting. The Court of Appeal, in reversing the trial judge's decision, held it was inappropriate to make an order under s 371 as to do so would be contrary to what the parties had agreed in the shareholders' agreement and would be in total disregard to the 'B' shareholders' rights which were akin to entrenched voting rights. Parties to a shareholders' agreement cannot, however, pick and choose those provisions that they wish to enforce[277].

[3.122] Some of the issues that can arise in the enforcement of shareholders' agreements are:

(a) Injunctions to enforce shareholders' agreements.

(b) Directors fettering their fiduciary powers.

(c) Binding companies through shareholders' agreements.

(a) Injunctions to enforce shareholders' agreements

[3.123] It is clear that an injunction will be granted[278] where one party to a shareholders' agreement has, or is about to, breach the agreement[279]. Where there is an anticipated breach of a shareholders' agreement a party to the agreement may seek relief from the

---

274 See *McAuliffe v Lithographic Group Ltd* (2 November 1993, unreported), Supreme Court where a pre-emption provision in a shareholders' agreement was the subject of an application under the Rules of the Superior Courts 1986 (SI 1986/15), Ord 83.

275 *Harman v BLM Group Ltd* [1994] 2 BCLC 674.

276 The similar Irish provision which would empower the court to make such an order is CA 1963, s 135.

277 See, for example, *Re Vocam Europe Ltd* [1998] BCC 396.

278 Of course, for an injunction to issue, the court must be satisfied that the requirements for an interlocutory injunction have been fulfilled. See Keane, *Equity and the Law Trusts in the Republic of Ireland* (1988), pp 205–243.

279 Cf *Russell v Northern Bank Development Corp Ltd* [1992] 3 All ER 161 considered at para **[3.127]**.

High Court which has discretion to grant an injunction to restrain the breach[280]. An example is provided by *Puddlephatt v Leith*[281] where Sargant J enforced an agreement that the defendant would vote as the plaintiff directed.

[3.124] In *TGM v Al Babtain Trading*[282] the plaintiffs were the sole distributors and assemblers in Ireland of Datsun (now Nissan), vehicles. The plaintiff and the first defendant formed a company called Datsun Ltd for the purpose of the acquisition of the franchise, and entered into a shareholders' agreement in respect of the venture. Differences arose between the plaintiff and the first defendant over the operations of the company and, in particular, the future role of the chief executive of the company. The first defendant, who owned 375,000 of the 500,000 shares subscribed for in the company, exercised its voting rights to terminate the appointment of the chief executive, managing director and deputy managing director. When the first defendant served notice of a meeting of the company, inter alia, dealing with the 'service agreements' of the managing director and deputy managing director, the plaintiff's solicitors wrote to the first defendant saying that such constituted a breach of the shareholders' agreement. The plaintiff then obtained an injunction restraining the defendants from exercising or procuring the exercise of their voting rights to grant service contracts to persons other than those named in the shareholders' agreement. Keane J continued the injunction on the basis that the shareholders' agreement seemed to prohibit the granting of service contracts, and so the plaintiff had established a prima facie case which would to be protected by an injunction until the full trial of the case, and the balance of convenience favoured the plaintiffs.

[3.125] Shareholders' agreements often provide that disputes between the parties are to be referred to arbitration. A shareholders' agreement in *Tellnor Invest AS v IIU Nominees Ltd and Esat Telecom Holdings Ltd*[283] so provided. In that case the agreement stated that so long as any party held not less than 10% of the company's equity share capital, that party would be entitled to nominate one person as a director. The second defendant initially held 20% of the equity share capital and on that basis had nominated a director. Subsequently, its shareholding fell to 1% and the plaintiff contended that the second defendant had lost its right to maintain its nominee on the board. This was disputed and it was contended that there was no onus on existing directors to resign. The first defendant sought a stay on the plaintiff's proceedings until the dispute had been determined by arbitration, as was provided for in the shareholders' agreement. O'Sullivan J accepted that the dispute was to be referred to arbitration as provided for in the agreement but stated this did not preclude parties from seeking interim relief pending the determination by arbitration. Hence, he stayed the proceedings and also granted an interim injunction restraining the defendant's nominee director from acting until the arbitration had been determined.

---

[280] As with all injunctions delay or acquiescence may incline the Court to refuse relief: *Re Pearce Duff & Co Ltd* [1960] 3 All ER 693.

[281] *Puddlephatt v Leith* [1916] 1 Ch 200.

[282] *TGM v Al Babtain Trading* [1982] ILRM 349.

[283] *Tellnor Invest AS v IIU Nominees Ltd and Esat Telecom Holdings Ltd* (20 July 1999, unreported), High Court (O'Sullivan J).

(b) Directors fettering their fiduciary powers

[3.126] While a shareholders' agreement will bind the signatory in his capacity *qua* member[284], there are difficulties where a shareholder binds himself in his capacity as a director (*qua* director) since a director is a fiduciary and because the office of director carries with it the requirement that a director should only act in the best interests of the company[285]. Thus it has been said[286] that:

> 'Unlike a shareholder, whose vote is a right of property he may exercise in furtherance of his own personal interests, a director is a fiduciary in respect of the powers entrusted to him by the company's articles of association, and he is accordingly bound to exercise those powers *bona fide* in the best interests of the company.'

It can sometimes arise in the context of a shareholders' agreement that a director is asked to fetter the future exercise of his fiduciary powers. The fettering of future discretion will not automatically amount to a breach of a director's duty. Directors will not act inconsistently with their fiduciary duties to the company where they fetter their discretion to act in the future in furtherance of a bona fide commercial agreement which confers substantial benefit on their company. So in *Fulham Football Club Ltd et al v Cabra Estates plc*[287] it was said:

> 'It is trite law that directors are under a duty to act *bona fide* in the interests of their company. However, it does not follow from that proposition that directors can never make a contract by which they bind themselves to the future exercise of their powers in a particular manner, even though the contract taken as a whole is manifestly for the benefit of the company. Such a rule could well prevent companies from entering into contracts which were commercially beneficial to them.'[288]

This matter is considered in detail in Chapter 10[289] where this case, and others such as *Thorby v Goldberg*, are examined[290]. Suffice it to say here that in entering into a shareholders' agreement, it may be the case that after due deliberation a company's directors can decide *bona fide* that it is in the best interests of the company to agree to act in a particular way in the future. Shareholders' agreements can be of great advantage

---

284 It will often be the case that the agreement will dictate that the signatories will exercise their vote in a particular manner: *Puddephatt v Leith* [1916] 1 Ch 200.

285 *Gabbett v Lawder* (1883) 11 LR Ir 295. See also *Motherwell v Schoof* [1949] 4 DLR 812; *Atlas Development Co Ltd v Calof and Gold* (1963) 31 WWR 575 and *Thorby v Goldberg* (1964) 112 CLR 597.

286 *The Encyclopaedia of Forms and Precedents* (5th edn), Vol 9, p 15, para 8.

287 *Fulham Football Club Ltd et al v Cabra Estates plc* [1994] 1 BCLC 363.

288 [1994] 1 BCLC 363 at 392a–b. Neill LJ said the 'true rule' was stated by the High Court of Australia in *Thorby v Goldberg* (1964) 112 CLR 597, the headnote of which read: '[i]f, when a contract is negotiated on behalf of a company, the directors bona fide think it in the interests of the company as a whole that the transaction should be entered into and carried into effect they may bind themselves by the contract to do whatever is necessary to effectuate it.'

289 At para **[10.034]** *ff*. For an interesting international survey of the courts' attitude to fettering directors' discretion in the context of shareholders' agreements, see further Reece Thomas & Ryan, *The Law and Practice of Shareholders' Agreements* (1999), pp 69–78.

290 Reece Thomas & Ryan, *The Law and Practice of Shareholders' Agreements* (1999), pp 69–78.

to a company: by assisting the controlled and orderly management of the company; by underscoring the basis of the participant's relationships; and by serving the company's economic advantage, particularly in a joint venture. Clearly, this general statement cannot be said to be true of all shareholders' agreements and each fetter on the directors' discretion will have to be considered individually.

(c) Companies bound by shareholders' agreements

[3.127] Often shareholders' agreements attempt to maintain the *status quo* in a company by preventing any alteration in shareholdings. Moreover, this will sometimes include not only the prohibition of share transfers, but also the prohibition on a company increasing its share capital. The prohibition on a company increasing its share capital may be unenforceable, as was held in the English House of Lords' decision in *Russell v Northern Bank Development Corp Ltd*[291]. In that case, four persons entered into a shareholders' agreement to which the company itself was also a party. The agreement provided, inter alia, that its terms and conditions would take precedence over the company's articles of association. In particular, it provided that the company would not create or issue any further share capital without the consent in writing of all parties to the agreement. A dispute arose when the directors of the company gave notice to its shareholders of an extraordinary general meeting ('EGM'), the purpose of which was to increase its share capital. The company was empowered to do this under its articles, the equivalent Irish regulation being model reg 44 of Part I of Table A. The plaintiff, who was a shareholder and a party to the shareholders' agreement, sought an injunction to prevent the other shareholders considering or voting on the proposed resolution at the EGM. At trial the injunction was refused and it was held that the company could not be prevented from increasing its share capital as that was an improper fetter on the statutory power of the company, contained in the UK equivalent to CA 1963, s 68. This view was upheld by the Court of Appeal.

In the House of Lords the appeal succeeded in part. It was held that the shareholders' agreement was binding on all parties to it, *except the company*. In so holding the House of Lords made a distinction between private persons who were parties to a 'private agreement'[292] and the company. As for the private persons who were party to the agreement, the dictum of Lord Davey in *Welton v Saffeny*[293] was cited by Lord Jauncey:

> 'Of course, individual shareholders may deal with their own interests by contract in such way as they may think fit. But such contracts, whether made by all or some only of the shareholders, would create personal obligations, or an *exceptio personalis* against themselves only, and would not become a regulation of the company, or be binding on the transferees of the parties to it, or upon new or non-assenting shareholders. There is no suggestion here of any such private agreement outside the machinery of the Companies Acts.'

The enforceability of the agreement against the shareholders stands in marked contrast to the position of the company. The House of Lords upheld the old principle in *Allen v*

---

[291] *Russell v Northern Bank Development Corp Ltd* [1992] 3 All ER 161.

[292] [1992] 3 All ER 161 at 167.

[293] *Welton v Saffeny* [1897] AC 299 at 331, [1895–9] All ER Rep 567 at 585.

Gold Reefs of West Africa Ltd[294] and *Bushell v Faith*[295] that a company 'cannot by its articles or otherwise deprive itself of the power by special resolution to alter its articles or any of them'. Applied to the present case, Lord Jauncey said:

> '[The company] on the other hand agreed that its capital would not be increased without the consent of each of the shareholders. This was a clear undertaking by [the company] in a formal agreement not to exercise its statutory powers for a period which could, certainly on one view of construction, last for as long as any one of the parties to the agreement remained a shareholder and long after the control of [the company] had passed to shareholders who were not party to the agreement. As such an undertaking it is, in my view, obnoxious as if it had been contained in the articles of association and therefore is unenforceable as being contrary to the provisions of [CA 1963, s 68].'[296]

However, while the company's promise not to increase its share capital was unlawful, it could be severed from the other party-shareholders' promises, which were enforceable against them inter se.

[3.128] Where shareholders decide to attempt to maintain the status quo by preventing an increase in share capital, it may be possible to join-in the company by ensuring that certain steps are first taken. Although CA 1963, s 68 empowers a company to increase its share capital, it does so on the condition that the company has internal power to do this in its articles of association. Thus, by ensuring ab initio, that reg 44 is purged from the company's articles, it is thought that the statutory power contained in s 68 and defended in the *Russell* case would not exist. On the authority of the *Russell* case a shareholders' agreement can oblige the members, personally, to refrain from voting in favour of altering the company's articles, thereby ensuring that reg 44 cannot be reinstated.

---

[294] *Allen v Gold Reefs of West Africa Ltd* [1900] 1 Ch 656, [1900–3] All ER Rep 746.

[295] *Bushell v Faith* [1969] 1 All ER 1002.

[296] [1992] 3 All ER 161 at 167.

Chapter 4

Incorporation and its Consequences

[4.001] As a *corporation*, or *body corporate*, a private company is regarded in law as having a separate legal personality from its shareholders (owners) and directors (managers). This chapter examines how the private company achieves corporate status (and how the status may be lost) and the consequences which flow from it. These topics are considered under the following headings:

[A] The acquisition of corporate status; and

[B] The consequences of incorporation.

[A] THE ACQUISITION OF CORPORATE STATUS

Registration, and issue of the certificate of incorporation

[4.002] The private company acquires corporate status through the process of *incorporation by registration*, ie registration of the company with the Companies Registration Office ('CRO') by the Registrar of Companies in accordance with the procedure detailed in Chapter 2[1]. Where the Registrar of Companies is satisfied that the documents filed are formally in order, and that the purpose for which the incorporators are associated is lawful[2], he must register the company and issue *a certificate of incorporation* certifying that the company is incorporated, and in the case of a limited company, that the company is limited[3]. The certificate serves as a kind of 'birth certificate' evidencing the existence of the company as a corporate body and the date upon which it acquired corporate status.

Continuing the analogy between registration and birth, it will be recalled that companies are capable of being reincarnated in a different form[4]. A certificate of incorporation thus, will, *also* be issued by the Registrar where:

— an unlimited company is re-registered as a limited company[5];

— a public limited company is re-registered as a private company[6];

— a limited company is re-registered as an unlimited company[7];

— a private company is re-registered as a public limited company[8];

---

1 See Chapter 2, *Formation, Registration and Conversion of Private Companies*, para **[2.010]** *ff.*

2 See CA 1963, s 5(1).

3 CA 1963, s 18(1). Where the company is a public limited company, the certificate must also contain a statement to that effect: C(A)A 1983, s 5(3).

4 See Chapter 2, *Formation, Registration and Conversion of Private Companies*, para **[2.060]** *ff.*

5 CA 1963, s 20; C(A)A 1983, s 53.

6 C(A)A 1983, s 14.

7 C(A)A 1983, s 52.

8 C(A)A 1983, s 9.

— a company incorporated under some other Act becomes registered under the Companies Acts[9];

— a company changes its registered name[10].

The principles which govern the original certificate of incorporation are largely applicable to these certificates also.

Failure or refusal by the Registrar of Companies

[4.003] If the Registrar fails or refuses to register the company where all the requirements for registration have been complied with, he may be compelled to do so by order of mandamus[11]. The Registrar may validly refuse to register where incorporation is sought to perpetrate an unlawful activity. Thus, in *R v Registrar of Joint Stock Companies*[12] the Court of Appeal refused an application for an order of mandamus to compel the Registrar to register a company formed for the sale in England, contrary to English law, of Irish Hospital Lottery tickets. It would appear that the Registrar might also refuse to register where the business of the company is unlawful on the grounds of being contrary to public policy[13].

Effect of the certificate of incorporation

[4.004] The certificate of incorporation is, by virtue C(A)A 1983, s 5(4):

> '...*conclusive evidence* that all the requirements of the Companies Acts in respect of registration and of matters precedent and incidental thereto have been complied with, and that the association is a company authorised to be registered under the Companies Act[s].'[14]

Similar effect is given to the certificates of incorporation issued upon re-registration in most of the circumstances outlined in paragraph **[4.002]** above[15]. Where a certificate is issued in respect of a change of registered name the Acts do not provide, however, that the new certificate is to constitute conclusive evidence of a valid incorporation. Whether, as one might expect, the courts will give that certificate such an effect by extending the conclusiveness of the original certificate to the new one still remains to be seen. In practice, it is customary to seek the original certificate and any certificates subsequently issued upon change of name as evidence of a valid incorporation. Where a public limited company is re-registered as a private company the certificate has the additional effect of constituting conclusive evidence that the company so re-registered is

---

9 C(A)A 1983, s 19; CA 1963, s 336.

10 CA 1963, s 23(3).

11 *R v Registrar of Companies, ex p Bowen* [1914] 3 KB 1161.

12 *R v Registrar of Joint Stock Companies* [1931] 2 KB 197.

13 *R v Registrar of Companies, ex p Her Majesty's Attorney General* [1991] BCLC 476. See para **[4.017]**.

14 C(A)A 1983, s 5(4) replacing CA 1963, s 19 (emphasis added).

15 See C(A)A 1983, ss 53(5), 14(5), 52(5), 9(9), and 19(6) respectively.

a private company[16], even though the company may not meet the requirements[17] for the formation of a private company.

[4.005] The conclusive evidence provision prevents inquiry into matters prior to and contemporaneous with the registration. In *Jubilee Cotton Mills v Lewis*[18], where the date of incorporation as stated in the certificate was patently earlier than the date upon which it was signed by the Registrar, the court was obliged to accept the date certified in the certificate as being the true date of incorporation. Consequently a contract entered into by the company on the day following the date certified in the certificate was held to be binding on the company – even though the certificate had not in fact been issued at that time.

A peculiar abstraction of the conclusiveness is its extension to matters concerning the validity of clauses contained in the company's memorandum or articles of association. In *Cotman v Brougham*[19], the conclusiveness of the Registrar's certificate was thought to preclude the courts from disputing the validity of an 'independent objects clause' in the company's memorandum of association, since the certificate was conclusive evidence that the memorandum, and the clauses contained therein, were valid and in accordance with the Companies Acts. Despite such conclusiveness, the Registrar's certificate does not lend legality to activities contemplated by the company in its memorandum or articles which are patently unlawful or which conflict with the Companies Acts[20].

Rationale for the conclusive effect of the certificate of incorporation

[4.006] The rationale for the conclusiveness of the certificate of incorporation was explained by Lord Cairns in *Peel's Case, Re Barned's Banking Co*[21], as follows:

> 'When once the memorandum is registered and the company is held out to the world as a company undertaking business, willing to receive shareholders and ready to contract engagements, then it would be of the most disastrous consequences, if, after all that has been done, any person was allowed to go back and enter into an examination (it might be years after the company had commenced trade) of the circumstances attending the original registration and the regularity of the execution of the document.'[22]

'Were such a thing permissible,' said Palmer[23], 'a company's foundation would be built not on a rock but on sand.' In *Peel's Case* the memorandum of association had, after signature by the requisite number of subscribers, but before registration, been altered significantly without the privity of the signatories. After registration and the issue of a

16 C(A)A 1983, s 14(5)(b).

17 See Chapter 1, *The Private Company in Context*, para **[1.114]** *ff*.

18 *Jubilee Cotton Mills v Lewis* [1924] AC 958.

19 *Cotman v Brougham* [1918] AC 514. See further Chapter 7, *Corporate Contracts, Capacity and Authority*, para **[7.050]**.

20 *Bowman v Secular Society Ltd* [1917] AC 406 at 435 per Sumner LJ. See also *Ayre v Skesley's Adamant Cement Co Ltd* (1904) 20 TLR 587; and *Gaiman v National Association for Mental Health* [1971] Ch 317.

21 *Peel's Case, Re Barned's Banking Co* (1867) LR 2 Ch App 674.

22 (1867) LR 2 Ch App 674 at 682.

23 *Company Law* (12th edn, 1924), p 51.

certificate by the Registrar, the question arose as to whether the company had been validly incorporated, since s 6 of the Companies Act 1862 required the memorandum of association to be subscribed 'by seven or more persons' whereas the signatures had been entirely overtaken by events. Lord Cairns held the certificate to be conclusive evidence of the company's incorporation, stating 'once the certificate of incorporation is given, nothing is to be inquired into as to the regularity of the prior proceedings.' [24]

[4.007] By treating the Registrar's certificate as conclusive evidence of a valid incorporation, Irish company law is relieved of the difficulties once encountered in Continental and US jurisdictions. In such jurisdictions, incorporated companies having traded under the banner of a corporation for some time have, on occasion, had their corporate status rendered null and void, with disastrous consequences for third parties dealing with them[25].

The First EU Directive on Company Law

[4.008] The aforementioned hazards were the principal concern of Section III of the First EU Directive on Company Law ('the Directive')[26]. Article 11.2 of the Directive provides:

> 'Nullity may be ordered only on the following grounds:
>
> (a) that no instrument of constitution was executed or that the rules of preventative control or the requisite legal formalities were not complied with;
>
> (b) that the objects of the company are unlawful or contrary to public policy;
>
> (c) that the instrument of constitution or the statutes do not state the name of the company, the amount of the individual subscriptions of capital, the total amount of the capital subscribed or the objects of the company;
>
> (d) failure to comply with the provisions of the national law concerning the minimum amount of capital to be paid up;
>
> (e) the incapacity of all the founder members;
>
> (f) that, contrary to the national law governing the company, the number of founder members is less than two.
>
> Apart from the foregoing grounds of nullity a company shall not be subject to any cause of non-existence, nullity absolute, nullity relative or declaration of nullity.'

Article 12.2 of the Directive requires member states to introduce provisions allowing the winding up of companies whose corporate status has subsequently been found to have been a nullity, and Article 12.3 further requires member states to provide that 'nullity shall not of itself affect the validity of any commitments entered into by or with the company'.

---

24 (1867) 2 Ch App 674 at 681. See also *Oakes v Turquand* (1867) LR 2 HL 325.

25 See Drury, 'Nullity of Companies in English Law' (1985) MLR 644; Van Bodungen, 'The Defective Corporation in American and German Law' 15 Am J Comp L 313 (1967).

26 Council Directive 68/151. See generally Chapter 1, *The Private Company in Context*, para **[1.093]**.

Effect of the First EU Directive's nullity provisions in Ireland

[4.009] So settled was the principle of conclusiveness thought to be in Ireland that the European Communities (Companies) Regulations 1973[27], which were introduced to implement the provisions of the Directive, do not contain any regulations implementing Section III of the Directive dealing with the nullity of companies.

[4.010] Though not implemented by national law, the Directive's provisions on nullity continue to have some legal effect in Ireland. First, it should be noted that the provisions dealing with nullity are *not* binding on private individuals[28] – because they have not been implemented here by way of statute or statutory instrument. Consequently, private individuals are not prohibited from seeking to have the incorporation of an Irish company declared a nullity on grounds other than those listed in the Directive. Secondly, the Directive's provisions *are* binding on the State[29], and the State and its agents may not seek to have the incorporation of a company declared a nullity *except* on the grounds listed in the Directive. Thirdly, where private individuals successfully obtain an order declaring the incorporation of a company to be a nullity on grounds other than those listed in the Directive, the State will be liable to compensate the members of the nullified company. Such liability relates to the loss caused to the members by the State's failure to limit the grounds of nullity to those specified in the Directive[30].

[4.011] In addition, when interpreting the provisions of Irish law, the courts will be obliged under European law to have regard to the wording and purpose of the Directive and should choose whichever interpretation best gives effect to it. In *Marleasing SA v La Comercial Internacional de Alimentacion SA*[31], a reference to the European Court of Justice from the Spanish courts, the question to be determined was how should the Spanish courts interpret ss 1261 and 1275 of their Civil Code? Those sections provided for the nullification of contracts made 'without cause'. The Directive had not yet been implemented in Spain, though the date for its implementation there had passed. Marleasing had argued that the incorporation of La Comercial should be declared void under those sections on the basis that the motive for La Comercial's formation was to place the assets of one of its founders beyond the reach of his creditors. The national courts were uncertain of whether they could interpret ss 1261 and 1275 so as to allow a company to be declared void simply because of the motive for which it was formed, particularly since that does not appear as a ground listed in Article 12 of the Directive. Hence the reference to the European Court of Justice.

The European Court held that since the Directive had not yet been implemented in Spain, and since Marleasing was a private company and not an organ of State, Marleasing was not precluded from seeking to have La Comercial declared void under

---

27 SI 1973/163.

28 See *Marshall v Southampton and South West Hampshire Area Health Authority (No 1)* [1986] 1 CMLR 688.

29 *Marshall v Southampton and South West Hampshire Area Health Authority (No 1)* [1986] 1 CMLR 688.

30 *Francovich v Italian Republic* [1993] 2 CMLR 66; *Brasserie du Pecheur SA v Germany (Factortame)* (C46/93) [1996] 1 CMLR 889.

31 *Marleasing SA v La Comercial Internacional de Alimentacion SA* [1992] 1 CMLR 305.

Spanish national law on grounds other than those listed in the Directive. The court stressed, however, that since Article 189 of the Treaty of Rome obliges member states to take appropriate measures to implement directives, the Spanish courts, as organs of state, were obliged to interpret the provisions of their existing law in accordance with the wording and purpose of the Directive. This, in effect, meant that the Spanish courts could not interpret ss 1261 and 1275 of the Spanish Code in such a way as to allow nullification of a company simply by reference to the motives for its formation, since that is not a ground listed in the Directive[32].

Impeachment of incorporation

[4.012] Conventional wisdom suggests that the conclusiveness of the certificate of incorporation prevents the reopening of matters prior to and contemporaneous with the registration of the company, and places the corporate existence of the company beyond question[33]. There is at least one (albeit rare) situation in which the certificate certainly will not have that effect – that is in the case of a trade union which is also registered as a company. Furthermore, the full field of challenges which may be made against the certificate has not yet been explored. These situations will now be examined under the following headings:

(a) Trade unions registered as companies.

(b) Judicial review of the Registrar's decision to issue a certificate of incorporation.

(c) Constitutionality of the conclusive effect of the certificate of incorporation.

(a) Trade unions registered as companies

[4.013] Section 3(4) of CA 1963 provides that nothing in that Act shall affect 'the provisions of s 5 of the Trade Union Act 1871'. The Trade Union Act 1871, s 5 provides, in turn, that the Companies Acts 'shall not apply to any trade union, and the registration of any trade union under any of the said Acts shall be void'.[34] The definition of 'trade union' for the purposes of the Trade Union Acts 1871–1982 is very broad, and includes bodies which are not regarded as trade unions in the general sense. For example, employers' associations, associations of self-employed persons, manufacturing associations and trade protection societies may all qualify as trade unions under the Acts[35].

[4.014] Where a trade union is both registered as a company and registered as a trade union under the Trade Union Acts 1871-1982, revocation of its company status and of its certificate of incorporation will not deprive it of its corporate status, because registered

32 Marleasing's argument that 'objects' in Article 11.2(b) of the Directive could be interpreted as including 'motives' was rejected. The court held that 'objects' refers to the objects of the company as described in the instrument of incorporation.

33 See para **[4.005]**.

34 The analogous English provisions were applied in *British Association of Glass Bottle Manufacturers (Limited) v Nettlefold* (1911) TLR 527: see Drury, 'Nullity of Companies in English Law' (1985) MLR 644 at 649-650; for a Scottish example see *Edinburgh and District Aerated Water Manufacturers Defence Association v James Jenkinson & Co* (1903) 5 SC 1159.

35 See Kerr & Whyte, *Irish Trade Union Law* (1985), p 39; Hickling, 'Trade Unions in Disguise' (1964) 27 MLR 625; see also generally Kerr, *Trade Union and Industrial Relations Acts, 2001*.

trade unions are themselves bodies corporate[36]. Where, however, the trade union has *not* been registered as a trade union under those Acts, revocation of its certificate of incorporation will deprive it of corporate status, since unregistered trade unions are unincorporated associations similar in legal nature to a social club[37]. Of course where a trade union is initially registered as a company under the Companies Acts it will have slipped through the Registrar's net - because he should not have permitted its registration according to the Trade Union Act 1871, s 5. One may expect such errors never to occur; but, conversely, where a company formed for other purposes subsequently adopts the mantle of a trade union, it will have evaded such scrutiny.

If the Trade Union Act 1871, s 5 is ever put to use so as to avoid the registration of a company which is not a registered trade union, the State may regret its decision not to implement Section III of the First EU Directive – because anyone suffering loss as a result of the State's failure to implement those provisions (which would have preserved the validity of transactions entered into by the company) may sue the State for compensation[38].

(b) Judicial review of the Registrar's decision to issue a certificate of incorporation

[4.015] The conclusive effect of the certificate of incorporation appears to preclude parties from obtaining judicial review of the Registrar's decision to register a company and to issue a certificate of incorporation[39].

The Registrar's functions may be classed as administrative or quasi-judicial in nature[40]. Ordinarily, administrative functions can be made the subject of judicial review proceedings, since they must be exercised without excess of jurisdiction and in accordance with principles of fundamental procedural fairness[41]. Thus, as was already observed[42], where the Registrar, in breach of fair procedures or in excess of jurisdiction, fails or refuses to register a company, he may be compelled to do so by the courts. However, once a certificate has been issued, the courts and the Companies Acts both say that it is the certificate rather than the Registrar's actions to which one must look. The approach of the courts is clearly evidenced in the case of *Irish Permanent Building Society v Registrar of Building Societies*[43].

---

36 *R(IUDWC) v Rathmines UDC* [1928] IR 260.

37 *Bonsor v Musician's Union* [1956] AC 101.

38 *Francovich v Italian Republic* [1993] 2 CMLR 66; *Brasserie du Pecheur SA v Germany (Factortame)* (C46/93) [1996] 1 CMLR 889.

39 *Princess of Reuss v Bos* (1871) LR 5 HL 176. See also *R v Registrar of Companies, ex parté Central Bank of India* [1986] QB 1114 and *Lombard & Ulster Banking (Ireland) Ltd v Amurec* [1976-7] ILRM 222 where the statutory conclusiveness of the registrar's certificate as to the validity of the registration of a company charge (see CA 1963, s 104) was held to preclude judicial review of that certificate.

40 *Bowman v Secular Society* [1917] AC 406 at 439–440 per Lord Parker of Waddington. See generally *McDonald v Bord na gCon (No.2)* [1965] IR 217; *Goodman International v Hamilton* [1992] 2 IR 542.

41 See *State (Crowley) v Irish Land Commission* [1951] IR 250; *Foley v Irish Land Commission* [1952] IR 118.

42 See para **[4.003]**.

43 *Irish Permanent Building Society v Registrar of Building Societies* [1981] ILRM 242.

[4.016] The *Irish Permanent* case concerned a certificate of incorporation issued *not* by the Registrar of Companies but by the Registrar of Building Societies under the Building Societies Act 1976. The matter in issue was whether or not the Irish Life Building Society, a society established and controlled by the Irish Life Assurance Co, was registrable under the Building Societies Act 1976. The Registrar of Building Societies had issued a certificate of incorporation under the 1976 Act to the Irish Life Building Society. The plaintiffs, alleging that the wrongful incorporation of a new building society had caused, and would cause them, loss, sought inter alia a declaration that the Registrar had exceeded his jurisdiction by registering the society when its internal rules as to voting contravened the provisions of the Act. The plaintiffs also sought a declaration that, consequently, the society had been invalidly registered.

Barrington J found that the rules did indeed contravene the provisions of the Act and that the Registrar had mistakenly construed the Act's provisions. But he declined to give any decision as to whether the Registrar's mistake amounted to an excess of jurisdiction, because Building Societies Act 1976, s 11 provided that the Registrar of Building Societies' certificate is *sufficient* evidence, until the contrary is shown, that the society is authorised to be incorporated. He observed:

> '...it appears to me to be a fair conclusion that the Act contemplates that notwithstanding the vigilance of the Registrar, societies with defective rules will get on to the register and also that societies may be validly incorporated notwithstanding that their rules are in some particular defective...I would be very surprised if the incorporation of a society could be invalidated by an honest mistake such as was made by the founders and the Registrar in the present case. If the law were otherwise people might in good faith deal with a society for many years only to find that because of some defect in its rules the society did not exist as a corporate body. Such a society, not being a building society incorporated under the Act could not even be wound up in accordance with the provisions of the Act...To hold that the society was not validly incorporated would clearly cause great damage to many innocent people.'[44]

Whereas the certificate in that case was merely 'sufficient evidence until the contrary is shown' of a valid incorporation, the Registrar of Companies' certificate is 'conclusive evidence' of a valid incorporation. This must, it is submitted, strengthen the proposition that the statutory conclusiveness of the Registrar's certificate precludes judicial review of his decision to issue it.

[4.017] The English courts have held the Registrar of Companies' certificate of incorporation to be amenable to judicial review by way of certiorari at the instance of the Attorney General where the objects of the company contemplate the perpetration of a public wrong. In *Bowman v Secular Society*[45] it was held that the Attorney General, as the Crown's servant, could obtain an order of *certiorari* to quash the registration of a company incorporated for unlawful purposes since the provisions of the Companies Acts, while binding on English citizens, are not binding on the Crown. Consequently the Crown is not bound to treat the Registrar's certificate as conclusive evidence of a valid incorporation.

---

44 [1981] ILRM 242 at 269-270.

45 *Bowman v Secular Society* [1917] AC 406.

This was taken to extremes in *R v Registrar of Companies, ex p Her Majesty's Attorney General*[46], where the registration of a company incorporated under the name of 'Lindi St Claire (Personal Services) Ltd' was quashed by the court at the instance of the Attorney General since the company's primary object – 'to carry on the business of prostitution' – was contrary to public policy, though prostitution itself was not a criminal offence.

It is doubtful whether similar proceedings could successfully be brought by the Irish Attorney General in the Irish courts. In *Byrne v Ireland*[47] the Supreme Court held that the State was not heir to a Crown privilege of immunity from the provisions of statutes. Rather, the court held, the wording of a statute would have to be such as to give rise to the implication that the State is not bound by its provisions before the State could ignore them. The wording of the Companies Acts 1963–2001 appears to give rise to no such implication; it is probable then that the State must respect the Registrar's certificate as being conclusive evidence of a valid incorporation just as private individuals must.

(c) Constitutionality of the conclusive effect of the certificate of incorporation

[4.018] Since the conclusiveness of the certificate of incorporation appears to prevent the courts from questioning the fairness of the Registrar's decision to issue a certificate, it might be argued that the statutory conclusiveness leads to a denial of individuals' rights to constitutional justice and to vindication of their constitutional rights[48]. However, if such a challenge were mounted, the courts would have to weigh the rights of the individual challenger against the interests of the common good[49]. In doing so, the court would probably be swayed in favour of upholding the constitutionality of the conclusiveness by the principles explained by Lord Cairns in *Peel's Case*, above[50]. Furthermore, it has been suggested that such a challenge might be answered by an assertion that the Registrar's actions, whilst impinging upon the constitutional rights of the challengers, do not interfere with them directly[51].

[4.019] The broad question[52] of whether the 'conclusive evidence' provision offends the constitutional prohibition against ousting the jurisdiction of the courts[53] has also not been judicially determined. Again, it would appear that even this avenue of challenge is closed.

In *Maher v Attorney General*[54], the Supreme Court struck down as unconstitutional Road Traffic Act 1968, s 44(2), which provided that an analyst's certificate as to the concentration of alcohol in a blood or urine sample should be 'conclusive evidence' as to

---

46 *R v Registrar of Companies, ex p Her Majesty's Attorney General* [1991] BCLC 476.

47 *Byrne v Ireland* [1972] IR 241.

48 Under Article 40.3 of Bunreacht na hÉireann.

49 *Murray v Ireland* [1985] IR 532.

50 See para **[4.006]**. See also *Abbey Films Ltd v Attorney General* [1981] IR 158.

51 This point is made by Ussher, *Company Law in Ireland* (1986), pp 469–470, in relation to the conclusiveness of the registrar's certificate that the formalities for registration of a company charge - under CA 1963, Part IV, as amended - have been complied with.

52 The question is raised by Power, *Irish Company Law 1973–1983 – A Guide and Handbook* (1984), p 51.

53 Article 34.1 of Bunreacht na hÉireann.

54 *Maher v Attorney General* [1973] IR 40.

the concentration of alcohol in the body of the person from whom the sample was taken. However, that case was concerned only with the administration of *criminal* justice, which the Constitution entrusts *exclusively* to the courts. All that follows from *Maher*'s case is that where a company is prosecuted in criminal proceedings, for example, for an illegal activity contemplated by its objects clause, it cannot rely on the Registrar's certificate as conclusive evidence of the legality of its activities. Indeed, where a company is prosecuted, it may, following *Maher*, try to challenge the validity of its *own* incorporation so as to evade criminal liability.

Where *civil* proceedings are concerned, however, it appears that it will be difficult to ignore the conclusiveness of the Registrar's certificate. The functions of the Registrar, as administrative or quasi-judicial functions[55] rather than judicial functions, may be exercised, under Article 37 of the Constitution:

> '...in matters other than criminal matters, by any person or body of persons duly authorised to exercise such functions and powers, notwithstanding that such person or body of persons is not a judge or a court appointed or established as such under t[he] Constitution.'

Consequently, in civil cases, the question of whether a company has satisfied the requirements for a valid incorporation is one which may constitutionally be left to the determination of the Registrar, whose decision will be final and binding, and 'conclusive'.

Cesser of corporate status

[4.020] Leaving the aforementioned possibilities aside, a private company validly incorporated in accordance with the Companies Acts continues to exist as a corporation until it is dissolved. Indeed, it continues even though it is in the process of being wound up, or though its membership has fallen below the legal minimum of two[56]. The Companies Acts provide that a company will be dissolved only when one of the following events occurs:[57]:

- in the case of a winding up by the court, an order is made by the court under CA 1963, s 249, dissolving the company; or
- in the case of a members' voluntary winding up, the period of three months, or such other time as the court thinks fit, from the registration of the liquidator's final return under CA 1963, s 263, has expired; or
- in the case of a creditors' voluntary winding up, the period of three months, or such other time as the court thinks fit, from the registration of the liquidator's final return under CA 1963, s 273, has expired;
- in the case of a company which has been struck off the companies register by the Registrar of Companies, for failure to carry on business[58] or for failure to

---

55 See para **[4.015]**.

56 See *Jarvis Motors (Harrow) Ltd v Carabbott* [1964] 1 WLR 1101. See further Chapter 5, *Disregarding Separate Legal Personality*.

57 See generally Chapter 25, *Winding Up Companies*.

58 CA 1963, s 311, as amended.

make an annual return[59], the Registrar publishes a notice to that effect in *Iris Oifigiúil*.

Any of the above dissolutions may, however, within a period of two years, be declared void by the court upon the application of the liquidator or any interested person[60]. Furthermore, where a company has been struck off the companies' register, the court may, within 20 years, on the application of the company or any member or creditor, restore the company to the register[61]. The effect of the court's order in both cases is that the company is treated as never having been dissolved. These matters are discussed in greater detail in Chapter 12.

[B] THE CONSEQUENCES OF INCORPORATION

[4.021] A company registered under the Companies Acts 1963-2001 becomes a body corporate as and from the date mentioned in the certificate of incorporation[62]. Incorporation under the Companies Acts carries with it a number of significant consequences, not all of which are set out in CA 1963, s 18(2), which, perhaps vaguely, provides:

> 'From the date of incorporation mentioned in the certificate of incorporation, the subscribers of the memorandum, together with such other persons as may from time to time become members of the company, shall be a body corporate with the name contained in the memorandum, capable forthwith of exercising all the functions of an incorporated company, and having perpetual succession and a common seal, but with such liability on the part of the members to contribute to the assets of the company in the event of its being wound up as is mentioned in this Act.'

[4.022] The courts have elaborated on the consequences of the company becoming, as CA 1963, s 18(2) puts it, a 'body corporate...capable forthwith of exercising all the functions of an incorporated company'. The consequences are considered in the following paragraphs under these headings:

1. Separate legal personality.
2. Limited liability.
3. Transferability of interests.
4. Perpetual succession.
5. Common seal.
6. Floating charges;
7. Formation of large associations.
8. Taxation.
9. Other consequences of incorporation.

---

59 C(A)A 1982, s 12 as inserted by C(A)(No 2)A 1999, s 46.

60 CA 1963, s 310.

61 CA 1963, s 311; and C(A)A 1982, s 12 as inserted by C(A)(No 2)A 1999, s 46.

62 CA 1963, s 18(2).

Separate legal personality

[4.023] The separate legal personality of the private company infiltrates almost every aspect of the company's dealings – whether these are between the company and its participants or between the company and third parties. Five significant aspects of the concept of separate legal personality are explored here as follows:

(a) Artificial or fictional personality.

(b) *Salomon*'s case.

(c) Corporate property.

(d) Suing and being sued.

(e) Privileges and obligations.

(a) Artificial or fictional personality

[4.024] A body corporate, unlike a partnership or other unincorporated association, is more than a mere aggregation of individual units: it constitutes a juristic or legal *person* with a legal identity separate and distinct from that of its individual shareholders or members. It is, of course, a metaphysical person - it has no physical manifestation: it has no body, limbs or brains. Thus, while it maintains a distinct legal existence from other persons such as its members, the corporation suffers from the complication that it is only ultimately capable of acting, thinking and deciding through other persons. Here we encounter one of the fundamental idiosyncrasies of corporate dealings - they may only ever be carried out by human intervention - and it is this aspect of corporate dealing with which much of our company law is concerned[63].

[4.025] Corporations are sometimes described as *artificial* or *fictional* persons, or as a 'mere abstraction of law' [64]. But to describe them as such is somewhat of a misnomer, for in the eyes of the law, corporations are no more artificial or fictional than natural human persons[65]. As far as the law is concerned, a person is something which is capable of being the subject of rights and duties, regardless of its physical form. For example, in many ancient (and, sadly, not so ancient[66]) societies slaves were not recognised as persons by the law, though they patently had physical existence; while in other societies even religious idols are recognised as persons who may sue and be sued and hold property in their own right[67]. That said, however, there is a disturbing air of artificiality about regarding corporations as full legal persons in certain contexts. Though corporations can comfortably be considered persons in the eyes of commercial law (where the concept of corporate personality was born through convenience) it is far from settled that they enjoy similar personhood under criminal or constitutional law. Any attempt to accord such rights or duties to corporations must inevitably come to terms

---

[63] See Chapter 7, *Corporate Contracts, Capacity and Authority*, paras **[7.001]** and **[7.096]** and Chapter 8, *Corporate Governance: Management by the Directors*.

[64] *Flitcroft's Case, In Re Exchange Banking Co* (1882) 21 Ch D 519 at 536, per Cotton LJ.

[65] Except, perhaps, where constitutional rights are concerned, see para **[4.059]** *ff*.

[66] See the American case of *Dredd Scott v Sandford* 60 US 393.

[67] See *Pramatha Nath Mullick v Pradyumna Kumar Mullick* (1925) LR 52 Ind App 245; Duff, 'The Personality of an Idol' (1927) 3 Camb LJ 43; also *Bumper Development Corporation v Commissioner of the Metropolis* [1991] 4 All ER 638 and note by Carter (1991) 62 BYIL 452.

with the fact that a corporation is in reality *not* a person but an association of persons bound by a common contractual purpose and is consequently itself incapable of manifesting the morality or humanity which is integral in many crimes and constitutional rights.

(b) Salomon's case

[4.026] The concept of the registered company as a separate legal person, capable of being the subject of rights and obligations, was firmly established by the House of Lords in *Salomon v A Salomon & Co Ltd*[68].

Aron Salomon had been operating prosperously as a boot manufacturer and leather merchant for some 30 years when, in 1892, bowing to pressure from members of his family who wanted to share in the business, and wishing to expand, he decided to transfer his operation to a registered company owned and controlled by himself and his family. Of the 20,007 shares issued by the company - Salomon & Co Ltd - Aron Salomon held 20,001, the remaining six being held one-each by six other members of his family[69]. These six shares were, however, held by the family members as *nominees* for Salomon, so the company was de facto a 'one-man company'. The contract for the sale of his business to the company provided that the purchase price was to be £38,782 - a price which overvalued the true worth of the business and 'represented the sanguine expectations of a fond owner'.[70] Part of the purchase price was to be satisfied by the issue to Salomon of 20,000 fully paid £1 shares, and the payment to him of £8,782 in cash. The remaining £10,000 was to stand as a debt to Salomon, secured by debentures creating a floating charge over all the company's assets. Therefore, not only was Salomon the principal shareholder of the company but he was also its principal creditor.

When the company subsequently fell upon hard times, Salomon attempted to get the company back on its feet by mortgaging his debentures to obtain funds which he could lend to the company. His efforts to save the company were in vain and, ultimately, the debenture holder appointed a receiver to the company. The company was subsequently put into liquidation. At that stage, the company's liabilities, including the debt secured in the debentures by the floating charge, exceeded its assets by £7,733, and if the debenture holder were to be paid, the unsecured trade creditors, who were owed some £11,000, would get nothing.

[4.027] The liquidator took up the torch of the unsecured trade creditors, arguing that the debentures were invalid on the grounds of fraud. Vaughan Williams J, at first instance[71], found in favour of the liquidator, holding that Salomon's sole purpose in transferring his business to the company was to use it as an agent for himself, and therefore Salomon as principal should have to indemnify the company in respect of its debts to the unsecured creditors. He said:

> '...the company was a mere nominee of Mr Salomon's...and therefore I wish, if I can, to deal with this case exactly on the basis that I should do if the nominee, instead of being a

---

68 *Salomon v A Salomon & Co Ltd* [1897] AC 22.

69 The Companies Act 1862 required a registered company to have at least seven members.

70 [1897] AC 22 at 49, per Lord Macnaghten.

71 Reported sub nom *Broderip v Salomon* [1895] 2 Ch 323.

company, had been some servant or agent of Mr Salomon's to whom he had purported to sell his business.'[72]

[4.028] On appeal[73], the Court of Appeal, affirming Vaughan Williams J's decision, took a slightly different tack and held that Salomon had abused the privileges of incorporation and limited liability. The court felt such privileges were intended by the Companies Act 1862 only to be conferred on:

> 'independent *bona fide* shareholders, who had a mind and a will of their own, and were not the mere puppets of an individual who, adopting the machinery of the Act, carried on his old business in the same way as before, when he was a sole trader.'[74]

This abuse was sufficient to render Salomon a sort of constructive trustee for the company and thereby liable to indemnify it against its liabilities in full. Lord Lindley explained:

> '...Mr Aron Salomon's liability to indemnify the company in this case is, in my view, the legal consequence of the formation of the company in order to attain a result not permitted by law. The liability does not arise simply from the fact that he holds nearly all the shares of the company...His liability rests on the purpose for which he formed the company, on the way he formed it, and the use which he made of it.'[75]

[4.029] The House of Lords unanimously reversed the rulings of Vaughan Williams J and the Court of Appeal. The Law Lords held that since the Companies Act merely required that there should be seven subscribers to the memorandum - each holding at least one share - and said nothing about whether those subscribers should be independent of the majority shareholder or that they should have a mind and will of their own, the company was validly incorporated and capable of exercising all of the functions of an incorporated company. 'I cannot understand,' said Lord Macnaghten, 'how a body corporate thus made "capable" by statute can lose its individuality by issuing the bulk of its capital to one person.' Furthermore, Salomon had not perpetrated a fraud on the company by wilfully selling his business to it at an overvalue because all the shareholders were made fully aware of these circumstances. As to Vaughan Williams J's hypothesis that the company must be treated as Salomon's agent, Lord Halsbury trenchantly remarked:

> 'I confess it seems to me that the very learned judge becomes involved by this argument in a very singular contradiction. Either the company was a legal entity or it was not. If it was, the business belonged to it and not to Mr Salomon. If it was not, there was no person and no thing to be an agent at all; and it is impossible to say at the same time that there is a company and there is not.'[76]

Lord Macnaghten, in words now regarded as a legal classic, endorsed this view and at the same time put to rest the Court of Appeal's hypothesis that Salomon's use of the company was contrary to the intentions of the Companies Act. He stated unequivocally:

---

72 Reported sub nom *Broderip v Salomon* [1895] 2 Ch 323 at p 323.

73 Reported sub nom *Broderip v Salomon* [1895] 2 Ch 323

74 Reported sub nom *Broderip v Salomon* [1895] 2 Ch 323 at 341 per Lopes LJ.

75 Reported sub nom *Broderip v Salomon* [1895] 2 Ch 323 at 338.

76 [1897] AC 22 at 31.

> 'The company is at law a different person altogether from the subscribers to the Memorandum and, although it may be that after incorporation the business is precisely the same as it was before, and the same persons are managers, and the same hands receive the profits, the company is not at law the agent of the subscribers or a trustee for them. Nor are the subscribers as members liable, in any shape or form, except to the extent and in the manner provided by the Act. That is, I think, the declared intention of the enactment.'[77]

Thus, priority was given to Salomon's debentures.

[4.030] The principles enunciated by the House of Lords in *Salomon*'s case have a particular significance for the private company. It was that case which first established that the de facto one-man company fell within the policy of the Companies Acts; so much so, that the Companies Act 1907 subsequently reduced the minimum number of subscribers required for the incorporation of a private company from seven to two - without adding a requirement that the subscribers should be independent of each other or that one of the subscribers should not be the nominee of the other. Furthermore, the decision shows that the sole trader can limit his liability to the amount which he has invested in the company *and* can protect this investment by subscribing for secured debentures, rather than shares, so as to rank in priority to subsequent debenture holders, unsecured creditors and other shareholders.

[4.031] The decision has, nevertheless, been the subject of some criticism. A contemporary view of it was one of amazement that a legal person could be created simply through observance of the machinery of the Companies Acts, regardless of the fact that there was *really* only one person involved[78]. *Kahn-Freund* later described the decision as 'calamitous'; the courts had failed to see through the 'rigidities of the "folklore" of corporate entity in favour of the legitimate interests of the company's creditors'.[79] Interestingly, he suggested that the legislature should mitigate the effects of *Salomon*'s case by raising the cost of incorporation; by introducing a minimum capital requirement and minimum subscription on incorporation; by deeming companies under the control of less than ten persons to be the agents of those persons; and by abolishing private companies! Despite such criticism, the courts have generally applied the principles in *Salomon*'s case assiduously[80], though both they and the legislature have established a number of exceptions to the principles so that the separate legal personality of companies may sometimes be disregarded[81]. These exceptions are considered in Chapter 5.

(c) Corporate property

[4.032] As a separate legal person, a company that owns property owns and holds it in its own right[82] - not (necessarily) as an agent or trustee for the members. As Lord Halsbury

---

77 [1897] AC 22 at 51.

78 See the comment at (1897) 13 LQR 6.

79 Kahn-Freund, 'Some Reflections on Company Law Reform' (1944) 7 MLR 54.

80 See, for example, the citation with approval of Salomon's case in the High Court in *Re Frederick Inns Ltd* [1991] ILRM 582 at 587, per Lardner J.

81 See Chapter 5, *Disregarding Separate Legal Personality.*

82 *Short v Treasury Commissioners* [1948] AC 534; *Lee & Co (Dublin) Ltd v Egan (Wholesale) Ltd (1979)* (18 October 1979, unreported), High Court (Kenny J).

observed in *Salomon*'s case, if the company existed (as it did in that case) then 'the business belonged to it and not to Mr Salomon.' A shareholder then, does not by mere virtue of his shareholding, have any proprietary interest in the company's assets

[4.033] The distinction between the members' and the company's property is one which members and persons dealing with companies (in particular de facto one man companies) would do well to remember. It is now well established that the controlling shareholders of a company may be convicted of stealing from the company[83]. Likewise, if the directors withdraw assets from the company then they may, in the course of a subsequent winding up, be found liable in misfeasance proceedings under CA 1963, s 298, and be compelled to repay or restore any money or property to the company with interest[84]. Indeed, even if the misfeasance proceedings under that section are unsuccessful, the costs of the application may still be awarded against the directors personally because of any confusion they may have caused[85].

[4.034] Third parties dealing with the company should also be wary of the distinction between the company's property and the members' property. This is illustrated by the case of *AL Underwood Ltd v Bank of Liverpool*[86]. In that case, Mr A L Underwood, who was the controlling shareholder of A L Underwood Ltd, would from time to time indorse cheques which were payable to the company over to himself, and pay them into his private bank account. The bank thought nothing strange of this, failing to appreciate the distinction between the company and Mr Underwood. The bank was punished for its indifference by a successful suit in conversion against it by the company.

[4.035] Some further repercussions of the distinction between the company's and its members' property are considered here as follows:

- (i) Transfer of property.
- (ii) Insurable interests.
- (iii) Compensation.
- (iv) Statutory tenancies.

(i) Transfer of property

[4.036] The transfer of property by the controlling shareholders to the company is a transfer to a distinct body[87]. As Lindley LJ observed in *Farrar v Farrars Ltd*[88]:

> 'A sale by a person to a corporation of which he is a member is not, either in form or in substance, a sale by a person to himself. To hold that it is would be to ignore the principle which lies at the root of the legal idea of a corporate body, and that is that the corporate body is distinct from the members composing it. A sale by a member of a corporation to the corporation itself is in every sense a sale valid in equity as well as at law.'

---

83 *Pearlberg v O'Brien* [1982] Crim LR 829; *Attorney General's Reference (No 2 of 1982)* [1984] QB 624; *Re Sullivan* [1984] Crim LR 405.

84 See Chapter 10, *Duties of Directors and Other Officers*, para **[10.129]**.

85 *Re David Ireland & Co Ltd* [1905] 1 IR 133; see Chapter 10, *Duties of Directors and Other Officers*, para **[10.131]**.

86 *AL Underwood Ltd v Bank of Liverpool* [1924] 1 KB 775.

87 *Ryhope Coal Co Ltd v Foyer* (1881) 7 QBD 485.

88 *Farrar v Farrars Ltd* (1888) 40 ChD 395 at 409.

One important consequence of this is that the transfer of the controllers' assets to the company may be viewed as a conveyance on sale for which ad valorem stamp duty may be payable[89]. Conversely, the transfer of assets by the company to the shareholders is a transfer between distinct bodies, and so the requisite formalities of conveyance must be observed. In *Re Strathblaine Estates Ltd*[90], where the shareholders, in a distribution of a company's assets in a voluntary winding up, were given merely the title deeds to freehold estates held by the company, it was held that the shareholders had not been conveyed the legal estate in the properties. However the distinction between the company's property and its controlling shareholder's property worked to the controller's advantage in *Torbett v Faulkner*[91], where a company owned and controlled by a houseowner purported to let the house to an employee. The houseowner was held to be entitled to recover possession of the house on the basis that the company had no title to grant the tenancy in the first place.

Where the legal title to property is vested in a company, in circumstances where the property was acquired with money provided by a shareholder, the shareholder will be the equitable or beneficial owner of the property unless it can be established that the property was gifted to the company. In *Fitzpatrick v Criminal Assets Bureau*[92] it was said that the proposition that there is a presumed intention to advance a gift:

> '...is untenable as between an individual, whether a shareholder, employee or officer of a company and such company. If there is a gift this intention must be proved.'

It should be noted that all substantial property transactions between a company and its directors must comply with the requirements of the Companies Act 1990, as amended. These are discussed in detail in Chapter 11.

(ii) Insurable interests

[4.037] The distinction between the company's and the members' property may occasionally work to deprive the controllers of a right or a remedy which they might have had if they had not transferred their property to a company. This is clearly illustrated in *Macaura v Northern Assurance Co Ltd*[93]. Macaura sold all of the timber from his Co Tyrone estate to The Irish Canadian Saw Mills Ltd for £42,000, which was paid for by the allotment to him of all of that company's 42,000 fully paid £1 shares. When the wood was subsequently destroyed by fire, it was held that Macaura could not recover on an insurance policy taken out in his name. 'No shareholder', Lord Buckmaster explained, 'has any right to any item of property owned by the company, for he has no legal or equitable interest therein'. Since the company owns company property in its own right, a shareholder cannot insure company property, because he has no insurable interest in it[94].

---

89 *John Foster & Sons v IRC* [1894] 1 QB 516.

90 *Re Strathblaine Estates Ltd* [1948] Ch 228.

91 *Torbett v Faulkner* [1952] 2 TLR 659.

92 *Fitzpatrick v Criminal Assets Bureau* [2000] 1 IR 243, [2000] 1 ILRM 299.

93 *Macaura v Northern Assurance Co Ltd* [1925] AC 619. Cf the Canadian case of *Kosmopolous v Constitution Insurance Co of Canada* (1984) 149 DLR (3d) 77, where a sole shareholder was held to have an insurable interest in the company property.

94 See *Verderame v Commercial Union Assurance Co plc* [1992] BCLC 793, discussed in further detail at para **[4.046]**.

A shareholder can, however, cover himself against loss by the company by insuring his shares (rather than the company's assets) against a drop in their value, for it is the shares, and not the company's assets, in which the shareholder has any legal or equitable interest. This was successfully done in *Wilson v Jones*[95].

(iii) Compensation

[4.038] Where compensation is payable in respect of loss suffered by a company, the shareholders have no right to payment. In *Stewarts Supermarkets Ltd v Secretary of State*[96], a holding company was held not to be entitled to recover compensation under the Northern Ireland criminal injuries compensation scheme for damage to its subsidiary's business in a terrorist attack, since the damage suffered was to the property of the subsidiary – not the holding company, its majority shareholder. In *Roberts v Coventry Corporation*[97], the defendant had compulsorily purchased the plaintiff's freehold interest in a building which the plaintiff had leased to a company of which she was the majority shareholder. The court refused to allow her claim for compensation in respect of the diminution in the value of her shares resulting from the company's relocation, since the loss was the company's, and not hers. This principle was relied upon by the Irish Supreme Court in *O'Neill v Ryan, Ryan Air Ltd, Aer Lingus plc, Kennedy, GPA Group Ltd and Transport Analysis Inc*[98]. In that case, the plaintiff alleged that breaches of competition law by the last four named defendants had caused a diminution in the value of his shares in the second named defendant, Ryan Air Ltd. The Supreme Court struck out his action for damages on the basis that such actions by the defendants could not cause personal loss to the shareholder. Blayney J quoted from the English Court of Appeal's decision in *Prudential Assurance Co Ltd v Newman Industries Ltd (No 2)*[99] as follows:

> 'What [the shareholder] cannot do is recover damages merely because the company in which he is interested has suffered damage. He cannot recover a sum equal to the diminution in the market value of his shares, or equal to the likely diminution in dividend, because such a loss is merely a reflection of the loss suffered by the company. The shareholder does not suffer any personal loss...The plaintiff's shares are merely a right of participation in the company on the terms of the articles of association. The shares themselves, his right of participation, are not directly affected by the wrongdoing. The plaintiff still holds all the shares as his own absolutely unencumbered property. The deceit practised upon the plaintiff does not affect the shares; it merely enables the defendant to rob the company.'[100]

(iv) Statutory tenancies

[4.039] The distinction between the company's and the members' property is of particular relevance as far as the rights of tenants to statutory leases are concerned. In

95 *Wilson v Jones* (1866) LR 1 Exch 193.

96 *Stewarts Supermarkets Ltd v Secretary of State* [1982] NI 286.

97 *Roberts v Coventry Corporation* [1947] 1 All ER 308.

98 *O'Neill v Ryan, Ryan Air Ltd, Aer Lingus plc, Kennedy, GPA Group Ltd and Transport Analysis Inc* [1993] ILRM 557.

99 *Prudential Assurance Co Ltd v Newman Industries Ltd (No 2)* [1982] Ch 204 at 222.

100 [1993] ILRM 557 at 569. See further Chapter 19, *Shareholders' Remedies*.

Tunstall v Steigman[101] a landlord applied to resist the grant of a statutory tenancy to her tenant on the ground that she needed the premises for the expansion of her business which was carried on in an adjoining premises. Her application failed on the basis that the business was not carried on by her, but by a company of which she was the controlling shareholder.

Conversely, in *Pegler v Craven*[102], an application by a tenant to obtain a statutory tenancy was refused because the premises had not been occupied by him but by a company of which he was the majority shareholder. Indeed, the company was held not to be entitled to such a tenancy either, because it was a mere licensee of the tenant and not a tenant itself. The rigours of that decision have been tempered in Ireland by the Landlord and Tenant (Amendment) Act 1980, s 5(3), which allows a tenant to obtain rights to a statutory tenancy where occupation is by a company which is controlled by him and which occupies the premises under a licence from him.

(d) Suing and being sued

[4.040] Since the company is a separate and distinct legal person, and is not per se the agent of its shareholders, only the company (and not its members) can be sued for its obligations and can sue to enforce its rights. Here, the following matters are considered:

(i) Contracts.

(ii) Torts.

(iii) Crimes.

(iv) Constitutional rights and duties.

(v) Legal rights and duties.

Further practical aspects of corporate litigation are considered in Chapter 6.

(i) Contracts

[4.041] 'Only a person who is a party to a contract can sue on it...[but] a principal not named in the contract may sue upon it if the promisee really contracted as his agent.' So held Viscount Haldane LC in *Dunlop Pneumatic Tyre Co Ltd v Selfridge & Co Ltd*[103]. A shareholder cannot sue to enforce a contract made by his company simply by virtue of the fact that he is a shareholder, because he is not a party to the contract. Nor can he claim as a principal not named in the contract, because companies are not per se the agents of their shareholders[104]. Likewise a shareholder cannot be sued on contracts, including loan contracts, made by the company[105]. A significant practical consequence is that third parties dealing with the company - notably financial institutions - will often

101 *Tunstall v Steigman* [1961] AC 12.

102 *Pegler v Craven* [1952] 2 QB 69.

103 *Dunlop Pneumatic Tyre Co Ltd v Selfridge & Co Ltd* [1915] AC 847.

104 Per Macnaghten LJ in *Salomon*'s case; see para **[4.029]**.

105 *Daimler Co Ltd v Continental Tyre & Rubber Co (Great Britain) Ltd* [1916] 2 AC 307; *Maclaine Watson & Co Ltd v Department of Trade and Industry* [1990] BCLC 102 - 'Members of a body corporate are not liable for the debts of a body corporate because they are not parties to the corporation's contracts', per Templeman LJ at 108.

require the controlling shareholders and/or directors personally to guarantee the performance of the company's obligations[106].

[4.042] Controllers of newly incorporated companies should be aware that they may continue to be liable for existing obligations to customers who have dealt with them in their capacity as sole traders or partners. In *The Pitner Lighting Co of Ireland v Geddis and Pickering*[107], the defendants had been partners for a few months before incorporation, during which time they contracted to purchase goods from the plaintiffs on account. No monies were paid to the plaintiffs on the account during this period. Upon incorporation, the plaintiffs continued to supply goods to the new company on the same account, and the new company paid some, but not all, of the balance outstanding on the account. The plaintiffs then re-arranged their accounts, appropriating the amount paid by the company as being in respect of goods supplied to the company after incorporation. They then sued the defendants for payment in respect of the goods supplied prior to incorporation. The court found the defendants liable.

[4.043] Contracts by companies are subject to the ultra vires doctrine, whereby the contract will be void if not contemplated in the company's objects clause as stated in the memorandum of association. Legislative intervention has done much, however, to temper the rigours of this doctrine, which is discussed in detail in Chapter 7.

[4.044] A company cannot, as a separate person, be sued for the contractual obligations of its members, and a misrepresentation or failure to disclose relevant information to a third party by a shareholder does not affect a contract entered into by the third party with the company, since the misrepresentation or non-disclosure must come from the company itself[108]. But the possibility of a company being liable for the contractual activities of its directors through agency principles (eg ostensible authority) should not be forgotten. This is also discussed in further detail in Chapter 7. Attention should be paid to the intentions of the contracting parties. Persons who negotiate contracts with controlling shareholders may intend to contract with them in their personal capacity - particularly if they have dealt with them before as sole traders or partners - while the shareholder may intend to act on the company's behalf. In such cases no contract will be formed because the parties will not be ad idem[109].

(ii) Torts

[4.045] A corporation has the same capacity as an individual to sue for torts committed against it[110]. Since the company is a separate legal person, it is the company, not its shareholders, who may sue in respect of torts committed against it[111].

---

106 See Chapter 5, *Disregarding Separate Legal Personality*, para **[5.015]** *ff*.

107 *The Pitner Lighting Co of Ireland v Geddis and Pickering* [1912] 2 IR 163.

108 *Bell v Lever Brothers Ltd* [1932] AC 161. Where a question of knowledge or intention arises in relation to whether the misrepresentation was fraudulent, negligent or innocent, the company's knowledge or ignorance must be found in the minds of its agents: *Regina Fur Co Ltd v Bossom* [1958] 2 Lloyd's Rep 466; *UBAF Ltd v European American Banking Corporation* [1984] QB 713.

109 *J Smallman Ltd v O'Moore & Newman* [1959] IR 220.

110 See generally, McMahon & Binchy, *Law of Torts* (3rd edn, 2000), Ch 39.

111 *Rainham Chemical Works Ltd (In Liquidation) v Belvedere Fish Guano Co Ltd* [1921] AC 465; *British Thomson-Houston Co v Sterling Accessories Ltd* [1924] 2 Ch 33.

It appears settled that a company may sue even though the tort occurred in connection with an activity which was ultra vires[112]. Naturally, some torts (eg assault and battery, false imprisonment, etc) cannot, by their nature, be committed against a corporation. A company may, however, sue for an injury to its reputation in the way of its business by libel or slander, such as, for example, an allegation that the company is insolvent[113]. In *Wiggins v Rigby*[114] the Supreme Court of Victoria held that an imputation concerning a director of a company can reflect upon the company itself, depending upon the part the director is claimed to have played in the company's operations and upon the extent to which the director and the company are associated or considered to be each other's alter egos.

[4.046] Where the tort complained of has its foundation in *negligence*, ie breach of a duty of care[115], it is quite possible for the one act of negligence to amount both to breach of a duty owed to the company and, at the same time, to breach of a duty owed to a shareholder. This will be so if both the company and the shareholder can be regarded as 'neighbours'[116] whom the tortfeasor ought reasonably to have had in his contemplation when directing his mind towards the act or omission in question.

Where, however, a third party provides services involving skill, advice or judgment to a company, the duty of care owed by the provider of the service to the company will not, in general, extend to the shareholders - especially where the shareholder suffers only economic loss[117]. This is well illustrated in *McSweeney v Bourke*[118], where a financial consultant, engaged by a group of companies in financial difficulties, advised the group that one prudent course of action open to it was to obtain an injection of further capital from two of its controlling shareholders. The two shareholders in question had been in close consultation with the consultant during the formulation of his proposal. The group of companies obtained the investment from the shareholders in line with the consultant's proposal. When the group failed to recover from its financial difficulties, the two shareholders brought an action against the consultant for negligent misstatement giving rise to economic loss. Carroll J dismissed their action, holding on the facts that the consultant had not been negligent in any way[119]. She added, however, that if the consultant had been negligent, his negligence could only have been in relation to his client, the group of companies, and not to the two shareholders. She explained:

---

[112] *National Telephone Company Ltd v The Constables of St Peter Port* [1900] AC 317. See Jenkins, 'Corporate Liability in Tort and the Doctrine of Ultra Vires' 5 Ir Jur (ns) 11 (1970).

[113] *South Hetton Coal Co v North Eastern News Association* [1894] 1 QB 133; *Irish People's Assurance Society v Dublin City Assurance Co* [1929] IR 25; *D & L Caterers and Jackson v D'Ajou* [1945] KB 364; *Gormanstown Equestrian Centre Ltd v Anglo Irish Bank Corporation plc* (14 July 1994, unreported), Circuit Court (McGuinness J).

[114] *Wiggins v Rigby* (10 August 2000, unreported), Supreme Court of Victoria.

[115] See generally McMahon & Binchy, *The Irish Law of Torts* (3rd edn, 2000), Ch 6.

[116] See Lord Atkin's famous dictum in *Donoghue v Stevenson* [1932] AC 562 at 580.

[117] See *Securities Trust Ltd v Hugh Moore & Alexander Ltd* [1964] IR 417; *Hedley Byrne & Co Ltd v Heller & Partners Ltd* [1964] AC 465; and, generally, McMahon & Binchy, *Law of Torts*, (3rd edn, 2000), Ch 10.

[118] *McSweeney v Bourke* (24 November 1980, unreported), High Court (Carroll J).

[119] (24 November 1980, unreported), High Court at p 22.

> '[I]rrespective of contract, the adviser has a primary duty of care to the client and there may or may not be a duty to third parties. If the advice given is not given negligently *vis-à-vis* the client in the first instance but is given with all due care, there is no breach of duty to the client. If an adviser is not negligent *vis-à-vis* the client and does not purport to advise any person other than the client, I do not see how a third party who knows the advice given to the client and who carries out the steps outlined in that advice (ultimately to his own detriment) can claim that the advice was negligent in relation to him...[T]he only reliance the two shareholders, as such, could place on the advice was that it was good advice for the group as a whole. They were intended to act on the advice but in the context that the advice was given with the interest of the group in mind. Once [the consultant] did not hold himself out as advising the shareholders as well as the group there was no additional duty placed on [him] to add any words of warning in relation to the risks attached to further capital investment in the group. There is no evidence that [the consultant] undertook an additional and separate duty of advising the shareholders, as such, with a conflicting interest.' [120]

Controlling shareholders should seek independent assurances from parties advising the company before relying on advice given to the company - or they should seek independent advice from third parties. This, as shall be seen[121], is of particular importance where reliance is placed by the shareholders on advice given to the company by its accountants or auditors. Similar steps should also be taken where other services are provided to the company, as may be seen from *Verderame v Commercial Union Assurance Co plc*[122]. There, a company engaged the services of an insurance broker to obtain insurance cover. The broker obtained cover in the name of one of the controlling shareholders. When some of the company property was subsequently stolen, the controlling shareholder-director was unable to recover on the policy because he had no insurable interest in the stolen property[123]. Instead, he and his wife, a fellow controlling shareholder-director, sued the insurance broker for damages for loss of business, alleging that the broker owed them a duty of care when effecting insurance for the company. The Court of Appeal unequivocally rejected the contention that any such duty of care existed. Balcombe LJ explained:

> '...the directors are seeking to go behind the corporate status of the company. In effect they are saying to the brokers, "By failing to arrange proper insurance cover for the company you broke a duty which you owed to us as directors and shareholders of the company and you are liable to us for our loss of emoluments"...if this submission were to succeed the principles of the leading case of *Salomon v Salomon & Co Ltd* would become a dead letter.'[124]

The fact that the company was a small private company made no difference to the court. Nourse LJ added:

> 'It being accepted that there was a contract between the brokers and the company alone, the proposition that the brokers also came under a duty of care in tort to the directors is not

---

[120] (24 November 1980, unreported), High Court at pp 17-18.

[121] See Chapter 13, Accounts and Auditors, para **[13.235]** *ff.*

[122] *Verderame v Commercial Union Assurance Co plc* [1992] BCLC 793.

[123] See para **[4.037]**.

[124] [1992] BCLC 793 at 802.

only novel but to my mind startling. If it was sustained it would have very wide-ranging consequences, not only in relation to insurance brokers, but also to others who provide services to small private companies, for example, solicitors, accountants, estate agents and so forth. Not only would it pierce the corporate veil on a vast scale, it would lead to quite unjustifiable procedural impracticabilities and rights or potential rights of double recovery. In my view it is simply unarguable that a duty of care can arise in such circumstances.'[125]

[4.047] A corporation may also, of course, be sued in respect of torts committed by it. The fact that a company's objects clause does not contemplate commission of tortious acts does not enable the company simply to avoid liability on the grounds that the activity complained of is ultra vires[126]. To say otherwise would be 'to say that no corporation can ever be sued for a public wrong'[127], and that would be absurd. Similarly, where the tort occurs in connection with the commission of an ultra vires activity, (eg where a bus knocks someone down and the bus is owned and operated by a company whose objects do not contemplate the operation of a bus business) a claim in tort will not be prohibited[128].

[4.048] Most commonly, a company's tortious liability arises *vicariously* through the operation of the principle of *respondeat superior*. Where a wrong is committed in the course of the company's employees' activities, the company will be vicariously liable as employer in much the same way as a natural employer would, regardless of whether the company consented to the particular act in question[129]. The company may be entitled to an indemnity from the servant or agent in such circumstances[130]. On the other hand, some torts may properly be said to be the result of the company's *own* acts - such as where they are done or authorised under the direction of the board of directors or the shareholders in general meeting. In such cases the courts will look to the actions of those who control the company. In *Lennard's Carrying Co v Asiatic Petroleum Co*[131], Viscount Haldane LC said:

> 'My lords, a corporation is an abstraction. It has no mind of its own any more than it has a body of its own; its active and directing will must consequently be sought in the person of somebody who for some purposes may be called an agent, but who is really the directing mind and will of the corporation, the very ego and centre of the personality of the corporation...[T]he fault or privity is the fault or privity of somebody who is not merely a servant or agent for whom the company is liable upon the footing of *respondeat superior*; but somebody for whom the company is liable because the action is the very action of the company itself.'[132]

---

[125] [1992] BCLC 793 at 804.

[126] See Jenkins, 'Corporate Liability in Tort and the Doctrine of Ultra Vires' 5 Ir Jur (ns) 11 (1970); Goodhart, 'Corporate Liability in Tort and the Ultra Vires Doctrine' (1926) 2 Cam LJ 350; Warren, 'Torts by Corporations in Ultra Vires Undertakings' (1925) Cam LJ 180.

[127] Per Avory J in *Campbell v Paddington Corporation* [1911] 1 KB 869 at 875.

[128] See Jenkins, 'Corporate Liability in Tort and the Doctrine of Ultra Vires' 5 Ir Jur (ns) 11 (1970), pp 17–19.

[129] See eg *Pearson & Son Ltd v Dublin Corporation* [1907] 2 IR 27. See generally McMahon & Binchy, *Law of Torts* (3rd edn, 2000), para 35.10 *ff.*

[130] *Lister v Romford Ice and Cold Storage Co Ltd* [1957] AC 555.

[131] *Lennard's Carrying Co v Asiatic Petroleum Co* [1915] AC 705.

[132] [1915] AC 705 at 713–714.

The above statement of principle was quoted with approval by McCarthy J in *Taylor v Smith*[133]; and was later applied by the Supreme Court in *Superwood Holdings plc v Sun Alliance and London Assurance plc*[134] with the qualification that the directing mind and will of a corporation was not necessarily that of the person or persons who had general management and control since the directing mind and will could be found in different persons in respect of different activities[135]. The Supreme Court in *Superwood* accepted the artificiality of the approach 'in seeking to force complex and varying corporate structures into a uniform human mould.'[136] One notable shortcoming of the doctrine, which was alluded to by the Supreme Court, is that it where power is diffused through a corporation it may be impossible to identify any one person as representing the directing mind and will.

[4.049] The principle is well illustrated in *The Lady Gwendolen*[137], where a ship owned by Arthur Guinness & Son Co (Dublin) Ltd was involved in a collision through failure to use radar during heavy fog. The ship had failed to use radar largely because the captain had never been fully instructed in its use. The company was vicariously liable for the captain's negligence, but the Merchant Shipping Act 1894, ss 502 and 503 allowed the company's liability to be limited if the damage occurred without the 'actual fault or privity' of the company. The court was able to find such fault or privity by the company by looking at its management structure. The responsibility for transport and transport staff had been delegated by the board of directors to an assistant managing director, who was at fault by having failed to ensure that the captain was properly instructed. His fault was imputed as the actual fault of the company; and the company, accordingly, could not limit its liability under the Merchant Shipping Act 1894. Therefore, where the tort complained of requires malicious intent to be proved, or where some defence[138] to an action in tort requires that the act not be done maliciously, the courts will show no hesitation in imputing malice of the controllers of the company to the company itself. It appears that proof of the company's liability in tort does not automatically prove that all the controlling members of the company are liable as well unless they can be shown to have actually participated in the commission of the tort or they have authorised or directed its commission[139].

(iii) Crimes

[4.050] An important common law power available to members of the public is the power to institute criminal prosecutions - whether or not they themselves have been the victims - as 'common informers'[140]. This power to act as a common informer, however,

[133] *Taylor v Smith* [1991] IR 142 at 166.

[134] *Superwood Holdings plc v Sun Alliance and London Assurance plc* [1995] 3 IR 303.

[135] Following *El Ajou v Dollar Land Holdings plc* [1994] 2 All ER 685.

[136] See Ussher, *Company Law in Ireland* (1986), p 39.

[137] *The Lady Gwendolen* [1965] 2 WLR 91.

[138] Eg the defence of qualified privilege to an action in defamation: see generally McMahon & Binchy, *The Irish Law of Torts* (3rd edn, 2000), para 34.134 *ff.*

[139] *Rainham Chemical Works Ltd (In Liquidation) v Belvedere Fish Guano Co Ltd* [1921] 2 AC 465; *Williams v Natural Life Health Foods Ltd* [1998] BCC 428.

[140] See *The People v Roddy* [1977] IR 177.

is not available to corporations. In *Cumann Luthchleas Gael Teo v District Justice Windle*[141], Dublin Corporation, acting as a common informer, had obtained an order from the respondent sending the GAA forward for criminal trial for breaches of the Fire Services Act 1981 arising out of the occupation and management of its premises at Croke Park. The Supreme Court quashed the order, Finlay CJ saying:

> '...a body corporate cannot, under a general common law principle, prosecute as a common informer or a private prosecutor either in relation to summary offences or in relation to indictable offences up to the stage of return for trial.'

[4.051] Though companies may not prosecute, it is well established that in appropriate circumstances they may *be prosecuted*, whether vicariously or personally, for criminal offences. The field of corporate criminal liability is fraught, however, with theoretical and practical difficulties[142], and outside of the regulatory regimes imposed by statute for the protection of health and safety, the environment, or the security of financial markets, for example, there is no real tradition in Ireland of companies being prosecuted for general crimes[143].

The criminal law has traditionally been concerned primarily with the responsibility of individuals rather than organisations. Old aphorisms that corporations are not capable of being subjected to the criminal law since it punishes 'violations of the social duties that belong to men and subjects'[144] and corporations cannot be expected to have a conscience when they have 'no soul to be damned, and no body to be kicked'[145] have partially fallen from favour in the modern context since corporations can be, and are, subjected to the criminal law under the regulatory regime. A fundamental difficulty remains, however: should the general focus of criminal law be confined to the individuals acting within the company rather than the company itself?

[4.052] Proponents of corporate criminal responsibility argue that the synergies of corporate organisation are not fully reflected in an individualistic approach. Many companies, it is argued, promote themselves as distinct *personae*, through advertising or otherwise. To fail to attach blame to the publicly perceived wrongdoer creates a perception that the real wrongdoer is getting away with criminal activity. Conversely, it is argued that a conviction of an individual within the company should not result in automatic conviction of the company itself where there is an absence of significant corporate participation in the crime or substantial policy considerations such as would justify the imposition of liability on one person (ie the corporation) for the acts of another (ie the individual)[146]. Such policy considerations are considered justified under our legal tradition only in the regulatory field.

---

141 *Cumann Luthchleas Gael Teo v District Justice Windle* [1994] 1 IR 533.

142 See generally Wells, *Corporations and Criminal Responsibility* (2nd edn, 2001); also Fisse & Braithwaite, *Corporations, Crime and Accountability* (1993).

143 See Law Reform Commission of Ireland, *Consultation Paper on Corporate Homicide* (2002).

144 Per Denman LCJ in *R v Great North of England Railway Company* (1846) 9 QB 315 at 326.

145 Per Edward, First Baron Thurlow (1731–1806), Lord Chancellor. See Coffee, '"No Soul to Damn: No Body to Kick:"' An Unscandalised Inquiry into the Problem of Corporate Punishment' (1981) 79 Mich L Rev 386.

146 *Re Article 26 and the Employment Equality Bill 1996* [1997] IR 321.

Secondly, it is said that a focus on individual wrongdoers within the corporate structure deflects attention from the fact that corporations may have a 'momentum and dynamic'[147] of their own which seriously influences individual conduct. As against such concerns, it is said that all human activity – whether within the corporate environment or otherwise - is influenced by a variety of factors (social and cultural, familial, institutional, political, economic, etc)[148]. Such external influences do not offer a defence to individual liability, though they can be given substantial weight in mitigation of sentence.

A third, related, argument is that it just may not be possible to attach liability to any individual within a corporation since the fault may lie in the system of management - a 'management failure' - so that the responsibility for the conduct is dispersed throughout the organisation and diluted rather than concentrated in any individual[149]. In such cases nobody – corporation or individual - can be prosecuted. The fundamental question in such cases, however, is whether management failure is an inherently criminal thing, or whether it ought to be so where it has serious or fatal consequences – particularly given that 'management failure' is difficult to define. Within the relatively new science of organisational understanding there is still no uniform concept of what exactly management failure is[150]. If management failure is considered to be a mischief, it can be argued, then, that it is better to tackle it at its roots by introducing measures designed to improve management practices (eg the system of education, monitoring and supervision employed by the Health and Safety Authority in the context of safety-related issues, or the Corporate Governance Codes which were adopted following the *Turnbull*, *Cadbury* and *Hampel* Reports in the context of investor protection[151]). The role of the criminal law in supporting such measures is to follow with sanction for serious breach of the regulatory code rather than to impose vague prohibitions on little understood areas of activity. And even if management failure is criminalised, there remains the issue of whether it is the corporation itself or the individuals within it who should be penalised[152].

Finally, it is argued that corporations should be the subject of criminal responsibility because it is they, rather than their individual constituents, who are best placed to prevent

147 Ashworth, *Principles of Criminal Law* (2nd edn, 1991).

148 See Wells, *Corporations and Criminal Responsibility* (2nd edn, 2001), pp 147 *ff*.

149 See Fisse & Braithwaite, *Corporations, Crime and Accountability* (1993), Ch 1 & 4; Wells, *Corporations and Criminal Responsibility* (2nd edn, 2001), pp 70 and 148.

150 See Wells, *Corporations and Criminal Responsibility* (2nd edn, 2001), Ch 8.

151 See Chapter 28, *The Public Company in Context*, para **[28.063]**.

152 The Law Commission of England and Wales proposed, in 1996, a new offence of homicide aimed specifically at corporations. The offence, 'corporate killing,' would be committed where a 'management failure' was a cause of death and the failure fell far below what could reasonably have been expected of the corporation. The Commission recommended, however, that the proposed offence be aimed at corporations only: Law Commission of England and Wales, Legislating the Criminal Code: Involuntary Manslaughter, Law Comm 237 (HC 171) 4 March, 1996. For an Irish response see Law Reform Commission of Ireland, *Consultation Paper on Corporate Homicide* (2002).

or remedy the defects in their operations which led to the incident. Such 'rehabilitative' arguments assume, of course, that corporations will react to criminal sanction by mending their ways and by adopting remedial policies. There is no evidence of such a trend, however. Corporations, like any other offender, measure the impact of criminal sanction against a variety of scales: the risk of offending; the risk of detection; the cost of compliance; and the cost of sanction *versus* the potential for profit, etc. Such balancing exercises are a function in the response to all criminal liability, and they vary little whether the offence is part of a regulatory regime or part of the 'mainstream' criminal law. Accordingly, the 'rehabilitative' argument is of little assistance in the argument that the criminal liability of corporations should be extended beyond the regulatory regime - where, as it happens, there is greater scope for the imposition of remedial measures

[4.053] Beyond such fundamental difficulties, the circumstances in which companies will be criminally liable are limited by a number of practical considerations.
First, certain crimes, such as bigamy or rape, cannot physically be attributed to corporations without absurdity. That is not to say, however, that they could not be made criminally liable as secondary parties for such crimes. For example, where a film company supervises intercourse between a 15-year-old girl and a 15-year-old boy, there seems to be no reason why the company and its controllers could not be convicted as secondary parties to unlawful sexual intercourse.

Secondly, punishments involving death, corporal punishment, or imprisonment are incapable of being suffered by corporations[153]. Therefore, a company cannot be convicted of crimes, such as murder, which carry mandatory sentences of imprisonment. Indeed, the only possible *direct* punishment for companies in the modern Irish repertoire of criminal penalties seems to be a fine or an order for sequestration[154]. The use of the fine is sometimes criticised[155]. It is argued that some companies are well placed to 'buy their way out of justice,' and that fines in any event punish innocent shareholders rather than the 'real' wrongdoers - the management.

[4.054] Most regulatory offences for which corporations can be prosecuted are offences of *strict liability*, so it is not necessary for the prosecution to prove any mental attitude or mens rea on the part of the offender[156]. The strict liability approach is of particular significance in the prosecution of corporate defendants because it dispenses with the need to attribute to the corporation the mens rea of some individual closely associated with it[157]. Furthermore, the liability is commonly *direct* rather than vicarious. Professor JC Smith has explained it thus[158]:

---

153 See *The King (Cottingham) v The Justices of County Cork* [1906] 2 IR 415, per Johnson J at 427; *Pearks, Gunston and Tee, Ltd v Ward* [1902] 2 KB 1; *Hawke v E Hulton & Co* [1909] 2 KB 93; *R v The Daily Mirror Newspapers Ltd* (1922) 16 Cr App R 131.

154 Sequestration is the appropriate order where a company is in contempt of court: *Re Hibernia National Review* [1976] IR 388: see Chapter 6, *Corporate Civil Litigation*, para **[6.093]**.

155 See eg. Wells, *Corporations and Criminal Responsibility* (2nd edn, 2001), p 31.

156 *R v British Steel plc* [1995] 1 WLR 1356.

157 See para **[4.056]**.

158 [1995] Crim LR 654 at 655.

> 'Where a statutory duty to do something is imposed upon a particular person (here, "an employer") and he does not do it, he commits the *actus reus* of an offence. It may be that he has failed to fulfil his duty because his employee or agent has failed to carry out his duties properly but this is not a case for vicarious liability. If the employer is held liable, it is because he, personally, has failed to do what the law requires him to do and he is personally, not vicariously, liable. There is no need to find someone – in the case of a company, the 'brains' and not merely the "hands" – for whose act the person with the duty can be held liable. The duty on the company in this case was to "ensure" - i.e. to make certain – that persons are not exposed to risk. They did not make it certain. It does not matter how; they were in breach of their statutory duty and, in the absence of any requirement of *mens rea*, that is the end of the matter.'

Some of the offences are qualified, however, by a defence of 'reasonable practicality'[159]. In *R v Gateway Foodmarkets Ltd*[160], the Court of Appeal held that the onus is on the defence to prove that such reasonably practicable precautions have been taken. The court further held that the 'identification doctrine' and 'directing mind and will' concepts[161] have no application in establishing such a defence. Accordingly, the corporation will be liable for breaches of health and safety legislation by any persons for whom it is responsible, even where there had been no failure to take practical precautions at higher levels of management. In *Gateway*, the company was convicted of the offence of failing in its duty to ensure, as far as reasonably practicable, the health and safety of its employees when an employee at a supermarket site fell to his death down an unguarded lift shaft. The company had employed an experienced and highly reputable firm of lift contractors to maintain the lift, and the head office was unaware of an informal arrangement at store level whereby company employees would themselves adjust the lift mechanism when it became stuck. The employee was killed when carrying out this informal procedure. The Court of Appeal found that the failure at store level was attributable to the company without any need to consider whether head office knew or ought to have known of the informal procedures.

Corporations cannot evade liability for offences under the regulatory regimes merely by issuing injunctions at board level prohibiting illegal activity: what is required is a proactive response at all levels of operation. In *R v British Steel plc*[162] the Court of Appeal rejected the company's argument that taking reasonable care at board level should lead to an acquittal. In that case a worker for an independent contractor was killed because of the collapse of a steel platform during a repositioning operation which a competent supervisor would have recognised was inherently dangerous. The defence was that the workmen had disobeyed instructions and, even if the supervisor was at fault,

---

[159] Eg, Safety, Health and Welfare at Work Act 1989, s 6(1) provides that 'it shall be the duty of every employer to ensure, so far as is reasonably practicable, the safety, health and welfare at work of all his employees.'

[160] *R v Gateway Foodmarkets Ltd* [1997] 2 Cr App R 40.

[161] Ie the prevailing concepts involved in the attribution of liability to corporations for crimes requiring mens rea: see further para **[4.056]**.

[162] *R v British Steel plc* [1995] 1 WLR 1356. The approach of the Court of Appeal was endorsed by the House of Lords in *R v Associated Octel Co Ltd* [1996] 1 WLR 1543.

the company at the level of its directing mind had taken reasonable care. An appeal against conviction was dismissed by the Court of Appeal. Steyn LJ said[163]:

> 'If it be accepted that Parliament considered it necessary for the protection of public health and safety to impose, subject to the defence of reasonable practicability, absolute criminal liability, it would drive a juggernaut through the legislative scheme if corporate employers could avoid criminal liability where the potentially harmful event is committed by someone who is not the directing mind of the company...That would emasculate the legislation.'

[4.055] A corporation will occasionally be *vicariously* liable for the crimes of its employees and agents committed within the scope of their employment where a natural person would similarly be vicariously liable. Although at common law there is not generally any vicarious liability for criminal acts[164], a company may be made vicariously liable for public nuisance at common law[165], or indeed where a statute provides for vicarious criminal liability[166]. Where the offence for which the company is to be made vicariously liable is a crime of strict liability the company may easily be found guilty[167]. The essential prerequisite is that the offence concerns an activity such as 'selling', 'offering' or 'using' which falls within the scope of the employee's or agent's activities[168]. Where the company is to be made vicariously liable for an offence which *does* require a *mens rea* to be proved - such as intent to defraud the Revenue[169] - the courts will impose liability provided that the *mens rea* in question is not so personal to the perpetrator as to break the link between the company and its employee or agent[170]. Thus, in *R v Cory Brothers & Co*[171], Finlay J quashed an indictment against a limited company which contained a count of manslaughter, partly, it seems, because the offence was too personal to the individual perpetrator to be attributed to the company. However, *in R v ICR Haulage Ltd*[172], Stable J pointed out that this was a branch of the law which had developed and, if the matter came before the courts today, the result might well be different[173].

---

[163] [1995] 1 WLR 1356 at 1362–1363.

[164] *Tesco Supermarkets Ltd v Natrass* [1972] 2 AC 153 at 199, per Diplock LJ.

[165] *R v Great North of England Railway Company* (1846) 9 QB 315.

[166] *Griffiths v Studebakers Ltd* [1924] 1 KB 102.

[167] *R v Birmingham and Gloucester Railway Co* (1841) 2 QB 47; *R v Great North of England Railway Co* (1846) 2 Cox CC 70.

[168] See *Pearks, Dunston & Tee Ltd v Ward* [1902] 2 KB 1; *Tesco Stores Ltd v Brent London Borough Council* [1993] 2 All ER 718.

[169] *Mousell v London & North Western Railway Co* [1917] 2 KB 836.

[170] Where the company is found personally criminally liable, the individual perpetrators may also be found liable as secondary parties: *McMahon v Murtagh* [1982] ILRM 342; *DPP v Roberts* [1987] IR 268.

[171] *R v Cory Brothers & Co* [1927] 1 KB 810.

[172] *R v ICR Haulage Ltd* [1944] KB 551.

[173] [1944] KB 551 at 556. In *R v P&O European Ferries (Dover) Ltd* (1991) 93 Cr App R 72 it was accepted that a company may be personally liable for manslaughter. See further Law Reform Commission of Ireland, *Consultation Paper on Corporate Homicide* (2002).

[4.056] A corporation will be *personally*, as opposed to vicariously, liable for criminal activity where the criminal act and the state of mind of a controlling officer or officers can be identified or attributed to the corporation in the same way as the tortious acts and intent of controlling officers can be attributed to a company[174]. As Denning LJ explained in *HL Bolton (Engineering) Ltd v TJ Graham & Sons Ltd*[175]:

> 'A company may in many ways be likened to a human body. They have a brain and nerve centre which control what they do. They also have hands which hold the tools and act in accordance with directions from the centre. Some of the people in the company are mere servants and agents who are nothing more than hands to do the work and cannot be said to represent the mind or will. Others are directors and managers who represent the directing mind and will of the company, and control what they do. The state of mind of these managers is the state of mind of the company and is treated by the law as such.'

In the Canadian Supreme Court in *Canadian Dredge & Dock Co Ltd v R*[176], Estey J put the principle thus:

> 'The identity doctrine merges the board of directors, the managing director, the superintendent, the manager or anyone else delegated by the board of directors to whom is delegated the governing executive authority of the corporation, and the conduct of any of the merged entities is thereby attributed to the corporation.'

The courts often encounter what is considered by many to be difficulty in applying the 'identification doctrine' to find the 'directing mind and will of the company.' The problem, if it be such, is that not every person who exercises some managerial discretion can be said to control the company. Thus, in *Tesco Supermarkets Ltd v Natrass*[177], where the company was charged with an offence under the Trade Descriptions Act 1978 (UK), it was held not to be personally liable since the commission of the offence was due to the act or default of a branch supermarket manager, of which the company employed hundreds, ie the branch manager was the hands, and not the brains, of the company. Similar difficulty was encountered in *R v P & O European Ferries (Dover)*[178], a prosecution arising out of the capsize of the car ferry 'Herald of Free Enterprise' at Zeebrugge, when the assistant bosun and the chief officer were found not to be sufficiently high-up in the management hierarchy of the company for their carelessness to be held against the company. Who then is high-up enough to think and act as the company? In *Tesco Supermarkets Ltd*, Lord Reid said:

---

[174] See para **[4.048]**.

[175] *HL Bolton (Engineering) Ltd v TJ Graham & Sons Ltd* [1957] 1 QB 159 at 173.

[176] *Canadian Dredge & Dock Co Ltd v R* (1985) 19 DLR (4d) 314 at 336–337.

[177] *Tesco Supermarkets Ltd v Natrass* [1972] AC 153.

[178] *R v P & O European Ferries (Dover)* (1991) 93 Cr App R 72. The company had been slated in an official inquiry arising out of the disaster as having been 'infected with the disease of sloppiness' from top to bottom: Sheen, *The Merchant Shipping Act 1894, MV Herald of Free Enterprise, Report of Court* No 8074 (1987), para 14.1 Similar difficulty was encountered in the prosecution of Great Western Trains Company for manslaughter following the Southall rail crash in England in which seven persons lost their lives. No member of senior management could be identified as having had the requisite gross negligence to fix the company with liability for manslaughter: see *Attorney General's Reference (No 2 of 1999)* [2000] QB 796.

> 'Normally the board of directors, the managing director and perhaps other superior officers of a company carry out functions of management and speak and act as the company. Their subordinates do not.'[179]

Viscount Dilhorne felt that the person should be one who:

> '...is in actual control of the operations of a company or part of them and who is not responsible to another person in the company for the manner in which he discharges his duties in the sense of being under others.'[180]

Lords Diplock and Pearson felt that only persons drawing their authority from the memorandum of association (whether directly, or indirectly through the positive sanction of the board of directors or the general meeting) could be said to represent the will of the corporation. Lord Diplock identified them as:

> '...those natural persons who by the memorandum and articles of association or as a result of action taken by the directors or by the company in general meeting pursuant to the articles are entrusted with the exercise of the powers of the company.'[181]

On this approach the person who will be identified as representing the company must be a *directive* rather than an *executive* employee or agent of the company[182]. But the exact limits of this are uncertain. An uncontroversial case is *DPP v Kent and Sussex Contractors Ltd*[183], where a transport manager knowingly produced a false return under certain Defence Regulations in order to acquire petrol coupons. The Divisional Court held that there was ample evidence that the company had done the act in question through the only person who could act or speak or think for it. That decision was approved in *R v ICR Haulage Ltd*[184], where a company and nine other persons were convicted of common law conspiracy to defraud, it being held that the fraudulent acts of the managing director were the fraudulent acts of the company. The conspiracy was thus between the company, acting through its managing director, and the nine others.

A more controversial case, however, is *Moore v I Bresler Ltd*[185], where a company was convicted of making certain returns in respect of UK purchase tax, which were false in material particulars, with intent to deceive contrary to the Finance (No 2) Act 1940 (UK). The returns were physically made by the company secretary and the sales manager of a branch of the company in their own interests and with the intention of defrauding the company itself. Viscount Caldecote LCJ found that[186]:

> 'These two men were important officials of the company, and when they made statements and rendered returns which were proved in this case, they were clearly making those statements and giving those returns as the officers of the company, the proper officers to make those returns. Their acts, therefore, as indeed the Recorder seems to have been

[179] [1972] AC 153 at 171.
[180] [1972] AC 153 at 187.
[181] [1972] AC 153 at 200.
[182] Glanville Williams, *Criminal Law, The General Part* (1953), p 857.
[183] *DPP v Kent and Sussex Contractors Ltd* [1944] 1 KB 146.
[184] *R v ICR Haulage Ltd* [1944] KB 551.
[185] *Moore v I Bresler Ltd* [1944] 2 All ER 515.
[186] [1944] 2 All ER 515 at 517.

> prepared to agree, were the acts of the company. It is only because, for some reason which I am not able to fathom, he thinks that they have converted the goods of the company and made them their own and so acted without authority, that the Recorder came to the conclusion that the appeal ought to be allowed. How he came to base his decision upon the fallacious reasoning contained in his opinion, if I may say so with great respect to him, I do not know. It is sufficient for us, I think, to say that he went wrong on a point of law and on the facts stated in this case these two people acting as officers of the company made the company liable for the offence which was committed.'

The decision has been heavily criticised as going too far[187]. In *Canadian Dredge & Dock Co Ltd v R*[188], Estey J observed:

> 'Where the corporation benefited or was intended to be benefited from the fraudulent or criminal activities of the directing mind, the rationale for the identification rule holds. Where the delegate of the corporation has turned against his principal, the rationale fades away.'

Nevertheless, the acts at least involved the company secretary. *Kent and Sussex Contractors*[189] may, on another reading, appear more doubtful since that case involved merely a transport manager.

A practical consequence of the identification doctrine is that it is far easier to convict small closely-held companies than it is to convict larger ones having diffuse organisational structures. The outcome of the *P&O* case[190], for example, seems to contrast starkly with that of *R v Kite and OLL Ltd*[191], where an outdoor leisure company was convicted of manslaughter for the death of a canoeist during a negligently-managed canoeing expedition. The company was essentially a one-man operation, and the company's liability was established automatically upon his conviction for manslaughter in connection with the same events since he was its managing director and directing mind and will - its 'brains' *and* its 'hands'. Though such outcomes in the case of smaller companies may appear at first unjust, it should not be overlooked, however, that larger companies avoid conviction in similar circumstances because no crime has been committed *by the corporation*. Though much attention has of late been given to devising mechanisms whereby larger corporations might nonetheless be convicted in such circumstances, one may ask whether the better approach would be to remove corporate criminal liability for the smaller corporation where little seems to be gained by making the corporation liable?

[4.057] The narrow focus of the identification doctrine may be contrasted with the broader principles of attribution which have been developed since *Tesco* by the English Courts to deal with statutory offences by corporations. In *Re Supply of Ready Mixed*

---

187 Glanville Williams, *Criminal Law, The General Part* (1953), p 859; Welch 62 LQR 345 at p 360.

188 *Canadian Dredge & Dock Co Ltd v R* (1985) 19 DLR (4d) 314.

189 *DPP v Kent and Sussex Contractors* [1944] 1 KB 146.

190 *P&O case* (1991) 93 Cr App R 72.

191 *R v Kite and OLL Ltd* Winchester Crown Court, 8 December 1994, The Independent, 9 December, 1994.

Concrete (No 2)[192] the House of Lords found companies to be in contempt of court when their employees implemented anti-competitive practices in breach of injunctions against the company and the Restrictive Practices Act 1976 (UK). The Law Lords held that the employees were carrying on the business of the company in the course of their employment, and liability would attach despite instructions from senior management - the directing mind and will - not to engage in such practices.

A similar approach was adopted by the Privy Council in *Meridian Global Funds Management Asia Ltd v Securities Commission*[193] where a company was convicted for failing to issue a notice disclosing a substantial shareholding, contrary to New Zealand securities legislation. The shares were acquired by employees acting on behalf of the company, but without the knowledge of the board of directors and the managing director. Lord Hoffmann held that where the 'primary' principles of attribution of responsibility, such as those derived from the company's constitution or implied by company law, would defeat the intended application of a particular provision to companies, it is necessary for the courts to devise a special rule of attribution which will give effect to the provision[194]. What that rule should be depends in each case upon an interpretation that is appropriate to the offence involved and the policies behind it. In the instant case, the rule of attribution should not require consideration of whether the board and managing director knew of the infringements, since such an interpretation would defer any enforceable reporting obligation until senior executives became aware.

Meridian was considered significant in the law relating to corporate criminal liability not merely because it involved a displacement of the identification principle in favour of a broader approach in cases where statutory provisions are concerned, but because the purposive approach to attribution gave recognition to the complexities of diffuse management structures and the fact that corporations do not always operate on a purely hierarchical or vertical model[195]. Its promise was short-lived, however: in *Attorney General's Reference (No 2 of 1999)*[196] the Court of Appeal firmly rejected the argument that Meridian admitted of any principle of attribution other than the identification doctrine in the general criminal liability of corporations. Rose J, speaking for the court, said that 'Lord Hoffmann's speech in *Meridian*...is a re-statement, not an abandonment, of existing principles.'[197]

[4.058] While it has been held that a company may be guilty in conspiring with others[198], the English courts have held that the company cannot conspire with the person who

---

[192] *Re Supply of Ready Mixed Concrete (No 2)* [1995] 1 AC 456. See, further, Chapter 6, *Corporate Civil Litigation*, para **[6.079]**.

[193] *Meridian Global Funds Management Asia Ltd v Securities Commission* [1995] 2 AC 500.

[194] [1995] 2 AC 500 at 507.

[195] See eg Gray, 'Company Directors and Ignorance of the Law' (1996) 17 Co Law; Grantham, 'Corporate Knowledge: Identification or Attribution?' (1996) 59 MLR 732; and Robert-Tissot, 'A Fresh Insight into the Corporate Criminal Mind: Meridian Global Funds Management Asia Ltd v Securities Commission' (1996) 17 Co Law 99.

[196] *Attorney General's Reference (No 2 of 1999)* [2000] QB 796.

[197] [2000] QB 796 at 814.

[198] *DPP v Kent and Sussex Contractors Ltd* [1944] 1 KB 146.

represents the controlling mind and will of the company, because conspiracy requires two minds. In *R v McDonnell*[199], Nield J observed:

> '...in the particular circumstances here, where the sole responsible person in the company is the defendant himself, it would not be right to say that there were two persons or two minds. If it were otherwise, I feel it would offend against the basic concept of a conspiracy, namely, an agreement of two or more to do an unlawful act and I think it would be artificial to take the view that the company, although it is clearly a separate legal entity, can be regarded here as a separate person or a separate mind, in view of the admitted fact that this defendant acts alone so far as these companies are concerned...'

That case was concerned with criminal conspiracy. The Irish Supreme Court, however, has taken the opposite view as far as civil conspiracy is concerned, and it would seem logical that the same view could be applied to criminal conspiracy[200]. This view was expressed in *Taylor v Smyth*[201], where the question was whether Mr Smyth could conspire with companies he controlled and in which he was the only active participant. McCarthy J noted that *R v McDonnell* had not been extended to civil cases, and then went on to hold that Mr Smyth had in fact and in law conspired with his companies. He said:

> 'In principle, it would seem invidious, for example, that the assets of a limited company should not be liable to answer for a conspiracy where its assets had been augmented as a result of an action alleged to constitute the conspiracy. Essentially, it would be permitting the company to lift its corporate veil if and when it suits...I see no reason why the fact that one individual controls the company of limited liability should give immunity from suit to both that company and that individual in the case of an established arrangement for the benefit of both company and individual to the detriment of others. If such were the case, it would follow that a like arrangement to the advantage of two companies of limited liability, both controlled by the same individual, would give an equal immunity from suit to both companies and so on.'

(iv) Constitutional rights and duties

[4.059] In the first edition[202] it was noted that, in contrast to some other jurisdictions[203], the Irish courts have been markedly reluctant to accord corporations personal rights under the Constitution - largely because those rights are an emanation of Natural Law, which is a system of rights derived from man's inherent humanity[204]. The landscape has changed[205] somewhat since then. The reluctance remains in respect of certain rights, such as the right to equality, which is guaranteed by Article 40.1 of Bunreacht na hÉireann, which provides:

> 'All citizens shall, as human persons, be held equal before the law. This shall not be held to mean that the State shall not in its enactments have due regard to differences of capacity, physical and moral, and of social function.'

---

199 *R v Mc Donnell* [1966] 1 QB 233.

200 See MacCann, 'Companies and Conspiracy' (1990) ILT 197.

201 *Taylor v Smyth* [1991] IR 142.

202 Courtney, *The Law of Private Companies* (1st edn, 1994), para 3.054.

203 See 'Constitutional Rights of the Corporate Person' (1982) 91 Yale LJ 1641.

204 See generally, Kelly, *The Irish Constitution* (3rd edn, 1994) (Hogan and Whyte, eds), pp 671 *ff*.

205 See para **[4.060]**.

Corporations are considered by the courts to be unable to rely on the constitutional protection of this right since they are not human persons; as Walsh J observed in *Quinn's Supermarket Ltd v Attorney General*[206]:

> '...under no possible construction of the Constitutional guarantee could a body corporate or any entity but a human being be considered to be a human person for the purposes of this provision.' [207]

The same can be said of the right to communicate, which has been held to exist by virtue of man's human personality[208] and cannot be enjoyed by corporations. Certain other constitutional rights are of no personal relevance to corporations; for instance the right to *habeas corpus*[209]; the right to inviolability of the dwelling[210]; the unenumerated rights to marry and found a family[211], to marital privacy[212], and the right to bodily integrity[213]. There seems to be no bar, however, on the corporation acting to protect such constitutional rights *of others*, once it is shown to have sufficient locus standi[214].

[4.060] It does not automatically follow, however, that the 'inherent humanity' approach should extend to all personal rights guaranteed by the Constitution. An area of particular concern in this regard is the personal right to property. Article 40.3.2° of Bunreacht na hÉireann provides:

> 'The State shall, in particular, by its laws protect as best it may from unjust attack and, in the case of injustice done, vindicate the life, person, good name and property rights of every citizen.'

Prior to 1969, the ability of bodies corporate to rely on these provisions was not questioned in decisions in which the constitutionality of legislation was challenged by such bodies[215], though in that year O'Keeffe P adverted to the question in *East Donegal Co-Operative Livestock Mart Ltd v Attorney General*[216] merely as follows:

[206] *Quinn's Supermarket Ltd v Attorney General* [1972] IR 1.

[207] [1972] IR 1 at p 14. In *Abbey Films Ltd v Attorney General* [1981] IR 158, a company alleged that certain legislation was an unconstitutional breach of the equality guarantee because it required a company to retain a solicitor whereas individual citizens could appear in person. The Supreme Court, sidestepping the issue of whether the company could rely on that guarantee, held that even if it could, the differing treatment would be justified according to differences in capacity and social function.

[208] *Attorney General v Paperlink Ltd* [1984] ILRM 343.

[209] Article 40.4.2°.

[210] Article 40.5. 'Dwelling' appears to refer only to the living quarters of a human person. See *The People (Attorney General) v O'Brien* [1965] IR 142; *DPP v Corrigan* [1986] IR 190; *O'Mahony v Shields* (22 February 1988, unreported), High Court.

[211] *Murray v Attorney General* [1985] IR 532.

[212] *McGee v Attorney General* [1974] IR 284.

[213] *Ryan v Attorney General* [1965] IR 294.

[214] Eg *Quinn's Supermarket Ltd v Attorney General* [1972] IR 1; *Educational Company of Ireland v Fitzpatrick* [1961] IR 323.

[215] *Attorney General v Southern Industrial Trust* (1957) 94 ILTR 161; *Educational Company of Ireland Ltd. v Fitzpatrick (No 2)* [1961] IR 345.

[216] *East Donegal Co-Operative Livestock Mart Ltd v Attorney General* [1970] IR 317.

> 'Artificial persons may possibly not be entitled to rely on the constitutional guarantees...(although they have been held to be so entitled in the United States).'

In *Private Motorists' Provident Society v Attorney General*[217] Carroll J reasoned that the property rights guaranteed by Article 40.3.2° are incapable of being enjoyed by corporations since those rights are, she reasoned, in turn derived from Article 43 of the Constitution, which recognises that 'man, in virtue of his rational being, has the natural right, antecedent to positive law, to the private ownership of external goods' and corporations do not enjoy such inherent humanity[218]. The Supreme Court in that case was less unequivocal, and did not express any opinion as to whether the corporation, as a creature of positive law, enjoyed the constitutional guarantees accorded to citizens, but Carroll J's reasoning was later applied by Murphy J in the High Court in *Chestvale Properties Ltd v Glackin*[219].

The decision in the *Private Motorist's* case gave rise to the use of an artificial practice to circumvent the issue. In that case this was done by joining a member of the corporation as a co-plaintiff, who, as a natural person and a citizen, could maintain an action on the grounds that *his* constitutionally guaranteed property rights constituted by his membership of the corporation would be indirectly affected if the corporation were injured. This indirect means of protecting the corporation and its members against unconstitutional attack was open to criticism[220], however, and appeared to contradict the approach of the courts in respect of the invocation of other constitutional rights by companies[221].

[4.061] Carroll J's doubts in *Private Motorists' Provident Society v Attorney General*[222] about the ability of corporations to invoke the constitutionally guaranteed property rights in Article 40.3.2° have since been challenged by Keane J in the High Court in the 1995 case of *Iarnród Éireann v Ireland*[223]. In that case the learned judge reasoned, following a number of Supreme Court decisions[224], that the property rights guaranteed by Article 40.3.2° are not derived from Article 43, since the latter is concerned with the

---

217 *Private Motorists' Provident Society v Attorney General* [1983] IR 339.

218 [1983] IR 339 at 349.

219 *Chestvale Properties Ltd v Glackin* [1993] 3 IR 35 at 45. In *MMDS Television Ltd and Suir Nore Relays Ltd v South East Community Deflector Association Ltd and Kirwan* (8 April, 1997, unreported), High Court, an application for an interlocutory injunction relating to a planning matter, the argument was raised before Carroll J that the plaintiffs, being corporate bodies, had no constitutional rights. The learned judge did not consider the issue, however, deciding in the plaintiff's favour on other grounds. See also *Carrigaline Community TV v Minister for Transport Energy and Communication* [1997] 1 ILRM 241, [1996] DULJ 139 (Keane J); *Cork Communications Ltd and Kerr v Dennehy* (4 October 1993, unreported), High Court (Lynch J).

220 See Courtney, *The Law of Private Companies* (1st edn, 1994), para 3.056. Also Ussher, *Company Law in Ireland* (1986), pp 54–56.

221 See para **[4.061]**.

222 *Private Motorists' Provident Society v Attorney General* [1983] IR 339.

223 [1996] 3 IR 321.

224 The learned judge relied on the Supreme Court's judgments in *Blake v Attorney General* [1982] IR 117 and *Attorney General v Southern Industiral Trust Ltd* (1957) 94 ILTR 161.

institution of private property (the sanctity of which institution the State guarantees only to human persons). He said[225]:

> 'It is, accordingly, clear that the rationale on which Carroll J based her rejection of the locus standi of the corporate plaintiff in *Private Motorists' Provident Society v Attorney General* [1983] IR 339 can no longer be supported. In contrast to Article 40, s. 1 and Article 43, Article 40, s. 3, sub-s. 2, in enumerating the rights which are thereby guaranteed, refers simply to "the property rights of every citizen". If the decision in *PMPS* is to be supported, it must be on the ground that the "property rights of every citizen" thereby guaranteed are confined to rights enjoyed by the citizens as human persons.
>
> Undoubtedly, some at least of the rights enumerated in Article 40, s. 3, sub-s. 2 - the rights to life and liberty - are of no relevance to corporate bodies and other artificial legal entities. Property rights are, however, in a different category. Not only are corporate bodies themselves capable in law of owning property, whether movable or immovable, tangible or intangible. The "property" referred to clearly includes shares in companies formed under the relevant companies' legislation which was already a settled feature of the legal and commercial life of this country at the time of the enactment of the Constitution. There would accordingly be a spectacular deficiency in the guarantee to every citizen that his or her property rights will be protected against "unjust attack", if such bodies were incapable in law of being regarded as "citizens", at least for the purposes of this Article, and if it was essential for the shareholders to abandon the protection of limited liability to which they are entitled by law in order to protect, not merely their own rights as shareholders but also the property rights of the corporate entity itself, which are in law distinct from the rights of its members.
>
> Article 43 undoubtedly treats the general right of private property, the abolition of which in its entirety is expressly prohibited, as one inhering in "man in virtue of his rational being" and, in that sense, as being "antecedent to positive law", including the Constitution itself. But it does not necessarily follow that the property rights of the individual citizens which are protected against 'unjust attack' by Article 40, s 3 are confined to rights enjoyed by human persons. Had the framers of the Constitution wished to confine the comprehensive guarantee in Article 40, s 3. in that manner, there was nothing to prevent them including a similar qualification to that contained in Article 40, section 1.'

The learned judge went on to reveal the deficiencies of the approach commonly adopted since the *Private Motorists'* case of joining a human co-plaintiff[226]:

> 'The present case demonstrates that the restriction on the property rights of the citizen which would logically result from confining the protection of Article 40, s 3 to individual citizens would not necessarily be eased in every case by joining the shareholders as plaintiffs in the proceedings. If this case were to depend on the *locus standi* of the second plaintiff, it would appear that his property rights as an individual arising out of his ownership of one share in the first plaintiff are of so nominal a nature as not to afford him any such locus standi. It is unnecessary at this point to consider how many other corporate bodies would be in a similarly impotent state, although they would clearly include some in the private sector, such as companies limited by guarantee. It is sufficient to say that, although the strategy adopted in *Private Motorists' Provident Society v Attorney General* [1983] IR 339 of joining the shareholder as a plaintiff was accepted by the Supreme Court

---

[225] *Iarnród Éireann v Ireland* [1996] 3 IR 321 at 344–345.

[226] [1996] 3 IR 321 at 345–346

> as obviating any constitutional difficulty that might have arisen in that case, it is of critical importance that the Court expressly refrained from holding that the corporate plaintiff had no locus standi. In the result, I consider that I am not bound to hold that where, as here, it is not possible to make effective use of such a strategy, the claim of a corporate plaintiff must necessarily fail.'

Keane J concluded that the expression 'every citizen' in Article 40.3.2º is not confined to citizens in their capacity as human beings, and that artificial legal entities must also be protected by the laws of the State against unjust attacks on their property rights. It is peculiarly the role of the courts to vindicate the property rights of such entities in accordance with Article 40.3.2º.

[4.062] The Supreme Court in *Iarnród Éireann v Ireland*[227] declined, however, to consider the locus standi issue, and it remains to be seen whether that court will ultimately favour the approach adopted by Carroll J or that proffered by Keane J[228]. The appeal of the latter is that it gives protection to the constitutional rights of the members of companies with due regard to the manner in which they have lawfully chosen to exercise them. It further accords with the approach of the courts in relation to other constitutional rights guaranteed by Article 40 of Bunreacht na hÉireann.

[4.063] The other personal rights guaranteed by Article 40, including the *unenumerated rights* judicially identified as emanating from Article 40.3.1º[229], are conferred simply on 'citizens' without expressly requiring that the citizens be human persons. Are these rights conferred on corporations? [230] It has been argued[231] that if this were so it would be to make too odd and arbitrary a distinction between those rights and the others protected by the Article[232]. The courts have recognised, however, that corporations may invoke such rights.

---

227 *Iarnród Éireann v Ireland* [1986] 3 IR 370.

228 Keane J's reasoning was applied by the High Court in *Lancefort Ltd v An Bord Pleanála, Ireland, Attorney General and Treasury Holdings Ltd (Notice Party)* [1997] 1 ILRM 508 (Morris J); *An Blascaod Mór Teoranta v Commissioners of Public Works in Ireland and Minister for the Arts Culture and the Gaéltacht* (27 February 1998, unreported), High Court (Budd J); and *Lancefort Limited v An Bord Pleanala, Ireland and the Attorney General and Treasury Holdings Limited (Notice Party)* (12 March 1998, unreported), High Court (McGuinness J).

229 See generally Casey, *Constitutional Law in Ireland* (3rd edn, 2000).

230 It may be argued that a corporation is a 'citizen' since it is capable of having a nationality: see, for example, *Daimler Co Ltd v Continental Tyre and Rubber Co (Great Britain) Ltd* [1916] 2 AC 307.

231 By Ussher, *Company Law in Ireland* (1986), pp 53–54.

232 In support of his submission, Ussher cites Costello J in *Attorney General v Paperlink* [1984] ILRM 373 at 385, where the learned judge advised that the courts should not, in interpreting the Constitution, 'place the same significance on differences in language used in two succeeding sub-paragraphs as would, for example, be placed on differently drafted sub-sections of a Finance Act. A purposive, rather than a literal approach...is appropriate.' See also *Cafolla v Ireland* [1986] ILRM 177 at 183.

The personal unenumerated[233] right of access to the courts[234] was invoked by a company in *Bula Ltd v Tara Mines Ltd*[235], where Murphy J rejected the defendant's argument that the plaintiff (a body corporate) should make out a prima facie case before being granted an order for the inspection of the defendant's mining activities, saying:

> 'It is the right of citizens under the Constitution to have access to the courts for the resolution of justiciable controversies...If, then, a citizen is free to institute proceedings he must be at least equally free to invoke the procedures of the court to present his case properly. In my view the right of a party to seek and obtain an order for inspection (or indeed an order for discovery which may be equally burdensome) is in no way dependent upon the court being satisfied as to the strength of the plaintiff's case.'[236]

Again, in *Society for the Protection of Unborn Children (Ireland) Ltd v Coogan*[237], where the plaintiff was a company limited by guarantee formed with the object of protecting human life, particularly the life of the unborn, the Supreme Court held that the company had sufficient *locus standi* to commence proceedings to enforce compliance with the provisions of Article 40.3.3° of the Constitution (which deal with the right to life of the unborn). Walsh J said:

> 'One of the fundamental political rights of the citizen under the Constitution, indeed one of the most valued of his rights, is that of access to the courts...The citizen's right of access to the courts in the appropriate case will include not only access in defence of his own personal and direct rights which are being threatened by the Executive or by his fellow citizens, but also the right to seek to restrain the acts of the Executive or other persons from breaching the constraints imposed by the Constitution if the public interest requires that such breaches or attempted breaches should be restrained.'[238]

The fact that the 'citizen' in this case happened to be a limited company did not prevent the court from finding that it had a constitutional right of access to the courts.

[4.064] The mere existence of a constitutional right of access to the courts does not guarantee that the corporate constitutional litigant will have *locus standi* in any given case: it must further be shown that the corporation has a *bona fide* interest to invoke the constitutional right. This was explained in the context of the corporate constitutional litigant by Walsh J in the Supreme Court in *Society for the Protection of Unborn Children (Ireland) Ltd v Coogan*[239]:

> 'In a case such as this the essential question is have the plaintiffs a *bona fide* interest to invoke the protection of the courts to vindicate the constitutional right [of the unborn] in question. It would be an ironic situation if our law, which permits a citizen to bring a petty thief before the courts even though the citizen himself is not a victim of the theft, could yet

---

233 First recognised in *Macauley v Minister for Posts and Telegraphs* [1966] IR 345.

234 See *SEE Co Ltd v Public Lighting Services Ltd* [1987] ILRM 255 at 258. But the right of a company to appear in court, as opposed to its right of access to the courts, is restricted, see Chapter 6, *Corporate Civil Litigation*, para **[6.061]**.

235 *Bula Ltd v Tara Mines Ltd* [1987] IR 85.

236 [1987] IR 85 at 92–93.

237 *Society for the Protection of Unborn Children (Ireland) Ltd v Coogan* [1989] IR 738.

238 [1989] IR 738.

239 [1989] IR 738.

deem the citizen unqualified to invoke the court's protection to prevent the destruction of the constitutional right to life.'

In *Lancefort Limited v An Bord Pleanála, Ireland and the Attorney General and Treasury Holdings Limited*[240], a limited company was formed to pursue judicial review proceedings generally and, more particularly, to challenge the constitutionality of the Local Government (Planning and Development) Act 1976, s 14(8), while at the same time affording the true applicants a shield against an award of costs. McGuinness J held that while the corporate plaintiff enjoyed locus standi to pursue a judicial review application in respect of a planning decision, it lacked locus standi on the constitutional issue:

> '...I find the learned Keane J's survey and analysis [in the *Iarnród Eireann* case] both impressive and convincing and I would accept that in principle a corporate body, or juristic person, can possess *locus standi* to impugn legislation by invoking the relevant provisions of the Constitution.
>
> However, that is not the end of the matter. The second question then arises as to whether the Applicant in the present proceedings has "sufficient interest" in the proceedings in the sense used in *Cahill v Sutton* [1980] IR 269 to acquire the necessary *locus standi*...
>
> In the instant case the Applicant seeks to rely on Article 43 of the Constitution. While in its Statement of Grounds the Applicant relies on the reference in Article 43.2 to the concepts of social justice and the common good, this must be seen in the context of the main purpose of the Article which is to uphold the right of private property and to forbid its abolition. The Applicant is a company limited by guarantee with effectively no assets. It maintains no commercial or profit making activity which could enable it to acquire property. It owns no property in the area affected by the proposed development - or indeed anywhere else. It was not an objector to the planning permission at the time nor did it take any part in the oral hearing by the inspector appointed by An Bord Pleanála. It was not even in existence at the time of An Bord Pleanála's decision on 11 December, 1996. At the time of An Bord Pleanála's decision, therefore, the Applicant was neither a property owner in the area affected by the development nor an upholder of social justice and the common good which was affected by that decision. The applicant cannot be compared with SPUC in the *SPUC v Coogan* case: it is by no means impossible that a Plaintiff whose actual property interests were affected by this or any other decision of An Bord Pleanála could mount a challenge to the impugned section. In the context of social justice and the common good there were a number of individual objectors to both the planning authority's decision and to An Bord Pleanála's decision who could as Plaintiffs challenge the Section.
>
> The Applicant also cannot be compared with Iarnród Éireann, the corporate plaintiff in the case of that name. Iarnród Éireann was definitely and seriously financially affected by the legislation which it sought to challenge.
>
> It does not appear to me that the Applicant has established the proper interest to provide it with *locus standi* to challenge section 14(8) of the 1976 Act.'

The use of the corporate form exclusively as a means of shielding constitutional litigants from potential awards of costs may, consequently, result in *locus standi* being denied.

---

[240] *Lancefort Limited v An Bord Pleanala, Ireland and the Attorney General and Treasury Holdings Ltd* (12 March 1998, unreported), High Court (McGuinness J).

[4.065] The constitutional right to freedom of expression under Article 40.6.1°.i has also been invoked by companies to allow the dissemination of factual information in appropriate circumstances. The matter of the company's expression rights was skirted in *Attorney General v Paperlink Ltd*[241], where the constitutional claim was maintained by the directors and members of the company, it being accepted that the company had no constitutionally guaranteed personal rights upon which to found a cause of action. But in *Attorney General for England and Wales v Brandon Book Publishers Ltd*[242], Carroll J held that the defendant had a constitutional right under Article 40.6.1°.i to publish information which does not involve any breach of copyright provided that the public interest in this jurisdiction is not affected by the publication and there was no breach of confidentiality.

[4.066] Whatever a corporation's constitutional rights, there is no doubt that the corporation, as a creature of positive law, is obliged to observe constitutional *duties*[243]. Breach of the duty may even give rise to an award of compensation against the company. *Thus, in Meskell v CIÉ*[244], where the defendant company made membership of a trade union a condition of employment, the company was held to have breached the plaintiff employee's constitutional right of dissociation[245], and was made liable to pay such damages as might, upon inquiry, be proved to have been sustained by him.

(v) Legal rights and duties

[4.067] As a legal person, the corporation is capable of enjoying rights and being the subject of duties and obligations - just as natural persons can. Indeed, for the purposes of legislation, bodies corporate are treated as falling within the definition of 'person' wherever that word appears in a statute, unless the context otherwise requires[246]. Where a statute does not clearly stipulate whether its provisions are to apply to companies, the courts will consider the general background and purpose of the legislation in question[247]. Certain statutes, however, prohibit companies from acting in situations where natural persons are permitted to act. The Companies Acts 1963-2001 prohibit bodies corporate from acting as examiners[248], liquidators[249], receivers[250] or auditors[251]; and other statutes forbid them from providing services as solicitors[252], doctors or dentists[253], or veterinary

---

241 *Attorney General v Paperlink Ltd* [1984] ILRM 373.

242 *Attorney General for England and Wales v Brandon Books Publishers Ltd* [1986] IR 579.

243 See eg *Irish Times Ltd and Others v Ireland* [1998] 1 IR 359; *Byrne v Judge Scally and Dublin Corporation* (12 October 2000, unreported), High Court (O'Caoimh J).

244 *Meskell v CIÉ* [1973] IR 121.

245 Which is a necessary corollary of the right to freedom of association under Article 40.6.1°.iii of Bunreacht na hÉireann: *Educational Company Ltd v Fitzpatrick (No 2)* [1961] IR 345.

246 Interpretation Act 1937, s 11(c).

247 See, for example, *R (Cottingham) v The Justices of Cork* [1906] 2 IR 415.

248 C(A)A 1990, s 28.

249 CA 1963, s 300.

250 CA 1963, s 314.

251 CA 1990, s 187(2)(g).

252 Solicitors Act 1954, s 64.

253 Medical Practitioners Act 1978, ss 59 and 61; Dentists Act 1985, s 52.

surgeons[254]. A certificate of personal fitness to operate bookmaking premises may not be held by a company[255].

(e) Privileges and obligations

[4.068] A consequence of gaining separate legal personality is that it may alter relations between the enterprise and the world at large - including the company's relations *vis-à-vis* its controllers. Consequently, a sole trader who incorporates his business may find himself to be an employee of the legal person he has created, and may thereby become entitled to avail of the statutory protection given to employees. A good illustration is *Lee v Lee's Air Farming Ltd*[256], in which Mr Lee, who held the beneficial interest in all of the shares in the defendant company, and who was also its sole governing director, was employed by it as a salaried pilot. When he was killed while flying on company work, his wife claimed compensation under the Worker's Compensation Act 1922 (New Zealand) as the widow of a 'worker' of the company. The Privy Council, applying *Salomon's* case, held that she should succeed. The company and Lee were separate legal persons, and the mere fact that Lee was governing director of the company should not preclude him from entering into a contract of service with it - even though, paradoxically, this duality of roles could lead to Lee, as governing director, giving orders to himself as an employee.

Reasoning similar to that applied in *Lee*'s case was employed recently by the English Court of Appeal in *Secretary of State for Trade and Industry v Bottrill*[257] to hold that the controlling shareholder director of a small insolvent company was entitled to redundancy payments under the Employment Rights Act 1996 (UK) despite the argument that as controlling shareholder he could have prevented his own dismissal. Lord Woolf MR added, however, that the courts should inquire into whether the company was established purely for the fraudulent motive of entitling the director to redundancy payments. The Master of the Rolls suggested that the size of the individual's shareholding should be taken into account as an indicator of whether such a motive existed. A literal application of this test could lead unfairly to the separate legal personality of small companies being ignored, and the benefits of Lee's case being denied[258].

It follows from *Lee*'s case that a controlling shareholder may maintain an action against the company where a winding up of the company would cause the breach of a service contract between the shareholder and the company. In *Fowler v Commercial Timber Co Ltd*[259] it was held that such an action for breach of contract would not be precluded by the fact that the shareholder had voted in favour of the winding up.

---

254 Veterinary Surgeons Act 1931, s 47.

255 Betting Act 1931, s 4(1). A natural person may, however, hold such a certificate as agent for the company: *McDonnell v Reid* [1987] IR 51.

256 *Lee v Lee's Air Farming Ltd* [1961] AC 12.

257 *Secretary of State for Trade and Industry v Bottrill* [2000] 1 All ER 915. Cf *Buchan v Secretary of State for Employment* [1997] BCC 145.

258 See Howell, 'Salomon under Attack', (2000) 21 Co Law 312.

259 *Fowler v Commercial Timber Co Ltd* [1930] 2 KB 1.

[4.069] Another good example of how the incorporation of a company may be used to gain a privilege which would have been unavailable to the individual shareholders is to be found in *Farrar v Farrars Ltd*[260]. In that case it was held that a mortgagee may exercise his power of sale by selling the property which forms the subject matter of the mortgage to a company of which he is the controlling shareholder - despite the rule that he may not sell the property to himself[261] or to an agent or nominee acting on his behalf[262].

[4.070] The separate legal personality of the company may also be relied upon effectively to avoid obligations which would otherwise fall on the controlling shareholders. However, it is advisable to tread warily, for the courts may find it necessary to disregard the separate personality of the company where incorporation is used fraudulently to evade existing legal obligations[263]. But where the legal relation does not amount to an obligation, or where the intention is to avoid *future* obligations, incorporation can be a successful avoidance mechanism. In *Roundabout Ltd v Beirne*[264] a limited company, 'Marian Park Inn Ltd', owned and operated a public house when, in May 1958, all of the staff joined a trade union. The controllers of the company, unwilling to operate with a unionised staff, caused the company to close the public house and to dismiss all the staff. The union, arguing that the closure was effected to force staff-members to leave the union, responded by placing a peaceful picket on the premises, something it was entitled to do under the Trade Disputes Act 1906. Meanwhile, the controllers of the company formed a second company, called 'Roundabout Ltd', of which they were permanent directors with a controlling interest in its shares. Roundabout Ltd then leased the public house from the first company. Three new non-union barmen were made directors of Roundabout Ltd, and it was they who carried out the day-to-day business of the public house when it opened for business three weeks after its closure. Since the new company had no employees (only barmen-directors, who, under the articles of association of the company, could be removed by the controllers at any time) it could not be classed as an 'employer'; consequently it could not be the subject of a trade dispute. The new company then sought an injunction against the union to restrain the picketers on the basis that the business was being conducted by a different legal person to that with which the ex-employees had a trade dispute. Dixon J, granting the injunction said:

> 'The new company is in law a distinct entity, as is the old company. Each company is what is known as a legal person. I have to regard the two companies as distinct in the same way as I would regard two distinct individuals. I must, therefore, proceed on the basis that a new and different person is now in occupation of the premises and carrying on business there.'

[4.071] It should be noted that the European Communities (Safeguarding of Employees' Rights on Transfer of Undertakings) Regulations 1980[265] automatically transfer any

---

260 *Farrar v Farrars Ltd* (1888) 40 Ch D 395.

261 *Henderson v Astwood* [1894] AC 150.

262 *Downes v Grazebrook* (1817) 3 Mer 200.

263 See Chapter 5, *Disregarding Separate Legal Personality*, para **[5.038]** *ff*.

264 *Roundabout Ltd v Beirne* [1959] IR 423.

265 SI 1980/303. See generally Kerr & Whyte, *Irish Trade Union Law* (1985), pp 158–159.

obligations arising under collective agreements entered into by the transferor to the transferee of a business undertaking. Incorporation may not, therefore, be used to evade obligations under collective agreements.

Limited liability

[4.072] Limited liability is an extremely significant consequence of incorporation, and one of the principal reasons why most businesses decide to incorporate in the first place. It must be stressed at the outset that it is only the members' liability which is limited: the company remains liable down to its last penny for all its debts and liabilities.

[4.073] By definition, the expression 'limited liability' connotes some form of liability. The expression is sometimes incorrectly used to describe the 'immunity' (which connotes no liability whatsoever) which members enjoy from direct liability to the company's creditors. As we have seen[266], the members of the company are not liable to the company's creditors in respect of the company's obligations, since the company's obligations are separate and distinct from those of its members[267]. This 'immunity' stems from the separate legal personality of the company, and as such, it exists regardless of whether the company is registered with or without limited liability. Clearly, then, it is not this immunity which the Companies Acts refer to when they speak of limited liability, though the immunity is, of course, a consequence of incorporation of paramount importance.

[4.074] What the expression 'limited liability' refers to in fact is the *liability* of the members towards the company, rather than towards the company's creditors. This liability is of statutory origin, and does *not* stem from the fact that the company is a separate legal person. Where the company is liable for its obligations to third parties, it is entitled to look to its members for a contribution to enable it to discharge its obligations. The limit to the members' liability to contribute to the company is stated in the company's memorandum, and it is calculated by reference 'to the amount, if any, unpaid on the shares respectively held by them.'[268] If the shareholders have additionally undertaken in the memorandum to guarantee the company, their liability is limited to the amount which they 'respectively thereby undertake to contribute to the assets of the company in the event of its being wound up.'[269] The extent of a shareholder's liability to contribute in a winding up is further regulated by CA 1963, s 207(1) which provides:

> 'In the event of a company being wound up, every present and past member shall be liable to contribute to the assets of the company to an amount sufficient for payment of its debts and liabilities, and the costs, charges and expenses of the winding up, and for the adjustment of the rights of the contributors among themselves...subject to the following qualifications:

---

[266] At para **[4.041]** *ff*.

[267] Statute and common law have intervened, however, to provide for situations in which the members' immunity from liability for corporate debts may be eroded, see Chapter 5, *Disregarding Separate Legal Personality*.

[268] CA 1963, s 5(2)(a).

[269] CA 1963, s 5(2)(b).

(a) a past member shall not be liable to contribute if he has ceased to be a member for one year or more before the commencement of the winding up;

(b) a past member shall not be liable to contribute in respect of any debt or liability of the company contracted after he ceased to be a member;

(c) a past member shall not be liable to contribute unless it appears to the court that the existing members are unable to satisfy the contributions required to be made by them in pursuance of this Act;

(d) in the case of a company limited by shares, no contribution shall be required from any member exceeding the amount, if any, unpaid on the shares in respect of which he is liable as a present or past member;...'[270]

The liability of shareholders to contribute to the assets of the company is thus limited to the amount, if any, unpaid on their shares. This liability exists both while the company is a going concern[271], and also continues where the company is being wound up. Where the liability is limited by guarantee in the memorandum of association, it is limited to the amount undertaken to be contributed in the guarantee - but the guarantor is not obliged to pay under the guarantee until the company is being wound up[272]. By way of contrast, where the company is registered as an unlimited company, the members' liability to contribute to the assets of the company is unlimited[273].

[4.075] It may be observed that limited liability is not logically a necessary attribute of separate legal personality but is, rather, a statutory development. In *Revenue Commissioners v Bank of Ireland*[274], Murnaghan J observed:

> 'There is at common law no liability upon the members of a body corporate in respect of the debts and liabilities of the body corporate, and such liability in respect of the corporate acts must be created by statute.'[275]

This principle was again to the fore in the English case of *Maclaine Watson v Department of Trade and Industry*[276], where Lord Templeman observed that[277]:

> '...by custom or by legislation the members of some corporations in some countries are not free from personal liability. But no such custom exists in the United Kingdom as a general rule and s 4 of the Partnership Act 1890, which preserves for a Scottish partnership some of the benefits of incorporation and some of the attributes of an unincorporated association, does not prove the existence of any general custom in any part of the United Kingdom that members of a corporation or of a body analogous to corporations shall be

---

270 Paragraphs (e), (f) and (g) of the subsection deal with companies limited by guarantee; policies of insurance; and dividends and profits due to a member, respectively. For an outline of the history leading to the introduction of limited liability to company law see Chapter 1, *The Private Company In Context*, para **[1.045]** *ff.*

271 See Chapter 15, *Shares and Membership*, para **[15.038]** *ff.*

272 CA 1963, s 207(1)(e).

273 Except as regards past members who ceased to be members over a year before the commencement of the winding up: CA 1963, s 207(1)(a).

274 *Revenue Commissioners v Bank of Ireland* [1925] 2 IR 90.

275 [1925] 2 IR 90 at 108.

276 *Maclaine Watson v Department of Trade and Industry* [1990] BCLC 102.

277 [1990] BCLC 102 at 108–109.

liable for the debts of the corporation. Parliament, of course, may provide that members of a corporation shall bear liability for or shall be bound to contribute directly or indirectly to payment of the debts of the corporation to a limited or an unlimited extent in accordance with express statutory provisions. The history of the Companies Acts illustrates the power of Parliament, if it pleases, to impose some liability on shareholders as a condition of the grant of incorporation.'

Transferability of interests

[4.076] One of the significant advantages of incorporation as a registered company is that the members' interests may easily be transferred. This is especially so where, as with the private company, the company has a share capital. The transfer and registration of shares is discussed in detail in Chapter 16, *Share Transfers in Private Companies*, so at this stage we may simply observe that a member's shares are items of his personal property[278], the transfer and registration of which in the transferee's name relieves the transferor of all[279] of his obligations to the company, and which places the transferee in the shoes of the transferor. The transfer of shares in a private company must, of course, be subject to restrictions on transfer and the public may not be invited to participate[280]. The significance of the ease of transfer of interests may be understood by contrasting it with the transfer of interests in a partnership or the transfer of a sole trader's interests. The transfer of a partner's interest does not entitle the person to whom the interest is transferred to interfere in the management or administration of the partnership business or affairs, or to require any accounts of the partnership transactions, or to inspect the partnership books[281]. The transferee of the transferring partner's interest is only entitled to receive the share of the profits to which the transferring partner would otherwise have been entitled[282]. Unless the partners have agreed otherwise, the transferee may only be admitted as a partner if all the other partners agree[283]. Notably, the transferring partner will continue to be liable for the obligations of the firm until the firm's creditors agree to release him[284].

The sole trader who wishes to transfer his interest will also encounter difficulty. Many of the existing obligations of the sole trader will be personal in nature and may not be easily transferred to others without the agreement of the parties to whom the obligations are owed.

Perpetual succession

[4.077] As one writer has observed[285], 'one of the principal advantages of an artificial person is that it is not susceptible to "the thousand natural shocks that flesh is heir to".' Since a company only ceases to exist as a legal person upon the occurrence of one of the

---

[278] See, generally, Chapter 15, *Shares and Membership*.

[279] Subject, of course, to the possibility of liability under CA 1963, s 207(1)(a) where a winding up follows within a year and the shares were not fully paid up.

[280] CA 1963, s 33(1); see Chapter 1, *The Private Company in Context*, para **[1.115]**.

[281] PA 1890, s 31(1).

[282] PA 1890, s 31(1) and s 31(2).

[283] PA 1890, s 24(7).

[284] PA 1890, s 17(2) and 17(3).

[285] Gower, *Principles of Modern Company Law* (5th edn, 1992), p 92.

dissolving events referred to earlier[286], its existence remains unaffected by the insanity, bankruptcy, or other incapacities of any or all of its members. Likewise, where all the members of the company die, the company will survive[287] - though its membership will necessarily fall below the statutory minimum until the registration of some new persons as members under a transfer by the deceased's executors or administrators.

Perpetual succession has particular advantages where the sale of a business is concerned as the company remains there to perform existing contracts whereas when a sole trader or a firm of partners sells a business as a going concern problems may arise concerning the performance of existing contracts and the validity of contracts entered into by customers ignorant of the change of ownership.

Common seal

[4.078] CA 1963, s 18(2) requires the company to have a common seal. The use of the common seal is discussed in further detail in Chapter 7.

Floating charges

[4.079] Banks and financial institutions often prefer to lend to a company than to a sole trader or firm of partners because a company registered under the Companies Acts 1963-2001 is capable of granting a floating charge over its assets to secure the company's indebtedness. A *charge*, very simply, is an equitable interest in goods which entitles the chargee to look to the goods for repayment in the event of a default by the debtor. A *floating charge* may be described as an equitable charge which floats or hovers over the assets from time to time which match a certain description, eg 'stock in trade', 'book debts and other debts', etc, but which does not restrict the company's ability to deal with the charged assets in the usual course of business until something occurs to cause the charge to become crystallised or fixed. Where, prior to such crystallisation, the assets which are subject to the charge are sold and replaced with new assets of that description the floating charge attaches to those new assets. A *fixed charge*, by way of contrast, attaches to specific, identifiable and defined property and restricts the ability of the company to deal with, or dispose of, the assets which are subject to the charge[288].

[4.080] A floating charge may not, in practice, be granted by a sole trader or a partnership. Though legally speaking there is no prohibition on their doing so, it is impractical for them to do so because a charge given by an individual or partnership over personal chattels[289] amounts to a *bill of sale* within the meaning of the Bills of Sale

---

[286] See para **[4.020]**.

[287] See, for example, *Re Tedman Holdings* [1967] QR 561.

[288] The topic of floating and fixed charges is discussed more fully in Chapter 20, *Corporate Borrowing: Debentures and Security.*

[289] 'Personal chattels' is defined in the Bills of Sale (Ireland) Act 1879, s 4. Notably, the definition does not include interests in land, shares or interests in the stock, funds or securities of a government or an incorporated company, or choses in action. Ships are excluded from the definition by the Mercantile Marine Act 1955, as are agricultural machines, stock and crops by the Agricultural Credit Act 1978, s 36(1). See Maguire, 'The Bill of Sale: The Forgotten Relation?' (1997) 4 CLP 3.

(Ireland) Acts 1879-1883 (which do not apply to companies)[290] and must therefore comply with certain registration formalities[291]. If not registered with a detailed inventory of the charged chattels in the form required by the 1883 Act, the bill of sale, the security *and the loan* will be invalid[292] - indeed, this will be so if the inventory supplied is not very specific about the precise identity of the chattels. Thus, in *Davies v Jenkins*[293], an inventory which stated 'Stock: 2 Horses, 4 Cows' was held not to satisfy the Act's requirements, and in *Witt v Banner*[294], an inventory describing two paintings by reference to the place in which they were hanging was held to be equally inadequate. The requisite specificity would be impossible to achieve in the case of a floating charge by a sole trader or partnership because the charged assets would be changing from day to day[295].

Formation of large associations

[4.081] A practical consequence of incorporation under the Companies Acts is that it enables members to form an association consisting of more than 20 persons, with a view to the acquisition of gain, which would otherwise have been prohibited by CA 1963, s 376. This provides:

> No company, association or partnership consisting of more than twenty persons shall be formed for the purpose of carrying on any business (other than the business of banking), that has as its object the acquisition of gain by the company, association or partnership, or by the individual members thereof, unless it is registered as a company under this Act or is formed in pursuance of some other statute[296].

A private company, however, may not have more than 50 members[297].

Taxation

[4.082] A major consequence of incorporation is the differing tax treatment which companies receive as opposed to individuals and partnerships. A comprehensive analysis of the taxation advantages of incorporation is beyond the scope of this work. However the following features may briefly be noted: first, companies are taxed on the whole of their income and capital gains under a single rate of Corporation Tax[298],

---

290 Bills of Sale (Ireland) Act 1879 (Amendment) Act 1883, s 17; *Re Standard Manufacturing Co* [1891] 1 Ch 627.

291 See Chapter 21, *Corporate Borrowing: Registration of Charges*, para **[21.037]**.

292 Bills of Sale (Ireland) Act 1879 (Amendment) Act 1883, s 9.

293 *Davies v Jenkins* [1900] 1 QB 133.

294 *Witt v Banner* (1887) 20 QBD 794.

295 A second impediment to the creation of floating charges by sole traders and partnerships was the doctrine of 'reputed ownership' which applied in the bankruptcy of individuals. Under this doctrine the court was empowered to order the sale and disposal of any goods or chattels of which the bankrupt was the 'reputed owner' for the benefit of the creditors, despite the interests of floating charge holders: Irish Bankrupt and Insolvent Act 1857, s 313. The doctrine was repealed and not replaced by the Bankruptcy Act 1988.

296 C(A)A 1982, s 13, however, permits partnerships consisting of more than twenty solicitors or qualified accountants.

297 CA 1963, s 33(1).

298 Corporation Tax Act 1976, as amended.

whereas individuals are taxed separately on their income and capital gains and at varying rates. Secondly, if the company engages in the 'manufacture' of goods within the State it may further qualify for a reduced rate of corporation tax on the profits from the sale of those goods[299]. Finally, the controlling shareholders of the company should also note that company directors are not insurable as employees for the purposes of calculating Pay Related Social Insurance (PRSI) contributions, and may, consequently, be entitled to reduced social insurance benefits.

Other consequences of incorporation

[4.083] To the list of consequences already discussed may be added the *practical* statutory consequences of incorporation already listed in Chapter 2, namely:

— the requirements to carry on an activity within the State;

— to deliver certain particulars to the Revenue Commissioners;

— to maintain certain registers;

— to have at least two directors and a secretary;

— to display certain information; and

— to make annual returns to the Companies Registration Office[300].

A further major consequence of incorporation is the application of doctrines such as the ultra vires rule[301], and the rules governing the raising and maintenance of capital[302], to companies.

---

[299] Finance Act 1980, s 38, as amended.

[300] See Chapter 13, *Accounts and Auditors*.

[301] See Chapter 7, *Corporate Contracts, Capacity and Authority*, para **[7.043]** *ff*.

[302] See Chapter 18, *The Maintenance of Capital*.

Chapter 5

Disregarding Separate Legal Personality

Introduction

[5.001] This chapter is concerned with situations in which the separate legal personality of a private company may be disregarded. It will be recalled that in *Salomon*'s case[1] it was not only established that an incorporated company is a legal person, but that it is a *separate and distinct* legal person from its members. Therefore, companies should not be regarded as agents or trustees of their members (or vice versa), and the motives of those who form a company should be of no consequence to its separate corporate existence.

[5.002] Many jurists have described the principle of separate legal personality through the use of metaphors such as 'mask', 'cloak', 'shell', and, most popularly, 'veil' of incorporation[2]. The terms 'lifting the veil' or 'piercing the veil' are frequently used to describe situations in which the separate legal personality of a company is disregarded[3]. Even the courts have shown a penchant for such imagery[4]. The problem, however, is that the use of such vague metaphorical language often obscures precisely which aspect of the principle of separate legal personality (if any) is in issue[5]. As Cardozo J said in an American case[6], 'metaphors are in law to be narrowly watched, for starting as devices to liberate thought, they often end by enslaving it.' The 'veil' image, for example, has been described as 'a singularly unhelpful and confusing metaphor'[7] because it gives the impression that regard may never be had to the identity and character of those who control a company when its affairs are in issue – an impression which is falsely grounded[8]. The use of such metaphors will be avoided in this chapter.

[5.003] What has sometimes been overlooked is the fact that *Salomon*'s case itself recognises the possibility of departure from the principle of separate legal personality.

---

1 *Salomon v Saloman & Co* [1897] AC 22. See Chapter 4, *Incorporation and its Consequences*, para **[4.026]** *ff.*

2 For a detailed list of metaphors in this context see Pickering, 'The Company as a Separate Legal Entity' (1968) 31 MLR 481 at 482.

3 See, for example, Davies (ed), *Gower's Principles of Modern Company Law* (6th edn, 1997); Forde, *Company Law* (3rd edn, 1999), p 67 *ff.*

4 See para **[5.040]** *ff.*

5 See, for example, Mayson, French and Ryan, *Company Law* (1989), p 100; Ussher, *Company Law in Ireland* (1986), p 25.

6 *Berkley v Third Avenue Railway* 50 ALR 599 at 604 (1926).

7 Keane, *Company Law* (3rd edn, 2000), p 122.

8 Keane, *Company Law* (3rd edn, 2000), p 122. The learned author points out that the great principle underlying modern companies legislation is the requirement that the identity of those who control the company should be ascertainable to the public. In that regard see Chapter 15, *Shares and Membership*, para **[15.017]** *ff.*

Lord Halsbury said that the principle was to be of application *provided that* there was '...no fraud and no agency and if the company was a real one and not a fiction or a myth.'[9]

A company, thus, is a legal person which should not per se be regarded as an agent or trustee of its members (or vice versa), and the motives of those who formed it should not per se affect its separate corporate existence. Where additional factors exist, the separate legal personality of the company may be disregarded. This chapter is primarily concerned with identifying those additional factors.

[5.004] In the first edition[10] it was noted that as the law then stood the courts had failed to identify in a systemic manner the additional factors permitting the disregard of the separate legal personality of a company. This failure produced an amorphous and unprincipled body of jurisprudence where each case was treated, to a large degree, on its own merits and according to convenience rather than legal principle. An Australian judge described the situation thus:

> 'The threshold problem arises from the fact that there is no common, unifying principle which underlies the occasional decision of courts to pierce the corporate veil. Although an *ad hoc* explanation may be offered by a court which so decides, there is no principled approach to be derived from the authorities.'[11]

Decided cases contain abundant reference to metaphors such as 'veil,' 'façade,' 'cloak,' 'alias,' 'alter ego', 'agent', 'fiction', 'instrumentality', 'puppet', and 'sham'[12] which do not serve to enlighten. Attempts by commentators to disentangle and rationalise the cases in the hope of identifying a unifying underlying principle have resulted in little more than the unhelpful observation that the courts will disregard the principle of separate legal personality where some injustice is intended, or would result, to a party dealing with the company or its members[13]. Thus, in *Re a Company (1985)*[14], the English Court of Appeal stated:

> 'In our view the cases ... show that the court will use its power to pierce the corporate veil if it is necessary to achieve justice irrespective of the legal efficacy of the corporate structure...'

The 1970s and 1980s in particular had witnessed a tendency in the courts to disregard the separate legal personality of companies by giving regard to the economic realities of the situation rather than legal formality on the basis that the 'justice of the case' so

---

9 [1897] AC 22 at 22–23.

10 Courtney, *Law of Private Companies* (1st edn, 1994), para [4.015].

11 Per Rogers AJA in *Briggs v James Hardie & Co Pty Ltd* [1989] 16 NSWLR 549 at 567, cited by Farrar, Furey and Hannigan, *Farrar's Company Law* (3rd edn, 1991) Butterworths, at p 73.

12 See Pickering, 'The Company as a Separate Legal Entity' (1968) 31 MLR 481.

13 See eg Gallagher and Zeigler, 'Lifting the Corporate Veil in the Pursuit of Justice' [1990] JBL 292; 'The Company as a Separate Legal Entity' (1968) 31 MLR 481 at p 22. For an empirical study of the circumstances in which the English courts have disregarded the separate legal personality of companies, including a comparison with American and Australian studies in the field, see Mitchell, 'Lifting the Corporate Veil in the English Courts: An Empirical Study' (1999) 3 CFILR 15.

14 *Re a Company (1985)* [1985] BCLC 333 at 337, 338.

required[15]. Though the courts were cautious in the application of this approach, it gave the impression that *Salomon's* case was losing importance.

[5.005] The intervening years, however, have seen a concerted effort on the part of the English and Irish courts (and some commentators) to restate the importance of *Salomon*'s case in an attempt to restore principle to this area. The process has not altogether been completed, but the direction is clear. In his 1997 Hamlyn Lecture on *Salomon*'s case, Lord Cooke of Thorndon revealed this trend, saying:

> 'In the main, the concept that a duly incorporated limited liability company, if not a real thing, is at least not to be identified with its shareholders, has been faithfully followed by British and other Commonwealth courts ever since *Salomon's* case. But there has been some gnawing away at the edges of the doctrine, a process commonly described as piercing or lifting the corporate veil. I believe that there is only one broad class of cases where this is truly consistent with the *Salomon* reasoning. They are all cases where, under enactments such as those against fraudulent or wrongful trading, or on the permissible interpretation of an enactment or contract, or for the purposes of the common law or equitable principles against fraud or oppression or relating to agency, it is necessary to look at what has happened in fact, rather than in form.' [16]

Evidence of a retrenchment was solidly apparent by 1990, however. The Court of Appeal in *Adams v Cape Industries*[17] held that the courts were not generally free to disregard separate legal personality on the vague and elusive 'justice of the case' criterion; Gower[18] summarised the decision as giving rise to the conclusion that the courts may only disregard the separate legal personality of a company in the following circumstances:

- When the court is construing a statute, contract or other document;
- When the court is satisfied that a company is a 'mere façade' concealing the true facts;
- When it can be established that the company is an authorised agent of its controllers or its members, corporate or human.

Adams was followed by Walker J in *Re Polly Peck International plc (In Administration) (No 4)*[19], where he added that the courts must look to the legal substance of any transaction and not its economic substance when deciding whether the company is a mere façade, regardless of any perceived injustice that arose when the company became insolvent. Again in *Ord v Belhaven Pubs Ltd*[20] the Court of Appeal indicated that the disregard by the courts of the separate legal personality of companies should be

---

15 See para **[5.050]**.

16 Lord Cooke of Thorndon, *Hamlyn Lectures – Turning Points of the Common Law* (1997), p 13. See, eg, *Trustor AB v Smallbone et al (No 2)* [2001] 3 All ER 987 where *Re A Company* [1985] BCLC 333 was not followed.

17 *Adams v Cape Industries* [1990] Ch 433. See para **[5.048]**.

18 Gower, *Principles of Modern Company Law* (5th edn, 1992), pp 125–133.

19 *Re Polly Peck International plc (In Administration) (No 4)* [1996] 2 All ER 433. See para **[5.060]**.

20 *Ord v Belhaven Pubs Ltd* [1998] 2 BCLC 447. See para **[5.044]**.

exercised with restraint, and generally should only occur where some impropriety is found.

The Irish Supreme Court, in *Allied Irish Coal Supplies Ltd v Powell Duffryn International Fuels Ltd*[21] showed similar restraint, holding that the principles enunciated by the House of Lords in *Salomon*'s case remain the 'corner stone of company law'[22] and that the proposition that the assets of a parent company should be generally available to meet the liabilities of a trading subsidiary was so fundamentally at variance with those principles as to be 'wholly unstateable'. [23]

[5.006] Following a review of the law, Keane[24] lately suggests (with some hesitation) that the following principles can now be said to summarise the existing law in this area:

> '(1) The rule in *Salomon's* case is still the law. The company and its shareholders are separate legal entities and the courts normally cannot infer from the degree of control exercised by a shareholder a relationship of principal and agent or beneficiary and trustee between the shareholders and the company.
>
> (2) The courts, however, will not permit the statutory privilege of incorporation to be used for a fraudulent, illegal or improper purpose. Where it is so misused, the court may treat the company thus incorporated as identical with its promoters.
>
> (3) In certain cases, where no actual misuse of the privilege of incorporation is involved, the courts may nonetheless infer the existence of an agency or trust if to do otherwise would lead to injustice or facilitate the avoidance of tax liability.
>
> (4) In the case of a group of companies, the court may sometimes treat the group as one entity, particularly where to do otherwise would have unjust consequences for outsiders dealing with companies in the group.
>
> (5) The rule in *Salomon's* case does not prevent the court from looking at the individual members of the company in order to determine its *character* and *status* and where it legally resides.'

This summary is much to be welcomed as a principled map of the prevailing legal landscape, and it can be expected to have a significant effect on future judicial decisions. It is submitted that, *for the future*, the true principles of *Salomon's* case will better be reflected by the abandonment of the 'justice of the case' criterion, as there is nothing in the case to suggest such a special rule. It is further submitted that the true principle of *Salomon's* case is that, where the corporate form has not in fact been misused and where statute does not expressly allow the disregard of separate legal personality, *ordinary* principles of contract, agency, or the law of trusts etc should be applied when inferring the existence of a connecting relationship between the members of a company and the company itself. It is not sufficient to suggest, for example, that a company can be regarded as the agent of its members simply because injustice might otherwise be done:

---

21 *Allied Irish Coal Supplies Ltd v Powell Duffryn International Fuels Ltd* [1998] 2 IR 519. See para **[5.045]**.

22 *Allied Irish Coal Supplies Ltd v Powell Duffryn International Fuels Ltd* [1998] 2 IR 519 at 535 per Murphy J, approving the comments of Laffoy J in the High Court in the case.

23 *Allied Irish Coal Supplies Ltd v Powell Duffryn International Fuels Ltd* [1998] 2 IR 519 at 537.

24 Keane, *Company Law* (3rd edn, 2000), pp 139–140.

injustice would likewise be done to the company, its members, and its creditors were the courts to ignore the legal formalities establishing an agency relationship[25].

[5.007] Some have suggested that the legislature should lay down definite rules in this area[26]. As shall be seen, however, the legislature has not responded to such pleas; though it has provided for disregard of separate legal personality in a number of particular circumstances[27].

The manner in which separate legal personality may be disregarded

[5.008] The separate legal personality of a company may be disregarded in a number of different ways, and to varying degrees. It may be, and commonly is, disregarded without ignoring the fact that the company still exists as a legal person; instead, the *separateness* of its existence is compromised by the identification of the company with its members, or by regarding it as an agent or trustee for them. Four means of disregarding the separate legal personality of a company have been identified[28], and it is to these which discussion now, briefly, turns.

First, the separate legal personality of the company may be disregarded merely by looking at its controlling members in order to characterise it, ie to attribute to it some characteristic, such as residence, negligence, or mens rea, which cannot comfortably be associated with a purely metaphysical entity having no physical manifestation. In such cases, the legal existence of the company is not ignored, but the separateness of its existence is compromised to the extent that the characteristics of its controllers are attributed to it[29].

Secondly, the separate legal personality of the company may be disregarded by making other persons, particularly its members, *in addition to the company itself*, responsible for the debts and other obligations of the company. It should be noted that such disregard is not limited merely to making *members alone* liable for the company's debts; other persons who are *not members* may also be made liable[30]. Again, in such cases, the legal existence of the company is not forgotten, but the separateness of its existence is

---

25 See the comments of Murphy J in *Allied Irish Coal Supplies Ltd v Powell Duffryn International Fuels Ltd* [1998] 2 IR 519 at 537; also those of Walker J in *Re Polly Peck International plc (In Administration) (No 4)* [1996] 2 All ER 433.

26 'The Legislature might, but no Court could possibly, lay down a hard and fast rule...': *Daimler v Continental Tyre & Rubber Co* [1916] 2 AC 307 at 346 per Lord Parker; see also Wedderburn, 'Multinationals and the Antiquities of Company Law' (1984) 47 MLR 87 at 90.

27 See para **[5.073]** *ff*.

28 See Ottolenghi, 'From Peeping Behind the Corporate Veil to Ignoring it Completely' (1990) 53 MLR 338. The author describes these four means as 'peeping behind the veil'; 'penetrating the veil'; 'extending the veil'; and 'ignoring the veil', respectively.

29 See, for example, *The King (Cottingham) v The Justices of County Cork* [1906] 2 IR 415, discussed at para **[5.072]**.

30 See, for example, CA 1990, s 297A(1)(b), discussed in detail in Chapter 10, *Duties of Directors and Other Officers*, para **[10.104]** *ff* which empowers the court to impose personal liability for the company's debts and other liabilities on '*any person*...knowingly a party to the carrying on of any business of the company with intent to defraud...' (Emphasis added). See also *O'Keeffe v Ferris* [1993] 3 IR 165 at 174 per Murphy J.

compromised to the extent that its responsibilities are *shared*, whether jointly or severally, by other persons. Such disregard of separate legal personality is most commonly permitted by legislative provision[31], though the same effect can be obtained through contract[32] or agency[33], and through the courts' power to order enforcement of their orders against anyone in respect of another's obligation[34].

Thirdly, the separate legal personality of the company may be disregarded by regarding it as a mere constituent of a larger legal entity, such as a group of companies. In such cases the legal existence of the company is not ignored, but its identity is consumed by a larger entity. This kind of disregard is sometimes employed by the courts where a group of corporate entities is regarded as a 'single economic unit'[35]. Certain legislative provisions permit similar disregard[36]. In such cases, the disregard directly affects the other members of the larger entity, notably, one of the company's principal members – its 'parent' or holding[37] company.

The final type of disregard of the separate legal personality of the company involves ignoring the existence of the company completely, so that liability will fall on some other person - often a member. The courts have regularly stated that they will disregard the legal personality of a company in this manner where it is erected merely as a 'sham', 'device', or 'façade' designed as a means to defraud or to avoid a person's existing legal obligations[38]. Unfortunately the courts have been unable to come up with uniform criteria for identifying whether a company is such a sham, device or façade, etc. Furthermore, in many cases where these circumstances *have* been identified by the courts, the courts have then proceeded to give a determination of the case which could be justified *without* disregarding the separate legal personality of the company[39]. Disregard of the existence of the company has the disadvantage of estopping a court from directing orders against the company itself, and it has been suggested that, as a means of preventing or remedying injustice, it goes too far[40].

---

31 See the statutory provisions discussed at para **[5.073]** *ff*.

32 Such as a contact of guarantee. See para **[5.015]**.

33 Agents who do not disclose the fact that they are acting as agents may be made liable for the obligations of their principals. See para **[5.027]**.

34 See para **[5.063]**.

35 See, for example, *Power Supermarkets Ltd v Crumlin Investments Ltd* (22 June 1981, unreported), High Court (Costello J), discussed at para **[5.052]**.

36 See, for example, CA 1990, s 141, considered in detail in Chapter 27, *Realisation and Distribution of Assets in a Winding Up*, para **[27.112]** *ff*. The section permits two or more related companies to be wound up as though they were a single company.

37 On holding companies and subsidiary companies see generally Chapter 17, *Groups of Companies*.

38 See, for example, *Jones v Lipman* [1962] 1 All ER 442, and *Gilford Motor Company Ltd v Horne* [1933] Ch 939, both discussed at para **[5.040]** *ff*.

39 See, for example, *Cummings v Stewart* [1911] 1 IR 236, discussed at para **[5.040]** *ff*.

40 Ottolenghi, 'From Peeping Behind the Corporate Veil to Ignoring it Completely' (1990) 53 MLR 338 at 351.

With whom will the company be identified?

[5.009] When the separate legal personality of a company is disregarded, the question becomes 'with whom will it be identified?' The answer varies depending on the manner of disregard, but in most situations the focus shifts to the controllers of the company[41]. The persons or entities most likely to be identified with a company where the company's separate legal personality is disregarded are its day-to day controllers, whether they are directors of the company or not[42]. This factor should be of particular concern to the many Irish private companies which are beneficially owned and controlled by only one person, and is of even greater significance to the sole member of a single-member private limited company[43].

It is essential to note, however, that control is *not* the determining factor in the decision to disregard the separate legal personality of a company[44]. Some additional circumstances must be shown to exist which would justify the controllers being identified with the company. It is to a review of these circumstances that discussion now turns.

The circumstances in which separate legal personality may be disregarded

[5.010] The circumstances in which the separate legal personality of a company may be disregarded are considered in this chapter under the following headings:

[A] Contract, tort, agency and trusts.

[B] Misuse of the corporate form.

[C] The single economic entity.

[D] Injunctions and orders.

[E] Characterisation.

[F] Statute.

[A] CONTRACT, TORT, AGENCY AND TRUSTS

[5.011] *Salomon*'s case[45] established that a company is to be regarded as a separate legal person, and that a company is not per se to be regarded as entitled to or responsible for the rights and obligations of its members, and vice versa. The law has long recognised, however, that persons (natural or artificial) are generally free to assume the rights and responsibilities of others through ordinary principles of contract, tort, agency or trusts. Thus, for example, a person can become responsible for the debts of another by agreeing to a guarantee; a person can become responsible in tort to another where they have personally assumed a duty of care; a principal will be responsible to another for the acts of his agent; and a beneficiary under a trust will be entitled to property held by another

---

41 See especially *Smith, Stone & Knight Ltd v Birmingham Corporation* [1939] 4 All ER 116, discussed at para **[5.024]**.

42 See *Gilford Motor Co v Horne* [1933] Ch 939, discussed in further detail at para **[5.041]**, where the controller was neither a director nor even a member of the company.

43 See Howell, 'Salomon under Attack' (2000) 21 Co Law 312.

44 *Allied Irish Coal Supplies Ltd v Powell Duffryn International Fuels Ltd* [1998] 2 IR 519.

45 *Salomon v Saloman & Co* [1897] AC 22.

in trust. The law also recognises that such relationships can arise unwittingly – the parties to an agency or a trust, for example, do not have to appreciate that they are entering such a relationship, though they commonly do. Here, we consider the circumstances in which such relationships may arise under the following headings:

1. Contracts.
2. Torts.
3. Agency.
4. Trusts.

Contracts

[5.012] The separate legal personality of a company is subject to easy circumvention by agreement. There is no legal objection to an agreement whereby a member agrees to be liable in respect of the company's obligations – provided the normal formalities for the making of such agreements are observed[46]. Most institutional lenders, for example, would insist on the director-members of smaller private companies contracting around the separate (limited) liability of the company by getting them to agree to personal guarantees or other securities – so that they assume personal responsibility for the debts of the company.

Likewise, a company may agree to be liable for the obligations of its members if the usual formalities are observed – provided, however, that the transaction is: not ultra vires; not beyond the scope of the directors' authority[47]; does not amount to a fraudulent preference[48]; and does not amount to a breach of statutory regulations governing transactions between directors and companies[49].

[5.013] The courts will be slow to imply such agreements, however, as both the High Court and Supreme Court noted in *Sweeney v Duggan*[50]. The plaintiff in that case was seriously injured whilst employed by a quarrying company. His action in negligence against the company succeeded, but the company went into voluntary liquidation during the proceedings and was unable ultimately to satisfy the judgment against it. The plaintiff then commenced proceedings against the defendant, who was principal shareholder in the company and quarry manager within the meaning of the Mines and Quarries Act 1965. The two broad planks of his case against the defendant were that in reality he was the company (or its *alter ego*) and that as quarry manager he owed the plaintiff duties in contract and tort to take reasonable care to ensure that the company had adequate insurance cover to meet any claims in respect of injuries to employees. Barron J in the High Court refused to hold the defendant liable, saying:

---

[46] See *Ford & Carter Ltd v Midland Bank Ltd* (1979) 129 New LJ 543.

[47] See Chapter 7, *Corporate Contracts, Capacity and Authority*, para **[7.096]** *ff*.

[48] CA 1963, s 286, as amended. See Chapter 27, *Realisation and Distribution of Assets in a Winding Up*, para **[27.072]** *ff*.

[49] See, generally, Chapter 11, *Statutory Regulation of Transactions Involving Directors and their Companies*.

[50] *Sweeney v Duggan* [1991] 2 IR 274.

'Neither of these matters is a ground for imposing liability on the defendant personally. He is in law a different person from the company and there are no circumstances from which it could be inferred that the company was a sham or should be treated as an instrument of fraud. Undoubtedly, as quarry manager the defendant was personally liable for breach of any of the statutory duties imposed upon the holder of that office. But such duties relate only to safety. There is no statutory duty of the type which the plaintiff seeks to establish...The reality of the plaintiff's claim is that the defendant was the person in control of the company. He can certainly have no greater liability than that of the company itself. However it does seem to me that perhaps this claim should be answered by saying that to allow it as against the defendant would in effect be depriving the defendant of his protection under company law and to nullify all the essential principles of that law.'

Each case will, however, turn on its own facts and in *Shinkwin v Quin-Con Ltd and Quinlan*[51], a case said by Fennelly J to bear a superficial resemblance to Sweeney, a manager was held to be liable in tort for an employee's injuries[52].

[5.014] The types of agreement which cause the separate legal personality of a company to be disregarded include:

(a) Personal guarantees.

(b) Indemnities.

(c) Comfort Letters.

(a) Personal guarantees

[5.015] It is common for lending institutions to require personal guarantees from third parties, often director-members, where a company seeks credit facilities. A guarantee is a contract whereby a person agrees to become answerable *himself* to the lending institution in the event that the company fails to meet its obligations. In many Irish private companies the directors will be members, and the contract of guarantee may be viewed by the lending institution as a means of circumventing the separate legal personality of the company and the limited liability of the member. A detailed review of the law relating to guarantees is outside the scope of this work[53]; however the following features may briefly be noted:

— A guarantee must be evidenced in writing[54].

— A guarantee is an *ancillary* obligation, ie no obligation arises under it until the company has defaulted. Additionally, anything which terminates the company's obligation (eg release[55], notice of death, bankruptcy, insanity,

51 *Shinkwin v Quin–Con Ltd and Quinlan* [2001] 1 IR 514, [2001] 2 ILRM 154.

52 See para **[5.018]**.

53 See further Johnston, *Banking and Security Law in Ireland*, (1998), ch 9; Breslin, *Banking Law in the Republic of Ireland* (1998), ch 27; Marks and Moss, *Rowlatt on Principal and Surety* (5th edn, 1998); Goode, *Legal Problems of Credit & Security* (2nd edn, 1988), ch 7; Lingard, *Bank Security Documents* (3rd edn, 1993), ch 13.

54 Statute of Frauds (Ireland) 1695, s 2. See generally Clark, *Contract Law in Ireland* (4th edn, 1998), ch 4. The equitable doctrine of part performance may not generally be relied upon where guarantees are concerned: *Madison v Alderson* (1883) 8 App Cas 467; cf *Steadman v Steadman* [1976] AC 536.

55 See, however, *Tempany v Royal Liver Trustees Ltd* [1984] ILRM 273, where it was held that where a liquidator disclaims any of the company's continuing obligations, under CA 1963, s 290, the disclaimer will *not* relieve the guarantor of his obligations under the guarantee.

misrepresentation, etc) likewise terminates the guarantor's obligations. However, standard form letters of guarantee issued by lending institutions frequently modify this principle[56].

— Standard letters of guarantee issued by lending institutions may stipulate that the guarantee is a 'continuing security'. By this it is meant that the guarantor agrees to guarantee not only the company's liability in respect of the initial advance, but also in respect of any future advances made to the company. In contractual terms, a continuing guarantee is a standing offer which is accepted by the lending institution each time a new advance is made[57]. The offer may be revoked by the guarantor in respect of future advances before acceptance by notifying the lending institution in accordance with the provisions of the guarantee[58]. In *Bank of Ireland v McCabe*[59] the Supreme Court held that a continuing security clause in a standard letter of guarantee could be ousted by oral agreement between the parties at the time of contracting.

— Since it is an agreement, a guarantee may be invalidated by want of capacity, or by mistake, misrepresentation, duress, undue influence, etc. The circumstances in which guarantees are given may render them susceptible to invalidation on grounds of misrepresentation[60] or duress and undue influence[61]. Lending institutions will normally require a guarantor to sign a declaration that he has been given an opportunity to obtain independent legal advice to mitigate the chances of such invalidation[62]. Guarantees may also be avoided by statute[63].

Standard form letters of guarantee regularly contain covenants by the guarantor entitling the lending institution to enforce the guarantee by exercising a lien over any monies held by it in the guarantor's account; by setting-off the amount due under the guarantee against those monies; or by exercising any other form of security right (eg mortgage of the family home) it may have against the guarantor. Where the guarantor is himself a creditor of the company, the lending institution may additionally require him to agree to subordinate any security he holds in the company's assets in favour of a security held by the institution. Under such a subordination agreement, the guarantor agrees not to realise his security until any securities held by the lending institution in the company's assets have been realised in full[64].

---

56 See *Moschi v Lep Air Services* [1973] AC 331; *Heald v O'Connor* [1971] 2 All ER 1105; *Yeoman Credit v Latter* [1961] 2 All ER 294; *Garrard v James* [1925] Ch 616.

57 *Lloyds v Harper* (1880) 16 Ch D 290.

58 See *Bradbury v Morgan* (1862) 1 H & C 249; *Bradford Old Bank v Sutcliffe* [1918] 2 KB 833; *Morrisson v Barking Chemicals Ltd* [1919] 2 Ch 325.

59 *Bank of Ireland v McCabe* (19 December 1994, unreported), Supreme Court.

60 See *Lloyds Bank v Bundy* [1975] QB 326.

61 See *Barclay's Bank v O'Brien* [1993] 4 All ER 417; *Bank of Ireland v Smyth* [1993] 2 IR 102. See Sanfey, 'Undue Influence and the 'Tender Treatment' of Wives' (1994) CLP 99.

62 See *CIBC Mortgages v Pitt* [1993] 4 All ER 433 and *Banco Exterior Internaçional v Mann* [1995] 1 All ER 936. For a discussion of the legal principles surrounding the giving of independent legal advice see Johnston, *Banking and Security Law in Ireland*, (1998), Ch 8.

63 See Courtney, 'The Latest Hazard to Guarantees: Inter–Company Guarantees and s 31 of the Companies Act 1990' (1991) Gazette ILSI 261, and Chapter 11, *Statutory Regulation of Transactions Involving Directors and their Companies*; also Johnston, *Banking and Security Law in Ireland*, (1998), pp 626 *ff;* and Breslin, 'Guarantees under Attack' (1996) CLP 243.

64 On debt subordination generally see Wood, *The Law of Subordinated Debt* (1990).

(b) Indemnities

[5.016] Lending institutions may additionally require an *indemnity* from the controlling members of a company seeking credit facilities. Strictly speaking, an indemnity differs from a guarantee in that it is a *primary* obligation, personal to the individual and independent of the company's obligation. Most standard form letters of guarantee contain provisions creating the same effect as an indemnity – thus rendering the distinction between guarantees and indemnities somewhat academic[65]. Indeed the current practice is for banks to describe their standard suretyship agreement as a 'guarantee and indemnity.' An indemnity need not, however, be evidenced in writing[66].

(c) Comfort letters

[5.017] Where credit facilities are sought by a subsidiary[67] of a holding company, a lender may seek a comfort letter from the holding company instead of a full guarantee. The comfort letter will usually state that the holding company will not reduce its shareholding in the subsidiary during the term of the loan; that it will ensure that the subsidiary remains in a position to repay the loan; and that it will not do anything which could result in the subsidiary defaulting in its repayments under the loan[68]. The terms of such comfort letters vary from case to case, as does their legal effect[69].

A comfort letter, depending upon its terms, may have the effect of creating a *binding* contractual obligation on the holding company to observe any terms making it liable for the default of the subsidiary. Indeed, in appropriate circumstances, an officer of a company may even become personally liable for the commitment given in a comfort letter[70]. In order to avoid such liability, the letter should not evidence an intention to

---

65 *Moschi v Lep Air Services* [1973] AC 331; *Heald v O'Connor* [1971] 2 All ER 1105; *Yeoman Credit v Latter* [1961] 2 All ER 294; *Garrard v James* [1925] Ch 616. Also, CA 1990, s 25(1) interprets 'guarantee' as including 'indemnity' for the purposes of CA 1990, Part III, which concerns transactions between a company and its directors.

66 See, for example, *Barnett v Hyndman* (1840) 3 Ir LR 109, where an indemnifier was held liable on an oral promise to indemnify.

67 On holding and subsidiary companies see Chapter 17, *Groups of Companies*.

68 See, for example, the terms of the letter examined in *Re Atlantic Computers Ltd (In Liquidation); National Australia Bank Ltd v Soden* [1995] BCC 696.

69 For more detailed discussion on the topic see Johnston, *Banking and Security Law in Ireland* (1998), para 9.123–9.130. For recent comparative review see Trichardt 'Chameleonic Documents in Law – A Comfort Letter Trilogy' (2001) 16 BJIB & FL 416; Von Diessl 'US Comfort Letters: Purpose and Content' (2001) PLC 45; and Vernerson 'Sweden: Company Law – Letters of Comfort – Recent Case Law' (1996) ECL 58.

70 See *Paulger v Butland Industries Ltd* [1989] 3 NZLR 549, where the managing director of D Ltd., which was facing financial difficulties, circulated a letter, written on the firm's letterhead, in which he asked for the 'tolerance' of all creditors whilst a certain deal concerning the acquisition of a part of the firm's business by another entity was being finalised. He advised that D Ltd. 'would make good all outstanding matters within 90 days' and added: 'The writer personally guarantees that all due payments will be made.' The Court of Appeal of New Zealand confirmed the finding of the Master on summary judgment that the letter constituted a personal guarantee.

create legal relations[71]. In *Kleinwort Benson Ltd v Malaysia Mining Corporation Berhad*[72], a comfort letter stated, inter alia that 'It is our policy to ensure that the business of [the subsidiary] is at all times in a position to meet its liability to you'. At first instance, Hirst J held that the letter evidenced an intention to be legally bound, and consequently, was actionable. The Court of Appeal, however, overturned Hirst J's findings on the basis that the letter confined itself to a representation of existing fact, ie 'it is our policy'. It would seem, then, that careful phrasing of the acknowledgements contained in the letter, and use of the present tense, might avoid the creation of a contractual obligation. The decision has been criticised, however, as a 'semantic and textual analysis' in the Australian courts[73].

Torts

[5.018] A third party (eg, director, member, controller) may become responsible for the torts (ostensibly) of a company where it is found to owe an 'independent duty' to the victim[74]. Whether such an independent duty exists depends upon the elements of the tort in question, and will involve an inquiry into the centrality of the third party in the events generating corporate liability. Where the third party has knowingly authorised, directed or procured the tort in question, personal liability may be imposed[75]. In *Fairline Shipping Corporation v Adamson*[76] the plaintiff claimed damages for negligence sustained to ships' provisions which were not kept adequately refrigerated. The defendant, who was managing director of the company providing the cold storage, denied liability arguing that sole responsibility lay with the company. Kerr J noted that the mere fact that the defendant was managing director of a company, and that the company alone was the contracting, party did not mean that the director's personal duty to the plaintiffs was excluded. On the evidence it was clear that the defendant was the only director to concern himself with the goods following delivery to the cold store, which was in his personal ownership. Correspondence indicated that he, rather than the company, was responsible for storage. Kerr J imposed personal liability on the defendant, saying:

> '...the defendant ... assumed and owed a duty of care to the plaintiffs in respect of storage of their goods in his premises and was in breach of that duty with the result that the plaintiff's goods were damaged.'[77]

---

71 A mere statement that 'This letter is not intended to create any legal obligations' will not be conclusive: *Wilson Smithett & Cape Sugar v Bangladesh Sugar and Food Industries* [1986] 1 Lloyds' Rep 378.

72 *Kleinwort Benson Ltd v Malaysia Mining Corporation Berhad* [1989] 1 All ER 785. See also *Chemco Leasing SPA v Rediffusion* [1987] FTLR 201.

73 *Banque Brussels Lambert SA v Australian National Industries Ltd* (1989) 21 NSWLR 502.

74 See generally Hawke, *Corporate Liability* (2000), Ch 4.

75 *Rainham Chemical Works Ltd and Others v Belvedere Fish Guano Co Ltd* [1921] 2 AC 465; *Wah Tat Bank Ltd v Chan Cheng Kum* [1975] AC 507; *Reitzman v Grahame–Chapman and Derustit Ltd* (1950) 68 RPC 25.

76 *Fairline Shipping Corporation v Adamson* [1975] 1 QB 180.

77 *Fairline Shipping Corporation v Adamson* [1975] 1 QB 180 at 191.

A significant element in the decision is that the managing director had positively, personally and voluntarily assumed (and not excluded) a duty to the plaintiff.

A similar approach was taken by the Supreme Court in *Shinkwin v Quin-Con Ltd and Quinlan*[78]. There, the plaintiff lost three fingers and part of his thumb when his hand slipped and came into contact with the circular saw that he had been operating. The plaintiff succeeded in the High Court against the defendant employer-company and also against the second defendant who was the manager of the factory. It was held that the second defendant, who was the sole owner of the company, had failed in his duty by not providing proper training or warnings in relation to the operation of the saw. The decision of the High Court was appealed to the Supreme Court. Fennelly J reduced the question of liability to whether the manager had involved himself 'so closely in the operation of the factory and, in particular, in the supervision of the plaintiff as to make himself personally liable for any of the acts of negligence which injured the plaintiff?'. Fennelly J went on to note the significance of the manager being in undisputed control of the factory. In finding the manager liable in negligence, Fennelly J said:

> '...the second defendant, on the particular facts of this case, placed himself in a relationship of proximity to the plaintiff. He had personally taken on a young and untrained person to work in a factory managed by him and personally put him to work upon a potentially dangerous machine over which he exercised control to the extent of giving some though completely inadequate instructions to the workers. He was bound to take appropriate steps to warn the plaintiff of such obvious dangers...In his supervision and instruction of the plaintiff, he failed to do these things and was consequently negligent'.[79]

This case did not involve the 'lifting of the veil' of incorporation. Fennelly J made it quite clear that the claim against the second defendant was made directly in negligence, 'not as employer or as shareholder but as a person who had placed himself by his own actions in such a relationship to the plaintiff as to call upon himself the obligation to exercise care'.

[5.019] In *Williams v Natural Life Health Foods*[80] the plaintiffs approached a one-man company, which operated franchises in the retail health food sector, with a view to obtaining a franchise. The defendant managing director, Mr Mistlin, advised them of his expertise and experience in the sector, and he produced for them various financial projections predicting their turnover and profits. In the event, turnover and profits failed to match the projections, and the plaintiffs sued the company for damages in respect of financial loss arising from negligent misstatement. The company was later wound up, and Mistlin was joined as second defendant. The Court of Appeal found Mistlin liable on an application of the ordinary principles of negligent misstatement in tort, given his substantial participation in the events. The House of Lords, however, reversed that decision, holding that an independent duty on the part of Mistlin could only arise if he had positively and voluntarily assumed responsibility so that a special relationship of care could be said to exist between him and the plaintiffs. The primary focus in that

---

78 *Shinkwin v Quin–Con Ltd and Quinlan* [2001] 1 IR 514, [2001] 2 ILRM 154.

79 [2001] 1 IR 514 at 519.

80 *Williams v Natural Life Health Foods* [1998] 2 All ER 577.

regard had to be on the personal exchanges between Mistlin and the plaintiffs. The House of Lords held that while the plaintiffs had been given a brochure promoting the company's expertise as being derived from Mistlin's own expertise, that was insufficient to constitute a voluntary assumption of responsibility on Mistlin's part. Applying an objective test, their Lordships held that the plaintiffs could not reasonably have relied on the brochure as constituting a voluntary assumption of personal liability by Mistlin.

Agency

[5.020] Although a company is not per se to be treated as the agent or trustee of its members, there is also no objection in principle to a company *agreeing* to act and be treated as an agent or trustee of its members. And, of course, as shall be seen, the corollary whereby members who are directors or other officers of the company agree to act as agents in particular circumstances of the company is an essential feature of all companies[81].

[5.021] An agent is a person who has authority to do acts affecting the legal position of another person, termed the principal. When an agent acts on behalf of his principal, the law treats the act as being that of the principal himself, and renders the principal liable for it[82].

A comprehensive treatment of the law of agency is beyond the scope of this work[83]; suffice it to say that agents commonly obtain the authority to alter their principal's legal position from an *agency agreement*, to which both the agent and the principal are parties. Where the agent is a company and the principal is a member, the agency agreement has the effect of circumventing the company's separate legal personality to the extent that the member, as principal, will be liable for the acts of the company, his authorised agent.

Little controversy can be said to arise where there exists an express agency agreement whereby a company agrees to act as a member's agent, because the principal's liability for the acts of the agent must clearly have been in the contemplation of both parties to the agreement when they first entered into it[84]. Greater controversy arises, however, concerning the extent to which the courts are prepared to *infer*, in the absence of an express agency agreement, that a company is in fact the agent of its principal, and this is discussed below. Additionally, there remains, however, another situation in which the members of a company may be made personally liable for the company's obligations

[81] See Chapter 7, *Corporate Contracts, Capacity and Authority*, para **[7.096]**.

[82] The maxim *qui facit per aliam facit per se* (he who does through another does by himself) applies.

[83] See Freidman, *Law of Agency* (7th edn, 1996); Reynolds, *Bowstead on the Law of Agency* (17th edn, 2001).

[84] See, for example, *Rainham Chemical Works Ltd v Belvedere* [1921] 2 AC 465, where an agency agreement provided that a company should take possession of land as an agent of its members; also *Southern v Watson* [1940] 3 All ER 439 where a company agreed, as part of a contract for the purchase of the business of its incorporators, to act as agent for the incorporators in the fulfilment of their outstanding commitments stemming from the time when they ran the business in the form of a partnership.

through the operation of the law of agency: this is where the member is acting as agent of the company and he fails to disclose that he is acting on the company's behalf.

[5.022] Specific aspects of the law of agency insofar as it concerns the separate legal personality of companies are considered here under the following headings:

(a) Implied agency.

(b) Undisclosed agency.

(a) Implied agency

[5.023] Though a company is not to be regarded per se as the agent of its members, there is nothing to prevent the *creation* of an agency relationship between the two. Some controversy has arisen about the extent to which the courts are willing to imply that a company is an agent of its members.

[5.024] In *Smith, Stone and Knight v Birmingham Corporation*[85], a subsidiary of the plaintiff company took over a waste business. The waste business was carried out on land owned by the plaintiff. The subsidiary was beneficially owned by the plaintiff company, and it was treated in day-to-day running as a mere department of the plaintiff's business. The arrangement between the subsidiary and the plaintiff company was such that the plaintiff company was entitled to all the profits of the subsidiary without any need for a dividend to be declared[86]. When the lands of the parent company were compulsorily acquired by the defendant corporation, the plaintiff successfully claimed compensation in respect of the disturbance caused to the subsidiary. Atkinson J accepted that the subsidiary was carrying on business as the agent of the plaintiff company. He observed:

> '[T]he Corporation rest their contention on *Salomon's* case and their argument is that the waste company was a distinct legal entity. It was in occupation of the premises, the business being carried on in its name, and the claimant's only interest in law was that of holders of the shares. It is well settled that the mere fact that a man holds all the shares in a company does not make the business carried on by the company his business, nor does it make the company his agent for the carrying on of the business. That proposition is just as true if the shareholder is itself a limited company. It is also well settled that there may be such an arrangement between the shareholders and a company as will constitute the company the shareholders' agent for the purpose of carrying on the business and make the business the business of the shareholders.'[87]

The learned judge considered that six factors should be weighed in determining whether such an agency may be deemed to exist, namely:

— Were the profits of the subsidiary treated as the profits of the holding company?

— Were the persons who were conducting the business of the subsidiary appointed by the holding company?

— Was the holding company the 'head and brains' of the trading venture?

[85] *Smith, Stone and Knight v Birmingham Corporation* [1939] 4 All ER 116.

[86] On shareholders' entitlements to dividends see Chapter 15, *Shares and Membership*, para **[15.069]** *ff*.

[87] [1939] 4 All ER 116 at 120.

- Did the holding company govern the adventure?
- Were the profits made by the subsidiary company made by the skill and direction of the holding company?
- Was the holding company in effective and constant control of the subsidiary?

Atkinson J considered that all six questions should be answered in the plaintiff's favour. He continued:

> 'Indeed, if ever one company must be said to be the agent or employee or tool or *simulacrum* of another, I think the waste company was in this case a legal entity because that is all that it was. There was nothing to prevent the claimants at any moment saying "we will carry on the business in our own name." They had but to paint out the waste company's name on the premises, change their business paper and form and the thing would have been done. I am satisfied that the business belonged to the claimants; they were, in my view, the real occupiers of the premises.'

Notably, most of Atkinson J's criteria for the determination of an agency relationship between a subsidiary and its holding company concentrate on the issue of *control* of the subsidiary's day to day operations. If such a criterion is to be applied to every case in which the day-to-day affairs of a company are controlled by a member, then a significant number of companies may be regarded as agents of their members, and the principle of separate legal personality would be the exception rather than the rule. The courts, however, seem reticent to imply such agency where the company is controlled by a natural person, and most cases in which agency has been implied have been concerned with subsidiaries and holding companies.

[5.025] Some explanation for this may be found in *Munton Bros Ltd v Secretary of State*[88], where the facts were not dissimilar to the *Smith, Stone & Knight* case. A parent company made a claim for compensation in respect of criminal damage done to the property of its subsidiary, alleging that the loss was really its own because of the close relationship between the two companies. The subsidiary's business was to make up cloth supplied by the parent company and return the cloth to it. Its finances were arranged so that it never made a profit or incurred a loss in any year. Gibson J found in favour of the parent company, holding that the subsidiary was in fact its agent. He observed that while the courts are extremely reluctant to hold that a company is its shareholder's agent or acts as trustee for them, even though the shareholder may be a sole proprietor:

> '...the same objections do not apply where it is sought to demonstrate that a subsidiary company is in fact the agent of its parent company because the conception of incorporation remains intact.'

While the judge's words may be taken as an indication of the courts' reluctance to regard companies as agents of their *natural* members, and of the courts' readiness to regard companies as agents of their *corporate* members, the judge's reasoning is less than convincing, because the concept of incorporation remains intact where a company is treated as agent of its member *regardless* of the member's attributes. This flaw deprives the observations as to the reluctance of the courts to regard companies as agents of their natural members of much weight.

---

[88] *Munton Bros Ltd v Secretary of State* [1983] NI 369.

[5.026] A case where a subsidiary has been found to be an agent of its parent or holding company is *Firestone Tyre and Public Co v Llwellin*[89]. In that case, an American company formed a wholly-owned subsidiary in England for the purpose of manufacturing tyres and supplying them to the European market. The English company received the payment for the tyres, and, after deducting a sum representing 5% of the payment, transferred the balance to the American company. When the American company was assessed for English tax on the profits of the business, it sought to deny liability on the basis that it was a legal person separate from its subsidiary. Indeed, the circumstances of the case seemed to lie in its favour: the English company was independent in its day-to-day operations, and only one of the English company's directors was also a director of the American company. Nevertheless, the Court of Appeal and the House of Lords found the English company to be an agent of the American company on the basis of the actual manner in which the companies had arranged their affairs. In the Court of Appeal, Evershed MR said:

> 'My conclusion does not involve the proposition that [the subsidiary], instead of being an independent legal entity, is a mere branch of [the American company]; but [the subsidiary], though a separate entity, is in fact wholly controlled by [the American company], and in the making of what may be described as [the American company's] proprietary branded articles it acts under the close direction of [the American company] in all respects, and in selling those articles to [the American company's] customers it does so on terms fixed by [the American company], so that after allowing [the subsidiary] its costs and a percentage thereon the whole of the profits on the transactions go to [the American company].'[90]

Similarly, in *Re FG (Films) Ltd*[91], a company was incorporated in England to enable films produced in its name to qualify as British under the Cinematograph Films Act 1938 (UK). The company was promoted by an American company. Two of its three directors were English, one of whom was also the president of the American company. The third director, an American, held 90% of the company's issued shares. The English company contracted with its American parent to make the film in question, but the money for the purpose was to be found by the American company, and all contracts and arrangements for making the film were made by the American company in the name of the English company. It was clear, then, that the English company was under-capitalised for the business which it conducted under the guise of a separate legal entity. The court held that the film did not qualify as British, because it had not been made by the English

---

89 *Firestone Tyre and Public Co v Llwellin* [1957] 1 All ER 561.

90 [1956] 1 All ER 693, at 700. Cf *Kodak Ltd v Clark* [1902] 2 KB 450, where an English company held 98% of the shares in its American subsidiary. The court refused to hold that the subsidiary was agent of the English company so as to render the latter liable for tax on the subsidiary's profits. In the course of his judgment, Phillimore J said (at 459): 'A company may control another company; but it does not necessarily follow because an individual controls the company, or the company controls the individual, that the business carried on by the person or company controlled is necessarily a business carried on by the controller; and particularly is that the case when the machinery of companies is used and the controller is a company.'

91 *Re FG (Films) Ltd* [1953] 1 All ER 615.

company at all; what little the English company did, it did as a mere nominee of the American company.

(b) Undisclosed agency

[5.027] Where the agents of a company fail to disclose that they are acting on behalf of the company, they will, under ordinary principles of agency, become personally liable for their acts – even though, legally speaking, the acts are done by the company[92]. As far as the third party is concerned, the agent is really a principal, dealing in his own name, and on his own behalf, and there is no obligation on the third party to inquire whether there is an undisclosed principal. At common law, both the agent and the undisclosed principal, once discovered, may be sued upon contracts concluded in such circumstances[93]. These principles apply, however, only where the existence of the principal has not been disclosed *at all* at the time the contract is concluded. If the agent represents that he is acting as agent of a principal, but misdescribes or misidentifies the principal, the principal will not be undisclosed, and the agent will not be liable[94]. The Companies Acts expand upon these common law principles, however, by providing for liability of the company's agents in certain circumstances where they have misdescribed or misidentified their principal. These circumstances are examined in further detail at para **[5.078]** below.

Trusts

[5.028] There is no legal objection to a company formally agreeing to act as trustee for all or some of its members, provided all the requisite formalities are observed. But even where no such formal trust may be found, the courts will, on occasion, disregard the separate legal personality of a company so as to *imply* that it acts as trustee for its members. This approach is most clearly evident in those cases concerning incorporated social clubs.

[5.029] In *Re Parnell GAA Club Ltd*[95], McWilliam J found that the club held its stock and assets on trust for its members. Accordingly, when it sold drink to the members, the 'sale' was really a distribution of the members' common property. Such a distribution would not require an intoxicating liquor licence. The learned judge quoted from Lord

---

92 See generally Goodhart & Hamson, 'Undisclosed Principals in Contract' (1931) 4 Cam LJ 320; Müller–Frienfels 'The Undisclosed Principal' (1953) 16 MLR 299; Fridman, *Law of Agency* (7th edn, 1996), pp 228–244.

93 *Short v Spackman* (1831) 2 B & Ad 962; *Hersom v Bernett* [1955] 1 QB 98. The obligations of the principal and agent are not joint. Once the third party discovers the existence of the undisclosed principal he must elect whether to sue the principal or the agent, and once a final judgment has been obtained by the third party against one, he cannot then sue the other: *Kendall v Hamilton* (1879) 4 App Cas 504. Similarly, a settlement with one may discharge the other: *Coates v Lewes* (1808) 1 Camp 444.

94 *Finzel, Berry & Co v Eastcheap Dried Fruit Co* [1962] 1 Lloyd's Rep 370.

95 *Re Parnell GAA Club Ltd* [1984] ILRM 246.

Hewart's judgment in *Trebanog Working Men's Club v MacDonald*[96], where the it was said that:

> '...once it is conceded that a members' club does not necessarily require a licence to serve its members with intoxicating liquor because the legal property in the liquor is not in the members themselves, it is difficult to draw any legal distinction between the various legal entities which may be entrusted with the duty of holding the property on behalf of the members, be it an individual, or a body of trustees, or a company formed for the purpose, so long as the real interest in the liquor remains, as it clearly does, in the members of the club. In this connection, there is no magic in the expression "trustee" or "agent". What is essential is that a holding of property by the agent or trustee must be a holding for and on behalf of, and not a holding antagonistic to, the members of the club.'

[B] Misuse of the Corporate Form

[5.030] Misuse of the corporate form can occur in a variety of ways. Here we consider the topic under the following headings:

1. Concealment of impropriety.
2. Mismanagement.
3. Evasion of existing legal obligations.
4. Avoidance of future legal obligations.

Concealment of impropriety

[5.031] In many instances the courts have threatened to disregard the separate legal personality of a company where to do otherwise would result in the use of the corporate personality as a cloak to conceal impropriety.

[5.032] The case of *Re Darby; ex p Brougham*[97], serves as an example of judicial disregard of the separate legal personality of a company where the company was being used to conceal fraudulent profits. Darby and Gyde, both of whom were undischarged bankrupts, registered a company in Guernsey in the Channel Islands. That company then promoted and registered a second company in England. Finances were raised by the English company on foot of debentures, and these monies were paid to the Guernsey company, where they were distributed directly to Darby and Gyde. When the English company failed, its liquidator claimed in Darby's bankruptcy for the secret profits Darby and Gyde had made through the Guernsey company. The court allowed the liquidator's claim, rejecting the argument that the profits had been made by the Guernsey company and not Darby himself.

---

96 *Trebanog Working Men's Club v MacDonald* [1940] 1 KB 576. See also *Newell v Hemmingway* (1888) 60 LT 544.

97 *Re Darby; ex p Brougham* [1911] 1 KB 95. See also *R v Goodwin* (1980) 71 Cr App R 97, where a bankrupt who had obtained credit for himself through the vehicle of a company was held to have committed an offence under the UK equivalent of the Bankruptcy Act 1988, s 129, even though normally the offence is not committed if the credit is obtained for another person.

[5.033] Likewise, in *Re Bugle Press Ltd*[98], the use of a company as a device to expropriate a minority was struck down by the courts as a 'hollow sham,' but in that case the impropriety complained of consisted of an attempt to abuse a fundamental principle of company law, namely that a majority of shareholders should not, unless permitted by the articles, be allowed to expropriate a minority. The Companies Act 1948 (UK), s 209(1) - their equivalent of the Companies Act 1963, s 204(1) ('CA 1963')[99] - permitted a company which had acquired a 90% shareholding in a takeover of another company to compulsorily acquire the remaining 10%, unless the court, in its discretion, thought fit to order otherwise. Two majority shareholders of Bugle Press Ltd, holding 90% of its issued share capital, formed a company, which then made a takeover bid for all the shares of Bugle Press Ltd. The purpose of this was to enable the company to compulsorily acquire the shareholding of a third minority shareholder under s 209. The third shareholder applied to the court for relief. Harman LJ disregarded the separate legal personality of the new company, describing it as nothing but a 'little hut' built around the two shareholders and 'a bare faced attempt to evade that fundamental rule of company law which forbids the majority of shareholders unless the articles so provide, to expropriate the minority.'[100]

[5.034] A not dissimilar instance of disregard of the separate legal personality of a company formed for a fraudulent purpose is the case of *Re Shrinkpak Ltd*[101]. In that case, a company, Shrinkpak Ltd, was established using monies which had been fraudulently converted from the use of a company which had gone into voluntary liquidation, Contract Packaging Ltd. Both companies were under the control of the same person, Mr Waldner, and Barron J found that the liquidation of Contract Packaging Ltd and the subsequent establishment of Shrinkpak Ltd had been choreographed by Waldner so as deliberately to defraud the creditors of Contract Packaging Ltd. The learned judge granted an order winding up Shrinkpak Ltd on the application of the liquidator of Contract Packaging Ltd.

[5.035] Recently, the English Court of Appeal in *Re (H) (Restraint Order: Realisable Property)*[102] allowed the separate legal personality of a company to be disregarded where the company's owners had used the company as a device or façade to conceal criminal activities, including fraud on the Commissioners of Customs and Excise. A receiver appointed to the assets of the controllers under the Criminal Justice Act 1988, s 77 (UK) was permitted to treat the company's assets as the 'realisable property' of the controllers. Likewise, in *Trustor AB v Smallbone (No 3)*[103] receipt by a company of funds was

---

98 *Re Bugle Press Ltd* [1961] Ch 270. The case is also examined in Chapter 16, *Share Transfers in Private Companies*, para **[16.092]** *ff.*

99 See Chapter 16, *Share Transfers in Private Companies*, para **[16.084]**. Note that in Ireland the magic figure is 80%.

100 [1961] Ch 270 at 288.

101 *Re Shrinkpak Ltd* (20 December 1989, unreported), High Court, The Irish Times 21 December, 1989. See also the related decision in *Re Contract Packaging Ltd* (1992) The Irish Times, 16, 17, 18 January discussed in Chapter 10, *Duties of Directors and Other Officers*, para **[10.109]**.

102 *Re (H) (Restraint Order: Realisable Property)* [1996] 2 All ER 391.

103 *Trustor AB v Smallbone (No 3)* [2001] 3 All ER 987.

treaded as receipt of those funds by its owner-director. The funds were caused to be paid to it by its owner-director who was using the company as a vehicle to siphon off substantial funds from another company of which he was also managing director.

Mismanagement

[5.036] Where the controllers of a company have been guilty only of *mismanagement*, it appears that the courts will not disregard the separate legal personality of the company so as to make them personally liable for the company's obligations. In *Dublin County Council v Elton Homes Ltd*[104], a company which had been granted planning permission for a housing development went into liquidation before it was able to comply with the conditions of the planning permission. The plaintiff County Council sought an injunction under the Local Government (Planning and Development) Act 1976, s 27 compelling the company *and* its directors, Mr Keogh and Mr English, to carry out the necessary works. Barrington J refused the plaintiff's application, saying:

> 'What is suggested is that because they were directors of the company at the time when the company obtained planning permission that they should be ordered to complete the development at their own expense. I am not saying that there might not be a case where the court would be justified in making such an order. If the case were one of fraud, or if the directors had siphoned off large sums of money out of the company, so as to leave it unable to fulfil its obligations, the court might be justified in lifting the veil of incorporation and fixing the directors with personal responsibility. But that is not this case. The second and third named respondents appear to be fairly small men who having failed in this particular enterprise are now back working for others. The worst that can be imputed against them is mismanagement.
>
> They gave personal guarantees to the insurance company which supplied the bond for £10,000 and to the company's bankers. They therefore stand to lose heavily arising out of the transaction. Moreover...the liquidator and his officials entertain no suspicion that there has been any impropriety on the part of the directors in dealing with the assets of the company.
>
> It appears to me that Mr Keogh and Mr English traded with the benefit of limited liability in this case and that in the absence of any evidence of impropriety on their part, I would not be justified in attempting to make them liable for the default of the company.'

[5.037] Again, in *Dublin County Council v O'Riordan*[105], even though the affairs of the company had been carried on with 'scant disregard for the requirements of the Companies Acts', Murphy J refused to grant an injunction against the company's directors requiring them personally to fulfil the planning obligations of the company since no evidence of 'fraud or the misapplication of monies' had been established. That case was relied upon by Hamilton P in *Dunlaoghaire Corporation v Park Hill Developments*[106] where the learned judge refused to grant an injunction against a director

---

104 *Dublin County Council v Elton Homes Ltd* [1984] ILRM 297.

105 *Dublin County Council v O'Riordan* [1986] ILRM 104.

106 *Dun Laoghaire Corporation v Park Hill Developments* [1989] IR 447. See also *Ellis v Nolan* (6 May 1983, unreported), High Court, where McWilliam J refused to grant an injunction under the Local Government (Planning and Development) Act 1976, s 27 against a director in respect of whom no 'fraud, misrepresentation, improper application of money or negligence' had been established.

of the respondent company. It was contended by the applicant in that case that the company and Mr Parkinson Hill, the director, were indistinguishable in law for the following reasons: in contravention of CA 1963, s 131, no annual general meeting was ever held; no formal directors' meeting was ever convened; no director's fees or dividends on his shares were paid to Mr Kearns, the other director; in contravention of CA 1963, s 148 no financial reports were ever issued to the shareholders; Parkinson Hill was the only person with knowledge of the financial affairs of the company; and he was in total control of the company and managed it without regard for the requirements of the Companies Acts. Hamilton P observed[107]:

> 'I have no doubt, having heard the evidence of [Parkinson Hill], that he was in effective control of the first respondent and he failed to comply with the requirements of the Companies Act 1963, but I have found no evidence of any fraud or misrepresentation on his part; any siphoning off or misapplication of the funds of the said company; nor of negligence in the carrying out of the affairs of the said company... As I have found no evidence of any impropriety by the second respondent in the conduct of the affairs of the first respondent, I am satisfied that he traded with the benefit of limited liability in this case and I would not be justified in attempting to make him personally responsible for the admitted default of the first respondent.'

It should be noted that despite the reluctance of the courts to disregard the separate legal personality of a company where the controllers are guilty of mismanagement, the legislature has also made provisions to protect creditors of the company from abuse of the corporate form through either fraudulent *or reckless* trading. These are considered in Chapter 10, *Duties of Directors and Other Officers*.

Evasion of existing legal obligations

[5.038] The courts have shown an apparent willingness to disregard the separate legal personality of a company where to do otherwise would allow a controller to evade an existing legal obligation. Such a case is *Cummings v Stewart*[108], where Cummings entered into a patent licensing agreement whereby he agreed to license his patent for reinforced concrete to Stewart. Clause 2 of the agreement required Stewart to pay Cummings a minimum sum annually in respect of royalties. Clause 5 of the agreement forbade Stewart from subletting, assigning, or transferring the licence without Cummings' consent; but the clause also contained a proviso permitting Stewart to transfer the licence to any limited company he might form to carry on his business or the business connected with the licence. Stewart was unable to make a profit from his use of the patents, and in an attempt to evade his liability to Cummings for royalties on the patents, he transferred the licence to a limited company formed by him. It was not intended that this new company should work the patents. Cummings successfully claimed that Stewart should be regarded as being liable for all arrears of royalty payments, *including those due for the period during which the licence was held by the company*. Meredith MR said:

[107] *Dunlaoghaire Corporation v Park Hill Developments* [1989] IR 447 at 450–452.

[108] *Cummings v Stewart* [1911] 1 IR 236.

> 'In my opinion, the Companies (Consolidation) Act 1908 embodies a code framed (inter alia) for the purposes of preserving and enforcing commercial morality and it would be strange indeed, if that code could be turned into an engine for the destruction of legal obligations and the overthrow of legitimate and enforceable claims. The most casual reader of the speeches of the House of Lords in the case of *Salomon v Salomon & Co* cannot fail to observe that there is nothing in any of those speeches contrary to the view that I have just expressed...
>
> The defendant says he has formed the company within the meaning of [clause 5 of the licensing agreement] and that the intention with which the company was formed and with which the two holders of £1 shares come into this concern is not for me, and I have no right to comment on it. I have no right at all except for the fact that it is demonstrated that the company was formed not to carry on the business of the plaintiff – not, in the words of the proviso, to carry on the business "connected with and arising out of said patents and this licence", but for the purpose of extinguishing the patent rights or at all events – and this is sufficient to justify the plaintiff in persisting in his claim in this case – for the purpose of refraining from carrying on any work connected with the reinforced concrete patents of the plaintiff.'

The fact that no order appears to have been made against the company, coupled with the opening sentiments expressed in the passage quoted, would suggest that the learned Master of the Rolls was prepared to ignore completely the existence of the company. On the other hand, it has been suggested that this was not a case of disregard of separate legal personality at all, but was, rather, a case of mere contractual interpretation[109]. Nevertheless, other cases involving avoidance of existing legal obligations illustrate some disregard by the courts of the separate legal personality of a company.

[5.039] The decision in *Mastertrade (Exports) Ltd v Phelan*[110] shows that there must be some evidence that a company was used 'as an engine for the destruction of legal obligations or the overthrow of legitimate or enforceable claims'. The facts there were that P sold 50% of his interest in the Master Meat Group of companies to T and subsequently, in breach of their joint-venture agreement, T disposed of his shares to G. P was not aware that T had disposed of his shares to G. After the group encountered financial difficulties P and T entered into negotiations, T's agents in fact acted on behalf of G and offered to acquire the group for IR£2.5 million but a counter-offer of IR£2.75 million was made and under the terms of the joint venture agreement, that became binding. Subsequently, P commenced proceedings against T, G and the Master Meat Group of companies. These companies countered with an action against P, alleging 32 allegations of misappropriations by P. The application before the court was brought by P to strike out the proceedings against him by the Master Meat Group of companies having regard to G's alleged wrongdoing. In particular, P alleged that the effect of the actions was to ensure that an entirely unlawful and improper benefit would be obtained by G as beneficial owner of the companies because although the companies' complaints against P predated G's involvement, G would still benefit from any award made. P also contended that G's alleged wrong doing constituted fraud and was a factor the court

---

[109] Ussher, *Company Law in Ireland*, (1986), p 27.

[110] *Mastertrade (Exports) Ltd v Phelan* (4 December 2001, unreported), High Court (Murphy J).

must consider in lifting the corporate veil. Murphy J refused to disregard the companies' separate legal personality saying that the respondent companies:

> 'have not been in breach of any agreement, have not induced a breach of an agreement nor are in any way tainted with illegality, deceit or fraud. They are the proper plaintiffs in relation to the allegations that they make in these proceedings.'

In finding that the companies were not used as an engine for the destruction of legal obligations or the overthrow of legitimate or enforceable claims (as referred to in *Cummings v Stewart*) Murphy J also held that whilst there may have been concealment, which did mislead the public, 'there is no evidence before the Court that the sole object of the concealment was to "cheat and mislead the public"'.[111] Having regard to the documentary evidence before the court, Murphy J concluded that it was inappropriate to lift the corporate veil and he refused to strike out the proceedings.

[5.040] One case where the courts have disregarded the separate legal personality of a company is *Jones v Lipman*[112]. In that case, Lipman entered into a legally enforceable contract to sell his house to Jones. Subsequently, Lipman changed his mind, and, in an attempt to avoid having to convey the house to Jones, he acquired a ready-made company, which had been incorporated with the object of acquiring land, and transferred the house to it. Lipman was the beneficial owner of all the shares of the company. Russell J, awarding specific performance to Jones and thereby compelling Lipman to sell the house, said that the company was 'the creature of the first defendant, a device and a sham, a mask which he holds before his face in an attempt to avoid recognition by the eye of equity.'[113]

An order for specific performance was also made against the company. This last fact indicates that the learned judge was not prepared to ignore altogether the existence of the company he had so recently described as a sham; but appears to have disregarded its separate legal personality to the extent that he considered the company to be bound by the obligations of a member. Sadly, the terms 'device', 'sham', and 'mask' serve merely to cloud the true reasoning in the case, and it has been suggested that the outcome in that case might have been achieved by applying more conventional legal methods[114].

[5.041] In the *Jones* case, orders were directed against both the company and its controlling member. In *Gilford Motor Co Ltd v Horne*[115], the use of a company to avoid existing legal obligations caused the courts to make an order against the company and a person who was not one of its members. In that case, Horne's contract of employment contained a covenant whereby he agreed that should he leave his employment he would not compete with the plaintiff employers for a period of six years from 1 September 1928. Before this period had expired, Horne left the plaintiff's employ. A week later his wife and son set up a company to carry on business in competition with the plaintiff. Horne was neither a registered shareholder nor a director of the company, but it acted in

---

[111] An expression used in *Scott v Brown, Douring McNab and Company* (1892) 2 QB 724.

[112] *Jones v Lipman* [1962] 1 All ER 442.

[113] *Jones v Lipman* [1962] 1 All ER 442 at 445.

[114] Ussher, *Company Law in Ireland,* (1986), p 28.

[115] *Gilford Motor Co Ltd v Horne* [1933] Ch 939.

accordance with his instructions[116]. The plaintiffs succeeded in obtaining an injunction against Horne and the new company, restraining them from carrying on business in competition. Lord Hanworth said that the new company[117]:

> '...was formed as a device, a stratagem in order to mask the effective carrying on of the business of Mr Horne. The purpose of it was to try to enable him under what is a cloak or a sham to engage in business in respect of which he had a fear that the plaintiffs might intervene and object...'

[5.042] An even less convincing, though nonetheless similar, finding was made in *Creasey v Breachwood Motors Ltd*[118]. In that case a company, Breachwood Welwyn Ltd, wrongfully dismissed Creasy, its general manager. Creasey then commenced an action for wrongful dismissal against the company. The company ceased trading, paid off all its creditors apart from Creasey, and transferred its assets to a new company, Breachwood Motors Ltd. Creasey subsequently obtained judgment against Breachwood Welwyn Ltd, which by then had no assets. Richard Southwell QC, sitting as deputy High Court judge in the Queen's Bench Division, held that the takeover of Breachwood Welwyn Ltd's assets by the new company was carried out by the directors in total disregard of their duties as such, and in an attempt to ensure that Creasy would not recover anything if successful in his claim. Accordingly, he disregarded the separate identity of Breachwood Motors Ltd and allowed Creasey to proceed in enforcing his judgment for wrongful dismissal against it. The decision may be criticised[119], however, on the basis that the facts did not justify a finding that the arrangement between Breachwood Welwyn Ltd and Breachwood Motors Ltd was a façade concealing the actual facts. The directors were under a common law duty to act bona fide and in the best interests of the company as a whole. By transferring the business to Breachwood Motors Ltd and paying off all the old company's existing creditors, they were able to produce a stronger balance sheet in the members' interest. If there was evidence of a fraudulent motive or desire on the part of the incorporators of the new company to evade an existing legal obligation, it was not relied upon by the learned Judge in his reasoning; nor was it suggested that the new company was established as a façade concealing the true facts. Unfortunately, the new company, Breachwood Motors Ltd, decided not to defend the case, so the reasoning was not challenged. It is also important to note that the court decided merely that Breachwood Motors Ltd, the new company, could be substituted as a defendant in Creasy's action against his former employer – no liability was imposed on the directors. *Creasey*'s case was recently rejected by the Court of Appeal in *Ord v Belhaven Pubs Ltd*[120], considered below.

[5.043] Though not traditionally viewed as such, the decision of Costello J in *Power Supermarkets Ltd v Crumlin Investments Ltd and Dunnes Stores (Crumlin) Ltd*[121] may be

[116] Nowadays, he would be classed as a 'shadow director'; see Chapter 8, *Corporate Governance: Management by the Directors*, para **[8.058]**.

[117] *Gilford Motor Co Ltd v Horne* [1933] Ch 939 at 956.

[118] *Creasey v Breachwood Motors Ltd* [1993] BCLC 480.

[119] See Png, 'Lifting the Veil of Incorporation: Creasey v Breachwood Motors: A Right Decision for the Wrong Reasons' (1999) 20 Co Law 122.

[120] *Ord v Belhaven Pubs Ltd* [1998] 2 BCLC 447.

[121] *Power Supermarkets Ltd v Crumlin Investments Ltd and Dunnes Stores (Crumlin) Ltd* (22 June 1981, unreported), High Court.

seen as an Irish example of judicial willingness to ignore the separate legal personality of a company when its substantial purpose and effect is to evade an existing legal obligation. The decision was made at a time when the 'single economic entity' theory was in vogue, and the major part of the judgment is devoted to an application of the then popular view that the separate identity of companies in a group could be ignored where the 'justice of the case' so required. What is clear from the learned judge's reasoning is that the justice of the case required the group to be regarded as a single entity because to do otherwise would lead to the evasion of an existing legal obligation to respect the terms of a commercial lease. The case is considered in further detail at para **[5.052]** below.

[5.044] An important element in the decision of whether to disregard the separate legal personality of a company for evasion of legal obligations is whether, as a matter of fact, the company was incorporated for that purpose, and whether the true facts were concealed. In *Ord v Belhaven Pubs Ltd*[122], the facts (which may be likened to those in *Creasy*'s case, above) were that the plaintiffs who bought a 20-year lease of a public house from Belhaven Pubs Ltd, subsequently claimed that the vendor had misrepresented the turnover and profitability of the pub. They commenced proceedings against the company in 1991. In 1992, however, following a general collapse in property values, the defendant's parent company decided to restructure group operations with the ultimate effect that, by 1995, the assets of Belhaven Pubs Ltd had been bought by other members of the group at a price in excess of the net book value, and its creditors had been satisfied, so that the company became nothing more than a dormant company, having no assets and no liabilities. The Court of Appeal allowed an appeal against an order of the English High Court that the parent company be substituted as defendant in the plaintiffs' action against Belhaven Pubs Ltd. The Court of Appeal held that nothing improper had been done by the directors and there was no evidence to suggest that the company was a mere façade or that the true facts were concealed.

[5.045] Another Irish analogue is to be found in the case of *Allied Irish Coal Supplies Ltd v Powell Duffryn International Fuels Ltd*[123]. In that case the plaintiff alleged that the defendant, a wholly-owned subsidiary of Powell Duffryn plc, was in breach of a commercial contract to supply coal. When the plaintiff later became aware that the parent company was about to sell the subsidiary it sought an order joining the parent as co-defendant. Laffoy J in the High Court rejected the application, noting that the plaintiff had traded with the defendant knowing that it was a subsidiary, and that there was no suggestion of any privity of contract between the plaintiff and the parent company. The learned judge concluded that the mere fact alone that the defendant subsidiary was financially dependent on its parent was insufficient to render the parent responsible for the contractual obligations of the subsidiary:

> 'The proposition advanced by the plaintiff seems to me to be so fundamentally at variance with the principle of separate corporate legal personality laid down in *Salomon v Salomon & Co* [1897] AC 22, and the concept of limited liability, that it is wholly unstateable.'

---

122 *Ord v Belhaven Pubs Ltd* [1998] 2 BCLC 447.

123 *Allied Irish Coal Supplies Ltd v Powell Duffryn International Fuels Ltd* [1998] 2 IR 519.

The Supreme Court upheld Laffoy J's decision. Murphy J, contrasting *Power Supermarkets Ltd v Crumlin Investments Ltd and Dunnes Stores (Crumlin) Ltd*, pointed to the fact that the defendant subsidiary company was more than a mere shell: it carried on a very substantial business and its employees reported to the board of the subsidiary rather than directly to the board of the parent.

[5.046] The courts have shown themselves willing to disregard the separate legal personality of a company where it has been used to avoid statutory obligations, or where it would otherwise frustrate the purpose of a statute. In *Merchandise Transport Ltd v British Transport Commission*[124], a holding company attempted to use its subsidiary company[125] as a vehicle to avoid a statutory provision designed to protect the public from unfair competition. The provision prohibited licensed public hauliers from using their vehicles to carry their *own* goods; and private hauliers were likewise prohibited from using surplus capacity to carry the goods of others. The holding company wished to transfer vehicles which it owned and used privately to a subsidiary engaged in the public haulage business. The subsidiary was to use the vehicles to carry the holding company's goods, and to use surplus capacity to carry third parties' goods. An application by the subsidiary for a public haulier's licence was refused by the licensing authority, and the refusal was upheld by the Court of Appeal, because to grant the licence would put the holding company in the position of a manufacturer who could use his own vehicles to deliver his goods and then solicit return loads from the public. Here, the court disregarded the separate legal personality of the subsidiary by looking at the motives of its controllers.

[5.047] A similar approach appears to have been adopted by the Supreme Court in *The State v District Justice Donnelly*[126], where the holders of a wine licence established a company, to which they transferred the premises. They were the company's only directors and shareholders, and they had formed the company in the hope that they could transfer to it the licence which had been indorsed twice already, and which, if it continued in their hands, was about to suffer a third indorsement, whereupon it would be revoked. The transfer of the licence required a certificate of no objection from the District Justice[127], and the justice refused to issue such a certificate. The Supreme Court upheld the refusal, stating that the wide discretion given to the Justice by the Revenue Act 1862 justified him in disregarding the separate legal personality of the company by examining the motivations of those who had formed it.

Avoidance of future legal obligations

[5.048] The courts will *not*, however, disregard the separate legal personality of a company where it is used merely to avoid prospective or *future* obligations. This is evident in the judgment of the House of Lords in *Adams v Cape Industries*[128]. In that

---

124 *Merchandise Transport Ltd v British Transport Commission* [1962] 2 QB 173.

125 On holding and subsidiary companies see Chapter 17, *Groups of Companies*, para **[17.006]** *ff*.

126 *The State v District Justice Donnelly* (1977) The Irish Times, 5 November noted by Ussher, *Company Law in Ireland* (1986), p 33.

127 Revenue Act 1862, s 15.

128 *Adams v Cape Industries* [1990] Ch 433.

case, Cape Industries, a large multinational company based in England, was engaged in the asbestos industry. At one stage, Cape had a supply subsidiary (the North American Asbestos Corporation) in America, but after that company was involved in a $20 million settlement for injuries suffered by its employees, it was put into liquidation and its operations taken over by CPC. CPC was an American company which was established with financial assistance from Cape. Though not a subsidiary of Cape, CPC was instructed from time to time by AMC, a Liechtenstein incorporated company, which acted as Cape's agent.

In a subsequent tort action, workers at the CPC asbestos plant who had suffered illness as a result of exposure to asbestos obtained judgment in default against Cape in the American courts to the tune of some $15.64 million, and sought to have the judgment enforced in the English courts. In order to succeed in their application, they had to establish either that Cape had established and maintained, at its own expense, a fixed place of business in America and for more than a minimal time carried on business there through its servants and agents, or that Cape had, through its representative, carried on business at some fixed place in America. The plaintiffs contended that Cape had carried on business in America through CPC, which, they said, though not technically a subsidiary of Cape, was established and controlled indirectly by Cape in an attempt to evade future tortious liability.

The Court of Appeal found that CPC had indeed been established with a view to minimising the appearance of Cape's involvement in the sale of asbestos in America, and also with a view to lawfully reducing the possibility of Cape being made liable for US taxes or for future tort claims. But the court was equally satisfied that CPC was an independent corporation, wholly owned by its chief executive, and carrying on its *own* business in America. Slade LJ said[129]:

> 'We do not accept as a matter of law that the court is entitled to lift the corporate veil as against a defendant company which is the member of a corporate group merely because the corporate structure has been used so as to ensure that the legal liability (if any) in respect of particular future activities of the group (and correspondingly the risk of enforcement of that liability) will fall on another member of the group rather than the defendant company. Whether or not this is desirable, the right to use a corporate structure in this manner is inherent in our corporate law... [Counsel for the plaintiffs] urged on us that the purpose of the operation was in substance that Cape would have the practical benefit of the group's asbestos trade in the United States...without the risks of tortious liability. This may be so. However, in our judgment Cape was in law entitled to organise the group's affairs in that manner and (save in the case of AMC to which special considerations apply) to expect that the court would apply the principle of [separate legal personality].'

[5.049] An earlier Irish analogue is to be found *Roundabout Ltd v Beirne*[130] where the High Court held that a company which was incorporated with a view to evading potential future pickets was in law a distinct entity not to be identified with its

---

[129] *Adams v Cape Industries* [1990] Ch 433 at 544.

[130] *Roundabout Ltd v Beirne* [1959] IR 423. See Chapter 4 *Incorporation and its Consequences*, para **[4.070]**.

predecessor. The case is considered in detail in Chapter 4, *Incorporation and its Consequences*.

[C] The Single Economic Entity

[5.050] In the 1970s and 1980s the courts put forward a novel apparent justification for disregarding the separate legal personalities of related companies. In a number of cases the courts disregarded the separate legal personality of the company *where justice required*[131] by regarding it as a mere constituent of a larger legal entity, or 'single economic entity'. This kind of disregard may be distinguished from the implied agency cases discussed earlier, for where a number of companies are regarded as a single legal entity, only one legal person is recognised, whereas agency recognises the existence of at least two persons. This means of disregarding separate legal personality has been employed in the past by the Irish courts, and has received approval in general terms from the Supreme Court[132], but its scope has been severely restricted by the English Court of Appeal[133], and more recently by the Irish Supreme Court[134]. The recent trend of the courts reveals a significant reluctance to introduce any general rule of disregard of the separate legal personality of companies in groups beyond those enunciated in *Salomon*'s case.

The single economic entity approach never took root firmly in Ireland. Though it was taken in its time as evidence of a new exception to *Salomon's case*, it is appears now that the courts will only apply it to determine who should be identified with a company when its separate legal personality is being disregarded in accordance with the *Salomon* principles.

[5.051] The single economic entity approach has its roots in an observation by Gower that there was 'evidence of a general tendency to ignore the separate legal entities of companies within a group, and to look instead at the economic entity of the whole group.'[135] This statement was accepted without question by Lord Denning in *DHN Food Distributors Ltd v Tower Hamlet London Borough Council*[136], a case which arose out of a compulsory acquisition of property. A holding company conducted business on land owned by one of its wholly-owned subsidiaries. When the council compulsorily acquired the land, the holding company entered a claim for compensation in respect of the disturbance caused to it. The Court of Appeal upheld the claim for compensation. Lord Denning MR held that the court could look to the economic entity of the whole group and treat the business as being carried on by that group. He said[137]:

---

131 See *Power Supermarkets Ltd v Crumlin Investments Ltd* (22 June 1981, unreported), High Court (Costello J), discussed at para **[5.052]**.

132 *Re Bray Travel and Bray Travel (Holdings) Ltd* (13 July 1981, unreported), Supreme Court, discussed at para **[5.052]**.

133 *Adams v Cape Industries* [1990] Ch 433.

134 *Allied Irish Coal Supplies Ltd v Powell Duffryn International Fuels Ltd* [1998] 2 IR 519.

135 Gower, *Principles of Modern Company Law* (3rd edn; 1969), p 216. Perhaps the effect which the author's remarks had on subsequent jurisprudence prompted him to take the especially measured view which appears in later editions of his work. See para **[5.005]**.

136 *DHN Food Distributors Ltd v Tower Hamlet London Borough Council* [1976] 3 All ER 462.

137 *DHN Food Distributors Ltd v Tower Hamlet London Borough Council* [1976] 3 All ER 462 at 467.

> 'We all know that in many respects a group of companies are treated together for the purpose of general accounts, balance sheet and profit and loss account. They are treated as one concern. Professor Gower in his book on company law says: "there is evidence of a general tendency to ignore the separate legal entities of various companies within a group, and to look instead at the economic entity of the whole group". This is especially the case when a parent company owns all the shares of the subsidiaries, so much so that it can control every movement of the subsidiaries. These subsidiaries are bound hand and foot to the parent company and must do just what the parent company says...This group is virtually the same as a partnership in which all the three companies are partners. They should not be treated separately so as to be defeated on a technical point...They should not be deprived of the compensation which should justly be payable for disturbance. The three companies should, for present purposes, be treated as one and the parent company, DHN, should be treated as that one.'

Lord Denning MR also found that the holding company was entitled to compensation on other grounds, namely, that the subsidiary had given an irrevocable licence to the holding company to conduct business on the land, and that this licence conferred an equitable interest in the land on the holding company. Goff LJ and Shaw LJ were of the view that the case should be decided on the basis that the holding company was the owner in equity of the property under a resulting trust. Nevertheless, it was Lord Denning's observations concerning the disregard of separate legal personality which attracted later attention to the case.

[5.052] Lord Denning's views on the disregard of separate legal personality were adopted in Ireland by Costello J in *Power Supermarkets Ltd v Crumlin Investments Ltd and Dunnes Stores (Crumlin) Ltd*[138]. In that case, Crumlin Investments Ltd were landlords of a large shopping centre. Power Supermarkets Ltd, controllers of the Quinnsworth chain of supermarkets, entered into a lease of one of the units in the shopping centre. Since it was important to Power Supermarkets Ltd that no other large supermarket should be allowed to set up in the shopping centre in competition with them, Crumlin Investments Ltd covenanted inter alia:

> '...not during the term to grant a lease for or to sell or permit or suffer the sale by any of its tenants or so far as within [Crumlin Investments Ltd's] control any sub or under tenants of groceries or food products in or over an area exceeding 3000 square feet in any one unit ... forming part of the shopping centre...'

The shopping centre failed in those early days to be a financial success for Crumlin Investments Ltd, and the company decided to sell it. A sale was agreed with Cornelscourt Shopping Centre Ltd, and the sale was subsequently carried out by way of a transfer of all the shares in Crumlin Investments Ltd to Cornelscourt Shopping Centre Ltd. Cornelscourt Shopping Centre Ltd was one of the Dunnes Stores group of companies, operators of a rival chain of stores to Power Supermarkets Ltd. The 150 or so individual companies making up the Dunnes Stores group were, in many respects, only notionally separate companies. All the affairs of the group were managed by members of

138 *Power Supermarkets Ltd v Crumlin Investments Ltd and Dunnes Stores (Crumlin) Ltd* (22 June, 1981, unreported), High Court (Costello J). See Hannigan, 'Piercing the Corporate Veil', (1983) DULJ (ns) 111.

the Dunne family. It was vital from the Dunne family's point of view that a Dunnes Stores retail outlet be established in the shopping centre. The family policy was that a new company should operate each separate retail unit, and so a new company, Dunnes Stores (Crumlin) Ltd, was incorporated for the purposes of acquiring a lease in the shopping centre and establishing a retail outlet there in direct competition with Power Supermarkets Ltd. Upon incorporation of this new company, Cornelscourt Shopping Centre Ltd caused Crumlin Investments Ltd to convey the freehold of a large unit in the shopping centre to Dunnes Stores (Crumlin) Ltd for a nominal consideration, and without any of the usual covenants which would accompany a transaction of this kind when carried out between strangers at arm's length.

When Dunnes Stores (Crumlin) Ltd began to trade in the shopping centre, Power Supermarkets Ltd sought an injunction restraining them. Costello J found for the plaintiffs, holding that Dunnes Stores (Crumlin) Ltd were bound by the covenant contained in the plaintiff's lease, *even though* they were not a party to that lease. He found that the covenant was a restrictive covenant, the burden of which, according to well-established principles, ran with the land. Significantly, he also found that Dunnes Stores (Crumlin) Ltd were bound by the terms of the lease to which they were not formally a party because Dunnes Stores (Crumlin) Ltd, Crumlin Investments Ltd, and Cornelscourt Shopping Centre Ltd were all part of a single economic entity. Having cited the views of Lord Denning MR and Shaw LJ in *DHN Ltd v Tower Hamlets London Borough Council*, Costello J continued:

> 'It seems to me to be well established...that a court may, if the justice of the case so requires, treat two or more related companies as a single entity so that the business notionally carried on by one will be regarded as the business of the group or another member of the group if this conforms to the economic and commercial realities of the situation. It would, in my view, be very hard to find a clearer case than the present one for the application of this principle. I appreciate that Crumlin Investments is a property owning not a trading company but it is clear that the creation of the new company and the conveyance to it of the freehold interest in a unit in the shopping centre were means for carrying out the commercial plans of the Dunne family in the centre. The enterprise had a two-fold aspect (a) the creation of a new retail outlet for the Dunnes Stores Group in the shopping centre and (b) the enhancement of the rents in the centre as a whole which the creation of such an outlet would hopefully produce. To treat the two companies as a single economic entity seems to me to accord fully with the realities of the situation. Not to do so could involve considerable injustice to the plaintiffs as their rights under the covenant might be defeated by the mere technical device of the creation of a company with a £2 issued capital which had no real independent life of its own. If it is established that the covenant is breached there should in my opinion be an injunction against both defendants.'

[5.053] This passage was, along with Lord Denning's observations in the *DHN* case, subsequently cited with approval by the Supreme Court in *Re Bray Travel and Bray Travel (Holdings) Ltd*[139], and may thus still be regarded as a correct statement of the law

139 *Re Bray Travel and Bray Travel (Holdings) Ltd* (13 July 1981, unreported), Supreme Court. The judgment was delivered *ex tempore* and no written judgments were handed down. Its value as an authority may be questioned to this extent. The case is, however, noted by Keane, *Company Law* (3rd edn, 2000), p 135, and Ussher, *Company Law in Ireland* (1986), p 52, fn 65–66. See also MacCann, *A Casebook on Company Law*, (1991), pp 135–136. The 'justice' criterion was also applied by Barron J in *H Albert De Bary & Co NV v TF O'Mullanel* (2 June 1992, unreported), High Court, but without much explanation.

in this jurisdiction. In that case, the court granted an injunction to the liquidator of Bray Travel Ltd freezing the assets of its subsidiaries. Henchy J and Kenny J, with whom Hederman J concurred, both observed that the injunction was equally justified on ordinary tracing principles without the necessity for disregarding the separate legal personality of the company, there being evidence that the company had transferred properties to its subsidiaries at a gross undervalue[140].

[5.054] A common feature of all of the cases discussed in the two preceding paragraphs is that in each case the disregard of the separate legal personality of the companies was justified on traditional grounds in accordance with the principles in *Salomon*'s case.

[5.055] Accordingly, in *Rex Pet Foods Ltd v Lamb Bros (Dublin) Ltd*[141], Costello J refused to disregard the separate legal personalities of a group of companies under common ownership or control. The case arose on a claim by the receiver and manager of Rex Pet Foods Ltd that its assets and the assets of the defendant companies should be aggregated and that the businesses of all the companies should be treated as one. Lamb Bros (Dublin) had acquired a 52% shareholding in Rex Pet Foods. Some of Lamb Bros (Dublin)'s directors joined Rex Pet Foods' board of directors, but the management of Rex Pet Foods Ltd remained unaltered. A number of contracts were entered into between Rex Pet Foods and Lamb Bros (Dublin) whereby the defendant group of companies became sole distributors for Rex Pet Foods' goods, and under which the defendants would supply management services to Rex Pet Foods. Separate books of account were maintained by the companies. When Rex Pet Foods got into financial difficulties Lamb Bros (Dublin) acquired the remaining shares in Rex Pet Foods. At this stage there were some management changes to Rex Pet Foods whereby managers from the defendant group joined its board. When Rex Pet Foods went into receivership, the receiver sought to have the assets of all the companies treated as one. Costello J, refusing the application, said:

> 'It is alleged that the plaintiff company should be regarded merely as a branch of the defendant group as its manufacturing arm because, firstly, the defendants discharged the creditors of the plaintiff company from time to time. The evidence establishes that this in fact occurred...but this to my mind did not in any way affect the separate legal entity of the plaintiff company and was a normal enough arrangement for companies trading in a group such as these companies were trading. Secondly, it is suggested that the claim is supported by the fact that invoices from suppliers of the plaintiff company were sent direct to the defendant company. Factually this is so. From time to time creditors of the plaintiff company, in particular suppliers of goods and raw materials to the plaintiff company, sent invoices to one or other of the defendant companies but this does not raise any claim or sustain any claim that the two companies should be treated as one legal entity. It does perhaps, reflect some confusion but not to the extent which would justify the claim now being made on the plaintiff's behalf. Thirdly, it is suggested that the management of the plaintiff company was such that the claim being made is justified. The management changed in the way I have indicated. The explanation for the change is a reasonable one and in my view does not of itself justify the claim that has been made. Fourthly, it was

[140] See Courtney, *Mareva Injunctions and Related Interlocutory Orders* (1998), pp 9–19.

[141] *Rex Pet Foods Ltd v Lamb Bros (Dublin) Ltd* (5 December, 1985, unreported), High Court (Costello J).

suggested that there were no regular meetings of the board of directors of the plaintiff company. There were meetings of the board of directors and meetings were held up to March 1982. Thereafter it seems that no inference such as is being sought to be drawn arises from the fact that the board of directors comprised members of the parent company for this is a situation which is normal and is to be found where a group of companies is controlled by a parent company.

Finally, the point was raised that the defendant company was sole distributor for the plaintiff company, but this was a situation which was in no way unique or which raises the inference which the plaintiffs seek to raise.

The question arises whether all these factors taken together raise the inference sought to be raised but I cannot agree that this is so. There have been some cases which counsel have referred me to where the courts have treated companies as being one legal entity but these have been cases in which the facts are very different to those which the evidence establishes in the circumstances of this case.

So in my view the plaintiffs have failed to make out a case which would justify me in making the declaration which is sought. I should add that even if the situation were different and there were circumstances in which the court should regard these companies as being one for some reason or other, this would not justify the court making another order which, indeed, is a separate order in relation to the aggregation of assets because it seems to me there has been *no evidence to suggest that any funds of the plaintiff company were siphoned off into any of the defendant companies in such circumstances as would raise an equitable claim to the assets of any of the defendant companies...*'.[142]

Much seems to have been made by Costello J of the fact that no equitable claim to the assets of any of the defendant companies arose, and he refused to disregard the separate legal personality of the plaintiff company on that basis. If an equitable claim had been established permitting such disregard of the company's separate legal personality, then doubtless it would have been actionable in equity without a need to disregard separate legal personality.

[5.056] Likewise, in *The State (McInerney & Co Ltd) v Dublin County Council*[143], Carroll J refused to regard two subsidiaries of the same holding company as part of a single economic entity so that one could, when refused planning permission, compel the defendant council to purchase lands owned by the other. No recognised legal relationship between the subsidiaries could be identified which might establish a proprietary relationship in the first subsidiary. Had a proprietary interest been found, it is submitted, there would have been grounds other than the single economic entity principle upon which to afford the applicants relief. Carroll J said:

'In my opinion the corporate veil is not a device to be raised and lowered at the option of the parent or group. The arm which lifts the corporate veil must always be that of justice. If justice requires (as it did in the *DHN* case) the courts will not be slow to treat a group of subsidiary companies as one. But can it be said that justice requires it in this case? We have here a parent company with 30 subsidiary companies forming the McInerney Group. According to Mr Cody, the finance director of the parent company, it is group policy,

[142] Emphasis added.

[143] *The State (McInerney & Co Ltd) v Dublin County Council* (12 December 1984, unreported), High Court (Carroll J).

depending on circumstances to operate in the name of one of these companies on various sites throughout the country. He says that McInerney Construction Ltd (the registered owner) has no resources other than those supplied by another subsidiary. The purchase moneys were provided by the applicant, (it being the intention that such moneys be repaid in due course out of the proceeds of realisation).

When those averments are considered, it appears to me that here is a group of companies operated so as to maximise the benefits to be gained from the individual corporate identity of each subsidiary. If the purchase money was to be repaid out of the proceeds of realisation, it follows that the profits of losses remained with the registered owner. If the development was not profitable the loss would be confined within the assets of that one company...In my opinion this is not a case where justice demands that the corporate veil be lifted...It is not for a corporate group to claim that the veil should be lifted to illuminate one aspect of its business while it should be left *in situ* to isolate the individual actions of its subsidiaries in other respects.'

[5.057] As Carroll J observed in *The State (McInerney & Co)* case, a controller must not be allowed to disregard the separate legal personality of a company simply when it suits him. In *Gresham Industries Ltd v Cannon*[144], Finlay P refused to regard a company and its controller as a single economic entity. He refused to allow a debtor to set off, against a debt which was owed to a creditor, a debt owed by that creditor to Paulcar Ltd, one company in a group of companies, all of which were beneficially owned by the debtor. He said:

'It seems to me...a fundamental principle of the law that if a person decides to obtain and use the benefit of trading through limited liability companies and if for any purposes whether the limitation of his liability, tax purposes or otherwise he transfers assets from one company to another or makes drawings from one company and invests them in his own name in another company that he cannot subsequently be heard to ignore the existence of the legal entities consisting of the different companies and to look upon the entire transaction as a personal one...All these claims were put forward by the defendant upon the basis that he was the effective beneficial owner of Paulcar Ltd which he asserted was a solvent company and that therefore he must be identified with the rights and liabilities of Paulcar Ltd as if they were his own rights and liabilities and that therefore he was entitled to these as a set-off or credit against the amounts due by him to the plaintiff company in liquidation...I am satisfied that as a matter of law even a 100% beneficial shareholder in a company cannot for the purposes of the settling of an account between him and another individual or company be identified with the company.' [145]

[5.058] English authorities suggest that the justice of the case will only permit a company to be regarded as part of a single economic entity where it is established merely as a 'façade' to conceal improprieties, or where the court is interpreting a statute or contract. Doubts about the scope of Lord Denning's observations in the *DHN* case

144 *Gresham Industries Ltd v Cannon* (2 July 1980, unreported), High Court (Finlay P).

145 *Gresham Industries Ltd v Cannon* (2 July 1980, unreported), High Court at p 19 of the transcript. Contrast *Munton Bros Ltd v Secretary of State* [1983] NI 369 where Gibson LJ stated that the members of a group may apply to have their separate legal personality disregarded where justice so requires.

were expressed in the English House of Lords by Lord Keith of Kinkel in *Woolfson v Strathclyde Regional Council*[146], where he said:

> 'I have some doubts whether...the Court of Appeal properly applied the principle that is appropriate to pierce the corporate veil only where special circumstances exist indicating that it is a mere façade concealing the true facts.'

[5.059] In *Adams v Cape Industries*[147], discussed above, the Court of Appeal determined:

> '...the relevant parts of the judgments in the *DHN* case ... must, we think, likewise be regarded as decisions on the relevant statutory provisions for compensation even though these parts were somewhat broadly expressed and the correctness of the decision was doubted by the House of Lords in *Woolfson v Strathclyde Regional Council* ...'

The Court of Appeal concluded that:

> '...save in cases which turn on the wording of particular statutes or contracts, the court is not free to disregard the principles of *Salomon v Salomon* merely because it considers that justice so requires. Our law, for better or worse, recognises the creation of subsidiary companies which though in one sense the creatures of their parent companies, will nevertheless under the general law fall to be treated as separate legal entities with all the rights and liabilities which would normally attach to such legal entities.'

[5.060] *Adams* was followed by Walker J in *Re Polly Peck International plc (In Administration) (No 4)*[148], where he added that the courts must look to the legal substance of any transaction and not its economic substance when deciding whether the company is a mere façade, regardless of any perceived injustice that arose when the company became insolvent.

In that case the court was required to determine the legal status of a wholly-owned subsidiary company which had been established within the Polly Peck group as a special-purpose financial vehicle, to raise funds through bond issues from the group. The subsidiary had a very small paid-up capital (which would not have covered even the transaction costs); it had no independent management; and had no bank account or separate financial records. Once it received funds pursuant to a bond issue, the subsidiary on-loaned the money to its holding company. The holding company guaranteed the subsidiary's obligations and pursuant to the relevant agreements became the principal obligor in regard to the bonds. The holding company went into administration and in the subsequent scheme of arrangement it was provided that no creditor should prove more than once in respect of any scheme claim. The subsidiary company then itself went into liquidation and sought to claim from the scheme supervisors for sums on-loaned to the holding company. Banks which had taken up the bonds also lodged claims against the holding company pursuant to its guarantees. The supervisors, after accepting most of these claims by the banks, applied to the court for directions as to whether the subsidiary company was entitled to maintain a claim in the

146 *Woolfson v Strathclyde Regional Council* (1978) SC 90.

147 *Adams v Cape Industries* [1990] Ch 433 at 536. See para **[5.048]**.

148 *Re Polly Peck International plc (In Administration) (No 4)* [1996] 2 All ER 433.

arrangement separate to those of the banks in respect of which it was essentially the same debt.

Walker J held that the claims of the subsidiary and of the banks were *not* so closely connected as to be, in substance, claims in respect of the same debt. He observed that it was not open to the court to disregard the principle of separate corporate personality and treat a closely integrated group of companies as a single economic unit on the basis merely of perceived injustice, particularly in cases where the separate legal existence of these companies assumed greater importance once they became insolvent. One company in the group could not properly be considered to be a nominee or agent of another, since neither agency nor nomineeship could be inferred simply because a subsidiary company has a small paid-up capital and has a board of directors all or most of whom are also directors or senior executives of its holding company.

The court held that full force had to be given to the legal meaning of the documents in question, for to regard them otherwise would be to deprive them of any legal meaning and would be at variance with the intentions of the parties. Nor was the subsidiary a sham. Walker J thought that there was a considerable difference between the creation and operation of a single-purpose financial vehicle, and the creation of a sham or façade simply to cloak the true character of certain transactions.

[5.061] The Irish courts, as has been stated above, have lately reaffirmed the importance of *Salomon*'s case in instances where the single economic entity approach has been argued. In *Allied Irish Coal Supplies Ltd v Powell Duffryn International Fuels Ltd*[149], discussed above, both the High Court and the Supreme Court rejected any possibility of a general rule that the mere existence of a close relationship between companies in a group could lead per se to their separate legal personalities being disregarded. What is especially interesting in the judgment of Murphy J in the Supreme Court in that case is his consideration of Costello J's decision in *Power Supermarkets Ltd v Crumlin Investments Ltd and Dunnes Stores (Crumlin) Ltd*[150]. Murphy J said:

> '...apart from the distinctions which may be drawn between this and other cases, the crucial feature of *Power Supermarkets Ltd v Crumlin Investments Ltd* is that Costello J did not purport to question the authority of *Salomon v Salomon & Co* [1897] AC 22. Indeed no reference was made to that case in the course of his judgment nor, as far as I am aware, the argument on which it was based. Again it is clear from the judgment in *Rex Pet Foods Ltd v Lamb Brothers (Ireland) Ltd* ... that Costello J had not intended in *Power Supermarkets Ltd v Crumlin Investments Ltd* to lay down any revolutionary principle of law. ..
>
> While it would be impossible to say that there are no circumstances in which the members of a company, whether corporate or individual, could not conduct, or purport to conduct the business of a company in such a way as to render their assets liable to meet claims in respect of the business normally carried out by the company, I believe that this would be an altogether exceptional state of affairs and difficult to reconcile with the seminal judgment in *Salomon v Salomon & Co*...'

[149] *Allied Irish Coal Supplies Ltd v Powell Duffryn International Fuels Ltd* [1998] 2 IR 519. See para **[5.045]**.

[150] See para **[5.043]**.

There is, of course, a hole in Murphy J's interpretation of *Power Supermarkets Ltd v Crumlin Investments and Dunnes Stores (Crumlin) Ltd*: as Costello J never referred to *Salomon*'s case in his judgment in that case, a fairer assessment would be that *Salomon*'s case was ignored by him rather than applied. Regardless, this merely serves to strengthen the proposition that the Supreme Court is keen to relegate the single economic entity approach to circumstances in which the exceptions identified in *Salomon*'s case are shown to exist. It is submitted that that is where it rightly belongs.

[5.062] The European Courts have held on more than one occasion that the EU Commission enjoys a degree of discretion in the choice of which company in a group ought to have a fine imposed on it for breaches of EU competition law. In *BPB Industries and British Gypsum*[151] the Court of First Instance confirmed the Commission's decision to impose fines on a subsidiary, 'whilst it is indeed true that the Commission could have imposed those fines on the parent company.'[152] And in Commercial Solvents[153], the Court of Justice established that the Commission can choose to impose the fine jointly and severally on a parent company and its subsidiary. Whilst such decisions on the face of them appear to indicate a general disregard for the principles of *Salomon*'s case, it must be remembered that EU competition law focuses on economic personality rather than legal personality by directing its provisions to 'undertakings' rather than to individuals or companies[154].

[D] Injunctions and Orders

[5.063] The courts retain an inherent jurisdiction to order enforcement of their judgments or orders against *any* person whom they think ought to be named therein to ensure observance of the order. In such cases the courts may disregard the separate legal personality of the company and issue an order or injunction against its directors or controlling members (as third parties), in addition to the company itself, in order to ensure that the company meets its obligations. This is well illustrated in cases involving injunctions under the Local Government (Planning and Development) Act 1976, s 27, though the principle is the same for many other types of order. In *Dublin County Council v Elton Homes Ltd*[155], Barrington J observed:

> 'Let me say at once that I think it may be quite proper, in certain circumstances to join the directors of a company as respondents when an application is made by a planning authority against a company pursuant to the provisions of s 27...There may be many cases particularly in the case of small companies where the most effective way of ensuring that the company complies with its obligations is to make an order against the directors as well as against the company itself. But in such a case the order against the directors would be a way of ensuring that the company carried out its obligations. A body corporate can only

151 *BPB Industries and British Gypsum* Case T– 65/89 [1993] ECR II–442.

152 *BPB Industries and British Gypsum* Case T– 65/89 [1993] ECR II–442.

153 *Commercial Solvents* Joined Cases 6 and 7/73 [1974] ECR 254.

154 See Wils 'The Undertaking as Subject of EC Competition Law and the Imputation of Infringements to Natural or Legal Persons' (2000) 25 EL Rev 99.

155 *Dublin County Council v Elton Homes Ltd* [1984] ILRM 297.

act through its agents and the most effective way of ensuring that it does in fact carry out its obligations might be to make an order against the persons in control of it.'

[5.064] The converse scenario, whereby the court issues an order or injunction against a company in respect of the obligations of its controlling members, is likewise possible. In *TSB Private Bank International SA v Chabra*[156], a Mareva injunction was made against a company even though the cause of action was not against it, but rather was against its controlling shareholder. Mummery J found that the court had jurisdiction so to order, saying:

> 'In the present case there are two defendants. There is one defendant, Mr Chabra, against whom the plaintiff undoubtedly has a good arguable cause of action: the claim on the guarantee. That is justiciable in the English court; Mr Chabra is amenable to the jurisdiction of the English court to make a final judgment against him on the guarantee. The claim for an injunction to restrain disposal of assets by Mr Chabra is ancillary and incidental to that cause of action. In my judgment, the claim for a similar injunction against the company is also ancillary and incidental to the claim against Mr Chabra and the court has power to grant such an injunction in an appropriate case. It does not follow that, because the court has no jurisdiction to grant a *Mareva* injunction against the company, if it were the sole defendant, the court has no jurisdiction to grant an injunction against the company as ancillary, or incidental, to the cause of action against Mr Chabra...I agree that such course of action is an exceptional one, but I do not accept that it is one that the court has no jurisdiction to take.'

The granting of the injunction against the company was, according to the judge, the most practical form of relief in the circumstances[157].

[E] CHARACTERISATION

[5.065] The courts regularly look behind the separate legal identity of a company in order to attribute to it a human characteristic required by law. It must be stressed that in such circumstances the courts *do not* ignore the separate legal existence of the corporation; rather, they examine its background in order to be able to say more about its separate personality. A number of such instances may be examined as follows:

1. Residence.
2. Culpability and mens rea.
3. Character for licensing purposes.

Residence

[5.066] Questions of *residence* arise very frequently, especially in relation to taxation, when, for example, a company is registered in one country and makes profits in another[158]. The actual residence of companies *incorporated* in Ireland is now irrelevant

---

156 *TSB Private Bank International SA v Chabra and Another* [1992] 2 All ER 245.

157 See also *Re A Company* [1985] BCLC 333 and *International Credit and Investment Co (Overseas) Ltd v Adham* [1998] BCC 134 and, generally, Courtney, *Mareva Injunctions and Related Interlocutory Orders* (1998), para [4.20] *ff.*

158 See Goldstein, 'The Residence and Domicile of Corporations with Special Reference to Income Tax' (1935) 51 LQR 684; Corrigan, 'Place of Abode Test in Establishing Tax Residence' (1988) 6 ILT 106.

for the purposes of the Tax Acts and the Capital Gains Tax Acts. This is because the Finance Act 1999, s 82(2) provides that 'subject to certain limited exceptions, '...a company which is incorporated in the State shall be regarded...as resident in the State'[159]. *Actual residence*, however, continues to be relevant, for example, for companies not incorporated in Ireland and for companies that come within the exceptions to s 82(2). The governing factor for determining the actual residence (as opposed to deemed residence) of a company is the place where its *control* abides[160]; but in each case it is a question of fact as to who actually controls the company, and the courts will disregard the separate legal personality of the company to find the answer to that question.

[5.067] The test for determining actual residence was established in *De Beers Consolidated Mines Ltd v Howe*[161]. The issue in that case was whether a South African registered company was resident for tax purposes in England. Lord Loreburn, in the House of Lords, rejected the argument that a company resides where it is registered and nowhere else, and said:

> 'Now, it is easy to ascertain where an individual resides, but when the inquiry relates to a company, which in a natural sense does not reside anywhere, some artificial test must be applied...In applying the conception of residence to a company, we ought, I think, to proceed as nearly as we can upon the analogy of an individual. A company cannot eat or sleep, but it can keep house and do business. We ought, therefore, to see where it really keeps house and does business. An individual may be of foreign nationality, and yet reside in the United Kingdom. So may a company...I regard that as the true rule; and the real business is carried on where the central management and control actually abides.'[162]

The head office of the company was in Kimberly, South Africa, and it was there that the general meetings of the company were held. Some of the directors also lived in Kimberly and directors' meetings were occasionally held there. But it was clearly established that the majority of directors and life governors of the company resided in England. The main directors' meetings were held there, at which all the important business of the company, such as negotiation of contracts, determination of policies of disposal of assets and the working of the mines, the application of profits, and the appointment of directors, were decided. Thus, since the company was controlled from England, it was held to reside there.

---

[159] See Chapter 2, *Formation, Registration and Conversion of Private Companies*, para **[2.052]**.

[160] The residence of a company is less easy to establish than its *nationality* or *domicile*, both of which are determined simply by reference to the *place* of incorporation. Domicile may be determined by reference to other criteria for the purposes of certain legislation; see, for example, the Jurisdiction of Courts and Enforcement of Judgments (European Communities) Act 1988, s 13(2) which provides that for the purposes of that legislation the domicile of a company is determined by where the corporation has its seat. See also Gill, 'The Seat of a Company and the EEC Judgments Convention' (1988) ILT 30.

[161] *De Beers Consolidated Mines Ltd v Howe* [1906] AC 455. See Young, 'The Legal Personality of a Foreign Corporation' (1906) 22 LQR 178.

[162] *De Beers Consolidated Mines Ltd v Howe* [1906] AC 455 at 458.

[5.068] In *John Hood & Co Ltd v Magee*[163], a company was held to be controlled by its shareholders in general meeting. Accordingly, it was held to be resident in Belfast, where the general meetings took place, rather than New York, where its managing director resided. Madden J referred to Lord Loreburn's test for residence in the *De Beers* case, and continued:

> 'Applying the test supplied by Lord Loreburn I ask in the first instance where does this company keep house? Assuredly in Belfast, for here the registered office must be, under the provisions of the memorandum of association, and here the general meetings of the company are in fact held. Where does it do business? Some of the business transactions are carried on in Ireland and some in New York, and this divided business leaves unsolved the question which Lord Loreburn regards as the true test as to where the real business is carried on. This, he says, is where the central management and control actually abides. In my opinion, the central management and control of this company abides with the general meeting of shareholders in Belfast, where the registered office of the company is situated and where the general meetings of the company are held... If the shareholders in general meeting were to consider it more in the interests of the company that the managing director should reside where the goods in which they deal are manufactured and bought, they might refuse to re-elect him, except on the terms of his residing in Belfast. Adopting the analogy suggested by Lord Loreburn, the movement would proceed from the heart and brain of the organisation in Belfast by which the action of its organs is controlled.' [164]

The shareholders' power to remove and replace the managing director, thus, was indicative of where the control of the company actually resided.

[5.069] The importance of this kind of control was also in evidence in the celebrated First World War case of *Daimler v Continental Tyre Co*[165], where the matter of residence was considered for purposes other than taxation. The issue in that case was whether the defendant, a British registered company, should pay the debt it owed the plaintiff, another British registered company, even though directors and shareholders of the defendant company were all German residents. The Proclamation against Trading with the Enemy Act 1914 (UK) forbade trade with enemies and rendered contracts with the enemy void, but as regards companies it stated that 'in the case of incorporated bodies, enemy character attaches only to those incorporated in an enemy country.' The courts of first instance found that the defendants should pay the plaintiff, since the legislation in question set out the decisive factor in determining the character of the plaintiff company. On appeal, however, the House of Lords found the plaintiff company to be an enemy[166]. Lord Parker, with whom Lords Paramoor and Kinnear, and Viscount Mersey, agreed, said:

> 'The acts of a company's organs, its directors, managers, secretary and so forth, functioning within the scope of their authority, are the company's acts and may invest it definitively with enemy character. It seems to me that similarly the character of those, who

[163] *John Hood & Co Ltd v Magee* [1918] 2 IR 34.

[164] *John Hood & Co Ltd v Magee* [1918] 2 IR 34 at 49–50.

[165] *Daimler v Continental Tyre Co* [1916] 2 AC 307.

[166] The finding on this matter, admittedly, was obiter, since the court's main ground for allowing the appeal was their finding that the secretary of the plaintiff company had no authority to commence litigation in the company name.

> can make and unmake those officers, dictate their conduct mediately or immediately, prescribe their duties and call them to account, may also be material in a question of the enemy character of the company. If not definite and conclusive, it must at least be *prima facie* relevant, as raising a presumption that those who are purporting to act in the name of the company are in fact, under the control of those whom it is their interest to satisfy...[A] company may assume an enemy character. This will be the case if its agents or the persons in *de facto* control of its affairs...are resident in an enemy country...The character of individual shareholders cannot of itself affect the character of the company...[it] may, however, be very material on the question of whether the company's agents, or the persons in *de facto* control of its affairs, are in fact adhering to, taking instructions from, or acting under the control of enemies. This materiality will vary with the number of shareholders who are enemies and the value of their holding.'[167]

Thus, the residence of the company's principal officers will be of prima facie importance in determining the residence of a company, but the extent to which they are controlled, removable, and replaceable, by the other members of the company may cause the focus to shift to the persons exercising such control.

[5.070] From the foregoing examination of the manner in which the courts disregard the separate legal personality of a company in order to determine its actual residence it should be clear that a company may, at one and the same time, be resident in a number of jurisdictions. This will be so where its control is exercised from a number of different states[168]. It should also be noted that in *Unit Construction Ltd v Bullock*[169] it was held that a stipulation in the company's constitution that it was to be managed only from a specified jurisdiction was not conclusive as regards its place of residence.

Culpability and mens rea

[5.071] The circumstances in which the courts will look to the character of a company's controllers in order to attribute the company with culpability or mens rea have already been discussed in detail in Chapter 4, *Incorporation and its Consequences*[170].

Character for licensing purposes

[5.072] Certain licensing statutes require the applicant to be of 'good character', and where a company is the applicant the courts will look for that character in the character of the company's agents or controllers. Such was the case in *The King (Cottingham) v The Justices of County Cork*[171], where the issue was whether a wholesale beer dealer's licence could be granted to a brewing company, Beamish and Crawford Ltd, when one of

---

[167] [1916] 2 AC 307 at 345.

[168] *Swedish Central Railway v Thompson* [1925] AC 495; *Egyptian Delta Land & Investment Co Ltd v Todd* [1929] AC 1.

[169] *Unit Construction Ltd v Bullock* [1960] AC 351.

[170] At para **[4.045]** *ff*

[171] *The King (Cottingham) v The Justices of County Cork* [1906] 2 IR 415. See also *R v LCC, ex parté London and Provincial Electric Theatres Ltd* [1915] 2 KB 466 where a local authority was held justified in its decision not to renew a cinematograph licence held by an English company because most of its shares were held by Germans and three of its six directors were Germans.

the prerequisites of granting such a licence was that the applicant be of good character. The company was granted a licence by the judges of the Petty Sessions District of Macroom, the licence stating that the magistrates found the company to be of 'good character, and that their house in the Main Street, Macroom...has been conducted in a peaceable and orderly manner in the past year...'. The licence was objected to by Mr Cottingham, the District Inspector, and he obtained a conditional order of certiorari to quash the licence. Palles CB found no difficulty in refusing to make the order absolute. He said:

> '...the only difficulty which presents itself...[is] the alleged impossibility of an incorporated company being able to have a good character, or a character at all. But I cannot appreciate the difficulty. I cannot see why a public Company cannot have a character. No doubt it has no soul; but it can act by others, and through others do acts which in the case of a natural person would affect conscience, and be the foundation of that reputation which the law knows as "character", be it good or bad. It can be guilty of fraud, of malice, and of various criminal offences, some of commission, others of omission; some punishable summarily, others by indictment. "Character" as used in the section means "reputation". Reputation is acquired by conduct. *The conduct of the authorised agents of a company is its conduct. Why should not that conduct give rise to a reputation as to its character, good, bad, or indifferent?*.'[172]

Thus, where 'good character' is sought to be established, the courts may disregard the separate legal personality of the company by examining the conduct of its agents.

[F] STATUTE

[5.073] Private companies are creatures of statute; thus, the principles which pertain to them may be modified by statute, provided the modification is made within the bounds permitted by the Constitution. The legislature has introduced a number of statutory provisions which cause the principle of separate personality to be disregarded in particular circumstances. A number of such provisions appear in the Companies Acts 1963–2001 and secondary legislation implementing EU company law directives. More are contained in taxation legislation. The principal legislative provisions requiring disregard of the separate legal personality of companies are discussed here as follows:

1. The Companies Acts 1963–2001.
2. Other legislation.

The Companies Acts 1963–2001

[5.074] The Companies Acts 1963–2001 provide for several instances in which the separate legal personality of a private company may be ignored. Some of these provisions require a company to be identified with other companies in a group. For example, groups of companies will be required to show accounts which reflect the

[172] *The King (Cottingham) v The Justices of County Cork* [1906] 2 IR 415 at 422–423. Emphasis added. See also *The State (Hennessy and Chariot Inns Ltd) v Commons* [1976] IR 238; and *McMahon v Murtagh Properties Ltd* (20 October 1981, unreported), High Court (Barrington J) where this passage was cited with approval.

financial position of the group as a whole[173]. Similarly, the court appointing an examiner to a company is empowered to appoint an examiner to other related companies[174].

Other provisions provide for several instances in which members, directors, or other officers may be made personally liable for the debts or other obligations of the company. Many of these provisions are not directed specifically at members, but at directors or other officers. The making of persons other than members personally liable for corporate debts and obligations is one of the most extreme forms of disregard of the principle of separate legal personality.

Some of the more significant provisions of the Companies Acts 1963–2001 which create personal liability[175] will be considered here under the following list of headings, which is not exhaustive:

(a) Reduction of number of members below the legal minimum.

(b) Failure to state correctly the company's name.

(c) Breach of restriction or disqualification order.

(d) Failure to meet capital requirements.

(e) Failure to keep proper books of account.

(f) Unreasonably inaccurate declaration of solvency.

(g) Liquidation of related companies.

(h) Fraudulent or reckless trading.

(a) Reduction of number of members below the legal minimum

[5.075] Section 36 of CA 1963 provides:

> 'If at any time the number of members of a company is reduced, in the case of a private company, below two, or, in the case of a public company, below seven, and it carries on business for more than 6 months while the number is so reduced, every person who is a member of the company during the time that it so carries on business after those 6 months and knows that it is carrying on business with fewer than two members, or seven members, as the case may be, shall be severally liable for the payment of the whole debts of the company contracted during that time, and may be severally sued therefor.'

The application of this section to private companies limited by shares has been discontinued by the European Communities (Single-Member Private Limited Companies) Regulations 1994[176], reg 7(1) of which provides that CA 1963, s 36 shall not apply to a private company limited by shares or by guarantee. It should be noted that s 36 continues to apply to unlimited private companies. Regulation 7(2) further provides that:

> 'Without prejudice to paragraph (1), a person who, before the coming into force of these regulations, is liable by virtue of s 36 of the 1963 Act (Members severally liable for debts where business carried on with fewer than, in the case of private company, two members) for the payment of the debts of a private company limited by shares or by guarantee, shall

[173] See Chapter 13, *Accounts and Auditors*, para **[13.109]** *ff*.

[174] See Chapter 23, *Examinerships*, para **[23.045]** *ff*.

[175] See generally MacCann, 'Personal Liability for Corporate Debts' (1991) ILT 206 and (1991) ILT 232.

[176] SI 1994/275.

> not be so liable for the payment of the company's debts contracted on or after the date on which these regulations come into force.'

Regulation 7(2) is, thus, a transitional provision, continuing the application of CA 1963, s 36 to acts done prior to 1 October 1994 by a private company with fewer than two members.

[5.076] It must be stressed at the outset that a company continues to exist as a legal person despite any reduction in membership below the legal minimum, even where no members remain[177]. Since CA 1963, s 36 makes only the remaining members – not the withdrawing members – liable, it has no application where there are no members left. In such circumstances, however, it appears that a single new member will be caught by the section for the debts of the company incurred until a second member joins to bring the number of members back up to the statutory minimum. It should also be noted that the remaining member must *know* that the company is carrying on business with fewer than two members.

The personal liability imposed by the section is several: thus, the creditors of the company may proceed *directly* against the liable member. But such liability arises only in respect of those *debts* of the company which have been *contracted* for subsequent to the expiration of six months from the reduction in membership. This seems to encompass only pecuniary obligations of a contractual nature, and would not include other liabilities such as claims for damages in tort or claims arising under statute, eg claims for damages for unfair dismissal. In addition, where a member does incur liability under the section he will be entitled to seek an indemnity from the company since the company, as a separate legal person, remains primarily liable for the debt[178].

[5.077] There is much to be said in favour of the disapplication of CA 1963, s 36 to all companies. In *Nisbett v Shepherd*[179], Moulton, one of the members of a two member company, Moulton & Co Ltd, transferred his shares to the other member, Shepherd, and resigned as director. This transfer was duly recorded in the company's register of members. No other transfer of shares was made until 1990 when Shepherd transferred a single share to his wife so that a resolution for the winding up of the company could be made. The liquidator successfully applied to have Shepherd made liable under the UK equivalent of s 36. The Court of Appeal rejected Shepherd's argument that the transfer of Moulton's shares to him was defective[180]. Hoffmann LJ observed:

> 'I have considerable sympathy with the appellant, who has fallen into a trap created by an ancient and obsolete rule. Section [36 of the 1963 Act] requires that a company should have at least two members. In default of compliance it strips the remaining member of the protection of limited liability. The rule goes back to s 48 of the Companies Act 1862 when the minimum number of members was seven. This reflects the evolution of company law from partnership, but the reason why it has survived through successive Companies Acts is obscure. It seems to serve no purpose in protecting the public or anyone else.'[181]

---

[177] See Chapter 4, *Incorporation and its Consequences*, para **[4.020]** .

[178] *Brook's Wharf Ltd v Goodman Brothers* [1937] 1 KB 534.

[179] *Nisbett v Shepherd* [1994] 1 BCLC 300.

[180] See further Chapter 16, *Share Transfers in Private Companies*, para **[16.006]** *ff*.

[181] [1994] 1 BCLC 300 at 305.

The section continues to apply to unlimited private companies, and to public companies. It is to be hoped that future legislation might remove it from the statute books altogether[182].

(b) Failure to state correctly the company's name

[5.078] Sectoin 114(4) of CA 1963 provides that if an officer of a company or any person on its behalf:

> '...signs or authorises to be signed on behalf of the company any bill of exchange, promissory note, endorsement, cheque or order for money or wherein its name is not mentioned [in legible characters]...he shall be liable to a fine...and shall further be personally liable to the holder of the bill of exchange, promissory note, cheque or order for money or goods for the amount thereof unless it is duly paid by the company.'

Section 114(5)[183] continues:

> 'The use of the abbreviation "Ltd" for "Limited" or "Teo" for "Teoranta" or "plc" for "public limited company" or "cpt" for "cuideachta phoiblí theoranta" shall not be a breach of the provisions of this section.'

The effect of these provisions is that where the correct and full registered name of the company does not appear on a bill of exchange, promissory note, cheque or order for money or goods[184] the signatory will be personally liable to pay the holder[185] if the company defaults in payment - even though the holder has not been misled by the misdescription. Thus, in *Atkins & Co v Wardle*[186], where a company whose registered name was 'South Shield Salt Water Baths Co Ltd' was described in a bill of exchange as 'Salt Water Baths Co Ltd', the directors who had signed the bill on the company's behalf were held to be personally liable to the holder of the bill. Similar principles were applied in *Nassau Steam Press v Tyler*[187], where 'The Bastille Syndicate Ltd' was described as 'Old Paris and Bastille Syndicate Ltd'. Two examples of the harshness of the rule are *Barber & Nicholls Ltd v R & G Associates (London) Ltd*[188] and *Hendon v Adelman*[189]. In the former case, liability was imposed where '(London)' was left out of the company name on a cheque; in the latter case liability was imposed on a cheque where '&' was left out of the company name, 'L & R Agencies Ltd'. The use of the abbreviation 'Co' for 'Company' has been held not to offend against the provisions[190], but a failure to

[182] The Company Law Review Group, *First Report*, (2001) recommends the repeal of CA 1963, s 36: recommendation 4.9.3.

[183] As amended by the C(A)A 1983, Sch 1, para 13.

[184] But not an order for the supply of services, as Gower, *Principles of Modern Company Law* (3rd edn, 1969), notes at p 116.

[185] The holder is the person to whom the document is addressed and who is to benefit by it: *Civil Service Co–Operative Society Ltd v Chapman* (1914) TLR 376.

[186] *Atkins & Co v Wardle* (1889) 61 LT 23.

[187] *Nassau Steam Press v Tyler* (1894) 70 LT 376.

[188] *Barber & Nicholls Ltd v R & G Associates (London) Ltd* (1981) 132 NLJ 1076.

[189] *Hendon v Adelman* (1973) 117 JJ 631.

[190] *Banque de l'Indochine v Euroseas Group Finance Co Ltd* [1981] 3 All ER 198.

indicate by the use of the appropriate word at the end of the company's name that the liability of the members is limited will fall foul of these statutory requirements[191].

The officer or agent will be liable under CA 1963, s 114(4) even where the misdescription of the company's name in the document is made by the holder of the document, because it is the duty of the officer or agent to ensure that the name is accurately stated on the document before he signs it or authorises it to be signed. Thus, in *Lindholst & Co A/S v Fowler*[192], where bills of exchange prepared by the plaintiffs referred to a company named 'Corby Chicken Co Ltd' simply as 'Corby Chicken Co' the defendant, who had signed the bills on behalf of the company without correcting the misdescription, was made personally liable on the bills. By way of contrast, in *Durham Fancy Goods Ltd v Michael Jackson (Fancy Goods) Ltd*[193], where a bill of exchange was drawn by the plaintiffs on the defendant company, and the bill and the form of acceptance had both been prepared by the plaintiff, the plaintiffs were held to be estopped from invoking the personal liability of the signatory for a misdescription of the company as 'M Jackson (Fancy Goods) Ltd.' In the *Lindholst* case, Donaldson MR distinguished the decision in the *Durham Fancy Goods* case on the basis that in that case the form of words for the acceptance had been prescribed by the plaintiffs and they were estopped by what they had prescribed whereas in the case before him the form of words for the acceptance had not been prescribed by the plaintiffs.

Clearly then, the officers and agents of a company must take great care to ensure that the company name is accurately stated *before* signing or authorising the signature of a bill of exchange, promissory note, cheque or order for money or goods. A mistake of the slightest nature may expose them to personal liability - whether or not they knew of the misdescription. The courts have made it clear that they will provide little assistance *after* signature: rectification will not be granted where the motive is to avoid personal liability under CA 1963, s 114(4)[194].

[5.079] The liability of the officer or agent is dependent upon his being a signatory to the document in question or his having authorised the signature of the document. If there is no signature on behalf of the company there can be no liability[195]. Where there is such a signature, but it is sought to impose personal liability not on the actual signatory but on the person who authorised the signing of the document, it must be shown that he not only authorised the signing of the document but also authorised it to be signed in such a way that the name of the company did not properly appear thereon[196]. The giving of such authority may, however, be inferred by the courts in appropriate circumstances, such as where the person who authorised the signature knew at the time of a misprint of the company's name on the document[197].

---

191 *Penrose v Martyr* (1858) EB & E 499; *British Airways Board v Parish* [1979] 2 Lloyd's Rep 361; *Blum v OPC Repartition SA* [1988] BCLC 170.

192 *Lindholst & Co A/S v Fowler* [1988] BCLC 166.

193 *Durham Fancy Goods Ltd v Michael Jackson (Fancy Goods) Ltd* [1968] 2 QB 839.

194 *Blum v OCP Repartition SA* [1988] BCLC 170; *Rafsanjan Pistachio Producers v Reiss* [1990] BCLC 352.

195 *Oshkosh B'Gosh Inc v Dan Marbel Inc Ltd* [1989] BCLC 507.

196 *John Wilkes Footwear Ltd v Lee International Footwear Ltd* [1985] BCLC 444.

197 *John Wilkes Footwear Ltd v Lee International Footwear Ltd* [1985] BCLC 444.

If the signatory is authorised to act on behalf of the company, the company will remain primarily liable on the document, despite the misdescription, so long as it can be identified[198]. The officer's or agent's liability under CA 1963, s 114(4), then, is *secondary* or collateral to that of the company. It is not in the nature of a guarantor's or surety's liability; thus the defences which are available to guarantors and sureties are not available[199]. And, it would appear, the signatory may be entitled to recover an indemnity from the company itself in respect of any personal liability incurred[200].

(c) Breach of restriction or disqualification order

[5.080] Part VII of the Companies Act 1990 ('CA 1990') is designed to prevent the directors of a company which is in an insolvent liquidation from forming a new company and carrying on business as before[201]. To this end, CA 1990, ss 150 and 160 provide for the making of a *restriction order* and a *disqualification order* against directors, shadow directors, and other officers of the company, in appropriate circumstances. These are discussed in further detail in Chapter 12, *Company Law Compliance and Enforcement.* Contravention of either order may render a person liable for the debts and liabilities of the company. Such liability qualifies as an exception to the principle that others, particularly members, are not normally to be made liable for the debts and other obligations of the company. Personal liability for contravention of these orders may arise in two ways:

(i) Where the restricted or disqualified person contravenes the order *in person.*

(ii) Where another person acts on the directions of a restricted person.

(i) Restricted or disqualified person acting in person

[5.081] Section 163(3) of CA 1990 provides that where any person who is subject to these restrictions or disqualifications acts in breach of them, and the company with which he then became concerned commences an insolvent winding up, either while he is involved or within twelve months of his so being involved, then:

> '...the court may, on the application of the liquidator or any creditor of the company, declare that such person shall be personally liable, without any limitation on liability, for all or any part of the debts or other liabilities of the company incurred in the period during which he was acting in such a manner or capacity.'

(ii) Acting on the directions of a disqualified person

[5.082] Where a director, officer, member of a committee of management, or trustee of any company acts *in accordance with the instructions* of a restricted or disqualified person while knowing that they are so restricted or disqualified, he will be guilty of an offence under CA 1990, s 164(1)[202]. In addition, CA 1990, s 165(1) provides that any person convicted under s 164(1) for acting in accordance with the directions of a

---

198 *Goldsmith (Sicklesmere) Ltd v Baxter* [1970] Ch 85.

199 *British Airways Board v Parish* [1979] 2 Lloyd's Rep 361.

200 Following *Brook's Wharf and Bull Ltd v Goodman Brothers* [1937] 1 KB 534. Such a right will, more often than not, prove worthless, since the company will (if the holders are choosing to move against the officers of the company rather than the company itself) probably be insolvent.

201 See further Chapter 12, *Company Law Compliance and Enforcement,* paras **[12.043]** *ff* and **[12.090]** *ff.*

202 Chapter 12, *Company Law Compliance and Enforcement*, para **[12.087]** *ff.*

disqualified[203] person will automatically become 'personally liable for the debts of the company concerned incurred in the period during which he was so acting'. He may, however, seek such relief from this personal liability as the court, having regard to the circumstances of the case, considers to be just and equitable[204].

Curiously, the liability of persons acting on the directions of disqualified persons seems to arise independently of whether the company is insolvent – even though the disqualified persons themselves only become personally liable if the company enters an insolvent liquidation. Whether the solvency of the company is a factor which will spur the courts to grant relief from the rigours of s 165(1) remains to be seen.

(d) Failure to meet capital requirements

[5.083] Where a person becomes the subject of restrictions under CA 1990, s 150 he may not accept appointment or act in any manner, whether directly or indirectly, as a director or secretary or take part in the promotion or formation of any company unless the company satisfies certain capital requirements. Furthermore, he must, within the fourteen days immediately preceding such appointment or so acting, send to the registered office of the company a notice stating that he is subject to such restrictions[205], If, having received such notification, the company carries on business without fulfilling these capital requirements within a reasonable period and subsequently enters an insolvent liquidation, then, by virtue of CA 1990, s 163(4):

> '...the court may, on the application of the liquidator or any creditor or contributory of the company, declare that any person who was an officer of the company while the company so carried on business and who knew or ought to have known that the company had been so notified shall be personally responsible, without any limitation of liability, for all or any part of the debts or other liabilities of the company as the court may direct.'

This personal liability, unlike the liability of a restricted or disqualified person under CA 1990, s 163(3)[206], is not restricted to the debts or other liabilities of the company arising during any specific period. The persons made personally liable may, however, apply to the court for such relief, in whole or in part, from personal liability as the court, having regard to the circumstances of the case, appears fit[207].

(e) Failure to keep proper books of account

[5.084] Section 202 of CA 1990 requires every company to keep proper books of account, whether in the form of documents or otherwise (for example, on computer). These requirements are discussed in detail in Chapter 13, *Accounts and Auditors*.

Where a company has contravened s 202, and the court is satisfied that the contravention has either:

— contributed to the company's inability to pay all of its debts; or

---

203 Notably, conviction for acting on the instructions of a restricted person does not attract the operation of CA 1990, s 165.

204 CA 1990 s 165(2).

205 CA 1990, s 155(5). See Chapter 12, *Company Law Compliance and Enforcement*, para **[12.049]**.

206 See para **[5.081]**.

207 CA 1990, s 163(5).

— resulted in substantial uncertainty as to the assets and liabilities of the company; or

— substantially impeded the orderly winding up of the company,

then, under CA 1990, s 204, the court may, on the application of the liquidator or any creditor or contributory of the company, impose personal liability for the debts and other liabilities of the company without limitation on any one or more officers and former officers of the company who are in default. The principles governing such liability are discussed further in Chapter 10, *Duties of Directors and Other Officers*.

(f) Unreasonably inaccurate declaration of solvency

[5.085] A statutory *declaration of solvency*, made by the directors in the prescribed form, will be required for a members' voluntary winding up[208]. The particulars required to be stated in such declarations are discussed elsewhere in this work.

[5.086] Where such a declaration has been made, and it is subsequently proved to the satisfaction of the court that the company is unable to pay its debts, CA 1963, s 256(8) provides that:

> '...the court on the application of the liquidator or any creditor or contributory of the company may, if it thinks it proper to do so, declare that any director who was a party to the declaration without reasonable grounds for the opinion that the company would be able to pay its debts in full within the period specified in the declaration shall be personally responsible, without limitation of liability, for all or any of the debts or other liabilities of the company as the court may direct.'[209]

The only defence available to the director against such personal liability is to show that he had reasonable grounds for making the declaration; and it is to be presumed until the contrary is shown that there were no such reasonable grounds for the opinion[210]. What amounts to reasonable grounds is not altogether clear, since there appear to be no judicial decisions on this point[211]. But one thing *is* clear: directors should take the utmost care *and* should seek independent professional advice[212] before making a declaration of solvency. This is especially so considering that where the debts are not paid or provided for in full within the period stated in the declaration the court may also make such further directions as it thinks proper to give effect to the declaration of personal liability[213]. This could, it has been suggested[214], include charging all or part of the company's debts and other liabilities on the assets of the defaulting directors.

---

208 See Chapter 25, *Winding Up Companies*, para **[25.004]** *ff*.

209 CA 1963, s 256(8), inserted by CA 1990, s 128.

210 CA 1963, s 256(9), as amended by CA 1990, s 128.

211 Nor, indeed, does there appear to be any judicial decision on what was meant by reasonable grounds under the old CA 1963, s 256 (now repealed and replaced by CA 1990, s 128) which provided for criminal penalties, as opposed to civil liability, in such circumstances: see Keane, *Company Law* (3rd edn, 2000), para 40.7.

212 From an independent practising liquidator, if possible, since it will most likely be the liquidator of the company who will raise any subsequent challenges to the accuracy of the statement.

213 CA 1963, s 256(10) as amended by CA 1990, s 128.

214 MacCann, 'Personal Liability for Corporate Debts' (1991) ILT 206 and (1991) ILT 232 at 234.

(g) Liquidation of related companies

[5.087] The principles enunciated by Costello J in *Power Supermarkets Ltd v Crumlin Investments Ltd*[215] are to a large extent reflected in CA 1990, ss 140. Section 140 of the 1990 Act allows the court to order a company to make a contribution to the liquidator of a *related company* equivalent to the debts of that company. Section 141 of CA 1990 allows the court to order, where two or more related companies are being wound up, that the companies be wound up together as if they were the one company. Each of these provisions is considered in detail in Chapter 27, *Realisation and Distribution of Assets in a Winding Up.*

(h) Fraudulent or reckless trading

[5.088] Section 297A of CA 1963, as inserted by CA 1990, s 138, provides that if, during the course of a winding up or an examinership, a person is found to have been guilty of reckless or fraudulent trading, the court may declare such person to be personally responsible, without limitation of liability, for all or any part of the debts or other liabilities of the company as the court may direct. The circumstances in which such a declaration may be made are discussed in further detail in Chapter 10, *Duties of Directors and Other Officers*.

Other legislation

[5.089] Among other legislative provisions which involve disregard of the principle of separate legal personality are the Capital Gains Tax Act 1975, the Corporation Tax Act 1976, and the Capital Acquisitions Tax Act 1976, as amended. A detailed review of these complex provisions lies outside the scope of this work; however, it may be observed that the provisions endeavour to prevent persons from using companies to conceal taxable personal income and gains. The provisions place heavy emphasis on the degree of control a person exercises over a company, and a special feature of the legislation is the concept of a 'close company,' which, broadly speaking, is a company under the control of five or fewer persons, or under the control of its directors[216]. A large number of Irish private companies fall within this definition. Onerous taxation regulations govern the provision of benefits or loans by a close company to its controllers.

[5.090] A trend in some regulatory statutes is the inclusion of provisions rendering company directors, secretaries, managers and other such officers personally criminally liable where the company is shown to have committed an offence. Such provisions adopt a common formula:

> 'Where an offence committed by a body corporate…is proved to have been committed with the consent or connivance of, or to have been attributable to any neglect on the part of any director, manager, secretary or other similar officer of the body corporate or a person who was purporting to act in any such capacity, he as well as the body corporate shall be guilty of that offence and shall be liable to be proceeded against and punished accordingly.'

---

[215] *Power Supermarkets Ltd v Crumlin Investments Ltd* (22 June 1981, unreported), High Court; see para **[5.052]**.

[216] Corporation Tax Act 1976, ss 94 and 103.

Provisions of this nature are to be found, for example, in the Safety, Health and Welfare at Work Act 1989, s 48, and the Competition (Amendment) Act 1996, s 3(4)[217]. Similar provisions are to be found in statutes extending at least as far back as the Customs Consolidation Act 1876[218]. They have been described by the English courts as 'parasitic'[219] because they make substantial inroads into the principle of the separate legal personality, and, it seems they have been introduced by the Legislature with scant regard for the principles of *Salomon*'s case, so dear to the courts.

[5.091] It should be noted, however, that the provisions do not impose automatic or strict liability on the directors etc[220]. The onus on the prosecution is to prove first that the company's offence was committed. There does not have to be a corporate conviction however, so that if the company is disbanded or wound up so that there is no undertaking left to convict, personal liability might still be imposed if the prosecution proves that an offence was committed by the company while in existence[221]. There is no advantage, therefore, in hurriedly winding up a company[222] in the hope that personal liability might thereby be avoided.

[5.092] The prosecution must also prove that the individual *consented* to or *connived* in the corporate offence, or that it was attributable to their *neglect*. Various definitions of consent and connivance in the context of provisions such as these have been given by the courts over the years, and the following propositions emerge:

— Consent and connivance both involve some *deliberate* and *conscious* complicity in the acts constituting the offence[223].

— A person consents to the commission of an offence by his company when he is '*well aware of it and he agrees to it*'[224].

— *Consent* requires simply that you consent to the doing of the acts; you do not have to know that the acts were criminal[225].

— '*Connivance* ... suggests to my mind some form of knowledge by the defendant that something was wrong, because you cannot connive at something unless you have mental knowledge that something is going wrong'[226].

---

217 See Hutchinson, 'Criminal Liability of Directors, Managers and Other Similar Officers Under the Competition Amendment Act, 1996,' (1997) 4 CLP 47.

218 Customs Consolidation Act 1876, 39 and 40 Vict c 36, ss 191 and 259; also the Merchandise Marks Act, 1877, 50 & 51, Vict c 28, ss 2(2) and 5 as amended); and the Stamp Act 1891, s 54 and 55 Vict c 39, s 13. More recent examples from the Irish Statute Books include the Redundancy Payments Act 1966, s 52; the Protection of Employment Act 1977, s 21(3); the Factories Act 1955, s 100(5); and the Office Premises Act, 1958, s 31(4).

219 Per Evans LJ in *R v Wilson* [1997] 1 All ER 119.

220 *Huckerby v Elliott* [1970] 1 All ER 189.

221 See *R v Dickson* [1991] Crim LR 854, [1991] BCC 719.

222 And, perhaps, transferring its business to another company.

223 *Southend Borough Council v White* 156 JP 463 (1991).

224 *Huckerby v Elliott* [1970] 1 All ER 189.

225 *R v McMillan Aviation* Crown Court, Kingston upon Thames, 4 June 1981.

226 *R v McMillan Aviation* Crown Court, Kingston upon Thames, 4 June 1981, per Reuben J; also *Secretary of State for Trade v Markus* [1976] AC 35.

The upshot of these statements of principle is that in order to consent to or connive at with acts constituting an offence a person must *know* of those acts. In other contexts in the criminal law the term connivance has been held to connote 'wilful shutting of the eyes', 'wilful blindness', 'purposefully abstaining from ascertaining'; 'wilfully abstaining from knowing'; 'deliberately refraining from making enquiries the results of which he might not care to have' and 'shutting his eyes to the obvious'[227]. In order to connive, therefore, there must have been facts (which one purposefully ignored) which would raise suspicion or would put one on inquiry.

Neglect, which may be proved in the alternative, requires proof of a breach of duty. Whether a duty exists depends on the individual's position in the company and his professional responsibilities. Such duties may properly be delegated to another. In *Huckerby v Elliott*[228] the Court of Appeal allowed an appeal against the conviction of a director who, it was held, had properly left matters of licensing to another director of the company. Lord Parker CJ said[229]:

> '...I know of no authority for the proposition that it is the duty of a director to, as it were, supervise his co-directors or to acquaint himself with all the details of the running of the company.'

Not all such delegation will relieve the individual of neglect however. If the individual knew of the particular circumstances of the corporate offence, or had reasonable grounds to believe that it might be committed, he would be obliged to act to prevent it. In *Hirschler v Birch*[230], accordingly, the defendant director was convicted for neglect for failing to consult an authoritative source before confirming a purchase of high level brake lights, the legality of which was open to doubt in the UK. Nor will the mere issuing of injunctions at board level prohibiting illegal activity necessarily relieve an individual of liability[231]. The size of the company will be of significance. In *Lewis v Bland*[232], a managing director was acquitted on a charge of neglect giving rise to the corporate offence of providing false particulars of car servicing contrary to the Trade Descriptions Act 1968. The company in question was a large company, and the court felt that he was entitled to delegate work to his senior staff and could expect that the work would be conducted in accordance with his instructions.

[5.093] Even though some other legislative provisions do not so clearly permit disregard of the separate legal personality of a company, it has been suggested by Diplock LJ, in the House of Lords in *Dimbleby & Sons v National Union of Journalists*[233], that a purposive interpretation of the provisions of a statute may give rise to the inference that Parliament intended the provision to permit such disregard. He observed:

[227] See Edwards, *Mens Rea in Statutory Offences*, (1955), pp 196–203.

[228] *Huckerby v Elliott* [1970] 1 All ER 189.

[229] *Huckerby v Elliott* [1970] 1 All ER 189 at 194.

[230] *Hirschler v Birch* [1987] RTR 13.

[231] *Southend Borough Council v White* 156 JP 436 (1991).

[232] *Lewis v Bland* [1985] RTR 171.

[233] *Dimbleby & Sons v National Union of Journalists* [1984] 1 WLR 427 at 435.

'My Lords, the reason why English statutory law, and that of all other trading countries, has long permitted the creation of corporations as artificial persons distinct from their individual shareholders and from that of any other corporation even though the shareholders of both corporations are identical, is to enable business to be undertaken with limited financial liability in the event of the business proving to be a failure. The "corporate veil" in the case of companies incorporated under the Companies Acts is drawn by statute and it can be pierced by some other statute if such other statute so provides: but in view of its *raison d'être* and its consistent recognition by the courts since *Salomon v Salomon and Co Ltd* [1897] AC 22, one would expect that any parliamentary intention to pierce the corporate veil would be expressed in clear and unequivocal language. I do not wholly exclude the possibility that even in the absence of express words stating that in specified circumstances one company, although separately incorporated, is to be treated as sharing the same legal personality of another, a purposive construction of the statute may nevertheless lead inexorably to the conclusion that such must have been the intention of Parliament.'

Indeed, the learned judge's observations reveal that which has already become apparent from earlier discussion in this chapter, namely, that the courts may, when construing the provisions of a statute, find it necessary to ignore the separate legal personality of a company in order to give effect to the statutory provisions.

Chapter 6

Corporate Civil Litigation

[6.001] As was considered in Chapter 4, one of the consequences of incorporation is that a company can sue and be sued in its own name. In very many respects, the laws of civil litigation as apply to companies are on a par with individuals. In many other respects, however, the laws (and more often the practice and procedures) applicable to proceedings commenced by or taken against companies can differ markedly to those applicable to individuals or partnerships. Although corporate litigation is not generally perceived to be a distinct area of company law, it is thought to be a useful clustering of issues that are illustrative of the principles of company law in a practical setting or, if you like, applied company law. Here, the following issues are considered:

[A] The proper plaintiff where a company is wronged.

[B] Authority to institute proceedings by a company.

[C] Service of proceedings.

[D] Security for costs.

[E] Discovery and interrogatories against a company.

[F] Appearance in court by a company.

[G] Enforcing judgments and orders against a company.

[A] The Proper Plaintiff Where a Company Is Wronged

[6.002] The proper plaintiff in an action in respect of a wrong alleged to be done to a company is, prima facie, the company[1]. This is the primary consequence of the rule in *Foss v Harbottle*[2] and as a principle of company law ranks alongside the principle of separate legal personality, conclusively established in *Salomon*'s case[3]; indeed, it can be viewed as an inevitable consequence of the principle of separate legal personality. In *O'Neill v Ryan et al*[4] O'Flaherty J and Blayney J cited, inter alia, the following passage from the English Court of Appeal's decision in *Prudential Assurance Co Ltd v Newman Industries Ltd*:

> '[The rule in *Foss v Harbottle*] is not merely a tiresome procedural obstacle placed in the path of a shareholder by a legalistic judiciary. The rule is the consequence of the fact that a corporation is a separate legal entity...The company is liable for its contracts and torts; the shareholder has no such liability. The company acquires causes of action for breaches of contracts and torts which damage the company. No cause of action vests in the shareholder.'[5]

---

1 See *Prudential Assurance Co Ltd v Newman Industries Ltd* [1982] 1 Ch 204 at 210 per Jenkins LJ.

2 *Foss v Harbottle* (1843) 2 Hare 461.

3 *Salomon v A Saloman & Co Ltd* [1897] AC 22.

4 *O'Neill v Ryan* [1993] ILRM 557.

5 *Prudential Assurance Co Ltd v Newman Industries Ltd* [1982] 1 Ch 204 at 224.

Suffice it to say for present purposes that it is well established that where a wrong is committed against a company (eg breach of contract, a tort, etc) it will be the company, and not its shareholders or others, who will have locus standi to bring proceedings[6]. The converse is equally true and a company will not be the proper defendant where one of its directors commits a tort, unless the company is as a matter of law vicariously liable for the tort: *Crofter Properties Ltd v Genport Ltd (No 3)*[7]. As fundamental as this principle is, it can be overlooked particularly in small private companies involving proprietary-directors who have a tendency to confuse corporate property (in all of its forms) with their own personal property.

[6.003] The importance of joining, in litigation, all relevant parties is illustrated by *Re New Ad Advertising Ltd*[8]. In that case a petition was brought alleging oppression pursuant to the Companies Act 1963, s 205 ('CA 1963'), where the only named party was the company, although the details of the oppression were directed against a Mr McNulty whom, it was alleged, was the controlling force in the company. Mr McNulty was not, however, joined as a notice party and was not in any other sense a party to the petition proceedings. Notwithstanding this, the High Court ordered Mr McNulty to pay over a total of £67,200 being the value that had been placed on the petitioner's shareholding in the company. On appeal to the Supreme Court, O'Flaherty J said:

> '...the petition proceeded on the basis, presumably, that there was such an identity of interest between the company and Mr McNulty that, in effect, any order that was being made would be on the basis that Mr McNulty was the company: this seems to be the way that the case was approached. There is no doubt that the company and Mr McNulty availed of the same firm of solicitors. But it is trite law to say that the identity of a company is distinct from the individuals who comprise it: that is *Salomon v Salomon & Co* [1897] AC 22. While in modern company legislation there is a tendency on occasion to allow the veil to be lifted on a corporation, that companies have a separate existence is still basic law.'[9]

The result was that the Supreme Court ordered Mr McNulty to be made a notice party to the proceedings; that he be furnished with all documents in the case; and that he should be given an opportunity to put in a defence if he was of such a mind.

[6.004] The doctrine of res judicata operates to estop parties from denying not only the state of affairs established by a judgment but also the grounds upon which that judgment was based; res judicata can be either cause of action estoppel or issue estoppel. One question that arises in the context of company law is whether a company will be estopped from taking proceedings against a defendant in circumstances where a director

---

6 This principle is consistently applied: see, eg, *DBP Construction Ltd v ICC Bank plc* (21 May 1998, unreported), Supreme Court (Keane J; nem. diss.). There, Keane J said 'in the light of the rule in *Foss v Harbottle* [1843] 2 Hare 461 as applied by this court in *O'Neill v Ryan* [1993] ILRM 557, [the individual plaintiffs], as shareholders and directors of the company, could not recover losses which were in fact the losses of the company itself' (at p 24).

7 *Crofter Properties Ltd v Genport Ltd (No 3)* (23 April 2002, unreported), High Court (McCracken J).

8 *Re New Ad Advertising Ltd* (26 March 1998, unreported), Supreme Court (O'Flaherty J and Lynch J).

9 (26 March 1998, unreported), Supreme Court at p 4, 5.

and shareholder of the company has previously taken an action in the same matter that was determined against him by a court. This was the issue at stake in *Belton v Carlow County Council; Prendergast & Prendergast (third parties)*[10]. In that case, a factory owned by WJ Prendergast & Son Ltd (the company) was destroyed by fire. The third parties were shareholding directors of the company. The company had brought a claim for compensation under the Malicious Injuries Act 1981 and had been successful in the Circuit Court but unsuccessful, on appeal, to the High Court. The defendant county council had asserted that the fire had been deliberately started by the third parties. Subsequently, the plaintiff (who was the owner of an adjoining premises that had been damaged by the fire) sought and received compensation from the Circuit Court. The defendant county council claimed to be indemnified by the third parties in respect of the decree of IR£4,500. The question that arose was whether the third parties were estopped by the earlier High Court judgment from litigating the issue as to whether they had deliberately started the fire. One of the key issues to be determined by the Supreme Court was whether there was sufficient 'privity of interest' between the company and the third parties as to satisfy the requirements of issue estoppel. After noting the definition of privity given by Lord Lowry LCJ in *Shaw v Sloan*[11] that 'a party is the privy of another by blood, title or interest when he stands in his shoes and claims through or under him', Keane J stated that the enquiry in hand was solely concerned with whether there was 'privity of interest'. Keane J held:

> 'Assuming that the third parties are the owners of all the shares in the company and are the only directors (as to which there is no finding of fact in the case stated), I am satisfied that there is no such privity of interest between them and the company. It has, of course, been settled law since the decision in *Salomon v Salomon* that the company on the one hand and its shareholders on the other are separate and distinct legal entities. Moreover, while the interest of the company and its controlling shareholders may very often coincide, that is not always the case. The interest of the shareholder is to receive a dividend, in the event of the company's profits allowing it to be paid, and to share in any surplus assets of the company on a winding up. The company's affairs must, however, be conducted by the directors, not merely in the interests of the shareholders, but of those of any persons who may have an interest in its financial well being: specifically the creditors, whether secured or unsecured. In the event of the company becoming insolvent (and it should be said that there is no evidence that this was at any stage the case with this company) the latter's interests will become paramount: see the decision of this court in *Re Frederick Inns Ltd* [1991] ILRM 582.'

Keane J went on to say that even assuming that the third parties had some control over the proceedings brought by the company, their interests were not identical to the company's: 'the proceeds of a successful application would become the assets of the company and would fall to be dealt with in accordance with the memorandum and articles and the applicable legislation'. On this point Keane J concluded:

> 'Similarly, in the event of the application being unsuccessful, the consequent liability for costs would be that of the company alone and in no sense the personal liability of the third

---

10 *Belton v Carlow County Council; Prendergast & Prendergast (third parties)* [1997] 2 ILRM 405.

11 *Shaw v Sloan* [1982] NI 393.

> parties. By contrast, in the present proceedings, the third parties alone will be liable, in the event of the local authority's claim succeeding and the company has no interest, present or contingent, in the outcome.'

On that basis Keane J answered the case stated in the negative and found that the third parties were not estopped from adducing facts to establish the cause of the fire on the company's premises.

[6.005] It would have been difficult for the Supreme Court to have permitted the invocation of an old doctrine which would have had the effect of denying individuals the right to defend allegations made against them that would have rendered them liable to pay compensation. In few cases involving companies and their shareholders is justice so acutely balanced. Yet, the decision of the Supreme Court in *Belton* clearly establishes that a shareholding in a company is not per se sufficient to give rise to the privity of interest necessary to invoke the doctrine of res judicata. An example of a different approach is seen in the English decision in *Barakot Ltd v Epiette Ltd*[12]. In that case the controlling director of the plaintiff-company personally sued the defendant for repayment of a loan allegedly made by him for £1.2 million on foot of an oral agreement. This claim had been dismissed because at the time of the alleged agreement, the defendant-company had not been incorporated. The plaintiff-company subsequently instituted proceedings for the repayment of the loan against the defendant-company, which applied to have the proceedings struck out on the basis of the doctrine of res judicata, by virtue of the parties' identities. It was held by a deputy High Court judge that the doctrine of res judicata did apply because there was sufficient identity between the plaintiff and its controlling director to ground privity of interest by reason of the fact that the plaintiff-company was wholly owned by the controlling director and there was also sufficient identity of subject matter. It is thought that, intellectually, the decision of the Supreme Court in *Belton* (which of course represents the law in Ireland) is to be preferred.

[B] Authority to Institute Proceedings by a Company

[6.006] Where model Table A, reg 80 (CA 1963, Sch 1) is adopted[13] the authority to institute any legal proceedings will be vested in the board of directors as, by this regulation, the members delegate the general power of management to the directors. Generally, a resolution should be passed by the directors at a properly convened and constituted meeting of the board of directors. Where it is found that a meeting of the directors was not properly held, as in the case of *Re Aston Colour Print Ltd*[14], any purported decision to commence proceedings – in that case a petition to have an examiner appointed to the company – will be invalidated.

[6.007] Even where model reg 80 has been adopted by a company (and its management thereby delegated to its directors) it is arguable that its members may, notwithstanding, direct the directors to institute legal proceedings. This is because the delegation of the

---

12 *Barakot Ltd v Epiette Ltd* [1997] 1 BCLC 303.

13 See Chapter 8, *Corporate Governance: Management by the Directors*, para **[8.004]** *ff*.

14 *Re Aston Colour Print Ltd* (21 February 1997, unreported), High Court (Kelly J). See Chapter 9, *Corporate Governance: Meetings*, para **[9.093]**.

powers of management to directors is, inter alia, subject to 'such directions, being not inconsistent with the aforesaid regulations or provisions, as may be given by the company in general meeting.' There is a view that because there is no specific, express, delegation of power to directors to institute legal proceedings, the effect is to permit the members to make a 'direction' to the directors in that regard[15]. This point can be significant where a company's members wish the company to institute proceedings but where its directors are not inclined to do so: rather than take the more drastic step of removing the directors, the members may in general meeting (or by written resolution) purport to issue a direction to institute proceedings.

[6.008] Where there are no directors (or none, at least, capable of acting) the authority to institute proceedings will vest in a company's members. In such circumstances, an ordinary resolution must be passed in either an annual general meeting ('AGM') or an extraordinary general meeting ('EGM') or, where permitted by the company's articles, by means of a written resolution as permitted by CA 1963, s 141(8). As in the case of a directors' meeting, a members' meeting at which it is proposed to pass a resolution authorising the institution of proceedings, must be validly convened and held. Where a meeting is not properly constituted, any litigation instituted might be found to be unauthorised: see *Colthurst and Tenips Ltd v La Touche Colthurst and Colthu*rst[16].

[6.009] Once a company goes into liquidation, its directors' powers to institute legal proceedings are displaced and any litigation must be instituted by the company's liquidator. In an official winding up the liquidator is empowered to bring or defend legal proceedings in the name and on behalf of the company, subject to the sanction of the court or committee of inspection[17]. The exercise of an official liquidator's powers to bring or defend litigation on a company's behalf is subject to the control of the court and any creditor or contributory may apply in relation to any exercise of those powers[18]. The difference between directors' and liquidators' powers to continue proceedings was commented upon by Laffoy J in *Re Greendale Developments Ltd*[19] in the following terms:

> 'The decision of the court on a contested application to continue proceedings under s 231 is qualitatively different from the decision of a board of directors of a solvent company in relation to prosecuting litigation. The decision of the board of directors should be informed by the interests of the company, not by the sectional interests of individual shareholders or creditors. Once a winding-up order is made, the company is doomed to extinction. The winding up process is the process of the administration of the assets of the company: their collection, realisation and distribution in discharge of the liabilities of the company to the creditors and of the entitlement of its contributories in accordance with the scheme of priorities prescribed in the Companies Acts. Insofar as the Companies Acts give an entitlement to a creditor or a contributory to be heard by the court in relation to a

15 See Chapter 8, *Corporate Governance: Management by the Directors*, para **[8.010]**.

16 *Colthurst and Tenips Ltd v La Touche Colthurst and Colthurst* (9 February 2000, unreported), High Court (McCracken J). See Chapter 9, *Corporate Governance: Meetings*, para **[9.031]**.

17 CA 1963, s 231(1). See Chapter 26, *Liquidators*, para **[26.027]**.

18 CA 1963, s 231(3).

19 *Re Greendale Developments Ltd* [1997] 3 IR 540 (Laffoy J).

> matter arising in the winding up, in my view, the court is required to have regard to the sectional interest of that creditor or contributory and, in particular, to the protection of his legal entitlement to a distribution from the assets of the company as defined by the Companies Acts.'[20]

Liquidators' power to bring and defend proceedings by and on behalf of companies is considered in detail in Chapter 26[21].

[C] SERVICE OF PROCEEDINGS

[6.010] In order to commence legal proceedings in either the District, Circuit or High Courts, it is necessary, after issuing the papers, to serve the requisite process[22] on the defendant in the action. It is useful to distinguish the following types of corporate defendant:

- (a) Companies formed and registered under the Companies Acts 1963–2001;
- (b) Bodies corporate having no connection with Ireland;
- (c) Foreign companies with an established place of business in the State; and
- (d) Foreign companies that have established a branch within the State.

Where service of proceedings is not effected within the limitation period prescribed by the Statute of Limitations 1957, a claim will not be statute barred where the cause of the failure to institute proceedings is due to a defendant company's failure to comply with CA 1963, s 22(1)[23].

(a) Companies formed and registered under the Companies Acts 1963-2001

[6.011] The service of proceedings (and, for that matter, any document) on companies formed and registered under the Companies Acts 1963-2001 is governed by CA 1963, s 379(1) which provides:

> 'A document may be served on a company by leaving it at or sending it by post to the registered office of the company or, if the company has not given notice to the registrar of companies of the situation of its registered office, by registering it at the office for the registration of companies.'

For example, a High Court summary summons applicable to a simple contract debt can validly be served on a company by sending it by ordinary post to its registered office. If the Companies Registration Office ('CRO') has not been notified of the company's registered office, the summons may be sent to the CRO itself[24]. In *National Gas Engine Co Ltd v Estate Engineering Co Ltd*[25] it was held that 'summons' in this regard includes 'default summons'. Service need not be by post[26] and a summons can simply be 'left' at

---

20 [1997] 3 IR 540 at 547.

21 At para **[26.028]**.

22 In the District Court, a Civil Process; in the Circuit Court, a Civil Bill; and in the High Court, a Summons (Summary, Special or Plenary) or an originating notice of motion. See, generally, Courtney, *Mareva Injunctions and Related Interlocutory Orders* (1998), paras [8.14] – [8.24].

23 See *Tierney v Midserve Ltd et al* (23 January 2002, unreported), High Court (Kinlen J).

24 Cf *Bank of Ireland v North City Providers Ltd* (1953-1954) Ir Jur Rep 16, where Murnaghan J allowed service on the directors at their home addresses where a company had ceased to occupy its registered office and place of business.

25 *National Gas Engine Co Ltd v Estate Engineering Co Ltd* [1913] 2 IR 474.

the company's registered office. Service on a company's solicitor will only be good service where the solicitor has been authorised by the company to accept service[27].

[6.012] The decision in *O'Shea v DPP*[28] shows that whilst service on a body corporate may be effected thought service on an officer of that body corporate, service on an individual in that individual's own right, cannot be effected by service on a body corporate of which he is a director. In that case Murphy J said:

> 'Service on a company secretary is good service on the company. It is not good service on a director of the company. While an argument could be made that service on a director, as agent of the company (see s 8 of the Companies Act 1963 and SI 1973/163) is service on the company, the reverse cannot be so. The company is not an agent of the director or member of the company.'

The facts in that case were that a defendant (who happened to be director of a company) was prosecuted for certain road traffic offences. Summonses were served on his workplace and, in his absence, were served by the gardaí on another individual at his workplace. The defendant was convicted of the offences and this was upheld in the Circuit Court. The defendant sought a judicial review of this decision and Murphy J held that he had not been properly served and remitted the matter back to the District Court. In that case the service provision under consideration was the District Court Rules 1948, Ord 47, r 2(a)[29] which deals with individuals. Murphy J's comment that service on a company secretary is good service needs to be contextualised. Service on a company secretary of a company within the meaning of CA 1963, s 2 is not, per se, good service. Where the company is a company to which CA, s 379 applies, the provisions of s 379 must be complied with. This can involve addressing the notice to the company secretary, but must involve 'leaving it at or sending it by post to the registered office of the company', etc.

[6.013] Where a company actually operates from its registered office, it would appear that little injustice can result from CA 1963, s 379. However, in reality, very many private companies have as their registered office the office of their accountant or

---

26 The question of service by fax remains contentious: see Hall, 'Service of Documents by Fax' (1989) Gazette ILSI 318.

27 *Re Denver United Breweries Ltd* (1890) 63 LT 96.

28 *O'Shea v DPP* (30 November 2000, unreported), High Court (Murphy J).

29 This provided:

> 'A summons may be served on a defendant to whom it is directed by delivering to him a copy thereof issued for service or by leaving such copy for him at his last or most usual place of abode, or at his office, shop, factory, home or place of business with the husband or wife of the defendant or with the child or other relative (residing with the defendant)...or with any agent, clerk or servant of the defendant, or with the person in charge of the house or premises wherein the defendant usually resides, provided that any person (other than the defendant himself) with whom such copy is left for the defendant is not under sixteen years of age and is not the complainant'.

This was amended by the District Court Rules (No 1) 1962 (SI 1962/7), Ord 5. These rules have now been replaced by the District Court Rules 1997 (SI 1997/93) ('DCR'). Service on companies is now addressed in DCR Ord 6, which mirrors the wording of CA 1963, s 379.

solicitor, which is normally the office where the company was formed. In such cases, the company obviously does not operate from its registered office. Consequently, a summons could validly be served on a company at its registered office without the company ever in fact being aware of service. This potential for injustice is compounded by CA 1963, s 379(2), which provides:

> 'For the purposes of this section, any document left at or sent by post to the place for the time being recorded by the registrar of companies as the situation of the registered office of a company shall be *deemed* to have been left at or sent by post to the registered office of the company notwithstanding that the situation of its registered office may have been changed.'[30]

This subsection creates a general presumption that a document is served on a company once it is delivered or posted to the company's registered office. However, the presumption may be rebutted in appropriate circumstances: where, for example, it is proved that the document never in fact reached its destination. Such were the circumstances in *Re J Bird Moyer & Co (Ireland) Ltd*[31], where an Irish registered company was sued by an American company for £6,446 5s.10d. The American company sent the summons to the registered office of the Irish company by registered mail, but the letter was retained by the post office and was never delivered. The American company subsequently obtained summary judgment in default of appearance and proceeded to register the judgment as a judgment mortgage against the Irish company's property. When the Irish company was being wound up, the liquidator sought to have the judgment mortgage set aside. Budd J, in granting the relief sought by the liquidator, held that the presumption was rebutted in this case because of the admitted fact that the summons had never been delivered to the registered office. Thus, he held, time had not begun to run for the entry of an appearance and so the summary judgment in default of appearance had been wrongly awarded.

(b) Bodies corporate having no connection with Ireland

[6.014] In the case of High Court proceedings, it should be noted that the Rules of the Superior Courts 1986, Ord 9, r 7 ('RSC') provides a procedure for the service of originating summonses on corporations[32]. This provides:

> 'In the absence of any statutory provision regulating service, every summons issued against a corporation aggregate may be served on the mayor or other head officer, or on the town clerk, clerk, treasurer, or secretary of such corporation; and every summons issued against the inhabitants of a county district or other like district may be served on any officer of the Gárda Síochána not below the rank of superintendent stationed in the county in which such district is situate and every summons issued against the inhabitants of any county or any city or town, or the inhabitants of any franchise, liberty, city, town, or place not being part of the county district or other like district on some peace officer thereof: provided always that in all such cases a sufficient notice of the issuing of the summons shall be given in Iris Oifigiúil and in one of the local newspapers of the county,

---

30 Italics added.

31 *Re J Bird Moyer & Co (Ireland) Ltd* 98 ILTR 202.

32 See Courtney, *Mareva Injunctions and Related Interlocutory Orders* (1998), para [12.14]. See also O'Floinn, *Practice and Procedure in the Superior Courts* (1996), p 52.

city, or district in which the defendant or defendants or the officer or other person to be served shall reside, the times for appearing to run in such cases from the day of the publication of such notice in Iris Oifigiúil or such newspaper, whichever shall be the latest; and where, by any statute, provision is made for service of any proceedings upon any corporation, or upon any society or fellowship, or any body or number of persons, whether corporate or incorporate, every summons may be served in the manner so provided.'[33]

However, by its very terms, this provision only applies 'in the absence of any statutory provision regulating service'. Accordingly, by virtue of CA 1963, s 379, RSC Ord 9, r 7 has no application to companies 'formed and registered' under the Companies Acts 1963–2001 or to existing companies, as defined by CA 1963, s 2. It will have application only to bodies corporate, to which CA 1963, s 379 does not apply and also foreign bodies corporate to which CA 1963, s 356[34] do not apply.

(c) Foreign companies with an established place of business in the State

[6.015] A different regime operates in respect of foreign or overseas companies which, having established a place of business within the State, are registered on the 'external register' under CA 1963, s 352[35]. Where such companies are concerned, CA 1963, s 356 provides that:

> '(1) Subject to subsection (2), any process or notice required to be served on a company to which this Part applies shall be sufficiently served if addressed to any person whose name has been delivered to the registrar of companies under the foregoing provisions of this Part and left at or sent by post to the address which has been so delivered.
>
> (2) A document may be served on any such company by leaving it at or sending it by post to any place of business established by the company in the State -
>
> (a) where the company makes default in delivering to the registrar the name and address of a person resident in the State who is authorised to accept on behalf of the company service of process or notices; or
>
> (b) if at any time all the persons whose names and addresses have been so delivered are dead or have ceased so to reside, or refuse to accept service on behalf of the company, or for any reason cannot be served.'

Where a company has established a place of business in the State but, contrary to its obligations, fails to register as an external company, CA 1963, s 356 will nevertheless apply to the service of any notice or process on such a company[36].

---

33 Note the wording of the English Rules is different. In *Kuwait Airways Corp v Iraqi Airways Co* [1995] 3 All ER 694 the House of Lords held there was good service of a process where it had been served on an employee in England who was in charge of its business there on the basis that he fell within the description of 'other similar officer' on whom personal service on the body corporate could be effected pursuant to the English Rules of the Supreme Court 1965, Ord 65, r 3(1).

34 See para **[6.015]**.

35 See generally Binchy, *Irish Conflicts of Law* (1988), pp 128–129; also Chapter 2, *Formation, Registration and Conversion of Private Companies*, para **[2.046]** *ff.*

36 It is thought that the question of service is analogous to the principle applying to the '*Slavenburg* file': see Chapter 21, *Corporate Borrowing: Registration of Charges*, para **[21.079]**.

[6.016] It is a prerequisite to good service that the foreign or overseas company must have actually established a place of business within the State. In *Donovan v North German Lloyd Steamship Co*[37], it was held by the High Court that a plenary summons served upon a foreign company was invalid because the company, while having connections with Ireland, did not appear to have a place of business in Ireland. Moreover, the person upon whom the summons had been served was not an agent or an employee of the company. It was held in *Rakusens Ltd v Baser Ambalaj Plastik Sanayi Ticaret AS*[38] that where it is sought to prove that a company has established a place of business within the State by the conduct of persons who are merely its agents as opposed to its employees, it is not sufficient to show that the agent had established a place of business at the relevant address. In that case the English Court of Appeal found that, when seeking to establish that an overseas company has established a place of business through the conduct of its agent, whether or not the agent had the authority to conclude contracts on behalf of the overseas company will be a relevant factor. The court, in that case, found that the service on an agent was not proper service because the agent was merely a commission agent who passed on orders to the overseas company and had no authority to conclude contracts on its behalf.

The courts, however, have an inherent power, recognised by RSC Ord 11, r 15, to treat service actually effected as being sufficient where there are just grounds for doing so[39]. A similar power was exercised by the English High Court in *Boocock v Hilton International Co*[40] to validate a service on a foreign defendant-company. The writ was not served in accordance with the English equivalent of CA 1963, s 356, since service had not been effected against a person whose name had been registered with the Registrar of Companies, but was instead simply posted to the defendant's UK offices. Neill J found that, in the interests of justice, there were grounds for treating this service as valid and deemed the posting to the UK office as good service.

[6.017] Substituted service under CA 1963, s 356(2) is only possible when attempts to serve under CA 1963, s 356(1) have been unsuccessful[41]. In *Rome v Punjab National Bank (No 2)*,[42] the English Court of Appeal held service to have been validly effected on a foreign overseas company once addressed to and left at the home of a person registered under the English equivalent of the Irish CA 1963, s 352[43] who was authorised to accept service on behalf of the company. This was held to be so notwithstanding that the company might have ceased to have an established place of business within the State and that it might have notified the Registrar of Companies of this fact, who, in turn, might have marked the company's file as closed. Parker LJ observed that:

---

[37] *Donovan v North German Lloyd Steamship Co* [1933] IR 33.

[38] *Rakusens Ltd v Baser Ambalaj Plastik Sanayi Ticaret AS* [2002] 1 BCLC 104, [2001] EWCA Civ 1820.

[39] See RSC Ord 11, r 15.

[40] *Boocock v Hilton International Co* [1993] BCLC 1363.

[41] See Binchy, *Irish Conflicts of Law* (1988), p 129.

[42] *Rome v Punjab National Bank (No 2)* [1990] 1 All ER 58.

[43] Companies Act 1985, s 695 (UK).

'...any injustice which may result from reliance on the provisions of [the section] when, for instance, the foreign company has long since left our shores, can always be remedied by a stay of the proceedings under the inherent jurisdiction of the English courts.'[44]

The judge conceded that this interpretation resulted 'in what may appear to be an absurdity'[45]. The Irish provision appears open to a similar interpretation - indeed, any other interpretation would appear to do violence to the plain words of the section.

(d) Foreign companies that have established a branch within the State

[6.018] Regulation 17 of the European Communities (Branch Disclosures) Regulations 1993[46] makes almost identical provision for the service of documents on limited companies incorporated outside the State which have established a branch within the State. Regulation 17 provides:

'(1) Subject to paragraph (2), any process or notice required to be served on a company to which these Regulations apply shall be sufficiently served if addressed to any person whose name has been delivered to the registrar under Regulation 4(2)(g) or 7(2)(h) (or any changes notified thereto) and left at or sent by post to the address which has been so delivered.

(2) A document may be served on any such company by leaving it at or sending it by post to any branch established by the company in the State—

(a) where the company makes default in delivering to the registrar the name and address of a person resident in the State who is authorised to accept on behalf of the company service of process; or

(b) if at any time all the persons whose names and addresses have been so delivered are dead or have ceased to so reside, or refuse to accept service on behalf of the company, or for any reason it cannot be served.'

Companies to which those regulations apply are companies which are incorporated outside the State, which are of a legal form comparable to any company to which Article 1 of the 1968 Directive applies and which establishes a branch in the State[47]. By mirroring the wording of CA 1963, s 356 in reg 17, we have avoided the difficulties that have been caused in England by the English decision to limit their branch disclosure service regime to matters 'in respect of carrying on of a business of the branch'. These difficulties were highlighted in *Saab v Saudi American Bank*[48] where Tuckey J had to decide whether service on a branch was good where the action was concerned only in part with the branch's business and also with the foreign company's other business. In the event, it was held that service was good and this was upheld by the Court of Appeal[49] which held there was no good reason for construing the words 'in respect of the carrying

---

44 [1990] 1 All ER 58 at 63.

45 [1990] 1 All ER 58 at 64. See also *Boocock v Hilton International Co* [1993] BCLC 1363; *Camera Care Ltd v Victor Hasselblad* [1986] FTLR 347.

46 SI 1993/395. See Chapter 2, *Formation, Registration and Conversion of Private Companies*, para **[2.046]**.

47 SI 1993/395, regs 3 and 6.

48 *Saab v Saudi American Bank* [1998] 2 BCLC 13.

49 [2000] BCC 466.

on of the business' of the branch in the Companies Act 1985, s 694A(2) (UK) narrowly as if they read 'arising out of the operations' of the branch.

[D] Security For Costs

[6.019] When a limited company appears as plaintiff in any proceedings, CA 1963, s 390 allows the defendant to apply to court for an order requiring the plaintiff-company to provide security for costs[50]. Where granted the plaintiff-company must pay into court a sum that can be looked to, in order to discharge the defendant's costs, should the defendant be successful in defending the proceedings. The effect of CA 1963, s 390 is that the court may, at its discretion[51], stay proceedings commenced by a limited company until such time as sufficient[52] security for the defendant's costs has been provided. Section 390 provides:

> 'Where a limited company is plaintiff in any action or other legal proceeding, any judge having jurisdiction in the matter, may, if it appears by credible testimony that there is reason to believe that the company will be unable to pay the costs of the defendant if successful in his defence, require sufficient security to be given for those costs and may stay all proceedings until the security is given.'

Section 390 gives the courts jurisdiction to grant an order for security for costs against a limited company. An order for security for costs affords protection to defendants who might incur substantial legal costs in successfully defending an action, only to be faced with an impecunious limited company or a person living outside the jurisdiction[53]. Where the plaintiff is an individual, as opposed to a limited company, the only grounds upon which he may be required to give security for costs is where he resides outside of the State or where one appeals an order or judgment made by a court[54]. As Keane J held, however, in *Pitt v Bolger*[55], the discretion to order security for costs against a person resident outside of the State will never, save in the most exceptional of circumstances, be exercised against an EU resident plaintiff[56]. The High Court of Northern Ireland in *McAteer v Lismore*[57] has rejected the claim that an order for security for costs infringed Article 6 of the European Convention on Human Rights, holding that it was a proportionate response designed to safeguard defendants' rights. Before embarking

---

50 See generally Garvey, 'Security for Costs and Corporate Plaintiffs – Law and Practice' (1994) CLP 105; Delany, 'Security for Costs in Relation to Corporate Plaintiffs' (2000) ILT 58; Milman, 'Security for Costs; Limited Liability in Litigation', (1995) Palmer's In Company, Issue 10/1995, 16 November 1995; and Doolan, 'The Insolvent Company and Security for Costs' (1986) ILT 218.

51 As to the court's discretion, see para **[6.040]**.

52 See para **[6.054]**.

53 In relation to security for costs in proceedings brought by foreign plaintiffs see Binchy, *Irish Conflicts of Law* (1988), pp 652–669.

54 RSC Ord 58, r 17. See para **[6.030]**.

55 *Pitt v Bolger* [1996] 1 ILRM 68. See also *Lough Neagh Exploration Ltd v Morrice* [1998] 1 ILRM 205 (Laffoy J).

56 See also *European Fashion Products Ltd v Eenkhoorn et al* (21 December 2001, unreported), High Court (Barr J).

57 *McAteer v Lismore* [2000] NI 477.

upon a review of the jurisdiction to grant orders for security for costs against limited companies, we shall first consider the circumstances in which such orders will be granted against non-resident natural and artificial persons.

The jurisdiction to order security for costs against non-residents

[6.020] The rules relating to applications for security for costs against non-resident plaintiffs (whether natural persons or bodies corporate) are set out in RSC Ord 29 which provides:

> '1. When a party shall require security for costs from another party, he shall be at liberty to apply by notice to the party for such security; and in case the latter shall not, within forty-eight hours after service thereof, undertake by notice to comply therewith, the party requiring the security shall be at liberty to apply to the Court for an order that the said party do furnish such security.
>
> 2. A defendant shall not be entitled to an order for security for costs solely on the ground that the plaintiff resides in Northern Ireland.
>
> 3. No defendant shall be entitled to an order for security for costs by reason of any plaintiff being resident out of the jurisdiction of the Court, unless upon a satisfactory affidavit that such defendant has a defence upon the merits.
>
> 4. A plaintiff ordinarily resident out of the jurisdiction may be ordered to give security for costs though he may be temporarily resident within the jurisdiction.
>
> 5. If a person brings an action for the recovery of land after a prior action for the recovery of the same has been brought by such person or by any person through or under whom he claims, against the same defendant, or against any person through or under whom he defends, the Court may at any time order that the plaintiff shall give to the defendant security for the defendant's costs, whether the prior action has been disposed of by discontinuance or by non-suit or by judgment for the defendant.
>
> 6. Where the Court shall have made an order that a party do furnish security for costs, the amount of such security and the time or times at which, and the manner and form in which, and the person or persons to whom, the same shall be given shall, subject to rule 7, be determined by the Master in every case.
>
> 7. Where a bond is to be given as security for costs, it shall, unless the Master shall otherwise direct, be given to the party or person requiring the security, and not to an officer of the Court. Provided that in any matrimonial cause or matter where security for costs is to be given by bond the bond shall be given to the Master.'

As shall be seen below, RSC Ord 29 is relevant to non-resident bodies corporate, against which application cannot be made under CA 1963, s 390 because they are not 'companies' within the meaning of CA 1963, s 2[58].

The justification for treating limited companies differently to individuals

[6.021] The law is less favourable to limited liability companies, since, regardless of whether they are resident in the State, they may be ordered to give security for costs where there is reason to believe that they may be unable to pay the defendant's costs. It is

---

58 See para **[6.027]**.

public policy, rather than any rational imperative, that has decided that a corporate plaintiff's winding up does not carry sufficient stigma as to dissuade the institution of frivolous proceedings. The rationale for this discrimination between natural and corporate plaintiffs seems to draw largely on the stigma that is perceived to accompany an individual's bankruptcy. The prospect of bankruptcy may deter an individual litigant from taking frivolous proceedings, whereas those behind a limited company - who may, after all, have their total liability limited to as little as two cent - have nothing to lose personally should the company lose the action. Nevertheless, as Murphy J observed in *Bula Ltd v Tara Mines Ltd*[59]:

> 'It is clear beyond doubt that section 390 aforesaid may impose a serious handicap on an impecunious limited liability company where a lack of funds would not create the same problem for an individual litigant.'

In *Harrington et al v JVC (UK) Ltd*[60] O'Hanlon J cited with approval the following passage from the decision of Megarry V-C in *Pearson v Naydler*[61].

> 'In the case of a limited company, there is no basic rule conferring immunity from any liability to give security for costs. The basic rule is the opposite; s 447 [of the Companies Act 1948 (UK)] applies to all limited companies, and subjects them to the liability to give security for costs. The whole concept of the section is contrary to the rule developed by the cases that poverty is not to be made a bar to bringing an action. There is nothing in the statutory language (the substance of which goes back at least as far as the Companies Act 1862, s 69) to indicate that there are any exceptions to what is laid down as a broad and general rule for all limited companies. Nor is it surprising that there should be such a rule. A man may bring into being as many limited companies as he wishes, with the privilege of limited liability; and s 447 provides some protection for the community against litigious abuses by artificial persons manipulated by natural persons. One should be slow to whittle away this protection as one should be to whittle away a natural person's right to litigate despite poverty.'

It is clear that the courts will therefore try to maintain a balance between the interests of limited liability companies and those of defendants when considering applications for orders for security for costs.

The test for an order for security for costs under s 390 of CA 1963

[6.022] Notwithstanding that, since the first edition of this book, security for costs applications have given rise to more judgments of both the Irish High and Supreme Courts than any other area of company law and practice, the circumstances in which an application will be successful are relatively straightforward. The circumstances in which security for costs will be ordered against a limited company may be stated in the following, sequential, test:

(a) Section 390 can be invoked by the defendant in any 'action or other legal proceeding',

---

59 *Bula Ltd v Tara Mines Ltd* [1987] IR 494.

60 *Harrington v JVC (UK) Ltd* (16 March 1995, unreported), High Court (O'Hanlon J).

61 *Pearson v Naydler* [1977] 3 All ER 531.

(b) The respondent-company must have limited liability and must also be a 'company' within the meaning of CA 1963, s 2,

(c) The respondent-company must be a 'plaintiff'; although this term will be broadly interpreted to include an appellant (who might be a plaintiff or defendant in an action) or a counterclaiming-defendant, for a substantial amount,

(d) The applicant will normally be a 'defendant' but can also include such other persons as are added to an action commenced by the plaintiff, who might be liable to have costs, should the plaintiff be unsuccessful,

(e) There is an onus of proof on the applicant who invokes CA 1963, s 390 to establish by credible testimony that there is a proven or admitted inability to discharge the applicant's costs, should the respondent-company fail in its action,

(f) There is also an onus of proof on the applicant to satisfy the court that he has a prima facie defence to the respondent-company's claim,

(g) The jurisdiction to order a respondent-company to give security for costs is discretionary, and is not available to an applicant as of right; and notwithstanding that the applicant discharges all of the foregoing proofs, the court may decline to make an order security for costs if the respondent-company can satisfy it that special circumstances exist. These include:
   (i) The applicant's lack of bona fides,
   (ii) The respondent-company's insolvency having been caused by the applicant,
   (iii) The respondent-company seeking to vindicate the public interest,
   (iv) The existence of a natural co-plaintiff,
   (v) The applicant's delay in applying for an order for security for costs,

(h) If satisfied that it is proper to make an order for security for costs, the court must determine what it considers to be sufficient security.

The commentary that follows will explore each of the foregoing limbs and sub-limbs of the test for an order for security for costs.

(a) Section 390 may be invoked in any 'action or other legal proceedings'

[6.023] Although CA 1963, s 390 is not expressly confined to civil actions or proceedings, it is in that context that the section has, to date, invariably been invoked; it is conceivable that a limited company in proceedings other than civil might be ordered to give security for a respondent's costs. The same words as used in the similar English provision, the Companies Act 1985, s 726(1) (UK) were given a wide interpretation in *Re Unisoft Group*[62]. There, 'action' was considered to be broad enough to include a petition for unfair prejudice so that a corporate petitioner under the Companes Act 1985, s 459 (UK) could be ordered to give security for costs.

[6.024] It may also be noted that it is not necessary that an applicant for an order for security for costs under CA 1963, s 390 must first ask the plaintiff to provide them, only

---

[62] *Re Unisoft Group* [1994] BCC 11.

proceeding by motion upon receiving a refusal. This was established in *Lancefort Ltd v An Bord Pleanála*[63] where Morris J found that the requirement in RSC Ord 29, r 1 (that a demand to the respondent-company for security must have been made before applying to court for an order) was not a precondition to an application under CA 1963, s 390.

(b) The respondent-company must have limited liability and be a 'company'

[6.025] An application for security for costs cannot be brought under CA 1963, s 390 against an unlimited company. Before CA 1963, s 390 can be invoked, the members of the respondent-company must have limited liability. Normally, liability will be limited by shares, but it was held in *R v Westminster, ex p Mayfair Residents*[64] that companies limited by guarantee can also be ordered to provide security under the English equivalent to CA 1963, s 390.

[6.026] Section 390 does not apply to all 'bodies corporate' and is expressly confined to limited liability 'companies' as defined by CA 1963, s 2. In England and Wales it has been held that the Companies Act 1985, s 726 (UK) does not apply to companies that are incorporated in Northern Ireland[65] and, similarly, CA 1963, s 390 does not apply to Northern Ireland registered companies or indeed to any body corporate other than a company that is formed and registered in the State. So, in *Harrington v JVC (UK) Ltd*[66] O'Hanlon J said:

> 'As the statutory provision relates only to situations in which a limited company incorporated within the jurisdiction is plaintiff in any action or other legal proceeding, and there is reason to believe that the company will be unable to pay the costs of the defendant if successful in his defence, the application for this relief can only be sought as against the second and third-named plaintiffs and not against the first-named plaintiff who is suing in his personal capacity, or against the fourth-named plaintiff, which is a company incorporated in Northern Ireland.'[67]

The matter arose again in *Windmaster Developments Ltd v Airoglen Ltd*[68] where at the hearing for the purpose of assessing the amount of security for costs (ie after an order for security had been made) it was contended that because the plaintiff was registered in England and Wales, s 390 did not apply as that section only applied to Irish companies. McCracken J refused to consider the matter of jurisdiction anew because first, he had already determined the matter which the plaintiff was not permitted to reopen, secondly, because no evidence of the plaintiff's status as an English registered company was put before the court; and thirdly, because the plaintiff had not raised the matter at the original hearing. Accordingly, whilst in that case an order pursuant to CA 1963, s 390

---

63 *Lancefort Ltd v An Bord Pleanála* (23 June 1997, unreported), High Court (Morris J).

64 *R v Westminster, ex p Mayfair Residents* (1991, unreported) High Court (Eng), but referenced in Milman, 'Security for Costs; Limited Liability in Litigation' (1995) Palmer's In Company, Issue 10/1995, 16 November 1995.

65 *DSQ Properties v Lotus Cars* [1987] 1 WLR 127; cf *Wilson Vehicle Distribution Ltd v Colt Car Co Ltd* [1984] BCLC 93.

66 *Harrington v JVC (UK) Ltd* (16 March 1995, unreported), High Court (O'Hanlon J).

67 (16 March 1995, unreported), High Court at p 15.

68 *Windmaster Developments Ltd v Airoglen Ltd* (10 July 2000, unreported), High Court (McCracken J).

was, apparently, made against an English registered company, it was in very exceptional (even, accidental) circumstances. It is clearly the case that CA 1963, s 390 applies only to 'companies' which expression has by virtue of CA 1963, s 2, a very clear and precise meaning[69].

[6.027] It should be noted, however, that even if CA 1963, s 390 cannot be invoked, one may seek to place reliance upon RSC Ord 29 which can be invoked against either corporate or individual plaintiffs who are ordinarily resident outside of the jurisdiction. So, in *Lough Neagh Exploration Ltd v Morrice*[70] although the plaintiff was not a company within the meaning of CA 1963, s 2 (being a company incorporated pursuant to the laws of Northern Ireland) application for security for costs was brought pursuant to RSC Ord 29, r 1. Further, where application is made under RSC Ord 29 the results may not be all that different than if it were made under CA 1963, s 390 since, in that case Laffoy J said:

> 'However, it is common case that, in broad terms, the same principles govern the determination whether a plaintiff should be ordered to furnish security for a defendant's costs under s 390 and under Ord 29.'[71]

It will be appreciated, however, that there is a lacuna here since neither RSC Ord 29 nor CA 1963, s 390 apply to an Irish resident body corporate with limited liability that is not a company within the meaning of CA 1963, s 2.

[6.028] It was Ireland's membership of the European Union that prompted Keane J in *Pitt v Bolger*[72] to say that the discretion under RSC Ord 29 to order security for costs against a person resident outside of the State will never, save in the most exceptional of circumstances, be exercised against an EU resident plaintiff. What of the position in relation to applications under RSC Ord 29 against EU registered bodies corporate? The English Court of Appeal in *Chequepoint SARL v McClelland*[73] decided that there is jurisdiction to order an EU registered body corporate to provide security for costs in an action in England in such a way as not to constitute unlawful discrimination contrary to EU law. Their reasoning was because a similar power could be exercised against an English company under the Companies Act 1985, s 726 (UK). It is thought that a limited liability EU legal entity that commences an action in Ireland is amenable to RSC Ord 29 where it is not resident in Ireland. Of course, where such an EU body corporate is resident in Ireland, an order cannot be made under RSC Ord 29.

[6.029] The question of the residence of a body corporate was considered by the English High Court in *Re Little Olympian Each Ways Ltd*[74]. Like RSC Ord 29, r 4, the English Rules of the Supreme Court 1965, Ord 23, r 1(1)(a) refers to a plaintiff being 'ordinarily resident' outside of the jurisdiction. In that case Lindsay J held that a corporate plaintiff

69 See Chapter 2, *Formation, Registration and Conversions of Private Companies*, para **[2.054]**.

70 *Lough Neagh Exploration Ltd v Morrice* [1998] 1 ILRM 205 (Laffoy J).

71 [1998] 1 ILRM 205 at 207.

72 *Pitt v Bolger* [1996] 1 ILRM 68. See also *Lough Neagh Exploration Ltd v Morrice* [1998] 1 ILRM 205 (Laffoy J).

73 *Chequepoint SARL v McClelland* [1997] 1 BCLC 117.

74 *Re Little Olympian Each Ways Ltd* [1994] 4 All ER 561.

will be ordinarily resident outside of the jurisdiction if the central control and management of the company actually abides and is exercised overseas[75].

(c) The respondent-company can be a 'plaintiff', an 'appellant' or a 'counter-claiming defendant'

[6.030] The most usual situation in which a respondent-company will be faced with an application for security for costs is where it is the plaintiff in an action. By reason of the reference to 'any action or other legal proceedings' it is thought to be clear that CA 1963, s 390 can be invoked against a company that is appealing a decision of a court of first instance[76]. This view was accepted by the Supreme Court in *Bula Ltd v Tara Mines Ltd*[77]. In that case Lynch J had, in the High Court, found against the plaintiffs on the substantive issues. The plaintiffs, however, appealed that decision to the Supreme Court and the defendants then brought motions to the Supreme Court seeking orders for security for costs against the corporate plaintiffs (pursuant to CA 1963, s 390) and against both the corporate and individual plaintiffs (pursuant to RSC Ord 58, r 17). Whilst RSC Ord 58, r 17 makes express provision for the making of an order for security for costs on an appeal[78], Keane J saw no jurisdictional issues in making an order under both CA 1963, s 390 and RSC Ord 58, r 17, saying:

> '...this is clearly a case in which an order providing for security for costs should be made under Ord 58, r 17. I am also satisfied that, in the case of the corporate plaintiffs, it would be reasonable to make such an order under s 390 of the Companies Act 1963. An application for security under that section was made at a far earlier state of the proceedings and refused by Murphy J in the High Court on the ground that [the plaintiffs] had made out an arguable case that their insolvency was the result of the wrongdoing of the defendants, a conclusion which was upheld on appeal by this court...The position at this stage, however, is radically different: there has been a prolonged trial in the High Court in the course of which the claim that the insolvency of [the plaintiffs] was caused by the wrongdoing of the defendant was rejected. While the plaintiffs are, of course, entitled to challenge that conclusion on the hearing of the appeal, the trial judge's findings, coupled with the other circumstances discussed at an earlier stage of this judgment, make it clear that this is a case in which the corporate plaintiffs should be required to furnish security for costs.'[79]

It is thought that CA 1963, s 390 can be invoked in any action or other legal proceedings in which it is possible to have costs awarded against the plaintiff to the defendant.

---

75 Following *De Beers Consolidated Mines Ltd v Howe* [1906] AC 455 and *Unit Construction Co Ltd v Bullock* [1959] 3 All ER 831. See, generally, Chapter 5, *Disregarding Separate Legal Personality*, para **[5.067]**.

76 Cf *Electro Services Ltd v Issa Nicholas (Grenada) Ltd* [1998] 1 WLR 202 where the Privy Council held that the Grenada Companies Act, s 584 only permitted the making of an order for security for costs in respect of first instance proceedings although it was acknowledged that in exceptional circumstances the court had an inherent jurisdiction to order security for costs.

77 *Bula Ltd v Tara Mines Ltd* (26 March 1998, unreported), Supreme Court (Keane J; nem diss).

78 RSC Ord 58, r 17 provides: 'Such deposit or other security for the costs to be occasioned by any appeal shall be made or given as may be directed under special circumstances by the Supreme Court.'

79 (26 March 1998, unreported), Supreme Court at p 28.

[6.031] Where an appellate court is asked by an appealing-plaintiff to exercise its discretion against making an order for security for costs, the circumstances which should be taken into account were stated by McCarthy J in *SEE Co Ltd v Public Lighting Services*[80] to be:

> 'Without attempting to make an exhaustive list, it would seem relevant to consider such matters as:
>
> (i) Has a prima facie case been made to the effect that the inability identified by the section flows from the wrong allegedly committed by the party seeking the security?
>
> (ii) Is there an arguable case stated in the notice of appeal?
>
> (iii) Has there been undue delay by the moving party?
>
> Countervailing circumstances would include the very fact that the insolvent company has lost the case in the High Court and is now an appellant.'

The question of the exercise of the court's discretion to make or decline an order for security for costs is considered in detail below[81]. It is important to note here, however, that in *Lismore Builders Ltd v Bank of Ireland Finance Ltd*[82] Barron J elaborated on the meaning of the second point, namely, whether there is an arguable case in the notice of appeal. He said:

> 'What may or may not be an arguable case has not been precisely defined in the cases. However it would seem to me that since the application is heard on affidavit that there must be at least a case which would be sufficiently strong as that which would entitle a defendant in a motion for liberty to enter final judgment to be permitted to defend.'[83]

Barron J later added, that 'once an arguable case has been established the strength of that case is immaterial unless it leads to showing that in reality the defendant has no real defence'[84]. The first[85] and third[86] points of this test are considered below. The test was applied in *Superwood Holdings plc et al v Sun Alliance and London plc et al*[87] where an order for security for costs was made against an appellant-plaintiff.

(d) The applicant can be a 'defendant' or notice party

[6.032] The typical applicant for an order for security for costs is the defendant in the action or other legal proceedings commenced by the plaintiff. Other persons too, who are not strictly 'defendants', may apply for security for costs. In *Broadnet Ireland Ltd v Office of the Director of Telecommunications Regulation and Eircom plc*[88] the plaintiff in a security for costs motion had applied for a broadband fixed wireless point to multi-point access licence and had been advised that it had been unsuccessful. The plaintiff

---

80 *SEE Company Ltd v Public Lighting Services* [1987] IRLM 255.

81 See para **[6.040]**.

82 *Lismore Builders Ltd v Bank of Ireland Finance Ltd* [1999] 1 IR 501 (Barron J).

83 [1999] 1 IR 501 at p 529.

84 As to the defendant's defence, see para **[6.038]**.

85 See para **[6.045]**.

86 See para **[6.052]**.

87 *Superwood Holdings plc v Sun Alliance and London plc* [1995] 3 IR 303.

88 *Broadnet Ireland Ltd v Office of the Director of Telecommunications Regulation and Eircom plc* [2000] 3 IR 281, [2000] 2 ILRM 241 (Laffoy J).

had then sought a judicial review of the decision of the Director of Telecommunications Regulation. By subsequent order of the court, Eircom was joined as a defendant and three other companies (who were successful in their applications for a licence) were joined as notice parties in the judicial review proceedings. Five motions were brought for, inter alia, security for costs. These were brought by the Director of Telecommunications Regulation, Eircom and three notice parties. Laffoy J noted that it was all but conceded that the Director of Telecommunications Regulation was entitled to security for costs but the plaintiff contested any order in favour of Eircom and the notice parties. The plaintiff contended that as the core issue on the substantive application was apparent bias on the part of the Director of Telecommunications Regulation, in which it was not alleged that the other parties were implicated, those parties had no role to play in the resolution of the core issue and that if they wished to participate in the substantive application, the plaintiff should not be required to give security for the costs of that participation, which it considered to be unnecessary. Laffoy J noted that RSC Ord 84, r 22 required that the originating notice of motion in judicial review proceedings 'must be served on all persons directly affected'. Laffoy J held:

> 'It is not disputed that these parties are directly affected and it was on that basis that they were joined in the proceedings as notice parties and, in the case of Eircom, as a respondent. If these parties are directly affected and have a right to be served with the proceedings, they have a right to participate in the proceedings and to be heard in order to protect their respective interests…The fact that in this case the alleged wrongdoer, the Director, is defending the proceedings, in my view, cannot as against the acknowledged innocent parties who are directly affected by the proceedings, Eircom and the Notice Parties, constitute a special circumstance for refusing to award security for costs to those parties.'

Laffoy J went on to note that even if it was subsequently found by the trial judge on deciding costs that the notice parties only required limited participation, the plaintiff would not be prejudiced as it would be entitled to a return of any surplus of the funds lodged in court by way of security.

(e) Onus on the applicant to adduce credible testimony of the plaintiff's inability to pay costs

[6.033] It is a prerequisite to making an order under CA 1963, s 390 that it appears by credible testimony that there is reason to believe that a respondent-company will be unable to meet the costs of a successful applicant. The requisite testimony will concern the solvency (or, more appropriately, the insolvency) of the respondent-company. In its initial consideration of whether there is reason to believe that a respondent-company will be unable to pay the costs of the applicant or defendant if successful in his defence, the court will be exclusively concerned with the respondent-company's factual ability to pay and not with the reasons why it might be unable to pay. Once it is established that the respondent-company is likely to be unable to pay the defendant's costs, the court has jurisdiction to make an order under s 390. Where it is alleged that the respondent-company's impecuniosity has been caused by the defendant's wrongdoing, the onus will be on the respondent-company to prove that to the court. Moreover, this will merely be a special circumstance as to why the court might exercise its discretion against making an order and establishing this will not mean that an order will be declined automatically;

this and other special circumstances are considered below[89]. In this section, however, we are concerned with the initial enquiry into the plaintiff's solvency.

[6.034] The essence of the enquiry into whether there is reason to believe that the respondent-company will be unable to pay the defendant's costs is the respondent-company's (ie plaintiff's) solvency. Insolvency may either be proved by the defendant or conceded by the respondent-company[90] and the latter course is taken with surprising frequency[91]. Where the plaintiff is a 'shelf company' which has no significant assets it has been held by the Supreme Court that:

> '...it follows therefore, that, undoubtedly if the [company] is unsuccessful in its claim before the High Court, it will be unable to pay the costs of the defendant and it therefore appears to be clearly within the jurisdiction of the High Court to make the order for security for costs.' [92]

Where insolvency is not admitted, it will be necessary to enquire into the plaintiff's finances. In *Bula Ltd v Tara Mines Ltd*[93] Murphy J said:

> 'However, I do not think it is necessary for me to enter into a detailed analysis of the assets and liabilities of Bula Ltd. All that the section requires is that it should appear by credible testimony "that there is reason to believe that the company would be unable to pay the costs of the defendant if successful in his defence".'[94]

Where solvency is hotly disputed, however, it will be necessary to outline the financial situation of the plaintiff. The plaintiff's alleged inability to pay the defendant's costs was disputed in *Irish Press plc v EM Warburg Pincus & Co International Ltd*[95]. In that case McGuinness J considered the assets and liabilities of the plaintiff and of its seven subsidiaries. The learned judge found that some of the companies did hold valuable assets and, notwithstanding that they were held by legal entities separate from the plaintiff, included them in reckoning the plaintiff's ability to meet any order for costs. McGuinness J said:

> 'While Irish Press plc is not in a particularly happy position and while its assets appear to be diminishing, it is not insolvent and continues to hold reasonably substantial assets through its subsidiary companies. I must also take account of the fact that Mr McHugh, a partner in the firm of Messrs Deloitte and Touche, who is not a director or member of the plaintiff company but the audit partner with overall responsibility for the plaintiff's audit,

---

89 See para **[6.042]**.

90 Per Finlay CJ in *Jack O'Toole Ltd v MacEoin Kelly Associates* [1986] IR 277 at 283; see also *Campbell Seafoods Ltd v Brodene Gram A/S* (21 July 1994, unreported), High Court (Costello J).

91 See, eg, *Bula Ltd v Tara Mines Ltd* [1987] IR 494; *SEE Co Ltd v Public Lighting Services Ltd* [1987] ILRM 255; *Society for the Protection of Unborn Children (Ireland) Ltd v Grogan* [1992] ILRM 461; *Comhlucht Páipear Ríomhaireachta Teo v Údarás na Gaeltachta* [1990] ILRM 266.

92 Per Keane CJ in *Hot Radio Co Ltd v IRTC and NP* (14 April 2000, unreported), Supreme Court (ex tempore), p 2.

93 *Bula Ltd v Tara Mines Ltd* [1987] IR 494.

94 [1987] IR 494 at 498.

95 *Irish Press plc v EM Warburg Pincus & Co International Ltd* [1997] 2 ILRM 263.

> is prepared as a professional accountant with full knowledge of the plaintiff's financial affairs to aver that in his opinion the assets of the plaintiff will be sufficient to discharge the costs of the defendants.'[96]

Accordingly, in that case the defendant's application for an order that the plaintiff should provide security for its costs was refused because of the factual finding that the plaintiff-company would be able to meet the defendant's costs.

[6.035] The estimated amount of the defendant's costs will be in respect of the present action. In *Irish Press plc v EM Warburg Pincus & Co International Ltd*[97] the defendant submitted that the possible costs of an appeal to the Supreme Court should also be considered. This was rejected by McGuinness J who held:

> 'It is my view that I am here dealing only with an action in this court and the costs that may arise therefrom. It is too uncertain a matter to look into the future to try to assess the plaintiff's ability to meet the costs of a putative appeal to the Supreme Court which may not in fact take place. If there is such an appeal, an appropriate application in regard to costs may be brought to the Supreme Court itself, as has been done in previous cases.'[98]

One such previous case in point is *Bula Ltd v Tara Mines Ltd*[99]. At the trial of the action an order for security for costs was refused. In the trial of the substantive issues, the defendant was successful. The plaintiff, however, appealed to the Supreme Court and once again the defendant applied for an order that the plaintiff provide security for costs. This time the Supreme Court acceded to the defendant's new application that security for costs be provided for the appeal. Generally, the precise amount of the defendant's costs will not be known at the hearing of the motion for security for costs and it will frequently happen that if a defendant is successful in his application, the actual amount of costs will be fixed by the Master of the High Court, although it may come back to the High Court[100]. The question of 'sufficient security' is considered below[101].

[6.036] The appropriate time in respect of which the court must determine inability to pay a defendant's costs is when the defendant has been successful in his defence. This was held to be the correct interpretation of CA 1963, s 390 by O'Neill J in *Ochre Ridge Ltd v Cork Bonded Warehouses Ltd and Port of Cork Company Ltd*[102]. In that case the plaintiff's solvency was contested and the plaintiff argued that no evidence had been adduced which would prove on the balance of probabilities that it was insolvent at the time of the making of the security for costs application. The plaintiff also argued that it had a valuable asset, namely the benefit of the contract in dispute that was worth

---

96 [1997] 2 ILRM 263 at p 274.

97 *Irish Press plc v EM Warburg Pincus & Co International Ltd* [1997] 2 ILRM 263 (McGuinness J).

98 [1997] 2 ILRM 263 at p 270.

99 *Bula Ltd v Tara Mines Ltd* (26 March 1998, unreported), Supreme Court (Keane J; nem diss).

100 See, eg, *Windmaster Developments Ltd v Airoglen Ltd and Kelly* (10 July 2000, unreported), High Court (McCracken J).

101 See para **[6.054]**.

102 *Ochre Ridge Ltd v Cork Bonded Warehouses Ltd and Port of Cork Company Ltd* (20 December 2000, unreported), High Court (O'Neill J).

£775,000. O'Neill J held that the appropriate reference point for determining ability to pay was the time when the defendant was successful in his defence. Accordingly, if the defendant were successful, the plaintiff would not be entitled to the benefit of the contract and so it appeared to the learned judge 'to be probable' that it would have no assets or income out of which to meet an order for costs.

[6.037] Where an action is brought by a company after commencement of its liquidation, the costs of a successful defendant against the company will rank in priority to the claims of all creditors (other than creditors secured by a mortgage or charge). This is because, as McCarthy J explained in *Comhlucht Páipear Ríomhaireachta Teo v Údarás na Gaeltachta*,[103] it would be:

> '...a great injustice if a company were free, after liquidation, to maintain an action for the benefit of the general body of creditors and, if unsuccessful, successfully to contend that the costs of the successful litigant against the company should only rank pari passu with the claims of the creditors.'

Accordingly, where a company that is in the course of being wound up has sufficient funds to pay the defendant's costs, the defendant will not normally be granted an order that the company being wound up must provide security for the defendant's costs. This will be the case even where the company is insolvent in the sense that its liabilities exceed its assets, provided that what assets it has are sufficient to pay the defendant's costs. In this way, money otherwise earmarked for unsecured or preferential creditors will, instead of going to them, be earmarked for the defendant's costs[104]. Priority aside, where a company that is in the course of being wound up would not be able to pay the defendant's costs, then normal principles will apply.

(f) Onus on the applicant to establish a prima facie defence

[6.038] Although not averred to in all Irish decisions on CA 1963, s 390, it would still seem to be accepted that there is an onus on a defendant, who brings an application under s 390 to show that he has a prima facie defence to the plaintiff's claim[105]. This requirement is more established in the context of an application under RSC Ord 29; so in *Fares v Wiley*[106] it was held by the Supreme Court that a defendant who establishes a prima facie defence to a claim made by a plaintiff residing outside of the State has a prima facie right to an order for security for costs[107]. Lynch J in the Supreme Court in

[103] *Comhlucht Páipear Ríomhaireachta Teo v Údarás na Gaeltachta* [1990] ILRM 267 at 274.

[104] See the discussion by McGuinness J in *Irish Press plc v EM Warburg Pincus & Co International Ltd* [1997] 2 ILRM 263 at 269-270.

[105] *Inter Finance Group Ltd v KPMG Peat Marwick* (29 June 1998, unreported), High Court (Morris J); *Wexford Rope and Twine Co Ltd v Gaynor and Modler* (6 March 2000, unreported), High Court (Laffoy J).

[106] *Fares v Wiley* [1994] 2 IR 379.

[107] This decision was referred to by Laffoy J in *Lough Neagh Exploration Ltd v Morrice* [1998] 1 ILRM 205, immediately after commenting that in broad terms the same principles govern the determination of applications brought under both CA 1963, s 390 and RSC Ord 29.

Lismore Homes Ltd v Bank of Ireland Finance Ltd[108] formulated the prima facie defence requirement in different terms, namely:

> 'The strength or otherwise of the parties' case is not an appropriate consideration unless the plaintiff's case is unanswerable in which circumstance security should be refused.'[109]

As McCarthy J observed in *Comhlucht Páipear Ríomhaireachta Teo v Údarás na Gaeltachta*[110]:

> 'The fact that the plaintiff appears to have a very strong case is not a ground for refusing an order for security, unless the strength is such as to show that the defendant has no real defence.'

A plaintiff's case will not be 'unanswerable' where a defendant establishes that he has a prima facie defence. The courts will look simply at whether each side has a prima facie case without turning a blind eye to the obvious. If the plaintiff has what appears to be an unanswerable case, no order will be made[111]. An example at the other extreme is provided by *Kerry Tree Ltd v Sun Alliance and London Insurance plc*[112]. There Carroll J granted the order for security sought by the defendant, holding that the plaintiff's 'claim for damages for delay in paying damages' was not known in law and that as a result the plaintiff did not have a statable claim either in contract or in tort.

[6.039] Although the onus lies on the defendant to establish that he has a prima facie defence, this may be admitted by the plaintiff[113] or the defendant's averment of a good defence not contested[114]. Where this is not admitted by the plaintiff, the defendant will have to show that he has a prima facie defence and that the plaintiff's case is, therefore, answerable. It is not appropriate to adduce voluminous evidence on a motion for security for costs which, it must be remembered, is an interlocutory application. In *Bula Ltd v Tara Mines Ltd*[115], Murphy J explained as follows:

> '...I repeat now that it is no part of my function as I see it to forecast the outcome of the litigation or to prejudice the facts or express an interim view on the questions of law involved. On behalf of the defendants it was argued that the weakness of the plaintiff's case is a factor to which regard should be had. Whilst it must be established that the plaintiffs do have an arguable case it does not seem to me that it is either necessary or proper to evaluate the prospects of success.'

---

108 *Lismore Homes Ltd v Bank of Ireland Finance Ltd* [1999] 1 IR 501 (Lynch J, Barrington J and Barron J). It will be noted that all three judges gave written judgments.

109 [1999] 1 IR 501 at p 513.

110 *Comhlucht Páipear Ríomhaireachta Teo v Údarás na Gaeltachta* [1990] ILRM 266 at 275.

111 See, eg, *Society for the Protection of Unborn Children (Ireland) Ltd v Grogan* [1992] ILRM 461; *Irish Commercial Society Ltd v Plunkett* [1985] IR 1.

112 *Kerry Tree Ltd v Sun Alliance and London Insurance plc* (3 October 2001, unreported), High Court (Carroll J).

113 See *Beauross Ltd v Kennedy* (18 October 1995, unreported), High Court at p 3 (Morris J).

114 See *Johnstown Ltd v Thiennez Ltd* (21 March 2001, unreported), High Court (McCracken J).

115 *Bula Ltd v Tara Mines Ltd* [1987] IR 494 at 501.

In *Lismore Homes Ltd v Bank of Ireland Finance Ltd*[116], an application which involved an appeal to the Supreme Court and gave rise to three judgments from that court, Barrington J said:

> 'The most important thing to remember about an application for security for costs is that it is an interlocutory motion. It will usually be made when the facts of the dispute have yet to be established. Our law recognises an oral hearing and cross-examination as the primary method of resolving disputed questions of fact. It is dangerous to attempt to resolve such questions on affidavit unless there is objective evidence which points conclusively in one direction or the other. Normally there is no reason why a motion for security for costs should occupy four days in the High Court or seven days in the Supreme Court as happened in this case.'[117]

Where the strength of the parties' claims is in contention, a balance must be struck. In *Inter Finance Group Ltd v KPMG Peat Marwick*[118] the plaintiff had conceived an idea of developing a software package that would assist large organisations in running their accounts' departments. The plaintiff had entered into a contract with the defendant under which the defendant agreed to design a software package to the plaintiff's specification. Subsequently, the plaintiff sued the defendant claiming that it had, in breach of contract, purported to sell and install the software system in a number of other sites, had held itself out as owner of the software system and had failed to take the necessary steps to put the plaintiff in a position to exploit the software package. On the motion for security for costs, Morris J held that there was an onus on the defendant to establish, inter alia, 'that he has a prima facie defence to the plaintiff's claim'. On this point Morris J considered the plaintiff's claim that it was part of the contract that it would become beneficially entitled to the software package; the defendant claimed that, since the contract was silent on the point, it as author of the software was beneficially entitled to it. Morris J held on the prima facie defence point:

> '...I am satisfied, for the purposes of determining this application, that the beneficial ownership in the program was not affected by any term of any contract entered into between the parties. It remains therefore to decide, at the hearing of this action, in whom the beneficial ownership is vested. Both...[parties]...claim beneficial ownership. Each has supported their claim with a variety of arguments and submissions.
>
> In determining the issue, for the purposes of this motion, I am satisfied that the defendants have established a prima facie defence to the plaintiff's claim. I consider it is undesirable to elaborate upon the nature of this defence as to do so might well prejudice the ultimate hearing. Accordingly, I am of the view that the defendants have overcome the second of the two necessary proofs in order to succeed in this motion.'[119]

---

[116] *Lismore Homes Ltd v Bank of Ireland Finance Ltd* [1999] 1 IR 501 (Lynch J, Barrington J and Barron J). It will be noted that all three judges gave written judgments.

[117] [1999] 1 IR 501 at p 506 of the judgment. Barrington J went on to cite with approval the decision of Sir Nicholas Browne-Wilkinson VC in *Porzelac KG v Porzelac (UK) Ltd* [1987] 1 WLR 420 at 423 and of Purchas LJ in *Trident International Freight Services v Manchester Ship Canal Co* [1990] BCLC 263 at 271 and noted that the quoted passages had been expressly approved of by O'Hanlon J in *Shortt v Ireland* [1996] 2 IR 195.

[118] *Inter Finance Group Ltd v KPMG Peat Marwick* (29 June 1998, unreported), High Court (Morris J).

[119] (29 June 1998, unreported), High Court at p 5, 6.

Again, in *Wexford Rope and Twine Co Ltd v Gaynor and Modler*[120] the question of whether the defendant had a prima facie defence was considered. There, the plaintiff had sued the defendants (who were former directors of the plaintiff-company) for, inter alia, damages for breach of fiduciary duty, breach of contract, fraud and passing off. Barr J held that he was satisfied that the defendants had met the condition that they establish a prima facie defence to the plaintiff's claim. It is interesting to see that Barr J struck the balance between overcoming this evidential hurdle and not determining the substantive matter, by speaking in terms of the defendants' contentions having the 'appearance of credibility'.

(g) Judicial discretion and 'special circumstances'

[6.040] The jurisdiction to make an order for security for costs under CA 1963, s 390 is entirely discretionary. A defendant cannot demand as of right that an order is made against a plaintiff. In *Peppard & Co Ltd v Bogoff*[121] Kingsmill Moore J observed in relation to the predecessor of s 390 that:

> '...the section does not make it mandatory to order security for costs in every case where the plaintiff company appears to be unable to pay the costs of a successful defendant, but that there still remains a discretion in the court which may be exercised in special circumstances.'[122]

As McCarthy J said in *SEE Co Ltd v Public Lighting Services Ltd*[123], the 'discretionary nature of the order is emphasised when read in the light of the constitutional right of access to the courts'. The importance of the discretionary nature of the remedy cannot be over-emphasised. In *Irish Press plc v EM Warburg Pincus & Co International Ltd*[124] McGuinness J said she got the impression from reading the Irish judgments on security for costs that the courts have tended to lean against the making of such orders. McGuinness J went on to refer to the comments of McCarthy J as follows:

> 'While I accept, as was submitted by counsel for the defendants in this case, that the constitutional right of access to the courts is primarily available to natural persons and that the courts must be careful not to render s 390 nugatory, it seems to me that in his judgment the learned McCarthy J is expressing the general tenor of judgments in this court and in the Supreme Court in regard to security for costs under s 390 of the Companies Act 1963'.[125]

Whilst it is thought that the learned judge put the case against making orders for security for costs somewhat too far, it is clear, that the court will actively exercise its discretion

[120] *Wexford Rope and Twine Company Ltd v Gaynor and Modler* (6 March 2000, unreported), High Court (Barr J).

[121] *Peppard & Co Ltd v Bogoff* [1962] IR 180.

[122] [1962] IR 180 at 188. The learned judge repeated this view in *Personal Service Laundry Ltd v The National Bank Ltd* [1964] IR 49 at 62. His dictum in the latter case was cited with approval in the English Court of Appeal in *Sir Lindsay Parkinson & Co Ltd v Triplan Ltd* [1973] 2 All ER 273.

[123] *SEE Co Ltd v Public Lighting Services Ltd* [1987] ILRM 255 at 258.

[124] *Irish Press plc v EM Warburg Pincus & Co International Ltd* [1997] 2 ILRM 263.

[125] [1997] 2 ILRM 263 at 274.

and endeavour to do so in the interests of justice. Moreover on appeal, the appellate court's discretion will be exercised independently of the lower court[126].

[6.041] The burden of proving that 'special circumstances' exist lies on the respondent-company. This is because it will be the respondent-company which is asserting that special circumstances do exist and although the defendant might be prima facie entitled to an order, an order should not in fact be made because of these special circumstances. As Finlay CJ observed in *Jack O'Toole Ltd v MacEoin Kelly Associates*[127]:

> '...if the plaintiff-company seeks to avoid an order for security for costs...it must, as a matter of onus of proof, establish to the satisfaction of the judge the special circumstances which would justify the refusal of an order.'

The onus of proof will, therefore, shift from the applicant to the respondent-company once the applicant has established that the respondent-company is unlikely to be able to pay the defence costs and that the applicant has a prima facie defence[128]. So, in *Wexford Rope and Twine Co Ltd v Gaynor and Modler*[129] Barr J said:

> 'Where it is established, as in the instant case, that the defendants appear to have a prima facie defence to the claim or claims made against them the onus passes to the plaintiff company to satisfy the court on the balance of probabilities that there are *special circumstances* which the court should take into account and accept in exercising its discretion whether or not to accede to the defendant's application for security for costs.'[130]

It is to those matters which have to date been considered 'special circumstances' that next we turn.

[6.042] The reported judgments show that the following matters have been held to constitute so-called special circumstances:

(i) The applicant's lack of bona fides,

(ii) The respondent-company's insolvency having been caused by the applicant,

(iii) The respondent-company seeking to vindicate the public interest,

(iv) The existence of a natural co-plaintiff,

(v) The applicant's delay in applying for an order for security for costs.

The significance of these special circumstances is that, notwithstanding the fact that the defendant has proved everything required by CA 1963, s 390[131] and seems to be prima facie entitled to an order for security for costs, the court may still exercise its discretion and refuse to order the respondent-company to provide security.

---

126 *Lismore Homes Ltd v Bank of Ireland Finance Ltd* [1999] 1 IR 501 at 529 (Barron J at p 13).

127 *Jack O'Toole Ltd v MacEoin Kelly Associates* [1986] IR 277 at 283.

128 *Ochre Ridge Ltd v Cork Bonded Warehouses Ltd and Port of Cork Co Ltd* (20 December 2000, unreported), High Court (O'Neill J).

129 *Wexford Rope and Twine Co Ltd v Gaynor and Modler* (6 March 2000, unreported), High Court (Barr J).

130 (6 March 2000, unreported), High Court at p 4; italics added.

131 As set out in paras **[6.022]**– **[6.039]**.

(i) The applicant's lack of bona fides

[6.043] Defendants commonly seek security for costs against corporate plaintiffs as a first line of defence in the hope that it will put off the plaintiff from continuing with the proceedings. Consequently, if there is evidence that an application for security for costs is not bona fide, as, for example, where the defendant has made a partial admission or lodgment into court[132], the court may refuse to grant the order.

[6.044] Where a defendant has established a prima facie defence, the court will be loath to find that the defendant lacks bona fides in making application for security for costs. This was one of the matters alleged in *Village Residents Association Ltd v An Bord Pleanála and McDonald's Restaurants of Ireland Ltd*[133]. There, the plaintiff-company had been incorporated for the very purpose of seeking judicial review of the first defendant's decision to grant planning permission to the second defendant (McDonalds) for a change of use from a hotel to a restaurant with a drive-through facility. The incorporators were residents in the locality of the drive-through restaurant. As a special circumstance, the plaintiff-company argued that the order for security for costs should not be granted as the true purpose was to stifle its legitimate claim. This was rejected by Laffoy J who said:

> 'It is quite clear that the impetus for the incorporation of the applicant, and I think it is reasonable to infer that its immediate sole raison d'être was to constitute a vehicle for bringing these proceedings. By its very nature, the applicant can have no assets or finances other than those its members put into it or procure for it.'

Laffoy J went on to note that the members of the plaintiff-company could finance the company to meet the order and found that the action would only come to a halt if they failed to do so. It should be noted that in *Lancefort Ltd v An Bord Pleanála*[134] Keane J had, in the Supreme Court, recognised the right of persons to organise themselves as a company with limited liability to shield themselves against an order for costs but had noted the existence of CA 1963, s 390 and the corresponding right of defendants to apply for an order for security for costs.

(ii) The respondent-company's insolvency having been caused by the applicant

[6.045] The fact that the insolvency of the respondent-company has been caused by the applicant's actions has proven to be the most contentious and frequently relied upon special circumstance that the court is asked to accept as a basis for refusing the applicant's applications for security. Kingsmill Moore J observed in the seminal decision of the former Supreme Court in *Peppard and Co Ltd v Bogoff*[135], that in such circumstances:

[132] *Sir Lindsay Parkinson & Co Ltd v Triplan Ltd* [1973] 2 All ER 273.

[133] *Village Residents Association Ltd v An Bord Pleanála and McDonald's Restaurants of Ireland Ltd* [2000] 4 IR 321, [2001] 2 ILRM 22.

[134] *Lancefort Ltd v An Bord Pleanála* [1998] 2 ILRM 401.

[135] *Peppard and Co Ltd v Bogoff* [1962] IR 180 at 187. See also *Personal Service Laundry Ltd v National Bank Ltd* [1964] IR 49 at 62.

> '...to order security would be to allow the defendants to defend an action by reason of an impecuniosity which they have themselves wrongfully and deliberately produced, a result which a court would strive to avoid.'

This defence to an otherwise proven application for an order that security be provided is a classic example of the exercise of the court's discretion to achieve justice between the parties. In the *Peppard* case Kingsmill Moore J referred to the case of *Gill All Weather Bodies Ltd v All Weather Motor Bodies Ltd*[136] where Maugham J was reported as saying:

> 'The section only confers a discretion on the court. There may be many cases where a company is insolvent, and yet the court would not order security to be lodged. I will take as an example a defendant-company which is alleged to have stolen the plaintiff company's business. It is quite clear that the court would not ask the plaintiff-company to give security.'

So, in *SEE Co Ltd v Public Lighting Services Ltd*[137], the Supreme Court refused to make an order for security for costs where it found that accountants' and auditors' evidence linked the failure of certain equipment (in respect of which the claim was being made against the defendants) with the financial collapse of the company[138]. Likewise, in *Campbell Seafoods Ltd v Brodene Gram A/S*[139], the plaintiff-company admitted that it would be unable to meet the defendant's costs in the event of a successful defence, and it attributed this inability to the defendant's actions. The plaintiff alleged that machinery which it had acquired in reliance upon the defendant's representations as to fitness for purpose was, in fact, grossly unsatisfactory for the purposes for which it was required, and that this had led ultimately to the appointment of a receiver. Costello J accepted the plaintiff-company's contention and refused to make an order for security for costs. Again, in *Inter Finance Group Ltd v KPMG Peat Marwick*,[140] Morris J said that it is 'well settled that the plaintiff must do more than merely state this to be a fact. It must support this assertion with details' and the judge concluded that the evidence adduced in that case, far from supporting the allegation, had discredited it[141].

[6.046] It is necessary that a plaintiff (ie respondent-company in an application for security) claiming this special circumstance of insolvency due to the defendant's wrongdoing must make out a prima facie case[142]. It has been said, time after time, that a mere 'bald assertion' by the plaintiff-company that its insolvency has been brought

---

[136] 77 LJ 123.

[137] *SEE Co Ltd v Public Lighting Services Ltd* [1987] ILRM 255.

[138] See also *Bula Ltd v Tara Mines Ltd* [1987] IR 494, and *Aquila Design v Cornhill Insurance* [1988] BCLC 134, where, after the plaintiff's factory was burnt down, the defendant insurance company refused to pay on the policy, thus causing the plaintiff's insolvency.

[139] *Campbell Seafoods Ltd v Brodene Gram A/S* (21 July 1994, unreported), High Court (Costello J).

[140] *Inter Finance Group Ltd v KPMG Peat Marwick* (29 June 1998, unreported), High Court (Morris J).

[141] (29 June 1998, unreported), High Court at pp 6, 7.

[142] See *Harrington v JVC (UK) Ltd* (16 March 1995, unreported), High Court at p 18 (O'Hanlon J).

about by the defendant will not suffice[143]. In *Jack O'Toole Ltd v MacEoin Kelly Associates*[144], Finlay CJ said:

> 'It is clear that s 390 of the Act of 1963 deals with the situation where an insolvent company is suing for damages or money due. That very circumstance in itself would appear to me to make it probable that in a very high majority of cases which would come within that section recovery of the amount claimed would make a significant contribution towards the solvency of the company concerned and a corollary of that is that its insolvency is being probably contributed to, though possible not entirely caused, by the delay in the payment of the amount alleged to be due.
>
> Having regard to these circumstances, it does not seem to me a sufficient discharge of the onus of proof which I deem to be on a company against whom an application is made under section 390, to make a mere bald statement of fact that the insolvency of the company has been caused by the wrong the subject-matter of the claim. On the facts of this instant case, in particular, it seems to me that if the plaintiff company were to satisfy even the duty of establishing a prima facie special circumstance, it would be necessary for some accounts, even though they might be in an informal form, such as bank accounts or the state of a bank overdraft, of the plaintiff company to be produced. It seems to me that some information would necessarily have to be established as to what other sources of income the plaintiff company had at the material time when this contract was being concluded. Apart from a mere statement that the company was in the course of building houses for the Dublin County Council, no concept at all of the extent of that contract or the monies due and owing or capable of being earned on it has been afforded.'[145]

The reason why a 'bald' or 'vague' assertion will not suffice is because there is an onus on the plaintiff-company that asserts the defendant's wrongdoing has caused its 'impoverished condition' to prove that assertion[146]. The reference in the decided cases to a prima facie case that the plaintiff's inability is caused by the defendant is a reasonable marker that the plaintiff must overcome[147].

[6.047] In *Johnstown Ltd v Thiennez Ltd*[148] the plaintiff-company did not establish to McCracken J's satisfaction that its insolvency had been caused by the defendants, and the learned judge found that the direct cause of the plaintiff's financial problems arose from the refusal of an insurance company to pay monies to the plaintiff. On the other hand, in *Beauross Ltd v Kennedy*[149] Morris J said that he had no doubt but that the plaintiff had established a prima facie case that its inability to pay the defendant's costs

---

143 In *Lismore Homes Ltd v Bank of Ireland Finance Ltd* [1999] 1 IR 501 at 524 (Lynch J).

144 *Jack O'Toole Ltd v MacEoin Kelly Associates* [1986] IR 277.

145 [1986] IR 277 at 284; cited as being the relevant law on this point by the Supreme Court (per Barron J) in *Lismore Homes Ltd v Bank of Ireland Finance Ltd* [1999] 1 IR 501.

146 See, eg, *Harrington v JVC (UK) Ltd* (16 March 1995, unreported), High Court (O'Hanlon J) .

147 See, eg, *Wexford Rope and Twine Co Ltd v Gaynor and Modler* (6 March 2000, unreported), High Court (Barr J) where despite adducing some evidence of this defence to an order for security for costs, Barr J held that the plaintiff's evidence did not go 'sufficiently far as to establish a prima facie case that the fall in profits was caused by the wrong doing on the part of the defendants or either of them. The alternative case which they put forward was at least equally credible'.

148 *Johnstown Ltd v Thiennez Ltd* (21 March 2001, unreported), High Court (McCracken J).

149 *Beauross Ltd v Kennedy* (18 October 1995, unreported), High Court (Morris J).

had arisen from the wrong allegedly committed by the defendant. In that case the plaintiff's case against the defendant was that he had, as a director of another company, traded recklessly; the plaintiff was a creditor of the company of which the defendant was a director. The essence of the plaintiff's case was that the defendant had made representations to the plaintiff which were designed to induce it to continue to provide credit to the company in circumstances where he ought to have known that such were unrealistic. Morris J said of the evidence adduced by the plaintiff:

> 'I am satisfied that the plaintiff has fulfilled this requirement in this case. It is not necessary for him, in my view, to answer every criticism or query raised by the defendant on these accounts. This may well arise at a future date and indeed I may say at this stage many of the criticisms raised by the defendant would appear to me to require answers. However, on the level of proof which is required of the plaintiff at this stage, I am satisfied that he has established special circumstances which the court in its discretion should exercise in his favour.'[150]

In *Irish Conservation and Cleaning Ltd v International Cleaners Ltd*[151] the plaintiff's action against the defendant claimed it was owed over IR£377,000 in respect of works done and services rendered. The defendant was the plaintiff's only customer and the plaintiff's directors had been employees of the defendant-company. The plaintiff had ceased to trade owing to its financial difficulties and it was not disputed that, if unsuccessful, it would be unable to pay the defendant's costs. The plaintiff resisted an application for an order for security for costs on the grounds that there were special circumstances, those circumstances being that the very financial situation which rendered them unable to pay the defendant's costs was created by the defendant's failure to pay their accounts in a timely manner. The Supreme Court found that what the plaintiff was saying was 'if that issue is resolved against us in the High Court so be it, but if it is resolved in favour of us in the High Court it would inevitably follow that indeed the very inability on our part to provide security for costs is due by the actions of the defendants'. Keane CJ identified that as the real issue and said:

> 'Neither the High Court nor this Court on this motion can determine that issue. It will have to be resolved in the proceedings, but it would in effect mean that if the Court was to accede to the application for security for costs that it would be resolving that very issue against the plaintiffs. It would be holding that there was no set of special circumstances in this case of the nature alleged by the plaintiff which brought about their particular financial difficulties.'

Keane CJ refused to make an order for security for costs and affirmed the earlier order of the High Court.

[6.048] If the plaintiff-company was already insolvent before the events forming the basis of the action, it is not acceptable to allege that the defendant's wrongdoing caused (or even contributed or increased) the plaintiff's inability to pay the likely costs. So in *Lismore Homes Ltd v Bank of Ireland Finance Ltd*[152] Lynch J said:

---

150 (18 October 1995, unreported), High Court at p 7, 8.

151 *Irish Conservation and Cleaning Ltd v International Cleaners Ltd* (19 July 2001, unreported), Supreme Court (Geoghegan, Murray JJ and Keane CJ).

152 *Lismore Homes Ltd v Bank of Ireland Finance Ltd* [1999] 1 IR 501 (Lynch J).

> 'If the plaintiff is insolvent before the events complained of then the plaintiff cannot resist the claim for security for costs on the basis that the defendant contributed to or increased the insolvency.'[153]

This was one of the reasons why the Supreme Court in that decision upheld an order for security for costs brought by some of the defendants – a receiver to the plaintiff-company and auctioneer who sold the company's property – because it was held that the company could not sustain the argument that the first defendant bank had caused the insolvency and simultaneously claim that the receiver appointed to the company (by the bank) had also wronged the company so as to make it unable to pay the defendants' costs. Where a plaintiff is unsuccessful at trial, appeals that decision, and the defendant seeks security for costs for the appeal[154] the plaintiff will be hard pressed to convince the Supreme Court that the plaintiff's inability to pay the defendant's costs was as a result of the defendant's wrongdoing. So in *Bula Ltd et al v Tara Mines Ltd*[155] Keane J said, after noting that an application for security for costs had been refused by the High Court at trial upon the judge accepting that the plaintiffs had made out an arguable case that their insolvency was the result of the defendants' wrongdoing:

> 'The position at this stage, however, is radically different: there has been a prolonged trial in the High Court in the course of which the claim that the insolvency of the [first plaintiff] was rejected. While the plaintiffs are, of course, entitled to challenge that conclusion on the hearing of the appeal, the trial judge's findings, coupled with the other circumstances discussed at an earlier stage of this judgment, make it clear that this is a case in which the corporate plaintiffs should be required to furnish security for costs.'[156]

This is an eminently sensible decision: the converse – that an appellate court would completely disregard the finding of a full trial hearing – would be perverse.

[6.049] In *Lismore Homes Ltd v Bank of Ireland Finance Ltd*[157] Barron J stressed the need for a plaintiff, appealing to the Supreme Court having been unsuccessful in the High Court action, who is alleging that the defendant's wrongdoing caused his impecuniosity, to establish, inter alia, that there 'is a prima facie case of a causal connection between the wrong alleged and the inability to furnish security for costs'.[158] On this point, which was identified by Barron J as the real issue on the appeal, the learned judge said it was necessary to establish how the plaintiffs had come to arrive at their present financial situation. As against the five defendants, Barron J held that there was prima facie evidence to support the plaintiff's allegation that its business collapsed because of the manner in which it was managed by an employee of the second defendant accountants who was answerable to the first defendant bank, and that security would not

---

153 [1999] 1 IR 501 at 513. See also *Lough Neagh Exploration Ltd v Morrice* [1998] ILRM 205 (Laffoy J) where Laffoy J held that the plaintiff was in substantially the same financial position prior to the commission of the acts complained of on the part of the defendant as it was at the time of the hearing for security for costs.

154 See para **[6.030]**.

155 *Bula Ltd v Tara Mines Ltd* (26 March 1998, unreported), Supreme Court (Keane J; nem diss)

156 (26 March 1998, unreported), Supreme Court at p 28.

157 *Lismore Homes Ltd v Bank of Ireland Finance Ltd* [1999] 1 IR 501 (Barron J).

158 [1999] 1 IR 501 at 529.

be ordered for their costs. Barron J refused to find a causal connection between the plaintiff's insolvency and the third, fourth and fifth defendants (quantity surveyors, estate agents and receivers respectively) and he made an order that they would get security for their costs. Barrington J concurred with this result based on the same reasons. The minority judgment of Lynch J would have given all five defendants orders for security for costs as on the evidence he found that the plaintiffs had made no more than bald assertions against them.

(iii) The respondent-company seeking to vindicate the public interest

[6.050] Another factor which may influence the court in the exercise of its discretion is where the respondent-company (or plaintiff) seeks to litigate a matter of such gravity and importance as to transcend the interests of the parties actually before the court, or where it is in the interests of the common good that the law on a point be clarified so as to enable it to be administered in the instant case and in future cases[159]. It is only in exceptional cases, however, that this will be a real factor that will influence the court's discretion. This special circumstances was rejected in both *Broadnet Ireland Ltd v Office of the Director of Telecommunications Regulation and Eircom plc*[160] and in *Village Residents Association Ltd v An Bord Pleanála and McDonald's Restaurants of Ireland Ltd*[161]. The proffering of this ground as a special circumstance will not be permitted to override legitimate commercial interests. This proposition was made clear by Keane CJ in the Supreme Court in *Hot Radio Co Ltd v IRTC and NP*[162]. There, the Chief Justice said:

> 'Now in cases involving planning considerations, it is undoubtedly the case that this court has on more than one occasion indicated that the court would be concerned that in the case of decisions of public importance concerning planning and development and the environment, affecting the interests of the public in many ways, bodies who are formed solely for the purpose of protecting the public interest, voluntary associations, should not be unduly and unfairly impeded in bringing challenges to the decisions of bodies such as An Bord Pleanála or planning authorities before the courts. That may also arise in other branches of the law but this is plainly not such a case because, while undoubtedly the public have a considerable interest in seeing that the provisions of this type of legislation are operated in a fair, and as people like to say nowadays, in a transparent manner and which is very right and no one would question, I think, that it is anything but appropriate that persons in the position of the disappointed applicants in this case should, if they have an arguable case, be in a position to bring it before the court, the fact remains at the end of the day that there are commercial interests at stake in this case...They are doing it in their own interest and there is nothing wrong with that. But they are not to be equated with the sort of applicants who have been looked on benevolently by the courts in other areas of

---

159 See *Fallon v An Bord Pleanála* [1992] 2 IR 380 and *Lancefort Ltd v An Bord Pleanála* [1998] 2 ILRM 401.

160 *Broadnet Ireland Ltd v Office of the Director of Telecommunications Regulation and Eircom plc* [2000] 3 IR 281, [2000] 2 ILRM 241 (Laffoy J).

161 *Village Residents Association Ltd v An Bord Pleanála and McDonald's Restaurants of Ireland Ltd* [2000] 4 IR 321, [2001] 2 ILRM 22.

162 *Hot Radio Co Ltd v IRTC and NP* (14 April 2000, unreported), Supreme Court (Keane CJ; ex tempore ruling).

> law, who are doing a public service by litigating matters which would otherwise not be litigated and who have simply not the financial resources to meet orders for costs given against them.'[163]

There Keane CJ upheld an order for security for costs against a disappointed applicant (being a shelf company) for an independent radio licence, in circumstances where it sought a judicial review of the IRTC's decision not to grant it a licence.

(iv) The existence of a natural co-plaintiff

[6.051] Where the plaintiff-company has a natural (ie human) co-plaintiff, a further complication arises. On the one hand, the individual's fear of the stigma accompanying bankruptcy might be thought to come into play, so that neither the court nor the defendant need be concerned about frivolous litigation. In *Peppard and Co Ltd v Bogoff*[164], Kingsmill Moore J said:

> 'There is no doubt that where an application for security for costs is made on the ground that a plaintiff is outside the jurisdiction it will be refused if there is another plaintiff within the jurisdiction who would be answerable for costs...There is, as far as I have been able to ascertain, no case in which this principle has been applied where the ground for seeking security was based on the section of the Companies Act and not on residence without the jurisdiction, but in principle the same arguments would seem applicable in both cases.'

On the other hand, the natural co-plaintiff might also be impecunious, so that the fear of having nobody to answer for costs remains. Thus, in *Bula Ltd v Tara Mines Ltd*[165] Costello J said the involvement of a human co-plaintiff should:

> '...have no direct bearing on the question of whether a corporate co-plaintiff would be required to give security. It might be argued, however, that the position would be different if it was shown that the individual plaintiffs were a good mark because it is only in that way that their inclusion would provide an answer to the defendant's concern of facing proceedings against an impecunious corporate body.'

The learned judge was concerned that 'nominal' co-plaintiffs could be named as parties 'in the confidence that they were so impecunious that an order for costs against them would no more increase their problems than solve those of the defendants.' However, the fact that the same scenario may arise in respect of a human plaintiff resident abroad, whereby 'a man of straw' lends his name to that plaintiff's action, was not addressed.

It is submitted that the correct approach lies somewhere between the two views outlined in these cases, and that the courts should ascertain whether the individual co-plaintiff is bona fide rather than a 'good mark.'[166] Certainly, it would seem essential to establish that the natural co-plaintiff has a statable case in his personal right against the defendant and has not been added to the action as a ruse.

---

163 (14 April 2000, unreported), Supreme Court at p 3.

164 *Peppard and Co Ltd v Bogoff* [1962] IR 180.

165 *Bula Ltd v Tara Mines Ltd* [1987] IR 494.

166 See *In Bonis Mooney* [1938] IR 354 at 358 where Hanna J stressed the importance of establishing the bona fides of a resident individual co-plaintiff when deciding whether or not to order security for costs against a non-resident individual plaintiff.

(v) The applicant's delay in applying for an order for security for costs

[6.052] Excessive delay on the part of the defendant may likewise indicate a lack of genuine concern about the plaintiff's ability to pay costs[167]. It is well established that where it is shown that a defendant has been guilty of unreasonable delay in bringing an application for security for costs, this is something that may constitute a special circumstance that is cognisable by the court when exercising its discretion[168]. This special circumstance was articulated by Morris J in *Beauross Ltd v Kennedy*[169] in the following terms:

> '...as I understand the principle it is this. If the party seeking security has delayed to such an extent as to commit the other party to an amount and a level of costs which it would never have become committed to had it known that it was to be required to provide security for costs and thereby altered its position to its detriment, then the court will not make the order.'[170]

This particular special circumstance is therefore in the nature of an estoppel, which prevents a defendant from prejudicing a plaintiff-company that alters its position on the basis of the defendant's actions. In that case, the plaintiff-company was a creditor of a company that had become insolvent and the defendant was a director of that company, which the plaintiff was pursuing for reckless trading, Morris J noted that there had been a time lapse from mid-November 1994 to late-February 1995. Although that was a relatively short period, Morris J held that this was a basis for refusing the applicant the order for security for costs that had been sought because 'comprehensive legal costs had been incurred in [that] short period of time' due to the defendant's attendance and cross-examination before the Master of the High Court on the substantive issues. It is implicit that, if the defendant had wanted to seek an order for security for costs, he ought to have done so before the plaintiff-company had embarked upon the litigation process, thereby incurring its own costs.

[6.053] It is necessary that a plaintiff-company should be proved to have 'altered its position' in order to successfully invoke this shield to order for security for costs. So, in *Village Residents Association Ltd v An Bord Pleanala and McDonald's Restaurants of Ireland Ltd*[171] Laffoy J held that there was no evidence that the plaintiff-company had 'altered its position to its detriment'. Accordingly, the plaintiff-company's invocation of that ground as a basis for refusing an order for security for costs was rejected. The message is clear: to successfully invoke unreasonable delay as a defence to an otherwise prima facie case for granting security for costs, the plaintiff-company must have altered its position as a direct result of the defendant's inertia.

---

167 *Lismore Homes Ltd v Bank of Ireland Finance Ltd* [1992] ILRM 798.

168 *Oakes v Lynch* (27 November 1953, unreported), Supreme Court and *SEE Co Ltd v Public Lighting Services Ltd* [1987] ILRM 266.

169 *Beauross Ltd v Kennedy* (18 October 1995, unreported), High Court (Morris J).

170 (18 October 1995, unreported), High Court at p 8.

171 *Village Residents Association Ltd v An Bord Pleanála and McDonald's Restaurants of Ireland Ltd* [2000] 4 IR 321, [2001] 2 ILRM 22.

(h) The amount required as security

[6.054] Once an order for security for costs has been made by the court, it falls to the Master of the High Court to fix the sum which the plaintiff-company will be required to in fact provide as security[172]. The security, as Kingsmill Moore J observed in *Thake v Soares*[173] is not 'intended either as an indemnity against all costs or as an encouragement to luxurious litigation.' Until recently, the practice was that the amount fixed by way of security would approximate to one-third of the amount which it would cost the defendant to defend the proceedings; although this practice was departed from in particular circumstances[174]. The general rule of one-third was, however, turned on its head by the decision of McCracken J in *Lismore Homes Ltd v Bank of Ireland Finance Ltd*[175]. There, the statutory expression of 'sufficient security' was interpreted to mean such security as must approximate to the (full) probable costs of the defendant, should he succeed. In that case, which had a long and chequered history[176], McCracken J set his task as deciding what constituted 'sufficient security', and in that regard accepted the distinction between CA 1963, s 390 and RSC Ord 29 – as determined in *Thalle v Soares* – as being governed by a deciding factor, namely: 'the wording of the section when contrasted with the rule', quoting Kingsmill Moore J as follows:

> 'The statute lays down reasonably precise instructions as to the measure of security while the rule makers and the judges seem studiously to have avoided any approach to definitiveness, leaving each case to be decided by an uncontrolled discretion.'[177]

McCracken J went on to cite the consideration of the expression 'sufficient security' in the English Court of Appeal decision in *Innovare Displays plc v Corporate Broking Services Ltd*[178] where Leggatt LJ said, inter alia:

> 'However, the section does not mean, in my judgment, complete security. It can only mean security of a sufficient in all the circumstances of the case to be just.'

McCracken J held that the statutory nature of s 390 and the use of the words 'sufficient security' were significant. The learned judge went on to hold:

> 'It is certainly arguable that the use of the word "may" in s 390 gives a general discretion to the court, but on the whole I think it more likely that that word refers to the *making of the order for security for costs* rather than the amount thereof. In other words, even if there is credible testimony that there is reason to believe the company will be unable to pay the costs, there is still a discretion in the court whereby an order for security for costs may be refused. If the discretion was intended to be in relation to the amount, I think the word "*sufficient*" would not have been used, but it is in the section and it must have a meaning. The question can be posed: *sufficient for what*? I think that question is answered in the section by saying "*for those costs*", that is the costs of the defendant if successful in his

172 RSC Ord 29, r 6.

173 *Thake v Soares* [1957] IR 152 at 194.

174 See, eg, *Fallon v An Bord Pleanála and Burke* [1991] ILRM 779.

175 *Lismore Homes Ltd v Bank of Ireland Finance Ltd* (24 March 2000, unreported), High Court (McCracken J).;

176 See paras **[6.031]**, **[6.038]**, **[6.039]**, **[6.048]**and **[6.049]**.

177 (24 March 2000, unreported), High Court at p 2.

178 *Innovare Displays plc v Corporate Broking Services Ltd* (1991) BCC 726.

defence. This seems to me to be the only logical construction of the section. Where the court orders security for costs to be given in other circumstances, such as where the plaintiff is out of the jurisdiction, it is customary to require security of approximately one-third of the probable costs. I do not see how under any circumstances this could be called "*sufficient security*" and I think the section can only mean that the security required must approximate to the probable costs of the defendant should he succeed.'[179]

This interpretation of 'sufficient security' was questioned, but followed, by the Supreme Court (per Keane CJ) in *Hot Radio Co Ltd v IRTC and NP*[180] where the Chief Justice found that even though McCracken J was speaking obiter dictum, it was just in the instant case to order the full measure of security 'because there is no suggestion that the action would be stifled by the award of security for costs in the sum actually awarded as opposed to awarding security for costs in the more conventional measure of one-third'[181]. Keane CJ's concern with awarding full costs was that the plaintiff's action might be stifled, and bears out the overriding concern of the judiciary when confronted with applications for security for costs, that plaintiffs' constitutional rights to access to the courts are not unjustly limited. There can be no other reason for the existence of so many written judgments of both the High and Supreme Court on a topic that is normally disposed of as a matter of mere practice and procedure.

[6.055] Any remaining questions as to the meaning of 'sufficient security' were put beyond doubt by the Supreme Court in the actual appeal against McCracken J's decision in *Lismore Homes v Bank of Ireland*[182]. In delivering the judgment of a five-judge court, Murphy J reviewed the Irish and English authorities and concluded that the plain meaning of the words 'sufficient security' were inescapable.

> 'The word "sufficient" in its plain meaning signifies adequate or enough and it is directly related in the section to the defendant's costs. The section does not provide – as it might have – a sufficient sum "to meet the justice of the case" or some such phrase as would give a general discretion to the Court. Harsh though it may be, I am convinced that "sufficient security" involves making a reasonable estimate or assessment of the actual costs which it is anticipated that the defendant will have to meet. Much of the injustice which may be anticipated by the operation of the section can be avoided by the application of the established principles in granting or withholding the order for security. Insofar as the quantum of the security may be oppressive in a case where security is in fact ordered this must be seen in the context in which it arises. It applies only to limited liability companies who are shown to be insolvent. Legislation has conferred many benefits on limited liability companies including, in particular, the very limitation and it is not surprising to find that some burdens are likewise cast by the legislature on corporators who enjoy those advantages. It is with hesitation that I disagree with the conclusions reached by the Court

[179] (24 March 2000, unreported), High Court at p 3. Italics added.

[180] *Hot Radio Co Ltd v IRTC and NP* (14 April 2000, unreported), Supreme Court (Keane CJ; nem diss).

[181] (14 April 2000, unreported), Supreme Court at p 7. In *Windmaster Developments Ltd v Airoglen Ltd and Kelly* (10 July 2000, unreported), High Court (McCracken J), McCracken J applied the same test as to the amount of security in ordering that the full amount of the defendant's costs should be provided for.

[182] *Lismore Homes v Bank of Ireland* [2002] 1 ILRM 541.

of Appeal in England[183] but I am greatly comforted to find myself in full agreement with the views expressed by Kingsmill Moore J in *Thalle v Soares* so many years ago.'

Murphy J went on to hold that he considered the assessment made by the trial judge to be as realistic an assessment as could be made and rejected the plaintiff's appeal (and the defendant's cross-appeal on the quantum of costs). Where the effect of making an order that full security be provided would be to stifle a plaintiff-company's action, it remains to be seen whether the courts will opt to exercise their discretion against making any order. The effect of the Supreme Court's decision may prove to be less favourable to defendant-applicants for orders for security for costs than might at first appear to be the case.

[E] Discovery and Interrogatories against Companies

[6.056] 'Discovery is a process generally available in civil proceedings whereby one party may, by way of certain pre-trial devices, obtain information in writing and on oath from the opposite party in the proceedings.'[184] Interrogatories is also a pre-trial process whereby one party can obtain an order directing the opposite party in the proceedings to answer on affidavit a series of written questions relating to the matter in question[185]. RSC Ord 31 deals generally with discovery and interrogatories. In the case of interrogatories against companies and other bodies corporate, RSC Ord 31, r 5 provides:

> 'If any party to a cause or matter be a body corporate or a joint stock company, whether incorporated or not, or any other body of persons, empowered by law to sue or be sued, whether in its own name or in the name of any officer or other person, any opposite party may apply for an order allowing him to deliver interrogatories to any member or officer of such corporation, company, or body, and an order may be made accordingly.'

It will be noted that this rule prevents members (and indeed directors and other officers) from relying on the fact that a company is a separate legal entity to resist an order for interrogatories. That said, it is important to appreciate that where interrogatories are directed at officers and members, such persons will be answering *on behalf of the company* and not on their own behalf. This is clear from the following comments of Walsh J in the Supreme Court decision in *J and LS Goodbody Ltd v The Clyde Shipping Co Ltd*[186]:

> 'Prima facie the secretary is the person to whom they [the interrogatories] should be delivered and in the absence of any order to the contrary it is to be assumed that that was

[183] In *Innovare Displays plc v Corporate Broking Services Ltd* [1991] BCC 174; *Roburn Construction Ltd v William Irwin (Sough) & Co Ltd* [1991] BCC 726; *Unisoft Group Ltd (No 2)* [1993] BCLC 532 and *Keary Developments Ltd v Tarmac Construction Ltd* [1995] 2 BCLC 400.

[184] Cahill, *Discovery in Ireland* (1996), p 1. See also O'Floinn, *Practice and Procedure in the Superior Courts* (1996), p 236 *ff* and Courtney, *Mareva Injunctions and Related Interlocutory Orders* (1998), p 373 *ff*.

[185] See *Mercantile Credit Co of Ireland and Highland Finance (Ireland) Ltd v Heelan* [1994] ILRM 406 and, generally, Courtney, *Mareva Injunctions and Related Interlocutory Orders* (1998), p 399 *ff*.

[186] *J and LS Goodbody Ltd v The Clyde Shipping Co Ltd* (9 May 1967, unreported), Supreme Court (Walsh J; O'Dalaigh CJ concurring).

what was intended in the present case. It is important to bear in mind, however, that it is not the secretary who is being interrogated but the company. The secretary is not answering for himself but for the company and in doing so he must get such information as he can from the other servants of the company who have personally conducted the transaction in question and have personal knowledge of the facts sought. The secretary's function is to give the answer of the company. When the secretary answers on the basis of information obtained from other servants of the company he is answering according to information. On behalf of the company he is bound to answer according to information and belief acquired or formed from personal knowledge or from information obtained from others who are servants or agents of the company and have acquired the information in that capacity.'[187]

In *Money Markets International Stock Brokers Ltd v Fanning*[188] O'Sullivan J held that where information can be said to be properly at the disposal of people to whom interrogatories are directed, it matters not that 'they are being interrogated as individuals rather than as officers of a company'. In either case, persons may not avoid giving answers to interrogatories merely on the grounds that the subject matter thereof is not within their personal knowledge[189]. Generally, a party is only obliged to disclose documents that are in his possession, custody or power. The general rule is that documents held by one separate legal entity will not be discoverable by another separate legal entity unless an agency can be established[190].

[6.057] It should also be noted that in an action against a company, directors and other officers and members are amenable to so-called third-party discovery, pursuant to RSC Ord 31, r 29[191]. Notwithstanding a company's separate legal personality, it will not always be appropriate to consider the company a third party for the purposes of discovery in an action between warring shareholder-directors. *Re Murray Consultants Ltd and Nocrumb Ltd; Horgan v Murray and Milton*[192] concerned a number of points that arose in discovery motions. The first point raised by the petitioner was that the respondents had failed to refer to files of advices received by the companies by several categories of third-party advisors. O'Sullivan J said:

'The relevance of the documents sought being accepted, the precise question is whether these are within the power or possession of the respondents who claim that these are advices given to a third-party, (namely the companies referred to in the title of these proceedings) and not to themselves. It is submitted that the petitioner can bring a third-

187 (9 May 1967, unreported), Supreme Court at p 5.

188 *Money Markets International Stock Brokers Ltd v Fanning* [2000] 3 IR 215, [2001] 1 ILRM 1 (O'Sullivan J).

189 See, eg, *Re Holborne Investments Trust Ltd* Irish Times, 9 October 1991 (Barron J) where a managing director was ordered to make full discovery of both his own and the company's assets and liabilities, in circumstances where a Mareva injunction – preventing the company, the director and his wife from reducing their assets below £300,000 – had been made.

190 *Johnson v Church of Scientology, Mission of Dublin Ltd* [2001] 1 IR 689. Cf *Northern Bank Finance v Charlton* (26 May 1977, unreported), High Court (Finlay P).

191 See Courtney, *Mareva Injunctions and Related Interlocutory Orders* (1998), p 381.

192 *Re Murray Consultants Ltd and Nocrumb Ltd; Horgan v Murray and Milton* [1999] 1 ILRM 257 (O'Sullivan J).

party discovery motion compelling the relevant companies to furnish him with the documents but that the respondents themselves should not be obliged in these proceedings as part and parcel of the general obligations under discovery principles to refer to these documents and to produce them for the petitioner.

This case is a "Section 205" petition. The petitioner alleges that the affairs of the above entitled companies have been operated oppressively against him by the two respondents. I do not think the company is a "third-party" in the usual sense of that term in these circumstances. If the advices furnished to the companies are relevant, as I have held, then they should be produced as part of discovery unless they are privileged. In my opinion the documents are within the power of the respondents in the circumstances of this case and they should be referred to in the affidavit and I so direct'.[193]

So in a section 205 petition it was held that advices to the company are discoverable unless they are privileged.

[6.058] Ordinarily, legal professional privilege entitles a legal entity that has received legal advice to refuse to disclose that advice to any other legal entity. It is, however, a well-established rule of practice, in the case of companies, that:

'There is no doubt that matters passing between solicitors to a company and a company are prima facie entitled to be produced to all shareholders of the company'.

Per Harman J in *Re Hydrosan Ltd*[194]. This is the so-called 'disclosure rule'. The basis of this rule is trustee law[195]. The rule was rationalised by Simonds J in *Dennis & Sons Ltd v West Norfolk Farmers' Manure and Chemical Co-Op Co Ltd*[196] where he quoted from the 1943 English Annual Practice note:

'A cestui que trust…is entitled to see cases and opinions submitted and taken by the trustee for the purpose of the administration of the trust; but where stated and taken by the trustees not for that purpose, but for the purpose of their own defence in litigation against themselves by the cestui que trust they are protected…'[197]

The fact that the disclosure rule is based on principles of trust law was re-emphasised in *CAS (Nominees) Ltd v Nottingham Forest plc*[198] where Evans-Lombe J said:

'As the authorities show the rule is based on principles of trust law, an analogy being drawn between the position of directors as fiduciaries and trustees. As the authorities show, directors though not properly described as trustees of the assets of the company within their charge, none the less owe fiduciary duties to the shareholders which prevent them from applying those assets save for the purposes of the company. Directors are subject to the same duty to shareholders regardless of the size of the company concerned.'[199]

---

[193] [1999] 1 ILRM 257 at 259.

[194] *Re Hydrosan Ltd* [1991] BCLC 418 at 420f.

[195] *Tugwell v Hooper* (1847) 10 Beav 348.

[196] *Dennis & Sons Ltd v West Norfolk Farmers' Manure and Chemical Co-Op Co Ltd* [1948] 2 All ER 94.

[197] [1948] 2 All ER 94 at 96.

[198] *CAS (Nominees) Ltd v Nottingham Forest plc* [2001] 1 All ER 954.

[199] [2001] 1 All ER 954 at 959.

The exception to the disclosure rule, as instanced by Simonds J in the passage quoted above, is referred to as the 'Rule in *Woodhouse & Co*'[200]. The exception to the rule is, perhaps, as important as the rule itself. In *Woodhouse* Phillimore LJ and Lush J took it to be a clear exception to the disclosure rule (ie that where a company takes the opinion of counsel and pays for it out of the funds of a company a shareholder has a right to see it) that it does not apply where the company has brought an action against a shareholder. In *Re Hydrosan Ltd*[201], however, it was held by Harman J that for the purposes of the exception to the rule, a petition to wind up a company on the 'just and equitable' grounds, was not properly to be regarded as hostile litigation because the nature of such allegations involved wrongs by those in control of the company rather than by the company itself, even though such a petition might produce severe results. The disclosure rule has been refined to state that a shareholder in a company is entitled to obtain from it otherwise privileged documents provided that they relate to the company's administration and not to litigation between the parties. In that case it was also held, a further exception to the disclosure rule arose where, from the nature of the relations between the parties, it was reasonable to be contemplated that litigation would arise.

[6.059] It was established in *CAS (Nominees) Ltd v Nottingham Forest plc*[202] that the disclosure rule applies to all companies and not just small private companies. In that case the facts were that at an EGM of the shareholders in the first defendant-company, the shareholders approved of an agreement relating to the disposal of shares in a wholly-owned subsidiary. The claimants in the case were minority shareholders who contended that the agreement was unfairly prejudicial to them and in the proceedings that they instituted, they sought disclosure of certain documents between the first defendant-company and its legal advisers which had come into existence in connection with the first defendant's board of directors' decision to support the agreement to dispose of the shares in the subsidiary and the preparations for the EGM. At that time the directors had realised that litigation was likely and all of the defendants contended that the documents were protected by legal professional privilege and not amenable to disclosure. The claimant-minority shareholders sought to rely upon the disclosure rule but the defendants claimed that it only applied to 'small private companies'. That contention that the disclosure rule was confined to small private companies was categorically rejected by Evans-Lombe J who held that:

> 'Nothing in the *Woodhouse & Co* case or the subsequent authorities down to and including *Re Hydrosan Ltd* supports the proposition that the rule is to be differently applied depending on the size and importance of the company concerned...Directors are subject to the same duty to shareholders regardless of the size of the company concerned.' [203]

In that case it was held that the documents had been created by the company's lawyers for the purpose of procuring the first defendant to take certain actions and that it had been anticipated that such might give rise to litigation in which the claimant-minority shareholders would challenge the propriety of those actions. In the instant proceedings –

[200] *Rule in Woodhouse & Co* (1914) 30 TLR 559.

[201] *Re Hydrosan Ltd* [1991] BCLC 418 at 420f.

[202] *CAS (Nominees) Ltd v Nottingham Forest plc* [2001] 1 All ER 954.

[203] *CAS (Nominees) Ltd v Nottingham Forest plc* [2001] 1 All ER 954 at 959.

in which the first-defendant appeared in a nominal capacity so as to be bound by any court order in the substantive issue – it was held that there was no reason why the claimant-minority shareholders should not be entitled to see the advice and guidance given to the board by the company's solicitors when those transactions had been embarked upon. In this respect the claim of legal professional privilege was rejected.

[6.060] In *Re Hydrosan Ltd*[204] the facts were that after a petition alleging unfair prejudice had been presented the petitioner then applied orders for discovery. The basis of that petition was the petitioner's complaint that the company's money had been expended in defending an earlier unfair prejudice petition. First, the petitioner sought discovery of solicitors' bills arising from the earlier petition. Secondly, the petitioner sought discovery of documents relative to a certain 'rights issue' proposed by the company in a particular circular. The English Registrar had ruled that none of these documents were discoverable and the petitioner appealed to the English High Court. Harman J accepted the propriety of the discovery rule and that there were exceptions where there was hostile litigation between the company and its shareholders (but finding that a petition to have a company wound up on the just and equitable ground was not hostile litigation in that sense); and where from the nature of the relations between the parties it was reasonable to contemplate that litigation would arise. In respect of the first ground, he held that all documents relating to the earlier petition were discoverable; and in relation to the second, he held that all documents and communications prior to the circular and notice of meetings relating to the proposed rights issue were discoverable, coming within the general rule relating to discovery of documents between a company and its shareholders.

[F] Appearance in Court by a Company

[6.061] A consequence of the corporate right to sue and be sued is that a company cannot appear in court except through its solicitor or counsel[205]. In *Battle v Irish Art Promotion Centre Ltd*[206] the managing director and majority shareholder of the defendant-company applied to the court for leave to defend an action against the company on foot of an alleged debt, on the grounds that the company had not the means to employ counsel and that a successful judgment in default of defence would reflect badly on his personal reputation. The Supreme Court refused his application on the basis that the company was a different person, separate and distinct from its controlling shareholder. O'Dálaigh CJ explained:

> '...in the absence of a statutory exception, a limited company cannot be represented in court proceedings by its managing director or other officer or servant. This is an infirmity of the company which derives from its very nature. The creation of the company is the act of its subscribers; the subscribers, in discarding their own personae for the persona of the company, doubtless did so for the advantages which incorporation offers to traders. In

---

[204] *Re Hydrosan Ltd* [1991] BCLC 418.

[205] Unless the company is being prosecuted on indictment, when it may appear in court by a representative appointed by the company: CA 1963, s 382. See para **[6.065]**.

[206] *Battle v Irish Art Promotion Centre Ltd* [1968] IR 252.

seeking incorporation they thereby lose their legal right of audience which they would have as individuals; but the choice has been their own. One sympathises with the purpose which the appellant has to mind, to wit, to safeguard his business reputation; but, as the law stands, he cannot as major shareholder and managing director now substitute his persona for that of the company. The only practical course open to him would, it appears, be for him personally to put the company in funds for the purpose of presenting its defence.'[207]

It appears that this prohibition does not amount to a breach of a constitutional right of access to the courts[208].

[6.062] The principle outlined in the *Battle* case may undoubtedly be the cause of great hardship, especially where the cost to the shareholder of personally putting the company in funds to employ lawyers is great. There are signs, however, that the courts may be able to depart from the strict rule where hardship would otherwise be caused. In *Arbuthnot Leasing Ltd v Havelet Leasing Ltd*[209] Scott J in the English Companies Court concluded, after a review of many authorities, including the *Battle* case, that while companies cannot appear in court except through their advocate, the courts have the inherent power to permit any person to appear as advocate for a litigant if the exceptional circumstances of the case so warrant. Thus, another party to the case, such as a shareholder, may be permitted to address the court both on behalf of the company as well as on his own behalf. Scott J stated:

'One of the great topical questions concerning the administration of justice in England is what, if anything, can be done about the burdens that exceptionally heavy legal costs lay on ordinary individuals who find themselves (not always, I accept, through no fault of their own) enmeshed in litigation. The financial implications faced by individuals who become parties to complex civil litigation are very serious. The cost burden is one that the courts should endeavour, in so far as is consistent with principle and practice, to mitigate...

In all these circumstances I can see no reason why a director should not, in an appropriate case (I would certainly not say in every case and I emphasise "in an appropriate case"), be allowed to become a party to litigation in which the company of which he is director is defendant in order to make an application in that litigation in relation to orders which have been made against that corporate defendant. Take as an example an action in which the company is the only defendant and a Mareva injunction has been granted against the company freezing its assets. Why should not a person who stands in relation to that corporate defendant [as beneficial owner of all the shares in the company] be permitted to become a party to the action and to apply in person for a variation or discharge of the injunction? I can see no sound reason of practice, procedure or policy which obliges the court to say to the director who desires to make such an application, "your only remedy is to put your hand in your pocket and instruct solicitors and counsel to appear on the company's behalf." I repeat, I see no reason why an individual should be forced to incur the horrendous cost of commercial litigation if he is willing to appear in person.'[210]

---

207 [1968] IR 252 at 254.

208 *Abbey Films Ltd v Attorney General* [1981] IR 158.

209 *Arbuthnot Leasing Ltd v Havelet Leasing Ltd* [1990] BCLC 802.

210 *Arbuthnot Leasing Ltd v Havelet Leasing Ltd* [1990] BCLC 802 at 810–811. See also *Re a Company, ex p F Ltd* [1991] BCLC 567.

This discretionary approach has been followed in other common law jurisdictions, such as Australia, as the decision of the Supreme Court of Western Australia in *Eastern Metropolitan Regional Council v Four Seasons Construction Pty Ltd*[211] shows. In that case, after reviewing *Arbuthnot Leasing Ltd* and a number of Australian authorities[212], the court exercised its discretion to permit a former director to represent the company. A distinction was, however, made in that case between 'defending an action' and 'appearing for a company'. Unlike the Irish Rules of the Superior Courts 1986, the Western Australia Rules of Court expressly provide that a defendant to an action which is a body corporate may not enter an appearance in the action or defend it otherwise than by a solicitor. Applying this distinction, the court held that an individual could not submit affidavits in relation to a security for costs application as such would be to allow him to defend the proceedings. The court also held it had no jurisdiction to make any exception to this because it was a Rule of Court. The court went on, however, to permit the individual to appear as advocate on behalf of the company, having satisfied itself that that was one of the rare and exceptional circumstances where such should be permitted[213].

[6.063] Whether the Irish courts will be so willing to depart from the strict rule in *Battle* remains to be seen. There was some evidence of a relaxation of the rule (or at the least, evidence of judicial pragmatism) in the Supreme Court's decision in *DBP Construction Ltd, Hennerty & Hennerty v ICC Bank plc et al*[214]. In that case the first plaintiff-company and the Hennertys (who were the company's sole shareholding-directors) were

---

211 *Eastern Metropolitan Regional Council v Four Seasons Construction Pty Ltd* [2000] (13 July 2000, unreported), WA Supreme Court.

212 Cases reviewed were: *Hubbard Association of Scientologists International v Anderson & Just* [1972] VR 340; *Bay Marine Pty Ltd v Clayton Country Properties Pty Ltd* (1986) 8 NSWLR 104; *Molnar Engineering Pty Ltd v Burns* (1984) 3 FCR 68; *ACT General Cleaning Pty Ltd v Naoum* (1996) 67 FCR 361; *Alice Springs Abattoirs Pty Ltd v Northern Territory of Australia* (1996) 134 FLR 440; *Schagen v The Queen* (1993) 8 WAR 410; and *NR & NJ Gardiner & Sons Pty Ltd v Osborne Cold Stores (WA) Pty Ltd* (1988) 7 SR (WA) 62.

213 *Eastern Metropolitan Regional Council v Four Seasons Construction Pty Ltd* [2000] (13 July 2000, unreported), WA Supreme Court. The court held (at para 55 of the judgment):

> 'The weight of the evidence establishes on the balance of probabilities that the company is impecunious and cannot afford or arrange legal representation. Mr Mavlian is closely involved with the affairs of the company and has a legitimate interest in making known to those called upon to adjudicate upon the current procedural issues his view of the matters in controversy and his detailed knowledge of the history of the dispute. As mentioned earlier, I am also influenced by the precept that a party in litigation should generally not be denied an opportunity to be heard. In the exceptional circumstances of this case, where there is a very close affinity between the party to the litigation and the person who is to speak on the company's behalf, bearing in mind that the company has undertaken one project only, and that Mr Mavlian was directly involved in the implementation of the project in question, the precept I have just mentioned weighs in favour of leave being granted.'

214 *DBP Construction Ltd, Hennerty & Hennerty v ICC Bank plc* (21 May 1998, unreported), Supreme Court (Keane J; nem diss).

unsuccessful in a High Court action for negligence, breach of duty and breach of contract in respect of the sale of the plaintiff-company's premises. The company and the Hennertys lodged an appeal and at the hearing of the appeal the company was not represented by solicitor or counsel. In the written submissions of two of the defendants, objection was taken to the locus standi of the Hennertys to conduct an appeal on behalf of the company. Nevertheless, in giving the decision of the Supreme Court, Keane J reviewed extensively the findings of the trial judge and concluded that the Supreme Court could not interfere with the findings of fact and that, accordingly, the trial judge was correct in holding that there was no negligence, breach of duty or breach of contract. Keane J said:

> 'While the merits of the case were fully argued before us and it is, accordingly, appropriate that the court should come to a conclusion on them, it must, of course, be pointed out that, having regard to the decision of this court in *Battle v Irish Art Promotion Centre Ltd* [1968] IR 252 Mr Hennerty was not entitled to represent the company on the hearing of this appeal.'[215]

Later, Keane J said of this and other points, that in view of the conclusions already reached, he did not find it necessary to express any view on those arguments. Accordingly, it may be concluded, that where an Irish court has substantive grounds for finding against a company, it will do so in preference to non-suiting its directors who seek to represent the company in person[216].

[6.064] It must, of course, be noted that an appeal of an earlier decision that was fully argued is more amenable to this pragmatic approach. Indeed, it is unlikely that a court of first instance would adopt the approach taken by the Supreme Court. In practice, therefore, a company which cannot afford a solicitor or counsel should seek financial assistance from its shareholders who share an interest in the success of the company.

[6.065] An exception of sorts to the above arises where a company is charged with an indictable criminal offence and it may, by virtue of CA 1963, s 382, appear in court by a representative. The representative may answer questions, enter any plea, and exercise any right of objection or election on the company's behalf. The representative must be authorised by the company to appear on its behalf. Any natural person may be appointed to act as a representative, but he must be appointed in writing - although the appointment need not be under seal. Where a natural person is to be returned for trial for an indictable offence, it is generally necessary that he appear in person, so that questions may be put to him[217]. This rule no longer applies to companies, however, since CA 1963, s 382(2) empowers the District Justice to proceed, in the absence of a representative, to take depositions and to send the company forward for trial.

---

[215] (21 May 1998, unreported), Supreme Court at p 23, 24.

[216] See also *Re Motor Racing Circuits Ltd* (31 January 1997, unreported), Supreme Court (Blayney J; nem diss).

[217] See *The State (Batchelor & Co Ireland Ltd) v O'Leannain* [1957] IR 1, where, prior to the enactment of CA 1963, s 382, Murnaghan J held that a company could not be returned for trial on indictment because it could not appear 'in person'.

[G] ENFORCING JUDGMENTS AND ORDERS AGAINST A COMPANY

[6.066] Common law and statute provide a variety of means by which judgments and orders may be enforced. Generally, the same principles apply in relation to enforcement against companies as apply to enforcement against natural persons. The aim here is to highlight the idiosyncrasies of and peculiarities in the enforcement of judgments and orders obtained against companies. In considering the issues arising, it is considered useful to distinguish between the enforcement of money judgments from the enforcement of court orders and non-money judgments.

Enforcing money judgments against companies

[6.067] Many remedies for the enforcement of money judgments have no appreciable differences in their application to companies as compared with natural persons. Examples here include orders for possession (in the case of secured creditors), receivers by way of equitable execution, garnishee orders, charging orders, stop notices on shares, etc[218]. Some examples of remedies where there are peculiarities in their application to companies, include:

(i) Seizure and sale of goods by the sheriff,

(ii) Judgment mortgages,

(iii) Winding up,

(iv) Sequestration.

The primary difference between money judgments and non-money judgments is that the remedies of attachment and committal are not available in the case of judgments that require defendants to pay money[219].

(i) Seizure and sale of goods by the sheriff

[6.068] The primary method of enforcement of a judgment for the payment of money, whether into court or otherwise, is for the judgment creditor to obtain an order directed to the sheriff[220] commanding him to seize whatever goods are within his bailiwick belonging to the judgment debtor and to procure the sum due, including interest and costs, out of their sale[221]. In the High Court, the order directed to the sheriff is known as a writ of fieri facias (commonly abbreviated to 'fi fa'); in the Circuit Court it is known as an execution order against the goods; and in the District Court the decree of the court itself is sent to the sheriff for execution. There are few peculiarities in the law on this method of judgment enforcement as it applies to companies. The clearest difference in the law as it applies to companies is contained in CA 1963, s 292, which provides that where the execution is for €25.39 or upwards, the sheriff must, after disposing of the seized assets, hold the proceeds for 14 days to allow for notice of a winding up of the company to be served on him. If such notice is served within that time, he must, after the deduction of his costs, pay the balance to the liquidator, who is entitled to retain it as against the execution creditor. If, however, the sheriff receives notice of the winding up

---

218 On receivers by way of equitable execution and garnishee orders, see generally, Courtney, *Mareva Injunctions and Related Interlocutory Orders* (1998), para [10.77] *ff* and [10.83] *ff*, respectively.

219 RSC Ord 42, r 7.

220 Or, outside of Dublin or Cork, the County Registrar.

221 See RSC Ord 42, rr 13-25, and Appendix F, Part II; CCR Ord 33; and DCR r 136.

before the sale or the completion of the execution by the receipt or the recovery of the full amount of the levy, he must deliver the goods or any money received to the liquidator without deducting the costs of the execution[222]. The costs of the execution will be a first charge on the goods or the monies so delivered, and the liquidator may sell the goods or a sufficient part thereof in order to satisfy the charge[223].

[6.069] Where a judgment creditor issues execution proceedings against a company and the company is subsequently wound up, then, under CA 1963, s 291, he shall not be entitled to retain the benefit of the execution against the liquidator in the winding up of the company unless he has completed the execution before commencement of the winding up. An execution will be deemed to be completed only where the goods have been seized and sold, or, in the case of land, where it is seized[224]. Where, however, an execution creditor has received the proceeds of the execution prior to the commencement of the winding up, his judgment will have been discharged to that extent, and he may keep the proceeds even though the remainder of the execution has not been completed[225]. At any time after the presentation of the petition and before the winding up the court may, under CA 1963, s 217, restrain any action or proceeding, including execution proceedings[226], against a company.

(ii) Judgment mortgages

[6.070] A judgment creditor may apply to have his judgment or order converted into a mortgage against the land of the company under the Judgment Mortgage (Ireland) Act 1850, as amended by the Judgment Mortgage (Ireland) Act 1858[227], provided that the judgment or order requires the payment of a sum of money to the judgment creditor[228]. There are no special conditions on the registration of judgment mortgages against companies as opposed to natural persons, but it should be noted that a judgment mortgage over property comprised in a previously crystallised floating charge will rank subordinate to that floating charge[229]. It may also be noted that where a judgment mortgage is obtained against a company, CA 1963, s 102(1)[230] provides that two copies (certified by the Land Registry or Registry of Deeds) of the affidavit required for the purpose of registering the judgment mortgage should be delivered by the judgment creditor to the company within 21 days after the date of registration; and within 3 days from the receipt thereof, the company must deliver one copy to the Registrar of Companies[231].

---

[222] CA 1963, s 292(1). See Chapter 27, *Realisation and Distribution of Assets in a Winding Up*, para **[28.051]***ff*.

[223] CA 1963, s 292(1).

[224] CA 1963, s 291(5). See Chapter 27, para **[28.050]** *ff*.

[225] *Re Andrew, ex p Official Receiver* [1937] Ch 122.

[226] *Re Artistic Colour Printing Co* (1880) 14 Ch D 502; see also *Pierce v Wexford House Co* [1915] 2 IR 310.

[227] See generally Wylie, *Irish Land Law* (3rd edn, 1975), pp 792 *ff*.

[228] Debtors (Ireland) Act 1840, ss 27 and 28; Judgment Mortgage (Ireland) Act 1850, s 6.

[229] *Eyre v McDowell* (1861) 9 HL Cas 619.

[230] See, generally, Chapter 21, *Corporate Borrowing: Registration of Charges*, para **[21.071]**.

[231] The Land Registry and the Registry of Deeds are also obliged to deliver a copy of the affidavit to the Registrar of Companies.

(iii) Winding-up

[6.071] One means of enforcing a judgment that is exclusive to company-debtors is a creditor's ability to petition to have the company wound up. This is comprehensively considered in Chapter 25, *Winding Up Companies.*

(iv) Sequestration

[6.072] Sequestration can be used as a remedy in the case of a money judgment, but treatment of this remedy is deferred to its use in the enforcement of court orders (such as injunctions) and other non-money judgments[232].

Enforcing court orders and judgments[233]

[6.073] The enforcement of High Court court orders and judgments against companies is regulated by RSC Ord 42, r 32. This provides:

> 'Any judgment or order against a company wilfully disobeyed may, by leave of the court, be enforced by sequestration against the corporate property, or by attachment against the directors or other officers thereof, or by order of sequestration of their property.'

Central to the operation of RSC Ord 42, r 32 is that a judgment or order is 'wilfully disobeyed', a matter considered in detail below[234]. Where a judgment or order is *not* wilfully disobeyed, the party who obtained it against the company will have to look elsewhere to enforce the judgment or order. Further, a company's inability to pay a money judgment against it will not result in 'wilful disobeyance' and will not give rise to its officers being attached[235].

The most obvious example of a court order is an injunction of any nature. Here, the following issues are considered:

(i) Proving 'wilful disobeyance' of judgments and orders by companies.

(ii) Wilful disobeyance due to employees' acts or omissions.

(iii) Breach of undertakings given in lieu of court orders.

(iv) Attachment of a company's officers.

(v) Sequestration of companies' and their officers' assets.

(vi) Fining companies and their officers.

(i) Proving 'wilful disobeyance' of judgments and orders by companies

[6.074] The use of the word 'wilful' in the English Rules of the Supreme Court has proven troublesome[236] and was removed from their Rules in 1965. The preferred

---

232 See para **[6.093]**.

233 The remainder of this chapter is based upon Ch 12 of Courtney, *Mareva Injunctions and Related Interlocutory Orders (*1998).

234 See para **[6.074]**.

235 See paras **[6.075]**.

236 See Courtney, *Mareva Injunctions and Related Interlocutory Orders* (1998), para [12.24]-[12.26] where the decisions in *AG v Walthamstow UDC* [1895] 11 TLR 533, *Fairclough & Sons v Manchester Ship Canal Co (No 2)* [1897] WN 7 and *Stancomb v Trowbridge UDC* [1910] 2 Ch 190 are considered.

interpretation of the expression is seen in the judgment of Warrington J in *Stancomb v Trowbridge*[237] where he said:

> 'In my judgment, if a person or a corporation is restrained by injunction from doing a particular act, that person or corporation commits a breach of the injunction, and is liable for process for contempt, if he or it in fact does the act, and it is no answer to say that the act was not contumacious in the sense that, in doing it, there was no direct intention to disobey the order...
>
> ...I think the expression "wilfully"...is intended to exclude only such casual or accidental and unintentional acts...'.

This interpretation was endorsed by the House of Lords in *Heatons Transport (St Helens) Ltd v Transport and General Workers' Union*[238] where Lord Wilberforce said that Warrington J's view as to the meaning of 'wilful':

> '...has thus acquired high authority. It is also the reasonable view, because the party in whose favour an order of a court has been made is entitled to have it enforced, and also the effective administration of justice normally requires some penalty for disobedience to an order of a court if the disobedience is more than casual or accidental or unintentional.'

As stated elsewhere[239], it is thought that this is the correct interpretation of the meaning and significance of 'wilful' and that RSC Ord 42, r 32 would be so construed by the Irish courts. Indeed, support for this can be taken from the Supreme Court's decision in *Irish Shell Ltd v Ballylynch Motors Ltd and Morris Oil Company Ltd*[240] where RSC Ord 42, r 32 was in issue. There, Costello P had found three of the directors of the second defendant-company to be in contempt of court and had fined each of them £1,000. Their contempt arose from an injunction made by the High Court which restrained the second defendant-company from providing to the first defendant-company or any other persons, motor fuels for resale from premises bearing the plaintiff's livery, trademark and logo and which were also under contract to the plaintiff for the exclusive sale of 'Shell' brand motor fuels. In breach of the injunction the second defendant had supplied motor fuels to a third party whose premises was also under contract with the plaintiff for the exclusive sale of 'Shell' products. The defence tendered was that the third party who had been supplied by the second defendant had represented that it was out of contract with the plaintiff. On appeal to the Supreme Court, the second defendant's directors' counsel argued that none of the directors were wilfully in breach of the injunction, as was required by RSC Ord 42, r 32[241]. The plaintiff's counsel contended that the directors had a duty to be aware of what was being done by their company and that because they had taken no steps in that behalf, they were, accordingly, answerable for the breach of the

---

237 *Stancomb v Trowbridge* [1910] 2 Ch 190.

238 *Heatons Transport (St Helens) Ltd v Transport and General Workers' Union* [1972] 3 All ER 101.

239 See Courtney, *Mareva Injunctions and Related Interlocutory Orders* (1998), para [12.26].

240 *Irish Shell Ltd v Ballylynch Motors Ltd and Morris Oil Company Ltd* (5 March 1997, unreported), Supreme Court (Lynch J; nem diss).

241 Relying upon *Ronson Products Ltd v Ronson Furniture Ltd* [1966] 2 All ER 381 and 9 *Halsbury's Laws of England* (Simmonds edn), p 26.

injunction[242]. In his judgment for the Supreme Court Lynch J held that Costello P was entitled to conclude that the second defendant had wilfully disobeyed the order and that the directors were liable to attachment or fine in lieu thereof. He said that once the second defendant had been requested to supply motor fuels to a premises which bore the plaintiff's 'Shell' logo then:

> '...they must as a matter of common sense make all necessary and proper enquiries to ensure that the premises are no longer tied to the plaintiffs and are free to accept the second defendant's motor fuels. If a company operating tied premises in the plaintiff's livery, trademark and logo requests the second defendants to supply motor fuels to them for resale it is wholly inadequate to rely solely upon that company's assurances that they are not tied...
>
> ...Nothing whatever was done by the [appellant-directors] to check the accuracy and reliability of the assurances given to them by the consignee company ... and to ensure that a delivery of motor fuels to them did not contravene the order...'[243]

A breach of an injunction will be 'wilful' if it is anything other than casual, accidental or unintentional. 'Wilful' is not to be construed as intentional; a careless disregard as to whether a court order is respected or breached can amount to a wilful breach. On the contrary, the applicable test is objective.

[6.075] In *Sligo Corporation v Cartron Bay Construction Ltd, Maguire and Maguire*[244] the applicant local authority applied for an order of attachment and sequestration against the first respondent-company and the second and third respondents who were two of its directors. The application arose out of the failure to complete certain works detailed in a schedule to a previous High Court order, in accordance with a planning permission that had been issued to the respondent-company. The required works related to a particular housing estate and included works relating to roads, footpaths, sewers and manholes. The applicant local authority claimed that the company had failed to comply with the terms of the order and asserted its belief that the respondent-company and its directors were in 'wilful disobedience' of the court's order. It was also claimed that the disobedience with the order was not caused by reason of any negligence or mismanagement but by premeditated wilfulness and an anxiety to frustrate the applicant's rights and those of the residents. Moreover, it was claimed that the directors had an intimate knowledge of the company's affairs and that they were solely responsible for deciding the recalcitrant policy of wilful disobedience. In addition to denying all impropriety and asserting that the court order had not been wilfully disobeyed, it was contended that the company was insolvent and therefore unable to carry out the terms of the order. Citing *Lewis v Pontypridd Caerphilly and Newport Railway Company*[245] O'Caoimh J accepted that an order or judgment cannot be said to have been wilfully disobeyed if compliance was impossible on account of a lack of funds. It was, however,

---

242 Relying upon Borrie & Lowe, *The Law of Contempt* (3rd edn, 1996), p 567 and *Biba Ltd v Stratford Investments Ltd* [1972] 3 All ER 1041.

243 (5 March 1997, unreported), Supreme Court at p 5, 6.

244 *Sligo Corporation v Cartron Bay Construction Ltd, Maguire and Maguire* (25 May 2001, unreported), High Court (O'Caoimh J).

245 *Lewis v Pontypridd Caerphilly and Newport Railway Company* 1 ITLR 203.

also noted that the burden of proving impossibility of compliance rested on the company and its directors[246]. O'Caoimh J concluded that the company's directors had not accounted to the company for certain money, that this had resulted in the company being unable to pay for the construction of the works in question and, on that basis, that a case had been made for the sequestration and attachment of the respondents.

[6.076] In order for a company to wilfully breach a court order or judgment, it must be on notice of the terms of that order or judgment. Service of any order or judgment on a company is regulated by CA 1963, s 379, considered above[247]. In addition to formally serving a company with the terms of an order or judgment, it is thought that persons who obtain such orders are well advised to seek to place a company's directors and other officers on actual notice of the order or judgment and to indicate to them that, if the injunction is breached, they may be attached and fined and their property sequestrated[248]. Unlike England and Wales, there is no Irish equivalent to the English Rules of the Supreme Court 1965, Ord 45, r 7, which provides, inter alia, for the personal service of a court order, such as an injunction, on an officer of the company. The indication that a person is liable to be imprisoned for breach of an order is termed a 'penal notice'[249].

[6.077] The standard of proof required to find that a defendant has breached an injunction or other order of the court - and thereby committed civil contempt of court - could either be the usual criminal standard of 'beyond reasonable doubt' or the usual civil standard of 'on the balance of probabilities'. In England[250] it has been established that the standard of proof required to be shown in order that a defendant be found to be in contempt of court is that applicable to criminal cases, namely, 'beyond all reasonable doubt.' [251] It is thought that the same is the standard of proof in Ireland[252].

(ii) Wilful disobeyance due to employees' acts or omissions

[6.078] Where it is found that a court order or judgment, directed at a company, is 'wilfully disobeyed', it must also be shown that the conduct which led to the breach was the act of the company and not, say, the act of an employee of the company acting outside the scope of his employment or, to use the colloquial favoured in this context,

---

246 See *Guilford Borough Council v Smith* (1993) The Times, 18 May 1993.

247 See para **[6.011]**.

248 For an instance of where directors were fined where their company breached the terms of an injunction see *Irish Shell Ltd v Ballylynch Motors Ltd* (5 March 1997, unreported), Supreme Court.

249 The foregoing paragraph is, in the main, a verbatim transcript of para [12.14] of Courtney, *Mareva Injunctions and Related Interlocutory Orders* (1998).

250 See generally, Lowe & Sufrin, Borrie & Lowe, *The Law of Contempt*, (3rd edn, 1996), pp 565-569.

251 See also *Re Bramblevale Ltd* [1970] Ch 128; see Courtney, *Mareva Injunctions and Related Interlocutory Orders* (1998), para [12.21].

252 See *Cooke v Cooke & Cooke* [1919] 1 IR 227 at 249 and *Orion Pictures Corporation v Hickey* (18 January 1991, unreported), High Court at p 2 where Costello J said of the defendant in a motion for committal for contempt of court (through breach of an Anton Piller order) that he was '...satisfied beyond a reasonable doubt that Mr Hickey was in very serious contempt of both of these orders.'

'on a frolic of his own.'[253] Although a company can only act through its directors, officers and employees, not every act of its directors, officers or employees can be attributed to the company[254]. It seems reasonably straightforward that where a company's board of directors cause a company to act in breach of an injunction or other court order, the company itself will be found to have been in breach of the order and in contempt of court[255]. What is less clear is where the breach of an injunction or other court order is occasioned by the actions of persons, such as employees, who may not have authority to bind the company. Moreover, the legal consequences which follow where a company's shareholders vote in such a manner so as to cause their company to breach a court order or undertaking is considered below[256].

[6.079] Where the act or omission which amounts to a breach of the injunction or other court order is caused by a company's employee, as opposed to a director or senior manager with power to bind the company, difficult questions are raised. Should a company be found to be in contempt of court if its directors or other senior management expressly instruct the company's employees not to act in breach of a court order? This was the question in issue in *Director General of Fair Trading v Smiths Concrete Ltd*[257]. In that case the company was subject to orders of the English Restrictive Practices Court which restrained it from, inter alia, 'giving effect to or enforcing or purporting to enforce, whether by itself, its servants or agents or otherwise', agreements with other companies relating to the supply of ready-mixed concrete in contravention of the Restrictive Practices Act, 1976, s 35(1) (UK). It was held by the English Court of Appeal that the company itself did not breach the order because, inter alia, there should be a mens rea on the part of the contemnor. There, Lord Donaldson MR said:

> 'It is an essential prerequisite to a finding of contempt that the factual basis shall have been proved beyond all reasonable doubt and that there shall have been mens rea on the part of the alleged contemnor. Mens rea in this context does not mean a wilful intention to disobey the court's order, but an intention to do the act which constitutes the disobedience with knowledge of the terms of the order, although not necessarily an understanding that the act is prohibited.'[258]

In relation to a company's employees, the Court of Appeal, per Lord Donaldson MR said:

> 'Whether X is doing an act by the instrumentality of its servants or agents will depend upon the scope of their mandate. This will be judged in the light of reality rather than

[253] Cf *Stancomb v Trowbridge UDC* [1910] 2 Ch 190. In the course of his judgment in that case Warrington J had said of a body corporate that: 'Such a body can only act by its agents or servants, and I think, if the act is in fact done, it is no answer to say that, done, as it must be, by an officer or servant of the council, the council is not liable for it, even though it may have been done by the servant through carelessness, neglect, or even in dereliction of his duty.'

[254] See generally, Chapter 7, *Corporate Contracts, Capacity and Authority*, para **[7.096]** *ff*.

[255] A company's directors or other officers may also be liable for the breach: see para **[6.088]**.

[256] See *Northern Counties Securities Ltd v Jackson & Steeple Ltd* [1974] 2 All ER 625 and generally, para **[6.084]**.

[257] *Director General of Fair Trading v Smiths Concrete Ltd* [1991] 4 All ER 150.

[258] [1991] 4 All ER 150 at 168.

> form. If X should have appreciated that the servant or agent would be likely to do the prohibited act unless dissuaded by X, the act will be regarded as being within the scope of that mandate if X has not taken all reasonable steps to prevent it. Such steps may in appropriate cases involve far more than express prohibition and extend to elaborate monitoring and compliance machinery and procedures and the creation of positive incentives designed to dissuade the servant or agent.
>
> If the mandate of the servant or agent has been effectively restricted, ie all reasonable steps have been taken to achieve this objective, X may nevertheless be answerable to third parties for damage suffered in consequence of the acts of the servant or agent, if it can be said that X put him in a position to do them. This is to be distinguished from answerability for acts done by X personally through the instrumentality of his servants or agents and does not involve a disobedience by X of the court's orders or any liability in contempt.'[259]

This was the state-of-the-art English judicial thinking on this point when the first edition of this work was published. The decision of the Court of Appeal was, however, overruled by the House of Lords in *Re the Supply of Ready Mixed Concrete (No 2); Director General of Fair Trading v Pioneer Concrete (UK) Ltd*[260]. Following the Court of Appeal's decision, certain other companies which had at first instance been found to be in contempt of court for breach of the order, were given leave to appeal out of time and were successful before the Court of Appeal[261]. The matter eventually came before the House of Lords. After reviewing the authorities against[262] and for[263] finding the companies liable for contempt of court, the House of Lords held that where a breach of a court order is committed by an employee, a company *will* be liable for the breach even though the employee was expressly forbidden by the company to do the act prohibited by the court order, provided that the employee was acting within the scope of his employment. In so holding, Lord Nolan expressly endorsed the decision of Warrington J in *Stancomb v Trowbridge UDC*[264] and held that Lord Wilberforce's judgment in *Heatons Transport (St Helens) Ltd v Transport and General Workers' Union*[265] was not inconsistent with Warrington J's decision. Lord Nolan said:

> 'Given that liability for contempt does not require any direct intention on the part of the employer to disobey the order, there is nothing to prevent an employing company from being found to have disobeyed an order "by" its servant as a result of a deliberate act by the servant on its behalf. In my judgment, the decision in *Stancomb v Trowbridge UDC* is good law and should be followed in the present case.'

---

259 [1991] 4 All ER 150 at 168.

260 *Re the Supply of Ready Mixed Concrete (No 2); Director General of Fair Trading v Pioneer Concrete (UK) Ltd* [1995] 1 All ER 135.

261 [1994] ICR 57.

262 The earlier Court of Appeal decision in *Smith*'s case [1994] 4 All ER 150; *Tesco Supermarkets Ltd v Natrass* [1971] 2 All ER 127.

263 *Rantzen v Rothchild* (1865) 14 WR 96; *Stancomb v Trowbridge UDC* [1910] 2 Ch 190; *Heatons Transport (St Helens) Ltd v Transport and General Workers' Union* [1972] 3 All ER 101.

264 *Stancomb v Trowbridge UDC* [1910] 2 Ch 190.

265 *Heatons Transport (St Helens) Ltd v Transport and General Workers' Union* [1972] 3 All ER 101. See para **[6.074]**.

It is thought by this writer that to find a company liable for contempt for its employees' acts or omissions, in circumstances where there is clear evidence that the company expressly prohibited those employees from doing such acts, is wrong in principle and it is further submitted that the decision of the House of Lords in *Re the Supply of Ready Mixed Concrete (No 2)* ought not be followed in Ireland.

[6.080] As this writer has already written elsewhere[266], the following criticisms may be made of the House of Lords' decision in *Re the Supply of Ready Mixed Concrete (No 2)*. In the first place, the *Stancomb* case is only authority for the proposition that the sole significance attaching to the word 'wilfully' is to exclude casual, accidental and unintentional acts which constitute disobedience. Secondly, Warrington J did not say that a company or other body corporate would be in contempt of court where its employees acted in breach of a court order in circumstances where those in authority expressly prohibited such employees from doing such acts. Thirdly, it is thought that there is much sense in the following statement of the law by Slade J in *Hone v Page*[267] (a passage cited with approval by the English Court of Appeal in *Attorney General for Tuvalu and another v Philatelic Distribution Corp Ltd et al*[268]):

> 'I think that a man must be deemed to do a relevant act "by his servants or agents"...if (a) the persons who did the acts were his servants or agents, (b) the acts were done in the course of the service or agency, and (c) he either (i) authorised the acts or (ii) could reasonably have foreseen the possibility of such acts and failed to take all reasonable steps to prevent them.'

It would seem that the House of Lords paid no regard at all to basic agency principles[269]. Fourthly, the 'deliberate act' of a company's employee cannot, in justice, be the sole determinant for holding that company to have been in contempt of court. Matters such as whether the employee was acting within the course of his employment, his or her 'apparent competence'[270] and whether the company genuinely exhorted the employee not to act in breach of an injunction or other order of the court must be material considerations. It is thought that where these circumstances are found to exist, the appropriate finding is that the company as principal is not in contempt of court, although the employee personally may well be in contempt of court as a third party who knowingly obstructs or frustrates the object of the injunction or other order[271].

---

266 See Courtney, *Mareva Injunctions and Related Interlocutory Orders* (1998), para [12.30]. This paragraph has been reproduced verbatim.

267 *Hone v Page* [1980] FSR 500.

268 *Attorney General for Tuvalu v Philatelic Distribution Corp Ltd* [1990] 2 All ER 216 at 222.

269 See generally Wickins & Ong, 'Confusion Worse Confounded: The End of the Directing Mind Theory?' [1997] JBL 524.

270 Where a firm of solicitors employed an 'apparently competent' solicitor it was found that they had taken all reasonable care and that they were not in contempt of court: see the decision of Skinner J in *TDK Tape Distributor (UK) Ltd v Videochoice Ltd* [1985] 3 All ER 345.

271 The liability of companies as third-parties to a court order or judgment in respect of the default of their employees is considered in Courtney, *Mareva Injunctions and Related Interlocutory Orders* (1998), para [12.38]-[12.42], generally, but with particular emphasis on Mareva injunctions.

(iii) Breach of undertakings given in lieu of court orders

[6.081] Undertakings given on behalf of companies raise particular issues. Insofar as it is accepted that an undertaking by a company has the same effect as a court order, it was held in England in *Biba Ltd v Stratford Investments Ltd*[272] that the Rules of the Supreme Court 1965 should be construed as applying to undertakings. In Ireland under the RSC it is a prerequisite to a company, or its directors or other officers, being sanctioned for contempt of court that the order of the court has been 'wilfully disobeyed'[273]. On this basis it is thought that the same principles apply to a breach of an undertaking.

[6.082] An undertaking given by or on behalf of a company must be properly authorised by those with authority in the company. In most private companies the board of directors will be the most appropriate organ to authorise (by resolution) the giving of an undertaking. A company's board may, however, delegate the actual authority to any person to give such an undertaking. It is thought that a director of a private company, present in court at the hearing of an application, may be said to have ostensible (if he does not, in fact, have actual) authority to bind his company[274]. By contrast, an ordinary employee would not have ostensible authority, although if properly authorised, he may have the actual authority to give an undertaking. An undertaking given by a company's solicitor or counsel is enforceable against a company because they are the company's agents in the cause or matter.

[6.083] Notwithstanding English authority, apparently to the contrary[275], it is thought that a company will not be liable in contempt for breaching an undertaking in lieu of an injunction or other court order where breach is occasioned by employees acting contrary to express instructions. It is thought that the situation whereby a company fails to take 'adequate and continuing steps to ensure'[276] that its obligations under an undertaking are complied with, must be distinguished from a situation whereby a company's employees cause an undertaking to be breached when acting outside the scope of their employment[277].

[6.084] It has been held that where a company's shareholders cause a company to act in breach of an undertaking they, the shareholders, will not be liable for contempt of court[278]. In *Northern Counties Securities Ltd v Jackson & Steeple Ltd*[279] the defendant-

272 *Biba Ltd v Stratford Investments Ltd* [1972] 3 All ER 1041.

273 RSC Ord 42, r 32, see para **[6.074]**.

274 On actual and ostensible authority of corporate officers see Chapter 7, *Corporate Contracts, Capacity and Authority*, para **[7.097]**.

275 In *Re Garage Equipment Associations' Agreement* (1964) LP 4 RP 491 Megaw J said (at 504):

> 'The court is prepared to accept that none of the officers of the company individually knew or realised that an undertaking given to the court was being broken or had been broken. But that does not in any way detract from the fact that the company - and this motion is only concerned with the company - was in contempt of court by these things being done when an undertaking had been given on behalf of the company and the company was aware of the existence of that undertaking.'

276 *Re Galvanised Tank Manufacturers' Association's Agreement* [1965] 2 All ER 1003.

277 Cf *Re the Supply of Ready Mixed Concrete (No 2)* [1995] 1 All ER 135.

278 The principle here is equally applicable to a court order made against a company.

279 *Northern Counties Securities Ltd v Jackson & Steeple Ltd* [1974] 2 All ER 625.

company undertook to the court to use its best endeavours to apply for a Stock Exchange quotation, and within 28 days of such quotation being obtained, to allot and issue shares to the plaintiff and not to increase the authorised share capital of the company or to do any other thing requiring the shareholders' authority in general meeting. Subsequently, the defendant-company discovered that the Stock Exchange required that the issue of shares be subject to the consent of the 'company in general meeting'. The defendant-company's directors initially failed to give notice of an EGM. At the plaintiff's prompting, they did eventually convene the meeting. Contrary to the company's undertaking the resolutions proposed: first, that the company's share capital be increased by 370,000 ordinary shares ranking pari passu as to dividend with the existing ordinary shares; and secondly, that the directors be authorised to issue those shares fully paid to the plaintiff. The text of the proposed resolutions was accompanied by a circular which stated that having taken a leading counsel's advice on the court order and the company's undertaking, the shareholders were free to vote as they wished. The directors also said that they were making no recommendation to the shareholders and were leaving the decision on how to vote to their individual judgment. Moreover, the directors advised that if the resolutions were passed the company would have to pay £300,873 for an asset it had acquired from the plaintiff but that if they were not passed, the cost would be circa £183,873. The plaintiff objected to the terms of what was circulated by the directors to the shareholders. Walton J held that the circular did not comply with the undertaking of the company to use its best endeavours to have the shareholders pass a resolution to issue shares to the plaintiff and that it ought to have been couched in more positive terms; he also held, inter alia, that the resolution to increase the company's share capital was a breach of the company's undertaking. More significantly for present purposes, however, was the finding by Walton J that the shareholders would not be in contempt of court if they voted against the resolution to issue shares to the plaintiff. In distinguishing the position of a director who votes, at a directors' meeting, against his company complying with a court order or undertaking to court, Walton J rejected the submission that a shareholder who votes, at a members' meeting, against a course of action required to comply with a court order or undertaking would be 'a step taken by him knowingly which would prevent the company from fulfilling its undertaking to the court'[280]. Walton J said:

> 'When a director votes as a director for or against any particular resolution in a directors' meeting, he is voting as a person under a fiduciary duty to the company for the proposition that the company should take a certain course of action. When a shareholder is voting for or against a particular resolution he is voting as a person owing no fiduciary duty to the company who is exercising his own right of property to vote as he thinks fit. The fact that the result of the voting at the meeting (or subsequent poll) will bind the company cannot affect the position that in voting he is voting simply as an exercise of his own property rights.
>
> ...a director is an agent, who casts his vote to decide in what manner his principal shall act through the collective agency of the board of directors; a shareholder who casts his vote in general meeting is not casting it as an agent of the company in any shape or form. His act,

[280] [1974] 2 All ER 625 at 635a.

therefore, in voting as he pleases cannot in any way be regarded as an act of the company.'[281]

In so finding he concluded:

'It is, I think, equally clear that the shareholders are not abetting the company to commit a contempt of court; the company is, indeed, by convening the requisite meeting and putting a positive circular before the members duly complying with the obligations which rest on it. It will have done its best, and the rest is in the lap of the gods in the shape of the individual decisions of the members.

It would, of course, be otherwise if one could envisage any circumstances in which an order was made by the courts on a company to do something, for example, to increase its capital (as distinct from using its best endeavours to increase its capital), which must of necessity involve the shareholders voting in a particular manner. But I at any rate cannot envisage any ordinary resolution (as distinct from, for example, a situation where all the shareholders were before the court and bound by the order) where such an order would ever be made.'[282]

[6.085] This decision might at first appear to be at odds with the general principle that a third party will be in contempt of court for aiding and abetting the breach of a court order or obstructing or frustrating a court order[283]. All other things being equal, however, it is thought that there is no conflict between these two principles. First, an individual shareholder who casts his vote in such a manner as to indirectly cause a company to act in breach of a court order is acting in furtherance of his own property rights - it would be unjust to expect a shareholder who is not directly party to the matter which gave rise to the court order or undertaking by the company to sacrifice his own interests in favour of another party's interests. Secondly, it may be considered that a court order or undertaking in such circumstances implicitly acknowledges that the company will abide by same to the extent that such is within its own remit - because it must be acknowledged that a shareholder can act in his own interests, to so act cannot be a contempt of court.

[6.086] In circumstances where a company's shareholders are different persons to a company's directors, the foregoing seems to the writer to represent good law. What may be seen as less clear is where the directors and shareholders are one and the same persons, as may be the case in a small, closely-held private company, which may even be run on the basis of a 'quasi-partnership'. In such a case it may be argued that it would be unconscionable for the directors, wearing their shareholders' hats, to cast their vote in such a manner as to cause the company to breach a court order or undertaking. To that extend, the finding by Walton J in *Northern Counties Securities Ltd v Jackson & Steeple Ltd*[284] that a director may, wearing his shareholder's hat, vote as he pleases, can be doubted. He said there that:

'I think that a director who has fulfilled his duty as a director of a company by causing it to comply with an undertaking binding on it is nevertheless free, as an individual

[281] [1974] 2 All ER 625 at 635e-g.

[282] [1974] 2 All ER 625 at 636a-b.

[283] See Courtney, *Mareva Injunctions and Related Interlocutory Orders* (1998), para [12.31] *ff.*

[284] *Northern Counties Securities Ltd v Jackson & Steeple Ltd* [1974] 2 All ER 625.

> shareholder, to enjoy the same unfettered right of voting at general meetings of the members of the company as he would have if he were not also a director.'

Where, on the facts of a case, the director's conduct is found to be fraudulent or unconscionable, it is thought that it is open to a court to disregard which particular 'hat' a person is wearing on the same grounds as a court can disregard a company's separate legal personality. In so finding that a director/shareholder is in contempt of court, the court would, in effect, be lifting the corporate veil on grounds of fraud or circumvention of an existing legal obligation[285].

[6.087] Another possible situation where a company's shareholders may be found to be in contempt of court is where they vote to cause a company to breach a court order or undertaking, without any personal gain, and where the dominant purpose of their action was spiteful or malicious. Were this basis to be found sufficient to deem shareholders to be in contempt of court, it could apply to large companies with unconnected membership and not be confined to small closely-held companies. One practical problem with this ground as a basis for finding shareholders in contempt of court is that it is notoriously difficult to establish a 'dominant intention'.

(iv) Attachment of a company's officers

[6.088] It will be noticed that RSC Ord 42, r 32 only makes provision for 'attachment' and not the 'more stringent remedy'[286] of committal[287] of a company's officers. An order for attachment directs the person against whom the order is directed to be brought before the court to answer the contempt in respect of which the order is issued[288]. An order for committal directs that upon the arrest of the person against whom the order is directed, he 'shall be lodged in prison until he purge his contempt and is discharged pursuant to further order of the Court'[289]. It has been said, however, that the only practical difference between attachment and committal concerns the manner of enforcement: attachment was enforced by the sheriff and committal was enforced by the tipstaff[290]. Even this distinction no longer holds true in Ireland, since the Rules of the Superior Courts 1986 provide that every order of attachment or committal shall be directed to the Commissioner and members of the Garda Síochána[291]. In the case of an application for an order of either 'attachment' or 'committal' the effect may be the same: the contemnor may be committed to prison. RSC Ord 44, r 4 concerns attachment. It provides:

> 'When the person against whom an order of attachment is directed is brought before the Court on his arrest, the Court may either discharge him on such terms and conditions as to costs or otherwise as it thinks fit or commit him to prison for his contempt either for a

---

[285] On the grounds for lifting the veil and disregarding a company's separate legal personality, see Chapter 5, *Disregarding Separate Corporate Personality*, para **[5.030]**.

[286] Per Ronan LJ in *Cooke v Cooke & Cooke* [1919] 1 IR 227 at 241.

[287] As to the distinction between 'attachment' and 'committal' see Courtney, *Mareva Injunctions and Related Interlocutory Orders* (1998), para [12.54].

[288] RSC Ord 44, r 1.

[289] RSC Ord 44, r 2.

[290] *R v Lambeth County Court Judge and Jonas* (1887) 36 WR 475.

[291] RSC Ord 44, r 7.

definite period to be specified in the order, or until he shall purge his contempt and be discharged by further order of the Court'.

In the case of an order of attachment, an alleged contemnor is brought before the court to answer his contempt. He is thereby given an opportunity, prior to being incarcerated, to explain his actions or omissions which are alleged to have caused the court's order to have been breached[292]. An order of committal directs that a contemnor be summarily lodged in prison: he will not have an opportunity to answer his contempt unless he applies to vary the order. Although it may well transpire to be the prelude to committal, an 'attachment' order can therefore be considered to be a lesser order than a 'committal' order[293]. An order for either committal or attachment for contempt of court requires the leave of the court which is applied for by motion on notice, save in the case of a criminal contempt 'in the face of the court'[294]. The purpose of a contemnor's imprisonment is considered only to be coercive: the court has made an order which the contemnor has not obeyed and, in these circumstances, the contemnor is liable to be visited with an indefinite term of imprisonment until he agrees to comply with the order or the plaintiff agrees to his release[295].

[6.089] Where a company wilfully disobeys an injunction or other court order those persons liable to be attached are its directors and other officers: RSC Ord 42, r 32. 'Officer' of a company is defined by CA 1963, s 2 to include its directors and the company secretary. Where a director or other officer of a company actively assists the company in disobeying an injunction or other court order he will be in contempt of court, as would any third party, on the basis that he has either aided and abetted the breach of the court's order or that he obstructed or frustrated the court's order[296]. This much is clear from cases such as *Ronson Products Ltd v Ronson Furniture Ltd*[297] *and Biba Ltd v Stratford Investments Ltd*[298].

[6.090] The circumstances in which a director or other officer can be attached for his company's breach of a court order must, however, be distinguished from cases where the

---

[292] See, eg, *M Ltd v T* (1991) *The Irish Times*, 19 September (Johnson J). There Johnson J ordered that the defendant be brought to court to explain why he should not be sent to prison for failing to comply with an order of Carroll J which directed him to make discovery on oath concerning various goods within 14 days from the making of the order. The plaintiff claimed that it had never been paid by the defendant or the company of which he was manager for tea and coffee-making equipment which it had supplied and which was valued at over Stg£99,000. It appears from the newspaper report that the plaintiff had obtained the order from Carroll J as ancillary relief to either a Mareva application or a claim for a proprietary injunction and *The Irish Times* report said that Carroll J had also made an order restraining the sale of or disposing of any interest in goods which had been supplied by the plaintiff.

[293] See *Piper v Piper* [1876] WN 202.

[294] RSC Ord 44, r 3.

[295] *The State (Commins) v McRann* [1977] IR 78 at 89.

[296] See generally, Courtney, *Mareva Injunctions and Related Interlocutory Orders* (1998), para [12.31] *ff*.

[297] *Ronson Products Ltd v Ronson Furniture Ltd* [1966] 2 All ER 381.

[298] *Biba Ltd v Stratford Investments Ltd* [1972] 3 All ER 1041 at 1045c.

director or other officer does not actively participate in the breach of the order or undertaking[299] given by the company. The question here is whether a director or other officer who has not actively participated in the breach of a court order and who has adopted a purely passive role will be liable to be attached. The English authorities are equivocal on this point. On the one hand, in *Director General of Fair Trading v Buckland and another*[300] Anthony Lincoln J held that a person is not liable in contempt merely by virtue of his office ie by simply being a director. In so finding he said:

> '...I reach the conclusion that Ord 45, r 5 does not render an officer of a company liable in contempt by virtue of his office and his mere knowledge that the order sought to be enforced was made. Resort can be had to r 5 only if he can otherwise be shown to be in contempt under the general law of contempt. In the circumstances set out in the preliminary issue neither Mr Buckland not Mr Stone could be liable in contempt in the absence of mens rea or an actus reus.'[301]

On the other hand, in *Biba Ltd v Stratford Investments Ltd*[302], the director whom it was sought to be found in contempt was a solicitor who had taken only a superficial interest in the day-to-day affairs of the defendant company and had nothing to do with staffing, advertising, selling or stocking. There, although it was accepted that he had, as director, played a 'purely passive role' Brightman J held that he was liable to proceedings for contempt, although he failed to support his finding with reasons. In Ireland, it is thought that 'wilful disobeyance' is a prerequisite to finding an individual officer in contempt.

[6.091] The decision of Anthony Lincoln J in *Buckland* was, however, distinguished by Woolf LJ in the Court of Appeal decision in *Attorney General for Tuvalu v Philatelic Distribution Corp Ltd*[303]. In that case the defendant-company contracted with the plaintiff-government to design, produce and sell Tuvalu postage stamps. The plaintiff-government subsequently suspected that the security printer company (which was owned by the defendant's managing director) had deliberately printed flawed stamps; the plaintiff-government obtained injunctions restraining the managing director and his companies from producing any more Tuvalu stamps or selling or dealing in stamps or other articles of philately or printing materials bearing the name Tuvalu. The injunction was subsequently varied and the managing director and the defendant both undertook not to make use of the printing materials. Prior to the variation of the injunction, an employee of the defendant-company gave an order to the security printer to produce stamps and the printing materials were used to this end. The plaintiff-government proceeded against a number of persons, including the managing director of the defendant-company for contempt of court and the employee who ordered the stamps. The managing director was found to be in contempt of the injunction by, inter alia,

---

299 As to attachment of directors and other officers following the breach of an undertakings by a company see *Biba Ltd v Stratford Investments Ltd* [1972] 3 All ER 1041.

300 *Director General of Fair Trading v Buckland* [1990] 1 All ER 545.

301 [1990] 1 All ER 545 at 549j.

302 *Biba Ltd v Stratford Investments Ltd* [1972] 3 All ER 1041.

303 *Attorney General for Tuvalu v Philatelic Distribution Corp Ltd* [1990] 2 All ER 216. This was cited in passing in *Cork County Council v CB Readymix Ltd and Cronin* (15 June 1999, unreported), High Court (McGuinness J).

causing or permitting the further production of Tuvalu stamps after the injunction was made and also in giving the later undertaking without making sure than no prohibited stamps were on order or were in the process of being printed. The managing director was fined £3,000 and committed to prison for three months. It was against this that he appealed to the Court of Appeal. In his judgment, Woolf LJ held that:

> 'In our view where a company is ordered not to do certain acts or gives an undertaking to like effect and a director of that company is aware of the order or undertaking he is under a duty to take reasonable steps to ensure that the order or undertaking is obeyed, and if he wilfully fails to take those steps and the order or undertaking is breached he can be punished for contempt. We use the word "wilful" to distinguish the situation where the director can reasonably believe some other director or officer is taking these steps.'[304]

Later, it was said:

> 'There must, however, be some culpable conduct on the part of the director before he will be liable to be subject to an order of committal under Ord 45, r 5; mere inactivity is not sufficient.'[305]

In this regard the Court of Appeal distinguished *Buckland* on the grounds that, there, no finding of culpable conduct on the part of the director had been found and the decision should not be taken as meaning that a director must actively participate in the breach before he is liable in contempt. A director's failure to supervise or investigate or his deliberate blindness will be regarded as being 'wilful' and he may be found to be in contempt[306].

[6.092] An undertaking given to the court is equivalent to a formal court order and its breach will be a contempt of court which can result in the contemnor being attached or committed. In *A-G v Wheatley & Co Ltd*[307] Warrington J said:

> 'The practice of the Court of Chancery was not to treat an undertaking as distinct from an injunction with regard to breach, and for the purpose of enforcing an undertaking that undertaking is equivalent to an order - that is to say, an undertaking, if broken, would involve the same consequences on the persons breaking the undertaking as would their disobedience to an order for an injunction.'[308]

(v) Sequestration of companies' and their officers' assets

[6.093] Sequestration is 'essentially penal in effect'[309]. It is a 'process of contempt'[310] by which a person or persons known as sequestrators are empowered to take a contemnor's property into their possession until such time as the contemnor purges his contempt.

---

304 [1990] 2 All ER 216 at 222c.

305 [1990] 2 All ER 216 at 223e.

306 *Re Galvanized Tank Manufacturers' Association's Agreement* [1965] 2 All ER 1003 cited.

307 *AG v Wheatley & Co Ltd* (1903) 48 Sol Jo 116. Applied in *Biba Ltd v Stratford Investments Ltd* [1972] 3 All ER 1041.

308 Warrington J went on to cite *London and Birmingham Railway Co v Grand Junction Canal Co* (1835) 1 Ry & Can Cas 224 where it was said that: '...an undertaking is equivalent to an injunction, and, if violated, may be the subject of an application to this court.'

309 *Larkins v NUM* [1985] IR 671 at 688.

310 *Pratt v Inman* (1889) 43 Ch D 175 at 179; *Romilly v Romilly* [1963] 3 All ER 607 at 609f-g.

Sequestration of an individual defendant's assets is facilitated by RSC Ord 43, r 2 which provides:

> 'Where any person is by any judgment or order directed to pay money into Court or to do any other act in a limited time, and after due service of such judgment or order refuses or neglects to obey the same according to the exigency thereof, the person prosecuting such judgment or order shall, at the expiration of the time limited for the performance thereof, be entitled, without obtaining any order from the Court for that purpose, to issue an order of sequestration in the Form No 17 in the Appendix F, Part II, against the estate and effects of such disobedient person.'

Sequestration is primarily available as a remedy to a plaintiff where a defendant or other person breaches a mandatory court order or injunction. Sequestration is also available to enforce a judgment or order for the recovery of property other than land[311]. Although sequestration in these circumstances is 'of right' ie without the leave of the court, before issuing an order for sequestration against a contemnor, the plaintiff must apply to the Master of the High Court to approve one or more sequestrators and to obtain directions as to his or their security and accounting[312].

[6.094] Where a company 'wilfully disobeys'[313] a judgment or order of the court RSC Ord 42, r 32 provides that the judgment or order may, by leave of the court, be enforced, inter alia, by sequestration against the corporate property or by order of sequestration of its directors' or other officers' property. Again, sequestration is not 'of right' and must be by leave of the court.

[6.095] A person appointed a sequestrator is an officer of the court. As a process, sequestration can only ever be effective against a contemnor of substance. Upon his appointment, a sequestrator will take possession of a contemnor's real and personal estate and collect, receive and get into his hands the rents and profits of the real estate and personal estate and keep same in his possession until such time as the contemnor purges his contempt. Unlike a fine, which is considered below[314], sequestration does not permit the indefinite retention of a contemnor's assets. This was made clear in *Con-Mech Ltd v Amalgamated Union of Engineering Workers*[315] where Sir John Donaldson MR said:

> 'If someone is fined the money is lost to him for ever. If his assets are sequestrated the money remains his but he cannot use it. The money stays in the sequestrator's possession until the court orders what shall be done with it. The man can come to court at any time and ask for the money to be returned to him, but if he does so the court will require some explanation of his conduct.'[316]

---

311 RSC Ord 42, r 6.

312 RSC Ord 43, r 3.

313 See para **[6.074]**.

314 See para **[6.098]**.

315 *Con-Mech Ltd v Amalgamated Union of Engineering Workers* [1973] ICR 620 at 627.

316 See further Lowe & Sufrin, Borrie & Lowe, *The Law of Contempt*, (3rd edn, 1996), p 606 *ff* where this and other cases such as *Australian Consolidated Press Ltd v Morgan* (1965) 112 CLR 483 are considered.

While a sequestrator has possession of a contemnor's assets, he owes the contemnor a duty of care in respect of those assets[317].

[6.096] Sequestration as of right arises where a company neglects or refuses to obey a judgment or order requiring the payment of money into court, or requiring the doing of any act within a limited time. In such case, the person prosecuting is, by virtue of RSC Ord 43, r 2:

> '...entitled, without obtaining any order from the court for that purpose, to issue an order of sequestration.'

It must be stressed that the judgment or order which has been disobeyed must require either the payment of money into court or the doing of an act within a limited time (and, of course, in the case of the latter, the time limit must have expired).

[6.097] Sequestration as a result of wilful disobeyance is said to be with leave of the court. Any judgment or order against a company may be enforced by sequestration with the leave of the court if it has been wilfully disobeyed. Significantly, in appropriate circumstances the sequestration may be against the property of the directors or other officers as well as that of the company: RSC Ord 42, r 32. Where a company is in wilful disobedience of any judgment or order, enforcement may be brought against the company by way of sequestration, or against the company's directors or officers by way of attachment or sequestration.

(vi) Fining companies and their officers

[6.098] The Rules of the Superior Courts 1986 are silent as to the jurisdiction to fine a person or a company who or which is found to be in contempt of court. It is, however, accepted practice that the High Court has jurisdiction to impose a fine where it considers attachment, committal, or sequestration to be inappropriate. The jurisdiction to impose a fine in lieu of attachment or committal was considered by Cross J in *Phonographic Performance Ltd v Amusement Caters (Peckham) Ltd*[318]. There, he said:

> 'I cannot for myself see the logic of saying that in a case of civil contempt the court has no alternative to sending the defendants to prison...I think that the court must have power, if there has been contumacious behaviour, to impose the lesser penalty of a fine'.[319]

Where a company's directors are being fined for their company's contempt of court it has been said by the English Court of Appeal in *McMillan Graham Printers v RR (UK) Ltd*[320] that each individual director's circumstances should be examined separately and that the directors should not be fined jointly and severally.

[6.099] One of the more recent Irish cases where the court fined persons who were found to be in contempt was in *Irish Shell Ltd v Ballylynch Motors Ltd and Morris Oil Co Ltd*[321] where the Supreme Court, per Lynch J, held that the President of the High

---

[317] *Inland Revenue Commissioners v Hoogstraten* [1984] 3 All ER 25.

[318] *Phonographic Performance Ltd v Amusement Caters (Peckham) Ltd* [1963] 3 All ER 493.

[319] [1963] 3 All ER 493 at 497.

[320] *McMillan Graham Printers v RR (UK) Ltd* [1993] TLR 152.

[321] *Irish Shell Ltd v Ballylynch Motors Ltd and Morris Oil Company Ltd* (5 March 1997, unreported), Supreme Court (Lynch J; nem diss).

Court had power to fine a defaulting company's directors in lieu of attachment[322]. Furthermore, RSC Ord 44, rr 4 and 5 provide that with regard to attachment and committal, the Court may discharge a person 'on such terms and conditions as to costs or otherwise as it thinks fit'. It is thought that this is broad enough to empower the making of a fine in lieu of imprisonment[323].

[322] (5 March 1997, unreported), Supreme Court at p 6.

[323] RSC Ord 36, r 22 provides that the officer having the management of the Central Office of the High Court is the proper officer to make entries and render accounts of all fines or penal sums imposed by the Court.

Chapter 7

Corporate Contracts, Capacity and Authority

[7.001] While natural persons are said to be 'only flesh and blood', they can think and act for themselves[1]. Companies, on the other hand, cannot think and act for themselves and are totally reliant upon natural persons to think and act for them. To grasp this point at the outset is not merely to acknowledge the obvious, but is to understand the central theme of this chapter: the involvement of human agents is a prerequisite to corporate contracting.

[7.002] Corporate contracts are considered in this chapter in four sections:

[A] Corporate contracts: form and formalities.

[B] Pre-incorporation contracts.

[C] Contractual capacity and ultra vires.

[D] The authority of corporate agents.

Section A of this chapter examines the nature of the corporate contract and the basic legal formalities required to create a binding corporate contract. Section B considers pre-incorporation contracts, ie contracts which purport to be made by a company prior to its incorporation. The remaining two sections look at two fundamental limitations on corporate contracting. Section C considers corporate contractual capacity and in particular the consequences where a company acts outside of its objects clause, or ultra vires. Finally, Section D addresses the application of the law of agency to corporate contracts which arises by virtue of the fact that a company can only act through its human agents.

[A] Corporate Contracts: Form and Formalities

[7.003] Of the thousands of contracts entered into every day by companies, the vast majority are concluded without formality, often orally, and the majority that are in writing tend to be signed 'for and on behalf of' companies by their agents. Formalities are at a minimum and as a general rule the company seal is not required to bind the company. Section 38 of the Companies Act 1963 ('CA 1963') provides the form which corporate contracts may take, and in so doing makes a threefold distinction: those required to be under seal, those required to be in writing and those which may be oral or parol. The changes to contract law effected by the Electronic Commerce Act 2000 ('ECA 2000') are considered as part of the treatment of written contracts and contracts that require to be under seal.

[7.004] Here, the form and formalities of corporate contracts are considered under the following headings:

1 See the colourful passage from the judgment of Buckley J in *Continental Tyre & Rubber Co (GB) Ltd v Daimler & Co* [1915] 1 KB 893 at 916, quoted at para **[7.096]**.

1. Oral contracts.
2. Written contracts.
3. Contracts and other instruments required to be under seal.
4. Delivery of a deed by a company.
5. Execution by power of attorney.

Oral contracts

[7.005] Section 38(1)(c) of CA 1963 provides the general rule that all contracts which can be made orally, or by parol, by an individual can also be made orally by a company, acting through its authorised agents. The authority of the contracting corporate agent to enter into contracts on behalf of the company is considered in Section D, below[2].

[7.006] Not all contracts which can be made orally by an individual should be made orally by a company. The Companies Acts 1963–2001 provide that certain contracts entered into by companies with certain persons must be in writing, or evidenced in writing, notwithstanding the provisions of CA 1963, s 38 and the ordinary laws of contract. An example is provided by the European Communities (Single-Member Private Limited Companies) Regulations 1994[3]. Regulation 13(1) provides that, save in respect of contracts entered into in the ordinary course of a company's business[4]:

> '...where a single-member company enters into a contract with the sole member of the company and the sole member also represents the company in the transaction, whether as a director or otherwise, the company shall, unless the contract is in writing, ensure that the terms of the contract are forthwith set out in a written memorandum or are recorded in the minutes of the first meeting of the directors of the company following the making of the contract.'

Although the company and every officer of the company who is in default will be guilty of an offence where reg 13(1) is not complied with[5], the failure to comply will not affect the validity of that contract[6]. Furthermore the provisions of reg 13 are expressed to be without prejudice to any other enactment or rule of law applicable to contracts between a company and its director[7].

Written contracts

[7.007] Section 38(1)(b) of CA 1963 provides that:

> '...a contract which if made between private persons would be by law required to be in writing, signed by the parties to be charged therewith, may be made on behalf of the company in writing, signed by any person acting under its authority, express or implied.'

Where the law requires a contract entered into by an individual to be in writing and signed, such a contract entered into by a company must also be in writing and signed. An

---

2 At para **[7.096]** *ff*.
3 SI 1994/275.
4 SI 1994/275, reg 13(2).
5 SI 1994/275, reg 13(3).
6 SI 1994/275, reg 13(5).
7 SI 1994/275, reg 13(4).

example of a contract required to be in writing is a contract which is going to operate over a number of years such as seen in *Henley Forklift (Ireland) Ltd v Lansing Bagnall & Co Ltd*[8]. The principle here is clear: corporate contracts are on a par with individual contracts.

[7.008] Many diverse types of contract are required by law to be made or evidenced in writing, examples of which are: contracts for the sale of land or an interest therein; contracts of guarantee (but not indemnity); contracts that are not intended to be performed within one year[9]; and legal assignments of choses in action[10], etc[11]. The requirement that a contract be in writing under hand (as opposed to oral or under seal) arises from statute, the agreement of the parties or in equity[12]. Although these contracts are merely required to be evidenced in writing, in practice these contracts are actually made in writing.

[7.009] The dual requirements of 'in writing' and 'signed' are both affected by ECA 2000. Section 19 of ECA 2000 permits certain[13] contracts, that would otherwise require to be in writing, to be instead in electronic form[14]. Section 19 provides:

> 'An electronic contract shall not be denied legal effect, validity or enforceability solely on the grounds that it is wholly or partly in electronic form, or has been concluded wholly or partly by way of an electronic communication.
>
> In the formation of a contract, an offer, acceptance of an offer or any related communication (including any subsequent amendment, cancellation or revocation of the

---

8 *Henley Forklift (Ireland) Ltd v Lansing Bagnall & Co Ltd* [1979] ILRM 257, where O'Higgins CJ said in relation to the contract in question: 'I find it very difficult to say in the circumstances whether the suggested execution of this scheduled agreement by any of the companies involved was such as to comply with the provisions of Companies Act 1963, s 38. It was, by reason of its terms, an agreement which was going to operate over a number of years and therefore was required to be in writing.'

9 Statute of Frauds (Ireland) 1695 (7 Will 3 c 12), s 2 provides:

> '...no action shall be brought...whereby to charge the defendant upon any special promise to answer for the debt, default or miscarriage of another person, or to charge any person upon an agreement made upon consideration of marriage, or upon any contract or sale of lands, tenements or hereditaments or any interest in or concerning them, or upon any agreement that is not to be performed within the space of one year from the making thereof, unless the agreement upon which such action shall be brought, or some note or memorandum thereof, shall be in writing, and signed by the party to be charged therewith, or some other person thereunto by him lawfully authorised.'

See Clark, *Contract Law in Ireland* (3rd edn, 1992), p 78 *ff*. Other examples of contracts which must be in writing are consumer lending contracts within the meaning of the Consumer Credit Act 1995, Part III.

10 Supreme Court of Judicature Ireland Act 1877, s 28: see para **[7.014]**.

11 See further, Kearney, 'Execution of Commercial Documents' (1994), 16 DULJ 1 at pp 6–7.

12 There is no common law requirement that any contract be in writing 'under hand' because, as Kearney, 'Execution of Commercial Documents' (1994), 16 DULJ 1, points out at p 5, the common law required instruments in writing to be executed under seal.

13 Not all contracts can be concluded electronically: see ECA 2000, s 10, considered at **[7.010]**.

14 See Coleman, 'The Irish Electronic Commerce Bill 2000' (2000) 7 CLP 139.

offer or acceptance of the offer) may, unless otherwise agreed by the parties, be communicated by means of an electronic communication.'

This section confirms the acceptability of 'electronic form' for contracts that would otherwise require to be 'in writing'. Generally, matters required to be 'in writing' may now be in electronic form[15]. In addition, ECA 2000, s 13(1) modifies the meaning of what has traditionally been taken to be meant by 'signed' and recognises an 'electronic signature'[16]. It provides:

> 'If by law or otherwise the signature of a person or public body is required (whether the requirement is in the form of an obligation or consequences flow from there being no signature) or permitted, then, subject to subsection (2), an electronic signature may be used.'

Section 13(2) enshrines the principle of consent. Where a signature is required or permitted to be given to a person who is not (and does not act for) a 'public body'[17] that person must consent to the use of an electronic signature. A public body must also consent but can also specify that an electronic signature conforms to certain information technology and procedural requirements[18].

[7.010] Because ECA 2000, s 19(1) permits individuals to conclude certain contracts electronically, by a curious inverted operation CA 1963, s 38(1)(b) applies this law to companies. Those contracts that are excluded from the operation of ECA 2000, ss 12–

---

15 ECA 2000, s 12(1): see para **[7.016]** (fn 62).

16 'Electronic signature' is defined by ECA 2000, s 2(1) to mean 'data in electronic form attached to, incorporated in or logically associated with other electronic data and which serves as a method of authenticating the purported originator, and includes an advanced electronic signature'. An 'advanced electronic signature' is defined by the same section to mean 'an electronic signature — (a) uniquely linked to the signatory, (b) capable of identifying the signatory, (c) created using means that are capable of being maintained by the signatory under his, her or its sole control, and (d) linked to the data to which it relates in such a manner that any subsequent change of the data is detectable.'

17 'Public body' is defined by ECA 2000, s 2(1) to mean: '(a) a Minister of the Government of a Minister of State, (b) a body (including a Department of State but not including a non-government organisation) wholly or partly funded out of the Central Fund or out of moneys provided by the Oireachtas or moneys raised by local taxation or charges, or (c) a commission, tribunal, board or body established by an Act or by arrangement of the Government, a Minister of the Government or a Minister of State for a non-commercial public service or purpose.'

18 ECA 2000, s 13(2)(a) provides: an electronic signature may be used as provided in sub-s (1) only -

> '...where the signature is required or permitted to be given to a public body or to a person acting on behalf of a public body and the public body consents to the use of an electronic signature but requires that it be in accordance with particular information technology and procedural requirements (including that it be an advanced electronic signature, that it be based on a qualified certificate, that it be issued by an accredited certification service provider or that it be created by a secure signature creation device) – if the public body's requirements have been met and those requirements have been made public and are objective, transparent, proportionate and non-discriminatory.'

23, specifically relevant to companies[19], are: the law governing the creation, execution, amendment, variation or revocation of trusts[20]; the law governing the making of an affidavit or a statutory or sworn declaration, or requiring or permitting the use of one for any purpose[21]; and the law governing the manner in which an interest in real property (including a leasehold interest in such property) may be created, acquired, disposed of or registered 'other than contracts (whether or nor under seal[22]) for the creation, acquisition or disposal of such interests'[23]. That latter exclusion thus draws a distinction between contracts for the acquisition or disposal of interests in real property (which can be concluded electronically) on the one hand, and instruments that actually effect the disposal or acquisition of interests in real property on the other, such as conveyances, assignments and transfers (which cannot be concluded electronically as they do not attract the protection of ECA 2000, ss 12–23). Accordingly, all of the examples cited earlier[24] of contracts that require to be in writing and signed may be concluded electronically.

[7.011] Where contracts are required to be made or evidenced in writing it is sufficient in law for any person so authorised by the company to sign either the contract or a written memorandum of the contract 'for and on behalf' of the company. A similar requirement pertains in the case of an electronic contract. The meaning of 'signing' was considered by Finnegan J in *Dundalk AFC Interim Company Ltd v The FAI National League*[25]. There, Finnegan J quoted with approval the following passage from the decision of Romer LJ in *London County Council v Vitamins Ltd*[26]:

> 'It is established in my judgment as a general proposition that at common law a person sufficiently "signs" a document if it is signed in his name and within his authority by somebody else and in such case the agent's signature is treated as being that of the principal.'

Where a director signs on behalf of a company his authority must derive from the board of directors who will have the authority to manage the company under model reg 80 of CA 1963, Sch 1, Table A (the 'model regulations')[27]. An authorised person's authority need not be in writing[28]. It will suffice for the authorised person to 'rubber stamp' such contracts. In *McDonald v John Twiname Ltd*[29] Evershed MR said:

---

[19] Also excluded are wills, codicils and other testamentary instruments, enduring powers of attorney and the rules practices and procedures of a court or tribunal: see ECA 2000, s 10(1).

[20] ECA 2000, s 10(1)(a)(ii).

[21] ECA 2000, s 10(2)(c).

[22] As to sealing, see para **[7.013]**.

[23] ECA 2000, s 10(1)(b).

[24] See para **[7.008]**.

[25] *Dundalk AFC Interim Co Ltd v The FAI National League* [2001] 1 IR 434.

[26] *London County Council v Vitamins Ltd* [1955] 2 All ER 229 at 232.

[27] See Chapter 8, *Corporate Governance: Management by the Directors*, para **[8.004]** *ff*.

[28] *Coles v Trecothick* (1804) 9 VES 234, cited by Finnegan J in *Dundalk AFC Interim Co Ltd v The FAI National League* [2001] 1 IR 434.

[29] *McDonald v John Twiname Ltd* [1953] 2 All ER 589 at 594A.

'A limited company can sign a document by means of some duly authorised person putting its printed signature to it or impressing the printed name of the company on it. That will suffice as a proper execution except in cases where the common seal must be affixed...'

It may be obvious, but where an agent contracts 'for and on behalf of' a company, they should sign just that, ie 'A for and on behalf of A & B Company Ltd'. The absence of these qualifying words could leave the contracting agent personally liable to perform the contract. Moreover, the exact registered name of all companies should be correctly stated in all contracts. If a spelling or other typographical error is made, resulting in A purporting to contract for and on behalf of a non-existent entity, the error may not be fatal provided that there is no misrepresentation or uncertainty. In *F Goldsmith (Sicklesmere) Ltd v Baxter*[30] Stamp J said:

'I would find it impossible to hold that a company incorporated under the Companies Acts has no identity but by reference to its correct name, or that, unless an agent acts on its behalf by that name, or a name so nearly resembling it that it is obviously an error for that name, he acts for nobody.'

This limited saver[31] ought not to encourage complacency, and the general rule is that precision is required to avoid such a contract being held to be void for uncertainty. Moreover, by virtue of CA 1963, s 114(4), the failure to correctly state the company's name in a written contract can render the company's agent personally liable. This has already been discussed at length in Chapter 5[32].

[7.012] To use the abbreviation 'Co' for the word 'company' has been held to be an insufficient deviation to cause personal liability to be imposed pursuant to CA 1963, s 114(4) on officers of the company who use or authorise the use of that abbreviation. This was the case in *Banque de l'Indochine et de Suez SA v Euroseas Group Finance Co Ltd*[33] where Goff J said:

'"Co" is an abbreviation of "Company"...we all know this to be true as a matter of ordinary commercial usage, "Co" is a generally and commonly accepted abbreviation of the word "Company", and is so to such an extent that it is treated as equivalent to "Company" and there is no possibility of it meaning anything else.'[34]

It is thought that CA 1963, s 114 will operate to impose personal liability only where it is shown that the other contracting party was misled to their detriment[35].

---

30 *F Goldsmith (Sicklesmere) Ltd v Baxter* [1969] 3 All ER 733 at 736G. In this case a Mr Brewster, director of F Goldsmith (Sicklesmere) Ltd, purported to contract 'for and on behalf of Goldsmith Coaches (Sicklesmere), Ltd.' The defendant refused to complete the sale arguing that there was no such legal entity. Stamp J rejected this and gave the order for specific performance sought.

31 [1969] 3 All ER 733 at 737G, where Stamp J said '...it is not essential to the validity of a contract made on behalf of a limited company that the company should be described with precision...' However, in an age when there are very many companies with very similar sounding names, particularly containing initials, precision should be striven for. See also *Badgerhill Properties Ltd v Cottrell* [1991] BCLC 805 at 813.

32 Chapter 5, *Disregarding Separate Legal Personality*, para **[5.078]** *ff*.

33 *Banque de l'Indochine et de Suez SA v Euroseas Group Finance Co Ltd* [1981] 3 All ER 198.

34 [1981] 3 All ER 198 at 201(b–c).

35 See *Badgerhill Properties Ltd v Cottrell* [1991] BCLC 805.

Contracts and other instruments required to be under seal

[7.013] Section 38(1)(a) of CA 1963 provides that contracts which are required by law to be in writing and to be under seal in the case of an individual 'may be made on behalf of the company in writing under the common seal of the company'. Again, there is equality of contractual formality between companies and individuals[36]. As with written and oral contracts, a contract which is under seal can be 'varied or discharged in the same manner in which it is authorised' to be made: CA 1963, s 38(3). However, it should be noted that in addition to those circumstances in which individuals are required to execute a document under seal, a company may use its seal in other instances, such as for authenticating a share warrant[37].

[7.014] In the case of an individual, those contracts that are required by law to be under seal, are deeds of various kinds[38] and certain other instruments. At common law there are three requirements to constitute a deed: it must be written on paper or parchment, it must be sealed and it must be delivered[39]. It has been noted that not every instrument under seal will be a deed because, for an instrument to be a deed, it must 'effect the transfer of an interest, right or property, or create an obligation binding on some person or persons, or confirm some act whereby an interest, right or property has already passed'[40]. Irish law requires a deed to be used in relation to transactions dealing with estates or interests in land[41]; to give a valid release or discharge of a right in personal property or cause of action[42]; and to make a valid contract and enter into a valid guarantee[43] where there is no valuable consideration[44]. While the necessity isdebatable[45],

---

36 It should be noted that as with CA 1963, s 38(1)(c) and (b) the provision here is not couched in mandatory terms. Rather, the provisions of the section are facilitatory, through the use of the word 'may'.

37 CA 1963, s 88(1).

38 The modern deed of conveyance being to the fore, its origin being an alternative to the cumbersome and quaint ancient forms of conveyance, such as feoffment with livery of seisin: see Wylie, *Irish Land Law* (3rd edn, 1997), para 3.023. Other documents which are required to be by deed under seal are grants of easements: see Wylie, para 6.54, and deeds of partition, see Wylie, para 7.35.

39 See Barnes and Kershaw, 'Executing Deeds – Signed, Sealed and Delivered?' (1995) Practical Law for Companies; whilst a useful article, care must be taken to distinguish the differences between Irish and English law.

40 See Chitty on Contracts, (26th edn) Vol 1 para 20, and quoted by Kearney, 'Execution of Commercial Documents' (1994), 16 DULJ 1, at p 3.

41 See Real Property Act 1845, ss 2 and 3: Wylie, *Irish Land Law* (3rd edn, 1997), para 3.026. See also, Pearce, *Land Law* (1985), pp 102–103 for a succinct treatment.

42 See Kearney, 'Execution of Commercial Documents' (1994) 16 DULJ 1 at 2.

43 Cf a guarantee which is supported by consideration, which does not have to be under seal: *Re PMPA Garage (Longmile) Ltd* [1992] ILRM 337 at 345.

44 *Drimmie v Davies* [1899] 1 IR 176, which held that promises under seal between partners were enforceable without the need to show consideration. See Clark, *Contract Law in Ireland* (3rd edn, 1992), p 36; see Cheshire, Fifoot and Furmston, *Law of Contract* (12th edn, 1986), p 26.

45 Prior to 1860, it was clear that a grant of a lease required a deed: the Real Property Act 1845, s 3. However, in that year, the Landlord and Tenant Law Amendment Act s 4, Ireland, known as Deasy's Act, muddied the water somewhat as regards the requirements for 'contracts for leases' and 'leases'.

leases of land for a term exceeding one year are normally under seal. Only debentures secured by a mortgage over land or an interest therein must be by deed under seal[46]. Certain other instruments executed by individuals, that are not deeds, are also required to be under seal[47]. These include: security bills of sale[48]; transfers and mortgages of Irish registered ships or shares in ships[49]; perfection of share certificates where so required by a company's articles of association; transfers of shares (in some cases)[50]; execution of bonds[51]; extensions of the standard contract and tort limitation period from 6 to 12 years; avoiding the need for consideration; and effecting a legal assignment of a chose in action under Supreme Court of Judicature Ireland Act 1877, s 28[52]. A power of attorney is no longer required to be under seal[53] nor is it necessary to impress the seal in order for a company to authenticate documents[54]. The central point is that the company is generally on a par with an individual and where the law requires an individual's contract to be under seal, so too must a corporate contract be under seal.

[7.015] As noted earlier, at common law for an instrument to be a deed all that was required was that it was sealed and delivered[55] ie a deed does not, theoretically, require to be signed. Universal practice is, however, to sign a deed and it is considered that not to sign is to court danger. Indeed, modern practice is to sign, but not to physically seal, deeds. In the case of contracts required to be by deed under seal by individuals, there is a growing recognition that the use of a seal is in reality ignored[56]: the practitioner who insists upon an individual stamping a blob of molten wax with his signet ring or caressing a plastic wafer will be met with incredulity. Only the meticulous remain so

---

45 *(contd)* What is clear, is that in respect of a 'lease...for any definite period of time not being from year to year or any lesser period [it] shall be by deed executed, or note in writing signed...' Hence, although practice is to have a lease under seal, simple writing will suffice.

46 CA 1963, s 39 provides that bills of exchange or promissory notes can be made, accepted or endorsed 'on behalf of a company...by a person acting under its authority.'

47 See, generally, Kearney, 'Execution of Commercial Documents' (1994) 16 DULJ 1 at 3, 4.

48 Note, the Bills of Sale Acts do not, per se, apply to companies: see generally, Chapter 21, *Corporate Borrowing: Registration of Charges*, para **[21.037]**.

49 Merchant Shipping Act 1894, s 31.

50 See Chapter 16, *Share Transfers in Private Companies*, para **[16.010]**.

51 See *British India Steam Navigation Co v IRC* (1881) 7 QBD 165 at 173 per Lindley J.

52 As Kearney, 'Execution of Commercial Documents' (1994) 16 DULJ 1, at 5fn points out, although the Supreme Court of Judicature Ireland Act 1877, s 28 refers to an assignment 'in writing, under the hand of the assignor', in *Re A Debtor's Summons* [1929] IR 136 Murnaghan J in the Supreme Court said (at 151) that an assignment 'would in the case of a company require to be under seal because the seal of an incorporated body is the equivalent of the hand of a natural person'.

53 See para **[7.028]**.

54 CA 1963, s 42 provides that a document or proceeding may be authenticated by being signed by a director, secretary or other authorised officer.

55 See para **[7.014]**. See Wylie, *Irish Conveyancing Law* (2nd edn, 1996), para [18.122].

56 See *Stromdale and Ball Ltd v Burden* [1952] All ER 59; *First National Bank Ltd v Jones* [1978] 2 All ER 221 and *TCB Ltd v Gray* [1986] 1 All ER 587. Indeed, in times past, it was the seal and not the signature which was most important. Danckwerts J in *Stromdale and Ball Ltd*, at 62, attributes the present importance of the signature to the 'spread in education'.

disposed[57]. While more radical dicta[58] suggest that sealing is simply unnecessary, it would seem that a deed that is not sealed is enforceable against a natural person by virtue of the seemingly ubiquitous doctrine of estoppel[59] where the deed is expressed to be a deed, contains a testimonium[60] and is signed[61].

[7.016] Section 16 of ECA 2000 facilitates the sealing of documents by electronic means. Section 16(1) provides:

> 'If by law or otherwise a seal is required to be affixed to a document (whether the requirement is in the form of an obligation or consequences flow from a seal not being affixed) then, subject to subsection (2), that requirement is taken to have been met if the document indicated that it is required to be under seal and it includes an advanced electronic signature, based on a qualified certificate, of the person or public body by whom it is required to be sealed.'

The other requirement for a deed or instrument to be under seal – that it is in writing – is addressed by ECA 2000, s 12(1)[62].

As in the case of ordinary electronic contracts, ECA 2000, s 16(2) again enshrines the principle of consent. Where a document to be under seal is required or permitted to be given to a person who is not (and does not act for) a 'public body'[63] that person must consent to the use of an advanced electronic signature based on a qualified certificate. A public body must also consent but it can also specify that an advanced electronic signature conforms to certain information technology and procedural requirements[64]. The essential difference between ordinary contracts and documents under seal is that

---

57 See Danckwerts J in *Stromdale and Ball Ltd* [1952] All ER 59 at 62 where he said: 'Meticulous persons executing a deed may still place their finger on the wax seal or wafer on the document, but it appears to me that at the present day if a party signs a document bearing wax or wafer or other indication of a seal with the intention of executing the document as a deed, that is sufficient...'

58 Eg *First National Securities Ltd v Jones* [1978] 2 All ER 221.

59 See *TCB Ltd v Gray* [1986] 1 All ER 587 at 595 per Browne Wilkinson VC. See also *Re Sean Hussey, A Bankrupt* (23 September 1987, unreported), High Court where Hamilton P found that a bankrupt was estopped from objecting to his original adjudication as a bankrupt notwithstanding that the company seal of the petitioning creditor was improperly attested.

60 Eg that part of a deed that provides 'In witness whereof the parties hereto have, where natural persons, set their hands and affixed their seals and, where bodies corporate, have caused their common seals to be affixed, the day and year first herein written.'

61 Land Registration Rules 1972, r 58 provides that in the case of transfers by natural persons, the registrar is entitled to assume that every deed expressed to be sealed by any party executing it has, in fact, been sealed, notwithstanding that no trace of sealing appears on the deed.

62 ECA 2000, s 12(1) provides: 'If by law or otherwise a person or public body is required (whether the requirement is in the form of an obligation or consequences flow from the information not being in writing) or permitted to give information in writing (whether or nor in a form prescribed by law) then, subject to subsection (2), the person or public body may give the information in electronic form, whether as an electronic communication or otherwise.'

63 'Public body' is defined by ECA 2000, s 2(1), see para **[7.009]**.

64 ECA 2000, s 16(2)(a) provides: an advanced electronic signature based on a qualified certificate may be used as provided in sub-s (1) only:

whereas the former can be concluded with an electronic signature simpliciter, documents under seal require an advanced electronic signature[65] based on a qualified certificate[66]. It is opined that where a company seeks to utilise ECA 2000, s 16, its articles of association ought to envisage such a means for sealing documents. This is because reg 115 is in the nature of an internal control on the use of a seal: where a company's articles require (as in reg 115) two persons to attest the use of the seal, it is to be assumed that two persons, rather than one, are required for reasons of control. Therefore, whilst because of ECA 2000, s 16, the validity of an electronic sealing may not be disputed, the question of corporate authority is not addressed by s 16: an officer acting alone who causes a document, to be sealed electronically may well be liable for breach of duty by acting beyond his authority and in breach of the company's articles of association.

[7.017] Not all deeds and instruments that require to be under a company's seal can be sealed electronically. For many private companies, the most frequent use of the seal is in relation to the acquisition or disposal of real property and from ECA 2000, s 10(1)(b), it is clear that ECA 2000, s 16 is without prejudice to the law governing the manner in which an interest in real property may be created, acquired, disposed of or registered. The deeds and instruments, other than those relating to real property, that can now be sealed electronically are those listed above[67].

[7.018] Again, it should be noted that ECA 2000, s 16 applies to companies 'by proxy' since although it does not specifically mention companies, by virtue of CA 1963, s 38(1)(a) the laws relating to the sealing of deeds and documents by individuals is applied to companies.

The requirement for a company to have a seal

[7.019] Section 114(1)(b) of CA 1963 provides that every company 'shall have its name engraven in legible characters on its seal'. This is the common seal referred to in CA 1963, s 18(2), which provides that on becoming incorporated a company shall, inter alia, have a common seal. The use of the term 'common seal', distinguishes the basic form of seal from an 'official seal'[68] (which can be used for transacting business outside the

---

64 *(contd)*

'where the document to be under seal is required or permitted to be given to a public body or to a person acting on behalf of a public body and the public body consents to the use of an electronic signature but requires that it be in accordance with particular information technology and procedural requirements (including that it be an advanced electronic signature, that it be based on a qualified certificate, that it be issued by an accredited certification service provider) – if the public body's requirements have been met and those requirements have been made public and are objective, transparent, proportionate and non-discriminatory'.

65 See para **[7.009]** (fn 16).

66 ECA 2000, s 2(1) defines 'qualified certificate' to mean a certificate which meets the requirements set out in ECA 2000, Annex I and is provided by a certification service provider who fulfils the requirements set out in ECA 2000, Annex II.

67 See para **[7.008]**.

68 If a company decides to have an 'official seal', CA 1963, s 41 provides that it 'shall be a facsimile of the common seal of the company with the addition on its face of the name of every territory, district or place where it is to be used'.

State: CA 1963, s 41). These are the only two possible forms of seal in the case of a private company[69]. Despite the uncertainty[70], in principle it is thought that there can be no objection to a company having two or more common seals (ie duplicate seals) which all comply with CA 1963, s 114(1)(b). Such a scenario might be expedient in a large company (most likely a public limited company ('PLC')) which has a high volume of deeds that require to be sealed so that, for example, two directors in Dublin might validly attest one seal whilst two other directors in Cork may attest a second seal, provided that all executions are authorised by the directors in accordance with Table A, model reg 115, considered below[71].

[7.020] A company whose objects include the transaction of business outside the State may, if authorised by its articles[72], have an official seal for use in any territory, district or place not situate in the State: CA 1963, s 41(1). The official seal must be a facsimile of the common seal of the company with the addition on its face of the name of every territory, district or place where it is to be used. A deed or other instrument to which an official seal is duly affixed shall bind the company as if it has been sealed with the common seal of the company[73]. Where a company has an official seal, it may by writing under its common seal[74] authorise any person appointed for the purpose in that territory, district or place to affix the seal to any deed or document to which the company is party in that place[75]. The authority of a person so appointed will last for the period specified in the appointment or, if no period is specified, until the notice of revocation or determination of the agent's authority has been given to the person dealing with him[76]. The person affixing any such official seal shall by writing under his hand certify on the deed or other instrument to which the official seal is affixed, the date on which and place at which it is so affixed[77].

Attestation of the company seal

[7.021] Usually, a company's articles of association make provision for the affixing and attestation of the company seal. It was held by the High Court in *Safeera Ltd v Wallis*

---

69 It should be noted that a company other than a private company may, by C(A)A 1977, s 3, also have a 'securities seal': see Chapter 28, *Public Companies in Context*, para **[29.058]**.

70 Note that the matter was considered by the English Law Commission in its report, *Execution of Deeds and Other Documents by or on behalf of Bodies Corporate* (1998) Law Com No 253, considered in Millerchip, 'Execution of Deeds and Documents – Proposals for Clarity' (1998) Practical Law for Companies 41. After noting that there was considerable uncertainty as to whether companies could have duplicate seals, it concluded that it would not recommend that companies should be permitted to have more than one common seal.

71 See para **[7.022]**.

72 The requisite authority will be present where CA 1963, Sch 1, Table A, model reg 82 is adopted.

73 CA 1963, s 41(2).

74 Note the anomaly in that since the Powers of Attorney Act 1996, it is no longer necessary as a matter of law to appoint an attorney by deed under seal: see para **[7.028]**.

75 CA 1963, s 41(3).

76 CA 1963, s 41(4).

77 CA 1963, s 41(5).

and O'Regan[78] that the failure to execute a conveyance of property in accordance with a company's articles will mean that the conveyance will not be effective to convey the company's interest in the property. It must be stressed that the sealing requirements in any particular company will depend, entirely, upon its particular articles[79].

(i) Companies formed and registered under CA 1963

[7.022] It is usual for a private company to adopt the provisions of model reg 115. Model reg 115 provides:

> 'The seal shall be used only by the authority of the directors or of a committee of directors authorised by the directors in that behalf, and every instrument to which the seal shall be affixed shall be signed by a director and shall be countersigned by the secretary or by a second director or by some other person appointed by the directors for that purpose.'

Where a person holds both the offices of director and secretary, his sole signature will not suffice: CA 1963, s 177[80]. It is not necessary under the model regulation for either a director or the secretary to physically affix the seal and the physical affixing can be effected by someone else[81]. When the sealing provisions in a company's articles are observed, and the corporate officers have the requisite authority to act for the company, then the deed so sealed will be invalidated only where it contravenes the law or is ultra vires the company's objects clause[82].

[7.023] Where the sealing provisions in a company's articles are not observed, and the company or its liquidator seeks to avoid the contract, an outsider[83] may be able to enforce the contract where he satisfies the requirements of the Rule in *Turquand*'s case[84] or comes within the European Communities (Companies) Regulations 1973, reg 6[85]. Where there is no evidence of the directors resolving to sanction the use of the seal, the rule in *Turquand*'s case may be invoked: *Ulster Investment Bank Ltd v Euro Estates Ltd and Drumkill Ltd*[86]. In *Re Motor Racing Circuits Ltd*[87] an appeal was brought to the Supreme Court against the trial judge's finding that an irregularity in the execution of a debenture created by the company (it would appear to have been claimed that one of the persons who attested the seal was not in fact a director) was covered by the rule in *Turquand*'s case. Blayney J said:

---

78 *Safeera Ltd v Wallis and O'Regan* (12 July 1994, unreported), High Court (Morris J).

79 It is possible that a company's articles could require all of the company's directors and the secretary to attest the company seal.

80 Cf *Re David Wright & Co Ltd* (1905) 39 ILT 204.

81 See *Savage River Pty Ltd v Fordcorp Industries Pty Ltd* (14 August 1998, unreported), Supreme Court of Victoria, Australia.

82 *Power v Hoey* (1871) 19 WR 916.

83 The term 'outsider' is often used to denote persons who deal with the company.

84 *Royal British Bank v Turquand* (1855) 5 EL & BL 248, considered at para **[7.118]**.

85 SI 1973/163, reg 6 considered at para **[7.126]** *ff*.

86 *Ulster Investment Bank Ltd v Euro Estates Ltd and Drumkill Ltd* [1982] ILRM 57, considered at para **[7.119]**.

87 *Re Motor Racing Circuits Ltd* (31 January 1997, unreported), Supreme Court (Blayney J; nem diss).

> 'The position under the articles of association of the company is that the seal had to be affixed in the presence of the director and the secretary of the company. If one looks at the manner in which the debenture was executed it is clear that it purports to have been executed by a director and the secretary. In so far as the bank were concerned, all they were required to check was that the debenture appeared to have been executed in accordance with the requirements of the articles of association. The bank was not required to investigate as to whether the particular individual who executed as a director was in fact a director or whether the particular individual who executed as the secretary was in fact the secretary. They were entitled to assume that what is called the internal management of the company has been correctly complied with'. [88]

Similarly, where a debenture was attested by a solicitor acting under a power of attorney and countersigned by the secretary in contravention of the company's articles[89], the equivalent UK provision to reg 6 saved the validity of the debenture[90].

(ii) Pre-1963 Irish companies

[7.024] Particular care should be taken when attending to the sealing of a deed or document by a company formed and registered under the Companies (Consolidation) Act 1908 ('C(C)A 1908') for, although a 'company' within the meaning of CA 1963, s 2, unless expressly disapplied, its governing articles of association will be Table A of the First Schedule to the 1908 Act[91]. A trap for the unwary is provided by model reg 76 of Table A of C(C)A 1908 . This provides:

> 'The seal of the company shall not be affixed to any instrument except by the authority of a resolution of the board of directors, and in the presence of at least two directors and of the secretary or such other person as the directors may appoint for that purpose; and those two directors and the secretary or other person as aforesaid shall sign every instrument to which the seal of the company is so affixed in their presence.'

Accordingly, where sealing is regulated by that regulation three signatures must appear: of two directors and of the secretary (or another person appointed for that purpose).

[7.025] Regulation 76 of Table A of C(C)A 1908 was considered by the High Court in the case of *Safeera Ltd v Wallis and O'Regan*[92]. In that case – which arose out of a vendor and purchaser's summons – the defendant-purchasers had refused to complete the purchase of a property on the grounds that a deed on title had not been properly

---

[88] (31 January 1997, unreported), Supreme Court at pp 6–7. The internal management rule (ie the rule in *Turquand's* case) is considered in detail at para **[7.118]**.

[89] The articles were in the same form as the Irish CA 1963, Sch 1, Table A, model reg 115. While reg 115 provides that 'some other person appointed by the directors' may countersign, this is an alternative to the secretary countersigning and not an alternative to a director signing. It should further be noted that in Ireland there is no prohibition on the directors granting a power of attorney even where the articles do not expressly authorise this: *Industrial Development Authority v Moran* [1978] IR 159.

[90] *TCB Ltd v Gray* [1986] 1 All ER 587. For a short note see Fish (1987) Gazette ILSI 287. See para **[7.128]**.

[91] See *Re Sean Hussey, A Bankrupt* (23 September 1987, unreported), High Court at p 6 (Hamilton P).

[92] *Safeera Ltd v Wallis and O'Regan* (12 July 1994, unreported), High Court (Morris J).

executed. Under the deed in question, a company that had been incorporated under the C(C)A 1908, had purported to convey the property to the plaintiff-vendor. The point was that the deed had only been countersigned by one director and the secretary. Although the plaintiff-vendor's solicitor had initially contended that the defendant-purchasers were not entitled to look behind the deed and were to assume that the seal had been properly affixed, eventually, the conveyance had been countersigned by a second director. However, although it was no longer disputed that there was a valid conveyance in existence, the issue remained of relevance in determining interest and costs on the delay in closing the sale. The plaintiff-vendor's counsel contended that since CA 1963 had repealed C(C)A 1908, one must construe CA 1963, s 324 as applying CA 1963, Table A to companies formed under C(C)A 1908. It was also contended that it was appropriate to interpret the Companies Acts as mercantile documents and on that construction and upon the application of Table A of CA 1963 to C(C)A 1908, the execution of the deed 'was at all times valid and properly attested'. This argument did not find favour with Morris J who said:

> 'I reject this argument. In my view the position is clear. *The indenture was not executed in accordance with the articles of association and was not effective to convey the company's interest in the property to the vendors.*
>
> The Land Purchase Act 1925 clarified this matter in the United Kingdom where at s 74 it provided, in favour of a purchaser, that a deed should be deemed to be duly executed by a corporation aggregate if its seal had been affixed thereto in the presence of and attested by a clerk, secretary or other permanent officer or his deputy or a member of the board of directors, council or other governing body of the corporation had been affixed to a deed attested by persons purporting to be persons holding office as aforesaid, the deed should be deemed to have been executed in accordance with the requirements of the section and to have taken effect accordingly. However, I accept as a correct statement of the law the statement at p 531 of the 13th edition of Volume 1 of *Emmett on Title* that "as regards deeds executed before 1926 and also cases not coming within subsection (1) above, it will still be necessary to inspect the articles of association or other authority for the purpose of ascertaining how the seal should have been affixed and to see that it has been so affixed".
>
> Since no section corresponding to s 74 exists in this jurisdiction in my view the onus still remains upon a company to strictly comply with its articles of association in the affixing and attestation of its seal and upon a purchaser investigating title to ensure such compliance.'[93]

In that case it was held that the purchasers had been justified in refusing to complete the contract up to and including the date upon which they were informed that the third signatory to the seal had been added. A matter not considered in that case was where the beneficial or equitable interest in the property lay up to the valid execution of the deed by adding a third signatory. In such a case, notwithstanding that the legal title to the property in question remains vested in the company, where that company has been paid full consideration for the property, it seems clear that the purchaser will be the equitable or beneficial owner. So if, for example, the company that defectively executes a deed subsequently goes into liquidation, the property the subject matter of the deed would be owned beneficially by a purchaser who has paid full consideration and would not be

[93] (12 July 1994, unreported), High Court at pp 3, 4. Emphasis added.

available for distribution as part of the company's assets, being effectively held on trust[94].

(iii) Foreign companies

[7.026] The laws of many foreign jurisdictions do not require companies to execute deeds under seal. So, for example, the laws of England and Wales permit a company to execute a deed, without requiring the affixing of a seal, where two directors or a director and the secretary sign the document and express it to be signed by the company as a deed[95]. Difficulties can arise in Ireland where it is sought to register a transfer of registered land, executed by such a company because the Land Registration Rules 1972, r 77(4) envisage that a company will use a seal[96]; moreover, the presumption in r 58 that deeds expressed to be sealed can be treated as being sealed does not apply to deeds executed by bodies corporate[97]. In practice, this is often dealt with by the Land Registry requiring a certificate from a solicitor that the deed was duly executed in accordance with the laws of the jurisdiction of the body corporate's incorporation.

Delivery of a deed by a company

[7.027] After a company has caused its common seal to be affixed to a deed, the deed may not be effective until such time as it has been delivered. Where a deed is held in escrow the effect is to suspend its delivery, and therefore its effectiveness[98]. 'Deliver' has a technical meaning and a deed may be delivered even though it has not been physically handed over[99]. In the case of deeds executed by individuals, the practice is to recite in the deed that it has been 'signed, sealed and delivered' and it has been held that this is prima facie evidence that the person delivered the deed[100]. Where a company executes a deed, the attestation clause will usually provide 'present when the common seal of X Ltd was affixed hereto'. Although 'delivery' is not expressly mentioned, there is a rebuttable presumption at common law that the affixing of the common seal imports delivery[101]. Wylie[102] has reasoned that, whilst arguable that a company cannot deliver a deed as an

---

94 For property held in trust on a liquidation, see Chapter 27, *The Realisation and Distribution of Assets in a Winding Up*, para **[27.136]** *ff.*

95 Companies Act 1985 (UK), s 36A(4), introduced by the Companies Act 1989, s 130 (UK). See, generally, Barnes and Kershaw, 'Executing Deeds – Signed, Sealed and Delivered?' (1995) Practical Law for Companies 15.

96 Land Registration Rules 1972 (SI 1972/230), r 77(4) provides: 'On a disposition by a company where the seal appears to have been affixed in the presence of an attested by the secretary, deputy secretary or a member of the board of directors of the company, the Registrar shall be entitled to assume that the deed was duly executed by the company.'

97 Land Registration Rules 1972 (SI 1972/230), r 58 provides: 'The Registrar shall be entitled to assume that every deed expressed to be sealed by the parties (other than a corporate body) executing same shall have in fact been so sealed notwithstanding that the deed bears no trace of such sealing at the time of lodgment in the Registry.'

98 See Wylie, *Irish Land Law* (3rd edn, 1997), para [18.125].

99 *Evans v Grey* (1882) 9 LR Ir 539.

100 *Evans v Grey* (1882) 9 LR Ir 539 per Sullivan MR at 546.

101 See Wylie, *Irish Land Law* (3rd edn, 1997), para [18.128] where the cases of *McArdle v Irish Iodine Co* (1864) 15 ICLR 146 and *Willis v Jermin* (1590) Cro Eliz 167 are cited in authority.

102 *Irish Conveyancing Law* (2nd edn, 1996), para [18.128].

escrow[103], there is no reason in principle why a company (or other corporation) cannot deliver a deed in escrow if it so wishes, providing its intention is made clear[104].

Execution by power of attorney

[7.028] Section 15(2) of the Powers of Attorney Act 1996 provides that a power of attorney is not required to be made under seal. This is, however, without prejudice to any requirement in or under any other enactment as to the execution of instruments by bodies corporate: Powers of Attorney Act 1996, s 15(3). Section 40(1) of CA 1963 facilitates a company granting a power to any person to act on the company's behalf outside the State. It provides:

> 'A company may, by writing under its common seal, empower any person, either generally or in respect of any specified matters, as its attorney, to execute deeds on its behalf in any place outside the State.'

Accordingly, an appointment of an attorney under CA 1963, s 40(1) (ie to execute deeds *outside* the State) must be under a company's common seal. When a deed is executed by an attorney pursuant to a valid power of attorney, such a deed is as binding on the company as if it were executed under the company's common seal[105].

[7.029] Any doubts that a company could appoint an attorney to act on its behalf within the State were dispelled by the decision in *Industrial Development Authority v Moran*[106] where it was decided that CA 1963, s 40(1) was intended to clarify the law as to a company's power to act by attorney outside of the State, and that its specificity did not lead to an inference that a company could not act by attorney within the State. Therefore, Kenny J held that 'a company has power to act by attorney to execute deeds within the State'. As to the exercise of the power, he cited *Palmer's Company Precedents*[107]:

> 'Whether, however, in any particular case the directors of a company have power to execute a power of attorney on the company's behalf depends on the articles. The general rule is delegatus non potest delegare. But directors are generally invested with wide general powers, and in virtue of such powers they are usually in a position to grant a power of attorney: otherwise the sanction of a general meeting must be obtained.'

Although Kenny J held that an article with the equivalent wording to the present model reg 80[108] was sufficient to empower the directors to appoint an attorney, where model reg 81 is adopted, a company will have specific authority to appoint an individual or a company to act as its attorney. Model reg 81 provides:

> 'The directors may from time to time and at any time by power of attorney appoint any company, firm or person or body or persons, whether nominated directly or indirectly by the directors, to be the attorney or attorneys of the company for such purposes and with

---

[103] *Gartside v Silkstone* (1882) 21 Ch D 762.

[104] *Lloyd's Bank v Bullock* [1896] 2 Ch 192 and *Beesly v Hallwood Estates Ltd* [1961] Ch 105 cited by Wylie.

[105] CA 1963, s 40(2).

[106] *Industrial Development Authority v Moran* [1978] IR 159 at 164 per Kenny J.

[107] *Palmer's Company Precedents* Vol 1 (17th edn, 1956) at p 950.

[108] See para **[7.109]**, and Chapter 8, *Corporate Governance: Management by Directors*, para **[8.004]** *ff*.

such powers, authorities and discretions (not exceeding those vested in or exercisable by the directors under these regulations) and for such period and subject to such conditions as they may think fit, and any such power of attorney may contain such provisions for the protection of persons dealing with any such attorney as the directors may think fit, and may also authorise any such attorney to delegate all or any of the powers, authorities and discretions vested in him.'

It is curious that this regulation can be interpreted to mean that the directors may appoint an attorney by resolution as opposed to under the seal of the company[109]. It is thought that the creation of a power in favour of a person to act as a company's attorney *within* the State (as opposed to outside of the State) does not require to be by deed under seal. Since no enactment prescribes the manner of execution of a power of attorney by a company for use within the State, and since CA 1963, s 38(1)(a) equates companies with individuals, the Powers of Attorney Act 1996, s 15(3) has no application and so s 15(2) applies, meaning that such a power of attorney is *not* required to be made under the company's common seal. Notwithstanding this, it is thought to be prudent for companies to appoint all donees of powers under their common seals since any such appointment would be susceptible to challenge were the donee, by chance, to execute a deed outside of the State.

[7.030] The execution of instruments by the donee of a power (ie the attorney) has been clarified by the Powers of Attorney Act 1996, s 17. Section 17(1) provides that the donee of a power of attorney may execute any instrument with his own signature and, where sealing is required, his own seal and do any other thing in his own name by the authority of the donor of the power. This section goes on to provide that 'any instrument executed or thing done in that manner shall be as effective as if executed or done by the donee with the signature and seal, or, as the case may be in the name of the donor.' As to the execution of conveyances by a donee for a donor-company, the Powers of Attorney Act 1996, s 17(2) provides:

'A person who is authorised under a power of attorney to convey any estate or interest in property in the name or on behalf of a corporation sole or aggregate may either execute the conveyance as provided in subsection (1) or, as donee of the power, execute the conveyance by signing his or her name as acting in the name or on behalf of the corporation in the presence of at least one witness and, in the case of a deed, by affixing his or her own seal, and such execution takes effect and is valid in like manner as if the corporation had executed the conveyance.'

It has been suggested by a leading conveyancer that whenever a conveyance of real property is executed by an attorney on behalf of a corporation, it is prudent to use the special method of execution provided for in the Powers of Attorney Act 1996, s 17(2) rather than the general method provided for in s 17(1)[110]. The same author suggests that best practice in relation to the execution of deeds by an attorney for a company (or other body corporate) is that:

---

[109] *The Company Law Review Group's First Report* (2000–2001), recommendation 4.8.13, p 70 recommends that CA 1963, Sch 1, Table A, model reg 81 be repealed on the grounds that an attorney can already be appointed under CA 1963, Sch 1, Table A, model reg 80.

[110] See Gallagher, *Powers of Attorney Act 1996* (1998), p 23.

— the deed is prepared in the company's name;
— the attestation clause states that the deed is executed on behalf of the company by the attorney; and
— the attorney executes by writing in his own hand: AB (the donor-company) by its attorney CD (the donee) who then signs his or her own name[111].

[7.031] Where a company (or other body corporate – not being a corporation sole) is appointed as an attorney, whether for an individual or another body corporate, the attorney-company (or donee) may appoint a person for the purpose of executing the deed or other instrument in the name of the donor-company: the Powers of Attorney Act 1996, s 17(3). Moreover, that subsection also provides that where an instrument appears to be executed by a person so appointed then, in favour of a purchaser, the instrument is deemed to have been executed by the person, unless the contrary is shown.

[7.032] Powers of attorney should not be given lightly. Although a company may revoke a power of attorney, protection is afforded to the donee[112] and third parties who deal with the donee[113] where they are unaware that the power has been revoked. Moreover, the Powers of Attorney Act 1996, s 20(1) provides that where a person (whether a natural person or a company) creates a power of attorney which is expressed to be irrevocable and given to secure either a proprietary interest of the donee of the power, or the performance of an obligation owed to the donee, then for the duration of the interest or obligation, the power shall not be revoked by the donor without the consent of the donee or even by the winding up or dissolution of the donor-company[114].

[B] PRE-INCORPORATION CONTRACTS

[7.033] Business opportunities often arise unexpectedly. Sometimes it may not be practical for individuals to form or acquire a company before the exigencies of business require a contract to be signed.

To take an example, a new shopping centre is in the course of construction and the developers are approaching potential tenants. A and B are interested in starting up a business for themselves and agree in principle to take a 35-year lease and their solicitors are furnished with all necessary documentation. The centre is due to open in two months, and it will take that time for A and B to fit out the unit. The developers' solicitors insist that an agreement for lease[115] be signed before allowing A and B to occupy the unit to fit it out. Time is of the essence. A and B do not have a company and, moreover, are not yet decided as to whether they want to take the lease in their own names or that of a company. Tempus fugit. In such circumstances A and B may safely sign the agreement for lease 'for and on behalf of A and B Company Ltd'. If they do form such a company, in due course the company can, by virtue of CA 1963, s 37, take

[111] See Gallagher, *Powers of Attorney Act 1996* (1998), p 23.

[112] Powers of Attorney Act 1996, s 18(1).

[113] Powers of Attorney Act 1996, s 18(2).

[114] See, further, Chapter 22, *Corporate Borrowing: Receivers*, para **[22.014]**.

[115] An agreement for lease is a contract whereby a tenant agrees to take, and a landlord agrees to give, a lease of a premises at a future date.

the lease by resolving to ratify the agreement for lease. However, if A and B decide to take the lease in their own personal names, in the absence of an express agreement to the contrary, they can sue and be sued on foot of the agreement for lease.

Prior to the coming into force of CA 1963, s 37, the implications of signing 'for and on behalf of' an unincorporated company were a legal quagmire. In this section pre-incorporation contracts are considered under the following headings:

1. The old quagmire.
2. Section 37 of CA 1963.
3. Liability of corporate agents.
4. Limitations on the application of CA 1963, s 37.

The old quagmire

[7.034] The problems that existed before 1963 were based on two principles of the law of contract. The first principle was privity of contract: on the facts of our example in para **[7.033]** the company 'A and B Company Ltd' could not sue or be sued in law or in equity[116] on the agreement for lease since it was not party to that contract. The second principle was the rules governing the ratification of contracts in the law of agency. Agency was at first thought to be the solution to the problems raised by the rule on privity of contract, and into this round hole a square peg was hammered. If A and B could be said to be the agents of A and B Company Ltd, could not the company as principal, ratify the agreement for lease contract ? The answer was No. It is a basic principle of ratification that a principal can only ratify an agent's actions where the principal itself could have entered into the contract at that time: A and B Company Ltd could not have entered into the agreement for lease since it did not itself exist at the time the agreement for lease was entered. The principles governing the ratification of contracts were stated by Wright J in *Firth v Staines*[117] to be as follows:

> 'To constitute a valid ratification three conditions must be satisfied: first, the agent whose act is sought to be ratified must have purported to act for the principal; secondly, at the time the act was done the agent must have had a competent principal; and, thirdly at the time of ratification the principal must be legally capable of doing the act himself.'

Although now modified in the context of pre-incorporation contracts, the principles of ratification set out in *Firth v Staines* continue to apply to ratification of contracts generally in Ireland[118].

Section 37 of CA 1963

[7.035] The problematic second condition for ratification of pre-incorporation contracts in *Firth v Stains* was reversed by CA 1963, s 37(1). As far as pre-incorporation contracts are concerned, only the first and third conditions in *Firth v Stains* now remain. Section 37(1) of CA 1963 provides:

116 See Vaughan Williams LJ in *Re English Colonial Produce Co Ltd* [1906] 2 Ch 435.

117 *Firth v Staines* [1897] 2 QB 70 at 75.

118 *Bank of Ireland v Rockfield* [1979] IR 21.

> 'Any contract or other transaction purporting to be entered into by a company prior to its formation or by any person on behalf of the company prior to its formation *may be ratified* by the company after its formation and thereupon the company shall become bound by it and entitled to the benefit thereof as if it had been in existence at the date of such contract or other transaction and had been a party thereto.'[119]

Several points arise for consideration. First, the section is not confined to 'contracts' but applies to 'transactions', which includes conveyances, trusts, covenants, but not (it has been held) grants of planning permission[120]. Secondly, CA 1963, s 37(1) not only applies to transactions entered into by persons 'on behalf of' a company, but also to transactions where an unincorporated company itself purports to enter into the transaction.

[7.036] Post-incorporation ratification of pre-incorporation contracts may be effected by either the resolution of the board of directors or of the members of the company in general meeting. The authority of both the board or the members to ratify will depend upon what the articles of association of a given company provide. Under model reg 80[121] the powers of management of the company are given to the directors. Where this is adopted by a company the appropriate organ to ratify a pre-incorporation contract will be the company's board of directors.

[7.037] In *HKN Invest OY v Incotrade PVT Ltd*[122] Costello J made a number of interesting observations on the question of corporate ratification of pre-incorporation contracts. In the first place he held that ratification may be effected informally:

> 'I do not think that any formal meeting to ratify must be shown to have taken place before [s 37] can be applied. Each case must depend on its own facts, but it seems to me that ratification can in certain circumstances occur informally, for example, in a one man company[123] where after incorporation the controlling shareholder, implements the contract without the benefit of a formal board meeting.'[124]

In that case, Costello J felt that he could not infer ratification of the pre-incorporation contracts from the mere acceptance by the principal shareholder of sums paid by commission. Costello J also held that in appropriate circumstances a company's liquidator could ratify a pre-incorporation contract under CA 1963, s 231(2)(i)[125]. This was appropriate in the instant case and meant, according to Costello J that:

> 'Ratification in this case will mean that as a matter of law the pre-incorporation contracts will have existed from their date of execution – it will not affect the rights of either party arising from the manner in which the contract has or has not been performed since then.'[126]

---

[119] Emphasis added.

[120] See *State (Finglas Industrial Estate Ltd) v Dublin County Council* (17 February 1983, unreported), High Court where a planning permission was held not to be a ratifiable transaction within the meaning of CA 1963, s 37.

[121] See Chapter 8, *Corporate Governance: Management by the Directors*, para **[8.004]**.

[122] *HKN Invest OY v Incotrade PVT Ltd* [1993] 3 IR 152.

[123] A reference to de facto single-member companies.

[124] [1993] 3 IR 152 at 160.

[125] See Chapter 26, *Liquidators*, para **[26.031]** and Chapter 27, *Realisation and Distribution of Assets in a Winding Up*, para **[27.009]**.

[126] [1993] 3 IR 152 at 161

[7.038] The facts in *HKN Invest OY v Incotrade PVT Ltd* were that two German nationals came to Ireland, established a bogus loan brokerage, defrauded a number of Irish and foreign nationals and departed 'this country hurriedly only a few steps ahead of the Irish and German police. They left behind them a number of angry creditors and a cluster of legal problems as to who is now entitled to the benefit of certain assets which they failed to take with them'[127]. The plaintiffs were judgment creditors of both the individuals and their company. The liquidator of the fraudsters' company claimed the assets left behind for the benefit of the company's creditors. The fraudsters incorporated the defendant company but prior to its incorporation had carried on business. Persons who had conducted business with the company and had entered into contracts in respect of loans to be obtained and commission to be paid believed that the fraudsters had been acting on the company's behalf. The main fraud appears to have been that the fraudsters would undertake to procure a loan and would in return obtain a commission. In most cases this commission was paid to the defendant company on foot of contracts entered into before the company had been incorporated. One of the fraudsters opened a personal bank account and caused the commission, payable to the defendant company, to be paid into this account. Sums continued to be paid into the fraudster's personal account even after the company's incorporation and no monies were transferred from the personal account to the company's account. Some of the monies in the personal accounts were used to purchase two Mercedes cars and a Porsche car which were registered in the fraudsters' personal names. The matter before Costello J was: who was beneficially entitled to the remainder of the monies in the personal account?

Having held that the liquidator of the company was entitled to ratify the pre-incorporation contracts, Costello J went on to hold that the company was beneficially entitled to the commission paid to the fraudsters, who held such payments under a constructive trust[128]. Costello J said:

> 'It seems to me therefore that the court should hold that the promoter of a company who received payment on behalf of a company which he is incorporating and pursuant to a pre-incorporation contract which the company is empowered to ratify holds the commission as a constructive trustee for the company.'[129]

Costello J also said that this would remain the case even if the company did not ratify the contract as the monies obtained were held on trust for the company.

Liability of corporate agents

[7.039] Once a contract or other transaction has been validly ratified the company will become bound by its terms and its agents normally will drop out of the picture. However, prior to ratification, CA 1963, s 37(2) provides:

> '...the person or persons who purported to act in the name or on behalf of the company shall in the absence of any express agreement to the contrary be personally bound by the contract or other transaction and entitled to the benefit thereof.'

---

127 [1993] 3 IR 152 at 155.

128 [1993] 3 IR 152 at 162, citing *Hussey v Palmer* [1972] 3 All ER 744 as authority.

129 [1993] 3 IR 152 at 163.

A similar UK provision was considered in the case of *Phonogram Ltd v Lane*[130]. In that case Lord Denning MR construed the word 'purports' (note that s 37 uses the word 'purported') as not implying any question that the outsider should believe that the company was in existence. So, it can be common knowledge to all contracting parties that at the time the contract is entered into there is no company in existence. However, it is important to note that an agent will be liable where the company is ultimately not formed and there is no express agreement that he is not to be liable. It is clear from CA 1963, s 37(2) that the persons who purport to act in the name of an incorporated company are 'entitled to the benefit' of the contract or other transaction (in the absence of agreement to the contrary)[131]. In *Badgerhill Properties Ltd v Cottrell*[132] the obvious point was made that for the transaction in question to be ratifiable, it must purport to be made by the company in question.

[7.040] Before the enactment of CA 1963, s 37(2), the liability of corporate agents prior to the incorporation of the company and ratification of the transaction was uncertain. In *Kelner v Baxter*[133] three agents purported to buy wine 'on behalf of' a company which had not been incorporated. In due course the company was formed, the wine was delivered and drunk and, as if in vino veritas, the company went into liquidation before the wine had been paid for. The three agents were held to be personally liable. In the oft quoted words of Erle CJ:

> 'Where a contract is signed by one who professes to be signing "as agent", but who has no principal existing at the time, and the contract would be altogether inoperative unless binding on the person who signed it, he is bound thereby: and a stranger cannot by a subsequent ratification relieve him from that responsibility.'[134]

While in that case the individual agents sought to avoid liability, the quagmire was such as to render the outcome of every case a matter of speculation. So in *Newborne v Sensolid (Great Britain) Ltd*[135] the hapless Newborne was unsuccessful in seeking to enforce a pre-incorporation contract. His error was not signing 'for and on behalf of' the company. Rather, he signed his own name over the name of the company, thus making it unclear as to whether he signed for himself, as agent for the company to be, or as a future director of the company. As the company could not in law ratify the contract, and the court could not decide in what capacity Newborne had signed, it was held that the

[130] *Phonogram Ltd v Lane* [1981] 3 All ER 182. This interpreted the European Communities Act 1972 (UK), s 9(2), a provision which provided that where a contract purports to be made by a company, or an agent on behalf of the company, prior to incorporation, subject to any agreement to the contrary, the person who purported to act for the company or as agent for it is personally liable.

[131] Although the English equivalent (CA 1985, s 36C(1)) is not so explicit as to persons being entitled to the benefit of a pre-incorporation contract that is not subsequently ratified, it has been held that such is the case: *Braymist Ltd v Wise Finance Company Ltd* [2002] 1 BCLC 415; [2002] EWCA Civ 127.

[132] *Badgerhill Properties Ltd v Cottrell* [1991] BCLC 805 at 813.

[133] *Kelner v Baxter* (1866) LR 2 CP 174.

[134] (1866) LR 2 CP 174 at 183.

[135] *Newborne v Sensolid (Great Britain) Ltd* [1954] 1 QB 45.

whole contract was void for uncertainty. It is to be welcomed that CA 1963, s 37(2) renders such case law obsolete in the context of pre-incorporation contracts entered into by companies to which the Companies Acts 1963–2001 apply[136].

Limitations on the application of CA 1963, s 37

[7.041] The reference in CA 1963, s 37 to a 'company' must be strictly construed. A strict construction of s 37 precludes a foreign company which enters into a contract in Ireland prior to its foreign formation and registration from relying upon its provisions. This is because 'company' is defined by CA 1963, s 2 as meaning 'a company formed and registered under this Act, or an existing company'[137]. Section 37 will not extend to companies outside of the s 2 definition[138]. This was indeed the construction given to the similar English section[139] in *Rover International Ltd v Cannon Film Sales Ltd*[140] where it was held that it had no application to foreign companies. Harman J held

> 'In my judgment, that contention [ie that it was intended the provision should apply to foreign companies since the common law applied the "pre-incorporation" rule to both United Kingdom and foreign companies] does not create a sufficient context to show a "contrary intention" so that s 36(4) would refer to companies wherever incorporated. Parliament has plainly legislated for United Kingdom companies and the subsection is effective in that regard. I do not find any convincing reason for believing that Parliament intended to legislate for foreign companies.'[141]

It may be noted that in England pre-incorporation contracts made by foreign companies, including Irish companies, are now treated as having been validly created if done in the manner prescribed by the law of the country in which the company is incorporated[142].

[7.042] A further limitation arises where a contract purports to be made by a company which was once incorporated, but which is subsequently struck off the register of companies. In *Cotronic (UK) Ltd v Dezonie*[143] it was held that the similar English provision had no application where a company had been dissolved. It has also been held in *Oshkosh B'Gosh Inc v Dan Marbel Inc Ltd*[144] that the similar English section has no application to a situation where a company changes its name, and trades before a new certificate of incorporation on change of name has been issued. It is thought that in both

136 CA 1963, s 37(1) and (2) is applied to certain unregistered companies by CA 1963, s 377. Compare the old 'half-solutions' such as the company re-entering a new contract on the same terms after its incorporation, or entering a conditional contract; both of which exposed people to the vicissitudes of trusting the other contracting party to co-operate. These may still have relevance where a transaction does not fall within CA 1963, s 37: see **[7.041]** *ff*.

137 See Chapter 2, *Formation, Registration and Conversion of Private Companies*, para **[2.054]**.

138 CA 1963, s 37(3) provides specifically that the section is not of general application to all companies, providing that the section should 'not apply to a company incorporated before the operative date'.

139 Companies Act 1985, s 36(4) (UK).

140 *Rover International Ltd v Cannon Film Sales Ltd* [1987] BCLC 540.

141 [1987] BCLC 540 at 543.

142 Foreign Companies (Execution of Documents) Regulations 1994 (SI 1994/950) (UK).

143 *Cotronic (UK) Ltd v Dezonie* [1991] BCLC 721. See 'Editorial' (1991) 12 Co Law 113.

144 *Oshkosh B'Gosh Inc v Dan Marbel Inc Ltd* [1989] BCLC 507.

situations CA 1963, s 37 would be held to have no application to contracts entered into by the companies in such circumstances.

[C] CONTRACTUAL CAPACITY AND ULTRA VIRES

The objects clause and ultra vires

[7.043] Section 6(1)(b) of CA 1963 provides that the memorandum of association must state 'the objects of the company'. Accordingly, every company has to have an objects clause, which states the purposes for which the company was formed and the legitimate activities it can pursue.

When a company purports to enter into a contract which is neither expressly nor impliedly in furtherance of its objects, such a contract is said to be ultra vires, or beyond the company's capacity[145]. Such contracts are void at common law. In *Ashbury Railway Carriage and Iron Co v Riche*[146] a company was incorporated with the object, inter alia, of making and selling railway carriages. Without regard to the company's objects, its directors purported to contract to buy a concession for constructing a railway in Belgium. It was held by the House of Lords that the contract was ultra vires and void and, furthermore, was unratifiable by the shareholders because the contract was a nullity. Today, while ultra vires contracts remain unratifiable[147], CA 1963, s 10 permits the alteration of the objects clause.

[7.044] The rationale of the doctrine of ultra vires was and remains the protection of the company's shareholders and creditors. Indeed, received wisdom is that it is thought to be part and parcel of limited liability that, upon a company being incorporated, its activities should be confined to its stated objects. In fact the doctrine often does more harm than good. As we shall see, the effects of the doctrine have been considerably modified by CA 1963, s 8[148]. Moreover, the Company Law Review Group has recently recommended that the doctrine be disapplied to private companies limited by shares which should be given the same contractual capacity as a natural person[149].

Restraining ultra vires activities

[7.045] So established is the doctrine of ultra vires that there is a statutory right to have recourse to the courts for an injunction to prevent a company from acting ultra vires. Section 8(2) of CA 1963 provides:

> 'The court may, on the application of any member or holder of debentures of a company, restrain such company from doing any act or thing which the company has no power to do.'

It may appear to be somewhat anomalous to confine locus standi to members and debenture holders. Members – Yes; debenture holders – Yes, but what about other

---

145 See generally MacCann, 'The Capacity of a Company' (1992) ILT 79 and 151.

146 *Ashbury Railway Carriage and Iron Co v Riche* (1875) LR 7 HLC 653.

147 See *Northern Bank Finance Corporation Ltd v Quinn and Achates Investment Company* [1979] ILRM 221.

148 See para **[7.077]**.

149 See para **[7.093]**.

creditors? On the one hand one may think that this ought to be extended to all creditors; on the other hand, however, one would not wish the legislature to afford a right of recourse to the courts of nominal unsecured creditors, with a frivolous or vexatious claim against a company. The anachronism is, however, found in the reference to 'debenture holders' and it might be more appropriate to refer to 'secured and preferential creditors'. In exercising its discretion to make an order under this section the courts will apply the same principles as in an application for any interlocutory injunction[150]. In *McGilligan and Bowen v O'Grady*[151] O'Donovan J, in the High Court, had granted an injunction against the third defendant. The third defendant was a company and it was restrained from 'acting ultra vires the objects set forth in its memorandum of association and, in particular, from engaging in activities that did not come within those objects'[152]. The company had wished to become involved in a manufacturing process and although such was not expressly permitted by its objects clauses, there was power to 'do all such other things as are incidental or conducive to the attainment of the above objects or any of them' which it was thought might permit the company to engage in manufacturing. At a meeting of the members to amend the objects clause the requisite qualified majority to pass a special resolution was not forthcoming and it was against this background that O'Donovan J restrained the company from acting ultra vires. That part[153] of the order was discharged on appeal to the Supreme Court. Keane J held that he was not satisfied that the balance of convenience required the company to be restrained from becoming involved in a manufacturing process and that irreparable damage could be caused to the company.

Contractual capacity

[7.046] In this section the following issues relating to corporate capacity to contract are considered:

- (a) Judicial construction of the objects clause.
- (b) Classifying corporate capacity.
- (c) Gratuitous dispositions of company property.
- (d) Companies Act 1963, s 8.
- (e) European Communities (Companies) Regulations 1973, reg 6.
- (f) Corporate enforcement of ultra vires contracts.
- (g) Recovery of money given by a company ultra vires.
- (h) Reform of the doctrine of ultra vires.

(a) Judicial construction of the objects clause

[7.047] In view of the drastic effects which can result from a contract being ultra vires[154], draughtsmen submit companies for registration with a veritable plethora of 'so-called'

---

150 As to which see, Courtney, *Mareva Injunctions and Related Interlocutory Orders* (1998), para [5.03]–[5.11].

151 *McGilligan and Bowen v O'Grady* [1999] 1 IR 346, [1999] 1 ILRM 303.

152 [1999] 1 IR 346 at 349.

153 See further Chapter 19, *Shareholders' Remedies*, para **[19.062]**.

154 See Shapira, 'Ultra Vires Redux' (1984) LQR 468.

objects. The hope is that whatever activity the company might possibly engage in will be intra vires. Hence, the 'admirable brevity' of the objects clause seen in the model objects clause in CA 1963, Sch 1, Table A bears no relation to the realities of life[155]. In the early days, the judiciary was not impressed by the multiplicity of so-called objects with which companies were formed. It was felt that such a practice was contrary to the spirit of the Companies Acts, since it defeated the purpose of requiring a company to set out, up-front, what it was formed to do. Thus, Lord Wrenbury in *Cotman v Brougham*[156] spoke of the 'pernicious practice', namely that of '...registering memoranda of association which, under the clause relating to objects contained paragraph after paragraph not specifying or delimiting the proposed trade or purpose...'.

What follows is an analysis of the 'cat and mouse' game played by the judiciary and the draughtsmen. The following are considered:

(i) The main objects rule.

(ii) The independent objects clause.

(iii) The 'Bell Houses' clause.

(i) The main objects rule

[7.048] The judiciary could not declare elongated objects clauses to be void on account of the statutory predecessors of Companies (Amendment) Act 1983, s 5 ('C(A)A 1983'). Like s 5, these provided that a company's certificate of incorporation shall be conclusive evidence that '...all the requirements of the Companies Acts in respect of registration and of matters precedent and incidental thereto have been complied with...'.[157]

Although the Registrar of Companies might try to refuse to register a company which contains an elongated objects clause, thus far this has not been done, presumably because the registrar's right to do so is far from clear. As for the judiciary, as Lord Finlay LC said in *Cotman v Brougham*[158] that 'all the courts can do is construe the memorandum as it stands'.

[7.049] Judicial construction has been, however, inventive and of devastating effect. The particular device used by the courts to defend what they perceived to be the legislative intention was the ejusdem generis rule of interpretation, which says that, when particular words are followed by general words, the general words are limited so as to have the same import implicit in the particular words. Accordingly, where the perceived 'main objects' of a company were followed by wider powers, the latter would be construed as being capable only of exercise in furtherance of the 'main objects'. This is the essence of the main objects or 'substratum rule'. The rule was described in *Anglo-Overseas Agencies Ltd v Green*[159] as follows:

---

155 See Ussher, *Company Law in Ireland* (1986), p 112.

156 *Cotman v Brougham* [1918] AC 514, [1918–19] All ER Rep 265.

157 On the conclusiveness of the certificate of incorporation see Chapter 4, *Incorporation and its Consequences*, para **[4.004]**.

158 *Cotman v Brougham* [1918-19] All ER 265 at 267.

159 *Anglo-Overseas Agencies Ltd v Green* [1961] 1 QB 1, [1960] All ER 244.

> '...where the memorandum of association expresses the object of the company in a series of paragraphs, and one paragraph, or the first two or three paragraphs, appear to embody the "main object" of the company, all the other paragraphs are treated as merely ancillary to the "main object", and as limited or controlled thereby.'

Not only will a contract which is not in furtherance of the main objects be ultra vires, but so also might a company which does not pursue its main objects be wound up for failure of substratum: *Re German Date Coffee Co Ltd*[160]. But the draughtsmen were not to be outdone.

(ii) The independent objects clause

[7.050] The draughtsmen rallied by devising so-called independent objects clauses which oust the main objects rule. A typical independent objects clause provides:

> 'It is hereby expressly declared that each sub-clause of this clause shall be construed independently of the other sub-clauses hereof, and that none of the objects mentioned in any sub-clause shall be deemed to be merely subsidiary to the objects mentioned in any other sub-clause.'

The validity of such a clause was upheld by the House of Lords in *Cotman v Brougham*[161], on the basis that the Registrar of Companies had issued the company (that had been registered with such an objects clause) with a certificate of incorporation which was conclusive evidence as to the validity of the contents of the memorandum of association[162]. In that case the objects clause contained 35 sub-clauses which, if valid, would have permitted the company to pursue almost any object. Were it not for the insertion of an independent objects clause, the main object would have been found to be the development of rubber plantations. However the twelfth sub-clause permitted the buying of stocks or shares in any company. The thirtieth sub-clause was an independent objects clause which said that all sub-clauses should be construed as substantive clauses. The company underwrote and had allotted to it shares in an oil company. Problems arose when the oil company was wound up and the company was placed on the list of contributories. In spite of protests to the contrary from both sides of the bench, it was held that the contract in respect of the shares was intra vires the company. Almost begrudgingly, Lord Wrenbury held:

> 'The language of c 13(30) is such that I cannot say that such a transaction was ultra vires because it was not ancillary to or connected with or in furtherance of something which I find elsewhere in the company's memorandum to have been "its business".'

An independent objects clause is found in the objects clause of most companies formed today.

---

160 *Re German Date Coffee Co Ltd* [1882] 20 Ch 169, [1881-85] All ER 372. Here a company acquired a Swedish patent for manufacturing a substitute for coffee from dates. The objects expressly referred to a German patent and Lindley LJ said (at 375): '...the real object of this company...was to manufacture a substitute for coffee in Germany under a patent which is valid according to German law. All the rest is subordinate to that main object and that is what the people subscribe their money for...'.

161 *Cotman v Brougham* [1918] AC 514.

162 [1918–19] All ER 265 at 267, per Lord Finlay LC.

(iii) The 'Bell Houses' clause

[7.051] A 'Bell Houses clause' – so called after a case of that name – gives a company the capacity to pursue any business which the directors believe would be advantageous to the company[163]. Accordingly, the company's capacity to pursue a particular business will be determined by the directors' subjective discretion. An example is:

> 'To carry on any other trade or business which can, in the opinion of the board of directors, be advantageously carried on by the company in connection with or as ancillary to any of the above businesses or the general business of the company, or further any of its objects.'

In *Bell Houses Ltd v City Wall Properties Ltd*[164] the principal business set out in the company's memorandum was the development of housing estates. However, the objects clause contained a clause which empowered the directors to pursue any business they considered advantageous to the company. The objects clause also contained an independent objects clause similar to that in the *Cotman* case. The company contracted to introduce a financier to another company for a procuration fee. The Court of Appeal held that in view of the clause used, the transaction was intra vires. Danckwerts LJ said that the impact of the clause was '...to make the bona fide opinion of the directors sufficient to decide whether an activity of the plaintiff company is intra vires.'[165]

When this clause is coupled with an independent objects clause, the potential ambit of the doctrine of ultra vires is considerably reduced: almost any object can validly be pursued.

(b) Classifying corporate capacity

[7.052] Companies' objects clauses frequently contain a multiplicity of sub-clauses. The courts have held that not all of these sub-clauses may actually be substantive objects which the company can pursue, independently. Some sub-clauses may be found to be *mere ancillary powers* which are incapable of being exercised otherwise than in furtherance of the company's substantive objects. Moreover, it may be found that in addition to these express clauses the company will have implied powers, ancillary to the company's substantive objects. The labelling of the various combinations is threefold:

(i) Substantive objects.

(ii) Express ancillary powers.

(iii) Implied ancillary powers.

(i) Substantive objects or ancillary powers?

[7.053] Most companies formed today have in excess of 20 sub-clauses within their objects clause. Many are merely ancillary powers, which a company would be implied to have eg the power to borrow, provide security in respect of borrowings, etc. The effects of the main objects rule and the use by draughtsmen of the independent objects clause

---

[163] See Wedderburn, (1966) MLR 191 and Pollock, (1966) CLJ 174.

[164] *Bell Houses Ltd v City Wall Properties Ltd* [1966] 2 All ER 674.

[165] *Bell Houses Ltd v City Wall Properties Ltd* [1966] 2 All ER 674.

have already been considered[166]. How do these bear on the question of whether or not something is an object or a power?

Whether a particular sub-clause is properly a substantive object or an ancillary power will, in every case, be a matter of construction for the courts. It has been held in *Rolled Steel Products (Holdings) Ltd v British Steel Corporation*[167] that some sub-clauses are incapable of constituting a substantive object. Where this is found to be the case, the sub-clause in question must be construed as being an express ancillary power. In the *Rolled Steel* case Slade LJ said:

> '...the question whether [the sub-clause which inter alia allowed the company to give guarantees] of RSP's memorandum contains a separate independent object of the company is purely one of construction of that memorandum. The decision of the House of Lords in *Cotman v Brougham* [1918] AC 514, [1918–19] All ER 265 requires that, in answering it, full force must be given, so far as possible, to the provision at the end of [the objects clause] which directs that each sub-clause shall be construed independently of the other sub-clauses. I accept counsel's submission...that [the sub-clause which inter alia allowed the company to give guarantees] must be treated as containing a substantive object unless either (i) the subject matter of this sub-paragraph is by its nature incapable of constituting a substantive object (as was the power to borrow in *Re Introductions*...), or (ii) the wording of the memorandum shows expressly or by implication that the sub-clause was intended merely to constitute an ancillary power only...'.[168]

Slade LJ, while accepting that a company could have as its main object the giving of guarantees, held that on the true construction of the objects clause in that case, the giving of guarantees was but an ancillary power and not a substantive object[169].

[7.054] The distinction between 'true objects' and 'mere powers' has been made in many cases. In *Re Horsley & Weight Ltd*[170] Buckley LJ said:

> 'It has now long been a commercial practice to set out in memoranda of association, a great number and variety of "objects", so called, some of which (for example, to borrow money, to promote the company's interests by advertising its products or services or to do acts or things conducive or incidental to the company's objects) are by their very nature incapable of standing as independent objects which can be pursued in isolation as the sole activity of the company. Such "objects" must, by reason of their very nature, be interpreted merely as powers incidental to the true objects of the company and must be so treated notwithstanding the presence of a separate objects clause...Where there is no separate objects clause, some of the express "objects" may upon construction fall to be treated as no more than powers which are ancillary to the dominant or main objects of the company.'[171]

---

166 See para **[7.048]** and **[7.050]**.

167 *Rolled Steel Products (Holdings) Ltd v British Steel Corporation* [1985] 3 All ER 52.

168 [1985] 3 All ER 52 at 81.

169 [1985] 3 All ER 52, where Slade LJ said: 'The references in [the sub-clauses] to the giving of credit and to customers of and persons having dealings with the company, make it additionally clear that the sub-clause in its context was intended to comprise merely a series of ancillary powers.'

170 *Re Horsley & Weight Ltd* [1982] 3 All ER 1045. See generally, (1983) MLR 204.

171 [1982] 3 All ER 1045 at 1050.

It seems clear that not even the presence of a separate or independent objects clause can 'save' what purports to be an object from being construed as a power if in fact that is what it is. Often, the giving of guarantees will be the action under scrutiny[172]. This may happen where Company A gives a guarantee to a bank in respect of money loaned to Company B. Unless the companies are members of a group of companies, it might be argued that Company A acted ultra vires in that it only had power to give guarantees in furtherance of its own objects. If, on construction of its objects clause the giving of guarantees is found to be only an ancillary power the next question to be asked is, what is the significance of this distinction?

(ii) Express ancillary powers: exercise conditional on the existence of commercial benefit

[7.055] While express ancillary powers can be subject to express limitations which go to the very root of the power itself, the most common express limitation is that they are expressly said to be exercisable only 'as may seem expedient for the furtherance of the objects of the company'[173] ie that there is commercial benefit to the company. However, even if they are not so qualified, such limiting conditions will always be implied[174]. Hence, express ancillary powers are always conditional and the board of directors must ensure that they are only exercised in furtherance of the objects of the company.

[7.056] Difficulties can arise in respect of groups of companies. One question that has arisen is whether there is commercial benefit to one member of the group where it enters into a guarantee for the benefit of another member of the group?[175] An example of where the power to guarantee in such circumstances was found to be exercised in furtherance of the objects of a company is *Re PMPA Garage (Longmile) Ltd*[176]. In that case a number of members in a group of companies gave guarantees for the benefit of another company, the Private Motorists Provident Society Ltd ('PMPS'), in return for a loan to only some of them. While recognising that the giving of guarantees can sometimes be a substantive object, it was stated that in this case it could not be so described, and was merely an ancillary power of all the companies[177]. The questions which arose were, first, could a guarantee in respect of very substantial sums advanced to associate companies benefit the guarantor companies, and, secondly, was there an abuse by the directors of their powers in giving guarantees without ostensibly receiving consideration? Murphy J said that the purpose of the guarantees was to secure payment to the PMPS by all members of the group of the amounts loaned by the PMPS, although he admitted that it was not easy to see why companies which did not get a loan from the PMPS gave guarantees. For

---

[172] On inter-company guarantees see generally, Andrews and Millett, *Law of Guarantees* (1992), pp 138–139.

[173] Per Slade LJ in *Rolled Steel Products* [1985] 3 All ER 52.

[174] [1985] 3 All ER 52 at 84a, where Slade LJ referred to *Re Introductions Ltd* [1969] 1 All ER 887 and *Re David Payne & Co Ltd* [1904] 2 Ch 608 at 612.

[175] See, generally, Price, 'Intra-Group Guarantees – Who Benefits?' (1997) Practical Law for Companies 15.

[176] *Re PMPA Garage (Longmile) Ltd* [1992] ILRM 337.

[177] [1992] ILRM 337 at 340, where Murphy J cited with approval *Rolled Steel Products (Holdings) Ltd v British Steel Corporation* [1985] 3 All ER 52.

example, there was no record of the directors of one of the companies having directed their minds to whether or not the execution of the guarantee could in some way further the business interests of that company or in any way resound to its benefit. However, this was no surprise to the judge who recognised the automatic nature of such decision making: in practice such resolutions would be prepared in advance by a company's solicitors. Murphy J further recognised that while directors of subsidiary companies cannot be excused from discharging their duties to the company of which they are directors:

> '...the analysis which the director or directors make of routine problems and the nature of the record made of the ultimate decisions must vary with the circumstances of particular cases and the dearth of records and even the failure of the directors to address problems which others can see clearly with the benefit of hindsight cannot be necessarily condemned as an abuse of fiduciary duty. It is clear...that those having control of the business interests of the companies constituting the group discussed the business problems on a day to day basis and fitted their decisions into the complex corporate structure that existed...there was considerable co-operation between the garage companies. One company which had surplus funds might transfer it to another in need. One company would, as one might expect, transfer potential customers to another. But as to the PMPS advances and the guarantees therefor [it was] simply explained that the PMPS required, as the auditors advised, further security for the advances made to the individual members of the group and this was given on the basis that it was "one for all and all for one"...There were advantages and disadvantages of acting in the group. "You guaranteed others and others guaranteed you".'[178]

Having thus examined the circumstances of this particular case, Murphy J concluded that:

> 'In the nature of things companies associated with each other as parent and subsidiary or through common shareholders or who share common management and common titles or logos can not safely ignore the problems of each other. Even the most independently minded director of any such related company seeking to advance the interests of a particular company would necessarily recognise that he should and perhaps must protect the interests of the group as a whole or else take steps to secure that the particular company disassociates itself from the group.
>
> In the circumstances of the present case it seems to me that whilst the directors of the Debtor Companies [the guarantors] may have accepted the need to give the guarantee without giving serious consideration to the benefits or burdens which could arise therefrom that their almost intuitive reaction to the request from the auditors for such a guarantee and its renewal each year was justifiable as a matter of law although as a matter of commerce it ultimately proved a disaster for the Debtor Companies.'

Accordingly, Murphy J held that the act of giving guarantees by certain companies in a group in respect of loans to other members of the group was intra vires the guarantor companies. It should be noted, however, that Murphy J also found that the purported

[178] [1992] ILRM 337 at 342, 343.

lending by the PMPS to different companies within the group was ultra vires the PMPS[179].

[7.057] Establishing commercial benefit is more difficult when a guarantee is given to a person other than a company that is part of the same group, particularly where the person who benefits from the guarantee is a director or person connected with a director of the guarantor company. Although it is now possible for a company to enter into a guarantee in such circumstances without breaching the Companies Act 1990, s 31 ('CA 1990'), by following the validation procedure provided for in CA 1990, s 34, it is necessary to establish and state, inter alia, 'the benefit which will accrue to the company directly or indirectly from entering into the guarantee or providing the security'.[180]

[7.058] The significance of express or implied conditions attaching to an express ancillary power has given rise to great confusion. Until relatively recently, it was thought that the exercise of an express ancillary power for a purpose not in furtherance of a company's main objects was ultra vires the capacity of the company[181]. Implicit in this old school of thought is the idea that the doctrine of constructive notice should be extended, and the outsider deemed to have notice not only of the company's objects clause but also of the existence of a condition attached to the exercise of a power and to whether or not the condition was fulfilled. This analysis, it is submitted, imposes too onerous a burden on an outsider dealing with the company, who ought only to suffer where he has notice of the directors' misfeasance. Since a wrongful exercise of any express ancillary power will result from the directors' abuse of their powers, it is thought that it is more appropriate to apply the legal principles relating to the authority of corporate agents to the resulting legal problem[182]. If the outsider can be saved by the rule in *Turquand*'s case, or by European Communities (Companies) Regulations 1973[183], reg 6, then the outsider ought to be able to enforce the transaction. If he cannot be saved, the transaction should fall as being a case where the directors abused their delegated powers, to the knowledge of the outsider.

[7.059] The new school of thought holds that the exercise of an express power contrary to the express or implied conditions attached to its exercise will always be intra vires the capacity of the company. Central to this analysis is the idea that an outsider is entitled to assume that the directors of a company will only exercise their powers, and those of the company, in furtherance of the company's objects. However, whilst the exercise of the power will not be ultra vires, the transaction at the centre of a wrongful exercise of that power will be unenforceable by an outsider where he is aware of the abuse by the

---

179 The fact that the PMPS was registered under the Industrial and Provident Societies Act 1893 was central to Murphy J's finding that the lending was ultra vires: the PMPS's power to lend was limited to members and 'on receiving proper security therefor'. See para **[7.065]**.

180 CA 1990, s 34(3)(e), as inserted by CLEA 2001, s 78. See Chapter 11, *Statutory Regulation of Transactions Involving Directors and their Companies*, para **[11.081]** *ff.*

181 See generally, *Re Introductions Ltd* [1968] 2 All ER 1221; *Thomas Williamson Ltd v Bailieborough Co-Operative Agricultural Society Ltd* (31 July 1986, unreported), High Court per Costello J.

182 See para **[7.096]** *ff.*

183 SI 1973/163.

directors of their powers and their lack of authority to authorise such a transaction[184]. A power is, of itself, neutral. It can be put to either ultra or intra vires purposes. Since it is the function of the directors to channel the exercise of a power, a strong case can be made that where the exercise of a power is not in furtherance of the company's main objects, the validity of the exercise of that power should be determined by reference to the legal principles applicable to the authority of corporate agents.

(I) The old school of thought on express powers

[7.060] The old school may be said to have thought that where the board of directors did not exercise express powers in furtherance of the objects of the company (through either mala fide intentions or simple non-advertence to the question) such an exercise was ultra vires. So in *Thomas Williamson Ltd v Bailieborough Co-Operative Agricultural Society Ltd*[185] it was contended that the guarantee given by the defendant co-operative was invalid. It was this guarantee which the receiver of the plaintiff-company wished to enforce. The co-operative's power to guarantee was expressly conditional, being limited to '...where the giving of such guarantee is in the opinion of the Board of Directors directly or indirectly conducive or incidental to the business or trade of the Society.' Costello J interpreted this to mean that:

> 'The Society could, therefore, only enter into certain types of guarantees, namely, those in respect of which the opinion referred to in [the rules] has been expressed by the board of directors; any other type of guarantee would be ultra vires the Society's powers.'[186]

In *Re Introductions Ltd*[187] a similar view was taken. In that case, the company was incorporated for the purpose of offering tourist services to visitors to Britain from 1951–1953 and for providing accommodation to tourists. From then until 1958 its business was the provision of deckchairs and amusement machines for tourists. Late in 1958, 398 of its 400 shares changed hands, as did the composition of the board of directors. In 1960, the only business pursued was pig-breeding. However, the company needed finance and borrowed money from the National Provincial Bank Ltd, which was actually aware of both the objects clause and the actual business pursued. Contrary to the old adage of 'where there's muck, there's luck', the pig-breeding business failed and the company was placed in liquidation. At trial, the issue arose as to whether or not the borrowing was ultra vires the company's capacity.

It was clear that the pig-breeding business was prima facie ultra vires, but the bank sought to rely on one of the sub-clauses in the company's objects clause, which provided, inter alia, that the company could borrow money. It argued that when read in conjunction with the independent objects clause, it meant that any act of borrowing was per se intra vires. At trial, Buckley J construed the sub-clause as being an ancillary power and not a substantive object, and said '...the moneys that were borrowed from the bank were not

184 See *Rolled Steel Products (Holdings) Ltd v British Steel Corp* [1985] 3 All ER 52.

185 *Thomas Williamson Ltd v Bailieborough Co-Operative Agricultural Society Ltd* (31 July 1986, unreported), High Court, per Costello J.

186 (31 July 1986, unreported), High Court at p 13.

187 *Re Introductions Ltd* [1968] 2 All ER 1221.

borrowed for legitimate purposes of the company; they were borrowed for ultra vires activities.'

This case and others seemed to support the belief that where such ancillary powers are exercised in circumstances other than in pursuit of the company's substantive objects, such an exercise was ultra vires and void.

(II) The new school of thought on express powers

[7.061] More recent case law views the foregoing analysis as based on a grave misunderstanding of the relationship between actions which are truly ultra vires a company's capacity and those which are an abuse of the directors' powers. Some current judicial thinking views any exercise of express ancillary powers as being intra vires[188]. A contract resulting from an exercise of an express ancillary power can founder if the directors exercise it in circumstances which are not in furtherance of that company's objects. Though not ultra vires the capacity of the company, to exercise a power otherwise than in furtherance of the company's objects is an abuse of the directors' powers, since directors must always act bona fide and in the interests of the company. If an outsider acts in good faith and is unaware of the internal irregularity, the contract will be enforceable against the company[189]. On the other hand, if outsiders do not act in good faith and/or are aware of the abuse of the directors' powers[190] the company will not be estopped from denying the contract because the outsider had notice of the irregularity. This is the principle of law which led to the unfortunate use of the phrase, 'ultra vires the powers of the directors'. Using ultra vires in this context is inaccurate and ought to be laid to rest. 'Ultra vires' refers only to actual corporate contractual capacity and ought never be used in the context of an abuse of directors' powers.

[7.062] The switch in judicial thinking is clearest in the English Court of Appeal decision in *Rolled Steel Products (Holdings) Ltd v British Steel Corp*[191]. In that case, two directors of the plaintiff-company caused the company to give a guarantee with a supporting charge in respect of the debts of another company owned by one of its directors. The plaintiff-company had an express power to guarantee, namely:

> '...to lend and advance money or give credit to such persons, firms or companies and on such terms as may seem expedient, and in particular to customers of and others having dealings with the company, and to give guarantees or become security for any such persons, firms or companies.'

There was also an independent objects clause in the memorandum of association. As was seen above[192], Slade LJ construed the foregoing clause as being an ancillary power

---

[188] *Rolled Steel Products (Holdings) Ltd v British Steel Corp* [1985] 3 All ER 52.

[189] Under the rule in *Turquand*'s case, and/or SI 1973/163, reg 6. While the memorandum and articles of association are public documents of which the outsider is deemed to have notice, they: '...would find, not a prohibition from [for example] borrowing, but a permission to do so on certain conditions', per Jervis CJ in *Royal British Bank v Turquand* (1856) 6 E & B 327, [1843–60] All ER Rep 435.

[190] As the bank was in *Re Introductions Ltd*. See also *Re MJ Cummins Ltd; Barton v Bank of Ireland* [1939] IR 60.

[191] *Rolled Steel Products (Holdings) Ltd v British Steel Corp* [1985] 3 All ER 52, [1986] 1 Ch 246.

[192] At para **[7.053]**.

to, inter alia, give guarantees. The qualifying words 'as may seem expedient', were interpreted as meaning 'as may seem expedient for the furtherance of the objects of the company[193]. Here the crucial point emerges. The court held that the giving of guarantees per se was intra vires the capacity of the plaintiff-company. Whether or not the exercise of the power to guarantee was in furtherance of the objects of the company did not affect the company's capacity to guarantee. Slade LJ was at pains to distinguish the use of the phrase ultra vires and clearly discouraged its usage in circumstances other than in respect of corporate capacity.

Of assistance to Slade LJ was the judgment of Buckley J in *Re David Payne & Co Ltd, Young v David Payne & Co Ltd*[194]. In that case the company had an express power to borrow, and did so, issuing a debenture to secure the loan. Later, the company's liquidator sought to have the debenture declared ultra vires because there was evidence that, contrary to the express condition attached to the power, the borrowing was not for the purposes of the company's business. While Buckley J did say 'a corporation cannot do anything except for the purposes of its business, borrowing or anything else; everything else is beyond its power, and is ultra vires', Slade LJ interpreted[195] this as the use of the phrase 'ultra vires' in the sense of 'ultra vires the directors' powers' or abuse of their powers. Slade LJ was fortified in his interpretation by the conclusion of Buckley J that:

> 'If this borrowing was made...for a purpose illegitimate so far as the borrowing company was concerned, that may very well be a matter on which rights may arise between the shareholders and directors of that company. It may have been a wrongful act on the part of the directors. But I do not think that a person who lends to the company is by any words such as these required to investigate whether the money borrowed was for a proper purpose or an improper purpose. The borrowing being effected, and the money passing to the company, the subsequent application of the money is a matter in which the directors may have acted wrongly; but this does not affect the principal act, which is the borrowing of the money.'

The decision in *Re Introductions Ltd* was distinguished likewise by Slade LJ who said that what was meant there was that the borrowing was ultra vires the directors' powers, in that it was an abuse of their powers, but was not ultra vires the capacity of the company.

[7.063] Where an outsider enters into a transaction with a company knowing that the directors are wrongfully exercising their powers, the transaction will not be enforceable by him. Slade LJ observed:

> 'The directors of the borrowing company in fact had no authority from the company to take the loan and grant the debenture because these transactions were not effected for the purposes of the company. Nevertheless as a general rule, a company incorporated under the Companies Acts holds out its directors as having the ostensible authority to do on its behalf anything which its memorandum of association, expressly or by implication, gives the company the capacity to do. In *Re David Payne & Co Ltd* the company's memorandum

---

193 *Rolled Steel Products (Holdings) Ltd v British Steel Corp* [1985] 3 All ER 52 at 81f.

194 *Re David Payne & Co Ltd, Young v David Payne & Co Ltd* [1904] 2 Ch 608.

195 [1985] 3 All ER 52 at 82h.

gave it the capacity to borrow. As a matter of construction of the company's memorandum, the court was not prepared to construe the words "for the purposes of the company's business" as limiting its corporate capacity, but construed them simply as limiting the authority of the directors. In the absence of notice to the contrary, the lenders would thus have to assume, on the authority of the principle in [*Turquand*'s case] and on more general principles of the law of agency, that the directors of the borrowing company were acting properly and regularly in the internal management of its affairs and were borrowing for the purposes of the company's business...However, a party dealing with a company cannot rely on the ostensible authority of its directors to enter into a particular transaction, if he knows they in fact have no such authority because it is being entered into for improper purposes. Neither the rule in *Turquand*'s case nor the more general principles of the law of agency will avail him in such circumstances...The various passages in the judgments in both courts in the *David Payne* case which refer to the extent of the lenders obligations (if any) to inquire as to the purposes for which the loan is to be used, in my opinion, are not directed at all to the corporate capacity of the borrowing company: they are directed to the right of the lender to rely on the ostensible authority of the borrower's directors.'[196]

That the validity of such contracts is to be governed by the law of agency was earlier stated in *Charterbridge Corp Ltd v Lloyds Bank Ltd*[197]. This proposition received the obiter dictum support of Johnston J in *Re MJ Cummins Ltd: Barton v Bank of Ireland*[198]. There, a Mr Cummins obtained a loan from the defendant-bank to enable him to purchase the shares in a company which subsequently changed its name to MJ Cummins Ltd. That company then borrowed from the defendant-bank and used the proceeds of the loan to discharge the indebtedness of Cummins to the bank on foot of the first loan. The loan by the company was ultra vires its objects clause. In fact the company exercised 'its general borrowing powers', an ancillary power of the company which was subject to the implied condition that any exercise of this power had to be in furtherance of its objects clause. Johnston J held that:

'This exercise by the company of its borrowing powers was...clearly an act ultra vires the powers of the company, and it is contended on behalf of the liquidator that the bank, at the time when they advanced this sum were well aware that the company was exceeding its powers and that no valid debt was thereby incurred which...can be relied upon by the bank.

Now, there are certain propositions of the law which have been advanced on behalf of the bank with which I entirely agree. For instance, it is the law that while a proposed lender in

---

196 [1985] 3 All ER 52 at 83e–j.

197 *Charterbridge Corp Ltd v Lloyds Bank Ltd* [1969] 2 All ER 1185 at 1189. Pennycuick J said:

'The memorandum of a company sets out its objects and proclaims them to persons dealing with the company and it would be contrary to the whole function of a memorandum that objects unequivocally set out in it should be subject to some implied limitation by reference to the state of mind of the parties concerned. Where directors misapply the assets of their company, that may give rise to a claim based on breach of duty. Again a claim may arise against the other party to the transaction, if he has notice that the transaction was effected in breach of duty. Further, in a proper case, the company concerned may be entitled to have the transaction set aside. But all that results from the ordinary law of agency and has not of itself anything to do with the corporate powers of the company.'

198 *Re MJ Cummins Ltd: Barton v Bank of Ireland* [1939] IR 60.

his dealings with a public company must be presumed to have notice of the provisions of its memorandum and articles of association, he is not called upon in the case of a company which has a general power of borrowing, to make any inquiries as to the purpose of the loan in order to make sure that that purpose is within the powers of the company. That proposition is very conveniently illustrated in the case of In *Re David Payne & Co Ltd*, where it was further decided that knowledge on the part of the lender that the money was intended to be misapplied will avoid the loan...

The main question in the case, therefore, is whether the bank had knowledge of the wrongful purpose for which this money was being raised: and, having analysed all the circumstances connected with the loan, I am satisfied that not only had the bank the fullest knowledge of that purpose, but the local Agent of the bank...was the person who arranged the ingenious plan by which the loan was carried through...'[199]

The foregoing analysis seems firmly predicated upon the law of agency, since the enforceability of the transaction turned on whether the bank had knowledge of the wrongful purpose of the loan, ie the abuse by the directors of their powers.

[7.064] The distinction between ultra vires a company's capacity and an abuse of the directors' powers has been accepted by Blayney J in *Parkes & Sons Ltd v Hong Kong and Shanghai Banking Corporation*[200]. In that case a Mr Collier, owner of a company called Walsh Kavanagh & Company Ltd, acquired control of the plaintiff-company ('Parkes'). Later, the stock and premises of Parkes were destroyed by fire, and the business of Parkes was transferred to the premises of Walsh & Kavanagh & Company Ltd ('Walsh'). Walsh owed the defendant-bank £200,000 and Collier guaranteed the indebtedness of the company up to this sum. Shortly after, the company ceased trading and its entire stock was bought by Parkes. The defendant-bank pressed for repayment of the money owed, and eventually, Parkes, inter alia, gave a guarantee to the defendant-bank, supported by a mortgage over its property. At this point in time, both companies were insolvent. Eventually, Parkes was wound up and, inter alia, Hamilton P ordered that the question of whether or not the guarantee and mortgage was ultra vires Parkes should be tried in liquidation proceedings.

Blayney J held that the guarantee and mortgage were not ultra vires Parkes simply because the company was insolvent at the time they were made. In respect of the case before him, he said 'The court is not being asked to consider whether Mr. Collier, as director of [Parkes], was in breach of duty, but whether the guarantee and mortgage were ultra vires [Parkes].'[201] Having said that, simply because a company is insolvent, does not mean that any disposition of its assets is ultra vires, Blayney J held 'While a disposition in such circumstances may constitute a breach of duty on the part of the directors, it does not follow that it would be ultra vires the company.'[202] Here the distinction between ultra vires the company, and abuse of the directors powers, was recognised[203]. In *Re Frederick Inns Ltd*[204] the Supreme Court, per Blayney J also

---

199 [1939] IR 60 at 64.

200 *Parkes & Sons Ltd v Hong Kong and Shanghi Banking Corporation* [1990] ILRM 341.

201 [1990] ILRM 341 at 349.

202 [1990] ILRM 341 at 249.

203 In support of this proposition, see Keane, *Company Law in the Republic of Ireland* (2nd edn, 1991), para 12.05.

204 *Re Frederick Inns Ltd* [1994] 1 ILRM 387.

distinguished between an abuse of directors' powers from questions of corporate capacity[205].

[7.065] Certain ancillary powers will contain express limitations on their exercise which are so fundamental as to mean that they are properly described as limited powers. An example of such a limited power is seen in *Re PMPA Garage (Longmile) Ltd et al*[206] where the power to lend was 'To advance or lend to members or others...any of the capital or other monies of the Society on receiving proper security therefor.'
In that case, the Private Motorists Provident Society Ltd ('PMPS') lent money to a number of subsidiary companies in return for unsecured guarantees. When the PMPS and other subsidiary companies were wound up, the liquidator of the PMPS sought to recover the sums due on the guarantees but this was disputed by the liquidators of the other companies on the grounds, inter alia, that the guarantees by the other companies were ultra vires as was the lending by the PMPS. Murphy J held that the giving of the guarantees by the other companies in the group were intra vires[207]. Accordingly, the remaining question concerned the validity of the loan advances made by PMPS to the other companies in the group.

The argument in respect of the alleged ultra vires lending was that the advances were made to persons who were not members of the PMPS and, moreover, were made without any security, real or personal. It is important to note that but for a particular statutory provision[208] the PMPS would not have power to lend at all. Murphy J held that for the PMPS to advance monies in these circumstances was ultra vires the PMPS. It is submitted that it is because of the fundamental restriction, coupled with the statutory provisions governing the powers of industrial and providential societies, that the exercise of this power by the PMPS was ultra vires. In effect, the power was a limited power ab initio and so differed fundamentally from those express ancillary powers considered above[209].

(iii) Implied ancillary powers

[7.066] Although companies are invariably incorporated with voluminous objects clauses, the truth is that this results more from a nervous adherence to practice than from legal necessity. It has long been the case that the courts will imply powers to a company

---

205 [1994] 1 ILRM 387 at 398 where Blayney J cited with approval Slade LJ in *Rolled Steel Products* where he distinguished both situations in the context of recovery of assets wrongly transferred by a company. In this regard he quoted the following passage of Slade LJ: 'The *Belmont* principle thus provides a legal route by which a company may recover its assets in a case where its directors have abused their fiduciary duties and a person receiving assets as a result of such abuse is on notice that they have been misapplied. The principle is not linked in any way to the capacity of the company; it is capable of applying whether or not the company had the capacity to do the acts in question.'

206 *Re PMPA Garage (Longmile) Ltd* [1992] ILRM 337.

207 See para **[7.056]**.

208 Industrial and Provident Societies Act 1893, s 40.

209 Although the lending was ultra vires the PMPS, Murphy J allowed the liquidator of the PMPS recover the amounts loaned: *Re PMPA Garage (Longmile) Ltd (No 2)* [1992] ILRM 349. See para **[7.086]** *ff*.

which 'may fairly be regarded as incidental to, or consequential upon', a company's express objects[210].

Certain powers are obviously incidental and necessary eg borrowing to finance the company's main business, hiring employees, acquiring business premises[211]. Others have traditionally been contentious: corporate gifts[212] and other gratuitous payments, such as political donations, pensions, sponsorships, scholarships and even redundancy payments in excess of those which are required by law.

[7.067] Whether or not any given power will be implied depends upon whether or not its exercise can be said to be reasonably incidental to the furtherance of the company's objects. This test will determine the very existence of an implied power and is the sole test today notwithstanding the case of *Re Lee Behrens & Co*[213] where Eve J set out a tripartite test:

> '...whether [gratuitous payments] may be made under an express or implied power, all such grants involve an expenditure of the company's money, and that money can only be spent for purposes reasonably incidental to the carrying on of the company's business, and the validity of such grants is to be treated as is shown in all the authorities by the answers to three pertinent questions: (i) Is the transaction reasonably incidental to the carrying on of the company's business? (ii) Is it a bona fide transaction? and (iii) Is it done for the benefit and to promote the prosperity of the company?'[214]

The reality is that the foregoing passage confuses corporate incapacity (ultra vires) with an abuse of the directors' powers. Limbs (ii) and (iii) are heresy when the existence of an implied power is in question[215]. All that now remains of the test is whether or not the exercise of a power is reasonably incidental to or consequential upon the company's substantive objects.

(c) Gratuitous dispositions of company property

[7.068] It is in the context of alleged gratuitous dispositions of company property that the doctrine of ultra vires is often frequently considered in modern judgments. Here the following issues are considered:

---

210 *Attorney General v Great Eastern Railway* (1880) 5 App Cas 473.

211 In *Halifax Building Society v Meridian Housing Association Ltd* [1994] 1 BCLC 540 it was held by Arden J that the development of office units was a transaction of a category that, was capable of being performed as reasonably incidental to the defendant's main objects which was that of carrying 'on the industry, business or trade of providing housing or any associated amenities'.

212 Bastin 36 Conv (ns) 89.

213 *Re Lee Behrens & Co* [1932] All ER 889, [1932] 2 Ch 46.

214 [1932] All ER 889 at 891A–B.

215 In *Rolled Steel Products (Holdings) Ltd v British Steel Corp* [1985] 3 All ER 52 at 81–82, [1986] 1 Ch 246, Slade LJ said of Eve J's test that it: '...should, in my opinion, now be recognised as being of no assistance and indeed positively misleading when the relevant question is whether a particular gratuitous transaction is within a company's corporate capacity'. See also *Northern Bank Finance Corporation Ltd v Quinn and Achates Investment Company* [1979] ILRM 221 where Keane J said the observations of Rowen LJ in *Hutton* 'may have been taken too far in *Re Lee, Behrens and Co*', and went on to refer to *Charterbridge*.

(i) Implicit power to make a gratuitous disposition where reasonably incidental.

(ii) Express object or power to make a gratuitous disposition.

(iii) No express object and not in furtherance of the company's interests.

(i) Implicit power to make a gratuitous disposition where reasonably incidental

[7.069] In appropriate circumstances the power to make a gratuitous disposition can be implied. In *Parke v Daily News Ltd*[216] a company sold its newspaper business for £2 million, which had constituted its main business. It subsequently purported to give £1.5 million to its then redundant employees in the form of pensions and retirement plans. It was held that these ex gratia payments were not permitted by the company's express objects and the company had no implied power to give them. As Plowman J said:

> '...the essence of this matter is this, that the directors of the defendant company are proposing that a very large part of its funds should be given to its former employees in order to benefit those employees rather than the company...'.

Hence the payments were not reasonably incidental to or consequential upon the company's objects.

[7.070] As Keane J said in *Re Greendale Developments Ltd*[217] 'it has been settled law since the decision in *Hutton v West Cork Railway Co*[218] that a company cannot spend money or dispose of its property except for purposes which are reasonably incidental to the carrying on of the business of the company'[219]. In *Hutton v West Cork Railway Co* it was held that it could not be said that there was any implied power to give gratuities to servants or directors of the company. While prima facie the gratuities were in the interests of the company because goodwill was generated, this did not apply there since the company was being wound up. On the general issue of corporate charity, Bowen LJ said:

> 'A railway company, or the directors of the company, might send down all the porters at a railway station to have tea in the country at the expense of the company. Why should they not? It is for the directors to judge, provided it is a matter which is reasonably incidental to the carrying on of the business of the company and a company which always treated its employees with Draconian severity...would soon find itself deserted...The law does not say that there are to be no cakes and ale, but that there are to be no cakes and ale except such as are required for the benefit of the company...Charity has no business to sit at boards of directors qua charity. There is, however, a kind of charitable dealing which is for the interest of those who practice it, and to that extent and in that garb (I admit not a very philanthropic garb) charity may sit at the board, but for no other purpose.'

In that case corporate charity was not reasonably incidental to or consequential upon the company's objects since the company was being wound up. When a company is solvent it will usually be the case that gratuitous dispositions to charities or to a company's employees or officers will be found to pass the foregoing test, such dispositions being tantamount to money spent on public relations or remuneration, respectively.

---

216 *Parke v Daily News Ltd* [1962] Ch 927, [1962] 2 All ER 929.

217 *Re Greendale Developments Ltd* [1998] 1 IR 8.

218 *Hutton v West Cork Railway Co* [1883] 23 Ch D 654.

219 [1998] 1 IR 8 at 22.

(ii) Express object or power to make a gratuitous disposition

[7.071] The general rule is that a company cannot make a gratuitous disposition of its property unless such a disposition is an express object in a company's memorandum of association. It has already been noted that certain forms of disposition – such as a guarantee – will rarely properly fall to be construed as a true object and will almost invariably be a 'mere' power which must be exercised in a manner that is in furtherance of an express object[220]. Other dispositions can, however, be express objects and where they are expressly authorised by the objects clause, they will not be ultra vires. So in *Re Horsley & Weight Ltd*[221] Oliver J said:

> 'The objects of a company do not need to be commercial, they can be charitable or philanthropic; indeed, they can be whatever the original incorporators wish, provided that they are legal. Nor is there any reason why a company should not part with its funds gratuitously or for non-commercial reasons if to do so is within its declared objects...Of course if the memorandum of association expressly or by implication provides that an express object only extends to acts which benefit or promote the prosperity of the company, regard must be paid to that limitation; but where there is no such express or implied limitation, the question whether an act done within the terms of an express object of the company will benefit or promote the prosperity of the company or of its business is...irrelevant.'[222]

In *Barclays Bank plc v British & Commonwealth Holdings plc*[223] Harman J said that in *Brady v Brady*[224] Nourse LJ had accepted that the law 'imposes a limit on even an express power such as he envisaged to give away all a company's assets so that such a power could only be exercised by a company with available distributable profits'[225].

[7.072] The courts will strictly construe any object which it is claimed authorises a company to make a gratuitous disposition of its property. The decision in *Re Frederick Inns Ltd*[226] is instructive in this regard. In that case three companies – Frederick Inns Ltd, The Rendezvous Ltd and The Graduate Ltd – all operated public houses in Dublin and were wholly-owned subsidiaries of Motels Ltd. All companies were in a constant state of indebtedness to, inter alia, the Revenue Commissioners, and owed in total, by June 1986, circa £2.8 million. Meetings were held between the company's representatives and the Revenue Commissioners, but the Revenue Commissioners were dissatisfied and threatened to wind up each of the four companies. A further meeting was held and it was decided that the public houses owned by Frederick Inns Ltd, The Rendezvous Ltd and The Graduate Ltd would be sold and the proceeds of sale paid to the Revenue Commissioners. In total, £1.2 million was paid over. In the High Court Lardner J found that this money was appropriated in reduction of the tax liabilities of not only these four

220 See para **[7.054]**.

221 *Re Horsley & Weight Ltd* [1982] 1 Ch 442.

222 [1982] 1 Ch 442 at 450, 452.

223 *Barclays Bank plc et al v British & Commonwealth Holdings plc* [1996] 1 BCLC 1.

224 *Brady v Brady* [1988] BCLC 20.

225 [1996] 1 BCLC 1 at 17a.

226 *Re Frederick Inns Ltd* [1991] ILRM 582 (High Court) and [1994] 1 ILRM 387 (Supreme Court).

companies, but also the tax liabilities of six other companies which were also subsidiaries of Motels Ltd. The liquidator contended that 'when any company is insolvent it is beyond its powers gratuitously to alienate its property or to make a gift to a third party out of its assets'[227]. After citing the most basic principle of company law, the concept of separate legal personality[228], Lardner J held:

> 'Insofar as payments to the Revenue were made by companies out of their assets, which exceeded their liabilities for tax, and were intended to be applied in reduction of the tax liabilities of other companies in the group, they can only be regarded as voluntary payments made without consideration for the benefit of third parties and as such in the absence of any evidence that such excess payments were for the benefit of the paying companies they are clearly ultra vires.'[229]

Lardner J also held that there was a breach of the directors' duties in applying the proceeds of sale as they did[230]. He concluded:

> 'that payment to the Revenue Commissioners by any of the companies of any sum in excess of its particular tax liability was ultra vires the paying company insofar (a) as it effected a gratuitous reduction or alienation of its assets and (b) it was done when the company was insolvent.'[231]

---

[227] [1991] ILRM 582 at 588. Reliance for this was placed upon *Hutton v West Cork Railway Company* (1883) 23 Ch D 654; *Parke v Daily News* [1962] 2 All ER 929; and *Charterbridge Corporation Ltd v Lloyds Bank Ltd* [1970] Ch 407.

[228] [1991] ILRM 582 at 587 where, Lardner J said:

> 'A fundamental attribute of a company in Irish law is that of corporate personality. A company is a legal entity distinct from its members, capable of enjoying rights and of being subject to duties which are not the same as those enjoyed or borne by its members. This was finally established in *Salomon v Salomon & Company Limited* [1897] AC 22 and the principle has been recognised and applied in many decisions of the Irish courts. Generally speaking this principle and the statutory rules of company law in which the principle is implicit apply to the relationship between holding companies and subsidiaries and to transactions between them and third parties. The assets of such companies are treated as owned by them legally and beneficially as distinct legal entities. And except where circumstances enable a court to discover an agency or trustee relationship between them, a holding company is not treated as owner of its subsidiaries' assets. And the liabilities of companies which are members of the same group are those of the individual companies which incur them. There is no common group liability for the obligations of individual members of the group imposed by law. The principle is reflected in many aspects of company law; for example in s 147 of the Companies Act 1963 every company (whether a holding company or a subsidiary) is required to keep proper books of account which must include accounts of all sums of money received and expended by the company...'.

[229] [1991] ILRM 582 at 588, supported by reference to *Trevor v Whitworth* [1887] 12 AC 414; *Hutton v The West Cork Railway Company Ltd* (1883) 23 Ch D 654; and *Roper v Ward* [1981] ILRM 408.

[230] See generally, Chapter 10, *Duties of Directors and Other Officers*. It is important to note that the reference to the abuse by the directors of their powers and their duty owed to the creditors on the insolvency of a company and the question of ultra vires were treated very separately by Lardner J. In this the eternal distinction between corporate capacity and directors' authority was underscored.

[231] [1991] ILRM 582 at 591.

[7.073] The decision of Lardner J was appealed to the Supreme Court[232]. Blayney J giving the judgment of the court dismissed the appeal. On the question of the gratuitous dispositions of funds in the reduction of the liabilities of other companies, Blayney J held that those payments were ultra vires because they were not within the contemplation of the companies' objects that were relied upon by the Revenue Commissioners. Of the two clauses[233] claimed to give the companies the power to pay other companies' debts Blayney J said:

> 'In my opinion neither of these clauses gives the power to pay the debts of an associate company, which is what happened here. What the first clause gives is a power "to establish or promote or concur in establishing or promoting" another company in certain circumstances. That could not be construed as a power to pay the debts of another company. And the second clause gives the power "to purchase or otherwise acquire and undertake all or any part of the...liabilities...of any company etc." The companies here were neither "purchasing" nor "acquiring and undertaking" the liabilities of the other companies. They were paying part of their debts. This clause did not give any power to do this.'[234]

Blayney J also rejected the submission that the power to lend money could be relied upon to validate the payments and concluded that the payments were ultra vires[235].

(iii) No express object and not in furtherance of the company's interests

[7.074] It will be difficult, if not impossible, to uphold the validity of a gratuitous disposition by a company where its objects clause contains no express object to make such a disposition and it is not argued that the payments were for the benefit of the company and where the disposition is not out of 'distributable profits'. In *Aveling Barford Ltd v Perion*[236] Hoffmann J said:

> 'A company can only lawfully deal with its assets in furtherance of its objects. The corporators may take assets of the company by way of dividend, or with the leave of the court, by way of reduction of capital, or in a winding up. They may of course acquire them for full consideration. They cannot take assets out of the company by way of voluntary

---

232 [1994] 1 ILRM 387.

233 The clauses were:

> '(1) To establish or promote or concur in establishing or promoting any other company whose objects shall include the acquisition and taking over of all or any assets and liabilities or, or the promotion of which shall be in any manner calculated to advance directly or indirectly the objects or interests of this company, and to acquire and hold, or dispose of shares, stock or securities of, and guarantee the payment of any securities issued or any other obligation of any such company.
>
> (2) To purchase or otherwise acquire and undertake all or any part of the business, property, liabilities and transactions of any person, firm or company carrying on or proposing to carry on any business which this company is authorised to carry on, or possessed of property suitable for the purpose of the company or to promote any company or companies for the above purpose.'

234 [1994] 1 ILRM 387 at 393–394.

235 As to the reliance placed by the Revenue Commissioners on CA 1963, s 8, see para **[7.080]**.

236 *Aveling Barford Ltd v Perion* [1989] BCLC 626.

disposition, however, described, and if they attempt to do so, the disposition is ultra vires the company.'[237]

In *Brady v Brady*[238] Nourse LJ said:

'In its broadest terms the principle is that a company cannot give away its assets. So stated, it is subject to the qualification that in the realm of theory a memorandum of association may authorise a company to give away all its assets to whomsoever it pleases, including its shareholders. But in the real world of trading companies, charitable or political donations to widows of ex-employees and the like apart, it is obvious that such a power would never be taken. The principle is only a facet of the wider rule, the corollary of limited liability, that the integrity of a company's assets, except to the extent allowed by its constitution, must be preserved for the benefit of all those who are interested in them, most pertinently its creditors.'[239]

Harman J cited both of these decisions in *Barclays Bank plc v British & Commonwealth Holdings plc*[240] and accepted that a company cannot make a gratuitous disposition of its assets save where this is for the benefit of its business (and so not really gratuitous) or where it is made out of distributable profits with the approval of its shareholders applied very widely[241].

[7.075] This same issue was at the centre of the decision in *Re Greendale Developments Ltd*[242] which concerned an appeal from an order of the High Court that a director of a company was obliged to repay over £435,000 to the company's liquidator. The circumstances were that the company had three equal shareholders: Mr and Mrs Fagan and Mr Burgess; Mr Fagan and Mr Burgess were its directors. The company had been formed to carry out a development at Islandbridge, Dublin and 80 houses had been built and sold, as also had an office building on the site. Following disputes between Mr Fagan and Mr Burgess, Mr Burgess presented a section 205 petition; Mr Fagan countered with a petition to wind up the company on the just and equitable ground and the company was wound up. The liquidator appointed to the company formed the view that substantial sums were owed by Mr Fagan to the company and instituted proceedings for misfeasance pursuant to CA 1963, s 298. It was as a result of these proceedings that the High Court order was made against Mr Fagan and this was appealed to the Supreme Court. On appeal it was argued by Mr Fagan's counsel that all payments made to Mr and Mrs Fagan or benefits obtained had been made with the assent of all the shareholders, with the result that the misfeasance proceedings were misconceived and since there was no evidence that the company had been insolvent, the payments could not constitute any form of wrongdoing or breach of trust. On the question of the assent of the shareholders to the impugned transactions, Keane J in the Supreme Court accepted the propriety of the principle summarised by Kingsmill Moore J in *Buchanan Ltd v McVey*[243] that where

---

[237] [1989] BCLC 626 at 631.

[238] *Brady v Brady* [1988] BCLC 20.

[239] [1988] BCLC 20 at 38.

[240] *Barclays Bank plc v British & Commonwealth Holdings plc* [1996] 1 BCLC 1.

[241] [1996] 1 BCLC 1 at 17.

[242] *Re Greendale Developments Ltd* [1998] 1 IR 8.

[243] *Buchanan Ltd v McVey* [1954] IR 89: see Chapter 9, *Corporate Governance: Meetings*, para **[9.081]**.

all corporators agree to a certain course of action, such is an act of the company and binds the company subject to two prerequisites:

> '(1) that the transaction to which the corporators agree should be intra vires the company;
>
> (2) that the transaction should be honest.'

It was in these circumstances that Keane J considered whether the making of payments by a solvent company to its director was ultra vires. Two very important aspects of the circumstances in this case should be noted. First, Keane J noted that ex hypothesi the company had obtained no benefits whatever from the impugned payments but that it was, nevertheless, contended that the payments were intra vires. Secondly, there was no express object or authorisation in the memorandum or articles of association to make the payments in question and it appears there was no attempt to argue that any of the company's objects envisaged the making of such payments[244]. As Keane J said, were it otherwise, 'different considerations might apply.'[245]

[7.076] Keane J addressed the issue by noting that it was 'settled law' since the decision in *Hutton v West Cork Railway Co* that a company cannot spend money or dispose of its property except for purposes that are reasonably incidental to the carrying on of the company's business. Thus, having noted that the transaction was not 'expressly authorised' by the company's objects clause, Keane J discarded any suggestion that it could be said that the company had an implied power to effect the transaction[246] because it received no benefit. The genesis of the Supreme Court's finding that the payments by the company were ultra vires was that there was no express or implied power for the company to make payments of the sort made to the director. Mr Fagan's counsel's purported reliance upon the principle that all of the corporators of a solvent company can do that which they like to its assets fell down on the simple fact that for that principle to operate, the thing which is done must be intra vires. Equally, there is no conflict between Keane J's judgment and that of Gavan Duffy P in *Re SM Barker Ltd*[247] upon which Mr Fagan's counsel relied heavily. In that case it was held that misfeasance proceedings did not lie against shareholders who had caused a company to voluntarily release a number of debts due to it by the company's three directors. The judgment of Gavan Duffy P was, however, predicated on the fact that in that case the voluntary release of indebtedness was not ultra vires; in *Re Greendale Developments Ltd* it was found as a matter of fact that the payments made there were ultra vires. As Keane J said:

---

[244] See Forde, *Company Law* (3rd edn, 1999), p 103 where he states that the objects clause of Greendale Developments Ltd said that the company could 'grant…gratuities, bonuses or other payments to the officers…or the dependants or connections of such persons'. This is, however, irrelevant since it was not argued and the judgment proceeded on the basis that there was no authority in the objects clause for such payments.

[245] [1998] 1 IR 8 at 22.

[246] In addition to citing the *Hutton* case, Keane J cited *Re Lee, Behrens and Company Ltd* [1932] 2 Ch 46; *Parke v Daily News Ltd* [1962] Ch 927; and *Roper v Ward* [1981] IRLM 408.

[247] *Re SM Barker Ltd* [1950] IR 123.

'*Re SM Barker Ltd* is, accordingly, not authority for the proposition that a company may spend money or apply property for purposes which are ultra vires the company provided all the shareholders agree to the ultra vires transaction...

...On the proved or admitted facts of this case, the impugned payments were made by the company to or for the benefit of the appellants in circumstances where the company derived no benefit in return. They were not expressly authorised by the memorandum or articles of association of the company. They were, accordingly, ultra vires the company and their fundamental illegality cannot be cured by the fact, if it be the fact, that all the shareholders assented to each and every one of the payments in question.'[248]

The decision in *Re Greendale Developments Ltd* was clearly in accordance with sound legal principle and established authority[249]. As far back as 1931, the principles in issue were considered by Orde JA in *Plain Ltd v Kenley*[250].

'...a limited joint stock company cannot do what it likes with its property...It cannot lawfully give away its property, either to shareholders or others. I am speaking broadly, because there are cases where, in the interests of its own business, a company may [make gifts] but transactions of that character either depend upon the fact that they are prudent and proper expenditures or are made out of accumulated profits and with the consent of the shareholders.'[251]

The suggestion that, if shareholders can agree to a company acting ultra vires, the ultra vires action will not be improper, is entirely misplaced and results from a failure to recognise the legitimate interests of creditors and the fact that the doctrine of ultra vires is intended to protect both shareholders and creditors. Only the existence of the clearest of express objects to make gratuitous dispositions, which will, of course, be a matter of public record, will allow companies to gratuitously divest themselves of their assets in favour of their owners and controllers. Even then, dispositions can only be made out of 'distributable profits' and, yes, the consent of the shareholders is required. The fallacy lies in elevating shareholder consent to the sole prerequisite. Were it otherwise, creditor protection measures such as the controls on loans to directors[252], capital maintenance rules[253], the very concept of 'distributable profits'[254], and the statutory declaration of solvency in a winding up would all be rendered meaningless. Moreover, vires aside, all dispositions of corporate property must be made for the benefit of the company; where not made for the benefit of the company, the directors may be found to have acted in breach of their duties to the company, as fiduciaries.

(d) Section 8 of CA 1963

[7.077] Section 8(1) of CA 1963 provides:

'Any act or thing done by the company which if the company had been empowered to do the same would have been lawfully and effectively done, shall, notwithstanding that the

[248] [1998] 1 IR 8 at 24.

[249] For a contrary view, see Forde, *Company Law* (3rd edn, 1999), p 104– 07.

[250] *Plain Ltd v Kenley* [1931] 1 DLR 468.

[251] [1931] 1 DLR 468 at 479.

[252] CA 1990, s 31.

[253] See generally, Chapter 18, *The Maintenance of Capital*.

[254] CA 1963, s 45.

> company had no power to do such act or thing, be effective in favour of any person relying on such act or thing who is not shown to have been actually aware, at the time when he so relied thereon, that such act or thing was not within the powers of the company. but any director or officer of the company who was responsible for the doing by the company of such act or thing shall be liable to the company for any loss or damage suffered by the company in consequence thereof.'

This statutory provision tempers the severity of the doctrine of ultra vires as seen in cases such as *Re Jon Beauforte (London) Ltd*[255]. There, the company's main object was to operate the business of costumiers and gown makers. Contrary to this it carried on the business of veneer panel makers. The transaction in issue was a contract to supply coke from a fuel merchant, a substance which could apparently be used in either business. Because of the fact that the company's objects clause was a matter of public knowledge, being registered in the Companies Registration Office ('CRO'), and because the notepaper on which the order was sent to the fuel merchant was headed 'Veneered Panel Manufacturers', the fuel merchant was held to have constructive notice of the ultra vires purpose for which the coke was intended, and so the contract was unenforceable and was not admitted as a debt when the company went into liquidation. Today, the doctrine of constructive notice is ousted and the contract would only be unenforceable if the fuel merchant was actually aware of the ultra vires purpose for which the coke was to be used.

[7.078] On the foregoing analysis of express ancillary powers, the scope of CA 1963, s 8 must now be seen to have been considerably reduced. Only the pursuit of non-objects and the purported exercise of powers not stated in the objects clause will attract the doctrine of ultra vires, and so be capable of being mitigated by CA 1963, s 8. Section 8 of CA 1963 may most usefully be considered by parsing its provisions:

(i) 'Lawfully and effectively done'.

(ii) 'In favour of any person'.

(iii) 'Actually aware'.

(i) 'Lawfully and effectively done'

[7.079] The use of these words show that acts or things prohibited by the Companies Acts and the general law of the land cannot be validated by CA 1963, s 8(1). Accordingly, a contract which unlawfully assists the purchase of the company's own shares cannot be saved: *Bank of Ireland Finance Ltd v Rockfield Ltd*[256]. The use of the word effectively, shows that contracts void for uncertainty or other defect can not be validated.

[7.080] 'Lawfully and effectively done' was interpreted by the Supreme Court in *Re Frederick Inns Ltd*[257]. There, on the facts considered above[258], Lardner J in the High Court had said of CA 1963, s 8(1) that:

---

[255] *Re Jon Beauforte (London) Ltd* [1953] 1 All ER 634.

[256] *Bank of Ireland Finance Ltd v Rockfield Ltd* [1979] IR 21.

[257] *Re Frederick Inns Ltd* [1994] 1 ILRM 387.

[258] See para **[7.072]**.

> 'By its terms this section refers to acts or things done which, if the company had been empowered to do the same, would have been lawfully and effectively done. I do not find the section capable of assisting the Revenue Commissioners in relation to companies which were insolvent, to their knowledge, even if one supposes that in the present case these companies had been empowered by their memoranda and articles to make gratuitous payments to or for the benefit of third parties out of their assets (and it is a supposition which in this case is so inconsistent with some of the basic principles of company law as to be hardly made). For insolvent companies such payments constitute a misapplication of the companies' assets and could not have been lawful or effective as against the general unsecured creditors, since they would effectively defraud them of assets to which the creditors were entitled to have recourse.'

This was upheld by Blayney J in the Supreme Court. He also held that at the time the ultra vires payments were made by the companies to the Revenue Commissioners, the companies were insolvent. Moreover, the learned judge held that one effect of a company being insolvent was that 'the company had ceased to be the beneficial owner of its assets with the result that directors would have had *no power* to use the company's assets to discharge the liabilities of other companies'. [259] He held that in consequence:

> '...I think it is clear that it could not be held that the payments by the four companies were "lawfully and effectively done". At the time the payments were made, the four companies were under the management of their directors pending imminent liquidation. Because of the insolvency of the companies the shareholders no longer had any interest. The only parties with an interest were the creditors. The payments made could not have been lawful because they were made in total disregard of their interests. And since the payments were not lawfully made, the Revenue Commissioners cannot rely on s 8 of the Companies Act 1963 to remedy the fact that the payments were ultra vires.'[260]

The effect of the Supreme Court's decision is that ultra vires dispositions of assets cannot be rendered effective by CA 1963, s 8 where the company is insolvent. The decision in *Re Frederick Inns Ltd* was on that basis distinguished by Laffoy J in *Ulster Factors Ltd v Entonglen Ltd and another*[261], the facts of which are considered below[262]. There the liquidator of a company had sought to claim that payments made to a third party (at the request of a person who was director and secretary of the company) was ultra vires and that no reliance could be placed on CA 1963, s 8. Since the company was not insolvent at the time the payments were made, Laffoy J held that reliance upon s 8(1) was not precluded.

[7.081] The decision in *Re Frederick Inns Ltd* greatly curtails the scope of CA 1963, s 8(1). The preclusion of reliance upon s 8, to make effective ultra vires dispositions of corporate assets when a company is insolvent, totally emasculates s 8(1). The propriety of the 'act or thing' that is done must not be assailable on any ground other than it being 'ultra vires' the company's capacity.

---

[259] *Re Frederick Inns Ltd* [1994] 1 ILRM 387 at 396.

[260] [1994] 1 ILRM 387 at 397.

[261] *Ulster Factors Ltd v Entonglen Ltd* (21 February 1997, unreported), High Court (Laffoy J).

[262] See para **[7.102]**.

(ii) 'In favour of any person'

[7.082] The reference to 'in favour of any person' shows that CA 1963, s 8 is not confined to 'outsiders', but can also apply to 'insiders', such as directors. Although from an evidential stance it will be hard to show that insiders were not 'actually aware' of the lack of company power, their reliance on CA 1963, s 8(1), is not per se automatically excluded.

(iii) 'Actually aware'

[7.083] In ordinary speech, actual awareness indicates an advertence to something and the consequent realisation of the consequences. In law, however, it has been decided that a person will be 'actually aware' where they see something but do not appreciate its consequences.

In *Northern Bank Finance Co Ltd v Quinn and Achates Investment Co*[263] the defendant-company purported to enter into a contract of guarantee with the plaintiff-bank on behalf of a Mr Quinn. Keane J held that the guarantee was ultra vires because the memorandum of association 'conferred neither expressly nor by implication any power on the Company to execute a Guarantee for the purpose of securing the payment of a bank loan to Mr Quinn'[264]. Nevertheless, the bank sought to rely on CA 1963, s 8(1), arguing it was not actually aware of the corporate incapacity. However, the bank's solicitor had been sent the memorandum and articles of association. Although the solicitor could not recall reading them, Keane J found that:

> 'I think that the probabilities are that [the solicitor] did read the objects clause...and came to the conclusion that the execution of the Guarantee and the mortgage was within the powers of the company.'[265]

Having so held, Keane J said s 8(1) did not apply, as 'the bank, because of the knowledge of their agent...which must be imputed to them, were aware of the objects of the company.' [266]

To the argument that this was not the 'actual awareness' contemplated by the section, Keane J said:

> 'I think it is clear that the section was designed to ensure that...persons who had entered into transactions in good faith with the company without ever reading the memorandum and accordingly with no actual knowledge that the transaction was ultra vires were not to suffer. I can see no reason in logic or justice why the legislature should have intended to afford the same protection to persons who had actually read the memorandum and simply failed to appreciate the lack of vires.'[267]

Keane J concluded by saying that:

---

[263] *Northern Bank Finance Company Ltd v Quinn and Achates Investment Co* [1979] ILRM 221.

[264] [1979] ILRM 221 at 226. Even with the recent developments in respect of express ancillary powers, such a view would still be correct today as the power to guarantee was in relation to 'the company', and furthermore, it appears there was no independent objects clause.

[265] [1979] ILRM 221 at 228.

[266] [1979] ILRM 221 at 229.

[267] [1979] ILRM 221 at 229.

'...where a party is shown to have been actually aware of the contents of the memorandum but failed to appreciate that the company were not empowered thereby to enter the transaction in issue, s 8(1) has no application.'[268]

Even at its most restrictive, this decision provides that a person who has not seen the memorandum will have the protection of CA 1963, s 8(1). Academic focus has largely been on Keane J's restrictive construction of the section, and the decision has been criticised on this basis[269]. Criticism has principally been directed at the finding that the clear meaning of the words 'actually aware', appear to have been confused for actual notice. In law, actual, constructive and imputed notice have very particular meanings[270]. 'Notice' does not mean 'awareness'. If being 'actually aware' of the provisions of a company's memorandum of association was intended to equate with 'actual notice' of such, one would have thought that the legislature ought to have used the words 'actual notice'.

As the law stands, a person who has not seen a company's memorandum and articles, will be protected by s 8(1). Ironically, a person who reads a company's memorandum and articles of association, but fails to understand the lack of vires, will not be protected by s 8(1). Notwithstanding this, it is *not* recommended that constitutional documents are ignored[271].

(e) European Communities (Companies) Regulations 1973, reg 6

[7.084] Regulation 6 of the European Communities (Companies) Regulations 1973 was introduced into Irish law as a result of Article 9 of the First EU Directive on Company Law[272]. The regulation concerns defects both in corporate agents' authority and in corporate capacity. Just as the rule in *Turquand*'s case is overlapped by reg 6, also overlapped is CA 1963, s 8(1). However, while there is an overlap, s 8(1) provides more protection to persons dealing with the company. First, the requirement of 'good faith' in the regulation imposes a greater standard of care than does the concept of being 'actually aware', even on its restrictive interpretation, because the former would seem to impose a duty to investigate. Secondly, reg 6 only affords protection where one deals with the board of directors or a registered person[273]. Thirdly, the regulation applies only to

268 [1979] ILRM 221 at 230.

269 Ussher, *Company Law in Ireland* (1986), p 126; see also Ussher (1981) DULJ 76.

270 Wylie, *Irish Land Law* (3rd edn, 1997), para 3.069.

271 See Johnston, *Banking and Security Law in Ireland* (1998), para [18.40].

272 See Chapter 1, *The Private Company in Context*, para **[1.093]**.

273 It was for this reason that the Revenue Commissioners could not rely upon SI 1973/163, reg 6 in *Re Frederick Inns Ltd* [1994] 1 ILRM 387. Blayney J said (at 394) that:

'I think it is clear that none of the companies had any person registered under the regulations as a person authorised to bind the company, so if the Revenue Commissioners are to get the benefit of the article [SI 1973/163, reg 6] they would need to show that the payment to them was a transaction entered into by the board of directors of each of the companies. There is no evidence of this in any of the affidavits filed by either side. The payment appears to have been agreed to be made as a result of informal meetings between accountants acting on behalf of the companies and Mr Patrick Burke acting on behalf of the Revenue Commissioners. In these circumstances it seems to me that the Revenue Commissioners cannot rely on Article 6 as validating the payment.'

limited companies. Regulation 6 is considered in detail in the context of corporate authority, below[274].

(f) Corporate enforcement of ultra vires contracts

[7.085] It might seem logical that if a company wishes to enforce a contract which is invalid according to its objects clause it should be able to amend its objects clause. However, in law a company cannot ratify an ultra vires act[275]. Furthermore, CA 1963, s 8(1) affords no remedy to the company as its saving provisions apply only in favour of any person relying on an act or thing done by a company. Although an ultra vires contract is void at common law, where s 8(1) can be relied upon the contract is unilaterally enforceable at the option of the person dealing with the company.

(g) Recovery of money given by a company ultra vires

[7.086] It has long been debated whether or not a company that has lent or advanced money in an ultra vires transaction can recover that money. The matter was addressed in detail by the High Court in *Re PMPA Garage (Longmile) Ltd (No 2)*[276]. This judgment arose out of the earlier finding by Murphy J, considered above[277], that certain loans made by the PMPS were ultra vires. As to the rights of the parties in these circumstances, Murphy J held that 'there are four possible solutions', ie: that the loans were unenforceable; recoverable in an action in rem; recoverable on the basis of quasi-contract; or recoverable on the basis of an estoppel. Each of the four possible solutions are next considered.

(i) The loan is unenforceable[278]

[7.087] This alternative provides that because the lending of the money was ultra vires, the loan is unenforceable and the borrowers can retain benefit of the loan for themselves. In *Re PMPA Garage (Longmile) Ltd (No 2)*[279] Murphy J dismissed this as a solution in the following terms:

> 'The monstrous injustice which would flow from the acceptance of such an audacious proposition would certainly render it unattractive to any court seeking to achieve justice in accordance with law.'[280]

Accordingly, the learned judge rejected the argument that a party who holds money paid on foot of an ultra vires contract can retain it, although he noted that the authorities differ as to the means which a court can avail of to restore such property to the company who gave it.

---

274 See para **[7.096]**.

275 *Ashbury Railway Carriage & Iron Co v Riche* (1875) LR 7 HLC 653; and *Re Balgooley Distillery Co* (1886) 17 LR Ir 239.

276 *Re PMPA Garage (Longmile) Ltd (No 2)* [1992] ILRM 349.

277 See para **[7.056]** and **[7.065]**.

278 *Re PMPA Garage (Longmile) Ltd (No 2)* [1992] ILRM 349.

279 [1992] ILRM 349 at 351.

280 [1992] ILRM 349.

(ii) The loan is recoverable in an action in rem: constructive trusts and the Belmont principle[281]

[7.088] In *Re PMPA Garage (Longmile) Ltd (No 2)*[282] Murphy J accepted the existence of this remedy which allows the lender to recover property in an action in rem on the basis that the monies available were never validly lent and as such remained the property of the lender. This solution has the disadvantage that the lender cannot recover interest on those sums and can only recover that which can be specifically traced and identified. This was established in the case of *Sinclair v Brougham*[283], where the facts bore an extraordinary resemblance to the facts of the case in question, save that there it was ultra vires borrowing which was in issue while in the PMPA case the question concerned ultra vires lending. In *Sinclair* it was said that the doctrine of ultra vires excluded any claim in personam and accordingly, in the words of Viscount Haldane LC:

> '...the only possible remedy for the person who has paid the money would on principle appear to be in rem and not in personam, a claim to follow and recover specifically any money which could be earmarked as never having ceased to be his property. To hold that a remedy will lie in personam against a statutory society, which by hypothesis cannot in the case in question have become a debtor or entered into any contract for repayment, is to strike at the root of the doctrine of ultra vires as established in the jurisprudence of this country.'[284]

Murphy J also noted that this case rejected the possibility that such monies could be recovered on a quasi-contract basis, based on the principle of unjust enrichment and a promise implied by law to repay.

[7.089] In *Re Frederick Inns Ltd*[285] the Supreme Court, considered the principle enunciated in *Belmont Finance Corporation Ltd v Williams Furniture Ltd*[286]. The *Belmont* principle states that where the directors of a company breach their fiduciary duties and misapply company funds and those funds come into the hands of a stranger to the trust with knowledge (actual or constructive) of the breach, the stranger cannot conscientiously retain them against the company unless he has some better equity[287]. In

281 [1992] ILRM 349 at 351.

282 *Re PMPA Garage (Longmile) Ltd (No 2)* [1992] ILRM 349.

283 *Sinclair v Brougham* [1914] AC 398.

284 [1914] AC 398 at 414.

285 *Re Frederick Inns Ltd* [1994] 1 ILRM 387.

286 *Belmont Finance Corporation Ltd v Williams Furniture Ltd* [1980] 1 All ER 393. See [1980] 1 All ER 393 at 398 where Blayney J cited with approval Slade LJ in *Rolled Steel Products* where he distinguished both situations in the context of recovery of assets wrongly transferred by a company.

287 The *Belmont* principle does not turn on corporate capacity but the abuse of fiduciary duties. In *Re Frederick Inns Ltd* Blayney J quoted the following passage from Slade J in *Rolled Steel Products* where he said: 'The *Belmont* principle thus provides a legal route by which a company may recover its assets in a case where its directors have abused their fiduciary duties and a person receiving assets as a result of such abuse is on notice that they have been misapplied. The principle is not linked in any way to the capacity of the company; it is capable of applying whether or not the company had the capacity to do the acts in question.'

applying the *Belmont* principle to the ultra vires payments in favour of the Revenue Commissioners, Blayney J said:

> 'The ultra vires payments in the present case were made on the authority of the directors of the four companies and, being ultra vires, they constituted a misapplication by the directors of the companies' funds...This misapplication was a breach by the directors of their fiduciary duties and the monies were received by the revenue commissioners with constructive knowledge of the breach since, if they had read the memorandum of association of the four companies, as they could have done since they are documents of public record, they would have seen that the companies had no power to make the payments. It follows in my opinion that the revenue commissioners are constructive trustees of the sums which were the subject of the ultra vires payments and must repay them to the official liquidator for each of the companies.'[288]

This was applied in *Ulster Factors Ltd v Entonglen Ltd and Maloney*[289]. In that case the liquidator of the first defendant-company sought to impugn a transaction whereby the defendant-company had authorised the plaintiff to pay a sum to a firm of Northern Irish solicitors. Laffoy J was not satisfied that the liquidator had established that the payment was ultra vires or, if it was, that CA 1963, s 8(1) would not be available. Laffoy J held that even if the liquidator was right on both counts, the *Belmont* principle as applied by the Supreme Court in *Re Frederick Inns Ltd* was not available. The learned judge said:

> 'Under the *Belmont* principle, as applied by the Supreme Court, what renders the recipient of or the dealer with funds which are being misapplied in breach of the fiduciary duties of the directors of a company liable as a constructive trustee is knowledge, actual or constructive, of the breach of trust. The factual position in this matter is that on the morning of 21 June 1990 the plaintiff acknowledged that it held at least IR£37,839.83 which, in accordance with the terms of the Agreement, was payable at the request of the company to the company or to its order and, later that morning, the plaintiff received a request on the letter-heading of the company showing its trading name and signed by a director of the company, who was also the financial director and secretary of the company, to make a payment equivalent to IR£37,839.83 to Messrs King & Gowdy and the plaintiff duly made that payment. Even if the payment was ultra vires the company and in breach of the directors' fiduciary duties, it is clear from the evidence that Mr Murray did not have actual knowledge of the purpose for which the payment was being made or of the breach. The agreement specifically provided that the plaintiff was objected to make payments to third parties at the request of the company. There was no obligation on the plaintiff to enquire as to the purpose for which any payment which the company requested the plaintiff to make to a third party was being made or to satisfy itself that the payment was intra vires the company and, even if the payment was ultra vires, constructive knowledge of a breach of trust cannot be imputed to the plaintiff for failure to make such enquiries.'[290]

---

[288] [1994] 1 ILRM 387 at 399.

[289] *Ulster Factors Ltd v Entonglen Ltd and Maloney* (21 February 1997, unreported), High Court (Laffoy J). See para **[7.102]**.

[290] (21 February 1997, unreported), High Court at pp 8, 9.

(iii) The loan is recoverable on basis quasi-contract

[7.090] In *Re PMPA Garage (Longmile) Ltd (No 2)*[291] Murphy J noted that recovery on the basis of quasi-contract[292] was at conflict with the decision in *Sinclair v Brougham*, 'inasmuch as it does involve recognising the availability of an action other than an action in rem', but the learned judge went on to recognise the evolution of the law relating to quasi-contract. Referring to *East Cork Foods v O'Dwyer Steel*[293] Murphy J noted that there Henchy J had said:

> '...the plaintiff succeeds in this type of action because, it is said, the law imputes a promise to pay the debt...In most cases it is in the teeth of the facts to impute to the debtor a promise to pay...Nowadays, however, when the forms of action have long since been buried, the concept of implied contract is an unreal and outdated rationale for the action for money had and received. Judges in modern times generally prefer to look at the reality of the situation rather than engage in the pretence that the defendant has promised to pay the debt.'[294]

Thus, the need[295] for an express or imputed promise to pay is no longer a necessary ingredient of the action for money had and received. Accordingly, Murphy J said:

> '...there is no impediment in availing of that remedy against a corporate body to recover monies received by it as a result of a transaction which was outside its corporate powers.'[296]

As to the case in hand, Murphy J said that the difference between the parties in dispute was whether the PMPS could recover the money on a basis other than an action in rem or a contract between the parties.

(iv) The loan is recoverable on the basis of an estoppel

[7.091] In *Re PMPA Garage (Longmile) Ltd (No 2)*[297] the fourth possible solution was that the PMPA companies were committed to repaying the money to the PMPS by virtue of their promises to repay. As authority for this proposition, Murphy J first referred to the decision of the English Court of Appeal in *Re Coltman*[298] which allowed recovery of monies in similar circumstances. However whilst this decision has been criticised[299] Murphy J referred to an Australian decision, *Re KL Tractors Ltd*[300] where the company concerned bought machinery from the Commonwealth Government of Australia. When the company subsequently became insolvent, its creditors disputed the right of the

---

[291] *Re PMPA Garage (Longmile) Ltd (No 2)* [1992] ILRM 349.

[292] [1992] ILRM 349 at 353.

[293] *East Cork Foods v O'Dwyer Steel* [1978] IR 103.

[294] [1978] IR 103 at 110.

[295] Note that Murphy J held that he would in any event have imputed such a promise on the facts of the case in hand.

[296] [1992] ILRM 349 at 354.

[297] *Re PMPA Garage (Longmile) Ltd (No 2)* [1992] ILRM 349.

[298] *Re Coltman* [1881] 19 Ch D 64.

[299] For not recognising the authority of *Ashbury Railway Carriage and Iron Co v Riche* (1875) LR 7 HL 653. See also the decision of Mocatta J in *Bell Houses Ltd v City Wall Properties Ltd* (1966) 1 QB 207, which although reversed on appeal, held at first instance that money paid was not recoverable.

[300] *Re KL Tractors Ltd* (1961) 106 CLR 318.

Commonwealth to recover, arguing that the contract was ultra vires the company. In what was 'very solid judicial support for the estoppel-type argument' it was held that the company could not plead ultra vires to avoid payment of the debt due and owing[301].

[7.092] Having thus canvassed the four possible alternatives, Murphy J admitted that the conflicting, but persuasive, authorities placed him in considerable difficulty. He concluded, however:

> 'I recognise the force of the simple cogent proposition that a body corporate cannot enforce a contract which it never had the capacity to make. It is demonstrated with equal clarity that all judicial authorities have set their face against any party who seeks to prevent the recovery from him of goods or monies which he has retained under an ultra vires transaction. The precise grounds on which such claims have been defeated have varied over the century during which the debate has spasmodically taken place but the result has been the same. No court would permit the manifest injustice which such a contention would involve...There is no inconsistency between the proper application of the ultra vires doctrine and the recovery by means of an action in rem or on a quasi contractual basis of monies or goods in the hands of the party receiving the same in consequence of the transaction. The problem which must be faced is whether there is any other basis on which such goods can be recovered. It seems to me that the alternative basis is something akin to an *estoppel*.'[302]

The basis of this finding can only be that the courts will not countenance injustice when it is within their power to prevent it. In the case in hand it was held that the PMPS were entitled to be admitted as creditor of the PMPA companies, since it would be unconscionable to allow the borrowing companies to rely on any want of authority to lend by the PMPS.

(h) Reform of the doctrine of ultra vires

[7.093] The traditional reason why a company had to have an objects clause was, first, to make its shareholders aware of its objectives, and secondly, to let its creditors know the nature of its business[303]. In this day and age such reasons are anachronistic. For both creditors and shareholders, the modern realities of company practice, as opposed to company law, have meant that the doctrine has done more harm than good. If the decision in *Rolled Steel Products* is followed, the scope of the doctrine of ultra vires will be greatly diminished[304].

[7.094] In the UK, the Companies Act 1985, s 35 (UK)[305] attempts to abolish the doctrine of ultra vires. One way could have been to dispense with the requirement to have an objects clause at all thus allowing a company to do as it pleased. This was not the chosen reform. Rather, s 35 (as amended) provided that 'the validity of an act done

301 Murphy J also referred to the Alberta Supreme Court, of Canada in *Breckenridge Speedway Ltd* 64 DLR 488 and the Supreme Court of Canada in *Rolland v La Caisse d'Economie Notre-Dame de Quebec* (1895) 24 SCR 405.

302 [1992] ILRM 349 at 362. Emphasis added.

303 See Pennington, 8 Co Law at 103–104, where the Prentice Report on Ultra Vires is reviewed.

304 Note Clark (1985) 6 Co Law 155 who says: 'the modern corporation will effectively have full contractual capacity'.

305 As amended by the Companies Act 1989 (UK), s 108.

by a company shall not be called into question on the ground of lack of capacity by reason of anything in the company's memorandum.'

It has been suggested[306] that such a reform seeks the most just solution in that while the doctrine of ultra vires cannot now apply in the UK, nevertheless a director who is responsible for the company pursuing an object which is not within the capacity of the company will be guilty of an abuse of power. Hence, English legislative focus has been on the imposition of responsibility on the internal management of the company: a previously ultra vires act will not invalidate the contract but will ground an action against the directors, at the suit of the company's members.

[7.095] In Ireland, the Company Law Review Group has recommended that the doctrine of ultra vires be abolished for private companies limited by shares, which accounts for some 89% of all companies registered. The Review Group's recommendation is that such companies should 'be given the legal capacity of a natural person'[307]. It remains to be seen whether the Review Group's recommendation will be accepted.

[D] THE AUTHORITY OF CORPORATE AGENTS

[7.096] Although a company is a separate legal entity[308], because of both de jure and de facto limitations, it does not have the same contractual capabilities as human persons. The most colourful expression of this is found in the dictum of Buckley J in *Continental Tyre & Rubber Co (GB) Ltd v Daimler & Co*[309] where he said:

> 'The artificial legal person called the corporation has no physical existence. It exists only in contemplation of law. It has neither body, parts, nor passions. It cannot wear weapons nor serve in wars. It cannot be neither loyal nor disloyal. It cannot compass treason. It can be neither friend nor enemy. Apart from its corporators it can have neither thoughts, wishes, nor intentions, for it has no mind other than the mind of the corporators.'

The root source of corporate authority in general, and contractual authority in particular, lies with the members of a company. However, it is usual for the members to divest themselves of almost all power through the adoption of model reg 80[310]. By model reg 80 the members delegate the management of the company to the board of directors. The board may in turn delegate its authority to a managing director where model reg 112 has been adopted.

The company's members can, where permitted by the articles of association, resolve in general meeting to enter into a contract. In practice, however, this is not the norm, and the vast majority of contracts are entered into by the board or the managing director without reference to the members. The board or managing director will be acting on delegated authority as agents for the company. Where authority is not delegated to the directors, and where the members resolve to enter into a contract, the only restrictions on

---

306 Pennington, *Pennington's Company Law* (6th edn, 1990), p 97.

307 *The Company Law Review Group's First Report, (2000–2001)*, recommendation 10.9.2 at p 226.

308 *Salomon v Salomon & Co Ltd* [1897] AC 22.

309 *Continental Tyre & Rubber Co (GB) Ltd v Daimler & Co* [1915] 1 KB 893 at 916.

310 See Chapter 8, *Corporate Governance: Management by the Directors*, para **[8.004]**.

their authority are the company's constitutional documentation and the general law. However, where the directors enter into a contract on behalf of a company they can only act within their permitted delegated authority. Much of the case law on the authority of corporate agents is consequently concerned with situations where the chain of authority breaks down. The issues which arise here for consideration are examined under the following headings:

1. Actual and implied authority of corporate agents.
2. Ostensible authority of corporate agents.
3. The usual and ostensible authority of particular corporate organs.
4. Constructive notice of public documents.
5. The indoor management rule.
6. The scope of the rule in *Turquand*'s case.
7. European intervention.

Actual and implied authority of corporate agents

[7.097] The legal principles applicable to the actual authority of corporate agents are found in the laws of agency[311]. Where an agent acts within the limits of his actual authority and the capacity of the company[312], the company as principal will be bound by all contracts entered into by the agent[313]. The basis of actual authority is the 'consensual arrangement' between the company and the agent[314]. No special formalities are required to appoint an agent[315]. In the case of corporate employees, the basis of the consensual arrangement will usually be rooted in their contract of employment. It should also be

---

311 See *Halsbury's Laws of England* (4th edn, 1974); Frideman, *The Law of Agency* (6th edn, 1990), *Bowstead & Reynolds on Agency* (16th edn, 1996); and Cheshire, Fifoot &Furmston, *Law of Contract* (12th edn, 1986), p 469.

312 The company will not be bound by the ultra vires acts of an agent: *Thomas Williamson Ltd v Bailieborough Co-operative Agricultural Society Ltd* (31 July 1986, unreported), High Court, per Costello J, considered at para **[7.060]**.

313 *Freeman & Lockyer v Buckhurst Park Properties (Mangal) Ltd* [1964] 2 QB 480, [1964] 1 All ER 630. Lord Diplock LJ said (at 502–503):

> 'An "actual" authority is a legal relationship between principal and agent created by a consensual agreement to which they alone are parties. Its scope is to be ascertained by applying ordinary principles of construction of contracts, including any proper implications from the express words used, the usages of trade, or the course of business between the parties. To this agreement the contractor is a stranger; he may be totally ignorant of the existence of any authority on the part of the agent. Nevertheless, if the agent does enter into a contract pursuant to the "actual" authority, it does create contractual rights and liabilities between the principal and the contractor.'

314 *Kett v Shannon & English* [1987] ILRM 364 at 366 per Henchy J, following Diplock LJ in *Freeman & Lockyer* [1964] 2 QB 480, [1964] 1 All ER 630.

315 CA 1964, s 38. That said, however, a commercial agent, within the meaning of the European Communities (Commercial Agents) Regulations 1994 (SI 1994/33), must be appointed, or his appointment evidenced, in writing: reg 5.

noted that an agent may have implied actual authority. In *SMC Electronics Ltd v Akhter Computers Ltd*[316] *the following passage*[317] was cited with approval:

> 'An agent who is authorised to do any act in the course of his trade, profession or business as an agent has implied authority to do whatever is normally incidental, in the ordinary course of such trade, profession or business, to the execution of his express authority, but not to do anything which is unusual in such trade, profession or business, or which is neither necessary not incidental to the execution of his express authority.'

In *Thomas Williamson Ltd v Bailieborough Co-operative Agricultural Society Ltd*[318] Costello J said:

> 'Actual authority can be expressly conferred on a company's board of directors or it can be expressly conferred by the board of directors on an agent or it can impliedly be conferred by them on an agent. Thus when a board of directors appoints a "managing director" or a "secretary" it impliedly confers on the person so appointed the powers usually associated with holders of such offices.'[319]

Where an agent's authority is conferred in ambiguous terms, his company might be bound by his actions where he acts reasonably and in good faith[320]. The concern of company law and agency is with the authority of corporate officers and corporate organs. The basis of the consensual arrangement between the agent and principal-company will be found in the company's articles of association, the resolutions of its members and directors and any contracts between the company and its agents. However, even where there exists no actual authority based on a consensual arrangement, the company may still be bound by an agent's actions where the agent is found to have acted within his *ostensible or apparent authority*[321].

Ostensible authority of corporate agents

[7.098] Actual and ostensible authority were distinguished by Henchy J in the Supreme Court in *Kett v Shannon & English*[322] where he said:

---

316 *SMC Electronics Ltd v Akhter Computers Ltd* [2001] 1 BCLC 433.

317 From *Bowstead & Reynolds on Agency* (16th edn, 1996) art 30.

318 *Thomas Williamson Ltd and Another v Bailieborough Co-operative Agricultural Society Ltd* (31 July 1986, unreported), High Court, per Costello J.

319 (31 July 1986, unreported), High Court at p 8.

320 In *SMC Electronics Ltd v Akhter Computers Ltd* [2001] 1 BCLC 433 the English Court of Appeal cited with approval the following passage from *Bowstead & Reynolds on Agency* (16th edn, 1996) art 26 at p 116 at para 3-106: 'Where the authority of an agent is conferred in such ambiguous terms, or the instructions given to him are so uncertain, as to be fairly capable of more than one construction, an act reasonably done by him in good faith which is justified by any of those constructions is deemed to have been fully authorised, though the construction adopted and acted upon by him was not that intended by the principal.'

321 In *Ulster Factors Ltd v Entonglen Ltd and Maloney* (21 February 1997, unreported), High Court (Laffoy J) it was held that, although the director in question did not have actual authority to make certain payments under scrutiny, he did in fact have ostensible authority: see para **[7.102]**.

322 *Kett v Shannon & English* [1987] ILRM 364 at 366.

> 'Actual authority exists when it is based on an actual agreement between the principal and the agent...Ostensible authority, on the other hand, derives not from any consensual arrangement between the principal and the agent, but is founded on a representation made by the principal to the third party which is intended to convey, and does convey, to the third party that the arrangement entered into under the apparent authority of the agent will be binding on the principal.'

The doctrine of apparent or ostensible authority may be seen as a form of estoppel which prevents the company from denying an agent's ostensible authority, which the company represented the agent as having. The law views the company as 'misrepresenting' the agent's authority, or lack of it. In consequence the company is estopped from later denying that agent's authority to bind the company. Implicit in this analysis is that there must be a representation from someone with actual authority[323].

[7.099] The definition of ostensible authority set out by Henchy J in *Kett v Shannon & English* is a para-phrase of the universally cited dictum of Diplock LJ in *Freeman & Lockyer v Buckhurst Park Properties (Mangal) Ltd*[324]. In this, the leading case on ostensible authority, the facts were that the defendant company was formed by Kapoor to buy and sell an estate of land. The articles of the company provided that the directors could appoint a managing director. Although Kapoor, who was a director, acted to the knowledge of the other directors as if he were managing director, he had never been formally appointed as such. When Kapoor engaged the plaintiff architects to apply for planning permission to develop the estate of land the question which arose was whether the company was liable on the contract to pay their fees. It was held that the company was liable to pay their fees, because Kapoor had ostensible or apparent authority to engage the plaintiffs since the board had represented that he was the managing director who had the actual authority to bind the company in a contract.

[7.100] If an outsider is to enforce a contract against a company by arguing that the agent who made it had ostensible authority to contract, the matters set out by Lord Diplock in *Freeman & Lockyer v Buckhurst Park Properties (Mangal) Ltd*[325] must be proved:

> '(1) that a representation that the agent had authority to enter on behalf of the company into a contract of the kind sought to be enforced was made to the contractor;
>
> (2) that such representation was made by a person or persons who had "actual" authority to manage the business of the company either generally or in respect of those matters to which the contract relates;
>
> (3) that he (the contractor) was indeed induced by such representations to enter into the contract, that is, that he in fact relied upon it; and

---

323 On corporate representations, see para **[7.101]**.

324 *Freeman & Lockyer v Buckhurst Park Properties (Mangal) Ltd* [1964] 2 QB 480.

325 *Freeman & Lockyer v Buckhurst Park Properties (Mangal) Ltd* [1964] 2 QB 480. Lord Diplock LJ said (at 503): 'An "apparent" or "ostensible" authority...is a legal relationship between the principal and the contractor created by a representation, made by the principal to the contractor, intended to be and in fact acted upon by the contractor, that the agent has authority to enter on behalf of the principal into a contract of a kind within the scope of the "apparent" authority, so as to render the principal liable to perform the obligations imposed upon him by such contract.'

(4) that under its memorandum or articles of association the company was not deprived of the capacity either to enter into a contract of the kind sought to be enforced or to delegate authority to enter into a contract of that kind to the agent.'[326]

It is well established that this is a correct statement of the law in Ireland[327]. Each of these requirements in order to establish that a person had ostensible authority are next considered, namely:

(a) Corporate representations.

(b) The actual authority of the representor.

(c) Relying on the representation.

(d) The contract was within the permitted capacity and authority of the company.

(a) Corporate representations

[7.101] In *United Bank of Kuwait Ltd v Hammond*[328] Lord Donaldson MR said '...it is trite law that an agent cannot ordinarily confer ostensible authority on himself. He cannot pull himself up by his own shoelaces...'.[329]

In order for the doctrine of ostensible authority to apply, the company must represent or 'hold the agent out as having' authority to do the act in question. No amount of 'self-representation' by the 'agent' will estop the company: *ESS-Food Eksportlagtiernes Sallgsforening v Crown Shipping (Ireland) Ltd*[330]. That this represents Irish law was made clear by the Supreme Court in *Kett v Shannon & English*, where Henchy J cited with approval *Freeman & Lockyer*, and went on to quote the following passage from the dictum of Goff LJ in *Armagas Ltd v Mundagas SA*[331]:

> 'It appears from that judgment [*Freeman & Lockyer*] that ostensible authority is created by a representation by the principle, to the third party that the agent has the relevant authority, when acted on by the third party, operates as an estoppel, precluding the principal from asserting that he is not bound. The representation which creates ostensible authority may take a variety of forms, but the most common is a representation by conduct, by permitting the agent to act in some way in the conduct of the principal's business with other persons, and thereby representing that the agent has the authority which an agent so acting in the conduct of his principal's business usually has.'

---

326 [1964] 2 QB 480 at 506, per Diplock LJ.

327 See, eg, *Kett v Shannon & English* [1987] ILRM 364 and *Ulster Factors Ltd v Entonglen Ltd and Maloney* (21 February 1997, unreported), High Court (Laffoy J).

328 *United Bank of Kuwait Ltd v Hammond* [1988] 1 WLR 1051 at 1066.

329 See also *AG for Ceylon v Silva* [1953] AC 461 at 479.

330 *ESS-Food Eksportlagtiernes Sallgsforening v Crown Shipping (Ireland) Ltd* [1991] ILRM 97. Of the requirement for a corporate representation, Costello J said (at 108): 'This means that although Ballybay [the agent] in this case certainly represented to the defendants [the outsider] that they had authority from third parties to enter into the contract on their behalf this is of no avail to the defendants – they must show some representation made by the plaintiffs which now estops them from denying the existence of the contract and the term conferring a right of lien on the defendants. But no such representation was made by the plaintiffs in this case and none can be inferred from their conduct...'.

331 *Armagas Ltd v Mundagas SA* [1985] 3 All ER 795 at 805.

The most common way in which a company represents is by conduct: the other directors hold the agent out as having the usual authority of a person in a particular position, or holding a particular office[332]. The paradigm situation is where a director acts like a managing director and the company (ie the other directors) acquiesces in outsiders believing this. Where a director has 'the airs' of a managing director and the company acquiesces in outsiders so believing that he is, the outsider can assume that the person has as much power as a real managing director would usually have *in that company*[333].

[7.102] In *Ulster Factors Ltd v Entonglen Ltd and Maloney*[334] it was held that a 'tacit representation' by a company's board of directors that a particular director had authority to authorise a draw down of funds could bind the company. The dispute in that case was between the plaintiff and the defendant-company's liquidator, who challenged the validity of a payment made by the plaintiff on the order of the defendant-company, to a third party on foot of a factoring agreement. In return for the defendant-company assigning all of its debts to the plaintiff, the plaintiff agreed, on request, to make payment 'to or to the order of' the defendant-company of a sum not exceeding the balance available to it under the terms of the agreement. By side-letter it was agreed that the defendant-company would advise the plaintiff as to which of its officers had been nominated to 'call off factor's funds' and these terms were accepted by the defendant-company by the same two directors who had countersigned the affixing of its seal to the factoring agreement. Moreover, the factoring agreement also provided that the defendant-company would provide the plaintiff with the names and specimen signatures of all persons authorised to sign documents on its behalf.

Laffoy J found that notwithstanding these agreements, no instructions or written mandate as to the formalities to be complied with in relation to the draw down of funds was ever given to the plaintiff. Laffoy J also found that for a period of three years, in all but three draw downs (one of which was the disputed one) the plaintiff had been instructed to make the payments directly to the defendant-company. The draw down that was disputed concerned an instruction from a Mr Holland to the plaintiff to make a cheque in the sum of Stg£35,000 payable to a firm of Northern Irish solicitors. Holland, who was a director, financial director and secretary of the defendant-company faxed the plaintiff, directing that the sum be paid to 'King Goddy Solicitors'. The plaintiff queried this by telephone and on foot of this received a second fax, amending the instruction to read 'King and Gowdy Solicitors'. Holland signed both faxes. The plaintiff complied with the instruction and paid the money to the designated solicitors and sent a statement, recording the draw down, to the defendant-company. The statement was not queried.

---

332 See *Allied Pharmaceutical Distributions Ltd v Walsh* [1991] IR 8 at 17, per Barron J. The totality of a company's conduct must always be considered: *Ebeed v Soplex Refson* [1985] BCLC 404; *First Energy (UK) Ltd v Hungarian International Bank Ltd* [1993] BCLC 1409.

333 The reason for the stress on 'in that company' is because, as we shall see an outsider will be deemed to have constructive notice of the company's articles of association which will say what authority a managing director will have in that company. This is because the articles are 'public documents', and any member of the public can examine them in the CRO. See para **[7.116]**.

334 *Ulster Factors Ltd v Entonglen Ltd and Maloney* (21 February 1997, unreported), High Court (Laffoy J). See Linnane, 'Corporate Capacity and Ostensible Authority and their "Inextricable" Entwinement on Display' (2000) 7 CLP 37.

Over six months' later, the defendant-company's then secretary, at the request of its auditors, requested a copy of the cheque for Stg£35,000, which the then secretary thought had been paid to 'Gaul & Knowlton Solicitors'. The plaintiff furnished the copy of the cheque, pointing out the correct name of the payee. Again, this was not queried by the defendant-company. Business continued to be transacted between the plaintiff and the defendant-company until the company was wound-up. The defendant-company's liquidator realised the debts due to the defendant-company, and paid over to the plaintiff all of them, with the exception of the Stg£35,000, which he disputed. The liquidator contended that that payment was ultra vires and also made without the authority of the defendant-company[335]. The defendant-company's managing director testified that Holland, in fact, had no authority to direct payments of funds to third parties on his own, because his authority was as one of two signatories.

[7.103] On this evidence, Laffoy J held that Holland did not have actual authority. The learned judge went on to find, however, that Holland had ostensible authority and she was satisfied that the four conditions laid down by Diplock LJ in *Freeman and Lockyer v Buckhurst Park Properties (Mangal) Ltd* had been fulfilled, in that:

> '(1) there was a representation that Mr Holland, as a director and as company secretary, had authority to request draw down of funds to the company or to a third party,
>
> (2) such representation was made by the board of directors of the company, which had actual authority under its articles of association to manage its business,
>
> (3) the plaintiff actually relied on such representation, and
>
> (4) under its memorandum or articles of association, the company was not deprived of the capacity to request payment of its funds to a third party or to delegate authority to do so.'[336]

As to the nature of the representation by the defendant-company that Mr Holland had authority to request draw down of the funds to the third parties, Laffoy J said:

> 'The representation on which the ostensible authority of Mr Holland, as a director and as company secretary, was founded was a tacit representation. The Agreement specifically provided for monies due to the company being drawn-down either by payment to the company directly or to a third party. The Agreement itself and the terms and conditions contemporaneously agreed to by the company in relation to the method of the operation of the Agreement required the company to advise the plaintiff as to which officers of the company had authority to draw-down funds due to the company. The evidence establishes that in the early states of the operation of the Agreement it was verbally agreed, in the context of a draw-down of funds to the company, that draw-downs would be advised by the directors and the company secretary. In the operation of the Agreement prior to [the disputed draw-down], subject to one exception, every draw-down was requested by one officer of the company only. In failing to communicate to the plaintiff that draw-downs to the order of the company were to be authorised in a different manner to draw-downs into the company, in my view, the company tacitly represented that all draw-downs were to be authorised in the same manner – by one officer of the company.'[337]

---

[335] The ultra vires claim was considered at para **[7.080]** and **[7.089]**.

[336] (21 February 1997, unreported), High Court at p 10.

[337] (21 February 1997, unreported), High Court at pp 10, 11.

Laffoy J found that the fact that the first authorisation to make a payment to the order of the company (in the nature of a payment to a director) had been authorised by both the managing director and Mr Holland, did not negate that tacit representation as it was made in the early stages of the agreement and, being a payment to a director, might well have been perceived as being in a special category. Laffoy J also thought it significant that the propriety of the payment in question was not questioned for some considerable time, and, ultimately, only after the commencement of the winding up. Accordingly, Laffoy J upheld the validity of the payment on the grounds that the director/company secretary had ostensible authority to authorise it. It can be seen that the court will normally look to the totality of a company's express and tacit representations and not confine its remit to what is normal or usual authority for a particular agent[338].

(b) The actual authority of the representor

[7.104] The person or organ which makes the representation must themselves have the actual authority to make such a representation either generally, or in respect of the particular transaction in issue[339]. In a company where model reg 80 is adopted, the board will be entrusted to manage the business of the company and so will have the requisite actual authority to represent an agent as having authority. In the absence of such a provision in the articles, residual actual authority can only lie with the members of the company: *Mahony v East Holyford Mining* Co[340].

[7.105] Not only must the representor have actual authority to enter into the transaction in hand, but so too must the company have the *capacity* to enter into such a transaction. The fourth condition in *Freeman & Lockyer* is that the company's objects clause must allow a contract of the sort made by the agent. This is but a reminder that contracts which are ultra vires the company's powers are void. So in *Thomas Williamson Ltd v Bailieborough Co-operative Agricultural Society Ltd* Costello J did not have to decide whether or not the board had held out the financial controller and chief executive as having power to enter into contracts of guarantee (or authorise others to do so) because he had held that such contracts of guarantee were ultra vires the defendant society.

(c) Relying on the representation

[7.106] The third condition in *Freeman & Lockyer* is that the outsider must have relied upon the representation if the company is to be estopped from disclaiming the transaction. To admit in evidence that one did not rely on the representation, is fatal to establishing that a company is bound by ostensible authority of one of its officers[341].

---

338 See, eg, *Ebeed (t/a Egyptian International Foreign Trading Co) v Soplex Wholesale Supplies Ltd (The Raffaella)* [1985] BCLC 404.

339 So in *British Bank of the Middle East v Sun Life Assurance Co of Canada* [1985] BCLC 78, it was found by the House of Lords that the representors did not themselves have the actual authority to make the representation.

340 *Mahony v East Holyford Mining Co* (1875) LR 7 HL 869. See also *Kilgobbin Mink and Stud Farms Ltd v National Credit Company Limited* [1980] IR 175, and generally, Chapter 8, *Corporate Governance: Management by the Directors*, para **[8.015]**.

341 See *Dunn v MBS Distribution Ltd* (1990) EAT/132/89, 12 June 1990 (UK).

(d) The contract was within the permitted capacity and authority of the company

[7.107] Even where all other elements exist, a person will not have ostensible authority to do something that is ultra vires the company's capacity or precluded by the company's articles of association. Outsiders will be deemed to be aware of any such restrictions on capacity and authority in companies' memoranda and articles of association because these are documents of public record of which they will be deemed to have constructive notice. Constructive notice is considered below[342].

The usual and ostensible authority of particular corporate organs

[7.108] It is important to consider what the usual authority of any given corporate agent is, and this can be gleaned from the articles of association of the particular company. In view of the fact that it is open to a company to vary its articles of association from those set out in CA 1963, Sch 1, Table A, what follows is necessarily a specific analysis of the powers given to various corporate officers in a company which has adopted the model articles in Table A. The authority of the following organs and officers is next considered:

- (a) The board of directors.
- (b) The managing director.
- (c) The chairman of the board.
- (d) The directors.
- (e) The company secretary.
- (f) The sole member of a single-member private company.

(a) The board of directors

[7.109] The model articles in CA 1963, Sch 1, Table A confer a wide variety of powers on the board of directors ('the board')[343]. Of these, model reg 80 is the widest, providing:

> 'The business of the company shall be managed by the directors, who may...exercise all such powers of the company as are not, by the Act or by these regulations, required to be exercised by the company in general meeting...'

It is common for most companies incorporated today to adopt model reg 80 in an undiluted form. Accordingly, the board potentially has the widest possible actual authority to enter into contracts on behalf of the company. Even where a particular board does not have actual authority, it may be found that it has ostensible authority. In *Mahony v East Holyford Mining Co*[344] the articles provided that the directors of the company should manage the business of the company and that all sums paid on behalf of the company were to be paid by cheque, signed as directed by the board. The subscribers to the articles acted as directors, and one acted as secretary although nobody was ever formally appointed to these posts. A letter to a bank claimed that the board had resolved that cheques would be signed by two of three named directors and countersigned by the secretary. A cheque was drawn and the bank which honoured it was protected when the company sought to avoid liability. The board had acted within the ostensible authority

---

[342] See para **[7.116]**.

[343] See generally, CA 1963, Sch 1, Part I, Table A, art 79–90.

[344] *Mahony v East Holyford Mining Co* (1875) LR 7 HL 869, [1874–80] All ER 427.

which could have been conferred upon them by the articles and the company was estopped from avoiding liability.

[7.110] Model reg 79 of Table A, which permits borrowing, is a very important power of the board. However, it is usual to exclude model reg 79 from a company's articles as it contains restrictions on the directors' powers to borrow[345]. It is usual, in lieu, to give to the directors an unfettered power to borrow, in anticipation of a lending institution requiring a company to have this at a later stage[346]. However, one can never assume that model reg 79 has been dropped and an examination of the articles of every company must be undertaken[347]. In *Re Shannonside Holdings Ltd*[348] the company's articles of association contained a model reg 79 type restriction on the directors' powers to borrow. This provided that the directors could not borrow in excess of the company's issued share capital without first obtaining the consent of the company's members in general meeting. What is notable is that Costello J held obiter dictum that 'in the absence of express notice' outsiders would not be bound where the directors borrowed in excess of the company's issued share capital[349]. This decision is considered further, below[350].

(b) The managing director

[7.111] Where model reg 112 of the model articles is adopted, the directors can delegate their authority to the managing director. In such a case the potential for actual authority of the managing director is high, and practice shows that it is usual to adopt model reg 112 in full. One can only assume that the managing director has as much authority as the board has and so one should ensure that model reg 80 also exists. Where both model regs 80 and 112 exist, the managing director will have very wide ostensible authority. Because a managing director's ostensible authority is very wide, a person who is represented as being a managing director will be assumed to have a wide ostensible authority too. Thus in the *Freeman & Lockyer* case, although one of the directors had not in fact been appointed managing director, he acted as such and it was represented by the company that he was managing director. Accordingly, it was held that he had the ostensible authority of a managing director. A further example is *Hely-Hutchinson v Brayhead Ltd*[351] where the chairman of the board acted as de facto managing director of a company. The articles would have permitted the appointment of a managing director,

345 See Chapter 3, *Private Constitutional Documentation*, para **[3.060]**.

346 A standard replacement for reg 79 is: 'The directors may exercise all the powers of the company to borrow money, and to mortgage or charge its undertaking, property and uncalled capital, or any part thereof and to issue debentures, debenture stock and other securities, whether outright or as security for any debt, liability or obligation of the company or of any third party without any limit.'

347 Eg *Re Burke Clancy & Co Ltd* (23 May 1974, unreported), High Court (Kenny J) especially at pp 10–11 of transcript. In that case an equivalent to reg 79 provided that the directors could not borrow in excess of the nominal issued share capital without the sanction of the members in meeting.

348 *Re Shannonside Holdings Ltd* (20 May 1993, unreported), High Court, per Costello J.

349 (20 May 1993, unreported), High Court at p 7.

350 See para **[7.117]** *ff*.

351 *Hely-Hutchinson v Brayhead Ltd* [1968] 1 QB 549.

but one was never appointed. The company entered into an arrangement to assist the plaintiff's company and bought £100,000 of shares from the plaintiff who was appointed a director of the company. Later the chairman signed letters to the plaintiff 'on behalf of' Brayhead Ltd purporting to indemnify him against a personal guarantee he had given for a loan of £50,000 to his company. The chairman further purported, on behalf of Brayhead Ltd, to guarantee a personal loan given by the plaintiff to his company in the amount of £45,000. When the company became insolvent, the plaintiff honoured his guarantee to the bank but the company refused to indemnify him, arguing that the chairman had no authority to sign the letters. The Court of Appeal held that the chairman had implied actual authority 'implied from the circumstance that the board by their conduct over many months had acquiesced in his acting.'[352]

This decision is open to criticism for engendering further confusion in an already confused area and it is submitted that it ought to have been decided on the basis of ostensible authority. It could not be said that the test for the finding of 'implied actual authority' was satisfied since the acts of the chairman were not 'necessary and incidental' to his chairmanship[353].

(c) The chairman of the board

[7.112] Model reg 104 of the model articles provides that 'the directors may elect a chairman of their meetings...'. While sometimes the office of chairman can have wide-ranging actual authority[354] this will only arise because he has been given a high degree of authority by the articles of association of the company in question.

It was held in *Kilgobbin Mink and Stud Farms Ltd v National Credit Company Ltd*[355] that a chairman had both ostensible and implied actual authority to request the company's landlord to pay £8,500 into the account of another company in return for surrendering the company's lease in circumstances in which it seemed that the articles of that company had no potential for conferring such wide authority on the chairman. The decision has been criticised[356] on the ground, inter alia, that there was no corporate representation that the chairman had the authority to do what he did. Apart from saying that the decision was one decided on its own facts, it may have been that since a company resolution was required to surrender the lease[357] the authority of the board was in question. Hence, while an agent cannot as a rule 'hold himself out' it may be possible to say that the chairman, who held 49,999 of the 50,000 shares in the company, could be said to have acted qua member in representing himself as a chairman to the outsider. The finding may, of course, simply have been wrong. The reality is that in general, the chairman will have very little potential actual authority under the CA 1963, Sch 1, Table A model articles of association[358].

---

352 [1968] 1 QB 549 at 584, per Lord Denning MR.

353 See 1 *Halsbury's Laws of England* (4th edn, 1974), p 441.

354 A chairman had 'full and complete plenipotentiary powers' in *Nash v Lancegaye Safety Glass (Ireland) Ltd* (1958) 92 ILTR 11.

355 *Kilgobbin Mink and Stud Farms Ltd v National Credit Company Limited* [1980] IR 175.

356 See Keane, *Company Law in the Republic of Ireland* (2nd edn, 1991), para 12.14.

357 *Kilgobbin Mink and Stud Farms Ltd v National Credit Company Limited* [1980] IR 175 at 176.

358 Note however that CA 1963, s 145(2) provides that where a chairman signs the minutes of a board meeting, such is a standing representation that the meeting was held, and of what happened.

(d) The directors

[7.113] As to the ostensible authority of other officers, a director has little or no potential actual authority in the model articles other than the authority to attest the company seal in model reg 115. Whether or not any given director has more authority will depend on that company's articles.

(e) The company secretary

[7.114] Similarly, the secretary has little actual authority in the model articles (and so, little ostensible authority), but again, this will depend on the circumstances of any given case[359]. Any actual authority enjoyed by a company secretary will have been given to him by the company. It may be noted, however, that being a company's chief administrative officer, a secretary will have ostensible authority to enter into certain contracts on behalf of the company eg employing staff, ordering office machinery and stationery, etc[360].

(f) The sole member of a single-member private company

[7.115] The sole member of a single-member private company[361] would appear to have no ostensible authority in his capacity as member. In such companies there may well be a tendency for the sole member to think that he has full plenipotentiary powers for the company, but this will remain wishful thinking unless the company's articles of association vest such powers in him. Even at that, where model reg 80 is adopted and delegates the management of the company to its directors, a sole member's ostensible authority will derive from his status as a shadow director, and not as a member[362].

Constructive notice of public documents

[7.116] The foregoing analysis of ostensible authority has been predicated on the basis that the outsider is aware of the actual authority accorded the company's officers and organs by its articles of association. By virtue of the doctrine of constructive notice, whether or not an outsider is in fact aware of what the articles say, in law he will be deemed to be aware of the provisions in a company's articles of association[363]. The rationale is that, since the documents are public, the public are on notice of their existence, and the public are further deemed to be aware of their contents[364]. Thus, for example, a person dealing with a company is deemed to be aware:

---

359 See *Panorama Developments (Guilford) v Fidelis Furnishing Fabric Ltd* [1971] 2 QB 711.

360 See Palmer's *Company Law*, p 8226, paragraph 8.1107.

361 As permitted by SI 1994/275, the European Communities (Single-Member Private Limited Companies) Regulations 1994. See generally, Chapter 1, *The Private Company in Context*, para **[1.119]**.

362 See Chapter 8, *Corporate Governance: Management by the Directors*, para **[8.004]***ff*.

363 See *Mahony v East Holyford Mining Co* (1875) 7 HL 869 at 893, *Ernest v Nicholls* (1857) 6 HL Cas 401 at 419; and *Re Jon Beauforte (London) Ltd* [1953] 1 All ER 634. A company's memorandum and articles of association are public documents in the sense that any member of the public can visit the CRO, and see, inter alia, a copy of these documents, a copy of the company's certificate of incorporation, all accounts filed and special resolutions passed.

364 For a justifiably critical analysis, see Ussher, *Company Law in Ireland* (1986), pp 148-151.

— that a given company does not have an model reg 112-type regulation, so that a person purporting to be the managing director has no ostensible authority, since in that company, there can be no managing director!

— that a particular company has no model reg 80-type regulation, so that the board has no potential actual authority to manage the business of the company.

— that a particular company has an unmodified model reg 79-type regulation, and that the members must pass a resolution if the directors are to borrow in excess of the issued share capital.

In its unmodified form, the doctrine of constructive notice of a company's articles has the potential to lead to draconian consequences.

[7.117] The obiter dictum finding by Costello J in *Re Shannonside Holdings Ltd*[365] that an outsider would not be bound by the provisions of a company's articles of association unless he has express notice of their provisions is thought not to be a sufficient authority to displace the albeit unruly but firmly established doctrine of constructive notice. Although it would be difficult to argue against the common sense of such a stance, it is thought that the learned judge was mistaken in his application of the legal principles applicable to ultra vires acts to the law applicable to the authority of corporate agents. In so finding Costello J said:

> 'Once the company in general meeting had decided to issue this debenture, even if it was for a sum in excess of the issued share capital, there was nothing *ultra vires* in the company so deciding to do this and so there was nothing *ultra vires* in the issuing of the debenture. Even if this was not so, I accept the submissions made on behalf of the [debentureholder]. I am not satisfied on the evidence that [the debentureholder] had any express notice of [the article which restricted the directors' borrowing powers]. It seems to me that I would have to have some evidence on which to conclude that [the debentureholder] that[366] some express notice of that article before I could adopt the submissions made on behalf of [the creditor seeking to set the debenture aside]. In the absence of express notice, the debenture granted to [the debentureholder] could not be invalidated even if the directors had exceeded their powers, which they had not, in my opinion.'[367]

It is respectfully submitted that the fact that the creation of the debenture was not ultra vires the company's capacity had no bearing on the question of the directors' *authority* to issue a debenture in excess of the company's issued share capital. It is further suggested that the subsequent references to 'express notice' of the company's articles must be viewed in the context of transactions which might be ultra vires but capable of being saved by reliance on CA 1963, s 8[368].

---

[365] *Re Shannonside Holdings Ltd* (20 May 1993, unreported), High Court.

[366] It would appear that the word 'that' is a typographical error. It is suggested that the learned Costello J intended to use the word 'had'.

[367] (20 May 1993, unreported), High Court, pp 6,7.

[368] On the doctrine of ultra vires and the effects of CA 1963, s 8, see para **[7.077]**.

The indoor management rule[369]

[7.118] Thankfully, the doctrine of constructive notice has been modified at common law by the rule in *Royal British Bank v Turquand*[370]. This relieves outsiders from any duty to satisfy themselves that any *internal requirement* necessary to perfect an agent's actual authority has been complied with. In *Turquand*'s case a company issued a bond to borrow money under seal. Its rules authorised this to be done where an ordinary resolution was passed. However, no such resolution was passed. Subsequently, the company argued that the bearer of the bond could not enforce it because it had constructive notice of the requirement in the company's articles that a resolution must be passed in support of the issuing of such a bond. This argument was rejected and it was held that the company was bound by the bond because, on reading the company's rules, an outsider:

> '...would find, not a prohibition from borrowing but a permission to do so on certain conditions. Finding that the authority might be made complete by a resolution, he would have a right to infer the fact of a resolution authorising that which on the face of the document appeared to be legitimately done.'[371]

In *Re Motor Racing Circuits Ltd*[372] Blayney J said in the Supreme Court:

> '...*Turquand's* case says that where a matter appears to be regular then the party dealing with the company is not affected if in fact by reason of some error in the internal management of the company there is an irregularity.'[373]

In that case the validity of a debenture given by a company was challenged on the basis that although the company's seal had been affixed to the debenture, one or other of the counter signatories was not in fact a director or secretary. The Supreme Court upheld the validity of the debenture on the basis that the bank (in whose favour the debenture had been created) was 'entitled to assume that what is called the internal management of the company had been correctly complied with'[374].

[7.119] The rule in *Turquand*'s case has been applied in many Irish cases. In *Allied Irish Banks Ltd v Ardmore Studios International (1972) Ltd*[375] a lending bank had notice, through the company's articles of association, that the company had three directors and that two directors were required for a quorum. The bank was given a copy of a resolution signed by a director and the secretary-cum-managing director. This certified that a meeting had been held at which a resolution had been passed which allowed, inter alia, the company to borrow from the bank. The company then drew a cheque and the bank

---

369 See generally, McCormack, 'The Indoor Management Rule in Ireland' (1985) Gazette ILSI 17 and Prentice, *The Rule in Turquand's* case, (1991) MLR 14.

370 *Royal British Bank v Turquand* (1856) 6 E & B 327, [1843-60] All ER Rep 435.

371 [1843–60] All ER Rep 435 at 437–438.

372 *Re Motor Racing Circuits Ltd* (31 January 1997, unreported), Supreme Court (Blayney J; nem diss).

373 (31 January 1997, unreported), Supreme Court at p 7.

374 (31 January 1997, unreported), Supreme Court at p 7.

375 *Allied Irish Banks Ltd v Ardmore Studios International (1972) Ltd* (30 May 1973, unreported), High Court, per Finlay J.

honoured it. However, there was an irregularity in the meeting which had been held to pass the resolution. Although two directors had attended the meeting, in fact a third director had not been given notice of the meeting. Finlay J said that this along with other invalid procedures were, merely 'classic examples of an irregularity in the internal management of the company'[376]. Accordingly the bank was permitted to rely on the rule in *Turquand's* case and the company was held to be bound to repay the bank[377]. Similarly in *Ulster Investment Bank Ltd v Euro Estates and Drumkill Ltd*[378] a mortgage was invalidly sealed by reason of the fact that there had been no valid directors' meeting to approve and authorise the sealing of the mortgage deed because the meeting had been invalid by reason of being inquorate. Nevertheless Carroll J held that the bank were:

> '...entitled to rely on the rule in the *Royal British Bank v Turquand* and to assume that the mortgage prepared by it and which on its face is duly executed in accordance with the articles, is the deed of the company.' [379]

It is significant that Carroll J held that the bank had not disentitled itself to rely on the rule in *Turquand's* case by requiring in its facility letter the right to receive and approve copies of the various board resolutions authorising the borrowing[380].

---

[376] (30 May 1973, unreported), High Court at p 8.

[377] Finlay J accepted that the rule in *Turquand's* case was more far-reaching than the case in hand. Referring to the case of *Duck v The Tower Galvanising Co Ltd* [1901] 2 KB 314 Finlay J said:

> 'The facts...were that a debenture had been issued by the defendant company without authority, no directors of the company having been appointed and no resolution to issue debentures having been passed. The holder of the debenture, however, had, on the findings of the court, no notice of any irregularity in the issue of the debenture. It was there held that the debenture was good and prevailed over the rights of an execution creditor. It seems to me that the irregularities found to have existed in the case which I have just quoted were far more fundamental than those which I assumed to exist in this case.'

[378] *Ulster Investment Bank Ltd v Euro Estates and Drumkill Ltd* [1982] ILRM 57.

[379] [1982] ILRM 57 at 67 Carroll J cited with approval the judgment of Lindley LJ in *County of Gloucester Bank v Rudry Merthyr Steam and House Coal Colliery Co* [1895] 1 Ch 629 where he said (at 636) that:

> 'Here the directors may make any quorum they like – it may be two, or it may be three. They did apparently appoint three. The mortgage in question is under the seal of the company, signed by two directors and countersigned by the secretary. Now what could anybody think of that? What is there to put them upon inquiry? What is there to give them notice of anything irregular? If a person looked at the deed and looked at the articles he would not see anything irregular at all; he would be at liberty to infer, and any one in the ordinary course of business would infer, that if the directors had appointed a quorum they appointed the two who signed that deed. But supposing that three were wanted, he is not bound to go and look at the directors' minutes; he has no right to look at them except as a matter of bargain. The directors' minutes unless he knows what they are, do not affect him at all. There is nothing irregular on the face of the deed even taken with the articles – there is nothing illegal in it. As to a plea of non est factum, that could not be sustained for a moment and I have not the slightest doubt myself that that deed is as good as any deed that ever was sealed.'

[380] See also the judgment of McWilliam J in *Re Irish Grain (Trading Board) Ltd* (26 November 1984, unreported), High Court and the Supreme Court decision of Lynch J in *Hyland v Ireland* (22 October 1998, unreported), Supreme Court (Lynch J; nem diss), p 7.

The scope of the rule in *Turquand*'s case

[7.120] While *Turquand*'s case will certainly save certain transactions, there are limits to its scope and operation[381]. Many of the so-called 'exceptions' to the rule are but examples of its definitional limits. Where, for example, an agent acts beyond his ostensible authority the rule in *Turquand*'s case cannot redeem the situation for an outsider, since one may only assume that an agent has the authority associated with the officer whom he is held out as being. Similarly, there must be reliance by an outsider on the articles which show the potential authority of any given agent. Thus in *Rama Corporation Ltd v Proved Tin & General Investments Ltd*[382] a director of the defendant-company, who had no actual authority to do so, contracted with the plaintiff-company. The defendant-company's articles provided that the directors could delegate power to one director but since there had been no reliance upon the articles by the plaintiffs who had not read them, they could not enforce the contract against the defendant-company. Constructive notice of the articles will not suffice: there must be *actual reliance* on the existence of the power to delegate. The other limitations on the scope of the rule in *Turquand*'s case are:

(a) Where the irregularity is of public record.

(b) The outsider must act in good faith.

(a) Where the irregularity is of public record

[7.121] While *Turquand*'s case allows one to assume that internal matters necessary to perfect authority have been done, it cannot apply to situations where the act needed to perfect authority becomes an act of public record. Consequently, where a company's articles require a resolution of the members to be passed before the directors can borrow above a certain amount, whether the rule in *Turquand*'s case will apply depends upon the nature of the required resolution. Although one can assume that an ordinary resolution was passed, one cannot assume that a special resolution was passed. This is because a copy of any special resolution passed must, pursuant to CA 1963, s 143(4)(a) be registered in the CRO, and once registered become a document of public record. Once something becomes a matter of public record, the rule in *Turquand's* case ceases to apply.

In *Irvine v Union Bank of Australia*[383] the company's articles required the members to pass a special resolution authorising the directors to borrow in excess of a specified amount. The directors caused the company to borrow an amount in excess of the specified amount without the sanction of the members by special resolution. It was held that the rule in *Turquand*'s case did not apply because the outsider had constructive notice that a special resolution had not been passed in accordance with the company's articles, since no copy had been filed in the CRO.

(b) The outsider must act in good faith

[7.122] Where a person is *actually aware* that a company's internal procedures have not been followed, he cannot rely upon the rule in *Turquand*'s case because the rule only

---

[381] See Prentice, (1991) LQR 14.

[382] *Rama Corporation Ltd v Proved Tin & General Investments Ltd* [1952] 1 All ER 554.

[383] *Irvine v Union Bank of Australia* (1877) 2 Ap Cas 366 Privy Council.

assists those who deal with the company in good faith. This limit on the scope of the rule will often, but not inevitably[384] mean that *insiders* cannot rely on the rule because they ought to know whether or not the articles of association have been complied with. Thus, in *Cox v Dublin City Distillery Co (No 2)*[385], a company's articles required a quorum of two directors and further precluded directors from voting on matters in which they were personally interested. Notwithstanding this, the directors issued debentures, both to themselves and to others, as security for advances. Barton J held that the debentures in favour of the 'outsiders' were valid by virtue of the rule in *Turquand*'s case and that the company was estopped from denying their validity. However, the loans to the directors were held not to be binding on the company because the directors were aware of the company's articles and thus could not rely on *Turquand*'s case 'the resolution was a nullity, and the two other directors cannot be regarded as outsiders who took without notice of the board's meetings.'
In that case, the resolutions were invalid because two of the three directors were personally interested and because the meeting was inquorate.

[7.123] Similarly, where the contract is of an exceptional nature, the outsider may be on notice that there may be an irregularity and so under a duty to satisfy himself that the company's articles were indeed complied with. Again, the central point is that the outsider should deal in good faith. Accordingly, in *AL Underwood Ltd v Bank of Liverpool & Martins*[386] the director of the plaintiff-company endorsed cheques which were made payable to the plaintiff-company into his own bank accounts with the defendant bank. The receiver to the plaintiff-company successfully sued the defendant-bank in conversion. The bank was prohibited from relying on *Turquand*'s case because it failed to make ordinary enquiries as to the director's actions. As Bankes LJ said, 'the strangeness of his conduct...is material'.[387] In the case of *Houghton & Co v Nothard Lowe & Wills Ltd*[388] a director entered into a contract with an outsider which entitled the outsider to sell goods owned by the company and to keep the proceeds to secure another debt of the company. Here the transaction was so unusual as to put the outsider on inquiry as to whether the contract was authorised. The outsider failed to make reasonable inquiries and consequently the company was held not to be bound by the contract purportedly made by the director on the company's behalf.

European intervention

[7.124] The European Communities (Companies) Regulations 1973[389] brought Article 9(2) of the First EU Directive on Company Law (68/151 of 9 March 1968) into Irish law.

---

[384] Sometimes the duty of directors to ensure compliance with the company rules is elevated to a rule that *Turquand*'s case can never assist 'insiders': *Morris v Kanssen* [1946] AC 459. However, cf *Hely-Hutchinson v Brayhead Ltd* [1968] 1 QB 549, where the plaintiff, although a director, was permitted to enforce a contract against his company by relying on the rule.

[385] *Cox v Dublin City Distillery Co (No 2)* [1915] IR 345. See also *Howard v Patent Ivory Manufacturing Co* [1883] 3 Ch D 156.

[386] *AL Underwood Ltd v Bank of Liverpool & Martins* [1924] All ER 230, [1924] 1 KB 775.

[387] [1924] All ER 230 at 234E.

[388] *Houghton & Co v Nothard Lowe & Wills Ltd* [1927] 1 KB 246; [1927] All ER 97.

[389] SI 1973/163.

These regulations have the effect of modifying the doctrine of constructive notice in two respects.

(a) Regulation 10 of the First EU Directive on Company Law

[7.125] Regulation 10 has the effect of limiting those documents of which an outsider will be deemed to have constructive notice. In respect of those documents listed in reg 4[390] a company cannot rely on these documents as against a person dealing with the company unless either notice has been published in *Iris Oifigiúil* of their delivery to the Registrar of Companies, or the person dealing with the company had knowledge of them[391]. Although the list of documents is very comprehensive it at least has the effect that persons dealing with the company have certainty as to what documents they shall be deemed to have notice of. The effects of the regulation are that simple filing in the CRO will not be sufficient in itself to put a person dealing with the company on notice: notice of the delivery must also be published in *Iris Oifigiúil*[392].

(b) Regulation 6 of the First EU Directive on Company Law

[7.126] Regulation 6, when read in conjunction with reg 10, modifies the doctrine of constructive notice. It provides:

> 'In favour of a person dealing with a company in good faith, any transaction entered into by any organ of the company, being its board of directors or any person registered under these regulations as a person authorised to bind the company, shall be deemed to be within the capacity of the company and any limitation of the powers of that board or person, whether imposed by the memorandum or articles of association or otherwise, may not be relied upon as against any person so dealing with the company.

Furthermore, there is a presumption[393] that the person dealing with the company acted in *good faith*. Regulation 6 raises several points for consideration.'

[7.127] In the first place, reg 6 does not affect the doctrine of ostensible authority because it only applies to transactions entered into by the board of directors and persons registered under the regulations. This prevents a person from relying upon the regulations where he transacts with a body whom he *mistakenly thinks* is the board of

---

390 SI 1973/163, reg 4(1) provides that notice that the following documents have been delivered to the Registrar of Companies shall be published in Iris Oifigiúil: (a) any certificates of incorporation; (b) memoranda and articles of association or charters; (c) documents amending/altering the documents at (b); (d) the amended text of the memoranda & articles; (e) returns relating to directors/change in directors; (f) returns regarding persons other than the board of directors, authorising such other persons to enter transactions binding the company and changes in respect of such persons; (g) annual returns; (h) notice of, or change in, the registered office; (i) any winding up order; (j) any order for the dissolution of the company; (k) returns by liquidator of final meeting on winding up. Regulation 4(2) provides that notice of the foregoing shall be published within six weeks of the relevant delivery.

391 SI 1973/163, reg 10 provides also that as regards: 'transactions taking place before the sixteenth day after the date of publication, they shall not be relied upon against a person who proves that it was impossible for him to have knowledge of them.'

392 This could well be an onerous task for companies, but the Registrar of Companies in practice normally obliges by giving the requisite notice to *Iris Oifigiúil*.

393 SI 1973/163, reg 6(2).

directors or believes to be a person registered under the regulations. The regulations only apply where one transacts with any organ of the company '*being* its board of directors or any person registered...'. In *Smith v Henniker-Major & Co*[394] it was held by Rimer J that the Companies Act 1985, s 35A (UK)[395] did not apply to validate a resolution passed by an inquorate board of directors. In that case one director purported to resolve in favour of an assignment of a cause of action from the company to himself. By reason of the company's articles, the meeting was inquorate. Rimer J held that in such circumstances it could not be said that the board of directors had in fact acted at all.

It should be noted that the case law on ostensible authority remains intact. Rather, it is the doctrine of constructive notice which has been modified by the regulations in that now qualifications in the articles on the *authority* of the board of directors or person registered under the regulations will not upset a transaction entered into by a person acting in good faith.

[7.128] In the second place, reg 6 applies only to persons dealing *in good faith*[396]. Clearly, insiders as well as outsiders can act in good faith. While there are no Irish authorities in point, the concept of dealing in good faith in this context has received consideration by the English courts. In *International Sales and Agencies Ltd v Marcus*[397] Lawson J said:

> '...the test of good faith in somebody entering into obligations with a company will be found either in proof of his actual knowledge that the transaction was ultra vires the company or where it can be shown that such a person could not in view of all the circumstances, have been unaware that he was party to a transaction *ultra vires*.'

A more pragmatic view of the law was taken by Browne Wilkinson VC in *TCB Ltd v Gray*[398]. In that case the company's articles required that all debentures securing a loan were to be under seal, with the usual attestation provisions[399]. While the secretary did sign, the other signatory was a solicitor acting under a power of attorney. Inter alia, it was argued that the debenture was invalid because a director ought to have attested the company seal. The plaintiff-bank successfully relied upon the English provision similar to reg 6. Notwithstanding that the bank did not look at the company's articles, it was held that they had acted in good faith:

> 'The last words of the second part of the sub-section expressly provide that good faith is to be presumed; the second part further provides that the person dealing with the company is *not* bound to inquire as to limitations on the powers of directors. In my judgment it is

394 *Smith v Henniker-Major & Co* [2002] BCC 544 noted by Howell, 'Section 35A of the Companies Act 1985 and an Inquorate Board: One Won't Do' (2002) 23 Co Law 96.

395 This provides: 'In favour of a person dealing with a company in good faith, the power of the board of directors to bind the company, or authorise others to do so, shall be deemed to be free of any limitation under the company's constitution.'

396 For further consideration of good faith or bona fides and an analysis of case law, in the context of CA 1990, s 38(1)(b), see Chapter 11, *Statutory Regulation of Transactions Involving Directors and Companies*, para **[11.100]**.

397 *International Sales and Agencies Ltd v Marcus* [1982] 3 All ER 551.

398 *TCB Ltd v Gray* [1986] 1 All ER 587.

399 As per model reg 115.

> impossible to establish lack of "good faith" within the meaning of the section solely by alleging that inquiries ought to have been made which the second part of the sub-section says need not be made.'[400]

While the existence of the requirement that a person must act in good faith means that there is no blanket protection, it is submitted, as has been suggested elsewhere, that[401] a subjective honesty is required: the fact that a *reasonable man* may have done otherwise than the person dealing with the company did is but an evidential factor in deciding whether or not good faith existed[402]. It is thought that good faith must also have been influential in the decision of *Smith v Henniker-Major & Co*[403] since there, not only was it possible to find out that a quorum for directors' meetings was two and that only one person had in fact attended the board meeting but the person who sought to rely upon the protection was himself a director.

[7.129] In the third place, Regulation 6 refers to 'any transaction'. This means that its scope is wider than mere contract. However, it is not necessary that the transaction be validly authorised by the company, indeed, it is fundamental to the nature of the regulation's intention, that it be a 'purported transaction'[404].

[7.130] Fourthly, it should be noted that in accordance with reg 3, the regulations only affect *limited liability* companies. Consequently, the regulations do not have application to all three types of private company and can only be invoked in transactions with a private company limited by shares or limited by guarantee and having a share capital.

[7.131] Finally, in *Coöperatieve Rabobank 'Vecht en Plassengebied' BA v Minderhoud (receiver in bankruptcy of Mediasafe BV)*[405] the European Court of Justice held that the rules governing the enforceability of acts as against third parties by a company's relevant organs where there is a conflict of interest fall outside the normative framework of Article 9 of the First EU Directive on Company Law (68/151 of 9 March 1968), which was implemented in Ireland by the European Communities (Companies) Regulations 1973. Previously the Advocate General had held that Article 9 did not afford protection where there was a conflict of interest, saying that it:

> '...concerns only the enforceability of the limits, laid down by law, the statutes or resolutions of the company, on the powers conferred on the company representatives.
>
> ...A conflict of interests entails a defect of intention on the part of the representative, thus preventing him from lawfully carrying out certain acts because the *contemplatio domini* is absent.'[406]

---

400 [1986] 1 All ER 587 at 596 e–f. Emphasis added.

401 See Ussher, *Company Law in Ireland* (1986), pp 135–136.

402 Cf *Crowley v Flynn* (13 May 1983, unreported), High Court per Barron J where it was suggested that 'in good faith' implied that a person would take reasonable steps and was not absolved from all enquiry.

403 *Smith v Henniker-Major & Co* English (unreported), Eng High Court, transcript HC 0102108 noted by Howell, 'Section 35A of the Companies Act 1985 and an Inquorate Board: One Won't Do'(2002) 23 Co Law 96.

404 See *TCB Ltd v Gray* [1986] 1 All ER 587 at 596g–h.

405 *Coöperatieve Rabobank 'Vecht en Plassengebied' BA v Minderhoud (receiver in bankruptcy of Mediasafe BV)* [1998] 2 BCLC 507.

406 [1998] 2 BCLC 507 at 511a–d.

In that case, a Dutch company's articles provided that in the event of a conflict of interests between the company and its directors, those director(s) without a conflict would be empowered to bind the company; and moreover, where there was only one director or if all of the directors had a conflict of interest, the company should be represented in such transactions by a 'board of commissioners'. The company had only one director and he caused the company to enter into a transaction that involved a conflict with his own interests. On the company's insolvency, the receiver appointed sought to avoid the transaction and he succeeded in avoiding the transaction in the Dutch courts. On appeal to the Dutch Supreme Court, the question was referred to the European Court of Justice. The Advocate General held that Article 9 had no application to a conflict of interests so that the person who would have been affected by the avoidance of the transaction could not use it as a shield. This was upheld by the European Court of Justice, which stated:

> '...the rules governing enforceability as against third parties of acts done by members of company organs in circumstances where there is a conflict of interest with the company fall outside the normative framework of the First Directive and are matters for the national legislature.'[407]

Accordingly, it would seem that on its true interpretation Article 9 of the First Directive cannot be relied upon by a third party to enforce a transaction or arrangement entered into by a company in circumstances where the board of directors had a conflict of interest. In such circumstances, the third party's defence would seem to be confined to the rule in *Turquand*'s case[408]. In some respects this decision is similar to that of the Irish courts in their interpretation of 'lawful and effectively done' as used in CA 1963, s 8[409]. The international judicial trend is to refuse protection in cases where there is an abuse of directors' powers.

---

[407] [1998] 2 BCLC 507 at 516de.

[408] See para **[7.118]**.

[409] See para **[7.080]**.

Chapter 8

Corporate Governance: Management by the Directors

Introduction

[8.001] In any company, the theoretical baseline is that corporate governance is divided between the members in general meeting and the directors acting as a board. One of the central concepts in company law is the distinction between corporate *ownership* and corporate *management*[1]. Ownership is considered in Chapter 15, *Shares and Membership*. In this chapter, corporate *management* and those responsible for management, the *directors* and other officers are considered. In the context of private companies, it is important to recognise that the distinction between ownership and management remains the baseline and that corporate governance is divided between the members and the directors. However, while this is the de jure position, the de facto position will often be that the directors and the members will be one and the same persons. In this sense, the division of powers can be something of a sham, since the players on both sides are quite often the same persons. The formalities imposed on directors and members that may seem to do no more than pay homage to the apparent sham, can – especially when relations are harmonious – be a source of irritation (or even jest) in small companies where the members and directors are one and the same people. If, however, relations become acrimonious these same formalities can become a battleground for warring factions, each side scrutinising the running of the company for transgressions of the Companies Acts and culpability on the other's part.

[8.002] In this chapter, corporate governance and the management of companies by the directors is considered in three separate sections:

[A] Delegating Managerial Power to the Directors.

[B] The Directors.

[C] The Secretary.

[A] Delegating Managerial Power to the Directors

Root authority begins with the members

[8.003] Root, or residual, authority in a company vests in the members by virtue of the Companies Act, 1963, s 18(2) ('CA 1963')[2]. This provides, inter alia, that:

---

1 For commentary on how even more acute these issues become in public companies, see, generally, Clarke, 'Corporate Responsibility in Light of the Separation of Ownership and Control' [1997] 19 DULJ 50 and Chapter 28, *Public Companies in Context*, para **[28.062]**.

2 See Flynn, 'The Power to Direct' [1991] 13 DULJ 101.

> 'From the date of incorporation...the subscribers of the memorandum, together with such other persons as may from time to time become members of the company, shall be...capable forthwith of exercising all the functions of an incorporated company...'

Accordingly, the members of a company are entitled to appoint the board of directors and to dictate, whether ab initio or by future alteration, the specific provisions in the company's articles and memorandum of association. In this way the members are the *root authority* in a company. It should be remembered that the members are free to adopt any internal regulations they see fit and are certainly not obliged to adopt the model articles contained in CA 1963, Sch 1, Table A (the 'model regulations'). It is, for example, possible – albeit extremely unlikely in practice – that a company might be incorporated which leaves all power with the members, and does not make any delegation of powers to the directors. Typically, however, the members will adopt the model articles and where model reg 80 is adopted, ironically, the very document to which the members give life typically emasculates them where it operates to divest them of the powers of management. What can be given can also be taken away and having considered the usual delegation of the powers of management to the directors, this section shall then consider the circumstances in which members' powers can resurface.

Delegation of powers of management to the directors

[8.004] The vast majority of private companies incorporated in Ireland contain model reg 80[3] (imported from CA 1963, Sch 1, Table A, Part I) in their articles of association. This most important of articles provides:

> 'The business of the company shall be managed by the directors, who may pay all expenses incurred in promoting and registering the company and may exercise all such powers of the company as are not, by the Act or by these regulations, required to be exercised by the company in general meeting, subject, nevertheless, to any of these regulations, to the provisions of the Act and to such directions, being not inconsistent with the aforesaid regulations or provisions, as may be given by the company in general meeting; but no direction given by the company in general meeting shall invalidate any prior act of the directors which would have been valid if that direction had not been given.'

The effect of model reg 80 is to vest the powers of management of the company's business in the directors, *exclusively*. Subject to the reservations contained in model reg 80, considered below[4], and the members' ability to amend model reg 80 by special resolution, the members cede to the directors the powers of management. So in *Howard Smith Ltd v Ampol Petroleum Ltd*[5] Lord Wilberforce said:

> 'The construction of a limited company normally provides for directors, with powers of management, and shareholders with defined voting powers having power to appoint the directors, and to take, in general meetings, by majority vote, decisions on matters not reserved for management...directors, within their management powers, may take decisions against the wishes of the majority of shareholders, and indeed the majority of

3 Individual provisions in the articles of association may be referred to either as a 'regulation' or as an 'article'.

4 At para **[8.007]**.

5 *Howard Smith Ltd v Ampol Petroleum Ltd* [1974] AC 821.

shareholders cannot control them in the exercise of these powers while they remain in office.'[6]

This principle was applied in *Scott v Scott*[7]. There, the members passed, in general meeting, two resolutions: one as to the interim payment of dividends before the dividends were declared, and the other as to the investigation of the company's financial affairs. It was held that both resolutions were invalid as they were attempts to dictate the financial direction of the company which, under the articles, was the sole remit of the directors.

[8.005] Model reg 80 delegates the powers to the 'directors', making no mention of the *board of directors*. However the fact that a company must have at least two directors (CA 1963, s 174), that the directors will generally act by majority (model reg 101) and that model reg 80 delegates powers to the 'director*s*', plural, implies that the delegation is to the board of directors.

[8.006] It should also be noted, for completeness, that in many companies the powers of management, delegated to the directors by model reg 80, will be further delegated by the directors to managers and employees of the company. This delegation will take effect either by resolution of the board of directors or, where a managing director has been appointed (or other director conferred with authority to make such a delegation) by his authorised act in favour of the employee. Where directors effect such a delegation of managerial power, they have a duty to ensure it is properly exercised and they will remain accountable for any misuse of the delegated power[8].

The express reservations of power to members in model reg 80

[8.007] The delegation of the powers of management is, however, subject to the three express qualifications contained in model reg 80:

(a) Subject to the Companies Acts 1963–2001.

(b) Subject to the other regulations in the articles of association[9].

(c) Subject to *directions* given by the members in general meeting where such are not inconsistent with the Companies Acts 1963–2001 or the other articles of the company concerned.

Of these three qualifications it is (c) which causes most controversy. The fact that the members do not, under model articles, fully divest themselves of all powers gives rise to the problem of the division of powers. Two distinct areas of debate are opened. The first is, in view of the extensive delegation of power to the board of directors, what powers remain with the members acting in general meeting? The second is, what is the effect of the members being empowered to make directions to the directors?

---

6 [1974] AC 821 at 837.

7 *Scott v Scott* [1943] All ER Rep 582.

8 See Chapter 10, *The Duties of Directors and Other Officers*, para **[10.024]** *ff*.

9 Of course, if the articles of a company specifically give the members certain powers, or fetter the exercise of certain powers of the directors by making member-consent a prerequisite, the powers of management of the company by the directors are thus qualified.

(a) Subject to the Companies Acts 1963–2001

[8.008] Even where model reg 80 has been adopted, the Companies Acts 1963–2001 provide that certain fundamental matters of corporate governance still require the assent of the members. This can be rationalised on the grounds that certain matters are so fundamental as to require the sanction of the *owners* of the company. In most private companies, the members and the directors will be one and the same, but nevertheless the law requires them to implement certain actions by voting in general meeting, wearing their shareholders' hats. An example is where it is proposed that a company provide financial assistance in connection with the purchase of its own shares pursuant to CA 1963, s 60[10]. In this instance, the directors alone cannot legally sanction the action: the members of the company are required to pass a *special resolution*. Similarly, Companies Act 1990, s 29 ('CA 1990') requires the members to pass an *ordinary resolution* to sanction a substantial property transaction between a director and the company.

(b) Subject to other regulations in the articles of association

[8.009] The clearest example of a regulation in the articles of association that confers a power on directors, subject to a claw-back in favour of the members, is model reg 79. The undiluted version of this article provides, inter alia, that the directors may exercise all the company's powers to borrow provided that the amount of the monies borrowed shall not exceed the nominal amount of the share capital of the company for the time being issued, 'without the previous sanction of the company in general meeting'. As considered in a previous chapter, this article is typically modified on incorporation to give the directors an unfettered power to borrow[11]. In those rare companies where model model reg 79 has been adopted, and the directors borrow in excess of the limits prescribed therein, it has been held that the members may ratify such unauthorised borrowing where the act of borrowing was itself within the capacity of the company ie it was not ultra vires[12].

(c) Subject to directions given by the members

[8.010] Typically the members will delegate the power to manage the company to the directors. Under model articles this delegation is qualified inter alia by the proviso contained in model reg 80 that the directors' powers are subject to '...such directions, being not inconsistent with the aforesaid regulations or provisions, as may be given by the company in general meeting.' The effects of this qualification and the extent to which the members in general meeting can control the directors have been the subject of some speculation[13]. It should be noted at the outset that any *directions* made by the members to the directors will not invalidate prior acts of the directors[14].

---

10 See Chapter 18, *The Maintenance of Capital*, para **[18.041]** *ff*.

11 See Chapter 3, *Private Constitutional Documentation*, para **[3.060]**.

12 See, for example, *Irvine v The Union Bank of Australia* (1877) 2 App Cas 366

13 For a view which sees model reg 80 as being a potential power base for the members, see Temple Lang, 'Shareholder Control in Irish Companies' (1973) Gazette ILSI 241; and for a contrary view see Ussher, 'Directing the Directors' (1975) Gazette ILSI 303. See generally, Ussher, *Company Law in Ireland* (1986), pp 85–91 and Flynn, 'The Power to Direct' [1991] 13 DULJ 101.

14 Model reg 80.

[8.011] Model reg 80 must be considered in its historical context. Prior to the passing of CA 1963, companies adopted a slightly different article under previous legislation. This provided for the members to give *regulations* as opposed to *directions*[15]. Indeed, the corresponding English modern provision still contains the word 'regulations', and consequently English case law must be viewed with caution. Judicial interpretation of the words 'such regulations' has held that the exclusive management of the company is vested in the directors and that the shareholders cannot interfere in the exercise of the directors' powers unless the shareholders amend the articles of association by inserting a new 'regulation', the effect of which is to wholly or partially oust the directors' powers of management. The old authorities in the UK[16] were applied in the case of *Breckland Group Holdings Ltd v London and Suffolk Properties Ltd*[17]. In that case the members of a company sought an injunction to prevent its directors from passing a board resolution to ratify the action of commencing a law suit. Harman J refused the injunction on the basis that:

> '...where matters are confided by the articles such as Article 80 to the conduct of the business by the directors, it is not a matter where the general meeting can intervene...The principle, as I see it, is that Article 80 confides the management of the business to the directors and in such a case it is not for the general meeting to interfere.'[18]

This case marks the present state of the English courts' interpretation of their corresponding model article to our model reg 80. In *Alexander Ward and Co Ltd v Samyang Navigation Co Ltd*[19] Lord Kilbrandon said that '...the directors, and no one else, are responsible for the management of the company, except in the matters specifically allotted to the company in general meeting.' This interpretation means that exclusive power vests in the directors, save in respect of functions which are specifically reserved to the members in general meeting.

[8.012] Irish authorities have similarly interpreted the predecessor of model reg 80, which used the phrase 'such regulations'. In *Clark v Workman*[20] Ross J said:

> '...the powers given to directors are powers delegated to the directors by the company, and when once given the company cannot interfere in the subject-matter of the delegation unless by special resolution.'

However, the use of 'such directions' in the modern model model reg 80 casts some doubt on whether the management of the company exclusively vests in the directors. The word 'directions' implies a member's directive, other than an actual special resolution, the effect of which is to amend the articles of association by the insertion of a new article or 'regulation'. Although the judgment of Buckley LJ in *Gramophone and Typewriter*

---

15 Companies (Consolidation) Act 1908, s 71.

16 *John Shaw & Sons (Salford) Ltd v Shaw* [1935] 2 KB 113; *Salmon v Quin & Axtens Ltd* [1909] AC 442; *Automatic Self-Cleansing Filter Syndicate Co Ltd v Cunningham* [1906] 2 Ch 34.

17 *Breckland Group Holdings Ltd v London and Suffolk Properties Ltd* [1989] BCLC 100.

18 [1989] BCLC 100 at 106.

19 *Alexander Ward and Co Ltd v Samyang Navigation Co Ltd* [1975] 2 All ER 424; see also *Scott v Scott* [1943] 1 All ER 582.

20 *Clark v Workman* [1920] IR 107. See also *Nash v Lancegaye Safety Glass (Ireland) Ltd* (1958) ILTR 11 at 26, per Budd J.

Ltd v Stanley[21] shows the deficiency in the use of the word 'regulations', so too does it demonstrate the significance of the use of the word 'directions'. In the course of his judgment Buckley LJ said:

> '...even a resolution of a numerical majority at a general meeting of the company cannot impose its will upon the directors when the articles have confided to them the control of the company's affairs. The directors are not servants to obey directions given by the shareholders as individuals; they are not agents appointed by and bound to serve the shareholders as their principals. They are persons who may by the regulations be entrusted with the control of the business, and if so entrusted they can be dispossessed from that control only by the statutory majority which can alter the articles.'[22]

The result of the use of the word 'directions' can be said to be as follows[23]: the members can direct the directors to do or refrain from doing certain acts only where to do so is not inconsistent with the articles of that company. Hence, where the articles themselves (apart from model reg 80) expressly give the directors certain powers, the members cannot act in disregard of those powers by directing the directors as to how such powers should be exercised. Accordingly, the members cannot direct the directors to register shares against their wishes, where model reg 3 of Part II has been adopted[24].

An example of where the Irish article might allow the members to direct the directors (where its English counterpart would not) is where the members wished the directors to commence or desist from litigation because the power to commence litigation is not *specifically* delegated to the directors. Accordingly, the powers of members may be said, in practice, to be dependent upon chance: they can only give directions to the directors upon matters that the articles have not exclusively remitted to the directors. That said, it is thought that maximum latitude will be given by the courts to the expression 'the business of the company', which is what model reg 80 entrusts to the management of the directors.

[8.013] Where the directors refuse to follow the members' wishes, one solution may be for the members to muster sufficient support to pass a special resolution amending the articles. In this respect, the Irish reality is in practice not all that different to the scenario outlined in *John Shaw & Sons (Salford) Ltd v Shaw*[25] where it was said that 'The only way in which the general body of the shareholders can control the exercise of the powers

---

21 *Gramophone and Typewriter Ltd v Stanley* [1980] 2 KB 89, [1908–10] All ER 833.

22 [1989] BCLC 100 at 105–106.

23 See Ussher, *Company Law in Ireland* (1986), p 87 *ff*.

24 In *Scott v Scott* [1943] All ER 582 at 584, Lord Clauston, after referring to an model reg 117 type regulation, (which provides that 'The directors may from time to time pay to the members such interim dividends as appear to the directors to be justified by the profits of the company') said: 'It is quite clear, accordingly, that the payment of an interim dividend is a matter which, by that article, is placed within the exclusive power of the directors, unless I can find some other article which limits that...I do not think it is suggested that, if this was a resolution for the payment of an interim dividend, that it could possibly be held to be valid, it having been passed by the company in general meeting. If it was, then the annual general meeting impinged upon the sphere of activity which, in the most express terms, is confined to the directors.'

25 *John Shaw & Sons (Salford) Ltd v Shaw* [1935] All ER 456 at 464, per Greer LJ.

vested by the articles in the directors is by altering their articles...'. Only by altering by special resolution the articles of association of a company can the members safely reassume the powers of management in the company. Where a separation of corporate powers exists the members will seldom have to exercise their legislative powers in this manner. This is because the directors' knowledge of the members' power to regain control will often be sufficient to ensure they comply with the members' wishes because, otherwise, there is every reason to expect that they (the directors) will be ousted by ordinary resolution[26]. More frequently, there will not be a complete separation of corporate powers and disputes may arise where the members are not a united body, and some or all of their number are also the company's directors.

The resurgence of members' powers

[8.014] Notwithstanding that the members delegate most of their powers to the directors, the members' powers may resurface. The three most common occasions when this will happen are:

(a) Where there are no directors capable of acting.

(b) Where the directors exceed their delegated authority.

(c) Where directors act in breach of their duties.

(a) Where there are no directors capable of acting

[8.015] In the first place, the members will always be the persons to whom power *reverts in default*. So, where the directors resign or die or become incapacitated, it is the members to whom power will revert in default. An example of this 'power in default' is *Mahony v East Holyford Mining Co*[27], where it was held that where there was no official board of directors the members of the company had the power to 'hold out' certain of their number as being directors. The ability to hold-out persons as something that they are not is the essence of authority. Similarly, in *Alexander Ward and Co Ltd v Samyang Navigation Co Ltd*[28], two individuals issued a summons against the defendant-company on behalf of the plaintiff-company which had no directors. The defendant-company later sought to have the action set aside on the ground that the plaintiff-company had not authorised the action. The plaintiff-company contended that it was open to the company subsequently to ratify the action under ordinary principles of agency. The articles of association of the plaintiff-company contained a model reg 80-type regulation which delegated the powers of management to the directors. Lord Hailsham held that where no directors had been appointed, residual authority to do such things reverted to the members in general meeting. Accordingly, the action on behalf of the company was capable of ratification. He said:

> 'In my opinion at the relevant time the company was fully competent...to raise proceedings...The company could have done so either by appointing directors or as I think by authorising proceedings in general meeting which, in the absence of an effective board,

---

26 In accordance with CA 1963, s 182(1): see para **[8.076]**.

27 *Mahony v East Holyford Mining Co* (1875) LR 7 HL 869, considered in Chapter 7, *Corporate Contracts, Capacity and Authority*, para **[7.109]**.

28 *Alexander Ward and Co Ltd v Samyang Navigation Co Ltd* [1975] 2 All ER 424.

> has a residual authority to use the company's powers...it was competent to do so, and in my view it was therefore a competent principal...'.[29]

(b) Where the directors exceed their delegated authority

[8.016] The second set of circumstances in which the members' powers resurface is where the directors exceed their delegated authority. An example in point is the case of *Re Burke Clancy & Co Ltd*[30]. In that case the directors of the company purported to borrow more money than they were authorised, under the articles of association, to borrow[31]. However, the members of the company approved of the accounts of the company in general meeting. Of this, Kenny J said:

> 'It is established law that the members of a company may ratify acts which are outside the powers of the directors but are *intra vires* the company...the approval of the accounts showing the amount borrowed was a ratification by the company of the action of the directors in borrowing an amount in excess of the [authorised limit]. '[32]

In one of the decisions relied upon by Kenny J, *Grant v United Kingdom Switchback Railways Company*[33], the articles of a company authorised the sale of part of its undertaking to another company; they also contained a provision, prohibiting any director from voting in respect of any contract in which he was interested. The directors of the company caused the company to enter into a contract for the sale of part of its undertaking to another company, of which all of the directors of the first company, except one, were also directors. At a general meeting of the company an ordinary resolution was passed approving and adopting the agreement for sale. Lindley LJ held that the adoption of the contract was within the objects of the company, did not amount to an alteration of the articles of association and thus could be sanctioned by an ordinary, as opposed to a special, resolution. He said:

> 'The appellant contends that the company could not ratify this contract except by special resolution. In my opinion that contention is unfounded. There is a broad distinction between altering the articles and merely saying "this act was not authorised by the articles, but we will ratify it". The shareholders can ratify any contract which comes within the powers of the company, and this contract clearly does, for the articles expressly authorise selling any part of the undertaking of the company'.[34]

The raison d'être for the members in general meeting being able to validate unauthorised acts of the directors which are intra vires the company's capacity is because the

---

29 [1975] 2 All ER 424 at 428.

30 *Re Burke Clancy & Co Ltd* (23 May 1974, unreported), High Court.

31 See the present model reg 79, which limits the borrowing powers of the directors, to borrow an amount which does not exceed the issued share capital. This is typically deleted by companies upon formation, but if it is not deleted ab initio, when that company decides to approach a bank to borrow money, then the bank or other financial institution will insist that it is deleted. See also *Re Shannonside Holdings Ltd* (20 May 1993, unreported), High Court, per Costello J.

32 (20 May 1993, unreported), High Court at pp 9, 10. Kenny J followed the cases of *Irvine v Union Bank of Australia* (1877) 2 App Cas 366 and *Grant v United Kingdom Switchback Railways Company* (1888) 40 Ch D 135.

33 *Grant v United Kingdom Switchback Railways Company* (1888) 40 Ch D 135.

34 (1888) 40 Ch D 135 at 139–140.

directors' powers derive from the members. The members of a company cannot, however, ratify acts that are ultra vires the company[35]. Were the directors to cause the company to engage in ultra vires activities, then not only would they be exceeding the ambit of the authority conferred upon them by the members, but they would also be acting beyond the company's capacity to act.

After the commencement of a company's winding-up, a liquidator is competent to ratify acts done without authority[36].

(c) Where directors act in breach of their duties

[8.017] The third set of circumstances in which the inherent powers of the members may resurface is where the members ratify breaches of directors' duties at all times before a company is wound up. In most circumstances, the members in general meeting can absolve the directors of their wrongdoings, provided those wrongdoings are *intra vires*. A good example of this is seen in *Bamford v Bamford et al*[37]. In that case 90% of a company's authorised capital had been issued and the articles provided that the power to issue shares was vested in the directors. When a takeover bid was made, the directors allotted the remaining 10% of the unissued capital at par value to a principal distributor of the company's products. The plaintiffs – who were two shareholders in the company – instituted proceedings, claiming that the allotment was invalid as in making the allotment the directors had not acted bona fide, but with an improper motive, namely to stymie the takeover bid. The directors responded by convening an extraordinary general meeting ('EGM') of the company and, despite the plaintiffs issuing further proceedings for a declaration that any ratifying resolution would be invalid, a majority of the company's members passed an ordinary resolution, ratifying the allotment of the unissued 10% of the company's shares by the directors. At trial, Plowman J held that the directors' allotment was capable of being ratified and that the actions of the members in ratifying the allotment had validated it and this was upheld by the Court of Appeal. Harman LJ said:

> 'I am expressing the view which I have held throughout – that this is a tolerably plain case. It is trite law, I had thought, that if directors do acts, as they do every day, especially in private companies, which, perhaps because there is no quorum, or because their appointment was defective, or because sometimes there are no directors properly appointed at all, or because they are actuated by improper motives, they go on doing for years, carrying on the business of the company in that way in which, if properly constituted, they should carry it on, and then they find that everything has been so to speak wrongly done because it was not done by a proper board, such directors can, by making a full and frank disclosure and calling together the general body of the shareholders, obtain absolution and forgiveness of their sins; and provided the acts are not ultra vires the company as a whole everything will go on as if it had been done all right from the beginning. I cannot believe that that is not a commonplace of company law. It is done every day. Of course, if the majority of the general meeting will not forgive and approve, the directors must pay for it.'[38]

---

35 *Ashbury Railway Carriage and Iron Co v Riche* (1875) LR 7 HL 256. For criticism of the members' inability to ratify ultra vires acts, see Ussher, *Company Law in Ireland* (1986), p 131.

36 *Alexander Ward & Co Ltd v Samyang Navigation Co Ltd* [1975] 1 WLR 673.

37 *Bamford v Bamford* [1970] 1 Ch 212.

38 [1970] 1 Ch 212 at 237, 238.

Moreover, the English Court of Appeal in that case rejected the contention that a special resolution was required to ratify the wrongs of directors. The wrong there involved an action (allotment of shares) that was within the contemplation of the articles of association; it was only 'wrong' because the directors exercised their powers to allot shares for an improper purpose. In these circumstances, Russell LJ said that since it would be a matter for the company by ordinary resolution to decide whether to proceed against the directors for compensation for misfeasance, the company could validly decide by ordinary resolution not to institute proceedings. This, he said, supported entirely the view that an ordinary resolution 'would be effective, having as it would in substance the same purpose and effect as a resolution not to bring the proceedings to avoid the allotment'[39].

[8.018] The members need not wait until there has been a breach of duty and they can act in anticipation of a breach of duty and prospectively release the directors from their duties. Perhaps the best example of this is seen in the leading case on directors' conflicts of interest – *Regal (Hastings) Ltd v Gulliver*[40]. There, Lord Russell said of the options open to the directors whom, it was held, had made a profit from their relationship with their company that:

> 'They could, had they wished, have protected themselves by resolution (either antecedent or subsequent) of the Regal shareholders in general meeting. In default of such approval, the liability to account must remain.'

It should be noted, however, that while the members in general meeting may absolve the directors of breaches of their duties to the company, they cannot release the directors of breaches of duties owed to individual members or to a minority of shareholders[41]. There is a principle that an act authorised by all of the shareholders is in law an act of the company[42]. In *Re D'Jan of London Ltd*[43] Hoffmann LJ held that that principle required that the shareholders should have, whether formally or informally, mandated or ratified the act in question and that it was not enough that they probably would have ratified if they had known or thought about it before the appointment of a liquidator[44].

[B] THE DIRECTORS

[8.019] The term 'director'[45] has no technical meaning. It is defined by CA 1963, s 2(1) to include 'any person occupying the position of director by whatever name called'. As seen above, the powers of management are delegated by the members to the directors

39 [1970] 1 Ch 212 at 242G.

40 *Regal (Hastings) Ltd v Gulliver* [1967] 2 AC 134, the facts of which are considered in Chapter 10, *Duties of Directors and Other Officers*, para **[10.050]**.

41 For members' personal rights see Chapter 15, *Shares and Membership*, para **[15.083]** and Chapter 19, *Shareholders' Remedies*, para **[19.089]**.

42 *Multinational Gas and Petrochemical Co v Multinational Gas and Petrochemical Services Ltd* [1983] Ch 258.

43 *Re D'Jan of London Ltd* [1993] BCC 646.

44 [1993] BCC 646 at 648.

45 See, generally, Sealy et al (eds), *British Company Law and Practice* (1983; loose leaf) at 29,001.

and, therefore, those who occupy the position of director, are those persons who are appointed to manage the business of the company. The definition of 'director' is robust. Were the members not to delegate management to the directors and, instead, to exercise the powers of management themselves, they could also be said to 'occupy the position of directors' and would be accountable under the Companies Acts just as directors proper would. However, it is almost invariably the case that the board of directors will be the organ within a company, which is the recipient of the members' delegated powers. While the members in general meeting retain certain powers, it is the board of directors who under the model articles are deemed to have the important powers of management of the business of the company. However, the board itself has no separate existence and is but the sum of its member-directors.

[8.020] In this section, the following issues concerning directors are considered:

1. Two directors, one resident in the state, and all natural persons.
2. Persons disqualified from and restricted in becoming directors.
3. The number of directorships that can be held by one person.
4. The formally appointment of directors.
5. Types of formally appointed directors.
6. De facto directors.
7. Shadow directors.
8. The status of directors.
9. The remuneration of directors.
10. Ceasing to be a director.
11. Disclosures concerning directors and secretaries.

Two directors, one resident in the state, and all natural persons

[8.021] Every company, including single-member companies, must have at least two directors[46], and while there is no statutory upper limit on the number of directors that can be appointed to a company, a company's articles of association may set a maximum number[47]. A director of a company may also be its secretary: CA 1963, s 175. However, CA 1963, s 177 provides that where the law requires something to be done by both a director and the secretary, this will not be satisfied by its being done by or to the same person acting both as director and as, or in place of, the secretary. The most obvious example of this is the attestation of the company seal: where the articles require two directors or one director and the secretary, an attestation by one person alone who is both director and secretary will be invalid.

[8.022] In an attempt to prevent Ireland being used as a jurisdiction of incorporation of choice by nefarious foreigners, the Companies (Amendment) (No 2) Act 1999, s 43(1) ('C(A)(No 2)A 1999') was enacted. The background to this was the utilisation of Irish registered non-resident (IRNR) companies in international money laundering and

46 CA 1963, s 174.

47 Model reg 97 provides that the members can by ordinary resolution increase of decrease the number of directors.

various other scams in foreign countries, as far apart as Mexico and Latvia and many in between. Although essentially tax driven, the view taken was that company law changes were also required to prevent these non-resident Irish companies from tarnishing Ireland's international reputation[48]. Though clearly motivated by the best of intentions, the remedial legislation makes for tortious reading, trying to batten down the hatches whilst, simultaneuously provisioning for fire escapes, necessitated by EU membership. Section 43(1) of C(A)(No 2)A 1999 provides that, subject to certain exceptions, at least one of the directors for the time being of a newly-incorporated company shall, from 18 April 2000[49], be a person who is resident in the State. In the case of companies formed and registered under the CA 1963 and existing[50] companies, they had 12 months from 18 April 2000 to ensure that at least one of their directors is a person resident in the State[51]. Moreover, any provision of a company's articles that prohibits a person resident in the State from being a director of the company is void[52]. The failure to comply renders the company and every officer in default guilty of an offence[53] and summary proceedings may be brought and prosecuted by the Registrar of Companies[54]. Moreover, a defaulting company may be struck off the register[55].

[8.023] Section 44(8) of C(A)(No 2)A 1999 provides that for the purposes of s 43, a person is resident in the State at a particular time ('the relevant time') if:

> '(a) he or she is present in the State at—
>
> > (b) any one time or several times in the period of 12 months preceding the relevant time (the "immediate 12 month period") for a period in the aggregate amounting to 183 days or more, or
> >
> > (c) any one time or several times—
>
> (d) in the immediate 12 month period, and
>
> (e) in the period of 12 months preceding the immediate 12 month period (the "previous 12 month period"),
>
> (f) for a period (being a period comprising in the aggregate the number of days on which the person is present in the State in the immediate 12 month period and the number of days on which the person was present in the State in the previous 12 month period) in the aggregate amounting to 280 days or more, or
>
> (e) that time is in a year of assessment (within the meaning of the Taxes Consolidation Act 1997) in respect of which the person has made an election under s 819(3) of that Act.'

---

48 See generally, Chapter 2, *Formation, Registration and Conversion of Private Companies*, para **[2.052]**.

49 The commencement date for C(A)(No 2)A 1999, s 43(1): SI 2000/61.

50 As defined by CA 1963, s 2.

51 C(A)(No 2)A 1999, s 43(2).

52 C(A)(No 2)A 1999, s 43(12).

53 C(A)(No 2)A 1999, s 43(13).

54 C(A)(No 2)A 1999, s 43(14).

55 C(A)(No 2)A 1999, s 43(15): on strike-off, see Chapter 12, *Company Law Compliance and Enforcement*, para **[12.143]**.

Moreover, notwithstanding C(A)(No 2)A 1999, s 44(8)(a)(ii), where in the immediate 12 month period concerned a person is present in the State at any one time or several times for a period in the aggregate amounting to not more than 30 days, the person shall not be resident in the State for the purposes of C(A)(No 2)A 1999, s 43 and no account shall be taken of the period for the purposes of the aggregate mentioned in C(A)(No 2)A 1999, s 44(8)(a)(ii)[56]. References to a person being present in the State means being 'personally present in the State' and a person is deemed to be present for a day if the person is present at the end of the day[57].

[8.024] The main exception to the general rule that every company must have at least one director who is a person resident in the State is set out in C(A)(No 2)A 1999, s 43(3). This provides that the general rule in sub-ss (1) and (2) will not apply to a company that holds a bond, in the prescribed form, in force to the value of €25,394.76[58]. This bond must provide for payment to a person nominated by the Registrar of Companies or the Revenue Commissioners of a sum of money to discharge the whole or part of the company's liability in respect of certain fines and penalties. The fines and penalties to which the bond must relate are:

— a fine, if any, imposed on the company in respect of an offence under the Companies Acts, committed by it, being an offence that is prosecutable by the Registrar of Companies; and

— a fine, if any, imposed on the company in respect of an offence under the Taxes Consolidation Act 1997, s 1078 committed by it, being an offence that consists of a failure by the company to deliver a statement which it is required to deliver under s 882 of that Act or to comply with a notice served on it under s 884 of that Act, and

— a penalty, if any, which the company has been held liable to pay under the Taxes Consolidation Act 1997, ss 1071–1073.

The nominated person is obliged by C(A)(No 2)A 1999, s 43(3) to apply any sum that becomes so payable to such fine or penalty. The nominated person is obliged to keep all proper and usual accounts, including an income and expenditure account and a balance sheet of all monies received by him on foot of the bond and of all disbursements made by him[59]. The Minister for Enterprise, Trade and Employment may, following consultation with the Minister for Finance, Revenue Commissioners and other concerned or interested persons, prescribe that arrangements in relation to bonds shall only be entered into with persons of a prescribed class or classes; the Minister for Enterprise, Trade and Employment may also prescribe the form of the bond and the

---

56 C(A)(No 2)A 1999, s 44(9).

57 C(A)(No 2)A 1999, s 44(10)(a) and (b).

58 In addition to the sum of £20,000, the bond must also make provision for the payment of a sum of money (not exceeding such sum as the Revenue Commissioners and the Minister for Enterprise, Trade and Employment may sanction) for the purpose of defraying such expenses as may have been reasonably incurred by the nominated person in carrying our his duties under C(A)(No 2)A 1999, s 43(3).

59 C(A)(No 2)A 1999, s 43(6).

minimum term of the bond[60]. Where a company is required to have such a bond it must append it to the statement required by Companies (Amendment) Act 1982, s 3 ('C(A)A 1982') (where there is a no resident director on the company's incorporation); to any notification by a person ceasing to be a director that the company has no resident directors (as required by C(A)(No 2)A 1999, s 43(9)); to its annual return where during the period to which it relates, none of the directors are resident in the State (unless notification has already been made under s 43(9))[61]. As noted, where a person ceases to be a director and he knows that he was the only resident director at that time, he is under a direct obligation to notify in writing the Registrar of Companies of those facts[62]. Where a former director fails to comply with the aforementioned requirement, he shall become jointly and severally liable with the company to pay any of the fines or penalties referred to in subsection (3) above, that are subsequently imposed upon the company[63]. Section 43(4) of C(A)(No 2)A 1999 exempts the bond from the laws of champerty.

[8.025] A further, discretionary, exemption from the requirement that every company must have at least one director who is a person resident in the State is provided for in C(A)(No 2)A 1999, s 44(1), which states that sub-ss (1) and (2) of s 43 shall not apply 'in relation to a company in respect of which there is in force a certificate under this section'. Such a certificate may be granted by the Registrar of Companies, on application being made in the prescribed form, where the registrar has been tendered proof[64] that '...the company has a real and continuous link with one or more economic activities that are being carried on in the State'.

An example of a case where the Registrar may grant such a certificate might be where a foreign multinational incorporates an Irish company in connection with the multinational locating a factory or other industry in Ireland. In such a case, the Registrar may exempt the Irish company from the requirement that one of its directors be resident in the State. A written statement[65] to the company from the Revenue Commissioners made within two months of application for a certificate which states that the Revenue have 'reasonable grounds to believe that the company has a real and continuous link with one or more economic activities being carried on in Ireland' is deemed to be proof for the registrar[66]. Where the Registrar, in consequence of information that has come into his possession, is of opinion that the company has ceased to have such a link, he must revoke the certificate[67] and likewise if the Revenue obtain such information, they

60 C(A)(No 2)A 1999, s 43(7).

61 C(A)(No 2)A 1999, s 43(8).

62 C(A)(No 2)A 1999, s 43(9). Such notification is deemed not, of itself, to be regarded as constituting defamatory matter: C(A)(No 2)A 1999, s 43(10).

63 C(A)(No 2)A 1999, s 43(11), which goes on to provide that any such fine or penalty may be recoverable by the Registrar of Companies or the Revenue Commissioners, as appropriate, from the former director, as a simple contract debt in any court of competent jurisdiction.

64 C(A)(No 2)A 1999, s 44(3).

65 Within the meaning of C(A)(No 2)A 1999, s 44(5).

66 C(A)(No 2)A 1999, s 44(4).

67 C(A)(No 2)A 1999, s 44(6).

may (but are not obliged) to give notice in writing of this to the registrar[68]. Where the Registrar receives such notice from the Revenue, such is deemed to constitute information in his possession[69].

[8.026] In Ireland, only natural persons can become directors of companies, as CA 1963, s 176(1) prohibits companies from having a body corporate as a director. It should be noted that there is no prohibition under the Companies Acts on an Irish company (or indeed any body corporate) from becoming a director: the prohibition is on Irish companies having as a director, a body corporate. Accordingly, an Irish company can validly be a director of a company incorporated in another jurisdiction where the laws of that jurisdiction do not prevent companies from having as directors, bodies corporate eg an Irish company may validly be the director of a company formed and registered in England and Wales.

Persons disqualified from and restricted in becoming directors

[8.027] The office of director requires no formal qualifications[70]. Qualifications, such as they are, are purely negative and the Companies Acts 1963-2001 merely state that certain persons may not become directors, or may only do so subject to specific restrictions. A fourfold classification can be made between:

(a) Persons debarred from being directors.

(b) Qualification shares.

(c) Persons restricted in their directorships.

(d) Disqualification of directors and others.

(a) Persons debarred from being directors

[8.028] An undischarged bankrupt cannot lawfully become a director, and for a bankrupt to do so is a criminal offence: CA 1963, s 183[71]. It was held in *R v Brockley*[72] that to act as a company director whilst being an undischarged bankrupt is an absolute offence of strict liability and that it was no defence for the accused to claim that he genuinely believed that he had been discharged as a bankrupt before becoming a company director. A person convicted of an indictable offence concerning his involvement with a company or of fraud or dishonesty can be prevented by the courts from being a director of a company[73]. It should also be noted that an auditor is debarred from being a director of the company of which he is auditor[74].

(b) Qualification shares

[8.029] As a general rule, a director is not obliged to hold so-called 'qualification shares' in a company. While model reg 77 allows a company to have a shareholding qualification for its directors, it goes on to provide that where the company in general

---

68 C(A)(No 2)A 1999, s 44(7).

69 C(A)(No 2)A 1999, s 44(7).

70 See Chapter 10, *The Duties of Directors and Other Officers*, para **[10.067]**.

71 As amended by CA 1990, s 169.

72 *R v Brockley* [1994] 1 BCLC 606.

73 CA 1990, s 160(1).

74 CA 1963, s 162(5), as amended by C(A)A 1982, s 6.

meeting does not fix any, none shall apply. Under CA 1963, s 180, a director, who by resolution of the members is required to have a share qualification must obtain and maintain such shares within two months from his appointment or a lesser time if the company's articles so provide. It may of course be provided in the articles that a share qualification is a condition precedent to the appointment of a director. It should be noted that this issue will not generally arise since, in many Irish private companies, the directors will perhaps themselves be the only shareholders of the company.

(c) Persons restricted in their directorships

[8.030] The law relating to the making of restriction orders pursuant to s 150 is comprehensively addressed in Chapter 12, *Company Law Compliance and Enforcement*[75], and it is sufficient to simply note here the existence of the restriction. Section 150 of CA 1990 provides that, subject to certain qualifications in sub-s (2), on an insolvent company being wound up, the court shall declare that a person to whom the chapter applies shall not for five years:

> '...be appointed or act in any way, whether directly or indirectly, as a director or secretary or be concerned or take part in the promotion or formation of any company unless it meets the requirements set out...'.

In the case of a private company, these requirements are set out in CA 1990, s 150(3), which provides that any company in which such a person is involved should have a nominal value of allotted[76] and fully paid up, in cash, share capital of €63,486.90[77]. On application being made to court, the court may grant relief to a restricted company under CA 1990, s 157. However, the rule remains that such companies are debarred from joining in the near shibboleth which was the Irish 'two pounds company' – whether it will in future be known as a one or two euro company remains to be seen. Before a 'restricted' person accepts an appointment as a director or secretary in another company, he must, within 14 days of his appointment or his acceptance, notify that company that he is a restricted person[78]. This latter provision will prove inappropriate in many Irish private companies since, far from it being the case that a restricted person will be 'head-hunted' by an innocent company looking for a director, it is quite likely that it will be the restricted director himself who will form the company which will, by his involvement, thereby become a restricted company.

(d) Disqualification of directors and others[79]

[8.031] The law relating to the making of disqualification orders pursuant to CA 1990, s 160 is comprehensively addressed in Chapter 12, *Company Law Compliance and Enforcement*[80], and it is sufficient to again note here that persons who are disqualified may not act as directors of companies.

---

75 See para **[12.043]** *ff*.

76 See CA 1990, s 156 as to the requirements for allotting shares in a restricted company.

77 CA 1990, s 150(3)(a)(ii) as amended by CLEA 2001, s 41(1)(b). See also CA 1990, s 158, which empowers the Minister for Enterprise, Trade and Employment to vary the amounts mentioned in CA 1990, s 150(3).

78 CA 1990, s 150(5).

79 Linnane, 'Restrictions on and Disqualification of Directors' (1994) ILT 132.

80 See para **[12.090]** *ff*.

The number of directorships that can be held by one person

[8.032] In addition to the requirement that Irish companies have at least one resident director[81], another measure taken to curb the abuse of Irish companies was to limit the number of directorships which any one person can hold. The perceived danger was that by requiring one Irish resident director, unscrupulous Irish residents might have facilitated the foreign controllers of companies wishing to locate in Ireland by allowing their name go forward and to act as multiple nominee directors. An acute example of what might have been is seen in the case of *Official Receiver v Vass*[82]. There, Blackburne J disqualified a resident of the jurisdiction of Sark who had acted as nominee director to 1,313 companies and as company secretary to 513 companies. When one of the companies went into liquidation two years after its formation, owing over £571,000 disqualification proceedings were taken against the nominee director. Blackburne J held that in holding himself out as a director to so many companies the person had abrogated his responsibilities for those companies by merely acting as a nominee and that he deserved to be disqualified for a substantial period.

[8.033] Section 45(1) of the C(A)(No 2)A 1999 provides that a person shall not, at a particular time, be a director or shadow director[83] of more than 25 companies. It will be noted that this provision is directed at the person, not the company, and that an Irish company may have more than 25 directors, unlikely though that might be. It is an offence for a person to become a director of one or more companies in contravention of the limit in s 45(1)[84], and such person may be summarily prosecuted by the Registrar of Companies[85]. Any appointment of a person as a director to a company in breach of s 45(1) is void[86], but the legislation attempts to provide that the first 25 directorships shall not become unlawful or rendered void or cease to have effect by reason of a subsequent invalid appointment[87]. Where a director holds in excess of 25 directorships after the commencement of s 45[88], the appointments having been made before the commencement of s 45, at the expiry of 12 months following its commencement, such appointments in excess of the 25-directorship limit, shall cease to have effect[89]. Where

---

81 See para **[8.022]**.

82 *Official Receiver v Vass* [1999] BCC 516.

83 CA(No 2)A 1999, s 45(2) provides that in sub-s (1) – but not any other sub-s of s 45 – 'director' includes a 'shadow director' within the meaning of the 1990 Act.

84 CA(No 2)A 1999, s 45(8). Each appointment in excess of the 25 directorship limit is deemed to constitute a separate contravention: CA(No 2)A 1999, s 45(11)(a).

85 CA(No 2)A 1999, s 45(13).

86 CA(No 2)A 1999, s 45(9).

87 CA(No 2)A 1999, s 45(11)(b).

88 18 April 2000: SI 2000/61.

89 CA(No 2)A 1999, s 45(10). Subsection (11)(c) provides that 'in determining whether one particular appointment referred to in sub-s (10), as distinct from another such appointment, has ceased to have effect by virtue of that sub-s or whether a person's remaining in office under one such appointment, as distinct from another such appointment, constitutes an offence under sub-s (8), the provisions of this section (other than sub-s (3)(b), (5), (6), (7) and (8) shall be deemed to have been in operation at the time of the making of that appointment.'

appointments of a person as director of two or more companies are made simultaneously and their timing is incapable of being distinguished, their timing will be deemed to be as per their order of registration under the Companies Acts[90].

[8.034] Just as there are exceptions to the general rule that every company must have at least one Irish resident director, so too are there exceptions to the general rule that no person may hold more than 25 directorships. Section 45(3) of C(A)(No 2)A 1999 provides that in reckoning whether a person has 25 directorships, the following directorships are not to be included, namely directorships of:

- — public limited companies ('PLCs')[91];
- — public companies (eg companies limited by guarantee without a share capital)[92];
- — companies in respect of which a C(A)(No 2)A 1999, s 44(2) certificate is in force[93]; and
- — any company that is the holder of a licence under the Central Bank Act 1971, s 9 or exempt from holding such a licence or that is referred to in the C(A)(No 2)A 1999, Sch 2, provided that before assuming such a directorship, and following notice[94] to the Registrar of Companies, the Registrar certifies that such company is within one of these categories or the Minister for Enterprise, Trade and Employment directs that such a company is not to be included amongst the companies that shall be reckoned for the purposes aforesaid[95].

It should be noted that if a person is director of both a holding company and its subsidiary, those two (or more if there is more than one subsidiary) directorships are treated as one directorship for the purposes of reckoning the number of directorships a person holds[96]. There was also a transitional provision in respect of the period from commencement of the section to 12 months after commencement[97].

---

90 CA(No 2)A 1999, s 45(12).

91 CA(No 2)A 1999, s 45(3)(a)(i).

92 CA(No 2)A 1999, s 45(3)(a)(ii); public company as within the meaning of C(A)A 1983.

93 CA(No 2)A 1999, s 45(3)(a)(iii): see Chapter 2, *Formation, Registration and Conversion of Private Companies*, para **[2.039]**.

94 Such notice may be delivered to the Registrar of Companies before the person concerned becomes a director of the company to which the notice relates: CA(No 2)A 1999, s 45(7).

95 CA(No 2)A 1999, s 45(3)(b)(i) and (ii). The Registrar of Companies may accept as sufficient evidence that the company falls within a recognised category, a statutory declaration in the prescribed form to that effect made by an officer of the company of the putative director: CA(No 2)A 1999, s 45(5). An appeal to the Minister for Enterprise, Trade and Employment can be taken from the refusal of the registrar to issue a certificate. The Minister may either: confirm the registrar's decision; certify that the company falls within a category; or (c) direct that the company shall not be included: s 45(6). The direction referred to in CA(No 2)A 1999, s 45(6)(c) can only be made where the director was a director of the company before the commencement of s 45; where the Minister forms the opinion that the section would result in serious injustice or hardship for the director and where the giving of the direction would not operate against the common good.

96 CA(No 2)A 1999, s 45(3)(c).

97 CA(No 2)A 1999, s 45(4) provides:

The formal appointment of directors

[8.035] First, it may noted that the restrictions contained in CA 1963, s 179 on the appointment of or advertisement for directors do not apply to private companies by virtue of CA 1963, s 179(5)(b). The statutory restrictions on the appointment of a director to a private company are, relatively speaking, minimal. A person can be formally appointed a director of a company in either of two ways. In the first place, the person can be appointed as one of the first directors of a company; in the second place, a person can be appointed a director to an existing company. In either case it is a prerequisite that the person first consents to becoming a director.

(a) Consent to act as a director

[8.036] A person is required to consent on a statutorily prescribed form to his or her appointment as a director to either a new[98] or to an existing company[99]. In addition, and statutory form aside, a person must in fact consent to acting as a director in a particular company. One of the issues here concerns age. The Companies Acts prescribe neither a minimum nor a maximum age requirement for company directors. In the context of minors, the fact that directors must consent to act as such must (as a matter of practical fact) require the director to be of a sufficient age and development to understand the nature of the consent. It is a sad fact of life that many parents have put forward their infant children to act as directors of the companies they control. The ability of a two-year old to sign, let alone to understand, the nature of such a consent is not even debatable. But where does one draw the line? If age alone is the criterion by which the consent is to be assessed, one can only say with certainty that an 18-year-old will be deemed to give a valid consent. But what about a 17-year-old, or a 15-year-old of above average intelligence? The result is to place the Companies Registration Office ('CRO') in an invidious position, to accept or reject the validity of the consent. Even where the CRO register a minor director, the validity of the consent given is open to challenge, subsequently.

[8.037] Of course, consent to act as a director may be vitiated for other reasons. Where a person signs the consent on the appropriate statutory form, this will be strong prima facie evidence that he has in fact consented to act as a director – for the purposes of both the statutory requirement and his agreement to act generally as a director of a particular company. In this regard the decision in *Re CEM Connections Ltd*[100] is instructive. The facts in that case were that the English Official Receiver applied to have a woman

---

[97] *(contd)* 'Without prejudice to sub-s (3), in reckoning, for the purposes of sub-s (1), the number of companies of which the person concerned is a director at a particular time, being a time that is before the expiration of the period of 12 months from the commencement date of this section, there shall not be included any company of which the person is a director at that time if he or she was such a director immediately before such commencement.' The effect would appear to have been to disapply the 25-directorship limit for a 12-month period following commencement, but only in respect of directorships held prior to commencement ie no new directorships in excess of the limit could be taken on after commencement.

[98] C(A)A 1982, s 3(3).

[99] CA 1963, 195(7).

[100] *Re CEM Connections Ltd* [2000] BCC 917.

disqualified from acting as a director and the question arose as to whether she had been formally appointed as a director of the company. There was no evidence that the woman had been appointed as a director of the company at any meeting of the company. As proof that she had been a director, however, the Official Receiver sought to rely upon the fact that she had signed the statutory consent to act as a director. The woman accepted that the signature was hers but claimed that at the time she had not knowingly signed it. Hers was, by any standard, a sorry story and the vitiating factors asserted were many: her grandfather, to whom she had been very close, had just died; her mother was seriously ill with cancer; and she herself was clinically depressed, anorexic and addicted to cocaine. In addition to signing the statutory consent, she also acknowledged that the signature on the company's VAT registration form and bank mandate was hers. However, it was claimed that that had been signed the day after she had tried to commit suicide and at a time when she claimed that she did not know whether she was 'coming or going'. Mr Registrar Rawson said:

> 'In my judgment, for the appointment of a director of a company to be valid it is necessary that the person appointed should give informed consent to that appointment…I do not think that the cases on non est factum are of any real assistance in resolving this question. The fact that a person signs a form of consent is, of course, strong prima facie evidence that consent was given, but it is not in my view conclusive and may be rebutted by evidence which indicates that the signature was obtained without the person signing the document appreciating what he or she was doing. I am satisfied that Miss Prowse did not realise that she was giving consent to being appointed a director...'[101]

In these circumstances, the disqualification application was dismissed. It is thought, however, that where a person's capacity is impaired at the time of signing the statutory consent or agreeing to becoming a director, he will only be excused if he removes himself from the position as soon as capacity is regained. If a person does not recant and if, upon regaining capacity, he continues to hold himself out as a director and continues to 'occupy the position' of director, that person is likely to be deemed a de facto director[102].

(b) Appointment as a first director

[8.038] The formal appointment of a director is governed by a company's articles; model reg 75 provides that the number of directors and the names of the first directors shall be determined in writing by the subscribers of the memorandum of association, or a majority of them. As noted above, the C(A)A 1982, s 3(1) requires that the names of the first directors and secretary and their consent[103] to their appointment must be sent to the CRO with the memorandum of the company. Such persons are then deemed to have been appointed as directors by the subscribers[104]. Model reg 92, which provides for the retirement of directors at the first annual general meeting ('AGM') is usually deleted by

---

[101] [2000] BCC 917 at 919.

[102] See para **[8.053]**. The liabilities of reluctant directors who might be said to contract a 'sexually transmitted debt' is considered in Chapter 10, *Duties of Directors and Other Officers*, para **[10.042]**.

[103] C(A)A 1982, s 3(3).

[104] C(A)A 1982, s 3(5).

most private companies[105]. Where this article is retained and an AGM is not, for whatever reason, held the result can give rise to considerable ambiguity as to the status of the directors[106].

(c) Appointments to an existing company

[8.039] Directors can, of course, also be formally appointed subsequent to a company's formation. Post-incorporation, directors may be appointed either by the company's members in general meeting or by the existing directors, acting as a board. Where at a general meeting it is proposed by persons other than the directors to appoint a person director (other than a retiring director) notice should be sent to the company's registered office, signed by the proposing member, not less than three nor more than 21 days before the meeting: model reg 96. Where the members in general meeting remove[107], by ordinary resolution, a director the vacancy thereby created may be filled at that meeting, or if not so filled may be filled as a casual vacancy[108] by the board of directors. Section 181 of CA 1963 provides that at a general meeting, directors must be elected individually unless the members unanimously agree to vote them in en bloc[109].

[8.040] Model reg 98 provides that casual vacancies can be filled by the board of directors who can (subject to the total number of directors not exceeding any limit imposed by the articles) also appoint an additional director; in either case, their appointment will last until the next AGM. Where a director is appointed by the existing directors, a resolution of the directors at a board meeting is required. In practice, for very many private companies, this is by far the most frequent way in which directors are appointed.

[8.041] Whether or not a person is appointed on a company's incorporation, as a first director, or subsequently, to an existing company, he will only be a formally appointed, or de jure, director where his appointment is in accordance with the company's articles of association. So, for example, for a person to be appointed as a formal director to fill a casual vacancy, his appointment requires a formal resolution of the board of directors, pursuant to model reg 98. Moreover, his appointment must comply with all other requirements contained in the articles, for example, that he holds any requisite share qualification, as envisaged by model reg 77 (where adopted). If a person's appointment does not comply with such requirements, he will not be a formally appointed director although, as is considered below, he may be found to be a de facto director[110].

---

105 As are model regs 93, 94 and 95.

106 See, for example, *Phoenix Shannon plc v Purkey* [1998] 4 IR 597, [1997] 2 ILRM 381 (Costello J), considered in Chapter 9, *Corporate Governance: Meetings*, para **[9.011]**.

107 See para **[8.076]**.

108 CA 1963, s 182(5). A person appointed a director in place of a removed director shall be treated, for the purpose of determining the time at which he or any other director is to retire, as if he had become a director on the day on which the person in whose place he is appointed was last appointed director: CA 1963, s 182(6).

109 See *Moylan v Irish Whiting Manufacturers Ltd* (14 April 1980, unreported), High Court, per Hamilton J, where the validity of the appointment of the directors of a company was doubted since they had been appointed en bloc, without evidence that there was an unanimous resolution.

110 See para **[8.053]**.

[8.042] Companies are obliged to notify the Registrar of Companies, within 14 days, from the happening of any change among its directors or in its secretary[111]. Although the failure to notify a change in directors is an offence, the actual validity of a director's appointment is unaffected by the failure and where a director is appointed on foot of a board resolution, the appointment will date from the passing of the resolution or such other time specified in the resolution. Judicial recognition of this long-standing position is seen in the decision of Jacob J in *POW Services Ltd and another v Clare et al*[112] where he said:

> 'The general rule is that the fact of registration or not has nothing whatever to do with whether a person is in fact a director or company secretary. Subject to one exception there is no deeming provision arising from registration. It is the company, acting by the procedures under the articles, which makes or sacks a director or company secretary. There are statutory requirements for registration of the persons whom the company has made a director or secretary with sanctions for non-compliance. It may well be that where a company has permitted registration of a person who is not in fact a director or secretary, the company would be estopped as against a third party who relied upon the registration from denying it, but that is as far as the matter goes. The only exception relates to the first directors and secretaries. By s 13(5) of the 1985 Act[113] the persons named on the appropriate form (Form 10) as these persons are deemed to be such.'[114]

Unless the Companies Acts provides otherwise, a requirement for the registration of a particular matter does not touch upon the validity of that matter and is solely intended to facilitate the inspection of a public register.

Types of formally appointed directors[115]

[8.043] In corporate practice, businessmen often add an adjectival label to formally appointed directors. Some have a statutory basis and some do not. To the uninitiated, these can be confusing. Here, the different types of formally appointed directors are considered and explained under the following headings:

(a) Managing directors.
(b) Chairmen.
(c) Executive directors.
(d) Non-executive directors.
(e) Nominee directors.
(f) Caretaker directors.
(g) Alternate directors.
(h) Assignee directors.
(i) Associate directors.

---

[111] CA 1963, s 195(6)(a).

[112] *POW Services Ltd v Clare* [1995] 2 BCLC 435.

[113] C(A)A 1982, s 3(5) also deems the persons specified in the form delivered to the CRO, as having been appointed as the first directors and secretaries.

[114] [1995] 2 BCLC 435 at 440–441.

[115] See generally, Lipton & Hertzberg, *Understanding Company Law* (9th edn 2000), pp 236 – 240.

(a) Managing directors

[8.044] Model reg 110 of Table A provides that:

> 'The directors may from time to time appoint one or more of themselves to the office of managing director for such period and on such terms as to remuneration and otherwise as they think fit, and, subject to the terms of any agreement entered into in any particular case, may revoke such appointment...'

Managing directors are not subject to the normal rules as to rotation of directors[116] but their appointment will be automatically terminated if they cease to be directors, for any reason. Their remuneration shall be as the directors determine[117]. Under model articles, managing directors will have such powers as the directors determine: Model reg 112 provides:

> 'The directors may entrust to and confer upon a managing director any of the powers exercisable by them upon such terms and conditions and with such restrictions as they may think fit, and either collaterally with or to the exclusion of their own powers, and may from time to time revoke, withdraw, alter or vary all or any of such powers.'

It is this standard provision which, if adopted, will result in persons held out as managing directors having ostensible or apparent authority to exercise all of the powers of management that would ordinarily be exercisable by the board of directors[118]. In *Shirlaw v Southern Foundries (1926) Ltd*[119] Lord Greene MR said:

> 'A managing director is...a director to whom the board, being empowered to do so by the articles of association, delegates its powers of management, or some of them, and this delegation is usually, if not invariably, made subject to the overriding authority of the board. Management here means management of the company's business, or part of it, as the case may be. There is no delegation of the remaining powers of the board. Such important matters [include] the financial policy of the company, the dividends to be declared and the issue of new shares are all reserved to the board'.

The precise powers retained by the board of directors will depend upon the arrangements made in particular companies, but 'outsiders' to the company will not normally have notice of these as the articles will be silent, and the matter one of internal management.

(b) Chairmen

[8.045] The board of directors may appoint a chairman[120]; notwithstanding perceived political correctness, in the absence of a company's articles expressly so providing, the term 'chairperson' has no reference point in company law. The function of a chairman is largely confined to the management of directors' and members' meetings. In the Australian case of *AWA Ltd v Daniels*[121] Rogers CJ said:

> 'The chairman is responsible to a greater extent than any other director for the performance of the board as a whole and each member of it. The chairman has the primary

---

116 See para **[8.073]**.

117 Model reg 111.

118 See, further, Chapter 7, *Corporate Capacity and Authority*, para **[7.111]** *ff.*

119 *Shirlaw v Southern Foundries (1926) Ltd* [1939] 2 All ER 113.

120 Model reg 104.

121 *AWA Ltd v Daniels* (1992) 10 ACLC 933.

responsibility of selecting matters and documents to be brought to the board's attention, for formulating the policy of the board and promoting the position of the company.'

Model articles do not confer any particular powers of management on chairmen and, accordingly, they do not have any particular ostensible or usual authority over and above that of ordinary directors[122].

(c) Executive directors

[8.046] The position of executive director has no statutory definition. In simple terms, an executive director is a director who participates in the day-to-day management of a company. Executive directors will – especially in larger companies – usually be employed by their company on a full-time basis and be in receipt of a salary (as opposed to simply directors' fees).

(d) Non-executive directors

[8.047] The position of non-executive director has no statutory definition. By non-executive director is usually meant a director who has no direct or personal role in the day-to-day management of a company. The non-executive director's role tends to be confined to the boardroom, where he will receive information from the executive directors and managers of the company. Usually, non-executive directors will only receive directors' fees and no salary as such. The value of non-executive directors is in their input to decisions of the company which are widely thought to be enhanced by their impartiality, objectivity and independence.

(e) Nominee directors

[8.048] A nominee director is a director who is 'expected to act in accordance with some understanding or arrangement which creates an obligation or mutual expectation of loyalty to some person or persons other than the company as a whole'[123]. This term does not have a statutory definition. Nominee directors do not owe any lesser duties to their company than do other directors and their particular predicament is considered in Chapter 10, *Duties of Directors and Other Officers*[124].

(f) Caretaker directors

[8.049] Caretaker directors are directors who were appointed by shareholders who have subsequently disposed of their shares in circumstances where the new shareholders are likely to replace the existing directors with their own nominees. This so-called type of director has been recognised in a number of Australian[125] and New Zealand[126] cases. As in the case of nominee directors, caretakers do not owe any lesser duties to their company. It has, however, been suggested that the powers of such directors might be found to be limited – particularly where a members' meeting has been called at which they may be voted from office. In such an event it has been suggested that caretaker

---

[122] See, further, Chapter 7, *Corporate Capacity and Authority*, para **[7.112]** *ff*.

[123] Companies and Securities Review Committee (NSW, Australia), Nominee Directors and Alternate Directors, Report No 8 (2 March 1989) at p 7.

[124] At para **[10.040]** *ff*.

[125] *Paringa Mining and Exploration Co PLC v North Flinders Mines Ltd* (1989) 7 ACLC 153.

[126] *Utilicorp Nz Inc v Powerer New Zealand Ltd* (1997) 8 NZCLC 261.

directors may be restrained from taking decisions that are fundamental or significant, outside of the ordinary course of the company's day-to-day business, and which are not otherwise necessary for the proper running of the company[127]. It remains to be seen whether an Irish court would accept that such limitation on directors' powers exists, or even recognises the concept of caretaker director.

(g) Alternate directors

[8.050] An alternate or substitute director does not hold office in his own right. An alternate director is a person appointed to act in the place of a director when that director is unable to act. Model reg 9 of Part II of Table A empowers the appointment of an alternate director and, in this respect, the model articles of private and public companies are different. Model reg 9 (which applies to private companies) provides:

> 'Any director may from time to time appoint any person who is approved by the majority of the directors to be an alternate or substitute director. The appointee, while he holds office as an alternate director, shall be entitled to notice of meetings of the directors and to attend and vote thereat as a director and shall not be entitled to be remunerated otherwise than out of the remuneration of the director appointing him. Any appointment under this regulation shall be effected by notice in writing given by the appointer to the secretary. Any appointment so made may be revoked at any time by the appointer or by a majority of the other directors or by the company in general meeting. Revocation by an appointer shall be effected by notice in writing given by the appointer to the secretary.'

Where appointed, an alternate director will, where this article is adopted, only hold office for as long as the principal director, whom he represents, determines.

(h) Assignee directors

[8.051] Directors who assume office as the result of the assignment of that office by another director are rare creatures indeed. Section 199 of CA 1963 envisages the office of director being assigned, and provides that where the articles of association so permit (and it may be noted that model articles make no provision one way or the other) any assignment of the office of director will be of no effect 'unless and until it is approved by a special resolution of the company' in general meeting.

(i) Associate directors

[8.052] The term 'associate director' has no statutory definition or particular meaning. One leading English commentator[128] has said of the practice of appointing associate directors that it is normally 'to allow the person concerned the dignity and standing of a title which included the word "director", without conferring upon him the full authority and duties of a director'. In *Secretary of State for Trade and Industry v Tjolle*[129] Jacob J recognised that the title 'director' can be used as a motivational tool and its usage did not necessarily mean that a person was holding himself out as a director. Notwithstanding that employees so labelled may not be penalised for corporate failure, their companies may be exposed. Although an associate director does not have the same actual authority

---

[127] *Woonda Nominees Pty Ltd et al v Chng* [2000] Western Australia Supreme Court of 19 October 2000.

[128] Sealy et al (eds), *British Company Law and Practice* (1983; loose leaf), at 28–250.

[129] *Secretary of State for Trade and Industry v Tjolle* [1998] BCC 282.

enjoyed by an ordinary director, it is thought that a company that so designates individuals may well expose itself to a finding that such persons have the same ostensible or apparent authority as an ordinary director and may thus find itself bound by their actions.

De facto directors

[8.053] De facto directors are persons 'occupying the position of director'[130] but who have not been formally appointed as directors, whether on incorporation or subsequently. The reasons for extending the definition of 'directors' to include persons who occupy the position of director have been expressed to be:

> '...to impose legal duties on a person described therein and to give other persons, including the company itself, legal rights against such a person. The justification for this is no doubt that, in some way, the powers or conduct of the person, or the practical necessities of commercial life, if the device of the limited liability company is to play a part in such life, warrants so treating the person.'[131]

A prime example of where a person will be deemed to be a de facto director is where he has been appointed a director but where his appointment does not satisfy other requirements of a company's articles of association, for example, where he does not hold a requisite share qualification. In that event such a person's appointment will be invalid, but if he assumes the position of director, he can be found to be a de facto director. This was precisely the issue in hand in what must be one of the earliest cases in which an individual was deemed to be a de facto director, *Re Canadian Land Reclaiming and Colonizing Co*[132]. In that case, Sir George Jessel MR said of two persons who had been appointed as directors, and had acted as such, but who lacked the share qualification required by their company's articles of association:

> 'No doubt they were not properly elected, and were, therefore, not de jure directors of the company; but that they were de facto directors of the company is equally beyond all question. The point I have to consider is whether the person who acts as de facto director is a director within the meaning of this section, [the Companies Act 1862, s 165, which made officers liable for misfeasance] or whether he can afterwards be allowed to deny that he was a director within the meaning of this section. I think he cannot. We are familiar in the law with a great number of cases in which a man who assumes a position cannot be allowed to deny in a Court of Justice that he really was entitled to occupy that position. The most familiar instance is that of executor de son tort. In like manner, it seems to me, in an application under this section, the de facto director is a director for the purposes of the section'. [133]

Although this decision was delivered over 120 years ago little judicial attention was given to de facto directors until the courts of England and Wales were called upon to

---

[130] CA 1963, s 2(1) in its definition of director refers to persons 'occupying the position of director'.

[131] Per Madgwick J in *Deputy Commissioner of Taxation v Austin* Federal Court of Australia, 27 August 1998.

[132] *Re Canadian Land Reclaiming and Colonizing Co* (1880) 14 Ch D 660.

[133] (1880) 14 Chapter D 660 at 664–665. See also *Corporate Affairs Commission v Drysdale* (1978) 141 CLR 236 where the Australian courts found that a director who had been deemed to retire at an AGM but who had continued to participate in the management of the company, was a de facto director.

disqualify persons who were de facto directors. Nowadays, it is the shadow director[134] who attracts the attention of the legal chattering classes. It is thought that as it becomes apparent that it is sometimes more easy to prove a person was a de facto director than a shadow director, more attention will be paid to the test for a de facto director. Although by CA 1963, s 297, such de facto directors could be made personally liable for fraudulent trading, where they were involved in the 'carrying on [of the company's] business' in a fraudulent manner, there have to date been no decisions on this point[135]. In *Re Lynrowan Enterprises Ltd*[136] the High Court accepted that de facto directors could be restricted under CA 1990, s 150[137]. All of the judicial authorities next considered derive from applications to disqualify from acting as director, persons who were alleged to have been de facto directors[138].

[8.054] One of the leading modern authorities on the meaning of de facto director is the decision of Millett J in *Re Hydrodam (Corby) Ltd*[139], which is also the leading authority on the meaning of shadow directors. In that case Millett J said that the terms 'de facto' director and 'shadow director' do *not* overlap; they are in most cases mutually exclusive alternatives. Of a de facto director Millett J said:

> 'A de facto director is a person who assumes to act as a director. He is held out as a director by the company, and claims and purports to be a director, although never actually or validly appointed as such. To establish that a person was a de facto director of a company it is necessary to plead and prove that he undertook functions in relation to the company which could properly be discharged only by a director. It is not sufficient to show that he was concerned in the management of the company's affairs or undertook tasks in relation to its business which can properly be performed by a manager below board level.'[140]

As noted by Robert Walker LJ in the English Court of Appeal decision which reviewed all of these authorities, *Re Kaytech International plc*[141], a number of subsequent applications to have persons disqualified from being directors on the grounds that they were de facto directors, were unsuccessful. In *Re Richborough Furniture Ltd*[142] it was held that a business consultant who had provided computer and other management

---

134 See para **[8.058]**.

135 Note also that CA 1963, s 178 provides that actions of directors shall be valid notwithstanding that there may be a defect in their appointment. However, in *Morris v Kanssen* [1946] AC 459 it was decided that this merely covered 'slips or irregularities' in the appointment of a director and did not refer to 'a total absence of appointment'.

136 *Re Lynrowan Enterprises Ltd* (31 July 2002, unreported), High Court (O'Neill J).

137 See Chapter 12, *Company Law Compliance and Enforcement*, para **[12.052]**.

138 In one of the first decisions on this point, *Re Lo–Line Electric Motors Ltd* (1988) 4 BCC 415 at 422, Sir Nicholas Browne–Wilkinson VC said: '...the plain intention of Parliament in [the Companies Act 1985 (UK), s 300] was to have regard to the conduct of a person acting as a director, whether validly appointed, or just assuming to act as a director without any appointment at all.'

139 *Re Hydrodam (Corby) Ltd* [1994] 2 BCLC 180, [1994] BCC 161.

140 [1999] BCC 161 at 163.

141 *Re Kaytech International plc* [1999] BCC 390.

142 *Re Richborough Furniture Ltd* [1996] 1 BCLC 507, [1996] BCC 155.

services to a furniture-making company, was not a de facto director, although he had undertaken extensive negotiations with creditors and had performed certain functions of a finance director. Similarly, in *Secretary for State for Trade and Industry v Tjolle*[143] Jacob J held that a manager employed by a holiday company who had been given the courtesy title of 'deputy managing director' and sometimes had attended board meetings, was not in a position of real power and was not, accordingly, a de facto director. In *Re Kaytech International plc*, the trial judge, Rimer J, following a review of the authorities cited the following passage from the decision of Mr Timothy Lloyd QC in *Re Richborough Furniture Ltd*:

> 'It seems to me that for someone to be made liable to disqualification ...as a de facto director, the court would have to have clear evidence that he had been either the sole person directing the affairs of the company (or acting with others all equally lacking in valid appointment, as in *Morris v Kassen* [1946] AC 459) or, if there were others who were true directors, that he was acting on equal footing with the others in directing affairs of the company. It also seems to me that, if it is unclear whether the acts of the person in question are referable to an assumed directorship, or to some other capacity such as a shareholder or, as here, consultant, the person in question must be entitled to the benefit of the doubt.'[144]

The foregoing is thought not to be a correct test for the finding that a person was, or was not, a de facto director, notwithstanding the decision in *Re Lynrowan Enterprises Ltd*[145], where the foregoing passage was cited with apparent approval by O'Neill J[146]. In particular it is thought to be erroneous to say that to be a de facto director a person must either have sole charge of the affairs of a company or that he was on *equal* footing with the de jure directors. Even where a person is not on an equal footing it is thought that this will not preclude his designation as a de facto director where other factors are present[147]. In *Kaytech International plc* the trial judge, Jacob J, had found that the person in question had been a de facto director and this was upheld on appeal. Robert Walker LJ said that that conclusion seemed to him to be inevitable and incontrovertible, having regard to the nature of the evidence heard. The evidence included that the person: had been the moving spirit in giving instructions for the incorporation of the company; had pretended to raise the necessary capital; had described himself as a director on at least one occasion; and had allowed himself to be held out as a joint founder and chief executive at a meeting with suppliers.

143 *Secretary for State for Trade and Industry v Tjolle* [1998] BCC 282.

144 [1999] BCC 161 at 169–170.

145 *Re Lynrowan Enterprises Ltd* (31 July 2002, unreported), High Court (O'Neill J).

146 The decision in *Re Lynrowan Enterprises Ltd* (31 July 2002, unreported), High Court (O'Neill J) is considered at para **[8.057]**.

147 See para **[8.057]**.

[8.055] In *Re Kaytech International plc*[148] the English Court of Appeal endorsed the view expressed by Jacob J in *Secretary for State for Trade and Industry v Tjolle*[149], that there was not one single test for whether a person was, or was not, a de facto director. In that case Jacob J said:

> '...it may be difficult to postulate any one decisive test. I think what is involved is very much a question of degree. The court takes into account all the relevant factors. Those factors include at least whether or not there was a holding out by the company of the individual as a director, whether the individual used that title, whether the individual had proper information (eg management accounts) on which to base decisions, and whether the individual had to make major decisions and so on. Taking all these factors into account, one asks "was this individual part of the corporate governing structure?", answering it as a kind of jury question. In deciding this, one bears very much in mind why one is asking the question. That is why I think the passage I quoted from Millett J is important. There would be no justification for the law making a person liable to misfeasance or disqualification proceedings unless they were truly in a position to exercise the powers and discharge the functions of a director. Otherwise they would be made liable for events over which they had no real control, either in fact or law.'[150]

It is thought that this is the correct approach. The difficulty with the judicial analysis in all of the foregoing authorities is that there is an implicit assumption that the person whose status is in question, disputes that he is or was a de facto director. Any truly generic test for de facto directors must recognise that a person whose status is in question may actually claim that he is or was a de facto director.

[8.056] In *Re Lynrowan Enterprises Ltd*[151] an application to have a person restricted under CA 1990, s 150, O'Neill J said that a person would be a de facto director where:

> '1. Where there is clear evidence that that person has been either the sole person directing the affairs of the company, or
>
> 2. Is directing the affairs of the company with others equally lacking valid appointment, or
>
> 3. Where there were other validly appointed directors that he was acting on an equal or more influential footing with the true directors in directing the affairs of the company.
>
> 4. In the absence of clear evidence of the foregoing and when there is evidence that the role of the person in question is explicable by the exercise of a role other than director, the person in question should not be made amenable to the section 150 restriction.
>
> 5. Where the object of the section is the protection of the public from dishonest or irresponsible persons the absence of a valid appointment should not permit an escape from the restriction in section 150. It would be nonsensical if a person who had been validly appointed a director was to be treated differently to someone who lacked valid appointment but nevertheless assumed in all other respects the role of

---

148 *Re Kaytech International plc* [1999] BCC 390.

149 *Secretary for State for Trade and Industry v Tjolle* [1998] BCC 282.

150 [1998] BCC 282 at 290.

151 *Re Lynrowan Enterprises Ltd* (31 July 2002, unreported), High Court (O'Neill J).

> director. I would agree that "liability cannot sensibly depend upon the validity of the defendant's appointment".
>
> 6. In the light of all the foregoing then in my view the Companies Acts 1963 to 1990 recognise and embrace in the provision of s 2(1) of the Act of 1963 and s 150 of the Act of 1990, the concept of "de facto director".'

For the reasons given above[152] it is thought to be erroneous to require that a person whom it is alleged is a de facto director must either be the sole person directing the company or that he acts with others on an equal footing. It is thought that many of the foregoing are, however, evidential factors which will indicate whether a person is a de facto director.

In order to find that a person is a de facto director, it is submitted that the following test applies, namely that:

— Although the person was not, in fact, a formally appointed director, he 'occupied the position of director'; and

— The company held him out as a director and he acquiesced in this or, in the alternative, he held himself out as a director and the company acquiesced in this.

It is thought that in order to be a de facto director, it is essential to show that a person was held out as such. It follows that a person should have some appreciation of the fact that he occupies the position of director. This is not to say that a subjective test applies and that a person can avoid being a de facto director by averting their mind from the possibility. If, from a person's actions, it is reasonable to assume that he was or ought to have been conscious that he occupied the position of director, this should suffice[153]. It is thought, however, that the paradigm circumstances giving rise to a person being found to be a de facto director is where a person put himself forward as a director, was accepted as such by the company but his appointment is found to be in some way defective eg as in *Re Canadian Land Reclaiming and Colonizing Co*[154].

[8.057] Factors, that indicate a person is or was a de facto director, *include*:

— The person had been appointed by the directors or members in general meeting as a director, but his appointment was invalid on grounds that it did not comply with the Companies Acts (eg because he was disqualified by operation of law or court order from acting as director or a restriction order had been made against him etc) or by virtue of the company's articles of association (eg because he did not hold qualification shares, his appointment as director meant

---

[152] At para **[8.054]**.

[153] In *Re Kaytech International plc* [1999] BCC 390 Robert Walker LJ noted that there a person had mistakenly convinced himself that he was not a director but went on to hold that even such an honest belief was not reasonable in the circumstances as the person was a professional man who made his living by holding nominee directorships. In *Deputy Commissioner of Taxation v Austin* Federal Court of Australia of 27 August 1998 (Madgwick J) a person who had resigned as a director but who had stayed on to assist the company had stayed so long as to have became a de facto director.

[154] *Re Canadian Land Reclaiming and Colonizing Co* (1880) 14 Ch D 660.

that the number of directors was in excess of the maximum number ordained by the articles, etc).

— The person sought to be called (or he acquiesced in the title of) a 'director', with or without an adjectival[155] label, but especially where the title 'managing director'[156] is used[157].

— The person was an authorised signatory on the company's bank mandates[158].

— The person attended board meetings by invitation or by uncontested choice, or was otherwise one of those who took managerial decisions, whether by formal resolution or otherwise on matters reserved for the board of directors or where the articles permitted the appointment of a managing director, he acted as such and took decisions permitted to be taken by a managing director.

— The person had as much information as any de jure director had or might reasonably be expected to have concerning the affairs and business of the company.

— The person held a substantial shareholding in the company in circumstances where one or more of the foregoing circumstances also exist[159].

The foregoing is a non-exhaustive list of some of the circumstances in which it is thought that a recalcitrant (or indeed, desirous) person may be found to be (or to have been) a de facto director.

---

[155] As to the various adjectival labels that a director may have, see para **[8.043]** *ff*.

[156] See, for example, in *Secretary for State for Trade and Industry v Jones* [1999] BCC 336 where on appeal it was held that the title 'joint managing director' had a significance far greater than that accorded to it by the District Judge.

[157] Evidence of title alone will not normally suffice. In *Re Red Label Fashions Ltd* [1999] BCC 308 it was held that although there was evidence that a woman was described in draft accounts as a director, there was no clear or unequivocal reference or indication that she 'was or acted as a director rather than as a manager or dutiful wife' (at 313) per Lightman J. See also *Secretary for State for Trade and Industry v Tjolle* [1998] BCC 282 where Jacob J held that there, the use of the title 'director', did not necessarily mean that the person was holding herself out as a director and could have been merely a motivational tool for staff to do better.

[158] *Re Lynrowan Enterprises Ltd* (31 July 2002, unreported), High Court (O'Neill J). The fact that a person was a signatory on the company's bank mandate alone should not, however, suffice as this is not the exclusive preserve of directors and could be done by an employee or manager in a company's finance department; see, however, *Re Sykes (Butchers) Ltd* [1998] 1 BCLC 110.

[159] Evidence of a substantial shareholding should not alone be considered sufficient. It is considered to ignore the realities of many private companies to entirely disregard evidence of shareholding as was done by Rimer J in the trial decision in *Re Kaytech International plc* [1999] BCC 390 at 401 on the grounds that where a model reg 80 type article is adopted and management delegated to the directors, evidence of shareholding is irrelevant. Indeed in *Secretary for State for Trade and Industry v Jones* [1999] BCC 336 it was held that where a substantial shareholder in a small company wished to take an active part in running the company's affairs in order to protect his investment, that raised the question as to whether in so doing he might not be constituting himself as a de facto director.

Shadow directors

[8.058] A shadow director[160] is a person who is neither formally appointed, nor necessarily held out as a director, but to whom certain sanctions and regulations, normally reserved for directors, can be applicable. Shadow directors existed in Ireland long before the passing of the Companies Act 1990, although they were only christened as such by s 27 of that Act, which defines a shadow director as:

> '...a person in accordance with whose directions or instructions the directors of a company are accustomed to act...unless the directors are accustomed so to act by reason only that they do so on advice given by him in a professional capacity.'

Section 195(12)(a) of CA 1963, however, always required every company to keep a register of formally appointed directors and the men not then christened, 'in accordance with whose directions or instructions the directors of a company are accustomed to act'. A finding that a person is a shadow director can have far-reaching consequences for the individual concerned: he or she can, for example, be made liable for reckless trading; can be made the subject of a disqualification[161] or restriction[162] order; and will be subject to the CA 1990, s 31 prohibition of loans, quasi-loans, credit transactions and guarantees and the provision of security in connection with such loans, quasi-loans and credit transactions.

[8.059] Shadow directors are considered under the following sub-headings:

(a) The professional advice exception.

(b) The proofs required to establish a person is a shadow director.

(c) 'Directed or instructed'.

(d) 'Acted in accordance with such directions or instructions'.

(e) 'Were accustomed so to act'.

(f) Can bodies corporate be shadow directors?.

(a) The professional advice exception

[8.060] Before considering who is a shadow director, it is necessary to consider who will *not* be deemed to be such. The 'professional advice' exception means that a person who gives directions or instructions to the directors of a company on foot of which they are accustomed to act, but only by way of advice given in a professional capacity, will not be deemed to be a shadow director. It is important to note that a person can act in many capacities and it is only where a person acts in a professional capacity that he or she can invoke this exception. In the Irish decision in *Re Vehicle Imports Ltd (in liquidation)*[163] a liquidator sought to have an order pursuant to CA 1990, s 150 made against the company's accountant. The liquidator was satisfied that the accountant had a significant involvement in and control over the management of the company's business during its short trading life and that the accountant had – on his own evidence – received

[160] See further Chapter 10, *Duties of Directors and Other Officers*, para **[10.095]** *ff.*

[161] CA 1990, s 159.

[162] CA 1990, s 149(5).

[163] *Re Vehicle Imports Ltd (in liquidation)* (6 December 2000, unreported), High Court (Murphy J).

substantial monies in that period. Murphy J held that although the evidence in relation to the accountant fell short of constituting him a shadow director, the uncontroverted evidence of a director that the director had signed blank cheques to be filled in by the accountant 'does sit with the definition of shadow director in CA 1990, s 27. Murphy J accepted that the accountant could well have a plausible explanation but in the absence of a denial that he was a shadow director in his affidavit, Murphy J made an order pursuant to CA 1990, s 150 against the accountant on the basis that he was a shadow director, granting a stay of 21 days to enable the accountant to make application if he deemed fit.

(b) The proofs required to establish a person is a shadow director

[8.061] The proofs required to be established in order to find that a person is a shadow director were set out by Millett J in *Re Hydrodam (Corby) Ltd*[164]. In the course of his judgment he said:

> 'To establish that a defendant is a shadow director of a company it is necessary to allege and prove:
>
> (1) who are the directors of the company, whether de facto[165] or de jure[166];
>
> (2) that the defendant directed those directors how to act in relation to the company or that he was one of those persons who did so;
>
> (3) that those directors acted in accordance with such directions; and
>
> (4) that they were accustomed so to act.
>
> What is needed is, first, a board of directors claiming and purporting to act as such; and secondly, a pattern of behaviour in which the board did not exercise any discretion or judgment of its own, but acted in accordance with the directions of others.'[167]

In keeping with CA 1990, s 27, to this formulation should be added, at point (2), that the defendant 'directed or instructed' the directors how to act. Notwithstanding the English Court of Appeal's decision in *Secretary of State for Trade and Industry v Deverell*[168] which qualifies, to an extent, the decision in *Re Hydrodam*, it is thought that this test represents good law as far as the definition of shadow director in the context of CA 1990, s 27 is concerned. The concepts of de jure director and de facto director have been considered previously. In relation to these proofs it is (2), (3) and (4) that give rise to further concern and which are next considered.

---

164 *Re Hydrodam (Corby) Ltd* [1994] 2 BCLC 180, [1994] BCC 161. Whilst consistently referred to as Hydrodam in the BCLC (Butterworths Company Law Cases) series, it is referred to as Hydrodan in the BCC (CCH's British Company Cases) series.

165 See para **[8.053]**.

166 See para **[8.035]**.

167 [1994] 2 BCLC 180 at 183.

168 *Secretary of State for Trade and Industry v Deverell* [2000] BCC 1057.

(c) 'Directed or instructed'

[8.062] One of the key questions concerning shadow directors is whether or not they must be more dominant than the de facto or de jure directors. In *Re Unisoft Group Ltd*[169] Harman J said that:

> '...the shadow director must be, in effect, the puppet-master controlling the actions of the board. The directors must be (to use a different phrase) the "cat's-paw"[170] of the shadow director. They must be people who act on the directions or instructions of the shadow director...'

In the first edition of this book it was suggested that to be a shadow director a person must be in a higher position of authority than an ordinary director and that perhaps the required standard of authority could best be described as being akin to that of a 'managing director'[171]. This was the view taken by Judge Cooke at first instance in the case of *Secretary of State for Trade and Industry v Deverell*[172]. He said:

> 'Directions or instructions are both words with a mandatory effect. Coupled with the word "accustomed" they...contemplate a situation where the board has cast itself in a subservient role to the "shadow" ie it does what it is told or to borrow an expression from trust law it "surrenders its discretion" to the shadow. Being accustomed to follow what somebody says does not of itself make what is said a direction/instruction...what the court has to find, whether on direct evidence or inference, is that the board does what [the shadow] tells it and exercises no (or at least no substantial) independent judgment.'[173]

In the Court of Appeal, Morritt LJ doubted Judge Cooke's view that the board of directors should be subservient to the shadow director. He said:

> 'It will, no doubt, be sufficient to show that in the face of "directions or instructions" from the alleged shadow director the properly appointed directors or some of them cast themselves in a subservient role or surrendered their respective discretions. But I do not consider that it is necessary to do so in all cases. Such a requirement would be to put a gloss on the statutory requirement that the board are "accustomed to act in accordance with" such directions or instructions. It appears to me that Judge Cooke, in looking for the additional ingredient of a subservient role or the surrender of discretion by the board, imposed a qualification beyond that justified by the statutory language.'[174]

It is thought that this cannot be taken as a correct interpretation of CA 1990, s 27 and that the interpretation placed on the similar words used in the English legislation by Judge Cooke and Harman J are to be preferred as being correct. The legislation is unequivocal: the real directors must act in accordance with the 'directions or instructions' of the shadow director. The statutory words must be given their natural and

---

169 *Re Unisoft Group Ltd* [1994] BCC 766.

170 The use of such epithets has been discouraged by Morritt LJ in *Secretary of State for Trade and Industry v Deverell* [2000] BCC 1057 at 1068 on the basis that such imply 'a degree of control both of quality and extent over the corporate field in excess of that the statutory definition requires'.

171 See Courtney, *The Law of Private Companies* (1st edn, 1994), para [7.055].

172 *Secretary of State for Trade and Industry v Deverell* [2000] BCC 1057.

173 [2000] BCC 1057 at 1.066.

174 [2000] BCC 1057 at 1067.

unstrained meaning and to the extent that they have been construed otherwise[175], this writer disagrees. For a person to be found to be a shadow director of a company, he or she must 'direct or instruct' the real directors as to how they act ie how they exercise their powers as directors and to that extent the real directors must be subservient to the 'shadow'. This may not rest comfortably with a mindset eager to penalise perceived wrongdoers, but it is submitted that this is the correct interpretation of s 27.

[8.063] In *Secretary of State for Trade and Industry v Deverell* Morritt LJ held that non-professional advice – which does not constitute a direction or instruction – can come within the definition, saying:

> 'the proviso excepting advice given in a professional capacity appears to assume advice generally is or may by included. Moreover the concepts of "direction" and "instruction" do not exclude the concept of "advice" for all three share the common feature of "guidance".'[176]

It is thought that this is incorrect. Section 27 of CA 1990 plainly requires a shadow director to issue 'directions or instructions': 'advice' is not part of the primary requirement; all that s 27 says on 'advice' is that such, given in a professional capacity, is insufficient to render its maker a shadow director. The significance of the professional advice exception can be grasped by accepting that a professional adviser does not direct or instruct a company on what it should do: he advises the company on what he perceives, in his professional judgment, to be the best course of action. The legislature clearly intended to preclude such 'advice' from being construed, as a result of judicial gymnastics of the sort seen in the judgment of Morritt LJ, a reckonable 'direction or instruction' for the purposes of CA 1990, s 27.

(d) 'Acted in accordance with such directions or instructions'

[8.064] The real directors of the company in question must, in fact, act in accordance with the shadow director' directions or instructions. This means that a person will not be deemed to be a shadow director, even if he or she makes directions or instructions, if the real directors do not, in fact, act in accordance with such directions or instructions. As Finn J said in *Australian Securities Commission v AS Nominees Ltd*[177] the idea of the section is that 'the third party [shadow director] calls the tune and the directors dance in their capacity as directors'[178].

[8.065] In *Secretary of State for Trade and Industry v Deverell*[179] Morritt LJ held that whether any particular communication from an alleged shadow director, whether by

[175] In the Court of Appeal in *Deverell* Morritt LJ expressly said (at 1.067) that 'the definition of a shadow director is to be construed in the normal way to give effect to the parliamentary intention ascertainable from the mischief to be dealt with and the words used. In particular the purpose of the Act is the protection of the public and as the definition is used in other legislative contexts it should not be strictly construed because it also has quasi–penal consequences…'.

[176] [2000] BCC 1057 at 1067.

[177] *Australian Securities Commission v AS Nominees Ltd* (1995) 133 ALR 1, (1995) 13 ACLC 1822.

[178] (1995) 133 ALR 1 at 52, (1995) 13 ACLC 1822 at 1838.

[179] *Secretary of State for Trade and Industry v Deverell* [2000] BCC 1057.

words or by conduct, is to be classified as a direction or instruction, 'must be objectively ascertained by the court in the light of all the evidence'[180]. It is thought that this is a correct statement of the law and that the subjective intentions of an alleged shadow director – unlike, perhaps, those of a de factor director – are irrelevant[181], as are the subjective impressions of the real directors who receive such a direction or instruction. As Morritt LJ said, 'In many, if not most, cases it will be sufficient to prove the communication and its consequence. Evidence of understanding or expectation may be relevant but it cannot be conclusive'.

(e) 'Were accustomed so to act'

[8.066] Section 27 of CA 1990 expressly envisages that the actual directors of a company must not only act on a shadow director's directions or instructions, but must be 'accustomed so to act'. The plain meaning is that the shadow director must have issued more than one direction or instruction that was acted upon: there must be a pattern. It is thought to be clear that a single direction or instruction, acted upon by a company's actual directors is not sufficient to cause the person who made that direction or instruction being deemed to be a shadow director. It is thought, however, that whilst a solitary 'direction or instruction' is insufficient, it is not necessary that the real directors act in accordance with all directions or instructions made by the alleged shadow director. The decision in *Australian Securities Commission v AS Nominees Ltd*[182] is instructive. There, Finn J said:

> '...the reference in the section to a person in accordance with whose directions or instructions the directors are "accustomed to act" does not in my opinion require that there be directions or instructions embracing all matters involving the board. Rather, it only requires that, as and when the directors are directed or instructed, they are accustomed to act as the section requires'.[183]

Later in his judgment Finn J said:

> 'The question the section poses is: Where, for some or all purposes, is the locus of effective decision making? If it resides in a third party...and if that person cannot secure the "adviser" protection...then it is open [to the court] to find that the person is a [shadow director].'

A single or solitary direction or instruction will not make the alleged shadow director the locus of effective decision making. Section 27 of CA 1990 requires a pattern of cause (direction or instruction) and effect (action on foot of same). This was accepted to be the legislative intent by Morritt LJ in *Secretary of State for Trade and Industry v Deverell*[184].

---

180 [2000] BCC 1057 at 1067.

181 See para **[8.054]**.

182 *Australian Securities Commission v AS Nominees Ltd* (1995) 133 ALR 1, (1995) 13 ACLC 1822.

183 (1995) 133 ALR 1 at 52, (1995) 13 ACLC 1822 at 1838.

184 *Secretary of State for Trade and Industry v Deverell* [2000] BCC 1057 at 1067.

(f) Can bodies corporate be shadow directors?

[8.067] In *Ex p Copp*[185] the question of whether a bank could be deemed a 'shadow director' arose in the context of wrongful trading[186] and it was held by the English court that a sustainable case had been made out that the bank was a shadow director[187]. In the first edition of this book it was suggested that whilst CA 1990, s 27 defines a shadow director as a 'person' in accordance with whose directions or instructions the directors of a company are accustomed to act, it was arguable that a body corporate could not be a shadow director[188]. On further reflection it is thought that whatever a body corporate incorporated in a foreign jurisdiction, an Irish company (within the meaning of CA 1963, s 2) can be a shadow director. The reason is that whilst CA 1963, s 176 prohibits a company from having a body corporate as a director, it does not prohibit an Irish company from acting as a director[189]. So, an Irish company can be validly appointed a formal, de jure, director of an English registered company because in England and Wales a registered company can have a body corporate as a director. Some residual injustice must, however, remain in the notion that an Irish company can be visited with the penalties liable to be imposed upon shadow directors, since they cannot lawfully benefit from being the de jure director of an Irish company[190].

The status of a director

[8.068] A director is an office holder, and is not per se an employee[191]. In the final instance, and absent the finding that he has a contract for service or of employment, a director holds office under the instrument which created that office, namely the memorandum and articles of association[192]. Were a director's status to be entirely dependent upon his being an office holder, his rights, independent of the company's constitutional documentation, would be slim since rights in the articles and memorandum are subject to the vicissitudes of the members' right to vote in general meeting as they see fit. However, it is often the case that the rights of the director will also be rooted in contract, and so, unless waived or otherwise void at law, are enforceable by the directors.

---

185 *Ex p Copp* [1989] BCLC 12; *Re a Company (No 005009 of 1987).*

186 In England and Wales it was decided to penalise those who engaged in 'wrongful trading', while in Ireland, 'reckless trading' was introduced: see Ussher, *Company Law in Ireland* (1986), p 530.

187 See further Chapter 10, *Duties of Directors and Other Officers*, para **[10.095]**.

188 See Courtney, *The Law of Private Companies* (1st edn, 1994), para [8.082].

189 See Courtney, *The Law of Private Companies* (1st edn, 1994), para [8.082].

190 In the Australian case of *Standard Chartered Bank of Australia Ltd v Antico* (1995) 13 ACLC 1381 it was held by the New South Wales Supreme Court that a holding company was a shadow director of its subsidiary because of the extent of control it exercised over the subsidiary's board of directors in which the subsidiary's directors had acquiesced.

191 See Redmond, *Dismissal Law in Ireland*, (1999), paras [3.08]–[3.21].

192 *Glover v BLN Ltd* [1973] IR 388 at 414, per Kenny J.

The remuneration of directors

[8.069] As officers, the directors of a company are not automatically entitled to be remunerated for their services[193]. To be entitled to remuneration, the directors' contract for services or of employment must authorise payment to directors. Model reg 76 provides that the remuneration and expenses of the directors shall be determined by the members in general meeting of the company, a convenient provision in view of the fact that, as repeatedly pointed out, the directors will in most Irish private companies be the shareholding-members[194]. A provision in the articles that there be a fixed sum paid to the directors seems to be insufficient unless the members pass a resolution or the director can show an express or implied contract: *Re New British Iron Co*[195]. However, once the members of a company pass a resolution to the effect that a sum or sums should be paid to the directors, then the directors can sue the company for such sums as a debt due and owing from the company[196]. Where the director does not have a controlling or even a substantial interest in a company, then it is best for him to have an express contract of employment. Where all else fails, a director may be able to claim payment on a quantum meruit basis[197].

[8.070] Section 28 of CA 1990 imposes restrictions on directors' service contracts with a company[198]. Sub-section (2) provides:

> 'This section applies to any term by which a director's employment with the company of which he is the director or, where he is the director of a holding company his employment within the group is to continue, or may be continued, otherwise than at the instance of the company (whether under the original agreement or under a new agreement entered into in pursuance of the original agreement), for a period exceeding five years during which the employment —
>
> (a) cannot be terminated by the company by notice, or
>
> (b) can be so terminated only in specified circumstances.'

In accordance with sub-s (1) a company shall not incorporate in an employment agreement such a term, unless the term is first approved by a resolution of the company in general meeting and, in the case of a director of a holding company, by a resolution of that company in general meeting. To avoid a situation where contracts are terminated and new ones entered into, sub-s (3) provides for an anti-avoidance measure whereby the period of employment in the further agreement is added to the unexpired period of the original agreement. Before the general meeting at which it is proposed to pass such a

---

193 *Hutton v West Cork Railway Co* (1883) 23 Ch D 654.

194 Members may not amend a company's articles of association so as to remove a director's entitlement to accrued remuneration, but a prospective amendment may be valid: *Swabey v Port Darwin Gold Mining Co* (1889) 1 Meg 385. See MacCann, *A Casebook on Company Law* (1991), p 415.

195 *Re New British Iron Co* [1989] 1 Ch 324.

196 *Re Richmond Gate Property Co Ltd* [1964] 2 All ER 936.

197 *Craven–Ellis v Cannons Ltd* [1936] 2 KB 403. See generally, Clark, *Contract Law in Ireland* (3rd edn, 1992), p 487 *ff*.

198 By CA 1990, s 28(7), 'employment' is deemed to include employment under a contract for services.

resolution, a written memorandum setting out the proposed agreement incorporating the relevant term must be available for inspection by members of the company for not less than 15 days before the meeting at the company's registered office and also at the meeting itself[199]. Any term in an agreement in contravention of s 28 shall to the extent of the contravention, be void, and in respect of agreements within the meaning of sub-s (3), shall be deemed to contain a term entitling the company to terminate it at any time by the giving of reasonable notice[200]. The effects of CA 1990, s 28 would seem destined to be of far greater significance for public companies than private companies. In private companies where the shareholders and directors are one and the same people, it will merely add a further paper procedure that must be complied with.

Ceasing to be a director

[8.071] The circumstances in which a person can cease to be a director and the issues attendant upon such cessation are next considered as follows:

(a) Resignation.
(b) Retirement by rotation.
(c) Removal of directors.
(d) Notification to Companies Registration Office of cessation of a directorship.
(e) Compensation on loss of office.

(a) Resignation

[8.072] A director may, of his or her own volition, resign as a director at any time by giving notice to the company. Where model reg 91(e)[201] is adopted, this will be expressly provided for but, even in the absence of such an article, this provision will apply as a general rule of law. It was held in *POW Services Ltd v Clare*[202] that whether a company has notice of the resignation of a director is a question of fact and in that case, the fact that all of a company's directors had notice of a director's letter of resignation was sufficient, notwithstanding that it had not been served upon the company's registered office. This decision is also authority for the fact that resignation is a matter entirely between the director and his company and the validity of a resignation is entirely unaffected by whether or not notice of the director's resignation has been filed in the CRO[203].

(b) Retirement by rotation

[8.073] Under the model articles of association, provision is made for the retirement by rotation of directors. Model reg 92 provides:

> 'At the first annual general meeting of the company all the directors shall retire from office, and at the annual general meeting in every subsequent year, one-third of the directors for the time being, or, if their number is not three or a multiple of three, then the number nearest one-third shall retire from office.'

---

199 CA 1990, s 28(4).
200 CA 1990, s 28(5).
201 See para **[8.074]**.
202 *POW Services Ltd v Clare* [1995] 2 BCLC 435.
203 See generally, para **[8.081]**.

Model regs 93–100 also make provision for the rotation of directors. Such articles will often be found unsuitable in private companies, especially where ownership and management are not divorced. In such companies it may, following legal review, be prudent to purge such regulations from the articles because unforeseen consequences can flow where such an article exists and, for example, an AGM is not, for whatever reason, held[204].

(c) Removal of directors

(i) Automatic removal

[8.074] Directors can be automatically removed if they are made the subject of a disqualification order under CA 1990, s 160[205]. In addition, model reg 91 of Table A provides that the office of director shall be vacated if the director:

> '(a) ceases to be a director by virtue of s 180 of the Act; or
>
> (b) is adjudged bankrupt in the State or in Northern Ireland or Great Britain or makes any arrangement or composition with his creditors generally; or
>
> (c) becomes prohibited from being a director by reason of any order made under s 184 of the Act; or
>
> (d) becomes of unsound mind; or
>
> (e) resigns his office by notice in writing to the company; or
>
> (f) is convicted of an indictable offence unless the directors otherwise determine; or
>
> (g) is for more than 6 months absent without permission of the directors from meetings of the directors held during that period.'

(ii) Removal by directors

[8.075] Where the articles of a company so permit, a director may be removed by resolution of the board of directors. Where the directors resolve to expel one of their number from the board of directors, they must exercise this power bona fide and in the interests of the company and not for ulterior purposes: *Lee v Chou Wen Hsien et al*[206]. Of course, where a director has rights under a contract of employment or in a quasi-partnership company, removal will be without prejudice to the director's rights.

(iii) Removal by members

[8.076] It is a basic principle of company law that the shareholders of a company can dismiss or remove a director by passing an ordinary resolution in a general meeting. So, CA 1963, s 182(1) provides:

> 'A company may by ordinary resolution remove a director before the expiration of his period of office notwithstanding anything in its articles or any agreement between it and him, so, however, that this subsection shall not, in the case of a private company, authorise the removal of a director holding office for life.'

---

204 See *Re Consolidated Nickel Mines Ltd* [1914] 1 Ch 883; cf *Phoenix Shannon plc v Purkey* [1998] 4 IR 597, [1997] 2 ILRM 381 (Costello J) both of which are considered in Chapter 9, *Corporate Governance: Meetings*, para **[9.011]** *ff*.

205 See Chapter 12, *Company Law Compliance and Enforcement*, para **[12.090]**.

206 *Lee v Chou Wen Hsien* [1985] BCLC 45.

Life directors, notwithstanding that they are permanently appointed by the memorandum or articles of association, can only be ousted from office by a special resolution which alters the company's constitutional documents, unless the memorandum of association itself prohibits their removal[207]. Where the resolution of the members to oust a director is invalid or the director is deprived of his statutory rights to notice, he may seek an injunction declaring that his removal was invalid. In *Coubrough v James Panton & Co Ltd*[208] an ordinary resolution was passed instead of the special resolution (as required under that particular company's articles) and accordingly the removal of the director was declared invalid. Similarly, an injunction may be sought to prevent the holding of an EGM for the purposes of passing such a resolution to remove a director where the notice of the EGM is invalid[209].

[8.077] Shareholding-directors may also bolster the likelihood of their staying in office through the use of a *Bushell v Faith*[210] clause in the articles of association. Such clauses can give certain members loaded voting rights which apply generally or simply where it is proposed to dismiss a director. Accordingly, the articles of association could provide that on a vote to dismiss a director, the voting rights of the director concerned are loaded, thus allowing him to thwart any resolution to remove him. Furthermore, shareholding-directors may enter into a shareholders' agreement containing a similar provision. Alternatively, the directors may simply retain sufficient shares, either holding legal or equitable/beneficial title, to ensure that they retain sufficient control over the company.

[8.078] Although a company acting through its members has an express statutory right to dismiss a director, certain factors may deter shareholders from exercising this power[211]. It is inappropriate to consider at length those disincentives rooted in labour law and treatment here is confined to specific company law issues. However, it should be said that while s 182(1) allows the member-shareholders to dismiss, s 182(7) provides that the right to compensation or damages payable to the director in respect of the determination of his appointment remains intact. To have rights against the company, a director must have been employed on a contractual basis as opposed to having been merely appointed as a director by resolution. Where there is such a contract, either express or implied, and the director is dismissed in contravention of that contract, or in breach of the terms of the Unfair Dismissals Acts 1977–1993, or simply wrongfully dismissed[212], then the director's right to compensation may be invoked[213]. Essentially, the question of compensation may be reduced to a finding that there were terms in the

---

207 CA 1963, s 28(3). See Chapter 3, *Private Constitutional Documentation*, para **[3.047]**.

208 *Coubrough v James Panton & Co Ltd* [1965] IR 272.

209 See *Currie v Cowdenbeath Football Club Ltd* [1992] BCLC 1029 (Court of Sessions), where inter alia, this grounded the granting of the Scottish equivalent of an interlocutory injunction.

210 *Bushell v Faith* [1970] AC 1099. See Chapter 3, *Private Constitutional Documentation*, para **[3.062]**.

211 See Ussher, *Company Law in Ireland* (1986), p 91 *ff*. And see generally, Chapter 19, *Shareholders' Remedies*, para **[19.060]**.

212 *Glover v BLN Ltd* [1973] IR 388.

213 *Industrial Yarns Ltd v Greene* [1984] ILRM 15; *Carvill v Irish Industrial Bank Ltd* [1968] IR 325; *Read v Astoria Garage (Streatham) Ltd* [1952] Ch 637; *Glover v BLN Ltd* [1973] IR 388.

appointment of the director which were irreconcilable with the right of summary dismissal.

[8.079] In a private quasi-partnership type private company, there is a danger that summary dismissal could give rise to an application by the dismissed director-shareholder for an order pursuant to CA 1963, s 213(f), directing that the company be wound up on just and equitable grounds[214]. Indeed, a director could seek relief under s 205 for oppression[215].

[8.080] A number of recent Irish cases have considered the correct interpretation of CA 1963, s 182 in circumstances where the director of a private company who has commenced proceedings under CA 1963, s 205, claiming oppression, seeks an injunction to prevent his removal[216]. In *Feighery v Feighery et al*[217] Laffoy J had, in the High Court, held:

> 'In my view, even assuming that the petitioner has an arguable case of relief under s 205 and an arguable case that that the respondents as shareholders and directors, owe him fiduciary duties and are in breach of those duties, I must nonetheless be satisfied that I have jurisdiction to override the shareholders' statutory power under s 182 to remove the petitioner from the board. I am not satisfied that I have such jurisdiction…'.[218]

The Supreme Court in *McGilligan & Bowen v O'Grady* did not follow this decision[219]. After stating that the effect of CA 1963, s 205 was to curb the majority's power to act in a manner which was harsh and oppressive, Keane CJ held:

> 'Why then should the court, on an application for an interlocutory injunction, be unable to restrain the company from removing a director pending the hearing of a petition under s 205 where he has established that there is a serious question to be tried as to whether his exclusion from the affairs of the company constitutes conduct which would entitle shareholders to relief under s 205?
>
> It should be noted that in *Bentley-Stevens v Jones* [1974] 1 WLR 638 there does not appear to have been any proceedings in existence under the English equivalent of s 205 at the time the application for an interlocutory injunction was made. However, apart from that consideration, I am bound to say, with all respect, that I do not understand why it should be thought that, because the relief sought in the interlocutory proceedings is not the same as the relief which will ultimately be sought in the s 205 proceedings, an interlocutory injunction should not be granted on that ground alone. If it is desirable, in accordance with the principles laid down in the *American Cyanamid Company* and *Campus Oil* cases[220] to

---

214 See *Ebrahimi v Westbourne Galleries* [1973] AC 360 and for an Irish example, *Re Murph's Restaurants Ltd* [1979] ILRM 141. See generally Chapter 25, *Winding Up Companies*, para **[25.076]**.

215 See Chapter 19, *Shareholders' Remedies*, para **[19.006]**.

216 See Dunleavy, 'The Power of Shareholders to Remove Directors Under s 182 of the Companies act 1963' (1999) Bar Law Review 265.

217 *Feighery v Feighery* (25 February 1998, unreported), High Court (Laffoy J).

218 (25 February 1998, unreported), High Court at p 28.

219 *McGilligan & Bowen v O'Grady* [1999] 1 IR 346, [1999] 1 ILRM 303.

220 As to which, see generally, Courtney, *Mareva Injunctions and Related Interlocutory Orders* (1998), para [5.03]–[5.10].

> preserve the plaintiff's rights pending the hearing of the s 205 proceedings and the balance of convenience does not point to a different conclusion, I see no reason why interlocutory relief should not be granted to cite but one example, the relief in many Mareva cases is very often not the relief which is sought in the substantive proceedings. I am satisfied that, to the extent that *Bentley-Stevens v Jones* and *Feighery v Feighery et al* suggests a different view of the law, they should not be followed.'[221]

It should be stressed that it will not be every case in which the shareholders' statutory right to remove a director will be injuncted and that the Supreme Court's decision would appear to be confined to injunctions sought as ancillary relief in a s 205 petition.

(d) Notification to Companies Registration Office of cessation of a directorship

[8.081] Section 195(6) of CA 1963 imposes a duty on companies to notify the CRO, within 14 days from the happening of any change among its directors or secretary. Originally, s 195(8) allowed directors the right to file notice of their resignation where their former company was remiss in complying with s 195(6). This was not particularly liked by the CRO because the result was, in many cases, a proliferation of registered companies without any apparent directors. In consequence, s 195 was amended by C(A)(No 2)A 1999, s 47, which introduced new sub-ss 11A–11E. The main change is now contained in CA 1963, s 195(11A), which provides:

> 'If a company fails to send, in accordance with subsection (6), a notification, in the prescribed form, to the Registrar of Companies of the fact of a person's having ceased, for whatever reason, to be a director or secretary of the company and of the date on which that event occurred that person may serve on the company a notice —
>
> (a) requesting it to send forthwith the notification of that matter, in the prescribed form, to the registrar, and
>
> (b) stating that if the company fails to comply with that request within 21 days of the service of the notice on it, he will forward to the Registrar of Companies and to every person who, to his knowledge, is an officer of the company a copy of any notice of resignation by him as a director or secretary of the company or any other documentary proof of his having ceased to be such a director or secretary together with—
>
> (i) in the case of the Registrar of Companies, such additional information as may be prescribed (which may include a statutory declaration made by the person stating the names of the persons who, to his knowledge, are officers of the company), and
>
> (ii) in the case of every other person as aforesaid, a written request of the person that he take such steps as will ensure that the failure of the company to comply with the notice continues no further.'

The effect of this subsection is that where a company does not comply with its obligation to notify the CRO, the rights of a director or secretary to make notification is preserved but made expressly subject to such director or secretary complying with certain conditions. The main condition is that the ex-director or ex-secretary must first request the company to notify the CRO and state that, if it fails to do so within 21 days, the ex-

---

[221] [1999] 1 IR 346 at 352. An injunction was also granted in *O'Gorman v Kelleher* (19 July 1999, unreported), High Court (Carroll J) where there were section 205 proceedings in train.

director or ex-secretary will send to the CRO and to every person who is to his knowledge an officer of the company, a copy of his resignation (or other documentary proof of his cessation to act as director or secretary)[222] together with such additional information as the CRO might require. The CRO will require a statutory declaration stating the names of the person who 'to his knowledge' are officers of the company. The ex-director or ex-secretary must also send to those whom he believes to be officers, a written request that they take such steps as will end the failure of the company to comply with the notice.

[8.082] Where the company does not comply with the ex-director's or ex-secretary's request, he can proceed to notify the CRO[223]. There was a concern that to misrepresent an individual as being a director of a company that was, say, insolvent or known to be engaged in nefarious activity, might expose the ex-director or ex-secretary to an action for defamation, so it is expressly provided that any representation made will not, of itself, constitute defamatory matter[224]. Any person may give notice (accompanied by such proof as may be prescribed) of the death of a director or secretary[225].

[8.083] The sole purpose behind this provision is to try to ensure that companies will have some persons registered as their directors. Of course, if there are no directors remaining that cannot stop an ex-director or ex-secretary from demanding that the register be amended accordingly, it just makes matters more difficult. No doubt the additional bureaucracy was considered justified by the greater good of making it difficult for registered companies to appear to have no directors.

(e) Compensation on loss of office

[8.084] Section 186 of CA 1963 provides that the approval of the members of a company is necessary for the payment of compensation by a company to a director for loss of office. It provides:

> 'It shall not be lawful for a company to make to any director of the company any payment by way of compensation for loss of office, or as consideration for or in connection with his

---

[222] CA 1963, s 195(11C) provides: 'No notice of resignation or other documentary proof of a person's having ceased to be a director or secretary of a company which is forwarded to the Registrar of Companies by that person (other than such a notice or other proof which is forwarded by him under and in accordance with sub-ss (11A) and (11B), or Companies Amendment (No 2) Act 1999, s 43(9)) shall be considered by the registrar.'

[223] CA 1963, s 195(11B) provides: 'If a company fails to comply with a request made of it under a notice referred to in sub-s (11A) the person who served the notice may forward to the Registrar of Companies and to every person who, to his knowledge, is an officer of the company a copy of the notice of resignation or other documentary proof referred to in sub-s (11A) if, but only if, there is forwarded together with that notice or proof, in the case of the registrar, the additional information referred to in that sub-s and, in the case of every other person as aforesaid, the written request referred to in that sub-s.'

[224] CA 1963, s 195(11D) provides: 'No additional information referred to in sub-s (11A)(b)(i) that is included in a notice of resignation or other documentary proof referred to in this section which is forwarded, under and in accordance with the foregoing provisions, to the Registrar of Companies shall, of itself, be regarded as constituting defamatory matter.'

[225] CA 1963, s 195(11E).

retirement from office, without particulars relating to the proposed payment (including the amount thereof) being disclosed to the members of the company and the proposal being approved by the company in general meeting.'

The materially identical UK provision[226] was considered by the Scottish Court of Session in *Mercer v Heart of Midlothian plc*[227]. The facts in that case were that Mercer had been majority-shareholder and chairman of the defendant football club and part of the agreement that he would be elected life president was that he would be granted certain privileges including seats in the directors' box at a football stadium on match days, access to the boardroom and a car park pass. When Mercer retired shortly thereafter, the board of directors sought to withdraw his privileges on the grounds that, pursuant to the Companies Act 1985 (UK), s 312, they had not been approved by the members. It was held that the payments in question were not within the contemplation of s 312 for two reasons. In the first place, it was held that the directors had regarded the privileges as being conferred on the life president and they were firmly attached to his future enjoyment of that position – not his leaving office. In the second place, it was held that although the privileges were of benefit to the recipient, it was not obvious that it would actually cost the defendant anything to allow Mercer to enjoy them; accordingly, it was held that the privileges did not constitute a 'payment'. It is also of note that the court held that the disclosure in a company's accounts of any payments within the contemplation of the section could not be said to be disclosure and approval to members because disclosure and approval was required to be prior to the making of any such payments, not ex post facto.

[8.085] It should also be noted that it is unlawful, in connection with the transfer of the whole or any part of the undertaking or property of a company, for any payment to be made to a director by way of compensation for loss of office or as consideration for or in connection with his retirement from office, without the prior disclosure to, and approval by, the members in general meeting[228].

Disclosures concerning directors and secretaries

[8.086] A company is obliged to disclose certain aspects of its relationship with its directors and secretary. These disclosure requirements may be considered under the following two headings:

(a) The register of directors and secretary.

(b) Disclosure and registration of directors' and others' interests in shares.

(a) The register of directors and secretary

[8.087] Section 195 of CA 1963, as replaced by CA 1990, s 51, provides that every company shall keep at its registered office a register of its directors and secretary, which should keep the prescribed details of such officers. Within 14 days of any change in either the directors or secretary or any change in any of the particulars in the register, the

---

226 Companies Act 1985 (UK), s 312.

227 *Mercer v Heart of Midlothian plc* (2001) SLT 945, noted by Goddard, (2002) 23 Co Law 23.

228 CA 1963, s 187. It should also be noted that tax free payments to directors are also prohibited: CA 1963, s 185.

company[229] must send the Registrar of Companies notification in the prescribed form[230]. Where the notification is of the appointment of a person as director or secretary/joint secretary, then the new officers must sign a consent[231].

The register of directors and secretary must be kept open for inspection for not less than two hours per day during business hours, subject to whatever reasonable restrictions the company's articles of association or resolution of the members in general meeting may impose[232]. Those who may inspect the register are the members of the company, who may do so without charge, and the general public, on payment of €1.27[233]. Section 195 of CA 1963 imposes a duty on the directors and secretary to give information to the company in writing to enable the company to comply with the section[234]. A refusal to permit inspection, or any default in complying with the operative subsections is liable to be visited by a fine on the company and every officer who is in default[235].

[8.088] The matters required to be detailed in relation to each director are set out in CA 1963, s 195(2). These are as follows:

- his present forename, surname and any former names[236];
- his date of birth;
- his usual residential address;
- his nationality;
- his business occupation, if any; and
- particulars of other directorships of other bodies corporate, Irish or foreign, past or present.

It is unnecessary to record particulars of other directorships that have not been held by a director during the ten years preceding inspection. Also excluded are directorships of bodies corporate of which the company is or was a wholly-owned subsidiary, or which are or were wholly-owned subsidiaries either of the company or of another body corporate of which the company is or was the wholly-owned subsidiary[237].

[8.089] The matters required to be detailed in relation to the secretary are set out in CA 1963, s 195(4) and are considered below[238].

---

229 CA 1963, s 195(8) provides that a person who has ceased to be a director may himself notify the Registrar of Companies.

230 CA 1963, s 195(6).

231 CA 1963, s 195(7).

232 CA 1963, s 195(10).

233 CA 1963, s 195.

234 CA 1963, s 195(11). A person who fails to comply with this is guilty of an offence and liable to a fine.

235 CA 1963, s 195(12), which provides for a fine not exceeding €1269.74 and for up to a €63.49 daily default fine. CA 1963, s 195(13) provides that the court may by order compel an immediate inspection of the register.

236 See generally, CA 1963, s 195(15).

237 CA 1963, s 195(3).

238 See para **[8.100]**.

(b) Disclosure and registration of directors' and others' interests in shares

[8.090] Prior to the Companies Act 1990 directors were only obliged to register with the company their interests in shares and debentures to which they held the legal title. On account of there being no obligation to register their interest in shares to which they held equitable or beneficial title, there was a black spot on such registers. This has now been addressed by CA 1990, Part IV (which applies to directors, shadow directors[239] and the secretary). The effect of CA 1990, Part IV has been to turn an arc light on the black spot and it is generally considered by practitioners that the disclosure requirements in Part IV have placed a significant burden of compliance on companies, their shareholders and officers[240]. Section 53 of CA 1990 contains the basic obligation to notify interests in shares and debentures held by directors or secretaries in a company or its subsidiary or holding company, at the commencement of the section[241] or on becoming a director or secretary, of:

— the subsistence of his interests at that time; and

— of the number of shares of each class in, and the amount of debentures of each class of the company or the holding or subsidiary company[242].

Although a person may be an existing director or secretary of a company, he is obliged to notify the company of the occurrence of any of the events set out in CA 1990, s 53(2):

'(a) any event in consequence of whose occurrence he becomes, or ceases to be, interested in shares in, or debentures of, the company or any other body corporate, being the company's subsidiary or holding company or a subsidiary of the company's holding company;

(b) the entering into by him of a contract to sell any such shares or debentures;

(c) the assignment by him of a right granted to him by the company to subscribe for shares in, or debentures of, the company; and

(d) the grant to him by another body corporate, being the company's subsidiary or holding company or a subsidiary of the company's holding company, of a right to subscribe for shares in, or debentures of, that other body corporate, the exercise of such a right granted to him and the assignment by him of such a right so granted;

stating the number or amount, and class, of shares or debentures involved.'

It is clear from the detail of the foregoing that few interests will escape the CA 1990's provisions since it captures interests in shares and debentures as well as share options not only in Irish but also overseas companies.

[8.091] Section 54 of CA 1990 gives a very wide definition to the 'interests' which require to be notified to the company under s 53. Section 54(4) provides that a person shall be taken to have an interest in shares or debentures, if:

'(a) he enters into a contract for their purchase by him (whether for cash or other consideration); or

---

239 CA 1990, s 53(9).

240 See, Nolan, 'Disclosure of Interests in Securities under Part IV of the Companies Act 1990' (2000) 7 CLP 31.

241 1 August 1991, by SI 1991/117.

242 CA 1963, s 195(1).

(b) not being the registered holder, he is entitled to exercise any right conferred by the holder of those shares or debentures or is entitled to control the exercise of any such right.'

Furthermore, by s 54(5), where a body corporate is interested in shares, a person shall be taken to be interested in them where:

'(a) that body corporate or its directors are accustomed to act in accordance with his directions or instructions; or

(b) he is entitled to exercise or control the exercise of one-third or more of the voting power at general meetings of that body corporate.'

In addition, s 54(6) provides:

> 'Where a person is entitled to exercise or control the exercise of one-third or more of the voting power at general meetings of a body corporate and that body corporate is entitled to exercise or control the exercise of any of the voting power at general meetings of another body corporate (the 'relevant voting power'), then, for the purposes of subs (5)(b), the relevant voting power shall be taken to be exercisable by that person.'

There are also further provisions governing the determination of the question of an interest in shares and debentures[243].

[8.092] Having established whether a relevant person has an interest in shares or debentures, CA 1990, s 53 obliges that person to notify the company in writing of the acquisition and the cessation of his interest and the number of shares of each class and the amount of debentures of each class in which he is interested in that company and its holding and subsidiary companies. He is also obliged to notify the company where he enters into a contract to sell any such shares or debentures, assigns or exercises a right granted to him to subscribe for shares or debentures in the company, or receives a right to subscribe for shares or debentures in the company's holding company, subsidiary or fellow subsidiary. In addition to the requirement that notice be given to the company, there is a corollary obligation on the company itself to 'keep a register for the purposes of s 53, by virtue of CA 1990, s 59 which goes on to make specific provisions and requirements.

[8.093] The requirements contained in CA 1990, s 53 apply to all dealings after 1 August 1991[244] and persons affected by s 53 were obliged to notify the company of their interests within five days of that date. A person is obliged to notify within five days of his becoming aware of his obligations: s 56. Section 57 of CA 1990 states the conditions which must be fulfilled with regard to the requirement to notify. Section 58(3) of CA 1990 provides a sanction where the relevant persons do not comply with the requirements, and provides that to fail to notify within the prescribed time will mean that the rights and interests in the shares and debentures are unenforceable. Section 58(3) provides:

> '...no right or interest of any kind whatsoever in respect of the shares or debentures concerned shall be enforceable by him whether directly or indirectly by action or legal proceedings.'

---

[243] See generally, CA 1990, s 54(7)–(13).

[244] SI 1991/117.

So as not to unduly penalise inadvertence, CA 1990, s 58(4) empowers the court to grant relief where satisfied that the default was accidental, due to inadvertence or some other sufficient cause, or on just and equitable grounds. The propriety, however, of CA 1990, Part IV is questionable. Just how important can it be in private companies that the 'company' is notified of interests in shares held by its directors when in reality the directors and shareholders are one and the same people? Such law demonstrates the worst excesses of the failure to understand that management and ownership in the vast majority of Irish private companies are not divorced. It is bad enough to put small enterprises to the trouble of paper exercises but it is entirely wrong to penalise non-compliance by rendering rights unenforceable.

[C] THE SECRETARY

The requirement to have a secretary

[8.094] By CA 1963, s 175, every company, including single-member companies, must have a secretary, who may be one of the directors Section 175(2) of CA 1963 provides:

> 'Anything required to be done by or to the secretary may, if the office is vacant or there is for any other reason no secretary capable of acting, be done by or to any assistant or deputy secretary or, if there is no assistant or deputy secretary capable of acting, by or to any officer of the company authorised generally or specially in that behalf by the directors.'

It should be noted that the prohibition[245] against companies having a body corporate as a director has no parallel in the case of secretaries, and indeed many incorporated companies provide secretarial services for many other Irish companies. Although it is permissible for a company to have more than one secretary[246], it would be unusual for a private company to have more than one secretary.

Appointment and cessation

[8.095] It should be noted that no formal qualifications are required to become secretary of a private company[247]. The name of the first secretary must be notified to the CRO in the Form A1, as in the case of a company's first directors[248], accompanied by their consent to act as such[249]. The subsequent appointment of a company secretary will be in accordance with the articles of association of each company and changes must be notified to the CRO[250]. In this regard, it is common for companies to adopt model reg 113. This provides:

> 'The secretary shall be appointed by the directors for such term, at such remuneration, and upon such conditions as they think fit; and any secretary so appointed may be removed by them.'

---

245 CA 1963, s 176(1).

246 CA 1963, s 195(4), as substituted by CA 1990, s 51.

247 Cf public limited companies: see Chapter 28, *Public Companies in Context*, para **[28.066]**.

248 C(A)A 1982, s 3(1)(b). See Chapter 2, *Formation, Registration and Conversion of Private Companies*, para **[2.039]**.

249 C(A)A 1982, s 3(3).

250 CA 1963, s 195(6).

Companies are obliged to notify the CRO of any cessation in the office of secretary and where the company fails to do this, an ex-secretary may effect notification, subject to the provisions of CA 1963, s 195(11A), considered above[251].

Status and remuneration

[8.096] A company's secretary, like its directors, is an office holder[252]. He will not necessarily have a contract of employment with the company. A company secretary's entitlement to remuneration and conditions of appointment will be set by the directors. A company secretary may have a contract of service or a contract of employment with the company.

Functions and duties

[8.097] The functions and duties of a company secretary are essentially administrative, as opposed to managerial[253]. They typically involve the keeping of the various registers required to be kept under the Companies Acts 1963-2001[254]. In many private companies no clearly-defined office of secretary will exist and many companies charge the performance of statutory tasks to the other 'secretary' who answers the telephone and does the typing! However, in the current environment of corporate compliance, companies who acquiesce in such practices do so at their peril[255].

[8.098] In *Barnett, Hoares & Co v South London Tramways Co*[256] Lord Esher MR said:

> 'A secretary is a mere servant; his position is that he is to do what he is told and no person can assume that he has any authority to represent anything at all.'

Commenting upon this passage, Lord Denning MR in *Panorama Developments (Guilford) Ltd v Fidelis Furnishing Fabrics Ltd*[257], noted that times have changed since it was uttered by Lord Esher in 1887. Lord Denning MR observed that the company secretary is a 'much more important person nowadays', being an officer with extensive duties and responsibilities. While this may be true in large private companies or PLCs, it hardly reflects the reality in the vast majority of Irish private companies.

[8.099] The duties of the secretary are considered in Chapter 10, *Duties of Directors and Other Officers*[258].

Disclosure requirements for secretaries

[8.100] Section 195(4) of CA 1963 requires the register of directors and secretaries to contain the following particulars in relation to the secretary:

---

251 See para **[8.081]**.

252 See para **[8.068]**.

253 See Keane, *Company Law* (3rd edn, 2000), para 30.02.

254 See Chapter 2, *Formation, Registration and Conversion of Private Companies*, para **[2.038]** *ff*.

255 See, generally, Chapter 12, *Company Law Compliance and Enforcement*.

256 *Barnett, Hoares & Co v Sough London Tramways Co* (1887) 18 QBD 815 at 817.

257 *Panorama Developments (Guilford) Ltd v Fidelis Furnishing Fabrics Ltd* [1971] 3 All ER 16.

258 At para **[10.132]** *ff*.

- in the case of an individual, his name, former names and his usual residential address;
- in the case of a body corporate, its name and registered office.

Company secretaries are also required to disclose their interests in shares held in the company, the details of which are set out in CA 1990, Part IV, and considered in the context of company directors, above[259].

[259] See para **[8.090]** *ff.*

Chapter 9

Corporate Governance: Meetings

[9.001] Where management (the directors) and owners (the shareholders) of a company are different people, the holding of meetings of both members and directors can be the cornerstone of sound corporate governance. It is a statutory requirement that all companies (except single-member private limited companies)[1] must hold an annual general meeting ('AGM') of their members; extraordinary general meetings ('EGM') will be required from time to time where the statutory approval of members (by ordinary or special resolution) is required. As was considered in the previous chapter, the management of companies is invariably vested in the directors; meetings of the directors, whether formal or informal, will be required in order to take particular decisions.

[9.002] The practice of corporate governance in many Irish private companies differs greatly from the prevailing practices in public companies, particularly those regulated by the Irish Stock Exchange[2]. More often than not, the pomp and ceremony of formal meetings of the board of directors and of the members, as portrayed in television drama, bears no relation to the practice of meetings in small Irish private companies. For a substantial number of Irish private companies, meetings of the members and of the directors will more often be held in a public house or over the breakfast table than in any 'board room'! Formal notice of meetings, in particular, is often forgotten unless a company is involved in a transaction with a credit institution, which makes the observance of formalities a prerequisite to the draw down of loan facilities.

[9.003] Another feature of many Irish private companies is that the relationship between members and directors is frequently blurred by reason of their being one and the same person. This duality of roles can even result in participants at meetings not being sure whether they are attending a members' general meeting or a directors' meeting[3]. This recognition of the reality for many companies should not be taken as an endorsement of such practices: the formalities imposed by the Companies Acts must be complied with and defective practices can result in resolutions, that were thought to have been passed, being set aside. This chapter considers meetings of both members and of directors.

---

1 See para **[9.013]**.

2 See Chapter 28, *Public Companies in Context*, para **[28.063]** *ff* where the requirements of the Combined Code are discussed.

3 See, for example, *Re Aston Colour Print Ltd* (21 February 1997, unreported), High Court, considered at para **[9.093]**.

[A] MEMBERS' MEETINGS[4]

[9.004] Members' general meetings are the fora at which the will of a company's members can be elicited and at which members are formally provided with certain information on the company. With the exception of the AGM, which is a statutory requirement, the holding of members' meetings is largely at the discretion of the company[5]. One of the most common – although not exclusive – reasons for convening EGMs is for the purposes of 'considering and if thought proper, adopting' a particular resolution. With a few notable exceptions[6], most resolutions can be passed without holding a members' meeting by using the written resolution procedure. This is facilitated by the Companies Act 1963, s 141(8) ('CA 1963') and practitioners would do well to bear this provision in mind. In appropriate cases, where the articles of association[7] so permit, s 141(8) can substantially alleviate what might reasonably be considered as excessive bureaucracy in small companies. The written resolution procedure and resolutions in general, are considered below[8].

[9.005] In this section the legal issues arising in members' meetings are considered under the following headings:

1. The annual general meeting.
2. Extraordinary general meetings.
3. Notice of members' meetings.
4. Notice of business to be conducted at a meeting.
5. The quorum.
6. Postponing and adjourning meetings.
7. Voting at members' meetings.
8. Minutes of members' meetings.
9. Resolutions.

The annual general meeting

[9.006] It is mandatory[9] that every multi-member company holds an AGM and CA 1963, s 131(1) provides that companies must, in each calendar year[10], hold an AGM.

4 See generally, Shearman, *Shackleton on The Law and Practice of Meetings* (9th edn, 1997), pp 105–220; Jones and Jacobs, *Company Meetings: Law and Procedure* (1991), pp 1–102. For a brief overview of Irish law see Maloney & Spellman, *The Law of Meetings* (1999), p 135–147.

5 An exception is the requirement to convene an EGM where a company suffers a serious capital loss: C(A)A 1983, s 40.

6 Resolutions to appoint or remove auditors (CA 1963, s 160) or to remove directors (CA 1963, s 182) cannot be passed as written resolutions: see para **[9.078]**.

7 This is where model reg 6 of Part II of Table A, or a bespoke equivalent, is adopted.

8 See para **[9.076]**.

9 An elective, as opposed to mandatory, regime applies in the case of single-member private limited companies: see para **[9.013]**.

10 'Year' has been held to mean a calendar year and not a period of 12 months from the date of incorporation: *Gibson v Barton* (1875) QB 329.

The primary requirement in s 131(1) for an annual general meeting is further limited – and not relaxed[11] – by the requirement that not more than 15 months may elapse between AGMs. There is one exception to this general rule, contained in CA 1963, s 131(2), which provides that so long as a company holds its first AGM within 18 months of its incorporation, it is not obliged to hold an AGM in the year of its incorporation or in the following year[12].

[9.007] Here, the AGM is considered under five sub-headings:

(a) The purpose of the AGM.

(b) AGMs must generally be held within the State.

(c) Ministerial direction to call an AGM.

(d) Possible consequences where AGM not held.

(e) AGMs in single-member private limited companies.

(a) The purpose of the AGM

[9.008] Historically, the AGM was intended to give the investing public an opportunity to meet the directors of their company, to receive certain information and to ask questions. In many private companies (especially those where the directors and members are one and the same) little remains of this rationale; indeed the Company Law Review Group has recommended that all companies except public limited companies ('PLCs') should be permitted to dispense with holding an AGM where the members unanimously so resolve[13]. The purpose behind the statutory obligation on companies to hold an AGM is primarily to provide an annual forum at which the directors can comply with their statutory duties. Accordingly, in each financial year, company directors must lay before the company's members in general meeting the annual accounts, the directors' report and the auditors' report on the accounts. These requirements are considered in detail in Chapter 13, *Accounts and Auditors*. Moreover, where a company's articles of association require directors to retire by rotation, the election or re-election of directors will typically occur at the AGM.

(b) AGMs must generally be held within the State

[9.009] By virtue of CA 1963, s 140, and CA 1963, Sch 1, Table A, Part I, model reg 47 ('the model regulations), the AGM of a company must be held within the State[14]. This,

---

11 This does not mean that companies are entitled to hold their AGM every 15 months as the primary obligation is that an AGM is held each calendar year. So, for example, if a company holds an AGM on 30 November 2001, its next AGM must be held not later than 31 December 2002 (a period of only 13 months), since there must be an AGM in the calendar year 2002.

12 CA 1963, s 131(1) and (2) is mirrored by model reg 48.

13 See the *Company Law Review Group's First Report, (2000–2001)*, recommendation 4.5.6, p 66.

14 CA 1963, s 140(1) provides: 'Subject to subsection (2), the annual general meeting of a company shall be held in the State and any business transacted at a meeting held in breach of this requirement shall be void unless—(a) either all the members entitled to attend and vote at such meeting consent in writing to its being held elsewhere or a resolution providing that it be held elsewhere has been passed at the preceding annual general meeting; and (b) the articles do not provide that the annual general meeting shall be held in the State.' This is, however, subject to CA 1963, s 140(2), which provides: 'Subsection (1) shall not apply to the first annual general meeting of a company held on or after the operative date.'

however, is subject either to the company's articles providing otherwise, a resolution being passed or the members' unanimously resolving in writing that it be held elsewhere[15].

(c) Ministerial direction to call an AGM

[9.010] Under CA 1963 a member of a company can request the Minister for Enterprise, Trade and Employment to call or direct the calling of an AGM, but such requests are rare[16]. Section 131(3) provides:

> 'If default is made in holding a meeting of the company in accordance with subsection (1), the Minister may, on the application of any member of the company, call or direct the calling of a general meeting of the company and give such ancillary or consequential directions as the Minister thinks expedient, including directions modifying or supplementing in relation to the calling holding and conducting of the meeting, the operation of the company's articles, and it is hereby declared that the directions which may be given under this subsection include a direction that one member of the company present in person or by proxy shall be deemed to constitute a meeting.'

The obligation is placed upon the officers of the company to hold the meeting by virtue of CA 1963, s 131(6), and where a failure to hold the meeting is detected, the officers can be fined[17]. Although the instances of criminal prosecutions under the Companies Acts have been rare, prosecutions are not unknown[18], and the advent of the Director of Corporate Enforcement is likely to give rise to more prosecutions for this and other company law offences.

(d) Possible consequences where AGM not held

[9.011] In certain circumstances the failure to hold an AGM may, depending upon the company's articles of association's provisions on rotation and retirement of directors, mean that some or all of the directors will cease to hold office. The clearest example of this in action is seen in *Re Consolidated Nickel Mines Ltd*[19]. In this case a company's directors made claims for remuneration against the company's liquidator but the liquidator denied the claims on the grounds that the directors had vacated office. The basis of the liquidator's contention was that the company's articles provided that 'At the ordinary meeting in 1906 all directors and in every subsequent year one-third of all the directors shall retire from office. A retiring director shall retain office until the dissolution of the meeting at which his successor is elected.' No general meetings were

---

15 See CA 1963, s 140(1) and (2).

16 CA 1963, s 131(3)–(5).

17 CA 1963, s 131(6), as increased to €634.87, by the C(A)A 1982, Sch 1. See *Smedley v Registrar of Joint Stock Companies* [1919] 1 KB 97.

18 See, for example, *Re Muckross Park Hotel Ltd* (21 February 2001), District Court, reported in (2001) The Irish Times, 22 February 2001 where it was reported that a company and its directors were successfully prosecuted for failing to hold an AGM of the company in 1999. This was despite having been notified by the Department of Enterprise, Trade and Employment, on a number of occasions. The defendants were fined a total of IR£1,200 and ordered to pay expenses of IR£400 at Killarney District Court.

19 *Re Consolidated Nickel Mines Ltd* [1914] 1 Ch 883.

held in either 1906 or 1907 and it was held that the meaning of that particular article was that:

> '...the holding of office of director was only to last until the end of 1906, or until the earlier date on which the ordinary meeting for that year was held...The duty of the directors was to call a meeting in 1906 and 1907, and they cannot take advantage of their own default in that respect and say that they still remain as director.'[20]

In *Phoenix Shannon plc v Purkey* [21] Costello J accepted that the court's construction in *Consolidated Nickel Mines* of the article in question was correct. In *Kanssen v Rialto (West End) Ltd*[22] the company's articles of association were materially identical to model reg 92, which provides:

> 'At the first annual general meeting of the company all the directors shall retire from office, and at the annual general meeting in every subsequent year, one-third of the directors for the time being, of if their number is not three or a multiple of three, then the number nearest one-third shall retire from office.'

In that case the court hear that an AGM at which a certain Mr Cromie should have retired as director, was not held in the year 1942. It was held that he had vacated office on 31 December 1941 by reason of this article. Similarly in *Re Zinotty Properties*[23] it was held that the effect of a materially identical article was that since no AGMs had been held, the original directors must be deemed to have retired.

[9.012] This line of authority was distinguished by Costello J in *Phoenix Shannon plc v Purkey* [24]. In that case the plaintiff-company did not hold an AGM for the year 1996. The second and third plaintiffs (who were directors) decided that since an AGM had not been held, all of the directors who had been co-opted in 1996 (the six defendants) had automatically vacated office by reason of the application of a bespoke article which provided:

> 'The directors may from time to time and at any time appoint any person to be a director wether to fill a casual vacancy or as an additional director provided that the total number of directors shall not exceed the maximum number fixed by or in accordance with these Articles. Subject to the provisions of the Acts, a director so appointed shall hold office only until the commencement of the annual general meeting following next after his appointment, when he shall retire. A director who retires under this article shall be eligible for re-appointment at the meeting at which he retires.'[25]

It was not argued (or mentioned in judgment) that the company had in fact an article equivalent to model reg 92, which contained the wording that had been interpreted by the foregoing authorities. The second-named plaintiff director conceded that he too had vacated office on this ground. The third-named plaintiff director then purported to

---

20 [1914] 1 Ch 883 at 888.

21 *Phoenix Shannon plc v Purkey* [1998] 4 IR 597, [1997] 2 ILRM 381 (Costello J).

22 *Kansen v Railto (West End) Ltd* [1944] Ch 346.

23 *Re Zinotty Properties* [1984] 1 WLR 1249. See also *Alexander Ward and Co Ltd v Samyang Navigation Co Ltd* (1973) SLT 80.

24 *Phoenix Shannon plc v Purkey* [1998] 4 IR 597, [1997] 2 ILRM 381 (Costello J).

25 The company's bespoke article was largely based on what is model reg 98.

exercise the powers conferred by another bespoken article (similar in effect to model reg 103) and re-appointed the second-named plaintiff as director and four others were subsequently co-opted onto the board. Costello J said:

> 'I agree that the "annual general meeting next following" the date of co-option referred to in article 92 must refer to the annual general meeting which should be held under article 52 and section 131. But the article is silent as to what is to happen if the directors fail in their duty to convene the meeting. In effect the plaintiff requires the court to imply a provision in article 92 to the effect that should the directors fail to convene an annual general meeting as required by the article the co-opted directors will automatically vacate office on the last day on which the meeting should lawfully have been held.'[26]

Costello J assigned two reasons for deciding that the court should not imply such a provision. In the first place, he found it significant that CA 1963, s 131(3) makes express provision as to what is to happen should the directors default in convening an AGM and said that:

> '...these provisions not only provide a practical remedy should the directors fail to convene an annual general meeting but also a means by which the default can be legally rectified...In the light of this express statutory provision should default occur I do not think the court should imply into the article the suggested provision of automatic resignations.'[27]

The second reason Costello J gave for refusing to imply such a provision into the company's regulation was because the company's bespoke article dealing with the circumstances in which the office of director shall be vacated did not cite as a ground the failure to hold an AGM. Costello J went on to say that the same arguments applied to the company's article dealing with rotation of directors. Without giving the wording of that article (so we do not know whether it was bespoken or identical to model reg 92 which was interpreted in the English line of authorities mentioned at the outset) Costello J said:

> 'At "each annual general meeting" one third are required to retire from office, but I do not think that the court should imply a provision into their articles to the effect that should the company fail to hold an annual general meeting the directors whose turn it is to retire should be deemed automatically to have vacated office.'[28]

It is thought that this decision gives rise to considerable uncertainty. Costello J seemed at pains to prevent the plaintiffs from deriving benefit from the *Consolidated Nickel Mines* line of authorities without going so far as to expressly decline to follow them.

(e) AGMs in single-member private limited companies

[9.013] Notwithstanding CA 1963, s 131, the European Communities (Single-Member Private Limited Companies) Regulations 1994, reg 8(1)[29] provides:

> 'The sole member of a single-member company may decide, in the manner provided for in Regulation 9, to dispense with the holding of annual general meetings and, if he or she does so, s 131 of the Principal Act shall not apply to the company.'

---

26 [1998] 4 IR 597 at 603.

27 [1998] 4 IR 597 at 604.

28 [1998] 4 IR 597 at 604, 605.

29 SI 1994/275.

Regulation 8(1) is an elective provision whereby the sole member of a single-member company can hold or dispense with holding an AGM if he so wishes. The sole member or the company's auditor may subsequently call an AGM under reg 8(3), which provides:

> 'In any year in which an annual general meeting would, but for a decision pursuant to paragraph (1) be required to be held, and in which no such meeting has been held, the sole member or the auditor of a single-member company may, by notice to the company not later than three months before the end of the year, require the holding of an annual general meeting in that year.'

When such notice is given to the company, the provisions of CA 1963, s 131 are again applied with respect to the calling of the meeting and the consequences of default[30]. It may be noted here[31] that corporate accounting requirements in the Companies Acts that require accounts[32] and other matters to be laid before the AGM are deemed to be satisfied where such accounts and reports are sent to the sole member within twenty one days before the appropriate date[33], in accordance with CA 1963, s 159[34].

Extraordinary general meetings

[9.014] An EGM has the potential to be the most dynamic of the two varieties of members' meetings since it will be convened where it is proposed to do something new, even if not quite 'extraordinary', in the vernacular sense of that word[35]. Four particular circumstances in which EGMs can be called are next considered:

(a) EGMs convened by the directors.

(b) EGMs convened on the requisition of qualified members.

(c) EGMs convened by order of the court.

(d) EGMs convened on the requisition of retiring auditors.

(a) EGMs convened by the directors

[9.015] Model reg 50 provides that an EGM can be called in either of two ways. In the first place, the directors of the company may call an EGM. In this regard model reg 50 goes on to provide:

> '...If at any time there are not within the State sufficient directors capable of acting to form a quorum, any director or any 2 members of the company may convene an extraordinary general meeting in the same manner as nearly as possible as that in which meetings may be convened by the directors.'

An EGM may be called at the directors' behest where, for example, they wish to obtain the prior approval of the shareholders before taking a certain course of action. By virtue of s 40 of the Companies (Amendment) Act 1983, directors are obliged to convene an EGM where a company suffers a serious loss of capital[36].

---

30 SI 1994/275, reg 8(4).

31 See further Chapter 13, *Accounts and Auditors*, para **[13.017]**.

32 CA 1963, s 148.

33 CA 1963, s 148, as defined by SI 275/1994, reg 8(9).

34 SI 275/1994, reg 8(5).

35 For single–member companies, see para **[9.074]**.

36 See Chapter 18, *The Maintenance of Capital*, para **[18.098]**.

(b) EGMs convened on the requisition of qualified members

[9.016] The second circumstance in which an EGM may be called is pursuant to CA 1963, s 132. Section 132(1), which empowers a member, or several members, holding not less than 10% of the paid up share capital with voting rights of the company 'qualified members' to compel the directors of a company to call an EGM[37], provides:

> 'The directors of a company, notwithstanding anything in its articles, shall, on the requisition of members of the company holding at the date of the deposit of the requisition not less than one-tenth of such of the paid up capital of the company as at the date of the deposit carries the right of voting at general meetings of the company, or, in the case of a company not having a share capital, members of the company representing not less than one-tenth of the total voting rights of all the members having at the said date a right to vote at general meetings of the company, forthwith proceed duly to convene an extraordinary general meeting of the company.'[38]

The formal requirements are that the requisition for an EGM must be signed by the requisitionists[39] and deposited at the registered office of the company and may consist of several documents in like form, each signed by one or more requisitionists[40]. However, directors, faced with a members' requisition, should have regard to both the subject matter of the requisitioned meeting and, also, the manner in which it is summoned.

[9.017] A member's requisition for an EGM should not misrepresent the circumstances which the member requisitioning the EGM holds out as the reason therefor. However, some latitude will be granted to members in respect of what they represent to be the case when seeking support for the requisitioning of an EGM. The facts in *Rose v McGivern*[41] were that the plaintiff was a member of the Royal Automobile Club Ltd (a friendly society) and he wrote a letter to other members of the company, proposing that it be demutualised. It was further proposed that an EGM be summoned and that two resolutions be put to the meeting: resolution (1) to elect a new board of directors; and resolution (2) to authorise the board to proceed with the demutualisation. The plaintiff's letter received sufficient support from the members to require the directors to convene and hold an EGM. It was held by Neuberger J that the fact that the plaintiff's letter to his fellow members might have given the impression that the company's directors were against the sale of the company's subsidiary's assets – which the directors denied was the case – merely expressed the plaintiff's opinion. Neuberger J said:

---

37 *Re Downs Wine Bar Ltd* [1990] BCLC 839.

38 This is underscored by CA 1963, s 134 which provides: 'The following provisions shall have effect in so far as the articles of the company do not make other provision in that behalf— … (b) two or more members holding not less than one–tenth of the issued share capital or, if the company has not a share capital, not less than 5 per cent. in number of all the members of the company may call a meeting.'

39 Where the requisite number of shares are held jointly, the requisition must be signed by all of those entitled to those shares: *Patenwood Keg Syndicate Ltd v Pearse* [1906] WN 164.

40 CA 1963, s 132(2).

41 *Rose v McGivern* [1998] 2 BCLC 593.

> '...I have reached the conclusion that this [the "impression" given by the plaintiff] is not a ground for validly challenging the March letter which gave rise to the requisitions. First, the March letter does not state in terms the attitude of the board [of the subsidiary]. It merely identifies [the plaintiff's] opinion at the date of the March letter as to the likely attitude of the board...In other words, the sentence centrally complained of is a statement of opinion on the part of the person seeking the requisitions on an assumed state of facts based on past knowledge. The letter represented [the plaintiff's] honest opinion.'[42]

Neuberger J held that the requisitions obtained for summoning the EGM were properly obtained and so were valid.

[9.018] A members' requisition must state the objects of the meeting. Great care should be taken in framing the objects of the meeting because at the meeting no business, other than that stated in the requisition, may be introduced by other members, as opposed to the vdirectors[43], for consideration at a meeting so requisitioned. Again, the case of *Rose v McGivern* [44], the facts of which have just been considered, is instructive. There, Neuberger J held that the proposals for resolutions, put forward by the plaintiff, could not constitute the subject matter of valid resolutions as they were too vague and ambiguous. In particular, he found that resolution (1) failed to identify the persons to be elected as directors, the exact size of the board, or which members of the old board were to be removed. In addition, resolution (2) failed too as, inter alia, it was meaningless as the board of the company had the power, regardless of such a resolution, to demutualise. Member-requisitionists would do well to bear this in mind and to consult with lawyers before attempting to frame the resolutions which they seek to propose at an EGM requisitioned by them. The notice of the business intended to be conducted at a meeting (AGM or EGM) is considered further, below[45].

[9.019] The directors of a company would be ill-advised to ignore a properly constituted requisition. Section 132(3) of CA 1963 provides that:

> 'If the directors do not within 21 days from the date of the deposit of the requisition proceed duly to convene a meeting to be held within 2 months from the said date, the requisitionists, or any of them representing more than one half of the total voting rights of all of them, may themselves convene a meeting, but any meeting so convened shall not be held after the expiration of 3 months from the said date.'[46]

---

[42] [1998] 2 BCLC 593 at 601, 602.

[43] *Ball v Metal Industries Ltd* [1957] SLT 124. This case also suggests (at 125) that 'it would be perfectly competent for the board of a company when they are sending out a notice convening an extraordinary general meeting pursuant to s 132 [of the Companies Act 1948 (UK)] to incorporate in the notice provisions relating to business which could competently have been put before the company by the directors at an extraordinary general meeting of the company ...'.

[44] *Rose v McGivern* [1998] 2 BCLC 593.

[45] See para **[9.037]**.

[46] Note that CA 1963, s 132(6) provides: 'For the purposes of this section, the directors shall, in the case of a meeting at which a resolution is to be proposed as a special resolution, be deemed not to have duly convened the meeting if they do not give such notice thereof as is required by section 141.'

Where a meeting is convened by the requisitionists it must be convened in the same manner as nearly as possible as that in which meetings are to be convened by directors[47]. In England it has been held that where the directors simply convened a meeting they were not in breach of the provisions of the English section notwithstanding that they did not actually hold the meeting until some months later[48]. The position is different in Ireland in that not only must the directors convene a meeting within 21 days from the date of the requisition, but they must convene a meeting to be *actually held* within two months from the date of the deposit of the members' requisition to hold the meeting. Where the directors fail to convene an EGM and the member-requisitionists decide to convene it themselves, they should be careful to comply with the provisions of the Companies Acts, lest any meeting they convene and hold be declared invalid for want of compliance with the requisite formalities. So, for example, the Supreme Court of New South Wales in *Howard v Mechtler*[49] declared that an EGM held by requisitionists was invalid because the notice convening the meeting was short of that required by statute. In that case, however, it was held that to convene a meeting for 6.00 pm on the 30 December was not an inherently unreasonable time.

(c) EGMs convened by order of the court

[9.020] A problem can arise where the holding of an EGM is thwarted because the other member or members do not attend a convened meeting. In such circumstances, CA 1963, s 135(1) can be invoked. This provides that:

> 'If for any reason it is impractical to call a meeting of a company in any manner in which meetings of that company may be called, or to conduct the meeting of the company in manner prescribed by the articles or this Act, the court may either of its own motion or of any member of the company who would be entitled to vote at the meeting, order a meeting of the company to be called, held and conducted in such manner as the court thinks fit, and where any such order is made may give such ancillary or consequential directions as it thinks expedient; and it is hereby declared that the directions that may be given under this subsection include a declaration that one member of the company present in person or by proxy shall be deemed to constitute a meeting.'[50]

---

47 CA 1963, s 132(4). CA 1963, s 134(5) provides: 'Any reasonable expenses incurred by the requisitionists by reason of the failure of the directors duly to convene a meeting shall be repaid to the requisitionists by the company and any sum so repaid shall be retained by the company out of any sums due or to become due from the company by way of fees or other remuneration in respect of their services to such of the directors as were in default.'

48 See *McGuinness v Bremmer plc* [1988] BCLC 673, following *Re Windward Islands (Enterprises) UK Ltd* [1983] BCLC 293. Note that the Companies Act 1985 (UK), s 386 has been amended by Companies Act 1989 (UK), Sch 19, para 9 so that the directors will be deemed not to have convened a meeting where they hold it more than 28 days after the notice convening it.

49 *Howard v Mechtler* (1999) New South Wales Supreme Court 232 (16 March 1999).

50 It should be noted that the wording here is more narrow than the corresponding UK provision in the Companies Act 1985 (UK), s 371 which also permits the court to order a meeting of the directors of a company: see *Re Sticky Fingers Restaurant Ltd* [1992] BCLC 84.

This is an exceptional jurisdiction and one that will be exercised sparingly on account of the judiciary's reluctance to interfere in the internal affairs of companies[51]. Where the court's jurisdiction is invoked, it has the consequence that

> 'Any meeting called, held and conducted in accordance with an order under subsection (1) shall for all purposes be deemed to be a meeting of the company duly called, held and conducted.'[52]

[9.021] The general rule is that one person cannot by him or herself hold a meeting[53]. A member may, however, be permitted by order of the court under CA 1963, s 135 to convene and hold a meeting by himself. It was emphasised, however, in *Arulchelvan v Wright*[54] that the general rule was that there cannot be a 'meeting' held by just one person. The facts of the case were that MW was the 100% beneficial owner of Company A. The legal ownership of the shares in Company A were held by MW (as to 49%), by the first defendant (as to 49% but in trust for MW) and by two solicitors (as to 2%, again in trust for MW). MW was also the 50% legal and beneficial owner of another company, Company B; its other shareholder being the first defendant. After MW died, probate of his will was granted to the first and third-named defendants who were named as his executors. MW had been a director of both companies; after his death the directors were the two plaintiffs and the first defendant and meetings were not held. Subsequently, the first and third defendants (MW's executors) and the first defendant in her own right as a member, convened EGMs of both Company A and Company B for the purpose of co-opting the second and third defendants to the boards of both companies. Notwithstanding that only one member (the first defendant) was present it was insisted that the meeting was quorate and the resolutions were passed. Whilst the executors had served notice of election to be registered as members the directors had not made a decision and the two-month period had not elapsed. The plaintiffs successfully challenged the validity of the meeting and the resolutions purportedly passed, and Carroll J held that the meetings were not quorate[55]. In the event that they were unsuccessful on that point, the defendants had also sought an order under CA 1963, s 135 for the convening of an EGM with a declaration that one member was deemed to constitute the meeting. On this point Carroll J said:

> 'The basic general rule is that there cannot be a meeting held by one person. Section 135 of the 1963 Act specifically provides that where the court on its own motion orders a meeting of the company to be held it can direct that one member of the company present in person or by proxy be deemed to constitute a meeting. While there are some exceptions to the general rule (eg such as where one person holds all of a class of shares) the exceptions do not in my opinion extend to the case where there is only one voting shareholder in a company and where the shares of a deceased member have not yet been registered in the name of a personal representative.'[56]

---

[51] See note by Milman, 'The Courts and Company Meetings' (1997) Palmer's In Company, Issue 8/97, 18 September 1997.

[52] CA 1963, s 135(2).

[53] *Re London Flats Ltd* [1969] 1 WLR 711.

[54] *Arulchelvan v Wright* (7 February 1996, unreported), High Court (Carroll J).

[55] See para **[9.042]**.

[56] (7 February 1996, unreported), High Court at p 9.

Carroll J went on to say:

> 'I will not order a meeting to be held under s 135 on my own motion as I think that it is premature to do so. The directors have yet to consider and deal with the application of the first and third defendants to be registered as members. If this application is granted, the problem concerning the holding of general meetings is solved. If their application to be registered is refused, the defendants can apply under s 205 of the 1963 Act, with all that entails'.[57]

It is thought that Carroll J's decision was undoubtedly correct and that an order under CA 1963, s 135 with a declaration that one member would constitute the meeting was inappropriate there. Her decision should not, however, be too narrowly construed, particularly the exceptions to the general rule that there cannot be a meeting held by one person. In *Re El Sombrero*[58], the applicant member held 90% of the issued shares, where the two directors who held the remaining 10% thwarted the holding of a members' meeting. Wynn Parry J made an order under the corresponding English section because otherwise the applicant member would have been unable to exercise his statutory right to remove the directors. More recently, in the case of *Re Opera Phonographic Ltd*[59], Morritt J exercised his discretion and ordered a meeting to be convened and held in similar circumstances.

[9.022] The making of an order under CA 1963, s 135 is discretionary, and, as was observed by Kenny J in *Angelis v Algemene Bank Nederland (Ireland) Ltd*[60], the court's power will not be exercised where there is no evidence that the directors of the company have shown themselves unwilling to comply with the requisition for the meeting. If of course there are no directors, the matter will be more straightforward. In *Re The Cambridge Group plc*, an ex tempore application to the Irish High Court, reported in The Irish Times[61], it was reported that application was brought by 12% of the company's shareholders to convene an EGM. The report stated that the once publicly quoted company appeared to have no directors following their resignation and that of the company secretary and in these circumstances Kinlan J granted the application, agreeing to direct the convening of an EGM for a particular date, time and venue[62].

[9.023] The facts in *Re British Union for the Abolition of Vivisection*[63] provide a classic example of the sort of situations in which CA 1963, s 135 was intended to be of

57 (7 February 1996, unreported), High Court at pp 9–10.

58 *Re El Sombrero* [1958] 3 All ER 1, [1958] Ch 900.

59 *Re Opera Phonographic Ltd* [1989] BCLC 763. See also *Re H & R Paul & Son Ltd* (1974) 118 Sol Jo 166, where the court held that the requirement to have a quorum for a meeting could not be allowed 'to frustrate the wishes of the majority.'

60 *Angelis v Algemene Bank Nederland (Ireland) Ltd* (4 July 1974, unreported), High Court, per Kenny J.

61 *Re The Cambridge Group plc* (1998) The Irish Times, 10 February (Kinlan J).

62 See also *Re Kenoughty Ltd*, an application reported in (1995) The Irish Times, 16 October (Carroll J) where an order under s 135 was sought by a director and member of a company in circumstances where the only other director and member's whereabouts were unknown and the purpose of the EGM was to appoint another director.

63 *Re British Union for the Abolition of Vivisection* [1995] 2 BCLC 1.

assistance. In this case the applicant-company (the BUAV) was a company limited by guarantees which opposed vivisection. Its articles of association only permitted voting by members in person, not permitting proxies. Its membership was, however, seriously factionalised, some of the factions being very militant. A previous AGM was long and confrontational and a previous EGM for the purpose of introducing voting by proxy had degenerated into tumult so badly that the police had had to intervene and close the meeting, apprehending a breach of the peace. The BUAV's board of directors brought an application under the similar English provision for an order that the court convene a meeting to vote on a special resolution to alter the company's articles of association to permit voting by proxy, and that the only persons entitled to attend this meeting should be the board (known in BUAV as its executive committee). However, the voting on the resolution to alter the articles by the company's other members should be by way of postal ballot and that the requirement for personal attendance in the company's articles should be dispensed with. Rimer J granted the application, saying that because of the genuine apprehension of violence it was clear to the court that it was impracticable to hold a meeting of the members in person as required by the company's articles.

[9.024] Section 135 of CA 1963 can also have application where all persons concerned are willing to convene and hold a meeting, but where problems arise in complying with the Companies Acts. An example of a non-contentious application can be seen in *Re Waterford Foods plc*, another ex tempore Irish order. There, because of the Irish postal dispute in mid-1992, the company felt it would be impractical to advise all its shareholders of a forthcoming EGM to consider proposed acquisitions of shares in other companies. The directors had agreed to make the share acquisitions subject to ratification by the company's members in general meeting. In lieu of postal notification, Lardner J gave leave to the company to advertise notice of the meeting in the national newspapers and some weekly newspapers in the South East[64]. Failure to take the prudent step of making such an application to court could have resulted in any subsequent ratification being impugned.

[9.025] It has been held by the English Court of Appeal that the similar provision in the UK[65] was procedural in nature and was not intended (and should not be used) to resolve a deadlock between two equal shareholders by affecting substantive voting rights. The facts in *Ross v Telford*[66] were that there were two companies, whose only directors and equal shareholders were an estranged husband and wife. As the quorum for meetings of the directors and members was two, there was deadlock. The husband had claimed that the wife had fraudulently amassed undisclosed assets at the expense of one of the companies, but this claim was rejected in the acrimonious divorce proceedings. Subsequently, having commenced proceedings in the company's name against the wife, the husband sought to have the initiation of these proceedings ratified and to this end sought an order under the English provision, requiring the convening of an EGM for the purposes of considering and voting on a resolution to appoint a third director for a

64 On the service of notices on members, see model reg 133–136. See Jones and Jacobs, *Company Meetings: Law and Procedure* (1991), p 46.

65 Companies Act 1985 (UK), s 371.

66 *Ross v Telford* [1998] 1 BCLC 82.

period of one year. This application was granted and the judge ordered that the third director (the husband's representative) could attend and vote at the EGM. This was appealed to the Court of Appeal, which allowed the appeal, as set out above, on thegrounds that the section should not be used to resolve a shareholders' deadlock[67]. Nourse LJ also pointed out that this section has nothing whatsoever to do with board meetings and is exclusively concerned with meetings of members.

[9.026] The courts will also probably refuse to exercise their discretion where no concrete purpose can be shown for the meeting. In *BML Group Ltd v Harman*[68] the Court of Appeal refused to convene an EGM where it would have been contrary to a shareholders' agreement which had been entered into by the company's shareholders. The shareholders' agreement provided that a members' meeting would not have a quorum unless a 'B' shareholder was present. The requisitionists held in excess of 50% of the shares carrying voting rights and wished to dismiss two of their opponent directors. In this they were thwarted by the only 'B' shareholder who refused to attend any members' meetings. The Court of Appeal reversed the decision of first instance and refused to convene a meeting of the members. To do so, it was held, would be in breach of the freely-contracted shareholders' agreement and the rights of the 'B' shareholder which were akin to rights entrenched in a company's articles of association.

(d) EGMs convened on the requisition of retiring auditors

[9.027] Section 186(1) of the Companies Act 1990 ('CA 1990') provides that a notice served by a resigning auditor (pursuant to CA 1990, s 185) may also requisition the convening of a general meeting by the directors of the company. The purpose of such a meeting is to receive and consider such account and explanation of the circumstances connected with the auditor's resignation as the resigning auditor may wish to give to the meeting. Where such a requisition is made the directors of the company must, within 14 days of the service on the company of the auditor's notice, proceed to convene a general meeting for a day not more than 28 days after such service[69]. Where the reason for the auditor's resignation is due to circumstances which the auditor considers should be

---

67 A remarkably similar application was brought in the Irish High Court in *Re a Company*, an ex tempore application reported in (1997) The Irish Times, 18 November (Costello P). There, application was brought for an order directing the convening of an EGM and an order that one director of the company be deemed a valid meeting. The sole directors and shareholders of the company were an estranged husband and wife. The applicant husband claimed that the company was in financial difficulties and was required to dispose of certain property but that his spouse, the other director and shareholder, had refused to agree to the sale and that he had attempted to convene an EGM to discuss the situation and appoint a third director but his spouse had refused to attend. The newspaper report stated that the applicant's spouse's counsel claimed that she objected to the appointment of the third director, whom it was claimed was in a relationship with the applicant and was 'perhaps the reason for the marital breakdown'. On hearing that the spouse had agreed to attend a board meeting to discuss the sale of the company's property, Costello P made no order but gave liberty to re–enter in the event of agreement not being reached on the sale of the property.

68 *BML Group Ltd v Harman* (1994) Times, 8 April 1994 (Court of Appeal).

69 CA 1990, s 186(2).

brought to the notice of the members or creditors[70], the auditor may request the directors to circulate to the company's members prior to any requisitioned meeting[71] a further statement prepared by the auditor of circumstances connected with his resignation. The directors of a company so requested must record the fact of the statement having been made in the notice convening the meeting and members must be sent a copy of the statement[72]. So as to protect innocent companies against gratuitously vindictive auditors, CA 1990, s 186(4) allows companies and other aggrieved persons to apply to court and for the court to excuse the company from having to issue such a statement, where:

> '...the court is satisfied that the rights conferred by this section are being abused to secure needless publicity for defamatory matter and the court may order the company's costs on an application under this section to be paid in whole or in part by the auditor concerned notwithstanding that he is not a party to the application.'

The similar English section was considered by Lightman J in *Jarvis plc v PricewaterhouseCoopers*[73]. In that case, a company applied to court to be excused from issuing its auditors' statement and although the company subsequently discontinued its application, the auditors contended that the court should consider the matter. Lightman J held that the effect and purpose of this provision was to impose:

> '...upon auditors an important duty in the public interest and in the interest of the persons interested and indirectly of creditors and the investing public: to make a statement. Indeed, it is a duty of such importance that a failure to comply constitutes a criminal offence. The auditor is the judge of whether there are relevant circumstances: he must exercise his judgment and, uninfluenced by any collateral considerations, make up his own mind and state whether he considers that there are circumstances which ought to be brought to the attention of the persons interested to whom for this purpose he must owe a duty of care. He is uniquely placed to judge. The requirement is not designed to protect the auditors or give the auditors an opportunity to say something which protects their goodwill or reputation when they cease to be the auditors, and the court will presume that the auditors who make a statement under [the section] are acting in faithful discharge of their duty and not in pursuit of any private or collateral interest, unless the contrary is shown.'[74]

In that case it was held that the effect of the discontinuance of the company's application was to bring the matter to an end and, specifically, it was held that the court was not required to issue a decision on the matter. It was also held that the company was liable to pay the auditors' costs on an indemnity basis.

Notice of members' meetings

[9.028] In this section, the following matters concerning the convening of members' meetings and the notice required to be given are considered:

---

70 CA 1990, s 186(3).

71 And indeed other general meetings: a general meeting at which apart from the notice his term of office would expire, or, a general meeting at which it is proposed to fill the vacancy caused by the auditor's resignation.

72 CA 1990, s 186(3).

73 *Jarvis plc v PricewaterhouseCoopers* [2001] BCC 670.

74 [2001] BCC 670 at 677.

(a) Those who should receive notice;
(b) Notice periods for AGMs and EGMs;
(c) Extended notice;
(d) Accidental omission to give notice;
(e) Summary of notice provisions.

(a) Those who should receive notice

[9.029] Section 134(a) of CA 1963 requires that, subject to individual companies' articles of association, all members – as defined by CA 1963, s 31[75] - should receive notice of a meeting.[76] To be entitled to receive notice, a member must be registered as a member in the register of members. This is considered further, below, in the context of those entitled to vote at general meetings[77]. It should be noted that the personal representatives of a deceased member and the official assignee of a bankrupt member are entitled, under model reg 136 to receive notice of every general meeting. Personal representatives and the official assignee in bankruptcy are not, however, entitled to vote and will not be counted for the purposes of determining whether the meeting is quorate[78].

[9.030] Notice of general meetings must also be given to the company's auditors. By virtue of CA 1990, s 193(5)[79] the auditors of a company are entitled to attend and to receive notices and other communications relating to any general meeting of a company, which any member of the company is entitled to receive. Moreover, the same section entitles auditors to be heard at any general meeting, which they attend on any part of the business of the meeting, which concerns them as auditors. Moreover, CA 1990, s 186(5) provides that an auditor of a company who has resigned shall be permitted to attend (and shall receive notices[80] of) the AGM at which, but for his resignation as auditor, his term of office would have expired and any EGM at which it is proposed to fill the vacancy caused by his resignation or convened by him pursuant to CA 1990, s 186(1)[81]. An auditor also has a right to be heard at any such meeting on any part of the business of the meeting that concerns him as a former auditor of the company.

[9.031] Save in the case of an accidental omission to give notice[82], a meeting held for which notice was not given to those entitled to notice, will be invalid. An example of this

[75] See Chapter 15, *Shares and Membership*, para **[15.004]** *ff*.

[76] CA 1963, s 134 provides that: 'The following provisions shall have effect in so far as the articles of the company do not make other provision in that behalf—(a) notice of the meeting of a company shall be served on every member of the company in the manner in which notices are required to be served by Table A and for the purpose of this paragraph 'Table A' means that Table as for the time being in force.'

[77] See para **[9.049]**.

[78] See *Arulchelvan and Wright v Wright* (7 February 1996, unreported), High Court (Carroll J) considered at para **[9.044]**.

[79] And model reg 136.

[80] An other communications relating to any such meeting as a member would be entitled to receive.

[81] See para **[9.027]**.

[82] See para **[9.035]**.

is seen in *Colthurst and Tenips Ltd v La Touche Colthurst and Colthurst*[83]. The plaintiffs in the proceedings had sought the recission of an earlier settlement and of an earlier court consent order in which the parties purported to settle various outstanding disputes. The second plaintiff-company was owned as to 49% of its shares by the first plaintiff, 1% by his wife and the remaining 50% by his mother, the second-named defendant. The shareholders were also the company's three directors. The second-named defendant claimed that the instant proceedings had never been authorised by her as a director nor had the second plaintiff-company resolved to set aside the settlement. In what McCracken J described as a charade, the first plaintiff had sought to 'put a gloss of legality on issuing these proceedings in the name of the company' by authorising the plaintiffs' solicitors to issue the proceedings by letter. The operative part of the letter provided that the husband and wife as 'directors and shareholders' authorised the solicitors to issue the proceedings. What in fact happened was that a meeting of the directors had been convened for the purposes of convening an EGM, the purpose of which was to authorise the issue of the proceedings[84]. No notice of either the directors' meeting nor of the EGM had been given to the second-defendant director and 50% shareholder. The minutes of the EGM provided that the resolution to initiate proceedings had been proposed and seconded and passed on a show of hands. McCracken J said that the only explanation he was given for the failure to give the notices was that the first plaintiff and his wife were aware that second-defendant would vote against the resolution, but were also aware that they would out-vote her. The judge also noted that the first plaintiff claimed that he had been advised by his accountants not to give his mother notice. McCracken J found that claim 'astonishing':

> '...both that in general his accountant would not have been aware of the necessary formalities in calling an extraordinary general meeting, and in particular that he would advise [that] a director and 50% shareholder would not be notified of either a directors' meeting or a general meeting of the company in which it was intended to pass a resolution authorising the company to issue proceedings against her'.

This, the judge found, was a deliberate attempt to prevent the defendants from finding out about the plaintiffs' intention to issue proceedings against them. On the consequences of the failure to give notice, McCracken J said:

> 'Lest there be any doubt as to the validity of the meeting...I would point out that it purported to be an extraordinary general meeting of the company, and that under s 134 of the Companies Act 1963 notice of a meeting of the company must be served on every member of the company, and further under s 193 of the Companies Act 1990 the auditor of the company is entitled to attend any general meeting of the company and to receive all notices in relation thereto. In view of the statutory provisions, quite clearly the resolution which was purported to be passed is invalid, and the second plaintiff has no standing in these proceedings.'[85]

---

83 *Colthurst and Tenips Ltd v La Touche Colthurst and Colthurst* (9 February 2000, unreported), High Court (McCracken J).

84 Notwithstanding model reg 80, the members in general meeting can by resolution, arguably, cause a company to initiate legal proceedings: see Chapter 8, *Corporate Governance: Management by the Directors*, para **[8.012]**.

85 (9 February 2000, unreported), High Court at p 8.

This must, of course, be contrasted with an accidental omission to give notice of a meeting[86].

(b) Notice periods for AGMs and EGMs

[9.032] In the case of all companies, for an AGM CA 1963, s 133 provides that at least 21 days' notice must be given in writing. In the case of a private company, for an EGM at least seven days' notice must be given in writing[87]. It is important to note, however, that seven days' notice for an EGM only applies where it is not proposed to pass a special resolution at the EGM: otherwise, 21 days' notice is required. Section 133(2) of CA 1963 provides:

> 'Save in so far as the articles of a company make other provision in that behalf (not being a provision avoided by subsection (1)) a meeting of the company (other than an adjourned meeting) may be called—
>
> (a) in the case of the annual general meeting by 21 days' notice in writing; and
>
> (b) in the case of a meeting (other than an annual general meeting or a meeting for the passing of a special resolution), by 14 days' notice in writing where the company is neither a private company nor an unlimited company and by 7 days' notice in writing, where it is a private company or an unlimited company.'

Any provision in a company's articles of association that provides for shorter notice shall be void[88]. Consequently, model reg 4[89], which will usually be adopted by most private companies, contains the same notice periods[90].

[9.033] Section 133(3) of CA 1963 contains a very important proviso to the prescriptive provisions of s 132(1) and (2) as regards notice for meetings (both the AGM and EGMs). This provides:

---

86 See para **[9.035]**.

87 Or, for any unlimited company. Note that in the case of a PLC at least 14 days' notice of an EGM is required to be given.

88 CA 1963, s 133(1) provides: 'Any provision of a company's articles shall be void in so far as it provides for the calling of a meeting of the company (other than an adjourned meeting) by a shorter notice than—(a) in the case of the annual general meeting, 21 days' notice in writing; and (b) in the case of a meeting (other than an annual general meeting or a meeting for the passing of a special resolution) 14 days' notice in writing where the company is neither a private company nor an unlimited company and 7 days' notice in writing where it is a private company or an unlimited company.'

89 Which applies in the case of a private company. Note that Regulation 51 of Part I applies only to public companies limited by shares.

90 Thus model reg 4 provides:

> 'Subject to sections 133 and 141 of the Act, an annual general meeting and a meeting called for the passing of a special resolution shall be called by 21 days' notice in writing at the least and a meeting of the company (other than an annual general meeting or a meeting for the passing of a special resolution) shall be called by 7 days' notice in writing at the least. The notice shall be exclusive of the day on which it is served or deemed to be served and of the day for which it is given and shall specify the day, the place and the hour of the meeting and, in the case of special business, the general nature of that business and shall be given in manner authorised by these regulations to such persons as are under the regulations of the company entitled to receive such notices from the company.'

> 'A meeting of a company shall, notwithstanding that it is called by shorter notice than that specified in subsection (2) or in the company's articles, as the case may be, be deemed to have been duly called if it is so agreed by the auditors of the company and by all the members entitled to attend and vote thereat.'

The basis for this provision – the consent of all members entitled to attend and vote – is the old notion that all of a company's members can waive a protection intended for them. The requirement that the consent of the auditors of the company is needed, however, renders the section a limited concession to the exigencies of commercial life[91]. The reason why the auditor's consent is also required is because CA 1990, s 193 and model reg 136 requires that companies give notice of general meetings to their auditors.

(c) Extended notice

[9.034] In respect of certain meetings, extended notice is required to be given. Section 142(1) of CA 1963 provides:

> 'Subject to subsection (2), where by any provision hereafter contained in this Act extended notice is required of a resolution, the resolution shall not be effective unless (except when the directors of the company have resolved to submit it) notice of the intention to move it has been given to the company not less than 28 days before the meeting at which it is moved, and the company shall give its members notice of any such resolution at the same time and in the same manner as it gives notice of the meeting or, if that is not practicable, shall give them notice thereof, either by advertisement in a daily newspaper circulating in the district in which the registered office of the company is situate or in any other mode allowed by the articles, not less than 21 days before the meeting.'

Section 142(2) of CA 1963 provides that:

> 'If, after notice of the intention to move such a resolution has been given to the company, a meeting is called for a date 28 days or less after the notice has been given, the notice though not given within the time required by subsection (1) shall be deemed to have been properly given for the purposes of that subsection.'

Extended notice is required, for example, for a resolution at an AGM to appoint a person other than a retiring auditor as auditor or a resolution not to re-appoint an auditor[92] and a resolution to remove a director[93].

(d) Accidental omission to give notice

[9.035] Model reg 52 provides that:

> 'The accidental omission to give notice of a meeting to, or the non-receipt of notice of a meeting by, any person entitled to receive notice shall not invalidate the proceedings at the meeting.'

Furthermore, model reg 133 provides that where notice is sent by post, service of the notice shall be deemed to be effected 'by properly addressing, prepaying and posting a letter containing the notice, and to have been effected in the case of the notice of a meeting at the expiration of 24 hours after the letter containing the same is posted'. This

---

91 Cf CA 1963, s 141(8), para **[9.076]**, which permits informal resolutions in writing.

92 CA 1963, s 161(1)(a). See also CA 1963, s 161(1)(b) and (1)(c).

93 CA 1963, s 182.

has, however, been interpreted in England as not entitling those who serve such notices to disregard reality. Thus, in *Bradman v Trinity Estates plc*[94], a company sent to members notice of an impending meeting during a postal strike. Those shareholders who lived within London were notified by courier, but those outside London were mailed their notices, and it transpired that, in some cases, the notices did not arrive until after the meeting had been held. As in the Irish model articles, the articles of the company allowed notices to be served by post[95]. One shareholder sought an injunction to restrain the holding of the meeting on the grounds, inter alia, that the meeting had not been validly summoned under the provisions of the company's articles. It was held by Hoffmann J that the equivalent article to the Irish model reg 133 was open to an interpretation other than a literal interpretation. In particular, it was arguable that in the circumstances of a postal dispute, the posting of notices could not be deemed to have been effective service on all the shareholders. It was also convenient to grant an injunction because if it subsequently transpired that the meeting had been convened invalidly, it would be very difficult to unravel business transacted thereat. In the instant case he granted an injunction preventing the meeting from being held, and suggested that the chairman should adjourn it[96].

(e) Summary of notice provisions

[9.036] The Companies Acts 1963–2001 provide for different notice provisions where it is proposed to consider a special resolution as opposed to an ordinary resolution. The provisions of CA 1963 may be summarised thus:

— In the case of an AGM, 21 days' notice must be given[97].

— Although in the case of an EGM only seven days' notice is generally required, where it is proposed to consider a special resolution, 21 days' notice is required[98].

— However, a lesser time than 21 days' notice may be given in respect of a special resolution, where at least 90% of the members of the company agree to shorter notice[99].

— Furthermore, in the case of an EGM, other than one for the passing of a special resolution, a period of notice less than seven days may be given where the members and the company's auditors agree to such shorter notice[100].

— Where any resolution, whether ordinary or special, is being proposed by persons other than the directors of the company, to either remove a director or to replace an auditor at an AGM, then extended notice, of 28 days, is required to be given[101].

---

[94] *Bradman v Trinity Estates plc* [1989] BCLC 757.

[95] Model reg 133. However, the articles of that company also allowed notices to be served by an alternative method, where there was a 'total suspension or curtailment of postal services.'

[96] See *Re Waterford Foods plc* (1992) The Irish Times, 12 May, at para **[9.024]**.

[97] CA 1963, s 133. See para **[9.032]**.

[98] CA 1963, s 141(1). See para **[9.070]** *ff*.

[99] CA 1963, s 141(2). See para **[9.071]**.

[100] CA 1963, s 133(3). See para **[9.033]**.

[101] CA 1963, s 142.

Notice of business to be conducted at a meeting

[9.037] The notice requirements for the convening of members' meetings last considered concern simple notice of the fact that a meeting is intended to be held. Here we examine notice of the business that it is proposed to consider at meetings. Where the business before the meeting will be either a 'special resolution', or 'special business', notice of the intention to transact such specific business must also be given in the notice convening the meeting.

[9.038] Where it is proposed to pass a special resolution, CA 1963, s 141(1) provides that the notice should also specify the wording of the proposed special resolution[102]. In the English case of *Re Moorgate Mercantile Holdings Ltd*[103] Slade J held that:

> '...if a special resolution passed at a general meeting is to be valid, it must be the same resolution as that which the requisite notice has specified the intention to propose...If, however, there is any difference whatsoever of substance between the two I would not, in the absence of authority, have regarded the later resolution, which was actually passed, as having been preceded by proper notice...'.

In that case, a special resolution purportedly passed by a company's members was held not to have been validly passed as it differed not only in form but also in substance from the one set out in the notice for the meeting. Unless the difference between the proposed resolution which has been notified and the actual resolution laid before the members is of a mere grammatical or clerical nature or otherwise inconsequential[104], the notice given may be deemed to be invalid[105]. Where notice of a special resolution has been given, its terms may be amended by ordinary resolution moved at the meeting provided that the terms of the resolution as amended will still be such that adequate notice of the intention to pass the same can be deemed to have been given[106]. Such a waiver by the members was found not to have been given in *Re Moorgate Mercantile Holdings Ltd*[107]. Moreover, in that case it was held by Slade J that in giving notice of a special resolution to be passed, nothing would be achieved by the addition of such words as 'with such amendments and alterations as shall be determined on at the general meeting'. Special resolutions are considered in more detail, below[108].

[9.039] Whether a meeting (AGM or EGM) is convened by the directors or by the members (pursuant to CA 1963, s 132, considered above[109]) it beholds those convening it or requisitioning its convening to represent accurately the basis for the need to propose

---

102 See para **[9.071]**.

103 *Re Moorgate Mercantile Holdings Ltd* [1980] 1 All ER 40.

104 See *Re Willaire Systems plc* [1987] BCLC 67.

105 It has been said that '[a]s far as ordinary resolutions are concerned, there is a greater latitude for amendments to be proposed and passed at a general meeting, even though they were not notified to members in advance in the same way as the original resolution': Jones and Jacobs, *Company Meetings: Law and Procedure* (1991), p 93. See *Baillie v Oriental Telephone & Electric Co Ltd* [1915] 1 Ch 503. Cf *Henderson v Bank of Australasia* (1890) 45 Ch D 330.

106 CA 1963, s 141(5).

107 *Re Moorgate Mercantile Holdings Ltd* [1980] 1 All ER 40.

108 See para **[9.070]**.

109 See para **[9.016]**.

resolutions. This has already been considered in the circumstances of members requisitioning an EGM, but the principle applies equally to where directors convene a meeting for the purposes of passing a resolution. In *Re European Home Products plc*[110] Mervyn Davies J held that it was not easy to secure the court's confirmation for resolutions passed on the strength of a circular that contained inaccurate information; in that case the court made an exception since it found that although reasonable shareholders could have been misled, they were not in fact misled. The finding in the case must be seen as very much the exception, and every care should be taken to accurately represent the facts upon which shareholders are asked to base their judgment when voting on a resolution.

[9.040] Sometimes in the case of AGMs, but *always* in the case of EGMs, notice must be given where it is proposed to consider special business. Model reg 53[111] provides that all business at a meeting shall be deemed to be special business with the exception of routine matters conducted at an AGM, namely:

- the declaration of a dividend;
- the consideration of accounts and reports;
- the election of directors and replacement of those retiring;
- the re-appointment and remuneration of directors.

In practice this means that the notice convening the meeting must state what the meeting is going to be asked to consider. Where insufficient particulars of the special business to be conducted are given, an injunction to restrain the holding of the meeting may be obtained[112]. Where such a meeting is held, it is open to disgruntled members to seek a declaration that any resolution passed is invalid.

[9.041] Issues arise where notice of a resolution has been given and on the holding of the meeting it is desired to amend the resolution to be put to the meeting. Where notice has been given of an ordinary resolution, it can be amended at the meeting provided that the proposed change does not alter the essential intention of the original resolution[113]. A resolution to wind up a company where notice was given of a resolution to wind up the company for the purpose of a reconstruction, has been held to be invalid[114]. On the other hand, a resolution to wind up a company and appoint X as liquidator instead of winding up and appointing Y as liquidator has, however, been held to be valid[115]. A stricter test applies in the case of an amendment to a special resolution and in such cases, there can

[110] *Re European Home Products plc* (1988) 4 BCC 779.

[111] Model reg 53 states: 'All business shall be deemed special that is transacted at an extraordinary general meeting, and also all that is transacted at an annual general meeting, with the exception of declaring a dividend, the consideration of the accounts, balance sheets and the reports of the directors and auditors, the election of directors in the place of those retiring, the re-appointment of the retiring auditors and the fixing of the remuneration of the auditors.'

[112] See *Jackson v Munster Bank* (1884–85) 13 LR 118.

[113] See generally Shearman, *Shackleton on the Law and Practice of Meetings* (9th edn, 1997), pp 171, 172.

[114] *Re Teele & Bishop* (1901) 70 LJ 409.

[115] *Re Trench Tubeless Tyre Co* [1900] 1 Ch 408.

be no amendment to the substance (however slight) of the resolution of which notice was given[116].

The quorum

[9.042] Every company may validly decide in its own articles the requisite quorum for a general meeting of the company[117]. Under model reg 5, the quorum for a general meeting of the members of a private company limited by shares is two members, 'present in person or by proxy'. Section 134(c) of CA 1963 provides that (in so far as the articles of the company do not make other provision in that behalf) ...in the case of a private company two members, and in the case of any other company three members, personally present shall be a quorum...

Model reg 55 provides that 'if within half an hour from the time appointed for the meeting a quorum is not present, the meeting, if convened upon the requisition of members, shall be dissolved'. If otherwise convened:

> '...it shall stand adjourned to the same day in the next week, at the same time and place or to such other day and at such other time and place as the directors may determine, and if at the adjourned meeting a quorum is not present within half an hour from the time appointed for the meeting, the members present shall be a quorum.'

Where a quorate meeting is convened, it was held in *Re Hartley Baird Ltd*[118], that where members leave during the course of the meeting, it will remain validly constituted and subsequent decisions taken will be valid. It may be observed that in *Re Hartley Baird* the company's articles required a quorum of ten members; in the case of a company requiring a quorum of two members and where only one member is left, it is questionable as to whether the courts would uphold business subsequently transacted[119].

[9.043] In the case of single-member companies, the European Communities (Single-Member Private Limited Companies) Regulations 1994, reg 10[120] provides 'Notwithstanding any provision to the contrary in the articles of a single-member company, one member present in person or by proxy shall be a quorum.'

By virtue of CA 1963, s 134(c), unless the articles of the company provide otherwise, the quorum shall be two. Notwithstanding s 134(c), in the case of single-member companies, reg 10 shall apply as otherwise a meeting could never be held or more importantly, the business required to be transacted at a meeting could not be transacted. Except as provided for by s 135, and reg 10, above, it has been held that a single person cannot as a rule constitute a quorate meeting[121].

[9.044] A meeting will not be quorate where the quorum is two members and only one member is present, even if a deceased member's executors are present. This was

---

116 *Re Moorgate Mercantile Holdings* [1980] 1 All ER 40, considered at para **[9.038]**.

117 The requisite quorum for a members' meeting may be agreed between the members in a shareholders' agreement: *BLM Group Ltd v Harman* (1994) Times, 8 April (Court of Appeal).

118 *Re Hartley Baird Ltd* [1954] Ch 143.

119 See *Re London Flats Ltd* [1969] 1 WLR 711.

120 SI 1994/275.

121 See *Arulchelvan v Wright* (7 February 1996, unreported), High Court (Carroll J) at para **[9.021]**; *Re London Flats Ltd* [1969] 1 WLR 711; and *Sharp v Dawes* [1876] 2 QBD 26.

confirmed by Carroll J in *Arulchelvan v Wright* [122] on the grounds that, by virtue of CA 1963, s 31, a person is not a member unless his name is on the register of members and, specifically, that a personal representative is not a member until such time as he is registered as such. Interpreting the articles of association, Carroll J held that although a personal representative is recognised as having title to a deceased member's shares (model reg 29) and is entitled to dividends (model reg 32) he is not entitled to exercise any right conferred by membership (model reg 32). Carroll J went on to hold that as the deceased member's personal representatives had not been registered as members, they could not be counted as forming part of the quorum and since no quorum was present, no business had been transacted at the purported meeting.

Postponing and adjourning meetings

[9.045] In *Smith v Paringa Mines Ltd*[123] it was held that a company's directors may not postpone a general meeting that has been validly convened, unless the articles of association expressly empower them to so postpone. In that case, a company's directors convened an AGM. Later that day one of its shareholders (who was also a director) initiated proceedings against the company and, on learning of this, the directors purported to postpone the AGM pending the outcome of the litigation. The shareholder wrote to the company and advised that he had taken advice that the AGM could not be postponed and advertised in the press that the AGM would be held. On the appointed day for the AGM the shareholder (and others) attended but the directors and secretary did not. At this meeting the shareholder and certain others were elected directors and the existing directors and secretary voted out of office. The case arose out of the plaintiff-shareholder's action against the old directors and secretary in which an order was sought directing them to deliver up the company's books, records and seal. The court granted the order sought, finding that the AGM had been validly convened and held and that it could not be postponed. Kekewich J held:

> '...it was not competent for the board to postpone the meeting. The articles provide for the adjournment of a general meeting in certain events, but they contain no provision for postponement. It is said that the directors must be able to postpone the meeting because they may fix the time and place at which the meeting is to be held; but in my opinion that is not so. On the other hand, if the directors had power to postpone, and a meeting adverse to the directors was called, they might postpone it for a week or a month, or perhaps sine die.'[124]

Where a meeting has been convened, and circumstances arise which make it undesirable to hold the meeting, then – in the absence of the articles expressly providing for postponement – the appropriate course of action would be to meet but then immediately adjourn the meeting[125].

[9.046] Adjournment of meetings is regulated by model reg 58 which states:

---

[122] *Arulchelvan v Wright* (7 February 1996, unreported), High Court (Carroll J).

[123] *Smith v Paringa Mines Ltd* [1906] 2 Ch 193.

[124] [1906] 2 Ch 193 at 197–198.

[125] See Shearman, *Shackleton on The Law and Practice of Meetings* (9th edn, 1997), p 137.

> 'The chairman may, with the consent of any meeting at which a quorum is present, and shall if so directed by the meeting, adjourn the meeting from time to time and from place to place, but no business shall be transacted at any adjourned meeting other than the business left unfinished at the meeting from which the adjournment took place. When a meeting is adjourned for 30 days or more, notice of the adjourned meeting shall be given as in the case of an original meeting. Save as aforesaid it shall not be necessary to give any notice of an adjournment or of the business to be transacted at an adjourned meeting.'

[9.047] Where a resolution is passed at a meeting of a company which had been adjourned at an earlier meeting, the resolution shall for all purposes be treated as having been passed on the date on which it was in fact passed and shall not be deemed to have been passed on any earlier date[126]. It was held in *Holmes v Keyes*[127] that a resolution on which a poll was taken, had been passed on the date the result became known. In that case a poll was taken on the election of directors on 23 December but the result was not known until 24 December. The directors, who were obliged to hold qualification shares within two months of their appointment, only acquired their shares on 24 February of the following year. The question arose as to whether they had acquired them within the requisite period of two months. The Court of Appeal held that the directors had been elected on 24 December, the date upon which the result became known. Jenkins LJ held:

> 'In my judgment, the ascertainment of the result should be considered as part of the poll, and, consequently, there can be no appointment of a director by a general meeting until the result of the poll is ascertained. It is only then that the appointment can become in any sense effective. I think that, in effect, the meeting should be treated as continuing until the result of the voting on the poll is ascertained. Unless the appointment begins when the result of the poll is ascertained and on no earlier date, it would be impossible for the company to know who its directors were. It seems to me that produces a really quite impossible result.'[128]

Voting at members' meetings

[9.048] To be entitled to vote at a general meeting a member's name must be registered on the register of members[129]. In this respect, a company is not obliged to await the registration of particular persons as shareholders and members, before convening and holding a meeting. There is no obligation on the chairman of a meeting to adjourn it pending the registration of share transfers, in order to facilitate a person acquiring voting rights[130]. The decision as to when to hold a general meeting is, however, an exercise of directors' powers which must be exercised in a bona fide manner and there is authority

---

126 CA 1963, s 144.

127 *Holmes v Keyes* [1959] 1 Ch 199.

128 [1959] 1 Ch 199 at 216.

129 CA 1963, s 31. Where the articles of association prescribes a procedure for admission as a member, it must be followed. In *POW Services Ltd v Clare* [1995] 2 BCLC 435 it was held an EGM had not been validly constituted because admission to membership required a decision of the company's council as to whether a person should be admitted, and the procedure adopted was defective since it conferred membership on a virtual automatic administrative basis which was insufficient to comply with the company's articles.

130 *Kinsella v Alliance and Dublin Consumers Gas Company* (5 October 1982, unreported), High Court per Barron J: see Chapter 16, *Share Transfers in Private Companies*, para **[16.023]**.

for saying that the company must have some regard for the interests of its shareholders[131]. Here, the following issues are considered:

(a) 'One member one vote' or one vote per share.

(b) Voting on a poll.

(c) Voting by representatives.

(d) Voting by proxy.

(a) 'One member one vote' or one vote per share

[9.049] Voting at general meetings will be effected in either of two ways: on a show of hands or on a poll. The norm is on a show of hands, which will apply unless a poll is called[132]. Where voting is by a show of hands, the general rule is that of 'one member, one vote'; on a poll the general rule is one vote for each share held. Model reg 63 states:

> 'Subject to any rights or restrictions for the time being attached to any class or classes of shares, on a show of hands every member present in person and every proxy shall have one vote, so, however, that no individual shall have more than one vote, and on a poll every member shall have one vote for each share of which he is the holder.'

Section 134(e) of CA 1963 provides that, in so far as the articles of the company do not make other provision in that behalf, in the case of a company originally having a share capital, every member shall have one vote in respect of each share or each £10 of stock held by him, and in any other case, every member shall have one vote. Of course it is open to companies to decide what voting rights each share or class of share shall have and in what circumstances such arises[133]. If there is an equality of votes, whether on a show of hand or on a poll, the chairman of the meeting at which the show of hands takes place or at which the poll is demanded, shall be entitled to a second or casting vote[134].

[9.050] On a vote on a show of hands, the amount of shares held by a member will not, unless the articles provide otherwise, add to or take from his voting power, the general rule being one member, one vote. Unless a poll is demanded[135], model articles of association provide that a declaration by the chairman that a resolution has, on a show of hands, been carried or carried unanimously, or by a particular majority, or lost, and an entry to that effect in the book containing the minutes of the proceedings of the company shall be conclusive evidence of the fact without proof of the number or proportion of the votes recorded in favour of or against such resolution: model reg 59. A similar provision to model reg 59 was interpreted in *Re Hadleigh Castle Gold Mines Ltd*[136]. In that case Cozens Hardy J held that in the absence of fraud, or the valid requisition of a poll, the declaration of the chairman of a meeting that a special resolution has been passed, is conclusive. The learned judge said that:

---

[131] In *Cannon v Trask* (1875) 20 Eq 669 an injunction was granted restraining the holding of an AGM in circumstances where the directors had convened the AGM several weeks earlier than was usual and before the plaintiff's voting rights under recently effected transfers had been registered.

[132] Model reg 59. See para **[9.054]**.

[133] *Bushell v Faith* [1970] AC 1099.

[134] Model reg 61.

[135] See para **[9.053]**.

[136] *Re Hadleigh Castle Gold Mines Ltd* [1900] 2 Ch 419.

> '...unless a poll is demanded by at least five members a declaration of the chairman that the resolution has been carried shall be deemed conclusive evidence of the fact without proof of the number or proportion of the votes recorded in favour of or against the same. "Conclusive" seems to me to be a clear word ...I cannot regard "conclusive" as equivalent to "sufficient". I think the legislature intended, in the case of a special or extraordinary resolution, that the chairman's declaration should be conclusive unless challenged by means of a poll demanded by five members.'[137]

[9.051] Care must be taken, however, not to be complacent when following such an apparently informal voting method as a show of hands. In *Re The Citizens' Theatre Ltd*[138] an EGM was convened to consider a special resolution to effect a change in the company's memorandum. The resolution was proposed and seconded, and when there was no counter-motion the chairman, without calling for a show of hands, declared that the resolution had been passed as a special resolution. It was held that as there had been no show of hands, the resolution had not been effectively submitted to the meeting and that, in those circumstances, reliance could not be placed upon wording similar to model reg 59.

[9.052] Model articles provide that where there are joint holders of shares, the vote of the senior (as determined by the order of the joint holders' names in the register of members) who tenders a vote, whether in person or by proxy, shall be accepted[139]. Again, the model articles disenfranchise any member where there are outstanding calls or other sums immediately payable by him in respect of the shares he holds[140]. Objections to the qualification of voting members can only be raised at the meeting or adjourned meeting at which they vote and every vote not disallowed shall be valid; objections must, by the model articles, be referred to the chairman whose decision is final and conclusive[141].

(b) Voting on a poll

[9.053] In the Irish High Court decision in *Duggan v The Governor and Company of the Bank of Ireland*[142] McCracken J described the purpose of a poll:

> 'It is important to recognise the purpose of the taking of a poll at meetings of shareholders or stockholders. Largely for reasons of convenience, if a motion is put to a general meeting, it is initially decided on a show of hands, on the basis that each person present has one vote, irrespective of the number of shares they hold. When that result is known, normally any member ...[or number of members, depending upon the articles] ...or the chairman may demand a poll. This is frequently done where the persons who are defeated on a show of hands feel that in fact they have a greater shareholding than those who succeeded. In the present case, the chairman decided to hold a poll because he was not prepared to determine whether the resolution has been passed or not on a show of hands. However, the essence of a poll is that, instead of there being a principle of one vote for

---

137 [1900] 2 Ch 419 at 421–422. Note that Cozens Hardy J distinguished *Young v Sough African and Australian Exploration and Development Syndicate* [1896] 2 Ch 275.

138 *Re The Citizens' Theatre Ltd* (1948) SC 14.

139 Model reg 64.

140 Model reg 66.

141 Model reg 67.

142 *Duggan v The Governor and Company of the Bank of Ireland* (29 July 1998, unreported), High Court (McCracken J).

each shareholder, there is one vote for each share ...Thus the purpose of a poll is to allow those with the greatest financial interest in the company ultimately to determine the outcome of any vote.'[143]

Unlike a vote on a show of hands – where the rule of one member one vote applies – in the case of a vote on a poll, the general rule (subject to the articles is) one vote per share.

[9.054] An article that excludes the right to demand a poll on any question other than the election of the chairman of the meeting is void[144]; provided however that companies can (within certain parameters)[145] regulate when a poll can be demanded. The usual manner in which the calling of a poll is regulated is provided for in model reg 59, which states:

> 'At any general meeting a resolution put to the vote of the meeting shall be decided on a show of hands unless a poll is (before or on the declaration of the result of the show of hands) demanded—
>
> (a) by the chairman; or
>
> (b) by at least three members present in person or by proxy; or
>
> (c) by any member or members present in person or by proxy and representing not less than one-tenth of the total voting rights of all the members having the right to vote at the meeting; or
>
> (d) by a member or members holding shares in the company conferring the right to vote at the meeting being shares on which an aggregate sum has been paid up equal to not less than one-tenth of the total sum paid up on all the shares conferring that right...'

In addition to providing for the conclusiveness of a chairman's declaration, this article also provides that a poll may be withdrawn. In *The Second Consolidated Trust Ltd v Ceylon Amalgamated Tea & Rubber Estates Ltd*[146] it was held that the right of a chairman to demand a poll was not a personal right and that the chairman of a meeting had an obligation to demand a poll where such was necessary to give effect to the real sense of the meeting.

[9.055] Where a poll is demanded by members, it should be noted that a proxy's demand counts equally with that of a member because an instrument of proxy is deemed by CA 1963, s 137(2) to confer authority to demand or join in demanding a poll[147]. On a poll, a member entitled to more than one vote need not, if he votes, use all his votes or cast all the votes he uses in the same way[148]. The manner in which a poll is taken will, under

---

143 (29 July 1998, unreported), High Court at p 4.

144 CA 1963, s 137(1).

145 CA 1963, s 137(1)(b) provides that a demand for a poll cannot be deemed ineffective where it is made '(i) by not less than five members having the right to vote at the meeting, or (ii) by a member or members representing not less than one–tenth of the total voting rights of all the members having the right to vote at the meeting, or (iii) by a member or members holding shares in the company conferring a right to vote at the meeting, being shares on which an aggregate sum has been paid up equal to not less than one–tenth of the total sum paid up on all the shares conferring that right.'

146 *The Second Consolidated Trust Ltd v Ceylon Amalgamated Tea & Rubber Estates Ltd* [1943] 2 Ch 567.

147 See also model reg 72.

148 CA 1963, s 138.

model articles, be as directed by the chairman[149]; where, however, the poll is taken on the election of a chairman, it shall be taken forthwith, but otherwise a poll will be taken at such time as the chairman directs, whether before or after any other business[150]. The result of a poll is deemed to be the resolution of the meeting[151].

[9.056] In *Duggan v The Governor and Company of the Bank of Ireland*[152] the defendant-company – that is established by charter and not a company regulated, per se[153], by the Companies Acts 1963–2001 – proposed to amend its articles of association (known in the case of the defendant-company as its byelaws) to provide that on a poll, each member should have one vote for each £1 of ordinary stock of the defendant-company without limit. This had the effect of removing a 'cap' then contained in the byelaws limiting a member's right to vote to the extent that he held stock exceeding 1% of the defendant-company's shares. At the AGM the resolution was considered by the meeting, a number of people from the floor spoke against the resolution and the plaintiff put forward an amendment that would have had the effect of retaining the cap but increasing it to 3% of stock. On a vote on a show of hands, the chairman refused to call the vote on the basis that it was too tight to call and that he did not see a discernible majority either way. Accordingly, the chairman called a poll, saying:

> 'There are 122,803,863 votes in favour of the resolution for supporting the directors. Only those who oppose the resolution need vote, to speed up the process. If you wish to vote No, you may get a ballot from the stewards along each row and if you have any query, ask the stewards.'[154]

The plaintiff asked in respect of the 120 million qualified votes, could the defendant-company's proxy exercise all the one-percents and was told they had been vetted and approved by the auditors. Those who wished to vote were given a ballot paper, the votes were cast and counted and ultimately the chairman declared the resolution carried, saying that the final position was that there were circa 122.8 million for and 0.68 million against. As regards the expeditious means employed by the chairman – only inviting votes from those who wished to vote against the resolution – and after noting that one of the byelaws gave the chairman the discretion to direct how the will of those with a majority financial interest was to be determined, McCracken J said of the chairman, that:

> 'He was, of course, aware that he held such a large number of proxies that the resolution was in fact going to be passed, however he had an obligation to allow those who disagreed with the resolution to exercise their vote. I think it is unfortunate that he tried to cut corners by only seeking votes against the resolution, but that does not necessarily invalidate the poll or affect the question of whether he did in fact exercise the votes

[149] Model reg 60.

[150] Model reg 62.

[151] Model reg 60.

[152] *Duggan v The Governor and Company of the Bank of Ireland* (29 July 1998, unreported), High Court (McCracken J).

[153] The Governor and Company of the Bank of Ireland is an 'unregistered company' within the meaning of CA 1963, s 377, to which the provisions set out in the CA 1963, Sch 9, as amended, apply.

[154] (29 July 1998, unreported), High Court at p 2.

contained in the proxies. In my view the discretion given to him was so wide as to allow him to give the discretion which he gave…'.[155]

It seems clear that it would, accordingly, be prudent on a poll to invite both those for and against a resolution to vote and not to merely to seek the side most likely to lose to vote.

[9.057] In *Duggan v The Governor and Company of the Bank of Ireland*[156], another point raised by the plaintiff was whether in fact the chairman had cast the votes to which he was, undoubtedly entitled to cast, pursuant to proxies received. In this case the chairman had simply said 'there are 122,803,863 votes in favour of the resolution for supporting the directors'. Having said that he had no doubt but that the chairman had intended to exercise them and that this was clear to everybody present at the meeting, McCracken J said of the words used by the chairman that:

> 'I do not think that could be interpreted as anything other than his exercising the vote contained in those proxies. It should be noted that he did not merely state that he held proxies of this number of votes, but he specifically said that there were those number of votes in favour, and he said it having already declared that there was going to be a poll. In that context, I think there was a clear exercise of the votes by him.'[157]

The final question considered by McCracken J was whether the casting of votes by a proxy is required to be in writing. In this respect the learned judge said:

> 'I know of no general proposition, nor is there anything contained in the bye-laws [articles of association], which require votes in a poll to be cast in writing. The only reason why there might be such an implied requirement would be to ensure that there is a record of the votes cast. In the present cast there was such a record, as the proxies existed and were in writing, and furthermore were actually signed by the stockholders themselves. If there is any need for there to be a record in writing of votes cast at a poll, and I do not have to determine that matter, any such requirement is satisfied by the existence of the proxy documents which are of course available to the scrutineers who are counting the votes.'[158]

It is recommended that wherever any decision (particularly an exercise of discretion) is taken, it is preferable that there is a written record of that decision. A simple letter from the chairman or other person entitled to act as proxy, indicating that he is casting those votes in favour or against the resolution in question, is thought to be desirable.

(c) Voting by representatives

[9.058] Not all members will be able to vote in person and in certain limited instances members may appoint representatives. Persons of unsound mind may vote, on a show of hands or on a poll, by their committee, receiver, guardian or other person appointed by the court and such persons may in turn, like bodies corporate, also appoint proxies[159].

[9.059] In the case of members that are bodies corporate, CA 1963, s 137(1)(a) provides that a body corporate may:

---

155 (29 July 1998, unreported), High Court at p 4, 5.

156 (29 July 1998, unreported), High Court (McCracken J).

157 (29 July 1998, unreported), High Court at p 5.

158 (29 July 1998, unreported), High Court at p 5.

159 Model reg 75.

> 'if it is a member of a company, by resolution of its directors or other governing body authorise such person as it thinks fit to act as its representative at any meeting of the company or at any meeting of any class of members of the company...'[160]

A person authorised as aforesaid shall be entitled to exercise the same powers on behalf of the body corporate which he represents as that body corporate could exercise if it were an individual member, creditor or holder of debentures of the company[161]. Where a corporate member is in liquidation, the liquidator may appoint a person to represent it[162]. A body corporate may, instead of appointing a representative, appoint a proxy. It should be noted that there are differences between a corporate representative and a proxy appointed by a body corporate. While both natural and legal persons can appoint proxies, only bodies corporate can appoint representatives. Blanchard J explained the rationale for this in *Mauri Development Corporation Ltd v Power Beat International Ltd*[163] thus:

> 'A corporation, which is an entirely abstract concept, clearly cannot attend meetings in person so in its case the legislation provides for attendance on its behalf by a representative who acts as the agent of the company and can do anything at the meeting which the corporation could have done if it were a human shareholder.
>
> A corporation is thereby given an advantage not available to a human being, who cannot be represented at a meeting except by means of a proxy…in respect of whom a notice of appointment has to have been given to the company up to 48 hours prior to the meeting, if the articles so provide.'[164]

In that case a company's board of directors appointed a person as its proxy 'to attend and act on its behalf' at an EGM of the company in which it was a shareholder and the proxy was given verbal instructions as to how to vote. The member-company made a failed attempt to fax a proxy through to the company holding the EGM. Subsequently, the 'proxy' attended the meeting, signed in as agent of the member-company and addressed the meeting as the 'representative' of the member-company; he signed the polls on the resolutions under consideration as 'proxy' of the member-company. The chairman of the meeting disallowed his votes for want of compliance with the relevant statute and the company's articles. It was held by the New Zealand High Court that the person had attended the meeting not only as a purported proxy, but as a representative within the meaning of s 143 of the New Zealand Companies Act 1955 (which was materially identical to CA 1963, s 137(1)(a)). In so finding, the court held that the right to attend and vote depended upon whether the member-company had validly resolved to authorise him to act as representative and that this was a matter of fact. Unlike CA 1963 or the model articles therein, the articles of the company holding the EGM provided that where a representative was appointed, the chairman of the meeting could seek evidence of a representative's authority. However, here the court held that the chairman and board knew full well that he was not a proxy – since no proxy form had been appointed – and that under the articles he was only obliged to produce evidence of his authority if so called upon by the chairman. Blanchard J went on to say:

---

160 This is echoed in model reg 74.

161 CA 1963, s 137(2).

162 See *Hillman v Crystal Bowl Amusement Ltd* [1973] 1 WLR 162.

163 *Mauri Development Corporation Ltd v Power Beat International Ltd* [1995] 2 NZLR 568.

164 [1995] 2 NZLR 568 at 574.

> 'The right to vote does not depend upon the evidence offered (if any) but rather upon whether a valid resolution of the shareholder appointing the representative has in fact been passed. Further, if no objection is taken to the representation and no inquiry made as to the status of the representative prior to the declaration by the chairman of the result of the poll, the representative must be taken to have validly cast the vote of the corporate shareholder. The company cannot later rely upon a ground of invalidity not then specified by the chairman.' [165]

While the Irish model articles of association are silent on a company's authority to seek evidence of a representative's authority, it seems clear that the chairman of a meeting can seek such to establish not only a purported representative's authority, but also his bona fides. One learned English commentator has said that 'the company may be unwise to debar the representative from attending and voting unless it has, after careful enquiry, formed the view that no resolution had been passed'.[166] It is thought, however, that it is more accurate to say that to allow a person to attend and vote without careful enquiry would be imprudent.

(d) Voting by proxy

[9.060] Section 136(1) of CA 1963 and model reg 68 provide that members entitled to attend and vote at a meeting (whether a general meeting or a class meeting) may cast their votes in person or by proxy[167]. Moreover, a member's proxy (a contraction of 'procuracy'[168]) shall have the same right as the member to speak at the meeting and to vote on a show of hands and on a poll[169]. Unless the articles provide otherwise, members of companies not having a share capital are not entitled to appoint proxies and, in every company, unless the articles provide otherwise, members are not entitled to appoint more than one proxy[170]. Where members have a right to appoint proxies, a statement to this effect must appear with reasonable prominence on the notice calling the meeting[171]. Companies cannot insist upon receiving an instrument appointing a proxy or other document necessary to show the validity of or otherwise relating to the appointment of a proxy more then 48 hours before a meeting or adjourned meeting[172]. Model reg 70 makes provision for proxies to be delivered not less than 48 hours before the meeting at which a member appoints a proxy. Companies are also prohibited from inviting, at the

---

165 [1995] 2 NZLR 568 at 576, citing *ANZ Nominees Ltd v Allied Resources Corporation Ltd* (1984) 2 ACLC 783 at 788 as authority for the last sentence.

166 Shearman, *Shackleton on The Law and Practice of Meetings* (9th edn, 1997), p 146.

167 Statutory intervention modified the common law rule that shareholders could only attend and vote at meetings in person, save to the extent that the articles provided otherwise: *Harben v Phillips* (1883) 23 Ch D 14.

168 *Mauri Development Corporation Ltd v Power Beat International Ltd* [1995] 2 NZLR 568 at 575.

169 See generally, Jones and Jacobs, *Company Meetings: Law and Procedure* (1991), p 76.

170 CA 1963, s 136(2)(a) and (b) respectively.

171 CA 1963, s 136(3). Default renders the company and every officer in default liable to be fined.

172 CA 1963, s 136(4).

company's expense, only certain members to appoint a particular person as their proxy[173].

[9.061] Model reg 69 provides that the instrument appointing a proxy must be in writing under the hand of the appointer or of his attorney duly authorised in writing, or, if the appointer is a body corporate, either under seal or under the hand of an officer or attorney duly authorised. Moreover, a proxy need not be a member of the company. An instrument appointing a proxy shall be in the form of that in model reg 71 (or a form as near thereto as circumstances permit). The model articles do not require that proxies be attested by a witness, but this may vary from company to company[174].

[9.062] Companies will generally be afforded a measure of comfort where they act on foot of proxies. So model reg 73 provides:

> 'A vote given in accordance with the terms of an instrument of proxy shall be valid notwithstanding the previous death or insanity of the principal or revocation of the proxy or of the authority under which the proxy was executed or the transfer of the share in respect of which the proxy is given, if no intimation in writing of such death, insanity, revocation or transfer as aforesaid is received by the company at the office before the commencement of the meeting or adjourned meeting at which the proxy is used.'

Were it otherwise, it would be very unsafe for companies to act on foot of proxies.

Minutes of members' meetings

[9.063] There is a statutory obligation on a company as soon as may be to cause minutes of all proceedings of general meetings to be entered in books kept for that purpose[175]. Where minutes have been made of the proceedings at any general meeting in accordance with CA 1963, s 145(3), then:

> '...until the contrary is proved, the meeting shall be deemed to have been duly held and convened, and all proceedings had thereat to have been duly had, and all appointments of directors or liquidators shall be deemed to be valid'.[176].

Model reg 89 obliges the directors to cause minutes to be made in books provided for the purpose, inter alia, of all resolutions and proceedings at all meetings of the company. Where signed by the company's chairman, all minutes made in accordance with CA 1963, s 145 are prima facie evidence of the proceedings[177].

---

173 CA 1963, s 136(5) provides: 'Subject to subsection (6), if for the purpose of any meeting of a company invitations to appoint as proxy a person or one of a number of persons specified in the invitations are issued at the company's expense to some only of the members entitled to be sent a notice of the meeting and to vote thereat by proxy, every officer of the company who knowingly and wilfully authorises or permits their issue as aforesaid shall be liable to a fine not exceeding €126.97.' This is subject to sub-s (6), which provides: '(6) An officer shall not be liable under subsection (5) by reason only of the issue to a member at his request in writing of a form of appointment naming the proxy or of a list of persons willing to act as proxy if the form or list is available on request in writing to every member entitled to vote at the meeting by proxy.'

174 See, for example, *Harben v Phillips* [1883] Ch 14.

175 CA 1963, s 145.

176 CA 1963, s 145(3).

177 CA 1963, s 145(2). See *Re Indian Zoedone Co* (1884) 26 Ch D 70; *Re Fireproof Doors* [1916] 2 Ch 142; and *Kerr v John Mottram Ltd* [1940] 1 Ch 657.

[9.064] Section 145(1) of CA 1963 requires[178] that every company shall, as soon as may be practicable cause minutes of all proceedings of general meetings to be entered in books kept for that purpose. Extreme care should be taken when recording the minutes of a meeting so as to ensure, not only that all decisions taken are properly recorded but also that the record does not appear to show (through sloppy drafting, carelessness or loose use of language) any illegality or impropriety. This injunction is even more important since the enactment of CLEA 2001, s 19 which inserted the following sub-s (3A) into CA 1963, s 145:

> 'A company shall, if required by the Director, produce to the Director for inspection the book or books kept in accordance with subsection (1) and shall give to the Director such facilities for inspecting and taking copies of the contents of the book or books as the Director may require.'

Not alone will the Director of Corporate Enforcement be empowered to demand sight of minutes, but so too will the proceedings at the meeting be deemed, by s 145(3), to be duly had.

[9.065] Section 146(1) of CA 1963 provides that the books containing the minutes of proceedings of any general meeting of a company shall be kept at the registered office of the company, and shall during business hours (subject to such reasonable restrictions as the company may by its articles or in general meeting impose, so that not less than two hours in each day be allowed for inspection) be open to the inspection of any member without charge[179]. Default renders the company and every officer in default liable to be fined[180]. It is also significant that where there is a refusal or default under CA 1963, s 146, the court may by order compel an inspection of the books in respect of all proceedings of general meetings or direct that copies be sent to the persons requiring them[181].

[9.066] Section 134(d) of CA 1963 provides that, in so far as the articles of a company do not make other provision in that behalf, any member elected by the members present at a meeting may be chairman thereof. Model reg 56 provides that:

> 'The chairman, if any, of the board of directors shall preside as chairman at every general meeting of the company, or if there is no such chairman, or if he is not present within 15 minutes after the time appointed for the holding of the meeting or is unwilling to act, the directors present shall elect one of their number to be chairman of the meeting.'

Model reg 57 provides:

> 'If at any meeting no director is willing to act as chairman or if no director is present within 15 minutes after the time appointed for holding the meeting, the members present shall choose one of their number to be chairman of the meeting.'

---

[178] CA 1963, s 145(4) provides that the company and every officer of the company who is in default shall be liable to a fine.

[179] Where a member requires a copy of the minutes, he 'shall be entitled to be furnished within 7 days after he has made a request in that behalf to the company with a copy of any such minutes as aforesaid at a charge not exceeding one shilling for every 100 words': CA 1963, s 146(2).

[180] CA 1963, s 145(3).

[181] CA 1963, s 145(4).

Resolutions

[9.067] Resolutions are the means used to effect decisions of the members of a company in general meeting[182]. A duly passed resolution represents the will of the majority of a company's members, or in the case of a special resolution, the will of a qualified majority of members. The various aspects to members' resolutions are considered here as follows:

(a) Ordinary resolutions.

(b) Special resolutions.

(c) Decisions by sole members of single-member private companies.

(d) The written resolution procedure.

(e) Estoppel where all corporators agree to a particular course of action.

(f) Filing of resolutions.

(a) Ordinary resolutions

[9.068] To pass an ordinary resolution, a simple majority of the members present in person or by proxy and entitled to vote must vote in favour of the resolution. Abstainers are not counted[183]; it is sufficient that a simple majority in number of those who actually vote, vote in favour of the resolution. In *Bushell v Faith*[184] Lord Upjohn said of the term 'ordinary resolution':

> 'An ordinary resolution is not defined nor used in the body of the Act of 1948 though the phrase occurs in some of the articles of Table A in the First Schedule to the Act. But its meaning is, in my opinion, clear. An ordinary resolution is in the first place passed by a bare majority on a show of hands by the members entitled to vote who are present personally or by proxy and on such a vote each member has one vote regardless of his shareholding. If a poll is demanded then, for an ordinary resolution still only a bare majority of votes[185] is required.'[186]

Two practical examples may be instructive. First, if there are ten shareholders in a company, all being entitled to vote on an ordinary resolution, that resolution will be passed where six vote in favour and four vote against. This remains the case even if the four who voted against are together entitled to, say, 90% of the issued equity share capital. Secondly, if there are again ten shareholders, all being entitled to vote, an ordinary resolution will be passed if five abstain, two vote against and three vote in favour. The ordinary resolution demonstrates one of the most fundamental principles of company law, majority rule, as seen in cases such as *Foss v Harbottle*. In an age of exceptions and ubiquitous 'special circumstances', it is important to remember that the general rule in a company is that the will of a majority shall prevail. The norm is that companies are democracies and, save to the extent to which their articles of association

---

[182] Note that in single–member companies a written decision of the sole member is used: see para **[9.074]**.

[183] *Re William Dixon Ltd* (1948) SLT 423.

[184] *Bushell v Faith* [1970] AC 1099.

[185] Calculated on the basis of one vote per share and not one vote per member.

[186] [1970] AC 1099 at 1108.

provide otherwise[187], the minority will be bound by the will of the majority acting bona fide[188].

[9.069] As compared with special resolutions, ordinary resolutions are typically required to carry out routine, non-contentious, business. That said, their importance should not be under estimated and it should be remembered that all that is required to legitimate an action outside the directors' authority, is an ordinary resolution. Where the Companies Acts 1963-2001 refers simpliciter to the company in general meeting being permitted or required to do something, such will be effected by an ordinary resolution.

(b) Special resolutions

[9.070] Although for either an ordinary or a special resolution to be passed a majority is required to vote in favour of the resolution, the essential difference between an ordinary and a special resolution is that in the case of an ordinary resolution a bare majority of 51% is required, while for a special resolution a qualified majority of 75% is required[189]. Pursuant to CA 1963, s 141(3), where it is proposed that a special resolution be passed, the declaration of the chairman shall, unless a poll is demanded, be conclusive evidence that the requisite number voted in its favour. That the chairman's declaration is conclusive evidence has been interpreted literally by the courts: *Re Graham's Morocco Co*[190].

[9.071] Section 141(1) of CA 1963 defines what is meant by a special resolution:

> 'A resolution shall be a special resolution when it has been passed by not less than three-fourths of the votes cast by such members as, being entitled so to do, vote in person or, where proxies are allowed, by proxy at a general meeting of which not less than 21 days' notice, specifying the intention to propose the resolution as a special resolution, has been duly given.'

Central to the definition of a special resolution is the fact that 21 days' notice must be given of the intention to pass the resolution. This requirement is, however, mitigated by sub-s (2), which provides:

> 'A resolution may be proposed and passed as a special resolution at a meeting of which less than 21 days' notice has been given if it is so agreed by a majority in number of the members having the right to attend and vote at any such meeting being a majority together holding not less than ninety per cent in nominal value of the shares giving that right or, in the case of a company not having a share capital, together representing not less than ninety per cent of the total voting rights at that meeting of all the members.'

---

[187] As Lord Upjohn went on to say, in *Bushell v Faith* [1970] AC 1099 at 1108–1109: 'But whether a share or class of shares has any vote upon the matter and, if so, what is its voting power upon the resolution in question depends entirely upon the voting rights attaching to that share or class of shares by the articles of association.'

[188] See, further, Chapter 19, *Shareholders' Remedies*, para **[19.082]**.

[189] CA 1963, s 141(1).

[190] [1932] SC 269. Where manifest error is shown the chairman's declaration may be set aside: *Re Caratal (New) Mines Ltd* [1902] 2 Ch 498.

To be effective, those who invoke this remedial provision must appreciate the fact that they are invoking it. In *Re Pearce Duff & Co Ltd*[191] Buckley J said:

> 'Section 141(2) of the Companies Act 1948 [UK], requires 21 days' notice in the case of a special resolution, with the proviso as to resolutions being passed on short notice which is to be found in that subsection. In my judgment, that proviso requires the persons who agree to a resolution being passed on short notice to appreciate that the resolution is being passed on short notice and to agree to its being so passed with that consideration in their minds.'[192]

In that case over 90% of the members of a company consented at a general meeting to receiving short notice there and then of a special resolution ancillary to the special resolution in respect of which the meeting had been convened. In fact, the directors had given short notice for the primary resolution and it was held that the members' consent to short notice for the second would not be taken as consent for the short notice that had been given for the primary resolution[193].

[9.072] Notice will be deemed to be duly given and the meeting duly held when the notice is given and the meeting is held in the manner provided for by the Companies Acts or the company's articles of association[194]. At any meeting at which a special resolution is submitted to be passed, a declaration of the chairman that the resolution is carried shall, unless a poll is demanded, be conclusive evidence of the fact without proof of the number or proportion of the votes recorded in favour of or against the resolution[195].

[9.073] Those matters that are specifically required by the Companies Acts to be effected by special resolution are:

- alteration of the articles of association[196];
- most alterations of the memorandum of association – namely the alteration of the objects clause[197], the name clause[198], the capital clause (but only where the effect is to reduce the share capital)[199], rendering unlimited the liability of directors[200] and any other clause that could be in the articles of association[201];
- the variation of class rights attaching to classes of shares[202];

---

[191] *Re Pearce Duff & Co Ltd* [1960] 1 WLR 1014.

[192] [1960] 1 WLR 1014 at 1016.

[193] In that case the two resolutions were in fact upheld on the grounds that the unanimous written consent of the members was subsequently obtained.

[194] CA 1963, s 141(4).

[195] CA 1963, s 141(3).

[196] CA 1963, s 15.

[197] CA 1963, s 10.

[198] CA 1963, s 23.

[199] CA 1963, s 72.

[200] CA 1963, s 198.

[201] CA 1963, s 28.

[202] C(A)A 1983, s 38.

- conversions – from private company to PLC[203], from unlimited (public) company to PLC[204], from PLC to private company[205], limited companies to unlimited companies[206] and unlimited companies to limited companies[207];
- the provision of financial assistance in connection with own-share purchase[208];
- approving a scheme of arrangement[209];
- resolving that a company be wound up by court[210];
- resolving in favour of a members' voluntary winding-up[211];
- the disapplication of statutory pre-emption rights on allotment[212];
- setting the price of treasury shares[213];
- the purchase off-market of own shares[214] and of shares in holding company[215];
- the provision of guarantees and security in connection with loans, quasi-loans and credit transactions in favour of directors of a company, its holding company or persons connected with such directors[216].

These are the main circumstances in which special resolutions of the members in general meeting are required.

(c) Decisions by sole members of single-member private companies

[9.074] In single-member companies it would be absurd to require the sole member to go through the motions of 'passing a resolution'. Consequently, it was necessary for the European Communities (Single-Member Private Limited Companies) Regulations 1994[217] to provide that resolutions are replaced by written decisions of the sole member. Regulation 9(1) provides:

> 'Subject to paragraph (2), all the powers exercisable by a company in general meeting under the Companies Acts or otherwise shall be exercisable, in the case of a single-member company, by the sole member without the need to hold a general meeting for that purpose.'

Again, this provision is not mandatory and it is open to a sole member to hold a general meeting. Regulation 9(2) provides that the foregoing paragraph does not entitle the sole

203 C(A)A 1983, s 9.
204 C(A)A 1983, s 11.
205 C(A)A 1983, s 14.
206 C(A)A 1983, s 52.
207 C(A)A 1983, s 53.
208 CA 1963, s 60.
209 CA 1963, s 210.
210 CA 1963, s 213.
211 CA 1963, s 251.
212 C(A)A1983, s 24.
213 CA 1990, s 209.
214 CA 1990, s 213.
215 CA 1990, s 224.
216 CA 1990, s 34, as substituted by CLEA 2001, s 78.
217 SI 1994/275.

member to exercise the power to remove an auditor[218]. The issue of resolutions is addressed by reg 9(3) which provides that, subject to reg 9(2):

> '...any provision of the Companies Acts which—
>
> (a) enables or requires any matter to be done or to be decided by a company in general meeting, or
>
> (b) requires any matter to be decided by a resolution of the company,
>
> shall be deemed to be satisfied, in the case of a single-member company, by a decision of the member which is drawn up in writing and notified to the company in accordance with this Regulation.'

[9.075] Where the sole member of a single-member company takes a decision which may be taken by the company in general meeting, he must provide the company with a written record of that decision, unless the decision is taken by way of written resolution which he has already forwarded to the company[219]. The company is obliged to record and retain such resolutions in a book or other suitable means maintained for the purpose[220]. Where the decision taken would ordinarily be required to be notified to the Registrar of Companies, this must be done by the company within 15 days[221]. The failure by a sole member to notify the company as set out above, does not affect the validity of any decision referred to above[222].

(d) The written resolution procedure

[9.076] At common law it was always the case that the unanimous agreement of the shareholders in a company, expressed informally, was sufficient to adopt a resolution and, indeed, this remains good law. The Jenkins Committee recommended that there should be an express statutory provision governing such matters, which should provide that a resolution in writing signed by all of the members would have the same effect as an ordinary or special resolution. The recommendation was that total informality would be formalised by a lesser informality, which required writing. This became law in CA 1963, s 141(8)(a), which provides:

> 'Notwithstanding anything to the contrary in this Act, in any case in which a company is so authorised by its articles, a resolution in writing signed by all the members for the time being entitled to attend and vote on such resolution at a general meeting...shall be as valid and effective for all purposes as if the resolution had been passed at a general meeting of

---

218 CA 1963, ss 160(2)(b), 160(5) and 160(6).

219 European Communities (Single-Member Private Limited Companies) Regulations 1994 (SI 1994/275), reg 9(4).

220 European Communities (Single-Member Private Limited Companies) Regulations 1994 (SI 1994/275), reg 9(5).

221 European Communities (Single-Member Private Limited Companies) Regulations 1994 (SI 1994/275), reg 9(6).

222 European Communities (Single-Member Private Limited Companies) Regulations 1994 (SI 1994/275), reg 9(8). A failure to comply with paragraph (4) will render the sole member liable to a fine and a failure to comply with paras (5) or (6) will render the company liable to fine. Such a fine, on summary conviction, cannot exceed €1,269.74: reg 14.

> the company duly convened and held, and if described as a special resolution shall be deemed to be a special resolution within the meaning of this Act.'

It will be noted that in order to avail of s 141(8), a company must be so authorised by its articles of association. In this regard model reg 6 of Part II of Table A provides:

> 'Subject to s 141 of the Act, a resolution in writing signed by all the members for the time being entitled to attend and vote on such resolution at a general meeting (or being bodies corporate by their duly authorised representatives) shall be as valid and effective for all purposes as if the resolution had been passed at a general meeting of the company duly convened and held, and if described as a special resolution shall be deemed to be a special resolution within the meaning of the Act.'

Unless expressly excluded by a company's articles of association, this will automatically apply in the case of private companies, incorporated under the Companies Acts 1963-2001. It should be noted that there is no similar provision in the Companies (Consolidation) Act 1908 and care should be taken when dealing with companies incorporated under that Act as the model articles contained in the CA 1963, Sch 1 do not automatically apply to such companies[223].

[9.077] The written resolution procedure can be used to pass both ordinary resolutions and special resolutions. Section 141(8) of CA 1963 is intended to give effect to the unanimous voice of those whose authorisation is required before a resolution can be passed. It follows that even though a simple majority of members is all that is required in order to pass an ordinary resolution, all of the members entitled to attend and vote on the resolution must sign the written resolution if CA 1963, s 141(8) is to be utilised. Where the written resolution procedure is followed, a resolution will be deemed to have been passed on the date on which it was signed by the last member to sign. Moreover, 'where the resolution states a date as being the date of his signature thereof by any member the statement shall be prima facie evidence that it was signed by him on that date'.[224] Where the resolution passed is a special resolution or other designated resolution, it should be filed in accordance with CA 1963, s 143(1), considered below[225].

[9.078] It is important to remember that the written resolution procedure may not be utilised for passing all resolutions. By its very terms, its application is excluded in the case of resolutions for any of the purposes of CA 1963, s 160 or 182[226]. Moreover, the practice of the legal community was to interpret CA 1963, s 60(6) as implicitly excluding the application of CA 1963, s 141(8)(a)[227], thereby precluding its use on the passing of a special resolution authorising the provision of financial assistance in connection with the purchase of a company's own shares. Any doubts over the use of the written resolution procedure when utilising the validation procedure in s 60 have now been dispelled by Company Law Enforcement Act 2001, s 89(b) ('CLEA 2001')[228].

---

223 See *Safeera Ltd v Wallis & O'Regan* (12 July 1994, unreported), High Court (Morris J).

224 CA 1963, s 141(8)(b).

225 See para **[9.084]**.

226 CA 1963, s 141(8)(c).

227 See Chapter 18, *The Maintenance of Capital*, para **[18.063]**.

228 CLEA 2001, s 89(b) substituted the following new CA 1963, s 60(6) for the old s 60(6): 'The special resolution referenced in subsection (1)(a) may be passed in accordance with section 141(8)'.

Notwithstanding the limited exclusions, the written resolution procedure provides private companies with a welcome relief from the otherwise proscriptive formalities of the Companies Acts.

(e) Estoppel where all corporators agree to a particular course of action

[9.079] The unanimous agreement of members, whether oral or implicit from their acts or omissions, can have the same consequences as if the members had passed a formal resolution to that effect. It cannot be said, however, that such an agreement amounts to a resolution that complies with the Companies Acts, as there is no written record of a resolution, nor document that can be filed. This is especially so in the case of resolutions that require to be filed pursuant to CA 1963, s 143. In effect, an estoppel arises from the members' unanimous agreement against the company and, indeed, any subsequently dissenting member[229]. The estoppel that arises from the unanimous agreement of members has come to be known as the 'Duomatic principle'[230]. In *Re Duomatic Ltd*[231] a company's articles of association made the payment of compensation to a director for loss of office, conditional upon the members authorising this by resolution; in addition the members were required to determine the director's remuneration. A claim by the company's liquidator for the repayment of a sum paid on a director's loss of office and for the repayment of certain remuneration paid to the company's directors, by reason of neither having been approved by the company's members in general meeting, failed. Buckley J held:

> '...where it can be shown that all shareholders who have a right to attend and vote at a general meeting of the company assent to some matter which a general meeting of the company could carry into effect, that assent is as binding as a resolution in general meeting would be.'[232]

In *Cane v Jones*[233] the court applied the Duomatic principle and held that an unsigned shareholders' agreement was sufficient to override a company's articles of association, and to deprive the chairman of the board of directors of his casting vote. It was acknowledged to be a basic principle of company law that all the corporators of a

[229] In *Re Greenore Trading Co Ltd* [1980] ILRM 94 it was argued that an allotment of shares was invalid because it had not been authorised by the board of directors in accordance with the articles, but by the members in general meeting. All of the members who were entitled to be present at the directors' meeting were present, and the petitioner had not challenged the decision for some time. Keane J held that: 'The Petitioner is clearly estopped in my opinion, from asserting the irregularities of a transaction which he tacitly approved of when it was being implemented, which does not offend against any principle of law and which was entirely for the benefit of the company and indeed its creditors.'

[230] See, generally, Burton, 'Dispensing with Formalities: The Duomatic Principle', (2000) 21 Company Lawyer 186 and Cabrelli, '*BDG Roof Bond Ltd v Douglas*: Further Observations on the Application of *Re Duomatic* Relief' (2001) 22 Co Lawyer 130.

[231] *Re Duomatic Ltd* [1969] 2 Ch 365.

[232] [1969] 2 Ch 365 at 373.

[233] *Cane v Jones* [1981] 1 All ER 533, see also Chapter 3, *Private Constitutional Documentation*, para **[3.089]**. See also *Re Horsley & Weight Ltd* [1982] 3 All ER 1045; *Re Oxted Motor Co* [1921] 3 KB 32; and *Re Fletcher Hunt (Bristol) Ltd* [1989] BCLC 109.

company, acting together, can do anything that is intra vires the company, and the statutory provisions on the alteration of the articles did not affect this position[234].

[9.080] Where the legal and beneficial/equitable ownership of shares is split, there is authority for the proposition that the Duomatic principle can be invoked where there is the agreement of the beneficial owners of shares. So in *Deakin v Faulding*[235] Hart J rejected the submission that 'as a matter of law, the assent of the shareholder himself must be proved, and that it was not sufficient simply to show that assent had been given by the beneficial owner of a share held by a nominee.'[236] Hart J said that he did not see why as a matter of principle it should be regarded as correct, and that where a person 'has an equity to compel a consent, I see no reason why equity should not have regard to the position of the beneficial as opposed to the legal owner in its application of the rule.'

[9.081] The most authoritative decision in point in Ireland is that of Kingsmill Moore J in *Buchanan Ltd v McVey*[237] where he said:

> 'If all the corporators agree to a certain course then, however informal the manner of their agreement, it is an act of the company and binds the company subject only to two pre-requisites: *Re Express Engineering Works Ltd* [1920] 1 Ch 466, *Parker and Cooper Ltd v Reading* [1926] 1 Ch 975[238].
>
> The two necessary pre-requisites are (1) that the transaction to which the corporators agree should be intra vires the company; (2) that the transaction should be honest: *Parker and Cooper Ltd v Reading* [1926] 1 Ch 975.'

In *Parker and Cooper Ltd v Reading* Astbury J went so far as to say that the unanimous consent was sufficient even if the corporators did not all meet together in one place, but merely discussed it and agreed 'to it one with another separately'[239]. The decision of Kingsmill Moore J was cited with approval by the Supreme Court in *Re Greendale Developments Ltd*[240], although in that case, it was deemed not to apply because the court found that the agreements in question were ultra vires the company's capacity.

---

234 In *Re Shannonside Holdings Ltd* (20 May 1993, unreported), High Court Costello J said: 'In my opinion, non–compliance with...Regulation [47] does not invalidate any resolutions passed at the meeting. It seems to me that the members of the company can mutually decide to have meetings anywhere they like, even though the Articles indicate that they are to be held in the State. Should they decide to hold meetings outside the State, they are entitled to do so provided there is agreement. If there was no formal indication that such agreement was forthcoming, it would be clear that it was to be implied in the circumstances of this case.'

235 *Deakin v Faulding* [2001] EWHC Ch 7 (31 July 2001).

236 *Re New Cedos Engineering Co Ltd* [1994] 1 BCLC 797 had been cited as authority for that proposition.

237 *Buchanan Ltd v McVey* [1954] IR 89.

238 In *Parker and Cooper Ltd v Reading* [1926] 1 Ch 975 at 982 Astbury J had said: '… where a transaction is intra vires the company and honest, the sanction of all the members of the company, however expressed, is sufficient to validate it, especially if it is a transaction entered into for the benefit of the company itself'.

239 [1926] 1 Ch 975 at 984.

240 *Re Greendale Developments Ltd* [1998] 1 IR 8 (per Keane J; nem diss).

[9.082] The fact that an estoppel might arise should, however, never be considered to be a sufficient basis for deliberately proceeding in a manner that is prima facie at variance with the requirements of company law. The Duomatic principle is best regarded as a remedial shield, the successful reliance upon which can never be guaranteed. So in *Re RW Peak (Kings Lynn) Ltd*[241] a company purchased its own shares contrary to the English statutory provisions on own-share purchase. In particular, the articles of association made no provision for the purchase of its own shares. Lindsay J held that the purported own-share purchase was void and that the provisions in the Companies Act 1985 (UK) could not be overridden by the Duomatic principle. One of the reasons given was that the statutory protection in question was intended to protect 'future shareholders'. It must be questioned whether the interests of future shareholders should be considered since persons becoming shareholders should take the company as it is. In *Demite Ltd v Protec Health Ltd*[242] Park J said that he was not convinced that s 320 of the Companies Act 1985 (UK) – which is similar to CA 1990, s 29 in Ireland and regulates substantial property transactions between directors and their companies – could be satisfied by a Duomatic-type assent. It is thought, however, that even on a restrictive application of the Duomatic principle, there is no reason why it should not apply in such a case since the statutory provision is exclusively concerned with shareholder protection. There is, however, a compelling case for ascertaining whether creditors' rights are lessened since statutory provisions designed to protect creditors should not be capable of being overridden by members. This should be the case whether the members act by passing a resolution at a properly-convened meeting, by passing a unanimous written resolution or in accordance with the Duomatic principle[243].

[9.083] Although it may be argued that the realities of the Irish private company should be accommodated by law, there are valid reasons for requiring the members to resolve in writing to carry out certain acts. Thus, where the resolution changes the company's constitution, unless there is something in writing, the Registrar of Companies cannot record the change, in order to make it ascertainable by the public. Accordingly, a balance must be struck between the exigencies of private company business, the necessary administration of the Companies Registration Office and the interests of creditors and, indeed, members.

(f) Filing of resolutions

[9.084] Special resolutions and certain ordinary resolutions must within 15 days of their passing be forwarded to the Registrar of Companies for recording: CA 1963, s 143(1)[244].

241 *Re RW Peak (Kings Lynn) Ltd* [1998] BCC 596.

242 *Demite Ltd v Protec Health Ltd* [1998] BCC 638.

243 In applying the Duomatic principle the English court in *BDG Roof Bond Ltd v Douglas* [2000] 1 BCLC 401 at 417 observed that the provision that the company's members had waived (making available a share repurchase agreement at the company's registered office) involved 'no element of creditor protection at all'. See also *Precision Dippings Ltd v Precision Dippings Marketing Ltd* [1985] 3 WLR 812 where a different treatment for provisions designed to protect creditors was mooted.

244 CA 1963, s 143(1) provides: 'A printed copy of every resolution or agreement to which this section applies shall, within 15 days after the passing or making thereof, be forwarded to the registrar of companies and recorded by him.'

Those ordinary resolutions that must be forwarded to the Registrar are listed in s 143(4) as being:

'(a) resolutions which have been agreed to by all the members of a company, but which, if not so agreed to, would not have been effective for their purpose unless they had been passed as special resolutions;

(b) resolutions or agreements which have been agreed to by all the members of some class of shareholders but which if not so agreed to, would not have been effective for their purpose unless they had been passed by some particular majority or otherwise in some particular manner, and all resolutions or agreements which effectively bind all the members of any class of shareholders though not agreed to by all those members;

(c) resolutions increasing the share capital of a company;

(d) resolutions that a company be wound up voluntarily passed under paragraph (a) or paragraph (c) of subsection (1) of section 251;

(e) resolutions attaching rights or restrictions to any share;

(f) resolutions varying any such rights or restrictions;

(g) resolutions classifying any unclassified share;

(h) resolutions converting shares of one class into shares of another class;

(i) resolutions of the directors of a company passed by virtue of ss 12(3)(a) and 43(3) of the 1983 Amendment Act.'

In this way such resolutions become public documents, and the public at large will be deemed to have constructive notice of their contents. Failure to register a resolution to which the section applies does not taint the validity of the resolution, which will have full force and effect without being registered. It should be noted, however, that a failure to file a copy of a resolution renders the company, and every officer in default, liable to a fine[245].

[9.085] There is also a requirement that where articles have been registered, a copy of every such resolution or agreement for the time being in force shall be embodied in or annexed to every copy of the articles issued after the passing of the resolution or the making of the agreement[246]. Members are entitled to receive a copy of every such resolution or agreement[247].

[B] DIRECTORS' MEETINGS

[9.086] The law governing the convening and holding of meetings of members is very prescriptive. Both statute and the model articles of association are deliberately intended

[245] CA 1963, s 143(5). Subsection (6) provides that the failure to comply with sub-s (2) or sub-s (3), renders the company and every officer of the company who is in default shall be liable to a fine not exceeding €1.27 for each copy in respect of which default is made. Moreover, sub-s (7) provides that for the purposes of sub-ss (5) and (6), a liquidator of a company shall be deemed to be an officer of the company.

[246] CA 1963, s 143(2).

[247] CA 1963, s 143(3) which provides that this is in return for the payment of one shilling or such less sum as the company may direct.

to safeguard members' rights to attend and vote at general meetings and to thwart any attempt by company directors to stymie the exercise of these rights. Moreover, it is important to bear in mind that general meetings of members are invariably sporadic, almost ritualistic events when the owners of a company are asked to either note certain statutory matters (as in the case of an AGM) or to decide an important course of action for the company, where such a decision is reserved for the members' judgment (as in the case of an EGM, or, indeed at an AGM). Directors' meetings[248] are usually far more frequent and informal affairs. These are the fora at which the day-to-day management decisions for a company are taken – especially where a company's board is comprised of executive directors who are personally involved in the management of the company. In consequence of this, the law relating to directors' meetings, such as it is, is far less prescriptive in terms, for example, of the notice required, notice of business to be conducted thereat, etc. In place of rigid notice provisions, and in deference to the exigencies of commerce, the key requirement underlying the law on directors' meetings is reasonableness.

[9.087] In this section, directors' meetings shall be considered under the following headings:

1. Regulation of directors' meetings.
2. Convening and notice of a directors' meeting.
3. Holding directors' meetings.
4. The business transacted.
5. The quorum.
6. The chairman.
7. Adjourned meetings.
8. Minutes of directors' meetings.
9. Committees.
10. Resolutions and voting.

Regulation of directors' meetings

[9.088] The regulation of directors' meetings is largely a matter for the directors themselves. Such provisions in the Companies Acts as concern meetings of directors tend to be in the nature of model articles – that can be amended or purged by a company – rather than prescriptive statutory requirements. Accordingly, model reg 101 provides:

> 'The directors may meet together for the dispatch of business, adjourn and otherwise regulate their meetings as they think fit. Questions arising at any meeting shall be decided by a majority of votes. Where there is an equality of votes, the chairman shall have a second or casting vote. A director may, and the secretary on the requisition of a director shall, at any time summon a meeting of the directors. If the directors so resolve, it shall not

[248] See generally, Shearman, *Shackleton on The Law and Practice of Meetings* (9th edn, 1997), pp 221–258; Jones and Jacobs, *Company Meetings: Law and Procedure* (1991), pp 105–193. For a brief overview of Irish law see Maloney & Spellman, *The Law of Meetings* (1999), pp 148–151. See also, Creamer & Michie, 'Board Meetings: Best Practice and New Trends' (1997) Practical Law for Companies 31 for an excellent review of the law and modern practice of directors' meetings.

be necessary to give notice of a meeting of directors to any director who, being resident in the state, is for the time being absent from the state.'

This omnibus regulation is adopted by most private companies, which are incorporated in Ireland today. The light touch in the legislative approach to directors' meetings is evident in the fact that, unlike the many articles that govern aspects of members' meetings, as regards directors' meetings the one article addresses voting, casting votes, the convening of meetings and notice of meetings.

Convening and notice of a directors' meeting

[9.089] Model reg 101 provides that the directors may meet together as they think fit. Any one director may, of his own right, summon a meeting and the company secretary must summon a meeting where a director requisitions a meeting. Unlike members' meetings, there is no express statutory equivalent to CA 1963, s 135[249] that enables persons to apply to court to order the requisition a directors' meeting. There are two reasons for this absence of specific jurisdiction. In the first place, any one director can summon a directors' meeting. Secondly, an impasse on the board of directors can be cured by the members in general meeting voting out the existing board and replacing it, so it can be said that the members' ability to requisition a general meeting is sufficient recourse.

[9.090] Model articles are silent on the length of notice required to be given for a directors' meeting. This is in recognition of the fact that the exigencies of business may dictate that, in particular circumstances, the directors of a company may be required to meet on a daily basis. Notwithstanding the absence of a fixed notice period, notice must be given to directors of forthcoming meetings and if notice is not given to all directors entitled to receive notice, any meeting held will be deemed irregular and any business purportedly effected deemed a nullity[250]. Here, common sense accords with the law, and it was held in *Holland v McGill*[251] that due notice, namely reasonable notice, must be given. In addition, there is no requirement in the model articles that notice be given of the business which it is proposed to conduct at a directors' meeting. However, as seen in the *Holland* case, a director will have cause to complain where he can show that he was misled as to the business which it was proposed to transact or consider at a meeting. Where what was transacted would have been done in any event through the force of majority voting, and in the absence of any finding of abuse of directors' powers, the meeting may not be invalidated[252].

An old example of the need for reasonable notice is seen in *Re Homer District Consolidated Gold Mines, ex p Smith*[253]. There a company had invited application for 106,000 preference shares in the company but had resolved that there would be no allotment until at least 14,000 had been applied for. The company had five directors and the articles provided that the quorum was two. Upon receiving applications for some

---

249 See the Companies Act 1985 (UK), s 371, considered *Ross v Telford* [1998] 1 BCLC 82. Cf *Re Sticky Fingers Restaurant Ltd* [1992] BCLC 84.

250 *Re Portuguese Consolidated Copper Mines Ltd* [1889] 42 Ch 160.

251 *Holland v McGill* (16 March 1990, unreported), High Court (Murphy J).

252 (16 March 1990, unreported), High Court at p 12 *ff*.

253 *Re Homer District Consolidated Gold Mines, ex p Smith* (1888) 39 Ch 546.

3,000 shares, one of the directors sought the approval of the board to reverse its earlier decision and to allot the circa 3,000 shares applied for. A board meeting was called on a particular day at 2.00 pm, on a few hours' notice. It was attended by two directors who purported to resolve that the earlier resolution be cancelled and that the shares applied for should be allotted. Of the three directors who did not attend, one was absent from the jurisdiction (and so not entitled to notice under the company's articles), another received notice but had said he could not make the meeting until 3.00 p.m. and the third did not receive the notice until the day after the meeting had been held. North J held that the allotments of shares were invalid and did not bind the company because the meeting had been improperly constituted without adequate notice of either the meeting or the business intended to be considered at the meeting[254].

[9.091] Where model reg 101 is adopted, it will not be necessary to give notice of a meeting to any director who, being resident in the State, is for the time being absent from the State, provided that the directors have previously resolved that such be the case. If the directors do not so resolve, the default position is that all directors must receive notice. Whilst there is some ambiguity, it is thought that model reg 106 will not override the requirement for a quorum and that even where the directors have previously so resolved, a valid meeting cannot take place (nor written resolution be passed) where the number of directors within the State is insufficient to make up the quorum[255].

[9.092] Resolutions passed and decisions taken at an invalidly convened, held and constituted board meeting can be subsequently validated by a valid board meeting. Alternatively, they can be ratified by the members in general meeting[256].

Holding directors' meetings

[9.093] If a meeting is to be a valid meeting of the board of directors, those present should appreciate or have a basis for appreciating that fact, the chairman of the board should chair it and it should be referred to as such in notices convening it[257]. Notwithstanding this, it has long been established that directors' meetings can be held in informal circumstances[258]. One of the inherent difficulties of informal regimes, however, is that there can be uncertainty as to whether a particular meeting was, in fact, a directors' meeting or some other kind of meeting. Whether or not a board meeting had taken place, was one of the issues before the High Court in the case of *Re Aston Colour Print Ltd*[259]. It was claimed that a directors' petition to have a company placed under the

254 Cf *La Compagnie de Mayville v Whitley* [1896] 1 Ch 788 which suggests that it is not necessary to specify in a notice convening a directors' meeting the business that it is intended will be transacted thereat.

255 See also *Hood Sailmakers Ltd v Axford* [1996] 4 All ER 830, considered at para **[9.108]**.

256 See *Bamford v Bamford* [1970] 1 Ch 212 and *Re D'Jan of London Ltd* [1993] BCC 646. See further, Chapter 8, *Corporate Governance: Management by the Directors*, para **[8.014]** *ff*.

257 *Re Aston Colour Print Ltd* (21 February 1997, unreported), High Court (Kelly J).

258 See *Smith v Paringa Mines* [1906] 2 Ch 193 where a valid board meeting was held to have taken place in the corridor outside a director's office.

259 *Re Aston Colour Print Ltd* (21 February 1997, unreported), High Court (Kelly J).

protection of the court had not been authorised by the company's board of directors because there had neither been a board meeting not an authorising resolution. Kelly J heard that meetings, known as executive or management meetings, had been held, attended by the company's two directors with some or all of its shareholders and its financial controller, on a weekly basis to discuss the day-to-day running of the company. No formal notices were issued convening these meetings. The meeting under scrutiny was to consider the company's financial difficulties. The company's options – more investment, the appointment of a liquidator or the appointment of an examiner – were all discussed. The meeting was attended by the company's only two formally appointed directors (C & B), two shareholders (McC and P) and by its financial controller (L). P, one of the shareholders present, chaired the meeting. Subsequently, a petition was presented in the names of the two directors, to have an examiner appointed. One of the directors, B, did not regard the meeting as having been a board meeting and irrespective of the nature of the meeting held (it was not disputed that there had been a meeting) did not believe a decision had been taken to appoint an examiner. Giving four reasons, Kelly J concluded that the meeting in question was not a board meeting:

> '1. Whilst board meetings may be held on an informal basis, the directors must at least appreciate or have a basis for appreciating that they are attending such a meeting.[260]. Mr B did not so appreciate, nor was there any reason why he should. The meeting was not so described; it did not differ from other management or executive meetings; it was not chaired by the chairman of the board.
>
> 2. If the meeting was that of the board, why was it not chaired by [C]? He was the chairman of the board yet it was Mr P, a non-director, who presided at the meeting.
>
> 3. Mr L [the financial controller], who is a man of some experience on the financial side, told me in evidence that he did not consider that he was attending a board meeting of the company.
>
> 4. Mr P who chaired the meeting, as he did the other executive meetings, believed he was presiding over a meeting of the company in general meeting which subsequently became a board meeting, to quote his evidence. But subsequent to what? And when did this change occur? And how was Mr B to know when the metamorphosis occurred?'[261]

This case underscores the importance of observing what might at first appear to be mere formalities[262].

[9.094] Modern technology facilitates, with ease, meetings to take place over the telephone, provided that all persons participating can hear each other. The question is whether this is sufficient to come within the expression, 'the directors may meet together' as provided for in model reg 101. There is old authority for the proposition that the directors need not be in the same physical location at the time they reach a decision,

---

[260] See, for example, *Barron v Potter* [1914] 1 Ch 895.

[261] (21 February 1997, unreported), High Court at pp 6, 7.

[262] See Canniffe, 'More than Mere Formalities: *Re Aston Colour Print Ltd and the Companies Acts*' (1997) 4 CLP 280.

but the possibilities of audio or audio-visual meetings could not have been even dreamed of in 1871[263]. Modern authority is provided by the Australian case of *Bell v Burton*[264], in which Tadgell J said:

> 'No doubt there is no necessity nowadays – if there ever was – that directors should gather physically together at a directors' meeting. In appropriate circumstances they can meet by assenting to a document, or by telephone, video link, or other electronic means which caters for a meeting of their minds.'

This was adopted by Santow J in *Wagner v International Health Promotions*[265] who went on to say: 'I agree that the words "meet together" connote a meeting of minds made possible by modern technology and not of bodies.' Both of these cases were followed by the Federal Court of Australia in *GIGA Investments Pty Ltd (in admin) v Ferguson*[266] which added:

> 'In my view, provided that each participating director is able to be aware of the contributions to the meeting made by each other director, and to contribute himself or herself to the meeting without significant impediment, it is not of importance that the meeting together of the directors is achieved with the assistance of the telecommunications industry. I conclude that directors can, generally speaking, meet together by video links or by using telephone conference connections. A meeting of two directors only can by analogy of reasoning, in my view, generally speaking, be held using an ordinary telephone connection.'

[9.095] Although there is authority for saying that the expression 'meet together' as used in model reg 101 encompasses telephone and other electronic meetings because it means a meeting of minds, it is preferable to expressly provide for such in a company's articles of association. One suggested wording[267] is:

> 'A meeting of the directors or of a committee of the board may consist of a conference between directors and any alternate directors who are not all in one place, but each of which is able (directly or by telephonic communication) to speak to each of the others, and to be heard by each of the others simultaneously. A director or an alternate director taking part in such a conference shall be deemed to be present in person at the meeting and shall be entitled to vote or be counted in a quorum accordingly. Such a meeting shall be deemed to take place where the largest group of those participating in the conference is assembled,

263 See *Re Bonelli's Telegraph Company; Collie's Claim* (1871) LR 12 EQ 246 where a letter committing the company to a course of action was found to be a decision of the company in circumstances where it was signed by each of the directors, some in different locations.

264 *Bell v Burton* (1993) 12 ACSR 325. Cf the earlier Australian cases of *Re Southern Resources* (1989) 15 ACLR 770 at 792–794 and *Magna Crete Ltd v Douglas–Hill* (1988) 48 SASR 565 at 603 where Perry J concluded that a company's articles did not contemplate a telephone meeting.

265 *Wagner v International Health Promotions* [1994] 12 ACLC 986.

266 *GIGA Investments Pty Ltd (in admin) v Ferguson* [1995] 13 ACLC 1050.

267 See the very interesting article by Creamer and Michie, 'Board Meetings – Best Practice and New Trends', (1997) Practical Law for Companies, 31 at 34.

> or, if there is no such group, where the chairman of the meeting is. The word meeting in these articles shall be construed accordingly.'[268]

The adoption of such an article will remove any uncertainly arising from simply relying upon the line of cases that affords a 'meeting of the minds' interpretation to the phrase 'meet together'.

The business transacted

[9.096] Depending upon the size of a company, pre-board meetings may be held to determine the agenda for the next board meeting. Individual directors should raise, with the chairman, items for consideration, as it is the chairman who will normally determine the agenda. As to the business transacted at meetings, the directors can take items on the agenda in whatever order they wish[269]. Obstructive directors can be suspended if their conduct is so disorderly as to impede the proceedings at a board meeting[270].

The quorum

[9.097] Model reg 102 provides that the quorum necessary for the transaction of the business of the directors may be fixed by the directors, and unless so fixed shall be two. If, due to a death or vacancy, the number of directors falls below the number necessary to have a quorate meeting, no business may be transacted at a directors' meeting, except for the purpose of increasing the number of directors to satisfy the quorum or of summoning a general meeting of the company[271].

[9.098] The general rule is that there must be a disinterested quorum, by which is meant those directors making up the quorum are not personally interested in, say, a transaction under consideration. However, it should be noted that most private companies will have adopted reg 7 of Part II of Table A, which provides that directors can vote in respect of any contract, appointment or arrangement in which they are interested and shall be counted in the quorum present at the meeting.

[9.099] In Ireland, it remains the law that every company must have at least two directors. As noted earlier, this position was unchanged by the European Communities (Single-Member Private Limited Companies) Regulations 1994[272]. It may be noted, however, that in jurisdictions – such as England and Wales – where one director companies are permitted, it has been held that self-dealing transactions which require directors to disclose their interests in particular transactions continue to apply, even

---

[268] For an Irish example, see (1991) The Irish Times, 17 April, where it was reported that Woodchester Investments plc proposed the following new regulation for its articles: 'Any director or alternative director may participate in a meeting of the directors or any committee of the directors by means of a conference telephone or of other telecommunications equipment by means of which all persons participating in the meeting can hear each other and such participation in a meeting shall constitute presence in person at the meeting.' This was subsequently passed by special resolution of the shareholders in general meeting.

[269] *Re Cawley & Co* [1888] 42 Ch 209.

[270] *Barton v Taylor* [1886] 11 App Cas 197.

[271] Model reg 103.

[272] SI 1994/275.

though this requires a director to disclose to himself his interest in a particular transaction! [273]

The chairman

[9.100] Model reg 104 provides that:

> 'The directors may elect a chairman of their meetings and determine the period for which he is to hold office, but if no such chairman is elected, or, if at any meeting the chairman is not present within 5 minutes after the time appointed for holding the same, the directors present may choose one of their number to be chairman of the meeting.'

Accordingly, the 'chairman' referred to in model reg 101 can be appointed in accordance with model reg 104, and apart from having the casting vote, his formally prescribed functions are few. One role of the chairman is signing the minutes of meetings; when signed by the chairman, the minutes are prima facie evidence of what took place at a meeting[274]. Where a chairman's period of office is not specified, the other directors can remove the chairman and appoint an alternative[275] – subject to any right the chairman may have under any executive contract.

Adjourned meetings

[9.101] Where a resolution is passed at a metting of the directors which had been earlier adjourned, the resolution shall for all purposes be treated as having been passed on the date on which it was in fact passed and shall not be deemed to have been passed on any earlier date[276].

Minutes of directors' meetings

[9.102] Section 145(1) of CA 1963 requires[277] that the minutes of all proceedings at meetings of directors and of committees of directors should be entered in a minute book as soon as may be possible. Model reg 89 enumerates the matters that should be entered in the minutes of directors' meetings, these being:

- all appointments of officers made by the directors;
- the names of the directors present at each board meeting and of any committee meetings;
- all resolutions and proceedings at members' meetings and at all meetings of the directors and of committees of directors.

---

[273] See *Neptune (Vehicle Washing Equipment) Ltd v Fitzgerald* [1995] 1 BCLC 352 where Lightman J held that it was necessary for a sole director to show that he had declared to himself his interest in a transaction at a director's meeting. It is to be hoped that such nonsense will be obviated by statute, should Ireland ever decide to allow one-director companies.

[274] CA 1963, s 145(2). See *Re Indian Zoedone Co* (1884) 26 Ch D 70; *Re Fireproof Doors* [1916] 2 Ch 142 and *Kerr v John Mottram Ltd* [1940] 1 Ch 657.

[275] *Foster v Foster* [1916] 1 Ch 532.

[276] CA 1963, s 144.

[277] CA 1963, s 145(4) provides that the company and every officer of the company who is in default shall be liable to a fine.

Section 145(3A) of CA 1963 empowers the Director of Corporate Enforcement to obtain copies of all minutes[278].

[9.103] Where the minutes are signed by the chairman of the meeting (or by the chairman of the next succeeding meeting) the minutes shall be evidence of the proceedings[279]. A further consequence of keeping minutes is that, until the contrary is proved, the meeting shall be deemed to have been duly held and convened, and all proceedings had thereat to have been duly had, and all appointments of directors or liquidators shall be deemed to be valid[280].

[9.104] Where meetings are held informally, there will often be no record of the meeting other than individual directors' recollections. Minutes of meetings, where taken, tend to be mechanical formulae to satisfy statutory requirements or the requirements of lending institutions who require a written record of certain board decisions before advancing finances. This was recognised in *Re PMPA Garage (Longmile) Ltd (No 1)*[281] where Murphy J said[282]

> '...one would not expect to find in any case the minute book of a company recording divergent views of directors and managers in relation to commercial documentation. The minute book of Longmile records, as does probably most minute books of comparable companies, the basic decisions which must be taken in accordance with the requirements of the Companies Acts from time to time. I think it may be assumed confidently that minutes of this nature and any record of any decision or resolution made for statutory or financial purposes would be prepared in advance by the secretary in case of routine matters or by legal advisers in relation to more important matters but in either event the purpose of the meeting would be to approve a preordained formula so that the minutes would reflect that formula and not the discussion, if any, which might take place.'

That said, it is very important that basic minutes are kept. Where no record exists of what has taken place, directors can find themselves exposed, especially when a board's decisions become the subject of judicial scrutiny in establishing the motive behind taking a particular course of action[283]. It should also be noted that the general rule applied to minutes is that they should record 'decisions not discussions'[284].

Committees

[9.105] In the absence of an empowering article, there can be no delegation by the board to a committee[285]. Model reg 105 provides that directors may delegate any of their

---

[278] See para **[9.064]**.

[279] CA 1963, s 145(2).

[280] CA 1963, s 145(3).

[281] *Re PMPA Garage (Longmile) Ltd (No 1)* [1992] ILRM 337.

[282] [1992] ILRM 337 at 342.

[283] See *Re Shrinkpak Ltd* (20 December 1989, unreported), High Court per Barron J, reported in (1989) The Irish Times, 21 December.

[284] On the lackadaisical approach of many small Irish private companies to keeping minutes, see the comments of Murphy J in *Irish Microforms Ltd v Browne* (3 April 1987, unreported), High Court.

[285] *Howard's Case* (1866) 1 Ch 561.

powers to committees consisting of such member or members of the board as they think fit; any committee so formed shall, in the exercise of the powers so delegated, conform to any regulations that may be imposed on it by the directors. Committees may elect their own chairs[286]. Committees may meet and adjourn as they think proper and questions arising at any meeting shall be determined by a majority of votes of the members present, and where there is an equality of votes, the chairman shall have a second or casting vote[287]. There is authority for the proposition that a sole director can validly constitute a committee[288].

Resolutions and voting

[9.106] Formal decisions of the board of directors are referred to as resolutions. In *Municipal Mutual Insurance Ltd v Harrop*[289] Rimer J said:

> 'The fundamental principle is, however, that a company is an artificial legal person the validity of whose operations is governed by its constitution. The ordinary rule is that the acts of a company's board must be authorised by resolutions properly passed at a duly convened board meeting. If the directors purport to act in accordance with the decisions of their majority, but without the prior authority of a board meeting, their acts are not those of either the board or the company.'[290]

In that case it was held that a company's directors had not amended the rules of a pension scheme, which required the passing of a resolution. Rimer J held that an oral assent in response to a memorandum sent to the board was not a resolution, which satisfied the company's articles.

(a) Formal resolutions at board meetings

[9.107] The general rule on voting at directors' meetings is that each director has one vote and that voting will take place by a show of hands. Model reg 101 provides that all questions are to be decided by simple majority and that where there is an equality of votes, the chairman will have a second or casting vote[291]. It is unusual even in PLCs for actual formal voting to take place, companies preferring to proceed on the basis of consensus. In *Re Aston Colour Print Ltd*[292], the facts of which have been considered above[293], Kelly J went on to consider whether a resolution of the board had been passed. To the extent that he had already decided that a board meeting had not been held, this aspect of his judgment is obiter, but nonetheless instructive. Having noted that there was no formal resolution and certainly no vote taken, he went on to say:

---

[286] Model reg 106.

[287] Model reg 107.

[288] *Re Fireproof Doors Ltd* [1916] 2 Ch 142.

[289] *Municipal Mutual Insurance Ltd v Harrop* [1998] 2 BCLC 540.

[290] [1998] 2 BCLC 540 at 551b–c. *Re East Norfolk Tramways Co, Barber's Case* (1877) 5 Ch D 963, cited.

[291] Unless the chairman has been invalidly appointed: *Clark v Workman* [1920] 1 IR 107.

[292] *Re Aston Colour Print Ltd* (21 February 1997, unreported), High Court (Kelly J).

[293] See para **[9.093]**.

> 'A decision by a board of directors to take such a step [ie presenting a petition to appoint an examiner] must be made in a manner which makes the will of the board clear. The usual way to do that is by the proposal of a resolution and its being voted upon.'[294]

Accordingly, formal resolutions should be proposed (may be seconded) and should be voted upon at a properly convened board meeting and, if passed, recorded in the minutes as having been adopted by the board. In that case, Kelly J found there had been no formal resolution nor, indeed, any informal resolution put to the meeting and he believed that what had occurred was that 'there was a general understanding arrived at between four of the five people present at the meeting'. Kelly J concluded:

> 'But the fifth person was of course the second director. He did not appreciate what was to happen. The level of informality was such that I do not think that he can be blamed or criticised for this. There was no resolution put before him nor was there any question put in such a way as to alert him as to what was to occur. Such being so, I do not accept that there was any resolution, formal or informal, passed by the board.'[295]

(b) Written resolutions without a board meeting

[9.108] There is also an informal means of passing directors' resolutions, provided for in model reg 109 which states:

> 'A resolution in writing signed by all the directors for the time being entitled to receive notice of a meeting of the directors shall be as valid as if it had been passed at a meeting of the directors duly convened and held.'

The effect of this article is to dispense with the need to convene and hold a board meeting, in order to have a resolution passed. Accordingly, it will suffice if a resolution is in writing and signed by all of the directors who are entitled to receive notice of a directors' meeting. It is thought that even if a particular director is not entitled to vote on a particular resolution, his signature to the resolution will still be required as the regulation refers to a resolution 'signed by all the directors' without qualification. It should be noted, though, that model reg 109 will not override a company's quorum requirements. So, in *Hood Sailmakers Ltd v Axford*[296] one director of a two director company, purported to pass a written resolution by signing it himself. His co-director was at that time out of the jurisdiction and the company's articles provided that where directors were out of the jurisdiction, they need not receive notice of a directors' meeting. The company's articles of association included regulations that were identical to the Irish model reg 109 (on written resolutions) and the Irish model reg 102 (on quorum)[297]. Its regulation on notice of directors' meetings differed from the Irish model reg 101[298] in that it simply stated that it was not necessary to give notice 'to any director for the time being absent from the United Kingdom', so that this applied automatically, without the need for the directors to resolve that this be the case, as is required in Ireland where model reg 101 is adopted without modification[299]. Carnwath J said:

---

[294] (21 February 1997, unreported), High Court at p 8.

[295] (21 February 1997, unreported), High Court at p 8.

[296] *Hood Sailmakers Ltd v Axford* [1996] 4 All ER 830.

[297] See para **[9.097]**.

[298] See para **[9.088]**.

[299] See para **[9.091]**.

> 'It seems to me that [model reg 109] is ambiguous. The reference to the meeting being "duly convened and held" could be taken as a reference, not only to the establishment of the meeting, but also to the validity of the business conducted at it. On the other hand, it might simply be indicating that the document is to be treated as equivalent to a meeting, without prejudice to any other requirement relating to the actual business transacted at it. I note that [model reg 102] refers specifically to the quorum required "for the transaction of business". This tends to suggest that, even if the meeting is validly convened and held, the requirement for a quorum is to be treated as a separate matter relating to the particular items of business on which reliance is placed. This view also accords with what I take to be the purpose of the provisions. As suggested by the textbooks[300], the object of [model reg 109] appears to be to avoid the need for a meeting where it would otherwise be superfluous. It does not appear to be directed to making a fundamental change to the quorum requirements. It would be odd if a director could evade the quorum requirements simply by waiting for his fellow director or directors to leave the country.'[301]

The same conclusion appears to have been independently arrived at by the Scottish Court of Session in *Davidson & Begg Antiques Ltd v Davidson*[302], a judgment handed down a few weeks prior to Carnwaith J's decision. In that case the company's articles made similar provision to those just discussed. In reliance upon them, one of the company's two directors resolved by written resolution that the company would institute proceedings against the other director, the other director being absent from the jurisdiction. Lord Roger held that the proceedings had been commenced on the basis of a resolution that did not comply with the company's quorum requirements. Specifically, he held that the equivalent to model reg 109, which commenced 'a resolution in writing signed by *all of the directors*', suggested the need for more than one signature and also that it had to be read in the context of the other articles. Moreover, he held that the company had set a quorum 'for the transaction of the business of the directors', that the initiation of litigation was part of the company's business[303] and so the quorum requirement applied to any resolution in that context. In reconciling the apparent conflict, Lord Roger said of the equivalent to model reg 102 that its terms are more general than simply laying down the quorum for a meeting of the directors, since it prescribes the quorum 'for the transaction of business of the directors'. He found:

> 'Especially since other regulations refer specifically to meetings of the directors, the inference must be that [model reg 102] has been framed deliberately in these wider terms in order to cover any means by which the directors are to transact business. [model reg 102] therefore applies to business transacted by means of resolutions under [model reg 109]. The result is that a resolution under [model reg 109] is valid provided not only that it is signed by all the directors who are entitled to receive notice of a meeting but also that the number of directors signing is at least two [where that is the quorum].'[304]

---

[300] Carnwath J had previously referred to Gower, *Principles of Modern Company Law* (5th edn, 1992), p 160; Pennington, *Pennington's Company Law* (7th edn, 1995), p 768; and Schmittoff (ed), *Palmer's Company Law* (1993) Volume 2 at para 8.301.

[301] [1996] 4 All ER 830 at 834e–g.

[302] *Davidson & Begg Antiques Ltd v Davidson* [1997] BCC 77.

[303] Cf whether this is the case in Ireland: see Chapter 8, *Corporate Governance: Management by the Directors*, para **[8.012]**.

[304] [1997] BCC 77 at 80D.

It is thought that this is the correct interpretation of these articles and that neither model reg 109 nor 101 can override a company's quorum requirements.

(c) Unanimous acts of the directors

[9.109] In *Municipal Mutual Insurance Ltd v Harrop*[305] Rimer J recognised that there was an exception to the general rule that resolutions must be either formal or written. Where the directors act unanimously in a matter, without either the prior sanction of a resolution of the board or a unanimous written resolution, there is authority for saying that their acts will, ordinarily, still be regarded as those of the company[306]. In *Harrop* it had been sought to extend that exception to a situation where a certain course of action was not unanimous, but this was rejected by Rimer J who said of the exception that:

> '…its essence is unanimity. Once an inroad is made into it so as to enable it to operate where there is something less than unanimity, the need for board meetings might as well be dispensed with altogether.'[307]

It is thought that this principle, such as it is, should only ever be considered to be a shield and that full formality (or, at the very least, the informality permitted by the articles) should never be sacrificed in reliance upon it.

[305] *Municipal Mutual Insurance Ltd v Harrop* [1998] 2 BCLC 540.
[306] *Runciman v Walter Runciman plc* [1992] BCLC 1084.
[307] [1998] 2 BCLC 540 at 551b.

Chapter 10

Duties of Directors and Other Officers

Introduction

[10.001] The duties owed by directors and other officers to their company are wide and diverse[1]. The source of such duties is found at common law, in equity and in statute. In many Irish private companies, the directors will often be the shareholders of the company. Consequently, directors' recognition of their duties as directors will often be blurred by the belief that their shareholdings entitle them to the company's assets. Sometimes the only interest which directors will look after will be their own self-interest. Into what has become, for many directors, this misguided reality, intrude the Companies Acts 1963–2001, the common law and equity, which together impose a myriad of duties on company directors and other officers.

[10.002] This chapter is mainly concerned with the duties owed by company directors. In law a director stands in a fiduciary position[2] to the company of which he is an officer. The duties of all fiduciaries are onerous. A fiduciary may be defined, simply, as a person in a special relationship of trust to another, whether a real person, or a legal person. No matter who is the subject of the fiduciary duties[3], the same principle applies: a fiduciary must act in a manner which is legally becoming of his office and which places the interests of the subject ahead of his own. Consequently, in many private companies where the directors are themselves the only shareholders, there is a real potential for conflict between their legal duties as directors and their selfish interests as shareholders.

[10.003] In this chapter, the duties of directors and other officers are considered in five sections:

- [A] The subject of directors' and other officers' duties.
- [B] Directors' duties at common law.
- [C] Directors' statutory duties arising on insolvency.
- [D] Secretaries' duties.
- [E] Promoters' duties.

It is the duty of each director and secretary 'to ensure that the requirements of the Companies Acts are complied with by the company'[4]. The myriad of statutory duties, both negative and positive, many of which are also criminal offences are considered in Chapter

1 See, generally, Keane, *Company Law* (3rd edn, 2000), p 350.

2 For an analogy of a director's status with that of a fiduciary, see the comments of Farwell J in *Re City Equitable Fire Insurance Co Ltd* [1925] Ch 407.

3 On the relevance of the law of 'trustee and beneficiary', to the law of 'director and company', see para **[10.048]**.

4 CA 1963, s 383(3), as replaced by CLEA 2001, s 100.

12, *Company Law Compliance and Enforcement*[5]. It should also be noted that the duties of company liquidators (voluntary and official) are considered separately in Chapter 26, Liquidators[6] and the duties of auditors are considered in Chapter 13, *Accounts and Auditors*[7].

[A] THE SUBJECT OF DIRECTORS' AND OTHER OFFICERS' DUTIES

[10.004] The general rule has always been that the directors' duties are owed to the company itself, and not to the shareholders, creditors or employees of the company. In this section the following matters are considered:

1. The general rule: duties are owed to the company.
2. The expansion of directors' duties.

The general rule: duties are owed to the company

[10.005] Directors have long been considered to stand in a fiduciary relationship to their company, and accordingly to owe duties to their company[8]. The rationale for directors being in a fiduciary relationship to the company is that, inter alia, they are agents of the company and the relationship of agent and principal will give rise to fiduciary duties[9]. Where directors act in breach of their duties the general rule is that the so-called 'proper plaintiff' in an action against the directors is the company itself[10]. Where the directors and the shareholders are one and the same persons, the duality of roles will often have the effect of preventing the company from taking legal action against errant directors. Action to enforce directors' duties is more likely to be taken where the company acts at the instigation of a liquidator, examiner or receiver. Furthermore, it should be recognised that the happiest of families and friendships can fall apart, especially where there is money at stake, and even where there are only two shareholding-directors one of the duo can embark upon a solo career in breach of his duties as a director. In such cases the problem of to whom are directors' duties owed takes on a very real significance, because for the company to take action, common form articles of association require a majority of the directors to instigate litigation[11]. However, there appears to be an increasing number of exceptions[12] and clarifications[13] to the general principle that directors' duties are only owed to the 'company'.

---

5 See para **[12.029]**.

6 See para **[26.018]** *ff*.

7 See para **[13.208]** *ff*.

8 See MacCann, 'Directors' Duties: To Whom Are They Owed?' (1991) ILT 3 and 30.

9 *Dawson International plc v Coats Paton plc* [1989] BCLC 233 at 243, per Lord Cullen. See para **[10.007]**.

10 *Foss v Harbottle* (1843) 2 Hare 461. See generally Chapter 19, *Shareholders' Remedies*, para **[19.082]** *ff*.

11 See model reg 80.

12 See para **[10.008]**.

13 See *Brunninghausen v Glavanics* (1999) 32 ACSR 294, considered at para **[10.021]**.

[10.006] The case of *Percival v Wright*[14] is the accepted authority for the proposition that directors' duties are owed to the company and not to its shareholders. In that case the plaintiff-shareholders sold their shares to three directors of the company. They discovered later that the directors intended to sell the entire of the company's undertaking to another person at a greatly inflated share price to that received by the plaintiffs. Although the sale never proceeded, had it done so, the directors would have profited handsomely. The plaintiffs alleged that the directors were in breach of their fiduciary relationship to the plaintiffs as shareholders through not disclosing the fact that it was proposed to sell the company at a greater price. It was held by Swinfen Eady J that no fiduciary duty was owed to the shareholders in such circumstances and that the directors had the power to negotiate the sale of the company and that the shareholders were deemed to be aware of the powers of the directors. Accordingly, the directors were under no obligation to disclose their negotiations to the plaintiff-shareholders.

[10.007] The Court of Session in *Dawson International plc v Coats Paton plc*[15] restated this general rule. In that case, the directors of the plaintiff and defendant-companies agreed that the plaintiff-company should take over the defendant-company by way of a share purchase. It was further agreed that the directors of the defendant-company would recommend the plaintiff-company's bid to the defendant's shareholders and that the directors of the defendant-company would not assist any other prospective purchaser. In breach of this agreement, the defendant's directors co-operated with a different purchaser and the plaintiff-company sued the defendant-company's directors for breach of the agreement. The defendant's directors claimed in their defence that they owed a duty to the shareholders of the defendant-company to advise them of the advantages and disadvantages of all takeover bids. It was held that the directors owed no such duty to the shareholders and that their duties were owed to the company itself. Consequently, their only concern should have been which takeover bid was in the best interests of the company. Lord Cullen said:

> 'It is well recognised that directors owe fiduciary duties to the company. Thus the directors have the duty of fiduciaries with respect to the property and funds of the company...These fiduciary duties spring from the relationship of the directors to the company, of which they are its agents...In contrast I see no good reason why it should be supposed that directors are, in general, under a fiduciary duty to the shareholders, and in particular current shareholders with respect to the disposal of their shares in the most advantageous way. The directors are not normally the agents of the current shareholders...The cases and other authorities to which I was referred do not seem to me to establish any such fiduciary duty [to the shareholders]...
>
> What is in the interests of current shareholders who are sellers of their shares may not necessarily coincide with what is in the interests of the company. The creation of parallel duties could lead to conflict. *Directors have but one master, the company.*'[16]

It should be remembered that the company in question was a public limited company ('PLC'). Although the principle that directors' duties are owed to the company remains

---

[14] *Percival v Wright* [1902] 2 Ch 421.

[15] *Dawson International plc v Coats Paton plc* [1989] BCLC 233.

[16] [1989] BCLC 233 at 243. Emphasis added.

true in the case of private companies, it is suggested that in private companies it is more likely that the directors may (by virtue of collateral contracts) be found to be the agents of the shareholders and consequently to owe fiduciary duties to the shareholders[17].

The expansion of directors' duties

[10.008] The current trend would seem to be towards the broadening of directors' duties towards persons beyond the company. Although the Supreme Court has refused to stretch the expansion to include shareholders' interests in the value of their shareholdings[18], recent developments have extended directors' duties to creditors[19] and, by statute, to employees and members[20]. At this juncture it is proposed to consider the extension of directors' duties to the following categories of persons:

(a) Duties to creditors.

(b) Duties to employees and members.

(c) Duties to shareholders.

(a) Duties to creditors

[10.009] A series of Irish judgments have held that when a company is insolvent, even if not in liquidation, the directors of the company will owe a duty to the company's creditors[21]. The principle relied upon by the Irish judges in all of these judgments was explained by Street CJ in the Court of Appeal in New South Wales, in the case of *Kinsella v Russell Kinsella Property Ltd*[22] where he said:

> 'In a solvent company the proprietary interests of the shareholders entitled them as a general body to be regarded as the company when questions of the duty of directors arise. If, as a general body they authorise or ratify a particular action of the directors there can be no challenge to the validity of what the directors have done. But where a company is insolvent the interests of the creditors intrude. They become prospectively entitled, through the mechanism of liquidation, to displace the power of the shareholders and the directors to deal with the company's assets. It is in a practical sense their assets and not the shareholders' assets that, through the medium of the company, or under the management of the directors pending either liquidation, return to solvency, or the imposition of some alternative administration.'[23]

This principle may be taken as representing the modern Irish law on the duties owed by directors to an insolvent company's creditors, having been cited with approval by Blayney J in the Supreme Court decision in *Re Frederick Inns Ltd*[24]. One consequence,

---

17 See para **[10.017]**.

18 *O'Neill v Ryan* [1993] ILRM 557. See Chapter 19, *Shareholders' Remedies*, para **[19.096]**.]

19 When a company becomes insolvent: *Re Frederick Inns Ltd* [1994] 1 ILRM 387, see para **[10.012]**.

20 Directors must have regard to the interests of employees: CA 1990, s 52(1), see para **[10.016]**.

21 *Parkes v Hong Kong & Shanghai Bank Corp* [1990] ILRM 341, per Blayney J (High Court), *Re Frederick Inns Ltd* [1991] ILRM 582, per Lardner J (High Court) and [1994] 1 ILRM 387, per Blayney J (Supreme Court); *Jones v Gunn* [1997] 2 ILRM 245, per McGuinness J.

22 *Kinsella v Russell Kinsella Property Ltd* [1986] 4 NSWLR 722.

23 [1986] 4 NSWLR 722 at 730.

24 *Re Frederick Inns Ltd* [1994] 1 ILRM 387.

identified by McGuinness J in *Jones v Gunn*[25], is that the directors of an insolvent company 'may not make payments which benefit either closely connected companies or themselves personally to the detriment of the general and independent creditors'. It is submitted that this is merely illustrative, and is not an exhaustive statement of directors' duties to creditors arising on insolvency.

[10.010] As will be considered, those Irish judgments as have cited the foregoing passage in *Kinsella* have taken it as authority for the imposition of duties on directors of insolvent companies, in favour of creditors. There is another interpretation open, as identified by Tulson J in *Yukong Line Ltd of Korea v Rendsburg Investments Corp of Liberia (No 2)*[26]. In that case it was held that the transfer of assets in disregard of creditors' interests was a breach of duty owed to the company, the only redress for which was the statutory remedies available in any liquidation. The judge concluded:

> 'Where a director, or person having the management, of an insolvent company acts in breach of his duty to the company by causing assets of the company to be transferred in disregard of the interests of its creditor or creditors, under English law he is answerable through the scheme which Parliament has provided. In my judgment he does not owe a direct fiduciary duty towards an individual creditor, nor is an individual creditor entitled to sue for breach of the fiduciary duty owed by the director to the company.'[27]

It is thought that the interpretation given by the Irish courts is to be preferred.

[10.011] The first[28] Irish judgment to recognise this principle was that of Blayney J in *Parkes v Hong Kong & Shanghai Bank Corp*[29]. The facts in that case have already been given in Chapter 7, *Corporate Contracts, Capacity and Authority*[30], but in summary the issue was, inter alia, whether the fact that a company was insolvent meant that a disposition of its assets was ultra vires. The liquidator relied upon the English case of *West Mercia Safetywear Ltd. v Dodd*[31]. In that case the defendant was a director of the plaintiff-company and another company, which was a wholly-owned subsidiary of the former. The plaintiff-company owed the defendant £30,000, and although an accountant advised both companies not to operate their bank accounts, the defendant transferred £4,000 from the plaintiff's account into the account of the other company. Later, both companies went into liquidation, and the liquidator of the plaintiff-company issued misfeasance proceedings against the defendant, alleging inter alia that the defendant owed a fiduciary duty to the plaintiff-company. This was accepted by the Court of

---

25 *Jones v Gunn* [1997] 2 ILRM 245 at 263.

26 *Yukong Line Ltd of Korea v Rendsburg Investments Corp of Liberia (No 2)* [1998] 4 All ER 82.

27 [1998] 4 All ER 82 at 99e–f.

28 An earlier statement of the Irish law on directors' duties to creditors is found in the judgment of O'Hanlon J in *Byrne v Shelbourne FC Ltd* (8 February 1984, unreported), High Court, where he said: '...before any limited company can dispose of all its assets, it must do the best it can for the creditors and explore all reasonable possibilities of obtaining a better offer before selling out to a particular bidder.' In that case the plaintiff unsuccessfully claimed that the company made a sale at an undervalue to the detriment of the creditors, of which he was one.

29 *Parkes v Hong Kong & Shanghai Bank Corp* [1990] ILRM 341.

30 Chapter 7, *Corporate Capacity and Authority*, para **[7.064]**.

31 *West Mercia Safetywear Ltd. v Dodd* [1988] BCLC 250.

Appeal, which held that the director '...was guilty of breach of duty when, for his own purposes, he caused the £4,000 to be transferred in disregard of the interests of the general creditors of this insolvent company.'

In the *Parkes* case Blayney J went on to cite the principle of law stated by Street CJ in the *Kinsella* case, but although he quoted both *Kinsella* and *West Mercia* cases with approval, the learned judge went on to distinguish them from the case in hand. In both cases, he said, the question concerned breach of directors' duties or abuse of directors' authority, while in the case in hand the question concerned lack of corporate capacity, or the doctrine of ultra vires. In addition, Blayney J distinguished the case in hand by saying:

> '...the defendant in the *West Mercia* case was aware that the company whose money he transferred was insolvent whereas, in the present case, there is no evidence that [the defendant] knew the claimant company was insolvent.'[32]

It would appear that in the *Parkes* case Blayney J accepted the distinction between solvent and insolvent companies, and that the directors of insolvent companies owed duties to that company's creditors. This distinction marked a novel departure in company law, since it represented the first inroad in Irish common law corporate jurisprudence to the general principle that officers' duties are only owed to their company.

[10.012] The other landmark Irish case on the duties of directors to creditors where a company is insolvent is *Re Frederick Inns Ltd*[33] where, in both the High Court and the Supreme Court, Street CJ's statement of principle was cited with approval. In that case, the directors of a group of companies caused certain of those companies to sell their principal assets and to pay the Revenue Commissioners not only the individual company's debts, but also debts owed by other companies within the group, in flagrant disregard of the concept of separate legal personality. After citing the judgments of Street CJ in the *Kinsella* case and of Dillon LJ in the *West Mercia* case, Lardner J in the High Court held that the statements of law therein seemed to him:

> '...to be consonant with the intent of Irish company legislation and to be appropriate and applicable to insolvent companies in Irish law. In my judgment therefore the payments to the Revenue which are in question were also misapplications of the respective companies' assets because they were made when the companies were insolvent and the payments were in disregard of the rights and interests of the general creditors.'[34]

Lardner J also said that:

> '...the payments to the Revenue which are in question were made by the authority of the directors of the respective companies in breach of the duty which the company and the directors owed to the general creditors of these insolvent companies.'[35]

The Revenue Commissioners unsuccessfully appealed to the Supreme Court against Lardner J's decision. Blayney J, who gave the Supreme Court's judgment, held that the

32 [1990] ILRM 341 at 349.

33 *Re Frederick Inns Ltd* [1991] ILRM 582 (High Court) and [1994] 1 ILRM 387 (Supreme Court). See Fealy, 'The Role of Equity in the Winding Up of a Company' [1995] 17 DULJ 18.

34 [1991] ILRM 582 at 590.

35 [1991] ILRM 582 at 589. Emphasis added.

companies' directors owed duties to the companies' creditors when the company became insolvent. After citing an old authority[36] for the proposition that a company's property is trust property when a company is being wound up, Blayney J said:

> 'It is clear from this case that as soon as a winding-up order has been made the company ceases to be the beneficial owner of its assets, with the result that the directors no longer have power to dispose of them. Where, as here, a company's situation was such that any creditor could have caused it to be wound up on the ground of solvency, I consider that it can equally well be said that the company had ceased to be the beneficial owner of its assets with the result that the directors would have had no power to use the company's assets to discharge the liabilities of other companies. Once the company clearly had to be wound up and its assets applied pro tanto in discharge of its liabilities, the directors had a duty to the creditors to preserve the assets to enable this to be done, or at least not to dissipate them.'[37]

After referring to the judgment of Street CJ in the *Kinsella* case, Blayney J adopted and followed the statement of principle quoted above[38]. Indicative of the strength of the principle that directors of an insolvent company owe duties to creditors is Blayney J's conclusion that the directors could not lawfully and effectively have made the payments to the Revenue Commissioners. Thus, where directors act in breach of their duties to the creditors of an insolvent company their actions will properly be termed 'unlawful'.

[10.013] It is only where a company is insolvent that directors will owe duties to creditors. In *Parkes v Hong Kong & Shanghai Bank Corp*[39] Blayney J appears to have adopted a subjective test by distinguishing the facts of the case in hand case from those in the *West Mercia* case, saying that there was no evidence that the defendant in the *Parkes* case knew that the company was insolvent[40].

[10.014] It may be noted that while the authorities in England are equivocal they are leaning towards the finding of a duty to the creditors of a company by the directors[41].

---

36 *Re Oriental Inland Steam Co* (1874) 9 Ch App 557, cited by Templeman J in *Ayerst v C & K (Construction) Ltd* [1974] 1 All ER 676.

37 [1994] 1 ILRM 387 at 396.

38 See para **[10.009]**.

39 *Parkes v Hong Kong & Shanghai Bank Corp* [1990] ILRM 341.

40 [1990] ILRM 341 at 349.

41 See *Lonrho v Shell Petroleum Ltd* [1980] 1 WLR 627; *Multinational Gas & Petrochemical Co v Multinational Gas & Petrochemical Services Ltd*; *Charterbridge Corp Ltd v Lloyds Bank Ltd* [1969] 2 All ER 1185; *Re Halt Garage (1964) Ltd*; and *Re Horsley & Weight Ltd* [1982] 3 All ER 1045. The cases of *West Mercia Safetywear Ltd v Dodd* [1988] BCLC 250 and *Winkworth v Edward Baron Developments Ltd* [1987] 1 All ER 114 must be distinguished. In the latter case the House of Lords per Lord Templeman said:

> '...a company owes a duty to its creditors, present and future. The company is not bound to pay off every debt as soon as it is incurred and the company is not obliged to avoid all ventures which involve an element of risk, but the company owes a duty to its creditors to keep property inviolate and available for the repayment of its debts. The conscience of the company is confided to its directors. A duty is owed by the directors to the company and to the creditors of the company to ensure that the affairs of the company are properly administered and that its property is not dissipated or exploited for the benefit of the directors themselves to the prejudice of the creditors.'

This case was cited with approval in *Jones v Gunn* [1977] 2 ILRM 245 at 260.

Several commonwealth cases also strongly endorse this trend. The extension of the duty can be explained on the basis of the general extension of the duty of care to one's neighbours in tort law. In the New Zealand case of *Nicholson v Permakraft (NZ) Ltd*[42] Cooke J heard a misfeasance suit[43] against the directors of a company resulting from the distribution to shareholders of a profit arising from the revaluation of certain properties owned by the company. On the facts, it was held that the directors had no reason to doubt the solvency of the company and so the remainder of the judgment is obiter dicta. Even so, the learned judge's rationale for the directors owing a duty of care is instructive. It was said that the creditors of a company are entitled to consideration in the following circumstances: where the company is insolvent; where it is near insolvent; where it is of doubtful solvency; or where a proposed course of action places the creditors in jeopardy, based on business ethics and upon general principles of the duty of care[44].

[10.015] It is interesting to note that Cooke J believed that where the shareholders ratify the actions of the directors the acts done cannot be challenged by the liquidator or creditors. Perhaps time will show that the inherent power of the shareholders to ratify the actions of directors will be confined to situations where the company is solvent, and that the concept of solvency will surpass the notion of the commencement of the winding up as the sole determinant of the shareholders' power to do this[45]. In the context of the Irish private company, where the directors will often be the shareholders, it is submitted that if the expansion of the duties owed by directors to creditors is to have any teeth, this further step must be taken, and the shareholders cannot be permitted to ratify the wrongs of the directors when the company is insolvent. It must not be forgotten, however, that the need for such a shift is to some extent obviated by the enactment of the provisions on reckless trading, since the difference between trading recklessly and breaching a duty to creditors is narrow[46].

(b) Duties to employees and members

[10.016] The statutory duty introduced by the 1990 Act that directors should have regard to the interests of the company's employees and members is of dubious value to its intended beneficiaries. Section 52 of the Companies Act 1990 ('CA 1990') provides:

---

42 *Nicholson v Permakraft (NZ) Ltd* [1985] 1 NZLR 242.

43 See para **[10.129]**.

44 Note that Sealy, *Cases and Materials in Company Law* (4th edn, 1989), p 250 believes that Cooke J's judgment is too wide.

45 Such may be said to be implicit in the judgment of Blayney J in *Re Frederick Inns Ltd* [1994] 1 ILRM 387 at 396 where he quoted from the judgment of James LJ in *Re Oriental Inland Steam Co* (1874) 9 Ch App 557 who said: 'The English Act of Parliament has enacted that in the case of a winding–up the assets of the company so wound up are to be collected and applied in discharge of its liabilities [there is a similar provision in CA 1963, s 235]. That makes the property of the company clearly trust property. It is property affected by the Act of Parliament with an obligation to be dealt with by the proper officer in a particular way. Then it has ceased to be beneficially the property of the company; and, being so, it has ceased to be liable to be seized by the execution creditors of the company'.

46 See para **[10.081]**.

'(1) The matters to which the directors of a company are to have regard in the performance of their functions shall include the interests of the company's employees in general, as well as the interests of its members.

(2) Accordingly, the duty imposed by this section on the directors shall be owed by them to the company (and the company alone) and shall be enforceable in the same way as any other fiduciary duty owed to a company by its directors.'

Truly, what the legislature gave by sub-s (1), it took away by sub-s (2). What began as a flame of potentially far greater significance than the Supreme Court's extension of directors' duties to creditors of an insolvent company in *Re Frederick Inns Ltd*[47], became a wet squib. The net effect of s 52 may be said to be: directors are obliged to have regard to the interests of employees and members but the recipients of the statutory favour may not themselves enforce the directors' duty. Only where an altruistic liquidator is appointed to the company may the duty to employees be vindicated; only where the aggrieved members can muster sufficient voting power in general meeting to compel the directors to have regard to them, may the duty owed to them by s 52 be vindicated[48]. The difficulty, of course, with extending the categories of persons with locus standi to sue directors is the possibility of a multiplicity of actions, something which, in this litigious age, must be a concern.

(c) Duties to shareholders

[10.017] Judicial attempts to expand directors' duties to shareholders have been varied and can often be seen as stopgap attempts to avoid an inequity or injustice caused by the general rule that duties are only owed to the company[49]. Such attempts can best be seen as a recognition of the principle that, although directors are agents of the company and in consequence automatically owe fiduciary duties to the company, there is no rule of law that directors cannot also be agents of the shareholders and so stand in a fiduciary relationship to them[50]. Keane J put the matter thus in the Supreme Court decision of *Crindle Investments v Wymes* [51]:

'There can be do doubt that, in general, although directors of a company occupy a fiduciary position in relation to the company, they do not owe a fiduciary duty, merely by virtue of their offices, to the individual members. That was the effect of the decision in the leading case of *Percival v Wright* [1902] 2 Ch 421 but it has been emphasised in subsequent decisions that, in particular circumstances, a company director may indeed be in a position where he owes a fiduciary duty to individual shareholders. A helpful example is the decision of the New Zealand Court of Appeal in *Coleman v Myers* [1977] 2 NZLR 225, which is referred to in the judgment under appeal.'[52]

---

47 *Re Frederick Inns Ltd* [1994] 1 ILRM 387. See para **[10.012]**.

48 See Chapter 8, *Corporate Governance: Management by the Directors*, para **[8.013]** *ff*.

49 See *Coleman v Myers* [1977] 2 NZRL 225, considered at para **[10.019]**.

50 See *Re Chez Nico (Restaurants) Ltd* [1992] BCLC 192; *Platt v Platt* [1999] 2 BCLC 745; *Peskin and another v Anderson* [2000] 2 BCLC 1; and *Brunninghausen v Glavanics* (1999) 32 ACSR 294.

51 *Crindle Investments v Wymes* [1998] 2 ILRM 275.

52 [1998] 2 ILRM 275 at 288.

In that case the Supreme Court held that mutual trust and confidence was not a feature of the relationship between the parties which led to the proceedings and, accordingly, no fiduciary duties were owed by the defendant-directors to the members. Again, in the English case of *Peskin v Anderson*[53] where Neuberger J said:

> 'I am satisfied, both as a matter of principle and in light of the state of the authorities, that *Percival v Wright* [1902] 2 Ch 421 is good law in the sense that a director of a company has no general fiduciary duty to shareholders. However, I am also satisfied that, in appropriate and specific circumstances, a director can be under a fiduciary duty to a shareholder. It seems to me that as a general proposition a director's primary fiduciary duty to shareholders (a) would involve placing an unfair, unrealistic and uncertain burden on a director and (b) would present him frequently with a position where his two competing duties, namely his undoubted fiduciary duty to the company and his alleged fiduciary duty to shareholders, would be in conflict.'[54]

So in *Platt and another v Platt*[55], a case involving three brother-shareholders, it was held that the defendant brother shareholder did owe fiduciary duties to his brothers, the plaintiffs. The circumstances giving rise to this duty were that the defendant had induced the plaintiffs to sell their shares to him for a nominal amount at a time when the company was in financial difficulties. The defendant had told the plaintiffs that this was necessary to enable the business to be sold at the insistence of BMW and that if the sale did not proceed their shares would be re-transferred. The defendant refused to transfer the shares back and when he eventually sold the business himself, the plaintiffs successfully sued for, inter alia, breach of fiduciary duty.

[10.018] The clearest situation in which directors will stand in a fiduciary relationship to the shareholders is where they expressly undertake certain obligations to the shareholders. Authority here is *Allen v Hyatt*[56] where the directors of a company induced the shareholders to give them options to buy their shares, on the pretext that this would assist the directors who were negotiating an amalgamation with another company. A dispute arose when, upon the terms of the amalgamation being agreed, the directors exercised the options to sell the shares and made a personal profit. It was held by the Privy Council that the directors were obliged to account to the shareholders for the profit made by them. Viscount Haldane LC distinguished this case from the general rule that directors' duties were owed to the company, saying:

> 'The [directors] appeared to have been under the impression that [they] were entitled in all the circumstances to act as though they owed no duty to individual shareholders. No doubt the duty of the directors was primarily one to the company itself. It might be that in circumstances such as those in *Percival v Wright* they could deal at arm's length with a shareholder. But the facts in the present case were widely different from those in *Percival v Wright*, and their Lordships thought that the directors must here be taken to have held

[53] *Peskin and another v Anderson* [2000] 2 BCLC 1. The decision was upheld by the Court of Appeal: [2001] 1 BCLC 372.

[54] [2000] 2 BCLC 1 at 14c–e.

[55] *Platt v Platt* [1999] 2 BCLC 745.

[56] *Allen v Hyatt* (1914) 30 TLR 444 (Privy Council).

> themselves out to the individual shareholders as acting for them on the same footing as they were acting for the company itself, that was, as agents...'[57]

Because of the factual finding of agency, the court was able to hold that the directors stood in a fiduciary relationship to the shareholders.

[10.019] It has been said that the 'traditional authorities are now on the retreat'[58] and evidence that the Irish courts may be inclined towards extending directors' duties to shareholders is seen in *Securities Trust Ltd v Associated Properties Ltd*[59]. In that case, McWilliam J suggested that the directors of a company were 'to some extent in a fiduciary position' to the shareholders who were entitled to be given reasonably full particulars by the directors of a takeover of the company being proposed to be financed by the company itself[60]. In the New Zealand case of *Coleman v Myers*[61] the retreat of the general rule that directors' duties are only owed to the company is also evident. Of particular interest is that that case concerned a family-type private company. One of the defendant directors acquired a controlling interest in the company and the plaintiff minority shareholders were forced to sell their shares by virtue of a statutory provision, similar to the Companies Act 1963, s 204 ('CA 1963')[62], whereupon the plaintiff-shareholders alleged that the directors were in breach of fiduciary duties owed to them. In the New Zealand Court of Appeal the fact that the company was a closely-held private company was crucial to the court in deciding that the directors were in a fiduciary position to the shareholders, since the latter often looked to the directors for advice. By withholding information on the value of the shares the directors were found to have breached their duty to the shareholders. It is submitted that the true authority of this case is that directors are not automatically precluded from standing in a fiduciary relationship to the shareholders of a company, and where they are agents of the shareholders they may, on the facts of the case, be in a fiduciary position to them. As Woodhouse J said:

> 'In my opinion it is not the law that anybody holding the office of director of a limited liability company is for that reason alone to be released from what otherwise would be regarded as a fiduciary responsibility owed to those in the position of shareholders of the same company...it is my opinion that the standard of conduct required from a director in relation to dealings with a shareholder will differ depending upon all the surrounding circumstances and the nature of the responsibility which in a real and practical sense the director has assumed towards the shareholder.'[63]

This would seem to be an eminently sensible position to adopt, because unlike the position between a director and his company, the relationship between a director and a shareholder does not per se give rise to fiduciary duties: such will only arise where there are special circumstances which give rise to a fiduciary duty[64]. Whether or not a

57 Cf *Dawson International plc v Coats Paton plc* [1989] BCLC 233, considered at para **[10.007]**.

58 See Ussher, *Company Law in Ireland* (1986), p 205.

59 *Securities Trust Ltd v Associated Properties Ltd* (19 November 1980, unreported), High Court.

60 See also *Heron International Ltd v Lord Grade* [1983] BCLC 244, where it was held that a duty can be owed to shareholders where a takeover bid has been made.

61 *Coleman v Myers* [1977] 2 NZLR 225.

62 See Chapter 16, *Share Transfer in Private Companies*, para **[16.084]** *ff*.

63 [1977] 2 NZLR 225 at 324.

64 See *Re Chez Nico (Restaurants) Ltd* [1992] BCLC 192. See also *Platt v Platt* [1999] 2 BCLC 745 and *Peskin v Anderson* [2000] 2 BCLC 1.

fiduciary duty exists will therefore depend upon the circumstances in each case. As Neuberger J said in *Peskin v Anderson*[65] useful guidance as to whether a fiduciary duty exists is seen in the observations of Millett LJ in *Bristol and West Building Society v Mothew*[66] where he said:

> 'A fiduciary is someone who has undertaken to act for or on behalf of another in a particular matter in circumstances which give rise to a relationship of trust and confidence. The distinguishing obligation of a fiduciary is the obligation of loyalty. The principal is entitled to the single-minded loyalty of his fiduciary. The core liability has several facets. A fiduciary must act in good faith; he must not make a profit out of his trust; he must not place himself in a position where his duty and his interest may conflict; he may not act for his own benefit or the benefit of a third person without the informed consent of his principal. This is not intended to be an exhaustive list, but it is sufficient to indicate the nature of fiduciary obligations..'[67]

[10.020] In private companies the relationship between the directors and the shareholders can sometimes ground a fiduciary relationship[68]. The dicta in *Coleman v Myers*[69] clearly show the possibility of a fiduciary relationship arising in the context of a private company. In a passage, cited with approval by Keane J in the Supreme Court in *Crindle Investments v Wymes*[70], Woodhouse J said:

> '...the courts can and should find some practical means of giving effect to sensible and fair principles of commercial morality in the cases that come before them; and while it may not be possible to lay down any general test as to when the fiduciary duty will arise for a company director or to prescribe the exact conduct which will always discharge it when it does, there are nevertheless some factors that will usually have an influence upon a decision, one way or the other. They include, I think, dependence upon information and advice, the existence of a relationship of confidence, the significance of some particular transaction for the parties and, of course, the extent of any positive action taken by or on behalf of the director or directors to promote it. In the present case each one of those matters had more than ordinary significance and when they are taken together they leave me in no doubt that each of the two directors did owe a fiduciary duty to the individual shareholders.'[71]

It may be noted, however, that in *Peskin v Anderson*[72] Neuberger J cautioned against compartmentalising a type of company – such as a private company or a family company – and saying that fiduciary duties to shareholders can only arise in such companies and not in others[73].

---

65 *Peskin v Anderson* [2000] 2 BCLC 1. The decision was upheld by the Court of Appeal: [2001] 1 BCLC 372.

66 *Bristol and West Building Society v Mothew* [1996] 4 All ER 698.

67 [1996] 4 All ER 698 at 711–712.

68 See Keane, *Equity and the Law of Trusts in the Republic of Ireland* (1988), ch 29.

69 *Coleman v Myers* [1977] 2 NZLR 225.

70 *Crindle Investments v Wymes* [1998] 2 ILRM 275 at 288.

71 [1998] 2 ILRM 275 at 325.

72 *Peskin and another v Anderson* [2000] 2 BCLC 1. The decision was upheld by the Court of Appeal: [2001] 1 BCLC 372.

73 [2000] 2 BCLC 1 at 15a–b.

[10.021] More recently, in *Brunninghausen v Glavanics*[74] the New South Wales Court of Appeal refused to follow *Percival v Wright*[75] and found that the directors did owe a duty to the company's shareholders. The circumstances were that the company had two shareholding-directors and, following a disagreement, one became passive in the running of the company. The other director agreed to buy the passive director's shares, but did not disclose that he was in discussions with a third party concerning the sale of the entire shareholding. The passive director was paid ten-times less for his shares than the active director obtained from the third party. Handley JA held that the decision in *Percival v Wright* did not stand in the way of the recognition of a fiduciary duty by directors. This case went further than both *Coleman v Myers* and *Allen v Hyatt*. Unlike *Coleman v Myers*, there was no relationship of actual trust and confidence and no such relationship invited by the defendant-director; unlike *Allen v Hyatt*, the defendant-director had not placed himself in a fiduciary relationship with the shareholders akin to that owed by agents to principals[76]. Handley JA's reasoning is compelling. Whilst the statement that directors owe a duty to their company is undoubtedly correct and its validity is undiminished, he said that:

> 'Any statement that the defendant owed a duty to the company in relation to his dealings with the plaintiff over his shares is meaningless. Such a duty would lack all practical content. The company could not suffer any loss from the breach of such a duty, and had no interest in its loyal and disinterested performance. Where a director's fiduciary duties are owed to the company this prevents the recognition of concurrent and identical duties to its shareholders covering the same subject matter. *However this should not preclude the recognition of a fiduciary duty to shareholders in relation to dealings in their shares where this would not compete with any duty owed to the company.*'[77]

This is precisely what Handley JA went on to find, namely: that directors can owe a fiduciary duty 'to the shareholders where there are negotiations for a takeover or an acquisition of the company's undertaking' which 'would require the directors to loyally promote the joint interests of all shareholders'. Any conflict that might arise would be if they sought to prefer their personal interests to the joint interest and Handley JA said that this was 'the very conduct which would be proscribed by the duty.'[78] On the facts it was found that the defendant-director did owe the plaintiff as shareholder a fiduciary duty, which had been breached by his non-disclosure of the negotiations for the sale of the company's assets before the purchase of the plaintiff's shares.

[B] DIRECTORS' DUTIES AT COMMON LAW

The nature and source of directors' common law duties

[10.022] Having explored the question of to whom the fiduciary duties of the directors are owed, it next falls to examine the nature of such fiduciary duties. The fiduciary duties of directors may be reduced to three broad principles:

---

74 *Brunninghausen v Glavanics* (1999) 32 ACSR 294. See Comment, 'The Last Rites for Percival v Wright' (2000) 21 Co Lawyer 261.
75 *Percival v Wright* [1902] 2 Ch 421.
76 See para 53 of the judgment.
77 At para 58 of the judgment. Emphasis added.
78 At para 106–107 of the judgment.

— Directors must exercise their powers[79] in good faith and in the interests of the company as a whole.

— Directors are not allowed to make an undisclosed personal profit from their position as directors, and must account[80] for any profit which they secretly derive from their position.

— Directors are obliged to carry out their functions with due care, skill and diligence[81].

The sources of directors' duties are diverse[82]. They can be summarised as follows:

— *Duties arising from a director's position as an agent*: Since a company must act through its agents, the directors under common form articles of association[83] are appointed the company's agents. As agents, the directors have fiduciary obligations to their principal, the company.

— *Duties arising from a director's status as a trustee and fiduciary*: Company directors are in charge of property which is not their own and accordingly, they are quasi-trustees for the legal owner: the company[84]. As trustees, directors are also fiduciaries.

— *Duties arising from a director's status as an employee*: Directors may have a written or oral contract of employment and will thus owe the normal duties owed by employees to their employer. While not fiduciary in nature, an employee owes duties of loyalty and fidelity which are important concepts in the context of competition with the company.

— *Duties arising from a director's proximity to a 'neighbour'*: By virtue of Lord Atkin's analysis in *Donoghue v Stevenson*[85] directors may be said to owe a duty of care in tort to those who are their neighbours, and so must take reasonable care to avoid acts or omissions which they can reasonably foresee would be liable to injure their neighbour.

The diverse sources of directors' duties has been recognised by the Company Law Review Group, which has said:

> 'the fiduciary duties of directors have been enunciated on a case by case basis rather than in a codified form…the Review Group has come firmly to the view that inaccessibility and incomprehensibility of the law concerning the duties of directors can be remedied by their being stated in statute law. Such inaccessibility and incomprehensibility can in

79 Ie the powers expressly delegated to them by the shareholders of the company pursuant to the company's articles of association, and powers which directors implicitly have.

80 To 'account' in law has a very specific meaning: see Keane, *Equity and the Law of Trusts in the Republic of Ireland*, p 291 *ff*.

81 See para **[10.063]** *ff*.

82 See generally, Loose & Yelland, *The Company Director* (6th edn, 1987), ch 4.

83 Typically, model reg 80: see Chapter 8, *Corporate Governance: Management by the Directors*, para **[8.004]**.

84 See *JJ Harrison (Properties) Ltd v Harrison* [2002] 1 BCLC 162, [2001] EWCA Civ 1467.

85 *Donoghue v Stevenson* [1932] AC 562.

practice be a disincentive to compliance or a ready excuse to the indolent who have no wish to comply with such duties.'[86]

[10.023] At the outset it is important to remember that only persons who are directors owe directors' duties. So, a person who is a 'director elect' will not, generally, owe the duties to a company of which he is a prospective director[87]. Directors' duties will, however, be owed by de facto directors, executive and non-executive directors; and nominee directors[88]. In this section the following aspects of directors' duties at common law are considered:

1. The exercise of directors' powers.
2. Fiduciary duties: conflicts of interests.
3. Fiduciary duties: competition with the company.
4. Directors' duties of skill, care and diligence.
5. Judicial relief for directors and indemnities.

The exercise of directors' powers

[10.024] The powers of directors must be exercised bona fide and in the interests of the company. This test for the proper exercise of directors' power also applies in other circumstances, such as in the exercise of the shareholders' powers to alter a company's constitutional documentation[89]. Eight specific matters are considered here:

(a) In the interests of the company as a whole.

(b) Good faith.

(c) The exercise of discretion.

(d) Fettering directors' discretion.

(e) The duties of nominee directors.

(f) Token directors in family companies and 'sexually transmitted debt'.

(g) The delegation of directors' powers.

(h) The consequences of abuse of directors' powers.

(a) In the interests of the company as a whole

[10.025] The concept of company as a whole has been examined in Chapter 3[90]. In essence, this concept means, in the first place, the company as a separate legal entity, and in the second place, the shareholders as a whole. It is submitted that in the context of a private company it is central to the nature of such ventures that the company as a whole ought to mean the shareholders as a whole because this recognises that the

86 See the *Company Law Review Group's First Report (2000–2001)*, para 11.3.1 at p 238. See, further, the Review Group's Report at para 11.3.7 where a proposed statement of statutory duties is set out.

87 *Lindgen v L & P Estates Ltd* [1968] 1 Ch 572.

88 See para **[10.040]**.

89 See Chapter 3, *Private Constitutional Documentation*, para **[3.065]** *ff*.

90 See Chapter 3, *Private Constitutional Documentation*, para **[3.077]** *ff*.

shareholders hold ultimate control of a company. In *G & S Doherty Ltd v Doherty*[91] Henchy J said of the exercise of the directors' powers to issue shares:

> '...directors are in a fiduciary position, and must exercise their power bona fide for the benefit of the company as a whole, that is to say, the shareholders as a whole : see *Greenhalgh v Arderne Cinemas Limited* [1951] 1 Ch 286 at 291. Where, as in the present case, directors issue shares for the ulterior purpose of benefiting themselves to the detriment of other shareholders, then it cannot be said that the issue of shares is bona fide or for the benefit of the company as a whole.'

This reference to fiduciary duties being owed to 'the shareholders as a whole' does not detract from the principle that those duties are owed to the company. Rather, such a statement is indicative of a recognition of the reality that the shareholders are the ultimate owners of the separate entity which is the company.

[10.026] It follows from this that directors must not exercise their powers in furtherance of their own personal interests. In practice, often the most blatant flouting of this duty is relatively common, particularly where proprietary-directors 'forget' that the company's assets are not theirs. Directors may not misapply their companies' assets in favour of themselves or their nominees[92] or acquire assets at an undervalue[93]. A straightforward example of this is seen in *Re Ashclad Ltd; Forrest v Harrington and Culleton*[94] where upon the expiry of a financial lease of valuable machinery a company was entitled to acquire the machinery for the nominal sum of £121. Instead of the company acquiring the machinery for that amount, one of its directors paid the £121 and subsequently claimed, after the company had gone into liquidation, that the machinery was not a company asset. This was rejected by Geoghegan J who held that because the director owed the company a fiduciary duty, he was a bare trustee of the machinery and the judge made an order vesting the machinery in the company's liquidator[95].

(b) Good faith

[10.027] Directors must exercise the powers which are entrusted to them in good faith, or bona fide[96]. The exact meaning of the phrase 'in good faith', appears to be relatively straightforward. Where a director exercises his powers, his intention is the paramount consideration. In determining a director's intention, a court will take cognisance of the evidential circumstances surrounding the director's action[97]. The question of good faith

[91] *G & S Doherty Ltd v Doherty* (19 June 1969, unreported), High Court, per Henchy J.

[92] *Gwembe Valley Development Co Ltd v Koshy* [1998] 2 BCLC 613.

[93] *Daniels v Daniels* [1978] Ch 406.

[94] *Re Ashclad Ltd; Forrest v Harrington and Culleton* (5 April 2000, unreported), High Court (Geoghegan J).

[95] (5 April 2000, unreported), High Court at p 17.

[96] See generally Chapter 16, *Share Transfer in Private Companies*, para **[16.037]** where the exercise of directors' powers in good faith is considered in the context of refusing to register a share transfer.

[97] See *Re Smith & Fawcett Ltd* [1942] 2 All ER 542 at 543, where Lord Greene MR said of the exercise of directors' powers that: 'They must exercise their discretion bona fide in what they consider not what the court may consider to be in the interests of the company...'.

usually arises in the negative in deciding not what is the proper exercise of the directors' powers, but rather what constitutes an abuse of the directors' powers.

[10.028] In determining a director's intention, many cases have made it clear that the courts will not interrogate the directors[98]. In *Re North City Milling Co Ltd*[99] Meredith MR said:

> 'I am of the opinion that the law allows the directors to hold their tongues. It allows them to say that everything was done honestly and bona fide in the interest of their company;...and according to my view I have no power to make them say more.'

In *Re Hafner*[100] Black J said of the directors' failure to explain the reasons for their actions:

> 'They are not bound to assign their reasons, and the court is not entitled to infer merely from their omission to do so that their reasons were not legitimate. Hedging around with the privilege of remaining mute and the prima facie presumption of rectitude the astutely silent director who wishes to exercise [his powers] illegitimately may well consider himself all but invulnerable.'

However, silence in the face of questions does not result in mandatory answering, but can lead to an adverse inference (namely bad faith) being drawn by the courts.

[10.029] The duty imposed on directors to act bona fide in the interests of the company is a subjective duty[101]. As Jonathan Parker J said in *Regentcrest plc v Cohen and another*[102]:

> 'The question is not whether, viewed objectively by the court, the particular act or omission which is challenged was in fact in the interests of the company; still less is the question whether the court, has it been in the position of the director at the relevant time, might have acted differently. Rather, the question is whether the director honestly believed that his act or omission was in the interests of the company. The issue is as to the director's state of mind. No doubt, where it is clear that the act or omission under challenge resulted in substantial detriment to the company, the director will have a harder task in persuading the court that he honestly believed it to be in the company's interest; but that does not detract from the subjective nature of the test.'[103]

In *Regentcrest* it had been claimed that a director had not acted bona fide in the interest of the company in waiving a contractual provision which would have entitled the company to claim £1.5 million against the vendors of land to the company. In that case it was held that there were good commercial reasons for agreeing to release the vendor

98 For example, see *Re Dublin North City Milling Co Ltd* [1909] 1 IR 179; *Re Hafner, Olhausen v Powderley* [1948] IR 426; *Clark v Workman* [1920] 1 IR 107. See also, Ussher, *Company Law in Ireland* (1986), p 222 *ff*.

99 *Re North City Milling Co Ltd* [1909] 1 IR 179.

100 *Re Hafner* [1943] IR 426.

101 *Re Smith & Fawcett Ltd* [1942] 1 All ER 542 at 543; *Bristol and West Building Society v Mothew* [1996] 4 All ER 698 at 712.

102 *Regentcrest plc v Cohen* [2001] 2 BCLC 80.

103 [2001] 2 BCLC 80 at 105b–d; para 120.

from the strict contractual provisions and that the director had not been in breach of his fiduciary duties.

[10.030] One way of determining a director's bona fides is to look to his perceived intentions. Another means is to scrutinise the proper purpose of the powers exercised. A wide variety of powers are given to directors and the essence of the delegation of such powers by the members is that the directors should use such powers in furtherance of the objects of the company. However, powers, being intrinsically neutral, can be put to either good or bad purposes.

Since any exercise of power can have two or more purposes, in deciding whether or not a power was properly or improperly exercised, the courts will look at the substantial purpose behind the exercise. Consequently, in *Smith (Howard) Ltd v Ampol Petroleum Ltd*[104] Lord Wilberforce said that the court must:

> '...examine the substantial purpose for which it was exercised, and...reach a conclusion whether that purpose was proper or not. In doing so it will necessarily give credit to the bona fide opinion of the directors, if such is found to exist, and will respect their judgment as to matters of management; having done this, the ultimate conclusion has to be as to the side of a fairly broad line on which the case falls.'

In the context of private companies, where often the same persons will be both the directors and the shareholders, it is difficult to believe that the exercise of all the directors' powers will be altruistically directed to further the company's interest[105].

[10.031] Of all directors' powers, the power to issue new shares has given rise to the most litigation. This is because intrinsic to the exercise of such power is the potential to alter the control of the company. The case of *G & S Doherty Ltd v Doherty*[106] illustrates how the issue of shares can marginalise certain shareholders. Where this happens, the directors' resolution authorising the exercise of the power to allot shares is liable to be set aside as being an abuse of power, and so invalid. In *Nash v Lancegaye (Ireland) Ltd*[107] an allotment of shares was made in favour of one shareholder. The result was that he obtained 51% of the shares in the company. While it was conceivable that the allotment could have been made for the benefit of the company (ie to increase its capital), it was held that it was an abuse of the directors' fiduciary powers and so the resolution authorising it was invalid. Recognising that the exercise of a power could have a dual purpose, Dixon J held:

---

[104] *Smith (Howard) Ltd v Ampol Petroleum Ltd* [1974] AC 821.

[105] See *Mills v Mills* (1938) 60 CLR 150, where the directors made an issue of bonus shares out of company profits, instead of by way of dividend. The incidental effect of this was that the managing director's voting power was increased, but it was held that this was not the substantial purpose of the exercise of the directors' powers, which was to act in the interests of the company. Latham CJ said that a director is not: '...required by law to live in an unreal region of detached altruism and to act in a vague mood of ideal abstraction from obvious facts which must be presented to the mind of any honest and intelligent man when he exercises his powers as a director. It would be setting up an impossible standard...'.

[106] *G & S Doherty Ltd v Doherty* (4 April 1968, unreported), High Court. See Chapter 3, *Private Constitutional Documentation*, para **[3.079]**.

[107] *Nash v Lancegaye (Ireland) Ltd* (1958) 92 ILTR 11.

> 'Having the two-fold object...of conferring a privilege or advantage on [one shareholder] and also increasing the voting strength of [that shareholder], is it of any avail to the defendant directors that they may also have had the object, other things being equal, of benefiting the company. This was certainly not their sole object and I cannot say that it, in fact, contributed to their decision. Even if it did, it was conceded in argument that would not suffice to validate the resolutions if the motives were partly improper.'[108]

In other cases, the directors' exercise of the power to allot fresh shares has been found to have been predominantly motivated by bona fide motives[109]. An example is the case of *Re Jermyn Street Turkish Baths Ltd*[110] where the allotment of shares to a director which gave her a majority stake in the company was held to be valid in that it was part of a rescue package for the company, and very much in the interests of the company.

[10.032] One contentious area concerns allotments which are designed to fight off takeover bids for the company's shares. In *Hogg v Cramphorn Ltd*[111] an allotment in such circumstances was held to be invalid as a breach of the directors' fiduciary duties. Buckley J said:

> 'Accepting, as I do, that the board acted in good faith and that they believed that the establishment of a trust would benefit the company and that avoidance of the acquisition of control by [an outsider] would also benefit the company, I must still remember that the essential element of the scheme, and indeed its primary purpose, was to ensure control of the company by the directors and those whom they could confidently regard as their supporters.'

However, *Teck Corporation Ltd v Millar*[112] has suggested that the matter is not cut and dried, because the directors may reasonably:

> '...consider who is seeking control and why. If they believe that there will be substantial damage to the company's interests if the company is taken over, then the exercise of their powers to defeat those seeking a majority will not necessarily be categorised as improper. I think the courts should apply the general rule in this way: the directors must act in good faith. Then there must be reasonable grounds for their belief. If they say that they believe there will be substantial damage to the company's interests, then there must be reasonable grounds for that belief. If there are not, that will justify a finding that the directors were actuated by an improper purpose.'

It is submitted that in a private company especially, the substratum of the company could be destroyed if the control held by the founders were upset by one of their number leaving the quasi-partnership and selling his shares to an outsider. For this reason most private companies will act prospectively and prevent such a situation arising by providing for pre-emption rights in their articles of association or in a shareholders'

---

108 See also *Whitehouse v Carlton Hotel Party Ltd* [1976] 2 All ER 268.

109 See *Mutual Life Insurance Co of New York v The Rank Organisation Ltd* [1985] BCLC 11; and *Afric Sive Ltd v Gas and Exploration Ltd* (30 January 1989, unreported), High Court per Carroll J.

110 *Re Jermyn Street Turkish Baths Ltd* [1971] 1 WLR 1042.

111 *Hogg v Cramphorn Ltd* [1966] 3 All ER 420.

112 *Teck Corporation Ltd v Millar* (1972) 33 DLR 288.

agreement. The effect of such provisions is that one shareholder cannot sell his shares without first offering them, usually on a pro rata basis, to the existing shareholders[113].

(c) The exercise of discretion

[10.033] Company directors have a positive duty to exercise their discretion, and inaction by directors in circumstances where action is required in order to further their company's interests will amount to a breach of duty[114]. This duty requires directors to exercise their judgment and discretion in relation to whether there are sufficient reserves to pay dividends[115], in the approval of the drawing of company cheques[116], etc. Often, the failure to exercise discretion will leave directors liable in negligence for breach of their duties of care, skill and diligence, considered below[117].

(d) Fettering directors' discretion[118]

[10.034] The general rule is that directors, as fiduciaries, may not in their capacity as directors[119], fetter their discretion ie agree that they will act in a particular way into the future. Problems can arise, however, where the exigencies of business require directors to agree to a future course of action. This can arise on the entering into of share sale agreements, shareholders' agreements and joint-venture agreements. Examples here include: agreeing to convene and hold meetings for the purpose of allotting shares in particular amounts to particular persons[120]; agreeing to vote in favour of the registration of a share transfer[121]; agreeing not to declare a dividend for a particular period[122]; or, generally, having taken a particular business decision, agreeing not to reverse that decision[123].

[10.035] The leading Irish case on the exercise of directors' powers in bad faith, *Clark v Workman*[124] is also authority for the proposition that directors cannot fetter their discretion. The facts there were that the directors of a private company approved of a transfer of shares by a majority shareholder to a non-member. The chairman of the board

113 See Chapter 16, *Share Transfers In Private Companies*, para **[16.063]**.

114 See, generally, Gregory, 'Directors' Duty to Exercise Discretion' (1998) Special Report, British Company Law Library Service, CCH for a very useful analysis of this aspect of directors' duties.

115 *Leeds Estate Building and Investment Co v Shepherd* (1887) 36 Ch D 787.

116 *Re Railway and General Light Improvement Col Marzetti's Case* (1880) 42 LT 206.

117 See para **[10.063]**.

118 See generally, Courtney, 'Fettering Directors' Discretion' (1995) 16 Co Laywer 227. See also Reece Thomas & Ryan, *The Law and Practice of Shareholders' Agreements* (1999), pp 69–78.

119 Persons may, however, fetter their discretion in their capacity as members or in another non–fiduciary capacity as members are generally free to act as they wish: *Northern Counties Securities Ltd v Jackson & Steeple Ltd* [1974] 2 All ER 625. See also *Coronation Syndicate Ltd v Lilkienfield* (1903) TS 489 where a South African court made this distinction in the context of a comparison with directors and their duties.

120 See, for example, *Thorby v Goldberg* [1965] 112 CLR 597, considered at para **[10.038]**.

121 See, for example, *Clark v Workman* [1920] 1 IR 107, considered at para **[10.035]**.

122 Such may be a covenant in a joint–venture agreement.

123 As in *Fulham Football Club Ltd v Cabra Estates plc* [1994] 1 BCLC 363.

124 *Clark v Workman* [1920] 1 IR 107.

of directors had promised the outsider transferee that he would do all that he could to obtain board approval for the transfer. The plaintiff-shareholders argued that this was wrong because the board had inadequate time to consider the matter and had acted in breach of their fiduciary duty by fettering their sacred discretion to act in the best interests of the company. Ross J stated that 'in all cases bona fides is the test of the valid exercise of powers by trustees'[125], and that an opportunity for deliberation of a proposed exercise of power was required in law. This was found not to be present notwithstanding that the result would have such an important bearing on the future of the company[126]. In view of the fact that an uncontradicted statement of a witness showed that the chairman director had promised to use his best endeavours to approve of the transfer of shares to the outsider it was held that this must be taken to represent the motives and intentions of the chairman director. Accordingly, Ross J said 'By acting thus he had fettered himself by a promise to the [outsider] and had disqualified himself from acting bona fide in the interests of the company...'.[127]

Thus, the general rule must be that, being in a fiduciary position, directors should not contract, undertake or otherwise agree in advance to exercise their discretionary powers in a particular way[128]. So, in *John Crowther Group plc v International plc*[129] the plaintiff instituted proceedings against the defendant-company when its directors recommended to the company's shareholders not to accept a bid made by the plaintiff for the defendant-company's shares. The circumstances were that the directors had entered into a prior agreement with the plaintiff to, inter alia, procure the satisfaction of the conditions in the agreement but had changed their recommendation to the shareholders when a more attractive bid was received. Vinelott J held in favour of the defendant-company on the grounds that the directors' obligations under the agreement must be read in the light of their duties to act in the interests of the company. He said:

> 'The terms of the agreement must clearly be read in the light of the fact known to all parties that directors owe a fiduciary duty to act in the interests of their company…and to make full and honest disclosure to shareholders before they vote on such a resolution. It seems to me that it must have been understood by all that if the undertaking was to use reasonable endeavours to procure the passing of the resolution it was necessarily subject

---

125 [1920] 1 IR 107 at 113.

126 [1920] 1 IR 107 at 113, Ross J said: 'It is a strong proposition to assert that a majority is to overbear and stifle a minority when the intention is to do such a serious thing as to give a controlling interest in one company to another company that is engaged in the same line of business, and that may be to some extent a rival company.'

127 [1920] 1 IR 107 at 118.

128 See, for example, the dissent of Lord Denning MR in *Boulting v Association of Cinematography, Television and Allied Technicians* [1963] 2 QB 606 at 626 where he said: 'It seems to me that no one, who has duties of a fiduciary nature to discharge, can be allowed to enter into an engagement by which he binds himself to disregard those duties or to act inconsistently with them. No stipulation is lawful by which he agrees to carry out his duties in accordance with the instructions of another rather than on his own conscious judgment; or by which he agrees to subordinate the interests of those whom he must protect to the interests of someone else.'

129 *John Crowther Group plc v International plc* [1990] BCLC 460.

> to anything which the directors had to do in pursuance of that fiduciary duty…It seems to me plain beyond question that directors are under a duty to disclose the facts to the shareholders.'[130]

Later, Vinelott J said that it was for the directors to decide what was in the best interests of the company and to take whatever steps they considered in furtherance of that[131].

[10.036] There are, however, exceptions to this general rule and it is fallacious to suggest that directors can never agree to fetter their discretion. Case law indicates that there are at least two possible justifications for directors to agree to fetter their discretion. In the first place, it is open to the members of a company to release directors from the strict application of the general rule. This was confirmed by majority in the English Court of Appeal in *Boulting v Association of Cinematography, Television and Allied Technicians*[132] which is also authority for the proposition that this directors' duty cannot be used as a shield by the directors: 'it is a sword and as such only can it be used by the person entitled to the benefit of it, and he may sheath the weapon'[133]. Thus, in that case it was not open to directors to assert the general rule as such was the sole preserve of the company[134]. In order for directors to be validly released, however, the company acting by its shareholders must fully understand in what they are approving[135].

[10.037] In the second place, it is submitted that directors may validly and lawfully decide, at the time when they enter into a contract, what is in the best interests of their company and, to this end, agree to fetter their future discretion. Authority here is the decision of the English Court of Appeal in *Fulham Football Club Ltd v Cabra Estates plc*[136]. The facts in this case were that a subsidiary of the defendant-company which owned the freehold in certain lands applied for planning permission to develop the lands for residential purposes. The plaintiff-company, through another subsidiary, had a leasehold interest in the lands. The local council also wished to develop the lands for its own purposes and issued a compulsory purchase order ('CPO') in respect of the lands and itself applied for planning permission. An agreement was entered into between the defendant-company and its subsidiary and the plaintiff-company and its directors and shareholders, concerning the future development of the lands, under which the plaintiff-company was to receive a large amount of money. Contemporaneous to the entering into of this agreement, the plaintiff-company's directors and shareholders entered into a letter of undertaking whereby they agreed to use their powers and rights as directors and members to ensure that:

---

130 [1990] BCLC 460 at 464.

131 See also *Rackham v Peel Foods Ltd* [1990] BCLC 895; *Motherwell v Schoof* [1949] 2 WWR 529, [1949] 4 DLR 812; *Alder v Dobie and Gallop* (1999) Supreme Court of British Columbia of 8 April 1999 (Burnyeat J).

132 *Boulting v Association of Cinematography, Television and Allied Technicians* [1963] 2 QB 606.

133 [1963] 2 QB 606 at 637, per Upjohn LJ.

134 See also the Canadian case of *Ringuet v Bergeron* (1960) 24 DLR (2d) 449.

135 *Knight v Frost* [1999] 1 BCLC 364.

136 *Fulham Football Club Ltd v Cabra Estates plc* [1994] 1 BCLC 363.

— the plaintiff-company would do nothing to prevent the withdrawal of the existing CPO and would not support any new CPO as might be substituted therefor;

— the plaintiff-company would not object to the current planning applications on behalf of the defendant or any other applications for redevelopment of the land; and

— the plaintiff-company would, if called upon by the defendant-company, write to the planning authority and the English Secretary of State, in support of the defendant-company's application for development of the land for residential purposes.

Following an inquiry into the CPO and the planning applications, the CPO was not confirmed and both planning applications were refused. The defendant-company's subsidiary made a fresh application, which was refused, and following this a further public enquiry was held. At this time the plaintiff-company did not wish to be bound by the undertaking that had been given, and instituted proceedings seeking a declaration that they were entitled to give such evidence at the inquiry as they considered to be in the plaintiff-company's best interests. The plaintiff-company also refused to provide a letter of support for the defendant-company's subsidiary's revised application. It was argued, inter alia, by the plaintiff-company that the undertaking was unenforceable as it conflicted with its directors' fiduciary duties.

At trial, Chadwick J rejected the contention that the undertaking was in breach of the directors' duties. He said:

> 'It is said…[that]…an obligation which seeks to fetter the exercise by directors of their fiduciary duties in the future is unenforceable as a matter of law. Whether or not that would be so in circumstances where the obligation is assumed by directors in that capacity alone, there is, in my judgment, no such principle where the obligation is assumed by directors who are at the time, and intend to continue to be, together the only members of the company; or where it is assumed with the approval of all those who are the members of the company.'[137]

Chadwick J also rejected the plaintiff-company's contention that there ought to be implied into the undertaking, a limitation that the directors would not thereby be required to do anything that would be inconsistent with their fiduciary duties. In distinguishing the cases of *Crowther* and *Rackham*, considered above[138], Chadwick J held there was no room for such an implication where the undertaking was given by persons who had been acting in their capacity as members[139].

[10.038] Both of the points upon which Chadwick J had held against the plaintiff-company were appealed to the Court of Appeal. Whilst upholding the decision of Chadwick J, Neill LJ rejected his reasons, namely that the members could release the directors from their strict duties. He did this on the grounds that directors owed common

137 [1994] 1 BCLC 363 at 376.

138 At para **[10.035]**.

139 [1994] 1 BCLC 363 at 375–376.

law duties to creditors[140] and because there were statutory duties to employees[141]. This finding is open to criticism[142] on the grounds that duties to creditors only arise where companies are insolvent[143] and duties to employees are only enforceable by the company and directors can, therefore, be released by the company acting through its members. Neill LJ preferred a more general reason for upholding Chadwick J's decision. He said:

> 'It is trite law that directors are under a duty to act bona fide in the interests of their company. However, it does not follow from that proposition that directors can never make a contract by which they bind themselves to the future exercise of their powers in a particular manner, even though the contract taken as a whole is manifestly for the benefit of the company. Such a rule could well prevent companies from entering into contracts which were commercially beneficial to them.'[144]

Neill LJ relied heavily on the decision of the Australian case of *Thorby v Goldberg*[145]. There, Kitto J had said:

> 'There are many kinds of transactions in which the proper time for the exercise of directors' discretion is the time of the negotiation of the contract, not the time at which the contract is to be performed. A sale of land is a familiar example. Where all the members of a company desire to enter as a group a transaction such as that in the present case[146], the transaction being one which requires action by the board of directors for its effectuation, it seems to me that the proper time for the directors to decide whether their proposed action will be in the interests of the company as a whole is the time when the transaction is being entered into, and not the time when their action is required. If at the former time they are bona fide of the opinion that it is in the interests of the company that the transaction should be entered into and carried into effect, I see no reason in law why they should not bind themselves to do whatever under the transaction is to be done by the board.'[147]

In the *Fulham Football Club* case Neill LJ found that the directors had exercised their discretion at the time of entering into the agreement and giving the undertaking and had concluded such was in the best interests of their company. Moreover, he found that the plaintiff-company had received substantial benefits from the original agreement and that it could not be said that the directors had acted improperly in agreeing to fetter the future exercise of their discretion.

[10.039] Where it is proposed to enter into a contract or other agreement which clearly does fetter directors' discretion, or could be so construed, good corporate housekeeping would suggest that a transparent and recorded procedure is followed. Without attempting to be definitive, companies should ensure:

140 See para **[10.009]**.
141 See para **[10.016]**.
142 See Courtney, 'Fettering Directors' Discretion' (1995) 16 Co Lawyer 227 at 234–235.
143 See para **[10.012]**.
144 [1994] 1 BCLC 363 at 392.
145 *Thorby v Goldberg* [1965] 112 CLR 597.
146 A transaction involving the demolition and redevelopment of a building.
147 [1965] 112 CLR 597 at 605, 606.

— that the directors explicitly acknowledge that they are agreeing to fetter their fiduciary discretion and in particular consider whether such is in the company's best interests;

— where it is decided to proceed, the decision (and, perhaps departing from the normal rules of minute taking, their deliberations) should be minuted and the minutes of the board meeting signed by the chairman;

— it may be prudent to allude to the directors' decisions in the recitals to the contract or other agreement; and

— if practicable, a resolution in support of the proposed course of action by the members of the company might be procured.

(e) The duties of nominee directors

[10.040] A nominee director[148] is a director who is 'expected to act in accordance with some understanding or arrangement which creates an obligation or mutual expectation of loyalty to some person or persons other than the company as a whole'[149]. The nominee director can find himself caught between a rock and a hard place being contemporaneously under some obligation to a third party and continuing to owe the same duties to the company as any other director. Traditionally, courts have been loath to acknowledge the commercial reality of nominee directors and have considered it wrong to have regard to anyone's interest but the company's. This is most vividly illustrated by the views of Street J in the Australian case of *Bennets v Board of Fire Commissioners of New South Wales*[150] where he said:

> 'It is entirely foreign to the purpose for which this or any other board exists to contemplate a member of the board being representative of a particular group or a particular body. Once a group has elected a member he assumes office as a member of the board and becomes subject to the overriding and predominant duty to serve the interests of the board in preference, on every occasion upon which any conflict might arise, to serving the interests of the group which appointed him. With this basic position there can be no room for compromise.'[151]

This has been described as imposing a standard that makes the position of nominee directors impossible[152]. The position of nominee directors is perhaps most precarious in the context of a joint venture, where two separate companies come together to jointly pursue a particular business opportunity and form a third company for that purpose. Where each of the joint venturers nominates, say, a director each, one must ask whether

148 See, generally, Boros, 'The Duties of Nominee and Multiple Directors' (1989) 10 Co Lawyer 211 and (1990) 11 Co Lawyer 6; Crutchfield, 'Nominee Directors: The Law and Commercial Reality' (1991) 12 Co Lawyer 136; Yeung, 'Corporate Groups: Legal Aspects of the Management Dilemma' [1997] Lloyd's Maritime and Commercial Law Quarterly 208; and Reece Thomas & Ryan, *The Law and Practice of Shareholders' Agreements* (1999), p 78.

149 Companies and Securities Review Committee (NSW, Australia), *Nominee Directors and Alternate Directors, Report No 8*, (2 March 1989) at p 7.

150 *Bennets v Board of Fire Commissioners of New South Wales* (1967) 87 WN (NSW) 307.

151 (1967) 87 WN (NSW) 307 at 311.

152 See Crutchfield, 'Nominee Directors: The Law and Commercial Reality', (1991) 12 Co Lawyer 136 at 137.

it is realistic to think that these directors will have no regard for the wishes of their appointing joint venturer. The directors of a joint-venture company are in such an invidious position that there is a strong case to put the matter beyond doubt in statute[153].

[10.041] In *Irish Press plc v Ingersoll Irish Publications Ltd*[154] Barron J took a more commercially focused and sympathetic approach to the plight of the nominee director, saying:

> 'The position of nominee directors can be a difficult one if they disagree with the views of the person or body appointing them. Their duty is to act in the interests of the company. They have also got a duty to act on the instructions of their nominating party. But acting in the interests of the company is no more than acting in the interests of all its shareholders. If what they are asked to do involves seeking to damage the interests of one section of the shareholders in favour of another then as a director they have a duty not to do that. However, if what they are required to do is merely something that they themselves personally think is not the way to approach the mater then they must give way. There is nothing wrong with the appointing body or party having a view as to where the interests of the company lie and ensuring that its nominees follow that direction provided that in so doing they are not seeking to damage anybody else's interest in the company.'[155]

In the foregoing passage Barron J recoiled from the absolutist position of Street J in the *Bennets* case. In the Australian case of *Levin v Clark*[156] it was held that a nominee director could act primarily in the interests of his principal and take steps to enforce his principal's security, the reasoning being that the duty could be modified by the company's constitutional documents and the members' wishes[157]. It is thought that this decision accords more with the realities of commercial life[158]. However, in the House of Lords decision in *Scottish Cooperative Wholesale Society Ltd v Meyer and another*[159], in

[153] See Lower, 'Do We Need a Joint Venture Act?' (1995) Palmer's In Company, Issue 5/95 (17 May 1995) where the author refers to the New Zealand Companies Act, s 131(4) which expressly allows the constitution of a joint venture company to be altered so that nominee directors can act in the best interests of their appointor even where this is not in the best interests of the joint-venture company. Note that the *Company Law Review Group in its First Report*, (2000–2001) has recommended that 'a director appointed or nominated for appointment by a member with an entitlement to so appoint or nominate under the articles of association or a shareholders' agreement may have regard to the interests of that member': see paragraph 11.3.7 at p 241.

[154] *Irish Press plc v Ingersoll Irish Publications Ltd* (15 December 1993, unreported), High Court.

[155] (15 December 1993, unreported), High Court at p 77.

[156] *Levin v Clark* [1962] NSWR 686.

[157] See Boros, 'The Duties of Nominee and Multiple Directors' (1989) 10 Co Lawyer 211 and (1990) 11 Co Lawyer 6, p 214.

[158] See MacCann, 'Directors' Duties: To Whom Are They Owed?' (1991) ILT 3 and 30, p 106, and see also *Berlai Hestia (NZ) Ltd v Fernyhough* [1980] 2 NZLR 150 where it was said that where a director is appointed nominee by a particular group of shareholders he may also owe duties to them. Cf *Kuwait Asia Bank EC v National Mutual Life Nominees Ltd* [1991] 1 AC 187 at 222 where the Privy Council said of nominee directors that 'the could not plead any instruction from the bank (that appointed them) as an excuse for breach of their duties…'.

[159] *Scottish Cooperative Wholesale Society Ltd v Meyer* [1959] AC 324.

a passage quoted by Barron J, Viscount Simonds said that nominee directors were not entitled to remain silent and inactive with full knowledge of the majority shareholder's intention to strip their company of its assets. It is interesting that Viscount Simonds extended his comments to the appointor of the nominee directors and said it was 'incumbent on the parent company to behave with scrupulous fairness to the minority shareholders and to avoid imposing upon their nominees the alternative of disregarding their instructions or betraying the interests of the minority.[160] In conclusion, it is thought, on the authority of Barron J, that whilst a nominee director will owe duties to his company, he can have regard to his appointor's interests where this does not harm any other party's interests.

(f) 'Token directors' in family companies and 'sexually transmitted debt'

[10.042] Although nominee directors are expected to act on an understanding or arrangement which creates an obligation or mutual expectation of loyalty to some person, the concept most certainly does not, per se, imply that the nominee director will abdicate all responsibility in relation to the company's management. It is thought that a different label is required for such directors, and that 'token director' is more apt. A token director is a nominee director who abdicates all responsibility for the company's management and whose sole purpose in being a director is to meet the statutory requirement that all companies must have at least two directors. A token director can sometimes assume that position at the behest of his or her spouse. In *Re Hunting Lodges Ltd*[161] Carroll J said of the wife of one of the directors concerned, who was a nominee director, that in the context of fraudulent trading[162] she could not:

> '...evade liability by claiming that she was only concerned with minding her house and looking after the children. If that was the limit of the responsibilities she wanted, she should not have become a director of the company, or having become one she should have resigned. Any person who becomes a director takes on the responsibilities and duties, particularly where there are only two...A director who continues as a director but abdicates all responsibility is not lightly to be excused.' [163]

A more liberal approach is apparent in the Supreme Court of New South Wales' decision in *Southern Cross Interiors Pty Ltd and another v Deputy Commissioner of Taxation*[164]. There, the liquidator of a company sought to have payments made by the company to the Australian Revenue Commissioners declared unlawful as an 'unfair preference'. The Revenue Commissioners, in addition to defending the liquidator's claim, sought a declaration that the company's two directors (a husband and wife) should be declared liable to indemnify the Revenue Commissioners on grounds of having traded whilst the company was insolvent. The wife-director sought to defend the claim against her by relying upon a provision in Australian legislation that created the defence of not taking

[160] See, Lower, 'Good Faith and the Partly–Owned Subsidiary' [2000] Journal of Business Law and, further, Chapter 19, *Shareholders' Remedies*, para **[19.011]**.

[161] *Re Hunting Lodges Ltd* [1985] ILRM 75.

[162] See para **[10.104]** *ff*.

[163] See also *Cronje No v Stone* (1985) (3) SA 597 (T) considered at para **[10.091]**.

[164] *Southern Cross Interiors Pty Ltd v Deputy Commissioner of Taxation* [2001] NSWSC 621 (31 August 2001).

part in the management of the company for a 'good reason'. The wife-director contended that she had only accepted the appointment at her husband's request, that she had been unaware of the duties of a company director and that it was for those reasons that she had not participated in the management of the company. The essence of her claim was that she had only agreed to become a director because of the trust and confidence she had placed in her husband. The court held that the wife-director had established 'good reason' for not participating in the management of the company. Palmer J said:

> 'I hold that [the wife-director] accepted appointment as a director of [the company] with no understanding at all of the duties and responsibilities which that office entailed. That lack of understanding was not due to any fault on her part. Her husband failed to explain to her anything of the responsibilities which directorship involved and did not suggest that she seek advice or further information. She accepted the appointment at his request because of the trust and confidence which she had in him, believing, at his suggestion, that the appointment was only a formal requirement. She did not participate in the management of the company because she did not believe that she was required to do so. That belief was induced by her husband's statements at the time he requested her to become a director and by his subsequent conduct in not discussing the company's affairs with her. She acted upon that belief because of the trust and confidence she placed in her husband because she thought that he was knowledgeable in such matters. Nothing was brought to her attention during her directorship which should have put her upon enquiry as to [the company's] financial position or as to her responsibilities as a director.'[165]

There is, of course, no such defence as 'good reason' to an action for reckless trading in Irish law. Nevertheless, the foregoing represents the other end of the spectrum in the approach to token directors' liabilities to that seen in *Re Hunting Lodges Ltd*[166] and it remains to be seen whether it will find favour, generally, in relation to actions against token directors. Somewhat surprisingly, in *Re Lynrowan Enterprises Ltd*[167], an application to have persons restricted under CA 1990, s 150, O'Neill J declined to make a restriction order for the following reason:

> 'All of the evidence before the Court suggests that [the first respondent] although a de jure director of the company took no part whatsoever in its affairs and does not appear to have been expected so to so. In those circumstances in the absence of any evidence of specific irresponsibility or dishonest behaviour on his part I am of the view that the granting of the relief sought against him would be inappropriate and I make no declaration pursuant to s 150(1) in respect of [the first respondent]'

One might have thought that allowing one's name to be used as a token director of a company in circumstances where one was not expected to take part in the affairs of that company is, in and of itself, an act of gross irresponsibility. It is thought that the sentiment expressed by Carroll J in *Re Hunting Lodges* is to be preferred.

[10.043] What was particularly novel about the decision in *Southern Cross Interiors Pty Ltd v Deputy Commissioner of Taxation*[168] was the judicial recognition afforded to the

---

165 At para 137 of the judgment.

166 *Re Hunting Lodges Ltd* [1985] ILRM 75.

167 *Re Lynrowan Enterprises Ltd* (31 July 2002, unreported), High Court (O'Neill J).

168 *Southern Cross Interiors Pty Ltd v Deputy Commissioner of Taxation* [2001] NSWSC 621 (31 August 2001).

so-called phenomenon of 'sexually transmitted debt' or the less salacious 'emotionally transmitted debt'. This has been described by the Australian Law Reform Commission in the following terms:

> 'The key feature of sexually transmitted debt is the relationship of dependence and the emotional ties that dominate the transaction. These are often found, for example, in wife/husband, parent/child and de facto relationships. The dependent party in the relationship accepts responsibility for the other party's debt primarily because of that relationship. If the other party becomes unable or unwilling, for example, through bankruptcy or divorce, to meet the debt, the dependent party is liable for that debt. In that way the debt is "transmitted" to the dependent party. A useful generic definition of sexually transmitted debt is the transfer of responsibility for a debt incurred by a party to his/her partner in circumstances in which the fact of the relationship, as distinct from an appreciation of the reality of the responsibility for the debt, is the predominant factor in the partner accepting liability.'[169]

As a phenomenon, sexually transmitted debt has a wider application than company law. In *Southern Cross Interiors Pty Ltd and another v Deputy Commissioner of Taxation* Palmer J held it was applicable to cases where wives (not, it will be noted, 'spouses')[170] become directors at their husbands' behest, saying:

> '…if a woman, inexperienced in business and completely unaware of the responsibilities of company directorship, is told by her husband, whom she trusts and believes to be honest and to be knowledgeable in such matters, that some formality requires her to be appointed as a director to a family company and that management of the company may be left entirely to him, then, in my view, she has a "good defence" for not participating in management for such time as she remains in ignorance of her duties.'[171]

Palmer J's view that recognition of sexually transmitted debt will not undermine the policy of the law that those who accept office as director are expected to act with competence and diligence in discharging the duties of their office is debatable. Whether this defence for token directors is just and proper or whether it is a charter that ignores culpability and furthers the in-vogue 'nobody is to blame' culture is a moot point. It is this writer's view that rather than operate as a defence to negligently acting as a second statutory director, the fact that some spouses are prevailed upon to meet a statutory

---

[169] *Equality Before the Law: Women's Equality* (1994) Report No 69 Part II at para 13.4.

[170] Much of the legal commentary on this phenomenon is feminist in origin. A sample of the legal literature in Australia includes: Fehlberg, 'Sexually Transmitted Debt' (1997) Clarendon Press; Bailey, 'Sexually Transmitted Debts: Criticisms and Prospects for Reform' (1999) 8(4) Auckland University Law Review 1001; Kaye, 'Equity's Treatment of Sexually Transmitted Debt' (1997) 5(1) Feminist Legal Studies 35; Howell, 'Sexually Transmitted Debt: a Feminist Analysis of Laws Regulating Guarantors and Co–Borrowers' (1995) 4 Australian Feminist Law Journal 93; Baron, 'The Free Exercise of Her Will: Women and Emotionally Transmitted Debt' (1995) Law in Context 23; and Fehlberg, 'Money and Marriage: Sexually Transmitted Debt in England' (1997) 11 International Journal of Law, Policy and Family 320.

[171] *Southern Cross Interiors Pty Ltd v Deputy Commissioner of Taxation* [2001] NSWSC 621 (31 August 2001) at para 135.

minimum of two directors should instead cause us to consider whether private companies should be required to have two directors[172].

(g) The delegation of directors' powers

[10.044] In many private companies it will commonly be the case that the directors are executives in their company, responsible alone or with employees for its day-to-day management. The larger the company, however, the greater the likelihood that the directors will be forced to delegate some of their powers to others. As shall be considered, the delegation of powers does not exonerate directors from their responsibilities or mitigate the duties they owe to their company.

[10.045] A particularly vexed question arises where one director relies upon another director to perform the first director's functions. While it is undoubtedly true that a director can rely upon his co-directors, it has been suggested that where a director does so, but fails to investigate the activities being undertaken, that director may very well cross the line and breach his positive duty. Irish authority here is *Jackson v Munster Bank Ltd*[173] where a director was held liable for breach of duty when he did not make proper enquiry upon being put on notice of irregular loans. Mere objection has been held to be insufficient, and to be certain of absolution, a director would be best advised to cease participation in the company.

[10.046] A more recent Irish case to consider this issue is the High Court decision of *Re Vehicle Imports Ltd*[174] where Murphy J held that the obligation[175] to keep proper books of account was not limited to where one director had a reputed responsibility for keeping the books and that the responsibility was a joint and separate liability on each of the directors. In the course of that case – which concerned CA 1990, s 150 and is considered in detail in Chapter 12, – Murphy J adopted the head note to the judgment of Jonathan Parker J in *Re Barings plc; Secretary of State for Trade and Industry v Baker*[176]. This states:

> '(a) Each individual director owed duties to the company to inform himself about its affairs and to join with his co-directors in supervising and controlling them[177].

[172] See the *Company Law Review Group's First Report, (2000–2001)*, recommendation 11.8.11 at page 247 where it is recommended that private companies limited by shares should be permitted to have just one director.

[173] *Jackson v Munster Bank Ltd* (1885) 15 LR Ir 356.

[174] *Re Vehicle Imports Ltd* (23 November 2000, unreported), High Court (Murphy J).

[175] Whilst this comment may have been made in the light of CA 1990, s 202(10) – which criminalises the failure to keep proper books of account and applies to every person who is a director of a company – it is thought to have a more widespread application.

[176] *Re Barings plc (No 5); Secretary of State for Trade and Industry v Baker (No 5)* [1999] 1 BCLC 433. See Parry, 'Delegation of Directors' Duties after Re Barings plc' (1999) CCH's Company Law News Issue 25, 11 February 1999.

[177] Jonathan Parker J quoted from the decision in *Re Westmid Packing Services Ltd* [1998] 2 BCLC 646 where Woolf MR went on to say (at 654): 'It is of the greatest importance that any individual who undertakes the statutory and fiduciary obligations of being a company director should realise that these are inescapable personal responsibilities.'

(b) Subject to the articles of association of the company, a board of directors might delegate specific tasks and functions. Some degree of delegation was almost always essential if the company's business was to be carried on efficiently; to that extent, there was a clear public interest in delegation by those charged with the responsibility for the management of a business[178].

(c) The duty of an individual director, however, did not mean that he might not delegate. Having delegated a particular function it did not mean he was no longer under any duty in relation to the discharge of that function, notwithstanding that the person to whom the function had been delegated appeared both trustworthy and capable of discharging the function.

(d) Where delegation had taken place the board (and the individual directors) remained responsible for the delegated function or functions and retained a residual duty of supervision and control. The precise extent of that residual duty will depend on the facts of each particular case, as will the question of whether it had been breached.

(e) A person who accepted the office of director of a particular company undertook the responsibility of ensuring that he understood the nature of the duty a director was called upon to perform. That duty would vary according to the size and business of that particular company and the experience or skills of the director held himself or herself out to have in support of appointment to the office. The duty included that of acting collectively to manage the company[179].

(f) Where there was an issue as to the extent of a director's duties and responsibilities in any particular case, the level of reward which he was entitled to receive or which he might reasonable have expected to receive from the company might be a relevant fact in resolving that issue. It was not that the unfitness depended on how much he was paid. The point was that the higher the level of reward, the greater the responsibilities which might reasonably be expected (prima facie, at least) to go with it[180].

(g) The following general propositions could be stated[181] with respect to the director's duties:

   (i) Directors had, both collectively and individually, a continuing duty to acquire and maintain a sufficient knowledge and understanding of the company's business to enable them properly to discharge their duties as directors.

   (ii) Whilst directors were entitled (subject to the articles of association of the company) to delegate particular functions to those below them in the

178 The authority here was *Dovey v Cory* [1901] AC 477 where Halsbury LC said (at 486): 'The business of life could not go on if people could not trust those who are put in a position of trust for the express purpose of attending to details of management.'

179 The authority given here was *Daniels v Anderson* (1995) 16 ACSR 607; see para **[10.068]**.

180 *Re Barings plc; Secretary of State for Trade and Industry v Baker* [1998] BCC 583.

181 The authorities cited by Jonathan Parker J were: *Re Brazilian Rubber Plantations and Estates Ltd* [1911] 1 Ch 425; *Re City Equitable Fire Insurance* [1925] Ch 407; *Re Norman Holding Co Ltd* [1991] BCLC 1; *Re D'jan of London Ltd, Copp v D'jan* [1994] BCLC 561; *Bishopsgate Investment Management Ltd v Maxwell (No 2)* [1993] BCLC 1282; *Martin v Webb* 110 US 7; *Briggs v Spaulding* 141 US 132; *Rankin v Cooper* 149 F 1010; *Atherton v Anderson* 99 F 2nd 883 and *Federal Deposit Insurance Corp v Bierman* 2 Fed Rep (3rd series) 1424.

management chain, and to trust their competence and integrity to a reasonable extent, the exercise of the power of delegation did not absolve a director from the duty to supervise the discharge of the delegated functions.

(iii) No rule of universal application can be formulated as to the duty referred to in (ii) above. The extent of the duty, and the question whether it had been discharged, depended on the facts of each particular case, including the director's role in the management of the company.'[182]

As Murphy J said, this is indeed a convenient summary of directors' duties on delegation[183]. In the absence of specific restrictions, directors can – and often, probably should – delegate particular duties to employees and others. It must always be borne in mind, however, that overall accountability is not delegable and just as a tenant remains responsible to his landlord where he carves out a sub-lease in favour of a sub-tenant, so too does a director remain accountable to his company where he delegates responsibility for the performance of some or all of his duties to others.

(h) The consequences of abuse of directors' powers

[10.047] Where directors abuse their powers, then the consequence is that any action taken is invalid, but can be cured by the company in general meeting ratifying the actions of the directors[184]. Where an outsider enters into a contract which is an abuse of the directors' powers, provided that he does not have notice of the abuse, the company will remain bound: *Rolled Steel Products Ltd v British Steel Corporation Ltd*[185].

Fiduciary duties: conflicts of interests

[10.048] The principle that a director shall not place himself in a position whereby his paramount duty to the company comes into conflict with his own personal interests arises from his status as a fiduciary vis-à-vis his company. Here we consider situations where a director abuses his position, fails to disclose a personal interest and gains a personal advantage. Other situations involve transactions and arrangements between a director and his company and the many statutory provisions that regulate such transactions and arrangements are considered in Chapter 11.

[10.049] Being a fiduciary, a director is bound to avoid a situation whereby his own personal interests conflict with those of the company[186]. One judicial statement of this principle is found in *Bray v Ford*[187] where Lord Herschell said:

> 'It is an inflexible rule of a Court of Equity that a person in a fiduciary position, such as the respondent's, is not, unless otherwise expressly provided, entitled to make a profit; he is not allowed to put himself in a position where his interest and duty conflict. It does not appear to me that this rule is, as has been said, founded upon principles of morality. I regard it rather as based on the consideration that, human nature being what it is, there is danger, in such circumstances, of the person holding a fiduciary duty being swayed by

---

182 [1999] 1 BCLC 433 at 435, 436.

183 *Re Vehicle Imports Ltd* (23 November 2000, unreported), High Court at p 10.

184 See Chapter 8, *Corporate Governance: Management by the Directors*, para **[8.014]** *ff*.

185 *Rolled Steel Products Ltd v British Steel Corporation Ltd* [1985] 3 All ER 52.

186 See MacCann, 'Directors' Fiduciary Duties' (1991) ILT 80 at 81.

187 *Bray v Ford* [1896] AC 44 at 51–52, [1895–9] All ER Rep 1009 at 1011.

> interest rather than duty, and thus prejudicing those whom he was bound to protect. It has, therefore, been deemed expedient to lay down this positive rule. But I am satisfied that it might be departed from in many cases, without any breach of morality, without any wrong being inflicted, and without any consciousness of wrongdoing.'[188]

Accordingly, the principle that directors must avoid conflicts of interest is a general one, designed to counteract human nature, and is especially applicable in a private company in which the directors and the shareholders are one and the same. However, as this is but an application of the general fiduciary principle of agent and principal or trustee and beneficiary, it follows that the company can make an informed and free decision to release the fiduciary director from his duty. Provided that the breach of a director's duty does not involve an act which is ultra vires, the company can prospectively or retrospectively release a director from his obligations by absolving him of his wrongdoing in general meeting[189].

(a) The general rule

[10.050] The principle that a director cannot gain from his fiduciary position is best illustrated by the leading case of *Regal (Hastings) v Gulliver*[190]. There, the plaintiff-company was in the cinema business, owning one cinema, which the directors decided to sell. The directors decided that it would be best to sell the cinema as part of a chain and so they decided to acquire a number of other cinemas and to sell them altogether. To this end, a subsidiary company was formed having a share capital of £5,000, divided into 5000 £1 shares. The landlord of two other cinemas would only offer leases to the new company if the new company had a paid up share capital of £5,000, or alternatively, if the directors would provide personal guarantees. The directors were not inclined to provide such guarantees and the plaintiff-company could not afford to raise any more than £2,000. Consequently, the plaintiff-company subscribed for £2,000 worth of shares in the new company and the directors personally subscribed for £3,000 worth of shares in the new company. The new company then acquired a lease of the two cinemas. Ultimately, it was decided to sell the shares in both companies rather than selling the assets themselves, and in this way the cinemas were indirectly sold. Upon the sale of the shares in the new company, the entire profit did not accrue to the plaintiff-company, but instead to the new company's shareholders. Of course, this meant that the directors made a personal profit since they held some of the shares in the new company. The matter became contentious when it was discovered by the new owners of both companies that the directors had made such profits through their office, and the new owners alleged that the directors had breached their fiduciary duties to the company.

It was held by the House of Lords that the directors were obliged in law to account for the profit made by them. In the words of Viscount Sankey, the directors:

> '...were in a fiduciary position and their liability to account does not depend upon proof of mala fides. The general rule of equity is that no one who has duties of a fiduciary nature to perform is allowed to enter into engagements in which he has or can have a personal

---

[188] This quotation was cited with approval by the Court of Appeal in *Guinness plc v Saunders* [1990] 1 All ER 652 at 660. See also *Aberdeen Railway Co v Blaikie Bros* (1854) 1 Macq 461.

[189] See generally, *Re Burke Clancy & Co Ltd* (23 May 1974, unreported), High Court per Kenny J.

[190] *Regal (Hastings) v Gulliver* [1942] 1 All ER 378.

> interest conflicting with the interests of those whom he is bound to protect. If he holds any property so acquired as trustee, he is bound to account for it to his cestui que trust.'[191]

Accordingly, the motives of the directors were immaterial to the outcome: in the course of their management of the company they entered into a transaction from which they made a personal profit. As fiduciaries, the directors were obliged to account for that profit.

[10.051] Since there were no mala fides on the part of the directors, it seems on first sight that the decision in the *Regal (Hastings)* case was harsh. However, had the directors formally notified the company of the proposal, they could have been released from their fiduciary duty by the members of the company passing a resolution (either antecedent or subsequent) to the directors' actions[192]. Where a director purports to disclose his interest in a particular matter to the members, that disclosure must be sufficient as to enable the members to make an informed decision as to whether or not to release the director from his duty[193]. In the context of many private companies, the directors will often also be the shareholders, and so it could be said that obtaining the shareholders' absolution is a mere technicality. However, since even in a two director, fifty-fifty shareholding company, one director could act in breach of the quasi-partnership relationship of trust, the point is far from moot[194].

[10.052] The general rule will not, however, apply where the company is aware that its directors are involved in exit-negotiations with a third party and the company expressly tells its directors that it is not interested in knowing of their private negotiations. In *Framlington Group plc v Anderson*[195] three directors decided to leave their company to join a competitor in circumstances where their contracts of employment permitted them to join or set up a competing business on leaving. The company to which they were going agreed with their company to acquire part of its business, represented by the clients who were serviced by the three directors. The plaintiff-company received by way of consideration shares in the company. The three directors were told by the company not to take part in these negotiations and further told that it was not interested in hearing about the terms of their remuneration package. Subsequently, on learning that the three directors had received shares in the company to which they were going, the plaintiff claimed that they had been in breach of their fiduciary duty which, it alleged, was to assist the plaintiff obtain the best price possible for its assets. It also claimed that they had earned secret profits and that they were accountable to it for the profits they had made. The plaintiff's action failed and it was held that the three directors had not, in the circumstances, been in breach of their duties because their company had expressed itself to be disinterested in their negotiations.

---

191 [1942] 1 All ER 378 at 381. The case of *Keech v Sandford* (1726) Sel Cas Ch 61 was cited as authority for this point.

192 [1942] 1 All ER 378 at 389d–e, per Lord Russell.

193 *JJ Harrison (Properties) Ltd v Harrison* [2001] 1 BCLC 158.

194 Similarly, in a single–member company, one of the two directors could embark on a personal frolic to the detriment of the company.

195 *Framlington Group plc v Anderson* [1995] 1 BCLC 475.

(b) Rejected business opportunities

[10.053] It would seem to be sensible for the law to relax directors' liability to account in circumstances where the company's board of directors has considered the transaction but rejected it. There seems to be nothing wrong in principle in permitting one of the directors to personally take up that rejected transaction or contract. In law where the company bona fide rejects a business opportunity, and one of the directors takes it for himself, then the director will not be liable to account for any profits made. This is borne out by *Peso Silver Mines Ltd v Cropper*[196]. In that case one of the directors of the plaintiff-company became aware that several mining claims were up for sale. He advised the board of directors of this and they decided not to acquire the claims because of cash-flow difficulties. The director, who was a geologist, formed a syndicate involving some of the other directors, and together they acquired the mining claims for themselves. The control of the plaintiff-company changed, and the new owners were peeved that the syndicate of directors had made a profit out of an opportunity which was the company's initially and which had come to the directors' notice in the course of their work for the plaintiff-company. However, it was held by the Supreme Court of Canada that the case was distinguishable from the *Regal (Hastings)* case since in the *Peso* case the company had rejected the 'business chance'. Consequently, the court refused an order to compel the directors to account for the profit[197].

[10.054] Some commentators[198] have espoused the general principle that directors should be obliged to account for any profits made where their self-interests conflict with those of the company. This view satisfies itself with the knowledge that the entrepreneurial director could always have disclosed his intentions to the company, and obtained its prior approval. There is much merit in this view since the principal difficulty with a more lenient approach is that it is dependant upon the court being able to satisfy itself that the board acted bona fide in rejecting the contract. Indeed, there is authority to suggest that the decision in *Peso Silver Mines* may not be followed in England where the strict duty to account was recently restated in *Gencor ACP Ltd v Dalby*[199]. In that case the plaintiffs were three group companies engaged in the design, manufacture and sale of asphalt plant and equipment. After the group was taken over, its new owners investigated certain transactions and instituted proceedings against the defendants who were the group's managing director (previously a substantial shareholder in the group) and the company secretary, alleging misfeasance in the misapplication of group money and assets and in diverting business opportunities. It was claimed, in particular, that the managing director had arranged for orders by foreign companies for second-hand refurbished plant and equipment and for equipment ancillary to plant previously supplied by the group to be placed with a company controlled by him. The sales of such second-hand equipment were often to group customers; group notepaper was often used for correspondence; and group staff had

---

196 *Peso Silver Mines Ltd v Cropper* (1966) 58 DLR 1.

197 See *Queensland Mines Ltd v Hudson* (1978) 18 ALR 1, and generally, MacCann (1991) ILT 104 at 105, for a thorough analysis of the cases and principles involved.

198 See Ussher, *Company Law in Ireland* (1986), p 215, and MacCann (1991) ILT 104 at 105.

199 *Gencor ACP Ltd v Dalby* [2000] 2 BCLC 734.

sometimes been used to fit the second-hand equipment. The managing director sought to excuse his actions on the grounds that the group did not, itself, deal in second-hand equipment. Rimer J rejected this, holding:

> 'The principles are well established. It is no answer to them that the company could not or would not have taken up the business opportunity that the director took up for his own benefit. Nor is it an answer that the director's own skill or property were also used in the course of making the profit. The only escape from potential accountability is the obtaining of the prior approval of the company's shareholders after full disclosure of all the facts and circumstances.'[200]

In so holding, Rimer J expressly purported to apply the principle in *Regal (Hastings) Ltd v Gulliver*.

[10.055] Where, however, a company has not even had a chance to consider the business opportunity and where there is no disclosure, the law is clear in providing that the director will be bound to account for any profit gained. This point is illustrated by the case of *Industrial Development Consultants v Cooley*[201] where Mr Cooley, the managing director of the plaintiff-company, tried, on behalf of the company, to secure a construction contract with the Eastern Gas Board, an English public body. Whilst Cooley was unsuccessful from the view point of the company, he himself very much impressed the gas board, who offered the contract to him in his private capacity. Feigning illness, Cooley resigned his position as managing director of the plaintiff-company and took up a job as project manager with the gas board. The plaintiff then sought to make Cooley account for the profit made by him. He refused, countering that there was no breach of fiduciary duty and that at best the plaintiffs could only get damages, although they did not suffer any damage since they could not have obtained the contract themselves in any event. It was held that there was a fiduciary duty owed, and there had been a breach of that duty by the director in using for his own ends the information obtained by him while working for the company[202]. Accordingly, the director was ordered to account for all personal profit made by him.

(c) The remedies available where directors profit from their office

[10.056] The normal remedy available to companies where directors wrongly profit from their office will be an account for profits. There must be a reasonable connection between the breach of duty and the profits for which it is sought to make a fiduciary accountable[203]. The underlying basis of a director's liability for exploiting a business opportunity is that the opportunity is treated as if it were the company's property and the director becomes a constructive trustee of the fruits of his abuse[204]. In the Australian High Court in *Chan v Zacharia*[205] Deane J had said, of the duties of a fiduciary:

---

200 [2000] 2 BCLC 734 at 741, [17].

201 *Industrial Development Consultants v Cooley* [1972] 2 All ER 162.

202 See also *Canadian Aero Service Ltd. v O'Malley* [1973] 40 DLR 371, where a similar situation occurred.

203 See *CMS Dolphin Ltd v Simonet* [2001] 2 BCLC 704.

204 *CMS Dolphin Ltd v Simonet* [2001] 2 BCLC 704.

205 *Chan v Zacharia* (1984) 154 CLR 178 at 198; quoted with apparent approval by Morritt LJ in *Don King Productions Inc v Warren* [2000] 1 BCLC 607 at 629.

'...the principle of equity is that a person who is under a fiduciary obligation must account to the person to whom the obligation is owed for any benefit or gain (i) which has been obtained or received in circumstances where a conflict or a significant possibility of conflict existed between his fiduciary duty and his personal interest in the pursuit or possible receipt of such a benefit or gain or (ii) which was obtained or received by use or by reason of his fiduciary position or of opportunity or knowledge resulting from it. Any such benefit or gain is held by the fiduciary as constructive trustee…'

The English Court of Appeal in *Paragon Finance plc v DB Thakerar & Co*[206] and in *JJ Harrison (Properties) Ltd v Harrison*[207] has observed that where a director receives property in breach of trust he is described as a constructive trustee but in a different position to a 'stranger' who acquires trust property. On the fiduciary duties of directors Chadwick LJ said in *JJ Harrison (Properties) Ltd v Harrison*[208]:

'...a director, on appointment to that office, assumes the duties of a trustee in relation to the company's property. If, therefore, he takes possession of that property, his possession "is coloured from the first by the trust and confidence by means of which he obtained it." His obligations as a trustee in relation to that property do not arise out of the transaction by which he obtained it for himself. The true analysis is that his obligations as a trustee in relation to that property predate the transaction by which it was conveyed to him. The conveyance of the property to himself by the exercise of his powers in breach of trust does not release him from those obligations. He is trustee of the property because it has become vested in him; but his obligations to deal with the property as a trustee arise out of his pre-existing duties as a director; not out of the circumstances in which the property was conveyed.'

[10.057] The Irish decision in *Aerospares Ltd v Thompson*[209] shows that an account for profits will not be the invariable result and that damages alone may be found to be the appropriate remedy. In that case, Kearns J agreed to grant a Mareva injunction to the plaintiff-company against the defendants in circumstances where the first two defendants were former directors of the plaintiff-company whom, it was alleged, had diverted monies from the company to their own use. The plaintiff's contention was that the first three defendants had perpetrated a fraud against the plaintiff by diverting monies due to the plaintiff from its customers and trading connections to the fourth defendant using an account in the name of the fifth defendant. The fifth defendant was a company incorporated in the Seychelles that had exactly the same name as the plaintiff. In addition, the plaintiff claimed further for as then unascertained losses for business allegedly poached by the first three defendants, both whilst still working for the plaintiff and thereafter. Kearns J found that while the plaintiff might well recover damages, it would not extend to profits obtained over a virtually indefinite period from a 'poached client'. Kearns J distinguished the case in hand from *Canadian Aeroservices v O'Malley*[210], where two senior officers were ordered to return profits to their company after they had established the benefit of a contract with a former customer of their company. Kearns J said:

---

206 *Paragon Finance plc v DB Thakerar & Co* [1999] 1 All ER 400.

207 *JJ Harrison (Properties) Ltd v Harrison* [2002] 1 BCLC 162, [2001] EWCA Civ 1467.

208 *JJ Harrison (Properties) Ltd v Harrison* [2002] 1 BCLC 162 at 175, [2001] EWCA Civ 1467 at [29].

209 *Aerospares Ltd v Thompson* (13 January 1999, unreported), High Court (Kearns J).

210 *Canadian Aeroservices v O'Malley* [1973] 40 DLR 371.

> 'That situation seems quite difference on the instant case where two of the three first named defendants were on routine service contracts terminable by one month's notice in writing, in a non-exclusive area of commercial trade and where in any event they could not have been restrained from competing for the same business under either the terms of their employment of under the Competition Acts. Accordingly, while the plaintiff-company may well recover damages in this case, it seems to me that such damages must in reality be confined to "poached" business…rather than the ongoing indefinite time contended for.'[211]

Whether such a distinction will be maintained in future cases on this point, remains to be seen.

[10.058] Transactions entered into by directors with their companies in breach of their duties can be set aside by the company, subject to the defence of laches, acquiescence and the rights of bona fide third parties acquired for value without actual notice of the breach[212]. It should be noted, however, that the English Court of Appeal in *JJ Harrison (Properties) Ltd v Harrison*[213] disallowed the defence of laches and a defence based on the Limitations Act 1980 (UK) to a claim for breach of trust against a director on the grounds that it was not intended to permit a trustee to retain something that he ought not to have.

Fiduciary duties: competition with the company

[10.059] As a general principle, it is not per se a breach of a director's fiduciary duties to be involved in a business which competes with that of his company[214]. The leading authority on an analogous point (concerning the law relating to trustees) is the Irish case of *Moore v M'Glynn*[215] where Chatterton V-C said that he was:

> '...not prepared to hold that a trustee is guilty of a breach of trust in setting himself up in a similar line of business in the neighbourhood, provided that he does not resort to deception, or solicitation of custom from persons dealing at the old shop.'

In that case, an executor and trustee was put in charge of the deceased's shop, which he held in trust and ran for the beneficiaries of the trust. When he set up in business himself, the question arose as to whether or not he was in breach of his trust. It was held that he was not per se in breach of his trust, provided that he did not divert custom from the 'trust shop' to his own shop[216]. The leading English authority on this point is *London and Mashonaland Exploration Co v New Mashonaland Exploration Co*[217]. The entire judgment reads:

---

211 (13 January 1999, unreported), High Court at p 12.

212 See *Aberdeen Railway Co v Blaikie Bros* (1854) 1 Macq 461; *Movites Ltd v Bulfield* [1988] BCLC 104; and *JJ Harrison (Properties) Ltd v Harrison* [2001] 1 BCLC 158.

213 *JJ Harrison (Properties) Ltd v Harrison* [2002] 1 BCLC 162, [2001] EWCA Civ 1467.

214 *Bell v Lever Brothers Ltd* [1932] AC 161.

215 *Moore v M'Glynn* [1894] 1 IR 74 at 89.

216 However, Chatterton VC held that while there was no breach of trust, there was an inconsistency in the trustee's interests under the trust and his own self–interest, and so removed him from the office of trustee.

217 *London and Mashonaland Exploration Co v New Mashonaland Exploration Co* [1891] WN 165.

'Chitty J said, even assuming that Lord Mayo had been duly elected chairman and director of the plaintiff-company, there was nothing in the articles which required him to give any part of his time, much less the whole of his time, to the business of the company, or which prohibited him from acting as a director of another company; neither was there any contract, express or implied, to give his personal services to the plaintiff-company and to no other company. No case had been made out that Lord Mayo was about to disclose to the defendant-company any information that he had obtained confidentially in his character of chairman; the analogy sought to be drawn by the plaintiff-company's counsel between the present case and partnerships was incomplete; no sufficient damage had been shown, and no case had been made for an injunction; the application was wholly unprecedented, and must be dismissed with costs.'

The general principle that it is not per se a breach of a director's fiduciary duty to compete with his company has been criticised by a number of commentators[218].

[10.060] The issue of conflict of interests must always be borne in mind by a director of a company in such situations. The basis for the application of this principle to the office of company director is because both directors and trustees are fiduciaries. So, in *Spring Grove Services (Ireland) Ltd v O'Callaghan*[219] Herbert J said:

'A director of a company owes strict obligations of good faith, fair dealing and honesty to the company of which he is a director. Aspects of these obligations commonly referred to as "fiduciary duties", include a duty not to compete with the company, a duty to act in the best interests of the company and a duty not to use confidential information obtained as such director otherwise and for the benefit of the company.'

[10.061] Where a director is employed under a contract of employment, or service contract, he will have certain duties to his company-employer. For example, where a director has a written contract of employment, there may be an express restraint of trade, non-competition and anti-solicitation clause in his contract[220]. In addition, whether a director's contract is in writing or not, the director-employee owes implied duties of fidelity and loyalty to his company-employer for so long as the contract of employment is in existence[221].

---

218 See, for example, Christie, 'The Director's Fiduciary Duty Not to Compete' [1992] 55 MLR 506.

219 *Spring Grove Services (Ireland) Ltd v O'Callaghan* (31 July 2000, unreported), High Court (Herbert J); [FL3114].

220 See Brearley & Bloch, *Employment Covenants and Confidential Information* (1993); Cheshire, Fifoot & Furmston, *Law of Contract* (12th ed, 1991), ch 12.

221 Cf *Dawnfleet Ltd t/a TES Technology v Shorte and McGowan* reported in (1991) The Irish Times, 6 September, where an interim injunction was granted to the plaintiff-company restraining the defendant directors (who resigned) from competing with the company from termination of their employment until the end of the required notice period. The order granted also required the directors to hand over confidential documents in their possession, not to destroy them, to refrain from soliciting customers and suppliers obtained from the company's confidential information and from publishing matters defamatory to the plaintiff company. Both directors had been responsible for marketing and sales. See also, Wedderburn, *The Worker and The Law* (3rd edn, 1986), p 183.

[10.062] The duty of fidelity owed by an employee will often surface in the context of the abuse of confidential information which is learnt by the director-employee in the course of his employment. It is important to note that where information cannot be classified as a 'trade secret' or 'confidential information' the common law duty of fidelity will not survive the termination of employment. In *Faccenda Chicken Ltd v Fowler*[222] the defendants, who were former employees (but not directors) of the plaintiff-company, were sued when they began to compete with the plaintiff-company by selling fresh chickens from refrigerated vans. The information used by them in their business included: the company's pricing policy, customers' names and addresses, routes taken by salesmen and other such matters. Using this information they proceeded to undercut the plaintiff-company. It was held that the plaintiff-company could not invoke an implied term of fidelity because the contract of employment had ended, and so the information used could not be classified as being legally confidential.

Breach of the implied duty of fidelity may justify the dismissal of an employee-director. In *Fairbrother v Stiefel Laboratories (Ireland) Ltd*[223] the dismissal of an employee was held to be fair where he had double-jobbed with his wife, another pharmaceutical researcher, who had her own business making a product similar to that made by her husband's employers[224].

Directors' duties of care, skill and diligence

[10.063] Directors owe duties of care, skill and diligence to their company[225]. A director must not act negligently or conduct the business of his company in an inept manner. These duties arise not only from the directors' fiduciary duties as agents, and from the fact that directors will often be employees, but also because directors owe duties of care in tort to persons who forseeably rely on their actions. Like other directors' duties, these are primarily owed to the company, but can sometimes be owed to third parties. It has been said[226] that unlike the principles involved in fiduciary duties which are largely prohibitive or negative, the duties under discussion here are in the nature of positive duties. As regards the enforcement of these duties it will invariably be the case that the controllers of a company will be slow to sue themselves. Often, action will only be taken against inept directors where, upon a company being wound up, a liquidator instigates such action or, alternatively, where following a change in a company's ownership, the control of the company shifts to outsiders. It will frequently be the case that directors'

---

222 *Faccenda Chicken Ltd v Fowler* [1986] 1 All ER 617.

223 *Fairbrother v Stiefel Laboratories (Ireland) Ltd* (1985) UD665/1985. See also, *Mulchrone v Feeney* (1983) UD1023/1982.

224 See also, *Conachey v Little Chic Knitwear* (1985) UD342/85.

225 See generally, Trebilcock, 'The Liability of Company Directors For Negligence' (1969) 32 MLR 499; Stanton & Dugdale, 'Recent Developments in Professional Negligence – IV: Directors' Liability' (1982) NLJ 251; Loose & Yelland, *The Company Director* (6th edn, 1987), para 4.8; Keane, *Equity and the Law of Trusts in the Republic of Ireland* (1988), para 29.29; Forde, *Commercial Law* (2nd edn, 1997), para 5.35 *ff*; and Ussher, *Company Law in Ireland* (1986), p 228 *ff*.

226 See Loose & Yelland, *The Company Director* (6th edn, 1987), para 4.8.1.

duties of care, skill and diligence will be enforced by CA 1963, s 298, in a misfeasance suit[227]. It is proposed to consider the various facets of such duties as follows:

(a) General principles of care, skill and diligence.
(b) Qualifications: their presence or absence.
(c) The need for diligence.
(d) Reliance on others for advice.
(e) Tortious liability to third parties.

(a) General principles of care, skill and diligence

[10.064] In the absence of an indemnity of the type envisaged by CA 1963, Sch 1, Table A, Part I, model reg 138 (the'model regulations')[228], a company director is liable in tort for negligent behaviour. One of the oldest statements on this point is found in the case of *Charitable Corporation v Sutton*[229] where Lord Hardwicke said:

> '[Directors] may be guilty of acts of commission or omission, of malfeasance or non-feasance...By accepting a trust of this sort, a person is obliged to execute it with fidelity and reasonable diligence; and it is no excuse to say that they had no benefit from it, but that it was merely honorary; and therefore, they are within the case of common trustees.'

In that case, 50 committee members of a company formed by charter were found liable for losses to the company which were occasioned by the failure of a person who was employed by the corporation to require adequate security for loans made to impecunious peasants. However, this promising start, from the viewpoint of the imposition of liability, plummeted in subsequent cases. The 'low point'[230] has been said to be the case of *Turquand v Marshall*[231] where the so-called 'business management' rule came into vogue[232]. According to Lord Hatherley LC, provided that the directors acted bona fide and within their authority they could not be liable for loss occasioned to the company. In that case the directors had caused the company to make a loan to one of their number, who subsequently died insolvent without repaying the loan. The directors were held not to have been negligent or liable for the loss to the company. Subsequent judicial statements have tempered the extremities of both the 'high' and 'low' points of directors' negligence. The current thinking is that it remains difficult to establish actionable negligence, and the standard of care required of directors has certainly not kept pace with developments in the law of tort since the landmark case of *Donoughue v Stevenson*[233]. It may also be noted that even where negligence is proven, the court may grant relief under CA 1963, s 391[234].

[227] Note that in *Re B Johnson & Co (Builders) Ltd* [1955] Ch 634 it was suggested that so-called 'mere-common-law-negligence' would not ground a misfeasance suit and that the negligence involved would have to have been such as to force the company into liquidation.

[228] See para **[10.079]** n 275.

[229] *Charitable Corporation v Sutton* (1742) 2 Atk 400, at 405,406.

[230] See Trebilcock, 'The Liability of Company Directors For Negligence' (1969) 32 MLR 499 at 500.

[231] *Turquand v Marshall* (1869) LR 4 Ch App 376.

[232] See Rhoads, 'Personal Liability of Directors for Corporate Mismanagement' (1916) 65 U of Pa LR 128.

[233] *Donoughue v Stevenson* [1932] AC 562.

[234] See para **[10.076]** *ff*.

[10.065] The leading case on directors' duties in the context of negligence remains *Re City Equitable Fire Insurance Co Ltd*[235]. The facts there were that the company concerned had lost £1.2 million because of bad investments and the fraudulent activity of one director, a 'daring and unprincipled scoundrel'. When the company went into liquidation, it was sought to make the other honest directors personally liable for the losses of the company. Although the action ultimately failed because of a specific exclusion in the company's articles of association for losses not caused by the wilful neglect or default of the directors, the judgment of the learned Romer J remains instructive. The essence of his judgment (which is worthy of being quoted in extenso) was that to establish directors' duties in the context of negligence:

> '...it is necessary to consider not only the nature of the company's business, but also the manner in which the work of the company is in fact distributed between the directors and other officials of the company, provided that this distribution is a reasonable one in the circumstances, and is not inconsistent with the provisions of the articles of association. In discharging the duties of his position thus ascertained a director must, of course[236],
>
> (a) act honestly; but he must also exercise some degree of both skill and diligence...
>
> (b) The care that he is bound to take has been described...as "reasonable care" to be measured by the care an ordinary man might be expected to take in the circumstances on his own behalf...
>
> (c) A director need not exhibit in the performance of his duties a greater degree of skill than may reasonably be expected from a person of his knowledge and experience[237].
>
> (d) A director is not bound to give continuous attention to the affairs of his company. His duties are of an intermittent nature to be performed at periodical board meetings, and at meetings of any committee of the board upon which he happens to be placed. He is not however, bound to attend all such meetings though he ought to attend whenever, in the circumstances, he is reasonably able to do so.
>
> (e) In respect of all duties that, having regard to the exigencies of business, and the articles of association, may properly be left to some other official, a director is, in the absence of grounds for suspicion, justified in trusting that official to perform such duties honestly.'

The most contentious of these is the principle encapsulated in (c), namely that the standard of care appropriate to a company director is a subjective standard. Subjectivity in this context has been interpreted as meaning that an idiot, provided he is honest, can avoid liability. The existence of professional and quasi-professional qualifications among company directors will mean that their actions will be judged by standards which accord with their increased subjective ability. The effect is that the modern spread of education and the rise of the executive director will mean that there is an increasing probability that liability may be imposed on modern directors.

---

[235] *Re City Equitable Fire Insurance Co Ltd* [1925] Ch 407.

[236] In the interests of clarity the dictum is broken down into point form, with sections of text omitted. The reader is referred to the actual judgment of Romer J at 407–408.

[237] As Romer J said by way of an example, 'A director of a life insurance company, for instance, does not guarantee that he has the skill of an actuary or physician.'

[10.066] There is modern precedent for findings of negligence against directors. In *Daniels v Daniels*[238] Templeman J held that the disposal of company land to a director for its probate value (£4,250) where he subsequently sold the land for £120,000 was negligence and the minority shareholders could bring an action against him, notwithstanding that there was no actual fraud. In *Cohen v Selby*[239] the Court of Appeal allowed an appeal against a trial judge's finding that a director had been negligent in delegating to his then 19-year-old son the decision of whether or not to effect insurance against loss or theft in respect of stock that was outside the UK. Having purchased jewellery worth some £393,000, the jewellery had been stolen or lost in the course of a ferry crossing. The company was subsequently wound up insolvent. The Court of Appeal held that the pleaded case against the director went no further than to allege negligence in delegating to his son the power to decide whether or not to insure the company's property outside of the UK, that the allegation of breach of duty lay not in the decision to delegate per se but in the decision to delegate to the 19-year-old director and student, and that in the circumstances there was no evidence touching upon the 19-year-old director's unsuitability.

(b) Qualifications: their presence or absence

[10.067] In law, a company director may be as thick as two short planks. The palpable lack of business acumen seen in two of the directors in *Re Brazilian Rubber Plantations & Estates Ltd*[240] could still be equalled today. There, Neville J described two of the directors in the following terms:

> 'Sir Arthur Aylmer was absolutely ignorant of business. He only consented to act because he was told the office would give him a little pleasant employment without incurring any responsibility. HW Tugwell was a partner in a firm of bankers in a good position in Bath; he was seventy-five years of age and very deaf; he was induced to join the board by representations made to him...'.

Neville J went on to hold that neither of the directors was liable in negligence when the company lost substantially after investing badly in the speculative business of rubber plantations in North Brazil. Thus, it was said of a director that he was:

> '...not bound to bring any special qualifications to his office. He may undertake the management of a rubber company in complete ignorance of everything connected with rubber, without incurring responsibility for the mistakes which may result from such ignorance.'

This may be seen as the 'country gentleman syndrome', since the older cases are typically concerned with the squire turned businessman whose company got into dire straits[241].

[10.068] However, while the foregoing remains true in theory, the modern practice is for directors to have more qualifications than in the past and the modern trend is for company directors to have a certain business acumen. While qualifications are not

---

[238] *Daniels v Daniels* [1978] 2 All ER 89.

[239] *Cohen v Selby* [2001] 1 BCLC 176.

[240] *Re Brazilian Rubber Plantations & Estates Ltd* [1911] 1 Ch 425.

[241] See *Re Denham & Co* (1884) 25 Ch D 752.

necessary their presence will raise the standard of care which an educated director will be expected to exercise. In what has been described as a case involving an exhaustive analysis[242] of directors' duties of skill, care and diligence, *Daniels v Anderson*[243], the Supreme Court of New South Wales said:

> 'A person who accepts the office of director of a particular company undertakes the responsibility of ensuring that he or she understands the nature of the duty a director is called upon to perform. That duty will vary according to the size and business of the particular company and the experience or *skills that the director held himself or herself out to have in support of appointment to the office*. None of this is novel. It turns upon the natural expectations and reliance placed by shareholders on the experience and skill of a particular director.' (Emphasis added)

So whilst a director may in fact be intellectually challenged, he may forfeit his immunity on this basis if he musters the intelligence to dupe the company into believing that he has particular experience or skills.

(c) The need for diligence

[10.069] The degree of diligence required of a director is dependent upon his abilities and is subjectively ascertained. Again, the older cases are instructive, the case of *Re Cardiff Savings Bank (the Marquis of Bute's case)*[244] being an example in point. In that case the Marquis became president of a bank at the tender age of six months, inheriting the office from his father in a singularly blatant display of nepotism. Of course, the diligence which could have been expected of the child Bute could not have been much. His involvement in the affairs of the company did not keep pace with his own development, and his diary only permitted him to attend one meeting after he reached the age of majority. Some 20 years later the liquidator of the company sought to make the adult Bute liable to reimburse the funds which were fraudulently taken from the company by one of the officials of the bank. It was held by Stirling J that he was not liable, was not expected to attend board meetings, and indeed the fact that he received regular notice of the company's meetings meant that he could assume that business was being transacted as usual!

[10.070] An Irish case on the question of directors' diligence is *Jackson v Munster Bank Ltd*[245]. There the respondent bank lent money to several of its own directors notwithstanding that loans to directors were proscribed by the bank's articles of association. One of the directors, whom it was sought to have made personally liable for the lending, did not participate in the meetings at which the loans were sanctioned. In fact the bank had two branches, one in Dublin and one in Cork. The director concerned worked in Dublin and had attended meetings held there. However, it was in Cork that the meetings were held at which the loans were sanctioned. His liability was in fact ultimately held to be limited. He was not liable for the loss arising from the Cork

242 Per Jonathan Parker J in *Re Barings plc (No 5); Secretary of State for Trade and Industry v Baker (No 5)* [1999] 1 BCLC 433 at 488b.

243 *Daniels v Anderson* (1995) 16 ACSR 607 at 668.

244 *Re Cardiff Savings Bank (the Marquis of Bute's case)* [1892] 2 Ch 100.

245 *Jackson v Munster Bank Ltd* (1885) 15 LR Ir 356.

meeting, but was liable in respect of a subsequent loss because he was shown a letter which should have alerted him to the possibility of the 'systematic fraudulent misappropriation of the property of the bank', and because of his inertia, from this point onward he was held to be liable. Had he been more diligent, he might have escaped liability entirely.

[10.071] The modern position must be taken to be tempered, and whether or not a director is guilty of not being diligent must depend upon the circumstances of each case. Clearly, where the director is a professional person and he abdicates his responsibilities to the company resulting in the management of the company being left to another director who causes losses to be incurred, there is a strong likelihood that inert directors will be responsible as they were in the case of *Dorchester Finance Co Ltd v Stebbing*[246]. There, two professional men who were non-executive directors, were made liable for the debts of the company occasioned when a third director caused the company to make loans which were never repaid. While it would seem that such liability may be restricted to instances in which, had the directors intervened, loss would have been avoided[247], indications to date are that the Irish courts might impose a stricter liability [248]. The directors of an Irish 'two-person' or single-member private company should exercise great caution and where an active role is not taken, resignation should be seriously considered. Indeed it seems there are greater duties of diligence owed in the context of a private company than in a public company[249]. This is particularly true because of the new legislation on disqualification of directors, reckless trading and the general possibilities of incurring personal liability which loom ominously before all directors, shadow directors and non-participating nominee directors alike. An even more recent example is the case of *Re Contract Packaging Ltd*[250] where Flood J imposed personal liability on the wife of one of the directors under CA 1963, s 297 for fraudulent trading and CA 1963, s 298 for breach of fiduciary duty. Indeed, it was ordered that the family home of the husband and wife directors be delivered up to the liquidator. Although these examples of increased liability do not arise from tortious duties it is thought they are still relevant to the present discussion.

[10.072] When a director is present at a meeting it is no defence for him to claim to have not been listening, asleep or otherwise inattentive while the meeting was being held and when improper decisions were taken by the other directors. It is one thing not to be present, but once present, one cannot claim not to have paid attention: *Land Credit Co of Ireland v Lord Fermoy*[251].

---

246 *Dorchester Finance Co Ltd v Stebbing* [1989] BCLC 498, a case which was heard in 1977 but went unreported for 12 years. See also, (1980) 1 Co Law 38.

247 See Trebilcock, 'The Liability of Company Directors For Negligence' (1969) 32 MLR 499.

248 See, for example, *Re Hunting Lodges Ltd* [1985] ILRM 75 considered, para **[10.042]**.

249 See also *Brenes & Co v Downie* (1914) SC 97 at 104.

250 *Re Contract Packaging Ltd* (16 January 1992, unreported), High Court per Flood J, reported in (1992) The Irish Times, 17 January. The author wishes to thank Mr Michael McInerney, Solicitor for bringing this case to his attention.

251 *Land Credit Co of Ireland v Lord Fermoy* (1870) LR 5 Ch App 763.

(d) Reliance on others for advice

[10.073] Not only is a director permitted to obtain, and rely upon, advice from other officers (*Re City Equitable Fire Insurance Co Ltd)*, but he is also obliged to seek such advice[252]. Where a director signs a company cheque, Romer J stated in *Re City Equitable Fire Insurance Co Ltd* that the director should satisfy himself that there is an authorising resolution, which should preferably specify the proposed payee. It has been said that such suggestions are impracticable for large companies[253].

(e) Tortious liability to third parties

[10.074] The question of a director being held liable to third parties is a difficult one and its answer is largely dependent upon the extension of the general principles of foreseeable liability in the law of negligence. Here, we are concerned with liability to outsiders of the company. In *WB Anderson & Sons v Rhodes*[254] a director was held liable for negligently supervising the accounts of his company and for not realising that one of the company's debtors had amassed dangerously large debts to the company. The buyer of shares in the company was thus duped, as was a subsequent third party supplier who was told that the company was financially healthy[255]. However, it was said in *Mutual Citizens' Assurance Co Ltd v Evatt*[256] that for a person to be liable to third parties the person must give his advice in a professional capacity, meaning that a director must hold himself out as having the requisite knowledge to advise the third party.

[10.075] In *Williams v Natural Life Health Foods Ltd*[257] the English House of Lords overruled a Court of Appeal decision that would have had significant adverse consequences for directors of companies. The Court of Appeal had held[258] that a franchisee had been persuaded to take on a franchise in reliance upon the personal expertise of the director of the franchisor-company and that there were special circumstances that displaced the presumption that the company alone was responsible. This was reversed by the House of Lords, which held, on the evidence, that there was an insufficient relationship between the franchisee and the director as to result in the director assuming responsibility. It further held that the appropriate test was an objective test as to whether or not the franchisee (who claimed the director had made representations) could reasonably rely on the director's assumption of personal liability in respect of the representations. Lord Steyn said:

---

[252] See *Fry v Tapson* (1884) 28 Ch D 268, where directors were said to be correct in seeking independent advice in respect of the valuation of a property which it was proposed to take as security for a mortgage.

[253] See Loose & Yelland, *The Company Director* (6th edn, 1987), para 4.8.2.

[254] *WB Anderson & Sons v Rhodes* [1967] 2 All ER 850.

[255] See also *Hedley Byrne & Co Ltd v Heller & Partners Ltd* [1963] 2 All ER 575.

[256] In *Mutual Citizens' Assurance Co Ltd v Evatt* [1971] 1 All ER 150.

[257] *Williams v Natural Life Health Foods Ltd* [1998] BCC 428. For comment on the House of Lords' decision, see Milman, 'Personal Liability of Directors: Aiding an Enterprise Culture?' (1999) Palmer's In Company, Issue 2/99, 12 February 1999.

[258] For comment, on the Court of Appeal decision see Milman, 'Directors Under Fire' (1997) Palmer's In Company, Issue 4/97, 16 April 1997.

'In the present case a triangular position is under consideration: the prospective franchisees, the franchisor company, and the director. In such a case where the personal liability of the director is in question the internal arrangements between a director and his company cannot be the foundation of a director's personal liability in tort. The enquiry must be whether the director, or anybody on his behalf, conveyed directly or indirectly to the prospective franchisees that the director assumed personal responsibility towards the prospective franchisees.'[259]

It was also held that the director could not be regarded as a joint tortfeasor with the company as to do so would expose directors, officers and employees of companies carrying on business to a plethorah of new tort claims[260].

Judicial relief for directors and indemnities

(a) Judicial relief for directors and other officers

[10.076] Section 391 of CA 1963 confers discretion on the court to relieve directors from liability in certain circumstances. It provides:

'(1) If in any proceeding for negligence, default, breach of duty or breach of trust against an officer of a company or a person employed by a company as auditor, it appears to the court hearing the case that that officer or person is or may be liable in respect of the negligence, default, breach of duty or breach of trust, but that he has acted honestly and reasonably, and that, having regard to all the circumstances of the case, including those connected with his appointment, he ought fairly to be excused for the negligence, default, breach of duty or breach of trust, that court may relieve him, either wholly or partly from his liability on such terms as the court may think fit.

(2) Where any such officer or person as aforesaid has reason to apprehend that any claim will or might be made against him in respect of any negligence, default, breach of duty or breach of trust, he may apply to the court for relief, and the court on any such application shall have the same power to relieve him as under this section it would have had if it had been a court before which proceedings against that person for negligence, default, breach of duty or breach of trust had been brought.

(3) Where any case to which subsection (1) applies is being tried by a judge with a jury, the judge, after hearing the evidence, may, if he is satisfied that the defendant ought in pursuance of that subsection to be relieved, either in whole or in part, from the liability sought to be enforced against him, withdraw the case in whole or in part from the jury, and direct judgment to be entered for the defendant on such terms as to costs or otherwise as the judge may think proper.'

[10.077] Section 391 of CA 1963 would seem not to have received scrutiny by an Irish court[261]. The circumstances in which relief may be granted is seen in a number of

---

[259] [1998] BCC 428 at 433. Lord Steyn gave, as an example where this had been proved, *Fairline Shipping Corp v Adamson* [1975] QB 180.

[260] Cf *AWA Ltd v Daniels* [1995] 16 ACSR 607 where an Australian court held that directors can be guilty of negligence and thus joint tortfeasors. For comment, see Marks, 'Taking Responsibility: The New Regime for Directors', (1998) In House Lawyer 36.

[261] For a concise note on the invocation of the similar English provision in the courts of England and Wales, see Linklater, 'Section 727 Relief From Liability – Redundant or Relevant' (2002) Company Law Newsletter, Issue 3/2002.

English decisions. In *Duckwari plc v Offerventure Ltd (No 2)*[262] Nourse LJ held that a statutory liability arising under the Companies Act 1985, s 322(3)(b) (UK) (see CA 1990, s 29) was 'a liability in respect of default' within the meaning of the equivalent English section (Companies Act 1985, s 727 (UK))[263]. In *Coleman Taymar Ltd v Oakes*[264], however, it was stated that relief under the similar English provision[265] could be granted in respect of a liability occasioned by a breach of fiduciary duty or arising out of an account for profits or an inquiry as to damages[266].

[10.078] It is an absolute precondition to the grant of relief under CA 1963, s 391 that a supplicant-officer has acted 'honestly and reasonably'[267]. But how does the latter reference to 'reasonableness' sit against a claim for relief where the officer has been negligent? Interpreting the similar English provision, Companies Act 1985, s727 (UK), Hoffmann LJ said in *Re D'Jan of London Ltd*[268] that the section:

> '...gives the court a discretionary power to relieve a director wholly or in part from liability for breaches of duty, including negligence, if the court considers that he acted honestly and reasonably and ought fairly to be excused. It may seem odd that a person found to have been guilty of negligence, which involves failing to take reasonable care, can ever satisfy a court that he acted reasonably. Nevertheless, the section clearly contemplates that he may do so and it follows that conduct may be reasonable for the purposes of s 727 despite amounting to lack of reasonable care at common law.'

In *Bairstow v Queens Moat Houses plc*[269] a director was found to be liable for unlawfully paying dividends where the company had insufficient distributable reserves. Nelson J said that 'even if under the rules of negligence a director ought to have known of the facts which rendered the payments unlawful, the court may nevertheless relieve him from liability if considering his personal situation it was reasonable that he did not in fact know.'[270] The 'guilty of negligence but relieved on account of reasonableness' paradox can therefore be resolved by focussing upon the degree of culpability of the director's conduct. In that case Nelson J said that 'if his conduct was honest but he was nevertheless guilty of negligence, he might still be relieved from liability if his negligence was not gross but the 'kind of thing which could happen to any busy man.'[271]

262 *Duckwari plc v Offerventure Ltd (No 2)* [1999] BCC 11 (Court of Appeal).

263 See Chapter 11, *Statutory Regulation of Transactions Involving Directors and their Companies*, para **[11.049]**.

264 *Coleman Taymar Ltd v Oakes* [2001] 2 BCLC 749.

265 Companies Act 1985 (UK), s 727(1).

266 Cf in *Customs and Excise Commissioners v Hedon Alfa Ltd* [1981] 1 QB 81 it was held that relief under the similar English provision was only available in respect of a claim against a director for breach of duty, negligence default or trust in an action brought by the company.

267 *National Trustees Co of Australia v General Finance Co of Australia* [1905] AC 373. See also *Bairstow v Queens Moat Houses plc* [2001] 2 BCLC 531, [2001] EWCA Civ 712 where the English Court of Appeal held that 'honesty and reasonableness are absolutely necessary preconditions' and held that it was not open to a judge, having found former directors to have been guilty of dishonesty in preparing false accounts, to find that they had acted honestly and reasonably in paying any dividends on the strength of those accounts.

268 *Re D'Jan of London Ltd* [1993] BCC 646 at 648H–649B.

269 *Bairstow v Queens Moat Houses plc* [2001] 2 BCLC 531, [2001] EWCA Civ 712.

270 [2001] EWCA Civ 712 at 1.034.

271 [2001] EWCA Civ 712 at 1.035, incorporating a quotation from Hoffmann LJ in *Re D'Jan of London Ltd* [1993] BCC 646 at 649C.

In that case the court did not grant relief because it found that the directors had not acted honestly or reasonably. In *Re Brian D Pierson (Contractors) Ltd*[272] the court excused directors from liability for certain misfeasance claims, but not others. There it was held that a failure to obtain payment for goodwill in selling part of the company's business could not be regarded as reasonable but the making redundant of two senior employees was reasonable, although only to the extent that proper redundancy payments had been granted to them.

The position is, therefore, a legislative fudge that vests in the courts a discretion to take all circumstances into account in deciding whether or not to make an officer personally liable. The court is indeed expressly directed by s 391 to have 'regard to all the circumstances of the case'. So in *Coleman Taymar Ltd v Oakes and another*[273] it was said:

> 'It does not follow that merely because a director has acted (subjectively) honestly and (objectively) reasonably the court is bound to excuse him. Proof that a director has acted honesty and reasonably are preconditions of the court's jurisdiction. Once the conditions are fulfilled, the court must consider whether in all the circumstances the director ought fairly to be excused, and if so may (not must) relieve him either absolutely or partly on the terms the court thinks fit.'[274]

In that case a director had used company confidential information to negotiate the purchase of leases personally, had failed to disclose his interest to the company and had competed with the company. It was found that the company was entitled to an inquiry as to any benefit that had accrued to the director from the breach of duty and to nominal damages for the director's breach of contract. It was, however, held that the director was entitled to relief from liability for engaging in competition since he had acted honestly and reasonably.

(b) Indemnities for directors and other officers

[10.079] Directors may not rely upon provisions in companies' articles of association which have the effect of exempting or indemnifying company officers from any liability in respect of negligence, default, breach of duty or breach of trust[275]. Section 200 of CA 1963 provides:

> 'Subject as hereinafter provided, any provision whether contained in the articles of a company or in any contract with a company or otherwise for exempting any officer of the company or any person employed by the company as auditor from, or indemnifying him against, any liability which by virtue of any rule of law would otherwise attach to him in respect of any negligence, default, breach of duty or breach of trust of which he may be guilty in relation to the company shall be void, so, however, that—
>
> (a) nothing in this section shall operate to deprive any person of any exemption or right to be indemnified in respect of anything done or omitted to be done by him while any such provision was in force; and

---

[272] *Re Brian D Pierson (Contractors) Ltd* [1998] BCC 26.

[273] *Coleman Taymar Ltd v Oakes* [2001] 2 BCLC 749.

[274] [2001] 2 BCLC 749 at 770.

[275] See Passmore, 'Directors' Indemnities', (1995) 16 Co Lawyer 243.

(b) notwithstanding anything in this section, a company may, in pursuance of any such provision as aforesaid, indemnify any such officer or auditor against any liability incurred by him in defending proceedings, whether civil or criminal, in which judgment is given in his favour or in which he is acquitted, or in connection with any application under section 391 in which relief is granted to him by the court.'

Accordingly, whilst any exemption or indemnity for directors will be void, a company may indemnify an officer for that officer's legal costs incurred in civil or criminal proceedings taken against him provided he is successful in defending such proceedings. Model form articles of association provide such an indemnity in model reg 138.[276] Although the general rule is that the articles are only enforceable between the company and its members, qua member inter se, the courts have been easily satisfied that the indemnity in model reg 138 has been incorporated into contracts between companies and their directors and auditors[277].

[C] DIRECTORS' STATUTORY DUTIES ARISING ON INSOLVENCY

[10.080] Generally, all directors owe a statutory duty to their companies to ensure that the requirements of the Companies Acts are complied with by the company[278]. This chapter is concerned with the statutory duties owed by directors where a company is insolvent. The following matters are considered:

1. Reckless trading.
2. Criminal fraudulent trading.
3. Civil fraudulent trading.
4. Personal liability for failure to keep proper books of account.
5. Section 251 of CA 1990: invocation of statutory remedies where a company is not being wound up.
6. Misfeasance.

Reckless trading

[10.081] The civil remedy of reckless trading arising out of proceedings under the Companies (Amendment) Act 1990 ('C(A)A 1990') was first introduced by s 33 of that Act. This has now been repealed by CA 1990, s 180(3) which inserted CA 1963, s 297A. Proceedings for reckless trading can arise in two distinct circumstances[279]:

---

[276] Model reg 138 provides: 'Every director, managing director, agent, auditor, secretary and other officer for the time being of the company shall be indemnified out of the assets of the company against any liability incurred by him in defending any proceedings, whether civil or criminal, in relation to his acts while acting in such office, in which judgment is given in his favour or in which he is acquitted or in connection with any application under section 391 of the Act in which relief is granted to him by the court'.

[277] See *John v Price Waterhouse* [2001] TLR 533.

[278] CA 1963, s 383(3), as replaced by CLEA 2001, s 100.

[279] See Flynn, 'Reckless Trading' (1991) ILT 186; MacCann, 'Reckless Trading Revisited' (1993) ILT 31; Kettle, 'Improper Trading in Ireland and Britain' (1994) ILT 91. For a prospective analysis of the possibilities of reckless trading coming into Irish law, see Ussher, *Company Law in Ireland* (1986), p 530 *ff*.

— during an examinership, or

— during a winding up.

Before considering the circumstances in which proceedings for reckless trading can be brought, it is proposed to first consider the actual principles of law applicable to reckless trading.

[10.082] The principal section on reckless trading is CA 1963, s 297A which provides that:

> '(1) If in the course of winding up of a company or in the course of proceedings under the Companies (Amendment) Act 1990, it appears that—
>
> (a) any person was, while an officer of the company, knowingly a party to the carrying on of any business of the company in a reckless manner...
>
> the court, on the application of the receiver, examiner, liquidator or any other creditor or contributory of the company, may, if it thinks it proper to do so, declare that such person shall be personally responsible without any limitation of liability, for all or any part of the debts or other liabilities of the company as the court may direct.'

Irish law now encompasses the concept whereby the officers, including the directors and shadow directors[280] of a company can be made personally liable for the debts of the company where it is shown that they acted recklessly. The first question which must be addressed on an application for reckless trading is: was the respondent a party to the carrying on of the business in a reckless manner?

(a) The meaning of 'knowingly' reckless

[10.083] Before personal liability can be imposed upon an officer it must be shown that he has been knowingly a party to the carrying on of any business of the company in a reckless manner. Under this heading, the circumstances in which a person can be found to have in fact been knowingly reckless is considered. This contrasts with the situation where a person may not have been in fact knowingly reckless but where he is deemed in law to have been reckless[281].

[10.084] The meaning of the word 'reckless' poses great difficulties of interpretation. Traditionally, a person would only be said to be reckless if he actually contemplated the particular consequences of his actions, and went on to consciously run the risk of such consequences ensuing. This is known as the *Cunningham* test of recklessness[282]. However there is another possible test, known as the *Cauldwell* test[283] which holds that a person will be reckless even where he does not appreciate the risks consequential upon his actions, where such risks would have been appreciated by a reasonable man. The difference between the two tests is that the former is subjective and the latter objective. The leading Irish case on recklessness is in the context of criminal law: *People v Murray*[284]. In that case the Supreme Court delivered five opinions, each of which

280 CA 1963, s 297A(10).

281 See para **[10.087]** *ff*.

282 *R v Cunningham* [1957] 2 All ER 412.

283 *R v Cauldwell* [1982] AC 341.

284 *People v Murray* [1977] IR 360. See McAleese, 'Just What is Recklessness' (1981) DULJ 29.

involved different tests of recklessness. One foreign judgment on recklessness which comes from the Republic of South Africa is *State v Goertz*[285]. That case concerned the meaning of recklessness in the context of the South African provision of reckless trading[286]. There, an objective test was favoured and it was not necessary for the person to have actually adverted to the risk involved, it being merely required that the person 'acted recklessly judged by the standards of reasonable businessmen'.

[10.085] The leading Irish decision on reckless trading is *Re Hefferon Kearns Ltd*[287]. The facts were that the respondents in the proceedings for personal responsibility for the debts and liabilities of the company were the directors of an ill-fated building company called Hefferon Kearns Ltd. Incorporated in 1988, it commenced trading in 1989 with an issued share capital of £202, the majority of the shares being held by the respondent directors. The company had three main contracts, in respect of construction work at Simmonscourt, Malahide and Rathgar. Six months after the company commenced trading, management accounts were prepared, which showed that to June 1989, the company had suffered a net loss of £73,101. In his judgment, Lynch J remarked that while indicating insolvency:

> '...the summer had arrived: the company had good contracts on hand: and the defendants as directors, having considered the position, were confident that the losses could be reversed and were proved right in that the audited accounts for the year ending the 31st December 1989 showed a net loss of only £8,113.'[288]

Optimism had reasonably prevailed. Because of the loss in 1989 the directors sought and obtained bi-monthly management accounts so as to keep the trading position of the company under control and scrutiny. Those accounts, up to 31 July 1990, showed total losses (including the losses carried from 1989) of £142,507. In the opinion of Lynch J, the accounts 'indicated a very serious crisis as to the viability of the company at that time'[289]. Previously, in May of 1990, two of the directors had borrowed £45,000 personally which was indirectly used to finance the company and the net effect of which was to result in their incurring personal liability 'in order to improve the company's cash flow.'[290]

The directors usually met for an informal directors' meeting each Monday. Immediately after the building trade holidays in August 1990, the directors met and considered the position of the company in the light of the accounts available. It was agreed that an urgent review of the company's trading position was required and it was resolved at that meeting that each of the four respondent directors would be assigned different tasks, the cumulative effect of which was designed to examine work on hand. At that meeting it was decided to continue trading to give priority to the Rathgar contract but to complete the others and to try to control and reduce costs in so far as possible. The company's

[285] *State v Goertz* (1980) (1) SA 269.

[286] Companies Act 1973 (RSA), s 424(1).

[287] *Dublin Heating Company Ltd v Hefferon Kearns Ltd* [1993] 3 IR 191 at 200, per Lynch J .

[288] [1993] 3 IR 191 at 200.

[289] [1993] 3 IR 19 at 201.

[290] [1993] 3 IR 19 at 201.

auditors were also instructed to prepare further accounts, on a doomsday basis, so as to assist the directors in deciding whether the company was viable.

The directors managed to discharge debts to the end of August, but realised by mid-September that they would have great difficulty in meeting payments at the end of September. Accordingly, another meeting was convened for 17 September 1990, at which one of the directors collapsed and was removed to hospital. On his discharge from hospital on 27 September the meeting was reconvened at his home (against medical advice). At that meeting their review was completed: the contracts at Simmonscourt and Malahide would be abandoned or rescinded and Rathgar would be pursued as the best chance to get money for their creditors. It was also decided that two of the directors would commence approaching creditors individually in an attempt to secure their co-operation for a moratorium. The minutes of the meeting indicated that achieving fairness amongst the creditors was paramount in the directors' minds.

The meetings with the company's creditors did not run smoothly and creditors began calling on some of the directors at their homes. Lynch J accepted one director's description of this as 'involving extreme pressure and a nightmare'[291]. Eventually, it was resolved that individual meetings with the creditors was futile, and so it was resolved to call a general meeting of the creditors. At that meeting the creditors by a majority decided to apply for the appointment of an examiner. The application was successful, an examiner was appointed and arising from that appointment, proceedings for reckless trading were instituted against the four director-respondents under C(A)A 1990, s 33.

[10.086] Having set out in full C(A)A 1990, s 33, and the submissions by both the plaintiffs and the defendants, Lynch J reviewed the meaning of 'reckless'. In particular, he noted[292] that the Supreme Court considered the meaning of 'reckless' in *Donovan v Landys Ltd*[293] and that Kingsmill Moore J had quoted Megaw J in *Shawinigan v Vokins*[294], Lynch J said that this seemed to him 'to go to the root of the matter and to constitute the best and most realistic test of recklessness which has yet been propounded in cases of tort'. What Kingsmill Moore J (and Lynch J) thought worthy of quoting in extenso was the following:

> 'In my view reckless means grossly careless. Recklessness is gross carelessness – the doing of something which in fact involves a risk whether the doer realises it or not: and the risk being such having regard to all the circumstances that the taking of that risk would be described in ordinary parlance as reckless. The likelihood or otherwise that damage will follow is one element to be considered not whether the doer of the act actually realised the likelihood. The extent of the damage which is likely to follow is another element not the wisdom or folly happens to foresee. If the risk is slight and the damage which will follow if things go wrong is small it may not be reckless however unjustified the doing of the act may be. If the risk is great and the probable damage great recklessness may readily be a fair description however much the doer may regard the action as justified and reasonable. Each case has to be viewed on its own particular facts and not by reference to any formula.

291 [1993] 3 IR 19 at 205.

292 [1993] 3 IR 19 at 220.

293 *Donovan v Landys Ltd* [1963] IR 441.

294 *Shawinigan v Vokins* [1961] 1 WLR 1206.

> The only test in my view is an objective one. Would a reasonable man knowing all the facts and circumstances which the doer of the act knew or ought to have known describe the act as reckless in the ordinary meaning of that word in ordinary speech? As I have said my understanding of the ordinary meaning of that word is a high degree of carelessness.'[295]

The foregoing test of recklessness is expressly objective and follows that described in *R v Cauldwell*, above[296]. What is notable is that having implicitly adopted this to be the appropriate meaning of the word 'reckless' in C(A)A 1990, s 33(1), Lynch J went on to hold that such could not be juxtaposed onto reckless trading within the meaning of that section. Thus he said:

> 'The inclusion of the word "knowingly" in sub-s (1) (a) of s 33 must have been intended by the Oireachtas to have some effect on the nature of the reckless conduct required to come within the sub-section. I think that its inclusion requires that the director is party to carrying on the business in a manner which the director knows very well involves an obvious and serious risk of loss or damage to others and yet ignores that risk because he does not really care whether such others suffer loss or damage or because his selfish desire to keep his own company alive overrides any concern which he ought to have for others.'[297]

In the present case, Lynch J held that there was no evidence of recklessness within the meaning of the section and that he was not satisfied that the directors were knowingly a party to the carrying on of any business of the company in a reckless manner within the meaning of C(A)A 1990, s 33(1)(a). Indeed, on the contrary he found that the directors were: concerned about the effects of a forced liquidation on creditors and traded in the hope and belief they would do better by the company so trading than by immediate liquidation; had diligently tried to achieve profitable trading; had guaranteed the company's debt; and were willing to surrender their shareholding in another company for the benefit of Hefferon Kearns Ltd. Accordingly, this first test for reckless trading, whilst appearing to be objective, must be construed in the light of the word 'knowingly', and is thus tempered by subjectivity.

(b) Deemed reckless trading

[10.087] Even if a person is not, in fact, found to have been knowingly a party to the carrying on of business in a reckless manner, he can be deemed in law to have been reckless in either of the two circumstances detailed in CA 1963, s 297A(2). This subsection provides:

> 'Without prejudice to the generality of subs (1)(a), an officer of a company shall be deemed to have been knowingly a party to the carrying on of any business of the company in a reckless manner if—
>
> (a) he was a party to the carrying on of such business and, having regard to the general knowledge, skill and experience that may reasonably be expected of a person in his position, he ought to have known that his actions or those of the company would cause loss to the creditors of the company, or any of them, or

295 [1961] 1 WLR 1206 at 1214.

296 See para **[10.084]**.

297 [1993] 3 IR 191 at 222.

> (b) he was a party to the contracting of a debt by the company and did not honestly believe on reasonable grounds that the company would be able to pay the debt when it fell due for payment as well as all its other debts (taking into account the contingent and prospective liabilities).'

This was considered by Lynch J in *Re Hefferon Kearns Ltd (No 2)*[298] who, after finding no recklessness in fact, said of C(A)A 1990, s 33(2) (now CA 1963, s 297A(2)):

> 'Sub-s (2) does not affect or extend the meaning of sub-s (1)(a) but it extends the application of sub-s (1)(a) to the cases mentioned in paragraphs (a) and (b) of sub-s (2) even though the director was not guilty of reckless trading within the meaning of sub-s (1)(a) itself as interpreted by me above. Sub-s (2) deems a director to be guilty of reckless trading in the circumstances set out in paragraphs (a) and (b) and that presupposes that otherwise he would not be so guilty.'[299]

Interpreting this provision involving 'deemed recklessness' Lynch J considered that the essential question was whether a person ought to have known that his actions or those of the company would cause loss to the creditors of the company or any of them? Lynch J said it was crucial to a finding of deemed reckless trading that there be found:

> '...knowledge or imputed knowledge that the...defendant's actions or those of the company would cause loss to creditors: it is not sufficient that there might be some worry or uncertainty as to the ability to pay all creditors. The requirement is that the...defendant knew or ought to have known that his actions or those of the company would cause loss to creditors.'[300]

While this is an objective test, on the facts of the case Lynch J found that the director concerned 'had good reason to believe that the company would be able to pay all its creditors falling due for payment' at the relevant time; had 'reasonably expected extra monies' arising from the company's contracts and that the directors '...reasonably expected that no further losses would be incurred on those contracts but rather gains...' Accordingly, there was no evidence within CA 1963, s 297A(2)(a) by which to deem the directors guilty of reckless trading.

[10.088] Section 297A(2)(b) of CA 1963 sets out the second limb of the second test by which a person may be deemed to have been knowingly guilty of reckless trading. Where a person did not honestly believe on reasonable grounds that the company would be able to pay its debts, as they fell due, he will be deemed to have been knowingly guilty of reckless trading. Of the application of this ground, Lynch J said that he was:

> '...not satisfied that as at the 29th of August 1990 and the weeks immediately thereafter the...defendant did not honestly believe on reasonable grounds that the company would be able to pay the debt when it fell due for payment as well as its other debts (taking into account the contingent and prospective liabilities).'

Here too, although an objective test applied, Lynch J held on the facts of the case that the individual director concerned honestly believed that, at that time, the debts of the company could be paid as they fell due. After that time (28 September), the continued

---

298 *Re Hefferon Kearns Ltd (No 2)* [1993] 3 IR 191.
299 [1993] 3 IR 191 at 222, 223.
300 [1993] 3 IR 191 at 223.

trading of the company was still 'mainly in the interests of the creditors because...[he]...believed that an immediate winding-up would be far more detrimental to creditors than continuing to trade...'

However, Lynch J went on to hold that by continuing to trade after 28 September the director was deemed to have traded recklessly. This was the case although the director had acted honestly and bona fide in what appeared to be the best interests of the creditors. The learned judge said that the director:

> '...was in fact a party to the contracting of debts, by the company at a time when he knew that those debts, together with all the other debts of the company, including contingent and prospective liabilities, could not be paid by the company as they fell due. In these circumstances in respect of the period from the 28th of September to the 11th of October 1990 the...defendant falls within the ambit of paragraph (b) of sub-s (2) though not necessarily within the ambit of paragraph (a) because he believed that the loss (if any) to be caused to creditors or any of them would be less than immediate liquidation.'[301]

Notwithstanding that the defendant was guilty of reckless trading, albeit of the deemed variety, Lynch J went on to absolve him by invoking his discretionary jurisdiction provided in the equivalent of CA 1963, s 297A(6)[302].

[10.089] The judgment of Lynch J is welcome not least for its understanding of the realities of commercial life. Indeed, the judgment may be seen as a reaction against the rigours of CA 1963, s 297A(2)(b). In the course of his judgment Lynch J said[303]:

> 'Paragraph (b) of sub-s (2) appears to be a very wide ranging and indeed draconian measure and could apply in the case of virtually every company which becomes insolvent and has to cease trading for that reason. If, for example, a company became insolvent because of the domino effect of the insolvency of a large debtor, it would be reasonable for the directors to continue trading for a time thereafter to assess the situation and almost inevitably they would incur some debts which would fall within paragraph (b) before finally closing down. It would not be in the interests of the community that whenever there might appear to be any significant danger that a company was going to become insolvent, the directors should immediately cease trading and close down the business. Many businesses which might well have survived by continuing to trade coupled with remedial measures could be lost to the community.'

It is submitted that where a company gets into difficulties which, it is thought, may result in the company having to cease business, it would be prudent for the directors to record and minute all business decisions taken in as detailed a fashion as possible up to the time of cessation of trading. This would have the effect of focusing the minds of the directors on the harsh realities of their plight; hastening the demise of a hopelessly insolvent company; and of providing the directors with a documentary record of the last weeks which could become evidence of their bona fides in any future reckless trading proceedings.

---

[301] [1993] 3 IR 191 at 224.

[302] See para **[10.097]**.

[303] [1993] 3 IR 191 at 224, 225.

(c) The requirement that the company is insolvent

[10.090] Section 297A(3)(a) of CA 1963 provides that a court can only grant a declaration of personal responsibility if the requirements provided for in CA 1963, s 214 (a),(b) or (c) apply to the company concerned. By this is meant that the company is unable to pay its debts (of at least €1,269.74) when demanded under the 21 day demand procedure[304], or, execution on the company is returned unsatisfied, or, it is proved to the court that the company is unable to pay its debts.

(d) The meaning of 'a party' and 'business'

[10.091] In respect of all possible respondents to an action for reckless trading, CA 1963, s 297A(1)(a) provides that they must have been 'knowingly a party to the carrying on of any business of the company in a reckless manner'. Previously, we have considered the meaning of 'knowingly' and 'reckless'. Two further concepts now require examination.

The first is that the respondent must have been 'a party to' the reckless conduct. As we have already seen, the view taken by some of the Irish High Court judges is such as to indicate that where a person becomes a director, they undertake the responsibilities and duties of directors. In *Re Hunting Lodges Ltd*[305] (a case which concerned fraudulent trading) Carroll J accepted the meaning of to be 'a party to' as indicating no more than 'participates in', 'takes part in' or 'concurs in', as was stated by Pennycuick VC in *Maidstone Buildings Provisions Ltd*[306]. Carroll J went on to observe, and apparently adopt, Pennycuick VC's observation that some positive steps were required. It remains to be determined whether or not inert disinterest will constitute being knowingly a party. In the South African case of *Cronje No v Stone*[307] a director who was also a large shareholder in the company, never became actively involved in the business of the company. It was held that she had recklessly refrained from exercising proper control over the company and that her inertia had facilitated the mismanagement by her co-director.

[10.092] The second concept is the 'carrying on of the business[308] of the company'. It is thought that one single act of recklessness will constitute the carrying on of a company's business in a reckless manner. So in *Re Hunting Lodges Ltd*[309] Carroll J said (in the context of fraudulent trading) that:

> 'In the course of the conduct of its affairs, a company will have many different aspects of its business. One single transaction can properly be described as "business of the company" and so also can constituent parts of a transaction.'[310]

---

[304] See Chapter 25, *Winding Up Companies*, para **[25.062]**.

[305] *Re Hunting Lodges Ltd* [1985] ILRM 75.

[306] *Maidstone Buildings Provisions Ltd* [1971] 3 All ER 363 at 368.

[307] *Cronje No v Stone* (1985) (3) SA 597 (T).

[308] '...most any form of activity, apart from one pursued for pleasure or as a hobby can be described as "business"...', per Mann J in *Corfield v Stenvwaus Garage Ltd* (1985) RTR 109 at 117.

[309] *Re Hunting Lodges Ltd* [1985] ILRM 75.

[310] See also *Re Gerard Cooper Chemicals Ltd* [1978] 2 All ER 49 at 53.

This seems a common sense approach since, were it otherwise, then one large transaction alone could not ground proceedings, whereas several minor ones could[311]. Support for this view is found in *Morris v Banque Arabe et Internationale d'Investissment SA (No 2)*.[312] In that case, Neuberger J held – in the context of fraudulent trading – that while it was necessary to prove that a respondent had participated in the fraudulent acts of the company, it was not necessary to show that such a person carried on or assisted in carrying on the company's business.

(e) The requirement to be an applicant

[10.093] Furthermore, CA 1963, s 297A(3)(b) provides that an applicant, being a creditor or contributory or any person on whose behalf application is made, must have '...suffered loss or damage as a consequence of any behaviour mentioned in subs (1).' In the absence of such proof, a court has no power to grant a declaration of personal responsibility against a respondent[313]. It should be noted that the meaning of 'creditor' in the context of fraudulent trading was considered in *R v Smith*[314]. In that case the English Court of Appeal gave the broadest possible interpretation of the meaning of 'creditor', saying, obiter dictum, that it included contingent and prospective creditors who might come into existence after the fraudulent trading had commenced.

[10.094] Where a creditor relies upon CA 1963, s 297A(2)(b), above, then by CA 1963, s 297A(4) the court shall have regard to whether or not that creditor was at the time that the debt was incurred:

> ...aware of the company's financial state of affairs and, notwithstanding that awareness, nevertheless assented to the incurring of the debt[315].

This will be a question of fact to be decided in each case[316]. The applicant under this provision can give evidence themselves or call witnesses[317]. Where the Director of Corporate Enforcement applies under CA 1990, s 251 for an order under CA 1963,

311 See also *Re Sarflax Ltd* [1979] 1 All ER 529 at 534 where Oliver J held: '...I feel quite unable to say that the expression "carrying on any business" in the section is necessarily synonymous with actively carrying on trade or that the collection of assets acquired in the course of business and the distribution of the proceeds of those assets in the discharge of business liabilities cannot constitute the carrying on of "any business" for the purposes of the section.'

312 *Morris v Banque Arabe et Internationale d'Investissment SA (No 2)* [2000] TLR 749.

313 See Lynch J in *Re Hefferon Kearns Ltd (No 2)* [1993] 3 IR 191at 225, 226. In that case insufficient proof was adduced to the court that the claimants had suffered loss or damage as a consequence of the behaviour of the respondents mentioned in C(A)A 1990, s 33(1).

314 *R v Smith* [1996] 2 BCLC 109.

315 CA 1963, s 297A(4). The use of the word 'assented' seems to indicate that consent in the formal written sense is unnecessary, and that mere tacit awareness is sufficient for the court to take cognisance. See *DKG Contracting Ltd* (1990) where it was held that ignorance of a company's financial position was no defence to proceedings for wrongful trading under the Insolvency Act 1986 (UK), s 214, see (1990), Irish Times, 13 December.

316 In *Re Hefferon Kearns Ltd (No 2)* [1993] 3 IR 191, 215, Lynch J found that the plaintiffs were not sufficiently aware of the company's financial state of affairs to be affected by C(A)A 1990, s 33(4), which was equivalent to CA 1963, s 297A(4).

317 CA 1963, s 297A(5).

s 297A, CA 1990, s 251(4)(a) provides that CA 1963, s 297A(7)(b) shall apply in relation to any order made pursuant to an application brought by the Director, except that no order shall be made in favour of the Director 'otherwise than as to his costs and expenses'.[318]

(f) Potential respondents

[10.095] Section 297A(1)(a) of CA 1963 is expressly directed at persons who are, or were, officers of the company. The term 'officers', for the purposes of the section is deemed, by s 297A(10), to include any auditor, liquidator, receiver, or shadow director. In *Ex p Copp*[319] the question of whether a bank could be deemed a 'shadow director' arose in the context of wrongful trading under English law[320]. When the company concerned exceeded its overdraft, the lending bank sought security and successfully obtained a fixed charge on the company's book, and other, debts. This was done in furtherance of a report which was commissioned by the bank. Also in furtherance of the report, the bank appointed a receiver. Eventually, the company went into liquidation. Inter alia, the liquidator to the company sought an order that the bank concerned was a shadow director of the company and had traded wrongfully. One of the grounds relied upon by the liquidator was that, 'at an early stage, the bank was aware that the company was insolvent with no reasonable prospect of avoiding insolvent liquidation'[321]. On the facts, Knox J held that the claim against the bank was sustainable, and that it was possible that the bank may have been a shadow director which had traded wrongfully.

[10.096] Another potential class of respondents are nominee directors[322]. In *Kuwait Asia Bank EC v National Mutual Life Nominees Ltd*[323] the Privy Council considered the question of nominee-directors. In that case a company operated as a money broker, accepting deposits from the public. To protect investing depositors, the respondent company was appointed trustee, to which the company covenanted to provide information. The appellant bank, which was a shareholder in the company, nominated two persons as directors. A depositor sued the respondent company for breach of trust and on this action being settled, the respondent sought contribution from, inter alia, the appellant bank. It was alleged that the nominee directors had acted in breach of their duties of care, skill and diligence and other statutory duties to the company. Following from this, the respondent alleged that the appellant bank was vicariously liable for the actions of its employee-nominee directors. It was held by the Court of Appeal that the facts disclosed a cause of action. It was against this decision that the appellant appealed

---

318 See para **[10.122]**.

319 *Ex p Copp* [1989] BCLC 12; *Re a Company (No 005009 of 1987)*.

320 In England and Wales it was decided to penalise those who engaged in 'wrongful trading', while in Ireland, 'reckless trading' was introduced: see Ussher, *Company Law in Ireland* (1986), p 530.

321 [1989] BCLC 12 at 18.

322 See *Cronje No v Stone* (1985) (3) SA 597, and see generally, Flynn, 'Reckless Trading' (1991) ILT 186, for an excellent analysis of the comparative law on this question. As to so-called 'token directors' see para **[10.042]**.

323 *Kuwait Asia Bank EC v National Mutual Life Nominees Ltd* [1990] 3 All ER 404, [1990] BCLC 868. See also *Re Tasbian Ltd (No 3)* [1991] BCLC 792.

to the Privy Council. The Privy Council held that there was not a good arguable case against the appellant bank, refusing to hold that the bank was vicariously liable for the acts or omissions of its employees, or that the appellant bank was a shadow director:

> 'In the performance of their duties as directors...[the two directors] were bound to ignore the interests and wishes of their employer, the [appellant] bank. They could not plead any instruction from the bank as an excuse for breach of their duties to [the company] and [the respondent]. Of course, if the bank exploited its position as employees of [the two directors] to obtain an improper advantage for the [appellant] bank or to cause harm to [the respondent] then the [appellant] bank would be liable for its own misconduct. But there is no suggestion that the [appellant] bank behaved with impropriety. Its duty to refrain from exploiting its influence over its employees is not different in principle from the duty of a father not to exploit his influence over a son who is a director or the duty of a businessman not to exploit his influence over a business associate who is a director.'[324]

Where the person who nominates a director causes the nominee to wrongly fetter his discretion as a fiduciary, that person may be vicariously liable for the actions of the nominee-directors. This will not invariably be the case: directors may fetter the future exercise of their powers where this is in the company's interests[325].

(g) Defences to reckless trading

[10.097] Section 297A(6) of CA 1963 provides a quasi-subjective defence. This provides that where it appears to the court, that an officer:

> ...acted honestly and responsibly in relation to the conduct of the affairs of the company or any matter or matters on the ground of which such declaration is sought to be made, the court may, having regard to all the circumstances of the case, relieve him either wholly or in part, from personal liability on such terms as it may think fit.

Consequently, where it appears to the court that a person acted honestly and responsibly in relation to the conduct of the affairs of the company, the court may, by s 297A(6), relieve him in whole or in part from personal liability on such terms as it may think fit. This jurisdiction was first invoked in *Re Hefferon Kearns Ltd (No 2)*[326] by Lynch J who considered that it was not proper to impose personal responsibility for the debts of the company on the defendant-directors. The 'draconian' effect of CA 1963, s 297A(2)(b), was considered by the judge to justify the exercise of this discretion:

> 'I think that it is because sub-s (2) and especially paragraph (b) is so wide-ranging that sub-s (6) was included...The English Insolvency Act 1986 at s 214(3) is not quite as widely drafted as sub-s (6)...and accordingly in the *Produce Marketing Consortium* case it was held that, while the court could take account of the absence of any fraudulent intent so as to lessen the amount ordered to be paid by the directors, unless the evidence showed that the directors had taken every step to minimize loss to creditors that they ought to have taken, an order should be made against them. It seems to me that the expression "acted honestly and responsibly in relation to the conduct of the affairs of the company" is wider than the corresponding provisions in sub-s (3) of s 214 of the English Act and the court in

[324] [1990] 3 All ER 404 at 424.

[325] *Fulham Football Club Ltd v Cabra Estates plc* [1994] 1 BCLC 363. See para **[10.034]**.

[326] *Re Hefferon Kearns Ltd (No 2)* [1993] 3 IR 191 per Lynch J.

> this jurisdiction is given specific power to relieve such a director from any personal liability whatsoever.
>
> I am satisfied that the...defendant acted honestly and responsibly in relation to the conduct of the affairs of the company to such an extent that having regard to all the circumstances of the case I relieve him wholly from any personal liability without imposing any terms.'[327]

Through this interpretation, the judiciary have retained their discretion in the face of very strict statutory guidelines on the circumstances in which a person will be deemed to have been a party to the carrying on of the company's business in a reckless manner[328].

(h) The scope of the court's order

[10.098] Section 297A(7)(a) of CA 1963 empowers the court when making an order for personal responsibility to:

> '...give such further directions as it thinks proper for the purpose of giving effect to that declaration and in particular may make provision for making the liability of any such person under the declaration a charge on any debt or obligation due from the company to him, or on any mortgage or charge or any interest in any mortgage or charge on any assets of the company held by or vested in him or any company or person on his behalf, or any person claiming as assignee from or through the person liable or any company or person acting on his behalf, and made from time to time make such further order as may be necessary for the purpose of enforcing any charge imposed under this subsection;'

In addition, by virtue of CA 1963, s 297A(7)(b), the court may:

> '...provide that sums recovered under this section shall be paid to such person or classes of persons, for such purposes, in such amounts or proportions at such time or times and in such respective priorities among themselves as such declaration may specify.'

Consequently, where a company owes an officer who has been made personally responsible for the company's debts, any sum of money, the court can order that the sum can be made the subject of a charge. Moreover, the court can order that any mortgage or charge held by him, or a person (human or artificial claiming on his behalf, or any person claiming to be an assignee) can be itself made the subject of a charge. Hence, this section empowers the court to create a security in respect of the personal responsibility imposed upon an officer.

(i) The date of the conduct complained of

[10.099] It has been conclusively established that the provisions on reckless trading are not retrospective, ie only conduct after the passing of the two 1990 Companies Acts, (31 August 1990 for C(A)A 1990, and 1 August 1991 for CA 1990) can be considered for the purposes of reckless trading proceedings. This was confirmed in *Re Hefferon Kearns Ltd (No 1)*[329]. There, Murphy J reviewed the nature of retrospective legislation and concluded that having regard to Article 15.5 of the Constitution[330]:

327 [1993] 3 IR 191 at 225.

328 See para **[10.088]**.

329 *Re Hefferon Kearns Ltd (No 1)* [1992] ILRM 51.

330 Which provided that, 'The Oireachtas shall not declare acts to be infringements of the law which were not so at the date of their commission'.

'In my view reckless trading is now an infringement of the law and to declare retrospectively innocent actions as constituting that wrong would necessarily amount to a breach of Article 15. Accordingly it seems to me for that reason also to be clear that the Oireachtas did not intend (nor could it have intended) to make s 33 operate retrospectively.'[331]

Re Hefferon Kearns Ltd (No 2)[332] established that not only is conduct prior to the coming into force of the legislation not cognisable, but where a person is guilty of reckless trading, neither can he be made personally liable for debts or liabilities incurred before the coming into effect of the legislation.

(j) Reckless trading proceedings in an examinership

[10.100] Section 33 of the C(A)A 1990 enabled proceedings to be taken for reckless trading in circumstances where a company had been placed in examinership. This has now been repealed by CA 1990, s 180(3) and replaced by CA 1990, s 138 which inserted CA 1963, s 297A. The appropriateness of a provision on reckless trading during an examination of a company has been questioned, both by practitioners[333] and by the court in *Re Hefferon Kearns Ltd*[334]. In that case, Murphy J said:

'As already demonstrated the...[C(A)A 1990] is designed essentially to empower the courts to appoint a new form of officer as examiner of a company enjoying certain statutory powers in the hope that by so doing it may be possible to preserve as a going concern a company which would be wound up otherwise. In practice a successful examinership would appear to entail a moratorium whilst the examiner conducted an examination and designed proposals under which creditors would compromise existing claims so as to facilitate the survival of the business. It is difficult to reconcile that scheme of things with a situation in which a creditor (amongst others) could pursue an officer of a company on the basis of an allegation of reckless trading at a time when the company is deemed to be under the protection of the court. It is even more difficult to reconcile the institution of such proceedings with the embargo imposed on proceedings and execution by paragraph (f) of subs (2) of s 5 of [C(A)A 1990]... However these apparently conflicting provisions must be reconciled.'

Murphy J went on to reconcile the provisions by saying that C(A)A 1990, s 5 which prevents proceedings from being taken generally when a company is under the protection of the court, does not prevent a creditor from taking proceedings for reckless trading, although he felt that evidentially, it would be difficult for a creditor to derive benefit from C(A)A 1990, s 33 and that it was difficult to envisage the effective operation of s 33 otherwise than in the context of insolvent liquidation. It remains the

331 [1992] ILRM 51 at 59.

332 *Re Hefferon Kearns Ltd (No 2)* [1992] ILRM 51 at 59.

333 See (1991) The Irish Times, 6 April, where Mr Peter Fitzpatrick (the first Irish examiner) is reported as having said that: 'My view is that litigation is not compatible with reconstruction...The aspects of fraudulent or reckless trading are those which will more likely be found within the company which is beyond financial redemption and are issues which would more appropriately be left for pursuit by any subsequent receiver or liquidator rather than by an examiner'.

334 *Re Hefferon Kearns Ltd* [1992] ILRM 51.

case, however, that CA 1963, s 297A can be invoked in either the course of a winding up or in the course of proceedings under the C(A)A 1990.

Criminal fraudulent trading

[10.101] Section 297 of CA 1963 as replaced by CA 1990, s 137 provides that it is a criminal offence to trade fraudulently[335]. Thus s 297(1) provides:

> 'If any person is knowingly a party to the carrying on of the business of a company with intent to defraud creditors of the company or creditors of any other person or for any fraudulent purpose, that person shall be guilty of an offence.'

On summary conviction the penalty is imprisonment for 12 months and/or a fine not exceeding €1,269.74. On conviction on indictment, the penalty is a term of imprisonment not exceeding seven years and/or a fine not exceeding €63,486.90. Fraudulent trading is an offence for which a suspect can be arrested without warrant and detained for six hours (and a further six hours in certain circumstances) for questioning under the Criminal Justice Act 1984, s 4.

[10.102] The first successful prosecution for fraudulent trading occurred in 1996. This arose from the infamous case of *Re Mark Synnott (Life and Pensions) Brokers Ltd*. The facts as emerged from the newspaper reports[336] were that over a number of years a brokerage business had consistently mismanaged clients' funds. Investors had been attracted to Mr Synnott's company on foot of its claims of having discovered a brilliant investment strategy which could net returns of at least 20% per annum. It transpired, however, that monies received for investment were in fact often simply put into a bank account and when an investor was looking for a return, money was simply withdrawn from the bank account. It emerged that the company had been trading at a loss for at least eight years. Many investors successfully applied for Mareva injunctions to restrain the dissipation of the managing director's assets[337]. Arising from these facts a director of the company, Mark A Synnott, was prosecuted for fraudulent trading in the Circuit Court in *People (DPP) v Mark A Synnott*[338]. The report in *The Irish Times* stated that charges against Synnott alleged that between 2 September 1990 and 3 June 1991 he was knowingly a party to the carrying on of the business of the company with intent to defraud the creditors of the company by falsely pretending that he, as director, was engaged in the bona fide business of investing monies entrusted to him when he knew that the company was insolvent. Synnott was also charged with fraudulently converting two sums of money to his own use, one in 1990 and one in 1991. Three of the charges were admitted from a total of 39 on the indictment and a nolle prosequi was entered on the remaining charges. The defendant was sentenced to four years and three months' imprisonment and disqualified from acting as a director.

---

335 See generally, Ussher, *Company Law in Ireland* (1986), p 516 and Pennington, *Corporate Insolvency Law*, (1991), p 229.

336 For newspaper coverage of various interlocutory and interim applications and orders (eg for Mareva injunctions) in the *Synnott* case, see (1991) The Irish Times of 15, 18, 19, 25, 27 June, 3, 4, 6, 9 July and 6, 7, 8, 9 November.

337 See Courtney, *Mareva Injunctions and Related Interlocutory Orders* (1998), para [6.50].

338 *People (DPP) v Mark A Synnott* Circuit Court, of 7 May 1996 (Judge Cyril Kelly).

[10.103] In *Aktieselskabet Dansk Skibsfinansiering v Brothers* [339] the Hong Kong Court of Final Appeal held that the offence of fraudulent trading requires proof that someone carried on the business of the company with a fraudulent intention and that the other directors whom it was sought to make liable were knowingly party to that fraud. As in civil fraudulent trading, considered next, it was stated that the question of 'fraud' was subjective in that the defendant must have been dishonest. The court also held that an inquiry into the conduct of the particular defendants was required in preference to invoking the concept of the 'hypothetical decent honest man'. It is thought that this is preferable to the approach taken by the English Court of Appeal in *R v Grantham*[340]. In that case, involving a criminal prosecution, the accused's intentions seem to have been objectively ascertained. Lord Lane CJ held than in order to prove an 'intent to defraud', actual 'fraud' is unnecessary, and it is sufficient that a respondent obtained credit from a creditor, where he knew there was no good reason for believing that the company would have funds to repay the credit when it became due, or soon after. Referring to the dicta of Buckley J just quoted, Lord Lane said:

> 'In so far as Buckley J was saying that it is never dishonest or fraudulent for directors to incur credit at a time when, to their knowledge, the company is not able to meet its liabilities as they fall due, we would respectfully disagree...In the present case it was open to the jury to find, if not inevitably that they would find, that whoever was running this business was intending to deceive or was actually deceiving [the creditor] into believing that he would be paid in 28 days or shortly thereafter, when they knew perfectly well that there was no hope of that coming about. He was plainly induced thereby to deliver further [goods] on credit. The potential or inevitable detriment to him is obvious.'[341]

It is by no means certain that an Irish court would follow the reasoning of the English Court of Appeal even in the context of a criminal prosecution, particularly in view of the clear wording of the section.

Civil fraudulent trading

[10.104] Section 297A of CA 1963[342] provides a civil remedy for fraudulent trading in addition to the civil remedy for reckless trading considered above[343]. Section 297A(1) provides:

> 'If in the course of winding up of a company or in the course of proceedings under the Companies (Amendment) Act 1990, it appears that—
>
> (b) any person was knowingly a party to the carrying on of any business of the company with intent to defraud creditors of the company, or creditors of any other person or for any fraudulent purpose;
>
> the court, on the application of the receiver, examiner liquidator or any creditor or contributory of the company, may, if it thinks it proper to do so, declare that such person

[339] *Aktieselskabet Dansk Skibsfinansiering v Brothers* [2001] 2 BCLC 324.

[340] *R v Grantham* [1984] 3 All ER 166.

[341] [1984] 3 All ER 166 at 170e–j.

[342] As inserted by CA 1990, s 138.

[343] See para **[10.081]** *ff.*

shall be personally responsible, without any limitation of liability, for all or any part of the debts or other liabilities of the company as the court may direct.'

Central to understanding CA 1963, s 297A(1)(b) is that the test for fraudulent trading is doubly subjective. Before personal responsibility can be imposed[344] it must be proved that the person alleged to have traded fraudulently: (1) was knowingly a party to the (2) carrying on of any business of the company[345], (3) with intent to defraud creditors of the company or of any other person or for any other fraudulent purpose. The use of 'knowingly' imports a subjective test into reckless trading[346]. In the case of fraudulent trading the requirement that there also be shown an intention to defraud provides a second, even stronger, subjective test.

(a) The intention to defraud

[10.105] The requirement of an intention to defraud has beleaguered liquidators in their pursuit of delinquent officers of Irish companies. The difficulty in proving fraudulent trading is because of the subjective nature of the test. In the case of *Re William C Leitch Bros Ltd*[347] Maugham J said:[348]

'In my opinion, I must hold with regard to the meaning of the phrase carrying on business "with intent to defraud creditors" that, if a company continues to carry on business and to incur debts at a time when there is, to the knowledge of the directors, no reasonable prospect of the creditors ever receiving payment of those debts, it is in general a proper inference that the company is carrying on business with intent to defraud.'

This test requires that the directors had actual knowledge that there was no reasonable chance that the creditors of the company would be paid[349]. Similarly, in *Re White & Osmond (Parkinstone) Ltd*[350] Buckley J said:

'...there is nothing wrong in the fact that directors incur credit at a time when, to their knowledge, the company is not able to meet its liabilities as they fall due. What is manifestly wrong is if the directors allow a company to incur credit at a time when the business is being carried on in such circumstances that it is clear that the company will never be able to satisfy its creditors. However, there is nothing to say that directors who genuinely believe that the clouds will roll away and the sunshine of prosperity will shine

344 Note that those who can be made personally responsible for fraudulent trading are the same individuals who can be made personally responsible for reckless trading, namely: directors, secretaries, and 'officers', as defined by CA 1963, s 297A(10) to include an auditor, liquidator, receiver or shadow director.

345 *Morris v Banque Arabe et Internationale d'Investissment SA (No 2)* [2000] TLR 749; see para **[10.092]**.

346 See para **[10.086]**.

347 *Re William C Leitch Bros Ltd* [1932] All ER 892.

348 [1932] All ER 892 at 895, of his widely-quoted but only two-page judgement.

349 Lingard, *Corporate Rescues and Insolvencies* (2nd edn, 1989), para 2.9. See also *Re Patrick & Lyon Ltd* [1933] Ch 786, where Maugham J also held that fraudulent trading requires 'actual dishonesty involving, according to current notions of fair trading among commercial men, real moral blame'.

350 *Re White & Osmond (Parkinstone) Ltd UK* (30 June 1960, unreported), English High Court, per Buckley J.

> upon them again and disperse the fog of their depression are not entitled to incur credit to help them to get over the bad time.'

Consequently, for a person[351] to be held personally responsible for the debts of the company on the grounds of fraudulent trading, it is necessary to prove a subjective intention to defraud[352]. A mere 'intention to prefer' one creditor over another does not amount to an 'intention to defraud'[353].

[10.106] In *O'Keeffe v Ferris*[354] the plaintiff sought a declaration that the old CA 1963, s 297(1) was unconstitutional since it created a criminal offence which was not minor in nature and that it should only be tried before a jury. The plaintiff also claimed that, even if it did create only a civil cause of action, it could not be pursued unless and until the conclusion of criminal proceedings under s 297(3). This was rejected by Murphy J who held that the old s 297(1) did not create a criminal offence and that the section was properly construed as creating only a civil wrong. He also held that civil proceedings need not be postponed pending a criminal prosecution. In the course of his judgment Murphy J held:

> 'The subsection confers a wide discretion on the court and it must be assumed that the court will exercise those powers, not merely in a responsible but also in a constitutional fashion. If the Constitution does require that in civil proceedings the burden imposed on the defendants should in general be commensurate with the loss suffered by the plaintiff (or the class whom the plaintiff represents) then it must be assumed that the subsection will be so construed and applied.'[355]

This was upheld by the Supreme Court[356] which held (per O'Flaherty J) that:

> '...the section does not create a criminal offence; it does not involve civil proceedings being dressed up to involve criminal procedures and the sanctions available do not trench on the Constitution in any respect'.[357]

(b) Proving fraudulent trading

[10.107] Proving fraudulent trading is a difficult, although not impossible task, as is illustrated by four Irish cases in which successful actions were taken. The first of these is *Re Kelly's Carpetdrome Ltd*[358] where debts were incurred by the company at a time when it failed to keep proper books of account and where records were actually

---

351 It should be noted that, unlike in reckless trading, persons other than 'officers' can be respondents in an action for fraudulent trading. CA 1963, s 297A(1)(b) refers to 'any person' who was knowingly a party to the carrying on of any business of the company, with intent to defraud creditors.

352 See also *Hardie v Hanson* (1960) 105 CLR 451 (Australia), where Dixon CJ stressed the need for: '...the intent to defraud creditors must be express or actual and real: nothing constructive, imputed or implied will do.'

353 See *Re Sarflax Ltd* [1979] 1 All ER 529 at 535f.

354 *O'Keeffe v Ferris* [1994] 1 ILRM 425. See Duffy, 'Fraudulent Trading and the Decision in O'Keeffe v Ferris' (1994) CLP 255.

355 [1994] 1 ILRM 425 at 432.

356 [1997] 3 IR 463, [1997] 2 ILRM 161.

357 [1997] 3 IR 463 at 473.

358 *Re Kelly's Carpetdrome Ltd* (1 July 1983, unreported), High Court, per Costello J.

destroyed. Indeed, assets were actually transferred to other companies when the main creditor, the Revenue Commissioners, began to pursue the company vigorously. Costello J held that it was proper in the circumstances for personal responsibility for the debts of the company to be imposed, not only on the officers, but also on persons who beneficially owned the company. In respect of one outsider (being neither a director nor a member) Costello J ordered that he too was personally responsible for the debts of the company[359].

In *Re Aluminium Fabricators Ltd*[360] the fraud involved the keeping of two sets of books of account, one for the benefit of the controllers of the company and the other for the Revenue Commissioners. The intention and effect of this was to enable the controllers of the company to siphon off company assets for their own benefit, to the obvious detriment of the creditors. Again, it was held by O'Hanlon J that an order for full personal responsibility for the debts of the company should be made against those responsible.

[10.108] The most helpful case is that of *Re Hunting Lodges Ltd*[361]. There, a single act – namely the sale at an under value of 'Durty Nellies' public house, the company's principal asset - was deemed to constitute fraudulent trading[362]. The company sold the public house, disguising the true price of the sale by paying a substantial part of the consideration to one of the directors 'under the counter'. Although the sale price was £480,000, a secret payment of £160,000 was also paid by the purchaser to the controllers. This money was then lodged by one of the directors into various building society accounts. This single fraudulent act was held to constitute the carrying on of the company's business in a fraudulent manner. There was an intention to defraud found by Carroll J who said:

> 'In my opinion, in order for the section to apply it is not necessary that there should be a common agreed fraudulent intent. If each of the participants acts for a fraudulent purpose then each may be liable.'

In the case of all four parties, a fraudulent intent was found, namely defrauding the creditors, defrauding the Revenue of stamp duty and depriving the company of money which rightly belonged to it.

[10.109] Another case is *Re Contract Packaging Ltd*[363]. There the liquidator to the company learnt through his investigations into the company's affairs of several instances of fraudulent trading. Amongst the instances of fraud detected were the existence of a number of deposit accounts which were excluded from the company's audited accounts, books and records. The money in these accounts had been siphoned off by some of the directors, action which resulted in the Revenue Commissioners being defrauded and company funds being misappropriated. In total over £384,000 was discovered in these accounts and the beneficiaries of withdrawals from them were one particular director

359 See Ussher, *Company Law in Ireland* (1986), p 520.

360 *Re Aluminium Fabricators Ltd* [1984] ILRM 399.

361 *Re Hunting Lodges Ltd* [1985] ILRM 75.

362 See para **[10.110]**.

363 See *Re Contract Packaging Ltd* (1992) The Irish Times, 16, 17, 18 January.

(Mr W), a company controlled by him, (Shrinkpak Ltd) and genuine creditors. The liquidator had evidence that W withdrew over £160,000 for his own personal use. Furthermore, the liquidator unearthed a VAT fraud, whereby the value of goods at point of importation was underestimated, a second invoice stating the true value issued by the company, and VAT credits sought on the basis of the second invoice. Evidence was also heard that when the company became insolvent, in addition to money being misappropriated by the directors, company business was diverted to Shrinkpak Ltd, W's company. The court also heard that the equitable ownership of the company's premises was fraudulently diverted to Shrinkpak Ltd. It was held by Flood J that it was proper to impose personal liability under CA 1963, s 297 on some of the directors involved. So it was ordered that W and his common law wife give up their home to the liquidator[364], and W was also ordered to give his interest in a Jaguar car, two boats and funds held in various financial institutions to the liquidator.

(c) The extent of personal responsibility imposed

[10.110] The extent of personal responsibility imposed by the court will depend upon the circumstances of each case. Thus, while full liability for the debts of the company was imposed in both the *Re Kelly's Carpetdrome Ltd* and *Re Aluminium Fabricators Ltd* cases, the extent of judicial discretion is seen in the judgment of Carroll J in *Re Hunting Lodges Ltd*[365]. There, there were four respondents, Mr and Mrs Porrit, Mr O'Connor and a company called Plage Services Ltd, which was owned by Mr O'Connor. The actions of each were stated by Carroll J[366] to be as follows:

> Mr Porrit—
>
> '...participated from start to finish. He was involved in all the negotiations; he required the payment on the side; he produced at closing the resolution of the directors authorising the sale at £480,000; he countersigned the affixing of the seal to the conveyance; he took the additional £160,000 and he opened the accounts with the building society under false names.'
>
> Mrs Porrit—
>
> '...participated in the sale. While she denied any knowledge of the resolution of the directors, she attended at the closing of the sale and countersigned the affixing of the seal to the conveyance without objection. She signed a false name to the signature cards in respect of the building society accounts. Therefore, she took an active part in the closing of the sale and the disposition of part of the purchase money.'
>
> Mr O'Connor—
>
> '...participated in the sale up to and including the closing. He negotiated directly with Mr Porrit and agreed to provide the money on the side. He co-operated by providing the three bank drafts in false names together with cash and the endorsed bank draft for the deposit and handed them over secretly to Mr Porrit without the knowledge of their solicitors or the company's auditor.'

364 Note though that in respect of the family home, a stay was put on the order for two months when Flood J heard that the family were homeless: (1992) The Irish Times, 17 January.

365 *Re Hunting Lodges Ltd* [1895] ILRM 75.

366 [1985] ILRM 75 at 83.

PS Ltd—

> '...is the actual vehicle which Mr O'Connor used to take the conveyance. It was therefore a party to the sale at closing.'

Having established the requisite element of fraudulent intent, Carroll J decided that it was proper to make a declaration of personal responsibility for the debts of the company. She then went on to consider the extent to which the participants should be made personally liable, stressing the importance of looking at the entire circumstances of the case. That the imposition can be punitive in nature was accepted ab initio[367]. However, looking at all the circumstances, Carroll J apportioned the extent of personal liability on the basis of individual culpability. Thus, in the case of Mr Porrit she held that he:

> '...should be personally responsible without any limitation for all the debts of the company. The benefit of limited liability should, in my opinion, be totally withdrawn and he should be put in the same position as if he were a trader carrying on business personally.'

Accordingly not only was he liable for the sums siphoned off from the company, but also all of the other debts of the company. Since the Revenue Commissioners were owed over £750,000, this decision is a prime example of the punitive discretion of the High Court in such matters.

However, in respect Mrs Porrit, her liability was somewhat less, ie all of the debts of the company not exceeding the value of advancements made by her husband six years thence, a decision which has been criticised as exposing Mrs Porrit to a double indemnity[368]. Mr O'Connor and Plage Services Ltd fared best of all and their liability was only in the sum of £12,000, jointly and severally. This figure represented the cash sum given by Mr O'Connor which had disappeared.

(d) The beneficiary of an award

[10.111] In *Re Esal (Commodities) Ltd v Punjab National Bank*[369] it was held by the English Court of Appeal that any recovery for fraudulent trading had to be in favour of the company's liquidator and not an individual shareholder. Where an individual shareholder (or indeed creditor) successfully brings an action any award will, at the court's discretion, be for the benefit of the general body of shareholders and creditors.

[10.112] It has been held that whilst it is imperative to establish an intention to defraud, it is not a pre-condition to a finding of such intent or purpose that the victim had in fact relied on the fraud[370].

---

367 Carroll J relied on the judgment of Maugham J in *Re William C Leith Bros Ltd* [1932] All ER 892 at 896 where he said: 'I am inclined to take the view that [the corresponding section in England and Wales] is in the nature of a punitive provision, and that where the court makes such a declaration in relation to "all or any of the debts or other liabilities of the company", it is in the discretion of the court to make an order without limiting the order to the amount of the debts of those creditors proved to have been defrauded by those acts of the director in question, though, no doubt, the order would in general be so limited'.

368 See Ussher, *Company Law in Ireland* (1986), pp 522–523.

369 *Re Esal (Commodities) Ltd v Punjab National Bank* [1997] 1 BCLC 705.

370 *Morphites v Bernasconi* [2001] 2 BCLC 1.

[10.113] Where the Director of Corporate Enforcement applies under CA 1990, s 251 for an order under CA 1963, s 297A, CA 1990, s 251(4)(a) provides that CA 1963, s 297A(7)(b) shall apply in relation to any order made pursuant to an application brought by the Director, except that no order shall be made in favour of the Director 'otherwise than as to his costs and expenses'.[371]

Personal Liability for Failure to Keep Proper Books of Account

[10.114] Section 202(1) of CA 1990 provides that every company must keep proper books of account that:

> '(a) correctly record and explain the transactions of the company;
>
> (b) will at any time enable the financial position of the company to be determined with reasonable accuracy;
>
> (c) will enable the directors to ensure that any balance sheet, profit and loss account or income and expenditure account of the company complies with the requirements of the Companies Acts; and
>
> (d) will enable the accounts of the company to be readily and properly audited.'

This duty is fully considered in Chapter 13, *Accounts and Auditors*. In this chapter the concern is the personal liability that can be visited upon officers of a company where CA 1990, s 202(1) is breached.

(a) The power to declare officers personally liable where proper books of account not kept

[10.115] Section 204(1) of CA 1990 provides:

> 'Subject to subsection (2)[372], if—
>
> (a) a company that is being wound up and that is unable to pay all of its debts has contravened section 202, and
>
> (b) the court considers that such contravention has contributed to the company's inability to pay all of its debts or has resulted in substantial uncertainty as to the assets and liabilities of the company or has substantially impeded the orderly winding up thereof,
>
> the court, on the application of the liquidator or any creditor or contributory of the company, may, if it thinks it proper to do so, declare that any one or more of the officers[373] and former officers of the company who is or are in default shall be personally liable, without any limitation of liability, for all, or such part as may be specified by the court, of the debts and other liabilities of the company.'

---

371 See para **[10.122]**.

372 CA 1990, s 204(2) provides: 'On the hearing of an application under this subsection, the person bringing the application may himself give evidence or call witnesses.'

373 In CA 1990, s 204, the term 'officer' is deemed to include: 'a person who has been convicted of an offence under CA 1990, ss 194, 197 or 242 in relation to a statement concerning the keeping of proper books of account by the company.'

The object of this section was stated by Shanley J in *Mehigan v Duignan; Re Mantruck Services Ltd*[374] not to be the removal of the benefit of limited liability and the placing of the person (on whom liability is imposed) in the same position as if he were a sole trader. This is because those against whom such a declaration can be made is not confined to officers, but extends beyond executives, and can embrace a company's auditors and members of a company.

[10.116] Upon making such a declaration, the court's powers are far-reaching. Section 204(3)(a) of CA 1990 provides that the court may:

> 'give such directions as it thinks proper for the purpose of giving effect to the declaration and in particular may make provision for making the liability of any such person under the declaration a charge on any debt or obligation due from the company to him, or on any mortgage or charge or any interest in any mortgage or charge on any assets of the company held by or vested in him or any company or other person on his behalf, or any person claiming as assignee[375] from or through the person liable under the declaration or any company or person acting on his behalf, and may from time to time make such further order as may be necessary for the purpose of enforcing any charge imposed under this subsection.'

The court's power to declare that an officer is personally liable where there has been a breach of CA 1990, s 202 is without prejudice to the fact that such a person may be criminally liable under s 202(10)[376].

(b) The imposition of personal liability is discretionary

[10.117] It does not follow, automatically, that where a company has failed to keep proper books of account as required by CA 1990, s 202, a declaration of personal liability will be made against its officers. Section 204(4) provides a defence:

> 'The court shall not make a declaration under subsection (1) in respect of a person if it considers that—
>
> (a) he took all reasonable steps to secure compliance by the company with section 202, or
>
> (b) he had reasonable grounds for believing and did believe that a competent and reliable person, acting under the supervision or control of a director of the company who has been formally allocated such responsibility, was charged with the duty of ensuring that that section was complied with and was in a position to discharge that duty.'

---

374 *Mehigan v Duignan; Re Mantruck Services Ltd* [1997] 1 ILRM 171. For comment, see Garvey, 'Being Brought to Book under Section 204 of the Companies Act 1990' (1997) 4 CLP 27 and Sanfey, 'Personal Liability of Directors under Section 204 of the Companies Act 1990' (1996) The Bar Review 50.

375 CA 1990, s 204(3)(b) defines 'assignee' to include: 'any person to whom or in whose favour, by the directions of the person liable, the debt, obligation, mortgage or charge was created, issued or transferred or the interest created, but does not include an assignee for valuable consideration (not including consideration by way of marriage) given in good faith and without notice of any of the matters on the ground of which the declaration is made.'

376 CA 1990, s 204(5).

It should be noted, however, that in *Re Vehicle Imports Ltd*[377] Murphy J held that the obligation[378] to keep proper books of account was not limited to where one director had a reputed responsibility for keeping the books and that the responsibility was a joint and separate liability on each of the directors. Accordingly, whilst delegation to a competent person will be a defence to an application to have one made personally responsible for a company's debts, it will not be a defence to a criminal prosecution or indeed any comfort, necessarily, in an application to have a director restricted under CA 1990, s 150.

(c) The proofs required for an order under CA 1990, s 204

[10.118] The first case in which CA 1990, s 204 was considered was *Mehigan v Duignan; Re Mantruck Services Ltd*[379] where Shanley J usefully set out the proofs required for an order under s 204. The facts of this case were that Mantruck Services Ltd was placed into creditors' voluntary liquidation, which was subsequently converted into an official liquidation. An employee of the official liquidator collected some books and records of the company from its premises. He did not collect certain books referred to as the 'red cathedral books'; those that he did receive were delivered to the liquidator's solicitor. Later, the High Court ordered the directors to hand-in all books, records documents and assets of the company to the official liquidator. This order had been sought by the official liquidator after he had examined the books and records received from the voluntary liquidator and having formed the view that there were 'significant and extensive' omissions in the company's records and that these resulted in substantial uncertainty as to the company's assets and liabilities that had impeded its orderly winding up. No further records were forthcoming and the respondent declared that proper books and records were duly made available to the official liquidator. At the hearing of a motion to have the respondent restricted under CA 1990, s 150 and an order for personal liability under s 204, it was indicated by the respondent that there might be certain other records at the company's old premises. The motion was adjourned and an order made that these be delivered up; following this 28 computer disks and the five red cathedral books were recovered. The applicant-liquidator continued to assert that certain basic information was still missing covering a period of some 18 months. The liquidator claimed that because of this he could not determine the company's financial position, that the company could not be readily and properly audited, there was no proper record of the assets and liabilities, no proper record of invoices and no proper record of money received or expended. The liquidator also claimed that these omissions impeded the orderly winding up of the company and gave evidence that some 80% of the time spent by him and his staff related to efforts to overcome these deficiencies. The respondent claimed that additional information was available on the computer disks and that he had thought that the 'red cathedral books' had been given to the voluntary liquidator.

[10.119] Shanley J made an order under CA 1990, s 204(1) against the respondent, restricted to 80% of the liquidator's costs in overcoming the deficiencies occasioned by

[377] *Re Vehicle Imports Ltd* (23 November 2000, unreported), High Court (Murphy J).

[378] On pain of criminal sanction in the light of CA 1990, s 202(10) – which criminalises the failure to keep proper books of account and applies to every person who is a director of a company.

[379] *Mehigan v Duignan; Re Mantruck Services Ltd* [1997] 1 ILRM 171.

the absence of proper books and records. Shanley J held that the requisite proofs, before an order could be made under s 204 were:

> '(a) The company in question is being wound up.
>
> (b) The company is unable to pay all its debts.
>
> (c) The company has contravened CA 1990, s 202.
>
> (d) Such contravention has contributed to the company's inability to pay all of its debts or has resulted in substantial uncertainty as to the assets and liabilities of the company or has substantially impeded the orderly winding up of the company.
>
> (e) The officer (or former officer) of the company knowingly and wilfully authorised or permitted the contravention by the company of s 202, or, the "officer" is a person convicted under ss 194, 197 or 242 in relation to a statement concerning the keeping of proper books of account.'[380]

Focusing on proof (d), Shanley J held:

> 'The section, on its face, does not require that there be any causal relationship between the s 202 contravention and the liability declared under s 204. Nor does the section, on its face, make any allowance for different degrees of blameworthiness which might attend contraventions of s 202. As to the absence of a causal connection between a contravention of s 202 and the liability imposed under s 204, there may well be a significant number of situations where the contravention bears little or no relationship to the amount of the debts of the insolvent company. For example, where the insolvency is the direct result of unwise foreign exchange transactions and it is discovered that the auditors and directors have knowingly and consistently undervalued the assets of the company (thereby resulting in a contravention of s 202) such that, while insolvent, the company's indebtedness is less than it would have been had the assets been properly valued. Where such an undervaluation results in substantial uncertainty as to the assets of the company or substantially impedes the orderly winding up of the company liability under s 204 is established, yet it would be clearly unjustifiable in principle to impose liability for all the debts of the company…On the other hand, where a particular contravention of s 202 can be seen to have a particular financial consequence resulting in a particular debt of the insolvent company, it is difficult to see how it could be argued that imposing liability for such a debt works any injustice.'[381]

Shanley J concluded that although s 204 could be read as to permit the imposition on a person of unlimited liability for all of a company's debts such could, where the s 202 contravention has not in itself resulted in any loss to the company but has substantially impeded the orderly winding up of the company, constitute an unjust attack on the person's personal rights. Accordingly, the court must exercise its discretion in a responsible and constitutional fashion and have regard to the extent to which the officer's involvement in the s 202 contravention resulted in financial loss and, if it did, whether or not such losses were reasonable foreseeable by the officer as a consequence of the contravention. Shanley J said that only in exceptional circumstances would liability be imposed where the contravention of s 202 did not result in loss or for losses not reasonably foreseeable as a consequence of the breach of s 202. Shanley J said that

[380] [1997] 1 ILRM 171 at 187.

[381] [1997] 1 ILRM 171 at 188–189.

he thought that the three factors suggested by Tompkins J in *Maloc Construction Ltd v Chadwick*[382] - causation, culpability and duration – in his interpretation of the almost identical provisions of the New Zealand legislation, were relevant to the principles that should guide the court's discretion and in assessing liability under CA 1990, s 204. As to the standard of proof, Shanley J considered this to be in the context of a civil wrong and held that no higher degree of probability of a contravention of CA 1990, s 202 is required than in any other civil wrong.

On the facts of the case in hand, Shanley J held that the company was in contravention of CA 1990, s 202 for some period of time and that the respondent was an officer of the company who had wilfully authorised and permitted the contraventions and could not avail of any defence under CA 1990, s 204(4). He concluded that he should exercise his discretion and declare the respondent personally liable for 80% of the cost of the liquidator's time as the losses that flowed from that expenditure of time were reasonably foreseeable as a consequence of the contravention of s 202.

[10.120] The decision in *Mehigan v Duignan* was followed by Geoghegan J in *Re Ashclad Ltd; Forrest v Harrington and Culleton*[383]. In this case the official liquidator (who took the action) found deficiencies to a greater or lesser degree in the available bank statements, purchases' book, sales' ledger, cheque payments' books, PAYE and PRSI records, audited accounts for certain years and VAT records. Geoghegan J said that as a consequence of these deficiencies, there was quite obviously substantial uncertainty as to the company's assets and liabilities and its orderly winding up was being impeded. Again, the liquidator estimated that 80% of his time related to his efforts to assess the company's books and records and to overcome deficiencies. Geoghegan J did not find the respondent's evidence impressive, particularly in relation to the explanations proffered for certain discrepancies in monies belonging to the company. He concluded that as a matter of probability sums amounting to at least £100,000 had been wrongly withdrawn from the company and appropriated for other purposes. Geoghegan J went on to say:

> 'I have read and considered the judgment of Shanley J in *Mehigan v Duignan* [1997] 1 IR 341. I broadly accept the approach which he adopted and the principles which he said had to be applied particularly having regard to the Constitution. To some extent he lays down quite a strict onus of proof in relation to causality. But the facts of that case are not the same as the facts of this case and I am satisfied that as a matter of probability the liabilities of the company were very substantially affected by cash withdrawals which were not for the benefit of the company.'[384]

Geoghegan J went on to declare that the respondent be made personally liable to the extent of £112,000 for the company's debts. His grounds were that the company had failed to keep proper books of account as required by CA 1990, s 202, that such contravention had resulted in substantial uncertainty as to the company's assets and

[382] *Maloc Construction Ltd v Chadwick* [1986] 3 NZCLC 99.

[383] *Re Ashclad Ltd; Forrest v Harrington and Culleton* (5 April 2000, unreported), High Court (Geoghegan J).

[384] At p 15.

liabilities; and/or had impeded the orderly winding up of the company; and/or contributed to the company's inability to pay all of its debts.

Section 251 of CA 1990: Invocation of statutory remedies where a company is not being wound up

[10.121] It is not a prerequisite to issuing proceedings for fraudulent trading, failing to keep proper books of account, etc that a company is being wound up. Section 251 of CA 1990 facilitates the invocation of various statutory remedies where a company is insolvent[385] even though it is not being wound-up. Section 251 applies to companies which are not being wound up but where:

— execution or other process issued on a judgment, decree or order of any court in favour of a creditor of the company is returned unsatisfied in whole or in part; or

— it is proved to the satisfaction of the court that the company is unable to pay its debts, taking into account the contingent and prospective liabilities of the company

and it appears to the court that the reason or principal reason for its not being wound up is the insufficiency of its assets. The purpose of this provision is to confer jurisdiction upon the court to make any one of a series of orders that could otherwise only be made where a company is being wound up, thereby making the directors of a hopelessly insolvent company amenable to the court. The legislative intention was to provide redress in cases of the so-called 'scorched earth' syndrome[386], which refers to a situation where the directors of a company so deplete its assets as to make it unattractive for any creditor to cause a liquidator to be appointed because of the absence of funds, in the hope that nobody will investigate any wrongdoing and pursue the directors. This provision is examined under the following headings:

(a) Those with locus standi to apply under CA 1990, s 251.

(b) The orders that can be made under CA 1990, s 251.

(c) The insufficiency of assets as a precondition to jurisdiction.

(d) The operation of the section.

(a) Those with locus standi to apply under CA 1990, s 251

[10.122] The original CA 1990, s 251 was silent as to who could apply for an order. It would seem, however, that creditors and members must have jurisdiction to apply for an order under s 251 as these are the two constituencies most likely to be adversely affected by corporate wrongdoing. The Director of Corporate Enforcement also has locus standi to apply for an order by reason of CA 1990, s 251(2A)[387] which provides:

---

385 Ie where the company is unable to pay its debts, taking contingent and prospective liabilities into account, or where the company has had execution or other process issued on judgment which is returned unsatisfied: CA 1990, s 251(1)(a) and (b).

386 See the *Report of the Working Group on Company Law Compliance and Enforcement* (1998), para 4.42 (the 'McDowell Report').

387 Inserted by CLEA 2001, s 54(b).

> 'The Director may apply to the court pursuant to this section for an order or judgement, as the case may be, under any of the sections which apply to a company to which this section relates.'

Accordingly, it is only the Director who has express locus standi to bring application under this provision. The role of the Director in this regard very much remains to be seen, particularly as regards those provisions that facilitate the making of an order rendering directors personally liable for some or all of a company's debts. On this issue, the Working Group on Company Law Compliance and Enforcement (the 'McDowell Group') clearly stated that:

> 'the Director's right to seek a declaration of personal liability or damages pursuant to s 251 should not extend to receiving or distributing any assets as may be recovered from persons pursuant to the relevant sections, as the Group considers this to be a matter for aggrieved creditors'.[388]

In this regard it is to be noted that s 251(4)(a) provides that CA 1963, s 297A(7)(b)[389] shall apply in relation to any order made pursuant to an application brought by the Director, except that no order shall be made in favour of the Director 'otherwise than as to his costs and expenses'. The rights of the 'aggrieved creditors', mentioned in the McDowell Report are, however, vindicated and s 251(4)(b) provides:

> 'A person having a claim against the company may apply for an enforcement order for a share of any sums or assets recovered or available following a successful action by the Director pursuant to subsection (2A), provided that the order is sought within a period of one month from the date of judgment on behalf of the Director.'

In view of the very short limitation period, it is important that aggrieved creditors closely follow any action for recovery taken by the Director, lest they be statute barred in seeking an enforcement order for a share of sums or assets recovered or available.

(b) The orders that can be made under CA 1990, s 251

[10.123] Section 251(2) of CA 1990 permits a court to hear application for any of the following orders:

- an order directing the return of assets improperly transferred[390];
- a contribution order[391];
- a restriction order[392];
- criminal failure to keep proper books of account[393];

---

[388] See the *Report of the Working Group on Company Law Compliance and Enforcement* (1998) at pp 60, 61, point 8 of Annex 4.1.

[389] CA 1963, s 297A(7)(b) provides that on making a declaration the court may: 'provide that sums recovered under this section shall be paid to such person or classes of persons, for such purposes, in such amounts or proportions at such time or times and in such respective priorities among themselves as such declaration may specify.'

[390] CA 1990, s 139. See Chapter 27, *Realisation and Distribution of Assets in a Winding Up*, para **[27.092]**.

[391] CA 1990, s 140. See Chapter 27, *Realisation and Distribution of Assets in a Winding Up*, para **[27.106]**.

[392] CA 1990, s 149. See Chapter 12, *Company Law Compliance and Enforcement*, para **[12.051]**.

[393] CA 1990, s 203. See Chapter 13, *Accounts and Audit*, para **[13.010]**.

- — civil failure to keep proper books of account[394];
- — inspection of books by creditors or contributories of the company[395];
- — power to summon persons for an examination[396];
- — an order against property as a result of an examination[397];
- — the arrest of absconding persons[398];
- — fraud by officers of companies in liquidation[399];
- — criminal fraudulent trading[400];
- — civil fraudulent trading[401];
- — power to assess damages against directors[402].

The orders that can be sought under s 251 are the essential tools of any liquidators' armoury which facilitate the furnishing of information, preservation of assets and recovery of assets in cases of wrongdoing.

[10.124] One apparent gap in s 251 is that proceedings for reckless trading are not permissible under the section. Inter alia, CA 1990, s 251(2)(b) provides that 'the provisions of the Principal Act mentioned in the Table to this section' shall apply notwithstanding that the company is not being wound up. This Table provides, inter alia, that CA 1963, s 297A shall apply but delimits its application by the further description: 'Civil liability for fraudulent trading'. Section 297A contains two limbs: civil liability for fraudulent trading and civil liability for reckless trading. Accordingly, if one applies a strict construction to this provision, the specific reference prejudices the general reference and precludes an applicant from relying on CA 1990, s 251 to ground an application for reckless trading where the company is not in liquidation or under the protection of the court.

(c) The insufficiency of assets as a precondition to jurisdiction

[10.125] The grounds which must be satisfied in order for CA 1990, s 251 to become operational are similar in part to the grounds for petitioning to have a company wound up under CA 1963, s 213. It is submitted that proving to the court that the company is unable to pay its debts is likely to be the most common reason relied upon to ground a s 251 application. Essential to the success of any application is that the reason or principal reason for the company not being wound up is the insufficiency of its assets.

---

394 CA 1990, s 204. See para **[10.115]**.

395 CA 1963, s 243.

396 CA 1963, s 245, as amended by CA 1990, s 126. See Chapter 27, *Realisation and Distribution of Assets in a Winding Up*, para **[27.022]**.

397 CA 1963, s 245A, as inserted by CA 1990, s 127.

398 CA 1963, s 247. See Chapter 27, *Realisation and Distribution of Assets in a Winding Up*, para **[27.041]**.

399 CA 1963, s 295.

400 CA 1963, s 297.

401 CA 1963, s 297A, as inserted by CA 1990, s 138 and CA 1963, s 297 as inserted by CA 1990, s 137.

402 CA 1963, s 298, as amended by CA 1990, s 142.

Since the main reason for a liquidation is to enable the orderly realisation and distribution of assets, it follows that where there are insufficient assets, there operates a strong financial disincentive to commencing costly liquidation proceedings. However, a court will not accede to a request under s 251 if there are sufficient assets available for the economical winding up of the company. It is submitted that this ground will be strictly adhered to by the courts to prevent abuse of this innovative legislative device.

[10.126] In *Alba Radio Ltd v Haltone (Cork) Ltd*[403] an order for examination under CA 1963, s 245 was sought pursuant to CA 1990, s 251 and it was argued, inter alia[404], that it had not been proved that that company had not been wound up by reason of insufficiency of its assets. Prior to the commencement of CA 1990 the plaintiff had obtained a judgment against the defendant-company. On this point Barron J said:

> 'The evidence shows that the judgment obtained by the plaintiff has not been satisfied at all and that such assets as may have belonged to the defendant-company have been transferred to the company presently using the same premises. In the absence of any denial as to the facts alleged in the [plaintiff's affidavit], I am satisfied that the company is unable to pay its debts and that the reason it is not being wound up is the insufficiency of its assets.'[405]

(d) The operation of the section

[10.127] It was held in *Jones and Tarleton v Gunn*[406] that CA 1990, s 251 was not retrospective. In that case, because the transactions complained of were completed prior to the commencement of s 251, and because the company was not being wound-up, the plaintiffs' claim under CA 1963, s 297A and s 298 must fail because their application in circumstances where a company was not being wound up would involve retrospection.

[10.128] Not every order made under CA 1990, s 251 will, however, violate the rule against retrospection. So, in *Alba Radio Ltd v Haltone (Cork) Ltd*[407] application was brought under s 251 for an examination order under CA 1963, s 245 against a person who was a director of a company that was not being wound up. The plaintiff-company had obtained a judgment against the defendant-company, prior to the commencement of CA 1990, s 251. To the director's claim that to make an order pursuant to CA 1963, s 245, under CA 1990, s 251, would be to give the CA 1990 retrospective effect, Barron J held:

> 'There is nothing new in that procedure [ie an order for examination under CA 1963, s 245]. What is new is that the application can be made even though the company is not being wound up. In effect what s 251 is doing is to permit a form of procedure which existed before the passing of the Act to be adopted in slightly different circumstances. Admittedly until the Act was passed, it was necessary to put the company into liquidation or to have a provisional liquidator appointed before the relief could be obtained. In my view that is not creating a retrospective effect to the section.

---

403 *Alba Radio Ltd v Haltone (Cork) Ltd* [1995] 2 IR 170, [1995] 2 ILRM 466 (Barron J).

404 As to retrospectivity, see para **[10.099]**.

405 [1995] 2 IR 170 at 172, 173.

406 *Jones and Tarleton v Gunn* [1997] 2 ILRM 245.

407 *Alba Radio Ltd v Haltone (Cork) Ltd* [1995] 2 IR 170 (Barron J).

> Whether or not an Act is retrospective in its effect is determined by the proper construction of the provisions of that Act. Where rights have been acquired or duties imposed in respect of completed transactions prior to the passing of the Act in question, then those rights or those duties cannot be affected by the Act unless it is to be retrospective in its operation. In the present case there is no right vested in [the director] not to be examined under s 245 of the Principal Act unless the company is being wound up. Because the law has been altered as to the circumstances in which an application may be made under s 245 and its provisions have been altered to some extent does not mean that the Act is being operated retrospectively.'[408]

It followed that Barron J granted in part the order sought. The question was left open as to whether any order seeking to impose personal liability which might be sought, subsequently, would involve retrospection.

Misfeasance

[10.129] Section 298(1) of CA 1963 provides[409]:

> 'Subsection (2) applies if in the course of winding up a company it appears that any person who has taken part in the formation or promotion of the company, or any past or present officer, liquidator, receiver or examiner of the company, has misapplied or retained or become liable or accountable for any money or property of the company, or has been guilty of any misfeasance or other breach of duty or trust in relation to the company.

Section 298(2) of CA 1963 provides

> 'The court may, on the application of the liquidator, or any creditor or contributory, examine into the conduct of the promoter, officer, liquidator, receiver or examiner, and compel him -
>
> (a) to repay or restore the money or property or any part thereof respectively with interest at such rate as the court thinks just, or
>
> (b) to contribute such sum to the assets of the company by way of contribution in respect of the misapplication, retainer, misfeasance or other breach of duty or trust as the court thinks just.'

This section can be invoked 'in the course of winding up a company' or under CA 1990, s 251[410]. It must be remembered that CA 1963, s 298 is merely a procedural measure and does not impose any additional duties on officers, nor confer any additional remedies on creditors[411]. Section 298 enables existing duties of officers to be enforced[412].

---

[408] [1995] 2 IR 170 at 173.

[409] As amended by CA 1990, s 142.

[410] See para **[10.123]**.

[411] In *Re Kirby's Coaches Ltd* [1991] BCLC 414 it was held by Hoffmann J that a petitioner did not specifically have to plead misfeasance, and it could arise at trial for the first time.

[412] See *Re Irish Provident Assurance Company Ltd* [1913] IR 352, where Cherry LJ said of the old section similar to CA 1963, s 298, that 'it applies only to cases where a cause of action would, independently of the section, exist, at the suit of the company...', and went on to quote *Cavendish–Bentinck v Fenn* [1887] 12 AC 652 at 669: '...it has been settled, and I think rightly settled, that that section creates no new offence, and that it gives no new rights, but only provides a summary and efficient remedy in respect of rights which, apart from that section, might have been vindicated either in law or in equity.'

[10.130] Section 298 of CA 1963 can only be used against an officer who has been guilty of a breach of trust which has caused his company to suffer a pecuniary loss[413]. That pecuniary loss must arise from the officer's breach of duty. In *Re SM Barker Ltd*[414] the three directors (and beneficial shareholders) of a company caused the company to voluntarily release a number of simple contract debts due to the company, arising out of transactions between the company and them in their personal capacities. Later, they sold their shares to another group of persons. When the company went into insolvent liquidation, the official liquidator sought an order under a section similar to CA 1963, s 298 for a declaration that the former directors were liable to contribute to the assets of the company by way of restitution or as damages for misfeasance. It was held that no order would be made since the gains made by the directors were made in their personal capacity, and not qua director nor qua trustee of the shareholders. Gavin Duffy J held:

> 'To succeed in this motion the liquidator must prove damage to the company at the hands of the respondent directors. So far, I think no such damage has been proved, unless the cancellation in the Latchmans' interest of an asset worth nearly £12,000, as I assume, so that the company thereafter had nothing to show for that asset, is itself such an actual loss as to justify this claim under [CA 1963, s 298]. At this point, it cannot be stressed too emphatically that on the evidence the three Latchmans were in truth the owners of the entire share capital, so that they were at liberty to do virtually whatever they chose, short of acting dishonestly or ultra vires. The transaction was the honest result of negotiations between the Latchmans and an external group of businessmen, eager for their own ends to gain control of the company and its assets without paying an excessive price for the shares which carried control. And I discern no moral obliquity in the deeds and omissions of the Latchmans as directors in this transaction...
>
> Here was a small private company, owned and controlled by a family group, who acted unanimously, and in concert with the incoming members about to replace them, at the...meetings, and what they did they did in good faith and in natural reliance for the technical mechanics of their operations and of the deal upon an accountant-auditor belonging to a firm of high repute. However improvident the resolution releasing the Latchmans' indebtedness and however regrettable the failures to observe the requirements and formalities of company law, quite beyond their ken, I think, the outstanding fact is the fact that the true owners of the property, acting with the full assent of their prospective assignees, all concurred at the two meetings and throughout in every step taken.'[415]

Hence, only losses occasioned by breach of directors' duties can be pursued under CA 1963, s 298[416]. An example of an order being made under s 298 is *Re Contract Packaging Ltd*[417]. After finding that the directors were, inter alia, in breach of their fiduciary duties, Flood J declared that pursuant to the section, two of the directors held a house (their family home) in trust for their company, and ordered that they convey it to the liquidator.

---

[413] See *Re B Johnson & Co (Builders) Ltd* [1955] 2 All ER 775.

[414] *Re SM Barker Ltd* [1950] IR 123.

[415] Gavan Duffy J (at 135 *ff*) went on to state that the actions were not ultra vires.

[416] See also *Derek Randall Enterprises Ltd v Randall* [1991] BCLC 379.

[417] *Re Contract Packaging Ltd* (16 January 1992, unreported), High Court, per Flood J reported in (1992) The Irish Times, 17, 18 January.

[10.131] It should be noted that where confusion is caused because of the intermingling of a 'sole director's' assets with those of the company, thereby provoking a liquidator to take misfeasance proceedings, it is open to the court to exercise its discretion and hold the director concerned liable for the costs of the action. This is what happened in *Re David Ireland & Co Ltd*[418] where the sole controller and beneficial owner of a company intermingled his personal finances with those of the company and treated the company's bank account as if it were his own. In fact the man concerned acted honestly, and always ensured that the company was reimbursed. Nevertheless, because it was his 'messing' which provoked the bewildered liquidator to institute misfeasance proceedings, he was held liable to pay the costs of the liquidator in taking the proceedings. In the words of Fitzgibbon LJ:

> 'It has been said that this is "an extremely hard order". The hardship, if any, is the result of the 'one man company' system. In my opinion anyone who chooses to give the support of his name as a director to a company of that class, and who neglects his duty by allowing "one man" to do as he pleases, and actively assists him by paying away the company's money at will, deserves to bear the expense of investigating what has been done, and any practical judicial lesson against undertaking such directorships should not be lightly set aside by a Court of Appeal.'[419]

Such has been said to remain 'a salutary reminder in the Ireland of today in which mere figurehead second directors are compulsory'[420]. Indeed, one could go further and say that not only is it a salutary reminder to figurehead or token[421] directors, but also to all controllers involved in conducting business through a private company, who tend to be most astute at realising the advantages of the limited liability company, but ignorant of the duties owed by corporate officers, and particularly, by directors.

[D] SECRETARIES' DUTIES

[10.132] The appointment and powers of the company secretary have been considered in a previous chapter[422]. In *Barnett, Hoares & Co v South London Tramways Co*[423] Lord Esher MR said:

> 'A secretary is a mere servant; his position is that he is to do what he is told and no person can assume that he has any authority to represent anything at all.'

Commenting upon this passage, Lord Denning MR in *Panorama Developments (Guilford) Ltd v Fidelis Furnishing Fabrics Ltd*[424] noted that times have changed since it was first mooted by Lord Esher in 1887. Lord Denning observed that the company secretary is a 'much more important person nowadays', being an officer with extensive duties and responsibilities. While Lord Denning's comments are indeed true in the

418 *Re David Ireland & Co Ltd* [1905] IR 133.

419 [1905] IR 133 at 141.

420 See Ussher, *Company Law in Ireland* (1986), p 241.

421 See para **[10.042]** *ff*.

422 See Chapter 8, *Corporate Governance: Management by the Directors*, para **[8.094]** *ff*. See generally, Doyle, *The Company Secretary* (1994).

423 *Barnett, Hoares & Co v South London Tramways Co* (1887) 18 QBD 815 at 817.

424 *Panorama Developments (Guilford) Ltd v Fidelis Furnishing Fabrics Ltd* [1971] 3 All ER 16.

context of PLCs and large private companies, they hardly reflect the reality in the vast majority of small Irish private companies.

[10.133] The secretary is the chief administrative officer of a company; by not having a management role as of right, it follows that his duties are equally circumscribed in terms of scope and to whom they are properly owed. It is important to consider, however, the actual duties and powers conferred on secretaries in any particular company. In the vast majority of small Irish private companies the office of secretary will be held by a person who is also a director. Large and medium-sized private companies will frequently employ the services of an accountancy firm to act as company secretary and to perform the requisite secretarial functions.

The subject of secretaries' duties

[10.134] The duties of secretaries are only owed to the separate legal entity that is the company: *Kelly v Kelly*[425]. Unlike the law in relation to directors, there has been no judicial extension of secretaries' duties to persons other than the company, such as shareholders, creditors, or employees. This is explained by reason of the fact that a company secretary is not, qua secretary, involved in the management of a company.

Secretaries' common law duties

[10.135] On account of the secretary's limited managerial role, his duties are also limited. As with any employee, a secretary has duties of fidelity and confidentiality. A secretary can be restrained by injunction from disclosing confidential information or trade secrets belonging to his company[426]. The company secretary owes the company duties of skill, care and diligence and can be liable in negligence for failure to exercise the necessary skill, care and diligence. Because a company secretary does not, usually or ex officio, have powers of management or decision making, it is thought that a company secretary is not a fiduciary to the same extent as directors and that the secretary does not owe the same fiduciary duties as are owed by directors. As an employee, however, a secretary must not make a secret profit by virtue of his office. Whether it is correct to say, as the authors of *Palmer's Company Law* do, that the principle in *Regal (Hastings) v Gulliver* applies to company secretaries, is thought to be debatable[427]. This is because the secretary has neither a vote at meetings of the board nor even the right to participate in discussions. If the principles concerning conflict of interest were extended to secretaries, then why not also to ordinary employees?

Secretaries' statutory duties

[10.136] The Companies Acts 1963-2001 provide that the company secretary is expressly named as the person responsible for certain specific matters, which include:

- Ensuring (with the directors) 'that the requirements of the Companies Acts are complied with by the company'[428];

---

[425] *Kelly v Kelly* [1986] SLT 101.

[426] *Robb v Green* [1895] 2 QB 315.

[427] *Palmer's Company Law*, p 8236; para 3.1118.

[428] CA 1963, s 383(3) as replaced by CLEA 2001, s 100.

— Co-signing (with a director) the annual return[429].

— Certifying (with a director) the copy of the balance sheet to be annexed to the annual return as being a true copy[430].

— Signing the certificate required in the case of a private company that the company has not issued any invitation to the public to subscribe for shares or debentures and where the number of members is over 50, that those persons over 50 are not reckonable in accordance with CA 1963, s 33 (with a director)[431].

— In a banking company, signing the balance sheet (with a director)[432].

— Giving notice in writing to the company as soon as may be of such matters relating to himself and to his spouse and children as may be necessary for the purposes of section 190 (register of shareholdings)[433].

— Giving information in writing to the company as soon as may be of such matters as may be necessary to enable the company to comply with CA 1963, s 195[434].

— Giving notice to a person who is to become a director with unlimited liability of that fact[435].

— Filing and verifying the statement of affairs required under CA 1963, s 224(1), where the court has made a winding-up order or appointed a provisional liquidator[436].

— Submitting and verifying the statement of affairs required under CA 1963, s 319, where a receiver has been appointed[437].

— Certifying (with a director) the copy of the balance sheet, profit and loss account, or auditor's report, as the case may be, laid before the annual general meeting of the company held during the period to which the return relates to be annexed to the annual return as being true copies[438].

— Signing a written statement (with a director) which contains the information required to be given by C(A)A 1986, s 16(1), in lieu of being stated in a note to the accounts, to be annexed to the annual return[439].

— Certifying (with a director) that the copy of the statement required by C(A)A 1986, s 16(3)(b) annexed to the annual return is a true copy[440].

---

429 CA 1963, s 127(1).
430 CA 1963, s 128(1)(a).
431 CA 1963, s 129.
432 CA 1963, s 156(2).
433 CA 1963, s 193(1).
434 CA 1963, s 195(11), as inserted by CA 1990, s 51.
435 CA 1963, s 197(2).
436 CA 1963, s 224(2).
437 CA 1963, s 320(2).
438 C(A)A 1986, s 7(1)(a).
439 C(A)A 1986, s 16(3)(a).
440 C(A)A 1986, s 16(3)(b).

— Certifying the copy of the report of the auditors under C(A)A 1986, s 18(3) to be furnished to the Registrar of Companies as being a true copy[441].

— Notifying the company in writing of the subsistence of his interests in shares or debentures and other information as required by CA 1990, s 53[442].

— Disclosing interests in shares or debentures[443].

— Notifying the company in writing if the secretary's spouse or children are granted a right to subscribe for shares in, or debentures of, the company and of the exercise by the spouse or minor child of such a right[444].

The foregoing statutory duties relate to matters that are exclusive duties of the company secretary in respect of which no other officer or person can perform.

[10.137] In addition, common form articles of association impose the following express duties on the company secretary:

— To summon a meeting of the directors, where called by a director[445];

— Countersigning (with a director) the affixing of the company's common seal where authorised by the directors or a committee thereof[446].

Again, the foregoing duties under standard form articles relate to matters that are exclusive duties of the company secretary in respect of which no other officer or person can perform.

[10.138] The Companies Acts 1963-2001 impose a myriad of duties on companies. Where a company defaults, the company secretary is liable to be penalised as being an 'officer in default'[447].

[10.139] Being a company's chief administrative officer, company secretaries will in practice be given a number of other duties. It is important to recognise that these are not statutory duties but, because they are commonly performed by company secretaries, they are noted here. These include:

— Attending and keeping minutes at meetings of the board of directors and members' meetings.

— Filing with the Company Registration Office and all other governmental agencies, all returns.

— Keeping all statutory books.

— Administering share registrations.

— Causing all notices to be published.

— Receiving all correspondence and legal notices on behalf of the company.

441 C(A)A 1986, s 18(5).
442 CA 1990, s 53(1) and (2).
443 CA 1990, s 63(1) and (5).
444 CA 1990, s 64(3).
445 Model reg 101.
446 Model reg 115.
447 See Chapter 12, *Company Law Compliance and Enforcement*, para **[12.032]** *ff*.

The actual duties of individual company secretaries will vary according to the practices adopted by their particular board of directors. In many small Irish private companies, there must be a suspicion that the duties of company secretary are taken more lightly, perhaps, than is prudent.

[E] PROMOTERS' DUTIES

Corporate promoters

[10.140] The persons who undertake the formation of a company are termed its promoters. Although often a promoter may be a professional advisor, it must not be forgotten in this context that A and B, who incorporated their garage business back in Chapter 2[448], are in law also 'promoters'. It has been said[449] that a promoter is '...one who undertakes to form a company with reference to a given project, and to set it going and who takes the necessary steps to accomplish that purpose.'

In the context of private companies, people who are involved in all but a purely professional or advisory capacity in the formation and ultimate registration of a company are liable in law to be deemed promoters.

Fiduciary duties of promoters

[10.141] Promoters owe fiduciary duties both to the shareholders and to the company itself. It has been said in *Whaley Bridge Calico Printing Co v Green & Smith*[450] that the duties owed by a promoter are based on general principles of equity. Thus, Bowen J said[451]:

> 'The relief afforded by equity to companies against promoters, who have sought improperly to make concealed profits out of the promotion, is only an instance of the more general principle upon which equity prevents the abuse of undue influence and of fiduciary relations. The term promoter is a term not of law, but of business, usefully summing up in a word a number of business operations familiar to the commercial world by which a company is generally brought into existence. In every case the relief granted must depend on the establishment of such relations between the promoter and the birth, formation and floating of the company, as render it contrary to good faith that the promoter should derive a secret profit from the promotion. A man who carries about an advertising board in one sense promotes a company, but in order to see whether relief is obtainable by the company what is to be looked to is not a word or name, but the acts and the relations of the parties.'

[10.142] Turning from the general to the specific, like a company director a promoter is considered to be a trustee, so where he acquires assets 'on behalf of the company', he does so in trust[452]. The duties owed by a trustee are of a fiduciary nature. As such, a

---

448 See Chapter 2, *Formation, Registration and Conversion of Private Companies*, para **[2.008]**.

449 *Twycross v Grant* (1877) CPD 469 at 541, per Cockburn CJ.

450 *Whaley Bridge Calico Printing Co v Green & Smith* (1879) 5 QBD 109.

451 (1879) 5 QBD 109 at 111.

452 For the duties of trustees, see Keane, *Equity and the Law of Trusts in the Republic of Ireland* (1988), pp 108–130.

promoter is bound to account for any profits made. So in *Erlanger v New Sombrero Phosphate Co*[453] Lord Cairns said:

> '[The promoters] stand, in my opinion, undoubtedly in a fiduciary position. They have in their hands the creation and moulding of the company; they have the power of defining how, and when, and in what shape, and under what supervision, it shall start into existence and begin to act as a trading corporation.'

By accounting for profits is meant that where a company's promoter, for example, buys a piece of property he will be liable to account for any profits made where he sells that property to the company. A good example in point is the case of *Gluckstein v Barnes*[454], where a syndicate was formed to purchase a particular company. The syndicate, of which Gluckstein was a member, formed another company called the Olympia Company Ltd. A prospectus[455] was issued by the company and stated that the property was purchased for £180,000 and disclosed a profit of £40,000. However, what the prospectus did not disclose was that the syndicate had purchased the shares of the company at a price which was below the market value and as a result made an additional profit of £20,000. When Olympia Company Ltd went into liquidation, the liquidator, mindful of the duties of promoters, sought to make the promoters account to the company for the additional profit as an undisclosed profit. The House of Lords held that the promoters were obliged to disclose the additional profit, to account to the company for it, and were accordingly bound to pay it to the liquidator. Although in that case the company was a public company, the rule that a promoter of a private company must disclose all profits to the shareholders of his company holds true. So where a person has a bright and apparently commercially viable idea, forms a company and invites his friends to join in with him to exploit this idea, and makes a 'secret profit' in the course of his promotional activities, he will be liable to account for this profit to the company and the other shareholders[456].

Breach of the promoter's fiduciary duty

[10.143] Where a promoter acts in breach of his fiduciary duties he will be liable to compensate the company. This is true whether the promoter acquired any property with a sale on to the company in mind, or not[457]. The remedies available to a company where a promoter acts in breach of his duties encompass the equitable, tortious and contractual.

[10.144] In equity, a claim can be made for rescission of a contract prejudicial to the company, but this will only succeed where restitutio in integrum is possible[458]. An example of where restitution was held to be impossible is *Re Cape Breton*[459] where a number of individuals, one of whom was a director of the company concerned, financed

---

[453] *Erlanger v New Sombrero Phosphate Co* [1878] 3 AC 1218 HL.

[454] *Gluckstein v Barnes* [1900] AC 240.

[455] See Chapter 28, *Public Companies in Context*.

[456] See also *Re Leeds and Hanley Theatres of Victoria Ltd* [1902] 2 Ch 809.

[457] *Ladywell Mining Co v Brookes* [1887] 35 Ch D 400 and *Re Cape Breton Co* [1885] 29 Ch D 795.

[458] Ie where all parties can be restored to their original position.

[459] *Re Cape Breton* [1885] 29 Ch D 795.

the purchase of certain coal fields which were taken in the name of a nominee. After the company in question was formed, the nominee agreed to sell the coalfields to the company. The director never disclosed his interest to the company. When the company went into liquidation, the coalfield was sold at a loss. The liquidator sought to make the director liable for breach of duty and although the Court of Appeal accepted that the contract could previously have been rescinded, restitution at the date of the hearing was impossible because the coalfield had been sold by the company. Accordingly, the company could not rescind the contract to purchase the coalfield from the promoter's nominee.

[10.145] Where a promoter has acted in breach of his duties to a company, the company can claim restitution of the benefit obtained by the promoter. Such can be done in equity on the basis of a constructive trust. Where a promoter receives commission on pre-incorporated contracts he will hold this as constructive trustee and not as a fiduciary agent to the company: *HKN Invest OY v Incotrade PVT Ltd.* Such a trust arises where a trustee obtains a benefit or derives a profit to which he is not entitled from his trusteeship[460]. A promoter is a trustee of the company he promotes, and where he acts in breach of his duties, he will hold any profit or other benefit in trust for the company. In such a situation a company may seek a declaration from the court that such profit or other benefit is held in trust by the promoter for the company. It should also be remembered that a delinquent promoter may also be pursued in tort for deceit or negligent misstatement[461].

[10.146] A promoter can be pursued in misrepresentation for damages for breach of contract, or damages for breach of trust. An example of an action for damages is *Re Leeds and Hanley Theatre of Varieties Ltd*[462]. In that case, a director and promoter did not disclose his interest in a transaction with the company through a nominee third party. The Court of Appeal held that not only could the company retain the property, but the company was entitled to recover damages from the promoter for breach of fiduciary duty. In the course of his judgment, Vaughan Williams J said:

> 'The authorities are not all perfectly conclusive that there is no remedy by way of an account for profits, but I prefer to say that, whether there is such a remedy or not, I am clear there is a remedy in the shape of damages.'

Insofar as this decision provides authority for promoters being liable in damages for breach of fiduciary duty, as opposed to breach of contract, it has been suggested that it is 'at least questionable'[463].

[10.147] The law of evidence may also provide a remedy in that a promoter may be estopped from denying that he purchased property on his own behalf. This is clear from

---

460 See generally, Keane, *Equity and Trusts in the Republic of Ireland*; ch 13, *Constructive Trusts*. See also *HKV Invest OY v Incotrade PVT Ltd* [1993] 3 IR 153 at 162 where Costello J cited *Hussey v Palmer* [1972] 1 WLR 1286.

461 See McMahon & Binchy, *The Law of Torts* (3rd edn, 2000), Chs 35 and 10, respectively.

462 *Re Leeds and Hanley Theatre of Varieties Ltd* [1902] 2 Ch 809.

463 Meagher, Gummow, Lehane, *Equity – Doctrines & Remedies* (3rd edn, 1992), p 150. See also *Tracy v Mandalay Party Ltd* (1952) 88 CLR 215.

Jacobus Marler Estates Ltd v Marler[464] where the House of Lords held that a promoter of a company could not assert that he bought property in his own capacity while acting as a promoter, and was estopped from denying that the property was bought on behalf of the company.

[10.148] A 1972 Irish case concerning the duties of promoters and the foregoing principles, which was only unearthed in the late-1980s[465], is *Hopkins v Shannon Transport Systems Ltd*[466]. In that case the plaintiff had a dream and floated the idea of a new project for a ferry across the Shannon. The support of another individual was secured when suitable vessels were located. Finance for the venture was sought from two sources: share subscriptions and grants from the Department of Finance. Unknown to some of the directors of the company, the plaintiff and the other individual, who were the promoters of the company, bought as a partnership some of the vessels which were subsequently sold to the company after it had been formed and registered. When the Department of Finance decided not to proceed, the plaintiff decided to pull out of the project. Later, he sought through the courts, his share of the profits of the partnership. When the matter came before the High Court, Pringle J held that because they were promoters, they were under a duty to make full disclosure, and so the contract entered by the company with the partnership was voidable at the instance of the company.

Promoters' transactions with a company

[10.149] Where there is full disclosure by a promoter of his interest or involvement in a contract entered by him with the company, his position will be safeguarded. The extent of the disclosure required by a promoter was examined in a number of cases, such as *Gluckstein v Barnes*[467] *and Erlanger v New Sombrero Phosphate Co*[468]. In the latter case Lord Cairns said:

> 'I do not say that the owner of property may not promote and form a joint stock company, and then sell his property to it, but I do say that if he does he is bound to take care that he sells it to the company through the medium of a board of directors who can and do exercise an independent and intelligent judgment on the transaction.'[469]

Caution should thus be exercised by promoters. Care must always be taken where an existing business is sold to a new company. Where an appropriate objects clause is adopted by the promoters and they as directors resolve in favour of the acquisition, they can be assured that they will not be guilty of a breach of their duties as promoters.

---

464 *Jacobus Marler Estates Ltd v Marler* [1916–17] All ER Rep 291.
465 See O'Dowd (1989) DULJ 120.
466 *Hopkins v Shannon Transport Systems Ltd* (10 January 1972, unreported), High Court.
467 *Gluckstein v Barnes* [1900] AC 240.
468 *Erlanger v New Sombrero Phosphate Co* [1878] 3 AC 1218.
469 [1878] 3 AC 1218 at 1236.

Chapter 11

Statutory Regulation of Transactions Involving Directors and their Companies

Introduction

[11.001] The fiduciary nature of the relationship between directors and their companies provides the justification for the statutory regulation of transactions and arrangements involving directors and their companies[1]. The legislature has ordained that common law fiduciary duties are not a sufficient protection of companies' assets when it comes to transactions involving directors and their companies. Directors are in a special position vis-à-vis their company and the temptation to abuse their position is particularly acute where the directors and shareholders are one and the same persons, as is often the case in private companies. In such companies, the usual control on directors abusing their position, namely the shareholders, does not exist. Where the directors and shareholders are one and the same persons the 'watchdog' that is the shareholders acting in general meeting in the interests of the company (and in their own interests, indirectly) is stood down.

Part III of the Companies Act 1990 ('CA 1990') was described in the explanatory memorandum to the Bill as containing 'a series of detailed provisions to deal with recognisable situations where a company director might be tempted to put his personal interest before that of the company'. In so providing, CA 1990, Part III amplifies by statute the common law regulation of transactions involving directors and their companies; the principle, however, is as old as company law itself. As was said in *Re Duckwari plc*[2] in the context of the very similar English provisions:

> 'None of the provisions introduce any novel concept into the law for it has long been recognised that the relationship of a director to his company is a fiduciary one, akin to that between trustee and beneficiary, though not identical with it. The specific topic of sales by the company to its directors at an undervalue or purchases by the company from its directors at an inflated value had been the subject of a number of cases, of which *Daniels v Daniels* [1978] Ch 406 is an example, but it was not tackled by the legislature until the Companies Act 1980, section 48.'

The abuse which CA 1990, Part III seeks to curtail is the gratuitous use of corporate assets for the benefit of directors and persons connected with them, to the detriment of the company, its creditors and its members.

[11.002] The statutory regulation of transactions involving directors and their companies arises under three main statutory provisions: CA 1990, ss 29 and 31 (which are the two main[3] regulatory provisions in CA 1990, Part III) and Companies Act 1963, s 194 ('CA

1 See generally, Chapter 10, *Duties of Directors and Other Officers*.

2 *Re Duckwari plc* [1997] 2 WLR 48 at 51 (per Judge Paul Baker QC).

3 Other transactions between directors and their companies that are regulated by CA 1990, Part III, and addressed in other chapters, are: s 28; directors' contracts of employment (Chapter 8, *Corporate Governance: Management by the Directors*, para **[8.070]**, and s 41; disclosure of substantial contracts (Chapter 13, *Accounts and Auditors*, para **[13.101]**).

1963'). Of the three provisions, CA 1990, ss 29 and 31 are the most far-reaching and comprehensive regulations. Notwithstanding its legitimate design, s 31, in particular, has caused severe difficulties for businesses and frequently rendered many bona fide commercial transactions unduly complicated, convoluted and costly. Indeed, many such transactions and arrangements have been rendered impossible[4]. Arising from concerns voiced by business and the legal and accounting professions, the section 31 regime was substantially amended by Part 9 of the Company Law Enforcement Act 2001, ('CLEA 2001') and whilst it remains complicated legislation, it is now more workable. Part 9 of CLEA 2001 was commenced on 1 October 2001[5].

[11.003] The provisions of CA 1990, ss 29 and 31 extend beyond directors to persons connected with directors and this chapter begins by identifying all of the persons who are regulated by CA 1990, ss 29 and 31. Thereafter, the main regulatory provisions are considered.

[A] Directors and persons connected with directors.

[B] Substantial property transactions.

[C] Loans, quasi-loans, credit transactions, guarantees and the provision of security in favour of directors and other relevant people.

[D] Disclosure of interests in contracts with companies.

These statutory provisions are given particular prominence in this work because of the frequency with which they arise in the practice of Irish company law and the far-reaching consequences of contravention[6].

[A] Directors and Persons Connected with Directors

[11.004] Both CA 1990, ss 29 and 31 regulate transactions and arrangements between companies and their directors, directors of their holding company (if any) and persons connected with such directors. It is the inclusion of *persons connected with directors* which causes CA 1990, Part III to be a minefield. Three distinguishable classes of 'relevant person' – a non-statutory term that, when used in this chapter, includes directors and persons connected with directors – can be identified:

1. Directors of the company and of its holding company.
2. Natural persons that are connected persons.
3. Bodies corporate that are connected persons.

Each of these are now considered and the results summarised, at para **[11.022]**.

4 See, for example, Editorial, 'When Can you Not Do Business – When Section 31 of the Companies Act 1990 Prevents You from Doing Business' (1995) 2 CLP 2.

5 See the Company Law Enforcement Act 2001 (Commencement) (No 2) Order 2001 (SI 2001/438), reg 3.

6 The English equivalent of CA 1990, s 31 – the Companies Act 1985, s 330 (UK) – has not affected English companies or company law practitioners to the same extent as s 31 has affected their Irish counterparts: see para **[11.052]**.

Directors of the company and of its holding company

[11.005] Both CA 1990, ss 29 and 31 apply to transactions and arrangements between companies and persons who are directors of such companies. 'Directors' here includes formally appointed or de jure directors[7] and de facto[8] directors. In addition, CA 1990, s 27(1) provides that CA 1990, Part III (containing ss 29 and 31) and CA 1963, s 194 apply to shadow directors[9].

[11.006] Sections 29 and 31 of CA 1990 also regulate transactions and arrangements between a company and the directors of its holding company. The reference to 'holding company' means a company so defined in accordance with CA 1963, s 155[10]. Again, it is thought that the reference to a director of a holding company will include a person who is either a de jure director, a de facto director or a shadow director of a company's holding company.

Natural persons that are connected persons

[11.007] Both CA 1990, ss 29 and 31 apply to transactions and arrangements between companies and 'persons connected with directors.' This was a new concept, introduced by the CA 1990. Section 26(1) of CA 1990,(as substituted by CLEA 2001, s 76(a)) defines the term as follows:

> 'For the purposes of this Part, a person is connected with a director of a company if, but only if, the person (not being himself a director of the company) is –
>
> (a) that director's spouse, parent, brother, sister or child;
>
> (b) a person acting in his capacity as the trustee of any trust, the principal beneficiaries of which are the director, his spouse or any of his children or any body corporate which he controls; or
>
> (c) in partnership within the meaning of section 1(1) of the Partnership Act 1890, with that director.'

A practical section 29 example here is that a company must obtain the approval of its members before it can convey a property to the child of one of its directors where the value of the property is in excess of €63,486.90[11]. Similarly, a section 31 example would be that a company cannot guarantee a loan made to the sister of one of its directors, unless the transaction comes within one of the exceptions to the s 31 prohibition[12]. It is also important to note that the spouses, parents, brothers, sisters, children etc of *shadow directors* are also persons connected with directors. Moreover, where a company is a subsidiary, the spouses, parents, siblings, etc of the directors of the subsidiary's holding company will also be persons connected with directors.

[11.008] Where a director's spouse is also a director of a company, he or she will not be deemed to be a person connected with a director, whose dealings with the company are

---

7 See Chapter 8, *Corporate Governance: Management by the Directors*, para **[8.035]** *ff*.

8 Chapter 8, *Corporate Governance: Management by the Directors*, para **[8.053]** *ff*.

9 Chapter 8, *Corporate Governance: Management by the Directors*, para **[8.058]** *ff*.

10 See Chapter 17, *Groups of Companies*, para **[17.006]** *ff*.

11 See para **[11.023]**.

12 See para **[11.051]**.

regulated on that basis. Instead, of course, their dealings with the company will be regulated on the basis that they are themselves directors of the company. If a director's spouse is a director of a subsidiary's holding company but not a director of the subsidiary, he or she will be a person connected with a director.

[11.009] The CLEA 2001 also clarified the meaning of 'partner'. It has now put beyond all doubt that by 'partner' is meant a business partner within the meaning of s 1(1) of the Partnership Act 1890[13].

[11.010] Regulation 12 of the European Communities (Single-Member Private Limited Companies) Regulations 1994[14] used to operate to deem the sole member of a single-member company to be a connected person[15]. This has now been replaced[16] with a *presumption* by CLEA 2001, s 76(c), which inserted a new CA 1990, s 26(6), providing:

> 'It shall be presumed for the purposes of this Part, until the contrary is shown, that the sole member of a single-member private limited company within the meaning of the European Communities (Single-Member Private Limited Companies) Regulations, 1994 (S.I. No. 275 of 1994) is a person connected with a director of that company.'

Although sole members will often properly fall to be classed as persons connected with directors, this will no longer be the case automatically. Like all presumptions, the presumption created by CA 1990, s 26(6) is rebuttable. On the one hand it can be said that the effect of s 26(6) is minimal since, whatever about a presumption, as a matter of fact a sole member can only be a person connected with a director if he (or it, in the case of a body corporate sole member) meets the requirements in s 26. Whilst this is of course true, the significance of the presumption is to shift the onus from the person claiming that a sole member is a connected person, to the sole member to refute that he (or it) is a connected person.

Bodies corporate that are connected persons

[11.011] Companies are also prohibited from entering into certain transactions or arrangements *in favour of another body corporate*. This is because CA 1990, s 26(2) provides: 'A body corporate shall also be deemed to be connected with a director of a company if it is controlled by that director.'

It is significant that the term 'body corporate' is used and not merely 'company'. As has been considered in an earlier chapter, 'company' means an Irish company ie one formed and registered under the Companies Acts or an existing company[17]. 'Body corporate', on the other hand, is more generic and refers to any entity that has a separate existence from

13 See Twomey, *Partnership Law* (2000), ch 2.

14 European Communities (Single–Member Private Limited Companies) Regulations 1994 (SI 1994/275).

15 Whilst dealt with under the heading of 'natural persons that are connected persons' for convenience, it is of course the case that a sole member of a private limited company can be a body corporate.

16 SI 1994/275, reg 12 was repealed by the European Communities (Single–Member Private Limited Companies) Regulations 1994 (Amendment) Regulations 2001 (SI 1994/275), reg 3.

17 CA 1963, s 2: see Chapter 2, Formation, *Registration and Conversion of Private Companies*, para **[2.054]**.

its members eg companies, building societies, industrial and provident societies etc. Section 2(2) of CA 1963 expressly states that references in the Companies Acts to a body corporate or to a corporation shall be construed as 'including a company incorporated outside the State'. The consequence is that an Irish company will be prohibited from entering into a transaction or arrangement of a kind envisaged by CA 1990, ss 29 or 31 *in favour of a foreign company* that is controlled by a director. Again, it should be noted that where a company is a subsidiary, regard must be had not only to bodies corporate that are controlled by directors of the subsidiary, but also to those that are controlled by directors of the subsidiary's holding company.

(a) The meaning of 'control'

[11.012] A body corporate will only be a person connected with a director if that director *controls* it. There is a statutory definition of 'control' in CA 1990, s 26(3) (as substituted by CLEA 2001, s 76(b)) which provides:

> 'For the purposes of this section, a director of a company shall be deemed to control a body corporate if, but only if, he is, alone or together with any other director or directors of the company, or any person connected with the director or such other director or directors, *interested in* one-half or more of the equity share capital of that body or entitled to exercise or control the exercise of one-half or more of the voting power at any general meeting of that body.' (Emphasis added)

The amended s 26(3) has clarified an issue that caused trouble to practitioners trying to interpret the old version. The question was – where two directors of Company A are *equally* interested in all of the shares issued in Company B, could Company B be said to be 'controlled' by either director? The uncertainty stemmed from the fact that since both directors had an equal interest, it seemed that, individually, neither could be said to be interested in 'more than one half' of the equity share capital[18], as provided for in the original s 26(3). The revised wording now puts beyond doubt that, in such a situation, Company B will be deemed to be controlled by both directors and so Company B will be a person connected with both directors. The consequence of this is that transactions or arrangements entered into by Company A in favour of Company B will be regulated by CA 1990, Part III.

[11.013] Where a director is interested in one-half or more of the equity share capital or entitled to exercise or control the exercise of one-half or more of the voting power at a general meeting of a body corporate, he will be deemed to control that body corporate. The other important change effected by the CLEA 2001 concerns aggregation of interests. So, in determining whether a body corporate is controlled by a given director, that director's interests will be aggregated with those of any other director or directors; and also with those of any person connected with him or any other director or directors. It should be noted that this latter aggregation pool includes other bodies corporate which a director controls and, to some extent, overlaps with CA 1990, s 26(4)(b)[19].

---

18 Or, indeed, entitled to control the exercise of 'more than one half' of the voting power as provided in the original s 26(3).

19 See para **[11.020]**.

[11.014] It may also be noted that one of the two relevant aspects of 'control', *equity share capital* is assigned the same meaning as it has under CA 1963, s 155[20].

(b) 'Interested in' one-half or more of the equity share capital

[11.015] Where a person is the legal and beneficial owner of one-half or more of the shares in a body corporate, it will be connected with him. A person need not, however, be the legal and beneficial owner and lesser interests will satisfy the test of 'interested in one-half or more of the equity share capital of that body or entitled to exercise or control the exercise of one-half or more of the voting power at any general meeting of that body'. Section 54 of CA 1990 defines the expression 'interested in' shares, for the purpose of s 26(3)[21].

[11.016] Where a director is interested in one-half or more of the shares in a body corporate it does not matter whether or not such shares carry full rights. Section 54(2) of CA 1990 provides:

> 'Any reference to an interest in shares or debentures shall be read as including a reference to any interest of any kind whatsoever in shares or debentures; and accordingly there shall be disregarded any restraints or restrictions to which the exercise of any right attached to the interest is or may be subject.'

---

[20] CA 1990, s 26(4)(a). See Chapter 17, *Groups of Companies*, para **[17.018]**, and generally, Warnock, 'Inter–Company Relationships and Section 31 of the Companies Act 1990' (1994) CLP 243.

[21] CA 1990, s 54 is subject to CA 1990, s 55, which expressly disregards certain interests:

> '(1) The following interests shall be disregarded for the purposes of section 54 and sections 56 to 58 – (a) where property is held on trust and an interest in shares or debentures is comprised in that property, an interest in reversion or remainder or of a bare trustee and any discretionary interest; (b) an interest of a person subsisting by virtue of—(i) his holding units in— (I) a registered unit trust scheme within the meaning of section 3 of the Unit Trusts Act, 1972; (II) a unit trust to which section 31 of the Capital Gains Tax Act, 1975, as amended by section 34 of the Finance Act, 1977 relates; (III) an undertaking for collective investment in transferable securities, within the meaning of the European Communities (Undertakings for Collective Investment in Transferable Securities) Regulations, 1989 (SI 1989/78); (ii) a scheme made under section 46 of the Charities Act, 1961; (c) an interest for the life of himself or another of a person under a settlement in the case of which the property comprised in the settlement consists of or includes shares or debentures, and the conditions mentioned in subsection (3) are satisfied; (d) an interest in shares or debentures held by a member of a recognised stock exchange carrying on business as a stock broker which is held by way of security only for the purposes of a transaction entered into by the person or body concerned in the ordinary course of business of such person or body; (e) such interests, or interests of such a class, as may be prescribed for the purposes of this paragraph by regulations made by the Minister. (2) A person shall not by virtue of section 54(4)(b) be taken to be interested in shares or debentures by reason only that he has been appointed a proxy to vote at a specified meeting of a company or of any class of its members and at any adjournment of that meeting, or has been appointed by a body corporate to act as its representative at any meeting of a company or of any class of its members. (3) The conditions referred to in subsection (1) (c) are, in relation to a settlement— (a) that it is irrevocable, and (b) that the settlor (within the meaning of section 96 of the Income Tax Act, 1967) has no interest in any income arising under, or property comprised in, the settlement.'

This means that where one-half or more of the shares in a body corporate are held, it is irrelevant that the holder or holders of the remaining shares *in fact* control the company. The person who holds one-half or more of the issued equity share capital is, in effect, deemed to control the company (or body corporate) for the purposes of CA 1990, s 26(3) and it will be a person connected with him for the purposes of s 26(2).

[11.017] Where shares are held by a trustee, it will be the real beneficiary who will be deemed to be 'interested in' them. Section 54(3) of CA 1990 provides:

> 'Where any property is held on trust and any interest in shares or debentures is comprised in that property, any beneficiary of that trust who, apart from this subsection, does not have an interest in the shares or debentures shall be taken to have such an interest; but this subsection is without prejudice to the following provisions of this section.'

The effect of this subsection is that if one-half or more of the shares in a body corporate are held in trust for a beneficiary, it is the beneficiary and not the trustee who is deemed to be interested in those shares.

[11.018] It follows, therefore, that in order for a person to be '*interested in*' shares, it is not necessary that legal title in the shares is actually vested in that person. Section 54(4) of CA 1990 furthers the philosophy in CA 1990, s 54(3), last considered, by providing:

> 'A person shall be taken to have an interest in shares or debentures if—
>
> (a) he enters into a contract for their purchase by him (whether for cash or other consideration); or
>
> (b) not being the registered holder, he is entitled to exercise any right conferred by the holding of those shares or debentures or is entitled to control the exercise of any such right.'

This makes two distinct provisions, the effect of both being to render reckonable inchoate interests. In the first place, a person who has merely *contracted* to acquire one-half or more of the shares in a body corporate will be deemed to be interested in those shares. There is no restriction on this and it would seem to apply even if the existence of pre-emption rights might thwart a person's legal registration as a shareholder. In the second place, CA 1990, s 54(4)(b) is a catch-all measure, whereby a person who is entitled 'to exercise any right conferred by the holding' or 'to control the exercise of any such right' will also be taken to have an interest in shares in circumstances other than where he has entered into a contract to acquire them (CA 1990, s 54(4)(a)) or where he is the beneficiary of any trust of them (CA 1990, s 54(3)). Section 54(7) of CA 1990 provides further specific detail on when a person will be taken to be 'interested in' shares:

> 'A person shall be taken to have an interest in shares or debentures if, otherwise than by virtue of having an interest under a trust—
>
> (a) he has a right to call for delivery of the shares or debentures[22] to himself or to his order; or

[22] CA 1990, s 54(13) provides: 'Delivery to a person's order of shares or debentures in fulfilment of a contract for the purchase thereof by him or in satisfaction of a right of his to call for delivery thereof, or failure to deliver shares or debentures in accordance with the terms of such a contract or on which such a right falls to be satisfied, shall be deemed to constitute an event in consequence of the occurrence of which he ceases to be interested in them, and so shall the lapse of a person's right to call for delivery of shares or debentures.'

(b) he has a right to acquire an interest in shares or debentures or is under an obligation to take an interest in shares or debentures;

whether in any case the right or obligation is conditional or absolute.'

It should be noted, however, that 'rights or obligations to subscribe for any shares or debentures shall not be taken for the purposes of sub-s (7) to be rights to acquire, or obligations to take, any interest in shares or debentures' and that this is without prejudice to CA 1990, s 54(2)[23]. Moreover, CA 1990, s 54(8) and (9) provide:

'(8) For the purposes of subsection (4)(b) a person shall be taken to be entitled to exercise or control the exercise of any right conferred by the holding of shares or debentures if he has a right (whether subject to conditions or not) the exercise of which would make him so entitled or is under an obligation (whether so subject or not) the fulfilment of which would make him so entitled.

(9) A person shall not by virtue of subsection (4)(b) be taken to be interested in any shares or debentures by reason only that he has been appointed a proxy to vote at a specified meeting of a company or of any class of its members and at any adjournment of that meeting or has been appointed by a body corporate to act as its representative at any meeting of a company or of any class of its members.'

[11.019] Section 54(5) of CA 1990 concerns situations where one body corporate is 'interested in' the shares in another body corporate. This provides:

'A person shall be taken to be interested in shares or debentures if a body corporate is interested in them and—

(a) that body corporate or its directors are accustomed to act in accordance with his directions or instructions; or

(b) he is entitled to exercise or control the exercise of more than half[24] of the voting power at general meetings of that body corporate.'

This is a particularly far-reaching measure. It means that Body Corporate A will be connected with a director of Body Corporate B if Body Corporate C is interested in more then one-half of the shares in Body Corporate A and the director is a shadow director of Body Corporate C or is entitled to exercise/ control the exercise of more than half of the voting power at general meetings of Body Corporate C. This provision rests uneasily with CA 1990, s 26(4)(b), considered above, in that there is some overlap with CA 1990, s 54(5)(b). Further elaboration is provided by CA 1990, s 54(6), which provides:

'Where a person is entitled to exercise or control the exercise of more than half[25] of the voting power at general meetings of a body corporate and that body corporate is entitled to

---

23 CA 1990, s 54(1).

24 CA 1990, s 26(5) directs that 'one–third or more', as appears in s 54, should be replaced by 'more than half' when s 54 is being applied to the construction of s 26(3). It would appear to be a minor oversight not to have amended s 26(5) to refer to 'one–half or more' when substituting the new s 26(3).

25 Again, CA 1990, s 26(5) directs that 'one–third or more', as appears in s 54, should be replaced by 'more than half' when s 54 is being applied to the construction of s 26(3). It would appear to be a minor oversight not to have amended s 26(5) to refer to 'one–half or more' when substituting the new s 26(3).

> exercise or control the exercise of any of the voting power at general meetings of another body corporate (the "relevant voting power"), then, for the purposes of subsection (5)(b), the relevant voting power shall be taken to be exercisable by that person.

Generally, it should be noted that where persons have a joint interest, each of them shall be deemed to have that interest[26] and it is provided that it is immaterial that shares or debentures in which a person has an interest are unidentifiable[27].

(c) Body corporate controlled by body corporate controlled by a director

[11.020] A body corporate that is controlled by a body corporate that is itself controlled by a director of a company will also be a person connected with such a director. This is apparent from the extensive definitions given to 'interested in' shares in CA 1990, s 54 which is applied to CA 1990, s 26(3) but is also the case pursuant to CA 1990, s 26(4)(b), which provides that 'references to voting power exercised by a director shall include references to voting power exercised by another body corporate which that director controls.'

This means that where A Ltd is a wholly-owned subsidiary of B Ltd and B Ltd is controlled by a director of C Ltd, then A Ltd is a person connected with a director of C Ltd, with the consequence that transactions between C Ltd and A Ltd will be regulated by CA 1990, ss 29 and 31.

(d) A subsidiary can be a body corporate controlled by a director

[11.021] A body corporate can be a subsidiary company – within the meaning of CA 1963, s 155[28] - and, contemporaneously, a body corporate controlled by a director within the meaning of CA 1990, s 26(2). It is, however, important to stress that a subsidiary will not invariably be a person connected with a director of its holding company. In the case of a wholly-owned subsidiary, such a subsidiary could only be a person connected with a director of its holding company if that director 'controlled' the holding company by, for example, being interested in all of the issued shares in the holding company.

Summary

[11.022] In the context of CA 1990, Part III, the expression 'director and any person connected with a director' includes all of the following persons:

Persons who are directors and other 'relevant people'	
- directors of a company, - shadow directors of a company, - directors of a holding company, - shadow directors of a holding company, - the spouse, parent, brother, sister, child of a director of a company or of its holding company,	- a body corporate controlled by a director of a company or of its holding company, - a body corporate controlled by a body corporate that is itself controlled by a director of a company or of its holding company,

26 CA 1990, s 54(11).

27 CA 1990, s 54(12).

28 See Chapter 17, *Groups of Companies*, para **[17.008]** *ff*.

- the partner of a director of a company or of its holding company, - trustees where the principal beneficiaries of the trust are a director (whether of the company or of its holding company), his spouse, any of his children or any body corporate he controls,	- there is a *presumption* that the sole member of a single-member private limited company is a person connected with a director.

[B] SUBSTANTIAL PROPERTY TRANSACTIONS[29]

[11.023] Section 29 of CA 1990[30] is designed to provide protection to the *members of a company*, not its creditors. It achieves this goal by requiring the members of a company to approve, by means of an ordinary resolution, all substantial property transactions entered into between companies and their directors. It therefore provides a safeguard against directors abusing their position in corporate transactions involving themselves in their personal capacities. Section 29 is a derogation from the directors' powers to manage the business of the company, conferred by CA 1963, Sch 1, Table A, Part I, model reg 80 ('the model regulations). A failure to comply with s 29 would not appear to be a criminal offence; it does, however, render an unapproved transaction *voidable* at the instance of the company (and not ab initio[31]) and exposes the directors involved to unpleasant personal consequences[32]. Whilst the effect may be to maintain the value of a company's assets, any protection afforded to creditors is incidental and not by design. This is because s 29 does not prohibit any corporate transaction involving directors that the members of the company are not capable of approving by ordinary resolution. This remains the case even where the directors and the members are one and the same, meaning that two shareholding directors can approve of a substantial property transaction (wearing their members' hats) although it is to the manifest disadvantage of the company without contravening s 29[33]. Section 29 gives no voice to creditors in whether or not substantial property transactions between directors and their companies are validated. Where the members and directors are one and the same persons – as is frequently the case in many Irish persons – there will be no difficulty in complying with s 29 which, in such cases, is no more than a paper exercise. The real issue, however, is whether companies and their advisors *realise* that s 29 has application. As Hodgson J observed in *Joint Receivers and Managers of Niltan Carson v Hawthorne*[34] in the context of a 'family company'[35]:

29 See generally, Courtney, '"Substantial Property Transactions" Between Directors and Companies: Section 29 of the Companies Act 1990', (1996) 3 CLP 142 and for a note on s 320 of the Companies Act 1985 (UK): Milman, 'Problems with Substantial Property Transactions' (1998) Palmer's In Company, Issue 8/98 17 September 1998.

30 See Keane, *Company Law* (3rd edn, 2000), para 29.19.

31 See para **[11.043]**.

32 See para **[11.046]**.

33 Of course, regard must be had to the directors' common law duties, considered in Chapter 10, *Duties of Directors and Other Officers* and otherwise unlawful transactions may be avoided on a winding up: see generally Chapter 27, *The Realisation and Distribution of Assets in a Winding Up*.

34 *Joint Receivers and Managers of Niltan Carson v Hawthorne* [1988] BCLC 298.

35 [1988] BCLC 298 at 303j.

> 'Plainly there would not have been the slightest difficulty in obtaining approval at the time, but as I have said, I am sure that Mr Nelson did not then know of the section at all.'[36]

Where the members and directors are different persons and the members refuse to approve a particular transaction, the section is doing as was intended – providing a safeguard against directors' abuses – and cannot be objectively criticised for so doing. In *British Racing Drivers' Club Ltd v Hextall Erskine & Co (a firm)*[37] Carnwath J said of the purpose of the materially identical s 320 of the Companies Act 1985 (UK):

> 'The thinking behind that section is that if directors enter into a substantial commercial transaction with one of their number, there is a danger that their judgment may be distorted by conflicts of interest and loyalties, even in cases where there is no actual dishonesty. The section is designed to protect a company against such distortions. It enables members to provide a check. Of course, this does not necessarily mean that the members will exercise a better commercial judgment; but it does make it likely that the matter will be more widely ventilated, and a more objective decision reached.'[38]

Of course the transaction need not be a 'substantial commercial transaction' and CA 1990, s 29 has considerable implications for routine conveyancing where a director proposes to sell or lease property of the requisite value to or from a company.

[11.024] Section 29(1) of CA 1990 has been in force since 1 February 1991; it does not apply to arrangements entered into before that date[39]. As to its territoriality, it is important to note that s 29, like Part III generally, has effect in relation to an arrangement whether or not that arrangement is governed by the law of the State or the law of another country[40]. The decisive criterion is that it only applies to arrangements entered into by an Irish *company*[41].

[11.025] Section 29 of CA 1990 is now analysed under the following headings:

1. The regulation of substantial property transactions.
2. The meaning of 'non-cash asset'.
3. The meaning of 'requisite value'.
4. Exceptions.
5. Compliance by approving resolution.
6. The consequences of breaching CA 1990, s 29(1).
7. Liability of directors and others for breach.

The regulation of substantial property transactions

[11.026] Section 29(1) of CA 1990 is a two-way valve. It regulates substantial property transactions in which a director acquires assets from his company *and* in which a company acquires assets from its director. It provides that, subject to certain exceptions[42]:

---

36 [1988] BCLC 298 at 320e–f.

37 *British Racing Drivers' Club Ltd v Hextall Erskine & Co (a firm)* [1996] 3 All ER 667.

38 [1996] 3 All ER 667 at 681.

39 CA 1990, s 25(7).

40 CA 1990, s 25(8).

41 As defined by CA 1963, s 2.

42 See para **[11.034]** *ff*.

'...a company shall not enter into an arrangement—

(a) whereby a director of the company or its holding company or a person connected with such a director acquires or is to acquire one or more non-cash assets of the requisite value from the company; or

(b) whereby the company acquires or is to acquire one or more non-cash assets of the requisite value from such a director or a person so connected;

unless the arrangement is first approved by a resolution of the company in general meeting and, if the director or connected person is a director of its holding company or a person connected with such a director, by a resolution in general meeting of the holding company.'

The arrangement need not be contractually binding; it includes agreements and understandings[43]. It should also be noted that where a subsidiary company enters into an arrangement with a director or other relevant person, if that person also happens to be a director of the subsidiary's holding company, the members of the holding company will also be required to approve of the arrangement by resolution *even though the holding company does not itself enter into any arrangement with any person.*

[11.027] It is difficult to appreciate fully the scope of CA 1990, s 29 without also appreciating the meaning of the defined terms used therein. The concept of *a person connected with a director* is defined by CA 1990, s 26, and has been considered above[44]. The statutory definitions of *non-cash assets* and *requisite value* are equally fundamental to understanding what transactions are affected by CA 1990, s 29.

The meaning of 'non-cash asset'

[11.028] As might be expected, 'non-cash asset' is defined by CA 1990, s 29(9)(a) as any property other than cash and for the purposes of the definition, cash is deemed to include foreign currency. Moreover, any reference to the acquisition of a non-cash asset includes a reference to the creation or extinction of an estate or interest in, or a right over, any property and also a reference to the discharge of any person's liability other than a liability for a liquidated sum[45]. In *Re a Company (No 0032314 of 1992); Duckwari plc v Offerventure Ltd*[46] the defendant-company (which was controlled by a director of the plaintiff-company) agreed to buy a freehold property, from a third-party, for £495,000 and paid a deposit of £49,500 to stakeholders. On completion of the sale, the property was in fact conveyed to the plaintiff-company, which paid the balance of the purchase price and reimbursed the defendant-company for the deposit. At trial it was held that there had been a transfer to the plaintiff of the defendant's interest under the contract of sale. This finding was, inter alia, appealed on the basis that the transaction did not involve the acquisition of an asset by the plaintiff from the defendant and that what had occurred was a novation of the contract. In the Court of Appeal Millett LJ held, after quoting the English equivalent of

[43] In *Duckwari plc v Offerventure Ltd (No 2)* [1999] BCC 11 Nourse LJ said: '"Arrangement" is a word which is widely used by Parliament to include agreements or understandings having no contractual effect. Further there is no misuse of language in describing a transaction contemplated by such an agreement or understanding as one which is entered into "pursuant to" it'.

[44] See para **[11.004]** *ff.*

[45] CA 1990, s 29(9)(b).

[46] *Re a Company No 0032314 of 1992; Duckwari plc v Offerventure Ltd* [1995] BCC 89.

CA 1990, s 29(9)(b)[47] that 'it is arguable that Duckwari acquired an asset from Offerventure even if the transaction was carried out by novation'[48].

In *Micro Leisure Ltd v County Properties & Developments Ltd (No 1)*[49], the facts of which are given below[50], Lord Hamilton made the following observation on the English equivalent to s 29(9)(b):

> 'The concept of a person acquiring an asset from the company (or vice versa) imports, in my view, as a matter of ordinary language that immediately prior to the time of acquisition the asset is in existence – though, given that s 320 covers arrangements under which a party "is to acquire" an asset, it may be that it can apply where an asset comes into existence between the making of the arrangement and the acquisition of the asset under it. [CA 1990, s 29(9)(b)] defines "non-cash asset" as meaning any property or interest in property. That is, as Lord Osborne observed in *Lander v Premier Pict Petroleum & another* [1998] BCC 248 at 254, a comprehensive definition. That definition…does not, however, in my view embrace property or an interest in property which is brought into existence only by the "acquisition" itself. It matters not that the property or interest in property then brought into existence is itself capable of transmission, by assignment or otherwise.'[51]

In *Lander v Premier Pict Petroleum*[52] the plaintiff had claimed the right (under his contract of employment) to terminate his contract as managing director when another party obtained more than 50% of the company's equity share capital and in such an event he became entitled to a sum of three-times his gross salary. The defendant-company claimed, inter alia, that this was an arrangement concerning a substantial property transaction with a non-cash asset of the requisite value and was required to be approved by the company's members. Lord Osborne held, inter alia, that the nature of the rights in question was to cash payments which could not be described as 'property or interest in property other than cash' and so were not 'non-cash assets'.

The meaning of 'requisite value'

[11.029] Not all transactions involving the acquisition or disposal of non-cash assets come within the scope of CA 1990, s 29(1). 'Requisite value' is defined by s 29(2), which provides that for the purposes of s 29, a non-cash asset is of the requisite value:

> '...if at the time the arrangement in question is entered into its value is not less than £1,000 but, subject to that, exceeds £50,000 or ten per cent of the amount of the company's *relevant assets...*'

'Relevant assets' is in turn defined by s 29(2)(a) and (b) as being:

---

47 Companies Act 1985, s 739(2) (UK).

48 [1995] BCC 89 at 96.

49 *Micro Leisure Ltd v County Properties & Developments Ltd and another (No 1)* (1999) (19 January 1999, unreported), Scottish Court of Sessions.

50 See para **[11.031]**.

51 (1999) (19 January 1999, unreported), Scottish Court of Sessions at p 8.

52 *Lander v Premier Pict Petroleum* [1998] BCC 248 at 254.

'(a) except in a case falling within *paragraph (b)*, the value of its net assets[53] determined by reference to the accounts prepared and laid in accordance with the requirements of section 148 of the Principal Act in respect of the last preceding financial year in respect of which such accounts were so laid;

(b) where no accounts have been prepared and laid under that section before that time, the amount of its called-up share capital.'

Since, frequently, private companies will not be capitalised by shares – eg the subscription for and issue of one or two €1 shares is commonplace – for 'relevant assets' to amount to a meaningful figure in such companies, regard will have to be had to their annual accounts[54]. Where the value of relevant assets is in issue in a proposed transaction, it is thought prudent to have it certified by the company's auditors.

[11.030] The provisions on requisite value may be summarised thus. First, there is a de minimis provision – if the value of a non-cash asset is less than €1,269.74 it falls outside of CA 1990, s 29(1). If the value of the non-cash asset is greater than €63,486.90 *or* greater than 10% of the company's relevant assets – *whichever is the lesser*[55]– s 29(1) will apply. All transactions where the value of the non-cash assets exceeds €63,486.90 must comply with s 29(1). Where the value of the non-cash asset is between €1,269.74 and €63,486.90, whether or not the transaction is caught by s 29(1) will depend upon the value of its relevant assets[56]. In a company where relevant assets are, say, €100,000 a transaction involving an assets valued at more than €10,000 will be caught. By contrast, in a company with relevant assets of €634,869 all transactions involving assets, the value of which does not exceed €63,486.90, will fall outside of s 29(1). It is clear from CA 1990, s 29(2) that the *punctum temporis* for the valuation of the non-cash asset is the time at which the arrangement is question is made[57].

[11.031] The onus of establishing that a non-cash asset is of the requisite value is on the person who invokes the section[58]. Placing a value on a particular asset the subject matter of an arrangement will usually be straightforward. An example of where, however, this posed a particular difficulty was *Micro Leisure Ltd v Country Properties & Developments Ltd*[59]. There, it was held by Lord Hamilton in the Scottish Court of Session (Outer House) that

53 CA 1990, s 29(9) provides: '"net assets", in relation to a company, means the aggregate of the company's assets less the aggregate of its liabilities, and for this purpose 'liabilities' includes any provision for liabilities or charges within paragraph 70 of the Schedule to the Companies (Amendment) Act, 1986.'

54 See, generally, Chapter 13, *Accounts and Auditors.*

55 CA 1990, s 29(2) does not use the words 'whichever is the lesser' but it is thought that this must be implied from the language used. This interpretation of the similar English legislation (Companies Act 1980 (UK), s 48(2) which pre-dates the Companies Act 1985, s 320 (UK)) has been thus construed by Hodgson J in *Joint Receivers and Managers of Niltan Carson Ltd v Hawthorne* [1988] BCLC 298 at 321g.

56 See the Company Law Review Group's *First Report*, (2000–2001), at para 6.11.3 at p108 where it is recommended that the monetary limit of €63,486.90 be removed for PLCs, leaving only the greater than 10% limit.

57 See also *Lander v Premier Pict Petroleum* [1998] BCC 248 at 254.

58 *Joint Receivers and Managers of Niltan Carson v Hawthorne* [1988] BCLC 298.

59 *Micro Leisure Ltd v Country Properties & Developments Ltd* [2000] BCC 872.

s 320 of the Companies Act 1985 (UK) was to be broadly construed and the value of a particular asset meant the true market value of the asset to the director or person connected with him, as subjectively ascertained. The facts[60] in that case were that the plaintiff sourced land available for purchase and development. The defendant provided funds for its acquisition and in return would receive title to part of the property and a half-share in the subsequent development of the property. The plaintiff took title at first but subsequently transferred it to the defendant, pursuant to an alleged trust, and thereafter the defendant mortgaged the entire of the property and then re-transferred a portion of it to the plaintiff, but subject to the mortgage in favour of a High Street bank. This occurred in 1993–1994 and at all material times the defendant was a person connected with a director of the plaintiff. Subsequently, in 1996 an agreement was put in place between the plaintiff and defendant whereby they agreed to develop lands owned by both companies, the development being carried out by the defendant and both companies sharing in the profits, the greater proportion going to the defendant. In *Micro Leisure Ltd v County Properties & Developments Ltd (No 1)*[61] it was held by Lord Hamilton that the 1996 Agreement could, in certain circumstances, apply to the rights acquired by the first defendant but he went on to say that the existing pleadings did not contain averments apt to satisfy the statutory provisions. The instant case arose from the plaintiff's amended proceedings. On the question of the requisite value, Lord Hamilton noted that the first defendant-company owned two sites, adjacent to the plaintiff's site. When taken together as one large site the plaintiff's site and one of the defendant's sites had a significantly greater value than had their values in isolation. The question to be determined was whether the non-cash asset had an 'objective market value' or a more subjective value, based on its utility to the director or person connected with a director. Lord Hamilton favoured the subjective approach, holding:

> 'Parliament has not defined the criteria by which "its value" in s 320(2), ie the value of the non-cash asset, is to be determined. That state of affairs is to be contrasted with definitions of "value" given for other statutory purposes. It is also to be contrasted with the prescribed criteria for determining whether the relevant threshold of value has been reached. The absence of definition suggests, in my view, that Parliament intended the value of the non-cash asset to be determined, having regard to the statutory purposes, in the context of the particular circumstances of the transaction or arrangement. I figured in the course of argument a situation in which a company owned a strip of land which a director of it sought to acquire, the director already being proprietor of adjacent land. In circumstances in which it was quite evident both to the company (ie its board) and to the director that the land proposed to be acquired was a random strip, the acquisition of which would markedly enhance the development value of the director's existing property, it is difficult to see why the 'value' of the strip should, for the purposes of s 320(2), be assessed without reference to that circumstance. Otherwise, not only would the director be acquiring the strip at an advantageous price but the company would be failing to take advantage of the known circumstance that its property could on sale to a particular purchaser realise a significantly higher price than its value treated in isolation. That enhanced price would in such

60 As elicited from the earlier decision of Lord Hamilton in *Micro Leisure Ltd v County Properties & Developments Ltd (No 1)* (1999) (19 January 1999, unreported) Scottish Court of Sessions.

61 (1999) (19 January 1999, unreported) Scottish Court of Sessions.

circumstances, in my view, represent the true market value or worth of the property. Such an example is not, in my view, so fanciful or unusual that taking account of it would distort the true purpose and intent of the statutory provisions.'[62]

It is thought that the application of the finding in this decision must be limited to circumstances where no contract of sale has been executed by the parties and where the valuation of a particular non-cash asset is, to some extent, notional. The facts in the instant case were unusual as it was even arguable that the arrangement in question did not give rise to an arrangement within the meaning of the legislation.

[11.032] In Ireland, guidance as to the meaning of the *value* of an arrangement is provided by CA 1990, s 25(4)(c). This provides that, for the purposes of CA 1990, Part III, the value of an arrangement is:

> '...the price which it is reasonable to expect could be obtained for the goods, land or services to which the transaction or arrangement relates if they had been supplied at the time the transaction or arrangement is entered into in the ordinary course of business and on the same terms (apart from price) as they have been supplied or are to be supplied under the transaction or arrangement in question.'

It is thought to be significant that, although the English legislation does contain a similar definition of 'value', that definition[63] does not apply to s 320 and is confined to the interpretation of ss 330–339 of the Companies Act 1985 (UK) which relate to loans to directors. Generally speaking, if the market value of a non-cash asset is greater than the consideration paid pursuant to the arrangement then, being a transaction at an undervalue, it is more appropriate to seek to have the arrangement set aside on the grounds of misfeasance under CA 1963, s 298 for being in breach of the directors' duties[64]. To the extent that the decision in *Micro Leisure Ltd* conflicts with the objective definition of value provided for in s 25(4)(c), it is thought that it ought not to be followed in Ireland.

[11.033] It should also be noted that where the value of a transaction or arrangement is not capable of being expressed as a specific sum or money (because the amount of any liability arising under the transaction is unascertainable, or for any other reason), it shall, whether or not any liability under the transaction has been reduced, *be deemed* to exceed €63,486.90[65].

Exceptions

[11.034] There are three exceptions which exempt certain transactions notwithstanding that non-cash assets of the requisite value are acquired from (or disposed of to) relevant people from companies. These are:

(a) Inter-group arrangements.

(b) Arrangements in insolvent windings up;

(c) Acquisitions by members acting 'qua member'.

---

62 [2000] BCC 872 at 874–875.

63 See the Companies Act 1985 (UK), s 340.

64 See *Daniels v Daniels* [1978] 2 All ER 89 and, generally, Chapter 10, *Duties of Directors and Other Officers*, para **[10.066]**.

65 CA 1990, s 25(5).

(a) Inter-group arrangements

[11.035] Section 29(7)(a) of CA 1990 provides that neither of the two limbs in CA 1990, s 29(1) apply where non-cash assets are acquired by a holding company from a wholly-owned subsidiary, *or* by a wholly-owned subsidiary from its holding company *or* by one wholly-owned subsidiary from another wholly-owned subsidiary. Implicit in this is the recognition that arrangements between companies will be caught by s 29(1) where one of the companies is controlled by a director of the other; and that *control* for the purposes of CA 1990, s 26(2) does not, per se, exclude a company that is controlled by a director within the meaning of s 26 from also being controlled by another company to the extent that it is its subsidiary within the meaning of CA 1963, s 155[66]. However, one should not assume that because a group relationship exists that members of that group will automatically be persons connected with directors and before looking to see whether s 29(7)(a) applies, one should first establish whether a particular company is in fact a person connected with a director. It is also important to note that not every transaction between a holding company and a subsidiary is automatically exempted. In order to avail of the section 29(7)(a) exemption, it is insufficient to merely show that the companies in the transaction are holding companies and subsidiaries, within the meaning of CA 1963, s 155. Only transactions involving *wholly-owned subsidiaries* can avail of the section 29(7) exemption. It should be noted that 'wholly-owned subsidiary' is not defined by s 29 of CA 1990, and s 150(5) of CA 1963[67] can be taken to be a guide only as to the meaning of wholly-owned subsidiary in the context of CA 1990, s 29(7)[68]. It cannot, in particular, be assumed that a wholly-owned subsidiary for the purposes of s 29(7) can have more than one member although two members are acceptable for the purposes of CA 1963, s 150(5) where the second member is itself a wholly-owned subsidiary of the first member.

(b) Arrangements in insolvent windings up

[11.036] Section 29(7)(b) exempts arrangements for the acquisition of a non-cash asset where the arrangement is entered into by a company which is being wound up, 'unless the winding-up is a members' voluntary winding up'. This means that neither court appointed liquidators nor voluntary liquidators in creditors' voluntary windings up must comply with CA 1990, s 29(1) in disposing of assets to directors or other relevant people. A voluntary liquidator in a *members' voluntary winding up must*, however, comply with s 29(1) and the members must approve of any arrangements whereby directors (and other relevant people) are to acquire non-cash assets from the company, or vice versa. This exception underscores the purpose of s 29, namely, the protection of members, since where a company is insolvent its members can have no legitimate interest in the company's assets which, as has been said in another context, are held 'in trust' for the company's creditors[69].

---

66 See para **[11.021]**.

67 CA 1963, s 150(5) provides: 'For the purposes of this section, a body corporate shall be deemed to be the wholly–owned subsidiary of another if it has no members except that other and that other's wholly–owned subsidiaries and its or their nominees'. See Chapter 17, *Groups of Companies*, para **[17.027]**.

68 See the Company Law Review Group's *First Report* (2000 – 2001), at para 6.11.4 at p108 where it is recommended that CA 1990, s 29(7)(a) should be amended to identify a 'wholly-owned subsidiary' as per CA 1963, s 150(5).

69 See *Parkes v Hong Kong & Shanghai Bank Corp* [1990] ILRM 341 considered in Chapter 10, *Duties of Directors and Other Officers*, para **[10.011]**.

[11.037] It has been held by the English High Court in *Demite Ltd v Protec Health*[70] that s 320 of the Companies Act 1985 (UK) applies to disposals by receivers of non-cash assets to directors or other relevant people[71]. The facts there were that Demite, the plaintiff-company, had been established in 1995 by s and WP who were its directors, with a view to exploiting a product called Z-Net which, when used with mattresses and pillows, gave protection from house dust mites. Demite had three shareholders: Integro Fiduciaire Sarl, an offshore holding vehicle for s which held 58.5% of Demite's shares; Schroder Asia Nominees Ltd, an offshore holding company for WP which held 40.5% of Demite's shares and P, a senior employee, who held 1% of Demite's shares. Demite borrowed £215,000 from L, a friend of WP, who contemporaneously lend £35,000 to a sister-company called Pioneer Biosciences Ltd ('Pioneer'). Cross guarantees were given and Demite executed a debenture in favour of L. After Demite encountered financial difficulties the relationship between s and WP broke down. The holder of the debenture, L, appointed administrative receivers and the receivers sold Demite's business to the defendant, Protec Health Ltd ('Protec'). The case proceeded on the basis that Protec was a company controlled by WP and so was 'a person connected with a director'. Demite argued, inter alia, that the prior approval of its members was required before its business (a non-cash asset of the requisite value) was sold to a person connected with one of its directors and sought to have the sale voided. Protec argued that s 320 of the Companies Act 1985 did not apply to receivers and that, if it did apply, there had been prior approval by informal agreement. It was held by Park J that s 320 did apply and that the sale of Demite's business was voidable. In rejecting that he should *imply* an exception to s 320 in the case of a sale by a receiver to a relevant person, Park J said:

> 'For me to do that would be to go beyond anything that I can properly do as an exercise in construction of the statute, and to assume the role of a legislator. [Counsel for Protec and the receivers] say that section 320 should be construed so as to exclude sales by companies in receivership. In my judgment, however, the argument is effectively ruled out by section 321(2)(b), which I have quoted above. That creates an express statutory exception for sales by companies acting by liquidators (except in the case of members' voluntary windings up). The presence of that provision leaves no room for me to find an implied statutory exception for sales by companies acting by receivers.'[72]

In accepting that s 320 applied to the sale by Demite's receivers, Park J went on to reject Protec's assertion that there had been compliance by means of an informal shareholders' agreement. Neither did Park J consider that it was open to find that lapse of time (in

[70] *Demite Ltd v Protec Health* [1998] BCC 638.

[71] See Courtney, 'Receiverships in Ireland in the Wake of Demite Ltd v Protec Health Ltd' (1998) 5 CLP 255.

[72] [1998] BCC 638 at 646E. Park J also said (at 647B–C): 'I think that that is true, but it is not the case that, where there is a hole to be patched, the patch must exactly fit the hole. Statutory patches are commonly bigger than the holes. In any case, where an express exclusion from the section has been enacted for one kind of sale by insolvent companies – sales by companies in insolvent liquidation (see section 321(2)(b)) – I do not think that I can invent another one for a different kind of sale by insolvent companies – sales by companies in receivership'.

seeking to avoid the sale) would operate to prevent avoidance and he was not prepared to imply such a fourth[73] exception to avoidance[74].

[11.038] It is submitted that the decision in *Demite* ought not to be followed in Ireland[75]. In the first place, sales of company assets by receivers to officers, directors and persons connected with directors are already regulated by CA 1963, s 316A(3) and the application of the decision in *Demite* in Ireland would give rise to an unnecessary duplication. To apply CA 1990, s 29 in such situations would be wrong in principle and there is a clear case for implying into s 29 that it only applies to arrangements by companies *where effected at the behest of their directors*. In this regard the pragmatism seen in the decision of Barr J in *Bula Ltd v Crowley*[76] is significant. In that case, commenting on the nature of a receivership Barr J said:

> 'In practical terms vis-à-vis mortgagee and mortgagor the control over the company's assets exercised by the receiver amounts to possession of the debtor's secured assets by him which in turn in practical terms is possession by the mortgagee who appointed him.'

Secondly, Irish receivers have a statutory obligation to 'exercise all reasonable care to obtain the best price reasonably obtainable for the property as at the time of sale'[77]. Thirdly, the appointment of a receiver will often imply insolvency and where a company is insolvent it is the interests of its creditors, not of its members, which require protection. Finally, it is an affront to common sense to apply CA 1990, s 29 to a sale by a receiver in circumstances where a company is insolvent: its members have nothing to protect and its creditors are left short. It is thought that the decision in *Demite* can be distinguished on the grounds that there, the debenture holder was a personal friend of one of the directors and that it would not apply where a receiver is appointed by an entirely independent third party. If practitioners acting for debenture holders believe that there is a possibility that, on a forced sale, the only interest in an asset being taken as security from a company is likely to come from the company's directors or other relevant people, it may be wise to insist upon members' prior approval to the creation of the debenture[78]. It may be noted that the

---

73 On bars to avoidance: see CA 1990, s 29(3), considered at para **[11.044]**.

74 Protec successfully applied for leave to appeal but withdrew the appeal when faced with an application for security for costs. It subsequently applied for leave to appeal out of time but the Court of Appeal rejected this: *Demite Ltd v Protec Health Ltd (No 2)* [1999] English Court of Appeal of 24 June 1999 (Gibson LJ).

75 For a fuller argument on this point, see Courtney, 'Receiverships in Ireland in the Wake of Demite Ltd v Protec Health Ltd' (1998) 5 CLP 255 at 259–261.

76 *Bula Ltd v Crowley* (1 February 2002, unreported), High Court (Barr J).

77 CA 1963, s 316A(1). See generally Chapter 22, *Corporate Borrowing: Receivers*, para **[22.014]** *ff*.

78 The operative part of such a resolution might provide:

> 'We, being all of the members of ABC Ltd ("the company"), entitled to attend and vote at a general meeting to pass a resolution envisaged by section 29(1) of the Companies Act, 1990 have seen a copy of a [mortgage] debenture with XYZ Bank plc which the company proposes to enter and **HEREBY RESOLVE**, for the purpose of section 29(1) to approve of any future sale of all or any of the company's assets by any receiver appointed pursuant to that mortgage debenture to any director of the company or person connected with a director of the company for whatever consideration is, at the time of the sale of the assets, the best price reasonably obtainable.'

Company Law Review Group have recommended that s 29 should be amended by the addition of a further exception regarding the disposal of a company's assets by a receiver[79].

(c) Acquisitions by members acting 'qua member'

[11.039] Section 29(8) of CA 1990 provides:

> 'Subsection (1)(a) shall not apply in relation to any arrangement whereby a person acquires or is to acquire an asset from a company of which he is a member if the arrangement is made with that person in his character as such member.'

It is important to note that this exception only applies to one limb of the two fold regulation of arrangements, namely those whereby a director or other relevant person acquires or is to acquire non-cash assets *from his company.* It has no application where companies acquire non-cash assets from directors. The only clear situation in which a person can be said to be acting *qua member* is in a voluntary winding up where a company's assets are distributed *in specie* amongst its members[80].

Compliance by approving resolution

[11.040] In order to comply with CA 1990, s 29(1), the members of the company must approve in advance of the proposed arrangement by passing an ordinary resolution. Thus s 29(1) provides that companies shall not enter into a substantial property transaction with a director or other relevant person:

> '*...unless the arrangement is first approved by a resolution* of the company in general meeting and, if the director or connected person is a director[81] of its holding company or a person connected with such a director, by a resolution in general meeting of the holding company.' [Emphasis added]

Where a company is a subsidiary company and it proposes to enter into an arrangement with a director or other relevant person, not only must its members approve of the arrangement by resolution, but so too must the members of its holding company give their approval *if the director or other relevant person* is a director of the holding company. Frequently, there will be common directors of subsidiary companies and holding companies and where a subsidiary enters into an arrangement with such a common director (or person connected with him) it will be the case that *two approving resolutions* will be required. This remains the case notwithstanding that the holding company does not itself actually enter into any arrangement[82].

[11.041] Although CA 1990, s 29(1) specifically refers to a resolution passed in general meeting, it will not be necessary to formally convene and hold a members' meeting where the company's articles of association incorporate CA 1963, Sch 1, Table A, Part II, model

---

79 See the *Company Law Review Group's First Report*, (2000 – 2001), at paragraph 6.11.4 at page 108.

80 See Chapter 27, *The Realisation and Distribution of Assets in a Winding Up*, para **[27.181]**.

81 Note that not all 'connected persons' can be directors; specifically, bodies corporate cannot be directors of Irish companies.

82 An example of this is provided by *British Racing Drivers' Club Ltd v Hextall Erskine & Co (a firm)* [1996] 3 All ER 667, considered at para **[11.050]**.

reg 6 (the 'model regulations')[83] which entitles one to rely upon CA 1963, s 141(8)[84]. Accordingly, where the company's articles of association so permit, all the members for the time being entitled to attend and vote on such a resolution may simply resolve in writing to approve of the arrangement[85]. The form the resolution takes will obviously depend upon the nature of the proposed transaction. The operative part of a simple form of written resolution might provide:

> 'We, being all of the members of ABC Ltd, entitled to attend and vote at a general meeting to pass a resolution envisaged by section 29(1) of the Companies Act 1990 **HEREBY RESOLVE**, for the purpose of that section, in favour of the proposed arrangement between ABC Ltd and Joe Bloggs, a director of ABC Ltd, whereby ABC Ltd is to acquire the property comprised in folio 12345 Co Dublin from Joe Bloggs for the sum of €100,000. We make this written resolution in accordance with Regulation 6 of Part II of Table A of the First Schedule to the Companies Act 1963 which has been adopted into the articles of association of the ABC Ltd, as permitted by section 141(8) of the Companies Act 1963.'

Where model reg 6 has not been adopted by a company it will be necessary for the company's directors to convene and hold an Extraordinary General Meeting ('EGM') of the company's members and to comply with the notice provisions for EGMs as provided for by the Companies Acts[86].

[11.042] Where CA 1990, s 29 applies in a conveyancing transaction, regard should be had to the Law Society's conveyancing committee's practice note[87]. The essence of the recommendation is that in transactions between a natural person and a body corporate, and in transactions between bodies corporate, a certificate should be included in the purchase deed showing that the parties are either not connected[88] or that they are connected and the

83 Private companies that adopt model reg 6 will be authorised by their articles of association to pass informal resolutions. Regulation 6 provides: 'Subject to section 141 of the Act, a resolution in writing signed by all the members for the time being entitled to attend and vote on such resolution at a general meeting (or being bodies corporate by their duly authorised representatives) shall be as valid and effective for all purposes as if the resolution had been passed at a general meeting of the company duly convened and held ...'. See Chapter 9, *Corporate Governance: Meetings*, para **[9.076]**.

84 CA 1963, s 141(8), provides that where a company is so authorised by its articles of association: '... a resolution in writing signed by all the members for the time being entitled to attend and vote on such resolution at a general meeting ... shall be as valid and effective for all purposes as if the resolution had been passed at a general meeting of the company duly convened and held ...'

85 This procedure has been referenced in the Law Society's Conveyancing Committee's Practice Note on substantial property transactions: see 'Practice Notes' (1991) Gazette ILSI 419.

86 See Chapter 9, *Corporate Governance: Meetings*, para **[9.032]** *ff*.

87 'Practice Notes' (1991) Gazette ILSI 419.

88 The Law Society's recommended certificates are: 'IT IS HEREBY CERTIFIED for the purposes of s 29 of the Companies Act 1990 that the [vendor/purchaser] is not a director or a person connected with a director of A or its holding company', and 'IT IS HEREBY CERTIFIED for the purposes of s 29 of the Companies Act 1990 that the vendor and the purchaser are not bodies corporate connected with one another in a manner which would require this transaction to be ratified by resolution of either.'

requisite resolution has been passed by the appropriate company[89]. In other arrangements involving non-cash assets *other than real property* it is also prudent to insert a suitable certificate into the deed or other document which evidences that CA 1990, s 29 either does not apply or has been complied with.

The consequences of breaching CA 1990, s 29(1)

[11.043] Arrangements that contravene CA 1990, s 29(1) are not voidable *ab initio*. So, in *Joint Receivers and Managers of Niltan Carson v Hawthorne*[90] Hodgson J said in respect of the predecessor of s 320 of the Companies Act 1985 (UK):

> 'That subsection seems to me to show clearly that a contract entered into contrary to [s 29] is not illegal *ab initio*. It remains valid and binding until it is avoided at the instance of the company.'

Where a company acts in contravention of s 29(1) the arrangement entered into is deemed by CA 1990, s 29(3) to be *voidable* at the instance of the company. This is the primary remedy for unlawful arrangements. In *Re Duckwari plc*[91], Judge Paul Baker QC said:

> 'The primary remedy of the company for a contravention of section 320 is avoidance of the arrangement and of any transaction entered into pursuant to it with consequential repayment of the money paid and retransfer of the asset.'

Not only will the 'arrangement' be voidable, but so too will 'any transaction entered into in pursuance of the arrangement (whether by the company or any other person)'.

[11.044] A company's ability to avoid an arrangement which does not comply with CA 1990, s 29(1) is dependent upon certain conditions being met. So, by CA 1990, s 29(3) avoidance will not be permitted where:

> '(a) restitution of any money or other asset which is the subject-matter of the arrangement or transaction is no longer possible or the company has been indemnified in pursuance of subsection (4)(b) by any other person for the loss or damage suffered by it; or
>
> (b) any rights acquired bona fide for value and without actual notice of the contravention by any person who is not a party to the arrangement or transaction would be affected by its avoidance; or
>
> (c) the arrangement is, within a reasonable period, affirmed by the company in general meeting and, if it is an arrangement for the transfer of an asset to or by a director of its holding company or a person who is connected with such a director, is so affirmed with the approval of the holding company given by a resolution in general meeting.'

Accordingly, a company's ability to avoid an arrangement that contravenes s 29(1) is conditional upon a finding that none of the foregoing 'savers' apply. Section 29(3)(a) and

[89] The Law Society's recommended certificate here is: 'IT IS HEREBY CERTIFIED for the purposes of s 29 of the Companies Act 1990 that the transaction hereby effected has been approved by a resolution passed (at an Extraordinary General Meeting of the members of [A/B being the holding company of A]) or (as a written resolution of the members of [A/B being the holding company of A]).'

[90] *Joint Receivers and Managers of Niltan Carson v Hawthorne* [1988] BCLC 298 at 322b.

[91] *Re Duckwari plc* [1997] 2 WLR 48 at 53.

(b) of CA 1990 (which are identical to CA 1990, s 38(1)(a) and (b)) are examined in the context of loans and other transactions made in favour of directors and other relevant people[92]. The reference contained in s 29(3)(a) to s 29(4)(b) enables the company to make the director concerned and any other director of the company who authorised the arrangement, account for any gain made, whether directly or indirectly, and to indemnify the company for any loss or damage resulting from the arrangement or transaction and this is considered below[93].

[11.045] Section 29(3)(c) of CA 1990 again demonstrates the purpose behind the section: the safeguarding of members' interests since the members may retrospectively validate an otherwise voidable arrangement involving a company and its directors and other relevant people[94]. The ability of a company's members to retrospectively validate an arrangement is subject to their so resolving 'within a *reasonable* period'. No guidance is provided for what is meant by 'reasonable'. In *Re Duckwari plc (No 2)*[95] Judge Baker QC said of the reference to 'a reasonable period' that the term suggested to him:

> '...that avoidance has to be pursued promptly once members have been made aware of the transaction, otherwise there is no point in limiting the time within which members can affirm it.'

In *Demite Ltd v Protec Health Ltd*[96] Park J said of this passage, that 'If the judge is saying that the statutory right to avoid a transaction may be lost on grounds of passage of time alone, I respectfully disagree'. It is thought that Park J's analysis is correct and that the passage from Judge Baker's decision confuses the members' right to affirm with the company's right to avoid. Where CA 1990, s 29(1) is not complied with, it is voidable at the instance of the company, but valid until it is avoided; if, within a reasonable period of time, the members affirm the arrangement then it is no longer voidable and is valid. It follows that if the members' affirmation is not effected within a reasonable period of time, then the right to affirm it disappears; it does not follow from the language used in s 29 that the company must act promptly in avoiding the transaction. If the members do not act promptly their power to affirm disappears and the default position continues, namely, that the arrangement is voidable[97]. What will be reasonable in one situation will be unreasonable in another: what will be found to be a 'reasonable period' will vary from

92 See para **[11.098]–[11.104]**.

93 See para **[11.046]**.

94 Of course, members may decline to retrospectively approve an arrangement. In *British Racing Drivers' Club Ltd v Hextall Erskine & Co (a firm)* [1996] 3 All ER 667, when a section 320 arrangement was put to the company's members they declined to give it their retrospective approval.

95 *Re Duckwari plc (No 2)* [1997] 2 WLR 48. Note: 'No 2' is not used in the official name of the case but is used here to distinguish the case from *Re a Company No 0032314 of 1992*; *Duckwari plc v Offerventure Ltd* [1995] BCC 89. Note also that the decision of Judge Paul Baker QC in *Re Duckwari plc* was successfully appealed (on another point than that made here) to the Court of Appeal and is reported as *Duckwari plc v Offerventure Ltd (No 2)* [1999] BCC 11.

96 *Demite Ltd v Protec Health Ltd* [1998] BCC 638 at 650.

97 See (1998) 5 CLP 255 at 258.

case to case[98]. It is thought, however, that the reasonable period will only begin to run from the time the members become aware of the transaction.

Liability of directors and others for breach

[11.046] Where an arrangement contravenes CA 1990, s 29(1), the director and other relevant people for whom it was made together with any other director who authorised the arrangement or transaction entered into in pursuance of such an arrangement can be made account to the company for any gain made and made indemnify the company against any loss suffered. Section 29(4) of CA 1990, provides:

> 'Without prejudice to any liability imposed otherwise than by this subsection, but subject to *subsection (5)*, where an arrangement is entered into with a company by a director of the company or its holding company or a person connected with him in contravention of this section, that director and the person so connected, and any other director of the company who authorised the arrangement or any transaction entered into in pursuance of such an arrangement, shall (whether or not it has been avoided in pursuance of *subsection (3)*) be liable—
>
> (a) to account to the company for any gain which he had made directly or indirectly by the arrangement or transaction; and
>
> (b) (jointly and severally with any other person liable under this subsection) to indemnify the company for any loss or damage resulting from the arrangement or transaction.'

The distinction between CA 1990, s 29(4)(a) and (b) is that (a) applies to a situation where, in breach of s 29(1)(a) a *gain is made by a director* or other relevant person arising from the acquisition of an asset from the company. On the other hand (b) applies where, in breach of s 29(1)(b), a *loss is made by the company* arising from the acquisition of an asset from a director or other relevant person. In the former case the company's remedy is *an account* for the profit made, whereas in the latter case it is *an indemnity* for the loss suffered.

[11.047] The Court of Appeal extensively reviewed the materially identical English provision in the leading English case on s 320 of the Companies Act 1985 (UK), *Duckwari plc v Offerventure Ltd (No 2)*[99]. The facts in that case were the defendant (Offerventure) agreed to buy a freehold property for £495,000 and paid a deposit of £49,500 to the stakeholders. At the completion of the sale, by agreement with the plaintiff (Duckwari), the property was conveyed to Duckwari, which repaid the deposit to Offerventure. A director of Duckwari, was also a director of Offerventure and he and his wife owned all of

---

98 See the Company Law Review Group's *First Report*, (2000–2001), at para 6.11.4 at p108. There, it is recommended that 'reasonable period' should be subject to ratification taking place at the next AGM and in any event not later than 15 months unless all of the members at any time unanimously consent in writing to the transaction.

99 *Duckwari plc v Offerventure Ltd (No 2)* [1999] BCC 11 (CA). See also *Re Duckwari plc* [1997] 2 WLR 48 which was the decision of Judge Paul Baker QC which was successfully appealed to the Court of Appeal. The original case – *Re a Company No 0032314 of 1992*; *Duckwari plc v Offerventure Ltd* [1995] BCC 89 – where the decision of Robert Reid QC that the transaction in question was a substantial property transaction within the meaning of CA 1985, s 320 (UK) involving a non–cash asset of the requisite value – was upheld by the Court of Appeal.

the shares in Offerventure, making it a person connected with a director of Duckwari. The transaction was not approved by the members of Duckwari in general meeting as required by s 320 of the Companies Act 1985 (UK). Subsequently, Duckwari sought to avoid the transaction and sought to do so on the basis that it was a substantial property transaction within the meaning of s 320. Offerventure and the director argued that the transaction did not involve the acquisition of an asset by Duckwari from Offerventure; that the transaction involved a novation of the purchase contract; that the asset was not a non-cash asset; and that its value was not £49,500. As considered above[100], these arguments were rejected by the Court of Appeal. The subsequent proceedings were concerned with the consequence of the contravention of s 320 and, in particular, the ambit of the indemnity against loss and damage. In *Re Duckwari plc*[101], Judge Paul Baker QC was asked to determine the amount of compensation and damages payable to Duckwari pursuant to s 322(3) which is couched in similar terms to CA 1990, s 29(4). The judge held that the loss or damage suffered by a company must result from the transaction, 'not from the holding of the property acquired pursuant to it'[102]. He said:

> 'The primary remedy of the company for a contravention of s 320 is avoidance of the arrangement and of any transaction entered into pursuant to it with consequential repayment of the money paid and retransfer of the asset. The personal liability of the director or connected person is to account for profits and indemnify against losses. The statutory remedies are thus analogous to equitable remedies in which the common law rules as to damages play no part. We are not here concerned with a breach of any contractual or tortious duty, giving rise to an award of damages at common law. We are concerned with the unauthorised acquisition or disposal of a non-cash asset. This is akin to an unauthorised investment by a trustee, but with the difference that directors of a company can and are expected to take risks which would be unacceptable in the case of a trustee. Accordingly, as I see it, the mischief, and only mischief, addressed by these provisions is acquisition[s] by the company at an inflated value or disposals by the company at an undervalue.'[103]

He also held that a successful claim would call for the accounting to the company for any 'gain', not any 'profit'; and that the doctrine of mitigation had no place in a case under s 320. Accordingly, notwithstanding that the company had acquired the property in question for £495,000 and the fact that it was found that the value of the property in 1993 to the date of the judgment was £90,000, the loss or damage resulted from Duckwari retaining the property and not from the transaction.

[11.048] The decision of Judge Baker was successfully appealed to the Court of Appeal[104]. Nourse LJ said that an indemnity arises 'for any loss or damage resulting from the arrangement or transaction' and said such, in isolation, are capable of including *either* a loss incurred on realisation *or* a loss resulting from a fall in value of the acquired asset. Regard had to be had to the other provisions in ss 320 and 322 of the Companies Act 1985 (UK) and the general law in order to see what sort of loss was intended to be included. Nourse LJ concluded that:

---

[100] See para **[11.028]**.

[101] *Re Duckwari plc* [1997] 2 WLR 48.

[102] [1997] 2 WLR 48 at 54B.

[103] [1997] 2 WLR 48 at 49E.

[104] *Duckwari plc v Offerventure (No 2)* [1999] BCC 11.

> 'Bearing in mind the evident purpose of ss 320 and 322 to give shareholders specific protection in respect of arrangements and transactions which will or may benefit directors to the detriment of the company, I am unable to construe s 322(3)(b) as denying the company a remedy which appears to flow naturally from a combination of s 320(1)(b) and the general law. No doubt it is possible to cite instances where Parliament has been held to take away with one hand what it appears to give with the other. But I cannot conceive that one would be found where the result was to give a narrow effect to provisions plainly intended to afford a protection and equally amenable to being given some wider effect.'[105]

Nourse LJ went on to hold that the two defendants (Offerventure and the director with whom it was connected) were jointly and severally liable to make good to Duckwari the loss caused to it by the depreciation in value of the property. It is thought that Nourse LJ's interpretation is to be preferred.

[11.049] Where an arrangement is entered into in breach of CA 1990, s 29(1), it is a defence for a director to show that he took all reasonable steps to secure compliance. Section 29(5) of CA 1990 provides:

> 'Where an arrangement is entered into by a company and a person connected with a director of the company or its holding company in contravention of this section, that director shall not be liable under *subsection (4)* if he shows that he took all reasonable steps to secure the company's compliance with this section and, in any case, a person so connected and any such other director as is mentioned in that subsection shall not be so liable if he shows that, at the time the arrangement was entered into, he did not know the relevant circumstances constituting the contravention.

It should be noted that this defence does not apply to an arrangement entered into by a company *directly* with a director of that company or with a director of its holding company; sub-s (5) only applies where the arrangement is between 'a company and a person connected with a director'[106]. In precluding directors of the company and of its holding company from relying upon the defence the intention would appear to be that, as 'insiders' and officers, they ought to be aware of their duties under the Companies Acts. It is for this reason that, in *Duckwari plc v Offerventure Ltd (No 2)*[107] the director (with whom Offerventure was a connected person) could not seek relief under the equivalent English provision[108], and instead sought to rely upon the English equivalent to CA 1963, s 391(1)[109], namely s 727(1) of the English 1985 Act[110]. In the Court of Appeal Nourse LJ

---

[105] *Duckwari plc v Offerventure (No 2)* [1999] BCC 11 at 19H–20A.

[106] See the comments of Judge Paul Baker QC in *Re Duckwari plc* [1997] 2 WLR 48 at 56E–F.

[107] [1999] BCC 11 (CA).

[108] Companies Act 1985, s 322(5) (UK).

[109] See Chapter 10, *Duties of Directors and Other Officers*, at para **[10.076]** *ff*.

[110] Companies Act 1985, s 727(1) (UK) provides:

> 'If in any proceedings for negligence, default, breach of duty or breach of trust against an officer of a company or a person employed by a company as auditor (whether he is or is not an officer of the company) it appears to the court hearing the case that that officer or person is or may be liable in respect of the negligence, default, breach of duty or breach of trust, but that he has acted honestly and reasonably, and that having regard to all the circumstances of the case (including those connected with his appointment) he ought fairly to be excused for the negligence, default, breach of duty or breach of trust, that court may relieve him, either wholly or partly, from his liability on such terms as it thinks fit.'

held that a liability arising under s 322(3)(b) of the English 1995 Act was 'a liability in respect of default within s 727'. A more difficult question is whether or not the existence of a limited specific defence in s 29(5) precludes a director from relying on the *general* defence in s 391. At trial, Judge Baker had held that the existence of specific defences to s 322 did not exclude the operation of the English s 727. Nourse LJ said he did not wish to restrict the application of s 727 unless it was necessary to do so and did not express a view[111]. It is thought that the limitation in the specific defence in CA 1990, s 29(5) to persons connected with directors, gives rise to a clear legislative intention to prevent directors from being excused liability and that an Irish court would be loath to permit a director to rely upon the general defence in CA 1963, s 391.

[11.050] As in the case of other statutory provisions where companies look to their professional advisers for guidance, persons other than directors and relevant people can also be liable in negligence where a company acts in contravention of CA 1990, s 29(1). In England a firm of solicitors were held liable in negligence for failing to properly advise a company of the necessity to comply with the materially identical s 320 of the Companies Act 1985 (UK). In *British Racing Drivers' Club Ltd and another v Hextall Erskine & Co (a firm)*[112] W was a director and chairman of the first plaintiff-company and chairman of the second plaintiff-company, which was a wholly-owned subsidiary of the first plaintiff-company. The subsidiary entered into a joint venture with another company of which W was a substantial shareholder and which was a person connected with him. The company's solicitors did not advise that s 320 of the Companies Act 1985 (UK) required the prior approval of the members of the first plaintiff-company as the holding company of the company that entered into the substantial property transaction with the connected person. The second plaintiff-company invested £5.3 million. Subsequently, when the agreement was put to the members for their retrospective approval, the members refused to approve of the arrangement and ordered the directors to extract themselves from the joint venture. Eventually, a settlement was agreed whereby W acquired the company's interest for STG£3.2 million. In an action for negligence against the company's solicitors, it was held that the solicitors were liable for the loss as had they given proper advise, and the matter referred to the shareholders for approval, the deal would not have gone ahead. Carnwath J said:

> 'It was [the company's solicitor's] duty to advise the board of the need to comply with s 320. By failing to do so he deprived the company of the protection which that section offers, namely the protection of the approval of the members in general meeting. It was certainly foreseeable that such a decision was likely to have produced a more informed and objective commercial judgment on the joint venture agreement. In my view, the loss on the shares, while directly caused by the directors' decision to make a bad investment, was fairly within the scope of the dangers against which, having regard to s 320, it was [the company's

[111] There, Nourse LJ noted that Judge Baker had exercised his discretion not to permit the director from relying on Companies Act 1985, s 727(1) (UK). Assuming that s 727(1) did apply (without deciding the point) he went on to say that the arrangement in question was 'a one–sided arrangement detrimental to Duckwari' and that in the circumstances 'it cannot be said that [the director] acted reasonably or that he ought fairly to be excused' (at 21G).

[112] *British Racing Drivers' Club Ltd v Hextall Erskine & Co (a firm)* [1996] 3 All ER 667.

solicitor's] duty to provide protection. The defendants' negligence was accordingly an effective cause of the loss.'[113]

This decision provides a salutary lesson for professional advisers on the dangers of overlooking the application of s 29 to a particular transaction.

[C] Loans, Quasi-Loans, Credit Transactions, Guarantees and the Provision of Security in Favour of Directors and Other Relevant People[114]

[11.051] Loans by private companies to directors have long been used as sweeteners whereby directors were indirectly remunerated by receiving benefits in kind. Often, such loans were never re-paid to the company, thereby depriving the company's creditors of available assets on the insolvent winding up of the company. For years this abuse went unregulated allowing some unscrupulous company controllers to line their pockets with money and assets through loans, quasi-loans, credit transactions, guarantees and the provision of security being made in their favour. Only when such transactions went beyond the somewhat uncertain and ill-drawn line provided by the case law on directors' duties, would the beneficiaries of such loans be brought to task. Another prime example of such abuses was where directors caused companies to create long leases reserving below market or even nominal rent of company property in favour of themselves or their nominees. The enactment of CA 1990, s 31 drastically changed the laissez faire approach to such transactions, so much so that, following its commencement on 1 February 1991, the status quo was entirely reversed and many bona fide commercial transactions were stymied.

[11.052] Section 31 of CA 1990 beleaguered businessmen and practitioners alike. The general consensus amongst the users of company law was that the balance had swung too far and had rendered many legitimate commercial (and more mundane) transactions either possible only after costly restructuring or, sometimes, simply impossible. This contrasted sharply with the position in England and Wales. Although there is similar English legislation – s 330 of the Companies Act 1985 (UK) – this has never caused the same difficulties for English practitioners and businessmen. This is because s 330 of the English 1985 Act distinguishes between 'companies' and 'relevant companies'. All 'companies' – public and private – are prohibited from making loans *directly* to directors and entering into guarantees and providing security in connection with loans made to directors; it will be noted, though, that the prohibition there does not extend to persons connected with directors[115]. Only 'relevant companies' are prohibited from making quasi-loans to directors and persons connected with directors; entering into guarantees or providing

---

[113] [1996] 3 All ER 667 at 682e.

[114] See generally: Courtney & Johnston, *Structuring Company Lending after the Company Law Enforcement Act 2001*, (2001); Johnston, *Banking and Security Law in Ireland* (1998), pp 626–631; and Breslin, *Banking Law in the Republic of Ireland* (1999), pp 700–707. See also: Courtney, 'The Latest Hazard to Guarantees: The Effects of S.31, Companies Act 1990 on Inter Company Guarantees' (1991) Gazette ILSI 261 and Courtney, 'Credit Transactions and Section 31 of the Companies Act 1990' (1994) CLP 17.

[115] Companies Act 1985, s 330(2) (UK).

security in connection with quasi-loans for directors or persons connected with them, entering into credit transactions for directors or persons connected with them; or entering into guarantees or providing security in connection with credit transactions made for directors or persons connected with them[116]. In this context, 'relevant company' means a company that is a public company, a subsidiary of a public company, a company that has a sister-subsidiary of a public company and a company that has a subsidiary that is a public company[117]. It can be seen that, in England, private companies have been spared the worst excesses of this type of legislation.

[11.053] The first published government sponsored recognition that s 31 was in need of reform was in the *Report of the Working Group on Company Law Compliance and Enforcement*[118], more commonly known as the 'McDowell Report', which noted:

> '...the Company and Commercial Law Committee of the Law Society has for a number of years been proposing urgently needed change to Part III of the Companies Act, 1990, which deals with transactions involving directors and, in particular, to the effect of section 31 of the 1990 Act on credit institutions providing legitimate financial services to customers. The Law Society's concerns are shared by domestic credit institutions and have been the subject of considerable debate in legal and academic journals and circles.'[119]

Although it is undoubtedly ironic that the report which highlighted Ireland's dismal company law compliance (and enforcement) record also recognised legislative excesses. It was, however, only right and proper that in a zero-tolerance environment, only reasonable laws would be on the statute books. The result was the inclusion of CLEA 2001, Part 9 which remedied a number of the previous excesses and provided a more workable structure.

[11.054] The primary prohibition is contained in CA 1990, s 31(1), which provides:

> 'Except as provided by sections 32 to 37, a company shall not:
>
> (a) make a loan or quasi-loan to a director of the company or of its holding company or to a person connected with such a director;
>
> (b) enter into a credit transaction as creditor for such a director or a person so connected;
>
> (c) enter into a guarantee or provide any security in connection with a loan, quasi-loan or credit transaction made by any other person for such a director or a person so connected.'

It is impossible to even begin to understand the full import of these few lines of legislation without cross-referencing them to the various meanings and definitions afforded to particular terms used in CA 1990, Part III. Section 31 of CA 1990 may be summarised in the following manner:

— a *company* shall not;

— directly or *indirectly*;

---

[116] Companies Act 1985, s 330(3) and (4) (UK).

[117] Companies Act 1985, s 331(6) (UK).

[118] *Report of the Working Group on Company Law Compliance and Enforcement* (1998) (Pn. 6697).

[119] *Report of the Working Group on Company Law Compliance and Enforcement* (1998) (Pn. 6697), para 5.9 at p 64.

— make or enter into any of *five prohibited transactions and arrangements*;
— *to or for*;
— a *director or other relevant person*;
— unless any of *five exceptions* apply.

Each of the italicised words has a particular significance and meaning and each shall be considered in turn; in addition, the consequences – both civil and criminal – of contravening the s 31 prohibition are considered:

1. CA 1990, s 31 prevents companies from making or entering into transactions or arrangements.
2. Anti-avoidance by preventing indirect activity.
3. The five prohibited transactions and arrangements.
4. The meaning of 'for' a director or other relevant person.
5. The application of s 31 to directors and other relevant people.
6. The five exceptions to the s 31 prohibition.
7. Civil consequences of contravention: voidability.
8. Civil consequences of contravention: account and indemnity.
9. Civil consequences of contravention: personal liability.
10. The criminal consequences of contravention.

Section 31 of CA 1990 prevents companies from making or entering into transactions or arrangements

[11.055] Unlike CA 1990, s 29(1), which regulates arrangements whereby a company acquires or disposes of non-cash assets from or to a director or other relevant person, CA 1990, s 31 is not a two-way valve and is only concerned with prohibited transactions or arrangements made or entered into by a company. So, to take the most straightforward prohibited transaction – a loan – a company cannot[120] make a loan to a director or other relevant person but there is nothing to prevent a director or other relevant person making a loan to a company. Similarly, a director can enter into a credit transaction – another prohibited transaction – in favour of a company and whilst such may fall to be regulated by CA 1990, s 29(1), s 31 is irrelevant to that transaction.

[11.056] Another important aspect under this heading is that when CA 1990, s 31 prohibits a *company* from making or entering into certain transactions and arrangements to or for directors and other relevant people, it refers to an Irish 'company' as defined by CA 1963, s 2[121]. So, a company incorporated in England, which does business in Ireland, can make a loan to one of its directors without CA 1990, s 31 having any relevance. Of course, that transaction may well be regulated by the similar – but far from identical – s 330 of the Companies Act 1985 (UK)[122].

---

[120] Subject to the express statutory exceptions. See para **[11.068]** *ff*.

[121] Note too that by CA 1963, s 377(1), the CA 1963, Sch 9 (which specifies CA 1990, Part III), is applied to certain bodies corporate, other than those mentioned in CA 1963, s 377(2). See, generally, Chapter 2, *Formation, Registration and Conversion of Private Companies*, para **[2.057]**.

[122] See para **[11.052]**.

Anti-avoidance by preventing indirect activity

[11.057] Section 31(1) of CA 1990 prohibits companies from directly engaging in prohibited transactions and arrangements. Subsections (2) and (3) of s 31 operate to prohibit companies from *indirectly* taking part in such prohibited transactions and arrangements. Section 31(2) of CA 1990 provides:

> 'A company shall not arrange for the assignment to it or the assumption by it of any rights, obligations or liabilities under a transaction which, if it had been entered into by the company, would have contravened subsection (1); but for the purposes of this Part the transaction shall be treated as having been entered into on the date of the arrangement.

This operates, for example, to prohibit a company from taking an assignment of a loan made by another person to a director of that company because the company would itself be prohibited from making such a loan by reason of s 31(1). By treating the date of the transaction as the date of the assignment or assumption of rights, obligations or liabilities, it cannot be argued that a transaction effected before 1 February 1991 was not prohibited then, with a view to arguing that the assignment (or assumption) is not now prohibited. Moreover, CA 1990, s 25(7) provides that for the purposes of determining whether an arrangement is one to which CA 1990, s 31(2) applies, the transaction to which the arrangement relates shall, if it was entered into before the commencement of Part III, be deemed to have been entered into thereafter.

[11.058] A further measure of anti-avoidance is provided by CA 1990, s 31(3). This provides:

> 'A company shall not take part in any arrangement whereby—
>
> (a) another person enters into a transaction which, if it had been entered into by the company, would have contravened subsection (1) or (2); and
>
> (b) that other person, in pursuance of the arrangement, has obtained or is to obtain any benefit from the company or its holding company or a subsidiary of the company or its holding company.'

An example of the operation of this subsection might be where a third party makes a loan to the director of a company in circumstances where the third party obtains (or is to obtain) a benefit from the company. The '*benefit*' need not be an actual guarantee or an indemnity[123] (since these would be captured by CA 1990, s 31(1)(c)) and could conceivably include a concession, indulgence, waiver of a company's legal entitlement or something else which benefits the third party. It does not appear to be a precondition that the giving of the benefit must be contrary to the company's interests. It should also be noted that the benefit need not come directly from the company: it is sufficient for the purposes of s 31(3) that the benefit comes from its holding company, or subsidiary or subsidiary of its holding company (ie sister-subsidiary).

The five prohibited transactions and arrangements

[11.059] Section 31(1) of CA 1990 prohibits a company from doing any one of five things in favour of a director or other relevant person:

---

[123] See para **[11.064]**.

— making a loan or
— making a quasi-loan,
— entering into a credit transaction as creditor, or
— entering into a guarantee in connection with a loan, quasi-loan or credit transaction, or
— providing security in connection with a loan, quasi-loan or credit transaction.

(a) Loans

[11.060] Of all the prohibitions, the prohibition on making a loan is the most straightforward[124]. Although normally, when one speaks of 'loan', one assumes a cash-loan, a loan is not confined to cash. It is thought that any asset may be lent and that a loan of real or personal property, choses in action and, of course, cash will all be subject to the CA 1990, s 31(1)(a) prohibition. One of the few reported or unreported cases on the English equivalent of s 31 – s 330 of the Companies Act 1985 (UK) – is *Tait Consibee (Oxford) Ltd v Tait*[125]. In that case it was held that where a loan is made to a director in breach of s 330 of the English Act, the loan is illegal and is immediately recoverable by the company, irrespective of the terms and conditions on which it was made. This decision was followed in *Currencies Direct Ltd v Ellis*[126] where it was held that public policy did not prevent a company from recovering a loan that had been made to a director in breach of s 330 of the English Act.

(b) Quasi-loans

[11.061] A company cannot make a quasi-loan in favour of a director or other relevant person. Section 25(2)(a) of CA 1990 defines a quasi-loan as:

> 'a transaction under which one party ('the creditor') agrees to pay, or pays otherwise than in pursuance of an agreement, a sum for another ('the borrower') or agrees to reimburse, or reimburse otherwise than in pursuance of an agreement, expenditure incurred by another party for another ('the borrower') -
>
> (i) on terms that the borrower (or a person on his behalf) will reimburse the creditor; or
>
> (ii) in circumstances giving rise to a liability on the borrower to reimburse the creditor;

Section 25(2)(b) of CA 1990 states that any reference to the person to whom a quasi-loan is made is a reference to the borrower and s 25(2)(c) provides that the liabilities of a borrower under a quasi-loan include the liabilities of any person who has agreed to reimburse the creditor on behalf of the borrower. This definition tries to capture transactions which are loans in all but name, including where there is no formal agreement, whether written or oral, by which the company can be said to have agreed to repay the debts of any of the relevant people. An implicit understanding to discharge the

---

124 Whilst few might associate the boy-band 'Westlife' with CA 1990, s 31, it is interesting to note that it was alleged in the Sunday Independent of 1 April 2001 that a company controlled by members of 'Westlife' 'breached company law by dishing out too many directors' loans, according to latest accounts'.

125 *Tait Consibee (Oxford) Ltd v Tait* [1997] 2 BCLC 349.

126 *Currencies Direct Ltd v Ellis* [2001] TLR 654.

debts of a director or other relevant person would accordingly seem to constitute a quasi-loan.

(c) Credit transactions

[11.062] A credit transaction[127] is defined by CA 1990, s 25(3) as a transaction under which one party, defined as 'the creditor' (ie a company):

'(a) supplies any goods or sells any land under a hire-purchase agreement or conditional sale agreement;

(b) leases or licences the use of land or hires goods in return for periodical payments;

(c) otherwise disposes of land or supplies goods or services on the understanding that payment (whether in a lump-sum or instalments or by way of periodical payments or otherwise) is deferred.'

This is a very far-reaching definition. As regards *goods*, a company cannot:

— supply goods under a hire-purchase agreement or conditional sale agreement;

— hire goods in return for periodical payments; or

— otherwise supply goods or services on the understanding that payment (whether in a lump sum or instalments or by way of periodical payments or otherwise) is deferred

to a director or other relevant person.

As regards *real property* (eg land), a company cannot:

— sell any land under a conditional sale agreement;

— lease or licence the use of land in return for periodical payments; or

— otherwise dispose of land on the understanding that payment (whether in a lump-sum or instalments or by way of periodical payments or otherwise) is deferred

to a director or other relevant person.

One of the more common instances of credit transactions are leases of land, including a *bona fide* commercial or residential lease of land. Accordingly, a company may not grant a lease to any relevant person. The definitions in s 25(3)(a) and (b) are wide enough to include a conveyance where the full consideration is not paid to a company on the disposal of its interest, one indicator of which will be the absence or modification of the usual receipt clause in a purchase deed[128].

[11.063] Prior to the CLEA 2001 it had been thought to be strongly arguable that not all leases of land are credit transactions[129] and that long leases of say, 10,000 years which reserve a peppercorn rent do not properly fall to be termed as credit transactions. The reasoning was that where a long lease is granted in return for an initial capital payment it can not be said to be 'in return for periodical payments'. Any periodic payments made subsequent to the creation of such a lease are merely incidental to the real consideration passing. Such a view was further strengthened where the nominal rent reserved in the long

---

[127] See Courtney, 'Credit Transactions and Section 31 of the Companies Act' (1994) CLP 17.

[128] See Wylie, *Irish Conveyancing Law*, (2nd edn, 1996), para [18.43]–[18.44].

[129] Courtney, 'Credit Transactions and Section 31 of the Companies Act 1990' (1994) CLP 17 at 19.

lease is expressed to be 'if demanded'. This matter has been conclusively resolved by CLEA 2001, s 75, which amends CA 1990, s 25, by the insertion of a new sub-s (3A):

> 'For the purposes of this Part, a lease of land which reserves a nominal annual rent of not more than £10 is not a credit transaction where a company grants the lease in return for a premium or capital payment which represents the open market value of the land thereby disposed of by the company.

This reflects the conveyancing reality of long leases, since usually the sole reason for choosing to alienate property by way of a long lease, as opposed to a conveyance of the freehold, is to further the proper management of an apartment complex or retail development by facilitating the enforcement of positive covenants eg the payment of a service charge.

(d) Guarantees in connection with loans, quasi-loans or credit transactions [130]

[11.064] Section 31 of CA 1990 also prohibits a company from entering into a guarantee in connection with a loan, quasi-loan or credit transaction made by any other person for a director of the company or of its holding company or to a person connected with such a director. It should be noted that 'guarantee' includes 'indemnity' [131]. Guarantees in respect of loans and quasi-loans can be most readily recognised. Where a lending institution makes a loan to a director of a company, that company cannot guarantee that loan unless one of the exceptions, considered below[132], can be invoked. The prima facie prohibition on companies entering into guarantees in respect of credit transactions made by other persons for directors and other relevant people has proven to be particularly problematic. Again, unless one of the exceptions applies, a company cannot guarantee the performance of, say, a 35-year lease granted by a third party to a company controlled by a director.

(e) Providing security in connection with loans, quasi-loans or credit transactions

[11.065] The prohibition on companies giving security in connection with loans, quasi-loans and credit transactions made by third parties for directors or other relevant people operates in the same way as the prohibition on guarantees. In practice, third party security will frequently involve both a guarantee and security. The specific prohibition on the provision of security operates to capture cases where no guarantee is given as, for example, in the case of a surety mortgage over land, which can charge the surety's lands and property with the repayment of a borrower's debt in the absence of a guarantee.

The meaning of 'for' a director or other relevant person

[11.066] It is important to note the meaning assigned to the expression, 'a transaction or arrangement made for a person'. This is relevant in the interpretation of, for example, CA 1990, s 31(1)(b), which prohibits a company from entering into a credit transaction as creditor '*for*' a director or relevant person and the interpretation of s 31(1)(c), which prohibits the entering into of guarantees and the provision of security in connection with

130 See Courtney, 'The Latest Hazard to Guarantees: The Effects of S.31, Companies Act 1990 on Inter–Company Guarantees' (1991) Gazette ILSI 261.

131 CA 1990, s 25(1).

132 See para **[11.068]**.

loans, quasi-loans and credit transactions made by any third party '*for*' a director or relevant person[133]. Section 25(6) of CA 1990 provides:

> 'For the purposes of this Part, a transaction or arrangement is made for a person if –
>
> (a) in the case of a loan or quasi-loan, it is made to him;
>
> (b) in the case of credit transaction, he is the person to whom goods or services are supplied, or land is sold or otherwise disposed of, under the transaction;
>
> (c) in the case of a guarantee or security, it is entered into or provided in connection with a loan or quasi-loan made to him or a credit transaction made for him;
>
> (d) in the case of an arrangement to which section 31(2) or 31(3) applies[134], the transaction to which the arrangement relates was made for him; and
>
> (e) in the case of any other transaction or arrangement for the supply or transfer of goods, land or services (or any interest therein), he is the person to whom the goods, land or services (or the interest) are supplied or transferred.'

Because of the specific definitions afforded to the expression 'a transaction or arrangement made for a person' it is thought that in the case of a dispute, the section must be strictly construed.

The application of CA 1990, s 31 to directors and other relevant people

[11.067] Section 31(1) does not operate, generally, to prevent companies from making loans or quasi-loans or entering into credit transactions or guarantees or providing security in connection with loans, quasi-loans and credit transactions. The prohibition only applies in circumstances where such transactions or arrangements are made to or for *directors of the company and other relevant people*. In summary, those persons for whom a company is prohibited by s 31(1) from making or entering into a prohibited transaction or arrangement are:

Persons who are directors and other 'relevant people'	
- directors of a company, - shadow directors of a company, - directors of a holding company, - shadow directors of a holding company, - the spouse, parent, brother, sister, child of a director of a company or of its holding company, - the partner of a director of a company or of its holding company, - trustees where the principal beneficiaries of the trust are a director (whether of the company or of its holding company), his spouse, any of his children or any body corporate he controls,	- a body corporate controlled by a director of a company or of its holding company, - a body corporate controlled by a body corporate that is itself controlled by a director of a company or of its holding company, - there is a presumption that the sole member of a single-member private limited company is a person connected with a director.

[133] It is also relevant in the context of the definition of 'quasi–loan' (CA 1990, s 25(2)(a)) and in the context of civil remedies for breach of s 31 (CA 1990, s 38(2)) and the imposition of personal liability in certain cases (CA 1990, s 39(1)).

[134] See paras **[11.057]–[11.058]**.

The reader's attention is referred to the beginning of this chapter where the subjects of the statutory regulation provided for in CA 1990, Part III are considered in detail[135].

The five exceptions to the CA 1990, s 31 prohibition

[11.068] It now falls to consider the exceptions to the prohibition on a company entering certain transactions or arrangements in favour of directors or other relevant people under the following headings.

(a) Applicability of exceptions to prohibited transactions and arrangements.

(b) Section 32 of CA 1990: the *de minimis* exception.

(c) Section 34 of CA 1990: the validation procedure for guarantees and security.

(d) Section 35 of CA 1990: the group exception.

(e) Section 36 of CA 1990: directors' expenses.

(f) Section 37 of CA 1990: business transactions.

(g) The repealed exception.

It should be noted that, unless otherwise stated, all references to 's 34 of the 1990 Act' are to the 'new' CA 1990, s 34, as substituted by CLEA 2001, s 78 unless otherwise stated.

(a) Applicability of exceptions to prohibited transactions and arrangements

[11.069] There are in total five exceptions to the CA 1990, s 31 prohibition. However, whilst there are five aspects to the section 31 prohibition (loans, quasi-loans, credit transactions, guarantees and the provision of security), and there are five exceptions, not all five exceptions apply to all five aspects of the section 31 prohibition.

Prohibited Transactions or Arrangements	*Exceptions*
Loans, quasi-loans and credit transactions	Ss 32, 35, 36 and 37
Guarantees and the provision of security in connection with loans, quasi-loans and credit transactions	Ss 34, 35 and 36

In addition, not all five exceptions are available to all 'relevant people'.

'Relevant people'	*Exceptions*
Directors (de facto, de jure and shadow) of companies	Ss 32, 34, 36 and 37
Directors (de facto, de jure and shadow) of companies' holding companies	Ss 34, and 37
Natural persons that are connected persons	Ss 32, 34 and 37
Bodies corporate that are connected persons	Ss 32, 34, 35, 37

(b) Section 32 of CA 1990: the de minimis exception

[11.070] One of the most availed of exceptions in the context of loans to directors is CA 1990, s 32. This provides a de minimis exception, whereby if the value of an arrangement[136] is below a certain amount, it falls through the net on the grounds that it is of

[135] See para **[11.004]** *ff*.

[136] Note, the de minimis exception is confined to 'arrangements' as defined. See para **[11.074]**.

insufficient value to justify the invocation of the s 31 prohibition. Section 32(1) of CA 1990 provides that:

> '*Section 31* shall not prohibit a company from entering into an *arrangement* with a director or a person so connected with a director if—
>
> (a) the value of the arrangement, and
>
> (b) the total amount outstanding under any other arrangements entered into by the company with any director of the company, or any person connected with a director,
>
> together, is less than ten per cent of the company's *relevant assets*.' [Emphasis added]

Two figures are fundamental to determining whether or not the *de minimis* exception applies:

— the value of the arrangement, and

— the amount of the company's relevant assets.

[11.071] Looking first at the *value of the arrangement*, CA 1990, s 25(4) provides some assistance in determining what value means in either of the three possible arrangements that can be exempted by s 32. In the case of a loan, its value is the principal of the loan; in a quasi-loan it is the 'amount or maximum amount which the person to whom the quasi-loan is made is liable to reimburse the creditor'.[137] In the case of a credit transaction[138] its value is:

> '...the price which it is reasonable to expect could be obtained for the goods, land or services to which the transaction or arrangement relates if they had been supplied at the time the transaction or arrangement is entered into in the ordinary course of business and on the same terms (apart from price) as they have been supplied or are to be supplied under the transaction or arrangement in question;'

Where the value of a transaction or arrangement is not capable of being expressed as a specific sum of money, it shall be deemed to exceed €63,486.90.

[11.072] Turning next to the company's *relevant assets*, as referred to in s 32(1)[139], this expression has the meaning assigned to it in CA 1990, s 29(2). Section 29(2)(a) and (b) defines 'relevant assets' as:

> '(a) except in a case falling within *paragraph (b)*, the value of its net assets determined by reference to the accounts prepared and laid in accordance with the requirements of s 148 of the Principal Act in respect of the last preceding financial year in respect of which such accounts were so laid;
>
> (b) where no accounts have been prepared and laid under that section before that time, the amount of its called-up share capital.'

In the case of many private companies, reliance upon *paragraph (b)* will not provide it with much scope for reliance upon s 32. In the typical '€2 private company', it will mean

137 CA 1990, s 25(4)(a) and (b).

138 CA 1990, s 25(4)(c) is unhappily worded. Rather than specifically saying 'credit transaction', it refers to a transaction or arrangement 'other than a loan or quasi–loan or a transaction or arrangement within paragraph (d) or (e)'. Of course, the effect of this is that it applies to more than just credit transactions ie any 'arrangement' for the purposes of CA 1990, s 29(1).

139 By virtue of CA 1990, s 32(2)(b).

that the amount permitted to be, for example, loaned to a director, will be 20 cent. Notwithstanding that companies are obliged to prepare accounts, there can be some delay in the preparation of accounts in many companies[140]. Accordingly, if the de minimis exception is to be meaningful, the 10% will be of the company's net assets as determined by the profit and loss account/income and expenditure account spoken of in CA 1963, s 148.

[11.073] It may happen that a company's relevant assets are reduced either in the normal course of its business, or because they were deliberately inflated so as to bring an arrangement within the de minimis exception. Where this happens after an arrangement which is in breach of s 31 has been entered into and the company has relied upon s 32, the provisions of CA 1990, s 33 apply. Thus, CA 1990, s 33(2) provides:

> 'Where the directors of a company become aware, or ought reasonably to become aware, that there exists a situation referred to in subsection (1), it shall be the duty of the company, its directors and any persons for whom the arrangements referred to in that subsection were made, to amend, within two months, the terms of the arrangements concerned so that the total amount outstanding under the arrangements again falls within the percentage limit referred to in that subsection.'

Consequently, where the relevant assets are reduced and the amount of the transaction or arrangement is then no longer less than 10% of the company's relevant assets, the situation must be regularised within *two months*. Whilst the CA 1990 was silent on the consequences of relevant assets falling, CLEA 2001, s 77 has introduced a new CA 1990, s 33(3) which provides:

> 'Where the terms of the arrangements referred to in subsection (2) are not amended within the period specified in that subsection, the arrangements shall be voidable at the instance of the company unless section 38(1)(a) or (b) applies.'

[11.074] Finally, turning to the application of the section 32 exception, it is by its very terms confined to 'arrangements'. For the purposes of CA 1990, s 32(1), s 32(2)(a) provides 'a company enters an arrangement with a person if it makes a loan or quasi loan to, or enters into a credit transaction as creditor for, that person...'.
Accordingly, the 10% exception has no application to guarantees or the provision of security and only applies to loans, quasi-loans and credit transactions. It should also be noted that s 32(1) prohibits a company from entering into an arrangement 'with a director or a person connected with a director'. It would seem, therefore, on a strict interpretation that the de minimis exception cannot be availed of where a company proposes to enter into an arrangement with a director (de facto, de jure or shadow) of that company's holding company or a person connected with such a director.

(c) Section 34 of CA 1990: the validation procedure for guarantees and security

[11.075] In principle, there can be no public policy objection to a company making or entering into any transaction or arrangement in favour of anybody where its creditors' interests are safeguarded and the majority of its members consent. The 'new' CA 1990, s 34[141] exempts companies from the prohibition on entering into guarantees and providing

---

[140] See generally Chapter 13, *Accounts and Auditors.*

[141] As substituted by CLEA 2001, s 78. For the 'old' CA 1990, s 34, see para **[11.094]**.

security in favour of any relevant person, where the interests of the two fundamental constituencies – creditors and shareholders – are protected. Based on the procedure whereby certain companies can provide financial assistance in connection with the purchase of their own shares (CA 1963, s 60) the 'new' s 34 introduces a *validation procedure* which, if followed, will allow companies to enter into *guarantees* and provide *security* in connection with loans, quasi-loans and credit transactions made to relevant people. The validation procedure cannot be utilised to validate loans, quasi-loans or credit transactions, the relaxation in the CLEA 2001 being confined to transactions that involve only a *contingent* liability for companies.

[11.076] The operative part of this exception is contained in CA 1990, s 34(1) which provides:

> 'Section 31 does not prohibit a company from entering into a guarantee or providing a security in connection with a loan, quasi-loan or credit transaction made by any other person to a director of the company or of its holding company or to or for a person connected with such a director, if—
>
> (a) the entering into the guarantee is, or the provision of the security is given, under the authority of a special resolution of the company passed not more than 12 months previously; and
>
> (b) the company has forwarded with each notice of the meeting as which the special resolution is to be considered or, if the procedure detailed in subsection (6) is followed, the company has appended to the resolution, a copy of a statutory declaration which complies with subsections (2) and (3) and also delivers, within 21 days after the date on which the guarantee was entered into or the date on which the security was provided, as the case may be, a copy of the declaration to the registrar of companies for registration.'

It will be noticed that the validation procedure is very similar to that contained in CA 1963, s 60[142]. The various issues that arise in the context of the section 34 validation procedure are considered under the following headings:

(i) The special resolution.

(ii) The statutory declaration of solvency.

(iii) The independent person's report.

(iv) The consequences of swearing a declaration based on unreasonable grounds.

(i) The special resolution and shareholder protection

[11.077] The protection of shareholders – an essential feature of this exception – is provided by the requirement that the members must pass a special resolution approving of the giving of a guarantee and or security. Accordingly, there must be at least 75% shareholder support before a company can enter such a transaction in favour of a relevant person[143]. It will be noted that unlike the section 29 validation procedure, CA 1990, s 34 requires a qualified majority to approve of the transaction.

---

142 See, generally, Chapter 18, *The Maintenance of Capital*, para **[18.041]** *ff.*

143 On special resolutions generally, see Chapter 9, *Corporate Governance: Meetings*, para **[9.070]**.

[11.078] The special resolution must be passed not more than 12 months before the transaction is entered into. This is to provide a measure of protection against a change in circumstances. Section 34(6) of CA 1990 provides a very useful administrative shortcut which, it is thought, will be availed of by many private companies, especially those where there are very few members. This subsection provides that the special resolution referred to in s 34(1)(a) 'may be passed in accordance with s 141(8) of the Principal Act' ie the written resolution procedure which has been considered in Chapter 9, *Corporate Governance: Meetings*[144]. The advantage of this is that where a company is so permitted by its articles of association, the special resolution may be passed by a written resolution, thereby avoiding the artificialities inherent in convening on statutory notice and thereafter holding a meeting of perhaps as few as one or two persons, who might also be the company's only directors.

[11.079] As in the case of the procedure under CA 1963, s 60, there is also additional shareholder protection, over and above the fact that a qualified majority must resolve in favour of a company entering into a guarantee or providing security in favour of a director or other connected person. First, unless the transaction is unanimously approved of by the members (ie all of the members entitled to vote at general meetings of the company in favour of the special resolution), the company may not enter into the guarantee or provide the security before the expiry of 30 days after the passing of the resolution or, if an application is made to court, until the application has been disposed of by the court[145]. Secondly, members (who have *not* consented to, signed or voted in favour of the special resolution)[146] may make application to court for relief and where such application is made the special resolution shall not have effect except to the extent to which it is confirmed by the court[147]. The 'counter-counterbalance' to these safeguards is that the application by dissenting members must be brought within 28 days after the date on which the special resolution was passed[148] and an application must be made by the holders of not less in the aggregate than 10% in nominal value of the company's issued share capital or any class thereof[149]. Of course, where the written resolution procedure is adopted, none of the foregoing safeguards are relevant since CA 1963, s 141(8) requires unanimity.

(ii) The statutory declaration of solvency

[11.080] Creditor protection is provided by the requirement that the directors of a company proposing to enter into a guarantee or provide security in connection with a loan, quasi-loan or credit transaction in favour of a relevant person, must make a statutory declaration of solvency. The timing of the statutory declaration is regulated by CA 1990, s 34(2), which provides:

---

144 At para **[9.076]** *ff.*

145 CA 1990, s 34(7).

146 Members who have consented to, signed or voted for the special resolution are debarred from bringing application to court for relief: CA 1990, s 34(10).

147 CA 1990, s 34(8).

148 CA 1990, s 34(11) which goes on to state that the application may be made on behalf of the persons entitled to make the application by such one or more of their number as they may appoint in writing for the purpose.

149 CA 1990, s 34(9).

'The statutory declaration shall be made at a meeting of the directors held not earlier than 24 days before the meeting referred to in subsection (1)(b) or, if the special resolution is passed in accordance with subsection (6), not earlier than 24 days before the signing of the special resolution, and shall be made by the directors or, in the case of a company having more than 2 directors, by a majority of the directors.'

The content of the statutory declaration is also regulated by statute. Section 34(3) of CA 1990 provides that the statutory declaration must state:

'(a) the circumstances in which the guarantee is to be entered into or the security is to be provided;

(b) the nature of the guarantee or security;

(c) the person or persons to or for whom the loan, quasi-loan or credit transaction (in connection with which the guarantee is to be entered into or the security is to be provided) is to be made;

(d) the purpose for which the company is entering into the guarantee or is providing the security;

(e) the benefit which will accrue to the company directly or indirectly from entering into the guarantee or providing the security; and

(f) that the declarants have made a full inquiry into the affairs of the company and that, having done so, they have formed the opinion that the company, having entered into the guarantee or provided the security, will be able to pay its debts in full as they become due.'

The requirements at (a) and (b) are self-explanatory. Requirement (c) involves the disclosure of the beneficiary of the guarantee and or security. Requirement (d) involves stating the purpose for which the company is entering into the guarantee or providing the security.

[11.081] Requirement (e) in CA 1990, s 34(3) is very important. It requires the declaring directors to state the benefit that will accrue to the company (directly or indirectly) from entering into the guarantee or providing the security. Apart altogether from being a necessary disclosure, the effect of this requirement is to remind the declaring directors that a company should not enter into transactions where it does not itself derive benefit. For a company to give a gratuitous guarantee or security is likely to be both ultra vires[150] and in breach of the directors' duties[151]. It is thought to be insufficient to state that 'no benefit' will accrue to the company: it is implicit that some benefit must accrue since otherwise the legislature would have said 'the benefit (if any)' or, even, 'whether any benefit will accrue'. It is also thought to be unlikely that it could be claimed that any benefit would flow to the company where a guarantee is in respect of a loan made to a director or other relevant person, to enable him or it to set up a competing business or to further his exclusively personal interests. An example of benefit flowing to a company from its guaranteeing a loan from a bank to one of its directors, might be where the purpose of the loan is to on-lend the money to the company in support of its trading activities. In

[150] See Chapter 7, *Corporate Contracts, Capacity and Authority*, para **[7.068]** *ff*.

[151] See Chapter 10, *Duties of Directors and Other Officers*, para **[10.026]**.

Charterbridge Corp Ltd v Lloyds Bank Ltd[152] Pennycuick J said of the meaning of benefit that:

> 'The proper test ...must be whether an intelligent and honest man in the position of a director of the company concerned, could, in the whole of the existing circumstances, have reasonably believed that the transaction was for the benefit of the company.'

Where the directors believe that the entering into of a guarantee or the provision of security is for their company's benefit, it would be prudent to ensure a minute to that effect is recorded. The requirement for there to be 'benefit' to the company strikes a good balance between the interests of directors, their companies and companies' creditors.

[11.082] The final requirement, (f) in CA 1990, 34(3), provides the essential creditor-protection. This requires the directors to aver that they have made a full inquiry into the company's affairs and that, having done so, have formed the opinion that the company will be able to pay its debts in full as they become due. In other words, the company must be solvent following the entering into of the guarantee and or the provision of the security.

(iii) The independent person's report

[11.083] The possible temptation for directors to be overly optimistic about their company's solvency is addressed by CA 1990, s 34(4), which requires the directors' statutory declaration to be accompanied by a report drawn up in the prescribed form[153] by an independent person. To be an independent person, one must be qualified at the time of the report to be appointed or to continue to be the company's auditor[154]. The importance of the independent person's report is that is must state whether, in the opinion of the independent person, the statutory declaration is reasonable[155]. It may be noted that there is no such requirement in respect of a statutory declaration sworn by directors pursuant to the validation procedure under CA 1963, s 60. There are some concerns amongst auditors and the accounting profession that the independent person's report, as required by s 34 and as prescribed by statutory instrument, is too wide and might expose auditors to civil liability. Of particular concern is the open-ended nature of the directors' declaration[156]. Although the prescribed form cannot be added to or detracted from it is opined that auditors, anxious lest they incur civil liability, could legitimately attach a disclaimer to the prescribed form which will alert all readers as to the basis upon which they make the independent report.

(iv). The consequences of swearing a declaration based on unreasonable grounds

[11.084] It is with respect to the consequences of swearing a declaration based on unreasonable grounds that the section 34 validation procedure again departs significantly from the section 60 validation procedure. Where the directors of a company purposing to provide financial assistance in connection with the purchase of the company's own shares swear a declaration on unreasonable grounds and the company is wound up insolvent, the

[152] *Charterbridge Corp Ltd v Lloyds Bank Ltd* [1969] 2 All ER 1185 at 1194.

[153] As prescribed by the Companies Act 1990 (Section 34) Regulations 2001 (SI 439/2001).

[154] CA 1990, s 34(4)(a). On the qualifications to be a company's auditor, see Chapter 13, *Accounts and Auditors,* para **[13.190]**.

[155] CA 1990, s 34(4)(b).

[156] Strangely, this does not seem to have been an issue in relation to CA 1963, s 60(2) declarations by directors where companies assisted the purchase of their own shares, which is also 'open-ended'.

directors are liable to prosecution. In the case of the section 34 validation procedure the consequences of swearing a declaration that is based on unreasonable grounds are likely to be more of a deterrent than risk of prosecution as the directors run the risk of being made personally liable 'without limitation of liability, for all or any of the debts or other liabilities of the company': CA 1990, s 34(5)(a). So, where the directors make a statutory declaration 'without having reasonable grounds for the opinion that the company having entered into the guarantee or provided the security will be able to pay its debts in full as they become due' the court is empowered to make the directors personally liable on such application being made by a liquidator, creditor, member or contributory of the company. Moreover, where a company is wound up within 12 months after the making of the declaration and its debts are not paid or provided for in full within 12 months after the commencement of the winding up, there is a statutory presumption 'until the contrary is shown, that the director did not have reasonable grounds for this opinion'.[157]

(d) Section 35 of CA 1990: the group exception

[11.085] The original section 35 exception only applied to transactions and arrangements made or entered into by a subsidiary in favour of its holding company[158]. It provided a complete exemption for such transactions and arrangements but was greatly limited by the fact that it did not exempt transactions or arrangements made or entered into by holding companies in favour of subsidiaries or by subsidiaries in favour of sister-subsidiaries. The 'new' CA 1990, s 35[159] does not suffer from such disabilities. It provides:

> '*Section 31* shall not prohibit a company from—
>
> (a) making a loan or quasi loan to any company which is its holding company, subsidiary or a subsidiary of its holding company or entering into a guarantee or providing any security in connection with a loan or quasi-loan made by any person to any company which is its holding company, subsidiary or a subsidiary of its holding company;
>
> (b) entering into a credit transaction as creditor for any company which is its holding company, subsidiary or a subsidiary of its holding company or entering into a guarantee or providing any security in connection with any credit transaction made by any other person for any company which is its holding company, subsidiary or a subsidiary of its holding company.'

Accordingly, it is now the case that any member of a group of companies can, in favour of another member of that group, make or enter into any of the five transactions or arrangements that are otherwise prohibited by CA 1990, s 31.

---

157 CA 1990, s 34(5)(b).

158 CA 1990, s 35, as originally enacted, provided that: 'Section 31 shall not prohibit a company from – (a) making a loan or quasi loan to its holding company or entering into a guarantee or providing any security in connection with a loan or quasi-loan made by any person to its holding company; (b) entering into a credit transaction as creditor for its holding company or entering into a guarantee or providing any security in connection with any credit transaction made by any other person for its holding company.'

159 As amended by CLEA 2001, s 79. Section 79 of CLEA 2001 provides: 'Section 35 of the Act of 1990 is amended by the substitution for "its holding company" (wherever occurring) of "any company which is its holding company, subsidiary or a subsidiary of its holding company".'

[11.086] It is fundamental to the invocation of s 35 that both companies (or bodies corporate) are part of a group within the meaning of CA 1963, s 155 which alone defines what constitutes a 'holding company' and a 'subsidiary company' for the purpose of CA 1990, s 35. The definitions of 'holding company' and 'subsidiary company' are considered in detail in Chapter 17, *Groups of Companies*[160].

[11.087] To the first-time reader of CA 1990, Part III it is, on its face, an apparent contradiction to conceive of a subsidiary company being a 'person connected with a director' of a holding company. The assumption is that if a company is another's subsidiary it must be exclusively controlled by that other company and cannot be controlled by someone else for the purposes of CA 1990, s 26. The apparent contradiction dissipates, however, when one realises that on the proper construction of CA 1990, Part III and of CA 1963, s 155, it becomes clear that a given company can be a 'person connected with' a director and, contemporaneously, a subsidiary of another company. The two tests for control are not mutually exclusive. This said, one must not automatically assume that every subsidiary company (or holding company) will be a person connected with a director of its holding company (or subsidiary company) so that s 35 must be invoked to exempt an otherwise unlawful transaction or arrangement. This will not necessarily be the case. These issues have been considered above[161] at the beginning of this chapter.

[11.088] On the application of CA 1990, s 35, it is readily obvious that it can only have application where a company proposes to make or enter into an otherwise prohibited transaction or arrangement in favour of a *body corporate* and that s 35 has no application to relevant people who are natural persons. It should also be noted that it applies to all five transactions or arrangements that are prohibited by s 31.

(e) Section 36: directors' expenses

[11.089] Section 36 of CA 1990 provides:

> '(1) *Section 31* shall not prohibit a company from doing anything to provide any of its directors with funds to meet vouched expenditure properly incurred or to be incurred by him for the purposes of the company or the purpose of enabling him properly to perform his duties as an officer of the company or doing anything to enable any of its directors to avoid incurring such expenditure.
>
> (2) Where a company enters into a transaction pursuant to *subsection (1)*, any liability falling on any person arising from any such transaction shall be discharged by him within six months from the date on which it was incurred.
>
> (3) A person who contravenes *subsection (2)* shall be guilty of an offence.'

At first, it would appear that the section 36 exception saves transactions which form part of everyday commercial, and especially, banking life such as where a company guarantees a director's credit card, or his petrol account, or loans him money to pay his hotel/restaurant expenses. However, on a closer reading of sub-s (2) it is seen that such 'loans' must be repaid to the company within six months from the date on which any liability was incurred. Failure to comply with this provision results in the director concerned being

[160] In particular, see paras **[17.006]** *ff*.

[161] See para **[11.011]**.

guilty of an offence, and liable to be visited with the penalties set out in CA 1990, s 40, considered below[162].

[11.090] Section 36 of CA 1990 has application to all five transactions or arrangements prohibited by CA 1990, s 31. It should be noted, however, that as regards those relevant people who may rely upon this exception, only the directors (de facto and de jure) and shadow directors of the company concerned, in whose favour a transaction or arrangement is made, come within s 36.

(f) Section 37: business transactions

[11.091] Section 37 of CA 1990 provides:

> '*Section 31* shall not prohibit a company from making any loan or quasi-loan or entering into any credit transaction as creditor for any person if –
>
> (a) the company enters into the transaction concerned in the ordinary course of its business; and
>
> (b) the value of the transaction is not greater, and the terms on which it is entered into are no more favourable, in respect of the person for whom the transaction is made, than that or those which-
>
> (i) the company ordinarily offers, or
>
> (ii) it is reasonable to expect the company to have offered,
>
> to or in respect of a person of the same financial standing as that person but unconnected with the company.'

The reference to a company entering a transaction in the *ordinary course of its business*[163] implies a certain 'usualness' for that company to enter into such a transaction. For a company to make a loan or quasi-loan in the ordinary course of its business, may imply that the company is a credit institution, or if a loan to a director acting as a consumer, to be governed by the Consumer Credit Act 1995. A company would also require to have as one of its principle objects, the object of lending money, or entering another transaction or arrangement contemplated by CA 1990, s 31.

[11.092] It is also a requirement that such a transaction be made or entered into on terms which are no more favourable and for a value no greater than those which the company would both reasonably, and ordinarily, offer to others. Here, an objective test is applied by the use of the word 'reasonable', and so a transaction which has already been made in favour of an unconnected person may not be used as a touchstone, unless the transaction concerned is also objectively 'reasonable' for the company to have entered into.

[11.093] It is very important to recognise that CA 1990, s 37 applies to only three (loans, quasi-loans and credit transactions) of the five prohibited transactions or arrangements in the section 31 prohibition. Guarantees and the provision of security are excluded. It would

162 See para **[11.111]**.

163 A transaction will not be in the ordinary course of a company's business where the company has agreed to cease trading: *Re Ashmark Ltd (No 2)* [1990] ILRM 455. 'Insolvency' may also be relevant in deciding whether something is in the ordinary course of a company's business: *Williams v Quebrada Railway Land and Copper Co Ltd* [1895] 2 Ch 751, cited in *Murphy v Kirwan* (9 April 1992, unreported), High Court per Costello J.

seem, however, that s 37 can be invoked in transactions between a company and any relevant person, since it refers to a situation where a company is making a loan, quasi-loan or entering into a credit transaction, for 'any person'.

(g) The repealed exception

[11.094] The 'old' CA 1990, s 34, which was repealed by CLEA 2001, s 78 provided:

> 'Where a company is a member of a group of companies, consisting of a holding company and its subsidiaries, s *31* shall not prohibit that company from—
>
> (a) making a loan or quasi loan to another member of that group; or
>
> (b) entering into a guarantee or providing any security in connection with a loan or quasi loan made by any person to another member of the group;
>
> by reason only that a director of one member of the group is connected with another.'

In order to appreciate the intricacies of this exception, a number of concepts referred to therein require further consideration. This section was flawed in a two fundamental respects. First, whilst it could be invoked in respect of loans and quasi-loans and guarantees and the provision of security in connection with such transactions, it could not be invoked in respect of credit transactions and guarantees and security in connection with credit transactions. Secondly, the final proviso – 'by reason only that a director of one member of the group is connected with another' – was nonsensical. This was because Part III did not elsewhere envisage or contain any definition of a situation where a *director* was connected *with a company* ie with another member of the group; CA 1990, s 26 only defines a situation where a person is deemed to be connected *with a director*.

[11.095] Because companies may have relied upon the repealed CA 1990, s 34 between 1 February 1991 and 30 September 2001, it is necessary to retain reference to it here. Again, it is important to note that the repealed s 34 only applied where a company was part of a group of companies. This required one to have regard to CA 1963, s 155 and because 'group of companies' is not specifically defined, one must look to the meaning of 'holding' and 'subsidiary' companies. This is considered at length in Chapter 17, *Groups of Companies*[164].

Civil consequences of contravention: voidability

[11.096] There are three civil consequences for contravening CA 1990, s 31. The first is that, subject to certain 'savers', any contravening transaction or arrangement is voidable at the instance of the company. The second is that the directors (and other relevant people) are liable to indemnify the company for any loss it suffers and to account for any gain they make. The third consequence is that, in certain circumstances, certain people can be made personally liable if the company is subsequently wound up insolvent.

[11.097] The first civil consequence of the contravention of the prohibition contained in s 31 are drastic, in that CA 1990, s 38(1) provides that subject to certain exceptions 'where a company enters into a transaction or arrangement in contravention of s 31 the transaction or arrangement *shall be voidable at the instance of the company...*'.

However, the relevant transaction will not be voidable where one of the following savers can be relied upon:

164 See para **[17.006]** *ff*.

— restitution of any money or any other asset which is the subject matter of the arrangement or transaction is no longer possible: CA 1990, s 38(1)(a); *or*

— the company has been indemnified in pursuance of sub-s (2)(b) for the loss or damage suffered by it: s 38(1)(a); *or*

— any rights acquired *bona fide* for value and without actual notice of the contravention by any person other than the person for whom the transaction or arrangement was made would be affected by its avoidance: CA 1990, s 38(1)(b).

These 'savers' from voidability must be distinguished from exceptions. Although a voidable transaction may be capable of being saved, it remains the case that there has been a contravention of CA 1990, s 31, which will have criminal consequences[165]. Where a transaction or arrangement can be brought within an exception, then there will have been no contravention of s 31.

(a) Restitution in integrum is impossible

[11.098] A prohibited transaction shall not be rendered voidable at the instance of the company entering it where restitution of the money or other asset which is the subject matter of that transaction is no longer possible: CA 1990, s 38(1)(a). It would seem that this saver is somewhat anomalous in respect of both guarantees and the provision of security. It is certainly arguable that where a third party has, in good faith, made a loan to a director and that loan has been guaranteed by his company in breach of CA 1990, s 31, restitution is impossible unless the director can repay the loan to the third party.

(b) The indemnity

[11.099] Section 38(1)(a) of CA 1990 provides that a transaction or arrangement will not be voidable where the company concerned 'has been indemnified' in pursuance of CA 1990, s 38(2)(b). What exactly is meant by an indemnity poses some difficulty, and can only be resolved in the light of judicial interpretation. The indemnity which is required to be given is to be in accordance with s 38(2)(b), which provides that where an arrangement or transaction is made in contravention of s 31 for a relevant person, such relevant people together with any other director of the company who authorised the transaction or arrangement, shall (whether or not the transaction or arrangement has been avoided under s 38(1)) be '(jointly and severally with any other person liable under this subsection) to indemnify the company for any loss or damage resulting from the arrangement or transaction.'

Such persons are also liable to account to the company for any gain made, directly or indirectly, by the transaction or arrangement: CA 1990, s 38(2)(a). The excusing circumstances set out in s 38(3)[166] ought to be borne in mind, although they will not

[165] See para **[11.111]**.

[166] CA 1990, s 38(3) provides: 'Where an arrangement or transaction is entered into by a company and a person connected with a director of the company or its holding company in contravention of section 31 that director shall not be liable under subsection (2) if he shows that he took all reasonable steps to secure the company's compliance with that section and, in any case, a person so connected and any other such director as is mentioned in the said subsection (2) shall not be so liable if he shows that, at the time the arrangement or transaction was entered into, he did not know the relevant circumstances constitution the contravention.' See para **[11.049]**, where the similar defence in s 29(5) to a claim for an account or indemnity arising from a breach of s 29(1) is considered.

directly affect the question of whether or not a transaction or arrangement can be avoided or saved under s 38.

This particular exception is not without difficulty. In the first place, one must ask what exactly does 'has been indemnified' mean? 'Indemnified' can *either* mean to merely give a certificate or 'paper indemnity' that the company which enters the transaction or arrangement will not suffer any loss *or* it can mean that the company has *actually* been compensated or reimbursed for any loss or damage suffered. If the latter is the case, it seems to suggest that the company which enters into a prohibited transaction or arrangement, must have actually been compensated for the loss suffered[167].

(c) Bona fide and without actual notice

[11.100] Where the avoidance of the prohibited transaction or arrangement would affect any rights acquired bona fide for value and without actual notice of the contravention of s 31, being rights of persons other than the person for whom the transaction or arrangement was made, CA 1990, s 38(1)(b) provides that the transaction or arrangement *cannot be avoided*. This saver was recently invoked to prevent a transaction being voided in the case of *Ruby Property Company Ltd et al v Kilty and Superquinn*[168]. The facts in this case were that the second and third plaintiffs (both deceased at the hearing of the case) were a husband and wife who had owned the entire of the issued share capital in the first plaintiff ('Ruby') and were its only directors. Ruby's sole asset was a property, situate in Sutton, Co Dublin. The directors were indebted to a bank and by a collateral mortgage debenture, dated 3 August 1990, Ruby had charged the Sutton property with repayment of all monies owed by the directors to the bank. After the directors defaulted in their obligations to the bank, the bank demanded repayment and when this was not received, appointed a receiver (the first defendant) to Ruby. After realising other security, which the directors had owned personally, the bank sought to recover the shortfall of £15,554.08 from Ruby and consequent upon this, the receiver sold the Sutton property to Superquinn. In the instant proceedings, Ruby sought, inter alia, declarations that the collateral mortgage had lapsed and had no validity or effect and that the appointment of the receiver was invalid and an order that the conveyance of the Sutton property to Superquinn was of no effect. On the s 31 point, Ruby argued that although it had given the security before the date upon which s 31 became operative, the terms of the loan had been revised post-1 February 1991 and that this had created a new debt and that this 'in reality amounted to the giving of a new security'. It therefore contended that the collateral debenture contravened CA 1990, s 31(1)(c), being security given in connection with a loan to a director. McCracken J said that he thought it unlikely that the plaintiffs could succeed on that argument but acknowledged the possibility that more detailed evidence could lead to a finding that a new security had been given. McCracken J went on to point out that any such issue would be between Ruby and the Bank, not between the plaintiffs and the defendants and that unless and until the transaction had been avoided, the debenture and the appointment of the receiver remained valid. McCracken J went on to say, however, that he was quite satisfied that even if the debenture had been in breach of CA 1990, s 31(1)(c),

167 See para **[11.105]**.

168 *Ruby Property Company Ltd et al v Kilty and Superquinn* (1 December 1999, unreported), High Court (McCracken J) [First Law 2092].

the plaintiffs would have no remedy against either of the defendants by reason of CA 1990, s 38(1)(b). On this point, he said:

> '...I have no doubt whatever that the Second Defendant [Superquinn] acquired the property *bona fide* and for value without actual notice of any contravention of s 31, if there has been such a contravention. Therefore, any challenge to the sale on the basis of a possible contravention of s 31 must fail.'[169]

Accordingly, if a company seeks to set aside a transaction or arrangement for contravention of s 31 it should be aware that any subsequent purchaser is liable to seek to rely upon s 38(1)(b) and claim to be 'Equity's darling'. Not everyone can, however, rely on this saver and four observations are apposite as discussed below.

(i) Beneficiaries of the transaction or arrangement may not seek to rely upon s 38(1)(b)

[11.101] Only 'outsiders' can rely upon CA 1990, s 38(1)(b). The beneficiaries of a transaction or arrangement cannot rely on s 38(1)(b) and CA 1990, s 25(6) sets out the circumstances in which a transaction or arrangement is 'made for a person'[170]. Therefore, a director or other relevant person for whom a transaction or arrangement is made is disqualified from claiming to be bona fide purchasers for value without actual notice.

(ii) A person must not have actual notice of the contravention

[11.102] A person's rights will only be saved if he does not have actual notice of the contravention. Actual notice imposes a lesser standard than does constructive notice, in that actual notice turns upon a person's subjective knowledge of a contravention. However, although this aspect of the saver is subjective, a person seeking to rely upon CA 1990, s 38(1)(b) will be precluded from adopting a blinkered approach. In *Agra Bank Ltd v Barry*[171] Lord Cairns said in the context of the doctrine of priorities:

> 'Of course, you may have...conduct so reckless, so intensely negligent, that you are absolutely unable to account for it in any other way than this, that by reason of a suspicion entertained by the person whose conduct you are examining that there was a registered deed before his, he will abstain from inquiring into the fact, because he is so satisfied that the fact exists, that he feels persuaded that if he did enquire, he must find it out.'

Actual notice has also been considered by the Supreme Court in *Bank of Ireland Finance Ltd v Rockfield Ltd*[172]. There, CA 1963, s 60(14) was under consideration[173], which provides that any transaction in breach of CA 1963, s 60(1) would be voidable against all persons with notice of the facts which constitute a breach. Kenny J held that the 'notice' referred to therein was 'actual notice'. Of interest is his comment that:

> '...I wish to say that I use the term "actual notice" as meaning in this case that the plaintiff bank, or any of its officials, had been informed either verbally or in writing, that part of the advance was to be applied in the purchase of shares in the defendant company, or that they knew facts from which they must have inferred that part of the advance was to be applied for this purpose...I include in "actual notice" cases where the agent gets actual notice of the equity.'

---

169 (1 December 1999, unreported), High Court at p 7.

170 See para **[11.066]**.

171 *Agra Bank Ltd v Barry* (1874) LR 7 HL 135 at 149.

172 *Bank of Ireland Finance Ltd v Rockfield Ltd* [1979] IR 21 at 37.

173 See Chapter 18, *The Maintenance of Capital*, para **[18.044]**.

In practice this has caused legal practitioners great difficulties: to what extent should a solicitor for a lending institution, desirous to lend money to a company, enquire into the circumstances of the loan, particularly where a guarantee and collateral security is being advanced by another company, which may or may not be a *relevant person*[174]. It has been opined elsewhere[175] that extreme caution must be exercised in striking the appropriate balance, and that it will often be the case that in the course of other routine enquiries made in the course of the transaction, facts will come to the knowledge of both a lending institution and its lawyer which may give them notice that the company which proffers the guarantee or security, is doing so in favour of a relevant person.

(iii) Rights must be acquired 'for value':

[11.103] Section 38(1)(b) of CA 1990 is confined to non-gratuitous rights acquired, ie only where a person has given consideration for the rights he acquired.

(iv) The requirement of bona fides

[11.104] The person seeking to rely upon this saver must also have acted bona fide[176], ie in good faith. The question left unanswered is whether 'good faith' implies a duty to investigate and if it does, how does this lie with the 'actual notice' standard, since a duty to investigate is more consistent with constructive notice. In a different context, it was said in *International Sales and Agencies Ltd v Marcus*[177], by Lawson J that:

> '...the test of good faith in somebody entering into obligations with a company will be found either in proof of his actual knowledge that the transaction was ultra vires the company or where it can be shown that such a person could not in view of all the circumstances, have been unaware that he was a party to a transaction ultra vires.'

This interpretation is essentially objective, meaning that it is open to a court to find that even though a person claims not to have had actual notice, the incredibility of such in the circumstances of the case could mean that the court may find that he did not, in law, act bona fide. In a number of situations the Irish courts have held that to act bona fide, a person must not turn their face against the possibility of something being improper[178]. It is thought that the twin requirements of 'without actual notice' and 'bona fide' can only be

[174] See Courtney, 'The Latest Hazard to Guarantees: The Effects of S.31, Companies Act 1990 on Inter Company Guarantees' (1991) Gazette ILSI 261, on the question of inter–company guarantees.

[175] Courtney, 'The Latest Hazard to Guarantees: The Effects of S.31, Companies Act 1990 on Inter Company Guarantees' (1991) Gazette ILSI 261 at 264.

[176] See Chapter 7, *Corporate Contracts, Capacity and Authority*, para **[7.128]** where 'good faith' in the context of SI 163/1973, reg 6(1) is considered. It must be remembered that, by reg 6(2), there is a presumption that a person acts in good faith.

[177] *International Sales and Agencies Ltd v Marcus* [1982] 3 All ER 551 at 559. See also *TCB Ltd v Gray* [1986] 1 All ER 587.

[178] See also *In Re Vendor and Purchaser Act 1874; Crowley v Flynn* (13 May, 1983, unreported), High Court per Barron J. There, the Succession Act 1965, s 51(1) which protects a "purchaser" of a deceased person's estate from a personal representative, was interpreted as meaning a person who acts in "good faith", and further that this meant that such person ought to make reasonable inquiries if the protection was to be successfully invoked. See also *Re Molyneau and White* 13 LR Ir 382.

reconciled by interpreting 'bona fide' as merely requiring that the outsider must act honestly[179] and not recklessly. A duty to investigate should not be implied in circumstances where the legislature has clearly turned its face against constructive notice of a contravention.

Civil consequences of contravention: account and indemnity

[11.105] The second civil consequence of contravention of CA 1990, s 31 is that the person for whom a contravening transaction or arrangement was made, and any directors who authorised it, are liable to indemnify the company for any loss it suffers and to account to the company for any gain made. Section 38(2) of CA 1990 provides:

> 'Without prejudice to any liability imposed otherwise than by this subsection but subject to subsection (3), where an arrangement or transaction is made by a company for a director of the company or its holding company or person connected with such a director in contravention of section 31, that director and the person so connected and any other director of the company who authorised the transaction or arrangement shall (whether or not it has been avoided in pursuance of subsection (1)) be liable—
>
> (a) to account to the company for any gain which he has made directly or indirectly by the arrangement or transaction; and
>
> (b) (jointly and severally with any other person liable under this subsection) to indemnify the company for any loss or damage resulting from the arrangement or transaction.'

This provides an identical remedy to companies to that provided by CA 1990, s 29(4) where a substantial property transaction is entered into in contravention of s 29(1); and the English case law on s 322(3) of the Companies Act 1985 (UK), considered above[180], is equally relevant to interpreting CA 1990, s 38(2). It is also the case that a director may be relieved of liability where he can show that he took all reasonable steps to secure compliance with s 31. This is provided for by s 38(3), which states:

> 'Where an arrangement or transaction is entered into by a company and a person connected with a director of the company or its holding company in contravention of section 31 that director shall not be liable under subsection (2) if he shows that he took all reasonable steps to secure the company's compliance with that section and, in any case, a person so connected and any such other director as is mentioned in the said subsection (2) shall not be so liable if he shows that, at the time the arrangement or transaction was entered into, he did not know the relevant circumstances constituting the contravention.

This has also been considered above[181] in the context of CA 1990, s 29(5). The English High Court held in *Re Ciro Citterio Menswear plc*[182] that a loan to a director in contravention of s 330 of the Companies Act 1985 (UK) did not automatically make the

---

[179] In the context of the Fraudulent Conveyances Act 1634 (10 Chas 1 Sess 2, c 3), Hamilton P, held in *Re Thomas O'Neill, a bankrupt* [1989] IR 544, that: 'With regard to the use of the term 'bona fide' or 'in good faith' in th[at] statute ... I am satisfied that the use of the term must be taken to mean without notice of the intention to delay, hinder or defraud creditors of their lawful debts, rights and remedies.'

[180] See para **[11.046]** *ff*.

[181] See para **[11.049]**. See in particular, *Duckwari plc v Offerventure (No 2)* [1999] BCC 11, CA.

[182] *Re Ciro Citterio Menswear plc* [2002] 2 All ER 717, [2002] EWHR 293 (ch).

director a constructive trustee. It was said that a loan to a director was not per se the sort of transaction that was inevitably a misapplication of company money or a breach by a director of his trusteeship of company assets. The fact that a loan in breach of s 330 stood until it was avoided was inimical to the existence of a constructive trusteeship or to any form of tracing claim, at least in the absence of special circumstances. It was also said that s 341(2)(a) of the English 1985 Act (materially identical to CA 1990, s 38(2)(a)) supported this as it seemed to presuppose the absence of constructive trusteeship because it expressly provided for what would otherwise be one of the consequences of constructive trusteeship, namely an obligation to account for gains made. It followed that an administrator's claim to a share in a property bought by a director in part with money advanced by his company, failed.

Civil consequences of contravention: personal liability

[11.106] The third civil consequence of contravention of CA 1990, s 31 is that certain persons may be made personally liable for some or all of the company's debts in the event of its subsequently being wound up insolvent. Section 39(1) of CA 1990 provides that where a company being wound up is insolvent a court may, if it thinks proper to do so, declare that any person for whose benefit *an arrangement of a kind described in s 32 was made* shall be personally liable without limitation of liability for all or certain specified debts and other liabilities of the company.

[11.107] It can immediately be seen that by use of the word 'arrangement', the application of CA 1990, s 39(1) is limited by reason of the reference to 'of a kind described in section 32'. This means only persons for whose benefit the following prohibited transactions may be personally liable:

— loans;

— quasi-loans;

— credit transactions.

Accordingly, it would seem, that persons who benefit from guarantees and the provision of security are *not* liable to be made personally liable under CA 1990, s 39(1) because such are not 'arrangements' within the meaning of CA 1990, s 32.

[11.108] One question of interpretation which arises here is, can personal liability be imposed only where the exception in CA 1990, s 32 is relied upon? The reference to 'an arrangement of a kind described in section 32', can refer either to the more narrow interpretation of:

— an arrangement whereby the value of the arrangement is less than 10% of the company's relevant assets, *or*, the broader interpretation of

— an 'arrangement' which is defined by s 32(2)(a), ie a loan, quasi-loan or credit transaction.

The significance of this distinction is that where the former is applied, it means that only persons who benefit from an arrangement which comes within the s 32, 'less than 10%' exception, can be made personally liable under s 39. On the other hand, where the latter is applied, it means that anybody who benefits from a loan, quasi-loan or credit transaction which is in contravention of s 31, may be made personally liable under s 39.

[11.109] It should also be noted that beneficiaries of an 'arrangement' are not automatically personally liable for the debts of a company where that company goes into insolvent liquidation. Rather, on the application of the liquidator or any creditor or contributory of the company, personal liability under CA 1990, s 39(1) *may* be imposed where:

> '...the court considers that any arrangement of a kind described in s 32 has contributed materially to the company's inability to pay its debts or has substantially impeded the orderly winding up thereof...'

While the simple fact that an arrangement was made for a beneficiary's benefit is sufficient to make them a respondent, it is necessary to prove that the arrangement made in their favour either contributed materially to the company's insolvency, or substantially impeded the orderly winding up of the company[183].

[11.110] A court can make an order under CA 1990, s 39(1), 'if it thinks it proper to do so'. Some guidance is given by CA 1990, s 39(2) which provides:

> 'In deciding whether to make a declaration under *subsection (1)*, the court shall have regard to whether, and to what extent, any outstanding liabilities arising under any arrangement referred to in that subsection were discharged before the commencement of the winding up.'

Clearly, where the beneficiary of an arrangement has entirely repaid or reimbursed to the company, the court should have regard to this fact and be inclined to exercise its discretion against the making of an order under s 39.

Criminal consequences of contravention

[11.111] The contravention of CA 1990, s 31 is, by CA 1990, s 40, a criminal offence. Thus where a company enters into an arrangement or transaction in contravention of s 31, the officers of that company may be guilty of a criminal offence where they know, or have reasonable cause to believe, that the company was contravening the section: CA 1990, s 40(1). A second offence, which is less clear, is that created by CA 1990, s 40(2):

> 'A person who procures a company to enter into a transaction or arrangement knowing or having reasonable cause to believe that the company was thereby contravening s 31 shall be guilty of an offence.'

The concept of 'procurement' is not without difficulty; it is conceivable that a solicitor, accountant or other advisor acting for a company could in certain circumstances be charged with an offence under this section. It is thought, however, that any charges would only be brought where the advisor acted with mala fides as opposed to inadvertence or negligence. It is thought that procuring a company to make a loan to a director, in circumstances where the money was to be on-loaned to the procurer, is the chief mischief that s 40(2) intends to criminalise.

[11.112] The penalties prescribed for a person or corporation who commits either of the foregoing offences, are set out in CA 1990, s 240. For either offence in s 40, on summary

---

183 See *Re David Ireland & Co Ltd* [1905] IR 133, where a director's honest but confusing intermingling of his personal finances with those of the company provoked the liquidator of the company to issue misfeasance proceedings. See Chapter 10, *Duties of Directors and Other Officers*, para **[10.131]**.

conviction, one is liable to a fine not exceeding €1,269.74 or at the discretion of the court, to imprisonment for a term not exceeding 12 months, or both. On conviction on indictment one is liable to a fine not exceeding €12,697.38 or, again at the discretion of the court, to a term of imprisonment not exceeding 5 years, or both.

[11.113] It is important to note that CLEA 2001, s 104(b) has amended CA 1990, s 240. The effect has been to increase the penalty applicable to conviction on indictment from three years' to five years' imprisonment. The consequence is that the contravention of CA 1990, s 31 now renders a suspect liable to arrest without warrant and detention for up to 12 hours under the Criminal Justice Act 1984, s 4. It is thought that the result will be the elevation of the criminal consequences in the minds of practitioners so that they are held in at least the same fear as the civil consequences are currently held.

[11.114] Unlike a transaction or arrangement that comes within the exemptions listed above in CA 1990, ss 32–37, when there is a contravention of the prohibition in s 31 but it is not voidable by reliance on one of the savers in s 38, the transaction or arrangement remains a criminal offence.

[D] DISCLOSURE OF INTERESTS IN CONTRACTS WITH COMPANIES

[11.115] Section 194(1) of CA 1963 imposes a duty on a director[184] who is in any way, whether directly of indirectly, interested in a contract or proposed contract with the company, to declare the nature of his interest at a meeting of the directors of the company. This states:

> 'It shall be the duty of a director of a company who is in any way, whether directly or indirectly, interested in a contract or proposed contract with the company to declare the nature of his interest at a meeting of the directors of the company.'[185]

Although the section is silent as to the civil consequences where a director does not declare his interest in a contract, it has been held that 'under the ordinary principles of general law'[186] the contract would be voidable at the company's instance, provided that the parties can be restored to their original position. In *Craven Textile Engineers Ltd v Batley Football Club Ltd*[187] it was found that a director had not declared to his company his interest in a contract with his company. The contract had been performed and the company had work done for it and materials supplied to it. Clarke LJ held that it was inappropriate for the company to avoid the contract as the court could not restore the parties to the position they had been in before the work had been done and the materials supplied. In these circumstances, it was held that the company was obliged to pay on foot of the contract.

[11.116] Section 194(2) of CA 1963 is concerned with the timing of a director's declaration of interest. This recognises three different circumstances in which a director

[184] CA 1963, s 194 has application to shadow directors by CA 1990, s 27(3).

[185] As to conflicts of interest, see, generally, Chapter 10, *Duties of Directors and Other Officers*, para **[10.048]** *ff*.

[186] See *Guinness plc v Saunders* [1990] BCC 205 at 217G and *Hely–Hutchinson v Brayhead Ltd* [1968] 1 QB 549 at 594.

[187] *Craven Textile Engineers Ltd v Batley Football Club Ltd* [2001] BCC 679.

can be interested in a contract or proposed contract and prescribes the times at which such interests should be disclosed:

— in the case of a proposed contract – at the meeting at which the question of entering into the contract is first proposed;

— in the case of a proposed contract where the director was not, at the date of the first meeting at which it was considered, interested – at the next meeting of the directors held after he became interested;

— in the case where a director becomes interested in a contract after it is made – at the first meeting of the directors held after the director became interested.

Section 194(3) of CA 1963, as replaced by CA 1990, s 47(3), provides that a general notice of declaration of interest can be made by a director to the effect that he is a member of a specified company or firm or is connected[188] to a specified person, and is to be regarded as interested in any contract made with such a party after the date of the notice.

[11.117] Section 194(4) of CA 1963 provides that a notice shall be of no effect unless either given at a meeting of the directors or unless the director giving the notice takes reasonable steps to secure that it is brought up and read at the next meeting of the directors after it is given. Section 194(5) provides that such declarations of interests should be kept in a book which is to be available for inspection by the officers and members of the company[189]. Furthermore, by CA 1990, s 47 a transaction or arrangement of the type described in CA 1990, s 31 made by a company for a director of the company or a person so connected with such a director is to be treated as a transaction or arrangement in which a director is so interested[190].

[11.118] Where a director does not disclose his interests in shares or debentures, he is liable to a fine[191]. While it might be thought that for a director to vote on a contract in which he was interested would be in breach of his fiduciary duties as a director, in private companies where model reg 7 is adopted, a director can vote in favour of such a contract and be counted in the quorum[192]. The question of a director breaching the fiduciary duties which he owes his company are discussed in detail in Chapter 10, *Duties of Directors and Other Officers*[193].

---

[188] Ie 'connected' within the meaning of CA 1990, s 26.

[189] Failure to comply with sub–s (5) renders the company and every officer of the company in default, liable to a fine not exceeding £500 and the court may by order, compel an immediate inspection or production: CA 1963, s 195(5)(b).

[190] See para **[11.051]** *ff*. It is interesting to note that CA 1990, s 47 provides that such is to 'be treated as a transaction or arrangement in which the director is interested', and not the 'contract or proposed contract' spoken of in CA 1963, s 194.

[191] CA 1990, s 47(6).

[192] Cf *Hely–Hutchinson v Brayhead Ltd* [1967] 3 All ER 98 where on the construction of the specific articles of association of the company concerned, it was held that a contract entered into by the company without a declaration being made, was voidable (though not void) at the instance of the company. See also *Cox v Dublin City Distillery (No 2)* [1915] 1 IR 345.

[193] Chapter 10, *Duties of Directors and Other Officers*.

Chapter 12

Company Law Compliance and Enforcement

Introduction

[12.001] It is accepted by most commentators that transgressions of the Companies Acts became a ubiquitous feature of Irish commercial life in the closing decades of the twentieth century. Little more than lip-service had been paid to non-compliance with company law until the mid to late-1990s when, in the shadow of various tribunals of enquiry, the Government took the decision to adopt what has come to be known as a zero-tolerance stance on corporate transgressions. The impetus for the sea-change was the announcement[1], on 7 August 1998, of the establishment of the *Working Group on Company Law Compliance and Enforcement*, chaired by Michael McDowell SC, which came to be known as the McDowell Group[2]. In establishing the working group the Tánaiste said that:

> '...the Government decision to set up the Group was influenced by the recent emergence of strong indications of abuses of company law which pose a particular problem for the integrity of the system of company regulation. The consequential public concerns must be allayed if the social consensus and Ireland's standing as a reputable place to do business which underlies our present economic success are to be maintained in the future.'

The McDowell Group first met in September 1998 and produced its report on 30 November of the same year[3], a remarkable achievement by any standard. Even more extraordinary, by Irish legislative standards, was the speed with which the recommendations of the McDowell Group were adopted by the Oireachtas and passed into law in July 2001, in the form of the Company Law Enforcement Act 2001 ('CLEA 2001')[4].

[12.002] The most visible metric of abuse and disregard for company law is non-compliance with the registration requirements for companies formed and registered under, and therefore regulated by, the Companies Acts 1963–2001. The McDowell Group labelled these transgressions as registration-type cases; and concluded that:

> 'Irish company law has been characterised by a culture of non-compliance and a failure by companies and their officers to meet their obligations in respect of the filing of annual returns on time. For example, in 1997 only 13% of companies complied with their obligations to file annual returns on time.'[5]

---

1 By the then Tánaste and Minister for Enterprise, Trade and Employment, Ms Mary Harney TD and Mr Noel Tracy TD, the then Minister for Science, Technology and Commerce.

2 The McDowell Group was an ad hoc group drawn from amongst the social partners, interested bodies and those whom it was perceived might add value to its deliberations.

3 See *The Report of the Working Group on Company Law Compliance and Enforcement* (1998) (Pn 6697).

4 The CLEA 2001 was commenced piecemeal by various statutory instruments.

5 *The Report of the Working Group on Company Law Compliance and Enforcement* (1998), p ii, point 9.

The McDowell Group made a number of recommendations designed to strengthen registration-type compliance with the Companies Acts, the most significant being the introduction of on-the-spot fines[6].

[12.003] The McDowell Group distinguished these (objectively) less serious transgressions, which are policed by the Registrar of Companies, from what the group termed non-registration type cases, the enforcement of which was primarily vested in the Director of Public Prosecutions ('DPP') and the Minister for Enterprise, Trade and Employment. It was recognised that culpability for *non-registration* type offences is not as clear cut as in the case of registration-type offences. In addition to accepting that a strict three-year time limitation[7] on the prosecution of company law offences hampered prosecution, since many offences only came to light outside of the time limit, the McDowell Group recognised that the successful prosecution of such offences would require significant investment in staffing and resources. In respect of non-registration type offences, and in reference to the unprecedented number of appointments of inspectors to investigate alleged malpractice, the group said:

> 'Many of these investigations are the subject of intense public interest, and where they reveal possible breaches of the Companies Acts appropriate enforcement action will have to be taken if the framework of company law is not to be brought into disrepute. There has been limited enforcement of company law offences in the past, and in the circumstances, the Group has considered what form of response should be forthcoming from Government to allay public concern in the area of corporate affairs.'[8]

What must be remembered is that, notwithstanding the McDowell Group's two-fold classification, the second category identified – ie, *non-registration* type offences – does not necessarily mean more serious offences. As shall be considered below[9] non-registration offences can be further broken down into the following:

— potentially serious offences involving acts or omissions contrary to the Companies Acts 1963-2001;
— offences involving a failure to supply documents or provide information by and to various parties; and
— offences in relation to the failure to maintain various statutory registers.

The most far-reaching solution to the absence of an adequate State infrastructure for the detection and prosecution of serious company law offences, proposed by the McDowell Group, and accepted by the Government in CLEA 2001 was the establishment of the office of Director of Corporate Enforcement[10].

[12.004] In this chapter the law relating to the compliance with and enforcement of company law will be considered in five sections:

---

6 See para **[12.040]**.

7 It is very significant that CA 1990, s 240 was amended by the insertion of a new sub–s (5) to provide, inter alia, that the three–year time limit is now subject to discoverability: C(A)(No 2)A 1999, s 41: see para **[12.036]**.

8 At pp 39–40 at para 4.4.

9 See para **[12.190]**.

10 See para **[12.009]**.

[A] The agencies of enforcement and compliance.

[B] Enforcement and compliance: criminal sanctions.

[C] Enforcement and compliance: civil and administrative sanctions against officers and companies.

[D] Registration-type offences.

[E] Non-registration type offences.

Section A addresses the roles, powers and remits of those officers and agencies responsible for company law enforcement and compliance. Section B considers the various criminal sanctions (including prosecution and arrest) available to ensure compliance and enforcement. Section C considers the civil and administrative sanctions and remedies (restriction, disqualification and strike-off) that are available against both companies and their delinquent officers. Section D will consider registration-type offences, which are of primary concern to the Registrar of Companies. Section E considers non-registration type offences under the Companies Acts, many of which are indictable offences and accordingly, more serious.

[A] THE AGENCIES OF ENFORCEMENT AND COMPLIANCE

[12.005] Until the enactment of the CLEA 2001 the Registrar of Companies, the Minister for Enterprise, Trade and Employment and the DPP were the three agencies which shared the prosecution of offences under the Companies Acts. Since CLEA 2001, the prosecution of company law offences and the enforcement of the Companies Acts are now shared by the following:

1. The Registrar of Companies.
2. The Director of Corporate Enforcement.
3. The Director of Public Prosecutions.
4. The *locus standi* of private parties.

The Registrar of Companies

[12.006] The office of the Registrar of Companies dates back to the Joint Stock Companies Act 1844, which first permitted incorporation *by registration*. Necessarily incidental to that momentous legislative decision to permit incorporation by registration was the creation of the office of the Registrar of Joint Stock Companies: the keeper of the register[11]. In *Business Communications Ltd v Baxter and Parsons*[12], Murphy J observed:

> 'Since the introduction of legislation permitting people to incorporate with limited liability, it has been recognised that the protection which this conferred on those taking advantage of the privilege has to be counterbalanced by statutory provisions to protect and safeguard the interests of those dealing with them. The original and essential protection to those dealing with companies incorporated under the Companies Acts from time to time was the creation of a registration office in which would be filed the essential information in relation to companies incorporated under the legislation so that outsiders would have an opportunity of

[11] See Chapter 1, *The Private Company in Context*, para **[1.067]**.

[12] *Business Communications Ltd v Baxter and Parsons* (21 July 1995, unreported), High Court (Murphy J).

ascertaining the persons constituting the corporation and be in a position to form some estimate as to the assets which would be available to meet its liabilities.'[13]

One of the original functions of the Registrar of Joint Stock Companies – now called the *Registrar of Companies* – the importance of which survives to today, is the receipt, evaluation and (if in order) the acceptance for registration of the documents lodged by persons desirous of incorporating a company. The Registrar's primary function can thus be seen as the statutory procreator of the artificial legal entity that is the registered company. His grant of a certificate of incorporation signals the birth of a company; Companies Act 1963, s 18 ('CA 1963') provides that on the registration of the memorandum of association, the Registrar 'shall certify under his hand that the company is incorporated'. The other three core functions of the Registrar are: the receipt and registration of post incorporation documents; the enforcement of the Companies Acts in relation to the filing obligations of companies and the making of information available to the public[14]. Notwithstanding the establishment of the office of Director of Corporate Enforcement, the Registrar retains these four core functions.

[12.007] The Minister for Enterprise, Trade and Employment is responsible for the maintenance and administration of the companies registration office ('CRO')[15] and for the appointment of the Registrar of Companies and assistant registrars[16]. Section 368(4) of CA 1963 provided that whenever any act is, by CA 1963, or other statute, directed to be done to or by the Registrar, 'it shall, until the Minister otherwise directs, be done to or by the existing Registrar of Joint Stock Companies or, in his absence, to or by such person as the Minister may for the time being authorise'. It would appear that some doubt existed as to the validity of acts done to or by assistant registrars and others employed in the Registrar's office. Section 52(1) of the Companies (Amendment) (No 2) Act ('C(A)(No 2)A 1999') provides that any act referred to in CA 1963, s 368(4) which, before the commencement of the C(A)(No 2)A 1999, was done to or by such persons:

> '...shall be valid and be deemed always to have been valid as if the Minister had directed under that subsection (4) that such an act was to be done to or by such an assistant registrar or other such person (including in cases where the existing Registrar of Joint Stock Companies (or his or her successor) was not absent).'

To put matters beyond all doubt, C(A)(No 2)A 1999, s 52(2) provides:

> 'On and from the commencement of this section, any act required or authorised by the Companies Acts 1963 to 1999, the Registration of Business Names Act 1963 or the Limited Partnership Act 1907 to be done to or by the registrar of companies, the Registrar of Joint Stock Companies or, as the case may be, a person referred to in the enactment concerned as "the registrar" may be done to or by a registrar or assistant registrar appointed under s 368(2) of the Principal Act or any other person authorised in that behalf by the Minister.'

---

13 (21 July 1995, unreported), High Court at p 15 (Murphy J).

14 See the CRO website at www.cro.ie. See generally, the *Companies Report 1999*, Government Publications.

15 CA 1963, s 368(1).

16 CA 1963, s 368(2).

[12.008] The Registrar of Companies is the person charged with securing compliance with the filing and registration requirements under the Companies Acts. The means of enforcement available to the Registrar to ensure compliance (and to punish non-compliance) are:

- — the prosecution of companies and their officers for registration-type offences – considered in Section D, below;
- — the imposition of on-the spot fines;[17] and
- — the strike-off of non-compliant companies[18];

The Director of Corporate Enforcement

[12.009] The central recommendation of the McDowell Group was the establishment of a dedicated company law enforcement office, located within the Department of Enterprise, Trade and Employment, headed by a Director of Corporate Enforcement (the 'Director')[19]. In the light of its findings on the then existing enforcement regime, the McDowell Group recommended:

> 'An independent statutory officer – to be known as the Director of Corporate Enforcement – who would have general – but not exclusive – responsibility for the enforcement of company law should be appointed. The Director should have a similar role to that of the Director of Consumer Affairs, who has specific responsibility in law for the prosecution of offences under consumer legislation, and should be independent in the discharge of his functions.'[20]

Part 2 of CLEA 2001 gives legislative effect to the McDowell Group's recommendations. Here the following are next considered:

(a) The appointment, status and independence of the Director.

(b) The functions and powers of the Director.

(a) The appointment, status and independence of the Director of Corporate Enforcement

[12.010] Section 7(1) of CLEA 2001 establishes the office of the Director, who is appointed by the Minister for Enterprise, Trade and Employment[21], after his election (following competition) by the Civil Service Commissioners[22]. Section 7(3) provides that:

> 'The Director shall be a corporation sole and, notwithstanding any casual vacancy in the office from time to time, shall have perpetual succession and shall be capable in his or her

[17] See para **[12.040]**.

[18] See para **[12.132]**.

[19] See *Report of the Working Group on Company Law Compliance and Enforcement* (1998), para 4.7 *ff*. A less radical recommendation was made by the ad hoc, *Company Law Review Group*, (chaired by James Gallagher) which reported to the Government in February 1995 which recommended the establishment of an 'executive unit' within the Department of Enterprise, Trade and Employment (para 7.14) to pursue delinquent directors of insolvent companies. See Courtney, *Company Law Review 1995*, (1996), p 11.

[20] See *Report of the Working Group on Company Law Compliance and Enforcement* (1998), at ii (Summary).

[21] CLEA 2001, s 7(2).

[22] CLEA 2001, s 7(3).

corporate name of holding and disposing of real or personal property and of suing and being sued.'

Section 11 of CLEA 2001 facilitates the ministerial appointment of an Acting Director to perform the Director's functions during periods when the Director is absent from duty, out of the State, unable to perform the Director's functions, suspended from office or where there is a vacancy in the office[23].

[12.011] Although the Director is expressed to be 'independent in the performance of his or her functions'[24] and is expressly prohibited from holding any other office or employment in respect of which emoluments are paid[25], the Director is politically accountable in a number of ways[26]. In the first place, the Director is expressed to be a 'civil servant'[27]. Secondly, the Director's term of office is for a maximum period of five years[28] but he can be removed by the Minister at any time for stated reasons, whereupon the Minister must cause a statement of the reasons for the removal to be laid before each House of the Oireachtas[29]; moreover, the Director will cease to be Director where he enters politics[30]. Thirdly, the Director is required to submit annual reports to the Minister for Enterprise, Trade and Employment concerning the performance of his functions and other activities[31]. Although the Director's report under CLEA 2001, s 16(1) shall include information in such form and about such matters as the Minister may direct, s 16(2) provides nothing in either subsection:

> '...shall be construed as requiring the Director to include in such report information the inclusion of which would, in the opinion of the Director, be likely to prejudice the performance by him or her of any of his or her functions.'

---

23 CLEA 2001, ss 11(2) and (3) provide, respectively, that a person may not be appointed as Acting Director for a continuous period of more than six months during a vacancy in the office of the Director and that the Minister may, at any time, terminate the appointment of Acting Director.

24 CLEA 2001, s 12(5).

25 CLEA 2001, s 8(3).

26 Information obtained by the Director by virtue of the performance of his functions which has not otherwise come to the public's attention cannot be disclosed, save in accordance with law: see generally, CLEA 2001, s 17.

27 It is not clear as to whether the Director is a civil servant 'in the service of the Government' or 'in the service of the State', the latter importing a greater degree of independence: see Osborne, *The Company Law Enforcement Bill 2000 Seminar* (2002) Dublin Solicitors Bar Association paper at p 4 and Hogan and Morgan, *Administrative Law in Ireland* (3rd edn, 1998), pp 79–81.

28 CLEA 2001, s 8(1).

29 CLEA 2001, ss 10(1) and (2).

30 CLEA 2001, s 10(3) provides that a person shall cease to be Director if he is nominated as a member of Seanad Éireann, nominated as a candidate for election to either House of the Oireachtas, the European Parliament or becomes a member of a local authority, or is regarded under the European Parliament Elections Act 1997, Sch 2, Part XIII as having been elected to the European Parliament; and CLEA 2001, s 10(4) provides that a person who is entitled to sit in the Houses of the Oireachtas, or is a member of the European Parliament or is a member of a local authority is disqualified from being Director.

31 CLEA 2001, s 16(1).

Likewise, although the Director is obliged to furnish from time to time information as requested by the Minister and to account to an appropriately established committee of either House of the Oireachtas, he is not obliged to furnish any information or answer any question which would, in his opinion, be likely to prejudice the performance of his functions[32].

[12.012] It was envisaged by the McDowell Group and accepted by the Government that, in addition to clerical staff, the enforcement office would be staffed by a number of solicitors and accountants and that a number of members of the Garda Síochána would be seconded to the enforcement office[33]. The Office of the Director of Corporate Enforcement ('ODCE') has been up and running since 1 October 2001.

(b) The functions and powers of the Director

[12.013] Section 12(1) of CLEA 2001 states the Director's functions to be:

(a) to enforce the Companies Acts, including by the prosecution of offences by way of summary proceedings,

(b) to encourage compliance with the Companies Acts,

(c) to investigate instances of suspected offences under the Companies Acts,

(d) at his or her discretion, to refer cases to the Director of Public Prosecutions where the Director of Corporate Enforcement has reasonable grounds for believing that an indictable offence under the Companies Acts has been committed,

(e) to exercise, insofar as the Director feels it necessary or appropriate, a supervisory role over the activity of liquidators and receivers in the discharge of their functions under the Companies Acts,

(f) for the purpose of ensuring effective application and enforcement of obligations, standards and procedures to which companies and their officers are subject, to perform such other functions in respect of any matters to which the Companies Acts relate as the Minister considers appropriate and may by order confer on the Director, and

(g) to perform such other functions for a purpose referred to in *paragraph (f)* as may be assigned to him or her by or under the Companies Act or any other Act.

Just as a company has 'objects' and 'powers', so too does the Director have power to 'do all such acts or things as are necessary or expedient for the purpose of the performance of his or her functions' under CLEA 2001 or any other statute[34]. The Director's functions (and the statutory powers he is given to achieve them) can be classified as involving:

(i) supervision,

(ii) investigation though the appointment of inspectors,

(iii) criminal investigation, prosecution and on-the-spot fines,

(iv) civil enforcement and sanction.

---

32 CLEA 2001, s 16(3) and (4).

33 Gardaí seconded continue to be under the general direction and control of the Commissioner of the Garda Síochána: CLEA 2001, s 12(3).

34 CLEA 2001, s 12(2).

(i) Supervision

[12.014] The Director's supervisory function is expressly envisaged by CLEA 2001, s 12(1)(e) in the context of the activity of liquidators and receivers[35]. So CA 1963, s 323A[36] provides that the Director may direct the production of a receiver's books and by CLEA 2001, s 57, the Director may direct the production of a liquidator's books. Section 58 of CLEA 2001 provides:

> 'Where a disciplinary committee or tribunal (however called) of a prescribed professional body finds that a member conducting a liquidation or receivership has not maintained appropriate records, or it has reasonable grounds for believing that a member has committed an indictable offence under the Companies Acts during the course of a liquidation or receivership, the body shall report the matter, giving details of the finding or, as the case may be, of the alleged offence, to the Director forthwith and if the body fails to comply with this section it, and every officer of the body to whom the failure is attributable, is guilty of an offence.'

Although not expressly stated in CLEA 2001, s 12, the activity of examiners and auditors will also fall to be supervised by the Director to the extent at least that the Companies Acts imposes particular requirements on such persons. So by the Companies Act 1990, s 192(6) ('CA 1990')[37] there is a similar obligation to that in CLEA 2001, s 58 (last quoted) placed on bodies of accountants. By CA 1990, s 187(12)[38] the Director is empowered to demand of a person acting as an auditor of a company or as a public auditor or purporting to be qualified to so act, the production of evidence of his qualifications. The Director may also require auditors – who, pursuant to s 194, advise the Registrar and the Director that, in their opinion, proper books of account have not been kept – to furnish information, including an explanation of their reasons for forming their opinion and to give the Director access to documents, etc: CA 1990, s 194(3A)[39]. Finally, CA 1990, s 194(5)[40] provides:

> 'Where, in the course of, and by virtue of, their carrying out an audit of the accounts of the company, information comes into the possession of the auditors of a company that leads them to form the opinion that there are reasonable grounds for believing that the company or an officer or agent of it has committed an indictable offence under the Companies Acts, the auditors shall, forthwith and after having formed it, notify that opinion to the Director and provide the Director with details of the grounds on which they have formed that opinion.'

This provision became effective on 28 November 2001. Where auditors comply with this provision, there is express protection against any claim for breach of professional or legal duty owed as auditor to the company, its shareholders, creditors or other interested parties[41]. Notwithstanding this protection, the accounting profession expressed grave

---

[35] By CA 1963, s 319(2A), as inserted by CLEA 2001, s 52, the Registrar must provide a copy of a retiring receiver's statement to the Director; the Registrar must also notify the Director of the appointment of a receiver.

[36] As inserted by CLEA 2001, s 53.

[37] Inserted by CLEA 2001, s 73.

[38] As inserted by CLEA 2001, s 72.

[39] As inserted by CLEA 2001, s 74.

[40] As inserted by CLEA 2001, s 74.

[41] CA 1990, s 194(6). On auditors' responsibilities to report offences, see Chapter 13, *Accounts and Auditors*, at para **[13.215]** *ff*.

reservations on the operation of CA 1990, s 145(5). This relatively short provision raises many difficult questions of interpretation. In the first place it must be asked whether s 194(5) applies when an auditor is carrying out non-audit work? It would seem, clearly, that an accountant who is providing non-audit services has no obligations under s 194(5); neither it seems does an accountant have a legal obligation to inform the auditors in his firm of anything untoward.[42] The Director has stated[43] that the words 'information comes into the possession of the auditors of a company' are not regarded by him as 'requiring auditors to seek out possible indictable offences.' They will, however, be expected to react to information which suggests that a possible indictable offence has been committed and make enquiries to form a considered opinion. The Director recognises that auditors are likely to take legal advice on whether particular incidents are reportable. On the requirement that auditors must be satisfied that a company officer or agent 'has committed' an indictable offence, the Director has acknowledged that this is of a higher standard of certainty than 'might' or 'may have' committed[44]. The Director has also stated that he does not consider that a reporting obligation arises where a relevant prosecuting authority has initiated and concluded enforcement action in respect of circumstances giving rise to an indictable offence.[45] As regards what are indictable offences, the Director has published a list of same which are set out below[46]. The Director has also published an Indictable Offences Report Form, for use by auditors[47].

[12.015] Also relevant here is the Director's function to 'encourage' compliance with the Companies Acts, stated in CLEA 2001, s 12(1)(b). The use of the word 'encourage' is notable, since it connotes an almost educational role for the Director, which can only be meaningfully exercised following the ongoing supervision of the activities of all corporate players and the subsequent identification of deficiencies in compliance.

(ii) Investigation through the appointment of inspectors

[12.016] The Director's investigative function arises in a number of contexts. In the first place, the Director has taken over the functions of the Minister for Enterprise Trade and Employment in regard to the investigation of companies and appointment of inspectors under CA 1990, Part II. Although this was not one of the McDowell Group's recommendations, it was considered by the Government 'to be more cost-effective, more efficient and less politicised if the decision on whether to initiate a company law investigation or a criminal investigation in any particular case was centralised with the Director'[48]. The investigation of companies and the appointment of inspectors is considered in Chapter 14.

---

42 See *Decision Notice D/2002/2* issued by the Office of the Director of Corporate Enforcement entitled *The Duty of Auditors to Report to the Director of Corporate Enforcement*, p 5.

43 *Duty of Auditors to Report to the Director of Corporate Enforcement*, p 7.

44 *Duty of Auditors to Report to the Director of Corporate Enforcement*, p 11.

45 *Duty of Auditors to Report to the Director of Corporate Enforcement*, p 13.

46 See para **[12.194]**.

47 *Duty of Auditors to Report to the Director of Corporate Enforcement*, Appendix 3.

48 See *Explanatory and Financial Memorandum* to the Company Law Enforcement Bill (2000), at p 1.

[12.017] Section 12(1)(c) of CLEA 2001 specifically details as a function of the Director, the investigation of suspected offences under the Companies Acts. The Director's investigative powers are also implicit in s 12(1)(a) (the enforcement of the Companies Acts and prosecution of summary offences) and s 12(1)(d) (the reference of cases to the DPP where the Director has reasonable grounds for believing an indictable offence has been committed) as in either case, an investigation would be required. To aid the investigation of offences, it is expressly provided that information relating to offences under the Companies Acts, held by the Competition Authority, Gardaí or Revenue Commissioners, may be disclosed to the Director or an officer of the Director[49].

[12.018] In investigating suspected breaches of the Companies Acts, the Director has certain powers to obtain information and preserve assets and secure the presence of persons to make them available for examination. This has been achieved by giving the Director all of the investigative powers enjoyed by official liquidators, and then some. In an official liquidation, the Director can seek an order for civil arrest of absconding contributories and officers (CA 1963, s 247[50]); an order for the delivery-up of records in a winding up (CA 1963, s 245A[51]); and an order for examination in a winding up (CA 1963, s 245[52]). Section 49 of CLEA 2001 expressly extends certain powers of official liquidators to voluntary liquidators. Accordingly, the Director can also apply for an order under CA 1963, s 282A for the inspection of books in a voluntary winding up and for an order under CA 1963, s 282B to summon persons for examination in a voluntary winding up or for an order under CA 1963, s 282C for the payment or delivery of property against a person examined in a voluntary winding up or for an order under CA 1963, s 282D to arrest an absconding contributory or director in a voluntary winding up.

(iii) Criminal investigation, prosecution and on-the-spot fines

[12.019] The Director is specifically empowered to enforce the Companies Acts by the prosecution of offences by way of summary proceedings: CLEA 2001, s 12(1)(a). As to the meaning of 'summary proceedings', CA 1990, s 240(3) provides:

> 'Every offence under the Companies Acts made punishable by a fine not exceeding £1,500 [€1,904.61] or by imprisonment for a term not exceeding 12 months, or by both, may be prosecuted summarily.'[53]

In this respect the Director has taken over this power from the Minister and, in line with the McDowell Group's recommendations[54], the Minister has been divested of all power to prosecute summary offences under the Companies Acts in favour of the Director[55]. The prosecution of both summary and indictable offences is considered below[56]. The Director

49 CLEA 2001, s 18.

50 See Chapter 27, *Realisation and Distribution of Assets in a Winding Up*, para **[27.041]**.

51 See Chapter 27, *Realisation and Distribution of Assets in a Winding Up*, para **[27.035]**.

52 See Chapter 27, *Realisation and Distribution of Assets in a Winding Up*, para **[27.034]**.

53 As amended by CLEA 2001, s 104(a).

54 See *The Report of the Working Group on Company Law Compliance and Enforcement* (1998), para 4.24.

55 CLEA 2001, s 14.

56 See para **[12.031]**.

also has the power to impose on-the-spot fines, as an alternative to prosecuting for a summary offence; this too is considered below[57].

[12.020] Central to the success of the Director's investigations will be the role played by the members of the Garda Síochána who have been seconded to the Director's office. Being trained investigators, it is to be expected that the quality of evidence collected by the gardaí, that will support referrals under CLEA 2001, s 12(1)(d) to the DPP, will facilitate the initiation of more prosecutions on indictment. The McDowell Group noted that they had been 'assured that any decision by the DPP not to commence criminal proceedings for breaches of the Companies Acts is due entirely to the quality of the evidential material available at the time of decision'[58].

[12.021] It should also be noted that the powers of investigation of breaches of the Companies Acts that constitute indictable offences have been greatly bolstered by CLEA 2001. As has been alluded to already, one intentional[59] effect of increasing the maximum term of imprisonment for indictable offences under the Companies Acts to five years, is to cause the provisions of the Criminal Justice Act 1984, s 4 to apply to such offences. Previously, with certain limited exceptions[60], a person suspected of committing an indictable offence under the Companies Acts could – upon being approached by the gardaí – refuse to co-operate and 'refer' them to deal with his or her solicitor. Where the conditions of s 4 of the 1984 Act are met, the gardaí in the Director's office will have the power to arrest a suspect without warrant and detain him for up to 12 hours where such is necessary for the proper investigation of the offence. Although it is thought that the persons who will make arrests without warrant will be the seconded gardaí, it is notable that civilian staff within the enforcement office also have, in certain circumstances, a similar power of arrest under the Criminal Law Act 1997, s 4. The circumstances in which a civilian has the power of arrest of a person suspected of committing an offence that carries a maximum term of imprisonment of five years, is where that person with reasonable cause suspects that the person to be arrested 'would otherwise attempt to avoid, or is avoiding, arrest by a member of the Garda Síochana'.[61]

(iv) Civil enforcement and sanction

[12.022] The Director's statutory function to enforce the Companies Acts in CLEA 2001, s 12(1)(a) is considerable wider than the prosecution of summary offences and encompasses civil enforcement and sanction. As considered below[62], the Director has standing to apply under CA 1963, s 371 for an injunction to require a company or an

57 See para **[12.040]**.

58 See *The Report of the Working Group on Company Law Compliance and Enforcement* (1998), para 4.28.

59 The application of the Criminal Justice Act 1984, s 4 to all indictable offences under the Companies Acts upon the increase in the maximum term of imprisonment to five years was noted by the McDowell Group: see *The Report of the Working Group on Company Law Compliance and Enforcement* (1998), para 4.30.

60 See para **[12.192]**.

61 Criminal Law Act 1997, s 4(4); where such an arrest is effected, the arrested person must be transferred into the custody of the Garda Síochana as soon as practicable.

62 See para **[12.175]**.

officer in default to make good that default. The default can involve the commission of either a summary or indictable offence and the Director's lack of standing to prosecute indictable offences is no bar to his seeking a section 371 injunction. Moreover, the Director has express power to apply to court for: an injunction to freeze the assets of companies, directors and others (CLEA 2001, s 55[63]) and other extensive powers of inspection and preservation, as noted above[64]. The Director can also apply for an order under CA 1963, s 298(2) that officers and others repay or restore etc money or property in cases of misfeasance. Also, as considered below[65], the Director has power to apply to court to have a person disqualified under CA 1963, s 160 or restricted under CA 1990, s 150. The Director's powers to apply for certain orders under CA 1990, s 251 in cases where companies have not been wound up by reason of the insufficiency of their assets is considered in Chapter 10[66].

The Director of Public Prosecutions

[12.023] The Director of Public Prosecutions ('DPP') is the only person who may prosecute through to the end, proceedings in respect of an indictable offence. The office of the DPP was established by the Prosecution of Offences Act 1974. That Act also transferred most of the State's prosecution functions from the Attorney General to the DPP[67]. It may be noted in passing, that CLEA 2001 took the opportunity to remove references in CA 1963 to the 'Attorney General' and to replace them with references to the DPP[68].

[12.024] Prior to the enactment of CLEA 2001, the authority to prosecute indictable offences vested with the DPP; and because the McDowell Group accepted this was the correct way to proceed, this remains the case. On the assumption that the reason for the dearth of prosecutions for indictable offences under the Companies Acts was on account of the quality of evidential material available at the time of the DPP's decision, the McDowell Group said:

> 'This leads us to recommend that the Director of Corporate Enforcement should play an active role in assisting the preparation of cases for possible criminal proceedings for breaches of the Companies Acts. We envisage that the Director and his staff will work closely with An Garda Síochána in identifying the indictable offences in any particular case and in supporting Garda enquiries (see paragraph 4.62). Such support would, we believe, be useful prior to the Gardaí submitting a case for possible criminal proceedings to the DPP.'[69]

Accordingly, the role of the DPP in prosecuting indictable offences under the Companies Acts remains.

---

63 See Chapter 27, *The Realisation and Distribution of Assets in a Winding Up*, para **[27.046]**.

64 See para **[12.018]**.

65 See para **[12.062]**.

66 At para **[10.121]** *ff*.

67 See generally, Kelly, *The Irish Constitution* (3rd edn, 1994), Hogan and Whyte, eds, p 307 *ff*.

68 See CLEA 2001, s 51 which amends CA 1963, s 299, which was, of course, enacted prior to the passage of the Prosecution of Offences Act 1974.

69 See *The Report of the Working Group on Company Law Compliance and Enforcement* (1998), para 4.29.

[12.025] One of the functions that the DPP lost as a result of CLEA 2001 was the right to apply for the disqualification of directors and other persons. Here, the McDowell Group recommended:

> 'The Group similarly found that although section 160 of the Companies Act, 1990, gives the Director of Public Prosecutions power to apply to the court to disqualify persons from acting as directors, auditors, officers, receivers, liquidators, examiners or being involved directly or indirectly in the promotion, formation or management of any company, the Office of the Director of Public Prosecutions is not equipped or organised to investigate and institute civil proceedings for disqualification in the manner envisaged by the Act. The Group concluded that there was an anomaly in providing a civil role in the monitoring of company directors for the Director of Public Prosecutions in matters which may not amount to or disclose the commission of a criminal offence.'[70]

The McDowell Group went on to say that the responsibility for the making of disqualification applications was 'generally inconsistent with the primary functions of the Director of Public Prosecutions in prosecuting criminal offences'.[71] The Group went on to recommend that it would be more appropriate for such functions to be carried out by either the Registrar of Companies or the Director of Corporate Enforcement and that the DPP should 'prosecute indictable offences under the Companies Acts on foot of completed investigations either by the Gardaí or by' the Director, or both[72].

The locus standi of private parties

[12.026] As regard the prosecution of criminal offences, it has long been recognised that, at common law, a so-called 'common informer', or private party, has locus standi to institute proceedings[73]. It has been held, however, that at common law, a corporation has no power to prosecute as a common informer[74]. For natural persons, however, the right of private prosecution remains[75] although it will ordinarily be only an altruistic or fool-hardy individual who will embark upon such a course. For most people, it will be the civil law that provides the attraction.

[12.027] There are a number of statutory provisions that specifically *empower* third parties to institute proceedings to prevent acts or omissions that are contrary to the Companies Acts. The primary statutory provision is CA 1963, s 371[76], considered in detail below[77], which empowers any member, creditor, the Registrar or the Director to apply to the High Court for an order to direct a company and any officer to make good a default in complying with any provision of the Companies Acts.

---

70 See *The Report of the Working Group on Company Law Compliance and Enforcement* (1998), para 2.15.

71 See *The Report of the Working Group on Company Law Compliance and Enforcement* (1998), para 2.16.

72 See *The Report of the Working Group on Company Law Compliance and Enforcement* (1998), para 2.17.

73 See, generally, Kelly, *The Irish Constitution* (3rd edn, 1994), Hogan and Whyte, eds, p 310 *ff*.

74 *Cumann Luthchlas Gael Teo v Windle* [1994] 1 IR 533.

75 *The State (Ennis) v Farrell* [1966] IR 107.

76 As amended by CLEA 2001, s 96.

77 See para **[12.175]**.

[12.028] Other, more specific, civil remedies are also contained in the Companies Acts. One such remedy is seen in CA 1963, s 8(2)[78] which empowers a member or 'holder of debentures' of a company to apply to the High Court to restrain a company 'from doing any act or thing which the company has no power to do'. Where a creditor, secured by a debenture, or any member has reason to believe that a company is engaged in ultra vires activities, CA 1963, s 8(2) may be invoked and appropriate application made to the High Court.

[B] Enforcement and Compliance: Criminal Sanctions

[12.029] Compliance with the statutory obligations of the Companies Acts 1963–2001 has for over 40 years been interpreted by many companies and their directors as if it was optional: CLEA 2001 has put paid to that interpretation. It is fast becoming established that the statutory *quid pro quo* for being permitted to conduct business with the shelter provided by the registered limited liability company, is comprehensive and timely compliance with all statutory requirements imposed by the Companies Acts.

[12.030] In this section, the following criminal sanctions and remedies against both companies and defaulting officers are considered:

1. Criminal prosecution of companies and 'officers in default'.
2. On-the-spot fines.

The criminal sanctions for breaches of the Companies Acts can operate to deprive wrongdoers of their liberty and to impose fines on them.

Criminal prosecution of companies and 'officers in default'

[12.031] In Section D and Section E the many summary and indictable offences created by the Companies Acts are outlined. Here, it is proposed to review the mechanics of prosecution and other ancillary matters in respect of the offences created by the Companies Acts under the following headings:

(a) Prosecution of 'officers in default'.
(b) The penalties specified by the Companies Acts.
(c) The statutory limitation period for prosecution of company law offences.
(d) The venue for prosecution.
(e) Evidence to juries in trials for indictable offences.

(a) Prosecution of 'officers in default'

[12.032] There are over 90 offences under the Companies Acts that are expressed to apply to the company *and* 'to every officer who is in default'. The instance of prosecution of officers in default has been very rare[79], largely due to the high evidential hurdle set by the original CA 1963, s 383, which defined an officer in default as:

---

[78] See Chapter 7, *Corporate Contracts, Capacity and Authority*, at para **[7.045]**.

[79] Although rare, the prosecution of officers in default was not unheard of. So in *Minister for Enterprise Trade and Employment v The Muckross Park Hotel Ltd* (20 February 2001), District Court, reported in (2001) The Irish Times, 21 February, two directors of the defendant-company were fined for failing to hold the company's AGM in 1999, despite having been notified on a number of occasions by the Department of Enterprise, Trade and Employment.

> '…any officer of the company who *knowingly and wilfully* authorises or permits the default, refusal or contravention…' [Emphasis added]

The use of the words 'knowingly and wilfully' in the definition of the phrase 'officer in default' necessitated proof of a defendant's subjective state of mind[80]. The difficulties attendant upon the use of this wording seems to have been recognised in 1990 since, rather than use the concept of 'officer in default' in relation to breaches of CA 1990, Part III, the legislature opted to criminalise the conduct of 'an officer of a company *who authorises or permits* a company to enter into a transaction or arrangement knowing or having reasonable cause to believe that the company was thereby contravening' CA 1990, s 31[81]. The McDowell Group recommended a revised definition of the concept of 'officer in default'[82] and this was effected by CLEA 2001, s 100, which replaced the wording of CA 1963, s 383 with the following provisions:

> '(1) For the purpose of any provision of the Companies Acts which provides that an officer of a company who is in default shall be liable to a fine or penalty, an officer who is in default is *any officer who authorises or who, in breach of his duty as such officer, permits, the default mentioned in the provision.*
>
> (2) For the purposes of this section, an officer shall be presumed to have permitted a default by the company unless the officer can establish that he took all reasonable steps to prevent it or that, by reason of circumstances beyond his control, was unable to do so.
>
> (3) It is the duty of each director and secretary of a company to ensure that the requirements of the Companies Acts are complied with by the company.
>
> (4) In this section "default" includes a refusal or contravention.' [Emphasis added]

This is a very far-reaching provision. In the first place, the relevant test is now whether the officer *authorised* or, in breach of his duty as officer, *permitted* the default: this is substantially more easy to prove than that old formulation of knowingly and wilfully. In the second place, there is an evidential presumption in favour of the prosecution, since an officer is *presumed* to have permitted a default, and the onus of proof is firmly on a defendant-officer to prove that he took all reasonable steps to prevent the default or was unable to prevent it by reason of circumstances outside of his control. The prosecution is also assisted in proving that a defendant-officer permitted a default *in breach of his duty as such officer* by sub-s (3) which categorically imposes a positive duty on each director and

---

79 (contd) CA 1963, s 131(6) criminalises the failure to hold an AGM where committed by a company and every officer who is in default. See further, the *Companies Report 1999*, Department of Enterprise, Trade and Employment at pp 44–45 for examples of successful prosecutions of directors under CA 1990, ss 202; CA 1963, s 131; and CA 1963, s 116–124.

80 The meaning of 'wilful' is considered in Chapter 6, *Corporate Civil Litigation*, para **[6.074]** and the meaning of 'knowingly' is considered in Chapter 10, *Duties of Directors and Other Officers*, para **[10.083]**.

81 Emphasis added.

82 See *The Report of the Working Group on Company Law Compliance and Enforcement* (1998), para 7.30.

secretary to ensure that their companies comply with the requirements of the Companies Acts[83].

[12.033] The new definition of officer in default is expressed to apply for the purposes of any provision of the Companies Acts that provides that an officer of a company who is in default 'shall be liable to a fine or penalty'. When formulating charges against a person, care should be taken to ensure that the offence alleged is sufficiently described[84].

(b) The penalties specified by the Companies Acts 1963–2001

[12.034] Section 240(1) of CA 1990[85] sets out the penalties for offences 'for which no punishment is specified'. It provides:

> 'A person guilty under any provision of the Companies Acts of an offence for which no punishment is specifically provided shall be liable –
>
> (a) on summary conviction, to a fine not exceeding £1,500 [€1,904.61] or, at the discretion of the court, to imprisonment for a term not exceeding 12 months or to both, or
>
> (b) on conviction on indictment, to a fine not exceeding £10,000 [€12,697.38] or, at the discretion of the court, to imprisonment for a term not exceeding 5 years or to both.'

In addition, CA 1990, s 240(2)[86], which is concerned with offences punishable by 'a fine or an unspecified amount' provides:

> 'A person guilty under any provision of the Companies Acts of an offence made punishable by a fine or an unspecified amount shall be liable –
>
> (a) on summary conviction, to a fine not exceeding £1,500 [€1,904.61] or
>
> (b) on conviction on indictment, to a fine not exceeding £10,000 [€12,697.38].'

In addition, the Companies Acts are littered with references to specific monetary fines and to specific maximum terms of imprisonment. Prior to the enactment of CLEA 2001 this gave rise to an anomalous position: where particular sections of CA 1963 specified particular monetary amounts, they tended to be lower in terms of the maximum fine or term of imprisonment than those applicable to offences for which no punishment was specified and those expressed to be punishable by fine or an unspecified amount. This anomaly was removed by CLEA 2001, s 104(c), which introduced new sub-ss (7) and (8) into s 240 of CA 1990. These provide for an equalisation of penalties under the Companies Acts. Section 240(7) of CA 1990 provides:

> 'In any provision of the Companies Acts for which a fine of any amount of less than £1,500 [€1,904.61] is provided in respect of a summary conviction, the maximum amount of that fine shall be taken to be £1,500 [€1,904.61].'

---

83 In *R v McCredie and Re v French* [1999] TLR 671 it was held by the English Court of Appeal that the officers of a company that was being wound up owed a positive duty to comply with the provisions of the Insolvency Act 1986, s 208(1) (UK) which required them to co-operate proactively (and not merely reactively) with the company's liquidator. As to the delegation of responsibility by directors, see Chapter 10, *Duties of Directors and Other Officers*, para **[10.044]**.

84 See *Lillyman and Pinkerton* (1982) (23 December 1982), Federal Court of Australia.

85 As amended by CLEA 2001, s 104(a) and (b).

86 As amended by CLEA 2001, s 104(a).

Section 240(8) of CA 1990 now provides:

> 'In any provision of the Companies Acts for which a term of imprisonment of less than 5 years is provided in respect of a conviction on indictment, the maximum term of imprisonment shall be taken to be 5 years.'

In consequences of these measures, the maximum fine in the case of all summary offences has now been increased to €1,904.61 and the maximum term of imprisonment is 12 months.

[12.035] In respect of indictable offences, the maximum fine where none is set is €12,697.38 (but this can be more in relation to specified offences) and the maximum term of imprisonment is five years (save in relation to a number of specified offences which provided for a greater maximum term)[87]. As noted earlier[88], one of the most tangible effects of increasing the maximum term of imprisonment for indictable offences to five years means that a person suspected of having committed such an offence may be arrested without warrant and detained in a Garda station for up to 12 hours: Criminal Justice Act 1984, s 4[89].

(c) The statutory limitation period for prosecution of company law offences

[12.036] Prior to the enactment of C(A)(No 2)A 1999, s 41 the limitation period within which a *summary prosecution* could be initiated under the Companies Acts was three years from the date of commission. The standard three-year limitation period has been retained: CA 1990, s 240(5)(a). This is, however, subject to two extensions. First, under s 240(5)(b) proceedings may be commenced if, at the expiry of the three-year period, the person against whom the proceedings are to be brought is outside the State, within six months from the date on which he next enters the State. More far-reaching is s 240(5)(c), which provides that proceedings can be commenced:

> '...at any time within 3 years from the date on which evidence that, in the opinion of the person by whom the proceedings are brought, is sufficient to justify the bringing of the proceedings comes to that person's knowledge.'

It is thought that this may have a significant impact on the numbers of prosecutions. Frequently, the suspected commission of offences under the Companies Acts will only come to light long after their commission following an independent investigation by a liquidator during the course of a winding up. Prosecutors are further assisted by CA 1990, s 240(5A), which provides that a certificate signed by or on behalf of the prosecutor as to the date on which the evidence referred to in s 240(5)(c) came to his knowledge, 'shall be *prima facie* evidence thereof'[90].

---

87 See para **[12.192]**.

88 See para **[12.021]**.

89 See Charleton, McDermott and Bolger, *Criminal Law* (1999), p 143.

90 This subsection goes on to provide that 'in any legal proceedings a document purporting to be a certificate issued for the purpose of this subsection and to be so signed shall be deemed to be so signed and shall be admitted as evidence without proof of the signature of the person purporting to sign the certificate'.

[12.037] There is no statutory limitation period on the prosecution of indictable offences under the Companies Acts[91]. It has been noted[92], however, that Irish law has always recognised that inherent in the rights conferred on a person being investigated in respect of a crime is the right to reasonable dispatch: in *Hogan v The President of the Circuit Court*[93] the Supreme Court prohibited a prosecution for fraud where there had been a delay in excess of ten years. Each case will, however, turn on its own facts. In *R v Thames Magistrates' Court; ex p Hogan*[94] it was held by Pill LJ (Garland J concurring), that the time limit in s 731(2) of the Companies Act 1985 (UK), for prosecuting offences that were capable of being tried summarily or on indictment, applied only to those that were *solely* summary offences; in respect of those capable of being prosecuted on indictment, no time limits applied.

(d) The venue for prosecution

[12.038] One of the difficulties previously encountered in the bringing of summary proceedings under the Companies Acts was that under the District Court Rules, proceedings have to be brought either in the court area where the accused resides or in the court area where the alleged offence was committed. The difficulties became manifest where it was not possible to identify the place where an act or omission occurred and practice was to issue proceedings against directors in the court area of their home addresses and in the court area of a company's registered office, leading to unnecessary duplication of work and a waste of court time[95]. This anomaly is cured by CA 1990, s 240A[96]. This provides:

> 'For the purposes of any provision of the Companies Acts which provides that the company and every officer of the company is guilty of an offence, summary proceedings against the company or an officer of the company may be brought, heard and determined either —
>
> (a) in the court area in which the offence charged or, if more than one offence is stated to have been committed, any one of the offences charged, is stated to have been committed,
>
> (b) in the court area in which the accused has been arrested,
>
> (c) in the court area in which the accused resides,
>
> (d) in the court area specified by order made pursuant to section 15 of the Courts Act, 1971, or
>
> (e) in the court area in which the registered office of the company is situated.'

It remains to be seen how this will operate in practice. If it is decided to centralise the hearing of summary prosecutions under the Companies Acts in one district one beneficial side-effect that might be expected would be the building-up of company law enforcement expertise in that court.

---

91 *B v DPP* [1997] 2 ILRM 118.

92 See Charleton, McDermott and Bolger, *Criminal Law* (1999), p 666.

93 *Hogan v The President of the Circuit Court* (21 June 1994, unreported), Supreme Court.

94 *R v Thames Magistrates' Court; ex p Hogan* [1997] TLR 633.

95 See the *Explanatory and Financial Memorandum to the Company Law Enforcement Bill* (2000), pp 28–29.

96 As inserted by CLEA 2001, s 105.

(e) Evidence to juries in trials for indictable offences

[12.039] Section 110(1) of CLEA 2001 provides that in a trial on indictment of an offence under the Companies Acts, the trial judge may order that copies of any or all of the following documents may be given to the jury 'in any form that the judge considers appropriate':

> '(a) any document admitted in evidence at the trial,
>
> (b) the transcript of the opening speeches of counsel,
>
> (c) any charts, diagrams, graphics, schedules or summaries of evidence produced at the trial,
>
> (d) the transcript of the whole or any part of the evidence given at the trial,
>
> (e) the transcript of the trial judge's charge to the jury,
>
> (f) any other document that in the opinion of the trial judge would be of assistance to the jury in its deliberations including, where appropriate, an affidavit by an accountant summarising, in a form which is likely to be comprehended by the jury, any transactions by the accused or other persons relevant to the offence.'

This extremely practical provision is intended to facilitate the comprehension of evidence of possibly complex and intricate commercial dealings by a jury composed of ordinary members of the public with no particular expertise in law, accounting or finance. To safeguard the rights of an accused, CLEA 2001, s 110(2) provides that if the prosecutor proposes to apply to the trial judge for an order that a document mentioned in s 110(1)(f) should be given to the jury, the prosecutor must give a copy of the document to the accused in advance of the trial and, on the hearing of the application, the trial judge shall take into account any representations made by or on behalf of the accused in relation to it. Moreover, where the trial judge has made an order that an affidavit by an accountant pursuant to s 110(1)(f) be given to the jury, the judge may 'with a view to further assisting the jury in its deliberations, require the accountant who prepared the affidavit to explain to the jury any relevant accounting procedures or principles'.

On-the-spot fines

[12.040] The McDowell Group recommended the introduction of on-the-spot fines for a select number of registration-type offences, such as the failure to file an annual return and the failure to file a liquidator's return[97]. Effect was given to this recommendation by CLEA 2001, s 66(1) whereby now, the Registrar can serve notice on a company or person in default requiring the payment of a particular sum in order to avoid the institution of proceedings. Section 66 goes further than seems to have been intended by the McDowell Group since it can be invoked by the Registrar in the case of *all* returns or documents required to be delivered, filed or made to the Registrar under the Companies Acts, and not the 'select number' as recommended. This notice will state that the person has failed to deliver, file or make a specified return or similar document to be registered under a specified section of the Companies Acts and that the person may within 21 days remedy

97 See *The Report of the Working Group on Company Law Compliance and Enforcement* (1998), para 3.21.

the default and make a prescribed payment to the Registrar. The notice must also specify that, where the person complies with the notice:

> '...a prosecution in respect of the person to whom the notice is delivered will not be instituted during the period specified in the notice, or, if the default is remedied and the payment specified in the notice is made during that period, at all[98].'

The hope is that this will avoid the institution of costly proceedings. Where a default has been remedied before the hearing of a prosecution in respect of the default, there must be a tendency to be lenient to the defaulter. Section 66(1) of CLEA 2001 is, therefore, a welcome addition to the Registrar of Companies' armoury since it is designed to achieve compliance, without recourse to the courts.

[12.041] The Director of Corporate Enforcement also has the power to impose on-the-spot fines, as an alternative to prosecuting for a summary offence. This power – which is virtually identical to that of the Registrar – is contained in CLEA 2001, s 109(1). This provides:

> 'Where the Director has reasonable grounds for believing that a person has committed an offence under the Companies Acts which is subject to summary prosecution, the Director may deliver to the person or, where the person believed to have committed the offence is a company, to an officer of the company, a notice in the prescribed form stating —
>
> (a) that the person or company is alleged to have committed that offence,
>
> (b) that the person to whom the notice is delivered may during a period of 21 days beginning on the date of the notice —
>
> (i) remedy as far as practicable to the satisfaction of the Director any default that constitutes the offence, and
>
> (ii) make to the Director a payment of a prescribed amount which shall be accompanied by the notice,
>
> and
>
> (c) that a prosecution of the person to whom the notice is delivered in respect of the alleged offence will not be instituted during the period satisfied in the notice or, if the default is remedied to the satisfaction of the Director and the payment specified in the notice is made during that period, at all.'

Section 109(2) of CLEA 2001 provides that when such a notice is given and the person makes the specified payment during the specified period, the Director may receive and receipt the payment (which shall not be recoverable by the person who made it) and, in such a case:

> 'A prosecution in respect of the alleged offence shall not be instituted in the period specified in the notice and, if the default is remedied to the satisfaction of the Director and the payment specified in the notice is made during that period, no prosecution in respect of the alleged offence shall be instituted at all.'

---

[98] The 'promise' not to prosecute contained in the section 66(1) notice is given legal effect by CLEA 2001, s 66(2)(c).

Again, as in the case of the Registrar's power to issue on-the-spot fines, the hope is that this will prove to be an effective and efficient means of ensuring compliance with the Companies Acts, without recourse to the courts.

[C] Enforcement and Compliance: Civil and Administrative Sanctions against Officers and Companies

[12.042] In this section the following civil and administrative sanctions in the enforcement and compliance with company law are considered:

1. Restriction of directors.
2. Disqualification of directors and others.
3. Striking companies off the register.
4. Injunctions to compel compliance with the Companies Acts 1963–2001.

These sanctions and remedies can operate to prevent wrongdoers from unencumbered participation as directors of companies, prevent them completely from acting as directors, deny corporate existence to wayward companies and compel, on pain of contempt of court, compliance with the Companies Acts 1963–2001.

Restriction of directors

[12.043] One of the most effective ways of punishing culpable directors of insolvent companies and of protecting the public from their future wrongdoing is to have them *restricted* in the future directorships, primarily by insisting that companies with which they become involved must be capitalised to a particular amount. *Restriction* was introduced into Irish law by CA 1990, Part VII, Chapter 1[99] as a new means of combating the so-called 'phoenix syndrome'. The phoenix syndrome is the situation where the controllers of a company that becomes insolvent by reason of their acts or omissions, walk away from their failed company (and especially its debts) and immediately re-establish themselves in a new company doing the same business, again availing of all the advantages of limited liability[100]. As Murphy J said in *Business Communications Ltd v Baxter and Parsons*[101], the restriction provisions in CA 1990, Part VII, Chapter 1:

> '...contains provisions of the utmost importance to the commercial community generally and in particular to those who have undertaken or propose to undertake the duties of a director of a company.'[102]

---

[99] See Linnane, 'Restrictions on and Disqualification of Directors' (1994) ILT 132; Farren, 'Restrictions on Directors of Insolvent Companies' (1997) Bar Law Review 349; Courtney, *Company Law Review 1995*, (1996), pp 21–33; Walker, 'Creditors' Rights to have Directors Restricted' (1998) 5 CLP 159; Garvey, 'Restricting Directors – Recent Case Law on Section 150 of the Companies Act 1990' (1998) 5 CLP 289

[100] See *Report of the Working Group on Company Law Compliance and Enforcement* (1998) (Pn 6697), pp 71–82

[101] *Business Communications Ltd v Baxter and Parsons* (21 July 1995, unreported), High Court (Murphy J).

[102] (21 July 1995, unreported), High Court at pp 4–5.

In *Re La Moselle Clothing Ltd and Rosegem Ltd*[103] Shanley J described the 'primary purpose' of CA 1990, s 150 as being:

> '...the protection of the public from persons who, by their conduct, have shown themselves unfit to hold the office of, and discharge the duties of, a director of a company and, in consequence, represent a danger to potential investors and traders dealing with such companies.'[104]

In this can be seen the real purpose of CA 1990, Part VII, Chapter 1, albeit that it is the protection of *traders*, as opposed to *investors*, with which the law is most concerned.

[12.044] The original Companies (No 2) Bill 1987 proposed a drastic solution to the problem of the phoenix syndrome, namely, the *automatic* restriction of all directors of all insolvent companies, without any limitation on the period of restriction unless the new company met certain requirements. As noted by the McDowell Group[105] the 'outrage over those engaged in the practice of the phoenix syndrome was, ultimately tempered by the realistic recognition that it is unjust to penalise "honest" business failure' and the automatic restrictions were ultimately dropped from the 1987 Bill. As enacted, CA 1990, s 150 requires an application to be brought to the High Court in order to have a director restricted and also excuses directors from the restriction regime where the court is satisfied, inter alia, that they have acted *honestly and responsibly*. Where application was brought, the remedy was effective, but in the period 1991–1995 there was a complete absence of applications being brought. The problem was that as initially drafted, s 150 did not specifically require any person to bring application to have a director restricted; it was, in effect, left up to individual liquidators of insolvent companies to decide whether or not to bother to bring application. Although following a practice direction made by Murphy J in 1994 which required all official liquidators of insolvent companies to make application under s 150, it was not until CLEA 2001 that the lacuna, identified in *Business Communications Ltd v Baxter and Parsons*[106], was finally filled. CLEA 2001 also gave the Director of Corporate Enforcement a central role in the bringing of applications to have directors of insolvent companies restricted. The law governing the restriction of directors in their directorships is treated here under the following headings:

(a) The mandatory nature of CA 1990, s 150 and the purpose of restriction orders;

(b) The consequences of an order under CA 1990, s 150;

(c) Persons liable to be restricted and insolvent companies;

(d) The duties of liquidators of insolvent companies and the Director's role;

(e) The locus standi of liquidators, receivers, creditors and the Director;

(f) The defence of acting 'honestly and responsibly';

---

[103] *Re La Moselle Clothing Ltd and Rosegem Ltd* [1998] 2 ILRM 345.

[104] *Re La Moselle Clothing Ltd and Rosegem Ltd* [1998] 2 ILRM 345 at 350–351.

[105] McDowell Group Report, para 6.4.

[106] *Business Communications Ltd v Baxter and Parsons* (21 July 1995, unreported), High Court (Murphy J).

(g) The defences of being a financial institution's or a venture capital company's nominee and the non-statutory defences of delay and estoppel;

(h) Post-order relief on just and equitable grounds;

(i) The enforcement of restriction orders.

(a) *The mandatory nature of CA 1990, s 150 and the purpose of restriction orders*

[12.045] Section 150(1) of CA 1990 provides:

> 'The court shall, unless it is satisfied as to any of the matters specified in subsection (2), declare that a person to whom this Chapter applies shall not, for a period of five years, be appointed or act in any way, whether directly or indirectly, as a director or secretary or be concerned or take part in the promotion or formation of any company unless it meets the requirements set out in subsection (3)…'

In the paragraphs that follow, consideration shall be given to those persons who are liable to be restricted[107], the defences specified in CA 1990, s 150(2)[108] and to the requirements which a company must meet, where a restricted person becomes 'involved' with it[109].

The making of a restriction order for a five-year period is mandatory where application is brought against the directors of an insolvent company and where the defences in s 150(2) do not apply. In the seminal decision of *Business Communications Ltd v Baxter and Parsons*[110], Murphy J observed:

> 'It is clear that Chapter I [of Part VII] of the Companies Act, 1990 contains provisions of the utmost importance to the commercial community generally and in particular to those who have undertaken or propose to undertake the duties of a director of a company. In appropriate circumstances the Chapter applies to every insolvent company which is being wound up, whether compulsorily or voluntarily, and – in consequence of s 154 aforesaid – to companies not being wound up but over which a receiver has been appointed. The next significant feature of the code created by Chapter I aforesaid is that the introductory words to s 150, that is to say, the phrase 'the court shall' are clearly mandatory and leave the Court with no discretion in those cases to which the Chapter applies unless the persons concerned establish that the case falls within one or other of the three exceptions set out in sub-section (2) of s 150. Again it is notable that the period of the restriction is a fixed period of five years and that, in the first instance at any rate[111], the court has no discretion to impose a lesser restriction.'[112]

Again in *Re Cavan Crystal Group Ltd*[113] Murphy J said that it was well accepted that:

---

[107] See para **[12.051]**.

[108] See para **[12.065]** *ff* and **[12.078]** *ff*.

[109] See para **[12.048]**.

[110] *Business Communications Ltd v Baxter and Parsons* (21 July 1995, unreported), High Court (Murphy J).

[111] This is a reference to CA 1990, s 152 which permits applications for relief to be brought subsequent to the making of a restriction order: see para **[12.081]**.

[112] (21 July 1995, unreported), High Court at pp 4–5.

[113] *Re Cavan Crystal Group Ltd* (26 April 1996, unreported), High Court (Murphy J).

'...this section is mandatory and that the court must impose the full statutory restriction unless the directors concerned discharge the onus of proof squarely imposed upon them as to any of the matters specified in subsection (2)'.[114]

[12.046] The mandatory nature of CA 1990, s 150 is in contrast to disqualification orders which are made at the discretion of the court[115]. In *Business Communications Ltd v Baxter and Parsons*[116], Murphy J recognised the justification for the distinction between these two sanctions for misfeasance, saying:

'Clearly, it is the comprehensive nature of a disqualification order which is seen as constituting an appropriately severe sentence for conduct which is manifestly more blameworthy than merely failing to exercise an appropriate degree of responsibility in relation to an insolvent company in liquidation of which the person was a director. Financially and commercially this is clearly a well-founded distinction. It is hardly unreasonable to require a person who was a director of a failed company in respect of which he committed no misconduct but for which he neglected to exercise an appropriate degree of responsibility from resuming such an office in another company, again with the privilege of limited liability except on condition that a stipulated and not excessive sum was provided for the paid-up capital thereof. The figure of £20,000[117] must represent a very modest sum as the capital for any commercial enterprise and a very limited obstacle to anyone wishing to engage in trade through the medium of a limited liability company. Indeed, it might not be unreasonable to suggest that every limited liability company should be required to have paid-up capital of at least that amount. It would seem, that the more serious penalty which the restraining order imposes is the stigma which attaches as a result of the making of the order and its filing in the Companies Office. In any event I would regard it as a far lesser penalty than that which may be imposed under s 160 of the 1990 Act and certainly would not elevate it to the status of s 33 of the 1990 Amendment Act – the reckless and fraudulent trading provisions – under which a director may be held personally responsible without limitation of liability for all the debts or other liabilities of the company and which Mr Justice Lynch in *Re Hefferon Kearns (No 2) Ltd* [1993] 3 IR 191 described as a "draconian measure".'[118]

Murphy J went on to quote with approval a passage from the decision of Henry LJ in the case of *Re Grayan Building Services Ltd*[119]. Although that case concerned disqualification

[114] (26 April 1996, unreported), High Court at pp 7–8 of the judgment. See also *Mehigan v Duignan* [1997] 1 ILRM 171 at 194 where Shanley J accepted that he had no discretion but to impose the five-year restriction since the respondent did not bring himself within any of the three exceptions in CA 1990, s 150(2).

[115] See para **[12.104]**.

[116] *Business Communications Ltd v Baxter and Parsons* (21 July 1995, unreported), High Court (Murphy J).

[117] Now €63,486.90 following the amendment effected by CLEA 2001, s 41(1).

[118] (21 July 1995, unreported), High Court at pp 13–15.

[119] *Re Grayan Building Services Ltd* [1995] 2 WLR 1 where Henry LJ said (at 15):

'The concept of limited liability and the sophistication of our corporate law offers great privileges and great opportunities for those who wish to trade under that regime. But the corporate environment carries with it the discipline that those who avail themselves of those privileges must accept the standards laid down and abide by the regulatory rules and disciplines in place to protect creditors and shareholders.

of directors under English law, Murphy J said that the general thrust of the passage he quoted was equally applicable to the restriction provisions under CA 1990, s 150 and to the standards of commercial practice demanded by our legislature.

[12.047] The five-year period of restriction commences whenever the court says it commences. This was established by O'Donovan J in *Duignan v Carway*[120], rejecting the respondent-directors' claims that the five-year period should commence from the date of the proceedings. It was recognised that to interpret CA 1990, s 150(1) in this manner might be to encourage respondent-directors to employ delaying tactics.

(b) The consequences of an order under CA 1990, s 150

[12.048] Restriction orders have consequences for two distinct legal entities: restricted persons and restricted companies. As far as the restricted person is concerned the effect of a section 150 order is a simple injunction: he is restrained, for a period of five years, from being appointed or from acting in any way, whether directly or indirectly, as a director or secretary and from being concerned or taking part in the promotion or formation of any company unless that company meets certain requirements. The consequences for a restricted company are more complicated. The requirements that must be met by any company with which a restricted person becomes involved are specified in CA 1990, s 150(3). This provides:

> '(a) the nominal value of the allotted share capital of the company shall—
>
> (i) in the case of a public limited company, be at least £250,000 [€317,434.52],
>
> (ii) in the case of any other company, be at least £50,000 [€63,486.90],
>
> (b) each allotted share to an aggregate amount not less than the amount referred to in subparagraph (i) or (ii) of paragraph (a), as the case may be, shall be fully paid up, including the whole or any premium thereon, and

---

[119] *(contd)* And, while some significant corporate failures will occur despite the directors exercising best managerial practice, in many, too many, cases there have been serious breaches of those rules and disciplines, in situations where the observance of them would or at least might have prevented or reduced the scale of the failure and consequent loss to creditors and investors. Reliable figures are hard to come by, but it seems that losses from corporate fraud and mismanagement have never been higher. At the same time the regulatory regime has never been more stringent – on paper even if not in practice. The parliamentary intention to improve managerial safeguard and standards for the long term good of employees, creditors and investors is clear. Those who fail to reach those standards and whose failure contributes to others losing money will often both be plausible and capable of inspiring initial trust, often later regretted. Those attributes may make them attractive witnesses. But as s 6 [of the Companies Directors Disqualification Act 1986 (UK)] makes clear, the Court's focus should be on their conduct, on the offence rather than the offender, the statutory corporate climate is stricter than it has ever been, and those enforcing it should reflect the fact that parliament has seen the need for higher standards. Where serious breaches have been shown, tribunals when deciding the question of fitness should give clear reasons why they reached the decision they did on that question. I could not find such reasons here'.

[120] *Duignan v Carway* (27 July 2000, unreported), High Court (O'Donovan J).

(c) each such allotted share and the whole of any premium thereon shall be paid for in cash[121].'

Where a restricted person becomes involved in another company (referred to here as a 'restricted company'), and the restricted company allots a share which *is not fully paid up*, with certain exceptions[122], the share shall be treated as if its nominal value together with the whole of any premium had been received, but the allottee shall be liable to pay the company in cash the full amount that should have been received plus interest, less the consideration actually paid[123]. Also, where a restricted company allots a share that is not fully paid for *in cash*, the allottee is liable to pay the company in cash an amount equal to its nominal value plus the whole of any premium and interest[124]. By reason of the application of the Companies (Amendment) Act 1983, s 26(4) ('C(A)A 1983') to CA 1990, s 156[125], any person – other than a bona fide purchaser for value without actual notice[126] of the requirements – who acquires shares that have not been fully paid up in the prescribed manner becomes jointly and severally liable with the original allottee to pay the foregoing amounts.

[12.049] Notwithstanding that a restricted company is a separate legal entity, the sins of its directors (who were directors of some insolvent company) will be visited upon it. This is in recognition of the fact that in most cases, the directors of failed companies will attempt to re-establish themselves in a new company; in these circumstances, no injustice is considered to be done to the restricted company. Not only is it subject to the capital restrictions seen above, but by CA 1990, s 155 there are additional fetters imposed on the restricted company. Accordingly, a restricted company cannot avail of:

— the exceptions to the prohibition in CA 1963, s 60 on a company providing financial assistance in connection with the purchase of shares, contained in CA 1963, s 60(2)–(11)[127]; or

---

121 As amended by CLEA 2001, s 41(1)(a) and (b) which increased the monetary amounts from £100,000 [€126,973.81] to £250,000 [€317,434.52] and from £20,000 [€25,394.76] to £50,000 [€63,486.90], respectively. Note, however, that by virtue of CLEA 2001, s 41(2)2001, these revised monetary amounts do not apply to companies which are 'restricted companies' by reason of a declaration made under CA 1990, s 150(1) *prior* to the commencement of CLEA 2001, s 41. It may be noted that primary legislation was not required to effect these changes since by CA 1990, s 158 the Minister for Enterprise, Trade and Employment has power to vary the amounts mentioned in CA 1990, s 150(3)(a).

122 The exceptions relate (a) to the allotment of a bonus share which is not fully paid up unless the allottee knew or ought to have known that the share was so allotted (CA 1990, s 156(3)); and (b) to shares allotted in pursuance of an employees' share scheme within the meaning of C(A)A 1983, s 2.

123 CA 1990, s 156(1). 'Interest' is payable at the appropriate rate within the meaning of the C(A)A 1983, s 2.

124 CA 1990, s 156(2).

125 CA 1990, s 156(6).

126 As to the meaning of which, see Chapter 11, *Statutory Regulation of Transactions Involving Directors and their Companies*, para **[11.100]** *ff.*

127 CA 1990, s 155(2): see Chapter 18, *The Maintenance of Capital*, at para **[18.041]** *ff.*

— the exceptions to the prohibition in CA 1990, s 31 on a company making loans, quasi-loans and entering into credit transactions, etc in favour of directors and persons connected with a director, contained in CA 1990, ss 32 and 37[128].

Moreover, the restrictions that apply to allotments of shares in PLCs, other than in cash, contained in C(A)A 1983, ss 32 to 36, also apply to the restricted company even if it is not a PLC[129]. Finally, before a restricted person accepts an appointment as a director or secretary in another company, he must, within 14 days of his appointment or so acting, notify that company that he is a restricted person[130]. This latter provision will prove inappropriate in many Irish private companies, since, far from it being the case that a restricted person will be 'head-hunted' by an innocent company looking for a director, it is quite likely that it will be the restricted director himself who will form the company which will, by his involvement, thereby become a restricted company. Although in many cases inappropriate, this protection for restricted companies is a necessary safeguard to prevent the sins of what may be a mere employee, being visited on a company, the management of which may have a pristine compliance record. Although by virtue of CA 1990, s 157(1), the High Court can, if it deems it just and equitable to do so, grant relief to a restricted company in respect of any act or omission which contravenes the Companies Acts, but which would not have but for the provisions of s 155 eg providing financial assistance in connection with an own share purchase in reliance upon the exceptions contained in CA 1963, s 60(2)–(11). The court's ability to grant relief is, however, confined to cases where the company has *not* been put on notice by the restricted person that he is a restricted person as required by CA 1990, s 155(5)[131].

[12.050] It should also be noted that by CA 1990, s 153 the Registrar of Companies is obliged to keep a register of restricted persons who are notified to him by the court registrars and examiner, who were prescribed as the persons responsible for informing the Registrar[132]. Section 150(4) of CA 1990 obliges such prescribed officers of court to cause the Registrar to be furnished with the prescribed particulars to enable him keep the register.

(c) Persons liable to be restricted and insolvent companies

[12.051] Section 149 of CA 1990 provides that Chapter 1 of Part VII applies to any person who was either a director[133] or a shadow director[134] of an insolvent company at the date of, or within 12 months prior to, the commencement of its winding-up. Section 149 is rather tortuously drafted and rather than refer to an 'insolvent company', reference is made to a

128 CA 1990, s 155(4): see Chapter 11, *Statutory Regulation of Transactions Involving Directors and their Companies*, at para **[11.034]** *ff.*

129 CA 1990, s 155(3).

130 CA 1990, s 150(5).

131 CA 1990, s 157(2).

132 Companies Act 1990 (Parts IV and VII) Regulations, (SI 1991/209).

133 CA 1990, s 149(2).

134 CA 1990, s 149(5).

company to which Chapter 1 applies: by s 149(1), Chapter 1 is expressed to apply to any company[135] if –

— at the date of the commencement of its winding up (or receivership) it is proved to the court, or,

— during the course of the winding up the liquidator of the company certifies, or it is otherwise proved to the court,

— that the company is *unable to pay its debts*, ie that the company is insolvent[136].

Only the directors of insolvent companies in existence at the time of the commencement of CA 1990, s 150 (ie 1 August 1991) can be restricted as the legislation is not retrospective. However, in *Re Dunleckney Ltd*[137] it was held that the directors of a company that had been struck off and dissolved, but was subsequently reinstated after the commencement of s 150, were susceptible to being made the subject of a restriction order.

[12.052] Directors and shadow directors are expressly mentioned as possible respondents. 'Persons occupying the position of director by whatever name called' or *de facto* directors are also liable to be restricted, since such persons are by CA 1963, s 2(1) included in the definition of 'director'. The meanings of 'director' (both de facto and de jure) and 'shadow director' have been considered in Chapter 8[138]. It may be noted, however, that in *Re Vehicle Imports Ltd*[139] Roderick Murphy J made an order restricting a person whom it was claimed was a shadow director in circumstances where prima facie evidence as to his status as such had not been rebutted. So too in *Re Gasco Ltd*[140] McCracken J held that a person was liable to be restricted where there was evidence that he controlled the management of the company, was signatory to the company's cheques and when the only two directors of the company resigned, he had chosen not to appoint new directors but instead employed two persons to run the company. McCracken J held that there was 'no doubt' but that this person effectively ran the company on his own and 'in these circumstances, he was clearly a shadow director and therefore his position falls to be considered under s 150'[141]. But is it that clear? It is thought that in circumstances where there are no directors and a person who is not a formally appointed director directs the operations of a company, he is not and cannot be a shadow director and is instead a de facto director[142]. It is thought that the decision in *Re Lynrowan Enterprises Ltd*[143], which

[135] 'Company' in this context has a wider meaning than the definition in CA 1963, s 2(1), and by CA 1990, s 149(4) is deemed to include a company within the meaning of CA 1963, s 351 ie foreign or overseas companies that establish a place of business in Ireland.

[136] A company is unable to pay its debts when the provisions of CA 1963, s 214 are met: CA 1990, s 149(1).

[137] (18 February 1999, unreported), High Court (Carroll J).

[138] At paras **[8.035]** *ff* and **[8.058]** *ff*, respectively.

[139] (23 November 2000, unreported), High Court (Murphy J).

[140] *Re Gasco Ltd* (5 February 2001, unreported), High Court (McCracken J).

[141] (5 February 2001, unreported), High Court at p 4.

[142] See, generally, Chapter 8, *Corporate Governance: Management by the Directors*, at para **[8.053]** *ff*.

[143] *Re Lynrowan Enterprises Ltd* (31 July 2002, unreported), High Court (O'Neil J).

found that s 150(1) is available against de facto directors is to be preferred where the respondent is clearly not a shadow director. There, O'Neill J said:

> 'I am of opinion that a person although not validly appointed a director of a company may nonetheless be said to be a de facto director and thus deemed to be a "director" within the meaning of s 21(1) of the Companies Act 1963 and thus amenable to the restriction contained in s 150 of the Companies Act 1990, in the following circumstances:
>
> 1. Where there is clear evidence that that person has been either the sole person directing affairs of the company or
> 2. Is directing the affairs of the company with other equally lacking in valid appointment or
> 3. Where there were other validly appointed directors that he was acting on an equal or more influential footing with the true directors in directing the affairs of the company.
> 4. In the absence of clear evidence of the foregoing and when there is evidence that the role of the person in question is explicable by the exercise of a role other than director, the person in question should not be made amenable to the section 150 restriction.
> 5. Where the object of the section is the protection of the public from dishonest or irresponsible persons the absence of a valid appointment should not permit an escape from the restriction in section 150. It would be nonsensical if a person who had been validly appointed a director was treated differently to someone who lacked valid appointment but nevertheless assumed in all other respects the role of director. I would agree that 'liability cannot sensibly depend upon the validity of the defendant's appointment'.
> 6. In the light of all the foregoing then in my view the Companies Acts 1963 to 1990 recognise and embrace in the provision of s 2(1) of the Act of 1963 and s 150 of the Act of 1990, the concept of "de facto director".'

O'Neill J went on to find that one of the respondents in the application for a restriction order was a de facto director of the company, who had 'virtually complete control over the affairs of the company'.

[12.053] All persons who are directors at the date of the commencement of a company's winding up (or receivership)[144] may be restricted, but it is important to remember that not every past director is liable to be restricted. Only persons who were directors within the 12 months prior to the commencement of the winding up can be restricted. This point was noted in *Re Cavan Crystal Group Ltd*[145] where Murphy J held that one of the respondents in that case was not liable to be restricted because he had resigned as a director more than 12 months prior to the commencement of the receivership. It may also be noted that the fact that the director's resignation had not been notified to the CRO was found to be irrelevant[146]. In *Re Gasco Ltd*[147] McCracken J said that he thought it was:

---

[144] CA 1990, s 154 also applies s 150 to receiverships, 'with the necessary modifications': see para **[12.061]**.

[145] *Re Cavan Crystal Group Ltd* (26 April 1996, unreported), High Court (Murphy J).

[146] In *Re Outdoor Advertising Services Ltd* (28 January 1997, unreported), High Court (Costello J) it was held that the court was not required to make an order against a person who had ceased to act as a de facto director about nine months before the liquidation; to the extent that this suggests that a de facto director cannot be restricted it is thought to be incorrect.

[147] *Re Gasco Ltd* (5 February 2001, unreported), High Court (McCracken J).

> '... quite significant that no restrictions can attach to somebody who ceased to be a director of the company more than twelve months before the winding up. This seems to me to indicate that the primary aim of s 150 is to deal with directors who have behaved irresponsibly or dishonestly during the last twelve months of the life of the company, and that the actions of a director who is subject to s 150 are to be looked at primarily in the light of his actions during that period.'[148]

[12.054] The certificate of a liquidator or receiver that a company is unable to pay its debts (within the meaning of CA 1963, s 214)[149] is capable of being challenged and does not give rise to an irrebuttable presumption of insolvency. This was established in *Carway v The Attorney General*[150] where the plaintiff (who was a respondent in a section 150 application) claimed that CA 1990, s 149(1)(b) was unconstitutional on the basis that it precluded him from disproving the liquidator's certificate as to insolvency[151]. Carroll J held:

> 'In this case, there is no provision that the certificate is to be conclusive. It seems to me that the purpose of s 149 is to identify companies and persons to which Chapter 1 of Part VII applies. Section 149(1) applies to any company in liquidation that is unable to pay its debts within the meaning of s 214 of the Companies Act 1963. There are two categories, those which at the date of the commencement of the winding up are proved to the Court to be unable to pay their debts and, secondly, those which during the course of the winding up are certified by the liquidator to be unable to pay their debts or this fact is otherwise proved to the Court. It seems to me there is no basis for accepting the plaintiff's argument that the section must be construed as if the words "which certificate shall be irrebuttable" or words to that effect, were added after the word "certifies". It is straining the language of the section to do so. The section merely requires the certificate by the liquidator in order to trigger off the application of Chapter 1 of Part VII and the necessity for the court to be satisfied under s 150 that the directors concerned acted honestly and responsibly. I consider that the principle enunciated in *Re Haughey* [1971] IR 217 applies. In that case the Supreme Court held the certificate of the committee of Public Accounts of Dáil Éireann was a preliminary step to the commencement of a full trial of a criminal offence in the High Court. Since the certificate is a preliminary step, there is nothing in the section which would prevent a director from raising any issue in relation to the insolvency of the company or adducing any evidence in order to satisfy the Court that he/she acted "honestly and responsibly in relation to the conduct of the affairs of the company". In my opinion, there is nothing in the section which warrants the interpretation that the certificate is to be conclusive evidence of insolvency'.[152]

Accordingly, although CA 1990, s 149(1)(b) permits an application to go forward to the High Court, it is open to a director-respondent who believes that the company is not insolvent to challenge the liquidator's certificate. In such a case, the effect of s 149(1)(b) is to put an onus on a director to disprove the company's insolvency. It is thought that such a challenge may be more likely where a receiver purports to certify insolvency than where a liquidator does so.

---

148 (5 February 2001, unreported), High Court at p 7.

149 See Chapter 25, *Winding Up of Companies*, para **[25.062]**.

150 *Carway v The Attorney General* [1996] 3 IR 300, [1997] 1 ILRM 110.

151 Relying on *Maher v The Attorney General* [1973] IR 140 and *The State (McEldowney) v Kelleher* [1983] IR 289.

152 [1996] 3 IR 300 at 305–306.

(d) The duties of liquidators of insolvent companies and the Director's role

[12.055] By virtue of CLEA 2001, s 56, the liquidators of all *insolvent companies* are obliged to bring application under CA 1990, s 150(1) unless directed otherwise by the Director of Corporate Enforcement. This measure was necessary to address the deficiencies in CA 1990, as identified by Murphy J in *Business Communications Ltd v Baxter and Parsons*[153]. The basic problem with CA 1990 was that it did not expressly require anyone (whether liquidator, receiver or other) to bring an application under CA 1990, s 150(1) to have a director restricted. The dearth in applications under s 150(1) from its commencement in 1991 until 1994[154] was clearly influential in the Gallagher Company Law Review Group's implicit conclusion that s 150 was simply not working and that group's consequent focus on bolstering disqualification provisions. During the course of 1994 Francis Murphy J issued a practice direction to official liquidators (the only liquidators under the supervision of the court), the effect of which was to direct them to bring application under CA 1990, s 150(1) against the directors of the companies they were winding up. In *Business Communications Ltd v Baxter and Parsons*[155] Murphy J said of the original provisions on restriction:

> 'A particularly surprising feature of the novel provisions is that neither the legislation nor any rules made thereto imposes a duty on any party or person to bring a case before the court so that it can exercise the mandatory duty imposed upon it. In windings-up by the court this lacuna has been overcome by the court on further consideration of the order for liquidation directing the official liquidator to bring the appropriate application on notice to persons appearing to be directors thereof. In the case of voluntary liquidations the court does not have either the responsibility or the machinery for giving comparable directions. It may be that voluntary liquidators and receivers are not sufficiently conscious of the provisions of Chapter 1 of Part VII of the 1990 Act or else they do not see it as their function to bring relevant cases before the Court. Perhaps it will be necessary for the legislature to consider the provision of a particular sanction to ensure that the many cases which have obviously arisen since August 1991 are duly pursued. If not, there would be an apparent injustice to the directors of insolvent companies wound up by the court as against those wound up voluntarily.'[156]

Subsequently, Shanley J observed in La Moselle Clothing Ltd and Rosegem Ltd v Soualhi[157] that the court's direction in official windings up resulted in applications being brought in almost all such cases[158]. However, Shanley J went on to note that the injustice, envisaged by Murphy J, still remained unredressed and he noted that only a handful of

---

153 *Business Communications Ltd v Baxter and Parsons* (21 July 1995, unreported), High Court (Murphy J).

154 An inspection of the register would have disclosed that only 11 persons had been restricted: see *Report of the Working Group on Company Law Compliance and Enforcement*, (1998) Government Publications (Pn 6697) at para 6.13.

155 *Business Communications Ltd v Baxter and Parsons* (21 July 1995, unreported), High Court (Murphy J).

156 (21 July 1995, unreported), High Court at pp 5, 6.

157 *Re La Moselle Clothing Ltd and Rosegem Ltd* [1998] 2 ILRM 345.

158 As at 31 December 1997 there were 108 persons restricted: *Companies Report, 1997*, p 41; and as at 31 December 1999 there were 128 persons restricted: *Companies Report, 1999*, p 45.

cases of insolvent companies in receivership or creditors' voluntary liquidation had came before the courts. On the recommendations of the McDowell Group, CLEA 2001 redressed the injustice, concluding that 'insolvency, and not the legal route by which a company is wound up, should determine whether the directors should be the subject of sanctions.'[159]

[12.056] Section 56 of CLEA 2001 provides:

> '(1) A liquidator of an insolvent company shall, within 6 months after his or her appointment or the commencement of this section, whichever is the later, and at intervals as required by the Director thereafter, provide to the Director a report in the prescribed form.
>
> (2) A liquidator of an insolvent company shall, not earlier than 3 months nor later than 5 months (or such later time as the court may allow and advises the Director) after the date on which he or she has provided to the Director a report under subsection (1), apply to the court for the restriction under s 150 of the Act of 1990 of each of the directors of the company, unless the Director has relieved the liquidator of the obligation to make such an application.
>
> (3) A liquidator who fails to comply with subsection (1) or (2) is guilty of an offence.'

The consequence of s 56 is that there is now an express statutory duty on liquidators of *insolvent companies* (whether in official liquidation or in creditors' voluntary liquidation):

- to report to the Director of Corporate Enforcement (the 'Director') in the prescribed form within six months of their appointment[160];
- not to bring a s 150 application within the three months immediately following their report; and
- to bring application after the expiry of that three month period but before the expiry of five months following his initial report, unless the Director relieves him of the obligation to bring application under s 150.

The effect is to impose a positive obligation on liquidators of insolvent companies to make application under s 150 whilst simultaneously giving the Director a 'dead man's brake'. The reasoning behind this section is that the 'private' (ie not publicly sponsored) applications by official liquidators, was perceived to operate very effectively and efficiently and it was sought not to interfere with something that was working. The reason for allowing the Director to relieve liquidators from the obligation to bring a s 150 application is:

- to avoid inappropriate applications being forced into court (eg worker-directors; aged relations, persuaded to assume the role of director; celebrity non-executive directors who accepted the office for charitable or altruistic reasons)[161]; and
- to facilitate the Director making a decision as to whether application for a disqualification order is more appropriate.

Section 56 was commenced[162] on 1 June 2002 insofar as it applies to liquidators who were

---

[159] *McDowell Group's Report*, para 6.22.

[160] Or the commencement of CLEA 2001, so that it affects then *existing* liquidators.

[161] See *McDowell Group's* report, para 6.23.

[162] Company Law Enforcement Act 2001 (Winding Up and Insolvency Provisions) (Commencement) Order 2002 (SI 2002/263).

— appointed on or after 1 June 2002, or

— appointed on or after 1 July 2001 and before 1 June 2002 where, in respect of the company to which the liquidator was appointed, an order has not been made under CA 1963, s 249(1) or the meetings required under CA 1963, s 273(1) have not been held.

The form of the liquidator's report has been prescribed by statutory instrument[163] and is considered further in Chapter 26, *Liquidators.*[164]

[12.057] One of the consequences that flows from CA 1990, s 150 being mandatory in nature is that a liquidator would not have the authority to agree to refrain from bringing an application under CA 1990, s 150 for any reason, but particularly in return for a company director's undertaking to act as if an order had been made. The question of undertakings in lieu of disqualification orders has arisen in the UK and is noted below[165]. Authority for the proposition that liquidators cannot agree to refrain from bringing s 150 applications is *Re Verit Hotel and Leisure (Ireland) Ltd; Duignan v Carway*[166]. In that case it was claimed that the liquidator was *estopped* from bringing the s 150 application because it was closely interrelated to other proceedings that had been settled. Rejecting this contention, McCracken J held:

> '...there can be no estoppel in the present case because of the nature of the s 150 proceedings…the proceedings are mandatory, and the section provides that the court must be satisfied as to certain matters. That being so, there can be no question of such proceedings being settled, and there would have been no power in the liquidator to undertake as part of an overall settlement not to pursue the s 150 proceedings...There can be no question of the liquidator being estopped, as s 150 raises an issue between the directors and the courts and not between the directors and the liquidator.'

Although liquidators have no authority to agree not to make a s 150 application, it should be noted that CLEA 2001, s 56 confers statutory power on the Director to relieve liquidators from bringing application. It is thought that there would be no statutory bar to the Director accepting an undertaking from a director of an insolvent company to act or refrain from acting in a particular manner as a condition for the Director relieving a liquidator from bringing application under s 150.

[12.058] Section 151(1) of CA 1990 imposes a duty on the liquidator of an insolvent company to inform the court of his opinion that the interests of any other company or its creditors may be placed in jeopardy by reason of the fact that a restricted person is 'involved'[167] in it. This duty also applies to receivers: CA 1990, s 154. Breach of this duty is an offence, liable to fine[168]. Upon receipt of a liquidator's or receiver's report to this effect, the court is empowered to make whatever order it sees fit.

---

163 Company Law Enforcement Act 2001 (Section 56) Regulations 2002 (SI 2002/324).

164 See paras **[26.023]**, **[26.024]**.

165 See para **[12.101]**.

166 *Re Verit Hotel and Leisure (Ireland) Ltd; Duignan v Carway* (23 January 2002, unreported), High Court (McCracken J).

167 By 'involved' is meant: 'is appointed or is acting in any way, whether directly or indirectly, as a director or is concerned or is taking part in the promotion or formation of such other company': s 151(2).

168 CA 1990, s 151(3).

[12.059] Where a restricted person is or becomes a director of a company which commences to be wound up within five years of the commencement of the winding up of the originally insolvent company, and it appears to the liquidator that it is insolvent, the liquidator is obliged[169] to report those matters to the court and on receiving the liquidator's report, the court can if it considers proper to do so, make a disqualification order against that person for such period as it thinks fit[170]. Disqualification orders are considered below[171].

[12.060] Practice has been to bring s 150 applications by way of notice of motion. In *Re Verit Hotel and Leisure (Ireland) Ltd; Duignan v Carway*[172], it was acknowledged by McCracken J that the Rules of the Superior Courts 1986 do not provide for bringing application under s 150 by way of notice of motion. Although in that matter it was contended that the liquidator's application ought, instead, to have been brought by way of a plenary summons, this was rejected on the grounds that, in that case, the respondent-directors had up until then accepted the procedures followed by the liquidator and could not subsequently raise a procedural objection.

(e) The locus standi of liquidators, receivers, creditors and the Director

[12.061] Whereas the liquidators of insolvent companies have a legal duty (unless relieved by the Director) to bring application under CA 1990, s 150(1), other persons have locus standi to bring application without having an obligation to do so. In the first place, CA 1990, Part VII, Chapter 1 envisages that applications may be brought by receivers of insolvent companies. Section 154 of CA 1990 provides:

> 'Where a receiver of the property of the company is appointed, the provisions of this Chapter shall, with the necessary modifications, apply as if the reference therein to the liquidator and to winding up were construed as references to the receiver and to the receivership.'

As Murphy J said in *Re Cavan Crystal Group Ltd*[173] 'there is no doubt but that Chapter 1 of Part VII of the Companies Act 1990...applies or may apply to a company over which a receiver has been appointed'[174]. It should be noted, however, that unlike liquidators, receivers are not subject to any obligation to report to the Director.

[12.062] By virtue of CA 1990, s 150(4A)[175] there is now express authority for liquidators, receivers and the Director to make application for a restriction order, thereby remedying the deficiency in the original CA 1990, highlighted by Shanley J in *Re Steamline Ltd*[176]. In that case, in holding that the creditors of an insolvent company could bring application under s 150(1), he said:

---

169 On pain of fine: CA 1990, s 161(6).

170 CA 1990, s 161(5).

171 See para **[12.090]**.

172 *Re Verit Hotel and Leisure (Ireland) Ltd; Duignan v Carway* (23 January 2002, unreported), High Court (McCracken J).

173 *Re Cavan Crystal Group Ltd* (26 April 1996, unreported), High Court (Murphy J).

174 (26 April 1996, unreported), High Court at p 2.

175 As inserted by CLEA 2001, s 41(1)(c).

176 *Re Steamline Ltd* [2001] 1 IR 103. See, generally, Walker, 'Creditors' Rights to have Directors Restricted – A New Development' (1998) CLP 159.

> 'All enactments should be given a purposive construction: that is, a construction which promotes the remedy the Oireachtas has provided to cure a particular mischief. Armed with such a canon of construction, this Court approaches Part VII of the 1990 Act noting that the legislature has expressly provided a particular restriction for particular types of conduct; it is a restriction to be imposed by the Court, but which cannot realistically be imposed in the absence of a procedure whereby applications for such a restriction are made to the Court by parties with an interest in making such an application. I believe that the Court ought to construe s 150(1) in such a way as to promote, rather than restrict, the remedy provided for in that subsection: while the grounds for the disqualification of a director and other officers of a company differ from the grounds warranting restriction of a director, nonetheless, it does appear to me that the persons authorised by s 160(4)(b) to bring an application for a disqualification order are, broadly, the same category of persons who would have an interest in seeking an order for the restriction of a director. In promoting, rather than restricting, the remedy provided for in s 150(1), this court ought, in my view, construe the mandatory power provided therein as exercisable on the application of any one of the class of persons identified in s 160(4)(b) of the 1990 Act being persons identified by the legislature as having an interest in moving an application for a disqualification order and whom the legislature would have intended to have a like interest in relation to applications to restrict directors. Accordingly, in my view, Musgrave Ltd, as a creditor of Steamline Ltd is entitled to maintain this application.'[177]

Since the reasoning of Shanley J no longer holds true – ie the legislature *has now* specified who can bring application under s 150 – it is thought most probable that the effect of s 150(4A) is to reverse *Re Steamline Ltd* with the effect that creditors no longer have standing to bring application under s 150. In view of the duty imposed upon the liquidators of all insolvent companies and the role of the Director, it is thought that the circumstances in which aggrieved creditors would have felt inclined to bring their own application to have the directors of an insolvent company restricted, would, in any event, have been rare.

[12.063] Where a company is not being wound up but is insolvent, CA 1990, s 251(2A) (as amended by CLEA 2001, s 54) can be invoked by the Director to bring application for the restriction of a director of such an insolvent company. As to the conditions when s 251 can be invoked, see Chapter 10[178].

[12.064] As regards the costs of a restriction application, CA 1990, s 150(4A) (as inserted by CLEA 2001, s 41(c)) provides that the court, in hearing an application for a declaration under s 150(1) brought by the Director, a liquidator or a receiver, 'may order that the directors against whom the declaration is made shall bear the costs of the application and any costs incurred by the applicant in investigating the matter'. Even before CLEA 2001, the Court would have exercised its discretion in this regard: so in *Re Cavan Crystal Group Ltd*[179], although Murphy J held that the directors there had acted honestly and responsibly, he ordered that each party was to bear his own costs. In *Re Century Communications Ltd*[180] Carroll J found that nine directors – who included a number of celebrities, such as Terry Wogan and Chris de Burgh – had acted honestly and responsibly in relation to the collapse

177 [2001] 1 IR 103 at 105–106.

178 At para **[10.121]** *ff*.

179 *Re Cavan Crystal Group Ltd* (26 April 1996, unreported), High Court (Murphy J).

180 *Re Century Communications Ltd*, an application reported in (1996) The Irish Times, 12 October (Carroll J).

of Century Radio, but according to the newspaper report it was the liquidator's duty to bring application under s 150 and that each of the directors present should contribute £250 plus VAT to the liquidator's costs. At a later hearing[181] necessitated by Mr Wogan's failure to file an affidavit at the earlier hearing, Carroll J found that he too had acted honestly and responsibly; however, because of the delay in producing the affidavit, Carroll J is reported as having ordered that he should pay more than the other directors towards the liquidator's costs and he was ordered to pay £500 plus VAT. The effect of s 150(4B) is to reinforce the court's discretion in such matters.

(f) The defence of acting 'honestly and responsibly'

[12.065] Much – if not most – of the voluminous judicial interpretation and musings on CA 1990, s 150 has concerned the defence of having acted 'honestly and responsibly'. The basis of this defence is s 150(2)(a) which provides that one of the matters which the court can take into consideration in deciding whether or not to impose the otherwise mandatory restriction order is:

> '...that the director acted honestly and responsibly in relation to the conduct of the affairs of the company and there is no reason why it is just and equitable for restrictions to apply.'

This defence is obviously intended to save honest and responsible directors from being restricted where, through no fault of theirs, a company goes into insolvent liquidation. It was thought[182] that the use of the words 'honestly and responsibly' was, in the light of *Re Hefferon Kearns Ltd (No 2)*[183] a quasi-subjective defence; this has proven to be incorrect and it is now clear that directors' behaviour is measured against an objective standard. Moreover, it is clear that the onus is on the respondents to establish that they acted honestly and responsibly. As Murphy J said in *Business Communications Ltd v Baxter and Parsons*[184]:

> '…it does seem that the most important feature of the legislature is that it effectively imposes a burden on the directors to establish that the insolvency occurred in circumstances in which no blame attaches to them as a result of either dishonesty or irresponsibility. In this respect the legislation differs from the very numerous other provisions contained in the Companies Acts which create various criminal and civil wrongs or remedies. These other provisions generally entail the expenditure of considerable sums of money in relation to matters on which the moving party rarely has direct or adequate evidence and the proceedings are, in the nature of things, brought against persons who being associated with an insolvent company may well be impecunious themselves. Commercial history in this country shows that this wide range of remedies, whether criminal or civil, are rarely invoked and even less frequently successful'.[185]

[12.066] The considerable case law of the High Court and Supreme Court demonstrate that a number of distinct, but obviously related, matters consistently arise in the honest and

[181] Reported in (1997) The Irish Times, 15 January (Carroll J).

[182] In the first edition of this book, *The Law of Private Companies* (1994), para [7.065].

[183] *Re Hefferon Kearns Ltd (No 2)* [1993] 3 IR 191. See generally, Chapter 8, *Duties of Directors and Other Officers*, para **[10.085]** *ff*.

[184] *Business Communications Ltd v Baxter and Parsons* (21 July 1995, unreported), High Court (Murphy J).

[185] (21 July 1995, unreported), High Court at p 18.

responsible defence. In *Re La Moselle Clothing Ltd and Rosegem Ltd*[186] Shanley J said, in interpreting CA 1990, s 150(2)(a) that it was clear that there are three hurdles that a director, seeking to be exonerated, has to surmount:

> '(a) He must establish that he has acted honestly in relation to the affairs of the company.
>
> (b) He must establish that he has acted responsibly in relation to the affairs of the company.
>
> (c) He must satisfy the Court that there is no other reason why it would be just and equitable that he should be subject to the restrictions imposed by the section.'[187]

(i) Acting honestly

[12.067] As shall be considered below, judicial comment on whether respondent directors of insolvent companies have acted honestly and responsibly has tended to focus, almost exclusively, on whether they acted responsibly. Whether this is because in cases involving blatant dishonesty by directors, the courts have not considered it necessary to examine, in a written judgment, their actions or because liquidators' prefer to prove irresponsibility rather than dishonesty remains to be seen. One case in which it was found that the directors had acted dishonestly was *Re Outdoor Advertising Services Ltd*[188]. There, Costello J held that two of the respondent directors had not acted honestly as they had consciously and deliberately sought to benefit themselves personally and two companies owned by them, at the expense of the insolvent company's creditors[189].

(ii) Acting responsibly: the test adopted by the Supreme Court

[12.068] The seminal test for acting 'responsibly' was first promulgated by Shanley J in *Re La Moselle Clothing Ltd and Rosegem Ltd*[190] when he set out a five-fold test:

> 'It seems to me that in determining the "responsibility" of a director for the purposes of s 150(2)(a) the court should have regard to:
>
> (a) The extent to which the director has or has not complied with any obligation imposed on him by the Companies Acts.
>
> (b) The extent to which his conduct could be regarded as so incompetent as to amount to irresponsibility.
>
> (c) The extent of the directors' responsibility for the insolvency of the company.
>
> (d) The extent of the directors' responsibility for the net deficiency in the assets of the company disclosed at the date of the winding up or thereafter.
>
> (e) The extent to which the director, in his conduct of the affairs of the company, has displayed a lack of commercial probity or want of proper standards.'[191]

In that case the facts were that La Moselle and Rosegem were incorporated in 1984 and 1987 respectively, and Mr Soualhi owned 99% of the issued shares in La Moselle and was beneficial owner of Rosegem, also being a director of both. La Moselle was a wholesaler

186 *Re La Moselle Clothing Ltd and Rosegem Ltd* [1998] 2 ILRM 345.

187 [1998] 2 ILRM 345 at 351.

188 *Re Outdoor Advertising Services Ltd* (28 January 1997, unreported), High Court (Costello J).

189 (28 January 1997, unreported), High Court at p 11.

190 *Re La Moselle Clothing Ltd and Rosegem Ltd* [1998] 2 ILRM 345.

191 [1998] 2 ILRM 345 at 352.

of ladies' and children's clothing and some 65% of its sales were to retail companies owned and controlled by Soualhi. Rosegem was one such company, which operated a retail shop in Dublin that it rented from An Post. La Moselle financed the purchase of stock by entering into an agreement with a finance house called Cambridge Confirming Ltd ('CCL') which, in consideration for a fee/interest, discharged La Moselle's monthly liabilities on the understanding that all of La Moselle's liabilities to CCL were discharged at each year end. This facilitated La Moselle's cash flow in the two seasons in the clothing industry. Initially, in 1989, the facility was £250,000 per season, but in 1993 this was reduced to £165,000 per season. As a result Soualhi claimed that he had to close two retail shops in Galway and Limerick. Upon the facility being reduced, in June 1993 it was also agreed that La Moselle would clear all of its liabilities to CCL by 15 October 1993; CCL would issue a cheque for £20,000 to La Moselle on 1 August 1993 and it in turn would issue a cheque payable to CCL for £50,000 on 31 July 1993. Soualhi stopped the La Moselle cheque, claiming this was because CCL had refused to honour its agreement to pay La Moselle £20,000. A further La Moselle cheque dated 31 August 1993 was also stopped and La Moselle did not clear its indebtedness to CCL by 15 October as per the agreement. A further agreement was entered into but the indebtedness was still not discharged and in November 1994 CCL presented a petition in respect of some £219,000 owed to it and consequent upon that, a winding-up order was made in March 1995. La Moselle had ceased trading in November 1994 and Rosegem ceased in September 1994. Soualhi's statement of affairs for La Moselle disclosed gross assets (including a claim for £650,000 against CCL) of £695,075 and gross liabilities of £487,891. Rosegem had no assets and had liabilities of over £48,000.

[12.069] The liquidator of La Moselle and Rosegem claimed that La Moselle continued to trade and to supply Rosegem when Soualhi knew both were insolvent and the liquidator sought to establish that Soualhi had acted 'irresponsibly, if not dishonestly'.[192] The liquidator pointed to the following matters in support of this: no effort had been made to stop trading or wind up Rosegem when it was clearly insolvent; the unsecured creditors of La Moselle did not include any trade suppliers and it was argued Mr Soualhi had organised his affairs so that he could secure payment of suppliers at the expense of the Revenue and other creditors such as his landlords and Dublin Corporation; La Moselle wrote off debts to other companies owned by Soualhi in the sum of over £476,000; the liquidator had extreme difficulty in obtaining the books and records of both companies and that Soualhi had a cavalier attitude to the books and records of Rosegem; credit card statements disclosed payments of just under £100,000 of which over £35,000 were in respect of payments to restaurants and night clubs which had been described as 'motor and travel expenses'; substantial sums had been drawn from Rosegem and La Moselle without provision for tax being made; in a period when an analysis of cash flow disclosed a deficit of £21,000 Soualhi had paid himself a salary of some £106,800; an analysis of La Moselle's current account and deposit accounts indicated that the reason why its cheque for £50,000 to CCL had been stopped was because there were no funds to meet it.

192 [1998] 2 ILRM 345 at 355.

Soualhi disputed these matters[193] but Shanley J found his evidence unconvincing. Shanley J did not accept that Soualhi was a reliable witness; he did not accept the reasons given for La Moselle stopping the cheque to CCL. Shanley J also found him to be less than frank in his explanation of Rosegem's relationship with its landlord in relation to rent outstanding and did not accept the statement of affairs to be reliable. Other conclusions drawn were: that La Moselle had traded when Mr Soualhi knew both companies to be insolvent; that La Moselle forgave debts owed by associated companies without any apparent reason or justification; that Soualhi maintained a very busy and expensive lifestyle whilst the companies were insolvent and there was no evidence – other than oral – that any of the many exotic foreign trips made were business related and that even if they were, the travel and associated costs showed a 'want of commercial probity on Soualhi's part, having regard to the overall parlous financial state of La Moselle and Rosegem'.[194] Shanley J also found that the drawings made at a time when the companies were in very poor financial health were 'not the actions of a responsible director'[195]. In making an order under CA 1990, s 150(1), Shanley J said:

> 'In conclusion, I have no doubt whatsoever that Mr Soualhi traded at a time when he knew that Rosegem and La Moselle were insolvent. I am quite satisfied that he used monies due to the Collector-General and CCL to finance his trading activities and his travel. I have little doubt that he was aware that Rosegem and La Moselle could not trade and at the same time discharge their liabilities to the Collector-General and CCL. Such conduct was, in my view, improper conduct and if it was not to be described as actual dishonesty it was certainly irresponsible.'[196]

In another case, gratuitous or otherwise improper payments to persons was said to be a ground for making a restriction order: *Re Outdoor Advertising Services Ltd*[197].

[12.070] Shanley J's criteria for deciding 'responsibility' in *Re La Moselle* were found to be of 'considerable assistance' and generally adopted by the Supreme Court in *Re Squash (Ireland) Ltd*[198]. As to the criteria, Shanley J himself acknowledged that they overlap:

> 'These criteria necessarily overlap: for example a failure to keep proper books of account may directly contribute to the company becoming insolvent and may be caused by the incompetence of a director. But not all situations of a want of responsibility will result from a breach of obligations imposed by the Companies Acts: for example, a director's inability to see the "writing on the wall" (eg an inability to see from a perusal of the company's management accounts that the company was trading while insolvent) may result from sheer incompetence and justify a restriction (see *Re Continental Assurance Co of London plc; Secretary of State for Industry v Burrows* [1997] 1 BCLC 48 where an inability to read and understand the statutory accounts of a company was considered a ground for disqualification of a director). Equally, a director who takes excessive sums from the company by way of drawings for salary without regard to the financial state of health of the company may be

[193] [1998] 2 ILRM 345 at 356.
[194] [1998] 2 ILRM 345 at 359.
[195] [1998] 2 ILRM 345 at 359.
[196] [1998] 2 ILRM 345 at 359.
[197] *Re Outdoor Advertising Services Ltd* (28 January 1997, unreported), High Court (Costello J).
[198] *Re Squash (Ireland) Ltd* (8 February 2001, unreported), Supreme Court.

said to have acted without commercial probity although he did not necessarily fail to comply with his obligations under the Companies Acts.'

In *Re Squash (Ireland) Ltd* McGuinness J agreed with Shanley J in finding that the court should look at the entire tenure of the director and not merely the months in the run up to the liquidation[199]. In the earlier judgment of *Re Gasco Ltd*[200] McCracken J had said that there should be particular focus on the actions of the directors during the final months before winding up. His reasons were:

> 'I think it is quite significant that no restrictions can attach to somebody who ceased to be a director of the company more than twelve months before the winding up. This seems to me to indicate that the primary aim of s 150 is to deal with directors who have behaved irresponsibly or dishonestly during the last twelve months of the life of the company, and that the actions of a director who is subject to s 150 are to be looked at primarily in the light of his actions during that period. This indeed has a considerable practical logic, as it is presumably intended to focus attention on the behaviour of directors in the period leading up to the winding up, and to try to ensure that they deal responsibly with creditors when a company is in difficulties. In my view, therefore, there should be particular scrutiny on the actions of directors during the final months before winding up.'[201]

Are these two views compatible? To the extent that McGuinness J is saying that the court cannot ignore the totality of a director's tenure and should consider all aspects of his relationship with the company and to the extent that McCracken J is saying that, in practice, such dishonesty and irresponsibility as exists will be more visible and cause more significant damage in the final twelve months, it is thought that the findings are not mutually exclusive.

[12.071] One key feature of acting responsibly has been held to be compliance with the Companies Acts and the maintenance of proper books and records. In *Business Communications Ltd v Baxter and Parsons*[202] Murphy J said:

> 'Ordinarily "responsibility" will entail compliance with the principle features of the Companies Acts and the maintenance of the records required by those Acts. The records may be basic in form and modest in appearance. But they must exist in such a form as to enable the directors to make reasonable commercial decisions and auditors (or liquidators) to understand and follow the transactions in which the company was engaged.'[203]

The absence of books and records was one of the factors which persuaded the court to make restriction orders against some of the directors in *Re Vehicle Imports Ltd*[204]. In *Re Gasco Ltd*[205] the liquidator of the company gave evidence that he found virtually no books and records, no monthly accounts for a particular two-year period and that this contributed

199 (8 February 2001, unreported), Supreme Court at p 8.

200 *Re Gasco Ltd* (5 February 2001, unreported), High Court (McCracken J).

201 (5 February 2001, unreported), High Court at p 7.

202 *Business Communications Ltd v Baxter and Parsons* (21 July 1995, unreported), High Court (Murphy J).

203 (21 July 1995, unreported), High Court at p 18.

204 *Re Vehicle Imports Ltd* (23 November 2000, unreported), High Court (Roderick Murphy J).

205 *Re Gasco Ltd* (5 February 2001, unreported), High Court (McCracken J).

to the difficulties in collecting the company's debts both before and after its liquidation. McCracken J said that:

> '...the fact that no such records exist may make me suspect many things, but certainly is clear evidence of serious irresponsibility by [the director] during the last few months of the trading life of the company.'[206]

Putting the same proposition in a positive way, Murphy J said in *Re Costello Doors Ltd*[207]:

> 'On the face of it, the maintenance of proper books and accounts and the employment of appropriate experts in relation to them would go a long way to discharge the onus of showing that the directors behaved responsibly.'[208]

Re Costello Doors Ltd[209] was the second written judgment on CA 1990, s 150 and was handed down by Murphy J on the same day as his decision in *Business Communications Ltd v Baxter and Parsons*. In *Re Costello Doors Ltd*, the evidence showed that appropriate books and records were kept up to September or October 1992, the time when the company ran into trading difficulties. However, from then until January 1993, when the company was placed into official liquidation, the books were not written up but the primary records were retained. On this point Murphy J said:

> 'I accept the contention made on behalf of the official liquidator that the preservation of basic records is not an adequate compliance with the requirements of the Companies Acts nor does it provide information in a suitable fashion so as to enable the management to make appropriate decisions or auditors to certify accounts but it does not seem to me that it is irresponsible to fail to write up the appropriate books for a particular period in the circumstances which existed in the present case. The fact was that the employment of the persons whose task it was to write up the records had been terminated in October 1992...'[210].

It is thought to be significant that, in that case, it seemed clear that whilst the failure to maintain the company's books might have impeded the liquidation, it was not claimed that it contributed to the company's insolvency. Murphy J declined to make an order under s 150(1) against the company's directors.

[12.072] It should also be noted that the general rule is that the obligation to keep proper books and records is not limited to a period in which a fellow director has reputed responsibility for keeping the books and, as noted by Roderick Murphy J in *Re Vehicle Imports Ltd*[211] 'the responsibility is a joint and separate liability on each of the directors'. Where directors are made personally responsible for a company's debts under CA 1990, s 204 on the basis that they were responsible for the company not keeping proper books of account, it will almost certainly follow that they will be also restricted under s 150[212].

---

206 (5 February 2001, unreported), High Court at p 6.

207 *Re Costello Doors Ltd* (21 July 1995, unreported), High Court (Murphy J).

208 *Re Costello Doors Ltd* (21 July 1995, unreported), High Court at p 5.

209 *Re Costello Doors Ltd* (21 July 1995, unreported), High Court (Murphy J).

210 *Re Costello Doors Ltd* (21 July 1995, unreported), High Court at p 7.

211 *Re Vehicle Imports Ltd* (23 November 2000, unreported), High Court at p 14 (Roderick Murphy J).

212 See *Re Ashclad Ltd and Forrest v Harrington and Culleton* (5 April 2000, unreported), High Court (Geoghegan J) and *Mehigan v Duignan* [1997] 1 ILRM 171.

[12.073] In *Re Verit Hotel and Leisure (Ireland) Ltd; Duignan v Carway*[213] McCracken J held that the use of moneys deducted from employees' wages such as PAYE and PRSI contributions to keep a company going where it is short of funds is totally irresponsible and is sufficient, in itself, to justify the making of a restriction order.

[12.074] It is very important to remember that corporate insolvency does not *per se* mean that directors have acted either dishonestly or irresponsibly. In *Business Communications Ltd v Baxter and Parsons*[214] Murphy J said: 'Of course one must be careful not to be wise after the event. There must be no "witch hunt" because a business failed as businesses will.'[215]

Again in *Re La Moselle Clothing Ltd and Rosegem Ltd*[216] Shanley J said 'the simple fact that a business fails is not evidence of a lack of responsibility nor indeed is it evidence of dishonesty'[217]. In that case Shanley J quoted with approval from Re Lo-Line Motors Ltd[218]. Shanley J added that a director, broadly complying with his obligations under the provisions of the Companies Acts 'and acting with a degree of commercial probity during his tenure as a director of the company will not be restricted on the grounds that he has acted irresponsibly'[219].

[12.075] In *Re Squash (Ireland) Ltd*[220] McGuinness J in the Supreme Court said that respondent-directors:

> '... must be judged by an objective standard. In the case of all companies which have become insolvent it is likely that some criticisms of the directors may be made. Commercial errors may have occurred; misjudgments may well have been made; but to categorise conduct as irresponsible I feel that one must go further than this.'[221]

In this case the High Court had previously found that the two directors of Squash (Ireland) Ltd had acted irresponsibly and, accordingly, they had been restricted under CA 1990, s 150(1). The respondent-directors appealed to the Supreme Court. The facts were that the company had been in existence since the early-1970s, providing services of a sporting and leisure nature, especially squash; the two respondents had been directors for some 18 years. Members paid annual or other subscriptions. After successful beginnings it was noted that due to fashions in sporting and leisure activities changing, interest in membership declined and the company was forced to close some premises and by the late-1990s it was clearly in financial difficulties. In an attempt to assist the company, the respondent-directors had made loans themselves through a trust company, to the company.

---

213 *Re Verit Hotel and Leisure (Ireland) Ltd; Duignan v Carway* (23 January 2002, unreported), High Court (McCracken J).

214 *Business Communications Ltd v Baxter and Parsons* (21 July 1995, unreported), High Court (Murphy J).

215 (21 July 1995, unreported), High Court at p 17.

216 *Re La Moselle Clothing Ltd and Rosegem Ltd* [1998] 2 ILRM 345.

217 [1998] 2 ILRM 345 at 351.

218 *Re Lo–Line Motors Ltd* [1988] BCLC 698 at 703. See para **[12.110]**.

219 [1998] 2 ILRM 345 at 353.

220 *Re Squash (Ireland) Ltd* (8 February 2001, unreported), Supreme Court (McGuinness J; nem diss).

221 (8 February 2001, unreported), Supreme Court at p 6.

At a later stage one of the respondents did not draw his salary for a period of up to one year. One premises in Clontarf from which the company had operated was held on foot of a lease from the Department of Education and the directors believed that the company was entitled to a valuable interest in the property. The company contracted to sell this lease to a building firm for some £700,000. Upon enquiring as to the purchase of the freehold interest, it transpired, however, on 1 December 1997 that the Department of Education was not bound by the Landlord and Tenant (Amendment) Act 1980. The directors procured counsel's opinion which, when obtained on 10 December 1997, confirmed this was the case. It seems that the sole ground for alleging the directors were irresponsible was because in late-November/early-December 1997 they allowed the company's staff to issue reminders for subscriptions from members. The directors had believed that the members would have been able to use the premises until the contract was completed and that, upon its being sold, the company would be able to refund subscriptions. It is significant that upon receiving counsel's opinion that the company did not have a valuable asset, the directors immediately ceased to seek subscriptions from members. Not only did the directors not act dishonestly, but they had actually lost considerable sums of their own money.

[12.076] As noted above, McGuinness J quoted with approval the criteria for determining irresponsibility, as set out by Shanley J in *Re La Moselle Clothing Ltd and Rosegem*[222]. McGuinness J went on to apply these criteria to the conduct of the directors of Squash (Ireland) Ltd. It is useful to quote the learned judge's application of the criteria in full:

> 'It appears from the history of the company that [the directors] have always acted responsibly and honestly and have put the interests of the company in the forefront of their minds, even insofar as losing their own money in an effort to assist the continuation of the company. With regard to:
>
> (a) *The extent to which the director has or has not complied with the Companies Acts.* There is no suggestion that there has been a failure to comply with the Companies Acts and indeed it is clear that the company held many board meetings to deal with the problems that faced them. These board meetings were well documented by proper minutes and the company was run in a correct fashion[223].
>
> (b) *The extent to which his conduct could be regarded as so incompetent as to amount to responsibility.* Perhaps the plan put forward by the directors in this company was overly optimistic but, had their position in regard to the business lease on the Clontarf premises being correct, it was a sensible enough plan in view of the shrinkage of their business over the years. It is unfortunate that they did not identify the problem with regard to the lease at any earlier stage but it has to be said that at the time they had professional and legal advice which they took. They did not act contrary to the advice that was given to them. I do not feel that they could be described as incompetent to such a degree as would amount to irresponsibility.

---

222 See para **[12.068]**.

223 With respect to McGuinness J, the holding of board meetings is but one aspect of compliance with the Companies Acts; however, it may be that the fact that the company was 'run in a correct fashion' implies that all other aspects were also complied with. That board meetings were held regularly and minuted was also considered significant by Murphy J in *Re Cavan Crystal Group Ltd* (26 April 1996, unreported), High Court at p 13.

(c) [*The extent of the directors' responsibility for the insolvency of the company.*] The directors were not responsible in themselves for the insolvency of the company. This basically arose from the reduction in business.

(d) [*The extent of the directors' responsibility for the net deficiency in the assets of the company disclosed at the date of the winding up or thereafter.*] They certainly were not responsible for the net deficiency. I would expect this to include some degree of dishonesty or something very near dishonesty if a director is to be held responsible for the net deficiency in the assets of the company.

(e) [*The extent to which the director, in his conduct of the affairs of the company, has displayed a lack of commercial probity or want of proper standards.*] This is the factor that [the liquidator] lays most emphasis on in his argument to the court in regard to lack of commercial probity and indeed this is the heading under which the matter of the subscriptions would arise. [The liquidator] stresses that the directors should have told the members at an early stage the financial position of the company. It is clear as I have said that this was also the main and indeed the sole matter of concern to the learned President of the High Court.'[224]

In these circumstances, the Supreme Court allowed the appeal and reversed the order of the High Court, McGuinness J finding that 'what they did was open to criticism but I do not feel that it was sufficient to be categorised as irresponsible'[225]. Less than perfect behaviour will not automatically attract a restriction order[226].

(iii) Otherwise just or equitable to make restriction order

[12.077] There has been little focus on this particular issue in the reported judgments, largely because the evidence of dishonesty or irresponsibility (or lack of same) has usually determined the matter. As to the interaction of this ground with 'honesty' and 'responsibility', the following passage from the judgment of Shanley J in *Re La Moselle Clothing Ltd and Rosegem Ltd*[227] is instructive:

> 'Apart from satisfying the court that he as a director acted honestly and responsibly, the director must also satisfy the court that there are no other reasons why it would be just and equitable to restrict him from acting as a director of a company. It is to be noted that acting honestly and responsibly relates to "*the conduct of the affairs of the company*" and arguable such bears no relation to any period after the commencement of a winding up or receivership of the particular company where the person may not be involved any further in the conduct of the affairs of the company. That the director must satisfy the court that there is no other reason why it would be just and equitable to restrict the director, allows the court to take into account, in my view, any relevant conduct of the director after the commencement of the winding up or the receivership (for example failure to co-operate with the liquidator or receiver) in deciding whether or not to make an order under s 150(1) of the 1990 Act.'[228]

---

[224] (8 February 2001, unreported), Supreme Court at pp 8–10 of the judgment. Criteria detailed in square brackets added for completeness; emphasis also added.

[225] (8 February 2001, unreported), Supreme Court at p 10.

[226] See also *Re Steamline Ltd* [2001] 1 IR 103, where he found that the directors had acted 'honestly' and 'responsibly' even though a better explanation could have been tendered than that which was in the statement of affairs.

[227] *Re La Moselle Clothing Ltd and Rosegem Ltd* [1998] 2 ILRM 345.

[228] [1998] 2 ILRM 345 at 353.

This catch-all provision provides the court with maximum latitude in deciding to make a restriction order, notwithstanding that a director has established that he acted both honestly and responsibly in relation to the conduct of the company's affairs.

(g) The defences of being a financial institution's or a venture capital company's nominee and the non-statutory defences of delay and estoppel

[12.078] There are two other statutory defences that may be invoked by a director whom it is sought to restrict. These are contained in CA 1990, s 150(2)(b) and (c), namely:

> '(b) Subject to paragraph (a), that the person concerned was a director of the company solely by reason of his nomination as such by a financial institution in connection with the giving of credit facilities to the company by such institution, provided that the institution in question has not obtained from any director of the company a personal or individual guarantee of repayment to it of the loan or other forms of credit advanced to the company, or
>
> (c) Subject to paragraph (a), that the person concerned was a director of the company solely by reason of his nomination as such by a venture capital company in connection with the purchase of, or subscription for, shares by it, in the first mentioned company.'[229]

These are intended to save banks and other financial institutions from having their bona fide nominees being made restricted persons, and venture capital companies from being treated similarly. They are, on their face, self-explanatory. The question that does arise, however, is whether a director seeking to rely upon either defence in paras (b) and (c) must *also* satisfy the court that they acted *honestly and responsibly*? This was addressed in *Re Cavan Crystal Group Ltd*[230]. In that case it was argued early in the application that one of the directors could rely upon para (b) and another could rely upon para (c). The director seeking to rely upon para (c) could not do so, however, because the venture capital company concerned had not been prescribed as such as required by s 150(5) in order to come with the meaning of 'venture capital company' as used in s 150(2)(c). It appeared that the director seeking to rely upon the defence in para (b) – Mr Lynch – had in fact been appointed by a 'financial institution'[231]. On the question of whether a nominee director was also required to establish that he acted 'honestly and responsibly', Murphy J said, obiter:

> 'On the face of it one would expect to find three independent bases on which the applicant might escape the statutory sanction. In practice to date every director has sought to rely on paragraph (a) by proving that he acted "honestly and responsibly in relation to the conduct of the affairs of the company". Can a person in the position of Mr Lynch rely on paragraph (b) on the basis that he is that type of nominee director described therein? Counsel has pointed to the fact that paragraph (b) is expressed to be 'subject to paragraph (a)' so that in any event it would appear that whatever the status of the particular director he must always prove that he acted both honestly and responsibly. So construed it would seem to me that articles (b)

[229] For CA 1990, s 150(2)(a) see para **[12.065]**.

[230] *Re Cavan Crystal Group Ltd* (26 April 1996, unreported), High Court (Murphy J).

[231] Defined by CA 1990, s 150(5) as meaning – (a) a licensed bank, within the meaning of CA 1990, s 25, or, (b) a company the ordinary business of which includes the making of loans or the giving of guarantees in connection with loans.

> and (c) are entirely meaningless. If a director has satisfied the court under paragraph (a) he does not have to rely on paragraph (b) and if notwithstanding the circumstances to which he became a director he must comply with the provisions of paragraph (a) there is no purpose served by relying on his special status. If it were necessary for me to resolve this conflict I would prefer to conclude that the legislature intended that where a person concerned established that he fell within the particular category of director designated in paragraphs (b) or (c) and it was not necessary for him to establish that he acted honestly or responsibly.'[232]

In the end it was unnecessary for Murphy J to base his decision 'on any such dubious interpretation of the section' because he found that the directors had both acted honestly and responsibly and so neither were restricted[233]. In this respect s 150(2) is unhappily drafted: it is hard to see how the legislature could possibly have intended the interpretation that Murphy J would have placed upon the subsection, if forced to do so. Nevertheless, if paras (b) and (c) are to have any meaning, Murphy J's interpretation should prevail. Ideally, all persons – regardless of whether they were nominees or otherwise – ought to have acted 'honestly' in relation to a company's affairs; a case can, however, be made for relieving nominees from the requirement to act 'responsibly' in relation to a company's affairs to the extent that this recognises the commercial reality that their primary duty is to their appointor[234].

[12.079] Before leaving defences that may be invoked by directors when an application is brought against them, the non-statutory defence of *delay* may be noted. It was recognised by O'Donovan J in *Re Verit Hotel and Leisure (Ireland) Ltd; Duignan v Carway*[235] that an inordinate and inexcusable delay in proceeding with an application may require its dismissal where to allow it to proceed would be against the balance of justice. In that case application was first brought on 6 December 1994 but not proceeded with until some five years later. It was noted that in that period there had been constitutional proceedings in being brought by the directors and a claim for damages brought by the liquidator. O'Donovan J found, in the circumstances of the case that whilst there had been some unreasonable delays, overall the delay was both inordinate and inexcusable. The learned judge noted, however, that that was not the end of the matter and that the Supreme Court had held in *Primor plc v Stokes Kennedy Crowley*[236] that 'even where the delay has been both inordinate and inexcusable the court must exercise a judgment on whether, in its discretion, on the facts the balance of justice was in favour of or against the case proceeding'. O'Donovan J held that there was no reason why the decision in that case should not apply to applications brought under CA 1990, s 150(1)[237]. O'Donovan J noted that the respondent-directors did not claim to have suffered specific prejudice but went on to note that it was claimed that they had suffered a general prejudice arising from the fact

---

232 (26 April 1996, unreported), High Court at pp 8, 9.

233 Another director conceded that CA 1990, s 150(1) applied to him and did not seek to argue that the statutory defences in CA 1990, s 150(2)(a) – (c) applied to him.

234 On the duties of nominee directors, see Chapter 10, *The Duties of Directors and Other Officers*, para **[10.040]** *ff*.

235 *Re Verit Hotel and Leisure (Ireland) Ltd; Duignan v Carway* (27 July 2000, unreported), High Court (O'Donovan J).

236 *Primor plc v Stokes Kennedy Crowley* [1996] 2 IR 459.

that the motion brought against them implied that they were not honest or responsible people, but he also rejected this. In exercising his discretion, O'Donovan J held:

> 'As to the balance of convenience, I am also influenced by the fact that the public interest requires that unsuitable persons should not be directors. In that context I think that the public interest would overcome any delay in this case. I accept, as [counsel for the respondent-directors] said, that perhaps a conscientious liquidator might have been more diligent in bringing these proceedings. However, as I have said, I do not think that the delay, however reprehensible it might be, is going to affect the respondents' capacity to get a fair trial if the motion proceeds. In my view public interest demands it.'

O'Donovan J disallowed the respondent-directors' motion to dismiss the application on the grounds of delay. This decision was upheld on appeal to the Supreme Court[238], where Fennelly J said that 'prejudice' would not be presumed and held that O'Donovan J had correctly exercised his discretion. Only in the most exceptional of cases involving specific prejudice will delay in prosecuting a section 150 application justify dismissal.

[12.080] Another non-statutory defence is that of *estoppel*. Having unsuccessfully sought to rely upon the defence of delay, the respondent-directors of Re Verit Hotel and Leisure (Ireland) Ltd contended in different proceedings, *Re Verit Hotel and Leisure (Ireland) Ltd; Duignan v Carway*[239], that the liquidator was estopped from bringing the application under CA 1990, s 150 because it was closely interrelated to other proceedings that had been settled. As noted above[240] this defence was also rejected by McCracken J who said that an estoppel could not arise because a s 150 application was a matter between the court and the directors, not between the directors and the liquidator.

(h) Post-order relief on just and equitable grounds

[12.081] Where application is brought against a director of an insolvent company and the director is unsuccessful in seeking to invoke the defences contained in s 150(2), and an order is made against him, he has a right of appeal to the Supreme Court[241]. If the Supreme Court confirm the restriction order, or where the High Court's order is not appealed, a restricted director may apply for relief under CA 1990, s 152(1). This provides:

> 'A person to whom *section 150* applies may, within not more than one year after a declaration has been made in respect of him under that section, apply to the court for relief, either in whole or in part, from the restrictions referred to in that section or from any order made in relation to him under *section 151* and the court may, if it deems it just and equitable to do so, grant such relief on whatever terms and conditions it sees fit.'

---

237 In *Re Manlon Trading Ltd* [1995] 4 All ER 14 the English Court of Appeal held that the 'inordinate and inexcusable delay giving rise to serious prejudice' test applied to proceedings for disqualification under the Company Directors Disqualification Act 1986 (UK), subject to its modification by an additional consideration, namely the need to protect the public. Interestingly, O'Donovan J also stressed the public interest.

238 *Re Verit Hotel and Leisure (Ireland) Ltd*; *Duignan v Carway* (31 July 2001, unreported), Supreme Court

239 *Re Verit Hotel and Leisure (Ireland) Ltd; Duignan v Carway* (23 January 2002, unreported), High Court (McCracken J).

240 See para **[12.057]**.

241 As occurred in *Re Squash (Ireland) Ltd* (8 February 2001, unreported), Supreme Court.

An applicant under this section is required to give not less than 14 days' notice of his intention to seek relief to the liquidator of all companies, the insolvency of which caused him to be restricted[242]. Upon receiving such notification, the liquidator is obliged to notify forthwith such creditors and contributories of the company as have been notified to him or known to him[243]. Where a liquidator fails to notify such persons, the application is likely to be adjourned to permit notification[244]. On the hearing of an application for relief, the liquidator and any relevant creditor or contributory has a right to appear and give evidence[245].

[12.082] The first application made under CA 1990, s 152 was in the matter of *Re Ferngara Associates Ltd; Robinson v Forrest*[246]. In that case the High Court (Shanley J) had made an order pursuant to s 150(1) that the applicant should be restricted on the basis that it was not satisfied that he had acted responsibly in relation to the conduct of the affairs of the insolvent company of which he had been a director. Two separate applications brought by the liquidator under CA 1963, s 297A (reckless trading) and CA 1963, s 298 (misfeasance) were compromised by the liquidator with the leave of the court. Five months after the order had been made (although its operation had been stayed by Shanley J), the applicant brought an application under s 152. In this second case, before Laffoy J, on the preliminary questions of procedure, the learned judge said that on a section 152 application, the liquidator in discharge of his obligations under s 152(3) should personally swear an affidavit that he has notified all creditors and contributories. Laffoy J went on to compare the court's powers under s 152 with those under s 150(1) and noted that, unlike the mandatory provisions of s 150(1), s 152 gives the court a very broad discretion, allowing it to wholly negative the effect of a s 150 order, the only criterion being that such should be 'just and equitable'.

The applicant for relief contended that to grant relief was just and equitable on the following grounds. First, he bore a lesser level of culpability for the company's failure than his co-director. It was pointed out that Shanley J had found he had acted honestly and he claimed he had only acted irresponsibly because he was overborne by his co-director who had taken most management decisions. Secondly, he had personally contributed over £200,000 to meet the claims of the company's creditors and that this indicated that he had acted responsibly after the company was wound-up. Thirdly, since the winding up he had been trading through another company of which he was a director and that this company's liabilities to the Revenue Commissioners were up to date. Fourthly, his sole means of livelihood was derived from the business carried on by the new company, which had five employees and he contended that if the restrictions were imposed, his livelihood and those of his employees would be seriously jeopardised.

The Revenue Commissioners opposed the applicant being granted relief, taking issue with the applicant on the facts as stated by him. It was first contended that although the

---

242 CA 1990, s 152(2).

243 CA 1990, s 152(3). Failure to comply by the liquidator is an offence, which renders him liable to fine: CA 1990, s 152(5).

244 See *Re Ferngara Associates Ltd; Robinson v Forrest* [1999] 1 IR 426, [1999] 2 ILRM 169.

245 CA 1990, s 152(4).

246 *Re Ferngara Associates Ltd; Robinson v Forrest* [1999] 1 IR 426, [1999] 2 ILRM 169.

applicant had ultimately acknowledged that he acted irresponsibly he had, initially, not co-operated with the liquidator; Laffoy J would not take this into consideration in the absence of evidence from the liquidator or the Revenue Commissioners. Secondly, it was contended that the applicant deserved no credit for discharging the company's debts as his motive was to assuage certain creditors with whom he wished to continue to deal. Thirdly, it was pointed out that the company had been run as a fraudulent company, to which the applicant responded that he was less culpable than his co-director. Fourthly, the Revenue could not – in the absence of a revenue audit – verify that all taxes owed by the new company had been paid up to date. Finally, it was said that although Shanley J had indicated that the applicant could later apply under s 152, he had not indicated that the restriction would be removed.

[12.083] Laffoy J did not accept the Revenue Commissioners' contention that, in principle, the sanction in CA 1990, s 150 would be devalued if a restricted director was relieved from the restriction imposed after six months. The Revenue indicated that the policy they proposed adopting would be not to support a s 152 application unless the restriction was in place for at least two-and-a half years *and* that all of the company's debts had been fully discharged. Laffoy J said:

> 'This case, in my view, is an exceptional case, which falls to be determined on its own peculiar facts. It weighs heavily with me that the late Shanley J who dealt with the respondent's application for leave to compromise the substantive proceedings was aware of the issues of law and fact in the substantive proceedings and approved the compromise and who determined the applications under s 150 against both [directors] considered it appropriate to stay the order against the applicant for six months and to entertain the applicant's application for relief under s 152, which came before the court within the six month period, to the extent that he adjourned the matter to enable the liquidator to deal with the procedural shortcoming and, that, significantly, he extended the stay on the operation of the order. In the light of that factor and having regard to the facts as established on this application, for my part, I consider that it would be just and equitable to give the applicant relief in whole against the restriction contained in the order of 22 January 1998. In particular, it seems to me that the deterrent value of the restriction order highlighted in the passage from the judgment of Murphy J quoted above and such protection as it affords to current and prospective creditors of enterprises in which the applicant is or may become involved will not be undermined if the restriction is lifted now because, on the evidence, I am satisfied that the applicant has learned an expensive lesson from his involvement in the company.'[247]

It is opined that it was indeed an exceptional case. The applicant's apparent ability to pursue his livelihood as a sole trader would seem to the writer to be very significant, especially when taken with Murphy J's comments in *Business Communications Ltd v Baxter and Parsons*[248], that the amount to which a new company must be capitalised – then £20,000 – must represent a very modest sum[249]. The general rule must be that the courts will be loath, in the absence of compelling reasons (perhaps even to the extent of requiring new evidence as to the restricted director's behaviour or the fate of the employees of a

247 [1999] 1 IR 426 at 435–436.

248 *Business Communications Ltd v Baxter and Parsons* (21 July 1995, unreported), High Court (Murphy J).

249 See para **[12.046]**.

business that *must* operate through the medium of a limited liability company) to set at naught a restriction order.

(i) The enforcement of restriction orders

[12.084] The enforcement of the provisions on restricted directors is achieved in two ways, namely: against the director (civilly and criminally); and against those persons in the restricted company who become involved with a restricted director.

(i) Breach of an order under CA 1990, s 150 by restricted directors: criminal sanction

[12.085] The penalty for acting contrary to the provisions of Chapter 1 is contained in CA 1990, s 161(1), the relevant part of which provides:

> 'Any person who, in relation to any company, acts in a manner or capacity which, by virtue of being a person to whom *section 150* applies…he is prohibited from doing shall be guilty of an offence.'

This offence is punishable in accordance with CA 1990, s 240. Where convicted of such an offence, the person is also subject to automatic disqualification[250].

(ii) Breach of an order under CA 1990, s 150 by restricted directors: civil sanctions

[12.086] Where a restricted director acts contrary to the restrictions imposed upon him, he may well feel the disapproval in his pocket, since the *restricted company* can recover any consideration paid to him for services rendered: CA 1990, s 163(2). Furthermore, by s 163(3), if a restricted director becomes involved in a company which does not meet the requirements set out in s 150(3) and that company goes into insolvent liquidation, then on the application of a liquidator or creditor, the court can make the restricted director *personally liable* without limitation for the debts of the company incurred in the period in which he was acting in such manner or capacity[251]. In relation to proceedings brought under either s 163(2) or (3) the court may, having regard to the circumstances of the case and if it considers it just and equitable to do so, grant relief in whole or in part from the liability which would otherwise attach, subject to such conditions as it sees fit[252]. However, a director who has been restricted ought to ponder long and hard before acting contrary to the declaration made against him.

(iii) Criminal sanctions for officers of companies who act in accordance with the directions or instructions of restricted directors

[12.087] Section 164(1) of CA 1990 makes it an offence for officers[253] who act in accordance with the directions or instructions of a restricted director, knowing that such person is restricted. A person convicted of an offence under this section shall be deemed to be subject to a disqualification order from the date of conviction[254].

250 CA 1990, s 161(2).

251 See Chapter 5, *Disregarding Separate Legal Personality*, para **[5.081]**.

252 CA 1990, s 163(5).

253 CA 1990, s 164(1) applies to 'a director or other officer or a member of a committee of management or trustee of any company'.

254 CA 1990, s 164(2).

(iv) Civil sanctions for officers of companies with which restricted directors become involved which fail to comply with the requirements in CA 1990, s 150(3)

[12.088] The officers of a company with which a restricted director become involved and which does not comply with the requirements in CA 1990, s 150(3) can in certain circumstances be made personally liable for that company's debts. This is provided for in CA 1990, s 163(4). Before such officers can be made personally liable, it must be established that:

— the company received a notification under CA 1990, s 155(5)[255];
— the officer in question knew or ought to have known that the company had been so notified;
— the requirements in s 155(3) were not fulfilled within a reasonable period; and
— the company is subsequently wound-up and at the commencement of such winding up is unable to pay its debts.

Upon such being proved, s 163(4) provides that the court may:

> '... on the application of the liquidator or any creditor or contributory of the company, declare that any person who was an officer of the company while the company so carried on business...shall be personally responsible, without any limitation of liability, for all or any part of the debts or other liabilities of the company as the court may direct.'

As in the case of liability imposed under CA 1990, s 163(2) and (3) the court may grant relief where in the circumstances of the case it considers it just and equitable to do so[256].

[12.089] A conviction under CA 1990, s 164 will also render a convicted person liable to be held personally responsible under CA 1990, s 165 for the debts of the company while they were acting, subject to their right to apply for just and equitable relief[257].

Disqualification of directors and others[258]

[12.090] A disqualification order is an altogether more severe remedy than a restriction order. A disqualification order is defined by CA 1990, s 159 as being:

> '...an order under this Part [ie Part VII of the 1990 Act] that the person against whom the order is made shall not be appointed or act as an auditor, director or other officer[259], receiver, liquidator or examiner or be in any way, whether directly or indirectly, concerned or take part in the promotion, formation or management of any company, or any society registered under the Industrial and Provident Societies Acts 1893 to 1978.'

Accordingly, irrespective of how much another company is capitalised, a person against whom a disqualification order is made can have no involvement, whatsoever, in the promotion, formation or management of any company for the duration of the disqualification period. Discretionary disqualification (ie upon application being made to court and the court being satisfied as to the proof of certain matters, making a

255 See para **[12.049]**.
256 CA 1990, s 163(5).
257 CA 1990, s 165(2).
258 Linnane, 'Restrictions on and Disqualification of Directors' (1994) ILT 132.
259 'Officer' is defined by CA 1990, s 159 as including 'any director, shadow director or secretary'.

disqualification order) existed before the CA 1990 in CA 1963, s 184[260]. The grounds for disqualification were greatly extended by CA 1990, Part VII, Chapter 2 and a considerable increase in the numbers of applications to have persons disqualified was expected by most commentators. The expected increase never materialised, and the numbers of persons against whom a disqualification order had been made in 1994 was in single figures, a fact noted by the Gallagher *Company Law Review Group* which reported in November 1994. The Gallagher Group made ten recommendations on the area of disqualification and restriction, the thrust being that disqualification was a more appropriate sanction for the phoenix syndrome than was restriction[261]. The principal recommendations were for the establishment of an executive unit in the Department of Enterprise, Trade and Employment to apply, in appropriate cases, for the disqualification of directors of insolvent companies and that liquidators and receivers should be obliged to report appropriate cases to the executive unit. Following the McDowell Group's Report, CLEA 2001 has made a number of changes not only to the law on the restriction of directors, but also to disqualification. In particular, the office of the Director of Corporate Enforcement can be seen as meeting the need identified by the Gallagher Group, although the powers, responsibilities and functions of the Director are far more comprehensive than were ever envisaged for the considerably more low key 'executive office'. As at 31 December 1999 the total number of persons who stood disqualified under CA 1990, s 160 was two[262]. It remains to be seen what the effect of CLEA 2001 will be on the numbers of persons who are disqualified. Here, the following issues are considered in relation to disqualification:

(a) Deemed disqualification following conviction for fraud or dishonesty.

(b) The persons who may be disqualified and the meaning of 'company'.

(c) The locus standi to apply for a disqualification order and the role of the Director of Corporate Enforcement.

(d) Notice to persons where application is to be made to disqualify.

(e) The grounds for discretionary disqualification.

(f) The nature of the disqualification order and the period of disqualification.

(g) Relief for the disqualified.

(h) The enforcement of disqualification orders.

(a) Deemed disqualification following conviction for fraud or dishonesty

[12.091] Where a person is convicted on indictment of any indictable offence in relation to a company, or involving fraud or dishonesty, then during the period of five years[263] from the date of conviction[264] he shall be *deemed* to be subject to a disqualification order for that period and shall not, for that period, be appointed or act as auditor, director or other

[260] Such an order was made in *Re Kelly's Carpetdrome Ltd* (1 July 1983, unreported), High Court (Costello J).

[261] See Courtney, *Company Law Review 1995* (1996), p 4.

[262] *Companies Report 1999*, p 45.

[263] CA 1990, s 162.

[264] Or such other period as the court, on the application of the prosecutor and having regard to all of the circumstances of the case, may order.

officer, receiver, liquidator or examiner or be in any way, directly or indirectly, concerned or take part in the promotion, formation or management of any company[265]. This is provided for by CA 1990, s 160(1) and it will be noted that conviction of a relevant indictable offence will alone, and without the need for any judicial intervention, result in such a person's disqualification. The English Court of Appeal held in *Re Cedarwood Productions Ltd*[266] that the making of a disqualification order against a director on conviction for a relevant indictable offence did not bar discretionary disqualification proceedings being brought against the same director. The basis for this decision was that the court held that a deemed disqualification is a penal sanction against the director in person for proven misconduct whereas a discretionary disqualification order was aimed at protecting the public.

[12.092] Section 160(1A) of CA 1990[267] also provides for the deemed disqualification of a person who either:

— fails to state in the statement to the Registrar of Companies (on incorporation) or notification on change in directors that he is disqualified in another jurisdiction and to provide the other details as required by C(A)A 1982, s 3A[268] and CA 1963, s 195(8)[269]; or

— in purported compliance with the foregoing provisions, permits either statement or notification to be accompanied by a statement signed by him which is false or misleading in a material respect.

These sections require disclosure of any disqualification orders made by a foreign state. In such a case the person is deemed to be disqualified by the delivery of such to the Registrar of Companies. The period of the person's disqualification in such circumstances will equate with the outstanding period of the foreign disqualification and, if disqualified in more than one foreign state, the greater period outstanding.

(b) The persons who may be disqualified and the meaning of 'company'

[12.093] Any person who involves themselves in the affairs of a company and whose behaviour comes within one of the discretionary grounds enumerated in CA 1990, s 160(2)(a)–(i) is liable to be disqualified. That said, a number of *primary* respondents may be identified, namely: promoters, officers (which includes any director, shadow director[270]) or secretary of a company[271]), receivers, liquidators, and examiners[272].

---

265 Or any society registered under the Industrial and Provident Societies Acts 1893–1978.

266 *Re Cedarwood Productions Ltd* [2001] TLR 450.

267 As inserted by CLEA 2001, s 42.

268 As inserted by CLEA 2001, s 101.

269 As inserted by CLEA 2001, s 91.

270 On the application of the provisions concerning disqualification of directors in the UK to *shadow directors*, see *Official Receiver v Nixon* (1992) Financial Times Law Reports, 6 March (Court of Appeal)

271 CA 1990, s 159.

272 On the jurisdiction in England and Wales to make a disqualification order in respect of persons outside of the jurisdiction, see *Re Seagull Manufacturing Co Ltd (No 2)* [1994] 1 BCLC 273.

[12.094] Although the 'fraud' ground, the 'breach of duty' ground and the 'unfitness' ground only give jurisdiction to make a disqualification order against these named persons where such arises from *their conduct as such*, it is not necessary that a person should have been formally and properly appointed a director, liquidator, etc. In *Re CB Readymix Ltd; Cahill v Grimes*[273] it was held that there was jurisdiction to disqualify a de facto liquidator. In so holding the Supreme Court relied upon the decision of Sir Nicholas Browne-Wilkinson VC in *Re Lo-Line Electric Motors Ltd*[274] where it was held that in England there was jurisdiction to disqualify a de facto director:

> 'As a matter of construction, I would hold that the word "director" in s 300 does include a person who is *de facto* acting as a director even though not appointed as such. [It was] submitted that as the disqualification of a director is a penal process the words should be strictly construed. But, as I have said, the paramount purpose of disqualification is the protection of the public not punishment. I therefore approach the question of construction on the normal basis. Section 300 requires the court to have regard to "conduct as a director". I can see no reason why Parliament should have intended that the decision to disqualify should turn on the validity of his appointment. The conduct relevant to future suitability to act as a director depends upon a man's past record as a director irrespective of the circumstances in which he came to act as such.'

In the Supreme Court Murphy J said of the foregoing passage that it was 'fully vindicated by a purposive reading of the relevant English and Irish legislation and it is, in my view, as applicable to a *de facto* liquidator as it is to a *de facto* director.'[275] On this basis, there is no reason to distinguish receivers, examiners, promoters or company secretaries. It remains the case, however, that in order to be disqualified a person must at least have de facto acted in such a capacity and, in England, this enquiry has given rise to a considerable number of judgments on who is or is not a director[276]. It may be noted, however, that since a non-officer or other person directly involved in a company can be made the subject of a declaration of personal responsibility under CA 1963, s 297A, for fraudulent trading, such persons can also be disqualified where an order has been made against them under s 297A[277].

---

[273] *Re CB Readymix Ltd; Cahill v Grimes* (1 March 2002, unreported), Supreme Court.

[274] *Re Lo–Line Electric Motors Ltd* [1988] 2 All ER 692; [1988] BCLC 698.

[275] (1 March 2002, unreported), Supreme Court at p 13.

[276] See, eg, *Re Moorgate Metals Ltd* [1995] 1 BCLC 503; *Re Richborough Furniture Ltd* [1996] 1 BCLC 507; *Re H Laing Demolition Building Contractors Ltd* [1998] BCC 561; *Re Sykes (Butchers) Ltd; Secretary of State v Richardson* [1998] 1 BCLC 110; *Secretary of State v Tjolle* [1998] BCC 282; *Secretary of State v Jones et al* [1999] BCC 336; *Re Kaytech International plc* [1999] BCC 390; *Re Red Label Fashions Ltd* [1999] BCC 308; *Re CEM Connections Ltd* [2000] BCC 917; and *Secretary of State v Deverell* [2000] BCC 1057. See, generally, Chapter 8, *Corporate Governance: Management by the Directors*, para **[8.053]** *ff* and **[8.058]** *ff* where these cases are considered in the context of the meaning of de facto director and shadow director, respectively.

[277] CA 1990, s 160(2)(c). See also grounds (e) and (f) which provided for the disqualification of 'persons' in certain specific situations.

[12.095] It is important to note the extended meaning assigned to the term 'company' as it is used in CA 1990, Part VII, Chapter 2. Section 159 provides that, except where the context otherwise requires:

> '..."company" includes every company and every body, whether corporate or unincorporated, which may be wound up under Part X of the 1963 Act and, without prejudice to the generality of the foregoing, includes a friendly society within the meaning of the Friendly Societies Acts 1896 to 1977.'

Those companies that can be wound up under CA 1963, Part X are considered in Chapter 25[278].

(c) The locus standi to apply for a disqualification order and the role of the Director of Corporate Enforcement

[12.096] There are nine separate grounds that, if proved, will permit the court to exercise its discretion and make a disqualification order pursuant to CA 1990, s 160(2)(a)–(i)[279] and there are four persons or classes of persons who have locus standi to make an application; however, the effect of s 160(4), (5)[280], (6) and (6A)[281] is to provide that not all persons can make application under all nine grounds. The result is best expressed in tabular form:

Applicant under CA 1990, s 160(2)	***Permissible grounds detailed in CA 1990, s 160(2)***
Director of Corporate Enforcement	(a)–(i)
Director of Public Prosecutions	(a)–(g)
Members, contributories, officers, employees and creditors	(a)–(d)
Registrar of Companies	(f)

Of course, the court can act on its own initiative in respect of any of these grounds during the course of proceedings and no application is actually required before the court can make a disqualification order[282]. In the case of an application made by members, contributories, employees or creditors, the court may require such applicants to provide security for all or some of the costs of the application[283].

[12.097] It would seem to be clear that the reason for the dearth in the numbers of disqualification orders over the last decade is primarily attributable to the fact that no person or agency has seen fit to bother making application under CA 1990, s 160(2). This is understandable to the extent that an applicant for a disqualification order will, if successful in his application, have little more to show for his efforts than the satisfaction of knowing that he has made life somewhat more difficult for the respondent. In commercial life, the desire for retribution of this nature rarely influences behavior and the efforts in

---

278 At para **[25.031]**.

279 See para **[12.103]**.

280 As inserted by CLEA 2001, s 42(d).

281 As inserted by CLEA 2001, s 42(e).

282 On the striking-out of proceedings for want of prosecution, see *Official Receiver v B Ltd* [1994] 2 BCLC 1

283 CA 1990, s 160(4).

making application would be seen to be throwing good money after bad; equally, it is unreasonable to expect altruism from private parties who can justly believe that it is the State's role to pursue disqualification orders on grounds of public policy. Those State agencies which had, prior to CLEA 2001, locus standi to make application may have had the right but it is arguable that they did not have the responsibility, resources or investigative powers to make applications for disqualification orders. It is in recognition of these matters that the McDowell Group recommended that the Director of Corporate Enforcement should have the responsibility for bringing disqualification applications in appropriate cases.

[12.098] As alluded to in the reasons for the dearth of applications, the absence of investigative powers and information generally contributed to the reluctance on the part of the Registrar of Companies and the DPP to seek disqualification orders. The Director of Corporate Enforcement should not be impeded by a lack of information, since in all cases where a company goes into insolvent liquidation he is entitled to receive a report from the company's liquidator on the conduct of the directors under CLEA 2001, s 56(1)[284]. It is this report which should provide the Director with sufficient information to:

— relieve the liquidator from the obligation to make an application for a restriction order under s 150(1);

— issue no direction in which case the liquidator must make an application for a restriction order; or

— relieve the liquidator from the obligation to make application for a restriction order and, instead, for the Director himself to make application for a disqualification order, where he believes such to be more appropriate in the circumstances of the case.

[12.099] An example of the Director's powers to procure information with a view to making an application for a disqualification order is seen in CA 1963, s 183A[285]. Section 183A(1) provides that where the Director has reason to believe that a company director is an undischarged bankrupt, he can require[286] him to produce by a specified date a sworn statement of all relevant facts pertaining to his financial position within and without the State and to any matter pertaining to bankruptcy as at a particular date. Thereafter, the court can on the Director's application require the company director to appear before it to answer on oath any question in relation to the statement[287]. By s 183A(3) the Director can apply to court for a disqualification order against such a company director and the court has jurisdiction to make such an order on the grounds that the company director is an undischarged bankrupt[288].

---

284 See para **[12.056]**.

285 Inserted by CLEA 2001, s 40.

286 Failure to comply is an offence: CA 1963, s 183A(4).

287 CA 1963, s 183A(2).

288 In *Re Westminster Property Management Ltd* [2000] TLR 28 it was held by Sir Richard Scott V–C that disqualification proceedings are 'regulatory civil proceedings' and that European law did not bar the use of statements given under compulsion.

[12.100] Where an application is successful and the respondent is either disqualified or restricted, the court is empowered under CA 1990, s 160(9B)[289] to order that the persons disqualified or restricted shall bear the costs of the application and, where the applicant is the Director of Corporate Enforcement, the DPP, a liquidator, or an examiner, any costs incurred in investigating the matter.

[12.101] It remains to be seen whether an increase in the numbers of applications for disqualification orders will give rise to persons offering to undertake *not to act as directors* in lieu of a formal court order being made against them[290]. In an attempt to reduce the numbers of applications coming before the English courts, the legislature there introduced a statutory undertaking procedure in s 6 of the Insolvency Act 2000 (UK)[291].

(d) Notice to persons where application is to be made to disqualify

[12.102] In all cases involving an application under CA 1990, s 160(2) (ie other than where the court acts on its own initiative during the course of proceedings) notice must be given to the person whom it is sought to disqualify. Section 160(7) of CA 1990 provides that where it is intended to make an application under the section, the applicant must give not less than ten days' notice to the proposed respondent. The similarly worded English section has been interpreted in *Re Jaymar Management Ltd*[292] to mean that the period of ten days begins to run from the date on which proceedings are issued for an application to the court and not when the applicant addresses the court so as to obtain an order. Clearly, notice is required to protect the respondent's right to a fair trial. That the ordinary rules of natural justice apply in the case of making a disqualification order was stated in Re Churchill Hotel Ltd[293]. However, in *Secretary of State for Trade and Industry v Langridge*[294] the Court of Appeal said that the ten-day notice requirement is *directory as opposed to mandatory* in character. Thus, a failure to give the requisite ten days' notice was merely a procedural irregularity, and did not render an application for a disqualification order void. It is thought, however, that the Irish courts will interprete the 10-day notice to respondents requirement as being mandatory.

(e) The grounds for discretionary disqualification

[12.103] Section 160(2) of CA 1990, as amended by CLEA 2001, s 42, provides that the High Court[295] may of its own motion in any proceedings, or as a result of an application,

[289] As to the option to restrict respondents: see para **[12.105]**.

[290] *Secretary of State for Trade and Industry v Cleland* [1997] BCC 473 (undertaking accepted); *Secretary of State for Trade and Industry v Davies (No 2)* [1997] BCC 488 (undertaking refused). See, generally, 'To Disqualify or no to Disqualify Directors (by Accepting their Undertaking not to Act)? (1997) *CCH's Company Law Newsletter* Issue 9, 20 May 1997.

[291] Griffin, 'Reforming the Disqualification Process – The Introduction of a Statutory Undertaking Procedure', (2001) *Palmer's In Company*, Issue 5/01.

[292] *Re Jaymar Management Ltd* [1990] BCLC 617, which arose under the Company Directors Disqualification Act 1986, s 16(1) (UK).

[293] *Re Churchill Hotel Ltd* [1988] BCLC 341 at 344d–e.

[294] *Secretary of State for Trade and Industry v Langridge* [1991] 3 All ER 591.

[295] CA 1990, s 159 provides that 'the court' means the High Court except in relation to a disqualification order made by a court of its own motion under CA 1990, s 160(2)(a), (b), (c), (d) or (f), in which case it includes any court.

make a disqualification order against a person for such period as it sees fit, on the following grounds:

'(a) a person has been guilty, while a promoter, officer, auditor, receiver, liquidator or examiner of a company of any fraud in relation to the company, its members or creditors; or

(b) a person has been guilty, while a promoter, officer, auditor, receiver, liquidator or examiner of a company, of any breach of his duty as such promoter, officer, auditor, receiver, liquidator or examiner; or

(c) a declaration has been granted under section 297A of the Principal Act [ie CA 1963] (inserted by *section 138* of this Act) in respect of a person; or

(d) the conduct of any person as promoter, officer, auditor, receiver, liquidator or examiner of a company, makes him unfit to be concerned in the management of a company; or

(e) in consequence of a report of inspectors appointed by the court or the Minister [now Director] under the Companies Acts, the conduct of any person makes him unfit to be concerned in the management of a company; or

(f) a person has been persistently in default in relation to the relevant requirements; or

(g) a person has been guilty of 2 or more offences under section 202(10)[296]; or

(h) a person was a director or a company at the time of the sending, after the commencement of section 42 of the Company Law Enforcement Act, 2001, of a letter under subsection (1) of section 12 of the Companies (Amendment) Act, 1982, to the company and the name of which, following the taking of the other steps under that section consequent on the sending of that letter, was struck off the register under subsection (3) of that section[297]; or

(i) a person is disqualified under the law of another state (whether pursuant to an order of a judge or a tribunal or otherwise) from being appointed or acting as a director or secretary of a body corporate or an undertaking and the court is satisfied that, if the conduct of the person or the circumstances otherwise affecting him that gave rise to the said order being made against him had occurred or arisen in the State, it would have been proper to make a disqualification order otherwise under this subsection against him.'[298]

Of the three grounds added by CLEA 2001, (g) adds the ground of having been guilty of two offences for failing to keep proper books or account; (h) adds the ground of being a director of a company that is struck off the register[299]; and (i) adds the ground of having been disqualified in another jurisdiction. The addition of these grounds – although possibly unnecessary by reason of the breath of the 'unfitness' criterion in s 160(2)(d) which would seem to encompass any of the additional matters – are indicative of the new get-tough policy on non-compliance with the Companies Acts.

---

[296] Inserted by CLEA 2001, s 42(b)(ii).

[297] Inserted by CLEA 2001, s 42(b)(ii).

[298] Inserted by CLEA 2001, s 42(b)(ii).

[299] See para **[12.120]**.

[12.104] Section 160(2) of CA 1990 confers a discretionary jurisdiction on the High Court to make a disqualification order, after a court has been satisfied as to the existence of any of the foregoing grounds. Unlike restriction orders under s 150(1), s 160(2) is not mandatory. This was made clear by Murphy J in *Business Communications Ltd v Baxter and Parsons*[300] who said:

> 'The Chapter 2 disqualifications are not mandatory. Section 160 confers a discretion on the Court by the use of the word "may" (rather than the word "shall" which is used in s 150) with regard to the imposition of a disqualification order'.[301]

Neither is the period of disqualification prescribed and it is a matter for the court to determine the duration of a disqualification order[302].

[12.105] Disqualification orders will not be made lightly and in *Business Communications Ltd v Baxter and Parsons*[303] Murphy J said:

> '…in relation to a disqualification order it is clear that there is a substantial burden to be discharged before the court has jurisdiction to make the appropriate order.'[304]

In *Re CB Readymix Ltd; Cahill v Grimes*[305] the Supreme Court accepted in principle that there is a heavy onus on the applicant and a corresponding reluctance on the court to exercise its discretion and make a disqualification order. Where there is either insufficient evidence of wrongdoing or the evidence establishes that the respondent's conduct was not sufficiently culpable as to justify the making of a disqualification order, the court can make the lesser order that the respondent be subject to a restriction order under CA 1990, s 150. Section 160(9A) of CA 1990[306] provides that in considering the penalty to be imposed the court may, as an alternative where it adjudicates that disqualification is not justified, make a declaration under s 150. While very broad, it should be remembered that the grounds for disqualification in CA 1990, s 160(2) are exhaustive. In *Reynard v Secretary of State for Trade and Industry*[307] it was held by Blackburne J that a respondent-director's deceitful performance in the witness box did not constitute a separate head of misconduct, but could be highly relevant, evidentially, as to whether an allegation of misconduct was or was not established.

[12.106] Where made, a disqualification order can be a comprehensive order. In *Business Communications Ltd v Baxter and Parsons*[308] Murphy J said:

> 'Clearly, it is the comprehensive nature of a disqualification order which is seen as constituting an appropriately severe sentence for conduct which is manifestly more

300 *Business Communications Ltd v Baxter and Parsons* (21 July 1995, unreported), High Court (Murphy J).

301 (21 July 1995, unreported), High Court at p 12.

302 See para **[12.122]**.

303 *Business Communications Ltd v Baxter and Parsons* (21 July 1995, unreported), High Court (Murphy J).

304 (21 July 1995, unreported), High Court at p 13.

305 *Re CB Readymix Ltd; Cahill v Grimes* (1 March 2002, unreported), Supreme Court.

306 Inserted by CLEA 2001, s 42.

307 *Reynard v Secretary of State for Trade and Industry* [2001] TLR 441.

308 *Business Communications Ltd v Baxter and Parsons* (21 July 1995, unreported), High Court (Murphy J).

> blameworthy than merely failing to exercise an appropriate degree of responsibility in relation to an insolvent company in liquidation of which the person is a director.'[309]

A disqualification order may be made on grounds, which include matters other than criminal convictions even though the respondent may be criminally liable for those matters[310]. Each of the nine separate grounds listed in CA 1990, s 160(2), the proof of which will entitle the court to exercise its discretionary jurisdiction to make a disqualification order, shall next be considered.

(i) Guilty of any fraud: CA 1990, s 160(2)(a)

[12.107] The first ground is that the person whom it is sought to disqualify must be proved to have been guilty of any fraud in relation to the company, its members or directors, whilst that person was a promoter, officer, auditor, receiver, liquidator or examiner. The provisions on disqualification are not directed at directors alone and are primarily intended to provide a remedy against all persons who owe ex officio duties to a company. The use of the word 'guilty' implies that there should be a court conviction and, unlike CA 1990, s 160(1) that conviction may follow a summary prosecution as well as one on indictment, although proof of the latter is more likely to induce the court to exercise its discretion and make a disqualification order than the former. In England it has been held that where no disqualification order was sought during a criminal trial, it was not an abuse of process to commence, subsequently, civil proceedings for disqualification[311].

(ii) Guilty of breach of duty: CA 1990, s 160(2)(b)

[12.108] This is similar to the 'fraud' ground, but wider. Guilty of a breach of duty would imply that a criminal conviction is again a prerequisite to the exercise of the jurisdiction here too.

(iii) Proof of a declaration of liability for fraudulent trading: CA 1990, s 160(2)(c)

[12.109] Where a declaration is made under CA 1963, s 297A that a person has been party to the carrying on of the business of a company with intent to defraud its creditors, this too is a basis for the court making a disqualification order[312].

(iv) Unfit to be concerned in the management of a company: CA 1990, s 160(2)(d)

[12.110] In the first edition of this book it was opined that of all the grounds enumerated in CA 1990, s 160(2), the ground which would be most litigated would be s 160(2)(d)[313]. Indeed, in *Business Communications Ltd v Baxter and Parsons*[314] Murphy J said that of all

---

[309] (21 July 1995, unreported), High Court at pp 13, 14.

[310] CA 1990, s 160(9).

[311] *Re Dennis Hilton Ltd* [2001] TLR 431.

[312] On fraudulent trading, see Chapter 10, *Duties of Directors and Others*, para **[10.104]** *ff.*

[313] There have been very few disqualification orders made in Ireland. One, which is noted by MacCann, *Butterworth Ireland Companies Acts 1963–1990* (1993), p 1014, is *Re Christy Kenneally Communications Ltd* (July 1992, unreported), High Court where Costello J disqualified two directors who refused to comply with a court order to prepare annual accounts and hold an AGM. An example of a disqualification order by consent is noted by Courtney, 'Company Law Update' (1994) CLP 56. In neither case was a judgment delivered.

[314] *Business Communications Ltd v Baxter and Parsons* (21 July 1995, unreported), High Court (Murphy J).

the grounds, it was s 160(2)(h) which 'typifies the grounds for disqualification'.[315] The 'unfitness' ground relates to where the person whom it is sought to have disqualified has behaved in a manner from which an inference can be drawn that such makes him unfit to be concerned in the management of a company. Among the salient factors that go to determine this question in the English courts is the question of whether there has been a lack of probity in the conduct of the person concerned, or a lack of 'commercial morality'. The power to make a disqualification order is firmly rooted in policy.

> 'It is a power to be exercised to protect the public against those who display lack of commercial probity, "rip-off" the public in colloquial terms, or otherwise shelter a totally rash and unjustified venture behind the shield of limited liability so that they themselves do not suffer when their rash venture fails, as was predictable, but leave the creditors at large to suffer.'[316]

In *Re Dawson Print Group Ltd*[317] Hoffmann J said:

> 'There must, I think, be something about the case, some conduct which if not dishonest is at any rate in breach of standards of commercial morality, or some really gross incompetence which persuades the court that it would be a danger to the public if he were to be allowed to continue to be involved in the management of companies, before a disqualification order is made. Obviously every case must turn on its own facts.'[318]

In that case, the respondent was a director of two companies. The history of one company was that it suffered a setback in its first year of trading when one of its major creditors defaulted, and although it expanded it was finally wound up as insolvent. The other company was wound up also being insolvent, both companies owing debts to the English Revenue. After the winding up, the director set up another business which seemed to be trading profitably. It was held by Hoffmann J that on the facts there was no evidence that the director had behaved recklessly or in a manner that was commercially immoral, and in all the circumstances it was inappropriate to make a disqualification order. Similarly, in *Re CU Fittings Ltd*[319] it was held that no disqualification order ought to be made, as there was no lack of probity. Hoffmann J stated:

> 'It may be that ... a dispassionate mind would have reached the conclusion that the company was doomed. But the directors immersed in the day-to-day task of trying to keep their business afloat cannot be expected to have wholly dispassionate minds. They tend to cling to hope. Obviously there comes a point at which an honest businessman recognises that he is only gambling at the expense of his creditors on the possibility that something may turn up. But this is not such a case.'[320]

---

[315] (21 July 1995, unreported), High Court at p 13.

[316] *Re Cladrose Ltd* [1990] BCLC 204 at 213, per Harman J.

[317] *Re Dawson Print Group Ltd* [1987] BCLC 601.

[318] [1987] BCLC 601 at 604e–f.

[319] *Re CU Fittings Ltd* [1989] BCLC 556.

[320] [1989] BCLC 556 at 559. See also *Re McNulty's Interchange Ltd* [1989] BCLC 709 where Browne–Wilkinson V–C said: 'The Official Receiver says that although Mr McNulty was not aware that the company was insolvent when it was continuing to trade, he says that he ought to have been aware it was. I reject that allegation on the evidence before me. The evidence is that he was throughout advised by professional financial advisers. To suggest that somebody in those circumstances, who relies on his advisers, is in some way acting improperly, because he does not appreciate that his advisers' advise is wrong, seems to me untenable.'

In *Re CB Readymix Ltd; Cahill v Grimes*[321] the Supreme Court said that the following passage from the decision of Browne-Wilkinson VC in *Re Lo-Line Motors Ltd*[322] was a correct statement of the law and represents a proper approach to the application and interpretation of CA 1990, s 160:

> 'What is the proper approach to deciding whether someone is unfit to be a director? The approach adopted in all the cases to which I have been referred is broadly the same. The primary purpose of the section is not to punish the individual but to protect the public against the future conduct of companies by persons whose past record as directors of insolvent companies have shown them to be a danger to creditors and others…Ordinary misjudgment is in itself not sufficient to justify disqualification. In the normal case, the conduct complained of must display a lack of commercial probity, although I have no doubt that in an extreme case of gross negligence or total incompetence, disqualification could be appropriate.'[323]

It may therefore be surmised that an enquiry into whether a respondent displayed commercial probity or morality is likely to feature in any application to have a person disqualified under CA 1990, s 160(2)(d).

[12.111] Whether or not a respondent maintained proper books and records is as important in an application for a disqualification order as it is in an application for a restriction order[324]. In *Re CB Readymix Ltd; Cahill v Grimes*[325] the 'dumping' of the company's records was the basis of the official liquidator's grievance with the respondent voluntary liquidator. The facts were that the respondent, Dr Grimes, had acted as voluntary liquidator in a company when he had, in fact, not been validly appointed liquidator. Subsequently, the applicant was appointed official liquidator. There was evidence from the directors that all books had been handed over to Dr Grimes and there was evidence that Dr Grimes had perused the books. Meetings were held and correspondence exchanged but the company's books and records were not handed over to the official liquidator. At one meeting the official liquidator claimed he was told that the 'books could have an accident'. Subsequently, Dr Grimes claimed he had sought a meeting with the official liquidator to hand over the books but that the official liquidator had declined to meet with him. For this reason, by his own admission, Dr Grimes said he reasoned that only the company's officers were responsible for the books, that he had not been involved in running the company and was not even liquidator so he had no duty to keep the records. For these reasons Dr Grimes 'dumped' the records by filling two-and-a-half refuse sacks and putting them out for collection with the garbage. The Supreme Court noted that Dr Grimes

[321] *Re CB Readymix Ltd; Cahill v Grimes* (1 March 2002, unreported), Supreme Court. The same passage was quoted with approval in *Re La Moselle Clothing Ltd and Rosegem Ltd* [1998] 2 ILRM 345 and *Re Squash (Ireland) Ltd* (8 February 2001, unreported), Supreme Court (by McGuinness J).

[322] *Re Lo–Line Motors Ltd* [1988] BCLC 698.

[323] [1988] BCLC 698 at 703.

[324] See para **[12.071]**.

[325] *CB Readymix Ltd; Cahill v Grimes* (1 March 2002, unreported), Supreme Court.

admitted to a feud with the Revenue Commissioners and that certain extreme statements had been attributed to him in the High Court[326]. Murphy J said:

> 'It is common case that Dr Grimes destroyed – or dumped with a view to their destruction – documents relating to the financial affairs of Readymix. In my view the inescapable conclusion is that those documents included the books and records of that company and that this was done with a view to depriving the official liquidator of access thereto. An experienced liquidator – and Dr Grimes rightly claims to be such – would immediately appreciate the importance of the records to which Dr Grimes admits he had access.'[327]

It was claimed that Dr Grimes had been motivated by the desire to save the jobs of those employed by the company. The Supreme Court, however, upheld the decision of Smyth J, inter alia, to disqualify Dr Grimes for a period of seven years. Murphy J said:

> 'His apparent belief that the commendable motive of saving employment would justify the destruction of documents and the frustration of the liquidation of a company shows a completely mistaken view as to the duties of a liquidator and would undoubtedly raise concern as to the propriety of his being involved in the management of companies which are subject to detailed regulations for the protection of the public whether as shareholders, creditors or employees'.[328]

Upholding the decision of the High Court, Murphy J justified the making of a disqualification order arising from one incident in the following terms:

> 'Adequate records are necessary to enable a liquidator to perform his statutory functions properly and some records are necessary to enable him to perform his functions at all. Whilst I accept that Dr Grimes did not act maliciously, his decision to destroy or permit the destruction of the books and records of Readymix was a very serious wrong indeed. Dr Grimes did argue that a liquidator or director should not be severely penalised for one error in relation to a particular company in a context where no allegations of inappropriate conduct are made against him in respect of many other such offices held by him. That argument has considerable force. However, a significant feature of the judgment of Mr Justice Smyth was his statement that he allowed time to Dr Grimes to reconsider the argument which he made to the court and notwithstanding the opportunity given to him he, Dr Grimes, "continued in a vein as to betoken a total disregard in his conduct complained of". It was the fact that Dr Grimes could not then – and does not now – appreciate the gravity of his misconduct that justifies the conclusion that he is unfit to hold the office of liquidator and casts serious doubt upon his suitability to participate in the management of any company.'[329]

[12.112] The English courts have taken into account a variety of factors in finding that people have acted with a lack of commercial morality or probity. These include:

— acquiring the assets of a company which was insolvent for another company with which the same directors were involved[330];

[326] (20 July 2001, unreported), High Court (Smyth J), p 12 of the judgment. The statements attributed to Dr Grimes were: 'I was determined to screw the Revenue no matter what it took'; 'I was prepared to blow up anyone who got in my way'; 'I was going to make an example of Mr Cahill'; 'I would not obstruct the liquidator but I would not help'; and 'Whatever tactics it took I was going to bring the Revenue to book'.

[327] (20 July 2001, unreported), High Court at p 7.

[328] (20 July 2001, unreported), High Court at p 15.

[329] (20 July 2001, unreported), High Court at pp 16–17.

[330] See *Re Keypak Homecare Ltd* [1990] BCLC 440.

— failing to keep proper books of account or to make annual returns even if there was no personal gain to the directors responsible[331];

— gross incompetence[332]; and

— trading when there is no prospect of the company surviving ie recklessly[333].

It is thought that proof of dishonesty will also justify a finding of 'unfitness' but that 'irresponsibility' (as that term has been defined in the context of CA 1990, s 150(1) restriction orders) will not alone justify a finding of 'unfitness' in the context of an application for a disqualification order. Another factor which has been held by the English courts to be very important in deciding whether or not to make a disqualification order is where a person was responsible for the company avoiding the payment of debts to the Revenue. Thus in *Re Cladrose*[334] it was held that non-payment of Crown debts was to be treated as a more serious matter than the failure to pay ordinary debts[335]. This was also stated to be the case in *Re Stanford Services Ltd*[336] by Vinelott J who saw an onus on the directors of a company not to use moneys collected on behalf of the Crown for the financing of the company. More recently the Court of Appeal in *Re Sevenoaks Stationers (Retail) Ltd*[337] has stated that the non-payment of Crown debts is not to be treated as an automatic ground for disqualification. Rather, it is but a factor to be taken into consideration in determining whether a director is unfit. In the words of Dillon LJ:

> '[The director] made a deliberate decision to pay only those creditors who pressed for payment. The obvious result was that the two companies traded, when in fact insolvent, and known to be in difficulties, at the expense of those creditors who, like the Crown, happened not to be pressing for payment. Such conduct on the part of a director can well, in my judgment, be relied on as a ground for saying that he is unfit to be concerned in the management of a company. But what is relevant in the Crown's position is not that the debt was a debt which arose from a compulsory deduction...but that the Crown was not pressing for payment, and the director was taking unfair advantage of that forbearance on the part of the Crown [and]...was trading at the Crown's expense while the companies were in jeopardy. It would be equally unfair to trade in that way and in such circumstances at the expense of creditors other than the Crown.'[338]

---

[331] See *Re Sevenoaks Stationers (Retail) Ltd* [1990] BCLC 668 and *Re Chartmore Ltd* [1990] BCLC 673. On the duty to keep accounts, see MacCann 'Duty to Keep Proper Books of Account' (1991) ILT 177. Note that in respect of CA 1990, s 160(2)(f), in respect of which only the Registrar of Companies, the Director or the Director of Public Prosecutions can make application, CA 1990, s 160(3)(a) provides that persistent default can be proved conclusively where it is shown that in the five years ending with the date of the application, the person has been adjudged guilty of three or more defaults.

[332] *Re Churchill Hotel (Plymouth) Ltd* [1988] BCLC 341.

[333] *Re J & B Lynch (Builders) Ltd* [1988] BCLC 376 at 379.

[334] *Re Cladrose* [1990] BCLC 204.

[335] See *Re J & B Lynch (Builders) Ltd* [1988] BCLC 376; *Re Lo–Line Electric Motors Ltd* [1988] BCLC 698. Cf *Re CU Fittings Ltd* [1989] BCLC 556;

[336] *Re Stanford Services Ltd* [1987] BCLC 607 at 616.

[337] *Re Sevenoaks Stationers (Retail) Ltd* [1991] 3 All ER 578, [1991] BCLC 325.

[338] [1991] 3 All ER 578 at 589,590. See also *Re Tansoft Ltd* [1991] BCLC 339, where the decision in the Court of Appeal was applied by Warner J.

Accordingly, in England and Wales, for a company to trade, owing debts to the English Revenue is not any more heinous than to behave in that way to creditors generally. In the Irish High Court Smyth J said in *Re CB Readymix Ltd; Cahill v Grimes*[339] that whilst he did not consider it necessary to pronounce on the special nature of revenue debts, he contented himself to note that the legislature had laid down those debts, the payment of which is to have priority in a winding up and that, for the present, was 'sufficient indication of their special nature'.

[12.113] It has been held that the court can have regard to the fact that a director whom it is sought to disqualify has a professional qualification, as this will increase the standard of care expected of him. In *Re Cladrose Ltd*[340] where one of the directors was a chartered accountant, it was held that the other director without a professional qualification could reasonably rely on the accountant-director to comply with the requirements governing the filing of accounts and annual returns[341]. This case is also authority for the fact that where a director has personal problems, such as the break-up of his marriage, such will not be sufficient to exonerate him from the responsibilities attendant on being a director.

[12.114] The decision of McCracken J in *Re Newcastle Timber Ltd*[342] shows that the courts will not make a disqualification order lightly and that the onus of proof rests firmly with the applicant. In that case an application to have two directors of a company that was wound up insolvent, disqualified, failed, and the court contented itself with making a restriction order under CA 1990, s 150. The liquidator identified five matters that he claimed showed that the directors had not acted honestly and responsibly. In respect of three of those claims McCracken J held that the liquidator had discharged the onus on him in relation to the section 160 disqualification proceedings. These were: first, that the company had failed to make CRO returns (it had at one point been struck off); secondly, that the company had traded whilst insolvent for some four years; and thirdly, that after the company ceased to trade its directors had caused it to discharge trade creditors in priority to the Revenue Commissioners[343]. After quoting from the passage in the decision of Browne-Wilkinson VC in *Re Lo-Line Motors Ltd*[344] as to the 'proper approach' to deciding whether someone is unfit to be a director[345], McCracken J declined to exercise his discretion in favour of making a disqualification order. Taking into account one of the directors' involvement in another company – something that has been done also in England in *Re Bath Glass Ltd*[346] – McCracken J said of the respondent-directors:

339 *Re CB Readymix Ltd; Cahill v Grimes* (20 July 2001, unreported), High Court at p 18.

340 *Re Cladrose Ltd* [1990] BCLC 204.

341 Cf *Re Majestic Recording Studios Ltd* [1989] BCLC 1 where it was held that a director cannot turn a blind eye to the affairs of the company to the neglect of his duties.

342 *Re Newcastle Timber Ltd* (16 October 2001, unreported), High Court (McCracken J).

343 The other two grounds were not upheld. First, it was not established that the company had not kept proper books and records because owing to a fire caused by vandalism, it was impossible to say what books and records did exist. Secondly, it was found that any irregularities in the acquisition by one of the directors of a property from the company had not prejudiced the company's creditors and could even have been said to have benefited the directors.

344 *Re Lo–Line Motors Ltd* [1988] BCLC 698.

345 See para **[12.110]**.

346 *Re Bath Glass Ltd* [1988] BCLC 329.

'I have no doubt that they acted incompetently, and, particularly in relation to insolvent trading and preference of trade creditors, I think they behaved irresponsibly. However, the liquidator has not satisfied me that the directors were so much in breach of their duties, that they are unfit to be concerned in the management of a company, particularly in view of the undoubted discretion which I have in this regard. The liquidator did rely to a considerable degree on the fact that the revenue debts remained unpaid, and cited a number of authorities as to the importance of this aspect of the case, but taking the overall behaviour of the directors I do not think it could be said that a disqualification order is necessary to protect the public against their future conduct. I say this particularly as it is now some six years since Newcastle ceased trading, during which time [one of the respondent-directors] has been intimately concerned in the management of another company, which appears to be trading successfully and is complying with its obligations to the Revenue. Accordingly, I will refuse an order under s 160.'[347]

In that case a restriction order was, however, made against both of the directors. The making of a restriction order was virtually automatic following the finding that the respondent-directors had acted 'irresponsibly'. From this decision it would appear that the Irish courts have a higher threshold for incompetence and irresponsibility than do the English courts. Were it not for the Supreme Court's acceptance in *Re CB Readymix Ltd* that there is jurisdiction to disqualify *conditionally*, (see para **[12.122]**) McCracken J's decision was likely to have dissuaded liquidators from bringing disqualification proceedings because of the tolerance for incompetence and irresponsibility seen in the exercise of the court's discretion. The effect of the Supreme Court's decision, however, is likely to be that conditional disqualification orders will be made where perhaps no disqualification order might otherwise be made.

(v) Unfitness appearing from an inspector's report: CA 1990, s 160(2)(e)

[12.115] Where an inspector has been appointed to a company and it appears from his report, as all inspectors are required to produce at the end of their investigation[348], that the conduct of any person makes him unfit to be concerned in the management of a company, this will give jurisdiction to the court to make a disqualification order against such person.

(vi) Persistently in default in relation to 'relevant requirements': CA 1990, s 160(2)(f)

[12.116] The meaning of 'relevant requirements' is defined by CA 1990, s 159 to mean:

'...any provision of the Companies Acts (including a provision repealed by this Act) which requires or required any return, account or other document to be filed with, delivered or sent to, or notice of any matter to be given to, the Registrar of Companies.'

Accordingly, the civil remedy of a disqualification order may be invoked in addition to a prosecution for a failure to file offence[349]. It will be noted that this is the only ground for disqualification that the Registrar of Companies has locus standi to prosecute[350].

347 (16 October 2001, unreported), High Court at pp 7–8.

348 CA 1990, ss 7–9.

349 See para **[12.178]**.

350 See para **[12.006]**.

[12.117] The term 'persistently' is ambiguous: what is consistent to one might be occasional to another. Fortunately, guidance is given by CA 1990, s 160(3)(a) which provides:

> 'For the purposes of subsection (2)(f) the fact that a person has been persistently in default in relation to the relevant requirements may (without prejudice to its proof in any other manner) be conclusively proved by showing that in the five years ending with the date of the application he has been adjudicated guilty (whether or not on the same occasion) of three or more defaults in relation to those requirements.'

Moreover, the interpretation of 'default' is assisted by CA 1990, s 160(3)(b):

> 'A person shall be treated as being adjudged guilty of a default in relation to a relevant requirement for the purposes of this subsection if he is convicted of any offence consisting or a contravention of a relevant requirement or a default order is made against him.'

By 'default order' is meant an order or injunction made pursuant to CA 1963, s 371[351], by virtue of any contravention of or failure to comply with any relevant requirement (whether on his own part or on the part of any company)[352].

[12.118] Before making application on this ground, it would be prudent for the applicant to be able to prove that in the preceding five years, the respondent has been either convicted of three offences relating to filing requirements or has been enjoined under CA 1963, s 371 on three occasions to comply with a relevant requirement. It is thought that two convictions and one section 371 injunction, or vice versa, will suffice. It is important to note that a section 371 injunction can issue in respect of matters other than filing requirements, but that it seems only such an injunction compelling compliance with a filing requirement is cognisable under CA 1990, s 160(2)(f).

(vii) Guilty of two or more offences for failing to keep proper books of account: CA 1990, s 160(2)(g)

[12.119] The requirement in CA 1990, s 202 that companies cause proper books of account to be kept is considered to be a fundamental aspect of corporate compliance and for this reason CLEA 2001 took the opportunity of specifically providing that two convictions for failing to keep proper books or accounts will ground an application for disqualification. The requirement in CA 1990, s 202 is considered further in Chapter 13[353].

(viii) Directorship of a company that has been struck off: CA 1990, s 160(2)(h)

[12.120] This ground also was added by CLEA 2001, s 42 as an aid to bolster the remedy of strike-off[354]. Although strike-off will be a commercial disaster for the honest procrastinator, it can represent an opportunity for the delinquent director of an insolvent company to pursue a 'scorched earth'[355] policy and wrong-foot pursuing creditors. Being a director of a company that has been struck off pursuant to C(A)A 1982, s 12 will ground an application for disqualification but the court is not permitted to make an order in all

---

[351] See para **[12.175]**.

[352] CA 1990, s 159.

[353] At para **[13.004]**.

[354] On strike–off, see para **[12.132]** *ff*.

[355] As that term is used in the *Report of the Working Group on Compliance and Enforcement* (1998), para 4.42.

cases. Section 160(3A) of CA 1990 ensures, however, that those who avail of the voluntary (solvent) strike-off procedure[356] will not be thereby rendered liable to being disqualified. It provides:

> 'The court shall not make a disqualification order under paragraph (h) of subsection (2) against a person who shows to the court that the company referred to in that paragraph had no liabilities (whether actual, contingent or prospective) at the time its name was struck off the register or that any such liabilities that existed at that time were discharged before the date of the making of the application for the disqualification order'.

Accordingly, the legislature wisely employed a rapier as opposed to a cutlass by restricting this ground to directors of companies whose liabilities *have not been discharged* at the time it was struck off the register. This means that C(A)A 1982, s 12 can continue to facilitate persons who wish a swift end for a solvent company which has outlived its usefulness, without their exposure to a disqualification order.

(ix) The subject of a disqualification order made in a foreign state: CA 1990, s 160(2)(i)

[12.121] The final ground was also introduced by CLEA 2001, s 42. Section 160(3B) of CA 1990 provides that a disqualification order based on this ground may be made notwithstanding that at the time of the order, the person is deemed by virtue of CA 1990, s 160(1A) to be subject to a disqualification order.

(f) The nature of the disqualification order and the period of disqualification

[12.0122] In *Re CB Readymix Ltd; Cahill v Grimes*[357] the High Court had made a twofold order against the respondent. First, the respondent was disqualified from 'being concerned in the management of a company as a liquidator, receiver or examiner for a period of seven years'. Secondly, the respondent was restricted in his acting as auditor, director or secretary to the extent that (i) he had such professional qualifications as are necessary or required by law so to do; and (ii) that at no time was he to have in his possession, custody or control companies' seals, books or records provided always he was to have access to them to discharge his legal obligations[358]. On appeal to the Supreme Court it was claimed that there was no jurisdiction to make such an order and that CA 1990, s 160 was in the nature of 'an all or nothing section'. The Supreme Court rejected that contention and upheld the form of conditional order made by Smyth J in the High Court. Murphy J said:

> 'In my view this argument is refuted by the provisions of subs (8) of s 160...The express power of the court to grant relief to a person who is subject or deemed subject to a disqualification order "either in whole or in part" and to "grant such relief on whatever terms and conditions it see fit" would enable the court to review a disqualification order in the days immediately following the making thereof by imposing precisely those terms which Mr Justice Smyth had required in the first instance. In my view it would be unthinkable that the court could have a power to revise its own order in that way and in that time frame and not have the same powers in the first instance. I am fully satisfied that the learned trial judge did have the powers which he purported to exercise so humanely in disqualifying the respondent

---

356 See para **[12.140]**.

357 *Re CB Readymix Ltd; Cahill v Grimes* (1 March 2002, unreported), Supreme Court.

358 *Re CB Readymix Ltd; Cahill v Grimes* (20 July 2001, unreported), High Court (Smyth J).

from filling certain offices and yet permitting him to fill others subject to stipulated conditions.'[359]

It was also rejected by the Supreme Court that the restrictions on the respondent acting as auditor, director or secretary were either an impermissible intrusion into the affairs of a company or otherwise inappropriate.

[12.123] The periods of disqualification imposed by the English courts have varied greatly. An attempt was made to standardise disqualification periods by the Court of Appeal in the case of *Re Sevenoaks Stationers (Retail) Ltd*[360], where the court introduced the following classification:

> '(i) The top bracket of disqualification for periods over ten years should be reserved for particularly serious cases. These may include cases where a director who has already had one period of disqualification imposed on him falls to be disqualified yet again.
>
> (ii) The minimum bracket of two to five years' disqualification should be applied where, though disqualification is mandatory, the case is, relatively, not very serious.
>
> (iii) The middle bracket of disqualification for from six to ten years should apply for serious cases which do not merit the top bracket.'[361]

This scale continues to be applied in England[362] and was applied in Ireland by Smyth J in *Re CB Readymix Ltd; Cahill v Grimes*[363]. The maximum period of disqualification has, however, been found to be in excess of ten years, and 15-year periods of disqualification are not unknown. An extreme example is seen in *Official Receiver v Vass*[364] where two directors were disqualified, one for 15-years and the other for 12-years in circumstances where the first had been acting as a director whilst disqualified and the second, a resident of the island of Sark, was nominee director of 1,313 UK companies and secretary of 513 UK companies, even after having resigned 282 directorships and 113 secretarial appointments! The court took a particularly dim view of acting as a director whilst already disqualified and such was the seriousness of this that a 15-year disqualification period was deemed appropriate. The second director's conduct in holding himself out as director for so many companies on a token basis and totally abrogating responsibility was also considered to be an extremely serious matter and deserving of a substantial period of disqualification ie 12 years.

(g) Relief for the disqualified

[12.124] Section 160(8) of CA 1990 provides:

> 'Any person who is subject or deemed subject to a disqualification order by virtue of this Part may apply to the court for relief, either in whole or in part, from that disqualification and the court may, if it deems it just and equitable to do so, grant such relief on whatever terms and conditions it sees fit.'

There is English authority that although a person's conduct justifies them being disqualified, the existence of certain mitigating factors may make it just in the

359 (1 March 2002, unreported), High Court at pp 11–12.

360 *Re Sevenoaks Stationers (Retail) Ltd* [1991] BCLC 325

361 [1991] BCLC 325 at 328d–e.

362 See, eg, *Re Saver Ltd* [1999] BCC 221.

363 *Re CB Readymix Ltd; Cahill v Grimes* (20 July 2001, unreported), High Court at p 18.

364 *Official Receiver v Vass* [1999] BCC 516.

circumstances for them to be disqualified generally but permitted or continue to act as the director of a particular company[365]. This is clearly within the inherent competence and jurisdiction of the Irish courts where the circumstances require such a partial dispensation to achieve justice, and *conditional disqualification* has been upheld by the Supreme Court in *Re CB Ready Mix Ltd*[366]. There must, however, be a clear and convincing reason why a court that has determined that an individual is not fit to be a director and who disqualifies him from so acting, should do a volte-face and lift that order. Where a person is convicted of an offence under CA 1990, s 161(1), ie acting contrary to a disqualification order or restriction order, and his disqualification is extended by ten years (in accordance with s 161(3)) recourse cannot be had to s 160(8) for relief.

[12.125] In *Re Barings plc; Secretary of State for Trade and Industry v Baker*[367] Sir Richard Scott V-C cautioned against courts forgetting the original reasons for making a disqualification order in entertaining an application for relief, subsequently. In that case the applicant had been a director at the ill-fated Barings Bank group and had been disqualified for four years in circumstances where there were no allegations of dishonest or fraudulent impropriety. He subsequently set up business as a management and advisory consultancy in partnership with his wife; he applied for leave to be allowed to act as director of four companies of which he had been a director before being disqualified. Although that case involved the interpretation of the use of the word 'need' in s 17 of the Company Directors Disqualification Act 1986 (UK), it does provide guidance as to the court's general approach. Sir Richard Scott V-C said:

> 'It seems to me that the importance of protecting the public from the conduct that led to the disqualification order and the need that the applicant should be able to act as director of a particular company must be kept in balance with one another. The court in considering whether or not to grant leave should, in particular, pay attention to the nature of the defects in company management that led to the disqualification order and ask itself whether, if leave were granted, a situation might arise in which there would be a risk of recurrence of those defects.'[368]

On the facts of that case it was held that there was virtually no risk at all of such a recurrence and that it was appropriate to grant leave to the person to act as a director of the companies, subject to certain conditions[369].

---

365 See *Re Chartmore Ltd* [1990] BCLC 673 where a person was disqualified for two years but was allowed to act as director of another particular company for one year with permission to apply for an extension. See also *Re Majestic Recording Studios Ltd* [1989] BCLC 1 where although disqualified generally, the person was allowed to continue to act as a director of another company with a co–director approved by the court where audited accounts were filed. Clearly, one of the overriding reasons for this was the fact that otherwise, the jobs of his employees would be jeopardised.

366 *Re CB Ready Mix Ltd* (1 March 2002, unreported), Supreme Court. See para **[12.122]**.

367 *Re Barings plc; Secretary of State for Trade and Industry v Baker* [1999] BCC 960.

368 [1999] BCC 960 at 965.

369 See also *Shuttleworth v Secretary of State for Trade and Industry; Re Dawes and Henderson (Agencies) Ltd* [2000] BCC 204; and *Re Amaron Ltd* [1998] BCC 264; and *Re TLL Realisations Ltd* [2000] BCC 998

(h) The enforcement of disqualification orders

[12.126] Just as in the case of restriction orders, the enforcement of the provisions on disqualified directors, is achieved in two ways, namely: against the director (civilly and criminally); and against those persons in a company with whom he becomes involved, whilst disqualified.

(i) Breach of disqualification order: criminal sanction

[12.127] The penalty for acting contrary to the provisions of Chapter 2 is contained in CA 1990, s 161(1), the relevant part of which provides:

> 'Any person who, in relation to any company, acts in a manner or capacity which, by virtue of being…subject or deemed to be subject to a disqualification order, he is prohibited from doing shall be guilty of an offence.'

This offence is punishable in accordance with CA 1990, s 240[370]. Where convicted of such an offence, the person is also subject to automatic disqualification[371]. Moreover, where a person who is convicted of an offence under s 161(1) was subject or deemed to be subject to a disqualification order immediately prior to the date of such conviction, the period for which he was disqualified shall be extended for a further period of ten years from such date or such further period as the court on the application of the prosecutor and having regard to all of the circumstances, may order[372].

(ii) Breach of disqualification order: civil sanctions

[12.128] Where a disqualified director acts contrary to the order imposed upon him any company with which he becomes involved may recover any consideration paid to him for services rendered: CA 1990, s 163(2). Furthermore, by s 163(3), if a disqualified director becomes involved in a company and that company goes into insolvent liquidation, then on the application of a liquidator or creditor, the court can make the disqualified director *personally liable* without limitation for the debts of the company incurred in the period in which he was acting in such manner or capacity[373]. In relation to proceedings brought under either s 163(2) or (3) the court may, having regard to the circumstances of the case and if it considers it just and equitable to do so, grant relief in whole or in part from the liability which would otherwise attach, subject to such conditions as it sees fit[374].

(iii) Criminal sanctions for officers of companies who act in accordance with the directions or instructions of disqualified directors

[12.129] Section 164(1) of CA 1990 makes it an offence for officers[375] to act in accordance with the directions or instructions of a disqualified director where they know that he has been disqualified. A person convicted of an offence under this section shall be deemed to be subject to a disqualification order from the date of conviction[376].

---

370 See para **[12.034]**.

371 CA 1990, s 161(2).

372 CA 1990, s 161(3).

373 See Chapter 5, *Disregarding Separate Legal Personality*, para **[5.081]**.

374 CA 1990, s 163(5).

375 CA 1990, s 164(1) applies to 'a director or other officer or a member of a committee of management or trustee of any company'.

376 CA 1990, s 164(2).

(iv) Civil sanctions for officers of companies with which disqualified directors become involved

[12.130] Section 165(1) of CA 1990 provides that any person who is convicted of an offence under s 164 for acting in accordance with the directions or instructions of a disqualified person shall, subject to s 165(2), be personally liable for the debts of the company that were incurred in the period during which he was so acting.

[12.131] By virtue of CA 1990, s 165(2) the court may grant relief where in the circumstances of the case it considers it just and equitable to do so and relieve people who act in accordance with the directions or instructions of a disqualified person from being made personally responsible.[377].

Striking off the register

[12.132] Perhaps the most ignominious fate to befall a company is where it is struck off the register of companies. Being struck off the register is usually 'courted' by the company's controllers or advisors in their failure to file annual returns, as prescribed by CA 1963, s 125[378]. While striking off may be regarded as being almost the 'just desserts'[379] of dormant companies, often it befalls the careless company, whose controllers are more interested in conducting business than observing the Companies Acts. While certainly not intended to mitigate the omissions of such companies, it does explain why legislation also provides for the reinstatement of such companies.

[12.133] Strike-off is the Registrar's most powerful weapon in the war of attrition against non-compliance with filing and other requirements. In recent years there has been a dramatic increase in the numbers of companies that have been struck off the register, primarily for failure to file annual returns[380]. The increase followed the Registrar's commencement of an extensive strike-off regime in September 1998 whereby companies that were in default with their obligation to file annual returns were selected at random for the initiation of the strike-off procedure. During 1999, over 28,000 companies were involuntarily struck off, the majority being private companies limited by shares. In addition, nearly 4,000 companies were struck off following their own request that this be done and their representation that they had no outstanding creditors[381]. Involuntary strike-offs almost invariably resulted from companies' failure to file their annual returns for two consecutive years. In consequence of the changes effected by C(A)(No 2)A 1999, the Registrar now has power to strike off where annual returns have not been filed for just one year[382].

[377] CA 1990, s 165(2).

[378] See Chapter 13, *Accounts and Auditors*, para **[13.154]** *ff*.

[379] See McCormack, *The New Companies Legislation* (1991), p 11.

[380] See *Companies Report 1999*, pp 47–48.

[381] See para **[12.140]**.

[382] See para **[12.136]**.

[12.134] The power of the Registrar of Companies to strike a company off the register is found in C(A)A 1982, s 12[383] and CA 1963, s 311[384]. Both of these sections have been heavily amended by C(A)(No 2)A 1999. Here, the following issues are considered:

(a) The grounds for strike-off.

(b) The effect of strike-off on the liability of directors, officers and members.

(c) The effect of strike-off on corporate property.

(d) Trading whilst struck off.

(e) The winding up of dissolved companies.

(f) Restoration to the register.

(g) The effect of restoration.

Each of these shall be considered next.

(a) The grounds for strike-off

[12.135] There are five distinct circumstances in which the Registrar can cause a company to be struck off the register. These are:

(i) Failure to make an annual return.

(ii) Failure to deliver required particulars to the Revenue Commissioners.

(iii) Ceasing to carry on business.

(iv) Having no recorded directors.

(v) Failure to have at least one resident director.

It should be remembered that strike-off will not always be involuntary. Where a company ceases to trade and has no outstanding creditors, it is open to such a company to *voluntarily* initiate the strike-off procedure by requesting that the Registrar strikes-off the company under CA 1963, s 311. This is facilitated by coming within ground (iii) above ie *ceasing to carry on business*[385].

(i) Failure to make an annual return

[12.136] By far the most common ground for the involuntary striking-off of companies is where they fail to make their annual return. Section 12(1) of C(A)A 1982[386] provides:

> 'Without prejudice to the generality of section 311 of the 1963 Act, where a company does not, for one or more years, make an annual return required by section 125 or 126 of the 1963 Act, the Registrar of Companies may send to the company by post a registered letter stating that, unless all annual returns which are outstanding are delivered to him within 1 month of the date of the letter, a notice will be published in *Iris Oifigiúil* with a view to striking the name of the company off the register.'

Where the Registrar either receives an answer to the effect that the company is not carrying on business or does not within one month of the initial notice receive all outstanding annual returns, the Registrar may then publish a notice in *Iris Oifigiúil* stating that after one month from the date of the notice, the name of the company shall be struck off the

383 See generally, MacCann, 'Striking off the Register and Section 12 of the Companies (Amendment) Act 1982' (1990) Gazette ILSI 125.

384 As amended by the C(A)A 1982, s 11 and the C(A)A 1983, s 8(2) and (3).

385 See para **[12.140]**.

386 As replaced by C((A)(No 2)A 1999, s 46.

register, unless all annual returns are delivered to the CRO[387]. Subject to the foregoing, at the expiration of the time in the notice and unless cause to the contrary is shown, the Registrar then has statutory power to strike-off a company's name from the register whereupon he must publish a further notice in *Iris Oifigiúil* and on publication of that notice, the company is dissolved[388].

(ii) Failure to deliver required particulars to the Revenue Commissioners

[12.137] Section 882(1) of the Taxes Consolidation Act 1997 ('TCA 1997') (as inserted by the Finance Act 1999, s 83) requires that every company, incorporated in the State or which commences to carry on a trade, profession or business within the State, shall within 30 days either of certain stated events[389], deliver a written statement to the Revenue Commissioners[390]. This statement must declare:

— the name of the company;
— the company's registered office;
— the address of its principal place of business;
— the name and address of the secretary;
— the date of commencement of the trade, profession or business;
— the nature of such trade, profession or business;
— the date to which accounts relating to such trade, profession or business will be made up;
— such other information as the Revenue Commissioners may consider necessary.

In addition, in the case of companies that are incorporated, but not resident in the State, and companies that are neither incorporated nor resident in the State, certain additional information is required[391]. This measure, which along with TCA 1997, s 23A (as inserted by the Finance Act 1999, s 82) was intended to combat the problem posed by non-resident Irish companies[392] is considerably strengthened by C(A)A 1982, s 12A. Section 882(3) of the TCA 1997 provides:

> 'Where a company fails to deliver a statement which it is required to deliver under this section then, notwithstanding any obligations as to secrecy or other restriction upon disclosure of information imposed by or under any statute or otherwise, the Revenue Commissioners may give a notice in writing to the Registrar of Companies (within the meaning of the Companies Act 1963) stating that the company has so failed to deliver a statement under this section.'

387 C(A)A 1982, s 12(2).

388 C(A)A 1982, s 12(3).

389 The stated events are: (a) the date it commences to carry on a trade, profession or business, wherever carried on, (b) the date at which there is a material change in information previously delivered by the company under that section; and (c) the giving of a notice to the company by an inspector requiring a statement under that section: TCA 1997, s 882(2).

390 This section applies (a) in the case of companies that are incorporated on or after 11 February 1999, as on and from that date; and (b) in the case of companies that are incorporated before 11 February 1999, as on and from 1 October 1999: Finance Act 1999, s 83(2).

391 Finance Act 1999, s 83(2)(i) and (iii).

392 See Chapter 2, *Formation, Registration and Conversion of Private Companies*, para **[2.052]**.

Enter C(A)A 1982, s 12A. Section 12A(1) provides:

> 'Where the Revenue Commissioners give a notice in writing under subsection (3) of section 882 (inserted by the Finance Act, 1999) of the Taxes Consolidation Act, 1997, to the Registrar of Companies stating that a company has failed to deliver a statement which it is required to deliver under that section, then, without prejudice to section 311 of the 1963 Act or section 12 of this Act, the Registrar may send to the company by post a registered letter stating that, unless the company delivers to the Revenue Commissioners the said statement within 1 month of the date of the letter, a notice will be published in *Iris Oifigiúil* with a view to striking the name of the company off the register.'

Where the company does not deliver the required statement to the Revenue Commissioners within one month of the date of the Registrar's warning letter, the Registrar may publish a notice in *Iris Oifigiúil* stating that one month after the published notice, the name of the company will, unless the statement is delivered to the Revenue, be struck off the register and the company dissolved[393]. Subject to the foregoing, at the expiration of the time in the published notice and unless cause to the contrary is shown, the Registrar then has statutory power to strike-off a company's name from the register whereupon he must publish a further notice in *Iris Oifigiúil* and on publication of that notice, the company is dissolved[394].

[12.138] Protection against any action for breach of confidentiality against the Revenue Commissioners is afforded by C(A)A 1982, s 12D. This provides that the Revenue may disclose to the Registrar any information in their possession required by the Registrar for the purposes of determining whether or not to strike a company off the register under ss 12A-12C.

(iii) Ceasing to carry on business

[12.139] It will be noticed that both of the two grounds last considered are expressed to be 'without prejudice to' CA 1963, s 311, which contains the generic ground for striking companies off the register, namely that a company is not 'carrying on business'. Section 311(1) of CA 1963 provides:

> 'Where the Registrar of Companies has reasonable cause to believe that a company is not carrying on business, he may send to the company by post a registered letter inquiring whether the company is carrying on business and stating that, if an answer is not received within one month from the date of that letter, a notice will be published in *Iris Oifigiúil* with a view to striking the name of the company off the register.'

The consequences that follow from this warning are similar to those that flow where a warning is issued under both C(A)A 1982, ss 12 and 12A. So, if the Registrar either receives an answer to the effect that the company is not carrying on business or, does not receive any answer within one month after sending the letter, he may publish a notice in *Iris Oifigiúil* and send to the company a notice by registered post, stating that after one month from the date of the notice, the company will be struck off the register unless cause is shown to the contrary[395]. At the expiration of the time mentioned in the notice, the

393 C(A)A 1982, s 12A(2).

394 C(A)A 1982, s 12A(3).

395 CA 1963, s 311(2).

Registrar is again empowered, unless cause to the contrary is previously shown, to strike the company's name off the register, in which case he must publish notice thereof in *Iris Oifigiúil* and upon such publication, the company is dissolved.

[12.140] Section 311(1) of CA 1963 is the legal basis for the Registrar of Companies' *voluntary strike-off process*, which facilitates corporate euthanasia. This process acknowledges that companies can take the initiative to be struck off and that the Registrar can be approached to exercise his powers under s 311(1) by being tendered 'reasonable cause to believe that a company is not carrying on business'. In his administrative notices the Registrar has made clear that:

> '...this is a discretionary power which the Registrar is prepared to use only if a director of a company furnishes a statement to the effect that the company has ceased trading or has never traded, that it has no assets or liabilities and that it wishes its name to be struck off the register.'[396]

In addition to the foregoing statement, with effect from 12 October 2001 such a statement must be accompanied by:

— all outstanding annual returns, including accounts and relevant filing fees including late filing penalty (if any)[397];

— a letter of no objection from the Revenue Commissioners; and

— a copy of an advertisement in the approved form[398] published in one daily newspaper indicating the intention to apply to have the company struck off the register.

This is a very useful and pragmatic method of culling moribund companies.

[12.141] A particular application of the cessation of business ground is where a company is 'half-wound up' as is provided by CA 1963, s 311(3). This provides that where a company is being wound up and the Registrar has reasonable cause to believe either that no liquidator is acting, or that the affairs of the company are fully wound up and the returns required to be made by the liquidator have not been made for a period of six consecutive months, the Registrar may publish in *Iris Oifigiúil* and send to the company (or liquidator, if any)[399] a like notice as is provided for in s 311(2). In such circumstances, a company is clearly not carrying on business and this power permits the Registrar to put the company out of its misery, and tidy up the register, by striking it off the register.

(vi) Having no recorded directors

[12.142] This is a sub-set of the ground last considered in CA 1963, s 311(1). The essential prerequisite for the Registrar's exercise of his power to strike-off a company under s 311 is

[396] See the CRO's website at www.cro.ie under Enforcement: *Guide to Voluntary Strike Off Process*.

[397] The Registrar waived late filing penalties in respect of all applications received prior to 2 August 2002.

[398] The CRO's website provides the text for the approved form of notice.

[399] CA 1963, s 311(9) provides that a notice under that section to a liquidator may be addressed to him at his last known place of business and a letter or notice ot a company may be addressed to the company at its registered office or, if no office has been registered, to the case of some officer of the company, or if there is no officer of the company whose name is known to the register, to each of the persons who subscribed to the memorandum at the addresses given therein.

his having 'reasonable cause to believe that a company is not carrying on business'. In addition to companies failing to make their annual returns, the other compliance offence that causes the CRO much concern is the failure to keep the Registrar notified of changes in the particulars in directors as required by CA 1963, s 195[400]. Apart from the desire to have the register of companies completely up to date and a mirror image of the de facto particulars of companies, another reason why this is considered so important is that it facilitates the prosecution of defaulting companies' officers. Section 48 of C(A)(No 2)A 1999 enables the Registrar to exercise his statutory power of strike-off where it appears that a company has no directors. This is achieved by providing that where a copy of a notice of resignation or other documentary proof of a person's having ceased to be a director is forwarded to the Registrar pursuant to CA 1963, s 195(11A) and (11B) and the result is that there is no one recorded in the CRO as being officers, then this fact affords the Registrar 'good grounds for believing that the company is not carrying on business' and provides the requisite cause for the Registrar to exercise the powers of strike-off, conferred by s 311(1).

(v) Failure to have at least one resident director

[12.143] The requirement that, subject to certain exceptions, every Irish company must have at least one resident director has been considered in a previous chapter[401]. It is indicative of the seriousness with which the agencies of the State treated the problems caused by the proliferation of Irish registered non-resident companies that the failure to comply with the requirements in C(A)(No 2)A 1999, s 43(1) and (2) will cause the Registrar's power to strike-off to arise. In a curious drafting style, C(A)(No 2)A 1999, s 43(15), provides that the provisions of CA 1963, s 311 shall apply for the purposes of C(A)(No 2)A 1999, s 43 'as they apply for the purposes of that s 311', subject to certain modifications. Those modifications are to CA 1963, s 311(1), (2) and (8). The modified CA 1963, s 311(1) provides:

> 'Where the Registrar of Companies has reasonable cause to believe that subsection (1) or, as the case may be, subsection (2) of section 43 of the Companies (Amendment) (No 2) Act, 1999, is not being complied with in relation to a company, he may send to the company by post a registered letter requesting the company to furnish to him evidence that the provision concerned is being complied with and stating that, if that request is not complied with within 1 month from the date of that letter, a notice will be published in *Iris Oifigiúil* with a view to striking the name of the company off the register.'

In the style of the other grounds which allow the Registrar to exercise his powers of strike-off, the modified s 311(1), provides that if the register does not, within one month after sending the warning letter, receive evidence that satisfies him that C(A)(No 2)A 1999, s 43(1) and (2) are being complied with, he may publish notice in *Iris Oifigiúil*. Thereafter he can send written notice to the company by registered post, to the effect that at the expiration of one month from the date of such notice, the company's name will be struck off the register and the company dissolved unless cause is shown to the contrary.

400 See Chapter 8, *Corporate Governance: Management by the Directors*, para **[8.081]**.

401 See Chapter 8, *Corporate Governance: Management by the Directors*, para **[8.022]**.

(b) The effect of strike-off on the liability of directors, officers and members

[12.144] Both C(A)A 1982, s 12B(1) and CA 1963, s 311(6) provide that the dissolution of a company shall not affect the liability of directors, officers or members of that company 'which shall continue and may be enforced as if the company had not been dissolved'. Members who have an outstanding liability in respect of unpaid shares can also be called upon to honour them. Directors who are guilty of breaches of their duties to the company or contravention of the laws on fraudulent or reckless trading can be similarly pursued.

(c) The effect of strike-off on corporate property

[12.145] Where a company is struck off, many potentially drastic consequences befall it, or more particularly, its assets[402]. Once the company is struck off, it ceases to have any legal existence. The fate of its assets is not found in the Companies Acts, but rather in the State Property Act 1954. Section 28 of the State Property Act 1954 provides that where a company is dissolved all of its property, both realty and personalty, including choses in action automatically vests in the State and is held by the Minister of Finance on behalf of the State[403]. Section 28(2) of the State Property Act 1954 provides:

> 'Where a body corporate[404] is dissolved, either before, on or after the operative date, the following provisions shall apply and have effect and, in the case of a body corporate dissolved before the operative date, be deemed to have applied and to have had effect as from such dissolution, that is to say:—
>
> (a) all land which was vested in or held in trust for such body corporate immediately before its dissolution (other than land held by such body corporate upon trust for another person) shall, immediately upon such dissolution, become and be the property of the State, subject however to any incumbrances or charges affecting the land immediately before such dissolution,
>
> (b) all personal property (excluding chattels real but including choses-in-action) which is vested in or held in trust for such body corporate immediately before its dissolution (other than personal property held by such body corporate upon trust for another person) shall, immediately upon such dissolution become and be State property.'

Property that is held in trust *by* the company is expressly stated not to vest in the State, because the company is not the beneficial owner of that property. The operation of this principle is seen in the case of *Re Kavanagh & Cantwell*[405] where Costello J held, and the Attorney General conceded, that property which was held in trust by a company which was dissolved did not vest in the State. In that case the court went on to hold that trust

---

402 See, MacCann, 'Striking off the Register and Section 12 of the Companies (Amendment) Act 1982' (1990) Gazette ILSI 125.

403 Far from it being seen as a windfall to the State, the fact that the property of dissolved companies vests in the State ought to cause the State to ponder its liability. The most obvious example would be where a business premises becomes vested in the State; in the event of third-party injury whilst on such premises, there must be at least a potential liability for the State in tort.

404 Body corporate is defined so as *not* to include 'a body corporate dissolved by an enactment wherein it is provided that the property of that body corporate shall, on such dissolution, vest in some other person': State Property Act 1954, s 28(1).

405 *Re Kavanagh & Cantwell* (23 November 1984, unreported), High Court (Costello J).

property is beneficially owned by the cestui que trust, or beneficial owner, and the legal title to such property could be vested in the beneficiary by the court under the Trustee Act 1893, s 26 on the grounds that the trustees could not be found.

[12.146] Real property held by a company which is dissolved and which is subject to a mortgage or charge, vests with the State subject to the interest of the mortgagee or chargee by virtue of s 28(2)(a) of the State Property Act 1954. It will be noted, however, that there is no such explicit saver for creditors secured by a mortgage or charge over personalty, such as a floating or specific chattel mortgage or a floating charge over tangible or intangible personalty. In the case of personal property, s 28(2)(b) provides that such property shall vest in the State and makes no express provision for where a third party has a security interest over such personal property. It is thought, however, that the holder of a security interest in personal property will have a *beneficial interest* in such property and to that extent it does not, unconditionally, vest in the State. Rather, such property is properly excluded from vesting in the State because it is 'held by such body corporate upon trust for another person'. Any other interpretation would be an unconstitutional deprivation of the property interests of the holders of security interests in personal property. Such a provision would be especially likely to be found unconstitutional because that there is no justification for distinguishing between real and personal property and would be a clear arbitrary attack on property rights. Where a third party is prejudiced by the operation of s 28(2)(b) as it is open to him as creditor to petition the court to have the company reinstated to the register of companies, and where such an order is granted, it seems most likely that the court would make the order subject to the rights of that creditor being restored. In practice, it is opined that it is highly unlikely that the Minister for Finance would oppose a third-party's bona fide assertion to have a security interest over the personal property of a dissolved company.

[12.147] Many companies and their controllers were unaware that they had been dissolved arising from the Registrar's policy to pursue the remedy of strike-off in cases of failure to file annual returns, commenced in 1998. Often, it was only when the company wished to dispose of property or avail of credit facilities that the enormity of strike-off became apparent. Many solicitors attempting to convey lands and buildings on behalf of companies were, on learning of their dissolution from a companies search, obliged to inform their clients that the transaction could not complete by reason of the fact that title to the properties had vested in the Minister for Finance! So too were many companies' directors shocked to have credit facilities declined upon credit institutions learning that the companies no longer existed. Other companies, however, did not become aware of the fact that they had been dissolved because they or third parties on their behalf had no occasion to conduct a CRO search. Such companies may, inadvertently, continue to trade whilst struck off[406] and may even continue to operate banking facilities for industry practice is to search against a company only when it embarks upon a particularly significant transaction. It is not either usual or practical to obtain such a search before effecting a debit or credit to or from a company's account with a lending institution. Indeed, the world of commerce would grind to a halt were it to be suggested that in every corporate transaction, a credit institution was to cause a CRO search to be conducted. Where it is discovered that a

[406] See para **[12.149]**.

company has been dissolved, its directors will usually set about the process of seeking to have companies restored to the register[407]. One practical solution adopted by many Irish credit institutions in the intervening period was to make a personal loan to the directors in circumstances where it was agreed that the company would repay that loan from its assets upon their being unfrozen following its restoration.

[12.148] The effect of restoration is to re-vest a dissolved company's property in the restored company. Sometimes, however, it will prove virtually impossible to restore a dissolved company to the register eg all its directors and shareholders are long since dead, or where the company has been struck off for a period in excess of 20 years[408]. What is to be done where it transpires that a conveyance by a company, long since dissolved, is defective eg inoperative words of limitation mean that there is a resulting trust in favour of the defunct company? In such cases any interest previously held by the company now stands in the name of the Minister for Finance by reason of the State Property Act 1954, s 28. In such a case there are two avenues open to the conveyancer seeking to regularise the matter. In the first place, application can be made for the appointment of a trustee (usually a solicitor) under the Trustee Act 1893, as was done in the case of *Re Kavanagh & Cantwell*[409]. This will be appropriate where the company is a bare trustee of the property (as it would be in the example given where full consideration passed to the company but title to the purchaser failed for technical reasons). Such an application to correct a defect on title should be made on notice to the Minister for Finance and the support of the Chief State Solicitor's office should be obtained. In practice this procedure tends to be used where the property in issue is being sold by successors in title.

A different, possibly more time consuming but equally effective, route can also be pursued, usually where it is sought to simply remedy a defect in title and there is no immediacy about having to show good marketable title. In such a case application can be made to the Minister for Finance, through the Chief State Solicitor's office, under the State Property Act 1954, s 30 for the Minister to execute a waiver of the property in question. Section 30 provides:

> 'Whenever, either before, on or after the operative date, any property of whatsoever nature or kind devolves upon the State by way of escheat or becomes the property of the State as bona vacantia or by virtue of section 28, the Minister may, if he thinks proper so to do, waive, in whole or in part and in favour of such person and upon such terms (whether including or not including the payment of money) as he thinks proper having regard to all the circumstances of the case, the right of the State to such property.'

In practice neither of these options will, generally, be consented to by the Chief State Solicitor's office where it is reasonably possible for an applicant to apply to have a company restored to the register, with the consequence that the restored company can, itself, perfect title by deed.

---

407 See para **[12.152]** *ff*.

408 In all cases where the court is empowered to restore a company to the register, there is a maximum time limit within which the company must have been dissolved of 20 years. See para **[12.161]** *ff*.

409 *Re Kavanagh & Cantwell* (23 November 1984, unreported), High Court, per Costello J.

(d) Trading whilst struck off

[12.149] The McDowell Group did not favour the creation of a new offence of trading after having been struck off[410]. It did recognise, however, that the then existing offence under CA 1963, s 381 which prohibited the improper use of the words 'limited' or 'teoranta' were insufficient to address the phenomenon of trading whilst struck off, especially as the maximum fine was then limited to £500. The CLEA 2001 did, however, take the opportunity to revamp CA 1963, s 381 and it was revamped by CLEA 2001, s 98. It continues to be the case that if any person or persons trade or carry on business under a name or title of which 'limited' or 'teoranta' or any contraction or imitation of either is the last word, he or they will, unless duly incorporated, be guilty of an offence. It will be noted, however, that the maximum fine has been removed and the penalties for the offence now fall to be determined by CA 1990, s 240[411]. Moreover, the Director and the Registrar of Companies now have power to serve a discontinuance notice on persons in contravention of the prohibition and if, within 14 days thereafter they fail to comply, the Director or the Registrar may apply for a court order requiring the cessation of the contravention[412]. Where such an order is made, it may provide that all costs incidental to the application shall be borne by the persons against whom it is made[413].

[12.150] It has already been stated that where a company has been struck off and dissolved, its controllers have no authority to deal with the assets to which it was entitled prior to its dissolution since by operation of law the company is no longer the legal owner of these assets. It follows that to the extent that 'trading' involves the disposal of a dissolved company's 'assets', this is unlawful and technically exposes such controllers to civil and criminal liability. To the extent that 'trading' after strike-off involves the controllers of a dissolved company contracting with third parties, on first principles they will be contracting (and therefore liable) on their own behalf unless and until such time as both the company is restored to the register and the court makes an order which deems such post-dissolution contracts to have been made with the company.

(e) The winding up of dissolved companies

[12.151] Both C(A)A 1982, s 12B(2) and CA 1963, s 311(7) expressly provide that the fact a company has been dissolved, *shall not affect* the power of the court to wind up that company. However, in order for a winding up to have meaning the company must be reinstated to the register of companies. The reason why it is necessary to reinstate a company is because until reinstated the title to its assets remains vested in the State[414].

---

[410] See *The Report of the Working Group on Company Law Compliance and Enforcement* (1998), para 3.31.

[411] See para **[12.034]**.

[412] CA 1963, s 381(2).

[413] CA 1963, s 381(3).

[414] The dissolved company has standing by C(A)A 1982, s 12(6) and CA 1963, s 311(8) to apply for its own restoration.

(f) Restoration to the register[415]

[12.152] There are two methods of restoring a company to the register of companies:

(i) restoration by administrative action.

(ii) restoration by judicial order.

(i) Restoration by administrative action

[12.153] Two different statutory provisions permit application to the Registrar of Companies to restore a company to the register. Application will be brought under either provision, depending upon the ground upon which the Registrar struck off the company that is the subject of the application. Both regimes have in common the requirement that application can only be made to the Registrar (as opposed to court) *before the expiration of 12 months* from the publication in *Iris Oifigiúil* of the notice striking the company's name off the register[416].

[12.154] First, C(A)A 1982, s 12C(1) applies to applications for restoration where the company was struck off pursuant to C(A)A 1982, s 12A(3) ie for a *failure to deliver the required particulars to the Revenue Commissioners*. Section 12C(1) provides:

> '...if a member or officer of a company is aggrieved by the fact of the company's having been struck off the register under s 12A(3) of this Act, the Registrar of Companies, on application made in the prescribed form by the member of officer before the expiration of 12 months from the publication in *Iris Oifigiúil* of the notice striking the company name from the register, and provided he has received confirmation from the Revenue Commissioners that all outstanding, if any, statements required by s 882 of the Taxes Consolidation Act, 1997, have been delivered to the Revenue Commissioners, may restore the name of the company to the register.'

Upon the registration of an application under this subsection and on payment of the appropriate fee, 'the company shall be deemed to have continued in existence as if its name had not been struck off': C(A)A 1982, s 12C(2). Moreover, subject to any court order to the contrary, the restoration shall not affect the rights or liabilities of the company in respect of any debt or obligation incurred or any contract entered into by, to, with or on behalf of the company between the date of its dissolution and its subsequent restoration[417].

[12.155] The use of the expression 'is aggrieved' is not without significance and it was held in *Re Contiv Uebersee Bank AG*[418] that a director who had initially agreed with the

---

415 For an excellent, practical, guide for solicitors to restoring companies to the register, see O'Higgins, 'How to Restore a Struck–Off Company to the Register' (2001) Jan/Feb Gazette of the Law Society of Ireland 40. For a review of the proof required under the old restoration regime (ie pre the C(A)(No 2)A 1999) see Mooney, 'Restoring Companies to the Register' (1997) Bar Review 226.

416 Note the 'fast track' restoration process introduced by the CRO to address the huge increase in numbers for reinstatements, described by O'Higgins, 'How to Restore a Struck–Off Company to the Register' (2001) Jan/Feb Gazette of the Law Society of Ireland 40 at 41, whereby a director of a dissolved company which qualifies for administrative restoration can wait in the CRO's offices until such time as reinstatement has been effected.

417 C(A)A 1982, s 12C(3).

418 *Re Contiv Uebersee Bank AG* (1998) Times Scots Law Report, 12 October.

board's decision that a company should be dissolved but who later changed his mind, was not 'aggrieved' for the purposes of an application for restoration. In an Australian case, *Re Waldcourt Investment Co Pty Ltd*[419] it was said by Olney J that:

> 'I do not think that either a shareholder or a director as such must necessarily be aggrieved by the cancellation of the registration of a company. An applicant must, in my opinion, show that his interests have been or are likely to be prejudicially affected by the cancellation of registration.'

In *Casali v Crisp*[420] it was said that prejudice might be proved where a shareholder shows that he was also a creditor of the company or, alternatively, that there might well be a surplus of assets if the company were reinstated and certain events occurred.

[12.156] The Registrar's statutory power to restore a company on such application being made is made expressly subject to a number of other statutory provisions:

— a member's or creditor's right to apply to court for judicial restoration under CA 1963, s 311(8);

— a company's right to apply itself to the Registrar for restoration by administrative action under CA 1963, s 311A;

— a member's, officer's or creditor's right to apply to court for judicial restoration under C(A)A 1982, s 12B(3); and

— the right of the Registrar to apply to court for judicial restoration under C(A)A 1982, s 12B(7).

[12.157] It is important to note a number of points in relation to an application under C(A)A 1982, s 12(C)(1) for restoration by the Registrar. First, only members or officers may apply – in particular creditors and the company itself have no standing to apply. It is not readily apparent as to why the company itself should not be permitted to apply under this provision. Secondly, unless the Revenue Commissioners have been supplied with all outstanding statements and the Registrar has received confirmation of this fact, it is pointless to make application as it will be refused outright. Finally, it is again important to stress the 12-month time period within which application must be made: if in excess of 12 months from the publication in *Iris Oifigiúil* of the notice striking the company name from the register, application will have to be made to the courts for restoration by judicial order.

[12.158] The second method of restoration by administrative action is provided for by CA 1963, s 311A(1). This applies to applications for restoration to the Registrar where strike-off resulted from any of the *other four* grounds. Section 311A(1) provides that:

> '…if a company feels aggrieved by having been struck off the register, the Registrar of Companies on an application made in the prescribed form by the company before the expiration of twelve months after the publication in *Iris Oifigiúil* of the notice striking the company name from the register, and provided he has received all annual returns outstanding, if any, from the company, may restore the name of the company to the register.'

The Registrar's power to restore is again expressed to be without prejudice to CA 1963, s 311(8) and C(A)A 1982, ss 12B(3), 12B(7) and 12C(1). Again it is provided that, upon the registration of an application under this subsection and on payment of the appropriate

[419] *Re Waldcourt Investment Co Pty Ltd* (1986) 11 ACLR 12.

[420] *Casali v Crisp* [2001] Supreme Court of New South Wales 860 (3 October 2001).

fee, 'the company shall be deemed to have continued in existence as if its name had not been struck off': CA 1963, s 311A(2). Moreover, subject to any court order to the contrary, the restoration shall not affect the rights or liabilities of the company in respect of any debt or obligation incurred or any contract entered into by, to, with or on behalf of the company between the date of its dissolution and its subsequent restoration[421].

[12.159] The important points to remember here are, first, that only companies can make application to the Registrar under CA 1963, s 311A(1); secondly, it is imperative that all outstanding annual returns are filed; and thirdly, application to the Registrar must be brought within 12-months of dissolution.

(ii) Restoration by judicial order

[12.160] In all cases where a company has been struck off for a period *in excess of 12 months*, application for restoration must be made to court. There are three separate provisions under which application can be made to court for judicial restoration. In all cases where application is made for judicial restoration, it is appropriate to notify the Chief State Solicitor's office and to procure a letter to the effect that the Minister for Finance and the Minister for Enterprise, Trade and Employment have no objection to the restoration of the company.

1. Application by members, officers or creditors following a strike-off for failure to file annual returns or failure to deliver required particulars to the Revenue

[12.161] Section 12B(3) of C(A)A 1982 provides that any member, officer or creditor of a company 'aggrieved'[422] by the fact that the company has been struck off for failure to file annual returns (C(A)A 1982, s 12(3)) or for failure to deliver the required particulars to the Revenue (C(A)A 1982, s 12A(3)) may apply to court for restoration. Such application must be made on notice to the Registrar of Companies, the Revenue Commissioners and the Minister for Finance. Application must be brought before the expiration of 20 years after the company's dissolution. Provided that the foregoing conditions are met, s 12B(3) goes on to provide that the court may:

> '...if satisfied that it is just that the company be restored to the register, and, subject to subsection (4) of this section, upon an office copy of the order being delivered to the Registrar for registration, the company shall be deemed to have continued in existence as if its name had not been struck off; and the court may by the order give such directions and make such provisions as seem just for placing the company and all other persons in the same position as nearly as may be as if the name of the company had not been struck off or make such other order as seems just (and such other order is referred to in subsection (4) of this section as an "alternative order").'

With the exception of the possibility that an alternative order may be made by the court, the effect of judicial restoration is identical to the effect of administrative restoration. Deciding whether or not to grant an application for restoration is a matter for judicial

421 CA 1963, s 311A(3).

422 The authorities cited at para **[12.155]** that consider the significance of 'aggrieved' are equally relevant here.

discretion[423], and what will be considered to be 'just' will vary from case to case[424]. In deciding what is just, the court may have regard to the views of third parties and the English Court of Appeal has held that there is a wide discretion to allow third parties to be jointed in restoration applications[425].

[12.162] There is, however, a strong bias in favour of making a restoration order where strike-off was occasioned by a failure to file annual returns. Some of the factors that have been held to justify a court in exercising its discretion against ordering restoration were identified by the English High Court in *Re Priceland Ltd*[426] and include:

— the objector to restoration should demonstrate a substantial amount of prejudice;

— that such prejudice could be attributed to restoration; and

— that the objector changed its position on account of the strike-off.

In the English case of *Re Blenheim Leisure (Restaurants) Ltd (No 2)*[427] Neuberger J held that once the stated proofs – or gateways – in restoration provisions were satisfied, in the absence of special circumstances, restoration should follow and exercising the court's discretion against restoration should be the exception and not the rule. In *Re Blue Note Enterprises Ltd*[428] the company, the subject of an application for restoration, had been struck off the register following its failure to file annual returns. The subject-company had been retained to run three clubs in London for another company, the Mean Fiddler Holdings Ltd, but, subsequently, had been dropped. The subject-company had initiated proceedings for breach of contract but these had languished due to insufficient funds. Mean Fiddler Holdings Ltd was joined in the application for restoration, which it opposed, on the basis that the subject-company had no prospect of taking the contract claim to judgment because it could not fund the litigation. It was again stated that the approach to applications for restoration following strike-off for failure to file annual returns was that 'exercising the discretion against restoration should be the exception not the rule'[429]. In that case restoration was ordered.

A different approach to third-party *objections* to restoration is apparent from the Irish Supreme Court decision in *Re Bloomberg Developments Ltd*[430]. There, it was said by the Supreme Court (Murphy J) that 'restoration is primarily a matter between the petitioner on the one part and the regulatory authority – who has a duty to ensure compliance with the relevant provisions of the Companies Acts – and the Minister for Finance – in whom

[423] See as to the court's jurisdiction see, *Re Portrafram Ltd* [1986] BCLC 533.

[424] See *Re Workvale Ltd* [1991] BCLC 528 and 531 in regard to persons with a claim for unliquidated damages against a company which was dissolved; in *Re Forte's Manufacturing Ltd* [1994] BCC 84 the Court of Appeal restored a company to the register in order to reopen its liquidation and thereby admit new claims.

[425] See *Re Blenheim Leisure (Restaurants) Ltd* [1999] TLR 603.

[426] *Re Priceland Ltd* [1997] 1 BCLC 467.

[427] *Re Blenheim Leisure (Restaurants) Ltd (No 2)* [2000] BCC 821.

[428] *Re Blue Note Enterprises Ltd* [2001] 2 BCLC 427.

[429] [2001] 2 BCLC 427 at 432e, citing *Re Priceland Ltd* [1997] 1 BCLC 467 at 476 and *Re Blenheim Leisure (Restaurants) Ltd (No 2)* [2000] BCC 821 at 829.

[430] *Re Bloomberg Developments Ltd* (12 July 2002, unreported) Supreme Court.

would vest the assets of the company as bona vacantia – of the other part'[431]. In that case, however, it was held that an opposing third party (which was being sued by the dissolved company) had properly been allowed to appear on the petition for restoration. This was because an application was made by the petitioner to extend a stay that had been put on the order it had obtained to have the proceedings against it struck out because the plaintiff company had been dissolved. Moreover, the Supreme Court accepted that the third-party objector had been in a position to bring before the High Court evidence as to the petitioner's conduct, which the High Court attached considerable significance.

[12.163] Where application is brought by either a creditor or the Registrar of Companies, the court to which application is made is the Circuit Court, a provision inserted by C(A)(No 2)A 1999 to reduce the costs involved in applications for restoration which were previously brought in the High Court[432]. It was held by the Supreme Court in *Re Deauville Communication Worldwide Ltd*[433] that although the language used in C(A)(A) 1982, s 12B was capable of being construed so as to make it *obligatory* that application for restoration be brought in the Circuit Court as opposed to the High Court, a creditor was permitted still to bring an application for restoration in the High Court. Keane CJ held he was satisfied that '…when the subsection is placed in the appropriate context, it becomes clear that the intention of the Oireachtas was more likely to have been to enable the application to be brought either in the High Court or the Circuit Court.' It is very notable, however, that where application for restoration is brought by either members or officers, application must be brought to the High Court.

[12.164] An example of an application for restoration is seen in *Re Eden Quay Investments Ltd*[434]. In that application before Keane J, the directors of a company, which had been dissolved 18 years previously, successfully applied to have the company restored to the register. It had only been discovered that the company's 514,256 shares in Hibernian Transport Companies Ltd were not worthless, as previously had been thought. In May 1993 the Supreme Court held that the shareholders in the company were entitled to benefit from a surplus of IR£2.5 million arising from the liquidation of the Hibernian companies, which also included Palgrave Murphy Ltd[435]. The company had been struck off the register in 1976 for failing to file its annual returns. Keane J granted the application having heard that if the company were not restored to the register it would not be able to prove its claim in the winding up of Hibernian Transport Companies Ltd.

[12.165] The ability to make an 'alternative order' was introduced by C(A)(No 2)A 1999. Section 12B(4) of C(A)A 1982 provides:

> 'An alternative order may, if the court considers it appropriate that it should do so, include a provision that, as respects a debt or liability incurred by, or on behalf or, the company during

[431] Citing *Conrad Hall & Co Ltd* [1916] WN 275 as authority.

[432] C(A)A 1982, s 12B(9). C(A)A 1982, s 12B(10) and (11) deal with the appropriate circuit in which to bring application.

[433] *Re Deauville Communications Worldwide Ltd* (15 March 2002, unreported) Supreme Court.

[434] An ex tempore order of the High Court reported in (1994) The Irish Times, 12 April. See also *Stanhope Pension Trust Ltd v Registrar of Companies* [1994] 1 BCLC 628.

[435] In *Re Hibernian Transport Companies Ltd* [1994] 1 ILRM 48. See Chapter 27, ***Realisation and Distribution of Assets on Liquidation***, para **[27.167]**.

the period when it stood struck off the register, the officers of the company or such one or more of them as is or are specified in the order shall be liable for the whole or a part (as the court thinks just) of the debt or liability.'

Accordingly, officers who cause a company to trade and incur liabilities whilst it is dissolved may be rendered personally responsible for such liabilities. It is thought, however, that save in the most exceptional of circumstances (eg where the company is insolvent) the courts will be slow to make an alternative order. It is not clear as to whether the alternative order can be made *in addition* to a restoration order or whether such is only permitted *in lieu* of a restoration order. The use of the word 'alternative' suggests such an order would *not* be made where a restoration order is made. In such a case the effect is that where the court declines to restore a company it can, in that event, pacify its creditors by making its officers personally responsible for the debts incurred whilst the company was dissolved.

[12.166] The legislature is quite prescriptive in detailing the conditions which the court should impose on making a restoration order. So, C(A)A 1982, s 12B(5) provides that 'unless cause is shown to the contrary' the court shall include in a restoration order where application is brought by a *member or officer* a provision that the order shall not have effect unless within one month of the date of the order, all outstanding annual returns are delivered to the Registrar (where dissolved on foot of s 12(3)) or that all outstanding statements are delivered to the Revenue Commissioners (where dissolved on foot of s 12A(3)). The Supreme Court has made clear in *Re Bloomberg Developments Ltd*[436] that, on an application for restoration, the High Court has power to ensure that the power to restore a company to the register is used for the purpose for which it was intended[437]. So, the High Court can require an undertaking to wind up a restored company once a particular purpose has been achieved. The High Court does not, however, have power to impose a penalty on a petitioner company[438]. In that case the Supreme Court allowed an appeal against a High Court order that required a company (which the court had ordered to be restored to the register) to pay the costs of litigation incurred to that point by a company that was being sued by the petitioner company as a condition of its restoration. The Supreme Court held this order was in the nature of a penalty and it was inappropriate to make an order for costs "in proceedings which fall to be dealt with on their own merits independently of the application for restoration".

[12.167] The expression 'creditor' will be given a broad interpretation and in *Re Deauville Communications Worldwide Ltd*[439] the Supreme Court held that 'creditor' in C(A)(A) 1982, s 12B(3) should be read as extending to contingent and prospective creditors[440]. Where application is brought by a creditor for the restoration of a company, C(A)A 1982,

[436] *Re Bloomberg Developments Ltd* (12 July 2002, unreported) Supreme Court.

[437] *Langlaate Propriety Co Ltd* [1912] 28 TLR 529.

[438] *Brown, Bayley's Steelworks* [1905] 21TLR 374.

[439] *Re Deauville Communications Worldwide Ltd* (15 March 2002, unreported) Supreme Court.

[440] Keane CJ cited the following cases as authorities: *Re Harvest Lane Motor Bodies Ltd* [1969] IR 457; *Re Telegraph Construction Company* LR 10 EQ 384; *City of Westminister Assurance Company Ltd v Register of Companies* (28 June 1996, unreported) English Court of Appeal and *Re Industrial Glazing Systems Ltd* (6 November 2000, unreported) High Court (Barr J).

s 12B(6) provides that the court shall direct that one or more specified members or officers shall, within a specified period, deliver all outstanding annual returns to the Registrar or all outstanding statements to the Revenue, as appropriate. This change to the law on restoration will obviate the lacuna, identified (but circumvented) by O'Hanlon J in *Re Haltone (Cork) Ltd*[441]. In that case the petitioner applied for the restoration of the above-named company pursuant to the 'old' CA 1963, s 311(8) in circumstances where the petitioner claimed to have large unsatisfied debts against the company and had obtained judgment in England for over £40,000 plus costs. The petitioner said it wished to enforce the judgment against the company and also against its officers in reliance upon statutory personal liability provisions. The company in question had been struck off for failure to file annual returns and O'Hanlon J said that where application is made on behalf of the company itself it was normally granted upon condition that all outstanding annual returns would be filed. He noted:

> 'In the present case, however, the application is made, not by or on behalf of the company itself, but by a creditor who feels that there is greater scope for invoking the provisions of the Companies Acts against the officers of the company when the company has been restored to the register and is no longer to be regarded as a company which has been dissolved.
>
> Obviously, the petitioner is not in a position to file annual returns on behalf of the company to make good the default which has taken place in the past and is unlikely to secure the co-operation of the company or its officers in carrying out this procedure.'[442]

In the event O'Hanlon J acceded to the petitioner's application and restored the company so as to allow the petitioner a reasonable opportunity to pursue whatever remedy was available to it under the Companies Acts. O'Hanlon J went on to direct that the petitioner should be responsible for the payment of any fees payable to the Registrar and suggested (but did not direct) that the Registrar should give notice to the petitioner of any further attempt to strike the company off the register. Section 12B(6) of C(A)A 1982 alleviates the burden on creditors seeking to have a company restored where the reason for its strike-off was failure to file annual returns, a default that is almost invariably beyond the ability of a creditor to remedy.

2. Application by the Registrar following a strike-off for failure to file annual returns or failure to deliver required particulars to the Revenue

[12.168] Section 12B(7) of C(A)A 1982 gives locus standi to the Registrar of Companies to apply to court for a restoration order where a company has been struck off for either failure to file annual returns or failure to deliver required particulars to the revenue. Again, application must be brought within 20 years of dissolution and the application must be on notice to each person who, to the Registrar's knowledge, is an officer of the company. The consequences for the company of the court acceding to the Registrar's application are the same as where application is brought by members, officers or creditors under s 12B(3). Of significance is the fact that on such application being brought, the court is again empowered to make an 'alternative order'. Again, it would seem to be open to the court to make such an order instead of making a restoration order. It would seem that this might

[441] *Re Haltone (Cork) Ltd* [1996] 1 IR 32.

[442] [1996] 1 IR 32 at 35.

indeed be the primary motivation behind this provision, namely, to allow the Registrar to apply for an alternative order to make in officers personally responsible for post-dissolution debts. It is thought that it would only be in rare cases that the Registrar (who, after all, caused the company to be struck off) would want to bring application to have it restored.

3. Application by a company, member or creditor following a strike-off on the grounds of ceasing to carry on business, having no recorded directors and having no resident director

[12.169] Section 311(8) of CA 1963 is the applicable section where a judicial restoration order is sought in circumstances where the reason for the company being struck off was because it ceased to carry on business, (CA 1963, s 311(2)) or had no recorded directors (or had no resident director (C(A)(No 2)A 1999, s 43(15)). Those with locus standi to apply under this section are the company, any member and any creditor. Again, application must be brought within 20 years of the company's dissolution. Where application is brought – on notice to the Registrar – the High Court may:

> '...if satisfied that the company was at the time of the striking off carrying on business or otherwise that it is just that the company be restored to the register, order that the name of the company be restored to the register, and upon an office copy of the order being delivered to the Registrar for registration, the company shall be deemed to have continued in existence as if its name had not been struck off; and the court may by the order give such directions and make such provisions as seem just for placing the company and all other persons in the same position as nearly as may be as if the name of the company had not been struck off or make such other order as seems just (and such other order is referred to in subsection (8A) as an "alternative order".'

Again, an alternative order may include a provision that as respects a debt or liability incurred by or on behalf of the company during the period when it was dissolved, the officers of the company or any one or more of them, shall be personally responsible for the whole or part, as the court thinks just, of the debt or liability. It will be noted that there is no provision for application to be brought under this provision to the Circuit Court and all applications have to go to the High Court.

[12.170] Where the reason why the company was dissolved was on the ground of failure to have a resident director, CA 1963, s 311(8) is modified by C(A)(No 2)A 1999, s 43(15)(b). The effect is to provide that upon an application for restoration of such a company, the court should be

> 'satisfied that subsection (1) or, as the case may be, subsection (2) of section 43 of the Companies (Amendment) Act 1999, was at the time of the striking off being complied with in relation to the company'.

It will be noted that even if the dissolved company was not complying with s 43(1) or (2) at the time of dissolution, the court may – where it considers it to be just – order its restoration. Presumably this would only be granted where the company in question had at the time of the application a resident director or where there was an undertaking from a resident to act as a director.

(g) The effect of restoration

[12.171] On the restoration of a company to the register, it is deemed to have continued in existence, notwithstanding that it was dissolved. Thus, upon an office copy of the order being delivered to the Registrar for registration C(A)A 1982, s 12B(3) and s 12B(7) and CA 1963, s 311(8) all provide that the effect is that 'the company shall be deemed to have continued in existence as if its name had not been struck off.'

It is, however, important to appreciate the distinction between restoration where dissolution results from strike-off for failure to comply with the Companies Acts and restoration where dissolution results from the winding up of the company[443]. This distinction is significant in the context of the effect of a restoration order, particularly in relation to the consequence for proceedings by or against the company. The different effects of restoration, depending upon why a company was dissolved, was noted by O'Neill J in *Re Amantiss Enterprises Ltd; Framus Ltd v CRH plc*[444], considered below[445].

The potential for confusion was recognised by the English Court of Appeal in *Top Creative Ltd v St Albans District Council*[446]. There, a County Court judge had refused an application by the shareholders in a company that had been struck off the register, to remove an action from the 'warned list' and adjourn it pending the hearing of an application to restore the company. The Court of Appeal allowed the appeal and held that the judge had misdirected himself in two respects. The first misdirection was that the action involving the company was automatically and irrevocable at an end once the company was struck off and that the judge had no jurisdiction to grant the application sought by the dissolved company. The second misdirection was the judge's view that the company had no existence of any kind, once its name was removed from the register. In the Court of Appeal, Roch LJ accepted the appellant's contention that:

> 'Whereas the appellants accept that if a company is wound up by a liquidator that company ceases to have any existence, and existing actions by or against such a company when the winding up is complete and the company dissolved, cease to exist, the position is not the same when all that has occurred is that the company's name has been removed from the register by the administrative act of the Registrar.'[447]

Dissolution following a winding-up order is considered in a later chapter.

[12.172] The effects of C(A)A 1982, ss 12B(3), 12B(7) and CA 1963, 311(8) are very far-reaching, as seen in the case of *Re Dunleckney Ltd*[448]. In that case a company that had been struck off and dissolved on 6 November 1990 was subsequently restored to the register on 21 October 1991. On 6 January 1992 an office copy of the restoration order was sent to the Registrar for registration. Immediately thereafter, the company was wound up. The liquidator of the company had cause to believe that the directors had not acted honestly or responsibly and sought to have them restricted under CA 1990, s 150. The respondent-directors argued that CA 1990, s 150 had only been commenced on 1 August 1991 and, despite the fact that the company had been restored on 21 October 1991, no entitlement to

[443] Dissolution following a winding up is considered in CA 1963, s 310. See Chapter 25, *Winding Up Companies*, para **[25.110]**.

[444] *Re Amantiss Enterprises Ltd; Framus Ltd v CRH plc* (21 December 1999, unreported), High Court (O'Neill J).

[445] See para **[12.173]**.

[446] *Top Creative Ltd v St Albans District Council* [1999] BCC 999.

[447] [1999] BCC 999 at 1003.

[448] *Re Dunleckney Ltd* (18 February 1999, unreported), High Court (Carroll J).

pursue the directors under s 150 existed as it was not retrospective. Carroll J gave this argument short shrift:

> 'Under s 311(8) of the Companies Act 1963 where a company is struck off and the name is restored to the register upon an office copy of the order being delivered, the company is deemed to have continued in existence as if its name had not been struck off.
>
> Therefore when the office copy was lodged on 6 January[449] 1992, the company was deemed to have continued in existence. If follows since the company is deemed to have continued in existence, Part VII [CA 1990, containing s 150] applies to the company because that Part came into operation on the 1 August 1991 and the company was not wound up until 21 October 1991. It was therefore a company in existence at the time Part VII came into operation. Since it is a company which at the date of the commencement of the winding-up order was unable to pay its debts, s 149 applies'.

Although this judgment concerned the interpretation of the 'old' CA 1963, s 311(8), the wording under consideration is identical to that used in both the 'new' CA 1963, s 311(8) and C(A)A 1982, s 12B(3) and (7).

[12.173] All three[450] restoration provisions also provide that 'the court may by order give such directions and make such provision as seem just for placing the company and all other persons in the same position as nearly as may be as if the name of the company had not been struck off'. A truly miraculous judicial act indeed[451]. This effect of restoration was considered by the High Court in *Re Amantiss Enterprises Ltd; Framus Ltd v CRH plc*[452]. The facts were that the petitioner-company had ceased trading in March 1991 and had been placed into voluntary liquidation on 1 April 1994. On 4 December 1996, it (and other companies) commenced proceedings against the seven defendant-companies, alleging that they had engaged in anti-competitive practices. One of the defendant-companies motioned the court seeking, inter alia, to have the petitioner's name struck-out from the proceedings when it learned that the petitioner had been dissolved for failure to file annual returns with effect from 19 May 1993! To enable it to continue and validate the proceedings it had commenced, the petitioner petitioned the court, inter alia, to be restored to the register pursuant to C(A)A 1982, s 12(6)[453]. The petitioner also sought such directions as may seem just for placing the company and all persons in the same position as nearly as may be if the name of the company had not been struck off. The court was asked to construe the proper meaning of the words in C(A)A 1982, s 12(6) (now, s 12B(7)), namely:

> '...and upon an office copy of the order being delivered to the Registrar for registration the company shall be deemed to have continued in existence as if its name had not been struck off; and the Court may by order give such directions and make such provisions as seem just

449 The judgment says 'December' but it is thought this was a typographical error.

450 CA 1963, s 311(8) and C(A)A 1982, s 12B(3) and (7)

451 See *Re Boxco Ltd* [1970] Ch 442 where particulars of a charge created after the dissolution were delivered to the English CRO, it was held that the charge had been properly registered by reason of the company's subsequent restoration.

452 *Re Amantiss Enterprises Ltd; Framus Ltd v CRH plc* [2000] 2 ILRM 177.

453 Section 12(6) was repealed and substituted by C(A)(No 2)(A) 1999, s 46. The corresponding provision is now s 12B(7).

for placing the company and all other persons in the same position as nearly as may be as if the name of the company had not been struck off'.

The petitioner claimed that the effect of s 12(6) was to validate all acts done by the company between its dissolution and its restoration. The defendants rejected this, contending, that the effect of the words 'the company shall be deemed to have continued in existence as if its name had not been struck off':

'...have the effect merely of restoring the status of incorporation of the company and its identity but do not have the effect of validating retrospectively any acts done between dissolution and restoration to the register.' [454]

The defendants also contended that the remainder of the subsection had 'the effect of giving to the Court the power by specific order to validate retrospectively acts that may have been done during dissolution'[455], the defendant's point being that retrospective validation was not automatic but subject to the court's discretion.

[12.174] O'Neill J rejected the defendant's arguments and held that C(A)A 1982, s 12(6) operated to confer 'automatic retrospective validation'. In so holding O'Neill J followed the majority judgments of the English Court of Appeal in *Tymans Ltd v Craven*[456], which interpreted the materially identical s 353(6) of the Companies Act 1948 (UK). On this point he said:

'... I find the reasoning of the majority judgments in the *Tyman* case preferable, and hold that the words "*the company shall be deemed to have continued in existence as if its name had not been struck off*" have the effect of validating retrospectively all acts done in the name or on behalf of the company during the period between its dissolution and the restoration of its name to the register, and that the words "*and the court may by order give such directions and make such provisions as seems just for placing the company and all other persons in the same position as nearly as may be as if the name of the company had not been struck off*" are not expository qualifying the scope of the proceeding general word but are complementary only to those general words so as to enable the court to achieve to the fullest extent consistent with justice the '*as you were*' position of the company.'[457]

As to the justification for this finding, O'Neill J said:

'In my view the plain and very reasonable and sensible intendment of s 12(6) is to preserve the validity of transactions entered into during a period of dissolution where frequently that dissolution is unknown to either the company and its officers or third parties dealing with it, and who conduct their business with each other and enter into engagements with each other on the basis that the company enjoys lawful existence. To remove legal validity from all of these transactions in circumstances where the parties to them at the time of their making intended them to have legal validity would in a great many instances work injustices and would provide the unscrupulous with much opportunity for mischief. I have no doubt that the legislature, in selecting the very clear language used in s 12(6), intended that such

---

454 [2000] 2 ILRM 177 at 187.

455 [2000] 2 ILRM 177 at 188.

456 *Tymans Ltd v Craven* [1952] 1 All ER 613.

457 [2000] 2 ILRM 177 at 191. O'Neill J declined to follow *Re Townreach Ltd* [1995] Ch 8 and *Natural Nectar Products Canada Ltd v Michael Theodor* Court of Appeal of British Columbia of 6 June 1990.

unfortunate consequences would not occur by reason of an unintended dissolution where no orderly process of winding up had taken place.'[458]

Overly forgiving of corporate non-compliance? Possibly. Realistic and practical? Most certainly so. O'Neill J himself pointed to the fact (noted by Evershed MR in *Tymans*) that to hold to the contrary could give rise to a multiplicity of proceedings concerning the validation of all the multifarious engagements into which a dissolved company might have entered. O'Neill J went on to find that it was proper to order that the petitioner be restored to the register of companies. He also held that he did not accept that the institution of proceedings against the defendants at the time the company had been dissolved was a specific prejudice having regard to his conclusions as to the meaning and effect of C(A)A 1982, s 12(6). O'Neill J went on to say that he was impressed by the fact that counsel for the Registrar of Companies had no objection to the relief being sought in the petition being granted having regard to the uniqueness of the Registrar's position in assessing compliance with the relevant statutory requirement.

Injunctions to compel compliance with the Companies Acts 1963–2001

[12.175] Section 371 of CA 1963 seems never to have been used and, indeed, to have been practically forgotten about until 're-discovered' by the chair of the McDowell Group shortly after the group's formation. In its report the group said:

> 'The threat of fast track High Court civil proceedings and consequent costs would, in many cases, act as a major deterrent to non-compliance, not only in relation to the companies in question, but also in relation to individual officer defendants.'[459]

The group went on to recommend the expansion of the section in terms of breath and in respect to those who can bring application[460]. Section 96 of CLEA 2001 effected a number of changes to the originally drafted CA 1963, s 371, resulting in the following extended section:

> '(1) If a company or any officer of a company having made default in complying with any provision of this Act fails to make good the default within 14 days after the service of a notice on the company or officer requiring it or him to do so, the court may, on an application made to the court by any member or creditor of the company, by the Director or by the Registrar of Companies, make an order directing the company and any officer thereof to make good the default within such time as may be specified in the order.
>
> (2) Any such order may provide that all costs of and incidental to the application shall be borne by the company or by any officers of the company responsible for the default.
>
> (3) Nothing in this section shall be taken to prejudice the operation of any enactment imposing penalties (including restriction under section 150, or disqualification under section 160 of the Companies Act 1990) on a company or its officers in respect of any such default as aforesaid.
>
> (4) In this section, 'officer of a company' and cognate words include a director, shadow director, an officer, a promoter, a receiver, a liquidator or an auditor of a company.'

[458] (21 December 1999, unreported), High Court at pp 22–23.
[459] *McDowell Group Report*, para 3.22.
[460] *McDowell Group Report*, para 4.33.

[12.176] The revamped CA 1963, s 371 provides company law enforcers (the Director of Corporate Enforcement and the Registrar of Companies) as well as disgruntled creditors or aggrieved members with the right to have recourse to the High Court for an injunction to compel compliance *by a company or any officer of a company* with *any default in complying with a provision of the Companies Acts*. Consequent upon s 371(4) (added to the section by CLEA 2001, s 96(c)) it can be seen that officer of a company is very broadly defined although why examiners were excluded, in view of the fact that there are serious duties imposed upon them, is unclear.

[12.177] It would seem to be a prerequisite to the invocation of CA 1963, s 371(1) that the default complained of is capable of being 'made good'. It is a remedial measure, designed to ensure compliance rather than to punish non-compliance; of course non-compliance with the High Court order is punishable as a contempt of court[461]. Where a person who is entitled to make complaint wishes to initiate the section 371 injunction, he should first serve a notice on the company or officer, requiring it or him to make good the default complained of within 14 days of the date of the notice. It would be prudent to head up the notice, '*Notice Pursuant to Section 371(1) of the Companies Act, 1963 Requiring a Default under the Companies Acts to be Made Good*', or words to that effect, so that the addressee can be under do doubt but that the intention in serving the notice is to proceed to seek a court order should the default not be made good. Once this has been done the High Court has jurisdiction to make an order. It is notable that there is no guidance provided to the court when it comes to the exercise of its discretion – not even that such an order should be made where the court considers it 'just' or 'just and equitable'. The order will operate in much the same way as an ordinary injunction and should require that the default is made good by a particular time. Section 371(2) expressly provides that the court, on making an order, can, at the court's discretion, provide that all costs of and incidental to the application shall be borne by the company or by any officers of the company responsible for the default. It is also significant that the making of an order under this section is expressed to be without prejudice to the operation of any enactment imposing penalties, including restriction and disqualification orders.

[D] Registration-type Offences

[12.178] The Companies Acts 1963–2001 contain numerous requirements for companies (and their officers) to deliver various notices and documents to the Registrar of Companies ('the Registrar') at the CRO. Section 368(1) of CA 1963 requires the Minister for Enterprise, Trade and Employment to maintain and administer an office or offices (the CRO) for the purposes of the registration of companies and sub-s (2) provides that the Minister may appoint such registrars and assistant registrars as he thinks necessary[462]. Two of the primary functions of the Registrar are the registration of new companies and the registration of post-incorporation documents from, or in relation to, registered companies[463].

---

461 As to which see, Courtney, *Mareva Injunctions and Related Interlocutory Orders* (1998), ch 12.

462 The current Registrar of Companies is Mr Paul Farrell.

463 See para **[12.006]** where the Registrar's enforcement functions are considered.

The purpose of registration

[12.179] The statutory purpose in requiring companies and others to file, deliver or register certain documents in relation to companies is to effect public disclosure, which is, in this respect, the quid pro quo for registration of companies. Public disclosure of the register is provided for by CA 1963, s 370(1)(a), which provides that any person may, on payment of a fee, 'inspect the documents kept by the Registrar of Companies'[464]. It is considered proper for the public at large to be able to consult with a central registry (the CRO) in order to elicit certain organisational, constitutional and financial information about a registered company[465]. It should be remembered, however, that public documents can be a double-edged sword: whilst they make available information on companies the public at large will be deemed to have *constructive notice* of their existence and contents[466].

Summary and indictable registration offences

[12.180] Of the circa 283 specified criminal offences identified in *Appendix 2* to the McDowell Group's report[467] (which enumerate the criminal offences created by the Companies Acts 1963–1990 only) some 73 related to failures to file, deliver or lodge with the Registrar, certain specified documents by companies and specified individuals. Of those 73 offences, only 14 can be prosecuted on indictment, the remainder being summary offences. Not only that, but only one of the indictable offences relating to registration relates to an offence committed by a company: CA 1990, s 226 which makes it an indictable offence to fail to deliver to the Registrar within 28 days, a return relating to a company's own-purchase of shares. The other registration offences that are indictable relate to failures by: liquidators[468]; receivers[469], petitioners for orders for court protection[470]; examiners[471]; auditors[472]; and recognised bodies of accountants[473].

Failure to file annual return and notify changes in officers

[12.181] The most common non-registration offence in respect of which the Registrar has in recent years taken action is the failure by a company to file its *annual return* with the

---

464 CA 1963, s 370(1)(b) allows any person to require a certificate of incorporation of any company or a copy or extract of any other document or any part thereof to be certified by the register in return for a fee.

465 See, for example, the rationale behind the registration of charges created by companies given by Sargant J in *Esberg & Son Ltd v Capital Counties Bank* [1913] 2 Ch 366 at 374: see Chapter 21, *Corporate Borrowing: Registration of Charges*, para **[21.003]**.

466 For the relevant of this in the context of outsiders being bound by constitutional restrictions on corporate authority, see Chapter 7, *Corporate Contracts, Capacity and Authority*, para **[7.096]**.

467 *Appendix 2* was reproduced in the McDowell Group's report from McGahon, *Irish Company Law Index* (1991).

468 CA 1963, s 306(1); CA 1990, ss 145, 151.

469 CA 1963, ss 319(2), 321(1).

470 C(A)A 1990, ss 12(5).

471 C(A)A 1990, ss 12(5).

472 CA 1990, ss 185, 186 and 194

473 CA 1990, ss 199 and 200.

Registrar within the set periods[474]. The requirement for all Irish registered companies to file an annual return is considered in Chapter 13[475]. Non-compliance with this particular case of *non-registration* attracts the Registrar's 'nuclear remedy' for defaulting companies: the much feared, *strike-off*. Strangely, no public justification, apart from statutory right, has ever been advanced for the invocation of the remedy of strike-off against companies which fail to file an annual return. One can only surmise that it is considered to be a fundamental quid pro quo for corporate registration. The remedy of strike-off is comprehensively considered above[476].

[12.182] Perhaps, the second most commonly spoken of non-registration offence is the failure by companies to notify the Registrar of changes in their officers, particularly the *retirement* of company directors. Again, this is a summary offence: CA 1963, s 195[477]. Here, the reason for the Registrar's concern lies in his remedies against the directors of defaulting companies and other 'officers in default'[478]: without having identifiable officers to prosecute, the Registrar's powers of enforcement are rendered impotent. This is exacerbated by the fact that as a matter of company law, a director's status as such is dependent upon whether or not in fact he continues to be a director vis-à-vis his company: whether or not he is registered as a director does not determine his status as a director[479]. It is for that reason that statutory obstacles have been placed in the path of directors' attempts to self-notify the Registrar of their resignations[480], since if companies notify the Registrar of resignations they are duty bound to notify him of replacement directors of a sufficient number to satisfy the statutory minimum of two: CA 1963, s 174[481].

Other registration offences

[12.183] Many of the registration offences comprise of relative innocuous transgressions of the Companies Acts 1963–2001; others – insofar as the failure to comply means that the public is unaware of serious matters affecting a company – have the potential to be very serious. Registration offences can be committed by: companies, liquidators, receivers, petitioners for orders for court protection, examiners, auditors and recognised bodies of accountants.

(a) Registration offences by companies

[12.184] Most of the registration offences are directed at defaulting companies. In most cases, not only will the company be guilty of the offence, but so too will 'every officer in default'[482]. These *include* the failure to deliver/notify/file to or with the Registrar the following:

474 CA 1963, ss 125–127, as replaced by the CLEA 2001, ss 59 and 60.

475 At para **[13.154]** *ff*.

476 At para **[12.132]** *ff*.

477 See Chapter 8, *Corporate Governance: Management by the Directors*, para **[8.087]** *ff*.

478 See para **[12.032]**.

479 *POW Services Ltd v Clare* [1995] 2 BCLC 435: see Chapter 8, *Corporate Governance: Management by the Directors*, para **[8.042]**.

480 See Chapter 8, *Corporate Governance: Management by the Directors*, para **[8.081]**.

481 See Chapter 8, *Corporate Governance: Management by the Directors*, para **[8.021]**.

482 'Every officer in default' is considered at para **[12.032]**.

- the altered memorandum where objects clause amended: CA 1963, s 10(9);
- a notice of an increase in members of an unlimited company: CA 1963, s 12(3);
- an endorsed copy prospectus before issue: CA 1963, s 47(1);
- a statement in lieu of prospectus: CA 1963, s 53(1);
- return of allotment of shares: CA 1963, s 58(1);
- details of authorised commissions on allotment: CA 1963, s 59(1);
- notice of consolidation, etc of shares: CA 1963, s 69(1);
- notice of increase in authorised or nominal share capital: CA 1963, s 70(1);
- court order for cancellation of variation of shareholders' rights: CA 1963, s 78(5);
- particulars of a charge[483], acquisition of property subject to existing charges[484], and a copy of the affidavit of judgment mortgage[485];
- notice of change in registered office: CA 1963, s 113(3);
- notice of place/ change in place where register of members is kept: CA 1963, s 116(7);
- annual return: CA 1963, ss 125 and 127[486];
- copy court order extending time in which annual return may be delivered: CA 1963, s 127(4)[487];
- annex balance sheet (and auditors' report, if applicable) to annual return: CA 1963, s 128(1);
- copy resolution treating a meeting as an AGM: CA 1963, s 131(5);
- copy of special and certain other resolutions: CA 1963, s 143(2);
- notice of removal of an auditor: CA 1963, s 160(5A)(a)(ii)[488];
- list of persons consenting to be directors in prospectuses etc: CA 1963, s 179(1);
- consents of new directors or secretary: CA 1963, s 195;
- copy of court order regarding compromises/ arrangements: CA 1963, ss 201(1) and 203(3);
- copy of court order in remedy for oppression: CA 1963, s 205(5);
- copy winding-up order: CA 1963, s 221(1);
- copy of court order annulling or staying winding up: CA 1963, s 234(4);
- copy order annulling or staying the resolution to wind up: CA 1963, s 280(3).
- register particulars required of foreign companies: CA 1963, s 358;
- documents required of new unregistered companies: CA 1963, s 377(6);

483 CA 1963, s 100(1).

484 CA 1963, s 101(1).

485 CA 1963, s 102(1). It was also an offence not to register a charge created before the coming into operation of CA 1963 ie 1 April 1964: CA 1963, s 112(1).

486 As inserted by CLEA 2001, ss 59 and 60.

487 As inserted by CLEA 2001, s 60.

488 Note, notice of arising of Minister's power to appoint an auditor must be given to the Minister: CA 1963, s 160(5A)(a)(i).

- notice of court application to cancel special resolution for re-registration of a PLC as a private company: C(A)A 1983, s 15(5);
- copy court order cancelling/ confirming special resolution to re-register as a private company: C(A)A 1983, s 15(5);
- copy ordinary resolution and report in respect of payment of non-cash consideration (PLCs only): C(A)A 1983, s 33(2);
- statement of rights attaching to shares, where not stated in memorandum or articles: C(A)A 1983, s 39(1);
- statement of allotment of shares containing particulars of variation: C(A)A 1983, s 39(3);
- notice of the assignment of name or designation to any class of shares: C(A)A 1983, s 39(4);
- notice of petition to appoint an examiner (where presented by company itself): C(A)A 1990, s 12(5);
- copy of statement by auditor to members: CA 1990, s 186;
- return relating to purchase of own shares: CA 1990, s 226;
- notice of cessation of last remaining State resident director: C(A)(No 2)A 1999, s 43(9).

Offences that are obsolete in the sense that they concern notifications after the commencement of particular Companies Acts are excluded from the foregoing list as they can no longer be prosecuted. Not all of the foregoing offences are also offences by 'officers in default' and each particular section should be consulted individually. As indicated, the requirement in each case varies from 'deliver to' or 'file with' or 'give notice to' the Registrar and the precise requirement should, in each case, be scrutinised. It should also be remembered that in many of the above registration requirements, an offence will be committed even if delivery etc is effected, but is outside of particular *statutory time* limits. Where Ministerial regulations require the use of any symbol of classification on documents required to be delivered to the Registrar, it is an offence not to comply[489].

(b) Registration offences by liquidators, receivers and examiners

[12.185] Most of the remaining registration offences are directed at defaulting insolvency practitioners. These *include* the failure to deliver/notify/file to or with the Registrar (or others) the following:

- notice of appointment (by a receiver): CA 1963, s 107(1);
- notice of cessation to act (by a receiver): CA 1963, s 107(2);
- statement of affairs (by a receiver): CA 1963, s 319(1);
- abstract of receipts and payments every six months and statement as to whether the company is solvent (by a receiver): CA 1963, s 319(2) and (2A)[490];
- returns (by a receiver or liquidator): CA 1990, s 145;

[489] CA 1990, s 247(4). See, also, para **[12.188]**.

[490] CA 1963, s 319(2A) was inserted by CLEA 2001, s 53(a).

- — notify directors that they are persons to whom CA 1990, ss 149–158 applies (by a liquidator): CA 1990, s 151;
- — copy of court order for dissolution of company (by a liquidator): CA 1963, s 249(2);
- — deliver office copy of order applying provisions ordinarily only applicable to a creditors' winding up to a members' winding up (by a liquidator): CA 1963, s 256(6).
- — copy final report of final general meeting in both members' and creditors' windings-up (by a liquidator): CA 1963, ss 263(3) and 273(3);
- — notice of appointment (by a liquidator): CA 1963, s 278(3);
- — copy court order annulling or staying a winding up (by a liquidator): CA 1963, s 280(3);
- — particulars on the progress of a liquidation (by a liquidator): CA 1963, s 306(1);
- — office copy order permitting disposal of charged property (by an examiner): C(A)A 1990, s 11(7);
- — notice of appointment (by an examiner): C(A)A 1990, s 12(5);
- — copy court order s 24 of the 1990 Amendment Act (by an examiner): C(A)A 1990, s 30(2);

Again, many of the foregoing registration requirements must be effected within particular *statutory time* limits. There is anecdotal evidence that the Registrar has been less than pleased with the compliance by insolvency practitioners with their statutory obligations to register, but that the situation has greatly improved in recent years.

(c) Registration offences by auditors and auditors' representative bodies

[12.186] Auditors and accountancy bodies are also required to make particular returns and deliver particular documents to the Registrar. These offences include the failure to deliver/notify/file to or with the Registrar the following:

- — notice of resignation of auditor (by an auditor): CA 1990, s 185;
- — opinion that company is contravening or has contravened its requirement to maintain proper books of account (by an auditor): CA 1990, s 194;
- — notice and (if applicable statement) of resignation (by an auditor): CA 1990, s 186;
- — list of members qualified for appointment as auditors (by recognised body of accountants): CA 1990, s 199;
- — list of members qualified for appointment as auditors, within one month of their qualification (by recognised body of accountants): CA 1990, s 200.

None of the foregoing are particularly onerous or controversial obligations. The most significant reporting duty imposed upon auditors is pursuant to CA 1963, s 194(5), inserted by CLEA 2001, s 74. This obliges auditors to report to the Director of Corporate Enforcement, inter alia, the auditor's suspicion that a company or its officer or agent has committed an indictable offence under the Companies Acts[491]. The recommendation of

[491] See para **[12.014]**.

Report of the Review Group on Auditing, chaired by Senator Joe O'Toole, that external auditors should be required to report whether, in their opinion, the proposed new directors' report on compliance with company law, taxation and other relevant statutory or regulatory requirements, is reasonable[492], if implemented, will also prove to be more controversial than the existing obligations[493].

(d) Registration offences by others

[12.187] The remaining registration offences can be committed by applicants to court who secure a court order deferring the date of dissolution of a company and who fail to file a copy thereof with the Registrar[494]; and a petitioner for the appointment of an examiner who fails to deliver notice of the petition with the Registrar[495].

The form of documents filed, returned or delivered

[12.188] In addition to the various registration requirements under the Companies Acts, there are also qualitative provisions regarding what is filed. Documents (which include any periodic account, abstract, statement or return)[496] required to be delivered must, by CA 1990, s 248(2):

> '(a) state in a prominent position the registered number of the company to which it relates,
>
> (b) satisfy any requirements prescribed for the purposes of this section as to the form and content of the document, and
>
> (c) conform to such requirements as may be prescribed for the purpose of enabling the Registrar to copy the document.'

The form and content of documents that are required to be delivered to the Registrar have been prescribed by the statutory instrument, and are very prescriptive[497].

The 'public person' consent provisions in the Electronic Commerce Act 2000, which allow public bodies to specify their requirements if information is to be delivered electronically had a forerunner in CA 1990, s 249. Section 249(2) facilitates the delivery of documents in any non-legible form prescribed for the purposes. As in the case of legible documents, non-legible documents must meet similar qualitative requirements.

[12.189] Section 249A of CA 1990[498] amended both CA 1990, ss 248 and 249[499] and applies the 'rectify your return error' in CLEA 2001, s 66 (which applies to a complete failure to deliver) to qualitative errors in documents that have been delivered. This provides that the Registrar can serve on defaulting persons, a notice indicating the deficiency, where a document is delivered which does not comply with the requirements of ss 248 or 249, any other requirement in the Companies Acts (particularly those requiring

492 (2000) Government Publications (Pn 8683), recommendation 14.1 and 14.2.

493 See O'Reilly, 'Auditors' Responsibilities: Changed Responsibilities' (2002) 9 CLP 79.

494 CA 1963, ss 263(6), 273(6) and 310(2).

495 C(A)A 1990, s 12(5).

496 CA 1990, s 248(8).

497 Companies Act 1990 (Form and Content of Documents Delivered to Registrar) Regulations 2002 (SI 2002/039).

498 Inserted by CLEA 2001, s 107.

499 By the deletion of CA 1990, s 248(3)–(5) and s 249(5)–(7).

delivery of a document) and any requirements imposed by other legislation relating to the completion of a document and its delivery to the Registrar[500]. Where the Registrar serves such a notice, unless a replacement document is delivered to him within 14 days thereafter and it complies with the specified requirements, the original document shall be deemed not to have been delivered to the Registrar[501]. Again, this deeming provision will assist the Registrar in prosecuting a default. Where the failure to deliver the document gives rise to the imposition of a penalty for continued contravention, or a step-up-fee for late delivery, the 14-day notice period is discounted provided the document is delivered to the Registrar within the 14-day period[502].

[E] NON-REGISTRATION TYPE OFFENCES

[12.190] Three categories of other offences, termed here *non-registration type offences*, can be identified:

1. Indictable offences.
2. Failure to keep and maintain registers and records.
3. Miscellaneous offences.

Indictable offences

[12.191] Although well over 100 of the offences created by the Companies Acts are expressed to be *indictable* offences, some are more serious than others. By reason of CLEA 2001, s 104, all indictable offences punishable by imprisonment, now carry a maximum term of imprisonment of five years on conviction, the maximum term having been raised from three years[503]. The significance of this is to make very many indictable offences under the Companies Acts, *arrestable (without warrant)* offences under the Criminal Justice Act 1984, s 4 and the consequences of this are considered above[504].

[12.192] The most serious indictable offences, which carry maximum prison terms in excess of five years, are fraudulent trading[505], three specific offences in relation to insider dealing in shares and furnishing false information. Fraudulent trading carries a maximum term of imprisonment of seven years. Unlawful dealing in securities in contravention of CA 1990, s 108 (CA 1990, s 111), dealing within twelve months of conviction by a person convicted of insider dealing (CA 1990, s 112) and dealing on behalf of another person with reasonable cause to believe the deal would be unlawful (CA 1990, s 113) all carry a maximum term of ten years' imprisonment. Furnishing false information in purported compliance with the Companies Acts may, in certain circumstances, be liable to be visited with a term of imprisonment not exceeding seven years.

[12.193] The offences set out hereunder are all indictable offences that attract, on conviction, a maximum term of imprisonment of five years. The seriousness with which the legislature is now taking these offences is borne out by the fact that persons suspect of their contravention are liable to arrest without warrant. Such indictable offences *include*:

---

500 CA 1990, s 249A(1).

501 CA 1990, s 249A(2).

502 CA 1990, s 249A(3).

503 CLEA 2001, s 104 inserted a new sub-s (8) in CA 1990, s 240. See para **[12.034]**.

504 See para **[12.021]**.

505 CA 1963, s 297.

- delivering a statement in lieu of prospectus to the Registrar containing any untrue statement: CA 1963, ss 35 and 54(5);
- wrongly giving financial assistance in connection with the purchase of a company's own shares: CA 1963, s 60(15);
- false and deceitful impersonation of a shareholder etc: CA 1963, s 90;
- failure to ensure proper books of account are maintained on a continuous and consistent basis: CA 1990, s 202;
- failure to keep proper books of account where this contributes to the company's insolvency: CA 1990, s 203;
- acting as an officer, liquidator or examiner or being involved in the promotion, formation or management of a company whilst an undischarged bankrupt: CA 1963, s 183;
- the several offences listed in CA 1963, s 293(1) that can be committed whilst a company is in liquidation;
- destruction, mutilation, alteration or falsification of books, papers or securities by an officer or contributory: CA 1963, s 294;
- fraud by an officer of a company that is ordered or resolves to be wound up: CA 1963, s 295;
- failure by a receiver to submit a statement of affairs within two months of appointment: CA 1963, s 320A;
- issuing, circulating or distributing a prospectus of a foreign company knowingly in contravention of CA 1963, ss 361 to 364: CA 1963, s 365;
- knowingly or recklessly permitting the inclusion of misleading, false or deceptive material in a directors' statement circulated with a special resolution to propose the allotment of shares without applying pre-emption rights: C(A)A 1983, s 24(6).
- knowingly or recklessly making a misleading, false or deceptive statement to an expert carrying out a valuation or reporting on the consideration of a non-cash asset: C(A)A 1983, s 31(3);
- failure of directors to convene an EGM upon becoming aware that the company has suffered a serious capital loss:C(A)A 1983, s 40(1);
- knowingly and wilfully making a false statement in any return, report, balance sheet etc required by the 1986 Act: C(A)A 1986, s 22;
- failing to give information or knowingly or recklessly providing false information in relation to the ownership of shares/debentures in the context of an investigation: CA 1990, s 15;
- disposing etc of shares contrary to the Director's[506] restriction order in an investigation: CA 1990, s 16;
- issuing shares in contravention of the Director's restrictions in an investigation: CA 1990, s 16;

[506] Formerly the Minister for Enterprise, Trade and Employment, but replaced with the Director by CLEA 2001.

- failing to comply with the Director's direction to produce books or provide explanations: CA 1990, s 19;
- unauthorised publication of information etc: CA 1990, s 21;
- directors' dealing in right to call for or to make delivery at specified price etc of relevant shares and debentures: CA 1990, s 28;
- failure by director to repay surplus business expenses: CA 1990, s 36;
- making a prohibited loan, quasi-loan, credit transaction, guarantee or provision of security in connection with a loan, quasi-loan or credit transaction in favour of a director or person connected with a director contrary to CA 1990, s 31: CA 1990, s 40(1);
- procuring the contravention of CA 1990, s 31: CA 1990, s 40(2);
- failure of licensed bank to maintain (and allow inspection of) register of substantial contracts with directors: CA 1990, s 44;
- failure by director, shadow director or secretary to notify interest in shares or notification by agent of acquisitions or disposals: CA 1990, ss 53 and 58;
- failure by director etc to notify spouse's or minor children's grant of right to subscribe for shares/ debentures or exercise of such right: CA 1990, s 64;
- failure by listed company (PLC) to notify Stock Exchange of acquisitions or disposals by directors etc: CA 1990, s 65;
- failure to disclose acquisition of relevant own share capital exceeding notifiable level by a PLC: CA 1990, s 79;
- failure by persons acting together to acquire interests in PLC to keep each other informed and for purchaser to ensure notification by agent of acquisitions/ disposals: CA 1990, s 79;
- acting as a director whilst disqualified: CA 1990, s 161;
- failure to comply with court order to give information in relation to a restriction order under CA 1990, s 16: CA 1990, s 85;
- failure to observe professional secrecy in the context of insider dealing: CA 1990, s 118;
- failure by liquidators to comply with provisions of CA 1990, s 131 in relation to creditors' meetings: CA 1990, s 131;
- directors, etc acting in accordance with the instructions of a disqualified person: CA 1990, s 164;
- failure by director or shadow director charged with fraud to give court written notice of required particulars of directorships: CA 1990, s 166;
- auditors' failure to notify Registrar of his resignation and to include specified material in notice of resignation: CA 1990, s 185;

— failure to give notice pursuant to CA 1963, s 159(1) of auditors' resignation: CA 1990, s 185;

— auditor's failure to notify Registrar of opinion that company is not keeping proper books of account and failure to comply with Director's requests for information: CA 1990, s 194[507];

— failure to convene a general meeting within 14 days of auditors' notice: CA 1990, s 186;

— failure to send persons entitled further statements by a retiring auditor: CA 1990, s 186;

— failure to notify auditor or to permit auditor to attend a general meeting: CA 1990, s 186;

— becoming or remaining as a partner in a firm of auditors when disqualified: CA 1990, s 195;

— failure by subsidiary/ auditor to give holding company's auditors information and explanations: CA 1990, s 196;

— holding company's failure to obtain audit information from subsidiary: CA 1990, s 196;

— knowingly or recklessly making a misleading, false or deceptive statement to the auditor by an officer or employee: CA 1990, s 197;

— failure to provide an auditor with required information or explanations within two days: CA 1990, s 197;

— failure by recognised body of accountants to deliver list of members qualified to be auditors within one month of renewal/ recognition: CA 1990, s 199;

— failure by recognised accountancy body to supply list of new members qualified to be auditors: CA 1990, s 200;

— failure to retain and permit inspection of contracts for the purchase of own shares: CA 1990, s 222;

— failure to comply with ministerial direction relating to own share purchase: CA 1990, s 228;

— failure by listed company to notify stock exchange of own share purchase: CA 1990, s 229;

— contravention of procedures on own share purchase: CA 1990, s 234;

— destroying, mutilating or falsifying books or documents: CA 1990, s 243;

— fraudulently parting with, altering or making an omission in any book or document: CA 1990, s 243;

— improper use of word 'limited': CA 1963, s 381[508];

— disclosure of information other than that in the public domain by the ODCE: CLEA 2001, s 17(4);

[507] As amended by CLEA 2001, s 74.

[508] As replaced by CLEA 2001, s 98.

— failure by liquidator of insolvent company to provide report to the Director: CLEA 2001, s 56(3);
— failure by liquidator to produce books to the Director for examination etc: CLEA 2001, s 57(4);
— failure by professional body to report to Director a finding by disciplinary committee that a member conducting a receivership or liquidation failed to maintain appropriate records: CLEA 2001, s 58.

The foregoing is undoubtedly an onerous list of serious offences. It should be noted that only a short indicative description of each offence is given above and, as in all criminal proceedings, a careful analysis of each individual provision is required in order to establish contravention. Similarly, many of the foregoing offences are subject to time provisos and will only be committed where default arises after a particular period specified in the provision; again, careful scrutiny of the actual provision is required. Where fraud is a constituent element in the offence it should be remembered that the prosecution face a high onus of proof[509].

[12.194] For years, apart from recognising that there were a large number of indictable offences under the Companies Acts, few paid too much attention to the need for a precise list. Only upon the commencement of CA 1990, s 194(5) which requires auditors to report indictable offences to the Director did it become a pressing issue.[510] In an attempt to assist practitioners, the Director has published a list of indictable offences.[511] Those indictable offences identified by the Director are clustered under a series of headings and are set out in Appendix 1.

Failure to keep and maintain registers and records

[12.195] There are a number of offences that involve the failure to keep and maintain registers and records created by the Companies Acts. Offences here *include* a failure by companies to:

— keep and maintain a register of debenture holders: CA 1963, s 91;
— maintain a register of members: CA 1963, s 116;
— index the register of members: CA 1963, s 117(1);
— prepare minutes of general meetings and directors' meetings: CA 1963, s 145(1);
— ensure proper books of account are kept: CA 1990, s 202;
— maintain register of directors' and secretary's shareholdings, and in chronological order, and to record new information within three days, and maintain index, and to amend index: CA 1990, s 60;
— enter interests in contracts in book: CA 1963, s 194(5);

[509] See, generally the position in England: Scanlan, 'Dishonesty in Corporate Offences A Need for Reform?' (2002) 23 Co Law 114.

[510] See para **[12.014]**.

[511] See Decision Notice D/2002/2 issued by the Office of the Director of Corporate Enforcement, entitled *The Duty of Auditors to Report to the Director of Corporate Enforcement*, at Appendix 2 (reproduced here in Appendix 1).

— maintain register of directors and secretary: CA 1963, s 195;
— keep proper books of account where company is wound up insolvent: CA 1990, s 203;
— keep registers in the required manner: CA 1963, s 378;
— maintain register of substantial contracts with directors (by a licensed bank): CA 1990, s 44;
— keep copies to directors' service contracts: CA 1990, s 50;
— maintain register of interests in shares: CA 1990, s 80.

Miscellaneous offences

[12.196] There are numerous other company law offences which do not fall neatly within one or other of the foregoing categories[512]. Many of these can be classified as involving the failure to supply information or documents to persons other than the Registrar[513], the failure by persons such as liquidators, receivers or examiners to advertise their appointment, etc[514], the failure to comply with directions[515], failure to meet requirements of the Companies Acts[516] and the making of untrue statements, etc[517].

---

[512] The offences concerning prospectuses only relate to public companies: CA 1963, ss 35, 44, 46, 54, 56, 57 and 115; C(A)A 1983, ss 6, 21, 43, 47, 57, etc.

[513] Eg: failure to supply copies of memorandum and articles when requested by a member: CA 1963, s 29(1); failure to ensure memorandum and articles reflect all changes made: CA 1963, s 30(2); wilful concealment of creditors entitled to object to capital reductions: CA 1963, s 77; failure to permit inspection of the register of debenture holders: CA 1963, s 92; failure to provide share certificates: CA 1963, s 86; failure to permit inspection of security instruments: CA 1963, s 110; failure to permit inspection of members' register: CA 1963, s 119; failure to include proxy notice when convening members' meetings and to only issue to some members: CA 1963, s 136; failure to issue etc resolution with copy of articles it changes and to supply a copy to members on request: CA 1963, s 143; failure to permit inspection of members' meetings minutes book: CA 1963, s 146; failure to supply copy of subsidiary accounts to requesting members: CA 1963, ss 150 and 154; failure to have same parent and subsidiary financial years: CA 1963, s 153; failure to provide information on subsidiary in accounts: C(A)A 1986, s 22; issuing accounts in the wrong format, etc and not issuing in advance of AGM: CA 1963, ss 157–159; failure to disclose payments to directors in connection with transfer of shares: CA 1963, s 188; failure to produce registers at AGM: CA 1963, s 190; failure of directors to provide various information: CA 1963, ss 193, 194; failure to permit inspection of register of directors and secretary: CA 1963, s 195; failure to state directors' names in business letters: CA 1963, s 196; failure of directors to advise their liability is unlimited: CA 1963, s 197; failure to attach court order of scheme of arrangement: CA 1963, s 201; failure to supply notices of creditors' meeting, etc: CA 1963, s 202; failure to file statement of affairs on a winding up or on receivership: CA 1963, ss 224 and 320; failure to publish notice of resolution to voluntarily wind up: CA 1963, s 252; non-disclosure by creditors' representative and voting for connected person: CA 1963, s 301A; failure to include statement that company is in liquidation or receivership: CA 1963, ss 303 and 317; failure to maintain accounting principles and requirements in C(A)A 1986: C(A)A 1986, s 22; etc.

[514] Eg: failure to publish notice of appointment in *Iris Oifigiúil* by liquidator: CA 1963, s 227; failure by liquidator to hold final general meeting: CA 1963, ss 263 and 273; failure by liquidator to summon meeting of creditors: CA 1963, s 266; failure by liquidator to dispose of books etc in accordance with law: CA 1963, s 305; liquidator's failure to report that a disqualified person is a director: CA 1990, s 161; receiver's failure to notify appointment to company: CA 1963, s 319; receiver's failure to notify resignation, etc.

[515] Eg: failure to change company's name when directed: CA 1963, ss 23(2) and 24(8); failure to re–register as a public company when ceasing to be a private company: CA 1963, s 35(2); acting as a director or auditor or liquidator whilst disqualified: CA 1963, ss 180, 162 and 300A, etc.

[516] Eg: failing to have a registered office in the State: CA 1963, s 113; failure to have name outside company's place of business, or use seal which does not have company's name: CA 1963, s 114; failure to hold an AGM: CA 1963, s 131; body corporate acting as liquidator or receiver: CA 1963, ss 300 and 314 etc.

[517] Eg: making an unreasonable statutory declaration of solvency in the context of the CA 1963, s 60 validation procedure: CA 1963, s 60(5); inducing appointment of liquidator: CA 1963, s 301, etc.

Chapter 13

Accounts and Auditors

Introduction

[13.001] The Companies Acts 1963-2001 contain detailed provisions regulating company accounting. The rationale for such regulation is the protection of all persons dealing with companies, be they shareholders, officers, creditors, or employees. A number of fundamental rules of company law, such as the maintenance of capital in the calculation of profits available for distribution, could not be enforced effectively without the proper regulation of company accounts. Similar concerns apply to the distribution of assets and capital in a liquidation. Likewise, persons dealing with companies require fundamental information concerning the financial position of the company. Their lot is eased to some degree when details of the company's accounts, prepared in accordance with recognised standards of accounting practice, are made available.

[13.002] The regulation of corporate accounting operates at three principal levels. First, all companies are required to keep proper books of account which display the 'true and fair' state of the company's financial affairs. Secondly, companies are required annually to disclose details of their accounts at regular intervals, both to their members, at the annual general meeting ('AGM'), and, usually, to the public at large, in the annual return filed with the Registrar of Companies in the Companies Registration Office. Thirdly, companies are required to adhere to certain standards in the preparation of the accounts for disclosure to their members and the public at large. The accounts must follow specimen formats, and must contain information prepared in accordance with specified accounting principles. Adherence to these standards is enhanced by requiring company accounts to be audited at regular intervals by a qualified auditor or auditors, exercising professional integrity and following standard professional accounting practices. Indeed, the auditor must report to the members at the AGM, and his report is normally filed along with the annual return.

Gone are the days when companies could be indifferent about the state of their accounts. Failure to comply with the legislative regime governing corporate accounting can lead to severe penalties being imposed on the company, its officers, and, indeed, even its auditors. Late returns to the Registrar of Companies will lead to the imposition of a fine, and failure to file the annual return (and the necessary accounts along with it) will lead to the company being struck off the register of companies and dissolved. It cannot be overstated that under the law as it stands careful attention *must* be given to the maintenance of proper books of account, to the correct preparation and circulation of annual accounts, and to the diligent filing of proper annual returns. Whether this regime is too onerous for some types of company, particularly small private ones, has been the subject of some debate[1], and the Companies (Amendment) (No 2) Act 1999 now provides that small companies can opt to dispense with the requirement to have an auditor in a given financial year[2].

[13.003] In this chapter, the accounting requirements relating to private companies are considered under the following headings:

[A] The Books of Account.

[B] The Annual Accounts.

[C] Group Accounts.

[D] The Annual Return.

[E] Auditors.

[A] THE BOOKS OF ACCOUNT

Introduction

[13.004] The Companies Act 1990, s 202 ('CA 1990')[3] requires all companies to keep proper books of account, giving a true and fair view of the state of the company's affairs and explaining its transactions[4]. Section 202(1) provides:

> Every company shall cause to be kept proper books of account, whether in the form of documents or otherwise, that —
>
> (a) correctly record and explain the transactions of the company,
>
> (b) will at any time enable the financial position of the company to be determined with reasonable accuracy,
>
> (c) will enable the directors to ensure that any balance sheet, profit and loss account or income and expenditure account of the company complies with the requirements of the Companies Acts, and
>
> (d) will enable the accounts of the company to be readily and properly audited.

Such books must be kept 'on a continuous and consistent basis, that is to say, the entries therein shall be made in a timely manner and be consistent from one year to the next'[5].

Contents of the books of account

[13.005] The overriding requirement in respect of the books of account is that they must give a 'true and fair view of the state of affairs of the company and explain its transactions'.[6] What amounts to a 'true and fair view' in the context of the company's books of accounts has not been firmly established[7], but CA 1990, s 202(3) provides some indication of what is involved by requiring that in particular, and without prejudice to the generality of the provisions of s 202(1), the books of account shall contain:

---

1 See, for example, Donovan, 'The Audit of Small Companies – Why it Should be Retained' (1993) *Accountancy Ireland* 6; Freedman and Godwin, 'The Statutory Audit and the Micro Company – An Empirical Investigation' (1993) JBL 105.

2 See para **[13.185]**.

3 Displacing CA 1963, s 147.

4 See generally MacCann, 'Duty to Keep Proper Books of Account' (1991) ILT 177.

5 CA 1990, s 202(2).

6 CA 1990, s 202(4).

7 As to the annual accounts providing a 'true and fair view' of the company's affairs, see para **[13.021]**.

'(a) entries from day to day of all sums of money received and expended by the company and the matters in respect of which the receipt and expenditure takes place,

(b) a record of the assets and liabilities of the company,

(c) if the company's business involves dealing in goods —

(i) a record of all goods purchased, and of all goods sold (except those sold for cash by way of ordinary retail trade), showing the goods and the sellers and buyers in sufficient detail to enable the goods and the sellers and buyers to be identified and a record of all the invoices relating to such purchases and sales,

(ii) statements of stock held by the company at the end of each financial year and all records of stocktakings from which any such statement of stock has been, or is to be, prepared, and

(d) if the company's business involves the provision of services, a record of the services provided and of all the invoices relating thereto.'

All of this requires careful bookkeeping.

Location of the books of account

[13.006] The books of account may be kept at the company's registered office, or at such other place as the directors think fit[8]. If the books are kept at a place outside the State, CA 1990, s 202(6) requires that:

> '...there shall be sent to and kept at a place in the State and be at all reasonable times open to inspection by the directors such accounts and returns relating to the business dealt with in books of account so kept as will disclose with reasonable accuracy the financial position of that business at intervals not exceeding 6 months and will enable to be prepared in accordance with the Companies Acts the company's balance sheet, its profit and loss account or income and expenditure account and any document annexed to any of those documents giving information which is required by the said Acts and is thereby allowed to be so given.'

Details of the accounts and returns must be sent to a place within the State at least every six months, to enable the financial position of the company to be discerned, and to enable the company's annual accounts[9] and annual return[10] to be prepared.

Form of the books of account

[13.007] The books of account may be kept 'in the form of documents or otherwise'[11] (eg on computer). The books, and, if the books are kept outside the State, the accounts and returns, must be kept either in written form in an official language of the State or so as to enable the books of account and the accounts and returns to be readily accessible and readily convertible into written form in an official language of the State[12]. Thus, where the books of account are kept on computer, a 'hard copy' of the accounts is not required to be kept at all times, so long as one may be produced when necessary for inspection.

---

8 CA 1990, s 202(5).

9 See para **[13.014]** *ff*.

10 See para **[13.154]** *ff*.

11 CA 1990, s 202(1).

12 CA 1990, s 202 (7).

The books of account, and any accounts and returns, must be preserved by the company for a period of at least six years after the latest date to which they relate[13].

Inspection of the books of account

[13.008] The books of account, and any accounts and returns, must be made available in written form in an official language of the State at all reasonable times for inspection without charge by the officers of the company and by other persons entitled pursuant to the Companies Acts to inspect the books of account of the company[14].

This right of inspection is of particular importance to the directors of the company, for they need to be in a position to examine the books of account in order to perform properly their duties, including their duties to ensure that proper books of account are kept and to report on the annual accounts at the AGM[15]. Onerous penalties may be imposed on directors who fail to comply with their duties in relation to accounts[16]. In *Healy v Healy Homes Ltd*[17], Kenny J held that a director's statutory right to inspect the books of accounts is a right which may be enforced where necessary by means of an injunction. The learned judge further held that a director exercising his right may be accompanied by an accountant, since it would be unreasonable to expect a director having no formal training in accountancy to be able to decide whether proper books of account were being kept. He said[18]:

> 'The purpose of [what is now CA 1990, s 202] is to compel companies to keep proper books of account: one of the ways in which this important object is achieved is by imposing an obligation on each director to make sure that this is being done. But a director who has not had a training in accountancy cannot decide whether proper books of account are being kept unless an accountant is allowed to inspect them; the phrase 'proper books of account' means books which give a true and fair view of the state of the company's affairs and which explain its transactions. It follows that a director's right to inspect books of account necessarily involves that an accountant nominated by him may do this. The accountant may do this when he is accompanied by the director or when the accountant has been given a written authority to do so, and he may be required to give a written undertaking that the knowledge which he gets will not be used for any purpose except in relation to the matter in connection with which he has been retained...The right of a director to inspect the books of a company when he has an obligation imposed on him the breach of which may involve him in criminal liability, necessarily implies that he has the right to employ a qualified agent to advise him. The question whether proper books are being kept is one on which an accountant is the only person qualified to advise as most directors would not be able to form a correct judgment on

13 CA 1990, s 202(9).

14 CA 1990, s 202(8). Persons entitled by the Companies Acts to inspect the books of account include inspectors appointed under CA 1990, Part II; the Minister under CA 1990, Part II; and the Director of Corporate Enforcement under the CLEA 2001. See generally Chapter 14, *Investigations and Inspectors*. The members of the company have no statutory right to inspect the books of account; see below.

15 See para **[13.104]**.

16 See Chapter 5, *Disregarding Separate Legal Personality*, para **[5.084]**.

17 *Healy v Healy Homes Ltd* [1973] IR 309.

18 [1973] IR 309 at 311–312.

> the matter. The director and his accountant are also entitled to make copies of the books of account or any part of them.'

Thus, the director need not even exercise his right in person; a qualified accountant or such other person having the necessary accounting training may exercise it on his behalf, provided that person has written authority to do so, and gives a written undertaking to use the information he obtains only for the director's purposes. In addition, the director and his agent are entitled to make copies of the accounts.

The company's auditors are given an express statutory right of access at all reasonable times to the books of account[19]. The *members* of the company have no statutory or common law right to inspect the books of account unless the articles of association expressly confer such a right on them[20].

Liability for failure to keep proper books of account

(a) Criminal liability

[13.009] CA 1990, s 202(10) provides that both the company and any director who fails to take all reasonable steps to secure compliance with the requirements relating to proper books of account, or who has by his own wilful act been the cause of any such default by the company, shall be guilty of an offence. Such offences are punishable on summary conviction by a fine not exceeding €1,905 or, at the discretion of the court, by imprisonment for a term not exceeding 12 months, or to both[21]. Upon conviction on indictment, a fine not exceeding €12,697 or imprisonment for a term not exceeding five years, or both, may be imposed[22]. As with all offences that carry a maximum term of five years' imprisonment, it is important to remember that a person suspected of committing such an offence can be arrested without warrant and detained under the Criminal Justice Act 1984, s 4[23]. In either case, however, a director may not be sentenced to imprisonment unless the court is satisfied that the offence was committed wilfully[24].

In any such proceedings, it is a defence for the accused to prove that he had reasonable grounds for believing, and did believe, that a competent and reliable person was charged with the duty of ensuring that those requirements were complied with and that that person was in a position to discharge that duty[25].

[13.010] Under CA 1990, s 203, where a company which is being wound up and which is unable to pay all of its debts has failed to keep proper books of account, and the court considers that such contravention has either contributed to the company's inability to pay

19 CA 1990, s 193(3). See also para **[13.206]**.

20 *Burn v New London & South Wales Coal Co* [1890] WN 209. MacCann, 'Duty to Keep Proper Books of Account' (1991) ILT 177, suggests, however, that such a right may be found to exist under CA 1963, s 205, as to which see Chapter 19, *Shareholder's Remedies*, para **[19.006]***ff*. The members must, in any event, be given detailed annual particulars of the company's financial position; see para **[13.014]***ff*.

21 CA 1990, s 240(1), as amended by CLEA 2001, s 104.

22 CA 1990, s 240(1), as amended by CLEA 2001, s 104.

23 See Chapter 12, *Company Law Compliance and Enforcement*, para **[12.021]**.

24 CA 1990, s 202(10)(b).

25 CA 1990, s 202(10)(a).

all of its debts, or has resulted in substantial uncertainty as to the assets and liabilities of the company, or has substantially impeded the orderly winding up of the company, then every officer of the company who is in default shall be guilty of an offence. On summary conviction, the officer may be fined up to €1,905 or imprisoned for a term not exceeding six months, or both[26]. 'Officer', in this context, includes director or secretary[27], but note that the category of persons who constitute officers is not exclusive. Consequently, an auditor may be regarded as an officer of the company for the purposes of this section[28]. Upon conviction on indictment, the officer may be fined up to €12,697, or imprisoned for five years, or both[29].

It is a defence for the officer in such proceedings to prove that he took all reasonable steps to secure compliance with the obligation to keep proper books of account, or that he had reasonable grounds for believing, and that he did believe, that a competent and reliable person, acting under the supervision and control of a director of the company who has been formally allocated such responsibility, was charged with the duty of ensuring that proper books of account were kept and was in a position to discharge that duty[30].

(b) Civil liability

[13.011] Significant personal liability may be imposed on directors and officers of companies which fail to keep proper accounts. Such civil consequences have already been examined in detail in Chapter 5, *Disregarding Separate Legal Personality*[31] *and Chapter 10, Duties of Directors and Other Officers*[32]. It will suffice to stress again that extreme care must be taken by directors to ensure that the company keeps proper books of account. Indeed, the company's auditors are required to investigate whether proper books are being kept[33].

Concealment, destruction and falsification of books of account

[13.012] CA 1990, s 243(1) provides that an officer:

> who destroys, mutilates of falsifies, or is privy to the destruction, mutilation or falsification of any book or document affecting or relating to the property or affairs of the [company], or makes or is privy to the making of a false entry therein, shall, unless he proves that he had no intention to defeat the law, be guilty of an offence.

Likewise, under subs (2), any officer who fraudulently either parts with, alters or makes an omission in any such book or document, or who is privy to fraudulent parting with, fraudulent altering or fraudulent making of an omission in, any such book or document, will also be guilty of an offence. Such offences are punishable on summary conviction by

---

26 CA 1990, s 203(1)(b)(i).

27 CA 1963, s 2(1). CA 1963, s 383 provides that the phrase 'officer who is in default' means any officer who knowingly and wilfully authorises the default, refusal or contravention mentioned in the provision.

28 *R v Schacter* [1960] 2 QB 252. So also may an *employee*: CA 1990, s 197(5).

29 CA 1990, s 203(1)(b)(ii).

30 CA 1990, s 203(2).

31 See Chapter 5, *Disregarding Separate Legal Personality*, para **[5.084]***ff*.

32 See Chapter 10, *Duties of Directors and Other Officers*, para **[10.114]**.

33 See para **[13.212]**.

a fine not exceeding €1,905 or by imprisonment for a term not exceeding twelve months, or both[34]. Upon conviction on indictment, a fine not exceeding €12,697 or imprisonment for a term not exceeding 5 years, or both, may be imposed[35].

[13.013] Similar provisions are contained in the Companies Act 1963, s 293 ('CA 1963' – 'the 1963 Act'), which creates a number of offences which may be committed by officers of companies which have gone into liquidation. For the purposes of that section, the term 'officer' includes any person in accordance with whose directions or instructions the directors of the company have been accustomed to act. In relation to the books of account, CA 1963, s 293(1)[36] provides:

> '...if any person, being a past or present officer of a company which at the time of the commission of the alleged offence is being wound up, whether by the court or voluntarily, or is subsequently ordered to be wound up by the court or subsequently passes a resolution for voluntary winding up —...
>
> (c) does not deliver up to the liquidator, or as he directs, all books and papers in his custody or under his control belonging to the company and which he is required by law to deliver up; or...
>
> (f) makes any material omission in any statement relating to the affairs of the company; or...
>
> (h) after the commencement of the winding up prevents the production of any book or paper affecting or relating to the property or affairs of the company; or
>
> (i) within twelve months next before the commencement of the winding up or at any time thereafter conceals, destroys, mutilates or falsifies or is privy to the concealment, destruction, mutilation or falsification of any book or paper affecting or relating to the property or affairs of the company; or...
>
> (j) within twelve months next before the commencement of the winding up or at any time thereafter makes or is privy to the making of any false entry in any book or paper affecting or relating to the property or affairs of the company; or
>
> (k) within twelve months next before the commencement of the winding up or at any time thereafter fraudulently parts with, alters or makes any omission in, or is privy to the fraudulent parting with, altering or making any omission in, any document affecting or relating to the property or affairs of the company;...
>
> he shall ... be liable, on conviction on indictment, to imprisonment for a term not exceeding [five][37] years or to a fine not exceeding £2,500 [€3,174] or to both, or,...on summary conviction, to imprisonment for a term not exceeding 6 months or to a fine not exceeding [€1,905 (IR£1,500)][38] or to both.'

It is a good defence to a charge under paragraphs (c) or (f) if the accused proves that he had no intent to defraud. Likewise, it is a good defence to a charge under paragraphs (h),

34 CA 1990, s 240(1) as amended by CLEA 2001, s 104.

35 CA 1990, s 240(1) as amended by CLEA 2001, s 104.

36 As amended by C(A)A 1982, Schedule, Part I.

37 CA 1990, s 240(8) as inserted by CLEA 2001, s 140.

38 CA 1990, s 240(7).

(i) and (j) of the subsection if he proves that he had no intent to conceal the state of affairs of the company or to defeat the law.

[B] THE ANNUAL ACCOUNTS

Introduction

[13.014] As has already been observed[39], the members of a company have no right under statute or at common law to inspect the company's books of account, unless such a right has expressly been given to them in the articles of association. Few companies embody such rights in their articles. Yet it is essential for most shareholders to have a knowledge of the state of the company's financial affairs. To this end, the Companies Acts 1963–2001 require the directors of all companies to lay the following accounts and reports before the AGM[40] of the company's members:

— a profit and loss account (or, if the company is not trading for profit, an income and expenditure account)[41];

— a balance sheet as at the date to which the profit and loss account (or income and expenditure account) is made up[42];

— a directors' report, attached to the balance sheet, detailing the state of the company's affairs[43];

— an auditors' report on the accounts examined by them and on the balance sheet, profit and loss account, directors' report and any group accounts laid before the AGM[44].

In addition, 'parent undertakings' within the meaning of the European Communities (Companies: Group Accounts) Regulations 1992[45] are required to prepare consolidated group accounts, in addition to their own accounts, detailing the state of affairs of the group as a whole, and to lay these group accounts before the AGM at the same time as their own accounts.

[13.015] Failure to comply with these requirements renders the directors liable to conviction for an offence punishable on summary conviction by imprisonment for a term not exceeding six months or by a fine not to exceed €1,905 or to both[46]. It will, however, be a defence in any such proceedings for the director to prove that he had reasonable grounds to believe, and that he did believe, that a competent and reliable person was charged with the duty of seeing that the requirements were complied with and was in a position to discharge that duty[47]. Furthermore, a sentence of imprisonment may only be imposed if the court is of the opinion that the offence was committed wilfully[48].

39 At para **[13.008]**.

40 See Chapter 9, *Corporate Governance: Meetings*, para **[9.040]***ff*.

41 CA 1963, s 148(1).

42 CA 1963, s 148(2).

43 CA 1963, s 158, as amended by C(A)A 1986, ss 13 and 14.

44 CA 1990, s 193.

45 See Chapter 17, *Groups of Companies,* para **[17.028]***ff*.

46 CA 1990, s 240, as amended.

47 CA 1963, ss 148(3) and 158(7), as amended by the C(A)A 1982, Sch 1.

48 CA 1963, ss 148(3) and 158(7), as amended by the C(A)A 1982, Sch 1.

[13.016] Copies of the annual accounts must be signed by the directors and sent to every member and debenture holder of the company (regardless of whether they are entitled to notices of general meetings) not less than 21 days before the AGM[49]. If the copies of the accounts are sent less than 21 days before the AGM, the meeting can nevertheless deem the accounts to have been duly sent[50]. Every member is entitled to copies of the preceding year's annual accounts without charge[51].

Failure to comply with any of these circulation requirements renders the company and every officer in default liable to a fine not exceeding €1,905 unless, in the case of a demand for a copy of the previous year's accounts, it is proved that the member made an earlier demand and was furnished with a copy[52].

[13.017] A single-member company may dispense with the requirement to hold an AGM by virtue of the European Communities (Single-Member Private Limited Companies) Regulations 1994, reg 8[53]. Where it does so, the requirement to lay the profit and loss account, balance sheet, directors' report, auditors' report, and any group accounts before the AGM will be deemed to be satisfied where they are sent to the sole member of the single-member company in accordance with the preceding paragraph not less than 21 days before the 'appropriate date', ie where it has never held an AGM, the last day of the month in which the anniversary of its formation falls, and in all other cases, the last day of the month in which the anniversary of its last AGM falls[54]. If the decision to dispense with the AGM ceases to have effect, then the normal requirements as to the laying of the accounts and reports before the AGM apply[55].

[13.018] Specified accounting principles are to be observed in the preparation of the annual accounts, the accounts are required to follow specified formats, and must disclose certain information by way of note to the accounts. 'Medium-sized' and 'small' companies are exempted from some of the rigours of the requirements relating to the annual accounts[56].

Unlimited companies, by their nature, require less formal accounting practices and standards to be followed, since the members thereof cannot hide behind the cloak of limited liability where the failing financial state of the company leads to insolvent liquidation. Accordingly, the Companies Acts 1963–2001 impose lesser obligations concerning the preparation of annual accounts for unlimited companies. Those obligations are to be found in CA 1963, s 149 and the Sixth Schedule. Essentially, the annual accounts of an unlimited company must give a 'true and fair view' of the company's financial position and profit or loss at the end of the financial year, and must adopt the formats and

49 CA 1963, s 159(1). Any other persons entitled, for whatever reason, to copies of the annual accounts must also be sent the accounts not less than 21 days before the AGM: CA 1963, s 159(1).

50 CA 1963, s 159(3).

51 CA 1963, s 159(4).

52 CA 1963, s 159(5), and CA 1990, s 240, as amended.

53 SI 1994/275. See Chapter 1, *The Private Company in Context*, para **[1.124]** ff.

54 SI 1994/275, reg 8(5) and 8(9).

55 SI 1994/275, reg 8(7).

56 For the meaning of 'medium–sized' and 'small' company see para **[13.041]**.

follow the requirements set out in the Sixth Schedule. That said, however, an unlimited company should not be allowed to be used as a mask for limited liability companies seeking to avoid some of their accounting obligations by operating through an unlimited company. To this end, the European Communities (Accounts) Regulations 1993[57] require unlimited companies, all of whose members are limited liability companies or similar bodies established under the laws of an EU Member State, to follow the accounting regime which applies in respect of limited liability companies[58].

[13.019] Each of the following shall now be considered in turn:

1. Accounting principles.
2. Medium-sized and small private companies.
3. The profit and loss account.
4. The balance sheet.
5. The notes to the accounts.
6. The directors' report.
7. The auditors' report.

Accounting principles

[13.020] The Schedule to the Companies (Amendment) Act 1986 ('C(A)A 1986') sets out the formats which the profit and loss account and balance sheet of a limited liability company must take. The information contained in the annual accounts and the notes thereto must include the information set out in that Schedule[59]. Furthermore, specified accounting principles are required to be observed in the preparation of the accounts of limited liability companies[60]. Mere adherence to the strict letter of the specified formats and principles may not always suffice, for C(A)A 1986, s 3 imposes the overriding requirement that the accounts show 'a true and fair view of the state of affairs of the company.'[61]

(a) 'True and fair view'

[13.021] The annual accounts must give a 'true and fair view' of the affairs of the company. Where a balance sheet or profit and loss account which is drawn up in accordance with C(A)A 1986's scheduled formats and accounting principles does not provide sufficient information to give a 'true and fair view' of the company's state of affairs, C(A)A 1986, s 3(1)(c) requires that:

> '...any necessary additional information shall be provided in that balance sheet or profit and loss account or in a note to the accounts.'

In addition, where compliance with the 1986 Act's scheduled formats and accounting principles would prevent the accounts from giving a 'true and fair view' of the company's state of affairs, even if additional information were given as above, C(A)A 1986, s 3(1)(d) requires the directors to:

---

57 SI 1993/396.

58 SI 1993/396, reg 7(1).

59 C(A)A 1986, ss 3(1)(a) and 4.

60 C(A)A 1986, s 5, and C(A)A 1986, Schedule, Parts II and III. See paras **[13.023]** *ff.*

61 C(A)A 1986, s 3(1)(b) and (4).

> ... depart from the requirements of the Schedule to [C(A)A 1986] in preparing those accounts insofar as is necessary to [give a true and fair view].[62]

The combined effect of these requirements is that a three-pronged approach must be taken in the preparation of the annual accounts. First, the accounts should be prepared in accordance with the scheduled formats and accounting principles as set out in C(A)A 1986. Secondly, it must be asked whether additional information is required for the accounts to give a 'true and fair view' of the company's state of affairs. If so, such information should be included in the accounts or in a note to the accounts. Thirdly, if such additional information would still not enable the accounts to give a 'true and fair view' of the company's state of affairs, the scheduled format must be departed from so that the accounts may give such a 'true and fair view'. Details of the departure, the reasons and the effect which the departure will have on the accounts must be included in a note to the accounts.

[13.022] When will the accounts give a 'true and fair view' of a company's state of affairs? The Companies Acts 1963–2001 do not contain an answer. The weight of professional and legal opinion suggests that the accounts will give a 'true and fair view' when they are prepared in accordance with the Statements of Standard Accounting Practice ('SSAPs'), issued until 1990 by the Accounting Standards Committee of the Consultative Committee of Accounting Bodies of the UK and Ireland[63], and the Financial Reporting Standards ('FRSs'), issued since 1990 by the Accounting Standards Board, the independent[64] body which replaced the Accounting Standards Committee[65]. These standards consist of guidelines as to the recognised practices and standards of the accountancy profession as regards matters such as cash flow statements, accounting for subsidiary undertakings, reporting financial performance, current-cost accounting, and accounting for goodwill[66].

---

[62] Such departures are, in practice, rarely necessitated. Where the directors do make such a departure, they are required to attach a note to the accounts detailing and explaining the departures and their effect on the accounts: C(A)A 1986, s 3(1)(e).

[63] Which was made up of the major professional accountancy bodies in the UK and Ireland, namely: the Chartered Association of Certified Accountants (ACCA); the Chartered Institute of Management Accountants (CIMA); the Chartered Institute of Public Finance and Accounting (CIPFA); The Institute of Chartered Accountants in England and Wales (ICAEW); the Institute of Chartered Accountants in Ireland (ICIA); and the Institute of Chartered Accountants of Scotland (ICAS).

[64] The Accounting Standards Committee was susceptible to lobbying from members of the accountancy bodies.

[65] See O'Kane, 'The Changing Face of Accountancy' (1994) CLP 41 and O'Boyle & O'Kane, *Accounting Standards: A Quick Reference* (1993) Oak Tree Press. The Accounting Standards Board (ASB) has been given statutory recognition in the UK (but not in Ireland) by the Companies Act 1985 (UK), s 256 as amended. Accounts prepared according to the UK Companies Acts must state whether they have been prepared in accordance with the ASB's standards.

[66] Twenty–five SSAPs were issued by the ASC between January 1971 and June 1990. Many of these were withdrawn or revised. Nineteen FRSs were introduced in the period September 1991 to May 2002, and one further FRS 'SE' applicable to smaller entities. In addition to accounting and reporting standards, the professional bodies have issued a number of Statements of Recommended Practice ('SORPs', and 'Eds' or 'FREDs'). See the Accountancy Standards Board's website at http://www.asb.org.uk.

Compliance with these standards in the preparation of the company accounts will be strong – but not conclusive – evidence that the accounts give a 'true and fair' view of the company's affairs. In *Lloyd Cheyham & Co Ltd v Littlejohn & Co*[67], Woolf J observed of the standards:

> 'While they are not conclusive, so that a departure from their terms necessarily involves a breach of the duty of care, and they are not as the explanatory foreword makes clear, rigid rules, they are very strong evidence as to what is the proper standard which should be adopted and unless there is some justification, a departure from this will be regarded as constituting a breach of duty. It appears to me important that this should be the position because third parties in reading the accounts are entitled to assume that they have been drawn up in accordance with the approved practice unless there is some indication in the accounts which clearly state that this is not the case.'

Adherence to the standards would thus seem to constitute *prima facie* evidence that the accounts portray a 'true and fair view'. Conversely, it has been said that 'the issue of an SSAP has the effect...of creating a *prima facie* presumption that accounts which do not comply are not true and fair.'[68] In practice, then, adherence to the standards should be maintained wherever possible; and, indeed, members of the accounting professions are expected by their professional bodies to follow them. In some circumstances, however, adherence to these standards may provide a distorted view of the company's financial position, in which case the overriding requirement of the 'true and fair view' must be preferred[69].

(b) Statutory accounting principles

[13.023] Specified accounting principles are further required to be observed in the preparation of the company accounts. C(A)A 1986, s 5 provides[70]:

> '...the amount to be included in the accounts of a company in respect of the items shown shall be determined in accordance with the following principles:
>
> (a) the company shall be presumed to be carrying on business as a going concern,
>
> (b) accounting policies shall be applied consistently from one financial year to the next,
>
> (c) the amount of any item in the accounts shall be determined on a prudent basis and in particular —
>
> (i) only profits realised at the balance sheet date shall be included in the profit and loss account, and

[67] *Lloyd Cheyham & Co Ltd v Littlejohn & Co* [1987] BCLC 303 at 313. This case was decided before the standards were given statutory recognition in the Companies Acts (UK). See also *Dovey v Corey* [1901] AC 493; *Dolan v AB Co Ltd* [1969] IR 247; *IRC v Duple Motor Bodies Ltd* [1961] 1 WLR 739.

[68] Leonard Hoffman QC and Mary H Arden, in Sutcliffe and Patient, *Accounting Problems of the Companies Acts* (1984) Tolley. See also Kelleher, *The Companies (Amendment) Act 1986: A Guide to the Accounting, Reporting and Filing Requirements*, (1987) The Institute of Chartered Accountants in Ireland, Chapter 3.

[69] See Lasok and Grace 'The True and Fair View' (1989) 10 Co Law 13; McGee 'The 'True and Fair View' Debate: A Study in the Legal Regulation of Accounting' (1991) 54 MLR 874.

[70] See also SSAP 2, 'Disclosure of Accounting Policies', which identifies (a) to (d) as the 'four fundamental accounting concepts'.

(ii) all liabilities and losses which have arisen or are likely to arise in respect of the financial year to which the accounts relate, or a previous financial year, shall be taken into account, including those liabilities and losses which only become apparent between the balance sheet date and the date on which the accounts are signed in pursuance of section 156 of the 1963 Act,

(d) all income and charges relating to the financial year to which the accounts relate shall be taken into account without regard to the date of receipt or payment, and

(e) in determining the aggregate amount of any item the amount of each individual asset or liability that falls to be taken into account shall be determined separately.'

Realised profits, in the context C(A)A 1986, s 5(c), are such profits as fall to be treated as realised profits in accordance with generally accepted principles (ie accounting standards) for the determination of realised profits at the time when the accounts are prepared[71]. Note also that s 5(e) requires that when determining the aggregate amount of an item in the accounts, each individual component of that item must be considered separately. This means, in effect, that a company may not offset gains and assets occurring within a particular item or group of items in the accounts, and a write down for diminution in value of each component item must be recorded when required.

[13.024] Departure from these accounting principles is permitted by C(A)A 1986, s 6. Where it appears to the directors of a company that there are special reasons necessitating such departure, the directors may so depart, but particulars of the departure, the reasons for it and its effect on the balance sheet and profit and loss account of the company must be stated in a note to the accounts, for the financial year concerned, of the company[72].

(c) Statutory valuation rules

[13.025] The Companies Acts 1963–2001 do not restrict companies to any particular method of valuing assets. Companies might opt for either a 'current cost' method, whereby the value of an asset is assessed according to its current replacement cost, or an 'historic cost' method, whereby the value of an asset is assessed by reference to its original cost to the company. Current cost accounting may give a company a clearer view of the company's current worth; but it has the effect of producing a lower figure for profits than an historic cost method. This aspect of the choice between current and historic costing caused the Revenue Commissioners to challenge the valuation of assets on a current cost basis in *Carroll Industries plc v O'Cualacháin*[73], since current cost accounting produces a smaller figure for taxable profits. Carroll J held that accounts prepared *for taxation purposes* must follow an historic cost approach, since that is the accounting method which is envisaged by taxation legislation. However, as regards accounts prepared for other purposes – eg to be laid before the AGM – the learned judge concluded that a company was free to choose whichever accounting method it would adopt in the light of the nature of its business.

[13.026] C(A)A 1986, Schedule, Part II lays down rules to be followed where computation follows an historic cost approach. Where the company opts for a current cost approach,

---

[71] C(A)A 1986, Schedule, para 72.

[72] C(A)A 1986, s 6.

[73] *Carroll Industries plc v O'Cualacháin* [1988] IR 705.

those rules are modified by the provisions of Part III of the Schedule. In either case, all assets must be categorised as being either 'fixed' or 'current', and each individual asset must be valued separately[74].

(i) Fixed assets

[13.027] Fixed assets are defined as those assets:

> '...which are intended for use on a continuing basis in the company's activities.'[75]

[13.028] Fixed assets, on an historic cost valuation, must be valued at purchase price[76] or at production cost, less any depreciation calculated to write off that amount systematically over the period of the asset's useful economic life[77]. The purchase price of an asset includes any expenses incidental to its acquisition[78]. Production costs include the price of raw materials and consumables, and direct costs which are directly attributable to the production of the asset[79]. Production costs may also *include* costs indirectly attributable to the production of the asset during the period of its production, and interest on capital borrowed to finance the production of that asset[80].

Provisions for permanent diminutions in the value of fixed assets must be made[81]. Similar provision may be made for the non-permanent diminution in fixed financial assets[82]. If any improvement in the value of the written-down fixed assets subsequently occurs, the provision must be written back to the extent to which it is no longer necessary[83]. Additional rules apply to the valuation of fungible fixed assets (ie assets which are substantially indistinguishable from one another)[84]. Tangible assets whose overall value is not material to assessing the company's state of affairs and whose quantity, value and composition are not subject to material variation may be included at a fixed quantity and value[85]. Development costs may only be included in the valuation of fixed assets in special circumstances[86].

Where goodwill is treated as a fixed asset, then, in addition to the foregoing rules, the amount of the consideration for any goodwill acquired by the company must be depreciated over a period (not exceeding the useful economic life of the goodwill) chosen by the directors[87].

---

74 C(A)A 1986, s 5(e); see para **[13.023]**.

75 C(A)A 1986, Schedule, para 60.

76 Ie any consideration (whether in cash or otherwise) given by the company in respect of that asset: C(A)A 1986, Schedule, para 71.

77 C(A)A 1986, Schedule, paras 5 and 6.

78 C(A)A 1986, Schedule, para 14(1).

79 C(A)A 1986, Schedule, para 14(2).

80 C(A)A 1986, Schedule, para 14(3).

81 C(A)A 1986, Schedule, para 7(2).

82 C(A)A 1986, Schedule, para 7(1).

83 C(A)A 1986, Schedule, para 7(3).

84 C(A)A 1986, Schedule, para 15(6). See para **[13.032]**.

85 C(A)A 1986, Schedule, para 13.

86 C(A)A 1986, Schedule, para 8(1). SSAP 13 details the appropriate circumstances.

87 C(A)A 1986, Schedule, para 9.

[13.029] Where there is no record of the purchase price or production cost, or of the details required to calculate them, or where it would cause unreasonable expense or delay to produce them, the earliest available record may be used[88].

(ii) Current assets

[13.030] Current assets are defined as those assets which are not intended for use on a continuing basis in the company's activities[89].

[13.031] Current assets must, on an historic cost valuation, be valued at purchase price or production cost, and the same rules as apply to fixed assets apply in the computation of the purchase price or production costs of current assets[90]. However, distribution costs may not be included in the calculation of production costs[91]. If the net realisable value of any current asset is lower than its production price or its production cost, the amount included in respect of that asset may be written down to its net realisable value[92].

[13.032] The purchase price or production cost of stocks and all fungible assets (whether fixed or current) may be valued by the application of either:

— the first in, first out (FIFO) method; or

— the weighted average price method; or

— any method similar to these methods[93].

The method chosen must be the one which appears to the directors to be appropriate in the circumstances of the company[94]. The most recent actual purchase price or production cost may be substituted if the directors think it appropriate[95]. Raw materials and consumables whose overall value is not material to assessing the company's state of affairs and whose quantity, composition and value are not subject to material variation may be included at a fixed quantity and value[96].

[13.033] Where any amount repayable on any debt owed by the company is greater than the value of the consideration received in the transaction giving rise to the debt, the amount of the difference may be treated as an asset. It must, however, be written off by reasonable amounts each year so that it is completely written off before repayment of the debt[97].

[13.034] Again, where there is no record of the purchase price or production cost, or of the details required to calculate them, or where it would cause unreasonable expense or delay to produce them, the earliest available record may be used[98].

---

88 C(A)A 1986, Schedule, para 16.

89 C(A)A 1986, Schedule, para 60.

90 C(A)A 1986, Schedule, para 14. See para **[13.028]**.

91 C(A)A 1986, Schedule, para 14(4).

92 C(A)A 1986, Schedule, para 11(1). If the reasons for the write down no longer exist, provision must be made to write back the provision:C(A)A 1986, Schedule, para 11(2).

93 C(A)A 1986, Schedule, para 15.

94 C(A)A 1986, Schedule, para 15.

95 C(A)A 1986, Schedule, para 15(5).

96 C(A)A 1986, Schedule, para 13.

97 C(A)A 1986, Schedule, para 12.

98 C(A)A 1986, Schedule, para 16.

(iii) Alternative accounting rules permitting current cost accounting

[13.035] C(A)A 1986, Schedule, Part III allows current cost accounting in the valuation of fixed and current assets by permitting certain assets to be revalued according to current cost, market value, or any basis which appears to the directors to be appropriate in the circumstances of the company[99]. However, where historical cost accounting is not employed, para 21(3) of the Schedule requires that:

> 'In the case of each balance sheet item affected (except stocks) either —
>
> (a) the comparable amounts determined according to the historical cost accounting rules, or
>
> (b) the differences between those amounts and the corresponding amounts actually shown in the balance sheet in respect of that item,
>
> shall be shown separately in the balance sheet or in a note to the accounts.'

No matter which accounting rules are employed, the historical cost of assets must always be disclosed or ascertainable. Whatever the accounting basis adopted, the accounts must still provide a 'true and fair' view of the company's state of affairs[100].

[13.036] The following items may be included at current cost[101]:

— intangible fixed assets, other than goodwill;

— tangible fixed assets;

— stocks;

— investments falling to be classified in the balance sheet as current assets.

[13.037] The following items may, alternatively, be included at a *market value* determined as at the date of their last valuation[102]:

— tangible fixed assets;

— financial fixed assets.

[13.038] Financial fixed assets may, alternatively, be included at a value determined on any basis which appears to the directors to be appropriate in the circumstances of the company[103].

[13.039] Where any of these alternative accounting rules is employed in the valuation of an asset, depreciation must be calculated according to the value produced by that alternative rule rather than according to its purchase price or production cost[104]. The figure for depreciation in the profit and loss account may be either the amount written off the alternative value or the amount written off the historical cost; but where the amount provided for depreciation is the historical cost amount, the amount of any difference between the two must be shown separately in the profit and loss account or in a note to the accounts[105].

99 C(A)A 1986, Schedule, para 19.

100 See para **[13.021]** .

101 C(A)A 1986, Schedule, para 19.

102 C(A)A 1986, Schedule, para 19.

103 C(A)A 1986, Schedule, para 19.

104 C(A)A 1986, Schedule, para 20(1).

105 C(A)A 1986, Schedule, para 20(3).

[13.040] Any profit or loss arising on the revaluation of an asset on application of the alternative accounting rules must be applied to a separate reserve, known as the *revaluation reserve*, and must be shown in the company's balance sheet[106]. The revaluation reserve must be reduced when the directors are of the opinion that the amounts standing to its credit are no longer necessary for the company's accounting policies but an amount may only be transferred to the profit and loss account from the reserve if either the amount in question was previously charged to that account, or if it represents realised profit[107]. The taxation treatment of the revaluation reserve must be disclosed in a note to the accounts[108].

Medium-sized and small private companies

[13.041] Medium-sized and small companies are exempted from some of the rigours of the requirements relating to the annual accounts. Before considering the annual accounts in further detail, it is necessary to examine what is meant by 'medium-sized' and 'small' in this context.

[13.042] C(A)A 1986, s 8, as amended[109], defines 'medium-sized' and 'small'. A private company qualifies to be treated as a 'medium-sized' company for any financial year if, both in that year *and* in the immediately preceding financial year, it satisfies at least *two* of the following conditions:

— its balance sheet total did not exceed €7,618,438;

— its turnover did not exceed €15,236,857;

— its average number of employees did not exceed 250.

A private company qualifies to be treated as a 'small' company for any financial year if, both in that year *and* in the immediately preceding financial year, it satisfies at least *two* of the following conditions:

— its balance sheet total did not exceed €1,904,607;

— its turnover did not exceed €3,809,214;

— its average number of employees did not exceed 50.

It will be noted that all small companies are, by definition, also medium-sized companies and, accordingly, may avail of the reliefs available to medium-sized companies.

Balance sheet total is defined in C(A)A 1986, s 8 as the aggregate of fixed and current assets[110]. Turnover is defined in the Schedule as the amounts derived from the provision of goods and services falling within the company's ordinary activities, after deduction of trade discounts, value-added tax, and any other taxes on the amounts so derived[111]. The average number of employees is computed by calculating the total number of persons

106 C(A)A 1986, Schedule, paras 21(1) and 21(3). Note that a profit moved to this reserve is not realised, therefore it may not be used in the calculation of 'profits available for distribution' within the meaning of the C(A)A 1983, s 45. On distributions see Chapter 18, *The Maintenance of Capital*, para **[18.082]** ff.

107 C(A)A 1986, Schedule, para 22(4).

108 C(A)A 1986, Schedule, para 22(5).

109 By the European Communities (Accounts) Regulations 1993 (SI 396/1993), reg 4.

110 C(A)A 1986, s 8(4). As to the valuation of fixed and current assets see para **[13.027]** ff.

111 C(A)A 1986, Schedule, para 75.

under contracts of service with the company for each week of the financial year, adding the totals together, and dividing the result by the number of weeks in the financial year[112].

A company which satisfies the criteria for a medium-sized or small company in its first financial year will qualify for such categorisation despite the fact that it has no immediately preceding financial year[113], but thereafter the normal criteria apply.

[13.043] A company which qualifies as a medium-sized or small private company continues to qualify as such unless it fails to meet the relevant criteria in two consecutive financial years. If it fails to meet the criteria in two consecutive years, it changes category for the second year[114].

The profit and loss account

[13.044] The directors must, at some date not later than 18 months after the incorporation of the company, and subsequently at least once in every calendar year, lay before the AGM a profit and loss account[115]. The profit and loss account provides a record of the company's overall business activities for the period to which it relates. Section 4(14) of C(A)A 1986 provides that:

> 'Every profit and loss account shall show the amount of the profit or loss of the company on ordinary activities before taxation.'

In addition, s 4(15) requires the profit and loss account of a company for a financial year to show:

— separately, the aggregate amount of the dividends paid and the aggregate amount of the dividends proposed to be paid,

— any transfer between the profit and loss account and reserves,

— any increase or reduction in the balance on the profit and loss account since the immediately preceding financial year,

— the profit or loss brought forward at the beginning of the year, and

— the profit or loss carried forward at the end of the year.

In the case of the first profit and loss account, the account must cover the period since the incorporation of the company[116]. In every other case it must cover the period since the preceding profit and loss account up to a date not earlier than 9 months before the date of the AGM[117].

(a) The profit and loss account formats

[13.045] Section 4(1) of C(A)A 1986 requires every profit and loss account to show the items listed in any one of the four Profit and Loss Account Formats set out in Part I of the Schedule to that Act. The directors may choose which format to adopt, subject to the overriding requirement that the accounts must give a 'true and fair' view of the company's

112 C(A)A 1986, Schedule, para 42 and C(A)A 1986, s 8(9).

113 C(A)A 1986, s 8(7).

114 C(A)A 1986, s 9.

115 CA 1963, s 148(1).

116 CA 1963, s 148(1).

117 CA 1963, s 148(1).

state of affairs[118]. Whichever format is used, however, the directors must adopt the same format in subsequent years, unless, in their opinion, there are special reasons for a change[119]. Where such a change is made, the reasons for the change and full particulars of the change must be given in a note to the accounts in which the new format is adopted[120]. At the outset, it may be pointed out that Formats 1 and 3 adopt a functional approach, whereas Formats 2 and 4 show income and expenditure by nature rather than by function. There are no material differences between Formats 1 and 3 or between Formats 2 and 4.

[13.046] Section 4 of C(A)A 1986 contains some basic rules for the preparation of the profit and loss account in accordance with the formats. First, any item required in accordance with the formats may be shown in greater detail than required by the format adopted[121]. Secondly, any items to which an Arabic number (ie 1, 2, 3, etc) is assigned in any of the formats may be combined where the individual amounts of such items are not material to assessing the state of affairs or profit and loss of the company, or where such combination facilitates the assessment[122]. Thirdly, the corresponding amount for the previous financial year for every item in the profit and loss account must be shown, and if it is not comparable, an adjustment must be made[123]. Fourthly, if there is no amount to be shown for an item, no mention need be made of it in the profit and loss account, unless a figure is available for that item from the immediately preceding financial year[124]. Fifthly, amounts in respect of items representing income may not be set off against items representing expenditure (or *vice versa*)[125]. Finally, the profit and loss account may contain an item representing or covering the amount of any income or expenditure not covered by any of the items listed in the formats[126].

[13.047] Formats 1 and 3 require companies to show the following items in the annual profit and loss account:

- turnover;
- *cost of sales*;
- gross profit or loss;
- *distribution costs*;
- *administrative expenses*;
- other operating income;

---

[118] See para **[13.021]**.
[119] C(A)A 1986, s 4(3).
[120] C(A)A 1986, s 4(4).
[121] C(A)A 1986, s 4(5).
[122] C(A)A 1986, s 4(6). The individual amounts of any items so combined must, however, be disclosed by way of a note to the accounts: C(A)A 1986, s 4(7). The Arabic and Roman numerals as they appear in the scheduled formats are not shown in this work; accordingly the reader should refer to the 1986 Act itself where appropriate.
[123] C(A)A 1986, s 4(8). Particulars of the adjustment and the reasons therefor must be given in a note to the accounts: C(A)A 1986, s 4(8).
[124] C(A)A 1986, s 4(9) and (10).
[125] C(A)A 1986, s 4(11).
[126] C(A)A 1986, s 4(12).

— income from shares in group undertakings;
— income from shares in undertakings in which a participating interest is held;
— income from other financial assets;
— other interest receivable and similar income;
— amounts written off financial assets and investments held as current assets;
— interest payable and similar charges;
— tax on profit or loss on ordinary activities;
— profit or loss on ordinary activities after taxation;
— extraordinary income;
— extraordinary charges;
— tax on extraordinary profit or loss;
— other taxes not shown under the above items;
— profit or loss for the financial year.

Format 1 also requires the account to show any figure for extraordinary profit or loss. Turnover is defined as the amounts derived from the provision of goods and services falling within the company's ordinary activities, after deduction of trade discounts, value added tax, and any other taxes[127]. Cost of sales, distribution costs and administrative expenses must be stated after taking into account any necessary provisions for depreciation or diminution in the value of assets[128]. Income and interest from group undertakings[129] must be shown separately from income and interest derived from other sources[130], and the amount of interest payable to group undertakings must be shown separately from other interests and charges payable.

[13.048] Formats 2 and 4, which show expenses according to nature rather than according to function, require companies to show the following items in the annual profit and loss account (items shown in italics do not appear in Formats 1 and 3):

— turnover;
— *variation in stocks of finished goods and in work in progress*
— *own work capitalised;*[131]
— other operating income;
— *raw materials and consumables;*
— *other external charges;*
— *staff costs:*

---

[127] C(A)A 1986, Schedule, para 75.

[128] C(A)A 1986, Schedule, para 75. C(A)A 1986, Schedule, Part I, note 11 of the Notes on the Balance Sheet Formats.

[129] 'Group undertaking' is defined in C(A)A 1986, Schedule, para 64 as an undertaking which is '(a) parent undertaking or subsidiary undertaking of that undertaking; or (b) a subsidiary undertaking of any parent undertaking of that undertaking.' See further Chapter 17, *Groups of Companies* para **[17.028]***ff*.

[130] C(A)A 1986, Schedule, Part I, note 12 of the Notes on the Balance Sheet Formats.

[131] 'Capitalised' means treated as a fixed asset: C(A)A 1986, Schedule, para 62.

(a) *wages and salaries*;
(b) *social welfare costs*;
(c) *other pension costs*;

— depreciation and other amounts written off tangible and intangible fixed assets;
— exceptional amounts written off current assets;
— other operating charges;
— income from shares in group undertakings;
— income from shares in undertakings in which a participating interest is held;
— income from other financial assets;
— other interest receivable and similar income;
— amounts written off financial assets and investments held as current assets;
— interest payable and similar charges;
— tax on profit or loss on ordinary activities;
— profit or loss on ordinary activities after taxation;
— extraordinary income;
— extraordinary charges;
— tax on extraordinary profit or loss;
— other taxes not shown under the above items;
— profit or loss for the financial year.

Format 2 also requires the account to show any figure for extraordinary profit or loss. Turnover has the meaning ascribed to it in the previous paragraph[132], and income and interest received from or payable to group undertakings must, again, be shown separately[133].

[13.049] At first glance, it might appear that Formats 2 and 4 require greater disclosure than Formats 1 and 3, judging by the greater number of items required to be shown. However, when it is considered that Formats 1 and 3 require details of cost of sales, distribution costs and administrative expenses, whereas Formats 2 and 4 simply require details of 'other operating charges'; and when it is further considered that details of 'staff costs' and 'depreciation and other amounts written off tangible and intangible fixed assets' must be given in a note to accounts adopting Formats 1 or 3[134], it is arguable that Formats 1 and 3 require greater disclosure[135].

(b) Notes relating to the profit and loss account

[13.050] In addition to the items required to be shown by the Profit and Loss Account Formats, further information relating to items covered in the profit and loss account is required to be shown by way of notes to the accounts[136]. These matters cover:

---

132 See para **[13.047]**.

133 See para **[13.047]**.

134 C(A)A 1986, Schedule, Part I, note 14 of the Notes on the Balance Sheet Formats. See para **[13.051]**.

135 See Kelleher, *The Companies (Amendment) Act 1986: A Guide to the Accounting, Reporting and Filing Requirements* (1987) The Institute of Chartered Accountants in Ireland, p 26.

(i) Depreciation and other amounts written off fixed assets.
(ii) Improvements in the value of written down fixed assets.
(iii) Certain items of income and expenditure (including directors' emoluments).
(iv) Particulars of tax.
(v) Particulars of turnover.
(vi) Particulars of staff.
(vii) Extraordinary income and research and development.
(viii) Accounting policies and currencies.

(i) Depreciation and other amounts written off fixed assets

[13.051] Where Format 1 or 3 is adopted, the notes must disclose the amounts of any provisions for depreciation or diminution in the value of tangible and intangible fixed assets[137]. Furthermore, regardless of which of the four formats is adopted, if any of the alternative valuation rules is employed[138], and a figure for depreciation in the profit and loss account is the amount written off the historical cost, the difference between the amount written off the alternative value and the amount written off the historical cost value must be given in the profit and loss account or in a note to the accounts[139]. Provisions for permanent diminutions in the value of fixed assets, if not shown in the profit and loss account, must be stated in a note to the accounts[140]. Likewise, provisions for non-permanent diminution in fixed financial assets, if not shown in the profit and loss account, must be stated in a note to the accounts[141].

(ii) Improvements in the value of written down fixed assets

[13.052] Amounts written back must, if not shown in the profit and loss account, be disclosed in a note to the accounts.[142]

(iii) Certain items of income and expenditure

[13.053] Each of the following must be stated separately in a note to the accounts[143]:

— The amount of interest on or any similar charges in respect of -

— bank loans and overdrafts, and loans made to the company (other than bank loans and overdrafts) which —

- are repayable otherwise than by instalments and fall due[144] for repayment before the end of the period of five years beginning with the day next following the end of the financial year of the company, or

---

136 C(A)A 1986, Schedule, para 1.

137 C(A)A 1986, Schedule, Part I, note 14 of the Notes on the Balance Sheet Formats.

138 See para **[13.035]**.

139 C(A)A 1986, Schedule, para 20(3).

140 C(A)A 1986, Schedule, para 7(2).

141 C(A)A 1986, Schedule, para 7(1).

142 C(A)A 1986, Schedule, para 7(3).

143 C(A)A 1986, Schedule, para 39.

144 A loan is treated as falling due for payment on the earliest date on which the lender could require repayment or payment if he exercised all options and rights available to him: C(A)A 1986, Schedule, para 67.

- are repayable by instalments the last of which falls due for payment before the end of that period, and

— loans of any other kind made to the company, but not interest or charges on loans to the company from group undertakings.

— The amounts respectively provided for redemption of share capital and for redemption of loans.

— The amount of income from listed[145] and unlisted investments.

— The amount of the remuneration of the auditors (including any sums paid by the company in respect of the auditors' expenses).

— The aggregate amounts of the emoluments of, and compensation in respect of loss of office to, directors and compensation in respect of loss of office to past directors.

Both CA 1963 and CA 1990 contain further requirements as to disclosure by note of particulars relating to directors' emoluments and transactions and arrangements with directors. These requirements are considered below[146].

(iv) Particulars of tax

[13.054] The following particulars of tax must be stated separately in a note to the accounts[147]:

— The basis on which the charge for corporation tax, income tax and other tax on profits (whether payable in or outside the State) is computed.

— Particulars of any special circumstances which affect liability in respect of taxation on profits, income or capital gains.

— The amount of the charge for corporation tax, income tax and other taxation on profits or capital gains so far as charged to revenue in the profit and loss account.

(v) Particulars of turnover

[13.055] Where a company, in the opinion of the directors, carries on substantially different classes of business, or where the company has supplied, in the opinion of the directors, substantially different geographical markets, then particulars of turnover are required to be given in a note to the accounts[148]. These particulars must detail the amount of turnover attributable to each class of business or each geographical market. When analysing the geographical market, the directors are required to have regard to the manner in which the company's activities are organised. If the directors are of the opinion that disclosure of particulars of turnover would be seriously prejudicial to the interests of the company (eg where it is of use to competitors), then the disclosure need not be made, but the fact that disclosure has not been made must be noted.

(vi) Particulars of staff

[13.056] The following particulars of staff must be stated in the notes to the accounts[149]:

145 'Listed' means listed on a recognised stock exchange within the State or on any stock exchange of repute outside the State: C(A)A 1986, Schedule, para 66.

146 See para **[13.098]**.

147 C(A)A 1986, Schedule, para 40.

148 C(A)A 1986, Schedule, para 41.

149 C(A)A 1986, Schedule, para 42.

— the average number of employees[150] employed during the financial year;

— the average number of persons employed within each category of persons employed by the company.

The directors may choose whatever basis they wish (if any), having regard to the activities of the business, for categorising the employees. In addition, the following must be stated in the notes if they are not already shown in the profit and loss account:

— wages and salaries paid;

— social welfare costs;

— pension costs.

Wages and salaries are calculated by reference to payments made or costs incurred in respect of all persons employed by the company during the financial year who are taken into account in calculating the average number of employees[151]. Social welfare costs means any contribution to any State social welfare, social security or pension scheme or any fund or arrangement connected with such a scheme[152]. Pension costs include any other contributions established for the purpose of providing pensions employed by the company, and any sums set aside or paid in respect of such schemes[153]. It will be noted that Formats 1 and 3 do not cover these items in the profit and loss account. Consequently, companies adopting Formats 1 or 3 will have to disclose these matters in the notes to the accounts.

(vii) Extraordinary income and research and development

[13.057] Particulars of extraordinary income or charges arising in the financial year must be stated in the notes to the accounts[154]. Furthermore, the effect of any exceptional transactions must be stated in the notes. Any amounts expended on research and development must likewise be stated in the notes; but where the directors are of the opinion that this would be prejudicial to the interests of the company, they need not make such a statement, but can simply state that such disclosure was not made.

(viii) Accounting policies and currencies

[13.058] The accounting policies adopted by the company in determining the profit and loss of the company, including such policies with respect to the depreciation and diminution in value of assets, must be stated in the notes to the accounts[155]. Changes in accounting policies or fundamental errors in earlier accounts must be detailed in the notes to the accounts. Likewise, where sums originally denominated in foreign currencies have been translated into euro currency, that fact and the conversion basis must be stated in the notes.

(c) Exemptions for 'medium-sized' and 'small' private companies

[13.059] Section 11(1) of C(A)A 1986 permits (but does not oblige) medium-sized private companies to prepare a 'short form' profit and loss account, subject to the requirement that

150 As to calculation of the average number of employees, see para **[13.042]**.

151 C(A)A 1986, Schedule, para 74.

152 C(A)A 1986, Schedule, para 74.

153 C(A)A 1986, Schedule, para 74.

154 C(A)A 1986, Schedule, para 43.

155 C(A)A 1986, Schedule, paras 24 and 44.

the accounts give a 'true and fair' view of the state of affairs of the company[156]. In the short form profit and loss account, certain items appearing in the formats may be combined as a single item. Since 'small' companies are, by definition, medium-sized companies, small companies may also avail of this exemption.

[13.060] Where Format 1 or 3 of the Profit and Loss Account Formats (C(A)A 1986, Schedule, Part I) is adopted by 'medium-sized' or 'small' private company, the following items may be combined under the heading 'gross profit or loss' in a short form profit and loss account:

— Turnover
— Cost of sales
— Other operating income

Where Format 2 or 4 of the Profit and Loss Account Formats is adopted, the following items may be combined under the heading 'gross profit or loss' in a short form profit and loss account:

— Reduction in stocks of finished goods and work in progress
— Increase in stocks of finished goods and work in progress
— Raw materials and consumables
— Other external charges
— Turnover
— Own work capitalised
— Other operating income

[13.061] In addition to the foregoing, C(A)A 1986, s 12(2) relieves 'medium-sized' companies (and, accordingly, 'small' companies) from the obligation to disclose particulars of turnover[157] in the notes to the accounts.

(d) Exemptions for parent undertakings

[13.062] A parent undertaking, within the meaning of the European Communities (Companies: Group Accounts) Regulations 1992[158], need not prepare an individual profit and loss account where it has produced consolidated accounts in accordance with those regulations. The notes to the accounts must, however, disclose the fact that it is availing of the exemption. It should be noted that this exemption only applies to companies which are required to produce consolidated accounts. Companies which voluntarily prepare consolidated group accounts may not avail of the exemption.

(e) Signature and circulation of the profit and loss account

[13.063] The profit and loss account must be signed on behalf of the directors by two of the directors of the company[159]. Prior to signature, and before the annual accounts are circulated and laid before the AGM, the profit and loss account must be annexed to the balance sheet and approved by the board of directors[160]. If a profit and loss account which

156 C(A)A 1986, s 11(1). On 'true and fair' see para **[13.021]**.
157 See para **[13.055]**.
158 SI 1992/201. See para **[13.111]** ff.
159 CA 1963, s 156(1).
160 CA 1963, s 157.

has not been approved or signed in accordance with these requirements is issued, circulated, or published, the company and every officer of the company who is in default, shall be liable to a fine not exceeding €1,905[161]. The issue, circulation, or publication of an unsigned fair and accurate summary of the profit and loss figures for part of the financial year is not prohibited; neither is the issue, circulation or publication of an unsigned fair and accurate summary of a profit and loss account which has been signed by the directors[162].

The balance sheet

[13.064] Every calendar year, the directors must cause a balance sheet, as at the date to which the profit and loss account is made up, to be made out, and must lay it before the AGM[163]. The balance sheet is a statement of the company's assets and liabilities, as at the date upon which it is drawn up. It is designed to give some indication of the company's worth[164] and of how the shareholders' investments in the company have been employed.

(a) The balance sheet formats

[13.065] Just as the profit and loss account must comply with one of the scheduled formats[165], C(A)A 1986, s 4(1) requires every balance sheet to show the items listed in any one of the two Balance Sheet Formats set out in Part I of the Schedule to 1986 Act. Again, the directors may choose which format to adopt, subject to the overriding requirement that the accounts must give a 'true and fair' view of the company's state of affairs[166]. Whichever format is used, however, the directors must adopt the same format in subsequent years, unless, in their opinion, there are special reasons for a change[167]. Where such a change is made, the reasons for the change and full particulars of the change must be given in a note to the accounts in which the new format is adopted[168].

[13.066] The statutory rules for the preparation of the profit and loss account in accordance with the formats apply *mutatis mutandis* to the preparation of the balance sheet in accordance with the formats[169]. Thus, any item required in accordance with the formats may be shown in greater detail than required by the format adopted[170]. Secondly, any items

---

161 CA 1963, ss 156(3) and 157(2), as amended by the C(A)A 1982, Sch 1; also CA 1990, s 240, as amended.

162 CA 1963, s 156(4).

163 CA 1963, s 148(2).

164 As Keane, *Company Law* (3rd edn, 2000), p 400 points out, the balance sheet 'is not designed to provide a reliable guide to the worth of the company. Essentially, it is a historic document intended to indicate the extent of the investment of the shareholders in the company and how that investment has been employed.' The balance sheet might not indicate the true worth of the company because, inter alia, of the fact that the valuation of the assets may be calculated by reference to historic cost, rather than current cost; see para **[13.025]** ff.

165 See para **[13.045]**.

166 See para **[13.021]**.

167 C(A)A 1986, s 4(3).

168 C(A)A 1986, s 4(4).

169 C(A)A 1986, s 4. See para **[13.046]**.

170 C(A)A 1986, s 4(5).

to which an Arabic number (1, 2, 3 etc) is assigned in any of the formats may be combined where the individual amounts of such items are not material to assessing the state of affairs of the company, or where such combination facilitates the assessment[171]. Thirdly, the corresponding amount for the previous financial year for every item in the balance sheet must be shown, and if it is not comparable, an adjustment must be made[172]. Fourthly, if there is no amount to be shown for an item, no mention need be made of it in the balance sheet, unless a figure is available for that item from the immediately preceding financial year[173]. Fifthly, amounts in respect of items representing assets may not be set off against items representing liabilities (or vice versa)[174]. Finally, the balance sheet may contain an item representing or covering the amount of any asset or liability not covered by any of the items listed in the formats; however, preliminary expenses, expenses and commission on any issue of shares or debentures, and costs of research may not be treated as assets in the balance sheet[175].

[13.067] Format 2, which is chosen for the sake of convenience to be shown here, requires companies to adopt the following format in the preparation of the balance sheet:

ASSETS	LIABILITIES
A. Fixed Assets	***A. Capital and reserves***
Intangible assets	Called up share capital
Development costs	Share premium account
Concessions, patents, licences trade marks and similar rights and assets	Revaluation reserve
Goodwill	
Payments on account	
Tangible assets:	*Other reserves:*
Land and buildings	The capital redemption reserve fund
Plant and machinery	Reserve for own shares
Fixtures fittings tools and equipment	Reserves provided for by the articles of association
Payments on account and assets in course of construction	
Financial assets:	*Other reserves:*
Shares in group undertakings	Profit and loss account
Loans to group undertakings	
Shares in undertakings in which a participating interest is held	
Loans to undertakings in which a participating interest is held	
Other investments other than loans	
Other loans	

171 C(A)A 1986, s 4(6). The individual amounts of any items so combined must, however, be disclosed by way of a note to the accounts: C(A)A 1986, s 4(7). The Arabic and Roman numerals as they appear in the scheduled formats are not shown in this work; accordingly the reader should refer to the CA 1986 itself where appropriate.

172 C(A)A 1986, s 4(8). Particulars of the adjustment and the reasons therefor must be given in a note to the accounts: C(A)A 1986, s 4(8).

173 C(A)A 1986, s 4(9) and (10).

174 C(A)A 1986, s 4(11).

175 C(A)A 1986, s 4(12).

B. Current Assets	**B. Provisions for liabilities and charges**
Stocks:	Pensions and similar obligations
Raw materials and consumables	Taxation, including deferred taxation
Work in progress	Other provisions
Finished goods and goods for resale	*Creditors:*
Payments on account	Debenture loans
Debtors:	Bank loans and overdrafts
Trade debtors	Payments received on account
Amounts owed by group undertakings	Trade creditors
Amounts owed by undertakings in which a participating interest is held	Bills of exchange payable
Other debtors	Amounts owed to group undertakings
Called up share capital not paid	Amounts owed to undertakings in which a participating interest is held
Prepayments and accrued income	Other creditors including tax and social welfare
Investments:	Accruals and deferred income
Shares in group undertakings	
Other investments	
Cash at bank and in hand	

[13.068] There is no material difference in the items required by Format 1 and Format 2 of the Balance Sheet Formats: Format 1 arranges items in vertical form, and Format 2 merely rearranges those items in horizontal form. Because it appears in vertical form, Format 1 requires a figure to be given for 'net current assets (liabilities)' and a figure for 'total assets less current liabilities'. It also shows separate figures for 'creditors: amounts falling due within one year' and 'creditors: amounts falling due after more than one year'. Format 2 does not require these items to be shown separately in the balance sheet, but where Format 2 is adopted, equivalent information has to be disclosed in a note to the accounts if not shown in the balance sheet[176].

[13.069] Regard must be had to the following matters when addressing each of the items required in the balance sheet. First, amounts in respect of concessions, patents, licences, trade marks and similar rights and assets can only be included under that heading in the balance sheet if either the assets were acquired for valuable consideration and are not required to be shown under goodwill, or the assets in question were created by the company itself[177]. Secondly, amounts in respect of goodwill may only be included to the extent that the goodwill was acquired for valuable consideration[178]. Thirdly, as regards debtors, the amounts falling due after more than one year must be shown separately for each item included under that heading[179]. Fourthly, the amounts of any convertible loans must be shown separately under debenture loans[180]. Fifthly, as regards creditors, payments received on account of orders must be shown insofar as they are not shown as deductions

[176] C(A)A 1986, Schedule, Part I, note 10 of the Notes on the Balance Sheet Formats.

[177] C(A)A 1986, Schedule, Part I, note 1 of the Notes on the Balance Sheet Formats.

[178] C(A)A 1986, Schedule, Part I, note 2 of the Notes on the Balance Sheet Formats.

[179] C(A)A 1986, Schedule, Part I, note 4 of the Notes on the Balance Sheet Formats.

[180] C(A)A 1986, Schedule, Part I, note 5 of the Notes on the Balance Sheet Formats.

from stocks[181]. Sixthly, the amount for creditors in respect of taxation and social welfare must show the following separately[182]:

— Income tax payable on emoluments to which Chapter IV of the Income Tax Act 1967 applies;
— Any other income tax;
— Corporation tax;
— Capital gains tax;
— Value added tax; and
— Any other tax.

Seventhly, as regards accruals and deferred income, the amount in respect of any government grants must be shown separately in a note to the accounts if it is not shown separately[183]. Finally, as regards called up share capital, the amount in respect of allotted share capital and the amount in respect of called up share capital which has been paid up must be shown separately.

(b) Notes relating to the balance sheet

[13.070] In addition to the items required to be shown by the balance sheet, further information relating to the items shown therein is required to be stated by way of notes to the accounts[184]. These matters cover:

(i) Accounting policies;
(ii) Group undertakings;
(iii) Items relating to creditors;
(iv) Historical costs;
(v) Development costs;
(vi) Goodwill;
(vii) Taxation treatment of revaluation reserve;
(viii) Purchase price and production costs;
(ix) Debts owed to company
(x) Share capital and debentures;
(xi) Fixed assets;
(xii) Financial assets held as investments;
(xiii) Reserves and provisions;
(xiv) Restrictions on distributable profits
(xv) Provision for taxation;
(xvi) Details in indebtedness;
(xvii) Guarantees and other financial commitments;
(xviii) First valuations;
(xix) Section 60 loans;
(xx) Dividends.

[181] C(A)A 1986, Schedule, Part I, note 6 of the Notes on the Balance Sheet Formats.
[182] C(A)A 1986, Schedule, Part I, note 7 of the Notes on the Balance Sheet Formats.
[183] C(A)A 1986, Schedule, Part I, note 8 of the Notes on the Balance Sheet Formats.
[184] C(A)A 1986, Schedule, para 1.

(i) Accounting policies

[13.071] The accounting policies[185] adopted by the company in determining the amounts to be included in respect of items shown in the balance sheet, including such policies with respect to the depreciation and diminution in value of assets, must be stated in the notes to the accounts.

(ii) Group undertakings

[13.072] If the company is a parent undertaking[186] within the meaning of the European Communities (Companies: Group Accounts) Regulations 1992, the aggregate amounts of any items in the balance sheet relating to:

— amounts attributable to dealings with or interests in any parent undertaking or fellow or subsidiary undertaking; or

— amounts attributable to dealings with or interests in any subsidiary undertaking of the company;

must be stated separately in the notes if not shown separately in the balance sheet.

(iii) Items relating to creditors

[13.073] Where Format 2 of the Balance Sheet Formats is adopted, the notes to the accounts must show separately, for each item falling under the general heading 'creditors', amounts falling due within one year and after one year.[187]

(iv) Historical costs

[13.074] Where the alternative valuation rules are employed in the valuation of assets, the comparable amounts determined according to the historical cost accounting rules, or the differences between those amounts and the corresponding amounts actually shown in the balance sheet in respect of that item must be shown separately in the balance sheet or in a note to the accounts.[188]

(v) Development costs

[13.075] If development costs are included in the valuation of fixed assets, a note to the accounts must explain the period over which the amount of those costs originally capitalised is being or is to be written off, and the reasons for capitalising the costs in question.[189]

(vi) Goodwill

[13.076] Where goodwill is treated as a fixed asset, the period chosen for depreciation of that asset, and the reason for choosing that period, must be disclosed in a note to the accounts.[190]

---

185 C(A)A 1986, Schedule, para 24.

186 C(A)A 1986, Schedule, para 45, as amended by the European Communities (Companies: Group Accounts) Regulations 1992 (SI 201/1992); see para **[13.111]** ff.

187 See para **[13.068]**.

188 C(A)A 1986, Schedule, para 21(3).

189 C(A)A 1986, Schedule, para 8(2). See para **[13.028]**.

190 C(A)A 1986, Schedule, para 9.

(vii) Taxation treatment of revaluation reserve

[13.077] The taxation treatment of the revaluation reserve must be disclosed in a note to the accounts.[191]

(viii) Purchase price and production costs

[13.078] Where interest is included in the calculation of production costs, a note to the accounts must disclose that fact[192]. In addition, where the purchase price or production cost of stocks or fungible assets is determined according to the FIFO or weighted average methods, or any similar methods, and the amount shown in respect of any item so valued differs materially from its replacement cost, the difference between the two values must be disclosed in a note to the accounts[193].

(ix) Debts owed to company

[13.079] Where any amount repayable on any debt owed by the company is greater than the value of the consideration received in the transaction giving rise to the debt, the amount of the difference may be treated as an asset and must be disclosed either as a separate item in the balance sheet or in a note to the accounts.[194]

(x) Share capital and debentures

[13.080] The following details must be disclosed by way of note to the accounts[195]:

— The authorised capital;

— Where there is more than one class of shares, the number and aggregate nominal value of the shares of each class;

— The earliest and latest date upon which the company has power to redeem redeemable shares;

— Whether redeemable shares must be redeemable in any event or are liable to be redeemed at the option of the company;

— Whether any premium is payable upon the redemption of redeemable shares;

— The amount of any such premium payable;

— The reasons for any allotments made during the financial year;

— The classes of any shares so allotted;

— The number, aggregate nominal value, and consideration received for shares so allotted ;

— The reason for any issue of debentures[196] during the financial year;

— The classes of debentures so issued;

— The amount issued and the consideration received for debentures so issued;

— Particulars of redeemed debentures which the company has power to reissue;

[191] C(A)A 1986, Schedule, para 22(5).

[192] C(A)A 1986, Schedule, para 14(3).

[193] C(A)A 1986, Schedule, paras 15(3) and 15(4).

[194] C(A)A 1986, Schedule, para 12.

[195] C(A)A 1986, Schedule, para 26.

[196] As to the meaning of 'issue of debentures' see Chapter 21, *Corporate Borrowing: Registration of Charges*, para **[21.035]**.

— Where debentures are held by a nominee or trustee for the company, the nominal amount of debentures and the amount at which they are stated in the company's accounting records in accordance with CA 1963, s 147[197].

[13.081] Where the company is a parent undertaking within the meaning of the European Communities (Companies: Group Accounts) Regulations 1992, the number, description and amount of the shares in, and debentures of, the company held by its subsidiary undertakings or their nominees must be stated in a note unless held as personal representative or trustee[198].

(xi) Fixed assets

[13.082] The notes must show all movements in fixed assets[199]. It was observed above[200] that items appearing with an Arabic number in the scheduled formats may be combined in the balance sheet where the individual amounts are not material to the assessment of the company's state of affairs, or where such combination facilitates that assessment. Where items shown under Fixed Assets in the formats are combined in this way, the notes must state:

— The 'appropriate amounts'[201] in respect of each item as at the beginning of the financial year and the date of the balance sheet, respectively;

— The effect of any application of the alternative valuation rules[202], acquisitions, disposals or transfers of assets, on the value of each item;

— The cumulative amount of provisions for depreciation or diminution in value of assets as at the beginning of the financial year and the date of the balance sheet, respectively;

— The amount of any provisions for depreciation or diminution in value made in the financial year;

— The amounts of any adjustments made in respect of depreciation or diminution in value made during the financial year in consequence of the disposal of any assets;

— The amounts of any other adjustments made in respect of depreciation or diminution in value during the financial year.

[13.083] Valuation particulars must also be given in the notes where any fixed assets of the company are valued according to the alternative valuation rules[203]. The notes must state the

---

197 CA 1963, s 147 contained requirements relating to the keeping of books of account. The section has since been repealed CA 1990, but the note requirements in the 1986 Act were not amended to take cognisance of the repeal.

198 C(A)A 1986, Schedule, para 46, as amended by the European Communities (Companies: Group Accounts) Regulations 1992, (SI 201/1992); see para **[13.111]**. Where the subsidiary undertaking holds the shares or debentures as trustee, neither it, the parent, nor any subsidiary of the parent must be beneficially interested, except by way of security, in the ordinary course of business: C(A)A 1986, Schedule, para 46.

199 C(A)A 1986, Schedule, para 29.

200 At para **[13.066]**.

201 The appropriate amount is the aggregate amount determined according to the statutory valuation rules: C(A)A 1986, Schedule, para 29(2).

202 See para **[13.035]**.

203 C(A)A 1986, Schedule, para 30.

years in which the assets were severally valued and the several values. The names or particulars of qualification of any person who conducted any valuation during the financial year, and the basis of valuation used, must also be stated.

(xii) Financial assets and investments held as current assets

[13.084] Listed investments must be disclosed in the notes to the accounts, and a distinction must be made between investments listed on a recognised stock exchange and other listed investments[204]. Where items falling under the general headings 'financial assets' or 'investments held as current assets' in the formats are combined, the notes must state how much of the combined amount is ascribable to listed investments. The amount ascribable to listed investments must also be divided to show how much of that amount is ascribable to investments listed on a recognised stock exchange and how much is not. The notes must also state the aggregate market value of the listed investments, and the market *and* stock exchange value where the market value stated in the accounts is higher than the stock exchange value.

(xiii) Reserves and provisions

[13.085] Particulars of each provision included in the item 'other provisions' in the balance sheet must be given in the notes where the amount of that provision is material[205]. Furthermore, movements in reserves and provisions must be stated in the notes if they do not appear on the balance sheet. The amounts of reserves or provisions as at the beginning of the financial year and the date of the balance sheet must be stated, as must any amounts transferred to or from the reserves or provisions during the financial year and the source and application of any amounts so transferred.

(xiv) Restrictions on distributable profits

[13.086] A subsidiary may be a member of its holding company[206]. In such circumstances, CA 1990, s 224(b)(1) requires the profits of the subsidiary which are available for distribution to be restricted by a sum equal to the total cost of the shares acquired. Particulars of this restriction must be stated in the notes to the accounts[207].

(xv) Provision for taxation

[13.087] The amount of any provision for taxation, other than deferred taxation, must be stated in a note to the accounts[208].

(xvi) Details in indebtedness

[13.088] In respect of every item shown under 'creditors' in the balance sheet, the notes must state[209]:

— the aggregate amount of any debts included under that item which are payable or repayable otherwise than by instalments and fall due for payment or repayment

204 C(A)A 1986, Schedule, para 31.

205 C(A)A 1986, Schedule, para 32.

206 See Chapter 15, *Shares and Membership*, para **[15.011]**.

207 C(A)A 1986, Schedule, para 32(a), as inserted by CA 1990, s 233.

208 C(A)A 1986, Schedule, para 33.

209 C(A)A 1986, Schedule, para 34

after the end of the period of five years beginning with the day next following the end of the financial year;

- the aggregate amount of any debts so included which are payable or repayable by instalments any of which fall due for payment after the end of that period;
- the aggregate amount of any debts included under that item in respect of which any security has been given;
- an indication of the nature of the securities so given and the aggregate amount of instalments falling due after the end of that period.

[13.089] If any fixed cumulative dividends[210] are in arrears, the amount of the arrears and the period for which each class of dividends is in arrears must be stated in the notes[211].

(xvii) Guarantees and other financial commitments

[13.090] Particulars of any charge on the assets of the company which secures the liability of another person must be given in the notes[212]. Where practicable, the amount of that liability must also be stated. In addition, the following further information must be stated in the notes:

- The amount or estimated amount of contingent liabilities not provided for;
- The legal nature of contingent liabilities not provided for;
- Whether any security has been provided in respect of such contingent liabilities and, if so, what;
- The aggregate or estimated amount of contracts for capital expenditure not provided for;
- The aggregate or estimated amount of capital expenditure authorised by the directors which has not been contracted for;
- Any pension commitments included under any provision shown in the balance sheet;
- Any pension commitments for which no provision has been made;
- Any pension commitment relating wholly or partly to past directors;
- The nature of any pension scheme operated by or on behalf of the company, including whether it is a defined benefit scheme or a defined contribution scheme;
- Whether each such scheme is externally or internally funded;
- Whether any pension costs and liabilities are assessed by a professionally qualified actuary and, if so, the date of the most recent actuarial valuation;
- Whether any such actuarial valuation is available for public inspection;
- Any financial commitments which have not been provided for and which are relevant to assessing the company's state of affairs.

[13.091] Any of the above commitments which are undertaken on behalf of or for the benefit of any parent undertaking or fellow subsidiary undertaking, or any subsidiary

210 See Chapter 15, *Shares and Membership*, para **[15.100]** *ff.*

211 C(A)A 1986, Schedule, para 35.

212 C(A)A 1986, Schedule, para 36.

undertaking of the company, must be shown separately from the other commitments and separately from each other[213].

(xviii) First valuations

[13.092] Particulars of any case where purchase price or production cost of any asset is determined for the first time must be given in the notes.[214]

(xix) Section 60 loans

[13.093] As observed in Chapter 18, *The Maintenance of Capital*[215], a private company may give a loan to assist in the purchase of its own shares provided that either a special resolution permitting the loan is passed in accordance with CA 1963, s 60, or the loan is given to an employee or an employee of a subsidiary as part of an employee share scheme[216]. The aggregate amount of any such loans which are outstanding must be disclosed by way of note to the accounts, and a distinction must be made between loans permitted by special resolution, loans to employees, and loans to employees of a subsidiary.

(xx) Dividends

[13.094] The aggregate amount which is recommended for distribution by way of dividend must be stated in the notes[217].

(c) Exemptions for 'small' private companies

[13.095] Section 10(1) of C(A)A 1986 *permits* (but does not oblige) 'small'[218] private companies to draw up an abridged balance sheet for the purposes of the annual accounts, subject to the requirement that the balance sheet must give a 'true and fair' view of the company's state of affairs as at the end of its financial year[219]. 'Medium-sized'[220] private companies may *not* avail of this exemption in their annual accounts. Under s 10(1), the abridged balance sheet need show only those items preceded by letters or Roman numerals in Formats 1 and 2 of the Balance Sheet Formats set out in the Schedule to the 1986 Act. In Format 2, those items are as follows:

ASSETS	LIABILITIES
A. Fixed Assets	**A. Capital and Reserves**
I. Intangible Assets	I. Called up Share Capital
II. Tangible Assets	II. Share Premium Account
III. Financial Assets	III. Revaluation Reserve
	IV. Other Reserves
	V. Profit and Loss Account

[213] C(A)A 1986, Schedule, para 45A, inserted by the European Communities (Companies: Group Accounts) Regulations 1992, (SI 1992/201). As to the meaning of parent undertaking, subsidiary undertaking and fellow subsidiary undertaking see Chapter 17, *Groups of* Companies, para **[17.028]***ff*.

[214] C(A)A 1986, Schedule, para 37.

[215] See Chapter 18, *The Maintenance of Capital*, para **[18.041]** ff.

[216] C(A)A 1986, Schedule, para 37.

[217] C(A)A 1986, Schedule, para 37.

[218] See para **[13.042]**.

[219] See para **[13.021]**.

[220] See para **[13.042]**.

B. Current Assets	***B. Provisions for Liabilities and Charges***
I. Stocks	***C. Creditors***
II. Debtors	
III. Investments	
IV. Cash at Bank and in Hand	

Where Format 1 of the Balance Sheet formats has been adopted, the abridged balance sheet must also show amounts for 'net current assets (liabilities)' and 'total assets less current liabilities,' and the amounts for 'creditors' must distinguish between amounts falling due within and after one year. Where Format 2 of the Balance Sheet Formats has been adopted, the item 'creditors' in the abridged balance sheet must show separately amounts falling due within one year and amounts falling due after one year. In addition, where either of the two formats has been adopted, the item 'debtors' must show separately the total amounts falling due within one year and after one year[221].

The requirements for notes relating to the abridged balance sheet of a 'small' private company are considerably fewer than those relating to a full balance sheet, since fewer items requiring explanation appear in the abridged balance sheet. As a general rule, the notes need only concern themselves with items preceded by Arabic and Roman numerals. However, caution should be exercised when preparing the notes relating to the abridged balance sheet, because certain particulars, eg information regarding the period over which capitalised development costs are written off[222], must be included in the notes regardless of whether the item to which it relates is shown separately in the balance sheet[223].

(d) Exemption statement by directors

[13.096] Since 21 February 2000, certain private companies have been permitted to opt-out of the requirements to have an auditor and to have the company's accounts audited[224]. The balance sheet of such companies for the exempted year must contain a statement by the directors that the exemptions have been availed of, that the company satisfied the conditions for exemption, that no valid veto to the exemption was exercised, and that they acknowledge the requirements of the Companies Acts as to the keeping of proper books of account[225]. The statement must appear immediately above the signatures of the directors to the balance sheet. Failure to provide such a statement, or wilfully providing a false one, constitutes an offence[226] for which one will be liable, on summary conviction, to a fine of up to €1,905 or 12 months' imprisonment or both; or on indictment to a fine of up to €12,697 or five years' imprisonment or both[227].

(e) Signature and circulation of the balance sheet

[13.097] The balance sheet must be signed on behalf of the directors by two of the directors of the company[228]. Prior to signature, and before the annual accounts are

221 C(A)A 1986, s 10(1).
222 See para **[13.075]**.
223 See also para **[13.098]** *ff.*
224 C(A)(No 2)A 1999, Part III. See para **[13.185]** *ff.*
225 CA 1963, s 34.
226 CA 1963, ss 34(6) and 37.
227 CA 1990, s 240, as amended.
228 CA 1963, s 156(1).

circulated and laid before the AGM, the profit and loss account[229], any group accounts[230], and the auditors' report[231] must be annexed to the balance sheet, and the balance sheet and all the accounts so annexed approved by the board of directors[232]. If a balance sheet which has not been approved or signed in accordance with these requirements is issued, circulated, or published, the company and every officer of the company who is in default, shall be liable to a fine not exceeding €1,905[233]. The issue, circulation or publication of an unsigned fair and accurate summary of a balance sheet which has been signed by the directors is not, however, prohibited[234].

The notes to the accounts

[13.098] Not only must companies prepare annual accounts in accordance with the scheduled formats contained in the C(A)A 1986, Schedule, Part I, but they must also prepare notes to the accounts[235]. The notes may be contained in the accounts themselves or in a document annexed to the accounts[236]. Many of the note requirements as they relate to the profit and loss account and balance sheet have been examined above[237]. In addition to those requirements, further information relating to subsidiary undertakings, directors' emoluments, and transactions and arrangements with directors is required to be stated in the notes to the accounts[238].

(a) Subsidiary undertakings

[13.099] Where a company is a subsidiary undertaking within the meaning of the European Communities (Companies: Group Accounts) Regulations 1992, certain details must be stated in the notes concerning the parent undertakings of the largest and smallest group of undertakings for which group accounts are prepared and of which the company is a member[239], namely:

- — The name of the parent undertakings;
- — The places of incorporation of the parent undertakings, if incorporated;
- — The addresses of the principal places of business of the parent undertakings, if unincorporated;
- — Any addresses from where copies of the group accounts prepared by the parent undertakings may be obtained, if made available to the public.

---

229 See para **[13.044]** *ff*.
230 See para **[13.109]** *ff*.
231 See para **[13.107]** *ff*.
232 CA 1963, s 157.
233 CA 1963, ss 156(3) and 157(2), as amended by the C(A)A 1982, Sch 1, and CA 1990, s 240, as amended.
234 CA 1963, s 156(4).
235 C(A)A 1986, s 4(1) and C(A)A 1986, Schedule, para 23(1).
236 C(A)A 1986, Schedule, para 23(2).
237 See paras **[13.050]** ff and **[13.070]** ff, respectively.
238 Particulars of directors' and the secretary's interests in shares must also be disclosed in the notes if not given in the directors' report. See para **[13.104]**.
239 C(A)A 1986, Schedule, para 46A, as inserted by the European Communities (Companies: Group Accounts) Regulations 1992, (SI 1992/201).

(b) Directors' emoluments

[13.100] Section 191 of CA 1963 requires detailed particulars of directors' salaries and payments to be given in the annual accounts or in a statement annexed thereto. The particulars required relate to:

— the aggregate amount of the directors' emoluments;

— the aggregate amount of directors' or past directors' pensions;

— the aggregate amount of any compensation to directors or past directors in respect of loss of office.

The particulars must distinguish between emoluments[240], pensions[241], and contributions to pension schemes[242] payable in respect of services rendered as director of the company itself and as director of subsidiary companies. The amounts shown must include all sums paid or receivable from the company, the company's subsidiaries, and any other person[243]. Where the accounts fail to give such information, the auditors are required, so far as they are reasonably able, to state the particulars in the auditors' report[244].

(c) Transactions, arrangements and agreements with directors and connected persons

[13.101] Sections 41–45 of CA 1990 also require disclosure of substantial contracts and other transactions or arrangements with directors, shadow directors, and connected persons in the notes to the accounts[245]. Transactions and arrangements of the kind to which CA 1990, s 31 relates must be disclosed[246], as must agreements to enter into such transactions[247] and any other transactions or arrangements with the company or its subsidiary in which the director had a material interest[248]. The particulars to be disclosed are[249]:

— A statement that the transaction, arrangement or agreement was made or subsisted during the financial year;

---

240 'Emoluments' includes fees and percentages, any sums paid by way of allowance insofar as those sums are charged to income tax, any contribution paid in respect of pension schemes, and the estimated money value of any other benefits received otherwise than in cash which are charged to income tax: CA 1963, s 191(2).

241 'Pension' includes superannuation allowance and superannuation gratuity or similar payment: CA 1963, s 191(3).

242 'Pension scheme' means a scheme for the provision of pensions in respect of services as director or otherwise which is maintained by means of contributions, and 'contributions' means any payment, including insurance premia, paid for the purposes of the scheme: CA 1963, s 192(3).

243 CA 1963, s 192(5).

244 See para **[13.107]**.

245 As to shadow directors see Chapter 8, *Corporate Governance: Management by the Directors* para **[8.058]***ff*.

246 CA 1990, s 41(1)(a).

247 CA 1990, s 41(1)(b).

248 CA 1990, s 41(1)(c). A director is deemed to be interested in transactions between himself or connected persons and the company or its subsidiary; but an interest is not material if a majority of the other directors is of the opinion that it is not material – provided they have considered the matter: sub-s 5.

249 See CA 1990, ss 42 and 43.

- The name of the person or director with whom it was made, and, if a connected person, the director with whom they are connected;
- The name of any director having a material interest, and the nature of that interest;
- The amount of the liability, in respect of principal and interest at the beginning and end of the financial year, of the person to whom any loan, agreement for a loan, or s 31 type arrangement was made;
- The maximum amount of that liability during the financial year;
- The amount of any interest due but not paid;
- The amount of any provision made in respect of failure or anticipated failure to pay the loan or any part thereof;
- The amount, at the beginning and at the end of the financial year, for which the company or subsidiary is liable under any guarantee or in respect of any security;
- The maximum amount for which the company or its subsidiary may become liable;
- The amount paid and any liability incurred by the company or its subsidiary for fulfilling the guarantee or discharging the security;
- The value of such transactions, arrangements, or agreements;
- The aggregate value of arrangements to which CA 1990, s 32 relates;
- The terms of any amendment in accordance with CA 1990, s 33;
- The aggregate amounts outstanding at the end of the financial year and the number of officers involved in loans, quasi-loans or credit transactions; guarantees and securities relating to loans, quasi loans, or credit transactions; arrangements under CA 1990, s 31 relating to loans, quasi-loans and credit transactions; and agreements to enter any of the foregoing.

[13.102] Certain transactions, arrangements and agreements are exempted from the above requirements to be disclosed by way of notes. Where the aggregate of the values of each arrangement made for a director or connected person less the amount by which the liability of the person for whom the arrangement was made has been reduced does not at any time during the financial year exceed €3,175, particulars in respect of those arrangements need not be disclosed[250]. Furthermore, if the transaction, arrangement or agreement is one in which the person concerned has a material interest, particulars need not be disclosed if the amount involved in each transaction did not during the financial year exceed €1,270 in aggregate, or, if more, did not exceed €6,350 or 1% of the net assets of the company for the financial year, whichever is less[251].

[13.103] Where any of these requirements is not complied with, the auditors must, as far as they are reasonably able, include a statement giving the required particulars in the auditors' report[252].

---

250 CA 1990, ss 43(2) and 45(1).

251 CA 1990, s 45(2).

252 CA 1990, s 46.

The directors' report

[13.104] CA 1963, s 158, as amended by C(A)A 1986, ss 13 and 14, requires a report by the directors on the state of the company's, and its subsidiaries', affairs to be attached to the balance sheet laid before the AGM. In addition, the report must state:

— The amount, if any, which the directors recommend should be paid by way of dividend[253];

— The amount, if any, which they propose to carry to reserves;

— Details of any change in the nature of the business of the company and its subsidiaries during the financial year so far as is material for the appreciation of the state of its affairs;

— A list the company's subsidiaries and any other bodies corporate in which the company has a beneficial shareholding of more than 20% of the shares carrying voting rights[254];

— A fair review of the development of the business of the company and its subsidiaries during the financial year;

— Particulars of any important events since the end of the financial year which affect the company or its subsidiaries;

— An indication of likely future development, if any, in the business of the company and its subsidiaries;

— An indication of the research and development activities, if any, of the company or its subsidiaries;

— An indication of the existence of branches of the company located outside the State and the country in which each branch is located[255];

— The number and nominal value of any of the company's own shares acquired by way of forfeiture or surrender, lien, or charge, or in accordance with the Companies (Amendment) Act 1983 ('C(A)A 1983' – '1983 Act')[256];

— The maximum number and nominal value of shares so acquired held during the financial year;

— The number and nominal value of shares so acquired which are disposed of or cancelled during the financial year;

— The percentage of called-up share capital which any shares so acquired, disposed of, or cancelled represent;

— The reasons for the acquisition, lien, or charge[257];

---

[253] On dividends see Chapter 15, *Shares and Membership*, para **[15.069]***ff*.

[254] CA 1963, ss 158(3) and 158(4). The list must distinguish between subsidiaries and other bodies corporate, and must give the name, place of incorporation, and nature of business of all bodies contained in the list.

[255] Inserted by reg 25 of the European Communities (Accounts) Regulations 1993, (SI 1993/396). The regulation professes to amend 'C(A)A 1986, s 13, and raises an interesting question as to the validity of a delegated legislative provision which fails to identify correctly the legislative provision it professes to amend.

[256] See the C(A)A 1983, ss 44 and generally Chapter 18 *The Maintenance of Capital*, para **[18.093]** *ff*.

[257] Inserted by CA 1990, s 233.

— The amount of any such charge; and

— The value of the consideration received in each case where any of the shares so acquired are acquired or disposed of for consideration;

— An evaluation of the extent to which the policy set out in a safety statement was fulfilled during the period in time covered by the report[258];

— Particulars of whether a director or secretary was interested in shares or debentures of the company, its subsidiaries, its holding company, or subsidiaries of its holding company at the end of the financial year, and, if so, the body or bodies and the number and amount of shares or debentures of each body held, distinguishing numbers and amounts held at the beginning of the financial year from those at the end[259];

— Particulars of all donations for political purposes exceeding €5,079 in value made by the company in the year to which the report relates, including particulars sufficient to identify the value of each such donation and the person to whom the donation was made[260].

The directors' report must be signed on behalf of the directors by two of the directors of the company[261].

[13.105] Failure to comply with these requirements renders the directors liable to conviction for an offence punishable on summary conviction by imprisonment for a term not exceeding six months or by a fine not to exceed €1,905 or to both. It will, however, be a defence in any such proceedings for a director to prove that he had reasonable ground to believe, and that he did believe, that a competent and reliable person was charged with the duty of seeing that the requirements were complied with and was in a position to discharge that duty[262]. Furthermore, a sentence of imprisonment may only be imposed if the court is of the opinion that the offence was committed wilfully[263].

The auditors' report

[13.106] It should be noted that since 21 February 2000, small companies satisfying specified criteria can opt out of the requirements to have an auditor and to produce audited accounts[264]. In such circumstances it is obviously not necessary that an auditors' report be produced or read to the company in general meeting. It will be necessary, however, for the directors to append certain statements to the balance sheet[265].

[13.107] Where such exemptions have not been availed of, however, an auditors' report must be produced. CA 1990, s 193(1) provides:

---

258 Safety, Health and Welfare at Work Act 1989, s 12(6).

259 CA 1990, s 63. If this information is not stated in the directors' report, it must be given in the notes to the accounts.

260 Electoral Act 1997, s 26.

261 CA 1963, s 158(2).

262 CA 1963, s 158(7)(a).

263 CA 1963, s 158(7)(b).

264 See para **[13.185]**.

265 See para **[13.096]**.

'The auditors of a company shall make a report to the members on the accounts examined by them, and on every balance sheet and profit and loss account, and all group accounts, laid before the company in general meeting during their tenure of office.'

The report must state[266]:

— Whether they have obtained all the information and explanations which, to the best of their knowledge and belief, are necessary for the purposes of their audit;

— Whether, in their opinion, proper books of account have been kept by the company;

— Whether, in their opinion, proper returns adequate for their audit have been received from branches of the company not visited by them;

— Whether the company's balance sheet and (unless it is framed as a consolidated profit and loss account) profit and loss account are in agreement with the books of account and returns;

— Whether, in their opinion, the company's balance sheet and profit and loss account and (if it is a holding company submitting group accounts) the group accounts have been properly prepared in accordance with the provisions of the Companies Acts and give a true and fair view -

- in the case of the balance sheet, of the state of the company's affairs as at the end of its financial year;
- in the case of the profit and loss account (if it is not framed as a consolidated profit and loss account), of the company's profit and loss for its financial year; and
- in the case of group accounts submitted by a holding company, of the state of affairs and profit or loss of the company and its subsidiaries dealt with thereby, so far as concerns members of the company;

— Whether, in their opinion, there existed at the balance sheet date a financial situation which under C(A)A 1983, s 40(1), would require the convening of an extraordinary general meeting ('EGM');

— Particulars relating to transactions, arrangements and agreements involving directors insofar as those matters have not been disclosed in the notes to the accounts[267];

— Whether, in their opinion, the information given in the directors' report relating to the financial year is consistent with the accounts prepared by the company for that year[268].

[13.108] The auditors' report must be read (though not necessarily by the auditors) at the AGM of the company, and must be open to inspection by any member[269].

266 CA 1990, s 193(4).

267 See para **[13.100]**.

268 C(A)A 1986, s 15.

269 CA 1990, s 193(2).

[C] Group Accounts

Introduction[270]

[13.109] Until 1 September 1992, holding companies[271] were required to prepare group accounts in addition to their own annual accounts, unless the company was the wholly-owned subsidiary of another Irish company[272]. Private holding companies were exempt from the requirement provided that they made copies of all the subsidiaries' annual accounts available to every member on request. The group accounts could take the form of a consolidated balance sheet, profit and loss account, and notes, detailing the consolidated amounts of each item for the group as a whole, but the directors were permitted to adopt a different form for the accounts where they were of the opinion that it would show a better picture of the group's affairs[273].

[13.110] That regime still operates in respect of unlimited companies, provided all the members of which are not limited companies or equivalent bodies governed by the laws of another State.

[13.111] As regards all other companies, the legislative regime governing group accounts has since been altered by the European Communities (Companies: Group Accounts) Regulations 1992[274] (the '1992 Regulations'), which implement the EU Seventh Company Law Directive[275]. To some extent, the regulations reflect accounting practice going back a number of years[276]. Most significantly, the obligation to prepare group accounts has shifted from companies which *own* other companies to 'undertakings' which *control* other undertakings. Thus, in addition to preparing their own annual accounts, parent undertakings[277] within the meaning of the regulations are required to prepare group accounts in accordance with those regulations and to lay them before the AGM at the same time as their own annual accounts are so laid.

[13.112] The directors of the parent undertaking no longer have a choice as to the form which the group accounts will take. The group accounts *must* comprise of a consolidated balance sheet, dealing with the state of affairs of the whole group; a consolidated profit and loss account, dealing with the profit or loss of the group as a whole; and notes to the accounts giving additional information. The consolidated accounts must combine in full the individual information contained in the separate accounts of each of the undertakings in the group, subject to adjustments which are required or permitted by the regulations.

---

270 See generally Rue, *Guide to The 1992 Group Accounts Regulations* (1992).

271 See Chapter 17, *Groups of Companies*, para **[17.006]***ff*.

272 CA 1963, s 150.

273 CA 1963, s 151.

274 SI 1992/201.

275 83/349/EEC, 13 June 1983. See Chapter 1, *The Private Company in Context*, para **[1.099]**; and generally Woolridge, 'The EEC Council Seventh Directive on Consolidated Accounts' (1988) 37 ICLQ 714.

276 Notably, accounting for subsidiary undertakings is dealt with by FRS 2 July 1992, which imposes similar, if not more stringent, requirements to the 1992 Regulations.

277 See Chapter 17, *Groups of Companies*, para **[17.028]**.

[13.113] The general formats for the preparation of consolidated group accounts follow those contained in the C(A)A 1986 in respect of individual accounts, but with necessary modifications to take into account the aims of group accounting. Likewise, the note requirements in respect of individual companies apply, and are expanded upon. Furthermore, in determining the amounts to be included in the group accounts, the accounting principles and valuation methods contained in C(A)A 1986 are to be applied, and must be applied consistently from one year to the next. If the assets and liabilities of an undertaking have been valued on a different basis to those adopted by the group accounts, they must be revalued according to the group's basis. There is limited scope for departure from some of these requirements.

[13.114] The 1992 Regulations contain special provisions governing the circumstances in which acquisition accounting principles and merger accounting principles are to be employed when arriving at consolidated figures[278]. They further permit the use of proportional consolidation as a method of accounting for joint ventures where the parent undertaking or one of its subsidiary undertakings manages the joint venture undertaking with another undertaking not represented in the group accounts (provided the joint venture is not a body corporate or a subsidiary of the parent undertaking).

[13.115] Where an undertaking in the group is involved with an associated undertaking, the 1992 Regulations require the equity method of accounting to be followed when accounting for those interests so that profits, losses, assets and liabilities arising out of such involvement are reflected in the group's accounts.

[13.116] The following matters shall now be considered:

1. Undertaking, parent undertaking and subsidiary undertaking;
2. The obligation to prepare group accounts;
3. Form, format and contents of group accounts;
4. Acquisition and merger accounting;
5. Joint ventures;
6. Associated undertakings.

Undertaking, parent undertaking and subsidiary undertaking

[13.117] The meaning of 'undertaking,' 'parent undertaking' and 'subsidiary undertaking'[279] is considered in full detail in Chapter 17, below[280].

The obligation to prepare group accounts

[13.118] The obligation to prepare consolidated group accounts under the 1992 Regulations applies, subject to certain exemptions, only to a parent undertaking which is:

— A company limited by shares[281];

— A company limited by guarantee[282];

---

[278] See para **[13.148]**.

[279] See generally Rue, *Guide to The 1992 Group Accounts Regulations* (1992), pp 3–8, and Warnock, 'Inter–Company Relationships and Section 31 of the Companies Act 1990' (1994) CLP 243.

[280] See Chapter 17, *Groups of Companies*, para **[17.028]**.

[281] SI 1992/201, reg 5(3).

[282] SI 1992/201, reg 5(3).

— An unlimited company or partnership, where all the members which do not have a limit on their liability are either —
  - companies limited by shares or guarantee;
  - equivalent bodies not governed by the law of the State;
  - any combination of (a) or (b);
  - themselves unlimited companies or partnerships of this kind, governed by the law of the State;
  - themselves equivalent bodies of this kind, governed by the laws of an EU Member State[283].

Group accounts must be drawn up as at the same date as the annual accounts of the parent undertaking[284]. Section 153 of the 1963 Act provides that the directors of *a* holding company[285] must secure that the financial year of each of its subsidiaries coincides with its own, unless there are good reasons against it. The Minister may extend the financial year of a holding company[286]. The 1992 Regulations provide that where the financial years of a parent undertaking and its subsidiaries do not coincide, interim accounts must be drawn up by the subsidiary if the end of its financial year precedes the end of the parent's financial year by more than three months[287]. Where the financial years of parent and subsidiary do not coincide, the reasons therefor and the dates must be disclosed in the parent's accounts and in any group accounts[288]. A parent undertaking to which the regulations apply is required by Regulation 5(1) to lay the group accounts before the AGM at the same time as which its own annual accounts are so laid.

[13.0119] Certain parent undertakings are exempt from the requirement to prepare group accounts. Three types of exemptions arise:

(a) Exemptions related to size of group;

(b) Exemptions for parent undertakings that are fully or 90% owned subsidiary undertakings of EU undertakings;

(c) Exemptions for other parent undertakings that are subsidiary undertakings of EU undertakings.

(a) Exemptions related to size of group

[13.120] This exemption is not unlike the exemptions which relate to 'small' and 'medium-sized' private companies in relation to their own annual accounts. Only private companies may avail of this exemption. Regulation 7 of the 1992 Regulations provides that a private company which is a parent undertaking will be exempt from the requirement to prepare group accounts in any financial year if at the date of its balance sheet for that financial year and the immediately preceding financial year, the group as a whole satisfies *two* of the following three conditions:

283 European Communities (Accounts) Regulations, 1993, (SI 1993/396), reg 6 and 9.
284 SI 1992/201, reg 26.
285 Note that not all parent undertakings are holding companies: See Chapter 17, *Groups of Companies*, para **[17.028]***ff*
286 CA 1963, s 153(2), as amended by CLEA 2001, s 61.
287 SI 1992/201, reg 26.
288 C(A)A 1986, Schedule, para 55.

— The balance sheet total of the group as a whole does not exceed €7,618,428;
— The amount of turnover of the group as a whole does not exceed €15,234,857;
— The average number of employees for the group as a whole does not exceed 250[289].

Where the financial period to which the accounts relate is not in fact a year, the size exemption for turnover must be proportionally adjusted[290]. It would appear that the balance sheet total may be computed without reference to set offs and other adjustments to be made in the preparation of group accounts where such accounts have not been previously prepared[291]. This means that private companies need not go through the process of preparing consolidated group accounts just to see whether they meet the size exemption.

In the first financial year of becoming a parent undertaking, the exemptions may be calculated by reference to the figures for that year only; subsequently the undertaking must meet the requirements in both its present and immediately preceding financial year[292]. If it fails to meet the requirements in any subsequent financial year, it may avail of the exemption for that year – but may not rely on the exemption again until it has met the criteria in any immediately preceding financial year[293].

[13.121] The size exemption does not apply where[294]:

— Any shares, debentures or other debt securities of the parent undertaking or one of its subsidiary undertakings have been admitted to official listing on a stock exchange established in the EU; or
— The parent undertaking or any of its subsidiary undertakings is an undertaking to which the 90% subsidiary of EU undertakings exemption applies.

(b) Exemptions for parent undertakings that are fully or 90% owned subsidiary undertakings of EU undertakings

[13.122] The obligation to prepare consolidated group accounts does not apply to parent undertakings which are themselves wholly or more than 90% owned subsidiary undertakings of undertakings established according to the laws of a Member State of the EU[295]. The exemption is not available to any parent undertaking whose shares, debentures or debt securities have been listed on an official stock exchange in the EU[296]. In the case of a non-wholly-owned undertaking coming within this category, the remaining shareholders must approve of the exemption[297]. Shares held by directors in the exempted parent undertaking by virtue of operation of law or a provision in the memorandum or articles must be disregarded in the calculation[298].

289 On calculation of the average number of employees, see para **[13.042]**.
290 SI 1992/201, reg 7(4).
291 Rue, *Guide to The 1992 Group Accounts Regulations* (1992), pp 14–15.
292 SI 1992/201, reg 7, paras (5), (6) and (10).
293 SI 1992/201, reg 7(7).
294 SI 1992/201, reg 7(8).
295 SI 1992/201, reg 8(1).
296 SI 1992/201, reg 8(4).
297 SI 1992/201, reg 8(1)(b).

[13.123] Furthermore, the following conditions must be met[299]:

— The exempted parent and all of its subsidiary undertakings must be dealt with in group accounts prepared by a parent undertaking which is established under the law of a Member State, and of which the exempted parent is a subsidiary undertaking;

— The EU undertaking's group accounts and directors' report must be prepared and audited according to the law of the Member State in which that undertaking is established and in accordance with the Seventh EU Directive on Company Law;

The following must be annexed to the annual return of the exempted parent after the EU undertaking's group accounts have been prepared:

— The EU undertaking's group accounts;

— The EU undertaking's directors' report; and

— The report of the person responsible for auditing the EU undertaking's accounts;

The notes on the annual accounts of the exempted parent must disclose;

— The name and registered office of the EU undertaking that draws up the group accounts; and

— The exemption from the obligation to draw up group accounts and a directors' report;

If the EU undertaking's group accounts, directors' report or auditors' report are in a language other than the English language or the Irish language, there shall be annexed to each such document a translation in the English language or the Irish language certified in the prescribed manner to be a correct translation.

(c) Exemptions for other parent undertakings that are subsidiary undertakings of EU undertakings

[13.124] Under reg 9 of the 1992 Regulations, a parent undertaking which does not qualify for exemption under the previous exemption (eg because it is not wholly or more than 90% owned by an EU undertaking) but which is nevertheless a subsidiary of an EU undertaking may avail of the exemption if the shareholders or members holding not less than 10% or more in aggregate of the nominal value of the total share capital of the undertaking have not requested the preparation of group accounts within the six months preceding the end of the financial year. The further conditions set out in paragraph **[13.123]** above must be met, and the exemption will not apply if any of the undertaking's shares are listed on an official stock exchange in the EU.

Form, format and contents of group accounts

[13.125] The directors of a parent undertaking to which the 1992 Regulations apply no longer have a choice as to the form which the group accounts shall adopt. Regulation 5(4) requires the accounts to be in the form prescribed by the regulations, and supersedes corresponding provisions of the Companies Acts 1963–2001.

[298] SI 1992/201, reg 8(2).

[299] SI 1992/201, reg 8(3).

(a) Form of group accounts

[13.126] Regulation 13 of the 1992 Regulations provides that the group accounts are to comprise of:

— A consolidated balance sheet dealing with the state of affairs of the parent undertaking and its subsidiaries as a whole;

— A consolidated profit and loss account dealing with the profit and loss of the parent undertaking and its subsidiaries as a whole;

— Notes to the accounts giving additional information required by the regulations.

The group balance sheet and profit and loss account must combine in full the information contained in the separate balance sheets and profit and loss accounts of the parent and subsidiary undertakings with adjustments required or permitted under the regulations[300].

The group accounts must present a 'true and fair view' of the state of affairs and profit and loss of the group as a whole for the financial year to which they relate[301]. In this regard, compliance with FRS requirements would seem tantamount to providing a 'true and fair view'.[302]. If the accounts drawn up in accordance with the regulations would not provide a 'true and fair view', necessary additional information must be given in the accounts[303]. Departure from preparation of the accounts in accordance with the regulations is permitted, indeed required, only in exceptional circumstances when the accounts so prepared would not give a 'true and fair view'[304]. Any such departure must be disclosed by way of a note to the group accounts, explaining the reason therefor and the effect on the group accounts[305].

(b) Format of group accounts

[13.127] Regulation 15(1) of the 1992 Regulations provides that the general format rules which apply to the preparation of individual annual accounts[306] also apply to group accounts with any necessary modifications; in particular[307]:

— Any subsidiary undertakings of the parent undertaking not dealt with in the group accounts are to be treated as a subsidiary undertaking of the group;

— If the parent undertaking is itself a subsidiary undertaking, the group is to be treated as a subsidiary undertaking of any parent undertaking of the parent undertaking, and the references to fellow subsidiary undertakings are to be construed accordingly; and

300 SI 1992/201, reg 16.

301 SI 1992/201, reg 14(1).

302 *Lloyd Cheyham Ltd v Littlejohn & Co* [1987] BCLC 303; *Dovey v Cory* [1901] AC 493; *Dolan v AB Co Ltd* [1969] IR 247; *IRC v Duple Motor Bodies Ltd* [1961] 1 WLR 739. See para **[13.021]**. FRS 2, as amended, is the current reporting standard dealing with accounting for subsidiary undertakings.

303 SI 1992/201, reg 14(2).

304 SI 1992/201, reg 14(3).

305 SI 1992/201, reg 14(4).

306 See para **[13.045]** ff.

307 SI 1992/201, reg 15(2) and (3).

— Where, in the opinion of the directors, undue expenses would be incurred in showing separately different categories of stocks, namely raw materials and consumables; work in progress; finished goods and goods for resale; and payments on account, those items may be combined in the group balance sheet and shown as a single item under the heading 'stocks'.

A parent undertaking need not prepare an individual profit and loss account detailing its own income and expenditure separately where it produces consolidated accounts in accordance with the regulations and the notes to the individual balance sheet show the profit and loss for the financial year determined in accordance with the C(A)A 1986[308]. The notes to the consolidated accounts *and* the individual accounts must disclose the fact that this exemption has been availed of[309].

(c) Contents of group accounts

[13.128] The contents of the group accounts bear many similarities to accounts prepared by individual companies, except that the figures shown will be consolidated for the group as a whole. In addition to the items required to be shown in the accounts by the scheduled formats to the C(A)A 1986, amounts for minority interests must be stated in the consolidated balance sheet and consolidated profit and loss account[310]. The amount shown must be the amount of capital and reserves attributable to shares in subsidiary undertakings dealt with in the group accounts held by or on behalf of persons other than the parent undertaking and its subsidiary undertakings[311].

The methods of consolidation of the group accounts are to be applied consistently from one financial year to the next, unless it appears to the directors that there are special reasons for departure, whereupon the fact of the departure, the reasons and its effect on the accounts must be disclosed in a note to the accounts[312].

[13.129] The group accounts must not take intra-group transactions into account – for to do so would give an untrue view of the group as a whole. Accordingly, reg 25 of the 1992 Regulations requires the accounts to show the assets, liabilities, state of affairs as at the end of the financial year and profit or loss of the parent undertaking and its subsidiary undertakings dealt with in the accounts as if they were a single undertaking. In particular:

— debts and claims between the undertakings dealt with in the group accounts must be eliminated from the accounts;

— income and expenditure relating to transactions between the undertakings dealt with in the group accounts must be eliminated from the accounts;

— where profits and losses resulting from transactions between the undertakings dealt with in the group accounts are included in the book values of assets, they must be eliminated from the accounts;

but these requirements need not be complied with where the amounts involved are not material for the purpose of giving a 'true and fair view.'

---

308 C(A)A 1986, s 3(2).

309 C(A)A 1986, s 3(3).

310 SI 1992/201, Sch, Part 1, paras 8 and 9.

311 SI 1992/201, Sch, Part 1, para 8(2).

312 SI 1992/201, reg 24.

[13.130] Regulations 10 and 11 of the 1992 Regulations permit the exclusion of a subsidiary undertaking from consolidation where:

— Its inclusion is not material for the purpose of the group accounts showing a 'true and fair view'; or

— Severe long-term restrictions substantially hinder the parent undertaking in the exercise of its right over the assets or management of that subsidiary undertaking; or

— The information necessary for the preparation of group accounts in accordance with the regulations cannot be obtained without disproportionate expense or undue delay; or

— The shares of the subsidiary undertaking are held by the parent undertaking exclusively with a view to their subsequent resale.

In addition, reg 12(1) requires the exclusion of subsidiary undertakings from consolidation when their activities are so different from those of other undertakings to be dealt with in the group accounts that their inclusion would be incompatible with the obligation to give a 'true and fair view'.

As regards materiality, the exclusion of two or more undertakings from consolidation is prohibited if, when taken together, they are material for the purposes of giving a 'true and fair view'[313]. Severe long-term restriction is not defined, but an explanation is to be found in FRS 2[314]. Disproportionate expense and delay appears to refer to situations where the value of the information is disproportionate to the expectations of the members[315]. 'View to subsequent resale' is not defined, but a definition may be found in FRS 2[316]. As regards differing activities, reg 12(2) states that activities are not different for the purposes of the exemption merely because some are industrial, others commercial, and some provide services while others deal with products or provide different services. Where a subsidiary is excluded from consolidation on the basis of different activities, that fact and the reasons therefor must be disclosed in a note to the accounts[317].

[13.131] Where the composition of undertakings dealt with in the group accounts has changed significantly in the course of the financial year, the group accounts must include information which makes the comparison of successive sets of group accounts meaningful[318].

[13.132] The valuation methods contained in the C(A)A 1986, Schedule must be applied in computing the amounts to be stated in the group accounts, and must be applied consistently within those accounts[319]. A parent must employ the same valuation rules in the preparation of the group accounts as it employs in the preparation of its own accounts,

[313] SI 1992/201, reg 24.

[314] See paras 25(a) and 78(c) of FRS 2.

[315] This was certainly the test under CA 1963, s 150(2)(b). It is not clear whether the new regulations require the interests of persons other than the members to be taken into account.

[316] See para 11 of FRS 2.

[317] SI 1992/201, reg 12(3).

[318] SI 1992/201, reg 27.

[319] SI 1992/201, reg 28.

unless departure is necessary to give a 'true and fair view'[320]. If the assets and undertaking of a member of the group have been valued according to a different method than that being used by the group accounts, they must be revalued, unless such revaluation is immaterial[321]. All departures must be stated in a note to the accounts[322]. Account must be taken in the consolidated accounts of any difference on consolidation between the tax chargeable for the financial year and for preceding financial years and the amount of tax payable in respect of those years, provided it is probable that the actual charge to tax will arise within the foreseeable future for one of the undertakings dealt with in the group[323].

(d) The notes to the group accounts

[13.133] In addition to the information required by the Companies Acts 1963–2001 to be stated by way of note to the accounts[324], the 1992 Regulations specifically require the notes to the group accounts to state certain information. These requirements relate to:

(i) Acquisitions;
(ii) Foreign currencies;
(iii) Details of indebtedness;
(iv) Particulars of staff;
(v) Directors' emoluments;
(vi) Transactions involving directors and others;
(vii) Miscellaneous matters.

(i) Acquisitions

[13.134] The requirements for notes relating to acquisitions are discussed at para **[13.149]** below[325].

(ii) Foreign currencies

[13.135] The conversion basis on which sums have been translated into the currency in which the group accounts are drawn up is to be stated[326].

(iii) Details of indebtedness

[13.136] The regulations require a statement in respect of the aggregate of the amounts shown in the balance sheet[327] under the heading 'creditors' which is the same as that required of individual companies by the 1986 Act[328].

(iv) Particulars of staff

[13.137] The regulations require the same information to be given in respect of persons employed by the undertakings[329] dealt with in the group accounts as is required of

---

320 SI 1992/201, reg 29.
321 SI 1992/201, reg 30.
322 SI 1992/201, reg 30.
323 SI 1992/201, reg 31.
324 See para **[13.098]** ff.
325 SI 1992/201, Schedule, para 12.
326 SI 1992/201, Schedule, para 13.
327 SI 1992/201, Schedule, para 14.
328 See para **[13.073]**.
329 SI 1992/201, Schedule, para 15.

individual companies by the C(A)A 1986[330], except that the aggregate amount of staff costs (save insofar as this amount is stated in the group profit and loss account) can be given in the group account notes instead of wages and salaries paid; social welfare costs; and other pension costs. The regulations also require that the average number of persons employed during the financial year by an undertaking proportionally consolidated be stated in the group accounts.

(v) Directors' emoluments

[13.138] The provisions of the C(A)A 1986 in respect of directors' emoluments[331] in individual companies apply equally to group companies[332]. In the case of group accounts, the disclosures relating to the pension commitments, and the emoluments and compensation in respect of loss of office to directors or past directors are to encompass such commitments, emoluments and compensation relating to directors or past directors of the parent undertaking in respect of duties relating to the parent undertaking, to any of its subsidiary undertakings, to any undertakings proportionally consolidated, or to associated undertakings. Most significantly, CA 1963, s 191, which also deals with directors' emoluments[333], does not apply to group accounts.

(vi) Transactions involving directors and others

[13.139] The 1992 Regulations extend the provisions of CA 1990, ss 41–43 to group accounts[334]. Transactions, arrangements and agreements[335] entered into by a director of the parent undertaking with an undertaking proportionally consolidated[336] or an associated undertaking[337] must also be stated. Note especially, however, that ss 41–43 of the 1990 Act speak of holding companies and their subsidiaries rather than parent undertakings and their subsidiary undertakings.

(vii) Miscellaneous matters

[13.140] The following information is to be given in relation to undertaking dealt with in the group accounts (including the parent undertaking where appropriate)[338] -

(1) The name and registered office of the undertaking;

(2) The aggregate of the qualifying capital interests[339] held in that undertaking by the undertakings dealt with in the group accounts as a proportion of the total of such interests;

(3) Which of the provisions of reg 4[340] gave rise to the undertaking being dealt with in the group accounts.

330 See para **[13.056]**.
331 SI 1992/201, Sch, para 16.
332 See para **[13.056]**.
333 See para **[13.100]**.
334 See para **[13.101]**.
335 SI 1992/201, Schedule, para 17.
336 See para **[13.150]**.
337 See para **[13.151]**.
338 SI 1992/201, Schedule, para 18.
339 See para **[13.117]**.
340 See para **[13.112]**.

The information required by (3) above may be omitted where the undertaking has been dealt with in the group accounts by virtue of the parent undertaking holding or controlling alone a majority of the voting rights, or controlling the composition of the board of directors provided the proportion of capital and the proportion of voting rights held are the same.

[13.141] The information referred to in (1) and (2) above is also to be given in respect of:

— Each undertaking which is excluded from the group accounts by virtue of the exemptions[341];

— Each associated undertaking[342];

— Each undertaking that has been proportionally consolidated[343];

— Each undertaking of substantial interest.

An undertaking of substantial interest for the purposes of the note disclosure requirements is defined in para 22(1) of the Schedule to the regulations[344] as an undertaking, *other than* a subsidiary undertaking, associated undertaking or joint venture, in which:

— undertakings dealt with in the group accounts and undertakings not so dealt with because their activities are so different[345]; or

— persons acting in their own name but on behalf of such undertakings,

between them hold a qualifying capital interest[346] representing 20% or more of such interests.

[13.142] The nature of the joint management of each joint venture proportionally consolidated must be stated. In addition, the amount of capital, reserves, and profit or loss for each undertaking of substantial interest must be stated, unless it is of negligible importance, or the undertaking is not required to attach a balance sheet to its annual return[347] and the qualifying capital interest is less than 50%.

Acquisition and merger accounting

[13.143] The 1992 Regulations set out the accounting principles which must be employed where a subsidiary undertaking is acquired: namely the acquisition method and the merger method. Where an undertaking becomes a subsidiary undertaking, that event is referred to in the regulations as its 'acquisition.'[348] An acquisition is to be accounted for by the acquisition method unless the conditions for accounting for it as a merger are met and the merger method of accounting is adopted. Where the acquisition is of a group, as opposed to an individual undertaking, the following regulations apply *mutatis mutandis*[349].

341 See para **[13.119]**.

342 See para **[13.151]**.

343 See para **[13.150]**.

344 SI 1992/201.

345 See para **[13.130]**.

346 See para **[13.117]**.

347 See para **[13.154]** ff. In this jurisdiction, the only companies which are not required to annex a balance sheet to their annual return are private unlimited companies which are not wholly owned by limited companies or by equivalent bodies not governed by the law of the State.

348 SI 1992/201, reg 17.

349 SI 1992/201, reg 23.

FRS 6, first adopted in September 1994 and twice since amended, sets out the circumstances in which the two methods of accounting are to be used. The objective of FRS 6 is to ensure that merger accounting is used only for those business combinations that are not, in substance, the acquisition of one entity by another but the formation of a new reporting entity as a substantially equal partnership where no party is dominant. To this end the FRS sets out five criteria that must be met for merger accounting to be used. If those five criteria are *not* met then acquisition accounting should be used. The FRS also sets out the disclosures to be made under acquisition and merger accounting. At the time of writing the Accounting Standards Board is working on a current project that may in time supersede FRS 6.

(a) Acquisition accounting

[13.144] Regulation 19 of the 1992 Regulations defines the acquisition method as follows:

— The identifiable assets and liabilities of the undertaking acquired shall be included in the consolidated balance sheet at their fair values as at the date of acquisition. In this paragraph the "identifiable assets or liabilities" means the assets or liabilities which are capable of being disposed of or discharged separately, without disposing of a business of the undertaking.

— The income and expenditure of the undertaking acquired shall be brought into the group accounts only as from the date of acquisition.

— There shall be set off against the acquisition cost of the interest in the shares of the undertaking held by the undertakings dealt with in the group accounts, the interest of the undertakings dealt with in the group accounts in the adjusted capital and reserves of the undertaking acquired.

The qualification cost means the amount of any cash consideration and the fair value of any other consideration, together with such amounts (if any) in respect of fees and other expenses of the acquisition as the parent undertaking may determine; and the adjusted capital and reserves of the undertaking acquired means its capital and reserves at the date of the acquisition after adjusting the identifiable assets and liabilities of the undertaking to fair values as at that date. If the resulting amount is positive it must be treated as goodwill and treated in the manner in which goodwill is treated under the C(A)A 1986[350], but if it is negative it must be treated as a negative consolidation difference.

Where a parent undertaking acquired a subsidiary undertaking before the introduction of the 1992 Regulations, but has not previously included that subsidiary in the group accounts, and there is no record of the fair values as at the date of acquisition[351] of the identifiable assets or of the acquisition cost of the interest in shares of the acquired undertaking held by the undertakings dealt with in the group accounts, the earliest available record of those costs may be used[352]. Similar steps may be taken where such records cannot be obtained without unreasonable expense or delay.

FRS 7, adopted in September 1994 and since amended on three occasions, sets out how the fair values of identifiable assets and liabilities should be determined and what 'identifiable

350 See para **[13.028]**.
351 See paras 6 and 45 of FRS 2.
352 SI 1992/201, reg 20.

assets and liabilities' means. The difference between the sum of these fair values and the cost of acquisition is recognised as goodwill or negative goodwill. The standard also gives guidance on the period available to investigate and identify the fair values of assets and liabilities of an acquired entity and how to account for any subsequent adjustments.

(b) Merger accounting

[13.145] Merger accounting is a system of accounting which has been popular in the United States for some time[353]. Essentially, it is used where shares in a target undertaking are acquired in exchange for shares in the acquiring undertaking. The two balance sheets of the undertakings are then simply added together, the nominal value of the two types of shares exchanged cancelling each other out as far as possible. Any difference is adjusted in reserves. Consequently, no share premium account is created, and the pre-acquisition profits of the subsidiary undertaking are accounted for as distributable reserves.

[13.146] The merger method of accounting is defined by reg 22 of the 1992 Regulations as follows:

— The assets and liabilities of the undertaking acquired are to be brought into the group accounts at the figures at which they stand in the undertaking's accounts, subject to any adjustment authorised or required by the regulations.

— The income and expenditure of the undertaking acquired is to be included in the group accounts for the entire financial year, including the period before the acquisition.

— The group accounts are to show corresponding amounts relating to the previous financial year as if the undertaking had been included in the consolidation throughout that year.

— The nominal value of the issued share capital of the undertaking acquired held by the undertakings dealt with in the group accounts is to be set-off against the aggregate of:

(a) the appropriate amount in respect of shares issued by the undertakings dealt with in the group accounts as part of the merger arrangement in consideration for the acquisition of shares in the undertaking acquired; and

(b) the fair value of any other consideration for the acquisition of shares in the undertaking acquired, determined as at the date when those shares were acquired.

— The resulting amount is to be shown as an adjustment to the consolidated reserves.

[13.147] Regulation 21 of the 1992 Regulations sets out the conditions for accounting for an acquisition as a merger as follows:

— At least 90% of the nominal value of the relevant shares in the undertaking acquired is held by or on behalf of the undertakings dealt with in the group accounts;

— The 90% was attained pursuant to the arrangement providing for the issue of equity shares by the undertakings dealt with in the group accounts; and

353 See Schmitthoff (ed), *Palmer's Company Law*, para 74.04; and Filfis, 'Accounting for Mergers, Acquisitions and Investments in a Nutshell: The Interrelationships of, and Criteria for, Purchase or Pooling, the Equity Method, and Parent–Company Only and Consolidated Statements' (1981) 37 Business Lawyer 89.

— The fair value of any consideration other than the issue of equity shares given pursuant to the arrangement by the undertakings dealt with in the group accounts did not exceed 10% of the nominal value of the equity shares issued.

'Relevant shares' are those carrying unrestricted rights to participate both in distributions and in the assets of the undertaking upon liquidation.

[13.0148] No provision has been made for merger relief, which raises the question as to whether the merger method of accounting breaches the rules of capital maintenance[354]. In *Henry Head v Ropner Holdings Ltd*[355] it was held in England that a share for share exchange where the nominal value of the bidder's shares was less than the market value of the target's shares, the difference had to be transferred to a share premium account by virtue of the English equivalent of CA 1963, s 62(1). The amounts provided for in the share premium account may only be applied in accordance with the provisions of that section, and do not constitute profits available for distribution. Thus, in the later English case of *Shearer (Inspector of Taxes) v Bercain Ltd*[356], where the merger method of accounting was used so that differences were transferred to distributable reserves, it was held that an unauthorised reduction of capital had occurred. This effectively prohibited the merger method of accounting in the UK, and legislative steps were taken to introduce merger relief[357]. The effect of this relief was to supplant the requirement that the subsidiary's pre-acquisition profits be transferred to a share premium account which can only be applied in special circumstances. Instead, the relief permits pre-acquisition profits to be distributed to the parent company which can then distribute them to the shareholders. Although no such relief has been introduced in this jurisdiction, CA 1963, s 149(5), for which there was no English counterpart at the time of the *Henry Head* and *Shearer* decisions, provides that where the directors and auditors are satisfied and certify that it would be fair and reasonable and would not prejudice the rights of any person, the pre-acquisition profits or losses attributable to any shares in a subsidiary may be treated in the holding company's accounts as revenue profits or losses. Arguably, it would seem reasonable for the directors and auditors to so certify where the 1992 Regulations permit merger accounting[358] – provided, of course, that the parent undertaking is a holding company within the meaning of the CA 1963[359], and that the rights and interests of any person would not be prejudiced.

(c) Disclosures in notes relating to acquisitions and mergers

[13.149] Paragraph 12 of the Schedule, Part I to the 1992 Regulations requires the following disclosures concerning acquisitions of subsidiary undertakings to be made in the notes to the group accounts:

— As regards positive and negative goodwill, the methods used in calculating those amounts and the reasons for any significant difference between such amounts for

354 See Chapter 18, *The Maintenance of Capital.*

355 *Henry Head v Ropner Holdings Ltd* [1952] Chapter 124.

356 *Shearer (Inspector of Taxes) v Bercain Ltd* [1980] 3 All ER 295.

357 CA 1985 (UK), ss 131–135.

358 See Rue, *Guide to The 1992 Group Accounts Regulations* (1992), p 39.

359 See Chapter 17, *Groups of Companies*, para **[17.006]** ff.

the financial year to which the group accounts refer and those for the preceding financial year; and

— As regards acquisitions taking place in the financial year:

(a) the name and registered office of the undertaking acquired during the financial year, or where a group was acquired, the name and registered office of the parent undertaking of that group; and

(b) whether the acquisition has been accounted for by the acquisition or the merger method of accounting.

It should be observed that the note disclosure requirements in the relevant FRSs are more onerous, and that failure to observe these could amount to a breach of the 'true and fair view' requirement.

Joint ventures

[13.150] Where a parent undertaking or one of its subsidiary undertakings dealt with in the group accounts manages another undertaking (ie the joint venture) jointly with one or more undertakings not dealt with in the group accounts, the joint venture may, if it is not a body corporate or a subsidiary undertaking of the parent undertaking, be proportionally consolidated in the group accounts in proportion to the rights in its capital held by the parent undertaking or the subsidiary undertakings dealt with in the group accounts as the case may be[360]. Note that proportional consolidation in such circumstances is permitted, but is not mandatory. Where a joint venture is proportionally consolidated, information concerning the qualifying capital interests held in the joint venture by the undertakings dealt with in the group accounts as a proportion of the total of such interests[361]. Where a joint venture is not proportionally consolidated, the same information may be required if it is an associated undertaking or an undertaking of substantial interest[362].

Associated undertakings

[13.151] Since the coming into operation of the 1992 Regulations, group accounts following the scheduled formats[363] contained in the C(A)A 1986 must disclose interests and profits or losses arising from participating interests[364] and associated undertakings. The participating interest replaces the old concept of the 'related company' used by the 1986 Act[365].

An associated undertaking is an undertaking in which an undertaking dealt with in the group accounts has a participating interest and over whose operating and financial policy it exercises a significant influence[366]. The associated undertaking must not be a subsidiary of the parent undertaking, or a joint venture which has been proportionally consolidated[367].

---

360 SI 1992/201, reg 32.

361 SI 1992/201, Schedule, para 20–22.

362 As to undertakings of substantial interest for these purposes see para **[13.141]**.

363 See para **[13.045]** ff.

364 See para **[13.117]**.

365 See generally Warnock, 'Inter–Company Relationships and Section 31 of the Companies Act 1990' (1994) CLP 243.

366 SI 1992/201, reg 34.

367 SI 1992/201, reg 34(1).

Where an undertaking holds 20% or more of the voting rights in another undertaking it is presumed to exercise a significant influence unless the contrary is shown[368].

[13.152] Regulation 33 of the 1992 Regulations requires interests in associated undertakings to be shown in the group accounts and to be accounted for by way of the equity method of accounting, unless the amounts in question are immaterial for the purpose of providing a 'true and fair view,' and any goodwill must be dealt with in accordance with the provisions of the 1986 Act[369]. If the associated undertaking is itself a parent undertaking, the net assets and profits or losses to be taken into account are those of the associated-parent undertaking and its subsidiaries after the making of any consolidation adjustments[370].

What constitutes the equity method of accounting is not spelt out in the regulations; however, FRS 9 contains detailed provisions concerning the mechanics of equity accounting[371].

[13.153] Information in respect of each associated undertaking concerning the aggregate of the qualifying capital interests[372] held in that undertaking by undertakings dealt with in the group accounts as a proportion of the total of such interests is required to be stated in the notes to the group accounts[373].

[D] THE ANNUAL RETURN

Introduction

[13.154] Section 125 of CA 1963, as amended by the Company Law Enforcement Act, s 59 ('CLEA 2001'), requires every company to make, once at least in every year, a return (termed the 'annual return') in the prescribed form[374] to the Registrar of Companies. The purpose of the annual return is to provide information in relation to the affairs of the company which may be of relevance to the public, such as the address of the registered office, the location of the register of members, the total indebtedness of the company, etc. Certain other documents are required to be filed along with the annual return, notably, specified particulars of the annual accounts and reports annexed thereto[375].

Prior to 31 December 1986 private companies were exempt from the requirement of filing details of their accounts along with the annual return, but that exemption was lifted in respect of private companies having limited liability by the C(A)A 1986. The rigours of the requirement to file details of accounts are mitigated somewhat, however, in the case of 'small' and 'medium-sized' private companies.

---

368 SI 1992/201, reg 34(2). Voting rights are determined in the manner described in para **[13.115]**.

369 SI 1992/201, reg 33(1). As to the treatment of goodwill see para **[13.028]**.

370 SI 1992/201, reg 3(2).

371 See also FRS 2, para 56.

372 See para **[13.117]**.

373 SI 1992/201, Sch, para 20.

374 The Companies (Form and Content of Documents Delivered to the Registrar) Regulations 2002 (SI 2002/39) prescribe Form B1 as the required form. The form can be downloaded from the Companies Registration Office website http://www.cro.ie.

375 C(A)A 1986, ss 7–12.

Foreign limited companies and equivalent bodies corporate which are incorporated outside the State and which have established a branch within the State are required to file an annual return in accordance with Part IV of the European Communities (Branch Disclosures) Regulations 1993[376]. The regulations require the accounting documents of the company or body corporate, which are drawn up, audited, and, where so required, disclosed in accordance with the law of the State in which it is incorporated, to be delivered under cover of the prescribed form to the Registrar of Companies once in every year. If the company or body corporate is incorporated in an EU Member State, the accounting documents must be drawn up and audited in accordance with the Fourth, Seventh and Eighth EU Directives on Company Law[377]. If there is no requirement to prepare accounts in the state of incorporation, the documents must be drawn up and audited in accordance with the Fourth and Seventh Directives, and non-EU companies or bodies corporate may alternatively choose to draw up and audit the accounts on this basis instead of according to the law of the place of incorporation. If the documents are not in Irish or English, a certified translation must accompany them.

Foreign unlimited companies and equivalent bodies corporate incorporated outside the State but having an established place of business[378] within the State are obliged by CA 1963, s 354 to prepare and publish accounts as if they were companies formed and incorporated under the Companies Acts 1963-2001, unless they have provisions in their constitutions which would entitle them to rank as a private company had they been registered in the State. Accordingly, foreign unlimited *private* companies having an established place of business within the State are not required to submit an annual return to the Registrar of Companies.

Time for filing of the annual return

[13.155] Section 125 of CA 1963[379] requires the annual return to be made at least once a year. It need no longer be completed within 60 days after the AGM[380] - instead, it must now be filed within 28 days of the company's *annual return date* ('ARD'). Section 127 of CA 1963 provides[381]:

> '(1) The annual return of a company shall be made up to a date which is not later than its annual return date.
>
> (2) Subject to subsection (3), the annual return shall be delivered to the registrar of companies-

[376] SI 1993/395.

[377] SI 1993/395. As to the Fourth, Seventh and Eighth EU Company Law Directives (78/660/EEC, 83/349/EEC, and 84/253/EEC, respectively) see Chapter 1, *The Private Company in Context*, para **[1.091]***ff*.

[378] See Chapter 2, *Formation, Registration and Conversion of Private Companies* , para **[2.046]***ff*.

[379] As replaced by CLEA 2001, s 59. See Rice and Walker 'The New Annual Return Date ('ARD') Provisions under the Companies Acts' (2002) CLP 75.

[380] The old CA 1963, s 127 so required – but since it required details of the state of affairs on the fourteenth day after the AGM it could not be made for at least two weeks after the AGM.

[381] As replaced by CLEA 2001, s 60.

(a) in the case of the first annual return following the commencement date of a company incorporated before the commencement date - not later than 28 days after the annual return date or 3 months after the commencement date, whichever is the later, and

(b) in any other case - not later than 28 days after the annual return date, unless it is made up to an earlier date in which case it shall be delivered to the registrar not later than 28 days after that earlier date.'

For companies incorporated after 1 March 2002, the ARD falls six months after the date of incorporation[382]. For companies incorporated prior to that date, the ARD is the anniversary of the date on which the latest annual return prior to that date (if any) was filed, or (in the case of companies which had yet to file a first annual return by that date) six months after the anniversary of the incorporation of the company[383]. ARDs in subsequent years will fall on the anniversary of the ARD unless the ARD has been altered by the company.

The ARD can be brought forward by simply making an annual return up to a date which is more than 14 days earlier than the existing ARD[384]. Extending the ARD to a later date is only slightly more complicated – the company must notify the registrar of the new ARD which may be no later than six months after the original[385]. However, only one further extension of time will be allowed within the following five years[386]. In any case where the ARD is being extended it is important to remember that the accounts accompanying the return can predate the ARD by no more than nine months[387].

The ARD of a holding company or its subsidiary can also be extended with ministerial permission to allow the ARDs of each to correspond[388].

Consequences of failure to file annual return on time

[13.156] Late filing of the annual return will attract a penalty fee[389], and persistent late filing may attract an additional on-the-spot fine[390]. Furthermore, all failure by the company to comply with the filing requirements renders the company, every officer of the company who is in default, and any person in accordance with whose directions or instructions the directors of the company are accustomed to act and to whose directions or omissions the default is attributable, guilty of an offence[391]. Proceedings in relation to offences under the section may be commenced and prosecuted by the Registrar of Companies[392]. Since the enactment of the CLEA 2001, however, it appears that the registrar will precede most such prosecutions by issuing a notice under CLEA 2001, s 66 inviting the defaulter to remedy

382 CA 1963, s 127(6).
383 CA 1963, s 127(5).
384 CA 1963, s 127(8).
385 CA 1963, s 127(9).
386 CA 1963, s 127(10).
387 Rice and Walker, 'The New Annual Return Date ('ARD') Provisions under the Companies Acts' (2002) CLP 75 at 77.
388 CA 1963, s 153(2) as amended by CLEA 2001, s 61.
389 CLEA 2001, s 63(3).
390 CLEA 2001, s 66.
391 CA 1963, s 125(2).
392 CA 1963, s 125(3).

the default and to pay a prescribed fee within a specified period. No prosecution may be commenced during the currency of the notice; nor thereafter if the default is remedied in the interim[393].

Since 28 February 2002[394], all documents filed with the registrar which fail to comply with the requirements of CA 1990, ss 248 and 249, as amended, or with any other requirements prescribed by law, may be rejected for filing. The registrar may serve a notice on the person filing indicating the defect, and if not remedied within 14 days the original will be deemed not to have been delivered[395].

[13.157] A harsher penalty of last resort is provided in C(A)A 1982, s 12, as amended[396]. Where a company fails for one or more years to make an annual return, the registrar may take steps to have the company's name struck off the register of companies and to have the company dissolved. These procedures are discussed in further detail in Chapter 12, *Company Law Compliance and Enforcement*[397]. The liability of every director, officer and member of the company will survive such dissolution, as will the court's power to wind up the company while struck off .[398]

Contents and form of the annual return

[13.158] Section 125 of CA 1963 requires the annual return to specify the matters listed in Part I of the Fifth Schedule to the 1963 Act and to be in the form set out in Part II of that Schedule.

(a) Contents

[13.159] Part I of CA 1963, Fifth Schedule, lists the following details which must be contained in the annual return:

— The address of the registered office of the company;

— The address of the place where the register of members is kept, if it is not kept at the registered office;

— The address of the place where the register of debenture holders is kept, if it is not kept at the registered office.

— A summary, distinguishing between shares issued for cash and shares issued as fully or partly paid up otherwise than in cash, specifying the following particulars[399]:

  - The amount of the share capital of the company and the number of shares into which it is divided;
  - The number of shares taken from the incorporation of the company up to the date of the return;

[393] CLEA 2001, s 66(2)(c).

[394] Companies Act 1990 (Commencement) Order 2002 (SI 2002/57).

[395] CA 1990, ss 248 and 249A as amended. See also the Companies Act 1990 (Form and Content of Documents Delivered to Registrar) Regulations 2002 (SI 2002/39).

[396] By C(A)(No 2)A 1999, s 46.

[397] See Chapter 12, *Company Law Compliance and Enforcement,* para **[12.132]***ff*.

[398] See Chapter 12, *Company Law Compliance and Enforcement,* para **[12.144]***ff*.

[399] See generally Chapter 15, *Shares and Membership*.

- The amount called up on each share;
- The total amount of calls received;
- The total amount of calls unpaid;
- The total amount of the sums, if any, paid by way of commission in respect of any shares or debentures;
- The discount allowed on the issue of any shares issued at a discount or so much of that discount as has not been written off at the date on which the return is made;
- The total amount of the sums, if any, allowed by way of discount in respect of any debentures since the date of the last return;
- The total number of shares forfeited.

— Particulars of the total amount of the indebtedness of the company in respect of all mortgages and charges which are required to be registered with the Registrar of Companies under the Companies Acts 1963-2001[400].

— A list of members:

- containing the names and addresses[401] of all persons who, on the 14th day after the company's AGM for the year, are members of the company, and of persons who have ceased to be members since the date of the last return or, in the case of the first return, since the incorporation of the company;
- stating the number of shares held by each of the existing members at the date of the return, specifying shares transferred since the date of the last return (or, in the case of the first return, since the incorporation of the company) by persons who are still members and have ceased to be members respectively and the dates of registration of the transfers.

— Those particulars relating to the persons who are directors and the secretary at the date of the return which are required to be entered in the company's register of directors and secretary[402].

— Particulars of all donations for political purposes exceeding IR£4,000 (€5,079) in value made by the company in the year to which the report relates, including particulars sufficient to identify the value of each such donation and the person to whom the donation was made[403].

[13.160] If the names contained the list of members are not arranged in alphabetical order, it must be accompanied by an index sufficient to enable the name of any person named therein to be easily found. If each annual return for the immediately preceding five years has contained a full list of members, then, by virtue of CA 1963, s 125(1)(d), the list of members contained in its *next* annual return need only give particulars relating to persons who have ceased to be members since the last return; persons who have become new members since the last return; and the transfer of shares since the last return. It should be noted, however, that if the company does file such an abridged list in its next annual

[400] On the registration of charges see generally Chapter 21, *Corporate Borrowing: Registration of Charges*.

[401] The requirement to also state the occupations of these persons was removed by C(A)A 1982, s 22.

[402] On the registers of directors and secretary see Chapter 8, *Corporate Governance: Management by the Directors*, para **[8.087]**.

[403] Electoral Act 1997, s 26.

return, a full list of particulars relating to every member will be required again in the subsequent return[404]. By virtue of CA 1990, s 248(2)(a), the annual return must also state in a prominent position the registered number of the company to which it relates.

(b) Form

[13.161] Part II of CA 1963, Fifth Schedule, sets out the form of the annual return. Under s 395 of the 1963 Act, as amended[405], the Minister is empowered to alter or add to the form set out in Part II of the Fifth Schedule, and various versions of the form – Form B1 – have been prescribed by the minister, most recently in 2002[406]. Moreover, the annual return and all documents filed must comply with specific requirements as to size, print and paper colour, paper weight and quality, binding and stapling, and manner of information insertion[407]. The annual return is required to be signed by a director and by the company secretary[408].

[13.162] Section 249 of CA 1990 provides for the making of regulations permitting the delivery of documents, including the annual return, to the Registrar of Companies otherwise than in legible form, eg on computer disk. No such regulations, however, have been made to date.

Documents to be annexed to the annual return

[13.163] Section 7 of C(A)A 1986 sets out the documents which are required to be annexed to the annual return of a limited company as being:

- — a copy of the balance sheet;
- — a copy of the profit and loss account;
- — a copy of the directors' report;
- — a copy of the auditor's report.

Each of these documents must be certified by both a director and the company secretary to be a true copy of the document laid before the AGM for the period to which the return relates[409]. If the document is not in English or Irish it must be accompanied by a certified translation in either of those two languages[410]. If any of the documents does not contain the particulars required by law at the date of the relevant audit, it must be amended by the company to bring it into line with the legal requirements and must contain a statement that it has been amended for those purposes[411].

If a company fails to comply with the requirements of C(A)A 1986, s 7, it, and any officer in default, will be liable to a fine not exceeding €1,905[412]. Proceedings in this regard may

404 Because it will not have filed full particulars in the five *immediately preceding* years.

405 By C(A)A 1983, Sch 1, para 23.

406 Companies (Forms) Order, 2002 (SI 2002/38).

407 Companies (Form and Content of Documents Delivered to the Registrar) Regulations 2002 (SI 2002/39).

408 CA 1963, s 127.

409 C(A)A 1986, s 7(1)(a).

410 C(A)A 1986, s 7(1)(b).

411 C(A)A 1986, s 7(2).

412 C(A)A 1986, s 22(1).

be brought by the Registrar of Companies[413]. Furthermore, where any person wilfully and knowingly makes a false statement in any of the documents, he will be liable on conviction on indictment to imprisonment for a term not exceeding five years[414] or a fine not exceeding €3,174 or both[415], or on summary conviction, to imprisonment for a term not exceeding six months[416] or a fine not exceeding €1,905 or both[417].

[13.164] Where the company annexing accounts to its annual return is a member of an undertaking having unlimited liability, C(A)A 1986, s 16A[418] requires the name, head office or registered office, and the legal form of each such undertaking to be stated in a note to the accounts, unless such information is of negligible importance for the purposes of giving a 'true and fair view'.

[13.165] The requirements of C(A)A 1986, s 7 are modified by ss 10, 11 and 17 of that Act in respect of 'medium-sized' private companies, 'small' private companies, and private companies which are subsidiary undertakings of parent undertakings established under the laws of EU Member States, respectively. Unlimited private companies, apart from those coming within the scope of the European Communities (Accounts) Regulations 1993[419] (the '1993 Regulations), are *not* required to annex any documents to their annual returns[420]. The 1993 Regulations require unlimited companies, all the members of which having unlimited liability being:

— limited companies or equivalent bodies governed by the law of another State; or

— themselves unlimited companies or partnerships or equivalent bodies governed by the laws of an EU Member State, all the members of which having unlimited liability are limited companies or bodies equivalent to limited companies governed by the law of another state,

to make an annual return in accordance C(A)A 1986, s 7, and, if they are private companies, permit such unlimited companies to avail of the exemptions for 'medium-sized' and 'small' private companies[421]. It should also be noted that partnerships, all the members of which having limited liability being the kind of bodies described above, are now also required to file a balance sheet and profit and loss account drawn up in accordance with reg 12 of the 1993 Regulations, and copies of the auditor's and partners' reports, with the Registrar of Companies within six months from the end of their financial year[422].

---

413 C(A)A 1986, s 22(1).

414 CA 1990, s 240, as amended.

415 C(A)A 1986, s 22(3).

416 C(A)A 1986, s 22(3).

417 CA 1990, s 240, as amended.

418 Inserted by the European Communities (Accounts) Regulations 1993 (SI 1993/396), reg 23.

419 SI 1993/396.

420 See CA 1963, s 128 and SI 1993/396, reg 6.

421 SI 1993/396, reg 7.

422 SI 1993/396, reg 20.

(a) Exemptions for medium-sized companies

[13.166] 'Medium-sized' private companies are permitted by C(A)A 1986, s 11(2) to annex an abridged balance sheet to the annual return. The abridged balance sheet for the purposes of a 'medium-sized' company's annual return differs from the abridged balance sheet which a 'small' private company may lay before its AGM. 'Medium-sized' private companies may also annex to the annual return a short-form profit and loss account of the kind which such companies are permitted to lay before the AGM[423], *even where* they have not availed of the exemption as respects the AGM[424]. It should be recalled that since 'small' private companies are by definition also 'medium-sized', they too can avail of these exemptions. Where a company relies on these exemptions, a special auditors' report must be annexed to the return.

In addition to the above exemptions, C(A)A 1986, s 12(2) exempts 'medium-sized' companies from the requirement to disclose particulars of turnover by way of note to the accounts annexed to the annual return, abridged or otherwise.

(b) The abridged balance sheet of a medium-sized company

[13.167] The abridged balance sheet for the purposes of the annual return may show the items preceded by letters and Roman numerals in Formats 1 and 2 of the Balance Sheet Formats set out in the C(A)A 1986, Schedule. Additionally, however, the abridged balance sheet must show separately the *total* amounts falling due within one year and after one year in respect of:

— Trade debtors;
— Amounts owed by group undertakings;
— Amounts owed by undertakings in which a participating interest is held;
— Other debtors;
— Called up share capital not paid;
— Prepayments and accrued income;

and the *individual* amounts falling due within one year and after one year in respect of:

— Amounts owed by group undertakings;
— Amounts owed by undertakings in which a participating interest is held,

and where Format 2 of the Balance Sheet Formats has been adopted, the *individual* amounts due within one year and after one year in respect of:

— Debenture loans;
— Bank loans and overdrafts;
— Amounts owed to group undertakings;
— Amounts owed to undertakings in which a participating interest is held.

[13.168] Certain other amounts must also be disclosed separately, either in the abridged balance sheet itself, or in the notes to the accounts of the company, namely[425]:

423 See para **[13.060]**.
424 C(A)A 1986, s 11(3).
425 C(A)A 1986, ss 11(2)(a) and (b).

- Goodwill;
- Land and buildings;
- Plant and machinery;
- Fixtures, fittings, tools and equipment;
- Payments on account and assets in course of construction;
- Shares in group undertakings representing financial assets;
- Loans to group undertakings representing financial assets;
- Shares in undertakings in which a participating interest is held representing financial assets;
- Loans to undertakings in which a participating interest is held representing financial assets;
- Own shares representing financial assets;
- Amounts owed by group companies;
- Amounts owed by undertakings in which a participating interest is held;
- Prepayments and accrued income;
- Shares in group companies representing investments;
- Own shares representing investments;
- Debenture loans falling due within one year;
- Bank loans and overdrafts falling due within one year;
- Amounts owed to group companies falling due within one year;
- Amounts owed to undertakings in which a participating interest is held falling due within one year;
- Other creditors including tax and social welfare falling due within one year;
- Accruals and deferred income falling due within one year;
- Debenture loans falling due after one year;
- Bank loans and overdrafts falling due after one year;
- Amounts owed to group companies falling due after one year;
- Amounts owed to undertakings in which a participating interest is held falling due after one year;
- Other creditors including tax and social welfare falling due after one year;
- Accruals and deferred income falling due after one year.

(c) The short form profit & loss account of a medium-sized company

[13.169] The short form profit and loss account which may be annexed to the annual return of a 'medium-sized' private company is the same as that which may be laid before the AGM, and has been considered above[426].

(d) Special auditors' report

[13.170] Where a 'medium-sized' company relies on the provisions permitting it to file an abridged balance sheet or short-form profit and loss account, C(A)A 1986, s 18(3)

[426] See para **[13.060]**.

provides that a copy of the auditors' report on the unabridged accounts of the company need not be filed. Instead, a special report from the auditors is required to be filed, containing[427]:

- a statement that in the opinion of the auditors of the company, the directors of the company are entitled to annex abridged accounts to the annual return and that the accounts so annexed are properly prepared[428]; and
- a copy of the report of the auditors under CA 1963, s 163.

CA 1963, s 163 was repealed by CA 1990, s 6, and although s 193 of the 1990 Act replaces that provision, only references to s 163 of the 1963 Act appearing in the 1963 Act are to be construed as references to s 193 of the 1990 Act[429]. The upshot is that, perhaps through legislative oversight, arguably, no copy of the auditors' report seems to be required to be contained in the special auditors' report for the purposes of the annual return. The special auditors' report must be certified by both a director and the secretary to be true copies of the reports.

(e) Exemptions for small companies

[13.171] C(A)A 1986, s 10(2) permits 'small' companies to annex to the annual return a copy of the abridged balance sheet which it is allowed to lay before the AGM[430], and not to annex copies of:

- the profit and loss account; and/or
- the directors' report.

Essentially, then, all a 'small' private company is required to annex to its annual return are the abridged balance sheet and the special auditors' report. It should be recalled that a small company may alternatively rely on the exemptions which operate in respect of 'medium-sized' companies.

In addition to these exemptions, very few of the note requirements contained in the C(A)A 1986, Schedule need be complied by a small company when it comes to the accounts annexed to the annual return, abridged or otherwise. Note requirements appearing elsewhere must, of course, still be complied with, except those which are only required to be made when the information to which they relate appears in the accounts, and that information does not so appear in the filed accounts because exemptions have been relied upon. C(A)A 1986, s 12(1) identifies the requirements of the Schedule to C(A)A 1986 regarding notes which are to be complied with as follows:

- Details of accounting policies[431]
- Particulars of share capital and debentures[432]

---

427 C(A)A 1986, s 18(3).

428 C(A)A 1986, s 18(4).

429 CA 1990, s 193(7). The specificity of s 193(7) may be sufficient to displace the proviso in s 20(1) of the Interpretation Act 1937 that references to repealed and re-enacted provisions in other statutes shall be to the re-enacted provision 'unless the contrary intention appears.'

430 See para **[13.095]**.

431 C(A)A 1986, Schedule, para 24.

432 C(A)A 1986, Schedule, para 26. See para **[13.071]**.

— Details of allotments[433]

— Details of provision for taxation[434]

— Details of indebtedness[435]

— Details of foreign exchange; changes in accounting policy; or errors in accounts[436]

(f) Special auditors' report

[13.172] 'Small' companies must file a special report of the auditors in the same way as 'medium-sized' companies[437]. Note, however, that certain small companies may opt to dispense with the requirement to appoint an auditor, and in such circumstances they will be exempt from the requirement to file a special auditors' report[438]. This exemption is considered further below[439].

(g) Exemptions for subsidiaries of parent undertakings established under the laws of EU Member States

[13.173] C(A)A 1986, s 17, as amended by the 1992 Regulations, exempts private companies which are subsidiary undertakings of parent undertakings established under the laws of EU Member States from the requirement to annex a balance sheet, profit and loss account, and directors' and auditors' reports, to their annual returns. All of the following conditions must be satisfied:

— Every person who is a shareholder of the company on the date of the holding of the next AGM of the company after the end of that financial year, must declare his consent to the exemption;

— There is in force in respect of the whole of that financial year an irrevocable guarantee by the parent undertaking of the liabilities and losses which have arisen or are likely to arise in respect of that financial year, and the company has notified in writing every shareholder referred to above of the guarantee;

— The annual accounts of the company for that financial year are consolidated in the group accounts prepared by the parent undertaking and the exemption of the company under this section is disclosed in a note to the group accounts;

— A notice stating that the company has availed of the exemption under this section in respect of that financial year and a copy of the guarantee and notification referred to above, together with a declaration by the company in writing that every shareholder referred to above has declared his consent to the exemption, is annexed to the annual return for the financial year made by the company under the 1963 Act to the Registrar of Companies;

---

433 C(A)A 1986, Schedule, para 27. See para **[13.080]**.

434 C(A)A 1986, Schedule, para 33. See para **[13.080]**.

435 C(A)A 1986, Schedule, para 34. See para **[13.088]**.

436 C(A)A 1986, Schedule, para 44. See para **[13.058]**.

437 See para **[13.070]**.

438 C(A)(No 2)A 1999, s 32(2).

439 See para **[13.185]**.

— The group accounts of the parent undertaking are drawn up in accordance with the requirements of the Seventh EU Company Law Directive; and

— The group accounts of the parent undertaking are annexed to the annual return and are audited in accordance with Article 37 of the Seventh EU Directive on Company Law.

It has been suggested[440] that the first of these requirements is odd, considering that the shareholders would, in any event, be entitled to copies of the accounts under C(A)A 1963, s 159[441] – accordingly they would not be prejudiced by the non-disclosure of the accounts in the annual return. On the other hand, the withholding of consent could prove useful to minority shareholders where, say, the reason non-disclosure is sought is that the directors are anxious not to publicise the size of their emoluments, etc.

Additional disclosure requirements for certain group undertakings

[13.174] Additional information is required by C(A)A 1986, s 16 (as amended by the 1992 Regulations) to be stated by way of note to the accounts annexed to the annual returns of certain group undertakings. The undertakings affected by this requirement are companies which at the end of their financial year[442]:

— have a subsidiary[443]; or

— hold a qualifying capital interest[444] equal to 20% or more of all such interests in an undertaking that is not the company's subsidiary undertaking (in this section referred to as 'an undertaking of substantial interest')[445].

The information required to be stated in the notes must distinguish between the subsidiaries and the undertakings of substantial interests, and must state:

— The name and registered office of each subsidiary or undertaking of substantial interest and the nature of the business carried on by it;

— The identity of each class of shares held by the company in each subsidiary or undertaking of substantial interest and the proportion of the nominal value of the allotted shares in the subsidiary or undertaking of substantial interest of each such class represented by the shares of that class held by the company;

— The aggregate amount of the capital and reserves of each subsidiary or undertaking of substantial interest as at the end of the financial year of the subsidiary or undertaking of substantial interest ending with or last before the end of the financial year of the company to which the accounts relate; and

— The profit or loss of the subsidiary or undertaking of substantial interest for the financial year thereof mentioned above.

---

440 Ussher, *Company Law in Ireland* (1986), p 362.

441 See para **[13.016]**.

442 C(A)A 1986, s 16(1).

443 On subsidiaries see Chapter 17, *Groups of Companies*, para **[17.008]** *ff*.

444 Interests held by persons acting in their own name but on behalf of the company are deemed to be held by the company: C(A)A 1986, s 16.

445 Contrast the undertakings of substantial interest which are required to be dealt with in the notes to group accounts; see para **[13.141]**.

The third and fourth items, ie capital and reserves, and profit and loss, of the subsidiary or undertaking of substantial interest, are not required to be stated either[446]:

— In respect of a subsidiary undertaking of a company, if the company prepares group accounts in accordance with the 1992 Regulations and either —
  – the subsidiary undertaking is dealt with in the group accounts prepared by the company, or by a parent undertaking established under the laws of an EU member state provided the company itself and all its subsidiary undertakings are dealt with in that undertaking's accounts; or
  – the qualifying capital interest of the company in the subsidiary undertaking is included in or in a note to the company's accounts by way of the equity method of valuation;

— In respect of an undertaking of substantial interest of a company if the qualifying capital interest in the undertaking of substantial interest is included in, or in a note to, the company's accounts by way of the equity method of valuation;

— If the subsidiary undertaking or the undertaking of substantial interest is not required to publish its accounts, and the qualifying capital interest held in the subsidiary undertaking or the undertaking of substantial interest does not amount to at least 50% of all such interests;

— If that information is not material.

[13.175] The directors of a company to which these additional disclosure requirements relate do not have to state in their directors' report details of any change in the nature of the business of the company and its subsidiaries during the financial year so far as is material for the appreciation of the state of its affairs, or list the company's subsidiaries and any other bodies corporate in which the company has a beneficial shareholding of more than 20% of the shares carrying voting rights[447].

[13.176] Any of this additional information may, in lieu of being stated in a note to the accounts, be given in a statement in writing signed by a director and the secretary of the company and annexed to the first annual return made by the company next after its accounts for that year are laid before the AGM of the company if, in the opinion of the directors, compliance with the section would required a note to the accounts of excessive length[448]. However, this mechanism may not be used where the directors of the subsidiary or undertaking of substantial interest are of the opinion that the financial state of their company or undertaking has a substantial effect on the profit or loss or the amount of assets of the parent company and its subsidiaries[449].

[E] Auditors

[13.177] The word auditor comes from the Latin *audire*, to hear, and the office is an ancient one[450]. Originally, auditors were persons before whom persons who had a duty to account (in the sense of answering for their conduct) were heard. Nowadays, most

---

446 C(A)A 1986, s 16(2).

447 C(A)A 1986, s 16(5). On the directors' report generally see para **[13.104]**.

448 C(A)A 1986, s 16(3)(a).

449 C(A)A 1986, s 16(3)(b).

companies are required to appoint an auditor whose principal function is to examine the books of account, annual accounts, any group accounts, and directors' report made or kept by the directors and officers of the company, and to make a report on his findings to the owners of the company, the members. Accordingly, it is principally[451] the members who have the power to appoint or remove the auditor, and to fix his remuneration, and it is to them that the auditor owes a primary duty.

[13.178] The regulation of auditors has been the subject of recent review following a Parliamentary inquiry into the evasion of deposit income retention tax which concluded that more could be done by auditors to prevent or uncover tax evasion. The July 2000 Report of the Review Group on Auditing[452] ('RGA') chaired by Senator Joe O'Toole recommended the establishment of an oversight board, similar to that employed in the United States, to exercise the disciplinary and supervisory functions with respect to auditors which are currently vested in the Minister[453]. Other recommendations of the RGA include the recommendation that the audit reports of all companies (including unlimited companies) should be filed annually with the Registrar of Companies[454], and that non-audit work done for the same client should be disclosed as part of the audit report[455]. The recommendations of the RGA, though aimed principally at public limited companies, financial institutions, and public interest companies, have been endorsed with appropriate modification for other companies by the Company Law Review Group[456].

[13.179] In April 2001 the Irish Auditing and Accounting Supervisory Authority ('IAASA') was established pending introduction of legislation to implement the recommendations of the RGA. By December of 2001 the draft heads of the Companies (Audit and Accountancy) (Amendment) Bill 2001 were agreed by the Government. It is clear that the importance of the auditor in company law is increasing, and that the role is becoming more onerous[457].

[13.180] The law relating to auditors is considered further below as follows:

1. The requirement to appoint an auditor.
2. Exemption from the requirement to have accounts audited.

---

450 See Robinson, 'Auditors under the Companies Act 1963', a paper delivered to the student members of the Dublin Society of Chartered Accountants, October 1965. A statutory reference to auditors is found in a Statute of Edward I in 1285 (13 Edward I) which introduced the Statute of Westminster 1285 (2 Edward I) to Ireland, requiring 'sergeants, bailiffs, chamberlains, and all manner of receivers who are bound to yield account' to appear before the auditor appointed by the 'lord of such servants.' The bodies of any such persons 'in arrear upon their account' were to be arrested, and 'by the testimony of the said auditors of the said account they be sent and delivered to the next gaol.'

451 The directors may make the appointment to fill a vacancy pending the members' meeting – see para **[13.183]**.

452 Pn 8638.

453 July 2000 Report of the Review Group on Auditing, recommendations 7.2, 8.1, 8.2, 9.1 & 9.2.

454 July 2000 Report of the Review Group on Auditing, recommendation 11.7.

455 July 2000 Report of the Review Group on Auditing, recommendation 12.2.

456 First Report, 2001, Chapter 14.

457 See O'Reilly, 'Auditor's Responsibilities: Changed Responsibilities' (2002) CLP 79.

3. Qualification for appointment as auditor.
4. Persons who may not act as auditor.
5. Removal and replacement of auditors.
6. Remuneration and expenses of auditors.
7. The rights and powers of auditors.
8. Status and duties of auditors.
9. Civil liability of auditors.

The requirement to appoint an auditor

[13.181] Under CA 1963, s 160(1), every company is required to appoint an auditor or auditors at its AGM, to hold office from the conclusion of that AGM until the conclusion of the next AGM. By reason of the Companies (Amendment) (No 2) Act ('C(A)(No 2)A 1999'), certain private companies are permitted to depart from the requirement to appoint an auditor and to have accounts audited[458].

[13.182] The appointment of the auditor or auditors is principally a matter for the shareholders in general meeting. The appointment of auditors need not be on the agenda of every AGM. Section 160(2) and (3) of CA 1963 go on to provide that a retiring auditor shall automatically be re-appointed without any resolution being passed, unless one of the following conditions is satisfied:

- He is not qualified for re-appointment;
- A resolution has been passed at that meeting appointing somebody instead of him;
- Notice of a resolution to appoint somebody else instead of him has been given, but the proposed resolution cannot be passed because of the death, insanity, or disqualification of the replacement;
- A resolution has been passed at that meeting providing expressly that he shall not be re-appointed;
- He has given notice in writing of his unwillingness to be re-appointed.

Where the AGM fails to appoint an auditor, the company must, within one week, give notice of that fact to the Minister[459]. The Minister may then appoint an auditor to the company[460]. This provision is designed to ensure that companies do not frustrate the requirement to have an auditor by simply failing to appoint any auditors. Failure to notify the Minister renders the company and every officer in default liable to a fine not exceeding €1,905.

[13.183] Not all appointments of auditors need be made at the AGM. The first auditors of the company may be appointed by the directors at any time before the first AGM, and if they fail to do so, the company in general meeting may make the appointment[461]. Similarly, casual vacancies in the office of auditor may be filled by the directors or by the

[458] See para **[13.185]**.

[459] CA 1963, s 160(5A), inserted by CA 1990, s 183.

[460] CA 1963, s 160(4).

[461] CA 1963, s 160(6).

company in general meeting[462], but where there is more than one auditor, while the vacancy continues, the surviving or continuing auditor or auditors may continue to act[463]. Furthermore, the company in general meeting may also appoint an auditor to replace an auditor removed from office at that meeting[464].

[13.184] There seems to be no limit to the number of auditors a company may appoint; and, indeed, it is common for a firm of auditors rather than an individual to be appointed. The appointment of a firm by its firm name is deemed to be an appointment of those persons who, from time to time during the currency of the appointment, are the partners in that firm as from time to time constituted and who are qualified to be auditors of that company.

Exemption from the requirement to have accounts audited

[13.185] Under C(A)(No 2)A 1999, Part III, the directors of a small[465] private company having less than 50 employees, whose turnover does not exceed €317,435 and whose balance sheet total does not exceed €1,904,607, may elect to dispense with the requirement to appoint an auditor or to produce audited accounts in the following financial year[466]. The directors must be of the opinion that the company will continue to fall below these thresholds for the following year, and their decision must be minuted[467].
The exemption cannot be availed of if the company has failed to comply with the requirements as to filing of an annual return[468], nor can it be availed of by banking or insurance companies or companies within a group[469].

[13.186] Given that the function of the auditor is to act as a watchdog in the members' interests, it appears at first strange that the directors, and not the members, should be given the power to opt out of the requirement to have an auditor. However, C(A)(No 2)A 1999, s 33 gives members holding 10% in aggregate of the voting rights in the company the right to veto the directors' power to opt for an exemption. The veto, which is exercised by serving a notice on the company, must be exercised no later than one month in advance of the financial year in which the exemption would otherwise be claimed[470].

[13.187] The balance sheet of the company for the exempted year must contain a statement by the directors that the exemptions have been availed of, that no valid veto was

---

462 Extended notice must be given of the resolution to fill the casual vacancy, and a copy of the resolution must be sent to any person whose loss of office occasioned the vacancy: CA 1963, s 161.

463 CA 1963, s 160(7), as amended by CA 1990, s 183.

464 See para **[13.199]**.

465 See para **[13.042]**.

466 C(A)(No 2)A 1999, s 32. The exemption can be claimed in the first financial year of a company incorporated after 21 February 2000: C(A)(No 2)A 1999, s 32(1)(b) and the Companies (Amendment) (No 2) Act 1999 (Commencement) Order, 1999 (SI 1999/406).

467 C(A)(No 2)A 1999, s 32(1).

468 C(A)(No 2)A 1999, s 32(3).

469 C(A)(No 2)A 1999, s 32(3).

470 C(A)(No 2)A 1999, s 33.

exercised, and that they acknowledge the requirements of the Companies Acts as to the keeping of proper books of account[471].

[13.188] If, when availing of the exemption, the office of a sitting auditor is terminated, the auditor must provide a statement to the effect either that there are no circumstances which should be brought to the attention of the members or creditors, or else a statement setting out such circumstances. If the latter, the statement must be circulated to the Registrar of Companies and all other persons entitled to be sent copies of the company's accounts[472].

[13.189] Whenever the exemption ceases to have effect the directors are required to appoint an auditor to fill the vacancy until the next AGM[473].

Qualification for appointment as auditor

[13.190] Section 187(1) of CA 1990, as amended[474], provides that only the following may qualify for appointment as auditor of a company:

— a member of a body of accountants for the time being recognised by the Minister for the purposes of the section who holds a valid practising certificate from such a body;

— the holder of an accountancy qualification that is, in the opinion of the Minister, of a standard which is not less than that required for membership of a recognised body of accountants and which would entitle him to be granted a practising certificate by that body if he were a member of it, and is for the time being authorised by the Minister to be appointed;

— a person who, on 31 December 1990, was a member of one of the bodies of accountants recognised under CA 1963, s 162 and who holds a valid practising certificate from such a body;

— a person who was authorised by the Minister to be appointed to act as auditor before 3 February 1983;

— a person who was undergoing professional or practical accountancy training on 1 January 1990 and who is admitted to membership of one of the recognised accountancy bodies before 1 January 1996 and subsequently awarded a valid practising certificate;

— a person who holds a specified accountancy qualification, or a qualification entitling him to audit accounts, under the law of a specified country outside the State, where the Minister has declared that such persons are qualified to be appointed.

[13.191] Notwithstanding the statutory prohibition on bodies corporate acting as auditor in CA 1990, s 187, the Eighth EU Directive on Company Law[475] and the Companies Act 1990 (Auditors) Regulations 1992 provide that a firm can qualify to be appointed as

471 C(A)(No 2)A 1999, s 32(4).

472 C(A)(No 2)A 1999, s 34. As to the persons entitled to be sent copies of the accounts see CA 1963, s 159 and para **[13.016]**.

473 C(A)(No 2)A 1999, s 35. The directors may appoint notwithstanding CA 1963, s 160 which requires auditors to be appointed by the general meeting: C(A)(No 2)A 1999, s 35(1).

474 By CLEA 2001, s 72.

475 See Chapter 1, *The Private Company in Context*, para **[1.100]**.

auditor provided at least one member of the firm holds a practising certificate from one of the recognised bodies of accountants[476].

[13.192] The Director of Corporate Enforcement can demand a person acting as auditor to provide evidence of his or her qualification. Failure to produce such evidence within 30 days of the demand (or such longer period as the director may allow) constitutes an offence[477], and the presumption of innocence is reversed so that the onus is placed on the accused to prove that the demand was complied with[478].

[13.193] Sections 191 and 192 of CA 1990 deal with the recognition by the Minister of bodies of accountants and the granting of authorisations. Under s 191, bodies of accountants seeking recognition must satisfy the Minister that the standards relating to training, qualifications and repute required by that body for the awarding to a person of a practising certificate were not less than those specified in Articles 3 to 6, 8 and 19 of the Eighth EU Directive on Company Law[479], and as to the standards it applies to its members in the areas of ethics, codes of conduct and practice, independence, professional integrity, technical standards and disciplinary procedures. The six bodies which are currently recognised in this manner are:

— The Institute of Chartered Accountants in Ireland (ICAI);

— The Institute of Certified Public Accountants in Ireland (ICPAI);

— The Association of Chartered Certified Accountants (ACCA);

— The Institute of Chartered Accountants in England and Wales (ICAEW);

— The Institute of Chartered Accountants of Scotland (ICAS);

— The Institute of Incorporated Public Accountants Ltd (IIPA)[480].

Under CA 1990, s 192, the Minister may attach conditions to the recognition or authorisation, and amend, insert or delete conditions by notice in writing to the body or individual concerned. Likewise, he may revoke or suspend a recognition or authorisation. Section 192(4) empowers the Minister to require recognised bodies to prepare and submit to him a code of professional conduct, and he may apply the provisions of any such code

---

476 Companies Act 1990 (Auditors) Regulations 1992 (SI 259/1992), reg 4.

477 CA 1990, s 187(12), as inserted by CLEA 2001, s 72.

478 CA 1990, s 187(12)(b).

479 84/253/EEC. See generally Chapter 1, *The Private Company in Context*, para **[1.100]**. The relevant articles require the members to be of good repute and not to carry on incompatible activities, to attain university entrance level, to complete theoretical instruction, to undergo three years' practical training, and to pass an examination of professional competence covering: auditing, analysis and assessment of accounts, general accounting, consolidated accounts, cost and management accounting, internal audit, standards relating to the preparation of annual and consolidated accounts, legal and professional standards of auditing, and company law, insolvency law, tax law, civil and commercial law, social security law, employment law, information and computer systems, business, general and financial economics, mathematics and statistics, and basic principles of financial management and undertakings.

480 Judicial review proceedings were initiated in 1996 in respect of the Minister's recognition of the IIPA. The proceedings were brought by the ICAI, the ICPAI, the ACCA, and the Chartered Institute of Management Accountants (CIMA), a non–recognised body. These proceedings were still pending at the time of writing.

to an individual authorised by him. The Minister is empowered to make regulations providing for the monitoring of compliance with the code.

[13.194] Before granting, renewing, withdrawing, revoking, or suspending recognition of a body of accountants, the Minister may consult with any person or body of persons as to the conditions imposed or standards required by the body concerned in connection with membership of that body or the awarding to persons of practising certificates[481]. He may also consult with any person or body of persons before forming any opinion or making any declaration in relation to the qualifications held by any person or class of persons as respects qualification for appointment as auditor[482]. In making and relying on such consultations, the Minister should employ fair procedures and accord with the principles of natural justice.

[13.195] Since the enactment of the CLEA 2001, the accountancy bodies are required to notify the Director of Corporate Enforcement if a disciplinary committee or tribunal of the body has reasonable grounds for believing that an indictable offence under the Companies Acts may have been committed by a member[483]. Failure to notify the director is itself an offence[484].

[13.196] Section 198 of CA 1990 requires the Registrar of Companies to keep a register of persons notified to him to be qualified for appointment as auditor. The register must contain the names, business addresses, and names and addresses of the head office of any firm of which the persons are partner or employee[485]. The recognised bodies are required to notify the registrar in respect of any of their members so qualified; but recognised bodies outside the State need only inform the registrar of members practising within the State[486]. Failure by a recognised body to notify the registrar of these details constitutes an offence. Persons to whom the Minister has granted an authorisation must themselves notify the registrar.

Persons who may not act as auditor

[13.197] Persons who qualify for appointment as auditor under CA 1990, s 187(1) may nevertheless be disqualified from acting as auditor in particular circumstances where so to act might compromise their independence. Section 187(2) provides that none of the following persons shall be qualified for appointment as auditor of a company:

- An officer or servant of the company[487];
- A person who was an officer or servant of the company during the period to which the accounts to be audited relate;

---

481 CA 1990, s 190.

482 CA 1990, s 190.

483 CA 1990, s 192(6) as inserted by CLEA 2001, s 73.

484 CA 1990, s 192(7).

485 CA 1990, s 192(7), as construed by the Companies Act 1990 (Auditors) Regulations 1992 (SI 1992/259).

486 CA 1990, s 200.

487 Officer or servant includes directors, the secretary, and, it would seem, shadow directors. See generally Chapter 10, *Duties of Directors and Other Officers*.

— A parent, spouse, brother, sister or child of an officer of the company;

— A person who is a partner of, or who is in the employment of, an officer of the company;

— A person who is disqualified, for any of the above reasons, from acting as auditor of any other body corporate which is a subsidiary, holding company, or subsidiary of the company's holding company, whether that body corporate is a company or otherwise;

— A person disqualified for any of the above reasons from acting as public auditor of an industrial and provident society[488] which is a subsidiary, holding company, or subsidiary of the company's holding company.

[13.198] Persons who are the subject of a disqualification order[489] are also prohibited from being appointed to act as auditor of any company. Where any such person becomes or remains a partner in a firm of auditors after 28 days from the making of the disqualification order, and he gives directions or instructions in relation to the conduct of any part of the audit of the accounts of a company, or works in any capacity in the conduct of the audit, he is guilty of an offence. His disqualification order may, upon conviction, be extended for a further ten years or such further period as the court, on the application of the prosecutor and having regard to all the circumstances of the case, may order[490].

A shareholder or other person beneficially entitled to shares in the company is not disqualified by CA 1990, s 187(2) from acting as auditor of the company[491]; neither are auditors who rely substantially on the company for their livelihood. Nevertheless, persons who act as auditors in such circumstances will fall foul of the codes of practice of their respective accountancy bodies.

Removal and replacement of auditors

[13.199] An auditor, other than the first auditor of the company, may be removed by ordinary resolution of the company in general meeting, and another auditor, nominated by any member of the company, may be appointed in his stead[492]. In addition, any auditor may be removed at the AGM by way of a resolution appointing somebody instead of him, or by way of a resolution providing expressly that he shall not be re-appointed[493]. In any of the above cases, extended notice[494] of the intended resolution must be given to the members[495]. When the company receives notice of the proposed removal, it must send a copy of the resolution to the auditor proposed to be removed[496].

---

488 Within the meaning of the Industrial and Provident Societies Acts 1893–1978.

489 See Chapter 12, *Company Law Compliance and Enforcement*, para **[12.090]***ff*.

490 CA 1990, s 195.

491 See Fitzgerald, 'A Consideration of the Companies Acts 1948 and 1967, The Companies Act (Northern Ireland) 1960, and the Companies Act 1963: VIII' (1969) Ir Jur 315 for a description of some of the difficulties which may arise from permitting auditors to be shareholders.

492 CA 1963, s 160(5), as amended by CA 1990, s 183. Ordinary notice of the nomination of the replacement must be given to the members: CA 1990, s 183.

493 CA 1963, s 160(2)(b).

494 Ie at least 28 days' notice: CA 1963, s 142. See Chapter 9, *Corporate Governance: Meetings*, para **[9.034]**.

The first auditor may also be removed by the company in general meeting, and another auditor, nominated by any member of the company, appointed in his stead[497]. Not less than 14 days' notice of the nomination for replacement must be given to the other members of the company[498].

[13.200] During the course of his audit, it is quite possible that an auditor might uncover compromising information concerning the directors' handling of the company's financial affairs. To prevent the directors from causing the removal of the auditor in order to suppress such information, CA 1963, s 161(3) enables the auditor to contest his proposed removal and to explain the circumstances of his proposed removal to the members. An auditor wishing to contest his proposed removal may send written representations, not exceeding a 'reasonable length', to the company, and may request the company to notify the members of his representations. Unless it is too late for it to do so, the company is then obliged to state the fact that such representations have been made to it in any notice of the resolution which it gives to the members, and must send a copy of the representations to every member to whom any notice of the meeting is or has been sent[499]. Of course, the directors might cause the company not to circulate such representations, but if copies of the representations have not been sent out to the members, whether because they have been received too late for circulation or because of the company's default, the auditor may, without prejudice to his right to be heard orally, require them to be read out at the meeting at which it is proposed that he be removed[500]. If reading the representations at the meeting would secure needless publicity for defamatory matter, the company or an aggrieved person may prevent the reading by applying to court[501].

Section 161(2A) of CA 1963 expressly entitles the auditor to attend the AGM at which, but for his removal, his term of office would have expired, and the general meeting at which it is proposed to fill the vacancy occasioned by his removal[502]. In addition, the auditor is entitled to receive all notices and other communications relating to any such meeting which a member of the company is entitled to receive, and to address any AGM on any business of the meeting which concerns him as former auditor of the company. The provisions of s 161(2A) do not, however, extend to auditors removed from companies claiming an exemption under the C(A)(No 2)A 1999[503].

Remuneration and expenses of auditors

[13.201] Under CA 1963, s 160(8), the remuneration and expenses of an auditor appointed by the Minister or by the directors is fixed by the person or persons who appointed him. Where the auditor is appointed by members, whether at the AGM or otherwise, the

495 CA 1963, s 161(a) and (b), as amended by CA 1990, s 184.

496 CA 1963, s 161(2)(b).

497 CA 1963, s 160(6)(a).

498 CA 1963, s 160(6).

499 CA 1963, s 161(5).

500 CA 1963, s 161(5).

501 CA 1963, s 161(5). The auditor may be made liable for the costs of the company in any such application: CA 1963, s 161(5).

502 See further, Chapter 9, *Corporate Governance: Meetings*, para **[9.030]** *ff*.

503 C(A)(No 2)A 1999, s 34(5).

remuneration and expenses must be fixed at the AGM or in such manner as the AGM shall determine. Thus, the AGM may, and in practice commonly does, empower the directors to fix the auditors' remuneration and expenses.

[13.202] An auditor may, in appropriate circumstances, exercise a lien over the books of the company in respect of his fee. Since, however, the central requirement of all valid liens is that possession of the subject matter of the lien is taken by the person exercising the lien *with the consent of the debtor*, the auditor may *not* exercise a lien over books and documents which are required by the articles of association to be kept in the possession of the company. In *Re JJ Hopkins & Co*[504], the auditors claimed a lien over a number of books and documents belonging to the company. These included the petty cash book, the debtors' ledger, the sales book, the cash book, the cheques journal, the creditors' ledger, some wages books, the nominal ledger, the share register, and the certificate of incorporation. The company's articles of association required the books of account to be kept at the company's registered office. On the application of the liquidator of the company for an order that the auditors were not entitled to exercise a lien, Dixon J, granting the order sought, said:

> '...a lien is a matter of contract and if by reason of a prohibition in the articles of association the directors of a company have no power to create a lien, there cannot be an implied contract. It has been said that the auditors are not bound by the articles of association, but even if that is correct, it seems to me to be irrelevant. The articles of association restrict the power of the company to enter into an implied contract which is necessary to create a lien. It was submitted that a valid lien had been created because the books had been left with the auditors for a valid purpose. The purpose for which the books had been left with the auditors was a temporary purpose and it seems clear that the books would have to be returned to the company as soon as the purpose for which they had been left with the auditors was completed. There is no distinction in principle between books of account which come into the hands of the auditors for legitimate purposes and books of account which come into the possession of a solicitor. I think that the position is the same for solicitors and auditors. In either case, if the books are in the hands of an agent for a legitimate purpose a lien may exist but it cannot arise when the books are of a type that are required by the articles of association of the company to be kept at the registered office of the company or are books like the register of members which are incapable of being the subject of a lien.'

Where an auditor successfully exercises a lien over the company's books or records, he may nevertheless be required to deliver up the books to any liquidator, provisional liquidator, or examiner of the company, but without prejudice to his rights under the lien[505].

Resignation of auditors

[13.203] CA 1990, s 185(1) permits an auditor to resign from office before the expiry of his term of appointment by serving notice in writing on the company. The resignation takes effect on the date on which the notice is served or such later date as may be specified

---

504 *Re JJ Hopkins & Co* (1959) 93 ILTR 32. See also *Re Darion Fashions Ltd* [1981] 2 NZLR 47.

505 CA 1963, s 244A, inserted by CA 1990, s 125, and CA 1990, s 180(2). Cf *Kelly v. Scales* [1994] 1 IR 42. See also CA 1963 s 236 and Order 74, rule 91 of the Rules of the Superior Courts which require the delivery up of all such documents to the liquidator.

in the notice. Prior to the enactment of this section, an auditor could only resign from office by notifying the company of his unwillingness to be re-appointed at the next AGM[506]. The resignation procedure, as it then stood, provided no mechanism whereby the auditor could explain the reasons for his resignation which, in his opinion, ought to be made known to the members or creditors of the company, or the public at large. Consequently, where an auditor resigned because he had discovered improper practices in the conduct of the company's financial affairs, he took that information with him.

CA 1990, s 185(2) now requires a resigning auditor, or an auditor notifying the company of his unwillingness to be reappointed[507], on pain of criminal penalty, to state in the notice of resignation the circumstances connected with his resignation which he considers ought to be brought to the attention of the members and creditors, or, if there are none, that no such circumstances exist. Within 14 days of service, the notice must be sent by the auditor to the Registrar of Companies. If it contains a statement of circumstances which the auditor considers ought to be brought to the attention of the members and creditors (eg fraud, misfeasance or breach of duty) the company must, within 14 days of service, send a copy of the notice to the Registrar of Companies and to every person entitled to receive copies of the annual accounts[508].

Failure by the auditor to make a statement in his notice, and failure by the company to circulate such notices, constitutes an offence, rendering the auditor, or the company and every officer in default as the case may be, liable on summary conviction to a fine not exceeding €1,905 or to imprisonment for a term not exceeding 12 months, or to both, and on indictment to a fine not exceeding €12,697 or to imprisonment for a term not exceeding five years, or to both[509]. The company need not circulate the notice, however, if on the application of the company or any aggrieved person the court is satisfied it contains material which has been included to secure needless publicity for defamatory matter[510].

[13.204] If a resigning auditor's notice contains a statement of circumstances as set out above, he is further entitled by CA 1990, s 186 to requisition the directors to call a general meeting of the company for the purpose of receiving and considering any such circumstances as the auditor may wish to give. Where the auditor makes such a requisition in his notice, the directors must proceed duly to convene a general meeting for a day no later than 28 days after service of the notice. The auditor will be entitled to attend and be heard at such a meeting.

[13.205] An auditor who has resigned is also entitled to attend and be heard at the AGM at which, but for his resignation, his office would have expired, and at any meeting at which it is proposed to fill the vacancy caused by his resignation[511]. If his notice of resignation contained a statement of circumstances which the auditor considered ought to be brought to the attention of the members and creditors, he may also require the company to circulate

---

506 CA 1963, s 160(2)(c). See para **[13.181]**.

507 CA 1990, s 185(5).

508 As to the persons entitled to receive copies of the annual accounts see para **[13.016]**.

509 CA 1990, s 185(7) and s 240 (as amended).

510 CA 1990, s 185(4). The auditor may be made liable for the company's costs in such an application: CA 1990, s 185(4).

511 CA 1990, s 186(5).

a further statement of those circumstances to the Registrar of Companies and all persons entitled to receive copies of the company's annual accounts. The company must state that it has received such a further statement in any notice of the meeting given to the members. Again, failure to comply renders the company and any officer in default guilty of an offence[512] and the company or any aggrieved person may apply to prevent the circulation if it would secure needless publication of defamatory matter[513].

The rights and powers of auditors

[13.206] In addition to those rights which arise specifically upon resignation or removal, CA 1990, s 193(3) gives the auditor a general right of access at all reasonable times to the books, accounts and vouchers of the company, and further empowers him to require all officers and employees of the company to give such information and explanations within their knowledge or which they can procure which *he*[514] thinks necessary for the performance of his duties as auditor. Any person who fails, within two days of the request, to give such information while it is within their knowledge will be guilty of an offence, as will any person who knowingly or recklessly gives false, misleading or deceptive information[515]. It will be a defence, however, to show that the request was actually complied with within a reasonable time. Persons convicted of such offences may be made personally liable, without limitation of liability, for all or part of the company's debts and other liabilities in a winding up[516].

CA 1990, s 196 also imposes a duty on any of the company's subsidiary companies incorporated in the State, and their auditors, to supply information and explanations to the auditor upon request. Where the company has subsidiaries outside the State, the company itself is obliged to take all reasonable steps to obtain such information and explanations for the auditor. If the company or an auditor of a subsidiary fails to comply with such requests within five days, a fine not exceeding €1,905 on summary conviction, or not exceeding €12,697 on conviction on indictment, may be incurred, but it will be a defence to show that compliance was achieved as soon as was reasonably possible.

There is old authority for the proposition that an auditor who is denied access to the books of account can merely report that matter to the members: in *Cuff v London and County Land & Building Co Ltd*[517] it was held that the courts will not order by mandatory injunction the company to produce the books of account to the auditor where the shareholders do not wish him to act.

[13.207] The auditor is also entitled to attend any general meeting of the company and to receive the same notices and communications relating to meetings as the members[518]. He has a right to be heard at all general meetings, annual or otherwise, on any part of the business of the meeting which concerns him as auditor. Indeed, reg 8(4) of the European

512 The penalties are the same as those detailed in para **[13.203]**.

513 CA 1990, s 186(3) and (4).

514 Notably, the auditor's right is subjectively assessed.

515 CA 1990, s 197. The penalties are the same as those detailed in para **[13.203]**.

516 See Chapter 5, *Disregarding Separate Legal Personality*, para **[5.084]***ff*.

517 *Cuff v London and County Land & Building Co Ltd* [1912] 1 Chapter 440.

518 CA 1990, s 193(5). See Chapter 9, *Corporate Governance: Meetings*, para **[9.030]**.

Communities (Single-Member Private Limited Companies) Regulations 1994 empowers the auditor of a single-member company to *require* the holding of an AGM.[519]

Status and duties of auditors

(a) Status

[13.208] An auditor, unless there are special provisions in his contract of engagement with the company, is not normally an agent of the company. In *Re Transplanters (Holding Co) Ltd*[520] the applicant, one of two directors of the company, sought to prove as creditor in its liquidation, but his claim was opposed by the liquidator on the basis that the claim was statute barred. The applicant pointed in evidence to two balance sheets of the company which made reference to the debt, signed by himself and his fellow director, and certified by the auditor. The applicant alleged that the references constituted an acknowledgement of the debt for the purposes of the Statute of Limitations, so that time began to run afresh from the date of the references. Wynn-Parry J held that the auditor's certificate was not such an acknowledgement, saying:

> 'In my view an auditor of the company is not (apart from any special contract and there is none in this case) an agent of the company at any rate for the purpose of being able to bind the company by merely signing the normal certificate at the foot of the balance sheet...No doubt for certain purposes the auditors may be regarded as servants of the company so that the court will not by mandatory injunction force on the company auditors whom the shareholders do not desire to act: see *Cuff v London & County Land & Building Co Ltd* [1912] 1 Ch 440. Apart however, from any special contract, the relations between the company and its auditors are governed by the provisions of the Companies Act 1948 and their duty as expressed by s 162(1) is to make a report to the members on the accounts examined by them and on every balance sheet and every profit and loss account and their report is to contain statements as to the various matters mentioned in Schedule 9 to that Act...I cannot spell out of his relations with the company as to be extracted from the Companies Act 1948, any authority to do anything in the nature of giving an acknowledgement within the Limitation Act 1939 or any authority to do more than to perform the duties laid on him as auditor by the Companies Act 1948.'

The sources of the auditor's duties are the Companies Acts 1963–2001 and any contract of engagement under which he is appointed, and his authority from the company extends merely to the performance of those duties and for those purposes only. If in the course of his audit he is fixed with constructive notice of matters not connected with the performance of his duties, that notice may not be imputed to the company[521].

Though not normally an agent, an auditor may, however, be regarded as an *officer* of the company in relation to his duties, particularly where he has been guilty of, or has concurred in, the production of false or fraudulent accounts or the misappropriation of property. Accordingly, he may be made liable, either civilly or criminally, under any statutory provisions directed at 'officers'[522]. In *R v Shacter*[523] an auditor was convicted of larceny and misfeasance, offences which under the Larceny Acts and Companies Acts (UK) applied to officers. Parker CJ distinguished between auditors appointed to fill an

[519] SI 1994/275.

[520] *Re Transplanters (Holding Co) Ltd* [1958] 2 All ER 711.

[521] *Spackman v Evans* (1868) LR 3 HL 171.

office and those appointed *ad hoc* for a limited purpose, observing that the latter were not officers, but he could see no reason why the former should not be regarded as officers and made criminally liable as such. Conversely, an auditor who is regarded as officer should be entitled to rely on statutory provisions which relieve officers from liability, eg CA 1963, s 391 which empowers the court to excuse officers for negligence, default, breach of duty or breach of trust, even prospectively, where he has acted honestly and reasonably and it appears to the court that he ought to be so excused[524].

(b) Statutory duties

[13.209] The auditor's duties arise from statute, his contract of engagement, and the common law. His express statutory duties are five-fold, viz:

(i) To make a report to the members;

(ii) To exercise professional integrity;

(iii) To report failure to keep proper books of account;

(iv) To disclose directors' emoluments if they do not appear in the accounts;

(v) To report suspected indictable offences.

(i) To report to the members

[13.210] The auditor's principal statutory duty is to make a report to the members. Sections 193(1) of CA 1990 provides:

> 'The auditors of a company shall make a report to the members on the accounts examined by them, and on every balance sheet and profit and loss account, and all group accounts, laid before the company in general meeting during their tenure of office.'

The statements required to be contained in the report have been considered above. The statutory obligation to report to the members is not one which can be removed or limited by agreement or by the memorandum and articles. In *Newton v Birmingham Small Arms Co*[525] a special resolution changing the articles so as to provide that an internal reserve fund could be formed, which would not be disclosed in the balance sheet and which the auditors were not to report upon to the shareholders, was held to be invalid. Buckley J said:

> 'Any regulations which precluded the auditors from availing themselves of all the information to which, under the Act, they are entitled, as material for the report which under the Act they are to make, as to the true and correct view of the company's affairs, are, I think, inconsistent with the Act.'

---

522 See generally Chapter 10, *Duties of Directors and Other Officers*. Apart from those provisions aimed at officers by the Companies Acts, there appear a number of such provisions in the Larceny Act 1861, ss 82–84; the Larceny Act 1916, s 20; and the Falsification of Accounts Act 1875, ss 1 and 2.

523 *R v Shacter* [1960] 1 All ER 61. See also *Re London General Bank* [1895] 2 Ch 166, where Lindley LJ said of an officer: 'he is appointed by the company to check the directors and for some purposes and to some extent it seems quite impossible to say that he is not an officer of he company'; also *Re Western Counties Steam Bakeries & Milling Co* [1897] 1 Ch 617.

524 See Chapter 10, *Duties of Directors and Other Officers*, para **[10.076]**. Section 391 only excuses the auditor from liability to the company itself: *Commissioner of Customs and Excise v Hedon Alpha Ltd* [1981] QB 818.

525 *Newton v Birmingham Small Arms Co* [1906] 2 Ch 378.

(ii) To exercise professional integrity

[13.211] The auditor's general duty in the preparation of the report is to carry out his audit with 'professional integrity'[526]. It will be recalled[527] that the auditor is statutorily required to state in the report *inter alia* whether in his opinion, proper books of account have been kept by the company; whether the balance sheet and profit and loss account are in agreement with the books of account; whether the information in the directors' report is consistent with the accounts; and whether the balance sheet, profit and loss account, and any group accounts give a 'true and fair view'. Accordingly, it is not enough for the auditor merely to consider the annual accounts in isolation: rather, part of the auditor's reporting function is to carry out sufficient investigations to enable him to form an opinion as to whether proper books of account have been kept and whether the company's annual accounts are in agreement with the books of account.

The Companies Acts do not elaborate further upon what is required by professional integrity. It seems clear, however, that compliance with SSAPs and FRSs[528], and the Statements of Auditing Standards ('SASs') issued by the Auditing Practices Board of the Consultative Committee of Accounting Bodies will almost certainly amount to the exercise of 'professional integrity'. The guidance of the Ethical Standards Board of the Accounting Foundation in the UK will also be of influence[529].

(iii) To report a failure to keep proper books of account

[13.212] Where the auditor forms the opinion that proper books of account are not being kept, CA 1990, s 194, as amended, requires him to serve by recorded delivery[530] a notice stating his opinion on the company and, not less than seven days later, on the Registrar of Companies, who will forthwith notify the Director of Corporate Enforcement. Failure by the auditor so to do renders him guilty of a criminal offence[531], and upon conviction further renders him open to the prospect of being made personally liable, without limitation of liability, for all or part of the company's debts and other liabilities in a winding up[532].

[13.213] Where the auditor files a notice with the Registrar of Companies pursuant to CA 1990, s 194, the Director of Corporate Enforcement may require him to furnish information and an explanation of the reasons for the opinion[533]. Failure to comply with the request of the director or failure to allow the Director access to information and documents in the auditor's possession constitutes an offence.

Any written information given in response to a request of the director will be admissible in subsequent legal proceeding as evidence of the facts stated therein, at least until the contrary is proved[534].

---

526 CA 1990, s 193(6).

527 See para **[13.107]**.

528 See para **[13.022]**.

529 See the Report of the Review Group on Auditing, at p 48.

530 The recorded delivery requirement was added by CLEA 2001, s 74.

531 The penalties are those detailed in para **[13.203]**.

532 CA 1990, s 204. See Chapter 5, *Disregarding Separate Legal Personality*, para **[5.084]**.

533 CA 1990, s 194(3A).

534 CA 1990, s 194(3B).

(iv) To disclose directors' emoluments where they do not appear in the accounts

[13.214] As was observed above[535], CA 1990, s 191 requires detailed particulars of directors emoluments to be given in the annual accounts. If such details are not disclosed, s 191(8) provides:

> '...it shall be the duty of the auditors of the company by whom the accounts are examined to include in the report thereon, so far as they are reasonably able to do so, a statement giving the required particulars.'

(v) To report suspected indictable offences

[13.215] CA 1990, s 194(5), as inserted by CLEA 2001, s 74, provides:

> 'Where, in the course of, and by virtue of, their carrying out an audit of the accounts of the company, information comes into the possession of the auditors of a company that leads them to form the opinion that there are reasonable grounds for believing that the company or an officer or agent of it has committed an indictable offence under the Companies Acts, the auditors shall, forthwith after having formed it, notify that opinion to the Director and provide the Director with details of the grounds on which they have formed that opinion.'

The duty is to report suspected indictable offences to the Director of Corporate Enforcement. Failure so to do will itself constitute an offence[536], and it seems there is no discretion given to the auditors as to whether to report the suspicion – even when the misconduct has ceased.

[13.216] No professional or legal duty of the auditor (such as, for example, a duty of client confidentiality) is breached by reason of compliance with the duty to report suspected indictable offences, nor will compliance expose the auditor to liability to members, creditors and other interested parties[537].

[13.217] The duty to report arises in the course of the auditing function, and would seem to have no application where the suspicion is formed during non-audit work[538]. Moreover, the duty appears to end with the conclusion of duties as auditor.

The duty may prove difficult to comply with in practice, however. The problem for auditors is that the Companies Acts create a myriad of criminal offences, many of which are triable either summarily or upon indictment at the election of the prosecuting authorities. The publication[539] by the Director of Corporate Enforcement of a list of indictable offences may be of some assistance to auditors in complying with the spirit of the duty, but will not remove confusion that may follow where the auditor is of the opinion that only a summary offence has been committed[540]. And while the legislation does not place a positive duty on the auditor to obtain legal advice, it seems clear that the auditor is

---

535 See para **[13.100]**.

536 CA 1990, s 194(4), as amended.

537 CA 1990, s 194(6).

538 See O'Reilly, 'Auditor's Responsibilities: Changed Responsibilities' (2002) CLP 79 at 81.

539 Director of Corporate Enforcement, 'The Duty of Auditors to Report Suspected Indictable Offences under the Companies Acts to the Director of Corporate Enforcement via Section 74(e) of the Company Law Enforcement Act 2001' Consultation Paper C/2002/2.

540 O'Reilly, 'Auditor's Responsibilities: Changed Responsibilities' (2002) CLP 79 at 81.

not entitled to rely conclusively on legal advice that no indictable offence has been committed.

[13.218] Does the new duty place an onus on auditors to seek out and investigate possible offences? Probably not. The duty arises in the course of and by virtue of the audit function. As shall be seen below[541], the function of the auditor is to act as 'watchdog' rather than 'bloodhound'. In addition, the Director of Corporate Enforcement has indicated that the duty does not arise where a relevant enforcement authority has already initiated and concluded enforcement action in respect of the circumstances giving rise to the offence[542].

(c) Common law duties

[13.219] The auditor who breaches the duties contained in his contract of engagement may be made liable in contract for damages to the other party to the contract of engagement, ie the company, provided the company can prove consequential loss. Such loss can often be difficult to prove since it will be difficult to show that the company would not have suffered as it did if it had not relied on inaccurate figures, etc[543]. Individual members are not normally party to the contract of engagement; consequently, an individual member may not sue the auditor in contract unless he represents the company by way of a derivative action[544].

[13.220] The law of tort places a duty on the auditor not to breach his statutory duties, and to exercise reasonable skill and care in the performance of his duties, however they may arise. The standard of care required in such circumstances is 'to exercise such skill and care as a diligent, skilled and cautious auditor would exercise according to the practice of his profession.'[545] In *Irish Woollen Co v Tyson*[546] Fitzgibbon LJ said:

> 'The measure of duty is the bringing of reasonable care and skill to the performance of the business directed to be done, having regard first to the contract of employment, then to the character of the business itself, to the remuneration of the defendant and to all the other circumstances of the case. In strict rule, however, the measure of the duty is to be ascertained by applying to all the circumstances of the case the best consideration so as to ascertain what ought to have been done under the circumstances.'

[13.221] Accordingly, the auditor must not certify as true that which he does not believe to be true, and he must make inquiries in relation to any irregularities which come to his attention which affect the performance of his duty. In this regard it has been said that the auditor is 'a watchdog, not a bloodhound'[547], ie that he must be alert to irregularities which he may be expected to find in the performance of the audit, but that he need not search for them. In *Re Kingston Cotton Mills Co (No 2)* Lopes LJ said as follows[548]:

---

541 See para **[13.231]**.

542 Consultation Paper C/2002/2, p 9.

543 See Ford, 'The Company Auditor – Principles of Civil Liability', (1989) Gazette ILSI 385.

544 See generally Chapter 19, *Shareholders' Remedies*, para **[19.099]**ff.

545 Per Hanna J in *Leech v Stokes* [1937] IR 787, at 789.

546 (1900) 26 The Accountant LR 13, and MacCann, *A Casebook on Company Law*, (1991) at pp 489–490.

547 Per Lopes LJ in *Re Kingston Cotton Mill (No 2)* [1896] 2 Chapter 279 at 288.

548 [1896] 2 Chapter 279 at 288 at 288–289.

> '...it is the duty of an auditor to bear on the work he has to perform that skill, care and caution which a reasonably competent, careful and cautious auditor would use. What is reasonable skill, care and caution must depend on the particular circumstances of each case. An auditor is not bound to be a detective, or, as was said, to approach his work with suspicion or with a foregone conclusion that there is something wrong. He is a watchdog, but not a bloodhound. He is justified in believing tried servants of the company in whom confidence is placed by the company. He is entitled to assume that they are honest, and to rely upon their representations, provided he takes reasonable care. If there is anything calculated to excite suspicion he should probe it to the bottom; but in the absence of anything of that kind he is only bound to be reasonably cautious and careful.'

[13.222] The auditor must, however, be wary that mistakes might have been made. In *Fomento (Sterling Area) Ltd v Selsdon Fountain Co*[549] Lord Denning observed of an auditor that:

> 'His vital task is to take care that errors are not made, be they errors of computation or of omission or commission, or downright untruths. To perform this task properly he must come to it with an inquiring mind – not suspicious of dishonesty, I agree – but suspecting that someone may have made a mistake somewhere and that a check must be made to ensure that there has been none.'

[13.223] In modern times, it seems that the auditor will be required in the performance of his duties to make enquiries of customers and other third parties dealing with the company where he discovers an irregularity. In the *Irish Woollen Co* case Holmes LJ was of the opinion that an auditor discovering irregularities is entitled to ask for explanations, but 'is not called to seek for knowledge outside the company or to communicate with customers or creditors. He is not an insurer against fraud or error.' Fitzgibbon LJ, however, was of the opinion that the auditor, though a watchdog, 'is bound to keep his eyes open and his nose, too. As in the case of the hound, the auditor will follow up this trail to the end.'[550] In *Re City Equitable Fire Insurance Co*[551] Romer J held that an auditor could never be justified in omitting to make a personal inspection of company securities which were in improper hands. However, much depends here upon the prevailing standards of professional practice. Thus, in *Re Thomas Gerrard & Son Ltd*[552], where the explanations of a managing director as to irregular invoices concerning the purchases of stock had been accepted at face value by the auditor, Pennycuick J relied on expert evidence of prevailing practice in holding that the auditor had failed to perform his duties by not examining the suppliers' statements and, where necessary, communicating with the suppliers. Likewise, in *Kelly v Haughey Boland & Co*[553] Lardner J accepted that the standards of the profession have tended to become more exacting. He relied on SSAPs as evidence of the prevailing standard of care required of auditors in relation to stocktaking, and held that the auditor

549 *Fomento (Sterling Area) Ltd v Selsdon Fountain Co* [1958] 1 All ER 11.
550 See MacCann, *A Casebook on Company Law*, (1991) p 493.
551 *Re City Equitable Fire Insurance Co* [1925] Chapter 407.
552 *Re Thomas Gerrard & Son Ltd* [1967] 2 All ER 525.
553 *Kelly v Haughey Boland & Co* [1989] ILRM 373.

had not met those standards, even though the auditor in question had employed the same approach in the case as he might have legitimately employed 20 years' previously[554].

[13.224] The upshot of these cases, coupled with the statutory requirement to exercise 'professional integrity', is that auditors have a duty to maintain close adherence to SSAPs, FRSs and the related SASs issued by the Auditing Practices Board and the recognised accounting bodies. Professional standards may evolve and change over time so that the courts are bound to consider innovations and technical developments when assessing the standard of care required of auditors.

Civil liability of auditors

(a) Liability to the company

[13.225] As was observed in the preceding paragraphs, an auditor may be made liable by the company for breach of contract where he fails to observe the obligations imposed upon him by the contract of engagement, provided the company can prove consequential loss. Likewise, since the auditor is appointed by the company, his principal duty is to the company, and he may be made liable to the company in tort where his breach of duty causes loss[555]. As was also observed above, an auditor who has been convicted of an offence relating to failure to keep proper accounts may be made to contribute to the assets of the company in a subsequent insolvent liquidation.

(b) Liability to others

[13.226] An auditor's contractual liability to others depends upon whether the others are party to the contract. In may be recalled that an auditor's contract of engagement is normally between him and the company; accordingly, third parties, including shareholders and members, are not normally entitled to rely on the contract[556]. An auditor's liability to third parties in tort depends upon the existence of a duty of care owed to that party. Where a third party claims that reliance on inaccurate information negligently presented by the auditor led to economic loss, he must prove that he actually relied on the misstatement, and that:

— the loss was reasonably foreseeable;

— there was a sufficient degree of proximity between the auditor and the third party; and

— it was reasonable for the third party to rely on the accounts.

[13.227] In *Kelly v Haughey Boland & Co*[557] the plaintiffs claimed damages in respect of negligent misstatement by the auditors. The plaintiffs were the directors of Cavan Crystal Ltd, and wishing to purchase the company to which the auditors had been appointed, were given copies of the audited accounts for the period 1973–1976. The figures contained therein were explained by the auditors during a number of meetings prior to completion of

[554] As to the standard of care required according to current professional standards see Chua, 'The Auditor's Liability in Negligence in Respect of the Audit Report' (1993) 14 Co Law 203 and (1994) 15 Co Law 35.

[555] *Candler v Crane Christmas & Co* [1951] 1 All ER 426; *Caparo Industries plc v Dickman* [1990] 1 All ER 568.

[556] See para **[13.219]**.

[557] *Kelly v Haughey Boland & Co* [1989] ILRM 373.

the purchase. Subsequent to completion, the plaintiffs sought to sue the auditors in negligence because of inaccuracies in the accounts, arguing in particular that the auditors had not taken requisite care to ensure that stock figures were correct by attending the stocktaking. Lardner J held for the plaintiffs. In doing so he relied on the words of Lord Morris in *Hedley Byrne & Co v Heller & Partners Ltd*[558] and those of Woolf J in *JEB Fasteners v Mark Bloom & Co*[559], where it was said:

> '…without laying down any principle which is intended to be of general application on the basis of the authorities which I have cited, the appropriate test for establishing whether a duty of care exists appears in this case to be whether the defendants knew or reasonably should have foreseen at the time the accounts were audited that a person might rely on those accounts for the purpose of deciding whether or not to take over the company and therefore could suffer loss if the accounts were inaccurate. Such an approach does place a limitation on those entitled to contend that there has been a breach of duty owed to them. First of all, they must have relied on the account and second, they must have done so in circumstances where the auditors either knew that they would or ought to have known that they might. If the situation is one where it would not be reasonable for the accounts to be relied on, then in the absence of express knowledge, the auditor would be under no duty. This places a limit on the circumstances in which the audited accounts can be relied on and the period for which they can be relied on, the longer the period which elapses prior to the accounts being relied on from the date on which the auditor gave his certificate, the more difficult it will be to establish that the auditor ought to have foreseen that his certificate would in those circumstances be relied on.'

Lardner J found that the plaintiffs satisfied the foreseeable loss, proximity, and reasonable reliance criteria outlined above, since the auditors were aware of an imminent sale when they audited the accounts in 1976, and that they ought to have foreseen in the previous year, 1975, that reliance might be placed on the accuracy of the accounts in a subsequent sale of the business. However, although the plaintiffs established that the auditors owed them a duty of care, they failed to prove that their loss was actually incurred *as a result* of reliance on inaccuracies negligently stated in the audited accounts, and the action failed.

[13.228] A similar conclusion was reached by Woolf J in the *JEB Fasteners* case, observing that even if the plaintiffs had known the true financial position of the company at the time, they would not have acted any differently. In that case, even though the auditor did not actually know that the plaintiffs were going to rely on the accounts, Woolf J held that he owed them a duty of care since he *ought* to have foreseen that the subsequent purchaser might rely on his work, being one of a class of persons, known or unknown to him, who might reasonably be expected to rely on the accuracy of his audit.

[13.229] The scope of the duty of care has been radically restricted in the UK in the case of *Caparo Industries plc v Dickman*[560]. In that case, the plaintiff bought shares in a company, Fidelity plc. The plaintiff's involvement with Fidelity occurred in three stages: at first, they were merely potential investors, relying on information in the public domain; later,

558 *Hedley Byrne & Co v Heller & Partners Ltd* [1964] AC 465 at 502.

559 *JEB Fasteners v Mark Bloom & Co* [1981] 3 All ER 289.

560 *Caparo Industries plc v Dickman* [1990] 1 All ER 568. See Mulcahy 'Accountable to Whom? Auditors' Liability' (1994) CLP 295.

they became shareholders and received copies of the shareholders' accounts; and finally they became investors, by purchasing, in reliance upon the shareholders' accounts, shares in small batches on the open market until they could compel acceptance of their terms for the purchase of all the shares in Fidelity. Once they obtained control of Fidelity, they discovered its true worth, and issued proceedings against the defendant auditors.

At first instance, Sir Neil Lawson ruled that the auditors owed the plaintiffs no duty of care, either as potential investors, actual investors, or shareholders. Although the Court of Appeal overturned Sir Neil Lawson's finding on the duty of care to the plaintiffs as shareholders, the House of Lords restored his decision. The relationship as potential investor was not sufficiently proximate: Fidelity was a public limited company and its members could change from day to day. Moreover, the auditors did not know the plaintiffs' takeover plans when they became shareholders, nor ought they to have known then. As regards the plaintiffs' status as shareholder, their Lordships found that the auditors' statutory duties are owed to the shareholders as a whole – not to individual shareholders. The purpose of the audit was to protect the company itself. As a class the shareholders were determinate; but as individuals they could change identity from day to day and from time to time. To extend a duty to individual shareholders would open the auditor to liability for an indeterminate amount, for an indeterminate time, to an indeterminate class[561]. The interests of the shareholders could be protected by the bringing of an action by, or on behalf of, the company, but not through individual action. Indeed, Lord Bridge found it difficult to see how a shareholder's interest could not adequately be protected through the bringing of an action on the company's behalf.

[13.230] The *Caparo* decision, and the cases which follow it[562], illustrate a turn away from the broad principles for identifying the existence of a duty of care which Lord Wilberforce laid down in *Anns v Merton London Borough Council*[563] and which have been upheld in by the Irish Supreme Court in *Siney v Dublin Corporation*[564]. To this extent it is questionable whether the Irish courts would be prepared to go a similar route. *Caparo* may be distinguished from the *Haughey Boland* case on the basis that the auditors in the latter case actually knew the plaintiffs before they conducted the audit. Moreover, *Caparo* concerned a public limited company, and the relationship between auditors and shareholders or investors in a private company could hardly be more different. Private company auditors will often be aware of any on-going or prospective take over or investment negotiations, as in the *Haughey Boland* case, since they will be more acutely aware of the company's need for additional investment. Likewise, particularly in smaller private companies, banks and other lending institutions tend to rely more heavily on the audited accounts, as auditors may well know[565]. Consequently, it is easier to find foreseeability of loss, proximity, and reasonableness of reliance in a private company, and *Caparo* might be confined to its facts.

561 See *Ultramares Corporation v Touche* (1931) NY 170, per Cardozo J at 179.

562 Eg *James McNaughton Papers Group Ltd v Hicks Anderson & Co* [1991] 1 All ER 134; *Peach Publishing Ltd v Slater & Co* [1998] BCC 139.

563 *Anns v Merton London Borough Council* [1978] AC 728.

564 *Siney v Dublin Corporation* [1980] IR 400.

565 Cf *Ali Saudi Banque v Clark Pixley* [1989] 3 All ER 361, which was approved in *Caparo*, where auditors were held not to owe a duty of care to banks lending money on foot of the audited accounts, even though it was reasonably foreseeable that the banks would act on foot of the information contained therein.

[13.231] Since *Caparo*, auditors have been found to owe a duty of care in a case where the price of shares in a transfer was fixed as a multiple of profits in audited accounts procured *jointly* by purchaser and vendor[566], and in a case where an auditor assumed responsibility for the accuracy of the accounts through statements to a prospective purchaser, knowing all the time that the accuracy of the accounts was the final consideration in the purchaser's decision whether or not to bid[567].

(c) Excluding liability

[13.232] An auditor cannot exclude his liability to the company, nor can he get it to indemnify him in respect of his liability to third parties. CA 1963, s 200 provides that:

> '...any provision whether contained in the articles of a company or in any contract with a company or otherwise for exempting any officer of the company or any person employed by the company as auditor from, or indemnifying him against, any liability which by virtue of any rule of law would otherwise attach to him in respect of any negligence, default, breach of duty or breach of trust of which he may be guilty in relation to the company shall be void...'

He will, however, enjoy a limited right of indemnity from the company in respect of any liability incurred in defending proceedings, whether civil or criminal, in which judgment is given in his favour or in which he is acquitted, and in connection with any application for relief under CA 1963, s 391 or under C(A)A 1983, s 42[568]. Moreover, the company in general meeting may by resolution forgive or ratify a breach of duty by an auditor.[569]

[13.233] Unless there is a contractual relationship between the parties, an exclusion clause in the contract of engagement will not exclude the auditor from liability to third parties to whom he owes a duty of care, because there will be no privity of contract. Where, however, a qualification is placed in the accounts, the exclusion clause may prove effective. In *John Sisk & Son v Flinn*[570] the plaintiffs wished to purchase a 75% shareholding in a company, it being agreed that the purchase price would be determined according to the company's accounts. The auditors knew of the plaintiff's plans when auditing the accounts. The books of account were not made available to the plaintiffs before the purchase, so there was no way in which they could verify the accuracy of the accounts. The audited accounts contained the following clause:

> 'We have obtained all the information and explanations which to the best of our knowledge and belief were necessary for the purpose of our audit except that stock and work in progress at the beginning and end of the financial period are as certified by the management and have not been physically observed.'

---

[566] *Galoo Ltd v.Bright Grahame Murray Ltd* [1995] 1 All ER 16.

[567] *ADT Ltd v BDO Binder Hamlyn* [1996] BCC 808.

[568] See para **[13.208]**. On CA 1963, s 391, see Chapter 10, *Duties of Directors and Other Officers*, para **[10.076]**.

[569] See *Multinational Gas and Petrochemical Co v Multinational Gas and Petrochemical Services Ltd* [1983] Ch 258.

[570] *John Sisk & Son v Flinn* (18 July 1984, unreported), High Court (Finlay P).

Finlay P found that although the auditors had prima facie failed to comply with the prevailing standards of recognised accounting practice in relation to the work in progress figure, the clause in the accounts effectively excluded them from liability to the plaintiffs, because the defendants, seeing the statement, must have doubted whether the accounts contained the information sufficient to warrant reliance on them. The limits of such exclusions have not been judicially examined.

Chapter 14

Investigations and Inspectors

Introduction

[14.001] The Companies Act 1990 ('CA 1990'), as amended by Part 3 of the Company Law Enforcement Act 2001 ('CLEA 2001'), provides a number of means whereby the ownership, control or affairs of a company can be investigated. Such investigations fall into two broad categories. The first category includes the Director of Corporate Enforcement's powers to require a person to give information with regard to the ownership of shares or to require the production of books and documents relating to a company. That category of investigation may (though need not necessarily) be a precursor to the second, more invasive, category of investigation which involves the appointment of an inspector or inspectors to conduct a detailed investigation and to report on their findings.

[14.002] The investigatory regime exists to ensure compliance with company law:

> 'to ensure that companies incorporated under the Acts do not abuse the privileges which incorporation confers on them to the detriment of their members, their creditors or indeed the public in general[1].

Though the legislation is broadly worded, it seems unlikely that an investigation will be commenced in the absence of suspected abuse of the privilege of incorporation[2]. The information gathered in an investigation may be applied to various purposes, however. In particular, it may be used as evidence in subsequent criminal or civil proceedings[3]. A company may be wound up on foot of information contained in an inspector's report. The information can also be released to other regulatory authorities (such as the Competition Authority or the Revenue Commissioners) who may decide to act upon it accordingly.

Background

[14.003] The basic concept of appointing competent inspectors to investigate the books and affairs of a company is of venerable origin[4]. The power of the Board of Trade to appoint one or more competent inspectors was to be found in the Companies Act 1862[5].

---

1 Per Keane CJ in *Dunnes Stores Ireland Company v Ryan* (1 February 2002, unreported), Supreme Court at p 26.

2 The powers of the Director may be invoked to assist an investigation by a foreign company law authority: CA 1990, s 23A, as amended.

3 Indeed, an inspector's report will carry presumptive weight in civil proceedings, defying the hearsay rule: see para **[14.058]**. It would appear to remain subject to the normal exclusionary rules of evidence in criminal proceedings: see para **[14.044]**.

4 See *Chestvale Properties Ltd v Glackin* [1993] 3 IR 35; also generally McGrath, 'Investigations under the Companies Act' (1993) ILT 264; Fraser, 'Administrative Powers of Investigations into Companies' (1971) 24 MLR 260; and McCormack, *The New Companies Legislation* (1991).

5 CA 1862, s 56.

The power does not appear to have been invoked with any great frequency, though it was continued in the Companies (Consolidation) Act 1908[6] and in a more extended form in the Companies Act 1963 ('CA 1963'[7]), by which time the powers of the Board had become vested in the Minister.

In theory, these powers should have proved useful in checking abuse of duties by directors, and in controlling company fraud generally. By the 1980s, however, and probably for a long time before then, it was apparent that the investigation procedures as they then existed were not serving any useful purpose[8]. The principal problem seems to have been that no detailed procedures were outlined in the legislation and that, as a consequence, most investigations suffered from legal objections grounded on the requirements of natural justice[9]. Moreover, investigations tended to occur in private, and their findings were rarely published[10].

[14.004] The Companies Act 1990 introduced new and more detailed procedures to make investigations more meaningful. The principal innovation was that the High Court, rather than the Minister, was conferred with the power to appoint inspectors to investigate 'the affairs of a company'. This transfer of function, it was hoped, would enable the procedures to be determined in a more efficient manner. Additionally, two new and distinct powers were conferred on the Minister. The first was the power to appoint an inspector or inspectors to investigate and report on 'the membership of any company and otherwise with respect to the company for the purpose of determining the true persons who are or have been financially interested in the success or failure (real or apparent) of the company or able to control or materially to influence the policy of the company,'[11] or to investigate and report share dealings[12]. The second was to require the production of books or documents. CA 1990 gave inspectors more extensive powers, and the statutory effect of the inspector's report was extended.

[14.005] The reforms in CA 1990 had substantially the desired effect. A little over a month after Part II of CA 1990 came into force, the Minister appointed an inspector to investigate the ownership and control of a number of companies involved in the purchase of shares in Sugar Distributors (Holdings) Ltd and the subsequent resale of those shares to Siúcre Éireann cpt at a substantial profit (the so-called 'Greencore Affair'). Four days later the High Court, on the application of the Minister, appointed two more inspectors to

---

6 Companies (Consolidation) Act 1908, ss 109-111.

7 Companies (Consolidation) Act 1908, ss 165-173.

8 See especially McCormack, *The New Companies Legislation* (1991), p 37 where the author, writing in 1991, points out that the investigation procedures contained in CA 1963, ss 165-166 were employed only five times since their introduction in 1963, and with little success. It is apparent from the annual Companies Reports of the time that further applications were made for the appointment of inspectors during that time, but the outcome of those applications is not known.

9 McCormack, *The New Companies Legislation* (1991), p 37.

10 An exception is the *Report of the Enquiry into Irish Estates Ltd*, Stationery Office 23 October 1963, which enquiry was held under the provisions of the Companies (Consolidation) Act 1908.

11 CA 1990, s 14.

12 CA 1990, s 66.

investigate the affairs of Siúcre Éireann cpt. Less than a month later the Minister, acting on the recommendations of a committee of inquiry appointed by the Minister for Tourism, Transport and Communications, appointed an inspector to investigate the membership and control of Chestvale Properties Ltd and Hoddle Investments Ltd, two companies connected with the sale of a site in Ballsbridge, Dublin, to the state-owned telecommunications company Telecom Éireann at a price more than twice that which had been paid for it less than a year previously (the 'Telecom Affair'). Both investigations produced a number of judicial decisions interpreting the new procedures, and, in general, upholding the new investigatory scheme.

To date, the investigation procedures have been deployed on 20 occasions since the commencement of CA 1990[13]. The majority of these have been investigations requiring the production of books and documents, but inspections have been ordered on seven occasions in total: four by the High Court on the application of the Minister[14], and the remaining three by the Minister directly[15].

[14.006] Lately, CLEA 2001 has revised the detail of the investigatory regime while retaining its general structure. The principal innovation is the transfer of the Minister's investigatory functions to the Director of Corporate Enforcement ('the Director'). This transfer has the advantage of placing the investigation powers in the hands of a full-time, independent, specialist office. CLEA 2001 further enhances the investigatory regime by, *inter alia*, strengthening the powers of inspectors to examine the affairs of companies not named in the warrant of appointment; by increasing the powers of the Director with regard to the examination of books in respect of the production of books and documents; by introducing new offences in connection with the destruction of books and documents; by increasing the grounds on which a search warrant can be obtained where books and documents have not been produced; and by extending the categories of persons to whom information gathered in the process can be revealed.

Future

[14.007] Despite the increase in its popularity since it was revamped by CA 1990, the investigatory regime has yet to come of age. No other investigatory mechanism in Irish law is quite as powerful or severe. Though submission to its more Orwellian features may be seen as the price which must be paid for the concession to incorporate, doubts still linger about its constitutionality in many respects[16]. Nor has there been time yet for mature

13 *Companies Report 2000*, Appendix 2.

14 *Companies Report 2000*, Appendix 2. In addition to the companies involved in the Telecom Affair, the High Court has appointed inspectors to County Glen plc (1994); National Irish Bank Ltd and NIB Financial Services Ltd (1998); and to Ansbacher (Cayman) Ltd (1999).

15 *Companies Report 2000*, Appendix 2. In addition to the companies involved in the Telecom and Greencore affairs, the Minister appointed an inspector to Bula Resources (Holdings) plc in 1997.

16 See *Dunnes Stores v Ryan* (1 February 2002, unreported), especially the judgments of Keane CJ at pp 36-37 of the transcript, and Murray J, at p 19, in respect of CA 1990, s 19. In *Dunnes Stores v Ryan* (5 June, 2002) Kearns J in the High Court held the old s 19(6) to be unconstitutional, though that provision has since been replaced by an apparently more constitutionally robust provision. See para **[14.076]** *ff*. Laffoy J has alluded to similar concerns about the constitutionality of CA 1990, s 22; see *Countyglen plc v Carway* [1998] 2 IR 542 at 551-552. See also para **[14.060]**.

consideration of the regime's success or failure. Investigations are costly and complex affairs which it seems, as a practical matter, can only be justified where substantial wrongdoing is suspected and where a high profile is attached. Even then, such a sledgehammer may not crack every nut.

Should any pitfalls in the investigation procedure become apparent in the future, the Minister has purported power in CA 1990, s 24 to introduce regulations 'to do anything which appears to him to be necessary or expedient' to remove any difficulty, to bring provisions of Part II into operation, or secure or facilitate the operation of any provision in Part II, and any such regulations may modify the provisions of Part II insofar as may be necessary for the carrying into effect of the new regulations. That provision smacks of unconstitionality, however, as an over-broad delegation of the law-making function reserved exclusively to the Oireachtas by Article 15 of the Constitution[17]. Not surprisingly the section appears never to have been utilised.

Architecture of the investigatory regime

[14.008] The following table details generally the various types of investigation possible under the Companies Acts:

Statutory Provision	*Investigation*	*Scope*	*Persons who may initiate*	*Outcome*
CA 1990, s 7	Court-appointed Inspector	Affairs of the company	The company; a director; a creditor, or the requisite number of members	Report to Court
CA 1990, s 8	Court-appointed inspector	Affairs of the company	Director of Corporate Enforcement	Report to Court
CA 1990, s 14	Inspector appointed by Director of Corporate Enforcement	True persons involved or interested in membership or control	Director of Corporate Enforcement	Report to Director of Corporate Enforcement
CA 1990, s 15	Inquiry by Director of Corporate Enforcement	Interests in shares or debentures	Director of Corporate Enforcement	Information
CA 1990, s 19	Inquiry by Director of Corporate Enforcement	Books or documents	Director of Corporate Enforcement	Information
CA 1990, s 66	Inspector Appointed by Director of Corporate Enforcement	Share or debenture dealings	Director of Corporate Enforcement	Report to Director of Corporate Enforcement

[17] *City View Press v An Comhairle Oiliúna* [1980] IR 381; *Cooke v Walsh* [1984] IR 710.

[14.009] As was noted above[18], and as can be seen from the above table, investigations fall into either of two broad categories: those which involve the appointment of an inspector; and those which do not. We turn, now, to consider each of these categories in further detail under the following headings:

[A] Inspections.

[B] Other Investigations and Inquiries.

[A] INSPECTIONS

[14.010] Part II of CA 1990 envisages two types of inspections. The first, which is ordered by the High Court, involves the appointment of an inspector or inspectors to investigate and report on the 'affairs' of a company. The second, which is ordered by the Director, involves the appointment of an inspector or inspectors to investigate and report on the narrower question of the true ownership or control of a company or its shares.

Although there are some differences between Court-ordered inspections on the one hand and those ordered by the Director on the other, the powers and status of inspectors appointed by either means are the same, and the provisions of CA 1990, Part II dealing with inspectors' powers apply to both kinds of inspector. Accordingly we deal here with the law relating to both kinds of inspections under the following headings, distinguishing between the two types as necessary:

1. Appointment of an inspector.
2. Scope of the inspection.
3. Conduct of the inspection.
4. Powers of the inspector.
5. Inspector's report.
6. Costs of the inspection.
7. Concurrent investigations.

Appointment of an inspector

[14.011] An inspector may be appointed in one of two ways:

(a) by the Court, or

(b) by the Director.

Each of these methods will now be considered in turn.

(a) Appointment of inspector by the Court

[14.012] Sections 7 and 8 of CA 1990, as amended, empower the Court to appoint one or more competent inspectors to investigate *the affairs of a company* and to report thereon in such a manner as the Court directs. The Court's power of appointment is exercisable notwithstanding that the company or body corporate to which it relates is in the throes of being wound up[19]. Under CA 1990, s 7(1), the Court's power of appointment is exercisable:

---

18 At para **[14.001]**.

19 CA 1990, s 8(2)(a).

'(a) in the case of a company having a share capital, on the application either of not less than 100 members or of a member or members holding not less than one-tenth of the paid up share capital of the company;

(b) in the case of a company not having a share capital, on the application of not less than one-fifth in number of the persons on the company's register of members;

(c) in any case, on the application of the company;

(d) in any case, on the application of a director of the company;

(e) in any case, on the application of a creditor of the company.'

Notably, the Court is not given a power to appoint an inspector of its own motion. Since private companies must restrict their membership to 50 and must have a share capital[20], neither (b) nor the first limb of (a) applies to private companies. All of CA 1990, s 7(1) relates only to companies formed and registered under the Companies Acts[21].

[14.013] These provisions have never been invoked, and the question arises as to whether they are, in fact, redundant? Persons who are in a position to seek the appointment of an inspector under CA 1990 Act, s 7 already have a more direct remedy against the company or the officers in default, such as an action under CA 1963, s 205[22] or a petition to have the company wound up under CA 1963, s 213[23]. Also, the risks involved in applying to the Court for an investigation may be too great to warrant invocation of the Court's powers, since the Court may require the applicant to put up security for the costs of the investigation[24].

[14.014] An application under CA 1990, s 7(1) must be made by originating notice of motion[25] and must be supported 'by such evidence as the Court may require, including such evidence as may be prescribed.'[26] *Prescribed* in this context means prescribed *by regulations*[27], but since no such regulations have been made, the grounds upon which the Court may make an order under s 7(1) are at present a matter for the Court alone. Presumably, the Court would wish to be satisfied that there was at least prima facie evidence of some irregularity in relation to the company's affairs[28]. Indeed, the Court might have regard to the grounds for appointment enumerated in CA 1990, s 8(1), which apply where the Director is the applicant[29]. It seems unlikely that the Court would order an

20 CA 1963, s 33(1). See Chapter 1, *The Private Company in Context*, para **[1.115]**.

21 CA 1963, s 2(1). See Chapter 2, *Formation, Registration and Conversion of Private Companies* .

22 See generally Chapter 19, *Shareholders' Remedies*.

23 See Chapter 25, *Winding Up Companies*.

24 See para **[14.014]**.

25 RSC Ord 75B, r 3(a). If the application is brought by a member or creditor, the notice must be served on the company and all of its directors; where brought by the company, the notice must be served on the directors; and where brought by a director, the notice must be served on the company and all other directors.

26 CA 1990, s 7(2).

27 CA 1990, s 3(1).

28 *Re Miles Aircraft Ltd (No 2)* [1948] WN 178; *Sage Holdings Ltd v The Unisec Group Ltd* (1982) 1 SA 337.

29 *Sage Holdings v The Unisec Group* (1982) 1 SA 337. On CA 1990, s 8(1), see para **[14.015]**.

investigation where it is clear that no useful result is likely to be achieved[30], but no doubt it would be difficult for the Court to determine at the application stage whether a useful result is likely or not. To this end, CA 1990, s 7(3) seeks to deter vexatious applications by empowering the Court, if it so chooses, to require applicants to put up security for the costs of the investigation. Such security must not exceed €317,435, but may not be less than €6,359[31]. The net effect of CA 1990, s 7(3) may be to deter all but the most assured of potential applicants from seeking the appointment of an inspector, an effect which rather militates against the purpose of having an investigation procedure in the first place.

[14.015] The Director of Corporate Enforcement may apply to the Court for the appointment of an inspector, but in his case the grounds for the application are expressly limited by statute. Section 8(1) of CA 1990, as amended[32], provides:

> 'Without prejudice to its powers under *section 7*, the Court may on the application of the Director appoint one or more competent inspectors (who may be or include an officer or officers of the Director) to investigate the affairs of a company and to report thereon in such manner as the Court shall direct, if the Court is satisfied that there are circumstances suggesting -
>
> (a) that its affairs are being or have been conducted with intent to defraud its creditors or the creditors of any other person or otherwise for a fraudulent or unlawful purpose or in an unlawful manner or in a manner which is unfairly prejudicial to some part of its members, or that any actual or proposed act or omission of the company (including an act or omission on its behalf) is or would be so prejudicial, or that it was formed for any fraudulent or unlawful purpose; or
>
> (b) that persons connected with its formation or the management of its affairs have in connection therewith been guilty of fraud, misfeasance or other misconduct towards it or towards its members; or
>
> (c) that its members have not been given all the information relating to its affairs which they might reasonably expect.'

Section 8(1) relates not only to companies formed and registered under the Companies Acts 1963-2001, but also to all bodies corporate incorporated outside the State which are carrying on, or have carried on, business in the State[33].

[14.016] Taking each of the grounds contained in CA 1990, s 8(1) in turn, it should first be observed that the reference to 'members' in sub-s (1)(a) includes persons to whom shares have been transferred or transmitted by operation of law though they are not registered as members[34]. For example, the interests of transferees of shares whom the directors wrongfully refuse to register as members may be taken into account[35]. It has been observed[36] euphemistically that the reference to 'unfairly prejudicial' in CA 1990, s 8(1)(a) is 'surprising', since the concept of unfair prejudice, whilst familiar to English

30 CA 1990, s 8(1), see para **[14.015]**.

31 On security for costs generally see Chapter 6, *Corporate Civil Litigation*, para **[6.019]** ff.

32 By CLEA 2001, s 21.

33 CA 1990, s 17.

34 CA 1990, s 8(2)(b).

35 See generally Chapter 16, *Share Transfers in Private Companies*, para **[16.037]***ff*.

36 MacCann, *Butterworths Ireland Companies Acts 1963-1990* (1993) p 542.

company law[37], is novel to Irish company law. The similarity of s 8(1) to the corresponding UK section[38] may provide a clue to this incursion; how the Irish courts will construe it remains to be seen. The scope of sub-s (1)(a) is broad, though the interests of members are better protected than those of creditors. Notably, past, present *or future* conduct which was, is, *or will be* unfairly prejudicial to the members may ground the Director's application, whereas only past or present conduct may be taken into account where the interests of creditors (of the company or otherwise) are concerned. Note also that evidence that the company was formed for a fraudulent or unlawful purpose may ground an application by the Director[39].

Secondly, CA 1990, s 8(1)(b) is clearly directed at situations where the promoters, directors, or other officers connected with the management of the company have breached their duties to the company[40]. Although less clear, it would also seem to encompass breaches by shadow directors. Significantly, the fraud, misfeasance or other misconduct may be towards the company *or* 'towards its members.' Perhaps, then, breach of a shareholders' agreement between the directors and some or all of the members could ground an application by the Director.

Thirdly, CA 1990, s 8(1)(c) refers to information relating to the affairs of the company which the members 'might reasonably expect.' Such information could include the annual accounts of the company and any group accounts[41], and also the information contained in the registers of the company which the members are entitled to inspect[42].

(b) Appointment of inspector by the Director

[14.017] Section 14 of CA 1990, as amended[43], empowers the Director to appoint an inspector to investigate a company for the purposes of determining the identity of the true persons who are financially interested in it or who are able to shape its policy. Section 14(1)–(3) provide:

> '(1) The Director may, subject to subsection (2), appoint one or more competent inspectors to investigate and report on the membership of any company and otherwise with respect to the company for the purpose of determining the true persons who are or have been financially interested in the success or failure (real or apparent) of the company or able to control or materially to influence the policy of the company.
>
> (2) An appointment may be made by the Director if he is of the opinion that there are circumstances suggesting that it is necessary-
>
> (a) for the effective administration of the law relating to companies;

37 The concept was introduced by the Companies Act 1985 (UK), ss 459-461 to replace the concepts of 'oppression' and 'disregard of interests,' both of which live on Ireland: see Chapter 19, *Shareholders' Remedies*, para **[19.006]***ff*.

38 Companies Act 1985 (UK), s 432.

39 As to the remedies of creditors and members where the company is formed for an unlawful purpose see principally Chapter 25, *Winding-Up Companies*, para **[25.089]**.

40 See generally Chapter 10, *Duties of Direcors and Other Officers*.

41 See Chapter 13, *Accounts and Auditors*.

42 See Chapter 15, *Shares and Membership*, para **[15.018]***ff* . One might have thought that these situations are already covered by CA 1990, s 8(1)(b).

43 By CLEA 2001, ss 14 and 26.

(b) for the effective discharge by the Director of his functions under any enactment; or

(c) in the public interest.

(3) The appointment of an inspector under this section may define the scope of his investigation, whether as respects the matters or the period to which it is to extend or otherwise, and in particular may limit the investigation to matters connected with particular shares or debentures.'

It will be noted that the Director must be satisfied as to at least one of the conditions contained in CA 1990, s 14(2) before making an appointment.

[14.018] Section 66 of CA 1990, as amended, also confers on the Director the power to appoint an inspector to investigate and report on dealings in shares or debentures where there are circumstances suggesting a contravention of CA 1990, ss 30, 53, or 64(3)-(5). Those sections place limitations or prohibitions on certain types of share dealings involving directors and connected persons, and which impose an obligation on such persons to register their interests in shares and debentures.

[14.019] In reaching a decision in any case as to whether an inspector ought to be appointed, it is thought that the Director is not bound to observe the rules of natural justice or to notify the subject of his intention[44], nor is he required to state in the warrant of appointment the reasons for the appointment[45]. The Director must, however, act bona fide. In *Desmond v Glackin (No 2)*[46], a case arising out of the Telecom affair, O'Hanlon J observed of the above provisions:

'These provisions appear to me to confer a discretion on the Minister when making such an appointment and expressing it to be made in the public interest, to spell out the matters to which the investigation is to extend, if he thinks fit to do so. I do not interpret the statute as imposing an obligation on the Minister to define in express terms the nature of the public interest upon which he relies as justifying the appointment.

Following the decision of the Supreme Court in *The State (Lynch) v Cooney* [1982] IR 337 at 361, it appears that an appointment made under the section might be open to challenge if it could be shown that any opinion formed by the Minister and relied upon as justifying the appointment was not *bona fide* held, or not factually sustainable, or unreasonable.'

In that case, the applicant, Dermot Desmond, a stockbroker, was instrumental in negotiating the purchase of a site in Ballsbridge, Dublin, for £4 million, by United Property Holdings Ltd (UPH). After the purchase, the property became vested in Chestvale Properties Ltd, a wholly owned subsidiary of UPH. UPH subsequently sold its subsidiary, Chestvale, to Delion Investment Dealings Ltd, a Cyprus registered company, for apparently £2.75 million. Delion immediately sold on to Hoddle Investments Ltd for £9.3 million, and Hoddle sold on to Telecom Éireann for £9.4 million, a transaction which Mr Desmond was, again, instrumental in negotiating. Public disquiet was aroused when it became apparent that Telecom Éireann, a Semi-State company, had paid over twice what the property had sold for less than a year previously, and a good deal of speculation arose

---

44 *Norwest Holst Ltd v Secretary of State for Trade* [1978] 3 All ER 280.

45 *Desmond v Glackin (No 2)* [1993] 3 IR 67; *R v Secretary of State for Trade, ex parté Perestrello* [1981] QB 19.

46 [1993] 3 IR 67.

as to the identity of the parties who had benefited from this financial coup. A committee of inspection was appointed by the Minister for Transport and Communications, which, though it succeeded in establishing much background information, was stonewalled by a number of parties. The committee recommended to the Minister that he appoint an inspector under CA 1990, and the Minister did so. The warrant of appointment of the inspector recited that the Minister was 'of the opinion that there are circumstances suggesting that it is necessary in the public interest' and that:

> '…the investigation shall extend to the investigation of any circumstances suggesting the existence of an arrangement or understanding which, though not legally binding, is likely to be observed in practice and which is relevant to the purposes of the investigation.'

Mr Desmond, who was subjected to close scrutiny by the inspector, applied for judicial review of the warrant of appointment on the basis that it did not state the nature of the public interest relied upon by the Minister in making the appointment. O'Hanlon J observed that the appointment of the inspector followed the recommendation of a committee of inspection which had published an interim report making the nature of the public interest involved very clear, and that the applicant had at no stage of the investigation requested information as to the public interest involved. Additionally, wide publicity had already been given to the matters of public interest leading up to the appointment of the inspector. The learned judge concluded that the validity of the appointment under CA 1990, s 14 was not dependent on the recital in the warrant of the nature of the public interest influencing the Minister to make the appointment[47].

Scope of the inspection

[14.020] In *Chestvale Properties Ltd v Glackin*, Murphy J held that CA 1990, Pt II had retrospective effect so that an inspector appointed under that Part could investigate the affairs, membership or control of a company for periods prior to the enactment of CA 1990, and unless the investigation amounted to more than a limited intrusion on the contractual rights of persons it could not be seen as an unjust attack on the constitutional property rights of citizens.

The scope of a Court-ordered inspection differs from that of an inspection ordered by the Director. The scope of each type of inspection will now be considered in turn.

(a) The scope of a Court-ordered inspection

[14.021] The Companies Act 1990 states that an investigation by a Court-appointed inspector is into the affairs of the company in order to enquire into matters specified by the Court, but does not elaborate further as to what is meant by the 'affairs' of the company. In the absence of an Irish authority, English precedent may prove useful here. In *R v Board of Trade, ex p St Martins Preserving Co Ltd*[48], a creditor of a company to which an inspector had been appointed under the Companies Act 1948, s 165(a)(1) (UK) sought an order of mandamus compelling the inspector to investigate the conduct of a receiver-manager as agent of the company in disposing of its assets. The Board of Trade contested the application on the basis that the actions of a receiver-manager for a debenture-holder were

---

47 The learned judge repeated his observations in *Probets v Glackin* [1993] 3 IR 134 at 139.

48 *R v Board of Trade, ex p St Martins Preserving Co Ltd* [1965] 1 QB 603.

not the 'affairs' of the company. Rejecting the latter contention, Phillimore J granted the order sought, saying:

> 'What are "its affairs" when the company is in full control? They must surely include its goodwill, its profits or losses, its contracts and assets including its shareholding in and ability to control the affairs of a subsidiary, or perhaps in the latter regard a sub-subsidiary...How were "its affairs" changed on the appointment of a receiver and manager of the property of the applicant company by the debentureholders? Did its affairs cease to be its affairs and become solely the affairs of the receiver and manager or of the debentureholders? I think not. Could the debentureholder and/or its receiver and manager play "ducks and drakes" with "its affairs" without regard to any interests of the shareholders of the applicant company?...In short what the receiver and manager does may in a narrow sense be his affair, but it is also the affair of the company in the broad and natural meaning of the phrase "its affairs". He acts in the name of the company - what he does may ruin its shareholders or leave them with some prospect of future recovery. The fact that an action of the receiver and manager may be primarily designed to serve the interests of the debentureholder and to that extent be his affair does not in my judgment prevent it being an affair of the company, whose future may depend upon such action carried out in its name. If he is the agent as provided for in the debenture, why should he not be answerable for his conduct of "its affairs"?'

'Affairs', therefore, has a broad meaning: it extends to the conduct of receiver-managers appointed by creditors to the company; and may include the affairs of subsidiary companies under the company's control. Of course, the order appointing the inspector will state specific matters to be enquired into.

Where there is doubt, the inspector may from time to time apply to the Court under CA 1990, s 7(4) for such directions or otherwise as it thinks fit with a view to ensuring that the investigation is carried out as quickly and inexpensively as possible. Such applications may be heard otherwise than in public if there is a danger that disclosure of the application would prejudice sensitive enquiries. In *Re Countyglen plc*[49] Murphy J considered that the majority of such applications were administrative applications rather than administrations of justice and that, accordingly, the Constitution did not require them to be heard in public.

[14.022] As was observed in the preceding paragraph, the 'affairs' of a company may include the affairs of *subsidiaries* under its control. Whether the scope of a Court-ordered investigation extends *without more* to the investigation of the broader category of *related* companies (within the meaning of CA 1990, s 140(5))[50] and related bodies corporate is unclear, but would seem to depend upon whether the related company is under the control of the company under investigation, since the investigation must relate to the 'affairs' of the company under investigation.

[14.023] In this regard, CA 1990, s 9, as amended[51], comes to the assistance of the inspector who thinks it is necessary to investigate a related company. Section 9 provides:

> '(1) If an inspector appointed under section 7 or 8 to investigate the affairs of a company thinks it necessary for the purposes of his investigation to investigate also the affairs of any

---

49 *Re Countyglen plc* [1995] 1 IR 220.

50 CA 1990, s 3(1). See Chapter 27, *The Realisation and Distribution of Assets in a Winding Up*, para **[27.107]***ff*.

51 By CLEA 2001, s 22.

> other body corporate which is related to such company, he shall, with the approval of the Court, have power so to do, and shall report on the affairs of the other body corporate so far as he thinks the results of his investigation thereof are relevant to the investigation of the affairs of the first-mentioned company.
>
> (2) For the purposes of this section, a body corporate which is related to a company includes a body corporate with which the company has a commercial relationship, and a commercial relationship exists where goods or services are sold or given by one party to another.'

Thus, with the approval of the Court, the investigation can be extended to the affairs of related companies. Section 9, however, applies only to related companies and bodies corporate which are formed and registered within the State or which have been incorporated outside the State and are carrying on, or have carried on, business within the State[52]. Where the Court grants approval under CA 1990, s 9, the inspector must also report on the related company's or body corporate's affairs so far as he thinks the results of his investigation are relevant to his principal investigation[53].

(b) The scope of an inspection ordered by the Director

[14.024] Section 14(1) of CA 1990 states that an inspection ordered by the Director is to be into 'the *membership* of any company and otherwise with respect to the company *for the purpose of determining the true persons* who are or have been financially interested in the success or failure (real or apparent) of the company or able to control or materially to influence the policy of the company.' The purpose of such an investigation is to look behind the separate legal personality of the company, as McCarthy J observed in *Desmond v Glackin (No 2)*[54]:

> 'Since the decision in *Salomon v Salomon & Co Ltd* [1897] AC 22, efforts at lifting the corporate veil have largely come from the legislature rather than the courts. Section 14, in my judgment, clearly entitled the Minister through his inspector to tear the veil of secrecy of ownership from the company and identify those financially interested in the success or failure of the company, whatever *personae* any such person may have.'

Such an investigation may prove useful in establishing whether directors or other officers of a company have hidden behind another company when acting in breach of their duties to the company. Section 14(4) further provides:

> 'Subject to the terms of an inspector's appointment his powers shall extend to the investigation of any circumstances suggesting the existence of an arrangement or understanding which, though not legally binding, is or was observed or likely to be observed in practice and which is relevant to the purposes of his investigation.'

Clearly, then, the scope of an investigation ordered by the Director extends to the identification not only of the persons legally interested in the success or failure of a company, or in its control, but to those who *in practice* are so interested. Investigations under s 14 are not restricted to Irish companies: CA 1990, s 17 extends the scope of such

---

52 CA 1990, s 17; See also *Desmond v Glackin (No 2)* [1993] 3 IR 67 at 125, per McCarthy J, and *Minister for Justice v Siúcre Éireann, Greencore plc* [1992] 2 IR 215, which is discussed at para **[14.063]**.

53 CA 1990, s 9.

54 *Desmond v Glackin (No 2)* [1993] 3 IR 67 at 128-129.

investigations to all bodies corporate incorporated outside the State which are carrying on, or have carried on, business within the State, or have at any time carried on business therein as if they were companies registered under CA 1963, subject to any necessary modification[55].

[14.025] The special purpose of an investigation under CA 1990, s 14 has the effect of extending the scope of the investigation beyond the examination of the companies named or identified in the inspector's warrant of appointment. This is because the expression 'true persons' in CA 1990, s 14(1) refers to natural persons. In *Lyons, Keleghan and Murphy v Curran*[56], Blayney J explained:

> 'In my opinion the correct construction of this subsection is that an inspector appointed under it to investigate a particular company has the duty and power to investigate the membership of the company for the purpose of determining who are or have been financially interested in the success or failure of the company. And investigating the membership is not simply for the purpose of ascertaining who are the members. It is for the purpose of determining who are the true persons financially interested in the success or failure of the company. That would clearly cover ascertaining the identity of the beneficiary, where shares are held by a person or persons as trustees, or by a corporate trustee, but in my opinion it also covers ascertaining the identity of the persons entitled to the shares of a corporate member. Otherwise it would be necessary to conclude that where an inspector had ascertained that some or all of the shares in the company he was investigating belonged to another company, he had finished his investigation; he had determined the true persons financially interested in the success or failure of the company. In my opinion that could not be so. I am satisfied that the phrase "the true persons" means the real individuals who are financially interested, and cannot refer to a company. So, where an inspector finds a company as shareholder in the company he is investigating, he must go further and seek to determine the persons who are the beneficial owners of that company.'

Accordingly, an inspector appointed to investigate the membership of a company named in the warrant of appointment may, *without further approval of the Director*, investigate the membership of a company *not* named in the warrant, if such investigation is necessary for the purpose of enquiring into the identity of the natural persons interested in the success or failure, or involved in the control, of the company under investigation. Indeed, the inspector may, if needs be, extend his investigation to the personal business affairs of natural persons. In *Desmond v Glackin (No 2)*[57], O'Hanlon J found that the inspector was 'fully justified', having regard to the scope of his duty, in investigating the personal business affairs of the applicant. All the evidence made available to the inspector led him to believe that the applicant had master-minded all the relevant transactions in the Telecom Affair.

[14.026] These extended investigative powers create a curious interrelationship between CA 1990, ss 14(1) and 9[58] as applied to investigations under CA 1990, s 14 by s 14(5).

---

55 As to 'carry on business' see the observations of Lynch J in *Minister for Justice v Siúcre Éireann, Greencore plc* [1992] 2 IR 215, discussed at para **[14.063]**.

56 *Lyons, Keleghan and Murphy v Curran* [1993] ILRM 375. Blayney J's views were endorsed by McCarthy J in the Supreme Court in *Desmond v Glackin (No 2)* [1993] 3 IR 67 at 127-128.

57 [1993] 3 IR 67.

58 See para **[14.023]**.

That inter-relationship was considered by Blayney J in *Lyons, Keleghan and Murphy v Curran*. The respondent in that case, Mr Maurice Curran, was appointed by the Minster for Industry and Commerce under CA 1990, s 14 to investigate and report on the activities of a number of companies involved in the 'Greencore Affair', including a company called Gladebrook. That affair concerned the purchase of shares in Sugar Distributor Holdings Ltd by Gladebrook, and the subsequent resale of those shares to Siúcre Éireann cpt (Irish Sugar plc) at a substantial profit to Gladebrook. Gladebrook was part owned by Talmino, a foreign company, which was not named in the warrant of appointment. Mr Curran investigated Talmino - without obtaining prior approval under CA 1990, s 9 - and concluded in his report that Mr Chris Comerford, a director of Siúcre Éireann, was beneficial owner of Talmino. The applicants sought an order of certiorari quashing Mr Curran's report, on the grounds that Mr Curran had not been appointed to investigate Talmino nor had he obtained approval under CA 1990, s 9. They argued that if the inspector could proceed without the necessity to have regard to s 9, then that section was superfluous.

Blayney J held that the inspector had both the power and a duty to investigate Talmino under the terms of his appointment, and he rejected the argument that CA 1990, s 9 was superfluous. He said:

> 'In finding that the respondent was entitled to report on Talmino as he has done, I am necessarily rejecting the applicants' submission that if the respondent was entitled to investigate Talmino it meant that s 9 was unnecessary. I will give briefly my reasons for taking this view. In my opinion s 9 applies to a situation different from that in which the respondent found himself in regard to Talmino. The respondent had to investigate Talmino in order to fulfil the purpose for which he was appointed. That is very different from the position of an inspector availing of s 9. Such an inspector simply "*thinks* it necessary for the purposes of his investigation to investigate also the membership" of another body corporate. He does not *know* that it is necessary, which was the respondent's position. An inspector seeking to investigate another body corporate under s 9 might not be correct in his view that it was necessary, and because of this further authority in the form of the approval of the Minister is required. So there is a clear category of cases for which s 9 is needed, and an illustration of this is the respondent's application in the present case to the Minister for his approval to investigate Siúcre Éireann cpt.'[59]

Accordingly, where an inspector *knows* that the investigation of a related company not named in the order of appointment is necessary for the performance of his function, he may proceed to investigate it without obtaining prior approval under CA 1990, s 9, but where he merely *thinks, but does not know*, that such an investigation is necessary, he must obtain approval. In practice, of course, it will be almost impossible for anyone challenging the inspector's acts to prove that the inspector does not 'know' that investigation of the related company is not necessary for the purposes of his investigation[60], so CA 1990, s 9 may, in reality, be redundant after all.

---

[59] Emphasis added.

[60] See McGrath, 'Investigations under the Companies Act' (1993) ILT 264 at 265.

Where the inspector does obtain approval under CA 1990, s 9, the section requires him to report on his findings as regards the related company 'so far as he *thinks*[61] the results' of his investigation are relevant.

[14.027] The advantage of regarding CA 1990, s 9 in this way is that an inspector may extend his investigation to the membership of other companies which are *not* related *in any way* to the companies named in the warrant of appointment. In this respect, investigations under CA 1990, s 14 may be said to differ from Court-ordered investigations, since a Court-appointed inspector may only investigate the 'affairs' (in the broadly construed meaning of that word[62]) of the company to which he is appointed, and, with the approval of the Court, related companies which he 'thinks' necessary for the purposes of his investigation. It remains to be seen whether the subtleties of Blayney J's distinction between 'knowing' and 'thinking' will be applied to Court-ordered investigations.

Conduct of the inspection

[14.028] Is an inspector required to conduct his investigation in the same manner as a judicial inquiry in a Court? Must he adhere strictly to the rules of natural justice during the conduct of the investigation? It would appear that the answer is No – at least until the investigation reaches a stage where adverse conclusions are to be drawn against a person or body. Thereafter, persons in respect of whom such conclusions are to be drawn must be afforded an opportunity to review and test the evidence against them, and to give evidence themselves.

The general issue came before the Supreme Court in the 1970s in *Re Haughey*[63] in connection with the rights of a witness appearing before the Dáil Public Accounts Committee. The Court concluded that the applicant in that case, Mr Padraic Haughey, was entitled to representation where the proceedings had reached the stage where[64]:

> '...Mr Haughey is more than a mere witness. The true analogy, in terms of High Court procedure, is not that of a witness but of a party. Mr Haughey's conduct is the very subject matter of the committee's examination and is to be the subject matter of the Committee's report.'

In those circumstances, the Court held, the applicant was entitled not only to legal representation, but to cross-examine witnesses, to introduce rebutting evidence, and to address the committee in his own defence. While this approach represents the view of the Supreme Court, the case was not concerned with the duties of inspectors appointed under the Companies Acts. As shall be seen, however, it has had a significant influence on the Courts' approach to investigations under the Companies Acts.

---

61 If one were to maintain Blayney J's distinction between 'knows' and 'thinks', one might conclude that the inspector is under no obligation to report on his findings vis-à-vis the related company where he knows that the results are relevant to the investigation of the companies named in the warrant of appointment.

62 See para **[14.021]**.

63 *Re Haughey* [1971] IR 217. See also *Chestvale Properties Ltd v Glackin* [1993] 3 IR 35 at 50.

64 [1971] IR 217 at 263, per Ó Dálaigh CJ.

[14.029] In *Re Pergamon Press Ltd*[65] the English Court of Appeal was asked to consider whether the directors of Pergamon Press Ltd, which was under investigation by an inspector appointed by the Board of Trade, were entitled to assurances that the investigation would be conducted in the same manner as a judicial inquiry in a court of law, so that the directors could see the transcripts of the evidence of witnesses adverse to them and could cross-examine those witnesses. Counsel for the inspector submitted that the rules of natural justice did not apply to an investigation. Lord Denning rejected that argument, saying:

> 'I cannot accept counsel for the inspector's submission. It is true, of course, that the inspectors are not a court of law. Their proceedings are not judicial proceedings: see *Re Grosvenor and West End Railway Terminus Hotel Co Ltd* (1897) 76 LT 337. They are not even quasi-judicial for they decide nothing; they determine nothing. They only investigate and report. They sit in private and are not entitled to admit the public to their meetings: see *Hearts of Oak Assurance Co Ltd v AG* [1932] AC 392. They do not even decide whether there is a *prima facie* case...But this should not lead us to minimise the significance of their task. They have to make out a report which may have wide repercussions. They may, if they think fit, make findings of fact which are very damaging to those whom they name. They may accuse some; they may condemn others; they may ruin reputations or careers. Their report may lead to judicial proceedings. It may expose persons to criminal prosecutions or to civil actions. It may bring about the winding up of the company and be used itself as material for the winding up: see *Re SRA Properties Ltd* [1967] 2 All ER 615...When they do make their report the board are bound to send a copy of it to the company and the board may, in their discretion publish it, if they think fit, to the public at large. Seeing that their work and their report may lead to such consequences I am clearly of opinion that the inspectors must act fairly. This is a duty which rests on them, as on many other bodies, although they are not judicial nor quasi-judicial, but only administrative...The inspectors can obtain information in any way which they think best, but before they condemn or criticise a man they must give him a fair opportunity for correcting or contradicting what is said against him. They need not quote chapter and verse. An outline of the charge will usually suffice.'

In *Maxwell v Department of Trade & Industry*[66], a further case arising out of the Pergamon Press Affair, Lord Denning explained that a 'fair opportunity' meant *not* that the inspector must prepare a tentative report and circulate it to the persons to be criticised or condemned; *nor* did it mean that every relevant statement of other witnesses must be put to that person so as to give him an opportunity of answering them. Rather, the inspector is under a duty to do what is fair *to the best of his ability.* Consequently, where the inspector bona fide overlooks something of substance and fails to put it to the person to be criticised in the report, he has not failed in his duty to give a fair opportunity.

[14.030] A somewhat similar approach to the level of compliance with the rules of natural justice required of an inspector was taken by Murphy J in *Chestvale Properties Ltd v Glackin*[67]. In that case the applicant contended that the inspector, a solicitor by profession, was disqualified from acting as inspector because his firm had previously acted as

---

65 *Re Pergamon Press Ltd* [1970] 3 All ER 589.

66 *Maxwell v Department of Trade & Industry* [1974] QB 523, [1974] 2 All ER 122. See Pennington, 'Investigations under the Companies Acts and the Pergamon Affair' 118 Sol J 507.

67 *Chestvale Properties Ltd v Glackin* [1993] 3 IR 35.

solicitors for a Mr Doherty, one of the persons who claimed to be interested in one of the companies under investigation. Murphy J referred[68] to the Court of Appeal's decision in *Re Pergamon Press*, which he thought 'helpful', and to the decisions of the High Court in *The State (Shannon Atlantic Fisheries) v McPolin*[69] *and the Supreme Court in Re Haughey*[70]. He then continued:

> 'I think it would be correct to say that in every one of those cases the Court concluded that the investigating authority was bound to exercise an appropriate measure of natural justice. On the other hand it is, I believe, equally clear that *the findings in that regard were directed and relevant only to certain issues* within the various investigations and were not intended to be applied and could not in fact be applied to each and every inquiry or communication emanating from the investigating authority.'

The learned judge concluded that the claim in the case before him was premature, since it was commenced when the investigation was only at a very preliminary and exploratory stage, at which stage it was too early to say whether the inspector had to 'enter any verdict' on any issue concerning Mr Doherty in the report. He said:

> 'In these circumstances it must be presumed that the respondent (unlike Inspector McPolin in *The State (Shannon Atlantic Fisheries Ltd) v McPolin* [1976] IR 93) will not have to "enter a verdict" on any issue between claimants to the shares in question. Even if the presumption were otherwise and that one should anticipate a stage being reached at which the respondent would find it necessary to make a choice as between conflicting claims, it is clear that that stage has not yet been reached. Accordingly the present application is premature insofar as it is based upon the contention that the inspector is engaged in a task which at present involves him in a quasi-judicial function. The respondents also contend that the applicants have no locus standi to challenge the impartiality of the respondent vis-à-vis Mr Doherty. In my view this point too is well founded. The case based on bias is constructed solely by reference to the injustice which Mr Doherty foresees he would suffer if and when the respondent is called upon to adjudicate on a contentious issue between him and some other party as yet unidentified. Whilst I have accepted that circumstances could exist in which bias would be perceived, it is only the parties whose rights would be affected by the adverse decision who could challenge the procedure in which it was reached.'

Notably, in contrast to Lord Denning's view in *Re Pergamon Press*, above, the learned judge was of the opinion that the inspector's role could become quasi-judicial at some stage in the proceedings.

[14.031] In *Re National Irish Bank Ltd (Under Investigation)*[71] Shanley J adopted the approach employed by Murphy J in *Chestvale Properties Ltd v Glackin*, though this time in the context of inspectors appointed by the High Court rather than by the Minister (or now by the Director). The inspectors in this case had expressly proposed a two-stage process in their investigation: the first being an information gathering exercise, which would occur in private; the second, arising only when the first stage indicated the possibility that adverse conclusions might be drawn against any persons, would afford the

68 [1993] 3 IR 35 at 49.
69 *The State (Shannon Atlantic Fisheries) v McPolin* [1976] IR 93.
70 *Re Haughey* [1971] IR 217.
71 *Re National Irish Bank Ltd (Under Investigation)* [1999] 3 IR 145, [1999] 1 ILRM 321.

individuals at risk an opportunity to attend, hear evidence, cross-examine witnesses, and give evidence themselves. Shanley J considered that the procedures adopted by the inspectors accorded with the requirements of natural and constitutional justice and fair procedures. One of the employees of National Irish Bank Ltd disputed that the investigation could maintain its character as a mere information gathering exercise when the media had already levelled a wide range of criminal accusations against the bank and its employees. Shanley J noted, however, that such anonymous accusations had not arisen in the course of the investigation, nor were they accepted as evidence in the investigation. Accordingly the challenge on procedural grounds was unfounded.

[14.032] That approach was subsequently endorsed by Kelly J in further proceedings arising out of the same investigation. In *Re National Irish Bank Ltd and National Irish Bank Financial Services Ltd*[72], the companies contended that the investigations could not be considered to be a mere information gathering exercise given that the Oireachtas had passed the Comptroller and Auditor General and Committees of the Houses of the Oireachtas (Special Provisions) Act 1998 which provided for a special investigation by the Comptroller and Auditor General and the Revenue Commissioners into the evasion of Deposit Interest Retention Tax ('DIRT') by certain financial institutions, including the National Irish Bank companies.

By this stage the inspectors had produced their second interim report to the Court, in which they noted that some of the evidence of employees pointed to the willing opening and maintenance of fictitious non-resident bank accounts for Irish resident customers of the bank, and the facilitation of offshore bank accounts for customers in associated companies of the bank outside the State. Of particular significance was the fact that in their report the inspectors expressly emphasised that they had 'not yet formed any concluded view on these matters' and that they could not do so until they had had the opportunity of interviewing the relevant employees of the bank. Until such time, they said, 'it is not possible even to commence the process of considering whether the evidence should be accepted or not.'

Kelly J concluded that the companies' objections were unfounded. He quoted from Lord Denning's judgment in *Maxwell v Department of Trade & Industry*[73] as follows:

> 'Remember what it is not. It is not a trial of anyone, nor anything like it. There is no accused person. There is no prosecutor. There is no charge. It is not like a disciplinary proceeding before a professional body. Nor is it like an application to expel a man from a trade union or a club, or anything of that kind. It is not even like a committee which considers there is a *prima facie* case against a person. It is simply an investigation, without anyone being accused.'[74]

Kelly J continued as follows[75]:

---

72 *Re National Irish Bank Limited and National Irish Bank Financial Services Ltd* [1999] 3 IR 190, [1999] 2 ILRM 443.

73 *Maxwell v Department of Trade & Industry* [1974] 2 All ER 122.

74 [1974] 2 All ER 122 at 127.

75 [1999] 3 IR 190 at 215.

'Insofar as this jurisdiction is concerned, that, in my view, is a correct summary of the position which obtains at least insofar as the investigatory stage of the inspectors' task is concerned. Once one moves into the second stage then, whilst the investigation is not transformed into an adversarial hearing, nonetheless fair procedures have to be observed insofar as any adverse conclusions may be drawn in relation to individuals. The procedure which the inspectors have outlined as one which they will follow if such a stage is reached is in complete compliance with their obligations to observe fair procedures under the relevant jurisprudence. It follows therefore, that I take precisely the same view as Shanley J that there is no entitlement to invoke the rights established in *Re Haughey* at the information gathering stage of the inspectors' work.'

As the investigation had not entered the second stage, the companies' objections were, at best, premature. Moreover, the challenge that the investigation had in fact entered the second stage was held to be unfounded. Kelly J observed[76] that the mere making of an allegation under oath does not carry the investigation into the second stage:

'It is not the mere fact of making an allegation under oath which elevates the status of an accusation to one which calls for a response. What brings that about is a determination by the inspectors (a) that they will admit such an allegation as evidence and (b) that the admission of it may give rise to adverse conclusions being drawn against the party accused.'

[14.033] There are good reasons for this approach. Were an inspector bound to give every witness an opportunity of cross-examining the other witnesses, his ability to get to the heart of the matter efficiently would be substantially impaired. As one commentator[77] has observed, a requirement to proceed in accordance with the full rules of natural justice in the same manner as the Court would be:

'...a very impractical one, because when you are conducting one of these investigations, you don't know when you are getting evidence from the witnesses whether anybody has done anything wrong or whether it is just bad luck and it may not be until you have examined the fifty-fourth witness that you suddenly get the information which enables you to discover that the second, third or fourth witness has told you a pack of lies and that, in fact, he is the man who has stolen all the company's funds.

Of course, I am not suggesting that a fair investigator would not, in those circumstances, seek to recall the man whom he examined second, third or fourth. Of course, he would...'

Powers of the inspector

[14.034] Section 10 of CA 1990 confers three wide powers on inspectors appointed either by the Court or by the Director, namely:

(a) To require the production of books, documents and information relating to the company.

(b) To examine persons on oath.

(c) To certify refusal to comply with requests for the production of books, documents and information or attendance before the inspector.

Further, there is a fourth power, given only to Court-appointed inspectors:

76 [1999] 3 IR 190 at 215.

77 Judge Sir Richard Eggleston, Chairman of the Australian Company Law Reform Committee. See [1971] 45 ALJ 513 at 520.

(d) To require the production of books and documents relating to directors' bank accounts.

Each of these powers will now be considered in turn.

(a) Books, documents and information relating to the company

[14.035] Section 10(1) of CA 1990, as amended[78], places a duty on officers and agents of the company to produce books and documents, to attend before the inspector, and otherwise to assist with the investigation. It provides:

> 'It shall be the duty of all officers and agents of the company and of all officers and agents of any other body corporate whose affairs are investigated by virtue of section 9 to produce to the inspectors all books and documents of or relating to the company, or, as the case may be, the other body corporate which are in their custody or power, to attend before the inspectors when required so to do and otherwise to give to the inspectors all assistance in connection with the investigation which they are reasonably able to give; but where any such person claims a lien on books or documents produced by the person, the production shall be without prejudice to the lien.'

Section 10(7) of CA 1990 provides that the reference in sub-s (1) to 'officers and agents' includes past, as well as present, officers and agents, and that 'agents' includes the company's bankers, solicitors and persons employed as auditors, accountants, book keepers or taxation advisors, whether they are officers of the company or not.

[14.036] The obligations imposed by CA 1990, s 10(1) are two-fold[79]. First of all, there is an obligation to produce books and documents; and secondly, there is an obligation to attend and give viva voce evidence. When giving oral evidence, the obligation is to provide all assistance in relation to the investigation.

Of course, the inspector and the officer or agent may have differing views as to what information may be of 'assistance in connection with the investigation'. In this regard, it seems that the officer or agent must produce all information which in his *honest opinion* may be of assistance to the inspector[80]. While this test might at first appear to favour the ignorant or the naive, it would seem to be the case that the officer or agent must have regard to the information stipulated in the inspector's request when forming his opinion[81]. There is something to be said for the latter approach: where the inspector makes a broad request, the officer or agent must not withhold any such information which he honestly believes may be of assistance; but where, however, the inspector identifies particular books or documents, or a particular class of books or documents, the officer or agent must comply with the request - since it would be impossible for him to form an honest belief that the specified information *may not* be of assistance.

---

78 By CLEA 2001, s 23.

79 See McGrath, 'Investigations under the Companies Act' (1993) ILT 264, where the author discusses the views of Murphy J in *Chestvale Properties Ltd v Glackin (No 2)* [1993] 23 IR 35. Murphy J's construction of CA 1990, s 10(1) met with the approval of Costello J in *Glackin v Trustee Savings Bank* [1993] 3 IR 55.

80 McGrath, (1993) ILT 264.

81 McGrath here relies on the words of Murphy J in *Probets v Glackin* (25 May 1992, unreported), High Court.

[14.037] Section 10(2) of CA 1990, as amended, extends these duties to persons, who are *not* officers or agents, whom the inspector considers to be in possession of relevant information, books or documents. It provides:

> 'If the inspectors consider that a person other than an officer or agent of the company or other body corporate is or may be in possession of any information concerning its affairs, they may require that person to produce to them any books or documents in his custody or power relating to the company or other body corporate, to attend before them and otherwise to give them all assistance in connection with the investigation which he is reasonably able to give; and it shall be the duty of that person to comply with the requirement; but where any such person claims a lien on books or documents produced by the person, the production shall be without prejudice to the lien.'

[14.038] *Any* books and documents may be required by the inspector under CA 1990, s 10(1) and (2), regardless of whether they are the property of the company. As Murphy J observed in *Chestvale Properties Ltd v Glackin*[82]:

> '...the fact that particular books and documents may be properly identified as being the property of or relating to one company does not necessarily preclude them from relating also to another company.'

That said, however, CA 1990, s 23(1) expressly provides that nothing in Part II of the Act is to be taken as compelling any person to divulge information which, in the opinion of the Court, he would be entitled to refuse to produce on the grounds of legal professional privilege.

[14.039] Other duties of confidentiality are not so closely protected. In *Glackin v Trustee Savings Bank*[83] Costello J held that a bank may not refuse to co-operate on the basis that to do so would breach a duty of confidentiality which it owes a customer. In that case, the plaintiff-inspector formed the opinion that part of the proceeds of one of the transactions in the Telecom Affair had been credited to accounts in a branch of the defendant bank. In a wide-ranging request to the bank pursuant to CA 1990, s 10(2), he sought details of those accounts, including the name of the account holder and the mandate under which the accounts had been opened. The bank, on the advice of its solicitors, failed to respond to the requests. In an application by Mr Glackin to have the failure enquired into, Costello J said[84]:

> 'It seems to me that the bank has misunderstood its statutory duty. Its statutory duty has been made perfectly clear in the judgment of Murphy J in *Chestvale Properties Ltd. v Glackin (No 2)* (Unreported, High Court, Murphy J 10th March 1992). It is a duty to give assistance if requested to do so under s 10, sub-s 2 of the Act of 1990. It is not permitted to refuse assistance, because of a contractual arrangement with a customer which may have involved a term of confidentiality.
>
> The Oireachtas has made perfectly clear, to my mind, what people, statutory organisations such as the Trustee Savings Bank, are required to do. They are required to assist the inspector, who has been appointed by the Minister [or the Court, as the case may be]. They are not entitled to obstruct him and they must observe his requests. They have a statutory

82 *Chestvale Properties Ltd v Glackin* [1993] 3 IR 35 at 53.

83 *Glackin v Trustee Savings Bank* [1993] 3 IR 55.

84 [1993] 3 IR 55 at 62–63.

> obligation to do so. They are not entitled to ask their customer whether or not the customer objects. Whatever contractual arrangement there has been between the bank and the customer has been clearly over-ridden by the provisions put into this section by the Oireachtas and the manner in which it should comply with the request has been made clear by Mr Justice Murphy. They are to give assistance to the inspector when requested to do so...What the bank has to do, and other persons who are subject to a request by an inspector under the section, is to comply with the request and to assist the inspector in the work which he has to perform and which is clearly set out in the section.'

Accordingly, only that privilege which is expressly mentioned in CA 1990, namely, legal professional privilege, may be relied upon in refusing an inspector's request[85] - and even then only if the Court is of the opinion that it is so privileged.

[14.040] Where a person fails or refuses to produce books, documents or information in accordance with either of CA 1990, s 10(1) and (2), the inspector may certify the refusal and apply to Court for an order directing the production of the books etc[86].

[14.041] A demand by the inspector under CA 1990, sub-ss 10(1) or (2) will not amount to an abuse of his statutory powers if the demand follows closely the terms of the Act. In *Chestvale Properties Ltd v Glackin*[87] the applicants contended that the demand made by the inspector for books and documents was expressed in such general terms and imposed such time limits as to amount to an abuse of the inspector's statutory powers. Murphy J rejected that contention on the facts before him, saying:

> 'Whatever argument might be constructed on the basis of any such analysis, the reality is that both the bankers and the solicitors were able to comply with the demand and within the time limits prescribed by the inspector. Neither the bankers nor the solicitors raised any objection based upon administrative difficulties. Their only concern was to ensure that in performing the obligations which appeared to be imposed upon them by statute that they did not neglect the duty which they had to their clients or former clients as the case may be.
>
> In the circumstances it seems to me that there is no substance in this particular ground. Furthermore it would be difficult to sustain a challenge to the validity of the exercise of a statutory power which follows so closely the terms of the section by which it was conferred.'[88]

In so saying, however, it seems that the learned judge implicitly recognised the possibility that a substantial demand by the inspector might amount to an abuse of power in appropriate circumstances.

(b) Examination of persons on oath

[14.042] Section 10(4) of CA 1990 provides:

---

85 See also *Re an Inquiry under the Company Securities (Insider Dealing) Act 1985* [1988] AC 660 where it was held in England that a journalist could not rely on a wish not to disclose his sources as a ground for refusal to comply with a request from an inspector appointed under the Company Securities (Insider Dealing) Act 1985 (UK).

86 See para **[14.046]**.

87 *Chestvale Properties Ltd v Glackin* [1993] 3 IR 35.

88 [1993] 3 IR 35 at 54.

> 'An inspector may examine on oath, either by word of mouth or on written interrogatories, the officers and agents of the company or other body corporate and such person as is mentioned in subsection (2) in relation to its affairs and may –
>
> (a) administer an oath accordingly,
>
> (b) reduce the answers of such person to writing and require him to sign them.'

There is old authority in *Re Redbreast Preserving Co (Ireland) Ltd*[89] for the proposition that the examination does not have to be held in public; however the constitutional propriety of that decision was doubted by Walsh J in *Re R Ltd*[90] in the light of the constitutional requirement that justice, where possible, must be administered in public. It is hardly the case, however, that an inspector could be regarded as administering justice even though he may have quasi-judicial functions[91].

[14.043] In *Probets v Glackin*[92], another case arising out of the Telecom Affair, the applicant sought an order prohibiting the inspector from investigating the membership and control of Freezone Investments Ltd by taking evidence on oath on the basis that he had earlier voluntarily signed and submitted to the inspector a statutory declaration detailing the information in his possession. O'Hanlon J accepted that such a declaration *might* be sufficient for the inspector's purposes in the course of his investigation, but it could *not* be relied upon in judicial review proceedings such as this to prevent the inspector from seeking subsequent evidence on oath. He said:

> 'The applicants appear to take the view that the first respondent should accept at face value, and without further investigation, matters which have been deposed to by statutory declaration, or at least that there is some onus on him to show a *prima facie* case for disbelieving the averments made before continuing to seek further evidence to confirm or disprove the accuracy of what he has been told. In my opinion, this is not a correct interpretation of an inspector's functions when conducting an investigation.'

Accordingly, an examination under oath cannot be avoided by simply swearing a declaration or affidavit as to the facts in issue.

[14.044] The privilege against self-incrimination *cannot* be invoked by a witness as a valid basis for a refusal to answer a question put to him by the inspector. This is of particular significance, since CA 1990, s 18 provides that any answer given by a person to a question put to him in exercise of the powers under CA 1990, s 10 may be used in evidence against him.

In *Re National Irish Bank Ltd (Under Investigation)*[93] the Supreme Court held that the privilege against self-incrimination is a judge-made rule which can be abrogated by the legislature, and that CA 1990, ss 10 and 18 have the effect of so abrogating the privilege.

---

89 *Re Redbreast Preserving Co (Ireland) Ltd* 91 ILTR 12. See also *Hearts of Oak Assurance Co v AG* [1932] AC 392.

90 *Re R Ltd* [1988] IR 126.

91 See eg *McDonald v Bord na gCon (No 2)* [1965] IR 217.

92 *Probets v Glackin* [1993] 3 IR 134.

93 *Re National Irish Bank Ltd (Under Investigation)* [1999] 3 IR 169, [1999] 1 ILRM 321. See Dillon-Malone, 'Voluntariness, The Whole Truth, and Self-Incrimination after In Re National Irish Bank' (1999) Bar Review 237.

Accordingly, an individual cannot refuse to answer a question put to him by an inspector – unless it is covered by legal professional privilege which is expressly and separately protected by CA 1990, s 23.

The Supreme Court added the *caveat*, however, that a confession given involuntarily cannot be admitted in subsequent *criminal* proceedings. Barrington J, with whom the other members of the Court concurred, said[94]:

> '…a confession of a bank official obtained by the inspectors as a result of the exercise by them of their powers under s 10 of the Companies Act 1990 would not, in general, be admissible at a subsequent criminal trial unless, in any particular case, the trial judge was satisfied that the confession was voluntary.'

This saver provides cold comfort for those obliged to answer incriminating questions. The problem is how does one show that an answer given was done so involuntarily? It has been suggested that the only certain means of displaying involuntariness is to refuse to answer, whereupon the Court may be called upon to compel an answer to be given[95]. Such tactics will, however, inevitably result in sanctions of another kind for refusal to co-operate with the inspector[96].

[14.045] A similar approach is required from the perspective of European human rights. In *Saunders v United Kingdom*[97] the European Court of Human Rights found that the reliance by prosecuting authorities on transcripts of interviews between Saunders, a former Chief Executive of Guinness plc, and inspectors appointed by the English Department of Trade and Industry was a violation of Article 6.1 of the European Convention on Human Rights. Under English law, Saunders could not refuse to answer questions put to him by inspectors relating to his involvement in an illegal share support scheme[98], and he was effectively compelled to incriminate himself. Both the European Commission on Human Rights and the European Court of Human Rights considered this aspect of the criminal trial to have been in breach of the entitlement to a fair hearing by an impartial and independent tribunal. It should be noted, however, that the decision relates only to the use of transcripts of answers in subsequent criminal proceedings, and provides no real grounds for a refusal to answer an inspector's question. Nor would it seem to prohibit reliance in criminal proceedings on other information obtained as a consequence of a self-incriminatory answer.

(c) Certification of refusal

[14.046] The inspector's powers would be worthless if he were unable to see that they were enforced. Section 10(5) and (6) of CA 1990 as amended[99] enable the inspector to call upon the courts for assistance by certifying a refusal to co-operate with him. The Court is then empowered to conduct a hearing into the refusal and hear any witnesses that may be

94 *Re National Irish Bank Ltd (Under Investigation)* [1999] 3 IR 169, [1999] 1 ILRM 32.

95 Dillon-Malone, 'Voluntariness, The Whole Truth, and Self-Incrimination after In Re National Irish Bank' (1999) Bar Review 237.

96 See para **[14.046]**.

97 *Saunders v United Kingdom* [1997] BCC 872 (Case 43/1994/490/572).

98 *R v Harris* [1970] 3 All ER 746; *Bishopsgate v Maxwell* [1992] 2 All ER 856.

99 By CLEA 2001, s 23.

produced against or on behalf of the person who refused, and to make any order which it thinks fit, including an order that the person concerned re-attend before the inspector, or produce the information sought. Alternatively, the Court may direct that the person concerned need not produce the information sought.

[14.047] As originally enacted, CA 1990, s 10(5) gave the Court the power to punish the person certified by the inspector 'in like manner as if he had been guilty of contempt of Court'. However, in *Desmond v Glackin (No 2)*[100] O'Hanlon J, and on appeal, the Supreme Court, found the power to be unconstitutional since it enabled a person to be tried on a non-minor charge of contempt without a jury. The Supreme Court found that part of CA 1990, s 10(5) bore a direct similarity to the Dáil Éireann (Privilege and Procedure) Act 1970, s 3(4), which had been struck down as unconstitutional by the Supreme Court in *Re Haughey*[101] in 1971. Applying the 'severability' test laid down in *Maher v Attorney General*[102] the Court was able to sever the unoffending words in CA 1990, s 10(5) from the unconstitutional words. Section 10(6) of CA 1990 was likewise doctored, since it contained a passage referring to s 10(5). The Court seemed disappointed that the Oireachtas had allowed this situation to arise: CA 1990, s 10(5) was modelled on CA 1963, s 168(3), which had, since the decision in *Re Haughey*, been amended by the Companies (Amendment) Act 1982, s 7 ('C(A)A 1982') in a manner which made it constitutional. Had the Oireachtas modelled the new subsections on the amended section the constitutional problem would not have arisen.

[14.048] Section 10(5) and (6) of CA 1990 have been repealed and replaced by CLEA 2001, s 23 to give effect to the decision in *Desmond v Glackin (No 2)*. The new provisions are as follows:

> '(5) If an officer or agent of the company or other body corporate, or any such person as is mentioned in subsection (2), refuses or fails within a reasonable time to-
>
> (a) produce to the inspectors any book or document which it is his duty under this section so to produce,
>
> (b) attend before the inspectors when required so to do, or
>
> (c) answer a question put to him by the inspectors with respect to the affairs of the company or other body corporate as the case may be,
>
> the inspectors may certify the refusal or failure under their hand to the Court, and the Court may thereupon enquire into the case and, after hearing any witnesses who may be produced against or on behalf of the person alleged to have so refused or failed and any statement which may be offered in defence, make any order or direction it thinks fit.
>
> (6) Without prejudice to the generality of subsection (5), the Court may, after a hearing under that subsection, direct –
>
> (a) the person concerned to attend or re-attend before the inspectors or produce particular books or documents or answer particular questions put to him by the inspectors, or

100 *Desmond v Glackin (No 2)* [1993] 3 IR 67.

101 *Re Haughey* [1970] IR 217.

102 *Maher v Attorney General* [1973] IR 140.

(b) that the person concerned need not produce a particular book or document or answer a particular question put to him by the inspectors.'

(d) Books and documents relating to bank accounts

[14.049] Section 10(3) of CA 1990 contains a power which it seems is exercisable only by Court-appointed inspectors (since it refers to an investigation into the 'affairs' of a company), and then only against *a director* - which, for the purposes of the subsection, includes past or present directors, past or present *connected persons*[103], and past or present shadow directors. In this respect, the power is supplemental to those contained in CA 1990, s 10(1) and (2). Essentially, the power enables the inspector to require a director to give details of his or her *private* bank accounts, whether held solely or jointly, within or outside the State, where the inspector *reasonably believes* that accounts exist containing amounts which have not been disclosed to the company or which are connected with misconduct. Subsection (3) provides:

'If an inspector has reasonable grounds for believing that a director of the company or other body corporate whose affairs the inspector is investigating maintains or has maintained a bank account of any description, whether alone or jointly with another person and whether in the State or elsewhere, into or out of which there has been paid–

(a) any money which has resulted from or been used in the financing of any transaction, arrangement or agreement –

(i) particulars of which have not been disclosed in a note to the accounts of any company for any financial year as required by section 41; or

(ii) in respect of which any amount outstanding was not included in the aggregate amounts outstanding in respect of certain transactions, arrangements or agreements as required by section 43 to be disclosed in a note to the accounts of any company for any financial year; or

(iii) particulars of which were not included in any register of certain transactions, arrangements and agreements as required by section 44; or

(b) any amount which has been in any way connected with any act or omission, or series of acts or omissions, which on the part of that director constituted misconduct (whether fraudulent or not) towards that company or body corporate or its members,

the inspector may require the director to produce to him all documents in the director's possession, or under his control, relating to that bank account...'

'Bank account' is given an extended meaning by the section. The term relates not only to accounts held with licensed banks, but also to bodies exempt from the requirement in the Central Bank Act 1971, s 9 to hold a banking licence. Such exempted bodies include ACC Bank, ICC, the Post Office Savings Bank, certified Trustee Savings Banks, building societies, credit unions, friendly societies, industrial and provident societies, and unit trust schemes.

[14.050] Though the power is wide, it is not without its limitations. First, the inspector must have *reasonable grounds* for his belief. The absence of such grounds may lead to the inspector's exercise of the power being overturned by judicial review. Secondly, it has been

---

[103] As defined by CA 1990, s 26. See further Chapter 11, *Statutory Regulation of Transactions Involving Directors and their Companies*, para **[11.004]** *et seq*.

argued that the words '...relating to that bank account...' require the inspector to *specify* a particular bank account, a requirement which, if true, is particularly difficult to meet without a corresponding power to require the director to disclose accounts maintained by him generally[104]. It is submitted that the latter power is to be found in CA 1990, s 10(1) and (2). Thirdly, CA 1990, s 10(3) appears not to relate to pension schemes and other investment funds; but, again, details of such funds may be obtained under sub-ss (1) and (2). Indeed, on the whole it is difficult to see how sub-s (3) adds anything to the powers given to inspectors by sub-ss (1) and (2): directors may be required under sub-s (1) to give the information referred to in sub-s (3), and shadow directors and connected persons may be required under sub-s (2) to give such information[105]. It could not be argued that sub-s (3), unlike sub-ss (1) and (2), entitles the inspector to investigate matters other than those which may relate to the affairs of the company under investigation - for in such circumstances the investigator would be exceeding the scope of his brief under CA 1990, ss 7 and 8[106]. Section 10(3) mirrors the provisions of the Companies Act 1981 (UK), s 87, which has since been repeated and supplemented by the Companies Act 1985 (UK), ss 434–435. In the light of CA 1990, s 10(1) and (2), it is submitted that CA 1990, s 10(3) is redundant. Indeed, the Oireachtas thought it unnecessary to extend the powers in sub-s (3) to inspectors appointed by the Director under CA 1990, s 14.

The inspector's report

[14.051] An inspector, no matter how appointed, must make a report at the end of the investigation[107]. Indeed, where the inspector investigates the affairs, membership or control of a related company or body corporate with the approval of the Court or the Director as the case may be, he is *obliged* by CA 1990, s 9 to report on the findings which he thinks relevant to his investigation of the company or companies to which he was appointed[108]. In *Lyons, Keleghan and Murphy v Curran*[109], Blayney J held that an inspector who, within the scope of his investigation, investigates the membership or control of a company or body corporate not specified in the warrant of appointment, is *entitled* to report his findings. The inspector may also give a recommendation in the report as to who he thinks ought to bear the costs of the investigation[110].

Section 11(1) of CA 1990 also empowers the inspector to make an interim report, and, indeed, obliges him to make an interim report where so ordered by the Court or the Director as the case may be. He may also inform the Court, without having to make a report, of any matters coming to his attention which tend to show that an offence has been committed[111].

---

104 See Chaikin (1982) 3 Co Law 115.

105 *Desmond v Glackin (No 2)* [1993] 3 IR 67.

106 See para **[14.020]**.

107 CA 1990, ss 7, 8 and 14.

108 See para **[14.023]**.

109 *Lyons, Keleghan and Murphy v Curran* [1993] ILRM 375.

110 CA 1990, s 13(3).

111 CA 1990, s 11(2).

(a) Publication of the report

[14.052] The extent to which the report of a Court-appointed inspector is to be published or circulated is a matter for the Court, with the rider that *all* inspectors' reports must be furnished to the Director[112]. Section 11(3) of CA 1990, as amended[113], empowers the Court, if it thinks fit, to:

> '(a) forward any copy of the report made by the inspectors to the company' registered office;
>
> (b) furnish a copy on request and payment of the prescribed fee to
>
> (i) any member of the company or other body corporate which is the subject of the report;
>
> (ii) any person whose conduct is referred to in the report;
>
> (iii) the auditors of that company or body corporate;
>
> (iv) the applicants for the investigation;
>
> (v) any other person (including an employee) whose financial interests appear to the Court to be affected by the matters dealt with in the report whether as a creditor of the company or body corporate or otherwise;
>
> (vi) the Central Bank, in any case in which the report of the inspector relates, wholly or partly, to the affairs of the holder of a licence under section 9 of the Central Bank Act 1971;
>
> (ba) furnish a copy to —
>
> (i) an appropriate authority in relation to any of the matters referred to in section 21(1)(a) to (fb); or
>
> (ii) a competent authority as defined in section 21(3)(a) to (i);
>
> and
>
> (c) cause any such report to be printed and published.'

[14.053] Where the Court thinks it proper, it may direct that a particular part of a report be omitted from a copy of the report sent or published in the above manner[114]. The means by which the Court may be approached in this regard gives rise to a procedural conundrum, however.

In *Re Ansbacher (Cayman) Ltd*[115], the High Court was approached by solicitors for two unnamed persons, apparently clients of the bank, who had been informed by the inspectors that their names were soon to be published in the forthcoming inspector's report. Plainly, these persons intended to obtain a direction from the Court that their names be omitted from published copies of the report. Their difficulty, however, was that if the application for such a direction had to be made in open Court, their anonymity would be destroyed. McCracken J considered, as a preliminary matter, whether the application could be made *in camera*, but held that it could not be so heard given that it involved an administration of justice which the Constitution required to be conducted in public, and given the countervailing necessity that justice must not only be done but must be seen to be done.

---

[112] CA 1990, s 11(3).

[113] By CLEA 2001, s 24.

[114] CA 1990, s 11(4).

[115] *Re Ansbacher (Cayman) Ltd* (24 April 2002, unreported), High Court (McCracken J).

[14.054] The manner and extent of publication of a report produced by an inspector who has been appointed by the Director is a matter for the Director. Section 14 of CA 1990 confers the same powers on the Director as the Court has under CA 1990, s 11(3) above. A bona fide decision by the Director *not* to publish the report or any part thereof will survive challenge by way of judicial review[116], and the Director is empowered to cause a copy of the report or part thereof to be kept by the Registrar of Companies[117].

[14.055] The publication of the report is privileged[118], so that persons affected by the report have very limited recourse by way of an action for defamation against those responsible for its publication[119].

(b) Proceedings on foot of an inspector's report

[14.056] Section 12(1) of CA 1990 confers wide powers on the Court to make 'such order as it deems fit' on foot of a Court-appointed inspector's report, including:

> '(a) an order of its own motion for the winding up of a body corporate, or
>
> (b) an order for the purpose of remedying any disability suffered by any person whose interests were adversely affected by the conduct of the affairs of the company, provided that, in making any such order, the Court shall have regard to the interests of any other person who may be adversely affected by the order.'

The powers conferred on the Court by sub-s (1)(b) appear very wide indeed, and seem to envisage that the Court could order the restoration of property or the setting aside of transactions. The Court might even award damages to persons affected by the conduct of the company's affairs. Presumably, where granting relief to members of the company, the Court would have to have regard to the rule in *Foss v Harbottle*[120] so as not to provide individual members with redress for a wrong which was done to the company itself.

The Court's power to impose the corporate 'death-penalty' *of its own motion* by ordering the winding up of the company seems draconian. It is hard to imagine the circumstances in which the Court might feel confident to make such an order, though presumably it would apply the established principles applicable to winding-up petitions, including, perhaps, the 'just and equitable' criterion[121]. It seems plain at any rate that the Court would have to give full opportunity to be heard to all persons likely to be affected by such an order before proceeding.

[14.057] The Director is given the right by CA 1990, s 12(2) to petition the Court for the winding up of any body corporate to which the winding up provisions of the Companies Acts 1963–2001 apply, unless that body is already being wound up. The Court may order

---

[116] CA 1990, s 14(2); *Lonrho plc v Secretary of State for Trade and Industry* [1989] 2 All ER 609.

[117] CA 1990, s 14(5)(b).

[118] CA 1990, s 23(3).

[119] On the defence of privilege, see McMahon & Binchy, *Law of Torts*, (3rd edn, 2000) p 920.

[120] *Foss v Harbottle* (1843) 2 Hare 461. See Chapter 19, *Shareholders' Remedies*, para **[19.082]** *ff*. See also *Minister for Justice v Siúcre Éireann cpt, Greencore plc* [1992] 2 IR 215, discussed at para **[14.061]**.

[121] As regards windings up on the 'just and equitable' ground see Chapter 25, *Winding Up Companies*, para **[25.076]***ff*.

the winding up if it thinks it 'just and equitable to do so.'[122] The Director's right to petition may *only* be exercised where it appears to him, from either:

— any report of a Court-appointed inspector who was appointed *on the application of the Director*[123]; or

— any report of an inspector appointed by the Director; or

— any information or document obtained by the Director under the other investigatory procedures contained in CA 1990, Part II[124],

that a petition should be presented for the winding up of the body. Accordingly, the Director may not petition the Court on foot of information contained in a report of a Court-appointed inspector who was appointed on the application of someone else.

It appears that the Director must keep the public interest in mind when deciding whether or not to petition the Court for a winding-up order on foot of an inspector's report[125], and his decision may be overturned on judicial review if he has not acted bona fide in reaching his decision[126].

(c) Admissibility and presumptive evidentiary effect of the report in civil proceedings

[14.058] The inspector's report is admissible in evidence in *any* civil proceedings as proof of the facts set out therein, despite the hearsay rule which would ordinarily prevent it being put to such use. Section 22 of CA 1990 provides:

> 'A document purporting to be a copy of a report of an inspector appointed under this Part shall be admissible in any civil proceedings as evidence —
>
> (a) of the facts set out therein without further proof unless the contrary is shown, and
>
> (b) of the opinion of the inspector in relation to any matter contained in the report.'

The civil proceedings in which the report is to be relied upon may be brought by any party. In *Countyglen plc v Carway*[127], for example, the report was relied upon by the company under investigation to ground an application for a Mareva-type injunction against a number of persons alleged to have defrauded it[128].

Section 22 does not purport to extend to criminal proceedings. That is not to say, however, that an inspector's report can have no evidentiary value in such proceedings. It would, however, have to be subjected to the normal exclusionary rules of evidence in criminal trials, and confessions or self-incriminatory statements which are sought to be relied upon would at least have to satisfy the voluntariness requirement[129]. The better approach, given

---

122 As regards windings up on the 'just and equitable' ground see Chapter 25, *Winding Up Companies*, para **[25.076]***ff*.

123 See para **[14.015]**.

124 See para **[14.067]** ff.

125 *Re Lubin, Rosen & Associates Ltd* [1975] 1 WLR 122.

126 *Re Walter L Jacob & Co Ltd* [1989] BCLC 345.

127 *Countyglen plc v Carway* [1995] 1 IR 208.

128 See Courtney, *Mareva Injunctions and Related Interlocutory Orders* (1998), pp 187–189.

129 See para **[14.044]**.

the views of the European Court of Human Rights[130], might yet be to refrain from reliance on self-inculpatory statements in the report in criminal trials.

[14.059] It will be noted that the section does more than oust the hearsay rule – it further gives the report a presumptive evidentiary effect. In subsequent proceedings also entitled *Countyglen plc v Carway*[131], Laffoy J held that CA 1990, s 22 rendered the report of an inspector admissible in all civil actions to give all findings of primary fact clearly expressed as such in the report the status of proven fact unless disproved. The learned judge further held that the word 'facts' in s 22 did not extend to deductions of fact from the contents of the report, and that the word 'report' included the entire report, regardless of whether some of the report had been ordered not to be disclosed. She continued[132]:

> 'Section 22 does not prescribe that the facts thereby given the status of proven facts have any special probative value or that any particular weight should be attached thereto. Accordingly, the ordinary rules apply in determining whether an application for a direction should be acceded to at the end of the plaintiff's case and in determining the issues of fact when all the evidence is in.'

The point is, thus, that while the facts stated in the report are presumed to have been proved until the contrary is shown, the presumption can be rebutted by ordinary evidence.

[14.060] In *Countyglen v Carway*, Laffoy J raised the issue of whether CA 1990, s 22 might be constitutionally flawed; but since none of the parties had raised a constitutional challenge the section had to be presumed constitutional until some later occasion. The learned judge did not, however, elaborate on the reasons for her concerns about the constitutionality of the section. Presumably, they relate to the fact that the exclusionary rules of evidence are intimately bound up with the requirements of fair procedures.

It is submitted, in addition, that s 22 cannot have the effect of rendering admissible evidence in a report which was unconstitutionally obtained, for to allow it to be so used would be a failure to vindicate the constitutional rights of citizens.

The attendance of the inspector responsible for the report is not required in Court. The copy of the inspector's report need only 'purport' to be such, so that the inspector is not needed in Court to show that it is a true copy. Neither is he required in Court to give further evidence as to the opinions stated in the report.

Costs of the inspection

(a) The costs of Court-ordered inspections

[14.061] The costs, expenses and incidentals of a Court ordered inspection are, under CA 1990, s 13(1), as amended[133], to be defrayed initially by the Minister (or, in the case of inspectors appointed under CA 1990, s 7, by the Minister for Justice, Equality and Law Reform). The Court, however, may direct that any body corporate dealt with in the report, or the applicants for the investigation, should be liable to reimburse the relevant Minister;

---

130 See para **[14.045]**.

131 *Countyglen plc v Carway* [1998] 2 IR 540.

132 [1998] 2 IR 514 at 551.

133 By CLEA 2001, s 25.

provided that the aggregate amount for which the applicants are so made liable does not exceed €317,435.

In *Minister for Justice v Siúcre Éireann, Greencore Plc*[134] Lynch J observed that only persons 'dealt with in the report' may be made liable under CA 1990, s 13(1). He concluded that this meant that the only bodies corporate who could be made liable under the subsection were those which had been both under investigation and dealt with in the report; otherwise companies simply named in the report could be made liable to bear the costs of the investigation without being given the opportunity of putting their case to the inspector.

[14.062] In addition, under CA 1990, s 13(2), any person who is:

- (a) convicted on indictment of an offence on a prosecution instituted as a result of an investigation;
- (b) ordered to pay damages or restore any property in proceedings brought as a result of an investigation; or
- (c) awarded damages or to whom property is restored in proceedings brought as a result of an investigation;

may, in the same proceedings, be ordered to repay all or part of the expenses of the investigation to the relevant Minister or to any person who has already been ordered to pay such expenses under CA 1990, s 13(1). A person awarded damages or to whom property is restored may not be ordered to pay in excess of one-tenth of the amount of the damages awarded or the value of the property restored, and the order may not be executed until such time as the person has received his damages or property.

[14.063] In *Minister for Justice v Siúcre Éireann, Greencore plc*[135] an application was brought by the Minister for Justice under CA 1990, s 13(1)(a) to be reimbursed by the respondents. The expenses, totalling approximately £1,150,000 (€1,460,199), were incurred in a Court-ordered investigation into the affairs of Siúcre Éireann, which was commenced by an application by the Minister for Industry and Commerce to the Court under CA 1990, s 8[136]. Lynch J accepted that as a general rule, and subject to the facts in each case, the Minister for Justice should *prima facie* be reimbursed the expenses of an investigation by the company or companies dealt with in the report, whether adversely or not, who could, in turn, seek reimbursement from others under CA 1990, s 13(2). He found, however, that in the case before him the alleged wrongdoings which gave rise to the investigation had all taken place at a time when the Minister for Finance owned and controlled Greencore plc, of which Siúcre Éireann was a wholly-owned subsidiary. He had since sold 70% of his shares in Greencore to the public to facilitate a privatisation. The learned judge concluded that if the Minister were to be reimbursed by Greencore and Siúcre Éireann it would place an unjust liability on those who had purchased the shares in the meantime, the vast majority of whom had nothing to do with the companies under investigation at the time of the alleged wrongdoings and had been unaware of them at the

---

134 *Minister for Justice v Siúcre Éireann, Greencore Plc* [1992] 2 IR 215.

135 *Minister for Justice v Siúcre Éireann, Greencore Plc* [1992] 2 IR 215.

136 On the Director's power to apply to the court for the appointment of an inspector see para **[14.015]**.

time they purchased the shares. Furthermore, the State, through the Minister for Finance, had already benefited from the sale of the shares in Greencore at a time when the tax liabilities referred to in the report did not arise, and if the applicant were to get his order, the State would benefit doubly.

Moreover, the learned judge considered it just and equitable to take into account the factor of who was in ultimate control of the enterprise at the time of the wrongdoing, and he concluded that the rule in *Foss v Harbottle*[137] *did not prevent him in this regard. He said*[138]:

> 'Apart altogether from the fact that innocent shareholder owners of the enterprise would now be damnified by an order in favour of the State, there is the factor of who was in ultimate control of the enterprise at the material time. As between the body having ultimate control of the enterprise at the time of the alleged wrongdoing, and successors to that ultimate control, especially insofar as they are without any notice of the wrongdoing, it seems to me that it is more equitable that those in ultimate control at the time of the wrongdoing (even though unaware of it at that time) should bear the costs of the investigation rather than their successors especially to the extent that such successors were wholly unaware of any such wrongdoing. On this basis it might be suggested that the enterprise should pay 45% or 30% of the expenses seeing that the State retained ownership of those percentages as above but I do not think that that follows because the wholly innocent present shareholder owners will still be penalised to the benefit of the State.'

Accordingly, the controllers of the company at the time of the wrongdoings are more likely to be fixed with the expenses of the investigation if it is possible so to make them liable. In this regard it must be remembered that the controllers, whoever they may be, may only be fixed with the costs of the investigation if they fall into one of the categories of persons identified in CA 1990, s 13(1) and (2). Only bodies corporate incorporated in the State, or which, incorporated outside the State, carry on business within the State, fall into these categories. In the *Siúcre Éireann* case, Lynch J agreed that this was the conclusion to be drawn from CA 1990, s 17, and he added that the words 'carry on business' presupposed a sort of continuum of activity as opposed to one or two isolated transactions. Accordingly, Talmino, a company registered in Jersey, whose only transaction in the State was the purchase of 2,425 shares in a company in 1989 and the sale and transfer of those shares in 1990, could not be ordered to reimburse the Minister for Justice.

(b) The expenses of an inspection ordered by the Director

[14.064] Section 14 of CA 1990 was added to by CLEA 2001 to enable the Director to recoup the costs of an inspection ordered by him from the parties involved. The new provisions are similar in effect to those of CA 1990, s 13 relating to Court-appointed inspections, and presumably the principles developed in relation to s 13, above, will be applied to the new provisions *mutatis mutandis*.

Section 14(6)–(8) of CA 1990 provides:

> '(6) The Court may, on the application of the Director, direct that a company the subject of an investigation under this section shall be liable, to such extent as the Court may direct, to repay the Director the expenses of and incidental to the investigation.
>
> (7) Without prejudice to subsection (6) but subject to subsection (8), a person –

---

137 *Foss v Harbottle* (1843) 2 Hare 461. See Chapter 19, *Shareholders' Remedies*, para **[19.082]***ff*.

138 [1992] 2 IR 215 at 228.

(a) convicted on indictment of an offence on a prosecution instituted,

(b) ordered to pay damages or restore any property in proceedings brought, or

(c) awarded damages or to whom property is restored in proceedings brought,

as a result of an investigation under this section may, in the same proceedings, be ordered to repay the Director all or part of the expenses referred to in subsection (6).

(8) The Court shall not order a person to whom subsection (7)(c) relates to make payment in excess of one-tenth of the amount of the damages awarded or of the value of the property restored, as the case may be, and any such order shall not be executed until the person concerned has received his damages or the property has been restored.'

Concurrent investigations

[14.065] The circumstances giving rise to the ordering of an inspection may also give rise to some other form of investigation being ordered by other authorities in the State. What is the effect of a concurrent investigation on an inspection under the Companies Acts? In *Re National Irish Bank Ltd*[139] the applicants sought to limit the inspectors in their investigations into the compliance by the bank of its obligations concerning Deposit Interest Retention Tax ('DIRT'). They contended that the concurrent investigation by the Comptroller and Auditor General into the alleged evasion of DIRT by a number of financial institutions including the applicants involved a duplication of process which opened them to the threat of double jeopardy, and which placed them in an unfair position whereby the body reporting second was not bound by the findings of the body reporting first. Moreover, they claimed, the duplication of investigation was slowing up the work of the inspectors, and the Court was bound, under CA 1990, s 7(4), to give directions 'with a view to ensuring that the investigation is carried out as quickly and as inexpensively as possible.'

Kelly J dismissed the application, holding that the inspectors' focus was narrower than that of the Comptroller and Auditor General, who was concerned not merely with the applicants but with a number of other financial institutions. The learned judge further held that the question of double jeopardy did not arise as the investigations were only fact-finding exercises, not criminal trials in themselves. Likewise, the applicants' argument on the *res judicata* issue held force only in respect of criminal proceedings.

[14.066] While the decision in *Re National Irish Bank Ltd* may reveal a certain reluctance on the part of the Court to interfere with the terms of reference of appointed inspectors, it does seem clear from the judgment that where the focus of a concurrent investigation is the same, there is some leeway for such interference. The issue may fall to be determined at some stage in the future should an inspector ever be appointed on the application of the members, directors, or creditors of a company under CA 1990, s 7. The Act would not appear to forbid such an appointment even where an inspector has already been appointed by, or on the application of, the Director under CA 1990, ss 7 and 14 – or *vice versa*.

---

[139] *Re National Irish Bank Ltd* (19 March 1999, unreported), High Court (Kelly J).

[B] OTHER INVESTIGATIONS AND INQUIRIES

[14.067] The CA 1990, as amended, places two further investigatory processes – which do *not* involve the appointment of an inspector – at the Director's disposal. First, he is given the power in CA 1990, ss 19-20 to require the production of books and documents in circumstances where he thinks it may be necessary to make a decision whether an inspector ought to be appointed to investigate a company or body corporate, and in other specified circumstances. Secondly, where the Director is of the opinion that a company ought to be investigated but it appears to him that the appointment of an inspector is unnecessary, he may, under CA 1990, s 15, conduct an inquiry himself. The investigatory (and related) powers of the Director are considered here as follows:

1. Production of books and documents.
2. Inquiries by the Director.
3. The Director's power to impose restrictions on shares and debentures.

Production of books and documents

[14.068] Section 19(1) of CA 1990 as amended[140] gives the Director the power to direct the production of specified books and documents of a company or other body[141] at such time and place as may be specified in the direction. The Director may take copies of the books and documents so produced, *and* may require the person producing them, or any past or present officer or employee (including a professional or consultant) of the body at the relevant time, to provide any explanation of any of them, and of any omission.

[14.069] The constitutionality of s 19 of CA 1990 has yet to be copper-fastened. In *Dunnes Stores Ireland Company v Ryan*[142], Keane CJ expressed some regret[143] that the constitutionality of the section could not be considered by the Supreme Court on appeal since the issue had not been raised first at a lower level. The Court remitted the constitutional issue to the High Court, though it must inevitably be destined for the Supreme Court at some future stage.

(a) Grounds for investigation of books and documents

[14.070] The Director may exercise his powers under CA 1990, s 19(1) where he is of the opinion that there are circumstances suggesting that:

> '(a) it is necessary[144] to examine the books and documents of the body with a view to determining whether an inspector should be appointed to conduct an investigation of the body under the Companies Acts; or
>
> (b) the affairs of the body are being or have been conducted with intent to defraud –
>
> (i) its creditors,

---

[140] By CLEA 2001, s 29.

[141] The bodies which may be the subject of such a direction are listed in CA 1990, s 19(1) and include unincorporated bodies which appear to be insurance undertakings.

[142] *Dunnes Stores Ireland Company v Ryan* (1 February 2002, unreported), Supreme Court.

[143] (1 February 2002, unreported), Supreme Court at pp 36–37.

[144] 'Necessary' does not entail any extreme or compelling need, but could be equated to 'reasonably required': CA 1990, s 19(1).

(ii) the creditors of any other person[145], or

(iii) its members;

(c) the affairs of the body are being or have been conducted for a fraudulent purpose other than described in paragraph (b);

(d) the affairs of the body are being or have been conducted in a manner which is unfairly prejudicial to some part of its members[146];

(e) any actual or proposed act or omission or series of acts or omissions of the body or on behalf of the body are or would be unfairly prejudicial to some part of its members;

(f) that any actual or proposed act or omission or series of acts or omissions of the body or on behalf of the body are or are likely to be unlawful[147];

(g) that the body was formed for any fraudulent purpose;

(h) that the body was formed for any unlawful purpose; or

(i) the body may be in possession of books or documents containing information relating to the books or documents of a body which comes within the terms of one or more of paragraphs (a) to (h).'[148]

Whether such circumstances exist is a matter of subjective opinion for the Director. The Director is not required to give a person or body prior notice of his intention to make a direction[149].

[14.071] Such directions may be given to any person who appears to the Director to be in possession of the books or documents, or copies thereof, or books or documents relating thereto; but where that person claims a lien over the books, the production is not to prejudice their rights under the lien[150].
The power to require the production of books and documents relating to other books and document seems to be aimed at bookkeeping professionals and the like who may have second-hand information. Where the Director requires the production of such books or documents, however, the Director must be of the opinion that there are reasonable grounds for believing that the two sets of books or documents are related; he must notify the person in possession of the reasons for his belief; and he must allow them 21 days in which to controvert his opinion. Moreover, the production of such books or documents can be refused on the basis that it is privileged – whether by virtue of legal professional privilege or otherwise[151].

[14.072] The Director may have to provide reasons for his decision to require the production of books and documents. In *Dunnes Stores Ireland Company v Maloney*[152],

---

145 The Revenue Commissioners might be regarded as creditors for these purposes: CA 1990, s 19(1).

146 The Director may proceed on this ground even though none of the members complains of unfairly prejudicial treatment and opposes the direction: CA 1990, s 19(1).

147 The focus on present or future wrongdoing precludes the grounding of a decision solely on past unlawful conduct: CA 1990, s 19(1).

148 CA 1990, s 19(2).

149 *Dunnes Stores Ireland Company v Ryan* (1 February 2002, unreported), Supreme Court.

150 CA 1990, s 19(3).

151 CA 1990, s 19(4).

152 *Dunnes Stores Ireland Company v Maloney* [1999] 3 IR 542, [1999] 1 ILRM 119.

Laffoy J held that the decision of the Minister (as predecessor to the Director) under CA 1990, s 19 was one which was capable of being judicially reviewed. Accordingly, the person directed by the Minister was entitled to know the reasons for the decision to enable them to assess whether they should seek such review. Laffoy J said[153]:

> '...they are entitled to have the decision reviewed on the lines indicated above and, in my view, they are utterly stymied in the exercise of that right by reason of the refusal to give reasons for the decision. In my view, this is a case in which procedural fairness requires that the Minister give reasons for her decision. The Applicants have demonstrated that they bona fide believe that the Minister has misused her power in appointing an authorised officer. Whether that belief is well founded or not, they are entitled to explore the possibility of obtaining redress by way of judicial review. They have made a bona fide request for reasons. In the absence of reasons, they cannot explore the possibility of or pursue redress by way of judicial review. Consequently, they are suffering a significant detriment. I consider that the Minister is obliged to give reasons.'

Notably, however, Laffoy J did not quash the investigation on foot the failure to give reasons; instead she granted declaratory relief so that the Minister was given an opportunity to provide reasons. Moreover, the case was one in which reasons were sought by the recipient of the direction. It is unclear whether reasons are required in every case even if no such request is made.

[14.073] Another important element in the decision is the finding that the direction was excessive and unreasonable in the context of a lack of reasons. Without reasons, the applicants were unable to determine from the very broad demand precisely what books and documents were being sought. Laffoy J said[154]:

> 'In my view, the applicants' criticisms of the demand are well founded. Without knowing the reasons why the Minister thought it appropriate to appoint an authorised officer, it is impossible to form any view as to whether even the categories of documents sought which are specific fall within the ambit of the entitlement to seek documents under s 19. The inclusion of the categories which are of a general nature gives the demand as a whole the hallmark of a trawl. That being the case, the only reasonable inference is that the demand was excessive in content.'

On balance, therefore, it would seem sensible that the Director should give reasons along with every direction under CA 1990, s 19.

[14.074] The reasons so given must, of course, coincide with the statutory purposes listed in CA 1990, s 19; moreover, they must not be patently irrational[155].

(b) Limits of the procedure

[14.075] A practical limitation on these powers is that the Director is required to *specify* the books and documents required. It may well be that the Director will be unaware of some relevant books and documents which, consequently, may slip through the net. In this regard it may be observed, however, that since the enactment of CLEA 2001, a person directed to produce the books or documents under CA 1990, s 19 is now expressly obliged

---

[153] [1999] 3 IR 542 at 563.

[154] [1999] 3 IR 542 at 564.

[155] *Dunnes Stores Ireland Company v Ryan* (1 February 2002, unreported), Supreme Court.

to give 'all assistance' in the same way as he or she would be were the direction to come from an inspector[156].

A second limitation is to be found in CA 1990, s 23(2) which prohibits the Director from requiring a bank to disclose a document relating to the business of its customer unless either it appears to the Director that it is necessary to do so for the purpose of investigating the affairs of the bank or the customer – whether as a former or a current customer. As was observed above, an inspector is not so prohibited[157].

Legal professional privilege may be relied upon to justify a refusal to co-operate with a direction made under CA 1990, s 19[158].

(c) Consequences of failure to comply

[14.076] If the books or documents are not produced, the person who was required to produce them may be asked to state, to the best of his knowledge, where they are[159]. A statement made by a person in compliance with these requirements may be used in evidence *against* him in any proceedings *other* than criminal proceedings, (except those for an offence under s 19)[160]. Moreover, the making of a false statement is now itself an offence[161]. Persons making statements in response to a direction should, thus, do so advisedly. The shadow of unconstitutionality was cast over these provisions by the High Court in *Dunnes Stores and Others v Ryan*[162], but it would appear that the amendments made by CLEA 2001 will defend them from further such challenge. In *Dunnes Stores*, Kearns J held that the original provisions were unconstitutional because the examinee was required, on pain of punishment for a refusal, to answer questions which might be incriminating and which might be used in subsequent criminal proceedings. The learned judge observed that the provisions failed to immunise answers given from later use in criminal proceedings. The new provisions, however, expressly prohibit the use of answers given in later criminal proceedings. It will be noted, however, that the new provisions still permit use of the answers given in criminal proceedings brought under CA 1990, s 19(6) and 19(8). It is doubtful that such *use* would survive constitutional scrutiny following *Dunnes Stores v Ryan*.

[14.077] Failure to comply with any direction under CA 1990, s 19 is an offence[163]. The person charged with such an offence has a good defence, however, if he can prove that the books or documents in question were not in his possession or control and that it was not reasonably practical for him to comply with the requirement. In *Dunnes Stores v Ryan*[164] Kearns J upheld the constitutionality of similar provisions in the original s 19 of CA 1990. He held that parties enjoying the benefit of incorporation must also accept concomitant

[156] See para **[14.035]**.
[157] See para **[14.039]**.
[158] CA 1990, s 23(1).
[159] CA 1990, s 19(5), as amended by CLEA 2001, s 29.
[160] CA 1990, s 19(7), as amended by CLEA 2001, s 29.
[161] CA 1990, s 19(8), as amended by CLEA 2001, s 29.
[162] *Dunnes Stores and Others v Ryan* (5 June 2002, unreported), High Court (Kearns J).
[163] CA 1990, s 19(6), as amended by CLEA 2001, s 29.
[164] (5 June 2002, unreported), High Court (Kearns J).

duties and obligations, and the duty to produce documents and answer questions was unobjectionable and proportional in the light of the public interest and good corporate governance.

[14.078] The destruction, mutilation, falsification or concealment of any book or document which is the subject of a direction is also an offence if done by a person having notice of the direction[165], or if done by a person who knows or suspects that an investigation by the Director is being or is likely to be carried out. In the latter case the presumption of innocence is reversed so that the person is presumed to have known or suspected until reasonable doubt is established[166].

[14.079] A search warrant may issue under CA 1990, s 20 from a District Judge authorising a designated officer of the Director and such other persons as the officer thinks necessary, to enter premises specified in the warrant, using force if necessary; to search the premises; to require persons found on the premises to give details of their name, home address and occupation and to produce material in their custody or possession; to seize and retain any material or information so found; and to take any other steps considered necessary to preserve the material or to prevent interference therewith. The warrant retains its force for one month from its issue, and the books or documents obtained under it may be kept for a period of six months or for such further time as a District Judge may permit as being necessary for the conclusion of any criminal proceedings initiated during the six-month period.
Computer-based information may be searched and seized in this process, and disclosure of passwords and other technical assistance can be required of persons identified as having that knowledge[167].

Obstruction of an entry and search under CA 1990, s 20 is also an offence.

(d) Publication or disclosure of information, books and documents

[14.080] Under CA 1990, s 21(1), as amended[168], no information, book or document which has been obtained in accordance with CA 1990, ss 19 and 20 may be disclosed or published without the prior written consent of the body to which it relates unless the publication or disclosure is to a 'competent authority' *or* is required:

> '(a) with a view to the investigation or prosecution of any offence, being an offence –
>
> (i) under–
>
> (I) the Companies Acts;
>
> (II) the Central Bank Acts 1942 to 1998;
>
> (III) the Exchange Control Acts 1954 to 1986;
>
> (IV) the Insurance Acts 1909 to 1990;
>
> (V) the Taxes Consolidation Act 1997 or an offence under an enactment referred to in section 1078(1) of that Act;
>
> (VI) regulations relating to insurance made under the European Communities Act 1972;
>
> or

165 CA 1990, s 19(9) as inserted by CLEA 2001, s 29.

166 CA 1990, s 19A.

167 CA 1990, s 20(4).

168 By C(A)(No 2)A, s 53 and CLEA 2001, s 31.

(ii) entailing misconduct in connection with the management of the body's affairs or misapplication or wrongful retainer of its property;

(b) for the purpose of assessing the liability of a person in respect of a tax or duty or other payment owed or payable to the State, a local authority (within the meaning of the Local Government Act 1941) or a health board or for the purpose of collecting an amount due in respect of such a tax or duty or other payment;

(c) for the purpose of the performance by a tribunal (to which the Tribunals of Inquiry (Evidence) Acts 1921 to 1998, apply) of any of its functions;

(d) for the purpose of assisting or facilitating the performance by any Minister of the Government of any of his functions;

(e) for the purpose of assisting or facilitating any accountancy or other professional organisation in the performance of its disciplinary functions with respect to any of its members;

(f) for the purpose of the performance by the Irish Takeover Panel or any stock exchange established in the State of any of its functions in relation to the body or any other person who, in its opinion, is connected with the body;

(fa) for the purpose of the performance by the Competition Authority of any of its functions;

(fb) for the purpose of the performance by a committee (being a committee within the meaning of the Committees of the Houses of the Oireachtas (Compellability, Privileges and Immunities of Witnesses) Act 1997, to which sections 3 to 14 and 16 of that Act apply) of any of its functions;

(g) for the purposes of complying with the requirements of procedural fairness, to be made to –

(i) any company in relation to which an inspector has been appointed under section 14 or any person required by the Director to give any information under section 15, or

(ii) any body to which the Director has given a Direction under section 19 or any person named in a report relating to an examination under that section;

(h) for the purpose of complying with any requirement, or exercising any power, imposed or conferred by Part II of the 1990 Act with respect to reports made by inspectors appointed thereunder by the Court or the Director;

(i) with a view to the institution by the Director of proceedings for the winding-up under the 1963 Act of the body or otherwise for the purposes of proceedings instituted by him for that purpose;

(j) for the purposes of proceedings under section 20 or 160[169]'

A person who publishes or discloses any information, book or document in contravention of these provisions will be guilty of an offence.

[14.081] For these purposes, 'competent authority' includes[170] the Minister; a person authorised by the Minister; an inspector appointed under CA 1990; the Minister for Finance; an officer authorised by the Minister for Finance; any Court of competent

169 CA 1990, s 21(1).

170 CA 1990, s 21(2).

jurisdiction; the Central Bank, and any authority established outside the State in which there are vested

— functions of investigating or prosecuting an offence similar to an offence referred to in CA 1990, s 21(1), para (a) above; or

— functions of assessing the liability of a person in respect of a tax or duty or other payment owed or payable to the state in which it is established or any other authority established in that state or of collecting an amount due in respect of such a tax or duty or other payment; or

— functions which are similar to the functions referred to in CA 1990, s 21(1), para (c), (d), (e) or (f).

(e) Costs of the investigation

[14.082] The Director's costs and expenses incurred in an investigation under CA 1990, s 19 may be recouped by order of the Court upon application by the Director from any person convicted on indictment as a result of a direction, or ordered to pay damages as a result of a direction, or awarded damages or restored property as a result of a direction; but in the latter case the payment shall not exceed 10% of the amount of damages awarded or the value of the property restored[171].

Inquiries by the Director of Corporate Enforcement

[14.083] Section 15 of CA 1990 permits an inquiry into the ownership of shares and debentures in a company without the need for the appointment of an inspector. In any case where it appears to the Director that it is necessary to investigate the ownership of any shares or debentures in a company on the grounds contained in CA 1990, s 14, he may, under CA 1990, s 15(1), if he thinks it unnecessary to appoint an investigator, require instead:

> '...any person whom he has reasonable cause to believe to have or to be able to obtain any information as to the present and past interests in those shares or debentures and the names and addresses of the persons interested and of any persons who act or have acted on their behalf in relation to the shares or debentures, to give any such information.'

The subsection seems to require the Director to have reasonable cause to believe quite a number of things: first, that persons have, or are able to obtain, the information; secondly, that those persons also have, or are able to obtain, the names *and* addresses of interested persons; and thirdly, that those persons also have the names and addresses of any persons who have acted on behalf of interested persons. Surely the categories of persons who may be expected to have such information must be few in number.

[14.084] For the purposes of CA 1990, s 15(1) a person is deemed to have an interest in a share or debenture if he has:

— any right to acquire or dispose of the share or debenture or any interest therein;

— a right to vote in respect of the shares or debentures; if his consent is necessary for the exercise of any of the rights of other persons interested in the shares or debentures; or

---

171 CA 1990, s 19, ss 10–12.

— if the other persons interested in the shares or debentures can be required or are accustomed to exercise their rights in accordance with his instruction[172].

Any person who fails to give the required information, or who knowingly or recklessly gives materially false information, will be guilty of an offence.

Director of Corporate Enforcement's power to impose restrictions on shares and debentures

(a) Application of restrictions

[14.085] Finally, it should be noted that CA 1990, s 16 gives the Director additional powers exercisable in connection with an investigation. Where, in connection with an inspection under s 14 or an inquiry under CA 1990, s 15, it appears to the Director that there is difficulty in finding out the relevant facts about any shares or debentures (whether issued or to be issued), the Director may direct, by notice in writing, that the shares or debentures shall, until further notice, be subject to the following restrictions:

'(a) any transfer of those shares, or in the case of unissued shares any transfer of the right to be issued therewith and any issue thereof, shall void;

(b) no voting rights shall be exercisable in respect of those shares;

(c) no further shares shall be issued in right of those shares or in pursuance of any offer made to the holder thereof; and

(d) no payment shall be made of any sums due from the company on those shares, whether in respect of capital or otherwise.'[173]

In addition, any *agreement* to transfer the shares, debentures, or rights restricted by (a), (c) or (d) is deemed to be void[174]. The Director must, as soon as may be after the making of the direction, send notice of it to the company at its registered office and to the registrar of companies. Notice must also be published in *Iris Oifigiúil* and at least two daily newspapers.

[14.086] Under the provisions of CA 1990, s 16(14), any person who:

(a) exercises or purports to exercise any right to dispose of any shares which, to his knowledge, are for the time being subject to the said restrictions or of any right to be issued with any such shares; or

(b) votes in respect of any such shares, whether as holder or proxy, or appoints a proxy to vote in respect thereof; or

(c) being the holder of any such shares, fails to notify of their being subject to the said restrictions any person whom he does not know to be aware of that fact but does know to be entitled, apart from the said restrictions, to vote in respect of those shares whether as holder or proxy; or

(d) being the holder of any such shares, or being entitled to any such right as is mentioned in subsection (4) enters into an agreement which is void by virtue of [section 16],'

---

172 CA 1990, s 15(2).

173 CA 1990, s 16(17) applies the provisions of the section to debentures.

174 CA 1990, s 16(3)–(4).

will be guilty of an offence. In addition, where shares or debentures are issued in contravention of the said restrictions, the company and every officer in default will be guilty of an offence. Summary proceedings may not be instituted under CA 1990, s 16 except by or with the consent of the Director.

(b) Removal of restrictions and sale

[14.087] Where the Director directs that shares or debentures are to be subject to these restrictions, or refuses to direct that shares or debentures shall cease to be subject to such restrictions, any aggrieved person may apply to the Court for an order that the shares or debentures shall cease to be subject to the restrictions[175]. However, neither the Court nor the Director can order the restrictions to cease unless satisfied that the relevant facts about the shares or debentures have been disclosed to the company or the Director as appropriate, *or* the shares or debentures are to be sold and the Court or the Director approves the sale[176]. In the English case of *Re Westminster Property Group plc*[177] it was held that the words 'to be sold' in this context should be construed as meaning transferred for a money consideration. Thus, it would appear that neither the Court nor the Director has the authority to approve non-cash transfers of restricted shares or debentures, such as a share-for-share exchange.

[14.088] The company or the Director may apply to Court for an order directing the restricted shares or debentures to be sold, subject to Court approval[178]. The Court, in granting the order, may decide to release the shares or debentures from all of the restrictions, or may continue the restrictions on issue of further shares or debentures or on payments on those shares or debentures[179].

Once a Court-sanctioned sale takes place, the Director, the company, the person appointed to sell the shares or debentures, or any person interested in them may apply to the Court for any further order relating to the sale or transfer of shares or debentures[180]. The proceeds of sale of the shares or debentures less the costs of the sale must be paid into Court for the benefit of the persons who were beneficially interested in the shares or debentures, and any such person may apply to the Court for the whole amount of those proceeds to be paid to him[181]. The Court will order the payment to the applicant of that proportion of the proceeds of sale to which he is beneficially entitled, but may also order that the costs of the application by the Director or company for the sale be paid out of the proceeds of sale before any other sums are paid out[182].

---

175 CA 1990, s 16(5).

176 CA 1990, s 16(6). In *Re Greers Gross plc* [1987] 1 WLR 1649 the English Court of Appeal held that mere demonstration that the restricted shares were to be sold was of itself insufficient to justify the court in removing the restrictions, especially where the applicants had failed to disclose the identity of the owners of the shares. See McCormack, *The New Companies Legislation* (1991), pp 33-34.

177 *Re Westminster Property Group plc* [1985] 1 WLR 676.

178 CA 1990, s 16(7).

179 CA 1990, s 16(7) and (12).

180 CA 1990, s 16(8).

181 CA 1990, s 16(9).

182 CA 1990, s 16(10) and (11).

Chapter 15

Shares and Membership

Introduction

[15.001] Although a company is legally a separate person from the members who constitute it[1], it has no practical[2] or physical existence without its members, for the company is really nothing more than a conglomeration of their mutual rights, interests and obligations.

In a private limited company, a shareholder (ie a person who holds a share or shares in the company) is a member[3] of the company whose liability is limited to the extent of his investment in the share capital of the company. Every private company is required to have a share capital and to limit the maximum number of members to 50[4]. Each member contributes to the share capital of the private company by taking shares in it, secure in the knowledge that his liability to contribute to the assets of the company in the event of a winding up will be limited to the amount, if any, left unpaid on his shares[5]. In relation to the private company, then, it has been observed that the terms 'member' and 'shareholder' are synonymous[6]. But this statement is not unimpeachable - for a subscriber of the memorandum will become a member upon incorporation of the company without ever becoming a shareholder; and a person who acquires a share or shares upon transfer or transmission does not become a member until his name is entered on the register of members[7].

[15.002] Most of the rights, interests, and obligations associated with shares stem from the fact that a shareholder, properly registered as such, is a member[8]. Therefore, in this chapter shares and membership are considered in two separate sections, namely:

[A] Membership.

[B] Shares.

---

1 See Chapter 4, *Incorporation and its Consequences*, para **[4.023]** ff.

2 The company will, however, continue to exist legally even though it may have no members, for a company only ceases to exist as a separate legal person upon the occurrence of one of the circumstances detailed in Chapter 4, para **[4.020]**.

3 Provided, on becoming a shareholder, his name has been entered on the register of members; see para **[15.004]** ff.

4 CA 1963, s 33; see generally Chapter 1, *The Private Company in Context.*

5 CA 1963, s 207; see, however, Chapter 5, *Disregarding Separate Legal Personality* for exceptions to this statement.

6 Schmitthoff (ed), *Palmer's Company Law*, (24th edn, 1987), p 791.

7 See para **[15.004]** ff.

8 For an examination of the rights of a 'bare' shareholder whose name has not been entered on the register of members see para **[15.022]** and generally Chapter 16, *Share Transfers in Private Companies*.

[A] MEMBERSHIP

[15.003] The rights, interests and obligations of a shareholder are to a large extent dependent upon the shareholder's status as a member of the private company. Membership will be examined here under the following headings:

1. What constitutes membership?.
2. Persons who may become members.
3. The register of members.
4. Cesser of membership.

What constitutes membership?

(a) Definition of member

[15.004] The Companies Act 1963, s 31 ('CA 1963 – the '1963 Act') is unequivocal as to what constitutes a member of a private company. A member of a private company is someone who either:

(i) is an original subscriber of the memorandum of association[9]; or

(ii) has agreed to become a member and whose name has been entered on the register of members[10].

Only persons who fall into one of these categories acquire full status as members[11]. Each category will now be examined in further detail.

(i) Subscribers of the memorandum

[15.005] CA 1963, s 31(1) provides:

> 'The subscribers of the memorandum of a company shall be deemed to have agreed to become members of the company, and, on its registration, shall be entered as members on its register of members.'

The effect of this subsection is that the subscriber becomes a member *automatically* upon registration of the company. This will be so even if his name is not subsequently entered on the register of members[12]. No allotment[13] of shares to the subscriber is required to make him a member[14]; but in *Mackley*'s case[15], it was held that it will no longer be possible to regard the subscriber as a member if *all* the authorised shares have been issued to others without any shares being allotted to the subscriber.

---

9 CA 1963, s 31(1).

10 CA 1963, s 31(2).

11 See Schmitthoff (ed), *Palmer's Company Law*, (24th edn, 1987), p 792; also *Nicol's case* (1885) 29 Ch D 421. Membership may have other connotations in the context of other legislation however: see *Soden v British and Commonwealth Holdings plc* [1997] TLR 515 where the House of Lords held that a sum was due to a member of a company 'in his character as member' under the Insolvency Act 1986 (UK), s 74(2)(f) if the right to receive it was based on the contract implied between the members and the company by the English equivalent of CA 1963, s 25.

12 *Nicol's case* (1885) 29 Ch D 421; *Alexander v Automatic Telephone Co* [1900] 2 Ch 56.

13 See para **[15.049]**.

14 *Evan's case, Re London, Hamburg and Continental Exchange Bank* (1867) 2 Ch App 427.

15 *Mackley's* (1875) 1 Ch D 247.

While failure to enter the subscriber's name on the register of members is not fatal to a subscriber's membership, it amounts, nevertheless, to the commission of a criminal offence for which the company and every officer may be punished by a fine[16].

(ii) Other persons

[15.006] Section 31(2) of the 1963 Act provides:

> 'Every other person who agrees to become a member of the company, and whose name is entered in its register of members, shall be a member of the company.'

Therefore, in order for a person who is not a subscriber to the memorandum to become a member, two conditions must be fulfilled:

- — he must *agree* to become a member; and
- — his name must be entered on the register of members.

Both conditions must be fulfilled; merely agreeing to become a member does not make that person a member[17]. Likewise, where a person's name is entered on the register of members *without* his consent, he is not bound by it, and he may apply to have the register rectified and his name removed from it[18]; though he may, in certain circumstances, be *estopped* from denying his membership of the company[19].

(b) Membership agreements

[15.007] There is no difference in law between an agreement to become a member and any other type of agreement. All that is required is a valid offer and a valid acceptance[20]. An agreement to take shares will constitute an agreement to become a member. In general, no formal requirements need be fulfilled by an agreement to become a member, eg it need not be in writing, but the articles may, in particular circumstances, require certain formalities to be met. Model reg 31 of Table A, for example, requires a person who has become entitled to a share by way of *transmission*[21] and who elects to be registered as a member himself to 'deliver or send to the company a notice in writing signed by him stating that he so elects'.

(c) Estoppel

[15.008] In the absence of formal agreement to become a member, a person may still be regarded as a member through the operation of estoppel if his name is entered on the register of members. Estoppel can operate in two ways to make a member of someone who has not consented to the entry of his name on the register of members.

First, entry of names on the register entitles persons examining the register to rely on the truth of its contents; and they may subsequently rely on the results of their examination. As Lord Cranworth observed in *Oakes v Turquand*[22]:

---

16 CA 1963, s 116(9), as amended by C(A)A 1982, Sch 1. On the register of members see para **[15.017]**.

17 See *Re a Company* (No 003160 of 1986) [1986] BCLC 391 at 393; *Nicol's case* (1885) 29 Ch D 421.

18 See para **[15.022]**.

19 See para **[15.008]**.

20 See generally Clark, *Contract Law in Ireland* (4th edn, 1998), ch 1.

21 See Chapter 16, *Transfer of Shares in Private Companies*, para **[16.025]***ff*.

22 *Oakes v Turquand* (1867) LR 2 HL 325 at 366.

> 'When the legislature enabled shareholders to limit their liability, not merely to the amount of their shares but to so much of that amount as should remain unpaid, it is obvious that no creditor could safely trust the company without having a means of ascertaining, first, who the shareholders might be, and, secondly, to what extent they might be liable...The legislature took care to provide the register as a means of enabling persons dealing with the company to know to whom and to what they might trust.'

The person who knows that his name has been placed on the register of members without his consent will be treated as a member if he does not act quickly to have his name removed because the entry of his name on the register may have the effect 'of inducing other persons to alter their position'[23], eg they may extend credit to the company or they may subscribe for shares in it. Delay in seeking rectification of the register may estop the person so registered from denying his membership[24].

Secondly, where a person whose name has been entered on the register of members without his consent does some act which is consistent with membership he will be estopped from denying his membership and from having the register rectified. In *Linz v Electric Wire Co of Palestine*[25], Linz, an allottee of shares under a void allotment, sold the shares to third parties who were subsequently registered as members of the company. Linz then sought to recover from the company the money she had paid it for the shares, on the basis that she had not become a member because of the invalidity of the allotment. She was estopped from suing the company for the return of her consideration because, having sold the shares, she had acted in a manner consistent with membership.

Persons who may become members

(a) Natural members

[15.009] The law places few restrictions on natural persons becoming members. Foreigners may become members[26]. Likewise, a bankrupt may become a member, and his bankruptcy will not inhibit his membership rights[27]. Minors and persons of unsound mind may become members, but contracts by them for the purchase of shares will be subject to the ordinary rules of contractual capacity which pertain to persons not sui juris[28]. A minor enjoys all the benefits of membership, provided he appears on the register of members, until such time as the contract for the purchase of his shares is repudiated by either himself or the company[29]. A company's constitutional documents may, however, exclude certain persons from becoming shareholders. Furthermore, as shall be seen[30], the articles of a private company usually give the directors a broad discretion to refuse to register any person as a member.

---

23 *Per* Lord Cairns in *Lawrence's case, Re Cachar Co* (1867) LR 2 Ch 412 at 417.

24 *Sewell's case, Re New Zealand Banking Corporation* (1868) 3 Ch App 131; *Re Scottish Petroleum Co* (1883) 23 Ch D 413; *Re Railway Timetables Publishing Co* (1889) 42 Ch D 98.

25 *Linz v Electric Wire Co of Palestine* [1948] AC 371. See also *Crawley's case* (1869) LR 4 Ch 322.

26 *Princess of Reuss v Bos* (1871) LR 5 HL 176.

27 *Morgan v Gray* [1953] Ch 83; *Birch v Sullivan* [1957] 1 WLR 1247.

28 See generally, Clark, *Contract Law in Ireland*, (4th edn, 1998), ch 16.

29 *Capper's case* (1868) LR 3 458; *Pugh and Sharman's case* (1872) LR 13 566.

30 See Chapter 16, *Share Transfers in Private Companies*, para **[16.037]***ff*.

(b) Corporate members

[15.010] A company may become a member of another company provided its objects so permit[31]. If the company in which membership is sought is neither the company itself nor its holding company, no further restrictions apply.

There are significant restrictions, however, on the extent to which a company can become a member in itself by acquiring its own shares[32]. Likewise, a company cannot be a member of its holding company unless certain requirements are met.

The following matters in relation to corporate members are considered here as follows:

(i) Subsidiaries and holding companies.

(ii) Section 32 of the Companies Act 1963

(iii) Exceptions to the prohibition contained in s 32 of the Companies Act 1963;

(iv) Section 224 of the Companies Act 1990;

(v) Formalities required to be met for section 224 to apply;

(vi) Treatment of shares held by subsidiary.

(i) Subsidiaries and holding companies[33]

[15.011] The Companies Act 1990, s 224 ('CA 1990' – the '1990 Act') permits a subsidiary to acquire and hold shares in its holding company once authorised to do so in advance, and provided certain capital safeguards are met. The section largely supersedes CA 1963, s 32, which lays down a blanket prohibition, subject to specified exceptions, on a subsidiary becoming a member in its holding company. Section 32 of the 1963 Act remains in force, however.

Where membership of a subsidiary in its holding company is in issue, a two pronged examination will thus be required. First, it must be determined whether the membership falls within one of the exceptions to CA 1963, s 32. If it does, then the matter will end there. But if it does not, it must, secondly, be determined whether the membership is permitted in accordance with CA 1990, s 224. Each of these statutory provisions may now be considered in turn.

(ii) Section 32 of the Companies Act 1963

[15.012] CA 1963, s 32(1) provides:

> 'Subject to the provisions of this section, a body corporate cannot be a member of a company which is its holding company, and any allotment of shares in a company to its subsidiary shall be void.'

A nominee of the subsidiary is likewise prohibited from becoming a member of the subsidiary's holding company[34]. If the holding company is not a company limited by shares (eg a guarantee company or an unlimited company) then the reference to shares is to be construed as a reference to the interests of members, whatever the form of that

---

31 *Re Barned's Banking Co* (1867) LR 3 Ch 105.

32 See Chapter 18, *The Maintenance of Capital*, para **[18.017]***ff.*

33 On subsidiary and holding companies see further Chapter 17, *Groups of Companies.*

34 CA 1963, s 32(7).

interest[35]. The rationale behind the prohibition contained in s 32(1) is the prevention of companies from trafficking in their own shares by indirect means[36].

(iii) Exceptions to the prohibition contained in the Companies Act s 32

[15.013] There are four exceptions to the prohibition on a subsidiary becoming a member of its holding company. Three of these may be relied upon by most companies; the fourth, however, is applicable only to companies which were subsidiaries on or before 5 May 1959. The exceptions are as follows.

First, the prohibition does not extend to situations where a subsidiary is a personal representative under a will or an intestacy[37].

Secondly, the prohibition does not extend to situations where the subsidiary is a trustee, unless the holding company, or a subsidiary of the holding company, is beneficially interested in the trust, except by way of security issued in the ordinary course of a business which includes the lending of money[38].

Thirdly, a company which is a member of another company and subsequently becomes a subsidiary of that other company is not prohibited from continuing to be a member of that company[39]. It may even acquire further shares in the holding company, but only if those shares are issued to it for no consideration in the course of a capitalisation by the holding company[40]. The holding company may, when making an offer of shares to its members, sell any shares which the subsidiary could have taken up by virtue of its membership of the holding company, and pay the subsidiary the proceeds of the sale instead[41]. Furthermore, the subsidiary is prohibited from voting at meetings of the holding company or at class meetings of the holding company's shareholders[42]. The subsidiary is, thus, deprived of one of the advantages ordinarily associated with being a member[43].

Finally, a subsidiary which was a member of a holding company on 5 May 1959 is not prevented from continuing as member of its holding company[44], but the same restrictions apply to that company as apply to the subsidiary considered in the previous exception.

(iv) Section 224 of the Companies Act 1990

[15.014] CA 1990, s 224 provides:

> 'Notwithstanding ss 32 and 60 of the 1963 Act a company may, subject to the provisions of this section, acquire and hold shares in a company which is its holding company.'

---

35 CA 1963, s 32(9).

36 See Schmitthoff (ed), *Palmer's Company Law* (24th edn, 1987), para 50-09; Ussher, *Company Law in Ireland* (1986), p 104.

37 CA 1963, s 32(2).

38 CA 1963, s 32(2).

39 CA 1963, s 32(5).

40 CA 1963, s 32(5).

41 CA 1963, s 32(8).

42 CA 1963, s 32(6).

43 On voting rights see para **[15.076]** ff.

44 CA 1963, s 32(3).

The first point of note in relation to this provision is that it only permits a subsidiary to acquire *shares* in its holding company. The holding company must, therefore, be a company limited by shares before the provision may be relied upon; if it is not, then the subsidiary will be prohibited from becoming a member by CA 1963, s 32 unless the membership falls within the permitted exceptions to that section.

(v) Formalities required to be met for s 224 to apply

[15.015] Two formalities must be satisfied before a subsidiary may rely on the provisions of CA 1990, s 224(1) and hold shares in its holding company. Failure to comply with these requirements may render the directors of the subsidiary personally liable to repay the total amount paid by the subsidiary for the shares[45].

First, a contract for the acquisition of the shares must be authorised in advance both by the subsidiary and its holding company[46]. If the shares are to be purchased on a recognised stock exchange and subject to a marketing agreement, then an *ordinary resolution*[47] of the general meetings of both the holding and the subsidiary companies authorising the acquisition will suffice[48]. If, however, the shares are to be acquired in some other manner, such as in a private sale, or if the subsidiary proposes to enter into a contract whereby it will be obliged to take shares in its holding company on the occurrence of some contingency, special resolutions[49] will be required from both companies authorising the contracts[50]. In all cases, the authority may be revoked, varied or released only by the passing of a resolution of the kind which was necessary to authorise the acquisition in the first place[51].

Secondly, the consideration paid by the subsidiary for the shares in its holding company may only come out of those profits of the subsidiary which are available for distribution[52]. When calculating the profits which are available for distribution for the purposes of acquiring shares in its holding company, the subsidiary may not take into account any profits attributable to any shares in the subsidiary which are held by the holding company, insofar as they are profits relating to the period before the holding company became a member of the subsidiary[53].

---

45 CA 1990, s 225.

46 CA 1990, 224(3). Notably, such authority will only be required where the shares are to be acquired under a contract; if there is no contract - say, for example, the shares are a gift from the holding company - no advance authority appears to be required. In most cases, however, some kind of contract will be involved.

47 On ordinary resolutions generally see Chapter 9, *Corporate Governance: Meetings*, para **[9.068]**.

48 CA 1990, ss 212 and 215.

49 On special resolutions see Chapter 9, *Corporate Governance: Meetings*, para **[9.070]***ff*.

50 CA 1990, ss 224(3), 212–214. The special resolution will not be effective unless a copy of the proposed contract or, if it is not in writing, a memorandum of its terms, is available for inspection at the registered offices of the companies for at least 21 days before each meeting respectively, and at the meetings themselves: CA 1990, s 213(5).

51 CA 1990, ss 213(2), 215(1), and 214(2), respectively.

52 CA 1990, s 224(2). On the availability of profits for distribution see Chapter 18; *The Maintenance of Capital*, para **[18.081]***ff*.

53 CA 1990, s 224(4).

(vi) Treatment of shares held by subsidiary

[15.016] Once a subsidiary acquires shares in its holding company, two restrictions apply to how it may deal with them. First, the subsidiary's profits available for distribution must be treated as being reduced by the total cost of the shares acquired[54]. Secondly, the subsidiary may not exercise any voting rights in respect of the shares acquired by it in the holding company, and any purported exercise of those rights will be void[55]. This prevents the directors of the holding company from controlling the voting rights of shares held by the subsidiary in order, say, to perpetually vote themselves into office.

Regarding a holding company in which a subsidiary has acquired shares, the holding company must, for the purposes of preparing its consolidated accounts[56], treat the shares held by the subsidiary in the same manner as treasury shares[57].

The register of members

(a) Form and location of the register

[15.017] According to CA 1963, s 116[58], every company is required to keep a register of members (the 'register'). The register may be kept either 'by making entries in bound books or by recording the matters in question in any other manner'[59] or 'by recording the matters in question otherwise than in a legible form so long as the recording is capable of being reproduced in a legible form'[60] (eg computer disk, etc). Where the register is not kept in a bound book, 'adequate precautions' must be taken for guarding against falsification and facilitating its discovery[61]. Failure to take such precautions renders the company and every officer in default liable to a fine not to exceed €1,905[62].

The register is required to be kept at the company's registered office except when work is being done on it at another office of the company or an office of some person (eg the company's accountant) who undertakes work on the register on behalf of the company. The register must not be kept in any place outside the State[63], and the company is required to notify the Registrar of Companies of the place where the register is kept and of any change in that place[64]. Failure to comply with any of these requirements will render the company

54 CA 1990, s 224(2)(b)(i).

55 CA 1990, s 224(2)(b)(iii).

56 See Chapter 13, *Accounts and Auditors*, para **[13.109]** ff.

57 CA 1990, s 224(2)(b)(ii). On treasury shares generally see para **[15.109]**.

58 As amended by C(A)A 1982, s 20.

59 CA 1963, s 378(1).

60 C(A)A 1977, s 4(1) (the '1977 Act').

61 CA 1963, s 378(2). What is meant by 'adequate' in these circumstances is not clear. Where the register is kept on computer disk, a backup copy, made at regular intervals, should be password protected and kept on another disk to be placed in a secure and safe place. This serves the dual purpose of minimising the chances of falsification and preventing loss of information in the all too common event of corruption of the main disk.

62 CA 1963, s 378(2), as amended by C(A)A 1982, Sch 1, and CA 1990, s 240 as amended by CLEA 2001, s 104.

63 CA 1963, s 116(6).

64 CA 1963, s 116(7).

and every officer in default, and, if the books are being looked after by an agent of the company, the agent, liable to a fine not to exceed €1,905[65]. In practice, many private companies have been guilty of less than strict compliance with these requirements.

(b) Inspection of the register

[15.018] The register must be open for inspection for at least two hours each day to any member free of charge and to any other person upon payment of such reasonable fee which may not exceed six cent[66] except when the company has advertised in a newspaper circulating in the district of the company's registered office that the register will be closed[67]. The register may not be closed for more than 30 days in each year[68]. Again, it is thought that many private companies fail to comply with these requirements.

Any member or other person may obtain a copy of the register from the company on payment of a sum not to exceed three cent per one hundred words or fraction thereof[69]. Such copy must be sent to the member or other person requesting it within ten days[70].

Failure to comply with inspection requirements will render the company, every officer in default, and, where the register is being looked after by an agent, the agent, liable to a fine not to exceed €1,905[71]. A refusal by the company to allow inspection or copying must be distinct and definite before such liability will arise[72].

The right to inspect, and to receive copies of, the register terminates upon a winding up[73].

(c) Particulars to be registered

[15.019] CA 1963, s 116 provides that the register must contain the following particulars:

> '(a) the names and addresses of the members, and ... a statement of the shares held by each member, distinguishing each share by its number so long as the share has a number, and ... the amount paid or agreed to be considered as paid on the shares of each member;
>
> (b) the date at which each person was entered in the register as a member;
>
> (c) the date at which any person ceased to be a member.'

The register should also contain details of the class of share held by each member[74]. The particulars detailed in paragraph (a) are required to be entered on the register within 28

65 CA 1963, s 116(9), as amended by C(A)A 1982, Sch 1; and CA 1963, s 120, as amended by CA 1990, s 240, as amended by CLEA 2001, s 104.

66 CA 1963, s 119(1).

67 CA 1963, s 121.

68 CA 1963, s 121.

69 CA 1963, s 121(2). The Act describes the maximum fee for this purpose as 'sixpence,' which, since decimalisation, amounted to two-and-a-half-pence.

70 CA 1963, s 121.

71 CA 1963, s 119(3) as amended by C(A)A 1982, Sch 1 and CA 1963, s 120; as amended by CA 1990, s 240, as amended by CLEA 2001, s 104.

72 *R v Wiltshire and Berkshire Canal Navigation* (1835) 3 Ad & El 477.

73 *Re Kent Coalfields Syndicate* [1898] 1 QB 754.

74 *Re Performing Rights Society Ltd* [1978] 2 All ER 712.

days of the conclusion of the agreement to become a member, or, in the case of a subscriber to the memorandum, within 28 days after the registration of the company[75].

(d) Legal significance of the particulars registered

[15.020] CA 1963, s 124 provides that the register of members 'shall be prima facie evidence' of any of the matters authorised or directed by the Companies Acts to be inserted in it. The fact that it is prima facie evidence of the matters contained therein (and not conclusive evidence) means that a person relying on the contents of the register must remember that a person's name may have been improperly entered on the register because of some mistake, misrepresentation or accident, and that the name may subsequently be removed.

(e) Registration of changes in particulars

[15.021] The company should register any changes in the registered details, such as change of ownership, name, address etc, of which it has notice, lest the register should be as untrue as if false particulars had been registered in the first place[76]. Such registration should be carried out by the company secretary or the person appointed to keep the register, but no changes may be made without the prior approval of the board of directors[77].

(f) Rectification of the register

(i) Rectification by the company

[15.022] The company has a statutory power to rectify any error or omission in the register by CA 1963, s 122(5). Such rectification may be made without an application to the court, but rectification will not be allowed to affect adversely any person unless he agrees to the rectification being made[78]. The rectification will be made by the company secretary or the person appointed to keep the register, but no rectification may be made without the prior approval of the board of directors[79]. Notice of the rectification must be sent to the registrar of companies within twenty-one days of rectification if the error or omission appeared in any document previously sent to him[80].

(ii) Rectification through the court

[15.023] CA 1963, s 122 also gives the court the power to order rectification of the register where:

> (a) the name of any person is, without sufficient cause, entered in the register of members or omitted therefrom in contravention of ... s 116; or
>
> (b) default is made in entering on the register within the period fixed by ... s 116 of the fact of any person having ceased to be a member.

An application for rectification in such circumstances may be made to the court by any aggrieved person, member of the company, or, indeed, the company itself. The court's power to make an order under the section is discretionary[81], and the court has the power to

---

75 CA 1963, s 116(2).

76 See generally, Doyle, *The Company Secretary* (1994), pp 91–94.

77 *Wheatcroft's case* (1873) 29 LT 324; *Chapterida Mines Ltd v Anderson* (1905) 22 TLR 27.

78 CA 1963, s 122(5).

79 See para **[15.021]**.

80 CA 1963, s 122(5).

81 *Trevor v Whitworth* (1887) 12 App Cas 409 at 440, per Lord Macnaghten.

decide any question of the title of any party to the application and may decide any question necessary or expedient to be decided for the rectification of the register[82]. The court may award compensation for any loss suffered by the aggrieved person[83].

[15.024] The court's power to examine title in an application under CA 1963, s 122 makes the application attractive whenever a dispute arises concerning the title to shares. The application to the court for rectification may be invoked to compel the company to register particulars which it has improperly neglected or refused to register. In this regard it provides an appropriate procedure to the transferee of shares whom the directors refuse to register as a member of the company[84]. As shall be seen, however, it will be very difficult to show that the directors acted 'without sufficient cause' or in bad faith, as is required to be proved by the section, if the articles give the directors a general power to refuse to register a transfer[85]. The circumstances in which such an application might succeed are examined in Chapter 16, *Share Transfers in Private Companies*. Likewise, rectification may be sought to compel the company to register particulars where the company, acting on foot of a forged share transfer, has removed the name of the real owner and entered another's name[86], or where shares have been improperly forfeited[87].

An application under CA 1963, s 122 may also be used to compel the company to remove particulars from the register. Thus, an application may succeed where registration has been effected on foot of a misrepresentation[88], unless a winding up has commenced[89].

Failure to apply for rectification within a reasonable time, or otherwise acting inconsistently with a grievance, may estop an aggrieved person from proceeding with an application for rectification[90].

(g) Beneficial interests

[15.025] The register is only concerned with legal title to shares. CA 1963, s 123 succinctly provides that:

> 'No notice of any trust, express, implied or constructive, shall be entered on the register or be receivable by the registrar.'

In *Rearden v Provincial Bank*[91], Porter MR explained that the intention of the section is:

> '... to spare the company the responsibility of attending any trusts or equities whatever attached to their shares, so that they might safely and securely deal with the person who is registered owner, and with him alone, recognising no other person and no different right; freeing them, in short, from all embarrassing inquiries into conflicting claims as to shares,

---

82 CA 1963, s 122(3). See *Keene v Martin* [1999] TLR 777.

83 CA 1963, s 122(3).

84 On the power of the directors to refuse the register a transfer of shares see Chapter 16, *Share Transfers in Private Companies*, para **[16.037]***ff*.

85 CA 1963, s 122(3).

86 *Re Bahia and San Francisco Railway* (1868) LR 3 QB 584.

87 *Re Ystalyfera Gas Co* [1887] WN 30. On forfeiture of shares see para **[15.119]**.

88 *Stewart's case* (1886) 1 Ch App 74; *Components Tube Co v Naylor* [1900] 2 IR 1.

89 *Oakes v Turquand* (1867) LR 2 HL 325.

90 See para **[15.008]**.

91 *Rearden v Provincial Bank* [1896] IR 532.

transfers, calls, dividends, right to vote and the like; and enabling them to treat the registered shareholder as owner of the shares for all purposes, without regard to contract as between himself and third persons.'

This provision is of great significance, for it facilitates the de facto one-man company. A shareholder may appear in the register of members as owner of all but one share in the company, and his nominee, holding the remaining share on behalf of, or on trust for, the majority shareholder, may appear in the register as the other shareholder. Only the person registered can be made liable by the company in respect of payment for the shares or to contribute in a winding up. The practice of nominee shareholding has been, of course, very popular in Ireland to date.

The prohibition on the entry of trusts in the register of members also has the effect of making it unattractive for banks and other lending institutions to take equitable mortgages or charges of the shares as security for advances. This is because the registered owner of the shares can pass a good title to the shares to a bona fide purchaser for value without notice, thus depriving the lender of his security[92].

[15.026] CA 1963, s 123 must be read in conjunction with model reg 7 of Table A, which provides:

> 'Except as required by law, no person shall be recognised by the company as holding any share upon any trust, and the company shall not be bound by or be compelled in any way to recognise (even when having notice thereof) any equitable, contingent, future or partial interest in any share or any interest in any fractional part of a share (except only as by these regulations or by law otherwise provided) and any other rights in respect of any share except an absolute right to the entirety thereof in the registered holder: this shall not preclude the company from requiring the members or a transferee of shares to furnish the company with information as to beneficial ownership of any share when such information is reasonably required by the company.'

The effect of this article, in conjunction with s 123 of the 1963 Act, is to permit the company to ignore all equitable interests in its shares. The article goes beyond the statutory provision in that it relates not merely to registration of the equitable right but also to recognition of the right.

[15.027] It may also be observed that the provision does not prevent a company, if it so desires, from recognising an equitable interest in a share[93], though it may not, of course, enter the interest so recognised on the register of members because of CA 1963, s 123.

[15.028] It should be stressed that the provisions of CA 1963, s 123 and reg 7 *do not* prevent the creation of beneficial interests in the shares of a company. In *Société Générale de Paris v Walker*[94], James Walker, the registered owner of 100 in a tram company, created two equitable charges over the shares. The first charge arose by virtue of an equitable deposit of the share certificates with a Mr James Scott Walker as security for advances. The second and subsequent charge was in favour of the Société Générale de Paris and

---

92 *Société Generalé de Paris v Walker* (1885) 11 App Cas 20; *Ireland v Hart* [1902] 1 Chapter 522.

93 The article merely provides that the company is not 'bound,' nor can it be 'compelled,' to recognise the interests to which it refers.

94 *Société Générale de Paris v Walker* (1885) 11 App Cas 20.

arose on foot of a blank transfer form duly executed in their favour as security for advances. The Société tried to register as members of the tram company but were unsuccessful because they could not show that they possessed the share certificates. A dispute then arose as to whether the Société or the executors of James Scott Walker (by then deceased) had priority of equitable security interests. The Société argued that since a share is a chose in action[95], and since priority of interests in choses in action is given to the first person to notify the debtor or fundholder (or, in this case, the company) of his interest, then they should take in priority. By attempting to have their name entered on the register of members, they had been first to notify the company of their interest. The courts, however, held that the normal rules governing priorities of interests in choses in action did not apply to interests in shares. In the course of his judgment in the Court of Appeal, which was later affirmed by the House of Lords, Lindley LJ stated:

> 'If a shareholder in a company governed by the Companies Act ... does not transfer his shares, but agrees to transfer them or to hold them on trust for another, either absolutely or by way of security, there can be no doubt as to the validity of the agreement, nor as to the effect of it as between the parties to it. As between them the agreement or trust can be enforced; but as regards the company the shareholder on the register remains shareholder still. He is the person to exercise the rights of a shareholder, for example, to vote as such, to receive dividends as such, and to transfer the shares. On the other hand, he, and he alone, is liable for calls, and to be put on the list of contributories if the company is wound up.'

Thus, although the company may safely ignore the equitable interests of others in the shares held by a registered member, the interests remain valid as between the trustee and the cestui que trust. In *Re Harvard Securities Ltd*[96] it was further held that the law governing the equitable interests so created in the shares will normally be the 'lex situs' – the law of the place of incorporation.

[15.029] Despite the provisions of CA 1963, s 123 and model reg 7 of Table A, a company will *not* be allowed to ignore beneficial interests of which it has actual notice[97]. In *Rearden*'s case[98], Mr Barry, a trustee holding shares in the bank to which Mrs Rearden was beneficially entitled, became personally indebted to the bank. The bank had been told, in the course of correspondence, that Mr Barry held the shares on trust for Mrs Rearden, but despite this notification it nevertheless sought to exercise a lien[99] over the shares in respect of Mr Barry's personal debt. The bank argued that the combined effect of s 30 of the Companies Act 1862 (the precursor to CA 1963, s 123) and Clause 8 of its articles of association (the precursor to model reg 7 of Table A) was to permit the bank to ignore *all* equitable interests - even those of which it had been notified - so that it could exercise a lien on the shares in respect of the personal debts of the registered owner. The courts, however, found otherwise. Porter MR explained:

> 'It is right and necessary that a company should not be mixed up with outside claims and disputes. The company is to have one person, or one set of persons, alone to deal with as

95 See para **[15.037]**.

96 *Re Harvard Securities Ltd* [1997] 2 BCLC 369.

97 Though again, of course, it may not enter them on the register: CA 1963, s 123.

98 *Rearden v Provincial Bank of Ireland* [1896] IR 532.

99 On liens over shares see para **[15.117]**.

> shareholders; and it is to be unaffected by trusts, equities and the like, which they have no means of determining or knowing anything about. In such cases, apart from s 30 and special articles of association, they really could not protect themselves. But this immunity can have no reason to support it when it is claimed that the company may, for its own benefit, ignore facts within its own knowledge, as by creating liens in its own favour, contrary to good faith ... *In both cases the language is, I think, intended for the protection of the company; not to enable it to commit frauds; or knowingly take the benefit of them.*'[100]

On appeal to the Court of Appeal, Palles CB added:

> 'The effect and operation of the section, and of clause No 8 does not extend to extinguish or affect any obligation to which the company would otherwise have been subjected by reason of its own unconscientious conduct, although notice of the trust might be a material element in arriving at the conclusion that the conduct of the company was against conscience. The mere fact of notice does not convert the company into trustees for the persons whose beneficial interest they have notice; but if, having that notice, they advance money to the trustee, on the security of the trust property, their conduct is not protected by the section and they participate in a breach of trust. So, too, they seek to commit a breach of trust by claiming, under colour of a lien created after such notice, to appropriate to the payment of their own debt property which to their knowledge is trust property. Property thus acquired they cannot be permitted to hold against the *cestui que trust*.'

This principle was more recently to the fore again in *McGrattan v McGrattan*[101], where a resolution which had been carried with the votes of trustees of shares was held to be null and void because the company had knowledge of the fact that the trustees, in so voting, were acting in breach of trust.

[15.030] Although beneficial interests may not be recorded in the register of members, the beneficial interests of directors and secretaries must be disclosed and recorded in a register specially kept for that purpose. Likewise, the beneficial interests of other persons may be required to be disclosed on foot of a court order - though no register recording the fruits of such disclosure appears to be required. The topic of disclosure of interests in shares is considered at para **[15.123]** below.

[15.031] Order 46 of the Rules of the Superior Courts 1986 provides a mechanism whereby persons beneficially entitled to shares may protect their interests. Under this mechanism, the beneficiary, having filed a 'stop notice' and an affidavit of their interest in the Central Office of the High Court, may serve a copy of the stop notice and affidavit on the company, thus notifying it of his interest[102]. The company, in turn, upon receipt of the stop notice, must thereafter notify the beneficiary of any attempt by the legal owner to transfer the shares or to pay the dividends[103] payable thereon to another, and must delay the transfer or payment for eight days in order to allow the beneficiary to take steps to protect his position[104].

---

[100] [1896] IR 532 at 567–568. Emphasis added.

[101] *McGrattan v McGrattan* [1985] NI 28.

[102] RSC 1986, ord 46, rr 5-11, 13. See also Chapter 16, *Share Transfers in Private Companies*, para **[16.036]**.

[103] On dividends see para **[15.069]** ff.

[104] RSC 1986, rule 12.

Cesser of membership

[15.032] Membership may cease in many ways, each of which is considered in its proper context elsewhere in this work. Here it is necessary only to list the principal modes of cesser of membership and to add, as a rule of thumb, that membership may be treated as subsisting as long as the member's name appears on the register of members, with the consequence that failure on the part of the outgoing member to ensure prompt removal of his name from the register may result in the creation of an estoppel[105]. The principal ways in which membership ends include cesser:

- upon *dissolution* of the company[106];
- upon *transfer* of shares (whether voluntarily or compulsorily) and entry of the transferee's name on the register of members[107];
- upon *transmission* of shares upon death or bankruptcy and entry of another's name on the register of members in place of the deceased or bankrupt member[108];
- upon *redemption* of shares by the company[109];
- upon *forfeiture* or *surrender* of shares[110];
- upon sale by the company on foot of a *lien on shares*[111];
- upon *rescission*, for misrepresentation, of the contract for the acquisition of the shares[112];
- upon *repudiation*, by a minor, of the contract to take the shares[113];
- upon foot of a *court order*, such as an order under CA 1963, s 205 ordering the purchase of the shares of an oppressed minority by the company[114];
- upon a *takeover* by an 80% shareholder exercising its power under CA 1963, s 204 to acquire compulsorily the shares of a dissentient minority[115];
- upon a *sale of assets in a liquidation* to another company in consideration for shares or like interests in the other company, under CA 1963, s 260 the liquidator may elect to purchase the shares of a shareholder who does not wish to take shares in the other company[116].

105 See para **[15.008]**.
106 See Chapter 4, *Incorporation and its Consequences*, para **[4.020]**.
107 See further Chapter 16, *Share Transfers in Private Companies.*
108 See further Chapter 16, *Share Transfers in Private Companies.*
109 See further Chapter 18, *The Maintenance of Capital*, para **[18.012]***ff.*
110 See further para **[15.119]** ff.
111 See para **[15.117]**.
112 See para **[15.007]**.
113 See para **[15.009]**.
114 See Chapter 19, *Shareholders' Remedies*, para **[19.006]***ff.*
115 On compulsory acquisitions of shares see Chapter 16, *Share Transfers in Private Companies*, para **[16.080]***ff.*
116 See generally Chapter 25, *Winding Up Companies.*

[B] SHARES

[15.033] Shares are considered here in the following manner:

1. The legal nature of shares.
2. Formal requirements relating to shares.
3. Allotment of shares.
4. Shareholders' rights and duties.
5. Classes of shares.
6. Conversion of shares.
7. Liens on shares.
8. Forfeiture and surrender of shares.
9. Disclosure of interests in shares.

The legal nature of shares

[15.034] A share is an intangible accumulation of rights, interests and obligations. It is not a document – though a document (ie a share certificate) is used to certify that a person has the rights, interests and obligations of a shareholder[117]. The courts appear reticent when it comes to giving an exact description of the legal nature of shares; but certain features of shares are, by now, well established. Those features are examined here in the following manner:

(a) A share confers no interest in the company's assets.
(b) A share is an interest in the nature of personalty.
(c) A share is a *chose in action.*
(d) A share confers contractual rights and obligations.
(e) A share confers an interest in the company itself.
(f) A share confers statutory rights and obligations.
(g) A share confers interests and rights protected by the Constitution.

(a) A share confers no interest in the company's assets

[15.035] It used to be thought that a shareholder held beneficial ownership of the company's property, or, in other words, that the company held its assets on trust for the members[118]. This view stemmed from the fact that the property and assets of old deed of settlement companies were vested in trustees to hold for the benefit of the members[119]. But the modern company cannot ipso facto be regarded as a mere trustee for its members because of the separate legal existence which it enjoys - this was the crux of *Salomon*'s case[120]. Where the company holds property, it holds it in its own right. The shareholders have no interest in the property or any particular part of it. As Kenny J observed in *Attorney General for Ireland v Jameson*[121]:

---

[117] See para **[15.046]**.

[118] *Chapterild v Hudson's Bay Co* (1723) 2 P Wms 207; *Harrisson v Pryse* (1740) Barn Ch 324.

[119] See generally Chapter 1, *The Private Company in Context*, para **[1.064]**.

[120] *Salomon v Salomon & Co* [1897] AC 22; See generally Chapter 4, *Incorporation and its Consequences*, para **[4.026]** *ff.*

[121] *Attorney General for Ireland v Jameson* [1904] 2 IR 644 at 671. See also *Kerry Co-operative Creamery Ltd v An Bord Bainne Co-Op Ltd* [1990] ILRM 664.

'No shareholder has a right to any specific portion of the company's property, and save by, and to the extent of, his voting power at a general meeting of the company, cannot curtail the free and proper disposition of it.'

Thus, in *Short v Treasury Commissioners*[122], a case concerning the valuation of shares according to regulations which provided for payment of their value 'as between a willing buyer and a willing seller,' the English Court of Appeal rejected the argument that the shares should be valued according to the value of the company's assets and undertaking, since:

'The shareholders are not in the eye of the law part-owners of the undertaking. The undertaking is something different from the totality of the shareholdings.'[123]

(b) A share is an interest in the nature of personalty

[15.036] It follows from the foregoing that the nature of the share is not affected by the nature of the corporate assets, whether those assets are real property or personal property[124]. In fact, CA 1963, s 79 expressly states that:

'The shares or other interest of any member in a company shall be personal estate, transferable in a manner provided in the articles of the company, and shall not be of the nature of real estate.'

In *Lee & Co (Dublin) Ltd v Egan (Wholesale) Ltd*[125], it was argued that a contract for the sale of shares in a company owning land should be subject to the rule in Bain v Fothergill[126] so that only nominal damages could be recovered by the intending purchaser. Kenny J rejected that argument, observing[127] that that rule applies to the sale of land only, and not to the sale of shares in a company which owns land.

(c) A share is a chose in action

[15.037] Shares belong to that class of personal property known as *choses in action*[128]. What exactly a chose in action constitutes may be difficult to define, since the term is used to describe a wide range of interests. A simple description of a chose in action is an intangible interest which one can only protect by legal action rather than by taking possession of a physical thing[129]. Shares are affected by many of the idiosyncrasies which apply to the transfer or assignment of choses in action generally[130]. For example, shares do

---

122 *Short v Treasury Commissioners* [1948] 1 KB 116.

123 [1948] 1 KB 116 at 124, per Evershed J. On the valuation of shares generally see Chapter 16, *Share Transfers in Private Companies*, para **[16.108]***ff*.

124 See Rice, 'The Legal Nature of a Share' (1957) 21 Conv (ns) 433.

125 *Lee & Co (Dublin) Ltd v Egan (Wholesale) Ltd* (18 October 1979, unreported), High Court (Kenny J).

126 *Bain v Fothergill* (1874) LR 7 HL 158. See generally Wylie, *Irish Conveyancing Law* (2nd edn, 1996), p 431.

127 (18 October 1979, unreported), High Court at p 3.

128 *Colonial Bank v Whinney* (1886) 11 App Cas 426; *Re VGM Holdings* [1942] Ch 235. See also Halsbury's *Laws of England* (4th edn), Vol 6, para 6.

129 See *Re Cuff Knox (deceased)* [1963] IR 263, per Kingsmill Moore J at 291.

130 On the assignment of choses in action generally see Bell, *Modern Law of Personal Property in England and Ireland* (1989), ch 15.

not come within the definition of 'goods' under the Sale of Goods Act 1893[131]. As shall be seen in Chapter 16, *Share Transfers in Private Companies*, the transfer of shares is also subject to its own peculiar rules. Thus, unlike other choses in action, the legal title to shares may not be passed simply by notifying the company of the transfer[132].

(d) A share confers contractual rights and obligations

[15.038] One feature of shares which is repeatedly focused upon by the courts is the fact that shares embody contractual rights. The contractual rights and obligations associated with shares stem from the shareholder's status as a member of the company and the so-called 'section 25 contract'[133]. This contract 'of the most sacred character'[134] has already been considered in detail[135]. The contractual aspect of the interests constituted by a share was emphasised by Farwell J in his respected definition of a share in the case of *Borlands Trustee Co v Steele*[136]:

> 'A share is the interest of a shareholder in the company measured by a sum of money, for the purpose of liability in the first place, and of interest in the second, but also consisting of a series of mutual covenants entered into by all the shareholders *inter se* in accordance with [s 25 of the 1963 Act]. The contract contained in the articles of association is one of the original incidents of the share.'

In *Attorney General for Ireland v Jameson*[137] Kenny J amplified this definition, saying of a shareholder's rights and obligations that:

> 'He is entitled to a share of the company's capital and profits, the former ... being measured by a sum of money which is taken as the standard for the ascertainment of his share of the profits. If the company disposes of its assets, or if the latter be realised in a liquidation, he has a right to a proportion of the amount received after the discharge of the Company's debts and liabilities. In acquiring these rights - that is, in becoming a member of the company - he is deemed to have simultaneously entered into a contract under seal to conform to the regulations contained in the articles of association ... Whatever obligations are contained in those articles, he accepts the ownership of the shares and the position of a member of the company, bound and controlled by them. He cannot divorce his money interest, whatever it may amount to, from those obligations. They are inseparable incidents attached to his rights, and the idea of a share cannot, in my judgment, be complete without their inclusion.'

The *terms of issue* of a share enumerate the particular contractual rights associated with the share, but these terms must be authorised by the memorandum or the articles of association.

---

131 Sale of Goods Act 1893, s 62 defines 'goods' as including 'all chattels personal other than things in action and money'. See also *Lee & Co (Dublin) Ltd v Egan (Wholesale) Ltd*.

132 *Ireland v Hart* [1902] 1 Ch 522.

133 Arising under CA 1963, s 25.

134 Per Ross J in *Clark v Workman* [1920] IR 107 at 112.

135 See Chapter 3, *Private Constitutional Documentation*, para **[3.096]***ff*.

136 *Borlands Trustee Co v Steele* [1901] 1 CH 279 at 288. See also *Provincial Bank of Ireland Ltd v O'Connor* (23 July 1973, unreported), High Court 23 July 1973 (Kenny J).

137 *Attorney General for Ireland v Jameson* [1904] 2 IR 644 at 671.

(e) A share confers an interest in the company itself

[15.039] Shareholders are *members* of the company, and membership constitutes an interest *in the company itself*[138]. That a share confers an interest in the company itself is evident in Farwell J's definition in the *Borland's Trustee* case[139]. This interest stems from the contractual rights associated with membership, but it is more than a mere contractual right *in personam*[140]. Rather, it is a right *in rem*. In other words, the shareholder not only has rights *against* the company but he also, as member, has rights *in* the company itself. He, along with the other shareholders, owns the company, and, depending upon the extent of the interest he possesses, he has a hand in controlling its activities. The extent of his interest in the company is determined by reference to the contractual rights conferred by the memorandum and articles and the Companies Acts 1963-2001. Thus, Russell LJ, in *IRC v Crossman*[141], described a share as follows:

> 'It is the interest of a person in the company, that interest being composed of rights and obligations which are defined by the Companies Act and by the memorandum and articles of association of the company.'

In *Kerry Co-operative Creamery Ltd v An Bord Bainne Co-Op Ltd*[142], Costello J explained the shareholder's interests in a similar manner, emphasising that they are property rights[143]:

> 'The shareholder has rights which can properly be regarded as property rights (*PMPS Ltd & Moore v Attorney General* [1984] ILRM 88) but their nature and extent are to be ascertained by reference to the contract it has entered into with the society whose terms are contained in the society's rules.'

As property rights, the rights conferred on an individual member by a share may be exercised independently of the will of the majority of shareholders[144], and they are protected by the Constitution[145]. It is the fact that a shareholder holds property in the company itself which distinguishes him from a debentureholder who has rights against the company, and, if the debenture is secured, in the company property, but who has no rights in the company itself.

(f) A share confers statutory rights and obligations

[15.040] Apart from those rights which are conferred on shareholders by the company's memorandum and articles, the Companies Acts 1963–2001 confer certain other individual

138 Though not, of course, its assets. See para **[15.035]**.

139 See para **[15.038]**.

140 See *North Western Railway v M'Michael* (1851) 5 Exch 114; *Cork and Bandon Railway v Cazenove* (1847) 10 QB 935; *Steinberg v Scala (Leeds) Ltd* [1923] 2 Ch 452.

141 *IRC v Crossman* [1937] AC 26 at 66.

142 *Kerry Co-operative Creamery Ltd v An Bord Bainne Co-Op Ltd* [1990] ILRM 664.

143 [1990] ILRM 664 at 714. See also *Poole v Middleton* (1861) 29 Beav 646; *Private Motorist's Provident Society Ltd & Moore v Attorney General* [1984] ILRM 988.

144 *Carruth v ICI Ltd* [1937] AC 707 at 765, per Maugham LJ. It is important here, however, to distinguish a shareholder's personal rights from the rights of the company as a whole; see para **[15.083]**, and Chapter 19, *Shareholders' Remedies*, para **[19.089]**.

145 See para **[15.041]**.

and collective rights on shareholders as members of the company. These are considered at length at para **[15.085]** below.

(g) A share confers interests and rights protected by the Constitution

[15.041] The interests conferred by a share are interests which are protected by the Constitution. In *Private Motorist's Provident Society Ltd & Moore v Attorney General*[146], both the Society and Mr Moore, one of its major shareholders, sought a declaration that s 5(2) of the Industrial and Provident Societies (Amendment) Act 1978, which prohibited the Society from accepting or holding deposits, constituted an unjust attack on their constitutional property rights. Carroll J, in the High Court, for reasons discussed earlier[147], dismissed the Society's application; but in relation to Mr Moore's application she said[148]:

> 'Mr Moore is a shareholder in the Society. He invested his money with other shareholders in a society incorporated under the law which is entitled to carry on business *intra vires*. If the business of the society is affected by the Act of 1978 in such a way that the property rights of Mr Moore are affected, then he is entitled, *prima facie*, to make a claim that his constitutional rights that are protected by Article 40, s 3, and Article 43 have been infringed. Ownership of shares is one of the bundle of rights which constitute ownership of private property: *per* Mr Justice Kenny at p 84 of the report of *Central Dublin Development Association v The Attorney General* (1969) 109 ILTR 69.'

Carroll J's reference to 'ownership of shares' may be taken as a reference to the interests conferred by a share, since there was no question of the offending legislation divesting Mr Moore of his ownership of the shares in question. That was how the Supreme Court approached the matter on appeal. Delivering the court's judgment, O'Higgins CJ said[149]:

> '[A]s a shareholder and to the extent of his investment, Mr Moore has an interest in the Society and contractual rights arising therefrom. This interest and these contractual rights are property rights which belong to Mr Moore and they are capable of being harmed by injury done to the Society. The Court, therefore, rejects the submission made on behalf of the Attorney General that, as a shareholder in the Society, Mr Moore has no property rights capable of being invoked for the purposes of Article 40, s 3, of the Constitution.'

The range of effects of this constitutional aspect to shareholders' interests has yet to be fully explored in the courts. Apart from providing a convenient mechanism for indirectly enforcing rights which are not available to a company, it has been suggested[150] that the constitutionally protected property rights conferred by shares may also open the door for another exception to the rule in *Foss v Harbottle*[151], which is discussed in Chapter 19, *Shareholders' Remedies*.

---

146 *Private Motorist's Provident Society Ltd & Moore v Attorney General* [1983] IR 339.
147 See Chapter 4, *Incorporation and its Consequences*, para **[4.061]**.
148 [1983] IR 339 at 349.
149 [1983] IR 339 at 359.
150 See MacCann, 'The Rule in *Foss v Harbottle*, Recent Developments' (1990) 8 ILT 68 at 72.
151 *Foss v Harbottle* (1843) 2 Hare 461.

Formal requirements relating to shares

[15.042] Every share is required to have a nominal value[152], and, unless certain conditions are met, to be numbered[153]. In addition, each shareholder is entitled to a share certificate[154], certifying his title to the shares held by him. Each of these matters will now be considered in turn.

(a) Nominal value of shares

[15.043] CA 1963, s 6(4) requires the memorandum of a private company (or any other company having a share capital) 'to state the amount of share capital with which the company proposes to be registered, and the division thereof into shares of a fixed amount'[155]. In *Re Scandinavian Group plc*[156], Harman J held that the division into shares of a fixed amount need not be expressed in the currency of the realm - a foreign currency is equally acceptable[157].
The monetary value given to a share by the memorandum is referred to as its *nominal* or *par* value, for it need not represent the amount actually paid on the share and rarely does it reflect the true price which the share might obtain upon transfer or transmission[158]. The nominal value of a share, as may be seen from Farwell J's definition of a share in the *Borland's Trustee* case[159], serves merely as a yardstick by which the strength of the rights, interests and obligations of the shareholder may be measured.

In consequence of the euro changeover on 1 January 2002, the nominal value of shares previously denominated in Irish pounds (or in the currency of another participating Member State) became be re-denominated in euro[160]. The Economic and Monetary Union Act 1998, s 24 provides that the re-denomination takes place at the total issued or to be issued share capital (including each class of such capital where divided into separate classes) and the re-denominated nominal share par value is then calculated by dividing the total re-denominated amount by the number of shares authorised, issued or to be issued as appropriate, so that the nominal value is expressed in unrounded euro amounts. It is not simply a matter, therefore, of converting the nominal value as it appears on the face of any share certificate.

To avoid the complexities of such re-denomination and otherwise to neaten the nominal value following the introduction of the single currency, the Economic and Monetary Union

---

152 CA 1963, s 6(4).

153 CA 1963, s 80.

154 CA 1963, s 86.

155 The share capital as stated in the memorandum represents the limit of the capital which the company is authorised to issue, not the amount of capital actually issued; see Chapter 3, *Private Constitutional Documentation*, para **[3.017]**.

156 *Re Scandinavian Group plc* [1987] 2 WLR 752.

157 Cf Keane, *Company Law in the Republic of Ireland* (3rd edn, 2000), para 17.08, where the learned author, writing prior to the euro changeover, suggested that the better view is that the amount should be expressed in Irish pounds or pence.

158 On the valuation of shares see Chapter 16, *Share Transfers in Private Companies*, para **[16.108]**.

159 See para **[15.038]**.

160 EU Regulation 974/98, art 14.

Act 1998, s 26 further provides a mechanism whereby companies can re-nominalise their share capital to express it in a more convenient euro amount (other than zero). This mechanism could only be availed of until 30 June 2003.

(b) 'No par' shares

[15.044] Other jurisdictions, such as the USA and Canada, have allowed companies to issue *no par* shares, whereby a shareholder's rights, interests and obligations are measured as a fraction of the aggregate, without a misleading nominal value being attributed to the share capital and the individual shares in a manner which serves to confuse unsophisticated parties dealing with the company. While there is something to be said in favour of such measures, they might only compound confusion unless all companies were required to dispense with placing a nominal value on their shares. Although various commentators[161] and company law committees[162] have favoured the introduction of no par shares on this side of the Atlantic, nothing has yet come of their recommendations.

(c) Numbering of shares

[15.045] CA 1963, s 80 requires each share to be distinguished by an appropriate number, unless all the issued shares, or all the issued shares of a particular class, are fully paid up and rank *pari passu* (ie carry equal rights of participation in the benefits of membership) for all purposes and provided that those conditions continue to exist. In practice, those conditions usually exist in private companies, and, consequently, the numbering of shares is frequently dispensed with. Where shares are numbered the number does not, of course, appear on the share itself - since a share is not a tangible item - rather, the number of each share held by a member is registered in the register of members, and may also be recorded on the share certificate[163].

(d) Share certificates

[15.046] Under CA 1963, s 86 each shareholder is to be furnished with a share certificate which is prima facie evidence of his title to the shares held by him[164]. The share certificate must be completed and ready for delivery within two months of the allotment or transfer[165]. It is not necessary that a separate certificate be issued for each share held by the shareholder. Failure to comply with the requirements governing share certificates will render the company and its officers liable to make good the default, and the directors may be made liable to cover the costs of making good such default[166].

---

161 Eg Gower, *Principles of Modern Company Law*, (6th ed 1997).

162 Eg The Gedge Committee, Cmnd 9112 (1954); The Jenkins Committee, Cmnd 1749 (1962), paras 32–34. An attempt to introduce them in the UK in 1967 failed; see Cmnd 5391, para 49. Note, however, that an investment company within the meaning of CA 1990, Part III may have, in effect, no par shares.

163 CA 1963, s 116(1)(a); see para **[15.019]**.

164 CA 1963, s 87. Under CA 1990, s 239(3), however, the Minister is empowered to make regulations dispensing with the obligation of a company to issue certificates and providing for alternative procedures.

165 CA 1963, s 87. A transfer for these purposes means a transfer which is duly stamped and otherwise valid and not one which the company is entitled to refuse to register and has not registered. See also Chapter 16, *Share Transfers in Private Companies*.

166 CA 1963, s 86(3).

(i) Liability of the company for false information in certificate

[15.047] The company may be liable to third parties who suffer damage in respect of incorrect information appearing in share certificates. The company's liability in such circumstances stems from the equitable doctrine of estoppel. Under this doctrine, any person who makes or authorises a representation as to a certain fact is bound to accept the truth of that fact as regards a third party who relies upon it. In *Re Bahaia and San Francisco Railway Co*[167], Cockburn LJ said of a share certificate that it:

> '...is a declaration by the company to all the world that the person in whose name the certificate is made out, and to whom it is given, is a shareholder in the company, and it is given by the company with the intention that it shall be so used by the person to whom it is given, and acted upon in the sale and transfer of shares.'

Thus, the company will be liable to any person who purchases the share in good faith on the strength of the information contained in the certificate[168]. The purchaser in such circumstances will not be entitled, however, to have his name entered on the register of members - the original person named in the certificate will remain on the register - but the company must pay damages to the purchaser. Likewise, in the past it has been held that where a certificate states that the shares are fully paid up, the company cannot make a call[169] on the shareholder in respect of any amount actually unpaid on the share[170]. This decision has now, however, been superseded by s 27 of the 1983 Act, which prohibits the issue of shares at a discount[171].

It need hardly be said that the issue of share certificates is a matter which requires the utmost care and attention, for the company may incur serious liability as a result of an incorrect certificate.

(ii) Forged certificates

[15.048] The company will not, of course, be liable to third parties where the third party is aware of the fact that the information contained in the share certificate is incorrect, since no estoppel is created[172]. Likewise, the company will not be liable in respect of a share certificate which has been forged by a person having no authority to issue such a certificate, because the information contained therein does not amount to a representation which is made or authorised by the company[173]. A certificate which is issued by the company secretary without first obtaining the requisite authority of the board of directors may be regarded as a forgery[174], but this will depend upon whether the particular secretary can be viewed as having no ostensible authority to issue the certificate[175].

---

167 *Re Bahaia and San Francisco Railway Co* (1868) LR 3 QB 584 at 595.

168 *Re Bahaia and San Francisco Railway Co* (1868) LR 3 QB 584; *Balkis Consolidated Co v Tomkinson* [1893] AC 396.

169 See para **[15.090]** ff.

170 *Burkinshaw v Nicholls* (1878) 3 App Cas 1004.

171 See Chapter 18, *The Maintenance of Capital*, para **[18.091]***ff*.

172 *Re Caribbean Co* (1875) 10 Ch App 614.

173 *Ruben v Great Fingall Consolidated Co* (1875) 10 Ch App 614.

174 *South London Greyhound Racecourses Ltd v Wake* [1931] 1 Ch 496.

175 See Chapter 7, *Corporate Contracts, Capacity and Authority*, para **[7.098]**.

Allotment of shares

[15.049] There are three principal ways in which a person may become a shareholder; namely, upon *allotment* of newly issued[176] shares by the directors of a company; upon *transfer* by an existing shareholder; or upon *transmission* from a shareholder. Transfer and transmission of shares are considered in Chapter 16, *Share Transfers in Private Companies.* In this section, the allotment of shares by the company will be considered, and the following issues will be examined:

(a) Directors' authority to allot shares.

(b) Variation of invalid allotment.

(c) The mechanics of allotment.

(d) Statutory pre-emption rights on allotment.

(e) Consideration for shares on allotment.

(a) Directors' authority to allot shares

[15.050] Model reg 5 of Table A gives the directors the authority to make an allotment; however, this must be read in the light of C(A)A 1983, s 20 which provides that the directors shall not exercise the power of the company to allot shares unless they are authorised to do so either by the company in general meeting or by the articles of association.

Such authority may be given either for a particular allotment or it may be given unconditionally; but in either case it must state the maximum number of shares to be allotted and the date (not exceeding five years from the date of incorporation or the date of the resolution) upon which the authority will expire[177]. After the authority has expired, the directors may still make an allotment to any person who entered into an agreement with the company before the authority expired. The authority given may be revoked, varied or renewed for a further five years by an ordinary resolution of the company, even though this may have the effect of varying the company's articles of association.

An allotment in contravention of the C(A)A 1983, s 20 remains valid[178]; but any director knowingly and wilfully involved in the contravention will be guilty of an offence and liable to a fine not exceeding €3,174. The section does not apply to the allotment of shares pursuant to an employee share scheme, nor to a right to subscribe for or to convert any security into shares.

[15.051] In exercising their powers of allotment, the directors are required to act bona fide and in the best interests of the company. In *Nash v Lancegaye (Ireland) Ltd*[179], the plaintiff,

---

[176] 'Issued' is used colloquially in this context. As to the formal distinction between 'allotted' and 'issued' see *National Westminster Bank plc v Inland Revenue Commisisoners* [1994] 2 BCLC 239, where the House of Lords held that shares were not issued until they had been allotted and the allottee had been registered.

[177] C(A)A 1983, s 20.

[178] C(A)A 1983, s 8.

[179] *Nash v Lancegaye (Ireland) Ltd* (1958) 92 ILTR 11. See also *Hogg v Cramphorn Ltd* [1966] 3 WLR 254; *Smith (Howard) Ltd v Ampol Petroleum Ltd* [1974] AC 821; *Clemens v Clemens Brothers Ltd* [1976] 2 All ER 268; *Bamford v Bamford* [1969] 2 WLR 1107.

and certain proxies he had obtained, accounted for approximately 51% of the voting shares in the defendant company, the remaining 49% or so being held by a Mr Ryan and his associates. Ryan and his associates dominated the board of directors, and when differences arose between Ryan and the plaintiff, a fresh issue of shares was authorised by the board, allotted in such a way as to give Ryan and his associates 51% of the issued voting shares. Dixon J found that the resolutions authorising the allotment were not made in good faith. No agenda or notice of any resolution was circulated before the directors' meeting; and the only heading appearing on the notice circulated at the meeting under which the matter could be discussed was 'capital position' - an item appearing on the agenda of nearly every meeting. The plaintiff's plea for an adjournment to afford further consideration of the matter was summarily rejected. All these factors combined to indicate that the directors' true motive in making the allotment was to maintain their control over the affairs of the company and to defeat the wishes of the existing majority of shareholders[180].

(b) Variation of invalid allotment

[15.052] If it is apprehended for any reason that shares have been invalidly allotted, CA 1963, s 89, as amended by CA 1990, s 227, provides that the court can declare the allotment valid if it would be 'just and equitable' to do so. In *Re Sugar Distributors Ltd*[181] an application was brought under the section to validate an allotment where no authority to allot had been received from the members and no resolution of the board of directors had been passed, though the company secretary had prepared purported minutes for each documenting the requisite resolutions. The purpose of the purported allotment was to enable the company to avail of a tax advantage. Keane J refused the application, however, holding that the section must be exercised in a judicial manner and in accordance with appropriate criteria - and, in particular, with regard to the underlying policy of the section which was the avoidance of hardship to persons who had innocently subscribed for shares which were invalid due to a defect in their title. Under the section, shares could be validated by the court only in a manner which was not unjust or inequitable having regard to the interests of third parties who might be affected. Keane J found that the object of the application in this case was not to validate the defective title to the shares in question so as to protect the interests of innocent parties; rather it was to enable the company to gain tax advantage. This, held the learned judge, was not a purpose for which the procedure under s 89 was intended to be used. The learned judge further held, however, that it was within the competence of the members to ratify the allotment separately without recourse to the court.

(c) The mechanics of allotment

[15.053] In many small private companies, few formal steps are observed in the allotment of shares. However, since an allotment involves a contract for the sale of shares, a number

---

[180] Contrast *Re Jermyn Street Turkish Baths Ltd* [1971] 1 WLR 1042 where, in return for desperately needed cash, a director was allotted shares giving her control of the company. The net effect of the allotment, coupled with the director's management prowess, was the saving of the company. The Court of Appeal held the allotment to have been bona fide and for the benefit of the company as a whole.

[181] *Re Sugar Distributors Ltd* [1995] 2 IR 194.

of legal principles apply to each step taken in it. Once the directors announce their intention to make an allotment, a person may apply to them for shares. Such an application, whether made orally or in writing, amounts to an *offer*, and it will be subject to the normal legal principles applying to offers in contract[182]. For example, the application may be revoked by the applicant at any reasonable time up to acceptance. In the private company, this offer is often accepted by conduct, ie by issuing the applicant with a share certificate which indicates his title to the shares[183]. It may also be accepted by the company when the offeror is notified, whether orally or in writing, that he has been allotted the shares for which he has applied. Mere posting of a written notice of allotment, will, it appears, amount to acceptance[184].

It is also possible to issue a *renounceable letter of allotment*, under which the person to whom the shares have been allotted may renounce the allotment in favour of another. These are relatively rare as far as private companies are concerned.

[15.054] Within one month of the allotment, the company must, under CA 1963, s 58(1)(a), make a return to the registrar of companies stating the number and nominal amount of the shares comprised in the allotment; the names and addresses of the allottees; and the amount, if any, paid or due and payable on each share.

(d) Statutory pre-emption rights on the allotment of shares

[15.055] It will be recalled that a private company is not permitted to offer its shares to the public[185]. This requirement is, to some extent, enhanced by the provisions of C(A)A 1983, s 23, which gives the existing members of a private company a statutory *pre-emption* right, in proportion to their existing shareholding, on the allotment of new shares. These pre-emption rights may, however, be ousted by the provisions of the memorandum or articles. A pre-emption right is a right of first refusal, which arises either by way of statute or by way of agreement[186]. Under the statutory scheme, the offer of shares to existing shareholders must be served in the same way as notices[187] and must state a period of not less than 21 days during which the offer may be accepted and during which the offer may not be withdrawn[188].

The Companies Acts 1963–1990 do not contain any provisions regulating how the company may deal with shares which have not been taken up by existing members under the statutory pre-emption scheme. This should be dealt with in the company's memorandum and articles of association or in the resolution authorising the allotment. The relevant provision should stipulate whether the company is to be permitted to offer the 'refused' shares to persons who are not already members or whether it must first offer those shares to existing members.

---

182 See Clark, *Contract Law in Ireland* (4th edn, 1998), ch 1.

183 On share certificates see para **[15.046]**.

184 *Household Fire Insurance Co v Grant* (1879) 4 Ex D 216.

185 See Chapter 1, *The Private Company in Context*, para **[1.115]**.

186 As to pre-emption rights on transfer of shares see Chapter 16, *Share Transfers in Private Companies*, para **[16.063]***ff*.

187 See Chapter 3, *Private Constitutional Documentation* para **[3.050]***ff*.

188 C(A)A 1983, s 23(7) and (8).

[15.056] The memorandum and articles of a private company may exclude generally the operation of CA 1963, s 23[189]. Furthermore, even where the section is not excluded generally, the articles or a special resolution may exclude the section in respect of a particular allotment[190]. The notice of the meeting at which such a special resolution is to be passed must contain a written statement from the directors explaining their reasons for departing from the statutory pre-emption scheme, and the amount to be paid to the company in respect of the shares to be allotted. There is nothing, of course, to prevent a company from providing for its own pre-emption scheme in its memorandum or articles. In such cases, the statutory system will not apply, but any offers under the company's own scheme must still be made in the manner described above, or else they will be of no effect[191].

[15.057] Statutory pre-emption rights are *not* given:

- to the holders of *preference shares* which as respects dividend and capital carry a right to participate only up to a specified amount in a distribution[192];
- when the allotment is in respect of an *employees' share scheme*[193];
- when the allotment is an allotment of *preference shares* which, as respects dividend and capital, carry a right to participate only up to a specified amount in a distribution[194];
- when the allotment is to be paid for, either wholly or partly, in *non-cash consideration*[195];
- where the memorandum or articles of a private company, or a special resolution of the general meeting of a private company, *exclude* the operation of C(A)A 1983, s 23[196];
- where the memorandum or articles provide for the *company's own pre-emption scheme*[197].

[15.058] Failure to comply with the statutory requirements as to pre-emption will render the company and every officer who knowingly authorised or permitted the contravention jointly and severally liable to compensate any person to whom the offer should have been made[198]. Proceedings in respect of contravention may not, however, be commenced after the expiration of two years from the delivery to the Registrar of Companies of the return of allotments in question[199]. It may be observed that contravention of the statutory provision does not invalidate the allotment itself.

---

189 C(A)A 1983, s 23(10).
190 C(A)A 1983, s 24.
191 C(A)A 1983, s 23(9); see para **[15.055]**.
192 C(A)A 1983, s 23(13). As to preference shares see para **[15.098]** ff.
193 C(A)A 1983, s 23(6). On employees' shares see para **[15.111]**.
194 C(A)A 1983, s 23(13).
195 C(A)A 1983, s 23(4). On consideration for allotments see para **[15.057]** ff.
196 C(A)A 1983, s 23(10), s 24(1) and s 24(2).
197 C(A)A 1983, s 24(2), (9).
198 C(A)A 1983, s 23(10).
199 C(A)A 1983, s 23(10).

(e) Consideration for shares on allotment

[15.059] Shares may be issued for either a cash payment or for some other form of consideration. The allottee need not necessarily be required to pay the full amount of the consideration upon allotment: he may be allowed to pay in instalments, or he may be allowed to keep his money until it is needed by the company, when it can look to him for payment by way of a *call*[200]. He will normally be liable in a winding up only to the extent of any sums due or owing on his shares, and if he has transferred the shares to another person and that other person is registered as a member, then the new member becomes liable to pay the sums due.

(i) Non-cash consideration

[15.060] Shares in private companies may be paid for in kind; C(A)A 1983, s 26 expressly provides:

> '...shares allotted by a company and any premium payable on them may be paid up in money or money's worth (including goodwill and expertise).'

Where shares are allotted for a consideration other than cash, the company must, under CA 1963, s 58(1)(b), deliver to the Registrar of Companies the contract constituting the title of the allottee to the shares, or, if it is not in writing, particulars of the contract, and a return stating the number and nominal amount of the shares so allotted, the extent to which they are to be treated as paid up, and the consideration for which they have been allotted. Delivery of these particulars to the registrar must be effected within one month of allotment. Default in the delivery of particulars within the prescribed period renders every officer in default liable to a fine not exceeding €634.87[201], but the time for delivery of any document under the section may be extended by the court if it is satisfied that the omission was accidental or due to inadvertence or that it is just and equitable to grant relief[202].

[15.061] Goods or services will constitute good consideration for shares provided the company is prepared to accept them as payment. Thus, in *McCoy v Greene*[203], the provision of mediation services to a company which had been split by a family dispute was found to constitute valid consideration for an allotment. However, since under ordinary principles of contract law 'past consideration is no consideration'[204], services already performed, or services which the allottee is already bound to render to the company under an earlier contract with it, will not constitute valid consideration[205]. An allotment in consideration of the release of a debt due to the allottee by the company will be regarded as an allotment for cash, so no return to the registrar will be required[206]; but an allotment by way of accord and satisfaction will be regarded as an allotment for non-cash consideration[207].

---

200 See para **[15.090]** ff.

201 CA 1963, s 58(3), as amended by C(A)A 1982, Sch 1.

202 CA 1963, s 58(4).

203 *McCoy v Greene* (19 January 1984, unreported), High Court (Costello J).

204 See Clark, *Contract Law in Ireland* (4th edn, 1998), ch 2.

205 *Re Eddystone Marine Insurance Co* [1893] 3 Ch 9; *Re Leinster Contract Corporation* [1902] IR 349.

206 *Larocque v Beauchemin* [1897] AC 358.

207 *Re Johannesburg Hotel Co, ex parté Zoutpansberg Prospecting Co* [1891] 1 Ch 119.

[15.062] Ordinary principles of contract law forbid the courts from inquiring into the adequacy of consideration[208] and the same principles apply to consideration given for shares. Thus, in *Re Leinster Contract Corporation*[209] where shares were allotted in return for certain patents, the court refused to set aside the allotment even though the patents proved ultimately to be valueless. In *Re Wragg Ltd*[210], where a business run by two partners was acquired by a company formed by them in consideration of a sum of money and the allotment to them of fully paid up shares, the court refused to accede to the liquidator's argument that the shares be treated as unpaid because the business had been overvalued by £18,000. Lord Lindley said:

> 'It is not the law that persons cannot sell property to a limited company for fully paid-up shares and make a profit by the transaction. We must not allow ourselves to be misled by talking of value. The value paid to a company is measured by the price at which the company agrees to buy what it thinks is worth its while to acquire. While the transaction is unimpeached, that is the only value to be considered.'

However, where *convertible debentures* (ie debentures[211] which give the holder the right to convert his interest into shares in the company) are to be converted, the amount to be paid up, or actually paid up, on the debenture must at least equal the nominal value of the share into which it is to be converted - otherwise the conversion would amount to the issue of a share at a discount[212].

(ii) Issue of shares at a discount

[15.063] There is a general prohibition on the issue of shares at a discount, ie at a price below their nominal value, because such an issue causes a reduction of the company's share capital. Detailed consideration of the issue of shares at a discount is reserved for Chapter 18[213].

(iii) Issue of shares at a premium

[15.064] While there is a general prohibition on the issue of shares at a discount, there is nothing to prevent a company from issuing shares at a *premium*, ie at a price higher than their nominal value. In private companies it is particularly common to issue shares at a premium, since the price of the share will normally reflect the value of the business. A premium obtained from the issue of shares is *not*, however, part of the company's trading profit; instead, it is treated like the capital of the company and it is transferred to a special account called the *share premium account*.

[15.065] CA 1963, s 62 requires all such premia to be transferred into the share premium account and provides that the rules governing the maintenance of capital apply to the share premium account in the same way as they apply to the paid up share capital of the company. The section goes on to permit four applications of the share premium account:

---

[208] See Clark, *Contract Law in Ireland* (4th edn, 1998), ch 2.

[209] *Re Leinster Contract Corporation* [1902] IR 349.

[210] *Re Wragg Ltd* [1897] 1 Chapter 796.

[211] On debentures see further Chapter 20, *Corporate Borrowing: Debentures and Security.*

[212] *Mosley v Koffyfontein Mines Ltd* [1904] 2 Ch 108. On the prohibition against issue of shares at a discount see Chapter 18, *The Maintenance of Capital*, para **[18.091]***ff.*

[213] See Chapter 18, *The Maintenance of Capital*, para **[18.091]***ff.*

- — paying up unissued shares of the company and issuing them to members of the company as fully paid up *bonus* shares;
- — writing off the preliminary expenses of the company;
- — writing off the expenses of, or the commission paid on, any issue of shares or debentures in the company;
- — providing for the premium payable on redemption of any redeemable preference shares pursuant to CA 1990, s 220, or of any debentures of the company.

[15.066] Where shares in one company are allotted in consideration for shares in another company, and the nominal value of the shares in the allotting company is lower than the actual value of the shares in the allottee company, the difference in value constitutes a premium which must be transferred to the share premium account. This is so even though the difference represents profits made by the allottee company prior to the acquisition of its shares by the allotting company[214]. These pre-acquisition profits may not be distributed by the allotting company in any subsequent dividend, because to do so would amount to an unauthorised application of the share premium account[215]. English law, in line with the expectations of the accounting profession, has been altered to allow such distribution[216]; no such changes have been made in Ireland.

Shareholders' rights and duties

[15.067] Shareholders' rights and interests are determined by reference to the terms of issue of their shares, which, in turn, must be authorised by the company's constitutional documents and any necessary resolutions. Model reg 2 of Table A provides simply that shares may be issued 'with such rights or restrictions as the company may by ordinary resolution determine'. In each case, a shareholder's rights should be determined by reference 'to the terms of the instrument which contains the bargain which they have made with the company and each other.'[217] Too much reliance should not be placed on judicial decisions dealing with the rights of shareholders in other companies, unless the clause or term in question is identical[218].

[15.068] The principal rights which shares generally confer are:

(a) The right to *dividend*, if, while the company is a going concern, a dividend is duly declared.

(b) The right to attend and *vote* at meetings of the company.

(c) The right, in the winding up of the company, after the payment of the company's debts, to receive a proportionate part of the *capital* or otherwise participate in the distribution of the assets of the company.

---

[214] *Henry Head & Co v Ropner Holdings Ltd* [1952] Ch 124; *Shearer (Inspector of Taxes) v Bercain Ltd* [1980] 3 All ER 295. See Ussher, 'Doubts Remain on *Shearer v Bercain*' (1982) 3 Co Law 28.

[215] *Henry Head & Co v Ropner Holdings Ltd* [1952] Ch 124; *Shearer (Inspector of Taxes) v Bercain Ltd* [1980] 3 All ER 295.

[216] CA 1985 (UK), ss 131-134.

[217] *Scottish Insurance Corp v Wilson & Clyde Coal Co* [1949] AC 462 at 488.

[218] *Cork Electric Supply Co v Concannon* [1932] IR 314.

(d) Statutory rights to notices, information, and to seek relief against the company, which are conferred by the Companies Acts 1963–2001.

In addition we examine the following points:

(e) Shareholders' 'personal' rights.

(f) Shareholders' duties.

Each of the above will now be considered in turn; then consideration will be given the duties of a shareholder.

(a) Dividend

[15.069] A dividend is a distribution out of a company's profits[219] to its members. Every company has the implied power, subject to any restrictions which may be imposed by its memorandum, to apply its profits to the distribution of dividend amongst its members. This inherent power of a company to divide its profits amongst its members is a reflection of the fact that companies are vehicles through which profits may be made. That said, however, there is no legal obligation on the company to pay a dividend, even where there are sufficient distributable profits available, unless the company's constitutional documents provide otherwise. As Lord Davey said in *Burland v Earle*[220]:

> 'Their Lordships are not aware of any principle which compels a joint stock company while a going concern to divide the whole of its profits among its shareholders. Whether the whole or any part should be divided, or what portion should be divided and what portion retained, are entirely questions of internal management...and the court has no jurisdiction to control or review their decision.'[221]

(i) Entitlement to dividend where the company is a going concern

[15.070] A shareholder has no right to dividend while the company is a going concern until the dividend is *declared and payable*[222]. Once it is declared and payable, however, the shareholder is entitled to sue the company for arrears of his proportion as a contract debt in the same way as an ordinary creditor of the company may sue for a debt[223]. This debt is one which is personal to the shareholder; thus, after a dividend has been declared, a transfer of the share and registration of the transferee as a member of the company does not entitle the transferee to sue the company for the dividend. Whether he may sue the transferor, however, depends upon the terms of the transfer[224].

The holders of preference shares will generally be entitled to claim arrears of declared dividend out of subsequently declared dividends in priority to ordinary shareholders. Preference shares are examined at para **[15.098]** below.

---

219 The profits available for such a distribution are considered in Chapter 18, *The Maintenance of Capital*, para **[18.081]**.

220 *Burland v Earle* [1902] AC 83 at 95.

221 The court, since the introduction of CA 1963, s 205 in 1963, now appears to have some power of control in relation to dividends; see para **[15.074]** and, generally, Chapter 19, *Shareholders' Remedies*, para **[19.006]***ff*.

222 *Re Drogheda Steampacket Co Ltd* [1903] IR 512; *Bond v Barrow Haematite Steel Co* [1902] 1 Ch 353.

223 *Re Belfast Empire Theatre of Varieties* [1963] IR 41. The company does not hold the unclaimed dividend on trust for the shareholder.

224 *Black v Homersham* (1878) 4 Ex D 24; *Re Wimbush* [1940] Ch 92.

[15.071] The time limit for the bringing of an action against the company in respect of dividend is 12 years from the date of declaration or the declared date of payment, whichever is the later. In *Re Belfast Empire Theatre of Varieties*[225], a case where a company was unable to pay declared dividends to a number of shareholders who could not be traced, Kenny J explained:

> 'Section 11(1) of the Statute of Limitations 1957 provides:- "The following actions shall not be brought after the expiration of six years from the date on which the cause of action accrued...(a) actions founded on simple contract", while sub-s 5 of the same section provides:- "The following actions shall not be brought after the expiration of twelve years on which the cause of action accrued ... (a) an action on an instrument under seal...".The right of [a member of] a company to receive dividends is conferred by the articles of association of the company; it is a right derived from the contract which the articles create between the company and each of its members...and although the contract is not sealed by each member or by the company, the effect of [s 25 of the 1963 Act] is that the contract binds the company and the members as if it were under seal. The appropriate statutory period is the period of twelve years...'

The 12-year limitation period has been forsaken by the English courts in favour of the six year period applicable to simple contract debts. In *Re Compania de Electricidad de la Provencia de Buenos Aires Ltd*[226], Slade J held that the right of a shareholder to a properly declared dividend was a simple contract debt, since although the Companies Act 1985 (UK), s 14 (which is materially the same as CA 1963, s 25) deems the contractual effect of the articles to be under seal, it does not state that the company is deemed to have sealed the contract but only that the members are deemed to have sealed it. It remains to be seen whether the Irish courts will follow this decision.

(ii) Forfeiture of dividend

[15.072] The articles may provide for the forfeiture of dividends which are not claimed within any specified period less than twelve years. Such clauses will be construed strictly by the courts. In *Ward v Dublin North City Milling Co Ltd*[227], a limited company provided in its articles that:

> 'Notice of each dividend declared shall be given to each member in the manner hereinafter mentioned, and all dividends unclaimed for three years after having been declared may by a resolution of the directors be forfeited for the benefit of the company.'

Although notices of meetings at which dividends were to be declared were sent to one of two joint owners of certain shares (who was known to be dead), none were sent to the other joint owner. When the latter died, his executrix brought an action for arrears of dividends stretching back over five years. Upholding her claim, O'Connor MR said[228]:

> 'I read this article as meaning that the unclaimed dividends to be forfeited are dividends of which notice has been given, for I cannot read the earlier part of the article apart from the latter. Arts 140 and 141 prescribe how notices are to be given...Now, provisions such as these in arts 140 and 141 are absolutely necessary for the convenient despatch of business and a

[225] *Re Belfast Empire Theatre of Varieties* [1963] IR 41.

[226] *Re Compania de Electricidad de la Provencia de Buenos Aires Ltd* [1980] Ch 146.

[227] *Ward v Dublin North City Milling Co Ltd* [1919] 1 IR 5.

[228] [1919] 1 IR 5 at 11.

company's protection. But they should not be used dishonestly or unfairly, and if the officers of a company have actual knowledge that one of two joint shareholders is dead, and if with that knowledge present to their mind they issue notices to the deceased shareholder and no notice to the surviving registered shareholder, the company is in such default that it cannot rely upon a formal notice which in substance is no notice. That would be a perversion of the purpose for which the articles were framed.'

Furthermore, although the time limit for the bringing of an action against the company in respect of dividend has passed, the company may, by its conduct, revive the right of action. In *Re Compania de Electricidad de la Provencia de Buenos Aires Ltd*[229], Slade J held that a balance sheet showing an entry acknowledging unclaimed arrears of dividend may amount to an acknowledgment which will revive the right of action, provided that the person claiming the right can prove receipt of the relevant accounts. In such circumstances the time limit will begin afresh from the date of acknowledgement[230].

(iii) Entitlement to dividend where the company is being wound up

[15.073] A shareholder's entitlement to a dividend can arise only before a winding up commences. Declared dividends cease to be debts owed by the company once a winding up occurs, and the shareholder's right to sue in respect of the dividend is deferred until the debts owed to the company's ordinary creditors have been satisfied. This is because the capital available for distribution in the form of dividend ceases in a liquidation to be 'profit' and becomes instead part of the assets to be distributed in the winding up. In *Wilson (Inspector of Taxes) v Dunnes Stores (Cork) Ltd*[231], Kenny J explained this principle as follows:

'[W]hile what is distributed to the members in a winding up may be identified as having been profits, it is not distributed as profits but as a distribution in the winding up of the company or (as some call it) surplus assets. In a winding up of a company there may be liabilities which are related to the amount of the profits made before the company went into liquidation or the articles may confer on some shareholders a right to a dividend related to the amount of the profits before the company goes into liquidation but these are cases of the discharge of liabilities incurred before liquidation. What remains after discharge of liabilities is distributed among the shareholders not as profits but as surplus assets or as a distribution in the winding up. All the cases are consistent with this view and, on close examination, they refute the contention that what is distributed in a winding up is in any sense profits of the company.'[232]

This does not mean that the shareholder loses his entitlement to the dividend; it may be taken into account in calculating the extent of the shareholder's right of participation in the distribution of assets in the winding up. To this end, CA 1963, s 207(1)(g) provides:

---

229 *Re Compania de Electricidad de la Provencia de Buenos Aires Ltd* [1980] Ch 146.

230 Statute of Limitations 1957, s 56.

231 *Wilson (Inspector of Taxes) v Dunnes Stores (Cork) Ltd* (22 January 1976, unreported), High Court (Kenny J).

232 (22 January 1976, unreported), High Court at p 8. See also *IRC v Blott* [1920] 2 KB 657; *IRC v Burrell* [1924] 2 KB 52; *Re Lafayette* [1950] IR 100; and *Re Imperial Hotel (Cork) Ltd* [1950] IR 115.

> '...a sum due to any member of the company, in his character of a member, by way of dividends, profits or otherwise, shall not be deemed to be a debt of the company, payable to that member in a case of competition between himself and any other creditor not a member of the company, but any such sum may be taken into account for the purpose of the final adjustment of the rights of the contributories among themselves.

As shall be seen, the articles and the terms of issue of certain preference shares entitle the holders to rank ahead of other shareholders in the distribution of assets in a winding up[233].

(iv) Declaration of dividend

[15.074] The Companies Acts 1963–2001 do not provide who shall declare a dividend nor do they stipulate when a dividend shall become payable; these are matters of internal management. Model reg 116 of Table A provides simply that:

> 'The Company in general meeting *may* declare dividends, but no dividend shall exceed the amount recommended by the directors.'[234]

Since the recommendation of the general meeting must not exceed the amount, if any, recommended by the directors, the directors have, effectively, the last say as to when a dividend is to be declared and how much is to be made available for that purpose. There is no way in which the shareholders can force the directors to recommend a dividend[235]. The general meeting may get around this difficulty, however, by removing the directors through an ordinary resolution under CA 1963, s 182[236], or by altering the articles through a special resolution under CA 1963, s 15[237]. A failure by the directors to declare dividends may, in any event, amount to oppression within the meaning of s 205 of the 1963 Act, where, for example, the directors cause themselves to be paid excessive salaries which consume the profits which would otherwise be available for distribution in the form of dividend. The wide discretion given to the courts to award relief for a breach of that section may include the power to order that a dividend be declared[238].

Model reg 117 of Table A also allows the directors to pay *interim* dividends. It provides:

> 'The directors *may* from time to time pay to the members such interim dividends as appear to the directors to be justified from the profits of the company.'[239]

The power of the directors to pay interim dividends does not require the sanction of the general meeting.

(v) Form of dividend

[15.075] Dividends are prima facie payable in cash; but, if the articles permit, a company may pay them by the distribution of non-cash assets such as shares, debentures or specific

---

[233] See para **[15.098]** ff.

[234] Emphasis added.

[235] See eg *Scott v Scott* [1943] 1 All ER 582.

[236] See Chapter 9, *Corporate Governance: Meetings*, para **[9.078]***ff*.

[237] See Chapter 3, *Private Constitutional Documentation*, para **[3.065]***ff*.

[238] See generally Chapter 19, *Shareholders' Remedies*, para **[19.006]***ff*.

[239] Emphasis added.

items of property[240]. Model reg 123 of Table A authorises the payment of dividend by cheque.

(b) Attendance and voting at meetings

[15.076] Every shareholder who appears on the register of members is entitled to attend meetings of the company unless the terms of issue of his share and the company's constitutional documents provide otherwise. The mechanics of calling and attending meetings of the company have been considered in Chapter 9, *Corporate Governance: Meetings*. Unless a company's articles otherwise provide, notice of general meetings must be given to every shareholder of the company[241], even where the terms of issue of the shares and the articles confer no right on the shareholder to attend or to vote[242]. At common law, a meeting will be invalid unless each shareholder entitled to receive notice of the meeting has done so[243]. It is usual, therefore, for the articles to provide that accidental failure to give notice, or the non-receipt of notice, shall not invalidate the meeting[244].

A body corporate which is a member may authorise, by resolution of its directors or other governing body, such person as it thinks fit to act as its representative at any meeting of the company[245]. The representative is not a proxy and therefore there is no need to notify the company of his appointment before the meeting.

[15.077] Every shareholder who appears on the register of members and who is entitled to attend meetings of the company is also entitled to vote on any questions which are to be decided by the meeting, unless the terms of issue of their shares and the company's constitutional documents otherwise provide. It is not uncommon, however, for the terms of issue and the articles to restrict or abrogate the voting rights associated with certain classes of shares; conversely, some shares may be given loaded voting rights[246].

(i) Show of hands

[15.078] Questions arising at meetings are to be decided, in the first place, by a show of hands[247]. This is a common law rule which applies automatically unless the company's constitutional documents provide otherwise[248], and it is one which is repeated in model reg 59 of Table A. In the absence of a contrary provision in the company's memorandum or articles, each shareholder will be entitled on a show of hands to *only one vote*, regardless of the size of his shareholding[249].

---

240 *Hoole v Great Western Railway* (1867) 3 Ch App 262. The articles of public companies may commonly give their shareholders the choice of electing to take shares in the company in lieu of cash dividends.

241 CA 1963, s 134(a).

242 *Re MacKenzie & Co Ltd* [1916] 2 Ch 450.

243 *Smyth v Darley* (1849) 2 HL Cas 789.

244 See Chapter 9, *Corporate Governance:Meetings*, para **[9.035]**.

245 CA 1963, s 139. If the body corporate is in liquidation, it is the liquidator who makes the appointment: *Hillman v Crystal Bowl Amusements Ltd* [1973] 1 All ER 379.

246 See para **[15.106]**.

247 See Chapter 9, *Corporate Governance: Meetings*, para **[9.049]**.

248 *Re Horbury Bridge Co* (1879) 11 Ch D 109.

249 See also CA 1963, Table A, model reg 63.

(ii) Poll

[15.079] A show of hands is often an inadequate means for determining the wishes of the whole company; accordingly, common law and statute[250] both provide that a shareholder may demand a *poll*. Where voting takes place by poll, every member has one vote in respect of each share held by him, unless the articles otherwise provide[251]. Model reg 63 of Table A repeats the one share/one vote principle, but model reg 62 gives the chairman a casting vote where there is equality of votes. In practice, a poll is usually conducted by each shareholder signing a piece of paper stating whether he is for or against the motion and the number of votes held by him.

CA 1963, s 137 renders *void* any provision in the articles[252] as follows: which excludes the right to demand a poll on any question other than the election of a chairman or adjournment; or which requires a demand for a poll to be made by more than four[253] members having the right to vote at the meeting, or by members representing not less than one tenth of the total voting rights of all members entitled to vote at the meeting; or holding shares paid up to the extent of not less than one-tenth of the total sum paid up on all the shares conferring a right to vote at the meeting. Model reg 59 of Table A is more generous in allowing for a poll where demanded by at least three members. Where there are fewer than three shareholders who wish to demand a poll, they may, in advance of the meeting, vest some of their shares in nominees and obtain their proxies[254] for the meeting; but they may encounter difficulty if the directors refuse to register the nominees in the register of members[255].

(iii) Proxies

[15.080] At common law, there is no right to vote by proxy. However, as was seen in Chapter 9[256], this position has been modified by CA 1963, s 136.

(c) Participation in a winding up

[15.081] Where a company is being wound up, once the creditors and the expenses of the liquidator have been paid, shareholders are returned their capital investment in the shares and any remaining property of the company is distributed among the shareholders in proportion to their rights and interests in the company, unless the articles otherwise provide[257]. Where the memorandum (as opposed to the articles) provides that no part of the assets is to be distributed to the members, the surplus assets are still distributable amongst the members[258]. Where, however, the memorandum further provides that the surplus assets

---

[250] CA 1963, s 137.

[251] CA 1963, s 134(e).

[252] Notably, there seems to be no prohibition on such a provision appearing in the memorandum. Such a provision would not, apparently, be contrary to common law either: *R v Wimbledon Local Board* (1882) 8 QBD 459.

[253] The section refers to 'not less than five' members.

[254] See para **[15.080]**.

[255] See Chapter 16, *Share Transfers in Private Companies*, para **[16.037]**.

[256] See Chapter 9, *Corporate Governance: Meetings*, para **[9.060]**.

[257] See CA 1963, s 275.

[258] *Re Merchant Navy Supply Association Ltd* (1947) 177 LT 386.

are to be distributed in a special manner, such as to a charity, the courts have given effect to the provision notwithstanding the absence of equivalent provisions in the articles[259]. Prima facie, the distribution of surplus assets is to be in proportion to the nominal value of each share[260], and, as has been seen[261], sums due to a member which are not treated as creditors' claims in the liquidation (eg dividends etc) are to be taken into account when adjusting the rights of shareholders to participate in the surplus. The articles and terms of issue of some shares may provide for preferential rights of participation in a winding up; see para **[15.098]** *ff*, below. The topic of distribution in a winding up is considered in detail in Chapter 27[262].

(d) Shareholders' statutory rights

[15.082] Apart from the principal rights of shareholders discussed above, the Companies Acts 1963-2001 also confer a number of ancillary rights, which include the following:

- to receive a copy of the memorandum and articles of association and any Act of the Oireachtas which alters the memorandum[263];
- to inspect and obtain copies of the minutes of general meetings and resolutions[264];
- to inspect and receive a copy of the registers kept by the company, such as the register of members[265], the register of directors and secretaries[266], and the register of directors' shareholdings[267];
- to receive copies of balance sheets and directors' and auditors' reports[268];
- to demand and receive the balance sheets of a subsidiary company for the preceding ten years[269];
- to exercise pre-emption rights where the company proposes to allot unissued equity securities which are to be wholly paid up in cash[270];
- to petition the court for the winding up of the company[271];
- to petition the court for relief in cases of oppression[272].

---

259 *Liverpool and District Hospital for Diseases of the Heart v Attorney General* [1981] 1 All ER 994.

260 *Re London India Rubber Company* (1868) LR 5 Eq 519.

261 At para **[15.073]**.

262 See Chapter 27, *The Realisation and Distribution of Assets in a Winding Up.*

263 CA 1963, s 29.

264 CA 1963, s 143.

265 CA 1963, s 119.

266 CA 1963, s 195, as amended by CA 1990, s 51.

267 CA 1963, s 190, as amended.

268 CA 1963, s 159; see generally Chapter 13, *Accounts and Auditors.*

269 CA 1963, s 154; see generally Chapter 13, *Accounts and Auditors.*

270 C(A)A 1983, s 23; see para **[15.055]**.

271 CA 1963, s 213; see generally Chapter 25, *Winding Up Companies.*

272 CA 1963, s 205; see generally Chapter 19, *Shareholders' Remedies.*

(e) Shareholders' 'personal' rights

[15.083] Not all the rights associated with a share may be enforced by the shareholder in his personal or individual capacity. Yet the classification of certain rights as personal is of particular importance, for, as shall be seen in Chapter 19[273], company law has established a rule (known as the rule in *Foss v Harbottle*) that an individual shareholder cannot generally initiate proceedings in respect of a wrong done to the company, rather than to him personally. This is so even though the wrong suffered by the company will almost certainly impinge upon his rights as a shareholder. This rule is of no application where the individual is alleging that the wrong has been done to him *personally*[274].

[15.084] Neither the courts nor the legislature have provided a uniform formula for identifying whether a right associated with a share is personal or otherwise. At this juncture, it may prove useful to consider situations in which shareholders have been held to have personal rights. An examination of the case law shows that personal rights arise in at least the following situations:

(i) where those rights stem from the 'section 25 contract' and the particular right is considered *too fundamental to the individual* to be allowed to be abrogated by the majority of shareholders;

(ii) where those rights stem from the directors' fiduciary duties in the course of *direct dealings* between the directors and the individual shareholder;

(iii) where the right is given to the shareholder *by statute*.

A brief examination of these categories will now follow. However, it must be stressed that the list is neither conclusive nor closed - for these are no more than miscellaneous examples of situations in which a shareholder's rights have been held to be personal and actionable by a shareholder individually.

(i) Section 25 rights

[15.085] Shareholders have contractual rights by virtue of s 25 of the 1963 Act which makes them party to a contract with the company and the other shareholders which is contained in the memorandum and articles of association - provided that the right is given to them *qua* member, and not in another capacity such as solicitor or accountant of the company[275].

Many of these rights stem from the articles of association of the company, and, as has already been seen[276], many breaches of the articles can subsequently be regularised by ratification by the majority. In such circumstances, the courts will be slow to let an individual shareholder proceed against the company or the members in breach, because to do so would be to 'interfere in the domestic affairs of a company or association on the ground of mere irregularity in form in the conduct of those affairs'.[277] The following examples, however, have been held to be breaches of the articles which could not subsequently be regularised:

---

[273] See Chapter 19, *Shareholder's Remedies*, para **[19.085]***ff*.

[274] See eg *Edwards v Halliwell* [1950] 2 All ER 1064 at 1067, *per* Jenkins LJ.

[275] See Chapter 3, *Private Constitutional Documentation*, para **[3.103]***ff*.

[276] See Chapter 10, *Duties of Directors and Other Officers* para **[10.047]**.

[277] Per Jenkins LJ in *Edwards v Halliwell* [1950] 2 All ER 1064.

— breach of rules which provide that subscriptions may only be increased with the consent of a two-third majority of members[278];

— breach of articles requiring the directors to purchase an outgoing member's shares[279];

— breach of articles providing that no decision of the board of directors should be valid where either of two particular directors dissented[280];

To the extent that actions (for injunction and declaration) by individual shareholders in respect of these breaches were permitted, the breaches may be described as breaches of the shareholders' *personal* rights; but it must be stressed that the shareholder in each case was attempting to protect his personal interests, and not those of the company as a whole.

Where rights stem from the objects clause in the memorandum of association, retrospective regularisation will not be permitted. In such cases it is well established that an individual shareholder can bring injunctive or declaratory proceedings to restrain the company from acting ultra vires in breach of its objects[281].

[15.086] A shareholder's vote is an individual contractual right stemming from the company's constitutional documents. It is a kind of property right, which he may use as he pleases. Where the company denies him this right he may obtain an injunction or take some other form of legal action to restrain the company from so acting. In *Pender v Lushington*[282], Jessel MR proclaimed:

> 'In all cases of this kind, where men exercise their rights of property, they exercise their rights from some motive adequate or inadequate and I have always considered the law to be that those who have the rights of property are entitled to exercise them, whatever their motives may be for such exercise...This is an action by Mr Pender himself. He is a member of the company and whether he votes with the majority or the minority he is entitled to have his vote recorded - an individual right in respect of which he has a right to sue...He has a right to say, "Whether I vote in the majority or minority, you shall record my vote, as that is a right of property belonging to my interest in this company and if you refuse to record my vote I will institute legal proceedings against you to compel you." What is the answer to such an action? It seems to me it can be maintained as a matter of substance and that there is no technical difficulty in maintaining it...'.

(ii) Directors' fiduciary duties

[15.087] Case law has also established that in certain circumstances the directors owe certain fiduciary duties[283] to individual shareholders personally. This normally arises where the directors are involved in direct dealings with the shareholder concerned[284].

---

278 *Edwards v Halliwell* [1950] 2 All ER 1064.

279 *Rayfield v Hands* [1960] Ch 1.

280 *Quin & Axtons v Salmon* [1909] 1 Chapter 311.

281 CA 1963, s 8(2). See also *Simpson v Westminster Palace Hotel* (1860) 8 HLC 712; *Smith v Croft (No 2)* [1988] Ch 114. See Chapter 19, *Shareholders' Remedies*, para **[19.108]***ff*.

282 *Pender v Lushington* (1877) 6 Ch D 70.

283 See Chapter 10, *Duties of Directors and Other Officers*, para **[10.017]***ff*.

284 *Allen v Hyatt* (1914) TLR 444. See also *Coleman v Myers* [1977] 2 NZLR 225.

(iii) Statutory rights

[15.088] The statutory rights given to shareholders (listed at para **[15.081]** above) are enjoyed, exercisable, and enforceable by a shareholder in his personal capacity.

(f) Shareholders' duties

[15.089] The principal duty of the shareholder, *qua* shareholder, is to pay the company the amount, if any, which remains outstanding in respect of the price[285] agreed for the share in the original allotment[286]. Such moneys become payable by the shareholder when a *call* is made upon him by the company, or, where the terms of issue provide for payment in instalments, when the dates stated in the terms have arrived. Where shares are to be paid for by instalments, model reg 19 of Table A provides that all the provisions of the articles regulating payment of interest and expenses, forfeiture or other matters shall apply as if such sum had become payable by virtue of a call.
A shareholder's liability for past and future calls continues where the company is being wound up, since the uncalled amount forms part of the assets to be made available for distribution in the liquidation. In the private company, it may be recalled, a shareholder's liability to contribute to the company in a winding up is restricted to the amount, if any, unpaid on his shares[287].

Apart from the foregoing duty, the other duties of shareholders include the duty to account to the company for any dividend received in contravention of the rules governing profits available for distribution; and the duty to answer personally for the company's liabilities where statute or common law require. These topics are considered elsewhere in this book[288]. The topic of calls shall now be considered in further detail.

(i) Calls

[15.090] The shareholder's liability in respect of a call is contractual in nature, stemming from the terms of issue and the section 25 contract. After a call has been made and it has matured into a debt, the amount due on foot of the call may not be recovered by the company after the expiration of 12 years from the date upon which it became due[289].
The liability of a shareholder for future calls on his shares is transferred to any shareholder who takes the share by way of transfer or transmission once the latter's name is entered on the register of members, even though he may be a minor[290]. Where shares are transferred to a minor, however, the transferring shareholder continues to be liable for all future calls for so long as the minor is registered as a member. The company may not waive its right to uncalled capital if the waiver would cause the company to receive less than the nominal value of the shares, because to do so would result in the issue of those shares at a discount in breach of the rules of capital maintenance[291].

---

285 The price will exceed the nominal value of the share where it is issued at a premium; see para **[15.064]**.

286 See para **[15.049]**.

287 See Chapter 27, *Realisation and Distribution of Assets in a Winding Up*, para **[27.117]**.

288 See Chapter 18, *The Maintenance of Capital*, para **[18.081]**, and Chapter 5, *Disregarding Separate Legal Personality*, para **[5.073]** ff respectively.

289 CA 1963, s 25(2).

290 *Cork and Bandon Railway v Cazenove* (1847) 10 QB 935.

291 See Chapter 18, *The Maintenance of Capital*, para **[18.091]**.

[15.091] The procedure for the making of calls is usually contained in the articles. Model regs 15–21 of Table A contain provisions in relation to calls which are adopted by most private companies. Under those articles, the power to make calls from time to time is given to the directors, provided that no call shall exceed one-fourth of the nominal value of the share or be payable at less than one month from the date fixed for payment of the last preceding call[292]. Each shareholder is required to pay, subject to receiving at least fourteen days' notice) the amount of every call made on him to the persons and at the times and places fixed by the directors[293]. If a call is not paid before or on the date appointed by the directors, it carries interest at such rate not exceeding 5% *per annum* as the directors may determine[294].

The power of the directors to make calls must be exercised in good faith and for the benefit of the company as a whole[295]. Where it is exercised mala fide, an injunction may be obtained to restrain the call[296]. Such relief may be difficult to obtain in practice, however, since the onus of proving bad faith rests on the shareholder[297]. Calls should be made *pari passu* unless the articles otherwise provide, and should certainly not favour a shareholder who is a director above the other shareholders. Although model reg 20 of Table A allows directors to differentiate between the holders of shares as to the amount of calls to be paid and the time of payment, the principle of equal calls should still not be departed from unless there is very good reason[298]. Furthermore, the resolution of the directors making the call must be passed at a properly convened directors' meeting, and a proper entry must be made in the minutes; otherwise the call may be invalid[299].

[15.092] The directors, if the articles permit, may also receive payment in advance of calls from any shareholders willing to advance such sums, and may credit the sum with interest not to exceed a specified percentage *per annum*. The amount of interest allowed must not be excessive[300]. Model reg 21 of Table A permits directors to receive payment in advance of calls and permits the directors to pay such interest not exceeding 5% *per annum* (unless the company in general meeting otherwise directs) as may be agreed upon by the directors and the shareholder paying in advance. Such powers must be exercised *bona fide* and in the best interests of the company. Thus, in *Sykes*' case[301], where the directors of an insolvent company exercised the power to accept payment in advance of calls in respect of their own shares, and then used the money obtained to pay their own directors' fees, it was held that the power was not exercised in good faith. The entire transaction was held to be ineffectual and the directors were held to remain liable on their shares.

---

292 CA 1963, Table A, reg 15.

293 CA 1963, Table A, reg 15.

294 CA 1963, Table A, reg 18.

295 *Alexander v Automatic Telephone Co* [1900] 2 Chapter 56.

296 *Odessa Tramways v Mendel* (1878) 8 Ch D 235.

297 *Odessa Tramways v Mendel* (1878) 8 Ch D 235.

298 *Galloway v Halle Concerts Society Ltd* [1915] 2 Chapter 233.

299 *Garden Gully United Quartz Mining Co v McLister* (1875) 1 App Cas 39; *Cornwall Mining Co v Bennett* (1860) H & N 423.

300 *Poole, Jackson and Whyte's case* (1879) 9 Ch D 322.

301 *Sykes*' case (1872) LR 13 Eq 255.

[15.093] The articles generally provide for the forfeiture of shares for non-payment of calls. The topic of forfeiture is considered at para **[15.119]** below.

Classes of shares

(a) Preliminary presumptions

[15.094] All shares are presumed, *prima facie*, to rank *pari passu*, so that each share is presumed to carry the same rights, interests and obligations as every other share. This principle was expressed by Lord Macnaghten in *Birch v Cropper, Re Bridgewater Navigation Co*[302], as follows:

> 'Every person who becomes a member of a company limited by shares of equal amount becomes entitled to a proportionate part in the capital of the company, and, unless it be otherwise provided by the regulations of the company, entitled as a necessary consequence, to the same proportionate part in all the property of the company ...'

Often, it is simply the size of a shareholding which distinguishes the extent of a shareholder's interests and obligations from those of the other shareholders in the company. But where, for example, a company issues shares to persons who merely invest in the company without participating in its management, the company may wish to restrict the rights held by that shareholder, despite the size of his shareholding[303]. This it may do once the memorandum or articles permit the creation of different *classes* of shares with differing rights, since the rights associated with a share stem, largely, from the memorandum and articles in the first place.

(b) Power to create different classes of shares

[15.095] The power to create different classes of shares must appear in either the memorandum or the articles. The power may, but need not necessarily[304], be provided for in the capital clause of the memorandum[305]. More commonly, it is dealt with in the articles, for they are easier to alter than the memorandum. Therefore, model reg 2 of Table A provides:

> 'Without prejudice to any special rights previously conferred on the holders of any existing shares or class of shares, any share in the company may be issued with such preferred, deferred or other special rights or such restrictions, whether in regard to dividend, voting, return of capital or otherwise, as the company may from time to time by ordinary resolution determine.'

In *Andrews v Gas Meter Co*[306], it was held that where the power to create different classes of shares appears in the articles it must not conflict with any provision of the memorandum which expressly requires equality amongst all shareholders. Where such a conflict arises, the provisions of the memorandum will take precedence, but the memorandum itself may be altered to remove the requirement of equality amongst all shareholders. In *Campbell v*

---

302 *Birch v Cropper, Re Bridgewater Navigation Co* (1899) 14 App Cas 525 at 543.

303 Or, indeed, it may wish to enlarge certain of the rights associated with the share to encourage the shareholder to invest.

304 *Andrews v Gas Meter Co* [1897] 1 Ch 361.

305 See Chapter 3, *Private Constitutional Documentation*, para **[3.017]**.

306 *Andrews v Gas Meter Co* [1897] 1 Ch 361.

Rofe[307], the Privy Council summarised the principles governing the power to create different classes of shares as follows:

> 'While the memorandum must state the amount of capital, divided into shares of a certain fixed amount, provision as to the character of the shares and rights to be attached to them is more properly made by the articles of association, which may be altered from time to time by special resolution of the company. If equality of the shareholders is expressly provided in the memorandum, that cannot be modified by the articles of association. If nothing is said in the memorandum, the articles of association may provide for the issue of the authorised capital in the form of preference shares; if the articles do not so provide, or do provide for equality *inter socios*, the power to issue preference shares may be obtained by alteration of the articles.'

In *Re Powell Cotton's Settlement, Henniker Major v Powell Cotton*[308], Roxburgh J held that it was possible to have sub-classes within a class of shares; but this was not a company law case, and the better view seems to be that each sub-class should be regarded as a separate class[309].

Just as the power to create different classes of shares may be given by the company's constitutional documents, so too may the power to alter or vary class rights be given. In that respect it is important to note, however, that CA 1963, s 78, read with C(A)A 1983, s 38, require that such variations may only take place in accordance with the procedure set out in the memorandum or articles where so provided. If no procedure is provided, the variation must, according to s 38, be consented to in writing by the holders of three-quarters of the shares in that class or sanctioned by a special resolution of that class at a separate class meeting. The holders of not less than ten *per cent* in aggregate of the shares in that class may, however, apply to court to have the variation cancelled, and where such an application is made the variation can have no effect until approved by the court.

A cancellation will only follow, however, where the action complained of actually constitutes a variation or abrogation of right attached to a share as a matter of law, not as a matter of business. In *Greenhalgh Cinemas v Arderne Cinemas (No 2)*[310] for example, a subdivision of ordinary shares of 10 shillings each into five shares of 2 shillings each was held not to constitute a variation of rights of the holders of another class of holders of 2 shillings shares since no formal change was made to their shareholding - despite the fact that the effect of the change was to shift the balance of voting power within the company completely. Likewise in *White v Bristol Airplane Co Ltd*[311] the issue of new preference shares to the ordinary shareholders which gave them a majority over the existing preference shareholders was held *not*, as a matter of law, to vary the rights of the existing preference shareholders.

---

307 *Campbell v Rofe* [1933] AC 91 at 98.
308 *Re Powell Cotton's Settlement, Henniker Major v Powell Cotton* [1957] Ch 159.
309 See *Re Hellenic and General Trust Ltd* [1975] 3 All ER 382.
310 *Greenhalgh Cinemas v Arderne Cinemas (No 2)* [1945] 2 All ER 719.
311 *White v Bristol Airplane Co Ltd* [1953] Ch 65.

(c) Particular categories of shares

[15.096] Different classes of shares are usually given distinguishing descriptions, such as 'ordinary shares,' 'preference shares,' and 'deferred shares,' or, quite commonly, 'A shares,' 'B shares,' 'A ordinary shares,' 'B ordinary shares' etc. It must be stressed that the company is free to choose whatever description it wishes, and the law does not apply any rigid meaning to the description. The company's register of members should show the class of shares of each member[312].

Whatever the label given to a class of shares, company law has established a number of presumptions governing the extent of preferred rights in the absence of stipulation to the contrary. It may prove useful here to attempt a categorisation of some of the more common types of share. Accordingly, the following types of share will be considered here:

(i) Ordinary shares;
(ii) Preference shares;
(iii) Redeemable shares;
(iv) Deferred or founders' shares;
(v) Treasury shares;
(vi) Bonus shares;
(vii) Employee shares.

(i) Ordinary shares

[15.097] The description 'ordinary shares' is sometimes used to describe that class of shares which confer on their holders the residual rights which have not been conferred on other classes. There should be no mystery about the description - it is simply a means of distinguishing the shares from other classes of shares of restricted or preferred status. Where no separate classes of shares have been created, then all shares may be thought of as ordinary shares.

The rights and duties already considered will normally attach to ordinary shares; but, as has been seen, the rights and duties to be carried by shares are matters for the company. In every case, the terms of issue of the shares and the company's constitutional documents should be referred to when seeking to establish the extent of the shareholder's rights and duties.

(ii) Preference shares

[15.098] The description 'preference shares' is used to describe shares which carry preferential rights over those of the other classes of shares. Such preferential rights may be in respect of any of the rights and duties already discussed; the most common types of preference shares being either:

1. preferred as to dividend.
2. preferred as to capital.
3. preferred as to voting.

Any combination of the above preferences is, of course, possible. However, where the articles and the terms of issue of preference shares confer a preference in respect of only

[312] *Re Performing Rights Society Ltd* [1978] 2 All ER 712.

some of these rights, they do not imply a preference as regards the other rights, because of the principle expressed by Lord Macnaghten in *Birch v Cropper*[313], that prima facie all shares rank equally.

1. Preferred as to dividend

[15.099] Shares which are preferred as to dividend usually entitle the shareholder to be paid his dividend in priority to the ordinary shareholders. The terms of issue of such shares commonly express the preferential right as a right to a percentage *per annum* of the nominal amount of the share. Thus, for example, '10% preference shares' might carry a right to a fixed dividend amounting to 10% of the nominal amount of the share each year. The fact that the right to a preferential dividend is expressed to arise annually should not, however, be taken as meaning that the dividend is to be payable annually, for the terms of issue normally entitle the shareholder to claim his dividend only when a dividend has been declared. A contrary intention may, however, be divined from the relevant documents. In *Re Lafayette Ltd*[314], the company's articles provided:

> 'The holders of the preference shares shall be entitled to receive out of the profits of the company a cumulative preferential dividend for each year of 6 per cent. per annum on the amount for the time being paid on the preference shares held by them respectively, such dividend shall be cumulative, and arrears thereof shall be the first charge on the subsequent profits of the company.'

Kingsmill Moore J held that the effect of the articles was to give the preference shareholders:

> 'a right to their dividend, irrespective of any declaration, and again without any declaration, automatically charge arrears of preference dividends on any future profits.'[315]

[15.100] Preferred rights as to dividend are presumed to be cumulative. A preferential right as to a dividend is presumed to be a right to a *cumulative* dividend[316]. This means that if a dividend is not declared in any particular year, or if there is a shortfall in the payment in respect of a previously declared preferential dividend, then, when a dividend *is* declared, the shareholder may claim the arrears as well as his dividend in priority to the ordinary shareholders. This presumption can be rebutted by wording which indicates that the dividend is non-cumulative or that the dividend is to be paid only out of the 'profits available for dividends' of a particular year[317].

[15.101] Whether arrears of undeclared cumulative preference dividend are payable in a winding up depends upon the wording of the articles and the terms of issue. If the wording makes it clear that the entitlement extends to a winding up, the preference shareholders will be entitled to those arrears. Where the preference shares are also preferred as to capital[318] but the articles and the terms of issue are silent as to whether arrears of undeclared preference dividend are payable in a winding up, the courts may nevertheless

313 *Birch v Cropper* (1889) 14 App Cas 525; see also para **[15.094]**.

314 *Re Lafayette Ltd* [1950] IR 100.

315 [1950] IR 100 at 112.

316 *Webb v Earle* (1875) LR 20 Eq 556; *Re F de Jong and Company Ltd* [1946] Ch 211.

317 *Adair v Old Bushmills Distillery* [1908] WN 24.

318 See para **[15.104]**.

imply an entitlement to such arrears[319]. Where the preference shareholder's entitlement to dividend depends upon the existence of 'profits available for dividend', the shareholder's preferential right to arrears ceases, because 'profits' are no longer regarded as such where a winding up occurs[320].

[15.102] Claims for arrears of cumulative preference dividend may not be discharged in a winding up until the claims of non-member creditors have been discharged in full[321]. CA 1963, s 207(1)(g) provides that such claims shall not be payable to a member in competition between himself and any other creditor who is not a member of the company. Such claims may, however, be discharged in priority to the claims of the ordinary shareholders. In *Re Imperial Hotel (Cork) Ltd*[322], the articles gave preference shareholders a right to an annual 6% cumulative dividend, including all arrears, 'independent of any recommendation by the board of directors and independent of any declaration of dividend by the company in general meeting ...' Gavan Duffy J construed those provisions as giving rise to a *debt*, accruing annually, owed by the company to the preference shareholders. This debt, he found, survived the winding up of the company and was payable by the liquidator in preference to claims for arrears by the ordinary shareholders, but was deferred to the claims of the non-member creditors. He said:

> 'If in every financial year showing profits the company, under its articles, owed a dividend to its preference shareholders without any recommendation or declaration, it incurred a debt to those members under their contract with the corporate body, when the board declared the net profits, if not before...
>
> I have not overlooked the rule that dividends, properly so called, are not payable on a winding up, when, after payment of the liabilities, the mass of a company's assets, whatever their separate provenance, comes to be allocated among the members entitled; but that rule is immaterial here, if the application of the surplus assets under the [articles'] code for liquidation does not come into play at all, until the debt due to the preference shareholders is discharged out of the moneys available for its payment; and that is the position. I find that the claimants are seeking to enforce payment of a debt due to them by the company; I find that that is one of the liabilities that the liquidator ... is bound to discharge before he distributes the company's property among the members ...; and I find that this liability is in the peculiar position of not being payable *pari passu* with the liabilities generally, because the claimant's debt is deferred debt, not payable in competition with those creditors who are not members of the company, by virtue of [s 207(g) of the 1963 Act.]'

[15.103] Shares preferred as to dividend are presumed to be non-participatory. Shares which are preferred as to dividend are presumed to be *non-participatory* unless the company's constitutional documents and the terms of issue provide otherwise. This means that once the preference shareholders have been paid their fixed dividend they are not entitled to participate in the distribution of the remaining profits along with the ordinary

---

319 *Re F de Jong & Co Ltd* [1946] Ch 211; *Re E W Savory Ltd* [1951] 2 All ER 1036.

320 *Re Crichton's Oil Co* [1902] 2 Ch 86. See *Wilson (Inspector of Taxes) v Dunnes Stores (Cork) Ltd*, discussed para **[15.073]**.

321 CA 1963, s 207(1)(g); see para **[15.073]**.

322 *Re Imperial Hotel (Cork) Ltd* [1950] IR 115. See also *Re WJ Hall & Co Ltd* [1909] 1 Chapter 521 at 527, *per* Swinfen Eady J; and *Re Spanish Prospecting Co Ltd* [1911] 1 Ch 92 at 107, *per* Farwell LJ.

shareholders. Thus, where the profits available for distribution are large, the ordinary dividends may well exceed the preference dividends in value.

In *Will v United Lankat Plantations Co*[323], preference shareholders who had already been paid their preferential dividend of 10% per annum sought to participate *equally* with the ordinary shareholders in the distribution of the remaining profits made available for dividend, arguing that the principle in *Birch v Cropper*[324] required equality between all shareholders unless the contrary was stated. The House of Lords rejected their argument on the basis that an expression of preferential rights in relation to one or more of the particular rights of shareholders (eg dividend, capital, voting etc) must be taken as an exhaustive definition of those rights. Lord Haldene said[325]:

> '... when you turn to the terms on which the shares are issued you expect to find all the rights as regards dividends specified in the terms of issue. And when you do find these things prescribed it certainly appears to me unnatural to go beyond them.'

This presumption may, of course, be rebutted by appropriate wording[326].

2. Preferred as to capital

[15.104] Shares which are preferred as to capital entitle the shareholder to have his capital investment in the company repaid in full before the ordinary shareholders are returned their capital in a winding up. As has been seen, however, such preferential entitlement must be created by express provision, because of the presumption expressed in *Birch v Cropper* that *prima facie* all shares rank *pari passu*[327].

[15.105] Shares carrying preferred rights as to return of capital are presumed to be *participatory*, ie after the return of their capital, the shareholders are presumed to be entitled to participate in the distribution of any surplus assets in the winding up along with the other shareholders. This presumption was found to exist in *Birch v Cropper*, and was applied by the Supreme Court in the case of *Cork Electric Supply Co Ltd v Concannon*[328]. In that case, the preference shareholders were given preferred rights as to dividend (which were expressed to be non-participatory) and preferred rights as to return of capital. The company was being wound up and its assets compulsorily acquired by the ESB, and the company sought directions from the High Court as to whether the preference shareholders' rights of participation should be confined to those contained in the articles or whether they had any further rights of participation in the winding up. Johnson J held that the statement of the rights in the articles should be considered exhaustive; but on appeal the Supreme Court reversed his decision. Kennedy CJ said[329]:

> '...the right to participate in a distribution of surplus assets on a winding up will be taken from preference shareholders by a clause in the articles of association delimiting their rights

---

323 *Will v United Lankat Plantations Co* [1914] AC 11.

324 See para **[15.094]**.

325 [1914] AC 11 at 17.

326 See eg *Steel Company of Canada Ltd v Ramsay* [1931] AC 270; *Re Isle of Thanet Electricity Supply Co Ltd* [1950] Ch 161.

327 *Birch v Cropper* (1889) 14 App Cas 525; see para **[15.094]**.

328 *Cork Electric Supply Co Ltd v Concannon* [1932] IR 314.

329 [1932] IR 314 at 328.

> exhaustively to the exclusion of any other rights and...the question whether a particular clause does so exhaust the rights attached to the preference share exhaustively and exclusively is a question of construction of the particular articles of association in each case...'

The court found that no limitation on the right of the preference shareholders to participate in the distribution of surplus assets in a winding up existed in the articles, and, thus, held the preference shareholders were entitled to participate.

In England, however, this presumption has been departed from in favour of a presumption along the lines of *Will v United Lankat Plantations Co*[330], ie that a statement of a preference shareholder's right to participate in capital in a winding up will be exhaustive[331]. This approach has been said to reflect the view, commonly held in the commercial world, that a preference share is more like a debenture than a share, since it carries a fixed return[332]. Whether the Irish Supreme Court will move towards this approach remains to be seen.

3. Preferred as to voting

[15.106] Shares preferred as to voting have created little controversy and few special presumptions pertain to them[333]. Shares which are preferred as to capital or dividend are commonly given no voting rights, or are given voting rights only where their dividend is in arrears, but the extent of voting rights depends in each case on the terms of issue of the shares in question.

(iii) Redeemable shares

[15.107] Preference shares, commonly carrying a right to a fixed dividend, resemble debentures in many ways, and are regarded by companies and businessmen as a form of quasi-loan capital. In order to enable companies to continue to treat preference shares in a like manner to debentures, CA 1963, s 64 permitted the issue of *redeemable preference shares*, which allowed the company to obtain a capital injection when necessary, which could be redeemed or paid-off when finances improved. Special conditions applied to the redemption of redeemable preference shares. That section has now been repealed by CA 1990, s 220 and replaced by CA 1990, s 207. Under s 207, a company may, if authorised by its articles, issue redeemable ordinary or preference shares. The company cannot have only redeemable shares, and redemption can only take place if the shares are fully paid up. The conditions for the redemption of redeemable shares are discussed in further detail in Chapter 18, *The Maintenance of Capital*.

---

330 *Will v United Lankat Plantations Co* [1914] AC 11; see para **[15.103]**.

331 *Scottish Insurance Corporation v Wilsons and Clyde Coal Company* [1949] AC 462; *Prudential Assurance Co v Chapteratterly Whitfield Collieries Co Ltd* [1949] AC 462; *Re Isle of Thanet Electricity Supply Co Ltd* [1950] Ch 161. See Rice, 'Capital Rights of Preference Shares' (1962) Conveyancer (ns) 115; Pickering, 'The Problem of the Preference Share' (1963) 26 MLR 499.

332 See Schmitthoff (ed), Palmer's *Company Law*, (24th edn, 1987), pp 559–560.

333 As to the uses to which weighted voting rights may be put see Chapter 5, *Private Constitutional Documentation*, para **[5.078]**.

(iv) Deferred or founders' shares

[15.108] This category of shares, virtually obsolete nowadays, were at one time commonly given to the founders of the enterprise which became the company. They carried special rights, such as rights to a fixed dividend, which were deferred in priority to the ordinary shares in order to encourage others to invest in the shares of the company.

(v) Treasury shares

[15.109] Where shares are redeemed, the company, instead of cancelling them, may retain them as treasury shares. While retained as treasury shares, the company will be unable to exercise the rights as to dividend and voting associated with the shares. Treasury shares are discussed in further detail in Chapter 18, *The Maintenance of Capital*[334].

(vi) Bonus shares

[15.110] A 'bonus issue' (or 'capitalisation issue') of shares occurs where the company capitalises profits or revenue reserves or some permissible fund, such as the share premium account or the capital redemption reserve fund, and applies the proceeds in paying up bonus shares which are then given, normally, to existing members in proportion to their entitlement to dividend[335]. A capitalisation of this nature is essentially an accounting exercise which reduces the company's reserves but increases its share capital. One advantage of a bonus issue is that the funds in the share premium account may be applied to the funding of the issue - so that the shareholders receive the benefits of that account - whereas they may not be distributed by way of dividend. A bonus share, therefore, is a fully or partly paid up share in the company, paid for by the company out of permissible funds.

(vii) Employee shares

[15.111] Unlike some other jurisdictions, such as France, there is no legal requirement on companies in Ireland to allot shares to their employees. Some companies, however, take the view that allotting shares to their employees encourages them to participate more wholeheartedly in the company's affairs. Employees may find the possibility of participating in the profits of the company, and voting on its decisions, attractive. Accordingly, companies may wish not only to allot shares to their employees, but may wish, also, to assist them in doing so. The legislature has responded in a number of ways to the desires of companies to assist their employees in the purchase of shares in the company.

First, there are tax incentives facilitating the purchase of shares in a company by its employees. Consideration of such incentives lies outside the scope of this work, however.

Secondly, the statutory prohibition, contained in CA 1963, s 60, on a company assisting the purchase of its own shares does not apply where a company *provides money* in accordance with any scheme for the time being in force under which its shares are to be held by, or on behalf of, its employees (including directors who are salaried employees), former employees, or the employees of its subsidiary[336]. Nor does it apply to *loans* made

---

[334] See Chapter 18, *The Maintenance of Capital*, para **[18.014]***ff*.

[335] See CA 1963, Table A, model reg 130A, inserted by C(A)A 1983, Sch 1, para 24.

[336] CA 1963, s 60(13)(b).

by the company to *bona fide* employees (but not employees who are directors) to enable them to acquire shares in the company or its holding company[337].

Thirdly, as has already been observed[338], the statutory pre-emption rights given to the general body of shareholders by CA 1983, s 23 do not arise where the allotment is in respect of employee share schemes. An employee share scheme is defined by s 2(1) of that Act as:

> '...any scheme for the time being in force, in accordance with which a company encourages or facilitates the holding of shares or debentures in the company or its holding company by or for the benefit of employees of former employees of the company or of any subsidiary of the company including any person who is or was a director holding a salaried employment or office in the company or any subsidiary of the company.'

Whether or not a company should issue employee shares is a matter entirely for the company itself; but in making such a decision it should weigh up the benefits of employee participation against the non-desirability of employees hinging all their prospects on the fortunes of the company. Should the company collapse, then not only will they be out of a job, but their reserve investments will be lost as well. With this in mind, a limit on employee participation might be considered.

Conversion of shares

[15.112] As was observed in Chapter 3, *Private Constitutional Documentation*, CA 1963, s 68 permits a company, if so authorised by its articles, inter alia, to:

(a) *consolidate* and divide all or any of its share capital into shares of larger amount than its existing shares; or

(b) *convert* all or any of its paid up shares into stock, and re-convert that stock into paid up shares of any denomination; or

(c) *subdivide* its shares, or any of them into shares of smaller amount than is fixed by the memorandum, so that in the subdivision the proportion between the amount paid and the amount, if any, unpaid on each reduced share shall be the same as it was in the case of the share from which the reduced share is derived.

Model regs 40 to 45 of Table A provide that these alterations may be effected by ordinary resolution. It should also be remembered that the standard notification and disclosure requirements in relation to alteration of the company's constitutional documents also apply to these alterations[339]. Notice of any of the above conversions must be sent to the registrar of companies within one month of the conversion[340]. Failure to notify the registrar in the prescribed manner will render the company and every officer in default liable to a fine not exceeding €1,905[341].

---

337 CA 1963, s 60(13)(c).

338 See para **[15.057]**.

339 See Chapter 3, *Private Constitutional Documentation*, para **[3.023]***ff*.

340 CA 1963, s 69.

341 CA 1963, s 69(2), as amended by C(A)A 1982, Sch 1 and CA 1990, s 240 as amended by s 104 of the 2001 Act.

(a) Consolidation

[15.113] Consolidation means converting a number of shares into a new share of aggregate nominal value; eg the conversion of five €1 shares into one €5 share. This procedure is quite uncommon nowadays, but may be used where long-established companies wish to make their shares less unwieldy - because, say, inflation has caused there to be little point in having 10 cent shares. Consolidation has no financial impact on the shareholders, who now hold fewer shares but of greater nominal value, but it may affect their voting power in a poll.

(b) Conversion of shares into stock, and vice versa

[15.114] Shares may be converted into stock if they are fully paid up. Though it is uncommon to do so nowadays, they may be so converted to allow the stock to be dealt with in fractions. While this may be of some use to public companies whose shares are traded on the stock exchange, it is of little use to a private company which may not offer its shares to the public. Stockholders are given the same rights, privileges and advantages as if they held the shares[342].

(c) Subdivision

[15.115] Subdivision is merely the converse of consolidation. For example, the holder of one €5 share may find his shareholding converted into five €1 shares. This is usually done to improve the marketability of shares when a company feels that the nominal value of its shares is too high, though occasionally it may be done to change the control of the company[343].

(d) Conversion into redeemable shares

[15.116] CA 1990, s 210 permits a company, subject to the rules governing variation of rights and the alteration of a company's constitutional documents, to convert any of its shares into redeemable shares. A shareholder may notify the company before the conversion of his wish not to have his shares so converted. If he notifies the company in this manner, his shares may not be converted, and any attempt to convert them may be struck down by the courts.

No conversion of shares into redeemable shares will be permitted if as a result of the conversion the nominal value of the issued share capital which is not redeemable would be less than one-tenth of the total issued share capital of the company.

Liens on shares

[15.117] Model reg 11 of Table A provides:

> 'The company shall have a first and paramount lien on every share (not being a fully paid share) for all monies (whether immediately paid or not) called or payable at a fixed time in respect of that share but the directors may at any time declare any share to be wholly or in part exempt from the provisions of this regulation. The company's lien on a share shall extend to all dividends payable thereon.'

---

[342] See CA 1963, Table A, model reg 42.

[343] See *Greenhalgh v Arderne Cinemas Ltd* [1946] 1 All ER 512.

A lien is a right to withhold possession of an item of property, such as a share, until payment has been received either in respect of that piece of property (in which case the lien is described as 'particular') or in respect of some other claim which the person exercising the lien has against the owner of the property (in which case the lien is described as 'general'). A company has no power to exercise a lien over its shares in respect of monies outstanding on them or in any other respect unless the power to do so is expressly provided for in the articles.

[15.118] The company's lien will be enforceable against the shareholder in priority to all other claims (eg charges in favour of third parties) which may exist against the share[344] unless the company has notice of the other interests[345]. Enforcement of the lien normally involves a sale of the share to third parties[346]. Model reg 12 of Table A provides that the company may sell any shares on which it has a lien if it gives 14 days' notice to the shareholder and is not paid by him within that period. Of course the shareholder may be unwilling to execute a transfer[347] of the shares to the purchaser. Thus, model reg 13 of Table A authorises the directors to appoint some other person to execute, on the shareholder's behalf, a transfer of the shares to the purchaser.

Forfeiture and surrender of shares

(a) Forfeiture

[15.119] Model regs 33 to 39 of Table A empower the directors, by resolution, to forfeit shares in the event of the member failing to pay any call or instalment of a call on the day appointed for payment thereof. Such provisions are regarded as being penal in nature, and must be observed strictly or else the forfeiture will be invalid[348]. Fourteen days' notice to the member will be required, and the notice must state that in the event of payment not being made within that period, the shares in respect of which the liability arose will be liable to be forfeited.

[15.120] A forfeited share may be sold or otherwise disposed of in any manner which the directors think fit; or they may be cancelled before disposal on such terms as the directors think fit. Since the recalcitrant shareholder may refuse to return the share certificate in respect of the shares to the company, and since he may even attempt to deal with the forfeited shares by relying on the share certificate, model reg 38 provides that a statutory declaration by a director or the company secretary that a share has been forfeited is to be conclusive evidence of the facts stated therein against all persons claiming entitlement to the shares. Model reg 38 also provides that any irregularity or invalidity in the forfeiture

---

344 *New London and Brazilian Bank v Brocklebank* (1882) 21 Ch D 302.

345 *Rearden v Provincial Bank of Ireland* [1896] 1 IR 532; *Bradford Banking Co v Briggs* (1886) 12 App Cas 29.

346 See, however, *G & s Doherty Ltd v Doherty* (4 April 1968 and 19 June 1968, unreported), High Court (Henchy J), (19 December 1969, unreported), Supreme Court, noted by O'Dowd, (1989) 11 DULJ 120, where a lien was enforced by attaching special terms to an allotment of new shares, requiring the recalcitrant shareholder to pay any amounts outstanding on his existing shares before taking up the new shares.

347 See Chapter 16, *Share Transfers in Private Companies*, para **[16.006]**.

348 *Johnson v Lyttle's Iron Agency* (1877) 5 Ch D 687.

proceedings is not to affect the title of any person taking the forfeited shares under a sale or other disposition by the directors.

[15.121] Model reg 37 of Table A provides that a person whose shares have been forfeited shall cease to be a member. Notwithstanding such cesser, the regulation provides that he is to continue to be liable for all monies outstanding on the date of forfeiture until such time as the monies have been paid to the company in full.

(b) Surrender

[15.122] A shareholder may surrender his share to the company in order to avoid the formalities of forfeiture, provided the articles permit, and provided those provisions as to surrender are strictly observed. Failure to observe the provisions as to surrender constitutes an unlawful reduction of capital[349].

Disclosure of interests in shares

[15.123] The fact that beneficial interests may not be entered on the register of members would make it easy for directors and other officers, having inside knowledge about the affairs of the company, to buy and sell shares in the company through nominees without anyone noticing or being able to discover otherwise. This would, for example, enable the insider to acquire the shares of other members, secure in the knowledge that the shares can be sold at a large profit in an impending takeover of which the other members are unaware. As has already been observed[350], CA 1990, s 53 requires directors and secretaries to notify the company of any interests they may have in the shares or debentures of the company, and the company is required to keep a register for this purpose, ie the register of directors' and secretaries' share interests. 'Interests' for these purposes is defined broadly to encompass virtually every kind of legal or equitable interest in a share.

[15.124] CA 1990, Part IV also provides for a procedure enabling a wide variety of persons to obtain information about interests held by other persons in shares (or debentures) of the company. For this procedure to be put in motion, a court order must first be obtained. The order, called a *disclosure order*, may be applied for by any person who has 'a financial interest' in the company - which includes members, contributories, creditors, employees, co-adventurers, examiners, lessors, lessees, licensors, licensees, liquidators or receivers, of either the company itself or a related company[351]. The applicant must give ten days' notice of his application to the company, and to the person to whom the order is intended to be directed[352].

(a) Scope of disclosure order

[15.125] A disclosure order may require the person to whom it is addressed to give the court written particulars of his past and present interests in shares of the company, and, so far as such information lies within his knowledge, particulars of any other interests

---

[349] *Bellerby v Rowland & Marwood's SS Co* [1902] 2 Ch 14. On reductions of capital generally see Chapter 18, *The Maintenance of Capital.*

[350] See Chapter 8, *Corporate Governance: Management by the Directors* para **[8.090]** ff.

[351] On what constitutes a 'related company' see Warnock 'Inter-Company Relationships and Section 31 of the Companies Act 1990' (1994) CLP 243.

[352] CA 1990, s 99.

subsisting in the shares during the time at which he was interested, and of the identity of the person who became interested when he ceased to be interested[353].

[15.126] The interests which must be disclosed by the addressee of a disclosure order include 'any interest of any kind whatsoever in the shares'[354], and specifically includes the interests of a beneficiary under a trust[355], a purchaser under a contract[356], and a person who, though not a shareholder, is entitled to exercise or control the exercise of the rights of the shareholder[357]. A person will also be deemed to be interested where his spouse or minor child is interested, or where a body corporate which is accustomed to act in accordance with his instructions, or in which he controls more than one-third of the voting power, is interested[358].

[15.127] The following need *not* be disclosed:

— where property is held on trust, an interest in reversion or remainder, or of a bare trustee, or any discretionary interest[359];

— interests subsisting under unit trusts or UCITS[360];

— interests in schemes under s 46 of the Charities Act 1961[361];

— life interests under irrevocable settlements where the settlor has no interest in the income or the property[362];

— 'exempt security interests,' ie interests held as security for a loan by a bank, insurance company, post office savings bank, or a stockbroker carrying on business on a recognised stock exchange, etc.[363];

— interests held by the President of the High Court under s 13 of the Succession Act 1965[364];

— interests held by the Accountant of the High Court pursuant to the Rules of Court[365];

— any other interests exempted by the Minister[366].

---

353 CA 1990, s 100(1).

354 CA 1990, s 77, as applied by CA 1990, s 100(3).

355 CA 1990, s 77(2). A person on whose behalf a nominee holds shares is, thus, caught by the section.

356 CA 1990, s 77(4)(b).

357 CA 1990, s 77(4)(b).

358 CA 1990, s 72.

359 CA 1990, s 78(1)(a).

360 CA 1990, s 78(1)(b)(i).

361 CA 1990, s 78(1)(b)(ii).

362 CA 1990, s 78(1)(c) and s 78(3).

363 CA 1990, s 78(1)(d) and s 78(4). See also the Companies (Stock Exchange) Regulations 1990, SI 337/1990.

364 CA 1990, s 78(1)(e).

365 CA 1990, s 78(1)(f).

366 CA 1990, s 78(1)(g).

(b) Powers of the court in relation to disclosure orders

[15.128] The court may only make a disclosure order if it deems it just and equitable to do so and if it is of the opinion that the financial interest of the applicant is or will be prejudiced by the non-disclosure of any interest in the shares or debentures of the company[367]. The court may impose such restrictions or conditions on the rights attaching to the shares in respect of which the order is made as it sees fit[368]; but any person affected by conditions or restrictions may apply to the court for relief[369]. The court may subsequently, on cause shown, vary or rescind a disclosure order, or, if it is of the opinion that it would be just and equitable to do so and that the financial interests of the applicant would not be prejudiced, it may exempt any person or persons, share or class of shares, interest or class of interest, or debenture or class of debentures from the requirements of a disclosure order[370].

[15.129] The order must identify the person to whom it is directed and must give his address[371]. Notice of the making of an order must be given, within seven days of its making, by the applicant to the company, the Registrar of Companies, shareholders or debentureholders not resident in Ireland where the court considers they should be notified, and any such other person as the court sees fit[372]. Notice must also be published in two daily newspapers circulating in the district of the company's registered office[373].

Any information given to the court in compliance with the order must be given by a prescribed officer of the court to the applicant and to the company, unless the court otherwise directs[374].

(c) Consequences of contravention of a disclosure order

[15.130] Where a person fails to fulfil the obligations required by a disclosure order, or provides information which is false, no right or interest of any kind whatsoever in respect of any shares or debentures of the company held by him may be enforced, whether directly or indirectly, by action or legal proceeding, unless the court is satisfied upon an application for relief by any person that such default was accidental, or due to inadvertence or some other sufficient cause[375]. Notably, no criminal sanctions apply to contravention; however, breach of the order may also render the offender liable to contempt proceedings, including attachment and, ultimately, committal to prison[376].

---

367 CA 1990, s 98(5).

368 CA 1990, s 101(4).

369 CA 1990, s 101(5).

370 CA 1990, s 101(3).

371 CA 1990, s 103(1).

372 CA 1990, s 102.

373 CA 1990, s 102.

374 CA 1990, s 103(2).The examiner and registrars of the High Court have been so prescribed: SI 1991/209.

375 CA 1990, s 104.

376 See RSC 1986, ord 44.

Chapter 16

Share Transfers in Private Companies

Introduction

[16.001] In private companies, shares are transferred by the registered owner ('transferor') or someone on his behalf, executing a *stock transfer form* in favour of the purchaser ('transferee'). However, in order to comply with the statutory definition of a private company, the articles of association (the 'articles') of every private company must restrict the right of shareholders to transfer their shares[1]. Sometimes, the shareholders will go one step further and enter into a *shareholders' agreement* which will typically include extensive restrictions on the transfer of shares[2]. Restrictions will often extend not only to the transfer of shares, but also to their transmission and mortgaging. The *transmission* of shares is where shares pass by operation of law, on a member's death or bankruptcy, to his personal representatives or the official assignee in bankruptcy, respectively[3].

[16.002] Restrictions on the transfer of shares may be categorised as being either general or specific in nature. The objective of transferring shares is to place the transferee in the same position as the transferor vis-á-vis membership rights. As shall be considered below, to pass full title in shares, the transferee must not only be named in the stock transfer form, but must also have his name entered on the register of members by the company's directors. General restrictions are usually in the nature of the *power to refuse to register shares*, which is vested in the directors[4]. Specific restrictions on the transfer of shares invariably take the form of *pre-emption rights*, or rights of first refusal on the sale of shares usually in favour of the company's existing members. Pre-emption rights usually require proposing transferors first to offer their shares to the other members of the company before transferring them to outsiders.

[16.003] Where the transferee intends to acquire the entire of the company's business, perhaps the greatest choice facing him is the *share/asset purchase quandary*. This involves deciding whether to purchase all of the company's shares from the shareholders, or to purchase all of the company's assets and undertaking from the company itself. Where it is decided to purchase the shares in a private company a share purchase agreement should be prepared setting out the rights of the transferee and obligations of the transferor. Although this chapter is concerned only with the law relating to the transfer of shares, the factors influencing the choice between a share purchase and an asset purchase are outlined below[5].

---

1 CA 1963, s 33(1)(b). See generally, Ch 1, *The Private Company in Context*, para **[1.115]**.

2 For restrictions in shareholders' agreements, see para **[16.063]**. For shareholders' agreements, see generally, Ch 3, *Private Constitutional Documentation*, para **[3.109]**.

3 See para **[16.025]** *ff*.

4 See para **[16.037]** *ff*.

[16.004] Where the transferor and the transferee agree upon the consideration to be paid for the shares in sale, the *valuation of shares* will not be in issue. In cases where the consideration for the shares cannot be agreed or where the articles or a shareholders' agreement contain a valuation mechanism, recourse may be had to the courts by the transferee or transferor. The valuation of shares may arise also where the court makes an order to buy or sell shares pursuant to the Companies Act 1963, s 205 ('CA 1963'). The valuation of shares is considered below[6].

[16.005] The law of the transfer, transmission and general alienation of shares in private companies is considered here under the following headings:

[A] The mechanics of share transfer.

[B] Transferability and restrictions.

[C] Transmission of shares and security over shares.

[D] Directors' powers to refuse registration.

[E] Pre-emption rights on share transfer.

[F] Compulsory transfers of shares.

[G] Share purchase agreements.

[H] The valuation of shares in private companies.

[A] The Mechanics of Share Transfer

The requirement for a 'proper instrument of transfer'

[16.006] Save in public companies whose shares are in uncertificated form[7], in order to effect a transfer of shares[8] the transferor must execute a proper instrument of transfer[9]. Model reg 23 of CA 1963, Sch 1, Table A, Part I (the 'model articles') provides:

> Subject to such of the restrictions of these regulations as may be applicable, any member may transfer all or any of his shares by instrument in writing in any usual or common form or any other form which the directors may approve.

The need for a written instrument to transfer shares is also clear from CA 1963, s 81(1), which provides:

> 'Subject to subsection (2), and notwithstanding anything in the articles of a company, it shall not be lawful for the company to register a transfer of shares in or debentures of the company unless a proper instrument of transfer has been delivered to the company.'

---

5 See para **[16.100]** *ff.*

6 See para **[16.108]** *ff.*

7 See para **[16.009]**.

8 See Johnston, *Banking and Security Law in Ireland* (1998), Ch 16; Doyle, *The Company Secretary* (1994), Ch 7; Nicholson, *Table A Articles of Association* (1997), pp 53–73; and Egan, *Jordans Irish Company Secretarial Precedents* (1993), Ch 5B.

9 Contrast a contract for the sale of shares which can be oral: *Bowlby v Bell* (1846) 3 CB 284. In *Guardian Builders Ltd v Sleecon Ltd and Berville Ltd* (18 August 1988, unreported), High Court Blayney J distinguished a contract for the sale of shares from a contract for the sale of land and held that the former contract would not be within the Statute of Frauds (Ireland) 1695. See generally, Clark, *Contract Law in Ireland* (3rd edn, 1992), Ch 4.

Section 81(2) provides that the foregoing is without prejudice to a company's power to register as shareholder[10] any person to whom the right to any shares in the company[11] has been transmitted by operation of law. The transmission of shares is considered below[12]. It was held in *Re Greene*[13], however, that a transferor must always execute a share transfer. In that case, the company's articles provided that a shareholder's shares would be transferred automatically on death. It was held that this was impermissible and that the transferor's personal representatives must execute a share transfer form.

[16.007] One question that arises is whether the phrase 'proper instrument of transfer' as used in CA 1963, s 81 implies that a transfer must be stamped. It is thought, on balance, that it is lawful for a company to register an instrument transferring shares on which stamp duty has not been paid. In *Nisbet v Shepherd*[14] the English Court of Appeal had to consider whether the registration of a stock transfer form which omitted the consideration and which had not been stamped had been validly registered. Leggatt LJ said:

> 'The question is whether that omission [particulars of the consideration] in particular prevented the stock transfer form from constituting a proper instrument. In my judgment, the phrase does not mean an instrument complying in all respects with statutory requirements. In this context, "proper" means no more than "appropriate" or "suitable". What it had to be suitable for was stamping...That would no doubt have required the addition to the document of the amount of the consideration, so that the stamp duty might be ascertained, but because the document sufficiently recorded the transaction, the defects in the form were mere irregularities. It was an instrument chargeable with stamp duty. It was, therefore, a proper instrument, and the registration of the transfer was not invalid.'[15]

It is thought that the foregoing is the correct interpretation of the phrase 'proper instrument of transfer'. The failure to stamp a stampable document does not invalidate that document, as stamping is simply a Revenue requirement[16]. However, whilst a company has a *right* to register an unstamped instrument of transfer, it has no *duty* to issue a share certificate following receipt of an unstamped instrument of transfer. This is because CA 1963, s 86(1) provides in connection with the duties of a company in relation to the issue of share certificates following, inter alia, a transfer of shares:

> 'The expression "transfer" for the purpose of this subsection means a transfer duly stamped and otherwise valid, and does not include such a transfer as the company is, for any reason, entitled to refuse to register and does not register.'

---

10 Or, debenture holder.

11 Or, debentures of the company.

12 See para **[16.025]**.

13 *Re Greene* [1949] 1 All ER 167.

14 *Nisbet v Shepherd* [1994] 1 BCLC 300. See also *Re Paradise Motor Co Ltd* [1968] 2 All ER 625 at 630, per Danckwerts LJ and *Powell v London and Provincial Bank* [1893] 2 Ch 555.

15 [1994] 1 BCLC 300 at 305.

16 See *Re Motor Racing Circuits Ltd* (31 January 1997, unreported), Supreme Court (Blayney J; nem diss) considered in Chapter 20, *Corporate Borrowing: Debentures and Security*, para **[20.033]**.

[16.008] Where fully paid shares are transferred a standard pre-printed stock transfer form as permitted by the Stock Transfer Act 1963, s 2 is invariably used. Section 2(1) of the Act provides that shares '*may* be transferred by means of an instrument under hand in the form set out in the First Schedule to this Act'. Accordingly, shares can be validly transferred *without compliance* with that Act and without using the form provided. This is borne out by s 2(3) of the Act, which states that 'nothing in this section shall be construed as affecting the validity of any instrument which would be effective to transfer securities apart from this section'.

[16.009] Whilst the operation of the Companies Act 1990 (Uncertificated Securities) Regulations 1996[17] is not expressly confined to public companies, in practice it is. Indeed, the free transferability of shares in uncertificated (or, indeed, any) form is anathema to private companies which, by definition, must restrict the transfer of shares[18]. It is opined that, in a private company, it is not open to the directors to resolve that title to shares of a class issued or to be issued may be transferred by means of a 'relevant system' pursuant to reg 8(2) of the 1996 Regulations.

Execution of the instrument of transfer

[16.010] In the case of an individual, a stock transfer form can be executed under hand. In the case of a body corporate vendor of shares, it is debatable whether the form must be executed under hand or under seal. Although the Stock Transfer Act 1963, s 2(1) clearly states that shares 'may be transferred by means of an instrument *under hand* in the form set out in the First Schedule to this Act', the form in the said First Schedule[19] contains a note 'a body corporate *should* execute this transfer under its common seal or otherwise in accordance with applicable statutory requirements'. It is thought, on balance, that the prescribed stock transfer form does *not* strictly require to be under seal where executed by companies by reason of the following observations: the express general reference to 'under hand' in s 2(1); the equation of individuals with companies, in CA 1963, s 38(1)(a), as to when a seal is required[20]; and the use of 'should' as opposed to 'must' in the prescribed form. Of course, it is open to a party to a transaction to seek to insist that a stock transfer form be executed under seal.

[16.011] Although model reg 22 provides that a transfer should also be executed by the transferee, private companies commonly amend model reg 22 to dispense with the necessity of the transferee also executing the transfer.

[16.012] The execution of a stock transfer form need not be attested[21]. Unpaid or partly paid shares are not covered by the Stock Transfer Act 1963 which provides, in s 2(4) that 'this section applies to fully paid up transferable registered securities'[22].

---

17 SI 1996/68.

18 CA 1963, s 33: see para **[16.020]**.

19 As inserted by the Stock Transfer (Forms) Regulations 1996 (SI 1996/263).

20 See Chapter 7, *Corporate Contracts, Capacity and Authority*, para **[7.013]**.

21 Stock Transfer Act 1963, s 2(2).

22 See model reg 23.

The transferee's obligations on transfer

[16.013] Upon the execution of a share transfer the transferor is obliged to give the transferee the share certificate(s) relating to the shares transferred. A transferor of shares is also obliged to:

> '...execute a valid transfer of the shares and hand the same to the transferee, and do all that is necessary to enable the transferee to insist with the company on his right to be registered a member in respect of such shares.'[23]

Unless a contract for the sale of shares specifically provides otherwise, the general rule is that a transferor is not obliged to procure the *registration* of the shares in the name of the transferee[24]. Notwithstanding this general rule, a transferor who was a director has been held to be obliged to vote in favour of the registration of the transferee as a member of the company[25].

[16.014] Prudent transferees who purchase shares will require that a *share purchase agreement* is also prepared and executed. The raison d'être of a share purchase agreement is the protection of the transferee. It is sought to achieve this by the reduction to writing of warranties and indemnities from the transferor. Share purchase agreements are considered below[26].

[16.015] Where a transferor sells only some of his shares or sells all of his shares to different transferees, practical difficulties prevent him from handing over his share certificate to the transferee(s). In such cases the company may *certify* the transfer(s) pursuant to CA 1963, s 85. Such certification by the company is a representation to bona fide purchasers that the company has been furnished with such documents as are necessary to prove the transferor's prima facie title to the shares. As considered in the previous chapter, the company concerned may be liable where, on foot of a forged share transfer, it issues a share certificate[27].

[B] TRANSFERABILITY AND RESTRICTIONS

[16.016] The transfer of shares involves the consideration of a number of diverse matters. Although shares are prima facie transferable, by definition, private companies must impose restrictions on the transfer of their shares. Here the following matters are considered:

1. Shares are transferable but subject to restrictions.
2. The rationale for restrictions in private companies.

---

[23] *Skinner v The City of London Marine Insurance Corporation* (1885) 14 QBD 882 at 887, per Brett MR.

[24] For the consequences of the directors refusing to register a share transfer, see para **[16.058]** *ff*.

[25] *Lee & Company (Dublin) Ltd v Egan (Wholesale) Ltd* (27 April 1978, unreported), High Court at p 10, per Kenny J.

[26] See para **[16.099]**. For specialised treatments see: Sinclair, *Warranties and Indemnities on Share Sales*, (2nd edn, 1989); Patterson, *Private Company Share Sale Manual* (2nd edn, 1990); Longman, *Commercial Series*; and Wine, *Buying & Selling Private Companies and Businesses* (3rd edn, 1986).

[27] See Chapter 15, *Shares and Membership*, para **[15.046]**.

3. Registration by the directors.
4. Transferees' position pending registration.

Shares are transferable but subject to restrictions

[16.017] Shares in private companies are prima facie transferable. Section 79 of CA 1963[28] provides that:

> 'The shares or other interest of any member in a company shall be personal estate, transferable in manner provided by the articles of the company, and shall not be of the nature of real estate.'

It is crucial to recognise that s 79 cannot be read in isolation and in particular does not confer an absolute unfettered right to transfer shares. Rather, the provisions of other sections of the Companies Acts 1963–2001 and the company's articles must also be considered. Notwithstanding the principle of transferability in s 79, restrictions on either the transfer of shares and/or the registration of the transferee as a member are intrinsic to private companies.

[16.018] In *Weston*'s case[29] Selwyn LJ said of the materially similar[30] Companies (Consolidation) Act 1908, s 22 that it:

> '...merely refers the company to their own articles for determining the manner in which that transfer shall be effected, but leaves the general right to transfer to stand upon the provisions of the Act.'

Referring to this, in *Re Hafner*[31] the learned Black J said of the Companies (Consolidation) Act 1908, s 22:

> '...I think the section is plain itself, that a statutory right of transfer is given independently of the articles, but a right which may or may not be restricted by the articles. This is shown by the fact that articles cannot validly confer upon the directors a power to refuse to allow a member of the company to transfer his shares at all to anybody...
>
> The statute confers what Selwyn LJ called a general right of transfer, and what the statute has given, the articles cannot take away. On the other hand, the words of the sub-section which follow the word 'transferable' are 'in manner provided by the articles of the company,' and it is well settled that these latter words permit of various restrictions being imposed by the articles upon the general statutory right of transfer. It is by virtue of this power held to be given by s 22, [CA 1963, s 79] that a private company restricts the transfer of its shares by its articles, which, indeed, it is bound to do under s 121, [CA 1963, s 33] such restriction being one of the essential ingredients of a private company.'[32]

Accordingly, while shares per se are transferable, shares in private companies *must* contain restrictions. These restrictions are to be found in the company's articles[33].

---

28 For further consideration, see Ch 4, *Incorporation and its Consequences*, para **[4.076]**.

29 *Re Smith, Knight & Co* (1868) LR 4 Ch App 20 at 30.

30 Companies (Consolidation) Act 1908, s 22 omitted the final words of CA 1963, s 79, 'and shall not be of the nature of real estate.'

31 *Re Hafner* [1943] IR 426.

32 [1943] IR 426 at 448.

33 Although restrictions are also found in shareholders' agreements, where adopted, such restrictions are optional.

[16.019] Restrictions on the transfer of shares in private companies have been held not to fall foul of the rule against perpetuities. In *AG for Ireland v Jameson*[34] the alienation of shares was governed by an elaborate series of provisions in the company's articles. Inter alia, shares could only be transferred to members of the company where a member was willing to purchase the shares at the 'fair value thereof'. *Fair value* was defined as the sum of £100 per share or such other sum as was from time to time fixed as the fair value by resolution of the company in general meeting. When a member who held 750 shares died, his estate became liable to pay estate duty. His executors valued his shares on the basis of the right of pre-emption and the restrictions on transfer contained in the articles, ie £100 per share. The Revenue Commissioners sought a declaration from the court that the value of the shares was the value which they would obtain if they were sold on the open market. The Revenue Commissioners argued, inter alia, that the restrictions on share transfer in the articles were invalid either as infringing the rule against perpetuities or as being repugnant to the right of alienation inherent in absolute ownership. Kenny J rejected these suggestions, holding as follows:

- that it was only the shares which were subject to restrictions on alienation and not the company's assets;
- that shareholders' rights are enjoyed by entering into a statutory contract under seal and shareholders' rights are inseparable from shareholders' obligations;
- that there is no interest in land, legal or equitable, vested in the members or the members' executors; and
- that there existed no absolute prohibition on the alienation of shares[35].

The rationale for restrictions in private companies

[16.020] Restrictions on the transfer of shares in private companies exist for reasons beyond mere compliance with CA 1963, s 33(1). Restrictions on share transfers are frequently adopted by promoters of their own volition because a restriction on the transfer of shares is sympathetic to the underlying structure of many private companies. It is common for restrictions in the articles or shareholders' agreements in many private companies to extend further than the statutory requirement. Often the restrictions placed on the transfer of shares are the result of very elaborate and complex feats of draughtsmanship. The practical necessity for restrictions on the transfer of shares is underscored by the statutory restrictions on a company purchasing or assisting the purchase of its own shares in order to maintain control and prevent outsiders from entering the circle of members[36].

---

[34] *AG for Ireland v Jameson* [1904] IR 644. For an analysis of the policy considerations involving the question of the inalienability of shares, see Andre, 'Restrictions on the Transfer of Shares: A Search For A Public Policy' (1979) Tulane L Rev 776, where the case law of Louisiana is analysed. The differences between the corporations considered there and the Irish private company are striking.

[35] See also *Borland's Trustee v Steel, Bros & Co Ltd* [1901] 1 Ch 279; *Casey v Bentley* [1902] 1 IR 376 and *London & South-Western Railway Co v Gomm* 20 Ch D 562.

[36] See the dictum of Lord Macnaghten in *Trevor v Whitworth* [1887] 13 App Cas 409 at 428 and 436.

[16.021] Intrinsic to many Irish private companies are the ties of friendship, quasi-partnership, mutuality and kinship which exist between their members. The involuntary admission of an outsider to such a close circle could destroy the very fabric of the company and shatter a quasi-partnership understanding. As Lord Greene MR observed in *Re Smith and Fawcett Ltd*[37] of the directors' power to refuse registration:

> 'Private companies are in law separate entities just as much as are public companies, but from the business and personal point of view they are much more analogous to partnerships than to public corporations. Accordingly, it is to be expected that in the articles of such a company the control of the directors over the membership may be very strict indeed.'

Furthermore, restrictions on the transfer of shares can assist the maintenance of the status quo by restricting existing members from acquiring additional shares and so perhaps obtaining a controlling interest. Indeed, even in jurisdictions such as England and Wales where statutory restrictions on the transfer of shares in private companies have been abolished, the existence and importance of restrictions in private companies have continued regardless[38].

Registration by the directors

[16.022] A transfer of shares is inchoate until the transferee is registered as a member of the company[39]. In *Tangney v The Clarence Hotels Company Ltd*[40] Johnston J said '[a] transfer is not legally complete until the transferee has been registered in the books of the company...'. Accordingly, while the transferee has certain equitable rights to the shares, his legal title is not perfected until his name is placed on the company's register of members[41]. It is the transferee's responsibility to procure the registration of the transfer[42]. Directors have both powers and duties in regard to the refusal of registrations of share transfers. Where the articles give the directors a veto to refuse the registration of shares, the directors will have a power of refusal. On the other hand, the directors have a duty to refuse registration where there is non-compliance by a transferring member with a pre-ordained pre-emption procedure in the company's articles. There exists a considerable amount of case law on the directors' powers and duties of refusal to register share transfers, which is considered below[43].

---

37 *Re Smith and Fawcett Ltd* [1942] 1 Ch 304 at 306.

38 See Schmittoff (ed), *Palmer's Company Law* (24th ed 1987), para 40–14 and Fox & Bowen, *The Law of Private Companies* (1991), pp 63,64.

39 See *Powell v London and Provincial Bank* [1893] 2 Ch 555 where Lindley LJ said at 560 that '...in order to acquire the legal title to stock or shares in companies governed by the Companies Clauses Consolidation Act you must have a deed executed by the transferor, and you must have that transfer registered. Until you have got both you have not got the legal title in the transferee.' This passage was cited with approval by Barron J in *Kinsella v Alliance and Dublin Consumers' Gas Company* (5 October 1982, unreported), High Court at p 10 of the transcript.

40 *Tangney v The Clarence Hotels Company Ltd* [1933] IR 51 at 61.

41 On the register of members, see Chapter 15, *Shares and Membership*, para **[15.017]** *ff*.

42 See *Skinner's case* (1885) 14 QBD 882, cited with approval by Johnston J in *Tangey v The Clarance Hotels Company Ltd et al* [1933] IR 51 at 59,60.

43 See para **[16.037]**.

Transferees' position pending registration

[16.023] In principle, at any given time, only one person should be beneficially entitled to enjoy whatever rights attach to particular shares in a company[44]. This is particularly true of voting rights. By reason of this principle, before the transferor is removed from the register of members and the transferee is registered as a member, the transferee has none of the rights of membership[45]. This was found to be the position in *Kinsella v Alliance and Dublin Consumers' Gas Company*[46] where Barron J held that:

> 'Persons entitled to stock must be registered in the register of shareholders. Until they are, they are not entitled to vote. This is a well established principle and I would be wrong not to follow it.'[47]

Accordingly, the applicant-transferees were unsuccessful in their claim to be entitled to exercise the voting rights attaching to the shares transferred to them which had not yet been registered in their names. The fact that the transfers had been lodged with the company for registration did not alter the rule. It is thought that this common law rule may be displaced and that a company's articles may provide to the contrary so as to afford unregistered transferees with full rights of membership. Moreover, as is considered below[48] a transferee who has paid for shares enjoys equitable or beneficial rights to those shares.

[16.024] A number of cases show that the position of a transferee pending registration can be precarious. Care must be taken to apply for registration as soon as possible since pending registration a transferee has only *equitable rights* to the shares. Where another person also has an equity in the same shares, the rule governing priorities is that *where the equities are equal, the first in time prevails*[49]. This rule is said to apply unless the transferee has 'a present, absolute, unconditional right to have the transfer registered'[50]. In *Moore v NW Bank*[51] Romer J interpreted the foregoing statement as referring to a situation where an unregistered transferee acquires the full status of a shareholder or at least where all formalities have been complied with, there being only some purely administrative act remaining to be done by the company which the company could not

44 Where shares are in joint-ownership, the model articles restrict the rights attaching to the senior joint-owner: see, eg, model reg 64 which provides that 'the vote of the senior who tenders the vote...shall be accepted.'

45 Contrast CA 1963, s 205(6) which gives the personal representatives of a deceased member locus standi to petition the court under s 205(1). See generally, Chapter 19, *Shareholders' Remedies*.

46 *Kinsella v Alliance and Dublin Consumers' Gas Company* (5 October 1982, unreported), High Court, per Barron J.

47 (5 October 1982, unreported), High Court at p 12.

48 See para **[16.068]**.

49 *Moore v NW Bank* [1891] 2 Ch 599 at 602 per Romer J. See also *Ireland v Hart* [1902] 1 Ch 522 and *Société Generale de Paris v Walker* (1885) 11 App Cas 20, per Lord Selborne. See generally, Keane, *Equity and the Law of Trusts in the Republic of Ireland* (1988), para 5.04.

50 Per Lord Selborne in *Société Generale de Paris v Walker* (1885) 11 App Cas 20 at 29.

51 *Moore v NW Bank* [1891] 2 Ch 599.

refuse to do[52]. An example might be where the directors have voted in favour of the transferee's registration and only the perfection of the transferee's title remains.
Where a transferee cannot be registered as a member of a company by reason of a failure to comply with pre-emption rights, it is thought that his position pending registration is especially precarious. The attitude of the courts appears to be firmly in favour of assisting the enforcement of pre-emption agreements and recognising the rights of those to whom the shares should be offered[53].

[C] Transmission of Shares and Security over Shares

The transmission of shares on death

[16.025] The *transmission of shares* is where shares pass by operation of law on the death or bankruptcy of a member. The discussion here is confined to where shares pass on the death of a member[54]. Where the title to shares passes by transmission, it is typical for the articles to provide that the *same* restrictions shall apply as apply in the case of an inter vivos transfer of shares. Consequently, it is common for the directors' power to refuse to register the shares to apply in the case of a transmission[55]. Similarly, where pre-emption rights exist, they are commonly expressed in articles to apply to a deceased member's personal representatives who will, in consequence, be obliged to comply with such provisions[56].

[16.026] The principle that only one person should be legally entitled to particular shares holds good in the case of the *transmission* of shares. Model reg 29 provides that the:

> '...survivor or survivors where the deceased was a joint holder, and the personal representatives of the deceased where he was a sole holder, shall be the *only persons recognised by the company as having any title* to his interest in the shares.' [Emphasis added]

Personal representatives cannot be said to be in a similar position to transferees, as the rights of a personal representative per se are only legal[57]. The production of a grant of probate or letters of administration must be accepted by the company as sufficient evidence of the personal representative's title in the shares[58]. A transfer of a share of a

---

52 See also *Re Rose* [1949] Ch 78; *Milroy v Lord* (1862) 4 De GF & J 264; *Re Fry, Chase National Executors & Trustees Corp v Fry* [1946] Ch 312.

53 See *Lee and Co (Dublin) Ltd v Egan (Wholesalers) Ltd* (27 April 1978, unreported), High Court, per Kenny J, *Re Champion Publications Ltd* (4 June 1991, unreported), High Court and *Tett v Phoenix Property and Investment Co Ltd* [1987] BCLC 149. Cf *Hawks v McArthur* [1951] 1 All ER 22.

54 For the position on a member's bankruptcy, para **[16.030]**.

55 See model reg 30, at para **[16.028]**. In *Re Hackney Pavilion Ltd* [1924] 1 Ch 276 it was held that where the articles provided that the beneficiary of a deceased member's shares was entitled to be registered unless the directors declined registration, the beneficiary was entitled to be registered where the board of directors was deadlocked on the question of refusing registration.

56 *Re Benfield Greig Group plc* [2000] 2 BCLC 488.

57 It should be remembered that model reg 29 can be deleted or amended prior to incorporation.

58 CA 1963, s 87.

deceased member made by his personal representative shall, although the personal representative is not a member, be as valid as if he had been such a member at the time of execution of the transfer: CA 1963, s 82.

[16.027] A personal representative has two options. On the one hand, he can elect to be registered himself; on the other, he can elect to have another person registered. These options are addressed in model reg 31, which provides:

> 'If the person so becoming entitled elects to be registered himself, he shall deliver or send to the company a notice in writing signed by him stating that he so elects. If he elects to have another person registered, he shall testify his election by executing to that person a transfer of the share. All the limitations, restrictions and provisions of these regulations relating to the tight to transfer and the registration of transfers of shares shall be applicable to any such notice or transfer as aforesaid as if the death or bankruptcy of the member had not occurred and the notice or transfer were a transfer signed by that member.'

So, whether a personal representative elects[59] to be registered or not, model regs 30[60] and 31 provide that the directors have the same right to decline or suspend registration as if the death (or bankruptcy) had not occurred.

[16.028] Model reg 30 provides:

> 'Any person becoming entitled to a share in consequence of the death or bankruptcy of a member may, upon such evidence being produced as may from time to time properly be required by the directors and subject as hereinafter provided, elect either to be registered himself as holder of the share or to have some person nominated by him registered as the transferee thereof, but the directors shall, in either case, have the same right to decline or suspend registration as they would have had in the case of a transfer of the share by that member before his death or bankruptcy, as the case may be.'

The registration of a transfer executed by a personal representative is subject to the directors' discretion, where, of course, the articles give the directors such discretion[61]. In *Village Cay Marine Ltd v Acland (Barclays Bank plc third party)*[62] the Privy Council held that personal representatives were not in a more privileged position than ordinary transferors, saying:

> '[The articles of association] expressly say that applications for registration by personal representatives or trustees in bankruptcy, either of themselves...or of a nominated person…shall be treated as if they were transfers. They were accordingly subject to the [directors'] discretion…in the same way as any other transfer…'[63].

Under common form articles of association – where the registration of all share transfers is made subject to the directors' unfettered discretion – the registration of a transfer, executed by a personal representative, will be at the directors' discretion. Where,

---

59 Where a personal representative elects to be registered, model reg 31, where adopted, will govern the mechanics of registration. See *Stothers v William Steward (Holdings) Ltd* [1994] 2 BCLC 266.

60 See para **[16.028]**.

61 See para **[16.038]**.

62 *Village Cay Marine Ltd v Acland (Barclays Bank plc third party)* [1998] 2 BCLC 327.

63 [1998] 2 BCLC 327 at 336.

however, the articles of association direct that transfers to a particular class of person is not subject to the directors' discretion, then registration of a transfer by a personal representative in favour of a member of such class will not be subject to the directors' discretion, by reason of the use of the words 'have the same right to decline...as they would have had in the case of a transfer of the share by that member before his death'. This distinction was made clear in *Stothers v William Steward (Holdings) Ltd*[64]. In that case the company's articles provided that a transfer by a member to one of the following classes of member was *not* subject to the directors' general discretion to refuse registration: another existing member; a privileged relation (as defined); and trustees to be held upon family trusts (as defined). Upon the death of a shareholder, it was held by the English Court of Appeal that since the directors could not have refused to register a transfer by a member to his wife (who fell to be defined as a 'privileged relation'), the directors could not refuse to register a transfer from a deceased member's personal representatives in favour of that deceased member's wife[65].

[16.029] Pending registration, a personal representative has certain rights that are indicative of his fiduciary position and duty to account to the beneficiaries of the deceased shareholder[66]. Common form articles provide that a personal representative is entitled to receive notice of members' meetings[67]. Personal representatives cannot, however, vote at such meetings unless registered as members. In *Arulchelvan and Wright v Wright*[68] the question arose as to whether a meeting attended by a deceased's personal representatives was quorate and whether resolutions passed thereat were valid. It was contended that the personal representatives of a deceased shareholder were to be counted as shareholders at meetings. It was sought to support this contention by the fact that model reg 136 entitles personal representatives to be given notice of general meetings; that the articles of association must be construed together[69]; that a transmission of shares was to be treated differently from a transfer of shares[70]; that one member may be counted as two if he holds in different capacities[71]; and that CA 1963, s 141, which relates to a special resolution being passed by not less than three-fourths of the votes cast, draws a distinction between members entitled to vote and those not entitled to vote, which could therefore refer to personal representatives. This was rejected by Carroll J who held:

> 'A "member" is defined by section 31 of the 1963 Act. Unless his name is on the register of members, he is not a member. A personal representative who is entitled to be registered as a member of a company does not become a member unless his name is entered on the register of members. A personal representative is recognised as having title to the deceased member's interest in his shares (regulation 29) and is entitled to the same

64 *Stothers v William Steward (Holdings) Ltd* [1994] 2 BCLC 266.

65 See also the final 24 words of model reg 31 para **[16.027]**.

66 *Gabbett v Lawder* (1883) 11 LR Ir 295.

67 Model reg 136(b).

68 *Wright v Wright* (7 February 1996, unreported), High Court (Carroll J).

69 *Stothers v William Stewart (Holdings) Ltd* [1994] 2 BCLC 266 cited.

70 *Moodie v W & J Shepherd (Bookbinders) Ltd* [1949] 2 All ER 1044 cited.

71 *Neil M'Leod & Sons* [1967] SLT 46 cited.

> dividends and other advantages to which he would be entitled if he were the registered holder (regulation 32). But before being registered as a member in respect of a share he is not entitled in respect of it to exercise any right conferred by membership in relation to meetings of the company (see: Regulation 32, Part I of Table A).
>
> The regulations seem eminently clear to me. The right to attend a meeting is conferred by membership, as is the right to speak and to vote. Since the first and third defendants have not been registered as members, they could not be counted as forming part of the quorum at the two meetings in question. And since no valid quorum was present, no business was transacted[72].

The general rule under the model articles is that 'a person becoming entitled to a share' has the same entitlement to dividends and other advantages attaching to shares as he would have were he registered, save the right to vote[73].

Transmission of shares on bankruptcy

[16.030] On a person being adjudicated bankrupt any shares he holds in any company will automatically vest in the official assignee in bankruptcy by virtue of the Bankruptcy Act 1988, s 44(1). It is common for companies' articles to provide that the same restrictions shall apply on a member's bankruptcy as apply on death or the *inter vivos* transfer of shares. Private companies commonly adopt model regs 30, 31 and 32, already considered in the context of the transmission of shares on a member's death[74].

Security over shares

[16.031] Another form of alienation of shares is where the registered owner creates a mortgage over his shares[75]. Although often regarded by lending institutions as a less than perfect security, shares in private companies may be mortgaged and charged at law or in equity[76].

(a) Legal mortgage of shares

[16.032] A *legal mortgage of shares* involves the transfer of the legal title in shares to the mortgagee and the registration of the mortgagee as legal owner and full member of those shares[77]. By reason of CA 1963, s 123 the mortgagor's equity of redemption cannot be recorded in either the transfer instrument or the register of members[78]. A mortgagee of shares can, however, register a *stop notice*, considered below[79].

---

72 *Wright v Wright* (7 February 1996, unreported), High Court (Carroll J) at pp 8-9 of the transcript.

73 Model reg 32.

74 See para **[16.027]** to **[16.029]**.

75 See generally, Johnston, *Banking and Security Law in Ireland* (1998), Ch 16 and Lingard, *Bank Security Documents* (3rd edn, 1993), Ch 15.

76 Shares may also be *charged* and a debenture or deed of charge executed by the registered owner of the shares in favour of a chargee. The effect is to give the charge holder equitable rights over the shares in the private company. For the reasons set out at para **[16.033]** *ff*, this is considered to be a below average security.

77 See generally, Bell, *Modern Law of Personal Property in England and Ireland* (1989), p 183 (where mortgages are considered) and at p 173 (where charges are considered).

78 See Chapter 15, *Shares and Membership*, para **[15.017]**.

Accordingly, the transfer to the mortgagee must be outright, giving the mortgagee all of the rights to vote and to dividend, which attach to the shares. On the release of the security the shares must be re-transferred[80], giving rise to a double stamp duty liability. If the mortgagee becomes the registered shareholder before it advances money to the borrower, it can avoid the potential problems of pre-emption rights and of approaching the directors to be registered as a member on a foreclosure, both of which may be problematic in the case of equitable mortgages[81]. Written deeds of mortgage and charge over shares will typically permit the mortgagor to vote the shares and receive any dividends payable thereon, for as long as the mortgagor is not in default[82].

(b) Equitable mortgage of shares

[16.033] An *equitable mortgage of shares* typically arises where the mortgagor executes a blank stock transfer form and accompanies this by the deposit of the share certificate(s) with a mortgagee[83]. It is established that this transaction operates as an equitable mortgage and not a pledge of the share certificate, which is merely evidence of title: a share is a chose in action and cannot be pledged[84]. Where share certificates are deposited with a mortgagee, the onus of proof rests with the mortgagee to show that the deposit was intended to be as security[85]. In the absence of a written mortgage deed, a power of sale will be implied upon reasonable notice being given to the defaulting mortgagor[86].

---

79 See para **[16.036]**.

80 *Tutt v Mercer* (1725) 2 Bro PC 563; *Langton v Waite* (1868) LR 6 Eq 165; and *Ellis & Co's Trustees v Dixon–Johnson* [1925] AC 489.

81 See Johnston, 'Bank Finance – Searching for Suitable Security' (1994) CLP 3 at 5–6.

82 See further, Johnston, *Banking and Security Law in Ireland* (1998), pp 554–555.

83 No particular form of document is needed to create an equitable mortgage over shares. As Chernov J said in the Supreme Court of Victoria decision in *Whiting Inc v Prudential Bache Securities Australia Ltd and another* [1998] VSC 86 (18 September 1998), para 31 of the judgment: 'To create an equitable mortgage, no particular form of words is necessary. An equitable mortgage of legal property is based upon a contract between the parties. If that contract or agreement is supported by valuable consideration, equity treats it as an agreement to create a legal mortgage, and where consideration has been given…specific performance is available and the equitable maxim whereby equity regards as done that which ought to be done operates, thereby creating immediately a security in the property in question.'

84 In *Harold v Plenty* [1901] 2 Ch 314 at 316, Cozens–Hardy J said the deposit of a share certificate was properly construed as an *equitable mortgage* and not a pledge, saying that: 'I do not think that this is properly a case of pledge. A share is a chose in action. The certificate is merely evidence of title...I think I cannot treat the plaintiff as a mere pledgee. The deposit of the certificate by way of security for the debt....seems to me to amount to an equitable mortgage, or, to an agreement to execute a transfer of the shares by way of mortgage.' See also *Stubbs v Slater* [1910] 1 Ch 623 and *London and Midland Bank v Mitchell* [1899] 2 Ch 161. It may, however, be that a pledge exists in respect of the share certificate itself, as a document of title.

85 See *Re Alton Corporation* [1985] BCLC 27 at 31, 32 where Megarry VC stressed the need to find an agreement to create a mortgage in the context of the deposit of a land certificate.

[16.034] Where a blank stock transfer form is taken the mortgagee should also obtain a power of attorney[87] to enable it to complete the blank transfer. In *Powell v London and Provincial Bank*[88] Lindley LJ held that in the absence of a power of attorney a bank, with which a stock certificate and blank transfer had been deposited, was not entitled to complete the blank forms. In *Powell* the trustee of a trust had made the deposit and although the bank had no notice of the trust, the beneficiaries of the trust were held to have priority[89]. The power of attorney should be expressed to be irrevocable and where given to secure a proprietary interest of the donee of the power of the performance of an obligation owed to the donee, will attract the benefit of the Powers of Attorney Act 1996, s 20(1). A power within the meaning of that section cannot be revoked, for as long as the interest or obligation remains undischarged, by: the donor without the donee's consent or the death, incapacity, bankruptcy, winding up or dissolution of the donor.

[16.035] One difficulty with an equitable mortgage of shares is that should the mortgagee seek to enforce its security, it may be thwarted by the directors refusing registration or by pre-emption rights in the articles or a shareholders' agreement of which the mortgagee has notice[90]. For this reason, a mortgagee may insist upon the articles being amended to ensure its registration can be effected without the directors having the right of veto, to facilitate the enforcement of its security.

(c) Protection for mortgagees – stop notices[91]

[16.036] An equitable mortgagee of shares can bolster his position by serving a *stop notice* on the company. This is facilitated by the Rules of the Superior Courts 1986, Ord 46, rr 5–13[92] which enable a person claiming an interest in shares in a company to serve notice on the company itself, restraining the transfer of stock or shares and/ or the payment of dividends. This is done by the notice and a grounding affidavit being filed in the Central Office of the High Court and serving a duplicate of the filed notice and an

---

86 On reasonable notice, see *Deverges v Sandeman, Clark & Co* [1902] 1 Ch 579 and *Stubbs v Slater* [1910] 1 Ch 632.

87 A letter of authority will suffice where a pre-printed stock transfer form is permitted under the Stock Transfer Act 1963 and a power of attorney is only strictly necessary where the transfer must be by deed under seal. For reasons given above, a power of attorney is most certainly to be preferred. On the alteration of deeds without authority, see the *Rule in Pigot's Case* (*Winchcombe v Pigot* (1614) 2 Bulst 246) as recently applied by the High Court of Northern Ireland in *Northern Bank Ltd v Laverty* [2001] NI 315.

88 *Powell v London and Provincial Bank* [1893] 2 Ch 555.

89 See also *Ireland v Hart* [1902] 1 Ch 522.

90 Equitable mortgagees are well advised to insist upon the articles of the company being amended to provide that the directors are obliged to register a transfer of shares in their favour: see Lingard, *Bank Security Documents* (3rd edn, 1993), para 15.24 for a form of article. It must be remembered, though, that a company cannot contract that it will not alter its articles: see Chapter 3, *Private Constitutional Documentation*, para **[3.127]**, although it may be possible to injunct its shareholders where they act contrary to a contract not to cause the articles to be altered. Regard should also be had to pre–emption clauses, be they contained in the articles or in shareholders' agreements.

91 See generally, Johnston, *Banking and Security Law in Ireland* (1998), pp 555–559.

92 SI 1986/15.

attested copy affidavit on the company at its registered office. The effect of this is that after service of the notice it is unlawful[93] for the company to permit the specified shares to be transferred or to pay dividends on the shares. The company is obliged to notify the person named in the notice upon receiving a request to transfer the shares and to wait eight days before registering the transfer. Even where a stop notice lapses, it is possible that the equitable mortgagee's interests may continue to be protected by reason of the fact that the company has notice of its interest and a company's right to exercise a lien is suspended[94]. All of this is notwithstanding CA 1963, s 123, which prohibits companies from entering notice of any trust, express, implied or constructive, on the register. Where an equitable mortgagee of shares gives a stop notice, it has been held that such constitutes the taking of the necessary steps to perfect its title by putting the company on notice of its interest in the shares[95].

[D] Directors' Powers to Refuse Registration

[16.037] The directors' power to refuse registration of a share transfer is clearly a restriction directed at the *registration* of the transfer and not at the *transfer* of the share itself. The directors' power to refuse registration can take many forms. On the one hand there is model reg 3 of Table A, Part II, considered below[96]. This is a completely unfettered power with little by way of guidance as to how it should be exercised by the directors. Alternative restrictions empower the directors to refuse to register shares unless they are being transferred to existing members; or transferred or transmitted to family members of the transferring, bankrupt or deceased member; or to existing employees of the company. Such restrictions focus on the *status* of the transferee. Other restrictions focus on the *qualities* of the transferee, such as financial strength and other personal attributes. In all cases the powers of the directors to refuse registration must be exercised bona fide *and for the benefit of the company as a whole*. In addition, the powers of the directors will lapse unless exercised, whether for or against registration, within a *reasonable* period of time. Where a member-transferor feels that the directors have exercised their powers oppressively it is open to him to institute proceedings under CA 1963, s 205. In this section, the foregoing matters are considered under the following headings:

1. The model regulation 3 restriction.
2. The transferee's status.
3. The transferee's qualities.
4. The bona fides of the directors.
5. The lapsing of the directors' powers.
6. Relief under CA 1963, s 205.
7. The consequences of declining registration.

---

93 RSC Ord 46, r 10.

94 *Rearden v Provincial Bank of Ireland* [1896] 1 IR 532, considered in Chapter 15, *Shares and Membership*, para **[15.025]**.

95 See *Re Morrissey and Morrissey* [1961] IR 442.

96 See para **[16.038]** *ff*.

8. The procedure for challenging a refusal to register.

The model regulation 3 restriction

[16.038] The most common restriction on the transfer of shares in private companies is a provision in the articles which empowers the directors to veto the registration of any transfer. Model reg 3 of Part II of Table A provides:

> 'The directors may, in their absolute discretion, and without assigning any reason therefor, decline to register any transfer of any share, whether or not it is a fully paid share.'

The essence of this restriction on transfer is the power of the directors to decline the registration of a share transfer without giving reasons for their decision. This is the most unfettered of powers. Where registration is refused on the basis of model reg 3, the prospective transferee has few grounds upon which to contest the directors' decision. The only real basis for challenge is to claim that the directors have abused their powers. While the duties of directors are considered in detail in Chapter 10[97], the bona fides of the exercise of directors' powers in the context of declining registration of share transfers is further considered here.

[16.039] The difficulty in setting aside an exercise of the directors' powers is seen in *Re Smith and Fawcett Ltd*[98], where the articles of the company concerned provided that the directors could in their absolute discretion refuse to register any transfer of shares. The company had two shareholders and directors, Smith and Fawcett, who each held 4001 shares. On Fawcett's death, his son, as executor of the Will, applied to be registered as member in respect of his father's 4001 shares. Smith refused, offering to purchase 2000 of the shares and agreeing to register the remaining 2001 shares in Fawcett Jr's name. Fawcett Jr unsuccessfully applied to the court to have all 4001 shares registered in his name and the decision of the court was affirmed by the Court of Appeal. In the course of his judgment Lord Greene MR said of the model reg 3 type power:

> 'There is nothing, in my opinion, in principle or in authority to make it impossible to draft such a wide and comprehensive power to directors to refuse to transfer as to enable them to take into account any matter which they conceive to be in the interests of the company, and thereby to admit or not to admit a particular person and to allow or not to allow a particular transfer for reasons not personal to the transferee but bearing on the general interests of the company as a whole - such matters, for instance, as whether by their passing a particular transfer the transferee would obtain too great a weight in the councils of the company or might even perhaps obtain control...In the present case the article is drafted in the widest possible terms[99], and I decline to write into that clear language any limitation other than a limitation which is implicit by law, that a fiduciary power of this kind must be exercised bona fide in the interests of the company. Subject to that qualification, an article in this form appears to me to give the directors what it says, namely, absolute and uncontrolled discretion.'[100]

---

97 See Chapter 10, *Duties of Directors and Other Officers*.

98 *Re Smith and Fawcett Ltd* [1942] 1 Ch 304.

99 The article in question in Smith and Fawcett Ltd provided simply that: 'The directors may at any time in their absolute and uncontrolled discretion refuse to register any transfer of shares...'

100 [1942] 1 Ch 304 at 308.

Lord Greene MR rejected the argument that the directors' refusal to register a transfer of shares must always be limited to matters personal to the transferee[101]. That the directors were prepared to register 2001 shares, but not 4001, may have indicated that there was no personal objection to Fawcett Jr, but this fact did not affect or determine the directors' discretion to refuse to register whatever number of shares they wished.

[16.040] Another feature of the model reg 3 restriction is that the directors are not obliged to give reasons for declining to register a share transfer. It has been observed that these words 'are in fact surplusage'[102] by reason of the fact that directors, like trustees, are not obliged to assign reasons for their decisions. This general rule was acknowledged by Black J in *Re Hafner*[103]. In that case the directors of a company declined to register the plaintiff as a member of the company and refused to give reasons for their decision, astutely choosing to rely on the blanket power to refuse registration contained in the articles[104]. Black J recognised the general rule that the directors were entitled to remain mute, saying:

> 'It is well settled that under such an article as this the directors may refuse to register a transfer. It is equally well settled that the directors' power in this regard is a fiduciary one and must be exercised in the interest of the company as a whole. They must not exercise it arbitrarily, capriciously, or corruptly. They are not bound to assign their reasons, and the court is not entitled to infer merely from their omission to do so that their reasons were not legitimate.'[105]

Although the general rule[106] is that directors are not obliged to give reasons for declining to register a transfer or transmission of shares, there are exceptions to the rule. In *Re Hafner*, Black J put the matter succinctly:

> 'Hedged round with the privilege of remaining mute and the prima facie presumption of rectitude, the astutely silent director may well consider himself all but invulnerable. No need to speak and no unfavourable inference from reticence – that is the settled rule. Yet, like many another settled rule, I am persuaded that it is not proof against possible exceptions.'[107]

Having considered Chitty J's judgment in *Bell*'s case[108], Black J concluded that 'in order to interfere the court must not only find that the directors had an invalid motive, but it must also find that they had no valid motive that might be itself sufficient'.[109] The rule that the directors are not obliged to assign reasons for their decisions ceases to be good

---

101 This is, of course, unless a company's articles provide that such is to be the case.

102 Ussher, *Company Law in Ireland* (1986), p 191.

103 *Re Hafner* [1947] IR 426.

104 Regulation 6 of the company's articles of association provided: 'The directors may, in their absolute and uncontrolled discretion and without assigning any reason, refuse to register any transfer of shares, and clause 20 of Table "A" shall be modified accordingly.'

105 [1947] IR 426 at 439.

106 See also *Re Dublin North City Milling Co Ltd* [1909] 1 IR 179 at 184 where Meredith MR said that although he disliked mystery, the directors were entitled in law 'to hold their tongues'.

107 [1947] IR 426 at 440.

108 *Re Bell Brothers Ltd* 7 TLR 689.

109 [1947] IR 426 at 441.

where an invalid reason for declining to register the shares is proved to the satisfaction of the court. Black J accepted that the purpose of the directors acting as they did was to compel the plaintiff to sell his shares to them at an undervalue and to prevent him from questioning the directors' voting themselves large emoluments. It was held on this point that the acceptance of the allegation of an improper motive was sufficient to enable the court to draw an inference from the directors' silence[110].

[16.041] The significance of the exceptions to the rule that directors are not obliged to assign reasons for declining to register a transfer are somewhat equivocal. To come within the exception recognised by Black J in *Re Hafner* a transferee who is refused registration must establish an improper motive on the part of the directors which cannot be explained by reference to some valid motive. Where a prima facie case of invalid motive, otherwise inexplicable, is established, it is logical that the court will require some explanation from the directors. Where the directors remain silent and they do not counter the prima facie case, it seems inevitable that the transferee should succeed in establishing that the directors acted in bad faith. However, to establish a prima facie case of improper motive is tantamount to proving that there was an abuse of the directors' powers and accordingly, the exception to the rule that directors may remain mute may be seen as being of little practical value.

[16.042] Directors are not confined to the reasons they give at the time of a refusal: *Village Cay Marine Ltd v Acland (Barclays Bank plc third party)*[111]. In that case, P owned the entire issued share capital in the plaintiff, Village Cay Marine Ltd, which owned certain development land. Pursuant to a joint-venture agreement for the residential development of the land a joint-venture company – Landac Development Ltd ('the JVC') – was incorporated, P holding 49 shares and A holding 51 shares. A made a loan of $150,000 to the JVC, which it passed to the plaintiff in return for an option to require the grant of sub-leases of the proposed residential units to its nominees. P died and his 49 shares passed to his widow. Subsequently, the plaintiff granted underleases to a company nominated by the JVC. The shares in the plaintiff were subsequently acquired by E from P's widow. E also acquired the 49 shares in the JVC, P's administrators executing a transfer. A, the sole director of the JVC, declined to register E as a shareholder, saying in a letter that he did not regard it as beneficial to the company to involve third parties in its ownership at that stage of the development. At trial, further reasons for the refusal were given and it was accepted by the court that A was entitled to refuse to register the transfer on the basis of his knowledge that the plaintiff was over-indebted to banks and because it was owned by a holding company which could result in its beneficial ownership changing without the JVC's knowledge. The British Virgin Islands Court of Appeal reversed this but the trial judge's decision was, on appeal to the Privy Council, restored in this respect. The Privy Council, per Lord Hoffmann, held that there was no rule of law by which directors are confined to the reasons they have given. In so finding the Privy Council distinguished and explained – on the construction of the particular article – the dictum of Lord Cozens-Hardy MR in *Re Bede Steam Shipping Co Ltd*[112] where he had said that 'the directors ought not to be allowed to state their reason

[110] See also *Clark v Workman* [1920] 1 IR 107 at 118.

[111] *Village Cay Marine Ltd v Acland (Barclays Bank plc third party)* [1998] 2 BCLC 327.

in the certificate itself to the transferee and then to say that was not the only reason, but they had other and different reasons'.[113] The Privy Council went on to accept that A's reasons were bona fide and not 'obviously unreasonable', saying:

> '[The JVC] was a vehicle for a joint venture in the nature of partnership and it is not obviously unreasonable that [A] should have concerns about the financial standing of a prospective new partner or the possibility that he might lose any practical form of control over further transfers of the beneficial ownership in the shares.'[114]

The transferee's status

[16.043] The transferee's *status* will often be deemed a relevant, or indeed the determining factor, in the directors' exercise of their discretion to admit or decline the registration of a transfer of shares. In many private companies, *existing members* are accorded a favoured position in that it is sometimes provided that restrictions do not apply to transfers between members.

[16.044] In many Irish private companies, restrictions are expressed not to apply to a member's family. An example of such an exception based on the transferee's status is that model reg 3 of Part II of Table A is sometimes amended to provide that any share may be transferred to a member's, or deceased member's, spouse, child or grandchild[115]. Such exceptions to the directors' general right to decline registration are not as popular as positive *pre-emption* rights in favour of spouses, children and other family members of deceased or existing shareholders.

[16.045] Another possible exception to the directors' general power to refuse registration are transfers of shares to the company's *employees*. Such restrictions are appropriate where the company concerned is run on co-operative, or extended partnership, principles. Again, it is more usual to protect employees through a positive pre-emption right in their favour, rather than a carve-out from the directors' power to refuse registration.

The transferee's qualities

[16.046] Even where existing members are not expressly excluded from the operation of restrictions on transfer, it has been held that the restrictions will not apply to members where the directors' power to refuse registration is referable to the transferee's status as being a 'desirable person'. In *Tangney v The Clarence Hotels Company Ltd*[116] the articles of the company provided, inter alia, that members proposing to transfer shares had to notify the directors of the proposed transferee's name and address and that '...if the directors are of opinion that the proposed transferee is not a desirable person to admit to membership, they may decline to register the transfer of any such share...'.

---

[112] *Re Bede Steam Shipping Co Ltd* [1917] 1 Ch 123.

[113] [1917] 1 Ch 123 at 135.

[114] [1998] 2 BCLC 327 at 339.

[115] For further comment on a variation of this clause, see Ussher, *Company Law in Ireland* (1986), p 193, fn 66.

[116] *Tangney v The Clarence Hotels Company Ltd* [1933] IR 51.

In that case, the plaintiff, Denis Tangney had been a shareholder and member of the company for many years. However, on his purchasing further shares, the directors of the company refused to register those shares in his name on the ground that he was not a 'desirable person' to admit to membership. Johnston J noted that although the directors were entitled to decline registration, their power was not unlimited[117]. Rather, their power turned upon whether a proposed transferee was a *desirable person*. He held that an existing member's application for registration of additional shares could not be declined by the directors.

[16.047] Where the articles provide that the directors may decline registration if 'in their opinion it is contrary to the interests of the company that the proposed transferee should be a member thereof', the directors may only have regard to the transferee's personal qualities. In *Re Bede Steam Shipping Company Ltd*[118] where the articles so provided, it was held by the Court of Appeal that the directors could not decline to register shares on the ground that the person was an existing shareholder who already held a large shareholding or because registration would increase the number of shareholders and so alter the balance of power. Lord Cozens-Hardy held[119] that where a company's articles contain such a provision:

> 'You may look and see personally who the transferee is. There may be personal objections to him: it may be because he is an uncertain person, or it may be that he is acting in the interests of a rival company, or something of that kind. All those things are fairly incidental in the word "personal"; but to seek to say "We will not accept any transfer of a single share from a particular shareholder who holds a large number" is, it seems to me, an abuse of the power which was conferred by the clause in the articles.'[120]

It should be noted that the directors' lack of power to decline registration turned entirely upon the construction of the actual restriction in that company's articles.

The bona fides of the directors

[16.048] Irrespective of the wording of any particular restriction which empowers directors to decline to register shares, directors, as fiduciaries, must exercise their powers bona fide and for the benefit of the company as a whole[121]. Lord Greene MR said in *Re Smith and Fawcett Ltd*[122] that the principles to be applied to the directors' discretion to decline registration of a share transfer were clear:

> 'They must exercise their discretion bona fide in what they consider – not what a court may consider – is in the interests of the company, and not for any collateral purpose.'[123]

---

[117] [1933] IR 51 at 62. Of the power to decline registration in the case of undesirable persons, Johnston J said at 62–63: 'It seems to me that that clause was intended to meet the case of a stranger proposing to come into the family, as it were.'

[118] *Re Bede Steam Shipping Company Ltd* [1917] 1 Ch 123.

[119] Following Mellish LJ in *Ex p Penny* LR 8 Ch 446.

[120] [1917] 1 Ch 123 at 133.

[121] See generally, Ch 10, *Duties of Directors and Other Officers*, para **[10.024]**.

[122] *Re Smith and Fawcett Ltd* [1942] 1 Ch 304.

[123] [1942] 1 Ch 304 at 306.

Although the exercise of the power to refuse to register shares lies within the directors' subjective discretion, it is within the courts' competence to review the result of an exercise of their power where it is established that the directors of a company have acted otherwise than bona fide and for the benefit of the company.

[16.049] In *Popely v Planarrive Ltd*[124] a bitter feud existed between the plaintiff, on the one side, and his wife, children and nephew on the other, arising from his wife's discovery that he had had extra-marital relationships with two women, each of whom had borne him a child. Upon the plaintiff submitting certain shares that he had acquired, for registration, the directors refused to register but did not inform the plaintiff of this fact (this aspect of the decision is considered below[125]). On the question of the directors' bona fides in refusing registration and whether it was in the company's interests, it was contended by the plaintiff's counsel that the decision was taken for personal, not company, reasons and that personal feelings were so strong that the directors could never have acted bona fide in the company's interests and ought to have resigned and allowed new directors to make the decision. Laddie J rejected this, saying:

> 'Particularly in small private companies there are likely to be ebbs and flows of personal relationships between directors and shareholders. Opposing camps may form. Relationships may become strained. But such common occurrences do not mean that the directors are to be disqualified from exercising powers which may have impact on other directors or shareholders…
>
> In such companies the directors will normally have private views as to the suitability of new shareholders. It would be unrealistic and unworkable in many cases to require the directors to disqualify themselves in relation to the issue of registration of shareholdings merely because such views exist. No doubt if it can be shown that those private and personal feelings have been allowed to overcome the directors' views as to what is bona fide in the interests of the company, then a decision taken to refuse registration may be impeached. But if, say, directors believed that registration of a new shareholder's shares would give him control of the company and that would not be in the interests of the company because he was a fraudster and liar, the decision to refuse registration could not be challenged simply because the new shareholder had defrauded all of the current directors. The fact that the directors had a personal dislike of the new shareholder would not alter the fact that their decision was taken bona fide in the interests of the company.'[126]

On reviewing the evidence, Laddie J found that any reasonable board would have been likely to have taken the same decision as the directors had taken.

[16.050] In *Re Hafner*[127] it was established that the directors had acted in bad faith. In that case the directors of the company declined to register the plaintiff as a member of the company. In his claim the plaintiff had asserted that the directors had declined to register him because, were he a member, he would be in a position to query the 'bloated emoluments'[128] paid to the directors. Black J accepted that this was the real reason (or primary purpose) why the directors had declined registration and concluded that:

---

[124] *Popely v Planarrive Ltd* [1997] 1 BCLC 8.

[125] See para **[16.055]**.

[126] [1997] 1 BCLC 8 at 15–16.

[127] *Re Hafner* [1943] IR 426. Also discussed at para **[16.040]**.

[128] [1943] IR 426 at 443.

> '...if, and so far as, the defendants' refusal to register the plaintiff was based upon the discretion given them by Art 6[129] it was not the result of a bona fide or legitimate exercise of their discretion and if it cannot be justified apart from Art 6, it cannot be justified at all.'[130]

That finding was subsequently upheld by the Supreme Court[131].

[16.051] In *Re Dublin North City Milling Company*[132] the transferee was refused registration, even though he was an existing member. The facts of the case were that a Mr Edward Spicer held 25 shares in Dublin North City Milling Company but the directors of the company refused to register him in respect of a further 20 shares which he had acquired. The articles of the company provided that the transferee had to be approved of by the board of directors. One of the directors swore an affidavit stating that although the plaintiff had previously been registered as a member, having considered the matter carefully, the directors thought it detrimental and injurious to the company, its property and business to register a further transfer of shares in the plaintiff's name. Although the plaintiff already held 25 shares, he was managing director of another company, John Spicer & Co Ltd, millers and bakers.

Meredith MR considered that the Court of Appeal decision in *Re Coalport China Company*[133] summed up the 'true guiding principle' upon which the court should act. Meredith MR quoted with approval the judgment of Lindley LJ in that case, where he said[134]:

> '...I have not the slightest doubt that the court has ample power to control the refusal of directors, or the exercise by them of their power to refuse, provided there is some evidence which justifies the court in coming to the conclusion that they have not done their duty; but in the absence of all such evidence, the court has no right to presume – it is contrary to the ordinary principles of justice to do so – that they have done wrong, but it must be presumed that they have done right.'

Although Meredith MR admitted that he 'disliked mystery', he said that he thought it wise to refuse to compel directors to disclose their reasons for accepting or declining to register a transfer. He went on to say:

> '...I am of the opinion that the law allows the directors to hold their tongues. It allows them to say that everything was done honestly and bona fide in the interests of their company; and they have unanimously decided that it is not for the interest or advantage of the Company that their shares should be transferred to Mr Spicer: and according to my view I have no power to make them say more.'[135]

---

129 Regulation 6 of the company's articles of association provided: 'The directors may, in their absolute and uncontrolled discretion and without assigning any reason, refuse to register any transfer of shares, and clause 20 of Table "A" shall be modified accordingly.'

130 [1943] IR 426 at 445.

131 [1943] IR 426 at 471, per Sullivan CJ.

132 [1909] 1 IR 179.

133 *Re Coalport China Company* [1895] 2 Ch 404.

134 [1895] 2 Ch 404 at 409.

135 [1909] IR 179 at 184.

Had the applicant made any clear charge of corruption, conspiracy or dishonesty, such would have been examined by the court. Indeed such might on the authority of Black J in *Re Hafner* justify a departure from the general rule that no implication can be drawn from the directors' silence[136]. The burden of proof in such matters is clearly on the rejected transferee. As Meredith MR said, '[e]ach transferee who demands registration of a transfer must allege and prove some indirect motive on the part of directors in refusing application. The fact that he is already a shareholder does not prove this'.[137]

The lapsing of the directors' powers

[16.052] Directors are obliged to exercise their powers within a reasonable period of time of such powers arising. Where the directors neither effect nor decline registration of a share transfer within a reasonable period, their power to do so will lapse and the transferee will become entitled to be registered automatically. The reason for this can be seen in the fact that shares are prima facie transferable. It has been held that a transferor has a basic right to transfer his shares in a company[138], albeit one which can be ousted where the directors, in accordance with the articles, validly decline the registration of a share transfer. It must be questioned, however, whether this is good law in the context of a private company since the law provides that the transfer of shares must be subject to restrictions. Subject to this, it seems to be accepted that where the directors' powers to refuse registration lapse, the right of a transferee to be registered is resurrected.

[16.053] An example of where the transferee's right to become registered as a member was resurrected in the face of directors' inertia is *Re Hackney Pavilion Ltd*[139]. In that case the executrix of a deceased member sought to be registered as a member of the company. The directors of the company had an absolute right to decline registration under the company's articles. A meeting of the company's board of directors was called, but the two-man board was divided on the issue, there being no provision for a casting vote. Accordingly the resolution was neither approved nor rejected. Astbury J held that the directors had not declined to register the executrix's shares as the directors' power to decline registration must actively be exercised by a vote of the board of directors. In such a case the right of the transferee to be registered is resurrected and this is the status quo which has precedence where the directors' powers are not exercised[140].

---

136 See para **[16.040]** *ff.*

137 [1909] IR 179 at 183.

138 See *Re Discoverers Finance Corporation Ltd, Lindlar's case* [1910] 1 Ch 312 where Buckley LJ held, inter alia, that if the articles of association do not contain any restrictions, shareholders have the right the transfer their shares. See also *Stothers v William Steward (Holdings) Ltd* [1994] 2 BCLC 266.

139 *Re Hackney Pavilion Ltd* [1924] 1 Ch 276.

140 See also *Moodie v W & J Shepherd (Bookbinders) Ltd* [1949] All ER Rep 1044 where the principle was again applied, the court holding that the directors could only exercise their right to decline registration by passing a resolution to that effect: a mere failure to pass a resolution was not a formal exercise of the right to decline registration. In this case the deceased member's executors were held to be entitled to be registered as members since the directors had not exercised their power to decline registration.

[16.054] What will be considered to be a reasonable period of time, will depend upon the circumstances of each case. It is generally accepted, however, that a period of two months from the date on which the transfer is lodged for registration is reasonable[141]. This is because CA 1963, s 84 requires the company to notify a transferee within two months that his application has been refused by the directors, if that be the case. In *Re Swaledale Cleaners Ltd*[142], where the directors had delayed in either effecting or declining registration for four months, it was held that the directors' power to decline to register a transfer had lapsed and that the transferee was entitled to be registered as a member of the company. This rule continues to be applied[143].

[16.055] In *Popely v Planarrive Ltd*[144] a distinction was drawn between a situation where the directors do not exercise their discretion within two months and a situation where the directors do exercise their discretion within two months, but do not inform the transferee. The facts in this case, set out above[145], were that the plaintiff submitted shares for registration in his name. Were he so registered, he would have obtained control of the company as a shareholder with the entitlement to control the board of directors. The articles provided that the directors had an absolute discretion as to registration and also provided that if they refused to register shares they should send the transferee notice to this effect within two months from the date the transfer was lodged with them. Upon the plaintiff lodging the transfer with the directors, they refused to register it but failed to inform him of their decision. Consequent upon this happening, the plaintiff applied to have the share register rectified[146]. Laddie J found that although the directors had not notified the plaintiff of their decision to refuse registration, they had exercised their discretion within the requisite two months. He said:

> 'When a company's articles of association include an article like art 14[147] in this case, the directors' power to refuse to register will be narrowly construed. If they fall outside the time limit implicitly set in the articles then their decision is a nullity. That is all that was being considered in *Re Swaledale Cleaners Ltd*. As all the judgments in that case make clear, at the time the directors took their decision to refuse registration they had no power to take it. However, quite different considerations apply in a case where the decision is taken within the time set by the articles. If that happens then the decision itself is not a nullity. The subsequent failure to notify the shareholder in accordance with the procedure and timetable set by the articles may well expose the directors to civil[148] and criminal[149]

141 See *Re New Cedos Engineering Co Ltd* [1994] 1 BCLC 797.

142 *Re Swaledale Cleaners Ltd* [1968] 1 WLR 1710.

143 So in *Re Inverdeck Ltd* [1998] 2 BCLC 242, where the directors of a company failed to either register or refuse to register a transfer of shares within two months from its being lodged for registration, Carnwath J held that they had lost the power to refuse to register. This was notwithstanding that one of the directors claimed to be part beneficial owner of the shares in transfer, although it was said that registration would not prevent his asserting his beneficial ownership.

144 *Popely v Planarrive Ltd* [1997] 1 BCLC 8.

145 See para **[16.049]**.

146 See para **[16.061]**.

147 Regulation 14 provided: 'The directors may, in their absolute discretion and without assigning any reason therefor, decline to register the transfer of a share, whether or not it is a fully paid share…'.

liabilities, but I do not see how that failure can relate back so as to turn a proper exercise of the directors' powers into a nullity.'[150]

Laddie J went on to say that it might be open to a court to find an estoppel where the delay in notification was so long and where the shareholder took actions on the assumption that he had been registered, but that had not been advanced in the instant case.

Relief under CA 1963, s 205

[16.056] It should be remembered that the rights of a transferor of shares are not entirely dependent upon common law principles. Where the directors have exercised their powers in a manner oppressive to, or in disregard of, a *transferor-member's* interests he may bring a petition under CA 1963, s 205. Although normally only members of a company have standing to petition the court for s 205 relief, an exception exists in the case of deceased members' personal representatives who are given locus standi by s 205(6)[151].

[16.057] Section 205 of CA 1963 is considered in detail in Chapter 19. However, its possible application to situations where the directors of a closely-held private company unreasonably decline to register a share transfer should be remembered. The necessity for restrictions on the transfer of shares in closely-held companies has been discussed above[152]. The converse is that a quasi-partner should be able to dispose of his interest in the business venture. The result must be a balancing of interests. Where the directors cannot or will not strike the appropriate balance, the courts may be asked to do so.

The consequences of declining registration

[16.058] Where a share transfer is executed by the transferor but the directors of the company decline to register the transferee as a member of the company, a binding contract to sell the shares continues to exist[153]. The contract to sell the shares cannot be avoided unless the contract is expressly made conditional upon the transferee's registration.

[16.059] In the case of an unlimited public company, it has been held that there exists no implied term in a contract for the sale of shares that the transferee will be registered as a member of the company: *Casey v Bentley*[154]. In that case the transferee paid the

---

148 Presumably this refers to the breach of the 'section 25 contract'. Where an existing shareholder's application for registration of additional shares is refused, a civil action might be maintained; however, where the applicant–transferee is not a member it is thought that he would not be privy to the section 25 contract, although the existing shareholder who purported to transfer the shares to him would have privity of contract.

149 The failure to send to a transferee, within two months of lodgement of transfer, notice of refusal: CA 1963, s 84(1).

150 [1997] 1 BCLC 8 at 15a–c.

151 See Chapter 19, *Shareholders' Remedies*, para **[19.048]**.

152 See paragraph **[16.021]**.

153 See *Skinner v City of London Marine Insurance Corp* (1885) 14 QBD 882.

154 *Casey v Bentley* [1902] 1 IR 376.

transferor the consideration due under the contract for the sale of the shares in the public company, upon the transferor giving the transferee an executed transfer and the share certificate. The directors of the company were entitled to decline to register a transfer under the company's articles, and this they duly did upon the share transfer being presented for registration. The transferor issued proceedings claiming specific performance of the contract and an order that the transferee should be ordered to procure the shares to be registered in his own, or some other person's, name. Later, the transferor amended the proceedings seeking an indemnity and rescission of the contract. At trial, Madden J held that there was a condition subsequent in the contract that the transferee would be registered and the failure to do this meant that the transferor was entitled to treat the contract as at an end and that the shares should be re-transferred to the transferor on the return of the purchase money.

The Court of Appeal overruled Madden J by a majority, holding that the contract for the sale of shares on the Stock Exchange did not import an undertaking by the transferor that the company would register the share transfer. Lord Ashbourne noted that the reason for the transferor's concern was that she continued to have an exposure since she remained a member of an unlimited company but yet she was paying over the dividend on the 'sold' shares to the unregistered transferee.

The distinction between contracts made on the Stock Exchange from those made off it was crucial to the reasoning of the Court of Appeal[155]. Although this case is authority for the proposition that there is no implied term as to registration in contracts for the sale of shares on the Stock Exchange, that principle does not necessarily extend to the sale of shares in private companies. In the case of a contract for the sale of shares in a private company there is a strong case for implying a term that the contract is conditional upon the transferee's registration as a member of the company. Depending upon the type of private company there may well exist considerable overlap between those who own the shares and those who manage the company. It was established in *Lee & Company (Dublin) Ltd v Egan (Wholesale) Ltd*[156] that a director who sells shares must vote in favour of the transferee's registration as a member.

[16.060] Where registration is refused by the directors and the transferee has paid over the purchase price of the shares, the transferor remains the legal owner of the shares but is a trustee of the shares for the transferee who is the equitable owner[157]. By this rule of law, where consideration has passed the registered transferor must account to the unregistered transferee for dividends paid and must vote to the order of the unregistered transferee[158].

---

155 [1902] 1 IR 376 at 386–387, where Lord Ashbourne cited *Fry on Specific Performance*.

156 *Lee & Company (Dublin) Ltd v Egan (Wholesale) Ltd* (27 April 1978, unreported), High Court, per Kenny J at p 10.

157 *Stevenson v Wilson* (1907) SC 445 and *Hawks v McArthur* [1951] 1 All ER 22.

158 See *Musselwhite v CH Musselwhite & Son Ltd* [1962] Ch 964, considered at para **[16.067]**.

The procedure for challenging a refusal to register[159]

[16.061] Procedurally, where a transferee is declined registration, he will commonly seek rectification of the company's register of members under CA 1963, s 122. Section 122(1) provides:

> 'If—
>
> (a) the name of any person is, without sufficient cause, entered in the register of members or omitted therefrom, in contravention of subsections (1) and (2) of section 116; or
>
> (b) default is made in entering on the register within the period fixed by subsection (3) of section 116 the fact of any person having ceased to be a member;
>
> the person aggrieved, or any member of the company, or the company, may apply to the court for rectification of the register.'

On application being made, the court may either refuse or order rectification[160] of the register, and it may also order the payment by the company of compensation for any loss suffered by any party aggrieved[161]. On an application under s 122 the court may decide any question of title. The section 122 procedure is without prejudice to a company's own right to rectify its own register[162]. In bringing an application for rectification it is imperative that the company, whose register it is sought to have rectified, be joined as a party[163]. It has been observed[164] that these utilitarian provisions fill a gap in shareholder protection legislation, since the English Companies Act 1985 (UK) cannot be invoked by prospective or former members wishing to assert membership rights. With the exception of personal representatives[165], the same can be said of CA 1963, s 205.

[16.062] Rectification can be ordered under CA 1963, s 122(1)(a) only where a member's name is entered or omitted '*without sufficient cause*'. Where application is made for rectification based on the directors' refusal to register by reason of, for example, the failure to respect pre-emption rights or because the directors have absolute discretion to refuse registration, either of these grounds may give rise to 'sufficient

159 See also generally, Chapter 15, *Shares and Membership*, para **[15.022]**.

160 Where rectification is ordered CA 1963, s 122(4) provides: 'In the case of a company required by this Act to send a list of its members to the registrar of companies, the court when making an order for rectification of the register shall by its order direct notice of the rectification to be given to the registrar.'

161 CA 1963, s 122(2).

162 CA 1963, s 122(5) provides: 'A company may, without application to the court, at any time rectify any error or omission (whether occurring before, on or after the operative date) in the register but such a rectification shall not adversely affect any person unless he agrees to the rectification made. The company shall, within 21 days, give notice of the rectification to the registrar of companies if the error or omission also occurs in any document forwarded by the company to him.'

163 See *Autodata v Gibbons* [2000] 13 July 2000, unreported), Supreme Court, New South Wales.

164 Milman, 'Rectifying Share Registers' (1998) *Palmer's In Company*, Issue 10/98 20 November 1998.

165 See Chapter 19, *Shareholders' Remedies*, para **[19.048]**.

cause' for the refusal. The interaction between the UK's provisions similar to CA 1963, s 122(1) and s 122(3) has been the subject of recent consideration by the English courts. Section 122(3) of CA 1963 provides:

> 'On an application under this section the court may decide any question relating to the title of any person who is a party to the application to have his name entered in or omitted from the register, whether the question arises between members or alleged members, or between members or alleged members on the one hand and the company on the other hand, and generally may decide any question necessary or expedient to be decided for rectification of the register.'

In *Keene v Martin*[166] the English Court of Appeal held that the fact that a proper share transfer does not exist, does not automatically preclude the court from proceeding under s 122(1), as s 122(3) empowers the court to decide questions of title. At trial, (reported as *Re Hoicrest Ltd*[167]) Judge Rich QC had held that no ground for registration existed until the applicant could show legal title, which the company had failed to register. He had also held that the English equivalent to s 122(3) did not enlarge the jurisdiction conferred by s 122(1)[168]. This was rejected by the Court of Appeal, which found that an over-concentration on the equivalent to s 122(1) does not give full effect to the wide powers of the court under sub-s (3) and that it was circular to contend that sub-s (3) was subject to the prior limitations in sub-s (1). Mummery LJ said:

> 'The answer is to be found, in my view, in an appreciation of the distinction between jurisdiction and discretion. Jurisdiction to rectify is conferred by subsection (1). A general discretionary power is conferred on the court by subsection (3) so that a court, to which an application to rectify is made may, on such application, "... decide any question relating to the title of a person who is a party to the application to have his name entered in or omitted from the register...and generally may decide any question necessary or expedient to be decided for rectification of the register."
>
> There is such a question here: the title of Mr Keene to the 49 shares which he claims should be registered in his name. It is true that...Mr Keene must establish that he has title to be entered in the register as a member in respect of the 49 shares. But, if there is a dispute about that title, subsection (3) empowers the court 'on such an application' to decide that question. It is true that the court would not make an order which required the company or its board to act in contravention of s 183 [of the Companies Act 1985 (UK); CA 1963, s 81(1)] or the articles. But that inhibition on making an order does not prevent

[166] *Keene v Martin* [2000] BCC 904, [2000] TLR 777.

[167] *Re Hoicrest Ltd* [1998] 2 BCLC 175.

[168] Judge Rich QC said: 'Subsection (3) of the section seems to be to be very clear. The first half makes clear that the court may decide any question relating to the title of a party "to have his name entered or omitted". [It is suggested] that this latter phrase is concerned only with title, that is ownership, legal or equitable, of the shares. In my view the words "to have his name entered" cannot be disregarded. That is the title which Cotton LJ found in *Wernher*'s case. These words do not enlarge the jurisdiction to rectify when the company itself would be powerless to alter the register.' In *Re Kimberley North Block Diamond Co, ex p Wernher* (1888) 59 LT 579 Cotton LJ said 'Section 35 of the Companies Act 1862 imposes no limit on the jurisdiction thereby conferred on the court, though there may be cases in which it is not desirable that it should be executed'. It may be noted, though, that there the applicant had had a transfer executed in his favour.

> the court from resolving, prior to deciding whether or not to make an order for rectification, relevant disputes about the entitlement to the shares.'[169]

The Court of Appeal did, however, go on to caution against the exercise of the discretion to determine title disputes in what are, essentially, summary proceedings and indicated that proceedings for a declaration might often be more appropriate. In that case directions were made for the trial on the preliminary issue of whether the parties had agreed that 49 of the shares in the company would be held by the defendant on trust for the plaintiff, pending repayment of a loan by the defendant to the company.

[E] Pre-Emption Rights on Share Transfer

[16.063] In addition to the directors' rights to decline registration of share transfers, the articles of private companies commonly include pre-emption rights or rights of first refusal[170]. Because pre-emption clauses are creatures of the draughtsmen, any definition can only be general. However, it can be said that a pre-emption clause confers rights, usually in favour of existing members or the directors[171] of the company, which entitle them, usually on a pro-rata basis, to a right of first refusal to buy the shares which are for sale before they can be offered to an outsider. The primary purpose of a pre-emption provision is to control the admission of members to a private company and to obstruct the unregulated admission of outsiders to the circle of members. Pre-emption rights on the transfer of shares should be distinguished from pre-emption rights on allotment of shares, considered in Chapter 15[172].

[16.064] The following is a form of pre-emption clause which might be found in a private company's articles or a shareholders' agreement[173]:

> '(a) The legal, equitable, beneficial or other interest in a share (hereinafter called "a Share" or "Shares") shall not be transferred unless the following provisions are complied with.
>
> (b) Any member or any other person entitled to a Share by reason of the death or bankruptcy of any member or by operation of law who wishes to transfer a Share (hereinafter called "the Proposing Transferor") shall give notice in writing to the company (hereinafter called "a Transfer Notice"). Every such Transfer Notice shall constitute the directors as the Proposing Transferor's agents for the sale of the Shares specified in the Transfer Notice at a price to be agreed upon by the Proposing Transferor and the directors or in the absence of such agreement, at the price which the company's auditors shall certify to be, in their opinion, the fair value thereof, but without discounting or giving a premium to the value because the Shares constitute a minority or majority interest in the company[174], if that is the case ("the Share Price").

---

169 [2000] BCC 904 at 908B–E.

170 Where a shareholders' agreement exists, pre–emption rights are very commonly included and form an integral part of such agreements.

171 See *Dean v Prince* [1954] 1 Ch 409, considered at para **[16.117]**.

172 See Chapter 15, *Shares and Membership*, para **[15.055]**.

173 This clause is intended merely as an example of its genre and may not be suitable for use in some companies. It is not intended for use as a precedent.

174 This may be considered appropriate in a quasi–partnership private company but perhaps inappropriate to other forms of private company: see generally para **[16.113]** *ff*.

(c) A Transfer Notice served or deemed[175] to be served by a Proposing Transferor shall be irrevocable, save with the consent of the directors who may impose such conditions as they think fit in their absolute discretion.

(d) The certificate of the company's auditors as to the Share Price shall be final and binding upon all parties.

(e) When the Share Price has been determined in accordance with the provisions of clause (b) hereof, the directors shall within 7 days by notice in writing, offer to the existing members of the company the Shares specified in the Transfer Notice at the Share Price pro rata to their existing shareholdings in the company. Such offer shall be open to the existing members for a period of 28 days from the date of the offer (hereinafter called "the Acceptance Period"). If within the Acceptance Period the existing members apply for all or any of the Shares specified in the Transfer Notice the directors shall allocate the Shares, or such of them as are applied for, to the existing members in proportion or pro rata to their existing shareholdings in the company, as nearly as may be.

(f) If the existing members accept the offer within the Acceptance Period, the directors shall forthwith send a written notice to the Proposing Transferor (hereinafter called "the Acceptance Notice") of the acceptance and shall specify in the Acceptance Notice the completion date which shall be not more than 28 days from the date of the Acceptance Notice and details of the completion date for the sale of the Shares.

(g) The Proposing Transferor shall be bound to complete the sale of the Shares specified in the Transfer Notice in accordance with the terms of the Acceptance Notice and where the Proposing Transferor refuses or fails for any reason whatsoever to complete the sale of the Shares, the directors shall be deemed and are hereby appointed the Proposing Transferor's attorney with full power to execute, complete and deliver in the name and on behalf of the Proposing Transferor, a transfer of the Shares or such as are applied for to the existing members of the company on receipt of the Share Price. Upon the payment of the Share Price to the directors:

    (i) the transferee shall obtain good title to the Shares and shall be entitled to insist upon being registered as a member of the company; and

    (ii) the company shall pay the Share Price into a separate bank account and shall hold same on trust for the Proposing Transferor.

(h) If the existing members or any or all of them do not within the Acceptance Period accept the offer to purchase the Shares specified in the Transfer Notice, then the Proposing Transferor may on payment of the Share Price transfer all or any of those

---

[175] In *Re Sedgefield Steeplechase Company (1927) Ltd; Scotto v Petch et al* [2000] 2 BCLC 211, [2000] TLR 107 it was held that an agreement for the sale of shares that expressly precluded the purchaser from requiring the vendor to do anything which would contravene the company's pre–emption provisions, did not demonstrate the necessary intention to transfer the legal title so as to trigger the pre–emption rights. Lord Hoffmann also held that a shareholder who had done nothing inconsistent with an intention to comply with the existing provisions, at the appropriate moment, could not be required to serve a transfer notice before he had entered into arrangements which placed him under a contractual obligation to execute and deliver a transfer in violation of the rights of pre-emption.

Shares which are not applied for by the existing members to a person who is not a member of the company (hereinafter called "a Non-Member") PROVIDED THAT

(i) the directors shall be satisfied that the Non-Member is a person whom it is desirable to admit to membership of the company and unless they are so satisfied, shall not register the Non-Member as a member of the company,

(ii) the directors shall be satisfied that the Proposing Transferor does not transfer the Shares at a price less than the Share Price and that the transfer is a bona fide sale for the consideration stated in the transfer.

(i) The restrictions on the transfer of Shares contained in this article shall not apply to any transfer approved in writing by all the members.

(j) For the purposes of this article the following shall be deemed to give rise to and are deemed to be the service of a Transfer Notice:

(i) any direction by a member renouncing his right to an allotment of shares,

(ii) any sale or other disposition of any equitable or beneficial interest in a share whether for consideration or otherwise and whether or not effected by an instrument in writing,

(iii) the death or bankruptcy of any member,

(iv) in the case of a member which is a body corporate, 7 days before its going into liquidation, except a members' voluntary winding up for the purpose of a reconstruction or amalgamation, or, 7 days before the appointment of a receiver to the corporate member, or 7 days before an Examiner is appointed to the Company.

(k) Subject to compliance with the foregoing sub-clauses, the directors shall register any transfer made in pursuance of these provisions but shall refuse to register any other transfer.

[16.065] The foregoing clause is given to exemplify the sort of matters with which pre-emption clauses are concerned. The basic philosophy behind the clause is that a member who wants to sell his shares in the company must first offer them to the existing members in proportion to their existing shareholding. The pre-emption clause set out above contains a number of features common to many such clauses. First, there is a prohibition on the transfer of a share or any interest in a share, save in accordance with the provisions of the clause. Secondly, concepts central to the operation of the pre-emption procedure are defined, eg 'Transfer Notice', 'Proposing Transferor', etc. Thirdly, the person desiring to transfer his shares must serve notice of his wish to sell his shares on the directors of the company who are thereby constituted his agent for the sale of the shares. Fourthly, the price to be paid for the shares is the price agreed by the transferor and the directors, or in default of agreement, by the company's auditors whose determination of the shares' value is binding on all parties. Fifthly, the existing members of the company are offered the shares for sale in proportion to their existing shareholdings. Sixthly, strict time limits apply to the procedure. Seventhly, if the existing members do not take up the shares on sale, the transferor may sell them to a non-member, subject to the directors' powers to veto such in particular situations. Eighthly, certain circumstances will give rise to the deemed service of a transfer notice. Finally, provision is made for compulsory transfers of shares in particular specified circumstances.

[16.066] Pre-emption rights are a very important control on the transfer of shares in Irish private companies. Such clauses have been the subject of judicial scrutiny in a number of cases[176]. Pre-emption clauses are considered here as follows:

1. The need for pre-emption rights in private companies.
2. The judicial construction of pre-emption clauses.
3. Application to beneficial interests in shares.
4. The enforceability of pre-emption rights.

The need for pre-emption rights in private companies

[16.067] It is primarily because of the inadequacies of model reg 3 of Part II of Table A type restrictions on the registration of share transfers that some private companies favour the adoption of pre-emption rights. Although the directors can generally veto the registration of a share transfer, model reg 3 does not prohibit a member from transferring the equitable interest in his shares, whether outright[177] or by way of mortgage[178]. Although the equitable transferee or mortgagee may not be the registered owner of the shares in the company, it is well established that where consideration has passed, the legal owner holds the shares in trust. In this way *control* of a company can pass without the directors' consent.

The decision in *Musselwhite v CH Musselwhite & Son Ltd*[179] demonstrates the weakness of the model reg 3 type restriction on the transfer of shares. In *Musselwhite* the company had four shareholders: the plaintiff-husband and wife held 3599 shares and 1 share respectively and the defendant-husband and wife held 3599 shares and 1 share respectively. The plaintiff-husband was managing director and the other three shareholders were directors of the company. The plaintiff-husband and wife agreed to sell their shares in the company and in another company to the defendant for £10,000, to be paid partly by way of instalments. It was also agreed that the transfers of the shares should be executed and together with the share certificates, deposited with the company's solicitors until payment in full had been made to the plaintiffs. This was done but a dispute arose when the defendants erroneously believed that the plaintiffs were not entitled to receive notice of general meetings of the company, when in fact they remained on the register of members. When a general meeting was called without the plaintiffs being given notice, the plaintiffs applied inter alia for a declaration that the meeting was invalid.

Russell J rejected the defendants' contention that the plaintiffs were not entitled to notice of general meetings of the company. For as long as the plaintiffs were unpaid vendors in respect of their shares, they remained members of the company and were entitled to receive notice of meetings of the company. In this regard Russell J held that an unpaid vendor was in no weaker a position than a mortgagee:

176 See Hannigan, 'Share Transfer Problems in the Private Company' (1990) 11 Co Law 170, for an overview of some recent decisions of the Courts of England and Wales.

177 *Musselwhite v CH Musselwhite & Son Ltd* [1962] Ch 964.

178 *Wise v Landsell* [1921] 1 Ch 420.

179 *Musselwhite v CH Musselwhite & Son Ltd* [1962] Ch 964.

> 'The purchaser acquires the beneficial interest subject to the vendor's lien; the mortgagor retains the beneficial interest subject to the charge in favour of the mortgagee, in the form of an equity of redemption. In the one case the mortgagee is deliberately put on the register to safeguard his money lent: in the other case the vendor is deliberately left on the register until all is paid to safeguard his purchase-money due.
>
> In my judgment an unpaid vendor of shares remaining on the register after the contract for sale retains *vis-à-vis* the purchaser the prima facie right to vote in respect of those shares.'[180]

Conversely, where consideration has passed but the transferee has not been registered, the transferor will hold the shares in trust for the transferee and will be compelled to account for dividends paid in respect of the shares and to vote to the order of the transferee[181]. It is in this way that the reins of control in a company may change hands notwithstanding the directors' powers to refuse registration.

[16.068] The decision in *Musselwhite* was distinguished by the High Court in *O'Gorman v Kelleher*[182]. In this case, the plaintiffs and defendants were all directors of a company. The defendants were together entitled to 56.25% of the shares. The defendants had previously offered to buy the plaintiffs' shares and this offer was accepted but subsequently withdrawn when financial arrangements did not come through. The plaintiffs then offered to buy the first defendant's shareholding and the plaintiffs claimed that he agreed to sell his shareholding for £5.2 million. The first defendant disputed this. Subsequently, the defendants gave notice of their intention to remove certain persons as directors of the company and the proposed meeting was injuncted by interim order. On the interlocutory application the plaintiffs sought, inter alia, an injunction restraining the respondents from exercising rights in respect of the 160,000 ordinary shares that were alleged to be the subject of the agreement. Carroll J noted that if there was (as alleged) an enforceable agreement the effect would be to shift the balance of the voting power from the defendants to the plaintiffs. Citing *Musselwhite*, the defendants argued that even if the plaintiff was to succeed in the specific performance of the alleged contract for the sale of the shares, it was not open to the court to restrict the right of a registered owner to vote whichever way he wanted. Carroll J noted that there it was held that the 'unpaid vendors were entitled to exercise their voting rights in respect of the shares (it not being alleged that the rights would be exercised so as to damage the subject matter of the purchase)'. The learned judge distinguished the facts there from those in hand, saying:

> 'Here it is clear that the voting rights attached to the shares, the subject matter of the alleged contract, are being used to oust Michael O'Gorman, one of the purchasers, which is damaging to the plaintiffs' interests. If an unpaid vendor of shares were to vote deliberately so as to damage the purchaser, or contrary to the interests of the purchaser, who is the beneficial owner, it seems to me that he should be restrained by the court of Equity.'[183]

---

180 [1962] Ch 964 at 987.

181 *Ward and Henry's case* (1867) 2 Ch App 431; *Stevenson v Wilson* (1907) SC 445; and *Hawks v McArthur* [1951] 1 All ER 22.

182 *O'Gorman v Kelleher* (19 July 1999, unreported), High Court (Carroll J).

It is thought to be sound law for the courts of equity to restrain a *paid* vendor of shares from exercising the voting rights attaching thereto to the detriment of the purchaser. Whether a purchaser who has not parted with any consideration ought to be afforded protection is a more difficult matter. Some support can be found for saying that the voting rights of a vendor under an uncompleted contract are in abeyance, at least for certain purposes. In *Michaels v Harley House (Marylebone) Ltd*[184] Robert Walker LJ considered shareholders' rights to vote for the purposes of the definition of parent and subsidiary company. There, he said:

> 'A registered shareholder who is absolute beneficial owner can vote as he pleases, subject only to rather imprecise constraints imposed by company law (see *Smith v Croft (No 2)* [1987] 3 All ER 909 at 957-958. A registered shareholder who is a nominee must vote in accordance with the directions of the absolute beneficial owner, to whom his voting rights are attributed. A registered shareholder who is vendor under an uncompleted contract is in an intermediate position, a fiduciary but not a nominee, and his voting rights are for the purposes of s 736 [of the Companies Act 1985 (UK), which defines parent and subsidiary company] in abeyance.'

It would seem that the Irish (and perhaps the English) courts are prepared to protect a purchaser who has not parted with the consideration for the shares on the basis that the vendor is in a fiduciary relationship to the purchaser and the purchaser has an equity as a result of the unconcluded contract.

The judicial construction of pre-emption clauses

[16.069] Clauses which confer pre-emption rights on members can fall to be construed by the courts, directly or indirectly, in a number of situations. Pre-emption rights may result in a direct judicial hearing where application is made under RSC 1986, Ord 83, which facilitates application to be made to court for the determination of any question of construction arising under a written instrument. Pre-emption rights may fall to be indirectly construed by the courts in a variety of situations: in a minority shareholders' remedy action under CA 1963, s 205 and where decisions of the company are called into question by its members on the basis that the articles or a shareholders' agreement have been breached[185].

[16.070] In *McAuliffe v Lithographic Group Ltd*[186] the Supreme Court considered a member's right to purchase shares which was conferred by a pre-emption clause in a shareholders' agreement. In the High Court Costello J had construed a clause in a shareholders' agreement as requiring the plaintiff and his wife to purchase the shares held by the defendant in a company called Mac Publishing Ltd. The appeal to the Supreme Court arose from this decision. The facts of the case were that the McAuliffes and the defendant had entered into a shareholders' agreement whereby the McAuliffes

---

[183] (19 July 1999, unreported), High Court at p 4.

[184] *Michaels v Harley House (Marylebone) Ltd* [1999] 1 All ER 356. See further Ch 17, *Groups of Companies*, para **[17.022]** *ff*.

[185] See generally, Chapter 19, *Shareholders' Remedies*.

[186] *McAuliffe v Lithographic Group Ltd* (2 November 1993, unreported), Supreme Court, ex tempore recorded judgment per O'Flaherty J.

purchased 40% and the defendant purchased 60% of the shares in the company. O'Flaherty J said it was clear that each party was given a right of pre-emption, entitling them to purchase the other party's shares. The problem which required resolution in the case was whether the obligation to purchase the shares was a mutual obligation or a unilateral obligation?

When, pursuant to the clause, the defendant company served a purchase notice on the McAuliffes, the McAuliffes did not accept the offer but served their own purchase notice on the defendants. Were the obligation to purchase the shares mutual, the first in time would have prevailed. Costello J had held that the obligation was mutual and that the McAuliffes were obliged to purchase the defendant's shares. O'Flaherty J accepted that the clause in hand 'was quite a confused provision'.[187] However he acknowledged that the court must come to grips with the clause as best it may. He held that the clause imposed an obligation on the defendants to purchase the McAuliffes' shares and that the only binding purchase notice was the one served by the McAuliffes. Accordingly, the decision of the High Court was reversed. The importance of this case is that the wording of the pre-emption clause in hand was decisive; a cautionary note for the legal draughtsman.

[16.071] There is a tendency for the courts to construe pre-emption clauses strictly[188]. Shares are prima facie transferable and where the right to transfer is curtailed, the courts will strictly construe all restrictions. This is exemplified by the English Court of Appeal decision in *Safeguard Industrial Investments Ltd v National Westminster Bank Ltd*[189]. The plaintiff investment company and a deceased member of the company together held one-sixth of the issued shares in the subject company, M Wright & Sons Ltd. The remainder of the shares were held by the deceased member's two cousins and one of the cousin's two children, Y and Z. By his will the deceased member appointed the defendant bank as executor and named Y and Z as beneficiaries. The company's articles contained pre-emption rights in favour of the existing members where shares were transferred. No restriction was stated to apply to the transmission of shares[190]. The beneficiaries, Y and Z directed the executor-bank not to transfer the shares to them, preferring to rely on the bank's acknowledgement that it held the shares on trust for Y and Z. At trial the plaintiff unsuccessfully argued that the bank was bound to serve a transfer notice after it had completed the administration of the deceased member's estate and purported to assent to the vesting of the beneficial interest in the shares in Y and Z. The Court of Appeal upheld the trial judge's decision, holding that on a true construction

---

[187] (2 November 1993, unreported), Supreme Court at p 10.

[188] In *The Ocean Coal Company Ltd v The Powell Duffryn Steam Coal Company Ltd* [1932] 1 Ch 654 a pre-emption clause obliged any member desiring to sell his shares to notify the directors of the number of shares, the price and the proposed transferee and provided that the directors must offer such shares at that price to the existing members. It was further provided that if the shares or any of them were not so accepted, the proposing transferor could sell to the transferee of his choice. It was held by Farwell J that a subsequent offer to buy less than 4% of the shares at even the stated price was not sufficient and that the proposing transferor was entitled to sell all of the shares to the proposed transferee of his choice.

[189] *Safeguard Industrial Investments Ltd v National Westminster Bank Ltd* [1982] 1 All ER 449.

[190] [1982] 1 All ER 449 at 451, per Oliver LJ.

of the articles the bank was not obliged to serve a transfer notice and that until such was served the pre-emption machinery could not be triggered. Furthermore it was held that the term transfer only embraced the legal title to shares and not the equitable title[191]. It is because of decisions such as this that most properly-drafted pre-emption clauses are expressed to apply to the transmission of shares and, as shall be considered next, restrictions on the transfer of shares are deemed to apply to the disposal of an equitable interest in addition to a legal interest.

[16.072] Where a pre-emption clause contains a time limit within which action must be taken, this will be construed strictly by the courts. An example of this is *Re New Cedos Engineering Co Ltd*[192] where Oliver J held that a deceased member's personal representatives were only bound to transfer the shares where, within three months of receiving notice of the member's death, the company found a member willing to purchase the shares at fair value.

Application to beneficial interests in shares

[16.073] As has been seen, it was held by the Court of Appeal in *Safeguard Industrial Investments Ltd v National Westminster Bank Ltd*[193] that the pre-emption clause in question applied only to transfers of the legal interest in a share, and did not extend to the equitable interest in shares. As Harmon LJ said in *Re Swaledale Cleaners Ltd*[194], in a passage noted by Roderick Murphy J in *Phelan v Goodman*[195]:

> 'If the right of transfer, which is inherent in property of this kind, is to be taken away or cut down, it seems to me that it should be done by language of sufficient clarity to make it apparent that this was the intention.'

The case law on this point is somewhat ambiguous[196]. It was thought in the first edition of this book[197] that the dominant view was that that a simple prohibition on the *transfer* of shares will not prevent the disposition of the *equitable or beneficial interest* in shares[198]. Since then, the balance may be said to have tipped in favour of construing a restriction on transfer as preventing the equitable interest being transferred. In *Phelan v Goodman*[199] it was held by the Irish High Court that the disposition of a person's equitable interest in shares was in breach of a prohibition in the articles of association on the 'transfer' of shares without first offering them to the other member. In so finding,

[191] See also *Hunter v Hunter* [1936] AC 222 and *Lyle & Scott Ltd v Scott's Trustees* [1959] 2 All ER 661.

[192] *Re New Cedos Engineering Co Ltd* [1994] 1 BCLC 797.

[193] *Safeguard Industrial Investments Ltd v National Westminster Bank Ltd* [1982] 1 All ER 449.

[194] *Re Swaledale Cleaners Ltd* [1968] 1 WLR 1710. See also *Scotto v Petch*, (20 January 2000), English High Court.

[195] *Phelan v Goodman* (11 September 2001, unreported), High Court.

[196] See *Lyle & Scott Ltd v Scott's Trustees* [1959] 2 All ER 661, and generally, Stedman & Jones, *Shareholders' Agreements* (2nd edn, 1990), pp 23–26.

[197] Courtney, *The Law of Private Companies* (1994), para [10.057].

[198] For a distinction between *equitable* and *beneficial* ownership, see *J Sainsbury plc v O'Connor (Inspector of Taxes)* [1990] STC 516, per Millett J.

[199] *Phelan v Goodman* (11 September 2001, unreported), High Court.

Roderick Murphy J quoted the following passage from Lord Keith in *Lyle and Scott Ltd v Scotts Trustees*[200]:

> 'A share is of no value to anyone without the benefits it confers. A sale of a share is sale of the beneficial rights that it confers, and to sell or purport to sell the beneficial rights without the title to the share is, in my opinion, in plain breach of the provisions of [the relevant article].'

The learned High Court judge also quoted the following passage from Lord Keith, and in so doing, illustrated the attitude he took to the argument that legal and beneficial title could be distinguished for the purposes of pre-emption rights:

> 'A shareholder who has transferred, or pretended to transfer, the beneficial interest in a share to a purchaser for value is merely endeavouring by a subterfuge to escape from the peremptory provisions of the Article.'

In *Phelan v Goodman* the High Court would not countenance a technical argument that sought to distinguish legal from beneficial title. The company in that case had, however, only two shareholders and it remains to be seen whether future cases might not seek to distinguish this decision on the grounds that it ought to be confined to companies with so few members.

[16.074] *Hawks v McArthur*[201] is, however, authority for the proposition that a simple restriction on share transfer will not prevent the equitable interest in the shares passing where full consideration has passed to the transferor. The articles of the company contained rights of pre-emption. Notwithstanding the pre-emption rights in the articles, a retiring director, McArthur, executed two transfers of shares, one in favour of the chairman and one in favour of the manager of the company. The chairman and the manager paid McArthur the full purchase price for the shares, although they had not been registered as owners of the shares. The plaintiff, who was a member of the company, obtained a money judgment against McArthur and converted this into a charging order on his shares. The chairman and the manager of the company who had paid the full price for the shares claimed that notwithstanding that the pre-emption rights had not been complied with, they held the beneficial interest in the shares and that the charging order was ineffective.

Vaisey J reluctantly[202] upheld the manager's and the chairman's contention. The decisive factor was that they had both paid McArthur full consideration. Vaisey J considered that he could not bring himself to suppose that they got nothing from the bargain. Having accepted that the chairman and the manager had rights, the remaining question was that of priorities: McArthur had legal rights; the plaintiff with his charging order had an equity or quasi-equitable rights; and the chairman and the manager had equitable rights. In the clash between the equitable rights Vaisey J held that the first in time prevailed and reluctantly held for the manager and the chairman, whom he felt had acted in almost scandalous disregard of the company's articles[203].

---

[200] *Lyle and Scott Ltd v Scotts Trustees* [1959] AC 763 at 785.

[201] *Hawks v McArthur* [1951] 1 All ER 22.

[202] [1951] 1 All ER 22 at 27g–h.

[16.075] This decision appears to conflict with *Lee & Company (Dublin) Ltd v Egan (Wholesale) Ltd*[204] where Kenny J did not acknowledge that the purchaser had any equitable rights in shares which were contracted to be sold in breach of a company's pre-emption right provisions. The decision in *Lee & Company* may be distinguished on a number of grounds. First, a transfer of shares had not been executed, there being only a contract for the sale of the shares. Secondly, the purchaser had thought he was buying all the shares in the company when in fact the vendor did not own all the shares and so the purchaser may not have been well served had it been declared that he had merely an equitable interest in only some of the company's shares[205]. Finally, the purchaser had not yet paid the vendor for the shares as is required to claim an equitable interest.

[16.076] It has been held that that no rights, whether legal or equitable, can arise in favour of the equitable mortgagee where pre-emption rights are bypassed. Authority for this proposition is *Hunter v Hunter*[206] where Lord Atkin said:

> 'The effect of art 17 in my opinion is to provide the means and the only means by which a member of the company can form an agreement for the sale of shares, which can only be constituted by the act of the secretary as agent for seller and purchaser declaring a contract to be concluded at the price fixed by the auditor. That was not done in that case, and in my opinion no rights arose between the bank and Harry Hunter under any contract of sale either equitable or legal.'[207]

As a general proposition it must be doubted that the distinction between equitable mortgagees and other transferees can be sustained. Perhaps the matter should turn upon whether or not the transferee (or equitable mortgagee) had actual notice of the pre-emption provisions[208]. In view of the ambiguities in the law, when drafting a pre-emption clause extreme caution should be exercised. Although it would seem that a simple prohibition on the transfer of shares is sufficient to prevent an equitable mortgagee from acquiring either legal or beneficial title in shares, such might be ineffective to prevent the passing of the equitable or beneficial interest to a transferee for value. When restricting the transfer of a *share* it may be desirable to define *share* in the articles or in a shareholders' agreement[209] as including the legal and beneficial and equitable interest in the share.

---

203 See also *Theakston v London Trust plc et al* [1984] BCLC 390 where 'transfer' in the pre–emption clause in hand was defined by Harman J (at 397) as referring to actions disposing of the legal ownership of shares and 'not to mere dealings with equitable interests in the shares.'

204 *Lee & Company (Dublin) Ltd v Egan (Wholesale) Ltd* (27 April 1978, unreported), High Court, per Kenny J, considered at para **[16.077]**.

205 To have equitable rights in only some of the shares in a private company is a less than desirable position to be in, especially if the other shareholders are opposed to one's admission.

206 *Hunter v Hunter* [1936] AC 222. See *Re Hafner* [1943] IR 426, per Black J.

207 [1936] AC 222 at 261.

208 *Actual notice* is to be preferred to *constructive notice* in this context: were the pre–emption machinery contained in a company's articles, it is possible that because the articles are public documents, everybody would have constructive notice of their provisions.

209 See para **[16.064]**.

The enforceability of pre-emption rights

[16.077] Where the articles or a shareholders' agreement contain pre-emption rights, the courts of Ireland and the UK have shown that they will vigorously defend the rights of a company's members to first refusal to purchase the shares in the company[210]. One of the clearest examples is the case of *Lee and Company (Dublin) Ltd v Egan (Wholesale) Ltd*[211]. In that case the articles of the defendant-company included a right of pre-emption in favour of the existing members[212]. There were four members: Mr Roe who held 7,100 shares, his wife who held 900 shares, Mr Wallace who held 800 shares and Mr Mulligan who held two shares. Mr Roe was anxious to retire from the business and entered into negotiations, through an auctioneer, with a Mr Conroy who was managing director of the plaintiff-company, Lee and Company (Dublin) Ltd. Conroy believed that Roe owned 90% of the shares in the company and that he had authority to sell *all* the issued shares. A purchase price of £205,000 was agreed, the parties thinking in terms of the assets and liabilities of the company although Roe had no authority to sell all the shares in the company. Roe contracted to sell all the shares in the company to Conroy; the contract was not conditional and although the terms were never put in writing, they were set out in a letter to Roe dictated by the auctioneer.

It was not remembered that the articles gave the other members the right to acquire Roe's 7,100 shares in priority to any other person. Problems arose when Roe sought more money for the shares in the company. Conroy refused to pay more and sought an order for specific performance of the contract to sell the shares.

Kenny J held that the proper form of relief was to declare that the contract for the sale of the 7,100 shares owned by Roe ought to be performed. However, Kenny J held that if the plaintiff decided to purchase the shares, Roe, the proposing transferor had to give notice under the company's articles to the company's other members of the fixed price which had been agreed with Conroy. The right of first refusal of the existing members was thus vindicated by the court. Any other member of the company was accordingly entitled to purchase Roe's shares in accordance with the pre-emption machinery. Only if no other member elected to purchase the shares within the specified time period could Roe execute a transfer of shares in favour of Conroy. This decision clearly affords the members of the company, who have rights of first refusal, with equitable rights, or at the very least, equities. In *O'Gorman v Kelleher*[213], where an alleged contract to sell shares was claimed to be in breach of the company's pre-emption provisions, Carroll J declined to find that the pre-emption rights would render the contract inoperable. Following *Lee and Company Dublin Ltd v Egan Wholesale Ltd*, Carroll J found that Kenny J had held that the 'proper form of relief in such a case was to declare that the contract ought to be performed subject to the pre-emption rights of the members of the company'.[214]

---

[210] See *Attorney General for Ireland v Jameson* [1904] 2 IR 644.

[211] *Lee and Company (Dublin) Ltd v Egan (Wholesale) Ltd* (27 April 1978, unreported), High Court, per Kenny J.

[212] For the actual wording of the particular clause, see (27 April 1978, unreported), High Court, pp 2–5.

[213] *O'Gorman v Kelleher* (19 July 1999, unreported), High Court (Carroll J). The facts are given at para **[16.068]**.

[16.078] The willingness of the court to enforce the rights of pre-emption is seen also in Blayney J's judgment in *Re Champion Publications Ltd*[215]. In that case, the articles contained pre-emption rights in favour of existing members and Blayney J ordered that certain transfers be set aside because they were not carried out in accordance with the articles. The form of the pre-emption clause employed by the company was one which is in relatively common use in Ireland, and is favoured by a number of company formation firms. The part of the clause under examination concerned the method in which shares being transferred should be offered to the company's existing members. The clause provided that the members of the company in general meeting could make, and from time to time vary, the procedure to be followed and the rights of the members. It went on to provide that unless otherwise determined, 'every such share shall be offered to the members in such order as shall be determined by lots drawn in regard thereto and the lots shall be drawn in such manner *as the directors think fit*' [Emphasis added]. Blayney J refused to construe this so as to give the directors a free reign and held that it was the sensible course 'to allow the members themselves to decide the appropriate rules which should be formulated and in accordance with which shares contained in a transfer notice should be offered to the members'.

[16.079] In *Tett v Phoenix Property and Investment Co Ltd*[216] the defendant-company's articles contained pre-emption rights in favour of existing members and their families on both the transfer and transmission of shares. When a member died, her executors were instructed to sell her shares by the beneficiary under her Will. Due to a misunderstanding, notice was served on the company's other members advising them that 23 shares were on offer; in fact the deceased member had held 113 shares in the company. When the other members refused what they thought was an offer of 23 shares, the executors believed that the offer to sell *all 113* of the shares had been rejected by the existing members and they agreed to sell the shares to the plaintiff, Tett. The directors of the company refused to register the transfer in favour of the plaintiff on the basis that the pre-emption provisions had not been complied with properly. The directors then took the step of advising the members that a further 90 shares were in fact being offered, and before the trial of the matter at least one member indicated an interest in purchasing the shares. At trial Vinelott J ordered the company to register Tett as a member of the company. This was reversed by the Court of Appeal. The first question to be determined was identified by Slade LJ as being: did the clause on its true construction impose a valid and enforceable condition which has to be satisfied if the executors were to have the right to transfer the 90 shares to a non-member of the company? Slade LJ said that the clause was valid and effective:

> 'This condition was that the executors should have first taken reasonable steps to give all other members and their specified relatives a reasonable opportunity to make an offer to purchase the shares at a fair value to be determined by the auditors in default of agreement and that no such offer should have been made...I am satisfied that the executors before executing the transfer of their shares, did not take reasonable steps to give even *the other*

---

214 (19 July 1999, unreported), High Court at p 5.

215 *Re Champion Publications Ltd* (4 June 1991, unreported), High Court (Blayney J).

216 *Tett v Phoenix Property and Investment Co Ltd* [1986] BCLC 149.

members of the company a reasonable opportunity to make such an offer.'[217] [Emphasis added]

Although there were certain uncertainties with the clause, it was held to contain a sufficiently clear express restriction to cut down the prima facie right to transfer shares[218]. On account of the non-compliance with the required procedure, the directors were entitled to refuse to register the shares in the plaintiff's name.

[F] Compulsory Transfers of Shares

[16.080] Shares may be transferred compulsorily in either of three ways:

- in accordance with the provisions in a company's articles;
- by statute, pursuant to CA 1963, s 205(3); or
- also by statute, pursuant to CA 1963, s 204.

Section 205 of CA 1963 is considered in Chapter 19, *Shareholders' Remedies*. At this point, compulsory transfer under the articles and under CA 1963, s 204 are considered.

Compulsory transfer under the articles

[16.081] Sometimes the articles of private companies will provide that a member is obliged to transfer his shares upon the occurrence of certain events. One of the earlier cases which upheld the validity and enforceability of such a clause was *Borland's Trustee v Steel Brothers & Co Ltd*[219]. Extreme caution should be exercised by the members in altering the articles to provide for the compulsory transfer of a member's shares, lest the alteration be set aside as being mala fide and not in the interests of the company as a whole[220]. Even where the articles provide ab initio for the compulsory transfer of a member's shares, the courts will construe such provisions strictly. Where a member's shares are expropriated in an oppressive manner, he may petition the court under CA 1963, s 205[221].

[16.082] Although there is no compulsory transfer of shares clause in the model articles, some companies' articles provide that the following acts are triggers for requiring the compulsory transfer of shares:

- death;
- bankruptcy;
- conviction of an indictable offence;
- insanity or other mental incapacity;
- the commencement of a winding up or the appointment of a receiver or an examiner, where the member is a body corporate;

---

217 [1986] BCLC 149 at 161.

218 [1986] BCLC 149 at 157 recognised by Slade LJ, referring to *Re Swaledale Cleaners Ltd* [1968] 3 All ER 619 and *Greenhalgh v Mallard* [1943] 2 All ER 234. See also Robert Goff LJ at 163.

219 *Borland's Trustee v Steel Brothers & Co Ltd* [1901] 1 Ch 279.

220 See generally, Chapter 3, *Private Constitutional Documentation*, para **[3.074]** *ff*.

221 See generally, Chapter 19, *Shareholders' Remedies* at para **[19.006]** *ff*.

— the change in the control of a member which is a body corporate;

— the member's ceasing to be a director or an employee of the company;

— the disposal or attempted disposal of the equitable or beneficial ownership in shares in the company.

It is possible to include a compulsory transfer clause in a pre-emption clause[222]. Where this is done, the occurrence of one of the foregoing events will be deemed to constitute the service of a *transfer notice* in respect of that member's shares. Upon the service of that transfer notice, the usual pre-emption rights mechanism will then come into operation.

[16.083] When shares are compulsorily transferred it is prudent to provide that they are valued in a just and equitable manner. Where the auditors are entrusted with the valuation of shares sold pursuant to the pre-emption rights clause, it is often appropriate to apply the same valuation provisions to compulsory transfers. In *Re Castleburn Ltd*[223] the company concerned was a quasi-partnership private company. In addition to having pre-emption rights, there was a compulsory transfer provision. This provided that any member who was a director or employee and who ceased to be such could be compelled by a majority of the other members to sell his shares. When one of the original promoters who was a director and the owner of 44% of the shares was removed as an employee and a director, the compulsory transfer provisions were triggered. The valuation by the company's auditors, which discounted their value on the basis that they were a minority shareholding, was upheld as being reasonable by the court. The valuation of shares in private companies is considered in more detail below[224].

Compulsory transfer under CA 1963, s 204

[16.084] In particular limited circumstances, a member can be compelled by statute to transfer his shares[225]. The power to acquire shares from members arises under CA 1963, s 204. Section 204(1) provides an enabling mechanism whereby one company, ('the transferee-company') can compulsorily acquire shares held by members of another company ('the target company') where its offer to purchase the shares in the target company has been accepted by at least 80% of its members. The effect of s 204 is to facilitate a complete and efficient takeover of the target company by the transferee-company. Its exclusive application to *takeovers* is borne out by the fact that *only a company*[226] can compulsorily acquire the shares in the target company; a human person has no standing under s 204 to acquire shares compulsorily. It is important to note, however, that the transferee-company need not be a 'company' within the meaning of

222 See para **[16.064]** at sub–clause (j).

223 *Re Castleburn Ltd* [1991] BCLC 89.

224 See para **[16.108]**.

225 See generally, Clarke, *Takeovers and Mergers Law in Ireland* (1999), p 326 *ff.*

226 CA 1963, s 204(1). In this regard, it should also be noted that only 'companies' within the meaning of CA 1963, s 2 can have their shares compulsorily acquired. For the provisions of CA 1963, s 2, see Ch 2, *Formation, Registration and Conversion of Private Companies*, para **[2.054]**.

CA 1963, s 2, but the transferor or target company must be an Irish company within the meaning of s 2: *Re Fitzwilton plc; Duggan v Stoneworth Investment Ltd*[227].

[16.085] Although CA 1963, s 204 is a legitimate and useful means of taking over a company, if abused, it has the potential to give rise to unjust results. Even the notional agreement of members, which can by implication be said to exist when shares are compulsorily acquired in accordance with a company's articles, does not exist in a section 204 acquisition. Accordingly, it is only proper that the courts should construe s 204 strictly. Here it is proposed to consider the issues which arise in the context of s 204 under the following headings:

(a) The mandatory statutory requirements.

(b) The court's discretion.

(a) The mandatory statutory requirements

[16.086] Section 204(1) of CA 1963 provides:

> 'Subject to subsection (2), where a scheme, contract or offer involving the acquisition by one company, whether a company within the meaning of this Act or not (in this section referred to as "the transferee-company") of the beneficial ownership of all the shares (other than shares already in the beneficial ownership of the transferee-company) in the capital of another company, being a company within the meaning of this Act (in this section referred to as "the transferor company") has become binding or been approved or accepted in respect of not less than four-fifths in value of the shares affected not later than the date 4 months after publication generally to the holders of the shares affected of the terms of such scheme, contract or offer, the transferee-company may at any time before the expiration of the period of 6 months next following such publication give notice in the prescribed manner to any dissenting shareholder that it desires to acquire the beneficial ownership of his shares, and when such notice is given the transferee-company shall, unless on an application made by the dissenting shareholder within one month from the date on which the notice was given, the court thinks fit to order otherwise, be entitled and bound to acquire the beneficial ownership of those shares on the terms on which under the scheme, contract or offer, the beneficial ownership of the shares in respect of which the scheme, contract or offer has become binding or been approved or accepted is to be acquired by the transferee-company.'

In order to acquire the shares held by dissident shareholders, the transferee-company must publish details of the terms of the scheme, contract or offer generally to the holders of the shares affected by the scheme. The transferee-company's offer must relate to *all* of the shares in the company since the terms of s 204(1) do not extend to partial offers. It is only when a scheme, contract or offer ('the offer') has become binding or has been approved or accepted by the holders of 80%[228] in value of the shares in the target-company that the compulsory transfer of shares can be triggered. It is usual for offers to be made conditional upon the transferee-company receiving acceptances from the requisite four-fifths[229]. This offer must have been accepted by and become binding on the holders of the 80% not later than *four months* after the publication of the terms of the

[227] *Re Fitzwilton plc; Duggan v Stoneworth Investment Ltd* [2000] 2 ILRM 263. There the transferee company was a British Virgin Islands company; the target or transferor company was an Irish company.

[228] *Four-fifths* is the phrase used in CA 1963, s 204.

offer to the shareholders. Once notice has been served, dissenting shareholders become obliged to sell, and the transferee-company becomes obliged to purchase the shares[230]. Where, on application by the transferee-company, all of the mandatory statutory requirements have been met, dissenting shareholders will be bound to sell and the transferee-company will be bound to acquire remaining shares. A dissenting shareholder must act without delay in making objection because the offer will become binding on him without the sanction of the court unless he makes application to court within one month of receiving the notice aforesaid. The terms offered to dissenting shareholders (including the consideration) must be the same as those which the assenting shareholders received[231].

[16.087] Section 204(2) and (3) of CA 1963 provide:

> '(2) Where shares in the transferor company are, at the date of such publication, already in the beneficial ownership of the transferee-company to a value greater than one-fifth of the aggregate value of those shares and the shares affected, subsection (1) shall not apply unless the assenting shareholders besides holding not less than four-fifths in value of the shares affected are not less than three-fourths in number of the holders of those shares.
>
> (3) For the purpose of this section, shares in the transferor company in the beneficial ownership of a subsidiary of the transferee-company shall be deemed to be in the beneficial ownership of the transferee-company, the acquisition of the beneficial ownership of shares in the transferor company by a subsidiary of the transferee-company shall be deemed to be the acquisition of such beneficial ownership by the transferee-company and shares shall not be treated as not being in the beneficial ownership of the transferee-company merely by reason of the fact that those shares are or may become subject to a charge in favour of another person.'

Therefore, s 204(1) is subject to sub-s (2) which applies where at the date of publication of the terms of the offer, the transferee-company already has in its beneficial ownership, more than 20% of the aggregate value of the shares in the company and the affected shares. In such circumstances the transferee-company cannot apply for an order under

---

229 See further, Clarke, *Takeovers and Mergers Law in Ireland* (1999), pp 330, 331 where the Takeover Rules' provisions are also noted.

230 CA 1963, s 204(4).

231 CA 1963, s 204(10) provides:

> 'Where the scheme, contract or offer provides that an assenting shareholder may elect between 2 or more sets of terms for the acquisition by the transferee company of the beneficial ownership of the shares affected, the notice given by the transferee company under subsection (1) shall be accompanied by or embody a notice stating the alternative sets of terms between which assenting shareholders are entitled to elect and specifying which of those sets of terms shall be applicable to the dissenting shareholder if he does not before the expiration of 14 days from the date of the giving of the notice notify to the transferee company in writing his election as between such alternative sets of terms, and the terms upon which the transferee company shall under this section be entitled and bound to acquire the beneficial ownership of the shares of the dissenting shareholder shall be the set of terms which the dissenting shareholder shall so notify or, in default of such notification, the set of terms so specified as applicable.'

sub-s (1) unless those who are agreeable to sell their shares not only hold 80% in value of the shares but are also together not less than 75% of the holders of those shares[232].

(b) The court's discretion

[16.088] Where a dissenting shareholder makes an application for relief from compulsory acquisition of his shares the court has discretion *where it thinks fit* to order otherwise. It is notable that the court's discretion is not confined to a stark choice between confirmation or veto. Rather, it can make any order it thinks fit, and so could order that the dissenting shareholders be paid more than the assenting shareholders. That said, however, in general, the court will either confirm or veto the takeover. In exercising its discretion, it will have regard to a number of matters, which are considered here as follows:

(i) Disclosure of full particulars.

(ii) The onus of proof.

(iii) The bona fides and independence of the transferee-company.

(i) Disclosure of full particulars

[16.089] A transferee-company must disclose full details of the proposed transaction in publishing the terms of the offer to the target company's shareholders[233]. In *Securities Trust Ltd v Associated Properties Ltd and Estates Development Ltd*[234] McWilliam J said:

> 'I do not know what is the reason for the provisions of s 204 of the 1963 Act or why it should be thought desirable that minority shareholders may be compulsorily bought out, but I am of opinion that, on a compulsory purchase of this nature, the people whose shares are being compulsorily purchased are entitled to be given full particulars of the transaction, its purpose, the method of carrying it out and its consequences. The purpose of the transaction and its consequences have not yet been disclosed and the method of carrying it out was not disclosed to the persons concerned.'[235]

It was unnecessary to make an order in that case because the parties settled the action. Although it has been observed that this case marks a slight lightening of the burden on dissenting shareholders[236], this test is thought to be correct in the context of some private companies. Where there exists mutuality and understanding between a company's

---

232 Shares in the target company which are in the beneficial ownership of a subsidiary of the transferee company are deemed to be in the beneficial ownership of the transferee company: CA 1963, s 204(3).

233 Cf *Re Evertite Locknuts Ltd* [1945] 1 Ch 220 where Vaisey J said (at 224–225):

> 'I do not see how I can listen to the plea of the applicant, who refuses to tell me whether he regards the offer as fair or unfair, but merely asks the court to say that he is not bound, because he might have had more information than in fact was offered to him as to circumstances which were, or might have been, relevant when he was considering the terms of the offer he had received...it cannot be right that one shareholder, owning one–seven–hundredth part of the shares affected, should be entitled to stand out against the decision of the 699/700ths of the share capital, merely because he has, as he thinks, been left somewhat in the dark in regard to the material facts.'

234 *Securities Trust Ltd v Associated Properties Ltd and Estates Development Ltd* (19 November 1980, unreported), High Court, per McWilliam J.

shareholders, and especially where the company is in the nature of a quasi-partnership, the deprivation of relief to a dissenting shareholder must be withheld sparingly.

(ii) The onus of proof

[16.090] Where the statutory provisions embodied in CA 1963, s 204 have been complied with, case law establishes that the onus is on the dissenting shareholder to establish unfairness. An early case in point is *Re Hoare and Co Ltd*[237], where the transferee-company made an offer to the shareholders in the target company to acquire their shares. The holders of 99.62% of the total issued share capital in the target company had accepted the offer. Although 0.24% of the remaining shareholders went on to agree to compulsory purchase, 0.14% refused and they made application to court seeking a declaration that their shares could not be acquired compulsorily. Maugham J refused the declaration sought and ordered the sale of their shares. As to the court's exercise of its discretion he said:

> '...the mere circumstance that the sale or exchange is compulsory is one which ought not to influence the court. It has been called an expropriation, but I do not regard that phrase as being very apt in the circumstances of the case. The other conclusion I draw is this, that again prima facie the court ought to regard the scheme as a fair one inasmuch as it seems to me impossible to suppose that the court, in the absence of very strong grounds, is to be entitled to set up its own view of the fairness of the scheme in opposition to so very large a majority of the shareholders who are concerned. Accordingly, without expressing a final opinion on the matter, because there may be special circumstances in special cases, I am unable to see that I have any right to order otherwise in such a case as I have before me, unless it is affirmatively established that, notwithstanding the views of a very large majority of shareholders the scheme is unfair. There may be other grounds, but I see no other grounds available in the present case for the interference of the court.'[238]

Maugham J's judgment has been applied in many subsequent cases[239]. Where a large company with diverse membership is concerned, the reasoning of Maugham J is unimpeachable. However, reflected in his own allusion to 'special circumstances' and

---

235 (19 November 1980, unreported), High Court at pp 9–10 of the transcript. In the earlier case of *McCormick v Cameo Investments Ltd* [1978] ILRM 191 McWilliam J had said (at 193): 'I consider it unsatisfactory that they and I do not understand the full implications of the scheme and that a full and simple statement, elucidating the ramifications of the group or groups of companies involved and the purpose and effect of this scheme, has not been made, but I am only concerned with the scheme as it stands and the provisions of the statute enabling it to be put through, and, the statutory provisions being complied with, the onus is on the applicants to establish that it is unfair to them...'.

236 See Ussher, *Company Law in Ireland* (1986), p 300. At p 298 the author says:'[i]n dealing with these applications the courts reflect the attitude of the section itself which is, put bluntly, that 80 per cent of the offerees cannot be wrong, or, put another way, the resisting minority are merely being difficult.'

237 *Re Hoare and Co Ltd* (1933) 150 LT 374.

238 (1933) 150 LT 374 at 375.

239 In *Evertite Locknuts Ltd* [1945] 1 Ch 220 Vaisey J applied the principles in *Re Hoare*; as did McWilliam J in *McCormick v Cameo Investments Ltd* [1978] ILRM 191, citing also *Grierson, Oldham & Adams Ltd* [1968] 1 Ch 17.

'other grounds' is the recognition that the onus of proof may not be as strong on a dissenting shareholder in all cases. In *Re Hoare* the shareholdings were many and diverse. It should not be seen as settled that the same onus will be placed on dissenting shareholders in a private company with fewer members.

[16.091] In *McCormick v Cameo Investments Ltd*[240] the applicants were the personal representatives of a deceased shareholder in the target company who had dissented and made application under CA 1963, s 204(1). The scheme had been accepted by the holders of 90% of the shareholders of the target company. The applicants made a number of objections: that the provisions of CA 1963, s 60 had been breached; that the target company had made a loan of £800,000 to the transferee-company which had not been repaid at the date of the notice to them under s 204(1); and that the purported acquisition of their shares was oppressive and unfair to them. McWilliam J held that s 60 had not been breached[241] and that the making of an unsatisfactory decision by the directors was not oppressive[242]. In the context of s 204, McWilliam J applied Maugham J's decision in *Re Hoare* and held that the onus of proving that the scheme was unfair rested with the applicants. They did not prove to his satisfaction that the scheme was unfair and he rejected the arguments that the shares were worth more than was being offered and that it was a bad time to sell their shares as the market was poor or that there was evidence of oppression (or bad faith)[243]. From the facts of the case it would seem that the company concerned could not be said to have been of the quasi-partnership type and such does not appear to have been pleaded. In different circumstances, it is thought that such a plea might shift the onus, as in *Re Bugle Press Ltd*, discussed below, particularly where the applicants can also make out a case to have the company wound up on just and equitable grounds.

[16.092] In *Re Bugle Press Ltd*[244], which concerned a company in which there were only three shareholders, Buckley J said:

> 'In a case of this kind it seems to me that the onus must clearly be on the other side, and it must be incumbent on the majority shareholders to satisfy the court that the scheme is one with which the minority shareholders ought reasonably to be compelled to fall in.'[245]

This was cited by the Supreme Court in *Re Fitzwilton plc; Duggan v Stoneworth Investment Ltd*[246] but Murphy J went on to note that, in general, the onus falls on a dissenting shareholder to satisfy the court that it is an appropriate case in which to 'order otherwise'[247] and that it is reasonable as a matter of fact and established as a matter of

---

240 *McCormick v Cameo Investments Ltd* [1978] ILRM 191.

241 See Chapter 18, *The Maintenance of Capital*, para **[18.041]**.

242 See Chapter 19, *Shareholders' Remedies*, para **[19.020]**.

243 On bad faith, see para **[16.050]**.

244 *Re Bugle Press Ltd* [1961] 1 CH 270. See para **[16.094]**.

245 [1961] 1 Ch 270 at 227.

246 *Re Fitzwilton plc; Duggan v Stoneworth Investment Ltd* [2000] 2 ILRM 263.

247 Citing *McCormick v Cameo Investments Ltd* [1978] ILRM 191. See also *Elkington v Vockbay Pty Ltd* 10 ACSR 785 at 793–794 and *Super John Pty & Ors v Marsford Investments Pty Ltd*, (18 April 1997) Federal Court of Australia.

law[248] that 'the Court should pay great attention to the views of the majority who have accepted the bid'.[249] Murphy J went on to say:

> 'The Court of Appeal in England in the *Bugle* case held that the fact that the promoters of the transferee-company held 90% of the shares in the transferor company shifted the onus from the applicant to the respondents. A 27% shareholding would not necessarily have the same effect. On the other hand, it would clearly follow that the acceptance of an offer by the shareholders in the transferor company who were also associated directly or indirectly with the transferee-company would not carry the same weight or influence as acceptance by shareholders wholly independent of the transferee-company. In the present case the learned judge of the High Court adopted the prudent course of assuming – without deciding – that the onus lay on the respondents to prove that the offer made was a fair one and that the court should not exercise its discretion by "ordering otherwise".'[250]

The facts in *Re Fitzwilton plc* are considered, and the factors that influenced the Supreme Court in upholding the trial judge's decision not to 'order otherwise', are considered below[251].

(iii) The bona fides and independence of the transferee-company

[16.093] In establishing the bona fides of the transferee-company the courts will look at a number of factors such as the independence of the assenting shareholders and the intentions of the transferee-company. In *Esso Standard (Inter-America) Inc v JW Enterprises*[252] the Supreme Court of Canada refused to sanction a compulsory transfer of shares where the holding company of the transferee-company held over 96% of the shares in the target company. Its reason for doing so was based on the perceived lack of independence in the assenting shareholder, by reason of the connection between the transferee-company and the assenting shareholders in the target company.

[16.094] A blatant example of a sham is provided by *Re Bugle Press Ltd*[253]. In that case an attempt was made to rely on a section similar to CA 1963, s 204 to expropriate a minority shareholder in the target company, Bugle Press Ltd. The majority shareholders in the target company formed another company which became the transferee-company. The transferee-company served notice on all the shareholders in the target company of its desire to acquire their shares. The majority shareholders naturally agreed to transfer their shares in the target company, thus giving the transferee-company the requisite percentage to enable it to require any dissenting shareholders to transfer their shares[254]. The minority shareholder refused to transfer his shares and sought a declaration that he was not obliged to transfer his shares. The Court of Appeal made the declaration sought. Harman LJ, in a judgment which concurred with that of Lord Evershed MR, said:

---

248 Citing *Securities Trust Ltd v Associated Properties Ltd* (19 November 1980, unreported), High Court (McWilliams J).

249 [2000] 2 ILRM 263 at 274.

250 [2000] 2 ILRM 263 at 275.

251 See para **[16.095]**.

252 *Esso Standard (Inter-America) Inc v JW Enterprises* (1963) 37 DLR 598.

253 *Re Bugle Press Ltd* [1961] 1 Ch 270, [1960] 3 All ER 791. See also Chapter 5, *Disregarding Separate Legal Personality*, para **[5.033]**.

254 The requisite percentage under CA 1948, s 209 (UK) was 90%.

> 'In my judgment this is a barefaced attempt to evade that fundamental rule of company law which forbids the majority of shareholders, unless the articles so provide, to expropriate a minority. It would be all too simple if all one had to do was to form a £2 company and sell to it one's shares, and then force the outsider to comply...no serious attempt to comply with the section has ever been made here...[t]here is no sign anywhere of any scheme or contract...and therefore the section does not begin to operate.'[255]

Lord Evershed MR said:

> 'Even, therefore, though the present case falls strictly within the terms of [the English provision, similar to CA 1963, s 204], the fact that the offeror, the transferee-company, is for all practical purposes entirely equivalent to the nine-tenths of the shareholders who have accepted the offer, makes it in my judgment a case in which , for the purposes of exercising the court's discretion, the circumstances are special - a case, therefore, of a kind contemplated by Maugham J, to which his general rule would not be applicable.'[256]

It is thus clear that the courts will not allow CA 1963, s 204 to be used as an unlawful method of expropriation. So notorious is the decision in *Re Bugle Press Ltd* that it would be a very foolhardy individual who would attempt to mimic the machinations of the majority shareholders in that case.

[16.095] The independence of accepting shareholders was extensively reviewed by the Supreme Court in *Re Fitzwilton plc; Duggan v Stoneworth Investment Ltd*[257] where it was held that independence of shareholding is not an actual requirement, but merely a factor to be considered in the court's exercise of its discretion. The facts were that Fitzwilton plc, a company quoted on the Dublin and London stock exchanges, was owned as to 27.6% of its ordinary shares by Dr AJF O'Reilly and Mr PJ Goulandris and their immediate families. These men formed Stoneworth Investments Ltd, an investment company in the British Virgin Islands ('Stoneworth') and offered to buy the ordinary shares in Fitzwilton at 50 pence a share and the preference shares at £1 per share. This offer was accepted by 47% of the shareholders who, together, held 84% of the ordinary shares in Fitzwilton. Thereafter, Stoneworth notified the holders of the remaining 16% of the ordinary shares that, having obtained the requisite four-fifths (80%) of the ordinary shares, it intended to compulsory acquire the outstanding 16% in reliance upon CA 1963, s 204. The plaintiff, who held ten ordinary shares (0.0001% of the ordinary share capital) objected and applied to the High Court, asking that the court 'order otherwise' than to sanction the proposal.

The essence of the plaintiff's objection was that the requisite four-fifths had not been acquired. He asserted that by applying a teleological rather than literal interpretation[258], Stoneworth was not the true owner of the 84% of ordinary shares as it was O'Reilly's and Goulandris' 'alter ego', since Stoneworth was owned by them and they owned

---

[255] [1960] 3 All ER 791 at 796F.

[256] [1960] 3 All ER 791 at 795H.

[257] *Re Fitzwilton plc; Duggan v Stoneworth Investment Ltd* [2000] 2 ILRM 263; see Lysaght, 'The Compulsory Acquisition of Shares' (2000) 21 Co Law 221.

[258] On a literal interpretation s 204(2) did not apply to cause the 27.6% of ordinary shares held by O'Reilly and Gaulandris to be discounted as these shares were not held by the transferee-company, Stoneworth.

27.6% of the shares in Fitzwilton. The court was urged to 'tear aside the corporate veil' and to treat O'Reilly and Goulandris as being identical with Stoneworth in construing s 204(2), with the result that Stoneworth would not then have acquired the requisite four-fifths' shareholding. In the alternative it was argued that the court should not exercise its discretion because the majority of acceptances of the offer was achieved only by treating O'Reilly and Goulandris as separate and distinct from Stoneworth, when, he claimed, this did not correspond with the commercial reality of the situation.

[16.096] The decisions in *Esso Standard (Inter-America) Inc v JW Enterprises*[259] *and Re Bugle Press Ltd* were both cited by the plaintiff. Stoneworth, on the other hand, relied upon the decisions in *Sammel v President Brand Gold Mining Co Ltd*[260] *and Blue Metal Industries Ltd v Dilley*[261]. Beginning with the decision in *Re Bugle Press Ltd*, Murphy J analysed and contextualised all four decisions. On *Re Bugle Press Ltd* Murphy J noted that Harman LJ was critical of the procedure adopted by the majority shareholders to expropriate the minority shareholding, describing the procedure in the following terms:

> '... the transferee-company was nothing but a little hut built round his two co-shareholders, and the so-called scheme was made by themselves as directors of that company with themselves as shareholders and the whole thing, therefore is seen to be a hollow sham'.[262]

This was essentially what the plaintiff in *Re Fitzwilton plc* wanted the court to find and to then disregard shares held by Stoneworth in computing the four-fifths requirement. Murphy J rejected this finding, pointing out the importance of the basis on which the *Bugle* case was decided, namely, the complete absence of evidence from the transferee-company substantiating the valuation of the shares which the applicant sought to challenge[263] and not just on account of the fact that the shareholders in the transferee-company were not independent. Murphy J next considered the Supreme Court of Canada's decision in *Esso Standard (Inter-America) Inc v JW Enterprises*[264], quoting from the decision of Judson J, where he stressed the importance of shares being 'independently held' in the transferee-company[265]. Murphy J rejected that this favoured the plaintiff, saying:

> 'If the phrase "and that this 90% must be independently held" with which that quotation concludes was intended to convey or reinforce what Judson J had previously said as to the

---

[259] *Esso Standard (Inter-America) Inc v JW Enterprises* (1963) 37 DLR 598.

[260] *Sammel et al v President Brand Gold Mining Co Ltd* (1963) 37 DLR (2d).

[261] *Blue Metal Industries Ltd v Dilley* [1970] AC 827.

[262] *Re Bugle Press Ltd* [1961] 1 Ch 270 at 288, [1960] 3 All ER 791.

[263] Murphy J quoted the following passage from the conclusion of Lord Evershed MR ([1961] 1 Ch 270 at 288):

> 'It was then for the transferee company to show that nevertheless there was some good reason why the scheme should be allowed to go on. The transferee company, whether because the two members did not wish to go into the witness–box and be cross–examined or for some other reason, did not file any evidence at all; they merely purported to rely on a copy of a valuation said to have been made on their behalf by a firm of chartered accountants. That valuation was not sworn to, nobody was able to cross–examine the authors of it and there is in my judgment no case [to answer]. The minority shareholder has nothing to knock–down; he only has to shout and the walls of Jericho fall flat.'

[264] *Esso Standard (Inter–America) Inc v JW Enterprises* (1963) 37 DLR 598.

value of a transfer between closely related companies as an indication of the propriety of the transaction, I would respectfully agree with it. If, on the other hand, the learned judge was deciding that the section did not apply where the majority of the shares in respect of which the offer was made were held by a company associated with the transferee-company I would not accept that it is a proper interpretation of s 204 of the Irish Act nor does it accord, in my view, with the judgments in the *Bugle* case.'[266]

Murphy J then turned to the South African decision in *Sammel v President Brand Gold Mining Co Ltd*[267], and said that the judgment of the court delivered by Trollip JA was helpfully and correctly summarised in the head note to the judgment in the following terms:

'Section 103 of the [South African] Act does not require for its applicability that the holders of the nine-tenths majority of countable shares must be independent of or disinterested in the transferee-company. If such a majority does accept a take-over made in pursuance of a scheme or contract the existence of any connection, interest or dependence between that majority and the transferee-company is merely a factor to be taken into account by the court in exercising its discretion under the section, the weight to be given to it depending upon the circumstances of each case'.

Murphy J went on to hold that the foregoing passage represents a correct statement of the law as to the proper interpretation of CA 1963, s 204(1)[268].

[16.097] The relationship between CA 1963, s 204(1) and 204(2) was next considered and Murphy J held that there was no ambiguity in their interpretation, saying:

'The legislature determined clearly and unequivocally to apply the relevant subsections to the beneficial ownership of shares of the transferor-company other than shares "already in the beneficial ownership of the transferee-company". Subsection (3) extended that exclusion by providing that shares in the beneficial ownership of a subsidiary of the transferee-company should not be deemed to be in the beneficial ownership of the transferee-company itself. It is curious, as Mr Lyndon MacCann pointed out at p 201 of his book on the Companies Acts 1963–1990 that the deeming provisions were not extended to the case where shares in the transferor company were held by a holding company of the transferee-company. However, it is the very fact that the particular exclusionary provisions are expressed to relate to shares in the beneficial ownership of the transferee-company and that the legislature consciously extended that exclusion to capture only shares in a subsidiary which makes it impossible to infer an intention to exclude other

---

[265] Judson J had said (at 604): 'We have here 90% ownership in Standard Oil (New Jersey). The promoting force throughout is obviously that of Standard Oil and not its subsidiary. A transfer of shares from Standard Oil to Esso Standard is meaningless in these circumstances as affording any indication of a transaction which the court ought to approve as representing the wishes of 90% of the shareholders. This 90% is not independent. On this ground alone I would reject the appeal and hold that the section contemplates the acquisition of 90% of the total issued shares of the class affected and that this 90% must be independently held.'

[266] [2000] 2 ILRM 263 at 272.

[267] *Sammel v President Brand Gold Mining Co Ltd* (1963) 37 DLR (2d).

[268] Murphy J held that the purposive approach taken by the Privy Council in *Blue Metal Industries Ltd v Dilley* [1970] AC 827 was undertaken to resolve a conflict between the New South Wales Interpretation Act and the actual terms of s 185 of their Companies Act.

categories of share holdings. Moreover, the legislature must have addressed very consciously the particular terms in which the excluded share holdings were described. Those terms differ significantly from the comparable provisions contained in s 8 of the Companies Act [1959] which had been enacted only four years earlier. Furthermore even if s 204 expressly provided or this Court were, contrary to my views, to infer that shares in the holding company were deemed to be in the beneficial ownership of its subsidiary, that would not carry the applicant in the present case. The 27% of the ordinary shares which he asks the court to treat "as if" they were in the beneficial ownership of the transferee-company were not held by its holding company but by the shareholders therein. It is clear that the shares in question are not in the beneficial ownership of Stoneworth as a matter of fact or law. It is equally clear that they are not deemed by the provisions of s 204 to be in the beneficial ownership of Stoneworth. In those circumstances I can find no basis on which the court would be justified for the purpose of s 204(1) or (2) as treating those shares "as if" they were in that ownership'.[269]

[16.098] In upholding the refusal to order otherwise – and thereby upholding the expropriation of the dissenting minority – Murphy J listed the nine distinct factors in that case, which had entitled the trial judge to refuse to order otherwise[270]. It may be noted that costs were awarded against the plaintiff in this case, a fact which has provoked one commentator to forecast that 'the High Court and Supreme Court have almost certainly ensured that they will not again be troubled by applications by dissenting shareholders dissatisfied by the terms of takeover bids'.[271]

[G] SHARE PURCHASE AGREEMENTS

[16.099] A company's business may be acquired in either of two ways: by the purchase *from the shareholders* of their shares in the company or by the purchase *from the company itself* of the company's property, assets and undertaking. This is the *share/asset purchase quandary*, spoken of at the outset of this chapter. Although a full treatment of the two methods of acquiring a business is beyond the scope of this work, it is proposed to outline briefly the nature of a *share purchase agreement*[272]. First, however, we examine the relative merits of the share purchase versus the asset purchase.

---

269 [2000] 2 ILRM 263 at 274.

270 These were (at 275):

> '1. The offer was accepted by the overwhelming majority of shareholders. 2. The acceptance included all of the major institutional and all of the substantial shareholders in the transferor company. 3. The bankers, Deutsche Morgan Grenfel, advised the independent directors that the offer was fair and reasonable. 4. NCB Stockbrokers likewise expressed the opinion that the offer was "full and fair". 5. The independent directors, whose independence has been scrutinised by the Take-over Panel, unanimously recommended and accepted the offer in respect of the shares held by them. 6. Perhaps more important in relation to the offer price was the fact that it reflected a very significant premium over the then market price. 7. The objections of Mr Duggan to the bid were investigated by the Take-over panel and rejected. 8. The involvement of the O'Reilly Group in the transferee company was clearly and fully disclosed in all of the offer documentation. 9. That Mr Duggan held a mere ten ordinary shares in Fitzwilton representing 0.0001% of that share capital'.

271 See Lysaght, 'The Compulsory Acquisition of Shares' (2000) 21 Co Law 221 at 224.

The relative merits of the share purchase versus the asset purchase

[16.100] The advantages of a *share purchase* may be summarised as follows:

— there may be tax savings and, in particular, a stamp duty saving since, where real property used for commercial purposes is sold for in excess of €76,200, stamp duty is payable at 6%[273] – by contrast the standard rate of stamp duty payable on a share purchase is 1%;

— where the company is well established, the goodwill and identity of the company may more easily be preserved on a share transfer.

[16.101] The advantages of an *asset purchase* may be summarised as follows:

— the purchaser can be selective and purchase only those assets which he wants;

— the company's liabilities are not included in the purchase, one of the greatest disadvantages of a share purchase[274]; and

— the legal procedure and documentation involved in an asset purchase are generally more standardised and commonplace than in a share purchase.

The nature of a share purchase agreement

[16.102] Where it is agreed to purchase the shares in a private company[275] two documents are required: a simple share transfer form and a *share purchase agreement.* The purpose of a share purchase agreement is to afford protection to the transferee. The need for protection may be said to stem from the target company's separate legal personality. Where the target company has been trading for a number of years, there is the possibility that it may have hidden tax liabilities, law suits, contractual commitments, labour relation difficulties, defective title to its properties, etc. The title to the target company's shares will not disclose any of the foregoing problems and liabilities because such problems and liabilities belong directly to the company. Where a transferee purchases the shares in the company those problems become his problems.

(a) Disclosure letters

[16.103] Transferees will usually seek to be provided with detailed information of all matters affecting the company by being given a so-called 'disclosure letter'. Because the transferee of shares is not protected by any statutory provisions he must protect himself

---

272 The following books provide a specialised treatment of the topic: Wine, *Buying & Selling Private Companies & Businesses*, (3rd edn, 1986); Sinclair, *Warranties and Indemnities on Share Sales*, (2nd edn, 1989), Longman Commercial Series; and Patterson, *Private Company Share Sale Manual* (2nd edn, 1990) Longman Commercial Series.

273 In respect of residential property, where the value is in excess of €635,000 the applicable rate of duty is 9%.

274 When a business is acquired by purchasing the entire issued share capital in the company, the new owners of the company stand in no better a position than did the old owners. All debts, liabilities, claims and demands against the company whilst the old owners owned the company will continue to exist on the change of ownership. The separate legal personality of the company is uninterrupted and unaffected by the change in shareholdings.

275 The sale of shares in quoted public limited companies ('PLC') is not normally accompanied by a share purchase agreement.

by insisting that the transferor provide him with *warranties* and *indemnities,* discussed below. The subject matter of the warranties and indemnities provided by the transferor will often be dictated by the contents of the disclosure letter. Accordingly, disclosure letters can serve to put the transferee on notice of matters adversely affecting the company (and so affect the value of the shares being acquired) and also bind the transferor to the veracity of its contents which can be seen as representations to the transferee[276].

(b) Warranties on share sales

[16.104] The transferee seeking protection from hidden liabilities will require the transferor to make certain *warranties* in relation to the company's affairs. Warranties involve the transferor of the shares giving the transferee certain assurances in relation to all potential liabilities of the company concerned. In addition to creating a legal liability between the transferor and transferee, it has been accepted that the giving of warranties also serves to bring all factors affecting the value of the shares to the transferee's attention[277]. In practice, warranties may also serve to further the transferor's interests since problems that are identified may be excluded from the warranties, and this fact will commonly be reflected in the consideration paid for the shares.

[16.105] The warranties typically given by the transferor fall into the following generic categories:

— Taxation warranties;

— Property warranties;

— Company's constitutional documents warranties;

— Accounting and financial warranties;

— Labour warranties;

— Contractual and trading warranties.

Depending upon the company in question, while all of the foregoing warranties will be important, some will be more important than others. *Taxation* warranties are of particular importance in almost all companies. These will span the entire ambit of taxation and address corporation tax, capital acquisitions tax, capital gains tax, value added tax, stamp duty, etc. *Property* warranties can also be of enormous importance where the company owns any real property. Although it is possible for the transferee to rely entirely upon the property warranties offered by the transferor, it is more usual for the transferee's solicitor to conduct a full investigation of title to the property by raising objections and requisitions on title. Alternatively, the transferor's solicitor may certify that the company has good and marketable title to the property.

[16.106] It is common to delimit warranties in terms of time, and the share purchase agreement may provide that any claims must be brought within a period of, say, three years[278]. Where, having warranted something to be the case, and within the prescribed time limit, it later transpires that the warranty is materially false, the transferor becomes

---

276 For an example of the matters addressed in a disclosure letter, see Wine, *Buying & Selling Private Companies & Businesse* (3rd edn, 1986), Appendix C.

277 See Sinclair, *Warranties and Indemnities on Share Sales* (2nd edn, 1989), Ch 1, *History and Function of Warranties and Indemnities.*

liable to compensate the transferee[279]. The transferee may face difficulties where he has paid the full consideration to the transferor and subsequently discovers that there has been a breach of a warranty given[280]. For this reason transferees sometimes require security. This is commonly achieved by an agreed retention from the total consideration which will only be released after a certain period of time. Alternatively, the transferor may be required to effect insurance against a breach of a warranty.

(c) Indemnities on share sales

[16.107] Indemnities from the transferor are usually limited to taxation matters. It has been noted[281] that, originally, indemnities were only given by the transferor in respect of specific secondary taxation liabilities. This is now usually extended to all taxation liabilities of the company and indemnities are often given to the transferee and the company itself.

[H] The Valuation of Shares in Private Companies

[16.108] The valuation of shares[282] can be a contentious exercise in a number of distinct situations. Disputes as to the basis of valuation can arise where a member, who wants to sell his shares, is compelled to offer them for sale to existing members pursuant to a pre-emption clause. Similarly, where an event arises which compels a member to transfer his shares, disputes as to the value of such shares can arise. In addition, where a member is obliged to transfer his shares pursuant to a court order under CA 1963, s 205 the value of the interest to be transferred often becomes an issue. In this section it is proposed to consider the legal rules which apply to share valuations in private companies under the following headings:

1. The principles of share valuation.
2. Discounting share value for a minority holding.
3. Establishing fair value.
4. The appropriate valuation date.

The principles of share valuation

[16.109] The valuation of a shareholding in a private company may be said to involve a two-fold process:

(a) Determination of a company's total worth; and

---

278 Certain warranties, such as those in relation to taxation matters, may be extended in some cases to six years.

279 See *Eurocopy plc v Teesdale* [1992] BCLC 1067 which concerns a claim that the warrantors had failed in breach of warranty to disclose all relevant facts in the disclosure letter.

280 On warranty claims generally, see Fagan and McKendrick, 'Corporate Warranty Claims – How They Should be Handled' (1995) PLC 15.

281 Stedman & Jones, *Shareholders' Agreements* (2nd edn, 1990), p 3.

282 Clarke, *Takeovers and Mergers Law in Ireland* (1999), p 10 *ff*; Giblin, *Valuation of Shares in Private Companies* (3rd edn, 1999 The Institute of Taxation in Ireland); see also Fox & Bowen, *The Law of Private Companies* (1991), Ch 14, 'Valuing Shares in Private Companies'.

(b) Assessment of the value of the shareholding.

The responsibility for the valuation of a shareholding will often be given to the company's auditors or to some independent accountant. Where the value of shares cannot be agreed, conflicting valuations by opposing expert valuers will commonly result[283]. Where the matter cannot be resolved amicably and results in a court hearing, the valuation of the shareholding may be determined by the court[284].

(a) Determination of a company's total worth

[16.110] The determination of the total worth of a company can be a most difficult task, with conflicting evidence being adduced by both parties. Private companies can be valued in a number of different ways. One way is to value the company as a *going concern*. Whether or not a company can be said to be a going concern will obviously depend upon the finances of the company in question[285]. An interesting consideration of the fate of one company is seen in the judgment of O'Hanlon J in *Re Clubman Shirts Ltd*[286]. This case arose as a result of an order previously made under CA 1963, s 205 that the petitioner's shares in the company be bought out[287]. In all of the circumstances O'Hanlon J concluded that he was not prepared to say that the petitioner's shares should be valued on the basis that the company should be regarded as a going concern on the valuation date. In that case the company was running at a loss and was unable to meet its liabilities as they fell due. Because of this, O'Hanlon J said:

> '...I take the view that the Petitioner's shareholding as of the 31 July 1980, was unsalable in the open market; had no value if assessed on a dividend yield or earnings yield basis, and the Petitioner must fall back on a *net asset valuation* basis to support a claim for payment when the shares are to be acquired by the parties resisting his claim.'[288] [Emphasis added]

O'Hanlon J went on to say that in the circumstances, the company's assets should properly be valued on a 'break-up' basis and not in relation to their value to a company which could continue in business as a going concern'. Even on this basis he could not readily establish their value and he was convinced that they were of no great value. Due to the deficiencies in the evidence he was, however, unwilling to hold that the shares were worthless. In the circumstances he measured the value of the shares at 60 pence each and he refused to award interest, although over ten years had passed since the finding of oppression. He considered that in striking the figure of 60 pence he may have erred on the side of generosity.

---

283 An example in point being *Irish Press plc v Ingersoll Irish Publications Ltd* (13 May 1994, unreported), High Court, per Barron J.

284 See *Colgan v Colgan & Colgan* (22 July 1993, unreported), High Court, per Costello J, *Re Clubman Shirts Ltd* [1991] ILRM 43, per O'Hanlon J; and *Irish Press plc v Ingersoll Irish Publications Ltd* (13 May 1994, unreported), High Court, per Barron J.

285 See generally, *Buckingham v Francis* [1986] 2 All ER 738.

286 *Re Clubman Shirts Ltd* [1991] ILRM 43.

287 *Re Clubman Shirts Ltd* [1983] ILRM 323.

288 [1991] ILRM 43 at 54.

[16.111] The valuation of shares has been considered in a number of Irish cases. The first of these was *Colgan v Colgan*[289], a case which also arose on foot of an application under CA 1963, s 205. The companies in question were part of a very successful group of companies which owned a considerable number of unencumbered properties in and around Dublin, including the Lucan Spa Hotel and the County Bars Lucan. Costello J had the benefit of a valuation report on all of the companies' properties and found that the combined valuation figures totalled £7,370,000. From this figure Costello J deducted the sum of £300,000 to allow for current liabilities over current creditors. He then held that the share value should be calculated by reference to the net asset value of the group without deduction. This case is also important for holding that there should not be a discounting for a minority interest. The second case was *Irish Press plc v Ingersoll Irish Publications Ltd*[290]. The principal difficulty there was that conventional methods of valuation were considered unsatisfactory on account of the company's business and financial situation. The valuations from both the petitioner and the respondent, while different, were both non-asset based. In the end Barron J valued the companies without fully accepting the method advanced by either party's valuer. Generally, the market for shares in private companies will be very limited and accordingly a valuation based on the price payable by a willing buyer and a willing seller may be fraught with artificiality[291]. Where shares are valued on the basis of an order to purchase under CA 1963, s 205, it has been held in *Re Clubman Shirts Ltd*[292] that sub-s (3) of that section confers a wide discretion on the courts, having regard to all the circumstances of the case, in arriving at a fair valuation. In *Re New-Ad Advertising Company Ltd*[293] Laffoy J ordered that a shareholding director, whom she found to have engaged in oppressive conduct, should purchase the petitioner's shares. As to the value of the shares, the learned judge said:

> 'The evidence [of the accountant], is that, as explained in his report, ordinarily the value of a company is obtained by reference to its net asset position at a given date together with a review of its dividend policy over a period of three to five years. In this case there was insufficient evidence to show what the assets of the company were and no dividends were paid. In the alternative, what has to be done is to establish what the income of the company ought to have been and from this to reconstruct what the net asset position would have been if the income to which the company was entitled had been received'.[294]

In that case, the latter method was adopted by Laffoy J in valuing the petitioner's 10% shareholding in the company.

---

[289] *Colgan v Colgan* (22 July 1993, unreported), High Court, per Costello J.

[290] *Irish Press plc v Ingersoll Irish Publications Ltd* (13 May 1994, unreported), High Court, per Barron J.

[291] For a discussion of the concept of 'willing seller', see *Shortt v Treasury Commissioners* [1948] AC 534. See also *Attorney General v Jameson* [1904] 2 IR 644.

[292] *Re Clubman Shirts Ltd* [1991] ILRM 43 at 53 where O'Hanlon J approved of *Re Bird Precision Bellows Ltd* [1985] 3 All ER 523 at 529, per Oliver LJ.

[293] *Re New-Ad Advertising Company Ltd* (1 July 1997, unreported), High Court (Laffoy J).

[294] (1 July 1997, unreported), High Court at p 14.

(b) The assessment of the value of the shareholding

[16.112] Once the net worth of a company has been established, the second step is to ascertain the value of the shareholding in question. The fundamental question here will be: should the shares in question be valued on a pro rata basis, or should the shareholding be subject to a discount or a premium to reflect the fact that a minority or majority shareholding is being transferred?

Discounting share value for a minority holding

[16.113] It is generally accepted that in a quasi-partnership private company, a minority shareholding *should not be discounted*, nor a majority shareholding attributed a premium[295]. Rather, in quasi-partnership companies, all shareholdings should be valued on a pro rata basis. This has been accepted as the law in Ireland by Costello J in *Colgan v Colgan and Colgan*[296] where the learned judge said '...all the authorities indicate that there should not be a discount when dealing with a quasi-partnership'[297]. There are a number of good reasons for not discounting the value of a shareholding in quasi-partnership companies, and it is thought that these reasons extend beyond the case where shares are being sold pursuant to an order of the court under CA 1963, s 205.

[16.114] The accepted circumstance in which a minority shareholding will not be discounted is when it is sold pursuant to a court order under CA 1963, s 205. The rationale for this is seen in *Re Bird Precision Bellows Ltd*[298] where Nourse J said at trial:

> 'I would imagine that in a majority of cases where purchase orders are made under s 75 [CA 1963, s 205] in relation to quasi-partnerships the vendor is unwilling in the sense that the sale has been forced upon him. Usually he will be a minority shareholder whose interests have been unfairly prejudiced by the manner in which the affairs of the company have been conducted by the majority. On the assumption that the unfair prejudice has made it no longer tolerable for him to retain his interest in the company, a sale of his shares will invariably be his only practical way out short of a winding up. In that kind of case it seems to me that it would not merely not be fair, but most unfair, that he should be bought out on the fictional basis applicable to a free election to sell his shares in accordance with the company's articles of association, or indeed on any other basis which involved a discounted price. In my judgment the correct course would be to fix the price pro rata according to the value of the shares as a whole and without any discount, as being the only fair method of compensating an unwilling vendor of the equivalent of a partnership share. Equally, if the order provided, as it did in *In re Jermyn Street Turkish Baths Ltd* [1970] 1 WLR 1194, for the purchase of the shares of the delinquent majority, it would not merely not be fair, but most unfair, that they should receive a price which involved an element of premium.'[299]

Although the reasoning here is especially significant in a compulsory sale or purchase under CA 1963, s 205, it is thought that the rationale holds good in any sale of shares in

[295] See generally, Fox, 'Valuing Minority Holdings in Private Companies' (1985) 129 SJ 456.

[296] *Colgan v Colgan and Colgan* (22 July 1993, unreported), High Court.

[297] (22 July 1993, unreported), High Court at p 7. See also *Profinance Trust SA v Gladstone* [2000] 2 BCLC 516.

[298] *Re Bird Precision Bellows Ltd* [1984] Ch 409; for the Court of Appeal see [1986] 2 WLR 158.

[299] [1984] Ch 409 at 430.

a quasi-partnership private company. Even when a shareholder in a private company *voluntarily* decides to dispose of his shares in a true quasi-partnership private company, in the absence of agreement to the contrary, he should be entitled to have his share valued on a pro rata basis because his holding in the business is tantamount to a share in a partnership. If the shareholders are truly partners who chose to regulate their affairs through a limited liability private company, and they contribute to the quasi-partnership on the basis of a certain contribution, it is only proper that they should be attributed a similar fraction when selling their *interest* in the company. An exception, recognised by Nourse J, is where the reason for the break up of the quasi-partnership is attributable to the transferor's wrongdoing or where the transferor acquired the shares in question from an original quasi-partner at a discount[300]. It is thought that the principle of pro rata valuation holds good notwithstanding the dissent of Judge Paul Baker QC in *Re Castleburn Ltd*[301] from the proposal that *Re Bird Precision Bellows Ltd* is confined to valuations pursuant to section 205-type actions. There, he distinguished the finding of Nourse J on the grounds, inter alia, that the case concerned a court-ordered valuation.

[16.115] In *Re Bird Precision Bellows Ltd*[302] the company was established for the purpose of combining the expertise of one man (Bird) in the manufacture of precision bellows with the experience of two other men (Armstrong and Nin) in management, finance and industrial matters. All three were also directors of the company. After about five years, the company's business prospered but the relationship of mutual confidence between the shareholders began to deteriorate. Following the calling of an extraordinary general meeting, Armstrong and Nin were removed as directors. Armstrong and Nin petitioned the court under s 75 of the Companies Act 1980 (UK) which was broadly similar to our CA 1963, s 205, providing a remedy where the affairs of the company were conducted in a manner unfairly prejudicial to them. The relief sought by the petitioners was to have their shares purchased by the respondents *at the fair value thereof.* At trial Nourse J found that there was no universal rule applicable to the valuation of shares. He did, however, as considered in the last paragraph, hold that in valuing a shareholding in a quasi-partnership private company, a pro rata approach should be adopted and no discount should be made for the fact a minority shareholding was being valued.

Establishing fair value

[16.116] Where a shareholders' agreement or a company's articles provide for an extra-judicial mechanism for the valuation of shares, the courts generally decline jurisdiction and insist upon the parties exhausting the ordained procedure[303]. Establishing the *fair value* of shares will often be a task entrusted to the company's auditors. Often the document referring the determination of a shareholding's fair value to the company's auditors will provide that the auditors' certification will be conclusive evidence[304]. Save

[300] [1984] Ch 409 at 430–431.

[301] *Re Castleburn Ltd* [1991] BCLC 89 at 96–100.

[302] *Re Bird Precision Bellows Ltd* [1986] 2 WLR 158 and [1984] Ch 409, CA (Nourse J).

[303] See *XYZ Ltd* (1986) 2 BCC 520.

[304] See para **[16.064]**.

where there is manifest error, mistake or proof of some improper motive[305] or where the auditors give reasons for their valuation[306], the auditors' valuation will not be questioned by the courts[307]. The justification for this is that upon joining the company the members implicitly accept the provisions in a company's articles or internal rules. As Lord Denning MR said in *Campbell v Edwards*[308], *albeit in another context*[309]:

> 'If two persons agree that the price of property should be fixed by a valuer on whom they agree, and he gives that valuation honestly and in good faith, they are bound by it. Even if he has made a mistake they are bound by it. The reason is because they have agreed to be bound by it. If there were fraud or collusion, of course, it would be very different. Fraud or collusion unravels everything. It may be that if a valuer gives a speaking valuation - if he gives reasons or his calculations – and you can show on the face of them that they are wrong it might be upset.'

It has been held that such provisions in articles of association also bind deceased members' executors by virtue of the deceased's adherence to the articles.[310].

[16.117] One of the leading authorities on the concept of fair value is *Dean v Prince*[311]. There, the court held on the preliminary issue of jurisdiction that notwithstanding that an auditor's determination is conclusive, there was jurisdiction to review the valuation in that case by reason of the fact that the auditor had, in an attempt to achieve agreement, given reasons for his determination of the shareholding's fair value. The facts were that on the death of a director and controlling shareholder, his shares were subject to compulsory sale to the surviving directors of the company, at a price to be certified by an auditor as a fair value. The auditor certified a fair value for the deceased director's shareholding, but went further and stated his reasons for not valuing the company as a going concern on account of consistent losses. At trial, Harman J held the valuation invalid and not binding because the auditor had not attributed a premium to the shareholdings to reflect the fact that they represented a majority and controlling interest in the company.

The finding of Harman J was rejected by the Court of Appeal, which held that the auditor was correct in not attributing a premium to the value of the shares, which should be valued pro rata to the company's worth[312], and that he had rightly rejected valuing the company on the basis of a going concern because of the losses suffered[313].

---

305 *Collier v Mason* (1858) 25 Beav 200, per Sir John Romilly MR and *Johnston v Chestergate Hat Manufacturing Co Ltd* [1915] 2 Ch 338, per Sargant J. See also *Re Benfield Greig Group plc* [2000] 2 BCLC 488.

306 *Burgess v Purchase & Sons (Farms) Ltd* [1983] 1 Ch 217, considered para **[16.118]**.

307 See also *Arenson v Arenson* [1972] 2 All ER 939 concerning valuer's liability.

308 *Campbell v Edwards* [1976] 1 WLR 403 at 407.

309 The context of this decision was landlord and tenant law.

310 *Re Benfield Greig Group plc* [2000] 2 BCLC 488.

311 *Dean v Prince* [1954] 1 Ch 409.

312 [1954] 1 Ch 409 at 427–428 per Lord Denning.

313 In this regard it was accepted that although the company's worth had increased since the valuation date, this was irrelevant because the material date for the valuation was the date of the member's death, per Evershed MR at 416.

[16.118] Caution should to be exercised by auditors in valuing a company's shares pursuant to a pre-emption type provision that requires them to establish the fair value of a shareholding. Where acting as an expert, an auditor's determination can only be impugned in the limited circumstances set out above[314], unless the auditor states the basis of the valuation. Another case in point is *Burgess v Purchase & Sons (Farms) Ltd*[315]. There, the executors of a deceased member notified the company of their desire to sell the deceased member's shares pursuant to a pre-emption clause in the company's articles. Upon the happening of this the company became the executors' agent for the sale of the shares to any existing member at their fair value which was to be determined by the company's auditors. The auditors' determination was expressed to be final, binding and conclusive. Notwithstanding that the auditors could simply have advised the executors of the value they had assessed, they went on to explain by letter how they had arrived at that value. Nourse J held that 'a speaking valuation' could be impugned notwithstanding that the articles provided that it was final, binding and conclusive.

The appropriate valuation date

[16.119] Two broad situations must be distinguished in fixing the appropriate date for the valuation of shares in a private company, namely:

- where shares are valued pursuant to the company's articles or a shareholders' agreement;
- where shares are valued pursuant to an order of court, such as an order under CA 1963, s 205.

[16.120] Where shares are valued pursuant to the company's articles or a shareholders' agreement, the valuation date will be governed by the terms of the instrument giving rise to the valuation. On the valuation of shares pursuant to a pre-emption clause it will typically be provided that the valuation date will be either the date of the deceased member's death[316], the date of the service of a transfer notice by a proposing transferor, or the occurrence of an event giving rise to the compulsory sale of a member's shares[317].

[16.121] Difficulties can arise where an order for the sale of shares is made pursuant to CA 1963, s 205. If there can be said to be a general rule[318] it is that shares ordered to be bought should be valued as at the date of the making of the order. This is seen in the judgment of Nourse J in *Re London School of Electronics Ltd*[319] where he said:

> 'If there were to be such a thing as a general rule, I myself would think that the date of the order or the actual valuation would be more appropriate than the date of the presentation

[314] At para **[16.116]**.

[315] *Burgess v Purchase & Sons (Farms) Ltd* [1983] 1 Ch 216.

[316] See eg, *Dean v Prince et al* [1954] 1 Ch 409.

[317] See eg, *Re Castleburn Ltd* [1991] BCLC 89.

[318] It is not accepted that there is a general rule. In *Profinance Trust SA v Gladstone* [2000] 2 BCLC 516 it was held that there was no prima facie rule that the date of the court's order was the appropriate date on which to value a minority shareholding for purchase by the majority shareholder. See also *Re Regional Airports Ltd* [1999] 2 BCLC 30 and *Re DR Chemicals Ltd* (1989) 5 BCC 39.

[319] *Re London School of Electronics Ltd* [1983] 3 WLR 474.

of the petition or the unfair prejudice. Prima facie an interest in a going concern ought to be valued at the date on which it is ordered to be purchased. But whatever the general rule might be it seems very probable that the overriding requirement that the valuation should be fair on the facts of the particular case would, by exceptions, reduce it to no rule at all.'[320]

[16.122] Case law demonstrates that the *general rule* has been departed from in a great many situations. The courts have fixed the appropriate valuation date to be:

— the date of the oppression[321],

— the date of the petition if there had been no oppression[322],

— the date of valuation when the petitioner had previously unreasonably rejected fair offers to purchase the shares[323], and

— a date a few weeks before the court's order to purchase the shares[324].

[16.123] Barron J has held that different considerations apply to the fixing of a valuation date where an order is made under CA 1963, s 205 against a party who has acted oppressively, ordering him to sell his shares to an oppressed petitioner. In the course of his judgment in *Irish Press plc v Ingersoll Irish Publications Ltd*[325] Barron J said:

'It has been submitted on behalf of the respondent that the date of presentation of the petition should be the date at which the shares should be valued. This may be the correct approach when the wrongdoer is being compelled to buy the shares but not if their value has already fallen by that date by reason of the oppression. A totally different situation arises when it is the wrongdoer who is being compelled to sell his shares. His actions have caused loss and the value of the shares has gone down. This factor must be reflected in the price which the petitioner will be required to pay for the respondent's shares. Here this fall has taken place, not only in the value of the respondent's shares but also in the value of the petitioner's shares. Clearly the appropriate date for valuing the respondent's shares must be the date of valuation. In addition, additional compensation must be provided for any drop in value of the petitioner's shares.'[326]

The learned judge ordered that the appropriate valuation date was to be 21 December 1993, five days after he delivered the judgment in which he found that there had been oppression. Notwithstanding the Supreme Court's subsequent finding that compensation cannot be awarded pursuant to CA 1963, s 205(3)[327], it is thought that Barron J's comments on the appropriate valuation date remain valid.

---

320 [1983] 3 WLR 474 at 484B–C.

321 *Re Clubman Shirts Ltd* [1983] ILRM 323; *Re OC (Transport) Services Ltd* [1984] BCLC 251.

322 *Scottish Co-operative Wholesale Society Ltd v Meyer* [1959] AC 324.

323 *Re A Company (No. 002567 of 1982)* [1983] 1 WLR 927.

324 *Colgan v Colgan & Colgan* (22 July 1993, unreported), High Court, per Costello J.

325 *Irish Press plc v Ingersoll Irish Publications Ltd* (16 December 1993, unreported), High Court.

326 (16 December 1993, unreported), High Court at p 85.

327 See Chapter 19, *Shareholders' Remedies*, para **[19.065]**.

Chapter 17

Groups of Companies

[17.001] The commercial reality of business is that a great many corporate enterprises operate as groups of companies, comprised of two or more individual companies. It is very common to utilise a group structure. This is true whether in the context of a large public limited company with a plethora of divisional subsidiaries or a small private company, which is a holding company and has one subsidiary company. The purpose of this chapter is to consider the circumstances in which companies will, primarily[1] for the purposes of company law, be treated as being part of a group of companies, consisting of a holding company and its subsidiaries. In addition, a number of issues, which are specific to groups of companies, are considered here. The matters considered are:

1. The significance of the holding-subsidiary relationship in company law.
2. The definition of holding company in company law.
3. The definition of subsidiary company in company law.
4. Definitions of undertakings, parent undertakings and subsidiary undertakings for group accounting purposes.
5. Capital maintenance definitions of parent public companies and public company subsidiaries.
6. Taxation definitions of holding and subsidiary companies.
7. Select issues in the holding-subsidiary relationship.

The significance of the holding-subsidiary relationship in company law

[17.002] In Ireland and England there is no distinct body of law applicable to groups of companies; the Companies Acts 1963–2001 apply generally to groups of companies[2]. There are, however, consequences for companies in a group[3]. Some consequences involve possibly negative *impositions*, which do not apply to stand-alone companies – for example, the regulation of accounting in corporate groups[4] or lifting the veil at common law[5]. Other consequences allow group companies to avail of *exemptions* that do not apply to stand-alone companies – for example, the Companies Act 1990, s 35 ('CA 1990') which disapplies the prohibitions in CA 1990, s 31 to certain transactions and

---

[1] Note, however, that, for the purposes of comparison, the definition of holding company and subsidiary company in taxation legislation is considered at para **[17.041]** *ff*.

[2] See, generally, Wainman, *Company Structures* (1995), ch 6, 'Groups of Companies'; Farrar & Hannigan, *Farrar's Company Law*, (4th edn, 1998), p 529; Forde, *Company Law* (3rd edn, 1999), p 562.

[3] See Schmitthoff & Wooldridge, *Groups of Companies* (1991).

[4] See Chapter 13, *Accounts and Auditors*, para **[13.109]** *ff*.

[5] See, generally, Chapter 5, *Disregarding Separate Legal Personality*, para **[5.010]** *ff*.

arrangements between group companies[6]. Where the law provides exceptions, lawyers and their clients will seek to bring themselves within those exceptions. In this chapter, some of the many ways in which stand-alone companies can be brought into a group, are considered. An important caveat is appropriate: the slightest tinkering with the ownership and control of the shares in a company can, for the non-tax lawyer, have unforeseen financial repercussions and the creation of a group of companies must always be considered in totality, the short-term advantage in availing of a particular regime, weighted against the accounting and taxation implications of a re-structure.

[17.003] The Companies Acts 1963–2001 do not contain any definition of 'group of companies'. Accordingly, it is necessary to consider the definitions of the constituent elements of any group of companies, namely the meanings of 'parent' or 'holding' company and 'subsidiary' company. The practitioner must always be conscious of the eternal difference between the legal definition of a 'group of companies' and the vernacular meaning of that expression. So, for example, a businessman who holds the legal and beneficial ownership in all of the shares issued in five companies might legitimately refer to those companies as his 'group'. Because, however, the common connection is him, a natural person, and not a body corporate, his enterprise will not be a 'group of companies' within the meaning of the Companies Act 1963, s 155 ('CA 1963'). The potential for confusion is exacerbated by the fact that a partnership which controls a company may, for the purposes of group accounts, be deemed that company's parent undertaking by reason of the application of the European Communities (Companies: Group Accounts) Regulations 1992 (the '1992 Regulations')[7] to 'undertakings' and not just to bodies corporate[8].

[17.004] It is also important to recognise at the outset that a shareholding that gives rise to a parent-subsidiary relationship for the purposes of the Companies Acts 1963–2001, will not necessarily be sufficient for the purpose of enabling those companies to avail of certain advantages in revenue law which distinguishes between degrees of parent-subsidiary. The threshold degrees of connection and control in revenue law are outlined below[9].

[17.005] The term 'related company' is employed by the Companies Acts 1963–2001 in the context of investigations[10], examinerships[11] and contribution and pooling orders in windings up[12]. A related company will not, per se, be a holding company or a subsidiary company within the meaning of CA 1963, s 155 as in each case the definition of 'related company' is wider than that contained in s 155. Companies and other bodies corporate

6 See Warnock, 'Inter–Company Relationships and Section 31 of the Companies Act, 1990', 1 CLP 243; and, generally, Chapter 11, *Statutory Regulation of Transactions Involving Directors and their Companies*, para **[11.085]** *ff.*

7 SI 1992/201.

8 See para **[17.028]**.

9 See para **[17.041]**. See, generally, Feeney, *The Taxation of Companies 1998–99* (1998), p 51 *ff.*

10 See Chapter 14, *Investigations and Inspectors*, para **[14.023]**.

11 See Chapter 23, *Examinerships*, para **[23.045]**.

12 See Chapter 27, *The Realisation and Distribution of Assets in a Winding Up*, para **[27.107]**.

can be *connected*, but only with a director and not another body corporate[13]. The term 'associated company' or 'associated undertaking' is relevant in the context of company accounts[14], but not in the case of s 155 which governs the general company law definition of holding and subsidiary company.

The definition of holding company in company law

[17.006] 'Holding company' is circularly defined by CA 1963, s 155(4) in the following terms 'For the purposes of this Act, a company shall be deemed to be another's holding company if, but only if, that other is its subsidiary.' The consequence of this is that it is the definition of 'subsidiary', which will determine whether or not a company will be another's holding company.

[17.007] Ordinarily, where the Companies Acts 1963–2001 refer to a 'company' the reference is to a company within the meaning of CA 1963, s 2[15]. For the purposes of CA 1963, s 155, however, it is important to note that sub-s (5) provides that '"company" includes any body corporate'. Accordingly, to take as an example of a legal entity that is not a 'company' for the purposes of s 2, a company formed and registered in accordance with the laws of England and Wales, such an entity will be a 'company' for the purposes of s 155 and can be either the holding company or subsidiary company of an Irish registered company[16].

The definition of subsidiary company in company law

[17.008] 'Subsidiary company' is defined by CA 1963, s 155(1). This provides:

> 'For the purposes of this Act, a company shall, subject to subsection (3)[17] be deemed to be a subsidiary of another if, but only if—
>
> (a) that other—
>
> (i) is a member of it and controls the composition of its board of directors, or
>
> (ii) holds more than half in nominal value of its equity share capital, or
>
> (iii) holds more than half in nominal value of its shares carrying voting rights (other than voting rights which arise only in specified circumstances); or
>
> (b) the first-mentioned company is a subsidiary of any company which is that other's subsidiary.'

For general purposes of company law, there are, therefore, four circumstances in which one company shall be deemed to be the subsidiary of another company (the holding company). The issues that arise are now considered as follows:

---

13 CA 1990. s 26(2). See, generally, Chapter 11, *Statutory Regulation of Transactions Involving Directors and their Companies*, para **[11.011]**.

14 See Chapter 13, *Accounts and Auditors*, para **[13.151]**.

15 See Chapter 2, *Formation, Registration and Conversions of Private Companies*, para **[2.054]** *ff*.

16 Note that CA 1963, s 2(3) provides that 'references in this Act to a body corporate or to a corporation shall be construed as not including a corporation sole, but as including a company incorporated outside the State'.

17 See para **[17.021]**.

(a) The 'golden share': a member controlling the composition of the board of directors.

(b) Holding more than half in nominal value of the equity share capital or of the shares carrying voting rights.

(c) Shares held and powers exercisable in a fiduciary capacity, as nominee or pursuant to a debenture or trust.

(d) A subsidiary of a subsidiary.

(e) Wholly-owned subsidiaries.

(a) The 'golden share': a member controlling the composition of the board of directors

[17.009] It can sometimes come as a surprise to learn that a company will be deemed to be another company's subsidiary in circumstances where the holding company holds only one share in the subsidiary. The requirement in CA 1963, s 155(1)(a)(i) is twofold: a company shall be another's holding company if it is, first, a *member* of the subsidiary and, secondly, if it *controls the composition of its board of directors*. Membership, which is considered in Chapter 15, *Shares and Membership*[18], arises from either being an original subscriber of the memorandum of association or having agreed to become a member and having one's name entered on the register of members. Every shareholder whose name is entered on the register of members is a member. For the purposes of s 155(1)(a)(i) it matters not that a company is the holder of just one of ten thousand shares issued – provided it is registered as a member, it passes the first limb.

[17.010] If the first limb of the test in CA 1963, s 155(1)(a)(i) is a formality, the second limb contains the substantive basis for transforming such a potentially minor participant in a company into that company's holding company. To be another company's holding company, a corporate member must control the composition of the putative subsidiary's board of directors. Notwithstanding the fact that the first limb of the test is passed if the putative holding company is a nominal member, since the second limb requires that member to control the board of directors, the most obvious circumstances in which the complete test will be passed is where a corporate member holds in excess of 50% of the issued equity share capital where all shares carry equal voting rights for this will, all things being equal, permit that member to control the composition of the company's board of directors.

[17.011] As noted above, however, it will equally suffice for a corporate member to hold just one of, for example, 10,000 shares issued provided that the rights attaching to that one share entitle its holder to control the composition of the company's board of directors. This position is permitted by the definition afforded to '*control*' and companies' freedom to issue shares with '*loaded voting rights*'. Section 155(2) of CA 1963 defines 'control' for the purposes of s 155(1):

> 'For the purposes of subsection (1), the composition of a company's board of directors shall be deemed to be controlled by another company if, but only if, that other company by the exercise of some power exercisable by it without the consent or concurrence of any

[18] See para **[15.003]** *ff*.

> other person can appoint or remove the holders of all or a majority of the directorships; but for the purposes of this provision that other company shall be deemed to have power to appoint to a directorship in relation to which any of the following conditions is satisfied—
>
> (a) that a person cannot be appointed thereto without the exercise in his favour by that other company of such a power as aforesaid; or
>
> (b) that a person's appointment thereto follows necessarily from his appointment as director of that other company.'

The significance of s 155(2) is that the key factor in determining 'control' is the entitlement to *exercise some power without the consent or concurrence of any other person*. The source[19] of that power is irrelevant. It is also significant that the test in s 155(1)(a)(i) will be passed where there is power to appoint or remove the holders of a *majority* of the directorships. Finally, it may be noted that by containing a 'deeming' provision, s 155(2) operates to assist, rather than defeat, the creation of a parent-subsidiary relationship. So, the power to appoint to a directorship is *deemed* to exist where *either* of two situations exist. The first is where a person cannot be appointed as a director without the putative holding company exercising its power; the second is where a person's appointment as a director to the putative subsidiary 'follows necessarily' from his or her appointment as director of the putative holding company.

[17.012] There are a number of ways in which a corporate member holding just one share of, for example, the 10,000 issued shares can have the unilateral power to control the composition of the company's board of directors. In the first instance, the articles of association can provide that the holder of a particular class of shares is exclusively entitled to control the composition of the company's board of directors and the holders of all other classes of shares are expressly not so entitled. In *Bushell v Faith*[20], the House of Lords upheld the propriety of such 'golden shares'. An alternative source of a corporate member's entitlement to exercise the power to control the board of directors is a shareholders' agreement. This is because the source of the power is not confined to rights intrinsic to particular shares; the power can be contractual[21], whether by way of a shareholders' agreement or otherwise, and will be effective for the purposes of CA 1963, s 155(1)(a)(i) provided it is enforceable.

[17.013] In the Australian case of *Mount Edon Gold Mines (Aust) Ltd v Burmine Ltd*[22] it was stated that the most important feature of the power was that it must be legally enforceable. Accordingly, it was held that a practical or de facto power giving rise to control by reason of a significant shareholding (but legally insufficient shareholding to amount to an overall majority, if all entitled to attend and vote were to do so) would not

---

19 See para **[17.012]**.

20 *Bushell v Faith* [1970] AC 1099. See Chapter 3, *The Constitutional Documentation*, para **[3.062]** *ff*.

21 In *Kolotex Hoisely (Australia) Pty Ltd v Federal Commission of Taxation* (1973) 130 CLR 64 Mason J said: '(c)entral to the concept of control of a company is the capacity to control a general meeting. That capacity rests on majority voting power and it matters not whether the majority voting power is, or is not, attached to shares.'

22 *Mount Edon Gold Mines (Aust) Ltd v Burmine Ltd* (1994) 12 ACLC 185.

satisfy the test under their similar legislation[23]. In that case White J said of the similarly worded Australian provision that:

> '...each of the three sub-paragraphs of para (a) is concerned with legal power. It is difficult to see how, in the absence of a legal power, a body corporate could be said to control the composition of the board of another body corporate, by virtue of what it in fact does, when another body holds more than one-half the maximum number of votes that might be cast at a general meeting of the company. To take a hypothetical example, suppose that the shares of a company are held as to 80% by shareholder A, as to 15% by shareholder B and as to 5% by shareholder C, and that, perhaps as the result of apathy, shareholder A is customarily absent from general meetings of the company. In the result, shareholder B is accustomed to appoint his nominees to the board of directors of the company and to remove directors of the company as it may decide, whether or not shareholder C agrees. In such a case, if the plaintiff is correct, the company is a subsidiary of shareholder B, a situation that is liable to change on short notice if shareholder A decides at any time to exercise its rights. In my opinion, it cannot correctly be said, in the hypothetical case envisaged, that shareholder B controls the composition of the board of the company.'[24]

Burmine was followed by the Supreme Court of New South Wales in *Bluebird Investments Pty Ltd v Graf*[25] where it was held that the test for determining control of a subsidiary was one of *legal control* and not a present (de facto) ability to control. There, Santow J said:

> 'The test...is solely one of "control" not "present ability". This ordinarily connotes something intrinsically more durable and binding than an adventitious voting coalition, not reinforced by any legally enforceable arrangement. Such a coalition would be readily capable of changing at each shareholder meeting, providing additional reason for avoiding such a test falling short of legal enforceability, unless the language were clear.'[26]

[17.014] The capacity in which a power is exercisable is all-important. The foregoing assumes that the power to control the composition of the board of directors is *not* exercisable:

- in a fiduciary capacity;
- as nominee for some other person; or
- pursuant to a security debenture or trust.

The effect of a power being exercisable in a fiduciary capacity, or as nominee, or on foot of a security is considered at para **[17.020]** below.

[17.015] Although equally applicable to CA 1963, s 155(1)(a)(ii) and (iii), it is readily apparent from s 155(1)(a)(i) that a company may be a subsidiary of another company whilst at the same time being 'controlled' by another person, whether a natural person or

---

23 Cf *Re Federal Capital Press of Australia Pty Ltd* [1995] ACTAAT 102 (1 February 1995) where the Australian Administrative Appeals Tribunal distinguished *Mount Edon Gold Mines (Aust) Ltd v Burmine Ltd* found that 'effective control' was sufficient for purposes of taxation law.

24 *Mount Edon Gold Mines (Aust) Ltd v Burmine Ltd* (1994) 12 ACLC 185 at 196.

25 *Bluebird Investments Pty Ltd v Graf* (1994) 12 ACLC 724.

26 (1994) 12 ACLC 724 at 726.

a body corporate. Section 155 does not prevent a company from being the subsidiary of two separate and unrelated holding companies[27]. It is also trite[28] to say that a company can be a subsidiary but yet 'controlled' by a director of that company within the meaning of CA 1990, s 26 for the purposes of, for example, CA 1990, ss 29 or 31[29].

(b) Holding more than half in nominal value of the equity share capital or of the shares carrying voting rights

[17.016] It is convenient to consider together, the two bases for the existence of the holding/subsidiary company relationship that is set out in CA 1963, s 155(1)(a)(ii) and (iii). Three distinct issues arise here requiring elaboration:

(i) More than half in nominal value;
(ii) 'Of equity share capital';
(iii) 'Of shares carrying voting rights'.

(i) More than half in nominal value

[17.017] More than half is self-explanatory: a putative holding company must hold 50% or more in nominal value. The nominal value of shares is the monetary value assigned to a share in a company's memorandum of association; it is 'nominal' in the sense that it may bear no relation to the actual commercial value of a share in a company[30].

(ii) 'Of equity share capital'

[17.018] For the purposes of CA 1963, s 155, 'equity share capital' is defined by sub-s (5) to mean:

> '...in relation to a company, its issued share capital *excluding* any part thereof which, neither as respects dividends nor as respects capital, carries any right to participate beyond a specified amount in a distribution.' (Emphasis added)

Accordingly, to be a holding company under CA 1963, s 155(1)(a)(ii) a company must hold more than half in *nominal value* of the subsidiary's *issued* equity share capital. Not all of a company's issued equity share capital is reckonable for this purpose; issued share capital that does not have the right to participate in dividends or capital beyond a specified amount in a distribution must be excluded from the computation. An example of such share capital might be certain preference shares that entitle the holder to a higher dividend than ordinary shareholders but which limit the holder's rights to participate beyond a certain limit (as regards dividends or capital) in a distribution[31]. It is not clear

---

27 Warnock, 'Inter–Company Relationships and Section 31 of the Companies Act 1990', (1994) 1 CLP 243 at 244.

28 It is trite in the sense that CA 1990, ss 34 and 35 purport to exclude certain transactions and arrangements involving holding companies and subsidiary companies in circumstances where, since a body corporate cannot in Ireland be a director, it can only be a 'person connected with a director' which, in the case of a body corporate, is established by showing that it is 'controlled by a director'.

29 See Chapter 11, *Statutory Regulation of Transactions Involving Directors and their Companies*, para **[11.021]** *ff.*

30 See, generally, Chapter 15, *Shares and Membership*, para **[15.043]** *ff.*

31 On the different rights that may attach to shares see Chapter 15, *Shares and Membership*, para **[15.068]** *ff.*

from the definition as to whether the limitation must be as regards dividends *and* capital or whether a limitation in either respect is sufficient render such share capital unreckonable for the purposes of s 155.

(iii) 'Of shares carrying voting rights'

[17.019] Section 155(1)(a)(iii) of CA 1963 provides that a company will be another's holding company where it 'holds more than half in nominal value of its shares carrying voting rights (other than voting rights which arise only in specified circumstances)'. There is no statutory definition of the meaning of 'shares carrying voting rights', but the meaning is self-apparent. To be reckonable, the putative holding company's holding must be of shares which carry voting rights in *all circumstances* and not, for example, shares which have no voting rights on, say, a resolution to appoint or remove directors. Section 155(1)(a)(iii) is silent on the effect, if any, of different classes of shares having loaded or weighted voting rights in circumstances where all shares do have voting rights.

(c) Shares held and powers exercisable in a fiduciary capacity, as nominee or pursuant to a debenture or trust

[17.020] If CA 1963, s 155 had not given guidance as to when, for the foregoing purposes, a share will be considered to be 'held' or a power considered to be 'exercisable by', great confusion would have been occasioned due to the myriad capacities in which property can be held and powers exercisable. Not only must holding as 'legal' and 'equitable/ beneficial' owner be distinguished, so also must holding in a 'fiduciary capacity' be distinguished from holding as a 'nominee', as must rights accruing pursuant to a debenture or trust[32].

[17.021] For the purposes of CA 1963, s 155(1), where a company holds shares or exercises a power in a fiduciary capacity, the rule is that such shares or power will be treated as *not* held or exercisable by it. Section 155(3)(a) and (b) of CA 1963 provide:

> 'In determining whether one company is a subsidiary of another—
>
> (a) any shares held or power exercisable by that other in a fiduciary capacity shall be treated as not held or exercisable by it;
>
> (b) subject to paragraphs (c) and (d), any shares held or power exercisable—
>
> (i) by any person as a nominee for that other (except where that other is concerned only in a fiduciary capacity); or
>
> (ii) by, or by a nominee for, a subsidiary of that other, not being a subsidiary which is concerned only in a fiduciary capacity;
>
> shall be treated as held or exercisable by that other;...'
>
> [paragraphs (c) and (d) are considered at para **[17.025]** below]

To take an extreme example: if company A holds all of the equity share capital in company B, but does so in a fiduciary capacity or as nominee for X, company A will not be company B's holding company. A *nominee* is someone in whose name shares are

[32] On the splitting of legal and equitable/beneficial ownership, see Chapter 16, *Share Transfers in Private Companies*, para **[16.073]** *ff*.

registered, but who is not the beneficial or equitable owner of those shares: a nominee is a bare trustee. Holding shares in a *fiduciary capacity* will arise where the registered owner has sold those shares to a purchaser: pending the registration of the purchaser as registered owner of the shares, the vendor will hold the shares in a fiduciary capacity. In both cases, s 155(3) requires that the 'nominee' or 'fiduciary' cannot be considered the holder of the shares or of the power to control the board of directors for the purposes of s 155(1).

[17.022] The meaning of holding shares in a fiduciary capacity/as nominee was considered by the English Court of Appeal in *Michaels and another v Harley House (Marylebone) Ltd*[33]. In that case a company, called Taylor Woodrow Property Co Ltd ('Property'), owned a building in which the plaintiffs' flat was located. The plaintiffs sought to claim rights under English landlord and tenant legislation. In 1992, Property agreed to sell the building to its subsidiary, Taylor Woodrow Development Ltd ('Development'). Development paid Property but title in the building rested with Property. Subsequently, in 1993, two transactions were effected:

- Development agreed to sell the building to its subsidiary, Harley House (Marylebone) Ltd ('Marylebone') for £15.75m and, to this end, agreed to lend Marylebone that sum to enable it to complete the purchase.
- On the same day, Development entered into an agreement with Frogmore Estates plc ('Frogmore') to sell to Frogmore the two, £1 issued shares, held by Development in Marylebone and also the loan notes.

The share sale agreement was expressed to be dependent upon the prior completion of the property sale agreement. At a pre-completion meeting the parties' solicitors signed an escrow agreement which provided that the transfer of the building would be completed before the transfer of the shares and the necessary transfers were executed in escrow. Completion was ultimately effected and the transfers lodged for registration.

[17.023] The plaintiffs' application was for an order against Marylebone, obliging it to disclose full particulars of the terms and dates of all transactions whereby Property agreed to transfer ownership and control of the building to Marylebone. The plaintiffs also sought a declaration that the transfer involved a 'relevant disposal' within the meaning of s 4 of the Landlord and Tenant Act 1987 (UK). In the course of his judgment Robert Walker LJ said:

> 'It is…common ground that persons within the Taylor Woodrow group and the Frogmore group and their respective legal advisers set about producing a scheme under which they could achieve the commercial substance of a sale of the freehold in [the building] while in form and in law (as they hoped) avoiding triggering any relevant disposal for the purposes of the 1987 Act.'[34]

Robert Walker LJ noted that a disposal would not be a 'relevant disposal' if made to an 'associated company', which was defined by the Landlord and Tenant Act 1987 (UK) by reference to ss 736 and 736A of the Companies Act 1985 (UK). Section 736A(5) provided: 'rights held by a person in a fiduciary capacity shall be treated as not held by

33 *Michaels v Harley House (Marylebone) Ltd* [1999] 1 BCLC 670.

34 [1999] 1 BCLC 670 at 674.

him…'. The net question (for present purposes) was whether Marylebone was Development's subsidiary at the time of the disposal. It was contended that Marylebone was not Development's subsidiary because '…rights held by [Development] in [Marylebone] were held in a fiduciary capacity pursuant to the uncompleted share sale agreement.'[35]

At trial, it had been held by Lloyd J that Marylebone *was* Development's subsidiary at the time of the disposal and that it followed that the disposal was not a 'relevant disposal' within the meaning of the Landlord and Tenant Act 1987 (UK). Lloyd J had held that on the conclusion of the share sale agreement, Development had held the shares in Marylebone on trust for Frogmore but did not hold the voting rights in the shares in a fiduciary capacity within the meaning of s 736A(5). Lloyd J had held:

> '…this is not an ordinary trust and there is authority that, even where shares are the subject of an uncompleted, unconditional contract (as here), it is the vendor who can decide how to cast the relevant votes and he is not subject in this respect to any direction from the purchaser (see *Musselwhite v CH Musselwhite & Son Ltd* [1962] 1 All ER 210). It was argued in that case that the vendor, in exercising its voting powers in respect of the shares at any general meeting was, by virtue of the beneficial ownership of the purchaser in the shares, bound to comply with the directions of the purchaser as to how to vote, except in respect of a direction which would affect the value of the lien of the unpaid vendor, so that the vendor was (apart from that exception) in the same position as a bare trustee. Russell J rejected this argument and held that the unpaid vendor of shares remaining on the register after the contract retains, vis-à-vis the purchaser, the prima facie right to vote in respect of those shares (see [1962] 1 All ER 201 at 208). He could, no doubt, be restrained by injunction, or made liable after the event in damages, if the right were exercised in a manner inconsistent with the contract. But it seems to me that it is impossible to say, in those circumstances, that he holds the voting rights in a fiduciary capacity for the purchaser even if, because of the doctrines of equity, he holds the shares themselves in a fiduciary capacity. This is consistent with the proposition that the vendor's trusteeship of the property agreed to be sold does not extend to the pre-completion fruits of the property, or give the purchaser a right to possession. For that reason, it seems to me, [it cannot be established] that the terms and circumstances of the contracts have the result that when the transfer of the building was executed unconditionally, [Marylebone] was other than a subsidiary…'[36]

As Robert Walker LJ was later to comment[37] Lloyd J made a clear distinction 'between the shares themselves and the voting rights, which he seems to have regarded as equivalent or analogous to "fruits" of the shares, or to a right to possession of the shares'.

[17.024] The decision of Lloyd J was appealed to the English Court of Appeal. It was held that Lloyd J had erred in holding that Development did not hold the voting rights in Marylebone *in a fiduciary capacity* for Frogmore. Robert Walker J distinguished the case of *Musselwhite* on the grounds that, there, Russell J had upheld the unpaid vendor's 'prima facie right' to vote in respect of shares registered in his name but that the case

---

[35] [1997] 2 BCLC 166 at 172i per Lloyd J.

[36] [1997] 2 BCLC 166 at 178f–179b.

[37] [1999] 1 BCLC 670 at 680f.

was not authority for the proposition that an unpaid vendor did not owe a purchaser a fiduciary obligation. Robert Walker LJ succinctly summarised the law in England in the following terms:

> 'A registered shareholder who is absolute beneficial owner can vote as he pleases, subject only to rather imprecise constraints imposed by company law (see *Smith v Croft (No 2)* [1987] 3 All ER 909 at 957-958). A registered shareholder who is a nominee must vote in accordance with the directions of the absolute beneficial owner, to whom his voting rights are attributed. A registered shareholder who is vendor under an uncompleted contract is in an intermediate position, a fiduciary but not a nominee, and his voting rights are for the purposes of s 736 in abeyance.'[38]

It was, therefore, held that once Development had executed the uncompleted contract, its shares were held in a *fiduciary capacity* and its voting rights in respect of the shares in Marylebone were in abeyance and, therefore, Marylebone was *not* its subsidiary[39].

[17.025] Section 155(3)(c) and (d) of CA 1963 provides:

> 'In determining whether one company is a subsidiary of another—
>
> …
>
> (c) any shares held or power exercisable by any person by virtue of the provisions of any debentures of the first-mentioned company or of a trust deed for securing any issue of such debentures shall be disregarded;
>
> (d) any shares held or power exercisable by, or by a nominee for, that other or its subsidiary (not being held or exercisable as mentioned in paragraph (c)) shall be treated as not held or exercisable by that other if the ordinary business of that other or its subsidiary, as the case may be, includes the lending of money and the shares are held or power is exercisable as aforesaid by way of security only for the purposes of a transaction entered into in the ordinary course of that business.'

Section 155(3)(c) of CA 1963 requires that shares held or powers exercisable by any person by virtue of the provisions of a debenture given by the company or of a trust deed for securing any issue of debentures, must be disregarded. The effect of CA 1963, s 155(3)(d) is to preclude financial institutions from inadvertently being deemed to be the holding company of a company whose shares, for example, are held by the financial institution, its subsidiary or its nominee as security for a loan made to the company.

(d) A subsidiary of a subsidiary

[17.026] Section 155(1)(b) of CA 1963 provides that a company shall be another company's subsidiary where 'the first-mentioned company is a subsidiary of any company which is that other's subsidiary'. So, a subsidiary of a company that is itself a subsidiary of a third company, is deemed to be a subsidiary of the third company.

---

[38] [1999] 1 BCLC 670 at 682d–e. See, further, Chapter 16, *Share Transfers in Private Companies*, para **[16.068]**.

[39] Although the consequence was that the disposal was a 'relevant disposal' for the purposes of the Landlord and Tenant Act 1987 (UK), the court exercised its discretion (as permitted under the Act) and rejected the appeal on the grounds that the plaintiffs had not acted sufficiently promptly.

(e) Wholly-owned subsidiaries

[17.027] There are subsidiaries and there are subsidiaries. In places, the Companies Acts 1963–2001 refer to 'wholly-owned subsidiaries'. This term is defined by CA 1963, s 150(5) as follows:

> '…a body corporate shall be deemed to be the wholly owned subsidiary of another if it has no members except that other and that other's wholly-owned subsidiaries and its or their nominees.'

If the 'and' is read as a conjunction, it would seem to imply that a wholly-owned subsidiary *must* have two members. It must be remembered, of course, that s 150(5) dates from a time when the only single-member company was the de facto kind, one shareholder being the other's nominee. Section 150(5) is, however, expressly stated to be 'for the purposes of *this* section' ie CA 1963, s 150 which concerns the obligation to lay group accounts before a holding company[40]. One can only speculate at what precisely the legislature means by the reference to 'wholly-owned subsidiary' in CA 1990, s 29(6) and (7)(a)[41], where the term is used but not defined.

Definitions of undertakings, parent undertakings and subsidiary undertakings for group accounting purposes

[17.028] The obligation to prepare group accounts has been considered in Chapter 13[42]. That obligation arises under the European Communities (Companies: Group Accounts) Regulations 1992 (the '1992 Regulations')[43] and turns upon an entity being a 'parent undertaking', which is defined as 'an undertaking that has one or more subsidiary undertakings'[44]. The 1992 Regulations apply to an 'undertaking', which is defined by reg 3(1) as meaning:

> 'a body corporate, a partnership, or an unincorporated body of persons engaged for gain in the production, supply or distribution of goods, the provision of a service or the making or holding of investments.'

Just as CA 1963, s 155, in applying to bodies corporate, expands its scope beyond 'companies' within the meaning of CA 1963, s 2, so too are the 1992 Regulations widely cast.

[17.029] Central to the definition of 'parent undertaking' is the definition ascribed to 'subsidiary undertaking'. This is defined by reg 4(1) of the 1992 Regulations, which provides:

> 'For the purposes of these Regulations, an undertaking shall be deemed to be a subsidiary of another, if but only if—

---

40 See Chapter 13, *Accounts and Auditors*, para **[13.109]**.

41 See Chapter 11, *Statutory Regulation of Transactions Involving Directors and their Companies*, para **[11.035]**.

42 See para **[13.118]** *ff*.

43 SI 1992/201.

44 SI 1992/201, reg 3(1).

(a) that other—

(i) holds a majority of the shareholders' or members' voting rights in the undertaking, or

(ii) is a shareholder or member of it and controls the composition of its board of directors, or

(iii) is a shareholder or member of it and controls alone, pursuant to an agreement with other shareholders or members, a majority of the shareholders' or members' voting rights; or

(b) that other has the right to exercise a dominant influence over it—

(i) by virtue of provisions contained in its memorandum or articles, or

(ii) by virtue of a control contract; or

(c) that other has a participating interest in it and—

(i) that other actually exercises a dominant influence over it, or

(ii) that other and the subsidiary undertaking are managed on a unified basis; or

(d) the undertaking is a subsidiary of any undertaking which is that other's subsidiary undertaking.'

There are a number of similarities between the 1992 Regulations and CA 1963, s 155; there are, however, also a number of major differences. The principal differences concern the two extra circumstances in which one entity will be deemed to be the subsidiary of another entity. Regulation 4(1)(b) operates to deem one undertaking the subsidiary of another where that other has the right to exercise a 'dominant influence' over it. Regulation 4(1)(c) contains a basis that is even more removed than those in s 155, namely, where that other has a 'participating interest' in the undertaking. It is also noteworthy that the 1992 Regulations refer to 'parent' undertakings as opposed to 'holding' undertakings, the term used in CA 1963, s 155. Such is the inter-changeability of both terms in common speech, that it is not safe to assume that the use of either expression refers to a group within the meaning of either CA 1963 or the 1992 Regulations. The salient features of the regulation 4 definition are next considered:

(a) Controlling the composition of the board of directors.

(b) Shares held/powers exercisable by 'nominees'.

(c) Circumstances in which voting rights shall be discounted.

(d) The meaning of 'dominant influence'.

(e) The meaning of 'participating influence'.

(f) The meaning of associated undertaking.

(a) Controlling the composition of the board of directors

[17.030] Regulation 3(2) expressly provides that the definition of 'control' in CA 1963, s 155 applies to the use of that term in the 1992 Regulations:

> 'In determining whether one undertaking controls the composition of the board of directors of another for the purposes of paragraph 1(a)(ii), subsection (2) of section 155 of the Principal Act shall apply to undertakings subject to these Regulations as it applies to companies subject to that section.'

In this respect, the issues considered above are equally applicable to the 1992 Regulations[45].

(b) Shares held/ powers exercisable by 'nominees'

[17.031] The 1992 Regulations also distinguish between shares held and powers exercisable by persons who are both the legal and beneficial owner from those who are nominees, and so bare trustees. Regulation 3(3) provides:

> 'For the purposes of paragraph (1)(a)—
>
> (a) subject to paragraphs (c) and (d), any shares held or power exercisable—
>
> (i) by any person as a nominee for that other; or
>
> (ii) by, or by a nominee for, a subsidiary undertaking of that other, not being the subsidiary undertaking whose shares or board of directors are involved;
>
> shall be treated as held or exercisable by that other,
>
> (b) any shares held or power exercisable by that other or a subsidiary undertaking of that other, on behalf of a person or undertaking that is neither that other nor a subsidiary undertaking of that other shall be treated as not held or exercisable by that other,
>
> (c) any shares held or power exercisable by that other or a nominee for that other or its subsidiary undertaking shall be treated as not held or exercisable by that other if they are held as aforesaid by way of security provided that such power or the rights attaching to such shares are exercised in accordance with instructions received from the person providing the security,
>
> (d) any shares held or power exercisable by that other or a nominee for that other or its subsidiary undertaking shall be treated as not held or exercisable by that other if the ordinary business of that other or its subsidiary undertaking, as the case may be, includes the lending of money and the shares are held as aforesaid by way of security provided that such power or the rights attaching to such shares are exercised in the interests of the person providing the security.'

One of the most significant differences between CA 1963, s 155 and the 1992 Regulations is that the regulations are silent on the consequence of shares being held in a fiduciary capacity, as distinct from shares being held by a nominee. So, it would seem that the shares of a registered shareholder who is a vendor-undertaking under an uncompleted contract, which will be held in a fiduciary capacity but not as a nominee are considered to be held by the vendor-undertaking and not held in abeyance, as they would under s 155[46]. Again, the effect of this is to mean that undertakings will be deemed to be in a group for group accounting purposes in circumstances where they would not be a group within the meaning of s 155.

(c) Circumstances in which voting rights shall be discounted

[17.032] Regulation 4(4) of the 1992 Regulations details three specific circumstances in which the total of the voting rights of shareholders or members in a subsidiary undertaking shall be reduced. It provides:

---

45 See para **[17.011]**.

46 *Michaels v Harley House (Marylebone) Ltd* [1999] 1 BCLC 670. See para **[17.022]**.

'For the purposes of paragraphs (1)(a)(i) and (ii), the total of the voting rights of the shareholders or members in the subsidiary undertaking shall be reduced by the following—

(a) the voting rights attached to shares held by the subsidiary undertaking in itself, and

(b) the voting rights attached to shares held in the subsidiary undertaking by any of its subsidiary undertakings, and

(c) the voting rights attached to shares held by a person acting in his own name but on behalf of the subsidiary undertaking or one of its subsidiary undertakings.'

(d) The meaning of 'dominant influence'

[17.033] One of the grounds by which an undertaking shall, under the 1992 Regulations, be deemed to be a subsidiary undertaking is where another undertaking has the right to exercise a 'dominant influence' over it. The key to whether or not a dominant influence exists is whether one undertaking has the right to give directions 'with respect to the operating and financial policies' of another. That this is the guiding feature is made clear by reg 4(5), which provides:

'For the purposes of paragraph 1(b) an undertaking shall not be regarded as having the right to exercise a dominant influence over another undertaking unless it has a right to give directions with respect to the operating and financial policies of that other undertaking which its directors are obliged to comply with.'

It seems clear that, in order to be reckonable, an undertaking must have a legally enforceable *right* to give directions. A de facto 'right' will not suffice.

[17.034] Of particular significance is the fact that an undertaking will be deemed by this provision to be the parent undertaking of another *without being a member or holding any shares in the other undertaking*. This basis for the creation and subsistence of a parent-subsidiary relationship is unique to the 1992 Regulations and does not have a parallel in CA 1963, s 155. Accordingly, two companies that are required to prepare group accounts solely on the basis of the deeming provision in reg 4(1)(b) of the 1992 Regulations will not be a holding and subsidiary company for the purposes of s 155 and will not, for example, be able to avail of the benefits of being in a group for general company law purposes. The regulations state that the dominant influence can arise by virtue of either of two means: (a) provisions in its memorandum or articles (reg 4(1)(b)(i)) or (b) by virtue of a control contract (reg 4(1)(b)(ii)).

[17.035] The reference to the right to exercise a dominant influence by virtue of provisions contained in a body's memorandum or articles, would seem to refer to the memorandum or articles of the subsidiary undertaking. The circumstances in which reg 4(1)(b)(i) of the 1992 Regulations alone will give rise to a parent-subsidiary relationship are thought to be rare because, under Irish law, a right conferred by the memorandum and articles on a party who is not a member of the company is not enforceable[47].

---

[47] *Eley v Positive Government Security Life Assurance Co* (1876) 1 Ex D 88 and CA 1963, s 25. See Chapter 3, *The Constitutional Documentation*, para **[3.103]** where the case law that interprets s 25 is considered.

[17.036] The other way in which an undertaking will be considered to have a 'dominant influence' is where it has the right to exercise such by virtue of a 'control contract': reg 4(1)(b)(ii) of the 1992 Regulations. The meaning of a 'control contract' is provided by reg 4(6):

> 'A "control contract" as specified in paragraph 1(b) means a contract in writing conferring such a right which—
>
> (a) is of a kind authorised by the memorandum or articles of the undertaking in relation to which the right is exercisable, and
>
> (b) is permitted by the law under which that undertaking is established.'

An undertaking will, therefore, be the subsidiary undertaking of another undertaking where there is a contract, which gives the parent the right to exercise a 'dominant influence', without the parent ever having to hold shares in or be a member of the subsidiary.

(e) The meaning of 'participating influence'

[17.037] Another basis by which an undertaking will be deemed to be a parent undertaking is where it has a participating interest in, and *actually*[48] exercises, a 'dominant influence' or where both undertakings are managed on a unified basis. This basis is also foreign to the general definition in CA 1963, s 155. Regulation 35(1) of the 1992 Regulations defines what is meant by a 'participating interest':

> 'A "participating interest" means a qualifying capital interest held by one undertaking in another on a long term basis for the purpose of securing a contribution to that undertaking's own activities by the exercise of control or influence arising from or related to that interest.'

Unlike the 'dominant influence' basis considered above, to give rise to a parent-subsidiary relationship on this basis, the parent must have an interest in the capital of the subsidiary. Regulation 35(2) goes on to define what is meant by a 'qualifying capital interest' in the following terms:

> '(a) in relation to an undertaking with share capital means an interest in shares comprised in the allotted share capital of that undertaking,
>
> (b) in relation to an undertaking with capital but no share capital means an interest conferring rights to share in the capital of the undertaking,
>
> (c) in relation to an undertaking without capital means interests—
>
> (i) conferring any right to share in the profits or liability to contribute to the losses of the undertaking, or
>
> (ii) giving rise to an obligation to contribute to the debts or expenses of the undertaking in the event of a winding up; and
>
> (d) includes an interest which is convertible into a qualifying capital interest as well as an option to acquire any such qualifying capital interest.'

Regulation 35(3) provides that where an undertaking holds a qualifying capital interest in another undertaking and such an interest represents 20% or more of all such interests

48 See para **[17.038]**.

in the other undertaking it shall be presumed to hold that interest on the basis and for the purpose mentioned in reg 35(1) unless the contrary is shown[49].

[17.038] In addition to having a participating interest, the holder of such an interest must *actually exercise a dominant influence*. 'Dominant influence' has been considered above and it was observed that to be cognisable, reg 4(5) required it to be, inter alia, a legally enforceable right to give directions with respect to operating and financial policies. This is watered-down in the context of the nature of the dominant influence required where the holder has a 'participating interest'. Thus, reg 4(7) provides that reg 4(5) shall not be read as affecting the construction of the expression 'actually exercises a dominant influence' in reg 4(1)(c).

(f) The meaning of associated undertaking

[17.039] Another label, which arises from the 1992 Regulations, is that of an 'associated undertaking'[50]. Regulation 34 of the 1992 Regulations provides:

> '(1) For the purposes of these Regulations an "associated undertaking" means an undertaking in which an undertaking dealt with in the group accounts has a participating interest and over whose operating and financial policy it exercises a significant influence and which is not—
>
> (a) a subsidiary undertaking of the parent undertaking, or
>
> (b) a joint venture proportionally consolidated in accordance with Regulation 32.
>
> (2) Where an undertaking holds 20 per cent or more of the voting rights in another undertaking, it shall be presumed to exercise such an influence over it unless the contrary is shown.'

Moreover, reg 34(3) provides that paragraphs (3) and (4) of reg 4 shall apply in determining for the purposes of this Regulation whether an undertaking holds 20% or more of the voting rights in another undertaking.

Capital maintenance definitions of parent public companies and public company subsidiaries

[17.040] The European Communities (Public Limited Companies Subsidiaries) Regulations 1997 (the '1997 Regulations')[51] extends the meaning of 'subsidiary', as

---

49 SI 1992/201, reg 35(4) provides that the percentage of qualifying capital interests held in an undertaking with share capital shall be the percentage that the nominal value of the shares held represents of the nominal value of the allotted share capital of that undertaking. Regulation 35(5) provides that for the purpose of this regulation an interest held on behalf of an undertaking shall be treated as held by it. Moreover, reg 35(6) provides that for the purposes of the Regulation 35, as it applies in relation to the expression 'participating interest' in reg 4(1)(c) (subsidiary undertaking): '(a) there shall be attributed to an undertaking any interests held by any of its subsidiary undertakings, and (b) the references in paragraph (1) to the purpose and activities of an undertaking include the purpose and activities of any of its subsidiary undertakings and of the group as a whole.' Finally, reg 35(7) provides that in the Balance Sheet and Profit and Loss Account Formats set out in the C(A)A 1986, Schedule, as amended by the Schedule to these Regulations, 'participating interest' does not include an interest in a group undertaking.

50 For the significance of associated undertakings, see Chapter 13, *Accounts and Auditors*, para **[13.151]**.

51 SI 1997/67.

defined by CA 1963, s 155, for the purposes of CA 1990, Part XI which deals with the acquisition of own shares and shares in a company's holding company[52]. Regulation 4(1) of the 1997 Regulations provides:

> 'For the purposes of Part XI of the Act of 1990, in addition to the circumstances where a company (including a body corporate) is deemed to be a subsidiary of a public limited company by virtue of section 155 of the Principal Act, a limited company (including a body corporate) within the meaning of paragraph (2) shall also be deemed to be a subsidiary of a public limited company if, but only if, the public limited company is itself a shareholder or member of the said limited company and controls alone, pursuant to an agreement with other shareholders or members, a majority of the shareholders' or members' voting rights in the company in question.'

This extended definition borrows from the 1992 Regulations, considered above[53], the expression, a 'majority of the shareholders' or members' voting rights'. Again, it is important to note that where a company is deemed to be the subsidiary of another company (a parent public company) for the purposes of CA 1990, Part XI, solely by reason of the 1997 Regulations, it will not be a subsidiary within the meaning of CA 1963, s 155 and may not avail of the advantages conferred by other provisions of the Companies Acts 1963–2001 which are expressed to apply to a group of companies within the meaning of s 155.

Taxation definitions of holding and subsidiary companies

(a) Corporation tax

[17.041] The Taxes Consolidation Act 1997 distinguishes between three different types of subsidiaries[54], based on different degrees of ownership. The different types of subsidiary are:

(a) A 51% subsidiary;

(b) A 75% subsidiary;

(c) A 90% subsidiary.

Section 9(1) of the Taxes Consolidation Act 1997 provides:

> 'For the purposes of the Tax Acts, except where otherwise provided, a company shall be deemed to be—
>
> (a) a "51 per cent subsidiary" of another company if and so long as more than 50 per cent of its ordinary share capital is owned directly or indirectly by that other company,
>
> (b) a "75 per cent subsidiary" of another company if and so long as not less than 75 per cent of its ordinary share capital is owned directly or indirectly by that other company,
>
> (c) a "90 per cent subsidiary" of another company if and so long as not less than 90 per cent of its ordinary share capital is directly owned by that other company.'

52 See, generally, Chapter 18, *The Maintenance of Capital*, para **[18.017]** *ff*.

53 See para **[17.029]** *ff*.

54 See, generally, Feeney, *The Taxation of Companies 2002*, p 30 *ff*.

The main distinction between the three categories of subsidiary is that in the case of 51% and 75% subsidiaries, on the one hand, and 90% subsidiaries, on the other, in the case of the latter the shares must be *directly* owned by the holding company. In the case of both 51% and 75% subsidiaries, it is sufficient that the requisite percentage of shares held in the subsidiary is owned *directly or indirectly* by the holding company. 'Owned directly or indirectly' is defined by s 9(2) of the Act as meaning 'owned whether directly or through another company or other companies or partly directly and partly through another company or other companies.'

The reference to 'ownership' is defined to mean 'beneficial ownership'.[55]

[17.042] For the purposes of s 9 of the Taxes Consolidation Act 1997 the amount of ordinary share capital of one company owned by a second company through another company or other companies, or partly directly and partly through another company or other companies, shall be determined in accordance with sub-ss (5) to (10)[56]. These rules are:

> '(5) Where, in the case of a number of companies, the first directly owns ordinary share capital of the second and the second directly owns ordinary share capital of the third, then, for the purposes of this section, the first shall be deemed to own ordinary share capital of the third through the second and, if the third directly owns ordinary share capital of a fourth, the first shall be deemed to own ordinary share capital of the fourth through the second and third, and the second shall be deemed to own ordinary share capital of the fourth through the third, and so on.
>
> (6) In this section—
>
> (a) any number of companies of which the first directly owns ordinary share capital of the next and the next directly owns ordinary share capital of the next but one and so on, and, if there are more than 3, any 3 or more of them, are referred to as a 'series';
>
> (b) in any series—
>
> (i) that company which owns ordinary share capital of another through the remainder is referred to as "the first owner";
>
> (ii) that other company the ordinary share capital of which is so owned is referred to as "the last owned company";
>
> (iii) the remainder, if one only, is referred to as an "intermediary" and, if more than one, are referred to as, a chain of intermediaries;
>
> (c) a company in a series which directly owns ordinary share capital of another company in the series is referred to as an "owner";
>
> (d) any 2 companies in a series of which one owns ordinary share capital of the other directly, and not through one or more of the other companies in the series, are referred to as being directly related to one another.
>
> (7) Where every owner in a series owns the whole of the ordinary share capital of the company to which it is directly related, the first owner shall be deemed to own through the intermediary or chain of intermediaries the whole of the ordinary share capital of the last owned company.

55 Taxes Consolidation Act 1997, s 9(3).

56 Taxes Consolidation Act 1997, s 9(4).

(8) Where one of the owners in a series owns a fraction of the ordinary share capital of the company to which it is directly related, and every other owner in the series owns the whole of the ordinary share capital of the company to which it is directly related, the first owner shall be deemed to own that fraction of the ordinary share capital of the last owned company through the intermediary or chain of intermediaries.

(9) Where—

(a) each of 2 or more of the owners in a series owns a fraction, and every other owner in the series owns the whole, of the ordinary share capital of the company to which it is directly related, or

(b) every owner in a series owns a fraction of the ordinary share capital of the company to which it is directly related,

the first owner shall be deemed to own through the intermediary or chain of intermediaries such fraction of the ordinary share capital of the last owned company as results from the multiplication of those fractions.

(10) Where the first owner in any series owns a fraction of the ordinary share capital of the last owned company in that series through the intermediary or chain of intermediaries in that series, and also owns another fraction or other fractions of the ordinary share capital of the last owned company, either—

(a) directly,

(b) through an intermediary which is not a member, or intermediaries which are not members, of that series,

(c) through a chain or chains of intermediaries of which one or some or all are not members of that series, or

(d) in a case where the series consists of more than 3 companies, through an intermediary which is a member, or intermediaries which are members, of the series, or through a chain or chains of intermediaries consisting of some but not all of the companies of which the chain of intermediaries in the series consists,

then, for the purpose of ascertaining the amount of the ordinary share capital of the last owned company owned by the first owner, all those fractions shall be aggregated and the first owner shall be deemed to own the sum of those fractions.'

[17.043] It is beyond the scope of this book to consider the consequences in taxation law of a subsidiary being deemed to be in any of the three categories recognised by the 1997 Act. Suffice it to say that the availability of various reliefs under the Taxes Consolidation Act 1997 are determined by reference to which category a subsidiary belongs[57].

(b) Stamp duty

[17.044] It may also be noted here that exemptions and relief from certain stamp duties [58] between group companies is not based on the definition of CA 1963, s 155 [59]. Rather, the

57 See Feeney, *The Taxation of Companies 2002*.

58 Namely: (a) conveyance or transfer on sale of stocks or marketable securities; (b) conveyance or transfer on sale of a policy of insurance or a policy of life insurance where the risk to which the policy relates is located in the state; and (c) conveyance or transfer on sale of any property (eg land and buildings) other than stocks or marketable securities or a policy or insurance or a policy of life insurance: Stamp Duties Consolidation Act 1999, s 79(1).

59 See, generally, Donegan and Friel, *Irish Stamp Duty Law* (2nd edn, 1998), pp 169–182.

exemption and relief applies as respect dispositions between 'associated bodies'. 'Associated bodies' are defined by s 79(3) of the Stamp Duties Consolidation Act 1999 as:

> '...that is, one was the beneficial owner of not less than 90 per cent of the issued share capital of the other, or a third such body was the beneficial owner of not less than 90 per cent of the issued share capital of each and that this ownership was ownership either directly or through another body corporate or other bodies corporate, or partly directly and partly through another body corporate or other bodies corporate, and subsections (5) to (10) of section 9 of the Taxes Consolidation Act 1997, shall apply for the purposes of this section as if—
>
> (a) references to body corporate were references to company,
>
> (b) references to bodies corporate were references to companies, and
>
> (c) references to issued share capital were references to ordinary share capital.'

Accordingly, the Stamp Duties Consolidation Act 1999, s 79(4) creates a fourth category of subsidiary for the purposes of stamp duty exemption and relief, namely a 90% subsidiary in which the shares are held, whether directly or indirectly. The section provides that, in addition to meeting the conditions in sub-s (3), at the time of the execution of the otherwise stampable instrument, the holding company must be beneficially entitled to not less than 90% of any profits available for distribution to the shareholders of the subsidiary *and* to not less than 90% of any assets of the subsidiary[60] for distribution to its shareholders on a winding up[61]. It should be noted that there are other qualifying conditions too (eg that the consideration is not paid directly or indirectly by an outsider)[62].

[17.045] The important point to take from the foregoing brief excursion into revenue law is the reinforcement of the point that whilst one company may or may not be the subsidiary of another company as defined by CA 1963, s 155, it may or may not:

(a) have its own share purchases or those in its holding company regulated by CA 1990, Part XI; and

(b) be able to avail of exemptions or be subject to provisions of the tax code.

Select Issues in the holding-subsidiary relationship

[17.046] Throughout this book there are references to specific issues that apply only or primarily to groups of companies. These issues are best considered in the context of

60 Or, if the disposition is between two subsidiaries, that a third–party holding company is entitled to not less than 90% of any profits available for distribution to the shareholders of each and to not less than 90% of any assets available for distribution to the shareholders of each on a winding up.

61 Stamp Duties Consolidation Act 1999, s 79(4)(a) and (b). The percentage to which a body corporate is beneficially entitled of any profits available for distribution and of any assets on a winding up means 'the percentage to which the first body corporate is, or would be, so entitled either directly or through another body corporate or other bodies corporate or partly directly and partly through another body corporate or other bodies corporate.' See also Stamp Duties Consolidation Act 1999, s 79(8).

62 See, further, Donegan and Friel, *Irish Stamp Duty Law* (3rd edn, 2001), pp 175–188.

their natural generic environment. It is thought, however, that two group-specific issues should be alluded to here, by reason of their fundamental importance to groups of companies.

(a) The sanctity of the separate legal personality of group companies.

(b) Group companies' directors' and holding companies' duties.

(a) The sanctity of the separate legal personality of group companies

[17.047] The general circumstances in which the courts have disregarded separate corporate personality have been considered in detail in Chapter 5, *Disregarding Separate Legal Personality*[63], as have the circumstances when the courts have treated a group of companies as a single economic entity[64]. It is useful, however, to mention here the general or orthodox[65] principle that a parent company and its subsidiaries are to be treated as separate entities. So, in *Re Frederick Inns Ltd*[66], Lardner J said (and the Supreme Court endorsed):

> 'A fundamental attribute of a company in Irish law is that of corporate personality. A company is a legal entity distinct from its members, capable of enjoying rights and of being subject to duties which are not the same as those enjoyed or borne by its members. This was finally established in *Salomon v Salomon and Company Ltd* (1897) AC 22 and the principle has been recognised and applied in many decisions of the Irish courts. Generally speaking this principle and the statutory rules of company law in which the principle is implicit apply to the relationship between holding companies and subsidiaries and to transactions between them and third parties. The assets of such companies are treated as owned by them legally and beneficially as distinct legal entities. And except where circumstances enable a court to discover an agency or trustee relationship between them, a holding company is not treated as owner of its subsidiaries' assets. And the liabilities of companies which are members of the same group are those of the individual companies which incur them. There is no common group liability for the obligations of individual members of the group imposed by law. The principle is reflected in many aspects of company law; for example in s 147 of the Companies Act 1963 every company (whether a holding company or a subsidiary) is required to keep proper books of account which must include accounts of all sums of money received and expended by the company…'[67].

An example of the statutory recognition of group companies' separate legal personality is seen in the Companies (Amendment) Act 1986, s 17(1)(b). That provision exempts subsidiaries that are private companies from certain requirements of the Act provided their holding company have entered into an irrevocable guarantee of their subsidiaries'

---

63 See para **[5.010]** *ff*.

64 See para **[5.050]** *ff*.

65 See Milman, 'Groups: Recurrent Issues of Status' (1997) *Palmer's In Company*, Issue 2/97.

66 *Re Frederick Inns Ltd* [1991] ILRM 582 (HC), [1994] 1 ILRM 387 (SC).

67 [1991] ILRM 582 at 587.

liabilities[68], the clear implication being that a holding company is not automatically liable for its subsidiaries' liabilities.

[17.048] In *Allied Irish Coal Supplies Ltd v Powell Duffryn International Fuel Ltd*[69], after noting that CA 1963, ss 150-154 require, in certain circumstances, the production of group accounts, the Supreme Court (per Murphy J) said that whilst that legislation recognised that trading parents and subsidiaries 'may require to be viewed as an economic entity...there is no question of that legislation making the assets of one company within the group liable for the debts of another'[70]. The distinction between 'legal substance' and 'economic substance' has also been made in England: in *Re Polly Peck International plc (in administration)*[71] Robert Walker J said:

> '...I think that [counsel] is in one sense assuming what he seeks to prove, since the unjust or inequitable result which he asserts does not occur unless the group is recognised as being in substance a single economic entity, whose constituent members' internal rights and obligations are to be disregarded. But the authorities to which I have already referred show that substance means legal substance, not economic substance (if different), and that ...the separate legal existence of group companies is particularly important when creditors become involved. Injustice may be in the eye of the beholder, but I do not perceive any obvious injustice – certainly not such as the court can remedy – in the unpredictable consequences that may follow from the unforeseen insolvency of a large international group of companies such as the Polly Peck group'.[72]

There will be circumstances where a group of companies can be found to be an single economic entity such as to justify the disregard of their separate corporateness, but these will be exceptional[73].

---

68 Cf the apparent anomaly in CA 1990, s 34 which purports to exempt only certain guarantees, otherwise prohibited by CA 1990, s 31 from being made by a company that is a holding company in favour of its subsidiaries: see Chapter 11, *Statutory Regulation of Transactions Involving Directors and their Companies*, para **[11.094]**.

69 *Allied Irish Coal Supplies Ltd v Powell Duffryn International Fuel Ltd* [1998] 2 IR 519 .

70 (19 December 1997, unreported), Supreme Court at p 12. In *Allied Irish Coal Supplies Ltd v Powell Duffryn International Fuels Ltd* (19 June 1996, unreported), High Court Laffoy J rejected the notion that the companies there were a single economic entity and held that the principle 'cannot be utilised to render the assets of a parent company available to meet the liabilities of a trading subsidiary to a party with whom it has traded'. This was upheld by the Supreme Court (per Murphy J) who said that the proposition that the assets of a parent company should be available to meet the liabilities of a trading subsidiary was so fundamentally at variance with the principle of separate corporate personality as to be wholly unstatable.

71 *Re Polly Peck International plc (in administration)* [1996] 2 All ER 433.

72 [1996] 2 All ER 433 at 488e–g.

73 See generally *DHN Food Distributors Ltd v Tower Hamlet London Borough Council* [1976] 3 All ER 462; *Power Supermarkets Ltd v Crumlin Investments Ltd and Dunnes Stores (Crumlin) Ltd*, (22 June 1981, unreported), High Court; *Re Bray Travel and Bray Travel (Holdings) Ltd* (13 July 1981, unreported), Supreme Court; *Rex Pet Foods Ltd v Lamb Bros (Dublin) Ltd* (5 December 1985, unreported), High Court, *Adams v Cape Industries* [1990] Ch 433, discussed at Chapter 5, *Disregarding Separate Corporate Personality*, para **[5.050]** *ff*.

[17.049] In *Ringway Roadmarking v Adbruf Ltd*[74] the terms of a contract provided that either party could terminate it if a controlling shareholding in a party to the agreement passed to a new owner. The defendant-company wished to increase its prices to the plaintiff-company under the contract but the plaintiff declined. With the intention of triggering the provision in the contract that gave rise to its termination, the defendant-company's holding company transferred its shares in the defendant-company to another subsidiary. It was held that although the ownership of the shares in the defendant-company had been transferred, to read 'new owner' as referring to a subsidiary company which had bought shares from the holding company did not reflect the purpose and intention of the parties. Accordingly, the defendant-company was held not to be entitled to terminate the contract.

(b) Group companies' directors' and holding companies' duties

[17.050] Directors' duties are primarily owed to the company of which they are directors[75]. It follows from the principle in *Salomon v Saloman & Co Ltd*[76] that the duties owed by directors of group companies are to their individual companies. This can sometimes result in directors of group companies being placed in a 'difficult and delicate position'[77] which will be exacerbated where the subsidiary is not wholly owned by its parent. A stark example of an abusive relationship is provided by *Scottish Co-operative Wholesale Society Ltd v Meyer*[78] where it was observed that:

> '…in all the evidence I have not been able to find the least trace that they [the directors] regarded themselves as owing any duty to the company of which they were directors. They were the nominees of the society and, if the society doomed the company to destruction, it was not for them to put out a saving hand. Rather, they were to join in that work, and, when a frank and prompt statement to their co-directors might have enabled them to retrieve its fortunes, they played their part by maintaining silence.'[79]

The position of and duties owed by nominee directors have been considered in a previous chapter[80]. What is clear is that where a subsidiary company is fraudulently abused through the actions or at the sufferance of its nominee directors, not only will those directors be accountable, but so too will the holding company which appointed them. In the *Meyer* case it would seem that there was a special relationship between the company and the society which was analogous to partnership in substance, though not law[81]. This will not be so in every case. Neither is it true, in every case, that the apparently gratuitous act or omission by a subsidiary in favour of its holding company

---

[74] *Ringway Roadmarking v Adbruf Ltd* [1998] 2 BCLC 625.

[75] *Percival v Wright* [1902] 2 Ch 421. See, generally, Chapter 10, *Duties of Directors and Other Officers*, and, on nominee directors, para **[10.006]**.

[76] *Salomon v Saloman & Co Ltd* [1897] AC 222.

[77] See *Scottish Co-operative Wholesale Society Ltd v Meyer* [1959] AC 324 at 341, per Viscount Simonds.

[78] *Scottish Co-operative Wholesale Society Ltd v Meyer* [1959] AC 324.

[79] [1959] AC 324 at 341.

[80] See Chapter 10, *Duties of Directors and Other Officers*, para **[10.040]** *ff.*

[81] See, Lower, 'Good Faith and the Partly-Owned Subsidiary' [2000] JBL 232 at 246–247.

will mean that there has been an actionable (or even moral) breach of duty. In *Re PMPA Garage (Longmile) Ltd*[82] Murphy J observed:

> 'In the nature of things companies associated with each other as parent and subsidiary or through common shareholders or who share common management and common titles or logos cannot safely ignore the problems of each other. Even the most independently minded director of any such related company seeking to advance the interests of a particular company would necessarily recognise that he should and perhaps must protect the interests of the group as a whole or else take steps to secure that the particular company disassociates itself from the group.'

Equally it is thought that there will be occasions when it will be legitimate for the directors of a subsidiary (or holding company) to sacrifice either company's short term interests for the good of the group[83].

---

82 *Re PMPA Garage (Longmile) Ltd* [1992] ILRM 337.

83 See, Lower, 'Good Faith and the Partly–Owned Subsidiary' [2000] JBL 232 at 245.

Chapter 18

The Maintenance of Capital

Introduction

[18.001] This chapter is concerned with the rules of share capital maintenance. A company can acquire finance in one of three ways. In the first place it can acquire loan capital by borrowing money from either internal sources (members or directors) or external sources (lending institutions or private investors). This method of acquiring capital is considered below in Chapters 20, 21 and 22[1]. In the second place, a company can acquire capital through the issue of shares. This is referred to as share capital and it is the maintenance of share capital that is the concern of this chapter. Share capital is generally intended to be permanently[2] invested in a company. Here, a distinction may be drawn between the owner of the share capital, who may change, and the capital itself, which will generally remain intact. Loan capital, on the other hand, especially from external sources, is not intended to be permanently invested: loans mature and are repaid. In the third place, it must be remembered that a company can acquire finance by successfully conducting its business and making profits on its investments.

The rationale behind share capital maintenance rules

[18.002] It has always been a basic principle of company law that throughout a company's corporate existence its share capital must remain intact. The traditional rationale for the maintenance of capital is to ensure that a company's creditors can rely upon the existence of the company's share capital to satisfy their claims on a winding up. Furthermore, share capital maintenance rules are designed to protect shareholders from other shareholders, or classes of shareholders, redeeming their shares and getting back their capital.

[18.003] Companies acquire share capital through the issue of shares. The basic rationale for prohibiting a company from buying back its own shares is that the liability of a member of a private limited company is limited to the amount, if any, unpaid on the shares which he holds: were a member permitted to take back the share capital which he contributed to the company, the statutory liability contained in the Companies Act 1963, s 207 ('CA 1963') would be obviated[3]. Although the liability imposed by s 207 on the members of many private companies is largely illusory in practice, this would seem to continue to be the primary rationale behind the rules on capital maintenance. A judicial expression of the rationale behind share capital maintenance rules is seen in *Guinness v Land Corporation of Ireland*[4], where Cotton LJ said of a predecessor of CA 1963, s 207 that it:

---

1 Chapter 20, *Corporate Borrowing: Debentures and Security*; Chapter 21, *Corporate Borrowing: Registration of Charges*; and Chapter 22, *Corporate Borrowing: Receivers*.

2 Subject to the permitted methods of share capital reduction, considered below.

3 See Chapter 15, *Shares and Membership*, para **[15.074]**; and Chapter 27, *Realisation and Distribution of Assets in Winding Up*, para **[27.117]**.

4 *Guinness v Land Corporation of Ireland* (1882) 22 Ch D 349.

> '...provides that in the case of a company limited by shares being wound up, no contribution shall be required from any member exceeding the amount if any unpaid on the shares in respect of which he is liable as a present or past member; that the capital of the company as mentioned in the memorandum is to be the fund which is to pay the creditors in the event of the company being wound up. *From this it follows that whatever has been paid by a member cannot be returned to him*...[Capital]...is, of course liable to be spent or lost in carrying on the business of the company, but no part of it can be returned to a member so as to take away from the fund to which the creditors have a right to look as that out of which they are to be paid.'[5] [Emphasis added]

This is the basic rationale which underlies the rules of share capital maintenance. However, as shall be considered, in no other area of company law is the traditional rationale underlying the law more divorced from the commercial reality.

Private companies and capital maintenance rules

[18.004] The notion that the subscribed share capital in a private company is a creditors' fund will frequently be little more than a nonsense in many private companies. While a company may well have an *authorised* share capital of €1,000,000 divided into one million €1 shares, its *issued* share capital will often be as little as €1: because a private company may have as few as one shareholder, the result is that the 'creditors' fund' may be as little as €1[6]. Accordingly, there is a vast difference between private companies and public limited companies ('PLCs') because, by virtue of the Companies (Amendment) Act 1983, s 19, ('C(A)A 1983') PLCs must have a minimum *issued* share capital of €38,092.14[7]. However, the rules of capital maintenance still have relevance to many private companies because of the fact that the *nominal* value of a share will not, in a successful company, reflect the actual *market value* of that share. Accordingly, where a company has an issued share capital of two €1 shares, but an actual value (total assets *less* total liabilities) of €100,000, each €1 share may have a market value of €50,000. If the company was allowed to buy back one of its two issued €1 shares at market value, the company's worth would fall from €100,000 to €50,000.

[18.005] The foregoing example demonstrates that rules on capital maintenance exist to ensure that the capital of a company is preserved by preventing the dissipation of assets to members. Here the notion of *distributable profits*, as defined by C(A)A 1983, s 45, is important. As will be considered below, the controls on a company acquiring its own shares[8], redeeming its own shares[9] or paying a dividend on its shares[10], all provide that

---

5 (1882) 22 Ch D 349 at 373.

6 Indeed, a company's share capital can be as little as one cent, *ie* one one–cent share issued to the sole member of a single member private limited company as permitted by the European Communities (Single–Member Private Limited Companies) Regulations 1994 (SI 1994/275).

7 It should be noted, however, that not all of the minimum issued share capital of €38,092.14 must be fully paid up, and it is sufficient that only one quarter of the nominal value of shares be paid up: C(A)A 1983, s 28(1) and s 6(3)(b). See Chapter 28, *Public Companies in Context*, para **[28.038]**.

8 See para **[18.017]**.

9 See para **[18.012]**.

10 See para **[18.081]** *ff*.

such potential reductions of capital can be funded only from a company's distributable profits.

[18.006] The only departure from the general principle that a private company is not obliged by law to have a minimum issued share capital is the situation envisaged by the Companies Act 1990, s 150(3) ('CA 1990')[11]. This provides that where a court makes an order restricting a director or other officer of an insolvent company which goes into liquidation, any other company in which the restricted person acts as director or secretary or in which the restricted person is concerned or takes part in its promotion or formation, must meet certain minimum capital requirements. In the case of a private company, the minimum nominal value of the allotted share capital is €63,486.90, which together with any premium must be fully paid up in cash.

[18.007] Although the rationale behind the maintenance of capital in private companies is somewhat of an anomaly, practitioners will frequently encounter the rules on capital maintenance. Some of the most common situations where caution must be exercised include situations where it is proposed:

- to purchase a dissident shareholder's holding in order to maintain control;
- to acquire a business by means of a share purchase as opposed to an asset purchase; where the loan for the acquisition is guaranteed or otherwise secured by the company;
- to divide profits at the end of a joint venture; and
- to pay dividends to the company's members.

It must be remembered that the rules of capital maintenance continue to apply even where the company concerned has few, or even no, creditors.

[18.008] Capital maintenance rules have traditionally been considered to be a shield for shareholders. The rationale was that a shareholder who advanced monies for shares in the company was entitled to assume that his fellow shareholders would not dilute their shareholding in the company. Attempting to rationalise the rules of capital maintenance in the context of single-member companies[12] is consequently rendered even more difficult.

[18.009] If a schism occurs in a quasi-partnership type private company and if one of the members wants to separate from the others, where the remaining members cannot muster sufficient personal finances to buy him out, it may be suggested that the company would either buy back that member's shares or finance the purchase of his shares by the remaining members. This situation could also arise where, in an attempt to maintain control of a private company and to avoid a member selling his shares to an outsider, the remaining members seek to cause the company to purchase the departing member's shares by relying on whatever pre-emption rights are contained in the company's articles of association or in a shareholders' agreement[13]. However, it has

---

[11] See Chapter 12, *Company Law Compliance and Enforcement*, para **[12.043]**.

[12] As permitted by the European Communities (Single-Member Private Limited Companies) Regulations 1994 (SI 1994/275). See generally Chapter 1, *The Private Company in Context*, para **[1.119]** *ff*.

[13] See generally Chapter 16, *Share Transfers in Private Companies*.

been made clear as far back as 1887 in the leading case of *Trevor v Whitworth*[14] that the quite reasonable end of maintaining control in a private family company will not justify breaches of the capital maintenance rules. Lord Herschell said that one suggestion as to why the company in that case bought back its own shares was because the company:

> '...was intended to be a family company, and that the directors wanted to keep the shares as much as possible in the hands of those who were partners, or who were interested in the old firm, or of those persons whom the directors thought they would like to be amongst this small number of shareholders. I cannot think that the employment of the company's money in the purchase of shares for any such purpose was legitimate...I can quite understand that the directors of a company may sometimes desire that the shareholders should not be numerous, and that they should be persons likely to leave them with a free hand to carry on their operations. But I think it would be most dangerous to countenance the view that, for reasons such as these, they could legitimately expend the moneys of the company to any extent they please in the purchase of its shares. No doubt if certain shareholders are disposed to hamper the proceedings of the company, and are willing to sell their shares, they may be bought out; but this must be done by persons, existing shareholders, who can be induced to purchase the shares, and not out of the funds of the company.'[15]

The purchase of a company's shares in circumstances where the remaining shareholders wish to retain control of the company must be financed by persons other than the company itself. This was stated in trenchant terms by Lord MacNaghten who said:

> 'If shareholders think it worth while to spend money for the purpose of getting rid of a troublesome partner who is willing to sell, they may put their hands in their own pockets and buy him out, thought they cannot draw on a fund in which others as well as themselves are interested. That, I think, is the law and that is the good sense of the matter.'[16]

Whatever about the 'good sense' of the rule of law which prevents a company from buying back the shares of a disenchanted member, problems are caused for many private companies where the pockets of the individual shareholders are not deep enough to finance the buy-out of such a dissenting member.

[18.010] One of the more frequently encountered situations where the capital maintenance rules meet commercial practice is where it is proposed to buy the business of a private company by means of a share purchase, as opposed to an asset purchase[17]. Often, the purchasers will propose to finance the purchase of the shares through a lending institution which will be asked to accept, as security for the advance, a charge over the assets of the company. Because in such circumstances the company will be providing financial assistance for the purchase of its own shares, extreme care must be exercised. As shall be considered below[18], CA 1963, s 60 prohibits a private company

---

[14] *Trevor v Whitworth* (1887) 12 App Cas 409. See para **[18.018]**.

[15] (1887) 12 App Cas 409 at 417.

[16] (1887) 12 App Cas 409 at 436.

[17] See Chapter 16, *Share Transfers in Private Companies*, para **[16.099]** *ff.*

[18] See para **[18.041]** *ff.*

from providing such financial assistance, whether directly or indirectly, unless certain steps are taken.

Overview of capital maintenance rules

[18.011] The rules of capital maintenance, as they apply to private companies, shall be considered in this chapter under the following headings:

[A] Redemption of shares.

[B] Acquisition by a company of its own shares.

[C] Assisting the purchase of a company's own shares.

[D] Court sanctioned capital reduction.

[E] Court ordered capital reduction.

[F] Distributions and the payment of dividends.

[G] Miscellaneous capital maintenance rules.

[H] Meetings when there is a serious capital loss.

[A] REDEMPTION OF SHARES

[18.012] Section 207 of CA 1990 allows a company to issue redeemable shares. Redeemable shares lack the permanency normally associated with share capital. Companies are, however, only permitted to issue and redeem redeemable shares provided that the following conditions are met:

— the issue and redemption of redeemable shares is authorised by the company's articles of association[19]; and,

— the nominal value of issued share capital which is *not* redeemable is not less than one-tenth (10%) of the nominal value of the total issued share capital of the company[20]; and,

— the shares redeemed are fully paid[21]; and,

— the terms of redemption provide for payment on redemption[22]; and,

— the funds used to finance the redemption must be from profits which are available for distribution[23]; and,

— where shares are cancelled pursuant to CA 1990, s 208, such shares may also be redeemed out of the proceeds of a fresh issue of shares made for the purposes of redemption[24]; and,

— any premium payable on the redemption of the shares must be paid out of profits available for distribution[25]; and,

19 CA 1990, s 207(1).

20 CA 1990, s 207(2)(a).

21 CA 1990, s 207(2)(b).

22 CA 1990, s 207(2)(c).

23 CA 1990, s 207(2)(d)(i). See para **[18.081]** *ff*.

24 CA 1990, s 207(2)(d)(ii).

25 CA 1990, s 207(2)(e).

— where shares were issued at a premium, any premium payable on their redemption (being a redemption involving the cancellation of shares pursuant to CA 1990, s 208 and the fresh issue of shares for that purpose) may be paid out of the proceeds of a fresh issue of shares made for the purposes of the redemption, up to an amount equal to the aggregate of the premiums received by the company on the issue of the shares redeemed, or the current amount of the company's share premium account, whichever is less. In any such case the amount of the company's *share premium account*[26] shall, notwithstanding CA 1963, s 62(1), be reduced by a sum corresponding to the amount of any payment made by virtue of this provision out of the proceeds of the issue of the new issue[27].

Where an existing company wishes to issue redeemable shares, it must ensure that its articles of association authorise the issue of redeemable shares. Furthermore, subject to the conditions outlined in CA 1990, s 210, a company may convert any of its shares into redeemable shares.

[18.013] Where a company decides to redeem its shares it is presented with a number of options as to what to do with them. In the first place, a company may redeem its shares by cancelling them. Cancellation of redeemable shares is governed by CA 1990, s 208. Where shares are cancelled, the company's issued share capital is reduced, but the authorised share capital is maintained as it was before. Central to the maintenance of capital principle is the notion of a company's *Capital Redemption Reserve Fund.* Into this fund the company must pay the proceeds of the redemption. Where the redemption is funded from profits, a sum equal to the amount by which the company's issued share capital is reduced must be paid into the company's Capital Redemption Reserve Fund. Where the redemption is in whole or in part funded by a fresh issue of shares, and the amount of money obtained is less than the amount required to redeem the shares, then the difference must be paid from profits into the company's Capital Redemption Reserve Fund.

[18.014] In the second place, upon redeeming its shares a company may retain them, instead of cancelling them, in which case they become *treasury shares*[28]. This is facilitated by CA 1990, s 209(2)(a) which provides that the nominal value of treasury shares held by a company at any one time may not exceed 10% of the company's nominal issued share capital. The creation of treasury shares is an alternative to cancelling redeemed shares. A treasury share is different from all other types of share. The principal difference lies in its ownership. Central to the notion of a share is that some person or body corporate holds it, giving that person a share in the company[29]. A treasury share on the other hand is not owned by anyone other than the company and may be seen as existing in a state of limbo. Accordingly, although a treasury share may carry voting rights and the right to a dividend, such may not be exercised while the company holds them[30].

---

26 For a company's share premium account see para **[18.094]**.

27 CA 1990, s 207(2)(f).

28 See Chapter 15, *Shares and Membership*, para **[15.109]**.

29 See Chapter 15, *Shares and Membership*, para **[15.035]**.

[18.015] Treasury shares may be reissued or cancelled[31]. Where reissued by private companies, CA 1990, s 209(6) provides that a certain price must be obtained. The 'reissue price range', which is set by the members of the company in general meeting, sets a maximum and minimum price which must be obtained before any contract is formed for the reissue of treasury shares[32]. Where the treasury shares which are reissued are derived in whole or in part from *shares purchased by the company*, the reissue price range of the whole or such part of those shares must be determined by special resolution of the company passed at the meeting at which the resolution authorising the purchase has been passed and such determination shall remain effective with respect to those shares for the requisite period[33]. Where treasury shares which are reissued are derived in whole or in part from *shares redeemed by the company*, the reissue price range must be determined by special resolution of the company passed before any contract for the reissue of those shares is entered into and such determination shall remain effective for the requisite period[34]. The company may, from time to time by special resolution, vary or renew a determination of the reissue price range with respect to particular treasury shares before any contract for reissue of those shares is entered into and any such variation or renewal shall remain effective as a determination of the reissue price range of those shares for the requisite period of time[35]. Requisite period is defined as the period of 18 months from the date of the passing of the resolution determining the reissue price range or varying or renewing such determination, or such lesser period of time as the resolution may specify[36]. A reissue of treasury shares in contravention of CA 1990, s 209(6) will render the reissue unlawful[37].

By CA 1990, s 228(1) the Minister for Enterprise, Trade and Employment may make regulations governing the sale by companies of their own shares which are held as treasury shares. The Minister's regulations may relate to either companies in general or to a particular category or class of company. In this way, it is open to the Minister acting by statutory instrument to differentiate between public and private companies.

[18.016] Sections 218 of CA 1990 (payments with respect to purchase or redemption of own shares), 219 (effect of failure to purchase or redeem a company's own shares) and 228 (ministerial power to make regulations in respect to purchase/redemption of a company's own shares) all apply to the redemption of redeemable shares. These also apply to the acquisition of a company's own shares and are considered next.

---

30 CA 1990, s 209(3).

31 CA 1990, s 209(4).

32 CA 1990, s 209(6)(a).

33 CA 1990, s 209(6)(b).

34 CA 1990, s 209(6)(c).

35 CA 1990, s 209(6)(d).

36 CA 1990, s 209(6)(e)(ii).

37 CA 1990, s 209(7).

[B] Acquisition by a Company of its Own Shares

[18.017] Companies can directly or indirectly acquire their own shares. Here, the following issues in connection with the acquisition of a company's own shares are considered:

1. The common law prohibition.
2. The statutory prohibition on acquiring own shares.
3. Exceptions to acquiring own shares.
4. Acquiring shares in a company's holding company.

The common law prohibition

[18.018] It is a long-established rule at common law that a company may not purchase its own shares[38]. The cornerstone of the common law is *Trevor v Whitworth*[39]. In that case the executors of the late Mr Whitworth, a shareholder in James Schofield & Sons Ltd, sold back the shares which he had held in the company *to* the company. This was permitted by the company's articles of association. When the company subsequently went into liquidation, the executors sought to recover from the company the balance of the purchase price which was outstanding on the shares. This was resisted by the liquidator and the case eventually came before the House of Lords. It was held that because the purchase of a company's own shares was not permitted by the objects clause, the purchase of the company's own shares was ultra vires. Moreover, it was held by the House of Lords that whether or not the acquisition by a company of its own shares was authorised by its objects clause, the act of purchasing its own shares was in itself repugnant to the law. After referring to the law on the reduction of capital[40], Lord Watson said:

> 'One of the main objects contemplated by the legislature, in restricting the power of limited companies to reduce the amount of their capital as set forth in the memorandum, is to protect the interests of the outside public who may become creditors. In my opinion the effect of these statutory restrictions is to prohibit every transaction between a company and a shareholder, by means of which the money already paid to the company in respect of his shares is returned to him, unless the court has sanctioned the transaction. Paid-up capital may be diminished or lost in the course of the company's trading; that is a result which no legislation can prevent; but persons who deal with, and give credit to a limited company, naturally rely upon the fact that the company is trading with a certain amount of capital already paid up, as well as the responsibility of its members for the capital remaining at call; and *they are entitled to assume that no part of the capital which has been paid into the coffers of the company has been subsequently paid out, except in the legitimate course of its business.*'[41] [Emphasis added]

[38] See generally, Brennan, *A Company Purchasing its Own Shares* (1991); McCormack, *The New Companies Legislation* (1991), pp 40–61; and for a specific analysis of private companies acquiring their own shares, see Fox & Bowen, *The Law of Private Companies* (1991), pp 150–168.

[39] *Trevor v Whitworth* (1887) 12 App Cas 409. For a recent application, see *Barclays Bank plc et al v British & Commonwealth Holdings plc* [1996] 1 BCLC 1.

[40] Considered in Chapter 3, *The Constitutional Documentation*, para **[3.043]** *ff.*

[41] (1887) 12 App Cas 409 at 423, 424.

The case of *Guinness v Land Corporation of Ireland*, quoted above[42], was cited with approval. An old Irish case which restated the common law prohibition is *Re Irish Provident Assurance Company Ltd*[43]: that case demonstrates that the acquisition by a company of its own shares often arises in circumstances where it is agreed that one of the shareholders in a company should leave and his shares be acquired. There, differences of opinion arose between a company and one of its shareholders who also happened to be its managing director. A deal was struck and it was agreed that his shares would be purchased by the company for £2,000 in return for his waiving any claim he had against the company and agreeing not to compete with the company. It was held by Palles CB that the agreement was void because part of the consideration was the purchase by a company of its own shares. These authorities continue to hold good and prevent own-share purchase by a company unless a transaction can be brought within one of the statutory exceptions[44].

The statutory prohibition on acquiring own shares

[18.019] The old common law rule that a company cannot purchase its own shares was given statutory expression in CA 1963, s 72(1). It simply provided that 'Except insofar as this Act expressly permits, it shall not be lawful for a company limited by shares...to purchase any of its shares or reduce its share capital in any way.'

In what can only be seen as a spurt of 'blind' European fervour, the Oireachtas enacted a second statutory prohibition on a company purchasing its own shares in the guise of C(A)A 1983, s 41(1)[45]. This provides:

> 'Subject to the following provisions of this section, no company limited by shares or limited by guarantee and having a share capital shall acquire its own shares (whether by purchase, subscription or otherwise).'

It should be stressed that neither provision prohibits *unlimited companies* from acquiring their own shares.

[18.020] The direct acquisition of own-shares can be distinguished from a situation where a company acquires shares in a company whose principal asset comprises of shares in the acquiring company. In *Acatos & Hutcheson plc v Watson*[46] it was held by the English High Court that, as a general principle, a company is not precluded by either the common law rule in *Trevor v Whitworth* or statute[47] from acquiring the shares of another company in circumstances where the sole asset of the company whose shares are acquired is shares in the acquiring company[48]. This decision is soundly based on the fundamental principle of company law, established in *Salomon v A Salomon & Co Ltd*[49] and consistently applied by the Irish courts, that a company's separate legal personality

---

42 See para **[18.003]**.

43 *Re Irish Provident Assurance Company Ltd* [1913] IR 352 (Court of Appeal).

44 *Re RW Peak (Kings Lynn) Ltd* [1998] BCC 596.

45 As Ussher, *Company Law in Ireland* (1986), p 315 has most aptly said, 'Statute is not required to repeat itself for emphasis'.

46 *Acatos & Hutcheson plc v Watson* [1995] 1 BCLC 218.

47 CA 1985, s 143(1) (UK) which provides, in terms similar to C(A)A 1983, s 41(1), that: 'Subject to the following provisions, a company limited by shares…shall not acquire its own shares, whether by purchase, subscription or otherwise'.

should be respected. Although in the instant case the acquiring company's shares were not *directly* held, Lightman J recognised that the economic effect was the same and did sound a caution:

> 'I should add that, whilst such a purchase by one company of a shareholder in it is not absolutely prohibited, in view of the potential for abuse and for adverse consequences for shareholders and creditors, the court will look carefully at such transactions to see that the directors of the acquiring company have acted with an eye solely to the interests of the acquiring company (and not for example to the interests of the directors) and have fulfilled their fiduciary duties to safeguard the interests of shareholders and creditors alike.'[50]

In that case there were legitimate reasons for adopting the proposed course of action, which included the mitigation of taxes otherwise payable on a restructure. The independent directors of the acquiring company had obtained legal and accounting advice that the proposed transaction was in the interests of both the plaintiff and its shareholders. In particular, it should be noted, that the shares in the acquiring company had not deliberately been transferred to a shelf company with the sole intention of evading the statutory and common law prohibition on the acquisition of a company's own shares. In a case where a dummy company is incorporated with the sole or dominant intention of evading the prohibition on own-share acquisition, it is thought that a court would be sorely tempted to lift the veil of incorporation and deem the transaction a sham[51]. Insofar as the result of such a transaction is that the company whose shares are acquired in toto thereby becomes a subsidiary of the acquiring company in circumstances where it holds shares in, what has become, its holding company, regard must be had to CA 1963, s 32. It is thought that s 32(1) does not prevent such an acquisition because s 32(1) only renders void any allotment or transfer of shares in a company to its subsidiary: this must be read as referring to any future allotment or transfer. Moreover, s 32(4) expressly provides that the section shall not prevent a company, which at the date it becomes a subsidiary is already a member of the acquiring company, from continuing to be a member[52].

Exceptions to acquiring own shares

[18.021] Prior to the enactment of CA 1990, there were a number of limited exceptions to the statutory prohibitions on own-share purchase. Those exceptions, which still remain, are:

— the redemption of preference shares pursuant to CA 1963, s 65[53];

---

48 See also the supporting Australian authorities cited with approval by Lightman J: *Dyason v JC Hutton Pty Ltd* (1935) Argus LR 419; *August Investments Pty Ltd v Poiseidon Ltd and Samin Ltd* [1971] 2 SASR 71; and *Trade Practices Commission v Australian Iron & Steel Pty Ltd* (1990) 22 FCR 305, 92 ALR 395.

49 *Salomon v A Salomon & Co Ltd* [1897] AC 22.

50 [1995] 1 BCLC 218 at 225b–c.

51 On lifting the veil, see Chapter 5, *Disregarding Separate Legal Personality.*

52 See further McGee, *Share Capital*, (1999), pp 3 and 115.

53 C(A)A 1983, s 41(4)(a). Furthermore, it should be noted that the redemption or purchase of shares pursuant to CA 1990, Part XI now forms part of this exception by virtue of CA 1990, s 232(a) which amends C(A)A 1983, s 41(4)(a).

— the acquisition of any shares in a reduction of capital duly made pursuant to CA 1963, s 72[54];

— the purchase of any shares in pursuance of an order under C(A)A 1983, s 15, or CA 1963, ss 10 or 205[55];

— the forfeiture of any shares, or the acceptance of any shares surrendered in lieu, in pursuance of the articles of association for failure to pay any sum payable in respect of those shares[56].

Although these provisions remain in force, there now exists a further statutory exception to the general statutory rule that a company may not acquire its own shares. The statutory regime in CA 1990, Part XI is next considered:

(a) The rules governing own-share purchase under CA 1990, s 211

(b) Funding can only come from distributable profits.

(c) Authorised by articles of association.

(d) The requirement for a special resolution.

(e) Contingent purchase contracts

(f) Statutory safeguards.

(g) Repudiation by company and effect of winding-up.

(h) Ministerial regulations.

(a) The rules governing own-share purchase under CA 1990, s 211

[18.022] The new regime applicable to the purchase by a company of its own shares is set out in CA 1990, s 211, which provides:

> '(1) Subject to the following provisions of this Part, a company may, if so authorised by its articles, purchase its own shares (including any redeemable shares).
>
> (2) Sections 207(2)[57], 208[58] and 209[59] shall apply in relation to the purchase by a company under this section of any of its own shares as those sections apply in relation to the redemption of shares by a company under section 207.
>
> (3) A company shall not purchase any of its shares under this section if as a result of such purchase the nominal value of the issued share capital which is not redeemable would be less than one tenth of the nominal value of the total issued share capital of the company.'

The permitted mechanism by which a private company limited by shares or by guarantee can acquire its own shares is by means of an 'off market purchase' pursuant to CA 1990, s 213. Section 212 of CA 1990 defines an off market purchase as being one where the shares are purchased either:

— otherwise than on a recognised Stock Exchange; or

— on a recognised Stock Exchange but are not subject to a marketing arrangement on that Stock Exchange.

---

54 C(A)A 1983, s 41(4)(b).

55 C(A)A 1983, s 41(4)(c).

56 C(A)A 1983, s 41(4)(d).

57 See para **[18.012]**.

58 See para **[18.013]**.

59 See para **[18.014]**.

A company's shares are subject to a marketing arrangement on a recognised Stock Exchange if either they are listed on that Stock Exchange, or, the company has been afforded facilities for dealing in those shares to take place on that Stock Exchange without prior Stock Exchange permission for individual transactions and without limit as to the time during which those facilities are to be available[60]. *Market purchases* are considered in Chapter 28, below[61].

(b) Funding can only come from distributable profits

[18.023] Section 211(2) of CA 1990 provides that ss 207(2), 208 and 209 (which primarily apply to the redemption of shares) also apply to own-share purchases. Section 207(2)(d)(i) of CA 1990 provides that, except where shares are cancelled on redemption[62], '... no such shares shall be redeemed otherwise than out of profits available for distribution'. In England and Wales[63], a private company may, subject to certain safeguards, fund the purchase of its own shares from its capital[64], and only a public company is confined to using distributable profits or the proceeds of a fresh share issue to fund a redemption or purchase. In Ireland, there is no such distinction between private companies and PLCs. While Keane[65] expresses relief that 'we have at least been spared further provisions of tortuous complexity', it is thought to be unfortunate that the legislature did not take the opportunity of making a distinction between such vastly different legal structures. The concept of distributable profits is considered below[66], in connection with the payment of dividends. Furthermore, it should be noted that a company may use only distributable profits to fund premia or other payments upon an acquisition or redemption of shares as made clear by CA 1990, s 218(1) and (2), which provides that payments from a source other than distributable profits is unlawful.

(c) Authorised by articles of association

[18.024] In order to be able to purchase its own shares, a private company must first be authorised to do so by its articles of association. In England, this is considered to be an essential prerequisite and one that cannot be overridden by an informal resolution[67], and it it thought that this is likely to be followed in Ireland[68].

(d) The requirement for a special resolution

[18.025] The first step in a private company acquiring its own shares is that the members in general meeting must pass a special resolution authorising the terms of the proposed contract of purchase[69]. This special resolution[70] must be passed *before* the contract to

---

60 CA 1990, s 212(2)(a) and (b).

61 See Chapter 28, *Public Companies in Context*, para **[28.112]**.

62 In which case such shares can be redeemed out of the proceeds of a fresh issue of shares made for the purposes of the redemption: CA 1990, s 207(2)(d)(ii).

63 See generally, Wyatt, *Company Acquisition of Own Shares* (1989).

64 See Fox & Bowen, *The Law of Private Companies* (1991), p 153 *ff*.

65 Keane, *Company Law*, (2000) para 15.10.

66 See para **[18.081]**.

67 See Chapter 9, *Corporate Governance: Meetings*, para **[9.079]** *ff*.

68 See *R W Peak (Kings Lynn) Ltd* [1998] BCC 597.

69 CA 1990, s 211(1).

70 By CA 1990, s 213(4), notwithstanding anything in CA 1963, s 137 or in a company's articles, any member can demand a poll on such a special resolution.

purchase a company's own shares is entered into, and any such authority may be varied, revoked or from time to time renewed by special resolution. Although the fact that a special resolution is required ensures that a qualified majority of members is in agreement that the company purchase its own shares, a further safeguard is provided by CA 1990, s 213(3). This provides that the special resolution:

> '...shall not be effective for the purposes of this section if any member of the company holding shares to which the resolution relates exercises the voting rights carried by any of those shares in voting on the resolution and the resolution would not have been passed if he had not done so.'

Furthermore, a special resolution shall *not be effective* unless a copy of the proposed contract of purchase (or a written memorandum of the contract, where the proposed contract is oral) is available for inspection by members of the company both at the meeting itself, and at the registered office of the company for at least 21 days before the extraordinary general meeting ('EGM') at which the special resolution is proposed[71]. Any memorandum of the terms of a contract for the purchase of shares must include the names of any members who hold shares to which the contract relates and a copy of the contract which is made available must have annexed to it a written memorandum specifing any such names which do not appear in the contract itself[72]. The members in general meeting may agree to a variation of an existing contract to purchase shares only if the variation is authorised by special resolution before the variation is agreed to by CA 1990, s 213(7). Retrospective validation of a variation is not permitted. Whilst a company cannot assign its rights under a contract to purchase its shares, it can release its rights. In such a case, a private company is required to pass a further special resolution[73].

[18.026] It is clear that the nature and timing of the requisite special resolution is closely regulated. In England it has been held that the principle in *Re Duomatic Ltd* cannot override the statutory formalities involved in own-share purchases. *Re RW Peak (Kings Lynn) Ltd*[74] concerned an application for rectification of a company's register of members. The applicant had sold his shares in a company back to the company pursuant to an agreement signed by himself and the only other member of the company. The applicant sought to have this sale set aside on the grounds that it was invalid by reason of the rule in *Trevor v Whitworth*, by virtue of s 143 of the Companies Act 1985 (UK) and the fact that the validation procedure, permitted by Part V, Chapter VII of that Act, had not been followed. Against this, it was argued that the effect of the company's only two members signing the agreement under which the shares were bought back was tantamount to compliance by reason of the principle in *Re Duomatic Ltd*[75]. Lindsay J considered the problem from the perspective of the written resolution procedure; had that been utilised as permitted in England by s 381A of the Companies Act 1985 (UK), two resolutions would have been required: one to amend the articles of association and the other to authorise the proposed share purchase contract. That the similar English

---

71 CA 1990, s 213(5).

72 CA 1990, s 213(6).

73 CA 1990, s 217.

74 *Re RW Peak (Kings Lynn) Ltd* [1998] BCC 596.

75 *Re Duomatic Ltd* [1969] 2 Ch 365.

legislation (s 164(2) of the Companies Act 1985 (UK)) requires the resolution to be passed *before* the entering into of a contract for the purchase of shares was found to be fatal to the purported reliance on the *Duomatic* principle. Lindsay J said:

> 'If, on the hypothesis of any such written procedure being used, the only signed paper, instead of being two such resolutions, had been the contract itself, then, even if its language were generously to be regarded as if it were also effective as an alteration to the articles and as a resolution approving the company's entry into the contract, its effect could hardly antedate the entry into itself and hence it could not be regarded as a resolution passed "*before* the contract is entered into" within s 164(2). The contract would thus not have been approved 'in advance' within s 164(2)…
>
> If that is right then it is evidence that, in relation to such a supposed case, Parliament would have preserved and have retained as determinative of the efficacy of the related transactions at least some of the requirements of s 164, even in cases where written assent had been given by the only persons or person…who by statute is to have a voice in the decision of whether or not the company should enter into the particular contract to buy its own shares. That being so, can it sensibly be the case that, where there has been no approval of the contract *in advance* but where the shareholder whose shares are being bought also assents, and therefore brings assents up to 100% of the membership of the company, a transaction, ineffective in reliance upon s 381A, is thereupon to be given efficacy?
>
> I cannot think that Parliament can be taken to have countenanced an application of the *Duomatic* principle such that a transaction, even less formal than a written resolution under s 381A and which would have been ineffective as such, would become effective merely by reason of the further assent of the remaining shareholder, [the applicant], a person excluded by statute from having his votes on the subject counted had there been a vote (s 164(5)), and whose signature of approval was rendered unnecessary to any written resolution had there been one…A transaction otherwise ineffective, had s 381 been deployed in a corresponding way, would, were that so, have become effective upon the decision of the very person whom statute requires not to have a voice in its favour. So anomalous would that be that in the circumstances, rather than my ruling upon the application of the *Duomatic* principle more generally, I reject its applicability to cure this particular transaction.'[76]

It is thought that an Irish court, interpreting CA 1990, s 211 and CA 1963, s 148(1) would reach a similar conclusion[77].

[18.027] An interesting variation on the same theme, of compliance with the statutory regime, arose for consideration in *Vision Express (UK) Ltd v Wilson*[78]. The facts were that a 'Tomlin order'[79] had been made which provided, inter alia, that the plaintiff-company would purchase certain shares (in itself) from the defendant by a particular

---

[76] [1998] BCC 596 at 603C–H.

[77] On written resolutions, see generally, Chapter 9, *Corporate Governance: Meetings*, para **[9.076]** *ff.*

[78] *Vision Express (UK) Ltd v Wilson* [1998] BCC 173.

[79] A 'Tomlin order' is an order of a court which directs that all further proceedings in a matter be stayed upon specified terms (set out in a schedule to the order) save for the purpose of enforcing the said terms with liberty to apply for that purpose. The origin of the order is an English practice direction issued following the decision of Tomlin J in *Dashwood v Dashwood* [1927] WN 276. See, generally, Hardiman, 'Settlement of Actions' (1998) 5 CLP 247 at 253.

date and for a particular price. The purchase did not complete by the specified date so as to facilitate compliance with the statutory requirements where a company purchases its own shares. The defendant claimed that the plaintiff-company was in breach of the Tomlin order; the plaintiff-company refuted this. The defendant also claimed that the Tomlin order was a contract for the sale and purchase of the shares, which was illegal because no special resolution had been passed in advance. The instant case arose from the plaintiff-company's request that a clause be implied into the Tomlin order to the effect that the order was '...subject (in so far as necessary) to compliance with statutory provisions for the purchase by the company of its own shares'. In these circumstances, Judge Levy QC held that the court should do all it can to uphold an agreement which parties in litigation have come to unless there are obvious illegalities and that he would imply the terms sought by the plaintiff-company, with the result that there was no illegality with the agreement.

(e) Contingent purchase contracts

[18.028] The agreement by a company to purchase its own shares need not be acted upon immediately. So, the provisions considered above also apply to '*contingent purchase contracts*', defined by CA 1990, s 214(1) as meaning contracts entered into by a company which do not amount to a contract to purchase its shares but under which the company may become entitled or obliged to purchase those shares. So, a 'put' and 'call' contract is permitted, provided that the provisions contained in CA 1990, s 213(2)–(7) are complied with in full.

(f) Statutory safeguards

[18.029] Part XI of CA 1990 embodies certain additional safeguards in respect of own share acquisition by companies. These focus primarily on the disclosure to the public of particulars of contracts for own-share purchase. Section 222 of CA 1990 provides that copies of the purchase contracts must be kept at the company's registered office for a period of ten years after full performance of the contract, and that they must be made available for public inspection. Failure to comply can render the officers of the company liable to a fine or imprisonment or both. Another safeguard is seen in CA 1990, s 226 which provides that within 28 days of a company purchasing its own shares, it must deliver to the Registrar of Companies a return in the prescribed form stating each class purchased, the number and nominal value of the shares and the date upon which they were delivered back to the company. Again, failure to comply means that every officer who is in default is guilty of an offence.

(g) Repudiation by company and the effect of winding up

[18.030] A company that enters into a contract to purchase its own shares can repudiate the contract without a shareholder being able to sue the company for damages: CA 1990, s 219(2). Moreover, CA 1990, s 219(3) provides:

> 'The court shall not grant an order for specific performance of the terms of redemption or purchase of the shares to which this section applies if the company shows that it is unable to meet the cost of redeeming or purchasing the shares out of profits available for distribution.'

Although this provision weakens the enforceability of contracts for the purchase of a company's own shares, it is consistent with the spirit of the legislation which only permits a company to purchase shares out of distributable profits[80].

[18.031] Where the winding up of a company commences before a contract to purchase its shares has been completed, the contract may be enforced against the company by CA 1990, s 219(4). Where this happens, the shares purchased are to be treated as cancelled. However, to this provision there are two exceptions, and s 219(4) shall *not* apply if:

- the terms of the purchase provide for the purchase to take place at a date later than that of the commencement of the winding up (namely, the date of the presentation of the petition to have the company wound up); or
- the company could not have lawfully made a distribution equal in value to the price at which the shares were to have been purchased between the date on which the purchase was to have taken place and the commencement of the winding up.

Section 219(6) of CA 1990 provides that any payment made pursuant to sub-s (4) shall rank, in order of priority, *after* the payment of all other debts and liabilities of the company other than any due to members in their capacity as members, and if other shares have rights, after those shareholders' claims have been satisfied. However, any such payments shall rank in priority over any amounts due to members in satisfaction of their rights whether as to capital or income as members.

(h) Ministerial regulations

[18.032] Section 228(1) of CA 1990 empowers the Minister for Enterprise, Trade and Employment to make regulations by way of statutory instrument in respect of the purchase by a company of its own shares, just as he may make such regulations in respect of treasury shares, above[81], or a company purchasing shares in its holding company. Without prejudice to the generality of the Minister's power to make regulations, CA 1990, s 228(2) provides that such regulations may provide, in particular, for the following matters:

- the class or description of shares which may (or may not) be purchased or sold;
- the price at which they may be purchased or sold;
- the timing of such purchases or sales;
- the method by which the shares may be purchased or sold; or
- the volume of trading in the shares which may be carried out by companies.

Failure to comply with such Ministerial regulations means that the company and every officer in default shall be guilty of an offence[82].

Acquiring shares in a company's holding company

[18.033] Subject to certain exceptions, CA 1963, s 32 prohibits a body corporate from becoming a member of its holding company. This has been considered in Chapter 15[83].

---

80 On distributable profits see para **[18.081]** *ff.*

81 See para **[18.015]** *ff.*

82 CA 1990, s 228(3).

83 Chapter 15, *Shares and Membership*, para **[15.010]** *ff.*

That prohibition, and the prohibition found in CA 1963, s 60 against providing financial assistance in connection with the purchase of a company's own shares, are, however, subject to CA 1990, s 224. Section 224(1) of CA 1990 provides that, notwithstanding CA 1963, ss 32[84] and 60 a company[85] may, subject to the provisions of that section, acquire, and hold shares in a company which is its holding company.

(a) Conditions on the holding of shares in holding company by subsidiary.

(b) The meaning of subsidiary.

(c) Regulation of private companies that are 'public company subsidiaries'.

(a) Conditions on the holding of shares in holding company by subsidiary

[18.034] Section 224(2) of CA 1990 provides that the acquisition and holding by a subsidiary under sub-s (1) of shares in its holding company shall be subject to the following conditions:

> '(a) The consideration for the acquisition of such shares shall be provided for out of the profits of the subsidiary available for distribution.
>
> (b) Upon the acquisition of such shares and for so long as the shares are held by the subsidiary—
>
> (i) the profits of the subsidiary available for distribution shall for all purposes be restricted by a sum equal to the total cost of the shares acquired;
>
> (ii) the shares shall, for the purposes of the consolidated accounts prepared by the holding company in accordance with sections 150 to 152 of the Principal Act, be treated in the same manner as is required in respect of shares held as treasury shares under section 43A of the Act of 1983 (inserted by section 232 (c) of this Act); and
>
> (iii) the subsidiary shall not exercise any voting rights in respect of the shares and any purported exercise of those rights shall be void.'

Section 224(3) provides that a contract for the acquisition (whether by allotment or transfer) by a subsidiary of shares in its holding company shall not be entered into without being authorised in advance both by the subsidiary and its holding company and the provisions of ss 212–217 are applied, with the necessary modifications, to the granting, variation, revocation and release of such authority. This means that a special resolution is required in a private sale; an ordinary resolution suffices where the shares are to be purchased on a recognised Stock Exchange and subject to a marketing agreement. In the context of s 224, a subsidiary's profits available for distribution shall not include the profits attributable to any shares in the subsidiary for the time being held by the subsidiary's holding company so far as there are profits for the period before the date on or from which the shares were acquired by the holding company[86].

---

84 Note, though, that CA 1990, s 224 does not apply to shares held by a subsidiary in its holding company in the circumstances permitted by CA 1963, s 32: CA 1990, s 224(5). Neither does CA 1990, s 224 (except sub-s (2)(b)(iii)) apply to shares subscribed for, purchased or held by a subsidiary in its holding company pursuant to the Insurance Act 1990, s 9(1): CA 1990, s 224(6).

85 The reference to 'a company' here is deemed, by reg 4(4) of SI 1997/67 to include a body corporate.

86 CA 1990, s 224(4).

(b) The meaning of subsidiary

[18.035] The meaning of the expression 'subsidiary' for the purposes of CA 1990, Part XI was extended by reg 4 of the European Communities (Public Limited Companies Subsidiaries) Regulations 1997[87] (the '1997 Regulations')[88]. Accordingly, in addition to the circumstances set out in CA 1963, s 155, a limited company (including a body corporate)[89] is also deemed to be a subsidiary of a PLC if, but only if, the PLC is itself a shareholder or member of the said limited company and controls alone, pursuant to an agreement with other shareholders or members, a majority of the shareholders' or members' voting rights in the company in question. For the purposes of CA 1990, Part XI , a PLC exercises its control indirectly where the control of a subsidiary is exercised through another subsidiary, pursuant to CA 1963, s 155(1)(b)[90].

[18.036] Section 224 of CA 1990 was extended by reg 5 of the 1997 Regulations. Regulation 5 applies where any holding company is a PLC (referred to as a 'parent public company') and where its subsidiary (not being a subsidiary solely by virtue of CA 1963, s 155(1)(a)(ii) or (b)) is a limited company (including a body corporate) of the type referred to in reg 4(2) (referred to as a 'public company subsidiary'). For present purposes it is important to recognise that the definition of a public company subsidiary can include a private limited company.

(c) Regulation of private companies that are 'public company subsidiaries'

[18.037] Regulation 5(2) of the 1997 Regulations provides that a *public company subsidiary* shall not:

> '(a) subscribe for the shares of its parent public company, or
>
> (b) purchase shares in its parent public company which are not fully paid, or
>
> (c) provide financial assistance in accordance with subsections (2) to (11) of section 60 of the Principal Act for the purchase of or subscription for shares in its parent public company.'[91]

[18.038] The subscription for the shares of its parent public company by a public company subsidiary is a criminal offence and the purported subscription will be void[92]. Where, in contravention of the 1997 Regulations, reg (2)(a) a nominee of a public company subsidiary subscribes for shares in a parent public company, the shares will be

---

87 SI 1997/67. These Regulations implement Company Law Directive 92/101/EEC, which amended the EU Second Company Law Directive (Formation and Capital of Public Limited Companies). Although due for implementation on 1 January 1994, SI 1997/67 was only signed into law on 5 February 1997.

88 See, further, Chapter 17, *Groups of Companies*, para **[17.040]**.

89 A limited company (including a body corporate) is defined as a company (a) to which Article 1 of the Directive of 1968 applies, or (b) which is incorporated other than in a Member State of the European Union and is of a legal form comparable to the type of company referred to in paragraph (a): reg 4(2) of SI 1997/67.

90 SI 1997/67, reg 4(3).

91 See para **[18.041]**.

92 SI 1997/67, reg 5(3).

treated as being held by the nominee on his own account and the public company subsidiary will be regarded as having no beneficial interest in them[93].

[18.039] Where a public company subsidiary purchases, subscribes for or holds shares in its parent company and:

— the shares were not fully paid when they were purchased, or

— the authorisation required by CA 1990, s 224(3) has not been obtained, or

— the shares are held as treasury shares in excess of the limit referred to in CA 1990, s 209(2), or

— the purchase or subscription was in contravention of reg 5(2)(c).

The 1997 Regulations, reg 5(5) provides that, unless the shares or any interest of the public company subsidiary in them are previously disposed of, the provisions of C(A)A 1983, s 43(3), shall apply to the public company subsidiary in respect of such shares[94]. This is expressed to be without prejudice to any other requirements contained in or penalties imposed by the Companies Acts.

[18.040] The 1997 Regulations are expressly stated not to affect or prohibit certain subscriptions and allotments[95]. An offence under the 1997 Regulations is punishable, on

93 Moreover, the provisions of C(A)A 1983, s 42(2)–(6) are applied, with any necessary modifications.

94 With the modification that the 'relevant period' in relation to any shares shall be 12 months and with any other necessary modifications.

95 These are provided in SI 1997/67, reg 5(6):

> '(a) the subscription for, acquisition or holding of, shares in its parent public company by a public company subsidiary where the public company subsidiary is concerned as personal representative or where it is concerned as trustee unless the parent public company or a subsidiary thereof is beneficially interested under the trust and is not so interested only by way of security for the purposes of a transaction entered into by it in the ordinary course of a business which includes the lending of money; (b) the allotment to, or holding by, a public company subsidiary of shares in its parent public company in the circumstances set out in section 32(5) of the Principal Act, but where the shares so allotted are held as treasury shares and the nominal value of treasury shares held by the public company subsidiary exceeds the limit referred to in section 209(2) of the Act of 1990 then, unless the shares or any interest of the public company subsidiary in them are previously disposed of, the provisions of section 43(3) of the Companies (Amendment) Act, 1983, shall with the modification that the relevant period in relation to any shares shall be 3 years and with any other necessary modifications, apply to the public company subsidiary in respect of such shares; (c) the subscription, acquisition or holding of shares in its parent public company by a public company subsidiary where the subscription, acquisition or holding is effected on behalf of a person other than the person subscribing, acquiring or holding the shares, who is neither the parent public company itself nor a subsidiary within the meaning of Part XI of the Act of 1990 of the said parent public company; (d) the subscription, acquisition or holding of shares in its parent public company by a public company subsidiary which is a member of an approved stock exchange specified in section 17(2) of the Stock Exchange Act, 1995 (No. 9 of 1995), acting in its capacity as a professional dealer in securities in the normal course of its business.'

summary conviction, by a fine not exceeding €634.87 or to imprisonment for a term not exceeding six months, or both[96]. Where an offence has been committed by a public company subsidiary and it is proved to have been committed 'with the consent or connivance of or to be attributable to any neglect on the part of a person being a director, manager, secretary, or a person purporting to act in any such capacity', or a member where the affairs of the company are managed by its members, that person too shall be guilty of an offence[97].

[C] ASSISTING THE PURCHASE OF A COMPANY'S OWN SHARES

[18.041] One of the easiest ways in which a company can inadvertently breach the rules of capital maintenance is by directly or indirectly providing financial assistance for the purchase of its own shares[98]. The basic prohibition is contained in CA 1963, s 60(1), which provides that subject to certain exceptions:

> '...it shall not be lawful for a company to give, whether directly or indirectly and whether by means of a loan, guarantee, the provision of security or otherwise, any financial assistance for the purpose of or in connection with a purchase or subscription made or to be made by any person of or for any shares in the company, or where the company is a subsidiary company, in its holding company.'

The integrity of the basic prohibition is maintained despite a number of exceptions to the section, which do not detract substantially from the general prohibition. The exceptions to CA 1963, s 60(1) are considered here as follows:

1. Section 60 of CA 1963 and private companies.
2. The consequences of contravening CA 1963, s 60(1).
3. The meaning of 'financial assistance'.
4. The validation procedure: resolution and declaration.
5. Dividends and lawful liabilities: CA 1963, s 60(12).
6. Miscellaneous exceptions: CA 1963, s 60(13).

Section 60 of CA 1963 and private companies

[18.042] The application of CA 1963, s 60 to private companies is best illustrated by way of an example. A company, which shall be termed 'Borrowings Ltd', decides to acquire the business of another company called Investment Properties Ltd, which owns a property portfolio worth €1 million. In order to minimise stamp duty which would otherwise be payable at 6% of €1 million[99], Borrowings Ltd decides to acquire indirectly the property portfolio by purchasing the shares in Investment Properties Ltd from its shareholders, as opposed to purchasing its assets from the company. By doing

---

96 SI 1997/67, reg 5(7).

97 SI 1997/67, reg 8(a) and (b).

98 See Johnston, *Banking and Security Law in Ireland* (1998), paras [18.13]–[18.29]. Cotter, 'Section 60 of the Companies Act 1963' (2000) 7 CLP 111 and MacCann, 'Section 60 of the Companies Act 1963: Law and Procedure' (1994) 1 CLP 74. For a summary of recent English developments, see Dawson, 'Financial Assistance for the Acquisition of Shares' (1996) *Palmer's In Company*, Issue 7/96, 17 July 1996.

99 See Chapter 16, *Share Transfers in Private Companies*, para **[16.100]**.

this Borrowings Ltd will own the assets (and liabilities) of the company, *but only indirectly*; the title to those assets being vested in the separate legal entity which is Investment Properties Ltd. Borrowings Ltd strikes an agreement with the shareholders of Investment Properties Ltd to purchase their shares for €1 million, which a credit institution agrees to advance to it. Although Borrowings Ltd cannot itself offer any security for the loan, its controllers know that after acquiring Investment Properties Ltd, it can cause Investment Properties Ltd to offer its assets as security for the loan from the credit institution.

Before the credit institution issues its facility letter, it will ensure that one of the special conditions of the letter will be that 'all of the provisions of s 60 of the Companies Act 1963 are complied with in all respects'. This is because in providing security for the purchase of its own shares, Investment Properties Ltd would be directly providing financial assistance (ie to Borrowings Ltd) for the purchase of the shares in Investment Properties Ltd. Unless the provisions of CA 1963, s 60 are complied with in all respects the provision of security by Investment Properties Ltd to the credit institution would be voidable. Regard should also be had to CA 1990, s 31, as to which see Chapter 11.

The consequences of contravening CA 1963, s 60(1)

(a) Criminal consequences

[18.043] The criminal sanction for the contravention of s 60(1) is set out in CA 1963, s 60(15)[100]. This provides that where a company acts in breach of the prohibition every officer who is in default is liable, on summary conviction, to imprisonment for a term not exceeding six months or to a fine not exceeding €634.87, or both. Where convicted on indictment, an officer in default is liable to imprisonment for a term not exceeding two years or to a fine not exceeding €3,174.35, or both.

(b) Civil consequences – voidability

[18.044] For there to be a breach of CA 1963, s 60 there must be a finding of fact that the company concerned has directly or indirectly financed the acquisition of its own shares[101]. Where the prohibition in s 60(1) is contravened, CA 1963, s 60(14) provides that:

> 'Any transaction in breach of this section shall be voidable at the instance of the company against any person (whether a party to the transaction or not) who had notice of the facts which constitute such breach.'

In *Lombard & Ulster Banking Ltd v Bank of Ireland*[102] it was noted by Costello J that the consequence of a contravention of CA 1963 s 60(14) is that the transaction is merely voidable against persons having notice of the facts constituting the breach, and is not void ab initio. Accordingly, it is a matter for the company which provides such financial assistance to seek to avoid the transaction in question. Where a company which has unlawfully provided financial assistance in connection with the purchase of its own

---

[100] As amended by C(A)A 1983, s 15.

[101] *McCormick et al v Cameo Investments Ltd* [1978] ILRM 191 at 194.

[102] *Lombard & Ulster Banking Ltd v Bank of Ireland* (2 June 1987, unreported), High Court *per* Costello J.

shares goes into liquidation, the liquidator of the company may seek to have the transaction set aside in order to swell the company's assets[103]. However, it should be stressed that a contravening transaction is merely *voidable* against persons *who have notice* of the facts that constitute the breach.

(c) The meaning of 'any transaction'

[18.045] The meaning of 'any transaction' as used in CA 1963, s 60(14) was considered in *CH (Ireland) Inc (in liquidation) v Credit Suisse Canada*[104], the facts of which are set out below[105]. McCracken J said:

> 'A transaction in breach of the section must be one which is in breach of *subsection (1)*, which is the giving of financial assistance for the purpose of or in connection with the purchase or subscription of shares. Furthermore, it must be a transaction whereby the company gives the financial assistance. Furthermore, the use of the word "transaction" in the subsections dealing with the making of a declaration by the directors refers in both *subsections (4)* and *(5)* to "the company having carried out the transaction whereby such assistance is to be given". In my view the only transaction which can be attacked under *subsection (1)* is a transaction directly involving the company.'[106]

Applying this to the facts of the case in hand, McCracken J held that the relevant transaction there was the depositing of monies by or at the direction of the company and the consideration for that deposit. In that case, McCracken J found that there had been a provision of financial assistance in connection with the purchase of a company's own shares and that there was 'actual notice' of the facts that constituted the breach. The order of the court was to declare void the deposit of the monies by CHI with CSZ as security and the consideration for that deposit. The declaration was, however, made only as against CSC – a party to the proceedings – and not against any other company involved.

(d) The meaning of 'notice'

[18.046] In order for a company to avoid a transaction which is in breach of CA 1963, s 60(1) against any person it must be shown that the person concerned had notice of the facts which constitute such breach. 'Notice', in this context has been held to mean *actual notice*. Accordingly, in *Bank of Ireland Finance Ltd v Rockfield Ltd*[107] Kenny J in the Supreme Court held that:

> 'The notice referred to in s 60(14) is actual notice and not constructive notice. As there has been considerable confusion as to the meaning of the terms "actual notice" and "imputed notice" and "constructive notice" - a confusion which has been pointed out by many judges and text-book writers - I wish to say that I use the term "actual notice" as meaning in this case that the plaintiff bank, or any of its officials, had been informed either verbally or in writing, that part of the advance was to be applied in the purchase of shares in the defendant company, or that they knew facts from which they must have inferred that part

[103] See Chapter 27, *Realisation and Distribution of Assets in Winding Up*, para **[27.122]**.

[104] *CH (Ireland) Inc (in liquidation) v Credit Suisse Canada* [1999] 4 IR 542 (McCracken J).

[105] See para **[18.049]**.

[106] [1999] 4 IR 542 at 556.

[107] *Bank of Ireland Finance Ltd v Rockfield Ltd* [1979] IR 21.

of the advance was to be applied for this purpose...I include in "actual notice" cases where the agent gets actual notice of the equity.'[108]

In particular, Kenny J refused to extend the doctrine of constructive notice to CA 1963, s 60(14), citing with approval the case of *Manchester Trust v Furness*[109]. In the *Manchester Trust* case Lindley J, who was acknowledged by Kenny J to be 'a great authority upon company law', said:

'...as regards the extension of the equitable doctrines of constructive notice to commercial transactions, the courts have always set their faces resolutely against it. The equitable doctrines of constructive notice are common enough in dealing with land and estates, with which the court is familiar; but there have been repeated protests against the introduction into commercial transactions of anything like an extension of those doctrines, and the protest is founded on perfect good sense. In dealing with estates in land title is everything and it can be leisurely investigated; in commercial transactions possession is everything and there is not time to investigate title; and if we were to extend the doctrine of constructive notice to commercial transactions we should be doing infinite mischief and paralysing the trade of the country.'[110]

The fact that the transaction in question involved a mortgage of land was found to be immaterial; the learned judge held that it would be a ludicrous interpretation to read s 60(14) in one sense for financial assistance without security, and in another sense when a mortgage is involved.

[18.047] In the *Rockfield* case, two men wished to acquire an hotel and obtained an agreement from the plaintiff-bank to advance £170,400, the bank's security being the equitable deposit of the land certificate of the hotel. The bank understood that the hotel would in time be conveyed to a company called either 'Rockville Ltd' or 'Rockfield Ltd'. In fact the company was called Rockfield Ltd, it owned the hotel, and the deal involved the purchase of the company's shares by the two borrowers. A first advance of £150,000 was made by the bank, which the borrowers used to purchase the shares in Rockfield Ltd. The second advance was used to repay part of the initial advance. When the borrowers acquired control of the company, they authorised the deposit of the land certificate of the hotel with the plaintiff-bank by way of equitable mortgage by deposit of title deeds. The bank was aware that stamp duty at 1% was being paid on the acquisition, indicating a share transfer and not a transfer of land. The bank was also aware that the defendant-company had applied for and had obtained planning permission in respect of the land. On the second[111] question to be determined, Kenny J said:

'This is the first case, as far as I know, in which the meaning of sub-s 14 of s 60 has been considered by any court in this country. The onus of proving that the money was advanced

[108] [1979] IR 21 at 37. Kenny J quoted with approval Snell's *Principles of Equity* (27th edn), where 'imputed notice' was defined as: '...where his agent as such in the course of the transaction has actual or constructive notice of the equity'.

[109] *Manchester Trust v Furness* [1895] 2 QB 539.

[110] [1895] 2 QB 539 at 545.

[111] He also considered the question of ratification by the company, and held that this had been validly done.

for the purchase of shares in the defendant company lies on the person who alleges this. The plaintiffs do not have to prove that they had no notice of the facts which constituted a breach of s 60. What has to be established is that the plaintiffs had notice when lending the money that it was to be used for the purchase of shares in the defendant company. The fact which constituted such breach in this case was the application of £150,000 to the purchase of the shares in the defendant company. As the purchase followed the loan, the defendants must establish that the plaintiffs knew at the time when they made the loan that it was to be applied for this purpose. If they got notice of this subsequently, that is irrelevant.'[112]

As noted earlier[113], Kenny J rejected the application of the doctrine of constructive notice and in so doing, the Supreme Court tempered the effects of CA 1963, s 60(14). However, notice of the 'facts which constitute such breach' should be distinguished from notice of a breach. Section 60(14) uses the former expression and, consequently, even where a person does not have actual notice of a breach, it may be argued that they had notice of *facts which constitute* a breach. It is significant, however, that notwithstanding that the plaintiff-bank knew that the stamp duty was estimated at 1%, this fact was held by the Supreme Court *not* to be notice that the money was to be applied to purchase shares in the defendant-company. Accordingly, the Supreme Court held that the defendant-company was not entitled to avoid the transaction since the plaintiff-bank did not have notice of the facts which constituted a breach of s 60(1).

[18.048] In *Lombard & Ulster Banking Ltd v Bank of Ireland*[114] certain persons came together with a view to acquiring indirectly a school house by purchasing the shares in the company which owned it. The plaintiff-bank agreed to finance the acquisition of the shares in the company, its security being a guarantee supported by a charge over the school building from the company. Although at the time of the advance the bank was assured that the procedure set out in CA 1963, s 60(2)[115] had been complied with, it later transpired that this was not the case. In fact a special resolution of the members was not passed, nor had a statutory declaration of solvency been sworn by the company's directors. Costello J held that there had indeed been a breach of s 60(1) but that such merely rendered the transaction voidable against persons who had notice of the facts which constituted the breach. Costello J considered that there were three questions to be answered on the matter of notice.

First, he rejected the liquidator's contention that the phrase 'transaction in breach of the section' meant the carrying out of a transaction prohibited by CA 1963, s 60(1) and that since the plaintiff-bank knew that the transaction was prohibited by s 60(1), it had sufficient notice to enable the company to avoid the guarantee and charge. In order for a company to avoid a transaction, it is necessary to show that the bank knew of the facts which resulted in non-compliance with the section. It is not sufficient that it merely knows of the fact that a transaction that would contravene s 60(1) if the validation procedure is not followed, is proposed.

---

112 [1979] IR 21 at 36–37.

113 See para **[18.046]**.

114 *Lombard & Ulster Banking Ltd v Bank of Ireland* (2 June 1987, unreported), High Court *per* Costello J.

115 See para **[18.057]**.

Secondly, Costello J held that the company, or its liquidator, must establish as a matter of probability that the bank had notice that there was non-compliance with the exceptions to s 60(1). Therefore, the onus is on the liquidator or the company to prove his or its case. The failure to show that a person had actual notice will mean that a guarantee, mortgage, charge or other security, is enforceable and cannot be avoided by the company.

Thirdly, the learned judge applied the meaning of notice decided by the Supreme Court in *Bank of Ireland Finance Ltd v Rockfield Ltd*, and held that in order for the bank to have notice, they must have had actual notice, meaning:

> '(a) that they or their officials actually knew that the required procedures were not adopted or that they knew facts from which they must have inferred that the company had failed to adopt the required procedures, or (b) that an agent of theirs actually knew of the failure or knew facts from which he must have inferred that a failure had occurred..."Constructive Notice" of the failure is not sufficient for subs (14).'

[18.049] The question of notice – and in particular notice of the facts that constitute the breach – was most recently considered in *CH (Ireland) Inc (in liquidation) v Credit Suisse Canada*[116]. The facts, like many of these cases, are somewhat convoluted. The applicant-company was in liquidation and was suing by its liquidator. The litigation concerned a transaction whereby the respondent company ('CSC') made a loan of £18.8 million to Castor Holdings Ltd ('Castor') which was secured by a 'payment obligation' from the CSC's holding company, Credit Suisse ('CSZ'). Castor utilised the borrowed money to subscribe for shares in a company called CH Investments (New Brunswick) Inc ('CHNB'). CHNB, in turn, used the money to subscribe for shares in the applicant-company ('CHI'). CHI then deposited the purchase monies with CSZ, indemnified CSZ against any liability on foot of its payment obligation to CSC and pledged the deposited monies as security. CSZ then guaranteed the repayment of the loan made by CSC to Castor. In addition, CHI guaranteed all liabilities of Castor to either CSZ and CSC. It was CHI's liquidator's contention that the monies paid by CHNB to CHI as a subscription for shares were deposited by CHI effectively as the ultimate security for the monies advanced by CSC to Castor, and that this was a breach of CA 1963, s 60. McCracken J held that the depositing of monies by CHI with CSZ was to ensure that CSC (on CSZ's effective direction) would advance monies to Castor and then to CHNB to enable it to purchase the shares in CHI, and that the foregoing constituted 'financial assistance'[117]. However, McCracken J did not believe that the only or main purpose of the guarantee given by CHI was to give financial assistance for the purchase of shares. Turning to CA 1963, s 60(14), McCracken J considered the meaning of 'any transaction in breach of this section' as used therein and held that in the relevant transaction there was the depositing of monies by or at the direction of the company and the consideration for that deposit[118]. McCracken J noted that a transaction is only voidable under s 60(14) against any person who had notice of the facts which constitute the breach of s 60(1), and that the onus was on the liquidator to prove that CSC had such notice. After

[116] *CH (Ireland) Inc (in liquidation) v Credit Suisse Canada* [1999] 4 IR 542.

[117] See further, para **[18.050]**.

[118] See para **[18.045]**.

reviewing the finding of the Supreme Court in *Bank of Ireland Finance Ltd v Rockfield Ltd*[119] and the requirement that '*actual notice*' be shown, McCracken J considered the facts of the case in hand and found that CSC did in fact have actual notice of the facts that constituted the breach of s 60(1), ie it knew that:

— the monies it was advancing to Castor were going to be paid on to CHNB to acquire shares in CHI and that the words 'reference: capital subscription' had been used in correspondence;

— that CHI was going to make a fiduciary deposit with CSZ;

— that the fiduciary deposit was to be security for the payment obligation or guarantee by CSZ to CSC; and

— that the payment obligation or guarantee by CSZ to CSC was to cover the monies being advanced.

McCracken J concluded that, CSC had actual notice that the monies they were advancing were going to be ultimately used by CHNB to acquire shares in CHI and that those monies were being secured by a payment obligation or guarantee by CSZ which was countersecured by the deposit of the same monies by CHI with CSZ. McCracken J went on to say:

> 'As probably the most important link, or perhaps as it would be put by CSC as the weak link, in this argument, was the reference to capital subscription in the payment directions. I should comment on this further. The evidence of Mr McFarland was that as far as he was concerned this was simply a note put into the request by Castor and by CHNB respectively for the purpose of giving information to their auditors, and that it was of no relevance to CSC. However, even if one accepts that that was what Mr McFarland thought at the time, that does not take away from the fact that it is a clear statement of fact which directly informed CSC that the money was going to be used to subscribe for shares. I can appreciate that Mr McFarland may not have thought this was of any relevance, as of course I fully accept that Mr McFarland was totally unaware of the provisions of s 60 of the Companies Act 1963. However, what s 60(14) relates to is a person having notice of the facts which constitute the breach of s 60. It does not require that the person who had notice of the facts also had notice that it was in law a breach of s 60, or indeed that such person was aware of the existence of s 60. I am quite satisfied that CSC had notice of the facts which constituted the breach, and no doubt had they been aware of the provisions of s 60, they would have been aware that there was a breach of that section.'[120]

Ignorance of the law can never be a defence; hence what is only relevant is actual notice of the facts that constitute a breach of the prohibition against financial assistance.

The meaning of 'financial assistance'

[18.050] Section 60(1) of CA 1963 provides that it shall not be lawful for a company to give 'financial assistance' for the purpose of or in connection with a purchase or subscription made or to be made by any person of or for the shares in the company or its holding company. In examining the meaning of 'financial assistance' the following points are considered:

---

119 *Bank of Ireland Finance Ltd v Rockfield Ltd* [1979] IR 21; see para **[18.046]**.

120 [1999] 4 IR 542 at 558–559.

(a) The express forms of 'financial assistance'.

(b) The breadth of the prohibition: 'otherwise' and 'in connection with'.

(c) Warranties and covenants that constitute financial assistance.

(d) Actual versus potential financial assistance.

(a) The express forms of 'financial assistance'

[18.051] In *Charterhouse Investment Trust Ltd v Tempest Diesels Ltd*[121], in a passage quoted with approval by McCracken J in *CH (Ireland) Inc (in liquidation) v Credit Suisse Canada*[122], Hoffmann J said:

> 'There is no definition of giving financial assistance in the section, although some examples are given. The words have no technical meaning and their frame of reference is in my judgment the language of ordinary commerce. One must examine the commercial realities of the transaction and decide whether it can properly be described as the giving of financial assistance by the company, bearing in mind that the section is a penal one and should not be strained to cover transactions which are not fairly within it.' [123]

The express statutory examples referred to are 'by means of a loan, guarantee, the provision of security or otherwise'.

[18.052] In *CH (Ireland) Inc (in liquidation) v Credit Suisse Canada*, the facts of which are given above[124], it was held that the only or main purpose of the applicant-company depositing monies was to ensure that monies would be advanced to enable the applicant-company's shares be purchased. Therefore, McCracken J held that the applicant-company had clearly given financial assistance within the meaning of CA 1963, s 60. In *Re Northside Motor Co Ltd; Eddison v Allied Irish Banks*[125], an individual owned half of the shares in a company and wished to acquire the remainder. The defendant-bank advanced finance to another company which was owned by the individual, the bank's security being the provision by the plaintiff-company of a guarantee of the repayment of the loan taken out by the second company. Costello J held that the company had provided financial assistance for the purchase of its own shares because the transaction involved a promise to make a pecuniary payment to the bank if the borrower company defaulted in its obligations.

---

[121] *Charterhouse Investment Trust Ltd v Tempest Diesels Ltd* [1986] BCLC 1.

[122] *CH (Ireland) Inc (in liquidation) v Credit Suisse Canada* [1999] 4 IR 542.

[123] [1986] BCLC 1 at 10. Hoffmann J went on to say (in a passage also quoted by McCracken J):

> 'The *Belmont* case shows that the sale of an asset by a company at a fair value can properly be described as giving financial assistance if the effect is to provide the purchaser of its shares with the cash needed to pay for them. It does not matter that the company's balance sheet is undisturbed in the sense that the cash paid out is replaced by an asset of equal value. In the case of a loan by a company to a credit worthy purchaser of its shares, the balance sheet is equally undisturbed but the loan plainly constitutes giving financial assistance. It follows that if the only or main purpose of such a transaction is to enable the purchaser to buy the shares, the section is contravened.'

[124] See para **[18.049]**.

[125] *Re Northside Motor Co Ltd; Eddison v Allied Irish Banks* (24 July 1985, unreported), High Court (Costello J).

(b) The breadth of the prohibition: 'otherwise' and 'in connection with'

[18.053] Whether financial assistance can be said to have been provided will, in each case, depend upon the facts of the particular transaction. As Lord Denning MR said in *Wallersteiner v Moir*[126] 'you look to the company's shares and see into whose hands they have got. You will soon see if the company's money has been used to finance the purchase'. Such a broad statement can be substantiated by considering that the prohibition in CA 1963, s 60(1) is not just confined to the express forms of financial assistance in s 60(1), but also refers to financial assistance 'otherwise' provided. So too is the connection, between whatever the financial assistance given and the purchase or subscription of own-shares or shares in a company's holding company, widely drafted. Section 60(1) refers to the financial assistance being 'for the purpose of or in connection with'. As *Johnston* has said: 'the reference to 'directly or indirectly' and the words 'in connection with' are such as to render s 60 applicable to many transactions which are not at first sight obviously apparent'[127]. It is significant that the words 'in connection with' have been dropped from the English section that regulates the provision of financial assistance in connection with the purchase of shares[128].

[18.054] The words 'in connection with' were considered in the Australian case of *Sterileair Pty Ltd v George Ralph Papallo and another*[129]. In that case D Ltd was owned as to 75% by the defendants and as to 25% by W. The defendants loaned D Ltd Aust$100,000. Subsequently, W acquired the plaintiff-company, which was a shelf company. At this time the defendants and W were in dispute but notwithstanding, the first defendant became a director and shareholder in the plaintiff-company. After discussions, it was agreed that D Ltd's assets and liabilities (including the debt to the defendants) would be transferred to the plaintiff-company and a new loan agreement would be drawn up between the plaintiff and the defendants. After the loan agreement was executed, the first-defendant resigned from the plaintiff-company, transferred his share in that company to W's nominee and he and the second defendant also resigned from D Ltd and transferred their shares in D Ltd. The plaintiff-company subsequently sought to void the loan agreement on the ground, inter alia, that it breached the Australian Corporations Law by involving the giving of financial assistance for the

---

126 *Wallersteiner v Moir* [1974] 3 All ER 217.

127 Johnston, *Banking and Security Law in Ireland* (1998), at 18.14.

128 CA 1985, s 151(1) (UK) provides: 'Subject to the following provisions of this Chapter, where a person is acquiring or is proposing to acquire shares in a company, it is not lawful for the company or any of its subsidiaries to give financial assistance directly or indirectly for the purpose of the acquisition before or at the same time as the acquisition takes place.' Moreover, s 152(1) provides '(a) "financial assistance" means – (i) financial assistance given by way of gift, (ii) financial assistance given by way of guarantee, security or indemnity…(iii) financial assistance given by way of a loan…(iv) any other financial assistance given by a company the net assets of which are thereby reduced to a material extent or which has no net assets'. Section 152(2) provides that 'net assets' means 'the aggregate of the company's assets, less the aggregate of its liabilities…'. The differences are apparent; the English legislation is clearly less onerous than CA 1963, s 60(1).

129 *Sterileair Pty Ltd v George Ralph Papallo and another* [1998] 1446 Federal Court of Australia (16 November 1998).

purpose of or in connection with the acquisition of the plaintiff-company's shares. This was rejected at trial and that finding was upheld by the Federal Court of Australia, where the court held:

> 'Not only was there in our opinion no "financial assistance" for the acquisition of the share, there was not the necessary purpose of connection which s 205 [of the Australian Corporations Law] requires. (Counsel for [the plaintiff-company] put his case only on the 'in connection with' limb of the section.) While the covenant of [the plaintiff-company's] under the loan agreement undoubtedly involved a "diminution in the company's resources" (see *Burton v Palmer* [1980] 2 NSWLR 878 at 881), that was for the purpose of, or in connection with, the acquisition of the assets of [D Ltd]. The commercial reality was that for [W's] vehicle, [the plaintiff-company], to get access to the business of [D Ltd] so that he could carry it on free from interference by [the defendants], [the plaintiff-company] had to take over [D Ltd's] debt to them. Viewed in this light, the acquisition of [the first-defendant's] share in [the plaintiff-company] was no more than a tidying up.'[130]

Later the court said:

> 'We think therefore that it is not enough to satisfy the "in connection with" requirement to say, as counsel for [the plaintiff-company] argued, that 'but for' the [plaintiff-company's] covenant to pay the [defendants], the transfer of [the first-defendant's] one $1 share to [W's nominee] would not have taken place. Whilst 'but for' considerations are material, they are not conclusive – the issue remains whether in a practical business sense financial assistance was given by the company in connection with the acquisition of its shares.'[131]

(c) Warranties and covenants that constitute financial assistance

[18.055] It is sometimes questioned whether the giving of covenants, representations and warranties by a company in a share purchase/subscription agreement can amount to the provision of financial assistance in connection with the purchase of or subscription for its shares. It has been noted, though, that there are two views on this point[132]. One, seen in *Charterhouse Investment Trust Ltd v Tempest Diesels Ltd*[133], is that such does not amount to financial assistance as they are not financial in nature, merely contractual representations, albeit that they may ultimately have financial implications where a court of law finds that there has been a breach and awards damages. In the New South Wales case of *Burton v Palmer*[134] Mahony J said:

> 'The fact that a company undertakes obligations, absolute or contingent, in connection with the proposal for the transfer of its shares does not of itself constitute the giving of financial assistance. As I said, the fact that a company facilitates a proposal for such a transfer will not involve it necessarily in contravention of s 67. Thus, a company may answer requests for information relevant to the proposed transfer knowing that it does so in circumstances such that it will be liable for damages if, for lack of care, the information is incorrect (cf *Mutual Life and Citizens' Assurance Co Ltd v Evatt* [1971] 1 All ER 150, [1971] AC 793). But, by answering such requests, the company does not thereby give

---

130 [1998] 1446 Federal Court of Australia (16 November 1998) at p 7.

131 [1998] 1446 Federal Court of Australia (16 November 1998) at p 9.

132 See Cotter, 'Section 60 of the Companies Act 1963' (2000) 7 CLP 111.

133 *Charterhouse Investment Trust Ltd v Tempest Diesels Ltd* [1986] BCLC 1.

134 *Burton v Palmer* [1980] 2 NSWLR 878 at 889–890.

> financial assistance. There may, of course, be circumstances in which the obligations entered into by a company are entered into for a collateral purpose: in such circumstances it may be that the company will, in the particular case, be giving financial assistance. But, collateral purpose aside, if s 67 is to be relevant, there must be more than the incurring, in connection with the transfer of shares, of an obligation which may involve the company in the payment of money. The obligation must be such that it is properly to be categorised as financial assistance. An obligation of a different kind, eg, an obligation to permit inspection of books and records, will not constitute the giving of financial assistance simply because, if it is broken, the company will be liable to pay damages. I do not mean by this that the relevance of s 67 is to be determined by a schematic analysis of the obligation undertaken. The words "financial assistance" are words of a commercial rather than a conveyancing kind and the form of the obligation or transaction will not be conclusive. Thus a loan ostensibly given by a third party may, in the context of a 'round robin' of cheques, be seen as financial assistance in connection with the sale of shares: see *Wallersteiner v Moir* [1974] 3 All ER 217. And a loan given by the company after the sale has completed may, in particular circumstances be such: in the example given in the Greene Report, the Act might be contravened: cf *Glennon v Comr of Taxation* (1972) 127 CLR 503 at 510. Similarly, a warranty given with the intention that the company will be called upon to pay damages and to provide funds in connection with the transfer of its shares will contravene the section.'

This is considered to be the better view and is supported by the decision of the English Court of Appeal in *Barclays Bank plc v British & Commonwealth Holdings plc*[135]. In that case it was agreed that a major shareholder in a public company would, instead of placing such a large number of shares on the market, have the shares converted to redeemable shares, which would be redeemed in four tranches. This scheme of arrangement was approved by court. To safeguard the shareholder against the company not redeeming the shares, a special purpose company was formed and the shareholder given an option to sell the shares to that company, which was financed by a number of banks. As part of the arrangement the company whose shares were being sold covenanted to maintain certain asset rates. After the redemption of two tranches, the company redeeming the shares went into administration and the shareholder exercised its option to call upon the special purpose company to acquire the shares. The financing banks then claimed damages from the company for, inter alia, breach of the covenant to maintain the particular agreed asset rates. One of the questions that arose was whether the company had, in giving the covenants to the banks, provided *financial assistance* for the purchase of its own shares. The English Court of Appeal held, after quoting the passage in *Burton v Palmer* (quoted above):

> 'That statement of the way to approach s 67 of the Australian Companies Act 1961 is, I believe, applicable to s 151 of the 1985 Act. No doubt, as pointed out by Mahony J, there will be cases where the court will look behind the form to see whether there was a collateral purpose and if so conclude that financial assistance was provided; this is not such a case. The purpose of the covenants in the option agreement was to assure [the vendor of the shares]. The covenants were bona fide covenants the performance of which did not involve giving financial assistance. The fact that breach of the covenants might

[135] *Barclays Bank plc v British & Commonwealth Holdings plc* [1996] 1 BCLC 1.

> render [the company whose shares were being redeemed] liable to damages did not mean that [it] gave financial assistance thereby.'[136]

Even allowing for the difference between the Companies Act 1985, s 151 (UK) and CA 1963, s 60 (and, especially, the absence of 'in connection with' in the English Act) it is thought that this represents the law in Ireland. Covenants, representations and warranties can amount to financial assistance in particular cases[137], but not unless that is the dominant purpose behind them.

(d) Actual versus potential financial assistance

[18.056] In England there is also a tendency to interpret particular agreements and transactions in such a way as not to contravene the Companies Act 1985, s 151 (UK)[138]. In *Parlett v Guppys (Bridport) Ltd*[139] the plaintiff was chairman and managing director of the defendant-company and three other family companies; none of the companies were in a formal group. In 1988 it was agreed the plaintiff would, in return for an annual salary of £100,000, a pension and a bonus of 25% of the group of companies' profits, transfer his shares in one of the companies (Guppys (Estates) Ltd) into the joint names of himself and his sons. The companies agreed to share the cost of providing the package to the plaintiff, but did not set a percentage contribution. This operated for a number of years and some three years' later the plaintiff executed stock transfer forms in blank. These were subsequently completed in favour of another of the companies in the 'group', Guppys (Bridport) Ltd. Some five months' later, in December 1991, the plaintiff issued proceedings against his sons and the nominee company, claiming the balance of salary and bonus owed to him. The defendants contended that the agreement was unenforceable as it amounted to the provision of financial assistance by Guppys (Estates) Ltd in connection with the purchase of its own shares. It was held by the Court of Appeal that the agreement was not unenforceable as it did not have to be performed in a manner that contravened s 151(1) of the Companies Act 1985 (UK). This could have been done had Guppys (Estates) Ltd (the company whose shares were being sold) not contributed to the plaintiff's package; instead the other companies privy to the agreement – Guppys (Bridport) Ltd, Guppys (Properties) Ltd and Guppys (Builders) Ltd – could have provided the funds. Nourse LJ said:

> '...the directors of Bridport and Properties could, at the date of the 1988 agreement, reasonably and prudently have made provision for the whole cost to be borne by those two companies and, in discharge of their contractual and statutory duties to [the plaintiff] and Estates respectively as identified in *Lawlor v Gray*, they were bound to do so. On that footing there was no reduction in the net assets of Estates and no financial assistance within s 151(1).'[140]

---

[136] [1996] 1 BCLC 1 at 41.

[137] As to when 'break fees' (ie a sum agreed to be paid by a bidder to a target company in the event of specified events occurring which prevent a takeover bid proceeding) see: Charnley & Breslin, 'Break Fees: Financial Assistance and Directors' Duties' (2000) 21 Co Law 269.

[138] *Brady v Brady* (1988) BCC 390.

[139] *Parlett v Guppys (Bridport) Ltd* [1996] 2 BCLC 34, [1996] BCC 299.

[140] [1996] 1 BCLC 1 at 45c–d.

The reference to *Lawlor v Gray*[141] was to the English Court of Appeal's finding that an agreement which could have been, but did not have to be, performed in breach of a statutory provision, would be interpreted as not coming within its ambit. This was followed (although not expressly) in *Vision Express (UK) Ltd v Wilson*[142] in the context of the statutory provisions concerning the purchase of own shares. There it was held again that where an agreement could be performed in alternative ways, one lawful and the other not, it was presumed that the parties would perform it in accordance with the lawful means. In Ireland too this approach has been taken. So, in *McGill and another v Bogue*[143] the Supreme Court refused to strike out an application for specific performance of a share purchase agreement, which it was claimed contravened CA 1963, s 60(1) because it envisaged a company providing security in connection with the purchase of its own shares. Keane CJ refused to strike out the application because, inter alia, it could be argued that what had been envisaged was that when the share purchase was complete, the company would then provide financial assistance in the nature of security but strictly in compliance with the validation procedure in s 60(2).

The validation procedure: resolution and declaration

[18.057] The principal exception to the prohibition in CA 1963, s 60(1) is the validation procedure – or 'whitewash' procedure as it is sometimes referred to in England – contained in CA 1963, s 60(2)-(11). The validation procedure is considered under the following headings:

- (a) The validation procedure in practice.
- (b) Not all companies can utilise the validation procedure.
- (c) The directors' statutory declaration.
- (d) The shareholders' special resolution.
- (e) The importance of strict compliance in Ireland.
- (f) The validation procedure cannot be utilised retrospectively
- (g) Shareholder protection.

(a) The validation procedure in practice

[18.058] Section 60(2) of CA 1963 (as amended by the Company Law Enforcement Act 2001, s 89 ('CLEA 2001')) provides that the s 60(1) prohibition on a company providing financial assistance in connection with the purchase of its own shares, shall not apply where:

- — the directors of the company swear a statutory declaration of solvency containing the matters detailed below[144]; and
- — the members in general meeting pass a special resolution, not more than 12 months before the financial assistance is provided, giving the directors authority to provide such financial assistance[145], and,

[141] *Lawlor v Gray* (10 July 1979, unreported) English Court of Appeal.

[142] *Vision Express (UK) Ltd v Wilson* [1998] BCC 173.

[143] *McGill and another v Bogue* (11 July 2000, unreported), Supreme Court.

[144] See para **[18.062]**.

[145] CA 1963, s 60(2)(a).

- the company has forwarded, with each notice of the extraordinary general meeting where the special resolution is to be considered, a copy of a statutory declaration, which complies with CA 1963, s 60(3) and (4)[146]; and,
- the company delivers, within 21 days after the date on which the financial assistance is given, a copy of the directors' statutory declaration of solvency to the Registrar of Companies for registration[147]; and,
- where, the members do not unanimously vote in favour of the special resolution, the assistance must not be provided before 30 days after the special resolution is passed, or, until any application made to court has been disposed of by the court[148].

This is the traditional validation procedure that should still be followed as the norm. A more streamlined procedure may be followed where the proposed financial assistance is *unanimously approved* of by the company's members and the company's articles of association contains a model reg 6 type provision (from CA 1963, Sch 1, Table A, Part II (the 'model regulations')). In such cases, the following procedure might be adopted:

- the directors of the company swear a statutory declaration of solvency; and
- the members unanimously sign a written resolution, not more than twelve months before the financial assistance is provided, giving the directors authority to provide such financial assistance[149]; and,
- appended to the written resolution is a copy of a statutory declaration, which complies with CA 1963, s 60(3) and (4)[150]; and,
- the company delivers, within 21 days after the date on which the financial assistance is given, a copy of the directors' statutory declaration of solvency to the Registrar of Companies for registration[151].

These are the *key features* of the validation procedure. To understand where, when and how they arise in practice, an example is considered useful.

[18.059] Returning to the example given above[152] of Investment Properties Ltd providing a guarantee and security in connection with the purchase of its own shares, CA 1963, s 60(2) might be utilised in the following manner. Two individuals, A and B, who own all of the shares in Investment Properties Ltd, have agreed to sell their shares to Borrowings Ltd, a shelf company owned and controlled by C and D, for €1 million. C & D have arranged for Borrowings Ltd to borrow all of the monies from a credit institution on the security of the guarantee of Investment Properties Ltd and a mortgage debenture over its property portfolio. On the closing of such transaction, a typical chronology of events might be:

---

146 CA 1963, s 60(2)(b), as substituted by CLEA 2001, s 89(1).

147 CA 1963, s 60(2)(b).

148 CA 1963, s 60(7).

149 CA 1963, s 60(2)(a).

150 CA 1963, s 60(2)(b), as inserted by CLEA 2001, s 89(a).

151 CA 1963, s 60(2)(b), as inserted by CLEA 2001, s 89(a).

152 See para **[18.042]**.

— The solicitors for A & B and C & D (and both companies) will, in advance of the completion, agree the share transfer documentation and C & D will conduct (through their solicitors, accountants and tax advisers) a due diligence of the affairs of Investment Properties Ltd[153].

— On the day of completion, A & B and their solicitors and the C & D and their solicitors will attend at the offices of the lending bank[154].

— The solicitors for the share vendors (A & B) and the solicitors for Borrowings Ltd and C & D will prepare to close the share sale; A & B's solicitor will pass over all documentation (eg share certificates, stock transfer forms in favour of Borrowings Ltd, share purchase agreement, to mention but a few of the documents involved).

— The Bank will then advance the €1 million by way of a loan to Borrowings Ltd *after* Borrowings Ltd has executed a debenture. (Borrowings Ltd may not have any assets at this point in time and the reason for the debenture will be to acquire a floating security over the shares in Investment Properties Ltd which will shortly be acquired by Borrowings Ltd). Typically, the personal guarantees of C & D will also be required.

— Borrowings Ltd will then pay to A & C the consideration for the shares in Investment Properties Ltd.

— A & C (the shareholders in Investment Properties Ltd) may then execute a form of declaration of trust in favour of Borrowings Ltd. By this A & C will confirm that, although they continue to be the legal owners of the shares pending registration of the stock transfer, having received payment for the shares, they hold the shares in trust for Borrowings Ltd. The intention of this is to make Borrowings Ltd the holding company of Investment Properties Ltd so as to avoid any possible contravention of CA 1990, s 31 when it comes to Investment Properties Ltd giving security later on[155].

— Borrowings Ltd's auditors may then often be required to give the bank a certificate that the Investment Properties Ltd is a subsidiary of the Borrowings Ltd as defined by CA 1963, s 155.

— Borrowings Ltd's directors (C & D) will then be appointed as directors of Investment Properties Ltd by A & B who will meet as directors and appoint C & D as such. Immediately thereafter the existing directors of Investment

---

153 See Chapter 16, *Share Transfers in Private Companies*, para **[16.102]**.

154 The necessity to meet in the early morning to ensure there is time to file the directors' statutory declaration in the Companies Registration Office ('CRO') is no longer necessary since the statutory declaration no longer needs to be filed the same day. CA 1963, s 60(2)(b), as substituted by CLEA 2001, s 89(a), now provides that a copy of the statutory declaration must be delivered to the registrar 'within 21 days after the date on which the financial assistance was given'.

155 Borrowings Ltd will be the holding company of Investment Properties Ltd by reason of CA 1963, s 155(3)(b)(i): see, generally, Chapter 17, *Groups of Companies*, para **[17.021]** et seq. On CA 1990, s 31 see Chapter 11, *Statutory Regulation of Transactions Involving Directors and their Companies*, para **[11.051]** *ff*.

Properties Ltd (A & B) will resign, expressly stating that they have no claims for compensation for loss of office or under any contract of employment.

— C & D (as sole directors of Investment Properties Ltd) will then swear a statutory declaration of solvency for Investment Properties Ltd in accordance with CA 1963, s 60(2)-(5)[156].

— In the example given, where there is unanimous agreement to the provision of financial assistance, the written resolution procedure as envisaged by CA 1963, s 141(8) as now permitted by CA 1963, s 60(6)[157] may be availed of to pass the requisite special resolution. If this is utilised, the copy statutory declaration must be appended to the written special resolution. The written special resolution must then by signed by A & B (who are still the sole registered shareholders in Investment Properties Ltd). Although not strictly necessary, the cautious practitioner might seek to have the beneficial owner of the shares in Investment Properties Ltd, namely Borrowings Ltd, also execute the written special resolution under seal.

— The written special resolution should approve the provision of financial assistance in connection with the purchase of the company's (ie Investment Properties Ltd's) shares. If there is any doubt as to the capacity of Investment Properties Ltd to give a guarantee in favour of what is now its holding company (Borrowings Ltd) this opportunity may also be taken to pass a second special resolution to alter and bolster its objects clause[158].

— C & D, the sole directors of Investment Properties Ltd will then meet as directors and pass a board resolution in favour of entering into the guarantee and providing a mortgage debenture as security over its assets in respect of Borrowings Ltd's loan from the bank. Section 35 of CA 1990 will operate to exempt the guarantee and the provision of security from the provisions in CA 1990, s 31, to the extent to which it might be thought that they apply.

— C & D will then, as directors of Investment Properties Ltd, cause it to execute the bank's guarantee and mortgage debenture in favour of the bank.

— Within 21 days of the entering into of the guarantee and mortgage debenture by Investment Properties Ltd a copy of the directors' statutory declaration must be delivered to the Registrar of Companies in the Companies Registration Office (CRO)[159].

Where the written resolution procedure cannot be availed of (because, for example, some of the shareholders are unavailable) there will need to be additional steps. So, for example, an EGM will need to be convened after the directors swear the statutory declaration of solvency. Thereafter, C & D (as directors of the Investment Properties

[156] See para **[18.062]**.

[157] As substituted by CLEA 2001, s 89(b).

[158] See Chapter 7, *Corporate Contracts, Capacity and Authority*, para **[7.043]**.

[159] Of course particulars of both charges, created by both companies, must be delivered to the CRO within 21 days of their creation: CA 1963, s 99(1). See, generally, Chapter 21, *Corporate Borrowing: Registration of Charges*.

Ltd) would be required to give short notice of an EGM for the purpose of passing the requisite special resolution and this will, require the consent of the Investment Properties Ltd's auditors[160]. As the only registered members will still be A & B (Borrowings Ltd not yet being registered), they will upon the direction of Borrowings Ltd as the sole equitable and beneficial owner of the shares, pass the requisite special resolution at a general meeting. The resolution will approve the giving of authority to the directors to provide financial assistance in connection with the purchase of the Investment Properties Ltd's shares.

Although where there is unanimous agreement to proceed with the provision of financial assistance, the validation procedure will be very much a paper exercise, only the foolhardy would attempt to short-circuit the statutory procedures. As Costello J said in *Lombard & Ulster Banking Ltd v Bank of Ireland*[161], where reliance is placed on these exceptions '...then strict compliance with the procedures is necessary'.

(b) Not all companies can utilise the validation procedure

[18.060] In should be noted from the outset that the validation procedure may *not* be utilised by PLCs. Section 60(15A) of CA 1963 provides that sub-ss (2)–(11) shall not apply to a PLC originally incorporated as such or to a company registered or re-registered as a PLC under the C(A)A 1983 unless a special resolution as provided for in CA 1963, s 60(2) was passed before the company's application for registration or re-registration. Other companies that are precluded from availing of the validation procedure exception to the prohibition in CA 1963, s 60(1) include investment companies[162] and companies whose directors have been restricted pursuant to CA 1990, s 150[163].

[18.061] Although the general rule is that private companies can utilise the validation procedure, a private company which is a 'public company subsidiary' is precluded from providing financial assistance, in accordance with the validation procedure, for the purchase of or subscription for shares in its 'parent public company'[164].

(c) The directors' statutory declaration

[18.062] Section 60(2)(a) of CA 1963 requires that any financial assistance provided must be given under the authority of a special resolution. Section 60(2)(b) of CA 1963 (as substituted by CLEA 2001, s 89(a)) provides that the prohibition in s 60(1) shall not apply where, in addition to the special resolution being passed:

> 'the company has forwarded with each notice of the meeting at which the special resolution is to be considered or, if the procedure referred to in subsection (6) is followed, the company has appended to the resolution, a copy of a statutory declaration which

---

160 See Chapter 9, *Corporate Governance: Meetings*, para **[9.033]**.

161 *Lombard & Ulster Banking Ltd v Bank of Ireland* (2 June 1987, unreported), High Court, per Costello J.

162 See CA 1990, s 260(1).

163 CA 1990, s 155(2). See, further, Chapter 12, *Company Law Compliance and Enforcement*, para **[12.049]**.

164 Regulation 5(2)(c) of the European Communities (Public Limited Companies Subsidiaries) Regulations 1997 (SI 1997/67). See para **[18.037]**.

> complies with subsections (3) and (4) and also delivers, within 21 days after the date on which the financial assistance was given, a copy of the declaration to the Registrar of Companies for registration.'

The statutory declaration referred to in CA 1963, s 60(2)(b) must be made by a majority of the directors of the company. Although this statutory declaration is essentially one of *solvency*, it also contains reference to other matters. The statutory declaration of the directors must contain the following matters[165]:

— the form which such assistance is to take, and,

— the persons to whom such assistance is to be given, and,

— the purpose for which the company intends those persons to use such assistance, and,

— that the directors have made a full inquiry into the affairs of the company and that, having done so, have formed the opinion that the company, having carried out the transaction whereby such assistance is to be given, will be able to pay its debts in full as they become due, (ie that the company is solvent).

The directors' statutory declaration must be made at a meeting of the directors held not more than 24 days before the meeting of the members at which the requisite special resolution is to be passed[166]. In practice, it is common for this declaration to be made on the same day as the financial assistance is provided. Furthermore, the declaration must be made by two directors where a company has only two directors or, by a majority of the directors where there are more than two[167]. There is a strong incentive for the directors to ensure that their statutory declaration is correct since CA 1963, s 60(5) provides that the prohibition in s 60(1) shall not apply where, in addition to the special resolution being passsed:

> 'Any director of a company making the statutory declaration without having reasonable grounds for the opinion that the company having carried out the transaction whereby such assistance is to be given will be able to pay its debts in full as they become due, shall be liable to imprisonment for a period not exceeding 6 months or to a fine not exceeding £500 [€634.87] or to both; and if the company is wound up within the period of 12 months after the making of the statutory declaration and its debts are not paid or provided for in full within the period of 12 months after the commencement of the winding up, it shall be presumed until the contrary is shown that the director did not have reasonable grounds for his opinion.'

The severity of the provision in s 60(5) is one reason why it will be the *new* directors of the company providing the financial assistance who will swear the declaration of solvency, and not the *old* directors. Because they will have nothing further to do with the company, the old directors will be reluctant to expose themselves to the presumption in s 60(5) where the company is wound up insolvent within the following 12 months. Logically, it would seem to be more appropriate for the old directors and members to implement the CA 1963, s 60(2) validation procedure; where the new directors and

---

165 CA 1963, s 60(4)(a)–(d).

166 CA 1963, s 60(3).

167 CA 1963, s 60(3).

members implement the procedure, the timing of the transaction becomes paramount and the loan to purchase the shares will be have to occur momentarily before the provision of security.

(d) The shareholders' special resolution

[18.063] An example of the operative part of the special resolution might be:

> 'In connection with the purchase by Borrowings Ltd of all of the ordinary (and preference) shares in Investment Properties Ltd, it is **hereby resolved** by way of a special resolution and for the purposes of s 60(2)(a) of the Companies Act 1963 that Investment Properties Ltd should enter into a guarantee and provide security in the form of a Mortgage Debenture incorporating a floating charge and several fixed charges to include a specific fixed charge over its property in folio 12345678F Co Dublin (the 'Security') in favour of Big Bank PLC, bankers to Borrowings Ltd, to secure a loan to Borrowings Ltd, in circumstances where the provision of the Security constitutes the provision of financial assistance within the meaning of s 60(1) of the Companies Act 1963.'

Section 89 of CLEA 2001 substituted the following for the original CA 1963, s 60(6): 'The special resolution referred to in subsection (1)(a) may be passed in accordance with section 141(8).'

Accordingly, since 1 October 2001, the written resolution procedure[168] can be availed of to pass the special resolution and the formal convening and holding of a general meeting, whether on full or short notice, can be avoided. Prior to this change, it was common to rely upon the provisions in CA 1963 which permit the convening and holding of a members' EGM on short notice with the company's auditor's consent[169]. In this way, the resolution of the company's members and the declaration of solvency of the company's directors may both happen at the same meeting, shortly before the company provides the financial assistance in connection with the purchase of its own shares.

(e) The importance of strict compliance in Ireland

[18.064] It is important to recognise that there are differences in the form of (and judicial attitude to) the validation procedure between England and Ireland. Accordingly, great care must be taken of some English authorities that suggest that strict compliance with the validation procedure is not absolutely necessary[170]. An example, is *Re NL Electrical Ltd, Ghosh v 3i plc*[171] where a company provided financial assistance in

---

168 Chapter 9, *Corporate Governance: Meetings*, para **[9.076]**.

169 Chapter 9, *Corporate Governance: Meetings*, para **[9.033]**.

170 See, however, *Re SH & Co (Realisations) 1990 Ltd* [1993] BCLC 1309 where Mummery J stressed the need for strict compliance with the prescribed statutory procedure whereby companies may provide financial assistance in connection with the purchase of their own shares. In this case the statutory declaration sworn by the directors failed to provide details of the debenture which the company intended to provide. Although Mummery J found that the detail of the particulars provided satisfied the statutory requirements, it was a borderline case. In *Re RW Peak (Kings Lynn) Ltd* [1998] BCC 596 Lindsay J held that a failure to comply with the provisions of the Companies Act 1985 (UK) in the context of the *purchase of own shares* (as distinct from providing financial assistance in connection with the purchase of own shares) could not be overridden by the principle in *Re Duomatic Ltd* [1969] 2 Ch 365 on informal resolutions.

171 *Re NL Electrical Ltd, Ghosh v 3i plc*[1994] 1 BCLC 22.

connection with the purchase of its own shares within the meaning of s 156 of the Companies Act 1985 (UK). The directors of the company made a statutory declaration but did so in the form prescribed by an obsolete statutory instrument. In addition, a copy of the declaration was not delivered within the time limits prescribed by s 156 of the Act[172]. Notwithstanding these defects Harman J held that they were insufficient to render the financial assistance unlawful under the English legislation.

[18.065] In stark contrast stands the decision of Costello J in *Lombard & Ulster Banking Ltd v Bank of Ireland*[173] where it was held that the validation procedure in CA 1963, s 60(2) had not been complied with even though the shareholders had authorised their solicitor to take all necessary steps to enable the company to provide financial assistance for the purchase of its own shares, and the shareholders had agreed informally to what was done. In the words of the learned judge:

> 'The section makes illegal the granting of financial assistance (as defined) and if exemption for a transaction in breach of subs (1) is claimed because of the adoption of the procedures laid down in subs (2) and (3) and (4) then strict compliance with the procedures is necessary. It is not sufficient to show that all the shareholders had authorised their solicitor to take the necessary steps and that they subsequently ratified what in fact was done. If the procedural requirements were not adopted the transaction is an illegal one, if in fact it involved that granting of financial assistance contrary to subs (1).'

In so holding, Costello J rejected the application of the line of authorities on informal agreement by shareholders[174] to the statutory exception contained in s 60(2)[175]. In view of Costello J's judgment, it is thought Mummery J's advice that '[i]n future solicitors responsible for completing such a statutory declaration should err on the side of caution'[176] is equally applicable to solicitors in this jurisdiction[177].

(f) The validation procedure cannot be utilised retrospectively

[18.066] In *Re Northside Motor Co Ltd; Eddison v Allied Irish Banks*[178], an individual owned half of the shares in the plaintiff-company and wished to acquire the remainder. The defendant-bank advanced finance to another company which was owned by the

---

172 A copy of the declaration was delivered to the English Companies House 30 days after it had been made, which was clearly outside the 15-day statutory limit.

173 *Lombard & Ulster Banking Ltd v Bank of Ireland* (2 June 1987, unreported), High Court, per Costello J.

174 Best illustrated by *Cane v Jones* [1980] 1 WLR 1451. See also, *Re Duomatic Ltd* [1969] 2 Ch 365; *Re Bailey Hay* [1971] WLR 1352; and *Re Gee and Co (Woolich) Ltd* [1975] Ch 52. See generally, Chapter 9, *Corporate Governance: Meetings*, para **[9.079]**.

175 Cf *Re Shannonside Holdings Ltd* (20 May 1993, unreported), High Court where, in different circumstances, Costello J appears to have accepted the principle that all of a company's members may informally alter a company's articles of association. See Chapter 9, *Corporate Governance: Meetings*, para **[9.079]**.

176 *Re SH & Co (Realisations) 1990 Ltd* [1993] BCLC 1309 at 1318h.

177 On solicitors' liabilities and whether solicitors owed a company a duty of care, see *BDG Roof-Bond Ltd v Douglas et al* [2000] BCC 770.

178 *Re Northside Motor Co Ltd; Eddison v Allied Irish Banks* (24 July 1985, unreported), High Court (Costello J).

individual, the bank's security being the provision by the plaintiff-company of a guarantee of the repayment of the loan taken out by the second company. The bank later became aware that the procedure set out in CA 1963, s 60(2) had not been followed, and it demanded that the company pass the appropriate special resolution, and that the directors make the requisite declaration of solvency. These were done. Later, the company was called upon to honour its guarantee and paid money over to the plaintiff-bank. Subsequently, the company was wound up and the liquidator sought the recovery of the money paid on foot of the guarantee. It was accepted by Costello J that the company had provided financial assistance for the purchase of its own shares because the transaction involved a promise to make a pecuniary payment to the bank if the borrower company defaulted in its obligations. Costello J held that the declaration and special resolution could not retrospectively validate the breach of CA 1963, s 60(1) and he held that the liquidator was entitled to the recovery of the money paid by the company on foot of the guarantee.

[18.067] A person who is the beneficiary of a corporate transaction which is in breach of CA 1963, s 60(1) is placed in a very difficult position where facts constituting a breach of s 60(1) *subsequently* come to their notice. The judgment of Costello J in *Re Northside Motor Co Ltd* makes it clear that one cannot retrospectively validate a transaction through compliance with sub-ss (2). What is unclear from that judgment is whether the bank in question had notice of the facts which constituted a breach of s 60(1) *at the time* the guarantee was given. Where a bank or other person does not have the requisite notice at the time the transaction is entered into, the transaction may not subsequently be avoided by the company or its liquidator. The taking of steps to regularise the situation – even where these are proved to be ineffective – ought not retrospectively jeopardise a person's position[179].

(g) Shareholder protection

[18.068] Section 60(8) of CA 1963 enables a shareholder who does not approve of the provision of financial assistance to apply to court for relief in the form of an order for the cancellation of the special resolution. Where such an application is made to court the special resolution shall have no effect, except to the extent, if any, to which it is confirmed by the court. Those shareholders who are entitled to make application to court are the holders of 10% in nominal value of the company's issued share capital or any class thereof[180]. The equitable principle of estoppel finds statutory form in CA 1963, s 60(10), which provides that those who consented to or voted for the special resolution may not make an application under s 60(8). The only procedural provision in respect of this application[181] provides that the application must be made within 28 days after the date of the passing of the special resolution, and may be made on behalf of those entitled to make application by one person whom they appoint in writing for the purpose.

---

[179] Even had it been possible retrospectively to validate the transaction, Costello J held that the statutory declaration of solvency of the directors was 'materially inaccurate and misleading' and the members' special resolution invalid since its factual statements were incorrect, averring that the ownership of the shares were held by persons who were not in fact the owners.

[180] CA 1963, s 60(9).

[181] CA 1963, s 60(11).

Dividends and lawful liabilities: CA 1963, s 60(12)

[18.069] Section 60(12) of CA 1963 provides:

> 'Nothing in this section shall be taken to prohibit the payment of a dividend properly declared by a company or the discharge of a liability lawfully incurred by it.'

It is thought that the sort of transaction envisaged by the 'discharge of a liability lawfully incurred', is one where a company pays a person for a bona fide debt (whether for goods, services or otherwise) and that person uses those proceeds to acquire shares in that company. Notwithstanding that a somewhat different situation arose in *Eccles Hall Ltd v Bank of Nova Scotia*[182], Murphy J found that s 60(12) provided 'a complete answer to the plaintiffs' claim'[183] that the provision of finance to acquire shares in such a circumstance was contrary to s 60(1).

[18.070] In *Eccles Hall Ltd v Bank of Nova Scotia*[184] the plaintiff-company, Eccles Hall Ltd ('Eccles Hall') which was owned by Mr K and Mrs K, was the owner of a Knocklofty House. Mr K agreed to sell to Mr L 500 shares (being 50% of the company's equity share capital) for £180,000 and to redeem a mortgage affecting the property with the proceeds; Mr L agreed to advance £156,250 to Eccles Hall to complete the development of the property and it was agreed that that sum would be secured by a charge over most of the property, from the company in favour of Mr L. It was also acknowledged that Mr K had loaned the company £180,000. Subsequently the company purported to increase its share capital by the creation of an additional 40,000 ordinary shares of £1 each and 359,000 10% cumulative preference shares of £1 each, and to allot Mr K and Mr L 179,5000 of those preference shares. The company's records supporting the allotment of shares were scant. Later still, two charges were created in favour of Mr L, secured on the property. Just over a year later the relationship between Mr K and Mr L deteriorated dramatically and resulted in a breakdown in communications. To resolve the empasse an accountant sought to negotiate an arrangement, in effect to ascertain a price at which Mr L could be bought out of the company and also to find some way of financing that purchase and further development of the property. He was successful in brokering a deal and it was agreed that in consideration of £300,000 Mr L would, inter alia, transfer his interest in the share capital of the company to Mr K and vacate the two mortgages that he held. In his judgment, Murphy J said that it was essential to recognise that the agreement brokered was arrived at by reference to the amount 'put up' by Mr L in connection with the transaction and that he was concerned to be repaid the full amount contributed by him, whether by way of advance or investment in the company or as a result of the purchase of shares; and that the negotiations did not involve the discussion of the then value of the company's properties, less still the value of a 50% shareholding.

As Mr K did not have sufficient personal resources to finance the purchase, the accountant eventually found a willing purchaser, a Mr B. Mr B negotiated a facility with the first defendant – the Bank of Nova Scotia. The result was that Mr B would purchase

---

[182] *Eccles Hall Ltd v Bank of Nova Scotia* (3 February 1995, unreported), High Court (Murphy J).

[183] (3 February 1995, unreported), High Court at p 18.

[184] *Eccles Hall Ltd v Bank of Nova Scotia*(3 February 1995, unreported), High Court (Murphy J).

a 50% beneficial interest in the company, Mr L was to get £325,000 of which Mr B was to put up £100,000 and the Bank of Nova Scotia was to provide the remaining £225,000 to complete the purchase of the shares. The transaction proceeded as follows: the company – Eccles Hall – obtained a mortgage loan of £350,000 and an overdraft facility of £25,000. These were secured by a first fixed and floating charge over its assets with the exception of certain time-share units and the personal guarantees of Mr B, Mr K and Mrs K. The acquisition of Mr L's shares and the repayment of loans made by him to Eccles Hall was structured thus: the bank loaned the sum of £225,000 to a company called Paramount Enterprises Ltd ('Paramount'), a company wholly owned by Mr B. Paramount would then lend the £225,000 that it had borrowed to Eccles Hall which would charge its assets in favour of Paramount and that Paramount would in turn grant a sub-mortgage to the bank. Paramount would also obtain the sum of £100,000 from Mr B. The result of the various transactions ultimately effected was as follows:

— Mr L received £350,000; Paramount obtained 50% of the issued share capital in Eccles Hall;
— Eccles Hall's indebtedness to Mr L was discharged;
— Mr B provided £100,000 to the transactions and the Bank of Nova Scotia provided the remainder; and
— Eccles Hall provided security for the moneys advanced, otherwise than those from Mr B.

[18.071] Subsequently an official liquidator was appointed to Eccles Hall and he challenged the validity of the security given by it which he contended constituted the provision of security for the purpose of or in connection with the purchase of its own shares. Murphy J rejected that CA 1963, s 60 had been breached by reason of the fact that Mr L's shares were not sold for £325,000 as initially envisaged but for a mere £50. Although there was some dispute as to what the true value of the shareholding was, Murphy J said:

> 'Whilst the potential value of the shareholding is not without relevance, it is only a peripheral consideration in the present case. I am satisfied that the sum paid to secure the withdrawal of Mr L from the venture was not related to the value of his shareholding but to the amount of his contribution or the cost to him of his investment in the enterprise.'[185]

Murphy J went on to note that the official liquidator had sought to rely upon a number of case authorities: Irish[186], English[187] and South African[188]. He pointed out that the importance of the Irish cases was the decision in *Bank of Ireland Finance Ltd v Rockfield* which determined the meaning of 'notice' as used in CA 1963, s 60(14) to mean 'actual notice' as opposed to and distinct from 'constructive notice'. As to the English and South African cases he said that they established the following propositions:

---

185 (3 February 1995, unreported), High Court at p 12.

186 *Bank of Ireland Finance Ltd v Rockfield* [1979] IR 21; *Northside Motor Company Ltd: Eddison v Allied Irish Banks Ltd* (24 July 1985, unreported), High Court (Costello J).

187 *Charterhouse Investment Trust Ltd v Tempest Diesels Ltd* [1986] BCLC 1.

188 *Gradwell Property Ltd v Rostra* [1959] 4 SA 419.

'1. That such legislation being punitive in its nature "should not be strained to cover transactions which are not fairly within it".

2. That the words "in connection with" are of wide import. Indeed it was submitted on behalf of the plaintiffs that it was the wide ambit of that phrase which resulted in its deletion from the UK amending provisions of 1981.

3. That commercial transactions negotiated between a company and a person intending to purchase shares therein might constitute the provision of 'financial assistance'. Certainly the purchase by a company of an asset from the intending purchaser at an inflated price would constitute such assistance. In addition it would seem that the purchase of an asset at a fair price or any other sound commercial transaction negotiated at arms' length might constitute the giving of financial assistance if the purpose of such purchase or transaction was to put the purchaser in funds to buy shares in the company entering into the transaction.

4. That the legislation might be breached by the provision of financial assistance to the vendor of the shares as distinct from the purchaser thereof.'[189]

Murphy J repeated his belief that the vast bulk of the payment to Mr L represented the repayment of the company's indebtedness to him: 'The Bank had no notice and indeed I do not believe that it was the case that any part of the moneys provided by them was to be used for the purpose of purchasing shares in Eccles Hall Ltd.'[190]

[18.072] Murphy J went on to find that CA 1963, s 60(12) provided a complete answer to the plaintiff's claim because the payments made by the company (with money borrowed by the company and secured on its assets) were to discharge debts owed by the company to the shareholder. Notwithstanding this decision[191], it is thought that great care must be taken in satisfying oneself that a particular transaction falls squarely within the terms of, and intentions behind, s 60(12). Insofar as it is possible, the consideration for a share purchase should be kept separate from the repayment of a loan. The value attributable to the share purchase must reflect the true value and an appropriate valuation should always be obtained[192]. The fact that in the *Eccles Hall* case the vendor's shares were sold for a nominal sum of £50 and the balance paid in discharge of the company's indebtedness shows, in the words of Murphy J, an 'apparently extraordinary fall in the value of the 50% shareholding in Eccles Hall between February 1989 and May 1989 from £325,000 to £50.'[193] It is difficult to concur with Murphy J's conclusion that 'whilst the potential value of the shareholding is not without relevance, it is only a peripheral consideration in the present case.'[194]

---

[189] (3 February 1995, unreported), High Court at p 16, 17.

[190] (3 February 1995, unreported), High Court at p 17.

[191] The findings in *Eccles Hall Ltd* have been questioned by Breslin, *Banking Law in the Republic of Ireland* (1998), p 691: 'It is, with respect, hard to reconcile the decision with the wide ambit of section 60(1). Even if the discharge of the debt is part of the overall share purchase transaction, the granting of security to secure a loan to discharge that indebtedness is at least an indirect provision of financial assistance in connection with the purchase of the shares.'

[192] See Chapter 16, *Share Transfers in Private Companies*, para **[16.108]** *ff*.

[193] (3 February 1995, unreported), High Court at p 11.

[194] (3 February 1995, unreported), High Court at p 12.

[18.073] Irrespective of other considerations, if CA 1963, s 60(12) is to be of relevance, the liability that is discharged must be a liability of the company, which engages in activity that would otherwise be prohibited financial assistance. So, in *Armour Hick Northern Ltd v Armour Trust Ltd*[195] it was held that where company A owed money to company B, the discharge of that liability by company C (a subsidiary of company A) contemporaneously with the sale by company B of its shares in company A was outside the English equivalent to s 60(12).

[18.074] The fundamental principle, before CA 1963, s 60(12) will operate to exempt the discharge of a lawful liability incurred by a company from the prohibition in s 60(1), must be that the liability is bona fide incurred. The use of the word 'lawful', in the context of CA 1963, s 8(1), has been interpreted to mean not in breach of directors' duties[196] and there is no reason to distinguish its meaning in s 60(12)[197].
The payment of dividends from distributable profits is considered below[198].

Miscellaneous exceptions: CA 1963, s 60(13)

[18.075] Section 60(13) of CA 1963 provides that the general prohibition contained in s 60(1) shall not be taken to prohibit:

- — the lending of money by a company in the ordinary course of its business; or
- — the provision by a company, in accordance with any scheme for the time being in force, of money for the purchase of or subscription for fully paid shares in the company or its holding company where such is for the benefit of its employees or former employees of either it or a subsidiary. This exception includes a director holding salaried employment in either the company or a subsidiary; or
- — the making by a company of loans to persons, other than directors, *bona fide* in the employment of the company or a subsidiary with a view to enabling them to purchase or subscribe for fully paid shares in the company or its holding company to be held by them as beneficial owners.

The foregoing exceptions are self-explanatory. Extreme care must be exercised where the company proposes to assist directors, and persons connected with them, to purchase shares in the company; regard must also be had to CA 1990, s 31, as to which see Chapter 11, above.

[D] Court Sanctioned Capital Reduction

[18.076] The alteration of the capital clause contained in a company's memorandum of association has already been considered[199]. Here it is important to realise that although a

---

[195] *Armour Hick Northern Ltd v Armour Trust Ltd* [1980] 3 All ER 833.

[196] *Re Frederick Inns Ltd et al* [1994] 1 ILRM 387.

[197] In *Belmont Finance Corporation Ltd v Williams Furniture Ltd* [1979] Ch 250 an asset was acquired by a company at a grossly inflated value and the proceeds were then used to acquire the company's own shares. This was held by the Court of Appeal to be the unlawful provision of financial assistance in connection with the purchase of its own shares.

[198] See para **[18.081]**.

[199] See Chapter 3, *The Constitutional Documentation*, para **[3.032]** *ff*.

special resolution of the members of the company in general meeting is necessary, so too is confirmation by the court under CA 1963, s 72(2). It has been noted[200] that this provision is primarily concerned with the protection of the company's creditors thereby underscoring the notion that a company's capital is its 'creditors' fund'.

[E] Court Ordered Capital Reduction

[18.077] The Companies Acts 1963-2001 provide for certain situations in which the courts may *order* the reduction of a company's capital by ordering the company to purchase its own shares. Here, the following provisions which enable the court to order the reduction of a company's capital, are considered:

1. Section 10(6) of CA 1963,
2. Section 205(3) of CA 1963,
3. Section 15 of C(A)A 1983.

Section 10(6) of CA 1963

[18.078] Section 10(1) of CA 1963 enables a company to alter its objects clause[201]. Section 10(6) of CA 1963 provides that where application is made to court in circumstances where a company has by special resolution altered its objects clause, the court may, inter alia:

> '...provide for the purchase by the company of the shares of any members of the company and for the reduction accordingly of the company's capital and may make such alterations in the memorandum and articles of association of the company as may be required in consequence of that provision.'

The purpose behind this provision is to enable dissenting shareholders to be bought out where the majority of the company's shareholders decide to change its direction by altering its 'object'. Implicit in s 10(6) is the recognition that the majority of shareholders may not have sufficient resources to finance the purchase of the dissenting shareholders' shares. That such an order by the court may be made 'on such terms and conditions as it thinks fit' is thought to be sufficient safeguard to ensure that the rights of creditors will not be prejudiced by any order for the reduction of capital.

Section 205(3) of CA 1963

[18.079] A similar provision, which also enables dissenting shareholders to have their shares acquired by the company, is CA 1963, s 205(3). The protection of minority shareholders' interests is considered in Chapter 19, where the statutory right of shareholders to apply to court for relief is discussed. One of the powers of the court is to make an order:

> '...for the purchase of the shares of any members of the company by other members of the company or by the company and in the case of a purchase by the company, for the reduction accordingly of the company's capital, or otherwise.'

---

[200] See Ussher, *Company Law in Ireland* (1986), p 339.

[201] See Chapter 3, *The Constitutional Documentation*, para **[3.027]** *ff*.

Again, implicit in s 205(3) is the recognition that dissenting shareholders, whether they are a minority or a majority, can have their shares acquired in circumstances where the remaining shareholders have insufficient resources to acquire their shares. It is especially just that an oppressed minority should not be prejudiced by the majority's impecuniosity.

Section 15 of C(A)A 1983

[18.080] Section 15 of C(A)A 1983 is concerned with a situation where the members of a PLC pass a special resolution to have the company re-registered as a private company under C(A)A 1983, s 15. Section 15 is essentially a safeguard, which enables members to object to court and to have the special resolution cancelled by court. The court can make an order either cancelling or confirming the resolution, and again any order made may, if the court thinks fit, provide for the purchase by the company of the shares of any member and the consequent reduction of the company's capital.

[F] Distributions and the Payment of Dividends

[18.081] Section 45(1) of C(A)A 1983[202] provides that: 'A company shall not make a *distribution*...except out of profits available for the purpose.'
'Distribution' is defined by C(A)A 1983, s 51, as amended[203], as meaning every description of distribution of a company's assets to members of the company, whether in cash or otherwise, with the exception of the following distributions:

- an issue of shares as fully or partly paid bonus shares,
- the redemption of preference shares pursuant to CA 1963, s 65, out of the proceeds of a fresh issue of shares made for the purpose of the redemption,
- the redemption or purchase of shares under CA 1990, Part XI, out of the proceeds of a fresh issue of shares made for the purpose of the redemption or purchase and the payment of any premium out of the company's share premium account on a redemption under CA 1990, s 220,
- the reduction of share capital by extinguishing or reducing the liability of any of the members on any of its shares in respect of share capital not paid up or by paying off paid up share capital; and
- a distribution of assets to members of the company on its winding up.

Accordingly, the C(A)A 1983, s 45(1) prohibition on a company making a distribution otherwise than out of profits available for the purpose is subject to a number of exceptions, many of which have been considered previously.

[18.082] Central to C(A)A 1983, s 45(1) is that only distributions 'out of profits available for the purpose' are permitted. Section 45(2) of C(A)A 1983, defines profits available for distribution as meaning a company's:

> '...accumulated, realised profits, so far as not previously utilised by distribution or capitalisation, *less* its accumulated, realised losses, so far as not previously written off in a reduction or reorganisation of capital duly made.'

---

[202] See generally, Power, *Accounting Law and Practice for Limited Companies* (1983), Ch 14.
[203] By CA 1990, s 232.

Realised and unrealised profits and losses are not defined by the Companies Acts, although in a scattered way, certain subsections of C(A)A 1983, s 45 provide assistance to those desirous of understanding the rules on distributions. The central rationale behind these rules is that the only assets which a company can distribute are those assets which in the case of an individual very roughly accord with his 'disposable income'. Distributions cannot be made out of capital assets, only out of 'realised profits'.

[18.083] Great care should be taken when using the word 'distribute' in commercial agreements or even in articles of association. In *Igote Ltd v Badley Ltd*[204] a share subscription agreement that had been entered into by the parties provided that in any financial period of 12 months' duration, the company would 'distribute' at least £40,000 to the parties. The agreement went on to provide that such 'shall be *distributed* to the first subscriber and thereafter a similar amount shall be *distributed* to the second subscriber. Any dividend in excess of such amounts shall be split between the shareholders in proportion to their holdings of ordinary shares.' It was held by the Supreme Court that this was to be interpreted, not as a simple obligation to pay, but rather as an obligation to distribute monies by way of dividend which could only be paid out of distributable profits. Murphy J said:

> 'The learned trial judge expressed the view that the ordinary and natural meaning of the word 'distribute' as used in the paragraph in question was "pay". I would respectfully disagree with that view. The *Shorter Oxford Dictionary* gives the primary definition of 'distribute' as 'to deal out or bestow in proportions or shares amongst many; to allot or apportion as his share to each.'

In those circumstances it was held that the use of the word 'distribute' suggested the payment of a dividend, meaning that such could be paid, only, from distributable profits.

[18.084] For those unfamiliar with accounting terminology, the concepts of 'accumulated realised profits' and 'accumulated realised losses'[205], pose some difficulty. In essence, what a company can distribute are those profits remaining after its total losses for the current and previous years are subtracted from its total profits for the current and previous years. The distributable profits may be loosely described as unencumbered profits or 'real profits' as opposed to 'artificial profits'. By so legislating, an attempt has been made to ensure that a company's capital is maintained in situations where a company makes a distribution. The question of whether a distribution may be made by a company is to be determined by reference to the relevant items in the company's accounts[206].

[18.085] It should be noted that insofar as the prohibition under C(A)A 1983, s 45 applies to 'distributions', it includes the payment of dividends. Dividends have been considered previously in Chapter 15[207]. The payment of dividends by private companies is less entrammeled by restrictions than public companies. The rules on the payment of dividends by private companies have been succinctly summarised by Power[208]:

---

204 *Igote Ltd v Badley Ltd* (18 July 2001, unreported), Supreme Court.

205 On what is to be treated as a realised loss see C(A)A 1983, s 45(4).

206 C(A)A 1983, s 49(1). See generally Ch 13, *Accounts and Auditors*.

207 Chapter 15, *Shares and Membership*, para **[15.069]**.

208 Power, *Accounting Law and Practice for Limited Companies* (1983), p 129.

'Private limited companies may pay dividends:

(i) out of net realised profits,

(ii) but must make up past losses first,

(iii) need not cover net unrealised losses, and

(iv) may use unaudited interim accounts to justify payments. Such accounts need not be filed with the Registrar of Companies.'

[18.086] Whether or not directors are obliged to apply profits that are available to pay dividends to capital is a matter for individual companies' articles of association. So, in *Kehoe v The Waterford and Limerick Railway Company*[209] an injunction to restrain the defendant-company and its directors from paying dividends (declared and passed) to the preference shareholders before first replacing certain railway wagons was refused by Porter MR where the directors were under no legal obligation to set aside a fund for maintenance of capital assets.

[18.087] Where a company makes a distribution to its members in contravention of C(A)A 1983, s 45(1), and where at the time of the distribution a member-beneficiary knows or has reasonable grounds for believing that it is so made, that member shall by C(A)A 1983, s 50 be liable to repay what he receives to the company. Where a member receives a non-cash distribution, he shall be liable to pay the company a sum equal to the value of the distribution. Moreover, the directors who cause a company to pay dividends contrary to statute are accountable to the company for such unlawful payments[210]. In *Bairstow v Queens Moat Houses plc*[211] the English Court of Appeal, (per Robert Walker LJ) said:

'The basic rules about lawful and unlawful dividends, developed from the earliest days of company law and now elaborated in accordance with Community legislation, exist not only for the protection of creditors but also for the protection of shareholders. If directors cause a company to pay a dividend which is ultra vires and unlawful because it infringes these rules, the fact that the company is still solvent should not be a defence to a claim against the directors to make good the unlawful distribution.'[212]

In that case it was also held that the directors' liability was not limited to the difference between the unlawful dividends and the amount of dividends that could lawfully have been paid, but extended to the full amount paid. This was because although not trustees, directors were in a closely analogous position because of their fiduciary duties and trustee-like responsibilities. Accordingly, it was held that the directors in that case who were liable for deliberately, and, in one case, dishonestly, paying dividends out of the company's funds which were in their stewardship[213]. Neither could the directors in that case obtain relief under the English equivalent of CA 1963, s 391[214].

[209] *Kehoe v The Waterford and Limerick Railway Company* (1888) LR 21 (Ire) Ch 221.

[210] *Flitcroft's Case* (1882) 21 Ch D 519.

[211] *Bairstow v Queens Moat Houses plc* [2001 2 BCLC 531, [2001] EWCA Civ 712.

[212] [2001 2 BCLC 531 at 546, para [44].

[213] Cf *Target Holdings v Redferns* [1995] 3 All ER 785.

[214] See, further, Ch 10, *Duties of Directors and Other Officers*, para **[10.076]**.

[18.088] In *MacPherson v European Strategic Bureau Ltd*[215] it was held by Ferris J that a shareholders' agreement that provided for the payment to departing shareholders of a percentage of profits earned from contracts on which they had worked, was not an unlawful distribution within the meaning of s 263(1) of the Companies Act 1985 (UK). In that case the company was a quasi-partnership. The agreement in question provided for the payment of the company's overheads and Ferris J held that the balance over was more naturally to be regarded as deferred remuneration for past employees than as a gratuitous payment to shareholders.

[G] Miscellaneous Capital Maintenance Rules

[18.089] There exist a number of other situations where there is a potential for the capital of a company to be reduced. Here the following issues are considered:

1. Forfeiture of shares.
2. Issuing shares at a discount.
3. Liens on shares.
4. Shares issued at a premium.

Forfeiture of shares

[18.090] Model regs 33–39 of CA 1963, Table A, Part I concern the *forfeiture* of shares[216]. These provide that if a member fails to pay any call or instalment of a call on the day appointed for payment, the directors may serve a notice on the member and require payment on the call or instalment, together with interest[217]. The notice to a member should name a further day at least 14 days after the service of the notice, and state that unless payment is made by that day, the shares in respect of the call are liable to be forfeited[218]. The actual act of forfeiture is effected by a resolution of the directors[219]. Model reg 37 states:

> 'A person whose shares have been forfeited shall cease to be a member in respect of the forfeited shares, but shall, notwithstanding, remain liable to pay to the company all monies which, at the date of forfeiture were payable by him to the company in respect of the shares, but his liability shall cease if and when the company shall have received payment in full of all such monies in respect of the shares.'

Furthermore, C(A)A 1983, s 41(4)(d) expressly provides that the restrictions on a company acquiring its own shares shall not prevent a company from forfeiting its shares.

Issuing shares at a discount

[18.091] There is a general prohibition on a company issuing shares at a discount. The reason for concern is that where shares are issued at a discount, the result is that the company will end up having less actual capital than if it had issued shares at full price,

---

215 *MacPherson v European Strategic Bureau Ltd* [1999] TLR 144.

216 See also Chapter 15, *Shares and Membership*, para **[15.119]** *ff*.

217 CA 1963, Sch 1, Table A, model reg 33.

218 CA 1963, Sch 1, Table A, model reg 34.

219 CA 1963, Sch 1, Table A, model reg 35.

and at the same time, it will appear to outsiders that the company has received full payment for its shares[220]. Such a situation is worse than where shares are issued and partly paid for, since in such a case, there is a further unpaid liability outstanding. Where shares are issued at a discount, the shares held are not subject to any further claim for payment.

[18.092] The issuing of shares at a discount is prohibited by C(A)A 1983, s 27(1). This provides that '...the shares of a company shall not be allotted at a discount'. Where this prohibition is breached, the allottee is liable to pay the company the difference between the amount paid and the amount actually due, together with interest[221]. This general prohibition is subject to sub-s (4) and court approval.

Liens on shares

[18.093] A lien on shares is a security right in favour of a company which allots shares to a shareholder in respect of amounts remaining unpaid on those shares[222]. Liens on shares held in private companies remain unregulated, notwithstanding the restrictions imposed on public companies by C(A)A 1983, s 44. Such a situation is envisaged by common form model articles of association, and in particular regs 11-14. Accordingly, model reg 11 provides that a company has a first and paramount lien on all unpaid shares, subject to express exclusion by the directors, and model reg 12 gives the company an express power of sale of such shares. One common modification of the model articles of association is the inclusion of fully paid shares being subject to this lien in respect of all debts due by members to the company[223].

Shares issued at a premium

[18.094] Often, companies will issue shares at a premium[224]. Where shares are issued by a company at a premium, whether for cash or otherwise, CA 1963, s 62(1)[225] provides:

> '...a sum equal to the aggregate amount or value of the premium on those shares shall be transferred to an account, to be called 'the share premium account', and the provisions of this Act relating to the reduction of the share capital of a company shall, except as provided in this section and s 207(2) of the Companies Act 1990[226] apply as if the share premium account were paid up share capital of the company.'

Accordingly, where shares are issued at a premium it is not the full consideration received which must be paid into the share premium account, only the amount received

---

220 See *Ooregram Gold Mining Co of India v Roper* [1892] AC 92, where it was said that a shareholder could '...purchase immunity from liability beyond a certain limit on terms that there shall be and remain a liability up to that limit.'

221 C(A)A 1983, s 27(2).

222 See Chapter 15, *Shares and Membership*, para **[15.117]** *ff.*

223 See *Allen v Gold Reefs of West Africa Ltd* [1900] 1 Ch 656.

224 This is a matter for the company and companies are not obliged to issue shares at a premium: *Lowry (Inspector of Taxes) v Consolidated African Selection Trust Ltd* [1940] 2 All ER 545.

225 As amended by C(A)A 1983, Sch 1, para 11 and CA 1990, s 231(1).

226 See para **[18.012]**.

which is in excess of the nominal value of the shares. Monies held in a company's share premium account are not available for distribution[227].

[18.095] A company's share premium account may be utilised in either of the four circumstances provided for in CA 1963, s 62(2), namely:

- in paying up unissued shares of the company (other than redeemable shares) to be allotted to members of the company as fully paid bonus shares[228];
- in writing off the preliminary expenses of the company[229];
- in writing off the expenses of, or the commission paid or discount allowed on, any issue of shares or debentures of the company;
- in providing for the premium payable on redemption of any redeemable preference shares in pursuance of CA 1990, s 220, or of any debentures of the company.

In *Henry Head & Co Ltd v Ropner Holdings Ltd*[230] the defendant-company was incorporated for the acquisition, for amalgamation purposes, of two shipping companies which had previously been carried on separately under the same management. The means employed was that the shareholders in the two shipping companies sold their shares in exchange for shares in the new holding company. Each shareholder got one new share in the new holding company in exchange for each old share in the shipping companies. In consequence, although the new holding company had an authorised and issued share capital of £1,719,606, the real value of the shares was approximately £7 million. In these circumstances the directors were advised that the sum of circa £5 million had to be placed in the company's share premium account. The directors of the company objected to this because they were seriously fettered in their use of this money by virtue of the equivalent UK provision to CA 1963, s 62. Although Harman J was willing to limit the operation of the section he was constrained by the clear wording of the section and said:

> 'I have every desire to reduce the effect of this section to what I cannot help thinking would be more reasonable limits, but I do not see my way of limiting it in that way. It is

227 In *Shearer (Inspector of Taxes) v Bercain Ltd* [1980] 3 All ER 295 it was held that monies paid into a holding company's share premium account after the holding company issued its shares (nominal value of £4,100) in return for the entire issued share capital in two other companies (worth £96,000) was not distributable by the holding company. This was so although most of the value in the shares of the other two companies represented undistributable profits. Because it was held that the money in the share premium account was not distributable, this money was not taxable. See Ussher, 'Doubts Remain on *Shearer v Bercain*' (1982) 3 Co Law 28.

228 On bonus shares see Chapter 15, *Shares and Membership*, para **[15.110]**.

229 Keane, *Company Law*, (2000) para 9.24 has noted that shares in a private company which is incorporated to acquire an existing business are often issued at a premium to the company's controller as a means of avoiding capital duty. Were the controller to cause the company to allot to him shares equivalent to the value of the business being transferred, capital duty would be payable on the full value of the shares allotted. In such circumstances, the premium charged on the shares may be utilised to discharge the preliminary expenses incurred in the formation of the company.

230 *Henry Head & Co Ltd v Ropner Holdings Ltd* [1952] Ch 124.

> not stated to be a section which only applies after the company has been in existence a year or after the company has acquired assets or when the company is a going concern, or which does not apply on the occasion of a holding company buying shares on an amalgamation. Whether that is an oversight on the part of the legislature or whether it was intended to produce the effect it seems to have produced, is not for me to speculate. All I can say is that this transaction seems to me to come within the words of the section, and I do not see my way to holding as a matter of construction that it is outside it.'

Since CA 1963, s 62 is identical in all material respects to the section under consideration, s 56 of the Companies Act 1948 (UK), it is thought that an Irish court would be bound to follow this decision[231]. In Ireland, however, the provisions of CA 1963, s 149(5) should be noted[232]. This states that, the profits and losses attributable to any shares in a subsidiary held by its holding company may be treated in the holding company's accounts as revenue profits or losses, *provided that*, the directors and the auditors of a company are satisfied and so certify that it is fair and reasonable and does not prejudice the rights and interests of any person.

[H] Meetings Where There is a Serious Capital Loss

[18.096] It has long been recognised that no matter what the legislature provides, nothing can prevent a company from suffering a capital loss in the course of trading[233]. However, where a company does suffer a serious loss of capital, the directors of that company are under a duty, by C(A)A 1983, s 40, to call an EGM of the members.

[18.097] Section 40(1) of C(A)A 1983 provides that:

> '...where the net assets of a company are half or less of the amount of the company's called up share capital, the directors of the company shall, not later than 28 days from the earliest day on which that fact is known to a director of the company, duly convene an extraordinary general meeting of the company for a date not later than 56 days from that day for the purpose of considering whether any, and if so what, measures should be taken to deal with the situation.'

Clearly, not only is there an obligation of the directors to convene such a meeting, but the directors also have a statutory duty to consider what should be done. In so providing, the legislature has imposed a positive obligation on such a company's directors which prevents them from ignoring the situation faced by the company. What is also clear, however, is that should the members or the directors decide to do nothing, there is nothing which can be done to force them to take action.

[18.098] Section 40(2) of C(A)A 1983 provides that where there is a failure to convene an EGM, each of the directors of the company who knowingly and wilfully authorises or permits the failure to hold the meeting, or who knowingly and wilfully authorises or permits the failure to hold the meeting during the period in which it should be held, is guilty of an offence.

---

231 CA 1948, s 56 (UK) was modified by s 37 of the Companies Act 1981 (UK) to provide an exemption in these circumstances.

232 See also Chapter 13, *Accounts and Auditors*, para **[13.148]**.

233 See *Guinness v Land Corporation of Ireland* (1882) Ch D 349, cited at para **[18.003]** and *Trevor v Whitworth* (1887) 12 App Cas 409.

Chapter 19

Shareholders' Remedies

Introduction to shareholders' remedies

[19.001] This chapter is concerned with situations where relations between shareholders and directors, and between shareholders inter se, breakdown. In company law there exists a general rule, known as 'the rule in *Foss v Harbottle*', which states that where a company is wronged, the only person who can sue to redress that wrong is the company. This can cause considerable difficulty to minority shareholders where the directors and a majority of the other shareholders refuse to sue to redress the wrong to the company. The rationale of the rule is that the will of the majority of the shareholders ought to prevail. In a private company, particularly where the shareholders can be said to be quasi-partners, majority rule is more difficult to justify. It is for this reason that the Companies Act 1963, s 205 ('CA 1963') has become the most important shareholders' remedy, allowing shareholders to seek redress from the courts in cases of *oppression*. Section 205 allows petitioners to avoid the artificialities of the rule in *Foss v Harbottle* as it applies to private companies. In this work s 205 is elevated from being a mere statutory exception to the rule in *Foss v Harbottle* to being centre stage in this discussion of shareholders' remedies. It should, in addition, be remembered that there are other remedies available to shareholders as follows:

(a) Petitioning to wind up on just and equitable grounds.

(b) Miscellaneous statutory remedies in particular situations.

(c) Shareholders' personal rights.

(a) Petitioning to wind up on just and equitable grounds

[19.002] Another remedy, potentially more potent than CA 1963, s 205, that is also available to disgruntled shareholders, is to petition the court to have the company wound up on *just and equitable* grounds under CA 1963, s 213(f). Frequently, application is made to the High Court under ss 205 and 213(f) in double harness. Section 213(f) of CA 1963 and the principles of winding up on just and equitable grounds are considered in Chapter 25[1].

(b) Miscellaneous statutory remedies in particular situations

[19.003] The Companies Acts 1963–2001 afford several statutory remedies to shareholders in particular situations, primarily those involving serious constitutional changes and capital reorganisations. Shareholders may apply to court for relief in the following instances, all of which are considered elsewhere in this book:

— on the alteration of the objects clause[2];

— on the alteration of the articles of association, whether in respect of individual members' rights[3] or class rights;

[1] See Chapter 25, *Winding Up Companies*, para **[25.076]** *ff*.

[2] Chapter 3, *The Constitutional Documentation*, para **[3.027]**.

[3] Chapter 3, *The Constitutional Documentation*, para **[3.065]**.

— on the reduction of capital[4];
— on the provision of financial assistance in connection with the purchase of a company's own shares[5];
— on the entering into of a guarantee or the provision of security in connection with a loan, quasi-loan or credit transaction in favour of a 'relevant person'[6];
— in a scheme of arrangement[7];
— in a reconstruction on a voluntary liquidation[8]; and
— on the compulsory acquisition of shares[9].

(c) Shareholders' personal rights

[19.004] Finally, by virtue of their membership of a company, shareholders have *personal rights* by virtue of the articles of association and the Companies Acts 1963-2001. These rights are enforceable by the shareholders personally, and the rule in *Foss v Harbottle* does not apply to such actions. The personal rights of shareholders have been considered in Chapter 15 above[10]; but here the rights of members to vindicate their personal rights are distinguished from the rule in *Foss v Harbottle*.

[19.005] The primary shareholders' remedies, which are considered in this chapter, are addressed as follows:

[A] Oppression: Section 205 of CA 1963.
[B] The Rule in *Foss v Harbottle*.
[C] Derivative Actions and Exceptions to *Foss v Harbottle*.

[A] OPPRESSION: SECTION 205 OF CA 1963[11]

[19.006] Section 205 of CA 1963 provides a company's shareholders with their most powerful and far-reaching remedy against the company and its directors in cases of oppression and disregard of their interests. This statutory remedy was first introduced in Ireland in 1963 and, despite the dearth of early cases, has established itself today as the remedy most frequently resorted to by shareholders[12]. Many cases[13] demonstrate the effectiveness of section 205 actions in cases where relationships in quasi-partnership

---

4 Chapter 18, *The Maintenance of Capital*, para **[18.077]**.

5 Chapter 18, *The Maintenance of Capital*, para **[18.041]**.

6 Chapter 11, *Statutory Regulation of Transactions Involving Directors and their Companies*, para **[11.004]**.

7 Chapter 24, *Schemes of Arrangement*, para **[24.040]** *ff.*

8 Chapter 24, *Schemes of Arrangement*, para **[24.053]**.

9 Chapter 16, *Share Transfers in Private Companies*, para **[16.088]** *ff.*

10 Chapter 15, *Shares and Membership*, para **[15.083]**.

11 See generally, McCann, 'Minority Shareholder Protection: Sections 205 and 213(f) of the Companies Act, 1963' (1995) Dli – The Western Law Gazette 85.

12 See generally, Temple–Lang, 'Minority Shareholder Protection Under Irish Law' (1974) NILQ 387.

13 Such as *Colgan v Colgan* (22 July 1993, unreported), High Court and *Irish Press plc v Ingersoll Irish Publications Ltd* (15 December 1993, unreported), High Court.

companies have broken down. Section 205 is of particular utility where the members of a quasi-partnership type private company fail to cater prospectively for their relations in a shareholders' agreement[14].

[19.007] Section 205(1) of CA 1963 provides:

> 'Any member of a company who complains that the affairs of the company are being conducted or that the powers of the directors of the company are being exercised in a manner oppressive to him or any of the members (including himself), or in disregard of his or their interests as members, may apply to the court for an order under this section.'

This subsection demonstrates the fundamental objective of s 205: to provide members with relief where the *affairs of the company or the powers of the directors* are being conducted or exercised *oppressively or in disregard of their interests*. Here, s 205 shall be considered in the following manner:

1. The nature of the remedy.
2. Oppression.
3. Disregarding members' interests.
4. 'Affairs of the company' and 'powers of directors'.
5. Quasi-partnership companies and 'legitimate expectations'.
6. The locus standi to petition.
7. Abuse of process.
8. The position of the company.
9. *In camera* applications.
10. Remedies: restraining the removal of a shareholding-director.
11. Remedies: ending the matters complained of.
12. The unfairly prejudicial remedy contrasted.

The nature of the remedy

[19.008] Section 205 of CA 1963 may be resorted to in a wide variety of situations. In the context of quasi-partnership private companies, perhaps the paradigm situation in which s 205 is invoked is where one or more of the quasi-partner-members believes that the affairs of the company or the powers of the directors are being exercised *oppressively*, or in *disregard of his interests*. Of course s 205 has a wider application, and any member, whether he is a quasi-partner or not, can make application under the section. Where it is shown to the court's satisfaction that section 205 relief is available, the court has wide powers. Accordingly, the court is empowered to order any of the following courses of action:

— that the oppressor buy the petitioner's shares;
— that the petitioner buy the oppressor's shares;
— that the company buy either party's shares;

[14] Cf *Irish Press plc v Ingersoll Irish Publications* (15 December 1993, unreported), High Court, where there was in fact a substantial shareholders' agreement in existence.

— that the company's memorandum and/or articles of association are amended to provide as the court directs; or

— that the company be wound up.

These remedies are considered below[15].

[19.009] Section 205 petitions are a messy and expensive business. Putative petitioners would do well to heed the words of Murphy J in *Re Murray Consultants Ltd and Nocrumb Ltd; Horgan v Murray and Milton*[16] where he said:

> 'It has been observed before that there is a surprising parallel between matrimonial proceedings and proceedings under section 205 of the 1963 Act[17]. They both involve an examination of the conduct of the parties over a period of years and usually a determination by them to assert rights rather than solve problems. It may well be that the disparate forms of litigation are frequently fuelled by a bitterness borne of rejection: matrimonial or commercial. In neither discipline can the courts persuade the parties that it is in their best interests to direct their attention to solving their problems rather than litigating them.'

Oppression

[19.010] At this point, the concept of oppression is considered. The study of oppression involves the consideration of a number of matters:

(a) The test for oppression.

(b) Oppression need not be qua member.

(c) Isolated acts of oppression.

(d) Fraudulent and unlawful transactions.

(e) Oppressive management.

(f) Exclusion from management.

(g) Non-consultation with shareholders.

(h) Technical oppression.

(a) The test for oppression

[19.011] The concept of *oppression* is relatively new in company law, having first being introduced by the Companies Act 1948 (UK). In *Re Greenore Trading Company Ltd*[18] Keane J acknowledged that 'oppressive conduct' for the purposes of the corresponding s 210 of the English 1948 Act meant the exercise of the company's authority '...in a manner burdensome, harsh and wrongful.'

Acceptance of this definition of oppressive conduct is seen in the judgment of Viscount Simonds in *Scottish Co-operative Wholesale Society Ltd v Meyer*[19]. In that case, a

---

15 At para **[19.065]**.

16 *Re Murray Consultants Ltd and Nocrumb Ltd; Horgan v Murray and Milton* [1997] 3 IR 29 at 42.

17 Sentiment echoed by O'Flaherty J in *New Ad Advertising Ltd* (26 March 1998, unreported), Supreme Court at p 3.

18 *Re Greenore Trading Company Ltd* [1980] ILRM 94 at 100–101.

19 *Scottish Co–operative Wholesale Society Ltd v Meyer* [1959] AC 324.

subsidiary company was formed by a co-operative society, in which the plaintiff-company became a minority shareholder. The plaintiff became a minority shareholder in the subsidiary to facilitate the co-operative society because without the plaintiff's involvement a licence would have been required for the manufacture of raylon. When the law relating to such licences changed, the co-operative no longer needed the plaintiff as a minority shareholder and it sought to buy the plaintiff's shares. When the plaintiff refused to sell its shares, the co-operative transferred the subsidiary's business into its own name, rendering the subsidiary's shares valueless. The plaintiff succeeded in its action under s 210 of the English 1948 Act and the court ordered that the co-operative buy out the plaintiff's shares at the value they would have been, had the subsidiary's assets not been dissipated. In the course of his judgment, Viscount Simonds said:

> '...it appears to me incontrovertible that the society have behaved to the minority shareholders of the company in a manner which can justly be described as "oppressive". They had the majority power and they exercised their authority in a manner "burdensome, harsh and wrongful" – I take the dictionary meaning of the word.'[20]

In *Re Greenore Trading Company Ltd*[21] a company had three shareholders – the petitioner, a Mr Boyle and a Mr Vanlandeghem – each of whom owned 8,000 £1 shares. Shortly after the company was formed, a resolution was passed that no one shareholder should hold more than 8,000 shares in the company. Some years later, when the company was encountering financial difficulties, Vanlandeghem contributed £10,000 to it in return for a further 10,000 shares in the company. Subsequently, Boyle agreed to sell his shares to Vanlandeghem for £22,500, made up of £8,000 from Vanlandeghem, being par value for the shares, and £14,500 from the company as a severance payment. The petitioner brought proceedings under s 205 claiming that Vanlandeghem was using his control of the company in a manner that was oppressive. The petitioner sought, inter alia, the winding up of the company or an order requiring the oppressor to buy his shares. Keane J noted that the payment by the company of the £14,500 was contrary to CA 1963, s 60 and 'constituted conduct of such a nature as to justify, and indeed require, the making of an order under s 205(3)'.[22] Through his influence, Vanlandeghem had caused the company to part with its assets to provide indirect financial assistance to enable him purchase the company's shares. As Keane J said:

> 'The patent misapplication of the company's monies for the purpose of giving Mr Vanlandeghem a dominant position in its affairs seems to me to be properly described as "burdensome, harsh and wrongful" *quoad* the petitioner.'[23]

[19.012] An objective standard will be used in determining whether particular conduct should be deemed to be burdensome, harsh and wrongful. In the first Irish case to consider CA 1963, s 205, *Re Irish Visiting Motorists' Bureau Ltd*[24], Kenny J said:

---

20 [1959] AC 324 at 342. For a recent case concerning alleged 'unfairly prejudicial' conduct in the context of parent companies and their subsidiaries, see *Nicholas v Soundcraft Electronics Ltd* [1993] BCLC 360.

21 *Re Greenore Trading Company Ltd* [1980] ILRM 94.

22 [1980] ILRM 94 at 100.

23 [1980] ILRM 94 at 101.

24 *Re Irish Visiting Motorists' Bureau Ltd* (7 February 1972, unreported), High Court.

> 'The affairs of a company may be conducted or the powers of the directors may be exercised in a manner oppressive to any of the members although those in charge of the company are acting honestly and in good faith. If one defines oppression as harsh conduct or depriving a person of rights to which he is entitled, the person whose conduct is in question may believe that he is exercising his rights in doing what he does. One of the most terrifying aspects of human history is that many of those whom we now regard as having been oppressors had a fanatical belief in the rightness of what they were doing. The question then when deciding whether the conduct of the affairs of a company or the passing of a resolution is oppressive is whether, judged by objective standards, it is.'[25]

Although the conduct complained of is to be judged by objective standards, what will be oppressive will vary from company to company. What might be oppressive in the context of a quasi-partnership company may not be oppressive in a private company with unconnected membership. In *Crindle Investments v Wymes*[26] it was held that the rejection of offers to compromise proceedings in circumstances where such constituted 'an improvident gamble' amounted to oppression and a disregard of the interests of other shareholders within the meaning of CA 1963, s 205.

(b) Oppression need not be qua member

[19.013] One of the many problems with s 210 of the Companies Act 1948 (UK) was that the oppression suffered by a member had to be suffered by him in his capacity as a member, or qua member. This was established by a series of cases[27]. However, the provision which replaced s 210 — s 459 of the Companies Act 1985 (UK) — has been afforded a wider interpretation[28]. Further, in Ireland, CA 1963, s 205(1) provides that the court can grant relief where a member proves that the affairs of the company are being conducted, or that the powers of the directors of the company are being exercised, in a manner oppressive to him or *any of the members* (including himself).

[19.014] Implicit authority for the proposition that oppression can be suffered by a member in his capacity *as a director* is found in *Re Murph's Restaurants Ltd*[29]. The facts of this case are considered in detail in Chapter 25[30]. Of interest here is the fact that the

---

25 (7 February 1972, unreported), High Court at p 33.

26 *Crindle Investments v Wymes* [1998] 4 IR 578 at 582 where Keane J noted an earlier decision of Murphy J in the High Court (at p 7).

27 Eg *Elder v Elder* (1952) SC 49, *Re Lundie Brothers Ltd* [1965] 1 WLR 1051 and *Re Westbourne Galleries Ltd* [1971] 2 WLR 618.

28 See, eg, *Tay Bok Choon v Tahanson Sdn Bhd* [1987] BCLC 472 and *R & H Electrical Ltd v Haden Bill Electrical Ltd* [1995] 2 BCLC 280. Cf *Re JE Cade & Son Ltd* [1992] BCLC 213 where Warner J refused to make an order under the Companies Act 1985, s 459 (UK) where the company concerned occupied a farm owned by a minority shareholder and refused to deliver up possession. See also *Re Alchemea Ltd* [1998] BCC 964 where it was found that any alleged unfairly prejudicial conduct did not affect the petitioner's interests as a member in any material respect in circumstances where the company had been established as a cooperative under which members, like employees, could hope to derive nothing but wages, discretionary bonuses and expenses.

29 *Re Murph's Restaurants Ltd* [1979] ILRM 141. See Ussher, 'Company Law – Oppression, Justice and Equity' (1979–80) DULJ 92.

30 See Ch 25, *Winding Up Companies*, para **[25.078]**.

petitioner's claim was based on his oppression in his capacity as a director of the company. At the interlocutory hearing McWilliam J refused the order seeking to have the company wound up, saying that CA 1963, ss 205 and 213(g) only apply to members in their capacity as members. In that case the petitioner was both a shareholder and a director of the company. His complaint was, inter alia, that he was removed as a director of the company by the other two directors. At the actual hearing of the action Gannon J did not doubt his jurisdiction to make an order under s 205, although in the circumstances he ordered that the company be wound up under CA 1963, s 213(f)[31]. A definitive judicial statement from the Irish courts is awaited on this point, but it is thought on a literal interpretation of s 205(1) that it will be found that relief for oppression is not confined to members acting qua member.

(c) Isolated acts of oppression

[19.015] It is now generally accepted that an isolated act of oppression can give rise to relief under CA 1963, s 205: *Re Williams Group Tullamore Ltd*[32], per Barrington J. Often, the matters complained of can be said to be ongoing. In the *Williams* case Barrington J said:

> '...in the present case we are dealing with a transaction which is ongoing at the date of the hearing of this petition in the sense that it is one which will be implemented if the petitioners do not obtain the relief they are seeking.'[33]

In that case the company's authorised share capital was divided into 250,000 ordinary shares of £1 each and 150,000 8% preference shares of £1 each. There were 133,540 ordinary shares and 133,540 preference shares issued in the company. On the basis of the rights attaching to both classes of share, the ordinary shareholders fared much better than the preference shareholders on foot of the dividend paid. The company's directors decided to adjust the position by allowing the preference shareholders to participate in the profits of the company and a resolution was passed in general meeting to make a distribution of £267,000 between all of the shareholders. The ordinary shareholders, who could not vote at this meeting, petitioned the court on the grounds that the preference shareholders' actions were oppressive.

Barrington J held that the petitioners were entitled to relief under CA 1963, s 205 because, although it could not be said that the ordinary shareholders were oppressed, the transaction was in objective disregard to the ordinary shareholders' interests. As authority for the proposition that an isolated transaction can give rise to relief under CA

---

31 In *R & H Electrical Ltd and another v Haden Bill Electrical Ltd* [1995] 2 BCLC 280 the petitioner claimed to have been unfairly prejudiced by reason of his having been removed as a director in circumstances where a company controlled by the petitioner was a creditor of the subject company and was prejudiced. Robert Walker J said that the court should take a broad view of the petitioner's interest when considering the capacity in which a petitioner complained. There, it was found that the petitioner had a 'legitimate expectation' (see para **[19.034]**) of being able to participate in the management of the company for as long as the loan was outstanding to his company.

32 *Re Williams Group Tullamore Ltd* [1985] IR 613. Cf *Re Westbourne Galleries Ltd* [1970] 3 All ER 374 and *Re Greenore Trading Company Ltd* [1980] ILRM 94.

33 [1985] IR 613 at 620.

1963, s 205, Barrington J cited the judgment of Kenny J in *Re Westwinds Holding Company Ltd*[34]. In the *Westwinds* case, considered below, the sale of the company's assets was found to constitute oppression. After reciting the first in a series of acts by the oppressor, Kenny J said:

> 'The sale of the lands at Knocknacarra was an exercise by the directors of their powers in a manner which was fraudulent and oppressive to the petitioner and was in total disregard of his interest as a member of the company. On *this ground alone* the conditions for the exercise of the powers of the court under s 205(3) have been fulfilled.'[35] [Emphasis added]

By way of contrast, in *Re Greenore Trading Company Ltd*[36] Keane J said that an isolated act of oppression will not normally be sufficient to justify relief[37]. He overcame that requirement in that case by finding 'a multiplicity of unlawfulness in the same one act in order to raise it to the level of oppressive conduct'[38]. Although sometimes a distinction is drawn between lawful and unlawful actions, it is thought that such a distinction is artificial and that an isolated act of oppression or disregard of members' interests will be sufficient to grant relief[39].

(d) Fraudulent and unlawful transactions

[19.016] *Re Westwinds Holding Company Ltd*[40] provides one of the most vivid and dramatic examples of a case in which the Irish High Court found the petitioner to have been oppressed. The facts of the case are worthy of extensive summary. The company in question was incorporated in 1964 to take over the business of builders and public works contractors carried on by a Martin Hession, the promoter and defendant in the subsequent action. The company's articles of association provided for the appointment of a 'governing director', Hession, and went on to give him weighted voting rights. Two shares were issued in the company, one in Hession's name and one in another person's name. The following year Hession held discussions with the petitioner, on foot of which the second shareholder transferred her share to the petitioner who in turn was appointed director and the company secretary. Subsequently, at the offices of a solicitor, the petitioner, Hession and an auditor met. The solicitor made a written record of what transpired, and Kenny J noted that it had been agreed, inter alia, that 4,998 shares were to be issued to Hession in return for assets which were to become the company's property; 4,999 shares were to be issued to the petitioner for cash; Hession was to become chairman and the petitioner the company secretary; that there was to be no governing director; and that Hession and the petitioner were to be permanent directors. The company subsequently acquired three acres of land at Knocknacarra, Galway. Some time later two of these three acres were sold to a company in which Hession owned almost all the shares. The deed of transfer to that company bore the seal of Westwinds

[34] *Re Westwinds Holding Company Ltd* (21 May 1974, unreported), High Court.

[35] (21 May 1974, unreported), High Court at p 17.

[36] *Re Greenore Trading Company Ltd* [1980] ILRM 94 at 101.

[37] Citing *Re Westbourne Galleries* [1970] 1 WLR 1378.

[38] Ussher, *Company Law in Ireland* (1985), p 261.

[39] Ussher, *Company Law in Ireland* (1985), p 261.

[40] *Re Westwinds Holding Company Ltd* (21 May 1974, unreported), High Court.

Holding Company Ltd but the petitioner's signature had been forged by Hession. Although a number of justifications for Hession signing the petitioner's name were advanced by Hession's counsel, these were rejected by Kenny J. The two acres were again sold on to another company in which Hession was the owner of most of the shares. Subsequently, Hession disposed of his shares in that company to another individual for £15,000.

There was also a second transaction, whereby Hession caused Westwinds Holding Company Ltd to guarantee the overdraft of another company owned indirectly by him. Hession provided the bank concerned with a minute of a meeting, purportedly signed by Hession and the petitioner. Kenny J accepted that the petitioner's signature was a forgery. Even the Form 47 evidencing the creation of the equitable mortgage given by the company contained the forged signature of the petitioner. Kenny J said that he was:

> '...convinced that the petitioner would never have agreed to the creation of this charge and that he did not get notice of the meeting because Mr Martin Hession wished to conceal the business being transacted.'[41]

A number of meetings were purportedly held, the minutes of which were not signed by the petitioner. Finally, Hession purported to hold a meeting appointing himself company secretary and removing the petitioner as secretary and director of the company.

[19.017] Kenny J found that the sale of the lands at Knocknacarra was made at a gross undervalue 'and was a fraud on the other member of the company' and that the 'sale benefited Mr Martin Hession only at the expense of the company and the petitioner'[42]. As has been noted above[43] Kenny J held that this ground alone was adequate to justify an order under CA 1963, s 205(3). Similarly, the mortgage created by the company was not for the benefit of the company or the petitioner, but was to Hession's benefit. Again this was found to be an exercise of the directors' powers which was oppressive to the petitioner, being in total disregard of his interest as a member. Kenny J held that the appropriate remedy was to make an order directing Hession to purchase the petitioner's shares, to be valued on the basis that the lands sold were still the property of the company, and without regard to the fact that there existed restrictions on the transfer of shares in the company.

[19.018] Conduct does not need to be unlawful to be oppressive. In *Re Clubman Shirts Ltd*[44], O'Hanlon J found that the petitioner had been oppressed notwithstanding that the respondents had not acted unlawfully[45].

(e) Oppressive management

[19.019] It is sometimes said that mere incompetence or mismanagement of a company's affairs will not per se amount to oppression within the meaning of CA 1963, s 205. An authority in point is *Re Five Minute Car Wash Service Ltd*[46]. In that case the petitioner,

---

41 (21 May 1974, unreported), High Court at p 12.

42 (21 May 1974, unreported), High Court at pp 16, 17.

43 See para **[19.015]**.

44 *Re Clubman Shirts Ltd* [1983] ILRM 323 discussed at para **[19.026]**.

45 There had been a number of breaches of the Companies Acts such as failure to file accounts, hold annual general meetings and to furnish copies of the register of members and accounts, however such were found not to amount to oppression ([1983] ILRM 323 at 325).

who was a former director of the company, took proceedings under s 210 of the Companies Act 1948 (UK). The petitioner alleged that the managing director conducted the affairs of the company with complete disregard of the interests of any shareholders other than his wife and himself. Buckley J refused to find that there was oppression because, inter alia, even if the managing director was unwise, inefficient and careless in the performance of his duties as managing director there was no suggestion that he had acted unscrupulously, unfairly or with any lack of probity or had overborne or disregarded the wishes of the board of directors or that his conduct was harsh, burdensome or wrongful towards any member of the company.

[19.020] In *Re Clubman Shirts Ltd*[47] O'Hanlon J held:

> 'I would not classify as oppressive conduct within the meaning of the Act, the omission to comply with the various provisions of the Act referable to the holding of general meetings and the furnishing of information and copy documents. These were examples of negligence, carelessness, irregularity in the conduct of the affairs of the company, but the evidence does not suggest that these defaults or any of them formed part of a deliberate scheme to deprive the petitioner of his rights or to cause him loss or damage.'[48]

Similarly in *McCormick v Cameo Investments Ltd*[49] McWilliam J held that mere mismanagement by the directors of the company was not sufficient to constitute oppression. In contrast, in *Re a Company (No 00789 of 1987) ex p Shooter*[50] Harman J held that a repeated failure to hold annual general meetings ('AGMs') and to lay accounts before the members was conduct unfairly prejudicial to the interests of all the members. It is thought that irregularity in the conduct of a company's affairs will be oppressive where it is part of a *deliberate* scheme.

[19.021] One of the most striking cases of tyranny in the management of a company is *Re Harmer*[51]. In that case the sons of an octogenarian, Harmer Snr, who had incorporated his successful stamp-dealing business, grew increasingly frustrated by his totalitarian management of the company in which they were shareholders. Harmer Snr was deemed to be the company's 'governing director', but the office had no special or distinctive rights or powers. The sons alleged that Harmer Snr ran the business as if he owned it himself, disregarding the resolutions and wishes of the board of directors and the interests of the shareholders. An example of his actions was that he unilaterally, and against the wishes of the directors, founded an unprofitable branch of the business in Australia. The Harmer sons succeeded both at trial and in the Court of Appeal.

[19.022] In *Irish Press plc v Ingersoll Irish Publications Ltd*[52] the respondent was found to have acted in furtherance of its own agenda in managing the subject company. The background to the case was that in 1989 the petitioner and respondent agreed to enter

---

46 *Re Five Minute Car Wash Service Ltd* [1966] 1 All ER 242.

47 *Re Clubman Shirts Ltd* [1983] ILRM 323.

48 [1983] ILRM 323 at 327.

49 *McCormick v Cameo Investments Ltd* [1978] ILRM 191.

50 *Re a Company (No 00789 of 1987) ex p Shooter* [1990] BCLC 384.

51 *Re HR Harmer Ltd* [1958] 3 All ER 689.

52 *Irish Press plc v Ingersoll Irish Publications Ltd* (15 December 1993, unreported), High Court.

into a partnership to manage three newspapers, The Irish Press, The Evening Press and The Sunday Press. To that end two companies were formed – Irish Press Newspapers Ltd and Irish Press Publications Ltd – in which the petitioner and respondent held equal shareholdings. The parties also entered into a subscription and shareholders' agreement and a management agreement. Under the management agreement the respondent was engaged by Irish Press Newspapers Ltd. Although the relationship was initially good, it deteriorated and culminated in the petitioner instituting proceedings under CA 1963, s 205. The petitioner claimed, inter alia, that although management services ceased to be provided by the respondent, the respondent insisted upon the continuance of the management agreement; the respondent acted in furtherance of its own interests and contrary to the interests of the subject companies; and the respondent had acted oppressively towards the petitioner. In a lengthy judgment, Barron J found that the respondent had acted oppressively. Having quoted extensively from the case of *Scottish Cooperative Wholesale Society v Meyer*[53] he held that there were parallels between it and the case in hand and that:

> 'What it shows is that where a deliberate plan to damage the interests of a company is carried out by a shareholder in the manner by which it exercises its power to conduct the affairs of the company, such behaviour is oppression...
>
> Here there is also a deliberate plan. Though it was not a plan to destroy the business of the company, it was a plan of action against the interests of the petitioner and was carried out by the manner in which the affairs of the companies were exercised.'[54]

The failure by the respondent to properly operate the management agreement, which was held to be a repudiation of the agreement, was central to the finding of oppression. Barron J went on to hold that after the management agreement had come to an end:

> '...insistence that it still subsisted was oppression. But the real complaint was the *de facto* take over of the companies. This in reality was the placing in position of nominees by the respondent for the purpose of the interests of the respondent and not in the interests of the company. That is also oppression. Neither was done *bona fide*. Both were done in wilful disregard of the interests of the companies.'[55]

Barron J ordered the respondent to sell its shares in the companies to the petitioner at a price to be determined by the court[56]. Although on appeal to the Supreme Court it was held that damages could not be awarded pursuant to CA 1963, s 205(3), the foregoing findings were not disturbed.

[19.023] One particular issue in petitions alleging oppression in the management of a company concerns the position of *nominee directors*[57]. The duty of nominee directors was considered in the judgment of Viscount Simonds in *Scottish Cooperative Wholesale Society v Meyer*[58], which was cited with approval by Barron J in *Irish Press plc v*

---

[53] *Scottish Cooperative Wholesale Society v Meyer* [1959] AC 324.

[54] (15 December 1993, unreported), High Court at pp 79, 80.

[55] (15 December 1993, unreported), High Court at p 81.

[56] See *Irish Press plc v Ingersoll Irish Publications Ltd* (13 May 1994, unreported), High Court, per Barron J. See Chapter 16, *Share Transfers in Private Companies*, para **[16.111]**.

[57] See generally Chapter 10, *Duties of Directors and Other Officers*, para **[10.040]** *ff*.

Ingersoll Irish Publications Ltd above. Viscount Simonds, in a passage quoted by Barron J[59], said that nominee directors were not entitled to remain silent and inactive with full knowledge of the majority shareholder's intention to strip the company of its assets. He said:

> 'They were the nominees of the Society and, if the Society doomed the Company to destruction, it was not for them to put out a saving hand. Rather, they were to join in that work, and, when a frank and prompt statement to their co-Directors might have enabled them to retrieve its fortunes, they played their part by maintaining silence. That is how they conducted the affairs of the Company, and it is impossible to suppose that that was not part of the deliberate policy of the Society. As I have said, nominees of a parent Company upon the Board of a subsidiary company may be placed in a difficult and delicate position. It is, then, the more incumbent on the parent company to behave with scrupulous fairness to the minority shareholders and to avoid imposing upon their nominees the alternative of disregarding their instructions or betraying the interests of the minority. In the present case the Society pursued a different course. It was ruthless and unscrupulous in design and it was effective in operation, and, as I have said, it was promoted by the action or inaction of the nominee Directors.'[60]

Commenting on the nominee directors appointed by the respondent in the *Irish Press plc* case, Barron J said:

> 'The position of nominee directors can be a difficult one if they disagree with the views of the person or body appointing them. Their duty is to act in the interests of the company. They have also got a duty to act on the instructions of their nominating party. But acting in the interests of the company is no more than acting in the interests of all its shareholders. If what they are asked to do involves seeking to damage the interests of one section of the shareholders in favour of another then as a Director they have a duty not to do that. However, if what they are required to do is merely something that they themselves personally think is not the way to approach the matter then they must give way. There is nothing wrong with the appointing body or party from having a view as to where the interests of the company lie and ensuring that its nominees follow that direction provided that in so doing they are not seeking to damage anybody else's interest in the company.'

Nominee directors are frequently appointed to the boards of joint-venture companies, which can sometimes be found to be quasi-partnership companies. Barron J's comments in this regard are extremely instructive and are cautionary words for both nominee directors and for those who appoint them[61].

(f) Exclusion from management

[19.024] To exclude a director from the management of the company can amount to oppression in certain circumstances. This is apparent from the decision of Gannon J in *Re Murph's Restaurants Ltd*[62] where he said '...the purported exclusion of [the petitioner] by the [respondents] in an irregular and arrogant manner is undoubtedly oppressive.'[63]

---

58 *Scottish Cooperative Wholesale Society v Meyer* [1959] AC 324.

59 (13 May 1994, unreported), High Court at p 77.

60 [1959] AC 324 at 341.

61 See further Ch 10, *Duties of Directors and Other Officers*, para **[10.041]** *ff*.

62 *Re Murph's Restaurants Ltd* [1979] ILRM 141.

63 [1979] ILRM 141 at 152.

In that case, the respondent-directors had resolved to dismiss the petitioner as a director of the company, offering him three months' salary. In *Re Ghyll Beck Driving Range Ltd*[64] it was held that a petitioner (a shareholding-director) who had been excluded from a joint venture, which it was contemplated would be managed by all four participants, was unjustly excluded and that his exclusion had destroyed the trust between the parties[65]. It is believed that in similar circumstances such conduct could amount to oppression[66].

[19.025] The exclusion of a shareholding-director from the management of a quasi-partnership company may be found to destroy the trust, confidence and mutuality which theretofore subsisted. However, in *O'Neill v Phillips*[67], the facts of which are set out below[68], it was held that a shareholder in a quasi-partnership company does not have 'a stark right of unilateral withdrawal'[69] where trust and confidence breaks down. On this point it was said:

> 'Such breakdowns often occur (as in this case) without either side having done anything seriously wrong or unfair. It is not fair to the excluded member, who will usually have lost his employment, to keep his assets locked in the company. But that does not mean that a member who has not been dismissed or excluded can demand that his shares be purchased simply because he feels that he has lost trust and confidence in the others. I rather doubt whether even in partnership law a dissolution would be granted on this ground in a case in which it was still possible under the articles for the business of the partnership to be continued. And as Lord Wilberforce observed in *Re Westbourne Galleries Ltd* [1973] AC 360 at 380B, one should not press the quasi-partnership analogy too far: "A company, however small, however domestic, is a company not a partnership or even a quasi-partnership".'[70]

In an Irish context it is important to remember that before the remedies provided for in CA 1963, s 205(3) can be invoked, oppression or disregard of interests within the meaning of s 205(1) must first be established.

(g) Non-consultation with shareholders

[19.026] Although the directors' non-consultation with a company's shareholders will not per se amount to oppressive conduct, it may do so in certain circumstances. In quasi-partnership private companies, non-consultation can be indicative of a breakdown in the mutual trust associated with such companies. In *Re Clubman Shirts Ltd*[71] the petitioner

64 *Re Ghyll Beck Driving Range Ltd* [1993] BCLC 1126.

65 See also *Re Elgindata Ltd* [1991] BCLC 959 where the petitioner's expectation to take part in the management of the company was in issue. See also *Re Apollo Cleaning Services Ltd; Richards v Lundy et al* [1999] BCC 786.

66 In *Re Eurofinance Group Ltd*, unrept English High Court of 16 June 2000 (Pumfrey J) the exclusion of the petitioner from the management of a banking consultancy company amounted to unfair prejudice. See also *Re Tottenham Hotspur plc* [1994] 1 BCLC 655 for an example in the breakdown of a personal relationship between the company's chief executive and chairman.

67 *O'Neill v Phillips* [1999] BCC 600.

68 See para **[19.037]**.

69 [1999] BCC 600 at 611H.

70 [1999] BCC 600 at 612B. To the extent to which *Re Apollo Cleaning Services Ltd; Richards v Lundy et al* [1999] BCC 786 found otherwise, it should not be considered as correctly decided.

71 *Re Clubman Shirts Ltd* [1983] ILRM 323.

claimed that he was oppressed by the respondent directors because they had, inter alia, completed a transaction whereby the *entire* business of the company was transferred to another company without the petitioner's knowledge or consent. O'Hanlon J held that in such circumstances:

> '[a] minority shareholder is entitled to have such a transaction, completed without his knowledge or consent, subjected to the closest scrutiny to ensure that he has been dealt with fairly by those who controlled the destinies of the company.'[72]

(h) Technical oppression

[19.027] Section 205 of CA 1963 provides a very useful remedy where the relationship between shareholders has broken down. Where oppression is found, the court has many options open to it, although the usual order is for the purchase or sale of either party's shares. An order to wind up a company under CA 1963, s 213(f) on the ground that such is *just and equitable* may have disastrous consequences for all concerned. In practice, parties in dispute have occasionally *agreed* that the court has jurisdiction to make an order under s 205. In *Colgan v Colgan & Colgan*[73], Costello J began his ex tempore judgment by saying:

> 'I think that the court has jurisdiction on the evidence before it under s 205 of the Act. The parties agreed that I can make an order under this section, and I have jurisdiction to do so. I do not think that I need give any final conclusion as to the nature of the oppression that occurred.
>
> In that case very serious disputes arose. Certain actions were taken arising from these disputes and these actions do mean that I have got jurisdiction under the section to do what is fair between the parties to bring an end to the situation which exists. I do not think that my jurisdiction to do so has been challenged.'[74]

In that case, Costello J noted that the father of the petitioner and respondents had 'built up a fine commercial empire'[75], but that unfortunate differences had arisen amongst his sons, the successors to his enterprises. The empire consisted of a number of prime properties, including a number of hotels and public houses in Dublin, all unencumbered by mortgages. Costello J acknowledged that nobody wanted a winding-up order to be made, and in this, it is opined, he was objectively right. Had five hotels/public houses simultaneously come onto the property market, their realisable value, and the value of the shares in the companies concerned, would have been greatly diminished. The relief claimed by the petitioner was an order requiring his brother-respondents to buy out his shares, and Costello J concluded that the respondents should be required to buy out the petitioner at a valuation determined by him based on submissions from the parties' respective accountant-valuers[76].

---

72 [1983] ILRM 323 at 325.

73 *Colgan v Colgan & Colgan* (22 July 1993, unreported), High Court.

74 (22 July 1993, unreported), High Court at p 1.

75 (22 July 1993, unreported), High Court.

76 With regard to the valuation of the shares, see generally Chapter 16, *Share Transfers in Private Companies*, para **[16.108]**.

It is thought that the approach adopted by the learned Costello J was particularly suited to the case in hand. Whether the parties were satisfied with the valuation placed on the shares in sale is one thing; that it was appropriate for the court to end the matters complained of by ordering the purchase of the petitioner's shares seems indisputable.

Disregarding members' interests

[19.028] The second situation in which a member can petition the court under CA 1963, s 205 is where the affairs of the company or the powers of the directors are being exercised in *disregard of his interests*. Although, disregard of members' interests seems to be an easier ground than oppression upon which to succeed, the majority of Irish cases have turned upon whether or not there has been oppression.

[19.029] The reference to 'disregard of his or their *interests* as members' is wider than referring to a disregard of one's *rights* as a member[77]. This has been recognised in England in the context of s 459 of the Companies Act 1985 (UK). In *Re Sam Weller & Sons*[78] Peter Gibson J observed:

> 'The word 'interests' is wider than a term such as 'rights', and its presence as part of the test of s 459(1) to my mind suggests that Parliament recognised that members may have different interests, even if their rights as members are the same.'[79]

The reference to 'interests' enables the court to have regard to the widest possible matters, unconnected with the petitioner's purely legal rights as a member of the company.

[19.030] The leading Irish case on conduct in disregard of members' interests is *Re Williams Group Tullamore Ltd*[80]. The facts of that case are considered above[81]. There, Barrington J held that the preference shareholders in the company had acted within their formal powers and had acted honestly in resolving to allow the distribution between all shareholders; their conduct was found to be neither burdensome, harsh, wrongful nor lacking in probity or fair dealing and consequently did not amount to oppression. However, Barrington J recognised that there was an alternative to finding oppression:

> 'It is perhaps worth noting that the Irish section offers relief not only when the affairs of the company are being conducted in an oppressive manner but also (and alternatively) where they are being conducted *in disregard of the interests of some member or members*.'[82] [Emphasis added]

Of the resolutions passed by the preference shareholders, Barrington J said that it appeared to him that they:

> '...were carried in disregard of the interests of the ordinary shareholders. It appears to me that the implementation of these resolutions is an ongoing matter in the company and justifies the view that the affairs of the company are being conducted in disregard of the

77 See MacCann, *Butterworth Ireland Companies Acts 1963 – 1990*, (1993), p 203, *Note* 41.

78 *Re Sam Weller & Sons* [1990] BCLC 80.

79 [1990] BCLC 80 at 85b–c.

80 *Re Williams Group Tullamore Ltd* [1985] IR 613.

81 See para **[19.015]**.

82 [1985] IR 613 at 620.

> interests of the ordinary shareholders. I fully accept that the proposal put forward in the resolution...was put forward in good faith. Nevertheless, it appears to me that it is in objective disregard of the interests of the ordinary shareholders and that to persist in implementing it would, in the circumstances, be oppressive to the ordinary shareholders.'[83]

Although the learned judge grounded his jurisdiction to make an order on the basis that the affairs of the company were being conducted in disregard of the interests of the ordinary shareholders, it is remarkable that he tagged onto his view the observation that to implement the resolutions would be *oppressive*. It is thought that it was unnecessary to find that the implementation of the resolutions would be oppressive: sufficient jurisdiction existed to make an order pursuant to CA 1963, s 205 on the finding that the affairs of the company were being conducted in disregard of the ordinary members' interests.

[19.031] A petitioner claiming that the powers of the directors or the affairs of the company are being conducted in disregard of his interests as a member must show that the damage suffered was qua member or in his capacity as a member. The operative part of CA 1963, s 205(1) refers to 'in disregard of his or their interests *as members*'. As was considered above, oppression can be claimed by a member in his capacity as member or in some other capacity such as director[84].

'Affairs of the company' and 'powers of directors'

[19.032] Where a petition is brought under CA 1963, s 205, the oppression or the disregard of interests must result from either the conduct of the *affairs of the company* or the exercise of the *powers of the directors*. The '*powers of the directors*' refers to the directors' exercise of their delegated powers of management which typically arises on foot of model reg 80 of CA 1963, Sch 1, Table A, Part I (the 'model regulations').

[19.033] The 'affairs of the company' refers to the conduct of the member-shareholders when acting together as corporators. An example in point from decided case law is *Re Williams Group Tullamore Ltd* where the passing of the resolution by the preference shareholders was found to be in disregard of the interests of the ordinary shareholders. In the Australian case of *Weatherall v Satellite Receiving Systems (Australia) Pty Ltd*[85] the equal shareholders in the respondent-company agreed to admit W as third equal shareholder and director in consideration of his investing US$250,000 in the company. A third-party company ('UST') agreed by deed to procure the allotment to W of one-third of the shares in the company and his appointment as director upon his paying UST the consideration on the respondent-company's account, which UST would remit to the respondent-company. Although only US$150,00 was received and remitted to the respondent-company, W was allotted the shares and appointed as a director. The petitioner alleged oppression. It was held, in these circumstances, that W's failure to pay

[83] [1985] IR 613 at 622.

[84] See para **[19.014]**.

[85] *Weatherall v Satellite Receiving Systems (Australia) Pty Ltd* [1999] Federal Court of Appeal 218 (12 March 1999).

UST had nothing to do with his position as a director or member so as to constitute the company's 'affairs', and that the failure to pay the remaining US$100,000 was not 'corporation-related'. In *Re Leeds United Holdings plc*[86] it was held that the petitioner had no right to expect that another shareholder would not sell his shares without the consent of the petitioner, as such did not relate to the company's 'affairs'.

Quasi-partnership companies and 'legitimate expectations'

[19.034] Quasi-partnership companies[87] are referred to in various places throughout this book[88]. Where a relationship of *equality, mutuality, trust, and confidence*[89], based on a personal relationship[90], subsists in a private company[91] it may be appropriate that it be considered as a quasi-partnership[92]. Such a finding may result in members and directors being found to be restrained on equitable grounds from enforcing rights found in the 'black letter of the law'. In such companies, acts and omissions may be found to amount to oppression or disregard of members'[93] interests, by reason of equitable considerations; formal rights may be forced to give way to equitable principles implied from the law of partnership[94].

[19.035] Quasi-partnerships have been found to exist, notwithstanding the provisions of s 1(2)(a) of the Partnership Act 1890, which provides that the relationship between members of a registered company 'is not a partnership within the meaning of this Act.' Although there is a *presumption* that those who choose to incorporate have elected for

---

86 *Re Leeds United Holdings plc* [1996] 2 BCLC 545.

87 See, generally, Twomey, *Partnership Law* (2000) at [8.68] *ff*. See also Prime and Scanlan, *The Law of Private Limited Companies* (1996), p 298.

88 See Chapter 1, *The Private Company in Context*, para **[1.128]** and Chapter 25, *Winding-Up Companies*, para **[25.076]**.

89 See *Re Murph's Restaurant Ltd* [1979] ILRM 141 at 151.

90 See *Re Astec (BSR) plc* [1999] BCC 59 where Jonathan Parker J found (at 86) that in order to give rise to an equitable constraint based on 'legitimate expectations' 'what is required is a personal relationship or personal dealings of some kind between the party seeking to exercise the legal right and the party seeking to restrain such exercise, such as will affect the conscience of the former'. One of the best examples of a personal relationship is seen in *Re Apollo Cleaning Services Ltd; Richards v Lundy* [1999] BCC 786 and *Re Legal Costs Negotiators Ltd* [1999] BCC 547 where pre–existing partnerships had been converted into limited companies.

91 In England it has been said that there was no room for 'legitimate expectations' in public companies: *Re Blue Arrow plc* (1987) 3 BCC 618 at 623; *Re Astec (BSR) plc* [1999] BCC 59 at 87D.

92 In *Third v North East Ice & Cold Storage Co Ltd* [1998] BCC 242 it was held that where a company was a quasi–partnership, but circumstances changed rendering it not a quasi-partnership, 'legitimate expectations' would be displaced.

93 It is possible that some members will be found to be quasi–partners and some will not: see *Re Planet Organic Ltd* [2000] 1 BCLC 366.

94 In *Irish Press plc v Ingersol Irish Publications Ltd* (15 December 1993, unreported), High Court (Barron J) at p 70 of the judgment, Barron J said: 'Where there are equal shareholdings in a company and where the reality is that the shareholders have entered into a partnership the court will where necessary apply the principles of partnership law.'

the legislation governing companies to govern their relationship, that presumption can be rebutted by clear evidence[95]. An example of where the court found that the three shareholders in a company which had been incorporated over 20 years' previously, were not in a partnership arrangement, is *Horgan v Murray and Milton*[96]. This case concerned an application to strike out plenary proceedings seeking various declarations, including one that the plaintiff was a partner of the two defendants[97]. In striking out the proceedings, O'Sullivan J said:

> 'I cannot agree that there is any indication on the pleadings that clear evidence will be advanced to show that obligations or rights apart from or additional to those arising under the companies code were contemplated or agreed between the parties. On the contrary, [the plaintiff's counsel] has accepted in argument that the relationship between the parties under what is an independently subsisting partnership relationship are precisely the same as those which exist between them as fellow shareholding members of the company. In my view this is no case for a partnership: these parties conceived and promoted a public business to be conducted through the medium of [the company].'

[19.036] The existence of formalised agreements – such as shareholders' agreements – will generally operate to preclude the implication of unstated expectations, although this will not always be conclusive[98]. In England, it has been found to be possible for one member of a company to be considered a 'junior partner' to another member who was the 'dominant senior partner' so that despite the absence of complete equality, the company could still be considered to be a quasi-partnership where the characteristics of such a company had been found to exist[99].

[19.037] One twist to this is the categorisation of such equitable considerations as giving rise to so-called 'legitimate expectations'. Recent English authorities have discussed how, in such companies, a member may be entitled to have certain *legitimate expectations*, over and above those to which he would be entitled as a matter of strict contract and statute law[100]. Lord Hoffmann in *O'Neill v Phillips* described the term[101], as follows:

---

95 See the decision of Murphy J in *Crindle Investments v Wymes* [1998] 4 IR 567 at 576 where he said: '… I believe that the presumption must be that parties who elect to have their relationship governed by corporate structures rather than, say, a partnership, intend their duties – and where appropriate their rights and remedies – to be governed by the legal provisions relating to such structures and not otherwise. It would require, in my view, reasonable clear evidence to impose obligations on directors or shareholders above and beyond those prescribed by legislation or identified by long established legal principles.'

96 *Horgan v Murray and Milton* (17 December 1999, unreported), High Court (O'Sullivan J).

97 There already existed section 205 proceedings and other plenary proceedings for wrongful dismissal in being.

98 See, eg, *Re A Company (No 002015 of 1995)* [1997] 2 BCLC 1.

99 See *Quinlan v Essex Hinge Co Ltd* [1996] 2 BCLC 417.

100 See *O'Neill v Phillips* [1999] BCC 600; *Re Astec (BSR) plc* [1999] BCC 59; *Re Pectel Ltd* [1998] BCC 405 (the Court of Appeal decision in *O'Neill v Phillips*); *Richards v Lundy*; *Re Apollo Cleaning Services Ltd* [1999] BCC 786; *Third v North East Ice & Cold Storage Co Ltd and another* [1998] BCC 242.

101 *O'Neill v Phillips* [1999] BCC 600.

> 'In *Re Saul D Harrison & Sons plc* [1994] BCC 475 at 490A I used the term "legitimate expectation", borrowed from public law, as a label for the "correlative right" to which a relationship between company members may give rise in a case when, on equitable principles, it would be regarded as unfair for a majority to exercise a power conferred upon them by the articles to the prejudice of another member. I gave as an example the standard case in which shareholders have entered into association upon the understanding that each of them who has ventured his capital will also participate in the management of the company. In such a case it will usually be considered unjust, inequitable or unfair for a majority to use their voting power to exclude a member from participation in the management without giving him the opportunity to remove his capital upon reasonable terms. The aggrieved member could be said to have had a "legitimate expectation" that he would be able to participate in the management or withdraw from the company.'[102]

Lord Hoffmann went on to express his own misgivings with the term he had applied to quasi-partnership companies:

> 'It was probably a mistake to use this term, as it usually is when one introduces a new label to describe a concept which is already sufficiently defined in other terms. In saying that it was "correlative" to the equitable restraint, I meant that it could exist only when equitable principles of the kind I have been describing would make it unfair for a party to exercise rights under the articles. It is a consequence, not a cause, of the equitable restraint. The concept of a legitimate expectation should not be allowed to lead a life of its own, capable of giving rise to equitable restraints in circumstances to which the traditional equitable principles have no application. That is what seems to have happened in this case'.[103]

Despite Lord Hoffmann's misgivings, 'legitimate expectations' remains a useful label with which to describe certain shareholders' hopes, although it must be remembered that it is just a label for oppressive conduct or disregard of interests and is not an independent cause of action.

[19.038] The facts in *O'Neill v Phillips* were that O'Neill had been an employee of Pectel Ltd, a construction company, who had risen through the ranks to become a shareholding-director, holding 25% of the company's shares. Phillips was the other director and holder of 75% of the shares in the company. O'Neill alleged that, as a result of informal discussions, he had been led to believe that he would receive a full 50% shareholding in Pectel Ltd, upon the company achieving certain targets. Upon Phillips retiring, O'Neill became sole director and upon the company prospering, O'Neill was credited with half the profits by Phillips, who voluntarily waived a third of his 75% entitlement to dividends. During this time a number of relevant events happened: the company's share capital was increased by £100,000 by contributions in the proportions of 25:75; O'Neill guaranteed the company's bank account, secured by a charge on his residence; and Phillips indicated in principle his willingness to increase O'Neill's shareholding to 50% upon certain net-asset targets being achieved. Things turned sour when the construction industry went into recession. Phillips became dissatisfied with O'Neill's management of the company and resumed personal command. At one particular meeting Phillips criticised O'Neill's management and said that he would no

[102] [1999] BCC 600 at 609, 610.

[103] [1999] BCC 600 at 610.

longer receive 50% of the profits, just the 25% to which he was entitled as a 25% shareholder. O'Neill terminated his guarantee and arranged to set up a competing business in Germany (where Pectel Ltd also had operations). O'Neill then petitioned under s 459 of the Companies Act 1985 (UK), alleging unfairly prejudicial conduct by Phillips. O'Neill lost at trial but succeeded in the Court of Appeal[104] where it was found that despite the absence of a concluded agreement between the parties, O'Neill had a 'legitimate expectation' that he would receive a further 25% of the company's shares from Phillips when targets were reached.

[19.039] The House of Lords allowed the appeal and dismissed O'Neill's petition. Lord Hoffmann accepted that the Court of Appeal had found that the company had acquired the characteristics identified as commonly giving rise to equitable restraints upon the exercise of powers under articles, namely:

- an association formed on the basis of a personal relationship which involved mutual confidence;
- an understanding that certain shareholders would participate in the management of the business; and
- restrictions on the transfer of shares[105].

Lord Hoffmann held that it would have been unfair had O'Neill been excluded from participation in the management of the company without affording him the chance to sell his shares. Despite this the House of Lords went on to find that O'Neill had not been excluded from participating in the company's management, nor had he been driven out of the company. Lord Hoffmann found:

> '...the Court of Appeal said that Mr O'Neill had a legitimate expectation of being allotted more shares when the targets were met. No doubt he did have such an expectation...and no doubt it was legitimate, or reasonable, in the sense that it reasonably appeared to happen. Mr Phillips had agreed in principle, subject to the execution of a suitable document. But this is where I think that the Court of Appeal may have been misled by the expression "legitimate expectation". The real question is whether in fairness or equity Mr O'Neill had a right to the shares. On this point, one runs up against what seems to me the insuperable obstacle of the judge's finding that Mr Phillips never agreed to give them. He made no promise on the point. From which it seems to me to follow that there is no basis, consistent with established principles of equity, for a court to hold that Mr Phillips was behaving unfairly in withdrawing from the negotiation. This would not be restraining the exercise of legal rights. It would be imposing upon Mr Phillips an obligation to which he never agreed. Where, as here, parties enter into negotiations with a view to a transfer of shares on professional advice and subject to a condition that they are not to be bound until a formal document has been executed, I do not think it is possible to say that an obligation has arisen in fairness or equity at an earlier stage.'

The same reasoning applies to the sharing of profits. The judge found as a fact that Phillips made no unconditional promise about the sharing of profits'[106].

---

[104] *Re Pectel Ltd* [1998] BCC 405; also reported as *Re a Company (No 00709 of 1992)* [1999] 2 BCLC 739.

[105] See *Re Westbourne Galleries Ltd* [1973] AC 360.

[106] [1999] BCC 600 at 610H–611B.

Lord Hoffmann went on to find that Phillips had not acted unfairly. It would seem that the notion of 'legitimate expectations', as applied before the House of Lords' decision, bore some considerable relation to the doctrine of promissory estoppel[107]. As observed earlier, it is considered wise to confine its usage to a mere descriptive term for existing, independent, equitable obligations. The House of Lords' reluctance to interfere so in a statutory and contractual relationship is thought to be both understandable and correct.

[19.040] Notwithstanding the discrediting of the label, 'legitimate expectations' in a quasi-partnership company, where there are personal relationships and understandings[108] which give rise to equitable considerations over and above legal and statutory rights, the courts are more likely to deem *unconscionable* acts and omissions to be oppressive or in disregard of members' interests[109].

The locus standi to petition

[19.041] Only certain persons have locus standi to petition the court for relief under CA 1963, s 205. Those who have locus standi are the following:

(a) Members of the company.
(b) Personal representatives of deceased members.

[19.042] Section 205(2) of CA 1963 provides that the Minister for Enterprise, Trade and Employment can apply for an order under s 205 'in a case falling within subs (3) of s 170' of the 1963 Act. Sections 165–173, which governed the appointment of an inspector to a company, have now been repealed by the Companies Act 1990, s 6 ('CA 1990'). Section 12 of CA 1990 roughly corresponds to the repealed CA 1963, s 170. However, s 12 makes no specific mention of CA 1963, s 205 and makes no provision for the Minister's right to apply for an order under s 205. Although the Minister does not have express locus standi to seek relief under CA 1963, s 205, it is thought that s 20(1) of the Interpretation Act 1937 might allow s 205(2) to be construed as referring to CA 1990, s 12[110].

(a) Members of the company

[19.043] Any member of the company may petition the court for relief under CA 1963, s 205. Save as considered below, it is a prerequisite that the petitioner has been registered as a member of the company and that his name appears on the register of members[111]. A person whose name still appears on the register of members but who has disposed of his beneficial interest in the shares cannot, however, petition for section 205 relief. The Supreme Court has made this clear in *Re Via Net Works Ireland Ltd*[112]. In that case the

---

107 See McDermott, *Contract Law* (2001), pp 136–148.

108 See *Re a Company (No 002015 of 1996)* [1997] 2 BCLC 1.

109 See, eg, the seminal *Re Murphs Restaurants Ltd* [1979] ILRM 141.

110 Interpretation Act 1937, s 20(1) provides: 'Whenever any statute or portion of a statute is repealed and re–enacted, with or without modification, by an Act of the Oireachtas, references in any other statute or in any statutory instrument to the statute or portion of a statute so repealed and re-enacted shall, unless the contrary intention appears, be construed as references to the portion of such Act of the Oireachtas containing such re–enactment.'

111 See Chapter 15, *Shares and Membership*, para **[15.004]**.

112 *Re Via Net Works Ireland Ltd* (23 April 2002, unreported), Supreme Court.

respondents were section 205 petitioners who had agreed in a shareholders' agreement to transfer their shares to the appellants in the subject company. Giving the judgment of the court, Keane CJ held that the respondents did not have locus standi to petition under s 205. He said:

> 'Section 205 is a valuable protection against the misuse by shareholders, usually constituting the majority, of their powers in a manner which is oppressive to the other shareholders or fails to have regard to their interests. Persons, such as the respondents, who have voluntarily disposed of their entire shareholding in a company could not conceivably have been contemplated by the legislature as persons who would be entitled to relief under the section. Nor is it any answer to say that, because the respondents have not transferred their shares, as they are contractually bound to do, they remain registered as members of the company. It is undoubtedly the case that a person who has become entitled to be registered as a shareholder may be unable to exercise any of his rights as a shareholder until his name has been entered on the register. But it does not follow that a person who, conversely, has voluntarily divested himself of all his shares in the company, but remains on the register must be treated as a member of the company for all purposes. I have no doubt that, when the legislature enacted s 205(1), it was not envisaged that persons without any interest in the company but who, for whatever reason, remained on the register as members would be entitled to present a petition grounded on alleged oppression of them as members.'

This decision could, if taken literally, lead to injustice. It could not, for example, have been intended to suggest that a trustee of shares was debarred from petitioning under s 205 although he was not beneficially entitled to the shares. Equally, where the articles provide for the compulsory transfer of shares, it could not have been intended that once triggered an aggrieved transferor who claims that the effect of the expropriation was oppressive was denied the right to petition under s 205. In such a case it could be argued that the transferor had voluntarily agreed to the transfer because he became a member on the basis of the company's articles of association, which contained a compulsory transfer clause. It is thought that where the oppression or disregard of interest alleged is the expropriation of the petitioner's shares, the decision in *Re Via Net Works Ireland Ltd* will not preclude the petition being heard under s 205.

[19.044] 'Member' has the meaning assigned to it by CA 1963, s 31[113]. A person to whom shares have been transferred but whose name has not been entered by the directors on the register of members cannot petition under CA 1963, s 205[114]. An example in point is *Re Quickdome Ltd*[115] where the petitioner, a Mrs O'Callaghan claimed to be entitled to present a petition under s 459 of the Companies Act 1985 (UK). Her only claim to be a member was that she possessed a stock transfer form which had been executed in blank[116]. It was held that she had no standing to present the petition. It is important to note that unlike s 205, s 459 of the 1985 Act did allow an unregistered transferee to present a petition. However, Mervyn Davies J rejected her contention that

---

[113] See *Re Allied Metropole Hotel Ltd* (19 December 1988, unreported), High Court, per Gannon J.

[114] *Re A Company (No 003160 of 1986)* [1986] BCLC 391. See generally Chapter 10, *Share Transfers in Private Companies.*

[115] *Re Quickdome Ltd* [1988] BCLC 370.

she was even an unregistered transferee. Similarly, company employees[117] and ex-members of a company[118] cannot rely on s 205.

[19.045] The petitioning member does not have to be a *minority* member, notwithstanding the heading, 'Minorities', to the section. In *Re Westwinds Holding Company Ltd*[119] Kenny J dismissed the respondent's claim that the section had no application on account of the fact that the petitioner was an equal shareholder with the respondent:

> 'The word "minority" does not appear in any part of the section and the heading is merely a convenient way of describing the majority of cases in which the section will apply. In addition, Martin Hession was governing director and under Article 42 had five votes on a show of hands or on a poll for each share of which he was the holder, while every other member was to have one vote for every hundred shares held by him. Although the two share-holders held an equal number of shares, the petitioner was certain to be out-voted and so was a minority.'[120]

In so holding, Kenny J may be said to have been 'hedging his bets'. After holding that it was irrelevant to the wording of the section that a petitioner be a minority, he went on to hold that the petitioner was a minority through the operation of a *Bushell v Faith*-type clause. It is thought that a petitioner needs only to be a member, and not necessarily a minority member. In *Irish Press plc v Ingersoll Irish Publications Ltd*[121] it is notable that the petitioner and respondent were equal fifty-fifty shareholders in the joint-venture companies[122].

[19.046] Although a petitioner should be a member of the company, it is not necessary that his complaint should be in respect of conduct affecting him in his capacity qua member. In this regard it is crucial to distinguish between complaints based on oppression and those based on a disregard of interests. As has already been considered, whilst complaints based on disregard of interests must be made qua member[123], complaints based on oppression can and have been made in the petitioner's capacity as a director[124].

[19.047] Although, in general, those who have locus standi to petition the court for relief under CA 1963, s 205 may do so whenever they wish, petitions are blocked in certain

---

116 On stock transfer forms executed 'in blank' see the comments of Mervyn Davies J at 374–375 and *Re A Company (No 003160/1986)* [1986] BCLC 391. See generally, Chapter 16, *Share Transfers in Private Companies*, para **[16.033]**.

117 *Jaber v Science and Information Technology Ltd* [1992] BCLC 764.

118 *Re Baltic Real Estate Ltd (No 1)* [1993] BCLC 498.

119 *Re Westwinds Holding Company Ltd* (21 May 1974, unreported), High Court.

120 (21 May 1974, unreported), High Court at p 20.

121 (16 December 1993, unreported), High Court.

122 See also *Re Baltic Real Estate Ltd (No 1)* [1993] BCLC 498 where Knox J refused to strike out a petition simply because it was brought by a majority shareholder since it was arguable that a case could be made out.

123 See para **[19.031]**.

124 See para **[19.013]-[19.014]** and particularly *Re Murph's Restaurants Ltd* [1979] ILRM 141.

circumstances by the Companies (Amendment) Act 1990, s 5(4) ('C(A)A 1990'). This provides that:

> 'Complaints concerning the conduct of the affairs of the company while it is under the protection of the court shall not constitute a basis for the making of an order for relief under s 205 of the Principal Act.'

It is thought that this must be strictly construed and that, accordingly, relief may still be granted for complaints concerning the exercise of the *powers of the directors* (whether by the directors or, indeed, by an examiner) of a company under examination[125].

(b) Personal representatives of deceased members

[19.048] Were CA 1963, s 205 confined to *members* it would mean that under common form articles of association[126] the personal representatives of a deceased member could not rely on the section unless the directors acceded to their registration as members. Where the personal representatives were aggrieved, the directors would understandably be reluctant to register them as members. However, s 205(6) provides that the personal representatives of deceased members have standing to petition the court for relief. It provides:

> 'The personal representatives of a person who, at the date of his death was a member of a company, or any trustee of, or person beneficially interested in, the shares of a company by virtue of the will or intestacy of any such person, may apply to the court under subs (1) for an order under this section and, accordingly, any reference in that subsection to a member of a company shall be construed as including reference to any such personal representative, trustee or person beneficially interested as aforesaid or to all of them.'

There are no reported Irish cases involving such an application by a deceased member's personal representatives[127]. It should be noted, however, that in addition to personal representatives, trustees and persons beneficially interested in shares under a member's will or by intestacy also have standing. Accordingly, where such a person is refused registration by the directors of the company, it is open to them to petition the court for relief under s 205.

Abuse of process

[19.049] Upon the presentation of a petition under CA 1963, s 205 it may be open to the respondents to apply to have the petition struck out as being vexatious or otherwise constituting an abuse of process. One of the first Irish applications of this kind was made in *Re Murray Consultants Ltd and Nocrumb Ltd; Horgan v Murray and Milton*[128]. In this case the respondents applied to have a section 205 petition struck out as being an abuse of process and claimed that since the primary relief sought by the petitioner was to be bought out, that could be done more beneficially by adopting a procedure for the

---

125 On examinerships, see further Chapter 23, *Examinerships*.

126 Eg model reg 3: see generally, Chapter 16, *Share Transfers in Private Companies*, paras **[16.027]** *ff*.

127 For an English example, see *Re a Company* [1983] 2 All ER 36. See also *Re Jermyn Street Turkish Baths Ltd* [1971] 3 All ER 184.

128 *Re Murray Consultants Ltd and Nocrumb Ltd; Horgan v Murray and Milton* [1997] 3 IR 23 (HC) and 29 (SC).

valuation of shares which was contained in the company's articles of association. In the High Court Barron J refused to find that the petition was an abuse of process. In his judgment:

> 'Before the issue of proceedings can amount to an abuse of the process of the court, it seems to me that there must be some element of impropriety. So if a plaintiff who has a valid claim which has been admitted seeks to continue proceedings for further relief to which such plaintiff could not in any circumstances be entitled that would be an abuse of the process of the court. It is upon this basis that the respondents maintain that the petitioner would be abusing the processes of the court by refusing to accept the offer to value the shares being made by them.'[129]

Barron J accepted that if the articles of association contained a specific provision as to what should happen in the circumstances, to refuse to rely on the articles would be an abuse of process[130]. He noted that in England it had been held that a petition should not be struck out where there was impropriety on the part of the respondent[131] or where there was any risk to the petitioner that a proper valuation would not be made of his shareholding[132]. Barron J declined the respondents' application for four reasons:

- the articles did not provide for an involuntary sale;
- the articles form a contract between the shareholders and no party can impose altered terms on another party without their prior consent;
- no court valuation would arise unless oppression had been established; and
- the petitioner was seeking an equitable remedy and the level of the valuation to be determined by the court will take into account the court's view of the appropriate level of compensation having regard to the circumstances giving rise to the proceedings[133].

[19.050] On appeal, by a 2-to-1 majority, the Supreme Court upheld Barron J's decision and refused to strike out the petition. The majority judgment, given by Murphy J, reviewed in some detail several relevant English authorities[134]. Murphy J concluded that

---

[129] [1997] 3 IR 23 at 27.

[130] As held in *Re a Company* [1987] BCLC 562.

[131] *Re a Company; ex p Kremer* [1989] BCLC 365. There Hoffmann J said (at 368) '…there might be cases of impropriety on the part of the respondent which had so affected the value of the shares in the company as to make it inappropriate for the matter to be dealt with by a straightforward valuation.'

[132] *Re a Company; ex p Holden* [1991] BCLC 597. There, Harman J said (at 603): 'A petitioner is entitled to refuse to accept a risk – any risk – in an accountant's valuation of his interest if such risk can be seen to be one that would depreciate in any way the valuation.'

[133] In this latter respect Barron J noted that whilst *Irish Press plc v Ingersoll Irish Publications Ltd* [1995] 2 IR 175 had decided that damages as a common law remedy are not available to a section 205 petitioner, the Supreme Court had accepted that where a shareholder is bought out the price can include an element of compensation, as relief incidental to the main relief.

[134] *Re a Company* [1986] BCLC 362; *Re a Company* [1987] BCLC 94; *Re a Company* [1989] BCLC 365; *Re a Company* [1983] 1 WLR 927; *Re a Company* [1987] BCLC 563; *Re a Company* [1987] BCLC 80; *Re a Company; ex p Holden* [1991] BCLC 597; *Re a Company* [1996] 2 BCLC 192; and *Virdi v Abbey Leisure et al* [1990] BCLC 342.

in those cases in which petitions had been struck out, there was no oppression or wrongdoing proven. He held:

> 'If oppression had actually taken place…or was alleged, I believe that a court, in this jurisdiction at any rate, would not strike out the petition as being an abuse of process of the court. It is difficult to see how the court could be satisfied that the precise remedy offered by the oppressor was the appropriate means by which to bring to an end the oppression if it had occurred .'[135]

Murphy J refused to strike out the instant petition. He noted that the petitioner was asserting oppression 'above and beyond the mere breakdown of the previously harmonious relationship' and also asserting that the respondents' actions represent a deliberate and calculated decision by them to further their own ambitions and to oppress the petitioner. These assertions were for the trial judge to decide and it was inappropriate to strike out the petition.

[19.051] In *Re Vitara Foods Ltd*[136] a petition alleging unfairly prejudicial conduct was struck out on the ground of want of prosecution which amounted to an abuse of process. Lindsay J held that an application could be struck out where there was intentional and contumelious delay (which possibly included conduct amounting to an abuse of court) and proof of inordinate and inexcusable delay by a petitioner which gave rise to a substantial risk that there would not be a fair trial[137]. In *Arrow Nominees Inc v Blackledge*[138] it was held that a petition would not be automatically struck out where a petitioner committed a fraud on the court by disclosing forged documents if there was no substantial risk that a fair trial of the petitioner's claim would not follow. Evans-Loambe J held that to strike out such a petition where the court took the view that a fair trial would follow was likely to be a breach of Article 6.1 of the European Convention on Human Rights[139]. Application to strike out a petition may also be made where it is presented by a company without the authority of its directors[140].

The position of the company

[19.052] Disputes under CA 1963, s 205 are typically between the members inter se or the members and the directors. The separate legal entity which is the company will usually not play an active part in the litigation, although for practical reasons it may be separately represented at a section 205 hearing. In the particular context of disputes

---

135 [1997] 3 IR 29 at 40–41. See also *North Holdings Ltd v Southern Tropics Ltd; Re a Company No 004837 of 1998* [1999] BCC 746 where the Court of Appeal refused to strike out a petition alleging unfairly prejudicial conduct on the grounds that allegations that the company's assets had been used to capitalise and develop the respondent's business might extend to an account for profits and so the offer to purchase the petitioner's shares following a share valuation was not sufficient to remove any potential unfair prejudice.

136 *Re Vitara Foods Ltd* [1999] BCC 315.

137 See also *Re Marchday Group plc* [1998] BCC 800.

138 *Arrow Nominees Inc v Blackledge* [2000] 1 BCLC 709.

139 See also *Logicrose Ltd v Southend United Football Club Ltd* (1988) Times, 5 March and *Re Swaptronics Ltd* (1998) Times 17 August.

140 *Re Oriental Gas Co Ltd* [2000] 1 BCLC 209.

involving the exclusion of quasi-partners from the company's management it will be wrong for the company's controllers to utilise the company's resources in connection with the proceedings. In *Re Milgate Developments Ltd*[141] it was held that there was no justification for the companies concerned to incur expenditure in proceedings under s 459 of the Companies Act 1985 (UK) where the dispute was one between the shareholders based on the petitioner's exclusion from the companies' management. In *Re Murph's Restaurants Ltd*[142] Gannon J, after ordering that the company should be wound up, held that the company itself should bear its own costs, as they were *not* related to those of the respondents.

[19.053] In *Re Murray Consultants Ltd and Nocrumb Ltd; Horgan v Murray and Milton (No 2)*[143] the petitioner in an action under CA 1963, s 205 brought a discovery motion, objecting to the fact that the respondents had failed to refer to files of advice given to the companies involved by several categories of third-party advisers. In ordering that the advices be discovered, O'Sullivan J held:

> 'It is submitted that the petitioner can bring a third party discovery motion compelling the relevant companies to furnish him with the documents but that the respondents themselves should not be obliged in these proceedings as part and parcel of the general obligations under discovery principles to refer to these documents and to produce them for the petitioner.
>
> This is a "section 205" petition. The petitioner alleges that the affairs of the above entitled companies have been operated oppressively against him by the two respondents. I do not think the company is a "third party" in the usual sense of that term in these circumstances. If the advices furnished to the companies are relevant, as I have held, then they should be produced as part of discovery unless they are privileged.'[144]

In the light of O'Flaherty J's comments in *Re New-Ad Advertising Company Ltd*[145], the correctness of disregarding the company's separate legal personality is open to question and it is thought that, when in doubt, the company should be joined in the action whether as a respondent or notice party.

[19.054] Minority shareholders would do well to remember the so-called 'disclosure rule', which might be of assistance in obtaining copies of legal advice given to the company. In *Re Hydrosan Ltd*[146] Harman J said that 'There is no doubt that matters passing between solicitors to a company and a company are prima facie entitled to be produced to all shareholders of the company.' This has been considered in Chapter 6[147].

141 *Re Milgate Developments Ltd* [1993] BCLC 291.

142 *Re Murph's Restaurants Ltd* [1979] ILRM 141 at 155.

143 *Re Murray Consultants Ltd and Nocrumb Ltd; Horgan v Murray and Milton (No 2)* [1999] 1 ILRM 257.

144 [1999] 1 ILRM 257 at 259–260.

145 *Re New-Ad Advertising Company Ltd* (26 March 1998, unreported), Supreme Court at p 6 (O'Flaherty J).

146 *Re Hydrosan Ltd* [1991] BCLC 418 at 420f. See also *Dennis & Sons Ltd v West Norfolk Farmers' Manure and Chemical Co–Op Co Ltd* [1948] 2 All ER 94 and *Tugwell v Hooper* (1847) 10 Beav 348.

147 At para **[6.058]**.

In camera applications

[19.055] The basic rule governing the hearing of actions is set out in Article 34.1 of *Bunreacht na hÉireann*:

> 'Justice shall be administered in Courts established by law by judges appointed in the manner provided by this constitution, and, save in such special and limited cases as may be prescribed by law, shall be administered in public.'

One of the 'special and limited cases' referred to therein is CA 1963, s 205(7) which provides:

> 'If, in the opinion of the court, the hearing of proceedings under this section would involve the disclosure of information the publication of which would be seriously prejudicial to the legitimate interests of the company, the court may order that the hearing of the proceedings or any part thereof shall be in camera.'

In recent years there have been two Supreme Court decisions on the principles of law applicable to an application for proceedings to be *in camera*[148].

[19.056] The law applicable to the hearing of applications under CA 1963, s 205(7) *in camera* was conveniently summarised by Finlay CJ in *Irish Press plc v Ingersoll Irish Publications Ltd*[149]:

> '1. The court cannot even commence to exercise a discretion under s 205(7) unless it is of opinion that the hearing of the proceedings or of some particular part of the proceedings would involve the disclosure of information the publication of which would be seriously prejudicial to the legitimate interests of the company.
>
> 2. If it is of opinion that such a situation exists the court may then enter upon an investigation as to whether it should exercise its discretion under s 205(7) to hold the case *in camera*. In so doing, it will, however, be involved in considering a fundamental constitutional right vested in the public, namely, the administration of justice in public, and it cannot, therefore, make an order under s 205(7) merely on the consent of all the parties concerned in the petition before it.
>
> 3. The additional matter which a court would have to be satisfied of in order to direct a hearing of the whole or part of the petition otherwise than in public would be that a public hearing of the whole or of that part of the proceedings would prevent justice being done.
>
> 4. In reaching a conclusion as to whether this test has been satisfied in any particular case, it would be appropriate for the court, having regard to the terms of the provisions of Article 34.1 of the Constitution, to construe s 205(7) bearing in mind that the entitlement of the Oireachtas pursuant to Article 34.1 to prescribe by law for the administration of justice otherwise than in public is confined to special and limited cases.
>
> 5. It would appear to me to be probable that in most instances, at least, a successful application for a hearing *in camera* pursuant to s 205(7) would be:

---

148 *Re R Ltd* [1989] ILRM 757 and *Irish Press plc v Ingersoll Irish Publications Ltd* [1993] ILRM 747. For an analysis of *Re R Ltd* see Daly, 'Lifting the Veil of Secrecy' (1990) Dli – The Western Law Gazette 11.

149 *Irish Press plc v Ingersoll Irish Publications Ltd* [1993] ILRM 747 at 754–755.

(a) where the party seeking an *in camera* hearing is the petitioner, by establishing to the satisfaction of the court that, by reason of the making known to the public of information concerning the company involved, notwithstanding the very wide and varied jurisdiction which by virtue of s 205(3) the court would have to redress the wrong inflicted upon the petitioner by oppression, if that was proved, by reason of the extent of the damage to the asset consisting of the petitioner's shareholding in the company concerned that the court was incapable by reason only of the publication of the proceedings or some part thereof to render a just remedy to the wronged petitioner, or

(b) where the party seeking an *in camera* hearing is the respondent by establishing to the satisfaction of the court that by reason of the making known to the public of information concerning the company involved in the course of the hearing of the petition that even if the petition were to be dismissed by the court and the respondent awarded costs against the unsuccessful petitioner, that by reason of the extent of the damage to the asset consisting of the respondent's shareholding in the company concerned, or if the company were the respondent by reason of the damage to its value, that the court would, merely by dismissing the petition with costs, be incapable, by reason only of the publication of the proceedings, from rendering a just remedy to the wrongfully sued respondent, or

(c) by proving that either the petitioner to further his claim or the respondent to defend himself against the claim of the petitioner, in reasonable prudent protection of the asset which he owned consisting of his shareholding in the company, would be obliged to abstain from tendering evidence which would probably influence the resolution of the issues and the achieving of a just result by the court, by reason of the fact that the publication of it would do such damage, (irrespective of the result of the case and the remedy which he might obtain from the court) to the asset consisting of his shareholding so as to outweigh the advantage of succeeding in the petition.'

Although Finlay CJ formulated the law applicable to s 205(7) applications into five points, before the courts can exercise their discretion under s 205(7), a twin test must be satisfied.

[19.057] Section 205(7) of CA 1963 has been consistently construed strictly[150]. It is now well established that in order to have section 205 proceedings heard *in camera* an applicant must prove two matters to the court's satisfaction:

(1) that the hearing of the proceedings in public would involve the disclosure of information the publication of which would be seriously prejudicial to the legitimate interests of the company. This is a statutory condition precedent to the exercise of the court's discretion[151]; and

(2) that the hearing in public of the whole or that part of the proceedings which it is sought to have heard *in camera* would fall short of doing justice.

These two limbs are conjunctive: both must be proven to the court's satisfaction by the applicant.

---

[150] See the majority judgment of Finlay CJ in *Irish Press plc v Ingersoll Irish Publications Ltd* [1993] ILRM 747 at 754.

[151] Per Walsh J, giving the majority judgment of the Supreme Court in *Re R Ltd* [1989] ILRM 757 at 766.

[19.058] The first limb of this test is a difficult obstacle for an applicant to overcome. In *Re R Ltd*[152] the majority decision of the Supreme Court, delivered by Walsh J, noted that it had been agreed between the parties in dispute that the information in question related to the company's five-year business plan to the programme of the company, to details of its accounts and of one particular transaction and its commercial terms. Having considered the matters in question, Walsh J held that it was a condition precedent to the exercise of the court's discretion that the disclosure of these matters would seriously prejudice the company's legitimate interests. It was held on the facts that the first limb of the test was *not* met.
In *Irish Press plc v Ingersoll Irish Publications Ltd*[153] the judgments of Finlay CJ and Blayney J both concurred that there was not sufficient evidence to satisfy the first limb of the test. Blayney J in particular was most systematic in addressing the details of the company which had previously been published. Having reviewed the matters which had already been reported in the national newspapers, he concluded that in the circumstances the public was already aware of much of the companies' financial affairs and that the publication of audited accounts would not seriously prejudice the legitimate interests of the companies. Having so found, Blayney J held that it was not necessary to consider the second limb.

A good example of where the court held that it *would* be prejudicial to the company's legitimate interests to hear a section 205 petition in public is thought to be the case of *Re Bula Holdings; Roche v Wymes*[154]. Because it was held *in camera* neither the judgment of the High Court or Supreme Court was made public and the only references are in a related case involving the same parties. It can be surmised, however, that because the essence of the complaint of oppression/disregard of interests concerned the failure to compromise third-party litigation involving Tara Mines Ltd, Bula Holdings' legitimate interests would have been prejudiced had its shareholders' divergent views on the litigation between it and Tara Mines Ltd been made public.

[19.059] The second limb of the test is whether a hearing in public would prevent justice being done. The justification for this second limb arises from the requirement that all derogations from the principle enunciated by Article 34.1 must be construed strictly. This second limb is particularly difficult to overcome. The onus is firmly placed on the applicant to prove to the satisfaction of the court that to have the petition heard in public would prevent justice being done.

Remedies: restraining the removal of a shareholding-director

[19.060] The exclusion from management by the removal or intended removal of a shareholding-director as a director can form the basis of a claim of oppression under CA 1963, s 205[155]. In *Gilligan and Bowen v O'Grady*[156] the Supreme Court denied the

---

[152] *Re R Ltd* [1989] ILRM 757.

[153] *Irish Press plc v Ingersoll Irish Publications Ltd* [1993] ILRM 747.

[154] See references thereto in *Crindle Investments v Wymes* [1998] 4 IR 578, [1998] 2 ILRM 275.

[155] See para **[19.010]**.

[156] *Gilligan and Bowen v O'Grady* [1999] 1 IR 346, [1999] 1 ILRM 303. See Dunleavy, 'The Power of Shareholders to Remove Directors under Section 182 of the Companies Act, 1963' (1999) Bar Law Review 265.

sanctity of members' rights to remove a director, pursuant to CA 1963, s 182[157], and upheld the jurisdiction to restrain by injunction the removal of a director pending the hearing of a section 205 petition.

[19.061] A few months before the Supreme Court's decision in *Gilligan*, the High Court had decided in *Re SIAC Construction Ltd; Feighery v Feighery*[158] that there was no jurisdiction to enjoin the removal of a director pending the hearing of a section 205 petition. In that case the petitioner was a minority shareholder and director in a construction company where he had been employed for 16 years. His petition alleged oppression and in particular pointed to the convening of an extraordinary general meeting ('EGM') to consider a resolution to remove him as director. The petitioner claimed that the company had been operated as a quasi-partnership and that there was an understanding that he would be employed as a director for his working life. By way of interlocutory relief to preserve the status quo the petitioner sought an injunction to restrain his removal as director. Laffoy J refused to grant the injunction and in arriving at her decision noted the decision in *Bentley-Stevens v Jones*[159] where Plowman J had rejected that *Re Westbourne Galleries Ltd*[160] was authority for the jurisdiction to grant an injunction to interfere with shareholders' statutory right to remove a director. Laffoy J also noted the distinction between an injunction to restrain directors from excluding another director from office, on the one hand, and an injunction which interferes with shareholders' statutory power to remove directors, without prejudice to directors' rights (if any) to damages[161]. Laffoy J held that she did not have jurisdiction to override the shareholders' statutory power in CA 1963, s 182 to remove the petitioner as a director.

[19.062] In *Gilligan and Bowen v O'Grady*[162] the first-named plaintiff was managing director of Business and Trading House Investment Company Ltd ('BTH') which was in the business of arranging investment funds on behalf of various people under the Business Expansion Scheme. BHT decided to invest in Premier International Trading House Ltd ('PITH'); and it, PITH and the Bank of Ireland entered into an agreement (the 1989 Agreement) under which the Bank of Ireland applied for shares to the value of £600,000 on behalf of a number of investors. Under that agreement, BTH was to be kept fully informed of PITH's business and its financial affairs and the first-named plaintiff and another person were appointed directors of PITH. The first-named defendant was chairman, chief executive and secretary of Premier International Merchandising Ltd ('PIM'); the first and second-named defendants controlled the votes of at least a simple majority of the shareholders in PITH and PIM. The first-named plaintiff held circa 1% of the shares in PIM. Subsequent to the 1989 Agreement the Bank and BTH wished to

157 See Chapter 8, *Corporate Governance: Management by the Directors*, para **[8.076]**.

158 *Re SIAC Construction Ltd; Feighery v Feighery* (25 February 1998, unreported), High Court (Laffoy J).

159 *Bentley–Stevens v Jones* [1974] 1 WLR 638.

160 *Re Westbourne Galleries Ltd* [1973] AC 360.

161 Citing *Palmer's Company Law* (24th edn, 1987), p 901.

162 *Gilligan and Bowen v O'Grady* [1999] 1 IR 346, [1999] 1 ILRM 303. See Dunleavy, 'The Power of Shareholders to Remove Directors under Section 182 of the Companies Act, 1963' (1999) Bar Review 265.

realise their investments but since the 1989 Agreement contained no exit mechanism, a sub-committee was formed by PITH's board of directors and discussions took place with another company ('Seamar Ltd') that was in the same business as PITH. The first-named plaintiff was also a director of Seamar Ltd. In the Supreme Court Keane J found that the proposal became a source of acrimony between the parties to the proceedings. Subsequently, in 1995, the shareholders in PITH accepted an offer made by PIM to exchange their shares in PITH for an equivalent shareholding in PIM together with a loan note for £2.38 in respect of every seven shares held by them in PITH. As a result, PITH became a wholly-owned subsidiary of PIM and the first-named plaintiff was appointed non-executive director of PIM. Disagreements between the first-named plaintiff and the first and second named defendants ultimately led to the convening of an EGM of PIM for the purpose of considering a resolution that the first-named plaintiff be removed as director. This led to the plaintiffs instituting proceedings and presenting a petition pursuant to CA 1963, s 205 claiming that the affairs of PIM were being conducted in a manner oppressive to the plaintiffs and in disregard of their interests; the relief sought was an order directing PIM to purchase the beneficial shareholding of each of the petitioners or in the alternative an order winding up the company. The plaintiffs successfully applied for an injunction in the High Court to restrain the removal of the first-named plaintiff as director of the company. In so deciding, O'Donovan J distinguished the earlier decision of Laffoy J in *Feighery v Feighery*[163], accepting the plaintiffs' submission that by virtue of the 1989 Agreement, the first-named plaintiff was a director not merely to represent his own interests as shareholder but also to represent the interests of the Business Expansion Scheme investors. O'Donovan J held:

> 'There is no doubt in my mind that, in the absence of the said agreement of 25 July 1989, having regard to the decision of Laffoy J in *Feighery v Feighery*, these plaintiffs have no right to the injunctive relief sought herein. In this regard, I am satisfied that, were he a director of PITH and PIM in the ordinary sense in which one might be on the board of a limited company, I have no jurisdiction to deprive the shareholders of either company of the opportunity of considering resolutions to remove him from their respective boards. However, I think that there is substance to Mr Shipsey's submission that, by virtue of the terms of that agreement, Mr McGilligan is a director of each company; not merely in his own interests, but also representing the interests of BTH and the BES investors and in this regard, by the way, I think that there is also substance to the argument that, after the takeover of PITH by PIM in 1995, the rights and interests of BTH and the Bank under the said agreement of 1298 were transferred to PIM...I think that, in the event that a court were to conclude that BTH and the BES investors, through their nominee, the Bank were entitled to be represented on the boards of PITH and PIM by Mr McGilligan, the decision of Laffoy J in *Feighery v Feighery et al* is of no relevance in this case because she was only concerned with the rights of shareholders to remove a director who had no such special entitlement to be on the board of the company with which she was concerned.'

Accordingly, O'Donovan J granted the injunction sought, restraining the shareholders from removing the first-named plaintiff as a director of PIM and PITH.

[19.063] The Supreme Court rejected the defendants' appeal. Keane J did not seek to try to distinguish the case of *Feighery v Feighery* or *Bentley-Stevens v Jones* and instead

163 *Feighery v Feighery* (25 February 1998, unreported), High Court (Laffoy J).

contented himself with finding that they should not be followed to the extent that they held that there was no jurisdiction to make an injunction in such matters. After reviewing the purpose of s 205, Keane J held[164]:

> 'Why then should the court, on an application for an interlocutory injunction, be unable to restrain the company from removing a director pending the hearing of a petition under s 205 where he has established that there is a serious question to be tried as to whether his exclusion from the affairs of the company constitutes conduct which would entitle the shareholders to relief under s 205? It should be noted that in *Bentley-Stevens v Jones* there do not appear to have been any proceedings in existence under the English equivalent of s 205 at the time the application for an interlocutory injunction was made. However, apart from that consideration, I am bound to say, with all respect, that I do not understand why it should be thought that, because the relief sought in the interlocutory proceedings is not the same as the relief which will ultimately be sought in the s 205 proceedings, an interlocutory injunction should not be granted on that ground alone. If it is desirable, in accordance with the principles laid down in the *American Cyanamid Company* and *Campus Oil* cases, to preserve the plaintiff's rights pending the hearing of the s 205 proceedings and the balance of convenience does not point to a different conclusion, I see no reason why interlocutory relief should not be granted. To cite but one example, the relief granted in many *Mareva* cases is very often not the relief which is sought in the substantive proceedings. I am satisfied that, to the extent that *Bentley-Stevens v Jones* and *Feighery v Feighery et al* suggest a different view of the law, they should not be followed.'

Keane J went on to find that the balance of convenience favoured the granting of an injunction to preserve the status quo pending the outcome of the substantive proceedings[165].

[19.064] The converse to the removal of a director – the appointment of another director – which can also alter the status quo pending the outcome of the substantive proceedings can additionally be prevented by injunction of the court[166].

Remedies: ending the matters complained of

[19.065] Section 205(3) of CA 1963 provides in the widest possible terms that the court has power to *end the matters complained of.* Accordingly, where conduct oppressive or in disregard of a member's interests is found to exist:

> '...the court may, with a view to bringing to an end the matters complained of, make such order as it thinks fit, whether directing or prohibiting any act or cancelling or varying any transaction or for regulating the conduct of the company's affairs in future, or for the purchase of the shares of any members of the company or by the company and in the case of a purchase by the company, for the reduction accordingly of the company's capital, or otherwise.'

It is thought that the enormous width of the court's power is encapsulated in the words 'make such order as it thinks fit'. Although the particular powers set out in s 205(3) are

---

164 [1999] 1 ILRM 303 at 319.

165 Another injunction sought to restrain the company from becoming involved in a manufacturing process was refused.

166 See *Corbett v Corbett* [1998] BCC 93.

themselves extensive, they ought not be viewed as being exhaustive. The court's general power must not be viewed as prejudiced by the specificity of its particular powers. This is, of course, subject to the important limitation that the court may not award damages for oppression or disregard of members' interests, as established by the Supreme Court in *Irish Press plc v Ingersoll Irish Publications Ltd*[167] and discussed further below. Here, the following matters are considered:

(a) Section 205(3) of CA 1963 does not permit a general award of compensatory damages.

(b) Section 205(3) of CA 1963 does not justify orders requiring persons to desist from litigation.

(c) Futile orders will not be made.

(d) Permissible orders under of CA 1963, s 205(3) 'to end the matters complained of'.

(a) Section 205(3) of CA 1963 does not permit a general award of compensatory damages

[19.066] The Supreme Court in *Irish Press plc v Ingersoll Irish Publications Ltd*[168], the facts of which have been given previously[169], held that CA 1963, s 205(3) does not empower the court to award damages for oppression. In the High Court Barron J had held:

> 'Having regard to the nature of the oppression and the consequential losses to the companies as a result, the nature of the relief must be designed not only to bring an end to the matters complained of, but also to compensate the petitioner and the companies for the losses sustained. This can best be done by directing a purchase of the respondent's shareholding...
>
> ...The price to be paid for such shares shall be the present value of the respondent's shareholding having regard to the terms of the subscription and shareholders' agreement but not to the terms of the management agreement on the basis that there shall have been made good in money terms all actual financial loss to the company by reason of the oppression. In addition the petitioner shall be entitled to recover from the respondent the drop in value of its shareholding upon the same basis and the value of its shareholding on the 14 November 1991 being a date contemporaneous with the commencement of the oppression but before it commended having regard to the terms of both agreements.'[170]

Subsequently, the High Court made, inter alia, the following orders:

— that Ingersoll should repay £6 million to Irish Press Newspapers Ltd ('IPN') and Irish Press Publications Ltd (IPP) and £2.75 million to Irish Press plc ('PLC');

— Ingersoll's shareholdings were valued at £2.25 million and PLC was to pay this sum to Ingersoll after the sums of £6 million and £2.75 million were paid by Ingersoll; and

---

[167] *Irish Press plc v Ingersoll Irish Publications Ltd* [1995] 2 IR 175.

[168] [1995] 2 IR 175. See generally, Courtney, *Company Law Review 1995* (1996), pp 13–21.

[169] See para **[19.022]**.

[170] (15 December 1993, unreported), High Court at p 84.

— all shares held by Ingersoll in IPN and IPP were to be transferred to PLC.

On appeal to the Supreme Court, Ingersoll claimed, inter alia, that the court had no power to award damages in a section 205 petition.

[19.067] The Supreme Court held that the order to transfer the shares from Ingersoll to PLC would, of itself, 'bring to an end the oppression complained of' and went on to find that the court had no power to order the payment of compensation. Blayney J held:

> 'The relief which may be given under the section is that the Court may make such order as it thinks fit "with a view to bringing to an end the matters complained of". The Court is not at large as to what it may do. Whatever order it makes must have this object. It must be made with a view to bringing to an end whatever it was that was causing the oppression.'[171]

Blayney J went on to say:

> 'Could it be said that the order directing [Ingersoll] to pay £6 million to IPN and IPP and the £2.5 million to PLC was made with a view to bringing to an end the oppression of which PLC had complained? In my opinion it could not. The object of the order was clearly something quite different. It was to compensate IPN and IPP for the loss suffered by those companies and to compensate PLC for the reduction in the value of its shareholding. The object quite clearly was not to bring to an end the oppression which the learned trial judge had found to exist. The object was to compensate the three companies for the consequences of the oppression. Even if no other order had been made by the High Court, that would still have been the position, but the fact that [Ingersoll] was directed to transfer its shares to PLC, and that this put an end to the oppression, as referred to earlier, puts it beyond doubt that the order for the payment of compensation could not have also have been made with a view to bringing to an end the matters complained of. That object had already been achieved by the direction to transfer the shares.'

This finding is open to the criticism that it divorces the notion of a partial remedy from a complete remedy.

[19.068] It is important to note, though, that the decision of the Supreme Court does not *entirely* rule out an element of compensation when taken in conjunction with an order for the purchase of shares. Blayney J went on to recognise that in both *Re Greenore Trading Co Ltd*[172] and *Scottish Co-operative Wholesale Society Ltd v Meyer*[173] there had been an element of compensation in the courts' orders. Blayney J distinguished both of these cases from the case in hand on the grounds that in those cases the element of compensation was incidental to the main relief which was the purchase of shares. Blayney J expressed the distinction in the following terms:

> 'While compensation was included in the relief given in each of these two cases, it was given in an extremely limited context – where the oppressor had been directed to purchase the shares of the oppressed shareholder, and where the compensation resulted from the court's determination of what would be a fair price for the shares in the particular circumstances. The element of compensation was incidental to the main relief which was

---

171 [1995] 2 IR 175.

172 *Re Greenore Trading Co Ltd* [1980] ILRM 94. There Keane J had said (at 102): '...it is clear that in prescribing the basis on which the price is to be calculated, the Court can, in effect, provide compensation for whatever injury has been inflicted by the oppressors.'

the purchase of the shares. The cases are not authority for a general right to compensation for loss resulting from oppression...'[174].

Blayney J also went on to reject as a general proposition that damages might be awarded under CA 1963, s 205(3). In this regard he said:

'It was also submitted that the provisions of section 205(3) were so wide that they would permit damages to be awarded. I am unable to agree. Firstly, an award of damages would not satisfy the condition that the order be made 'with a view to bringing to an end the matter complained of', secondly, an award of damages is a purely common law remedy for a tort, breach of statutory duty or breach of contract, and acts of oppression would not come within any of these categories, and finally, if the Oireachtas had intended to include the remedy of damages as one of the reliefs which could have been granted, there would have been no difficulty in doing so, and it is quite clear that this was not done.'[175]

Whilst this passage is open to criticism[176] it is thought that the die has been cast and that it is unlikely, in the near future, that the courts in Ireland will recant. It is equally clear, though, that the price at which shares may be ordered to be purchased may contain an *incidental* element of compensation for the oppression suffered by the vendor of the shares.

(b) Section 205(3) does not justify orders requiring persons to desist from litigation

[19.069] In *Crindle Investments v Wymes*[177] an order was sought in proceedings under CA 1963, s 205 to require the defendants, whether as directors or personal litigants, to join in the acceptance of an offer in other proceedings, which had then been made to compromise those proceedings. In the High Court Murphy J declined to make such an order and this was upheld by the Supreme Court on appeal. Finlay CJ said:

'Having regard to the constitutional right to litigate and having regard in addition to the fact that the particular form of litigation with which we are involved in this case in part at least is a claim be it valid or otherwise, that constitutional rights of property have been interfered with, it seems to me that s 205 of the Act of 1963, so clearly designed and expressed to deal with the affairs of a company, could not by implication include the right to prevent a citizen from litigation. If it were established in any case that members of a company in addition to acts of oppression or disregard of interests to other members were

---

173 *Scottish Co-operative Wholesale Society Ltd v Meyer* [1959] AC 324. There Lord Denning had said (at 369):

'One of the most useful orders mentioned in the section – which will enable the court to do justice to the injured shareholders – is to order the oppressor to buy their shares at a fair price; and a fair price would be, I think, the value which the shares would have had at the date of the petition, if there had been no oppression. Once the oppressor has bought the shares, the company can survive. It can continue to operate. That is a matter for him. It is no doubt, true that an order of this kind gives to the oppressed shareholders what is in effect money compensation for the injury done to them; but I see no objection to this. The section gives a large discretion to the court and it is well exercised in making the oppressor make compensation to those who have suffered at his hands.'

174 [1995] 2 IR 175 at 190.

175 [1995] 2 IR 175 at 190.

176 See Courtney, *Company Law Review 1995* (1996), pp 18–19.

177 Supreme Court, per Finlay CJ (*in camera*) but noted at [1998] 4 IR 578, [1998] 2 ILRM 275.

maintaining or intending to institute proceedings which constituted an abuse of the process of the court in the sense that it was not being done for a valid intention or hope of obtaining relief but rather for some other indirect or improper motive then it might well be that the court might be entitled to intervene but, if it were, it would appear more probable that it could be entitled to intervene in order to prevent an abuse of its own processes. However, I am not satisfied that it is possible on the facts in this case and having regard to the terms of s 205 to grant the additional relief sought by the petitioner.'

Accordingly, it can be concluded that only in the rarest of cases will a court, on foot of s 205 order respondents to desist from exercising their constitutional right to litigate.

(c) Futile orders will not be made

[19.070] The court will only grant relief to a petitioner under CA 1963, s 205(3) where its order can bring to an end the matters complained of: the court will decline its jurisdiction under s 205 where it believes that it cannot make an order which will have this end result. In *Re Murph's Restaurants Ltd*[178] Gannon J declined to exercise his jurisdiction under s 205(3) because, although he had found that the petitioner had been oppressed, he held that:

> 'It is clear from the evidence that there is no form of order of the nature indicated in s 205(3) which could bring to an end the matters complained of by [the petitioner] in the proceedings or which could regulate the affairs of the company for the future. It appears to me that the circumstances in which by order under s 205 the court may direct the purchase of the shares of a member by other members or by the company are circumstances in which the court would do so 'with a view to bringing to an end the matters complained of' by the person applying to the court. It is my opinion that in that case the fundamental relationship between [the petitioner and the respondents was so] sundered that proceedings under s 205 would not in any circumstances be appropriate.'[179]

On the facts of the case in question Gannon J ordered that the company be wound up. Central to this decision was the fact that the company was a quasi-partnership company and that the relationship between the quasi-partners had broken down irretrievably.

(d) Permissible orders under s 205(3) 'to end the matters complained of'

[19.071] In *Re Forest Mill Investments Ltd; MacAvin v Fleming*[180] the petitioner claimed that she had been oppressed by the defendants. The petitioner claimed to have been ousted from her position as marketing director (holding 50% of the company's shares) by the first-named defendant who owned the remaining 50% and the second-named defendant who was also a director. The allegations were denied. Since the petition had been filed the company had been placed into liquidation and the High Court dismissed the petition for oppression on that basis. In dismissing the petitioner's appeal Barron J said:

> 'Where the conduct whether of the majority in general meeting or of the directors is oppressive of any shareholder, the Court has power to regulate the matter in one of three ways. It can direct that the decisions leading to the oppression be reversed or amended; it

[178] *Re Murph's Restaurants Ltd* [1979] ILRM 141.

[179] [1979] ILRM 141 at 152.

[180] *Re Forest Mill Investments Ltd; MacAvin v Fleming* (14 July 1998, unreported), Supreme Court (Barron J; nem diss).

> can direct a purchase of the shares of any member; or it can direct a winding up of the company.'[181]

Notwithstanding the reduction of the means of granting relief into three ways, it is thought to be convenient to consider particular relief in the following order:

(i) Purchasing the petitioner's shares.

(ii) Purchasing the respondent's shares.

(iii) The company purchasing shares.

(iv) Cancellation and variation of transactions.

(v) Alteration of constitutional documents.

(vi) Other relief except damages.

(i) Purchasing the petitioner's shares

[19.072] An order for the purchase of the petitioner's shares is the most commonly invoked remedy to end the matters complained of. Examples of cases in point include: *Re Greenore Trading Company Ltd*[182]*; Re Clubman Shirts Ltd*[183]; *Re Westwinds Holding Company Ltd*[184]; *Colgan v Colgan & Colgan*[185]; and *Re OC (Transport) Services Ltd*[186]. The principles upon which the shares will be valued have been considered in Chapter 16[187].

[19.073] An important procedural point to remember is that all persons against whom an order to purchase the petitioner's shares may be made, must be named parties in the petition or, at the very least, notice parties. In *New-Ad Advertising Company Ltd*[188] a petition alleging oppression was brought in which the only named party was the company. After the company sold all of its assets, the company advised that it did not wish to defend the proceedings and asked that the defence which it had previously delivered be struck out. Costello P held that a Mr McNulty, a director and majority shareholder in the company, had acted oppressively towards the petitioner and in disregard of his interests as a member. Costello P said:

> 'The usual order in a case of this kind is that the company or the oppressor should buy out the minority shareholder at a value the shares would have had but for the oppressive conduct. Alternatively, an order to wind up the company can be made. However, in this case it would not be just to order the winding up of the company because no relief would be given to the petitioner. Similarly, I see no point in ordering that the company should buy the petitioner's shares because the company has no assets with which to purchase them. In order to ensure that justice is done, it seems to me that the wrongdoer – in this

[181] (14 July 1998, unreported), Supreme Court at p 4.

[182] *Re Greenore Trading Company Ltd* [1980] ILRM 94.

[183] *Re Clubman Shirts Ltd* [1983] ILRM 323 and [1991] ILRM 43.

[184] *Re Westwinds Holding Company Ltd* (21 May 1974, unreported), High Court.

[185] *Colgan v Colgan & Colgan* (22 July 1993, unreported), High Court.

[186] *Re OC (Transport) Services Ltd* [1984] BCLC 251.

[187] See Chapter 16, *Share Transfers in Private Companies*, para **[16.108]**.

[188] *New-Ad Advertising Company Ltd* (1 July 1997, unreported), High Court (Costello P), (26 March 1998, unreported), Supreme Court.

instance Mr McNulty – should buy the petitioner's shares at the value which they would have had but for the oppressive conduct to which I have briefly referred.

I am aware of the fact that Mr McNulty has not been jointed as a notice party but he must have known that such an order might be sought, particularly in view of the fact that he, as a director, was instrumental in selling all the assets of the company. He must have been aware that it was highly likely, as claimed in the petition, that an order would be made against him personally. However, Mr McNulty did not seek separate representation. He could have brought a motion seeking to be separately jointed but he did not do so. It would therefore be unjust not to order that Mr McNulty, who was the person who committed the acts of which complaint is made, should remedy the injustice. And as Mr McNulty decided to sell the company's assets and not to contest the petition, it seems to me that it would be wrong for the court not to make the order sought by the petitioner.'[189]

Costello P went on to assess the value of the shares on the evidence presented and ordered McNulty to pay £67,200 to the petitioner in return for the petitioner's shares in the company. McNulty subsequently applied to be made a notice party but this was refused by Costello P who informed him that it was too late. On appeal to the Supreme Court it was held that McNulty should then be made a notice party to the proceedings and should be furnished with all documents in the case and given an opportunity to enter a defence if he was so minded. In the course of his judgment O'Flaherty J said that based on the basic constitutional principles of *audi alteram partem* and the necessity to give a party against whom allegations are being made the opportunity to take part in the proceedings, it was a matter of 'elementary and fundamental justice that Mr McNulty should have been a party to the proceedings.'[190]

(ii) Purchasing the respondent's shares

[19.074] In *Irish Press plc v Ingersoll Irish Publications Ltd*[191], on finding that the petitioner had been oppressed, the High Court ordered that the respondent sell its shares to the petitioner. This was one of the few occasions on which the High Court ordered that the petitioner should be at liberty to purchase the respondent-wrongdoer's shares[192]. In *Brenfield Squash Racquets Club Ltd*[193] Rattee J said in the English High Court that it would only be in exceptional circumstances that a majority shareholder would be obliged to sell his shares to an unfairly prejudiced minority.

(iii) The company purchasing shares

[19.075] Section 205(3) of CA 1963 empowers the court to order that the company itself should purchase the petitioner's or the respondent's shares. This may be the only remedy available where a party who is ordered to purchase the other's shares lacks the necessary

[189] (1 July 1997, unreported), High Court at pp 10–11.

[190] (26 March 1998, unreported), Supreme Court at p 6. O'Flaherty J also warned against the tendency to approach such matters on the basis that a controlling shareholder and director *is* the company and remarked that it was trite law to say that the identity of a company is distinct from the individuals who comprise it: *Salomon v A Salomon & Co* [1897] AC 22 (at p 4).

[191] *Irish Press plc v Ingersoll Irish Publications Ltd* (15 December 1993, unreported), High Court.

[192] Cf Ussher, *Company Law in Ireland* (1985), p 267–268 where the author criticises the situation whereby the wrongdoers could be left in 'sole control of the field of battle'.

[193] *Brenfield Squash Racquets Club Ltd* [1996] 2 BCLC 184.

resources and the company cannot avail of the validation procedure under CA 1963, s 60(2) and provide financial assistance for the purchase of its own shares by the party ordered to buy the shares[194]. In such circumstances, it is acknowledged by the wording of s 205(3) that the company's capital may be reduced and allows the court to so order. Where the funds to purchase shares come other than from distributable profits, the court must be extremely cautious lest the interests of the company's creditors' are prejudiced.

(iv) Cancellation and variation of transactions

[19.076] On a number of occasions the High Court has cancelled and/or varied transactions which have occurred. This remedy will frequently be coupled with an order to purchase either the respondent's or petitioner's shares[195]. Resolutions passed by the members have been cancelled by the court upon finding oppression or disregard of interests[196]. Sometimes it will not be necessary to cancel or vary a transaction which has been found to be oppressive because the court will order that the respondent purchase the petitioner's shares, and it will go on to value the shares on the basis that the impugned transaction never took place[197].

(v) Alteration of constitutional documents

[19.077] A less frequently employed remedy is for the court to order that the company's constitutional documents (ie its memorandum and articles of association) should be amended to safeguard the petitioner's rights. Perhaps one reason for such infrequent use is because such a remedy may only provide temporary relief: in the many companies where CA 1963, s 205 proceedings are taken the members will be quasi-partners and the institution of proceedings will mark the end of the mutuality which characterises such relationships. Where the court orders that the company's constitutional documents are to be altered, they may not subsequently be altered again without the consent of the court[198].

(vi) Other relief except damages

[19.078] It is considered that the relief which the court can grant is unlimited, with the important proviso that *damages* may not be awarded[199]. Examples of extreme relief can be seen in a number of cases. An example is *Re HR Harmer Ltd*[200], where the English Court of Appeal ordered that the octogenarian respondent be excluded from the management of the company[201].

---

194 For distributable profits see Ch 18, *The Maintenance of Capital*, para **[18.081]**.

195 *Re Westwinds Holding Company Ltd* (21 May 1974, unreported), High Court, per Kenny J.

196 *Re Williams Group Tullamore Ltd* [1985] IR 613 and *Re Irish Visiting Motorists' Bureau Ltd* (7 February 1972, unreported), High Court.

197 Eg *Re Westwinds Holding Company Ltd* (21 May 1974, unreported), High Court, per Kenny J.

198 CA 1963, s 205(4).

199 See para **[19.066]**.

200 *Re HR Harmer Ltd* [1958] 3 All ER 689. See para **[19.021]**.

201 See the ex tempore judgment in *Re Christy Kenneally Communications*, noted by MacCann, *Butterworth Ireland Companies Acts 1963–1990*, p 204 where Costello J disqualified the respondents from acting as directors and replaced them as court appointed directors.

The unfairly prejudicial remedy contrasted[202]

[19.079] At this point it is appropriate to consider briefly the statutory remedies for shareholders in England and Wales[203]. Because of the tendency to consider the case law of England and Wales and to cite such case law in the Irish courts, it is important to set out the differences between their statutory remedy and ours. Although English case law is extremely useful, it must be relied upon with caution. Section 210 of the Companies Act 1948 (UK) was the closest statutory remedy to CA 1963, s 205, employing the concept of '*oppression*'. The present English provision is s 459(1) of the Companies Act 1985 (UK) , as amended by the Companies Act 1989 (UK). This provides:

> 'A member of a company may apply to the court by petition for an order under this Part on the ground that the company's affairs are being or have been conducted in a manner which is unfairly prejudicial to the interests of its members generally or some part of the members (including at least himself) or that any actual or proposed act or omission of the company (including any act or omission on its behalf) is or would be so prejudiced.'

A number of comparisons with CA 1963, s 205 may be made.

[19.080] First and most significantly, s 459 of the Companies Act 1985 (UK) employs the test of *unfairly prejudicial* instead of *oppression*[204]. Secondly, there is no reference to the exercise of the *powers of the directors*. Thirdly, the section 459 remedy is expressed to apply to actual or *proposed* acts or *omissions*. While these are the main differences, others exist[205].

[19.081] The law relating to shareholders' remedies has been the subject of reform and further review in England and Wales. The English Law Commission's report on *Shareholders' Remedies*[206] made a number of far-reaching recommendations, which include: there should be active case management of shareholder-proceedings; there should be rebuttable presumptions introduced to assist proving unfair prejudice but also limitation periods; the model articles of association should encourage dispute resolution before litigation; and the derivative action should be replaced. Reform of shareholders' remedies has not yet, to date, been mooted in Ireland but is thought to be inevitable in

---

202 See generally, Griffin, 'The Statutory Protection of Minority Shareholders: Section 459 of The Companies Act 1985' (1992) 13 Co Law 83; Hollington, *Minority Shareholders' Rights* (1990), Ch 4, 'The Unfair Prejudice Remedy' and Gower, *Principles of Modern Company Law* (1992), p 662 *ff.*

203 Griggs & Lowry, 'Minority Shareholder Remedies: A Comparative View' [1994] JBL 463, for a comparative consideration of shareholders' remedies in England, Canada and the United States.

204 See *Re a Company (No 00477 of 1986)* [1986] BCLC 376; *Re Bovey Hotel Ventures Ltd* (31 July 1980, unreported), High Court England & Wales (Nourse J); and see generally, Griffin, 'The Statutory Protection of Minority Shareholders: Section 459 of The Companies Act 1985' (1992) 13 Co Law 83 and Griggs & Lowry, 'Minority Shareholder Remedies: A Comparative View' [1994] JBL 463 at 466–468.

205 Eg, unregistered transferees of shares in the company have locus standi to petition under the Companies Act 1985, s 459 (UK).

206 Law Com No 246, Cm 3769. For commentary, see *Palmer's In Company*, Issue 4/98, 28 April 1998 and CCH's *Company Law Newsletter* (1997) Issue 22, 15 December 1997.

view of the swell of reform witnessed in other common law jurisdictions and the advent in Ireland of the statutory Company Law Review Group[207].

[B] THE RULE IN *FOSS V HARBOTTLE*

[19.082] The rule in *Foss v Harbottle*[208] is one of the most established principles in company law. It has, however, been the cause of considerable confusion. The confusion has resulted largely from the failure to recognise that the rule has two *limbs*:

— the first is that where the company has been wronged, the company, and not its shareholders is the proper person to institute proceedings;

— the second is that an individual shareholder, or shareholders, may not bring proceedings to overturn a decision of the company where that decision is one which a majority of the members may confirm.

There is a further complication: members have *personal rights* which are always capable of being enforced by the members personally. In this section, the law is considered under a number of headings:

1. The principles behind the rule.
2. The rule in *Foss v Harbottle.*
3. The rule summarised.
4. Corporate rights distinguished from members' personal rights.
5. Personal rights and personal actions distinguished.

The principles behind the rule

[19.083] The basis of the rule in *Foss v Harbottle* is that the company is an independent legal entity which is separate from its shareholders[209]. Accordingly, wrongs committed against the company are generally actionable only by the company and not by its members. A further basis of the rule is that the members of a company generally[210] agree to majority rule in their relations inter se. Minority shareholders in a company are expected, and obliged, to respect the decision of the majority. In common sense, nothing more could be expected. As in any democracy, the corporate enfranchised must dictate the direction of the company. Although minority members undoubtedly have rights, their wishes must not override the bona fide wishes of the majority. The traditional rule must, however, be qualified where the majority acts inequitably. The two fundamental principles considered above are the basis of the rule which, although diluted by the many exceptions thereto and overridden by CA 1963, s 205, still retains a certain vitality and importance. Commenting on the leading cases of *Foss v Harbottle*, *Prudential*

---

207 See, eg, New Zealand's reforms: Fitzsimons, 'The Companies Act 1993: A New Approach to Shareholder Litigation in New Zealand' (1997) 18 Co Law 306.

208 *Foss v Harbottle* (1843) 2 Hare 461.

209 See generally, Chapter 4, *Incorporation and Its Consequences*, para **[4.023]** *ff.*

210 In certain circumstances, majority rule is tempered by the weighting of certain member's voting rights, as illustrated by the case of *Bushell v Faith* [1970] AC 1099.

Assurance Co Ltd v Newman Industries Ltd (No 2)[211] and *Burland v Earle*[212] O'Flaherty J said in *O'Neill v Ryan*[213]:

> 'The reasons are clear for the requirement established by this line of authority: otherwise there would be a multiplicity of actions, oppressive litigation and the company would cease to have proper control of its corporate destiny.'[214]

[19.084] The rationalisation of the rule in *Foss v Harbottle* on the basis of the company's separate legal personality, as seen in the judgment of the English Court of Appeal in *Prudential Assurance Co Ltd v Newman Industries Ltd (No 2)* and the Supreme Court's endorsement thereof in *O'Neill v Ryan*, is indicative of a 'back to basics' approach. Notwithstanding that CA 1963, s 205 has driven a horse and four through the rule, the Supreme Court's recent endorsement of the rule has ensured its immediate survival in Irish company law.

The rule in *Foss v Harbottle*

[19.085] The rule in *Foss v Harbottle* has its origins in the now relatively dated case of *Foss v Harbottle*[215]. The facts of the case were that a company was formed by Act of the English Parliament for the purposes of acquiring approximately 180 acres of land in Manchester. It was intended to develop the land by planting it in an ornamental and park-like manner and building houses with attached gardens. The land was purchased from one of the 13 defendants, a Joseph Denison, who had acquired the land only after the project had been agreed upon in principle. On foot of advertisements, the plaintiffs, Richard Foss and Edward Starkie Turton, subscribed for two shares and 12 shares respectively in the joint-stock company. Subsequently, to avail of the advantages of limited liability[216], application was successfully made for an Act of incorporation, and The Victoria Park Company began life.

The plaintiffs alleged inter alia: first, that the defendants, who had been appointed directors in the company, purchased the lands from themselves for the use of the company and had charged the company an exorbitant consideration; and, secondly, had raised finance for the company in a manner not authorised by its powers under the Act of incorporation since they created mortgages over the company's lands.

[19.086] The decision of the Vice-Chancellor in *Foss v Harbottle* incorporates a number of legal principles. The most important for present purposes is that where a company suffers a wrong, it is the company and not its shareholders which is the proper plaintiff in any subsequent action. Wigram VC said:

> 'It was not, nor could it successfully be argued, that it was a matter of course for any individual members of a corporation thus to assume to themselves the right of suing in the name of the corporation. In law, the corporation and the aggregate members of the

211 *Prudential Assurance Co Ltd v Newman Industries Ltd (No 2)* [1982] Ch 204.

212 *Burland v Earle* [1902] AC 83.

213 *O'Neill v Ryan* [1993] ILRM 557.

214 [1993] ILRM 557 at 559. See also the majority judgment of Blayney J at 570.

215 *Foss v Harbottle* (1843) 2 Hare 461.

216 Joint–stock companies were denied limited liability until the passing of the Limited Liability Act 1855. See Ch 1, *The Private Company in Context*, para **[1.069]**.

corporation, are not the same thing for purposes like this; and the only question can be, whether the facts alleged in that case justify a departure from the rule which *prima facie* would require that the corporation should sue in its own name and in its corporate character, or in the name of someone whom the law has appointed to be its representative.'[217]

Wigram VC justified the principle of majority rule on the basis that:

'...whilst the supreme governing body, the proprietors at a special general meeting assembled, retain the power of exercising the functions conferred upon them by the Act of incorporation, it cannot be competent to individual corporators to sue in the manner proposed by the plaintiff on the present record. This in effect purports to be a suit by cestui que trusts, complaining of a fraud committed or alleged to have been committed by persons in a fiduciary character. The complaint is, that those trustees have sold lands to themselves, ostensibly for the benefit of the cestui que trusts. The proposition I have advanced is, that although the Act should prove to be voidable, the cestui que trusts may elect to confirm it. Now, who are the cestui que trusts in that case? The corporation, in a sense, is undoubtedly the cestui que trust; but the majority of the corporators at a special general meeting assembled, independently of any general rules of law upon the subject, by the very terms of the incorporation in the present case, has power to bind the whole body, and every individual corporator must be taken to have come into the corporation upon the terms of being liable to be so bound. How then can this court act in a suit constituted as this is, if it is to be assumed, for the purposes of the argument, that the powers of the body of the proprietors are still in existence, and may lawfully be exercised for a purpose like that I have suggested? Whilst the court may be declaring the acts complained of to be void at the suit of the present plaintiffs, who in fact may be the only proprietors who disapprove of them, the governing body of proprietors may defeat the decree by lawfully resolving upon the confirmation of the very acts which are the subject of the suit. The very fact that the governing body of proprietors assembled at the special general meeting may so bind even a reluctant minority, is decisive to show that the frame of this suit cannot be sustained whilst that body retains its functions. In order then that this suit may be sustained, it must be shown either that there is no such power as I have supposed remaining in the proprietors, or, at least, that all means have been resorted to and found ineffectual to set that body in motion...'.[218]

In summary, under common form articles of association the management of the company is delegated to the company's directors and the company's directors act for the company which is the proper plaintiff in an action for a wrong committed against the company. The members of the company have the power to appoint and remove the board of directors and where the directors act in a manner at variance with the wishes of a majority of the members, the members are competent to remove the board, and to appoint a more sympathetic board in their stead.

The rule summarised

[19.087] In *Prudential Assurance Co Ltd v Newman Industries Ltd (No 2)*[219] the Court of Appeal remarked that 'the classic definition of the rule in *Foss v Harbottle* is stated in

[217] (1843) 2 Hare 461 at 490–491.

[218] (1843) 2 Hare 461 at 493–494.

[219] *Prudential Assurance Co Ltd v Newman Industries Ltd* [1982] 1 Ch 204 at 210.

the judgment of Jenkins LJ in *Edwards v Halliwell*'[220]. *Edwards v Halliwell* concerned the internal rules of a trade union which provided that the contributions of members should be as per the tables set out in the articles, unless these were varied by a members' ballot. Despite this rule, a delegate meeting of the trade union, without taking any members' ballot, increased the members' union subscriptions. The plaintiff-members sought a declaration that this alteration of the rules was invalid. Jenkins LJ found that the rights infringed were members' *personal rights* and, that accordingly, *Foss v Harbottle* had no application to the case. In a passage quoted with approval by the Supreme Court in *Balkanbank v Taher*[221], Jenkins LJ said:

> 'The rule in *Foss v Harbottle*, as I understand it, comes to no more than this. First the proper plaintiff in an action in respect of a wrong alleged to be done to a company or association of persons is, prima facie, the company or association of persons itself. Secondly, where the alleged wrong is a transaction which might be made binding on the company or association and on all its members by a simple majority of its members, no individual member of the company is allowed to maintain an action in respect of that matter for the simple reason that, if a mere majority of the members of the company or association is in favour of what has been done, then *cadit quaestio*, no wrong has been done to the company or association and there is nothing in respect of which anyone can sue. If, on the other hand, a simple majority of members of the company or association is against what has been done, then there is no valid reason why the company or association itself should not sue. In my judgment, it is implicit in the rule that the matter relied on as constituting the cause of action shall be a cause of action properly belonging to the general body of corporators or members of the company or association as opposed to a cause of action which some individual member can assert in its own right.'[222]

[19.088] In *Prudential Assurance Co Ltd v Newman Industries Ltd (No 2)*, the Court of Appeal summarised Jenkins LJ's statement of the rule in *Foss v Harbottle* in five propositions:

> '(1) The proper plaintiff in an action in respect of a wrong alleged to be done to a corporation is, *prima facie*, the corporation.
>
> (2) Where the alleged wrong is a transaction which might be made binding on the corporation and on all its members by a simple majority of the members, no individual member of the corporation is allowed to maintain an action in respect of that matter because, if the majority confirms the transaction, *cadit quaestio*; or, if the majority challenges the transaction, there is no valid reason why the company should not sue.
>
> (3) There is no room for the operation of the rule if the alleged wrong is ultra vires the corporation, because the majority of members cannot confirm the transaction.
>
> (4) There is also no room for the operation of the rule if the transaction complained of could be validly done or sanctioned only by a special resolution or the like, because a simple majority cannot confirm a transaction which requires the concurrence of a greater majority.

---

[220] *Edwards v Halliwell* [1950] 2 All ER 1064.

[221] *Balkanbank v Taher* (19 January 1995, unreported), Supreme Court at p 35 of the judgment.

[222] [1950] 2 All ER 1064 at 1066.

(5) There is an exception to the rule where what has been done amounts to fraud and the wrongdoers are themselves in control of the company. In that case the rule is relaxed in favour of the aggrieved minority, who are allowed to bring a minority shareholders' action on behalf of themselves and all others. The reason for this is that, if they were denied that right, their grievance could never reach the court because the wrongdoers themselves, being in control, would not allow the company to sue.'[223]

Points (3)–(5) are the so-called 'exceptions' to the rule in *Foss v Harbottle*, and are considered below. As shall be considered next, it is important to delimit the scope of the rule.

Corporate rights distinguished from members' personal rights

[19.089] Several judicial interpretations of the rule in *Foss v Harbottle* have engendered confusion for over 150 years[224]. The primary source of confusion has been the failure to distinguish actions by a member seeking to vindicate the *company's corporate rights* from actions by a member seeking to vindicate that *member's personal rights*[225]. A member's personal rights are always enforceable against his company by virtue of CA 1963, s 25. As has been considered in Chapter 3, s 25 creates a statutory contract between a member and his company and the company and its members[226].

[19.090] This confusion was encouraged by cases such as *MacDougall v Gardiner*[227]. In that case the articles of association of the company provided that a poll could be demanded on the question of whether a general meeting could be adjourned by five shareholders. At a general meeting, an adjournment of the meeting was moved and accepted by the chairman. A poll was demanded by the members[228]. However the chairman ruled that there would not be an adjournment. One of the shareholders issued proceedings against the company and its directors both on his own behalf and on behalf of all of the other shareholders. It was alleged that the course taken at the meeting by the chairman was the result of collusion with the directors with a view to stifling discussion and that the directors were intending to carry out certain measures injurious to the company. A declaration was sought that the chairman's conduct was illegal and improper together with an injunction restraining the directors from carrying out the proposed arrangements without submitting them to the shareholders for approval.
The Court of Appeal held that the action could not be sustained as it infringed the principles laid down in *Foss v Harbottle* and *Mozley v Alston*[229]. In short, the court

---

223 [1982] 1 Ch 204 at 210–211.

224 The most notably cases are *Mozley v Alston* (1847) 1 Ph 790 and *MacDougall v Gardiner* (1875) 1 Ch D 13. For a commentary, see Ussher, *Company Law in Ireland* (1986), pp 166–167, where the confusion is attributed as being a failure to distinguish duties owed to the company from internal irregularities. See also Gower, *Principles of Modern Company Law* (5th edn, 1992), p 643 *ff*.

225 For members' personal rights see Chapter 15, *Shares and Membership*, para **[15.067]** *ff*.

226 See Chapter 3, *The Constitutional Documentation*, para **[3.098]**.

227 *MacDougall v Gardiner* (1875) 1 Ch D 13.

228 On polls see Chapter 9, *Corporate Governance: Meetings*, para **[9.053]**.

229 *Mozley v Alston* (1847) 1 Ph 790.

would not interfere in the internal management of the company[230] even if that meant refusing to vindicate a member's personal rights. It is submitted that *MacDougall v Gardiner* makes bad law.

[19.091] Recognition of the members' right to vindicate their own personal rights has, however, been clearly recognised in a number of cases. In *Pender v Lushington*[231] the articles of association of the company provided that the votes of nominee shareholders would be counted at a general meeting. Contrary to this provision in the articles, the chairman of the company refused to count the votes of the plaintiff's nominees with the result that a resolution proposed by the plaintiff was not carried. The plaintiff applied, in both his own name and that of the company, for an injunction to restrain the directors from acting on foot of the invalid resolution. Jessel MR said in the course of his judgment that:

> 'This is an action by Mr Pender for himself. He is a member of the company and whether he votes with the majority or the minority he is entitled to have his vote recorded – an individual right in respect of which he has a right to sue. That has nothing to do with the question like that raised in *Foss v Harbott*le and that line of cases. He has a right to say, "Whether I vote in the majority or minority, you shall record my vote, as that is a right of property belonging to my interest in this company and if you refuse to record my vote I will institute legal proceedings against you to compel you." What is the answer to such an action? It seems to me it can be maintained as a matter of substance and that there is no technical difficulty in maintaining it...'.

A similar conclusion was arrived at in the case of *Edwards v Halliwell*[232]. There, in respect of the plaintiffs' rights not to have their membership subscriptions increased unless pursuant to a ballot, Jenkins LJ said:

> 'Those rights, these members claim, have been invaded. The gist of the case is that the personal and individual rights of membership of each of them have been invaded by a purported, but invalid, alteration of the tables of contributions. In those circumstances, it seems to me the rule in *Foss v Harbottle* has no application at all, for the individual members who are suing sue, not in the right of the union, but in their own right to protect from invasion their own individual rights as members.'[233]

Although sometimes considered to be an exception to the rule in *Foss v Harbottle*, the right of members to sue to vindicate their personal rights as members is entirely divorced from the rule.

Personal rights and personal actions distinguished

[19.092] The cases cited in the preceding paragraphs clearly demonstrate that a member can sustain an action to vindicate his personal *rights* as a member of the company. Action to vindicate the personal rights accorded a member under the company's articles of association and the Companies Acts 1963-2001[234] must be distinguished from a

---

[230] In *Carlen v Drury* (1812) 1 V & B 154 Lord Eldon said 'This court is not required on every occasion to take the management of every playhouse and brewhouse in the Kingdom.'

[231] *Pender v Lushington* (1877) 6 Ch D 70.

[232] *Edwards v Halliwell* [1950] 2 All ER 1064, considered at para **[19.087]**.

[233] [1950] 2 All ER 1064 at 1067.

[234] See Chapter 15, *Shares and Membership*, para **[15.067]**.

member instituting proceedings in respect of a diminution in the value of his shareholding, or a personal action unrelated to his personal rights.

[19.093] In *Prudential Assurance Co Ltd v Newman Industries Ltd (No 2)*[235] the plaintiff-company, which was a minority shareholder in the defendant-company, brought a derivative action[236] and a personal action against the defendant and two of its directors. The personal action alleged that the directors had acted fraudulently, causing the value of the company to diminish. The Court of Appeal held on this point, in a passage cited with approval by Blayney J in the majority Supreme Court decision in *O'Neill v Ryan*[237] that:

> 'In our judgment the personal claim is misconceived. It is of course correct, as the judge found and Mr Barlett did not dispute, that he and Mr Laughton, in advising the shareholders to support the resolution approving the agreement, owed the shareholders a duty to give such advice in good faith and not fraudulently. It is also correct that if directors convene a meeting on the basis of a fraudulent circular, a shareholder will have a right of action to recover any loss which he has been personally caused in consequence of the fraudulent circular; this might include the expense of attending the meeting. But what he cannot do is to recover damages merely because the company in which he is interested has suffered damage. He cannot recover a sum equal to the diminution in the market value of his shares, or equal to the likely diminution in dividend, because such a 'loss' is merely a reflection of the loss suffered by the company. The shareholder does not suffer any personal loss. 'Loss' is through the company, in the diminution in the value of the net assets of the company, in which he has (say) a 3% shareholding. The plaintiff's shares are merely a right of participation in the company on the terms of the articles of association. The shares themselves, his right of participation, are not directly affected by the wrongdoing. The plaintiff still holds all the shares as his own absolutely unencumbered property. The deceit practised upon the plaintiff does not affect the shares; it merely enables the defendant to rob the company.'[238]

The following passage from the Court of Appeal's decision was also cited by both O'Flaherty J[239] and Blayney J[240]:

> 'A personal action would subvert the rule in *Foss v Harbottle* and that rule is not merely a tiresome procedural obstacle placed in the path of a shareholder by a legalistic judiciary. The rule is the consequence of the fact that a corporation is a separate legal entity. Other consequences are limited liability and limited rights. The company is liable for its contracts and torts; the shareholder has no such liability. The company acquires causes of action for breaches of contracts and torts which damage the company. No cause of action vests in the shareholder. When the shareholder acquires a share he accepts the fact that the value of his investment follows the fortunes of the company and that he can only exercise his influence over the fortunes of the company by the exercise of his voting rights in general meeting. The law confers on him the right to ensure that the company observes the limitations of its memorandum of association and the right to ensure that other shareholders observe the rule, imposed upon them by the articles of association.'[241]

---

235 *Prudential Assurance Co Ltd v Newman Industries Ltd (No 2)* [1982] Ch 204.

236 See para **[19.099]**.

237 *O'Neill v Ryan* [1993] ILRM 557 at 569.

238 [1982] Ch 204 at 222.

239 [1993] ILRM 557 at 559 (minority judgment).

240 [1993] ILRM 557 at 569–570 (majority judgment).

241 [1982] Ch 204 at 224.

Blayney J opined that the foregoing passage is a correct statement of the law in regard to the status of a shareholder in a limited liability company[242].

[19.094] Notwithstanding that disgruntled shareholders in Irish private companies tend to rely on CA 1963, s 205, the rule in *Foss v Harbottle* has been accepted and continues to be applied in the Irish courts[243]. Recent acceptance of the rule is seen in the decision of the Supreme Court in *O'Neill v Ryan*[244] where the High Court decision of Lynch J was confirmed[245]. The plaintiff claimed, inter alia, damages and other relief for breach of contract and wrongful dismissal against the first and second defendants in the action. The claim arose from the plaintiff's allegation that the four last-named defendants had caused damage to Ryan Air Ltd, thereby reducing the value of his shareholding in that company. The defendants brought a motion to have the plaintiff's action dismissed or stayed on the basis that the pleadings disclosed no reasonable cause of action. In the High Court Lynch J dismissed the plaintiff's action against the last-four named defendants. This was upheld by the Supreme Court who endorsed the rule in *Foss v Harbottle* and went on to endorse the judgment of the Court of Appeal in *Prudential Assurance Co Ltd v Newman Industries Ltd (No 2)*, holding that the members of a company could not sue on account of a diminution in the value of their shareholding.

[19.095] In *Stein v Blake*[246] the first defendant was a 50% shareholder and the sole director (as permitted under English law) of a group of companies in which the plaintiff held the other 50% of the shares. The transaction in issue was one under which the assets belonging to the group of companies were transferred into the ownership of various other companies controlled by the first-defendant. The plaintiff objected, claiming that in breach of the first defendant's fiduciary duty and the companies' articles of association, the first defendant had misappropriated the assets by causing the assets to be sold at an undervalue. The plaintiff claimed that this action had deprived him of the ability to sell his shares at their fair value and that this had caused him personal loss. At trial, it had been held that the plaintiff had no cause of action in respect of any losses suffered by the group of companies in which he was shareholder and that those companies were the proper plaintiffs in any action against the defendants. This was upheld by the English Court of Appeal. There, Millett LJ distinguished the case of *Heron International v Lord Grade*[247] where the Court of Appeal had recognised that breach of directors' fiduciary duties may cause loss to the shareholders because 'they are deprived of the opportunity of realising their shares to greater advantage'[248]. Millett LJ pointed out that in the *Heron* case the court had been addressing a situation where, as a result of a breach of duty of care on the part of directors to advise their shareholders in relation to a prospective takeover bid, the plaintiff had been induced or compelled to

---

242 [1993] ILRM 557 at 570.

243 See *Duggan v Bourke et al* (30 May 1986, unreported), High Court, per Costello J.

244 *O'Neill v Ryan* [1993] ILRM 557.

245 The judgment of Lynch J is reported at [1990] ILRM 140.

246 *Stein v Blake* [1998] 1 All ER 724. See also *Giles v Rhind* [2001] TLR 497 and *Johnson v Gore Wood & Co* [2001] 2 WLR 72.

247 *Heron International v Lord Grade* [1983] BCLC 244.

248 [1983] BCLC 244 at 262.

dispose of his shares to a bidder at an undervalue. Millett LJ observed that in such a case 'no wrong is done to the company. Its assets are not depleted; its coffers remain unaffected'. On the distinction between the two scenarios, Millett LJ said:

> 'The distinction is between (i) loss sustained by a shareholder by a diminution in the value of his shares by reason of the misappropriation of the company's assets, and (ii) loss caused directly to a shareholder who has been induced to part with the shares at an undervalue. The shareholder has a personal cause of action to recover in respect of the second type of loss, but not the first.'[249]

Applying these principles to the case in hand, Millett LJ found that the wrong complained of had been done, if to anyone, to the companies whose assets were allegedly misappropriated. He concluded:

> 'In my judgment, this case indicated the distinction which must be made. Directors owe fiduciary duties to their company to preserve and defend its assets and to the shareholders to advise them properly so that they are not induced or compelled to part with their shares at an undervalue. No doubt other fiduciary duties are also owed to both the company and to its shareholders. Shareholders may suffer loss in the event of a breach of either duty, but in the first case the loss consists of a diminution of the value of their shares, is fully reflected in the loss suffered by the company, and is fully compensated by restitution to the company. In the second case the company suffers no loss. Its assets are unaffected, though they are changed from physical assets to a chose in action consisting of a claim against the wrongdoers.'[250]

It is thought that, with the exception of the final sentence, the foregoing paragraph clearly expresses the distinction between a claim by the company and a claim by shareholders. The final sentence does not, however, make clear sense: where shareholders are induced to sell their shares at an undervalue the company's assets are not changed from physical assets to choses in action and it is thought that Millett LJ must have been referring to the nature of the shareholders' claims, although this too is not without difficulty since shareholders' interests in shares are, by definition, choses in action, and never were physical assets.

[19.096] The refusal to allow a member to take a personal action against the directors in respect of the diminution of his shareholding or in respect of some other breach of the directors' duties is open to criticism on a number of grounds. First, the refusal fails to take on board the developments in the law of negligence and the greatly expanded categories of duties of care. Indeed the Supreme Court has recently accepted that directors can owe duties to creditors, upon the company becoming insolvent[251]. Moreover, as discussed in the context of Chapter 10, the Supreme Court in *O'Neill v Ryan et al* made no mention of the fact that there is case law to suggest that shareholders can be owed duties by the directors in certain circumstances[252]. Secondly, it was recognised in *Private Motorists' Provident Society v Attorney General*[253] that the

[249] [1998] 1 All ER 724 at 729g.

[250] [1998] 1 All ER 724 at 730c.

[251] *Re Frederick Inns Ltd* [1994] 1 ILRM 387.

[252] See Chapter 10, *Duties of Directors and Other Officers*, para **[10.017]**.

[253] *Private Motorists' Provident Society v Attorney General* [1983] IR 339.

shareholders in a company have certain constitutional rights in respect of their shareholding[254].

[C] DERIVATIVE ACTIONS AND EXCEPTIONS TO *FOSS V HARBOTTLE*

Preliminary considerations

[19.097] It now falls to consider the supposed[255] five recognised exceptions to the rule in *Foss v Harbottle* and the procedural mechanism of the derivative action. On a practical level, it should be remembered that the derivative action and the exceptions to *Foss v Harbottle* are normally only relied upon by members where they cannot bring themselves within CA 1963, s 205.

[19.098] The exceptions to the rule in *Foss v Harbottle* amount to a recognition that the rule does not prevent a member from bringing either of two types of action. First, a member is entitled to bring a personal action to vindicate an infringement of his personal rights. Secondly, a member *may* be entitled to bring a derivative action on behalf of the company. This may seem peculiar in that the analysis here of *Foss v Harbottle* has been predicated on the basis that the rule has *no* application to where a member's personal rights have been infringed. The reason for including this now as an exception to the rule is in recognition of the traditional view that actions to vindicate a member's personal rights are an exception to the rule[256]. Whether there is a real significance in this distinction or whether it can be passed off as an exercise in semantics does not detract from the fact that it engenders confusion. Before considering the supposed exceptions to the rule in *Foss v Harbottle* it is proposed to first consider the most usual procedural means of enforcing those exceptions: the derivative action.

The derivative action

[19.099] Where a wrong is committed against a company, whether by outsiders or by the directors, the proper plaintiff in the subsequent action is the company. The decision to institute proceedings will typically be taken by the company's board of directors who will usually be empowered to manage the company's business under model reg 80[257]. The problem of the minority shareholder arises:

— where the directors are themselves responsible for the wrong done to the company and refuse to take action against themselves; or

— where the aggrieved member or members cannot muster sufficient voting power in general meeting to compel the directors to institute proceedings.

Such situations arise less frequently in private companies than in public companies with large membership where the division of powers between members and directors is a reality. The central question at issue in deciding whether a minority member should be

---

[254] See generally, Chapter 4, *Incorporation and its Consequences*, para **[4.059]** *ff.*

[255] It shall be argued that when one property distinguishes the rule in *Foss v Harbottle* from a company's members' right to sue to vindicate their personal rights, the traditionally accepted *exceptions* are in some cases, not exceptions, but examples of situations in which the rule has no application whatsoever.

[256] Endorsed by the Supreme Court in *O'Neill v Ryan* [1993] ILRM 557.

[257] See generally, Chapter 8, *Corporate Governance: Management by the Directors*, para **[8.004]** where model reg 80 is considered in detail.

permitted to bring a derivative action is whether, unless the action is brought, a wrong committed against the company would otherwise go unredressed.

(a) The nature of a derivative action

[19.100] Although the rule in *Foss v Harbottle* precludes individual members from instituting proceedings where the company has been wronged, the rule does have a number of exceptions. Where such exceptions can be relied upon, a member or members may be allowed to institute a derivative action. A derivative action is where a shareholder, as representative of all of the other shareholders[258], institutes proceedings on behalf of the company in an attempt to redress a wrong perpetrated against the company. In *Wallersteiner v Moir (No 2)*[259] Lord Denning MR set out the general rule and the rationale for permitting derivative actions:

> 'It is a fundamental principle of our law that a company is a legal person, with its own corporate identity, separate and distinct from the directors or shareholders, and with its own property rights and interests to which alone it is entitled. If it is defrauded by a wrongdoer, the company itself is the one person to sue for the damage. Such is the rule in *Foss v Harbottle*...The rule is easy enough to apply when the company is defrauded by outsiders. The company itself is the only person who can sue. Likewise, when it is defrauded by insiders of a minor kind, once again the company is the only person who can sue. But suppose it is defrauded by insiders who control its affairs – by directors who hold a majority of the shares – who then can sue for damages? Those directors are themselves the wrongdoers. If a board meeting is held, they will not authorise the proceedings to be taken by the company against themselves. If a general meeting is called, they will vote down any suggestion that the company should sue them themselves. Yet the company is the one person who is damnified. It is the one person who should sue. In one way or another some means must be found for the company to sue. Otherwise the law would fail in its purpose. Injustice would be done without redress.'[260]

Accordingly, wrongs done to the company may be redressed by the minority members bringing a derivative action on the company's behalf[261]. In practice the company itself will be named as a party to the proceedings so as to ensure that any order made by the court may be enforced by or against the company.

[19.101] It is important to remember that in a derivative action a shareholder acts in a non-personal capacity, namely, he acts not only for himself but also for all the other shareholders. Accordingly, it was held in *Cooke v Cooke*[262] that where a shareholder sought to join in one action a claim for relief in his personal capacity with a derivative claim as representative of all of the other shareholders, leave was required to join those causes of action.

---

[258] See *Cooke v Cooke* [1997] 2 BCLC 28.

[259] *Wallersteiner v Moir (No 2)* [1975] 1 QB 373.

[260] [1975] 1 QB 373 at 390A–D.

[261] See generally, *East Pant Du United Lead Mining Co v Merryweather* (1864) 2 Hem & M 254, *Mason v Harris* (1879) 11 Ch D 97 and *Menier v Hooper's Telegraph* (1874) 9 Ch App 350.

[262] *Cooke v Cooke* [1997] 2 BCLC 28.

(b) The indemnity for costs

[19.102] Where a member is successful in a derivative action he will drop out of the action and the court will award judgment in favour of the company[263]. It is important to note that the member who instigates a derivative action may discontinue it at his own behest without the consent of his supposed principal[264]. The question of costs looms large for a member about to embark upon the institution of a derivative action. In *Wallersteiner v Moir (No 2)*[265] Lord Denning MR said:

> '...the minority shareholder, being an agent acting on behalf of the company, is entitled to be indemnified by the company against all costs and expenses reasonably incurred by him in the course of the agency. This indemnity does not arise out of a contract express or implied, but it arises on the plainest principles of equity. It is analogous to the indemnity to which a trustee is entitled from his cestui que trust who is *sui juris*.'[266]

Lord Denning MR went on to say that before being given leave to commence an action on behalf of the company, a putative plaintiff should first make application to the Master's Court for directions, supported by counsel's opinion as to whether such an action is reasonable. Although Lord Denning MR did say that application should be made ex parte, the English Court of Appeal has cast fatal doubts on this in *Prudential Assurance Co Ltd v Newman Industries Ltd (No 2)*.

[19.103] The importance of recognising early in proceedings that one's cause of action is to be framed as a derivative action is seen in the Supreme Court's decision in *Balkanbank v Taher*[267]. The facts in that case were that the plaintiff had commenced proceedings against the defendants alleging, inter alia, breach of trust, breach of duty and fraud by some of them against a joint venture company – Balkan International Ltd – in which the plaintiff-company was a shareholder. The essence of the dispute concerned the draw down and subsequent utilisation of the proceeds of credit facilities by Balkan International Ltd. In the High Court it had been held that the defendants had not been guilty of fraud or breach of duty in drawing down the credit facilities and that any irregularity in the utilisation of the credit facilities was actionable only by Balkan International Ltd, not the plaintiff, by reason of the operation of the rule in *Foss v Harbottle*. Notwithstanding that the proceedings had been commenced in the plaintiff's own name, the trial judge gave liberty to amend the statement of claim to include a derivative action, brought on behalf of the company based on the 'fraud on a minority'[268] exception to the Rule in *Foss v Harbottle*. The defendants appealed against this on the basis that to make such a change in the proceedings was unfairly prejudicial to their

---

263 *Spokes v Grosvenor Hotel Co Ltd* [1897] 2 QB 124. See also *Wallersteiner v Moir (No 2)* [1975] 1 QB 373 at 391–392 *per* Lord Denning MR.

264 *Re Alpha Co Ltd* [1913] 1 Ch 203.

265 *Wallersteiner v Moir (No 2)* [1975] 1 QB 373.

266 [1975] 1 QB 373 at 391G–H. This was endorsed by Buckley LJ who said (at 403G): 'It seems to me that in a minority shareholder's action, properly and reasonably brought and prosecuted, it would normally be right that the company should be ordered to pay the plaintiff's costs so far as he does not recover them from any other party.'

267 *Balkanbank v Taher et al* (19 January 1995, unreported), Supreme Court.

268 See para **[19.115]** *ff*.

defence. The Supreme Court agreed and allowed the appeal. In the course of his judgment Hamilton CJ found that the change was radical and not minor in nature and seriously prejudiced the defendants and that such was not in accordance with fair procedures which require that a party to an action be given notice of the nature of a claim and an adequate opportunity of defending all aspects thereof. Hamilton CJ also noted that the plaintiff's original claim, as pleaded, required the establishment of fraud and that the High Court had found that the plaintiff had failed to establish fraud; however, in a derivative action 'they were merely required to establish that, without any element of dishonesty or criminality, monies entrusted to the defendants/ appellants for a particular purpose were used by them for some other purpose.'[269]

(c) The twin test to bring a derivative action

[19.104] In *Prudential Assurance Co Ltd v Newman Industries Ltd (No 2)*[270] it was held by the English Court of Appeal that before a minority shareholder should be permitted to bring a derivative action on behalf of the company he:

> '...ought at least be required before proceeding with his action to establish a *prima facie* case (i) that the company is entitled to the relief claimed, and (ii) that the action falls within the proper boundaries of the exception to the rule in *Foss v Harbottle*.'[271]

The reason for this procedural hurdle was said by the Court of Appeal to be that it cannot be right to subject the company to a lengthy court action[272] only to decide whether the plaintiff had a proper right of action. Keane J in *Crindle Investments v Wymes*[273] appears to have accepted the propriety of the Court of Appeal's procedural requirements in *Newman*.

[19.105] In the *Newman* case[274] the facts were that two companies, Newman and TPG were substantial shareholders in each other. When TPG encountered financial difficulties a rescue plan was put together by a Mr Barlett and a Mr Laughton, who held prominent positions of management in both companies. It was proposed that Newman would buy the entire of TPG's assets, save its shares in Newman, at a price to be determined by Newman's auditors. To comply with Stock Exchange regulations, a circular was sent to the shareholders in both companies, convening separate general meetings and explaining the mechanics of the proposed transaction. Prudential Assurance, a minority shareholder in Newman, took objection to the proposed purchase price for TPG's assets and took further objection to the contents of the circular, claiming that it was difficult and misleading. Despite Prudential's protestations, the resolution approving of the transaction was passed by a small majority. At this point Prudential instituted proceedings against Newman: a personal action on its own and in other

---

269 (19 January 1995, unreported), Supreme Court at p 39.

270 *Prudential Assurance Co Ltd v Newman Industries Ltd (No 2)* [1982] 1 Ch 204.

271 [1982] 1 Ch 204 at 221, 222.

272 The *Newman* case lasted 64 days.

273 *Crindle Investments v Wymes* [1998] 4 IR 578 at 594. See further para **[19.124]**.

274 Considered by Gower, *Principles of Modern Company Law* (5th edn, 1992), under the heading of 'The "Calamitous" *Newman* case', at 647, although he attributes the label to the Court of Appeal at [1982] Ch 224 at 235C.

capacities, and a derivative action on behalf of the company. At the preliminary hearing, Vinelott J in a judgment[275] much criticised by the Court of Appeal, held that Prudential could proceed with its claim. At the subsequent trial[276] Vinelott J held that Prudential could bring a derivative action on behalf of Newman, and justified this on the basis of the fifth exception to the rule in *Foss v Harbottle*, considered below[277], namely that 'the interests of justice do require that a minority action should be permitted.'[278]

What followed was an appeal to the Court of Appeal which delivered such a lengthy judgment that only Chapter 5 (the law) and Chapter 7 (conclusions) were reported in the Chancery Reports. The personal actions brought by Prudential were unsuccessful, as considered above[279]. Because Vinelott J had allowed the derivative action to proceed and because this had not been appealed, the Court of Appeal refused to reopen the matter, saying that it would amount to 'a grave injustice to all parties to increase the already horrendous costs of this litigation by allowing time for argument on an interesting but irrelevant point'[280]. And so, despite the lengthy judgment, the law remained unsettled as to the principles of law applicable to derivative actions. What was put forward, though, was the twin test for establishing whether a member has standing to bring a derivative action, which has been set out above[281].

[19.106] In *Smith v Croft (No 3)*[282] Knox J delivered a judgment which applied the test promulgated by the Court of Appeal in the *Newman* case. The facts of the case were that Smith and others were minority shareholders in a company called Film Finance Ltd ('the company'). Between them, they held shares which carried 14.44% of the voting rights in the company. Croft and the other defendants together held between them 62.5% of the shares carrying voting rights in the company. The defendants did not belong to an homogenous class, there being three groups: the executive directors, companies associated with them, and the chairman and non-executive director who was a nominee of a company called Wren Trust Ltd ('the independent shareholder'). The independent shareholder held 19.66% of the shares which carried voting rights in the company. Disagreements arose between, inter alia, Smith and Croft. These culminated in Smith and others instituting proceedings to bring a derivative or minority shareholders' action on behalf of the company. In these proceedings it was alleged, inter alia, that the executive directors paid themselves excessive remuneration directly and indirectly and that those and other payments were ultra vires. It was also alleged that the company had been caused to provide financial assistance to the associated companies to enable them to purchase the company's shares, contrary to the English equivalent of CA 1963, s 60. Knox J ordered that the plaintiff's claim be struck out. He held that Smith et al had not satisfied the twin test promulgated by the Court of Appeal in the *Newman* case.

---

275 [1981] Ch 229.

276 [1981] Ch 257.

277 See para **[19.126]**.

278 [1981] Ch 257 at 327B.

279 See para **[19.093]**.

280 [1982] Ch 204 at 220.

281 See para **[19.104]**.

282 *Smith v Croft (No 3)* [1987] BCLC 355.

As to the first limb of the test the learned judge held that Smith et al had failed to establish, on behalf of the company, a prima facie case that the payments to the directors or their associated companies were ultra vires or in breach of their duties. However Knox J did find that there had been a breach of the English equivalent of CA 1963, s 60. This breach did satisfy the first limb of the test because it was ultra vires the company and illegal and was consequently unratifiable by the members.

The plaintiff was, however, unsuccessful in satisfying the second limb. Although the action was unratifiable, and although there was an exception to the rule that a derivative action could be brought to recover for any loss occasioned by an ultra vires act, Knox J held that if there was any reason why either the shareholder or the company would be debarred from taking action, a derivative action could not proceed. Knox J also held that it was proper to have regard to the views of a majority of the shareholders, who were independent of the defendants, as to whether the action should proceed. On the facts, Knox J found that the independent shareholder was opposed to the action. As the independent shareholder held a majority of the minority shares and opposed the action, Knox J ordered that the action should be dismissed. He said:

> '...I remain unconvinced that a just result is achieved by a single minority shareholder having the right to involve a company in an action for recovery of compensation for the company if all the other minority shareholders are for disinterested reasons satisfied that the proceedings will be productive of more harm than good. If the argument of counsel for the plaintiffs is well founded, once control by the defendants is established the views of the rest of the minority as to the advisability of the prosecution of the suit are necessarily irrelevant. I find that hard to square with the concept of a form of pleading originally introduced on the ground of necessity alone in order to prevent a wrong going without redress.
>
> I therefore conclude that it is proper to have regard to the views of independent shareholders. In that case it is common ground that there would be no useful purpose served by adjourning to enable a general meeting to be called. For all practical purposes it is quite clear how the votes would be cast...'.[283]

This additional test, after establishing control[284], imposes a further obstacle in the path of shareholders intent on bringing a derivative action on behalf of the company.

The exceptions to the rule in Foss v Harbottle

[19.107] Traditionally[285], the textbooks say that there are four exceptions to the rule in *Foss v Harbottle*. To these has been added a less settled fifth exception. The five *supposed* exceptions are said to be:

(a) Where an ultra vires or illegal act is perpetrated.

(b) Where more than a bare majority is required to ratify the 'wrong' complained of.

(c) Where the members' personal rights are infringed.

(d) Where a fraud has been perpetrated upon a minority by those in control.

---

283 [1987] BCLC 355 at 403.

284 See para **[19.119]**.

285 See eg, Keane, *Company Law* (3rd edn, 2000), para 26.10.

(e) Where the justice of the case requires a minority to be permitted to institute proceedings.

Notwithstanding the cold response[286] to suggestions of the fifth exception, it may be argued that it is at least as deserving of recognition as the traditional four exceptions. In that the fifth exception recognises the inherent jurisdiction of the courts to remedy unconscionable conduct, it is thought that it is well placed and deserving of recognition as a *true* exception to the rule. Indeed the *justice of the case* is perhaps the true reason for permitting all derivative actions to subsist, the other four exceptions being variations on this theme.

***(a)* Ultra vires *and illegal acts*[287]**

[19.108] Notwithstanding the rule in *Foss v Harbottle* an individual member may either:

(a) Seek an injunction to prevent the company committing an ultra vires act[288] and,

(b) Where an ultra vires act has been committed, sue on behalf of the company for a declaration that an act was ultra vires[289].

This is an exception to both limbs of the rule in *Foss v Harbottle* which exalts majority rule: a simple majority of the members cannot ratify action which is outside the company's capacity, and which is consequently ultra vires[290] and, it would appear, also that where a wrong is committed to the company, that the company is the proper plaintiff[291].

[19.109] A number of decisions have held that an individual member has a *personal right* to take an action to restrain the commission of an ultra vires act[292]. In *Simpson v Westminister Palace Hotel Co*[293] Lord Campbell LC said:

> 'The funds of a joint stock company established for one undertaking cannot be applied to another. If an attempt to do so is made, this act is ultra vires, and although sanctioned by

---

286 See the dicta of the Court of Appeal in *Prudential Assurance Co Ltd v Newman Industries Ltd (No 2)* [1982] 1 All ER 354 and *Estmanco Ltd v GLC* [1982] 1 All ER 437; and see para **[19.126]**.

287 See Chapter 7, *Corporate Contracts, Capacity and Authority*, para **[7.043]** *ff*.

288 See CA 1963, s 8(2); *Simpson v Westminister Palace Hotel Co* (1860) 8 HL Cas 712; *Maunsell v Midland Great Eastern (Ireland) Rly Co* (1863) 1 Hem & M 130; *Spokes v Grosvenor Hotel Co* [1897] 2 QB 4; and *Hoole v Great Western Rly Co* (1867) 3 Ch App 262.

289 See *Hennessy v National Agricultural and Industrial Development Association* [1947] IR 159, *Spokes v Grosvenor Hotel Co* [1897] 2 QB 124; and *Salomons v Laing* (1850) 12 Beav 377.

290 *Ashbury Railway Carriage and Iron Co v Riche* (1875) LR HL 653; *Buchanan Ltd v McVey* [1954] IR 89 and *Re Balgooley Distillery Co* (1886) 17 LR Ir 239; and see generally Chapter 7, *Corporate Contracts, Capacity and Authority*, para **[7.043]**.

291 See *Smith v Croft (No 3)* [1987] BCLC 355.

292 *Hutton v West Cork Rly Co* (1833) 23 Ch D 654.

293 *Simpson v Westminister Palace Hotel Co* (1860) 8 HL Cas 712. See also *Hoole v Great Western Railway Co* (1867) LR 3 Ch App 262 where Lord Cairns LJ said: '...if the arrangement which has been proposed is legal, is *intra vires*, the company, through their general meetings, have power to carry it into effect; if on the other hand, it is *ultra vires*, if it is illegal, any member of the company may dissent from it, and has a right to appeal to this court to be protected against its effects...'.

all the directors and by a large majority of the shareholders, any single shareholder has a right to resist it, and a court of equity will interpose on his behalf by injunction...'.

This common law statement has statutory backing in CA 1963, s 8(2) which provides:

> 'The court may on the application of any member or holder of debentures of a company, restrain such company from doing any act or thing which the company has no power to do.'

On the traditional analysis, this is seen as a common law/statutory exception to the rule in *Foss v Harbottle*. It is thought that such an analysis is misfounded and that this situation is in reality also an example of a situation to which the rule has no application in the first place. Rather, to sue to prevent the commission of an ultra vires act is a personal right of a company's members.

[19.110] Where an ultra vires act has taken place, it was held in *Hennessy v National Agricultural and Industrial Development Association*[294] that a member of the company may apply to court for a declaration to that effect. Similarly, a member may bring a derivative action to have an ultra vires act set aside and to recover money wrongly paid, as in *Russell v Wakefield Waterworks Co*[295]. There is authority that different principles apply to where a member institutes proceedings to have an ultra vires transaction set aside as opposed to where proceedings are taken to prevent the commission of a threatened ultra vires act.[296] On this analysis, a member's right to sue is by way of derivative action, and not by way of vindication of his personal rights. In *Smith v Croft (No 3)* [297], the facts of which have been considered above[298], Knox J said:

> '...the whole doctrine whereby a minority shareholder is permitted to assert claims on behalf of the company, is rooted in a procedural expedient, and adopted to prevent a wrong going without redress. Where what is sought is compensation for the company for loss caused by ultra vires transactions the wrong, in my judgment, is a wrong to the company which has the substantive right to redress. Where the minority shareholder is seeking to prevent an ultra vires transaction or otherwise seeking to enforce his personal substantive rights, the wrong which needs redress is the minority shareholder's wrong.' [299]

Such a distinction seems excessively legalistic. The principles of law applicable to the so-called exceptions to the rule in *Foss v Harbottle* are already a quagmire. It should also be noted that Knox J in *Smith v Croft (No 3)* held that a minority shareholder may be prevented from bringing a derivative action where a majority of the minority shareholders oppose the action being taken. It is difficult to reconcile this with Knox J's acceptance of the fact that ultra vires actions are not ratifiable[300]: if acts are not ratifiable, why should any disgruntled member be prevented from instituting proceedings?

---

[294] *Hennessy v National Agricultural and Industrial Development Association* [1947] IR 159.

[295] *Russell v Wakefield Waterworks Co* (1875) LR 20 Eq 474.

[296] See *Smith v Croft et al (No 3)* [1987] BCLC 355. This has been accepted by Pennington, *Pennington's Company Law* (6th edn, 1990), p 655, but found to be 'unconvincing' by Keane, *Company Law* (3rd edn, 2000), para 26.12.

[297] [1987] BCLC 355 at 389.

[298] See para **[19.106]**.

[299] Support for the distinction was found in the Court of Appeal judgments in *Towers v African Tug Co* [1904] 1 Ch 558.

[19.111] A member is at liberty to institute proceedings in respect of apprehended illegal acts or where illegal acts have been committed. The leading Irish authority on this exception is *Cockburn v Newbridge Sanitary Steam Laundry Company*[301]. The facts of that case were that the company's managing director paid bribes to officials in the War Office in return for lucrative contracts with the company. Two of the company's shareholders instituted proceedings to compel the managing director to pay the bribes to the company; the other shareholders were not inclined to such action. The managing director's defence was that any proceedings against him should be brought in the name of the company and because 'the company' was not disposed to bringing such proceedings no action against him was possible. O'Brien LC dismissed the defence that the matters complained of related to the company's 'internal management'. He went on to say:

> 'The rule of law and of good sense laid down in *Foss v Harbottle* is indisputable, but is subject to the exception that where the acts complained of are of a fraudulent character, or beyond the powers of the company, the action may be maintained by a shareholder suing on behalf of himself and the other shareholders, the company being made a defendant in the action...'[302].

The learned judge held also that it was 'not within the power of the company either to make, ratify or adopt a proceeding of the scandalous character sought to be cloaked over in the present case by...resolution', and was satisfied that the plaintiffs were entitled to the relief sought[303].

(b) Transactions unratifiable by a bare majority

[19.112] This exception may be said to derive from that limb of the rule which exalts *majority rule* in conflicts between shareholders. Where a bare majority of members purports to ratify an act which in fact requires the sanction of a special resolution, a dissenting member is not prohibited by the rule in *Foss v Harbottle* from bringing proceedings. Similarly where inadequate notice is given of a proposed resolution at a general meeting of the company any member can bring a derivative action to prevent the company from acting on any resolution passed[304].

---

300 [1987] BCLC 355 at 384e.

301 *Cockburn v Newbridge Sanitary Steam Laundry Company* [1915] 1 IR 237.

302 See also *Buchanan Ltd v McVey* [1954] IR 89 where a fraud on the Revenue Commissioners was held to be unratifiable by the company.

303 Holmes LJ said in the course of his judgment: 'There is, however, one well-recognised exception to this rule [ie the rule in *Foss v Harbottle*]. Where the question involves the investigation of misconduct or criminality on the part of the company and one or more of its officers, or something ultra vires the company itself, the arm of the law cannot be stayed by the rule of law to which I have referred.' When the company's shareholders subsequently refused to make the managing director account for the bribes, further application was made to court. This resulted in the making of an order for the winding up of the company on just and equitable grounds: see *Re Newbridge Sanitary Steam Laundry Ltd* [1917] 1 IR 67 and, generally, Chapter 25, *Winding Up Companies*, para **[25.076]**.

304 *Baillie v Oriental Telephone and Electric Co Ltd* [1915] 1 Ch 503, [1914–15] All ER Rep 1420.

[19.113] Where a bare majority of a company's members purports to act in breach of the company's memorandum or articles of association or purports to ratify a breach[305], a member can institute proceedings to restrain such a breach[306]. In such circumstances the majority must either abide by the articles of association or alter them in accordance with law. Where the alteration is not *bona fide* and in the interests of the company as a whole, the body of law considered in Chapter 3, above, may be invoked by the minority[307].

(c) Actions for infringement of personal rights

[19.114] Although this has been considered to be an exception to the rule in *Foss v Harbottle*, it is thought that this is not an exception at all, but rather an example of a situation in which the rule has no application whatsoever. Actions to vindicate a member's rights have been considered above and are entirely divorced from the rule[308].

(d) Fraud on a minority by those in control[309]

[19.115] This is the clearest and most exceptional case where the rule in *Foss v Harbottle* will not apply and has even been identified as the only true exception to the rule[310]. Accordingly, notwithstanding the rule, a minority of the company's shareholders may take a derivative action on behalf of the company where the majority in *control* of the company perpetrate a *fraud* on the minority. This is an exception to both limbs of the rule which provides that only the company has locus standi to take action on foot of a wrong committed against the company and that the will of the majority should prevail. In *Smith v Croft (No 3)*[311] Knox J said:

> 'Ultimately the question which has to be answered in order to determine whether the rule in *Foss v Harbott*le applies to prevent a minority shareholder seeking relief as plaintiff for the benefit of the company is: "Is the plaintiff being prevented improperly from bringing these proceedings on behalf of the company?" If it is an expression of the corporate will of the company by an appropriate independent organ that is preventing the plaintiff from prosecuting the action he is not improperly but properly prevented and so the answer to the question is No. The appropriate independent organ will vary according to the constitution of the company concerned and the identity of the defendants who will in most cases be disqualified from participating by voting in expressing the corporate will.'

[19.116] This exception can only provide relief to the company concerned: it is not intended to provide the minority shareholders with relief[312]. This exception must be

---

305 *Edwards v Halliwell* [1950] 2 All ER 1064.

306 *Mosely v Koffyfontein Mines Ltd* [1911] 1 Ch 73 and *Salomon v Quinn and Axtens Ltd* [1909] 1 Ch 311.

307 See Chapter 3, *The Constitutional Documentation*, para **[3.077]** *ff.*

308 See para **[19.089]**. For members' personal rights, see Chapter 15, *Shares and Membership*, **[15.083]** *ff.*

309 See generally, Wedderburn, 'Shareholders' Rights and the rule in *Foss v Harbottle*' [1958] Cam LJ 93.

310 See Farrar, *Farrar's Company Law* (3rd edn, 1991), p 449.

311 *Smith v Croft (No 3)* [1987] BCLC 355.

312 *Ferguson v Wallbridge* [1935] 3 DLR 66 (Privy Council). It has been noted by Wedderburn, 'Shareholders' Rights and the rule in *Foss v Harbottle*' [1958] Cam LJ 93 that the standard of service to be delivered to the company has not been very high.

clearly distinguished from situations where a minority institutes proceedings on foot of an alteration of a company's articles of association by a majority which does not act bona fide and in the interests of the company as a whole: in such situations the minority's remedy will usually be a *personal action*[313]. The alteration of the articles of association in such circumstances has been considered in Chapter 3[314].

[19.117] The case law which has built up around this exception typically involves the *expropriation* or *appropriation*, to use two expressions found in other textbooks, of corporate property by a majority who are in a controlling position. Other cases involve situations where a majority support the directors who act in breach of their fiduciary duties, or negligently or mala fide in the exercise of their powers. Again, it is important to distinguish the case law proper to a consideration of this exception to the rule from cases concerning the expropriation by majority shareholders of minority shareholders' shares in a company. In such cases a derivative action is usually inappropriate, the expropriated members having a personal action against the majority.

[19.118] One of the leading cases on the fraud on a minority exception is *Menier v Hooper's Telegraph Works Ltd*[315]. In that case the defendant-company manufactured telegraph cable. Another company was formed with the intention that the defendant would supply cable to that company which would then lay a transatlantic telegraph cable. The necessary government concession was obtained and was held by a trustee on behalf of the company. Subsequently, the defendant began to supply its cable to a third party at a better price and procured a trustee who held the requisite government concession to transfer this concession to the third party. To thwart the company from instituting proceedings to recover the government concession, the defendant procured the passing of a resolution that the company be placed into voluntary liquidation. A liquidator, friendly to the defendant, was appointed who would not sue the defendant for what it had done. The unfortunate Menier was a minority shareholder in the company who, presumably outraged at the scam which had been perpetrated, brought a derivative action on behalf of the company against the defendant to make it account for its fraudulent profit. It was held that Menier had standing to bring the derivative action against the defendant, James LJ saying:

> 'The minority of the shareholders say in effect that the majority has divided the assets of the company, more or less, between themselves, to the exclusion of the minority. I think it would be a shocking thing if that could be done, because if so the majority might divide the whole assets of the company, and pass a resolution that everything must be given to them, and that the minority should have nothing to do with it. Assuming the case to be as alleged in the bill, then *the majority have put something into their pockets at the expense of the minority.* If so, it appears to me that the minority have a right to have their share of the benefits ascertained for them in the best way in which the court can do it, and given to them.'[316] [Emphasis added]

313 *Greenhalgh v Arderne Cinemas* [1950] 2 All ER 1120 and *Sidebottom v Kershaw Leese & Co Ltd* [1920] 1 Ch 154. See generally, Ch 3, *The Constitutional Documentation*, para **[3.078]** *ff*. It should be noted though that some minority claims have been brought as derivative actions.

314 Chapter 3, *The Constitutional Documentation*, para **[3.065]**.

315 *Menier v Hooper's Telegraph Works Ltd* (1874) 9 Ch App 350.

This case demonstrates many of the factors properly associated with the *fraud on a minority* exception to the rule:

- The defendant majority perpetrated a *fraud* against the minority and the company.
- The defendant was in *control* of the company.
- The wrong committed to the company was unredressed and unless a derivative action was permitted, no proceedings could have been instituted.

It is proposed next to consider the concepts of *control* and *fraud*, the basic ingredients of the *fraud on a minority* exception. In addition, the other essential constituent – that *the defendant must derive benefit* – is also considered.

(i) Control

[19.119] The first constituent element in this exception to the rule is the requirement that the minority shows that those who have perpetrated the fraud are *in control* of the company[317]. To show that the majority holds in excess of 50% of the shares in the company which carry voting rights is the simplest way of satisfying this requirement. Where control is exercised by a majority through the use of nominees, trusts, etc, it is thought that the court can cut through the facade to the heart of where de facto control lies. Where simple voting control cannot be established, Fairweather J's[318] old test still has merit, namely that the minority shareholder:

> '...must '*account for the fact that the company has not seen fit to bring action on its own behalf.* This may be done by showing that the company has refused to allow the action to be brought on its own behalf, or that, by reason of the wrongdoer being in control of the company at the time of bringing the action, it would be idle to apply to the company.' [Emphasis added]

In *Smith v Croft (No 3)*[319] Knox J held that the word 'control' was placed in inverted commas by the Court of Appeal in *Prudential Assurance Co Ltd v Newman Industries Ltd (No 2)*[320] 'because it was recognised that voting control by the defendants was not necessarily the sole subject of investigation.'

[19.120] In *Smith v Croft (No 3)* Knox J went on to say that a further consideration exists, even after control is established. This further requirement is that the court must have regard to the views of other disinterested minority shareholders. Knox J said:

> '...I remain unconvinced that a just result is achieved by a single minority shareholder having the right to involve a company in an action for recovery of compensation for the company if all the other minority shareholders are for disinterested reasons satisfied that the proceedings will be productive of more harm than good. If the argument of counsel for

---

[316] (1874) 9 Ch App 350 at 353.

[317] See *Prudential Assurance Co Ltd v Newman Industries Ltd (No 2)* [1982] 1 Ch 204; *Birch v Sullivan* [1958] 1 All ER 56; *Russell v Wakefield Waterworks Co* (1875) LR 20 Eq 474; and *Pavlides v Jensen* [1956] 2 All ER 518.

[318] *Fisher v St John Opera House Co* [1937] 4 DLR 337 at 342, quoted approvingly by Wedderburn, 'Shareholders' Rights and the rule in *Foss v Harbottle*' [1958] Cam LR 93 at 95.

[319] *Smith v Croft (No 3)* [1987] BCLC 355 at 403b.

[320] *Prudential Assurance Co Ltd v Newman Industries Ltd (No 2)* [1982] 1 All ER 354 at 364.

> the plaintiffs is well founded, once control by the defendants is established the views of the rest of the minority as to the advisability of the prosecution of the suit are necessarily irrelevant. I find that hard to square with the concept of a form of pleading originally introduced on the ground of necessity alone in order to prevent a wrong going without redress.'[321]

In that case Knox J had regard to the views of an independent shareholder and concluded that the interests of the company would not be best served by allowing the action to proceed.

(ii) Fraud on the minority

[19.121] There exist many general judicial statements of what a majority of shareholders is not permitted to do: they may not 'appropriate to themselves money, property or advantages which belong to the company or in which the other shareholders are entitled to participate'[322] or may not 'put something into their pockets at the expense of the minority'[323]. The ordinary meaning of the word '*fraud*' has little application to the concept of 'fraud on the minority'. Rather, as *Keane* has said[324], 'fraud' in this context does not necessarily involve any element of dishonesty, let alone criminality'. This has been endorsed by the Supreme Court in *Balkanbank v Taher*[325]. Fraud on a minority has been found to exist in a number of diverse situations, involving varying degrees of moral turpitude.

[19.122] In *Estmanco (Kilner House) Ltd v Greater London Council*[326] the defendant, the GLC, had incorporated a non-profit making company with the object of selling long leases of refurbished council flats to GLC tenants. Although the GLC retained control of the company, it was intended that the company would manage the blocks of flats and that each owner would become a shareholder in the company. Until all of the leases were sold, flat-owning shareholders had no voting rights attaching to their shares. An agreement was entered into between the company and the GLC on these terms. Following an election, the GLC had a change of political heart and no longer believed home-ownership to be a desirable social goal. Consequently, the GLC acted in breach of the agreement between it and the company. Two directors of the company caused the company to institute proceedings against the GLC for breach of the agreement. The GLC convened a general meeting of the company and procured the passing of a resolution to discontinue the legal action. A shareholding flat-owner sought to take over, by way of a derivative action, the proceedings which had been instituted by the company. Sir Robert Megarry VC held that the GLC as a majority shareholder could not exercise its voting rights selfishly and:

---

321 [1987] BCLC 355 at 403e–f.

322 Per Lord Davey in *Burland v Earle* [1902] AC 83 at 93.

323 Per James LJ in *Menier v Hooper's Telegraph Works* (1874) LR 9 Ch App 350.

324 See Keane, *Company Law* (3rd edn, 2000), para 26.15.

325 *Balkanbank v Taher* (19 January 1995, unreported), Supreme Court.

326 *Estmanco (Kilner House) Ltd v Greater London Council* [1982] 1 All ER 437.

> '...with impunity...injure his voteless fellow shareholders by depriving the company of a cause of action and [thereby] stultifying the purpose for which the company was formed.'[327]

Although the GLC's actions were contrary to company law they could hardly be said to be truly *fraudulent* in the recognised sense of that word[328].

[19.123] A more blatant example of where a majority were found to have committed a fraud on the minority is seen in *Cook v Deeks*[329]. In that case the directors of a company, in gross disregard of their fiduciary duties to the company, diverted a contract belonging to the company to themselves. Mindful of their duties to the company, the directors, who together held a majority of the shares in the company, caused a resolution to be passed, approving of the transaction. The plaintiff, who was a minority shareholder, was successful in bringing a derivative action. Of the purported absolving resolution, the Privy Council held:

> '...a resolution that the rights of the company should be disregarded in this matter would amount to forfeiting the interests and property of the minority of shareholders in favour of the majority and that by the votes of those who are interested in securing the property for themselves.'

Such an example of *fraud on a minority* may be classified as an unratifiable appropriation of corporate property. Other examples include negligence[330], although some instances of negligence have been held to be ratifiable, and thus not amenable to a minority shareholder's derivative action[331].

(iii) The defendant must derive benefit

[19.124] This constituent of the exception was mooted by the Supreme Court in *Crindle Investments v Wymes*[332]. The facts of that complicated and drawn-out case were succinctly summarised by Keane J in the Supreme Court who referred throughout to the plaintiffs as 'the R Group' and the defendants as 'the W Group'. Over 25 years' prior to the decision the R Group and the W Group bought certain lands near Navan under which there lay a vast and valuable ore body. The ore body extended under adjoining lands and had been discovered by another company, Tara Mining Ltd ('Tara') which had been given a lease by the State. The State subsequently acquired a 49% interest in Bula Ltd ('Limited'), a company formed by the R Group and the W Group to exploit the ore body. Limited borrowed substantial sums from several banks, which took security from Limited and personal guarantees from the personal plaintiffs. There were considerable delays in exploiting the ore body and the banks ultimately appointed a receiver-manager to Limited and obtained judgment against the personal plaintiffs in the R Group.

327 [1982] 1 All ER 437 at 448.

328 In *Daniels v Daniels* [1978] Ch 406 a derivative action against the company's directors and majority shareholders was successful where they had caused the company to sell company land to themselves at an undervalue, although in that case fraud was not found.

329 *Cook v Deeks* [1916] 1 AC 554.

330 *Daniels v Daniels* [1978] Ch 406.

331 *Pavlides v Jensen* [1956] 2 All ER 518.

332 *Crindle Investments v Wymes* [1999] 4 IR 578, [1998] 2 ILRM 275.

Subsequently, Limited, an associated company called Bula Holdings ('Holdings'), the personal plaintiffs and defendants instituted proceedings against Tara and the State for, inter alia, conspiracy to cause economic loss, trespass etc ('the Tara Proceedings') and later against the receiver, four of the banks and a firm of consultant mining engineers for, inter alia, negligence ('the Bank Proceedings'). Some seven years' later – in 1993 – the Tara Proceedings were dismissed by Lynch J – this decision was still under appeal. Some eleven years' later – in 1997 – the Bank Proceedings were heard by Barr J but after a time he was informed that the plaintiffs accepted that if Lynch J's decision was upheld on appeal, the Bank Proceedings would also fail unless they could succeed on a particular Statute of Limitations point. In the circumstances, Barr J adjourned the Bank Proceedings to await the outcome of the appeal[333].
Differences had arisen between the R Group and the W Group and in 1993 a section 205 petition had been presented by the R Group, based on the manner in which the W Group (which held 60% of the shares in Holdings) was conducting the litigation and the manner in which possible compromises were being addressed. The section 205 petition was held *in camera*. Murphy J held that the actions of the W Group in rejecting particular offers of compromise in both proceedings was 'an improvident gamble' and amounted to oppression and a disregard of the interests of the other shareholders within the meaning of CA 1963, s 205. On appeal, the Supreme Court upheld this finding. It was ordered that the petitioning R Group should be in control of the negotiations on behalf of Holdings to settle the proceedings and should be entitled to settle them by negotiation if possible on terms broadly similar to those offered but no less advantageous unless agreed to by all of Holdings' members or approved by the High Court. The R Group also sought an order to require all of the parties, whether as directors or as personal litigants, to join in the acceptance of an offer which had then been made to compromise the proceedings (if still available). This was because the defendants in both the Tara Proceedings and in the Bank Proceedings had indicated that they were unwilling to enter into any compromise unless all the plaintiffs *including the personal plaintiffs* were bound by the settlement. As has been noted earlier[334] Murphy J declined to make such an order, a decision upheld on appeal by the Supreme Court.

The personal claims, that had been asserted in the Tara Proceedings and the Bank Proceedings by the R Group, were withdrawn. The W Group's personal claims – in the Tara Proceedings for monies lent to Holdings, embarrassment etc and in the Bank Proceedings to have the securities and personal guarantees set aside and for damages – were maintained.

[19.125] The R Group also instituted plenary proceedings against the W Group in an attempt to force the W Group to withdraw their personal claims. These plenary proceedings alleged, first, that the W Group owed a fiduciary duty to the R Group and that the maintenance and perseverance in the individual claims to the detriment of Limited and Holdings constituted a breach of trust. Secondly, it was contended that the exercise of the W Group's constitutional rights to assert individual claims was an abuse

---

333 The claim against the engineers was resolved and the proceedings against them were struck out.

334 See para **[19.069]**.

of the constitutional rights of the R group. In the High Court, Murphy J rejected the R Group's claims in the plenary proceedings. The subject matter of the instant case was an appeal from that decision. Keane J held that there was no fiduciary duty owed by the W Group, as alleged, as the requisite confidence and trust did not subsist between the parties at the relevant times. The R Group's next claim was that they could rely upon the damage allegedly caused to Holdings and Limited by the conduct of the W Group in pursuing their personal claims and were not prevented from so doing by the *Rule in Foss v Harbottle* by reason of the fourth and fifth exceptions. Keane J noted the ambit of the fourth exception, as stated in *Burland v Earle*[335] and the fact that it was not necessary to establish fraudulent conduct in the criminal sense, noting that there was, even, some doubt as to whether fraud in any sense needed to be established[336]. Keane J held, however, that the R Group's claim was bound to fail for failure to show that the W Group would derive benefit from the alleged wrongdoing. On this point he said:

> 'Should there be no reasonable offer forthcoming and approved by the court, the maintenance by the defendants of their personal claims will not constitute any form of wrongdoing *quoad* the company or anyone else. If there were such an offer forthcoming and the defendants maintained their personal claims, *no benefits would flow to the individual defendants – an essential constituent of the exceptions to the rule – since they would only derive such a benefit in the event of a victory in the Tara and Bank proceedings or a compromise of both*. In either event, far from any damage being caused to the company, benefits would accrue to it as a result of the persistence of the W Group in maintaining their claims and declining to co-operate in any offers of settlement, however ill-judged that course of conduct might now appear to be. This, even on the widest construction of the exceptions to the rule in *Foss v Harbottle* the maintenance of the personal claims does not come within them.'[337] [Emphasis added]

It is significant that Keane J also questioned the form of procedure adopted by the R Group in pursuing what was in substance, although not in form, a derivative action. In this regard Keane J seems to have accepted the requirement in *Prudential Insurance Company v Newman Industries Ltd (No 2)*[338] that before such an action can proceed 'the

---

335 *Burland v Earle* [1902] AC 83. There he said: 'The cases in which the minority can maintain such an action are … confined to those in which the acts complained of are of a fraudulent character or beyond the powers of the company. A familiar example is where the majority are endeavouring directly or indirectly to appropriate to themselves money, property, or advantages which belong to the company, or in which the other shareholders are entitled to participate …'.

336 Here Keane J noted the observations of Templeman J in *Daniels v Daniels* [1978] Ch 406 at 413 where he said:

> 'The authorities which deal with simple fraud on the one hand and gross negligence on the other do not cover the situation which arises where, without fraud, the directors and majority shareholders are guilty of a breach of duty which they owe to the company and that breach of duty not only harms the company but benefits the directors. If majority shareholders can sue if there is fraud, I see no reason why they cannot sue where the action of the majority and the directors, though without fraud, confers some benefit on those directors and majority shareholders themselves. It would seem to be quite monstrous – particularly as fraud is so hard to plead and difficult to prove – if the confines of the exception to *Foss v Harbottle* were drawn so narrowly that directors could make a profit out of their negligence.'

337 [1999] 4 IR 578 at 594.

fact of control by the alleged wrongdoers and a good prima facie case must first be established.'[339]

(e) Where justice requires a derivative action to be brought

[19.126] A number of cases have suggested that there exists a fifth exception to the rule in *Foss v Harbottle*[340]. This fifth exception to the rule is, however, less well established than the foregoing motley miscellany of supposed exceptions. In *Heything v Dupont*[341] Harmond LJ said:

> 'There are cases which suggest that the rule is not a right one and that an exception will be made where the justice of the case demands it.'

In *Moylan v Irish Whiting Manufacturers Ltd*[342] Hamilton J quoted this passage with approval and went on to say that:

> 'Having regard to the provisions of Bunreacht na hÉireann, I am satisfied that an exception to the rule must be made when the justice of the case demands it.'

On the facts of the particular case, the learned judge was not required to rely on this exception and so his comments were obiter dictum.

[19.127] Although the issue was raised before the Supreme Court in *O'Neill v Ryan*[343] Blayney J was not required to pronounce upon its validity[344], because the nature of the plaintiff's claim was such that it fell totally outside the rule in *Foss v Harbottle*. Similarly, in *Crindle Investments v Wymes*[345], the Supreme Court per Keane J acknowledged the existence of 'the less solidly' and 'less securely' based fifth exception, but did not directly pronounce upon its validity. The fifth exception was considered by the Court of Appeal in *Prudential Assurance Co Ltd v Newman Industires Ltd (No 2)*[346] to be an impractical test to adopt. However, as Knox J observed in *Smith v Croft (No 3)*[347]:

---

338 *Prudential Insurance Company v Newman Industries Ltd (No 2)* [1982] Ch 204.

339 [1999] 4 IR 578 at 594. It may be noted that Keane J also rejected the R Group's claims, based on negligence and infringement of constitutional rights.

340 See *Russell v Wakefield Waterworks Co* (1875) LR 20 Eq 474–480 which was cited with apparent approval by the Supreme Court in *O'Neill v Ryan* [1993] ILRM 557; *Edwards v Halliwell* [1950] 2 All ER 1064, 1067, *Baillie v Oriental Telephone and Electric Co Ltd* [1915] 1 Ch 503 at 518; *Cotter v National Union of Seamen* [1929] 2 Ch 58 at 69 and *Heything v Dupont* [1964] 1 WLR 843 at 851.

341 *Heything v Dupont* [1964] 1 WLR 843.

342 *Moylan v Irish Whiting Manufacturers Ltd* (14 April 1980, unreported), High Court.

343 *O'Neill v Ryan* [1993] ILRM 557.

344 Blayney J said (at 566) that: 'it was submitted that there was a fifth exception and [that the plaintiff] came within it. Such exception was where it was necessary to permit an exception "in the interests of justice." In my opinion, however, there is no need to consider whether such an exception exists as I am satisfied that for other reasons the plaintiff's claim to come within an exception to the rule in *Foss v Harbottle* is untenable...'.

345 *Crindle Investments v Wymes* [1999] 4 IR 578.

346 *Prudential Assurance Co Ltd v Newman Industries Ltd (No 2)* [1982] Ch 204, [1982] 1 All ER 354 at 366.

> 'But the fact that such a yardstick would or might be unsatisfactory because it does not give a practical guide to the limits of the rule and its exceptions, does not detract from the fact that the whole doctrine whereby a minority shareholder is permitted to assert claims on behalf of the company, is rooted in a procedural expedient, and adopted to prevent a wrong going without redress.'

This passage contains the correct focus on the nature of the derivative action and the exceptions to the rule in *Foss v Harbottle*. If the *justice of the case* criterion would provide a nebulous exception to the rule, it would be in good company with the other four *supposed* exceptions. The Supreme Court's continued references to the fifth exception, albeit neutral references, indicates that should a suitable case arise, the court is unlikely to recoil from its application.

---

[347] *Smith v Croft (No 3)* [1987] BCLC 355 at 389.

Chapter 20

Corporate Borrowing: Debentures and Security

Borrowing as a source of capital

[20.001] For the vast majority of Irish private companies there are three main ways in which they raise or acquire capital: by issuing shares[1], by generating profit or by borrowing money[2]. When many Irish private companies are incorporated, they are frequently capitalised to the princely sum of €2, representing one euro each from the two subscribers for one €1 share each[3]. It can be readily understood that this amount will not adequately capitalise a company's business. Accordingly, the first priority of a company on its incorporation is to acquire capital from another source to permit it to commence trading and, hopefully, to make a profit. Capital is typically acquired through the negotiation of finance internally, in the form of loans from its controllers or members, or externally, from financial institutions. In the case of a company with very little resources, it would be most unlikely for any commercial lending institution to advance facilities without first requiring security for the loan. Such security will often take the form of personal guarantees from the controllers of the company and, where the purpose of the loan is to acquire property with the funds provided, by the taking of a mortgage or charge over that property. The concern of this chapter is to consider the question of corporate capacity and authority to borrow, guarantee and provide security; the nature of the instruments of corporate borrowing; and the provision of different types of security in respect of that borrowing. This is done under the following headings:

[A] Corporate capacity and authority to borrow.

[B] Debentures and security.

[A] Corporate Capacity and Authority to Borrow

The capacity to borrow, guarantee and secure

[20.002] Corporate capacity has already been considered at length[4]. However, it is necessary to recapitulate briefly on that treatment before embarking upon the consideration of corporate borrowing.

(a) The capacity to borrow

[20.003] A company's capacity to borrow will be found, expressly or implicitly, in its objects clause. Here one must reconsider the question of whether the act of borrowing is

1 See generally Chapter 16, *Shares and Membership*.

2 There are, of course, other means available to companies in raising capital. More sophisticated companies can issue notes (whether domestically or internationally).

3 Of course in the case of single–member companies, as little as €1 share may be issued. Although it is permitted to issue one-cent shares, it is more usual to issue shares in €1 denominations.

4 See generally Chapter 7, *Corporate Contracts: Capacity and Authority*, para **[7.043]** *ff.*

authorised by an express object, an express ancillary power or an implied ancillary power. Few private companies will actually engage in borrowing as their main business, and most companies will simply borrow in the course and furtherance of their business. The capacity or power to do this will be implied where the purpose of borrowing is reasonably incidental to the company's main objects[5].

[20.004] Problems in a company's capacity to borrow arise, typically, where the act of borrowing is neither a main object, nor can it be considered to be reasonably incidental to the main objects of the company. A company's objects clause will often contain an express power to borrow. In such a case, notwithstanding the existence of an independent objects clause, the power to borrow can only be seen as an express ancillary power. Older case law suggested that where a company exercised the power to borrow other than in pursuit of its main objects, the act of borrowing was ultra vires, and void[6]. However, as considered above[7] the modern trend is to view the act of borrowing in such circumstances as being intra vires, but liable to be unenforceable as being an abuse of the directors' powers if the outsider is aware of the abuse[8].

(b) The capacity to guarantee

[20.005] Similar considerations apply to corporate guarantees. Although the giving of guarantees can be, in theory[9], a main object of a company[10], the giving of guarantees is more likely to be construed as being an express ancillary power. Most well-drafted objects clauses contain an express power to enter into guarantees. In certain circumstances, a company may be found to have an implied ancillary power to give guarantees where such is reasonably incidental to the furtherance of the company's main objects. Again, problems arise where the act of giving a guarantee can only be said to be an exercise of an express ancillary power in furtherance of an object other than the company's main object. Such a guarantee will on modern authority[11] be intra vires but unenforceable if the outsider is aware that the directors did not exercise the power in good faith.

[20.006] Guarantees entered into by companies in respect of loans and other transactions and arrangements made to or for directors and persons connected thereto (including inter-company guarantees) must also be considered in the light of the Companies Act 1990, s 31 ('CA 1990')[12]. The essential point is that where a guarantee is entered into by

---

5 See *Attorney General v Great Eastern Railway* (1880) 5 App Cas 473; *Re Lee Behrens & Co* [1932] 2 Ch 46, and generally, Chapter 7, *Corporate Contracts, Capacity and Authority*, para **[7.067]**.

6 See *Re Introductions Ltd* [1968] 2 All ER 1221.

7 See Chapter 7, *Corporate Contracts, Capacity and Authority*, para **[7.061]** *ff*.

8 *Rolled Steel Products (Holdings) Ltd v British Steel Corp* [1985] 3 All ER 52.

9 The giving of guarantees, bonds and contracts of suretyship is highly regulated. Only assurance companies, banks and credit institutions can freely provide guarantees. See, further, Johnston, *Banking and Security Law in Ireland* (1998), p 268 *ff*.

10 See *Rolled Steel Products (Holdings) Ltd v British Steel Corp* [1985] 3 All ER 52 at 81, per Slade LJ. See also the observations of Murphy J in *Re PMPA Garage (Longmile) Ltd* [1992] ILRM 337 at 340–341.

11 *Rolled Steel Products (Holdings) Ltd v British Steel Corp* [1985] 3 All ER 52 at 81.

12 See Chapter 11, *Statutory Regulation of Transactions Involving Directors and their Companies*, para **[11.051]** *ff*.

a company in favour of certain relevant persons[13], it may be rendered voidable by virtue of CA 1990, s 38[14]. Other legislation relevant to the enforceability of corporate guarantees includes CA 1963, s 60, also considered above[15].

(c) The capacity to secure

[20.007] The foregoing comments in relation to borrowing and giving guarantees apply generally to the provision of security. Unless a company is, however, specially incorporated to provide security, the circumstances in which a company will have the provision of security as its main object will seldom arise in practice; the ability to provide security will almost invariably fall to be categorised as a power.

The authority to borrow, guarantee and secure

[20.008] Having established whether or not a company has the *capacity* to borrow, guarantee or secure, the next question is whether or not the officers who act for the company have the requisite *authority* to cause the company to borrow, enter into guarantees or provide security. The issue here is the extent of authority of a company's agents[16].

(a) The authority to borrow and secure

[20.009] The express authority for directors to borrow and secure is contained in CA 1963, Sch 1, Table A, Part I, model reg 79 ('the model regulations'). However, it is common for this to be modified on incorporation[17], so that it will typically read (after modification) as follows:

> 'The directors may exercise all the powers of the company to borrow money, and to mortgage or charge its undertaking, property and uncalled capital, or any part thereof and to issue debentures, debenture stock and other securities, whether outright or as security for any debt, liability or obligation of the company or of any third party without any limit as to the amount.'

As noted in the next paragraph, this authority of directors will be implicitly subject to the directors exercising such powers bona fide and in the interests of the company[18].

---

13 'Relevant persons' include directors and shadow directors of the company concerned, directors and shadow directors of that company's holding company and persons connected with the foregoing persons, namely a spouse, parent, brother, sister, child, trustee, partner or a company controlled by the foregoing persons (CA 1990, ss 26 and 31(1)). There is a presumption that the sole member of a single–member private limited company is a person connected with a director: CA 1990, s 26(6).

14 See generally, Chapter 11, *Statutory Regulation of Transactions Involving Directors and their Companies*, para **[11.097]** *ff*.

15 Chapter 18, *The Maintenance of Capital*, para **[18.041]** *ff*.

16 See Chapter 7, *Corporate Contracts: Capacity and Authority*, para **[7.096]** *ff*.

17 The amendment is necessary so as to unfetter the power of directors, who otherwise could only borrow up to the nominal issued share capital of the company without obtaining authority from the members in general meeting. See Chapter 3, *Private Constitutional Documentation*, para **[3.060]**.

18 See Chapter 10, *Duties of Directors and Other Officers*, para **[10.024]** *ff*.

(b) Authority to guarantee

[20.010] Directors will have power to give guarantees where they are expressly authorised to do so, or where the giving of guarantees is necessary to further the business of the company, and so can be said to be authorised by the general powers of management contained in model reg 80[19]. Furthermore, it may be the case that the memorandum of association will authorise the directors to give guarantees 'where they see fit'. Whether or not the capacity to guarantee in the memorandum is so fettered, the power of directors to give guarantees will be implicitly subject to the directors exercising their powers bona fide and in the interests of the company.

[20.011] Where the directors do not exercise their authority to borrow, guarantee or secure bona fide and in the interests of the company, they abuse their authorised powers. Consequently, those acts, while not ultra vires, will be unenforceable where the outsider is either:

- — aware of the abuse of authority, and so cannot rely on the rule in *Turquand's* case which would otherwise allow an outsider to assume that the internal rules, including the rule that powers are properly exercised, are in order[20]; or,
- — aware of the abuse of authority, and so has not got the requisite 'good faith' required for the European Communities (Companies) Regulations 1973[21].

If the outsider is unaware of the fact that the directors have abused their authority, and in the absence of anything else untoward, the outsider should be able to call upon the company to honour the loan made and guarantee or security given.

[B] DEBENTURES AND SECURITY

The mechanics of secured borrowing

[20.012] The usual way in which a private company will obtain loan finance is through its directors approaching a lending institution and negotiating a loan facility. The principal matters under negotiation will usually be the amount of the facility, the interest to be paid, the term (ie duration) of the facility, the security to be given by the company, and any other security which the lending institution requires, such as personal guarantees from the directors/shareholders, guarantees from associated companies or the assignment of a life policy on the lives of the principal controller/controllers[22]. When a loan facility has been successfully negotiated the lending institution will issue a *facility letter* to the company's directors which will set out the terms of the facility to be granted. Certainly not later than this point in time[23], the respective legal advisers of both the lending institution and the borrowing company will become involved in the proposed transaction. The lending institution's solicitor will receive a copy of the facility letter

---

[19] See Chapter 8, *Corporate Governance: Management by the Directors*, para **[8.004]**.

[20] See Chapter 7, *Corporate Contracts, Capacity and Authority*, para **[7.118]** *ff*.

[21] SI 1973/163. Chapter 7, *Corporate Contracts, Capacity and Authority*, para **[7.124]** *ff*.

[22] Other matters that will usually be the subject of negotiations include the provision of financial covenants and events of default.

[23] Where the purpose of the facility involves something out of the ordinary, sometimes the solicitor for the lending institution will assist in the drafting of the facility letter.

and will in turn contact the borrowing company's solicitor. The lending institution's solicitor will then seek copies of the title to any real property being offered as security. In the majority of commercial loans to small and medium-sized Irish private companies, the lending institution's main security will be land and 'bricks and mortar'; floating charges too are taken – often on the understanding that they are 'for what they are worth'. However, where it is proposed to take personal property as security, the lending institution's solicitor will also seek information in respect of whatever personalty is to be mortgaged or charged. Upon receiving replies to these queries, he will then raise *requisitions and objections on title* in respect of the real property which will form the lending institution's security, information on the company[24], confirmation that insurance policies (if applicable) will be in place prior to draw-down of the facilities, and information on personal property which may form the basis of a floating charge.

When the lending institution's solicitor is satisfied that all matters are in order a closing appointment will be arranged. Where the borrower-company already owns the property being given as security the closing will be a straightforward two-way closing. In attendance will usually be both solicitors and the directors of the borrower-company. Where the company is acquiring the property which it is mortgaging the closing will (unless the lending institution is prepared to rely on the borrower-company's solicitor's undertaking) be a three-way closing because the vendor's solicitor will also attend. Title to the property being taken as security will be passed to the lending institution's solicitor and all security documentation will be executed under the seal of the company. Where searches[25] disclose no adverse acts by or against the borrower and the lending institution's solicitor's requirements have been satisfied, the facility may then be drawn down.

[20.013] The remainder of this chapter is concerned with the law relating to debentures and other consensual security, granted by companies in the context of corporate borrowing. The following matters are discussed:

1. Facility letters.
2. The debenture defined.

---

24 Typically, the following documents are sought: a certified copy certificate of incorporation; a certified copy memorandum and articles of association; a certificate from the secretary of the company, stating the following information: (a) the names and addresses of directors of the company including those of any shadow directors; (b) the names and addresses of shareholders; (c) the company's registered office; (d) the nominal and issued share capital of the company; (e) confirmation no orders have been made or resolutions passed to wind up the company; (f) and that no charges have been created other than those that have been registered pursuant to CA 1963, s 99(1).

25 Searches carried out against a borrowing company will invariably be done by a law searching firm. The usual searches sought are: a *Registry of Deeds hand search* where unregistered real property is taken as security, or a *Land Registry folio search* where registered property is taken as security, a *planning search* against the property being taken as security, a *judgments search*, *Sheriff's Office search* and *Companies Office search* against the borrower company and its directors to ensure they have not been restricted or disqualified. *Bankruptcy Office searches* may be made against the directors of the company.

3. Transfer of debentures.
4. Secured debentures: the four kinds of consensual security.
5. Mortgages and charges, defined and distinguished.
6. All sums due debentures.
7. Creating the appropriate kind of security.
8. Fixed charges on book debts.
9. Fixed charges on deposit accounts
10. Floating charges.
11. Negative pledge clauses.
12. Events which affect assets subject to floating charges.
13. Crystallisation of floating charges.
14. The causes of crystallisation.
15. The de-crystallisation of floating charges.

Facility letters

[20.014] A facility letter[26] is a letter from a lending institution addressed to the borrower which informs the borrower of the lender's willingness to advance credit facilities to the borrower and which sets out the terms and conditions of the facility. While it can be simple and succinct, a facility letter is a legal document and generally constitutes an offer by the lending institution to advance money on certain terms and conditions to the borrower, which can be accepted or rejected by the borrower.

[20.015] The contents of facility letters vary from lending institution to lending institution. One question which often arises is the extent and detail which the facility letter will devote to the legal terms of the advance, and whether or not such legal provisions should be catered for entirely in the security documentation ie the debenture. It is often considered to be best if the legal covenants as regards the actual protection of the security and rights of the lending institution are confined to the security documentation while financial covenants should be in the facility letter. One particular dilemma is whether or not to include a 'default clause' in the facility letter or in the security documents. On this point, Lingard[27] says:

> 'There is much merit in putting default clauses in the security documents. Each facility letter must incorporate the default clause by reference, but well-drawn default clauses tend to be lengthy and are out of place in a short facility letter. From a marketing standpoint, it is undesirable to highlight the default clause and to repeat it each time a facility is granted.'

While lending institutions will be pleased where solicitors manage to draft a facility letter that is not off-putting, care must be taken to ensure that legal formalities are not

26 Otherwise known as a sanction letter, offer letter or loan agreement. See, generally, Johnston, *Banking and Security Law in Ireland* (1998), Ch 7; Donnelly, *The Law of Banks and Credit Institutions* (2000), pp 376–384 and Lingard, *Bank Security Documents* (3rd edn, 1993), Ch 5.

27 Lingard, *Bank Security Documents* (3rd edn, 1993), para 5.2.

sacrificed for aesthetic niceties. It is outside the scope of this work to consider further facility letters and the reader is referred to specialist texts[28].

The debenture defined[29]

[20.016] The term 'debenture' is often misunderstood and is commonly ascribed a far greater meaning than in fact it has. The definition provided in the CA 1963 sheds little light on the true meaning of the term[30]. In truth, a debenture is but the written acknowledgement of a debt by a company. In *Edmonds v Blaina Co*[31] Chitty J said of the meaning of debenture, that:

> 'The term itself imports a debt - an acknowledgement of a debt - and speaking of the numerous and varied forms of instruments which have been called debentures without anyone being able to say the term is correctly used, I find that generally, if not always, the instrument imports an obligation to pay. This obligation is in most cases at the present day accompanied by some charge or security.'[32]

When people use the term 'debenture' they can mean:

- a written acknowledgement of a debt;
- an acknowledgement of a debt which incorporates a deed of mortgage and charge (commonly termed a 'mortgage debenture'); or
- an acknowledgement of a debt which includes a floating charge.

Often, people will mean all or a combination of the three.

[20.017] In the context of corporate borrowing, the modern debenture may be described as an instrument executed by or on behalf of[33] a company that acknowledges a debt, contains an obligation to repay that debt with interest, *will usually* create security and will contain a mechanism for enforcement in the event of default of repayment by the company.

[20.018] The person in whose favour a debenture is drawn (eg usually, though not invariably, a bank or other credit institution) is termed a debenture holder. Whilst debenture holders, like shareholders, advance funds to a company, unlike shareholders, they do not become a member of the company, and remain 'outsiders'. Although in

---

28 See Johnston, *Banking and Security Law in Ireland*, (1998), Ch 7; Donnelly, *The Law of Banks and Credit Institutions* (2000), at pp 376–384 and Lingard, *Bank Security Documents* (3rd edn, 1993), Ch 5.

29 See generally, Lingard, *Bank Security Documents* (3rd edn, 1993), Ch 5 and Hapgood, *Paget's Law of Banking* (11th edn, 1996).

30 CA 1963, s 2(1) defines 'debenture' to include 'debenture stock, bonds and any other securities of a company whether constituting a charge on the assets of the company or not'.

31 *Edmonds v Blaina Co* [1887] 36 Ch D 215 at 219.

32 See also *British India Co v IRC* [1881] 7 QBD 165; *Knightsbridge Estates Trust v Byrne* [1940] AC 613; and *Levy v Abercorris Co* [1887] 33 Ch D 260.

33 See *British India Co v IRC* [1881] 7 QBD 165, where a debenture was held to have been validly executed by two directors merely signing the debenture without the affixing of the common seal of the company. Note, though, that the company seal must be affixed where the debenture contains a mortgage over real property: see Ch 7, *Corporate Contracts, Capacity and Authority*, para **[7.013]** *ff*.

many Irish private companies the creation of debentures is almost invariably in favour of a lending institution, in return for that institution providing credit facilities to the company, a debenture can be drawn in favour of an individual, for example, a controller of the company, typically a director with a shareholding[34]. The concept of debenture stock is not really relevant to a discussion of corporate borrowing in the context of a private company, and must be distinguished in our present discussion. In practice, the issuing of debenture stock refers to a situation where, usually, a public limited company ('PLC') issues debentures and debenture stock certificates to the public[35]. Many of the statutory provisions concerning debentures are, in general, anachronisms and complete strangers to the modern Irish private limited company[36].

Transfer of debentures

[20.019] Debentures may be transferred by the debenture holder to some other person. The paradigm debenture created by a private company in favour of a lending institution will usually provide that it cannot be assigned by the borrowing company; although it may provide that the lending institution can transfer its interest[37]. Where a debenture is transferred, CA 1963, s 81 provides that the company cannot register the transfer unless a proper instrument of transfer has been delivered to the company.

[20.020] When a debenture is transferred, the law is that the transferee takes the debenture subject to any equities, ie rights enjoyed by others, and so the assignee is in no better a position than the assignor: *Re Brown & Grogory Ltd*[38]. However the case of *Hilger Analytical Ltd v Rank Precision Industries Ltd*[39] shows that a debenture can be transferred free from any equities which *the company* may have, where such is provided for in the debenture itself. In that case, the plaintiff purchased the defendant's entire business, which was the manufacture and sale of precision instruments. No money was paid, but the plaintiff gave the defendant a debenture comprising a fixed and floating charge over the plaintiff's assets. Later, the plaintiff-company got into financial difficulties, and commenced proceedings against the defendant for inter alia, misrepresentation, and claimed a set-off against the sums due under the debenture. Later

---

34 Eg *Salomon v A Salomon & Co* [1897] AC 22, considered in Chapter 4, *Incorporation and Its Consequences*, para **[4.026]** *ff.*

35 See Keane, *Company Law* (3rd edn, 2000), para 22.07.

36 Eg CA 1963, s 92 (rights of inspection of register of debenture holders and to copies of register and trust deeds); CA 1963, s 93 (liability of trustees for debenture holders); CA 1963, s 94 (perpetual debentures); CA 1963, s 95 (power to re–issue redeemed debentures); CA 1963, s 96 (saving of rights of certain mortgagees in case of re–issued debentures) and CA 1963, s 97 (specific performance of contracts to subscribe for debentures).

37 Such may be done by the lending institution where it is reorganising its business, and decides that one company within the group should hold all security taken by the lending institution. Well–drafted debentures will envisage the possibility of the future inclusion of the debenture and the loan it secures in a loan transfer and securitisation scheme. On securitisation generally, see Newby, 'Securitisation – A Lead Manager's Perspective' (2000) 7 CLP 264

38 *Re Brown & Grogory Ltd* [1904] 1 Ch 827, and *Re Palmer's Decoration and Furnishing Co* [1904] 2 Ch 743; but cf *Re Goy & Co Ltd* [1900] 2 Ch 149.

39 *Hilger Analytical Ltd v Rank Precision Industries Ltd* [1984] BCLC 301.

still, the defendant assigned the debenture free from all equities to an associated company, which would have had notice of the plaintiff's claims. It in turn assigned the debenture to the defendant's holding company, both assignments appearing to be at market value. While it was accepted that, ordinarily, an assignee took subject to any equities, it was held that this was dependant upon the terms of the debenture itself: where the grantee company agreed with the original debenture holder that it should have the right to transfer its debenture free from equities, the court will give effect to this agreement. Harman J held:

> 'I accept the basic proposition of law that transferees of debentures are subject to equities, but that, by agreement, that position can be altered. On the true construction of this debenture the parties agreed to allow the debenture holder to transfer free of equities. The transfers in that case are both so expressed. In my judgment any creditor would wish to agree with his debtor that the instruments securing the debt shall be as freely negotiable as possible. So far as the law permits this debenture is drawn so as to approximate to a negotiable instrument. The natural ambition of a creditor is thus satisfied by the terms of this debenture.'[40]

Accordingly, whether or not a debenture can be transferred free from equities will depend upon its construction. Whether the benefit of a debenture or, indeed, any other security document made in favour of a financial institution, can be transferred at all depends upon whether it contains the appropriate consents[41] on the borrower's part.

Secured debentures: the four kinds of consensual security

[20.021] While a debenture can be created which does not contain security (ie it operates merely to evidence a debt) this is almost unheard of in the context of modern commercial lending to private companies. The reason is simple, unless a loan is secured, then on a liquidation of the borrowing company, the lending institution is in no better a position than other unsecured creditors. The essence of the concept of a 'security' is that it means that the holder of that security is the person legally or equitably entitled to look to certain assets to satisfy the liabilities of the person who created the security. By consensual security is meant security which is freely given by a company to the person entitled to rely upon the security and not, for example, security that arises by operation of law eg a judgment mortgage.

[20.022] As Millett LJ said in *Re Cosslett (Contractors) Ltd*[42]:

> 'There are only four kinds of consensual security known to English law:
>
> (i) pledge;
>
> (ii) contractual lien;
>
> (iii) equitable charge and
>
> (iv) mortgage.'

---

40 [1984] BCLC 301 at 305.

41 Eg consent to disclosure of banker–customer information (where the debenture holder is a bank or other financial institution); consent to the disclosure of personal data under the Data Protection Act 1988, s 8 does not, however, apply where the data subject is a company.

42 *Re Cosslett (Contractors) Ltd* [1997] 4 All ER 115. Although overruled by the House of Lords, the decision of the higher court does not affect the propriety of this statement of the law.

Initially[43], the common law recognised only three ways in which a company could give security over its assets. These were: first, the granting of a legal mortgage over the assets (whether realty or personalty) in the legal ownership of a company; secondly, the delivery to a creditor of corporate assets in the form of a pledge[44]; and thirdly, the creation of a contractual lien involving the company's authority to seize and sell its realty or personalty so as to recover the money lent from the proceeds of sale. Nowadays, the equitable charge has been added to the list of kinds of consensual security and mortgages can be either legal or equitable.

(a) Pledge

[20.023] A pledge is a transaction under which a debtor (pledgor) delivers possession of goods (personalty) to his creditor (pledgee) to be retained by the pledgee as security and for as long as the pledgor has unsatisfied obligations to the pledgee[45]. A pledge is a *possessory security* in the sense that delivery of possession of the goods pledged must be given to the pledgee. Possession may be actual or constructive[46] where, for example, the pledgee holds documents of title to goods. There must also be an intent to pledge: *Dublin City Distillery (Great Brunswick Street, Dublin) Ltd v Doherty*[47]. A pledge confers a power of sale upon a pledgee in the event of the pledgor defaulting. In addition to the simplicity of its creation, one of the principal benefits of a pledge is that particulars of the pledge are not required to be delivered to the Companies Registration Office ('CRO') pursuant to CA 1963, s 99[48].

(b) Liens

[20.024] Liens are also a form of possessory security. A lien, has been defined by Bell[49] in the following terms:

---

43 Before considering the modern law of corporate security, it is important to understand the broad historical development of the law of security. See generally Keeton & Sheridan, *Equity* (2nd edn, 1976), Ch IV, p 95 *ff*, for a detailed treatment of the gradual development of the 'mortgage' from a fettered common law concept to its rise through the intervention of equity.

44 See generally, Johnston, *Banking and Security Law in Ireland* (1998), Ch 12. See also Bell, *Modern Law of Personal Property in England and Ireland* (1989), Ch 8 at p 136 *ff*. There Bell adopts the meaning of pledge as 'a transaction under which goods are delivered by a debtor (the pledgor) to his creditor (the pledgee) to be retained as security for the due discharge of the debt'.

45 See generally, Bell, *Modern Law of Personal Property in England and Ireland* (1989), p 136.

46 See *Official Assignee of Madras v Mercantile Bank of India Ltd* [1935] AC 53 at 58.

47 *Dublin City Distillery (Great Brunswick Street, Dublin) Ltd v Doherty* [1914] AC 823.

48 As Johnston, *Banking and Security Law in Ireland* (1998), p 446 has pointed out, when taking a pledge, care must be taken not to inadvertently create a bill of sale which will be void for want of registration. On the distinction between a pledge and a bill of sale Johnston cites Lord Esher MR in *Re Hardwick* (1886) 17 QBD 690 at 697 where he said: '... the essence of a pledge is that the grantee says to the grantor, I will lend you money if and when you deposit certain goods with me. It is not, I will lend you money on the security of an authority to take possession of certain goods.' On the registration of bills of sale, see Chapter 21, *Corporate Borrowing: Registration of Charges*, para **[21.037]** *ff*.

49 Bell, *Modern Law of Personal Property in England and Ireland* (1989), Ch 8, p 136. For liens, see, generally, Bell, *Modern Law of Personal Property in England and Ireland* (1989), p 138 *ff*. See also Hapgood, *Paget's Law of Banking* (11th edn, 1996), Ch 31.

> 'A lien…is not a transaction, but a right. It is a right given to a person (the lienee) who is in possession of goods belonging to another (the lienor) under a contract for the provision of services relating to them, and it entitles him to retain possession until paid for his services.'

Liens may arise in a number of ways but above all else it is the *possession* and *delivery of possession* of goods which is crucial in determining the existence of a lien. First, liens may arise by operation of law, from both the common law, equity and statute. Examples of these include the unpaid vendor's lien and the unpaid purchaser's lien and are considered in the next chapter in the context of whether such liens require to be registered under CA 1963, s 99[50]. Secondly, liens may arise by contractual arrangement between the parties. The primary difference between a lien and a pledge is that while, in both cases, the holder of the security has possession of the goods, '...in the case of a lien the creditor retains possession of goods which had previously been delivered to him for some other purpose'[51]. In the Court of Appeal decision in *Re Cosslett (Contractors) Ltd*[52], the facts of which are considered below[53], Millett LJ said of the difference between a pledge and a lien that:

> '…in the case of a pledge the owner delivers possession to the creditor as security, whereas in the case of a lien the creditor retains possession of goods previously delivered to him for some other purpose.'[54]

In that case it was held that the possession of the plant and materials in question was not attributable to any delivery of possession by way of lien. There, Millett LJ held that the company had brought (not *delivered possession*) the plant and materials onto the county council's site, exclusively, to enable it to use them in the completion of the construction works in question and that there was no question of it delivering them by way of lien:

> 'The council comes into possession of the plant and materials when it expels the company from the site leaving the plant and materials behind. But this does not amount to a voluntary delivery of possession by the company to the council…In my judgment, therefore, the council's rights are derived from contract, not possession and, in so far as they are conferred by way of security, constitute an equitable charge.'[55]

(c) Equitable charge

[20.025] It was in the eighteenth and nineteenth centuries that equity developed two new forms of security, namely the equitable charge and the equitable mortgage. The essence of an *equitable charge*[56], in its application to commercial transactions, is that the lender

---

50 Contractual liens may or may not be registrable under CA 1963, s 99. See, eg, *Re Hamlet International plc* [1998] 2 BCLC 164 and, generally, Chapter 21, *Corporate Borrowing: Registration of Charges*, para **[21.023]**.

51 Per Millett LJ in *Re Cosslett (Contractors) Ltd* [1997] 4 All ER 115 at 126c. See also *Young v Matthew Hall Mechanical and Electrical Engineers Pty Ltd* (1988) 13 ACLR 399.

52 *Re Cosslett (Contractors) Ltd* [1997] 4 All ER 115.

53 See para **[20.069]**.

54 [1997] 4 All ER 115 at 126c.

55 [1997] 4 All ER 115 at 126e.

56 See Coughlan, 'Equitable Mortgages and Charges' (1992) DULJ 171 and *O'Keeffe v O'Flynn Exhams and Partners and Allied Irish Bank* (31 July 1992, unreported), High Court (Costello J).

and the borrower agree that in return for the lender making credit facilities available to the borrower, certain property will be available to satisfy the debt owing in the event of the borrower defaulting in repayment. From what was essentially a mere contractual obligation (which of itself confers no interest in the borrower's property) the charge became a security, which would be enforced in equity, as a proprietary interest.

Equitable charges can be either *fixed* (on a specific asset or class or asset) or *floating* (over a body of assets). The fortunes of the holders of fixed and floating charges can differ immensely, particularly where the chargor-company becomes insolvent. So, the holder of a fixed charge (having claim to identifiable property) has a higher priority than has the holder of a floating charge. By contrast, the holder of a floating charge is, first, dependent upon there being sufficient assets available within the class of assets that are subject to the floating charge to meet his debts, and, secondly, dependent upon not being leap-frogged by a debtor-company's preferential creditors[57], eg a policy of insurance, a share etc.

(d) Mortgages: legal and equitable

[20.026] The early law of security only permitted the mortgaging of the legal interest in realty and personalty. In time, however, it came to be recognised that the equitable interest in both could also be mortgaged. Eventually it was recognised also that *choses in action* could be mortgaged. A chose in action 'is a known legal expression used to describe all personal rights of property which can be claimed or enforced by action, and not by taking physical possession'[58] eg a policy of insurance, a share etc.

[20.027] The *equitable mortgage* on the other hand developed where an agreement was reached to grant a legal mortgage, but there was in fact no legal instrument of mortgage. Here again, equity intervened and would, on application being made to court, grant a decree for specific performance of the agreement between the lender and the borrower[59]. Indeed, this remains the basis of many mortgages of land, where the borrower actually hands over the title deeds or land certificate to the property to the lender, who holds them until the loan is repaid. The act of depositing the deeds constitutes the 'agreement' between the parties[60].

Mortgages and charges, defined and distinguished

[20.028] A *legal mortgage* involves either the formal conveyance, assignment or demise of the legal title to real property, or the formal assignment of legal title to personal property which is specifically identifiable at the time the mortgage is created. In a legal mortgage, the mortgagee becomes the legal owner of the mortgaged property. The mortgagor will be protected by equity which will imply the right of the mortgagor to

---

57 See Chapter 27, *The Realisation and Distribution of Assets in a Winding Up*, para **[27.169]** *ff.*

58 *Per* Channell J in *Torkington v Magee* [1902] 2 KB 427. See also *Re Cuff Knox (deceased)* [1963] IR 263. On choses in action generally, see Bell, *Modern Law of Personal Property in England and Ireland* (1989), p 361 *ff.*

59 See Farrell, *Specific Performance* (1994); and generally, Keane, *Equity and the Law of Trusts in the Republic of Ireland* (1988), para 16.01 *ff* and Delaney, *Equity and the Law of Trusts in Ireland* (1996), p 434.

60 See Doyle, 'The Mortgage by Deposit for "Present and Future Advances"' (1990) Gazette of ILSI 141.

redeem or recover the mortgaged property on repayment[61]. An *equitable mortgage* may also be created[62] whereby the equitable mortgagee becomes the equitable owner of the mortgaged property[63]. Equity will continue to protect the mortgagor by acknowledging his right to redeem the mortgage. An equitable mortgage may be created formally or informally. A formal equitable mortgage involves the conveyance, assignment or demise of the equitable title in the mortgaged property[64]. An informal equitable mortgage typically involves the deposit of the title deeds of real or personal property that is specifically identifiable from the title deeds deposited[65]. It should be noted that whilst, in Ireland, it continues to be possible to create an equitable mortgage by deposit of title deeds without any written record thereof, such has not been possible in England and Wales since the enactment of the Law of Property (Miscellaneous Provisions) Act 1989, s 2[66]. The essential feature of a fixed or specific mortgage is that the mortgaged property is unambiguously identifiable.

[20.029] All fixed charges are essentially equitable in nature notwithstanding that, in practice, some are referred to as being *legal charges*. It is thought that the only charge over property which can even be considered to be a legal charge is a charge on real property that is registered in the Land Registry. Such a charge is more properly termed a registered charge. Where a charge over property, the ownership of which is registered in the Land Registry, is created informally by deposit of a land certificate this has a similar effect to an equitable mortgage by deposit of title deeds to unregistered land[67].

[20.030] The crucial distinction between a mortgage and a charge is that, unlike a mortgage, a charge does not operate to pass title in the secured assets to the chargee[68]. It

---

61 Although the mortgagor will have a *legal right* to redeem the mortgage, this will often be on a specific date; the mortgagor will have the *equitable right* to redeem for an indefinite time: *Burrough v Cranston* (1840) 2 Ir Eq R 203. See Wylie, *Irish Land Law* (1986), para 13.088 *ff*; Baker & Langan, *Snell's Equity* (29th edn, 1990), p 391 *ff*.

62 See Coughlan, 'Equitable Mortgages and Charges' (1992) DULJ 171.

63 On the distinction between an *equitable mortgage* and an *equitable charge*, see *O'Keeffe v O'Flynn Exhams and Partners and Allied Irish Banks* (31 July 1992, unreported), High Court, (Costello J), noted by Coughlan, 'Equitable Mortgages and Charges' (1992) DULJ 171. See also the decision of the Supreme Court [1994] 1 ILRM 137.

64 *Antrim County Land Building and Investment Co Ltd v Stewart* [1904] 2 IR 367.

65 See generally: *Russel v Russel* (1783) 1 Bro CC 269; *Eyre v McDowell* (1861) 9 HLC 619; *Re Hurley's Estate* [1894] 1 IR 488. See further, Johnston, *Banking and Security Law in Ireland* (1998), p 327–335 for an excellent review of the law and procedure on taking equitable deposits of title deeds. See also Hardiman, 'Deposit of Title Deeds' (1999) CLP 3 for a very perceptive analysis of the legal principles behind such security; Corscadded, 'Deposit of Title Deeds' (1953) 55 JIBI 253 and Doyle, 'The Mortgage by Deposit for 'Present and Future Advances' (1990) Gazette ILSI 141.

66 See Busby, 'Real Property as Security – Safe as Houses?' (1995) PLC 39 and *United Bank of Kuwait v Sahib*, (1994) Times, 7 July.

67 Registration of Title Act 1964, s 105(5). See *O'Keeffe v Russell and Allied Irish Banks plc* [1994] 1 ILRM 137.

68 *London County and Westminster Bank Ltd* [1918] 1 KB 515. See also *Burlinson v Hall* (1884) 12 QBD 347 where Day J said: 'A charge differs altogether from a mortgage. By a charge the title is not transferred, but the person creating the charge merely says that out of a particular fund he will discharge a particular debt.'

is for that reason that all charges are equitable: instead of getting legal title all that the chargee gets is the right in equity to look to the charged property for satisfaction of the secured debt[69]. In *Re Clare Textiles Ltd*[70] Costello J said:

> 'There is nothing special about the term "charge". It relates to a contract under the terms of which certain property is available as security to meet the performance of a liability, usually the payment of money. Its creation is dependent upon contract.'[71]

In *Re Charge Card Services Ltd*[72] Millett J said that:

> '...the essence of an equitable charge is that, without any conveyance or assignment to the chargees, specific property of the chargor is expressly or constructively appropriated to or made answerable for payment of a debt, and the chargee is given the right to resort to the property for the purpose of having it realised and applied in or towards payment of the debt. The availability of equitable remedies has the effect of giving the chargee a proprietary interest by way of security in the property charged.'[73]

It is fundamental to a fixed charge that the charged property is *specifically identifiable*. In *Illingworth v Houldsworth*[74] the 'great Irish judge Lord Macnaughton [said] with his usual lucidity'[75]*:* 'A specific charge, I think, is one that without more fastens on ascertained and definite property or property capable of being ascertained and defined...'.

It should be noted that a fixed charge may be created over future property ie property which the chargor-company acquires after the charge is created[76].

[20.031] An irrevocable agreement to grant a fixed charge operates to create an 'equitable' fixed charge. This was held to be the case in *Re Valley Ice Cream (Ireland) Ltd*[77]. In that case the company, the subject of its official liquidator's application, and certain associated companies were indebted to a creditor, Master Foods Ltd, in respect of goods supplied. To secure the indebtedness, the company agreed to provide the security set out in a debenture. The debenture provided in clause 5.4 that the company:

> '...irrevocably undertakes to [Master Foods Ltd] forthwith upon expiration or earlier determination of each lease to execute, or procure the execution of, a mortgage over the equipment to which the lease relates in the form attached hereto in the Fifth Schedule.'

---

69 In *Re Cosslett (Contractors) Ltd; Smith (Administrator of Cosslett (Contractors) Ltd v Bridgend County Borough Council* [2002] 1 All ER 292, [2001] UKHL 58 Lord Hoffmann said (at 303j; [41]) 'I do not see how a right to sell an asset belonging to a debtor and appropriate the proceeds to payment of the debt can be anything other than a charge.'

70 *Re Clare Textiles Ltd* (1 February 1993, unreported), High Court.

71 (1 February 1993, unreported), High Court at p 2.

72 *Re Charge Card Services Ltd* [1986] 3 All ER 289.

73 [1986] 3 All ER 289 at 309.

74 *Illingworth v Houldsworth* [1904] AC 355, cited with approval by the Supreme Court in *Welch v Bowmaker (Ireland) Ltd* [1980] IR 251 at 258, per Kenny J.

75 *Welch v Bowmaker (Ireland) Ltd* [1980] IR 251 at 258, per Kenny J.

76 *Welch v Bowmaker (Ireland) Ltd* [1980] IR 251.

77 *Re Valley Ice Cream (Ireland) Ltd* (22 July 1998, unreported), High Court (McCracken J).

The equipment referred to consisted of some vehicles and a large number of freezers located in various shops throughout the State. The vehicles and equipment were held by the company under leases, and at the expiration of each lease the company would be entitled to purchase the goods for a nominal sum. Therefore, at the time the debenture was created, the equipment was in the ownership of the lessor (Master Foods Ltd) and would continue to be in its ownership until the expiry of the leases. This was the reason why the company could only *undertake* to mortgage the equipment and could not then in fact mortgage the equipment. At the time of the application it was common case that there were a number of vehicles and freezers which came within clause 5.4 in respect of which no mortgage in the form set out in the fifth schedule to the debenture had been executed[78].

The net point to be decided was whether clause 5.4 created an equitable fixed charge or a floating charge over the equipment. Master Foods Ltd contended that it was the former; the official liquidator contended that it was the latter. On this point McCracken J said:

> 'Clause 5.4 clearly creates a legal and binding obligation on the Company to execute a mortgage as soon as any lease of equipment expires or terminates. It does not, and cannot, of itself create a legal mortgage over the equipment, as the equipment is not an asset of the Company at the time of execution of the debenture. However, at the moment that the lease of any one piece of equipment terminates or expires, there is no doubt that Master Foods [Ltd] would be entitled to obtain an immediate order of specific performance to enforce the execution of a legal charge or mortgage. Furthermore, the form of the charge as set out in the fifth schedule to the debenture quite clearly is intended to create a fixed charge over the goods, as it specifically assigns the goods and the benefit of any insurance thereon. I think it is beyond doubt that the clear intention of this document is that there will be a fixed charge on the specific goods as soon as the document is executed. The only question, therefore, is whether an irrevocable agreement to grant such a fixed charge does of itself create an equitable fixed charge.'[79]

After quoting with approval from Fisher & Lightwood's *Law of Mortgages*[80] McCracken J went on to hold:

> 'In the present case, there has not been a legal transfer of a proprietary interest, but there has been a binding undertaking to confer such an interest, which undertaking is

---

78 It was also heard that the Form 47 (the predecessor to the Form C1) which had been filed in the CRO in respect of the debenture, mistakenly referred to the mortgage, which the company undertook to execute, as being contained in the *first* schedule to the debenture. In fact it was contained in the *fifth* schedule. McCracken J found that this was of no material effect. See further Chapter 22, *Corporate Borrowing: Registration of Charges*, para **[21.014]**.

79 (22 July 1998, unreported), High Court at pp 4–5.

80 Fisher & Lightwood's *Law of Mortgages* (10th edn), p 12 where it is stated:

> 'Generally, the essence of any transaction by way of mortgage is that a debtor confers upon his creditor a proprietary interest in property of the debtor, or undertakes in a binding manner to do so, by the realisation or appropriation of which the creditor can procure the discharge of the debtor's liability to him, and that the proprietary interest is redeemable, or the obligation to create it is defeasible, in the event of the debtor discharging his liability.

specifically enforceable. I think it is entirely in keeping with the principles governing the creation of a fixed charge that such a charge should be created under these circumstances. The essence of a fixed charge is that property is irrevocably set aside in such a way that the creditor can have recourse to it to satisfy his debt. The clear intention of clause 5.4 was that, as each of the items came into the ownership of the company, it would immediately be subject to a legal charge in favour of Master Foods [Ltd], which was to be implemented by the execution of a deed. It is a well known maxim of equity, which is frequently enforced, that equity regards as being done that which ought to be done, and it is for this reason that the undertaking contained in clause 5.4 would be specifically enforceable. It must also be a consequence of the truth of that maxim that, while a legal charge may not have been created, equity will regard a charge as having been created because it ought to have been created under the terms of clause 5.4. That charge must be a fixed charge, as what clause 5.4 contemplates clearly is a fixed charge. Accordingly, I will grant a declaration that the debenture creates a fixed charge in equity over the leased assets to which it refers'.[81]

This judgment shows just how easy it is to create a security interest in property. It is thought that the same conclusion could have been arrived at had the undertaking been contained in a letter[82], as opposed to a debenture, provided, of course that CA 1963, s 99(1) was complied with.

All sums due debentures

[20.032] It is more common for debentures to provide that they secure 'all sums due or to become due on any account or accounts, whether present or future' or, more generically, 'all present and future indebtedness'. The courts have, traditionally, applied a wide construction to such expressions and have held that 'debt' includes not merely present debts but liabilities that may mature into debts[83]. So in *Banner Lane Realisations v Berisford*[84] the Court of Appeal held that 'future indebtedness' includes not only a present obligation to pay a sum certain in the future, but also a 'present obligation to pay an unquantified sum in the future or on a contingency'.[85]

---

80 (contd)

If there has been no legal transfer of a proprietary interest but merely a binding undertaking to confer such an interest, that obligation, if specifically enforceable, will confer a proprietary interest in the subject matter in equity. An equitable mortgage is a contract which operates as a security and is enforceable under the equitable jurisdiction of the court. The court carries it into effect either by giving the creditor immediately the appropriate remedies, or by compelling the debtor to execute a security in accordance with the contract. It is applicable to all property of which a legal mortgage can be made, even where statute provides, as, for example, in the case of ships, a particular method for passing the legal property therein.'

McCracken J noted that the first part of that statement is taken verbatim from the judgment of Buckley J in *Swiss Bank Corporation v Lloyds Bank Ltd* [1980] 2 All ER 419 at 426.

81 (22 July 1998, unreported), High Court at p 6.

82 Either supported by valuable consideration or under seal.

83 *Flint v Barnard* (1888) 22 QBD 90.

84 *Banner Lane Realisations v Berisford* [1997] 1 BCLC 380.

85 [1997] 1 BCLC 380 at 388b–c.

[20.033] Where a financial institution advances, say, €300,000 secured by an all-sums debenture and the financial institution subsequently advances a further €100,000 all that is required to be done is to 'stamp-up' the debenture to cover a total indebtedness of €400,000[86]. The validity of an 'all sums due' debenture will not be affected by its being 'stamped-up' subsequent to the date of the presentation of a petition to have the chargor company wound up. This was put beyond all doubt by the Supreme Court decision in *Re Motor Racing Circuits Ltd*[87]. In that case a chargee caused an 'all sums due' debenture to be stamped-up after a petition had been presented to have the company wound up. In the debenture, the company covenanted to pay to the chargee 'all such sums as may now be due or owing or at any time shall become due or owing'. In addition, the company also charged certain lands with all sums that might at any time be owing by the company. Blayney J said:

> 'The legal position is quite clear and that is initially such a debenture covers such amount as the mortgage is stamped in respect of but, where the amount exceeds the amount in respect of which the debenture is stamped, the bank is entitled to stamp up the debenture and that stamping up is simply a revenue requirement. The debenture from the beginning is valid to cover all sums which may at any time be due by the company to the bank. But if at any time the amount due under the debenture exceeds the amount in respect of which it has been stamped initially, the bank is free to increase the stamping so that the amount of the stamp duty will then cover the amount which is actually due at the time under the debenture.
>
> It is quite clear under the provisions of the Stamping Act and accordingly, the bank was perfectly free to stamp up the debenture so as to comply with the requirements of the Stamping Act. But as I said in the beginning the debenture itself covered all sums which at any time would be due by the company to the bank.'[88]

There was, therefore, no problem with the bank stamping-up the debenture *after* the petition to wind up the company had been presented. The same reasoning should apply equally to where an 'all sums due' debenture or other charge is stamped-up after the passing of a resolution to wind up a company, to the appointment of an examiner or indeed in any other eventuality.

Creating the appropriate kind of security

[20.034] Most borrowing by private companies is secured by a mortgage or charge over real property[89]. Whether a mortgage or a charge is created, depends in practice upon the nature of the property being offered as security. Where the title to property offered as security is unregistered title[90] (ie registered in the Registry of Deeds), a legal mortgage is

---

86 Up to a maximum stamp duty of €630. See Chapter 21, *Corporate Borrowing: Registration of Charges*, para **[21.114]**.

87 *Re Motor Racing Circuits Ltd* (31 January 1997, unreported), Supreme Court (Blayney J; nem diss).

88 (31 January 1997, unreported), Supreme Court at pp 5, 6 of the judgment.

89 See generally, Johnston, *Banking and Security Law in Ireland* (1998), Ch 10, 'Mortgages and Charges of Land' for an excellent review of this type of security.

90 Property, the title to which is registered in the Registry of Deeds, is referred to as *unregistered* property because it is *not* registered in the Land Registry.

almost invariably created. An equitable mortgage of property registered in the Registry of Deeds is usually only taken where either the exigencies of commercial lending require an immediate draw-down of loan facilities and there is not time to put in place a legal mortgage, or where the term of the loan facility is relatively short.

Where the title to property offered as security is registered land (ie registered in the Land Registry), the most common security taken is a registered charge. An informal charge by deposit of the land certificate to the property can also be taken as security.

[20.035] Where personal property is taken as a fixed security the most common method of doing so is by way of a fixed equitable charge[91]. A legal mortgage over personal property has a number of disadvantages, the principal one being that, usually, the borrower will wish to retain the legal title in the goods so as to facilitate their disposal in the usual course of business[92]. Other methods of taking security over personal property include taking it by way of a pledge[93] or by way of a letter of hypothecation[94], the latter being a form of equitable charge.

[20.036] Where a chose in action is taken as a fixed security the form of security will depend upon the nature of the chose in action in question. Two examples will illustrate. Shares may be the subject of either a legal mortgage or an equitable mortgage[95]. Where book debts are taken as a fixed security, this is usually effected by way of a fixed charge[96].

[20.037] Extreme care[97] should be taken in drafting a debenture that purports to create a mortgage or fixed charge over property. Where the property mortgaged or charged is not properly identified, or where its identity is ambiguous, then it is likely that the mortgage or charge will prove to be void and unenforceable where it purports to be *fixed*. Where property is intended to be the subject of a fixed mortgage or charge but is not properly identified, and where the mortgage debenture or deed of mortgage creates a floating charge over all property of the company, the property may consequently only be subject to a floating charge, which ranks lower in priority to a fixed charge[98]. This is illustrated by *Re Hi-Fi Equipment (Cabinets) Ltd*[99] where a bank took a secured debenture which provided that the borrowing company charged 'by way of first fixed charge all future freehold and leasehold property of the company together with all buildings fixtures (including trade fixtures) and fixed plant and machinery from time to time thereon' and went on to give the bank a floating charge over all of its other assets. It was held that the

---

91 *Tucker v Wilson* (1714) 1 P Wms 261; *Deverges v Sandeman Clark & Co* [1902] 1 Ch 579.

92 See further, Lingard, *Bank Security Documents* (3rd edn, 1993), para 17.10 *ff*.

93 *Dublin City Distillery Ltd v Doherty* [1914] AC 823.

94 *Re Slee, ex p North Western Bank* (1872) LR 15 Eq 69.

95 See Chapter 16, *Share Transfers in Private Companies*, para **[16.031]**.

96 See para **[20.038]**.

97 Cf *Re Cimex Tissues Ltd* [1995] 1 BCLC 409 where it was found that, although the particular debenture in that case was in a number of ways 'ineptly drafted' it did not permit the chargor to dispose of the charged property without the chargee's consent and so, there was no reason to hold that the charge was other than what it was described as, namely, a fixed charge.

98 On *floating charges*, see para **[20.063]** *ff*.

99 *Re Hi–Fi Equipment (Cabinets) Ltd* [1988] BCLC 65.

reference to *fixed* plant and machinery implied that the plant and machinery was in some way firmly attached to the company's premises, and thus, since the plant and machinery in question was *not* attached to the company's premises, it did not form part of the assets subject to the fixed charge. On account of the deficiency in the assets available to satisfy the claims against the company, the plant and machinery in question were applied in satisfaction of other creditors' debts.

Fixed charges on book debts

[20.038] The advantage of being a fixed charge holder is that if the chargor-company becomes insolvent and is placed into liquidation, the fixed chargee's position is more favourable than that of a floating chargee's position. Unlike the holder of a floating charge, the holder of a fixed charge *ordinarily* ranks ahead of the Revenue Commissioners and other preferential creditors[100]. Furthermore, although *all* securities are capable of being vitiated, unlike a floating charge, a fixed charge is not liable to be set aside where the company goes into liquidation within 12 months[101] of its creation. Consequently, credit institutions are more eager to take fixed charges than to take floating charges. It was the traditionally superior position of fixed charges, which provoked credit institutions to be imaginative in seeking to stretch the boundaries of the sort of assets that could be the subject of a fixed charge.

[20.039] Only in recent years has it been recognised that a fixed charge can be created over the book debts of a company[102]. Book debts have been defined in *Palmer*[103] as:

> '...debts owing to the company concerned with and arising out of the company's trade or business, which are entered, or commonly would be entered in the ordinary course of business, in well kept books of such a trade or business.'

By their nature, book debts would seem to be incapable of being the subject of a fixed charge since they will not continue to be specifically identifiable: old book debts will be paid and new book debts will be created. Indeed, for years, it was generally thought that the only suitable means of taking security over book debts was by way of a floating charge. A series of cases have shown this to be mistaken and now, when properly drafted[104], a fixed charge can be created over book debts. However, it should be noted at the outset that the primary rationale for creating fixed charges over book debts has, to a

---

100 As shall be seen, para **[20.052]**, in response to the courts upholding the validity of fixed charges on book debts, the State responded by giving the Revenue Commissioners priority in respect of such fixed charges.

101 Or, in the case of a floating charge given to a 'connected person', within two years: CA 1963, s 288, as amended by CA 1990, s 136.

102 See Byrne & Tomkin, 'Charges on Book Debts – Siebe Gorman in Ireland' (1985) NLJ 443.

103 Schmitthoff (ed), *Palmer's Company Law* (24th edn, 1987), para 46–06. See also *Re Brian Tucker Ltd* [1990] 2 IR 549, considered in Chapter 21, *Corporate Borrowing: Registration of Charges*, para **[21.048]**.

104 See generally, Houghton & Mercer, 'Fixed or Floating Charge? – Taking Security over Stock, Equipment and Other Movable Assets' (1995) PLC 43 for a thorough review of the concepts (and pointers) on taking an effective fixed charge over book debts.

large extent, been rendered otiose by statute since, subject to certain limited exceptions, fixed charges on book debts will not have priority to the Revenue Commissioners[105].

(a) Judicial acceptance of the validity of fixed charges on book debts

[20.040] The first breakthrough case was the English case of *Siebe Gorman v Barclays Bank Ltd*[106]. In that case, a company created a debenture in favour of Barclays Bank, secured by way of legal mortgage over all its freehold and leasehold property and all fixed plant and machinery, present and future. In addition, the company further charged '...by way of first fixed charge all book debts and other debts now and from time to time due or owing to the company.'

Since the construction of such charges is all-important, the restrictions on dealing with its book debts placed on the company by the bank in the mortgage debenture in that case are worth quoting:

> 'During the continuance of this security the company...shall pay into the company's account with the bank all moneys which it may receive in respect of the book debts and other debts hereby charged and shall not without the prior consent of the bank in writing purport to charge or assign the same in favour of any other person and shall if called upon to do so by the bank execute a legal assignment of such book debts and other debts to the bank.'

The court held that the effect of this clause was to create a fixed charge over the book debts of the company. Critical to the decision was the foregoing restriction on the rights of the chargor-company to deal with its collected book debts. Had the company not been restricted in its right to deal with its collected book debts, Slade J would have been inclined to accept that the charge could be no more than a floating charge. However, in the circumstances, he concluded that[107]:

> '...it is perfectly possible in law for a mortgagor, by way of continuing security for future advances, to grant to a mortgagee a charge on future book debts in a form which creates in equity a specific charge on the proceeds of such debts as soon as they are received and consequently prevents the mortgagor from disposing of an unencumbered title to the subject matter of such charge without the mortgagee's consent...I see no reason why the court should not give effect to the intention of the parties, as stated...that the charge should be a first fixed charge on book debts.'

It is fundamental, however, to the finding that a particular charge over book debts is a fixed charge, that it was created *as such*. A charge which is created as a floating charge over book debts can never become a fixed charge, no matter how a receiver – appointed pursuant to the charge – may have come to hold them[108].

(b) The importance of restrictions on the chargor's use of the debts

[20.041] If a charge over book debts is to be found to be a fixed charge it is crucial that the debenture should provide that the chargor-company is *restricted* in its dealings with

105 See para **[20.052]**.

106 *Siebe Gorman v Barclays Bank Ltd* [1979] 2 Lloyd's Rep 142.

107 [1979] 2 Lloyd's Rep 142 at 159.

108 *Re Pearl Maintenance Services Ltd; Re Pearl Building Contracts Ltd* [1995] BCC 657.

the collected book debts[109]. Where, as in *Re Armagh Shoes Ltd*[110] the debenture provided for no restrictions, the court will not imply restrictions and the charge will fall to be deemed a floating charge. Similarly, in *Re Brightlife Ltd*[111], although there was a prohibition on the chargor company selling, factoring or discounting the book debts in question, the absence of the positive requirement that the monies collected be paid into a separate bank account meant that the charge could only be a floating charge. This was because the absence of such a restriction meant that the company could use the assets as it wished, a freedom which is intrinsic to a floating charge, but anathema to a fixed charge. The nature of the restrictions placed on the chargor-company was also found to be the decisive test by Barron J in *AH Masser Ltd v Revenue Commissioners*[112], who held that the restrictions were consistent with the security being a fixed charge. Although the restrictions were less extensive than those in *Re Keenan Bros Ltd*[113], Barron J held:

> 'Nevertheless it seems to me that the essential provision is the restriction on the mortgagor which prevents it from purporting to charge, assign or otherwise dispose of its book debts and other debts. I regard this provision as acknowledging that the debts are in equity the property of the mortgagee and so not available to the mortgagor in the ordinary course of its business.'[114]

Today, such alone would probably not, in the light of recent Supreme Court pronouncements[115], justify a finding that a charge over book debts is a fixed charge.

[20.042] A case considered by many to have been even stronger than *Siebe Gorman*[116], is *Re Keenan Bros Ltd*[117]. In that case the Supreme Court pronounced upon the validity of a fixed charge over book debts, and in the process reversed the High Court judgment of Keane J who had held that the charge in question was a floating charge. However it is clear that mere terminology, or labelling, will not be sufficient to make what is in reality a floating charge, a fixed charge[118]. Neither will the declared intention of the parties be sufficient to make a charge properly construed as a floating charge, a fixed charge.

---

109 It was held in *William Gaskell Group Ltd et al v Highley (Nos 1, 2, 3)* [1994] 1 BCLC 197, *per* Morritt J, that the assignment of a fixed charge on book debts did not result in the charge becoming a floating charge since the same restrictions continued to bind the companies in question.

110 *Re Armagh Shoes Ltd* [1984] BCLC 405.

111 *Re Brightlife Ltd* [1986] BCLC 418.

112 *AH Masser Ltd v Revenue Commissioners* [1978–1987] 3 ITR 706.

113 See para **[20.042]**.

114 [1985] IR 401 at 552.

115 See para **[20.043]–[20.044]**.

116 See *Re Brightlife Ltd* [1986] BCLC 418 at 423, per Hoffmann J.

117 *Re Keenan Bros Ltd* [1985] IR 401; [1985] BCLC 302 (High Court) and [1986] BCLC 242 (Supreme Court).

118 See *Re Westmaze* (1998) (15 May 1998, unreported), High Court (Eng); *CCH's Company Law Newsletter* (1998) Issue 11, 12 June 1998 where it was accepted that there mere fact that a charge was described as 'fixed' was not determinative of the question as to whether it was, in fact, fixed or floating.

Rather, only on the true construction of the debenture in question will a charge on book debts be found to be a fixed charge. As in the cases cited in the preceding paragraph, the restrictions on the rights of the chargor-company over the book debts was decisive in the determination of the question. There, the debenture provided that:

> 'The company shall pay into an account with the Bank designated for that purpose all moneys which it may receive in respect of the book debts and other debts hereby charged and shall not without the prior consent of the Bank in writing make any withdrawals or direct any payment from the said account.'

In the judgment of McCarthy J:

> 'In my view, it is because it was described as a specific or fixed charge and was intended to be such, that the requirement of a special bank account was necessary; if it were a floating charge payment into such an account would be entirely inappropriate and, indeed, would conflict with the ambulatory nature of the floating charge...'[119]

In the second edition of his textbook[120], Keane states that there are limitations on 'the efficacy of this form of hybrid charge', and in particular refers to the judgment of Walsh J in *Re Keenan Bros Ltd*, saying that it appears from it that the charge would only attach to *uncollected* book debts, since once collected they cease to exist. He concludes from this, 'it would seem to follow that the money in the special bank account would not be subject to the fixed charge and would accordingly be available to the ordinary creditors'. If this statement is correct, it is submitted that it is specific to the debenture in *Re Keenan Bros Ltd* and that another debenture could go on to provide that the bank would have a first fixed charge on the separate bank account[121].

An alternative view to that propounded by Keane is, however, provided by Millett LJ in *Royal Trust Bank v National Westminster Bank plc*[122]. There he said: 'while it is possible to distinguish between a capital asset and its income, I do not see how it can be possible to separate a debt or other receivable from the proceeds of its realisation'. It is thought that there is considerable merit in this observation. This has been reiterated by Lord Millett (as he later became) in the Privy Council in *Re Brumark Investments Ltd;*

---

[119] [1985] IR 401 at 423, 424.

[120] Keane, *Company Law in the Republic of Ireland* (2nd edn, 1991), para 22.18.

[121] Care should be exercised in taking a charge over a bank account. In *Re Charge Card Services Ltd* [1986] 3 All ER 289 at 309 Millett J said that:

> '...in my judgment the benefit of a debt can no more be appropriated or made available to the debtor than it can be conveyed or assigned to him. The objection to a charge in these circumstances is not to the process by which it is created, but to the result. A debt is a chose in action; it is the right to sue the debtor. This can be assigned or made available to a third party, but not to the debtor, who cannot sue himself. Once any assignment or appropriation to the debtor becomes unconditional, the debt is wholly or partially released. The debtor cannot, and does not need to, resort to the creditor's claim against him in order to obtain the benefit of the security; his own liability to the creditor is automatically discharged or reduced.'

Cf Lingard, *Bank Security Documents* (3rd edn, 1993), para 18.29–18.30 where an effective means of obtaining security over cash in a deposit account is canvassed. See para **[20.060]**.

[122] [1996] 2 BCLC 682 at 704g–h.

Commissioner of Inland Revenue v Agnew[123]. In that case he said, in relation to the question as to whether a debt or other receivable can be separated from its proceeds:

> 'While a debt and its proceeds are two separate assets, however, the latter are merely the traceable proceeds of the former and represent its entire value. A debt is a receivable; it is merely a right to receive payment from the debtor. Such a right cannot be enjoyed in specie; its value can be exploited only by exercising the right or by assigning it for value to a third party. An assignment or charge of a receivable which does not carry with it the right to the receipt has no value. It is worthless as a security.'[124]

A fixed charge over book debts will operate as a charge on the uncollected book debts and if a company becomes insolvent, all uncollected book debts will be the subject of that charge and will be available to satisfy the chargee's debts. Where the proceeds are paid into a designated bank account the chargee can also have a fixed charge on that account, but to be a fixed charge the account must be subject to restricted access and the chargor must not be able to withdraw without the chargee's permission. Alternatively, the account can be a 'trust account' where the chargee is the sole beneficial owner[125].

[20.043] The requirement that money collected be paid into a separate bank account is probably the most decisive factor in concluding that a charge on book debts is a fixed charge. Where a debenture provides that a separate bank account must be maintained, it has been held that it will not be fatal to the charge on book debts being deemed a fixed charge where the separate bank account is not *in fact* maintained. So, Finlay CJ held in *Re Wogan's (Drogheda) Ltd*[126] that:

> 'If a lender, having availed of a debenture in these terms as a concession delays the designation of a bank account or suspends for some period the operation of direct control over the bank account into which the proceeds of book debts is paid, thus permitting the company issuing the debenture to carry on trading in a more normal fashion than strict compliance with the terms of a fixed charge would permit there does not appear to be any principle of law of justice which would deprive such a lender of the rights agreed by the debtor company of a fixed charge over the assets, whereas, a lender with a more draconian approach to the rights which were granted to it by a debenture would be in a more advantageous position.'[127]

In that case the terms of the debenture provided for, inter alia, the maintenance of a separate bank account. The clause in question provided:

> 'The company hereby covenants to pay into such banking account or accounts as may be designated for such purpose by the lender, and whether with the lender or with any other banking institution, designated by the lender, all monies which it may receive in respect of book debts and other debts or securities and not without the prior consent of the lender in writing to withdraw or deal with such monies or to assign or purport to assign the same in favour of any other person and if called upon to do so by the lender to execute a legal assignment of such book debts and other debts and securities to the lender.'

---

123 [2001] 2 BCLC 188, [2001] UKPC 28. See para **[20.048]**.

124 [2001] 2 BCLC 188 at 204c–d, para [46].

125 See Peterson, (2002) 23 Co Lawyer 24 at 25.

126 *Re Wogan's (Drogheda) Ltd* [1993] 1 IR 157.

127 [1993] 1 IR 157 at 170–171.

The requirement to have a designated bank account was held to be the decisive factor in determining whether the debenture created a fixed or floating charge over the company's book debts and the subsequent conduct of the parties was held not to be relevant for the purpose of construing the debenture[128]. In *Oakdale (Richmond) Ltd v National Westminster Bank plc*[129] a novel challenge was raised to the practice of insisting that book debts be paid into a designated bank account, based on Articles 85 and 86 of the EU Treaty which prevent anti-competitive practices. The challenge did not succeed. It was held by Chadwick J that the requirement that book debts be paid into the company's account with the chargee-bank 'far from being anti-competitive, is necessary in order that the fixed charge over book debts which the company has sought to create should be effective.'[130]

[20.044] The more recent Supreme Court decision in *Re Holidair Ltd*[131] is virtually impossible to reconcile with the decision in *Re Wogan's (Drogheda) Ltd*. In the *Holidair* case the Kentz group of companies were placed under the protection of the court and an examiner was appointed. A dispute arose between the examiner and the company's main creditors who were debenture holders, inter alia, on whether their debentures created fixed or floating charges over the company's book debts[132]. In the High Court, Costello J had held that on its proper construction, the debenture created a fixed charge over the company's book debts. This was reversed in the Supreme Court by Blayney J, who held that, upon its true construction, the debenture created a floating charge over the chargor-company's book debts. This was so found notwithstanding the existence of a clause which provided that the chargee could designate a bank account into which the proceeds of book debts were to be paid. The clause in question provided, inter alia, that:

> 'With reference to the book debts and any other debts hereby charged, the companies shall pay into such accounts with the banks or any of them as the trustee [the banks] may from time to time select, all monies which they may receive in respect of such debts and shall

---

[128] Following *Re Whitworth Street Estates Ltd* [1980] AC 583.

[129] *Oakdale (Richmond) Ltd v National Westminster Bank plc* [1997] 1 BCLC 63.

[130] [1997] 1 BCLC 63 at 75g. Similarly, Chadwick J upheld the prohibition in the debenture against selling, factoring, discounting or otherwise charging or assigning the book debts without the prior consent in writing of the bank, which he found to be an ancillary requirement to the requirement that the proceeds be paid into a specified account. On this point he said: 'The prohibition is not an absolute prohibition. It is a prohibition against dealing with debts without prior consent in writing of the bank. The requirement for prior consent ensures that the bank is given notice of what is proposed. It enables the bank to exercise its own commercial judgment in determining whether what is proposed will or will not prejudice its security and to reflect that determination by the giving or withholding of consent. The prohibition is necessary if the bank is to have the security which it sought and which the company was willing to provide'. (at 76b).

[131] *Re Holidair Ltd* [1994] 1 ILRM 481, considered by Connaughton, 'The Kentz Case – More Problems for Secured Lenders' (1994) CLP 110.

[132] A number of other issues are considered elsewhere: the effect of the negative pledge clause in the company's debenture on the examiner's powers to borrow without the debenture holders' consent: see para **[20.077]**; the effects of C(A)A 1990, s 5(2)(d) and the construction of C(A)A 1990, s 29(3) – see Chapter 23, *Examinerships*, para **[23.071]** and **[23.079]**, respectively.

> not without the prior consent in writing of the trustee sell, factor, discount or otherwise charge, assign or dispose of the same in favour of any other person or purport so to do and the companies shall if called upon to do so by the trustee from time to time execute legal assignments of such book debts and other debts to the trustee in such form as the trustee shall require and at the companies' own expense.'[133]

Blayney J rejected the notion that merely because the clause was described as a fixed charge it should be accepted as such unless there were other indications in the debenture consistent with this conclusion[134]. Moreover, he found that the charge under consideration had the three characteristics of a floating charge, as described by Romer J in *Re Yorkshire Woolcombers' Association Ltd*[135]. In particular, he found that the charge on book debts in the banks' debenture did not 'prevent the companies from using the book debts in the normal way for the purpose of carrying on their business.'[136] Finding that the existence of the particular clause in *Re Wogan's (Drogheda) Ltd*[137] 'clearly distinguishes that case from the present'[138] the learned judge concluded that the effect of the clause was to create a floating charge over the companies' book debts. The only significant difference between the two clauses was that the clause in *Re Wogan's (Drogheda) Ltd* specifically prohibited the company from withdrawing monies from the designated accounts[139]. Indeed, it appears that this was the only reasoning by which Blayney J could have found that the companies were not prohibited from using the book debts in the ordinary course of their businesses[140]. If this is so, it is within the power of the legal draftsman to ensure that such a fate will not befall all future fixed charges over book debts.

(c) The chargee must exercise control as of legal right

[20.045] Another important feature in determining whether a particular charge over book debts is a fixed or floating charge is the extent of the chargee's control over the book debts. In *Re Double S Printers Ltd*[141] it was held that the fact that a chargee was a director of the chargor-company and a signatory of the company's bank mandate was not sufficient to give rise to the requisite control over the chargor-company's book debts. Jonathon Parker J held that:

> 'In order for the debenture to take effect as a fixed charge over present and future book debts, there must, it seems to me, be some right of control over the debts, or their proceeds, exercisable by [the chargee] in *his capacity as chargee*, and not in some other capacity, e.g. as a director of the company. The opportunity for [the chargee] to exercise de

133 [1994] 1 ILRM 481 at 491.

134 Here, Blayney J relied on the High Court decision of Keane J in *Re Keenan Bros Ltd* [1985] BCLC 302.

135 *Re Yorkshire Woolcombers' Association Ltd* [1903] 2 Ch 284. See para **[20.064]**.

136 [1994] ILRM 481 at 493.

137 See para **[20.043]**, where the clause referred to is reproduced.

138 [1994] ILRM 481 at 494.

139 The Supreme Court decision in *Re Keenan Bros Ltd* [1986] BCLC 242 was distinguished in the same way.

140 See [1994] 1 ILRM 481 at 493.

141 [1999] BCC 303.

> facto control of the company's bank account in his capacity as a director of the company is, in my view, *nihil as rem*. He might, after all, cease to be a director during the continuance of the security; or he might assign the debenture, in which event the assignee would not be in a position to exercise control. In any event, as a director, [the chargee] was at all material times under a fiduciary duty to the company to act bona fide in the interests of the company, and not for a collateral purpose such as the maintenance of his rights as chargee. I therefore conclude that, despite its description as a fixed charge, the charge over book debts created by the debenture takes effect not as a fixed but as a floating charge.'[142]

Accordingly, for a charge to be a fixed charge on a company's book debts, the chargee must exercise the requisite control over the book debts, de jure, in his capacity as chargee and not in any other de facto capacity.

(d) Hybrid charges on book debts

[20.046] The difficulty with fixed charges on book debts is that the restrictions and controls that must be imposed upon a company on how it deals with its book debts can be most inconvenient for the company. Indeed, the holder of the charge too, is often happy to allow the company to deal with its book debts in the ordinary course of business – the real requirement being that in the event of the company's insolvency, its charge over those book debts that remain uncollected should have priority over any claim by the Revenue Commissioners. The best of both worlds is a fixed charge whilst the book debts are outstanding and a floating charge when they have been collected.

[20.047] The case of *Re New Bullas Trading Ltd*[143] broke new ground in allowing the creation of just such a hybrid charge on book debts. There, the charge provided that for as long as book debts remained uncollected, they were subject to a fixed charge but that as soon as they were paid into the designated bank account they became the subject of a floating charge[144]. The charge had the following features:

— the chargee could give instructions with respect to the manner in which the company dealt with the book debts and could also demand that the company assign the book debts to it;

— the chargor was obliged to pay the book debts into a designated bank account and the chargee could give directions with respect to the operation of the account;

— if the chargee failed to give directions in relation to the money in the designated account, then the moneys became released from the fixed charge and became subject to a floating charge, thereby permitting the company to deal with the money in the course of its ordinary business.

In the English Court of Appeal Nourse LJ made it clear that the issue to be decided was whether the law allowed book debts to switch from being the subject of a fixed charge to

---

142 [1999] BCC 303 at 306–307.

143 [1994] 1 BCLC 485.

144 Nourse LJ observed (at 487) that: 'Here, for the first time in a reported case, the draftsman has deliberately and conscientiously set out to subject [the book debts] to a fixed charge while they are uncollected and a floating charge on realisation.'

being the subject of a floating charge. Pronouncing upon the validity of the debenture, Nourse LJ said:

> '...just as it is open to contracting parties to provide for a fixed charge on future book debts, so it is open to them to provide that they shall be subject to a fixed charge while they are uncollected and a floating charge on realisation. No authority to the contrary has been cited and, the principle being as spacious as it has been expressed to be, no objection is on that account sustainable. For these reasons, I would...hold that the charge over book debts of the company, as created by the debenture, was, unless and until their proceeds were paid into the specified account, a valid fixed charge.'[145]

The acceptance of such hybrid clauses was not universal. At the heart of the debate was the propriety of treating charges on book debts as being divisible from charges on the proceeds of book debts[146]. Another concern was with the chargor's ability to end the chargee's fixed charge by paying the proceeds of the book debts into a bank account. The issue here was that a chargor should not, under a fixed security, be able to remove the charged assets from the chargee's security so as to be able to deal with the assets in the ordinary course of its business. Indeed, this concern goes back to the heart of the fixed/floating debate of the 1980s: the necessity for restrictions on the chargor's ability to deal with the book debts commensurate with a fixed security.

[20.048] The hybrid clause came to be used in debentures around the world and it was in New Zealand that its demise began. In *Re Brumark Investments Ltd; Commissioner of Inland Revenue v Agnew* the New Zealand Court of Appeal[147] and, subsequently, the Privy Council[148], both declined to follow *Re New Bullas Trading Ltd*[149]. The New Zealand Court of Appeal held that the charge (which was in all material respects identical to that in *Re New Bullas Trading Ltd*) was a *floating charge*. The trial judge, Fisher J, had drawn a distinction between the company's freedom to receive debts, thereby extinguishing the charge on the one hand and disposing of the debts to third parties on the other. This was not accepted by the Court of Appeal and Gault J held:

> 'In the present case, by excluding from the purported fixed charge created by the debenture (until intervention by the bank) proceeds of book debts, the bank and the company were merely emphasising the freedom of the company to collect the book debts on its own account. That is the usual manner of dealing with book debts. That the company was contractually bound not to dispose of, create or allow any interest in the uncollected debts does not detract from that. As created this was a floating charge over book debts.'[150]

---

145 [1994] 1 BCLC 485 at 493.

146 See Goode (1994) 110 LQR 592.

147 *Re Brumark Investments Ltd; Commissioner of Inland Revenue v Agnew* [2000] 1 BCLC 354.

148 [2001] 2 BCLC 188. See, generally, Berg, 'Brumark Investments Ltd and the 'Innominate Charge' [2001] JBL 532; Tribe, 'The Privy Council and Brumark: A Lingering Shadow over Book Debts?' (2001) 22 Co Lawyer 318; Sealy, 'Thumbs Down for New Bullas 'Down Under' (2000) Company Law Newsletter; Issue 53; 9 May 2000; Sealy, 'Company Charges: New Bullas Overruled – But is this the End of the Story?', (2001) Company Law Newsletter; Issue 76; 29 June 2001.

149 The decision in *Re New Bullas Trading Ltd* was distinguished by Hart J in *Chalk v Kahn* [2000] 2 BCLC 361.

150 [2000] 1 BCLC 354 at 364i, para [34].

The subsequent appeal to the Privy Council was dismissed. Giving the judgment of the Council, Lord Millett reviewed the history of the floating charge and the development of the fixed charge on book debts. He then turned to the hybrid charge that was upheld in *New Bullas Trading Ltd*, commenting:

> 'In every previous case the debenture had treated book debts and their proceeds indivisibly. Now for the first time in any reported case the draftsman set out deliberately to distinguish between them. As in the present case the debenture purported to create two distinct charges, a fixed charge on the book debts while they remained uncollected and a floating charge on their proceeds. It differed from the debenture in the present case only in that the proceeds of the debts were not released from the fixed charge until they were actually paid into the company's bank account, whereas in the present case they were released from the fixed charge as soon as they were received by the company...The intended effect of the debenture was the same in each case. Until the charge holder intervened the company could continue to collect the debts, though not to assign or factor them, and the debts once collected would cease to exist. The proceeds which took their place would be a different asset which has never been subject to the fixed charge and would from the outset be subject to the floating charge.'[151]

Lord Millett said that the 'net question' was 'whether the book debts which were uncollected when the receivers were appointed were subject to a fixed charge or a floating charge'.

[20.049] The Privy Council made a number of findings. In the first place, it was held that Nourse LJ's observation in *Re New Bullas Trading Ltd* that 'an uncollected book debt is a natural subject of a fixed charge; but once it is collected, the proceeds being needed for the conduct of business, it becomes a natural subject of a floating charge' was 'unsound'. In the second place, the Privy Council disagreed with Nourse LJ's approach to interpretation that the question was one of construction and that the intention of the parties as gleaned from the terms of the debenture should prevail. On this point Lord Millett said:

> 'Their Lordships consider this approach to be fundamentally mistaken. The question is not merely one of construction. In deciding whether a charge is a fixed charge or a floating charge, the court is engaged in a two-stage process. At the first stage it must construe the instrument of charge and seek to gather the intentions of the parties from the language they have used. But the object at this stage of the process is not to discover whether the parties intended to create a fixed or a floating charge. It is to ascertain the nature of the rights and obligations which the parties intended to grant each other in respect of the charged assets. Once these have been ascertained, the court can then embark on the second stage of the process, which is one of categorisation. This is a matter of law. It does not depend on the intention of the parties. If their intention, properly gathered from the language of the instrument, is to grant the company rights in respect of the charged assets which are inconsistent with the nature of a fixed charge, then the charge cannot be a fixed charge however they may have chosen to describe it. A similar process is involved in construing a document to see whether it creates a licence or tenancy. The court must construe the grant to ascertain the intention of the parties: but the only intention which is relevant is the intention to grant exclusive possession...So here, in construing a debenture

[151] [2001] 2 BCLC 188 at 199e–g, para [28].

> to see whether it creates a fixed or a floating charge, the only intention which is relevant is the intention that the company should be free to deal with the charged assets and withdraw them from the security without the consent of the holder of the charge; or, to put the question another way, whether the charged assets were intended to be under the control of the company or of the charge holder.'[152]

Turning from the general to the specific, the Privy Council rejected that the book debts were sufficiently under the chargee's control for the charge to be capable of being a fixed charge. In particular, Nourse LJ's reasoning that there was sufficient control was rejected. Nourse LJ had said it was wrong to say that assets ceased to be subject to a fixed charge at the chargor's will, but rather that they ceased to be subject to a fixed charge because this is what the parties had agreed would happen in the debenture. It is opined that, objectively, there is nothing intrinsically wrong with Nourse LJ's reasoning and that the Privy Council were primarily motivated by the policy considerations in the pecking order of priorities in an insolvency rather than the pursuit of conceptual possibility.

[20.050] The Privy Council also discredited the suggestion that it was sufficient to prevent the chargor from alienating its book debts, for the purposes of establishing the requisite degree of control for a fixed charge, but that it was not necessary to go further and also prohibit it from collecting and disposing of them[153]. Lord Millett said of that proposition:

> 'It makes no commercial sense because alienation and collection are merely different methods of realising a debt by turning it into money, collection being the natural and ordinary method of doing so. A restriction on disposition which nevertheless allows collection and free use of the proceeds is inconsistent with the fixed nature of the charge; it allows the debt and its proceeds to be withdrawn from the security by the act of the company in collecting it.'[154]

It was accepted that a company could exploit the characteristics inherent in the nature of the asset itself and that a wasting asset could be the subject of a fixed charge, provided always that whilst it subsists it cannot be destroyed or withdrawn from the security by the chargor[155]. The Privy Council also disapproved of the concept of two charges – one (fixed) over uncollected book debts and the other (floating) over the proceeds.

[20.051] The primary difficulty with the hybrid charge in *Re Brumark Investments Ltd* being a fixed charge was that the chargor was free to deal with the charge assets in a manner inconsistent with a fixed charge. As Lord Millett concluded:

> '...the debenture was so drafted that the company was at liberty to turn the uncollected book debts to account by its own act. Taking the relevant assets to be the uncollected book debts, the company was left in control of the process by which the charged assets were extinguished and replaced by different assets which were not the subject of a fixed charge and were at the free disposal of the company. That is inconsistent with the nature of a fixed charge.'[156]

---

152 [2001] 2 BCLC 188 at 200d–g, para [32].
153 Cf *Re ASRS Establishment Ltd* [2000] 2 BCLC 631.
154 [2001] 2 BCLC 188 at 201, para [36].
155 [2001] 2 BCLC 188 at 201, para [37].
156 [2001] 2 BCLC 188 at 205, para [49].

The question remains – can a debenture be drafted that achieves what it was thought had been achieved by the *New Bullas Trading* debenture? And what of the position in Ireland? Ironically, the Supreme Court has distinguished between uncollected debts and their proceeds, albeit in circumstances unfavourable to the chargee[157]. It would be a hardy prognosticator who would venture an opinion upon whether the Irish courts would endorse *Re New Bullas Trading Ltd* or *Re Brumark Investments Ltd* in a dispute of this nature.

***(e) Legislative curtailment of the priority of fixed charges on book debts*[158]**

[20.052] Shortly after it was accepted by the Irish courts that a fixed charge could be created over book debts the Finance Act 1986, s 115 was enacted. This provided that a fixed charge over a book debt does *not* enjoy preference in priority to one preferential creditor, the Revenue Commissioners. This section was very convoluted. It provided that where a company, which had created a fixed charge over its book debts, was unable to pay certain taxes owed to the Revenue Commissioners, the Revenue Commissioners could serve a notice on the holder of the fixed charge whereupon the holder of the fixed charge would become liable to pay such sums. This was subject to the proviso that the fixed charge holder would not be liable to pay more than it had received from the company which had created the fixed charge, and did not apply to amounts received by the fixed charge holder before it was notified by the Revenue Commissioners that he was liable for the chargor-company's liabilities.

[20.053] In March 1994 the Task Force for Small Business recommended that s 115 of the Finance Act 1986 be repealed[159]. As a result of this and other lobbying, the then Minister for Finance purported to reform the section so as to make fixed charges over book debts a more attractive security for banks, in the hope that there would be increased lending to small businesses. The result was the Finance Act 1995, s 174 which amended the original s 115 by the substitution and addition of certain subsections.

[20.054] Such were the origins of the Taxes Consolidation Act 1997, s 1001 ('TCA 1997') which provides:

---

157 See para **[20.042]**.

158 See Courtney, *Company Law Review, 1995* (1996), pp 33–40 and 'Editorial' (1995) 2 CLP 242.

159 Task Force for Small Business, *Report*, pp 83 and 84:

> 'For many trading companies, their book debts are a major, if not the main, source of collateral that they can offer to banks in negotiating a loan. As a result of section 115, the value of book debts as a security has been considerably diminished. We discussed the effects of this provision with representatives of the associated banks. All indicated that it had had an adverse effect on their willingness to lend to small business and on the terms on which they did so. As we have noted already, the operation of the Section has also led to as greater emphasis on fixed asset–backed loans under the Small Business Expansion Loan Scheme than we consider desirable. We believe that the Revenue Commissioners have adequate powers with which to protect their interests. The effect of section 115 is to confer on them a kind of super preferential status which is neither necessary or desirable. Though the legal position on book debts is similar in the United Kingdom, the authorities there have not legislated along the lines of section 115. We recommend that it should be repealed in the 1994 Finance Bill'.

'(2) Subject to this section, where a person holds a fixed charge (being a fixed charge created on or after the 27th day of May, 1986) on the book debts of a company (within the meaning of the Companies Act, 1963), such person shall, if the company fails to pay any relevant amount for which it is liable, become liable to pay such relevant amount on due demand, and on neglect or refusal of payment may be proceeded against in the like manner as any other defaulter.

(3) This section shall not apply –

(a) unless the holder of the fixed charge has been notified in writing by the Revenue Commissioners that a company has failed to pay a relevant amount for which it is liable and that by virtue of this section the holder of the fixed charge –

(i) may become liable for payment of any relevant amount which the company subsequently fails to pay, and

(ii) where paragraph (c) does not apply, has become liable for the payment of the relevant amount which the company has failed to pay,

(b) to any amounts received by the holder of the fixed charge from the company before the date on which the holder is notified in writing by the Revenue Commissioners in accordance with paragraph (a), and

(c) where, within the period from the 2nd day of June, 1995, to the 22nd day of June, 1995, or within 21 days of the creation of the fixed charge, whichever is the later, the holder of the fixed charge furnishes to the Revenue Commissioners a copy of the prescribed particulars of the charge delivered or to be delivered to the registrar of companies in accordance with section 99 of the Companies Act, 1963, to any relevant amount which the company was liable to pay before the date on which the holder is notified in writing by the Revenue Commissioners in accordance with paragraph (a).

(4) The amount or aggregate amount which a person shall be liable to pay in relation to a company in accordance with this section shall not exceed the amount or aggregate amount which the person has, while the fixed charge on book debts in relation to the company is in existence, received directly or indirectly from that company in payment or in part payment of any debts due by the company to the person.

(5) The Revenue Commissioners may, at any time and by notice in writing given to the holder of the fixed charge, withdraw with effect from a date specified in the notice a notification issued by them in accordance with subsection (3); but such withdrawal shall not –

(a) affect in any way any liability of the holder of the fixed charge under this section which arose before such withdrawal, or

(b) preclude the issue under subsection (3) of a subsequent notice to the holder of the fixed charge.

(6) The Revenue Commissioners may nominate any of their officers to perform any acts and discharge any functions authorised by this section to be performed or discharged by the Revenue Commissioners.'

If there were a prize for the most tortuous, rambling and cryptic legislative enactment, this would surely be a contender for first prize. The effect (and spirit) of this section is to punish those who dare to lend to small companies on the security of a fixed charge on book debts! By imposing a liability on a chargee to pay his chargor's liabilities to the Revenue Commissioners, it is possibly even unconstitutional.

[20.055] The approach of TCA 1997, s 1001 is to proceed by imposing a liability on the holder of a fixed charge on book debts to pay, in certain circumstances, his chargor's liabilities to the Revenue Commissioners and then to follow this with a series of qualifying provisos. The holder of a fixed charge on a company's book debts will, on due demand being made by the revenue, be liable to pay any PAYE and/or VAT[160] for which the chargor-company is liable to the Revenue, *unless* certain circumstances exist. Section 1001 goes considerably further than merely altering the long established priority that a fixed charge holder prevails over all other creditors. The section can be described as a unilateral statutory indemnity whereby the holder of a fixed charge on book debts is forced to stand in his debtor's shoes.

[20.056] The first of four provisos to the chargee's liability is provided by TCA 1997, s 1001(3)(a). This provides that the chargee will not be liable to pay the chargor's liabilities for PAYE and VAT unless he has been so notified in writing by the Revenue Commissioners. The notification must provide that the chargor has defaulted and that the chargee may become liable for payment of any relevant amounts which the company *subsequently* fails to pay, or, if the third qualification does not apply, has already become liable for relevant amounts that the company *has already failed* to pay. The effect of this qualification is that s 1001 will only become operational at the instigation of the Revenue Commissioners.

[20.057] The second proviso is provided for by TCA 1997, s 1001(3)(b). This provides that the section does not apply to any amounts received by the chargee from the chargor *before* the chargee is notified in accordance with paragraph 3(a), just considered. This proviso confuses the chargee's *actual* liability to pay anything with the *extent* of his liability. It would appear that this proviso provides that the chargee's liability does not apply to any amounts received by the chargee before he is notified as outlined. Therefore, regardless of the relevant amount that a chargee may be *liable* to pay, a chargee will only have to account for monies received by him *after* the Revenue Commissioners' notice is served on him.

[20.058] The third proviso, which was held out by the Department of Finance to be the panacea, is provided for in TCA 1997, s 1001(3)(c). This provides for a bastard procedure which seems intended to afford a chargee with some comfort where he notifies the Revenue Commissioners upon the creation of the fixed charge over the chargor's book debts. To avail of this, notification must be made within 21 days of the creation of the charge. The means of notification is by way of a copy to the Revenue Commissioners of the Form C1 that a chargee must deliver to the CRO within 21 days of the creation of a registrable charge pursuant to CA 1963, s 99. Where a chargee does this, then his liability for the chargor's liability for relevant amounts shall not apply 'to any relevant amount which the company was liable to pay before the date on which the [chargee] is notified in writing by the Revenue Commissioners in accordance with

---

160 TCA 1997, s 1001(1) defines 'relevant amount' as amounts due under the PAYE system or VAT Acts.

paragraph (a)'. Therefore, the amounts which the chargee is obliged to pay the Revenue Commissioners will, where this procedure is followed, only extend to *subsequent* relevant amounts. It is important to note that it is not relevant amounts which subsequently accrue, merely relevant amounts which the company fails to pay; so it would seem that relevant amounts which have accrued but are not actually due and owing are not excluded.

[20.059] The fourth proviso is provided for in TCA 1997, s 1001(4). This seeks to cap the *extent* of a chargee's liability. So, it is provided, that the amount which a chargee shall be liable to pay:

> '...shall not exceed the amount or aggregate amount which that person has, while the fixed charge on book debts in relation to the said company is in existence, received, directly or indirectly, from that company in payment or in part payment of any debts due by the company to the person'.

The extent of a chargee's liability under s 1001(4) is draconian and, most probably, unconstitutional. The principal difficulty is the failure to recognise that companies may pay chargees amounts other than on foot of a fixed charge on book debts. Where a chargee also holds, say, a fixed mortgage and charge over lands and premises, whilst s 1001 does not assail the priority of that charge, it would seem to seek to affect the proceeds of sale by possibly requiring a chargee to pay to the Revenue Commissioners such proceeds in discharge of a chargor's tax liabilities. It is thought that s 1001 should simply be repealed once and for all.

Fixed charges on deposit accounts[161]

[20.060] Companies that have credit balances at banks and other financial institutions rightly regard such as being a valuable asset. Generically, such assets fall to be classified as *choses in action*. They do not, however, fall to be classified as book debts[162]. In *Re Brightlife Ltd*[163] Hoffmann J said:

> '...I do not think that the bank balance falls within the term "book debts or other debts" as it is used in the debenture. It is true that the relationship between banker and customer is one of debtor and creditor. It would not therefore be legally inaccurate to describe a credit balance with a banker as a debt. But this would not be a natural usage for a businessman or accountant. He would ordinarily describe it as "cash at bank"...'[164].

In the instant case Hoffmann J had further reason for finding that the cash balances of the company in question were not part of its 'book or other debts'. The debenture in that

161 See generally, Johnston, *Banking and Security Law in Ireland* (1998), Ch 15; Donnelly, *The Law of Banks and Credit Institutions* (2000), pp 548–553; and Breslin, *Banking Law in the Republic of Ireland* (1998), p727. See also, Hutchinson, 'Charge–Backs, Set–Off and Flawed Assets: Taking Security Over Self–Held Cash Deposits' (1996) 3 CLP 55; Randell–Kahn and Graham, 'Charge Backs: Charge Card Overruled' (1998) PLC 21; de Lacy, 'The Legality of Charge–Back Security Interests' (1998) *Palmer's In Company* Issue 5/98, 19 May 1998.

162 *Watson v Parapara Coal Co Ltd* (1915) 17 GLR 791; and *Perrins v State Bank of Victoria* (1991) 1 VR 749, cited in Gough, *Company Charges* (2nd edn, 1996), p 684.

163 *Re Brightlife Ltd* [1986] BCLC 418.

164 [1986] BCLC 418 at 422.

case provided that the company was prohibited from dealing with such debts without the chargee's consent 'otherwise than in the ordinary course of getting in and realising the same'. Hoffmann J held that a credit balance in a bank account could not sensibly be got in or realised and so, in that case, found that the company's cash in its bank account was not included in the term 'book or other debts'. Subsequently, in *Re Permanent Houses (Holdings) Ltd*[165] Hoffmann J stated that the previous case was not authority for the proposition that cash at the bank could never amount to a book debt and that it depended upon the wording of each debenture. Notwithstanding the legal reality that a credit balance in a bank account is indeed a debt owed by the bank to a company, current judicial thinking is that the creation of security over a company's 'book debts' will not operate to capture a credit balance in a bank account. That said, however, the prudent practitioner will, in anticipation of a judicial revision or the interpretation of a particular debenture, register a charge on a bank deposit as a charge on book debts in the CRO[166].

[20.061] Leaving to one side the nature of such assets, the observation of Millett J in *Re Charge Card Services Ltd*[167] that 'a charge in favour of a debtor of his own indebtedness to the chargor is conceptually impossible'[168] made lenders to companies very wary about taking security over cash in an account. This, of course, only applied to cases where a bank or other credit institution sought to take a charge over a company's money held in an account *held with* that bank or other credit institution. Many lenders sought to avoid Millett J's 'conceptual impossibility' by causing borrowing-companies to deposit monies in subsidiary or otherwise associated companies before taking a charge over them. Others did, and still do, allow borrower-companies to deposit monies with them but take security by obtaining an assignment of the debt, a charge over the account, a contractual set-off against monies borrowed and the making of the credit balance in the account a 'flawed asset'.

[20.062] The decision in *Re Charge Card Services Ltd* was reconsidered by the House of Lords in *Morris v Rayners Enterprises Inc*; *Morris v Agrichemicals Ltd*; *Re BCCI (No 8)*[169]. There, Lord Hoffmann noted the doctrine of 'conceptual impossibility', first propounded by Millett J, and went on to depart from the stringency of the rule of interpretation thus propounded, saying that there seemed to him '...no reason for preventing banks and their customers from creating charges over deposits if, for reasons of their own, they want to do so'[170]. Speaking obiter, Lord Hoffmann said:

> 'In a case in which there is no threat to the consistency of the law or objection of public policy, I think that the courts should be very slow to declare a practice of the commercial

---

[165] *Re Permanent Houses (Holdings) Ltd* [1988] BCLC 563.

[166] See Johnston, *Banking and Security Law in Ireland*, (1998), p 581 and Hutchinson, 'Charge–Backs, Set–Off and Flawed Assets: Taking Security Over Self–Held Cash Deposits' (1996) 3 CLP 55 at 57, 58 and *Re BCCI SA (No 8)* [1997] 4 All ER 568 at 577. Cf *Northern Bank Ltd v Ross* [1990] BCC 883. See, generally, Ch 21, *Corporate Borrowing: Registration of Charges*, para **[21.047]**.

[167] *Re Charge Card Services Ltd* [1986] 3 All ER 289.

[168] [1986] 3 All ER 289 at 308.

[169] *Re BCCI (No 8)* [1997] 4 All ER 568.

[170] [1997] 4 All ER 568 at 577f.

community to be conceptually impossible. Rules of law must obviously be consistent and not self-contradictory...But the law is fashioned to suit the practicalities of life and legal concepts like "proprietary interest" and "charge" are no more than labels given to clusters of related and self-consistent rules of law. Such concepts do not have a life of their own from which the rules are inexorably derived. It follows that in my view the letter was effective to do what it purported to do, namely to create a charge over the deposit in favour of BCCI'.

It is thought that the pragmatism witnessed in this judicial interpretation would find favour with the Irish courts and that there should be no prohibition to the creation of a charge, whether fixed or floating, over a credit balance at a credit institution which is the chargee in such a transaction[171]. That said, there remain compelling reasons why an Irish lender who takes security over a 'self-held' credit balance would continue to take security by seeking a 'quadruple cocktail' in the form of a charge, an assignment, a right of set-off and a flawed asset.

Floating charges

(a) The nature and characteristics of a floating charge

[20.063] A floating charge is a charge over a company's present or future property, or classes of property, which hovers over that property until the moment of crystallisation whereupon the charge fastens onto the charged property or class of property, and becomes a quasi-fixed charge[172]. The 'crucial' distinction between a fixed charge and a floating charge has been described as relating to:

'...the nature of the interest of the [chargee] in the charged property immediately created by the debenture before any crystallising event occurred. A fixed charge attaches to the charged property *in specie* either immediately or as soon as it is acquired by the chargor. The interest of a floating chargee is not specific prior to crystallisation. The floating chargee is, in effect, given a security interest in the fund of assets over which the charge is created.'[173]

[20.064] The essence of a floating charge is that up until the moment of crystallisation the company is free to use the assets which are the subject of the charge in the ordinary course of its business. In the words of Lord Macnaghten in *Illingworth v Houldsworth*[174],

---

[171] Cf *Re Euro Travel Ltd; Dempsey v The Governor and Company of the Bank of Ireland* (28 May 1984, unreported), High Court [1963–93] Irish Company Law Reports 207 at 212 where Murphy J said: 'I find it difficult to accept the proposition that the company was purporting to charge monies in the hands of the bank itself with monies due by the company to the bank. This argument might have been more attractive when and so long as the sum of £75,000 was lodged by the company to the credit of the Bank of Ireland Finance Company Ltd, a legal entity separate from the respondents in the present proceedings.'

[172] The charge is a 'quasi–fixed charge' in the sense that although it becomes a fixed charge, it is in a different position to a charge which is fixed, ab initio. As we shall see, a floating charge can be upset in the order of priorities where it is created within 12 months, or two years in the case of a floating charge created in favour of a 'connected person', and a floating charge ranks after preferential creditors in priority.

[173] *Re Cimex Tissues Ltd* [1995] 1 BCLC 409 at 420, per Stanley Burnton QC, sitting as a deputy judge of the High Court.

[174] *Illingworth v Houldsworth* [1904] AC 355.

unlike a specific or fixed charge, which fastens ab initio onto ascertained or definite property, a floating charge:

> '...is ambulatory and shifting in its nature, hovering over and so to speak floating with the property which it is intended to affect until some event occurs or some act is done which causes it to settle and fasten on the subject of the charge within its reach and grasp.'[175]

From the view point of the chargor-company, the principal advantage of the floating charge is that it allows the company to continue to have the use and enjoyment of the assets which are the subject matter of the floating charge for so long as it remains uncrystallised. This was made clear in the judgment which is most cited by the judiciary, *Re Yorkshire Woolcombers' Association Ltd*[176], where Romer J made a pragmatic speech which has long-lingered upon the lips of the judiciary:

> 'I certainly do not intend to attempt to give an exact definition of the term 'floating charge', nor am I prepared to say that there will not be a floating charge within the meaning of the Act, which does not contain all the three characteristics that I am about to mention, but I certainly think that if a charge has the three characteristics I am about to mention it is a floating charge. (1) If it is a charge on a class of assets of a company present and future; (2) if that class is one, which in the ordinary course of the business of the company, would be changing from time to time; and (3) if you find that by the charge it is contemplated that, until some future step is taken by or on behalf of those interested in the charge, the company may carry on its business in the ordinary way so far as concerns the particular class of assets I am dealing with.'

Floating charges are the most common form of floating security taken by creditors. It may be noted, however, that while it is possible to create a *floating mortgage*, they are not very common. The most common form of floating mortgage is a *floating chattel mortgage*. Floating chattel mortgages are most frequently used in agricultural lending where they are taken over a farmer's stock, plant and machinery[177].

[20.065] It should be noted that there is some controversy as to whether or not a floating charge takes immediate effect over the property charged, and merely allows the chargor company to continue to deal with the property until the moment of crystallisation, or, on the other hand, whether it is a future charge, which does not take effect until crystallisation. While it was the case that, previously, the former was the preferred view[178], the latter has now been put forward as the answer[179]. It is submitted that the former is logically, the more attractive view, in that upon the execution of a floating charge, a present charge comes into immediate effect, which requires registration under

---

175 [1904] AC 355 at 358, approved of by Kenny J in *Welch v Bowmaker (Ireland) Ltd* [1980] IR 251 at 258.

176 [1903] 2 Ch 284 at 295, being the judgment of the court of first instance in the case which on appeal was entitled *Illingworth v Houldsworth* [1904] AC 355.

177 Floating chattel mortgages over agricultural stock must also be registered pursuant to the Agricultural Credit Act 1978. See Chapter 21, *Corporate Borrowing: Registration of Charges*, para **[21.109]**.

178 Pennington, 'Genesis of a Floating Charge' (1960) 23 MLR 630.

179 See Gough, *Company Charges* (2nd edn, 1996), pp 135–137.

CA 1963, s 99(1). Although inchoate or dormant[180], a floating charge is very definitely a 'present charge'. This view is supported by the decision of Blayney J in *Re Tullow Engineering (Holdings) Ltd*[181], where he held that a debenture which contained a floating charge over shares in another company constituted a present security[182] which was unaffected by the granting of an option to buy those shares. Blayney J quoted Buckley LJ in *Evans v Rival Granite Quarries Ltd*[183] where he said:

> 'A floating security is not a future security; it is a present security, which presently affects all the assets of the company expressed to be included in it...A floating security is not a specific mortgage of the assets, plus a licence to the mortgagor to dispose of them in the course of his business, but is a floating mortgage applying to every item comprised in the security, but not specifically affecting any item until some event occurs...which causes it to crystallise into a fixed security.'[184]

Accordingly, Blayney J held that the shares remained within the ambit of the floating charge, which did not crystallise until the appointment of a receiver. At that point, an equitable assignment of the shares to the debenture holder occurred[185]. In *Smith (Administrator of Cosslett (Contractors) Ltd v Bridgend County Borough Council*[186] Lord Scott in the House of Lords acknowledged that not all floating charges are the same and said that some may be drafted so as to operate as a present charge and others to operate as a future charge. Of course, in practice, most debentures merely provide that a class of assets are charged 'by way of floating charge'. The point is largely moot and the House of Lords held that irrespective of the nature of the charge, it required to be registered as a floating charge upon its creation[187]. One question, to which there seems

---

[180] In *Governments Stock and Other Securities Investment Co Ltd v Manila Railway Co* [1897] AC 81 at 86 Lord Macnaghten said: 'A floating security is an equitable charge on the assets for the time being of a going concern. It attaches to the subject charged in the varying condition in which it happens to be from time to time. It is of the essence of such a charge that it remains dormant until the undertaking charged ceases to be a going concern, or until the person in whose favour the charge is created intervenes.'

[181] *Re Tullow Engineering (Holdings) Ltd* [1990] 1 IR 452.

[182] [1990] 1 IR 452 at 458.

[183] *Evans v Rival Granite Quarries Ltd* [1910] 2 KB 979 at 999.

[184] See also *Wallace v Evershed* [1899] Ch 891 where Cozens–Hardy said (at 894): 'A floating security gives an immediate equitable charge on the assets, subject to a right to the company in the ordinary course and for the purposes of the business of the company, but not otherwise, to dispose of the assets as though the charge had not existed …'.

[185] See *Re Interview Ltd* [1975] IR 382.

[186] *Smith (Administrator of Cosslett (Contractors) Ltd v Bridgend County Borough Council* [2002] 1 All ER 292, [2001] UKHL 58. For comment, see Sealy, 'House of Lords Washes Floating Charges in Cosslett (Contractors) Ltd' (2001) Company Law Newsletter, (Issue 85; 12 November 2001).

[187] Lord Scott said: 'I do not think, however, that this analysis bars the clause 63(1) future security rights from constituting a floating charge for s 395 registration purposes. In my opinion, a charge expressed to come into existence on the occurrence of an uncertain future event and then to apply to a class of assets that cannot be identified until the event has happened would, if otherwise valid, qualify for registration as a floating charge.

no immediately clear-cut answer, is whether a floating charge confers (on the holder) an equitable interest over the property of the chargor. Notwithstanding that the effect of crystallisation is to give effect to an equitable assignment in the assets, the subject matter of a floating charge, it is logically attractive to conclude that, pending crystallisation, the holder has some form of equitable interest in assets so charged[188]. On this point *Gough*[189] is instructive:

> 'Even before crystallisation, under a floating charge there is from the very moment of its creation a present security immediately in existence. For this reason enforcement remedies are available before crystallisation. It may appear contradictory that a floating charge should be both a present security and also a security under which the assignor is free to deal with the assets and under which the assignee gains no proprietary interest over present or future property. The contradiction is in fact apparent, rather than real. The very nature of the floating charge postulates both security for the chargee and commercial freedom for the chargor.
>
> ...The combined features of a floating charge of a present security and a deferred proprietary interest for the chargee through lack of appropriation are fully consistent with general principle.'

It is thought that to describe pre-crystallisation rights as being 'proprietary'[190] is to overstate their importance[191]. If a label is to be attributed to the nature of the interest of a floating charge holder in the assets subject to such a charge, it is thought best described as 'an equity' and not 'an equitable interest'[192]. The definition of 'an equity', whether mere or naked, given by Kenny J in *Allied Irish Banks Ltd v Glynn*[193] seems apposite to

187 (contd) The future charge would have the essential characteristic of floating, remaining dormant, until the occurrence of the specified event. It would, I think, come within the mischief sought to be dealt with by the s 395 requirement of registration of floating charges. For the same reasons, it would also, in my view constitute a floating charge for Insolvency Act 1986 purposes ...' (at 307g–h; para [63]).

188 See, eg, Forde, *Company Law* (3rd edn, 1999), pp 16–21.

189 Gough, *Company Charges* (2nd edn, 1996), pp 97, 98.

190 In *Wily v George Partnership Banking Ltd* [1999] Federal Court of Appeal (29 January 1999) Finkelstein J said: 'One possible view of the effect of a floating charge is that it creates an immediate equitable interest over the property of the company and that the company is permitted (licensed) to deal with those assets free of the charge in order to carry on its business until the charge has crystallised...The opposing view is that because a floating charge does not specifically attract any asset until it crystallises into a fixed security it cannot confer a proprietary interest before crystallisation'. It was said, obiter dictum, that because the courts of equity will protect charged property, the rights of a floating charge holder are proprietary in nature.

191 Cf the views of Farrar & Hannigan, *Farrar's Company Law* (4th edn, 1998), p 633 where the authors take a different view.

192 In *Smith (Administrator of Cosslett (Contractors) Ltd v Bridgend County Borough Council* [2002] 1 All ER 292, [2001] UKHL 58 Lord Scott said that he did not think that the local authority, which he found to be secured by a floating charge, could be said to have had an equitable interest in the charged machinery. He said of their rights that they were a 'contractual operational right, not property rights' (at 307; para [62]).

193 *Allied Irish Banks Ltd v Glynn* [1973] IR 188 at 192.

the right in question. There, in distinguishing equitable interests from equities, Kenny J said: 'The main difference, I think, is than an "equity" does not create or give any estate in the land; it is a right against persons and is enforceable against those who were parties to the transactions which created it'[194]. Certainly, a floating charge immediately creates rights that are enforceable against the chargor[195], but it is thought that the rights may, in certain circumstances also be enforced against persons other than those who are parties to the transaction.

(b) The chargor's ability to deal with the charged property

[20.066] The ability of the chargor-company to actually deal with the charged property, including the right to dispose of the property in the ordinary course of business, is clearly the most advantageous feature of the floating charge. In *Re Lakeglen Construction Co Ltd*[196] the question which arose was whether a clause in a debenture in favour of some of the company's creditors created a fixed or floating charge. In charging the assets of the company, the debenture made certain assets subject to a fixed charge, and went on to further charge the company's 'book debts and all rights and powers of recovery thereof'. On account of the company having been insolvent when the debenture was created, the crucial question was whether the latter charge was fixed or floating. In his examination of the central question, Costello J said[197]:

> '...if it was intended that the charge was to remain dormant until some future date and that the company was permitted to go on receiving the book debts and using them until then, the security would contain the true element of a floating charge.'

In posing the central question[198] Costello J said that it was noticeable that the company concerned was a trading company and that the parties expressly agreed that the company was permitted to carry on its business since 'in the normal course of affairs it would obviously create difficulties for a trading company if it were required to hand over to its mortgagees its book debts as it received them from time to time'[199]. He went on to cite

---

194 Support for this view can be seen in the Australian case of *Landall Holdings Ltd v Caratti* [1979] WAR 97 where Wallace J said (at 114) '... the charge by way of floating charge or security, though equitable in nature, lies dormant...Granted there is an equity created upon execution of the debenture charge in favour of the debenture holder but it is a *mere equity* and does not vest or become fixed until crystallisation' (Emphasis added). See also *Latec Investments Ltd v Hotel Terrigal Pty Ltd* (1965) 113 CLR 265. Gough, *Company Charges*, p 230 supports this view of the nature of a floating chargee's right prior to crystallisation.

195 Eg *Re Woodroffes (Musical Instruments) Ltd* [1986] Ch 366 at 378 where an injunction was granted against the chargor to restrain it from dealing with the charged property otherwise than in the ordinary course of business.

196 *Re Lakeglen Construction Co Ltd* [1980] IR 347.

197 When he was referring to *Illingworth v Houldsworth* [1903] 2 Ch 284.

198 Namely, 'When they executed the debenture did the parties intend that in relation to its book debts the company was free to receive them and bring new book debts into existence as if the debenture had not been created – until such time as the debenture holder became entitled to intervene in the company's affairs ?'

199 *Re Lakeglen Construction Ltd* [1980] IR 347 at 353.

and apply the test of Romer J in *Illingworth v Houldsworth*, and found that the charge over the book debts was a floating charge.

[20.067] It should also be noted that the test in *Illingworth v Houldsworth* is not, nor was it ever intended to be, exhaustive in detailing the traits of a floating charge. So, a charge can be a floating charge even where the company does not, in fact, dispose of the class of property so charged in the ordinary course of its business. Such is shown in the case of *Welch v Bowmaker (Ireland) Ltd*[200]. There, a company created a debenture in favour of the defendant bank and gave a fixed charge over three parcels of property owned by the company specified in the schedule thereto, and a general charge on the company's undertaking and all its property and assets, present and future. There was, however, a condition in the debenture that, with regard to all of the company's specified property, the charge was to be a specific charge and with regard to other property, a floating charge. The company owned a fourth property which was not specified in the schedule to the debenture, and the question arose as to whether or not this was a fixed or floating charge. This became important when the company later gave an equitable mortgage on the fourth property to the Bank of Ireland. In the Supreme Court, Henchy and Parke JJ applied the old maxim, *generalia specialbus non derogant*, (the general does not derogate from the particular) and held that the specification in respect of the first three properties ought to prevail, meaning that the fourth property was merely subject to a floating charge. This meant that Bowmaker lost priority to Bank of Ireland, as the latter had obtained a fixed equitable mortgage before Bowmaker's floating charge of the fourth property had crystallised. It is noticeable that although the company would not ordinarily have disposed of land in the normal course of its business, the Supreme Court implicitly held by majority that this did not prevent the land from being the subject of a floating charge[201].

(c) Fixed or floating? – the Cosslett (Contractors) Ltd saga

[20.068] Whether or not a particular document or deed will give effect to the creation of a floating charge will depend upon its true construction. This is exemplified by the case of *Re Cosslett (Contractors) Ltd*[202] (as the English Court of Appeal decision is reported) or *Smith (Administrator of Cosslett (Contractors) Ltd) v Bridgend County Borough Council*[203] (as the House of Lords' decision is reported). In this case, a company entered

---

200 *Welch v Bowmaker (Ireland) Ltd* [1980] IR 251.

201 Note the dissenting judgment of Kenny J who said (at 258) that: 'The land owned by the company is capable of being ascertained and defined and this satisfies Lord Macnaghten's definition of a specific charge. It certainly is not a class of asset which would be changing from time to time. I have no doubt that the debenture given to Bowmaker created a specific charge on the [fourth property]'.

202 *Re Cosslett (Contractors) Ltd* [1997] 4 All ER 115. See Gregory, 'Floating Charge over Changing Asset – Statements of Principle' (1997) *CCH's Company Law Newsletter*, Issue 16, 11 September 1997.

203 *Smith (Administrator of Cosslett (Contractors) Ltd) v Bridgend County Borough Council* [2002] 1 All ER 292, [2001] UKHL 58. For comment, see Sealy, 'House of Lords Washes Floating Charges in Cosslett (Contractors) Ltd' (2001) Company Law Newsletter, (Issue 85; 12 November 2001).

into a building contract with a local authority to carry out certain land reclamation works involving the processing of coal bearing shale. The company acquired two coal washing machines with an advance of £1.8 million from the local authority. The building contract[204] provided, inter alia, that all 'plant' owned by the company when on the site would be deemed to be the property of the local authority (clause 53). The contract also provided that in the event of the company's insolvency or abandonment of the contract, the local authority could enter upon the site and complete or employ another contractor to complete the works and could use such of the plant which had been deemed to become its property; the local authority could also, at any time, sell the plant and apply the proceeds of sale in or towards the satisfaction of any sums due under the building contract (clause 63). Some two years into the contract the company encountered financial difficulties and abandoned the site. The local authority invoked clause 63 and engaged another contractor to complete the works. Eventually, the local authority sold the two machines to the new contractor.

[20.069] When an administrator was appointed to the first company, he contended that the effect of the building contract was that the local authority had contractual rights over the plant that gave it a proprietary interest in the plant. He also contended that this proprietary interest amounted to an equitable 'security interest' which was a floating charge[205]. The local authority argued that no equitable charge had been created and, alternatively, if a charge had been created it was a fixed or specific charge over the plant, which did not require registration under the English Companies Acts[206]. Arising from the several proceedings instituted, the following findings were made:

— The administrator brought summary proceedings seeking the delivery up of the machinery to him. Parker J held[207] that the effect of clause 63 was to create an equitable charge over the machinery which was, because of the controls reserved over the machinery, a fixed charge not a floating charge.

— The administrator appealed this decision and the English Court of Appeal held[208] that the charge was properly construed as a floating charge and so, because it had not been registered, was void. The administrator, however, lost

---

204 The contract was in standard English ICE (Institution of Civil Engineers Conditions of Contract) format. The fact that the clause in question was found to give rise to a floating charge was all the more incredible since this type of contract had been used for years without users suspecting that registration of a floating charge was required if the clause was not to be void. On registration of floating charges, see Ch 21, *Corporate Borrowing: Registration of Charges*, para **[21.052]**.

205 The basis of these contentions was, were the contract to have created a floating charge and were the floating charge not registered under CA 1985, s 395 (UK), it would be void as against the administrator.

206 As has been pointed out by Sealy, 'House of Lords Washes Floating Charges in Cosslett (Contractors) Ltd', (2001) Company Law Newsletter, (Issue 85; 12 November 2001), it is curious that nobody contended that even if the charge was fixed it would still require to be registered as a charge which, had it been created by an individual, would require registration as a bill of sale.

207 [1996] 4 All ER 46, [1996] 1 BCLC 407, [1996] BCC 515.

208 [1997] BCC 724.

the appeal because it was also held that regardless of the validity of the charge, clause 63 gave the local authority the right to retain possession of the machinery until the works had been completed. This is referred to as the First Court of Appeal decision.

— After the local authority sold the machinery, the administrator instituted proceedings for conversion against the local authority on the basis that they had no authority to sell the machinery since the contract had created a charge that was void for want of registration. The administrator obtained summary judgment from Judge Toulmin QC.

— The local authority appealed against the order for summary judgment and the English Court of Appeal[209] set aside the summary judgment on the grounds that the 'charge' was not void for want of registration[210]. This is referred to as the Second Court of Appeal decision.

— The administrator appealed against this decision to the House of Lords[211] which overruled the second Court of Appeal's decision and reinstated the order made by Judge Toulmin QC.

This legal saga gave rise to two really important issues concerning charges. The first issue, considered here, is whether the contract (clause 63) created a charge and, if so, whether that charge was fixed or floating. The second issue, considered in Chapter 21, concerned the effect of the failure to register a registrable charge[212].

[20.070] In the First Court of Appeal decision, the administrator's appeal was dismissed but it was held that a charge had been created, and that it was a floating charge. It was held that legal ownership in the plant did not pass to the local authority; neither did the contract constitute a possessory lien with a power of sale. After finding that the local authority's rights constituted an equitable charge, Millett LJ went on to hold that the charge was a floating charge, finding that the three characteristics of a floating charge identified by Romer LJ in *Yorkshire Woolcombers Association Ltd*[213] were all present. Of significance was his finding that:

> 'The chargor's unfettered freedom to deal with the assets in the ordinary course of his business free from the charge is obviously inconsistent with the nature of a fixed charge; but it does not follow that his unfettered freedom to deal with the charged assets is essential to the existence of a floating charge. It plainly is not, for any well-drawn floating charge prohibits the chargor from creating further charges having priority to the floating charge; and a prohibition against factoring debts is not sufficient to convert what would otherwise be a floating charge on book debts into a fixed charge…
>
> The essence of a floating charge is that it is a charge, not on any particular asset, but on a fluctuating body of assets which remain under the management and control of the chargor,

[209] [2000] BCC 1155.

[210] This was a rather bizarre finding which was, in fact, reversed by the House of Lords at [2002] 1 All ER 292. See Chapter 21, *Corporate Borrowing: Registration of Charges*, para **[21.007]**.

[211] *Smith (Administrator) of Cosslett (Contractors) Ltd v Bridgend County Borough Council* [2002] 1 All ER 292, [2001] UKHL 58.

[212] At para **[21.007]**.

[213] *Yorkshire Woolcombers' Association Ltd* [1903] 2 Ch 284.

> and which the chargor has the right to withdraw from the security despite the existence of the charge. The essence of a fixed charge is that the charge is on a particular asset or class of assets which the chargor cannot deal with free from the charge without the consent of the chargee. The question is not whether the chargor has complete freedom to carry on his business as he chooses, *but whether the chargee is in control of the charged assets*.'[214] [Emphasis added]

Millett LJ held that the contractual provision which prohibited the company from removing from the site plant and materials and from deploying them elsewhere did not have any relation to the local authority's security; it was designed to ensure that the company gave proper priority to the completion of the work and did not indicate that the charge was a fixed charge.

[20.071] The House of Lords in *Smith (Administrator of Cosslett (Contractors) Ltd) v Bridgend County Borough Council*[215] ultimately upheld the decision that clause 63 created a charge and also that the type of charge created was a floating charge. Lord Hoffmann said that he agreed with the reasons given by Millett LJ:

> 'I do not see how a right to sell an asset belonging to a debtor and appropriate the proceeds to payment of the debt can be anything other than a charge. And because the property subject to clause 63 (constructional plant, temporary works, goods and materials on the site) was a fluctuating body of assets which could be consumed or (subject to the approval of the engineer) removed from the site in the ordinary course of the contractor's business, it was a floating charge.'[216]

Notwithstanding Lord Hoffmann's confident, almost flippant, assertion as to the nature of the charge in hand, students and practitioners of company law can take some comfort that this outing to the House of Lords marked the end of a legal saga that had lasted several years.

(d) Floating charges are peculiar to companies

[20.072] In practice, floating charges tend only to be created by companies and other bodies corporate, and floating charges over personal chattels, within the meaning of the Bills of Sale Acts, cannot be created by an individual[217] without giving rise to considerable difficulties[218]. It is thought that there is no reason in theory or in practice why an individual cannot create a floating charge over 'non-personal chattels' such as classes of real property or of choses in action, or rights or interests therein. The High Court judgment of Keane J in *Re Keenan Bros Ltd*[219] shows the evolution and primary purpose of the floating charge:

---

[214] At 127d–f.

[215] *Smith (Administrator of Cosslett (Contractors) Ltd) v Bridgend County Borough Council* [2002] 1 All ER 292; [2001] UKHL 58. For comment, see Sealy, 'House of Lords Washes Floating Charges in Cosslett (Contractors) Ltd' (2001) Company Law Newsletter, (Issue 85; 12 November 2001).

[216] [2002] 1 All ER 292 at 302j, para [41].

[217] There is authority that all *corporations* are excluded from the Bills of Sale Acts: *NV Slavenburg's Bank v Intercontinental Natural Resources Ltd et al* [1980] 1 All ER 955 at 975 per Lloyd J who said his preferred view of such an issue was 'that the Bills of Sale Acts apply to individuals only and not to corporations at all'.

[218] See Chapter 4, *Incorporation and its Consequences*, para **[4.080]**.

[219] *Re Keenan Bros Ltd* [1985] IR 401 at 407.

> 'I think that one has to bear in mind at the outset that this form of charge made its first appearance in England as a by-product of the joint stock companies which began to flourish after the enactment of the Joint Stock Companies Act 1844. In order to borrow money, such companies offered as security not merely their fixed assets, but also assets which were regularly turned over in the course of business, such as the companies' stock in trade. It was obviously cumbersome and impractical to charge such assets specifically with the repayment of advances, since it would mean the constant execution and release of securities as the assets were disposed of and replaced. Hence the concept developed of a charge which did not attach to any specific assets of the company, remained dormant until the mortgagee intervened and in the interim did not prevent the mortgagor from using the assets in question in the ordinary course of his business.'

Stock, goods and other chattels and choses in action such as book debts are the assets most amenable to being the subject of a floating charge.

Negative pledge clauses

[20.073] Debentures often contain so-called 'negative pledge clauses' which provide that the chargor-company shall not create any other charges or mortgages without the chargee's permission[220]. Negative pledge clauses seek to prevent chargors from creating subsequent fixed securities which would, in the absence of such clauses, have priority to the holders of a prior floating charge. Typically, a negative pledge clause will state inter alia that:

> 'The Company hereby covenants that it will not without the prior consent in writing of the Lender, create or attempt to create or permit to subsist any mortgage, debenture, charge or pledge upon or permit any lien or other encumbrance to arise on or affect the goodwill, undertaking, property, assets, revenue and rights hereby charged or any part thereof.'

However, such a clause in a debenture is only a contractual promise between a floating chargor and a floating chargee and where the chargor acts in breach of it, eg by creating a subsequent charge, the prior floating chargee will not, by virtue of the negative pledge clause, automatically have priority ahead of a subsequently created charge.

(a) Priority of floating charges accompanied by negative pledge clauses

[20.074] In Ireland[221], the question of priorities will be determined by whether or not the subsequent chargee had *notice* of the existence of the negative pledge clause[222]. Most debate turns upon whether or not constructive or imputed notice will suffice. The most

---

220 See Gough, *Company Charges* (2nd edn, 1995), Ch 10 and Johnston, *Banking and Security Law in Ireland* (1998), p 470. See also Maxton, 'Negative Pledges and Equitable Principles', [1993] JBL 458.

221 Cf the United Kingdom: CA 1985, s 464 (UK). In *AIB Finance Ltd v Bank of Scotland* [1995] 1 BCLC 185 the Scottish Court of Sessions construed CA 1985, s 464 (UK) as conferring priority to a floating charge over a fixed charge on land, in circumstances when both charges were created the same day, but where the floating charge contained a negative pledge clause. The reason why this was held to be the case was because when read against the statutory history, the negative pledge clause regulated ranking for the purposes of CA 1985, s 464 (UK) and that its existence qualified the order of ranking of a fixed and floating charge.

222 For English authority that actual notice defeats the subsequent chargee's priority, see *Wilson v Kelland* [1910] 2 Ch 306; *English and Scottish Mercantile Investment Co Ltd* [1892] 2 QB 700; and *Re Castell and Brown Ltd* [1898] 1 Ch 315.

authoritative Irish case in point is *Welch v Bowmaker (Ireland) Ltd*[223], where the Supreme Court, per Henchy J, held that:

> 'Counsel for [the defendant] has argued that...the bank should be fixed with constructive notice of the provision in the debenture precluding the company from creating a mortgage (such as the bank got) which would have priority over the debenture. Since such a prohibition is more or less common form in modern debentures, there would be much to be said for applying the doctrine of constructive notice to such a situation were it not that it is settled law that there is no duty on the bank in a situation such as this to seek out the precise terms of the debenture...Actual or express notice of the prohibition must be shown before the subsequent mortgagee can be said to be deprived of priority.
>
> Whatever attractions there may be in the proposition that priority should be deemed lost because a duty to inquire further was called for but ignored, and that such inquiry would have shown that the company was debarred from entering into a mortgage which would have priority over the debenture, the fact remains that it would be unfair to single out the bank for condemnatory treatment because of their failure to ascertain the full terms of the debenture when what they did was in accord with judicially approved practice and when such a precipitate change in the law would undermine the intended validity of many other such transactions. If the proposed extension of the doctrine of constructive notice is to be made, the necessary change in the law would need to be made prospectively and, therefore, more properly by statute.'[224]

From the judgment of Henchy J, it would appear that the factor which decided that the subsequent chargee would not lose priority was that it was 'settled law that there is no duty on a bank in a situation such as this to seek out the *precise terms* of the debenture'.

[20.075] Although it would seem clear that the doctrine of constructive notice will not be extended and that subsequent chargees will not be deemed to have constructive notice of the existence of a negative pledge clause, it is thought that, in practice, many subsequent chargees will have the *actual or express* notice spoken of by Henchy J in the passage last quoted. In practice, a subsequent chargee will invariably conduct a CRO search against the chargor-company. Where the terms of a negative pledge have been inserted in a Form C1[225] the subsequent mortgagee will have *actual notice* of its existence. This will be *imputed* to the subsequent chargee through their solicitors[226] or other legal advisers[227]. In such circumstances, it is thought that equity will prevent the

---

[223] *Welch v Bowmaker (Ireland) Ltd* [1980] IR 251.

[224] [1980] IR 251 at 256.

[225] The form used to register a charge created by a company: see Chapter 21, *Corporate Borrowing: Registration of Charges*, para **[21.100]**.

[226] A distinction is drawn by Lingard, *Bank Security Documents*, (3rd edn, 1993), between a solicitor and, say a 'warehouse keeper', in respect of whether or not they should be deemed to have notice of the existence of a negative pledge clause by virtue of the Companies Registration Office register.

[227] Indeed, it will almost certainly be the case that the solicitor acting for the subsequent mortgagee/chargee will have sight of a search of the Companies Registration Office register, and may actually have in his possession the precise wording of the negative pledge clause. If he does not 'appreciate' the significance of this, then, presumably, the same reasoning as was applied by Keane J in *Northern Bank Finance Corporation v Quinn and Achates Investment Company* [1979] ILRM 221, would apply here too, so that the solicitor would be deemed to be actually aware of the negative pledge clause, and such knowledge imputed to his client.

subsequent chargee from obtaining priority. Moreover, there is authority that the burden of proof operates in favour of the prior floating charge[228].

[20.076] The Supreme Court decision in *Re Holidair Ltd*[229] demonstrates a further weakness in negative pledge clauses. According to Finlay CJ, the effect of the Companies (Amendment) Act 1990, ss 7 and 9 ('C(A)A 1990') was that an examiner appointed to a company under the protection of the court can exercise his borrowing powers granted by the court without obtaining the consent of the debenture holders[230]. Section 18 of the Companies (Amendment) (No 2) Act 1999 does nothing to alleviate this. This amends C(A)A 1990, s 7 to allow examiners to repudiate contracts which provide that a company shall not, inter alia, 'create or permit to subsist any mortgage, charge, lien or other encumbrance or any pledge over the whole or any part of the property or undertaking of the company'[231].

(b) Negative pledge clauses and competition law

[20.077] A novel challenge to debentures containing negative pledge clauses was made in *Oakdale (Richmond) Ltd v National Westminster Bank plc*[232]. In this case the plaintiff was a small company which obtained its supplies from EU Member States, other than the UK. Its indebtedness to its bank was secured by an all sums due debenture which was expressed to be repayable on demand. The debenture created a specific fixed charge over the company's book and other debts and a floating charge over its other assets. Monies payable on foot of its book debts were required to be paid into its account with the chargee-bank, and it was restrained from factoring, discounting, charging or assigning its book or other debts without the prior written consent of its bank, the chargee. Two loans under the UK Government's small firms loan guarantee scheme contained covenants prohibiting the company from borrowing and charging of assets. The company sued its chargee-bank seeking, inter alia, a declaration that its loan arrangements and the debenture were void for being contrary to Articles 85 and 86 of the EU Treaty of Rome. The chargee-bank countered for an injunction to restrain the company from paying its book debts into any account other than the chargor-company's account with the chargee-bank. The chargor-company contended:

- that the restrictions and prohibitions against borrowing and charging assets were anti-competitive since the company was obliged to give security because it was locked into borrowings with the chargee-bank;
- that the debenture was, itself, anti-competitive and void under Article 85 because it prevented the company from using property charged as security for a loan for further lending by a third party; and
- that the chargee-bank had abused its dominant position contrary to Article 86.

---

228 See Gough, *Company Charges*, p 226 who cites *Kay Hian & Co (Pte) v Jon Phua Ooi Yong* [1989] 1 MLJ 284 and *Nymph Products Ltd v Heating Centre Pty Ltd* (1992) 7 ACSR 365.

229 *Re Holidair Ltd* [1994] 1 ILRM 481.

230 Chapter 23, *Examinerships*, para **[23.091]** *ff.*

231 C(A)A 1990, ss 7(5A)–7(5C).

232 *Oakdale (Richmond) Ltd v National Westminster Bank plc* [1997] 1 BCLC 63.

These were, undoubtedly, novel and imaginative grounds for seeking to assail a standard form debenture and their formulation was, no doubt, occasioned by some necessity or other.

[20.078] Not surprisingly, Chadwick J held that the prohibition against borrowing and charging of assets without prior written consent was not anti-competitive for the reason that the company was always free to pay off its indebtedness to the chargee-bank with money borrowed from another source and thereby freeing itself from the restriction in the debenture. Moreover, it was held that the requirement that the proceeds of book debts be paid into a designated account was occasioned by the requirement that control be exercised over fixed charges over book debts and it did not have as its object the prevention, restriction or distortion of competition within the EU. The restrictions in the small loans agreements (guaranteed by the British Government) against unsecured borrowing without the bank's consent were held by Chadwick J to be a necessary incident of last resort lending and designed to enable the chargee-bank to protect itself from a material change in the credit risk. In this respect Chadwick J held[233]:

> 'In assessing whether to lend to such a company it is likely to be highly material to evaluate at the time the decision is taken what other borrowing commitments the company has; that is to say it is necessary for the lender to understand the extent to which the company's continued trading is dependent on loan finance. A decision by a bank, made on the basis of material put before it at the time of that decision, would be undermined if the borrower was in a position to increase its borrowings without referring the matter back to the bank. A lender who lends on the basis that the borrower has no other borrowing commitments is concerned to ensure that he does not find, some six or 12 months later, that he is lending to a borrower who has incurred substantial other borrowing commitments.
>
> A restriction, therefore, that the bank must be approached for consent before the company incurs further borrowing may be seen as a necessary incident of the small firms loan guarantee scheme. It is necessary that a bank which is to participate in a scheme of last resort lending has the means to protect itself from a material change in the credit risk which it has agreed to undertake.'

It is opined that this reasoning will apply, with equal force, to most loans made by banks to companies where there is any credit assessment since a company's liabilities and repayment capacity are central to most decisions to lend. Finally, it was held that the company had not established an arguable case that the bank enjoyed a dominant position within the relevant market since it was one of a number of lenders to the small trading company sector, within the UK.

Events which affect assets subject to floating charges

[20.079] In the intervening period between when a company creates a floating charge and when it crystallises, the company may deal with its assets as it sees fit in the ordinary course of its business[234]. Where a company disposes of its assets and receives

---

[233] [1997] 1 BCLC 63 at 76j–77b.

[234] Subject, that is, to any provisions as to the general protection of the assets which may well be found in a modern well-drafted debenture.

consideration, those assets will no longer be subject to the floating charge where the company retains bare legal title[235].

[20.080] In the same way, third parties may cause steps to be taken against the chargor-company which affect the assets of the company, including those assets which are subject to the floating charge[236]. This can happen in several ways, namely by the creation of subsequent charges, the application of the rules of set-off or by the existence of a lien[237].

(a) Subsequent mortgages and charges

[20.081] Since a floating charge is inchoate until the moment of crystallisation, if a company creates a subsequent fixed mortgage or charge over assets that are subject to a prior floating charge, the subsequent fixed mortgagee or chargee will have priority over the holder of the floating charge[238]. This will be the case unless the holder of the subsequent charge has notice of the existence of the prior floating charge, or has actual notice of the existence of a negative pledge clause[239]. Likewise, a subsequently created floating charge over part, but not all[240], of the assets of the class which is the subject of the first floating charge will have priority because the company has apparent authority to do this[241]. In a clash of priorities between floating charges it has been held that it is the date of crystallisation of the floating charges and not their date of creation that is critical[242]. The holder of a judgment registered as a judgment mortgage against a company's property which is subject to a floating charge will also have priority to the holder of the floating charge.

(b) Set-off

[20.082] The right to set-off arises[243] in favour of a debtor when the person or company to whom or which he owes money is also his debtor[244]. Before a floating charge crystallises, set-off can operate over assets that are subject to a floating charge, even if

---

235 In *Sharp v Woolwich Building Society* [1998] BCC 115 the House of Lords, on appeal from the First Division of the Inner House of the Court of Session of Scotland, held that where a company was paid the purchase price for an apartment it owned prior to the appointment of a receiver, the apartment was no longer part of the company's 'property and undertaking' and so took free of the floating charge.

236 Eg, when judgment is executed against a company, the judgment holder has priority over the holder of the uncrystallised floating charge.

237 See Lingard, *Bank Security Documents* (3rd edn, 1993), paras 9.4–9.10.

238 See the judgment of North J in *Wheatley v Silkstone and Haigh Moor Coal Co* [1885] 29 Ch D 715 at 724.

239 *Welch v Bowmaker (Ireland) Ltd* [1980] IR 251; *Wilson v Kelland* [1910] 2 Ch 306; and *English and Scottish Mercantile Investment Co Ltd v Bruton* [1892] 2 QB 700.

240 *Re Benjamin Cope & Sons Ltd* [1914] 1 Ch 800.

241 *Re Automatic Bottle Makers Ltd* [1926] Ch 412.

242 *Griffiths v Yorkshire Bank* [1994] 1 WLR 1427.

243 Note that parties can contract out of their right to set–off: *Hong Kong and Shanghai Banking Corp v Kloecker & Co AG* [1989] BCLC 776.

244 See, generally, Donnelly, *The Law of Banks and Credit Institutions* (2000), pp 506–518.

this means that those assets are consequently depleted. This is evidenced by the case of *Re Russell Murphy*[245] where Kenny J reviewed the law and held that:

> '...the debt due to the respondents was in existence when the receiver was appointed, and so the equitable assignment of the future asset (the right to payment of a terminal loss) was always subject to the right of set off.'[246]

The converse situation should also be noted, however, namely, that where a floating charge has crystallised, then the right of set-off no longer exists[247].

(c) Liens

[20.083] Where a lien arises before a floating charge crystallises, the lien will take priority over the floating charge. This is true in respect of liens which are contractual or which arise by operation of law.

Crystallisation of floating charges

[20.084] A floating charge may never crystallise eg where the debt secured by the floating charge is repaid. However, it may not 'float on' indefinitely and a time may come when it is said to crystallise. If this happens, it is as if a net drops over whatever assets the company has within the class or classes of assets, which are the subject of the floating charge. The *effect* is that the charge becomes a quasi-fixed charge[248]. As has been stated by Farrar in his frequently cited article[249], crystallisation is:

> '...the process whereby the charge attaches specifically to all the items of the class of mortgaged assets which the company owns at that date or subsequently acquires if future assets are within the scope of this particular charge. The latter assets become subject to a fixed charge as they come into existence. In relation to debts the fixed charge operates as an equitable assignment.'

The rights enjoyed by the holder of a floating charge are rights which exist in equity, and up until the moment of crystallisation are properly described as being *inchoate*[250]. After the occurrence of a crystallising event (considered next) the holder of the charge becomes entitled to fixed, tangible equitable rights. Existing assets within the ambit of the floating charge's net are said to be assigned to the holder of the charge, as are future assets which come into the class of property which is subject to the floating charge[251]. Statute law in some jurisdictions distinguishes between fixed charges originally created as such and (quasi) fixed charges that were originally created as floating charges. So, for

---

245 *Re Russell Murphy* [1976] IR 15.

246 [1976] IR 15 at 19. See also *Rother Iron Works Ltd v Canterbury Precision Engineers Ltd* [1974] QB 1, referred to by Kenny J.

247 See *Lynch v Ardmore Studios (Ireland) Ltd* [1966] IR 133, per Budd J.

248 Although it should be noted that it may be set aside where created within certain time scales, unlike a fixed charge.

249 Farrar, 'The Crystallisation of a Floating Charge' (1976) 40 Conv NS 397 at 398.

250 See Ussher, *Company Law in Ireland* (1986), p 431. See para **[20.065]**.

251 See *Lynch v Ardmore Studios (Ireland) Ltd* [1966] IR 133, and *Re Interview Ltd* [1975] IR 383, where Kenny J said: '[crystallisation] of a floating charge on the assets of a company operates as an equitable assignment of the property and goods owned by the company to the debenture holder'. See also *Tempany v Hynes* [1976] IR 101 at 116, per Kenny J.

example, s 251 of the Insolvency Act 1986 (UK) defines 'floating charge' to mean a 'charge which, as created, was a floating charge'.

The causes of crystallisation

[20.085] Two eventualities are well established as causing a floating charge to *crystallise*: the appointment of a receiver to a chargor company, and the commencement of a chargor-company's winding up. More contentious, however, are situations where a debenture purports to deem a floating charge to crystallise on the occasion of an event other than the established two, above. It is important to distinguish between situations where a debenture holder takes steps to cause a floating charge to crystallise and where it crystallises independently of any intervention by a debenture holder. Thus, the appointment of a receiver is an act of the debenture holder, while the commencement of a winding up may be an act independent of the debenture holder. *Ceasing to carry on business* can either be an event which is contained in the debenture and agreed to be an event which will crystallise a floating charge or could also be an event which will automatically cause the floating charge to crystallise.

(a) The appointment of a receiver

[20.086] It is beyond doubt that where a chargee causes a receiver to be appointed either by relying on the terms of the debenture or by order of the court, this will cause a floating charge to crystallise. One Irish authority on this point is *Halpin v Cremin*[252] where this was confirmed in the judgment of Lavery J[253]. The mere taking of steps to appoint a receiver will be insufficient to cause a floating charge to crystallise[254]. Where *another* debenture holder causes a receiver to be appointed to a company, this will usually have the effect of causing *all* floating charges created by that company to crystallise. This is because most debentures simply provide that the appointment of a receiver will cause the debenture holder's floating charge to crystallise and do not specify that the receiver must be appointed by them.

(b) The winding up of the chargor company

[20.087] Similarly, a floating charge will crystallise where the chargor-company goes into liquidation and the process of winding up commences. The reason for this has been given by Warrington J in *Re Crompton & Co Ltd*[255] where he said:

> '...I think there can be no question at all that according to ordinary principles the winding up puts an end to the period of suspension; and the reason that it does that is that the effect of the winding up is to put an end to the floating nature of the security.'[256]

---

[252] *Halpin v Cremin* [1954] IR 19 at 24.

[253] See also, *Re Panama, New Zealand and Australian Mail Co* (1870) 10 Ch D 530; *Nelson & Co v Faber & Co* [1903] 2 KB 367; *Evans v Rival Granite Quarries Ltd* [1910] 2 KB 979; *NW Robbie & Co v Witney Warehouse Co* [1963] 3 All ER 316; and *Farrar* (1976) 40 Conv NS 397 at 398.

[254] *Re Roundwood Colliery* Co [1897] 1 Ch 371.

[255] *Re Crompton & Co Ltd* [1914] 1 Ch 954.

[256] [1914] 1 Ch 954 at 963.

A floating charge will crystallise whether a company is wound up by its members or creditors voluntarily, or compulsorily, by the court[257].

(c) The giving of notice[258]

[20.088] The mere service of notice on the chargor-company that the floating charge is to crystallise forthwith, can cause a floating charge to crystallise where such is provided for in the instrument creating the floating charge. The giving of notice can be seen as a withdrawal of the licence to deal with the assets which are the subject of the floating charge. Since the ability to deal with the assets which are subject to a floating charge is the very essence of a floating charge, the withdrawal of that licence necessarily changes the nature of the charge. Although the giving of notice has not traditionally been seen as a crystallising event, it seems clear that it must be such, because the withdrawal of the licence to use the assets in the normal course of business removes the basic trait which distinguishes a floating from a fixed charge.

[20.089] Unlike the appointment of a receiver and the commencement of a winding up which will take effect unless the charge itself provides to the contrary, the *giving of notice* will only be such an event where the charge itself expressly contains such a clause. In practice it will take the form of a 'notice of conversion clause' which empowers the charge holder to *convert* the floating charge into a fixed charge. In *Re Wogan's (Drogheda) Ltd*[259] clause 8 of the debenture in question provided, inter alia:

> 'If the lender shall by notice in writing make a demand on the company as provided for in clause 8E hereof then the floating charge created by clause 4E hereof shall immediately on service of such notice on the company become crystallised and be a specific fixed charge on...[inter alia]...all book debts and other debts and securities due to the company...'

While the Supreme Court did not specifically comment upon the validity of this clause, Finlay CJ referred to clause 8 in the reasoning for his conclusion. It seems inconceivable that the Supreme Court could base its decision, albeit in part[260], on a clause which the law did not consider to be effective. Moreover, there is no sound policy reason why the giving of notice to that effect ought not effect crystallisation.

(d) Ceasing to carry on business[261]

[20.090] The fourth way in which a floating charge can crystallise is where the chargor company ceases to carry on business. While it has not been conclusively established in Ireland that such an event will cause a floating charge to crystallise, it is submitted that when it eventually falls to be decided by the Irish courts, it will be held to be a valid

---

[257] See *Re Colonial Trusts* Corp (1879) 15 Ch D 465 and *Re Crompton & Co Ltd* [1914] 1 Ch 954 which applied the principle to a members voluntary winding up, even for the purposes of reconstruction of the company.

[258] See Sealy, *Cases and Materials in Company Law* (4th edn, 1989), p 380.

[259] *Re Wogan's (Drogheda) Ltd* [1993] 1 IR 157.

[260] [1993] 1 IR 157 at 168.

[261] Gill, 'Ceasing to Carry on Business' and the Concept of Automatic Crystallisation of Floating Charges', (1986) ILT 160.

crystallising event[262]. The principle has now been accepted in England in the case of *Re Woodroffes (Musical Instruments) Ltd*[263]. There, a company created a debenture in favour of a bank, which contained a first fixed charge over certain property and also a floating charge on all the undertaking and assets of the company, present and future, which were not affected by the fixed charge. The debenture allowed the bank to convert the floating charge into a fixed charge upon the bank giving notice to the company. Later, a second floating charge was created by the company in favour of one of the directors of the company, which provided that it too could become *fixed* by the debenture holder giving notice to the company. This second debenture and charge was created in violation of a negative pledge clause contained in the earlier debenture. Shortly afterwards, the director-debenture holder gave the requisite notice that her debenture should crystallise. Some days later, the bank gave notice that all sums due on the debenture should be paid (although it did not give notice that its floating charge should crystallise) upon which the board of directors of the company resolved to invite the bank to appoint a receiver. The bank acted on this invitation. Later, the company went into liquidation and the net question was, which floating charge should have priority, since the company's assets did not satisfy both claims. It was assumed that the director's floating charge had crystallised upon her giving notice to the company.

The bank advanced two main arguments. In the first place it was argued that upon the director-debenture holder giving notice that her charge should crystallise, this had the result that their floating charge also crystallised, in that it should be implied into their debenture that crystallisation of a subsequent charge should also crystallise theirs. The giving of notice by the director-debenture holder, it was argued, had the effect of determining the company's licence to use the assets forming the subject matter of the charge, which would have the effect of *automatically* crystallising their floating charge. Nourse J rejected this argument[264] saying that it appeared to run contrary to 'fundamental principles of the law of contract'. Indeed, he could not see that such action by the director-debenture holder would necessarily cause the company to cease to carry on business. In effect, the motivation of Nourse J was that he was being asked to *imply* an automatic crystallisation clause on the happening of a certain event, into the debenture. This he refused to do, although as we shall see he accepted the validity of an *express* automatic crystallisation clause.

The second proposition of the bank is our present concern. In the words of Nourse J, they argued:

> '...that there was *in fact* a cessation of the company's business [on the giving of notice by the director debenture holder, or prior to their own action] and that that cessation caused an automatic crystallisation of the bank's floating charge.'[265]

---

[262] It is also unclear as to its effectiveness in England, although Lingard, *Bank Security Documents* (3rd edn, 1993), para 9.19 says that: 'The better view is that a floating charge crystallises not only on the appointment of a receiver or the commencement of winding up but immediately a company ceases to carry on business as a going concern'. Cf Keane, *Company Law* (3rd edn, 2000), para 20.67.

[263] *Re Woodroffes (Musical Instruments) Ltd* [1985] BCLC 227.

[264] [1985] BCLC 227 at 231–232.

[265] [1985] BCLC 227 at 232i.

This argument differs from the former, in that its acceptance hinged upon whether or not the judge accepted that cessation of business *in fact* caused a floating charge to crystallise. Having referred to several[266] authorities, Nourse J held that a factual cessation of business was a third circumstance (along with the appointment of a receiver and the commencement of a winding up) in which a floating charge would crystallise. While accepting that there were opinions which hold that 'automatic crystallisation clauses' are undesirable from a policy perspective, Nourse J held:

> 'On the state of the authorities it would be very difficult for me to question it, even if I could see a good reason for doing so. On the contrary, it seems to me that it is in accordance with the essential nature of a floating charge. The thinking behind the creation of such charges has always been a recognition that a fixed charge on the whole undertaking and assets of the company would paralyse it and prevent it from carrying on its business...On the other hand it is a mistake to think that the chargee has no remedy while the charge is still floating. He can always intervene and obtain an injunction to prevent the company from dealing with its assets otherwise than in the ordinary course of its business. That no doubt is one reason why it is preferable to describe the charge as "hovering", a word which can bear an undertone of menace, rather than as "dormant". A cessation of business necessarily puts an end to the company's dealings with its assets. That which kept the charge hovering has not been released and the force of gravity causes it to settle and fasten on the subject of the charge within its reach and grasp.'[267]

Thus, where a company 'ceases to carry on business'[268], any floating charge created by that company will crystallise, in just the same way as it would were a receiver appointed or were the company wound up. While this is the law in England, and other Commonwealth countries, it remains to be seen whether this reasoning will be accepted in Ireland. More recently in *Re The Real Meat Co Ltd*[269] it was held by Chadwick J that the effect of a company selling its business was to cause a floating charge to automatically crystallise because the sale of a company's business amounted to a cessation of business which was an implied ground for crystallisation.

[20.091] It has been questioned whether this is the law in Ireland[270]. Policy considerations aside, the bedrock of possible objection is the case of *Halpin v Cremin*[271]. In that case, the plaintiff sought a declaration that he owned certain lands, formerly owned by the Listowel and Ballybunion Railway Company ('the company'), by virtue

[266] *Government Stock and other Securities Investment Co v Manila Rly Co* [1897] AC 81; *Hubbuck v Helms* (1887) 56 LJ Ch 536; *Robson v Smith* [1895] 2 Ch 118, *Re Victoria Steamboats Ltd* [1897] 1 Ch 228; *Davey & Co v Williamson & Sons Ltd* [1898] 2 QB 194; *Re Yorkshire Woolcombers' Association Ltd* [1904] AC 355; *Edward Nelson & Co Ltd v Faber & Co* [1903] 2 KB 367; *Evans v Rival Granite Quarries Ltd* [1910] 2 KB 979; and *Re Crompton & Co Ltd* [1914] 1 Ch 954.

[267] [1985] BCLC 227 at 233, 234.

[268] As distinct from ceasing to be a going concern on which Nourse J did not comment, if there was a difference between the two concepts.

[269] *Re The Real Meat Co Ltd* [1996] BCC 254.

[270] See Ussher, *Company Law in Ireland* (1986) and Gill, 'Ceasing to Carry on Business and the Concept of Automatic Crystallisation of Floating Charges' (1986) ILT 160.

[271] *Halpin v Cremin* [1954] IR 19.

of a purchase made by him in 1942 and an order of the High Court which had vested in him the estate and interest theretofore vested in the company. The company had acquired those lands by virtue of an Act of 1886[272]. Two years later, the company executed a debenture in favour of the Debenture Corporation Ltd over the entire undertaking of the company. The company ran its last train in 1924, the track being removed from the land the following year. The defendant then entered on that land, and remained in exclusive and uninterrupted possession for many years. In 1928 the then owner of the debenture obtained a declaration that he was entitled to a lien or mortgage under the debenture on inter alia the lands in question. In 1942, the present plaintiff obtained the order referred to at the outset, but the defendant objected, claiming that he had acquired title through adverse possession. In the Circuit Court, the plaintiff lost his case for failing to show that the lands in question were part of the undertaking and premises owned by the company.

Lavery J held that nothing was done by the debenture holder or its successors and assigns to cause the floating charge to crystallise prior to when the squatter entered into adverse possession of the lands in question. In passing, he said[273] 'the charge becomes specific on the appointment of a receiver or on a winding up'. Since neither of these happened, Lavery J held that the floating charge had not crystallised. However, one cannot say with any conviction that this case is unequivocal authority for the proposition that a company's cessation of business does not cause a floating charge to crystallise.

[20.092] In the first place, it can only be implied into the judgment of Lavery J that the fact that the company ceased to carry on business prior to when the defendant squatter entered into occupation of the lands was not an event which in law would crystallise the floating charge. Nowhere in his judgment is this proposition canvassed by counsel for the plaintiff, nor indeed does Lavery J himself even allude to this point. Rather, that he made the point at all is pure surmise, particularly in that there is no statement that the appointment of a receiver or a winding up are the sole events which cause crystallisation: he does not purport to be exhaustive. In the second place, while citing authorities such as *Government Stock v Manila Ry Co*[274] *and Evans v Rival Granite Quarries Ltd*[275] he did not allude to the fact that these suggested that ceasing to carry on business can cause a floating charge to crystallise: see *Re Woodroffes (Musical Instruments) Ltd*[276]. In the third place, the decision of Lavery J can be seen as indicative of a judiciary eager to give full effect to the legislative intent found in the statute similar to the modern s 13 of the Statute of Limitations 1957. Such legislative enactments are intended to 'quieten title to land' and avoid doubts as to ownership. In order to upset that intention he would have had to presumably[277] raise a point which was not raised before him in argument by counsel. It is submitted that the decision in the case can thus be

272 49 Vict, c vii.

273 [1954] IR 19 at 24.

274 *Government Stock v Manila Ry Co* [1901] 1 Ch 326.

275 *Evans v Rival Granite Quarries Ltd* [1910] 2 KB 979.

276 *Re Woodroffes (Musical Instruments) Ltd* [1985] BCLC 227.

277 'Presumably', in view of the fact that while the argument of counsel is not reported in the law report, it is still possible that such could have been raised, though not reported.

explained. Finally, and most importantly, it is submitted that the fact that this decision was made in 1953 is of significance, particularly in view of the radical developments in both company and commercial law over even the last decade. In the view of the writer, the decision of *Halpin v Cremin* is not authority for the proposition that 'ceasing to carry on business' will not cause a floating charge to crystallise in Ireland[278].

(e) Automatic crystallisation clauses[279]

[20.093] An automatic crystallisation clause purports to deem in advance the occurrence of an event, other than the four preceding events, to cause the floating charge to crystallise. Such clauses are intended to mitigate the effects of the statutory limits placed on the floating charge, and while as yet untested in Ireland, are to be found in most Irish debentures. Among those events which are commonly stated to cause automatic crystallisation are:

- — the giving of notice by the debenture holder;
- — an attempt to create a subsequent charge;
- — any attempt by another to levy execution against the company;
- — non-payment of loan instalments.

There are of course many other events, and probably more which will be inserted into charges in the future.

[20.094] Of all the events which may cause a floating charge to crystallise, automatic crystallisation clauses are the most contentious. The essence of the objection is based on policy. As one commentator has observed[280]:

> 'There are two schools of thought on this question. One takes the view that the floating charge is not an established phenomenon having fixed characteristics, but is simply the creature of the draughtsman and that a creditor is free to strengthen his security in this way if he wants to. The other looks at the effect of such an arrangement on third parties and contends that it must be against public policy to have a charge crystallise in circumstances which may be unknown (and perhaps even unknowable) at the time, so that a company could not give a buyer a good title even though everyone was acting in good faith.'

Those opposed to the acceptance of automatic crystallisation clauses in charges, include Keane[281] who says:

> 'It is thought, however, that this line of authority is unlikely to be followed in Ireland. The courts here will probably incline to the view that such automatic crystallisation would present problems for other creditors who would have no actual notice of the terms of the debenture and that any such doctrine would need to be the subject of considered legislation and regulation.'

[20.095] The writer respectfully disagrees with the learned judge's views and it is to be hoped that, on full reflection, the Irish courts will accept the validity of such clauses.

---

278 Note the comments of Gill, 'Ceasing to Carry on Business' and the Concept of Automatic Crystallisation of Floating Charges' (1986) ILT 160 at 161.

279 See Lingard, *Bank Security Documents* (3rd edn, 1993), para 9.25 – 9.31.

280 Sealy, *Cases and Materials in Company Law* (4th edn, 1989), p 380.

281 Keane, *Company Law* (3rd edn, 2000), para 20.67.

This stance is based on three objections. In the first place, it is doubted that problems will necessarily be caused for creditors. Other opinion[282] suggests that notwithstanding that the chargor-company will have no legal power to deal with the assets which were subject of a floating charge, but are not subject to a fixed charge, it remains the case that the company will have *ostensible authority* to deal with those assets. Indeed, a subsequent bona fide legal purchaser for value of such assets will, where the equities are equal, take priority over the prior equitable owner of a fixed charge[283]. It will only be where the subsequent purchaser has notice, actual or constructive, of the prior equitable floating (now fixed) charge, that he will be defeated.

In the second place, it is submitted that it would be misconceived for a court to impose additional restrictions on floating charges when the legislature have already made encroachments. Thus floating charges created within certain time periods before a company is wound up are liable to lose priority[284], and floating charges rank behind certain preferential creditors in priority[285]. For the courts to impose an additional limitation, in the form of a fetter on the freedom of the parties to contract, would, it is submitted, be judicial law-making and unconstitutional. This is in effect the view of Hoffmann J in *Re Brightlife Ltd*[286] who commented on existing legislative limitations thus:

> 'These limited and pragmatic interventions by the legislature make it in my judgment wholly inappropriate for the courts to impose additional restrictive rules on grounds of public policy. It is certainly not for a judge of first instance to proclaim a new head of public policy which no appellate court has even hinted at before. I would therefore respectfully prefer the decision of the New Zealand Supreme Court in *Re Manurewa Transport Ltd* [1971] NZLR 909, recognising the validity of a provision for automatic crystallisation, to the contrary dicta in the Canadian case[287] I have cited.'

Hoffmann J did not feel it was necessary to decide the question of the validity of the clause, although in the later *Re Permanent Houses (Holdings) Ltd*[288] he upheld the validity of such a clause which effected the crystallisation of a floating charge when a stated event of default occurred. Since the legislature can impose a third statutory restriction, it could provide that the Form C1, used to register charges created by a company, should note whether or not the charge includes an automatic crystallisation clause. Such would give any subsequent outsiders ample opportunity to enquire further.

In the third place, the floating charge is a creation of the draftsman, and as such is a *right* and does not exist by virtue of any *licence*, granted by the legislature. As Hoffmann J said, 'I do not think that it is open to the courts to restrict the contractual freedom of parties to a floating charge...'.[289]. It is submitted that where a charge clearly contains an

---

282 See Goode, *Commercial Law* (1982), p 799.

283 See the discussion of priorities in equity, in Keane, *Equity and the Law of Trusts in the Republic of Ireland*, (1988), Ch 5.

284 See CA 1963, s 288.

285 See CA 1963, s 285(2).

286 [1986] BCLC 418 at 427–428.

287 *R v Consolidated Churchill Copper Corp Ltd* [1978] WLR 652.

288 *Re Permanent Houses (Holdings) Ltd* [1988] BCLC 56.

unequivocal automatic crystallisation[290] clause, there is no reason why the courts should not give effect to the parties' contractual agreement.

The de-crystallisation of floating charges

[20.096] Until recent times, it was a generally[291] held view that once a floating charge crystallised, it could not de-crystallise. The Supreme Court in *Re Holidair Ltd*[292] has turned this view on its head by holding that the appointment of an examiner pursuant to C(A)A 1990 will de-crystallise a crystallised floating charge. Having held[293] that the debenture in question created a floating charge over the companies' book debts, Blayney J acknowledged that it had crystallised upon the appointment of the receiver. However, he went on to hold that upon the appointment of an examiner, the crystallised floating charge de-crystallised. It is submitted that since floating charges are essentially matters of contract between the parties there is nothing in principle that should prevent the parties to a debenture from providing that a particular floating charge is *incapable* of de-crystallising, thereby distinguishing it from the floating charge (that was silent on that point) in *Re Holidair Ltd*. The decision in *Re Holidair Ltd* is considered further, and critiqued, in Chapter 23[294].

289 See Hoffmann J in *Re Brightlife Ltd* [1986] BCLC 418 at 427–428.

290 See the comments of Hoffmann J in *Re Permanent Houses (Holdings) Ltd* [1988] BCLC 563 at 567 d–e.

291 See Gough, *Company Charges*, (2nd edn, 1996), pp 404–407.

292 *Re Holidair Ltd* [1994] 1 ILRM 481.

293 See para **[20.044]**.

294 Chapter 23, *Examinerships*, para **[23.071]–[23.072]**.

Chapter 21

Corporate Borrowing: Registration of Charges

Introduction

[21.001] It is vital to realise that before certain mortgages and charges will be valid and have priority over subsequent mortgages and charges, they must be registered pursuant to the Companies Acts 1963–2001. Such charges are referred to here as registrable charges[1]. In addition to the Companies Acts, a number of other registration systems exist where mortgages and charges of certain types of property must also be registered. In this chapter the following issues are considered:

1. The register of charges.
2. The consequences of non-registration.
3. The conclusiveness of the certificate of registration.
4. Non-registrable security interests
5. Registrable charges.
6. Disguised registrable charges: retention of title clauses
7. Judgment mortgages
8. Charges over property outside of the State.
9. Charges created by foreign companies.
10. Late registration of registrable charges.
11. Registration.
12. Particulars required to be registered.
13. Satisfaction of charges
14. The chargor-company's obligations.
15. Other registration systems.
16. Stamp duty on security instruments.

The register of charges

[21.002] Section 103 of the Companies Act 1963 ('CA 1963') prescribes that the Registrar of Companies shall keep, in relation to each company, a register of all charges which are required to be registered under CA 1963, Part IV[2]. The basic principle to be remembered is

---

1 See Gough, *Company Charges* (2nd edn, 1996); Johnston, *Banking and Security Law in Ireland* (1998), Ch 17; Lingard, *Bank Security Documents* (3rd edn, 1993), Ch 3; and Schmitthoff (ed), *Palmer's Company Law*, (24th edn, 1987), para 46–01 *ff*.

2 CA 1963, s 103 goes on to provide that the Registrar of Companies shall on payment of a fee – currently €30 – enter certain details in the register. This register is open to the public for inspection, an invitation which is generally only availed of by law searchers on behalf of solicitors.

that where a company creates a registrable charge[3], particulars of such a charge must be delivered, in the prescribed form, to the companies registration office ('CRO'). The failure to deliver particulars within the prescribed 21 days will render the mortgage or charge *void* against a liquidator of the company or any creditor of the company. The basic requirement and most far-reaching sanction is contained in CA 1963, s 99(1), which provides:

> 'Subject to the provisions of this Part, every charge created after the fixed date by a company, and being a charge to which this section applies, shall, so far as any security on the company's property or undertaking is conferred thereby, be void against the liquidator and any creditor of the company, unless the prescribed particulars of the charge, verified in the prescribed manner, are delivered to or received by the registrar of companies for registration in manner required by this Act within 21 days after the date of its creation, but without prejudice to any contract or obligation for repayment of the money thereby secured, and when a charge becomes void under this section, the money secured thereby shall immediately become payable.'

(a) The rationale for the register of charges

[21.003] The rationale[4] behind the requirement that certain charges created by companies must be registered is to afford protection to creditors of the company by providing them with a means of discovering whether a particular company has secured creditors[5]. This protection is intended for both secured and unsecured creditors. However, this objective will not be realised unless subsequent creditors actually search against a company in the CRO. As Palmer has noted[6], the object of the legislation is to enable creditors to search the register. The result of such a search will show either that the company's property is encumbered or not with registrable charges. Thus, in the case of *Esberger & Son Ltd v Capital and Counties Bank*[7] Sargant J said that the object of registration was to:

> '... show what moneys are owing by the company on certain securities, so that the creditors may have some notion of how far the property of the company is unencumbered.'

Having this knowledge, the rationale continues that the creditor will then make an informed decision as to whether or not to deal with the company. Such a system of registration is not peculiar to companies. In the case of individuals, there is a somewhat similar, albeit infrequently used system under the Bills of Sale (Ireland) Acts 1879–1883[8]. However, even in the case of companies, while the object of the legislation aims for full consensual dealing by creditors with a company, the reality is somewhat different. In the first place, as we shall see below, not all security interests are registrable (not even all consensually created security interests). In the second place, to expect all

3 'Registrable charge' refers to those charges described in CA 1963, s 99(2), and which are considered at para **[21.033]** *ff*.

4 See generally Gough, *Company Charges* (2nd edn, 1996).

5 See *Re International Retail Ltd* (25 July 1974, unreported) High Court, per Kenny J.

6 Schmitthoff (ed), *Palmer's Company Law* (24th edn, 1987), para 46.03.

7 *Esberg & Son Ltd v Capital and Counties Bank* [1913] 2 Ch 366 at 374.

8 See para **[21.037]**.

creditors, particularly those who are unsecured such as suppliers of goods, to examine the register, assumes too much.

(b) Notice of the register of charges

[21.004] In various places throughout this work[9] it has been noted that documents registered with the CRO are *public documents* and that third parties dealing with a company will, generally, be deemed to have constructive notice of matters which are registered. The general rule is true in the case of charges that are registered pursuant to CA 1963, s 99. Accordingly, persons who deal with a company will be deemed to have notice of the existence of charges that are duly registered[10].

[21.005] The exception to the general rule that the public have constructive notice of matters registered with the CRO is that it has been consistently held that the 'unruly horse'[11] of constructive notice does not extend beyond the particulars which have been recorded. The seminal Supreme Court decision in *Welch v Bowmaker (Ireland) Ltd and the Governor and Company of the Bank of Ireland*[12], which has been considered in Chapter 20, decided that the public will not have constructive notice of negative pledge clauses[13].

The consequences of non-registration

[21.006] Where particulars of a registrable charge are not delivered within 21 days of its creation, CA 1963, s 99(1) provides that it shall be void against the liquidator and any creditor of the company[14]. It is vital to realise that non-registration of a registrable charge will not entirely vitiate that charge, which will still be enforceable against the company[15], and indeed the sum secured by the charge will become immediately payable[16]. Rather, it is the case that if another creditor of the company exists, secured or unsecured, then the holder of the unregistered charge will not have priority over that other creditor[17]. In *Re Monolithic Building Co*[18], Phillimore LJ said of the predecessor of s 99(1) that:

---

9 See Chapter 3, *Private Constitutional Documentation*, para **[3.112]** and Chapter 7, *Corporate Contracts, Capacity and Authority*, para **[7.116]**.

10 See, eg, *Siebe Gorman & Co Ltd v Barclays Bank Ltd* [1979] 2 Lloyds Rep 142 at 615.

11 Per Parke J in *Welch v Bowmaker (Ireland) Ltd and the Governor and Company of the Bank of Ireland* [1980] IR 251.

12 *Welch v Bowmaker (Ireland) Ltd and the Governor and Company of the Bank of Ireland* [1980] IR 251.

13 See Chapter 20, *Corporate Borrowing: Debentures and Security*, para **[20.068]** *ff*. See also Johnston, *Banking and Security Law in Ireland* (1998), pp 611–616.

14 See *Re Clarets Ltd; Spain v McCann* [1978] ILRM 215 at 217, per Costello J, where there is a statement of the obvious effect of non–registration under CA 1963, s 99.

15 *Wright v Horton* [1887] 12 AC 371.

16 CA 1963, s 99(1).

17 Of course priority will only be an issue where a company is insolvent and accordingly the security will stand as against the company when it is a going concern.

18 *Re Monolithic Building Co* [1915] 1 Ch 643.

> 'It makes void a security; not the debt, not the cause of action, but the security, and not as against everybody, not as against the company grantor, but against the liquidator, and against any creditor, and it leaves the security to stand as against the company while it is a going concern. It does not make the security binding on the liquidator as successor of the company.'[19]

[21.007] The reference there to the fact that an unregistered charge is void but 'not as against *everybody*' was taken to peculiar lengths by the English Court of Appeal before they were reigned-in by the House of Lords on appeal in *Smith (Administrator of Cosslett (Contractors) Ltd) v Bridgend County Borough Council*[20]. The facts in that case have been reviewed in Chapter 20[21] and it is sufficient for present purposes to note that a contract was found to have unintentionally created a floating charge. In the Court of Appeal it had been said by Laws LJ that:

> '…the failure to register the floating charge, which as this court found was constituted by cl 63, in my judgment conferred on the respondent administrator a purely adventitious potential claim in specie to recover or retain the plant as against the appellants if it lay in their hands after completion of the works. This inchoate claim had nothing to do with the true state of account between the company and the appellants as it would fall to be ascertained for the purposes of a just and reasonable approach to the administration or…liquidation of the company.'[22]

The Court of Appeal went on to say that the only circumstances in which an unregistered charge would be void would be where a liquidator or administrator was suing *in his personal name* as, for example, under CA 1963, s 236[23]. This, of course, not only over-turned a century of received judicial wisdom (and legitimate expectation of the commercial community) but also made a total mockery out of the purpose of registration. It was not conceivable that it would stand. In the House of Lords, Lord Hoffmann stated that he considered that the grounds upon which the Court of Appeal had decided the case to be 'startling and unorthodox', rejecting as it had the accepted effects of a failure to register a registrable charge. To the extent that the Court of Appeal had said that an unregistered charge was void only as against a liquidator or, under English law, an administrator, acting personally this was overruled. Lord Hoffmann restated that an unregistered charge is 'void against a company acting by its liquidator'.[24] Moreover, Lord Scott said that where a security is barred from being enforceable because of non-registration, it is no part of equity to provide, via equitable set-off, an alternative security[25].

---

[19] [1915] 1 Ch 643 at 667–668.

[20] *Smith (Administrator of Cosslett (Contractors) Ltd) v Bridgend County Borough Council* [2002] 1 All ER 292.

[21] At para **[20.069]** *ff*.

[22] [2000] 1 BCLC 775 at 791.

[23] The English Court of Appeal specifically referred to the similar English provision, Insolvency Act 1986, s 234 (UK).

[24] [2002] 1 All ER 292 at para [21]. And, in England, as against a company in administration: see [2002] 1 All ER 292 at para [31].

[25] [2002] 1 All ER 292 at para [79].

[21.008] A registrable charge that is not registered will be void against a subsequent creditor even where that creditor is aware of the prior charge. Authority for this is again the case of *Re Monolithic Building Co*[26] where the subsequent encumbrancer, who registered his charge notwithstanding his knowledge of the existence of a prior unregistered mortgage, was held, by the Court of Appeal, to have priority. His knowledge of the prior charge did not preclude him from insisting on his rights as a registered debenture holder[27].

[21.009] Serious problems can arise where a charge is created which is not perceived to be a registrable charge and which is consequently not registered. As will be considered in some detail later in this chapter[28], a retention of title clause in a contract for the sale of goods can, in certain circumstances, be found to be a registrable charge. An example of the consequences that befall the holder of such a charge is *Carroll Group Distributors Ltd v G & JF Bourke Ltd*[29]. In that case the plaintiff supplied goods to the defendant-company under a contract that allowed four weeks' credit. The contract also contained a retention of title clause which provided that the property in the goods would remain with the plaintiff until the defendants had discharged all sums due to the plaintiff. The clause gave the defendant an express right to sell the goods, subject to the defendant-company holding all proceeds of sale 'in trust' for the plaintiff. When the defendant-company went into liquidation, the issue arose as to whether or not this retention of title clause constituted a registrable charge. Holding that this particular clause was properly construed as a registrable charge, Murphy J said:

> '...parties cannot escape the inference that a transaction constitutes a mortgage registrable under s 99 aforesaid by particular labels to the transaction. The rights of the parties and the nature of the transaction in which they engage must be determined from a consideration of the document as a whole and the obligations and rights which it imposes on both parties...The description may be a material consideration but clearly it cannot be decisive. Specifically in relation to mortgages registrable under the Companies Acts it has been held that it is in the substance of the transaction as ascertained from the words used by the parties and the context in which the document is executed that determines registrability under the Companies Acts ... effectively [the defendant-company] were creating or conferring a charge on the proceeds of sale in substitution for the right of property which [the plaintiff] had previously enjoyed. The charge so created required registration under s 99 of the Companies Act 1963 and in the absence of such registration was invalid.'[30]

Accordingly, the plaintiff-company lost any security interest it claimed because the retention of title clause was void against the liquidator and other creditors of the defendant-company. What this case shows is that extreme caution ought to be exercised

26 *Re Monolithic Building Co* [1915] 1 Ch 643.

27 Cf *Re Clarets Ltd; Spain v McCann* [1978] ILRM 215 at 218 where Costello J distinguished this case from the case in hand.

28 See para **[21.057]** *ff*.

29 [1990] ILRM 285. For analysis, see Maguire, 'Romalpa Misinterpreted' (1989) DULJ 40 at 53 *ff*.

30 [1990] ILRM 285 at 290.

so as to ensure that any transaction does not result in a corporate party thereto unconsciously creating a registrable charge.

The conclusiveness of the certificate of registration

[21.010] When the Registrar of Companies receives particulars of a registrable charge he will in due course issue a certificate of registration that the charge has been registered in accordance with CA 1963, s 99. Section 104 of CA 1963 provides that the certificate of registration is conclusive evidence that the requirements of CA 1963, Part IV have been complied with.

[21.011] The certificate of registration remains conclusive evidence even where the parties creating the charge act in a manner that was not contemplated by the legislature. Thus, in *Lombard & Ulster Banking Ireland Ltd v Amurec Ltd*[31] the plaintiff-bank made loan facilities available to the defendant-company ('Amurec') to enable it to purchase property. On the completion of the conveyance in November 1972, Amurec gave the deed of conveyance of, and the deed of mortgage and charge over, the property, along with documents of title, to the plaintiff-bank's solicitors. Both deeds had been left undated. Amurec's solicitor gave an undertaking to give £3,500 to the plaintiff-bank's solicitors for the stamping of the deeds. There was a delay in providing the stamp duty and, eventually, in March 1974 when the plaintiff-bank's solicitors still had not received funds for stamping they decided to proceed and used their own funds, and so the conveyance and mortgage were stamped and dated 21 and 22 March 1974, respectively. The mortgage was then lodged with the Registrar of Companies who issued a certificate of registration. The certificate of registration of the charge certified that the date of the creation of the charge was 22 March 1974 and that the date of registration was 10 April 1974. The liquidator of Amurec contended that the plaintiff-bank's charge was void because particulars of the charge had not been delivered to the Registrar within the prescribed 21 days, as required by CA 1963, s 99(1). It was held by Hamilton J that the charge was valid because the certificate of registration was conclusive evidence that the requirements of CA 1963, Part IV had been complied with and in particular that the charge had been registered within the prescribed 21 days. In his judgment, he recited the wording of CA 1963, s 104 and accepted the argument of counsel for the plaintiff-bank that since it was expressly stated to be conclusive as to the fact that the requirements of CA 1963 had been complied with, this included the time within which charges had to be registered. While he had considerable sympathy with the submissions of the liquidator, he found himself bound by the express provisions of s 104. Thus he followed Pennycuick J in *Re Eric Holmes (Property) Ltd*[32] where he had held that the certificate was conclusive evidence that the delivery of particulars had been within 21 days, even though an incorrect date had been inserted. The reason why Hamilton J decided as he did was based on the fact that 'the wording of s 104 is clear and unambiguous.'[33]

[21.012] The rationale behind the conclusive evidence provision is seen in *Re CL Nye Ltd*[34], a case cited with approval by Hamilton J in the *Amurec* case. There again, a

31 *Lombard & Ulster Banking Ireland Ltd v Amurec Ltd* [1976–7] ILRM 222.

32 *Re Eric Holmes (Property) Ltd* [1965] Ch 1052.

33 [1976–1997] ILRM 222 at 228.

34 *Re CL Nye Ltd* [1970] 3 All ER 1061.

company had created a charge over property it had purchased and in February 1964 had handed the charge and the transfer to the solicitor for the chargee-bank, undated for the purpose of the solicitor vetting the title for the bank. In March 1964 the solicitor reported that the security was good and the bank then lent to the company. Through an oversight, the charge was not registered and it was only on 3 July 1964 that particulars were delivered to the Registrar of Companies, stating that the charge had been created on 18 June 1964 (ie a mere 15 days' previously). This was innocently accepted by the Registrar and a certificate of registration was issued to the bank. The Court of Appeal held that the charge was valid, again on the basis that the certificate of the Registrar was conclusive evidence that the requirements of the Companies Act had been complied with. In the course of his judgment, Harman LJ stated:

> 'In my judgment the certificate must be conclusive...The whole point of creating the register under [CA 1963, s 99] is to give security to persons relying on the certificate. If it were possible to go behind the certificate and show that the date of creation of the charge made it out of time, no lender on the face of the charge could be secure and sure that it would not thereafter be attacked by somebody who could successfully prove that there was in fact an interval of more than twenty-one days between the charge's creation and its registration. This would be disastrous in my opinion and is not a view to be taken unless the language positively compels it.'[35]

It is, therefore, accepted law that the certificate of registration of a charge is conclusive evidence that the relevant particulars were registered.

(a) The significance of mistakes in the Form C1

[21.013] *Re Mechanisations (Eaglecliffe) Ltd*[36] is authority for the proposition that even where the particulars of the amount charged in the debenture are incorrect, this will not invalidate the certificate of registration. This has been followed in Ireland by Costello J in *Re Shannonside Holdings Ltd*[37]. In that case it was claimed that the company had created a debenture in favour of the estate of the late Mr Barrett, who was the promoter of the company and, also, who had advanced substantial sums to the company. On 25 May 1973 the directors of the company met in Chicago and agreed to grant a debenture to Mr Barrett. The debenture was then executed in favour of Mr Barrett. On 14 June 1973, Irish solicitors acting for the company filed a Form 47 (the predecessor to the Form C1) in respect of the debenture. The debenture was subsequently lost. Costello J accepted, on the balance of probabilities, that the debenture had been executed. One of the issues which also arose for consideration concerned the amount secured by the debenture. Costello J said:

> 'I now come to the terms of the debenture. In light of the submissions made by counsel it is perfectly clear that the debenture which is now lost was not limited to the sum of £200,000 which appears in Form 47. The explanation for that figure being in the debenture is, I think, to be found in the documents which indicate that it was to be stamped at this figure and that is why this figure was inserted in Form 47.

35 [1970] 3 All ER 1061 at 1069.

36 *Re Mechanisations (Eaglecliffe) Ltd* [1964] 3 All ER 840.

37 *Re Shannonside Holdings Ltd* (20 May 1993, unreported) High Court.

> One of the authorities to which I have been referred, *Re Mechanisations (Eaglescliffe) Ltd* [1964] 3 All ER 840, makes clear that what the court is required to do is to give effect to the document creating the charge and not to the particulars given in Form 47.'[38]

Accordingly, while the certificate of registration will be conclusive evidence that particulars of the charge were delivered in accordance with the requirements of CA 1963, the actual terms of the debenture itself will always have precedence over the particulars contained in the Form C1[39].

[21.014] More recently in *Re Valley Ice Cream (Ireland) Ltd*[40], the facts of which were considered in Chapter 20[41], the liquidator of a company which had given an irrevocable undertaking to execute a mortgage on certain refrigerator equipment, challenged the registration of that charge. The basis of the challenge was that a Form 47 that had been filed in the CRO had incorrectly referred to '... the execution of a mortgage over the equipment in the form attached in the first schedule to the debenture'; in fact, the draft mortgage which the company undertook to procure to be executed was contained in the *fifth schedule* to the debenture. On this point McCracken J said:

> 'It is suggested that this is misleading, as any creditor looking at the file in the companies office would not realise or understand the form of the mortgage to be executed. In my view, this is not relevant, as what is registered is the fact that there is an irrevocable undertaking to procure the execution of a mortgage over the equipment, and the equipment is clearly set out in the Form 47. What s 99 requires to be registered is particulars of the charge, not the form which the charge is to take. In my view, it is quite clear from what was registered that there was a charge in the form of an irrevocable undertaking to execute a mortgage over this equipment, and that satisfies s 99.'[42]

It is thought that this was a pragmatic decision in which the validity of the charge was upheld in circumstances where to do so was just.

[21.015] A similar approach was taken in *Re Advantage Healthcare (T10) Ltd*[43]. In that case a certificate of registration of charge issued which contained one company's name but another company's registered number. Lightman J rejected the argument that the charge was valid on account of the conclusiveness of the certificate of registration because in providing that the wrong company has complied with the statutory requirements as to the registration of a charge that it had not created, it was 'meaningless and worthless'. Lightman J went on, however, to find that the charge created by the company was valid, saying:

> 'The company's registered number is a detail which the applicant for registration is required to complete, but it cannot fairly be described as 'a particular of the charge' to be registered. It is a particular of the mortgagor. The explanation for the existence of the registered number is to be found in the Companies Act 1985, ss 705 and 706 [UK].

---

38 (20 May 1993, unreported) High Court at p 8.

39 See *National Provincial & Union Bank v Charnley* [1924] 1 KB 431 where the precursor to Form C1 had omitted to contain the categories of property that had been charged.

40 *Re Valley Ice Cream (Ireland) Ltd* (22 July 1998, unreported) High Court (McCracken J).

41 See Chapter 20, *Corporate Borrowing: Debentures and Security*, para **[20.031]**.

42 (22 July 1998, unreported) High Court at p 4.

43 *Re Advantage Healthcare (T10) Ltd* [2000] BCC 985.

> Section 705 requires the registrar to allocate to every company a number to be known as the company's registered number; and s 706(2) requires documents delivered to the registrar under any provision of the Companies Acts to state in a prominent position the registered number of the company to which it relates. Section 706(3) and (4) provides that, on receipt of a document not including such number, the registrar may (but not must) serve notice on the person by whom the document is delivered pointing out the non-compliance, whereupon (in default of delivery of a replacement document complying with this requirement) the original document shall be deemed not to have been delivered to him. The registrar served no such notice in this case, no doubt because he did not appreciate the error. In the absence of such notice, the particulars delivered by the company remain duly delivered to the registrar.'[44]

As noted, below[45], it was suggested that a third party prejudiced by the error might have a cause of action against the Registrar of Companies or the company.

[21.016] Notwithstanding what might be taken as a concession to the human condition, the necessity for being nothing short of fastidiously accurate and timely in completing and filing the Form C1 cannot be over-stressed. Compliance with CA 1963, s 99 is one task in which pedantry is a definite virtue.

(b) The limits to the decision in the* Amurec *case

[21.017] Notwithstanding the judgment of the High Court in *Lombard & Ulster Banking Ireland Ltd v Amurec Ltd*, an alternative line of authority exists, which was cited by counsel for the liquidator in that case. So in *Esberger & Son Ltd v Capital and Counties Bank*[46], a company deposited an undated charge with a bank, which, some months' later was dated and registered by the bank. Sargant J held that the charge was void because it was not registered within the 21-day limit. In his words:

> 'I feel that on the true meaning of that section the date of the creation of the mortgage or charge is the date when that instrument was executed and is not the date when any money is subsequently advanced, so as to make an effective charge for the amount of that money.'[47]

This line of authority[48] is willing to ignore the conclusiveness of the certificate of registration and look behind it. As seen, however, this was not followed in the *Amurec* case.

[21.018] Another judgment which questions the sacrosanctity of the certificate of registration of charges is that of Mervyn Davies J in *R v Registrar of Companies, ex p Esal (Commodities) Ltd*[49]. There, he said that an error of law, made by the Registrar of Companies, could be subject to judicial review:

---

44 [2000] BCC 985 at 988c–d.

45 See para **[21.018]–[21.019]**.

46 *Esberger & Son Ltd v Capital and Counties Bank* [1913] 2 Ch 366.

47 [1913] 2 Ch 366 at 373.

48 See also *Re Defries N and Co Ltd* [1904] 1 Ch 366; *Re Stevenson* [1902] 1 IR 23 and [1903] 1 IR 403; and *Yolland v Husson & Birkett Ltd* [1908] Ch 152.

49 *R v Registrar of Companies, ex p Esal (Commodities) Ltd* [1985] BCLC 84. See generally O'Riordan and Pearce, 'The Conclusiveness of Certificates of Registration of Company Charges' (1986) ILSI Gazette 281.

> '... the decision of the registrar may be reviewed if it can be shown that he made his decision to register (and issued his certificate) in consequence of, in the course of examining the facts, having asked himself the wrong questions.'[50]

This was said in reliance on the notion that an error of law is always reviewable by the courts. However the modern trend in the English courts seems to be to follow the line of authority established in *Re CL Nye Ltd,* as did Hamilton J in the *Amurec* case. On appeal, the decision of Mervyn Davies J was overturned in *R v Registrar of Companies, ex p Central Bank of India*[51] and the view that the certificate of registration is conclusive was reaffirmed. In the words of Slade LJ:

> 'In the face of the "conclusive evidence" provisions...I am driven to the conclusion (which I think is strongly supported by the *Nye* decision) that [the relevant sections] on their true construction confer upon the registrar the power to decide finally and conclusively all ancillary questions, whether they be questions of fact or law, or mixed fact and law, which fall to be decided in determining whether the requirements of Part [IV] of the Act as to registration had been complied with in any given case. Even the clearest evidence that he had come to the wrong conclusion in answering any of these questions would not entitle anyone (except the Attorney General) to claim he acted beyond his powers, since [CA 1963, s 104] would preclude the court from considering such evidence...If these conclusions are correct, it must follow that even if the registrar erroneously registers a charge which should not have been registered and gives a consequent [CA 1963, s 104] certificate, such error may be incapable of correction.'[52]

However the judgment of Slade LJ went on to set out certain limitations of the scope of this principle, and so he went on to say:

> 'However, lest it be thought that this position may give rise to undue hardship or injustice, I would draw attention to two points. The first is the limited nature of the effect of registration and a consequent [CA 1963, s 104] certificate. It does not operate to confer validity on a charge which is invalid for reasons other than lack of registration. All it does is to give a chargee who has a valid charge protection against the statutory invalidation of that charge against a liquidator and creditors of the company which would occur by virtue of [CA 1963, s 99], if the company were to go into liquidation and the charge were unregistered ... Secondly, counsel for the registrar, has accepted that [CA 1963, s 104] does not bind the Crown, so that there might be nothing to prevent the Attorney General from interfering, if he saw fit, by way of an application for judicial review in what he considered an appropriate case, where evidence was available to show that the registrar had erred in the exercise of his functions as to registration. There is, therefore, in my opinion, no question of the registrar being wholly beyond the reach of the law.
>
> Two special cases may arise on which I wish to express no concluded opinion in this present judgment, because it is not necessary to do so. The first is the hypothetical case where a purported certificate given by the registrar discloses an error on the face of it. It may well be that even the protection afforded by [CA 1963, s 104] would not operate in that situation. The second special situation might arise where the certificate had been obtained by fraud[53]. Even in that case a direct attack on the certificate would, at least prima

[50] [1985] BCLC 84 at 97.

[51] *R v Registrar of Companies, ex p Central Bank of India* [1985] BCLC 465.

[52] [1985] BCLC 465 at 490.

[53] Note *Sun Tai Cheung Credits Ltd v AG of Hong Kong* [1987] 1 WLR 948, (Privy Council), per Lord Templeman.

> facie, be ruled out by [CA 1963, s 104] ... though it might well be that the court would act *in personam* against the fraudulent party so as to prevent him taking advantage of the fraudulently obtained certificate...and furthermore, a creditor personally damaged by the fraud might be able to take proceedings for damages...'[54].

Thus, Slade LJ's obiter dictum is that while the certificate is conclusive, in special cases injured parties may have recourse to the courts. In the first place it is recognised that an error on the face of the document might be so manifestly wrong as to invalidate registration. This was the reasoning of the court in *Re Advantage Healthcare (T10) Ltd*[55]. The second situation envisaged by Slade LJ was that of a fraudulently obtained certificate of registration. Slade LJ acknowledged the possible availability of an action in personam against persons who have fraudulently obtained a certificate of registration of a charge. By their very nature, if successful, they only attach to the person and not the property ie the successful plaintiff would be an unsecured creditor of the defendant, a situation that is most undesirable where an insolvent company is involved. However, since such an action could be taken against a lending institution which has acted fraudulently an aggrieved second charge holder may have a mark, should he be successful in establishing fraud. In establishing fraud here it is thought that, to be successful, the second charge holder would have to show that the charge holder who had delivered particulars of a charge which he had dated out of time so as to come within the 21 days, was aware of the second charge holder's rights and consciously intended to thwart those rights. In particular it is thought that a second charge holder whose charge came into being *after* the coming into existence of the first charge holder's charge would be unlikely to be successful.

[21.019] In the absence of fraud a claim may still lie against the Registrar of Companies. In *Re Advantage Healthcare (T10) Ltd*[56] it was recognised by Lightman J in the English High Court that a third party who was prejudiced by an error might have a claim against the Registrar (for registering the wrong particulars) or the company (for delivering, or allowing someone else to deliver, the wrong particulars) [57].

Non-registrable security interests

[21.020] The law provides that there are four kinds of consensual security which may be created: mortgages; charges; liens; and pledges. It is crucial to recognise at the outset that not all of these kinds of security interest are registrable pursuant to CA 1963, s 99. In order for mortgages and charges to be registrable they must be actually *created by* companies. Even still, not all charges are registrable. Moreover, liens and pledges are not, generally speaking, registrable. Here the following non-registrable security interests are considered:

(a) Charges which are not created by companies.

(b) Charges over proceeds of sale.

---

54 [1985] BCLC 465 at 490–491. The references to CA 1963 replace the similar English provisions.

55 *Re Advantage Healthcare (T10) Ltd* [2000] BCC 985. See para **[21.015]**.

56 *Re Advantage Healthcare (T10) Ltd* [2000] BCC 985.

57 See, also, *First City Corporation Ltd v Downsview Nominees Ltd* (1990) 5 NZCLC 66 at 303, [1990] 3 NZLR 265.

(c) Liens.

(d) Pledges.

(a) Charges which are not created by companies

[21.021] It is important to note that CA 1963, s 99(1) refers to 'every charge created...*by a company*'. Accordingly, where a charge arises other than through being created by a company, such as by operation of law[58], such a charge does *not* require to be registered[59]. It is this requirement – that in order for a charge to be registrable it must be created by a company – which is at the heart of the debate as to whether or not an aggregation type retention of title clause will constitute a 'registrable charge'[60]. Such an express aggregation clause[61] was included in the contract for the sale of goods in *Kruppstahl AG v Quitmann Products Ltd*[62]. There, Gannon J said of this agreement that it, along with the other clauses:

> '... constitute an immediate assignment of future interests and an agreement for security for whatever indebtedness on the part of Quitmann to Krupps might later arise ...'[63]

In *Somers v Allen*[64] Carroll J said, in referring to the *Quitmann* case, that:

> '... this case therefore illustrates that a seller can make an effective reservation of title to goods prior to manufacture, but if he requires security over the manufactured goods the *buyer will have to grant him* this and this would require registration as a Bill of Sale.'[65] [Emphasis added]

From the foregoing, it can be seen that the reason why an aggregation-type retention of title clause will be deemed a registrable charge, is because the purchaser-company grants back a charge over the goods which have undergone a manufacturing process. The courts seem to have taken the view that when goods sold undergo a manufacturing process, the property in them passes to the purchaser-company. Consequently, any security over those goods can only be *created by the company*, and so if it is within one of the heads of charge in s 99(2), it is a registrable charge under s 99(1).

(b) Charges over proceeds of sale

[21.022] Not all charges are registrable. By contrast with a mortgage or charge on land, a charge on *the proceeds of sale of lands* is not a registrable charge[66]. A charge on the

---

58 See para **[21.023]** *ff*.

59 *Lovell Construction Ltd v Independent Estates plc* [1994] 1 BCLC 31.

60 See para **[21.062]**.

61 Among the clauses in the contract, it was provided that: 'In the case of processing, blending and mixing of the reserved goods with other goods by the buyer, we acquire a joint title to the new goods in accordance with the ratio of the invoice value of the reserved goods to the invoice value of the other goods used. If our title lapses due to blending or mixing, the buyer assigns to us already at this stage his title to the new goods in accordance with the invoice value of the reserved goods, and holds them in trust for us, without charge.'

62 *Kruppstahl AG v Quitmann Products Ltd* [1982] ILRM 551.

63 [1982] ILRM 551 at 559.

64 *Somers v Allen* [1984] ILRM 437.

65 [1984] ILRM 437 at 441.

66 Such a charge may be registrable where it falls to be deemed a charge on a company's book debts if the company in question is a company which, in the ordinary course of its business, buys and sells land.

proceeds of sale of land can arise where, pending the sale of a business premises and the proposed purchase of another, a lender advances bridging finance to the company to enable it to purchase the other property. The lender's security will often be to require a solicitor to give an undertaking to hold the proceeds of sale on trust for the lender until the existing premises is sold. Such a charge is not registrable because, while ostensibly a charge on land, it has been construed as a charge on *the proceeds of sale of land*[67]. This was decided in *Re Kum Tong Restaurant (Dublin) Ltd; Byrne v AIB Ltd*[68] where a company contracted to sell its business premises. To enable it to continue its business until the completion of the sale of the premises, AIB advanced money on the strength of the contract to sell its premises. The company undertook to hold the documents of title on trust for the bank and to hand over sufficient monies out of the proceeds of sale to redeem the bridging finance. Subsequently, an order was made to wind up the company, the sale being closed with the approval of the court, and the money placed on deposit, pending the direction of the court. The applicant, who was the liquidator to the company, claimed the money for the ordinary creditors, saying that the bank had a charge which was void for want of registration. McWilliam J rejected this contention, saying:

> 'I am satisfied that an equitable mortgage was created in favour of the bank. A difficulty arises as to what was mortgaged. In so far as a charge was created on the premises, it was void against the liquidator as it was not registered in accordance with the provisions of s 99 of the Companies Act 1963 but I have always understood that, as from the date of a contract for sale, the vendor's interest is converted into personalty, that in equity the lands are the purchaser's lands from the date of the contract, and that the vendor is only entitled to the purchase money with a lien on the lands for it. Section 99 of the Act of 1963 does not appear to require registration of a mortgage of the purchase price.'[69]

The charge was not registrable as being a charge on land under CA 1963, s 99(2)(d) because it was a charge on the proceeds of sale of the company's land. It has been noted[70] that where a company is a property-investment company carrying on the business of buying and selling land, the creation of a charge on the proceeds of sale of the company's land might be registrable as constituting a charge on a company's book debts under CA 1963, s 99(2)(e).

(c) Liens

[21.023] Although liens confer proprietary rights they are not, generally speaking, registrable under CA 1963, s 99. The reason for this is because they arise by operation of law[71]. Examples of liens include:

(i) Common law liens.

(ii) General liens: bankers' and solicitors' liens.

---

67 In practice, it may be noted that it is still common to register such a solicitor's letter of undertaking.

68 *Re Kum Tong Restaurant (Dublin) Ltd; Byrne v AIB Ltd* [1978] IR 446.

69 [1978] IR 446 at 448.

70 See Ussher, *Company Law in Ireland* (1986), p 456.

71 This is somewhat peculiar in that liens are properly classified as a kind of consensual security. In this respect the consensual nature can only be seen as deriving from the decision to first enter into a relationship which might give rise to the subsequent existence of a lien based on the nature of the relationship.

(iii) Equitable liens: purchasers' and unpaid vendors' liens.

(iv) Contractual liens.

(i) Common law liens

[21.024] A number of common law liens can be identified. They have their origins in the rule of law that merchants may retain customers' goods as security for payment for services rendered. As Bell[72] explains it, because innkeepers and common carriers were, in times' past, required by law to provide services to the public, this was balanced by the early recognition of liens over guests' belongings and goods carried. The list of situations in which common law liens will arise has, however, been established and is now fossilised. This explains why the list of situations giving rise to common law liens has 'an archaic flavour, and in part seems somewhat arbitrary'[73]. Common law liens include: the common carrier[74]; the sea carrier[75]; the innkeeper[76]; and the 'improver'[77]. None of these liens are registrable under CA 1963, s 99.

(ii) General liens: bankers' and solicitors' liens

[21.025] A general lien must be distinguished from a particular lien. Common law liens are examples of *particular* liens which entitle the lienee to retain goods as security for the services rendered in respect of those particular goods. By contrast a general lien allows the retention of goods as security until the lienee has been paid for past and present services rendered.

[21.026] One of the most common examples of a general lien is the bankers' lien[78]. A general banker's lien arises where securities are deposited with a bank unless there is an express or implied contract which is inconsistent with the lien, such as where title deeds are left with a bank for safe keeping[79]. Bankers' liens arose for consideration in the case of *Re Farm Fresh Frozen Foods Ltd*[80] where, in return for a cash advance from a bank, a company agreed to deposit title deeds with the bank, although the property was at the time already charged. When the company went into liquidation, the bank sought to rely on the general banker's lien. It was held by Keane J that there was no general banker's lien in that case, since it was negatived by the express intention of the parties to create an equitable mortgage. This was found to be the case, because the transaction amounted to

---

72 Bell, *Modern Law of Personal Property in England and Ireland* (1989), p 138.

73 Bell, *Modern Law of Personal Property in England and Ireland* (1989), p 139.

74 *George Barker (Transport) Ltd v Enyon* [1974] 1 WLR 462.

75 *Wolf v Sumners* (1811) 2 Camp 631.

76 This is now a statutory lien by reason of the Hotel Proprietors Act 1963, s 8.

77 By 'improver' is meant someone who carries out work to goods. Bell, *Modern Law of Personal Property in England and Ireland* (1989), cites several examples as diverse as a mechanic who repairs a car, to accountants who draft ledgers and lawyers who work on documents.

78 See Donnelly, *The Law of Banks and Credit Institutions* (2000), p 500.

79 *Brandao v Barnett* (1846) 12 Cl & Fin 787 at 806, cited with approval in *Re Farm Fresh Frozen Foods Ltd* [1980] ILRM 131 at 134. See generally, Hapgood, *Paget's Law of Banking* (1996), Ch 31.

80 *Re Farm Fresh Frozen Foods Ltd* [1980] ILRM 131.

an agreement to create an equitable mortgage which was void against the liquidator for want of registration[81].

[21.027] Solicitors' liens are another common form of general lien[82]. In *Re Galden Properties Ltd*[83] McCarthy J said:

> 'A solicitor holds a general or retaining lien; in that respects it differs from the ordinary lien derived from possession of the article to which there attaches a lien for payment of the charges in respect of that added value. A solicitor's lien attaches to all documents and other personal property in his possession as such solicitor and relates to all outstanding charges, as solicitor, not merely those in respect of the particular documents over which the lien is claimed. The lien entitles the solicitor to retain the documents, or the personal property, till payment of the full amount of the bill...'

A solicitor's lien over property extends only to costs incurred by the client against whom it is claimed. So a solicitor owed costs by certain companies was found to have no lien on the title deeds to premises owned by individuals even though the companies were wholly owned and controlled by those individuals[84].

(iii) Equitable liens: purchaser's and unpaid vendor's liens

[21.028] Equitable liens arise in circumstances where the lienee has no possession of the property the subject of the lien but where the rules of equity give rise to a lien on account of the parties' relationship. As Gough[85] has said, 'an equitable lien gives the creditor a proprietary interest, although there is no transfer of the beneficial ownership and although it exists as a security right independent of possession by contrast with a legal lien'. Neither a purchaser's lien nor an unpaid vendor's lien is registrable under CA 1963, s 99. Of the purchaser's lien, Wylie[86] says:

> 'It is a principle of long standing that, once a contract for the sale of land has been entered into, the vendor becomes a constructive trustee of the land for the purchaser. To a large extent this notion seems to be based upon the special view taken of such contracts by the Courts of Equity, ie that a decree of specific performance will normally be granted to either party to the contract. Following on from this, it is then said that the purchaser may be regarded as the beneficial or equitable owner of the property until such time as completion takes place and the legal ownership is actually transferred to him by the conveyance.'

Consequently, where a person enters into a contract to buy land from another, the purchaser has a lien (ie a form of equitable charge) over the property in sale, to the extent of any deposit paid, which arises by operation of law. This is a purchaser's lien. Such a charge is not registrable by the purchaser against the vendor (where the vendor is

---

81 [1980] ILRM 131 at 136 where Keane J said: 'It follows that in the present case the documents of title came into the possession of the bank as equitable mortgagees and were not held by them at the relevant time on foot of any lien which survived the avoidance of the equitable mortgage for non-registration.'

82 See generally O'Callaghan, 'Safeguarding Solicitors' Fees' (1996) 3 CLP 167.

83 *Re Galden Properties Ltd* [1988] IR 213

84 *Ring v Kennedy* [1999] 3 IR 316, (1997) ITLR 6 October 1997.

85 See Gough, *Company Charges* (2nd edn, 1996), p 501.

86 Wylie, *Irish Land Law* (3rd edn, 1997).

a company). In addition, an unpaid vendor's lien, which entitles the vendor of property to a lien over the land in sale, to the extent of the outstanding purchase price, is also not registrable. Furthermore, where the vendor sells property to a company, and a lending institution advances money to that company to buy the land in question, then by subrogation[87] the lending institution is entitled to the unpaid vendor's lien, to the extent of the advance made, over the property. Authority here is *Bank of Ireland Finance Ltd v DJ Daly Ltd*[88] where the plaintiff-bank agreed to lend a sum of money to the defendant-company to enable it to buy lands, secured by the defendant agreeing to deposit the title deeds to the property with the plaintiff-bank as security for the loan. The sum was paid by the bank, and the defendant-company paid almost all of that money over to the vendor of the property in question. In turn, the property was conveyed to the purchaser-company, but the defendant-company did not hand the deeds over, nor did it repay the loan to the bank. The plaintiff-bank claimed, inter alia, that it was entitled by subrogation to the rights of the vendor of the property, ie to the money paid over by the defendant-company to the vendor which had been provided by the bank. McMahon J noted that Brightman J in *London Cheshire Co v Laplagrene Co*[89] had:

> '...held that an unpaid vendor's lien was the creature of the law; that it did not depend on contract but on the fact that the vendor had a right to a specific performance of his contract and that, accordingly, it was not registrable under s 95 of the Act of 1948. The learned judge pointed out that the provision in question had been in force since the Companies Act 1908, but no one had suggested that it was the practice for a vendor to register an unpaid vendor's lien when selling to a company. The lien is created on the formation of the contract of sale and the time for registration would expire twenty-one days thereafter. The lien is not discharged until the purchase money is paid on completion. If registration were necessary, every vendor selling to a company would be put to the inconvenience of having to register the unpaid vendor's lien as a matter of course on the off chance that circumstances might arise which would render it necessary for the vendor to rely on the unpaid vendor's lien. For the reasons of Brightman J I am satisfied that CA 1963, s 99 does not require registration of an unpaid vendor's lien arising on the purchase of property by a company.'[90]

The bank was entitled to the unpaid vendor's lien by virtue of the doctrine of subrogation, and so had priority in the winding up. In *Highland Finance (Ireland) Ltd v Sacred Heart College, McEllin and Bank of Ireland*[91] the Supreme Court made clear that although it was settled law that a party who lends money to another to buy land is prima facie entitled by subrogation to the unpaid vendor's lien on the property for the amount of the advance, there were circumstances which might prevent or preclude the application of the doctrine of subrogation. In that case it was found that subrogation was

87 Ie the right to stand into the shoes of another and claim as one's own, the rights which they enjoy. On the principles necessary for the right of *subrogation* to arise see *Highland Finance Ireland Ltd v Sacred Heart College of Agriculture Ltd* [1993] ILRM 260.

88 *Bank of Ireland Finance Ltd v DJ Daly Ltd* [1978] IR 79.

89 *London Cheshire Co v Laplagrene Co* [1971] Ch 499.

90 [1978] IR 79 at 84.

91 *Highland Finance (Ireland) Ltd v Sacred Heart College, McEllin and Bank of Ireland* [1997] 2 ILRM 87.

inconsistent with the parties' intentions and that justice and reason did not require that the doctrine be applied there.

[21.029] One particular form of purchaser's lien arises where a prospective purchaser pays a booking deposit in respect of the property which it is proposed to purchase. Again, such can amount to an equitable charge over the property which it is proposed to purchase, to the extent of the amount of the deposit. The case of *Re Barrett Apartments Ltd*[92] is instructive. In that case, putative purchasers paid booking deposits to a developer in respect of the apartments which they wished to buy following their construction. Subsequently, the developing company went into liquidation. The liquidator to the company alleged that the purchasers should only rank as unsecured creditors. However, the purchasers pointed out that in law they were entitled to a lien on the property. While the purchasers' contention was upheld in the High Court, the Supreme Court reversed the decision on the facts, holding that in the present case, there was no valid contract and that, consequently, there were no purchasers' lien.

(iv) Contractual liens

[21.030] Notwithstanding the central feature of a lien – namely, that it arises by operation of law – the general law recognises that liens can arise by virtue of express contract between parties. Such security interests are not registrable under CA 1963, s 99 for the simple reason that a lien is not a charge[93]; it is only 'charges' (and by virtue of CA 1963, s 99(10)(a), 'mortgages') that are registrable thereunder. In *Waitomo Wools (NZ) Ltd v Nelsons (NZ) Ltd*[94] Richmond J held that contractual liens are not registrable on the basis of the fundamental difference between a charge and a lien, namely that the latter relies exclusively on possession of the assets the subject matter of the security[95].

[21.031] In *Re Hamlet International plc (in administration)*[96] a freight forwarding and warehouse company (the applicant) sought leave to enforce its security under a general lien over stock held for and on behalf of two companies which were in administration. The applicant was owed over £1.8 million in respect of freight, warehousing and ancillary charges. The question which arose was whether the applicant's rights of lien coupled with its power of sale (granted under the British International Freight Association's and the Warehousing Association's conditions of sale) amounted to charges registrable under the Companies Act 1985, s 395 (UK). The administrators of the two companies claimed that because of the contractual power of sale given to the applicant, the lien also given by those conditions was turned into a charge. It was held

---

92 *Re Barrett Apartments Ltd* (15 July 1983, unreported) High Court (Keane J).

93 It is thought that the reference in C(A)A 1983, s 44(1) to 'a lien or other charge' cannot be taken as an indication that the legislature considers that a 'lien' was a 'charge'. Most likely there was a failure to distinguish their legal meaning and consequently treat them as synonymous. So, eg, the originally drafted C(A)A 1990, s 5(2)(d) appears to have assumed that mortgage, lien and pledge was included in the reference to 'charge'. Section 5(2)(d) was amended by C(A)(No 2)A 1999, s 14(b) and it now refers to 'mortgage, charge, lien or other encumbrance or a pledge of'.

94 *Waitomo Wools (NZ) Ltd v Nelsons (NZ) Ltd* [1974] 1 NZLR 484.

95 Cf *Re Wallis & Simmonds (Builders) Ltd* [1974] 1 All ER 561 at 573a–b, per Templeman J.

96 *Re Hamlet International plc (in administration)* [1998] 2 BCLC 164.

that the contractual right to retain possession and the right to sell did not operate to convert a lien to a charge. In the course of his judgment Eben Hamilton QC quoted from the last mentioned decision of Richmond J in *Waitomo Wools*:

> '...I think that in its ordinary and generally accepted meaning the word 'charge' is apt only to describe a situation in which some particular property, real or personal, is appropriated or set aside in favour of someone who is given by law, or by agreement, will or otherwise, the right to resort to the property to satisfy or discharge some obligation...A charge involves some deduction from the right of ownership in the property rather than mere interference with the right to possession which is normally an incident of ownership. It is not a word which is apt to describe a purely possessory lien as opposed to a lien of a non-possessory nature such as an equitable lien...the most essential distinction [between legal possessory liens and any transaction which gives rise to a charge on the ordinary and accepted meaning of that word] is that a true possessory lien depends entirely on possession and is lost with the loss of possession. A charge, on the other hand, exists independent of possession and confers an interest in the property which carries with it a right to resort to the property (as opposed to merely detaining it) to satisfy or discharge some obligation secured by the charge'.

It was held that all that the applicant had was a contractual possessory lien. It was also considered significant that the goods in question were not delivered into the applicant's possession by way of security but in order that they could be distributed to the company's customers.

(d) Pledges

[21.032] Pledges of chattels given by companies are not registrable under CA 1963, s 99[97]; neither are genuine pledges of chattels given by individuals registrable under the Bills of Sale (Ireland) Acts 1879–1883[98].

Registrable charges

[21.033] Only those charges that are enumerated in CA 1963, s s 99(2)[99] require by law to be registered. These 'registrable charges' are:

(a) Charges for the purpose of securing the issue of debentures.

(b) Charges on uncalled share capital of the company.

(c) Charges created or evidenced by an instrument which, if executed by an individual, would require registration as a bill of sale.

(d) Charges on land wherever situate, or any interest therein, but not including a charge for any rent or other periodical sum issuing out of land.

(e) Charges on book debts of the company.

(f) Floating charge.

---

97 *Highland Finance (Ireland) Ltd v Sacred Heart College, McEllin and Bank of Ireland* [1997] 2 ILRM 87.

98 See Lord Esher MR's observations on the distinction between a pledge and a bill of sale in *Re Hardwick* (1886) 17 QBD 690 at 697, quoted in Ch 20, *Corporate Borrowing: Debentures and Security*, para **[20.023]**.

99 As amended by CA 1990, s 122.

(g) Charges on calls of shares.

(h) Charges on – or any shares in – a ship or aircraft.

(i) Charges on goodwill and their intellectual property.

It should be noted that CA 1963, s 99(10)(a) provides that 'charge' includes 'mortgage' for the purposes of CA 1963, Part IV. It should also be remembered that in order for a charge to be a registrable charge it must be created by the company. This feature of registrable charges is considered above[100].

[21.034] By virtue of CA 1963, s 99(2A) and (2B), as inserted by Companies Act 1990, s 122 ('CA 1990') the Minister for Enterprise, Trade and Employment can, by statutory instrument, *add new* charges or remove or change the description of existing registrable charges. To date no order has been made under these provisions.

(a) Charges for the purpose of securing the issue of debentures

[21.035] This category of registrable charge is potentially very wide, since it could apply to any charge created which secures the issue of a single debenture. However, it has been held by the New Zealand Court of Appeal in *Automobile Association (Canterbury) Inc v Australasian Secured Deposits Ltd*[101] that the use of debentures in the plural, means that a charge securing the issue of a single debenture is not a registrable charge under this heading. Rather, this heading of registrable charge is only applicable to where a series of debentures are issued by a company, almost like an issue of shares. In Ireland, such a registrable charge will usually only be created by a public limited company ('PLC')[102].

(b) Charges on uncalled share capital of the company

[21.036] The ambit of this category of registrable charge is confined to a charge on the shares in the chargor-company itself. It has been identified as a noticeable gap in the legislation[103] that a company is not required to register charges which it creates over shares in a subsidiary company. Technically, this permits a company to transfer assets to a subsidiary and to then create a charge over the shares that it holds in the subsidiary, without having to register the charge in the CRO. In practice, this does not give rise to great abuses because charges on shares in Irish private companies are not a preferred form of security[104].

(c) Charges created or evidenced by an instrument which, if executed by an individual, would require registration as a bill of sale

[21.037] The inclusion in the Companies Acts of the requirement that certain charges must be registered to be enforceable, was not an original idea. Certain documents created by individuals in respect of their personal chattels were required to be registered

---

100 See para **[21.021]**.

101 *Automobile Association (Canterbury) Inc v Australasian Secured Deposits Ltd* [1973] 1 NZLR 417.

102 See CA 1963, s 99(8) which makes provision for registration of the issue of a series of debentures.

103 See *Fitzgerald* (1968) Ir Jur 258; *McCormack* (1984) ILT 67; and Ussher, *Company Law in Ireland* (1986), p 457.

104 See Chapter 16, *Share Transfers in Private Companies*, para **[16.031]**.

under the Bills of Sale (Ireland) Acts 1879–1883[105]. Section 99(2)(c) of CA 1963 requires the registration of charges created or evidenced by an instrument which, if executed by an individual, would require registration as a bill of sale. The Bills of Sale (Ireland) Act 1879 (the '1879 Act') and the Bills of Sale (Ireland) Act (1879) Amendment Act 1883 (the '1883 Act') were enacted with different purposes in mind. In *Manchester, Sheffield and Lincolnshire Railway Co v North Central Wagon Co*[106] Lord Herschell distinguished the different purposes behind the 1879 Act and the 1883 Act. Of the English Act, equivalent to the Irish 1879 Act, he said it was intended:

> '...for the protection of creditors, and to prevent their rights being affected by secret assurances of chattels which were permitted to remain in the ostensible possession of a person who had parted with his property in them. The bills were therefore made void only as against creditors or their representatives. As between the parties to them they were perfectly valid'. [107]

And of the English Act, equivalent to the Irish 1883 Act, he said it was designed:

> '...to prevent needy persons being entrapped into signing complicated documents which they might often be unable to comprehend, and so being subjected by their creditors to the enforcement of harsh and unreasonable provisions.'

The Bills of Sale Acts' provisions on security bills do not apply directly to companies[108]; neither do the Acts apply, in toto, indirectly to companies. Rather, it is the case that where a company creates a 'charge' over 'personal chattels', that charge will be registrable if the charge amounts to a 'bill of sale' which, if created by an individual, would be registrable under the 1879–1883 Acts.

(i) The meaning of 'bill of sale' and the necessity for it to operate as a charge

[21.038] A bill of sale[109] is a document which transfers the property in goods from one person to another but permits the property to remain in the possession of the person

---

[105] See Maguire, 'The Bill of Sale: The Forgotten Relation' (1997) 4 CLP 3 for a thorough analysis of the provisions of the Bills of Sale (Ireland) Act 1879 and Bills of Sale (Ireland) Act (1879) Amendment Act 1883.

[106] *Manchester, Sheffield and Lincolnshire Railway Co v North Central Wagon Co* (1888) 13 App Cas 554.

[107] (1888) 13 App Cas 554 at 560. In *Somers v Allen* [1984] ILRM 437 Carroll J said of the Bills of Sale (Ireland) Act 1879 that: 'The purpose of the Act was to prevent the owner of chattels defeating the claims of his creditors by making or giving a Bill of Sale which would entitle the holder or grantee to seize or take possession of chattels where those chattels remained in the possession or apparent possession of the giver.'

[108] Bills of Sale (Ireland) Act (1879) Amendment Act 1883, s 17 provides: 'Nothing in this Act shall apply to any debentures issued by any mortgage, loan, or other incorporated company, and secured upon the capital stock or goods, chattels, and effects of such company'. In *Re Standard Manufacturing Company* [1891] 1 Ch 627 it was held that the legislature could not have intended the Bills of Sale Act 1878 (UK) to apply to charges created by companies since registration of charges by such companies was governed by the Companies Clauses Acts 1845 and 1862. This was followed in Ireland in *Re Royal Marine Hotel Company Kingstown Ltd* [1895] 1 IR 368.

[109] Bills of Sale (Ireland) Act 1879, s 4 provides that:

transferring the goods. There are two types of bill of sale: security bills (given to secure the payment of money) and absolute bills (given other than to secure the payment of money). The 1879 Act applies to both security bills and absolute bills; the 1883 Act applies exclusively to security bills.

[21.039] In order for a charge to be a registrable as a bill of sale under CA 1963, s 99(2)(c) it is necessary that it be a security bill – ie in the nature of a charge to secure the repayment of money[110]. Accordingly, an absolute bill created by a company is not registrable under s 99(2)(c) because that subsection makes express reference to 'charges' created or evidenced by an instrument which if executed by an individual would require registration as a bill of sale. The usual authority cited is *Stoneleigh Finance Ltd v Phillips*[111] where Russell LJ said[112] of the English equivalent of s 99(2)(c) that:

> 'I would say at the outset that it is clear that this section has no application to a transaction unless it is one which operates to charge property as security for the payment of money...it is not sufficient under s 99(2)(c) to find an instrument which if executed by an individual would require registration as a bill of sale; it is necessary also to find a charge. It is however what is in fact a charge in form an absolute assignment or by otherwise adopting a form which does not accord with the real transaction between the parties.'

That particular case concerned a hire-purchase agreement which, it was held, did not require to be registered under s 99(2)(c) and so was valid against the company's liquidator.

[21.040] Whilst it is a requirement that a bill of sale must operate to *charge* property, it is sufficient that it operates to *mortgage* property because CA 1963, s 99(10)(a) states clearly that for the purposes of Part IV 'charge' includes mortgage. However, these terms will on account of their long-established meaning be strictly construed and a *lien*

---

109 (contd)

> '...the expression "bill of sale" shall include bills of sale, assignments, transfers, declarations of trust without transfer, inventories of goods with receipt thereto attached, or receipts for purchase moneys of goods, and other assurances of personal chattels, and also powers of attorney, authorities or licences to take possession of personal chattels as security for any debt, and also any agreement, whether intended or not to be followed by the execution of any other instruments, by which a right in equity to any personal chattels or to any charge or security thereon shall be conferred, but shall not include the following documents: that is to say, assignments for the benefit of the creditors of the person making or giving the same, marriage settlements, transfers or assignments of any ship or vessel or any share thereof, transfers of goods in the ordinary course of business or any trade or calling, bills of sale of goods in foreign parts or at sea, bills of lading, India warrants, warehouse–keepers certificates, warrants or orders for the delivery of goods, or any other documents used in the ordinary course of business as proof of the possession or control of goods, or authorising or purporting to authorise, either by indorsement or by delivery, the possessor of such documents to transfer or receive goods thereby repossessed.'

110 See Keane, *Company Law* (3rd edn, 2000), para 21.15.

111 *Stoneleigh Finance Ltd v Phillips* [1965] 1 All ER 513.

112 [1965] 1 All ER 513 at 525.

or a *pledge* in respect of personal chattels will not be registrable under this (or any other)[113] head of charge[114].

(ii) Personal chattels defined

[21.041] The Bills of Sale Acts do not apply to all assets; they are exclusively concerned with *personal chattels*. The Bills of Sale Act 1883, s 4 defines 'personal chattels' to mean:

> 'goods, furniture, and other articles capable of complete transfer by delivery, and (when separately assigned or charged) fixtures and growing crops, *but shall not include* chattel interests in real estate, nor fixtures (except trade machinery as hereinafter defined), when assigned together with a freehold or leasehold interest in the land on which they grow, nor shares or interests in the stock, funds, or securities of any government, or in the capital or property of incorporated or joint stock companies, nor choses in action, nor any stock or produce upon any farm or lands which by virtue of any covenant or agreement or of the custom of the country ought not to be removed from any farm where the same are at the time of making or giving of such bill of sale.' [Emphasis added]

Whilst stock and farm produce are excluded from the definition of *personal chattels* for the purposes of the Bills of Sale Acts, the registration of charges over such chattels (whether created by individuals or by companies) is regulated by the Agricultural Credit Act 1978[115]. In *Somers v Allen*[116], Carroll J said of the 1879 Act that:

> 'The Act applies to Bills of Sale of personal chattels, whether absolute or subject to a trust, whereby the holder or grantee has power, with or without notice, either immediately or at any future time, to take possession of such chattels. There must be a maker or giver of the Bill of Sale and a holder or grantee of the Bill.'[117]

That case concerned the issue of whether or not a particular retention of title clause was required to be registered under CA 1963, s 99(1) and in particular whether the clause was in fact a charge of the type described in CA 1963, s 99(2)(c). There, soya bean meal was sold to a company, subject to a so-called 'simple retention of title clause'[118]. The goods sold to the company were still identifiable, and it was held that the clause was not complex enough to create a charge over the goods in question. Accordingly, it was held that the clause was not an instrument which, if executed by an individual, would require registration as a Bill of Sale. The reason why the retention of title clause did not create a registrable charge was because the company did not, and could not, create[119] any charge because the clause did not permit the property in the goods to pass to the company

---

[113] See para **[21.042]**.

[114] On why liens, for example, do not come within s 99(2)(c), see *Waitomo Wools (NZ) Ltd v Nelsons (NZ) Ltd* [1974] 1 NZLR 484.

[115] See para **[21.109]**.

[116] *Somers v Allen* [1984] ILRM 437.

[117] [1984] ILRM 437 at 441.

[118] See para **[21.059]**.

[119] For a charge to be a registrable charge it must have been *created* by a company: see para **[21.021]** *ff*.

(iii) Charges liable to be registered under this head

[21.042] It follows that where a company creates a charge in respect of personal chattels to which it holds title, then if an individual would be required to register such a charge under the Bills of Sale Acts, so too will the company under CA 1963, s 99(2)(c). Although retention of title clauses commonly fall to be registered under this head of charge, they are but one example of the sort of transaction caught. Also capable of being deemed registrable charges of the sort described by s 99(2)(c) are conditional sale agreements. Such an agreement is where a company is sold goods on the terms that it buy goods but charge them back to the vendor until the purchase monies in whole or in part have been paid. If there is a genuine sale or hiring transaction, or otherwise if there is no charge involved, then registration will not be required. Section 4 of the 1879 Act provides that transfers of goods in the ordinary course of business are expressly excluded from being registrable charges under that legislation. Thus, it follows that in the case of a company, such transfers are also exempt from registration[120]. Although it has been argued in relation to retention of title clauses that, as their usage became more common, the basis upon which they were registrable as charges would collapse[121], nearly 20 years on from that observation, there has still been no suggestion of judicial acceptance. Indeed, if anything, the courts of Ireland and England – motivated by the perceived equity of *pari passu* amongst unsecured creditors and the preferential status of the Revenue Commissioners – are more likely to find retention of title clauses void against liquidators for being unregistered charges.

(d) Charges on land[122]

[21.043] The most popular (and by many considered the best) form of security is a first legal mortgage or a fixed charge over real property because, usually, land can be easily disposed of should the mortgagee or chargee wish to realise his security. A company which owns real property can create a mortgage or charge over its land in several ways[123]. In the case of registered land it can create a formal registered charge or an informal charge; in the case of unregistered land it can create a legal or equitable mortgage. In addition, a company may create a floating charge in respect of either registered or unregistered land[124]. All mortgages and charges over land, whether fixed or floating, legal or equitable and with or without the creation of a document, must be registered under CA 1963, s 99(2)(d). So too will an undertaking to create a mortgage or

---

120 See Green, *A Manual of the Law Relating to Bills of Sale in Ireland* (1882), p 129; Pearce, *The Bills of Sale Acts* (14th edn, 1926), pp 77–80.

121 See Ussher, *Company Law in Ireland* (1986), p 462; Farrar & Furey (1976) CLJ 27; and the words of Lord Summer in *Dublin City Distillery Ltd v Doherty* [1914] AC 823 at 867 that from the Bills of Sale legislation: '...it is plain that the legislature intended to save certain documents, already known in commerce, and others which, by the usage of business, might come into existence notoriously and for the same or similar purposes'.

122 See Keane, *Company Law* (3rd edn, 2000), para 23.09.

123 For the various means by which one can charge or mortgage real property, see Wylie, *Irish Land Law* (3rd edn, 1997), pp 685–806 and Pearce, *Land Law* (1985), p 218–221. See also Chapter 20, *Corporate Borrowing: Debentures and Security*, para **[20.021]**.

124 See Chapter 20, *Corporate Borrowing: Debentures and Security*, para **[20.068]**.

charge over land be registrable as such is itself an equitable charge[125]. It is beyond the scope of this book to consider in any detail the means by which a mortgage or charge over land can arise[126].

[21.044] In all cases where a mortgage or charge is created over land by an Irish company the mortgage or charge must be registered under CA 1963, s 99(2). This is the case wherever the land is situate, even if outside the State, although a charge on land for rent or other periodic sum issuing out of land is not registrable[127]. The registration of mortgages and charges over land under other systems of registration is considered, briefly, below[128].

[21.045] Where a company does not create a charge, but acquires property which is already subject to a charge, CA 1963, s 101(1) provides:

> 'Where a company acquires any property which is subject to a charge of any such kind as would, if it had been created after the acquisition of the property, would have been required to be registered under this Part, the company shall cause the prescribed particulars of the charge, verified in the prescribed manner, to be delivered to the Registrar of Companies for registration in manner required by this Act within twenty-one days after the date on which the acquisition is completed...'

Where such a charge is not registered its fate is akin to that of an unregistered judgment mortgage: an offence will have been committed, but the charge is not void. The sanction is again a fine of €634 by virtue of CA 1963, s 101(2)[129]. As Gough says, because of this, there is a temptation for a creditor to claim that a charge is registrable under CA 1963, s 101 and not CA 1963, s 99, a claim 'which is particularly strong where a company purchases property using funds borrowed for the purpose either from the vendor himself or from a third party'.[130] The authorities[131] suggest that a charge will be registrable under s 101 and not s 99 where the vendor of land directly transfers that land to the chargee-lender, as otherwise, the charge will normally arise out of an act of creation by the company.

[21.046] It may also be noted that CA 1963, s 99(7) states that the holding of debentures which entitles the holder of the debenture to a charge on land shall not be deemed to be an interest in land. It is thought that this relates to a series of debentures and not to one debenture which creates a charge.

---

125 *Re Valley Ice Cream (Ireland) Ltd* (22 July 1998, unreported) High Court (McCracken J) and *Fullerton v Provincial Bank of Ireland* [1903] 1 IR 483.

126 See Johnston, *Banking and Security Law in Ireland* (1998), Ch 10, 'Mortgages and Charges of Land' where the law on this matter is set out with admirable clarity.

127 Moreover, CA 1963, s 108 deems that CA 1907, s 10(1)(d) and C(C)A 1908, s 93(1) never applied to a charge for any rent or other periodical sum issuing out of land.

128 See para **[21.105]** *ff*.

129 As increased by C(A)A 1982, s 15.

130 See Gough, *Company Charges* (1978), p 230.

131 *Re Connolly Bros (No 2)* [1912] 2 Ch 25; *Church of England Building Society v Piskor* [1954] 1 Ch 553, [1954] 2 All ER 85; *Capital Finance Co Ltd v Stokes* [1968] 1 All ER 573, [1968] 3 All ER 625.

(e) Charges on book debts of the company

[21.047] As was considered in Chapter 20, it is quite common for a company to create a charge over its books debts, whether present or future[132]. As was also seen, charges on book debts may be the subject of either a fixed or a floating charge. Book debts have been defined by Palmer[133] as:

> '...debts owing to the company concerned with and arising out of the company's trade or business, which are entered, or commonly would be entered in the ordinary course of business, in well kept books of such a trade or business.'

In *Paul & Frank Ltd v Discount Bank (Overseas) Ltd*[134] Pennycuick J said that the test for whether something was a book debt was 'is it the practice to enter the debts in question in the ordinary course of business' in the company's books. In that case the benefit of a contract was held not to be a book debt[135]. Where a company makes an assignment of a book debt for the purpose of securing a loan made to that company it will create a charge which is registrable under CA 1963, s 99(2)(e).

[21.048] A book debt is more easily defined than its definition is applied to a given set of facts. In *Re Brian Tucker Ltd*[136] a company sought a cash advance from a bank to enable it to pay its insurance brokers the premiums due in respect of the company's insurance policies. This was advanced to the company and the company signed an irrevocable letter of authority to its brokers, authorising the brokers to pay over to the bank any monies received by the brokers on foot of such policies pending the repayment of the advance to the bank. It was expressly agreed that if the company was wound up, the bank could terminate the policies of insurance and take such part of the premium as may be refunded by the insurance company. The company went into liquidation and the liquidator claimed, inter alia, that there was no charge in favour of the bank, and in the alternative, that if there was a charge, it was void for want of registration as a book debt under CA 1963, s 99(2)(e). Lynch J cited the case of *Paul & Frank Ltd v Discount Bank (Overseas) Ltd*[137] and quoted Pennycuick J who said:

> 'It seems to me that, in order to ascertain whether any particular charge is a charge on book debts within the meaning of the section, one must look at the items of property which form the subject-matter of the charge at the date of its creation and consider

---

[132] See *Re Keenan Brothers Ltd* [1985] IR 401; *Siebe Gorman & Co Ltd v Barclays Bank Ltd* [1979] 2 Lloyds Rep 142; *Re Wogan's (Drogheda) Ltd* [1993] 1 IR 157; *Re Holidair* [1994] 1 ILRM 481. See generally, Chapter 20, *Corporate Borrowing: Debentures and Security*, at para **[20.038]** *ff*. See also Johnston, *Banking and Security Law in Ireland* (1998), p 575.

[133] Schmitthoff (ed), *Palmer's Company Law* (24th edn, 1987), p 739, referred to by Lynch J in *Re Brian Tucker Ltd* [1990] 2 IR 549. There, Lynch J cited the definition in *Halsbury's Laws of England* (4th edn) 3 Vol, para 376, fn 2 and para 525, fn 4.

[134] *Paul & Frank Ltd v Discount Bank (Overseas) Ltd* [1966] 2 All ER 922.

[135] In *Northern Bank v Ross* [1991] BCLC 504 cash at a bank was held *not* to be a book debt; in *Re Brian Tucker Ltd* [1990] 2 IR 549 refunds of insurance premiums were held *not* to be a book debt; in *Re Kum Tong Restaurants (Dublin) Ltd* [1978] IR 446 the proceeds of the sale of land was held *not* to be a book debt.

[136] *Re Brian Tucker Ltd* [1990] 2 IR 549.

[137] *Paul & Frank Ltd v Discount Bank (Overseas) Ltd* [1966] 2 All ER 922.

> whether any of those items is a book debt. In the case of an existing item of property, this question can only be answered by reference to its character at the date of creation. Where the item of property is the benefit of a contract and at the date of the charge the benefit of the contract does not comprehend any book debt, I do not see how that contract can be brought within the section as being a book debt merely by reason that the contract may ultimately result in a book debt.'[138]

Lynch J accepted this view of the law, saying:

> 'The mere possibility that future refunds of premiums might become payable in amounts that were wholly unascertainable and might never arise at the date of the creation of the charge does not make that transaction a book debt which must be registered pursuant to s 99 of the 1963 Act.'[139]

This does not mean that a future debt will not be registrable as a book debt, since, although it is unascertained it is the case that it will almost invariably arise after the creation of the charge.

[21.049] The essential trait which will give rise to a registrable charge on book debts is that the assignment of the book debts is intended to secure the repayment of a loan. The authorities on the question of whether or not a particular transaction will be deemed to be a charge on book debts show that each case must be viewed on its own particular facts. So in *Kent v Sussex Sawmills Ltd*[140] it was held that where a company obtained a loan from a bank secured by the company writing to a government department, authorising that department to pay moneys owed to the company due under a contract into the company's account at the bank, no outright assignment was intended. Rather, the letter from the company amounted to an equitable assignment by way of security and constituted a charge on the company's book debts. That charge was further found to be void for want of registration under the equivalent of CA 1963, s 99(2)(e) [141].
In *Re Kum Tong Restaurants (Dublin) Ltd; Byrne v Allied Irish Banks Ltd*[142] a company, in the process of selling its premises, obtained a loan from the defendant-bank to enable it to continue in business pending the sale. The company undertook:

> '…to hold such documents of title…in trust for the bank and to hand over sufficient monies out of the proceeds of the sale to redeem this bridging finance as soon as the sale is closed...'

Subsequently, the company was wound up and the sale of its premises closed with court approval. The liquidator applied to the court to have the undertaking of the company set aside on the basis that it constituted a charge on the company's book debts which was void for want of registration under CA 1963, s 99(2)(e). It was held by McWilliam J that the proceeds of sale were indeed charged to the bank, but were not a book debt within the meaning of the section and so the order was made in favour of the bank. The reason

138 [1966] 2 All ER 922 at 926.

139 [1990] 2 IR 549 at 554.

140 *Kent v Sussex Sawmills Ltd* [1946] All ER 638.

141 Note that in *Re Welsh Irish Ferries Ltd* [1985] BCLC 327 it was held that a lien on sub–freights created by a company pursuant to a time charter in favour of a shipowner was registrable under the equivalent of CA 1963, s 99(2)(e).

142 *Re Kum Tong Restaurants (Dublin) Ltd; Byrne v Allied Irish Banks Ltd* [1978] IR 446.

for McWilliam J's decision was that upon the company contracting to sell its premises, its interest was not in the property but in the purchase money to be paid to it on completion.

[21.050] In *Re Interview Ltd*[143] an Irish company contracted with a German company to buy goods from the German company. The contract provided that the Irish company would assign to the German company any claims which it might have against persons to whom it sold the goods. Kenny J said:

> 'The first question is whether the clause...created an absolute assignment (in which event it would not require registration) or was an assignment by way of security. I think it was an assignment by way of security. It was not an absolute assignment for if the purchaser had paid for the goods immediately, there would have been no assignment of the debt created by the sale to the purchaser. In addition the clause itself states that the assignment is "by way of security"...In my opinion, it follows that, as the terms for deliveries abroad were not registered under s 99 of the Act of 1963, they are void against any creditor in so far as they created an obligation to assign or gave a charge on the debts owing...'[144]

Accordingly, because the assignment was found to be by way of security and not an absolute assignment, it was held to be a registrable charge on the Irish company's book debts[145].

[21.051] Other instruments which may be registrable as a book debt include *letters of hypothecation*[146]. This is a security by way of equitable charge which is used where it is impractical to give possession of the goods because they are not yet available. Letters of hypothecation have been described as a notification by a bank that the bank shall have a charge on personal property which comes into the bank's possession[147]. However, a bill of exchange or other negotiable instrument given to secure the payment of a book debt where the instrument is deposited to secure an advance to the company is not a registrable charge: CA 1963, s 99(6). A charge on cash which is on deposit at a bank is thought by some[148] not to be a charge which requires registration under s 99(2)(e) because standard accounting practice is to show cash on deposit under a separate heading in balance sheets; notwithstanding this, others recommend that such charges are registered under s 99(2)(e)[149].

(f) Floating charges

[21.052] Floating charges have been considered in detail in the previous chapter[150]. All floating charges are registrable under CA 1963, s 99(2)(f) and in default will be void as

---

143 *Re Interview Ltd* [1975] IR 382.

144 [1975] IR 382 at 396–397.

145 [1975] IR 382 at 397 where Kenny J said: 'In my opinion, it follows that, as the terms for deliveries abroad were not registered under CA 1963, s 99, they are void against any creditor in so far as they created an obligation to assign or gave a charge on the debts owing to Interview and arising out of sales of goods delivered by AEG or Telefunken.'

146 See *Ladenburg & Co v Goodwin Ferreira Co Ltd & Garnett* [1912] KB 275.

147 See Hapgood, *Paget's Law of Banking* (11th edn, 1996), p 539.

148 See Lingard, *Bank Security Documents* (3rd edn, 1993), para 3.19 and *Re Brightlife Ltd* [1986] 3 All ER 673 at 676.

149 See, Johnston, *Banking and Security Law in Ireland* (1998), para [17.21].

150 Chapter 20, *Corporate Borrowing: Debentures and Security*, para **[20.063]** *ff.*

against a liquidator or any creditor of the company. In the case of real property, a floating charge will also fall to be registered as being a charge on land under CA 1963, s 99(2)(d).

[21.053] Most floating charges are over personalty and are also registrable. Again the existence of a retention of title clause in a contract for the sale of goods may constitute a charge which requires registration as a floating charge under CA 1963, s 99(2)(f)[151].

(g) Charges on calls of shares made but not paid

[21.054] Section 99(2)(g) of CA 1963 provides that charges on calls of shares made but not paid are registrable. Although these are a sort of book debt, they are independently registrable under CA 1963, s 99(2)(g)[152].

(h) Charges on – or any share in – a ship or aircraft

[21.055] Section 99(2)(h) of CA 1963[153] provides that a charge on a ship or aircraft or any share in a ship or aircraft is registrable. In *Barber v Burke*[154] the Supreme Court held that a 'yacht' was not a 'ship' within the meaning of this subsection. Some doubt must be cast upon this decision by reason of the definition afforded to 'ship' in the Jurisdiction of Courts (Maritime Conventions) Act 1989 (the '1989 Act') which in s 13(2) provides that it includes 'every description of vessel used in navigation' and defines 'vessel' to include 'any ship or boat, or any other description of vessel used in navigation'. It should also be noted that in *Targe Towing Ltd v The Owners and all Persons Claiming an interest in the Vessel 'Von Rocks'*[155] the Supreme Court (per Keane J) held that a 'dredger' was a 'ship' for the purposes of the 1989 Act[156]. Whilst specific to the 1989 Act, it is thought that some considerable doubt must be cast upon the earlier decision in *Barber v Burke* and that it is now prudent to register a charge over a yacht or any other 'vessel' pursuant to CA 1963, s 99(2)(h). Mortgages on ships must also be registered under the Mercantile Marine Act 1955, mentioned below[157].

---

151 See the dictum of Templeman LJ in *Borden (UK) Ltd v Scottish Timber Products Ltd* [1981] Ch 35 at 44 where he said: '... if the buyers created a charge on chipboard, such a charge is void against the liquidator and creditors of the buyer under [CA 1963, s 99] which makes void against the company or its creditors an unregistered charge created or evidenced by an instrument which if executed by an individual, would require registration as a Bill of Sale. If the interest floated from the chipboard to proceeds of sale and onwards, so floated the charge, and [the equivalent to CA 1963, s 99(2)] makes void any unregistered floating charge on the undertaking or property of the company.'

152 See Schmitthoff (ed), *Palmer's Company Law* (24th edn, 1987), para 46–06.

153 As amended by CA 1990, s 122.

154 *Barber v Burke* [1980] ILRM 186.

155 *Targe Towing Ltd v The Owners and all Persons Claiming an interest in the Vessel 'Von Rocks'* [1998] 1 ILRM 481.

156 Keane J said ([1998] 1 ILRM 481 at 491–492): 'The preponderance of judicial opinion would support the view that, provided the craft was built to do something on water and, for the purpose of carrying out that work, was so designed and constructed as to be capable of traversing significant water surfaces and did in fact regularly traverse them, it is capable of being classified as a "ship", despite the absence of any form of self–propulsion or steering mechanism, such as a rudder.'

157 See para **[21.112]**.

(i) Charges on goodwill and other intellectual property

[21.056] Section 99(2)(i) of CA 1963 requires that any charge on goodwill, patents or licences under patents, trademarks, copyrights or licences under copyright created by a company must be registered. These may also be registrable under the relevant statutes on such intellectual property rights[158].

Disguised registrable charges: retention of title clauses

[21.057] Certain retention of title clauses have been held by the courts of both Ireland and other common law countries to give rise to a charge on the property of a company[159], which will be void unless registered with the CRO. In the late-1970s and 1980s, such clauses were of grave concern to unsecured creditors of insolvent companies, who often found that assets which they thought were available to them and other unsecured creditors, were in fact still owned by the person who supplied them to the company[160]. The immediate relevance of retention of title clauses to company law is that the courts have been repeatedly asked to determine whether the vendor of goods actually retained ownership in them, or whether title in the goods passed to the purchaser-company which *then* created a charge over the goods. Where the purchaser-company creates a registrable charge over goods the charging retention of title clause must be registered pursuant to CA 1963, s 99(1). Where such charges are not registered, they will be void as against the company's liquidator and creditors[161]. The assets which are the subject of the retention of title clause will then be available to meet the claims of the Revenue Commissioners and the company's unsecured creditors.

[21.058] A retention of title clause[162] is a provision in a contract for the sale of goods which purports to reserve the title in the goods to the vendor until a future time when certain conditions have been fulfilled. The statutory basis of a retention of title clause is

---

158 See Hackett, 'Taking Security Over Intellectual Property Rights in Ireland' (1994) CLP 50.

159 See generally, Law Reform Commission *Debt Collection: (2) Retention of Title*, 28–1989; Dickson, 'Reservation of Title Clauses' (1978) SLS Legal Publications; Parris, *Effective Retention of Title Clauses*, Collins; Hanley, 'Reservation of Title' (1989) Gazette ILSI 213; Thomas, 'Retention of Title Clauses in Business Contracts' (1989) Dli (Western Law Gazette) Autumn 28; Phillips & Schuster, 'Reservation of Title in the Commercial Laws of England and Ireland' (1979–80) DULJ 1; Maguire, 'Romalpa Misinterpreted' (1989) DULJ 40; Bradgate, 'Reservation of Title Ten Years On' (1987) Conv 434; McCormack, 'Reservation of Title – The House of Lords Speaks With A Scottish Accent' [1991] LMCLQ 154, the foregoing being a mere taste of the academic literature written on this most intriguing of topics.

160 *The Irish Independent* reported on 23 October 1987 that 'A significant number of suppliers to the H Williams chain are finding that the legal arrangements they had made to protect their title to goods supplied by them to the troubled supermarket firm are proving anything but watertight. 'There is around £7m worth of stock in the hands of the H Williams receiver. We assumed it was ours...[but]...we are now finding that recovery of around £3m worth of stock is in serious doubt.'

161 See para **[21.006]**.

162 Also referred to as a 'reservation of title', or a 'Romalpa' clause, the latter after the first modern decision to consider such clauses, *Aluminium Industrie Vaasen BV v Romalpa Aluminium Ltd* [1976] 2 All ER 552.

the Sale of Goods Act 1893, s 17 which provides that property in goods in sale shall pass when the parties stipulate that it should. Since there are a variety of types of retention of title clauses in existence, it is proposed to systematically consider the four main generic forms which retention of title clauses may take.

(a) Simple retention of title clause

[21.059] A simple retention of title clause provides that property or title in specific goods shall not pass to the purchaser until the full purchase price of those goods has been paid to the vendor. It may be taken as established law that such clauses will, where properly drafted, be effective to retain title in the vendor, and that furthermore, for present purposes, will *not* constitute the creation of a registrable charge. So, in *Re Charles Dougherty*[163], animal feed was supplied to the purchaser-company subject to a simple retention of title clause[164] and when the company went into receivership the food was still identifiable. The vendor sought its return, but the receiver to the company argued, inter alia, that the clause created a charge, which in the case of an individual should have been registered under the Bills of Sale (Ireland) Act 1879, and so ought to have been registered by the company by virtue of CA 1963, s 99(2)(c)[165]. Carroll J rejected this saying that:

> 'If the goods are delivered to the buyer who has not paid for them, on terms that title remains with the seller until he is paid, the buyer's creditors cannot seize the goods. Even though the goods are in the apparent possession of the buyer, he is *not the maker or giver* of the Bill of Sale. He is the holder or grantee under the Bill...
>
> However, if a contract deals with the future title of the buyer in the goods to be manufactured from the goods supplied, then, as regards that future title, the contract would be a Bill of Sale in which the buyer is the maker or giver and the seller is grantee...
>
> In this case the clause in question is *not complex enough to create a charge* over future manufactured goods, the title to which cannot exist at the date of the contract. The contract deals only with the present title to the goods sold and not with future title of goods to be manufactured.'[166] [Emphasis added]

As seen above, the Sale of Goods Act 1893, s 17 allows the parties to decide amongst themselves when property is to pass, and so a simple title retention is permissible. This judgment makes it clear that a 'simple' retention of title clause will not create a charge registrable under CA 1963, s 99(1). It also demonstrates the fundamental principle that the creation of a charge is essentially *a matter of contract*, between the parties themselves. If the buyer never has title in the goods, then he cannot grant a proprietary right in those goods to someone else[167].

---

163 *Somers v Allen* [1984] ILRM 437.

164 It provided: 'The transfer of title to you of the goods as detailed in this contract shall not occur until the invoice covering same has been paid in full, and accordingly, the goods wherever situated shall be thereupon at your risk.'

165 See para **[21.037]**.

166 [1984] ILRM 437 at 441, 442.

167 See Jones, 'Retention of Title Clauses 10 Years from Romalpa' (1986) Co Lawyer 235. However contrast an alternative view put forward by McWilliams J in *Frigioscandia (Contracting) Ltd v Continental Irish Meat Ltd* [1982] ILRM 396 at 398 where he said:

[21.060] An entirely different situation arises where, in a simple retention of title clause, the vendor reserves the 'equitable and beneficial ownership' in the goods. It has been held in *Re Bond Worth Ltd*[168] that such a clause allows the legal title to pass to the purchaser, meaning that the net substance of the transaction is that the purchaser grants back the equitable title to the vendor[169]. This will create a charge, and where such a charge is of a kind described in CA 1963, s 99(2), will constitute a registrable charge.

[21.061] A supplier of goods sold on foot of a retention of title clause will have his claim defeated by a subsequent delivery of those goods to a bona fide third party without actual notice of the supplier's title. It has been held, however, that in order for a supplier's claim to be defeated, there must be an actual sale and that delivery under a mere agreement to sell is not sufficient[170]. Another issue to have been addressed by the courts is the effect of a retention of title clause, where the original goods are subsequently processed. The macabre question considered in *Chaigley Farms Ltd v Crawford, Kaye & Greyshire Ltd*[171] was whether the slaughtering and cutting into meat products of cattle, originally sold 'on the hoof' and subject to a retention of title clause, was sufficient to transfer title to the purchaser. It was held that there was an inescapable difference between a live animal and a dead one and that the effect of such processing was to transfer title to the purchaser[172]. Equally, where goods the subject of a retention of title clause become fixtures to real property, the title to them will pass with the title to the land, thereby defeating the supplier's in rem claim to them[173]. Where a supplier's in

---

167 (contd)

'A difficulty which arises with regard to clauses of this nature is that they are included in the contracts to secure the payment to the vendor of the price of the goods and therefore it may be said as has been argued that the goods once delivered, are intended to be held by the purchaser as security for such payment and that the transaction is in the category of a mortgage in that the vendor, although retaining ownership or an interest in the goods, cannot take possession of them provided that the specified instalments are paid, and that this leads to the conclusion that such a clause must be treated as creating a mortgage or a charge over the goods. In my opinion such a conclusion can have no general application to these clauses and each must depend on its own facts.'

168 *Re Bond Worth Ltd* [1979] 3 All ER 919.

169 Note that a clause which retained the equitable and beneficial ownership in goods was upheld in *Re Stokes & McKiernan* [1978] ILRM 240, by McWilliams J but the same judge accepted that there was a difference between a simple retention of title clause which retains *legal* ownership and one which retains *equitable* ownership in *Frigoscandia (Contracting) Ltd v Continental Irish Meats Ltd* [1982] ILRM 396.

170 *Re Highway Foods Ltd* (1994) Times 1 November; *Palmer's In Company*, Issue 1/95, 18 January 1995.

171 *Chaigley Farms Ltd v Crawford, Kaye & Greyshire Ltd* [1996] BCC 957. See de Lacy, 'Processed Goods and Retention of Title Clauses', (1995) *Palmer's In Company*, Issue 10/97, 20 November 1997.

172 Cf *Re Weddel (NZ) Ltd* (1996) 5 NZBLC 104 and *Pongakawa Sawmill Ltd v New Zealand Forest Products Ltd* [1992] 3 NZLR 304.

173 *Aircool Installations v British Telecommunications* (1995) Current Law Week, 19 May 1995; (1995) *Palmer's In Company* Issue 7/95, 19 July 1995. In this case the supplier of air conditioning equipment delivered on foot of a retention of title clause had its claim to the equipment defeated after it became a fixture to real property.

rem claim to goods is defeated, he may still have an in personam claim against the purchaser, or a person acting on the purchaser's behalf, such as its liquidator[174].

(b) An aggregation retention of title clause

[21.062] An aggregation retention of title clause typically provides that until such time as the goods in sale have been paid for, not only will the title in those goods not pass, but the title in goods manufactured from the goods supplied, even where mixed with other goods not subject to the retention of title clause, will rest with the vendor[175]. This type of clause has almost invariably been held to be a charge over the assets of the purchaser-company[176]. However, a distinction must be made between situations where the goods sold are irreversibly mixed with other goods as opposed to where they remain readily identifiable[177]. Where goods are still identifiable, although mixed with other goods, a simple retention of title clause has been held to retain the title in those goods, without necessarily being deemed to create a charge: *Hendy Lennox Ltd v Grahame Puttick Ltd*[178].

[21.063] Where goods supplied are irreversibly mixed it has been held by Bridge LJ in *Borden (UK) Ltd v Scottish Timber Products Ltd*[179] that the title in those goods is extinguished. There, resin was supplied to the purchaser-company and the terms of sale provided that property would not pass until full payment had been received and further provided that chipboard manufactured from the resin would be charged to the extent that it consisted of the resin. When the purchaser-company went into liquidation, the vendors sought to rely on this clause, but Bridge LJ held that as soon as the resin was used in the manufacturing process, 'it ceased to exist as resin and accordingly, the title to the resin simply disappeared'.

[21.064] While this case did not consider an actual aggregation clause, Bridge LJ in *Borden* envisaged such a clause saying:

> '... if a seller of goods to a manufacturer who knows that his goods are to be used in the manufacturing process before they are paid for, wishes to reserve to himself an effective security for the payment of the price, he cannot rely on a simple reservation of title clause

---

[174] In *Vale Sewing Machines v Robb* [1997] SCLR 797, *Palmer's In Company* Issue 1/98, 28 January 1998 it was held by a Scottish Sheriff Court that a liquidator who disposed of goods that were held subject to a title retention clause might be personally liable to an unpaid supplier where there were reasonable grounds for believing that the goods were not the company's property.

[175] See, generally, Webb, 'Title and Transformation: Who Owns Manufactured Goods?' [2000] JBL 513.

[176] See *Re Andrabell Ltd* [1984] 3 All ER 407; *Pfeifer Weinkellerei v Arbuthnot Factors Ltd* [1988] 1 WLR 150; *Re Weldtech Ltd* [1991] BCC 16; and *Compaq Computers Ltd v Abercorn Group Ltd* [1991] BCC 484.

[177] These different scenarios have been said to be to be analogous to the Roman concepts of '*accessio*'/'*confusio*' and '*commixtio*', respectively: see Parris, *Effective Retention of Title Clauses*, Collins, p 88.

[178] *Hendy Lennox Ltd v Grahame Puttick Ltd* [1984] 1 WLR 485.

[179] *Borden (UK) Ltd v Scottish Timber Products Ltd* [1979] 3 All ER 961.

> such as that relied on by the sellers. If he wishes to acquire rights over the manufactured product, he can only do so by express contractual stipulation.'[180]

However, while one can draft such a clause, it seems inescapable that it will be deemed to constitute a charge which requires registration under CA 1963, s 99(1). So in *Peachdart Ltd*[181], where leather was supplied to a company which was intended to be used to make handbags, Vinelott J refused to interpret such a clause as anything other than a charge. The Irish courts have also taken such a view. Hence, in *Kruppstahl AG v Quitmann Products Ltd*[182] while a simple reservation of title clause was upheld, an aggregation-type clause over processed steel was found to be a charge. Again, in *Re Charles Dougherty Ltd*[183] Carroll J said of the *Quitmann* case that it:

> '... therefore illustrates that a seller can make an effective reservation of title clause to goods prior to manufacture, but if he requires security over the manufactured goods the buyer will have to grant him this and this would require registration as a Bill of Sale.'[184]

Essentially, while it is arguable that careful drafting[185] can prevent the purchaser-company from ever acquiring full title in the goods, it is clear that the courts have turned their face against this and have held that in such circumstances, the purchaser *creates a charge* in favour of the vendor[186]. For an alternative view, however, see *Associated Alloys Pty Ltd v Metropolitan Engineering & Fabrication Ltd*[187], considered below[188], where a combined aggregation-proceeds of sale clause was found to be capable of being construed as a trust that is not required to be registered in order to be effective.

(c) Proceeds of sale clause

[21.065] This form of a retention of title clause purports to acknowledge that a purchaser-company can sell the goods in sale, but provides that the proceeds are to be held *in trust* for the vendor. Genuine trusts are not registrable. So in *Fitzpatrick v Criminal Assets Bureau*[189] it had been held by the High Court that a Mercedes motor car which was in the legal ownership of a company was, in fact, beneficially owned by a director of the company. The Supreme Court held that there was no merit in a submission that the beneficial interest was void for want of registration because 'a trust is not a charge'.[190] One of the earlier cases, *Sugar Distributors Ltd v Monaghan Cash &*

---

180 [1979] 3 All ER 961 at 971.

181 *Peachdart Ltd* [1984] 1 Ch 131, [1983] All ER 204.

182 *Kruppstahl AG v Quitmann Products Ltd* [1982] ILRM 551.

183 *Re Charles Dougherty Ltd* [1984] ILRM 437.

184 [1984] ILRM 437 at 441.

185 Cf *Aircool Installations vBritish Telecommunications* (1995) Current Law Week, 19 May 1995; *Palmer's In Company*, Issue 7/95, 19 July 1995 where the supplier of air conditioning equipment supplied on foot of a retention of title clause had its claim defeated by the application of the rule that if goods become fixtures to land, their title passes with the land.

186 *Ian Chisholm Textiles Ltd v Griffiths* [1994] BCC 96.

187 *Associated Alloys Pty Ltd v Metropolitan Engineering & Fabrication Ltd* [1998] NSWSC 442 of 21 September 1998 (Supreme Court of New South Wales); [2000] HCA 25 of 11 May 2000 (High Court of Australia).

188 See para **[21.067]**.

189 *Fitzpatrick v Criminal Assets Bureau* [2000] 1 ILRM 299.

190 [2000] 1 ILRM 299 at 305.

Carry Ltd[191], went so far as to imply a proceeds of sale clause into a simple retention of title clause. This enabled the vendor to demand that the purchaser-company account for the proceeds of sale. More recently, in *Re WJ Hickey Ltd*[192], electrical goods were sold to a company subject to a proceeds of sale clause. The clause provided:

> '(a) No property in any of the goods...shall pass until full payment for all goods supplied hereunder has been received by the seller and until such payment has been received by the seller the buyer shall hold the goods in trust for the seller in a manner which enables them to be identified as the goods of the seller and the buyer shall immediately return the goods to the seller, should the seller so request.
>
> (b) Notwithstanding paragraph (a) hereof the buyer shall be permitted to sell the goods to third parties in the normal course of business, but the proceeds of any such sale shall whenever any sum whatsoever is due from the buyer to the seller be held in trust for the seller in a manner which enables such proceeds to be identified as such.'

There, Barron J held that for a charge to be created, all the property in the goods must pass to the purchaser-company so that there could in fact be an assignment back to the chargee:

> 'I can find no ground for construing the clause in such a way that all the property must have passed to the company and that it assigned back an equitable interest in the goods by way of charge. The existence of such an assignment is essential to the applicant's case. Where charges have been found to exist...there was a clear assignment of such an interest. There can be none since the entire property never passed. The words "no property in any goods shall pass" must be given their literal interpretation.'[193]

Of particular importance was the fact that the vendor had stipulated that the goods be held *in trust* for him, thus giving rise to a *fiduciary relationship* between vendor and purchaser. Furthermore, it was significant for the learned judge that the purchaser-company was bound to keep a separate account.

[21.066] While the *Hickey* case suggested that proceeds of sale clauses will not amount to the creation of a charge by the purchaser-company, *Carroll Group Distributors Ltd v G&JF Bourke Ltd*[194], found to the contrary. In that case the court scorned the requirement that a separate account was to be kept. The vendor sold tobacco worth £54,000, subject to a clause which provided that property would not pass until all sums due were paid. Again, the clause allowed the purchaser a right to resell the goods in the normal course of business. In so doing, the purchaser-company acted on its own behalf. Proceeds of sale were to be held in trust for the vendor and the purchaser was obliged to keep a separate account[195] and provide details to the vendor on request. Murphy J took a very different view to that taken by Barron J and held that the substance of the

---

[191] *Sugar Distributors Ltd v Monaghan Cash & Carry Ltd* [1982] ILRM 399.

[192] *Re WJ Hickey Ltd* [1988] IR 126.

[193] [1988] IR 126 at 131.

[194] *Carroll Group Distributors Ltd v G&JF Bourke Ltd* [1990] ILRM 285.

[195] [1990] ILRM 285 at 289, where Murphy J said that no account was opened, and that the vendor was probably aware of this.

transaction was to create a charge, and he endorsed the views of McWilliam J in *Frigoscandia (Contracting) Ltd v Continental Irish Meat Ltd*[196]. He said:

> 'If one...analyses the bargain made between the parties it is clear that such arrangements properly implemented would result in a bank account with sums of money credited thereto which would probably be in excess of the amounts due by Bourkes to Carrolls. This would arise partly from the fact that the goods would be resold at a marked up price and partly from the fact that the proceeds of sale would include some goods the cost price of which had been discharged and some had not. In other words the bank account would be a fund to which Carrolls could have recourse to ensure the discharge of the moneys due to them even though they would not be entitled to the entire of that fund. Accordingly the fund agreed to be credited would possess all the characteristics of a mortgage or charge...'[197]

Murphy J deemed the transaction to constitute a charge in substance, which was void for want of registration under CA 1963, s 99(1). It is thought that the views of Murphy J will ultimately prevail, and that such contractual stipulations will be held to constitute the creation of a charge by the parties[198]. Indeed, in Ireland, it was this decision which sounded the death-knell for proceeds of sale clauses.

[21.067] The High Court of Australia has, however, in *Associated Alloys Pty Ltd v Metropolitan Engineering & Fabrication Ltd*[199] breathed life into the proceeds of sale clause. In that case the plaintiff-supplier sold steel to the defendant-purchaser on foot of a clause which provided as follows:

> '... in the event that the purchaser uses the goods/ product in some manufacturing or construction process of its own or some third party, then the purchaser shall hold such part of the proceeds of such manufacturing or construction process as relates to the goods/ product in trust for the vendor. Such part shall be deemed to equal in dollar terms the amount owing by the purchaser to the vendor at the time of the receipt of such proceeds'.

This is a form of hybrid clause, which amounted to a combined aggregation-proceeds of sale clause. When the defendant-purchaser went into liquidation the plaintiff-supplier sought a declaration that its liquidator held over US$197,000 due in respect of steel supplied on trust for it. At trial it was held that the clause amounted to a registrable charge which was void for want of registration. On appeal the Supreme Court of New South Wales upheld the trial judge's decision that the clause created a charge which was void for want of registration. It went on to hold that the charge which the clause gave rise to was, on proper construction, a charge on book debts and not a floating charge. In arriving at this conclusion Sheller JA considered the decision in *Borden (UK) Ltd v Scottish Timber*[200], where Templeman LJ had stated that if a supplier's 'interest floated from the chipboard to proceeds of sale and onwards, so floated the charge and s 95 [of

---

[196] See para **[21.059]** at fn 167.

[197] See para **[21.059]** at fn 167.

[198] See also *Compaq Computer Ltd v Abercorn Group Ltd* [1993] BCLC 602 and *Modelboard Ltd v Outer Box Ltd* [1993] BCLC 623.

[199] *Associated Alloys Pty Ltd v Metropolitan Engineering & Fabrication Ltd* [1998] NSWSC 442 of 21 September 1998 (Supreme Court of New South Wales), [2000] HCA 25 of 11 May 2000 (High Court of Australia).

[200] *Borden (UK) Ltd v Scottish Timber* [1981] Ch 25.

the Companies Act 1948 (UK)] makes void any unregistered floating charge on the undertaking or property of the company'. Sheller JA took a contrary view:

> 'What Templeman LJ said accords with the general concept of a floating charge as one "intended by the parties to cover *a class of property* but not to attach to specific items within the class until some future event occurs" with the consequence that until that event occurs the chargor is free to dispose of items within the class in the ordinary course of business so that the taker from the chargor acquires the property free of the charge...But the [subclause in question] of the [plaintiff's] standard clause provided for the part of the proceeds charged to be held in trust for [the plaintiff] which inhibited [the defendant] from dealing with that part of the proceeds in any way contrary to the terms of the trust, that is to say, in any way other than for the benefit of [the plaintiff]. Moreover...a person in whose favour property is charged has only a security interest in the property and has not the equitable ownership in the same way as a beneficiary under a trust. I agree with [the trial judge] that any charge on the proceeds was not a floating charge'.

Shellar JA went on to hold that the retention of title clause went on to create a charge on book debts and that it was void for want of registration.

[21.068] Against all odds, the High Court of Australia held that the clause did not have to be construed as a registrable charge and that, if there was sufficient supporting evidence, it could be found to be a trust[201]. On the meaning of the phrase, 'the proceeds' as used in the clause, the majority decision rejected the contention that it included book debts. On this point it was said:

> 'The phrase has the meaning employed by Sir George Jessel MR in his ex tempore judgment in *Re Hallett's Estate; Knatchbull v Hallett*[202] where the Master of the Rolls eloquently states the principles of tracing in equity. The phrase "the proceeds" is to be construed as referring to moneys received by the Buyer and not debts which may be set out in the Buyer's books (or computer records) from time to time[203]. The concluding sentence of the Proceeds Subclause would be strained if the phrase "the proceeds" were to include book debts...In contrast, limiting the phrase "the proceeds" to refer to payments made to the Buyer results in this equation operating with certainty.'[204]

Having determined what was meant by the phrase 'the proceeds' the majority went on to consider whether it was possible for the parties to have intended to create a trust over the proceeds. After examining the language used and the requirements for a trust, the majority held that 'there was an agreement effective in equity to bind, from time to time, the relevant "proceeds"'[205]. The majority decision concluded that:

---

[201] As it happened, it was held that there was insufficient evidence to support the finding that there was in fact a trust and despite the sea change in judicial attitude, the appeal was disallowed.

[202] *Re Hallett's Estate; Knatchbull v Hallett* (1880) 13 Ch D 696 at 798–709.

[203] The Court's footnote reads: 'Questions as to the application of moneys received, which it is unnecessary now to answer, may arise where a running account exists between a supplier (eg the seller) and purchaser (eg the buyer).'

[204] *Associated Alloys Pty Ltd v Metropolitan Engineering & Fabrication Ltd* [2000] HCA 25 of 11 May 2000 (High Court of Australia) at para 25.

[205] [2000] HCA 25 of 11 May 2000 (High Court of Australia) at para 42.

'The Proceeds Subclause is an agreement to constitute a trust of future acquired-property. It is therefore not a "charge"...and the detailed provisions of the law governing charges thus do not apply to it. The Proceeds Subclause is not a "registrable charge"...In turn, the Proceeds Subclause is not void as against the administrators or liquidator of the Buyer.'[206]

The Australian High Court recognised that the lack of any statutory obligation to register the Proceeds Subclause created commercial incentives to incorporate such clauses into purchase agreements. They went on to comment on the lacunae they had identified in the following terms:

'In the law, the legislature has chosen to select as the criterion of operation of the registration provisions that which it defines as a "charge". The contractual and trust arrangement with which this appeal is concerned did not involve the creation of such a charge or an agreement to create one. To treat the Proceeds Subclause as an agreement which falls foul of the law is to rewrite the statute. It is not for the courts to destroy or impair property rights, such as those arising under trusts, by supplementing the list of those rights which the legislature has selected for such treatment.'[207]

In the final analysis, however, the appeal was dismissed because there was a 'critical gap in the evidence' required to prove the receipt of 'the proceeds'. The decision of the majority[208] is certainly more in accord with the High Court decision in *Re WJ Hickey Ltd*[209] *than in Carroll Group Distributors Ltd v G&JF Bourke Ltd*[210]. There is an attractiveness to the decision of the Australian High Court, giving effect as it does to the clear words used by the parties.

(d) Current account clause

[21.069] Current account clauses are often appended to simple retention of title clauses and provide that title in the goods in sale shall not pass until such time as *all sums due* to the vendor have been paid. Often, sums due on foot of other contracts will also be included[211]. While these have been upheld in both Ireland[212] and England it was thought that they would ultimately be found to constitute a charge over the company's book debts or alternatively a floating charge over the company's assets. This is because the essence of the transaction is that the title in goods which are 'sold' to the purchaser-company are contractually retained by the vendor, *as security*, until other moneys are paid by the purchaser-company.

[21.070] Notwithstanding the foregoing reservations, the House of Lords have upheld the validity of a current account clause (which had not been registered) in *Armour v Thyssen Edelstahlwerke AG*[213]. There, it was held that the ownership of the goods in

---

206 [2000] HCA 25 of 11 May 2000 (High Court of Australia) at para 48.

207 [2000] HCA 25 of 11 May 2000 (High Court of Australia) at para 51.

208 The decision of the court was by a four (Gaudron, McHugh, Gummow and Hayne JJ) to one (Kirby J) majority.

209 *Re WJ Hickey Ltd* [1988] IR 126.

210 *Carroll Group Distributors Ltd v G&JF Bourke Ltd* [1990] ILRM 285.

211 See *Clough Mill Ltd v Martin* [1984] 3 All ER 982 at 987h.

212 See *Re Stokes & McKiernan* [1978] ILRM 240.

213 *Armour v Thyssen Edelstahlwerke AG* [1990] 3 WLR 810.

question did not pass to the purchaser-company. Lord Keith said that a charge or right in security would only arise where:

> '... the contract of sale gave it the property in the goods, but the contract of sale said that the property in the goods was not to pass until all debts due to the appellants had been paid. We are here very far removed from the situation where a party in possession of corporeal movable is seeking to create a subordinate right in favour of a creditor while retaining the ultimate right to himself.'[214]

It remains to be seen whether the Irish courts will accept this reasoning and hold that a current account retention of title clause does not constitute a charge that requires to be registered pursuant to CA 1963, s 99 if it is to be valid.

Judgment mortgages

[21.071] A judgment mortgage[215] is a peculiar form of security from a company because the company does not *create* the judgment mortgage; it cannot, therefore, be described as 'consensual security'. A judgment mortgage is created by a person, ('a judgment creditor') who obtains a court judgment against another person ('a judgment debtor') and who then registers that judgment against real property owned by the judgment debtor. Section 102(1) of CA 1963 provides that where a judgment is recovered against a company and is subsequently converted into a judgment mortgage affecting the property of the company, then:

> '...the judgment creditor shall cause 2 copies (certified by the Land Registry or the Registry of Deeds, as the case may be, to be correct copies) of the affidavit required for the purpose of registering the judgment as a mortgage to be delivered to the company within twenty-one days of such registration, and the company shall within 3 days of receipt of such copies deliver one of such copies to the Registrar of Companies for registration in manner required by this Act. By way of further precaution, the Land Registry or Registry of Deeds, shall as soon as may be deliver a copy of the said affidavit to the Registrar of Companies.'

The sanction for contravention of this section is contained in CA 1963, s 102(2) which provides that a judgment creditor who acts in default shall be liable to a fine not exceeding €634[216]. Although it has been suggested[217] that non-registration should make a judgment mortgage invalid, it is submitted that this should not be the case because such a mortgage is *not created by a company*, and moreover, for a mortgage or charge to be void if unregistered such must be expressly provided for by the legislature.

Charges over property outside of the State

[21.072] Section 99(3), (4) and (5) of CA 1963 concern situations in which Irish formed and registered companies create charges over foreign property (ie property situate outside the State). These subsections do not create any additional head of charge; they

---

[214] [1990] 3 WLR 810 at 815.

[215] See Wylie, *Irish Land Law* (3rd edn, 1997), para 13.163 *ff.*

[216] As increased by C(A)A 1982, s 15.

[217] Keane, *Company Law* (3rd edn, 2000), para 21.38.

are intended to make provision for procedural matters which arise when either a charge is created outside the State or the subject matter of the charge is situate outside the State.

[21.073] Section 99(3) of CA 1963 deals with the situation where a charge is created *outside* of the State in respect of property that is situate *outside* of the State. It provides that where a charge is created out of the State then particulars must be delivered to the CRO:

> '...21 days after the date on which the prescribed particulars could, in due course of post, and if despatched with due diligence, have been received in the State.'

By default[218], this requirement applies only to companies to which the Companies Acts 1963–2001 apply.

[21.074] Section 99(4) of CA 1963 is concerned with cases where a charge is created *within* the State over property that is situate *outside* of the State. This provides that, in such cases:

> '...the prescribed particulars *may* be sent for registration [ie to the Irish CRO] under this section, notwithstanding that further proceedings may be necessary to make the charge valid or effectual according to the law of the country in which the property is situate.' [emphasis added]

It is notable that by the use of the word 'may', this provision is facilitatory and not mandatory in nature. Accordingly, any obligation to deliver particulars of a charge to the CRO in the circumstances envisaged by s 99(4) will arise elsewhere.

[21.075] Section 99(5) of CA 1963 is concerned with where a charge comprises property situate *outside* the State, whether or not the charge is created inside or outside the State. Again, it is intended to provide for procedural matters associated with the registration of a charge over foreign property. It provides:

> 'Where a charge comprises property situate outside the State and registration in the country where the property is situate is necessary to make the charge valid or effectual according to the law of that country, a certificate in the prescribed form stating that the charge was presented for registration in the country where the property is situate on the date on which it was so presented shall be delivered to the Registrar of Companies for registration.'

This subsection might apply in the circumstances considered in either sub-ss (3) or (4) last considered as an additional consideration, since both envisage circumstances where charges are created over foreign property over property within the State. The necessity and desirability of such a provision in Irish companies' legislation has been questioned[219], but unless and until the law is changed on this point, practitioners should be cautious. It is doubted whether non-compliance with CA 1963, s 99(5) will render a charge void. It is thought that provided there is compliance with CA 1963, s 99(1) – ie

[218] See CA 1963, s 111 which, by specifying to what charges CA 1963, Pt IV (ss 99 to 112) applies, implicitly means that s 99(3) must be taken as referring only to charges on foreign property created by companies formed and registered within the State ie within the meaning of CA 1963, s 2.

[219] See Nolan, 'Registration of Company Charges Over Foreign Property – Who Needs s 99(5) of the Companies Act 1963?' (1995) ILT 9.

that particulars of the charge have been delivered within the prescribed 21 days from creation – the failure to deliver a certificate that the charge was presented for registration in the foreign country should not render the charge void as against a liquidator or creditor. It would remain the case, of course, that an offence would have been committed[220].

Charges created by foreign companies[221]

[21.076] Charges created by foreign companies over foreign property are of no concern to Irish law. The validity of such charges will be determined by the *lex situs* and not by the Companies Acts 1963–2001.

[21.077] Charges created by foreign companies over property in the State are, however, required to be registered under CA 1963, Part IV *if* such companies have an established place of business in the State[222]. Furthermore, this remains the case even though such foreign companies have not registered on the Irish external register of companies, as they should[223] if they have an established place of business within in the State[224]. Where such charges are not registered then they will be *void* against a liquidator or creditor of the company. Section 111 of CA 1963 provides:

> 'The provisions of [Part IV] shall extend to charges on property in the State which are created...and to charges on property in the State which is acquired ... by a company incorporated outside the State which has an established place of business within the State, and to judgment mortgages created...and affecting property in the State of such a company and to receivers, appointed...of property in the State of such a company, and for the purposes of those provisions, the principal place of business of such a company in the State shall be deemed to be its registered office.'

(a) Registered foreign companies

[21.078] Foreign or 'external' companies which establish a place of business in the State are obliged to register with the Registrar of Companies by CA 1963, s 352(1)[225]. Where a registered company creates a registrable charge over a property in the State, then the requisite particulars must be delivered to the Registrar of Companies using a Form 8E. Such charges are then registered on the CRO register of charges, by reference to the number assigned to it on its registration as an external company.

(b) Unregistered foreign companies: the Slavenburg file

[21.079] A foreign company which *has* an established place of business in the State but which does *not register* as an external company as it is required to do under CA 1963, s 352(1) is obliged to deliver particulars of a charge over property in Ireland to the CRO in the same way (by using a Form 8E) as a company which has registered under CA 1963, s 352. This was decided in the UK in *NV Slavenburg's Bank v Intercontinental*

[220] CA 1963, s 100.

[221] See Courtney, 'Registration of Charges: Foreign Companies and the *Slavenburg* File' (1992) Gazette ILSI 151.

[222] Gill, 'Foreign Companies and Establishing "A Place of Business" (1989) ILT 264.

[223] Pursuant to CA 1963, s 352.

[224] *NV Slavenburg's Bank v Intercontinental Natural Resources Ltd* [1980] 1 All ER 955.

[225] See Chapter 2, *Formation, Registration and Conversion of Private Companies*, para **[2.046]** *ff*.

Natural Resources Ltd[226]. In that case a company, which was incorporated in Bermuda, had an established place of business in England and created charges over assets which subsequently came to be reposited in England. The company was not registered in England nor were the particulars of the charges delivered to the English Companies House. The property in England was later sold, and the proceeds of sale paid into a joint account in the names of the parties' solicitors. Subsequently, a Bermudan court wound up the company. In subsequent proceedings before the English courts it was argued, inter alia, that the charges over the property situated in England were void for non-registration. It was held by Lloyd J that although there was no formal method for registering such charges because the foreign company did not have a company number which it would have had were it registered on the external register, particulars of such charges were nonetheless required *to be delivered* to the English Companies House. Where such were not delivered those charges would be void as against a liquidator or any creditor. The mere fact that such charges could not formally be registered was not a sufficient reason for failing to deliver particulars to the Registrar of Companies. In the words of Lloyd J:

> 'The fallacy in the argument lies in regarding registration of the charge under [CA 1963, Part IV] as a condition precedent to its validity. It is clear both from the language of [CA 1963, s 99]...that it is delivery of particulars of the charge, together with the instrument (if any) by which it is created or evidenced that saves that charge, and not its registration. In the *National Provincial Bank*[227] case Scrutton LJ said, after referring to the language of the section: 'That makes the avoidance dependant on the neglect to send in the particulars. The neglect to register the charge will not make it void'...So far as I am concerned, it seems to follow that the bank could have preserved the validity of its charges by delivering particulars within twenty-one days, despite the unwillingness of the registrar to register the charge without prior registration by the company under [CA 1963, Part XI]. In those circumstances ... [t]here is nothing certainly in [CA 1963, s 111] to suggest that the operation of that section is dependant in any way on the company having registered under [CA 1963, Part XI ie as an external company], and I am unwilling to imply any such limitation.'[228]

This was therefore the law in England[229]. It continues to be the law in Ireland that where a foreign company which has an established place of business in the State, but which has not registered as an external company under CA 1963, Part XI, creates a charge over property, real or personal, situate in Ireland, the company, or the holder of that charge, must deliver particulars of that charge to the Irish Registrar of Companies. Failure to do so will render that charge invalid[230].

---

226 *NV Slavenburg's Bank v Intercontinental Natural Resources Ltd* [1980] 1 All ER 955.

227 *National Provincial Bank* [1924] 1 KB 431 at 447.

228 [1980] 1 All ER 955 at 963–964. References to CA 1963 have been added.

229 The law in England has been changed by the CA 1989, although the new provisions on the registration of charges by *overseas companies* have not as yet been implemented.

230 It may be noted that this contrasts with the case of a judgment mortgage registered against a foreign company which has an established place of business in Ireland and which is not registered on the external register. It is submitted that the comments referred to above in the case of judgment mortgages against Irish registered companies applies here, and that the only sanction is a fine, the *charge* itself remaining valid.

[21.080] Ironically, the decision in *Slavenburg* has now been reversed by the British Parliament enacting the Companies Act 1989 (UK) Sch 15, which inserted new ss 703A to 703N into the Companies Act 1985 (UK)[231]. The effect of these changes is that a foreign company which has not applied to be a 'registered overseas company' is not obliged to register charges which it creates over property in England and Wales, notwithstanding that it may have an established place of business there[232].

[21.081] The decision in *Slavenburg* would appear to continue to be the law, and certainly the practice, in Ireland. Thus, charges created in such circumstances should be delivered to the CRO[233]. What is the Registrar and his staff to do in such circumstances? The plight of the Registrar was addressed in *Slavenburg*'s case where Lloyd J said:

> 'Before leaving the point, I should say that counsel for the defendants expressly disclaimed any criticism of the registrar's current practice. Nor would I, myself, wish to criticise it in any way. His reasons for insisting on the company first registering under [Part XI] are clear enough. But they cannot affect the outcome of this case.'[234]

Following the lead set by the English Registrar, the Irish Registrar opened a so-called, '*Slavenburg* file', in which he notes that he has received delivery of the required particulars[235]. In due course the Registrar will issue a letter to the person who delivered particulars of the charge to the effect that delivery of the particulars has been received, but because the company is not registered as an external company, *registration* of the charge cannot be effected. Such a letter is a sufficient safeguard for any lender who takes a charge in such circumstances, and this letter should be treated as if it were a certificate of registration[236]. Indeed, in that the common parlance of the Irish CRO is that delivery of such particulars have been noted on the *Slavenburg* file, the hibernisation of the decision and its implications is clear.

(c) Established place of business

[21.082] Unless a company has an established place of business[237] in the State, neither full registration on the ordinary register of charges nor informal 'notation' on the *Slavenburg* file is required. What then is meant by an 'established place of business'?

---

231 These provisions have not as yet been brought into law in England and Wales.

232 See generally, Dine, 'Registration of Company Charges' (1991) BLR 31 and Ferran & Mayo, 'Registration of Company Charges – The New Regime' (1990) JBL 152.

233 See also *Re Oriel Ltd* [1985] BCLC 343 where the liquidator contended, and Oliver LJ accepted, at 346 that: '... although the company was a foreign company which had never filed any of the documents required to be filed by an overseas company under [CA 1963, Part XI], it was nevertheless a company to which the provisions of [s 99] of the Act were applicable.' See also *Re Alton Corporation* [1985] BCLC 27.

234 [1980] 1 All ER 955 at 964b.

235 The Irish *Slavenburg* file has been assigned a number by the registrar and so, all particulars for all companies which are delivered to the CRO are assigned the same number, 950000.

236 However, it may be noted that this letter is different from a certificate of registration by reason of the fact that it does not have the advantage of being *conclusive evidence* that the requirements CA 1963, Pt IV have been complied with.

237 See Courtney, 'Registration of Charges: Foreign Companies and the Slavenburg File' (1992) Gazette ILSI 151 and Gill, 'Foreign Companies and Establishing 'A Place of Business' (1989) ILT 264.

[21.083] The definition of 'established place of business' has not been the subject of discussion proper in the Irish courts. The decision in *Donovan v North German Lloyd Steamship Co*[238] is, however, instructive. In that case it was held that service of proceedings on a foreign company were not satisfied by serving the summons on an address in Ireland, because although the defendant company did have an 'office' here, it did not have a *place of business* in the State. The defendant company's connection with Ireland was set out in the course of O'Byrne J's judgment:

> 'Apparently the defendant company is a foreign corporation, whose ships from time to time, make calls of port in this country, particularly at Cobh. At Cobh there is, and has been for some time, an office bearing the name of the defendant Company in large letters, and this fact and several others were relied upon for the purpose of showing that the defendant Company resided in this country in the sense in which a corporation can be said to reside in any country. Reliance was also placed on the fact that the name of the defendant Company appeared in the telephone directory, and on the fact, as alleged, that they were the rated occupiers of the premises in which the aforesaid office is situate.'

However, the lease of the premises used by the defendant-company was held by another company, which acted as 'agent' for not only the defendant-company, but also for other foreign companies[239]. Here, it was held that the defendant company could not have proceedings served upon it in this manner. However, whether the facts of this case would today justify an Irish court to hold that it did not have an *established place of business* in the context under consideration here is debatable.

[21.084] Regarded as 'the most apposite case in the present context'[240] is the Court of Appeal decision in *Re Oriel Ltd*[241]. In that case the issue of established place of business was considered where a foreign company delivered particulars of the charges it had created, where it had not registered under the English equivalent of CA 1963, Part XI. The company in question had been incorporated and registered in the Isle of Man. Its objects were the acquisition, mortgaging and management of a company which was controlled by a husband and wife who lived in England. Subsequently, the company acquired three garage sites in England and upon entering a solus agreement charged them to a petrol supplier. Subsequently, three more sites were acquired, and charged. The management of the company was conducted by the husband-director, who gave as an address the registered office of the company and his own personal address. When the company was wound up, the validity of the charges was questioned since they had never been registered nor particulars of them delivered to the English Companies House. Central to the argument of the liquidator was that the company had an established place of business in England, and as such the charges ought to have been registered, or at least

238 *Donovan v North German Lloyd Steamship Co* [1933] IR 33.

239 In *Rakusens Ltd v Baser Ambalaj Plastik Sanayi Ticaret Asi* [2002] 1 BCLC 104 it was held that where it was sought to establish that a foreign company had established a place of business by the conduct of persons who were agents (as opposed to employees) it was insufficient to merely show that the 'agent' had established a place of business in the State.

240 Per Hirst J in *Cleveland Museum of Art v Capricorn Art International SA* [1990] BCLC 546 at 550i.

241 *Re Oriel Ltd* [1985] 3 All ER 216, [1985] BCLC 343.

particulars delivered since the company had never registered on the external register. Arising from this case, the Court of Appeal decided two particularly contentious issues. First, it was decided that the relevant date for determining whether or not a company had an established place of business was the date on which it executed a charge over its property in the State, while having an established place of business.

Secondly, the concept of 'established place of business', was said by Oliver LJ to suggest[242]:

> '... that it is essential to an "established place of business" that there should be some visible sign or physical indication that the company has a connection with particular premises ...
>
> Speaking for myself, I think also that when the word "established" is used adjectivally, as it is in [CA 1963, s 111], it connotes not only the setting-up of a place of business at a specific location, but a degree of permanence or recognisability as being a location of the company's business. If, for instance, agents of an overseas company conduct business from time to time by meeting clients or potential customers in the public rooms of an hotel in London, they have, no doubt, "carried on business" in England, but I would for my part find it very difficult to persuade myself that the hotel lounge was "an established place of business". The concept, as it seems to me, is of some more or less permanent location, not necessarily owned or even leased by the company, but at least associated with the company and from which habitually or with some degree of regularity business is conducted.'[243]

On the facts of the case it was held that in respect of the first three charges, particulars were not required to be delivered to the Companies House because, on their creation, the company did not have an established place of business in England and Wales. However, in respect of the second three charges, particulars of these ought to have been delivered to the Companies House since on their creation, the company had an established place of business in England and Wales.

[21.085] The use of the word *established* connotes some ensconced or settled place of business: to have an established place of business, a place must have some degree of permanence. It must not be merely transitory or dependent upon, say, the chance presence of a representative of the foreign company in Ireland. In summary, some of the factors which will go towards the finding by a court that a foreign company has an established place of business include:

- having a specified or identifiable place at which it carries on business although the company does not necessarily have to own or lease a premises;
- having a visible sign or physical indication that the company is connected to a place;
- that the company's physical connections are more than merely fleeting or transitory;
- that there is a degree of permanence or ensconcement about the connection;
- a regularity of business being conducted there by the company.

---

242 On the authority of *Derverall v Grant Advertising Inc* [1954] 3 All ER 389.

243 [1985] BCLC 343 at 347.

Clearly, any precise definition of what is meant by established place of business is fraught with difficulty. Every case will turn on its own facts and the presence of the foregoing factors will merely influence the outcome.

[21.086] It has also been decided that a company will be deemed to have an established place of business even if the business carried on in the State is only incidental to its main business. This was decided in *South India Shipping Corp Ltd v Export-Import Bank of Korea*[244] where the English Court of Appeal, per Ackner J, said:

> 'The defendant bank are an export-import bank, not a high street bank. They have both premises and staff within the jurisdiction. They conduct external relations with other banks and financial institutions. They carry out preliminary work in relation to granting or obtaining loans. They seek to give publicity to the foreign bank and encourage trade between Korea and the United Kingdom, and they consult with other banks and financial institutions on the usual operating matters. They have therefore an established place of business within Great Britain and it matters not that they do not conclude within the jurisdiction any banking dealings with the general public as opposed to other banks or financial institutions.'

This has been recently been re-stated in *Rome v Punjab National Bank (No 2)*[245] where Hirst J noted that the *South India Shipping Corp* case had held:

> '... that it was sufficient to show the establishment of an office in Great Britain where activities incidental to the main business of the company were carried on, and that it was unnecessary to show that a substantial part of its business was conducted within the jurisdiction.'

In the *Rome* case a bank which was registered on the external register ceased to carry on business in the UK. A hiving-down operation began and while the company did no new business in the UK, two employees remained to finalise outstanding matters. These two persons were registered as persons upon whom proceedings could be served, satisfying the requirements of the English equivalent to CA 1963, Part XI[246]. The company subsequently served notice on the Registrar of Companies that, after a certain date, the company would cease to have a place of business in the UK. The registrar responded by closing the company's file. Even though this had been done, proceedings were served on one of the employees, and this was held to be a valid service. Incidental to this it was also held that at the time of service of the writ, the company did not have an established place of business. As to the determination of this question, Hirst J said:

> 'In my judgment, the correct approach is that adopted in the *South India case*, namely to examine the actual activities which are revealed on the evidence in order to decide whether or not they qualify.
>
> Examining those described above, I have no hesitation whatsoever in concluding that all but the last are no more than loose ends which needed to be tied up after the cessation of business; and the last, which... involves no more than maintaining a point of contact with English solicitors, does not in my judgment constitute a business activity at all.

---

244 *South India Shipping Corp Ltd v Export–Import Bank of Korea* [1985] 2 All ER 219, [1985] BCLC 163.

245 *Rome v Punjab National Bank (No 2)* [1989] BCLC 328.

246 See Chapter 6, *Corporate Civil Litigation*, para **[6.015]**.

> Consequently there was no business activity being carried out here by the defendants at the relevant date.'[247]

[21.087] A particular problem arises for the solicitor acting for a lending institution where a foreign company, without any property or established place of business in Ireland, borrows money for the express purpose of acquiring a business premises in Ireland. Is one to insist upon registration of the charge? Is the operative date, for determining whether a company has an established place of business, the date on which the charge is created? This point was considered in *Re Oriel Ltd*[248] where Oliver LJ said:

> '...It is difficult to see how, when premises are acquired for the first time and immediately charged, the established place of business which the company has can be the premises charged. There is, in fact, no evidence that the company had any connection with those premises prior to the charge beyond being designated, prior to its incorporation, as the intended owner.'

It is respectfully submitted that where there is any doubt, it is safest to insist that particulars of a charge are delivered to the CRO. It is better to be safe than leave oneself open to a court finding that particulars ought to have been delivered and that the charge is consequently void.

Late registration of registrable charges[249]

[21.088] Failure to deliver particulars of a registrable charge to the CRO within the prescribed 21 days results in what was a secured charge becoming void against a liquidator and any creditor of the company. An attempt, of dubious value to a secured creditor so affected, is made to lessen the severity of this by CA 1963, s 106(1) which facilitates court-approved late-registration. It states:

> 'The court, on being satisfied that the omission to register a charge within the time required by the Act or that the omission or mis-statement of any particular with respect to any such charge or in a memorandum of satisfaction was accidental, or due to inadvertence or to some other sufficient cause, or is not of a nature to prejudice the position of creditors or shareholders of the company, or that on other grounds it is just and equitable to grant relief, may, on the application of the company or any person interested, and on such terms and conditions as seem to the court just and expedient, order that the time for registration shall be extended, or, as the case may be, that the omission or mis-statement shall be rectified.'

Relief under s 106 is discretionary. The section makes reference to five separate grounds on foot of which the court may grant relief. There are many examples of cases where the courts have granted relief using each of the five grounds as a basis:

- accident[250];

---

247 [1984] BCLC 328 at 338–339.

248 [1985] 3 All ER 216 at 221.

249 See generally, Gough, *Company Charges* (2nd edn, 1996), pp 762–807. See also Johnston, *Banking and Security Law in Ireland* (1998), pp 600–605.

250 In *Re Chantry House Developments plc* [1990] BCLC 813 the mortgagee's solicitor's failure to deliver particulars was found to be accidental.

— inadvertence[251];

— some other sufficient cause[252];

— not of a nature to prejudice the position of creditors or shareholders[253]; and

— it is just and equitable to grant relief on other grounds[254].

(a) The discretionary nature of CA 1963, s 106

[21.089] Section 106 of CA 1963 is a discretionary relief[255]. Accordingly, the court will not grant relief where to do so would be futile. One example here of an Irish case where late registration was refused is *Re Farm Fresh Frozen Foods Ltd*[256]. There, Keane J said that late registration would not be granted because:

> 'It is acknowledged that no useful purpose would be served by making such an order if it included the usual saver for the rights of parties acquired prior to the date of actual registration. I have no doubt that there would be no justification for making such an order in the present case.'[257]

Where a creditor who is making an application for late registration of a charge is aware of matters that would influence the court's discretion, he should disclose these matters to the court. In *Re Telomatic Ltd*[258] a creditor's conduct was said to be 'deplorable' where it did not disclose to the court that at the time of making the application the company had been dissolved[259]. It should also be noted that it is unwise for an applicant to delay in making application under s 106 as in *Victoria Housing Estates Ltd v Aspurton Estates Ltd*[260] the English Court of Appeal refused an application for late registration on the ground that, fearing the application might precipitate the company's liquidation, the applicant had deliberately deferred his application 'to see which way the wind [was] going to blow'.

---

[251] In *Re Resinoid and Mica Products Ltd* [1983] Ch 132 the mortgagee's and mortgagor's solicitors each thought that the other was attending to the registration, when neither was, in fact. See also *Re RM Arnold & Co Ltd* [1984] BCLC 535.

[252] The failure to recognise that a particular charge was registrable, through ignorance of the law: *Re S Abrahams & Sons* [1902] 1 Ch 695. Illness too has been accepted as an excuse for non–registration within time: *Re Joplin Brewery Co Ltd* [1902] 1 Ch 79.

[253] In *Re Braemar Investments Ltd* [1989] Ch 54 it was observed that the company's solvency meant that the likelihood of prejudice to unsecured creditors was remote.

[254] See *Re Chantry House Developments plc* [1990] BCLC 813 and *Re Braemar Investments Ltd* [1989] Ch 54.

[255] *Re Kris Cruisers Ltd* [1949] Ch 138.

[256] *Re Farm Fresh Frozen Foods Ltd* [1980] ILRM 131.

[257] [1980] ILRM 131 at 136.

[258] *Re Telomatic Ltd* [1994] 1 BCLC 90.

[259] [1994] 1 BCLC 90 at 94, per Judge Micklem. As to the requirement for full disclosure of all material facts in *ex parte* applications, albeit from the perspective of Mareva applications, see Courtney, *Mareva Injunctions and Related Interlocutory Orders* (1998), pp 305–316.

[260] *Victoria Housing Estates Ltd v Aspurton Estates Ltd* [1982] 3 All ER 665.

(b) Distinguishing a complete failure to register from a mere misstatement or omission

[21.090] The error sought to be rectified by CA 1963, s 106 can be one of two kinds. In the first place, there may have been a complete failure to register the charge within the prescribed time ie 21 days. In the second place, a charge may have been registered, but may have omitted or misstated one of the particulars required to be stated, eg to misstate the total amount secured by stating that a charge which in reality secured €100,000, only secured €80,000. On the authority of Costello J in *Re Shannonside Holdings Ltd*[261] such an error will not affect the validity of the charge, nor preclude the chargee from having security up to the amount actually specified in the debenture[262]. Since the effect of an order under s 106(1) is that the charge becomes a valid charge ab initio from the date of registration but subject to such other conditions as the court may impose[263], on the authority of the decision of Costello J, a chargee who discovers that particulars of the charge were misstated in the Form C1 might be better served not to make an application for rectification under s 106[264].

(c) The Joplin proviso[265]

[21.091] Where a court exercises its discretion and allows a charge to be registered out of time, it is usual for the court to insist that late registration is to be without prejudice to rights acquired by others. Accordingly, the courts usually insert a proviso that the order for late registration under CA 1963, s 106 is '...without prejudice to the rights of parties acquired prior to the actual time of such registration and a copy of this Order to be left with the Registrar of Companies.' [266]

A revised form of proviso also used is '...this order is without prejudice to the rights of the parties acquired during the period between the date of creation of the said charge and the date of its actual registration'.[267]

The first proviso (still inserted by Irish courts[268]) is said to provide an immune period ie a charge created after an unregistered charge, but before the expiration of 21 days from

---

261 *Re Shannonside Holdings Ltd* (20 May 1993, unreported) High Court. See para **[21.013]**.

262 See also *Re Valley Ice Cream (Ireland) Ltd* (22 July 1998, unreported) High Court (McCracken J) and generally para **[21.014]**.

263 See *Re Clarets Ltd; Spain v McCann* [1978] ILRM 215 at 217.

264 Other misstatements may well be 'protected' by reason of the conclusiveness of the register: see para **[21.013]–[21.014]**.

265 After *Re Joplin Brewery Co* [1902] 1 Ch 79.

266 See *Re Clarets Ltd; Spain v McCann* [1978] ILRM 215 at 217.

267 A variant of the form of proviso noted in *Watson v Duff Morgan and Vermont (Holdings) Ltd* [1974] 1 All ER 794, [1974] 1 WLR 450, namely: 'That the time for registering the charge be extended until the ... day of ... and this order is to be without prejudice to the rights of parties acquired during the period between the creation of the said charge and the date of its actual registration.' Note also that this latter proviso is quoted in Keane, *Company Law* (3rd edn, 2000), para 23.15.

268 In *Re Manning Furniture Ltd (in receivership)* [1996] 1 ILRM 13 where the wording of the proviso inserted by Keane J is quoted as being '...without prejudice to the rights (if any) of parties acquired prior to the time when the said particulars shall actually be registered.

the creation of the unregistered charge (eg created later the same day) will rank after an unregistered charge which is subsequently registered out of time[269]. The revised proviso will, however, protect rights acquired *after the creation* of the unregistered charge, the late registration of which is subsequently permitted[270].

[21.092] Those most clearly saved are other secured creditors who will be assisted by the insertion of this proviso. The proviso will not invariably be inserted into an order and was, for example, omitted in the case of *Re Fablehill Ltd*[271] where in an application for late registration of a prior unregistered charge it was heard that the company had, subsequent to the creation of that charge, created a subsequent charge in favour of its own directors.

[21.093] The position of unsecured creditors will clearly be prejudiced where relief is granted pursuant to CA 1963, s 106 and the proviso to an order for late registration will not save them. In *Re Ehrmann Bros Ltd*[272] Romer J said:

> '...the true effect of that condition is that it was only intended to protect rights acquired against or affecting the property charged by debentures. In my opinion that condition did not mean that after registration the registration was to be of no effect whatever as a charge against all creditors then existing...I think that they were intended to be treated as valid charges subject only...to rights acquired which could have been enforced in some way against the property had not the extension of time been granted'.

Unsecured creditors may have relied upon the fact that there were no registered charges before giving the company credit, but it may not be said that they acquired any 'rights' in the company's assets, unless the company is being wound up[273].

[21.094] In Ireland, the position of preferential creditors may be different. In *Re Manning Furniture Ltd (in receivership)*[274] it was held that the effect of the proviso was to mean that the late registration of a charge was without prejudice to the rights of preferential creditors of a company which was in receivership. The background facts were that a receiver had been appointed pursuant to the provisions of a mortgage debenture and various other security documents which had been given in favour of ICC Bank plc. However, the company had earlier granted a prior first legal mortgage and charge over certain premises in favour of, what was then, First National Building Society. When it transpired that the First National's charge had not been registered, and subsequent to the appointment by ICC of the receiver, application was made by First National for late registration under CA 1963, s 106. An order was made under that section by Keane J in the High Court which contained a proviso which stated 'But this Order to be without prejudice to the rights (if any) of parties acquired prior to the time

[269] See, for example, *Watson v Duff Morgan & Vermont (Holdings) Ltd* [1974] 1 All ER 794.

[270] See Gough, *Company Charges* (2nd edn, 1996), p 799–801.

[271] *Re Fablehill Ltd* [1991] BCLC 830.

[272] [1906] 2 Ch 697 at 707.

[273] See Ussher, *Company Law in Ireland* (1986), p 465. *Re Spiral Globe Co Ltd* [1902] 1 Ch 396 and *Re Ehrmann Bros Ltd* [1906] 2 Ch 697. But see *Re Telford Motors Ltd* (27 January 1978, unreported) High Court, per Hamilton J, where it was said that creditors acquire 'rights' once a winding-up order is made.

[274] *Re Manning Furniture Ltd (in receivership)* [1996] 1 ILRM 13.

when the said particulars shall actually be registered'. After the receiver realised the chattels and contracted for the sale of the premises he sought directions under CA 1963, s 316 as to whether he was obliged to discharge the preferential creditors out of the surplus (after payment of ICC) before paying the balance to First National. McCracken J, in reliance upon *Re Eisc Teoranta*[275], held that the receiver was bound to discharge the preferential creditors. As to the priority between the preferential creditors and First National, a mortgagee permitted late registration under s 106, he said:

> 'If the judgment of Mr Justice Lardner in the *Eisc Teoranta* case is correct, then the liability to discharge the preferential creditors arose on the appointment of the receiver, and was an existing liability of the Company with a preferential status at the time of the Order extending time. It was sought to be argued that, while they may have been preferential creditors, they were simply ordinary creditors who where given some form of preferential treatment, but I do not think I can accept that argument. On the appointment of the receiver, the preferential creditors were given a priority under s 98, and that priority was a right acquired prior to the time of the registration of the particulars of the mortgage of the First National Building Society.'[276]

In this case the proviso was construed as to afford protection to preferential creditors on the basis that the proviso protected those who had rights and because the preferential creditors had rights upon the appointment of the receiver they had protection. If a receiver had not been appointed then, of course, the preferential creditors would not have had section 98 'rights' and would not be entitled to priority ahead of any late registered floating charge.

In making an order under s 106 it is open to the court to modify[277] the traditional wording of the Joplin proviso to expressly exclude any possible reference to preferential creditors. Indeed it is thought that justice will not, ordinarily, be served by allowing the Revenue Commissioners priority to a late registered prior fixed charge since the only reason why one would allow priority – the absence of informed consent through notice to dealing with the encumbered company – is not relevant to the Revenue Commissioners' relationship with the company. It is submitted that, in principle and save where a winding up has commenced[278], the only 'rights' which ought to be protected by a Joplin proviso are such rights as are consensually acquired for value without notice of the existence of a prior right which would affect the right acquired. The protection of rights acquired otherwise, for example, by statute, are not within the contemplation of the registration of charges provisions.

(d) Application for late registration where company being wound up

[21.095] A contentious question concerns the situation where the winding up of a company has commenced. In *Re International Retail Ltd*[279] Kenny J said that court practice was to insist upon evidence that no winding-up order had been made, pending

275 *Eisc Teoranta* [1991] ILRM 760. See Chapter 22, *Corporate Borrowing: Receivers*, para **[22.056]**.

276 [1996] 1 ILRM 13 at 16.

277 *Re S Abrahams & Sons* [1902] 1 Ch 695; *Re IC Johnson & Co Ltd* [1902] 2 Ch 101.

278 See para **[21.095]**.

279 *Re International Retail Ltd* (26 July 1974, unreported) High Court (Kenny J).

or contemplated and that there were no judgments against the company which were unpaid before the granting of an extension of the time in which to register[280]. Upon a company going into liquidation, its existing unsecured creditors become interested in all the assets of the company; it has even been said that the creditors are in effect cestui que trust with beneficial interests in the company's property[281]. It has been said by Keane[282] that:

> 'Unsecured creditors are not protected by the proviso: it only applies to creditors who have acquired some form of proprietary interest in the property the subject of the charge. But once the company is wound up, the position is different: all the creditors of the company have an interest at that stage in the property, whether secured or not. The proviso would in such circumstances have to extend to all the creditors and this would render the making of the order a futile exercise. It has accordingly been held in England...that an order extending the time cannot be made once the company has been wound up, save in the most exceptional circumstances.'

Once an actual order to wind up has been made, no extension of time in which to register can be granted[283]. Where no order to wind up has been granted, then evidence of the kind spoken of by Kenny J will be required[284]. However, in *Re Telford Motors Ltd*[285] a registrable charge was taken by a lender, but was not registered. When the lender received a notice that it was proposed to wind up the company, an extension of time in which to register was applied for. Hamilton J, as he then was, granted the order and particulars were delivered to the Registrar of Companies. When the company was being wound up, the liquidator again applied to Hamilton J, this time to have the extended registration set aside. This was granted because the unsecured creditors had then acquired rights in the winding up. While it has been held that the imminence of a winding-up order ought to preclude the court from extending time[286], it was held in *Re Ashpurton Estates Ltd*[287] and *Re Braemar Investments Ltd*[288] that the imminence of winding up is not an absolute bar to relief. The imminence of winding up is, rather, a

---

280 Following *Re LH Charles and Co Ltd* [1935] WN 15.

281 See *Re Ashpurton Estates Ltd* [1983] Ch 110; *Re Anglo-Oriental Carpet Manufacturing Co* [1903] 1 Ch 914 and *R v Registrar of Companies, ex p Central Bank of India* [1986] 1 All ER 105.

282 Keane, *Company Law* (3rd edn, 2000), para 21.44.

283 *Re Resinoid & Mica Products Ltd* [1983] Ch 132 and *Victoria Housing Estates Ltd v Ashpurton Estates Ltd* [1983] Ch 110.

284 See *Re RM Arnold & Co Ltd* [1984] BCLC 535 where Harman J held that the imminence of liquidation was a relevant factor to be considered in deciding whether or not to exercise judicial discretion.

285 *Re Telford Motors Ltd* (27 January 1978, unreported) High Court (Hamilton J).

286 The granting of an order for extension here would seem to follow the case of *Re MIG Trust Ltd* [1933] Ch 542. However, Keane, *Company Law* (3rd edn, 2000), para 21.45 notes a different view was taken in *Re LH Charles & Co Ltd* [1935] WN 15. See also *Re Resinoid and Victoria Housing Estates* [1983] Ch 132.

287 *Re Ashpurton Estates Ltd* [1983] Ch 54.

288 *Re Braemar Investments Ltd* [1988] BCLC 556.

ground for refusal to be considered with all other matters in deciding whether or not to exercise the court's discretion. In *Exeter Trust Ltd v Screenways Ltd*[289] the English Court of Appeal, per Nourse LJ, held that where leave is granted to register a charge out of time and where the Registrar of Companies acts on foot of this order and issues a certificate of registration this will be conclusive evidence that the charge was validly registered. Where a court order is subsequently made for the removal of the charge from the register this will not affect the validity of the original registration.

[21.096] One of the means which a court may employ to safeguard unsecured creditors' interests, where application is made for late registration of a charge created by a company which is insolvent and teetering on the brink of liquidation, is to make a so-called '*Charles form order*'[290]. The Charles form order permits extension of time for registration but gives liberty to the company, usually through its liquidator or unsecured creditors, to apply to discharge the order for late registration where a winding up occurs within a specified number of days of the order for late registration. Accordingly the applicant for late registration may effect registration on foot of the order but submits himself to the court's jurisdiction for review of that order in the event of application being made consequent to a winding up. The Charles form order recognises that most applications for late registration are made ex parte, without creditors having an opportunity to be heard, and so justice requires that, should circumstances change (eg a winding up occur) they ought to have a right to be heard. Most instructive on this form of order is the decision of Hoffmann J in *Re Braemar Investments Ltd*[291] where he said:

> 'The type of order made in this case appears to have been invented by Clauson J in *Re LH Charles & Co Ltd* [1935] WN 15. It was intended to meet a difficulty caused by two special features of applications to extend time for registration. The first is that they are essentially ex parte in character. The creditors who may be affected are not respondents to the summons and the company will not necessarily have an interest in protecting the position. Indeed, in cases such as the present, in which the company's directors have guaranteed the debt, their interests will be opposed to those of unsecured creditors. In a case in which the evidence shows that the company is solvent, the likelihood of prejudice to unsecured creditors is remote and the court is, therefore, not particularly concerned about their lack of representation. But this case is different when liquidation appears to be imminent. However – and this is the second special feature of these applications – the court cannot deal with this problem by adjourning the application to see whether a petition is presented or a resolution for winding up is passed. Once the resolution has been passed, the rights of the unsecured creditor crystallise and an order to extend time can no longer be made. An adjournment may, therefore, cause injustice to an applicant who turns out to have been entitled to an order at the time when the application first came before the court. An order in *Re LH Charles & Co Ltd* form enables the whole matter to be reconsidered without pre-empting the question by postponing registration until after the liquidation has supervened.'

---

289 *Exeter Trust Ltd v Screenways Ltd* [1991] BCLC 888.

290 So called after the case of *Re LH Charles & Co Ltd* [1935] WN 15. See Gough, *Company Charges* (2nd edn, 1996), p 782 *ff*.

291 *Re Braemar Investments Ltd* [1989] Ch 54.

To a court faced with an otherwise meritorious application for relief under CA 1963, s 106 against a company of dubious solvency, or even certain insolvency, the Charles form order will sometimes help it strike the appropriate balance between competing interests[292].

(e) Agreement to late registered charge taking priority to prior registered charge

[21.097] Normally the existence of the proviso as to the safeguarding of rights will mean that the registered secured creditor will have priority to the late registered charge, even if they were aware of the unregistered charge when their charge was created. However, where a prior registered chargee *agrees to take after* the late registered chargee, the court will give effect to this and the prior registered chargee will be estopped from arguing to the contrary. So in *Spain v McCann*[293] a charge which was allowed to be registered late had priority over a charge which had been registered in time. Costello J held that:

> '...it was expressly agreed between the company and the bank that the bank's mortgage debenture was subject to the plaintiff's mortgage. [ie the one which was allowed to be registered late] Thus, the bank's rights were at all times subject to those of the prior [then, unregistered] encumbrancer and therefore, the right to appoint a receiver, enforce their security by sale of the company's premises were expressly made subject to the defendant's rights under his prior mortgage. The effect of the court's order...was that the defendant's security became a valid one when registration was effected without prejudice to the bank's rights under their mortgage debenture. What were those rights? They were clearly limited and qualified ones - they were subject at all times to those of the first mortgagee. The bank, it seems to me, are bound by the words of their agreement and they cannot now obtain a priority which they expressly agree they would not have.'

Where parties agree to a particular arrangement the courts will, generally, be reluctant to upset such consensually agreed arrangements.

Registration

[21.098] Section 100(1) of CA 1963 provides that it is the duty of the company which creates the charge to send details of the particulars to the CRO. However, it goes on to provide that registration 'may be effected on the application of any person interested therein'. This allows the solicitor for the chargee to apply for registration. In practice, this represents the norm, as it would indeed be unusual for a chargee to entrust this most important task to the company creating the charge[294]. Failure to deliver particulars of a registrable charge is punishable by a fine of €634, although the threat of this is probably the last reason why compliance with CA 1963, Part IV tends to be so high[295].

---

[292] See *Barclays Bank plc v Stuart Landon Ltd and another* [2001] 2 BCLC 316 where the English Court of Appeal said that since it had not been shown that an application to set aside an extension order was bound to succeed, the proper course was to make an order with the *proviso* which protected the bank and unsecured creditors. See also, *Re Chantry House Developments plc* [1990] BCLC 813 which also shows how the respective periods within a Charles form order can be shortened where justified by the circumstances.

[293] *Spain v McCann* [1978] ILRM 215 at 218.

[294] The cost of registration can be recovered from the company which creates the charge. At present the cost of registration is €30.

Particulars required to be registered

[21.099] Section 103(1) of CA 1963 details the particulars which are required to be delivered to the CRO. These details are:

> In the case of a charge to the benefit of which the holders of a *series of debentures*[296] are entitled, such particulars as are specified in s 99(8), namely:
>
> — the total amount secured by the whole series;
> — the dates and resolutions authorising the issue, the date of the covering deed by which the security is created or defined;
> — a general description of the property charged; and
> — the names of the trustees (if any).
>
> In the case of any *other charge*,
>
> — the date it was created by the company;
> — if the charge exists on property acquired by the company, the date of the acquisition of the property;
> — for a judgment mortgage, the date of creation;
> — the amount secured by the charge;
> — short particulars of the property charged;
> — the persons entitled to the charge.

In practice, the most commonly filed particulars are those in relation to the 'other charges'. In private companies charges over a 'series of debentures' are rarely created.

[21.100] The orderly registration of charges is achieved through the use of official forms used to record the details specified above. Of these, the most common is the *Form C1* which is used to register particulars of a charge created by a company incorporated in the State[297]. An officer of the company which creates the charge should sign the form, by way of application for registration, and it is usual for the solicitor of the chargee to arrange for this to be done at the same time as the charge itself is executed, prior to draw down of the facilities. Once signed by an officer of the company, the particulars of the charge are *verified*, usually by the solicitor for the chargee. Alternatively, a certified copy of the instrument which creates or evidences the charge can be delivered with the Form C1 in which application for registration should be made by the solicitor for the chargee. In practice, some solicitors' firms create their own Form C1s on computer. Such are acceptable to the CRO although prior approval should be sought before using such a form.

[21.101] There are several other forms as follows:

— A *Form 47A* is used to register particulars relating to a series of debentures giving any charge to the debenture holders.

— A *Form 47B* is used to register particulars of a charge where a company acquires property which is already subject to a charge or mortgage.

---

295 Increased by C(A)A 1982, s 15. See CA 1963, s 100(3) and (4) which allows the Registrar of Companies to bring and prosecute proceedings in relation to an offence under this section.

296 See para **[21.035]**.

297 The Form C1 replaced the Form 47, which had been introduced by SI 1964/45. The Form C1 became the prescribed form by SI 2001/466 with effect from 23 October 2001.

— A *Form 47C* is a certificate that a charge over property outside the State has been presented for registration in the country where the property is situate, pursuant to CA 1963, s 99(5).

The prescribed form for registration of particulars of a charge created by a foreign company over property within the State is a *Form 8E*. This is also used to deliver particulars of a charge created by a foreign company over property in the State where that company has not registered on the external register, ie for filing on the *Slavenburg* file.

Satisfaction of charges

[21.102] When a charge created by a company is paid off, or satisfied, the register of charges should be brought up to date and this fact recorded. This is achieved by the delivery of a memorandum of satisfaction of charge to the CRO in a *Form 49*[298]. The Registrar of Companies is empowered to enter on the register a memorandum of satisfaction *in whole* or *in part* by virtue of CA 1963, s 105. Before entering a satisfaction he should have evidence that:

— the debt has been paid or satisfied in whole or in part; or

— part of the property or undertaking charged has been released from the charge or has ceased to form part of the company's property or undertaking.

Unlike the application to have a charge registered, a Form 49 must be under the seal of the chargor-company, and particulars of the satisfaction must be verified by a director and the secretary of the company, and sworn before a commissioner for oaths. Upon the registrar receiving a completed Form 49, before entering a satisfaction on the register of charges he will write to the holder of the charge giving it notice. It is thought that it would be better were s 105 to provide that the charge holder should execute the Form 49 to avoid the possibility that the notice might be overlooked.

The chargor company's obligations

[21.103] In accordance with CA 1963, s 109, every instrument which creates a charge which requires registration must be kept at the registered office of the chargor company, or in the case of foreign companies, at its principal place of business[299]. Section 110(1) of CA 1963 provides that copies of the instruments must be open for inspection by any creditor or member of the company, subject to reasonable restrictions which the company in general meeting may impose, provided that inspection is allowed for not less than two hours per day. Failure to allow inspection is punishable by a fine of €634[300] and a court may order immediate inspection upon an application being made[301]. On a practical note, it is rare for a creditor or member to invoke this right, more rare for a company to be aware of this obligation, and bordering on fantasy for the average Irish

[298] It is proposed that the Form 49 will be replaced by a Form C6 in late 2002 or early 2003. See www.info@cro.ie

[299] CA 1963, s 111.

[300] CA 1963, s 110(2).

[301] CA 1963, s 110(3).

private company to have a strategy which would roll into action should a knock come to the door seeking inspection of the company's register of charges.

Other registration systems

[21.104] Registration of a charge in the CRO may not be the only registration which will be required if a charge is to be valid or to have priority to other charges.

(a) Mortgages of unregistered land

[21.105] Mortgages, whether legal or equitable, are the most common method of taking security over unregistered land. Mortgages of unregistered land should be registered in the Registry of Deeds pursuant to the Registry of Deeds Act (Ireland) 1707. Registration is effected by the preparation of a short summary of the effect of the instrument creating the mortgage, called a memorial, which is then stamped[302] and lodged in the Registry of Deeds. When registration has been effected, the memorial is retained in the Registry and is available for inspection by members of the public.

[21.106] In the case of unregistered land, registration of the mortgage is required if the mortgage is to have priority. In the case of a legal mortgage of unregistered land, although such registration is not compulsory, the failure to register will mean that the mortgagee will lose priority in a subsequent 'clash of priorities'[303]. An equitable mortgage by deposit of title deeds will be *unregistrable* unless a memorandum of equitable deposit is signed (whether by the chargor or chargee). Whilst this somewhat defeats the purpose of an equitable deposit, where a memorandum is created it must be memorialised and registered in the Registry of Deeds. Thus, an agreement to create a mortgage is registrable[304].

(b) Charges of registered land

[21.107] Charges of registered land should be registered in the Land Registry under the Registration of Title Act 1964. Registration is effected by lodging a *Form 17,* as set out in the Land Registry Rules[305], together with the instrument creating the charge, the land certificate (if issued), ancillary documents, such as a statutory declaration pursuant to the Family Law Acts[306] and the appropriate fee[307]. Where the Land Registry are asked to register a charge which has been created by a company and a certificate of registration of the charge has not been produced, a notice to that effect is entered on the Land Registry register[308]. In practice a certificate of registration or charge is often not lodged by reason

---

302 Currently €44 for the registration of a memorial: the Registry of Deeds (Fees) Order 1999 (SI 1999/346) as amended by the Euro Changeover (Amounts) Act 2001.

303 See Keane, *Equity and the Law of Trusts in the Republic of Ireland* (1988), p 49 *ff.*

304 *Eyre v McDowell* (1861) 9 HL Cas 619.

305 (SI 1972/30).

306 Family Home Protection Act 1976, Family Law Act 1981, the Judicial Separation and Family Law Reform Act 1989, the Family Law Act 1995 and the Family Law (Divorce) Act 1996.

307 Since 1 May 2000 the flat fee for the registration of a charge is €125: see the Land Registration (Fees) Order 1999 (SI 1999/343) as amended by the Euro Changeover (Amounts) Act 2001.

308 Land Registration Rules 1972 (SI 1972/230), r 114.

of the delays in its issue and the chargee's desire to lodge his charge in the Land Registry as soon as is possible.

[21.108] As in the case of unregistered land, the reason for registering a charge on registered land is to ensure that the chargee has priority over subsequent encumbrancers. Section 62 of the Registration of Title Act 1964 provides that:

> '...the instrument of charge shall operate as a mortgage by deed within the meaning of the Conveyancing Acts, and the registered owner of the charge shall, for the purpose of enforcing his charge, have all the rights and powers of a mortgagee under a mortgage by deed, including the power to sell the estate or interest which is subject of the charge.'

A fixed legal charge of land must be registered as a burden on the folio in the Land Registry. In the case of a floating charge, the predominant view is[309] that it cannot be registered as a burden, and so the holder of a floating charge can only enter a *caution* on the folio[310]. Upon its crystallisation a floating charge may be registered as a burden being a quasi-fixed charge[311]. Before a receiver exercises his powers under a debenture creating a floating charge, he should register the new quasi-fixed charge as a burden[312]. It is also the case that a chargor company can create an informal charge by depositing the land certificate to Irish lands with the chargee[313].

(c) Charges over agricultural stock[314]

[21.109] Certain chattel mortgages, whether floating or specific[315], created by a recognised borrower[316] in favour of a recognised lender[317] shall not have effect until registered[318]. Those chattel mortgages which are affected by this provision (which applies to those created by either companies or individuals) are charges over 'stock' as defined by the Agricultural Credit Act 1978, s 23(1), and which includes:

- animals and birds of every kind and the progeny and produce of such animals and birds;
- insects and fish of every kind and the progeny and produce of such insects and fish;

---

309 See Keane, *Company Law* (3rd edn, 2000), para 21.20. See also McAllister, *Registration of Title in Ireland* (1973), pp 191–192 and Fitzgerald, *Land Registry Practice* (1989), p 128.

310 Land Registration Rules 1972 (SI 1972/230), rr 131–145.

311 Land Registration Rules 1986 (SI 1986/310), r 4.

312 *Re Mono Food Equipment Ltd* (21 May 1986, unreported) High Court (Flood J).

313 Registration of Title Act 1964, s 105(5).

314 See Maguire, 'Agricultural Chattel Mortgages' (1997) 4 CLP 170.

315 Agricultural Credit Act 1978, s 23(1).

316 As defined by the Agricultural Credit Act 1978, s 23 as meaning any person to whom money may be lent or advanced or who may be provided with other credit facilities by a recognised lender or who gives or agrees to give security to a recognised lender for the payment of money by himself or any other person.

317 As defined by the Agricultural Credit Act 1978, s 23(1), to mean the ACC Bank plc (formerly, the Agricultural Credit Corporation plc) or a recognised bank, defined by the Agricultural Credit Act 1978, s 25.

318 Agricultural Credit Act 1978, Part III, s 26(5).

— agricultural crops (whether growing or severed from the land);
— trees (whether growing or severed from the land);
— any product deriving from the foregoing; and
— machinery, implements, vehicles, fixtures, fittings and materials used in or for the production, manufacture, processing, preparation for sale or marketing of any agricultural or fishery produce.

The foregoing list is wider than might at first be thought and full understanding of the 1978 Act's implications is vital if valid security is to be taken over such stock.

[21.110] Registration must be completed in accordance with the Agricultural Credit Act 1978, s 26, sub-s (1) of which provides that a register of chattel mortgages must be kept and maintained in every Circuit Court Office, the County Registrar being the person to whom the particulars ought to be delivered. Registration must be effected within one month from the date of creation of the chattel mortgage[319] at the Circuit Court Office serving the land on which the mortgagor is situate.

[21.111] It should be noted that in *Re Castlemahon Poultry Products Ltd*[320] Costello J suggested that where a company registered a chattel mortgage under CA 1963, s 99, then, even if it is a mortgage over 'stock' within the meaning of the Agricultural Credit Act 1978, registration under the latter Act is unnecessary. The reasoning in this decision has been questioned elsewhere[321]. It is thought to be imprudent to disregard any statutory provision, since the 1978 Act does not expressly state that registration under CA 1963 will satisfy the registration requirements in the 1978 Act. Although the view of Costello J is thought to be correct in common sense, only statutory reform can safely remove the requirement to register under both the 1978 and CA 1963.

(d) Mortgages over ships

[21.112] Legal mortgages over ships are required to be registered under the Merchant Shipping Act 1894, as amended by the Mercantile Marine Act 1955. By s 78 of the 1955 Act no notice of a trust, express, implied or constructive may be entered on the register which is established under the 1955 Act. Without prejudice to this provision, equitable rights over ships may exist, but only legal mortgages may be entered on the register.

(e) Charges over aircraft

[21.113] Charges over aircraft are required to be registered under the Air Navigation and Transport (Nationality and Registration of Aircraft) Regulations 1963-1984 made under the Air Navigation and Transport Acts.

---

319 Agricultural Credit Act 1978, s 26(2).

320 *Re Castlemahon Poultry Products Ltd* (13 December 1985, unreported) High Court (Costello J).

321 See Johnston, *Banking and Security Law in Ireland* (1998), para 11.45 where three compelling reasons are given for not disregarding the registration procedure provided in the Agricultural Credit Act 1978 where the chargor is a company. See also Forde, *Commercial Law in Ireland* (1990), p 228.

Stamp duty on security instruments

[21.114] By virtue of the Stamp Act 1891 as amended by various Finance Acts, most particularly, the Finance Act 1991, instruments which are required by that legislation to be stamped, must be stamped by the Revenue Commissioners. Prior to 1991, the failure to stamp an instrument meant only that the instrument was inadmissible in a court of law. However, now by the Stamp Duties Consolidation Act 1999, s 2 it is compulsory to stamp a stampable instrument. Security documents which must be stamped include:

- Mortgages/charges over real property where the amount mortgaged or charged is over €254,000. At present, the stamp duty is €1 per €1,000, to a maximum of €630 duty payable.
- Documents that are required to be stamped collaterally to a primary security (eg counterpart mortgages, guarantees, assignments of life policy) are stamped at €12.50 provided that the primary security exceeds €254,000.

Stamp duty must be paid within 30 days of a stampable document being executed and delivered. Penalty duty may be payable where a stampable document is not stamped within the prescribed time limit.

[21.115] In *Allied Irish Banks plc v Bolger*[322] the defendant resisted the plaintiff-bank's application for an order for possession of the defendant's property. The defendant, who had mortgaged his property in favour of the plaintiff-bank, objected to the order for possession on the ground that the date inserted in the mortgages was not the true date on which he had executed the mortgages. He argued that the trial judge was accordingly obliged to exclude the deeds of mortgage pursuant to the Stamp Act 1891. The Supreme Court rejected the defendant's contention and held that the only relevance of the date of the mortgage was whether the deeds had been stamped late and whether penalty duty had been avoided. The court thus held that the defendant's liability to the plaintiff was not affected and that the mortgages were admissible in court.

[21.116] It should also be noted that the Supreme Court held in *Re Motor Racing Circuits Ltd*[323] that the validity of an 'all sums due' debenture will not be affected by its being 'stamped up' subsequent to the date of the presentation of a petition to have the chargor company wound up[324].

---

322 *Allied Irish Banks plc v Bolger* (28 January 1994, unreported) Supreme Court.

323 *Re Motor Racing Circuits Ltd* (31 January 1997, unreported) Supreme Court (Blayney J; nem diss).

324 See Chapter 20, *Corporate Borrowing: Debentures and Security*, at para **[20.033]**.

Chapter 22

Corporate Borrowing: Receivers

Introduction

[22.001] Where a company defaults on a financial obligation secured by a debenture that creates a legal mortgage or charge over land it is open to the secured creditor to seek possession of the property (either voluntarily or by court order) and then to sell the property (either with or without the help of the court)[1]. More often than not, however, a secured creditor whose debenture so allows will seek to appoint a receiver: the appointment of a receiver is one of the most popular remedies availed of by secured creditors against defaulting companies[2]. In this chapter the following issues are considered:

1. Receiver defined.
2. Considerations on the appointment of a receiver under a debenture.
3. Qualifications of receivers.
4. Appointment of a receiver.
5. The effect of the appointment of a receiver.
6. The status of a receiver.
7. Duties of receivers.
8. Liabilities of receivers.
9. Powers of receivers.
10. Applications for directions.
11. Multiple receivers to the same company.
12. Resignation and removal of receivers.

Receiver defined

[22.002] The appointment of a receiver is one of the oldest remedies known to equity[3] 'the term deriv[ing] from the Latin *recipiere* (re-capere, to take)'[4]. Howsoever they are appointed, receivers are persons whose function it is to 'receive' a debtor's assets and property for and on behalf of a creditor who is entitled to take them in satisfaction of the

---

1 See Wylie, *Irish Land Law* (3rd edn, 1997), para [13.013] *ff*.

2 See Lynch, Marshall & O'Ferrall, *Corporate Insolvency and Rescue* (1996), pp 119–164; Forde, *The Law of Company Insolvency* (1993), pp 21–75; and Breslin, *Banking Law in the Republic of Ireland* (1998), pp 855 – 872.

3 *Hoplins v Worcester and Birmingham Canal Proprietors* (1868) LR 6 Eq 437at 46–447, per Giffard V-C and, generally, in the context of court appointed pre–judgment and post–judgment receivers, Courtney, *Mareva Injunctions and Related Interlocutory Orders* (1998), pp 422–432.

4 Per Murphy J in *Re Bula Ltd* (20 June 2002, unreported) High Court.

debtor's obligations. In the case of a court appointed receiver, the receiver is appointed by order of the court to gather-up and take into his possession the assets of another. In the case of a receiver appointed on foot of a deed (eg a debenture) the purpose is the same: the receiver is appointed by the creditor to gather-up and take into his possession the debtor's assets for the purpose of selling them and applying the proceeds in satisfaction of the sums due to the creditor. This chapter is generally concerned with receivers appointed on foot of debentures.

[22.003] The term 'receiver', has been defined in *Re Manchester and Milford Railway Co*[5] where Sir George Jessell MR said:

> 'A "receiver" is a term which was well known in the Court of Chancery, as meaning a person who receives rents or other income paying ascertained outgoings, but who does not, if I may say so, manage the property in the sense of buying or selling or anything of that kind. We were most familiar with the distinction in the case of a partnership. If a receiver was appointed of partnership assets, the trade stopped immediately. He collected debts, sold the stock-in-trade and other assets, and then under the order of the court the debts of the concern were liquidated and the balance divided. If it was desired to continue the trade at all it was necessary to appoint a manager, or a receiver and manager as it was generally called. He could buy and sell and carry on the trade.'

This dictum clearly shows the distinction between two different types of receivers: the first type having the function of essentially 'collecting' property with a view to its sale (a 'receiver simpliciter'); the second of 'managing' the property, running it as a going concern and being more properly termed a 'receiver-manager'.

[22.004] A receiver is very different from either a liquidator or an examiner. A *liquidator* has the task of winding up a company, realising its assets and distributing those assets in accordance with law[6]. An *examiner* is appointed under the Companies (Amendment) Act 1990 ('C(A)A 1990') for the purpose of examining 'the situation, affairs and prospects of the company' and then reporting to the court on the company's prospects for survival[7]. A *receiver*, appointed on foot of a debenture, has the principal task of securing the assets of a company which have been mortgaged or charged in favour of the debenture holder which appointed him. A company which is *in liquidation* is in the process of being wound up. A company which is *in examinership* is being scrutinised by an examiner so that he may report back to the court with proposals for the company's survival. A company which is *in receivership* has had a receiver appointed, who is realising and receiving its assets and/or managing its affairs in the hope that the debts outstanding to the debenture holder which appointed him can be met.

Considerations on the appointment of a receiver under a debenture

[22.005] It is not unusual for companies to become gradually insolvent. Pleas for forbearance from insolvent companies' directors are common. The financial institutions

[5] *Re Manchester and Milford Railway Co* (1880) 14 Ch D 645 at 653.

[6] See generally Chapter 19, *Realisation and Distribution of Assets in a Winding Up*.

[7] *Re Atlantic Magnetics Ltd* [1993] 2 IR 561 at 572, per Finlay CJ. See generally Chapter 23, *Examinerships*.

which have advanced facilities to such companies will often be faced with the hard financial (and human) decision of when to call in the facilities by seeking repayment.

(a) Default: the basis for the appointment of a receiver

[22.006] Before a receiver can be appointed on foot of a debenture there must usually have occurred an *act or event of default* by the borrower-company. So-called 'events of default' will usually be set out in the debenture creating the mortgage or charge, although some may also be listed in the initial facility letter. While not exhaustive, the following[8] are a sample of the typical events of default which will be contained in either a facility letter or debenture (or a combination of both):

— if any of the money (principal and interest and all other sums) owing by the chargor-company is not paid or discharged when due; or

— if there is a breach by the chargor-company of any of the terms and conditions of the debenture or of any loan agreement with the chargee or of any offer letter or letter of sanction issued by the chargee to the chargor-company or of any facility from the chargee or any representation or warranty or undertaking from time to time made to the chargee by the chargor-company is or becomes incorrect or misleading in any material respect; or

— if (save for the purpose of and followed by an amalgamation or reconstruction which shall have first been approved in writing by the chargee) a petition is presented, or an order is made, or a resolution is passed, or a notice is issued convening a meeting for the purpose of considering a resolution, or analogous proceedings or action are taken, to wind up the chargor-company or to place the chargor-company under the protection of the court or to appoint an examiner, interim examiner, administrator, trustee or similar official to the chargor-company or to a related company (within the meaning of C(A)A 1990) or the chargee has reason to believe that any of the foregoing may be about to happen; or

— if an encumbrancer takes possession or exercises or attempts to exercise any power of sale or a receiver or similar official is appointed over the whole or any part of the undertaking, property, assets or revenues of the chargor-company; or

— if any judgment or order made against the chargor-company is not complied with within seven days or an execution, distress, sequestration or other process is levied or enforced upon or sued out against any part of the undertaking, property, assets or revenues of the chargor-company; or

— if the chargor-company without the prior consent in writing of the chargee ceases or threatens to cease to carry on its business or any material part thereof in the normal course or changes the nature or mode of conduct of its trading in any material respect or ceases to be a going concern; or

— if any indebtedness of the chargor-company is not paid when due or becomes or is capable of being declared payable prior to its stated maturity or any

---

8 See Lingard, *Bank Security Documents*, (3rd edn, 1993), para 7.21 *ff*; Picarda, *The Law Relating to Receivers, Managers and Administrators*, (2nd edn, 1990), Chapter 3; Forde, *The Law of Company Insolvency* (1993).

encumbrance from time to time created by the chargor-company becomes enforceable; or

- if the chargor-company commences negotiations to reschedule the whole or any part of its indebtedness which it would or might otherwise be unable to pay when due or is unable to pay its debts as they fall due within the meaning of s 214 of the Companies Act 1963 ('CA 1963')[9] or stops or threatens to stop payment or is deemed to be unable to pay its debts for the purpose of any law of any jurisdiction to which it is subject or enters into any compromise or arrangement for the benefit of its creditors generally; or
- if the debenture or any guarantee, indemnity or other security[10] for any of the money (principal and interest and all other sums) owing fails or ceases in any respect to have full force and effect or to be continuing or is terminated or is disrupted or becomes in jeopardy, invalid or unenforceable; or
- if any licence, authorisation, consent or registration at any time necessary or desirable to enable the chargor-company to comply with its obligations to the chargee or to carry on its business in the normal course shall be revoked, withheld or materially modified or shall fail to be granted or perfected or shall cease to remain in full force and effect; or
- if any material adverse change occurs in the affairs of the chargor-company which in the opinion of the chargee gives ground for belief that the chargor-company may not or may be unable to perform its obligations hereunder or under any facility from the chargee; or
- if there shall occur any event of default howsoever described under any document governing, regulating, securing, guaranteeing or supporting the obligations of the chargor-company to the chargee; or
- if any event analogous to any of the foregoing events occurs without the prior consent in writing of the chargee in relation to (a) any third party which now or hereafter has guaranteed or provided security for or given an indemnity in respect of the money (principal and interest and all other sums) owing or (b) any subsidiary or holding company (as defined by CA 1963, s 155) of the chargor-company or of any such third party or any subsidiary of any such holding company; or if any individual now or hereafter liable as such third party shall commit an act of bankruptcy, die or become of unsound mind; or
- if the chargor-company shall (without the prior written consent of the chargee) redeem or purchase any of its share capital or declare, make or pay any

---

9 See generally, Chapter 25, *Winding Up Companies*, at para **[25.062]**. See also *Re Creation Printing Company Ltd* [1981] IR 353 and *Byblos Bank SAC v AL Khudhairy* [1987] BCLC 232.

10 This can generally only apply to a floating security as opposed to a fixed security: Lynch, Marshall & O'Ferrall, *Corporate Insolvency and Rescue* (1996), pp 123. The advent of C(A)A 1990, s 29 must, however, bring this position into question which only held good for as long as a fixed mortgage or charge could not be assailed: see generally Chapter 23, *Examinerships*, at para **[23.077]**.

dividend or other distribution (in cash or in kind) in respect of any of its share capital.

[22.007] Upon the occurrence of one or more of the foregoing *an event of default* is said to occur. The effect of the occurrence of an event of default will depend upon the actual terms of a given debenture. The effect, in practice, will be that the loan to the company may be called in and if it is not repaid, steps can be taken to enforce any security given by the company. Some or all of the events listed in the preceding paragraph are often found in most debentures' 'default clauses', which provide that if any of these events occur, the chargor can forthwith demand repayment. Whilst, sometimes, default clauses are stated to operate automatically, it is nevertheless common not to take any steps against a borrower until notice (coupled with a formal demand for repayment, where appropriate) is given in the manner prescribed by the debenture.

[22.008] It is encumbant upon a creditor to comply with the terms of his security document before taking action on foot of it in the form of, for example, appointing a receiver. Where provisions governing the service of notice or provisions as to who can serve notice are not strictly complied with, creditors will leave their subsequent appointment of a receiver open to challenge. Such was in issue in the Australian High Court case of *Pan Foods Company Importers & Distributors Pty Ltd v Australia and New Zealand Banking Group Ltd*[11]. There, however, in upholding the receiver's appointment in circumstances where the creditor's entitlement to declare monies owing to be due and payable, the service of notice to that effect and the status of the person serving the notice were called into question, the importance of construing commercial agreements practically was stressed. In the course of his judgment Kirby J said of commercial documents:

> 'In my view, such documents should be construed practically, so as to give effect to their presumed commercial purposes and so as not to defeat the achievement of such purposes by an excessively narrow and artificially restricted construction. The law facilitates and upholds commercial contractual obligations and the expectations that derive from them. Statute and equity may sometimes come to the aid or parties where various forms of unfairness or inequity can be shown. None was invoked in this appeal. But as between a commercial enterprise and a finance provider, such as a bank, the law should be the upholder of agreements. It should eschew artificialities and excessive technicalities for these will not be imputed to the ordinary businessperson. Business is entitled to look to the law to keep people to their commercial promises. In a world of global finances and trans-border capital markets, those jurisdictions flourish which do so. Those jurisdictions which do not soon become known. They pay a price in terms of the availability and costs of capital necessary as a consequence of the uncertainties of the enforcement of agreements in their courts.'[12]

In the instant case Kirby J found that one could not doubt that a reasonably informed businessperson 'looking at the notice in this case, and by whom it was handed to the company, would conclude that it was 'a notice from the Bank to the Customer…given by

[11] *Pan Foods Company Importers & Distributors Pty Ltd v Australia and New Zealand Banking Group Ltd* High Court of Australia, 13 April 2000.

[12] High Court of Australia, 13 April 2000 at para 24.

an Authorised Representative, in writing'. He concluded that in the absence of substantial, persuasive and practical reasons (of which there were none) the law could not come to a contrary conclusion.

(b) Appointment following default in repaying money repayable on demand

[22.009] Perhaps the most common event to cause a chargee to appoint a receiver to a company is where money owed to the chargee becomes due. It is common for debentures to provide that the repayment of all money (principal and interest and all other sums) owing by the chargee-company is repayable '*on demand*'[13]. It has been held that where money is repayable on demand the amount need not be specified in any written demand[14]. Moreover, the debtor must have it ready and is not entitled to further time in order to look for the money[15] and a receiver can be appointed at any time thereafter[16]. The preferred test in England is the so-called 'mechanics of payment test'. In *Bank of Baroda v Panessar*[17] Walton J said:

> 'Money payable "on demand" is repayable immediately on demand being made...Nevertheless, it is physically impossible in most cases for a person to keep the money required to discharge the debt about his person. He may in a simple case keep it in a box under his bed; it may be at the bank or with a bailee. The debtor is therefore not in default in making the payment demanded unless and until he has had a *reasonable opportunity* of implementing whatever reasonable mechanics of payment he may need to employ to discharge the debt. Of course, this is limited to the time necessary for the mechanics of payment. It does not extend to any time to raise the money if it is not there to be paid.' [Emphasis added]

It is thought that the mechanics of payment test is correct and that no other reasonable interpretation can be placed on a document which provides that money is to be repayable 'on demand' as that term is understood in Ireland and the United Kingdom[18]. In

---

13 See Hapgood, *Paget's Law of Banking* (11th edn, 1996), pp 179–181.

14 *Bunbury Foods Pty Ltd v National Bank of Australasia Ltd* (1984) 51 ALR 609; *Bank of Baroda v Panessar* [1986] 3 All ER 751.

15 *Brighty v Norton* (1862) 122 ER 116.

16 *Bank of Baroda v Panessar* [1986] 3 All ER 751 where a receiver was found to have been validly appointed one hour after the making of the demand. See also *Lloyds Bank plc v Lampert* [1999] BCC 507 where this was followed by Kennedy LJ in the English Court of Appeal.

17 [1986] 3 All ER 751 at 759–760.

18 Cf the reasonable notice test applied in some Commonwealth countries such as Canada. So in *Lister (RE) Ltd v Dunlop Canada Ltd* [1982] 1 SCR 726 it was held that a bank was required to give a debtor reasonable notice of its intention to enforce the security and a reasonable time to pay following such notice of intention. In *Mister Broadloom Corp (1968) Ltd v Bank of Montreal* (1979) 25 OR (2d) 198 (HC) at 208 the following criteria were established in determining the length of time amounting to reasonable notice: (1) the amount of the loan; (2) the risk to the creditor of losing his money or the security; (3) the length of the relationship between the debtor and the creditor; (4) the character and reputation of the debtor; (5) the potential ability to raise the money required in a short period; (6) the circumstances surrounding the demand for payment; and (7) any other relevant factors. In *Royal Bank of Canada v W Got & Associates Electric Ltd* Supreme Court of Canada of 15 October 1999 the court upheld an earlier finding that a bank was, inter alia, in breach of contract for failing to give sufficient notice and that damages were payable for the wrongful appointment of a receiver in such circumstances.

Sheppard & Cooper Ltd v TSB Bank plc[19] the question which arose was the validity of an administrative receivership, the answer to which turned on whether the bank had allowed sufficient time to pass between making its demand of the plaintiff and its purported appointment of receivers, which happened not more than 60 minutes later. The facts were that the plaintiff owed over £618,000 which was secured on foot of a debenture incorporating a fixed and floating charge and the defendant was the bank then entitled to the loan and security, having acquired it from the original lender. The defendant's representatives met with the plaintiff's directors and at that meeting gave the directors a written demand requiring repayment of the plaintiff's indebtedness. During the course of the meeting one of the plaintiff's directors stated that the plaintiff was not in a position to meet the demand and that the best that he could hope for would be to pay half the excess on the company's overdraft over the following seven days. Within 60 minutes of the meeting ending, the defendant appointed administrative receivers. It was held by Blackburne J that whilst the mechanics of payment test required a creditor to give a debtor a reasonable opportunity to pay the amount demanded:

> 'If, however, he has made it clear to the creditor that the necessary moneys are not available, then, provided a proper demand has been made, I cannot see that the creditor need allow any time to elapse before being at liberty to treat the debtor as in default.'[20]

It must always be remembered, however, that a receiver can only be validly appointed on foot of a debenture *in accordance with the provisions of that debenture or other deed.* Accordingly, the contractual circumstances that permit the appointment of a receiver (eg the happening of an event of default) must have occurred. Where a receiver is wrongly appointed the chargor-company will have a cause of action against the secured creditor for breach of contract and possibly conversion occasioned by a wrongfully appointed receiver taking possession of the chargor-company's assets[21]. Interlocutory relief in the form of an injunction to restrain a receiver from purporting to act as a receiver of the company's assets, may be sought by a company which asserts that there is no entitlement to appoint a receiver[22].

(c) No additional duty of care over and above contract

[22.010] Subject to strict contractual compliance in the appointment of a receiver, case law indicates that a creditor owes no special duty to a company in deciding whether or not to appoint a receiver. The fundamental issue for the debenture holder is whether the appointment of a receiver will further the debenture holder's interests. However, where the appointment will not advance the debenture holder's interests, the appointment may be said to have been made in bad faith. So, in *Re Potters Oils Ltd (No 2)*[23] Hoffmann J said that:

> 'The debenture-holder is under no duty to refrain from exercising his rights merely because doing so may cause loss to the company or its unsecured creditors. He owes a duty

---

[19] *Sheppard & Cooper Ltd v TSB Bank plc* [1996] 2 All ER 654.

[20] [1996] 2 All ER 654 at 660b. See also *Massey v Sladen* (1868) LR 4 Exch 13 at 17, per Kelly CB.

[21] Eg, see *Royal Bank of Canada v W Got & Associates Electric Ltd* Supreme Court of Canada of 15 October 1999.

[22] See, eg, *Ferris v Ward; Ward's Wholesale Meats Ltd v Ferris* [1998] 2 IR 194.

[23] *Re Potters Oils Ltd (No 2)* [1986] BCLC 98.

of care to the company but this duty is subordinated to the protection of his own interests.'[24]

A similar statement can be found in *Shamji v Johnson Matthey Bankers Ltd*[25] where again Hoffmann J said:

> 'The appointment of a receiver seems to me to involve an inherent conflict of interest. The purpose of the power is to enable the mortgagee to take the management of the company's property out of the hands of the directors and entrust it to a person of the mortgagee's choice. That power is granted to the mortgagee by the security documents in completely unqualified terms. It seems to me that a decision by the mortgagee to exercise the power cannot be challenged except perhaps on grounds of bad faith. There is no room for the implication of a term that the mortgagee shall be under a duty to the mortgagor to "consider all relevant matters" before exercising the power. If no such qualification can be read into the security documents, I do not think that a wider duty can exist in tort: see *Tai Hing Cotton Mill Ltd v Liu Chong Hing Bank Ltd* [1985] 2 All ER 947 at 959...I might add that Harman J once remarked that the analogous power of the mortgagee to enter into possession may be exercised "before the ink is dry on the mortgage". Certainly there has never been any suggestion that the right to exercise the power, as opposed to the way in which the mortgagee deals with the mortgaged property once he is in possession, is qualified by a duty of care to the mortgagor...a mortgagee who acts in what he considers to be in good faith to be his own interests may exercise his contractual right to appoint a receiver without regard to the effect upon the mortgagor or a guarantor of the obligations of the mortgagor.'[26]

It is thought to be right and proper that a debenture holder's duties to a company are exhausted upon compliance with the underlying contract which facilitates and makes provision for the appointment of a receiver.

Qualifications of receivers

[22.011] Although the law relating to receivers was revamped by the Companies Act 1990 ('CA 1990'), it remains the case that the only qualifications that the law requires of receivers are negative, ie certain persons are barred from becoming receivers. In the first place, a body corporate is not qualified for appointment as receiver to the property of a company, a prohibition that carries with it a fine of up to €634.87 by CA 1963, s 314[27]. Furthermore, CA 1963, s 315[28] provides that none of the following persons qualify for appointment as receiver:

— an undischarged bankrupt;

— a person who is, or has been within 12 months of the commencement of the receivership, an officer or servant of the company[29];

---

24 [1986] BCLC 98 at 103a–g.

25 *Shamji v Johnson Matthey Bankers Ltd* [1986] BCLC 278.

26 [1986] BCLC 278 at 284.

27 As increased by C(A)A 1982, s 15.

28 As amended by CA 1990, s 170 and considered by McCormack, *The New Companies Legislation* (1991), Ch 10.

29 References to officer or servant are deemed to include references to an auditor: CA 1963, s 315. See *The Wise Finance Company Ltd v O'Regan* (26 June 1998, unreported), High Court (Laffoy J) where a person who was the company secretary of a chargee company was found to be ineligible for appointment as receiver.

- — a parent, spouse, brother, sister or child of an officer of the company;
- — a person who is a partner of or in the employment of an officer or servant of the company;
- — a person who is not qualified by virtue of CA 1963, s 315 for appointment as receiver of the property of any other body corporate which is that company's subsidiary or holding company or a subsidiary of that company's holding company, or would be so disqualified if the body corporate were a company.

Where, after his initial appointment, a receiver becomes disqualified by virtue of the application of any of the foregoing, he must vacate the office and give notice in writing of this within 14 days to the company, the Registrar of Companies, and either the debenture holder or the court, depending upon which appointed the receiver[30]. Contravention of this section is an offence and liable on summary conviction to a fine not exceeding €1,269.97, and for a continued contravention €63.49 per day, and on indictment to a fine not exceeding €6,348.69, and for continued contravention, to a daily fine of €317.43[31].

Appointment of a receiver

[22.012] A receiver can be appointed in either of two ways: on foot of the powers contained in a debenture, or on foot of a court order. Of these, by far the most common is an appointment pursuant to the express power of appointment by the debenture holder which is contained in the debenture.

(a) Appointment on foot of a debenture

[22.013] Today, almost every debenture created by a company in favour of an institutional lender will provide that the debenture holder can appoint a receiver, at any time after the principal money secured shall become payable. Such moneys will generally become payable upon the occurrence of *an event of default*, considered above[32]. A typical provision found in a debenture for the appointment of a receiver will read:

> 'At any time after the security hereby constituted has become enforceable [ie upon the occurrence of an event of default] or at any time after the Company so requests the Bank may from time to time appoint under seal or under hand of a duly authorised officer or employee of the Bank any person or persons to be receiver and manager or receivers and managers (herein called "Receiver" which expression shall where the context so admits include the plural and any substituted receiver and manager or receivers and managers) of the Secured Assets [this term will be defined elsewhere in the debenture] or any part or parts thereof and from time to time under seal or under hand of a duly authorised officer or employee of the Bank remove any Receiver so appointed and may so appoint another or others in his stead. If the Bank appoints more than one person as Receiver of any of the Secured Assets, each such person shall be entitled (unless the contrary shall be stated in the appointment) to exercise all the powers and discretions hereby or by statute conferred on Receivers individually and to the exclusion of the other or others of them.'

---

30 CA 1963, s 315(2).

31 CA 1963, s 315(5).

32 See para **[22.006]**.

It has been held that the appointment of a receiver will be valid even if the debenture takes effect under hand as opposed to under seal[33]. However, this will mean that the debenture will not create a valid mortgage over real property, since such deeds of mortgage are required to be under seal[34]. Since the enactment of the Powers of Attorney Act 1996, s 15(2), it has not been necessary to create a power of attorney under seal; accordingly, a receiver appointed on foot of a debenture executed under hand can validly be constituted the company's attorney[35].

[22.014] One bar to the appointment of a receiver to a company is where an examiner has been appointed. Section 5(2)(b) of C(A)A 1990 provides that where a company has been placed under the protection of the court no receiver over any part of the property or undertaking of the company shall be appointed, or if appointed before the presentation of the petition to place the company under the protection of the court shall be unable to act. An examiner can apply to have a receiver removed[36].
It is also thought that a receiver cannot be appointed to a company which has been dissolved; and that where a receiver is appointed to a company which is subsequently dissolved that the receiver's authority will cease[37]. By reason of the Powers of Attorney Act 1996, s 20 where a receiver is appointed attorney and the power is expressed to be irrevocable and given to secure either a proprietary interest of the donee of the power or the performance of an obligation owed to the donee then the company's winding up or dissolution will not revoke the power of attorney[38]. In such a situation a debenture holder may seek to have the company reinstated onto the register of companies[39].

[22.015] It is not a bar to the appointment of a receiver that a winding-up order has been made or that a provisional liquidator has been appointed. It had been argued in *Re Motor Racing Circuits Ltd*[40] that upon a winding-up order being made or a provisional liquidator appointed, CA 1963, s 222 barred a secured creditor from appointing a receiver over the assets of the company. It was held by the Supreme Court that the appointment of a receiver under a power contained in a debenture does not come within

---

33 See *Byblos Bank SAL v Al-Khudhairy* [1987] BCLC 232.

34 See Chapter 7, *Corporate Contracts, Capacity and Authority*, para **[7.014]**.

35 Powers of Attorney Act 1996, s 15(3) provides that 'This section is without prejudice to any requirement in or under any other enactment as to the witnessing of powers of attorney or as to the execution of instruments by bodies corporate.' It is thought that there is no obstacle to a company appointing an attorney by deed under hand. Indeed, CA 1963, Pt I, Table A, model reg 81 provides: 'The directors may…by power of attorney appoint any company, firm or person or body of persons…to be the attorney or attorneys of the company…'

36 See para **[22.080]**. See also Chapter 23, *Examinerships*, para **[23.064]** *ff*.

37 In *Salton v New Boston Cycle Co* [1900] 1 Ch 43 the dissolution of a company had the effect of terminating the company's solicitors' authority.

38 Care would need to be taken in drafting the debenture since the Powers of Attorney Act 1996, s 20 refers to a proprietary interest or obligation *owed to the donee* it would seem to require the power to be drawn in favour of the chargee, not the receiver. See para **[22.031]**.

39 See Chapter 12, *Company Law Compliance and Enforcement*, para **[12.152]**.

40 *Re Motor Racing Circuits Ltd* (31 January 1997, unreported), Supreme Court.

the meaning of an 'action or proceeding' as used in CA 1963, s 222 and, accordingly, there was no bar to the receiver's appointment.

[22.016] The distinction between a receiver simpliciter and a receiver-manager is important, and the appointment of either will be dependent upon the nature of the debenture under which the receiver was appointed. Where the primary property mortgaged or charged is a specific asset, or series of assets, the appropriate appointment is of a simple 'receiver'. However, where the debenture created charges over the entire undertaking and business of the company, the debenture holder may appoint a 'receiver-manager'[41].

[22.017] The validity of the appointment of a receiver is dependent upon compliance with the terms contained in the debenture and the capacity of the company and authority of its officers to create the debenture ab initio[42]; if the debenture is invalid, so too will the purported appointment of any receiver on foot thereof[43]. Where a company initially co-operates with a receiver but subsequently chooses to deny the validity of that receiver's appointment, such a company may be estopped from such a course[44].

From the viewpoint of the receiver, it is important that he receives an indemnity from the debenture holder who appoints him against any claims or other proceedings which may be brought against him. This is particularly true where the circumstances of the receivership indicate that it may be problematic[45]. However, it is commonplace for lending institutions which appoint receivers to resist the giving of such an indemnity, a stance which often prevails through market forces.

(b) Appointment on foot of a court order

[22.018] In an unusual case where a debenture does not empower the holder to appoint a receiver (or, indeed, where there is no debenture), recourse may be had to the courts. The High Court has an inherent equitable jurisdiction to appoint a receiver, upon application being made[46]. In addition the High Court has the power to appoint a receiver pursuant to the Supreme Court of Judicature (Ireland) Act 1877, s 28(8), to which effect is given by

---

41 See *Re Irish Oil and Cake Mills Ltd* (27 March 1983, unreported), High Court (Costello J).

42 See generally Chapter 7, *Corporate Contracts, Capacity and Authority*, para **[7.096]** *ff*.

43 See, however, *Madden v Anglo Irish Bank plc* (29 June 1998, unreported), Supreme Court (O'Flaherty J). where an appeal against a refusal to grant an injunction to restrain a receiver from completing a contract for the sale of charged assets was upheld. In that case the applicant had claimed that the debenture was illegal because it secured a loan made for the purpose of purchasing the company's own shares and was thus in breach of CA 1963, s 60. O'Flaherty J noted the claim that the proceedings were vexatious and that interest was running at £12,000 per month. Refusing the injunction he found that the applicant had been aware all along of what was happening and held that if there was anything in the applicant's points on the validity of the debenture they sounded in damages.

44 *Bank of Baroda v Panessar* [1986] 3 All ER 751.

45 See generally, Hayes and Moran, *Receiverships* (1988) Incorporated Law Society Continuing Legal Education Seminar Material, 13 June 1988 at p 17.

46 See *Angelis v Algemene Bank Nederland (Ireland) Ltd* (4 June 1974, unreported), High Court, per Kenny J at p 2. See also *Maclaine Watson & Co Ltd v International Tin Council* [1987] BCLC 653.

the Rules of the Superior Courts 1986, Ord 50, r 6(1). Although unusual, application for an order of confirmation may be made even in the case of a receiver appointed under the terms of a debenture[47]. It is beyond the scope of this work to consider pre- and post-judgment court appointed receivers[48].

(c) Notice of appointment

[22.019] Section 107(1) of CA 1963 provides that where an order is obtained for the appointment of a receiver, or a receiver is appointed pursuant to the terms of an instrument, the person appointing the receiver shall, within seven days after the date of the order or appointment, publish a notice of this in *Iris Oifigiúil*. The notice must also be published in one daily newspaper, circulating in the district where the registered office of the company is situated. Notice of a receiver's appointment must also be given to the Registrar of Companies who, in turn, is obliged to notify the Director of Corporate Enforcement[49]. Similarly, notice must be given where a receiver resigns[50]. Default can result in a fine[51] but will not, however, invalidate a receiver's appointment[52]. A notice of appointment of a receiver will not, on its own and without satisfactory evidence of the power and authority of the person purporting to make the appointment, be sufficient proof of the valid appointment of a receiver[53].

[22.020] Section 319 of CA 1963 provides that where a receiver of the whole, or substantially the whole, of the property of a company is appointed on behalf of the holders of any debentures of the company secured by a floating charge, then certain steps must be taken:

— the receiver must send notice of his appointment to the company;

— within 14 days after receipt of the notice, or such longer period allowed by court or by the receiver, the company must make a statement in accordance with CA 1963, s 320 as to the affairs of the company;

— within two months of his appointment, the receiver must send to the Registrar of Companies, the court, any trustees for debenture holders and to the company, a copy of the said statement, together with a note of whatever comments the receiver sees fit.

[22.021] The desire to put the public on notice that a receiver has been appointed is also borne out by CA 1963, s 317 which provides that after such appointment, every invoice, order for goods or business letters issued by or on behalf of the company or the receiver,

---

47 See *Re 'Slogger' Automatic Feeder Co* [1915] 1 Ch 478. See generally Keane, *Equity and the Law of Trusts in the Republic of Ireland* (1988), Ch 22.

48 See further, Courtney, *Mareva Injunctions and Related Interlocutory Orders* (1998), pp 422–432.

49 CA 1963, s 319(7), as inserted by CLEA 2001, s 51(b).

50 CA 1963, s 107(2). See also duties to supply information to the Registrar and the Director considered at para **[22.059]** *ff.*

51 CA 1963, s 107(3).

52 *Re Motor Racing Circuits Ltd* (31 January 1997, unreported), Supreme Court.

53 *The Wise Finance Company Ltd v O'Regan* (26 June 1998, unreported), High Court (Laffoy J) at p 9.

being a document in which the name of the company appears, shall contain a statement that a receiver has been appointed[54].

The effect of the appointment of a receiver

[22.022] Where a receiver is appointed in respect of the assets of a company, certain consequences follow. Keane has described these, succinctly, as follows:

(1) Any floating charges crystallises, and become fixed charges on the assets/undertaking over which it was created,

(2) The powers of the company and the directors' authority are suspended in relation to the assets affected by the receivership, and can only be exercised with the consent of the receiver,

(3) Where the receiver is appointed as manager, then he is entitled to carry on the business of the company,

(4) The receiver may, if he considers that the interests of the debenture holder so require, dispose of any asset of the company affected by the debenture, including the entire of its undertaking.[55]

The appointment of a receiver will not, however, automatically terminate contracts[56] unless, of course, individual contracts are expressed to terminate upon the appointment of a receiver.

(a) Effect on management

[22.023] The appointment of a receiver to a company does not operate to automatically displace its board of directors. The directors' powers will continue save to the extent that they are ousted[57] or otherwise superseded by the powers granted to a receiver in the debenture on foot of which his appointment is made. In the New South Wales decision in *Hawkesbury Development Co Ltd v Landmark Finance Pty Ltd*[58] Street J said:

> 'Receivership and management may well dominate exclusively a company's affairs in its dealings and relations with the outside world. But it does not permeate the company's internal structure. That structure continues to exist notwithstanding that the directors no longer have authority to exercise their ordinary business-management functions. A valid receivership and management will ordinarily supersede, but not destroy, the company's own organs through which it conducts its affairs. The capacity of those organs to function bears a direct inverse relationship to the validity and scope of the receivership and management.'

---

54 Default is visitable by a fine of €126.97: CA 1963, s 317, as increased from €25.39 by C(A)A 1982, s 15.

55 See Keane, *Company Law*, (3rd edn, 2000), para 22.04.

56 In *Triffit Nurseries v Salads Etcetera Ltd* [2000] BCC 98 it was held by the English Court of Appeal that an agency relationship did not automatically terminate upon the appointment of a receiver to one of the parties.

57 In *Village Cay Marine Ltd v Acland et al* [1998] BCC 417 it was noted that there the receiver had replaced the board of directors as the person having authority to exercise the company's powers, and by virtue of that position validly authorised the company's seal to be affixed to various under-leases.

58 *Hawkesbury Development Co Ltd v Landmark Finance Pty Ltd* (1969) 92 WN (NSW) 199 at 209.

[22.024] In *Lascomme Ltd v United Dominions Trust (Ireland) Ltd and James Gilligan*[59] Keane J held that company directors' powers to maintain proceedings, commenced against a debenture holder, were unaffected by the subsequent appointment of a receiver by the debenture holder. In that case a company had commenced proceedings against a debenture holder. The debenture holder subsequently appointed a receiver to the company, and the receiver applied to court to stay the proceedings commenced by the company. Keane J held that the directors' powers to maintain proceedings were not terminated by the appointment of the receiver. He also held, however, that the debenture holder's position must also be considered and that the directors were not permitted to interfere with the receiver dealing with the company's property which had been charged to the bank or otherwise imperiling the company's assets which were the subject of the debenture. In so holding. Keane J struck a balance between the rights of the company and the rights of the debenture holder[60]. This finding was in line with that of the New South Wales court in *Hawkesbury Development Co Ltd v Landmark Finance Pty Ltd*[61]. It should be noted that that decision has not received universal support and in England in *Tudor Grange Holdings Ltd v Citibank NA*[62], Browne-Wilkinson V-C distinguished it from the case in hand on the ground that the proceedings had been instituted in *Tudor Grange* on behalf of the companies in receivership which directly impinged on the companies' property in that no indemnity against costs had been offered by the directors[63].

(b) Effect on employees

[22.025] Contracts of employment between the company and its employees are not necessarily terminated by the appointment of a receiver out of court by a debenture holder[64]. This is, however, qualified by the fact that contracts of employment which are inconsistent with the appointment of a receiver, such as that of a managing director are terminated, where a receiver-manager takes over the management of the business. A receiver can, of course, terminate contracts of employment at his own discretion and his obligations will be thereby determined[65]. Where a receiver does not terminate contracts of employment, and allows employees to continue in employment, he does not himself

---

59 *Lascomme Ltd v United Dominions Trust (Ireland) Ltd and James Gilligan* [1994] 1 ILRM 227.

60 See also *Wymes v Crowley* (27 February 1987, unreported), High Court; *Newhart Developments Ltd v Cooperative Commercial Bank Ltd* [1978] 2 All ER 896; and *Grange Holdings Ltd v Citibank NA* [1991] 4 All ER 1.

61 (1969) 92 WN (NSW) 199 at 209.

62 *Tudor Grange Holdings Ltd v Citibank NA* [1992] Ch 53.

63 See *Deangrove Pty Ltd (Rec & Mgrs Aptd) v Commonwealth Bank of Australia* [2001] Federal Court of Australia 173, 6 March 2001.

64 See *Griffiths v Secretary of State for Social Services* [1974] QB 468. At common law, the appointment of a receiver pursuant to a court order did terminate contracts of employment: *Reid v Explosives Co Ltd* [1887] 19 QBD 264.

65 Receivers will be obliged to comply with employment legislation such as the Minimum Notice (Terms of Employment) Act 1973: see *Bolands Ltd (in receivership) v Ward et al* [1988] ILRM 382.

become personally liable for their wages from the date of his appointment because there is no new contract, and any contract which subsists does so between the company and the employees[66].

[22.026] Whilst it has been established that the European Communities (Safeguarding of Employees' Rights on Transfer of Undertakings) Regulations 1980[67] (which makes provision for the continuity of contracts of employment of employees on the transfer of an undertaking) does not apply in liquidations[68], the position regarding receiverships in Ireland[69] remains unclear. In *Mythen v The Employment Appeals Tribunal*[70] Barrington J held that just because the European Court of Justice has held[71] that the Directive[72] on which the Irish regulations are based does not apply to a particular form of Dutch liquidation procedure, one could not assume '... that it would also hold that the Directive would not apply to a sale by a receiver appointed by a debenture holder'. In *Brett v Niall Collins Ltd (in receivership) and Oyster Investments Ltd*[73] a receiver sought to sell a business (premises, equipment and goodwill) as a going concern but purported to dismiss the staff by paying redundancy with the intention that the undertaking could be sold without employees. It was held by the Employment Appeals Tribunal that there had been a transfer of an undertaking and that the receipt and retention of the redundancy payments by the employees did not break their service for the purposes of the Unfair Dismissals (Amendment) Act 1993, s 15. In the course of its determination the EAT said:

> 'It should be pointed out that where a company is put into liquidation or an employer is declared a bankrupt the selling on of the assets of the insolvent person, natural or legal, is not a transfer of undertaking for the purposes of the Directive. A receivership is however, because the appointment of a receiver does not indicate in law that the company is insolvent although it operates to that effect for the purposes of the Protection of Employees (Employers' Insolvency) Act 1984.'[74]

---

66 See *Nicoll v Cutts* [1985] BCLC 322.

67 SI 1980/306. See Lynch, Marshall & O'Ferrall, *Corporate Insolvency and Rescue* (1996), p 161 *ff* and Redmond, *Dismissal Law in Ireland* (1999), p 403. For a very thorough review of the Directive from a general employment law perspective, see Byrne, 'Business Sales and Transfers, The Contracting out of Services and Employee Rights' (1996) 3 CLP 139.

68 *HBM Abels v Administrative Board of Bedrijfsvereniging Voor De Metaal– Industrie en de Electrotechnische Industrie* 2 ELC 434, [1987] 2 CMLR 406. See also *Re Castle Brand Ltd (In liquidation)* (25 March 1985, unreported), High Court, per Hamilton J. In *Sanders v Europieces Case* C–399/96 (12/11/98) it was held by the European Court of Justice that the Directive also applies to voluntary liquidations.

69 It has been held in England in several cases, such as *Angus Jowett & Co v Taylors and Garment Workers Union* [1985] IRLR 326 (see also *Secretary of State for Employment v Spence* [1986] IRLR 248) that equivalent English regulations apply to receiverships and impose obligations on receivers eg to consult with employees.

70 *Mythen v The Employment Appeals Tribunal* [1989] ILRM 844.

71 In *HBM Abels v Administrative Board of Bedrijfsvereniging Voor De Metaal– Industrie en de Electrotechnische Industrie* 2 ELC 434, [1987] 2 CMLR 406.

72 European Council Directive 77/187/EEC.

73 *Brett v Niall Collins Ltd (in receivership) and Oyster Investments Ltd* [1995] ELR 69.

74 [1995] ELR 69 at 73.

Notwithstanding convincing argument to the contrary[75], it is thought, on balance, that it is unlikely that the Irish superior courts will exclude receiverships from the ambit of the regulations.

The status of a receiver

[22.027] As has been noted above[76], a receiver can be appointed to a company in either of two ways: by court appointment or by a debenture holder. The *status* of a receiver will depend initially upon how he has been appointed.

(a) Receivers appointed by the court[77]

[22.028] A receiver appointed by the court has the status of an officer of the court[78]. The significance of this is that such a receiver cannot concern himself exclusively with the interests of the creditor who procured his appointment. Rather, his concern ought to be the interests of all creditors of the company. It follows that, unlike the position considered next, the receiver will not be deemed to be the agent of any particular person.

(b) Receivers appointed by a debenture holder

[22.029] A receiver appointed pursuant to a debenture is essentially a creature of contract whose status will be determined by the debenture. Unless the contrary is stated in the debenture the receiver will be the *agent* of the debenture holder, and will only be the agent of the company through necessity[79]. However, it would be a most unusual debenture which did not provide to the contrary, namely that any receiver appointed will be the agent of the company. The effect of this will be to make the company responsible not only for the receiver's acts or defaults but even for his remuneration. So, in *Irish Oil and Cake Mills Ltd v Donnelly*[80] Costello J said:

> 'The receiver derives his appointment and his authority from the contract entered into between the parties. In that case, as is usual, the parties agreed that he is to be treated as the agent of the mortgagors, the plaintiff herein. This provision protects the debenture holders from the liability as mortgagees in possession and establishes the relationship between the receiver and the company.' [81]

(c) The receiver as agent of the company

[22.030] Most debenture instruments will contain a provision that on the appointment of a receiver, the receiver will have a *power of attorney* to do all acts necessary to enforce

---

75 The so-called ETO (economic, technical and organisational) defence. Note, though, that this defence was unsuccessfully invoked by a receiver in *Brett v Niall Collins Ltd (in receivership) and Oyster Investments Ltd* [1995] ELR 69.

76 See para **[22.012]** *ff.*

77 See Picarda, *The Law Relating to Receivers, Managers and Administrators* (2nd edn, 1990), p 339 *ff.*

78 See the dictum of Viscount Haldane LC in *Parsons v Soverign Bank of Canada* [1913] AC 160.

79 See *Robinson Printing Co Ltd v Chic Ltd* [1905] 2 Ch 123.

80 *Irish Oil and Cake Mills Ltd v Donnelly* (27 March 1984, unreported), High Court, per Costello J.

81 (27 March 1984, unreported), High Court at p 6. See also *W & L Crowe Ltd v Electricity Supply Board* (9 May 1984, unreported), High Court, per Costello J.

the security. The authority of a company to execute a power of attorney to do acts on its behalf inside the country was recognised in *Industrial Development Authority v Moran*[82].

[22.031] Until recently, it had been questioned whether or not a company could be said to continue to be bound by such a power of attorney after a winding up has commenced, in that at common law any agency created by the company would be terminated. One solution for the debenture holder is to include in the debenture a provision to the effect that the power of attorney granted to the donee is irrevocable although such a provision was, prior to the enactment of the Powers of Attorney Act 1996 ('the 1996 Act'), questioned[83]. Since the enactment of the 1996 Act the matter has been put beyond all doubt, s 20(1) providing:

> 'Where a power of attorney is expressed to be irrevocable and is given to secure—
>
> (a) a proprietary interest of the donee of the power, or
>
> (b) the performance of an obligation owed to the donee,
>
> then, so long as the donee has that interest[84] or the obligation remains undischarged, the power shall not be revoked—
>
> (i) by the donor without the consent of the donee, or
>
> (ii) by the death, incapacity or bankruptcy of the donor or, *if the donor is a body corporate, by its winding-up or dissolution*[85].'

In order to rely upon s 20(1), the power of attorney must be expressed to be '*irrevocable*'; moreover, it must be given to *secure* either *a proprietary interest* of the donee or *the performance of an obligation* owed to the donee. Subject to these requirements, s 20(3) provides that the section applies to powers of attorney 'whenever created'. As the receiver will not have a proprietary interest nor will the company's obligations be owed to the receiver, consideration may be given to constituting the chargee the donee of the power and to giving the donee power to appoint somebody (the receiver) to act on the donee's behalf as a substitute.

[22.032] It is accepted that the relationship of agency created by a debenture between a receiver and a company is an unusual one[86]. As Costello J said in *Irish Oil and Cake Mills Ltd v Donnelly*[87]:

---

82 *Industrial Development Authority v Moran* [1978] IR 159. See Chapter 7, *Corporate Contracts, Capacity and Authority*, para **[7.029]**.

83 See *Keane, Equity and the Law of Trusts in the Republic of Ireland* (1988), at para 24.04 and Schmitthoff (ed), *Palmer's Company Law* (24th edn, 1987), para 86.04.

84 Powers of Attorney Act 1996, s 20(2) provides: 'A power of attorney given to secure a proprietary interest may be given, and shall be deemed to have been capable always of being given, to the person entitled to the interest and persons deriving title under that person to that interest, and those persons shall be duly constituted donees of the power for all purposes of the power but without prejudice to any right to appoint substitutes given by the power.'

85 Emphasis added.

86 See *Bula Ltd v Crowley* (1 February 2002, unreported), High Court (Barr J) and also *Gomba Holdings UK Ltd v Minories Finance Ltd* [1989] BCLC 115 at 117.

87 *Irish Oil and Cake Mills Ltd v Donnelly* (27 March 1984, unreported), High Court, per Costello J.

> 'The agency here is of course very different from the ordinary agency arising every day in commercial transactions. Here the receiver has been appointed by the owner in equity of these companies' assets with the object of realising their security and for this purpose to carry on the companies' business. The exceptional nature of his status is to be seen from the fact that notwithstanding his appointment as agent he is to be personally liable under contracts entered into by him...'

This is an agency that has some peculiar incidents[88]. The reasons why receivership is an unusual agency can be said to be threefold: while the receiver is an agent of the company, he is personally liable on contracts entered into on behalf of the company[89]; the company (principal) is unable to dismiss this particular agent; and this relationship of agency is, to use the expression employed by Maitland to describe a mortgage, founded on an underlying *falsio assumpit*, since the primary duty of the receiver is to realise the security held by the person who appoints him, and often not to manage the company to any other end. One consequence of the unusual nature of the agency between receivers and the companies to which they are appointed is that the law imposes certain *duties* on receivers[90].

[22.033] It is important to recognise that receiverships involve two distinct relationships. The nature of a receivership was considered by Barr J in *Bula Ltd v Crowley*[91], where he made the following observations:

> 'The relationship between a receiver, the mortgagee who appoints him and the debtor company which owns the secured assets is exceptional, if not unique. The appointment of a receiver is one of the remedies open to a debentureholder in respect of a defaulting company whose assets are secured by the debenture. There are two distinct relationships involved. As between the mortgagee and the debtor company, the duty of the receiver is to take control of the latter with a view to realising its assets in discharge of debt owing by the company to the mortgagee. This is the fundamental objective of the receivership. The appointment of the receiver entails taking possession of the company lands and in practical terms vis-à-vis the Banks and Bula in the instant case it amounts to possession by the mortgagees. In short, the Banks' purpose for the appointment of the receiver is to put him into control and effective possession of the company assets so as to realise the mortgagees' security by sale of the lands. The fact that under the terms of the debentures the receiver is stated to be the agent of the company does not detract from the foregoing relationship as between the receiver, the Banks and Bula. The agency as stated in the debentures is one which is relevant to the third party claims on the company. It is a long-standing practice in financial and commercial life that debenture holders (commonly banks or other such institutions) generally prefer not to become directly involved in the conduct of receiverships with consequent risk of liability to third parties, and so, in the context of dealings between a receiver on behalf of a company and third parties who make

---

88 *Kerr on Receivers* (16th edn), p 304 states: '...the principal may not dismiss the agent, and his possession of his principal's assets is really that of the mortgagee who appointed him. He owes no prior duty to the principal other than that of a mortgagee in possession'. This was cited with approval in *Bula Ltd v Crowley* (1 February 2002, unreported), High Court (Barr J).

89 See para **[22.062]** *ff*.

90 See para **[22.034]** *ff*.

91 *Bula Ltd v Crowley* (1 February 2002, unreported), High Court (Barr J).

claims upon it, the debenture normally provides that the former is agent of the company. In short, a receivership, such as that in the instant case, involves two distinct relationships.

First, that between the appointing mortgagee and the receiver which relates to the fundamental objective of the receivership, being entry into possession of the company's assets for the purpose of sale in the interest of the mortgagee. In practical terms vis-à-vis mortgagee and mortgagor the control over the company's assets exercised by the receiver amounts to possession of the debtor's secured assets by him which in turn in practical terms is possession by the mortgagee who appointed him.

The second relationship is that between the receiver and third parties arising out of the receivership. Debentures normally provide, as in the instant case, that such dealings are conducted by the receiver as agent of the company in receivership. The mortgagees have no right to interfere in the receivership in that regard. In my view there is no inconsistency between the foregoing relationships which represent long established commercial good sense.'

The facts in that case were that the plaintiff had created a mortgage and debenture, as security for monies loaned to it by a number of banks. After it encountered major financial difficulties, the lending banks appointed the first defendant as receiver over its property, issued proceedings seeking the recovery of the principal and interest and also sought a well-charging order. The first plaintiff contended that the banks' title to its land had been extinguished by ss 33[92] and 38[93] of the Statute of Limitations 1957. The essence of the plaintiff's claim was that it had established adverse possession against the banks. It was submitted that the appointment of a receiver had placed the plaintiff-company under the receiver's managerial control and had dis-empowered the directors but had not dislodged the plaintiff's possession of the lands and did not bring about possession of the lands by the receiver to the plaintiff's exclusion. The plaintiff's case was that the title of the banks to its lands had become, after 12 years, extinguished, as had the banks' right to principal and interest; in short, it was contended that the banks were statute barred. This was strongly disputed by the defendants who contended that the receiver, having been lawfully appointed under the debentures and having taken effective possession and control of the plaintiff, was outside the scope of the Statute of Limitations 1957. Barr J held that the activation of rights under the debentures (eg appointing a receiver) did not create a situation of adverse possession within the meaning of s 18(1) of the Statute of Limitations 1957. This was because, having analysed[94] the relationship between the

---

92 This provides: 'At the expiration of the period fixed by this Act for a mortgagee to bring an action claiming sale of the mortgaged land, the title of the mortgagee to the land shall be extinguished.'

93 This provides: 'At the expiration of the period fixed by this Act for a mortgagee of land to bring an action to recover the land or for a person claiming as mortgagee or chargeant to bring an action claiming sale of the land, the right of the mortgagee or such person to the principal sum and interest secured by the mortgage or charge shall be extinguished.'

94 Barr J cited and quoted with approval from: *Gomba Holdings v Homan* [1986] BCLC 331 at 334; *Gomba Holdings v Minories Finance* [1989] BCLC 115 at 117; *Rottenberg v Monjack* [1993] BCLC 374; *Irish Oil and Cake Mills v Donnelly* [ICLR (1963–1990) 564]; *Lascomme Ltd v UDT Bank* [1993] 3 IR 412 at 416; *Re Johnson and Co* [1955] 1 Ch 634 and *Ardmore Studies (Ireland) Ltd v Lynch et al* [1965] IR 1.

plaintiff, the receiver and the banks, there was no possession (eg by the plaintiff) without right or authority which, it was said, is the essence of adverse possession within the meaning of the 1957 Act.

Duties of receivers

[22.034] Receivers owe an ever-increasing number of common law and statutory duties to the companies to which they are appointed. These duties include:

(a) The duty to provide information to the company.

(b) Duties of receiver-managers.

(c) Duties arising on the disposal of assets.

(d) Duties to guarantors.

(e) Duties in applying the proceeds of sale of assets.

(f) Duties to supply information to the Registrar of Companies and the Director of Corporate Enforcement.

(a) The duty to provide information to the company

[22.035] Although CA 1963, s 319[95] requires receivers to provide certain information to the Registrar of Companies, the law is somewhat unsettled upon whether or not a company is entitled to obtain further information from a receiver. On balance the authorities indicate that a company, while owed a certain duty of care by a receiver, is not generally owed a duty to be provided with information. In *McGowan v Gannon*[96] Carroll J said obiter that under the ordinary law of contract where a company is deemed to be a principal it is entitled to obtain information from a receiver where he is the agent of the company. This was later distinguished in *Irish Oil and Cake Mills (Manufacturing) Ltd v Donnelly*[97] by Costello J who said:

> 'Whilst in that case the receiver had vouchsafed information about a sale to the directors there is nothing to suggest that he gave them details of his trading accounts and the court was in no way concerned with the point raised in that case, namely, the existence of a receiver's duty to account to the board of directors whilst managing the company's business.'[98]

While accepting that the receiver does owe a certain duty of care to the company[99], Costello J held:

---

[95] Within seven months of his appointment and every six months subsequently, a receiver has to send to the Registrar of Companies an abstract showing the assets of the company of which he has taken possession since his appointment, the estimated value of the assets, the proceeds of sale of any such assets since his appointment, his receipts and payments during that period of six months or, where he ceases to act, the aggregated amounts of his receipts and payments during all the preceding period since his appointment.

[96] *McGowan v Gannon* [1983] ILRM 516.

[97] *Irish Oil and Cake Mills (Manufacturing) Ltd v Donnelly* (27 March 1984, unreported), High Court.

[98] (27 March 1984, unreported), High Court at p 7.

[99] To obtain the best price reasonably obtainable on a sale of the charged assets, considered at para **[22.040]** *ff*.

> 'It is said that apart from the special facts of this case the general duty on a receiver and manager to take reasonable steps to secure the best possible price for the companies' assets includes a duty "to keep the company apprised of how the business of the company is going". This is a very far-reaching proposition and I must reject it. There may well be special circumstances in which, to ensure that the best price possible is obtained for the assets, trading information since the appointment of the receiver should be given to the company's directors. But in the absence of special circumstances which might favourably affect the price, a receiver/manager is not under any duty of care which involves him in reporting as suggested to the directors on his management and business. It cannot be said that a receiver/manager is under *no* duty to account to the company whose affairs he is managing nor did the defendant so urge in that case. The extent and nature of the duty and the extent and nature of the accounts he must furnish will depend on the facts of each individual case.' [100]

An example of such 'special circumstances' is seen in *Smiths Ltd v Middleton*[101] where it was held that a receiver as agent was under an equitable obligation to account.

[22.036] In *Kinsella v Somers*[102] the applicant was a director and shareholder in the Dublin Gas Company, which had been in receivership since a debenture holder had appointed a receiver pursuant to a mortgage debenture some 15 years' previously. The matter came before the High Court by way of a motion for directions under CA 1963, s 316 when the applicant sought directions. The applicant's motivation was information. Specifically he sought information about the nature of the assets of the company since the inception of the receivership, the changing nature of such assets, their estimated value and the basis for such evaluation, the manner of sale of such assets as were sold and the presale method of advertisement, the proceeds of sale realised and an account of offers received for the sale of each asset. The applicant also sought accounts in respect of the receiver's fees, the receivership on a yearly basis and an opportunity to inspect the documents relating to the receivership. The receiver contended, inter alia, that he had already furnished appropriate information to the company in October 1993. The receiver maintained that the applicant neither as a director nor as a shareholder had an entitlement to the type of information sought and in any event the lapse of time and the company's insolvency were such that it would no longer be just or equitable for him to have to furnish such information, particularly since the applicant and the other directors had, in 1993, failed to take up his then invitation to give more information. On the receiver's duty to disclose information Budd J took as the law on a receiver's duty to provide information, to be that as stated by Costello J in *Irish Oil and Cake Mills (Manufacturing) Ltd v Donnelly*[103]. He went on to find that while there may be some room for debate as to the extent of a receiver's duty towards the company to which he is appointed receiver, no authority could be found to support the applicant's proposition

---

[100] *Irish Oil and Cake Mills Ltd v Donnelly* (27 March 1984, unreported), High Court, at pp 12–13.

[101] *Smiths Ltd v Middleton* [1979] 3 All ER 842.

[102] *Kinsella v Somers* (22 November 1999, unreported), High Court (Budd J).

[103] *Irish Oil and Cake Mills (Manufacturing) Ltd v Donnelly* (27 March 1984, unreported), High Court, considered at para **[22.035]**.

that he was entitled as a director or shareholder to be furnished with accounts and documents.

[22.037] A related, although essentially distinct, issue concerns the right of a company to documents in the possession of a receiver. It has been held in the UK that such a claim will only succeed where it is based on a proprietary claim to ownership of those documents. So, in *Gomba Holdings UK Ltd v Minories Finance Ltd*[104] the defendant-company had appointed receivers and managers over the plaintiff-companies pursuant to debentures. When the receiverships were discharged, the receivers, pursuant to a court order, handed back certain documents to the plaintiff-companies which belonged to them. However, other documents were retained on the basis that they never belonged to the plaintiff-companies. The plaintiff-companies argued that even documents which were actually created by the receivers belonged to them because the receivers were their agents and so the plaintiff-companies, as principals, were entitled to those documents. This was rejected by Hoffmann J[105] and also by Fox LJ in the Court of Appeal. Fox LJ said that the agency relationship between a receiver and a company was very far removed from the ordinary principal and agent situation[106]:

> 'The result is that the receiver, in the course of the receivership, performs duties on behalf of the debenture holder as well as the mortgagor. And these duties may relate closely to the affairs of the entity which is the subject of the receivership. It is, therefore, not satisfactory to approach the problem of the ownership of the documents which come into existence in the course of the receivership on the basis that ownership depends on whether the documents relate to the affairs of...the companies.'[107]

The correct test to be adopted here is to ask whether or not the documents were brought into existence in discharge of the receiver's duties to the company, the debenture holder or neither. This approach envisages three categories of document. As Hoffmann J said at first instance[108]:

> 'The ownership of the documents depends in my judgment on whether they were created or received in discharge of the receivers' duties to the companies, or to the debenture holder, or neither. In the first category would fall documents generated or received by the receivers pursuant to their duty to manage the businesses of the companies or dispose of their assets. These documents belong to the companies. In the second category come documents containing advice and information about the receivership or the companies, brought into existence by the receivers for the purpose of being communicated to [the defendant-company] or sent to the receivers to enable them to advise [the defendant-company]. These documents belong to [the defendant-company]. The third category will include notes, calculations and memoranda prepared by the receivers, their agents or employees not pursuant to any duty to prepare those specific documents but for the purpose of enabling them to discharge their professional duties to [the defendant-company]...These belong to the receivers themselves...'[109]

---

104 *Gomba Holdings UK Ltd v Minorities Finance Ltd* [1989] BCLC 115. This case was described as 'helpful' by Barr J in *Kinsella v Somers* (23 November 1999, unreported), High Court.

105 [1988] BCLC 60.

106 [1989] BCLC 115 at 117.

107 [1989] BCLC 115 at 117.

108 [1988] BCLC 60 at 62.

109 See also *Chantery Martin & Co v Martin* [1953] 2 All ER 691, [1953] 2 QB 286.

A company will, on this analysis, only be entitled to certain documents created by the receiver while managing the business of the company or selling its assets. It is submitted that such a stance makes eminent sense and places the agency relationship between the receiver and the company in perspective[110].

(b) Duties of receiver-managers

[22.038] The difference between managing a company for the benefit of a debenture holder and managing a company for the benefit of shareholders is clearly distinguished in case law. In *Downside Nominees Ltd v First City Corporation Ltd*[111] Lord Templeman said the remedy for a dissatisfied debenture holder was to revoke the receiver's appointment and the remedy for a dissatisfied shareholder was to either pay off the debenture holder or else place the company into liquidation. He went on to say:

> 'But if a receiver and manager decides at his discretion to manage and is allowed to manage and does manage in good faith with the object of preserving and realising the assets for the benefit of the debenture holder, he is subject to no further or greater liability.'

The breach of a duty of good faith requires some dishonest or improper motive or element of bad faith to be established[112]. The following passage (quoted with apparent approval by Barr J in *Kinsella v Somers*[113]) from the judgment of Jenkins LJ in *Re B Johnson & Co (Builders) Ltd*[114] is instructive as to the duties of receiver-managers:

> 'In a word, in the absence of fraud or mala fides...the company cannot complain of any act or omission of the receiver and manager, provided that he does nothing that he is not empowered to do, and omits nothing that he is enjoined to do by the terms of his appointment. If the company conceives that it has a claim against the receiver and manager for breach of some duty owed by him to the company, the issue is not whether the receiver and manager has done or omitted to do anything which it would be wrongful in a manager of a company to do or omit, but whether he has exercised or abused or wrongfully omitted to use the special powers and discretions vested in him pursuant to the contract of loan constituted by the debenture for the special purpose of enabling the assets comprised in the debenture holders' security to be preserved and realised.'[115]

Recently, in *Medforth v Blake*[116] the English Court of Appeal held that in failing to negotiate discounts on pig feed whilst running the plaintiff-mortgagor's pig-farming business, receiver-managers were liable for breach of a so-called 'equitable duty of care'. It was alleged that the farmer had reminded the receivers that it was normal commercial practice to give such discounts. It was accepted, though, that the receivers'

---

[110] See also *Casson Beckman & Partners v Papi* [1991] BCLC 299 where the Court of Appeal held that the company was only entitled to those documents which were created or received by the receiver in pursuance of his duties as receiver or liquidator, the receivers were owners of any working papers.

[111] *Downside Nominees Ltd v First City Corporation Ltd* [1993] BCC 46.

[112] *Medforth v Blake* [1999] BCC 771 at 785.

[113] *Kinsella v Somers* (22 November 1999, unreported), High Court (Budd J).

[114] *Re B Johnson & Co (Builders) Ltd* [1955] 1 Ch 634.

[115] [1955] 1 Ch 634 at 663.

[116] *Medforth v Blake* [1999] BCC 771.

failure to seek such discounts was not the result of any conscious or deliberate impropriety. Sir Richard Scott V-C said of a receiver's duties:

> 'In my judgment, in principle and on the authorities, the following propositions can be stated:
>
> (1) A receiver managing mortgaged property owes duties to the mortgagor and anyone else with an interest in the equity of redemption.
>
> (2) The duties include, but are not necessarily confined to, a duty of good faith.
>
> (3) The extent and scope of any duty additional to that of good faith will depend on the facts and circumstances of the particular case.
>
> (4) In exercising his powers of management the primary duty of the receiver is to try and bring about a situation in which interest on the secured debt can be paid and the debt itself re-paid.
>
> (5) Subject to that primary duty, the receiver owes a duty to manage the property with due diligence.
>
> (6) Due diligence does not oblige the receiver to continue to carry on a business on the mortgaged premises previously carried on by the mortgagor.
>
> (7) If the receiver does carry on a business on the mortgaged premises, due diligence requires reasonable steps to be taken in order to try to do so profitably.'[117]

[22.039] On the substantive point of the extent of a receiver's duty Sir Richard Scott V-C said:

> 'The proposition that, in managing and carrying on the mortgaged business, the receiver owes the mortgagor no duty other than that of good faith offends, in my opinion, commercial sense. The receiver is not obliged to carry on the business. He can decide not to do so. He can decide to close it down. In taking these decisions he is entitled, and perhaps bound, to have regard to the interests of the mortgagee in obtaining repayment of the secured debt. Provided he acts in good faith, he is entitled to sacrifice the interests of the mortgagor in pursuit of that end. But if he does decide to carry on the business why should he not be expected to do so with reasonable competence? The present case, if the pleaded facts are established, involves the failure of the receivers to obtain discounts that were freely available. Other glaring examples of managerial incompetence can be imagined. Suppose the receivers had decided to carry on the business but had not decided, through incompetence and not for any dishonest reason, that the pigs need not be fed or watered more than once a week, and, as a result a number of pigs had died. The receivers would, I suppose, be in trouble with the RSPCA but, if Mr Smith is right, although they might be liable to the mortgagee they would have no liability to the mortgagor. Or suppose, that, as may well be the case, it is common practice to inoculate weaners against disease to which pigs are prone but the receivers decide to save money by dispensing with inoculations, with the result that a number of the weaners contracted disease and died and that the rest had to be slaughtered. If Mr Smith is right, the receivers would have no liability to the mortgagor whose business they had, by incompetence, ruined. It is accepted that, if the mortgagee had gone into possession and carried on the business similarly incompetently, the mortgagee would have been accountable to the mortgagor for the loss caused to the mortgagor by the incompetence. But, it is submitted, not so the receivers.'[118]

[117] [1999] BCC 771 at 784–785.

[118] [1999] BCC 771 at 777.

The distinction between the equitable duty of good faith and an equitable duty of care has been roundly criticised[119]. The Court of Appeal went on to hold that a receiver has duties in equity to manage a business with due diligence. The difficulty with this finding is that, for good reason, it has always been accepted that a receiver's duty in managing a business is best confined to a duty of good faith. How else can a receiver be judged on the peculiarities in the management of a particular business? Is a mortgagee to be fettered in his appointment of receivers by confining his choice to those with particular speciality business acumen? Certainly, receiver-managers must be bound to comply with the law of the land (eg health and safety legislation, licensing laws, etc) in managing a business and to that extent owe duties over and above that of good faith. But to extend their duties to nebulous, perhaps even discretionary, matters is thought to go too far. A receiver cannot be expected to manage a business with the same care and dedication as a mortgagor; he might not, for example, be obliged to work 14 hours a day as a mortgagor, striving for his own benefit, might voluntarily work. This decision is likely to encourage frivolous and vexatious litigation by disgruntled mortgagors who believe that nobody but themselves has managed their business as well as they could manage it. It is thought that a receiver-manager's duty is best confined to that of good faith and, if necessary, mortgagees will seek, in their security documents, to confine it thus.

(c) Duties arising on the disposal of assets

[22.040] Prior to the passing of CA 1990 it had been established by a number of Irish and Commonwealth cases that receivers owed a duty to take reasonable care to try to obtain the best possible price on the disposal of charged assets. In this respect the law always distinguished between duties owed on the disposal of assets and duties owed on the management of charged assets[120]. Receivers' duties on the disposal of assets were accepted in a number of Irish cases[121], most notably, *McGowan v Gannon*[122], and in England this continues to be known as 'the *Cuckmere* duty of care'[123].

(i) The statutory duty to obtain the best price reasonably obtainable

[22.041] This position is now enshrined in statute and CA 1963, s 316A(1)[124] provides that:

> 'A receiver, in selling property of a company, shall exercise all reasonable care to obtain the best price reasonably obtainable for the property as at the time of sale.'

---

119 See Anderson, 'Receivers' Duties to Mortgagors – Court of Appeal makes a Pig's Ear of it', *CCH's Company Law Newsletter*, Issue 37, 13 August 1999.

120 See para **[22.038]**.

121 See also, *Irish Oil and Cake Mills Ltd v Donnelly* (27 March 1984, unreported), High Court, per Costello J; *Holohan v Friends Provident and Century Life Office* [1966] IR 1; *Casey v Intercontinental Bank* [1979] IR 364; *Standard Chartered Bank v Walker* [1982] 3 All ER 938 (extending this duty to guarantors: see para **[22.050]** *ff*). See generally *Re Bula Ltd* (20 June 2002, unreported) High Court (Murphy J) where the basis of receivers' duties is reviewed.

122 *McGowan v Gannon* [1983] ILRM 516.

123 See *Cuckmere Brick Co Ltd v Mutual Finance Ltd* [1971] Ch 949 where it was held that a mortgagee was obliged to obtain 'the true market value' of the property in sale.

124 As inserted by CA 1990, s 172.

It has been observed by McCracken J in *Ruby Property Company Ltd v Kilty*[125] that 'this is simply a statutory acknowledgement of the position at common law.' The legislature contemplated that such a provision, if left to stand alone, would be avoided through the employment of counteracting contractual provisions in debentures, and so by CA 1963, s 316A(2)(a), notwithstanding the provisions of any debenture, it is *not* a defence to proceedings brought against a receiver that he was acting as the agent of the company or under a power of attorney given by the company. Section 316A(2)(b) of CA 1963 provides that a receiver who breaches his duty in this regard is not entitled to be compensated or indemnified by the company for any liability which he may incur. The meaning of 'best price reasonably obtainable' was considered by Murphy J in *Re Bula Ltd*[126]. There he said that "best price":

> '...begs the question as to the norm by which "best" is measured. There is no statutory requirement for an independent valuation nor, indeed, a necessity to have more than one buyer. In the absence of a professional valuation or open market competition to establish a price how can a court approve of a sale as rendering a "best price"? The requirement is not simply to get the best price reasonably obtainable'.

In that case a receiver sought approval pursuant to CA 1963, s 316A for the sale of an ore body (a mine) to the company's adjoining landowner (and long time fellow litigant) Tara Mines Ltd. The company opposed the application. After examining the receiver's duties under s 316A(1), Murphy J held that:

> 'Section 316A refers not to value nor cost but to price. The receiver in selling the property of the company, which he is clearly entitled to do, must exercise all reasonable care to obtain the best price reasonably obtainable for the property at the time of sale... What the court has to do is to ascertain that, given that a receiver has exercised all reasonable care, that the ultimate price is the best reasonably obtainable. That is the market "best price".'

Murphy J concluded that the receiver had exercised all reasonable care necessary to obtain the best price and allowed his application to complete the sale of the mine to Tara.

[22.042] The requirement that a receiver should exercise all reasonable care in the sale of property entails a higher standard than merely acting in *good faith*. Where it is apprehended that a receiver is not endeavouring to obtain the best price reasonably possible, an injunction can be applied for to prevent the sale of the mortgaged or charged property. Such was successfully sought by a mortgagor in *Holohan v Friends Provident and Century Life Office*[127] against a mortgagee exercising his power of sale. There, the mortgagee had entered into a contract to sell the mortgaged property without vacant possession (ie it was subject to existing tenancies) and refused to consider an alternative. It was successfully argued by the mortgagor that if the mortgaged property was sold with vacant possession, a higher price could be obtained. A contrasting case is *Casey v Irish Intercontinental Bank Ltd*[128] where the Supreme Court again addressed this matter. There, an offer of £111,000 had been accepted by mortgagees who at the time of

---

125 *Ruby Property Company Ltd v Kilty* (1 December 1999, unreported), High Court (McCracken J).

126 *Re Bula Ltd* (20 June 2002, unreported) High Court.

127 *Holohan v Friends Provident and Century Life Office* [1966] IR 1. See Wylie, *Irish Land Law* (3rd edn, 1997), para 13.036, and Wylie, *A Casebook on Irish Land Law* (1984), p 447.

128 *Casey v Irish Intercontinental Bank Ltd* [1979] IR 364.

acceptance had considered that to be the best offer available. Later, an offer of £190,000 was received but rejected because of the prior contract. An application to order the mortgagee to rescind the first contract was rejected by Kenny J who said:

> 'The subsequent offer of £190,000 did not in any way invalidate that contract which, in my opinion, Intercontinental were bound to carry out. A mortgagee who enters into a contract for sale at a price which all the circumstances and valuations show is, *at the date of the contract*, the best price available is not discharged if a higher price is offered after the contract is made.' [Emphasis added]

From this it is clear that at common law, the operative time to see whether or not the best price was obtained is the date of the contract. This is now further supported by CA 1963, s 316A(1) which specifically refers to 'as at the time of sale', which is the contract date not the completion date (of a conveyance).

[22.043] The safest course of action which a receiver can take when selling an asset of a company is to take expert advice on the most efficient and valuable method of disposal[129]. Expert or professional advice however, will often not resolve a matter outright, since an equally reputable opinion may be obtained from another professional advising to the contrary. In such a situation, where there is conflicting professional advice, it is open to the receiver to make a commercial decision between the two. This was the case in *Lambert Jones Estates Ltd v Donnelly*[130]. There, one opinion on the disposal of the property charged would have involved the delay and expense of planning applications at a time when interest on the principal sum charged was running at over £3,000 per day. The receiver was entitled to follow another expert opinion which would mean the property would realise less, but would be sold more quickly. There, the receiver indicated that in any event he would be seeking court approval for the sale, a matter considered below[131].

[22.044] In *Re Edenfell Holdings Ltd*[132], the Supreme Court heard an appeal from a decision of Laffoy J in respect of an application for directions brought under CA 1963, s 316(1). The matter in dispute was whether a receiver had exercised all reasonable care to obtain the best price reasonably obtainable for the property as at the time of sale as required by CA 1963, s 316A. Laffoy J had held that the receiver had not exercised all reasonable care and she had directed that the receiver should not complete the contract of sale that had been signed. The facts of this case were that a receiver was appointed by a debenture holder to a company after it had been placed into liquidation. Subsequently, a company called Stormdust Ltd ('Stormdust') issued proceedings claiming specific performance of an alleged contract to sell the charged lands to it. In the High Court it

[129] In *American Express International Banking v Hurley* [1986] BCLC 52 it was held that a receiver was negligent in not seeking specialist advice in relation to the market value of specialist equipment.

[130] *Lambert Jones Estates Ltd v Donnelly* (5 November 1982, unreported), High Court (O'Hanlon J).

[131] See para **[22.071]**. See also Ussher, *Company Law in Ireland* (1986), p 442, where he agrees that a receiver when faced with such difficult choices should be able to have recourse to court to seek its '*imprimatur*'.

[132] *Re Edenfell Holdings Ltd* [1999] 1 IR 458 (SC).

was held that Stormdust did not have an enforceable agreement but Stormdust appealed. Subsequently, a company called Astra Construction Services Ltd ('Astra') made an offer of £1.5 million for the charged lands and agreed to pay Stormdust £100,000 to withdraw the appeal. The receiver was advised by the auctioneers to accept this. The receiver refused to sign contracts until all interested parties were invited to better that offer; the liquidator was advised of this and the fact that the receiver would not sign until Astra had procured the withdrawal of Stormdust's appeal to the Supreme Court. The liquidator was told that after the bank was discharged and costs paid in respect of the proceedings against Stormdust, £45,000 would be made available to the liquidator; the liquidator said he had insufficient information as to whether the proposed transaction would discharge the receiver's duty under CA 1963, s 316A and he sought certain information. In all, 15 parties who had expressed an interest in the property were notified and invited to submit a better offer than Astra's. Only two responses were received. One simply expressed an interest; the other was from another company ('Anglo Eire') which confirmed that their previous offer of IR£1.6 million stood but was expressed to be subject to being furnished with copies of all relevant legal documentation in respect of the appeal and subject to its being satisfied with the contents and opinions therein.

The receiver decided to accept the Astra offer and he signed the contracts with Astra and £100,000 was thereupon paid by Astra to Stormdust in full and final settlement of all actions etc against the company and in particular the appeal to the Supreme Court. Stormdust then withdrew the appeal. The receiver then applied for directions in relation to the contract of sale and, if necessary, an order directing him to complete the sale and an order directing the liquidator to join in the contract to convey such interest as he may have had in an unregistered strip of land adjoining the secured property. Another application was also made by a director and shareholder in the company, seeking an order that the receiver should not complete the contract, directing the manner and method of marketing or reselling the secured property and directions as to whether the receiver was entitled to deduct the sum of £105,000 representing the costs of the proceedings involving Stormdust from the proceeds of sale. It was against this background that Laffoy J had held[133] that that the receiver could not be regarded as being unreasonable in concluding that the offer from Astra was the more attractive. However, the learned judge went on to find that, on the evidence, she was not satisfied that the receiver had exercised all reasonable care to free the lands of the encumbrance (which the appeal constituted) and to obtain for the company the best price reasonably obtainable for the lands and she directed the receiver not to complete the contract and to return the deposit paid thereunder.

[22.045] The Supreme Court reversed this decision. In giving the judgment of the court, Keane J held that the receiver had exercised all reasonable care. Adopting a very commercial approach, Keane J stated:

> 'It is not the function of the court in a case such as this to decide, with the benefit of hindsight, whether it might have been better for the creditors and anyone else interested in the property had the receiver rejected the Astra offer and continued to deal with Anglo Eire or anyone else who might be interested. The court was dealing with the matter with

[133] *Re Edenfell Holdings Ltd* [1999] 1 IR 443 (HC).

> the advantage of hindsight: the receiver had to deal with the matter then and there and in the light of the expert evidence available to him from a valuer. Having tested the market again, without any response in the form of an unconditional offer, he was entitled, in all the circumstances, to take the view he did, that accepting the Astra proposal was the more prudent course.'[134]

This case clearly demonstrates the highly subjective nature of a receiver's decision as to whether or not a particular price is the best price reasonably obtainable. Receivers would do well to heed the advice of Laffoy J when she suggested that application under CA 1963, s 316 should be considered before committing oneself to a contract[135].

[22.046] In *Ruby Property Company Ltd v Kilty*[136] McCracken J said that where a receiver is appointed to a company that is not insolvent and where the sale of the charged asset will produce a surplus that will be repaid to the company:

> '…it is open for consideration by the court as to whether in those circumstances the receiver has some form of obligation at least to consider representations made to him by the company as to how to conduct the sale, provided he is satisfied it will, in any event, realise enough to discharge the debentureholder in full.'

In that case a receiver had been appointed to the plaintiff-company. The receiver had taken possession of the company's premises and set about selling it. Despite a number of requests in correspondence from the company the receiver had refused to advertise the premises for sale. Initially, the receiver's estate agents had advised him to advertise but this advice had changed, subsequently. The premises was eventually sold by tender to Superquinn for £102,500. In an unsuccessful application to have the plaintiff's proceedings against the receiver struck out, it was heard that some four months' later there was evidence that the property was worth over £160,000. McCracken J's suggestion that a receiver is obliged to have a greater regard for a plaintiff-company's wishes where the sale of assets is likely to produce a surplus over for the plaintiff-company is superficially attractive. It must be remembered, however, that there is a clear duty on receivers to obtain the best price reasonably obtainable and, to this extent, a company's interests are protected. It is thought that it would be an unnecessary fetter on the exercise of a receiver's powers to compel consultation with a company and that the statutory duty in CA 1963, s 316A is more than sufficient protection.

(ii) The extent of the duty to obtain the best price reasonably obtainable

[22.047] A receiver is not obliged to await an upturn in the market before selling, and that his duty is merely to obtain the best price reasonably obtainable in any given economic climate[137]. Since the enactment in Ireland of CA 1963, s 316A, English case law must be read with care. However, it has been held in a number of English cases –

---

134 *Re Edenfell Holdings Ltd* [1999] 1 IR 458 (SC).

135 *Re Edenfell Holdings Ltd* [1999] 1 IR 443 (HC).

136 *Ruby Property Company Ltd v Kilty* (1 December 1999, unreported), High Court (McCracken J).

137 See para **[22.040]** and see *Re Bula Ltd* (20 June 2002, unreported) High Court (Murphy J). See also *Bank of Cyprus (London) Ltd v Gill* [1980] 2 Lloyds' Rep 51 where it was held that a mortgagee was not obliged to await an upswing in the market; in *McGowan v Gannon* [1983] ILRM 516 where Carroll J raised the question but left it unanswered.

cited with apparent approval by Budd J in *Kinsella v Somers*[138] - that the scope of the so-called '*Cuckmere* duty of care' is to be interpreted narrowly. In particular, there is authority for the rule that any duty of care (whether arising at common law or by statute) only arises *after* 'the creditor has decided what and when to sell'[139]. So, in *Downside Nominees Ltd v First City Corporation Ltd*[140] Lord Templeman said:

> 'The general duty of care said to be owed by a mortgagee to subsequent encumbrancers and the mortgagor in negligence is inconsistent with the right of the mortgagee and the duties which the courts applying equitable principles have imposed on the mortgagee...If a mortgagee exercises his power of sale in good faith for the purpose of protecting his security, he is not liable to the mortgagor even though he might have obtained a higher price and even though the terms might be regarded as disadvantageous to the mortgagor. *Cuckmere Brick Co Ltd v Mutual Finance Ltd* [1971] Ch 949 is Court of Appeal authority for the proposition that, if the mortgagee decides to sell, he must take reasonable care to obtain a proper price *but is no authority for any wider proposition* ... The duties imposed by equity on a mortgagee and on a receiver and manager would be quite unnecessary if there existed a general duty in negligence to take reasonable care in the exercise of powers and to take reasonable care in dealing with the assets of the mortgagor company.'[141] [Emphasis added]

It is thought that the foregoing passage applies equally to where the duty to obtain the best price reasonably obtainable 'at the time of sale' arises by statute as it does in Ireland. This principle has been followed in subsequent cases, such as *Routestone Ltd v Minorities Finance Ltd*[142], where Jacob J held that once a power of sale arises, a receiver cannot be found to be negligent in exercising it. So he said:

> 'Alleging that a decision to exercise a power is negligent is itself tantamount to saying that the mortgagee or receiver is a trustee of the power of sale which he is admittedly not. *No duty of care is owed by the mortgagee or receiver in relation to the actual decision to sell.*'[143] [Emphasis added]

(iii) Sale of non-cash assets to past and present officers

[22.048] An additional feature of a receiver's duty to take reasonable care to obtain the best possible price obtainable in a sale is the negative duty contained in CA 1963, s 316A(3)(a) which provides:

> 'A receiver shall not sell by private contract a *non-cash asset* of the *requisite value* to a person who is, or who, within three years prior to the date of appointment of the receiver, has been, an officer of the company unless he has given at least 14 days' notice of his

---

[138] *Kinsella v Somers* (22 November 1999, unreported), High Court (Budd J).

[139] See Judge Raymond Jack in *Huis v Ellis* [1995] BCC 462 at 466, citing *Re B Johnson & Co (Builders) Ltd* [1955] Ch 634 and *Downside Nominees Ltd v First City Corporation Ltd* [1993] BCC 46.

[140] *Downside Nominees Ltd v First City Corporation Ltd* [1993] BCC 46. For comment see Milman, 'Receiverships Reviewed', *Palmer's In Company*, Issue 9/98; 21 October 1998.

[141] [1993] BCC 46 at 55–56.

[142] *Routestone Ltd v Minorities Finance Ltd* [1997] BCC 180.

[143] [1997] BCC 180 at 191.

intention to do so to all the creditors of the company who are known to him or who have been intimated to him.' [Emphasis added]

The expressions *non-cash asset* and *requisite value* have the meanings assigned to them by CA 1990, s 29[144]. The expression 'officer' includes a person connected to a director or shadow director within the meaning of CA 1990, s 26[145]. The consequences of a receiver contravening this provision are not spelt out in the legislation. Is such a sale, void, voidable at the instance of the creditors of the company or at the instance of the company itself or is the validity of the sale unaffected by a contravention, the consequences being personal to the receiver? It is thought that the validity of the sale is unaffected as the legislature has not expressly provided that a sale in breach of CA 1963, s 316A(3)(a) is void or voidable and such should not be implied. Notwithstanding this view, until such time as there has been a judicial consideration of this provision, it is thought that extreme care ought to be taken as it may well be found that where this provision is contravened, a subsequent purchaser might be affected.

[22.049] It has been decided in England and Wales that receivers are bound to comply with the English equivalent of CA 1990, s 29[146]. In *Demite Ltd v Protec Health Ltd*[147] it was held by Park J that a receiver, who had been appointed by a debenture holder, could not dispose of a company's property to a director or person connected with a director of that company without first obtaining the company's members' approval under s 320 of the Companies Act 1985 (UK). For a number of reasons it is thought that CA 1990, s 29 should not be so construed and that *Demite* should not be followed by the Irish courts. First, it is necessary to distinguish the differences in the statutory duties of receivers appointed under Irish and English legislation. Regard must be had to the fact that in Ireland a receiver has a statutory obligation to exercise all reasonable care to obtain the best price reasonably obtainable for property as at the time of sale: CA 1963, s 316A(1). The only legitimate statutory purpose of CA 1990, s 29 is to protect against possible distortions which may arise when directors self-deal; the obligation to exercise all reasonable care to obtain the best price reasonably obtainable for property as at the time of sale must surely be sufficient. Secondly, it is thought to be outside the spirit of CA 1990, s 29 to apply it to sales of company assets by receivers when it was clearly intended to regulate self-dealing by directors[148]. Thirdly, in a receivership (particularly where the company is insolvent) it is the interests of the company's creditors and not the

---

144 CA 1963, s 316A(3)(b)(I) and, see generally, Chapter 11, *Statutory Regulation of Transactions Involving Directors and their Companies*, paras **[11.028]** and **[11.029]**, respectively .

145 CA 1963, s 316A(3)(b)(ii). For a consideration of shadow directors, see Chapter 8, *Corporate Governance: Management by the Directors*, para **[8.058]**.

146 CA 1985, s 320 (UK). See generally Chapter 11, *Statutory Regulation of Transactions Involving Directors and their Companies*, para **[11.023]**.

147 *Demite Ltd v Protec Health Ltd* [1998] BCC 638. See generally, Courtney, 'Receiverships in Ireland in the Wake of *Demite Ltd v Protec Health Ltd*' (1998) 5 CLP 255.

148 On the purpose of CA 1990, s 29 see the decision of Carnwath J in *British Racing Drivers' Club Ltd v Hextall Erskine & Co (a firm)* [1996] 3 All ER 667 at 681j–682a and generally, Chapter 11 *Statutory Regulation of Transactions Involving Directors and their Companies*, para **[11.050]**.

company's members which must come first. So CA 1963, s 316A(3) regulates the sale of non-cash assets to past and present officers by ensuring that creditors have notice of any such proposed transactions. Fourthly, it can be convincingly argued that upon the appointment of a receiver to an insolvent company, the company has just a bare legal interest in its assets with the result that a sale of those assets might not be of the requisite value in order to trigger the application of CA 1990, s 29. Where the market for a particular asset over which it is proposed to take security is particularly small and there is a possibility that a receiver might find that only the company's directors are interested in acquiring the assets, a creditor might consider insisting that a validating resolution to any future sale to a director or other relevant person by the company acting by any receiver, be passed *prior* to draw down of credit facilities[149].

(d) Duties to guarantors

[22.050] A receiver has also been held to owe a duty of care to persons who have guaranteed the debts of a company which has been placed into receivership. The exposure of such guarantors is possible, where, for example, after the receiver sells off assets charged there is a shortfall in the amount owed to the debenture holder[150]. In such a case, the guarantor would be secondarily liable to pay the secured debt and so has an interest to ensure that the highest price possible is obtained for the charged assets.

[22.051] It had been held that a receiver does not owe a duty to provide any information to a guarantor of the company's debts, nor indeed to any other creditors of the company: *McGowan v Gannon*[151].

[22.052] At common law, it was established in the case of *Standard Chartered Bank v Walker*[152] that a receiver owes a duty of care to guarantors in disposing of mortgaged or charged assets. The following passage of Lord Denning MR was cited by Carroll J in the Irish High Court in *McGowan v Gannon*[153]:

> 'If it should appear that the mortgagee or receiver have not used reasonable care to realise the assets to the best advantage, then the mortgagor, the company *and the guarantor* are entitled in equity to an allowance. They should be given credit for the amount which the sale should have realised if reasonable care had been used.'[154] [Emphasis added]

Earlier, Carroll J had said that this case had held:

---

149 See Courtney, 'Receiverships in Ireland in the Wake of *Demite Ltd v Protec Health Ltd*' (1998) 5 CLP 255 at 261. It may be noted that the *Company Law Review Group* in its First Report (February 2002) recommended that CA 1990, s 29(7) be amended by the addition of a third exception regarding the disposal of a company's assets by a receiver. See recommendation at 6.11.4.

150 See generally, *Ashley Guarantee plc v Zacaria* [1993] 1 All ER 254.

151 *McGowan v Gannon* [1983] ILRM 516. On the duty to provide information, see para **[22.035]**. However, note that the receiver does owe a duty of care in selling mortgaged or charged property, to any guarantor: see para **[22.052]**.

152 *Standard Chartered Bank v Walker* [1982] 3 All ER 938. See also, *Shamji v Johnson Matthey Bankers Ltd* [1986] BCLC 278 and *American Express International Banking Corp v Hurley* [1986] BCLC 52.

153 *McGowan v Gannon* [1983] ILRM 516.

154 [1982] 3 All ER 938 at 942.

> '...that a guarantor could sue a receiver for negligence in disposing of the assets of a company whose debts were guaranteed as there was sufficient proximity between receiver and guarantor for the receiver to owe a duty of care to the guarantor.'[155]

Where a receiver does not exercise reasonable care to obtain the best price reasonably possible, with the result that a property realises less than it ought to have realised, the amount for which the guarantor of the loan, secured by the instrument which permitted the appointment of the receiver is liable, will be reduced *pro tanto*[156].

[22.053] It would appear that the general duty of receivers to realise the best price reasonably obtainable on the sale of mortgaged or charged assets, as set out in CA 1963, s 316A(1), is also of relevance to guarantors. Since this section does not say to whom that duty is owed, one can infer that it is owed to all who suffer direct loss as a result of a receiver contravening it. The duty can, however, only be owed to persons with an interest in the equity of redemption in the sold property. This was confirmed in *Burgess v Auger; Burgess v Vansstock Ltd*[157] where Lightman J said:

> 'The fiduciary duties of the mortgagee and receiver relate only to the equity of redemption and are owed only to those interested in the equity of redemption; and all the duties owed by a mortgagee or receiver are historically merely developments or expanded forms of the duty of good faith arising from the existence of the fiduciary relationship.'[158]

Those with an interest in the equity of redemption will be the mortgagor, and subsequent mortgagee and, by operation of the doctrine of subrogation, any guarantor of the primary debt. In the *Burgess* case the claim of a director, shareholder, employee and guarantor were struck out. Furthermore, leave to amend the guarantor's claim was also refused because the guarantor had not then made any payment to the appointing mortgagee under the guarantee which would give rise to his having an interest in the equity of redemption.

(e) Duties in applying the proceeds of sale of assets

[22.054] Ordinarily, the onus of discharging the general debts owed by the company is not the concern of a receiver since this is the primary function of a liquidator. However, to the general principle there is an exception. It is settled law that where a receiver realises assets which are the subject of a *fixed charge* or a *legal mortgage* his only obligation is to apply the proceeds of these in discharge of the amount due and owing to the debenture holder. Any surplus over from the realisation can be paid back to the company, and is not to be applied in discharge of any debts owed to preferential creditors. However, in respect of a *floating charge*, CA 1963, s 98 provides that before a receiver can apply the proceeds realised in discharge of the debts owed to the debenture holder, he is obliged to first pay the company's preferential creditors[159].

---

[155] [1983] ILRM 516 at 518.

[156] *Skipton Building Society v Bratley and another* [2000] TLR 15.

[157] *Burgess v Auger; Burgess v Vansstock Ltd* [1998] 2 BCLC 478.

[158] [1998] 2 BCLC 478 at 482.

[159] On *preferential creditors*, see Chapter 27, *Realisation and Distribution of Assets in a Winding Up*, para **[27.169]**.

[22.055] In *United Bars Ltd v Revenue Commissioners*[160] CA 1963, s 98 and its application to assets subject to a fixed and floating charge was considered. Section 98(1) of CA 1963 provides that:

> 'Where either a receiver is appointed on behalf of the holders of any debenture of a company secured by a floating charge, or possession is taken by or on behalf of those debenture holders of any property comprised in or subject to the charge, then, if the company is not at the time, in course of being wound up, the debts which in every winding up are, under the provisions of Part VI relating to preferential payments to be paid in priority to all other debts, shall be paid out of any assets coming to the hands of the receiver or other person taking possession as aforesaid in priority to any claim for principal or interest in respect of the debentures.'

In that case certain companies had created debentures which charged certain assets by both fixed and floating charges. The receiver successfully realised two properties, and having paid the debenture holder what was due and owing, was left with a surplus of £85,417. The issue to be decided by the court was whether the receiver was obliged to pay this money to the company, or to the Revenue Commissioners in discharge of sums due to them as a preferential creditor. In his judgment, Murphy J referred to *Re GL Saunders Ltd*[161], where Nourse J had held that where a company created both a fixed and floating charge over its assets, and the receiver was left with a surplus of £444,000 from the sale of assets subject to the fixed charge, that this money should be repaid to the company and not applied in payment of the preferential creditors. There, Nourse J had relied on *Re Lewis Marlty Consolidated Collieries*[162], where Tomlin J had held that a similar section applied only in respect of accounts coming to a receiver which were the subject of a floating charge and not to the sale of assets the subject of a fixed charge. Counsel for the Revenue Commissioners argued against this on two main grounds. First of all, it was argued that on a true construction of the debenture in hand, the charge was primarily a floating charge and so CA 1963, s 98 applied. Secondly, it was 'courageously' argued that the authorities cited were wrong in law and ought not be followed. Both arguments were rejected by Murphy J who held that the established authorities should prevail, one reason being that:

> '...it seems to me of the utmost importance in dealing with commercial matters to maintain some measure of consistency, and to proceed on the footing that parties to commercial transactions have organised their affairs on the basis of the law as they understand and believe it to be for many years, and any change to that law should be made preferably by the Oireachtas or at any rate by the final court of appeal in this country...'[163]

[22.056] A receiver's duty under CA 1963, s 98 survives the making of a winding-up order and compels a receiver to pay the Revenue Commissioners in discharge of preferential debts ahead of any liquidator. In *Re Eisc Teo*[164] a company created both a fixed charge over certain assets and a floating charge over other assets. When the

160 *United Bars Ltd v Revenue Commissioners* [1991] 1 IR 396.

161 *Re GL Saunders Ltd* [1986] BCLC 40, [1986] WLR 215.

162 *Re Lewis Marlty Consolidated Collieries* [1939] 1 Ch D 498.

163 [1991] 1 IR 396 at 401.

164 *Re Eisc Teo* [1991] ILRM 760.

company defaulted on the loan, the chargee caused a receiver to be appointed and the charged assets were realised. The receiver paid off the chargee in full out of the fixed charge and was left in possession of the proceeds of sale of the assets the subject of the floating charge. A liquidator was later appointed and sought to compel the receiver to deliver up those proceeds, less his expenses. The receiver refused, believing he was under a statutory duty to apply the proceeds of a floating charge in discharge of preferential creditors pursuant to CA 1963, s 98. The liquidator argued that this had no application once a winding-up order had been made and that in any event, the liquidator would be under a duty to apply that money to the preferential creditors[165]. It was held by Lardner J that the receiver *was under a statutory duty* to pay the preferential creditors, saying:

> '...in my judgment, in the present case the receiver was at the time of his appointment, the company at that time being in the course of being wound up, obliged by s 98 to make the preferential payments. This duty having once been imposed in unqualified terms by the section, was not terminated or affected by the circumstance either that a winding up order was made three months after the appointment of the receiver or that the receiver did not in fact require to make any payment out of the assets the subject of the floating charge. The section refers not to the payment out of the assets but to claims for principal or interest. I think such a claim clearly exists at the time of the receiver's appointment and that the duty was then imposed upon the receiver by the section.'[166]

In *Re Manning Furniture Ltd (in receivership)*[167] it was sought to draw a distinction between a liquidator and a mortgagee. The facts in this case were that a receiver had been appointed to a company on foot of a mortgage debenture (incorporating a floating charge) and several chattel mortgages in favour of ICC Bank plc. It transpired that, some years' previously, the company had created a mortgage in favour of what was then First National Building Society ('FNSB') but that mortgage had not been registered pursuant to CA 1963, s 99 and application was made for late registration under CA 1963, s 106[168]. The receiver sold the chattels and at the time of seeking directions had contracted to sell the premises and held a surplus of £150,000. The directions sought by the receiver was whether he was obliged to discharge the preferential creditors of the company before paying the balance to FNBS. After considering the finding in *Re Eisc Teoranta*[169], McCracken J noted that the counsel for FNBS had sought to distinguish that case on that basis that there the question was whether the receiver should pay the revenue or the liquidator, whereas in the instant case the question was whether the receiver should pay the Revenue Commissioners or a mortgagee. McCracken J refused to distinguish the two cases and went on to find that the *Joplin proviso*[170] in the order for late registration meant that the FNBS's mortgage took priority *after* the Revenue Commissioners who had,

---

165 Under CA 1963, s 285.
166 [1991] ILRM 760 at 763–764.
167 *Re Manning Furniture Ltd (in receivership)* [1996] 1 ILRM 13.
168 In this respect, see Chapter 21, *Corporate Borrowing: Registration of Charges*, para **[21.094]**.
169 *Re Eisc Teoranta* [1991] ILRM 760.
170 See Chapter 21, *Corporate Borrowing: Registration of Charges*, para **[21.091]**.

under CA 1963, s 98, 'a right acquired prior to the time of the registration of the particulars of the mortgage'[171].

[22.057] The Revenue Commissioners can make a preferential claim in a receivership and also in a subsequent liquidation of the same company. In *H Williams (Tallaght) Ltd (in receivership and liquidation)*[172] a receiver had been appointed to a company and, pursuant to CA 1963, s 98, treated the Revenue Commissioners as preferential creditors in relation to certain debts of the company in respect of PAYE and PRSI. Thereafter he discharged the entire debt of the debenture holders and had no further function to perform. Subsequently, the company went into liquidation and the Revenue Commissioners then claimed to be a preferential creditor under CA 1963, s 285, this time in respect of corporation tax due by the company. The liquidator was unsuccessful in arguing that the Revenue Commissioners could not claim to be a preferential creditor for a second time[173].

[22.058] It has been decided in a number of English and Australian cases that a receiver's duty to pay preferential creditors survives the satisfaction of his appointing debenture holder's claims. So in *Re Pearl Maintenance Services Ltd*[174] Carnwath J said of receivers' duties under s 40 of the Insolvency Act 1986 (UK):

> 'The cases show that s 40 creates a positive duty (not merely a restriction) in favour of the preferential creditors, and that it is a duty enforceable by action in tort for damages…Thus it is a duty which creates statutory private rights, enforceable as such by the preferential creditors. This being so, it would be very odd if those rights disappeared, merely because the debenture holder…had been paid off...'[175]

In *Lumsden v Long*[176] it was held by the Federal Court of Australia that a receiver was under a personal obligation to discharge the preferential creditors. Whilst this obligation survived his resignation as receiver, it was held that whether the realised assets of the company are passed to a debenture holder[177] or to a liquidator, they are impressed with a constructive trust.

(f) Duties to supply information to the Registrar of Companies and the Director of Corporate Enforcement

[22.059] In addition to the requirement that a receiver notify his appointment to the Registrar of Companies[178], a receiver is also obliged to furnish within one month of his

---

171 *Re Manning Furniture Ltd (in receivership)* [1996] 1 ILRM 13.

172 *H Williams (Tallaght) Ltd (in receivership and liquidation)* [1996] 3 IR 531.

173 The liquidator was, however, successful in arguing that the Revenue Commissioners' claim was out of time and so statute barred. See Chapter 27, *The Realisation and Distribution of Assets in a Winding Up*, para **[27.170]**.

174 *Re Pearl Maintenance Services Ltd* [1995] 1 BCLC 449.

175 [1995] 1 BCLC 449 at 457.

176 *Lumsden v Long* [1998] 1304 Federal Court of Australia (16 October 1998). See also *Stein v Saywell* (1969) 121 CLR 529 and *Chief Commissioner of Stamp Duties v Buckle* (1998) 151 ALR 1.

177 *Inland Revenue Commissioners v Goldblatt* [1972] 2 All ER 202.

178 CA 1963, s 107(1), see para **[22.019]**.

appointment and, thereafter, at six-monthly intervals, an abstract in the prescribed form[179] to the Registrar. The abstract must show the assets of the company of which he has taken possession since his appointment, their estimated value, the proceeds of sale of any such assets since his appointment, his receipts and payments during that period of six months or, where he ceases to act, during that period to the end of the period to which the last preceding abstract related up to the date of his ceasing and also the aggregate amounts of his receipts and of his payments during all preceding periods since his appointment.

[22.060] The Company Law Enforcement Act 2001, s 52(a) ('CLEA 2001') inserted CA 1963, s 319(2A) which provides:

> 'Where a receiver ceases to act as receiver of the property of the company, the abstract under subsection (2) shall be accompanied by a statement from the receiver of his opinion as to whether or not the company is solvent and the registrar shall, on receiving the statement, forward a copy of it to the Director.'

Although this duty is owed by receivers to the Registrar, the Director of Corporate Enforcement is also a beneficiary of the information. The purpose of this provision is to alert the Director as to whether or not a company that has been through a receivership is solvent. If the company is insolvent and it transpires that the company is not wound up, the Director has the opportunity to consider whether the case is an appropriate one in which to exercise his powers under CA 1990, s 251.

[22.061] In addition to the foregoing duties to supply information routinely, receivers can also be made amenable to provide specific information to the Director of Corporate Enforcement on a particular receivership or in relation to all receiverships undertaken by him. Section 323A(1) of CA 1963[180] provides:

> 'The Director may, where he considers it necessary or appropriate, request (specifying the reason why the request is being made) the production of a receiver's books for examination, either in regard to a particular receivership or to all receiverships undertaken by the receiver.'

Receivers are obliged[181] to furnish their books to the Director, answer any questions concerning their content and the conduct of a particular receivership or receiverships and 'to give to the Director all assistance in the matter as the receiver is reasonably able to give.' The failure to comply is an offence[182]. It is notable that the Director must specify 'the reason why the request is made'; if the Director fails to provide a reason it is thought that a receiver is not obliged to comply. Moreover, requests may not be made in respect of books relating to a receivership that has concluded more than six years' prior to the request[183].

---

179 CA 1963, s 319(2).

180 As inserted by CLEA 2001, s 53.

181 By CA 1963, s 323A(2).

182 CA 1963, s 323A(4).

183 CA 1963, s 323A(3).

Liabilities of receivers

[22.062] The liability of a receiver arises primarily[184] in respect of contracts entered into by him on behalf of the company. Section 316(2) of CA 1963 provides:

> 'A receiver of the property of a company shall be personally liable on any contract entered into by him in the performance of his functions (whether such contract is entered into by him in the name of such company or in his own name as receiver or otherwise) unless the contract provides that he is not to be personally liable on such contract, and he shall be entitled in respect of that liability to indemnity out of the assets; but nothing in this subsection shall be taken as limiting any right to indemnity which he would have apart from this subsection, or as limiting his liability on contracts entered into without authority or as conferring any right to indemnity in respect of that liability.'

From this it is clear that, unless personal liability is disclaimed ab initio, a receiver will be liable on any contract entered into by him in, for example, the sale of a business, or in respect of contracts entered into by him as manager while he is running the business. It seems to be commercial practice for receivers not to exclude their personal liability in contracts as a general rule. Even so, it should be noted that a person dealing with a company may insist upon the company/receiver paying sums owed prior to the receiver's appointment before agreeing to continue to contract with him or the company[185]. Where a receiver chooses not to fulfil a contract which has been entered into by a company, persons thereby affected may bring proceedings against the company for breach of contract. Where a receiver is appointed under an invalid debenture, it is open to the court to relieve him from incurring personal liability. Where such relief is granted, what was his liability will be juxtaposed onto those who appointed him, ie the debenture holder[186]. As to a receiver's liability under CA 1963, s 98, see above[187].

[22.063] A receiver will not as a general rule, in the absence of bad faith, while acting within his authority be liable for a breach of a contract by the company, nor be guilty of inducing breach of contract. This is illustrated by *Lathia v Dronsfield Bros Ltd*[188]. There, the first defendant-company contracted to supply the plaintiff with certain goods, and when the company failed to do so the plaintiff began to sue them, and joined the second and third defendants who were managers and receivers to the first defendant-company, alleging inducement to breach of contract. The receivers were successful in having the proceedings against them struck out for showing no reasonable cause of action. Sir Neil Lawson said:

> 'The receivers can adopt or decline to adopt a contract which the company has entered into and which is unexecuted. It follows from this, and the agency clause, that the agent is personally immune from claims for damages for breach of contract or procurement of breach of contract. The agent has an immunity from a claim for inducing breach of contract unless he has not acted *bona fide* or acted outside the scope of his authority, ie

---

[184] Apart, that is, from those circumstances considered above, where a receiver acts in breach of a duty owed.

[185] See *W & L Crowe Ltd et al v ESB* (9 May 1984, unreported), High Court (Costello J).

[186] See CA 1963, s 316(3).

[187] At para **[22.055]**.

[188] *Lathia v Dronsfield Bros Ltd* [1987] BCLC 321.

> had not acted as agent. In my judgment, a mere assertion in a pleading of lack of *bona fides* is not enough. Particulars must be given, and one must look at the particulars in that case. So far as the authority is concerned, the authority of the receivers is to be found in cl 8 of the debenture[189]. Furthermore their authority resides on a general obligation to act so as to effect the best realisation of the company's assets for the debenture holders. On authority, one must look at the context to determine to whom the duties are owed. Primarily, they owe a duty to the debenture holders, and also as agents to the company. In my judgment, they do not owe a duty to the general creditors, to contributories, to officers of the company, and members.'[190]

This case relied on *Re B Johnson & Co (Builders) Ltd*[191] and *Airlines Airspace Ltd v Handley Page Ltd*[192], both of which support the proposition that a receiver is not bound by contracts entered into by the company prior to his appointment.

[22.064] A receiver will not be liable in respect of a contract or agreement entered into by the company prior to his appointment. This is seen in the Irish case of *Ardmore Studios (Ireland) Ltd v Lynch*[193]. In that case it was held that an agreement entered into between a trade union and a company would not to bind the receiver to that company. McLoughlin J said:

> 'As agent for the company, the company is made responsible for his acts but it is not a corollary to this that he [the receiver] is bound by all company contracts entered into by the company before the date of his appointment.'[194]

In that case the receiver was found not to be bound by a collective agreement which had been entered into by the company. This position has, in that particular context, however, been altered by reg 4 of the European Communities (Safeguarding of Employees' Rights on the Transfer of Undertakings) Regulations 1980[195].

[22.065] A receiver will, where appointed an agent of the company by the debenture, be bound to comply with court orders made against the company such as, for example, Mareva injunctions. So, in *Creatanor Maritime Co Ltd v Irish Marine Management Ltd*[196] the English Court of Appeal held that, having been appointed agent, a receiver to a

---

189 Clause 8 of the debenture provided: 'At any time after the security shall have become enforceable the Bank may by writing under the hand of any area manager or manager of the Bank appoint any person (or persons) to be a Receiver of the property hereby charged and may similarly remove any Receiver and appoint another in his stead. Any Receiver so appointed shall be the agent of the Company and the Company shall be solely responsible for his acts or defaults and for his remuneration and any Receiver so appointed shall have power...'.

190 [1987] BCLC 321 at 324.

191 *Re B Johnson & Co (Builders) Ltd* [1955] 2 All ER 775.

192 *Airlines Airspace Ltd v Handley Page Ltd* [1970] 1 All ER 29 (where it was held that a receiver was entitled to adopt or decline to adopt any unexecuted contract).

193 *Ardmore Studios (Ireland) Ltd v Lynch* [1965] IR 1.

194 [1965] IR 1 at 40.

195 SI 1980/306. See Lynch, Marshall & O'Ferrall, *Corporate Insolvency and Rescue* (1996), p 135.

196 *Creatanor Maritime Co Ltd v Irish Marine Management Ltd* [1978] 3 All ER 164. See generally, Courtney, *Mareva Injunctions and Related Interlocutory Orders* (1998), paras [9.40]–[9.41].

company was not entitled to apply for the discharge of a Mareva injunction which bound the company. In that case, however, it was held that the debenture holder was entitled to apply to have the Mareva injunction discharged on the basis that his security took precedence over any Mareva-plaintiff's rights as Mareva injunctions act in personam and not in rem against a Mareva-defendant's assets.

Powers of receivers

[22.066] A court appointed receiver's powers are dependent upon the terms of the order of the court appointing him. These will usually be to collect, get assets in and receive those assets. This express power is supported by the implicit power to do all acts which are incidental and consequential upon the exercise of the express power[197].

[22.067] Where a receiver is appointed out of court on foot of a debenture, his powers will generally be found in the debenture instrument itself[198] coupled with certain statutory powers[199]. The extent of the powers enjoyed by a receiver appointed under a standard form of debenture will vary according to whether or not the receiver is a receiver simpliciter, or a receiver-manager. The powers of a receiver simpliciter include:

— the power to take possession of charged assets;

— the power to collect, get in and receive the charged assets;

— the power to sell the charged assets.

Although not divorced from the foregoing situation, a receiver-manager will often have the following express powers:

— the power to compromise debts of the company;

— the power to carry on the business of the company;

— the power to insure and repair property;

— the power to borrow money for the business;

— the power to employ and dismiss employees.

In addition, all receivers will have ancillary powers, which are incidental to or consequential upon the exercise of the foregoing powers[200]. One such implied power is the power to sue in the company's name[201] and this implied power survives the appointment of a liquidator[202].

---

197 See Lynch, Marshall & O'Ferrall, *Corporate Insolvency and Rescue* (1996), pp 153–156. See Picarda, *The Law Relating to Receivers, Managers and Administrators* (2nd edn, 1990), p 356.

198 See generally, Picarda, *The Law Relating to Receivers, Managers and Administrators* (2nd edn, 1990), p 93.

199 As found in, say, the Conveyancing Act 1881.

200 In *Medforth v Blake et al* [1999] BCC 771 at 785 Sir Richard Scott V–C said that a receiver's power to manage a business was not ancillary to the power of sale, but was independent.

201 *M Wheeler & Co Ltd v Warren* [1928] Ch 840.

202 *Gough's Garages Ltd v Pugsley* [1930] 1 KB 615. Cf *Re Nenry Pound, Son and Hutchins* (1889) 42 Ch D 402.

[22.068] The power to sue in the company's name gives a receiver locus standi to make application for a so-called 'proprietary injunction'[203] to preserve the charged property[204]. Such an injunction should be distinguished from a Mareva injunction. So whereas a Mareva injunction will operate to prevent a person from dealing with his own assets, an injunction sought by a receiver (as agent of his principal company) will be to prevent dealing with the company's own assets (by, say, its directors or indeed third parties) and so is in the nature of a proprietary injunction. An example of an application for a proprietary injunction restraining the disposal of assets is seen in *Rex Pet Foods Ltd and Murphy v Lamb Brothers (Dublin) Ltd*[205]. In that case the plaintiff-company and its receiver sought an injunction restraining the defendants from disposing of certain goods which had been produced by the plaintiff-company and were at the time of the application in the possession of one or other of the defendants. In the alternative, the plaintiffs sought an injunction preventing such goods being disposed of until trial otherwise than on terms that the proceeds of sale would be held in a suspense or trust account pending resolution of the substantive question. Finlay P granted the injunction in that case, accepting that there was a 'serious question to be tried' and that the 'balance of convenience' favoured the granting of the injunction. This case also serves to demonstrate the inherent dangers of obtaining injunctions on an undertaking as to damages, in that there, it was ultimately held that the plaintiffs had no title in the goods and liberty was granted to apply in respect of the undertaking as to damages[206].

[22.069] In particular circumstances a receiver may, on a company's behalf, make application for a Mareva injunction. Such might arise where a receiver believes that money or property is owed to a company by a third party and there is a risk that the third party will remove his assets from the jurisdiction or otherwise dissipate his assets with the intention of evading his obligations to the plaintiff and frustrating the anticipated order of the court. In such an event, the standard proofs for a Mareva injunction must be met before such an injunction will issue[207].

---

203 Proprietary injunctions must be distinguished from Mareva injunctions. Proprietary injunctions are available where the applicant can establish that he has a proprietary interest in a defendant's assets; Mareva injunctions can be granted where the applicant has no legal or equitable interest in a respondent's assets but where other criteria are met. See, generally, Courtney, *Mareva Injunctions and Related Interlocutory Orders* (1998), para [1.16]–[1.29]. This distinction was accepted in *OBA Enterprises Ltd v TMC Trading International Ltd* (27 November 1998, unreported), High Court (Laffoy J); on the evidence, however, the applicants did not establish that their claim was in the nature of a proprietary claim to the defendant's assets. This case is considered in Courtney, 'The Continuing Development of the Mareva Injunction in Ireland' (1999) 6 CLP 39.

204 The mortgagee will, in any event, have sufficient locus standi for an injunction to preserve secured property.

205 *Rex Pet Foods Ltd and Murphy v Lamb Brothers (Dublin) Ltd* (26 August 1982), High Court (Finlay P), Irish Company Law Reports (1963–1993) 549.

206 *Rex Pet Foods Ltd and Murphy v Lamb Brothers (Dublin) Ltd (No 2)* (5 December 1985, unreported), High Court (Costello J), Irish Company Law Reports (1963–1993) 585.

207 See generally, Courtney, *Mareva Injunctions and Related Interlocutory Orders* (1998), para [8.31].

[22.070] The foregoing power to apply for an injunction to preserve the charged property has now been supplemented by statute. Section 55 of CLEA 2001 confers locus standi on receivers to apply for an order directing a director or other officer not to remove his assets from the State or to reduce them within or without the State below a specified amount in certain circumstances. In addition to the requirement that the court must be satisfied as to the existence of a nefarious intention on the part of the respondent[208], the court must also be satisfied that an applicant receiver has a substantive civil cause of action against the respondent. The only circumstances in which it is thought that the court will make an order under this section is where a receiver seeks to recover charged property from a director or other officer which has been misappropriated of otherwise diverted away from the company (and so out of the receiver's grasp). In the light of the requirement to show a nefarious intention on the part of a respondent, receivers might, in such cases, be better served by seeking a proprietary injunction to preserve the company's assets.

Applications for directions

[22.071] A receiver who finds that he is uncertain about the exercise of any powers or purported powers which he has been granted in a debenture instrument, may apply to court for directions in 'relation to any matter in connection with the performance or otherwise...of his functions': CA 1963, s 316(1). Furthermore, so also may officers, members, employees (at least half in number of full-time employees); creditors of the company[209], a liquidator, or contributories apply to the court for directions as to the exercise of a receiver's powers. On such an application the court may give such directions or make such an order declaring the rights of persons before the court or otherwise as the court thinks just.

[22.072] Where an application is made by a person other than a receiver, it must be supported by such evidence as the court may require that the applicant is being unfairly prejudiced by any actual or proposed action or omission of the receiver[210]. In *Kinsella v Somers*[211], the facts of which have been considered above[212], a director brought an application for directions under CA 1963, s 316. Budd J held, on the question of jurisdiction, that the court's discretion to make any order it thinks just in response to an application under s 316 was limited by CA 1963, s 316(1A). Budd J said:

> 'Unless the receiver is the applicant, the application must be supported by such evidence that the applicant is being unfairly prejudiced by any actual or proposed action or omission of the receiver as the Court may require. Accordingly, the right to apply for directions is rather limited and would seem not to cover an application for clarification of the receiver's powers or other general application for directions. If the application is being made by a director or shareholder then it would appear that a prerequisite is that proof is adduced that

---

[208] CLEA 2001, s 55(b): see Chapter 27, *Realisation and Distribution of Assets in a Winding Up*, para **[27.046]**.

[209] Defined as meaning one or more creditors to whom the company is indebted by more in aggregate than €12,697.38: CA 1963, s 316(1A), as inserted by CA 1990, s 171.

[210] CA 1963, s 316(1B), as inserted by CA 1990, s 171.

[211] *Kinsella v Somers* (22 November 1999, unreported), High Court (Budd J).

[212] See para **[22.036]**.

> the applicant is being unfairly prejudiced by some action or omission on the part of the receiver.'

Accordingly, unless it is the receiver who brings the application, the application must be supported by evidence that the applicant is being 'unfairly prejudiced' by any actual or proposed action or omission of the receiver as the court may require. In that case Budd J found that the applicant had not satisfied the court that it should make an order and it had not been shown that the receiver had been acting unreasonably in refusing to give further information to the applicant qua director and shareholder. He also found that the refusal was not actuated by bad faith on the receiver's part.

Multiple receivers to the same company

[22.073] At any one time a company may have more than one receiver appointed to it. Indeed, where a company has created two debentures in favour of different lending institutions the appointment of a receiver under one of these debentures will invariably be an *event of default*[213], which will precipitate the appointment of a second receiver by the other debenture holder. Where two receivers have been appointed to the same company their respective functions and powers may be reduced to a question of priorities between the debenture holders who appointed them. A receiver may not have any greater priority to a company's assets than has his appointing debenture holder. Accordingly, where a receiver is appointed by the holder of a fixed mortgage or charge over specific land or property, it may well make sense for another debenture holder who holds a fixed mortgage or charge over different land or property to appoint another receiver. When it comes to receiving property which is subject to a floating charge the first validly created and registered floating charge to crystallise will generally have priority[214]. It follows that the receiver appointed by the holder of that floating charge should have priority to the company's assets which were within the class of asset subject to that floating charge. Where a conflict arises it will usually be open to one of the receivers to apply to court for directions under CA 1963, s 316(1)[215].

Resignation and removal of receivers

(a) Resignation

[22.074] Section 322C of CA 1963[216] alters the common law position which was that where a receiver resigned without the consent of the debenture holder which appointed him, he would be guilty of breach of contract, and thus liable in damages[217]. It is now the case that a receiver appointed by a debenture holder can resign upon giving one month's notice to holders of fixed and floating charges over the company's property, and to the company and (if applicable) to its liquidator. A receiver appointed by the court can only

---

213 See para **[22.006]**.

214 See Chapter 20, *Corporate Borrowing: Debentures and Security*, para **[20.082]**.

215 See para **[22.071]**.

216 As inserted by CA 1990, s 177.

217 See Picarda, *The Law Relating to Receivers, Managers and Administrators* (2nd edn, 1990), pp 250–251.

resign with the consent of the court: CA 1963, s 322C(3). A failure to comply with these requirements is liable to be visited by a fine[218].

[22.075] A receiver appointed by a debenture holder may be dismissed by that debenture holder pursuant to the terms of the receiver's appointment. The matter is essentially one of contract.

(b) Removal by the court

[22.076] Section 322A(1) of CA 1963[219] empowers the court, upon cause being shown, to remove a receiver and appoint another in his place[220].

[22.077] The power of the court under CA 1963, s 322A to remove a receiver is couched in wide and general terms. Clearly, misconduct on the part of the receiver will justify his removal and amount to the showing of sufficient cause[221]. However, misconduct on the part of the receiver is not necessary, and where it is shown that the interests of the general creditors are best served by removing the receiver, as it was in *Re Keypack Homecare Ltd*[222], the receiver will be removed.

[22.078] While the power to remove a receiver seems to be directed at a court appointed receiver, a number of cases suggest that a receiver appointed by a debenture holder can be similarly ousted[223].

(c) Removal of receiver at the instigation of a liquidator

[22.079] The appointment of a liquidator does not per se affect the appointment of a receiver to a company. Section 322B of CA 1963[224] introduced a new measure providing that a liquidator can apply to court to have a receivership which began either before or after the commencement of the winding up, to be determined or limited. Thus, the court may order that the receiver shall cease to act as such and order that no further receiver be appointed, or may order that the receiver shall from a certain time act only in respect of certain assets specified by the court[225]. It is noticeable that CA 1963, s 322B(4) provides that no order made under this section shall affect any security or charge over the undertaking or property of the company. Even so, this subsection radically changes the

[218] Not exceeding €1,269.74: CA 1963, s 322C(3).

[219] As inserted by CA 1990, s 175.

[220] Notice that application is being made to have a receiver removed must be served on the receiver and on the person who appointed him, not less than seven days before the hearing of such proceedings, and at the hearing both can appear and be heard: CA 1963, s 322A(2) as inserted by CA 1990, s 175.

[221] See *Re St George's Estate* (1887) 19 LR Ir 556, where dereliction of duty by the receiver was shown.

[222] *Re Keypack Homecare Ltd* [1987] BCLC 409.

[223] See *Re Maskelyne British Typewriter Ltd* [1898] 1 Ch 133; *Re 'Slogger' Automatic Feeder Company Ltd* [1915] 1 Ch 478; and McCormack, *The New Companies Legislation* (1991), p 174–175.

[224] As inserted by CA 1990, s 176.

[225] CA 1990, s 176(3) provides that a receiver must get seven days' notice of such an application. The order of the court is not written in stone, and can be rescinded or amended on application of the liquidator or receiver: CA 1963, s 322B(2).

law, particularly in so far as privately appointed receivers are concerned[226], as contrasted with court appointed receivers[227]. One remedy available to liquidators against receivers that stops short of removal is an injunction to prevent a receiver from acting.

(d) Removal of receiver at the instigation of an examiner

[22.080] A company cannot be placed under the protection of the court, and *ergo*, an examiner cannot be appointed to a company where a receiver stands appointed for a continuous period of at least three days, prior to the presentation of the petition to have the examiner appointed[228]. However, where an examiner is appointed within three days of the receiver's appointment the examiner may apply to court for an order under C(A)A 1990, s 6(1). The orders which may be made by the court under this provision are considered in Chapter 23, next[229].

---

226 See *Re Potters Oil Ltd (No 2)* [1986] BCLC 98.

227 See *Re Joshua Stubbs Ltd* [1891] 1 Ch 475.

228 C(A)A 1990, s 3(6).

229 See Chapter 23, *Examinerships*, para **[23.065]**.

Chapter 23

Examinerships

Introduction

[23.001] This chapter considers the law relating to examinerships[1]. An examinership is where the court places a company under its protection to enable a court appointed examiner to investigate the company's affairs and to report to the court on its prospects of survival. Where survival can be achieved, the court may sanction a scheme of arrangement which often involves the part-payment of the company's creditors and which enables the company to continue in business.

(a) The background to the Companies (Amendment) Act 1990

[23.002] The law relating to examinerships[2] has its origins in the Companies (Amendment) Act 1990 ('C(A)A 1990') which was passed in unusual circumstances. It initially began life as a part of the Companies Bill 1987. However, before that Bill could be passed into law, international events overtook the legislature. As a direct result of those events C(A)A 1990 was passed quickly into force[3]. When Iraq invaded Kuwait in 1990, one international response was a United Nations' trade embargo. This had potentially disastrous consequences for the Irish economy since an Irish company, Goodman International, exported most of the Irish beef produced to Iraq. Goodman International, which had borrowings on 17 August 1990 of £460 million, found itself in very serious difficulties[4]. Upon the viability of Goodman International coming into question, the government of the day decided to introduce as a stand-alone piece of legislation[5] what had been Part IX of the Companies (No 2) Bill 1987. This became C(A)A 1990. Subsequently, on 22 December 1990, the Companies Act 1990 ('CA 1990') was passed and made minor amendments to C(A)A 1990[6].

(b) The Gallagher Company Law Review Group

[23.003] There were many calls for a more far-reaching overhaul of C(A)A 1990 throughout the 1990s[7] than that effected by CA 1990. In April 1994 the then Minister for

1 See generally, O'Donnell, *Examinerships*, (1994) and Keane, *Company Law* (3rd edn, 2000), Ch 37.

2 Although the expression used in C(A)A 1990 is 'court protection', C(A)(No 2)A 1999 uses the term 'examinership'.

3 See McCormack, *The New Companies Legislation* (1991), p 185 *ff*. See also the background analysis in (1990) The Irish Times, 1 September.

4 See 126 *Seanad Debates* 1065 where the Minister for Industry and Commerce quoted a letter to him from IBI Corporate Finance Ltd. See also 401 *Dáil Debates* 2055–2291.

5 126 *Seanad Debates* 1059, per Mr Desmond O'Malley, the then Minister for Industry and Commerce.

6 CA 1990, ss 180 and 181.

Enterprise and Employment established an ad hoc Company Law Review Group under the chairmanship of James Gallagher. This Group reported in November 1994 and its report included 29 recommendations and conclusions on the area of examinerships. The basis of its recommendations and conclusions is alluded to in the Report:

> 'It is essential, however, while allowing for consideration of the individual merits of each case, to set limits to the availability of examinership, to set parameters for the operation of the legislation and to provide checks and balances. It is these parameters which can focus on viability and limit the impairment of the interests of individual creditors and competitors. Many of the submissions made to us criticised the existing legislation arguing, in particular, that it does not give sufficient focus to viable companies and that it does not give sufficient protection to the interests of creditors. We accept the thrust of these particular criticisms and many of our recommendations relate to these issues.'[8]

Notwithstanding the speed with which the Group reported, it was not until late 1999 and the passing of the Companies (Amendment) (No 2) Act 1999 ('C(A)(No 2)A 1999') that legislative effect was given to the Group's recommendations.

(c) The Companies (Amendment) (No 2) Act 1999

[23.004] C(A)(No 2)A 1999 made very substantial and significant changes to the examinership regime[9]. Three changes stand to the fore. First, C(A)(No 2)A 1999 introduced a stricter test for the appointment of an examiner: C(A)A 1990, s 2(1), as amended, now requires that an examiner shall not be appointed by the court unless it is satisfied that there is a reasonable prospect of the survival of the company and the whole or any part of its undertaking as a going concern[10]. It was previously the case that only '*some prospect*' of survival was required[11]. Secondly, the old requirement that an examiner make an initial report before his final report has been abolished and replaced with the requirement that a *pre-petition report* prepared by an independent accountant[12] be presented with the petition. Thirdly, in an attempt to mitigate the prejudice suffered by creditors secured by fixed security, expenses (such as 'borrowings') incurred by examiners no longer rank ahead of such creditors[13]. C(A)(No 2)A 1999's provisions on examinerships, contained in Part II of that Act, were brought into operation on 1 February 2000[14].

---

7 See Donnelly, 'Is There A Case For Corporate Rescue' (1994) CLP 8.

8 Report of the *Company Law Review Group*, December 1994 at para 2.12.

9 Specifically repealed were C(A)A 1990, ss 3(3)(b), (c), 14, 15, 16 and 17.

10 As replaced by C(A)(No 2)A 1999, s 5(b). See para **[23.019]**.

11 *Re Atlantic Magnetics Ltd* [1993] 2 IR 561 at 572, 573. There Finlay CJ adopted the following test: 'It seems to me that the standard it this: does the evidence lead to the conclusion that in all the circumstances it appears worthwhile to order an investigation by the examiner into the company's affairs and see can it survive, there being some prospect of survival?'

12 See para **[23.031]**.

13 C(A)A 1990, s 29(3A), inserted by C(A)(No 2)A 1999, s 28. See para **[23.078]**.

14 Companies (Amendment) (No 2) Act 1999 (Commencement) Order 1999 (SI 1999/406).

The purpose of the legislation

[23.005] The intention of the C(A)A 1990 is to provide a procedure for the rescue and return to financial health of ailing but potentially viable companies[15]. Section 2(2) of C(A)A 1990[16] provides the key to the appointment of an examiner. It provides, unambiguously, that the court 'shall not make an order under this section unless it is satisfied that there is a reasonable prospect of the survival of the company and the whole or any part of its undertaking as a going concern'. In *Re Atlantic Magnetics Ltd*[17] McCarthy J stated the purpose of the Act in the following passage:

> 'It is, I believe, of great importance to bear in mind in the application of the Act that its purpose is protection – protection of the company and consequently of its shareholders, workforce and creditors. It is clear that parliament intended that the fate of the company and those who depend on it should not lie solely in the hands of one or more large creditors who can by appointing a receiver pursuant to a debenture effectively terminate its operation and secure as best they may the discharge of the monies due to them to the inevitable disadvantage of those less protected. The Act is to provide a breathing space albeit at the expense of some creditor or creditors.'[18]

It is salutary to remember that Finlay CJ in the Supreme Court held that it is appropriate to approach the construction of any sections in C(A)A 1990 on the basis that the two objectives of the legislature were to provide a period of protection for a company and that a company should be continued as a going concern[19].

[23.006] Upon the appointment of an examiner, the company is placed under the protection of the court. During the period of protection, C(A)A 1990, s 5 provides inter alia that no proceedings may be instituted against the company, whether against the company's assets or to wind up the company. Court protection lasts for an initial period of 70 days but this can be extended by the court for an additional 30 days. The examiner's main function is to propose a scheme of arrangement to the court, which if approved by the court, and supported by a majority of creditors becomes binding.

[23.007] In this chapter, examiners and court protection are considered under the following headings:

[A]. The appointment of an examiner: presenting the petition.

[B]. The effects of court protection.

[C]. The position of creditors.

[D]. The powers of examiners.

[E]. The examiner's report and schemes of arrangement.

[F]. The examiner's remuneration, costs and expenses.

---

15 See the comments of the then Minister for Industry and Commerce, Desmond O'Malley at 126 *Seanad Debates* 1060.

16 As amended by C(A)(No 2)A 1999, s 5(b).

17 *Re Atlantic Magnetics Ltd* [1993] 2 IR 561.

18 [1993] 2 IR 561 at 578.

19 *Re Holidair Ltd* [1994] 1 ILRM 481 at 487.

[A] The Appointment of an Examiner: Presenting the Petition

[23.008] Here the following matters associated with the appointment of an examiner are considered:

1. The jurisdiction to appoint an examiner: presenting the petition.
2. Locus standi to petition the court and be heard on the petition.
3. The grounds for appointing an examiner.
4. The petition and grounding affidavit.
5. The pre-petition report.
6. Interim protection pending the submission of a pre-petition report
7. Presenting the petition.
8. The hearing of the petition.
9. Related companies.
10. Formalities in the appointment of an examiner.
11. The commencement of protection.

The jurisdiction to appoint an examiner: presenting the petition

[23.009] Although all petitions to have an examiner appointed must be presented to the High Court[20], the High Court may remit the matter to the Circuit Court under C(A)A 1990, s 3(9) where it appears that the total liabilities of the company, including contingent and prospective liabilities, do not exceed €317,434. The appropriate circuit will be the circuit in which the company has its registered office. Where such an order is made, the Circuit Court has full jurisdiction to exercise all the powers of the court conferred by the Act in relation to the company[21]. If, on being remitted to the Circuit Court, it subsequently appears that the total liabilities of the company exceed €317,434, the Circuit Court is obliged to remit the matter back to the High Court after making such interim orders as it thinks fit[22].

[23.010] C(A)A 1990 is silent as to what companies may be placed under the protection of the court. Because the Companies Acts are to be construed together, regard must be had to the Companies Act 1963, s 2 ('CA 1963') and its definition of a 'company'. Accordingly, all companies formed and registered under the Companies Acts and former Acts may be the subject of an application to have an examiner appointed.

As shall be considered later, application can be made under C(A)A 1990, s 4 to have a *related company* placed under the protection of the court. The scope of this jurisdiction is wider than that contained in CA 1963, s 2 and for the purposes of s 4 'company' includes any body which is liable to be wound up under the Companies Acts[23].

---

[20] RSC (SI 1991/147), Ord 75A, r 2 provides that all applications and proceedings in relation to examiners must be assigned to such judge or judges as the President of the High Court shall from time to time nominate to hear such. Where a nominated judge is unavailable, any judge may dispose of any such application.

[21] C(A)A 1990, s 3(9)(b).

[22] C(A)A 1990, s 3(9)(c).

[23] C(A)A 1990, s 4(6). See para **[23.046]**. Cf *Re Tuskar Resources plc* [2001] 1 IR 668 (McCracken J) where it was held that a 'related company' in C(A)A 1990, s 4(5) did not include a company registered outside the State.

Section 36(1) of C(A)A 1990 provides that any order made by a court of any country recognised for the purposes of that section[24], and made for or in the course of the reorganisation or reconstruction of a company[25], may be enforced by the High Court in all respects as if the order had been made by the High Court. Where an application is made under s 36(1) to the High Court, an office copy of any order sought to be enforced is deemed to be sufficient evidence of the order[26].

Locus standi to petition the court and be heard on the petition

[23.011] Just as in the case of the presentation of a petition to have a company wound up, C(A)A 1990, s 3 sets out a list of those persons who may present a petition to have an examiner appointed and a company placed under the protection of the court. The *company* itself can present a petition to have an examiner appointed[27]. An ordinary resolution of the members will suffice, although support permiting, in view of the far-reaching effects, a special resolution of the members should be procured where possible. The resolution of the members may be exhibited with their verifying affidavit to have the company placed under the protection of the court.

[23.012] The *directors* of the company can also present a petition to have an examiner appointed[28]. To date, company directors have proven to be the most usual petitioners. By giving the directors locus standi to present a petition, those who may petition to have a company placed under the protection of the court differ from those who may petition to have it wound up compulsorily[29]. It has been held in *Re Don Bluth Entertainment Ltd (No 1)*[30] that once there is a valid resolution of the directors of a company in favour of the presentation of a petition, one or all of them can present the petition[31]. Here too, the resolution of the directors can be exhibited with their verifying affidavit. The directors' resolution to petition the court must take place at a properly convened board meeting. In

---

24 A 'recognised' country is one recognised by order made by the Minister for Enterprise, Trade and Employment: C(A)A 1990, s 36(3). See *Dallhold Estates (UK) Pty Ltd* [1992] BCLC 621 where the High Court in the UK held that it had jurisdiction to make an order against an overseas company.

25 A 'company', in this context, means a body corporate incorporated outside the State: C(A)A 1990, s 36(3).

26 C(A)A 1990, s 36(2). On foreign proceedings against a company under administration by virtue of the UK Insolvency Act 1986, see *Barclays Bank plc v Homan* [1993] BCLC 680.

27 C(A)A 1990, s 3(1)(a).

28 C(A)A 1990, s 3(1)(b). See for example *Re Maxwell Communication Corporation* [1992] BCLC 465.

29 See Chapter 25, *Winding up Companies*, para **[25.033]** and *Re Galway and Salthill Tramways Co* [1918] 1 IR 62.

30 *Re Don Bluth Entertainment Ltd (No 1)* (27 August 1992, unreported), High Court per Murphy J. See also *Don Bluth Entertainment Ltd (No 2)* [1994] 3 IR 141.

31 See *Re Equiticorp International plc* [1989] BCLC 597. Cf *Re Instrumentation Electrical Services Ltd* [1988] BCLC 550, although it should be noted that there a petition to have a company wound up was presented without any formal resolution of the board of directors.

Re Cavan Crystal Glass Ltd[32] Kelly J noted the submission that a directors' petition was required to be presented by all of a company's directors, but expressed no view one way or the other. It is thought that a majority of the directors will suffice.

[23.013] In *Re Aston Colour Print Ltd*[33] a petition was presented which represented that a board resolution had been passed unanimously. Kelly J found that not only had no resolution, formal or informal, been passed by the board but neither had the meeting referred to been a board meeting. In this case management meetings had been informal affairs attended by directors and non-directors alike; at these meetings no formal vote was usually taken, the participants preferring to see a consensus reached. As a result of his finding, Kelly J concluded that the petition had been improperly presented to the court and must be struck out, the interim examiner being discharged[34]. Where irregularity is of a technical nature, it is open to the court to cure it and where it transpires that a person was not a director of a company at a particular time it is open to the court to allow him proceed in his own name and as a shareholder of the company[35].

[23.014] The *creditors* of the company are also given locus standi to present a petition[36]. C(A)A 1990 specifies that contingent or prospective creditors[37], including employees of the company can also present a petition. A contingent or prospective creditor's petition shall not be heard by the court until such security for costs has been given as the court thinks reasonable[38]. In practice, creditors have been very slow to petition the court to have an examiner appointed to a company.

[23.015] The *members* of the company may also petition to have the company placed under the protection of the court[39]. This right to petition is granted to members *qua* member, where such members hold, at the date of the presentation of the petition, not less than one-tenth of the paid-up capital of the company as carries, at that date, the right to vote at general meetings. In many private companies there will be a duplication between the categories of petitioner. In particular, the categories of company, directors and members will often overlap. Furthermore, a petition may be presented by any of the foregoing parties, either together or separately. In *Re Cavan Crystal Glass Ltd*[40] the original petitioners purported to be its directors but, on account of an irregularity, it was impossible for the petition to proceed on such a basis. One of the directors then sought for his name to be substituted for those of the initial petitioners and the petition presented by him as a members' petition by reason of the fact that he held in excess of 10% of the share capital of the company. This was objected to but Kelly J found that the petitioner could

---

32 *Re Cavan Crystal Glass Ltd* [1998] 3 IR 570.

33 *Aston Colour Print Ltd* (21 February 1997, unreported), High Court (Kelly J).

34 See further Chapter 9, *Corporate Governance: Meetings*, at **[9.093]**.

35 *Re Cavan Crystal Glass Ltd,* [1998] 3 IR 591 at 593 (O'Flaherty J). See para **[23.015]**.

36 C(A)A 1990, s 3(1)(c).

37 See Chapter 25, *Winding up Companies*, para **[25.036]** *ff*.

38 C(A)A 1990, s 3(5) as amended by C(A)(No 2)A 1999, s 8.

39 C(A)A 1990, s 3(1)(d).

40 *Re Cavan Crystal Glass Ltd* [1998] 3 IR 570.

rely upon Ord 28, r 12 of the Rules of the Superior Courts 1986[41] and C(A)A 1990, s 3(7)[42] and the court would cure the irregularity. On this point Kelly J said:

> 'There is no evidence to controvert the assertion made by [the petitioning member] to the effect that the failure to present this petition as a shareholder holding in excess of 10% of the capital of the company was a bona fide one. It is clear that this petition had to be prepared and presented as a matter of considerable urgency. I accept that the error made was a genuine one. In such circumstances it would be strange indeed if the court did not have the power to put right such an error. I am of the view that it does have such power under the provisions of Order 28, Rule 12 and s 3(7) of the Act.
>
> Needless to say, the Court must always be astute to ensure that its process is not abused. This is particularly so in petitions presented under the Act. The mere presentation of a petition in the Central Office of this court provides statutory protection to the company. No judicial determination is required for that protection to be afforded. Given that such protection brings about a drastic abridgement to the rights of creditors, the court must make certain that this procedure is not abused...Great care should therefore be given to the presentation of petitions under the Act. In the present case, however, I am satisfied that a genuine mistake was made and I therefore propose to allow the amendments sought.'[43]

In that case Kelly J went on to say that the amendment did not involve the substitution of new petitioners for the existing ones and merely changed the description applicable to one of the initial petitioners as petitioner.

[23.016] Special provisions apply to certain types of financial companies. In the case of an insurance company only the Minister for Enterprise, Trade and Employment can present a petition to have an examiner appointed.[44] Only the Central Bank of Ireland has standing to present a petition in respect of certain companies such as banks.[45] In the case of a company referred to in C(A)(No 2)A 1999, Sch 2[46] certain other provisions apply[47]. First, those with locus standi are the company, its directors, creditors or members[48], the Central Bank or one or more of such persons and the Central Bank of Ireland acting together. Secondly, if the Central Bank does not present such a petition, prior to presenting the petition, the petitioner must give prior written notice to the Central Bank of his intention to present the petition and must subsequent to presenting the petition, serve a copy thereof on the Central

---

41 Ord 28, r 12 provides: 'The court may at any time, and on such terms as to costs or otherwise as the court may think just, amend any defect or error in any proceedings, and all necessary amendments shall be made for the purpose of determining the real question or issue raised by or depending on the proceedings.'

42 See para **[23.040]**.

43 [1998] 3 IR 570 at 581–582.

44 C(A)A 1990, s 3(2)(a).

45 C(A)A 1990, s 3(2)(b), as amended by C(A)(No 2)A 1999, s 6, provides that a petition can only be presented by the Central Bank of Ireland in the case of certain companies, such as the holder of a licence under the Central Bank Act 1971, s 9 and a company which was a building society.

46 Excepting companies referred to in C(A)(No 2)A 1999, Sch 2, paras 18–20, or to which C(A)A 1990, s 3(2)(b) applies. The Second Schedule is reproduced in the Appendix to this work.

47 C(A)A 1990, s 3(2)(c), as amended by C(A)(No 2)A 1999, s 6.

48 See para **[23.011]**.

Bank. Moreover, the Central Bank shall be entitled to appear and be heard at any hearing relating to the petition.

[23.017] Section 3B(1) of C(A)A 1990[49] provides that the court shall not make an order dismissing a petition presented under s 2 or an order appointing an examiner to a company without having afforded each creditor of the company who has indicated to the court his desire to be heard in the matter an opportunity to be so heard. This is without prejudice to the court's power under s 3(7) to make an interim order[50].

The grounds for appointing an examiner

(a) The test for the appointment of an examiner

[23.018] Section 2(1) of C(A)A 1990[51] provides that:

> 'Subject to subsection (2), where it appears to the court that —
>
> (a) a company is or is likely to be unable to pay its debts, and
>
> (b) no resolution subsists for the winding-up of the company, and
>
> (c) no order has been made for the winding-up of the company,
>
> it may, on application by petition presented, appoint an examiner to the company for the purpose of examining the state of the company's affairs and performing such duties in relation to the company as may be imposed by or under this Act.'

This subsection sets out the general prerequisites which must exist before the court can appoint an examiner to a failing company. It is a prerequisite that the company in respect of which an application is made is neither perfectly solvent nor in the course of being wound up. Accordingly, the company must be ailing but not to the extent that it has been resolved to wind up the company. If an order has been made to wind up the company, it will be too late for the court to accede to an application to have the company placed under its protection. It will not, however, be fatal to an application that a petition has been presented to have a company wound up.

A company is deemed to be unable to pay its debts if: it is unable to pay its debts as they fall due; the value of its assets is less than the amount of its liabilities, taking into account both contingent and prospective liabilities, or where CA 1963, s 214(a) or (b) apply to the company[52]. It is not necessary that the company must be unable to pay its debts at the time of presentation of the petition to have an examiner appointed. Rather, it is sufficient that it is likely to be unable to pay its debts in the future. This permits the court to accede to an application where the petitioner can point to some future circumstance which is likely to result in the company's insolvency. Further guidance to the court is provided by C(A)A 1990, s 2(4) which says that in deciding whether or not to make an order, the court may also have regard to whether the company has sought from its creditors significant

---

49 Inserted by C(A)(No 2)A 1999, s 10.

50 C(A)A 1990, s 3B(2).

51 As amended by C(A)(No 2)A 1999, s 5.

52 C(A)A 1990, s 2(3). As to CA 1963, s 214, see Chapter 25, *Winding up Companies*, para **[25.062]** *ff*.

extensions of time for the payment of its debts, from which it could reasonably be inferred that the company was likely to be unable to pay its debts.

[23.019] Section 2(1) of C(A)A 1990 is a general power and does not of itself, give much guidance to either the petitioners or to the court. Prior to its amendment by C(A)A 1990, s 2(2)[53] provided guidance to the court by suggesting that the court may make an order if it considered that such would be likely to facilitate the survival of the company and the whole or any part of its undertaking as a going concern. What was previously intended as guidance is now mandatory and this has 'raised the bar' for petitioners. The revised C(A)A 1990, s 2(2) now provides:

> 'The court shall not make an order under this section unless it is satisfied that there is a reasonable prospect of the survival of the company and the whole or any part of its undertaking as a going concern.'[54]

This is a stricter test. Now, the court cannot appoint an examiner *unless* there is a *reasonable* prospect of the survival of the company itself *and* the whole or any part of its undertaking. This revision was made because of the fact that the appointment of an examiner, even for a short period of time, to an insolvent company, is likely to result in the incurring of considerable cost and expense to the company. If the company cannot be salvaged, the already ill-fated creditors are likely to have their losses compounded.

(b) The need to show a 'reasonable prospect of survival of the company'

[23.020] Prior to the revision of C(A)A 1990, s 2(2) the leading authority on the test for the appointment of an examiner was the Supreme Court decision in *Re Atlantic Magnetics Ltd*[55]. The statutory revision of s 2(2) has effectively reversed that decision. There, Finlay CJ had said:

> 'The basic purpose of the appointment of an examiner is to do precisely what the word involves, *examine* the situation, affairs and prospects of the company.
>
> Having regard to these considerations, it is quite clear that there cannot be on a petitioner seeking an order for the appointment of an examiner an onus of proof to establish as a matter of probability that the company is capable of survival as a going concern.'[56]

He therefore rejected that a petitioner must establish to the satisfaction of a court that there is 'a real prospect of survival of the company', saying:

> 'I accept that for a court to consider that there was a likelihood that an order would facilitate the survival of the company involves it in some evaluation as to the chances of the company surviving. The real importance of such an evaluation at the stage of the petition for the appointment of an examiner goes no further than that a court should be very slow indeed to make an order pursuant to either of the subsections of s 2, where it considers that there is no identifiable prospect of the survival of a company.'[57]

---

53 The former C(A)A 1990, s 2(2) provided: 'Without prejudice to the general power of the court under sub–section (1), it may, in particular, make an order under this section if it considers that such order would be likely to facilitate the survival of the company, and the whole or any part of its undertaking, as a going concern.'

54 As replaced by C(A)(No 2)A 1999, s 5(b).

55 *Re Atlantic Magnetics Ltd* [1993] 2 IR 561.

56 [1993] 2 IR 561 at 572.

57 [1993] 2 IR 561 at 572.

The test adopted by Finlay CJ is now obsolete[58]. The Supreme Court's concern that it would have sufficient information upon which to decide whether there was a prospect of survival has been met by the requirement for a pre-petition report, also introduced by C(A)(No 2)A 1999. Now, as a matter of law, a petitioner must show some justification for the appointment of an examiner.

[23.021] The foregoing views are supported by the decision of the High Court in *Re Tuskar Resources plc*[59], which was the first written decision on the appointment of an examiner since the changes effected by C(A)(No 2)A 1999 were commenced. The facts in that case were that an interim examiner had previously been appointed to the company, which was primarily engaged in the business of oil exploration and production. The company's activities for the previous two years had been solely in Nigeria, where it had operated through a subsidiary company that was Nigerian registered. Among the matters in dispute was whether the subsidiary was entitled to an oil mining licence that had been granted initially to another, unrelated, Nigerian company. A third party, which had provided certain services and facilities to the company, claimed that it was owed over US$11 million and wanted the company wound up. The basis upon which an interim examiner had been appointed included the production to McCracken J of an independent accountant's report. That report had expressed the opinion that the company and the whole or any part of its undertaking would have a reasonable prospect of survival as a going concern subject to certain conditions being met. Those conditions included the successful resolution of the difficulties with the Nigerian company that claimed to be entitled to the oil mining licence and also to the resolution of the claim by the third party to be owed US$11 million. Since the appointment of the interim examiner, McCracken J noted that there had been two important developments: first, at a meeting to resolve the oil mining licence dispute, it appeared that the Nigerian company and the third party claiming to be owed US$11 million were not prepared to enter into negotiations with the company or its

---

58 The test he had adopted was a modification of that put forward by Lardner J in the High Court. It provided:

> 'In some cases the evidence may make it clear that survival of the company is not a practical possibility and the order is likely to be refused. In other cases the evidence may give a strong possibility of requisite adjustment. With requisite adjustment the company will survive and prosper therein. Here, it may be clearly possible to make an order appointing the examiner. In other cases, such as the present, the evidence may not lead to a clear cut conclusion. There may, as here, be a conflict of evidence on matters concerning the company's affairs – in such a case by what standards should the court make its decision? It seems to me that the standard is this: does the evidence lead to the conclusion that in all the circumstances it appears worthwhile to order an investigation by the examiner into the company's affairs and see can it survive, there being some prospect of survival?'

In so deciding, Finlay CJ omitted from Lardner J's test the adjective 'reasonable' from before 'prospect of survival'. See also *Re Butlers Engineering Ltd* (1 March 1996, unreported), High Court (Keane J); *Westport Property Construction Company Ltd* (13 September 1996, unreported), High Court (Budd J); and *Re Cavan Crystal Glass Ltd* [1998] 3 IR 570 and [1998] 3 IR 591 where the test in *Atlantic Magnetics* was applied.

59 *Re Tuskar Resources plc* [2001] 1 IR 668.

subsidiary; and, secondly, it appeared that there was a serious prospect of an investor being available to assist the company.

[23.022] McCracken J began by analysing the changes effected to the test for the appointment of an examiner. He said that the new test in C(A)A 1990, s 2(2) was more in keeping with the decision of Lardner J in *Atlantic Magnetics* than with the decision in the Supreme Court. He also noted that the legislature did not accept the view of McCarthy J that no real decision could be reached on the question of survival until an examiner had been in place for some weeks and it was now clear that a decision must be made at the initial stages. Comparing the new test with the old test McCracken J said:

> 'In the *Atlantic Magnetics* case Finlay CJ also stated that there cannot be an onus of proof on a petitioner to establish as a matter of probability that the company is capable of surviving as a going concern. It seems to me that this is no longer the position under the 1999 Act by reason of the wording of the new subsection 2(2). Under [C(A)A 1990] as originally enacted there would appear to be a wide discretion given to the Court. However, the new subsection prohibits the court from making an order unless it is satisfied there is a reasonable prospect of survival. If the court is to be "*satisfied*", it must be satisfied on the evidence before it, which is in the first instance the evidence of the petitioner. If that evidence does not satisfy the court, the order cannot be made, and in my view this is tantamount to saying that there is an onus of proof on the petitioner at the initial stage to satisfy the court that there is a reasonable prospect of survival. For this reason, the court has to view the evidence in a different manner to that applicable prior to the [C(A)(No 2)A 1999].'[60]

After reviewing the evidence McCracken J declined to appoint an examiner because he was not satisfied that there was a reasonable prospect of the survival of the company and the whole and or any part of its undertaking as a going concern. Seven separate reasons were given. First, because the company was purely a holding company that he held did not have an undertaking[61]. Secondly, because he found that in this application where the company's subsidiary was Nigerian registered, the court would exercise its discretion against appointing an examiner. Thirdly, because he held that the company had no prospect of success unless it could resolve its serious disputes with its protagonists. Fourthly, because that the company owed an indeterminate but large sum of money to a third party. Fifthly, because although it was known that the company (or its subsidiary) owed considerable sums to the Revenue Commissioners and other authorities in Nigeria, the court had no information as to the status of the moneys owed ie were they preferential debts? Sixthly, because the proposal for survival involved the transfer of a new business undertaking to the company and this was outside the scope of the legislation. Finally, because no evidence had been given as to the financial position of the Nigerian company.

(c) The need to show a 'reasonable prospect of survival of the whole or any part of its undertaking as a going concern'

[23.023] Not only must there be a reasonable prospect of the survival of the company, but so too must there also be a reasonable prospect of the survival of the whole or any *part of its undertaking* as a going concern. In the context of the old s 2(2), in *Re Clare Textiles Ltd*[62] Costello J said that the examiner in that case could only have come to the conclusion

[60] [2001] 1 IR 668 at 676.

[61] See para **[23.024]**.

[62] *Re Clare Textiles Ltd* [1993] 2 IR 213.

that the company alone was capable of survival: the undertaking of the company was not since the examiner proposed to sell the company's business and assets[63].

[23.024] In *Re Tuskar Resources plc*[64], McCracken J expressed the view that an examiner cannot be appointed to a company that is purely a holding company because such a company has no undertaking to continue as a going concern. He said of the company under scrutiny:

> 'Its only undertaking is the holding of shares in the Nigerian company, and I do not think that under any circumstances that could be called "a going concern". It seems to me that the wording of the Act precludes the court from making an order appointing an examiner to a holding company simpliciter, and that indeed to do so, particularly in the circumstances of this case, would be totally contrary to the objects of the Act. The Act is intended to give a breathing space to try to get the affairs of an insolvent company put in order. This is frequently to the detriment of some creditors, particularly secured creditors, but the legislature has considered that their interest may sometimes have to suffer if there would be a general benefit to other creditors, to the shareholders, and to the employees of the company. However, these considerations are unlikely to apply to a pure holding company.'[65]

McCracken J went on to make it clear that the foregoing did not mean that a holding company could never have an examiner appointed and that under C(A)A 1990, s 4 a holding company (as a related company) could have an examiner appointed where an examiner had been appointed to one of its subsidiaries.

The petition and grounding affidavit

[23.025] The petition to have an examiner appointed should be accompanied by a grounding affidavit from the petitioner[66]. Typically, the petition will be extensive, making detailed disclosures of all relevant matters to the court. Having averred to the petitioner's locus standi, the affidavit should give as full and detailed a history of the company as possible. The company's difficulties and insolvency and the causes of insolvency should also be set out. Furthermore, a full and detailed list of the company's creditors, both secured, unsecured and preferential debtors should be disclosed. Where proposals for a compromise or scheme of arrangement in relation to the company's affairs have been prepared for submission to interested parties for their approval, a copy of these proposals should accompany the petition[67]. Such proposals, if any, should now be referred to in the accompanying pre-petition report[68].

[23.026] The petition should also nominate a person to be appointed as examiner[69]. Furthermore, the putative examiner must consent to his or her appointment[70]. In practice,

---

63 *Re Edenpark Construction Ltd* [1994] 3 IR 126, where Murphy J commented that it was important that some entity or business should be preserved. On the Insolvency Act 1986 (UK), see *Re Harris Simons Construction Ltd* [1989] BCLC 202 and *Re Primlaks (UK) Ltd* [1989] BCLC 734.

64 *Re Tuskar Resources plc* [2001] 1 IR 668. The facts are given at para **[23.021]**.

65 [2001] 1 IR 668 at 679.

66 See RSC, Ord 75A, r 3 as inserted by SI 1990/27.

67 C(A)A 1990, s 3(4)(b).

68 See para **[23.031]**.

69 C(A)A 1990, s 3(3)(a).

70 C(A)A 1990, s 3(4)(a).

an affidavit of fitness for the nominee to act as examiner will accompany the petition. Often, this will be sworn by another insolvency practitioner, such as an accountant or a solicitor.

[23.027] As to who is qualified to act as an examiner, McCracken J held in *Re Tuskar Resources plc*[71] that there was no bar on the person who provides the independent person's report from acting as examiner. Whilst the learned judge said he had considerable sympathy with the contention that on the general basis that justice must be seen to be done, there can be a question mark over how independent an accountant can be if the purpose of his report is to determine whether he personally should or should not be appointed examiner. McCracken J said:

> 'It should be noted that in *Re Wogans (Drogheda) Ltd (No 3)*[72] Costello J held that the court would be very slow to appoint an accountant previously associated with the company as examiner, as his impartiality could be questioned. However, on the other side it can be argued that there would be considerable additional expense involved if two accountants had separately to investigate the prospects of the company, and there is also merit in that argument. In view of the fact that the legislature did not take on itself to prohibit the independent accountant from acting as examiner, I do not think that there is any statutory restriction on the court in so appointing him, although I can see there may be cases where it would be undesirable to do so.'[73]

Whilst it would be preferable to have the examiner separate from the independent person, it is thought that the additional cost is too great a price, particularly since the company must be insolvent to qualify to have an examiner appointed.

[23.028] Where a petition is presented by either the company itself or its directors, it must include a statement of the assets and liabilities of the company, in so far as these are known, as they stand on a date not earlier than seven days before the presentation of the petition[74]. This requirement is confined to the directors and the company, presumably because it would be unfair to expect those not involved in the management of the company to have access to such details.

[23.029] Section 3(3)(b) of C(A)A 1990 provides that a petition to have an examiner appointed shall:

> '...be supported by such evidence as the court may require for the purpose of showing that the petitioner has good reason for requiring the appointment of an examiner.'

Accordingly, a petitioner must both show that the company is in immediate danger of failing and also identify how the appointment of an examiner may be able to reverse this process. To show that a receiver has been appointed, that secured creditors are about to take other steps to enforce their security or that any creditor is threatening to place the company into liquidation are examples of dangers facing the company. Where a company is placed under the protection of the court, these and other immediate dangers will be

---

[71] *Re Tuskar Resources plc* [2001] 1 IR 668.

[72] *Re Wogans (Drogheda) Ltd (No 3)* [1993] 1 IR 157.

[73] [1993] 1 IR 157.

[74] C(A)A 1990, s 3(3)(c).

temporarily stopped. Essentially, the matters which a petitioner must show will depend upon the circumstances of each case[75].

[23.030] The petition to have an examiner appointed and the grounding affidavit must be made *uberrimae fides*, that is, in the utmost of good faith. What was first decided by Costello J in *Re Wogans (Drogheda) Ltd (No 2)*[76] has now been given statutory force. Section 4A of C(A)A 1990[77] provides:

> 'The court may decline to hear a petition presented under section 2 or, as the case may be, may decline to continue hearing such a petition if it appears to the court that, in the preparation or presentation of the petition or in the preparation of the report of the independent accountant, the petitioner or independent accountant —
>
> (a) has failed to disclose any information available to him which is material to the exercise by the court of its powers under this Act, or
>
> (b) has in any other way failed to exercise utmost good faith.'

Where it is discovered that the court has been misled, the entire application will be tainted. If this is discovered early in the proceedings, the examiner will be discharged where the lack of good faith is sufficiently serious[78]. Furthermore, the court will not hesitate to refuse to confirm any subsequent proposals made by the examiner where this is justified in the circumstances[79]. However, a lack of candour and good faith will not always result in a refusal to confirm an examiner's proposals. In *Re Selukwe Ltd*[80] Costello J found there was a considerable lack of good faith but was swayed by the fact that there were 30 jobs at stake and confirmed the examiner's proposals. Notwithstanding this, petitioners should exercise the same caution as is required in the case of an ex parte interlocutory

---

75 See O'Donnell, *Examinerships* (1994), p 4.

76 *Re Wogans (Drogheda) Ltd (No 2)* (7 May 1992, unreported), High Court, per Costello J. There he said (at pp 5–6 of the transcript):

> 'When an application is made by a company for a protection order under the C(A)A 1990, it seems to me that the directors and all those associated with the application (including their professional advisers) are obliged to exercise the utmost good faith and that such a duty exists not just on an *ex parte* application to appoint an interim examiner but also on the application itself. This is because (a) of necessity, the court must depend to a considerable extent on the truth of what it is told by the company and (b) because of the potential injustice involved in the making of a protection order when the proper course is to wind up the company. This duty involves an obligation to disclose all relevant facts material to the exercise by the court of its discretion. *A fortiori*, it involves a duty not to deliberately mislead the court by false evidence.'

77 Inserted by C(A)(No 2)A 1999, s 13.

78 See the Court of Appeal decision in *Cornhill Insurance plc v Cornhill Financial Services Ltd* [1993] BCLC 914 where it was held that there was jurisdiction to discharge an administration order where full disclosure was not made to the court on the initial application. On the facts of this case, it was held that there was no non–disclosure as the court had been told all it needed to know.

79 *Re Wogans (Drogheda) Ltd (No.2)* (7 May 1992, unreported), High Court, per Costello J, considered at para **[23.134]**.

80 *Re Selukwe Ltd* (20 December 1991, unreported), High Court, per Costello J.

injunction[81]. Similarly, in *Re Tuskar Resources plc*[82] McCracken J said that he did 'not think that over-optimism is sufficient to show bad faith, and in any event there is clearly a wide discretion in the court under the subsection, as it uses the word "*may*" rather than "*shall*".' In that case he exercised his discretion in favour of hearing the petition, notwithstanding that it was claimed that the original grounding affidavit was misleading and had failed to disclose material matters.

The pre-petition report

[23.031] In addition to the introduction of a stricter test, C(A)(No 2)A 1999 also introduced the new requirement that a *pre-petition report* prepared by an 'independent accountant' must accompany the petition. Section 3(3A) of C(A)A 1990[83] requires that the independent accountant must be either the company's auditor or a person who is qualified to be appointed as an examiner of the company. Section 3(3B) of C(A)A 1990 requires that the report of the independent accountant must comprise the following:

> '(a) the names and permanent addresses of the officers of the company and, in so far as the independent accountant can establish, any person in accordance with whose directions or instructions the directors of the company are accustomed to act,
>
> (b) the names of any other bodies corporate of which the directors of the company are also directors,
>
> (c) a statement as to the affairs of the company, showing in so far as it is reasonably possible to do so, particulars of the company's assets and liabilities (including contingent and prospective liabilities) as at the latest practicable date, the names and addresses of its creditors, the securities held by them respectively and the dates when the securities were respectively given,
>
> (d) whether in the opinion of the independent accountant any deficiency between the assets and liabilities of the company has been satisfactorily accounted for or, if not, whether there is evidence of a substantial disappearance of property that is not adequately accounted for,
>
> (e) his opinion as to whether the company, and the whole or any part of its undertaking, would have a reasonable prospect of survival as a going concern and a statement of the conditions which he considers are essential to ensure such survival, whether as regards the internal management and controls of the company or otherwise,
>
> (f) his opinion as to whether the formulation, acceptance and confirmation of proposals for a compromise or scheme of arrangement would offer a reasonable prospect of survival of the company, and the whole or any part of its undertaking, as a going concern,
>
> (g) his opinion as to whether an attempt to continue the whole or any part of the undertaking would be likely to be more advantageous to the members as a whole and the creditors as a whole than a winding-up of the company,

[81] See generally Courtney, *Mareva Injunctions and Related Interlocutory Orders* (1998), paras [8.32]–[8.44].

[82] *Re Tuskar Resources plc* [2001] 1 IR 668.

[83] Inserted by C(A)(No 2)A 1999, s 7.

(h) recommendations as to the course he thinks should be taken in relation to the company including, if warranted, draft proposals for a compromise or scheme of arrangement,

(i) his opinion as to whether the facts disclosed would warrant further inquiries with a view to proceedings under section 297 or 297A of the 1963 Act,

(j) details of the extent of the funding required to enable the company to continue trading during the period of protection and the sources of that funding,

(k) his recommendations as to which liabilities incurred before the presentation of the petition should be paid,

(l) his opinion as to whether the work of the examiner would be assisted by a direction of the court in relation to the role or membership of any creditor's committee referred to in section 21, and

(m) such other matters as he thinks relevant.'

Whilst it had been practice for some time for the court to require certain of this information to be brought to its attention on the presentation of a petition, that was an informal practice without force of law. It is now the case that, save in the exceptional circumstances next considered where interim protection may be granted, such information *must* be provided to the court on the hearing of a petition. As to the content of the report, in *Re Tuskar Resources plc*[84] McCracken J said that C(A)A 1990, s 3(3) does not say that the independent accountant must set out *in detail* the evidence which leads him to the opinion that the company and the whole or any part of its undertaking would have a reasonable prospect of survival as a going concern. McCracken J acknowledged that it could only be a preliminary opinion and that if he is appointed, an examiner will usually find out a great deal more about the company and its prospects.

[23.032] The independent accountant must supply a copy of the pre-petition report to the company and to any interested party upon receiving written application[85]. On application being made to the court, the court may direct that in supplying copies of the report, such parts of the report as it directs may be omitted; in particular any information which would be likely to prejudice the survival of the company or the whole or any part of its undertaking as a going concern may be omitted[86].

Interim protection pending the submission of a pre-petition report

[23.033] In exceptional circumstances the court may grant a company interim protection pending the presentation of a pre-petition report. Section 3A(1) of C(A)A 1990[87] provides:

---

84 *Re Tuskar Resources plc* [2001] 1 IR 668.

85 C(A)A 1990, s 3C(1), inserted by C(A)(No 2)A 1999, s 11.

86 C(A)A 1990, s 3C(2) and (3). Where the company is one referred to in s 3(2)(c) (see para **[23.016]**) and the Central Bank has not and does nor propose to present a petition under C(A)A 1990, s 2, the independent accountant must, as soon as may be after it is prepared, supply a copy of the report to the Central Bank and in such case sub-s (2) and (3) shall not apply to the copy sent to the Central Bank: C(A)A 1990, s 3C(4).

87 Inserted by C(A)(No 2)A 1999, s 9.

'If a petition presented under section 2 shows, and the court is satisfied —

(a) that, by reason of exceptional circumstances outside the control of the petitioner, the report of the independent accountant is not available in time to accompany the petition, and

(b) that the petitioner could not reasonably have anticipated the circumstances referred to in paragraph (a),

and, accordingly, the court is unable to consider the making of an order under that section, the court may make an order under this section placing the company concerned under the protection of the court for such period as the court thinks appropriate in order to allow for the submission of the independent accountant's report.'

The first point to be noted here is that where a court grants interim protection, it does so under s 3A and not C(A)A 1990, s 2. Secondly, s 3A makes it very clear that there must exist *exceptional circumstances* that are *outside the petitioner's control* and which *could not have been reasonably anticipated*. It is thought that these requirements should be strictly construed as the clear thrust of the legislation is not to afford the exceptional remedy of interim protection to a petitioner who by reason of his own culpability cannot comply with the requirement to have a pre-petition report. Section 3A(3) provides that, for the avoidance of doubt, the fact that a receiver stands appointed to the whole or part of a company's property or undertaking at the time of the presentation of the petition shall not, in itself, constitute 'exceptional circumstances outside the control of the petitioner'. At the end of the interim protection period if an independent accountant's report is submitted to the court, the court shall then proceed to consider the petition and the report as if they were presented in accordance with s 2[88]; if the report is not submitted before the expiry of the interim protection period then the company shall cease to be under the protection of the court, but without prejudice to the presentation of a further petition under s 2[89].

[23.034] Section 3A of C(A)A 1990 contains a number of very important additional safeguards to abuse of process. First, s 3A(2) provides that the period of interim protection shall expire not later than the 10th day after the date of the making of the order[90]. Secondly, s 3A(8) provides that any liabilities incurred by a company that has been granted interim protection may not be the subject of a certificate under C(A)A 1990, s 10(2).

[23.035] One difficulty, identified by the Gallagher Company Law Review Group[91], was that creditors or members who wish to present a petition may find it difficult or impossible to ascertain the information required by an independent accountant to produce a pre-petition report, unless they have the directors' co-operation. Section 3A(4) of C(A)A 1990 provides that where a member or creditor has presented a petition and interim protection is

88 C(A)A 1990, s 3A(6).

89 C(A)A 1990, s 3A(7).

90 If the 10th day is a Saturday, Sunday or public holiday, then it will be the first following day that is not such a day.

91 Report of the Gallagher *Company Law Review Group*, December 1994 at para 2.19.

granted, the directors of the company are obliged to co-operate in the preparation of the independent accountant's report[92].

[23.036] Although the legislation is silent on the point, it is thought that the only circumstances in which an *interim examiner* can be appointed is where interim relief is granted pursuant to s 3A. There is no specific reference to an interim examiner in C(A)A 1990, although there is the general power in s 3(7) to make an interim order. Order 75A, r 5(2) of the Rules of the Superior Court 1986 (as amended), however, refers to an interim examiner, providing:

> On the hearing of such *ex parte* application, the Court may, if it thinks fit, treat the application as the hearing of the petition and may make such order or any other order it thinks fit including adjourning the hearing and may appoint any proposed examiner on an interim basis until such adjourned hearing and an examiner so appointed over any company or any related company shall be referred to as the Interim Examiner and shall have the same powers and duties in relation to such company until the date of the adjourned hearing as if he were an examiner appointed other than on an interim basis.

'Before an examiner can be appointed, whether interim or otherwise, the statutory conditions for such appointment must be met' [93]. One reason for this is because an interim examiner has the same powers of certification of expenses as has a full examiner[94] and so the court must be equally cautious in acceding to the appointment of an interim examiner. It has been suggested that where a petitioner seeks the appointment of an interim examiner, the justification for this should be set out in detail in the grounding affidavit[95].

Presentation of the petition

[23.037] On the presentation[96] of a petition to place a company under the protection of the court, the petitioner is obliged to apply to the court for directions[97]. Although the court may treat this application as the full hearing of the petition, it rarely exercises this discretion[98]. The purpose of this requirement is principally to enable the court to direct the advertisement of the petition and to fix the date for the hearing of the petition. As in the presentation of the petition to have a company wound up, it is usual for the court to direct that the petition be advertised in two national daily newspapers, and to fix a Monday as the day for the hearing of the petition. The court will also normally direct the service of notice on certain parties at this point[99]. Depending upon who the petitioner is, the court will

---

92 Under C(A)A 1990, s 3A(5), where the directors fail to comply with C(A)A 1990, s 3A(4) the petitioner or independent accountant can apply to court for an order requiring the directors to do specified things by way of compliance therewith and the court may, as it thinks fit, grant such an order accordingly.

93 Per Kelly J in *Re Advanced Technology College Ltd* (13 March 1997, unreported), High Court at p 2.

94 See paras **[23.096]–[23.101]**. See, however, s 3A(8) considered at para **[23.034]**.

95 See O'Donnell, *Examinerships* (1994), p 11.

96 The petition is presented by lodging it with the Central Office of the High Court.

97 RSC, Ord 75A, r 4(4) now provides that: 'On the same day as the petition shall have been presented, the petitioner shall apply ex parte to the High Court for directions as to proceedings to be taken in relation thereto'.

98 RSC, Ord 75A, r 5(2).

99 RSC, Ord 75A, r 5(1).

usually direct service on, inter alios, the following: the company; all secured creditors; a receiver, if one has been appointed; and where a receiver has been appointed, the creditor who appointed him; the Revenue Commissioners and some or all of the unsecured creditors. Once served, the parties served will become 'notice parties' who from then on should be served with all further affidavits, notices and other relevant documentation. Because of the court's reluctance to appoint examiners in all but the clearest of cases and the duty of petitioners to make full disclosure to the court, if in doubt as to what or who should be served, petitioners should serve everything conceivably relevant on everybody conceivably interested.

The hearing of the petition

[23.038] On the hearing of the petition, C(A)A 1990 and the Rules of the Superior Courts 1986 try to ensure that all interested parties have an opportunity to hear and be heard. The rationale here is the same as in the hearing of a petition to have a company wound up and is evidenced by the advertisement of the hearing of the petition. For this reason the court has discretion to refuse to hear the petition until such time as such parties as the court directs have been notified[100].

[23.039] Section 3(6) of C(A)A 1990 prohibits the court from hearing a petition for the appointment of an examiner where a receiver has been appointed to the company, and stands appointed for a continuous period of at least three days prior to the presentation of the petition. Secured creditors often try to take advantage of this provision by appointing a receiver on a Thursday or Friday[101]. The hope is that petitioners seeking to have an examiner appointed will not have ready access to the courts on a Saturday or Sunday. Determined petitioners however, will succeed in locating a High Court judge on such days, at their home if necessary.

[23.040] In practice, C(A)A 1990, s 3(6) is tremendously important, even post-C(A)(No 2)A 1999 because of the availability of interim protection under C(A)A 1990, s 3A,[102] pending the production of the report of an independent accountant. When a company is failing, the consequence of s 3(6) is often a game of cat-and-mouse between the directors of the company and its main secured creditor. The secured creditor's dilemma is whether the company has passed the point of no return, and if so should they rely upon their security and appoint a receiver under their security documentation? The 'point of no return' from a secured creditor's perspective may be very different to the court's perspective when it is asked to appoint an examiner to a company on the basis that there is a reasonable prospect for its survival.

The directors' dilemma will be different. The director's concerns will often be based upon a reluctance to admit the company's insolvency and a fear of the consequences of corporate failure. To this will be added the expectation that the main secured creditor is likely to appoint a receiver coupled with a natural reluctance to precipitate failure by petitioning the court to appoint an examiner. The result is often a stand-off. When the

[100] RSC, Ord 75A, r 5(3).

[101] It is the case, however, that receivers have traditionally been appointed on Thursdays or Fridays.

[102] Inserted by C(A)(No 2)A 1999, s 9. See para **[23.033]**.

secured creditor moves first and appoints a receiver, the race commences. The directors must not only present a petition to have the company placed under the protection of the court within three days of the receiver's appointment, but they must also present as full and persuasive a petition as possible. Unless the petition succeeds, the receivership is implicitly confirmed and if the company's prospects are slim, its demise will be imminent[103]. Directors of a company fearful that a receiver might be appointed should seek to procure the report of an independent accountant as early as possible or else their petition will not be granted; indeed, even interim protection under s 3A will be refused unless there are 'exceptional circumstances' outside the control of the petitioner as to why this report is not available to accompany the petition. It is not sufficient to proffer the reason that the company is seeking to thwart the consequences arising from the appointment of a receiver[104].

The foregoing scenario represents a common pattern: the assumptions and expectations of the directors of an insolvent company do not necessarily accord with reality. It can be generally surmised that the directors of an insolvent company will sometimes either be procrastinating or seeking the implementation of a scheme of arrangement which would enable the company to wipe part of its slate clean. Unfortunately, where procrastination of the inevitable is the result of a successful application to have an examiner appointed, the directors themselves and the secured creditors are often among the losers. Where an examinership fails, often, the only winners will be the lawyers and accountants for both sides who, usually, will be paid their fees in full.

[23.041] In *Cavan Crystal Glass Ltd*[105] Kelly J sanctioned an amendment to the name in which the petition had been brought so as to cure an irregularity[106]. This was objected to by one secured creditor on the grounds that unless there was a valid petition before the court at midnight on the third day subsequent to the appointment of the receiver, an amendment was useless to avoid the provisions of C(A)A 1990, s 3(6). This point was rejected by Kelly J, who held:

> 'In my view, there was at all times a valid petition before the court albeit one which had a defect in form insofar as [the petitioning-member] was concerned. At all times he could have presented the petition as a shareholder of the company holding in excess of 10% of its share capital but through what I have held to be a bona fide error, did so as a director of the company. The amendment which I am permitting merely puts that position right...I do not consider that by so doing and by regarding the petition as a valid one as of the date of its presentation, that I am in any way running counter to the provisions of s 3(6) of the Act. I cannot accept that it was ever the intention of the legislature that the making of a bona fide error, such as the one in suit, could have the drastic consequences for the company and its workforce as [the opposing creditor] suggest'.[107]

---

103 In this regard it may be noted that in recent times, relatively few petitions have been successful. See *Companies Report 2000* at p 37 where it is stated that there were only 2 applications to the courts for the appointment of an examiner in 2000, 1 in 1999 and 13 in 1998.

104 C(A)A 1990, s 3A(3).

105 *Cavan Crystal Glass Ltd* [1998] 3 IR 570.

106 See para **[23.015]**.

107 [1998] 3 IR 570 at 582.

[23.042] On the hearing of a petition to have an examiner appointed, the court has a wide discretion. It may hear the petition in full; it may adjourn the petition conditionally or unconditionally; or it may make any other order which the judge thinks fit[108]. It is also open for the petitioner to seek to have the application heard *in camera*. Section 31 of C(A)A 1990 provides that the whole or any part of any proceedings under the Act may be heard otherwise than in public '...if the court, in the interests of justice, considers that the interests of the company concerned or of its creditors as a whole so require.'

In such circumstances, the court will follow the guidelines set out by the Supreme Court in *Re R Ltd*[109] and recently endorsed in *Irish Press plc v Ingersoll Irish Publications Ltd*[110]. In *Re Chancery plc*[111] Harman J held that although ordinarily an administration petition under the Insolvency Act 1986 (UK) should rarely be heard *in camera*, this could be departed from in particular circumstances. The circumstances of that case were such that it was held that the petition should be heard *in camera* because of the commercially damaging nature of the evidence to be presented.

[23.043] After hearing the petition and the reading of the grounding affidavit and replying affidavit (if any), the court will then address the central question of whether there is a reasonable prospect of survival for the company and, if so, whether the court should exercise its discretion to appoint an examiner in accordance with s 2[112]. It is also open to the court to dismiss the petition, which it will do where there is no reasonable prospect of survival. Where this occurs, a receiver who has been appointed can continue to secure the best position to protect the secured creditor who appointed him. It is open to the court to award costs against the unsuccessful petitioner(s)[113].

[23.044] Where, at first instance, a petition for the appointment of an examiner is refused it is open to the petitioner to appeal that decision. It was said by the Supreme Court in *Re Cavan Crystal Glass Ltd*[114] that on appeal a fresh discretion must be brought to bear on the case.

Related companies

[23.045] Upon the appointment of an examiner to a company (the primary company), it is open to the court to accede to an application to extend the examinership to a related company or companies. This power has been exercised by the High Court on numerous occasions since the passing of C(A)A 1990. Section 4(1) of C(A)A 1990[115] provides that subject to sub-s (2), the court may make an order appointing the examiner of the primary company to be examiner to a related company and conferring on the examiner all or any of the powers or duties conferred upon him in relation to the primary company. In deciding

---

108 See C(A)A 1990, s 3(7).

109 *Re R Ltd* [1989] IR 126, see Chapter 19, *Shareholders' Remedies* at para **[19.055]** *ff*.

110 *Irish Press plc v Ingersoll Irish Publications Ltd* [1993] ILRM 747.

111 *Re Chancery plc* [1991] BCLC 712.

112 See para **[23.018]** *ff*.

113 In *Re Land and Property Trust Co (No 3)* [1991] BCLC 856 costs were awarded against the petitioners where they had acted irresponsibly.

114 *Re Cavan Crystal Glass Ltd* [1998] 3 IR 591 at 597 (O'Flaherty J).

115 As amended by C(A)(No 2)A 1999, s 12 (a).

whether or not to make such an order, guidance is given to the court by s 4(2), which provides that:

> '...the court shall have regard to whether the making of the order would be likely to facilitate the survival of the company, or of the related companies, or both, and the whole or any part of its or their undertaking, as a going concern and shall not, in any case, make such an order unless it is satisfied that there is a reasonable prospect of the survival of the related company, and the whole or any part of its undertaking, as a going concern.'[116]

In consequence, no order can be made appointing an examiner to a related company unless the court is satisfied that the survival of it and the whole or any part of its undertaking as a going concern, is also a reasonable prospect[117]. It is not a prerequisite that the related company is also unable to pay its debts, or insolvent. Sometimes the related company's financial health will be inter-dependent upon that of the primary company. This is particularly true where the related company has guaranteed some or all of the debts of the primary company. The fact that a related company has an examiner appointed to it has no bearing upon the question of either that company's separate legal existence being disregarded or its being directed to contribute to the assets of the primary company or the pooling of their assets on a winding up. These are separate questions that must be addressed in the context of a particular set of circumstances.

[23.046] Not every company, however, can have an examiner appointed to it on the grounds that it is a related company. Although a company may be owned by the same persons as the primary company, that by itself may be an insufficient connection. 'Related company' is very specifically defined by C(A)A 1990, s 4(5). This provides:

> 'For the purposes of this Act, a company is related to another company if—
>
> (a) that other company is its holding company or subsidiary; or
>
> (b) more than half in nominal value of its equity share capital (as defined in s 155(5) of the 1963 Act) is held by the other company and companies related to that other company (whether directly or indirectly, but other than in a fiduciary capacity); or
>
> (c) more than half in nominal value of the equity share capital (as defined in s 155(5) of the 1963 Act) of each of them is held by members of the other (whether directly or indirectly, but other than in a fiduciary capacity); or
>
> (d) that other company or a company or companies related to that other company or that other company together with a company or companies related to it are entitled to exercise or control the exercise of more than one half of the voting power at any general meeting of the company; or
>
> (e) the businesses of the companies have been so carried on that the separate business of each company, or a substantial part thereof, is not readily identifiable; or
>
> (f) there is another body corporate to which both companies are related;
>
> and 'related company' has a corresponding meaning.'

---

[116] As amended by C(A)(No 2)A 1999, s 12(b).

[117] In *Re Tuskar Resources plc* [2001] 1 IR 668 it was held that there was not sufficient evidence to show a reasonable prospect of survival of a Nigerian company; earlier, McCracken J had held that a foreign company could not be a related company: see para **[23.010]**.

Section 4(6) further provides that for the purposes of s 4, 'company' includes any body which is liable to be wound up under the Companies Acts[118]. Although a non-Irish formed and registered company cannot be placed under the protection of the court, such a company may be deemed to be a related company, and may have an examiner appointed to it[119].

[23.047] In *Re Edenpark Construction Ltd and Edenpark Homes Ltd*[120], Edenpark Homes Ltd ('Homes') had an examiner appointed on the basis that it was a related company to Edenpark Construction Ltd ('Construction'). Murphy J said of Homes that it was 'a company which was related to Construction to the extent that Construction owned 25% of the shareholding in Homes and two directors were common to both companies'.[121] Such, by itself, was not sufficient for Homes to be a related company to Construction. Although it does not appear in Murphy J's judgment, it is surmised that the businesses of both companies must have been carried on in a manner so that they were not readily identifiable.

[23.048] Where an examiner is appointed to a related company the protection extended to the related company dates from the appointment of an examiner to the related company and *not* to the appointment of the examiner to the primary company[122]. The obvious difficulty which may arise is that a receiver is appointed to the related company for a period in excess of three days or that an order is made to wind up the related company. An interim examiner may also be appointed to a related company. It is suggested that petitioners who believe that the protection of a related company may be required for the survival of the primary company ought, in their petition for the appointment of an examiner to the primary company, seek the appointment of an interim examiner to the related company.

Formalities in the appointment of an examiner

[23.049] A number of provisions exist relating to the publicity of an examiner's appointment and the fact that a company has been placed under the protection of the court[123]. Within three days from the presentation of a petition, notice of the petition must be delivered to the Registrar of Companies as must the order appointing the examiner[124]. The appointment of the examiner, together with the date, if any, set for the hearing of his

---

[118] See Chapter 25, *Winding Up Companies*, at para **[25.031]**.

[119] In this regard it is thought that McCracken J in *Re Tuskar Resources plc* [2001] 1 IR 668 was mistaken. There he said '...in my view the definition of a related company in s 4(5) does not include a company registered outside this jurisdiction, as it sets out the conditions in which "a company is related to another company", and the word "*company*" as defined in the Companies Act 1963 means a company formed and registered under that Act, or an existing company'. This was, however, apparently without reference to C(A)A 1990, s 4(6). As to those companies that can be wound up by the High Court, see Chapter 25, *Winding Up Companies*, at para **[25.031]**.

[120] *Re Edenpark Construction Ltd and Edenpark Homes Ltd* [1994] 3 IR 126.

[121] [1994] 3 IR 126.

[122] C(A)A 1990, s 4(3).

[123] Persons in default of these provisions are liable to be fined up to €1,269.74 on summary conviction and €12,697.38 on conviction on indictment: C(A)A 1990, s 12(5).

[124] See C(A)A 1990, s 12(1) and (3) respectively.

first report, must also be advertised. Advertisements must be placed in two daily newspapers circulating in the district where the company has its registered office within three days of the appointment and in *Iris Oifigiúil*, within 21 days of the appointment[125]. In *Re Advanced Technology College Ltd*[126] Kelly J adjourned the hearing of a petition and directed re-advertisement of it because of defects in the proofs put before him, the principal one concerning omissions advertising the petition. This order was appealed to the Supreme Court where Barrington J (with whom Keane and Murphy JJ agreed) said:

> 'One must ask what is the purpose of such advertisements. It is to give notice to members of the public and included amongst them may be persons with no legal representation and persons who have never been in court. They should be informed where and when the application is to be made and its fundamental purpose. To be valid the advertisement must state the time, date and place where the application is to be heard. If it can, it should name the court in the Four Courts where the application will be heard. The learned trial judge was perfectly correct in the decision which he made which is unimpeachable'. [127]

[23.050] Section 13(1) of C(A)A 1990 provides that an examiner may resign, or on cause shown, be removed by the court[128]. In either eventuality, the court has power to fill the vacancy[129]. Any committee of creditors established under C(A)A 1990, s 21, the company or any interested party have locus standi to seek a court order to fill the vacancy[130].

[23.051] Where an examiner is appointed he must be described as 'the examiner' of the particular company in respect of which he is appointed and not by his individual name[131].

The commencement of protection

[23.052] Court protection of a failing company commences upon the presentation of a petition for the appointment of an examiner under C(A)A 1990. As with the winding up of a company, the date upon which a company is deemed to be under the protection of the court is not the date of the court order, but the date upon which the petition is presented.

[B] THE EFFECTS OF COURT PROTECTION

[23.053] Section 5(1) of C(A)A 1990[132] provides:

> 'Subject to section 3A, during the period beginning with the date of the presentation of a petition under section 2 and (subject to subsections (3) and (4) of section 18) ending on the

---

[125] C(A)A 1990, s 12(2)(a) and (b).

[126] *Re Advanced Technology College Ltd* (13 March 1997, unreported), High Court at pp 7–8.

[127] Quoted in Kelly J's judgment of 13 March 1997 (at pp 7–8) on a subsequent application to, inter alia, reverse himself and the Supreme Court by dispensing with the need to further advertise the petition at all, which he described as 'wholly misconceived'.

[128] On the removal of an administrator appointed under the Insolvency Act 1986 (UK), see *Re Exchange Travel (Holdings) Ltd* [1993] BCLC 887 where the peculiarities of the UK legislation was considered.

[129] C(A)A 1990, s 13(2).

[130] C(A)A 1990, s 13(3).

[131] C(A)A 1990, s 13(4).

[132] As amended by C(A)(No 2)A 1999, s 14(a), the effect of such amendment being to shorten the period of examination from three months to 70 days from the date of presentation of a petition.

expiry of 70 days from that date or on the withdrawal or refusal of the petition, whichever first happens, the company shall be deemed to be under the protection of the court.'

The most immediate and dramatic effect of a company being placed under the protection of the court is that creditors of the company are prevented from taking any action to enforce their security. The protected company is given a respite. Section 5(2) of C(A)A 1990 sets out in detail the effect of court protection. Accordingly, for so long as a company is under the protection of the court:

'(a) no proceedings for the winding-up of the company may be commenced, or resolution for winding-up passed, in relation to that company and any resolution so passed shall be of no effect[133];

(b) no receiver over any part of the property or undertaking of the company shall be appointed, or, if so appointed before the presentation of a petition under s 2, shall, subject to s 6, be unable to act;

(c) no attachment, sequestration, distress or execution shall be put into force against the company, except with the consent of the examiner;

(d) where any claim against the company is secured by a mortgage, charge, lien or other encumbrance or a pledge of, on or affecting the whole or any part of the property, effects or income of the company, no action may be taken to realise the whole or any part of that security, except with the consent of the examiner[134];

(e) no steps may be taken to repossess goods in the company's possession under any hire-purchase agreement (within the meaning of s 11(8)), except with the consent of the examiner[135];

(f) where under any enactment, rule of law or otherwise, any person other than the company ie a surety, is liable to pay all or any part of the debts of the company—

(i) no attachment, sequestration, distress or execution shall be put into force against the property or effects of such person in respect of the debts of the company, and

(ii) no proceedings of any sort may be commenced against such person in respect of the debts of the company;

(g) no order for relief shall be made under s 205 of the 1963 Act against the company in respect of complaints as to the conduct of the affairs of the company or the exercise of the powers of the directors prior to the presentation of the petition.'[136]'

[23.054] Section 5 of C(A)A 1990 is so wide that, with minor exceptions, it may be considered to place a total embargo on creditors or other aggrieved persons taking any steps which would affect the protected company's assets. Although shareholders are

---

133 See *Re a Company (No 001992 of 1988)* [1989] BCLC 9.

134 As inserted by C(A)(No 2)A 1999, s 14(b)(i) to remedy the lacunae in the original C(A)A 1990, s 5(2)(d) which was capable of being interpreted as not preventing the enforcement of a mortgage, as was identified in the first edition of this work at para [17.043].

135 C(A)A 1990, s 11(8) provides: 'References in this section to a hire–purchase agreement include a conditional sale agreement, a retention of title agreement and an agreement for the bailment of goods which is capable of subsisting for more than 3 months.' On hire–purchase agreements in UK administrations, see *Barclays Mercantile Business Finance Ltd v Sibec Development Ltd* [1993] BCLC 1077.

136 C(A)A 1990, s 5(2)(h) was deleted by C(A)(No 2)A 1999, s 14(b)(ii). See **[23.062]**.

prevented from taking proceedings under CA 1963, s 205[137], it is primarily the company's creditors who are affected by the appointment of an examiner.

[23.055] Section 5(3) of C(A)A 1990 prohibits (subject to sub-s (2)) the issuing of all 'other proceedings' against a company that is under the protection of the court, except with leave of the court[138] and subject to such terms as the court may impose. Moreover, on the application of the examiner, the court may make such order as it thinks proper in relation to any existing proceedings, including an order to stay such proceedings. The prohibition on the commencement of 'other proceedings' other than with the leave of the court has been interpreted by the courts of England and Wales in the context of their, on this point, similarly worded administration legislation[139] and found to encompass criminal proceedings[140]. The English courts have also held that there is no basis upon which to restrict the prohibition on the commencement of 'other proceedings' to actions brought by creditors and in one case the court dismissed an application for a declaration that leave of the court was not required in order to bring proceedings for the infringement of a patent[141].

[23.056] Because proceedings cannot be issued, interlocutory injunctive proceedings can not be commenced without the leave of the court. In the first proceedings under C(A)A 1990, *Re Goodman International*, a Mareva injunction was refused by Hamilton P in an application brought by Banque Paribas of London[142]. Hamilton P is reported as having refused leave to issue proceedings against a number of subsidiary companies of the Goodman Group of companies and refused to grant the Mareva injunction sought to freeze the companies' assets. Although the plaintiff may have a substantive cause of action, the effect of C(A)A 1990, s 5(3) is that proceedings cannot be instituted without the leave of the court, and accordingly no ancillary Mareva (or other interlocutory) relief can be granted[143].

---

137 C(A)A 1990, s 5(4) also provides that complaints concerning the conduct of the affairs of the company while it is under the protection of the court, shall not constitute the basis of the making of an order for relief under CA 1963, s 205.

138 As to the court's discretion to give leave to institute proceedings under the Insolvency Act 1986 (UK), see *Royal Trust Bank v Buchler* [1989] BCLC 130.

139 Insolvency Act 1986, s 11(3)(d) (UK).

140 In *Re Rhondda Waste Disposal Company Ltd (in administration)* [1999] TLR 605 it was held that the English Environmental Agency could not bring criminal proceedings against a company in administration without the leave of the court. See also *A Straume (UK) Ltd v Bradlor Developments Ltd* [1999] TLR 478 where it was held that an adjudication procedure under the English Housing Grants, Construction and Regeneration Act 1986 constituted 'other proceedings'.

141 *Biosource Technologies Inc v Axis Genetics plc (in administration)* [1999] TLR 814. See also *Re Paramount Airways Ltd* [1990] BCC 130 and *Carr v British International Helicopters Ltd* [1994] 2 BCLC 474 where it was found that the word 'other' could not be construed eiusdem generis with what had gone before so as to confine 'other proceedings' to those relating to a debt. Cf *Air Ecossee Ltd v Civil Aviation Authority* [1987] 3 BCC 492.

142 An application reported in (1990) The Irish Times, 20 October.

143 See generally, Courtney, *Mareva Injunctions and Related Interlocutory Orders* (1998), para [4.10]–[4.13].

[23.057] An interesting issue arises where a Mareva injunction is granted against a company before an examiner has been appointed. In *Capital Cameras Ltd v Harold Lines Ltd*[144] Harman J held that in certain circumstances an administrative receiver appointed in England could apply for the discharge of a Mareva injunction which was granted before his appointment. The reasoning of the court was that the basis upon which the Mareva injunction was granted had changed substantially. The difference was that after the appointment of an administrative receiver, a licensed insolvency practitioner was in control of the company. In Ireland, it is thought that the appointment of an examiner cannot automatically result in the successful application to have a pre-protection period Mareva injunction discharged. Only where the directors' powers have been transferred to the examiner under C(A)A 1990, s 9 can the court be assured that the company's affairs are being controlled by an officer of the court. In such a case it is thought that there will be a very clear case to have the injunction discharged since the risk of removal of assets from the jurisdiction or their dissipation with the *intention* of avoiding judgment or frustrating an order of the court, must surely be remote.

[23.058] Where a company is by virtue of C(A)A 1990, s 5, deemed to be under the protection of the court, every invoice, order for goods or business letter issued by or on behalf of the company, being a document on or in which the name of the company appears, must immediately after the mention of that name include the words 'in examination (under the Companies (Amendment) Act 1990)'[145].

[C] THE POSITION OF CREDITORS

[23.059] In *Re Butlers Engineering Ltd*[146] Keane J said of the consequences for creditors of the appointment of an examiner:

> 'It is almost superfluous to point out that while the purpose of the Act is the protection of the company and, as a result, its shareholders, employees and creditors, the court must never lose sight of the drastic abridgement that the giving of protection effects to the rights of the last mentioned category and I do not think that the judgments to which I have referred would lend any support to the view that the court must disregard those consequences in deciding whether an examiner should be appointed. In particular, it should be borne in mind that even the comparatively short breathing space...given by the appointment may have serious consequences for the creditors, given the fact that their nominal remedies remain in abeyance, while the control of the company remains in the hands of those who, in some cases at least, have contributed to its insolvency'.

The creditors of a company are those who are most directly and severely affected by the appointment of an examiner. It is proposed to consider here the effects of C(A)A 1990, s 5

---

144 *Capital Cameras Ltd v Harold Lines Ltd* [1991] BCLC 884.

145 C(A)A 1990, s 12(4) as substituted by C(A)(No 2)A 1999, s 20(4). Previously, the required words were 'under the protection of the court'; the use of 'examinership' in the revised wording evidences a change in thinking as to the most appropriate description of the whole process.

146 *Re Butlers Engineering Ltd* (1 March 1996, unreported), High Court (Keane J) at p 10 of the transcript. See O'Donnell, 'Appointing and Examiner: Learning to Live with the Culture of Corporate Rescue' (1997) Bar Review 246.

on the company's creditors. It will also be necessary to consider some other relevant sections in the Act. The issues considered here are:

1. Ordinary and preferential creditors.
2. Provisional liquidators.
3. Receivers.
4. Secured creditors: general.
5. Negative pledge clauses in debentures.
6. De-crystallisation of floating charges.
7. Sureties and guarantors.
8. Priority of secured creditors and liquidators' costs, charges and expenses.

Ordinary and preferential creditors

[23.060] The main remedies ordinarily available to unsecured creditors are either to petition to have the company wound up on the basis that it is unable to pay its debts or to institute proceedings in order to obtain judgment against the company. Section 5(2)(a) of C(A)A 1990 prohibits the commencement of proceedings for the winding up of a company in examinership. As considered above[147], no proceedings against a company under the protection of the court can be commenced without the leave of the court. As such, the ordinary creditor is deprived of his principal remedies against a debtor-company. It is only fair that, upon the hearing of a petition to have an examiner appointed, ordinary creditors are afforded every opportunity possible to voice their concerns[148]. This is particularly true since even if the examinership is successful, the creditors will almost certainly be asked to write off part of the debts owing to them.

It should also be noted that not only is a creditor restricted in the enforcement of a liability owed by a company to which an examiner has been appointed, but so too is there a general restriction on the discharge of pre-petition liabilities by such a company[149].

[23.061] The courts frequently tend to pay particular attention to the Revenue Commissioners' position on an application for the appointment of an examiner. The Revenue Commissioners and secured creditors will frequently find themselves allies in opposing petitions for the appointment of examiners, both fearing that they will share the same fate: the writing-down of what they would otherwise be entitled to on the presumed inevitable liquidation. Where the Revenue Commissioners are neutral, this has been interpreted as being a 'sign of hope' for the ailing company[150].

[23.062] One substantial change arising from C(A)(No 2)A 1999 is the deletion[151] of C(A)A 1990, s 5(2)(h)[152]. That paragraph provided that no set-off between bank accounts of a company that had been placed under the court's protection could be effected, except with the consent of the examiner. The effect of this was to discriminate between banks and

---

147 See paras **[23.053]–[23.058]**.

148 As now provided for by C(A)A 1990, s 3A.

149 C(A)A 1990, s 5A(1).

150 Per O'Flaherty J in *Re Cavan Crystal Glass Ltd* [1998] 3 IR 591 at 594 (O'Flaherty J).

151 By C(A)(No 2)A 1999, s 14(b)(ii).

152 Itself inserted by CA 1990, s 181(1)(c).

other creditors ie only set-off between bank accounts was prohibited. As a result of the recommendation of the Gallagher Company Law Review Group, this paragraph was repealed so that set-off between bank accounts is now permitted, despite the fact that a company is under the protection of the court.

Provisional liquidators

[23.063] Where at the date of the presentation of a petition to appoint an examiner to a company, a provisional liquidator stands appointed to that company, C(A)A 1990, s 6(2)[153] provides that the court may make such order as it thinks fit, including an order as to any of the following matters:

'(a) that the provisional liquidator be appointed as examiner of the company,

(b) appointing some other person as examiner of the company,

(c) that the provisional liquidator shall cease to act as such from the date specified by the court,

(d) directing the provisional liquidator to deliver all books, papers and other records, which relate to the property or undertaking of the company or any part thereof and are in his possession or control, to the examiner within a period to be specified by the court,

(e) directing the provisional liquidator to give the examiner full particulars of all dealings with the property or undertaking of the company.'

The court is also empowered to include such conditions in the order and make such ancillary or other orders as it deems fit for the purpose of giving full effect to an order under s 6(2)[154]. In deciding to make an order under s 6(2)(c) the court is obliged to have regard to whether the making of the order would be likely to facilitate the survival of the company, and the whole or any part of its undertaking, as a going concern[155]. Where a petition is presented to have an examiner appointed subsequent to the presentation of a petition for the winding up of a company but before a provisional liquidator is appointed, C(A)A 1990, s 6(5) requires both petitions to be heard together.

Receivers

[23.064] As has been considered above[156], the presentation of a petition to have an examiner appointed cannot be heard where a receiver has been appointed, and stands appointed for a period of at least three days prior to the presentation of the petition. Furthermore, after the presentation of a petition and for as long as the company is under the protection of the court, C(A)A 1990, s 5(2)(b) provides that no receiver shall be appointed over any part of the property or undertaking of the company.

[23.065] Where a receiver has been appointed for a lesser period of time than three days and the company is successfully placed under the protection of the court, the position of

[153] As amended by C(A)(No 2)A 1999, s 16.

[154] C(A)A 1990, s 6(4).

[155] C(A)A 1990, s 6(3) as amended by C(A)(No 2)A 1999, s 16.

[156] C(A)A 1990, s 3(6). See paras **[23.039]**–**[23.041]**.

the receiver is affected greatly. Section 6(1) of C(A)A 1990[157] provides, inter alia, that a receiver shall cease to act where, at the date of the presentation of a petition to appoint an examiner, he stands appointed to all or any part of the property or undertaking of the company. This section provides that the court may make such order as it thinks fit including an order as to any or all of the following matters:

> '(a) that the receiver shall cease to act as such from a date specified by the court[158],
>
> (b) that the receiver shall, from a date specified by the court, act as such only in respect of certain assets specified by the court,
>
> (c) directing the receiver to deliver all books, papers and other records, which relate to the property or undertaking of the company (or any part thereof) and are in his possession or control, to the examiner within a period to be specified by the court,
>
> (d) directing the receiver to give the examiner full particulars of all his dealings with the property or undertaking of the company.'

This is a remarkable provision which displaces, without regard to both of the original parties' interests, a freely negotiated contract. The court is also empowered to include such conditions in the order and make such ancillary or other orders as it deems fit for the purpose of giving full effect to an order under s 6(3)[159]. Section 6(3)[160] provides that the court shall not make an order under paras (a) or (b) unless the court is satisfied that there is a reasonable prospect of the survival of the company, and the whole or any part of its undertaking, as a going concern. Whatever the merits or demerits, it seems irreconcilable with the rationale of examinerships to permit a receiver to enforce the appointing debenture holder's security. In all but the most exceptional of cases, the receiver will be held powerless during the period of the examinership.

[23.066] Upon his appointment a receiver owes duties under CA 1963, s 98 to a company's preferential creditors[161]. Where an examiner has been appointed to a company or where in the opinion of the court such is likely, upon application being made, the court may, in relation to a receiver who stands appointed to the whole or any part of the property or undertaking of a company, make an order providing that s 98 shall not apply as respects payments made by the receiver out of assets coming into his hands[162]. The court must be of the opinion that the making of the order would be likely to facilitate the survival of the company and the whole or any part of its undertaking as a going concern[163]. Moreover, such an order cannot be made without the company's preferential creditors being afforded an opportunity to be heard[164].

---

[157] As amended by C(A)(No 2)A 1999, s 16.

[158] This was what happened in *Re Holidair Ltd* [1994] 1 ILRM 481.

[159] C(A)A 1990, s 6(4).

[160] As amended by C(A)(No 2)A 1999, s 16.

[161] See Chapter 22, *Corporate Borrowing: Receivers*, para **[22.054]** *ff.*

[162] C(A)A 1990, s 6A(1)(a), inserted by C(A)(No 2)A 1999, s 17.

[163] C(A)A 1990, s 6A(1)(b).

[164] C(A)A 1990, s 6A(2).

Secured creditors: general

[23.067] Section 5(2)(d) of C(A)A 1990[165] provides that while a company is under the protection of the court:

> '...where any claim against the company is secured by a mortgage, charge, lien or other encumbrance or a pledge of, on or affecting the whole or any part of the property, effects or income of the company, no action may be taken to realise the whole or any part of that security, except with the consent of the examiner.'

This provision has been substantially extended by C(A)(No 2)A 1999 so that it is no longer possible to argue that only 'charges' of property (as distinct from 'mortgages') cannot be enforced during the period of protection. It is now the case that the enforcement of all forms of consensual security that can be created by a company is not permissible without the consent of an examiner. It is also clear that security which does not require to be registered pursuant to CA 1963, s 99 is also caught by the revised wording[166].

[23.068] In *Re Holidair Ltd*[167] the question before the court was whether a bank's direction to a borrower-company which was under the protection of the court, to lodge the proceeds of the company's book debts to a designated account was in breach of C(A)A 1990, s 5(2)(d). Finlay CJ held that the action of the bank in directing for the first time, the payment of moneys collected from the company's debtors, into a nominated account in the name of a trustee, was in breach of the originally worded s 5(2)(d). Reversing the decision of Costello J in the High Court, he said:

> 'It is clear that this sub-section does not merely prohibit the realisation of the whole or any part of a security but prohibits the taking of any action to realise the whole or part of any security. It is in my view clear that to attempt to provide for the lodgment of the proceeds of book debts into a bank account in the name of the trustee of the debenture which could not be operated by the companies except with the consent of the trustee is an action taken to realise the security consisting of the book debts making them immediately available on the conclusion of the period provided for in s 5(1) as a set-off in respect of part of the debt of the banks. It is in my view irrelevant that the banks had reserved to themselves in the debenture a right to take this step once they did not take it and took it for the first time after the appointment of the examiner.'[168]

Negative pledge clauses in debentures

[23.069] Most modern debentures contain a negative pledge clause. The purpose of this is to prevent the borrowing company from creating any other charge over its property without the prior consent in writing of the debenture holder[169]. Notwithstanding that C(A)A 1990 does not authorise the court to give an examiner any power which is not exercisable by the directors, the Supreme Court has held that an examiner is *not* bound by a negative pledge clause. In *Re Holidair Ltd*[170] Finlay CJ held:

---

[165] As amended by C(A)(No 2)A 1999, s 14(b)(i).

[166] See para **[23.053]** at fn 134.

[167] *Re Holidair Ltd* [1994] 1 ILRM 481.

[168] [1994] 1 ILRM 481 at 489.

[169] See Chapter 20, *Corporate Borrowing: Debentures and Security*, at para **[20.074]** *ff*.

[170] *Re Holidair Ltd* [1994] 1 ILRM 481.

'I am however satisfied that he has got a power to dispense with the necessity to obtain such consent which is provided by s 7, sub-s 5 of the Act of 1990...The words in this sub-section "actual or proposed" when attached to the word 'contract' of necessity means that the sub-section applies to contracts already in existence and must therefore include the contract of debenture entered into before the examiner was appointed. There can be no doubt that the portion of the contract of debenture providing for the necessity of the companies to apply for the consent of the debenture holders to borrowing and the stated intention of the debenture holders not to agree to the borrowing which is in issue in this case clearly constitutes a contract and conduct in pursuance of the contract which is likely to be to the detriment of the company and the examiner, I am satisfied, is therefore entitled to take such steps as are necessary to rectify, halt and prevent such effects. This must, it seems to me, include a power provided the sanction of the court for borrowing has been granted to carry out that borrowing without seeking or obtaining the consent of the debenture holders'.[171]

Such an interpretation was not inevitable. This interpretation has, however, now been enshrined in statute. Whilst C(A)A 1990, s 7(5A)[172] restricts examiners' powers to repudiate contracts entered into by the company prior to its being placed under the protection of the court, s 7(5B) specifically excludes negative pledge clauses from this restriction. Section 7(5B) provides:

'A provision referred to in subsection (5C) shall not be binding on the company at any time after the service of the notice under this subsection and before the expiration of the period during which the company concerned is under the protection of the court if the examiner is of the opinion that the provision, were it to be enforced, would be likely to prejudice the survival of the company or the whole or any part of its undertaking as a going concern and he serves a notice on the other party or parties to the agreement in which the provision is contained informing him or them of that opinion.'

Subsection (5C) provides:

'The provision referred to in subsection (5B) is a provision of an agreement entered into by the company concerned and any other person or persons at any time (including a time that is prior to the period during which the company is under the protection of the court) that provides that the company shall not, or shall not otherwise than in specified circumstances—

(a) borrow moneys or otherwise obtain credit from any person other than the said person or persons, or

(b) create or permit to subsist any mortgage, charge, lien or other encumbrance or any pledge over the whole or any part of the property or undertaking of the company.'

[23.070] Not only can an examiner, with the sanction of the court, ignore a negative pledge clause, but he can also borrow money[173]. Where such borrowing is 'certified' by the examiner under C(A)A 1990, s 10, it will have priority to all other claims (including a claim secured by a floating charge) but *after* 'any claim secured by a mortgage, charge, lien or other encumbrance *of a fixed nature* or a pledge': C(A)A 1990, s 29(3A)[174]. This important concession to the holders of fixed security was introduced by C(A)(No 2)A

---

[171] [1994] 1 ILRM 481 at 488.

[172] Inserted by C(A)(No 2)A 1999, s 18.

[173] C(A)A 1990, s 9.

[174] As inserted by C(A)(No 2)A 1999, s 28.

1999; it remains the case, however, that the holders of floating charges – for whose protection negative pledge clauses are primarily intended – may still be prejudiced where subsequent borrowing is certified by an examiner[175]. An examiner's power to borrow is considered further below[176].

De-crystallisation of floating charges

[23.071] Floating charges will crystallise upon the happening of certain events[177]. One such event is the appointment of a receiver to a company. It has been held by the Supreme Court that notwithstanding the crystallisation of a floating charge occasioned by the appointment of a receiver, upon the appointment of an examiner the crystallised floating charge will *de-crystallise*. The effect of this is that the assets which were once the subject of a quasi-fixed charge become once more available for use by the company in the course of its business. De-crystallisation was introduced into Irish law by the Supreme Court in *Re Holidair Ltd*[178]. In his concurring judgment, Blayney J accepted the submission on behalf of the companies under the protection of the court that a floating charge which crystallised on the appointment of a receiver, de-crystallised on the appointment of an examiner. He said:

> 'Once the examiner was appointed, the receiver could no longer act (s 5 subs (2)(b) of the 1990 Amendment Act). It would accordingly have been pointless to keep the book debts frozen. The receiver would have had no right to collect them. Apart from this, since the purpose of the 1990 Amendment Act, as emphasised by the Chief Justice in his judgment, is the protection of the company and consequently of its shareholders workforce and creditors, it would be wholly inconsistent with that purpose that the company would be deprived of the use of its book debts particularly as it appears that they are absolutely essential for its survival during the protection period. Furthermore, it is no injustice to the debenture holders who appointed the receiver since the companies are continuing to trade and so continuing to create new book debts to replace those that may be paid and the proceeds of which may be used by the companies. Finally, it seems to me that if the receiver were to insist upon the charge on the book debts remaining crystallised, he would be in breach of s 5 subs (2)(d) of the 1990 Amendment Act ...' .[179]

The writer finds the reasoning of Blayney J unconvincing[180]. It is clear from C(A)A 1990, s 5(2)(d) that the receiver could not realise the book debts (or their proceeds) which were the subject of a quasi-fixed charge, but he would not have been in breach of the section were he to sit out the examinership and enforce the fixed charge later.

[23.072] In particular it must be asked whether it was necessary to go so far as to say that the floating charge had de-crystallised? It is submitted not. It would not have been pointless to have kept the book debts frozen: the debenture holder would at least have the certainty that he had a fixed charge over a quantifiable sum. The view that the debenture

---

175 On 'certification' of expenses, see para **[23.096]** *ff*; on priority of expenses, see para **[23.077]** *ff*.

176 See para **[23.091]**.

177 See Chapter 20, *Corporate Borrowing: Debentures and Security*, para **[20.086]** *ff*.

178 *Re Holidair Ltd* [1994] 1 ILRM 481.

179 *Re Holidair Ltd* [1994] 1 ILRM 481.

180 For a critique of this decision, see Johnston, *Banking and Security Law in Ireland* (1998), para 13.17.

holders suffer no injustice because new book debts will be created, is open to question on the same basis: on the crystallisation of the floating charge the debenture holder had certainty. It is certain that a company in examinership would not replace book debts as quickly as it would dispose of them. To use one of the purposes of C(A)A 1990 (to protect creditors) as a justification for de-crystallisation seems most misplaced. Whatever about creditors generally, it is certainly not in the interests of the secured creditor in question to de-crystallise his fixed charge. Finally, to introduce the concept of de-crystallisation in the context of a freely negotiated debenture is at best an attack on the freedom on contract, and without specific legislative authority, amounts to judicial law-making. Where a debenture specifically provides that the crystallisation of a floating charge is irrevocable, a court should not, in the absence of express legislation, disregard such a freely contracted condition. The notion that a crystallised charge may de-crystallise has, until 1994, been a concept foreign to Irish law[181]. Without wishing to appear jingoistic, it is submitted that this concept ought to have remained foreign.

Sureties and guarantors

[23.073] During the period of protection, not only is the company itself cocooned from creditors, but so also are persons who guarantee the company's debts. Section 5(2)(f) of C(A)A 1990 provides:

> '...where, under any enactment, rule of law or otherwise, any person other than the company is liable to pay all or any part of the debts of the company;
>
> (i) no attachment, sequestration, distress or execution shall be put into force against the property or effects of such person in respect of the debts of the company, and
>
> (ii) no proceedings of any sort may be commenced against such person in respect of the debts of the company.'

It should be noted though, that s 5(2)(f) does not prohibit the making of a demand on foot of a guarantee. Although the guarantor may be safeguarded from proceedings being instituted, in practice he may think it politically expedient to pay the sum demanded[182].

[23.074] When a scheme of arrangement is put to the court for approval, it may be sought to have the personal guarantees of the company's directors set aside. In *Re Selukwe*[183] Costello J refused to sanction that part of the scheme which purported to release the directors from their personal guarantees because there was no justification for depriving the bank of its security. The reason given for seeking the release of the guarantees was that the new investors did not wish the directors to face possible bankruptcy. In modifying the scheme to leave the personal guarantees in place, Costello J held that such a proposal was not fair and equitable as far as the bank was concerned.

Re Presswell Ltd[184] demonstrates that in certain circumstances the court may confirm the setting aside of directors' personal guarantees as part of a scheme of arrangement. There,

---

181 The concept is recognised in Scotland by CA 1985, s 478(6) (UK). See Lingard, *Bank Security Documents* (3rd edn, 1993), para 9.30.

182 This is especially true of institutional guarantors who may find it embarrassing to resist a creditor's demand on foot of a guarantee entered by them.

183 *Re Selukwe* (20 December 1991, unreported), High Court.

184 *Re Presswell Ltd* (4 November 1991, unreported), High Court, per Murphy J.

one creditor, the Ulster Bank, objected to the examiner's proposed scheme of arrangement because the arrangement involved the bank abandoning, foregoing or losing the benefit of the directors' personal guarantees in respect of the company's indebtedness. For the learned Murphy J the real issue was:

> '...whether these guarantees are of significant value to the Ulster Bank so that the loss thereof would prejudice the Bank unfairly. Undoubtedly this is the very real type of objection which creates a particular problem. It does so where not merely is the liability of the primary debtor reduced or limited to the amount agreed by the creditors and approved by the court but where the carrying of the arrangement would necessarily release those guaranteeing the primary liability. That is one matter to be borne in mind.'[185]

Murphy J recognised that an examiner is not usually in a position to evaluate personal guarantees, because he will only have access to the company's books and records. In *Re Presswell* however, the directors had filed affidavits swearing to the extent of their assets. Although the Ulster Bank filed affidavits setting out their opinion, Murphy J found that in the event of the guarantees being called in, the guarantors would be liable to be adjudicated bankrupt. Murphy J held that the proposals were not unfairly prejudicial to Ulster Bank under C(A)A 1990, s 25(1)(d)[186]. He noted that the directors' evidence as to their assets was uncontradicted and that it seemed to him that Ulster Bank would recover only a modest dividend from the guarantors, perhaps only after protracted proceedings. Even so, one might have though that the beneficiary of the guarantee was the person best placed to say whether or not the guarantee had a value.

[23.075] Section 25A of C(A)A 1990[187] specifically addresses guarantees. In a nutshell, s 25A(1) provides that third parties' guarantees[188] are enforceable notwithstanding that a scheme of arrangement compromises the creditor's recourse to the company, which is the primary debtor[189]. The one exception to the general rule is that it does not apply if the guarantor is a company to which an examiner has been appointed[190]. This is, however, without prejudice to s 5(2)(f), namely, that guarantees, etc still cannot be enforced during the protection period[191].

---

185 (4 November 1991, unreported), High Court at p 9.

186 See para **[23.137]**.

187 Inserted by C(A)(No 2)A 1999, s 25.

188 C(A)A 1990, s 25A is cast wider than just guarantees and applies 'in relation to the liability of any person ("the third person") whether under a guarantee or otherwise, in respect of a debt ("the debt") of a company to which an examiner has been appointed...'. Here, references to 'the guarantor' are intended as a shorthand.

189 C(A)A 1990, s 25A(1)(a) provides that 'subject to paragraph (b) and save where the contrary is provided in an agreement entered into by the third person and the person to whom he is liable in respect of the debt ("the creditor"), the liability shall, notwithstanding section 24(6), not be affected by the fact that the debt is the subject of a compromise or scheme of arrangement that has taken effect under section 24(9).'

190 C(A)A 1990, s 25A(1)(b).

191 C(A)A 1990, s 25A(2)(a). Moreover, it is without prejudice to any rule of law whereby any act done by the creditor referred to in C(A)A 1990, s 25A(1) results in the guarantor being released from his obligations in respect of the liability concerned.

[23.076] Where a creditor opts to enforce a guarantee, any rights he has in the examinership arising from his debt can pass to the guarantor. Where a creditor proposes to enforce, by legal proceedings or otherwise, the obligation of a guarantor he must serve a notice on the guarantor. The notice should contain a written offer to transfer to the guarantor any rights the creditor has, so far as they relate to the debt, to vote in respect of proposals for a compromise or scheme of arrangement in relation to the company: C(A)A 1990, s 25A(1)(c). Strict time limits apply to the sending of such a notice[192]. The usual legal requirements for a valid assignment of a chose in action appear to have been displaced. Where the guarantor accepts the creditor's offer he should furnish it to the examiner at the meeting concerned and the offer will 'operate without the necessity for any assignment or the execution of any other instrument, to entitle the [guarantor] to exercise the said rights'[193]. The transfer of the voting rights (or the voting by the guarantor) is, however, without prejudice to the creditor's right to object to the proposals under C(A)A 1990, s 25. Where a creditor fails to make an offer, as described, to a guarantor he cannot enforce by legal proceedings or otherwise the obligation of the guarantor in respect of the liability[194] unless a compromise or scheme of arrangement is not entered into or does not take effect under C(A)A 1990, s 24(9) and the creditor has obtained the leave of the court to enforce the guarantor's obligation[195]. It should also be noted that where a guarantor makes a payment to a creditor in respect of the liability after the period of protection has expired, then any amount that would, but for that payment, be payable to the creditor in respect of the debt under a compromise or scheme of arrangement that has taken effect, shall become payable to the guarantor on the same terms and conditions as it would otherwise be payable to the creditor[196].

Priority of secured creditors and liquidators' costs, charges and expenses

(a) Secured creditors

[23.077] Prior to the commencement of C(A)A 1990, creditors whose debts were secured by a mortgage or charge over a company's property enjoyed priority over all other creditors where the company became insolvent. As shall be considered below, a scheme of arrangement, which involves the reduction of a secured creditor's claim can be sanctioned by the court.

In addition, it was held in *Re Atlantic Magnetics Ltd*[197] that notwithstanding that a bank or other lender may have a first fixed charge over the company's property, the examiner could, with the sanction of the court, borrow against the company's fixed assets.

---

[192] If 14 days' notice or more is given of such meeting, at least 14 days before the day on which the meeting concerned under s 23 to consider the proposals is held (C(A)A 1990, s 25A(1)(c)(i)(I)); or if less than 14 days' notice is given of such meeting, not more than 48 hours after he has received notice of such meeting (C(A)A 1990, s 25A(1)(c)(i)(II)).

[193] C(A)A 1990, s 25A(1)(c)(ii).

[194] C(A)A 1990, s 25A(1)(c)(iii).

[195] C(A)A 1990, s 25A(1)(c)(iv).

[196] C(A)A 1990, s 25A(1)(d).

[197] *Re Atlantic Magnetics Ltd* [1993] 2 IR 561.

[23.078] The priority of secured creditors to look to the company's assets in satisfaction of their claims was also changed by C(A)A 1990, s 29(3). The costs, remuneration and expenses of an examiner now have, in the words of Murphy J, 'an extraordinary priority'[198] over all other debts of the company. Section 29(3)[199] provides:

> 'The remuneration, costs and expenses of an examiner which have been sanctioned by order of the court (other than the expenses referred to in subsection (3A)) shall be paid in full and shall be paid before any other claim, secured or unsecured, under any compromise or scheme of arrangement or in any receivership or winding-up of the company to which he has been appointed.'

The 'carve-out', contained in C(A)A 1990, s 29(3A)[200], provides:

> 'Liabilities incurred by the company to which an examiner has been appointed that, by virtue of section 10(1), are treated as expenses properly incurred by the examiner shall be paid in full and shall be paid before any other claim (including a claim secured by a floating charge), but after any claim secured by a mortgage, charge, lien or other encumbrance of a fixed nature or a pledge, under any compromise or scheme of arrangement or in any receivership or winding-up of the company to which he has been appointed.'

The original s 29(3) was interpreted by the Supreme Court on a number of occasions. For creditors secured by a floating security, the result is exacerbated by virtue of the fact that virtually any expenditure, including further borrowings, can de deemed 'expenses' where so certified by the examiner under C(A)A 1990, s 10.

[23.079] In *Re Atlantic Magnetics Ltd*[201] Finlay CJ held that the remuneration, costs and expenses of an examiner which are sanctioned by the court, have priority even over a creditor whose debts are secured by a fixed charge. He rejected the submission that C(A)A 1990, s 29(3) affected all security other than a fixed charge. The Chief Justice repeated this view in *Re Holidair Ltd*[202]. There he said:

> '... the true interpretation of s 29(3) is that the remuneration, costs and expenses as defined in that section of an examiner which had been sanctioned by order of the court shall be paid in actual priority to the claims of any secured or unsecured creditor and that under the provisions of s 29(2) the court may if necessary and must if it has sanctioned such remuneration, costs and expenses in a case where unsecured assets are insufficient to pay the total of the amounts involved direct their payment out of secured assets.'[203]

It is for this reason that secured creditors were particularly vociferous in their opposition to petitions to have examiners appointed.

(b) Liquidators' costs, charges and expenses

[23.080] Section 29(3B) of C(A)A 1990[204] provides:

---

198 In *Re Edenpark Construction Ltd* [1994] 3 IR 126 at 133.

199 As substituted by C(A)(No 2)A 1999, s 28.

200 Inserted by C(A)(No 2)A 1999, s 28.

201 *Re Atlantic Magnetics Ltd* [1993] 2 IR 561.

202 *Re Holidair Ltd* [1994] 1 ILRM 481.

203 [1994] 1 ILRM 481 at 490.

204 [1994] 1 ILRM 481 at 490.

> 'In subsections (3) and (3A) references to a claim shall be deemed to include references to any payment in a winding-up of the company in respect of the costs, charges and expenses of that winding-up (including the remuneration of any liquidator).'

This subsection gives statutory effect to the decision of the Supreme Court in *Re Springline*[205] which had reversed the earlier High Court decision of Shanley J[206]. There, it had been successfully argued by the official liquidator of a company that had been under the protection of the court that the examiner's costs, expenses and remuneration did not have priority to those of the official liquidator[207]. In Keane J's judgment for the Supreme Court it was held that the word 'claim' in s 29(3) had to be given its ordinary meaning which it was held included the liquidator's remuneration costs and expenses and so these ranked after those of the examiner. For better or for worse, the matter has been put beyond all doubt by s 29(3B).

[D] THE POWERS OF EXAMINERS

[23.081] A wide range of statutory powers are conferred upon examiners. It is important to note that the acts of an examiner, and so the exercise of his powers, shall be valid, notwithstanding any defects that may afterwards be discovered in his appointment or qualification[208]. Some powers can be exercised unilaterally by an examiner. Other powers can be exercised only with the approval of the court. The following are some of the powers which an examiner may have:

1. To seek a transfer of the directors' powers.
2. To obtain information.
3. To seek directions from the court.
4. To discharge pre-petition debts.
5. To borrow.
6. To deal with charged property.
7. To certify expenses.
8. To regularise improper transactions.

---

205 *Re Springline* [1999] 1 IR 478, [1999] 1 ILRM 15. See O'Donnell, 'Examinerships After Springline – Another Line in the Sand' (1998) 5 CLP 279.

206 *Re Springline* [1999] 1 IR 467, [1998] 1 ILRM 301.

207 Shanley J had held that while the examiner was given a priority by C(A)A 1990, s 29(3) it was 'not a priority in respect of anything other than all other claims against the company whether secured or unsecured'. He had found that the references to a future 'claim' or a future 'debt' could not be argued to refer in any way to the costs, expenses, remuneration or charges of an official liquidator (at p 476 of the report).

208 C(A)A 1990, s 13(5). In the context of the appointment of directors, CA 1963, s 178 makes a similar provision. It has been held in *Morris v Kanssen* [1946] AC 459 that the section only applies where there are procedural errors in the appointment and will not save substantive defects in an appointment.

To seek a transfer of the directors' powers

[23.082] An examiner does not per se have an executive role in the company to which he is appointed and does not have functions akin to a receiver or liquidator. In the words of Murphy J in *Re Edenpark Construction Ltd*[209]:

> 'In the absence of some particular order of the High Court, he may not usurp the functions of the board of directors of the company over which he is appointed and it is the board or its officials who will continue to manage the business of the company during the period of protection and the continuance of the examinership.'

Usually, the directors of a company under the protection of the court will not be asked to relinquish their authority and where the directors have been delegated the power to manage the company's business (as invariably they will where model reg 80[210] has been adopted) they will continue to be the company's managers. However, it is open to an examiner to seek to have the directors' powers transferred to him by order of the High Court as alluded to by Murphy J in the foregoing passage. Where an examiner believes that it is necessary to take over the management of the company, he, and he alone, may apply to the court under C(A)A 1990, s 9:

> 'Contrary to some views, [an examiner] does not take over the running of the company or displace the directors. If he is to do so, then he must apply to the court for such powers under section 9 of the Act. That section makes it quite clear that only the examiner may make such an application'. [211]

[23.083] Section 9 of C(A)A 1990 provides that an examiner may apply to court to seek the transfer to him of some, or all, of the powers exercised by the directors. Section 9(1) of C(A)A 1990 states:

> 'Where it appears to the court, on the application of the examiner, that, having regard to the matters referred to in subsection (2), it is just and equitable to do so, it may make an order that all or any of the functions or powers which are vested in or exercisable by the directors (whether by virtue of the memorandum or articles of association of the company or by law or otherwise) shall be performable or exercisable only by the examiner.'

The matters which the court must have regard to are set out in C(A)A 1990, s 9(2):

> '(a) that the affairs of the company are being conducted, or are likely to be conducted, in a manner which is calculated or likely to prejudice the interests of the company or of its employees or of its creditors as a whole, or
>
> (b) that it is expedient for the purpose of preserving the assets of the company or of safeguarding the interests of the company or of its employees or of its creditors as a whole, that the carrying on of the business of the company by, or the exercise of the powers of, its directors or management should be curtailed or regulated in any particular respect, or

---

209 *Re Edenpark Construction Ltd* [1994] 3 IR 126 at 136.

210 CA 1963, Sch 1, Table A, Part 1, ('the model regulations') in the model articles of association by which the members of a company delegate the power to manage the business of the company to its directors: see Chapter 8, *Corporate Governance: Management by the Directors*, para **[8.004]**.

211 Per Kelly J in *Re Advanced Technology College Ltd* (13 March 1997, unreported), High Court at p 6.

(c) that the company, or its directors, have resolved that such an order should be sought, or

(d) any other matter in relation to the company which the court thinks relevant.'

Where the court grants the order sought by the examiner, it may include such conditions in the order for the transfer of powers as it sees fit[212]. Any powers exercised by an examiner must not be ultra vires the company's capacity[213].

[23.084] Even where an examiner does not seek the transfer of powers to him, he will still be entitled to supervise the management of the company under the protection of the court. Accordingly, an examiner has power to convene, set the agenda for and preside over meetings of the board of directors and general meetings of the members of the company, and he can propose motions or resolutions or give reports to such meetings[214]. In relation to meetings of the members and directors, the examiner is entitled to reasonable notice of, to attend and be heard at such meetings[215]. Reasonable notice in this context is deemed to include a description of the business to be transacted at any such meeting[216].

[23.085] Where an examiner assumes an executive role under C(A)A 1990, s 9 he may enter into contracts which purport to be on behalf of the company. Even where the directors' powers are not transferred to him, he may enter into contracts with third parties. Section 13(6) of C(A)A 1990 provides:

> 'An examiner shall be personally liable on any contract entered into by him in the performance of his functions (whether such contract is entered into by him in the name of the company or in his own name as examiner or otherwise) unless the contract provides that his is not to be personally liable on such contract, and he shall be entitled in respect of that liability to indemnity out of the assets; but nothing in this subsection shall be taken as limiting any right to indemnify which he would have apart from this subsection, or as limiting his liability on contracts entered into without authority or as conferring any right to indemnity in respect of that liability.'

This provision should always be borne in mind by an examiner, but it should also be read in conjunction with CA 1990, s 29 which deals with an examiner's remuneration, costs and expenses, considered below. As a general principle, an examiner must always be cautious not to exceed his power and authority[217].

To obtain information

[23.086] It is essential to the operation of C(A)A 1990 that the examiner is given all of the information he requires. Section 7(1) of C(A)A 1990 provides that any provision in the Companies Acts relating to the rights and powers of an auditor of a company and the supplying of information to and co-operation with such auditor shall with the necessary modifications apply to an examiner[218].

---

212 C(A)A 1990, s 9(3).

213 See *Re Home Treat Ltd* [1991] BCLC 705.

214 C(A)A 1990, s 7(2).

215 C(A)A 1990, s 7(3).

216 C(A)A 1990, s 7(4).

217 *Re Charnley Davies Ltd* [1988] BCLC 243.

218 See, generally, Chapter 13, *Accounts and Auditors*, para **[13.206]**.

[23.087] Section 8(1) of C(A)A 1990 imposes a duty on the officers and agents[219] of the company or of related companies to produce to the examiner all books and documents of, or relating to, such companies. This duty applies where such documents are in their custody or power. This section also provides that such officers and agents must attend before the examiner when required to do so and otherwise to give him all assistance in connection with his functions which they are reasonably able to give. An examiner may also require a person who is not an officer or agent of the company to attend before him and produce to him any books or documents in his custody or power[220]. An examiner also has powers to require directors to produce documents relating to bank accounts[221].

[23.088] Where an examiner finds that officers and agents of the company or related company are unco-operative, he may examine them in relation to the company's affairs on oath, either orally or on written interrogatories[222]. In such a case the examiner may administer an oath accordingly and reduce the answers of such person to writing and require the person to sign them. A refusal by any officer or agent of the company or other person to produce any book or document as required or to attend before the examiner or to answer any question put to him in respect of the affairs of the company can be so certified by the examiner under his hand to the court; thereupon the court may enquire into the case and, after hearing any witnesses who may be produced or any statement which may be offered in defence, make any order or direction it thinks fit[223]. Without prejudice to the foregoing, the court may, after such a hearing make a direction to the person concerned to attend or re-attend before the examiner or produce particular books or documents or answer particular questions put to him by the examiner, or, that the person concerned need not do all or any of the foregoing[224].

To seek directions from the court

[23.089] Section 7(6) of C(A)A 1990 provides that an examiner may apply to court to determine any question arising in the course of his office. Such a power is in practice, very important as an examiner would be unwise to embark upon any drastic action without first obtaining court approval. It is also important to note that a company to which an examiner has been appointed, or any interested party, may apply to the court for the determination of any question arising out of the performance or otherwise by the examiner of his functions: C(A)A 1990, s 13(7).

---

[219] Subsection (6) provides that any reference to officers or to agents shall include past as well as present officers or agents and that 'agents' in relation to a company shall include the bankers and solicitors of the company and any person employed by the company as auditors whether those persons are or are not officers of the company.

[220] C(A)A 1990, s 8(2).

[221] C(A)A 1990, s 8(3). See generally *British and Commonwealth Holdings plc v Spicer & Oppenheim* [1993] BCLC 168 and *Re Polly Peck International plc* [1992] BCLC 1025.

[222] C(A)A 1990, s 8(4).

[223] C(A)A 1990, s 8(5), as substituted by C(A)(No 2)A 1999, s 19.

[224] C(A)A 1990, s 8(5A), as substituted by C(A)(No 2)A 1999, s 19.

To discharge pre-petition debts

[23.090] C(A)(No 2)A 1999 introduced a general restriction on the discharge of pre-petition debts. So, C(A)A 1990, s 5A(1)[225] now provides:

> 'Subject to subsection (2), no payment may be made by a company, during the period it is under the protection of the court, by way of satisfaction or discharge of the whole or a part of a liability incurred by the company before the date of the presentation under section 2 of the petition in relation to it unless the report of the independent accountant contains a recommendation that the whole or, as the case may be, the part of that liability should be discharged or satisfied.'

Where the independent accountant's report does not contain such a recommendation, pre-petition debts cannot be discharged. However, an examiner may apply to the court for an order authorising the discharge or satisfaction, in whole or in part, or a pre-petition liability; the court can only make such an order where it is satisfied that a failure to discharge or satisfy such liability would 'considerably reduce the prospects of the company or the whole or any part of its undertaking surviving as a going concern'[226].

To borrow

[23.091] An examiner has power to borrow monies on behalf of the company under the protection of the court where he has the prior sanction of the court. The basis of an examiner's power to borrow money on behalf of the company is grounded in C(A)A 1990, s 9. This permits the court, on the examiner's application, to transfer any power enjoyed by the directors of the company to the examiner[227]. The court exercised its discretion to transfer the directors' borrowing powers to the examiner in *Re Holidair Ltd*. In that case the judgment of Costello J in the High Court[228] explained that the reason for the examiner's application to exercise the directors' borrowing powers was:

> '...his belief that the formulation and acceptance of a scheme of arrangement under the Act depended on securing a substantial equity investor and that the continued survival of the group in the short term was dependent upon the ability of the companies to fund their current operations for the following 6 to 8 weeks by raising loans'.[229]

Clearly, the court has discretion under s 9 to transfer such a power to an examiner. In the circumstances of *Re Holidair* the foregoing reasons were sufficient to justify the exercise of the court's discretion and the Supreme Court permitted the examiner to borrow.

[23.092] Few but the most altruistic of lending institutions would lend money to a company which is under the protection of the court without a special security. The fact that an examiner has been appointed to the company implies that it has been proved to the satisfaction of the court that the company is unable to pay its debts. Were the examiner with the sanction of the court to offer security to a lending institution, this would still be unsatisfactory because all securities can be set aside either in a subsequent scheme of

---

[225] Inserted by C(A)(No 2)A 1999, s 15.

[226] C(A)A 1990, s 5A(2).

[227] See paras **[23.082]**.

[228] *Re Holidair Ltd* [1994] 1 IR 416.

[229] [1994] 1 IR 416 at 425.

arrangement or in the discharge of the examiner's costs, expenses and remuneration. For this reason, upon sanctioning an examiner to exercise the directors' borrowing powers, the court will often order that the examiner may certify, under C(A)A 1990, s 10, that the sums borrowed are 'expenses' of the examinership. As shall be considered below, the effect of such certification is to give the lending bank priority even ahead of a previously secured creditor[230], subject to the provision in s 29(3A) that certified borrowings will now only rank ahead of a creditor secured by a floating security[231].

In *Re Don Bluth Entertainment (No 2)*[232] Blayney J, giving the unanimous decision of the Supreme Court, held that a loan in US dollars which was certified as an expense of the examinership should be converted to Irish pounds on the date it was repaid. He held that were the conversion made on the termination of the examinership, the lender would not have the loan repaid in full, as required by C(A)A 1990, s 29(3), because the Irish pound had lost value against the dollar since the termination of the examinership.

To deal with charged property

[23.093] Section 11 of C(A)A 1990 enables an examiner, with the sanction of the court, to deal with certain corporate property although it is charged in someone else's favour. It is crucial to distinguish between assets which are the subject of a fixed charge or mortgage and those which are the subject of a floating charge. Although the legislation is not so clear cut as to explicitly draw a distinction between fixed and floating charges, this classification shall be employed here in the consideration of s 11.

(a) Floating charges

[23.094] Section 11(1) of C(A)A 1990 provides:

> 'Where, on an application by the examiner, the court is satisfied that the disposal (with or without other assets) of any property of the company which is subject to a security which, as created[233], was a floating charge or the exercise of his powers in relation to such property would be likely to facilitate the survival of the whole or any part of the company as a going concern, the court may by order authorise the examiner to dispose of the property, or exercise his powers in relation to it, as the case may be, as if it were not subject to the security.'

The effect of this is to enable an examiner to sell assets which are the subject of a floating charge. It is a pre-requisite that the court sanctions the exercise of this power and in deciding whether or not to sanction, the court must be satisfied that to do so would be likely to facilitate the survival of the whole or any part of the company as a going concern. It is important, though, to note that the interests of the holder of a floating charge are not totally foresaken.

Section 11(3) of C(A)A 1990 provides:

---

[230] [1994] 1 IR 416 at 425.

[231] See para **[23.078]**.

[232] *Re Don Bluth Entertainment (No 2)* [1994] 3 IR 155.

[233] The reference to 'as created' implies that a debenture holder may not argue that although the debenture created a floating charge, that the charge had crystallised and is now a fixed charge.

'Where property is disposed of under sub-section (1), the holder of the security shall have the same priority in respect of any property of the company directly or indirectly representing the property disposed of as he would have had in respect of the property subject to the security.'

Whether this means that the holder of a floating charge is to be in exactly the same position as he was in before the power in s 11(1) is exercised is not clear from s 11(2)[234]. Upon the conversion of the property subject to a floating charge to another form of property, it is possible that its value may be less than the value which the debenture holder would have realised had crystallisation happened as envisaged by the debenture. The use of the expression floating *charge* is significant and, it is thought, a floating *chattel mortgage* would not fall within s 11(1).

(b) Fixed charges and mortgages etc

[23.095] The holder of a fixed charge or mortgage fares better than the holder of a floating charge. However, the examiner may also, with the sanction of the court, dispose or otherwise deal with property which is subject to a fixed charge. Section 11(2) of C(A)A 1990 states:

'Where, on the application by the examiner, the court is satisfied that the disposal (with or without other assets) of —

(a) any property of the company subject to a security other than a security to which sub-section (1) applies, or

(b) any goods in the possession of the company under a hire-purchase agreement,

would be likely to facilitate the survival of the whole or any part of the company as a going concern, the court may by order authorise the examiner to dispose of the property as if it were not subject to the security or to dispose of the goods as if all rights of the owner under the hire-purchase agreement were vested in the company.'

The wording of C(A)A 1990, s 11(1) and (2) are not dramatically different. However, what is different is the protection afforded to persons with a security other than a floating charge.

Section 11(4) of C(A)A 1990 provides:

'It shall be a condition of an order under subsection (2) that —

(a) the net proceeds of the disposal, and

(b) where those proceeds are less than such amount as may be determined by the court to be the net amount which would be realised on a sale of the property or goods in the open market by a willing vendor, such sums as may be required to make good the deficiency,

shall be applied towards discharging the sums secured by the security or payable under the hire-purchase agreement.'

The essential difference is that the fixed charge-holder or mortgagee is safeguarded to the extent that the court is empowered to determine the open market value of the property

---

234 See para **[23.095]**.

sold, and to order the company to make good the deficiency to the fixed charge holder[235]. In *Re Atlantic Magnetics Ltd*[236] McCarthy J said:

> 'In the case of a fixed charge, the court may authorise the examiner to dispose of the property as if it were not the subject of the security but requires as a condition of an order that the net proceeds shall be applied towards discharging the sum secured by the security with a provision for its shortfall.'

However, McCarthy J held, as did Finlay CJ, that s 11 does not qualify or restrict C(A)A 1990, s 29 and accordingly, an examiner's costs, expenses and remuneration will have priority over all other claims against the company. This includes a creditor's claim, even where secured by a fixed charge or mortgage[237], save examiner's expenses in the nature of certified borrowings.

To certify expenses[238]

[23.096] One of the most far-reaching and controversial powers of an examiner is to certify expenditure incurred during the period of court protection as *expenses* of the examination. The statutory basis of certification lies in C(A)A 1990, s 10 which provides that:

> '(1) Any liabilities incurred by the company during the protection period which are referred to in sub-section (2) shall be treated as expenses properly incurred, for the purpose of section 29, by the examiner.
>
> (2) The liabilities referred to in sub-section (1) are those certified by the examiner at the time they are incurred, to have been incurred in circumstances where, in the opinion of the examiner, the survival of the company as a going concern during the protection period would otherwise be seriously prejudiced.
>
> (3) In this section "protection period" means the period, beginning with the appointment of an examiner, during which the company is under the protection of the court.'

Even without any judicial interpretation it can immediately be seen that s 10 has the potential for drastic effects. This is seen to be the case when read in conjunction with C(A)A 1990, s 29. For the purposes of understanding the significance of an examiner's power of certification it is sufficient to realise that all expenses, so certified by an examiner, have priority over all other claims against a company, including sums secured by a fixed charge or mortgage and even a liquidator's fees, costs and expenses. In *Re Edenpark Construction Ltd*[239] Murphy J said that to elevate liabilities of the company to the status of expenses, the following must occur:

> '(1) The liabilities must be certified by the examiner to have been incurred in circumstances where the survival of the company as a going concern would otherwise be seriously prejudiced.

---

[235] See *Re ARV Aviation Ltd* [1989] BCLC 664.

[236] *Re Atlantic Magnetics Ltd* [1993] 2 IR 561 at 579.

[237] See para **[23.077]** *ff*.

[238] See generally, O'Donnell, 'Nursing the Corporate Patient – Examinership and Certification Under the Companies (Amendment) Act 1990' (1994) CLP 83.

[239] *Re Edenpark Construction Ltd* [1994] 3 IR 126.

(2) That the prejudice must be foreseen as occurring in the period which commenced with the appointment of an examiner and terminating with the cessation of the protection.

(3) That the certification by the examiner must take place at the time when the liabilities are incurred.'[240]

A number of points contained in s 10 require further consideration.

[23.097] In the first place, not all liabilities of the company can be certified by an examiner. Section 10(1) of C(A)A 1990 is quite explicit in specifying that only liabilities incurred *during the protection period* may be certified as expenses of the examination. Corporate liabilities, such as the cost of the presentation of a petition to have an examiner or interim examiner appointed, are *not* certifiable expenses. This is clear from the decision of Murphy J in *Re Don Bluth Entertainment Ltd*[241] where the fees of the firm of solicitors who presented the petition to have the examiner appointed were held not to be a certifiable expense of the examinership. In the words of Murphy J:

> 'The 1990 Amendment Act does not confer any priority on the costs of persons petitioning for the appointment of an examiner...Furthermore, the general scheme of the Act could not have envisaged the Petitioner procuring a priority for his costs by means of certification under s 10 as ordinarily the examiner would not be appointed until after the expense of the petition had been incurred. It would seem to me to be inappropriate to alter the scheme of the Act by the fortuitous event that a provisional or interim examiner might be appointed and that his certificate would give to the petitioner a priority which the legislation had withheld. In so far as the examiner purported to certify liabilities already incurred, it is clear that the certificate has no statutory effect. In so far as the liabilities related...to contemporaneous liabilities in respect of proceedings for the appointment of an examiner, it seems to me that the certificate is likewise invalid for the reason...that the protection period during which the survival of the company falls to be considered is a period which commences with and postulates the existence of an examiner so that the appointment of an examiner or proceedings for that purpose can have no bearing on the survival of the company during the relevant period.'[242]

It should be noted also that, generally, the costs of presenting a petition to have an examiner appointed to a *related* company will not be liabilities capable of being certified as expenses of the company already under the protection of the court. As Murphy J noted in *Re Edenpark Construction Ltd*[243], during the protection period the company is safeguarded by C(A)A 1990, s 5. Accordingly it could not be said that the failure to appoint an examiner over a related company would prejudice the primary company during the protection period.

[23.098] In the second place, the opinion of an examiner is not sacrosanct. It is subject to review by the courts[244]. The act of certification can be questioned by the court. This is clear

240 [1994] 3 IR 126 at 134.

241 *Re Don Bluth Entertainment Ltd* [1994] 3 IR 141.

242 [1994] 3 IR 141 at 151–152.

243 *Re Edenpark Construction Ltd* [1994] 3 IR 126 at 138.

244 See *Re Don Bluth Entertainment Ltd* [1994] 3 IR 141 and in particular the passage quoted in the preceding paragraph.

from s 29 which by using the word 'may', indicates that the court has a discretion. In *Re Don Bluth Entertainment Ltd* Murphy J said that an examiner should:

> '...exercise great care and professional expertise in issuing certificates under s 10. I would anticipate that an examiner from whom a certificate is sought would require the directors managing the business of the company to submit to him their proposals in relation to any particular liabilities which they proposed to incur and to satisfy him as to how the services or goods to be obtained would benefit the company and in particular how they would contribute to the survival of the company "during the protection period".'

Where an examiner has successfully applied to have the directors' powers transferred to him, he ought to exercise even greater care in certifying liabilities as expenses of the examination.

[23.099] In the third place, even within the protection period itself, the court may refuse, ab initio, to sanction all but certain expenses certified by the examiner. Such an order was made by Murphy J in *Re Don Bluth Entertainment Lt*[245] which prevented the examiner certifying liabilities other than those of certain creditors. This was felt necessary in the circumstances, due to the concern of those who opposed the petition that the motive behind the presentation of the petition was to achieve a position in which the examiner would prefer certain creditors by issuing section 10 certificates.

[23.100] In the fourth place, the manner of certification is important. Although oral certification would appear to have been sanctioned by the courts[246], written certification is to be preferred, from an evidential standpoint if nothing else. In *Re Edenpark Construction Ltd*[247] Murphy J held that:

> '...I would accept that ordinarily the word "certify" does not necessarily connote a document in writing. Where such is required a draftsman would be expected to include the words "in writing". However even accepting that a certificate in writing is not a legislative requirement, one would have thought that it was an obvious and inescapable administrative necessity. Even where written documentation exists in the present case, it is by no means clear that the examiner directed his mind to the essential ingredients of a certificate for the purposes of s 10 aforesaid. In the absence of such documentation it is difficult to ask those creditors whose rights are postponed to accept that the parol certification was correct in its terms and in its content'.[248]

Murphy J went on to hold that the examiner in that case erred in the manner in which he purported to certify the liabilities of the company under C(A)A 1990, s 10. He said that it was significant that:

> '... the examiner states that the liabilities were certified by him "at the time they were incurred" and goes on to say that he did so as he considered they were necessary to ensure the survival of the companies but he does not say that it was his opinion that the survival of the companies would be seriously prejudiced "during the protection period". It seems to me there is a vast different between these two situations.'[249]

---

245 *Re Don Bluth Entertainment Ltd* [1994] 3 IR 141.

246 See O'Donnell, *Examinerships* (1994), who notes that oral certification was given to some creditors in the *United Meat Packers* examinership

247 *Re Edenpark Construction Ltd* [1994] 3 IR 126.

248 [1994] 3 IR 126 at 134–135.

249 [1994] 3 IR 126 at 135.

The difference referred to by Murphy J is between forming an opinion that a company's survival might be seriously prejudiced during a period limited to six or seven weeks, as opposed to during a wholly indefinite period. Another point, which was also made by Murphy J in *Edenpark*, is the importance of an examiner maintaining a clear distinction between expenses which he himself incurred and those which were incurred by the corporate entity, whether or not those are certified by him.

[23.101] Fifthly, and finally, it should be noted that any liabilities incurred by a company during a period of interim protection, granted under C(A)A 1990, s 3A(1) (ie where exceptional circumstances exist as to why the report of an independent accountant is not available) may not be the subject of a certificate under C(A)A 1990, s 10(2)[250].

To regularise improper transactions

[23.102] Once appointed, an examiner has certain duties to the court to ensure that any improprieties in the company's affairs are regularised. One example of this is an examiner's locus standi to make application under CA 1963, s 297A, as amended, in respect of fraudulent and reckless trading[251].

[23.103] Section 139 of CA 1990[252] provides that on the application, inter alia, of an examiner, if it can be shown to the satisfaction of the court that:

> '(a) any property of the company of any kind whatsoever was disposed of in anyway whatsoever, whether by act or omission, direct or indirect, and
>
> (b) the effect of such disposal was to perpetrate a fraud on the company, its creditors or members,
>
> the court can, if it deems it just and equitable so to do, order any person who appears to have the use, control or possession of such property or the proceeds of sale or development of such property to deliver it, or a sum in respect of it, to the examiner on such terms as the court sees fit.'

Section 139(2) of CA 1990 provides that sub-s (1) has no application to fraudulent preferences which are governed by CA 1963, s 286. In deciding whether it is just and equitable to make such an order the court is obliged to have regard to the rights of persons who have bona fide and for value acquired an interest in the property concerned[253].

[E] The Examiner's Report and Schemes of Arrangement

[23.104] Once appointed, the examiner's primary duty is to conduct an examination into the company's affairs with a view to preparing his report under C(A)A 1990, s 18.

1. Examiners' duties.
2. Hearing regarding irregularities.
3. The formulation of proposals.
4. Restriction on compromise of leasing claims.
5. Meetings of creditors and members to consider the proposals.

---

[250] C(A)A 1990, s 3A(8), inserted by C(A)(No 2)A 1999, s 9.

[251] See Chapter 10, *Duties of Directors and Other Officers*, para **[10.081]** *ff*.

[252] See Chapter 27, *Realisation and Distribution of Assets in a Winding Up*, para **[27.092]**.

[253] CA 1990, s 139(3).

6. The examiner's report under C(A)A 1990, s 18.
7. Hearing the proposals: court confirmation or rejection.
8. Matters arising after court confirmation of the proposals.

Examiners' duties

[23.105] An examiner's primary duty is to conduct an examination of the company's affairs and to report with the results to the court. Where he feels he cannot comply with his statutory duties within the prescribed time limit of 70 days, the examiner may apply ex parte[254] to the court for an extension of up to 30 days under C(A)A 1990, s 18(3)[255]. The court will be cautious to grant an extension to the prescribed time limit, particularly when met with the objections of creditors[256].

[23.106] An examiner also owes ancillary duties. In general terms, an examiner must act honestly, reasonably, and with the fullest candour to the court in respect of all matters which on objective criteria could be material. Some of the duties owed by examiners were considered by Costello J in *Re Wogans (Drogheda) Ltd (No 3)*[257]. There, he found that the examiner was in breach of his duties to the court and/or behaved improperly, inter alia, for the following reasons: failing to take reasonable steps to ensure that the court was not misled; failing to inform the company's solicitors of under-the-counter payments to employees, the effect of which meant that the company's liabilities were greater than previously thought by reason of outstanding taxes; failing to bring to the court's notice that the company's statement of affairs was incorrect; failing to enquire into the extent of the under-the-counter payments; failing to disclose to the court that he, the examiner, had acted as an informal interim examiner; failing to disclose that fees had been paid to him for his work as an informal interim examiner; failing to report adequately to the court on legal problems raised by directors' guarantees and the manner in which he dealt with them; failing to inform the Revenue Commissioners of the proposed investor's proposals for a tax write-down; and failing to disclose to the court the prospect that not all of the company's employees were proposed to be retained by the proposed investor[258]. The effects of the examiners' breaches of duties disentitled him to any remuneration, costs or expenses for his work as an examiner[259].

[23.107] It should also be noted that the examiner, or such other person as the court may direct, is obliged within 24 days after the delivery to the Registrar of Companies of every order made under C(A)A 1990, ss 13A, 24 or 27 to cause to be published in *Iris Oifigiúil* notice of such delivery[260].

---

[254] RSC, Ord 75A, r 16.

[255] On extensions of time under the Insolvency Act 1986 (UK), see: *Re Newport County Association Football Club Ltd* [1987] BCLC 582.

[256] Cf *Re NS Distribution Ltd* [1990] BCLC 169.

[257] *Re Wogans (Drogheda) Ltd (No 3)* [1993] 1 IR 157.

[258] See *Re Hartlebury Printers Ltd (in liq)* [1993] BCLC 902 for a consideration of a UK administrator's duty to employees of the company concerned.

[259] This is considered further at para **[23.114]**.

[260] C(A)A 1990, s 30 as amended by C(A)(No 2)A 1999, s 29.

Hearing regarding irregularities

[23.108] Where it appears to the court that there is evidence of a substantial disappearance of property of a company that is inadequately accounted for or of other serious irregularities in relation to the company's affairs, it may hold a hearing to consider that evidence[261]. Such may arise out of the presentation of the independent accountant's report or, indeed, otherwise. To assist the investigative process the court may direct the examiner to prepare a report setting out such matters as he considers will assist it in considering the evidence concerned on a hearing[262]. A copy of any such examiner's report must be supplied to the company on the same day as he causes it to be delivered to the court[263]. Copies must also be given to persons mentioned in his report and, on written application, to any interested party[264]; on application being made to it, the court may direct that there may be an omission of such parts of the report as it specifies in any copy of the report supplied to such persons[265]. Guidance is given, in respect of such omissions, by C(A)A 1990, s 13A(6) which provides that the court may in particular direct the omission of such information as would be likely to prejudice the survival of the company or the whole or any part of its undertaking as a going concern. Section 13A(8) of C(A)A 1990 lists those who have standing to appear and be heard at a hearing[266]. Arising from any such hearing the court may make such order or orders as it deems fit, including where appropriate, an order for the trial of any issue relating to the matter concerned[267] and may direct that an office copy of any such order must be delivered to the Registrar of Companies by the examiner or such other person as it may specify[268].

The formulation of proposals

[23.109] The formulation of proposals is the most fundamental aspect of the examinership provisions. The examiner's report made pursuant to C(A)A 1990, s 18[269] is mandatory in nature. Section 18(1) provides that:

> 'An examiner shall —
>
> (a) as soon as practicable after he is appointed, formulate proposals for a compromise or scheme of arrangement in relation to the company concerned,

---

261 C(A)A 1990, s 13A(1), as inserted by C(A)(No 2)A 1999, s 21.

262 C(A)A 1990, s 13A(2).

263 C(A)A 1990, s 13A(3). Where the company is a company referred to in C(A)A 1990, s 3(2)(a) a copy of the report must also be supplied to the Minister and where the company is a company referred to in C(A)A 1990, s 3(2)(b) or (c) a copy of the report must also be supplied to the Central Bank and in either case C(A)A 1990, s 3(5) and (6) (considered next) shall not apply to such copy: C(A)A 1990, s 13A(7).

264 C(A)A 1990, s 13A(4).

265 C(A)A 1990, s 13A(5).

266 Namely, the examiner, an independent accountant where the court decided to hold a hearing by reason of matters contained in his report, the company concerned, any interested party, any person referred to in the report, and in the case of a company referred to in C(A)A 1990, s 3(2)(a), the Minister, and in the case of a company referred to in C(A)A 1990, s 3(2)(b) or (c), the Central Bank.

267 C(A)A 1990, s 13A(9).

268 C(A)A 1990, s 13A(10).

269 As amended by C(A)(No 2)A 1999, s 22(a).

(b) without prejudice to any other provision of this Act, carry out such other duties as the court may direct him to carry out.'

In *Re Clare Textiles Ltd*[270] Costello J said:

> 'In my opinion, it is quite clear that the only proposals he is permitted to formulate are those which make it likely that (a) the company and (b) the whole or part of its undertaking will survive as a going concern. The examiner has no authority to prepare proposals involving the sale of the company's assets and its business or its liquidation and in my opinion the court has no power to confirm proposals under s 24 which do not provide for the survival of the company and at least part of its undertaking as a going concern...'

As has already been seen, an examiner who proceeds otherwise will be in breach of his statutory duty.

[23.110] Where an examiner is unable to reach agreement with interested parties or formulate proposals he may apply to the court for directions. Thus C(A)A 1990, s 18(9)[271] provides:

> 'If the examiner is not able to enter into an agreement with the interested parties and any other persons concerned in the matter or formulate proposals for a compromise or scheme of arrangement in relation to the company concerned, he may apply to the court for the grant of directions in the matter and the court may, on such application, give such directions or make such order as it deems fit, including, if it considers it just and equitable to do so, an order for the winding up of the company.'

[23.111] Section 22(1) of C(A)A 1990 specifies a number of matters which an examiner's proposals for a compromise or scheme of arrangement must address. Accordingly, the proposal must:

'(a) specify each class of members and creditors of the company,

(b) specify any class of members and creditors whose interests or claims will not be impaired by the proposals,

(c) specify any class of members and creditors whose interests or claims will be impaired by the proposals[272],

(d) provide equal treatment for each claim or interest of a particular class unless the holder of a particular claim or interest agrees to less favourable treatment,

(e) provide for the implementation of the proposals,

(f) if the examiner considers it necessary or desirable to do so to facilitate the survival of the company, and the whole or any part of its undertaking, as a going concern, specify

---

270 *Re Clare Textiles Ltd* [1993] 2 IR 213.

271 As inserted by C(A)(No 2)A 1999, s 22(d).

272 C(A)A 1990, s 22(6) provides what is meant by the interests of members being impaired. It provides: 'For the purposes of this section and sections 24 and 25, the interest of a member of a company in a company is *impaired* if – (a) the nominal value of his shareholding in the company is reduced, (b) where he is entitled to a fixed dividend in respect of his shareholding in the company, the amount of that dividend is reduced, (c) he is deprived of all or any part of the rights accruing to him by virtue of his shareholding in the company, (d) his percentage interest in the total issued share capital of the company in reduced, or (e) he is deprived of his shareholding in the company.' As to the impairment of the interests of *creditors*, see para **[23.112]**.

whatever changes should be made in relation to the management or direction of the company,

(g) if the examiner considers it necessary or desirable as aforesaid, specify any changes he considers should be made in the memorandum or articles of the company, whether as regards the management or direction of the company or otherwise,

(h) include such other matters as the examiner deems appropriate.'

[23.112] It has been noted[273] that the notion of proposals for a compromise is not a new concept in company law and has a parallel in the context of 'arrangements' under CA 1963, s 201.

[23.113] In addition to the matters detailed in C(A)A 1990, s 22(1), the examiner's proposals must be accompanied by a number of other documents. Section 22(2) provides that a statement of the assets and liabilities (including contingent and prospective liabilities) of the company as at the date of the proposals must be attached to each copy of the proposals to be submitted to meetings of members and creditors. Furthermore, s 22(3) provides that there shall also be attached to each such copy of the proposals, a description of the estimated financial outcome of a winding up of the company for each class of members and creditors.

[23.114] In reality, while the foregoing matters will be relevant to any proposals for a compromise or scheme of arrangement, they do not touch upon what is often one of the most important issues: the availability and willingness of an outside investor and the willingness of the company's creditors to compromise their claims. The availability and willingness of an outside investor will be a matter of fact in the context of any particular company. Sometimes investors will be found, but their agreement to become involved in the company will depend upon the inducements offered to them. Potential investors in an ailing company will be even more cautious than they would be if approached to become involved in a new company or a joint venture. The fact that a company is in examinership means, by definition, that the company is unable to pay its debts, ie it is insolvent. Consequently, the probability of an investor coming on board is often slim. Nonetheless, investors are sometimes found and companies which were placed under the protection of the court have been saved.

Restriction on compromise of leasing claims

[23.115] Section 25B(1)(a) of C(A)A 1990[274] prohibits the compromise or scheme of arrangement from providing for the extinguishment or reduction in the amount of rent or other payment due in respect of a lease of land after the scheme is approved. Furthermore, s 25B(1)(b) addresses a failure to pay an amount of rent or other periodical payment reserved under a lease of land or to comply with any other covenant or obligation of such a lease that falls to be paid or complied with after a compromise or scheme of arrangement takes effect. This prohibits a compromise or scheme of arrangement from containing a requirement that restricts the exercise by a lessor of any right whether under the lease or otherwise to recover possession of the land, effect a forfeiture of the lease or otherwise

[273] See O'Donnell, *Examinerships* (1994), p 55.

[274] Inserted by C(A)(No 2)A 1999, s 26.

enter on the land or to recover the amount of such rent or other payment or to claim damages or other reliefs in respect of the failure to comply with any covenant or obligation in such a lease. In both respects, a compromise or scheme of arrangement cannot be modified by the court under s 24 if the result would be as outlined. Again, in both cases, a compromise or scheme of arrangement can only contain such provisions where a lessor or owner of the property concerned has consented in writing to such provisions[275].

[23.116] The application of the foregoing prohibitions is confined to leases of land. However, C(A)A 1990, s 25B(2) provides that:

> '...proposals for a compromise of scheme of arrangement in relation to a company shall not be held by the court to satisfy the condition specified in paragraph (c)(ii) of section 24(4) if the proposals contain a provision relating to a lease of, or any hiring agreement in relation to, property other than land and, in the opinion of the court-
>
> (a) the value of that property is substantial, and
>
> (b) the said provision is of like effect to a provision referred to in paragraph (a) or (b) of subsection (1).'

Some guidance is given to the court in deciding whether the value of property is substantial and s 25B(4) provides that it shall have regard to the length of the unexpired term of the lease or the hiring agreement concerned.

Meetings of creditors and members to consider the proposals

[23.117] Upon an examiner formulating proposals for a compromise or scheme of arrangement, he is obliged to convene a meeting of the creditors and members of the company for the purpose of considering such proposals. Section 18(2) of C(A)A 1990[276] provides for the convening and holding of meeting by examiners. This now provides:

> 'Notwithstanding any provision of the Companies Acts relating to notice of general meetings, (but subject to notice of not less than 3 days in any case) the examiner shall convene and preside at such meetings of members and creditors as he thinks proper, for the purpose of section 23 and shall report on those proposals to the court, within 35 days of his appointment or such longer period as the court may allow, in accordance with s 19.'

Order 75A, r 18 of the Rules of the Superior Courts 1986 details the appointed procedure for the convening and holding of members' and creditors' meetings. The essence of the procedure detailed in rule 18 is that members and creditors should receive proper notice of their respective meetings. With each notice summoning a meeting of the members or creditors the examiner must send a statement explaining the effect of the compromise or scheme of arrangement.

[23.118] Formalities and procedure aside, the usual situation is that at meetings of the creditors of the typical private company placed under the protection of the court, the creditors will be asked to compromise their claims against the company and to accept that what is owed to them will be reduced. Section 23(1) of C(A)A 1990[277] provides:

---

275 C(A)A 1990, s 25B(3).

276 As amended by C(A)(No 2)A 1999, s 22(b).

277 As amended by C(A)(No 2)A 1999, s 23(a).

> 'This section applies to a meeting of members or creditors or any class of members or creditors summoned to consider proposals for a compromise or scheme of arrangement; save where expressly provided otherwise in this section, this section shall not authorise, at such a meeting, anything to be done in relation to such proposals by any member or creditor.'

The purpose of such a meeting is to enable members and creditors to consider the examiner's proposals. Every notice summoning a meeting of creditors or members must be accompanied by a statement explaining the effect of the compromise or scheme of arrangement and, in particular, must state any material interest of the directors of the company, whether as directors or as members or as creditors or otherwise and the effect thereon of the compromise or arrangement, insofar as it is different from the effect on the like interest of other persons[278]. Proposals shall be deemed to have been accepted by a meeting of creditors where a majority in number representing a majority in value of the claims represented at that meeting have voted, in person or by proxy, in favour of the resolution for the proposals[279]. Section 144 of CA 1963 is deemed to apply to any resolution to which C(A)A 1990, s 23(4) relates if passed at any adjourned meeting. A creditor's abstention or other failure to cast a vote in respect of such proposals is not to be construed as a casting of a vote against the proposals[280].

For unsecured creditors, the prospect is often bleak. By agreeing to a compromise they will not recover in full what is due and owing to them. However, where the company concerned is their major or even a prominent customer, the alternative may well be that the company will no longer purchase their goods or services with the result that their interests will be harmed, in any event. The unsecured creditors may, for commercial reasons, vote for a scheme of arrangement. The unsecured creditor may decide to accept a compromise and thereby compromise financial recompense for goods or services rendered, in the anticipation of future business.

Prior to C(A)A 1990, State authorities[281] that are creditors could not compromise claims which were due and owing to them under statute. To do so would be ultra vires their statutory function and power. This has now been changed by C(A)A 1990, s 23(5). Often it will be the Revenue Commissioners who will be asked to bear the brunt of the compromise, the State being the creditor with the deepest pocket. The Revenue Commissioners tend to take a strong line in such cases and unreasonable proposals for a compromise of their claims will be rejected, both by them and by the court.

Secured creditors who have a fixed mortgage or fixed charge are also likely to suffer in a compromise or scheme of arrangement. As has been considered previously, secured creditors can have their previously unassailable security ignored and the proceeds used to discharge claims other than theirs. However, in the circumstances of a particular case a

---

[278] C(A)A 1990, s 23(8). In the case of companies referred to in C(A)A 1990, s 3(2)(b) and (c), without prejudice to sub–ss (1)–(8) of s 23, the examiner is obliged to also afford the Central Bank an opportunity to consider the proposals for a compromise or scheme of arrangement and for that purpose must furnish the Central Bank with a statement containing like information as that referred to in sub–s (8): C(A)A 1990, s 23(9), as inserted by C(A)(No 2)A 1999, s 23(e).

[279] C(A)A 1990, s 23(4).

[280] C(A)A 1990, s 23(4A), as inserted by C(A)(No 2)A 1999, s 23(c).

[281] C(A)A 1990, s 23(5). 'State authority' is defined to mean the State, a Minister of the Government, a local authority or the Revenue Commissioners.

secured creditor may well be of the opinion that it is in its long-term interests to agree to a form of compromise.

[23.119] The company's creditors may not accept all of the examiner's proposals for a compromise or scheme of arrangement. Any modification of the proposals must be agreed by the examiner[282]. It has been, quite sensibly, suggested that where modifications are suggested at the last meeting, the examiner should reconvene previously held meetings to put the modified proposals to those meetings also[283].

The examiner's report under C(A)A 1990, s 18

[23.120] The contents of the examiner's report must conform to C(A)A 1990, s 19. This provides that his report must include:

- the proposals placed before the required meetings,
- any modifications of those proposals adopted at any of those meetings,
- the outcome of each of the required meetings,
- the recommendation of the committee of creditors, if any,
- a statement of the assets and liabilities (including contingent and prospective liabilities) of the company as at the date of his report,
- a list of the creditors of the company, the amount owing to each such creditor, the nature and value of any security held by any such creditor, and the priority status of any such creditor under CA 1963, s 285 or any other statutory provision or rule of law,
- a list of the officers of the company,
- his recommendations,
- such other matters as the examiner deems appropriate or the court directs.

The examiner's report is designed to inform the court of his proposals for a compromise or scheme of arrangement and then to show whether the proposals have been accepted by the company's creditors. Where the proposals are acceptable to the company's creditors, the court's task will be made considerably easier than where the examiner's proposals are rejected by them.

[23.121] The examiner must on the same day as he delivers the report to court, also deliver a copy of it to the company and to any interested party who applies in writing[284]. On the examiner's ex parte application[285], the court will, in an administrative action[286], receive the

282 C(A)A 1990, s 23(2).

283 See O'Donnell, *Examinerships* (1994), p 62.

284 C(A)A 1990, s 18(5) as substituted by C(A)(No 2)A 1999, s 22(d). Where the company concerned is one referred to in C(A)A 1990, s 3(2)(a) or s 3(2)(b) or (c) the examiner must supply a copy of the report to the Minister and Central Bank, respectively: C(A)A 1990, s 18(6) as substituted by C(A)(No 2)A 1999, s 22(d).

285 This application should be grounded upon a verifying affidavit, the contents of which are detailed in RSC, Ord 75A, r 17, as inserted by SI 1991/147.

286 In receiving the examiner's report the court will not be approving or disapproving the report. This was made clear by Costello J in *Re Clare Textiles Ltd* [1993] 2 IR 213 in the context of what was the examiner's 'first report' under C(A)A 1990, s 15 (now repealed). There he said (at 219) of the action of receiving the examiner's report that:

section 18 report without approving or rejecting it and set a date for the hearing of the examiner's proposals. The examiner should confirm in his application that the petitioner has complied with C(A)A 1990, s 12(1)[287], and that he has complied with sub-ss 12(2)[288] and (3)[289].

[23.122] On application being made, the court may direct that there may be an omission of such parts of the report as it specifies in any copy of the report supplied to any interested party who has made written application to the examiner for a copy of the report[290]. Guidance is given, in respect of such omissions, by C(A)A 1990, s 18(8) which provides that the court may, in particular, direct the omission of such information as would be likely to prejudice the survival of the company or the whole or any part of its undertaking as a going concern.

[23.123] Where the 70 days of protection specified in C(A)A 1990, s 5, and any extended period conferred by s 18(3), would expire, the court may under s 18(4) extend the protection period until it has heard the examiner's proposals under s 24. This is to ensure that after the examiner has delivered his report, but before the court has heard the proposals, the company will continue to be protected until the court has the opportunity to either confirm the proposals or abandon the attempt to save the company.

Hearing the proposals: court confirmation or rejection

[23.124] All proposals for a compromise or scheme of arrangement must be sanctioned by the court before they become binding. Even where proposals are accepted by a majority of the company's creditors they cannot become binding without court approval. As soon as the examiner delivers his section 18 report, C(A)A 1990 provides that it shall be set down for hearing as soon as may be after receipt of it by the court[291]. After hearing the proposals and any objections which may be raised against them, the court is empowered by C(A)A 1990, s 24(3) to confirm the proposals. This provides:

---

286 *(contd)* 'The examiner has advanced the argument in support of his present application [for the sanction of the examiner's remuneration, costs and expenses] that the court had "approved" his s 15 report, that it had "approved" the course of action proposed in his s 15 report, and that the remuneration and costs which he now claims were incurred with the court's approval. But this is a misconception of the section. The court neither approves nor disapproves of the s 15 report when liberty to deliver it is given. It has no statutory function or power to express an opinion on the proposals (if any) for the company's survival contained in it. The order giving liberty to deliver the report has no relevance on the present application.'

287 Namely, that the petitioner has delivered notice of the examiner's appointment to the Registrar of Companies.

288 As substituted by C(A)(No 2)A 1999, s 20(1) ie whether the examiner has advertised a notice of his appointment and the date thereof in *Iris Oifigiúil* and in at least two daily newspapers.

289 An examiner shall within three days after his appointment, deliver a copy of the order appointing him to the Registrar of Companies.

290 C(A)A 1990, s 18(7), as inserted by C(A)(No 2)A 1999, s 22(d).

291 C(A)A 1990, s 24(1).

> 'At a hearing under sub-section (1) the court may, as it thinks proper, subject to the provisions of this section and section 25, confirm, confirm subject to modifications, or refuse to confirm the proposals[292].'

Where the court either refuses to confirm proposals under s 24, or, the examiner's section 18 report concludes that following the required meeting of creditors of a company it has not been possible to reach agreement on a compromise or scheme of arrangement, the court may, if it considers it just and equitable to do so, make an order for the winding up of the company, or any other order as it deems fit[293].

[23.125] The effect of the court confirming the examiner's proposals are most far-reaching. As far as the company and its members are concerned, C(A)A 1990, s 24(5) provides that upon the court confirming the proposals, with or without modification, the proposals shall be binding on all the members or class of members affected by the proposals and also on the company. In the vast majority of examinerships, the fate of the company's creditors is more important. Section 24(6) of C(A)A 1990 provides:

> 'Where the court confirms proposals (with or without modification), the proposals shall, notwithstanding any other enactment, be binding on all the creditors or the class or classes of creditors, as the case may be, affected by the proposals in respect of any claim or claims against the company and any person other than the company who, under any statute, enactment, rule of law or otherwise, is liable for all or any part of the debts of the company.'

This is explicit as to the consequences of the confirmation of proposals for a number of reasons. One central reason is that, previously, the Revenue Commissioners felt they were prevented by statute from acceding to requests from companies to write-off or write-down Revenue debts. It is also explicit because the court can, in confirming proposals, deprive a secured creditor of part of its claim against a company and prevent it from realising any security granted by the company over the reduced amount of the claim.

[23.126] Section 20(1) of C(A)A 1990 provides that where proposals for a compromise or scheme of arrangement are to be formulated, the company concerned can, with the approval of the court, affirm or repudiate any contract under which some element of performance, other than payment, remains to be rendered both by the company and the other contracting party or parties. One effect of this is to enable a company to renege on an onerous contractual obligation[294]. An application under this provision may be made by the company unilaterally, but where this is the case the examiner must be served with notice by the company and the examiner is entitled to appear and be heard on any such application[295]. In approving the affirmation or repudiation of a contract under this section the court may make such orders as it thinks fit for the purposes of giving full effect to its

---

292 C(A)A 1990, s 18(8) provides that where the court confirms proposals under C(A)A 1990, s 24, it may make such orders for the implementation of its decision as it deems fit. It should also be noted that C(A)A 1990, s 18(9*)* provides that a court confirmed compromise or scheme of arrangement shall come into effect from a date fixed by the court provided this shall not be later than 21 days from the date of their confirmation.

293 C(A)A 1990, s 24(11), as amended by C(A)(No 2)A 1999, s 24(d).

294 Note, however, that C(A)A 1990, s 25B(1) restricts the compromise of leasing claims. See para **[23.115]**.

295 C(A)A 1990, s 20(4).

approval, including orders as to notice to, or declaring the rights of, any party affected by such affirmation or confirmation[296].

[23.127] The effects of C(A)A 1990, s 20(1) have the potential to cause great loss to other parties. Persons who suffer loss or damage as a result of the repudiation of any contract shall stand as unsecured creditors of the company for the amount of such loss or damage[297]. Unlike the compromise of a financial claim against a company, the loss suffered by a person may not be readily quantifiable. In this regard sub-s (3) empowers the court, in order to facilitate the formulation, consideration or confirmation of a compromise or scheme of arrangement, to hold a *hearing* and to make an order determining the amount of any such loss or damage. The amount so determined shall be due by the company to the creditor as a judgment debt.

[23.128] Section 24(2) of C(A)A 1990 sets out those parties who have locus standi to appear and be heard at a hearing of the proposals. They are:

- — the company;
- — the examiner;
- — any creditor or member whose claim or interest would be impaired if the proposals were implemented;
- — the Central Bank (in the case of a company referred to in s 3(2)(b) or (c))[298].

These are the only specified persons who have an entitlement to he heard by the court at the hearing of the examiner's proposals although the court has a general discretion to hear any person where the dictates of equity and justice requires that person's presence[299].

(a) Substantive objections to court confirmation

[23.129] The hearing of the proposals will become contentious where the examiner's proposals are opposed by the company's creditors[300]. Creditors' objections are likely to be based on the factors set out in C(A)A 1990, ss 24 and 25 to guide the court's exercise of its discretion. Whereas s 25 may be said to contain procedural objections, s 24(4) contains substantive objections which prevent the court from confirming proposals. Section 24(4) of C(A)A 1990 provides:

> 'The court shall not confirm any proposals —
>
> (a) unless at least one class of creditors whose interests or claims would be impaired by implementation of the proposals has accepted the proposals, or[301]
>
> (b) if the sole or primary purpose of the proposals is the avoidance of payment of tax due, or

---

[296] C(A)A 1990, s 20(5).

[297] C(A)A 1990, s 20(2).

[298] As inserted by C(A)(No 2)A 1999, s 24(a).

[299] O'Donnell, *Examinerships* (1994), p 71 notes that in *Re 3V Multimedia Group* (20 August 1992, unreported), High Court, ex tempore, Costello J allowed a proposed investor to address the court on the extent of a modification which the court had made to a proposed scheme.

[300] It is conceivable that the company's members will oppose the examiner's proposals for a compromise or scheme of arrangement.

[301] As amended by C(A)(No 2)A 1999, s 24(b).

(c) unless the court is satisfied that —

(i) the proposals are fair and equitable in relation to any class of members or creditors that has not accepted the proposals and whose interests or claims would be impaired by implementation, and

(ii) the proposals are not unfairly prejudicial to the interests of any interested party.'

This section makes it very clear that the court's discretion is fettered. The court *cannot* confirm proposals where any of the matters set out in (a), (b), or (c) apply. The guiding principle for the court will be that the scheme should be fair and reasonable[302]. Moreover, C(A)(No 2)A 1999 introduced the following further safeguard to the interests of creditors in C(A)A 1990, s 24(4A), which provides:

> 'Without prejudice to subsection (4), the court shall not confirm any proposals in respect of a company to which an examiner has been appointed under section 4 if the proposals would have the effect of impairing the interests of the creditors of the company in such a manner as to favour the interests of the creditors or members of any company to which it is related, being a company to which that examiner has been appointed examiner under section 2 or, as the case may be, 4.'

Notwithstanding sub-s (4) or any other provision of C(A)A 1990, nothing therein shall prevent the examiner from including in a report under s 18, proposals which will not involve the impairment of the interests or members or creditors of the company, nor the court from confirming any such proposals[303].

[23.130] Many of the criteria contained in C(A)A 1990, s 24(4) were considered in *Re Wogan's (Drogheda) Ltd (No 2)*[304]. The judgment of Costello J commences by setting out the broad proposals made by the examiner. The background to the proposed scheme of arrangement is instructive and worth quoting in full:

> 'The scheme involves the investment in the company of a Dublin firm (Dublin Providers Limited) which has successfully traded in the hardware trade in different parts of Ireland. The scheme will involve the purchase by the new investor of the issued share capital and the appointment of new directors (although one former director will be retained as an employee). The scheme will materially affect the interests of the company's two major creditors, one of which is Hill Samuel (Ireland) Limited, which is owed approximately £462,300 which is secured by a mortgage and a fixed and floating charge. The scheme proposed will result in the debts being written down to £235,000 and the revised amount being restructured as a 7-year term loan with a moratorium on repayment of principal for one year, thereafter payments to be made by equal quarterly amounts with interest as specified on the reducing balance. The other major creditor is the Revenue Commissioners. The total due to the Revenue Commissioners on 13th January 1992 was £293,402.71p, of which only a portion was a preferential debt. Under the proposed scheme the preferential amount was to be £82,598. The scheme involved a total payment to the Revenue Commissioners (over a period of years) of £73,467, that is about 25 per cent of the total taxes due. Both the Bank and the Revenue Commissioners voted against the scheme and object to its confirmation. The total debt due to the unsecured creditors is £857,800 approximately. Most of these

---

302 See *Re John Power & Son Ltd* [1934] IR 412.

303 C(A)A 1990, s 24(12) as substituted by C(A)(No 2)A 1999, s 24(e).

304 *Re Wogan's (Drogheda) Ltd (No 2)* (7 May 1992, unreported), High Court, per Costello J.

creditors are small creditors and they are to be paid 10 per cent of the sums due to them. A majority in number and value of the unsecured creditors voted to accept the scheme.'[305]

Costello J refused to confirm the examiner's proposals and he exercised his discretion by rejecting the suggested scheme and refusing to make any modifications[306]. In his judgment he said:

'Having carefully considered the scheme (and the suggested amendments to it during the proposed hearing) and the submissions made, I have come to the conclusion that I should not confirm it (a) because the evidence discloses that there was an abuse of the processes of the court at the time of the original application for protection on 13th January 1992; (b) because confirmation is conditional on orders being made relating to certain taxation issues which I do not think I should make; (c) because there are defects in the scheme which the examiner negotiated with the new investor of such a nature which preclude its confirmation.'[307]

The exercise of Costello J's discretion was largely based on s 24(3) (general discretion) and s 24(4) (specific substantive objections).

[23.131] The first reason given by Costello J for refusing to confirm the scheme was because there had been an abuse of the court's process. He found that the details of the company's indebtedness which accompanied the petition to have the company placed under the protection of the court had been understated. He also found that at least two of the company's directors were aware of the deliberate untruth relating to the debt due to the Revenue Commissioners; and that had the court been informed of the true deficit and that the directors had for some time been consistently defrauding the Revenue Commissioners, it would not have made an order to place the company under the protection of the court. He found that two of the directors who had given personal guarantees had sought the protection order to obtain personal advantage and, in so doing, had abused the court's process. On the jurisdictional basis for his refusal to confirm the scheme, Costello J said:

'... the court's discretion under s 24(3) to confirm, or to confirm subject to modifications, or to refuse to confirm the scheme proposed is not limited by the grounds set out in s 25. If an abuse of the court's processes has been established, I do not think that the court should ignore it and consider on its merits a scheme which had subsequently been prepared. To do so would be to condone the abusive behaviour and encourage similar conduct in the future.

In my view the abuse of the processes of the court in this case is such as to require the court to refuse to make an order sanctioning the scheme of arrangement prepared consequent on an order of the court improperly obtained.'[308]

Only some companies deserve to be placed under the protection of the court. Where a company is not worthy, the directors cannot mislead the court at the petition stage as to the company's worthiness. Where this is done, it is clear that the remainder of the examinership will be tainted.

---

305 (7 May 1992, unreported), High Court at pp 1, 2.

306 It is worthy of note that were it not the case that a majority in number and value of the unsecured voted to accept the scheme, further consideration would have been precluded on the basis of C(A)A 1990, s 24(4)(a).

307 (7 May 1992, unreported), High Court, at p 3.

308 (7 May 1992, unreported), High Court at p 7.

[23.132] The second reason for refusing to confirm the proposals was because Costello J felt he should not make certain orders sought in relation to taxation matters. The new investor had sought a tax clearance certificate from the Revenue Commissioners, who had duly refused to provide him with one. Costello J found the revenue's attitude to be reasonable and refused to order them to do so. The new investor had also sought two specific orders in relation to corporation tax and value added tax. Costello J again refused to make the orders sought because such would be unfair to the Revenue Commissioners and to their further detriment and because the proposed order sought in relation to VAT had not been made clear to him. Because the new investor's involvement was dependant upon the court making the orders sought, Costello J said it followed that the scheme could not be confirmed.

[23.133] Finally, Costello J identified seven defects in the proposed scheme of arrangement, only some of which were capable of remedy:

1. The heads of agreement with the investor were not legally binding. This could be remedied because the investor had accepted that they were binding.
2. The heads of agreement were not made part of the scheme of arrangement and were not produced to the principal creditors until late in the proceedings. This precluded the confirmation of the scheme.
3. The investor's obligations were ambiguous and imprecise. However they were clarified by the investor and so the scheme could be confirmed.
4. The scheme ignored the existence of the directors' two personal guarantees. Such are relevant matters for the court to consider; unless guarantees are extinguished by the court, a contingent liability exists against the company after the scheme is confirmed as the guarantor may enforce his subrogation rights against the company; and the directors voted in favour of the scheme on an erroneous understanding of the law, namely that their guarantees would be extinguished by confirmation of the scheme.
5. It was unacceptable that the proposed new investor could unilaterally withdraw from the scheme or amend the proposed scheme. This was because it is unacceptable to incur the costs of a hearing where the proposed investor may decide not to proceed with the scheme and the court cannot confirm a scheme since it cannot conclude that the scheme as amended is likely to facilitate the survival of the company.
6. One particular creditor's claim against the company was not adequately dealt with by the examiner and it was possible that the creditor could upset the proposed scheme of arrangement.
7. A particularly serious defect was that the investor wished to compel the company's staff to accept a list of wage rates by providing that if they did not agree their employment with the company would be terminated. Costello J said on this point that C(A)A 1990 was not intended to provide investors with investment opportunities.

Notwithstanding that the foregoing list of defects in the proposed scheme were *obiter dicta*, they provide a very useful guide as to what to avoid for an examiner who is formulating proposals for a scheme of arrangement.

[23.134] It was made clear in the first case in which the court was asked to confirm a scheme of arrangement that it was open to the court to confirm a scheme which the court itself had modified. In *Re Goodman International*[309] Hamilton P said of C(A)A 1990, s 24(3) that:

> 'This section appears to me to give absolute discretion to the court in this regard. It is of course a discretion that must be exercised judicially and if the modifications suggested were to fundamentally alter the proposals which had been considered by the members and creditors of the companies, then a court would be slow to modify the scheme in a fundamental manner without having the modifications considered by the members and creditors.'[310]

Often, the court will modify a scheme to provide that it is fairer to the interests of the company's creditors. An example of this is *Re Selukwe Ltd*[311]. In that case the company's two major creditors, AIB and the Revenue Commissioners objected to the examiner's proposals for a scheme of arrangement.

AIB objected to the scheme because the scheme proposed would require the bank to revoke its personal guarantees so that the directors would be freed from any liability on foot of them and the security obtained from the two directors would be nullified. The bank objected to the scheme on the basis that there was no justification for releasing the directors' personal guarantees. This objection found favour with Costello J who held that for so long as the proposals contained that provision they were not fair and equitable as far as the bank was concerned. In this regard Costello J seems to have refused to confirm the scheme on the basis of s 24(4)(c)(i). Rather than simply refuse to confirm the scheme, Costello J exercised his jurisdiction to modify the proposal to read that 'nothing herein will affect the liability of the directors on foot of the personal guarantees to Allied Irish Bank'. He also limited the directors' subrogation rights against the company in the event that their guarantees were called in by the bank. Costello J did not accept that the proposals were invalid because they affected contracts entered into before C(A)A 1990 came into operation.

The Revenue Commissioners objected to the proposals on a number of grounds. These included the following: the directors managed the business without causing the company to keep proper books and records; the directors totally disregarded their obligations to the Revenue Commissioners; they acknowledged the company's true indebtedness to them before presenting the petition; they failed to pay current taxes after presentation of the petition until ordered to do so by the court and they held a creditors' meeting without informing the revenue. Although Costello J held those objections were well founded, he decided that they did not constitute grounds for non-confirmation of the proposals under s 24(4) or s 25. They did however constitute grounds for *modification* of the proposals under s 24(3). Accordingly, Costello J modified the proposals to provide that the directors of the company would cease to act as directors as soon as new directors were appointed.

---

309 *Re Goodman International* (28 January 1991, unreported), High Court (Hamilton P).

310 (28 January 1991, unreported), High Court at p 14.

311 *Re Selukwe Ltd* (20 December 1991, unreported), High Court (Costello J).

[23.135] Costello J's explanation for exercising his discretion is instructive. Having set out the reasons for his concern he said:

> '...the position in this case is such that these considerations to which I have referred are outweighed by what I consider to be the main consideration in this case, namely the fact that there are 30 jobs at stake. I do not think the court should turn down the proposals if there is any prospect of saving those jobs. So notwithstanding the doubts which I have expressed I have decided to confirm the proposals subject to the modifications to which I have referred.'[312]

What is interesting is the prominence of social policy in the exercise of the court's discretion under C(A)A 1990, s 24(3). It is suggested that the survival of the company and some or all of its undertaking, and not the fate of its employees are the paramount matters which should influence judicial discretion.

(b) Procedural and other objections to court confirmation

[23.136] Section 25(1) of C(A)A 1990 provides that dissenting members and creditors can object to court confirmation of the examiner's proposals on procedural and other grounds. These are:

> '(a) that there was some material irregularity at or in relation to a meeting to which section 23 applies,
>
> (b) that acceptance of the proposals by the meeting was obtained by improper means,
>
> (c) that the proposals were put forward for an improper purpose,
>
> (d) that the proposals unfairly prejudice the interests of the objector.'

Irregularity in a section 23 meeting must be material: not every deviation from the correct procedure will justify the court refusing to confirm the examiner's proposals. Examples of irregularity might include not notifying some creditors of the meeting or excluding certain creditors from voting. The ground of objection based on the fact that the acceptance of the proposals was obtained by improper means is wide. This could be invoked where, for example, creditors vote in favour of proposals on the basis of a misunderstanding of their position, encouraged by the examiner. It is thought that the ground stated in s 25(1)(c) relates to where the *examiner* puts forward proposals for an improper purpose, such as to favour the interests of the company's directors.

(c) Unfairly prejudicial proposals

[23.137] Section 25(1)(d) of C(A)A 1990 and the objector's view that proposals are unfairly prejudicial has been considered in a number of cases. In *Re Presswell Ltd*[313], AIB Leasing claimed that particular proposals were unfairly prejudicial to them because as a matter of principle the cost or price of future services should not be waived or reduced; the commercial analysis of what they would recover on a liquidation; and doubts cast upon the availability of a substantial investor.

As to the first ground, Murphy J held that in principle there was nothing special about leasing creditors which would put them outside the scope of C(A)A 1990. However they should constitute a separate class from either ordinary or secured creditors. Further, the

---

312 (20 December 1991, unreported), High Court at p 8.

313 *Re Presswell Ltd* (4 November 1991, unreported), High Court (Murphy J).

fact that their rights extend into the future must always be taken into consideration. The second ground was based on the discrepancy between the value ascribed to the leased equipment by AIB Leasing and the value ascribed by the examiner. On the evidence presented, Murphy J favoured the examiner's judgment. He said:

> 'I approach this matter on the footing that the examiner is an experienced and competent accountant appointed by the court to report on the affairs of this company, as he has done. In that way he is distinguished from an arranging debtor who might bring proposals before his own creditor in ease of himself. The examiner expresses an opinion for the benefit of the court and carries out research to enable the court to impose, where appropriate, a solution on the parties; so I think that an opinion of the examiner is entitled to particular respect.'[314]

In all the circumstances, Murphy J held that the proposals were not unfairly prejudicial to this leasing creditor[315].

[23.138] The impairment of the interests or claims of creditors has been considered in *Re Jetmara Teo*[316]. In that case an examiner claimed that the interests of a secured creditor who would be repaid in full, but by instalments and without interest, were not 'impaired'. Costello J, in interpreting C(A)A 1990, s 22(5), held the secured creditor's interests were impaired[317]. Section 22(5) of C(A)A 1990 provides:

> 'For the purposes of this section and section 24 and 25, a creditor's claim against a company is impaired if he receives less in payment of his claim than the full amount due in respect of the claim at the date of presentation of the petition for the appointment of the examiner.'

The same question arose in *Re Antigen Holdings Ltd*[318] and McCracken J held as Costello J did, that a bank-creditor's interests would be impaired where asked to accept what was due to it immediately, instead, by way of instalments. The judgment in that case arose from an application to approve a scheme of arrangement arising from a company having been placed under the protection of the court. Certain bank-creditors had abstained from voting on the proposals and then had sought to have the scheme modified on the grounds that the scheme was *unfairly prejudicial* to them. The basis of the objection was that although it was proposed to pay off the preferential creditors in 16 months and the ordinary creditors in 18 months, the bank-creditors would be paid off over 30 months. The bank-creditors also objected to the fact that the company's shareholders would be bought-out by an incoming investor ahead of the company's liabilities to the bank being discharged. McCracken J said:

> 'I have to consider whether the banks have been unfairly prejudiced. It is beyond doubt that if the company has to go into liquidation then the banks will receive considerably less than they would receive under the scheme and this is a consideration to be taken into account. But it is not the only one. It has to be said no creditors are getting paid interest. The banks' debt of course is by far the largest proportion of the creditors and they undoubtedly are not being treated in the same way as the ordinary creditors. They are being paid off over a longer

314 (4 November 1991, unreported), High Court at p 7.

315 On the question of whether the foregoing of directors' personal guarantees was unfairly prejudicial to another creditor, see para **[23.074]**.

316 *Re Jetmara Teo* [1992] 1 IR 147.

317 See also *Re British and Commonwealth Holdings plc (No.3)* [1992] BCLC 322, per Vinelott J.

318 *Re Antigen Holdings Ltd* (8 November 2001, unreported), High Court (McCracken J).

> period and there is some validity in their point that interest to a bank is the equivalent to the profit made by an ordinary trade creditor on selling his goods and the trade creditors are in fact getting paid that profit. However the question is; is this unfair?
>
> The purpose of the scheme is to ensure the viability of the company, This can only be done if there is a reasonable time span in which to discharge the debt and that there is an amount being paid which is within the capacity of the company to pay. Now the vast bulk of remaining creditors are trade creditors who are presumably going to continue trading with the company. I don't think it is unfair that should get some priority because they are going to keep the company going.'

McCracken J held that the scheme of arrangement should be approved and that bank-creditors' interests would not be impaired or unfairly prejudiced. The judge did not accept that the payment to the shareholders for their shares in the company was prejudicial to the interests to the bank-creditors. It was said that such would only be prejudicial if the consideration would go to the creditors if it were not paid to the shareholders. It was held by McCracken J that the investor would not acquire the shares unless the shareholders gave the investor warranties and because the court could not insist that the shareholders gave warranties, the sale would not proceed were the warranties not given. Accordingly, it was not within the court's power to ensure that the sale would proceed without the shareholders' assent. It was also accepted that there was a serious danger that the scheme would collapse without the implementation of the agreement between the shareholders and the investors. McCracken J was also influenced by the fact that the company employed over 300 people whose jobs were at risk and the fact that he found as a probability that all of the creditors would eventually be paid – even if there was a delay. Notwithstanding that the bank-creditors might stand to lose £700,000 in interest, the court did not think that they were unfairly prejudiced in the light of the benefits of this scheme if the scheme proceeded. On the question of what is 'unfair', McCracken J followed the approach taken by Costello J in *Re Holidair (No 2)*[319] where he said:

> 'My first task is to consider whether I should confirm the proposals. I have come to the conclusion the court should confirm them. I do not think I can come to the view the proposals are not fair and are in some way inequitable to the revenue and that the revenue are being unfairly prejudiced in some way by them. As I have already said this is a complex commercial situation. The revenue have got some benefits from the scheme of arrangement which they would not otherwise have got in that they are getting paid as preferential creditors some of their debt. Under the proposals a substantial dividend will be paid. In all the circumstances of the case including the substantial debt which the banks had to forgo and the costs which they are going to have to bear, I do not think it can be said that the scheme of arrangement is unfair to the revenue because they are disproportionately disadvantaged in comparison with the secured creditors. I agree that the revenue will have to wait for payment but this is not unreasonable in the difficult situation presented to those preparing this scheme of arrangement. Again I agree that they will not obtain any interest in their debt but I do not think that they are unfairly prejudiced. The undoubted fact which is not denied by anybody is not only would all the creditors be worse off but the 750 employees would be very severely prejudiced if the company goes into liquidation. The court should be very slow to turn down the scheme of arrangement once there is a chance of maintaining the positions of the employees.'

---

[319] *Re Holidair (No 2)* (6 May 1994, unreported), High Court (Costello J).

[23.139] Section 25(2) of C(A)A 1990 limits those who may object under sub-s (1). Accordingly, any person who voted to accept the proposals may not object to their confirmation by the court except on the grounds that their acceptance was obtained by improper means or that after voting they become aware that the proposals were put forward for an improper purpose. Where the court upholds an objection under s 25(1), the court may make such an order as it deems fit, including an order that the decision of any meeting be set aside and an order that any meeting be reconvened[320].

[23.140] Where a scheme of arrangement purports to affect parties who are outside the jurisdiction of the Irish courts, application may be brought in foreign courts for assistance by order of the foreign court that a scheme of arrangement and composition be made binding. Where the foreign jurisdiction is England and Wales, application can be brought pursuant to the Insolvency Act 1986, s 426 (UK). In *Re Business City Express Ltd*[321] Rattee J held that assistance ought to be granted by an English court unless it was satisfied that there was some good reason not to do so. In that case he granted an order which applied Irish law to certain English creditors as to the binding effect on creditors of a scheme approved by the Irish High Court. It should also be noted that the EU's Council Regulation on Insolvency Proceedings[322] can also be invoked by examiners[323].

Matters arising after court confirmation of the proposals

[23.141] After the court confirms the examiner's proposals, the protection period will come to an end on the coming into effect of a compromise or scheme of arrangement[324]. If the proposals are not confirmed or the examinership aborts at any earlier time, the period of protection will cease on such earlier date as the court may direct[325]. Where the company ceases to be under the protection of the court the appointment of the examiner terminates on the date of such cessation[326].

[23.142] Section 27(1) of C(A)A 1990[327] provides that the company or any interested party may apply to the court within 180 days after an examiner's proposals have been confirmed, for the revocation of the court's confirmation on the grounds that it was procured by fraud. Where, upon such application being made, the court is satisfied that this was the case, it may revoke the confirmation on such terms and conditions as it thinks fit. The court must in particular have regard to the rights of parties acquiring interests or property in good faith and for value in reliance on that confirmation. This section has not, to date, been relied upon by any interested party or any company. It is thought that this jurisdiction represents a final safeguard for the rights of all those affected by the confirmation of proposals and is unlikely to be exercised, save in the most extraordinary of

---

320 C(A)A 1990, s 25(3).

321 *Re Business City Express Ltd* [1997] BCC 826.

322 Council Regulation (EC) No 1346/2000 of 29 May 2000; see, also, SI 2002/333, which inserted the new s 1A in C(A)A 1990.

323 See, further, Chapter 26, *Liquidators*, para **[26.055]**.

324 C(A)A 1990, s 26(1)(a).

325 C(A)A 1990, s 26(1)(b).

326 C(A)A 1990, s 26(1)(2).

327 Formerly C(A)A 1990, s 27, but renamed as s 27(1) by C(A)(No 2)A 1999, s 27(a).

circumstances. In view of the fact that there will be many court hearings in an examinership, it is thought that only the most exceptional of cases will disclose, up to 180 days later, that the court was misled.

[23.143] Section 27(2) of C(A)A 1990[328] provides that as soon as practicable after the revocation under s 27(1) of such a confirmation, a copy of the order made by the court shall be delivered to the Registrar of Companies and to the Minister (in the case of a company referred to in C(A)A 1990, s 3(2)(a)) and to the Central Bank (in the case of a company referred to in s 3(2)(b) or (c)) by such person as the court may direct.

[F] THE EXAMINER'S REMUNERATION, COSTS AND EXPENSES

[23.144] The extraordinary priority[329] conferred upon the payment of an examiner's costs, remuneration and expenses by C(A)A 1990, s 29 has been already considered in the context of his certifications of expenses[330]. What remains to be considered is an examiner's costs and remuneration. It is fundamental to realise that the examiner's costs, remuneration and expenses will normally have priority unless the court provides to the contrary. An examiner will ordinarily be entitled to such, unless he acts in breach of his duties[331].

Examiner's costs

[23.145] Ordinarily, an examiner's full costs will be borne by the company under protection in priority to all other creditors' claims. Where the examiner acts in breach of his duties[332], he may be disentitled to his costs: *Re Wogans Drogheda Ltd (No 3)*[333]. Costello J held that the court did not have power to order the examiner to pay the creditors' costs under C(A)A 1990, s 29. However, he considered the Rules of the Superior Courts 1986, Ord 99, r 1(1) sufficiently wide as to give the court jurisdiction to make orders relating to the costs incurred by parties, including creditors, who appeared in proceedings under C(A)A 1990. In the circumstances of that case, Costello J held that the interests of justice did not require him to order the examiner to pay the costs of the aggrieved creditors. He did, however, think that such an order might be made in very exceptional circumstances.

Examiner's remuneration

[23.146] Again, an examiner's reasonable remuneration for work performed will ordinarily be accorded the priority bestowed by C(A)A 1990, s 29. Even where an examiner acts fully in accordance with his duties, the court may disallow his claimed remuneration where such is seen to be excessive. In *Coombe Importers Ltd*[334] Hamilton CJ said:

---

328 Inserted by C(A)(No 2)A 1999, s 27(b).

329 See Murphy J in *Re Edenpark Construction Ltd* [1994] 3 IR 126 at 133.

330 See para **[23.096]** *ff*.

331 See para **[23.106]**.

332 *Re Edenpark Construction Ltd* [1994] 3 IR 126.

333 *Re Wogans Drogheda Ltd (No 3)* [1993] 1 IR 157.

334 *Coombe Importers Ltd* (22 June 1995, unreported), Supreme Court (Hamilton CJ).

> 'There is no doubt that the court has jurisdiction to review and disallow the remuneration, costs and expenses of the examiner and in view of the priority given to such remuneration, costs and expenses there is an obligation on the court to be vigilant in scrutinising an examiner's application for sanction of payment'.[335]

In that case the court allowed reasonable remuneration, legal costs and most but not all expenses. What is considered excessive remuneration will depend upon the circumstances of each case. In *Re Don Bluth Entertainment Ltd*[336] Murphy J commented (in 1993) that the figure of £145 per hour was probably the highest hourly charge proposed by an accountant for services of that nature at that time. In the circumstances of that case, and in view of the fact that it was an important case involving enormous sums and an exceptional business with a large and highly-qualified labour force, Murphy J held that the examiner's fees were justified, especially in view of the fact that one of the company's major creditors did not object to the level of the examiner's fees[337].

Where the examiner ought to have concluded the examinership at a time when it was apparent that the company was not capable of surviving as a going concern, it has been held that the examiner will only be entitled to his remuneration (and costs) up to the time when he ought to have ceased acting as examiner[338].

Examiner's expenses

[23.147] An examiner's expenses and the certification of such expenses has been considered above[339].

---

335 (22 June 1995, unreported), Supreme Court at p 6.

336 *Re Don Bluth Entertainment Ltd* [1994] 3 IR 141.

337 [1994] 3 IR 141. See also *Re Irish Press Newspapers Ltd,* an application reported in (1995) The Irish Times, 27 October wherein Murphy J questioned an examiner's fees and sought an analysis of the hours worked.

338 *Re Clare Textiles Ltd* [1993] 2 IR 213.

339 See para **[23.096]** *ff.*

Chapter 24

Schemes of Arrangement and Reconstructions

Introduction

[24.001] Schemes of arrangement and compromises were a feature of Irish company law long before the passing of the Companies (Amendment) Act 1990 ('C(A)A 1990'), which gave birth to the examinership process. Section 201 of CA 1963 contains a procedure whereby claims against a company can be compromised or arrangements made by the company with its members or creditors. These schemes of arrangement are the concern of Section A[1]. Another option, available only to a company that is in, or proposes to be in, voluntary liquidation[2], is a reconstruction pursuant to CA 1963, s 260. Reconstructions are treated in Section B.

[A] Schemes of Arrangement

[24.002] In this section the following issues are considered:

1. The circumstances when CA 1963, s 201 can be utilised.
2. Examinership distinguished.
3. The meaning of 'company', 'creditors' and 'members'.
4. The meaning of 'arrangement', 'compromise' and 'between'.
5. Limitations to schemes of arrangement.
6. Meetings of members and creditors.
7. Court sanction.
8. Judicial powers to assist schemes in contemplation of reconstruction.
9. Setting aside a scheme for fraud.

The circumstances when CA 1963, s 201 can be utilised

[24.003] The Companies Acts confer a wide array of statutory rights on companies' members and creditors. Where it is proposed to compromise the rights of either members or creditors or enter into an arrangement, the effect of which will be to vary their strict rights, CA 1963, ss 201–203 may be used to formalise the proposals even where there is not unanimous consent by either members or creditors. These provisions provide a structure for negotiation of a scheme for either or both the rearrangement of a company's

---

1 See, generally, Lynch, Marshall & O'Ferrall, *Corporate Insolvency and Rescue* (1996), p 318; Clarke, *Takeovers and Mergers Law in Ireland* (1999), p 250, Morse et al (eds), *Palmer's Company Law* (25th edn, 1992; loose leaf), p 12009; Sealy et al (eds), *British Company Law and Practice* (1983; loose leaf) at 68,001 and Lingard, *Corporate Rescues and Insolvencies* (2nd edn, 1989), Ch 5.

2 As to which, see Chapter 25, *Winding Up Companies*, para **[25.002]** *ff*.

capital structure amongst its members and the rearrangement (including compromise) of a company's obligations and liabilities to its creditors. Upon application being made to the court, CA 1963, s 201 empowers it to order the convening and holding of meetings of creditors or members and, where a majority representing 75% in value at those meetings approve of the scheme, to subsequently order that the scheme be binding – even on dissenting, absent or untraceable members or creditors.

[24.004] A relatively recent Irish example of such a scheme of arrangement is seen in *Re McInerney Properties plc*[3]. There it was reported in *The Irish Times* that Costello J made an order under CA 1963, s 201(3), sanctioning a scheme of arrangement that had earlier been approved at meetings of creditors and members of the well-known Irish property company[4]. The company was the parent in a group of companies which, although at the time of the application traded at a small profit, had incurred substantial losses in previous years sustained in the English property development market and certain leisure developments in Spain and Portugal. Because of the losses, several members of the group had been placed into liquidation. It was reported that since the group was not trading in profit in respect of its core activities, accrued losses and liabilities had an adverse impact on its financial position and threatened the survival of the group unless appropriately restructured. Under the scheme of arrangement that had been approved by its members and creditors a new company, McInerney Holdings plc, had been incorporated with a nominal share capital of £3.5 million, and it intended to raise new equity finance of £6 million. The scheme involved the 'A' ordinary shares in the old company being exchanged for shares in the new company at the rate of 18.75 ordinary shares of 10 pence each in the new company for every 1,000 'A' ordinary shares in the old company. It was also reported that the Revenue Commissioners were to be paid in full at what were described as 'ordinary trade creditors'; certain unspecified creditors were to receive payments in cash at an approximate rate of 7 pence in the pound and other creditors were to receive shares in the new company at a similar rate.

[24.005] Statutory schemes of arrangement can be utilised in many other circumstances too: the merger of two or more companies, the sub-division of a company into two or more companies, certain takeovers and other amalgamations[5]. Care must be taken, however, not to abuse the statutory mechanism contained in CA 1963, ss 201–203 by, for example, attempting to compulsorily acquire the shareholding of dissenting shareholders in circumstances where there is not an 80% majority since such cases are properly brought under CA 1963, s 204[6].

---

3 An application reported in (1996) The Irish Times, 18 December (Costello J).

4 One is reminded of Lingard's comment that 'some of the major companies now listed on the Stock Exchange have in the past suffered the indignity of a scheme of arrangement!': Lingard, *Corporate Rescues and Insolvencies* (2nd edn, 1989), p 49.

5 See generally, Morse et al (eds), *Palmer's Company Law* (25th edn, 1992; loose leaf), pp 12009–12013. On takeovers and mergers, see further Clarke, *Takeovers and Mergers Law in Ireland* (1999), p 248.

6 *Re National Bank* [1966] 1 WLR 819 and *Re Hellenic & General Trust Ltd* [1976] 1 WLR 123. On compulsory purchase of dissenting shareholders' shares, see further Chapter 16, *Share Transfers in Private Companies*, para **[16.080]**.

Examinership distinguished

[24.006] The end result of either an examinership under the C(A)A 1990 and the procedure envisaged by CA 1963, ss 201–203 may be similar: a scheme of arrangement that is sanctioned by the court and is binding. There are, however, a great many differences[7]. First, each procedure is initiated in a very different way. In the case of an examinership, an independent officer of the court, an examiner, must be appointed by the court to put together proposals for a scheme of arrangement. In the case of a scheme put together under CA 1963, ss 201–203, the scheme is largely formulated in advance of court involvement and by the company itself (with, of course, professional advice and assistance). Secondly, the requirement for at least 75% in value of members and creditors to approve of a scheme of arrangement under CA 1963, ss 201–203 affords all parties with greater protection than in an examinership. Thirdly, under CA 1963, s 201(2) the court is empowered to stay all proceedings and restrain further proceedings against a company in respect of which application is made 'for such period as to the court seems fit'.

The meaning of 'company', 'creditors' and 'members'

(a) Company

[24.007] Section 201 of CA 1963 is expressly concerned with compromises or arrangements between a *company* and its *creditors* or between a *company* and its *members*. As far as the reference to 'company' is concerned, this is defined by CA 1963, s 201(7) to mean 'any company liable to be wound up under this Act'. Since a foreign company can in certain circumstances be wound up by the High Court, this is wider definition of 'company' to that contained in CA 1963, s 2[8].

(b) Members

[24.008] The reference to 'members' means to persons who were either an original subscriber to the memorandum of association or persons who have agreed to become members and whose names have been entered on the register of members[9]. It is opined that an option holder is not a 'member' for these purposes. Until such time as a person, even one who has paid valuable consideration for shares in a company, has been registered as a member, it is thought that they cannot be included in a scheme of arrangement pursuant to CA 1963, ss 201–203.

(c) Creditors: ordinary, secured and preferential

[24.009] All classes of creditor may be affected (and bound) by a court sanctioned scheme of arrangement. It has been held that the reference to 'creditors' ought to be widely construed[10], but it has been held too that a person who has relied upon a letter of comfort from a company is not a 'creditor' for the purposes of a scheme of arrangement[11]. A 'creditor' is any person with a pecuniary claim against the company, whether actual or contingent. A person with an unliquidated claim in tort against a company has been

---

7 See Lynch, Marshall & O'Ferrall, *Corporate Insolvency and Rescue* (1996), p 329.

8 See Chapter 25, *Winding Up Companies*, para **[25.031]**.

9 See Chapter 15, *Shares and Membership*, para **[15.017]**.

10 See *Re Midland Coal, Coke and Iron Co* [1895] 1 Ch 267.

11 *Re Atlantic Computers plc (in admin); National Australia Bank Ltd v Soden* [1995] BCC 696.

considered to be a creditor[12]. It has been said that the only workable test of who is a creditor, is any person who has the right to prove in a winding up[13].

[24.010] It should be noted that dissenting secured creditors can be bound by a scheme: *Re Alabama, New Orleans, Texas and Pacific Junction Railway Co*[14]. Lingard astutely observes, however:

> 'Secured creditors cannot usually be lumped together in one class because each will have different security which differently affects his judgment. Some secured creditors may be acutely conscious that their security is of little value; others may know that they are fully secured. Some secured creditors may have security which is readily saleable; others may know that it will be some time before they can realise their security.'[15]

[24.011] It was held in *Re Pye (Ireland) Ltd; Hogan*[16] that the Revenue Commissioners' claims against a company ought not to be compromised. Costello J said:

> 'The court should not regard the Collector-General as just another creditor similar to other creditors; he is charged with the collection of monies due to the State. In this case I do not think that the Collector-General should be required to surrender for the benefit of other creditors contingently money owed to the public. The debt owed to the State in respect of VAT, PRSI, PAYE and Customs and Excise is at least £522,000. In those circumstances if the Collector General has decided that this scheme is not in the public interest' I should be very slow indeed to order these meetings given the opposition of the Collector General. I see no reason to order this scheme to proceed.'[17]

It should be noted that any doubts as to the Revenue Commissioners' powers to compromise debts owed by companies in an examinership under C(A)A 1990 have been dispelled by statute[18]. It is thought that a similar declaratory provision could usefully be introduced in respect of CA 1963, s 201 schemes of arrangement and compromises.

The meaning of 'arrangement', 'compromise' and 'between'

[24.012] Not every proposal between a company and its creditors or its members, can be sanctioned by the court under CA 1963, ss 201–203. The legislation refers specifically only to an 'arrangement' and a 'compromise' 'between' a company and its members or creditors. The legislation itself gives little guidance as to the definition of these terms, although CA 1963, s 201(7) does provide that 'arrangement' 'includes a reorganisation of shares of different classes or by the division of shares into shares of different classes or by both those methods.'

---

12 See Sealy et al (eds), *British Company Law and Practice* (1983; loose leaf) at 68,152 where the Australian case of *Re RL Child & Co Pty Ltd* is cited as authority on this point and *Trocko v Renlita Products Pty Ltd* (1973) 5 SASR 207 is distinguished.

13 *Re North Bucks Furniture Depositories Ltd* [1939] 2 All ER 549-551. See also *National Australia Bank Ltd v Market Holdings Pty Ltd* (26 October 2000) Supreme Court of New South Wales.

14 *New Orleans, Texas and Pacific Junction Railway Co* [1981] 1 Ch 213.

15 Lingard, *Corporate Rescues and Insolvencies* (2nd edn, 1989), para 5.30.

16 *Re Pye (Ireland) Ltd; Hogan* (12 November 1984, unreported), High Court, Irish Company Law Reports 320.

17 Irish Company Law Reports 320 at 322.

18 See Chapter 23, *Examinerships*, para **[23.125]**.

This is not an exhaustive definition of 'arrangement' which merely 'includes' the foregoing. One can approach the definition of 'arrangement' and 'compromise' from the perspective of their ordinary meaning and conclude that 'a "compromise" is an adjustment of conflicting interests by a modification of each and an "arrangement" is a putting into order or a settlement of a dispute'[19]. Case law on the definition of 'compromise' shows that in order for there to be a compromise, there must first be a dispute[20]. Although it was held in *Mercantile Investment and General Trust Co v International Co of Mexico*[21] that the giving up of a secured debenture in exchange for a preference share 'in the absence of all disputes as to the rights of the creditor, of all difficulty in enforcing those rights, and of any suggestion that the full fruits of these rights could not be obtained'[22] was not a compromise, Fry LJ found such to be capable of being described as an arrangement.

[24.013] Section 201 of CA 1963 can be invoked where a company proposes to enter into an amicable arrangement by way of reconstruction. It is not necessary for the company to propose to compromise claims against it. This was made clear in *Re Guardian Assurance Company*[23]. At first instance, Younger J had held that, although the scheme was advantageous to the interests of the company, he would refuse to sanction it because the section necessarily involved some kind of dispute or difficulty to be resolved by a compromise or arrangement and that this was absent in the case in hand. The Court of Appeal reversed this finding. Lord Cozens-Hardy MR held that the arrangement proposed between the company and its members was in good faith, that a dispute was not necessary and that the section applied to any compromise or arrangement.

[24.014] An example of a proposal that was found not to be an arrangement or compromise is seen in *Re NFU Development Trust Ltd*[24]. In that case the company concerned was a guarantee company with the main object of encouraging and assisting the production of fatstock and other livestock. The costs in administering the company, which had 94,000 members, were considered to be prohibitive: the cost of maintaining the register, posting accounts and other related administrative matters was in excess of £11,000. A scheme of arrangement was proposed whereby the only members would be a company which represented the farmers, and six other nominees would represent the interests of various English farmers' unions. In consequence it was proposed that all other members would forfeit all membership rights and cease to be members. Although nearly 85% of the members approved of the scheme the court refused to sanction it because it was held that the proposal was neither an 'arrangement' nor a 'compromise'. Brightman J held:

> 'The word "compromise" implies some element of accommodation on each side. It is not apt to describe total surrender. A claimant who abandons his claim is not compromising it. Similarly, I think that the word "arrangement" in this section implies some element of give and take. Confiscation is not my idea of an arrangement'.

---

19 Sealy et al (eds), *British Company Law and Practice* (1983; loose leaf) at 68,003.

20 *Snead v Valley Gold Ltd* [1893] 1 Ch 477.

21 *Mercantile Investment and General Trust Co v International Co of Mexico* [1893] 1 Ch 484.

22 [1893] 1 Ch 484 at 491.

23 *Re Guardian Assurance Company* [1917] 1 Ch 431.

24 *Re NFU Development Trust Ltd* [1972] 1 WLR 1548.

The requirement of 'give and take' is also seen in the case of *Re Alabama, New Orleans, Texas and Pacific Junction Railway Co*[25], which additionally stressed the need for schemes of arrangement to be reasonable[26]. Indeed, Nourse J said[27] of *Re NFU Development Trust Ltd* that 'all that that case shows is that there must be some element of give and take. Beyond that it is neither necessary nor desirable to attempt a definition of "arrangement"'.

In *Commissioners of Inland Revenue v Adam & Partners Ltd*[28] the English Court of Appeal held that, having the requisite element of give and take, a moratorium on the prosecution of claims by creditors qualified as a 'scheme of arrangement'.

[24.015] The necessity for arrangements to be 'between' a company and its members was considered in *Re Savoy Hotel Ltd*[29]. In that case a company's share capital was divided into 'A' shares and 'B' shares which ranked pari passu in all respects save that the 'B' shares carried 40- times as many votes as the 'A' shares. In consequence, the 'A' shareholders were entitled to 51.45% of the votes whilst the 'B' shareholders were entitled to 48.55% of the votes notwithstanding that the 'A' shareholders held 97.7% of the equity in the company, the 'B' shareholders holding the remaining 2.3%. Furthermore, 65.26% of the 'B' shares which carried 31.68% of the votes were held either beneficially or in trust *by* the members of the board. The applicant, an 'A' shareholder who held 88,000 shares, wished to gain control of the company by means of a scheme of arrangement. Among the issues decided by Nourse J was whether the rights and obligations existing between the company and its members would be sufficiently affected by the proposed scheme for it to constitute an arrangement 'between' the company and its members. The company, which opposed the proposed scheme, had submitted that the scheme was outside the statutory provisions because it was not one 'between' the company and its members or any class of them since it did not propose to materially affect the rights and obligations existing between the company and its members. Nourse J rejected this contention and found that it was not necessary that the rights and obligations existing between the company and its members should be 'materially affected, if by that is meant that there should be something more material or more substantial than there is in the present case'[30].

In so finding Nourse J relied upon the decision in *Singer Manufacturing Co v Robinow*[31], where the same point had been made on a transfer scheme of the same general nature. To the argument that the scheme was not one between the company and its members but a sale between two members Lord Clyde said:

> 'This contention is unwarranted...the company had a very direct interest in the arrangement. If the arrangement was sanctioned by the court, they came under obligation...on being satisfied that the consideration…had been paid...forthwith to register...the shares in respect of which the consideration has been so paid. The courts have always interpreted section 206 [of the Companies Act 1948 (UK)] and its statutory predecessors broadly, so as to enable a

[25] *Re Alabama, New Orleans, Texas and Pacific Junction Railway Co* [1891] 1 Ch 213.

[26] See para **[24.044]**.

[27] In *Re Savoy Hotel Ltd* [1981] 1 Ch 351 at 359.

[28] *Commissioners of Inland Revenue v Adam & Partners Ltd* [2001] 1 BCLC 222.

[29] *Re Savoy Hotel Ltd* [1981] 1 Ch 351, [1981] 3 All ER 646.

[30] [1981] 1 Ch 351 at 361h.

[31] *Singer Manufacturing Co v Robinow* (1971) SC 11.

wide variety of different types of arrangements to be put forward, and it seems to us clear that the present scheme falls within what is competent to achieve under that section. The arrangement is an arrangement between the petitioning company and "its members or any class of them" within the meaning of section 206.'[32]

Support for the decision also appears in *Re Guardian Assurance Co*[33]. So too is there authority for this position in *Re Odhams Press Ltd*[34], where Eve J said that a scheme between classes of shareholders was a scheme inter socios but, for that, was none the less a scheme within the contemplation of the legislation.

Limitations to schemes of arrangement

[24.016] In order to avail of the provisions in CA 1963, ss 201–203, applicants must meet certain requirements:

(a) The applicant must have locus standi.

(b) The company must support the application.

(c) Schemes must not be contrary to law or ultra vires.

(d) Where capital is reduced the normal rules apply.

(e) Where relevant, there must be compliance with the rules of the Irish Takeover Panel.

(a) The applicant must have locus standi

[24.017] As shall be considered below[35], the statutory procedure involves application being made to the court under CA 1963, s 201(1) for the purpose of ordering a meeting or meetings of creditors or members to be summoned as directed. Section 201(1) of CA 1963 provides that application may be brought by:

— the company,

— any creditor of the company,

— any member of the company, or, in the case of a company being wound up, by

— the liquidator of a company.

(b) The company must support the application

[24.018] Although CA 1963, ss 201–203 are silent on the point, it has been decided that the court cannot sanction an arrangement that does not have the approval of the company concerned. This was decided in *Re Savoy Hotel Ltd*[36], the facts of which have been given above[37]. In that case the company's board of directors did not favour the proposed scheme of arrangement and withheld the company's consent to it. Nourse J held:

> '...the court has no jurisdiction to sanction an arrangement under section 206 [of the Companies Act 1948 (UK)] which does not have the approval of the company either through

32 (1971) SC 11 at 13–14.

33 *Re Guardian Assurance Co* [1917] 1 Ch 431.

34 *Re Odhams Press Ltd* [1924] WN 10.

35 See para **[24.023]**.

36 *Re Savoy Hotel Ltd* [1981] 1 Ch 351, [1981] 3 All ER 646.

37 See para **[24.015]**.

> the board or, if appropriate, by means of a simple majority of the members in general meeting.'[38]

Although the statutory provisions clearly require the consent of at least 75% in value of a company's members and creditors, because the company is itself a separate legal entity with its own rights (which can be adversely affected by a scheme), the requirement that it is agreeable to a scheme of arrangement is implied.

[24.019] Where a company is in liquidation, its liquidator must also approve of the scheme of arrangement[39].

(c) Schemes must not be contrary to law or ultra vires

[24.020] The general rule is that any proposed scheme of arrangement or compromise must not be contrary to law or ultra vires the company concerned. So in *Re Oceanic Steam Navigation Co Ltd*[40] Simonds J said:

> 'The question then is whether, under [the statutory provision], the company can make and the court sanction an arrangement which is in excess of the corporate powers as defined by the memorandum. There is nothing in the language of [the statutory provision] which even remotely suggests such a conclusion. It contemplates a compromise or arrangement between a company and its creditors or any class of them or its members or any class of them, and provides machinery whereby such a compromise or arrangement may be made binding on dissenting persons by an order of the court. I find nothing here which would indicate that the company can effect an arrangement which would be otherwise ultra vires…'[41].

There have been exceptions made to this general rule[42]. It is thought that where an arrangement is approved which is ultra vires it will generally be the result of an oversight, occasioned by a general consensus amongst the company and its members and creditors that the scheme of arrangement is desirable. It is very hard to see how, if met with an objection on the grounds of ultra vires, a court could sanction such a scheme, particularly since a member or secured creditor has locus standi to apply for an injunction to restrain the commission of an ultra vires act[43].

(d) Where capital is reduced the normal rules apply

[24.021] Where a scheme of arrangement involves the reduction of a company's capital, the requirements in CA 1963, s 72 must be complied with[44]. This was established in *Re Cooper, Cooper & Johnson Ltd*[45] where Byrne J held that where a scheme of arrangement

---

38 [1981] 1 Ch 351 at 366. Nourse J relied, inter alia, upon *Re International Contract Co (Hankey's Case)* (1872) 26 LT 358, 20 WR 506.

39 *Re International Contract Co (Hankey's Case)* (1872) 26 LT 358, 20 WR 506 and *Re Savoy Hotel Ltd* [1981] 1 Ch 351, [1981] 3 All ER 646.

40 *Re Oceanic Steam Navigation Co Ltd* [1939] Ch 41.

41 [1939] Ch 41 at 47. See also *Re Skinner* [1958] 3 All ER 273.

42 Eg, see *Barclays Bank plc v British & Commonwealth Holdings plc* [1996] 1 WLR 1, [1995] BCC 1,059 where the Court of Appeal held that an arrangement which was possibly ultra vires was not open to challenge once approved by the court.

43 CA 1963, s 8(2).

44 See Chapter 3, *Private Constitutional Documentation*, para **[3.045]**.

45 *Re Cooper, Cooper & Johnson Ltd* [1902] WN 119.

involved a reduction of capital, the reduction should be carried out in accordance with the statute specifically dealing with such[46]. Where a proposal will involve a reduction in capital, the applications may be brought in double-harness, under CA 1963, s 201 and s 73. In exceptional circumstances, it may even be permissible to reduce a company's share capital below the authorised minimum for a public limited company[47]. In such circumstances, however, the order under s 73 cannot be registered by the Registrar of Companies unless the company re-registers as a different type of company or *the court otherwise directs*[48].

(e) Where relevant, there must be compliance with the rules of the Irish Takeover Panel

[24.022] Section 201(6A) of CA 1963[49] provides that CA 1963, ss 201–203 are without prejudice to the jurisdiction of the Irish Takeover Panel under the Irish Takeover Panel Act 1997 in relation to a compromise or scheme or arrangement that is proposed between a relevant company (as defined by the 1997 Act) and its members or any class of them and which constitutes a takeover. Specifically, the Irish Takeover Panel has the same power to make rules under Irish Takeover Panel Act 1997, s 8 in relation to such takeovers as it has in relation to any other kind of takeover. The Irish Takeover Panel is, however, statutorily obliged to have due regard to the High Court's exercise of its powers under the 1997 Act[50].

Meetings of members and creditors

[24.023] The first procedural step is that application should be made to the court under CA 1963, s 201(1) to order a meeting of the creditors, or a class of creditors or members, or a class of members[51]. Whilst a company, its members, its creditors and its liquidator all have locus standi to initiate the summoning of meetings, as has been considered above[52], it is a prerequisite to the court sanctioning a scheme of arrangement that the company agrees to it and, if in liquidation, that the liquidator agrees to it. Here, the following matters are considered:

- (a) Applicant's responsibility to constitute proper classes.
- (b) Repeat applications under CA 1963, s 201 where first scheme proposed unacceptable.
- (c) Constituting proper classes.
- (d) Classes of members: shareholders' rights and interests.
- (e) Providing information to members and creditors.
- (g) Voting at meetings.

---

46 See also *Re St James' Court Estate Ltd* [1944] Ch 6.

47 *Re Allied Domecq plc* [2000] 1 BCLC 134.

48 C(A)A 1983, s 17(3).

49 As inserted by CLEA 2001, s 92.

50 CA 1963, s 201(6B), as inserted by CLEA 2001, s 92. See para **[24.046]**.

51 See *Re John Clarke & Co Ltd* [1912] IR 24.

52 See para **[24.017]**.

(a) Applicant's responsibility to constitute proper classes

[24.024] At a hearing under CA 1963, s 201(1) the court may order such meeting or meetings to be summoned in such manner as it directs[53]. However, the court itself does not at this time decide what classes of creditors or members should be made parties to the scheme. This is a matter for the applicant to decide. Different interests must be recognised and separate groups must be treated as separate classes for the purpose of the scheme. A separate class will be a group of persons whose rights are not so dissimilar as to make it impossible for them to consult together with a view to arriving at a common consensus of their position[54]. Where a class of members or a class of creditors will *not* be affected by a proposed compromise or arrangement, there is no requirement for a meeting of that class to be convened[55].

[24.025] 'Great care must be taken in considering what for the purpose of the scheme constitutes a class. If meetings of the proper classes have not been held, the court may not sanction the scheme.'[56] In *Nordic Bank plc v International Harvester Australia Ltd*[57] Lush J said:

> 'The application...for an order for meetings is a preliminary step, the applicant taking the risk that the classes which are fixed by the judge, usually on the applicant's request, are sufficient for the ultimate purpose of the section, the risk being that if in the result, and we emphasise the words "in the result", they reveal inadequacies, the scheme will not be approved.'

This warning – that applicants should, in forming appropriate classes proceed with due diligence – has been given by the courts on a large number of occasions. In *Re Hellenic Trust Ltd*[58], Templeman J said:

> 'Although s 206 [of the Companies Act 1948 (UK)] provides that the court may order meetings, it is the responsibility of the petitioners to see that the class meetings are properly constituted, and if they fail then the necessary agreement is not obtained and the court has no jurisdiction to sanction the arrangement. Thus in *In Re United Provident Assurance Co Ltd* [1910] 2 Ch 477 the court held that the holders of partly paid shares formed a different class from holders of fully paid shares. The objection was taken that there should have been separate meetings of the two classes, and Swinfen Eady J upheld the objection, saying at

53 In *Re RMCA Reinsurance Ltd* [1994] BCC 378 the court directed that a meeting of a class of member could be held abroad.

54 See *Re Hawk Insurance Co Ltd* [2001] BCC 57.

55 *Re Tea Corporation* [1904] 1 Ch 12; *Re Mortgage Insurance Corporation* [1896] WN 4.

56 *Palmer's Company Law*, (23rd edn), para 79-10, cited with approval by Costello J in *Re Pye (Ireland) Ltd* (11 March 1985, unreported), High Court. Costello J also quoted with approval the following passage from *Palmer*: 'The court does not itself consider at this point [ie when an application to convene meetings is brought] what classes of creditors or members should be made parties to scheme. This is for the company to decide...If there are different groups within a class the interests of which are different from the rest of the class, or which are to be treated differently under the scheme, such groups must be treated as separate classes for the purpose of the scheme.'

57 *Nordic Bank plc v International Harvester Australia Ltd* [1983] 2 VR 298 at 303 also cited by Morse et al (eds), *Palmer's Company Law* (25th edn, 1992; loose leaf), p 12016.

58 *Re Hellenic Trust Ltd* [1976] 1 WLR 123.

> page 481: "... the objection that there has not been proper class meetings is fatal, and I cannot sanction the scheme."
>
> Similarly Eve J issued a practice direction, *Practice Note* (1934) WN 142 in which he reminded the profession, in dealing with the predecessor of s 206, that the responsibility for determining what creditors are to be summoned to any meeting as constituting a class rests with the petitioner, and if the meetings are incorrectly convened or constituted, or an objection is taken to the presence of any particular creditors as having interests competing with the others, the objection must be taken on the hearing of the petition to sanction and the petitioner must take the risk of having the petition dismissed.'[59]

It is thought that this is also the position in Ireland. In one of the few Irish cases on schemes of arrangement where a written judgment was delivered, *Re Pye (Ireland) Ltd*[60], the facts of which are given below, Costello J cited the quotation from *Palmer* set out at the beginning of this paragraph[61] and the dictum of Templeman J last quoted.

(b) Repeat applications under CA 1963, s 201 where first scheme proposed unacceptable

[24.026] There is authority that, where an applicant applies to court under CA 1963, s 201(1) to summon meetings of creditors and members and subsequently realises or is told that meetings of differently constituted classes ought to have been summoned, only in very exceptional circumstances will a second application under s 201(1) be entertained. In *Re Pye (Ireland) Ltd; Hogan*[62] Costello J held:

> 'In my view the section as interpreted in normal circumstances is that a second application should not be entertained unless very exceptional circumstances arise, as to do so would be to allow the section to be used as a means of improving a bid, which had failed under the first scheme, in favour of dissenting creditors, and it would be undesirable if the section was to be so used. The consequences of defeat therefore should flow; I would depart from this view only in exceptional cases. I cannot find that exceptional circumstances exist in the present case and therefore I must decline to exercise my discretion in this case.'[63]

The applicants successfully appealed this decision to the Supreme Court which summoned meetings of certain classes of creditors and members on the applicants' undertaking to pay a sum to the Revenue Commissioners[64]. Unfortunately, there is no judgment in the appeal available and it is not clear whether Costello J's test was disapproved or whether the instant case was found to be 'very exceptional'. It is thought that repeated applications under s 201(1) for the purposes of improving bids is indeed undesirable; however, it must be questioned whether principle requires a general policy of refusing subsequent applications where a genuine mistake is made initially in constituting the meetings of appropriate classes.

---

59 [1976] 1 WLR 123 at 125.

60 *Re Pye (Ireland) Ltd* (11 March 1985, unreported), High Court, *Irish Company Law Reports* 323.

61 See note 56.

62 *Re Pye (Ireland) Ltd v Hogan* (12 November 1984, unreported), High Court, *Irish Company Law Reports* 320.

63 *Irish Company Law Reports* 320 at 321–322.

64 See *Reporter's Note* at 322.

(c) Constituting proper classes

[24.027] There are few hard and fast rules as to what constitutes proper classes of members and creditors: in each situation the position and proposed fates of a company's creditors and members must be considered and their division into classes determined by their common interests. The Irish decision in *Re Pye (Ireland) Ltd*[65] is instructive. The facts in this case were that in July 1984 it was ordered pursuant to CA 1963, s 201(1) that meetings of certain classes of creditors and members of the company concerned should be convened to consider a proposed scheme of arrangement. At the subsequent meetings, the Revenue Commissioners opposed the scheme and the statutory majority of 75% was not obtained. Subsequently, a second application was made under s 201(1) to discuss a new scheme of arrangement but this was refused when the High Court upheld the objections of the Revenue Commissioners who had been served as a notice party. On appeal the Supreme Court made an order summoning the convening of meetings upon the applicants' undertaking to pay a preferential debt to the Revenue Commissioners of over £52,000. In consequence, three meetings of creditors were convened: secured creditors; preferential creditors; and unsecured trade and sundry creditors. The three meetings were then held and the scheme of arrangement was approved by the 75% majority, albeit that in the case of the third meeting, the vote was close. The applicants then applied to the court to sanction the arrangement under CA 1963, s 201(3), but the Revenue Commissioners opposed their application. The Revenue Commissioners' had three objections to the applicants' classifications of creditors' meetings. Before addressing the specific classifications in that case, Costello J quoted the following from the dictum of Bowen LJ in *Sovereign Life Assurance Co v Dodd*[66] where he said:

> 'It seems plain that we must give such a meaning to the term "class" as will prevent the section being so worked as to result in confiscation and injustice, and that it must be confined to those persons whose rights are not so dissimilar as to make it impossible for them to consult together with a view to their common interest.'[67]

Costello J then went on to address the three points of objection to the classification of creditors.

[24.028] Costello J agreed in principle with the first objection raised by the Revenue Commissioners, which was that those unsecured creditors whom it was proposed would be paid in full ought to have been constituted as a distinctive class from other unsecured creditors who would not fare so well. On this point he said:

> 'As they are to be paid in full within one month of its sanction it is impossible to see how they would vote against it and obviously their interests are different to the less favoured body of unsecured creditors amongst whom is the Collector General.'[68]

Whilst accepting the point in principle, however, Costello J did not consider that, in the instant case, there was justification to refuse to sanction because he was not satisfied that if

[65] *Re Pye (Ireland) Ltd* (11 March 1985, unreported), High Court, *Irish Company Law Reports* 323.

[66] *Sovereign Life Assurance Co v Dodd* (1892) 2 QB 573.

[67] (1892) 2 QB 573 at 583.

[68] *Irish Company Law Reports* 320 at 326.

a separate class for the favoured creditors had been created that this would have meant that the scheme would have been defeated.

[24.029] The Revenue Commissioners' second objection was that one of the applicants was a director in a firm which was an unsecured creditor and which it was intended by the proposal would be paid in full. On this point Costello J found that the firm of unsecured creditor ought to have been in a class with the other 'favoured' unsecured creditors but he found that the connection between the firm and one of the applicants did not necessitate the creation of a further class of creditors.

[24.030] Finally, the Revenue Commissioners pointed out that one of the unsecured creditors was a company which owned a significant and substantial portion of the entire issued share capital of Pye (Ireland) Ltd. On this point Costello J held:

> 'Without its vote the statutory majority would not have been obtained. There is no doubt that if the scheme is successful that the prospect for the ordinary shareholders is very much better than in a liquidation (which is the alternative if the scheme is not adopted) in which it would appear the ordinary shareholders are likely to do very badly. So it seems to me that the interests of a substantial unsecured creditor who is also a substantial shareholder are very different to those of the general body of unsecured non-shareholding creditors and that there is in reality no common interest between them – the creditor/shareholder is almost certain to support the scheme, whilst the ordinary unsecured shareholder may have (as happened in the case of the Collector General [of the Revenue Commissioners]) what is considered as valid reasons for opposing it. I think therefore that there should have been a separate class created comprising unsecured creditors who are also shareholders in the company.'[69]

Costello J declined to order the summoning of fresh meetings of the correct classes of unsecured creditors on the grounds that such 'would be an otiose exercise'[70]. This was because, had the proper classes been constituted, the views of a major creditor, the Revenue Commissioners, would not have been defeated and the requisite majority of 75% would not have been obtained.

[24.031] There are many other cases that are helpful, but not conclusive, as to when separate class meetings should be held. An example is *Sovereign Life Assurance Company v Dodd*[71] where it was held that in the reorganisation of an insurance company, the insured persons whose policies had matured formed a distinct class of creditors from those whose policies had not matured. This case was distinguished in *Re Osiris Insurance Ltd*[72] where another insurance company proposing a scheme had only constituted one class of creditors, notwithstanding that those summoned had different types of insurance. On this issue Neuberger J said:

> '…while it is true that those who were summoned to attend the meeting might be said to have been in different "classes", in the sense that they had different types of insurance, it does not seem to me that, bearing in mind the nature of the proposed scheme, their interests could be said to be different, let alone positively to conflict with each other, as was held to be the case in *Sovereign Life*. Whatever the nature of the policies which they held with the

---

69 *Irish Company Law Reports* 320 at 327.

70 (11 March 1985, unreported), High Court at p 6.

71 *Sovereign Life Assurance Company v Dodd* (1892) 2 QB 573.

72 *Re Osiris Insurance Ltd* [1999] 1 BCLC 182.

> company, all actual or potential scheme creditors had policies which had expired some time ago, and were all "claims made" policies or "short tail" policies. Accordingly, claims under any of the policies issued by the company should, by the time of the meeting, at least in the absence of very unusual circumstances, have been the subject matter of notification to the company. The nature of the proposals embodied in the scheme apply equally to all former policyholders, to all scheme creditors. Furthermore, as Mr Snowden pointed out, once one starts dividing up former policyholders into different classes, it is not immediately obvious where one stops: one could argue that policyholders are in different classes not merely if their policies are of different types, if they were insured over different periods, or even through different brokers; even within a particular type of policy in a given year, there may be other differences which could similarly be invoked to justify sub-dividing into yet further classes.'[73]

Of course the sense in this passage is patent; as is the fine balance which must be struck between ensuring that a particular class is not composed of persons without a common interest on the one hand and, on the other, sub-dividing into such small classes as to effectively guarantee that one meeting of a disgruntled minority can scupper a scheme acceptable to a majority.

(d) Classes of members: shareholders' rights and interests

[24.032] In *Re Hellenic Trust Ltd*[74], where one company was proposing to take over another company, Templeman J held that a particular shareholder in the target company formed a separate class to other shareholders in the target company because it was a subsidiary of the bidder company. It is thought that there is considerable force in criticism of this decision on the basis that members or creditors should not be split into classes for reasons that are purely personal to them[75]. It is also thought that this decision is distinguishable from that of Costello J in *Re Pye (Ireland) Ltd*[76] where one creditor happened to also be a shareholder, as there the shareholder had two clearly discernible interests and rights in two separate capacities.

[24.033] The usual guide for constituting classes is 'conflicting interests'. In the context of shareholding members, it is thought that the correct approach is one based on *conflicting rights*. In *Re Industrial Equity (Pacific) Ltd*[77] Nazareth J in the High Court of Hong Kong said:

> 'Is every different interest to constitute a different class? Clearly not, but where then is the line to be drawn? The difficulties in identifying shareholders with such interests, as in the present case, could raise in terms of practicality virtually insuperable difficulties. It is

73 [1999] 1 BCLC 182 at 188c-f.

74 *Re Hellenic Trust Ltd* [1976] 1 WLR 123.

75 This decision has been criticised. Sealy et al (eds), *British Company Law and Practice* (1983; loose leaf) at 68,301 say: 'There is, however, room for doubt whether this ruling was correct, for if the shareholders or creditors are split into separate "classes" for reasons which are personal to them rather than for reasons which apply to the group as a whole, the chances that one sub-group having adverse interests may block the entire scheme are significantly enhanced. It is surely the better approach for the court to allow the group to vote at a single meeting and to review their decision on the grounds of bona fides and fairness.'

76 *Re Pye (Ireland) Ltd* (11 March 1985, unreported), High Court, *Irish Company Law Reports* 323.

77 *Re Industrial Equity (Pacific) Ltd* [1991] 2 HKLR 614.

> determination by reference to *rights* of shareholders that meets such difficulties, while leaving any conflict of interest which may result to a minority being overborne or coerced to be dealt with by the courts when their sanction is sought.'[78]

Nazareth J also suggested that the genesis for constituting classes ought to be *interests based on rights*[79]. In *Re BTR plc*[80] the scheme of arrangement involved the cancellation of the company's ordinary shares and the allotment to the holders of these shares of other shares in a company with which it was being merged. A meeting of all the ordinary shareholders was convened and held. It was argued that such shareholders had diverse interests and that a single meeting was inappropriate. In particular the hypothetical situation of an ordinary shareholder in BTR plc who also held shares in the company with which it was proposed to merge was posed and it was contended that such shareholders might well have very different interests in deciding whether or not to vote in favour of the scheme. This was rejected by Jonathan Parker J who, in so doing, distinguished the decision in *Re Hellenic Trust Ltd* and confined the ratio of that case to the point that the shareholder which was a subsidiary of the bidder company ought to have been in a separate class because the scheme only affected the other shareholders in the target company. Jonathan Parker J was not convinced by Nazareth J's analysis of 'interests based on rights' and found that the relevant test is that of 'differing rights rather than differing interests' and he also found that 'interest' was not synonymous with 'right'. He held:

> 'Shareholders with the same rights in respect of the shares which they hold may be subject to an infinite number of different interests and may therefore, assessing their own personal interests (as they are perfectly entitled to do), vote their shares in the light of those interests. But that in itself, in my judgment, is simply a fact of life: it does not lead to the conclusion that shareholders who propose to vote differently are in some way a separate class of shareholders entitled to a separate class meeting. Indeed a journey down that road would in my judgment lead to impracticability and unworkability.'[81]

In that case it was held that there was no call to convene more than one meeting of the holders of the ordinary shares[82].

(e) Providing information to members and creditors

[24.034] Section 202(1) of CA 1963 provides that where a meeting of creditors or members or any class of either is summoned certain information must[83] be given to the invitees. Section 202(1) provides that there shall:

> '(a) with every notice summoning the meeting which is sent to a creditor or member, be sent also a statement explaining the effect of the compromise or arrangement and in

---

78 [1991] 2 HKLR 614 at 625.

79 [1991] 2 HKLR 614 at 624 he said: 'Moreover, in the *Sovereign* case, upon which he primarily relied, although Lord Esher did refer to interests in the passage Templeman J quotes, as I have said, that reference in my view must be construed as a reference to *interests arising out of rights in the company*'. (Emphasis added).

80 *Re BTR plc* [1999] 2 BCLC 675.

81 [1999] 2 BCLC 675 at 682–683.

82 See further Morse et al (eds), *Palmer's Company Law* (25th edn, 1992; loose leaf), p 12024.

83 On pain of criminal sanction: CA 1963, s 202(4); cf the defence in CA 1963, s 202(5).

particular stating any material interests of the directors of the company, whether as directors[84] or as members or as creditors of the company or otherwise, and the effect thereon of the compromise or arrangement, in so far as it is different from the effect on the like interests of other persons; and

(b) in every notice summoning the meeting which is given by advertisement, be included either such a statement as aforesaid or a notification of the place at which and the manner in which creditors or members entitled to attend the meeting may obtain copies of such statement as aforesaid.'[85]

Special regard is had to the rights of debenture holders and CA 1963, s 202(2) provides:

> 'Where the compromise or arrangement affects the rights of debenture holders of a company, the said statement shall give the like explanation in relation to the trustees of any deed for securing the issue of debentures as it is required to give in relation to the company's directors.'

[24.035] The duty to provide information in the form of a statement explaining the effect of the compromise or arrangement (and in particular stating any material interests of the directors of the company) to members and creditors has been considered in a number of cases. In *Re National Bank Ltd*[86] the facts were that, although the company had its head office in London, 72% of its shareholders had addresses in Ireland. This gave rise to difficulties and disadvantages because the large Irish business had been subject to the policies of successive English chancellors of the exchequer, which differed, sometimes, from those of Ireland, for example, in regard to liquidity ratios and interest rates. The board of directors eventually came to the conclusion that it was desirable to promote a scheme which involved the division of the bank's business into two parts. Its assets and liabilities attributable to the Irish business were to be transferred to a new Irish company (The National Bank of Ireland Ltd) and those of the English business were to remain with National Bank Ltd. The National Bank of Ireland Ltd was then to be acquired by the Governor and Company of the Bank of Ireland; National Bank Ltd was to become a wholly-owned subsidiary of the National Commercial Bank of Scotland Ltd. Shareholding-members of the company were sent a circular explaining the scheme. However, it did not disclose the value of the company's assets and liabilities. The reason for this, deliberate, non-disclosure was on account of the fact that banks were exempt from disclosing, in their accounts, certain information[87]. On this basis, just over 5% of the company's shareholders opposed the scheme. It was held that the court had the widest discretion to approve any sort of scheme between a company and its members. Since the Companies Act 1948 (UK) exempted the disclosure, in companies' accounts, of such information, the court felt it was appropriate to approve of the scheme in question.

---

84 It is the duty of directors (and trustees for debenture holders) to give notice to the company of such matters relating to themselves as may be necessary for the purposes of the section: CA 1963, s 202(6).

85 Members and creditors entitled to attend are required to be furnished with a copy of the statement explaining the effect of a compromise or arrangement, free of charge: CA 1963, s 202(3).

86 *Re National Bank Ltd* [1966] 1 WLR 819.

87 CA 1948, Sch 8, Pt 3 (UK).

[24.036] In *Re John Power & Son Ltd*[88] a scheme was proposed whereby the share capital of the famous whiskey manufacturer was to be restructured. The background to the scheme was that the company's profits had been in steady decline, attributable to increases in the excise duty on proof spirit. The company's share capital was divided into 400,000 preference shares of £1 each and 400,000 ordinary shares of £1 each. The preference shareholders were entitled to a fixed cumulative preference dividend of 8% and, after the ordinary shareholders received 8%, to a further distribution of dividend pari passu with the ordinary shareholders up to a maximum of 10%. The proposed scheme involved the reduction of the ordinary share capital to £200,000 by the write down of the value of the ordinary shares from £1 to 10 shillings each. As regards the preference shares, it was proposed that £400,000 redeemable debenture stock bearing interest at 5% would be created, that the preference share capital would be extinguished and that the preferential shareholders would be issued with £1 of the debenture stock in satisfaction of each £1 preference share held by them. All shareholders were circulated with the proposals. Subsequently, on application being made the court summoned separate meetings of the ordinary and preference shareholders. The ordinary shareholders voted unanimously in favour of the proposed scheme. The preference shareholders by more than six to one, in value, were in favour of the scheme. It was subsequently argued in the High Court, inter alia, that the circular letter sent by the directors had been misleading. The High Court declined to approve the proposals. In reversing the High Court decision of Meredith J the Supreme Court held, inter alia (Fitzgibbon J):

> 'I can find nothing misleading in the circular, and the proposals seem to me quite intelligible to any person of ordinary intelligence. The only omission which has occurred to me is one which was not stressed, or even mentioned during argument, of a statement as to the probably market value of the new debenture stock, but as any expression of opinion on this point would be purely speculative, and might be challenged as misleading, I am satisfied that it was properly omitted, and that it was not unfair to leave the shareholders to form their own estimate of the merits of the exchange which the learned judge considered might "reasonably be regarded as a more attractive investment".'[89]

[24.037] A specific disclosure to members and creditors, required by CA 1963, s 202(1) is any material interests of the directors of the company, whether as directors or as members or as creditors of the company or otherwise, and the effect thereon of the compromise or arrangement, in so far as it is different from the effect on the like interests of other persons[90]. By reason of the manifest potential for a conflict of interests, inherent in such a proposal, it is not hard to see why the legislation contains such a specific requirement. Where material changes arise between the issue of the explanatory statement and the voting on the proposals, such material changes must be disclosed to the member and creditors[91].

---

88 *Re John Power & Son Ltd* [1934] IR 412.

89 [1934] IR 412 at 419.

90 See, eg, *Re Pye (Ireland) Ltd* (11 March 1985, unreported), High Court, *Irish Company Law Reports* 323 considered at para **[24.027]**.

91 *Re MB Group plc* [1989] BCLC 672 and *Re Minister Assets plc* [1985] BCLC 200.

(f) Voting at meetings

[24.038] The statutory majority, required by CA 1963, s 201(3), is 'three-fourths in value' at *each* class meeting held. Provided the statutory majority approves of a scheme at a meeting, it matters not that those present were only a fraction of those persons who were entitled to attend and vote provided that all who were entitled to attend were duly summoned under s 201(1)[92]. The meaning of 'three-fourths in value of the...members or class of members' was considered by Brightman J in *Re NFU Development Trust*[93]. There the company in question was limited by guarantee. It had been contended that since the company had no share capital, and the right of membership was non-transferable and ceased on death, it was impossible to ascertain whether a particular majority did or did not represent three-fourths in value of the members present and voting. This was rejected by Brightman J, who held:

> 'It appears to me that section 206(2) of the Companies Act 1948 [(UK)] in referring to "three-fourths in value of the...members or class of members" is directing attention to the size of the stake which each member has in the company. The purpose is to prevent a numerical majority with a small stake outvoting a minority with a large stake, eg to prevent 51 members with one share each outvoting 49 members with 10 shares each. In a case such as the present where each member has precisely the same financial stake in the company, namely, a right if he survives the liquidation of the company to be considered for a payment at the discretion of the board, and a right to an aliquot share of any assets not distributed pursuant to such discretion, every member has in law an identical stake. The position therefore is the same as if each member owned a single share in the company, with the result that a three-quarter majority of votes satisfies the statutory requirements.'[94]

[24.039] Where a resolution is passed at any adjourned meeting held under CA 1963, s 201, s 201(4) provides that CA 1963, s 144 shall apply to any such resolution[95].

Court sanction

[24.040] In order for a scheme of arrangement or compromise to be binding, it must first receive the sanction of the court. Section 201(3) of CA 1963 provides:

> 'If a majority in number representing three-fourths in value of the creditors or class of creditors or members or class of members, as the case may be, present and voting either in person or by proxy at the meeting, vote in favour of a resolution agreeing to any compromise or arrangement, the compromise or arrangement shall, if sanctioned by the court, be binding on all the creditors or the class of creditors, or on the members or class of members, as the case may be, and also on the company or, in the case of a company in the course of being wound up, on the liquidator and contributories of the company.'[96]

---

92 *Re Osiris Insurance Ltd* [1999] 1 BCLC 182.

93 *Re NFU Development Trust* [1972] 1 WLR 1548.

94 [1972] 1 WLR 1548 at 1553F–H.

95 See Chapter 9, *Corporate Governance: Meetings*, para **[9.047]**.

96 CA 1963, s 201(5) provides, *inter alia*, that an order made under sub-s (3) shall have no effect until an office copy of the order has been delivered to the Registrar of Companies. A copy of every such order must be annexed to every copy of the company's memorandum of association issued after the order is made.

In *Re John Power & Son Ltd*[97] the former Supreme Court, per Fitzgibbon J, quoted[98] with approval the following passage from the judgment of Lindley LJ in *Re Alabama, New Orleans, Texas and Pacific Junction Railway Company*[99]:

> 'What the court has to do is to see, first of all, that the provisions of that statute have been complied with; and secondly, that the majority have been acting *bona fide*. The court *also* has to see that the minority is not being overridden by a majority having interests of its own clashing with those of the minority whom they seek to coerce. *Further than that*, the court has to look at the scheme, and see whether it is one as to which persons acting honestly, and viewing the scheme laid before them in the interests of those whom they represent, take a view which can be reasonably taken by business men. The court must look at the scheme, and see whether the Act has been complied with, whether the majority are acting *bona fide*, and whether they are coercing the minority in order to promote interests adverse to those of the class they purport to represent; *and then* see whether the scheme is a reasonable one *or* whether there is *any reasonable objection* to it, *or such an objection* to it as that *any reasonable man* might say that he could not approve of it.'

Greater succinctness is perhaps seen in the judgment of Astbury J in *Re Anglo-Continental Supply Co Ltd*[100], upon which the passage in *Buckley on the Companies Acts*[101], cited with approval in a number of recent English cases[102], is largely based. There, Astbury J said:

> 'In exercising its power of sanction under s 120 the court will see: First, that the provisions of the statute have been complied with. Secondly, that the class was fairly represented by those who attended the meeting and that the statutory majority are acting bona fide and are not coercing the minority in order to promote interests adverse to those of the class whom they purport to represent, and, thirdly, that the arrangement is such as a man of business would reasonable approve …'.[103]

Buckley on the Companies Acts says:

> 'The court does not sit merely to see that the majority are acting bona fide and thereupon to register the decision of the meeting, but, at the same time, the court will be slow to differ from the meeting, unless either the class has not been properly consulted, or the meeting has not considered the matter with a view to the interests of the class which it is empowered to bind, or some blot is found in the scheme.'

The three points made by Astbury J are next reviewed:

(a) Compliance with statute;

(b) Class fairly represented and majority act bona fide;

(c) A man of business would reasonable approve.

---

97 *Re John Power & Son Ltd* [1934] IR 412.

98 [1934] IR 412 at 424. See also *Re English, Scottish and Australian Chartered Bank* [1893] 3 Ch 385.

99 *Re Alabama, New Orleans, Texas and Pacific Junction Railway Company* [1891] 1 Ch 213.

100 *Re Anglo-Continental Supply Co Ltd* [1922] 2 Ch 723.

101 *Buckley on the Companies Acts* (14th edn, 1981), Vol 1, pp 473–474.

102 *Re Osiris Insurance Ltd* [1999] 1 BCLC 182 at 188 and *Re BTR plc* [1999] 2 BCLC 675 at 680. See also *Re National Bank Ltd* [1966] 1 All ER 1006 at 1012.

103 [1922] 2 Ch 723 at 736.

(a) Compliance with statute

[24.041] The need for statutory compliance – with the provisions of CA 1963, s 201 – has already been considered. So all requirements concerning the summoning of meetings of members and creditors (and classes thereof) must have been complied with[104]; members and creditors must have been provided with a statement of the proposal which must have made full and proper disclosure[105]; and the requisite statutory majority of three-fourths (75%) in value must have approved of the scheme or compromise[106]. These are pre-requisites and the court should not sanction a scheme or compromise where there is non-compliance with these matters.

(b) Class fairly represented and majority act bona fide

[24.042] This is a more nebulous requirement. If a company proposing a scheme has 100 shareholding members, each of whom holds 1,000 shares and only 5 members answer the summons to a meeting, the court might consider that even if the 5 voted unanimously in favour of the proposal, 5 out of 100 did not *fairly* represent the class (which, in the example given, is composed of all the members).

[24.043] Any inducement given to a creditor or member to vote in favour of a proposal can operate to negative the required bona fides. Whilst a member can vote selfishly in furtherance of his own interests, it has been held that he must do so bona fide and in the interests of the class as a whole[107].

(c) A man of business would reasonable approve

[24.044] The scheme must appear to the court to be reasonable in the eyes of an intelligent, honest man of business. Generally, the court will have regard to the views of those members and creditors who have approved the scheme. As Lord Lindley said in *Re English, Scottish and Australian Chartered Bank*[108]:

> 'If the creditors are acting on sufficient information and with time to consider what they are about, and are acting honestly, they are, I apprehend, much better judges of what is to their commercial advantages than the court can be.'

That said, the court will not simply 'rubber stamp' a scheme of arrangement, simply because a majority in value of creditors (or members) approve it[109]. The reasonableness or otherwise of each scheme will often turn on the facts of a particular scheme. In *Re Alabama, New Orleans, Texas and Pacific Junction Railway Company*[110] Bowen LJ set out the grounds upon which a court should exercise its discretion to confirm a scheme. He said:

---

[104] See para **[24.024]**.

[105] See para **[24.034]**.

[106] See para **[24.040]**.

[107] *British America Nickel Corporation Ltd v MJ O'Brien Ltd* [1927] AC 369 at 371. See also *Re Wedgewood Coal and Iron Co* (1877) 6 Ch D 627 at 637.

[108] *Re English, Scottish and Australian Chartered Bank* [1893] 3 Ch 385 at 409.

[109] *Re Osiris Insurance Ltd* [1999] 1 BCLC 182 at 191 (*per* Neuberger J).

[110] *Re Alabama, New Orleans, Texas and Pacific Junction Railway Company* [1891] 1 Ch 213.

> 'I do not think myself that the point of jurisdiction is worth discussing at much length, because everybody will agree that a compromise or agreement which has to be sanctioned by the court must be reasonable, and that no arrangement or compromise can be said to be reasonable in which you can get nothing and give up everything. A reasonable compromise must be a compromise which can, by reasonable people conversant with the subject, be regarded as beneficial to those on both sides who are making it. Now, I have no doubt at all that it would be improper for the court to allow an arrangement to be forced on any class of creditors, if the arrangement cannot reasonably be supposed by sensible business people to be for the benefit of that class as such, otherwise the sanction of the court would be a sanction to what would be a scheme of confiscation. The object of this section is not confiscation...Its object is to enable compromises to be made which are for the common benefit of the creditors as creditors, or for the common benefit of some class of creditors as such.'[111]

In *Re Dorman Long and Company Ltd*[112] Maugham J said that the court's duty is to see whether the proposal is such that an intelligent and honest man, a member of the class concerned and acting in respect of his interests, might reasonably approve[113]. In *Re John Power & Son Ltd*[114] the Supreme Court, per Murnaghan J said of the proposed scheme in that case, and generally:

> 'The compromise or arrangement which can only be made binding against the wishes of the dissentient shareholders...requires the sanction of the court. In my opinion the court under this section can give all due weight to the opinion of the majority of the shareholders but the court is in no way bound merely to register the opinion of this majority. The sanction to be given by the court must be a real sanction, and to my mind the meaning of the section clearly is that no majority under the section can carry an arrangement which a fair and impartial mind would not sanction.'[115]

Fairness, reasonableness and impartiality are prerequisites of any scheme that may be sanctioned by the court.

[24.045] Where the court is generally speaking happy with a proposed scheme, but has one or two reservations, it is open to the court to sanction the scheme subject to receiving certain undertakings. This was the approach adopted by Neuberger J in *Re Osiris Insurance Ltd*[116] where two undertakings in relation to relatively minor matters were required before he sanctioned the scheme.

[24.046] In the case of compromises and schemes of arrangement proposed between a relevant company (for the purposes of the Irish Takeover Panel Act 1997) and its members or any class of them and which constitutes a takeover (within the meaning of that Act) the High Court is statutorily obliged in exercising its powers under CA 1963, ss 201, 203 and 204 to have due regard to the exercise by the Irish Takeover Panel of its powers under the

---

111 [1891] 1 Ch 213 at 243.

112 *Re Dorman Long and Company Ltd* [1934] 1 Ch 635.

113 See also *Re English, Scottish and Australian Chartered Bank* [1893] 3 Ch 385 where it was held that since there was nothing unreasonable or unfair about the proposed scheme, the court would defer to the expressed opinion of the great majority of creditors.

114 *Re John Power & Son Ltd* [1934] IR 412.

115 [1934] IR 412 at 432.

116 *Re Osiris Insurance Ltd* [1999] 1 BCLC 182.

Irish Takeover Panel Act 1997. Mutual regard is required and a similar obligation is imposed on the Irish Takeover Panel[117].

Judicial powers to assist schemes in contemplation of reconstruction

[24.047] Section 203 of CA 1963 contains provisions which can facilitate a compromise or arrangement proposed for the purposes of a scheme for the reconstruction of any company or companies or the amalgamation of any two or more companies. Where it is envisaged that the whole or any part of the undertaking or property of any company concerned in the scheme is to be transferred to another company, CA 1963, s 203(1) provides that the court may either by order sanction in the compromise or arrangement or by subsequent order, make provision for all or any of the following matters:

- the transfer to the transferee company of the whole or any part of the undertaking and of the property or liabilities of any transferor company;
- the allotting or appropriation by the transferee company of any shares, debentures, policies or other like interests in that company which under the compromise or arrangement are to be allotted or appropriated by that company to or for any person;
- the continuation by or against the transferee company of any legal proceedings pending by or against any transferor company;
- the dissolution, without winding up, of any transferor company;
- the provision to be made for any persons who, within such time and in such manner as the court directs, dissent from the compromise or arrangement;
- such incidental, consequential and supplemental matters as are necessary to secure that the reconstruction or amalgamation shall be fully and effectively carried out.

[24.048] The power of the court is considerable. Section 203(2) of CA 1963 provides:

> 'Where an order under this section provides for the transfer of property or liabilities, that property shall, by virtue of the order, be transferred to and become the liabilities of the transferee company, and in the case of any property, if the order so directs, freed from any charge which is, by virtue of the compromise or arrangement, to cease to have effect.'

Where application is made to the court under CA 1963, s 201(1) the court may on such terms as seem just stay all proceedings or restrain further proceedings against the company for such period as the court thinks fit[118]. This section is similar in intent, but not as broad as the protection afforded a company to which an examiner is appointed by C(A)A 1990, s 5.

Setting aside a scheme for fraud

[24.049] It is possible for a scheme of arrangement that has been sanctioned by the court to be subsequently set aside on grounds of fraud. So in *Fletcher v Royal Automobile Club Ltd* (the 'RAC case')[119] Neuberger J said that:

---

[117] See para **[24.022]**.

[118] CA 1963, s 201(1).

[119] *Fletcher v Royal Automobile Club Ltd* [2000] 1 BCLC 331.

> 'In the absence of authority, I would reject the suggestion that a court order sanctioning a scheme cannot be set aside for fraud, and if this resulted in the scheme having to be unravelled, the court and the parties would have to face that and deal with it as the justice of the case demanded and the law permitted.'[120]

He went on to say:

> 'I would have thought that if parliament had intended an order under s 425 to have the special characteristic of not being liable to be set aside for fraud, and its effect unravelled, it would have said so. Many statutes state that something can only be done with a court order, or provide for the effect of a court order. It does not seem to me that this would take it outside the power of the court to set aside the court order and, in effect, to reverse the effect of that order. Indeed, I would regard it as remarkable if a court, which had been clearly, deliberately and systematically misled by a litigant so as to get a particular order, was not able to set aside the order and its effect simply because Parliament had said what the effect of the order was. In my judgment, when Parliament states the effect of a court order, it does not mean that the order cannot be set aside where it has been obtained by fraud'.[121]

Neuberger J made it clear that the fact that an innocent third party may be affected by the setting aside of an order goes to the court's discretion, but not jurisdiction, in deciding whether or not to set aside an order that sanctioned a scheme of arrangement.

[24.050] The facts in the *RAC* case were that the rules of the club divided members into three classes: life members, full members and overseas members who resided outside of the UK. The life and full members were members of the company which effectively owned the RAC roadside service business. In 1996 it was decided by committee to amend the rules to redefine the classes of members: it was proposed that persons living in the EU would become full members and those living outside would remain overseas members. By an apparent oversight, the rule change was not put to the general meeting and by a further oversight, this went unnoticed. The effect was that the committee's decision did change the rules but only for a period: when the change was not put to the general meeting, it lapsed and the rules reverted to their original state, before the committee's decision to change them. On renewal of memberships in 1998, the proposal was implemented and EU members were renewed as full members. However, because, independently, any revision in subscription rates was not to affect overseas members aged over 65 years, such persons, though resident in the EU, continued to be treated as overseas members. When it was proposed to sell the roadside business, a scheme of arrangement was proposed under which life and full members would each receive circa £30,000. At least one EU resident member aged over 65 claimed he would be unfairly treated if he did not benefit from the change. Counsel on instructions told the court that there was no rule change and the court proceeded on that basis to sanction the scheme of arrangement. It subsequently became clear that there had been a rule change from the time of the committee's decision to change the rules to the lapsing of that change for want of subsequent approval in general meeting. The plaintiffs applied to set aside the order sanctioning the scheme of arrangement on the basis that it had been procured by misleading information.

---

[120] [2000] 1 BCLC 331 at 344c–d.

[121] [2000] 1 BCLC 331 at 344g–i.

[24.051] Neuberger J found that as a general rule the court would not set aside a judgment obtained by fraud if satisfied that the result would have been the same even if the fraud had not been perpetrated. On this point he said:

> 'If it is satisfied that some sort of fraud occurred, or may well have occurred, the court's powers are quite wide enough to ensure that appropriate sanctions are applied without having to incur the pointless cost, effort and court time in re-running a case whose result is a foregone conclusion.'[122]

On the facts of the *RAC* case Neuberger J found that there was insufficient evidence of any fraud, which he said must be shown to be actual dishonesty or recklessness – mere negligence or inadvertence was plainly not enough. Accordingly, the plaintiffs' application to set aside the earlier sanctioned scheme of arrangement was refused.

[B] RECONSTRUCTIONS[123]

[24.052] Section 260 of CA 1963 provides for a procedure whereby a liquidator of a company being voluntarily wound up can transfer the assets of the company to a new company in circumstances where the members of the old company will be given shares in the new company. One of the primary differences between a reconstruction pursuant to s 260 and a scheme of arrangement under CA 1963, s 201 is that s 260 makes no provision for the compromise of creditors' claims. Accordingly, the s 260 machinery makes no provision for meetings of creditors. Whilst a reconstruction under s 260 may affect creditors, it is essentially an internal procedure which facilitates the adjustment of shareholders' rights. Moreover, although there is no requirement for the court to sanction a reconstruction under s 260, neither can dissenting shareholders be bound and they can insist upon being paid their entitlements as contributories[124].

The CA 1963, s 260 machinery

[24.053] Section 260(1) of CA 1963 provides:

> 'Where a company is proposed to be, or is in course of being, wound up voluntarily, and the whole or part of its business or property is proposed to be transferred or sold to another company, whether a company within the meaning of this Act or not (in this section referred to as "the transferee company"), the liquidator of the first-mentioned company (in this section referred to as "the transferor company") may, with the sanction of a special resolution of that company, conferring either a general authority on the liquidator or an authority in respect of any particular arrangement, receive in compensation or part compensation for the transfer or sale, shares, policies or other like interests in the transferee company for distribution among the members of the transferor company, or may enter into any other arrangement whereby the members of the transferor company may, in lieu of receiving cash, shares, policies or other like interests, or in addition thereto, participate in the profits of or receive any other benefit from the transferee company.'

---

[122] [2000] 1 BCLC 331 at 340i.

[123] See, generally, Clarke, *Takeovers and Mergers Law in Ireland* (1999), p 248; Morse et al (eds), *Palmer's Company Law* (25th edn, 1992, loose leaf), p 12045; and Sealy et al (eds), *British Company Law and Practice*, (1983; loose leaf) at 68,200.

[124] As to the rights of contributories, see Chapter 27, *The Realisation and Distribution of Assets in a Winding Up*, para **[27.178]**.

It can be seen that the primary person vested with power under s 260 is the voluntary liquidator. Before any liquidator would even consider invoking his powers under s 260 he would, in practice, first need to have proposals from a company's shareholders whereby they are agreeable in principle to such a proposal. A number of points arise for consideration.

(a) Only available in a voluntary winding up

[24.054] It will be seen that the procedure is only available where a company proposes to be or is in the course of being wound up voluntarily; CA 1963, s 260 does not apply where a company goes into official, compulsory, liquidation. Indeed, if an order is made converting a voluntary winding up to a compulsory winding up within a year of the special resolution being passed, it shall not be valid unless sanctioned by the court[125]. Accordingly, within what has been described as this 'year of uncertainty'[126], it is open to both creditors and members to seek to convert to a compulsory winding up where they feel their interests are prejudiced[127]. If a company is in creditors' voluntary liquidation, CA 1963, s 271 provides that CA 1963, s 260 will apply '...with the modification that the powers of the liquidator under that section shall not be exercised except with the sanction either of the court or the committee of inspection'.

In such cases the requirement that the liquidator obtains the sanction of the court or committee of inspection is in addition to obtaining the sanction of a special resolution of the company.

(b) The proposal

[24.055] The purpose of CA 1963, s 260 is to give effect to a proposal whereby the whole or part of a company's business or property is proposed to be transferred or sold to another company. The transferee need not be a company within the meaning of CA 1963, s 2[128] and so can be a foreign company. Often times the transferee-company will be specially formed, but this is not a prerequisite and an existing company can be a transferee-company. Section 260 empowers a liquidator to:

- receive in compensation or part compensation shares, policies or other like interests in the transferee company for distribution among the members of the transferor company or
- enter into any other arrangement whereby the members of the transferor company participate in the profits of or receive any other benefit from the transferee company, in lieu of cash, shares or policies or other like interests.

(c) The requirement for sanction by special resolution of members

[24.056] Section 260 of CA 1963 confers certain powers upon a liquidator where he has the sanction of a special resolution of the company[129]. The special resolution put to the members must propose to confer upon the liquidator a general authority or an authority in

125 *Re Callao Bis Co* (1889) 42 Ch D 169.

126 Ussher, *Company Law in Ireland* (1986), p 289.

127 See, eg, *Re Consolidated South Rand Mines Deep Ltd* [1909] 1 Ch 491.

128 CA 1963, s 260(1).

129 See Chapter 26, *Liquidators*, para **[26.046]**.

respect of a particular arrangement[130]. It is advisable for the resolution to sanction the proposal to be accompanied by a resolution to wind up the company[131]. The usual notice provisions for special resolutions apply[132] but there is nothing to suggest that, where so permitted by a company's articles of association, the written resolution procedure provided for by CA 1963, s 141(8) cannot be availed of[133].

[24.057] Section 260(2) of CA 1963 provides that any sale or arrangement in pursuance of sub-s (1) shall be binding on the members of the transferor-company. This is, however, subject to s 260(3) which drives a horse and four through s 260(2). Section 260(3) of CA 1963 provides that a member[134] who has not voted in favour of the special resolution may dissent from it in writing within seven days after the passing of the resolution and require the liquidator to abstain from effecting the proposal or, alternatively, to purchase that member's interest at a price to be determined by arbitration[135], in the absence of agreement. Where a liquidator elects to purchase the member's interest, CA 1963, s 260(4) provides:

> '...the purchase money must be paid before the company is dissolved and, unless otherwise provided for, shall be deemed to be and shall be paid as part of the costs, charges and expenses of the winding up.'

It has been held that a company's articles of association cannot dilute dissenting members' statutory rights[136]. It has also been held that a member who does not dissent pursuant to s 260(3) cannot be compelled or bound to accept new 'shares, policies or other like interests' in the transferee-company[137], an option that may prove attractive where the proposed interest to be given to the member is encumbered by contingent liabilities.

(d) Distribution of shares, policies or other interests

[24.058] A liquidator is obliged to distribute any shares, policies or other interests in accordance with the entitlements of the company's members. Where there are different classes of members, the respective rights of the various classes must be respected and distribution made in accordance therewith[138].

---

130 This is the requirement where a company is in members' voluntary winding up. See para **[24.054]** in respect of a company that is in creditors' voluntary winding up.

131 *Cleve v Financial Corporation* (1873) LR 16 Eq 363.

132 *Imperial Bank of China, India and Japan v Bank of Hindustan, China and Japan* (1868) LR 6 Eq 91.

133 As to which, see Chapter 9, *Corporate Governance: Meetings*, para **[9.076]** *ff*.

134 This has been held to include a deceased member's personal representatives: *Llewellyn v Kasintoe Rubber Estates* [1914] 2 Ch 670.

135 As to which, see CA 1963, s 260(6).

136 *Payne v Cork Co Ltd* [1900] 1 Ch 308 and *Henderson's Transvaal Estates Ltd* [1908] 1 Ch 743.

137 *Re Bank of Hindustan, China and Japan; Higg's Case* (1865) 2 H & M 657. There Wood V-C said (at 665) that a member who does not dissent within time '...may have lost all his rights over his own shares by his delay; but he may nevertheless decline to take this consideration for his shares if he thinks that that consideration would prove burdensome rather than beneficial'.

138 See further Morse et al (eds), *Palmer's Company Law* (25th edn, 1992; loose leaf), p 12057.

Chapter 25

Winding Up Companies

Introduction

[25.001] This chapter is concerned with the winding up of companies[1]. The first two methods of ending corporate existence are by means of a *members' voluntary winding up* and a *creditors' voluntary winding up*. These have in common the fact that court involvement is minimal, and a majority of the members of the company precipitate the winding up by voting in favour of it in a general meeting. The essential difference between these two forms of voluntary winding up is that in a members' voluntary winding up the company must be *solvent,* while this will not be the case in a creditors' voluntary winding up. The third method of winding up is that of a compulsory court winding up, also referred to as an *official liquidation*. In addition, the circumstances in which the Irish courts will wind-up entities that are not 'companies' within the meaning of the Companies Act 1963, s 2 ('CA 1963') are also considered. In this chapter winding up is considered in the following sections:

[A] Members' voluntary winding up.

[B] Creditors' voluntary winding up.

[C] Compulsory court winding up.

[D] Conversion of windings up.

[E] The winding-up order.

The topic of *Liquidators* (voluntary, official and provisional) is considered separately in Chapter 26. The principal tasks of liquidators, the *Realisation and Distribution of Assets in a Winding Up* is also considered separately in Chapter 27.

[A] Members' Voluntary Winding up

[25.002] The essential feature of a *members' voluntary winding up* is that the company must be *solvent*, and, for whatever reason, the members of that company decide to end its existence. Section 251(1) of CA 1963, governs both members' *and* creditors' voluntary windings-up, by stating three separate circumstances in which a company may be wound up voluntarily. Two of these grounds concern members' voluntary windings up[2]. Of these two grounds, it is s 251(1)(b) that envisages the most common basis for a members'

---

1 See generally, Ussher, *Company Law in Ireland* (1986), p 472–535; Keane, *Company Law* (3rd edn, 2000), p 493–534 and 559–571; Lynch, Marshall & O'Ferrall, *Corporate Insolvency and Rescue* (1996); Schmitthoff (ed), *Palmer's Company Law* (24th edn, 1987), pp 1353–1524; Pennington, *Corporate Insolvency Law* (1991); Lingard, *Corporate Rescues and Insolvencies* (2nd edn, 1989).

2 The third circumstance in which a company can be wound up voluntarily is under CA 1963, s 251(1)(c) and this relates to a creditors' winding up: see para **[25.015]**.

winding up, namely 'if the company resolves by special resolution that the company be wound up voluntarily.'

In addition to this, the event envisaged by s 251(1)(a) can also form the basis of a members' voluntary winding up, namely:

> 'when the period, if any, fixed for the duration of the company by the articles expires, or the event, if any, occurs, on the occurrence of which the articles provide that the company is to be dissolved, and the company in general meeting has passed a resolution that the company be wound up voluntarily...'

The main difference between s 251(1)(a) and s 251(1)(b) is that where the circumstances envisaged by ground (1)(a) apply, an *ordinary resolution* will suffice; where ground (1)(b) is relied upon, a *special resolution* must be passed. As might be imagined, the scenario envisaged in sub-s (1)(a) above is a relatively rare occurrence, it being most unusual for a company's articles of association to provide that it should only last for a limited period of time. The most common catalyst for a members' voluntary winding up is, therefore, the passing of a special resolution by the members to wind up the company, as envisaged by s 251(1)(b). One reason why a solvent company may be wound up is where the members wish to legally take the assets out of the company by means of a *distribution in specie*, ie in the form of the assets as opposed to their cash proceeds[3].

[25.003] In this section the following issues in members' voluntary windings up of companies are considered:

1. Declaration of solvency.
2. Report of an independent person.
3. Personal liability of the directors.
4. Resolution to wind up.
5. Commencement of a members' voluntary winding up.
6. Termination of a members' voluntary liquidation.

Declaration of solvency

[25.004] An essential feature of a members' voluntary winding up is the *declaration of solvency* which must be sworn by the directors of a company, or a majority of them, at a meeting of the directors. This is required by CA 1963, s 256(1) as amended[4] which provides that the directors must make a statutory declaration to the effect that:

> '...they have made a full inquiry into the affairs of the company, and having done so, they have formed the opinion that the company will be able to pay its debts in full within such period not exceeding 12 months from the commencement of the winding up as may be specified in the declaration.'

Such a statutory declaration was required under the original CA 1963, s 256. The effect of the 1990 amendment lies in the consequences which ensue if the appropriate procedure is not followed and, more seriously, if the company is unable to pay its debts within 12

---

3 The distribution of assets *in specie* is considered in detail in Chapter 27, *Realisation and Distribution of Assets in a Winding Up*, para **[27.181]**.

4 As amended by CA 1990, s 128.

months from the commencement of the winding up: in such situations, the directors can be made personally liable for the company's debts[5].

[25.005] Section 256(2) of CA 1963 provides that a declaration of solvency will have no effect unless[6]:

- it is made within the 28 days immediately preceding the date of the passing of the resolution to wind the company up;
- it is delivered to the Registrar of Companies not later than 15 days of the delivery of a copy of the resolution to wind the company up;
- it embodies a statement of the company's assets and liabilities as at the latest practicable date before the making of it, and not more than three months before the making of the declaration;
- a report by an independent person is attached to the declaration of solvency;
- a statement from the independent person is embodied which gives his unrevoked consent to the issue of the declaration with the report attached; and
- a copy of the declaration is attached to the notice issued by the company of the general meeting at which it is intended to propose a resolution for voluntary winding up.

Where these provisions are not, or cannot be, complied with, the winding up cannot be a members' voluntary winding up.

The report of an independent person

[25.006] The requirement that an independent person become involved in the procedure for a members' voluntary winding up was introduced by the Companies Act 1990 ('CA 1990')[7]. An 'independent person' is 'a person qualified at the time of the report to be appointed, or to continue to be, auditor of the company'[8].

[25.007] The report of the independent person must, in accordance with CA 1963, s 256(4), state whether in his opinion, and to the best of his information and according to the explanations given to him, the following are both reasonable:

- the opinion of the directors in the declaration of solvency; and
- the statement of the company's assets and liabilities embodied in the said declaration.

In this way, the legislature has sought to protect creditors. The point is, that by requiring an independent person to report on these matters, the veracity and accuracy of the declaration of solvency are inextricably connected to the skill, integrity and potential liability of the independent person who will be a professional. A failure to comply fully with the provisions of CA 1963, s 256 concerning the statutory declaration of solvency will result in the ensuing liquidation being deemed *a creditors' voluntary winding up*. This was so held in *Re Favon Investments Co Ltd*[9] where the directors failed to annex the report of an

---

5 See para **[25.009]**.

6 CA 1963, s 256(2)(a)–(e). As to the qualifications of auditors, see Chapter 13, *Accounts and Auditors*, para **[13.190]**.

7 By CA 1990, s 128, which amended CA 1963, s 256.

8 CA 1963, s 256(3).

9 *Re Favon Investments Co Ltd* [1993] 1 IR 87 at 90.

independent person to their declaration of solvency. It was held by Costello J that the court has no jurisdiction under CA 1963, s 280 to extend the time for making and filing the report and so the winding up would become a creditors' voluntary winding up. Where the company is out of time for holding a creditors' meeting in accordance with CA 1963, s 266, the court may annul the resolution that the company be wound up where nobody is prejudiced.

[25.008] The report of the independent person should be made *after* the directors have sworn their declaration of solvency. This appears to be the case because CA 1963, s 256(4) provides that this report should make reference to the opinion of the directors in the statutory declaration and this presupposes the prior existence of the directors' statutory declaration of solvency.

Personal liability of the directors

[25.009] Where, contrary to the statutory declaration sworn by the directors, a company is in fact insolvent, CA 1963, s 256(8) provides for the imposition of personal liability for the debts of the company, on the directors[10]. This states:

> 'Where a statutory declaration is made under this section and it is subsequently proved to the satisfaction of the court that the company is *unable to pay its debts*, the court on the application of the liquidator, or any creditor or contributory of the company may, if it thinks it proper to do so, declare that any director who was a party to the declaration without having reasonable grounds for the opinion that the company would be able to pay its debts in full within the period specified in the declaration *shall be personally responsible*, without any limitation of liability, *for all or any of the debts or other liabilities of the company as the court may direct*. [Emphasis added]

Subsection (9) provides that where a company's debts are not paid or provided for in full within the 12-month period after the commencement of the winding up, there is a presumption that the director did not have reasonable grounds for his opinion. Since the independent person must state whether or not in his view the opinion of the directors was reasonable, it would seem that a court would, in the absence of collusion, be loath to impose personal responsibility on the directors where their opinion is stated in the independent person's report to be reasonable. It would thus seem that the crucial statutory control will be getting the independent person's favourable report.

It is thought that this provision will be more than sufficient to dissuade a voluntary winding up by members of all companies save those which are unequivocally solvent. The risk that a director could be made personally liable or responsible for the debts and other liabilities of the company will not, it is thought, be taken lightly.

The resolution to wind up

[25.010] After the directors of a company have made their declaration of solvency, and the independent person has given his report, the directors should then call an extraordinary general meeting ('EGM') of the company. This should be held within 28 days of the date of the declaration of solvency and the notice provisions specified for such in the company's articles of association must be adhered to[11].

---

[10] See Chapter 5, *Disregarding Separate Legal Personality*, para **[5.085]**.

[11] On notice periods for *general meetings*, see Chapter 9, *Corporate Governance: Meetings*, para **[9.028]**.

[25.011] At the EGM, the members must pass a special resolution to wind up the company. Where a meeting is held, as opposed to the written resolution procedure being followed[12], the normal rules associated with the convening and holding of meetings, the giving of notice, the passing of special resolutions and the holding of polls must be followed[13]. Within 14 days from the passing of the winding-up resolution, notice of the resolution must be published in *Iris Oifigiúil*[14].

Commencement of a members' voluntary winding up

[25.012] Section 253 of CA 1963 provides that a voluntary winding up 'shall be deemed to commence' at the time of the passing of the resolution for voluntary winding up. It does not lie within the gift of the members or anyone else to alter this statutory date of commencement[15]. In *Re Norditrack (UK) Ltd*[16] it was held that the resolution for voluntary winding up could not be passed conditionally on another event as it took effect, as statute provided, at the time when it was actually passed.

Termination of a members' voluntary liquidation

[25.013] Where a members' voluntary winding up continues for a period in excess of one year the voluntary liquidator must within three months of the end of that year and in each succeeding year, summon a general meeting of the company. The purpose of this meeting is to lay before it an account of his acts and dealings and of the conduct of the winding up during the preceding year. Furthermore, the liquidator must send a copy of that account to the Registrar of Companies[17]. Non-compliance with this provision will render the liquidator liable to a fine not exceeding €1,269.74[18].

[25.014] In a members' voluntary winding up, when the affairs of the company are fully wound up, the liquidator must, by CA 1963, s 263(1), make an account of the winding up. This account must show how the winding up was conducted and how the company's property was disposed of. The liquidator must then call a general meeting[19] and lay his account before the meeting, giving whatever explanations are required by the members. The meeting must be advertised in two daily newspapers, 28 days before it is held[20]. Within one week of the meeting the liquidator must send the account and make a return to the Registrar of Companies who will register them[21]. Three months later, the company is

12 There is, however, no reason why the resolution cannot be passed pursuant to CA 1963, s 141(8), as a written resolution, where the articles of a company so permit.

13 See, generally, Chapter 9, *Corporate Governance: Meetings*. So, for example, those present can demand a poll: *Re Hockerill Athletic Club Ltd* [1990] BCLC 921.

14 CA 1963, s 252(1). A failure to do so by a company and every officer (including a liquidator) in default is an offence: CA 1963, s 252(2).

15 *Re West Cumberland Iron and Steel Company* (1889) 40 Ch D 361.

16 *Re Norditrack (UK) Ltd* [1999] TLR 782.

17 CA 1963, s 262(1).

18 CA 1963, s 262(2).

19 Failure to call the meeting renders the liquidator liable to be fined up to €317.43: CA 1963, s 263(7).

20 CA 1963, s 263(2).

21 CA 1963, s 263(3).

deemed to be dissolved[22]. It should be noted that application can be made to court to have the dissolution of the company deferred[23]. Where such an order is granted it is the duty of the applicant to inform the Registrar of Companies, and to send him an office copy of the order for registration[24].

[B] Creditors' Voluntary Winding up

[25.015] A *creditors' voluntary winding up* will arise either on the conversion of a members' voluntary winding up[25], or, ab initio, pursuant to CA 1963, s 251(1)(c). Section 251(1)(c) provides that the members in general meeting can resolve that the company cannot by reason of its liabilities continue its business, and that it be wound up voluntarily. The essential features of a creditors' voluntary winding up are the absence of a declaration of solvency and also the fact that the winding up is precipitated by the members themselves, usually on the advice of the directors. In this section the following issues in creditors' voluntary windings up are considered:

1. Statement of the position of the company's affairs.
2. The members' general meeting.
3. The creditors' meeting.
4. The committee of inspection.
5. Termination of a creditors' voluntary liquidation.

Statement of the position of the company's affairs

[25.016] The winding up of an insolvent company is not invariably the result of its creditors' actions. The directors (and in small companies, the members) will often be the first to realise that a company is insolvent. Indeed, the directors have *a duty* to take the necessary steps to initiate the winding up of an insolvent company. In *Re Shannonside Holdings Ltd*[26] the members' resolution to wind up the company was challenged by secured creditors who claimed that the decision was not bona fide and was intended to defeat their judgment mortgage. The resolution to wind up the company had been passed two-and-a-half months after the judgment mortgage had been registered and, accordingly, the judgment mortgage was invalid where the company was wound up within three months of its creation[27]. Costello J held on this question of fact that he found no evidence to suggest that there was an improper motive in adopting a resolution to wind up the company. Moreover, he held:

> '...it is not denied that the company was insolvent and unable to pay its debts. The *directors had a duty* to wind up the company and the members of the company acceded to the request that a resolution to wind up be passed. Even though it may be advantageous to directors to pass a winding-up resolution, it seems to me that the resolution to wind up cannot be

---

22 CA 1963, s 263(4).

23 CA 1963, s 263(5).

24 CA 1963, s 263(6). Failure to do this can result in a person being fined up to €31.74.

25 See para **[25.096]**.

26 *Re Shannonside Holdings Ltd* (20 May 1993, unreported), High Court.

27 CA 1963, s 284(2).

> challenged on this ground once insolvency has been established and the *duty to wind up* shown to exist.'[28] [Emphasis added]

The duty of directors to resolve to wind up a company that is insolvent is consistent with their general duties to creditors when a company becomes insolvent, as established by the Supreme Court in *Re Frederick Inns Ltd*[29].

[25.017] Where there is an internal decision to wind up a company on the grounds that it is insolvent the directors of the company should meet and resolve to convene two meetings: one of the members of the company, and one of the creditors. The next step, set out by CA 1963, s 266(3)(a), requires the directors to address the state of the company's affairs and to:

> '...cause a full statement of the position of the company's affairs, together with a list of the creditors of the company and the estimated amount of their claims to be laid before the meeting of the creditors...'

The exact position of the company's affairs should be ascertained by the directors in conjunction with the company's financial advisors. The creditors will usually be divided into the categories of secured, preferential and unsecured. In addition, the directors must appoint one of their number to preside at the meeting of creditors, considered below[30].

The members' general meeting

[25.018] At this time, the directors will cause a general meeting of the members to be convened. The purpose of the general meeting is to pass an ordinary resolution, pursuant to CA 1963, s 251(1)(c), that the company cannot, by reason of its liabilities, continue its business and that it be wound up voluntarily. The directors must, subject to the company's own articles of association providing for longer[31] notice, give seven days' notice in writing to the members of the proposed EGM[32]. Again, this resolution must be advertised within 14 days of its passing in *Iris Oifigiúil*[33]. From the date of this resolution, the voluntary winding up of the company is deemed to commence[34]. The company should cease to carry on its business, save as may be required for the beneficial winding up of the company, but its corporate status and powers continue until its dissolution[35].

[25.019] At this meeting the members may nominate a liquidator under CA 1963, s 267(1) for the purpose of winding up the affairs and distributing the assets of the company. However, if the creditors nominate a different liquidator, as they are entitled to do, their nominee will prevail as the company's liquidator. This is subject to the application by any directors, members or creditors to court for an order that the liquidator nominated by the

28 (20 May 1993, unreported), High Court at p 10.

29 *Re Frederick Inns Ltd* [1994] 1 ILRM 387. See Chapter 10, *Duties of Directors and Other Officers*, para **[10.012]**.

30 See para **[25.022]**.

31 See CA 1963, s 133(1). See also Chapter 9, *Corporate Governance: Meetings*, para **[9.032]**.

32 CA 1963, s 133(2)(b).

33 Under CA 1963, s 252(2) a fine of €158.72 is the penalty in default, as increased from €31.74 by C(A)A 1982, s 15.

34 CA 1963, s 253.

35 CA 1963, s 254.

members shall be the liquidator or the joint liquidator with the liquidator nominated by the creditors[36].

[25.020] Where the general meeting of the members is adjourned for whatever reason, CA 1963, s 266(5) provides that any resolution passed at the creditors' meeting held on the same or the following day as the original members' meeting shall take effect as if it had been passed immediately after the passing of the resolution to wind up.

The creditors' meeting

[25.021] CA 1963, s 266(1) imposes an obligation on the company to summon a meeting of its creditors[37], providing:

> 'The company shall cause a meeting of the creditors of the company to be summoned for the day, or the day next following the day, on which there is to be held the meeting at which the resolution for voluntary winding up is to be proposed, and shall cause the notices of the said meeting of creditors to be sent by post to the creditors at least 10 days before the date of the said meeting of the company.'

The first point to note here is the timing of the creditors' meeting, which must be held on the same day, or the day next following, the members' general meeting. The second point is that notices of the creditors' meeting must be sent by post to the creditors at least ten days before the date of the meeting[38] together with two proxy forms[39] giving the creditors the right to appoint the chairman of the meeting or someone else as his proxy[40]. Thirdly, an advertisement should be placed at least ten days before the creditors' meeting, once at least, in two daily newspapers circulating in the district where the company has its registered office or principal place of business[41].

[25.022] The purposes of the creditors' meeting are generally accepted as being threefold:

- to consider the statement of affairs prepared by the directors;
- to consider the appointment of the liquidator appointed by the members and replace him if desired; and
- to appoint a committee of inspection.

Where, however, a liquidator has been appointed, his report must be presented to the meeting and the meeting advised as to whether or not he has exercised any powers since he was appointed by the members[42]. The creditors' meeting will be addressed by a director nominated by the board, who will usually give short reasons for the failure of the

---

36 CA 1963, s 267(2).

37 See generally, Comyn, 'The Calling and Conduct of a Creditors Meeting in a Voluntary Winding up' (1982) Gazette ILSI January/February and Comyn, 'Creditors' Meetings – Revisited' (1994) CLP 191.

38 CA 1963, s 266(1).

39 RSC, Ord 74, r 76 provides that a general and special form of proxy shall be sent to each of the creditors with the notice summoning the meeting.

40 RSC, Ord 74, r 77.

41 CA 1963, s 266(2).

42 CA 1990, s 131. On liquidators' powers, see Chapter 26, *Liquidations*, para **[26.025]** *ff* and, especially, para **[26.044]** for the restrictions on the powers of liquidators appointed by members at the initiation of a creditors' voluntary winding up.

company, and answer any questions, usually through his solicitor. This is the reading of the statement of affairs which also includes providing a list of the company's creditors and an estimate of the amount of their claims[43].

[25.023] The procedures to be followed at creditors' meetings are largely determined by the Rules of the Superior Courts 1986. Order 74, r 66 provides that the quorum is three creditors, provided that if there are less than three creditors present, those present must represent all of the company's creditors. Unless a quorum is present, a meeting may not act for any purpose except for the election of a chairman and the adjournment of the meeting.

[25.024] To be entitled to vote, a creditor must have an ascertained debt, and a creditor shall not vote in respect of any unliquidated or contingent debt, the value of which is not ascertained[44]. A secured creditor can vote at the creditors' meeting. However, to do so he must provide certain details as to his security, namely the date of its creation and the value at which he assesses it. He can then only vote in respect of the balance (if any) due to him after deducting the value of the security. If he votes in respect of the whole debt he shall be deemed to have *surrendered his security* unless the court, on application being made, is satisfied that this omission to value the security has arisen from inadvertence[45]. Where a secured creditor votes in respect of the value of his claim after deducting the value of his security the liquidator of the company may, within 28 days after the meeting, require the creditor to give up the security for the benefit of the creditors generally on payment of the value so estimated, but provided that the creditor may correct the valuation by a new proof, prior to giving up his security[46]. It is most unusual for secured creditors to surrender their security. Typically, secured creditors stand back from the liquidation and rely on their security.

[25.025] The chairman of the meeting can admit or reject a proof for the purpose of voting, subject to appeal to court. Where there is doubt the chairman should mark the proof as objected to and allow the creditor to vote subject to the vote being declared invalid in the event of the objection being sustained[47]. Creditors may attend and vote in person or by proxy[48] and companies may send a 'representative'[49].

[25.026] There are two different tests for the passing of a resolution at a creditors' meeting. In the case of a resolution to appoint the creditors' nominee as liquidator, as permitted by CA 1963, s 267(3) such a resolution:

> '...shall be deemed to be passed when *a majority, in value only*, of the creditors present personally or by proxy and voting on the resolution have voted in favour of the resolution.'

---

43 CA 1963, s 266(3)(a).

44 RSC, Ord 74, r 68.

45 RSC, Ord 74, r 69 which provides: '...if he votes in respect of his whole debt he shall be deemed to surrender his security unless the court on application is satisfied that the omission to value the security has arisen from inadvertence'.

46 RSC, Ord 74, r 70.

47 RSC, Ord 74, r 71.

48 Proxies are dealt with in RSC, Ord 74, rr 74 – 83. Proxies must be lodged with the company not later than 4 pm on the day before the meeting: RSC, Ord 74, r 82(1).

49 CA 1963, s 139.

This represents a change to the law brought about by the Company Law Enforcement Act 2001, s 47 ('CLEA 2001'), which inserted a new sub-s (3) into CA 1963, s 267[50]. For all other resolutions, they will be deemed to be passed when a *majority in number and value* of those present personally or by proxy vote in their favour[51]. The effect of this change in law is to make it easier to displace any liquidator ensconced by the members[52]. It should also be noted that CA 1990, s 131 restricted the powers that a members' liquidator can exercise prior to the holding of a creditors' meeting, the purpose of this provision being to prevent the practice of '*centrebinding*' in Ireland[53].

The committee of inspection

[25.027] The creditors of a company have the power to appoint a committee of inspection under CA 1963, s 268(1). The creditors' committee will consist of not more than five persons nominated by the creditors. Where such a committee is appointed, the company, acting through its members, may appoint three persons to act as members of the committee. The committee members nominated by the members in general meeting can be objected to by the creditors and, subject to appeal to court, can be disqualified from so acting[54].

[25.028] The proceedings of the committee of inspection are the same as a committee of inspection appointed in a compulsory or official winding up[55]. These are enumerated in CA 1963, s 233(2)–(9), which provides that:

- the committee can meet as it thinks fit;
- the liquidator can convene a meeting of the committee;
- a committee member can convene a meeting;
- the committee acts by majority, provided a majority are present;
- resignation is effected by notice in writing to the liquidator;
- a member is deemed to have vacated office on becoming bankrupt or by making an arrangement with his creditors or by being absent from five consecutive meetings without leave;
- a member of the committee can be removed by a majority of those who appointed him (members or creditors);
- on a vacancy arising the liquidator must convene a meeting of those who appointed the ex-member, save where he obtains a court order that it is unnecessary;
- on a vacancy, those left can continue if they number at least two.

In relation to liquidators, the committee of inspection has three other powers:

---

50 This provision commenced with effect from 1 October 2001: SI 2001/438.

51 RSC, Ord 74, r 62.

52 See Lynch, Marshall and O'Ferrall, *Corporate Insolvency and Rescue* (1996), para [3.22].

53 *Re Centrebind Ltd* [1966] 3 All ER 889. See Chapter 26, *Liquidators*, para **[26.044]**.

54 CA 1963, s 268(2).

55 See Chapter 26, *Liquidators*, para **[26.021]**.

— to fix the remuneration of the liquidator[56],
— to determine whether the liquidator should continue the business of the company,
— to determine whether the powers of the directors should continue[57].

Termination of a creditors' voluntary liquidation

[25.029] In a creditors' voluntary winding up, when the affairs of a company are fully wound up the liquidator must make an account of the winding up, showing how it was conducted and how the property of the company has been disposed of, and then call a general meeting of the members and a meeting of the creditors and lay his account before them, giving whatever explanations are necessary[58]. This meeting is convened by advertisement in two daily newspapers circulating in the district where the registered office of the company is located specifying the place, time and object of the meeting and published at least 28 days before the meeting[59]. After the meeting, the liquidator must report to the Registrar of Companies who will register the report. On the expiration of three months the company shall be deemed to have been dissolved[60].

[C] Compulsory Court Winding up

[25.030] A compulsory, or official liquidation, will arise where the High Court is petitioned to have a company compulsorily wound up[61]. Of the three processes by which a company can be wound up, compulsory winding up has given rise to the most case law as the petition will often be resisted by the company. In this section the following issues are considered:

1. Jurisdiction to compulsorily wind up companies.
2. Locus standi to petition the court.
3. Procedural issues in compulsory windings up.
4. Grounds for ordering a company to be wound up.

Jurisdiction to compulsorily wind up companies

(a) Irish companies

[25.031] CA 1963, s 212 provides that 'The High Court shall have jurisdiction to wind up any company'. 'Company' is defined by CA 1963, s 2 as a 'company formed and registered under this Act, or an existing company'. An 'existing company' is defined, also by CA 1963, s 2 as a company formed and registered under the Joint Stock Companies Acts, the Companies Act 1862 or the Companies (Consolidation) Act 1908.

---

56 CA 1963, s 269(1).

57 CA 1963, s 269(3).

58 CA 1963, s 273(1).

59 CA 1963, s 273(2).

60 CA 1963, s 273(4). The liquidator or another person may apply for an order deferring the date of the dissolution of the company (CA 1963, s 273(5)).

61 See generally, Keane, *Corporate Insolvency Law*; Ussher, *Company Law in Ireland* (1986), p 478 *ff*; Lingard, *Corporate Rescues and Insolvencies* (2nd edn, 1989), ch 8; Pennington, *Corporate Insolvency Law* (1991), ch 2; and Schmitthoff (ed), *Palmer's Company Law* (24th edn, 1987), ch 88.

(b) Other companies, bodies corporate and associations

[25.032] The companies which the High Court has *jurisdiction* to wind up are those which are formed or registered under the Companies Acts 1963–2001, former Companies Acts[62] and unregistered companies[63]. In certain circumstances the Irish courts also have jurisdiction to wind up *foreign companies*, formed or registered abroad[64]. Section 344 of CA 1963 applies Part X of that Act to 'unregistered companies' which are defined as:

> '...any trustee savings bank certified under the Trustee Savings Banks Acts 1863 to 1958, any partnership, whether limited or not, any association and any company with the following exceptions —
>
> (a) a company as defined by section 2;
>
> (b) a partnership, association or company which consists of less than eight members and is not formed outside the State.'

CA 1963, s 345(1) provides that all 'unregistered companies' may be wound up under the Companies Acts, the provisions of which shall apply to such companies. It must be noted, however, that unregistered companies may *not* be wound up voluntarily ie they can only be wound up by court[65]. Section 345(4) enumerates three circumstances in which an unregistered company may be wound up:

— if the company is dissolved, or has ceased to carry on business, or is carrying on business only for the purpose of winding up its affairs;

— if the company is unable to pay its debts[66];

— if the court is of opinion that it is just and equitable that the company should be wound up.

Moreover, where a company incorporated outside the State which has been carrying on business in the State, ceases to carry on business in the State, it may be wound up as an unregistered company notwithstanding that it has been dissolved or otherwise ceased to exist as a company under the laws of the country where it was incorporated[67]. It is not necessary that an unregistered company have assets within the State. In *Stocznia Gdanska SA v Latreefers Inc (No 2)*[68] the English Court of Appeal endorsed the finding of Lloyd J

---

62 CA 1963, ss 324 and 325.

63 See CA 1963, s 345. In *Western Counties Construction Ltd v Whitney Town Football and Social Club* (1993) Times, 19 November, it was held that a *club* was not an unregistered company and could not be wound up under the Insolvency Act 1986 (UK). For an example of where an unregistered company was wound up, see *Re Welsh Highland Railway Light Railway Co* [1993] BCLC 338.

64 See CA 1963, s 345. See also *International Westminster Bank plc v Okeanos Maritime Corp* [1987] BCLC 450. See generally Binchy, *Irish Conflicts of Law* (1988), pp 485–486.

65 CA 1963, s 345(3).

66 CA 1963, s 345(5) lists four circumstances in which an unregistered company shall be 'deemed' to be unable to pay its debts.

67 CA 1963, s 345(7).

68 *Stocznia Gdanska SA v Latreefers Inc (No 2)* [2000] TLR 182.

that as the law has evolved[69], there are three core requirements before a court will exercise its discretion to order the winding up if an unregistered company:

> '(1) There must be a sufficient connection with England and Wales which may, but does not necessarily have to, consist of assets within the jurisdiction.
>
> (2) There must be a reasonable possibility, if a winding-up order is made, of benefit to those applying for the winding-up order.
>
> (3) One or more persons interested in the distribution of assets of the company must be persons over whom the court can exercise a jurisdiction.'

There, the Court of Appeal rejected the contention that it was a requirement that an unregistered company must have assets within the jurisdiction. In that case it was held that potential claims for misfeasance and wrongful and fraudulent trading provided a reasonable possibility of benefit to those applying for a winding-up order and that this satisfied the second core requirement. In *Atlantic & General Investment Trust Ltd v Richbell Information Services Inc*[70] it was held that the first core requirement – sufficient connection – was satisfied where a company's directors were resident in England at the relevant time, it was a member of a group of companies that consisted of English companies, a particular transaction had taken place in England and that it had assets in England and conducted correspondence from the London address of the group of companies.

Locus standi to petition the court

[25.033] Only certain persons have locus standi to petition to have a company wound up by the court, and those who can bring a petition are only permitted to do so on certain grounds[71]. Those who are entitled to petition the court to have a company wound up are: the company itself; a creditor of the company; a contributory; a member; the Director of Corporate Enforcement; and the Registrar of Companies.

(a) The company

[25.034] The grounds on which a company can petition for its own winding up are set out in CA 1963, s 213(c)–(f)[72]. Although a company can petition for its own winding up, such is rare. For the members of most companies it is preferable to resolve in favour of a members' or creditors' voluntary winding up because these are cheaper and less public.

---

69 Lloyd J referred to the decisions of Megarry J in *Re Compania Merabello San Nicolas SA* [1972] 3 All ER 448, [1973] Ch 75; Nourse J in *Re Eloc Electro-Optiek and Communicatie BV* [1981] 2 All ER 111, [1982] Ch 43; and Peter Gibson J in *Re A Company (No 00359 of 1987)* [1987] Ch 210 (which he noted was also known, less enigmatically, *as International Westminster Bank plc v Okeanos Maritime Corp* [1987] BCLC 450, [1987] 2 All ER 137. Lloyd J also said that the statement of the relevant principles has evolved to the point at which they were summarised, most recently, by Knox J in *Real Estate Development Co* [1991] BCLC 210 at 217.

70 *Atlantic & General Investment Trust Ltd v Richbell Information Services Inc* [2000] BCC 111.

71 CA 1963, s 215, as amended by CA 1963, Sch 1, para 18, and C(A)A 1983, Sch 3 and by CLEA 2001, s 94.

72 See para **[25.054]**. In the case of a private company limited by shares or by guarantee, the European Communities (Single-Member Private Limited Companies) Regulations 1994 (SI 1994/275), reg 11 has provided that CA 1963, s 213(d) shall not apply; see para **[25.057]**

[25.035] The general power of the directors of a company to manage the business of the company in model reg 80 would appear to be insufficient authority for them to present a petition[73]. In *Re Galway & Salthill Tramways Co*[74] the petition to have the company wound up was presented by its directors, without the express authority of the shareholders in general meeting. Certain dissenting shareholders claimed that such an action exceeded the powers of the directors. The directors contended that they had power to present the petition, such being part of their general power to manage the company and to exercise all of the company's powers[75]. This contention was rejected by O'Connor MR who said:

> 'In my opinion that part of the section which gives the directors all the powers of the company...must be read along with the opening words giving powers of management, and is merely in aid of the proper and effective exercise of such powers...the powers of the directors are only powers of managing, and if the argument relied on is sound, a winding up of the company must come within the scope of its management. But the object of management is the working of the company's undertaking, while the object of a winding up is its stoppage. On this ground alone I would hold that the directors had no power to present the petition in the present case ...'[76]

Of course, such an outcome is dependent upon the provisions of a particular company's articles of association, and it is possible for a company to give its directors express power to present a petition. Similarly, a receiver appointed out of court may have power as agent for a company to present a petition where he is expressly authorised to do so in the debenture instrument where this appears necessary to secure the assets charged[77].

(b) Creditors

[25.036] The grounds upon which a creditor can petition for the winding up of a company are those set out in CA 1963, s 213(c)–(f)[78]. Section 215 provides that a creditor or creditors, including contingent or prospective[79] creditors, have locus standi to petition the court to have a company wound up[80]. However, for a creditor to be able to present a petition, he must have a present[81] liquidated debt due and owing to him, and so a bare claim in tort would not be sufficient[82]. Similarly, the debt owed must be to the creditor

---

73 See Chapter 8, *Corporate Governance: Management by the Directors*, para **[8.004]**.

74 *Re Galway & Salthill Tramways Co* [1918] 1 IR 62.

75 Under Companies Clauses Act 1845, s 90 which was similar to the present CA 1963, Table A, Pt I, model reg 80.

76 [1918] 1 IR 62 at 65.

77 See *Re Emmadart Ltd* [1979] 1 All ER 599, and Pennington, *Corporate Insolvency Law* (1991), pp 13–15.

78 See para **[25.054]**. In the case of private company limited by shares or by guarantee, the European Communities (Single–Member Private Limited Companies) Regulations 1994 (SI 1994/275), reg 11 has provided that CA 1963, s 213(d) shall not apply; see para **[25.057]**.

79 See para **[25.037]**.

80 On a dispute as to a person's status as a *creditor*, see *Re Bank of Credit and Commerce International SA (No 5)* [1994] 1 BCLC 429.

81 Where a judgment creditor's debt has been satisfied by a sheriff's successful execution, he ceases to be a creditor and has no standing to petition: *Debtor v Goacher* [1979] 1 All ER 870.

82 Note though that CA 1963, s 214(c) provides that in determining whether a company is unable to pay its debts, 'the court shall take into account the contingent and prospective liabilities of the company'.

himself, and so where the company has given a guarantee to the creditor this will not entitle that creditor to petition until the primary debtor has defaulted and the company has failed to pay on foot of the guarantee[83]. A liquidator of a company which is owed money by another company can petition the court to have the debtor company wound up[84]. In *Re Dollar Land Holdings plc*[85] Sir Donaldson Nicholls VC said of a 'prospective creditor' that: '...a person with an undisputed claim for unliquidated damages for more than a nominal amount qualifies as a prospective creditor.'[86]

In that case the petitioner had guaranteed a bank loan to a company in return for a 25% stake in property being acquired by the company. When the property was not purchased he sought the release of his guarantee. When that was not done he simultaneously commenced proceedings for a mandatory order that the guarantee be released, an order for damages and he presented a petition to have the company wound up. It was held that the petitioner was entitled to present the petition as he was a contingent or prospective creditor of the company with respect to any unliquidated damages that he might suffer arising from the company's failure to obtain the release of the guarantee.

[25.037] Section 215(c) of CA 1963 provides that a court shall not hear a winding-up petition presented by a contingent or prospective creditor unless such security for costs have been given as the court thinks reasonable and a prima facie case for winding up has been established[87]. In *Truck and Machinery Sales Ltd v Marubeni Komatsu Ltd*[88] Keane J held in the context of applications to restrain the presentation of petitions by creditors, that:

> 'It is also clear that, where the would-be petitioner is a contingent or prospective creditor, the court which is asked to restrain the petition is not concerned with whether the creditor will be able to meet the requirements of the proviso in s 215, under which such a creditor must give security for costs and satisfy the court that a *prima facie* case for winding up has been established. I agree entirely with the view expressed by Goulding J in *Hold Southy v Catnic Components Ltd*[89], that, where it is shown that the would-be petitioner is a prospective or contingent creditor, it is for the court which hears the petition to determine whether the statutory requirements for the granting of the reliefs sought in the petition have been met.'[90]

[25.038] A creditor who is owed a debt is entitled *ex debito justiciae* to a winding-up order[91]. To this general rule there are a number of exceptions. It has been held that a court will have regard to the wishes of other creditors where they are a majority in number and

---

83 See *Re Fitness Centre (South East) Ltd* [1986] BCLC 518.

84 *Re Shrinkpak Ltd* (20 December 1989, unreported), High Court, (*unapproved*), per Barron J.

85 *Re Dollar Land Holdings plc* [1994] 1 BCLC 404.

86 [1994] 1 BCLC 404 at 407.

87 On security for costs generally, see Chapter 6, *Corporate Civil Litigation*, para **[6.019]** *ff*.

88 *Truck and Machinery Sales Ltd v Marubeni Komatsu Ltd* [1996] 1 IR 12. For comment, see Canniffe, 'Restraining a Creditor's Winding-up petition – The Position Since *Truck and Machinery Sales Ltd v Marubeni Komatsu Ltd*' (1997) 4 CLP 30.

89 *Hold Southy v Catnic Components Ltd* [1978] 2 All ER 276.

90 (20 December 1989, unreported), High Court at p 21.

91 See *Re Camburn Petroleum Products Ltd* [1979] 3 All ER 297. There, Slade J said (at 303) where a contributory challenged the petition of a creditor:

value. In *Re RW Sharman Ltd*[92] the court exercised its discretion and refused an order to wind up a company, where a majority of creditors opposed the petition by a judgment creditor[93].

[25.039] Another exception to the rule that a creditor is entitled *ex debito justiciae* to a winding-up order is that the petition presented must not be seen as an abuse of the court's process: *Re Bula Ltd*[94]. *In Re Bula Ltd* the company owed money to various banks, its only asset being zinc and lead deposits in the ground. One of the creditors who had a judgment against the company, tried to become a secured creditor by way of registering a judgment mortgage, and this prompted the banks to petition for the winding up of the company. The purpose of this was, inter alia, to prevent the judgment mortgage from ranking with the banks[95]. The High Court order to wind up the company was discharged by the Supreme Court. McCarthy J said that, since there was nothing to be gained by the winding up:

> '...in my judgment, in this case of special facts, where a petition is brought by secured creditors whose security attaches to the entire assets of the debtor company and who have appointed a receiver whose power of sale is, effectively, at least as great as that of a liquidator, the court should refuse its aid.'[96]

Accepting that a creditor was prima facie entitled to a winding-up order[97], McCarthy J held that this had the effect of shifting the initial burden faced by those who present a petition to those who oppose a petition to have a company wound up.

(c) Contributories and members

[25.040] Contributories and members may petition for the winding up of a company upon the grounds set out in CA 1963, s 213(a)–(g)[98]. A *contributory* is defined by CA 1963, s 208 as:

> '...every person liable to contribute to the assets of a company in the event of its being wound up, and for the purposes of all proceedings for determining, and all proceedings prior

91 *(contd)* 'While I recognise that it would have the right...to pay regard to the wishes of contributories, in deciding whether or not to make a winding-up order on a creditors' petition, or to adjourn the hearing, in my judgement it can, and should, ordinarily attach little weight to the wishes of contributories, in comparison with the weight it attaches to the wishes of any creditor, who proves both that he is unpaid and that the company is "unable to pay its debts". See also *Re JD Swain Ltd* [1965] 1 WLR 909 at 915.

92 *Re RW Sharman Ltd* [1957] 1 All ER 737.

93 See also *Re Belfast Tailors' Co-partnership Ltd* [1909] 1 IR 49 and *Re Fitness Centre (South East) Ltd* [1986] BCLC 518. See however, *Re George Downs & Co Ltd* [1943] IR 420 which shows that where the interests of a creditor will be prejudiced by *not* winding up the company, the court will grant the petition notwithstanding that there is opposition from other creditors. For the significance of creditors' views, see para **[25.053]**.

94 *Re Bula Ltd* [1990] 1 IR 440.

95 [1990] 1 IR 440 at 447. On the invalidity of judgment mortgages, see CA 1963, s 284(2) and generally Chapter 27, *Realisation and Distribution of Assets in a Winding Up*, para **[27.052]**.

96 [1990] 1 IR 440 at 451.

97 [1990] 1 IR 440 at 448.

98 See para **[25.054]**. In the case of a private company limited by shares or by guarantee, the European Communities (Single-Member Private Limited Companies) Regulations 1994 (SI 1994/275), reg 11 has provided that CA 1963, s 213(d) shall not apply.

to final determination of, the persons who are to be deemed contributories, includes any person alleged to be a contributory.'

Any person who has a potential liability to contribute to the assets of a company is a possible petitioner, even where he has no actual liability[99].

[25.041] A contributory is restricted in his right to bring a petition by virtue of CA 1963, s 215(a) which prevents him from bringing a petition unless:

— the number of members is reduced, in the case of an unlimited private company[100] to one member; or

— his shares or some of them were either allotted to him, or have been held by him and registered in his name, for at least six months during the 18 months before the commencement of the winding up or have devolved on him through the death of the former holder.

The rationale for these restrictions is motivated by the desire to prevent past or present disgruntled members from petitioning unless they have good and substantial reason to do so[101].

[25.042] Although all past and present members are prima facie entitled to present a petition, if the contributory is the holder of fully paid up shares, the court will be reluctant to accede to the application, unless it can be shown that the company is solvent and that a substantial surplus of assets will be available to the members, as otherwise the member will have no tangible interest in the winding up[102]. The question as to whether or not a person is a contributory or member will often be apparent without judicial scrutiny. Where a petitioner's standing is not clear cut, it has been held by the English Court of Appeal that it will not automatically be the case that this will be deferred to the hearing of the petition and that, on occasion, this question will be answered as a preliminary question, particularly where to do so would leave a petitioner without an effective remedy were the petition to be struck out[103].

(d) The Director of Corporate Enforcement

[25.043] The Director of Corporate Enforcement ('the Director') can petition for the winding up of a company on the grounds set out in CA 1990, s 12[104]. The Minister for Enterprise, Trade and Employment's locus standi was, in this respect, transferred to the

---

[99] *Re Anglesea Colliery Co* [1866] 1 Ch App 555 at 559, per Turner LJ.

[100] European Communities (Single-Member Private Limited Companies) Regulations 1994 (SI 1994/275), reg 11 dis-applies CA 1963, s 215(a)(i) to private companies limited by shares or by guarantee; see para **[25.057]**.

[101] See Schmitthoff (ed), *Palmer's Company Law* (24th edn, 1987), para 88–15 where it is said that this is to 'prevent a person buying shares in order to qualify himself to wreck the company'.

[102] See Schmitthoff (ed), *Palmer's Company Law* (24th edn, 1987), para 88–16, citing, among other cases, *Re Expanded Plugs Ltd* [1966] 1 WLR 514 and *Re WR Willcocks & Co Ltd* [1973] 3 WLR 669. See also *Re Instrumentation Electrical Services Ltd* [1988] BCLC 550.

[103] *Re UOC Corp; Alipour v Ary* [1997] BCC 377.

[104] See para **[25.054]**. Surprisingly, CA 1963, s 215(d) which provides that the Minister can petition for a winding up in a case falling within CA 1963, s 170(3) – a section repealed by CA 1990, s 6(1) – was not also repealed by CA 1990. The result is that CA 1963, s 215 now contains a superfluous and redundant provision, albeit one which will not affect the Director's right to petition for a winding up.

Director by CLEA 2001, s 14. The Director's locus standi arises where the affairs of a company have been investigated by an inspector and it appears from the report or information obtained by the Director that the company should be wound up in the public interest[105]. The Director's power is, however, dependant upon the court finding that it is just and equitable for the company to be wound up[106].

(e) The Registrar of Companies

[25.044] The Registrar of Companies can petition the court to have a company wound up on the grounds set out in CA 1963, s 213(h) and (i). It is rare for the Registrar to petition to have a company wound up because of the registrar's power to strike a company off the register[107].

(f) Trustees of investment companies

[25.045] Section 215(g) of CA 1963[108] provides that the only person with locus standi to petition for the winding up of an investment company on the grounds that such is just and equitable (pursuant to CA 1963, s 213(fa))[109] is the trustee of an investment company ie the person nominated by the Central Bank under CA 1990, s 257(4)(c).

Procedural issues in compulsory windings up

[25.046] Much of the law relating to the compulsory winding up of companies is procedural in nature[110]. At this point it is proposed to review the procedural steps in compulsorily winding up a company.

(a) The petition

[25.047] When it is sought to have a company wound up compulsorily the applicant must proceed by petition. A petition is an application to court, whereby the petitioner *prays* the court for a specified relief. The Rules of the Superior Courts 1986 set out the procedural rules applicable to a winding up, and the Appendix to the Rules sets out three precedent forms of petition. Among the details which will have to be included are:

- the date on which the company was incorporated;
- the registered office of the company;
- the nominal and issued share capital of the company;
- the principal objects of the company; and
- the ground or grounds upon which the petition is based, these being one of those listed in CA 1963, s 213.

The purpose of requiring these details is to provide the court with a certain amount of basic information on the company. In addition, the petitioner must swear a verifying affidavit as to the truthfulness of the contents of the petition[111].

---

105 See generally Chapter 14, *Investigations and Inspectors*.

106 See para **[25.092]**.

107 See Chapter 12, *Company Law Compliance and Enforcement*, para **[12.132]**.

108 As inserted by CLEA 2001, s 94(c).

109 See para **[25.054]**.

110 See generally, the excellent account given by Marshall & MacDermott, 'Liquidations' (1991) Incorporated Law Society Continuing Legal Education Seminar of 27 June 1991.

111 In the case of a body corporate petitioner, an authorised officer should swear the verifying affidavit.

[25.048] Having prepared the petition, the petitioner then causes it to be *issued* by going to the Central Office of the High Court, where the Central Office will give it a hearing date, stamp and keep the original and a copy and endorse the date of hearing on a further copy of the petition. The Central Office will then direct the newspapers in which the petition is to be advertised. The verifying affidavit referred to must be filed within four days after the presentation of the petition.

[25.049] At this point, the petitioner must *serve* a copy of the petition on the company by ordinary post to the registered office of the company, or if there is none, at the principal or last known principal place of business of the company, or with a member, employee or officer of the company or some other place where the court on application, directs[112]. While there is no prohibition on the petition being served *after* the advertisement of the petition, it makes common sense to serve the company first so as to give it an opportunity to settle the demand before the other creditors become aware of the proceedings. An affidavit of service is also required to be sworn, stating that the petition was served on the company.

(b) Advertisement of the petition

[25.050] Next, the petitioner must cause the petition to be *advertised* in those newspapers which the Registrar of the High Court directs. Usually this will be in *Iris Oifigiúil*, and two national newspapers. The Rules of the Superior Courts 1986 provide that the advertisements must appear at least seven clear days prior to the date on which the petition is to be heard[113]. These advertisements must be then *vouched* in the Central Office of the High Court, before the hearing of the petition. Advertisements must be accurate and any errors will invalidate them[114]. Where the winding up of a company commences within one year after the company has changed its name, CA 1963, s 23(6) provides that the former name as well as the existing name of the company must appear on all notices and advertisements in relation to the winding up.

(c) Options for a respondent-company

[25.051] A company upon which a petition is served has a number of options open to it. It may *defend* the proceedings on all grounds open to it. This may involve the sometimes obstructive step of seeking security for costs against a corporate petitioner. Alternatively, it can *compromise* the claim against it. In such a case the petition can be struck out, although where the petition is advertised, another creditor can continue the process begun by the petitioner. Other creditors must notify the petitioner of their intention to appear at the

---

112 See RSC, Ord 74, r 11. In *Re Corbenstoke Ltd* [1989] BCLC 496 an application to have a petition struck out was refused where it had been served at the wrong address because of the Registrar of Companies' failure to register a change of the company's registered office in the Companies House.

113 On the matter of notifying persons, it is necessary to decide upon a liquidator and obtain from him a *letter of consent* to act as such, and prepare an *affidavit of suitability* to act as such, usually prepared by a solicitor. Also, the local sheriff should be notified as this compels him to hold goods seized from the company for proper distribution by the liquidator. See Chapter 26, *Liquidators*, para **[26.012]**.

114 See *Re London and Provincial Pure Ice Manufacturing Company* (1904) WN 136.

hearing of the petition[115] and the petitioner must give a list of these persons to the Registrar of the High Court prior to the hearing of the petition. Similarly, affidavits of opposition to the petition must be filed within seven days after the publication of the last advertisement, and notice must be given to the petitioner[116].

(d) Hearing the petition

[25.052] On the designated day the petitioner's legal advisors will attend at the High Court in the Four Courts. The company may, or may not be represented. It may seem trite, but the options open to the court are to either hear or adjourn the petition, and if it hears it, the court may either dismiss it or grant it[117].

[25.053] The courts will accede to a request to have the hearing of a petition *adjourned* in exceptional circumstances, only. In *Re Demaglass Holdings Ltd*[118] a petition was presented to wind up a company but the receivers who stood appointed sought to have the petition hearing adjourned so as to enable them to dispose of certain stock more advantageously. There, Neuberger J granted the adjournment sought for a period of ten weeks. The court made clear that where some creditors were in favour and some were against the making of a winding-up order, an order would be made where the majority supported the petition. A bare majority of creditors against the making of a winding-up order would not be sufficient to dissuade the court from granting a dissenting minority of creditors their prima facie right to a winding-up order. Neuberger J went on to hold that there was an onus on those creditors who opposed the making of a winding-up order to satisfy the court that there was good reason for refusing to order a winding up. Where the majority and minority had both established their respective cases, the court accepted that it would be forced to carry out a balancing exercise.

Grounds for ordering a company to be wound up

[25.054] The circumstances, or causes, which will ground a petition to wind up a company are set out in CA 1963, s 213. This section provides that a company *may* be wound up by the court if:

> '(a) the company has by special resolution resolved that the company be wound up by the court[119];
>
> (c) the company does not commence its business within a year from its incorporation or suspends its business for a whole year;
>
> (d) the number of members is reduced, in the case of a private company, below two, or, in the case of any other company, below seven[120];
>
> (e) the company is unable to pay its debts;

---

[115] See RSC, Ord 74, r 15.

[116] RSC, Ord 74, r 17.

[117] CA 1963, s 216.

[118] *Re Demaglass Holdings Ltd* [2001] 2 BCLC 633.

[119] CA 1963, s 213(b) was repealed by C(A)A 1983, Sch 3.

[120] Note that this is no longer a ground under which the court can be petitioned by single-member private companies, under the European Communities (Single-Member Private Limited Companies) Regulations 1994 (SI 1994/275), reg 11. See para **[25.057]**.

(f) the court is of the opinion that it is just and equitable that the company, other than an investment company within the meaning of Part XIII of the Companies Act 1990, or the European Communities (Undertakings for Collective Investments in Transferable Securities) Regulations 1989 (SI 1989/78), should be wound up[121];

(fa) the court is of opinion that it is just and equitable that the company, being an investment company within the meaning aforesaid, should be wound up and the following conditions are complied with —

(i) in the case of an investment company within the meaning of Part XIII of the Companies Act 1990

(I) the petition for such winding up has been presented by the trustee of the company, that is to say, the person nominated by the Central Bank of Ireland under section 257(4)(c) of the Companies Act 1990, in respect of that company;

(II) the said trustee has notified the investment company of its intention to resign as such trustee and six or more months have elapsed since the giving of that notification without a trustee having been appointed to replace it;

(III) the court, in considering the said petition, has regard to -

(A) any conditions imposed under section 257 of the Companies Act 1990, in relation to the resignation from office of such a trustee and the replacement of it by another trustee; and

(B) whether a winding up would best serve the interests of shareholders in the company;

and

(IV) the petition for such winding up has been served on the company (if any) discharging, in relation to the first-mentioned company, functions of a company referred to in conditions imposed under section 257 of the Companies Act 1990, as a 'management company';

and

(ii) in the case of an investment company within the meaning of the European Communities (Undertakings for Collective Investment in Transferable Securities) Regulations 1989, such conditions as the Minister may prescribe by regulations[122];

(g) the court is satisfied that the company's affairs are being conducted, or the powers of the directors are being exercised, in a manner oppressive to any member or in disregard of his interests as a member and that, despite the existence of an alternative remedy, winding up would be justified in the general circumstances of the case so, however, that the court may dismiss a petition to wind up under this paragraph if it is of opinion that proceedings under s 205 would, in all the circumstances, be more appropriate;

(h) after the end of the general transitional period, within the meaning of the Companies (Amendment) Act 1983, the company is an old public limited company within the meaning of that Act;

121 As amended by CLEA 2001, s 93(a).

122 As inserted by CLEA 2001, s 93(b).

(i) after the end of the transitional period for share capital, within the meaning of the Companies (Amendment) Act 1983, the company has not complied with the conditions specified in s 12(9) of 1983 Act.'

The main grounds are now considered in some detail.

(a) The company has resolved by special resolution to wind up the company

[25.055] For the members of a company to pass a special resolution to have the company wound up, and proceed to petition the court to have the company wound up is a rare occurrence. If the members can combine to pass a special resolution, they will, in all probability, opt to have their company wound up voluntarily, this being the most economical and discrete route to take.

(b) The company does not commence its business within a year from its incorporation or suspends its business for a whole year

[25.056] Again, this ground is rarely relied upon since only contributories, the company itself and creditors may rely on it. Such parties will often find other, more appropriate grounds, on which to petition to have a company wound up.

(c) The number of members is reduced, in the case of a private company, below two, or, in the case of any other company, below seven

[25.057] In the case of private companies limited by shares or by guarantee this is no longer a ground to petition the court to have such a company wound up. The European Communities (Single-Member Private Limited Companies) Regulations 1994, reg 11[123] provides:

> 'Sections 213(d) and 215(a)(i) of the 1963 Act shall not apply to a private company limited by shares or by guarantee.'

It may be noted, however, that this ground continues to apply with full force and effect in the case of an *unlimited private company.* Of course, its application to public companies also continues.

(d) The company is unable to pay its debts

[25.058] It is upon this ground that most petitions of creditors are based for the understandable reason that they believe the company to be *insolvent* with the consequence that their debts may not be paid. This ground is considered here under the following headings:

(i) A discretionary ground.
(ii) Deeming companies to be unable to pay their debts.
(iii) The '21-day letter'.
(iv) Service of the demand.
(v) The bona fides of the debt.
(vi) The existence of a valid cross-claim.
(vii) The test for injuncting a petition based on CA 1963, s 213(e).
(viii) Liability for improperly presenting petitions.

---

123 SI 1994/275.

(i) A discretionary ground

[25.059] Section 213 of CA 1963 is a discretionary provision and even though a person may prove conclusively that a company is unable to pay its debts, there is no automatic right to a winding-up order. So, for example, a petitioner may be estopped from presenting a petition on equitable grounds[124]. The discretionary nature of s 213 was stressed by McCracken J in *Re Genport Ltd*[125]. In that case the petitioner was one of several defendants in proceedings that had been taken by the respondent-company and others. The action against the petitioner had been dismissed and the petitioner was awarded two-thirds of her costs against the plaintiffs. After taxation of her costs the petitioner served a demand under CA 1963, s 214(a) for her costs plus interest, and when these were not paid, issued the petition to wind up the respondent-company. McCracken J noted that the proceedings that gave rise to the order for costs were part of a long-running series of disputes between the respondent-company and other parties, including a landlord and tenant dispute concerning the respondent-company's lease of Sachs Hotel in Dublin. McCracken J stated that s 213 sets out a list of circumstances in which a company *'may'* be wound up by the Court. As to the instant case he said that there was no doubt but that the petitioner had proved (by reason of s 214[126]) that the company had been unable to pay its debts. McCracken J went on to say 'however, it is quite clear that s 213 is not mandatory, and there remains a discretion in the court'. McCracken J stated that the correct approach in such cases was that set out by McCarthy J in *Re Bula Ltd*[127], where he said:

> 'I would hold that a creditor is prima facie entitled to his order so as to shift the initial burden to those who oppose the winding up; the petitioner does not have to demonstrate positively that an order for winding up is for the benefit of the class of creditors to which he belongs, but, if issue is joined on the matter, and a case made that the petition is not for that purpose but for an ulterior, though not in itself improper object, then the burden shifts back to the petitioner'.

Applying that reasoning to the facts of *Re Genport Ltd* McCracken J said of the claim that the petitioner had an ulterior motive (ie to prevent further litigation) that he did not think that that alone was sufficient to persuade him to exercise his discretion against the petitioner because the motive was not necessarily improper. What swayed the judge in deciding to refuse to allow the petition to proceed, however, was the fact that the respondent's lease to Sachs Hotel would be forfeited were it was wound up with the result that there would be little left by way of assets for the remaining creditors. McCracken J also considered it significant that four trade creditors who were the only trade creditors to appear on the petition, were opposed to the company being wound up. He was also influenced by the fact that there was substantial litigation in being which a liquidator

---

124 An estoppel from presenting a petition was claimed by a respondent-company but rejected by the English Court of Appeal in *Re Selectmove Ltd* [1995] 2 All ER 531 on the application of the decision in *Foakes v Beer* (1888) 9 App Cas 606 and the rule in *Pinnel's Case* (1605) 5 Co Rep 117a. The Court of Appeal's decision in *Selectmove Ltd* was applied by Keane J in *Truck and Machinery Sales Lt v Marubeni Komatsu Ltd* [1996] 1 IR 12.

125 *Re Genport Ltd* (21 November 1996, unreported), High Court (McCracken J).

126 See para **[25.062]**.

127 *Re Bula Ltd* [1990] 1 IR 440 at 448.

would have difficulty in taking over. In these circumstances McCracken J held that the combination of the ulterior (although not necessarily improper) motive and the fact that a winding up might not be of any real benefit to ordinary creditors were sufficient to persuade him to exercise his discretion to refuse to make a winding-up order[128].

[25.060] The wishes of other creditors can, as seen in *Re Genport Ltd*, influence the court's discretion. Indeed, in that case McCracken J relied upon CA 1963, s 309(1) as authority for the proposition that the court 'may, as to all matters relating to the winding up of a company, have regard to the wishes of the creditors or contributories'[129]. Where there is a divergence of opinion and some creditors favour winding up and others do not, the court will ordinarily be inclined towards the wishes of those with the most money owed to them (s 309(2) of the 1963 Act) but where the opposing creditors are not independent, being persons associated with the company or its directors, their views will, at the judge's discretion, be discounted[130].

[25.061] The discretionary nature of the court's powers and the desire to act in the interests of members and creditors can also be seen in *Re WMG (Toughening) Ltd*[131]. In that case the petitioner claimed that the respondent-company owed a company in which he owned all of the issued shares some £138,000 on foot of a loan. The respondent-company was owned as to 21% by another company called WMG Group Ltd, of which the petitioner was chairman. The petitioner demanded repayment of the loan and when this did not happen presented a petition to have the company wound up; the respondent-company resisted the petition. The respondent-company had been capitalised by a Forbairt grant of £125,000, the loan of £138,000 by the petitioner's company and by two tranches of Business Expansion Scheme ('BES') funds of £55,000 and £157,000. Murphy J said that it was clear that the respondent-company had been set up for the purpose of financing (by grant aid and BES funding) an operation that was entirely dependent on another subsidiary of

---

128 The petition was, however, stayed with liberty to re-enter, pending the outcome of the litigation.

129 In *Re Genport Ltd (No 2)* (6 November 2001, unreported), High Court (McCracken J) five years' later, to the month, McCracken J again adjourned the petition generally with liberty to re-enter. There, McCracken J held that it appeared 'beyond doubt that if a winding-up order is made, the benefit to the petitioner will be negligible, and the probability is that neither she nor any of the ordinary creditors will recover anything at all'. Again, McCracken J identified the company's landlord (which would recover vacant possession of the property leased to the company) as the principal beneficiary. On this point he said:

> 'This seems to me to be the motive of seeking a winding-up order at this state. It may well be said, as was in the *Bula* case, that the motive is not in itself improper, as the petitioner is an officer of Crofter Properties Ltd, and indeed Crofter Properties Ltd is almost certainly the largest creditor of the company. There is no doubt in my mind that this application is not being brought to benefit the ordinary creditors of the company, as such, but to benefit Crofter Properties in its position as lessor of the property to the company and as one particular general creditor. In those circumstances, while I am not taking the drastic remedy of dismissing the petition as was done in the *Bula Ltd* case, nevertheless I would propose to adjourn the petition generally, with liberty to re-enter'.

130 *Re Lummus Agricultural Services Ltd* [1999] BCC 953. As to a contested adjournment, see para **[25.053]**.

131 *Re WMG (Toughening) Ltd* (6 April 2001, unreported), High Court (Roderick Murphy J).

> 'Although I understand that it is sometimes the practice of the Companies Court to act on the basis of a statutory demand which has been sent through the post, it seems to me that once the point taken by counsel for the company has been taken, it seems to be a good one. Section 437(1)[140] [of the Companies Act 1948 (UK)] is in these terms: 'A document may be served on a company by leaving it at or sending it by post to the registered office of the company'. That shows clearly that sending it by post is not leaving it at the registered office within s 223(a). It may be that the provisions of the Companies Acts have not yet fully caught up with modern conditions and that there would be a case for allowing a statutory demand to be sent through the post, or indeed to be sent by telex. On the other hand a statutory demand is a solemn document with potentially serious consequences. I can well understand that the legislature might have consciously intended that the service of a document of that character should be carried out in much the same way as the service of a winding-up petition, which cannot be sent through the post and certainly cannot be sent on the telex machine.'[141]

This case is also authority for the proposition that the written demand made must be unequivocal, of a peremptory character and unconditional: in that case Nourse J held that the demand made did not meet these criteria.

(v) The bona fides of the debt

[25.066] In order for a demand to be valid, it must be bona fide. Pennington[142] puts it thus:

> 'If the company contends that it is not liable to the creditor for the whole or the unpaid part of his claim, and can satisfy the court that it has a substantial and reasonable defence to plead, the court will hold that it is not in default, and will refuse to make a winding-up order.'

Where a creditor attempts to use the petition for inappropriate purposes, the court has discretion to refuse to make the order to wind up the company[143]. To seek to have a company wound up for failure to pay a debt that is disputed on bona fide grounds is an abuse of process[144]. In *Re Pageboy Couriers Ltd*[145] a creditor instituted a petition seeking the winding up of a company and relied upon CA 1963, s 214(a) to prove insolvency. The petition was 'hotly contested' by the company which disputed the debt. The petitioner had also instituted proceedings against the company for the sum and although the company had sought particulars of the claim from the plaintiff, such were not forthcoming. The proceedings against the company were then allowed to lie dormant, the petitioner instead seeking to have the company wound up. The company claimed that it was well established that a creditor should not proceed by petition where he is well aware that the company has a substantial and reasonable defence, and in this regard relied on *Stonegate Securities Ltd v Gregory*[146]. The following extract from the judgment of Buckley J in that case was cited with approval by O'Hanlon J:

---

[140] See CA 1963, s 379(1), considered in Chapter 6, *Corporate Civil Litigation*, para **[6.011]**.

[141] [1985] BCLC 37 at 42.

[142] In Pennington, *Corporate Insolvency Law* (1991), p 39.

[143] See para **[25.039]**.

[144] *Re Bula Ltd* [1990] 1 IR 440; *Ringinfo Ltd* [2002] 1 BCLC 210.

[145] *Re Pageboy Couriers Ltd* [1983] ILRM 510.

[146] *Stonegate Securities Ltd v Gregory* [1980] 1 All ER 241.

> 'If a company in good faith and on substantial grounds disputes any liability in respect of the alleged debt, the petition will be dismissed, or if the matter is brought before a court before a petition is issued, its presentation will in normal circumstances be restrained. That is because a winding-up petition is not a legitimate means of seeking to enforce payment of a debt which is *bona fide* disputed. Ungood-Thomas J, put the matter thus in *Mann v Goldstein* [1968] 2 All ER 769 at 775: "For my part, I would prefer to rest the jurisdiction directly on the comparatively simple proposition that a 'creditor's petition can only be presented by a creditor, that the winding-up jurisdiction is not for the purpose of deciding a disputed debt (that is, disputed on substantial and not insubstantial grounds) since, until a creditor is established as a creditor he is not entitled to present the petition and has no locus standi in the companies' court: and that, therefore, to invoke the winding-up jurisdiction when the debt is disputed (that is on substantial grounds) or after it has become clear that it is so disputed is an abuse of the process of the court".'

O'Hanlon J accepted that 'the principles there enunciated as being applicable also when considering the propriety of proceeding by way of petition for the winding up of a company under the provisions of our own Companies Acts'. Accordingly, it was held that the petition was not well founded, and it was dismissed. Whether or not there is a genuine dispute will be a matter of fact in each case[147]; where there is disputed fact, the court is likely to conclude that the dispute will require to be determined in plenary proceedings with appropriate cross-examination of both sides and not on a petition to wind up[148].

(vi) The existence of a valid cross-claim Re Bayoil

[25.067] It has been established that even if the debt claimed by the petitioner is bona fide, a petition might be dismissed where the company has a legitimate cross-claim against the petitioner which would negate the amount owed to the petitioner[149]. In *Re WMG (Toughening) Ltd*[150] Murphy J quoted with approval the following passage from *Malayan Plant (PT) Ltd v Moscow Narodny Bank Ltd*[151]:

> 'There is no serious distinction in principle between a cross-claim of substance and the serious dispute regarding the indebtedness imputed against a company, which has long been held to constitute a proper ground upon which to reject a winding-up petition.'

---

147 See *Re FSA Business Software Ltd* [1990] BCLC 825. In *McDonald's Restaurants Ltd v Urbandivide Co Ltd* [1994] 1 BCLC 306 it was held that the debtor company had an arguable defence by way of equitable set-off to the petitioner's claim.

148 In *Re Millhouse Taverns Ltd* (3 April 2000, unreported), High Court (Finnegan J) the Revenue Commissioner's petition to wind up the respondent-company was disputed. It was held by Finnegan J that the affidavits filed on behalf of the respondent-company fell 'far short of showing that the company has a substantial and reasonable defence to the petitioner's claim which would enable it to defeat the entire of the claim brought against it'. See also *Re Amadeus Trading Ltd* [1997] TLR 184.

149 *Re Bayoil SA* [1999] 1 All ER 374, where the English Court of Appeal relied upon the earlier authorities for this proposition in *Re Portman Provincial Cinemas Ltd* (1964) 108 Sol J 581 and *Re LHF Woods Ltd* [1970] Ch 27. See also *Montgomery v Wanda Modes Ltd* [2002] 1 BCLC 289.

150 *Re WMG (Toughening) Ltd* (6 April 2001, unreported), High Court (Roderick Murphy J).

151 *Malayan Plant (PT) Ltd v Moscow Narodny Bank Ltd* (1980) MLJ 53 at 55.

The existence of a valid cross-claim will not, however, invariably cause the court to exercise its discretion to dismiss a winding-up petition[152]. Of course, it is also necessary for the respondent-company to establish that its cross-claim is 'genuine, serious and has substance'[153] and is for an amount in excess of that claimed by the petitioner[154]. In *Greenacre Publishing Group v The Manson Group*[155] the respondent-company had refused to pay for printing services for a monthly magazine that had been delayed for seven days, because it claimed that it had lost revenue and advertising contracts. It argued that the petitioner's claim would be met with a substantial cross-claim and applied to have the petition struck out. Lloyd J held that where there was an undisputed debt but a disputed cross-claim, the court had to be satisfied that the evidence was such that the court would dismiss the petition because the case was so strong. In the instant case, Lloyd J held that the evidence for the cross-claim was unsatisfactory and the court could not conclude that the cross-claim would be sufficient to extinguish or reduce below the limit the petitioner's undisputed debt.

(vii) The test for injuncting a petition based on CA 1963, s 213(e)

[25.068] It is one thing to successfully dispute the bona fides of a debt at the hearing of a petition; however, even where successful, the company is exposed to a glare of adverse publicity, wherein its solvency is questioned. Upon being served with a petition in respect of a genuinely disputed debt, therefore, a company might wish to restrain the advertisement of the petition and have the dispute out in interlocutory proceedings rather than on an advertised petition. Where the ground relied upon to present the petition is the inability of the company to pay its debts, the court may grant an injunction to prevent the advertisement of the petition as an abuse of process where the company disputes the claim of the petitioner on bona fide and substantial grounds[156]. At the outset, it should be noted that the courts will be slow to restrain a petitioner from advertising or presenting a petition. The first Irish case to consider an application for an injunction to restrain the advertisement of a petition which has been lodged is *Clandown Ltd v Davis*[157]. In that case the defendant had presented a petition to have the plaintiff-company wound up. She had been a shareholder, director and employee of the company but had been removed as a

---

152 See *Re Richbell Information Services Inc* [1999] TLR 49 where it was held by Judge Weeks QC that the interests of the company and its creditors during the litigation of the cross-claim would be better protected by the appointment of a liquidator.

153 See Laddie J in the English High Court in *Orion Media Marketing Ltd v Media Brook Ltd and another* [2002] 1 BCLC 184.

154 *Re Latreefers Inc* [1999] TLR 37. There, Lloyd J also commented that the respondent-company was required to show that it had been unable to litigate the cross-claim.

155 *Greenacre Publishing Group v The Manson Group* [2000] BCC 11.

156 See *Mann v Goldstein* [1968] 2 All ER 769. In *Re a Company* [1986] BCLC 127, Hoffmann J held that the court has jurisdiction to restrain a petitioner from not only advertising the petition, but also to otherwise publicise it. In *Re a Company (No 001448 of 1989)* [1989] BCLC 715, Millett J held that an advertisement could be restrained where an undertaking to make application to put the company into administration (examination in Ireland) had been given by the company. See also *Re Garton (Western) Ltd* [1989] BCLC 304 and *Re a Company (No 00962 of 1991), ex p Electrical Engineering Contracts (London) Ltd* [1992] BCLC 248.

157 *Clandown Ltd v Davis* [1994] 2 ILRM 536.

director at the company's annual general meeting ('AGM'). The defendant claimed that the company owed her £56,889.69. Having demanded this and upon its not being paid, she sought to have the company wound up on the basis that it was unable to pay its debts. The plaintiff-company claimed that this was an abuse of the court's process as there was a serious and genuine dispute as to the veracity of the defendant's assertion that the plaintiff was indebted to the defendant in the amount claimed or in any amount. Indeed, the plaintiff-company had counterclaimed that the defendant was indebted to it. Morris J said that the law was well settled on this point: where a company in good faith and on substantial grounds disputes any liability in respect of the alleged debt, the petition will be dismissed[158]. However, he commented that this was the first Irish case to his knowledge where the question concerned an injunction to restrain the advertisement of a petition which had been lodged. Citing the judgments of Hoffmann J in *Re a Company (No 008725 of 1991)*[159] and *Re a Company (No 0012209 of 1991)*[160] Morris J concluded that the law required that he consider the following:

> 'Is the defendant a "creditor" which would entitle her to present a petition to the court or put another way, is the plaintiff, the company, disputing this claim on bona fide and substantial grounds.'[161]

Applying this test to the facts of the case, Morris J considered the affidavits which had been filed. The defendant said that her claim in her letter was allegedly uncontradicted by the plaintiff-company; that it was again uncontradicted in a minute presented to the directors' meeting of the plaintiff-company; that the company's auditors checked off various amounts in the company's accounts and had passed them as accurate; that there were inaccuracies in the plaintiff-company's accounting and that even taking the plaintiff-company's figures there was a credit due to the defendant. Of this Morris J said:

> '...I am left with a very clear feeling that the plaintiffs have sought high and low to produce figures to challenge the defendant in her claim that there is money due to her. I am far from satisfied that the defendant's allegations of inaccurate accounting and improper bookkeeping have been made out to anything like the level necessary to satisfy a court trying the issues between the parties. However, that is not the test that I have to apply. I am satisfied that on the law I would have to be satisfied that the amount of the defendant's claim is clear and incapable of dispute. I am not satisfied of this. I am not satisfied how much of the matter contained in the defendant's affidavits will eventually be found to be accurate. I am unable to be satisfied that the defendant can be deemed to be a creditor of the plaintiff-company. In a matter of this complexity, in my view it would be inappropriate for a court at this stage to form a clear cut view on affidavits filed as to the parties' indebtedness to one another and accordingly, adopting the test of Thomas J in *Mann v Goldstein*, I am not prepared to say that

---

[158] Here, Morris J cited, and quoted from, *Re Pageboy Couriers Ltd* [1983] ILRM 510 and *Stonegate Securities Ltd v Gregory* [1980] 1 All ER 241. See para **[25.066]**.

[159] *Re a Company (No 008725 of 1991)* [1992] BCLC 633. Here, Hoffmann J said (at 634): 'It is agreed that in order to restrain advertisement, I must be satisfied on the evidence before me that it would appear on the hearing of the petition that the debt is disputed in good faith and on substantial grounds.'

[160] *Re a Company (No 0012209 of 1991)* [1992] BCLC 865.

[161] [1994] 2 ILRM 536 at 540.

> the defendant in this case is "a creditor" entitled to present a petition and who would have locus standi in the Companies Court.'[162]

Accordingly, the learned judge granted the injunction to restrain the publication of the petition to have the company wound up. One result of this decision is to reinforce the principle that the courts will not permit CA 1963, s 213 to be used as a method of debt collection.

[25.069] It should be noted, however, that the correctness of restraining a winding up even where only part of the debt was disputed was doubted by Keane J in what must now be considered to be the leading Irish case, *Truck and Machinery Sales Ltd v Marubeni Komatsu Ltd*[163]. The facts there were that the defendant sought to have the plaintiff wound up for non-payment of moneys allegedly due. The plaintiff had purchased second-hand machinery from the defendant for approximately £2.9 million; the consideration was not payable until a particular date. The machinery was shipped to the United Arab Emirates but the plaintiff was prevented from distributing the machinery there because a third party claimed it had an exclusive distribution agreement with the defendant, which prevented the sale of the machinery there. The defendant had known that the plaintiff proposed to sell the machinery in the United Arab Emirates but considered that the distribution agreement was irrelevant, since it only concerned new machinery. Both parties attempted unsuccessfully to negotiate the distribution of the machinery. By this time the plaintiff had paid the defendant some £600,000 but it was claimed that in excess of £2.3 million remained outstanding. The defendant advised the plaintiff that if the balance was not forthcoming, it would bring a winding-up petition against the plaintiff. The plaintiff's claim that the defendant had agreed in a facsimile to waive the balance of the debt until the outcome of legal proceedings in the United Arab Emirates, was denied by the defendant. The plaintiff then sought an injunction to restrain both the advertisement of the petition and the bringing of the petition.

[25.070] In the High Court Keane J began by distinguishing situations where a respondent-company disputes that it has *any* liability in respect of an alleged debt from those where a company admits an indebtedness in a sum exceeding €1,269.74. In relation to the former situation, he said:

> 'It is clear that, where the company in good faith and on substantial grounds, disputes *any* liability in respect of the alleged debt, the petition will be dismissed, or if the matter is brought before the court before the petition is issued, its presentation will in normal circumstances be restrained. This is on the ground that a winding-up petition is not a legitimate means of seeking to enforce payment of a debt which is *bona fide* disputed.'[164]

Where, however, a respondent-company admits to an indebtedness in a sum exceeding €1,269.74 different considerations apply. Keane J held that where the company 'disputes the balance, even on substantial grounds, the creditor should not normally be restrained

[162] [1994] 2 ILRM 536 at 540-541.

[163] *Truck and Machinery Sales Ltd v Marubeni Komatsu Ltd* [1996] 1 IR 12. For comment, see Canniffe, 'Restraining a Creditor's Winding-up Petition – The Position Since *Truck and Machinery Sales Ltd v Marubeni Komatsu Ltd*' (1997) 4 CLP 30.

[164] At p 16 of the judgment, citing *Mann v Goldstein* [1968] 2 All ER 769 and *Stongate Securities Ltd v Gregory* [1980] 1 All ER 241 as authorities.

from presenting a petition'. In this respect, Keane J preferred the authority of the decisions in *Re Tweeds Garage Ltd*[165] and *Taylor's Industrial Flooring Ltd v M&H Plant Hire (Manchester) Ltd*[166] to that in *Clandown v Davis*[167]. Keane J went on to acknowledge that even where a company is insolvent, the court could restrain the presentation of a petition where presented for an ulterior or collateral purpose and not in good faith.

[25.071] Citing *Bryanston Finance Ltd v De Vries (No 2)*[168], Keane J went on to state that the jurisdiction to restrain the presentation of a petition to wind up is one to be exercised with great caution. Keane J held that the normal test for an interlocutory injunction, laid down by the Supreme Court in *Campus Oil Ltd v Minister for Industry and Energy (No 2)*[169] was not applicable to an injunction to restrain the presentation of a winding-up petition. Keane J's reason for so holding was:

> '...the object of the application is to prevent the respondent from exercising his right of access to the courts, whether by way of ordinary process or a winding-up petition. In such a case, the factors which the court should take into account were also identified in *Bryanston Finance*. Thus, Buckley LJ said that: - "The plaintiff-company cannot assert such a right in respect of any particular anticipated litigation without demonstrating that, at least *prima facie*, that litigation would be an abuse".'

Keane J noted that in the English Court of Appeal in *Coulson Sanderson & Ward v Ward*[170] Slade LJ had said of the former case that:

> 'This decision, therefore, is clear authority for the proposition that the court should not, on the hearing of an interlocutory motion, interfere with what would otherwise appear to be the

---

165 *Re Tweeds Garage Ltd* [1962] 1 All ER 121.

166 *Taylor's Industrial Flooring Ltd v M&H Plant Hire (Manchester) Ltd* [1990] BCLC 21.

167 Keane J noted that he had applied the principle in *Re Tweeds Garage Ltd* in *Patrick Butterly and Sons Ltd v Top Security Ltd* (27 September 1995, unreported), High Court (ex tempore).

168 *Bryanston Finance Ltd v De Vries (No 2)* [1976] 1 Ch 63. Keane J quoted the following passage from the judgment of Buckley LJ:

> 'It has long been recognised that the jurisdiction of the court to stay an action *in limine* as an abuse of process is a jurisdiction to be exercised with great circumspection and exactly the same considerations must apply to a *quia timet* injunction to restrain commencement of proceedings. These principles are, in my opinion, just as applicable to a winding-up petition as to an action. The right to petition the court for a winding-up order in appropriate circumstances is a right conferred by statute. A would-be petitioner should not be restrained from exercising it except on clear and persuasive grounds. I recognise that the presentation of a petition may do great damage to a company's business and reputation, though I think that the potential damage in the present case may have been rather exaggerated. The restraint of a petition may also gravely affect the would-be petitioner and not only him but also others, whether creditors or contributories. If the presentation of the petition is prevented the commencement of the winding up will be postponed until such time as the petition is presented or a winding-up resolution is passed. This is capable of far reaching effects.'

169 *Campus Oil Ltd v Minister for Industry and Energy (No 2)* [1983] IR 88. See, generally, the discussion of this test in Courtney, *Mareva Injunctions and Related Interlocutory Orders* (1998), pp 173–179.

170 *Coulson Sanderson & Ward v Ward* [1986] BCLC 99.

> legitimate presentation of a winding-up petition by someone qualified to present it unless the evidence before it is sufficient to establish prima facie that the plaintiff-company will succeed in establishing that the proceedings sought to be restrained would constitute an abuse'.

Accepting this, Keane J thereby disapplied the *Campus Oil/American Cyanamid* test to injunctions to restrain the presentation of a winding-up petition. He said:

> 'I am satisfied that this is the approach which should also be adopted in this jurisdiction. The constitutional right of recourse to the courts should not be inhibited, save in exceptional circumstances, and this applies as much to the presentation of a petition for the winding up of a company by a person with the appropriate locus standi as it does to any other form of proceedings. The undoubted power of the courts to restrain proceedings which are an abuse of process is one which should not be lightly exercised. *In the context of winding-up petitions, I have no doubt that it should be exercised only where the plaintiff-company has established at least a prima facie case that its presentation would constitute an abuse of process.* In many cases, a *prima facie* case will be established where the plaintiff-company adduced evidence which satisfies the court that the petition is bound to fail or, at the least, that there is a suitable alternative remedy.' [Emphasis added.]

Keane J went on to state that in considering an application for an injunction to restrain the presentation of a petition, the court must approach the matter with the interests of the creditors in mind[171]. Applying the law thus enunciated to the facts of the case in hand, Keane J held that the defendant could not be restrained from presenting a petition. To the argument that it had agreed not to proceed against the plaintiff, Keane J held that it was settled law that a promise to pay part of a debt was not good consideration and he rejected that there was any enforceable agreement[172] or any estoppel that bound the defendant. The result of these findings was that Keane J had not been satisfied that the company had established a prima facie case that the presentation of the petition would be an abuse of process[173].

[25.072] In *Meridian Communications Ltd v Eircell Ltd*[174] the Supreme Court applied the same principles but this time held that the defendant should be enjoined from presenting a petition to wind up the plaintiff. The background facts were that the plaintiff had rented certain telephone lines from the defendant and had leased them to its own subscribers of whom there were about 20,000. The agreement to supply these lines was due to be terminated and it was argued that this would cause the plaintiff's customer base to evaporate. The defendant claimed to be owed money from the plaintiff and had served a 21-day letter. The plaintiff asked to be allowed to try to sell its subscriber base before its arrangements with the defendants was terminated ie while it still had a valuable asset to

---

171 In reliance upon the decision of Street CJ in *Kinsella v Russell Kinsella Property Ltd* [1986) 4 NSWLR 722, which Keane J noted had been expressly approved of by the Supreme Court in *Re Frederick Inns Ltd* [1994] 1 ILRM 387.

172 Applying *Foakes v Beer* (1888) App Cas 605.

173 In *Re J McLaughlin and Co Ltd*, an application reported in (1996) The Irish Times, 9 July (Barron J) it was reportedly held that it would be an abuse of process to issue a petition in that case when there was a dispute about the debt in question.

174 *Meridian Communications Ltd v Eircell Ltd* (10 May 2001, unreported), Supreme Court (McGuinness J; *nem diss*).

sell and claimed that a sale could generate £10 million, which would meet any indebtedness it had to the defendant and any other creditors. The defendant argued that the plaintiff had cancelled certain direct debits and appeared to be insolvent. Its argument was that it was both logical and reasonable to move to terminate the service it provided the plaintiff and to bring a petition under CA 1963, s 213 on the grounds of inability to pay the plaintiff's debts.

[25.073] McGuinness J held that the principles applicable to such injunctions had been fully and clearly set out by Keane J in *Truck and Machinery Sales Ltd v Marubei Komatsu Ltd*[175] and she quoted the head note from the reported decision which she said the Supreme Court accepted were in principle the correct standards to be applied:

> '(a) Since a winding-up petition was not a legitimate means of enforcing payment of a debt which was *bona fide* disputed, the presentation of a petition would in normal circumstances be restrained if the company, in good faith and on substantial grounds disputed all liability in respect of the debt claimed.
>
> (b) Where a company admitted its indebtedness to the creditor in a sum exceeding £1,000 [€1,269.74] but disputed the balance, even on substantial grounds, the creditor should not normally be restrained from presenting a winding-up petition.
>
> (c) Even where the company appeared to be insolvent the court might in the exercise of its equitable jurisdiction, restrain the presentation of the petition where it was satisfied that the petition was being presented for an ulterior or collateral purpose and not in good faith; but that the court must approach the position of such a company with the interests of the creditors particularly in mind.
>
> (d) The jurisdiction to restrain the presentation of the petition should be exercised only with great caution.
>
> (e) Since an application to restrain the presentation of a winding-up petition involved not the restraint of an alleged violation of a plaintiff's right but of the exercise by a creditor of his right of access to the courts, the normal considerations of a fair question to be tried, the adequacy of damages as a remedy and the balance of convenience did not arise; instead, it was for the plaintiff to establish at least a prima facie case, which would in many instances be established by evidence that the petition was bound to fail or, at the least that there was a suitable alternative remedy.'

The Supreme Court held that it was extremely unlikely that the plaintiff's alleged debt to the defendant could be reduced below the sum of £1,000 and McGuinness J said:

> 'if the proposed sale and settlement of indebtedness does not proceed in the near future, there would seem to be no proper grounds for restraining [the defendant] from bringing the proposed petition'.

The Supreme Court, however, granted the injunction to restrain the presentation of the petition to wind up the plaintiff until the expiry of the other injunction which prevented the defendant from terminating the service agreement – a period of a few weeks.

(viii) Liability for improperly presenting petitions

[25.074] Where a petition is wrongly presented, the company which it was sought to have wound up may have a remedy. So, it has been held that a solicitor who swore an affidavit

175 *Truck and Machinery Sales Ltd v Marubei Komatsu Ltd* [1996] 1 IR 12.

in support of a petition when no debt was in fact owed, had acted unreasonably as there were no grounds upon which a competent solicitor could have formed that view, and the solicitor was ordered to pay personally the company's wasted costs[176]. Petitioners are well advised to consider carefully the option of proceeding by winding-up petition instead of by ordinary action. Where a respondent-company is forced to make application to restrain the advertisement of a petition that has been presented and (on being furnished with evidence of solvency) the petitioner undertakes not to advertise the petition, the petitioner might only be able to halt the process by undertaking and submitting to an order that they pay the costs incurred by the respondent-company[177].

[25.075] It may also be noted that the tort of *malicious presentation of petition* was acknowledged by the English Court of Appeal in *Radivojevic v LR Industries Ltd*[178]. There it was said that in order to establish the tort, it is necessary to show three things:

— that the petition terminated in favour of the respondent-company;

— that there was an absence of reasonable or probable cause for presenting the petition; and

— that there was malice or improper motive on the part of the petitioner in presenting the petition[179].

(e) The court is of the opinion that it is just and equitable that the company should be wound up

[25.076] This is the most dynamic ground for petitioning to have a company wound up. Previously, it was thought that the use of the words 'just and equitable', ought to be construed ejusdem generis to the preceding grounds in CA 1963, s 213[180]. However, this restrictive interpretation has now been abandoned as seen in *Ebrahimi v Westbourne Galleries Ltd*[181]. Lord Wilberforce's judgment in that case was cited with approval by Gannon J in *Re Murph's Restaurants*[182]. Consequently, one can petition for the winding up of a company in a situation which is unrelated to any of the other grounds listed in s 213. An early Irish case which applied the liberal interpretation was *Re Newbridge Sanitary Steam Laundry Ltd*[183] where a company was ordered to be wound up on just and equitable grounds by Sir Ignatius O'Brien LC, because the controller of a company refused to account for money received by him for and on behalf of the company, notwithstanding that this action by the controller had been ratified by the members in general meeting. Despite the more recent restrictive interpretation in *Re Guidezone Ltd*[184] that the winding-up

176 See *Re A Company (No 006798 of 1995)* [1996] 1 WLR 491.

177 See *Re a Company (No 007356/98) (ITC Infotech Ltd)* [2000] BCC 214.

178 *Radivojevic v LR Industries Ltd* Unreported decision of 22 November 1984.

179 This test was applied, but found not to have been met, in *Partizan Ltd v OJ Kilkenny & Co Ltd* [1998] BCC 912.

180 See *Ex p Spackman* (1849) 1 Mac & G 170–174, per Lord Cottenham LC.

181 *Ebrahimi v Westbourne Galleries Ltd* [1972] 2 All ER 492, [1973] AC 360.

182 *Re Murph's Restaurants* [1979] ILRM 141.

183 *Re Newbridge Sanitary Steam Laundry Ltd* [1917] 1 IR 237.

184 *Re Guidezone Ltd* [2000] 2 CLC 321. For notation of this case, see *CCH's Company Law Update* (2001) 5 September 2001. For further commentary, see Acton, 'Just and Equitable Winding Up – The Strange Case of the Disappearing Jurisdiction' (2001) 22 *Company Lawyer* 134.

jurisdiction may be no wider than the jurisdiction in Companies Act 1985, s 459 (UK) – namely to wind up where it has been shown that a company's affairs have been conducted in a manner unfairly prejudicial to a petitioner – it is thought that the 'just and equitable' test is not so confined and is, rather, available in any of the circumstances referred in the paragraph next following[185].

[25.077] The decided cases can be grouped into certain categories and it is proposed to adopt the following structure notwithstanding the danger of fettering the perceived latitude of this ground[186]:

(i) The 'quasi-partnership' cases.

(ii) Deadlock in corporate management.

(iii) Failure of substratum.

(iv) Illegal objects.

(v) Corporate instruments of fraud.

(vi) Public interest.

A jurisdiction that is driven by what is 'just and equitable' is the very essence of what is dynamic. The practice of law has an uncanny tendency to present factual situations which differ from established authorities, and so other situations which do not fit neatly into the foregoing categories may still merit the winding up of a company on just and equitable grounds.

(i) The 'quasi-partnership' cases

[25.078] While certainly not always the case[187], the relations between the shareholders in many private companies can be tantamount to a partnership. So, of the three members of the company in *Re Murph's Restaurant Ltd*[188] Gannon J observed that it was clear from the evidence that the members were:

> '...equal partners in a joint venture, and that the company was no more than a vehicle to secure a limited liability for possible losses and to provide a means of earning and distributing profits to their best advantage with minimum disclosure.'[189]

Such companies have more in common with partnerships than they have with companies envisaged by the Companies Acts 1963–2001. Where the member-partners of such

---

185 It is relevant that, in England, CA 1985, s 125(2) (UK) provides that an order for the winding up of a company should not be made on just and equitable grounds where 'some other remedy is available to the petitioners and that they are acting unreasonably in seeking to have the company wound up instead of pursuing that other remedy'. See *Re Murray Consultants and Nocrumb Ltd; Horgan v Murray and Milton* (9 July 1999, unreported), Supreme Court at p 19. See, also, *Re Copeland & Craddock Ltd* [1997] BCC 294 where the English Court of Appeal refused to strike out a petition for winding up on the just and equitable ground, notwithstanding s 125(2) on the grounds that, inter alia, it was reasonable for the petitioner to pursue the winding-up remedy. See, further, *CCH's Company Law News* (1997) Issue 7/1997; 23 April 1997.

186 See *Ebrahimi v Westbourne Galleries Ltd* [1972] 2 All ER 492.

187 See Lord Wilberforce's observations in *Ebrahimi v Westbourne Galleries Ltd* [1972] 2 All ER 492 at 500d–h.

188 *Re Murph's Restaurant Ltd* [1979] ILRM 141.

189 [1979] ILRM 141 at 150.

companies 'fall out' and the stronger member-partners banish the weaker from the company by inappropriate reliance on provisions in the Companies Acts, the court may be inclined to grant a petition to have the company wound up on 'just and equitable' grounds.

[25.079] The facts in *Re Murph's Restaurant Ltd* are instructive. Three men – two brothers and a friend – began a snack bar business. One brother and the friend advanced £800 each and a further £400 each on behalf of the second, then unemployed, brother so as to create an equal partnership. In time, the friend left his well-paid employment and began to work full-time in the company. The business was successful and the company acquired a delicatessen and a restaurant in Dublin and Cork, the latter being run by the friend.
The finances and affairs of the company were conducted in a most irregular manner, company meetings of sorts being held on Monday nights on the business premises over meals. Neither dividends nor directors' fees were paid. Instead, regular drawings were taken and the appropriate share equalised annually. In addition, up to £200 per month was taken in cash, no record being kept, referred to in the proceedings as 'slush money'. Regular sums were also taken in cash and lodged into building society accounts. According to Gannon J, at all times, great care was taken to ensure 'equality was maintained as between the three of them'. The Cork premises, being run by the friend, was regularly visited by the brothers. The Midas touch of the trio prevailed, and the Cork restaurant flourished. Around this time, the brothers acquired an hotel called 'The Strawberry Hill' which was part-financed through loans from the company. They set about developing this into three houses for use by the brothers for themselves and their families. The friend was unaware of this loan. To emphasise the equality of the relationship, it was noted that the time off used by the brothers in their private ventures was allowed to the friend who took similar time off to purchase a house.

In time, the brothers decided that they did not want the friend working in the company any longer and sent him notice of a meeting to be held where it was intended to remove him from office. This action was found by Gannon J to be entirely irregular and that it was:

> '...a deliberate and calculated repudiation by both of them [the brothers] of that relationship of equality, mutuality, trust and confidence between the three of them which constituted the very essence of the company.'[190]

Gannon J rejected that there was any merit in the claim that they were getting rid of the friend because of alleged unsatisfactory work, because their complaint could:

> '...not relate to the talents or qualifications which he had shown, and must have been known to them to have had, at the time he was induced to join with them in a venture of strictly drawn equality'.

The friend petitioned to have the company wound up on the basis of *oppression* under CA 1963, s 205[191] and also on the just and equitable ground. Gannon J found that it would be inappropriate to make an order under CA 1963, s 205 in view of the fundamental breakdown in the relationship. On the question of just and equitable as a ground for winding up, Gannon J relied heavily on the judgment of Lord Wilberforce in *Ebrahimi v*

190 [1979] ILRM 141 at 151.

191 See Chapter 19, *Shareholders' Remedies*, para **[19.006]** *ff*.

Westbourne Galleries Ltd[192] and made the order sought to wind up the company. Several quotations of Lord Wilberforce and Lord Cross, cited with approval by Gannon J are relevant. One particularly salient paragraph considers the quasi-partnership nature of certain private companies, namely that:

> 'People do not become partners unless they have confidence in one another and it is of the essence of the relationship that mutual confidence is maintained. If neither has any longer confidence in the other so that they cannot work together in the way originally contemplated then the relationship should be ended - unless, indeed, the party who wishes to end it has been solely responsible for the situation which has arisen. The relationship between the [parties there] was, of course, in form that of partners; they were equal shareholders in a limited company. But the court considered that it would be unduly fettered by matters of form if it did not deal with the situation as it would have dealt with it had the parties been partners in form as well as in substance.'

[25.080] The judgment of Lord Wilberforce extensively reviewed a number of relevant English and Commonwealth authorities which touched upon quasi-partnership companies and the availability of the just and equitable ground in their winding up[193]. In his opinion:

> '...these authorities represent a sound and rational development of the law which should be endorsed. The foundation of it all lies in the words "just and equitable" and, if there is any respect in which some of the cases may be open to criticism, it is that the courts may sometimes have been too timorous in giving them full force. The words are a recognition of the fact that a limited company is more than a mere judicial entity, with a personality in law of its own: that there is room in company law for recognition of the fact that behind it, or amongst it, there are individuals, with rights, expectations and obligations inter se which are not necessarily submerged in the company structure. That structure is defined by the Companies Act 1948 and by the articles of association by which the shareholders agree to be bound. In most companies and in most contexts, this definition is sufficient and exhaustive, equally so whether the company is large or small. The 'just and equitable' provision does not, as the respondents suggest, entitle one party to disregard the obligation he assumes by entering a company, nor the court to dispense him from it. It does, as equity always does, enable the court to subject the exercise of legal rights to equitable considerations; considerations, that is, of a personal character arising between one individual and another, which may make it unjust, or inequitable, to insist on legal rights, or to exercise them in a particular way.'

Some of the factors which Lord Wilberforce identified as being salient in deciding whether or not a company was of the quasi-partnership kind included, whether it was an association formed or continued on the basis of a personal relationship involving mutual confidence, an agreement or understanding that all of the members will participate in the

192 *Ebrahimi v Westbourne Galleries Ltd* [1972] 2 All ER 492, [1973] AC 360.

193 Eg, *Re Yenidje Tobacco Co Ltd* [1916] 2 Ch 426, [1916–1917] All ER Rep 1050 (a 'deadlock' case, which Lord Wilberforce held was not so confined); *Re Wondoflex Textiles Pty Ltd* [1951] VLR 458 (an 'expulsion' case where a quarter owner was removed and the company was held to resemble a partnership); *Lewis v Haas* (1970) SLT 67 (where 'exclusion' was accepted as a possible ground for having a company wound up, though on the facts there was insufficient evidence to justify this remedy); and *Re Lundi Brothers Ltd* [1965] 2 All ER 692 (where a director-shareholder who was 'excluded' from the management of the company obtained an order that the company be wound up on 'just and equitable' grounds when Plowman J applied partnership principles).

management of the business and which had restrictions on the transfer of shares. In *Re Fildes Bros Ltd*[194] Megarry J said that the question is dependent upon both the contractual rights of the parties and the settled and accepted course of conduct between them. In that case, no order was made where the controlling director refused to permit another director to become involved in the day-to-day management of the company, because there was no such course of conduct in existence between the parties. It is important to note that Lord Wilberforce did warn against any automatic assumption that all private companies amounted to quasi-partnerships.

[25.081] Having established that a company may possess sufficient characteristics to amount to a quasi-partnership, and thus be liable to be wound up on just and equitable grounds, Lord Wilberforce then addressed the question of how the legal rights to expel a quasi-partner could be set aside. In a passage cited with approval by Gannon J in *Re Murph's Restaurants* he said:

> 'The question is, as always, whether it is equitable to allow one (or two) to make use of his legal rights to the prejudice of his associate(s). The law of companies recognises the right, in many ways, to remove a director from the board. Section 184 of the Companies Act 1948 confers this right upon the company in general meeting whatever the articles may say. Some articles may prescribe other methods: for example, a governing director may have the power to remove (compare in *Wondoflex Textiles Pty Ltd, In re* [1951] VLR 458). And quite apart from removal powers, there are normally provisions for retirement of directors by rotation so that their re-election can be opposed and defeated by a majority, or even by a casting vote. In all these ways a particular director-member may find himself no longer a director, through removal, or non-re-election: this situation he must normally accept, unless he undertakes the burden of proving fraud or mala fides. The just and equitable provision nevertheless comes to his assistance if he can point to, and prove, some special underlying obligation of his fellow member(s) in good faith or confidence, that so long as the business continues he shall be entitled to management participation, an obligation so basic that, if broken, the conclusion must be that the association be dissolved. And the principles on which he may do so are those worked out by the courts in partnership cases where there has been exclusion from management…'

It is clear that in appropriate circumstances, a court will grant an order to have a company wound up on just and equitable grounds where there was a relationship of confidence, partnership and mutuality between the members of that company which has been sundered.

[25.082] Case law provides a number of examples of situations where a company will be wound up on the basis that it is just and equitable. In *Re Zinotty Properties Ltd*[195] a company was ordered to be wound up where the majority shareholders refused to elect one particular individual to the board of directors although he had purchased shares in the company on the understanding that he would be elected. Similarly, in *Tay Bok Choon v Tahansan Sdn Bhd*[196] a person subscribed for shares in a company on its formation and became a director at the same time. He not only incurred personal liability on foot of

---

[194] *Re Fildes Bros Ltd* [1970] 1 All ER 923.

[195] *Re Zinotty Properties Ltd* [1984] 3 All ER 754.

[196] *Tay Bok Chapteroon v Tahansan Sdn Bhd* [1987] BCLC 472.

guarantees in respect of the company's debts, but lent other directors money so that they could increase their shareholdings. To exclude such a person from the management of the company in such circumstances, was held to be a breach of the principles of equity, and justified the winding up of the company.

(ii) Deadlock in corporate management

[25.083] Another instance of companies being wound up on just and equitable grounds is where there is deadlock in the management of the company. This may arise where the voting power in the company is evenly divided between two diametrically opposed camps. In such cases to wind up the company may be the only way to resolve the deadlock. In *Bluzwed Metals Ltd v Transworld Metals SA*[197] the High Court held that where a company's activities are 'effectively paralysed to the detriment of both the members and creditors' such clearly indicates 'that the company may be wound up on the "just and equitable ground", Lavan J citing as the leading case, that of *Re Yenidje Tobacco Company*[198] and noting that that principle was applied by Murphy J in *Re Vehicle Buildings and Insulations Ltd*[199] and by Kenny J in *Re Irish Tourist Promotions*[200].

[25.084] One of the first cases to establish this principle was *Re Yenidje Tobacco Company Ltd*[201]. There, a company was formed by two manufacturers of tobacco: Rothman and Weinberg, being equal shareholders and the only directors. Differences arose and they ceased to converse directly, only doing so through the company secretary. They also became engaged in costly litigation in respect of their differences. Although the company was profitable, the Court of Appeal granted an order to have the company wound up on the ground that it was just and equitable. The judgment of Lord Cozens-Hardy MR was formulated on the quasi-partnership nature of the relations between the two shareholders. During the course of his judgment, he said of the shareholders:

> 'They assumed, and it is the foundation of the whole agreement that was made, that the two would act as reasonable men with reasonable courtesy and reasonable conduct in every way towards each other, and arbitration was only to be resorted to with regard to some particular dispute between the directors which could not be determined in any other way. Certainly, having regard to the fact that the only two directors will not speak to each other, and no business which deserves the name of business in the affairs of the company can be carried on, I think the company should not be allowed to continue. I have treated it as a partnership, and under the Partnership Act of course the application for a dissolution would take the form of an action; but this is not a partnership strictly, it is not a case in which it can be dissolved by action. But ought not precisely the same principles to apply to a case like this where in substance it is a partnership in the form of the guise of a private company? It is a private company, and there is no way to put an end to the state of things which now exists except by means of a compulsory order.'

---

[197] *Bluzwed Metals Ltd v Transworld Metals SA* (9 May 2001, unreported), High Court (Lavan J).

[198] *Re Yenidje Tobacco Company* [1916] 2 Ch 426.

[199] *Re Vehicle Buildings and Insulations Ltd* [1986] ILRM 239.

[200] *Re Irish Tourist Promotions* (22 April 1974, unreported), High Court (Kenny J).

[201] *Re Yenidje Tobacco Company Ltd* [1916] 2 Ch 426.

While Lord Cozens-Hardy MR viewed this case as not being one of complete deadlock[202] he held that it was within the just and equitable jurisdiction of the court to grant the winding-up order.

[25.085] The leading Irish case is, as noted, *Re Vehicle Buildings and Insulations Ltd*[203]. In that case a company was formed for the purpose of repairing and dealing in motor vehicles. The petitioner was an equal shareholder in the company, and alleged that a state of deadlock existed in the management of the company and that it would be just and equitable for the company to be wound up, just as it would be in the case of a partnership. It was also alleged that the company would become insolvent if tax assessments which were raised against the company were not successfully challenged on account of the deadlock in the company's management. As against the other shareholder, it was alleged that he ran the business in an inefficient manner and harassed the petitioner. The other shareholder replied that the petitioner was not harassed, that he was not incompetent and that the rift between the parties was because of the 'highly dubious manner' in which the petitioner managed the company's financial affairs. In this regard, he alleged that the Garda Fraud Squad and the Revenue Commissioners were investigating the affairs of the company. While accepting there was a rift between the shareholders, he alleged that the petitioner was responsible for this. He also alleged that the petitioner seeking equitable relief was not coming to court with clean hands.

Murphy J ordered that the company be wound up and in doing so endorsed the principles established in *Re Yenidje Tobacco Company Ltd*. Although the onus of proving deadlock rested with the petitioner, Murphy J said that:

> '...in a case such as the present where the petitioner establishes equality of shareholding and equality of management and a complete unwillingness of each party to co-operate with each other it seems to me that to put it at its lowest that the onus shifts to the respondent or the company to show some means by which this apparently insoluble problem may be resolved.'[204]

In addressing the question of the 'clean hands' of a petitioner Murphy J said that a hearing on affidavit was not the appropriate place to establish the guilt of either party. So, he held that:

> '...the objective fact is that the shareholders/directors cannot legally or practically administer the company without the co-operation of each other and that in practice neither party would be able or willing at this stage to co-operate with the other.
>
> In these circumstances whilst I am not by any means prepared to exculpate the petitioner from any wrong doing I do not feel that I would be justified either in concluding that she was guilty of such misconduct as would dis-entitle her in the particular circumstances of this case to have an order made which seems to be required not only in her interest but in the interests of the creditors of the company.'[205]

---

[202] There was a written agreement between the shareholder-directors to submit disputes to arbitration.

[203] *Re Vehicle Buildings and Insulations Ltd* [1986] ILRM 239.

[204] [1986] ILRM 239 at 242.

[205] [1986] ILRM 239 at 243.

Expressing regret that a solvent business was going to be wound up, Murphy J granted the order sought[206].

[25.086] Several other cases have consistently accepted that deadlock in corporate management will merit winding up. In *Re Irish Tourist Promotions Ltd*[207] Kenny J ordered that a company be wound up on the basis that relations between the parties had become so bad that the business of the company had almost ceased[208].

(iii) Failure of substratum

[25.087] Failure of substratum is where the purpose for which a company was formed is no longer pursued, or where the company pursues a different venture to that originally envisaged. Frequently a company's substratum will equate with its main objects[209]. The intentions of the parties who come together to form the company are of crucial importance in determining a company's substratum. Where the substratum of a company disappears, it is open to bring a petition for the winding up of that company on just and equitable grounds[210]. Since the advent of the ability to alter a company's objects clause, this ground has become somewhat anachronistic, although it probably can be invoked still to prevent one camp from relying strictly upon their legal rights to alter the objects clause.

[25.088] To wind up a company on the basis of failure of substratum, it is necessary to show that the real purpose for which the company was formed has been lost. Accordingly, in *Re Kitson & Co Ltd*[211] a company was formed to acquire a business which engaged in general engineering. Forty-six years later a petition was presented to have the company wound up when it was proposed to sell this business. While the members had passed a resolution to discontinue the business of engineering, this was subsequently withdrawn. The Court of Appeal reversed an earlier order that the company be wound up on the basis that there remained an intention to carry on the business of general engineering. Accordingly, the abandonment of the main objects of the company must be total, if an application for such an order to wind up is to be granted.

(iv) Illegal objects

[25.089] The objects of a company must be legal. In *R v Registrar of Joint Stock Companies*[212] a company had as an object the sale of tickets in the Irish Sweepstakes

---

206 Note that in an ex tempore judgment of 10 March 1986, an appeal was dismissed and the decision of Murphy J was affirmed.

207 *Re Irish Tourist Promotions Ltd* (22 April 1974, unreported), High Court (Kenny J).

208 See *Re A & BC Chapterewing Gum Ltd* [1975] 1 All ER 1017 (where the relationship between the parties in the company was so destroyed that effective management could not be regained, thus justifying the winding up of the company); *Re Davis Investments (East Ham) Ltd* [1961] 3 All ER 926 (petitioner must show that deadlock is likely to remain); *Re American Pioneer Leather Co* [1918] 1 Ch 556 (the voting power of the parties at loggerheads need not be divided equally) and see also *Re Dublin and Eastern Regional Tourism Organisation Ltd* [1990] 1 IR 579.

209 See *Re German Date Coffee Co* [1882] 20 Ch D 169.

210 See also *Re Anglo-Continental Produce Ltd* [1939] All ER 99 and *Re Perfectair Holdings Ltd* [1990] BCLC 423.

211 *Re Kitson & Co Ltd* [1946] All ER 435.

212 *R v Registrar of Joint Stock Companies* [1931] 2 KB 197. See also *Bowman v Secular Society Ltd* [1917] AC 406 and *McEllistrim v Ballymacelligott Co–operative and Dairy Society Ltd* [1919] AC 549.

lottery. The English Registrar of Companies refused to register the company, and his decision was upheld in court on the basis that a company could not be formed where its object included an offence against the law. Where a company slips through the Registrar's net, it is open to petition for its winding up on just and equitable grounds where its objects are explicitly or implicitly, illegal[213].

(v) Corporate instruments of fraud

[25.090] Where it is proved that a company is being used as an instrument of fraud the court will order that the company be wound up on the just and equitable ground. An example of such is seen in the decision in *Re Shrinkpak Ltd*[214] where Barron J granted the petition of the liquidator of Contract Packaging Ltd ('CPL') to have another company, Shrinkpak Ltd, wound up. The liquidator gave evidence that the winding up of CPL had been engineered to defraud the creditors of CPL by the diversion of CPL's funds and business to Shrinkpak Ltd in blatant disregard of the duties owed by the directors to CPL. Although a separate legal entity, Shrinkpak Ltd was financed solely out of the assets of CPL. Whilst liabilities of Shrinkpak Ltd were attributed to CPL, assets of CPL were claimed to belong to Shrinkpak Ltd. On the evidence presented before him, Barron J was inclined to grant the petition to have the company wound up. He also rejected the contention that the liquidator of CPL was not a creditor and had no locus standi. On the question of the petition being presented on the just and equitable ground, Barron J appears to have held that if the company was being used as an instrument of fraud, it was preferable to have the company wound up than to have the claims litigated by way of plenary summons. Since he found on the evidence that the whole financial status of Shrinkpak Ltd was based on fraud, he granted the petition sought and ordered that Shrinkpak Ltd be wound up.

[25.091] Since the passing of CA 1990, s 141 it is thought that a similar result could be achieved by means of a *pooling order* which will allow two or more companies to be wound up together and their assets pooled[215]. Notwithstanding this statutory power, it is thought that the equitable jurisdiction exercised by Barron J may still be of use, particularly where a petitioner cannot bring his case within the terms of s 141.

(vi) Public interest

[25.092] By virtue of CA 1963, s 12, the Director of Corporate Enforcement can, following any report made under CA 1990, s 11 or by inspectors appointed under CA 1990 or any information obtained by the Director under CA 1990, Part II, bring a petition to have a company wound up on the grounds that such is just and equitable. This right of the Director is not confined to 'companies' within the meaning of CA 1963, s 2 and extends to all companies that are capable of being wound up under the Companies Acts[216]. In England

---

213 See *Re Thomas Edward Brinsmead & Sons Ltd* [1897] 1 Ch 45 where the promoters deceived the subscribers into buying into the company.

214 *Re Shrinkpak Ltd* (20 December 1989, unreported), High Court (unapproved), per Barron J. The author acknowledges with gratitude the help of Mr Michael McInerney, Solicitor, for locating this unreported decision.

215 See Chapter 27, *Realisation and Distribution of Assets in a Winding Up*, para **[27.112]** *ff*.

216 CA 1990, s 12(2) refers to a 'body corporate liable to be wound up under the Companies Acts'. See para **[25.032]**. As to the winding up of foreign companies in England, see *Re Normandy Marketing Ltd* [1993] BCC 879.

and Wales, this right to petition the courts has come to be known as applications to wind up *in the public interest*. Although the English Secretary of State for Trade and Industry has had the power to petition the English courts since the Insolvency Act 1986, s 124A (UK) was inserted by the Companies Act 1989 (UK), only in the last number of years have applications become commonplace[217]. Examples of when the English Secretary of State has sought to exercise his power to petition is where it is suspected that a company is being used to promote an illegal lottery[218] and where savings companies have sought to apply excessive charges that were allegedly concealed[219].

[25.093] The Irish High Court ordered a company to be wound up on just and equitable grounds on foot of CA 1990, Part II in *Re Rayhill Property Ltd, Home Affairs Ltd and Hilltop Catering Ltd*[220], an order which has only been reported in the daily newspapers. There, the companies in question were involved in the running of the ill-fated Clonmannon retirement village in Co Wicklow. The elderly residents had complained for some time previously that the nursing service and food they had allegedly paid for was not satisfactory and that the estate had not been properly managed. The newspaper report of the petition reported that in October 1994 an accountant and employee of the Department of Enterprise, Trade and Employment had been appointed to examine the companies' books and to report to the Minister. In the light of the fact that the basis for such a Ministerial petition (which would, today, be brought instead by the Director of Corporate Enforcement) is rooted in the just and equitable ground, it is instructive to note that the newspaper reported that counsel for the Minister claimed that there had been a:

> 'failure of the substratum upon which the company was to be based and upon which it held itself out to the public as trading; that the company's affairs had been mismanaged; and that assets of the company had been improperly misappropriated'.

It was reported that Costello P ordered the winding up of the three companies.

[25.094] One of the issues that has arisen when the similar legislation has been considered by the English Courts is whether the same practices regarding the advertisement of petitions apply to petitions brought on this basis. It would seem that the general rule remains, although the English Court of Appeal was sympathetic to the State-backed petitioner in *Secretary of State for Trade and Industry v North West Holdings plc*[221]. In that case it was concluded that the public was entitled to know that the Secretary for State had taken the view that it was expedient and in the public interest to present a petition – especially where a court had been satisfied to appoint a provisional liquidator. Moreover, in *Re Applied Database Ltd*[222] it was held that the fact that exceptional damage might be caused a company would not justify a restraint on advertisement where the petition was not an abuse of process.

---

217 See, generally, Milman, 'Winding Up in the Public Interest' (1999) *Palmer's In Company*, (1999) Issue 3/99, 9 March 1999.

218 *Re Senator Hanseatische Verwaltungsgessellschaft mbh* [1996] 2 BCLC 562.

219 *Re North West Holdings plc; Secretary of State for Trade and Industry v Blackhouse* (26 January 2001, unreported) CA (Eng).

220 An application reported in (1995), The Irish Times, 17 October (Costello P).

221 *Secretary of State for Trade and Industry v North West Holdings plc* [1998] BCC 997.

222 *Re Applied Database Ltd* (17 February 1995, unreported), High Court (Eng).

(f) Oppression

[25.095] Section 205 of CA 1963 allows disgruntled members of a company to petition the court where the company is being run in a manner oppressive to them. One of the remedies available to the court in such circumstances is to order that the company be wound up[223]. Often, such a petition will be taken in tandem with a winding-up petition on just and equitable grounds[224]. Section 205 is considered in detail in Chapter 19[225].

[D] CONVERSION OF WINDINGS UP

Converting a members' winding up to a creditors' winding up

[25.096] There are two ways in which a members' voluntary winding up can be converted to a creditors' voluntary winding up. Both of these methods of conversion have in common the fact that, notwithstanding the declaration of solvency, the company will not be able to pay its debts within 12 months of the commencement of the winding up. Where this occurs the company's creditors will usually wish to have a more active part in the liquidation.

[25.097] The first means of conversion is provided for in CA 1963, s 256(5) which provides that the court may convert the members' voluntary winding up into a creditors' voluntary winding up where certain conditions are met. Section 256(5) provides:

> 'If within 28 days after the resolution for voluntary winding up, has been advertised under subs (1) of s 252, a creditor applies to the court for an order under this subsection, and the court is satisfied that such creditor together with any creditors supporting him in his application represents one-fifth at least in number or value of the creditors of the company, and the court is of opinion that it is unlikely that the company will be able to pay its debts within the period specified in the declaration, the court may order that all the provisions of this Act relating to a creditors' voluntary winding up shall apply to the winding up.'

Where the court makes an order for the conversion of the winding up, any liquidator appointed by the members prior to this, or if none has been appointed, the company itself, shall deliver a copy of the court's order to the Registrar of Companies: CA 1963, s 256(6)[226].

[25.098] The second means of conversion is provided by CA 1963, s 261[227] which imposes a duty on a liquidator appointed by the members to call a meeting of the creditors where he is of the opinion that the company will not be able to pay its debts in full within the time specified in the declaration of solvency. Where this happens, he must:

- call a meeting of the creditors within 14 days from the day he formed his opinion;
- mail notices of the meeting to the creditors not less than seven days before the day of the meeting;

---

[223] See *Re Commercial and Industrial Insulations Ltd* [1986] BCLC 191.

[224] *Re Murph's Restaurants Ltd* [1979] ILRM 141.

[225] See Chapter 19, *Shareholders' Remedies*, para **[19.006]** *ff*.

[226] Default in this regard is liable to be visited with a fine not exceeding €1,269.74: CA 1963, s 256(7).

[227] As replaced by CA 1990, s 129.

- advertise in *Iris Oifigiúil* and in two daily newspapers at least ten days before the meeting;
- furnish reasonable information to any interested creditor who requests such information;
- state in the notice of the meeting that he was under a duty to call the meeting having formed the opinion that the company was unable to pay its debts on time[228].

In addition, where an inadequate declaration of solvency is made by the directors because they do not annex the report of an independent person, a liquidator will have seven days in which to apply to court for directions[229]. Costello J held in *Re Favon Investments Co Ltd*[230] that where the liquidation is out of time the court has no jurisdiction in which to extend the time for making and filing the report. In such circumstances, there will be an automatic conversion from a members' voluntary winding up to a creditors' voluntary winding up. Where the company is out of time for holding a creditors' meeting in accordance with CA 1963, s 266, the court may annul the resolution of the members to have the company wound up where to do so would not prejudice anybody.

[25.099] At the creditors' meeting the liquidator must present a statement of affairs of the company (including its assets, liabilities, a list of outstanding creditors and an estimate of their claims). He must also attend and preside at the meeting of the creditors[231]. From this time onwards, the winding up becomes a creditors' voluntary winding up[232]. The creditors can then replace the liquidator and appoint their own, and where there is a dispute over the costs, charges or expenses of the members' liquidator, application can be made to court[233]. The validity of any acts which were previously done by the members' liquidator is not affected[234].

Converting a voluntary winding up to a compulsory winding up

[25.100] The mere fact that a company is in voluntary liquidation is not an absolute bar to its being wound up by the court. On application being made either by a company's members or creditors, prior to a completion of a voluntary winding up, the court may order a conversion. CA 1963, s 282 provides, however, that in the case of an application being made by a contributory[235], the court must be satisfied that the rights of the contributories will be prejudiced by a voluntary winding up, were it allowed to continue.

[25.101] In order to petition the court to wind up any company, the petitioner must come within one of the grounds set out in CA 1963, s 213. This is also the case where it is sought to have a company in voluntary liquidation wound up by the court. In addition, however,

[228] See CA 1963, s 261(1).

[229] CA 1990, s 131(5).

[230] *Re Favon Investments Co Ltd* [1993] 1 IR 87. See para **[25.007]**.

[231] CA 1990, s 131(2).

[232] CA 1990, s 131(3).

[233] CA 1990, s 131(5).

[234] CA 1990, s 131(4).

[235] Defined by CA 1963, s 208 and considered at para **[25.040]**.

some ground must be advanced by the petitioner as to why the court ought to grant an order to have the company wound up compulsorily as opposed to allowing the company to continue to be wound up voluntarily[236]. In *Re Oakthorpe Holdings Ltd*[237] Carroll J advanced the view, obiter, that where the members of a trading company commenced a voluntary winding up by passing a resolution but did not deliver a statutory declaration of solvency or call a creditors' meeting, thereby creating an impasse, the creditors of the company could petition the court for a winding-up order[238]. Other situations where such a conversion might be sought include the case of a liquidator refusing to investigate the alleged wrongs of the directors[239], or where the shareholders of a company appeared not to be required to pay all that was owing on partly paid-up shares[240]. Where a creditor petitions for a conversion the court may refuse where a majority in number and value of other creditors are opposed to conversion to an official liquidation[241]. In *Re JD Swain Ltd*[242] Diplock LJ said that it was permissible to take cognisance of the objections of other creditors in an application to have a company wound up. This situation was distinguished from where there was no winding up at all in existence. In a petition for a conversion the creditor already has his remedy of winding up, and so must show cause as to why that is not adequate. By contrast, where there is no winding up in progress the views of creditors who oppose the petition will be disregarded in the absence of mala fides on the part of the petitioner as a creditor owed a debt is entitled to a winding-up order *ex debito justiciae.*

[25.102] In *Re Gilt Construction Ltd*[243] O'Hanlon J was asked to convert a creditors' voluntary winding up to an official winding up. The company concerned had only two shareholders whom the learned judge said could be loosely referred to as partners. On account of its insolvency, they resolved to wind the company up and agreed to appoint a named liquidator. Subsequently at the creditors' meeting, one of the men had a change of heart and supported the appointment of another liquidator; this liquidator was appointed with the support of all creditors voting personally or by proxy, other than the petitioning-shareholder and the company's solicitor who was also a creditor. The other shareholder's change of heart led to the petitioner bringing the petition and he also claimed that the other shareholder had been manipulating the assets of the company for his own benefit. The remedy claimed was to have the winding up converted to an official liquidation under the supervision of a court appointed liquidator. O'Hanlon J first noted that the court 'must be

---

236 See generally, Pennington, *Corporate Insolvency Law* (1991), pp 84–87.

237 *Re Oakthorpe Holdings Ltd* [1988] ILRM 62.

238 Alternatively, in such a situation, Carroll J recognised (at 64) that an order could be granted extending the time in which a creditors' meeting could be called, thus allowing the 'half–dead' company, to proceed to an orderly death, by a creditors' voluntary winding up.

239 *Re Gutta Percha Corpn* [1900] 2 Ch 665; *Re United Service Co* (1868) LR 7 Eq 76; and *Re Gold Co* (1879) 11 Ch D 701.

240 *Re Northumberland and Durham District Banking Co* (1858) 2 De G & J 357.

241 *Re Wicklow Textiles Ltd* (1953) 87 ILTR 72. See also *Re Lowerstoft Traffic Services Ltd* [1986] BCLC 81; *Re Palmer Marine Surveys Ltd* [1986] BCLC 106; and *Re HJ Tomkins & Son Ltd* [1990] BCLC 76. See also para **[25.053]** and **[25.060]** where the importance of creditors' wishes is considered.

242 *Re JD Swain Ltd* [1965] 1 WLR 909 at 915.

243 *Re Gilt Construction Ltd* (3 June 1994, unreported), High Court.

slow to dislodge a voluntary liquidator who has apparently been appointed to wind up the company with the concurrence of a majority, numerically and in value, of the creditors of the company'[244]. The learned judge next held that he did not consider that the credentials of the creditors' liquidator:

> '...either from the point of view of his professional qualifications and competence to carry out the task assigned to him, or in respect of his integrity and reliability in holding the scales evenly between the two partners when carrying out the winding up, have been impugned in any manner which would justify the court in taking the serious course of converting the voluntary liquidation into a liquidation under the direction of the court, and appointing a new liquidator...'[245]

In refusing the order sought by the petitioner, O'Hanlon J noted that the authorities to which he had been referred[246] had stressed that the amount of assets to be administered in the winding up was of great importance. Of these authorities, the learned judge said:

> 'The general approach taken in these cases is to have due regard to the costs involved in winding up by the court and the delays which will be incurred; to the over-all value of the assets to be administered and the complexity or simplicity of the task facing the liquidator, as well as to other relevant factors, such as those raised by the petitioner in the present case, having to do with questions of *mala fides* on the part of a person or persons involved in the dispute. In the present case the value of the assets is small by comparison with the general run of cases where winding up by the court is deemed appropriate. I have had the experience of seeing substantial sums raised by sale of assets in court liquidations, only to be told that the entire of the sum is only sufficient to pay the legal costs and the liquidator's charges and that nothing remains for distribution to the creditors. The winding-up process in the present case appears to be comparatively straightforward and simple, and if any unexpected problems should arise where the guidance of the court is needed by the voluntary liquidator or any contributor or creditor, access to the court is provided by s 280 of the Companies Act 1963.'[247]

The judgment of O'Hanlon J shows clearly that in the absence of a valid, compelling reason as to why it is inappropriate to continue the voluntary winding up of the company, the court will refuse to order a conversion.

[25.103] In two subsequent cases the Irish High Court was asked to convert a creditors' voluntary winding up into a court, compulsory, winding up. In *Re Naiad Ltd*[248] a company was in the process of being wound up in a creditors' voluntary liquidation when one of its creditors petitioned the court to have it converted to a compulsory liquidation. The petitioning-creditor sought the conversion on five stated grounds. First, notices convening creditors' meetings had not been received by him until the day before it was due to be held. Secondly, no notice of the meeting had been given to employee-creditors. Thirdly, it

---

244 (3 June 1994, unreported), High Court at p 3.

245 (3 June 1994, unreported), High Court at pp 3–4.

246 *Re Belfast Tailors' Co-Partnership Ltd* [1909] 1 IR 49; *Re JD Swain Ltd* [1965] 2 All ER 761; *Re Lowerstoft Traffic Services Ltd* [1986] BCLC 81; *Re Palmer Marine Surveys Ltd* [1986] 1 WLR 573; and *Re Falcon RJ Development* [1987] BCLC 437.

247 (3 June 1994, unreported), High Court at pp 4–5.

248 *Re Naiad Ltd* (13 February 1995, unreported), High Court (McCracken J).

was alleged that the chairman of the meeting had refused to adjourn it when requested to do so by SIPTU, a creditor of the company. Fourthly, it was alleged that the company had been trading insolvently and the directors might be found to be personally liable and that a voluntary liquidator would not prosecute such actions as diligently as an official liquidator. And fifthly, whilst a majority in number of creditors attending the meeting voted in favour of one liquidator, a different liquidator was proposed by the petitioner who was by far the largest ordinary creditor and so was supported by a majority in value. McCracken J held that it was hard to think that the petitioner's sense of grievance was justifiable and rejected each of the five grounds. To the individual grounds, in order, McCracken J held: (1) the creditors' meeting had been properly convened in accordance with CA 1963, s 266; (2) at the date of the meeting the company's employees were not creditors and had no entitlement to notice of the meeting; (3) the petitioner had not requested an adjournment and SIPTU did not support the petition; (4) there was no specific allegation against the independence of the liquidator who had been appointed; and (5) the chairman was correct in abiding by the decision of the majority in number[249]. As to the general approach of the court in such applications, McCracken J cited with approval the first sentence of the second passage quoted above from the decision of O'Hanlon J in *Re Gilt Construction Ltd*[250].

[25.104] Again, in *Re Eurochick (Ireland) Ltd*[251] McCracken J was asked to displace a voluntary liquidator and appoint a court liquidator. In that case the liquidator's appointment was approved by 10 votes to 3, the petitioner being one of the objectors. The petitioner did not criticise the liquidator's ability or impartiality and instead merely asserted a 'legitimate sense of grievance'. In that case the judge found that the company (in liquidation) had been set up at the instigation of the management of the petitioner to process chickens sold to it by the petitioner. McCracken J said that it was clear it had been intended that the petitioner would beneficially own all or a substantial part of the company and he said that the petitioner's solicitor and a brother of one of the managers in the petitioner were the company's only shareholders and that the company operated from the same premises as the petitioner. After the company collapsed those connected with the company severed their connection with the petitioner. The judge noted the petitioner's claims, which suggested that it had been funding the company in various ways, the result of which was that the company could owe the petitioner more than shown in its books. McCracken J noted that in English cases such as *Re Magnus Consultants Ltd*[252] and *Re Falcon RJ Development Ltd*[253] the courts were inclined to order the conversion to a compulsory liquidation where there was some wrongdoing in the company which needed to be investigated. McCracken J was satisfied that there was no such wrongdoing alleged

---

[249] This was prior to the enactment of CLEA 2001, s 47 which inserted CA 1963, s 267(3), whereby now the majority in value will prevail on a resolution as to the creditors' nominee as liquidator. See para **[25.026]**.

[250] *Re Gilt Construction Ltd* (3 June 1994, unreported), High Court. See para **[25.102]**.

[251] *Re Eurochick (Ireland) Ltd* (23 March 1998, unreported), High Court (McCracken J).

[252] *Re Magnus Consultants Ltd* [1995] 1 BCLC 203.

[253] *Re Falcon RJ Development Ltd* [1987] BCLC 437.

in the instant case and that the petitioner's complaint related to the conduct of its own affairs by its own management! The judge said of the petitioner's management that:

> 'they may have used funds of the petitioner to support the company, but there is no suggestion that they benefited personally in any way, or that they were guilty of any act which would reduce the assets of the company or increase its liability to its creditors, other than to the petitioner'.

McCracken J again cited the same passage from the decision of O'Hanlon J in *Re Gilt Construction Ltd*[254] and concluded:

> 'I can only repeat that it appears to me that the mala fides alleged in this case are the mala fides of the management of the petitioner itself, and it is not for the liquidator to investigate that matter. The assets in this case are very small compared with the liabilities, and I do not think there is any sense of grievance among the creditors generally which would justify the application of the principles in the English cases'.

In a number of English cases, a compulsory winding up has been ordered where it has been held that the creditors would otherwise have a 'genuine sense of grievance'. A totally unsatisfactory creditors' meeting was cited as sufficient reason in one case[255]. Generally, however, it would seem that the English courts are more inclined to accede to a creditor's petition than are the Irish courts[256].

[E] The Winding-up Order

[25.105] Upon the granting of an order for the winding up of a company the law treats the company as being analogous to a trustee of its own assets. The order to wind up the company dates back to the date of the presentation of the petition[257]. By CA 1963, s 222, another consequence of a winding-up order being granted is that no proceedings may be instituted against the company without the consent of the court. Once an order is made, the company's separate legal personality does not disappear until such time as it is actually *dissolved* by the court.

[25.106] On the granting of the order to wind the company up, the company must deliver to the Registrar of Companies a copy of the winding-up order under CA 1963, s 221. In addition, a statement of the company's affairs must be prepared by the directors or others ordered to do so by the court, which must be filed in court unless the court orders otherwise[258]. To put the public on notice that the company is being wound up, every invoice, order for goods or business letter issued by or on behalf of the company or liquidator, or receiver which bears the name of the company, must by CA 1963, s 303, contain a statement that the company is being wound up. From this point onwards, the

---

[254] *Re Gilt Construction Ltd* (3 June 1994, unreported), High Court. See para **[25.102]**.

[255] *Re Inside Sports Ltd* [2000] BCC 40.

[256] In *Re Zirceram Ltd; Brodie & So v Zirceram Ltd* [2000] BCC 1,048 it was said that a compulsory liquidation could be ordered so that there could be an investigation which was not only independent, but was seen to be independent.

[257] CA 1963, s 220(2). See *Burton v Deakin* [1977] 1 All ER 631.

[258] CA 1963, s 224.

liquidator assumes, and the directors usually lose, the functions and the authority which they previously held[259].

[25.107] By CA 1963, s 234(1) the court has power on its own or on the liquidator's application, to annul the order to wind the company up, on satisfactory proof. In addition, by s 234(2) it has jurisdiction to make an order to stay the winding-up proceedings.

Annulling a members' winding up

[25.108] The court's power to annul an order to wind a company up in a compulsory liquidation has a parallel in a voluntary winding up. In *Re Oakthorpe Holdings Ltd*[260] Carroll J held that the reference in CA 1963, s 280(3) to an order annulling the resolution to wind up means that by analogy with the power in CA 1963, s 234, 'the court can in a voluntary winding up annul the resolution to wind up in an appropriate case, just as it can stay proceedings.' In that case the company was not a trading company, and had no creditors and thus it was deemed appropriate to exercise the power of the court. Carroll J noted, however, that had there been creditors, an alternative remedy might have been the bringing of a petition to wind up the company by the court, so as to remedy the impasse[261].

Rescission of a compulsory winding-up order

[25.109] There would seem to be some uncertainty as to whether a compulsory winding-up order can be rescinded in Ireland. Prior to the coming into force of the Insolvency Rules 1986[262], the position in England and Wales seemed to be that a winding-up order could only be rescinded if application was made before the order was drawn up, ie within a few days of the making of the order. As a result of that order, every court in England and Wales 'having jurisdiction…to wind up companies may review, rescind or vary an order made by it in the exercise of that jurisdiction'. It would seem that the position in Ireland is that which prevailed in England before r 7.47. As to who has locus standi to apply for rescission of a winding-up order, further to the issue of a practice direction on 26 April 1971[263], the position in England and Wales is that only a creditor, a contributory or the company jointly with a creditor or contributory may apply to rescind an order[264].

Voiding dissolution following the making of a winding-up order

[25.110] Section 310 of CA 1963 confers a statutory power on the courts to declare a dissolution of a company void. This is a different jurisdiction to that contained in CA 1963, s 311A or C(A)A 1982, s 12C[265] because the dissolution envisaged by s 310 follows the making of a winding-up order, whether voluntary or compulsory, as opposed to dissolution following strike-off by the Registrar of Companies. As O'Neill J said in *Re*

---

259 See *Re Union Accident Insurance Co Ltd* [1972] 1 All ER 1105.

260 *Re Oakthorpe Holdings Ltd* [1988] ILRM 62.

261 Under CA 1963, s 282, considered at para **[25.098]**.

262 Insolvency Rules 1986, r 7.47.

263 [1971] 2 All ER 200.

264 See *Re Mid East Trading Ltd; Lehman Bros Inc v Phillips et al* [1997] 3 All ER 481.

265 As to which see Chapter 12, *Company Law Compliance and Enforcement*, para **[12.152]** *ff*.

Amantiss Enterprises Ltd; Framus Ltd v CRH plc[266], s 310 is in contra distinction to the other sections. Section 310(1) of CA 1963 provides:

> 'Where a company has been dissolved, the court may at any time within 2 years of the date of the dissolution, on an application being made for the purpose by the liquidator of the company or by any other person who appears to the court to be interested, make an order, upon such terms as the court thinks fit, declaring the dissolution to have been void, and thereupon such proceedings may be taken as might have been taken if the company had not been dissolved.'

Where an applicant is successful in applying for an order to void a dissolution, he has a statutory duty to deliver an office copy of the court's order to the Registrar of Companies, on pain of fine[267]. It will be noted that once a dissolution has been declared void, 'thereupon such proceedings may be taken as might have been taken if the company had not been dissolved'. As to the meaning of this expression, in *Re Amantiss Enterprises Ltd; Framus Ltd v CRH plc*[268] O'Neill J said:

> '...s 310 of the Companies Act 1963...deals with the situation where a dissolution occurs following a winding up in a voluntary or a court liquidation. Necessarily in these circumstances there will be no question of the company having, since dissolution, conducted trading or business operations. If acts were done in the name of the company following dissolution in these circumstances it is hard to imagine how they could have a lawful character and hence, as a matter of principle, retroactive validation could not ensue automatically on a declaration under s 310, that the dissolution was void. The use of the phrase in s 310: "*and thereupon such proceedings may be taken as might have been taken if the company had not been dissolved*" would seem intended to have the effect of enabling from that point, namely when the declaration is made, the company to sue or be sued'.

O'Neill J went on to note that s 310 of the 1963 Act was identical to the Companies Act 1908, s 223 and that that section was so construed by the English House of Lords in *Morris v Harris*[269].

[25.111] The present English provision (identical to CA 1963, s 310) is the Companies Act 1985, s 651 (UK). That section was interpreted in *Smith v White Knight Laundry Ltd*[270] as meaning that where a dissolved company is restored, a cause of action against the company accrued on the date on which it would otherwise have accrued but for the dissolution. The purported acts of a dissolved company were not validated by the operation of the section but that did not mean that a cause of action could not accrue on the date it would otherwise have accrued. As Jonathan Parker LJ said:

> '...a crucial distinction is made between on the one hand the corporate existence of the company, which is restored as from the date of the dissolution, and on the other hand proceedings which had taken place during the period of dissolution (referred by Lord Blanesburgh as "corporate activity"). In *Morris v Harris* the House of Lords decided that purported acts of a dissolved, and hence non-existent, company were not validated by the

---

[266] *Re Amantiss Enterprises Ltd; Framus Ltd v CRH plc* [2000] 2 ILRM 177.

[267] CA 1963, s 310(2).

[268] *Re Amantiss Enterprises Ltd; Framus Ltd v CRH plc* [2000] 2 ILRM 177.

[269] *Morris v Harris* [1927] AC 252.

[270] *Smith v White Knight Laundry Ltd* [2001] 3 All ER 862, [2001] EWCA Civ 660.

> subsequent avoidance of the dissolution. But that is not the instant case. In the instant case, all that is needed for the accrual of a cause of action against the company is corporate existence, no question of 'corporate activity', in the sense in which Lord Blanesburgh used that expression, arises.'[271]

It can be concluded that the period during which a company is dissolved will be counted in reckoning whether or not a particular cause of action is statute barred. It should be noted, however, that proceedings initiated against a company before its dissolution, which remained pending at the time of dissolution, or which were commenced during the period of dissolution, are a nullity and are not validated by a subsequent restoration[272].

---

[271] [2001] 3 All ER 862 at 876.

[272] *Morris v Harris* [1927] AC 252; *Re Philip Powis Ltd* [1997] 2 BCLC 481. See, generally, Keay, 'The Pursuit of Legal Proceedings Against Dissolved Companies' [2000] JBL 405.

Chapter 26

Liquidators

Introduction

[26.001] This chapter considers the persons who are charged by law with the winding up of companies and the realisation and distribution of their assets in accordance with law, namely, liquidators[1]. The law relating to liquidators is considered under the following headings:

1. The four types of liquidator.
2. Liquidators' qualifications.
3. The appointment and removal of liquidators.
4. Liquidators' duties.
5. Liquidators' powers.
6. The remuneration of liquidators.
7. Foreign liquidators and the EU Council Regulation on Insolvency Proceedings.
8. The Director of Corporate Enforcement's power to supervise liquidators.

The issues arising under these headings shall be considered, with appropriate distinctions being made between the various types of liquidator and winding up.

The four types of liquidator

[26.002] There are four distinct types of liquidators: members' voluntary liquidators; creditors' voluntary liquidators; official liquidators; and provisional liquidators. All liquidators are fiduciaries[2] of the company to which they are appointed.

(a) Voluntary liquidators

[26.003] In both members' voluntary liquidations and creditors' voluntary liquidations the person charged with the winding up of a company is called a *voluntary liquidator*. Although both types of liquidation are distinguished by the fact that in one the company is solvent, whereas in the other it is not, the commonality is that in both, the winding up is done privately and is not the subject of direct court supervision. Unlike an official liquidator, a voluntary liquidator is not, ex officio[3], an officer of the court and he is best considered as a simple *agent* of the company[4]. The general rule is that a voluntary

---

1 See, generally, Lynch, Marshall and O'Ferrall, *Corporate Insolvency and Rescue* (1996), and Bailey, Grove and Smith *Corporate Insolvency: Law and Practice* (2nd edn, 2001), ch 10.

2 *Re Gertzenstein Ltd* [1937] Ch 115.

3 A liquidator who is, by profession, a solicitor would be an 'officer of the court', but would be such by virtue of being a solicitor, not because of his position as a liquidator.

4 See *Re Tailteann Freight Services Ltd* [1975] IR 376.

liquidator contracts with others as agent of the company and does not have a personal liability[5].

(b) Official liquidators

[26.004] Liquidators appointed by the court in a compulsory winding up are termed *official liquidators*[6]. An official liquidator is simultaneously an officer of the court and an agent of the company, owing fiduciary and statutory obligations to both. However, a liquidator is not a trustee for the shareholders or creditors[7].

(c) Provisional liquidators

[26.005] The final type of liquidator is termed a *provisional liquidator*. Such liquidators are appointed where a petition has been presented to have a company wound up compulsorily, but before a winding-up order is made where it is apprehended that a company's assets require to be preserved immediately[8]. The position of a provisional liquidator is, by definition, provisional and an official liquidator will normally be appointed immediately upon the actual making of the winding-up order.

Liquidators' qualifications

[26.006] Notwithstanding that Irish company law does not impose any positive qualification requirement on liquidators, the vast majority of appointees are members of a recognised accountancy body[9]. Unless a person is specifically debarred from becoming a liquidator, in theory, anybody can. Considering that liquidators are fiduciary agents who administer other people's money, it is thought that this is a most unsatisfactory state of affairs[10]. The Companies Act 1963, s 300 ('CA 1963') merely says that a body corporate is not qualified to be a liquidator and any body corporate acting as a liquidator shall be liable to a fine, and the appointment will be void, ab initio.

[26.007] Persons who are specifically stated *not* to be qualified for appointment as liquidator of a company are contained in CA 1963, s 300A[11], which lists:

- a person who was an officer[12] or employee of the company in liquidation within 12 months prior to the commencement of the winding up.
- a parent, spouse, brother, sister or child of an officer of the company, save with leave of the court.
- a partner or employee of an officer or employee of the company.

---

5 *Stewart v Engel* [2000] BCC 741; [1999] TLR 804.

6 CA 1963, s 228(b).

7 *Re Belfast Empire Theatre of Varieties Ltd* [1963] IR 41.

8 See para **[26.016]**.

9 Solicitors will sometimes act as liquidator especially in a solvent members' voluntary winding up where the assets of a company are being distributed *in specie*: see Chapter 27, *The Realisation and Distribution of Assets in a Winding Up*, para **[27.181]**.

10 See the *Company Law Review Group's* First Report (31 December 2001), ch 13, 'The Regulation of Insolvency Practitioners' and para 13.3.

11 Inserted by CA 1990, s 146.

12 References to 'officer' or 'servant' are deemed to include references to 'auditor'.

— a person disqualified on the basis of the foregoing grounds for appointment as liquidator of any other body corporate which is that company's subsidiary or holding company, or a subsidiary of the company's holding company, or would be disqualified if the body corporate were a company.

Where a liquidator becomes disqualified by reason of the foregoing, he must vacate office and give notice to the company or the company and the creditors, depending on the type of winding up[13]. To act as a liquidator while disqualified is an offence[14]. The Minister for Enterprise, Trade and Employment may, by regulations, add to the list of persons set out in CA 1963, s 300A who shall not be qualified for appointment as a liquidator: CA 1990, s 237.

The appointment and removal of liquidators

(a) Members' voluntary liquidators

[26.008] Section 258(1) of CA 1963 provides that in a members' voluntary winding up, the members in general meeting shall appoint a liquidator for the purpose of winding up the affairs of the company. The steps leading up to that appointment are considered in the previous chapter[15]. All voluntary liquidators appointed in either a members'[16], or creditors'[17], winding up must give their prior written consent to the proposed appointment[18]. Section 276A(1) of CA 1963 provides that a liquidator's appointment is of no effect unless he gives his prior consent in writing. If the liquidator appointed by the members dies or resigns, the company in general meeting may fill the vacancy[19]. The court can appoint a voluntary liquidator where no liquidator is acting, or can remove one and appoint another where cause is shown[20].

(b) Creditors' voluntary liquidators

[26.009] In the case of a creditors' voluntary winding up, where a liquidator or his representative is not present at the meeting at which he is appointed, the chairman of the meeting is responsible for notifying him within seven days of his appointment to enable him to give his consent. The failure to comply can lead to a fine on conviction.

[26.010] Section 301A of CA 1963[21] provides that any creditor who has a connection with a liquidator proposed by the other creditors must make this known to the chairman, who must in turn inform the creditors' meeting. The chairman himself must inform the meeting of any connection which he may have with the proposed liquidator. 'Connection' in this regard means being the parent, spouse, brother, sister, child, partner or employee of the

13 Or to the court in a compulsory winding up.

14 CA 1963, s 300A(4). Note that s 300A is not retrospective: s 300A(5).

15 See Chapter 25, *Winding Up Companies*, para **[25.004]** *ff*.

16 CA 1963, s 276A(1).

17 CA 1963, s 274.

18 As inserted by CA 1990, s 133.

19 CA 1963, s 259(1). Such meeting can be convened by any contributory, or the other liquidators if there are more than one.

20 CA 1963, s 277(1) and (2). As to 'cause shown' see para **[26.013]**.

21 As inserted by CA 1990, s 147.

proposed liquidator[22]. The failure to disclose a connection can result in a fine on conviction and the court can take such non-disclosure into consideration on an application for the appointment or removal of a liquidator[23].

[26.011] Where the liquidator appointed by the company's creditors dies, resigns or otherwise vacates office, the creditors may appoint another in his stead unless the deceased liquidator was appointed by or at the direction of the court[24]. Again, it should also be noted that the court can appoint a voluntary liquidator where no liquidator is acting, or can remove one and appoint another where cause is shown[25]. Alternatively, a creditors' liquidator can be displaced by an official liquidator where, on application being made to court, it is ordered that a creditors' voluntary winding up be converted to an official liquidation[26].

(c) Official liquidators

[26.012] CA 1963, s 225 provides that for the purpose of conducting the proceedings in winding up a company and performing such duties in reference thereto as the court may impose, 'the court may appoint a liquidator or liquidators'[27]. It follows that a liquidator can only be appointed by the court where the court has ordered that a company be wound up, upon its being satisfied as to the application of one of the grounds listed in CA 1963, s 213[28]. Section 228(a) of CA 1963 empowers the court to require an official liquidator to enter into a bond by way of security for the performance of his functions[29]. An appointment is of no effect unless the person nominated has prior to his appointment signified his written consent to the appointment: CA 1963, s 276A(1)[30]. Once appointed by order of the court, the liquidator must within 21 days of his appointment publish in *Iris Oifigiúil* a notice of his appointment and deliver to the Registrar of Companies an office copy of the order appointing him[31]. The court can fill any vacancy in the office of official liquidator[32].

[26.013] A liquidator appointed by the court can resign or be removed by the court. CA 1963, s 228(c) provides that a liquidator appointed by the court 'may resign or, on cause shown, be removed by the court'[33]. Although statute is silent on who has locus standi to

---

22 CA 1963, s 301A(4).

23 CA 1963, s 301A(5) and (6) respectively.

24 CA 1963, s 270.

25 CA 1963, s 277(1) and (2). As to 'cause shown' see para **[26.013]**.

26 See Chapter 25, *Winding Up Companies*, para **[25.100]**.

27 Where the court appoints more than one liquidator, it is required, by CA 1963, s 228(f), to 'declare whether any act by this Act required or authorised to be done by the liquidator is to be done by all or any one of the persons appointed'.

28 See Chapter 25, *Winding Up Companies*, para **[25.054]** *ff*.

29 This provides: 'the court may determine whether any and what security is to be given by a liquidator on his appointment'.

30 See para **[26.008]**.

31 CA 1963, s 227(1). Failure to do so is punishable by a fine of €317.43: CA 1963, s 227(2).

32 CA 1963, s 228(e).

33 Conflict of interest (see *Re P Turner (Wilsden) Ltd* [1987] BCLC 149 and *Re Corbenstoke Ltd (No 2)* [1990] BCLC 60) or a preference of shareholders (*Re Rubber and Produce Investment Trust* [1915] 1 Ch 382) are both 'causes' where it has been held to be appropriate to remove a liquidator.

apply to have a liquidator removed, it has been held by the common law judicial equivalent of the universal-wrench – the Privy Council – in *Deloitte & Touche AG v Johnson*[34], that the proper persons to make application are those persons interested in the outcome of the liquidation. It was observed there that a contributory who was not a creditor could not apply to have a liquidator removed. In that case the applicants were a firm of accountants who had acted as auditors to a company in liquidation and who were being sued for negligence. Following various mergers of accountancy practices, the applicants alleged that the liquidators had a conflict of interest by reason of the fact that a firm of accountants whom the applicants claimed had failed to provide them with material information, had now merged with the liquidators' firm. The Lords upheld the Cayman Islands' Court of Appeal decision that the applicants' application be struck-out. If there was a conflict, that was a matter for those who would be affected, namely, the company's creditors.

[26.014] In the decision of the Federal Court of Australia in *City & Suburban Pty Ltd v Smith*[35], it was stated of the court's entitlement to remove a liquidator 'on cause shown' that:

> 'It has long been accepted that the section and its predecessors were not confined to situations where it is established that there is personal unfitness, impropriety or breach of duty on the part of the liquidator. Cause is shown for removal whenever the court is satisfied that it is for the better conduct of the liquidation or, put another way, it is for the general advantage of those interested in the assets of the company that a liquidator be removed.' [36]

Fair play to a liquidator is secondary to the expediency of the liquidation. In *Re Adam Eyton Ltd; ex p Charlesworth*[37], Bowen LJ said:

> 'Of course, fair play to the liquidator himself is not to be left out of sight, but the measure of due cause is the substantial and real interest of the liquidation.'

In the Australian case of in *City & Suburban Pty Ltd v Smith* it was held that cause had been shown to justify the removal of the liquidator where it had been established that:

— the liquidator had failed to conduct a proper investigation into allegations that the directors of the company had been in breach of their fiduciary duties;

— there were allegations that the liquidator had himself been in breach of his fiduciary duties to the company;

— there were allegations of over-delegation by the liquidator of his functions to his employees giving rise to his having an allegedly insufficient grasp of the issues involved in the liquidation; and

— the liquidator's insensitivity to the committee of inspection.

---

34 *Deloitte & Touche AG v Johnson* [1999] BCC 992.

35 *City & Suburban Pty Ltd v Smith* [1998] Federal Court of Australia of 9 July 1998.

36 Authorities cited included: *Re Adam Eyton Ltd; ex p Charlesworth* (1887) 36 Ch D 299 at 306; *Re The Mutual Life Stock Financial and Agency Company Ltd* (1886) 12 VLR 777; and *Dallinger v Halcha Holdings Pty Ltd* (1995) 134 ALR 178 at 183–184.

37 *Re Adam Eyton Ltd; ex p Charlesworth* (1887) 36 Ch D 299 at 306.

(d) Provisional liquidators

[26.015] After a petition to have a company wound up has been presented, and before the making of an order for the winding up of the company, the court may, on application being made, order the appointment of a provisional liquidator under CA 1963, s 226(1). Such an application will usually be made by the petitioning creditor[38] who is concerned that, unless the assets of the company are immediately preserved[39], they are likely to be spirited away by the controllers of the company, or other anxious creditors, in disregard of the law of distribution on an insolvency[40]. However, where a provisional liquidator is appointed on foot of the petitioning creditor's application, he will not represent that creditor alone and must act in the interests of all of the company's creditors[41]. The appointment of a provisional liquidator is intrinsically detrimental[42] to a company and is a jurisdiction that will be exercised by the courts in the clearest of cases only.

The fears of the applicant must be supported by affidavit, showing 'sufficient ground'[43]. It has been held that the appointment of a provisional liquidator has the effect of terminating automatically the authority of agents who had been appointed to act on the company's behalf by its directors[44]. In this regard, the application for the appointment of a provisional liquidator may be seen as analogous to the application for a Mareva injunction by a plaintiff fearful that his litigation, if successful, could result in a pyrrhic victory[45]. Indeed, such an injunction may also be sought in a winding up so as to hold the threat of contempt of court over anyone who chooses to disregard the order[46].

---

38 RSC, ord 74, r 14(1) permits application to be made by either a creditor, contributory or the company itself. In *Re a company (No 002180 of 1996)* [1996] 2 BCLC 409 it has said by Knox J that applicants for the appointment of a provisional liquidator should, as a general rule, establish their standing to present a petition.

39 Note, though, that by CA 1963, s 229(2), for as long as there is no liquidator, all property of the company shall be deemed to be in the custody of the court.

40 In *Re EAEL* an application reported in (1998) The Irish Times, 12 February, it was reported that a provisional liquidator was appointed on the application of the Revenue Commissioners in circumstances where it was claimed that the company proposed to sell (at fair value) its assets to another company ahead of its inevitable liquidation. The newspaper report stated that the Revenue Commissioners were unhappy with the proposed approach to the sale of the company's assets and alleged that there was a connection with the company to which it was proposed to sell the assets.

41 *Bank of Credit and Commerce International SA (No 2)* [1992] BCLC 579.

42 *Re a Company (No 002180 of 1996)* [1996] 2 BCLC 409.

43 *Bank of Credit and Commerce International SA (No 2)* [1992] BCLC 579

44 *Pacific and General Insurance Co Ltd v Hazell* [1997] BCC 400.

45 In *Cope v Destination Education Pty Ltd* [1999] 12 January 1999, unreported), Supreme Court, New South Wales of an application for a Mareva injunction was declined on the grounds that the proofs had not been made out, but in the circumstances of that case, the judge said that the plaintiff should give consideration to applying for the appointment of a provisional liquidator.

46 See eg, *Re Mark Synnott (Life and Pensions) Brokers Ltd* (1991) The Irish Times, 2 July where after the making of a winding-up order, Mareva injunctions were applied for, as was a *Bayer* order to prevent the directors from leaving the country. This latter order was agreed on consent.

[26.016] The primary purpose of the appointment of a provisional liquidator is to ensure the *preservation* of corporate assets, and thus to enable the official liquidator to effect an orderly *realisation* and subsequent *distribution* of those assets[47]. This is the purpose of the winding-up order itself, and the appointment of the provisional liquidator is merely to ensure that no assets are spirited away. Thus, CA 1963, s 229(1) provides that on either the making of the winding-up order *or* the appointment of a provisional liquidator, either the official or provisional liquidator 'shall take into his custody or under his control all the property and things in action to which the company is or appears to be entitled'.

The order of appointment must, by the Rules of the Superior Courts 1986, ord 74, r 14(2), describe the property which the provisional liquidator is ordered to take into his possession.

[26.017] A provisional liquidator is displaced by the appointment of an official liquidator, or he can be removed by order of the court where it refuses the petition to have the company wound up. In *Re Kingscroft Insurance Co Ltd*[48] it was held that upon the discharge of a provisional liquidator and the dismissal of the winding-up petition, any orders made against persons during the proceedings will also be discharged because the purpose behind the making of such ancillary orders no longer exists. The powers of provisional liquidators are considered below[49].

Liquidators' duties

[26.018] All liquidators, whether appointed by the members[50], the creditors[51] or the court[52] are appointed for the purpose of winding up the affairs of the company, which involves the realisation and distribution of a company's assets in accordance with law. The myriad issues arising in the discharge of liquidators' primary duties of *realisation* and *distribution* of assets on liquidation are considered comprehensively in Chapter 27.

(a) Fiduciary duties

[26.019] In the discharge of their statutory obligations and duties, liquidators owe fiduciary duties to the company, as opposed to the individual creditors[53]. Liquidators may not make a secret profit as a result of their office[54] and are liable to account to the company where they do so.

(b) Statutory duties to members

[26.020] Liquidators owe many duties to members and these are referred to throughout this chapter. One particular duty owed by the liquidator in a members' voluntary winding

---

47 The importance of the preservation of corporate property in a provisional liquidator's function was stressed in *Re Bank of Credit and Commerce International SA* [1992] BCC 83.

48 *Re Kingscroft Insurance Co Ltd* [1994] 2 BCLC 80.

49 See para **[26.039]**.

50 CA 1963, s 258(1).

51 CA 1963, s 267(1).

52 CA 1963, s 225.

53 *Knowles v Scott* [1891] 1 Ch 717. A liquidator can, however, assume direct duties to creditors: *A&J Fabrications (Batley) Ltd v Grant Thornton* [1998] 2 BCLC 227, [1999] BCC 807.

54 *Re Gertzenstein Ltd* [1936] 3 All ER 341.

up is that contained in CA 1963, s 261, which obliges a members' liquidator to call a meeting of the company's creditors where he is of the opinion that the company will not be able to meet its debts in full within the time specified in the directors' declaration of solvency[55]. This is probably the most important duty of voluntary liquidators in a members' voluntary winding up.

(c) Statutory duties to creditors

[26.021] Liquidators also owe many duties to creditors. In a creditors' voluntary winding up, the creditors can appoint a committee of inspection, pursuant to CA 1963, s 268(1)[56]. In addition to such meetings as the committee of inspection holds, the liquidator is under a duty to call a meeting of the creditors and of the company at the end of the first year of the winding up, and within three months from the end of each succeeding year. The liquidator is obliged to lay before these meetings an account of his acts and dealings and of the conduct of the winding up during the preceding year and within seven days to send a copy of such account to the Registrar of Companies.

[26.022] In an official or compulsory winding up, the court may direct the liquidator to summon a meeting of the creditors of the company, or separate meetings of the creditors and contributories, for the purpose of determining whether or not an application is to be made to court for the appointment of a committee of inspection[57]. Where a committee of inspection is appointed, it will act in conjunction with the liquidator. It has been said of a committee of inspection that:

> 'Their task is to superintend and assist the liquidator in the performance of his duties and to watch over the interests of particular groups of creditors or contributories whom they are appointed to represent.'[58]

When a company is insolvent, its creditors are the beneficiaries of the company's assets. Just as it has been held that directors of insolvent companies owe duties to creditors[59], it follows that where the directors are displaced, the person with supervening authority – the liquidator – should be amenable to creditor supervision. In an official liquidation, the court will determine who are to be the members of the committee. In respect of disputes that arise between the meetings of creditors and contributories, the court has jurisdiction to make any order[60]. The mechanics for the conduct of committees' of inspection are set out in CA 1963, s 233.

(d) The statutory duty to report to the Director of Corporate Enforcement

[26.023] Finally, it may be noted that by the Company Law Enforcement Act 2001, s 56 ('CLEA 2001') the liquidators of all insolvent companies are obliged to make a report to the Director of Corporate Enforcement on the conduct of the insolvent company's

---

55 See, further, Chapter 25, *Winding Up Companies*, para **[25.098]**.

56 See, further, Chapter 25, *Winding Up Companies*, para **[25.027]**.

57 CA 1963, s 232(1).

58 See the decision of the Federal Court of Australia in *City & Suburban Pty Ltd et al v Smith* [1998] Federal Court of Australia, 9 July 1998 where this passage was quoted from McPerson, *Law of Company Liquidation* (BH (3rd edn, 1997, J O'Donovan (ed)) at p 236.

59 *Re Frederick Inns Ltd* [1994] 1 ILRM 387.

60 CA 1963, s 232(2).

directors and, unless advised otherwise, must make application to have the directors restricted pursuant to the Companies Act 1990, s 150 ('CA 1990')[61]. Section 56 of CLEA 2001 was commenced[62] on 1 June 2002 insofar as it applies to liquidators who were:

— appointed on or after 1 June 2002; or
— appointed on or after 1 July 2001 and before 1 June 2002 where, in respect of the company to which the liquidator was appointed, an order has not been made under CA 1963, s 249(1) or the meetings required under CA 1963, s 273(1) have not been held.

The Director of Corporate Enforcement has indicated[63] that it is possible that the obligation to report may be extended, on 1 December 2002, to all liquidators who were appointed to an insolvent company pursuant to any provision of the Companies Acts between 1 July 2000 and 30 June 2001, where the liquidation is ongoing on 1 December 2002. Thereafter, it has also been suggested that the obligation to report will be extended, on 1 June 2003, to all liquidators who were appointed to an insolvent company pursuant to any provision of the Companies Acts between 1 July 1998 and 30 June 2000, where the liquidation is ongoing on 1 June 2003.

[26.024] Section 56(1) of CLEA 2001 provides that the form of the *liquidator's report* will be prescribed by statutory instrument. A statutory instrument[64] has prescribed the form of the liquidator's report, which is a ten-page document, divided into seven sections:

— Liquidator's details.
— Company details.
— Company directors.
— Statement of affairs, accounts and report to creditors.
— Proceedings.
— Final report.
— Liquidator's statement.

Liquidators – and their legal advisers – will find the Office of Director of Corporate Enforcement's *Guidance Notes for the completion of Liquidators' Reports under s 56 of the Company Law Enforcement Act 2001*, an invaluable guide to the completion of the report[65].

Liquidators' powers

[26.025] The far-reaching extent of liquidators' duties is underscored by the fact that, on their appointment, liquidators will, generally, displace companies' directors. On the appointment of a members' voluntary liquidator[66] the powers of a company's directors

---

61 See Chapter 12, *Company Law Compliance and Enforcement*, para **[12.043]**.

62 Company Law Enforcement Act 2001 (Winding-up and Insolvency Provisions) (Commencement) Order 2002 (SI 2002/263).

63 See the paper published by the Office of the Director of Corporate Enforcement entitled 'Liquidators' Consultation Paper'. See the ODCE's website at: http://www.odce.ie/publications/consultation.asp.

64 Company Law Enforcement Act 2001 (Section 56) Regulations 2002 (SI 2002/324).

65 This is also available from the ODCE's website.

66 CA 1963, s 258(2).

cease, except so far as the company in general meeting or the liquidator sanctions their continuance. On the appointment of a creditors' voluntary liquidator[67], the powers of a company's directors shall cease except so far as the committee of inspection or if there is no committee, the creditors, sanction their continuance. Similarly, the appointment of a provisional liquidator[68] and an official liquidator will displace the powers of the directors to manage the company. The powers of liquidators are considered here as follows:

(a) Powers of official liquidators.

(b) Powers of provisional liquidators.

(c) Powers of voluntary liquidators.

(d) Restrictions on the exercise of powers by members' voluntary liquidators and other restrictions.

(e) Seeking directions from the court.

(a) Powers of official liquidators

[26.026] The statutory powers of official liquidators[69] are detailed in CA 1963, s 231. A twofold distinction can be made between official liquidators' powers that are exercisable with the sanction of the court or of the committee of inspection and those that are exercisable without prior sanction but subject to the control of the court. In addition, it should be noted that the creditors and contributories of a company that is in official or compulsory court liquidation have a statutory right to make application in relation to the exercise or proposed exercise of an official liquidator's powers under s 231.

(i) Powers exercisable with the sanction of the court or committee of inspection

[26.027] CA 1963, s 231(1) provides that an official liquidator shall have power, with the sanction of the court or of the committee of inspection, to do the following:

> '(a) to bring or defend any action or other legal proceedings in the name and on behalf of the company;
>
> (b) to carry on the business of the company so far as may be necessary for the beneficial winding up thereof;
>
> (c) to appoint a solicitor to assist him in the performance of his duties;
>
> (d) to pay any classes of creditors in full;
>
> (e) to make any compromise or arrangement with creditors or persons claiming to be creditors, or having or alleging themselves to have any claim present or future, certain or contingent, ascertained or unascertained or sounding only in damages against the company, or whereby the company may be rendered liable;
>
> (f) to compromise all calls and liabilities to calls, debts and liabilities capable of resulting in debts, and all claims, present or future, certain or contingent, ascertained or sounding only in damages, subsisting or supposed to subsist between the company and a contributory or alleged contributory or other debtor or persons apprehending

---

67 CA 1963, s 269(3). On where no liquidator is appointed, see *Re A Company (No 006341 of 1992)* [1994] 1 BCLC 225.

68 *Re Mawcon Ltd* [1969] 1 WLR 78.

69 See Milman, 'Liquidators: Powers and Constraints' (1997) *Palmer's In Company*, Issue 7/97, 17 July 1997.

> liability to the company, and all questions in any way relating to or affecting the assets or winding up of the company, on such terms as may be agreed, and take any security for the discharge of any such call, debt, liability or claim, and give a complete discharge in respect thereof.'

Some of the more significant powers conferred but subject to the sanction of the court or a committee of inspection are considered in the paragraphs that follow.

[26.028] Legal proceedings cannot be brought or defended in the name and on behalf of the company without the sanction of the court or committee of inspection[70]. In *Re Greendale Developments Ltd*[71] the official liquidator to a company that was being wound up by the court applied for an order pursuant to CA 1963, s 231(1)(a), granting him liberty to continue two plenary actions. In the course of her judgment (see below[72]) Laffoy J said:

> 'The decision of the court on a contested application to continue proceedings under s 231 is qualitatively different from the decision of a board of directors of a solvent company in relation to prosecuting litigation. The decision of the board of directors should be informed by the interests of the company, not by the sectional interests of individual shareholders or creditors. Once a winding-up order is made, the company is doomed to extinction. The winding up process is the process of the administration of the assets of the company: their collection, realisation and distribution in discharge of the liabilities of the company to the creditors and of the entitlement of its contributories in accordance with the scheme of priorities in the Companies Acts. Insofar as the Companies Acts give an entitlement to a creditor or a contributory to be heard by the Court in relation to a matter arising in the winding up, in my view, the Court is required to have regard to the sectional interest of that creditor or contributory and, in particular, to the protection of his legal entitlement to a distribution from the assets of the company as defined by the Companies Acts.'[73]

Accordingly, when it comes to an application for liberty to bring or defend legal proceedings, the court will have regard to whether the interests of the ultimate beneficiaries of the fruits of that litigation will be furthered[74].

In *Cork County Council v CB Readymix Ltd*[75] the Supreme Court held that only the liquidator who had been appointed to a company that was in the course of being wound up had locus standi to bring an appeal against a court judgment on behalf of the company.

[26.029] Another power that requires the sanction of the court or of a committee of inspection is the carrying on of the business of the company, so far as may be necessary for the beneficial winding up of the company[76]. This power recognises that sometimes, to realise assets for their true value, it will be necessary to continue in business eg to convert

---

70 CA 1963, s 231(1)(a).

71 *Re Greendale Developments Ltd* [1997] 3 IR 540 (Laffoy J).

72 At para **[26.038]**.

73 [1997] 3 IR 540 at 547.

74 In *Re Greenhaven Motors Ltd* [1997] BCC 547 a contributory's challenge to a liquidator's right to settle legal proceedings against a third party was rejected on the grounds that it had not been shown that there would be a sufficient surplus after debts, to which he would be entitled.

75 *Cork County Council v CB Readymix Ltd* (12 December 1997, unreported), Supreme Court; noted in (1999) 17 ILT 2.

76 CA 1963, s 231(1)(b).

relatively worthless work in progress into valuable finished products[77]. One of the reasons why the court will be loath to allow business be carried on for any length of time is because debts and other liabilities incurred by the company in the course of such post-liquidation trading in the bona fide belief that they were necessary for the beneficial winding up of the company will have priority to pre-liquidation debts[78].

[26.030] Where there is no committee of inspection, the court may provide in any order that the liquidator may exercise the powers detailed in CA 1963, s 231(1)(a) (bringing or defending legal proceedings) or (b) (carrying on the company's business) *without the sanction* or intervention of the court: CA 1963, s 231(4)[79].

(ii) Powers exercisable without prior sanction but subject to the control of the court

[26.031] Certain other powers are exercisable by liquidators *without* the need to obtain the sanction of the court or of any committee of inspection. Section 231(2) of CA 1963 provides that official liquidators have the following powers:

> '(a) to sell the real and personal property and things in action of the company by public auction or private contract, with power to transfer the whole thereof to any person or company or to sell the same in lots and for the purpose of selling the company's land or any part thereof to carry out such sales by fee farm grant, sub fee farm grant, lease, sublease, or otherwise, and to sell any rent reserved on any such grant or any reversion expectant upon the determination of any such lease;
>
> (b) to do all acts and to execute, in the name and on behalf of the company, all deeds, receipts and other documents, and for that purpose to use, when necessary, the company's seal;
>
> (c) where any contributory has been adjudged bankrupt or has presented a petition for arrangement with his creditors in pursuance of the Bankruptcy Acts, to prove, rank and claim in the bankruptcy or arrangement for any balance against his estate, and to receive dividends in the bankruptcy or arrangement in respect of that balance, as a separate debt due from the bankrupt or arranging debtor, and rateably with the other separate creditors;
>
> (d) to draw, accept, make and endorse any bill of exchange or promissory note in the name and on behalf of the company, with the same effect with respect to the liability of the company as if the bill or note had been drawn, accepted, made or endorsed by or on behalf of the company in the course of its business;
>
> (e) to raise on the security of the assets of the company any money requisite;
>
> (f) to take out in his official name letters of administration to any deceased contributory and to do in his official name any other act necessary for obtaining payment of any money due from a contributory or his estate which cannot be conveniently done in the name of the company, and in all such cases the money due shall, for the purpose of enabling the liquidator to take out the letters of administration or recover the money, be deemed to be due to the liquidator himself;
>
> (g) to give security for costs in any proceedings commenced by the company or by him in the name of the company;

---

77 See Lynch, Marshall and O'Ferrall, *Corporate Insolvency and Rescue* (1996), para [3.54].

78 *Re Great Eastern Electric Co Ltd* [1941] 1 All ER 409; *Re Davis & Co Ltd* [1945] Ch 402.

79 *Re The 19th Ltd* [1989] ILRM 652.

(h) to appoint an agent to do any business which the liquidator is unable to do himself;

(i) to do all such other things as may be necessary for winding up the affairs of the company and distributing its assets.'

The foregoing powers are largely self-explanatory.

[26.032] One of the most important and frequently exercised power is the power to sell corporate property. This power, like all of those in CA 1963, s 231(2), is subject to the right of creditors and contributories to apply to court for a determination in relation to the exercise or proposed exercise of the power. As Laffoy J said in *Re Greendale Developments Ltd; McQuaid v Malone and Fagan*[80], the powers of official liquidators to deal with corporate assets other than with the sanction of the court or the committee of inspection are 'extremely circumscribed'.[81]

[26.033] Section 231(1A) of CA 1963[82] imposes a restriction on the power of liquidators to sell corporate property to officers of the company and persons that are connected to officers. This provides:

> 'The liquidator of a company shall not sell by private contract a non-cash asset of the requisite value to a person who is, or who, within three years prior to the date of the commencement of the winding-up, has been, an officer of the company unless the liquidator has given at least 14 days' notice of his intention to do so to all creditors of the company who are known to him or who have been intimated to him.'

On its face, s 231(1A) does not apply where a non-cash asset is sold to officers where the sale is at a public auction ie it only applies to sale by *private contract*. The key words are defined[83]. 'Non-cash asset' and 'requisite value' have the meaning assigned to them by CA 1990, s 29[84] and 'officer' is deemed to include a person connected with a director within the meaning of CA 1990, s 26 and a shadow director[85].

[26.034] One question which arises from a liquidator's statutory power to sell the 'real and personal property *and things in action*' is the extent to which a liquidator can enter into an arrangement that might be considered, in other circumstances, to be champertous. 'Champerty', has been described by the Irish House of Lords in *Kenny v Browne*[86], a case decided in 1796 to be '...maintaining a suit in consideration of having some part of the thing in dispute'.

In the Supreme Court decision of *Fraser v Buckle*[87] it was held that the law of maintenance (champerty has been described as an 'aggravated form of maintenance'[88]) and champerty

80 *Re Greendale Developments Ltd; McQuaid v Malone and Fagan* (2 July 1997, unreported), High Court (Laffoy J).

81 (2 July 1997, unreported), High Court at p 6.

82 Introduced by CA 1990, s 124.

83 CA 1963, s 231(1A)(b)(i) and (ii).

84 See Chapter 11, *Statutory Regulation of Transactions Involving Directors and their Companies*, para **[11.023]**.

85 Chapter 11, *Statutory Regulation of Transactions Involving Directors and their Companies*, para **[11.004]**.

86 *Kenny v Browne* (1796) 3 Ridg PC 462.

87 *Fraser v Buckle* [1996] 2 ILRM 34. See also *O'Keeffe and O'Keeffe v Scales* [1998] 1 ILRM 393.

88 See *Guy v Chapterurchill* (1888) 40 Ch D 481 at 489.

in Ireland have not undergone any change since the nineteenth century. The question that arises here is whether the laws on maintenance and champerty curtail a liquidator's power to dispose of corporate assets in the nature of causes of action?[89] The assignment of a right or cause of action closely associated with a debt is not considered to be champertous and a liquidator may legitimately dispose of a debt in circumstances where the ownership of that debt confers an immediate right to litigate. This must, however, be distinguished from a purported sale of a 'bare' cause of action which is prima facie champertous. It has, however, been held consistently by the English courts that there is an exemption from the law of champerty for liquidators and trustees in bankruptcy. In *Grovewood Holdings plc v James Capel & Co Ltd*[90] it was explained that because a liquidator and a trustee in bankruptcy have a statutory power to dispose of all corporate property (and, specifically, things in action), these powers necessarily preclude any challenge to the sale of a cause of action (on terms that the assignees, by way of consideration, would pay over a share of the recoveries) on the grounds of maintenance and champerty. In that case Lightman J traced the history of the exception:

> 'The Court of Appeal in *Seear v Lawson* (1880) 15 Ch D 426 held that a bare right to sue was included within the term 'property' for the purpose of both provisions and accordingly (by way of statutory exception to the rules against maintenance) the trustee [in bankruptcy] could sell a bare right of action. Jessel MR remarked (at 433):
>
> > "The proper office of the trustee is to realise the property for the sake of distributing the proceeds amongst the creditors. Why should we hold as a matter of policy that it is necessary for him to sue in his own name? He may have no funds, or he may be disinclined to run the risk of having to pay costs, or he may consider it undesirable to delay the winding up of the bankruptcy till the end of the litigation."
>
> The following year in *Re Park Gate Wagon Works Co* (1881) 17 Ch D 234 the Court of Appeal held that s 95 of the Companies Act 1862 (the ancestor of modern company legislation), which authorised a liquidator to sell the property (similarly defined) of the company, likewise permitted the liquidator to sell causes of action, notwithstanding the rule against maintenance.'[91]

Lightman J went on to hold, however, that the exemption for liquidators in relation to the sale of bare causes of action would *not* be extended to sales of the fruits of litigation. In *Grovewood Holdings plc* the plaintiff-company had instituted proceedings for negligence and misrepresentation against the defendant. After the plaintiff-company went into liquidation, the liquidator sought to continue the action but when the plaintiff-company's shareholders and creditors refused to provide financial support for the proceedings, the liquidator purported to enter into an arrangement with secret backers who agreed to finance the litigation in return for half of the recoveries in the action. Lightman J held that this was champertous. It is submitted that it is difficult to accept the rationale of the distinction made in this decision and it has been criticised by later cases[92]. It is also

[89] See, generally, Bailey, Grove and Smith *Corporate Insolvency: Law and Practice* (2nd edn, 2001), para 20.27–20.33.

[90] *Grovewood Holdings plc v James Capel & Co Ltd* [1994] 4 All ER 417.

[91] [1994] 4 All ER 417 at 421e–h.

[92] *Re Oasis Merchandising Services Ltd* [1997] 1 BCLC 689 and *Abraham v Thompson* [1997] 4 All ER 362.

important to recognise that it is, in essence, an exception to an exception and it remains the case that a liquidator can sell a cause of action, something which a person other than a liquidator or official assignee in bankruptcy cannot do. So, in *Re Edennote Ltd (No 2)*[93] Lightman J held that where a liquidator was not in funds to pursue a particular cause of action that was in being, the interests of the creditors required that he either compromise or sell the action. In that case the liquidator had sought (and was granted) the court's sanction to compromise the cause of action.

[26.035] In *Re Oasis Merchandising Services Ltd*[94] it was held that claims that arise in the course of a liquidation eg claims for fraudulent or reckless trading against an insolvent company's directors cannot be assigned as these have been held not to be the 'property' of the company. There, Peter Gibson LJ held that the property, the sale of which came within the exemption to champerty, was the property of the company at the commencement of a winding up and not post-liquidation property.

[26.036] The attitude of the Irish courts to these questions very much remains to be seen. Although the decision in *Grovewood Holdings plc* was mentioned by the Supreme Court in *O'Keeffe and O'Keeffe v Scales*[95], no reference was made to the statements concerning the well-recognised exception for liquidators and trustees in bankruptcy. It is thought, however, that the Irish courts will follow the old authorities such as *Re Park Gate Waggon Works Co*[96], which accept that liquidators can dispose of causes of action being 'things in property'. Support for this view is derived from the judgment of Lynch J in *O'Keeffe and O'Keeffe v Scales*, where he said:

> 'While the law relating to maintenance and champerty therefore undoubtedly still subsists in this jurisdiction it must not be extended in such a way as to deprive people of their constitutional right of access to the courts to litigate reasonably statable claims.'[97]

Equally, it is thought to be very much within the public interest to facilitate the maximum realisation of the assets of an insolvent company to enable the greatest number of creditors to recoup the debts owed to them.

(iii) Applications by creditors or contributories regarding the exercise of powers under CA 1963, s 231

[26.037] As with the powers contained in CA 1963, s 231(2), which were considered above[98], CA 1963, s 231(3) provides that the exercise by an official liquidator of the powers in s 231(1):

> '...shall be subject to the control of the court, and any creditor or contributory may apply to the court in relation to any exercise or proposed exercise of any of those powers.'

It will be noted that only creditors or contributories have locus standi to apply to court under this provision[99].

---

93 *Re Edennote Ltd (No 2)* [1997] 2 BCLC 89.

94 *Re Oasis Merchandising Services Ltd* [1997] 1 BCLC 689.

95 *O'Keeffe and O'Keeffe v Scales* [1998] 2 ILRM 393.

96 *Re Park Gate Waggon Works Co* (1881) 17 Ch D 234.

97 [1998] 2 ILRM 393 at 397.

98 See para **[26.031]**.

99 See *Mahomed v Morris* [2000] 2 BCLC 536.

[26.038] Any application made pursuant to CA 1963, s 231(3) by a creditor or contributory must be heard in public. In *Re Greendale Developments Ltd*[100] the official liquidator to a company that was being wound up by the court applied for directions in connection with the liquidation and in particular an order pursuant to s 231(1)(a), granting him liberty to continue two plenary actions. Both actions had been commenced by the company prior to the commencement of its winding up, one being against a bank and a firm of chartered accountants, and the other being an action against a firm of solicitors. One creditor did not object to leave to continue but another creditor strenuously objected. The particular matter that arose for decision in that case was whether or not the court had the power to hear the application for directions otherwise than in public. After noting that it was well settled that the effect of Article 34.1 of the Constitution was that justice must be administered in public, in the absence of an exempting statutory provision, Laffoy J said the essential question was whether the making of the decision in hand was 'an administration of justice'. Applying the fivefold test advanced in *McDonald v Bord na gCon*[101], Laffoy J held that a decision under s 231 did involve the administration of justice and that the court had no discretion to hear the application otherwise than in public. The reasoning was as follows:

> 'In my view, when an application by a liquidator under s 231 involves either of the following situations—
>
> (i) the liquidator advocating that the relief sought to be granted in the interests of the general body of creditors and of the contributories as a whole and one creditor or contributor disputing the appropriateness of granting such relief, or
>
> (ii) the liquidator, as it were, "throwing in the ball" and individuals or factions proposing opposite points of view as to whether the relief sought by the liquidator should be granted,
>
> there is a contest between the parties. Moreover, in my view the consequences of the resolution of the contest cannot be defined with certainty at the time of resolution or, in certain circumstances, at any time, because there is inherent in the resolution a prediction as to the outcome of the proceedings sought to be continued, which outcome will only be known in the future if at all, nonetheless, the resolution does involve "the infliction of some form of liability or penalty on one of the parties". This can be illustrated by reference to the second scenario suggested above. If the proponent of the continuation of the proceedings loses the contest, he is deprived of the possibility of the assets of the company being augmented by an award of damages to his advantage. If the proponent of abandoning the proceedings loses the contest, he has foisted on him the possibility of assets which would have been available for distributing to him and the other creditors being favoured by an award of costs if the action is unsuccessful.'[102]

In so deciding, Laffoy J distinguished the decision of Murphy J in *Re Countyglen plc*[103] where he had held that an application for directions by an inspector, appointed under CA 1990, Part II, did not involve the administration of justice. The basis for that distinction

---

[100] *Re Greendale Developments Ltd* [1997] 3 IR 540.

[101] *McDonald v Bord na gCon* [1965] IR 217.

[102] [1997] 3 IR 540 at 546–547.

[103] *Re Countyglen plc* [1995] 1 IR 220.

was that, in that context, 'there was no contest between parties whereas in the instant case subs (3) of s 231 provides the machinery for the initiation of a contest. When a contest is initiated, its resolution must be a justiciable issue'[104].

(b) Powers of provisional liquidators

[26.039] The powers of a provisional liquidator are closely delimited by the order appointing him, the essence of the appointment being to preserve the status quo[105]. He will always be a creature of the order which appoints him and by CA 1963, s 226(2) the court 'may limit and restrict his powers by the order appointing him'. While often his powers will simply be to preserve assets, in suitable circumstances, he may be allowed to go further. So, while his power to carry on the business of the company will usually be only as far as is necessary for the beneficial winding up of the company, this may involve the actual continuance of the business, for instance, of a restaurant, as happened in *Re Gourmet Restaurants Ltd* where the goodwill of the restaurant was the company's main asset[106]. Just as the court is reluctant to allow the provisional liquidator to continue the business of the company, so too is it reluctant to allow him to close down the business. However, here too, in appropriate circumstances, such as where the business or a part of the business is making huge losses, the court may allow a provisional liquidator to close a business, as happened in *Re Union Accident Insurance Co Ltd*[107]. Powers in aid of gathering information, more normally associated with an official liquidator[108], such as to apply for an examination under CA 1963, s 245, or for the arrest of an absconding contributory under CA 1963, s 247 or to get the statement of company affairs under CA 1963, s 224 or the Rules of the Superior Courts 1986, ord 74, r 19 are also available to a provisional liquidator. Where a winding-up order is made or a provisional liquidator is appointed, no action can be commenced without the sanction of the court: CA 1963, s 222.

[26.040] On the application for the appointment of a provisional liquidator, it is common to list the powers that he seeks from the court. The power to - take possession of the assets in danger; open a bank account; retain a solicitor's services; insure assets and hire security; retain or dismiss employees and continue trading are amongst the powers commonly sought[109]. To avoid unnecessary court applications, the order might contain a proviso that the provisional liquidator has power to sell assets up to a certain *de minimis* amount but above that, the sanction of the court is required[110].

---

104 [1997] 3 IR 540 at 548.

105 See Ussher, *Company Law in Ireland* (1986), p 487.

106 See (1984) The Irish Times, 3 August, per Egan J, considered by Ussher, *Company Law in Ireland* (1986), p 487.

107 *Re Union Accident Insurance Co Ltd* [1972] 1 All ER 1105. Here a provisional liquidator was permitted to close down a branch of the company's business and dismiss employees.

108 See generally, Chapter 27, *Realisation and Distribution of Assets in a Winding Up*, para **[27.071]** *ff*.

109 See Lynch, Marshall and O'Ferrall, *Corporate Insolvency and Rescue* (1996), para [1.61].

110 See *Re Goodwill Merchant Financial Services Ltd* [2001] 1 BCLC 259.

(c) Powers of voluntary liquidators

[26.041] The powers enjoyed by a voluntary liquidator are set out in CA 1963, s 276(1). This provides that a voluntary liquidator may —

> '(a) in the case of a members' voluntary winding up, with the sanction of a special resolution of the company, and, in the case of a creditors' voluntary winding up, with the sanction of the court or the committee of inspection or (if there is no such committee) a meeting of the creditors, exercise any of the powers given by paragraphs (d), (e) and (f) of subsection (1) of section 231 to a liquidator in a winding up by the court;
>
> (b) without sanction, exercise any of the other powers by this Act given to the liquidator in a winding up by the court;
>
> (c) exercise the power of the court under this Act of settling a list of contributories, and the list of contributories shall be prima facie evidence of the liability of the persons named therein to be contributories;
>
> (d) exercise the power of the court of making calls;
>
> (e) summon general meetings of the company for the purpose of obtaining the sanction of the company by resolution or for any other purpose he may think fit.'

Section 276(3) of CA 1963 provides that when several liquidators are appointed, 'any power given by this Act may be exercised by such one or more of them as may be determined at the time of their appointment, or, in default of such determination, by any number not less than two.'

[26.042] It will be noted that a members' voluntary liquidator can only exercise the following powers with the sanction of a special resolution of the company:

— to pay any class of creditor in full[111];

— to make any compromise or arrangement with creditors or persons claiming to be creditors[112];

— to compromise all calls and liabilities to calls, between the company and a contributory[113].

A creditors' voluntary liquidator can only exercise these three powers with the sanction of the court or the committee of inspection or (if there is no such committee) a meeting of the creditors.

[26.043] Without the sanction of the committee of inspection or a meeting of the creditors[114] or of the members by special resolution, a voluntary liquidator has the following powers, namely to:

— bring or defend any action or other legal proceeding in the name and on behalf of the company[115];

---

[111] CA 1963, s 231(1)(d).
[112] CA 1963, s 231(1)(e).
[113] CA 1963, s 231(1)(f).
[114] By virtue of CA 1963, s 276(1)(b).
[115] CA 1963, s 231(1)(a).

- carry on the business of the company so far as may be necessary for its beneficial winding up[116];
- appoint a solicitor to assist him in the performance of his duties[117];
- sell the real and personal property of the company and things in action by auction or private contract[118];
- do all acts and to execute in the name and on behalf of the company all deeds, receipts and documents and to use the company seal[119];
- prove, rank and claim in the bankruptcy of any contributory[120];
- draw, accept, make or endorse any bill of exchange or promissory note in the name and on behalf of the company[121];
- borrow money and give corporate assets as security[122];
- take out letters of administration for any contributory of the company[123];
- give security for costs in any proceedings commenced by the company or by him in the name of the company[124];
- appoint an agent to assist him[125];
- do all such other things as may be necessary for winding up the affairs of the company and distributing its assets[126];
- exercise the power of the court to settle a list of contributories, such list being prima facie evidence of the liability of the persons named therein as contributories[127];
- exercise the power of the court in making calls[128];
- summon general meetings of the company for the purpose of obtaining the sanction of the company by resolution or for any other purpose he may think fit[129].

It can be seen from the foregoing list of powers that voluntary liquidators enjoy considerable freedom to get on with the job of realising and distributing the assets of the company to which they are appointed. This is in keeping with the essential private nature of a voluntary winding up.

---

116 CA 1963, s 231(1)(b).
117 CA 1963, s 231(1)(c).
118 CA 1963, s 231(2)(a).
119 CA 1963, s 231(2)(b).
120 CA 1963, s 231(2)(c).
121 CA 1963, s 231(2)(d).
122 CA 1963, s 231(2)(e).
123 CA 1963, s 231(2)(f).
124 CA 1963, s 231(2)(g).
125 CA 1963, s 231(2)(h).
126 CA 1963, s 231(2)(i).
127 CA 1963, s 276(1)(c).
128 CA 1963, s 276(1)(d).
129 CA 1963, s 276(1)(e).

(d) Restrictions on the exercise of powers by members' voluntary liquidators and other restrictions

[26.044] By virtue of CA 1990, s 131(2) a liquidator who is appointed by the members at the initiation of a creditors' voluntary winding up cannot exercise the powers granted to him by CA 1963, s 276 *before* the creditors' meeting is held. An exception is provided by CA 1990, s 131(3) and the foregoing ban does *not* apply in relation to the liquidator's powers:

> '(a) to take into his custody or under his control all the property to which the company is or appears to be entitled;
>
> (b) to dispose of perishable goods and other goods the value of which is likely to diminish if they are not immediately disposed of;
>
> (c) to do all such things as may be necessary for the protection of the company's assets.'

This section was inserted to prevent the practice which came to be known in England as 'centre-binding', after the case of *Re Centrebind Ltd*[130]. In that case the members of an insolvent company put the company into voluntary liquidation and appointed a liquidator. Prior to the creditors' meeting, the liquidator prevented the English Revenue Commissioners from proceeding against the company's assets. Later, this was held to have been a valid exercise of his powers which were held to be unfettered until the creditors' meeting was held. While the actions of the liquidator in that case were *bona fide*, other, less scrupulous companies caused a members' meeting to be held with the sole purpose of appointing a liquidator with whom they could collude so as to have the assets of the company acquired by another company controlled by them. Section 131(4) of CA 1990 provides that at the creditors' meeting the liquidator appointed by the members shall report any exercise of his powers under CA 1990, s 131 or CA 1963, ss 276 or 280 to the creditors' meeting.

[26.045] Furthermore, if default is made by the company in complying with CA 1963, s 266(1) or (2) or by the directors in complying with sub-s (3) the liquidator shall, within seven days of the day he was nominated by the company or the day he becomes aware of the default (whichever is the later), apply to the court for directions as to the manner in which that default is to be remedied[131]. Failure to do this will make the liquidator liable to be convicted of an offence[132].

[26.046] The liquidator in a members' voluntary winding up has the power, subject to certain safeguards, to accept shares in another company as consideration for the sale of the property of the company being wound up[133]. Before a liquidator can accept shares in another company he must obtain the sanction of the company's members by means of a special resolution. The sale or arrangement is expressed to be binding on the members of the transferor company[134]. This reorganisation is also permitted in a creditors' voluntary

---

130 *Re Centrebind Ltd* [1966] 3 All ER 889, [1967] WLR 377, see McCormack, *The New Companies Legislation* (1991), p 236.

131 CA 1990, s 131(5) and (6).

132 CA 1990, s 131(7).

133 CA 1963, s 260.

134 CA 1963, s 260(2).

winding up, with the necessary modification that the powers of the liquidator may not be exercised except with the sanction of either the court or the committee of inspection[135]. Reorganisations under CA 1963, s 260 are considered in Chapter 24[136].

[26.047] While on his appointment a liquidator will generally assume the management of a company, any arrangement entered into between a company about to be wound up and its creditors is binding on the company where sanctioned by a special resolution in a members' meeting or three-quarters of the creditors in a creditors' meeting[137]. This is subject to a right of appeal to court by any creditor or contributory within three weeks from the completion of the arrangement[138].

[26.048] All liquidators' powers will be suspended where he is appointed to a company in respect of which an interim or interlocutory order or a disposal order has been made under the Proceeds of Crime Act 1996[139]. Section 13(1) of the 1996 Act provides:

> 'Where property the subject of an interim order, an interlocutory order or a disposal order made before the relevant time is in the possession or control of a company and an order for the winding up of the company has been made or a resolution has been passed by the company for a voluntary winding up, the functions of the liquidator (or any provisional liquidator) shall not be exercisable in relation to the property.'

Where a winding-up order has been made or a resolution passed to have a company wound up, an interim or interlocutory freezing order shall not be made in relation to any property held by the company in relation to which the functions of the liquidator are exercisable:

> '(a) so as to inhibit him or her from exercising those functions for the purpose of distributing any property held by the company to the company's creditors, or
>
> (b) so as to prevent the payment out of any property of expenses (including the remuneration of the liquidator or any provisional liquidator) properly incurred in the winding up in respect of the property.'[140]

In that section, 'company' is defined to mean any company which may be wound up under the Companies Acts[141].

(e) Seeking directions from court

[26.049] Section 280(1) of CA 1963, which applies to voluntary liquidators, provides:

---

135 CA 1963, s 271.

136 See Chapter 24, *Schemes of Arrangement and Reconstructions*, para **[24.053]**.

137 CA 1963, s 279(1).

138 CA 1963, s 279(2).

139 See, generally, Courtney, *Mareva Injunctions and Related Interlocutory Orders* (1998), Ch 3, 'Statutory Jurisdictions to Freeze Assets'.

140 Proceeds of Crime Act 1996, s 13(2).

141 Proceeds of Crime Act 1996, s 13(2). 'Relevant time' is also defined in that section to mean: '(a) where no order for the winding up of the company has been made, the time of the passing of the resolution for voluntary winding up, (b) where such an order has been made and, before the presentation of the petition for the winding up of the company by the court, such a resolution had been passed by the company, the time of the passing of the resolution, and (c) in any other case where such an order has been made, the time of the making of the order.'

> 'The liquidator or any contributory or creditor may apply to the court to determine any question arising in the winding up of a company, or to exercise in relation to the enforcing of calls or any other matter, all or any of the powers which the court might exercise if the company were being wound up by the court.'

An official liquidator is an officer of the court and as seen above[142] he is subject to the control of the court in the exercise of his powers by CA 1963, s 231(3). Official liquidators too can apply for court directions. It is always advisable for a liquidator who is in doubt to make such an application for directions[143]. In *Re William Pickles plc*[144] it was held that a liquidator of more than one company could bring a single application for directions where there was an issue that required resolution and which was common to all of the companies in liquidation.

Remuneration of liquidators

[26.050] The members in general meeting set the remuneration of a members' voluntary liquidator[145]. The committee of inspection – or if there is no such committee, the creditors – fix the remuneration of a creditors' voluntary liquidator[146].

[26.051] The remuneration of an official liquidator is a matter for the court[147], whose direction in this regard will turn upon what it considers fair. Keane[148] has noted the current practice whereby one creditor (usually the Revenue Commissioners) is appointed to represent the other creditors before the examiner of the High Court at an inquiry into a liquidator's remuneration. In such cases, the report of the examiner as to the amount of such remuneration will be furnished to the High Court[149]. Notwithstanding the court's wide discretion under CA 1963, s 228(d), in *Re Car Replacements Ltd*[150] Murphy J noted that the practice of the courts has been for many years to determine the remuneration of an official liquidator on the basis of the hours worked by him and his staff. In that case, the company in the title of the matter was one of 39 companies being wound up by the same official liquidator, it being one of ten companies that would have surplus assets available for distribution amongst its shareholders. All of the companies were directly or indirectly subsidiaries of the failed PMPA group of companies and were connected to each other. The official liquidator's fees were disputed, not on grounds of time worked or rate charged, but on the basis that 'the hours involved in such work had been allocated to the various companies by reference to their gross realisations'. The liquidator's justification was that such course of charging has been adopted by him on previous occasions with the

142 See para **[26.004]**.

143 *Roper v Ward* [1981] ILRM 408.

144 *Re William Pickles plc* [1996] 1 BCLC 681.

145 CA 1963, s 258(1). Where remuneration is not fixed, it can be fixed by the court on application: *Re Amalgamated Syndicates Ltd* [1901] 2 Ch 181.

146 CA 1963, s 269(1).

147 CA 1963, s 228(d).

148 See Keane, *Company Law* (3rd edn, 2000), para 36.83.

149 See *Re Merchant Banking Ltd* [1987] ILRM 163 where McCarthy J said that this inquiry was 'one of amount and not of nature or kind'.

150 *Re Car Replacements Ltd* (15 December 1999, unreported), High Court, (Murphy J).

consent of the interested parties and the approval of the Court. In both his seventh and eighth status reports the official liquidator had stated that certain hours worked were not attributable to a specific company and covered all companies involved and that he had allocated those hours by reference to gross realisations to date. As a general point of principle Murphy J stated that he had no doubt that it was correct to contend that an official liquidator of a group of companies was not entitled to deem or attribute hours worked by him in relation to the affairs of the group to different companies on the basis of the amount of the assets realised by them respectively, or indeed on any basis other than the hours actually worked in respect of the particular companies. In all of the circumstances of the case in hand, however, Murphy J accepted that it was appropriate to calculate the liquidator's remuneration on the basis proposed by the liquidator[151]. Ordinarily, provisional liquidators will go on to become official liquidators and will be remunerated in accordance with the foregoing rules[152].

[26.052] As regards the priority of voluntary liquidators' remuneration, CA 1963, s 281 provides that such is payable out of the assets of the company in priority to all other claims. Section 244 of CA 1963 applies to official liquidations and provides that where assets are insufficient to meet liabilities, the court may make an order as to payment as it thinks fit. In this regard, guidance is provided by the Rules of the Superior Courts 1986, ord 74, r 128(1). The priority of the costs and expenses in liquidations (including the remuneration of liquidators) is considered in Chapter 27[153] but it may be noted that it has been held that where there is more than one liquidator and there are insufficient assets available to discharge their remuneration in full then their remuneration will rank equally[154].

Foreign liquidators and the EU Council Regulation on Insolvency Proceedings

(a) Assistance to foreign liquidators in Ireland

[26.053] A foreign liquidator (ie one who is appointed by a foreign court or is appointed under the laws of another country to a body corporate incorporated there) may apply to the Irish High Court for assistance under CA 1963, s 250(1) which provides:

---

[151] Inter alia, it was noted that there were no records available by reference to which the hours worked in respect of the affairs of each individual company could be ascertained and that to create them retrospectively would involve a very subjective element and would involve further delay and very considerable expense. Murphy J also noted that solicitors for parties substantially interested in the distributions in respect of the other 37 companies had submitted that the liquidator's means of calculation was the most practical and had been approved by the companies' creditors and contributories.

[152] In *Re UOC Corporation; Alipour v UOC Corporation* [1998] BCC 191 an unusual situation arose whereby a provisional liquidator was discharged before a petition was presented to wind up the company. Carnwath J held that the court had power under the English Insolvency Rules (r 4.31(2)) to direct that a provisional liquidator be discharged before the hearing of the petition, subject to the control of the court.

[153] Chapter 27, *The Realisation and Distribution of Assets in a Winding Up*, para **[27.150]**.

[154] See *Re Salters Hall School Ltd; Merrygold v Horton* [1998] 1 BCLC 401.

> 'Any order made by a court of any country recognised for the purposes of this section and made for or in the course of winding up a company may be enforced by the High Court in the same manner in all respects as if the order had been made by the High Court.'

For the purposes of this section, 'company' means a body corporate incorporated outside the State, and 'recognised' means recognised by order made by the Minister[155]. To date, one such order has been made by the Minister and Great Britain and Northern Ireland were recognised[156]. Section 250(2) provides that an office copy of any order sought to be enforced shall be sufficient evidence of the order. It should be noted that this section has now been confined to applications by liquidators appointed by the courts of non-EU countries (except the State and Denmark)[157].

[26.054] A possible alternative to foreign liquidators is CA 1963, s 345. This has already been considered in the preceding chapter[158]. Of particular significance, however, is CA 1963, s 345(7), which provides:

> 'Where a company incorporated outside the State which has been carrying on business in the State ceases to carry on business in the State, it may be wound up as an unregistered company under this Part, notwithstanding that it has been dissolved or otherwise ceased to exist as a company under or by virtue of the laws of the country under which it was incorporated.'

(b) The European Council Regulation on Insolvency Proceedings

[26.055] The most recent development in this area is the EU's Council Regulation on Insolvency Proceedings[159] (the 'Insolvency Regulation'). Although Council regulations have direct effect in the State, they have been implemented here by regulations[160] which have amended CA 1963. The purpose of the Insolvency Regulation is to improve the efficiency and effectiveness of insolvency proceedings having cross-EU border effects by harmonising the provisions in each Member State concerning jurisdiction, recognition and applicable law. The Insolvency Regulation is, by definition, concerned with insolvent liquidations, not members' voluntary windings up[161].

[26.056] The Insolvency Regulation provides in Article 3(1) that the courts of the Member State where the debtor's main interests is situated 'shall have jurisdiction to open insolvency proceedings' and in the case of a company this is presumed to be the place where its registered office is situate. The Insolvency Regulation goes on to recognise that *secondary proceedings*[162] may be opened up in a different Member State. However, Article 3(2) provides that the courts of a Member State, other than the state in which a debtor has his main interests, will only have jurisdiction to open insolvency proceedings against a

---

155 CA 1963, s 250(3).

156 SI 1964/42.

157 Section 250(4) of CA 1963 as inserted by reg 3(d) of SI 2002/333.

158 See Chapter 25, *Winding Up Companies*, para **[25.032]** *ff*.

159 Council Regulation (EC) No 1346/2000 of 29 May 2000.

160 The European Communities (Corporate Insolvency) Regulations 2002 (SI 2002/333).

161 Whilst it is the case that the Insolvency Regulations are not confined to companies, and extends to insolvent individuals and partnerships, it is only companies that are the subject of this work.

162 Insolvency Regulations, Article 3(3).

debtor if he has an establishment there. And further, secondary proceedings can generally[163] only be opened after the main proceedings have been opened. From this it can be seen that the Insolvency Regulation introduces nothing new to Irish law, bearing as it does a remarkable similarity in effect to CA 1963, s 345(7) which facilitates the Irish courts opening 'secondary' proceedings.

[26.057] The law applicable to insolvency proceedings is deemed to be the law of the Member State where the proceedings are opened[164]. That law determines the conditions for the opening of those proceedings, their conduct and closure[165]. Articles 5–15 of the Insolvency Regulation make provision for specific matters such as rights in rem, set-off, reservation of title etc.

[26.058] Article 16(1) of the Insolvency Regulation is similar in effect to CA 1963, s 250. This provides:

> 'Any judgment opening insolvency proceedings handed down by a court of a Member State which has jurisdiction pursuant to Article 3 shall be recognised in all the other Member States from the time that it becomes effective in the State of the opening of proceedings.'

[26.059] Perhaps the most significant development is the extra-judicial powers afforded to all EU liquidators of insolvent companies. Article 18(1) of the Insolvency Regulations provides that the liquidator appointed by the courts of the member state where the debtor's main interests are situate (under Article 3(1)):

> '...may exercise all the powers conferred on him by the law of the State of the opening of proceedings *in another Member State*, so long as no other insolvency proceedings have been opened there nor any preservation measure to the contrary has been taken there further to a request for the opening of insolvency proceedings in that State. He may in particular remove the debtor's assets from the territory of the Member State in which they are situated, subject to Articles 5 and 7.'[166]

---

[163] See, however, the exceptions to this generality in Insolvency Regulations, Article 3(4)(a) and (b).

[164] Insolvency Regulations, Article 4(1).

[165] Insolvency Regulations, Article 4(2) provides that it shall determine, in particular:

> '(a) against which debtors insolvency proceedings may be brought on account of their capacity; (b) the assets which form part of the estate and the treatment of assets acquired by or devolving on the debtor after the opening of the insolvency proceedings; (c) the respective powers of the debtor and the liquidator; (d) the conditions under which set-offs may be invoked; (e) the effects of insolvency proceedings on current contracts to which the debtor is party; (f) the effects of the insolvency proceedings brought by individual creditors, with the exception of lawsuits pending; (g) the claims which are to be lodged against the debtor's estate and the treatment of claims arising after the opening of insolvency proceedings; (h) the rules governing the lodging, verification and admission of claims; (i) the rules governing the distribution of proceeds from the realisation of assets, the ranking of claims and the rights of creditors who have obtained partial satisfaction after the opening of insolvency proceedings by virtue of a right in rem or through a set-off; (j) the conditions for and the effects of closure of insolvency proceedings, in particular by composition; (k) creditors' rights after the closure of insolvency proceedings; (l) who is to bear the costs and expenses incurred in the insolvency proceedings; (m) the rules relating to voidness, voidability or unenforceability of legal acts detrimental to all the creditors.

[166] Emphasis added. Insolvency Regulations, Article 5 preserves third parties' in rem rights and article 7 preserves the rights of sellers of goods under reservation of title clauses.

So, a liquidator appointed by the Irish High Court to, say, an insolvent Irish company with assets in England can travel to England and will have authority to collect in any assets belonging to the insolvent company and expatriate them. Of course the liquidator will have to comply with the laws of England and Wales regarding the procedures on the realisation of assets and coercive measures are specifically excluded[167]. A liquidator appointed by a court in secondary proceedings (under Article 3(2)) may in any other Member State claim through the courts or out of court that moveable property was removed from the jurisdiction of the State of the opening of the proceedings and may bring any action to set aside which is in the interests of the creditors[168].

[26.060] Article 19 of the Insolvency Regulations provides that a liquidator's appointment shall be evidenced by a certified copy of the original decision appointing him or by any other certificate issued by the court which has jurisdiction and, whilst individual Member States may, in their own laws, require it to be translated into one of its official languages, 'no legislation or other similar formality shall be required'. Individual Member States are also allowed to require the publication of notification of a liquidator's appointment by a court opening insolvency proceedings in another Member State in respect of companies that have an establishment there[169]. Section 227B(2) of CA 1963[170] provides that liquidators must publish in *Iris Oifigiúil* and once at least in two morning newspapers circulating in the State the following:

> '(a) notice of the judgment opening the insolvency proceedings concerned,
>
> (b) where appropriate, the decision appointing the liquidator in those proceedings,
>
> (c) the name and business address of the liquidator, and
>
> (d) the provision (either paragraph 1 or paragraph 2) of Article 3 of the Insolvency Regulation giving jurisdiction to open the proceedings'.[171]

Publication must be as soon as practicable after the opening of an insolvency proceeding, where the debtor company has an establishment in the State[172]. Individual Member States may also require foreign liquidators to notify a central registry – such as the companies registration office in Ireland – of their appointment[173]. Judgments handed down by a court whose judgment concerning the opening of proceedings is recognised in accordance with Article 16 and which concern the court and closure of insolvency proceedings and compositions approved by that court must also be recognised with no further formalities[174]. Section 227A(1) of CA 1963[175] provides that, without prejudice to Article 16(1) of the Insolvency Regulation, a liquidator appointed in insolvency proceedings who intends:

---

167 Insolvency Regulations, Article 18(3).
168 Insolvency Regulations, Article 18(2).
169 Insolvency Regulations, Article 21.
170 As inserted by reg 3(c) of SI 2002/333.
171 CA 1963, s 227B.
172 CA 1963, s 227B(3).
173 Insolvency Regulations, Article 22.
174 Insolvency Regulations, Article 25.
175 As inserted by SI 2002/333, reg 3(8).

'(a) to request under Article 21 of the Regulation that notice of the judgment opens the proceedings and, where appropriate, the decision appointing him or her be published in the state, or

(b) to take any other action in the State under the Regulation,

shall deliver to the Registrar of Companies for registration a duly certified copy of the judgment and, where appropriate, of the decision appointing the liquidator.'

Application can also be made by a liquidator who does not intend to take any action in the State and the Registrar may also cause such an application to be registered[176]. The certified copy judgment and, where appropriate, decision mentioned in s 227A(1) must be accompanied by a certified translation into the English or Irish language, a prescribed form and the appropriate fee[177]. It is also provided that the Registrar shall issue a certificate of registration to the liquidator[178]. Although likely to arise infrequently, it is important to note the public policy exception contained in Article 26. This provides:

> 'Any Member State may refuse to recognise insolvency proceedings opened in another Member State or to enforce a judgment handed down in the context of such proceedings where the effects of such recognition or enforcement would be manifestly contrary to that State's public policy, in particular its fundamental principles or the constitutional rights and liberties of the individual.'

[26.061] Articles 27–38 of the Insolvency Regulations deal with secondary insolvency proceedings. Those with standing to apply for the opening of secondary proceedings are the liquidator in the main proceedings and anybody else who has jurisdiction under the laws of the Member State whose courts are being asked to open secondary proceedings[179]. The liquidator in the main proceedings and the liquidators in the secondary proceedings are, by Article 31, 'duty bound to' communicate information and co-operate with each other.

[26.062] Regulation 6 of SI 2002/333, the European Communities (Corporate Insolvency) Regulations 2002 expressly provides that an insolvency judgment within the meaning of Article 25 of the Insolvency Regulation (read in accordance with Articles 38-58 of the Brussels Regulation on jurisdiction and the recognition and enforcement of judgments in civil and commercial matters)[180] can be declared enforceable immediately on completion of the formalities in Article 53 of the Brussels Regulation by the Master of the High Court. The Master is required to grant any preservation measures as are applied for where the High Court has jurisdiction to grant such relief[181]. It should be noted, however, that a request under Article 38 of the Brussels Regulations to secure and preserve any of a debtor's assets in the State must be made to the High Court[182].

---

[176] CA 1963, s 227(A).

[177] CA 1963, s 227A(3).

[178] CA 1963, s 227A(4).

[179] Insolvency Regulations, Article 29.

[180] Council Regulation (EC) No 44/2001 of 22 December 2000(2).

[181] Regulation 6(7) and (8) of SI 2002/333.

[182] Regulation 9(1) of SI 2002/333.

[26.063] The foregoing is but a sample of the 47 articles contained in the Insolvency Regulations. As has been noted in the proceeding paragraphs, there is nothing especially novel about secondary windings up or enforcing the orders of foreign courts. What is, however, significant is the effects of EU-wide regulations which force a degree of harmony in the insolvency laws of individual Member States.

(c) Assistance to Irish liquidators abroad

[26.064] Prior to the commencement of the Insolvency Regulations, the ability of Irish liquidators to bring application in the courts of other EU jurisdictions depended upon the legislative regime applicable in those jurisdictions. In *Re Business City Express Ltd*[183] an examiner who had been appointed to a company that had been placed under the protection of the Irish High Court successfully applied under the Insolvency Act 1986, s 426 (UK) to the English Chancery Division for co-operation with the Irish High Court's decision. Specifically, the examiner required assistance in the form of an order that would bind English creditors. Rattee J said '...since the Irish court has requested assistance of this court, while I am not bound to give it, I should do so unless satisfied that there is some good reason not to do so.'[184]
Generally speaking the comity of the courts will prevail and courts will assist the enforcement of orders made by courts in other jurisdictions. Not only can Irish official liquidators avail of the Insolvency Regulation, so too can creditors' voluntary liquidators, who may obtain 'certification' of their status as such from the Master of the High Court. This is provided for by CA 1963, s 267A[185] which allows application to be brought to the Master after a creditors' voluntary liquidator has been appointed provided that 'the centre of the company's main interests is situate in the State.'

The Director of Corporate Enforcement's power to supervise liquidators

[26.065] The CA 1963 provides that the court can make such order for inspection of the books and papers of a company by its creditors and contributories as it thinks fit[186]. The advent of the office of the Director of Corporate Enforcement has made liquidators amenable to supervision and inspection. Section 57(1) of CLEA 2001 provides that the Director can on his own motion or where complaint is made to him by a member, contributory or creditor of the company, request, specifying the reason why the request is being made, the liquidator of a company to produce to the Director the liquidator's books for examination and the liquidator is obliged to comply with such request. Failure to

[183] *Re Business City Express Ltd* [1997] BCC 826.

[184] Citing *Re Dallhold Estates (UK) Pty Ltd* [1992] BCC 394; *Re Focus Insurance Co Ltd* [1996] BCC 659 and *Re Bank of Credit and Commerce International SA* [1993] BCC 787.

[185] As inserted by reg 3(e) of SI 2002/333.

[186] CA 1963, s 243(1). Note that by s 234(1A), inserted by CLEA 2001, s 43, the court can on the application of the Director of Corporate Affairs: '... make an order for the inspection by the Director of any books and papers in the possession of a company the subject of a winding-up order and the company, every officer of the company and the liquidator shall give to the Director such access to and facilities as are necessary for inspecting and taking copies of those books and papers as the Director may require'. It may also be noted that CA 1963, s 282A(1) and (2), inserted by CLEA 2001, s 49, expressly extends the provisions of CA 1963, s 243 (which primarily applies in official liquidations) to voluntary liquidations.

comply is an offence[187]. Requests in respect of liquidations concluded more than six years prior to the request are prohibited[188]. It is particularly significant that the books which the director can seek can be *either* 'in relation to a particular liquidation process or to all liquidations undertaken by the liquidator'. Liquidators are obliged to answer the Director's questions concerning the content of the books requested to be produced and the conduct of a particular liquidation or all liquidations and is further obliged to give the Director such assistance in the matter as he is reasonably able to do[189].

[26.066] Section 58 of CLEA 2001 imposes a statutory duty on liquidators' professional bodies to report misconduct to the Director. It provides:

> 'Where a disciplinary committee of tribunal (however called) of a prescribed professional body finds that a member conducting a liquidation or receivership has not maintained appropriate records, or it has reasonable grounds for believing that a member has committed an indictable offence under the Companies Acts during the course of a liquidation or receivership, the body shall report the matter, giving details of the finding or, as the case may be, of the alleged offence, to the Director forthwith and if the body fails to comply with this section it, and every officer of the body to whom the failure is attributable, is guilty of an offence.'

Ironically, by definition, liquidators who are not members of any profession are entirely unaffected by this provision.

---

[187] CLEA 2001, s 57(4).
[188] CLEA 2001, s 57(3).
[189] CLEA 2001, s 57(2).

Chapter 27

Realisation and Distribution of Assets in a Winding Up

Introduction

[27.001] To use the term 'liquidation' in the context of the winding up of a company is to tell but half the story. As Laffoy J acknowledged in *Re Greendale Developments Ltd*[1]:

> 'Once a winding-up order is made, a company is doomed to extinction. The winding up process is the process of the administration of the assets of the company: their *collection, realisation and distribution* in discharge of the liabilities of the company to the creditors and of the entitlement of its contributories in accordance with the scheme of priorities prescribed in the Companies Acts'. [Emphasis added]

The essential nature of the winding up of a company entails two distinct concepts: the *realisation* of all assets belonging to the company following a full investigation into the company's assets, and the subsequent *distribution* of the proceeds of that realisation in the priority determined by law.

[27.002] The investigation into a company's affairs is an integral part of the realisation of a company's assets because the primary purpose of an investigation is invariably to bolster or swell the assets of the company. At the outset, it should be noted that the Company Law Enforcement Act ('CLEA 2001'), which created the office of the Director of Corporate Enforcement, has allowed the Director to piggyback on many of the powers of investigation afforded to liquidators. This is notwithstanding the fact that the Director has a very different purpose in mind to that of liquidators, namely, investigation with a view to prosecution or other sanction[2].

[27.003] The realisation and distribution of assets must be the theme of any treatment of the winding up of a company, whether of the voluntary or compulsory variety. Whilst often, the law of the consequences of a winding-up order are treated under the heading of 'the powers of a liquidator' or the 'incidents of a winding-up order', the reality is that the point under discussion is the *realisation* of corporate assets. In this regard, the word realisation is used in its wider meaning and includes the gathering of assets by whatever means. On this analysis, issues such as fraudulent preference, invalid floating charges and pooling and contribution orders are all examples of the principle that *all* corporate assets must be *realised* so as to be available for their subsequent distribution in accordance with the scheme of priorities in the Companies Acts. Consequently, this chapter treats the law in two sections:

[A] The realisation of corporate assets.

[B] The distribution of corporate assets.

---

1 *Re Greendale Developments Ltd* [1997] 3 IR 540.

2 See Chapter 12, *Company Law Compliance and Enforcement*, para **[12.009]** *ff*.

[A] The Realisation of Corporate Assets

The liquidator's duty to realise corporate assets

[27.004] Liquidators, whether official or voluntary, are entrusted with the task of realising the company's assets. The term 'realise' does not have a specific statutory meaning and is used here in its dictionary sense. In *Re Private Motorists Provident Society Ltd; Horgan v Minister for Justice*[3] Murphy J said of the role of the official liquidator in the realisation of assets:

> 'An official liquidator is appointed under s 225 of the Companies Act 1963 to perform, *inter alia*, the statutory duty imposed in the court by s 235 of that Act which provides that the court shall cause "the assets of the company to be collected and applied in discharge of its liabilities". How assets will be "collected" will depend upon the nature of the particular assets and the circumstances of the case. The task may include litigation, sale or simply the reduction into possession by the official liquidator of "cash in hand". It seems to me that all or any of such procedures would be appropriate to make the assets of the company available for the discharge of its liabilities and indeed the payment of the costs and expenses of the litigation. All such procedures which make the assets of the company available for that purpose in my view constitute a "*realisation*" whether or not a sale of the assets is required.'[4]

In the context of the realisation of corporate assets, the duties of liquidators may be seen to include:

- taking possession of all corporate assets, and protecting them, pending the distribution of the proceeds in accordance with law;
- pursuing all assets which in law or in equity belong to the company, but which may be in the possession of others;
- realising claims for compensation and damages against wrong-doing corporate officers and others who owe the company money; and,
- realising and liquidating all assets so as to have the proceeds available for distribution in accordance with law.

The foregoing duties of liquidators and the way in which they are governed by the Companies Acts 1963–2001, shall be considered in detail in this chapter.

Officers' duties to assist liquidators

[27.005] Directors and other officers[5] have statutory duties to assist and co-operate with liquidators. It should be noted that by the Companies Act 1963, s 293(1) ('CA 1963'), if any person being a past or present officer of a company that is being wound up (whether

3 *Re Private Motorists Provident Society Ltd; Horgan v Minister for Justice* (23 June 1995, unreported), High Court (Murphy J).

4 (23 June 1995, unreported), High Court at p 7, 8. See also *Re Chipboard Products Ltd* (27 February 1997, unreported), High Court (Laffoy J).

5 For the purposes of CA 1963, s 293, s 293(4) provides that '"officer" shall include any person in accordance with whose directions or instructions the directors of a company have been accustomed to act'.

officially or voluntarily) does not, inter alia, co-operate with a liquidator he shall, subject to s 293(2)[6], be guilty of an offence. The 16 offences set out there are:

'(a) does not to the best of his knowledge and belief fully and truly disclose to the liquidator when he requests such disclosure all the property, real and personal, of the company and how and to whom and for what consideration and when the company disposed of any part thereof, except such part as has been disposed of in the ordinary way of the business of the company; or

(b) does not deliver up to the liquidator, or as he directs, all such part of the real and personal property of the company as is in his custody or under his control, and which he is required by law to deliver up; or

(c) does not deliver up to the liquidator, or as he directs, all books and papers in his custody or under his control belonging to the company and which he is required by law to deliver up; or

(d) within 12 months next before the commencement of the winding up or at any time thereafter conceals any part of the property of the company to the value of €12.69 or upwards, or conceals any debt due to or from the company; or

(e) within 12 months next before the commencement of the winding up or at any time thereafter fraudulently removes any part of the property of the company to the value of €12.69 or upwards; or

(f) makes any material omission in any statement relating to the affairs of the company; or

(g) knowing or believing that a false debt has been proved by any person under the winding up, fails for the period of a month to inform the liquidator thereof; or

(h) after the commencement of the winding up prevents the production of any book or paper affecting or relating to the property or affairs of the company; or

(i) within 12 months next before the commencement of the winding up or at any time thereafter conceals, destroys, mutilates or falsifies or is privy to the concealment, destruction, mutilation or falsification of any book or paper affecting or relating to the property or affairs of the company; or

(j) within 12 months next before the commencement of the winding up or at any time thereafter makes or is privy to the making of any false entry in any book or paper affecting or relating to the property or affairs of the company; or

(k) within 12 months next before the commencement of the winding up or at any time thereafter fraudulently parts with, alters or makes any omission in, or is privy to the fraudulent parting with, altering or making any omission in, any document affecting or relating to the property or affairs of the company; or

(l) after the commencement of the winding up or at any meeting of the creditors of the company within 12 mouths next before the commencement of the winding up

6 CA 1963, s 293(2) provides 'It shall be a good defence to a charge under any of paragraphs (a), (b), (c), (d), (f), (n) and (o) of subsection (1), if the accused proves that he had no intent to defraud and to a charge under any of paragraphs (h), (i) and (j) of subsection (1), if he proves that he had no intent to conceal the state of affairs of the company or to defeat the law.'

attempts to account for any part of the property of the company by fictitious losses or expenses; or

(m) has within 12 months next before the commencement of the winding up or at any time thereafter, by any false representation or other fraud, obtained any property for or on behalf of the company on credit which the company does not subsequently pay for; or

(n) within 12 months next before the commencement of the winding up or at any time thereafter, under the false pretence that the company is carrying on its business, obtains on credit for or on behalf of the company, any property which the company does not subsequently pay for; or

(o) within 12 months next before the commencement of the winding up or at any time thereafter pawns, pledges or disposes of any property of the company which has been obtained on credit and has not been paid for, unless such pawning, pledging or disposing is in the ordinary way of business of the company; or

(p) is guilty of any false representation or other fraud for the purpose of obtaining the consent of the creditors of the company or any of them to an agreement with reference to the affairs of the company or to the winding up'.

In *R v McCredie*[7] the Court of Appeal heard an appeal against a conviction of two directors for failing to deliver up company books contrary to the English equivalent to our s 293(1)(c)[8]. The Court of Appeal quoted the English provision and said:

> 'We quote that section in full, to make the obvious but sometimes overlooked point that company officers in a winding up owe a duty to the company to comply with that section. The immediate relevance here depends on two points. First, these subsections require officers of the company to be pro-active, and not merely reactive. They must co-operate with the liquidator actively in "discovering" (ie disclosing) company property unknown to the liquidator, and the delivery up requirements significantly are not dependent on a prior request from the liquidator. It is clear that the delivery up requirement in s 208 is covered by s 12(1) of the Interpretation Act 1978:[9] "Where an Act...imposes a duty it is implied, unless the contrary intention appears, that...the duty is to be performed from time to time as occasion requires". This was a continuing duty, and not a once for all time duty. It did not have to be triggered by a request from the liquidator'.

In that case the company's liquidator's agents had taken away the company's filing cabinets after emptying them of computer disks and documents. The directors had removed the disks and documents, compiled from them a list of the company's customers and had sold the list as part of the company's goodwill to another company. The directors' defence to the liquidator's demand for the return of the information was that the disks and documents had been 'abandoned' by the liquidator, acting through his agents. The Court of Appeal held that the liquidator had not abandoned the property as this could not be done without knowledge of its existence. Moreover, the directors had a statutory duty to make full

7 *R v McCredie* [2000] BCC 617.

8 Insolvency Act 1986, s 208(1) (UK).

9 The Irish Interpretation Act 1937, s 16(1) also provides: 'Every duty imposed by an Act of the Oireachtas or by an instrument made wholly or partly under any such Act shall, unless the contrary intention appears in such Act or instrument, be performed from time to time as occasion requires.'

discovery of the company's property to its liquidator[10]. That directors owe duties to liquidators to co-operate is, no doubt, a fact that liquidators should not be shy to point out to recalcitrant officers.

The liquidator's starting point: gathering in assets

[27.006] Upon his appointment, the liquidator should immediately set about ascertaining, securing and gathering the company's assets. Official and provisional liquidators have very specific duties and express powers to gather in assets.

(a) The duty to gather-in assets

[27.007] Official and provisional liquidators have a statutory obligation to take a company's property under their control. Section 229(1) of CA 1963 provides that where a winding-up order has been made or where a provisional liquidator has been appointed, an official or provisional liquidator:

> '...shall take into his custody or under his control all the property and things in action to which the company is or appears to be entitled.'

The reason why court appointed liquidators have such an express duty is because they are the agents of the court and the court is expressly charged with causing 'the assets of the company to be collected and applied in discharge of its liabilities'[11]. Indeed, in a compulsory winding up, where no liquidator has been appointed, s 229(2) provides that all the property of the company shall be deemed to be in the custody of the court.

[27.008] By CA 1963, s 239(1) the court can order any person who owes money to the company to pay it into a bank account of the liquidator:

> 'The court may order any contributory, purchaser or other person from whom money is due to the company to pay the amount due into such bank as the court may appoint to the account of the liquidator instead of to the liquidator, and any such order may be enforced in like manner as if it had directed payment to the liquidator.'

Pending their distribution, the only person who is entitled to control the assets of a company that is in liquidation is its liquidator.

[27.009] In a members' voluntary liquidation the liquidator's powers derive from the members' resolution appointing him as liquidator which must appoint him 'for the purpose of winding up the affairs and distributing the assets of the company'.[12] A liquidator appointed in a creditors' voluntary liquidation has an identical statutory purpose[13]. In order to discharge these requirements, voluntary liquidators will be obliged to begin to gather-in the company's assets, something that voluntary liquidators have power to do without the

---

10 The Court of Appeal's warning on the difficulties in a jury trial of explaining the defence of 'abandonment' should be noted. In that case, at trial, a nine-page paper had been prepared to assist the jury but had not been agreed by counsel. There, no issue had been taken with the document circulated to the jury but the Court of Appeal warned that such an omission might court disaster in another case.

11 CA 1963, s 235(1), acknowledged in *Re Private Motorists Provident Society Ltd; Horgan v Minister for Justice* (23 June 1995, unreported), High Court (Murphy J). See para **[27.004]**.

12 CA 1963, s 258(1).

13 CA 1963, s 267(1).

sanction of either the members (in a members' voluntary) or the creditors (in a creditors' voluntary), by virtue of CA 1963, ss 276(1)(b) and s 231(2)(i)[14].

[27.010] By CA 1963, s 230, on the application of the liquidator, the court may:

> '...direct that all or any part of the property of whatsoever description belonging to the company or held by trustees on its behalf shall vest in the liquidator by his official name, and thereupon the property to which the order relates shall vest accordingly, and the liquidator may, after giving such indemnity, if any, as the court may direct, bring or defend in his official name any action or other legal proceedings which relates to that property or which it is necessary to bring or defend for the purpose of effectually winding up the company and recovering its property.'

It is relatively unusual for the court to order that the title to a company's assets vest in the liquidator. In *Re Private Motorists Provident Society Ltd; Horgan v Minister for Justice*[15] Murphy J held that it was not necessary for an order to have been made under s 230 in order for stamp duty on monies 'received by the liquidator in realisation of the assets of the company' to become due. There, it had been argued that monies realised by the society, itself, were not subject to duty and that monies could only be said to have been received by a liquidator where an order under s 230 has been made. Murphy J rejected this, saying:

> 'Clearly the realisation was brought about by the liquidator and he was the proper party to give a receipt for the proceeds of sale thereof even though the ownership remained vested in the Society.'[16]

Whilst this decision accords with common sense, it is thought that the liquidator's contention was pedantically correct since monies received by a liquidator in the absence of an order being made under s 230 are received as agent of and on behalf of the company.

(b) The assets to be gathered: the meaning of 'property and things in action'

[27.011] An official liquidator's statutory obligation to gather-in, contained in CA 1963, s 229(1), relates to all 'property and things in action'. Tangible personalty, such as chattels, is the most easily recognisable property that the liquidator must gather up for later distribution in accordance with the priority determined by law. Choses in action can be very varied in form and include, for example, shares, insurance rights, cheques, goodwill, debts and causes of action[17]. Choses in action cannot be grasped or held and whilst they will invariably have some physical title document (eg an insurance policy, share certificate or piece of paper acknowledging a debt, etc) the chose itself, does not have a tangible manifestation. The courts in England have held that a milk quota is 'property' in a winding up and that the liquidators could direct its sale or other realisation[18]. So too was a waste management licence found to be 'property' only, this time, worthless property that could be disclaimed by the liquidator[19]. It has been held, also, that the fruits of a company's

---

14 CA 1963, s 231(2)(i) provides that the liquidator has power to 'do all such other things as may be necessary for winding up the affairs of the company and distributing its assets'.

15 *Re Private Motorists Provident Society Ltd; Horgan v Minister for Justice* (23 June 1995, unreported), High Court (Murphy J).

16 (23 June 1995, unreported), High Court at p 5.

17 See Chapter 26, *Liquidators*, para **[26.034]**.

18 *Swift v Dairywise Farms Ltd* [2000] BCC 642.

property are themselves the company's property[20]. It has been questioned, however, whether the proceeds of a successful action against company directors for breach of duty or, say, fraudulent trading, is 'company' property[21].

(c) No lien on company books and records

[27.012] The title to real property, evidenced by title deeds, may be in the possession of advisors or former advisors to the company. Similarly, files and other documents relating to company property may be held by third parties. Prior to the commencement of the Companies Act 1990 ('CA 1990') advisors to companies could retain possession of certain files and other documents until they had been paid for their services by exercising a lien. Now, by CA 1963, s 244A[22] no person can withhold possession of deeds, instruments, or other documents, books of account, receipts, bills, invoices or other papers of a like nature relating to the accounts or trade, dealings or business of the company from the liquidator by claiming possession or lien. This is, however, without prejudice to the rights of the persons in whose possession such documents are, and the section is intended to assist the gathering of information by the liquidator, which will go to aid the orderly realisation of the company's assets. Section 244A does not apply where the circumstances giving rise to the lien claimed arose prior to the enactment of CA 1990: *Kelly v Scales*[23].

(d) Assets not beneficially owned by the company

[27.013] Certain assets in the company's possession may not in fact belong to the company. Examples include goods that are subject to a valid and effective retention of title clause, leased property and property that is held by the company in trust. The issues arising in relation to such property are considered in the context of the distribution of corporate assets, below[24]. Alternatively, certain property that belongs in law and in equity to a company may be more of a liability than a benefit to the company, and the liquidator may wish to *disclaim* it, something that is permitted by statute in certain circumstances[25].

(e) Disputed assets

[27.014] Most problems for liquidators tend to arise in respect of assets that are not legally owned by the company but to which the company is nevertheless beneficially entitled. Often, the liquidator will have reason to believe that the total worth of the company's assets far exceeds those assets that he can readily lay his hands on. So, in a wide variety of situations, the liquidator will have to set about realising assets to which the company is beneficially entitled, thereby swelling the assets available for distribution in accordance with insolvency law. Particularly where wrongdoing by the controllers of the company is suspected, the liquidator may find that he requires more information on the affairs of the

---

19 *Official Receiver as Liquidator of Celtic Extraction Ltd & Bluestone Chemicals Ltd v Environment Agency* [2000] BCC 487.

20 *R v McCredie* [2000] BCC 617.

21 See *Re Floor Fourteen Ltd; Lewis v Inland Revenue Commissioners* [2001] 2 BCLC 392 considered at para **[27.126]**.

22 As inserted by CA 1990, s 125.

23 *Kelly v Scales* [1994] 1 IR 42.

24 See para **[27.129]** *ff*.

25 See para **[27.053]**.

company and the whereabouts and ownership of assets than that being offered by the controllers. He may in such situations seek an order for examination, an asset freezing order or even an arrest order against directors and others to enable him obtain the information he requires[26].

(f) Swelling assets through transaction avoidance and litigation

[27.015] In realising a company's assets a liquidator may find that some or all of the company's assets have been siphoned off through unlawful dispositions, either before or after the commencement of the winding up. He may indeed find that certain creditors have been *preferred* over the vast majority of other creditors[27]. He may find that certain persons have recently been granted floating charges as security for sums owed to them by the company, thus allowing them 'leap frog' the orderly queue which the liquidator will attempt to create on distribution[28]. Additionally, realisable assets may be increased by applying to have related companies contribute to the assets of the company which is being wound up by means of a contribution order[29]. Where the affairs of two companies have been intermingled the liquidator may apply to have both companies wound up together, and their assets pooled[30]. He may find that the company has suffered loss through breaches of duty by its officers, or is owed money in contract and he may decide to litigate to satisfy such claims. Other methods of swelling assets involve making a call on the contributories in limited companies in respect of outstanding payments on shares; and in the case of unlimited companies, on all the shareholders to make good any deficit between assets and liabilities. It is evident therefore that not only is the liquidator concerned with the gathering of assets, but also with their lawful distribution since what he takes from one creditor he will ultimately pay to another creditor who is entitled in law to be paid in priority[31].

The liquidator's starting point: gathering information

[27.016] Commonly, liquidators will commence the liquidation of a company by gathering information to facilitate the gathering of assets. These powers are considered under the following headings:

(a) Powers to obtain basic information.

(b) Power to obtain books and papers.

(c) Examination.

(d) Post-examination transfer and search and seizure orders.

(e) Powers of civil arrest.

(a) Powers to obtain basic information

[27.017] Information will often be the key to an effective realisation of corporate assets. Where it is suspected that assets were, or are in the process of being spirited away their

---

26 See paras **[27.022]**, **[27.045]** and **[27.036]** , respectively.

27 See para **[27.072]**.

28 See para **[27.097]**.

29 See para **[27.106]**.

30 See para **[27.112]**.

31 See para **[27.127]**.

very whereabouts and the circumstances of their removal from the company may be unknown. Similarly, where delinquent behaviour on the part of the company's controllers is suspected, the best way of obtaining evidence is often by calling upon those suspected to give an account of their behaviour. Sometimes, a liquidator will be given full co-operation. Other times, a liquidator will be starved of co-operation in general and of information in particular[32] and in such circumstances may need to rely on certain statutory powers to extract the required information[33].

[27.018] The least Draconian statutory measure designed to assist the liquidator to obtain information is contained in CA 1963, s 224[34]. Where a compulsory winding up has been ordered or a provisional liquidator has been appointed, the law prescribes that there shall, unless the court says otherwise:

> '...be made out and filed in the court a statement as to the affairs of the company in the prescribed form, verified by affidavit, and showing the particulars of its assets, debts and liabilities, the names, residences and occupations of its creditors, the securities held by them respectively, the dates when the securities were respectively given, and such further or other information as may be prescribed or as the court may require.'[35]

The statement of affairs must be filed within 21 days of the order being made to wind up the company or from the date of the appointment of a provisional liquidator[36]. The statement of affairs may be inspected, and a copy or extract taken, by any person who states in writing that he is a creditor or contributory of the company on payment of the prescribed fee[37]. Where a person untruthfully states that he is a creditor or contributory he is guilty of contempt of court[38]. The costs incurred by any person making or concurring in making the statement and affidavit will be allowed and will be paid out of the assets of the company as the court may allow[39].

[27.019] The persons who must file and verify the statement of affairs are those who at the making of an order to wind up the company, or on the appointment of a provisional liquidator, are the company's directors, secretary, or others who are so ordered by the court to file and verify the statement[40]. These other persons include past officers and promoters and employees within the previous year. Order 74, r 24(2) of the Rules of the Superior

32 Ussher, *Company Law in Ireland*, (1986), p 491 aptly comments that 'Often the item of which the liquidator of an insolvent company is most short, apart from funds, is information'.

33 See also para **[27.005]** where officers' duties to co-operate with liquidators are considered.

34 See also RSC, ord 24, rr 24–28.

35 See *Re Tipperary Self-Drive Ltd* reported in (1992) The Irish Times, 21 January, where Costello J ordered the preparation of a statement of affairs by two directors of companies which had been ordered to be wound up. So too in *Re Eurokabin Ltd* reported in (1991) The Irish Times, 19 September one of the directors, in a company where fraudulent and reckless trading were suspected of having occurred, was ordered by Lynch J to make a statement of the affairs of the company.

36 CA 1963, s 224(3) and (8).

37 CA 1963, s 224(6).

38 CA 1963, s 224(7).

39 CA 1963, s 224(4).

40 CA 1963, s 224(2).

Courts 1986 provides, in addition to CA 1963, s 224, that the court may require that these persons attend before the court at a set time.

[27.020] The directors in a members' voluntary winding up are required to embody in their declaration of solvency a statement of the company's assets and liabilities[41]. In a creditors' voluntary winding up the directors are required to cause a full statement of the position of the company's affairs together with a list of the creditors and the estimated amount of their claims to be laid before the creditors' meeting[42]. It is arguable that where they do not receive co-operation, voluntary liquidators can by virtue of CA 1963, s 280(1), apply to court for an order under CA 1963, s 224(1). Threatening to report non-compliant directors to the Office of the Director of Corporate Enforcement for breach of CA 1963, s 293(1) may also induce co-operation[43].

(b) Power to obtain books and papers

[27.021] Where liquidators experience difficulty in obtaining possession and control of corporate property, books or papers, recourse may be had to the court for an order under CA 1963, s 236, which provides:

> 'The court may, at any time after making a winding-up order, require any contributory for the time being on the list of contributories and any trustee, receiver, banker, agent or officer of the company to pay, deliver, convey, surrender or transfer forthwith, or within such time as the court directs, to the liquidator any money, property or books and papers in his hands to which the company is *prima facie* entitled.'

Both official and voluntary liquidators can apply to court for such an order[44]. It was held in *Re Industrial Services Company (Dublin) Ltd (No 2)*[45] that where a disposition from a company's bank account had been declared void under CA 1963, s 218[46], although s 218 did not permit the making of an order that the moneys disposed of should be repaid, it was open to the court to make an order under CA 1963, s 236 requiring the bank as banker to the company to pay the amount to the company 'being moneys which are prima facie an asset of the company'.

(c) Examination

[27.022] In addition to the power to require officers to attend meetings of the creditors, contributories or committee of inspection[47], application can be made to court to summon an officer and certain other persons and examine him and them on oath (whether by word of mouth or in writing). The power of the court to order an examination is found in CA 1963, s 245(1)[48] which provides that:

---

41 CA 1963, s 256(2)(b).

42 CA 1963, s 266(3)(a).

43 See para **[27.005]**.

44 CA 1963, s 280(1).

45 *Re Industrial Services Company (Dublin) Ltd (No 2)* (15 May 2002, unreported), High Court (McCracken J).

46 See para **[27.058]**.

47 CA 1963, s 246; voluntary liquidators could apply for an order under this section by virtue of CA 1963, s 280(1).

48 As amended by CA 1990, s 126 and CLEA 2001, s 44(a).

> 'The court may, of its own motion or on the application of the Director, at any time after the appointment of a provisional liquidator or the making of a winding-up order, summon before it any officer of the company or person known or suspected to have in his possession any property of the company or supposed to be indebted to the company, or any person whom the court deems capable of giving information relating to the promotion, formation, trade, dealings, affairs or property of the company.'

The actual information extraction mechanism is to be found in s 245(2), which provides:

> 'The court may examine such person on oath concerning the matters aforesaid, either by word of mouth or on written interrogatories, and may reduce his answers to writing an require him to sign them.'

Examination is an investigative tool. The court may require an examinee to produce any 'accounting records, deed, instrument, or other document or paper relating to the company that are in his custody'.[49] Prior to being examined, the court may order that an examinee place before it 'a statement, in such form as the court may direct, of any transactions between him and the company of a type or class which the court may specify'[50].

[27.023] Sometimes, the examination will both bolster existing information and suspicions and also provide new information on wrongdoing or, indeed, simply indicate why a company failed[51]. Failure to attend an examination, without reasonable excuse, is treated as contempt of court[52]. The court also has power to order the civil arrest of a person who without reasonable excuse has failed to attend or a person in respect of whom there are reasonable grounds for believing that he has or is about to abscond[53].

(i) Locus standi in official liquidations

[27.024] An application to court to order an examination of a person under CA 1963, s 245(1) will usually be made by an official liquidator in pursuit of information to assist him in piecing together what went wrong, who caused things to go wrong, and where company's assets might now be. Provisional liquidators also can apply under s 245(1).

[27.025] While usually it will be the official liquidator who will apply for an examination order, it is open to others to make application, although the circumstances in which a court will accede to such a request will be rare. In *Re Embassy Art Products Ltd*[54] an application was made by contributories of a company which, on the direction of its financing bank, caused inter alia, the appointment of a non-executive chairman, the granting of fixed and floating charges over its assets and the retention of a firm of management consultants. When the company failed to adhere to other terms of the facility, receivers were appointed. On the application of another creditor, the company was wound up. The application for the examination of the bank-nominated chairman was refused. Acknowledging the Draconian nature of such an order, Hoffmann J said:

---

49 CA 1963, s 245(3).

50 CA 1963, s 245(4).

51 As in *Irish Commercial Society Ltd v Plunkett* [1987] ILRM 504 at 506, per Henchy J.

52 CA 1963, s 245(7).

53 The court's powers of civil arrest in winding up are considered at para **[27.036]** *ff*.

54 *Re Embassy Art Products Ltd* [1988] BCLC 1.

> 'Any application to use the section, which is *prima facie* an invasion of the rights of privacy of the persons whom it is sought to examine, is subject to the overriding requirement that the examination must be necessary in the interests of the winding up and not oppressive or unfair on the respondent. It is clear, however, that in applying these principles there are significant differences in the court's approach to applications by liquidators, on the one hand, and contributories, on the other.'[55]

Hoffmann J gave four reasons for a different approach by the court to an application for an examination by a person other than a liquidator. First, an official liquidator is an officer of the court and has by virtue of that office locus standi to make application. A contributory or creditor on the other hand must show a probability of some benefit accruing to him, ie he must show a special interest in the outcome of the winding up. Secondly, courts tend to attach more weight to the application of a liquidator because he is an independent professional person. Thirdly, where a contributory is suing his company there is a presumption that he seeks to advance his personal interests unlike an application by a liquidator who is presumed to have no ulterior motive. Fourthly, while a contributory may feel he needs information, the main purpose of the order is 'to assist the liquidator to discover the facts concerning transactions of which he will have had no personal knowledge'[56]. Clearly, although it is possible for a person, other than a liquidator, to obtain an order for examination, other persons will have to discharge a much higher evidential burden.

(ii) Locus standi in voluntary liquidations

[27.026] In the case of either a members' or creditors' voluntary winding up, the voluntary liquidator or any contributory or creditor may apply to court for an order under CA 1963, ss 245(1)[57] or 282B[58]. In *Re Comet Food Machinery Company Ltd*[59] a creditor in a creditors' voluntary winding up successfully applied for an order for the examination of two of the company's directors. The facts in that case were that the company had been engaged in the supply of cooking machinery and the applicant-creditors had purchased machinery from the company which, they claimed, was defective. The applicant-creditors had been awarded IR£255,000 plus costs in uncontested proceedings. Subsequent to this the company was placed into voluntary liquidation and in the absence of a declaration of solvency, proceeded as a creditors' voluntary winding up. The applicant-creditors learned that a new company owned by the same two directors had been formed, which occupied the same premises as the original company, and which appeared to employ the original company's employees. The company was insolvent and the Supreme Court stated that the

---

55 [1988] BCLC 1 at 6–7.

56 [1988] BCLC 1 at 7.

57 CA 1963, s 280(1), which applies to voluntary windings up, provides that 'the liquidator or any contributory or creditor may apply to the court to determine any question arising in the winding up of a company, or to exercise in relation to the enforcing of calls or any other matter, *all or any of the powers which the court might exercise if the company were being wound up by the court*'.

58 It should be noted that this section mirrors the provisions of CA 1963, s 245. In the light of CA 1963, s 280(1), it is thought that it was unnecessary to state a separate power for voluntary liquidators.

59 *Re Comet Food Machinery Company Ltd* [1999] 1 IR 485.

conclusion, that all trade creditors other than the applicant-creditors, had been paid prior to the litigation, seemed inescapable. In the High Court Costello P granted the applicant-creditors' application for an order under CA 1963, s 245(1); the applicant-creditors had contended that the company had been liquidated and the new company formed with a view to carrying on effectively the same business and that the company's assets had been disposed of with a view to frustrating the applicant-creditors' claim for damages. On the appeal to the Supreme Court, Keane J began his interpretation of the law by stating that it was clear that High Court's power under s 245(1) was a discretionary one and also that it was clear that in the case of a voluntary winding up a creditor had, by virtue of CA 1963, s 280(1), the locus standi to make application[60]. Keane J went on to state that the considerations stated by Hoffmann J in *Re Embassy Art Products Ltd*[61] – namely, that creditor-applicants for an examination order need to demonstrate that the examination would probably result in some benefit accruing to them and also that their belief in the necessity of an examination would not carry the same weight as that of a liquidator – were 'undoubtedly applicable where, as here, the application is made in the course of a voluntary winding up'.[62] Noting that the applicant-creditors' reason for wanting an order under s 245(1) was because of their suspicion that the company's assets had been diverted with a view to avoiding the payment of the judgment they had recovered might or might not have been well founded but that if it was, the ground might be laid for an application under CA 1990, s 139[63]. Keane J held:

> 'It cannot be said that, in these circumstances, the application is one which is manifestly brought by the applicants without any hope of recovering any benefit but simply in order to initiate an unnecessarily intrusive inquiry because of pique arising from the fact that their proceedings against [the company] have so far proved fruitless.'[64]

It was concluded that the High Court was entitled to exercise its discretion in favour of the applicant-creditors by making the order sought and that the court should not interfere with the exercise by Costello P of his discretion.

(iii) Locus standi of the Director of Corporate Enforcement

[27.027] It should also be noted that an order for examination under CA 1963, s 282B can be sought by the Director of Corporate Enforcement (for example, to assist in deciding whether or not to make an application under CA 1990, ss 150 or 160 against the director of an insolvent company). Moreover, an order under s 245(1) can be sought where a company is not being wound-up where the conditions set out in CA 1990, s 251 are satisfied ie where a company is unable to pay its debts and the reason that it is not being wound up is the insufficiency of its assets[65]. In *Alba Radio Ltd v Haltone (Cork) Ltd*[66] it was held by Barron J that to order the examination of a director of a company that was not

[60] See note 57.

[61] *Re Embassy Art Products Ltd* [1988] BCLC 1.

[62] [1988] BCLC 1 at 7.

[63] See para **[27.092]**.

[64] [1988] BCLC 1 at 8.

[65] See Chapter 10, *Duties of Directors and Other Officers*, para **[10.121]** *ff*.

[66] *Alba Radio Ltd v Haltone (Cork) Ltd* [1995] 2 IR 170, [1995] 2 ILRM 466.

being wound up in respect of circumstances that took place prior to the commencement of CA 1990 was not the application of a retrospective penalty. Although the circumstances in which such an order might be made were changed by CA 1990, no new liability would be imposed by the making of the order[67].

(iv) The courts' attitude to making examination orders

[27.028] When application is made for an examination, the court will scrutinise the circumstances before exercising its discretion. Although Irish judicial pronouncement on the topic is scarce, it has been held in the UK that the order must not be oppressive. Accordingly, in *Re Adlards Motor Group Holding Ltd*[68] Harman J refused to make an order for an examination against a receiver because this would be oppressive in view of the amount of time which had elapsed since the receiver had been appointed.

[27.029] Common reasons for the ordering of an examination are that the person is suspected of having corporate property in his possession, is indebted to the company, or may generally be able to throw light on the affairs of the company. In *Re Mark Synnott (Life and Pension Brokers) Ltd*[69] an insurance company originally in voluntary liquidation was later placed into official liquidation. The provisional liquidator who was appointed to the company is reported as having told the court that, since he was appointed provisional liquidator by the court three weeks' previously, he had not identified any mitigating factor which would not warrant a conclusion that the affairs of the company had been conducted in a fraudulent and reckless manner, to the extreme detriment of the company's clients[70]. Later, an application for the examination of certain directors was granted and these examinations were reported in the press[71]. Again, in *Re Aluminium Fabricators Ltd*[72], arising from an examination under CA 1963, s 245, it was learnt that two sets of accounts were kept by the directors of the company concerned.

(v) The holding of and procedure in examinations

[27.030] An examination is usually heard before the Master of the High Court and is held in public. While it was stated by the former Supreme Court in *Re Redbreast Preserving Co (Ireland) Ltd*[73] that examination could be held in private because it was not an 'administration of justice' and so was outside Article 34.1 of Bunreacht na hÉireann, this may now be said to be overruled in the light of the comments of Walsh J in *Re R Ltd*[74]. Walsh J said:

> 'If the dictum of the former Supreme Court in *Re Redbreast Preserving Co Ltd* means that the constitutional requirement that justice is to be administered in public is satisfied by the

---

[67] It must be questioned whether, if an order was disobeyed thereby giving rise to a contempt of court, would it still be considered that no new liability was being imposed.

[68] *Re Adlards Motor Group Holding Ltd* [1990] BCLC 68.

[69] An application reported in (1991) The Irish Times, 15, 18, 19, 27, 29 June, 2, 3, 4, 6, 9, July and 6, 7, 8, 9 November.

[70] See (1991) The Irish Times of 2 July.

[71] See (1991) The Irish Times of 6, 7, 8 and 9 November.

[72] *Re Aluminium Fabricators Ltd* [1984] ILRM 399.

[73] *Re Redbreast Preserving Co Ltd* 91 ILTR 12.

[74] *Re R Ltd* [1988] ILRM 126.

> public pronouncement of a decision based on evidence taken other than in public, then where that is not expressly authorised by a post-constitutional statute it is clearly incorrect and ought not to be followed.'[75]

As Keane has commented[76], since CA 1963, s 245 contains no such express authorisation it would 'clearly be unsafe to hold the examination in private'. However, Keane seems to recognise that where it is anticipated that evidence obtained will not be required in court proceedings and will be solely for the benefit of the liquidator, examination in private may be allowed. Clearly, great care must be exercised by the courts in acceding to a request for a private examination because in all but the most clear-cut of cases, *other* evidence may well arise at the examination.

[27.031] During the examination the person being examined may be examined on oath, either orally or in writing, and he may be required to sign his written answers to the questions put to him[77]. The court may also require that he produce any accounting records, deed, instrument or other document or paper relating to the company that are in his custody or under his control or power[78]. Before an examination takes place the court may order the person to be examined to place before the court a statement, as directed by the court, of any transactions between him and the company of a type or class specified by the court[79]. Such a statement may provide the liquidator with evidence of voidable transactions which will enable him to swell the company's assets available for distribution[80]. Where it is the opinion of the court that it is just and equitable to do so, the court may order the person being examined to pay the costs of the examination[81].

(vi) Failure to co-operate

[27.032] The co-operation of the person being examined is required[82], and failure to answer questions can render the person liable for contempt of court[83].

(vii) Admissibility of evidence obtained in an examination

[27.033] Section 245(6) of CA 1963[84] prohibits the person being examined from refusing to answer any questions put to him on the ground that his answer might incriminate him, and any answer by him to such a question may be used in evidence against him in any proceedings whatsoever (save proceedings for an offence (other than perjury) in respect of

---

75 On *in camera* applications under CA 1963, s 205(7), see Chapter 19, *Shareholders' Remedies*, para **[19.055]**.

76 Keane, *Company Law* (3rd edn, 2000), para 36.173.

77 CA 1963, s 245(2).

78 CA 1963, s 245(3).

79 CA 1963, s 245(4).

80 This may occur where evidence is obtained of the contravention of CA 1963, s 60: see Chapter 18, *The Maintenance of Capital*, para **[18.041]** *ff* or; or in contravention of CA 1990, ss 29 or 31: see Chapter 11, *Statutory Regulation of Transactions Involving Directors and their Companies*.

81 CA 1963, s 245(5). Presumably, just as although a misfeasance suit may be successfully defended, if the examinee's conduct prompted the instigation of the application he may be directed to bear the costs of the examination: *Re David Ireland & Co Ltd* [1905] IR 133.

82 See the warning given by the Master of the High Court to a company director in *Re Europa Forklift Ltd* an application reported in (1991) The Irish Times, 22 November.

83 CA 1963, s 245(7).

84 As substituted by CLEA 2001, s 44(b).

such an answer) [85]. It was held in *Re Aluminium Fabricators Ltd*[86] that evidence obtained from an examination was not admissible in other proceedings arising from the same winding up, such as under CA 1963, s 297[87]. Admissions of liability are somewhat rare, but are occasionally seen[88]. The position with regard to the use of such evidence against third parties is different though. Accordingly, in the case of *Irish Commercial Society Ltd v Plunkett*[89] Costello J held that evidence given by a person being examined does not preclude its use in proceedings against a third party, thus construing the subsection literally[90].

(d) Post-examination transfer and search and seizure orders

[27.034] If it appears to the court from an examination under CA 1963, s 245 that any person being examined is indebted to the company, or, has in his possession or control any money, property, books or papers of the company, then by CA 1963, s 245A(1)[91] the court may, of its own motion or on the application of the Director of Corporate Enforcement, order such person:

> '(a) to pay to the liquidator the amount or any part of the debt, or
>
> (b) to pay, deliver, convey, surrender or transfer to the liquidator such money, property or books and papers or any part thereof,
>
> at such time and in such manner and on such terms as it may direct.'

This order can be utilised to enable a liquidator to realise the assets of a company, since, on proof of misappropriation, the court is empowered to direct an immediate transfer of assets to the liquidator. Whilst s 245A(1)–(6) applies to official liquidations, CA 1963, s 282C(1)–(6) (inserted by CLEA 2001, s 49) applies to voluntary liquidations and gives the Director of Corporate Enforcement locus standi to make application for such an order. The two sections are in all material respects identical[92]. Official liquidators will continue to apply directly under s 245A for an order under that section. It is thought that voluntary liquidators should apply for a s 245A order in reliance upon s 280(1) and that only the Director should apply for an order under s 282C.

[27.035] Section 45(c) of CLEA 2001 extended CA 1963, s 245A by the addition of five new subsections. Although thought to be intended primarily for the benefit of the Director of Corporate Enforcement, the new subsections are also of benefit to liquidators. So, the court is empowered to make an order in the nature of an Anton Piller – search and seizure – order[93]. Section 245A(2) provides:

---

85 For an English perspective, see *Re Mirror Group Newspapers* reported in (1992) The Irish Times, 30 January. See also, *Re Jeffrey S Levitt Ltd* [1992] All ER 509.

86 *Re Aluminium Fabricators Ltd* [1984] ILRM 399.

87 See Chapter 10, *Duties of Directors and Other Officers*, para **[10.104]** *ff*.

88 See the newspaper report of an examination in *Re Mark Synnott (Life and Pensions) Brokers Ltd* (1991) The Irish Times, 8 November.

89 *Irish Commercial Society Ltd v Plunkett* [1986] ILRM 624.

90 See also *Re Jeffrey S Levitt Ltd* [1992] 2 All ER 509.

91 As inserted by CA 1990, s 127, and as amended by CLEA 2001, s 45.

92 Again, in the light of CA 1963, s 280(1), the necessity for separate powers for voluntary liquidators is not obvious.

93 On Anton Piller orders, see generally, Courtney, *Mareva Injunctions and Related Interlocutory Orders* (1998), para [10.38] *ff*.

'Where the court has made an order under subsection (1), it may, on the application of the Director or the liquidator, make a further order permitting the applicant, accompanied by such persons as the applicant thinks appropriate, to enter at any time or times within one month from the date of issue of the order, any premises (including a dwelling) owned or occupied by the person the subject of the order under subsection (1) (using such force as is reasonably necessary for the purpose), to search the premises and to seize any money, property or books and papers of the company found on the premises.'

It is important to note that only money, property, books or papers *of the company* may be seized. The obstruction of a right of entry, search and seizure is an offence[94] but proceedings on foot of this offence will not prejudice the power of the court to issue proceedings for contempt of court for failure to comply with an order under s 245A[95]. This order has the potential to be Draconian and it is thought that the courts will exercise their jurisdiction very sparingly, especially when the property which it is sought to search is a person's dwelling house. Some safeguards are evident. So, s 245A(3) requires a successful applicant of a search and seizure order to report back to the court 'as soon as may be on the outcome of any action on foot of the court's order and the court shall direct the applicant as to the disposition of anything seized on foot of the order'[96].

(e) Powers of civil arrest

[27.036] Civil arrest[97] is an extraordinary and potentially Draconian remedy which is available to a liquidator. The effect of civil arrest is that a person is deprived of his liberty or prevented from leaving the State where such is necessary to assist the civil process. An application for the civil arrest of a person in winding-up proceedings can be made in three circumstances:

(i) By statute to facilitate an examination.

(ii) In equity to facilitate an examination.

(iii) By statute to arrest an absconding officer or contributory.

(i) By statute to facilitate an examination

[27.037] Under CA 1963, s 245(8), where a person without reasonable excuse:

— fails at any time to attend his examination under CA 1963, s 245, or

— there are reasonable grounds for believing that a person has absconded, or is about to abscond,

— with a view to avoiding or delaying his examination under CA 1963, s 245,

then the court may cause that person to be arrested and his books and property seized and both to be detained until such time as the court may order. This subsection was inserted by CA 1990, s 126. Notwithstanding the provisions of CA 1963, s 280(1) which allows the court in a voluntary liquidation to make any order it has power to make in an official

94 CA 1963, s 245A(5).

95 CA 1963, s 245A(6).

96 CA 1963, s 245A(4) provides, somewhat cryptically, 'A direction under subsection (3) shall not be made in favour of the Director except in respect of the Director's costs and reasonable expenses'. By this it is thought that the court is precluded from ordering that any property seized be retained by the Director but that the court may order that the Director's costs are paid.

97 See generally, Courtney, *Mareva Injunctions and Related Interlocutory Orders* (1998), Ch 11, *Restraining Defendants from Leaving the State*.

liquidation, s 282B(8) confers a separate statutory power to order the arrest of a person examined under s 282B(1) ie in a voluntary liquidation[98]. It is thought that a voluntary liquidator seeking an arrest order should proceed on foot of s 280(1) for an order under s 245(8) but that an application by the Director of Corporate Enforcement should proceed under s 282B(8).

[27.038] Previously, it was the case that no order for arrest could be made until after an order for examination had been made, and the person who had been summoned to attend failed to do so. It is now the case that an order for the arrest of a person in connection with a CA 1963, s 245 examination is *not* dependant upon an actual order for examination having being made. Rather, where there is evidence that a person is about to abscond, with a view to avoiding or delaying an examination then, even though no order for examination exists, an order for arrest can be made. The old position led to the anomaly seen in the English case of *Re Oriental Credit Ltd*[99] and the Irish case of *Re J Ellis Pharmaceuticals Ltd*[100] where the court had no statutory power to order the arrest of a person in respect of an examination unless the person had been summoned to attend an examination and refused without excuse to come before the court. In *Re Oriental Credit Ltd* an order for the defendant's examination had been made and there was a likelihood that the defendant would abscond. However, the court could not invoke its statutory power of arrest until after the time for the performance of the examination had passed. In *Re J Ellis Pharmaceuticals Ltd* no order for examination had been made but the liquidator apprehended that the defendant might abscond before he had been examined. In both cases, the Irish and English courts in the absence of a statutory power of arrest, invoked their inherent equitable jurisdiction to grant an injunction to prevent the persons concerned from leaving the jurisdiction. While equitable intervention is no longer necessary in cases of absconding examinees, it remains a useful jurisdiction.

(ii) In equity to facilitate an examination

[27.039] There is an equitable jurisdiction to enjoin a person from leaving the State[101]. This may be either on foot of an ordinary injunction, or by the writ of *ne exeat regno*[102]. The injunction is an ever-adaptable and flexible remedy. The courts' power in the Supreme

---

98 CLEA 2001, s 49.

99 *Re Oriental Credit Ltd* [1988] 1 All ER 892.

100 Reported in (1988) The Irish Times, 13 August.

101 *O'Neill and Chiswick Ltd v O'Keeffe et al* (19 February 2002, unreported), High Court (Kearns J). See para **[27.040]**.

102 The writ of *ne exeat regno* is an order whereby a person is directed not to leave the State. The best statement of the law relating to this writ is seen in *Felton v Callis* [1968] 3 All ER 673. The writ gives such relief in respect of 'equitable plaintiffs', whereas the Debtors (Ireland) Act 1872, s 7 provides relief to 'legal plaintiffs'. The conditions before the writ will issue are fourfold: first, there is an equitable or legal action which prior to the passing of the 1872 Act would have entitled the plaintiff to seek the arrest of the defendant; secondly, that the plaintiff has a good cause of action over £20 or has sustained damage to that amount; thirdly, that there is probable cause for believing that the defendant is about to quit Ireland; fourthly, the defendant's absence would materially prejudice the plaintiff in the prosecution of his action. See generally, Courtney, *Mareva Injunctions and Related Interlocutory Orders* (1998), paras [11.02]–[11.21].

Court of Judicature (Ireland) Act 1877, s 28(8) to grant an injunction is regulated by Ord 50, r 6 of the Rules of the Superior Courts 1986 which provides that the High Court 'may grant...an injunction...by an interlocutory order in all cases in which it appears to the court to be just or convenient so to do'. The novelty with this injunction concerns what the court is being asked to do, namely to prevent a person from leaving the State. It should be noted that the Rules of the Superior Courts do envisage such injunctions issuing; Ord 40, r 21 provides: 'where an injunction or order not to leave the jurisdiction has been granted' the person so enjoined is entitled to copies of the affidavit upon which the injunction was granted. English authorities have struggled to assert jurisdiction to prevent a person from leaving the country. In *Bayer AG v Winter*[103] such an injunction was sought to restrain a defendant in a counterfeit-pharmaceutical suit from leaving England. The Court of Appeal overturned the earlier High Court decision and granted the injunction sought, Fox LJ referring to the power to grant such injunctions said:

> 'Bearing in mind we are exercising a jurisdiction which is statutory, and which is expressed in terms of considerable width, it seems to me that the court should not shrink, if it is of the opinion than an injunction is necessary for the proper protection of a party to an action, from granting relief, notwithstanding it may, in its terms, be of novel character.'[104]

The Court of Appeal granted the injunction after applying the 'balance of convenience' test and finding that it favoured the making of the injunction. The court also ordered the defendant to deliver up his passport. Other English cases have also recognised this jurisdiction[105] and several such orders have been granted also by the Irish courts on the application of liquidators, in apprehension that persons necessary to the orderly winding up of a company will absent themselves from the State[106].

[27.040] In *O'Neill and Chiswick Ltd v O'Keeffe and another*[107] Kearns J adopted the following criteria for granting a Bayer injunction, as suggested by Courtney[108]:

---

[103] *Bayer AG v Winter* [1986] 1 All ER 733.

[104] [1986] 1 All ER 733 at 737F–G after citing *Smith v Peters* (1875) LR 20 Eq 511.

[105] See *Allied Arab Bank Ltd v Hajjar* [1987] 3 All ER 39.

[106] In *Re J Ellis Pharmaceuticals Ltd*, reported in (1988) The Irish Times, 13 August, a liquidator was reported in *The Irish Times* as stating on affidavit that his investigations of the defendant's pharmacy business made him desire to examine the respondent on oath in respect of several aspects of the company's property and that he believed that the director was about to leave the State. There, Blayney J granted the injunction sought, subject to the usual undertakings. In *Re Mark Synnott (Life and Pensions) Brokers Ltd*, reported in (1991) The Irish Times, 3 July, a liquidator was given leave by Carroll J to make an application to require one of the directors of the company to surrender his passport, thus preventing him from leaving the State and going to Spain as the liquidator feared that the director would not return. In the end no order was made because the director agreed not to leave the country (see (1991) The Irish Times, 4 July) Again, in *Re Tipperary Self-Drive Ltd et al*, reported in (1992) The Irish Times, 4 February, a liquidator sought an injunction to prevent two directors from leaving the State. He claimed that his preliminary investigations suggested that the companies were involved in obtaining finance in respect of non-existent vehicles. It was reported that Murphy J granted the orders sought.

[107] *O'Neill and Chiswick Ltd v O'Keeffe* (19 February 2002, unreported), High Court (Kearns J).

[108] Courtney, *Mareva Injunctions and Related Interlocutory Orders* (1998), pp 457–458.

> '(1) The court is satisfied that there is a probable cause for believing that the defendant is about to absent himself from the jurisdiction with the intention of frustrating the administration of justice and/ or an order of the court.
>
> (2) The jurisdiction should not be exercised for punitive reasons; a defendant's presence should be required to prevent a court hearing or process or existing order from being rendered nugatory.
>
> (3) The injunction ought not to be granted where a lesser remedy would suffice.
>
> (4) The injunction should be interim in nature and limited to the shortest possible period of time.
>
> (5) The defendant's right to travel should be out-balanced by those of the plaintiff and the proper and effective administration of justice.
>
> (6) The grant of the injunction should not be futile.'

The facts in that case were that the plaintiffs (a US national and his investment vehicle) alleged that the first defendant had offered himself to the plaintiffs as a personal investment manager with particular expertise in trading foreign debt instruments through Swiss banks. Allegedly relying on his representations, the plaintiffs paid US$5 million into a Swiss bank account. This was to serve as a guarantee against any investment losses; the idea was that the first defendant and a company with which he was involved, Manro Group International, would suggest investment ideas. The monies were lodged in a joint account with the plaintiff as 'participant' and the first defendant as 'asset manager'. The plan was initially to last just one year but the first defendant advised the plaintiffs that he had unilaterally extended the period. On seeking a statement from the bank, the plaintiffs were instead given a fax from the first and second defendants stating that the value of the investment was then US£9.8 million. When, subsequently, the plaintiffs demanded the return of the monies they were met with a variety of excuses following which the plaintiffs initiated inquiries to be made in Dublin. Those inquiries revealed that the Dublin address was a private residence and that there was no evidence of 'Manro Group International' being there; a title search did not disclose the first-defendant to be the owner of a farm in Cork as he had claimed. All requests for information and co-operation were unsuccessful and Kearns J noted that in the circumstances the plaintiff 'is apprehensive that his investment monies either have been or may be in the process of being dissipated or perhaps misappropriated altogether'. A Mareva injunction, proprietary injunction, Anton Piller order and an asset disclosure order were obtained by the plaintiffs and were faxed to the first defendant's Swiss and Dublin addresses. Entry to the first defendant's address in Ballsbridge could not be effected. A voice message from a man identifying himself as the first defendant was left on the plaintiffs' solicitor's telephone which, inter alia, claimed that the Ballsbridge address belonged to his daughter and not to him or Manro Group International. In these circumstances the plaintiffs applied for a Bayer injunction.

Kearns J quoted from *Bayer AG v Winter* with approval and also *House of Spring Gardens Ltd v Waite*[109] and concluded that 'it is clear from the foregoing that the jurisdiction to make such an order derives from the requirement to make court orders effective and is analogous to disclosure orders in aid of Mareva relief.' Kearns J also noted the Supreme

[109] *House of Spring Gardens Ltd v Waite* [1985] 11 FSR 173.

Court of Judicature (Ireland) Act 1877, s 28(8) and went on to say that such relief would only be granted in exceptional and compelling circumstances because such an order 'is prima facie in breach of the constitutional right to travel, placing that right in abeyance for the specified period.' Acknowledging that in *Lennon v Ganley & Fitzgerald*[110] O'Hanlon J had recognised that the defendants there 'should only be restrained from exercising such right [to travel] if it was in some way unlawful for them to act in the manner in which they seek to act' Kearns J went on to point out that the Bankruptcy Act 1988, s 124 criminalised the leaving of the State with the intention to defraud one's creditors[111]. After adopting the criteria set out in Courtney, Kearns J went on to conclude that it was appropriate that a Bayer injunction be made against the first defendant. Kearns J held:

> 'I am satisfied that the instant case requires the making of the orders sought, both in relation to the restriction on the defendant leaving the country and in requiring him to hand over his passport. A very substantial sum of money is unaccounted for in circumstances which give rise to considerable suspicion. The fact that two different solicitors consulted by Mr O'Keeffe within several days were denied instructions to enter an Appearance does nothing to allay one's concerns. The Court has a very real apprehension that the first-named defendant may be about to absent himself from the jurisdiction with the intention of frustrating the orders of the Court. Indeed, one concern is that he may already have done so, which brings into play the "futility" consideration last mentioned by Mr Courtney. However, this will often be a possibility in this sort of case and there is no positive evidence to this effect. Any order made cannot only be described as futile. It may prove quite effective. There is no punitive aspect to the order which I will qualify further by ordering that he shall not leave the jurisdiction before 4 March 2002 without leave of the court. From everything I have said I hope I have made it clear I have decided (at this point only) that the defendant's right to travel is out-balanced both by those of the plaintiff and the requirement to secure the proper and effective administration of justice.'

A Bayer injunction is an exceptional remedy and will be granted only in exceptional and compelling circumstances.

(iii) By statute to arrest an absconding officer or contributory

[27.041] The originally enacted CA 1963, s 247[112] provided that the court could make an order for the civil arrest of contributories. The purpose of this provision seemed intended to prevent contributories (ie past or present members) from absconding to avoid calls on them in respect of outstanding liabilities on shares or guarantees or examination about the affairs of the company. The greatest handicap to the use of the originally enacted s 247 was that it could be invoked only in respect of *contributories*. The arrest of directors was entirely dependent upon their also happening to be contributories. Reform was effected on

[110] *Lennon v Ganley & Fitzgerald* [1981] ILRM 84.

[111] See Courtney, *Mareva Injunctions and Related Interlocutory Orders* (1998), para [11.28].

[112] This provided: 'The court, at any time either before or after making a winding-up order, on proof of probable cause for believing that a contributory is about to quit the State or otherwise to abscond or to remove or conceal any of his property for the purpose of evading payment of calls or of avoiding examination about the affairs of the company, may cause the contributory to be arrested, and his books and papers to be seized and him and them to be detained until such time as the court may order.' See generally, Courtney, *Mareva Injunctions and Related Interlocutory Orders* (1998), paras [11.42] – [11.47].

foot of the recommendations contained in the McDowell Report and CLEA 2001, s 46 repealed and substituted a new section for the old s 247. The new s 247 provides:

> 'The court, at any time either before or after making a winding-up order, on proof of probable cause for believing that a contributory, director, shadow director or secretary or other officer is about to quit the State or otherwise to abscond or to remove or conceal any of his property for the purpose of evading payment of calls or of avoiding examination about the affairs of the company, may, of its own motion or on the application of the Director, a creditor of the company or any other interested person, cause the contributory, director, shadow director, secretary or other officer to be arrested, and his books and papers and movable personal property to be seized and him and them to be detailed until such time as the court may order.'

Moreover, although it is thought that it was always the case that an arrest order could be made in a voluntary liquidation[113], CA 1963, s 282D[114], which is couched in materially identical terms, is expressly available in a voluntary winding up. Those who have locus standi to apply for an arrest order are: official and voluntary liquidators, the Director of Corporate Enforcement, a creditor of the company or any other interested person. Those who can be arrested are contributories, directors, shadow directors, secretaries and other officers. The application should be made by motion and may be ex parte[115].

[27.042] The proofs required to obtain an order for arrest under CA 1963, s 247 were, and continue to be onerous. Accordingly, *probable cause* for belief that a person is about to leave the State is required, the high evidential standard being required in view of the Draconian effects of civil arrest[116]. In *Re Imperial Mercantile Credit Company*[117] the official liquidators of the company sought an order for the arrest of a contributory under the Companies Act 1862, s 118 which was similar in most material respects to the originally enacted CA 1963, s 247. It was heard that a letter had been received by one of the liquidators from a solicitor, which stated that the contributory had advertised his property for sale and that it was 'well known in the neighbourhood that he was about to proceed to Lisbon'. This hearsay evidence did not impress Sir W Page Wood VC who said:

> 'I am not disposed to take the very strong step of arresting this gentleman without some more definite information upon oath as to his being about to abscond; but I think there is enough to induce me to stop the sale of his property until further notice'.[118]

The official liquidators' subsequent application (grounded upon the actual affidavit of the solicitor referred to in the previous affidavit) to have the contributory arrested was also unsuccessful, although an order was made to seize his books, papers, moneys, securities for moneys, goods and chattels; in so ordering Sir W Page Wood VC thought it had been

---

[113] By reason of CA 1963, s 280(1).

[114] Inserted by CLEA 2001, s 49.

[115] RSC, Ord 74, r 135(2).

[116] See *Felton v Callis* [1968] 3 All ER 673; *Re Underwood* (1903) 51 WR 335; *Re Imperial Mercantile Credit Company* (1867) LR 5 Eq 264; and *Sichel v Raphael* (1861) 4 LT 114, all in the context of the writ of *ne exeat regno*.

[117] *Re Imperial Mercantile Credit Company* (1867) LR 5 Eq 264.

[118] (1867) LR 5 Eq 264 at 265.

sufficiently proved that the contributory was about to remove his goods from the jurisdiction and held that whilst the section contemplates arrest at the same time as seizure of goods, one can be ordered without ordering the other[119].

[27.043] Not only is probable cause for absconding required, it must be shown also that there is, so to speak, a mens rea, namely that the person does so for the purpose of evading payment of calls or examination. Cases where such probable cause was shown include *Re The Ulster Land, Building and Investment Company Ltd*[120] where, after a winding-up order had been made, a liquidator sought the arrest of two contributories and the seizure of their property. One had sent his furniture to auction, given up his house, was generally disposing of his interests in property and was negotiating his passage to America. The other acted in a similar fashion and had actually taken his passage to San Francisco. An ex parte order for arrest was made, although on inter partes hearing this was discharged on security being given by recognizance that the remaining contributory would not leave Ireland without the consent of the court.

[27.044] A more recent Irish example is *Re Central Trust Investment Society*[121] where Murphy J ordered the arrest of a director (who was, presumably, also a contributory) where the liquidator sought to have him examined about the affairs of the company. In *Re O'Sheas (Dublin) Ltd*[122] an order for arrest was granted where there was evidence that the person concerned had sold his Irish home, had accommodation in Spain and had recently been abroad. The liquidator had made many unsuccessful attempts to contact the person concerned. The order for arrest was directed by Keane J to the Garda Commissioner and it directed him to bring the director before the court at the earliest opportunity. In both of the last two cases the court ordered the defendants to hand their passports over to the court[123].

Freezing corporate assets in a liquidation

[27.045] Where a liquidator suspects that a director or other person is likely to remove corporate assets from the jurisdiction or to dissipate those assets within the jurisdiction, he can apply for a Mareva injunction[124]. A Mareva injunction may be defined as a (pre-judgment or post-judgment) court order which restrains a defendant from removing from the State, or otherwise disposing of his own assets, whether generally, or up to a specified amount, until further order of the court or until the trial of the matter. Before a Mareva will be granted, the following matters must be shown to exist to the satisfaction of the court:

---

[119] The requirement that there be 'probable cause' was also considered in the context of the Debtors Act (Ireland) 1872, s 7; the similarities between civil arrest under the Companies Act 1862, s 118 and the writ of *ne exeat* resulted in the remedies being referred to interchangeably in *Re Cotton Plantation Company of Natal* [1868] WN 79.

[120] *Re The Ulster Land, Building and Investment Company Ltd* (1887) 17 LR Ir 591.

[121] *Re Central Trust Investment Society* (1982) The Irish Times, 31 August.

[122] *Re O'Sheas (Dublin) Ltd* (1984) The Irish Times, 6 July and (1987) 5 May.

[123] For court orders on passports, see also *Re Mark Synnott (Life and Pension) Brokers Ltd* and *Re Bishopsgate Investment Management* (1991) The Irish Times, 10 December, where Kevin and Ian Maxwell were ordered by the English High Court to surrender their passports.

[124] After *Mareva Compania Naviera SA v International Bulk Carriers* [1980] 1 All ER 213. See generally, Courtney, *Mareva Injunctions and Related Interlocutory Orders* (1998); Capper, *Mareva Injunctions* (1988); and Ough and Flenley, *The Mareva Injunction and Anton Piller Order* (2nd edn, 1993).

— a substantive cause of action[125];

— a good arguable case [126];

— 'an intention on the part of the defendant to dispose of his assets with a view to evading his obligation to the plaintiff and to frustrate the anticipated order of the court'[127];

— the defendant's beneficial ownership of assets, situate whether inside[128] or outside[129] the jurisdiction; and

— a favourable balance of convenience[130].

Like all injunctions, a Mareva injunction cannot be demanded as of right, and its grant or refusal is dependent upon the discretion of the court[131]. There are many instances[132] where liquidators have availed of Mareva injunctions to preserve corporate assets in their efforts to make them amenable to realisation and distribution.

[27.046] There is also a statutory jurisdiction to restrain certain persons from disposing of their assets[133]. Section 55 of CLEA 2001 provides:

> 'The court may, on the application of a company, director, member, liquidator, receiver, creditor or the Director, order a director or other officer of a company not to remove his or her assets from the State or to reduce his or her assets within or outside the State below an amount to be specified by the court, where the court is satisfied that —

125 See *Caudron v Air Zaire* [1986] ILRM 10 and *The Siskina* [1977] 3 All ER 803.

126 *Fleming v Ranks* [1983] ILRM 541; *The Tatiangela* [1980] 2 Lloyd's Reports 193; *Derby v Weldon* [1989] WLR 276 and *The Niedersachsen* [1984] 1 All ER 398.

127 Per Hamilton CJ in the seminal Supreme Court decision in *Re John Horgan Livestock Ltd; O'Mahony v Horgan* [1995] 2 IR 411 at 419. See also *Fleming v Ranks* [1983] ILRM 541, *Larkin v NUM* [1985] IR 671; and *Powerscourt Estates v Gallagher* [1984] ILRM 123; *Moloney v Laurib Investments Ltd* (20 July 1993, unreported), High Court, per Lynch J.

128 *Ashtiani v Kashi* [1986] 2 All ER 970 considered by Gill, (1986) ILT 18 and *Phelan v Master Meats Ltd* an application reported in (1989)The Irish Times, 1 August, where Blayney J is reported as saying that the presence of assets within the jurisdiction was an issue in such an application.

129 *Deutsche Bank Aktiengesellschaft v Murtagh & Murtagh* [1995] 2 IR 122. *Babanaft International Co SA v Bassatne* [1989] WLR 232; *Republic of Haiti v Duvallier* [1989] WLR 261 and *Derby v Weldon* [1989] WLR 276 which suggest that a *Mareva* can issue in respect of assets abroad by virtue of the court's powers in respect of those within its jurisdiction and the fact that an injunction acts in personam: *Lett v Lett* [1906] IR 618, per Porter MR.

130 Such a consideration applies to all injunctions: *American Cyanamid Co v Ethicon Ltd* [1975] 1 All ER 504, accepted in principle in Ireland in *Campus Oil Ltd v Minister for Industry and Energy (No 2)* [1983] IR 88.

131 *Countyglen plc v Carway* [1995] 1 IR 208; *Fleming v Ranks* [1983] ILRM 541 at 546.

132 See, eg, *Re Mark Synnott (Life and Pensions) Brokers Ltd* an application reported in (1991) The Irish Times, 15 June; *Re Tipperary Self-Drive Ltd* an application reported in (1992) The Irish Times, 4 February and *Re Holbern Investments Ltd* an application reported in (1991) The Irish Times, 9 October (obtained by creditors).

133 See O'Reilly, 'Freezing Orders Under Section 55 of the Company Law Enforcement Act 2001' (2002) 9 CLP 109.

(a) the applicant has a substantive civil cause of action or right to seek a declaration of personal liability or claim for damages against the director, other officer or the company, and

(b) there are grounds for believing that the respondent may remove or dispose of his, her or the company's assets with a view to evading his, her or the company's obligations and frustrating an order of the court.'

This is an unusual jurisdiction, borne out of the desire to provide the Director of Corporate Enforcement and all other persons battling against delinquent company law players with the means necessary to ensure justice is done. A wide variety of persons can apply for a section 55 freezing order: a company, directors, members, liquidators, receivers, creditors and the Director of Corporate Enforcement. Those who can have their assets frozen are a company's directors or other officers. This statutory jurisdiction is very closely aligned to the existing common law Mareva jurisdiction, particularly as it has developed in Ireland. Accordingly, an applicant under CLEA 2001, s 55 must have an *independent* substantive civil cause of action (eg a claim for breach of duty, etc) or the right to seek a declaration of personal liability or claim for damages (eg for fraudulent or reckless trading or failure to keep proper books of account, etc). Just as a Mareva injunction will not be granted where the applicant does not have a legal or equitable right, neither will an order under s 55. Although s 55(a) is silent as against *whom* the applicant must have this substantive civil cause of action, it is submitted that such must subsist against the person against whom the order is sought. For example, if a creditor sought an order to freeze a director's assets, it would not be sufficient to show that he has a cause of action against the director's company: he must show he has a cause of action against the director. Any other construction would be Draconian and most likely, unconstitutional. The second similarity, which is also a curb on excesses, is s 55(b) which requires the proof of grounds for believing that the respondent may remove or dispose of his assets 'with a view to evading his, her or the company's obligations and frustrating an order of the court'. Just as applies in the case of Mareva injunctions, it is not sufficient to establish that the assets are likely to be dissipated in the ordinary course of business or in the payment of lawful debts. It is thought that, so powerful is this relief, in exercising its undoubted discretion (ie 'the court *may*') the courts will give short shrift to unworthy applicants and be mindful that, just as the Mareva jurisdiction, s 55, 'if improperly invoked will bring about an injustice, something that it was designed to prevent'[134].

[27.047] Mareva injunctions and CLEA 2001, section 55 asset freezing orders must, however, be distinguished from injunctions in defence of a proprietary interest[135]. Where a

---

[134] *Re John Horgan Livestock Ltd; O'Mahony v Horgan* [1995] 2 IR 411 at 422 per O'Flaherty J. See also the caution sounded by McCracken J in *Production Association Minsk Tractor Works and Belarus Equipment (Ireland) Ltd v Saenko* (25 February 1998, unreported), High Court (McCracken J).

[135] See, Courtney, *Mareva Injunctions and Related Interlocutory Orders* (1998), para [1.16]–[1.29]. The distinction between proprietary injunctions and Mareva injunctions was accepted in *OBA Enterprises Ltd (& Others) v TMC Trading International Ltd* (27 November 1998, unreported), High Court (Laffoy J), noted in Courtney, 'The Continuing Development of the Mareva Injunction in Ireland' (1999) 6 CLP 39.

liquidator believes that assets properly belonging to the company are in the hands of a third party and he has commenced proceedings for their return (eg tracing) [136], where he seeks to preserve those assets and prevent the third party from disposing of them his proper remedy is to apply for an 'ordinary' interlocutory injunction[137]. Proprietary injunctions are distinguishable from Mareva injunctions or section 55 asset freezing orders because in both of these cases the respondent will have his *personal assets* frozen in anticipation that the applicant will be found to have an enforceable claim against the respondent; at the time of the order, however, the applicant does not need to have a proprietary (or in rem) claim in order to obtain a Mareva injunction or a section 55 order. Applicants for injunctions in defence of proprietary claims will be more readily afforded a remedy than Mareva applicants[138]. In such circumstances, the basis of the test to be applied for the grant of the injunction is that established in *Campus Oil Ltd v Minister for Industry and Energy* [139]. This is, is there a fair or serious question to be tried, does the balance of convenience favour the injunction and has the applicant established reasonable grounds for claiming a proprietary interest in the property that is the subject matter of substantive proceedings?

No litigation, execution, attachment or new judgment mortgages

[27.048] In addition to gathering assets, liquidators must also preserve the existing assets of the company and, if necessary, take steps to prevent creditors jumping the queue of priorities ordained by the Companies Acts, by executing judgments and attaching company property after a winding up has commenced. Section 219 of CA 1963 provides:

> 'Where any company is being wound up by the court, any attachment, sequestration, distress or execution put in force against the property or effects of the company after the commencement of the winding up shall be void to all intents.'

The attachment, sequestration and execution against corporate assets generally has been considered in Chapter 6[140]. Once a winding up has commenced, judgment creditors must take their chances with the other creditors of an insolvent company and rely on the liquidator to pay them their lawful dividend from the assets that he has realised[141].

[27.049] Moreover, no new action can be commenced against a company that is being wound up. Section 222 of CA 1963 provides:

> 'When a winding-up order has been made or a provisional liquidator has been appointed no action or proceeding shall be proceeded with or commenced against a company except by leave of the court and subject to such terms as the court may impose.'

In *Re Motor Racing Circuits Ltd*[142] lay-litigants sought to argue that a receiver could not be appointed on foot of a debenture after the making of a winding-up order or, indeed, after

---

136 *Polly Peck International plc v Nadir (No 2)* [1992] 4 All ER 769.

137 RSC, Ord 50, r 4.

138 *Republic of Haiti v Duvalier* [1989] 1 All ER 456 at 464g.

139 *Campus Oil Ltd v Minister for Industry and Energy* [1983] IR 88.

140 Chapter 6, *Corporate Civil Litigation*, para **[6.066]** *ff.*

141 *Re United English and Scottish Life Insurance Co* (1868) Lr 5 Eq 300; *Re Tumacacori Mining Co* (1874) LR 17 Eq 534.

the appointment of a provisional liquidator. The Supreme Court rejected this point, Blayney J holding:

> 'For the appointment of the receiver to be excluded his appointment by the bank would have had to constitute an action or proceeding and in my view it is quite clear that the appointment of a receiver is not an action or proceeding. An action or proceeding is something which is commenced by way of a court action, in other words by a summons being issued or some proceedings being issued before the court. But the appointment of a receiver does not come into that category, it is simply an appointment under a power contained in a debenture. It does not come within the definition of an action or a proceeding…'.[143]

Of course the appointment of a receiver other than by contractual right eg a receiver by way of equitable execution would, by s 222, be prohibited without the leave of the court. Also prohibited would be any action in any court of law, howsoever initiated, whether by process, bill, summons or originating notice of motion.

[27.050] In addition to the foregoing provision, the rights of creditors as to execution or attachment are further restricted by CA 1963, s 291 where a company is being wound up. Section 291(1) provides:

> 'Subject to subsections (2) to (4), where a creditor has issued execution against the goods[144] or lands of a company or has attached any debt due to the company, and the company is subsequently wound up, he shall not be entitled to retain the benefit of the execution or attachment against the liquidator in the winding up of the company unless he has completed the execution or attachment before the commencement of the winding up.'

The thrust of this section is that a creditor must hand back any goods or land unless the execution or attachment has been completed[145] before the commencement of the winding up[146]. Subsection (2) provides that where a creditor has notice of a meeting called for the voluntary winding up of the company, the date he had this notice is substituted for the date of the commencement of the winding up. Subsection (3) provides that a person who purchases in good faith under a sale by the sheriff any goods of a company on which an execution has been levied shall *in all cases* acquire good title to them against the company's liquidator. By sub-s (4) the court may set aside the rights conferred on a liquidator by sub-s (1) 'in favour of the creditor to such extent and subject to such terms as the court thinks fit'. In *Caribbean Producers (Yam Importers) Ltd*[147] Russell LJ said that weighty reasons would be required before the court would exercise its validating jurisdiction under this subsection as the purpose of s 291-type provisions is to further the principle that unsecured creditors of an insolvent company are to be paid *pari passu*. Subsection (5) provides:

---

142 *Re Motor Racing Circuits Ltd* (31 January 1997, unreported), Supreme Court.

143 (31 January 1997, unreported), Supreme Court at p 3.

144 'Goods' are defined by sub-s (7) to include all chattels personal.

145 On 'completion' see *Caribbean Products (Yam Importers) Ltd* [1966] Ch 331 where Russell LJ said an attachment is only complete where there has been an actual receipt of money by the creditor. See also s 291(5) considered below.

146 *Re Andrew* [1937] Ch 122.

147 *Caribbean Producers (Yam Importers) Ltd* [1966] Ch 331.

'For the purposes of this section, an execution against goods shall be taken to be completed by seizure and sale, and an attachment of the debt shall be deemed to be completed by receipt of the debt, and an execution against land shall be deemed to be completed by seizure and, in the case of an equitable interest, by the appointment of a receiver.'

By sub-s (6), nothing in s 291 is expressed to give any validity to any payment which constitutes a fraudulent preference[148].

[27.051] Section 292 of CA 1963 reinforces the effects of s 291 by providing that a sheriff is obliged to deliver goods and money seized from a company to its liquidator where he has been served with notice that a provisional liquidator has been appointed or that either a winding-up order has been made or a resolution passed to have a company wound up voluntarily. Again, the sheriff is only obliged to deliver goods or money to a liquidator before their sale or before the completion of the execution by the receipt or recovery of the full amount of the levy[149]. The rights of the liquidator conferred by sub-s (1) may again be set aside by the court in favour of the creditor to such extent and subject to such terms as the court thinks fit[150].

[27.052] One effect[151] of CA 1963, s 284(2) applying the Bankruptcy Act 1988 to the winding up of companies is that judgment mortgages registered against a company's property within three months of the commencement of a winding up are invalid[152]. An example of the operation of this is *Re Shannonside Holdings Ltd*[153] where Costello J held that a judgment mortgage which was registered within three months of the resolution to wind up a company was invalid.

Disclaiming onerous property

[27.053] In a discussion of the means employed by a liquidator in realising corporate assets, it may seem strange to consider a measure whereby a liquidator can disclaim, or disown, 'assets' to which the company is entitled. However, certain assets may in fact be more of a liability than a benefit to the company. In such circumstances, a liquidator might decide that the company is better off without them and may make an application to disclaim them pursuant to CA 1963, s 290.

[27.054] CA 1963, s 290(1) provides that:

'...where any part of the property of a company which is being wound up consists of land of any tenure burdened with onerous covenants, of shares or stock in companies, of unprofitable contracts, or of any other property which is unsaleable by reason of its binding the possessor thereof to the performance of any onerous act or to the payment of any sum of money, the liquidator of the company, notwithstanding that he has endeavoured to sell or has taken possession of the property or exercised any act or ownership in relation thereto, may,

---

148 On 'fraudulent preference' see para **[27.072]** *ff*.

149 Subsection (2) provides a partial saver for the sheriff's costs: see *Bluston and Bramley Ltd v Leigh* [1950] 2 KB 548; *Re Walkden Sheet Metal Co Ltd* [1960] Ch 170.

150 CA 1963, s 292(3).

151 For the effects of the bankruptcy legislation on the distribution of corporate assets on liquidation, see para **[27.128]**.

152 The Bankruptcy Act 1988, s 51, formerly the Irish Bankrupt and Insolvent Act 1857, s 311.

153 (20 May 1993, unreported), High Court, per Costello J.

with the leave of the court and subject to the provisions of this section, by writing signed by him, at any time within 12 months after the commencement of the winding up or such extended period as may be allowed by the court, disclaim the property.'

When one thinks of a company holding property, this tends to imply that it holds something worth having. However, sometimes owning property entails being subject to obligations. Where such obligations are burdened by onerous covenants, the legislature provides that a liquidator may disclaim such property. The purpose of s 290 is to streamline the realisation and distribution of a company's assets.

[27.055] The effect of a legal disclaimer is set out in CA 1963, s 290(3) which provides that:

> 'The disclaimer shall operate to determine, as from the date of disclaimer, the rights, interests and liabilities of the company, and the property of the company, in or in respect of the property disclaimed, but shall not, except so far as is necessary for the purpose of releasing the company and the property of the company from liability, affects the rights or liabilities of any other person.'

This provision was interpreted by Keane J in *Tempany v Royal Liver Trustees Ltd*[154] as meaning that the obligations of persons other than the company are not affected by the disclaimer. Consequently, the obligations of a guarantor of a lease taken by a company are not affected by a liquidator's disclaimer of that lease: the right of a landlord to recover rent from a guarantor, or the original lessee in the case where a company is a sub-lessee, is not affected by a disclaimer[155]. In the *Tempany* case a liquidator sought to disclaim a lease held by a company. The lease represented a liability of £1.5 million because the rent paid by the company was greatly in excess of the market value; a schedule of dilapidations had been served; and there was no prospect of assigning the lessee's interest for value. The defendant was the guarantor of the company's obligations under the lease and opposed the application for disclaimer by the liquidator. Keane J allowed the liquidator to disclaim the lease: the exclusive concern of the court was the interests of the company, although the court would have some regard to the parties affected by the disclaimer. However, the release of the guarantor was not necessary in order to release the company from its liabilities. As one writer has observed:

> 'The only practical consequence of a disclaimer allowed in such circumstances is that the company's proprietary [in rem] right, an untidy item of undisposable property, disappears. The company's *in personam* liabilities in respect of the lease simply reappear in other guises as provable debts in the liquidation.'[156]

That the rights and liabilities of persons other than the company being wound up remain intact, is seen in other subsections of CA 1963, s 290. The courts will seek to construe the statutory provision in such a way so as to remove a company's onerous obligations whilst seeking to interfere with other parties' rights as little as possible[157]. The decision of Keane J in *Tempany v Royal Liver Trustees Ltd* previously distinguished the effects of a

---

[154] *Tempany v Royal Liver Trustees Ltd* [1984] ILRM 273.

[155] See Keane, *Company Law* (3rd edn, 2000), para 36.99.

[156] Ussher, *Company Law in Ireland* (1986), p 497.

[157] See, eg, *Capital Prime Properties plc v Worthgate Ltd* [2000] BCC 525.

disclaimer of a lease on guarantors in Ireland from the prevailing position in England. In England, a series of cases had held that the effect of a lease being disclaimed is to discharge any surety or guarantor from their liabilities[158]. These cases have, however, been overturned by the House of Lords in *Hindcastle Ltd v Barbara Attenborough Associates Ltd*[159], where Keane J's decision was cited and followed in the Lords' decision that a liquidator's disclaimer does not affect the obligations of an original tenant or guarantor.

[27.056] The legislature goes on to protect the rights of persons other than the company in various subsections of CA 1963, s 290. Subsection (4) provides that the court, either before or upon allowing disclaimer, must require that notice be given to persons interested. Subsection (5) expressly prohibits a liquidator from disclaiming where any interested persons make application in writing requiring him to decide whether or not to disclaim, and he has not within 28 days thereafter given the interested person notice that he intends to apply to court for leave to disclaim. Subsection (6) provides that where a person is entitled to the benefit or subject to the burden under a contract, the court may rescind the contract on such terms as it thinks just, and any order for damages made against the company shall be a debt due on distribution by the liquidator. In *Re Ranks Ireland Ltd*[160] Murphy J restated the principle that all those who had contracted with the company, and whose rights were affected by a disclaimer, could prove in a winding up. There, Irish Telephone Rentals Ltd agreed to install and lease certain telephone equipment for 14 years. The liquidator of Ranks Ireland Ltd sought to disclaim these agreements and this disclaimer was permitted by Murphy J who said the appropriate measure of damages was not that provided for in the contract disclaimed, but simply 'the difference between the rent which would have been paid by the company under the lease and the rent which the lessor is likely to obtain during the unexpired residue'.[161]

[27.057] In an attempt to tidy up loose ends, CA 1963, s 290(7) permits the court, on application by any person who either claims any interest in any disclaimed property or is under any liability not discharged by the Act, to make an order for the vesting of the property disclaimed. The vesting can take place without the need for a conveyance or assignment, to any person entitled thereto, or to whom it appears just. However, by sub-s (8):

> 'Where the property disclaimed is of a leasehold nature, the court shall not make a vesting order in favour of any person claiming under the company, whether as under-lessee or as mortgagee by demise, except upon the terms of making that person -
>
> (a) subject to the same liabilities and obligations as those to which the company was subject under the lease in respect of the property at the commencement of the winding up; or
>
> (b) if the court thinks fit, subject only to the same liabilities and obligations as if the lease had been assigned to that person at that date;

[158] See *Stacey v Hill* [1901] 1 KB 660; *Murphy v Sawyer-Hoare* [1994] 2 BCLC 59.

[159] *Hindcastle Ltd v Barbara Attenborough Associates Ltd* [1996] 2 BCLC 234.

[160] *Re Ranks Ireland Ltd* [1988] ILRM 751.

[161] Citing Keane, *Company Law in the Republic of Ireland* (1st edn, 1985) at p 321.

> and in either event (if the case so requires), as if the lease had comprised only the property comprised in the vesting order, and any mortgagee or under-lessee declining to accept a vesting order upon such terms shall be excluded from all interest in and security upon the property, and, if there is no person claiming under the company who is willing to accept an order upon such terms, the court shall have power to vest the estate and interest of the company in the property in any person liable either personally or in a representative character, and either alone or jointly with the company, to perform the lessee's covenants in the lease, freed and discharged from all estates, encumbrances and interests created therein by the company.'

The fact that, on application, the court has power by sub-s (7) to make an order for the vesting of the property has been held by Carroll J in *Re Erris Investments Ltd*[162] to make it unsafe for the Registrar of Titles to cancel the leasehold burden on a freehold folio where the leasehold has been disclaimed by a company-lessee. Furthermore, the learned judge also held that Deasy's Act 1860, s 7[163], concerning the surrender of a lease, does not operate because it is based on an agreement between the lessor and lessee: such agreement did not exist in a disclaimer since this was a unilateral act of the liquidator and the court[164].

Post-commencement dispositions

[27.058] At the heart of the principles behind the realisation of corporate assets on a liquidation is the notion that *all* assets which belong to the company at the *commencement* of the winding up should be applied and distributed in accordance with the priority determined by law. Section 275(1) of CA 1963 states the central principle that 'the property of a company on its winding up...shall...be applied in satisfaction of its liabilities *pari passu*'. The commencement of a winding up is deemed to occur, in an official or compulsory liquidation[165], at the time of the presentation of the petition to have the company wound up[166]. Section 218 of CA 1963 provides:

> 'In a winding up by the court, any disposition of the property, including things in action, and any transfer of shares or alteration in the status of the members of the company, made after the commencement of the winding-up, shall, unless the court otherwise orders, be void.'[167]

This gives further statutory force to the *pari passu* principle in s 275 which requires that all creditors should be placed on an equal footing and that none should 'leap frog' the creditors' statutory queue. The basic point is clear, *all* dispositions are *void* after the commencement of a winding up. However, the court may in its discretion, *validate* a disposition. One judicial statement of the rationale[168] behind the jurisdiction to validate a disposition is provided by Cairns LJ in *Re Wiltshire Iron Co*[169] who said:

---

162 *Re Erris Investments Ltd* [1991] ILRM 377.

163 Landlord and Tenant Law Amendment (Ireland) Act 1860 (23 & 24 Vict c 154).

164 Cf Ussher, *Company Law in Ireland* (1986), p 498 whose interpretation of the judgment of Keane J in *Tempany v Royal Liver Trustees Ltd* [1984] ILRM 273 at 289, was not followed.

165 In the case of a voluntary winding up, commencement of the winding up occurs when the resolution is passed to this effect: CA 1963, s 253(1). See Chapter 25, *Winding Up Companies, para* **[25.012]**.

166 CA 1963, s 220(2).

167 On the transfer of shares and the alteration in the status of the members made after the commencement of the winding up, see para **[27.119]**.

'This is a wholesome and necessary provision, to prevent, during the period which must elapse before a petition can be heard, the improper alienation and dissipation of the property of a company *in extremis*. But where a company actually trading, which it is in the interests of everyone to preserve, and ultimately to sell, as a going concern, is made the object of the winding-up petition which may fail or succeed, if it were to be supposed that transactions in the ordinary course of its current trade, *bona fide* entered into and completed, would be avoided, and would not in the discretion of the court, be maintained, the result would be that the presentation of a petition, groundless or well-founded, would *ipso facto*, paralyse the trade of the company, and great injury, without any counter-balance of advantage, would be done to those interested in the assets of the company.'

The ethos of this dictum ought to be continually borne in mind when considering the case law concerning the jurisdiction to validate dispositions. Here, the following issues are considered:

(a) The concept of disposition.

(b) Post-commencement banking transactions.

(c) The jurisdiction to validate dispositions.

(a) The concept of disposition

[27.059] The ordinary meaning of disposition is the passing of an interest in something, or the giving away of something. Clearly, sales with or without consideration, gifts, payments for goods or services received, etc are all dispositions. Where a company has entered into an unconditional contract before the presentation of a petition to wind up the fact that it completes that contract after the petition has been presented, has been held not to be a disposition[170].

[27.060] An interesting argument as to what constituted a disposition was advanced in *Re Motor Racing Circuits Ltd*[171]. In that case lay-litigants advanced the novel argument that the appointment of a receiver after the commencement of a winding up falls within CA 1963, s 218 because it entitled the receiver to take possession of the assets of a company. The Supreme Court rejected this. Giving the judgment of the court, Blayney J said:

'The position here is that there was no alteration in any way in the property of the company effected by the appointment of the receiver. The alteration in regard to the assets of the company was effected when the debenture was executed. As a result of the debenture being executed the bank had a charge on the particular property which was the subject of the debenture. So the bank from the date of the execution of the debenture was the mortgagee of the property in question. The property in question had been vested in the bank as security for the monies owing to the bank. The appointment of a receiver simply amounted to the normal way for a bank to recover what is due to it on foot of its charge. But there was no change whatsoever in regard to the ownership of the asset that had already been vested in the company under the debenture when the debenture was executed. The position is that the appointment of a receiver does not in any way come within s 218. It does not in any way

[168] See also the judgment of Mummery LJ in *Hollicourt (Contracts) Ltd v Bank of Ireland* [2001] 1 BCLC 233 at 238–239.

[169] (1868) 3 Ch App 443 at 446–447.

[170] See *Re French's (Wine Bar) Ltd* [1987] BCLC 499.

[171] *Re Motor Racing Circuits Ltd* (31 January 1997, unreported), Supreme Court.

> represent any disposition of the property of the company; this disposition had taken place when the debenture was executed.'[172]

Accordingly, any action taken on foot of security granted prior to a company being wound up will not amount to a disposition within the meaning of CA 1963, s 218.

(b) Post-commencement banking transactions

[27.061] In the case of the drawing of a cheque, it is now established that there will be no disposition until the cheque is honoured: drawing a cheque in itself is not a disposition. In *Re Ashmark Ltd (No 2)*[173] Blayney J said the fact that a cheque was drawn before the commencement of a winding up was immaterial: the fact was that it was paid after the commencement, and so was void, unless the court decided to validate it[174].

(i) Lodgments into an overdrawn account

[27.062] Lodgments by a company into its own overdrawn bank account are dispositions of that company's property in favour of the bank. In the English case of *Re Gray's Inn Construction Co Ltd*[175], after the commencement of its winding up, a company paid certain sums into its overdrawn bank account, thereby reducing its overdraft. At first hearing, Templeman J said these were not dispositions but this was rejected by Buckley LJ in the Court of Appeal who held:

> 'When a customer's account with his banker is overdrawn he is a debtor to his banker for the amount of the overdraft. When he pays a sum of money into the account, whether in cash or by payment in of a third party cheque, he discharges his indebtedness to the bank *pro tanto*. There is clearly in these circumstances, in my judgment, a disposition by the company to the bank of the amount of the cash or of the cheque.'[176]

There is sometimes a temptation for companies to pay money into an overdrawn bank account, after the commencement of a winding up, where company directors have given personal guarantees in respect of the company's overdraft. Therefore, the lower the overdraft, the less the directors may be called upon to pay on foot of their personal guarantees to the bank.

(ii) Payments out of a company's account

[27.063] Clearly, payments out of a company's bank account will amount to dispositions within the meaning of CA 1963, s 218[177]. But where the disposition is effected by means of a cheque, drawn on the company's account, is the disposition in favour of the bank that honours the cheque or the third party in whose favour it is drawn? This question has recently received attention from both the Irish and English courts. In *Hollicourt (Contracts) Ltd v Bank of Ireland*[178] the English Court of Appeal reversed the decision of Blackburne J that the defendant-bank was liable to reimburse a company for payments

---

[172] (31 January 1997, unreported), Supreme Court at pp 10–11.

[173] *Re Ashmark Ltd (No 2)* [1990] ILRM 455.

[174] A contention supported by the Bills of Exchange Act 1882, ss 3(1) and 73. In the words of Blayney J (at 457): 'The cheque was no more than an unconditional order by the company to its bankers to pay [the creditor] the sum named in it. Until [the Bank] made the payment in accordance with the order there was no disposition'.

[175] *Re Gray's Inn Construction Co Ltd* [1980] 1 All ER 814.

[176] [1980] 1 All ER 814 at 818e–f.

[177] See Costello J in *Re Pat Ruth Ltd* [1981] ILRM 51 at 52.

made in these circumstances. Blackburne J had held that the effect of the materially identical English provision[179] was to operate not only against third party recipients of cheques drawn by companies but also against the bank that made the payments. The Court of Appeal found that the provision was not intended by the legislature to impose a restitutionary liability on a bank. It was also held that the purpose – namely, to prevent directors from dissipating assets to the detriment of creditors – was accomplished without impinging upon the validity of the intermediate steps in a disposition by cheque. Mummery LJ rejected that there had been any disposition by the company to the bank, saying:

> 'Consistent with that legislative policy the only dispositions of the company's property affected by the section in this case are the payments to the payees of the cheques drawn, after the presentation of the petition, on the company's bank account. What is needed for the section to operate is a disposition amounting to an alienation of the company's property (see *Mersey Steel & Iron Co Ltd v Naylor, Benzon & Co* (1884) 9 App Cas 434 at 440 per Earl of Selborne LC). The bank in honouring the company's cheque obeys as agent the order of its principal to pay out of the principal's money in the agent's hands the amount of the cheque to the payee (see *Westminster Bank Ltd v Hilton* (1926) 136 LT 315 at 317 per Lord Atkinson). The beneficial ownership of the property represented by the cheque was never transferred to the bank, to which no alienation of the company's property was made.'

It is thought that the final sentence is compelling. Where a bank effects a payment on foot of a company's mandate there is no disposition to the bank as the bank is not a 'disponee' – merely an intermediary, acting as agent of the company. Mummery LJ went on to quote with approval the following passage from the decision of Street CJ in *Re Mal Bower's Macquarie Electrical Centre Pty Ltd*[180] where he said there was 'great force' in the argument that:

> '…the paying by a bank of a company's cheque, presented by a stranger, does not involve the bank in a disposition of the property of the company so as to disentitle the bank to debit the amount of the cheque to the company's account. The word 'disposition' connotes in my view both a disponor and a disponee. The section operates to render the disposition void so far as concerns the disponee. It does not operate to affect the agencies interposing between the company, as disponor, and the recipient of the property, as disponee…The intermediary functions fulfilled by the bank in respect of paying cheques drawn by a company in favour of and presented on behalf of a third party do not implicate the bank in the consequences of the statutory avoidance prescribed by [the similar Australian provision]…I consider that the legislative intention…is such as to require an investigation of what happened to the property, that is to say, what was the disposition, and then to enable the liquidator to recover it upon the basis that the disposition was void. It is recovery from the disponee that forms the basic legislative purpose…'[181]

[178] *Hollicourt (Contracts) Ltd v Bank of Ireland* [2001] 1 BCLC 233. See Sealy, 'Company Liquidations: When Should Post-Petition Banking Transactions be Avoided' (2000) CCH's Company Law Newsletter, Issue 57, 11 July 2000 and Moore, 'Payments Received by Cheque Drawn on Bank Account of Company Following Presentation of Winding-up petition' (2001) 8 CLP 10.

[179] Insolvency Act 1986 (UK), s 127.

[180] *Re Mal Bower's Macquarie Electrical Centre Pty Ltd* [1974] 1 NSWLR 245.

The Court of Appeal acknowledged that the decision of Buckley LJ in *Re Gray's Inn Construction Co Ltd*[182] did contain certain passages which, if read out of context supported the view that all post-presentation cheques drawn on a bank account were dispositions in favour of the bank and also that a bank had a liability to a liquidator to the extent that dispositions were irrecoverable from the third parties who cashed such cheques. It was held, however, that that judgment was not binding authority for either proposition because it concerned an overdrawn account. The Court of Appeal also favoured the interpretation given by Lightman J in *Coutts & Co v Stock*[183] where it was held that although the statute in question invalidated a disposition as between a company and a payee, it did not do so as against the company's bank where the bank merely fulfilled an agency or intermediary role between the company and the payee. It is thought that the decision of the Court of Appeal was correct in law and common sense.

[27.064] The current law in Ireland is the reverse. Shortly after the decision of the English Court of Appeal, the issue arose for consideration by the High Court. In *Re Industrial Services Company (Dublin) Ltd*[184] the official liquidator of the subject company objected to certain payments into and out of the company's bank account, after the presentation of a petition to wind up the company because the bank had failed to notice the advertisement. In finding for the liquidator, Kearns J began his exposition of the law by stating that in *Re Pat Ruth Ltd*[185] Costello J was in no doubt that 'such payments were 'dispositions' within the meaning of CA 1963, s 218, be they lodgments into a company's bank account or payments out'.[186] It is thought that no such inference that Costello J believed anything of the sort can be drawn: in that case the account in question was overdrawn whereas in the instant case the account had been in credit for much of the relevant time. Likewise, any reliance on the decision in *Re Gray's Inn Construction Co Ltd*[187] to find in favour of the liquidator is weakened by the fact that, in that case, the bank account under consideration was overdrawn, thereby rendering any postulation on accounts that are 'in credit', clearly obiter dictum. Although Kearns J went on to quote from the decision of Mummery LJ in *Hollicourt (Contracts) Ltd v Bank of Ireland*[188] and the passage from the judgment of Street CJ in *Re Mal Bower's Macquarie Electrical Centre Pty Ltd*[189], cited in the preceding paragraph, he went on to reject their conclusion[190]. Kearns J said:

---

181 [1974] 1 NSWLR 245 at 258.

182 *Re Gray's Inn Construction Co Ltd* [1980] 1 All ER 814.

183 *Coutts & Co v Stock* [2000] 1 BCLC 183.

184 *Re Industrial Services Company (Dublin) Ltd* [2001] 2 IR 118. See Moore, 'Section 218 of the Companies Act, 1963 Banks and Hollicourt: the Irish Perspective' (2001) 8 CLP 108.

185 *Re Pat Ruth Ltd* [1981] ILRM 51.

186 [2001] 2 IR 118 at 121.

187 *Re Gray's Inn Construction Co Ltd* [1980] 1 All ER 814.

188 *Hollicourt (Contracts) Ltd v Bank of Ireland* [2001] 1 BCLC 233. See Sealy, 'Company Liquidations: When Should Post-Petition Banking Transactions be Avoided' (2000) CCH's Company Law Newsletter, Issue 57, 11 July 2000 and Moore, 'Payments Received by Cheque Drawn on Bank Account of Company Following Presentation of Winding-up petition' (2001) 8 CLP 10.

189 *Re Mal Bower's Macquarie Electrical Centre Pty Ltd* [1974] 1 NSWLR 245.

> 'I feel that notwithstanding the passage just referred to, something more than a commercial desideratum as considered from the Bank's viewpoint would be required to persuade me to take a different view from that expressed by Costello J in *Re Pat Ruth Ltd*. I am not convinced that the reasoning by the Court of Appeal in *Hollicourt* is preferable to the different view taken by the same court in *Gray's Inn Construction Ltd* I do not see that some commercial interpretation advantageous to the Bank must be given to s 218 when its meaning on the fact of it, is plain and straightforward. Had the legislature intended that some sort of derogation or qualification would apply in the case of banks, it would have been easy to frame this section appropriately.
>
> ...banks discharge a dual function in their relationship with their customer. In one sense they act as agents, but, given that property in money passes to them, the true relationship is that of borrower and lender. Thus the bank can be both agent, creditor and debtor. They thus have a very special role of responsibility in winding up situations. Not the least part of that role is one of vigilance in respect of their client customers which, because of their assets and expertise, they are well placed to perform. Where they do exercise that role and function it seems to me at least they serve a wider commercial interest to the narrow commercial contention of the Bank's interest is not the issue. If the Bank in exercising its functions responsibly ensures greater protection for the general body of creditors, that surely is consistent with the policy of the section.'[191]

[27.065] To the extent that Kearns J's conclusions are based on judicial precedent, it is thought that they are based on a falsio assumpit. Once it becomes clear that neither *Re Pat Ruth Ltd* nor the *Re Grey's Inn Construction* cases are authorities for the conclusion reached by Kearns J, the legal basis for the decision collapses. It is thought that to find as the Court of Appeal did in *Hollicourt* or as the Supreme Court of New South Wales did in *Mal Bower's Macquarie Electrical Centre* is not to put 'some commercial interpretation advantageous to the Bank...to s 218 when its meaning on the fact of it, is plain and straightforward'. It is submitted that, given the extent of judicial disagreement, the meaning of CA 1963, s 218 can hardly be said to be 'plain' or 'straightforward'[192]. As for the interpretation being commercially advantageous to banks, if it is correct there is nothing to recoil from in that suggestion. It is submitted that the interpretation afforded to the term 'disposition' was incorrect and operates to perpetrate an injustice to a person who has not benefited from the transaction. Indeed, to the extent that the effect of that interpretation is to force the redistribution of property rights (ie afford to certain creditors additional monies that never formed part of the company's assets) it is possibly an unconstitutional intrusion upon property rights. It is thought that a payment into a bank account is only a disposition within the meaning of s 218 where that account is overdrawn, as the effect of such a payment is to reduce the company's indebtedness to the bank ie the position of the bank in that situation is that of creditor. Payments into an account in credit should not, however, be treated as dispositions because the payment is not in reduction of any indebtedness. Payments out are a different matter but again, the bank in acting as an

---

[190] Kearns J was also not swayed by the views in Breslin, *Banking Law in the Republic of Ireland* (1998), p 386.

[191] [2001] 2 IR 118 at 129.

[192] Indeed, in *Coutts & Co v Stock* [2000] 1 BCLC 183 at 185, Lightman J said that 'the authorities are in disarray and the state of the law is uncertain'.

agent of the company should not be made to pick up the tab: the payment out should be voidable and returnable by the recipient, subject only to the court deciding whether or not to validate the payment. The disposition should be void only as against the actual beneficiary of the payment out.

[27.066] It should be noted, however, that in *Re Industrial Services Company (Dublin) Ltd*[193] Kearns J did acknowledge that the court did retain the important power of validation and said that any problem with 'double accounting' can be dealt with on application to the court by the bank to validate dispositions made'[194]. He also said that it did not necessarily follow from his conclusions that liquidators could set their sights against banks alone or that they could ignore the ultimate recipients of the payments made[195]. The question of validation of dispositions is considered below[196].

(iii) Debiting of interest post-commencement

[27.067] In *Re Ashmark Ltd: Ashmark Ltd v Allied Irish Bank plc*[197] the question of interest payable to a bank in respect of a company's overdraft account was considered by Lardner J. In this application the company had an overdraft account with AIB, and on the date upon which the company's winding up commenced this account stood in credit. However, interest on the account, which had accrued on a day-to-day basis, was debited from the account after the commencement of the winding up. Lardner J held that the debiting of this interest was not a disposition within the meaning of CA 1963, s 218. Relying on the authority of Buckley LJ in *Halesowen Presswork and Assemblies Ltd v Westminster Bank Ltd*[198] Lardner J said:

> '...the company had incurred over a period a liability to pay interest to the bank on its overdraft. This liability accrued from day-to-day and constituted a debt due by the company to the bank over and above the amount of the overdraft. Then the company paid money into the account so that the account was in substantial credit. The overdraft debt was repaid by the company which became entitled to a credit in the computation of the account. The amount of the credit was not itself the property of the company but of the bank. The bank became a debtor to the company. At any time the amount of each party's liability to the other could only be ascertained by discovering the ultimate balance of their mutual dealings. Where interest has been accruing on a daily basis as in the present case which is a liability of the company to the bank and at the same time, the bank owes a debt in respect of the

---

193 [2001] 2 IR 118. See Moore, 'Section 218 of the Companies Act, 1963 Banks and Hollicourt: the Irish Perspective' (2001) 8 CLP 108.

194 [2001] 2 IR 118 at 130.

195 See para **[27.071]**.

196 See para **[27.068]**.

197 *Re Ashmark Ltd: Ashmark Ltd v Allied Irish Bank plc* [1994] 1 ILRM 223.

198 *Halesowen Presswork and Assemblies Ltd v Westminster Bank Ltd* [1971] 1 QB 1, where (at 46) Buckley LJ had said: 'Where the relationship of the banker and customer is a single relationship such as I have already mentioned, albeit embodied in a number of accounts, the situation is not in my judgment a situation of lien at all. A lien postulates property of the debtor in the possession or under the control of the creditor. Nor is it a set off situation which postulates mutual but independent obligations between the two parties. It is an accounting situation in which the existence and amount of the parties' liability to the other can only be ascertained by discovering the ultimate balance of their mutual dealings'.

> company's current account credit balance to the company, it is not in my judgment correct to treat the ascertainment of the ultimate balance as a disposition of property by the company on that date (or a disposition of a thing in action) within s 218 of the Companies Act. It seems to me properly considered as an account situation in which the existence and amount of the bank's liability in respect of the current account to the company can only be ascertained by discovering the ultimate balance of their mutual dealings.'[199]

Where interest accrues *after* the commencement of a winding up it cannot be debited but remains due to the bank. In such cases the bank can either prove for the debt in the subsequent liquidation or, where it is secured, it can stand outside the liquidation and recover principal and interest from the proceeds of sale of the secured property.

(c) The jurisdiction to validate dispositions

[27.068] There is some doubt as to the precise principles which a court should employ in exercising its jurisdiction to validate certain post-commencement dispositions. In *Re Lynch, Monaghan & O'Brien Ltd*[200] Costello J said that the discretionary validation jurisdiction conferred on the courts is intended primarily for dispositions to creditors whose debts arise after the presentation of the petition to have the company wound up. In *Re Ashmark Ltd (No 1)*[201] certain payments were made after the commencement of the winding up and all were dispositions within the meaning of CA 1963, s 218. The first disposition was by cheque in respect of legal fees before the commencement of the winding up but which, due to the company's inability to provide funds, was not cashed until after the commencement. The second disposition was also in respect of services to the company prior to the commencement of the winding up. In respect of both of these dispositions, it was argued:

- that the solicitor-disponee was unaware that the payment disposition in his favour was made after the commencement of the winding up; and
- that in so far as the payments were made to the solicitor who had an intimate knowledge of the affairs of the company, the dispositions in his favour were made in the best interests of the company and were beneficial to the creditors.

O'Hanlon J accepted that both of the foregoing were grounds which a court would consider in deciding whether or not to validate a disposition. However, on the facts of the case, he held that the evidence did not justify reliance on either of these grounds to validate the dispositions. He held that the disponee-solicitor had constructive notice that the petition had been presented. On the validation of dispositions by a company after the commencement of its winding up, O'Hanlon J said:

> '...while transactions taking place after the commencement of the winding up have been validated under the provisions of s 218 of the Companies Act 1963, and under the comparable provisions found in the English statutes, where no dissipation of the company's assets have resulted therefrom, I find it hard to envisage a situation where the court would validate a payment in full made after the commencement of a winding up, in respect of

[199] [1994] ILRM 223 at 226.

[200] *Re Lynch, Monaghan & O'Brien Ltd* (9 June 1989, unreported), High Court, the facts of which are considered by MacCann, 'Liquidation: *Pari Passu* Distribution and Section 218 of the Companies Act 1963' (1990) ILT 6 at p 8, 9.

[201] *Re Ashmark Ltd (No 1)* [1990] ILRM 330.

> services rendered, or goods sold, or other obligations incurred by the company *prior* to the winding up, and when similar treatment could not be accorded to the general body of unsecured creditors.'[202]

This raises an important point. The primary rationale of the validation mechanism in CA 1963, s 218 is to protect creditors. Creditors who, in return for money, advance goods or services to a company after the commencement of its winding up may do so for either of two reasons. First, they may be unaware of the fact that a petition has been presented. Secondly, they know that a petition has been presented but nevertheless continue to give the company credit thereby enabling the company to continue in business and not go-under merely because a petition is presented to which the company may have a defence[203].

[27.069] In *Re McBirney and Co Ltd*[204] Murphy J said that:

> '...the entire burden of the authorities is to the effect that the making of the payment (as opposed to the incurring of the expense) must be shown to be for the benefit of the company or at least desirable in the interests of the unsecured creditors as a body.'[205]

However, having stated the general principle Murphy J departed from it saying, 'I do not think that the court should confine itself rigidly to particular propositions isolated from the very special features of the present case'[206]. The special features to which he referred were that the dispositions were made by an administrator and receiver-manager (acting in his capacity of receiver-manager) who was appointed under the Insurance (No 2) Act 1983 to PMPA Insurance plc. The payments made were disputed by the company's liquidator. Although it was rejected that CA 1963, s 218 had no application to a company to which a receiver-manager is appointed under the Insurance (No 2) Act 1983, the fact that the payments had been made by a receiver-manager was recognised as being a special feature. As Murphy J said:

> 'In my view it is important to recognise, therefore, that the public were dealing with the receiver in the belief, as was the case, that he was an officer appointed by the court to control and carry on the business of the company.'[207]

The learned judge went on to exercise his jurisdiction and validated a number of payments made by the receiver-manager. Amongst the justifications given were the fact that some suppliers believed that they were supplying goods to a person whom they inferred was acting on the general authority of the court[208], and payments to employees did not prejudice the rights of unsecured creditors as the employees already had a preferential status[209]. Murphy J also distinguished payments which were made to *connected companies*

---

202 [1990] ILRM 330 at 333, 334.

203 See MacCann, 'Liquidation: *Pari Passu* Distribution and Section 218 of the Companies Act 1963' (1990) ILT 6, where the recent case law in both Ireland and England is perceptively analysed.

204 *Re McBirney and Co Ltd* (2 July 1992, unreported), High Court.

205 (2 July 1992, unreported), High Court at p 8.

206 (2 July 1992, unreported), High Court.

207 (2 July 1992, unreported), High Court at p 10.

208 (2 July 1992, unreported), High Court at p 11.

209 (2 July 1992, unreported), High Court at p 12.

from those which were made to *unconnected companies* and maintained this distinction in the subsequent decision of *Re McBirney and Company Ltd (No 2)*[210]. In this latter case he said of the decision in the earlier case that:

> 'Certainly it is difficult to justify the decision on the basis of any benefit accruing on the unsecured creditors as a body by reason of the payment. However the justification for my earlier judgment may be found in the fact that the non-connected companies were perhaps unaware of the presentation of the petitions for the winding up of the companies and certainly less well informed concerning their affairs than the connected companies and the persons by whom they were controlled.'[211]

With regard to the connected companies Murphy J ordered that they were obliged to repay the company in full all payments which had been made to them, notwithstanding that they were in liquidation.

[27.070] A clear example of a disposition which was for the benefit of the creditors is provided by *Re AI Levy (Holdings) Ltd*[212]. In that case a disposition was validated where, after the presentation of a petition to wind the company up, it sold its leasehold interest in a property because the lease was liable to be forfeited if it, as the tenant, was wound up. By reason of this, the company sold the lease at market value before this happened. A further disposition was the payment of arrears of rent to the landlord, this being a condition to the landlord's consent to an assignment of the lease. Such dispositions were clearly to the benefit of the creditors of the company in that the company was put in funds arising from the sale of the lease, whereas had the company not disposed of its interest, it would have had neither funds nor a leasehold interest available for distribution amongst the creditors[213].

[27.071] Other cases are less easy to reconcile with the foregoing principles. In *Re Pat Ruth Ltd*[214] while all dispositions by the company into its overdrawn account were held to be void and would not be validated by the court, the other side of these same dispositions which were payments out of the bank account in favour of other creditors of the company were validated. So while the payment by cheque of creditors was validated, the honouring of those cheques by the bank was void: in effect, the bank paid the creditors from its own resources, and not from the company's account, which remained to the same extent in overdraft as it had been at the presentation of the petition. The reason why the dispositions to other creditors were validated was said by Costello J to be because:

> '...being persons whose debts were paid by means of the dispositions to which I have referred in good faith and in the ordinary course of business, come within the principle to which I have referred.'[215]

---

[210] *Re McBirney and Company Ltd (No 2)* (15 June 1993, unreported), High Court.

[211] (15 June 1993, unreported), High Court at p 7.

[212] *Re AI Levy (Holdings) Ltd* [1963] 2 All ER 85.

[213] Where a disposition does not benefit the creditors, but at the same time does not deplete the assets of the company available for distribution, this fact will be a material consideration for the court: *Re Tramway Building and Construction Co Ltd* [1987] BCLC 632.

[214] *Re Pat Ruth Ltd* [1981] ILRM 51.

[215] [1981] ILRM 51 at 52, 53.

The principle earlier referred to by Costello J in his judgment was that stated by Buckley LJ in *Re Gray's Inn Construction Co Ltd*[216] namely, that:

> 'A disposition carried out in good faith in the ordinary course of business at a time when the parties are unaware that a petition has been presented may, it seems, normally be validated by the court...'

There are fewer truer examples of 'ordinary course of business' than a bank acting on foot of a customer's instruction to pay a cheque. This case has been criticised on several grounds. One critic[217] has said that it seems irreconcilable to distinguish between the bank and the other creditors in this fashion, and in particular to deny that the dispositions to the bank were not made in the ordinary course of business[218].

In *Re Industrial Services Company (Dublin) Ltd (No 2)*[219] the bank that had effected withdrawals from an account in credit after the commencement of the company's winding up, which withdrawals has been held by Kearns J to be voidable, applied to have them validated. The validation application was heard by McCracken J, who noted that the following payments were in issue:

- lodgments of £4,961.77 and withdrawals of £8,022.27 in the period from the presentation of the petition and the advertising of the petition; and
- lodgments of £11,041.76 and withdrawals of £8,761.97 in the period from the advertising of the petition and the making of the winding-up order.

As to the principles applicable to validating payments, the following passage from the decision of McCracken J is instructive:

> 'The view I take is that I should validate any payments made in the ordinary course of business which were in respect of current debts, whether these were before or after the advertisement, as these were payments which the liquidator would probably have to have made in any event. To that degree, they are payments which could be said to be made for the benefit of the general body of creditors. However, I do not think that I should validate any payments made which were not made in the ordinary course of business, and I note that many of these payments were in fact made to directors of the company or persons who were connected with directors…'

---

216 *Re Gray's Inn Construction Co Ltd* [1980] 1 All ER 814.

217 Ussher, *Company Law in Ireland* (1986), p 483.

218 As to the meaning of 'ordinary course of business', in *Countrywide Banking Corporation Ltd v Dean* [1998] 2 WLR 441 the Privy Council said at 451 (in the context of whether a transaction was a preferential one in the context of the Companies Act 1955 (NZ), s 266): 'Plainly the transaction must be examined in the actual setting in which it took place. That defines the circumstances in which it is to be determined whether it was in the ordinary course of business. The determination then is to be made objectively by reference to the standard of what amounts to the ordinary course of business…the transaction must be such that it would be viewed by an objective observer as having taken place in the ordinary course of business. While there is to be reference to business practices in the commercial world in general, the focus must still be the ordinary operational activities of businesses as going concerns, not responses to abnormal financial difficulties.'

219 *Re Industrial Services Company (Dublin) Ltd (No 2)* (15 May 2002, unreported), High Court (McCracken J).

McCracken J applied this by validating payments in the ordinary course of business but not those to directors or persons connected with directors. In all payments totalling £2,125.57 were validated. McCracken J went on to consider the question of payments into and out of the bank accounts:

> 'There is an argument to be made that I should declare all payments into the bank account to be void dispositions, and only validate the sums that I have mentioned above in relation to the payments out of the bank account. However, to do so would lead to a windfall for the liquidator of the sum of £2,125.57, and would really be a form of double accounting. Accordingly, I would also validate the payment into the bank account of the sum of £2,125.57 by the company. All other payments into and out of the account are accordingly void, but again I would like to prevent any form of double benefit to the liquidator, which would result if he were able to recover the moneys paid in from the Bank and the moneys paid out from the recipients of the payments. What I would propose to do to try to meet this situation is that, while I am not validating any of these payments, I will direct that if the liquidator recovers the moneys from the Bank, he shall not seek to recover them from the recipients, and shall not in any way hinder the Bank from making such recovery should they be entitled to do so. It is then up to the Bank whether they wish to pursue the recipients themselves.'

This, it is thought, was a reasonable attempt by the court to do justice arising from the finding that payments into an in-credit bank account were 'dispositions'. Of course, the only reason why the possibility of 'windfalls' and 'double accounting' arose in the first place was because the payments by the company to its bank were treated as dispositions within the meaning of CA 1963, s 218[220].

Fraudulent preference of creditors

[27.072] The corporate law of fraudulent preference has its origins in the laws of bankruptcy, applicable to insolvent individuals[221]. In the words of Lord Ellenborough in *De Tastet v Carroll*[222] the raison d'être of such legislation arose because:

> '...it occurred to those who presided in the courts that it was unjust to permit a party on the eve of bankruptcy to make a voluntary disposition of his property in favour of a particular creditor, leaving the mere husk to the rest; and therefore that a transfer made at such a period, and under such circumstances, as evidently showed that it was made in contemplation of bankruptcy, and in order to favour a particular creditor, should be void.'

To allow an insolvent company on the verge of being wound up to freely dispose of its property would create an unacceptable loophole in the law of corporate insolvency. Fraudulent preference is addressed by CA 1963, s 286(1)[223], which provides:

> 'Subject to the provisions of this section, any conveyance, mortgage, delivery of goods, payment, execution or other act relating to property made or done by or against a company which is *unable to pay its debts as they become due* in favour of any creditor, or of any

---

220 For a criticism of the earlier decision of the High Court, see para **[27.065]**.

221 For the law of fraudulent preference applicable to individual bankrupts as contained in the Bankruptcy Act 1988, s 57, see generally, Sanfey & Holohan, *Bankruptcy Law and Practice in Ireland* (1991), Ch 8.

222 *De Tastet v Carroll* (1813) 1 Stark 88.

223 As amended by CA 1990, s 135.

> person on trust for any creditor, *with a view* to giving such creditor, or any surety or guarantor for the debt due to such creditor, *a preference over the other creditors*, shall, if a winding-up of the company commences within *six months* of the making or doing the same and the company is *at the time of the commencement of the winding-up unable to pay its debts* (taking into account the contingent and prospective liabilities), be deemed a fraudulent preference of its creditors and be invalid accordingly.' [Emphasis added]

Although a number of points arise for consideration here, two points in particular must be stressed. In the first place, in order for s 286(1) to become operative the company making the preference must be *unable to pay its debts as they become due* at the time the disposition was made and on the commencement of the winding up of the company. The circumstances in which a company will be found to be unable to pay debts is considered below[224] in connection with the invalidity of certain floating charges on a winding up. Many cases stress the insolvency of the company at the time of the making of the preference[225] but it is clear that it is only where a company is insolvent on its winding up also, that an application under CA 1963, s 286 can be made.

[27.073] The following points arise for consideration in the treatment of the law of corporate fraudulent preference:

(a) The disposition of corporate property.

(b) The operative time for making a preference.

(c) The effect of a fraudulent preference.

(d) The onus of proof.

(e) The intention to prefer.

(f) The beneficiary of the disposition.

(a) The disposition of corporate property

[27.074] There must be a preferential disposition of the company's property before CA 1963, s 286 can be invoked. While this may seem obvious, an application to have a transaction set aside as being invalid failed in *Re Welding Plant Ltd; Cooney v Dargan*[226] because the transaction under scrutiny was held not to amount to a disposition of corporate property. There, it was intended that in consideration of the company transferring certain corporate property to the controllers of the company, the controllers would take two loans in their personal names. It was held that this transaction had not in fact or in law happened because nothing had been executed by the company which would give effect to this intention. The company continued to own the property and, therefore, there was no disposition.

[27.075] It should be noted also that the type of transaction or disposition which may be impugned by CA 1963, s 286(1) is any conveyance, mortgage, delivery of goods, payment, execution or other act relating to property made or done by or against a company.

---

224 See para **[27.098]**.

225 Eg, see *Parkes & Sons Ltd v Hong Kong and Shanghai Banking Corp* [1990] ILRM 341 at 345.

226 *Re Welding Plant Ltd; Cooney v Dargan* (27 June 1984, unreported), High Court, per McWilliam J.

(b) The operative time for making the preference

[27.076] Section 286(1) of CA 1963 provides that the crucial time limit for the making of fraudulent preferences is *six months* before the commencement of the winding up. However, under the CA 1990, a further time limit has been added to catch fraudulent preferences in favour of *connected persons*. Now, CA 1963, s 286(3) provides that where a preferential transaction is made in favour of a connected person, the transaction shall be invalid where made within *two years* of the commencement of the winding up. Furthermore, it is deemed to have been made with a view to giving such a person a preference over other creditors and to be a fraudulent preference, unless the contrary is shown. A connected person is defined by s 286(5) as a person who at the time of the transaction was:

— a director or shadow director of the company,

— a director's spouse, parent, sibling or child,

— a related company within the meaning of CA 1990, s 140(5), considered below[227],

— any trustee of, or surety or guarantor for the debt due to any person referred to above.

In this way the legislature has broadened the scope of the provision by targeting persons who are perceived to be in a special position of trust to the company.

(c) The effect of a fraudulent preference

[27.077] Where a fraudulent preference is deemed or found to have been made, then it is invalid. Elsewhere[228], it has been suggested that this must equate with 'void' as provided for in the Bankruptcy Act 1988. In spite of the legislature not reconciling this difference in its most recent review[229] of the laws of fraudulent preference, it is thought that the consequence is indeed that the transaction is void in the case of a company.[230]

[27.078] Section 286(2) of CA 1963 provides that any conveyance or assignment by a company of all of its property to trustees for the benefit of all its creditors shall be void to all intents. This provision clearly rejects the view that a company can come to a voluntary arrangement with its creditors which benefits them all, and implicitly insists that the liquidator of a company is the proper person to distribute the assets of an insolvent company[231].

[27.079] The familiar saver for the rights of that most favoured person, the bona fide purchaser for value, applies to fraudulent preferences. Section 286(4) of CA 1963 provides that the rights of any person taking title in good faith and for valuable consideration through or under a creditor of the company shall not be affected[232]. This saver is not

---

227 See para **[27.107]**.

228 See Ussher, *Company Law in Ireland* (1986), p 505.

229 In drafting CA 1990, s 135 and the Bankruptcy Act 1988, s 57.

230 Support for this interpretation can be determined from s 287(1)(b) which makes reference to the situation where something is 'void under section 286 as a fraudulent preference'.

231 Contrast the Bankruptcy Act 1988, s 57 following the recommendation of the *Bankruptcy Law Committee Report* (Budd Committee) 1972. See generally Sanfey & Holohan, *Bankruptcy Law and Practice in Ireland* (1991), para 8.3.

232 See *Butcher v Stead* (1875) LR 7 HL 839.

directed at the preferred creditor, but rather at a person taking under him who will not suffer by an avoidance of a disposition to a creditor unless he acquires property fraudulently preferred to his successor in title without valuable consideration or has notice of the fraudulent preference[233].

[27.080] Section 287(1) of CA 1963 provides that where a company is being wound up and anything made or done on or after the operative date is void under CA 1963, s 286 as a fraudulent preference of a person interested in property mortgaged or charged to secure the company's debt, then:

> '...the person preferred shall be subject to the same liabilities and shall have the same rights as if he had undertaken to be personally liable as surety for the debt to the extent of the charge on the property or the value of his interest, whichever is the less.'

The effect of this section is that where a person who is preferred has a mortgage or a charge on company property to secure a debt due by the company he will become personally liable as a surety for the debt to the extent of the security on the property or the value of his interest (whichever is the lesser). The value of a person's interest is determined at the date of the fraudulent preference and in determining the value of the interest the interest is taken to be free from encumbrances other than those to which the charge for the company's debt was then subject[234].

(d) The onus of proof

[27.081] Before a disposition of corporate property will be deemed to be a fraudulent preference, it must be shown that it was made with a view to giving a creditor a preference over the other creditors. As with other cases where an intention is sought to be attributed to a company, the law will look to the dominant intentions of the controllers of the company, usually its directors[235], but occasionally its members[236].

[27.082] The general rule is that the task of proving an intention to prefer falls on the liquidator, as seen in *Corran Construction Company v Bank of Ireland Finance Ltd*[237] and other Irish cases. [238] In a case where a disposition within the meaning of CA 1963, s 286(1) is made in favour of a connected person as defined above, then there is a presumption that the disposition was made with a view to giving that person a preference over other

---

233 See *Ex p Tate* (1876) 35 LT 531, and Sanfey & Holohan, *Bankruptcy Law and Practice in Ireland* (1991), para 8.7.

234 CA 1963, s 287(2).

235 Note though that in *Kelleher v Continental Irish Meat Ltd* (9 May 1978, unreported), High Court, Costello J held that the intention of an employee to prefer was sufficient where he acted within his actual or ostensible authority.

236 See *Corran Construction Company v Bank of Ireland Finance Ltd* [1976–7] ILRM 175 at 178, where McWilliam J held that: '...I am bound to consider the matter on the basis of the intentions of the member of the company who was at that time in sole control of the affairs of the company'. There, the individual concerned was also a director.

237 *Corran Construction Company v Bank of Ireland Finance Ltd* [1976–7] ILRM 175, where *Peat v Gresham Trust Ltd* [1934] AC 252 and *Re FLE Holdings Ltd* [1967] 1 WLR 1409 were cited.

238 See also *Re Welding Plant Ltd; Cooney v Dargan* (27 June 1984, unreported), High Court, per McWilliam J, in MacCann, *A Casebook on Company Law* (1991), para 20.47. See also *Re Station Motors Ltd v Allied Irish Banks Ltd* [1985] IR 756.

creditors and thus a fraudulent preference. This amendment introduced by the CA 1990 is helpful to liquidators who, upon adducing evidence of a disposition in favour of a connected person, will see the evidential burden shift to the disponee to prove that the disposition was not a fraudulent preference.

(e) The intention to prefer

[27.083] There is a presumption that transactions entered into in favour of connected persons within the statutory time limit were with the intention of being a fraudulent preference. CA 1963, s 286(3) provides:

> 'A transaction to which subsection (1) applies in favour of a connected person which was made within two years before the commencement of the winding up of the company shall, unless the contrary is shown, be deemed in the event of the company being wound up —
>
> (a) to have been made with a view to giving such person a preference over the other creditors, and
>
> (b) to be a fraudulent preference,
>
> and be invalid accordingly.'

The power of such a presumption is evident from the decision of the English High Court in *Re Shapland Inc*[239]. In that case, a liquidator was successful in applying to have a charge set aside on the grounds of being a preference in circumstances where a company had entered into the charge in favour of its holding company within two years of its being wound up. It was held that the statutory presumption had not been displaced by the holding company[240].

[27.084] Other than in the case of connected persons, a liquidator must prove the intention of the company was that of preferring one creditor over another. While the difficult burden of proving fraud[241] is not required there is an equally difficult proof, namely that the act of preference arose from the free volition of the company to prefer a particular creditor. It is well accepted that where a creditor exerts such pressure on the debtor company so as to overbear the free volition of the company, there will be no fraudulent preference. In *Re Daly & Co*[242] Porter MR said:

> 'Where pressure exists so as to overbear the volition of the debtor a payment is not made with a view to prefer the creditor exerting it, but because the debtor cannot help it. The view to prefer is absent; or at least is not the real view, or motive or reason actuating the debtor...'

This has been said to be 'absurdly at odds with the aim of achieving an equitable distribution of the assets of an insolvent' company[243]. However, this is the established law and there are many cases where, upon proof that the company's will was overborne, the disposition was held not to be a fraudulent preference. Therefore, a fear of losing clients[244]

239 *Re Shapland Inc* [2000] BCC 106.

240 The statutory presumption is contained in the Insolvency Act 1986 (UK), s 239(6).

241 See Carroll J in *Re Station Motors Ltd* [1985] IR 756 and Porter MR in *Re Boyd* [1885–1886] 15 LR Ir 521.

242 *Re Daly & Co* [1887-8] 19 LR Ir 83 at 93.

243 See Ussher, *Company Law in Ireland* (1986), p 508.

244 See *Assignees of Taylor v Thompson* (1869–70) IRCL 129.

or a fear that failure to make the preference would bring about the demise of another company owned by the controller were both held to be sufficient to overbear the will of company controllers.

[27.085] In *Parkes & Sons Ltd v Hong Kong and Shanghai Banking Corporation*[245] a company's controller caused the company to enter into a guarantee and provide a mortgage in respect of the debts of another company. The controller was said to have been pressed by the bank for information, had many meetings with the bank, had the appointment of a receiver threatened, and had his affairs monitored closely by the bank. Blayney J held:

> 'It seems to me that the correct inference to draw from these facts is that [the controller] was concerned to save the claimant company and that this was his dominant motive in giving the mortgage. In view of the threat by the bank to put in a receiver, he had no alternative but to comply with their demand for further security. And while the giving of the mortgage may have taken some pressure off [his] personal guarantees, it did not relieve him from it or reduce his liability on it. In my opinion it has not been established that the facts are such that I should infer that [the controller's] dominant motive was to reduce his liability on the guarantees.'[246]

This case shows that personal gain to the person responsible for the company taking the decision to make a preference is not the decisive factor in the court's decision. Nevertheless, it is thought that evidence that the dominant intention for making the preference was in furtherance of the controller's personal interest ought to be a particularly strong reason in finding that a transaction was a fraudulent preference.

[27.086] In *Corran Construction Company v Bank of Ireland Finance Ltd*[247] the plaintiff-company deposited certain title deeds with the defendant-bank by way of an equitable deposit as security for a loan. The mortgage was not registered under CA 1963, s 99(1)[248]. Later, the bank became aware that the mortgage had not been registered and became concerned about the company's account. The bank persuaded the company to give a fresh equitable mortgage by deposit of title deeds which was then registered under s 99. Within six months of giving the fresh equitable mortgage the company was wound up. During the course of the winding up, the liquidator of the company sought to have the equitable mortgage set aside on the ground that it was a fraudulent preference. McWilliam J held that the liquidator had not established that there was an intention to make a fraudulent preference:

> 'I am satisfied that [the member-director] was anxious to keep the company going notwithstanding the advice of the accountant and his knowledge of the unfortunate state of the company's affairs...Although the defendant was not using pressure in the ordinary sense, I got the impression from the evidence that [the member-director] was trying to avoid their representatives because they had been continually trying to get back the money due to the defendant and that, when they finally caught up with him when he was ill in bed, it was something of a relief to find they would be satisfied if he would remedy some defect in the

245 *Parkes & Sons Ltd v Hong Kong and Shanghai Banking Corporation* [1990] ILRM 341.

246 [1990] ILRM 341 at 347–348.

247 *Corran Construction Company v Bank of Ireland Finance Ltd* [1976–7] ILRM 175.

248 See, generally, Chapter 21, *Corporate Borrowing: Registration of Charges.*

> mortgage. Although he undoubtedly appreciated that this would give the defendants security in case the company would not be able to pay the money back and should have appreciated that there was no real likelihood of the company being able to pay it back, this falls a long was short of making the deposit with the dominant intention of preferring the defendant over the other creditors.'

On this evidence it was held that there was not a fraudulent preference of the bank. The member-director's will had been overborne by the pressure applied by the bank to give a fresh mortgage.

[27.087] However, in *Station Motors Ltd v Allied Irish Bank Ltd*[249] Carroll J followed the decision in *Re M Kushler Ltd*[250] and held that:

> '...where there is no direct evidence of intention [to prefer] there is no rule of law which precludes a court from drawing an inference of an intention to prefer, in a case where some other possible explanation is open.'

There, a husband and wife were the controllers of a company which had a large overdraft with the defendant-bank. Furthermore, they had personally guaranteed the company's overdraft with the bank. When the company became insolvent, the husband and wife passed a resolution to put the company into creditors' voluntary liquidation. Before this happened they caused certain payments to be made into the company's overdrawn account so as to reduce the company's indebtedness to the bank, this having the indirect effect of reducing their personal exposure under the guarantees. Carroll J held that these payments were a fraudulent preference as they were made with the intention of preferring both the bank as a direct creditor and the directors themselves as guarantors of the company's overdraft. Among the facts which supported this conclusion were that:

— where the disposition has the effect of reducing personal exposure on guarantees, the court will find this to be a significant issue of fact in view of the strong element of private advantage;

— since the dispositions were made after they had resolved to call an EGM and creditors' meeting to put the company into creditors' voluntary winding up, they were aware that the company was insolvent; and

— of the cheques presented to the bank, only those which were to pay off the company's overdraft were honoured by the bank.

As a result, Carroll J held that the overwhelming evidence was that the lodgments were made to prefer the bank directly and the guarantors indirectly and this was the dominant purpose of the payments into the overdrawn account.

[27.088] The *Station Motors* case is a paradigm for the so-called 'guarantee-cases', whereby the controllers of a company cause the company to pay from its few assets, a liability to a bank where the controllers have given personal guarantees in respect of the company's indebtedness. Clearly, their act is self-serving, and will often be found to be a fraudulent preference. However, where the dominant intention is not to reduce one's personal liability, but is for another purpose, such as a fear that failure to make the disposition will result in another company having the financial rug pulled from under it, as

[249] *Station Motors Ltd v Allied Irish Bank Ltd* [1985] ILRM 756.

[250] [1943] 2 All ER 22, per Lord Greene MR.

in *Parkes & Sons Ltd v Hong Kong and Shanghai Banking Corp*[251], the preference will not necessarily be a fraudulent preference.

(f) The beneficiary of the disposition

[27.089] It is crucial to distinguish between a situation whereby a disposition is a *fraudulent preference* of one creditor over another, from where it is a *fraudulent disposition*[252]. CA 1963, s 286 is only concerned with fraudulent preferences. Thus, s 286 is concerned with transactions which are:

> '...in favour of any creditor, or of any person on trust for any creditor, with a view of giving such creditor, or any surety or guarantor for the debt due to such creditor, a preference over the other creditors...'

Thus, a disposition in favour of a person who is not a creditor (or a trustee of a creditor) of the company cannot be a fraudulent preference.

[27.090] This point is neatly illustrated by the decision of Blayney J in *Parkes & Sons Ltd v Hong Kong and Shanghai Banking Corporation*[253]. In that case a company entered into a guarantee and provided a mortgage in favour of the defendant-bank within six months of the commencement of its winding up. The facts were that a company (Walshe Kavanagh) was acquired by a Mr Collier who was the controller of the plaintiff-company. After he acquired control, the plaintiff-company's premises were destroyed by fire, and its business transferred to the premises of Walshe Kavanagh. Walshe Kavanagh was indebted in the amount of £200,000 to the defendant-bank and its indebtedness was personally guaranteed by Collier. Subsequently, Walshe Kavanagh ceased trading and the plaintiff-company purchased its entire stock. When the bank pressed for repayment, Collier agreed to cause Walshe Kavanagh to give an equitable mortgage by way of deposit of the title deeds to its premises. It was also agreed that the plaintiff-company would guarantee the loan to Walshe Kavanagh. The proceeds of sale of the plaintiff-company's former premises were to be used to discharge the indebtedness, and the companies' solicitors confirmed that following the release of the charge on the premises they would hold the monies on trust for the bank. Because of a problem with title, the defendant-bank began to press the controller for repayment and said it would not continue its support unless the plaintiff-company gave a mortgage of its property and its guarantee of the other company's indebtedness. This was eventually given at a time when both of the companies were insolvent. The bank agreed not to call in its security for a period of time. When both companies went into liquidation, it was argued, inter alia, that the guarantee and mortgage were fraudulent preferences.
It was held by Blayney J that these dispositions could not be fraudulent preferences because the bank was not a creditor of the plaintiff-company: the plaintiff-company did not in its own right owe the bank money. Construing the wording of CA 1963, s 286, Blayney J said:

> 'In my opinion the references in this section to a creditor or creditors in phrases "in favour of any creditor", and 'with a view to giving such creditor...a preference over the other creditors' must be construed as being references to a creditor or creditors of the person unable to pay

[251] *Re M Kushler Ltd* [1990] ILRM 341.

[252] See para **[27.092]**.

[253] *Re M Kushler Ltd* [1990] ILRM 341.

> his debts. What the section is concerned with is the bankrupt giving one of his creditors a preference over his other creditors. It is not concerned with someone other than the bankrupt paying off one of the bankrupt's creditors because such a person would have no obligation towards the other creditors, and so neither they nor the trustees in bankruptcy on their behalf, could have any ground for setting aside such a payment.'[254]

The liquidator had attempted to split the giving of the guarantee and the giving of the mortgage into two separate transactions. By so arguing the liquidator had hoped that the court would find that the plaintiff-company was a creditor on foot of its guarantee to the bank and that it had then made a fraudulent preference in the form of the mortgage. This argument was rejected by Blayney J who found that the guarantee and the mortgage constituted a single security, and that the plaintiff-company was not a debtor of the plaintiff bank at the time the mortgage was created.

[27.091] In England it has been held that it is immaterial that the disposition by way of fraudulent preference is far in excess of the amount owed, provided that it is in made in favour of a creditor. Accordingly, in *Re Clasper Group Services Ltd*[255], although the beneficiary of the disposition was owed approximately £60 in respect of damages for being dismissed from the company[256], he was paid £2000. Warner J held this was a fraudulent preference in spite of the vastly different payment made, and refused to find that the disposition was a fraudulent disposition, as distinguished in *Expo International Proprietary Ltd v Torma*[257]. Helpful to Warner J was the argument of the liquidator that had a small creditor been given a motor car in satisfaction of his claim, the liquidator would be entitled to the return of the car, and would not be confined to recovering a sum equal to the amount of his claim. It is thought that the decision in *Clasper* is not persuasive, and that while the sum ought to be recoverable by the liquidator, fraudulent disposition as opposed to fraudulent preference, is the appropriate remedy.

Fraudulent dispositions of property

[27.092] A fraudulent disposition of corporate property is liable to be subject to a court order that the property so disposed of be returned to the company. Section 139 of CA 1990 provides that a liquidator (voluntary or official), creditor or contributory of a company being wound up[258] can in certain circumstances apply to court for the return of property. To be successful in applying for such an order, it must be shown to the satisfaction of the court that:

> '(a) any property of the company of any kind whatsoever was disposed of either by way of conveyance, transfer, mortgage, security, loan, or in any way whatsoever whether by act or omission, direct or indirect, and,
>
> (b) the effect of such disposal was to perpetrate a fraud on the company, its creditors or members…'

Where this is proved to the satisfaction of the court then the court may:

---

[254] [1990] ILRM 341 at 345.

[255] *Re Clasper Group Services Ltd* [1989] BCLC 143.

[256] The beneficiary was the 16-year-old son of the controller of the company when he was dismissed.

[257] *Expo International Proprietary Ltd v Torma* [1985] 3 NSWLR 225.

[258] Or, receivers, by CA 1990, s 178 and examiners, by CA 1990, s 180(2).

> '...if it deems it just and equitable to do so, order any person who appears to have the use, control or possession of such property or the proceeds of the sale or development thereof to deliver it or pay a sum in respect of it to the liquidator on such terms or conditions as the court sees fit.'

A 'return' of property, if ordered, is made to the liquidator making it clear that the purpose of this provision is to 'swell the assets of the insolvent company'.

[27.093] It should be noted that an applicant under CA 1990, s 139 is not required to prove an intention to defraud, a difficult and problematic proof at the best of times. Rather, what is required to be shown is that the *effect* of the disposal *was to perpetrate a fraud* on the company, its creditors or members. It matters not what the *object* or *intention* was if the effect is to perpetrate a fraud and it is thought that when this provision is finally subjected to judicial interpretation that the courts will not require evidence of a subjective intent to defraud on the part of the company's controllers. It must, however, be shown that the effect of the disposal was to perpetrate a fraud. In this context it is submitted that by 'fraud' is meant the diversion of property from the entity or person who is lawfully entitled to it. An example would be where a company was owed money for goods or services rendered by a third party and that third party's payment was diverted away from the rightful recipient, the company, to another person or entity. Equally, a gratuitous disposition of company property in favour of, say, its controllers would have the effect of perpetrating a fraud on the company. Because company property is just that, 'company' property, the circumstances in which the effect of a disposal will be to perpetrate a fraud on members and creditors will be more rare than where the effect is to perpetrate a fraud on the company. In the case of members, the diversion of a dividend, properly declared before it was paid would be to perpetrate a fraud on members. As to creditors, an example of what is envisaged under this section might be where a creditor has acquired an equitable or beneficial interest in property belonging to a company and that property is disposed of to another person.

[27.094] Section 139(3) of CA 1990 goes on to provide that in exercising its just and equitable discretion, the court shall have regard to the rights of persons who have bona fide and for value acquired an interest in the property that is the subject matter of the application. This is not limited to persons who take from creditors, and extends to those who are the direct recipients of the disposition.

[27.095] It should also be remembered that a fraudulent conveyance or mortgage may be avoided under the Conveyances (Ireland) Act 1634[259]. That statute was successfully invoked by a liquidator in *Re Kill Inn Motel Ltd*[260] to set aside a mortgage in favour of a company's controller. Murphy J noted that it was the first time that that statute had been applied to a body corporate but said he saw no reason why it would not so apply.

[27.096] There is a distinction between fraudulent preferences and fraudulent dispositions, as Warner J observed in *Clasper Group Services Ltd*[261] when he said:

---

259 10 Charles 1. See generally Wylie, *Irish Conveyancing Statutes* (1994), pp 14–21.

260 *Re Kill Inn Motel Ltd* [1978–1987] Vol 3 ITR 706, (16 September 1987, unreported), High Court, per Murphy J).

261 *Clasper Group Services Ltd* [1989] BCLC 143 at 148.

> '...there is a distinction between a payment to a creditor as such and a payment which, albeit made to a person who is a creditor, is a sheer misapplication of the company's money.'

Section 139 of CA 1990 does not apply to fraudulent preferences, which are addressed by CA 1963, s 286. Section 139 can be analysed by counter reference to the limits of s 286 of the 1963 Act. Accordingly, it is irrelevant for the purposes of s 139 that the company was insolvent at the time of the disposition or that it was made to a creditor, or that the disposition was made within a certain time frame. There needs only to be a disposal where the effect is to perpetrate a fraud on the company, its creditors or its members[262].

Invalidating certain floating charges

[27.097] As seen in Chapter 20, *Corporate Borrowing: Debentures and Security,*[263] the essential nature of a floating charge is that it allows a company to continue to deal with its assets notwithstanding that they have been charged. It has been recognised by the legislature that the granting of a floating charge over the assets of a company exposes other creditors to the risk of continuing to give credit to the company for goods supplied, notwithstanding that those goods become the subject of a floating charge held by another creditor. For this reason the legislature has imposed certain statutory restrictions on the operation of floating charges. One such restriction[264] is that contained in CA 1963, s 288(1)[265] which provides:

> 'Where a company is being wound up, a floating charge on the undertaking or property of the company created within 12 months before the commencement of the winding up shall, unless it is proved that the company immediately after the creation of the charge was solvent, be invalid, except as to money actually advanced or paid, or the actual price or value of goods or services sold or supplied, to the company at the time of or subsequently to the creation of, and in consideration for the charge, together with interest on that amount at a rate of 5 per cent per annum.'

The effect of this provision is that once the conditions contained in s 288 are satisfied, the security provided by the floating charge becomes invalid. However, it is vital to note that even though a floating charge may be found to be invalid, the validity of the debt that it secured is unaffected and continues to remain valid. Rather than be invalidated, the debt becomes unsecured and the holder of the charge is relegated to the ranks of the unsecured creditors. The law applicable to invalid floating charges is considered under the following headings:

- (a) Proof of insolvency.
- (b) The operative time limits.
- (c) Invalid only where security unrealised on winding up.

---

262 See para **[27.089]**.

263 Chapter 20, *Corporate Borrowing: Debentures and Security*, para **[20.063]** *ff.*

264 Another restriction is that contained in CA 1963, s 285(7)(b) which provides that the preferential debts of a company: 'so far as the assets of the company available for payment of general creditors are insufficient to meet them, have priority over the claims of holders of debentures under any floating charge created by the company, and be paid accordingly out of any property comprised in or subject to that charge.' See para **[27.174]**.

265 As amended by CA 1990, s 136.

(d) Valid to extent of money actually advanced or paid.

(e) Other circumstances in which a floating charge is invalid.

(a) Proof of solvency

[27.098] In respect of floating charges created within the operative time limits, the onus is on the holder of the floating charge to prove that the company was solvent at the time of its creation[266] or that money or goods or services were advanced contemporaneously with the creation of the floating charge[267]. The onus is on the holder of the floating charge to uphold its validity since CA 1963, s 288(1) creates a presumption of invalidity where a floating charge is created within the operative time limits. The concept of solvency has been considered by the Supreme Court in *Re Creation Printing Company Ltd*[268] where the proposition that 'solvency equals assets exceeding liabilities' was rejected. Holding that the rejection of that proposition was established by the decided cases[269] Kenny J said:

> '...the test to be applied in determining this question is whether immediately after the debenture was given, the company was able to pay its debts as they became due. The question is not whether its assets exceed the estimated value its liabilities, or whether a business man would have regarded it as solvent...The question whether a company was solvent on a specified date is one of fact and it involves many difficult inferences. If there is, or is likely to be, a large deficiency of assets when the liquidation starts, the temptation to hold that the company was not solvent is strong. But the deficiency may have been caused by some change in economic or market conditions happening after the charge was given. So an examination of the financial history of the company, both before and after the charges were given, is necessary.'

This approach to determining solvency has been described as a 'cash flow test' rather than a 'balance sheet test'.[270] In *Re Creation Printing Company Ltd*, the company which went into liquidation had granted a floating charge on the undertaking of the company to secure money advanced by a bank to its parent company. The Supreme Court held that it was wrong to include the value of the company's fixed assets in considering the company's solvency because such were required for the purpose of generating income and would not, in the normal course of things, be sold by a company which intended to stay in business. Although the total assets of the company exceeded its liabilities, the company was held to be insolvent because its assets consisted mainly of fixed plant and machinery.

(b) The operative time limits

[27.099] In the case of a floating charge held by a person who is at arm's length to the company creating the floating charge, the operative time limit is 12 months from the date of the commencement of the winding up. Where however, the holder of the floating charge

---

266 See *Re Creation Printing Company Ltd; Crowley v Northern Bank Finance Co* [1981] IR 353 at 358, per Kenny J.

267 See para **[27.102]** *ff*.

268 *Re Creation Printing Company Ltd* [1981] IR 353, [1978] ILRM 219.

269 See *Ex p Russell* [1882] 19 Ch D 588; *Re Patrick and Lyon Ltd* [1933] Ch 786 and *Re Panama, New Zealand, and Australian Royal Mail Co* [1870] 5 Ch App 318.

270 See *Melbase Corporation Pty Ltd v Segenhoe Ltd* (1995) 17 ACSR 187. See also *Cuthbertson & Richards Pty Ltd v Thomas* [1999] Federal Court of Australia of 30 March 1999.

is a connected person, as defined above in relation to the law of fraudulent preference[271], the operative time limit is two years from the commencement of the winding up[272].

(c) Invalid only where security unrealised on winding up

[27.100] Section 288(1) of CA 1963 is directed at a situation where the floating charge has not crystallised at the commencement of the winding up. Consequently, where a floating charge is created within twelve months of the commencement of the winding up, but crystallises three months from the commencement, then that floating charge is not liable to be deemed invalid under s 288(1) although in the appropriate circumstances, it could be a fraudulent preference[273]. The rationale behind this principle is that once the floating charge crystallises, previously inchoate rights become choate and the floating charge becomes a quasi-fixed charge. This principle is supported by the Court of Appeal case in *Mace Builders (Glasgow) Ltd v Lunn*[274] where the holder of a floating charge caused the charge to crystallise by appointing himself receiver under the debenture. He then sold the charged assets and repaid himself. It was accepted that the company was insolvent at the date of the creation of the floating charge. The Court of Appeal, per Glidewell LJ, concluded that the holder of the charge was not obliged to repay the money to the company although it was created within 12 months from the commencement of the winding up. The reasoning was based on a literal interpretation of the wording of the then corresponding English section:

> 'The opening words are "Where a company is being wound up..." The section thus has no application unless and until the company is being wound up. It would follow that if, for example, the company had mortgaged any part of its assets, otherwise than by a floating charge...after the creation of the floating charge and before the winding up, the defendant could have claimed, and would have been granted, a declaration that his rights had priority over those of a subsequent mortgagee...The application of [the section] at that time would have been entirely speculative. Yet if counsel's argument for the plaintiff is accepted, the result would be that...immediately following the commencement of the winding up, the same court would have to declare that, contrary to what it had previously declared, the defendant had no such priority and, retrospectively, had never had any such priority. I am loath to accept, in the absence of much clearer words, that Parliament intended so Gilbertian a situation, ie order, counter-order, disorder.'[275]

The court was further supported in its view by considering that no protection was given to a bona fide purchaser for value of the company's assets.

[27.101] Although uncertain, a distinction has been drawn between a situation where assets subject to a floating charge have been realised and paid over to the charge holder by the receiver and where the receiver still has possession of the realised proceeds of sale. In the New Zealand case of *Re Port Supermarket Ltd*[276] it was held that where a receiver had not completed the realisation of assets subject to a floating charge when a liquidator was

---

271 See para **[27.076]**.

272 By CA 1963, s 288(3), as inserted by CA 1990, s 136.

273 See para **[27.072]** *ff*.

274 *Mace Builders (Glasgow) Ltd v Lunn* [1987] Ch 191, [1987] BCLC 55. The trial judgment of Scott J is reported at [1985] BCLC 154.

275 [1987] BCLC 55 at 58–59.

276 *Re Port Supermarket Ltd* [1978] NZLR 330, noted by *Milman* [1980] NILQ 255.

appointed, the receiver was obliged to pay what he had over to the liquidator, and that the liquidator could set the floating charge aside. Perhaps the distinction lies in the fact that while the courts are disinclined to upset a charge holder's rights where he is in possession of realised proceeds, where a receiver has not paid the proceeds over, his status as agent for the company has a significance. Such a distinction is hard to justify, and is motivated by a judicial attitude, set against floating charges. It is arguable that courts are obliged to accept the priority of the charge holder for as long as the Irish legislature has not taken the step taken in England[277], defining 'floating charge' as including all charges which were '*originally created*' as floating charges.

(d) Valid to extent of money actually advanced or paid

[27.102] Section 288(1) of CA 1963 provides that a floating charge shall not be invalid as to money actually advanced or paid, or to the actual price or value of goods or services sold or supplied to the company at the time of or subsequent to the creation of and in consideration for the charge. However, the interest rate permitted in such circumstances is not that provided for in the debenture, but rather, is determined by s 288(1) as 5% per annum.

[27.103] This important saver for a floating charge operates on the rationale that there is a distinction between a situation where a previously unsecured creditor takes a floating charge to secure advances made in the past, and a situation where the floating charge holder advances *fresh* money to the company at the time of the creation of the charge. Although the company creates a floating charge over its assets, it also receives consideration. An example of the operation of this saver is provided by *Re Lakeglen Construction Ltd*[278] where a floating charge created in favour of theretofore unsecured creditors in consideration for their *past advances* of money to the company, was held to be invalid.

[27.104] Money advanced between the time it was agreed to create the floating charge and its actual creation has been held to be a fresh advance. In the Irish case of *Re Daniel Murphy Ltd*[279] it was said that the delay between the agreement to give the floating charge and the creation of the floating charge, must not have been with a view to deceive creditors. The delay there of 55 days was held not to have been unreasonable because the solicitors acting for both parties acted as fast as they would have done in any other transaction. The court also held that the requirement that the fresh advance be made, in consideration for the charge, does not mean that the advance must be given simultaneously with the charge. It has been accepted by the High Court in *Smurfit Paribas Bank Ltd v AAB Export Finance Ltd (No 2)*[280] that there is no one firm test to be applied in determining how long a time may elapse between the first payment and the execution of the charge for the proviso in CA 1963, s 288(1) to be excluded[281]. However, Barron J did give guidance as to what might validate a floating charge which was created within the operative time limit:

277 See the Insolvency Act 1986 (UK), s 251.

278 *Re Lakeglen Construction Ltd* [1980] IR 347.

279 *Re Daniel Murphy Ltd* [1964] IR 1.

280 *Smurfit Paribas Bank Ltd v AAB Export Finance Ltd (No 2)* [1991] 2 IR 19.

281 [1991] 2 IR 19 at 29, where Barron J cited Farwell LJ in *Re Columbian Fireproofing Co Ltd* [1910] 2 Ch 120 at 123; Powell J in *Re Olderfleet Shipbuilding & Engineering Co* [1922] 1 IR 26 at 41 and Maugham J in *Re F and E Stanton Ltd* [1929] 1 Ch 180 at 193–194.

> 'In order to treat payments made to the company before the execution of the charge as payments made at the time of the charge, the necessary elements to be established are:– an honest transaction; advances made before the execution of the charge and reasonable expedition in and about the preparation and execution of the charge. Whether or not these particular elements have been established will depend upon the circumstances of each case.'[282]

Barron J held that the security could not be validated in that case because, inter alia, of the unreasonable delay in putting the floating charge in place: two years and three months. There, two lenders had proposed entering into a deed of postponement whereby the second lender's debt would be postponed to the first lender's debt. However, this was never actually executed due to delay on the part of the first lender. In the circumstances, Barron J held that it would not be unconscionable for the second lender to insist on a strict construction of the contract, and so was entitled to priority in the company's subsequent liquidation. Forbearance to sue has been held not to constitute 'cash paid': *Re Lakeglen Construction Ltd*[283].

(e) Other circumstances in which a floating charge is invalid

[27.105] Section 289(1) of CA 1963 provides that where:

— a company is being wound up,

— and within 12 months of the commencement, the company was indebted to an officer of the company[284],

— and the indebtedness was discharged wholly or partly by the company or any other person,

— and the company created a floating charge on any of its assets or property within 12 months before the commencement of the winding up, in favour of the officer to whom the company was indebted,

then without prejudice to rights or liabilities arising apart from this section:

> '...such charge shall be invalid to the extent of the repayment referred to...unless it is proved that the company immediately after the creation of the charge was solvent.'

Subsection (3) provides that in this section 'officer' includes the spouse, child or nominee of an officer.

Contribution by related companies to the assets

[27.106] Section 140 of CA 1990 introduced a new means by which a liquidator can bolster or swell the assets of the company being wound up: by applying to court for an order directing that a related company contribute to its assets. Section 140(1) provides:

> 'On the application of the liquidator or any creditor or contributory of any company that is being wound up, the court, if it is satisfied that it is *just and equitable* to do so, may order that any company that is or has been related to the company being wound up shall pay to the liquidator of that company an amount equivalent to the whole or part of all or any of the

282 [1991] 2 IR 19 at 30.

283 *Re Lakeglen Construction Ltd* [1980] IR 347.

284 Defined by sub-s (3) as including 'the spouse, child or nominee of an officer'.

debts provable in the winding up. Any order under this section may be made on such terms and conditions as the court thinks fit.'

This far reaching provision, which strikes at the root of group trading and the principle in *Salomon v Salomon & Co*[285], is designed to prevent companies creating a number of subsidiaries, using them to make profit, and then casting them (and their creditors) aside when they become insolvent[286]. Now, the court is empowered to order companies which are, or were, related, to contribute to the assets of the subsidiary which is being wound up[287]. The following issues raised by contribution orders are next considered:

(a) The concept of related company.

(b) Retrospectivity of application.

(c) Jurisdiction to grant a contribution order.

(a) The concept of related company

[27.107] A company is *related* to another company under CA 1990, s 140(5) if:

(a) the other is its holding or subsidiary company; or

(b) more than half in nominal value of the equity share capital[288] is held of the other company, and companies related to that company, directly or indirectly, but not in a fiduciary capacity; or

(c) more than half in nominal value of the equity share capital[289] of each of them is held by members of the other company, directly or indirectly, but not in a fiduciary capacity; or

(d) that other company or a company or companies related to that company or that other company together with a company or companies related to it are entitled to exercise or control the exercise of more than one half of the voting power at any general meeting of the company; or

(e) the businesses of the companies have been so carried on that the separate business of each company, or a substantial part thereof, is not readily identifiable; or

(f) there is another company to which both companies are related.

'Related company' is deemed to have a corresponding meaning. Subsection (7) defines 'company' as a company which is liable to be wound up under the Companies Acts[290], and defines 'creditor' as one or more creditors to whom the company being wound up is indebted by more, in aggregate, than €12,697.38.

[27.108] By any standards, the scope of CA 1990, s 140 is very wide. Not only will a company be deemed to be related where (within the meaning of CA 1963, s 155) the company is part of a group of companies, but the reference in (e) means that companies which are members of a *de facto* group of companies may also be related companies. This

---

285 [1897] AC 22. See Chapter 4, *Incorporation and its Consequences*, para **[4.026]** *ff*.

286 A practice noted in *Re Southard & Co Ltd* [1979] 1 WLR 1198, per Templeman LJ.

287 See Templeman LJ's analogy and acknowledged mixed metaphor, *Re Southard & Co Ltd* [1979] 1 WLR 1198.

288 As defined by CA 1963, s 155.

289 CA 1963, s 155.

290 See Chapter 25, *Winding Up Companies*, para **[25.032]**.

could, for example, arise where two or more companies are owned and controlled by the same person or persons[291].

(b) Retrospectivity of application

[27.109] Although CA 1990, s 140 provides that an order to contribute can be made where a company is or was related, where the company was related *before* the coming into force of s 140, an order should not be made where the companies have not been related after the coming into operation of the Act. Such a view may be supported by the decisions in *Re Hefferon Kearns Ltd*[292] *and Re Chestvale Properties Ltd*[293] and the extreme implications for property rights resulting from a contribution order being made.

(c) Jurisdiction to grant a contribution order

[27.110] Section 140(2) of CA 1990 provides that in deciding whether or not it is just and equitable to make a contribution order against a related company, the court shall have regard to the following matters:

(a) the extent to which the related company took part in the management of the company being wound up,

(b) the conduct of the related company towards the creditors of the company being wound up,

(c) the effect which such order would be likely to have on the creditors of the related company concerned.

The first two guidelines for judicial discretion aim at establishing a causal link between the conduct of the related company and the misfortune of the company being wound up. The third guideline recognises that the creditors of the company which the order is made against stand to be prejudiced by the contribution order. In this regard, a court must surely be loath to make an order where innocent creditors will be prejudiced. To deem creditors to have constructive notice[294] of charges created by a company may be harsh; to have the debts of another company paid by the company with which they traded is draconian. Subsection (4) provides that it shall *not* be just and equitable if the *only* ground which would justify the order is either:

(a) the fact that a company is related to another company, or,

(b) that the creditors of the company being wound up have relied on the fact that another company is or has been related to the first mentioned company.

Notably, a court cannot make an order based on the mere fact that the company being wound up is related to another company. Being a related company grounds the jurisdiction to hear an application, but unless there is more, a court cannot exercise its discretion to make a contribution order.

[27.111] Although the court's jurisdiction to make a contribution order is broad, it is vital to recognise that some culpability on the part of the company which is sought to be made

---

[291] On groups of companies see Warnock, 'Inter-Company Relationships and Section 31 of the Companies Act 1990' (1994) CLP 243.

[292] *Re Hefferon Kearns Ltd* [1992] ILRM 51.

[293] *Re Chestvale Properties Ltd* [1992] ILRM 221.

[294] See Chapter 20, *Corporate Borrowing: Debentures and Security*, para **[20.075]**.

the subject of a contribution order is required. By CA 1990, s 140(3) the court is expressly prohibited from making a contribution order, *unless*:

> '...the court is satisfied that the circumstances that gave rise to the winding up of the company are attributable to the actions or omissions of the related company.'

From this it is clear that an applicant must prove that the related company was the cause of the other being wound up. Nevertheless, it is thought that this new provision will undoubtedly be of great importance in assisting a liquidator to realise assets of not only the company in liquidation but also of companies whose conduct caused the company in liquidation to fail.

Pooling the assets of related companies

[27.112] Another weapon in a liquidator's armoury is CA 1990, s 141 which goes further than merely ordering another company to contribute to the assets of a company being wound up. Section 141 allows a court to order that the assets of a related company which is also being wound up should be pooled between the creditors of both companies. The empowering provision is s 141(1), which provides that:

> 'Where two or more related companies are being wound up and the court, on the application of the liquidator of any of the companies, is satisfied that it is *just and equitable* to make an order under this section, the court may order that, subject to such *terms and conditions* as the court may impose and to the extent that the court orders, the companies shall be wound up together as if they were one company, and, subject to the provisions of this section, the order shall have effect and all the provisions of this Part and Part VI of the Principal Act shall apply accordingly.'

The net effect of this provision is that upon application to have a related company wound up, the assets of two or more companies can be realised together, and then distributed amongst the creditors of all the companies. Clearly, this will be of benefit to the creditors of the insolvent company, only where the related company is sufficiently solvent to pay the creditors of both companies. Because the rights and interests of related companies will be affected by the making of such an order, s 141(6) provides that notice of an application for such an order must be served on every company specified in the application and on such other persons as the court may direct not later than the eighth day before the day on which the application is heard. Here the following issues which arise in the context of pooling orders are considered:

(a) The court's terms and conditions.

(b) The jurisdiction to make a pooling order.

(c) The consequences of a pooling order.

(a) The court's terms and conditions

[27.113] Section 141(2) of CA 1990 provides that the court, in deciding upon what terms and conditions it should make a pooling order, should have particular regard to the interests of those persons who are members of some, but not all, of the companies which are the subject matter of the order. In this we see the recognition that in exercising its just and equitable discretion, the court may have regard to a wide number of factors.

(b) The jurisdiction to make a pooling order

[27.114] The jurisdiction to make a pooling order only applies to companies which are related within the meaning of CA 1990, s 140(5) considered above[295]. The discretion of the court is again based on a determination of what is just and equitable in the circumstances. Here, the factors which a court must consider in exercising its equitable discretion are:

— the extent to which any of the companies took part in the management of any of the other companies;

— the conduct of any of the companies towards the creditors of any of the other companies;

— the extent to which the circumstances that gave rise to the winding up of any of the companies are attributable to the actions or omissions of any of the other companies;

— the extent to which the businesses of the companies have been intermingled.

The first three factors are also relevant where the court is asked to make a contribution order, although the third is a basic prerequisite to the court making a contribution order whereas in the context of a pooling order it is but a factor in deciding what is just and equitable. The fourth factor, the concept of *intermingling*, is a new and strange concept to practitioners and academics alike. Just how broad or narrow this will prove to be remains in the realm of speculation pending judicial analysis. Again, s 141(5) provides that certain factors shall not alone warrant the remedy, namely that a company is, without more, related to another company, or that the creditors of a company being wound up have relied on the fact that another company is or has been related to the first mentioned company.

(c) The consequences of a pooling order

[27.115] Where the court makes a pooling order, CA 1990, s 141(3) provides that the court is empowered to remove any liquidator of any of the companies and appoint any person to act as liquidator of any one or more of the companies. The wide control and supervision which the court has after an order is made is seen in the fact that it may give such directions as it thinks fit for the purpose of giving effect to the order[296].

[27.116] Section 141(3)(c) of CA 1990 provides that nothing in the section or any court order shall affect the rights of any secured creditor of any of the companies. This implies that the security of both fixed and floating charge holders will remain unaffected. In particular, holders of floating charges will not have their charges placed after the claims of preferential creditors in companies other than their own debtor company: s 141(3)(d). As to the claims of unsecured creditors of the companies whose assets are pooled, unless the court orders otherwise their claims shall rank equally among themselves.

Claims against contributories

[27.117] One of the first duties of a liquidator is to settle a list of contributories of the company being wound up[297]. A contributory is a person who is liable under CA 1963,

---

[295] See para **[27.107]**.

[296] On the question of liquidator's conflict of interest where appointed to two companies, see: *Re P Turner (Wilsden) Ltd* [1987] BCLC 149.

[297] RSC, Ord 74, rr 86-89.

s 207 to contribute to the assets of a company that is being wound up[298]. Moreover, for the purposes of all proceedings for determining, and all proceedings prior to final determination of, the persons who are to be deemed contributories, includes any person alleged to be a contributory[299]. Section 207(1) of CA 1963 provides:

> 'In the event of a company being wound up, every present and past member shall be liable to contribute to the assets of the company to an amount sufficient for payment of its debts and liabilities, and the costs, charges and expenses of the winding up, and for the adjustment of the rights of the contributories among themselves, subject to subsection (2) and the following qualifications:
>
> (a) a part member shall not be liable to contribute if he has ceased to be a member for one year or more before the commencement of the winding up;
>
> (b) a past member shall not be liable to contribute in respect of any debt or liability of the company contracted after he ceased to be a member;
>
> (c) a past member shall not be liable to contribute unless it appears to the court that the existing members are unable to satisfy the contributions required to be made by them in pursuance of this Act;
>
> (d) in the case of a company limited by shares, no contribution shall be required from any member exceeding the amount, if any, unpaid on the shares in respect of which he is liable as a present or past member;
>
> (e) in the case of a company limited by guarantee, no contribution shall, subject to subsection (3), be required from any member exceeding the amount undertaken to be contributed by him to the assets of the company in the event of its being wound up;
>
> (f) nothing in this Act shall invalidate any provision contained in any policy of insurance or other contract whereby the liability of individual members on the policy or contract is restricted, or whereby the funds of the company are alone made liable in respect of the policy or contract;
>
> (g) a sum due to any member of the company, in his character of a member, by way of dividends, profits or otherwise, shall not be deemed to be a debt of the company, payable to that member in a case of competition between himself and any other creditor not a member of the company, but any such sum may be taken into account for the purpose of the final adjustment of the rights of the contributories among themselves.'

The liability of a contributory creates a debt accruing due from him at the time when his liability commenced, but payable at the times when calls are made for enforcing the liability[300]. An action to recover a debt from a contributory must be brought within 12 years from the date on which the cause of action accrued[301]. The personal representatives of a deceased contributory are liable to contribute to the assets of the company and are themselves deemed to be contributories[302]. Bankrupt contributories are represented by the official assignee in bankruptcy who is also deemed to be a contributory[303].

---

298 CA 1963, s 208. See Chapter 25, *Winding Up Companies*, para **[25.040]**.

299 CA 1963, s 208.

300 CA 1963, s 209(1).

301 CA 1963, s 209(2).

302 CA 1963, s 210(1).

303 CA 1963, s 211(a).

[27.118] It is CA 1963, s 207(1)(d) which means that the liability of members of private companies limited by shares is limited to the amount, if any, 'unpaid on the shares'; and s 207(1)(e) which limits the liability of members of private companies limited by guarantee to the amount undertaken to be contributed by him. Therefore, in the vast majority of private companies, liquidators will not realise much, if any, money from the contributories of insolvent companies. This is because: first, the vast majority of companies are limited companies which have a nominal paid-up share capital, and secondly, very few trading companies are unlimited companies. For many Irish private companies, this means that where a company has two €1 shares, the holders' liability is limited to €1 each, unless they have already paid this. Other persons liable to contribute are those rarest of creatures, directors with unlimited liability[304].

[27.119] Where contributories do, however, have a liability to contribute towards a company's debts, there may be a temptation to evade their liabilities. One means of preventing contributories from attempting to evade their liabilities is CA 1963, s 218, considered already in the context of post-commencement dispositions of property[305], which provides also that:

> 'In a winding up by the court...any transfer of shares or alteration in the status of the members of the company, made after the commencement of the winding up, shall, unless the court otherwise orders, be void.'

Section 255 of CA 1963 provides that any transfer of shares, *other than with the liquidator's sanction*, or any alteration in the status of members after the commencement of a voluntary winding up is also void. As in the case of any dispositions of property by a company, this aspect to s 218 does not become operational until the company is being wound up *ie* in an official liquidation, from the date of the presentation of the petition to have the company wound up[306]. In a voluntary winding up the operative time for s 255 is the time of the passing of the resolution to wind up the company.

[27.120] By CA 1963, s 238 the court is only empowered to make calls on any of the contributories to the extent of their liability:

> '...for payment of any money which the court considers necessary to satisfy the debts and liabilities of the company, and the costs, charges and expenses of winding up, and for the adjustment of the rights of the contributories amongst themselves, and make an order for payment of any calls so made.'

The court may make such calls even though it has not ascertained the sufficiency of the assets of the company. 'Calls' on contributories are governed by the Rules of the Superior Courts 1986[307]. This is however subject to a number of major qualifications contained in CA 1963, s 207.

---

304 By CA 1963, s 197 the directors of a limited liability company may themselves have unlimited liability where this is provided for in the company's memorandum of association. See also CA 1963, s 207(2).

305 See para **[27.058]**.

306 See *Re Tumacacori Mining Co* (1874) LR 17 Eq 534; *Caratti Holding Co Party Ltd v Zampatti* [1975] WAR 183.

307 RSC, Ord 74, rr 92–94.

[27.121] Section 209 of CA 1963 provides that the liability of a contributory creates a debt due from him at the time when his liability commenced, but payable at the times when calls are made by a liquidator for enforcing his liability. Calls against contributories survive their demise, and are payable out of their estate: CA 1963, s 210. Where a contributory becomes bankrupt the Official Assignee shall represent him: CA 1963, s 211. Section 236 of CA 1963 empowers the court to require a contributory on the list of contributories to pay, deliver, convey, surrender or transfer forthwith, or within such time as the court directs, any money, property or books and papers in his hands to which the company is prima facie entitled. Section 237 of CA 1963 empowers the court to order a contributory to pay any money due by him to the company.

Voidable transactions

[27.122] Most transactions entered into by companies in contravention of the provisions of the Companies Acts 1963–2001 are avoided when the company is in liquidation. Frequently, the instigator of such avoidance will be the liquidator. His motivation for seeking to invalidate transactions will be his desire to swell the assets of the company which is in liquidation to facilitate the distribution of those assets in accordance with law.

[27.123] In examining the affairs of a company which is being wound up, liquidators will often scrutinise transactions for evidence that they are ultra vires the company[308]; an abuse of the directors' powers or outside of the directors' authority[309]; or, in contravention of provisions such as CA 1963, s 60[310] or CA 1990, ss 29 or 31[311]. Where evidence of such abuses is found the liquidator may succeed in avoiding guarantees entered into by the company, mortgages or charges of the company's property or other dispositions of the company's property.

Litigating to swell corporate assets

[27.124] Closely related to where a liquidator will seek to invalidate transactions is where he institutes proceedings against individuals or companies who appear to have *wronged* the company that is in liquidation. A liquidator may continue or initiate such proceedings with the leave of the court[312]. In such proceedings he will have no greater rights than those enjoyed by the company.

[27.125] Often the liquidator may have reason to believe that those behind the company, whether directors, shadow directors or others, are responsible for causing the company loss. In such circumstances, he may issue proceedings against those persons under specific statutory provisions such as those on reckless trading or fraudulent trading and for other breaches of duty or trust in misfeasance proceedings under CA 1963, s 298[313]. In an appropriate case, a liquidator may seek an order for interrogatories under Ord 31, r 2 of the

---

308 See Chapter 7, *Corporate Contracts, Capacity and Authority*, para **[7.043]** *ff*.

309 See Chapter 7, *Corporate Contracts, Capacity and Authority*, para **[7.096]** *ff*.

310 See Chapter 18, *The Maintenance of Capital*, para **[18.041]** *ff*.

311 See Chapter 11, *Statutory Regulation of Transactions Involving Directors and their Companies*, para **[11.096]** *ff*.

312 CA 1963, s 231(1)(a). See, generally, Chapter 26, *Liquidators*, para **[26.028]** *ff*.

313 See generally Chapter 10, *Duties of Directors and Other Officers*.

Rules of the Superior Courts 1986[314]. Where a liquidator is successful in such proceedings, any claims that a director might have against the company cannot be set-off against what he is ordered to pay the company[315].

[27.126] Certain causes of action open to liquidators may not, however, fall properly to be classified as 'property' of the company. So in *Re Floor Fourteen Ltd; Lewis v Inland Revenue Commissioners*[316] Peter Gibson LJ accepted the following statement of law:

> 'In *Re Oasis Merchandising Services Ltd* [1997] 1 BCLC 689 this court drew a distinction between the property of the company existing at the commencement of the liquidation and assets which arise only after the liquidation of the company and are recoverable only by the liquidator pursuant to the statutory powers conferred on him. The right of action of a liquidator for preferences or wrongful trading and the fruits of such an action were said by this court not to be the property of the company but to be held on the statutory trust for distribution by the liquidator, and that distinction was said to be supported by a number of authorities including *Re MC Bacon Ltd (No 2)* [1990] BCLC 607'.[317]

The distinction between property of the company and property held on a statutory trust by a liquidator for distribution holds good here in the context of, say fraudulent trading, reckless trading, failure to keep proper books of account or indeed any statutory provision which allows application be made to impose personal liability 'for all, or such part as may be specified by the court, of the debts and other liabilities of the company'. In the case of other claims – claims that properly belong to the company – such as claims for breach of directors' duties, trust, negligence or other actionable wrong, including misfeasance under CA 1963, s 298, it is thought that such actions are properly classified as 'company property'. This is because at the commencement of the winding up the company had a right to sue the defendants. That right to sue is a chose in action that was the company's property and all that happens to it is that it is 'realised' by the liquidator.

[B] THE DISTRIBUTION OF CORPORATE ASSETS

Distribution of assets: basic principles

[27.127] Having realised all corporate assets, the task which next falls to the liquidator is the distribution of those assets amongst the creditors of the company in accordance with the Companies Acts 1963–2001. In *Re Lines Bros Ltd*[318] Brightman LJ said:

> '...the making of a winding-up order brings into operation a statutory scheme for dealing with the assets of a company which is being wound up. It matters not whether the winding up is by order or pursuant to a resolution. The assets of the company when realised provide a fund which the liquidator administers in many respects, but not in all, as if he were managing a trust fund. Creditors' contractual rights to be paid by the company become under the statutory scheme a statutory right to a share in the trust fund.'

---

[314] See *Money Markets International Stock Brokers Ltd v Fanning* [2000] 3 IR 437. See, generally, Courtney, *Mareva Injunctions and Related Interlocutory Orders* (1998), para [10.36].

[315] *Re Greendale Developments Ltd* [1998] 1 IR 8. See para **[27.141]**.

[316] *Re Floor Fourteen Ltd; Lewis v Inland Revenue Commissioners* [2001] 2 BCLC 392.

[317] [2001] 2 BCLC 392 at 404.

[318] *Re Lines Bros Ltd* [1983] Ch 1 at 14.

Having considered the realisation of assets, this section now considers the following issues in the distribution of assets:

1. The statutory basis for distribution.
2. Assets not available for distribution by liquidators.
3. The costs and expenses of winding up.
4. Proof of debts by the company's creditors.
5. Priorities in distribution.
6. Distributions in specie.

The statutory basis for distribution

[27.128] The process of distribution and the task of the liquidator is somewhat similar to that of the administrator of the estate of a deceased person, in that the latter must distribute the estate of the deceased in accordance with the Succession Act 1965. A more analogous situation is where the Official Assignee, after realising the assets of the bankrupt, must distribute them amongst the bankrupt's creditors[319]. Indeed, it is this process of the distribution of a bankrupt's estate[320] upon which the laws of corporate insolvent distribution are based. This is because CA 1963, s 284(1) provides:

> 'In the winding up of an insolvent company the same rules shall prevail and be observed relating to the prospective rights of the secured and unsecured creditors and to debts provable and to the valuation of annuities and future and contingent liabilities as are in force for the time being under the law of bankruptcy relating to the estates of persons adjudged bankrupt, and all persons who in any such case would be entitled to prove for and receive dividends out of the assets of the company may come in under the winding up and make such claims against the company as they respectively are entitled to by virtue of this section.'

The effect of this provision is that the laws of distribution of a bankrupt's estate embodied in the Bankruptcy Act 1988 (which replaced the ancient Irish Bankrupt and Insolvent Act 1857) apply in a corporate insolvency[321]. However, before considering distribution amongst the creditors of the insolvent company, it is necessary to consider those assets that are in the ostensible ownership of a company but which are beneficially owned by someone else.

Assets not available for distribution by liquidators

[27.129] Not all assets that a liquidator realises or which appear to be in the apparent ownership of a company in liquidation may be available, in fact, for distribution to its

---

319 In *Oakes v Turquand* (1867) LR 2 HL 325 Lord Cranworth said (at 363): 'The winding up is but a mode of enforcing payment. It closely resembles a bankruptcy, and a bankruptcy has been called, not improperly, a statutable execution for the benefit of all creditors. The same description may be given to a winding up'.

320 See generally, Sanfey & Holohan, *Bankruptcy Law and Practice in Ireland* (1991).

321 Many cases have applied the laws of bankruptcy to corporate insolvent distribution, for example, *Re McCairns (PMPA) Plc* [1990] ILRM 501, noted by Woulfe, (1989) DULJ 113; and *Re Hibernian Transport Company Ltd* [1990] ILRM 42 where different interpretations were given to the applicable laws of bankruptcy, discussed below. Cf the judgment of Nourse J in *Barclays Bank Ltd et al v TOSG Trust fund Ltd et al* [1984] BCLC 1 at 25g–h.

creditors and contributories. Certain assets are *not available* for distribution. Five classes of assets that are unavailable for distribution can be identified:

(a) Assets subject to a fixed mortgage or charge.

(b) Assets that are held in trust.

(c) Monies that must be set-off.

(d) Super-preferential debts that are trust monies.

(e) Stamp duty on monies received in realisation of company assets.

(a) Assets subject to a fixed mortgage or charge

[27.130] By reason of CA 1963, s 284(1) 'the same rules shall prevail and be observed relating to the respective rights of secured and unsecured creditors' in an insolvent winding up as are in force under the law of bankruptcy[322]. In the law of bankruptcy the general rule of creditors' rights is set out in the Bankruptcy Act 1988, s 136(1). This provides:

> 'On the making of an order of adjudication, a creditor to whom the bankrupt is indebted for any debt provable in bankruptcy shall not have any remedy against the property or person of the bankrupt in respect of the debt apart from his rights under this Act, and he shall not commence any proceedings in respect of such debts unless with the leave of the court and on such terms as the court may impose.'

However, there is an exception to this general rule in favour of *secured creditors*. Section 136(2) of the Bankruptcy Act 1988 provides:

> 'This section shall not affect the power of a secured creditor to realise or otherwise deal with his security in the same manner as he would have been entitled to realise or deal with it if this section had not been enacted.'

Accordingly, the power of a secured creditor[323] to realise or otherwise deal with his security is unaffected by the general rule. Secured creditors can proceed against their security and can remain outside the winding-up process.

[27.131] It may be noted that not all secured creditors are entitled to realise their securities in priority to all other creditors or to stand outside the winding up. Holders of floating charges are subordinated to the claims of preferential creditors[324]; holders of fixed charges over book debts may also be postponed and rank after the Revenue Commissioners[325]. Notwithstanding these legislative claw-backs, the holder of a fixed charge or fixed mortgage is entitled to remain outside a winding up and to rely on his own security to discharge the debt owed to him[326].

---

322 For the full text of CA 1963, s 284(1) see para **[27.128]**.

323 *Secured creditor* is defined by the Bankruptcy Act 1988, s 3 as meaning: 'any creditor holding any mortgage, charge or lien on the debtor's estate or any part thereof as security for a debt due to him'.

324 See para **[27.174]**.

325 See Chapter 20, *Corporate Borrowing: Debentures and Security*, para **[20.052]**.

326 See para **[27.132]**. On the question of the payment of court fees incurred in a court sale of charged property, see *Re McCairns (PMPA) plc* [1992] ILRM 19 where the Supreme Court reversed Costello J, reported at [1989] ILRM 501. See also *Re Michael Orr (Kilternan) Ltd* [1986] IR 273.

[27.132] Although a secured creditor can remain outside of a winding up he is *not obliged* to do so[327]. Where a company is wound up insolvent a secured creditor is afforded a number of options by virtue of the operation of the Bankruptcy Act 1988, Sch 1, para 24. These options are:

— Realise the security and prove for the shortfall.

— Value the security and prove for the shortfall.

— Surrender the security and prove for the whole debt.

Where a secured creditor opts to realise his security and prove for the shortfall, para 24(1) provides that any dividends he receives from the general creditors' fund cannot disturb any dividend which is then already declared. The second option is to value the security and prove for the shortfall. Where this option is chosen para 24(2) provides that, before ranking for dividend, he must state in his proof the particulars of his security, the date on which it was given and the value at which he assesses it. He shall then be entitled to receive a dividend only in respect of the balance due to him after deducting the assessed value of his security. Secured creditors will be slow to under-estimate the value of their security in the hope of a windfall. A number of deterrents exist: the liquidator may redeem it on payment of the assessed value or require that the property be put up for sale[328]; the creditor will only be able to amend the valuation where he shows to the court that the valuation and proof were made bona fide on a mistaken belief[329]; and where a valuation is amended, any excess dividend received must be repaid[330]. The third option open to a secured creditor is to surrender the security and prove for the whole debt. It can readily be imagined that this option will very rarely be taken. Only where the value of the security is virtually worthless will a secured creditor surrender his security and take his chances with the company's unsecured creditors.

[27.133] Often a secured creditor will choose to remain outside of the winding up and to realise his security. Obviously, he will not have to prove for the shortfall where there is none. Where there is a surplus over after his debt is paid from the realisation of the security, he will be obliged to repay this either to the liquidator or the preferential creditors[331].

[27.134] The validity of a secured creditor's mortgage or charge will depend upon a number of factors: the capacity of the company and the authority of the directors to create the charge[332], the legality of the charge[333], and whether it has been registered pursuant to CA 1963, s 99(1)[334]. Where a registrable charge has not been registered the security will be void against the liquidator and any other creditors of the company. The consequence is that

---

327 See Sanfey & Holohan, *Bankruptcy Law and Practice in Ireland* (1991), p 153; and Pennington *Corporate Insolvency Law* (1991), p 294 *ff.*

328 Bankruptcy Act 1988, Sch 1, para 24(4)(a).

329 Bankruptcy Act 1988, Sch 1, para 24(5).

330 Bankruptcy Act 1988, Sch 1, para 24(6).

331 See Chapter 22, *Corporate Borrowing: Receivers*, para **[22.054]**.

332 See Chapter 7, *Corporate Contracts: Capacity and Authority*, para **[7.096]** *ff* and Chapter 20, *Corporate Borrowing: Debentures and Security*, para **[20.008]** *ff.*

333 See generally CA 1990, s 31 and CA 1963, s 60.

although the money secured becomes immediately repayable, the creditor of the money ceases to be a secured creditor and so must prove with the other unsecured creditors.

[27.135] Finally, it should be noted that where there are a number of secured creditors whose security extends to the same assets, the entitlement of each creditor will be determined by the law of priorities and the registration of security interests[335]. This will be the case whether the secured assets comprise of real property[336] or personal property[337].

(b) Assets that are held in trust

[27.136] Property that is not beneficially owned by a company is not available for distribution by the liquidator. The equitable or beneficial owner of property held in trust by a company that is in liquidation does not have to prove for his property in the winding up. Accordingly, when property is held by the company in trust, the beneficial owner is entitled to the property and does not have to prove with other creditors. In *Re Shanahans Stamp Auctions Ltd*[338] it was found that where a company held postage stamps in trust for investors, the investors were entitled to the stamps as of right and did not have to prove in the winding up of the company[339]. The principles discussed in that case were applied by Laffoy J in *Re Money Markets International Stockbrokers Ltd (No 1)*[340] and it was held that a particular client of a failed stockbroking firm was entitled to the return of monies, that were in the liquidator's hands, in circumstances where they had been transferred to the company to complete a purchase of shares that had never completed. The applicant's claim was unusual because monies had been transferred to purchase the shares in advance of the settlement date and were identifiable in the client account of the company. Laffoy J considered whether, as between competing claimants to a client account the rule in *Clayton's Case* (ie last in first out – as seen in *Re Shanahans Stamp Auctions Ltd*[341]) or the so-called 'pari passu ex post facto solution' (pari passu distribution – as seen in *Barlow Clowes International Ltd v Vaughan*[342]) applied. Laffoy J applied the rule in *Clayton's Case* to the benefit of the applicant. Similarly, where goods are purchased by a company subject to a valid retention of title clause the liquidator must hand back such goods to the

---

334 Note however, that the security held by a creditor may on application by the liquidator be found to be a fraudulent preference or fraudulent disposition: see para **[27.072]** and **[27.092]**, respectively.

335 Eg registration under the Registration of Title Act 1964 in the case of charges on registered land, the Registry of Deeds (Ireland) Act 1707 in the case of unregistered land, the Agricultural Credit Act 1978 in the case of a charge over 'agricultural stock', and the other registration systems considered in Chapter 21, *Corporate Borrowing: Registration of Charges*, para **[21.109]** *ff*.

336 See Keane, *Equity and the Law of Trusts in the Republic of Ireland* (1988), p 49 *ff*.

337 See Bell, *Modern Law of Personal Property in England and Ireland* (1989), p 516 *ff*.

338 *Re Shanahans Stamp Auctions Ltd* [1962] IR 38. See also *Re Ellis Sons & Vidler Ltd* [1994] BCC 532.

339 Cf *Re Goldcorp Exchange Ltd* [1994] 2 All ER 806. See Collins, 'Tracing into a Vanishing Asset: High Expectations and Equitable Remedies' (1994) CLP 211 where this case and the principles of tracing are perceptively analysed.

340 *Re Money Markets International Stockbrokers Ltd (No 1)* [1999] 4 IR 267.

341 *Re Shanahans Stamp Auctions Ltd* [1962] IR 38.

342 *Barlow Clowes International Ltd v Vaughan* [1992] BCLC 1910.

vendor-creditor[343]. On the other hand, in another application brought arising from the collapse of the same firm, *Re Money Markets International Stockbrokers Ltd (No 3)*[344] another client's claim to be entitled to a trust over monies in the client account was rejected. There, Carroll J rejected that the monies in question were subject to a trust, constructive or otherwise and found that the applicant did not have a proprietary claim, or a right in rem, against the company's client account.

(c) Monies that must be set-off

[27.137] A further consequence of the incorporation of the laws of bankruptcy into liquidations[345] is the application of the rules dealing with set-off in bankruptcy[346]. The Bankruptcy Act 1988, Sch 1, para 17(1) provides:

> 'Where there are mutual debts or credits between the bankrupt and any person claiming as creditor, one debt or demand may be set off against the other and only the balance found owing is to be recoverable on one side or the other.'

Where set-off applies its effect is to disapply the normal principle of *pari passu* distribution of assets. A creditor who is owed money by the company can avoid proving for that debt where he owes the company money. Unlike England and Wales[347], in Ireland set-off in a winding up is not mandatory[348].

[27.138] In order for debts to be capable of being set off in a liquidation, there must be *mutuality* of debits and credits between the creditor and the company. Accordingly, set-off can operate only where the obligations to be set off arise between the same parties and in the same right[349]. The Australian High Court has held that there are three aspects to mutuality: in *Gye v McIntyre*[350] it was said:

> 'The first is that the credits, the debits, or the claims arising from other dealings be between the same persons. The second is that the benefit or burden of them lie in the same interests. In determining whether credits, debits or claims arising from other dealings are between the same persons and in the same interests, it is the equitable or beneficial interests of the parties which must be considered...The third requirement of mutuality is that the credits, debits or

343 *Re WJ Hickey Ltd* [1988] IR 126.

344 *Re Money Markets International Stockbrokers Ltd (No 3)* [2001] 2 IR 17.

345 CA 1963, s 284(1). See para **[27.128]**.

346 See, O'Callaghan, 'Set-off on Insolvency' (1998) 5 CLP 20.

347 See *Re Bank of Credit and Commerce International SA (No 8)* [1997] 4 All ER 568; *Stein v Blake* [1995] 2 All ER 961; and *MS Fashions v BCCI SA* [1993] BCC 360.

348 In *Deering v Hyndman* (1886) LR (Ir) 18 QBD 323.

349 See *McKinnon v Armstrong* (1877) 2 App Cas 531 where a trustee could not set off a debt owed to him personally against a debt owed to him in his capacity as trustee, and *Re Irish Shipping* [1986] ILRM 518 where a bank could not set off money paid to it by mistake against a debt owed, since it held the money as constructive trustee. By way of contrast, in *MS Fashions Ltd v Bank of Credit and Commerce International* (1993) Independent, 6 January, a depositor with a bank was permitted to set off a claim against him of foot of a guarantee to another bank against his deposit with his own, now insolvent, bank, since his bank was the debtor of the other bank and the contract of guarantee expressly stated him to be 'principal debtor'.

350 *Gye v McIntyre* (1990-1991) 171 CLR 609 at 623. See O'Callaghan, 'Set-off on Insolvency' (1998) 5 CLP 20 at 24.

claims arising in other dealings must be commensurable for the purposes of set-off under the section. That means that they must ultimately sound in money.'

Set-off was considered by the House of Lords in *Re Bank of Credit and Commerce International SA (No 8)*[351]. The facts were that BCCI had loaned money to a borrower on the security of a deposit, made by a surety. The surety was a controlling shareholder in the borrower-company. Importantly, the security document signed by the surety did not contain an obligation on the surety to discharge the borrower's indebtedness, merely providing that BCCI had a lien or charge over the deposit which it could utilise to reduce the borrower's liabilities and providing that the surety could not withdraw the deposit until the borrower's liability to BCCI had been discharged. When BCCI went into liquidation, the liquidators applied for directions as to whether BCCI could claim repayment from the borrower *without resorting to the deposit* that had been given as security and thereby leaving the surety to prove with the other creditors. In essence, the liquidators wanted to know whether they were obliged to set-off the deposit against the borrower's indebtedness. At trial, in the Court of Appeal and in the House of Lords the basis answer was the same: the liquidators were not required to set-off the deposit account against the borrower's loan with the result that the liquidators could pursue the borrower for the monies loaned whilst at the same time forcing the surety who had made the deposit to prove in the liquidation along with all other creditors for the monies owed to him. In the House of Lords, Lord Hoffmann said that set-off was 'strictly limited to mutual claims' and that there 'can be no set-off of claims by third parties, even with their consent' as 'to do so would be to allow parties by agreement to subvert the fundamental principle of *pari passu* distribution of the insolvent company's assets'[352].

[27.139] The effect of a creditor being allowed to set-off a debt which the company owes him against a debt which he owes the company is that the creditor does not have to prove with the other creditors in the winding up of the company for the debt the company owes him. The advantage of set off to a creditor is seen in *Re Money Markets International Stockbrokers Ltd*[353]. There, Laffoy J described the operation of the Bankruptcy Act 1988, Sch 1, para 17(1) by reference to one of the insolvent company's (MMI's) creditors, a Mr Murtagh:

'Mr Murtagh's position vis-à-vis MMI post-liquidation is that the credit balance on his ledger account with MMI is £288,291. However, by letter dated the 1st of March 1998 Mr Murtagh instructed MMI to use funds from that account to clear debts on certain other accounts, on two of which, according to the relevant ledger accounts, there were at the commencement of the winding-up debit balances which aggregate £231,061. Mr Murtagh, as a beneficiary of client funds has a trust or property claim, a right *in rem*, against the client funds and he also has a right in personam or a money claim, against the trustee, MMI (in

[351] *Re Bank of Credit and Commerce International SA (No 8)* [1997] 4 All ER 568. See Hutchinson, 'Taking Security over Cash Deposits: The House of Lords Confirms the Conceptual Possibility of Charge-Backs' (1998) 5 CLP 3; Bannister, 'Liquidation Set-off and Security over Bank Deposits – The Uncertainties Removed' (1997) *CCH's Company Law Newsletter*, 15 December 1997.

[352] [1997] 4 All ER 568 at 573g. Relying on the authority of *British Eagle International Airlines Ltd v Cie Nationale Air France* [1975] 2 All ER 390.

[353] *Re Money Markets International Stockbrokers Ltd* [2000] 3 IR 437.

liquidation). MMI has a claim in debt, a claim *in personam*, against Mr Murtagh under the letter of set-off in respect of the indebtedness to MMI on the two connected accounts. The mutuality required by paragraph 17(1) will only apply if Mr Murtagh decides not to pursue his trust claim, in which case by operation of paragraph 17(1) Mr Murtagh could prove for £57,320 in the liquidation of MMI. That illustration shows that a party who has a dual money/ property claim against an insolvent company in liquidation may by pursuing one claim or cause of action, bring about a situation in which the parties are claiming in the same right and the mutuality requirement of paragraph 17(1) is fulfilled. It is not so much a question of the party with dual claim electing for set-off: it is a question of the claim or cause of action pursued by that party giving rise to a situation in which paragraph 17(1) comes into play.'

A creditor must, of course, pay any balance owing to the company after the set-off to the liquidator[354] or, where the company still owes him, he will have to prove with the company's other creditors for the balance. The debt owed by the company may be set-off in full. This gives the creditor the advantage of making full use of that debt to offset his liability to the company. If he does not exercise the set-off, he faces the prospect of having to pay his debt to the company in full and whilst perhaps receiving only a percentage of the debt owed by the company to him.

[27.140] Any debt, which is capable of being proved in bankruptcy or a winding up, can be the subject of a set off in bankruptcy or a winding up[355]. The relevant date for set-off is the date on which a resolution is passed, or a court order made, to have the company wound up[356] and there must be mutual debts and credits in existence at that date[357]. Whether it is permissible to set off a debt which was a mere contingency or possibility at the relevant date is the subject of some doubt. In *Re a Debtor*[358], a guarantor, who was not called upon to pay under the guarantee until after the relevant date, was held not to be entitled to set off sums owed to him against his payment obligation, since, at the relevant date, his obligation to pay under the guarantee was a mere contingency. However, in *Re Charge Card Services Ltd*[359], Millet J said that it is sufficient merely that mutual dealings exist at the date of the winding up which involve rights and obligations, whether absolute or contingent, of such a nature that have developed into pecuniary demands capable of set off at the time the claim to set off is made[360]. This has been affirmed by the House of Lords in *Re Bank of Credit and Commerce International SA (No 8)*[361] where Lord Hoffmann said set-off under the English rules[362] 'requires at least the existence of a right to make a pecuniary demand'.

354 A secured creditor is not obliged to set off his claim against a debt owed to him: *Re Norman Holding Co Ltd* [1990] 3 All ER 757.

355 *Re DH Curtiss* [1978] 1 Ch 162.

356 CA 1963, s 220 and 253.

357 *Re Casey* (21 July, 1986, unreported), High Court (Hamilton P); See *Re Bank of Credit and Commerce International SA (No 8)* [1997] 4 All ER 568; and *MS Fashions v BCCI SA* [1993] BCC 360.

358 *Re a Debtor* [1956] 3 All ER 225. See also *Re Fenton* [1931] 1 Ch 85. Both cases feature in the judgment of the Supreme Court in *Dempsey v Bank of Ireland* (12 December 1985, unreported), Supreme Court.

359 *Re Charge Card Services Ltd* [1987] BCLC 17.

360 [1987] BCLC 17 at 42–43. For authority on this point Millett J cited *Hiley v Peoples Prudential Assurance Co Ltd* (1938) 60 CLR 468 at 496.

Whatever about contingent debts, it is well settled that debts which are unliquidated or unquantified at the relevant date may be set off. Thus, for example, a claim for damages in contract or tort may be set-off even though the amount of damages to be awarded has not been settled at the relevant date. To this end, the Civil Liability Act 1961, s 61 provides:

> '(1) Notwithstanding any other enactment or any rule of law, a claim for damages or contribution in respect of a wrong shall be provable in bankruptcy where the wrong out of which the liability to damages or the right to contribution arose was committed before the time of the bankruptcy.
>
> (2) Where the damages or contribution have not been and cannot be otherwise liquidated or ascertained, the court may make such order as to it seems fit for the assessment of the damages or contribution, and the amount when so assessed shall be provable as if it were a debt due at the time of the bankruptcy.'

[27.141] Where a liquidator recovers damages against a director in respect of misfeasance or breach of trust or duty, a director or other officer of the company is not entitled to set off any debts owed to him by the company. In the Supreme Court decision of *Re Greendale Developments Ltd*[363] Keane J stated that this has been treated as settled law in England since the decision of the Court of Appeal in *Re Anglo French Co-Operative Society; ex p Pelly*[364], where it was held that:

> '...an officer of a company who has been found liable to pay money to the company in misfeasance proceedings is not entitled to set off a debt owing by the company to him against that liability. It appears from the judgments in that and subsequent cases that the reason for the rule was that the right of set off only arose in the case of actions between parties. However, it was also pointed out by Hall VC in another case referred to in a footnote in *Pelly's* case that no right of set off would in any event arise unless the debts could be said to be mutual.'[365]

In that case Keane J held that there was no mutuality between the sums sought to be recovered by the liquidator as having been misapplied in breach of the director's fiduciary duties and the sums claimed by the director against the company. In such a case the director can prove for any sums owed to him as an unsecured creditor in the company's winding up.

[27.142] Section 237(1) of CA 1963 addresses the extent to which a contributory's right of set-off can be overridden:

> 'The court may, at any time after making a winding-up order, make an order on any contributory for the time being on the list of contributories, to pay in manner directed by the order, any money due from him or from the estate of the person whom he represents to the

---

[361] *Re Bank of Credit and Commerce International SA (No 8)* [1997] 4 All ER 568. See Hutchinson, 'Taking Security over Cash Deposits: The House of Lords Confirms the Conceptual Possibility of Charge-Backs' (1998) 5 CLP 3; Bannister, 'Liquidation Set-off and Security over Bank Deposits – The Uncertainties Removed' (1997) CCH's Company Law Newsletter, 15 December 1997.

[362] Insolvency Rules 1986, r 490 (UK).

[363] *Re Greendale Developments Ltd* [1998] 1 IR 8.

[364] *Re Anglo French Co-Operative Society; ex p Pelly* [1882] 21 Ch D 492.

[365] [1998] 1 IR 8 at 28.

company, exclusive of any money payable by him or the estate by virtue of any call in pursuance of this Act.'

Section 237(2) provides that in making such an order the court may:

'(a) in the case of an unlimited company, allow to the contributory by way of set-off any money due to him or to the estate which he represents from the company on any independent dealing or contract with the company, but not any money due to him as a member of the company in respect of any dividend or profit; and

(b) in the case of a limited company, make to any director whose liability is unlimited or to his estate a like allowance.'

Notwithstanding the foregoing, in any company, limited or unlimited, 'when all the creditors are paid in full, any money due on any account whatever to a contributory from the company may be allowed to him by way of set-off against any subsequent call'[366].

[27.143] In addition to set off in bankruptcy, a creditor may, in appropriate circumstances, exercise a contractual right of set off so as to set off his liabilities to the company against debts owed to him by the company[367]. In *Dempsey v Bank of Ireland*[368] the Supreme Court upheld the validity of a bank's contractual right to appropriate accounts (ie to set-off debit accounts against credit accounts) *after* the commencement of the account holders' winding up. The liquidator in that case argued that such a right ceased on the relevant date because on that date the assets of the company, including money kept in bank accounts, vested in him so that he might distribute them *pari passu* to the ordinary creditors. Henchy J, dismissing that argument, said:

> 'To say that when the liquidator takes over, the assets of his company vest in him is a less than complete statement of the legal position. The general rule is that because he acquires only such title to the assets as the company had – no more, no less. He cannot take any better title to any part of the assets than the company had. This means that he takes the assets subject to any pre-existing enforceable right of a third party in or over them. If that were not so, equities, liabilities and contractual rights validly and enforceably created while the assets were in the hands of the company would be unfairly swept aside and an unjust distribution of the assets would result.'[369]

The debts in that case were contractually subject to the possible exercise of a right of set off when they first arose. Consequently, when they came into the hands of the liquidator, they remained subject to that contractual right.

No mutuality of obligations need exist in cases of contractual set off – consequently, a creditor may contractually set off the obligations of another of the company's creditors against his own. In *British Eagle International Airlines Ltd v Compagnie Nationale Air France*[370] the English House of Lords opposed the exercise of a contractual set off in a

366 CA 1963, s 237(3).

367 See generally, Shannon, 'Contractual Set-Off as a Form of Bank Security from an Irish Incorporated Company', a lecture delivered at the Irish Centre for Commercial Studies, University College Dublin, 22 June, 1992.

368 *Dempsey v Bank of Ireland* (6 December 1985, unreported), Supreme Court.

369 (6 December 1985, unreported), Supreme Court at pp 8–9.

370 *British Eagle International Airlines Ltd v Compagnie Nationale Air France* [1975] 2 All ER 390.

liquidation where no mutuality existed, on the basis that the exercise contravened the requirement that the property of the company (in that case the debts owed to it) be distributed by the liquidator amongst the ordinary creditors pari passu in satisfaction of all its liabilities[371]. However, in *Glow Heating v Eastern Health Board*[372] Costello J held that the *pari passu* requirement did not render void every contract by which a creditor obtained rights over the company's assets superior to those given to the ordinary creditors, and that the liquidator took the subject matter of the set off subject to any liabilities which affected it in the company's hands. As a result, it would appear that non-mutual contractual set-off will be permitted in Irish liquidations.

[27.144] As was observed in Chapter 20[373], set-off can operate against debts which are the subject of a floating charge up until the moment of crystallisation[374]. Since crystallisation operates as an equitable assignment of the subject matter of the charge to the charge holder, once crystallisation occurs the mutuality of the debts secured by the charge is destroyed. Consequently, set-off in bankruptcy under the Bankruptcy Act 1988, Sch 1, para 17(1) will be precluded for want of mutuality in such circumstances[375].

(d) Super-preferential debts that are trust monies

[27.145] The Revenue Commissioners' claims in respect of employment contributions (PAYE and PRSI) that have actually been deducted from employees' remuneration but which have not been paid over to them, have what is referred to as a '*super preferential*' status. The Social Welfare (Consolidation) Act 1993, s 16(2) provides:

> 'The assets of a limited company in a winding up under the Companies Acts 1963–1990 *shall not include*:
>
> (a) any sum deducted by an employer from such remuneration of an employee of his as was paid prior to the winding up in respect of an employment contribution due and unpaid by the employer in respect of such contribution, or
>
> (b) any sum which would have been deducted from the remuneration of an employee in respect of an employment contribution for a period of employment prior to a winding up had such remuneration been paid prior to such winding up and in such a winding up a sum equal in amount to the sum so deducted and unpaid or which would have been deducted and payable, shall notwithstanding anything in those Acts be paid to the Social Insurance Fund in priority to the debt specified in section 285(2) of the Companies Act 1963.'

The effect of this provision is to impress a *statutory trust* on certain monies in a company's possession and to deem the revenue commissioners as beneficial owners. The result of this provision is the same as if the company held such monies on an express trust: they are not included in the company's assets and so are unavailable to preferential creditors, creditors secured by a floating charge and unsecured creditors.

---

371 See CA 1963, s 275, as amended.

372 *Glow Heating v Eastern Health Board* [1988] IR 110.

373 See Chapter 20, *Corporate Borrowing: Debentures and Security*, para **[20.083]**.

374 *Re Russell Murphy* [1976] IR 15.

375 *Lynch et al v Ardmore Studios (Ireland) Ltd* [1966] IR 133.

[27.146] In *Re Coombe Importers Ltd*[376] Shanley J considered what sums, precisely, fell within the meaning of Social Welfare (Consolidation) Act 1993, s 16(2)(a) and s 16(2)(b). As to s 16(2)(a) he said that it is:

> '...a condition precedent to the super-preferential status of any sum is that it be a sum *deducted* by the employer in respect of the employment contribution of the employee which remains due and owing by the employer...[It does not permit] a construction that super-preferential status can be afforded to sums which *ought* to have been deducted in respect of the employment contributions of an employee, but were not so deducted.'[377]

As to s 16(2)(b), Shanley J said:

> '...it appears to me that that section deals with and is restricted to situations where employees were due remuneration prior to a winding up but did not receive such remuneration from their employer. It has no application...where employees did receive remuneration from their employer without deductions being made.'

In that case, neither provision could be invoked to confer super-preferential status on particular sums claimed. The facts there were that monies had been paid to the company's employees prior to its winding up without the deduction of any PAYE or PRSI. In those circumstances, neither s 16 nor its predecessor[378], applied and the monies due to the revenue did not have super-preferential status under s 16(2)(a) – because the taxes were not in fact actually deducted – or under s 16(2)(b) – because it only applies where employees are owed wages that are not in fact paid[379].

(e) Stamp duty on monies received in realisation of company assets

[27.147] Stamp duty is payable on 'the monies received by the liquidator in realisation of the assets of the company'[380]. The current rate of duty is 2.5%. This tax is only applicable to official or compulsory liquidations. Where it is payable, it must be paid before any other distribution ie ahead of the preferential creditors, floating charge holders and ordinary creditors. In *Re Private Motorists Provident Society Ltd; Horgan v Minister for Justice*[381] it was held that monies would be 'received by the liquidator in realisation of the assets' even in the absence of an order under CA 1963, s 230, vesting a company's assets in the liquidator[382]. There, the liquidator had claimed that monies received by a company were not liable to duty. The argument was, in effect, that in order for duty to be payable monies had to be received by the liquidator in his own capacity (where a section 230 order was made) and not in his capacity as agent of the company. This argument was rejected by Murphy J who held that the liquidator in that case had brought about the realisation and he was the proper party to give a receipt for the proceeds of sale, even if the ownership of the assets was not vested in him.

---

376 *Re Coombe Importers Ltd* [1999] 1 IR 492.

377 [1999] 1 IR 492 at 500.

378 Social Welfare (Consolidation) Act 1981, s 120.

379 In that case it should also be noted that Social Welfare (Consolidation) Act 1993, s 16(2)(b) was disregarded on the grounds that it was not in force at the relevant time (it not having a counterpart in Social Welfare (Consolidation) Act 1981, s 120) and could not be invoked retrospectively.

380 Supreme Court and High Court (Fees) Order, 1989 (SI 1989/341), Sch 1, Part III, para 22 being the prescribed fees envisaged by the Courts of Justice Act 1936, s 65.

381 (23 June 1995, unreported), High Court (Murphy J).

382 See **[27.010]**.

[27.148] In *Re Private Motorists Provident Society Ltd; Horgan v Minister for Justice*[383] the court also held that duty would not be payable on all monies received by a liquidator, but only those received in realisation of the company's assets. Murphy J rejected that the word 'realisation' necessarily involves a sale of assets and neither was a sale of assets necessarily a 'realisation'[384]. Murphy J held that, logically, assets can only be 'realised' once in the course of any liquidation:

> 'To constitute a realisation the particular asset or property must be got in by the liquidator in such a fashion as to be available to meet the liabilities of the company (subject to the expenses of the liquidation). Once that has been achieved – and ordinarily its achievement can be verified by the lodgment of the proceeds into the Bank of Ireland to the account of the official liquidator – the realisation is complete and any further activities by the liquidator in relation to such proceeds may augment the available funds by an accrual of interest or otherwise but would not constitute a realisation of the assets of the company.'[385]

Applying that reasoning, Murphy J held, inter alia, that the following receipts of monies were not liable to stamp duty: repayments of VAT representing the reversal of a liability *created* during the course of the winding up; a rebate from the Department of Labour in respect of statutory redundancy resulting from the liquidator's retention of certain employees for upwards of two years after the commencement of the winding up; a sum refunded by the company's bank that had been deducted in error and which arose solely from the liquidator's activities, not being an asset of the company; the costs of litigation initiated by the liquidator; the repayment of a dividend mistakenly paid; monies refunded by creditors whose claims were withdrawn – because this 'was merely the restoration or regularisation of the status quo above and not the realisation of an asset'; and interest received by the liquidator on the proceeds of realisation.

[27.149] The following receipts of money were, however, held by Murphy J to be liable to stamp duty: the repayment of corporation tax that had been overpaid prior to the liquidation; and sums received from associated companies, also in liquidation, that belonged to the company being wound up, even though duty had already been paid on those monies by those companies. Murphy J also held that monies received by the official liquidator from a previously appointed receiver constituted assets of the company and were liable to stamp duty. This matter again arose for consideration in *Re Chipboard Products Ltd*[386]. There, a liquidator sought directions as to whether stamp duty was payable on cash paid over to him by a receiver appointed over the company's assets. It was sought to distinguish Murphy J's decision on the grounds that, in the instant case, there had been a mere transfer of monies by the receiver to the official liquidator. Laffoy J rejected the liquidator's contentions and held that although the receiver had realised the proceeds and although the liquidator had to do no more than receive and lodge the cheques drawn by the receiver 'nonetheless, in my view, the monies represented by those cheques were received by the official liquidator 'in realisation of the assets of the company'[387].

---

383 *Re Private Motorists Provident Society Ltd; Horgan v Minister for Justice* (23 June 1995, unreported), High Court (Murphy J).

384 See para **[27.010]** where Murphy J is quoted.

385 (23 June 1995, unreported), High Court at pp 8–9.

386 *Re Chipboard Products Ltd* (27 February 1997, unreported), High Court (Laffoy J).

The costs and expenses of winding up

[27.150] Liquidating a company is a costly business. Were the Companies Acts to provide that liquidators' expenses and remuneration were to be merely provable along with the claims of the general body of creditors there would, in the absence of the conscription of liquidators, be few insolvent windings up. For this reason, the Companies Acts provide for the disbursement of the costs and expenses of the winding up, *in priority* to the claims of the general creditors.

(a) Liquidators' versus examiners' remuneration, costs and expenses

[27.151] As shall be considered next, the payment of liquidators' remuneration, costs and expenses is afforded a high priority by RSC, Ord 74, r 128(1) and, being part of the costs and expenses of a winding up, will rank ahead of preferential creditors, creditors secured by floating charges and unsecured creditors. Of course liquidators' remuneration costs and expenses cannot be paid out of assets that do not belong to the company[388] and for that reason are not liable to be paid out of assets that are the subject of a fixed mortgage or a fixed charge. However, in the event of a deficiency in assets an examiner's remuneration, costs and expenses will have priority to those of a liquidator. In *Re Springline Ltd*[389] the Supreme Court, reversing the High Court decision of Shanley J[390], held that C(A)A 1990, s 29(3)[391] gave an examiner's remuneration, costs and expenses priority over those of a liquidator. The finding in this decision was given statutory effect by C(A)A 1990, s 29(3B)[392].

(b) Official liquidations

[27.152] In the context of official liquidations, CA 1963, s 244 provides:

> 'The court may, in the event of the assets being insufficient to satisfy the liabilities, make an order as to the payment out of the assets of the costs, charges and expenses incurred in the winding up in such order of priority as the court thinks just.'

Guidance is provided by RSC, Ord 74 r 128(1), which provides:

> 'The assets of a company in a winding up by the court remaining after payment of the fees and expenses properly incurred in preserving, realising or getting in the assets, including where the company has previously commenced to be wound up voluntarily such remuneration, costs and expenses as the court may allow to a Liquidator appointed in such voluntary winding up, shall, subject to any order of the court, be liable to the following payments which shall be made in the following order of priority, namely:

---

387 (27 February 1997, unreported), High Court at p 8.

388 See para **[27.129]** *ff.*

389 *Re Springline Ltd* [1999] 1 ILRM 15.

390 [1998] 1 ILRM 301

391 See Chapter 23, *Examinerships*, para **[23.080]** and para **[23.144]**.

392 Inserted by C(A)(No 2)A 1999, s 28. C(A)A 1990, s 29(3B) provides: 'In subsections (3) and (3A) references to a claim shall be deemed to include references to any payment in a winding-up of the company in respect of the costs, charges and expenses of that winding-up (including the remuneration of any liquidator).'

First	The costs of the petition, including the costs of any person appearing on the petition whose costs are allowed by the court.
Next	The costs and expenses of any person who makes or concurs in making the company's statement of affairs.
Next	The necessary disbursements of the Official Liquidator, other than expenses properly incurred in preserving, realising or getting in the assets hereinbefore provided for.
Next	The costs payable to the solicitor for the Official Liquidator.
Next	The remuneration of the Official Liquidator.
Next	The out-of-pocket expenses necessarily incurred by the committee of inspection (if any).'

As to the interaction between CA 1963, s 244 and Ord 74, r 128, in *Re CHA Ltd*[393] Laffoy J held that s 244 overrides the order of priority stipulated in the Order, which provision by its terms is 'subject to any order of the court'.[394]

(c) Voluntary liquidations

[27.153] Section 281 of CA 1963, which applies in the case of voluntary liquidations, provides that:

> 'All costs, charges and expenses properly incurred in the winding up, including the remuneration of the liquidator, shall be payable out of the assets of the company in priority to all other claims[395].'

Both provisions have been the subject of considerable litigation, which has focused, in particular, upon whether or not certain taxes are payable in priority to all other claims.

(d) The meaning of 'necessary disbursement'

[27.154] Corporation tax payable to the Revenue Commissioners after the commencement of the winding up was held by the courts not to be an 'expense' or a 'necessary disbursement' within the meaning of Ord 74, r 128, although this has been reversed by Finance Act 1983, s 56 (now the Taxes Consolidation Act 1997, s 571). In *Re Van Hool McArdle Ltd*[396] Carroll J said that corporation tax was merely a possible consequence of a sale where a profit was made by the company. In the Supreme Court[397] the meaning of 'necessary disbursements' was given some consideration. O'Higgins CJ said that by necessary disbursement was meant 'expenses such as necessary maintenance of buildings

[393] *Re CHA Ltd* (25 January 1999, unreported), High Court (Laffoy J).

[394] In *Secretary of State for Trade and Industry v Aurum Marketing Ltd* [2000] TLR 615 the English Court of Appeal held that it had the discretion to order a non-party – in that case the sole director and shareholder – to pay the costs of the winding up and that the company's costs should not be paid out of company assets until after the unsecured creditors had been paid.

[395] Note that *Re Redbreast Preserving Co (Ireland) Ltd* [1958] IR 234 held that the priorities provided for in RSC, Ord 74, r 129(1) also apply to voluntary liquidations with appropriate modification.

[396] *Re Van Hool McArdle Ltd* [1982] ILRM 340.

[397] Reported as *Revenue Commissioners v Donnelly* [1983] ILRM 329.

or wages for caretaking or for other purposes'.[398] Somewhat strangely, in *Re A Noyek & Sons Ltd; Burns v Hearne*[399] CA 1963, s 281 which applies to companies in voluntary liquidation was interpreted by the Supreme Court as meaning that corporation tax *was* a cost within the meaning of 'costs, charges and expenses properly incurred in the winding up', as is tax on deposit interest. The basis for the distinction between the *Van Hool McArdle* case was the reference to 'charges' in s 281 and the absence of that word in the RSC, Ord 74 r 129(1).

[27.155] Items which have been held to constitute 'necessary disbursements', include post-liquidation rent paid by a liquidator in respect of property the continual use of which is necessary to the winding up of the company[400]. An interesting dispute concerning the payment of post-liquidation rent arose in *Re CHA Ltd*[401]. In that case the official liquidator of a company continued on in occupation of the company's premises and on failing to pay rent to the landlord, the landlord was given leave to institute proceedings against the company and successfully recovered judgment against the company for £5,000 plus costs. The landlord immediately recovered the sum of £2,000, which had been lodged by the liquidator. As to the balance, the landlord claimed in the High Court that the balance of £3,000 were 'costs, charges and expenses incurred in the winding up', within the meaning of CA 1963, s 244. The landlord also claimed that it was entitled to be paid the taxed costs (a further £2,644.34) in priority to all other claims in the liquidation. On the question of taxed costs, Laffoy J held on the authority of the Supreme Court in *Comhlucht Paipear Riomhaireachto Teo v Udaras na Gaeltachta*[402], that the landlord was entitled to be paid in full the taxed costs of the rent recovery proceedings in priority to all other claims of the liquidation. In relation to the award of £3,000 by way of rent, it was conceded by the liquidator that that sum fell to be regarded as a debt contracted for the purpose of the winding up of the company and to be paid in full like any other debt or expense properly incurred by the liquidator[403]. Accordingly, Laffoy J declared that that sum represented 'costs, charges and expenses incurred in the winding up' within the meaning of s 244. As to the priority between the sum owing to the landlord and the liquidator's own legal expenses and remuneration, Laffoy J deferred ruling until the liquidator's application was brought.

---

398 Note that in *Re Hibernian Transport Companies Ltd* [1984] ILRM 583, Costello J held that tax claimed in respect of post liquidation deposit interest was not a 'necessary disbursement' and further could not be proved for by the Revenue who were in this regard, a *post*-liquidation creditor, meaning no tax was payable at all. It would appear that this position remains unchanged in spite of the TCA 1997, s 571 (formerly the Finance Act 1983, s 56).

399 *Re A Noyek & Sons Ltd; Burns v Hearne* [1989] ILRM 155 (SC), [1987] ILRM 508 (HC).

400 *Re Oak Pits Colliery Co* [1882] 21 Ch D 322.

401 *Re CHA Ltd* (25 January 1999, unreported), High Court (Laffoy J).

402 *Comhlucht Paipear Riomhaireachto Teo v Udaras na Gaeltachta* [1991] IR 320. Laffoy J also cited with approval *Halsbury's Laws of England*, (4th edn) Vol 7(2), para 1803: 'Similarly, where leave is given to bring an action against the company and to the liquidator to defend it, the successful plaintiff is entitled to have his costs in full out of the assets, including his costs of obtaining leave'. It was also noted that authority for that statement was stated to be *Bailey and Leetham's Case* (1869) LR 8 Eq 94 and *Re Wenborn & Company* (1905) 1 Ch 413.

403 On the authority of *Re GWI Ltd* (16 November 1987, unreported), High Court (Murphy J).

[27.156] The costs of necessary litigation have also been considered to be 'necessary disbursements'[404]. Not all litigation will, however, be necessary and therefore automatically held to be payable out of the company's assets as an expense of the liquidation. So in *Re Floor Fourteen Ltd; Lewis v Inland Revenue Commissioners*[405] a liquidator of a company that was hopelessly insolvent proposed to institute proceedings against its directors for wrongful trading and preference. The realised monies meant that preferential creditors would receive only 44 pence in the pound whereas unsecured creditors would receive nothing. The liquidator was authorised by the unsecured creditors to institute proceedings but the preferential creditors, obviously wishing to cut their losses, wanted the proposed 44 pence in the pound. The liquidator applied successfully to the English High Court for a direction authorising the use of the realised assets to fund the litigation and contending that the costs would be 'expenses properly incurred in the winding up' payable out of the company's assets in priority to all other claims. The Deputy Judge held in favour of the liquidator. That decision was reversed by the Court of Appeal, which held that the similar English provision[406] to CA 1963, s 244 did not provide that all expenses properly incurred in the winding-up were automatically payable out of the company's assets in priority to all other claims. Moreover it was stated that liquidators did not have a right to recoup the costs of proposed litigation against directors automatically[407]. Of particular interest was the Court of Appeal distinction between litigation to recover a company's assets and litigation to recover damages from directors and its consequent finding that costs incurred in the latter were not costs of the proceedings and could not receive priority under the English equivalent to Ord 74, r 128(1)[408]. The Court of Appeal did, however, appear to accept that the court had an inherent discretion to recover the costs of proposed litigation from the company's assets but declined to exercise the court's discretion in that case by reason of insufficient information.

(e) Costs payable to the liquidator's solicitor

[27.157] Where legal expenses have been incurred in preserving or realising assets these will have priority to all claims. The costs of a legal cost accountant retained by the liquidator's solicitor to tax their costs, have been held *not* to be a cost properly incurred by a liquidator. It would seem that the only way that such costs will receive priority is where the court exercises its discretion under Ord 74, r 129(2) [409].

Proof of debts by the company's creditors

[27.158] Life would indeed be wonderfully easy for liquidators if they could simply accept what a creditor claimed was owing to him and pay it out! In practice, however, before this can be done, all unsecured creditors must first *prove* what sums are due and owing to them. Those debts which may be proved are enumerated in CA 1963, s 283(1) which provides:

---

[404] *Re National Building and Land Co* (1885-86) 15 LR Ir 47.

[405] *Re Floor Fourteen Ltd; Lewis v Inland Revenue Commissioners* [2001] 2 BCLC 392.

[406] Insolvency Act 1986 (UK), s 115.

[407] Relying upon *Re MC Bacon Ltd (No 2)* [1990] BCLC 607.

[408] *Re Oasis Merchandising Services Ltd* [1997] 1 BCLC 689.

[409] See the judgment of Carroll J in *Re Castle Brand Ltd* [1990] ILRM 97.

'...all debts payable on a contingency, and all claims against the company, present or future, certain or contingent, ascertained or sounding only in damages, shall be admissible to proof against the company, a just estimate being made, so far as possible, of the value of such debts or claims which may be subject to any contingency or which sound only in damages, or for some other reason do not bear a certain value.'

A number of issues arise here, particularly in respect of contentious claims by creditors. The matters considered here are:

(a) Proving claims by creditors.

(b) Discounting claims.

(c) Contingent and periodical liabilities.

(d) Creditors' claims for interest.

(a) Proving claims by creditors

[27.159] The liquidator of a company must advertise to the creditors of the company at a time directed by the court, advising them of where they should send their claims. Section 241 of CA 1963 empowers the court to:

'...fix a time or times within which creditors are to prove their debts or claims or to be excluded from the benefit of any distribution made before those debts are proved.'

Creditors are asked to give their names and addresses, particulars of their debts and claims and the names and addresses of their solicitors[410]. Creditors will not be obliged to attend before the liquidator to prove their debts unless the liquidator so requires[411].

[27.160] The task then falls to the liquidator to investigate the claims sent to him, and to 'ascertain in so far as he is able which of such debts or claims are legally due from the company'. In an official liquidation the liquidator should notify the claims, identifying those which he considers valid, to the court Examiner, usually a Court Registrar or the Master of the High Court[412]. Claims which are illegal or contrary to public policy should be disallowed by the liquidator. At the time appointed, the Examiner will adjudicate upon the claims allowing them or requiring them to be proved further as the case may be. The liquidator must then notify those creditors whose claims were allowed and those whose claims require to be proved further within certain time limits[413]. The result of the adjudication process must be certified by the Examiner[414].

[27.161] Save in cases where the official liquidator or the court Examiner requires claims to be proven on affidavit[415], claims ought to be made in writing and sent by post to the liquidator[416]. Unless the liquidator requires a creditor to attend and prove his claim further, the costs of proving the claim shall be borne by the creditor[417]. Those required to prove their debts are entitled to their costs where the claim is proved[418].

---

410 RSC, Ord 74, r 95.

411 RSC, Ord 74, r 96.

412 RSC, Ord 74, r 97.

413 RSC, Ord 74, r 98.

414 RSC, Ord 74, r 101.

415 As to the form and content, see RSC, Ord 74, r 103.

416 RSC, Ord 74, r 102.

417 RSC, Ord 74, r 104.

418 RSC, Ord 74, r 99.

(b) Discounting claims

[27.162] Where a creditor has agreed to give the debtor company a discount in respect of, for example, the sale of goods, then the creditor must deduct from his claim any such trade discount to which the company would have been entitled if it had not gone into liquidation and, any interest in excess of two and a half per cent[419].

(c) Contingent and periodical liabilities

[27.163] Although a claim may be unascertained it may still be proved by a creditor. An example is provided by *Macfarlane's Claim*[420] where a person had taken out a fire insurance policy with the company concerned. Even though no claim had arisen under the policy, it was held the person's claim in respect of the premium paid should be admitted[421]. Such is a contingent claim and is provable[422].

[27.164] A person who is entitled to recurring or periodical payments from a company may also prove against the company[423]. The creditor may prove for a proportionate part of a periodic payment only up to the date of the commencement of the winding up, save in the case of rent due to a landlord under a lease of land or property where the liquidator remains in possession. In such a case, the creditor-landlord is entitled to further rent[424]. Even if the liquidator does not remain in possession, the creditor may claim for damages arising from the breach of, for example, a lease[425].

(d) Creditors' claims for interest[426]

[27.165] By reason of the application of the rules of bankruptcy to insolvent liquidations, the general rule is that creditors of a company may prove for interest. The sorts of interest for which a creditor can prove can be contractual interest[427], statutory interest on a judgment or interest under RSC, Ord 74 r 107[428]. The entitlement of a creditor to claim for interest in a winding up depends upon his status. In an insolvent liquidation unsecured creditors and preferential creditors are entitled to prove for interest up to the date of the resolution to wind up in a voluntary winding up. Either are entitled to prove for interest up to the date of the presentation of the petition in an insolvent official winding up[429].

[27.166] The general rule is that a secured creditor is entitled to claim for interest up to the date of repayment of the debt secured. By virtue of the incorporation of the laws of bankruptcy into the law of corporate insolvency, it has been held that interest is payable *after* the commencement of the winding up in priority to the claims of other creditors and

---

419 RSC, Ord 74, r 105.

420 *Macfarlane's Claim* (1880) 17 Ch D 337.

421 See also *Butler v Broadhead* [1974] 2 All ER 401.

422 See RSC, Ord 74, r 108.

423 RSC, Ord 74, r 106.

424 *Re CHA Ltd* (25 January 1999, unreported), High Court (Laffoy J). See para **[27.155]**.

425 See *Re House Property and Investment Co Ltd* [1953] 2 All ER 1525.

426 See Marshall, 'Interested in Interest? A Perspective on Liquidations' (1994) 1 CLP 35.

427 See *Trustee Savings Bank Dublin v Maughan* [1992] 1 IR 488.

428 *Re Car Replacements Ltd* (11 May 1992, unreported), High Court, per Murphy J.

429 *Re Amalgamated Investment and Property Company Ltd* [1984] 3 All ER 272; *Re Lines Bros Ltd* (No 4) [1982] 2 All ER 183.

of shareholders to the residue. In *Re McCairns (PMPA) plc*[430] the Supreme Court, reversing the judgment of Costello J, held that a bank was entitled to claim against its security for post-liquidation interest out of the proceeds of sale of a site after the liquidation. There, a chargee bank consented to the sale of a site by the liquidator of the company over which it held three charges. On the sale of the site, difficulties arose as to who was entitled to what monies. In the Supreme Court McCarthy J held[431]:

> 'In my judgment, not having brought the property the subject of the charge into the winding up and not having sought to prove any claim in the winding up, the bank is entitled to be paid interest up to the date of redemption, in accordance with the terms of the charging documents.'

It should be noted that the decision of the Supreme Court only applies to where a secured creditor stays outside the winding up[432].

[27.167] A different situation arises where a *solvent* company is wound up and a dispute arises between the creditors' claims for interest after the commencement of the winding up and the shareholders' claims to the company's surplus assets. In *Re Hibernian Transport Company Ltd*[433] it was held by the Supreme Court that where a company was wound up solvent, CA 1963, s 284 did not apply and accordingly, the normal bankruptcy rules did not apply. In that case it was held that creditors who were entitled to contractual interest could claim interest up to the date on which their debts were discharged. The company's shareholders were entitled to any balance remaining after the payment of contractual interest to creditors, all outstanding debts and liabilities, and all fees, costs and expenses of the liquidator pursuant to CA 1963, s 242[434].

Priorities in a distribution

[27.168] After the debts due to the holders of fixed mortgages and charges have been satisfied, trust property has been excluded, set-off has happened, super-preferential debts have been discharged, stamp duty paid on the proceeds of realisation and provision made for the costs and expenses of the winding up, the liquidator will be left with a sum available for distribution. Distribution of the realised assets must be carried out in accordance with the priorities dictated by law. The priority of distribution is as follows:

---

430 *Re McCairns (PMPA) plc* [1989] ILRM 19. See [1989] ILRM 501 for the judgment of Costello J considered by Woolfe, (1989) DULJ 113.

431 [1989] ILRM 19 at 25, reversing *Re Egan Electric Ltd* [1987] IR 398.

432 See para **[27.133]**.

433 *Re Hibernian Transport Company Ltd* [1994] 1 ILRM 48.

434 See generally *Re Lines Bros Ltd* [1984] BCLC 215; *Re Fine Industrial Commodities Ltd* [1956] Ch 256; *Re Rolls Royce Ltd* [1974] 1 WLR 1584; *Re Oldham Tradesmens' Insurance Company Ltd* High Court (UK) Vinelott J of 19 December 1980; *Re Humber Ironworks and Shipbuilders Co* [1869] 41 Ch App 643; *Re Contract Corporation* [1871] LR 5 Ch App 112; *Re Imperial Land Company of Marseilles* [1871] LR 11 Eq 478; *Re Joint Stock Discount Company* [1869] LR 5 Ch App 86; *Re Alfred O'Dwyer & Co Ltd* (11 November 1988, unreported), High Court, per Costello J; *Re Thomas Burgess* [1988] 23 LR Ir 5; *Re Michael Orr (Kilternan) Ltd [*1986] IR 273; and *Re Egan Electric Co Ltd* [1987] IR 398 which was reversed by the Supreme Court in *Re McCairns (PMPA) plc* [1992] ILRM 19.

(a) Preferential creditors.
(b) Floating charges.
(c) Unsecured creditors.
(d) Members and contributories of the company.

(a) Preferential creditors

[27.169] Section 275(1)(a) of CA 1963 provides that subject to the provisions of the Act as to preferential payments, the property of a company on its winding up shall be applied in satisfaction of its liabilities *pari passu*[435]. That principle is ousted, however, by CA 1963, s 285(2) in favour of preferential creditors which provides that in a winding up 'there shall be paid in priority to all other debts' certain preferential debts. Persons who are deemed by law to be preferential creditors enjoy an enviable position of priority. Without legislative demarcation, they would otherwise be mere unsecured creditors who would be entitled *pari passu* to share in the distribution of those assets available after the payment of the holders of floating charges. The Oireachtas has deemed certain persons and institutions to come within this select class of creditors, on grounds entirely based on public policy. To the fore in this favoured class are the revenue commissioners. Many will agree with the revenue's priority: we want to see others pay their taxes in much the same way as we all want to go to heaven. However, injustice is often perpetrated by this loaded ranking, and small creditors who have advanced credit to the company concerned and who rank *after* the preferred few may themselves face bankruptcy or liquidation as a result of the revenue's claims being *preferred* to theirs. However, other creditors who are members of this preferred club, such as employees who are owed wages, are more deserving of their membership. From this it must be recognised that the categorisation of certain persons as preferential creditors is based on purely normative factors.

[27.170] The claims of preferential creditors do not arise in liquidations alone and as noted in a previous chapter, a receiver is obliged by CA 1963, s 98 to discharge the claims of preferential creditors out of the proceeds of his realisation[436]. In *Re H William (Tallaght) Ltd*[437] a company had been in receivership and the receiver had discharged the preferential creditors' claims. The company subsequently went into liquidation and the liquidator resisted a further preferential claim by the Revenue Commissioners on the grounds that it was never intended that CA 1963, ss 98 and 285 should enable the same creditor to make a preferential claim in a receivership and claim preference again in a subsequent liquidation. Geoghegan J rejected the liquidator's contention, finding the proposition unsustainable in

[435] This is, however, subject to CA 1963, s 275(2) which provides that nothing in CA 1963, s 275(1)(a) 'shall in any way affect any rights or obligations of the company or any other person arising as a result of any agreement entered into (whether before or after the commencement of section 132 of the Companies Act, 1990) by any person under which any particular liability of the company to any general creditor is postponed in favour or subordinated to the rights or claims of any other person to whom the company may be in any way liable.' The effect is to allow creditors to agree to subordinate liabilities and, therefore, contract out of the *pari passu* principle.

[436] See Chapter 22, *Corporate Borrowing: Receivers*, para **[22.054]**.

[437] *Re H William (Tallaght) Ltd* [1996] 3 IR 531.

the light of the clear wording in CA 1963, s 285(2). As considered below[438], however, there it was found that the Revenue's claim was statute barred.

[27.171] Those claims which the law deems to be preferred are contained in CA 1963, s 285 and various Revenue and employee based statutes. These claims are:

(1) Rates levied by local authorities[439];

(2) Capital and income taxes levied by the Revenue[440];

(3) The wages and salaries of employees[441];

(4) Holiday payments owed to employees[442];

(5) Social welfare contributions[443];

(6) Compensation and damages for uninsured accidents to employees[444];

(7) Sickness and superannuation payments[445];

(8) Claims for unfair dismissal[446];

(9) Claims for minimum notice payments[447];

(10) Redundancy payments to employees.[448]

Although these are the 'preferred few' whose claims against the company rank only after the payment of the costs and expenses incurred in the winding up, this order of priority shall apply only to those debts which are notified, or 'have become known' to the liquidator within six months of his advertisement for claims in at least two daily newspapers[449]. In *Re H William (Tallaght) Ltd*[450] Geoghegan J held that the six-month time limit could not be extended. In that case the Revenue Commissioners did not notify the liquidator of its claim to corporation tax within the six-month period. The learned judge rejected the argument that the company's corporation tax liability must 'have become known' to the liquidator on the grounds that the liquidator's affidavit makes it clear that he was not aware of the tax liability within the six-month period. Moreover, it was held that there had to be either actual notification or actual knowledge: constructive knowledge would not suffice.

---

438 See para **[27.171]**.

439 CA 1963, s 285(2)(a)(i).

440 CA 1963, s 285(2)(a)(ii); Income Tax Act 1967; Capital Gains Tax Act 1975; Corporation Tax Act 1976, Value Added Tax Act 1972; and Finance Act 1972.

441 CA 1963, s 285(2); C(A)A 1982, s 10; see *Re Castlemahon Poultry Products Ltd* [1987] ILRM 222.

442 CA 1963, s 285(2).

443 CA 1963, s 295(2).

444 CA 1963, s 285(2).

445 CA 1963, s 285(2).

446 Unfair Dismissals Act 1977, s 12.

447 Minimum Notice and Terms of Employment Act 1973.

448 Redundancy Payments Acts 1967–1979.

449 CA 1963, s 285(14).

450 [1996] 3 IR 531.

[27.172] Where the assets are insufficient to go around amongst the preferential creditors, then all preferential creditors rank *pari passu* and will each receive so many cent for every euro owed[451].

[27.173] It has been held that directors who have valid contracts of employment with the company will be deemed to be employees for the purposes of bringing them within the category of preferential creditor. In *Re Dairy Lee Ltd*[452] a director who was held to be an employee under an oral contract of employment had his claim admitted as a preferential debt[453]. Even where a director does not have an express contract of employment, it may be proved on the facts that where he works full-time for the company and draws a salary, that he may be an employee under an implied contract of employment[454].

(b) Floating charges

[27.174] Although the holder of a floating charge is a secured creditor, his security is very much less than that enjoyed by the holder of a fixed charge or mortgage. What the legislature has given to secured creditors generally, the legislature has taken away from creditors secured by a floating charge. Section 285(7)(b) of CA 1963, provides that the preferential claims listed above[455], shall:

> '....so far as the assets of the company available for payment of general creditors are insufficient to meet them, have priority over the claims of holders of debentures under any floating charge created by the company, and be paid accordingly out of any property comprised in or subject to that charge.'

Accordingly, the effect of s 285(7)(b) is to oust the operation of the Bankruptcy Act 1988, s 136(2) considered above[456]. For this reason, claims secured by a floating charge take subsequent to preferential claims.

[27.175] Before crystallisation, assets which are the subject of a floating charge can be whittled away through set-off, execution of process, and subsequent fixed charges where the holder of the fixed charge does not have notice of the existence of the prior floating charge[457]. After crystallisation, the assets subject to the floating charge become subject to a quasi-fixed charge.

[27.176] If a surplus remains after the preferential creditors have been paid, the holder of a floating charge is next in line. Where there are insufficient assets to satisfy the claims of all those whose claims are secured by floating charges the priority of payment will usually be based on the priority of the creation of their security.

---

451 CA 1963, s 285(7)(a).

452 *Re H William (Tallaght) Ltd* [1976] IR 314.

453 See *Re Beeton & Co Ltd* [1913] 2 Ch 279 and *Lee v Lee's Air Farming Ltd* [1961] AC 12.

454 In this respect the court will apply a similar test to that applied in deciding whether or not a person is employed under a contract of service or contract for services, the latter making them an independent contractor, see *Re Sunday Tribune Ltd* [1985] ILRM 698.

455 See para **[27.171]**.

456 See para **[27.130]**.

457 See Chapter 20, *Corporate Borrowing: Debentures and Security*, para **[20.083]** *ff*.

(c) Unsecured creditors

[27.177] Next in line in an insolvent liquidation are those unfortunates who have advanced money, goods or services to the company without taking any security, or those whose security has been set aside. Their position is most vulnerable and in an insolvent liquidation, by definition, there will not be sufficient assets left to satisfy their claims. Where there are some but not enough assets to pay all of the claims of the unsecured creditors, the unsecured creditors will rank *pari passu* amongst themselves.

(d) Members and contributories of the company

[27.178] In a *solvent* liquidation, there may be a surplus remaining after all other creditors have been paid, and if there is that surplus will be available for distribution amongst the members of the company: CA 1963, s 275[458]. Members who are owed dividends by the company when it goes into liquidation do not lose their claims, although they will not rank as creditors of the company[459]. Rather, they will only be paid after all other creditors have been paid, whereupon, any sum so due to a member shall be taken into account for the purpose of finally adjusting the rights of the contributories of the company: CA 1963, s 207(1)(g)[460]. The basic rule here is that sums due to a member 'in his character of a member' will only be paid after all creditors have been paid. The equivalent English provision[461] was recently considered in *Soden v British and Commonwealth Holdings plc*[462]. In that case British and Commonwealth Holdings plc ('B&C') had acquired the entire issued share capital in Atlantic Computers plc ('A'). The acquisition proved to be disastrous for both companies and both were ultimately placed into administration. B&C instituted proceedings against A for alleged negligent misrepresentations in connection with its purchase of A's shares. A's liabilities greatly exceeded its assets – an arrangement was eventually approved by the court whereby all creditors would rank pari passu in the distribution of the company's assets. The administrators sought a declaration that, were B&C to be successful in its action for damages for negligent misrepresentation, it would not be entitled to share in that distribution. The basis for seeking the declaration was the Insolvency Act 1986, s 74(2)(f) (UK) which, like CA 1963, s 207(1)(g), subordinates sums due to a member 'in his character of a member'. In the High Court, Court of Appeal and eventually the House of Lords it was consistently held that B&C *would* be entitled to share pari passu with other creditors in the distribution of A's assets because if B&C were awarded damages, those damages would be owed to B&C as a creditor, and not in its capacity as a member. In the House of Lords Lord Browne-Wilkinson held:

> 'Section 74(2)(f) requires a distinction to be drawn between, on the one hand, sums due to a member in his character of a member by way of dividends, profits or otherwise and, on the other hand, sums due to a member otherwise than in his character as a member. In the absence of any other indication to the contrary, sums due in the character of a member must

458 See *Re Consolidated Gold Fields of New Zealand Ltd* [1953] All ER 791; *Re LB Holliday & Co Ltd* [1986] BCLC 227; and *Re Belfast Empire Theatre of Varieties Ltd* [1963] IR 41.

459 See *Wilson (Inspector of Taxes) v Dunnes Stores (Cork) Ltd* (22 January 1976, unreported), High Court, per Kenny J.

460 See Chapter 15, *Shares and Membership*, para **[15.073]**.

461 Insolvency Act 1986 (UK), s 74(2)(f).

462 *Soden and another v British and Commonwealth Holdings plc* [1997] 4 All ER 353.

> be sums falling due under and by virtue of the statutory contract between the members and the company and the members inter se constituted by s 14(1) of the Companies Act 1985 [ie CA 1963, s 25]…In my judgment, in the absence of any contrary indication sums due to a member 'in his character of a member' are only those sums the right to which is based by way of cause of action on the statutory contract'.[463]

In the circumstances, the House of Lords held that any damages payable were not due in the capacity of a member and that the claim against A stood on exactly the same footing as any other claim by other creditors.

[27.179] In an official or compulsory liquidation, it is the duty of the court to settle a list of contributories[464] and to cause the assets of the company to be collected and applied in discharge of its liabilities: CA 1963, s 235(1). Moreover, by CA 1963, s 242 it is provided that:

> 'The court shall adjust the rights of the contributories among themselves and distribute any surplus among the persons entitled thereto.'

Accordingly, in an official winding up it is the duty of the court to determine which member-contributories are entitled to which assets. By contrast, in a members' or creditors' voluntary winding up, it is the duty and function of the liquidator, after paying the debts of the company, to adjust the rights of the member-contributories, distributing any surplus among them by virtue of CA 1963, s 276(2).

[27.180] Section 275(1)(b) of CA 1963[465] provides that on every winding up'[466] the property of a company shall, unless the articles of association provide otherwise, be distributed among the members according to their rights and interests in the company. The rights of all members cannot, however, be assumed to be equal. Individual shareholders may have different rights by virtue of the class of shares held by them and the rights accorded to such shares by the company's memorandum or articles of association and any shareholders' agreements that subsist between the shareholding members. In particular, conflicts may arise between the holders of ordinary shares and the holders of preferential shares to participate in a surplus of assets after the payment of a preferential dividend[467].

Distributions in specie

[27.181] One reason why a solvent company may be wound up is where the members wish to legally take the assets out of the company by means of a *distribution in specie*, ie in the form of the assets and not in their equivalent in say cash. As Laffoy has commented:

---

463 [1997] 4 All ER 353 at 357.

464 Only if necessary to make calls on or adjust the rights of contributories, otherwise the court may dispense with the settlement of a list of contributories: CA 1963, s 235(2).

465 See also CA 1990, s 132.

466 CA 1963, s 274 provides that CA 1963, ss 275–282 shall apply to every voluntary winding up, whether a members' or a creditors' winding up.

467 See generally, Chapter 15, *Shares and Membership*, para **[15.105]** *ff*; and *Re Cork Electric Supply Co Ltd* [1931] IR 314.

'...in the case of a private company, for example, a property holding company, it is frequently more desirable to vest the company's lands and premises in the members in specie on a members' voluntary winding up than to realise the assets and distribute the proceeds of realisation.'[468]

[27.182] The first prerequisite to distributing a company's assets amongst its members, in specie, is that the company must be placed into members' voluntary liquidation. All of the formalities attendant upon this process and considered in Chapter 25[469] must be complied with in all respects[470]. In addition, it is necessary that the company's articles of association expressly provide for a distribution in specie. Model reg 137 of CA 1963, Sch 1, Table A provides:

> If the company is wound up, the liquidator may, with the sanction of a special resolution of the company and any other sanction required by the Act, divide among the members in specie or kind the whole or any part of the assets of the company (whether they shall consist of property of the same kind or not) and may, for such purpose, set such value as he deems fair upon any property to be divided as aforesaid and may determine how such division shall be carried out as between the members or different classes of members. The liquidator may, with the like sanction, vest the whole or any part of such assets in trustees upon such trusts for the benefit of the contributories as the liquidator, with the like sanction, shall think fit, but so that no member shall be compelled to accept any shares or other securities whereon there is any liability.

Care should be taken to ensure that such a provision is contained in a company's articles of association (or memorandum of association) before proceeding with a distribution in specie[471]. Since a liquidator is only entitled to make a distribution in specie where there are surplus assets, it is good practice to prepare a statutory declaration from the liquidator, for the members' benefit, confirming this fact[472]. It should be noted that where the effect of a distribution in specie is that a member-director is to acquire a non-cash asset of the requisite amount (within the meaning of CA 1990, s 29(1)(a)) such a substantial property transaction is expressly exempted by s 29(8) where the arrangement is made with a person 'in his character as such member', as would be the case in a distribution in specie[473].

[27.183] The great attraction with distributions in specie is that the company's real property can be conveyed or otherwise transferred to the company's members without the payment of *ad velorum* stamp duty. This is because *ad valorum* duty is not chargeable where a conveyance is from a trustee to a beneficiary[474]. In a distribution in specie, a

---

[468] Laffoy, *Irish Conveyancing Precedents* (looseleaf), E264.

[469] See paras **[25.002]** to **[25.008]**.

[470] See *Re Strathblaine Estates Ltd* [1948] Ch 228, mentioned in Chapter 4, *Incorporation and its Consequences*, para **[4.036]**.

[471] Laffoy, *Irish Conveyancing Precedents*, (at E264): 'in the absence of an express provision in either the memorandum or the articles of association, it is doubtful whether the liquidator has power to distribute the company's assets in specie on a winding-up'.

[472] See Laffoy, *Irish Conveyancing Precedents*, E264.

[473] See Chapter 11, *Statutory Regulation of Transactions Between Directors and their Companies*, para **[11.039]**.

[474] Stamp Duties Consolidation Act 1999, s 30(5).

liquidator will, owing fiduciary duties, be a trustee for the members[475]. Where there is no money passing (as might be the case, where, say, a member makes a money payment to recompense the company for an excess in the value of real property distributed). Moreover, even where money is not passing the Revenue Commissioners must be satisfied that the distribution to members is being carried our in proportion to their entitlement as members to participate[476]. Members' entitlement to participate will turn on their shareholding as at the date of the resolution to wind up the company and it should be noted that shareholdings are prima facie immutable after the commencement of a winding up on account of CA 1963, s 255 which provides that 'any transfer of shares, not being a transfer made to or with the sanction of the liquidator, and any alteration in the status of the members of the company' made after the commencement of a voluntary winding up, is void.

---

475 Cf *Wigan Coal and Iron Co Ltd v Inland Revenue Commissioners* [1945] 1 All ER 392 where it was held that a company could not be the trustee of its own assets for its members and that any disposition to them operated as an *inter vivos* disposition that attracted *ad velorum* stamp duty.

476 In Donegan & Friel, *Irish Stamp Duty Law* (2nd edn, 1998), p 289, it is noted that the deed must be adjudicated and the following matters lodged with the form ADJN9: (a) proof that the property is being transferred in direct proportion to the entitlement to participate; (b) the names and addresses of the participating members and their shareholdings as at the date of the resolution to liquidate; and (c) a copy of the winding-up resolution.

Chapter 28

Public Companies in Context

Introduction

[28.001] While much of the law applicable to private companies is also applicable to public companies, many differences exist in the practical application of the Companies Acts to different types of companies. It now falls to consider public companies and to examine those aspects of company law which are exclusively applicable to public companies. As shall be seen in this chapter, there are six distinct types of *public company.* At the outset it is important to note that these six types of public company have diverse traits and that some have more in common with private companies than they have with their fellow public companies. The public company that is most different from the private company is the *public limited company* (PLC). The differences are even more pronounced in the case of a PLC, limited by shares, which is *listed* on the stock exchange. PLCs are of paramount importance to the Irish economy, generating most of the wealth created and employing tens of thousands of people. When company law makes the news it is typically a PLC specific issue eg disclosure of directors' remuneration and other issues in corporate governance, protection of the investing public and volatility of share prices, accounting practices etc. PLCs are, however, relatively few in number. Of the 130,516 companies registered with the Companies Registration Office (CRO) as at 31 December 2001, a mere 0.6%, or 914 companies, were PLCs limited by shares[1]. Care must, therefore, be taken when legislating for companies or commenting on company law not to generalise for all companies from issues specific to a numerically small, albeit economically important type of company.

[28.002] Those aspects of the law applicable to public companies which are most diverse from the law and practice applicable to private companies relate to: formation, capitalisation, membership, corporate governance, transfer of shares, and accounting disclosure requirements. The law and practice on the *division of powers* between members and directors and *corporate governance* of PLCs differ most markedly from such in private companies[2]. In a public company, membership is invariably divorced from management since, even where the directors are also shareholders, their shareholding will not typically represent a controlling interest in the company. Accordingly, the *division of powers* between shareholders and directors, so notably absent in many private companies, is a reality in many public companies[3].

---

1 See the *Companies Report 2001*, Appendix 12, p 73.

2 See Chapter 8, *Corporate Governance: Management by the Directors*, for the division of powers between members and directors and corporate governance in private companies.

3 See Chapter 8, *Corporate Governance: Management by the Directors*, para **[8.003]**.

The public company defined

[28.003] Before the passing of the Companies (Amendment) Act 1983 ('C(A)A 1983') all companies were automatically public companies, unless their articles of association contained the restrictions set out in the Companies Act 1963, s 33 ('CA 1963'), whereupon they were private companies. Now, C(A)A 1983, s 2 provides in a circular manner that: 'public company' means a company which is not a private company.'

[28.004] There exist a number of different types of public company, some of which are more common in practice than others. The types of public company which may be formed today are:

- the public limited company limited by shares;
- the public limited company limited by guarantee and having a share capital;
- the public limited company with a variable share capital;
- the public company limited by guarantee that does not have a share capital;
- the public unlimited company having a share capital; and
- the public unlimited company not having a share capital.

All public companies are multi-member companies and cannot be single-member companies. These six types of public company may be considered as falling into three generic categories:

(a) Public limited companies (PLCs).
(b) Public companies limited by guarantee not having a share capital.
(c) Public unlimited companies.

(a) Public limited companies (PLCs)

[28.005] The most important type of public company is the *public limited company* or PLC. Public limited company is defined by C(A)A 1983, s 2 as being:

> '...a public company limited by shares or a public company limited by guarantee and having a share capital, being a company —
>
> (a) the memorandum of which states that the company is to be a public limited company; and
>
> (b) in relation to which the provisions of the Companies Acts as to the registration or re-registration of a company as a public limited company have been complied with on or after the appointed day[4]...

It should be noted that a PLC can be either limited by shares or limited by guarantee. However, all PLCs *must* have a share capital, even where they are limited by guarantee. A PLC can also have a variable share capital. PLCs which are limited by guarantee and which have a share capital are an endangered species: C(A)A 1983, s 7 provides that:

> 'On or after the appointed day, no company shall be formed as, or become, a public company limited by guarantee and having a share capital.'

---

4 The 'appointed day' means the day appointed by the Minister under C(A)A 1983, s 1(3) for the coming into operation of the Act: C(A)A 1983, s 2(1). The C(A)A 1983 was brought into operation on 13 October 1983: Companies (Amendment) Act 1983 (Commencement) Order 1983 (SI 1983/288).

The only public companies in existence, which are limited by guarantee *and* have a share capital, are those that were incorporated as such before 13 October 1983.

[28.006] In practice, the PLC limited by shares is by far the more common of the two possible forms of PLC envisaged by C(A)A 1983, s 2. The PLC limited by shares is the necessary vehicle if a company is to trade its shares on the Irish Stock Exchange. Of course, the many other requirements of the Stock Exchange must also be complied with. These are set out, in the main, in the so-called 'Yellow Book', *Admission of Securities to Listing.*

(b) Public companies limited by guarantee not having a share capital

[28.007] The prohibition in C(A)A 1983, s 7 on the formation of public companies limited by guarantee and having a share capital, does not, obviously, affect the formation of public companies limited by guarantee which *do not have a share capital.* Public companies limited by guarantee without a share capital are a relatively popular type of public company in Ireland today. Such public companies are typically used as *management companies* in retail shopping centres or residential apartment developments. The incorporation of such companies is usually necessary where the number of members of a management company is likely to exceed 50, since 50 is generally the maximum permitted number in a private company[5].

(c) Public unlimited companies

[28.008] Public unlimited companies may be incorporated either with or without a share capital. Unlimited companies which do not have a share capital cannot by definition be private companies since all private companies must have a share capital[6]. Public unlimited companies, whether with or without a share capital, are rarely incorporated in Ireland.

[28.009] In this chapter it is proposed to approach the examination of the public company in much the same way as the private company has been considered already. Accordingly, most of those areas which comprise Chapters 2-27 shall be considered here under similar headings. Much of the law will be the same, and the reader's attention shall be drawn to those issues where the law differentiates substantially between private and public companies. The following areas are considered:

1. Formation and registration of public companies.
2. Public constitutional documentation.
3. Incorporation and its consequences.
4. Disregarding separate legal personality.
5. Corporate civil litigation.
6. Corporate contracts: capacity and authority.
7. Corporate governance: management by the directors.
8. Corporate governance: meetings.
9. Duties of directors and other officers.
10. Statutory regulation of transactions involving directors and their companies.

---

5 See Chapter 1, *The Private Company in Context*, para **[1.115]**.

6 CA 1963, s 33. See Chapter 1, *The Private Company in Context*, para **[1.115]**.

11. Company law compliance and enforcement.
12. Accounts and auditors.
13. Investigations and inspectors.
14. Shares and membership in public companies.
15. Share transfer in public companies.
16. Groups of companies.
17. Maintenance of capital in public companies.
18. Shareholders' remedies.
19. Corporate borrowing by public companies.
20. Examinership and schemes of arrangement.
21. Winding up of public companies.

Formation and registration of public companies[7]

[28.010] Public companies may be formed afresh or can come into existence through the successful conversion of a private company. The formation of a public company is achieved in much the same way as a private company ie by lodging the appropriate documents in the companies registration office.

[28.011] A public company will normally be formed afresh, or a private company will be converted to a public company, where the constraints of CA 1963, s 33 conflict with operational requirements. Accordingly, a public company may be formed to enable a company to offer its shares for sale to the public or to extend its maximum membership beyond 50; both of which may not be done by private companies[8]. First, it may be decided to convert a private company to a public limited company to enable the company to raise finance from the general investing public and institutional investors by offering its shares for sale. Typically, this will be done where a strong private company is starved of sufficient financial reserves to finance its activities, and opts by choice or necessity for an injection of share capital as opposed to loan capital. In such a case a radical transformation of the private corporate structure will take place. Secondly, as has already been observed, public companies are frequently employed as management companies where the number of members is likely to exceed 50. The dichotomy gives rise to a two-fold practical classification of public companies: those which are PLCs limited by shares and those which are public companies limited by guarantee not having a share capital. Together, these two types of public company account for the greatest number of public companies on the register. Here, the focus is on the PLC.

[28.012] The formation and registration of public companies is considered here in the following manner:

(a) Formation of a public company.

(b) Flotation, the prospectus and Stock Exchange listing.

(c) Criminal sanctions for false particulars.

---

7 See generally Chapter 2, *Formation, Registration and Conversion of Private Companies*.

8 CA 1963, s 33. See Chapter 1, *The Private Company in Context*, para **[1.115]**.

(d) Civil sanctions for false particulars.

(e) Registration of public companies and commencement of business.

(f) Converting from a private company to a public company.

(a) Formation of a public company

[28.013] A public company may be formed in much the same way as a private company. The following documents must be filed in the companies registration office ('CRO'):

— the memorandum and articles of association,

— the Form No A1.

Those features of the memorandum and articles of association which are peculiar to public companies are set out later[9]. The details required to be completed in the Form No A1 have been set out in Chapter 2[10].

(b) Flotation, the prospectus and Stock Exchange listing

[28.014] Intrinsic to many public companies, and to all public limited companies, is that they will offer their shares to the public. The advertising of shares to the public is generally achieved by the issuing of a *prospectus*. Because of the potential for abuse of investors, both small and large, the legislature, the common law and the Stock Exchange have sought to regulate the issuing of shares to the investing public[11]. Here, the following matters require to be considered:

(i) Flotations.

(ii) Prospectuses.

(iii) The statement in lieu of prospectus.

(iv) Stock Exchange regulation and listing particulars.

(i) Flotations

[28.015] Although it is possible for a public company to sell its shares directly to the investing public, it is common for many such companies to sell their shares through the Stock Exchange and to *float the company* in this way. The flotation of a public company may be effected in, or in a combination of, any of the following ways[12]:

— *offer for sale* to the public, achieved by the sale of all shares to an 'issuing house', which will endeavour to sell on the shares to the investing public;

— *placing* the shares by offering them for sale to an issuing house, which will try to place them with an institutional investor;

— *sale by tender* where the shares are set at a minimum price and offered for sale;

— *rights issue*, where an existing public company raises additional capital through a fresh allotment of shares to existing members.

In this regard it is important to appreciate the very wide meaning assigned to 'offering shares or debentures to the public'. Section 61(1) of CA 1963 provides:

---

9 See para **[28.048]**.

10 See, Chapter 2, *Formation, Registration and Conversion of Private Companies*, para **[2.027]**.

11 See generally, Ussher, *Company Law in Ireland* (1986), p 390 *ff*, and Keane, *Company Law* (3rd edn, 2000), pp 85–94.

12 See Keane, *Company Law* (3rd edn, 2000), p 86.

> 'Any reference in this Act to offering shares or debentures to the public shall, subject to any provision to the contrary contained therein, be construed as including a reference to offering them to any section of the public, whether selected as members or debenture holders of the company concerned or as clients of the person issuing the prospectus or in any other manner, and references in this Act or in a company's articles to invitations to the public to subscribe for shares or debentures shall, subject as aforesaid, be similarly construed.'

The legal controls which exist on the flotation of a public company are next considered.

(ii) Prospectuses

[28.016] The first legal control on the issuing of shares to the public is that it is *unlawful* to issue any form of application to purchase shares in a company unless it is issued with the required *prospectus*[13]. A prospectus is defined in very broad terms by CA 1963, s 2(1) as meaning:

> '...any prospectus, notice, circular, advertisement or other invitation, offering to the public for subscription or purchase any shares or debentures of a company.'

Prospectuses can take the form of a newspaper advertisements which will describe the company and its prospects. The purpose of a prospectus is to provide a means whereby all relevant information is disclosed to the investing public. The issue and registration of prospectuses in Ireland is a rare enough business. In the period 1999-2001 a mere 560 prospectuses were submitted to the companies registration office of which 188 were domestic and 372 were foreign[14].

[28.017] The information which is required[15] to be contained in a prospectus is set out in CA 1963, Sch 3 as amended by the European Communities (Transferable Securities and Stock Exchange) Regulations 1992, reg 8[16]. Every prospectus must set out the matters specified in CA 1963, Sch 3, Part I and must set out the reports specified in Part II of that Schedule, both parts being subject to the provisions in Part III of that Schedule. CA 1963, Sch 3 and the Regulations interact unhappily and the Company Law Review Group's First Report recommends that the provisions in CA 1963 as to when a prospectus must be prepared and filed be repealed and the Regulations utilised[17].

In the case of a prospectus which is issued to the general public and not to existing members or debenture holders of the company, it must have endorsed on it, or attached to it, a copy of any contract required by CA 1963, Sch 3, Part I, para 14. Such contracts are those which are material and not in the ordinary course of the company's business in the previous five years. Where such contracts are not in writing, a memorandum giving full particulars must be endorsed or attached to the prospectus[18].

---

13 CA 1963, s 44(3).

14 See *Companies Report 2001*, Appendix 12, p 75.

15 By CA 1963, s 44(1) and the European Communities (Transferable Securities and Stock Exchange) Regulations 1992 (SI 1992/202), reg 6.

16 SI 1992/205.

17 Company Law Review Group, *First Report*, (2002) Government Publications, recommendation 9.4.1.

18 CA 1963, s 47.

[28.018] Where a prospectus contains a statement purporting to be made by an *expert*, then that expert's consent to its issue must also be attached or endorsed[19]. 'Expert' is defined as including any engineer, valuer, accountant and any other person whose profession gives authority to a statement made by him[20].

All prospectuses must also have a statement attached to them or endorsed on them relating to any adjustments which are deemed necessary by the company's auditors relating to profits, losses, assets or liabilities set out in any reports contained in the prospectus[21].

Amongst the other matters which require to be set out in prospectuses are particulars of the directors and auditors of the company; details of the expenses likely to be incurred in the floatation; details of the investment to be made; and details of the business and property of the company.

[28.019] Part II of CA 1963, Sch 3 provides that certain reports must be made by the company's auditors on matters such as the amount of dividends paid over the preceding three financial years; profits and losses; assets and liabilities; and general liabilities of the company and its subsidiaries, if any. Similar reports are required on any business to be acquired directly or indirectly by the proceeds of the issue. Where the proceeds will be used to acquire shares in another company being sufficient as to make that other company its subsidiary, similar reports are required. Part III of Sch 3 contains provisions which apply in the implementation and interpretation of the provisions in Parts I and II of Sch 3.

[28.020] In certain circumstances a prospectus is not required where a company is floated. Where the public is not involved or where the proposed investors are already familiar with the affairs of the company, the law views the flotation differently, and does not insist upon the company issuing a statutory prospectus. These situations are eight-fold:

- where there is a *bona fide* underwriting agreement[22];
- where shares or debentures are not offered to the public[23];
- where the issue of shares or debentures is limited to the company's existing members or debenture holders, whether such is renounceable or not[24];
- where the issued securities are 'in all respects uniform' with securities issued within the preceding two years and are dealt with or quoted on a recognised stock exchange[25];
- where the company gets a certificate or exemption from a recognised stock exchange, in which case the advertisement complying with the regulations of the stock exchange for a quotation will be deemed to be a prospectus in accordance with CA 1963[26];
- where an application has been made for an 'official listing'[27];

---

19 CA 1963, s 46.

20 CA 1963, s 46(3).

21 CA 1963, Sch 3, Part I, para 29.

22 CA 1963, s 44(4)(a).

23 CA 1963, s 44(4)(b).

24 CA 1963, s 44(7)(a).

25 CA 1963, s 44(7)(b).

26 CA 1963, s 45.

27 See the European Communities (Stock Exchange) Regulations 1984 (SI 1984/282), reg 12.

— where the Stock Exchange exempts a company on the basis that to require it to prepare a prospectus would be 'unduly burdensome'[28]; or

— in the circumstances set out in Article 2 and Article 5 of the Prospectus Directive[29].

[28.021] As regards the definition of 'the public', where an invitation or offer is intended to apply only to those receiving it, or where it is the 'domestic concern' of the persons making and receiving it, it shall not be taken as made to the public: CA 1963, s 61(1) and (2). In *Shwernell v Combined Incandescent Mantles Syndicate*[30] an invitation to a few friends of the directors was held not to be 'an issue to the public'. It is not sufficient that the document be drawn up for public circulation – it must actually be issued to the public. In *Nash v Lynde*[31] the directors of a private company prepared a document which was in the form of a general offer for shares. It was not advertised but a copy was shown to one person with a view to his subscribing to the company and becoming a director. It was held by the House of Lords that the document was not issued to the public as a prospectus, Lord Sumner holding:

> ' "The Public" in the definition section...is of course a general word. No particular numbers are prescribed. Anything from two to infinity may serve; perhaps even one, if he is intended to be the first of a series of subscribers but makes further proceedings needless by himself subscribing the whole. The point is that the offer is such as to be open to anyone who brings his money and applies in due form, whether the prospectus was addressed to him on behalf of the company or not. A private communication is thus not open...[to being deemed to be made to the public].'

Whether shares or debentures will be deemed to have been issued to the public will depend entirely upon the circumstances of each case[32].

(iii) The statement in lieu of prospectus

[28.022] Section 54 of CA 1963[33] provides that a public company[34] which has a share capital may not allot any of its shares or debentures unless it delivers to the Registrar of Companies, a statement in lieu of prospectus at least three days before its first allotment of shares or debentures where:

— it does not issue a prospectus on its formation (having raised capital by other means, such as loan capital), or,

— where it did issue a prospectus but did not allot any shares (ie where the issue of shares failed).

---

28 The European Communities (Transferable Securities and Stock Exchange) Regulations 1992 (SI 1992/202), reg 8(4).

29 89/298/EEC of 17 April 1989. See the European Communities (Transferable Securities and Stock Exchange) Regulations 1992 (SI 1992/202), reg 7.

30 *Shwernell v Combined Incandescent Mantles Syndicate* [1907] WN 110.

31 *Nash v Lynde* [1929] AC 158.

32 *Re South of England Natural Gas and Petroleum Co Ltd* [1911] 1 Ch 573.

33 As amended by C(A)A 1983, Sch 1, para 8.

34 See CA 1963, s 54(3)(a) and (b) which provides that private companies and PLCs, as defined by C(A)A 1983, are excluded from this requirement.

The statement must be signed by every person named as a director or a proposed director or his agent authorised in writing. The form of this statement must be in accordance with CA 1963, Sch 4, and the required details here are similar to those set out in Sch 3, considered above[35]. Adjustments made, or required to be made, in its reports must be highlighted by a statement attached to or endorsed on the statement in lieu of prospectus[36].

[28.023] Where a company acts in contravention of CA 1963, s 54(1) or (2), the company and every director who knowingly and wilfully authorises or permits the contravention shall be liable to a fine not exceeding €634.87[37]. Moreover, where a statement in lieu of prospectus includes any untrue statement any person who authorised the delivery of the statement for registration is liable on conviction on indictment, to imprisonment for a term not exceeding two years or a fine not exceeding €3,174.35, or both, or on summary conviction to imprisonment for a term not exceeding six months or a fine not exceeding €634.87, or both[38]. In either case, it is a defence to prove that the untrue statement was immaterial or that the person had reasonable grounds to believe, and did believe, up to the time of delivery of the statement that the untrue statement was true. A statement is deemed to be untrue if it is misleading in the form and context in which it is included[39]. A statement is deemed to be included in a statement in lieu of prospectus if it is contained therein or in any report or memorandum appearing on the face thereof or by reference incorporated therein[40].

[28.024] A statement in lieu of prospectus is also required to be delivered to the Registrar of Companies in another situation. Where a private company makes application to convert to an unlimited public company, CA 1963, s 35(3) provides that it must, unless it issues and delivers a full prospectus, or has applied for a Stock Exchange listing[41], deliver a statement in lieu of prospectus to the Registrar of Companies. The form and content of this statement must be in accordance with CA 1963, Sch 2.

[28.025] A default in making a statement in lieu of prospectus renders the company and every officer in default[42] guilty of an offence and liable on summary conviction to a fine not exceeding €634.87[43]. Where a statement in lieu of prospectus includes any untrue statement, any person who authorises its delivery shall be guilty of an offence, and liable to a fine of €3,174.35 or two years' imprisonment on conviction on indictment, or both; and €634.87 or six months on summary conviction, or both, unless the person proves either that the untrue statement was immaterial or that the person had reasonable grounds to believe, and did believe up to the time of delivery, that the untrue statement was true[44].

---

35 See para **[28.017]**.

36 CA 1963, s 54(2).

37 CA 1963, s 54(4) as amended by C(A)A 1982, Sch 1.

38 CA 1963, s 54(5)(a) and (b) as amended by C(A)A 1982, Sch 1.

39 CA 1963, s 54(6)(a).

40 CA 1963, s 54(6)(b).

41 CA 1963, s 35(4).

42 See Chapter 12, *Company Law Compliance and Enforcement*, para **[12.032]**.

43 CA 1963, s 35(6).

44 CA 1963, s 35(7). See also CA 1963, s 35(8).

(iv) Stock Exchange regulation and listing particulars

[28.026] Where a company has applied for an official listing on the Stock Exchange it need not issue a prospectus. An application for an official listing must be made to the appropriate committee of the Irish Stock Exchange. In such a case, a document must be prepared which sets out the requisite listing particulars. In effect this will surpass the requirement that a company must issue a prospectus, and misstatements contained therein will attract the same liability as would misstatements in a statutory prospectus[45]. The rationale of this exception is rooted in an inter-Member State faith in the integrity and comprehensive scrutiny of the Stock Exchange. As noted elsewhere[46] the content of CA 1963, Sch 3 has largely been surpassed by the more detailed requirements of the Irish Stock Exchange.

[28.027] The matters which are required to be addressed in the *listing particulars* are those set out in the Schedules to the European Communities (Stock Exchange) Regulations 1984[47] which implement the Listing Particulars Directive[48]. While much specific information is required to be provided in similar detail to that required by the CA 1963, Sch 3[49], Article 4 of the Listing Particulars Directive provides a general rationale:

> 'The listing particulars shall contain the information which, according to the particular nature of the issuer and of the securities for the admission of which application is being made, is necessary to enable investors and their investment advisers to make an informed assessment of the assets and liabilities, financial position, profits and losses, and prospects of the issuer and of the rights attaching to such securities.'

Accordingly, it is clear that the aim is to ensure full disclosure of all particulars which a prudent investor would require before making an investment in a public company.

[28.028] The European Communities (Stock Exchange) Regulations 1984 empowers the Stock Exchange to dispense, in whole or in part, with the publication of the foregoing listing particulars. Where they are wholly dispensed with, a statutory prospectus will be required to be published, unless one of the other exemptions[50] set out above can be invoked.

[28.029] Publication of all relevant information is the key objective of the European Community (Stock Exchange) Regulations 1984. Regulation 13(1) requires that the listing particulars be delivered to the Registrar of Companies. The regulations also oblige all companies which obtain an official listing to publish their latest annual accounts and annual reports, and to make known to the public as soon as possible all material changes which would otherwise not be public knowledge[51]. All material changes set out therein must be brought to the attention of the Stock Exchange and of the public by

45 See para **[28.032]**.

46 See Ussher, *Company Law in Ireland* (1986), p 393.

47 SI 1984/282.

48 80/390/EEC of 17 March 1980.

49 See para **[28.017]**.

50 See para **[28.020]**.

51 Regulation 3(1) and Schedules C and D, applying the Admissions Directive (79/279/EEC) of 5 March 1979.

advertisement[52]. The regulations also implement another directive, the Interim Reports Directive[53] which requires that all companies actually listed must publish interim reports in a similar fashion.

(c) *Criminal sanctions for false particulars*

[28.030] The law regulates the flotation of public companies by imposing both criminal and civil sanctions for the issuing of false or misleading particulars which are intended to or in fact induce the public to subscribe for shares or debentures in a public company.

[28.031] Since it is considered to be necessary to oblige companies to disclose certain information to the investing public, it necessarily follows that there is justification for the imposition of criminal sanctions where the public is misled by false or misleading misstatements[54]. The failure to issue a prospectus, where such is required by law, is itself an offence by reason of CA 1963, s 44. Section 50(1) of CA 1963[55] provides:

> 'Where a prospectus issued after the operative date includes any untrue statement, any person who authorised the issue of the prospectus shall be liable—
>
> (a) on conviction on indictment, to imprisonment for a term not exceeding 2 years, or a fine not exceeding €3,174.35 or both; or
>
> (b) on summary conviction, to imprisonment for a term not exceeding 6 months, or a fine not exceeding €634.87, or both;
>
> unless he proves either that the statement was immaterial or that he had reasonable grounds to believe and did, up to the time of the issue of the prospectus, believe that the statement was true.'

Furthermore, CA 1963, s 52 provides that:

> '(a) a statement included in a prospectus shall be deemed to be untrue if it is misleading in the form and context in which it is included; and
>
> (b) a statement shall be deemed to be included in a prospectus if it is contained therein or in any report or memorandum appearing on the face thereof or by reference incorporated therein or issued therewith.'

The severity of the putative penalties shows the determination of the legislature that the information contained in prospectuses be accurate. In view of the severity of the foregoing provision, s 50(2) provides that a person shall not be deemed to have authorised the issue of a prospectus by reason only of his acting as 'an expert' and having given the consent required by CA 1963, s 46 to the inclusion therein of a statement purporting to be so made by him as an expert.

(d) *Civil sanctions for false particulars*

[28.032] There exist three ways which a misstatement in a prospectus can give rise to civil liability considered here under the following headings:

---

52 Admissions Directive, art 17.

53 82/121/EEC of 15 February 1982.

54 See *R v Kylesent* [1932] 1 KB 442.

55 As amended by C(A)A 1982, s 15 and Sch 1.

(i) Statutory liability.
(ii) Liability and remedies in equity.
(iii) Liability at common law.

(i) Statutory liability

[28.033] A right to *statutory compensation* for untrue statements in a prospectus is given by CA 1963, s 49(1). This provides:

> '...where a prospectus invites persons to subscribe for shares in or debentures of a company, the following persons shall be liable to pay compensation to all persons who subscribe for any shares or debentures on the faith of the prospectus for the loss or damage they may have sustained by reason of any untrue statement included therein—
>
> (a) every person who is a director of the company at the time of issue of the prospectus;
>
> (b) every person who has authorised himself to be named and is named in the prospectus as a director or as having agreed to become a director either immediately or after an interval of time;
>
> (c) every person being a promoter of the company;
>
> (d) every person who has authorised the issue of the prospectus.'

An 'expert' whose consent is required to the issue of a prospectus and who has given that consent shall not per se be liable by reason of having given his consent; however, he shall be so liable in respect of an untrue statement purporting to be made by him as an expert[56]. Persons shall not be liable under sub-s (1) where they withdrew their consent to become directors, withdrew their consent to the issue of the prospectus and where it was issued without their authority and consent[57]; where the prospectus was issued without their knowledge or consent and they gave reasonable public notice that it was issued without their consent or knowledge upon their becoming aware of its issue[58]; where after the issue of the prospectus but before any allotment thereunder they withdrew their consent on becoming aware of any untrue statement contained therein and gave reasonable public notice of the withdrawal and the reason therefor[59]; that in respect of non-expert statements, they had reasonable grounds to believe and did believe that the statement was true[60]; that in respect of expert statements, the statement fairly represented the statement or copies of extracts from reports that were correct and fair copies of the report and they had reasonable grounds to believe that the expert was competent to make the statement and had given their consent which was not revoked[61]; or, that in respect of untrue statements made by official persons or contained in what purports to be a copy of or extract from a public official document, that it was a correct and fair representation of the statement or copy of or extract from the document[62]. However, the foregoing savers shall not apply in respect of an expert who authorised the issue of the prospectus in respect of an untrue

56 CA 1963, s 49(2).
57 CA 1963, s 49(3)(a).
58 CA 1963, s 49(3)(b).
59 CA 1963, s 49(3)(c).
60 CA 1963, s 49(3)(d)(i).
61 CA 1963, s 49(3)(d)(ii).
62 CA 1963, s 49(3)(d)(iii).

statement purporting to be made by him as an expert[63]. Further savers from liability are contained in CA 1963, s 49(5)–(7).

(ii) Liability and remedies in equity

[28.034] Rescission of the contract of allotment of shares is available to an investor where he has been induced by an erroneous misstatement in a prospectus to enter into a contract of allotment. It is crucial to realise that the contract of allotment will not be void ab initio, but voidable at the instance of the duped investor. In this respect, the misstatement has the same effect as does a misrepresentation which induces a person to enter into any contract. As with a misrepresentation, rescission will not be permitted where *restitutio in integrum* is impossible[64]. In *Components Tube Co v Naylor*[65] O'Brien LCJ said:

> 'It appears to me to be one of the most elementary obligations of law as well as of morality that a prospectus, upon which the public are invited to buy, should be an honest and a candid one. When an invitation is held out to the public to buy on the faith of a prospectus, candour, entire candour, becomes an essential element of honesty.'

An example of a situation which may give rise to the rescission of a contract of allotment is provided by *Aaron's Reefs v Twiss*[66]. There, the prospectus of the company described a gold mine, the intended venture which the flotation was to finance, as being rich in gold. The existence of a contract between the company and its promoters, whereby the company would purchase the mine from the promoters, was disclosed. What was not disclosed, however, was that the proposed consideration would expend three quarters of the proposed outside public investment, leaving the company with very little working capital with which to undertake the business of mining[67]. The defendant subscribed for 100 shares in the company and subsequently the company made a call of four shillings per share. The defendant refused to pay this because of the company's poor performance, whereupon he was sued by the company. His defence was that he was fraudulently induced to enter the contract of allotment, and this succeeded, the court allowing him to rescind the contract.

(iii) Liability at common law

[28.035] An action for *breach of contract* may also be available to a person who has suffered as a result of an erroneous misstatement. It has been held that it is not open to a person who remains a member of the company to sue for breach of contract and recover compensation[68]. In such a case the disgruntled member should repudiate the shares, distance himself from the company and then sue for compensation for breach of contract[69].

[28.036] An action for damages for the *tort of deceit* may be appropriate where a person suffers loss and damage on account of a fraudulent misrepresentation made to him which

---

63 CA 1963, s 49(4).

64 Such as where the company concerned has gone into liquidation: *Oakes v Turquand and Harding* (1867) LR 2 HL 325.

65 *Components Tube Co v Naylor* [1900] 2 IR 1.

66 *Aaron's Reefs v Twiss* [1895] 2 IR 207 (Court of Appeal) and [1896] AC 273 (House of Lords).

67 The modern prospectus requirements in CA 1963, Sch 3 and the Listings Directive would now require the detailed disclosure of all material terms of such a contract.

68 *Houldsworth v City of Glasgow Bank* (1880) 5 App Cas 317.

69 *Re Addlestone Linoleum Co* (1887) 37 Ch D 191.

induces him to enter into a contract for the allotment of shares. This action is open to a person while he is still a member of the company, unlike an action for damages for breach of contract. One of the most celebrated cases of an action for deceit is *Derry v Peek*[70]. There, the directors of a company issued a prospectus which led investors to believe that the company was empowered by statute to employ the use of automotive power to run the company's tramways, as opposed to the use of horses. Such authority was in fact solely dependant upon the *fiat* of the Board of Trade, which had not been granted. The plaintiff-subscriber sued when the Board of Trade subsequently refused permission. However, because the directors honestly believed the contents of the prospectus, they were not liable in the tort of deceit. Lord Herschell stated:

> 'First, in order to sustain an action of deceit, there must be proof of fraud, and nothing short of that will suffice. Secondly, fraud is proved when it is shown that a false representation has been made (1) knowingly, or (2) without belief in its truth, or (3) recklessly, careless whether it be true or false.'[71]

That case may be contrasted with the case of *Jury v Stoker & Jackson*[72] where the plaintiff successfully recovered damages for deceit where it was proved that the directors fraudulently misrepresented in the prospectus that a particular individual would invest £7,500 in the company[73].

[28.037] The final possible course of action for a person who is induced to enter into a contract for the allotment of shares is to sue for damages for the *tort of negligent misstatement*. The leading authority on the tort of negligent misstatement is *Hedley Byrne & Co v Heller & Partners*[74] which established that liability can arise in appropriate circumstances from a negligent misstatement[75].

(e) Registration of public companies and commencement of business

[28.038] There exist a number of restrictions on the commencement of business by public companies. Section 6(1) of C(A)A 1983 provides that a company registered as a PLC on its original incorporation, *shall not do business or exercise any borrowing powers* unless the Registrar of Companies has issued it with a certificate under that section or the company has been re-registered as another form of company. The reason for the restriction is to ensure compliance with the minimum authorised share capital requirements which exist for PLCs. Section 19 of C(A)A 1983 sets this amount at €38,092.14, although this

---

70 *Derry v Peek* (1889) 14 App Cas 337.

71 (1889) 14 App Cas 337 at 374.

72 *Jury v Stoker & Jackson* (1882) 9 LR Ir 385.

73 There Sullivan MR said: 'In my opinion, the prospectus was deliberately and fraudulently adopted to make the concern attractive. The plaintiff acted on the prospectus and took the shares. I have a very strong opinion that the representation was false and fraudulent, to induce men to take shares in this company, and if loss has resulted from it, the person who made the false representation should be made to answer for the loss...The representation was false, fraudulent and material, made to induce a man to take the shares and loss has resulted to the plaintiff.'

74 *Hedley Byrne & Co v Heller & Partners* [1964] AC 465. See generally, McMahon & Binchy, *Law of Torts* (3rd edn, 2000), pp 967-977.

75 See generally *Securities Trust Ltd v Hugh Moore & Alexander Ltd* [1964] IR 417.

sum may be altered by the Minister by statutory instrument. C(A)A 1983, s 6(2) provides that the Registrar of Companies:

> '...shall issue a public limited company with a certificate under this section if, on an application made to him in the prescribed form by the company, he is satisfied that the nominal value of the company's allotted share capital is not less than the authorised minimum, and there is delivered to him a statutory declaration complying with subsection (3).'

The appropriate form which is required to be filed with the Registrar of Companies is a *Form 70*. This sets out the following matters which are enumerated in C(A)A 1983, s 6(3):

- that the nominal value of the company's allotted share capital is not less than the authorised minimum;
- the amount paid up, at the time of the application, on the allotted share capital of the company;
- the amount, or estimated amount, of the preliminary expenses of the company and the persons by whom any of those expenses have been paid or are payable; and
- any amount or benefit paid or given or intended to be paid or given to any promoter of the company, and the consideration for the payment or benefit.

Where a statutory declaration is made in accordance with C(A)A 1983, s 6(2), it is deemed to be sufficient evidence of the matters stated therein[76]. Where the Registrar of Companies issues a certificate under this section, it is conclusive evidence that the company is entitled to do business and exercise any borrowing powers[77]. While C(A)A 1983, s 6(7) makes contravention of the section a criminal offence, the general provisions of the section are without prejudice to the actual validity of any transaction. However, where a company does enter into a contravening transaction and fails to comply with the section within 21 days from being called upon to do so, C(A)A 1983, s 6(8) provides that the directors of the company shall be jointly and severally liable to indemnify the other party to the transaction in respect of any loss or damage suffered by the other party, by reason of the failure of the company to comply with the obligations contained in C(A)A 1983, s 6.

[28.039] A PLC, registered as such, which does not obtain a '*section 6 certificate*' within one year from its original incorporation can be struck-off the register of companies by the Registrar in accordance with CA 1963, s 311(5).

[28.040] Section 115 of CA 1963 imposes restrictions on public companies other than PLCs. It should be noted that s 115 has no application to public companies which do not have a share capital ie public companies limited by guarantee which do not have a share capital such as most management companies. Here, a distinction is made between cases where a company issues a prospectus and those where it does not. Where a public company with a share capital has issued a prospectus to subscribe for its shares, CA 1963, s 115(1) prohibits it from *commencing business or exercising any of its borrowing powers* unless four conditions are satisfied. These are:

---

[76] C(A)A 1983, s 6(5).

[77] C(A)A 1983, s 6(6).

(a) Sufficient shares have been allotted for cash to cover the 'minimum subscription' amount[78];

(b) Every director has paid for any shares taken or agreed to be taken by him, in the same proportion in cash as payable by public subscribers;

(c) No money is or can become liable to be repaid for failure to apply for or obtain permission to deal in shares or debentures on the Stock Exchange;

(d) A statutory declaration of compliance with the foregoing conditions has been made by the company secretary or a director and has been delivered to the Registrar of Companies.

A different scenario applies where a public company which has a share capital does not issue a prospectus. Such companies may not commence business or exercise any borrowing powers until the following three conditions are fulfilled:

— it has delivered a statement in lieu of prospectus to the Registrar of Companies;

— every director has paid for any shares taken or agreed to be taken by him, in the same proportion in cash as payable by public subscribers;

— a statutory declaration of compliance with the foregoing conditions has been made by the company secretary or a director and has been delivered to the Registrar of Companies.

On receiving the appropriate statutory declaration the Registrar of Companies is obliged to certify that the company is entitled to commence business, and such a certificate is conclusive evidence that it is entitled to commence business[79]. To commence business or exercise borrowing powers in contravention of this section renders every person responsible for the contravention liable to a fine of €634.87, without prejudice to any other liability[80]. Section 115 does not apply to private companies, PLCs, public companies which do not have a share capital and certain old companies registered under earlier Companies Acts[81]. Nothing in s 115 operates to prevent the simultaneous offer for subscription or allotment of any shares and debentures or the receipt of any money payable on application for debentures[82].

[28.041] The statutory obligations incidental to registration, spoken of in the context of private companies in Chapter 2[83], apply to all public companies. It should be noted however, that by C(A)A 1983, s 55, PLCs are obliged to publish in *Iris Oifigiúil*, certain matters over and above those matters which other companies are obliged to publish.

(f) Converting from a private company to a public company

[28.042] As previously observed[84], many public companies commence corporate life as private companies and subsequently convert to public companies. The conversion

---

78 See CA 1963, Sch 3, Part I, para 4.

79 CA 1963, s 115(3). On conclusive evidence see Chapter 4, *Incorporation and its Consequences*, para **[4.004]** *ff*.

80 CA 1963, s 115(6).

81 CA 1963, s 115(7).

82 CA 1963, s 115(5).

83 See Chapter 2, *Formation, Registration and Conversion of Private Companies*, para **[2.036]** *ff*.

84 See para **[28.011]**.

procedure is now governed by C(A)A 1983, s 9. Section 9(1) provides that a private company may be registered as a public limited company, if:

— it passes a special resolution, which complies with s 9(2), to the effect that it should be so re-registered;

— it files in the CRO the requisite Forms 71 and 72 signed by a director and the secretary of the company;

— all other statutory requirements are complied with[85].

[28.043] The special resolution referred to in C(A)A 1983, s 9(1) must, by s 9(2), address certain matters. It must:

— alter the company's memorandum so that it states that the company is to be a PLC;

— make such other alterations in the memorandum as are necessary to bring it in substance and in form into conformity with the requirements of the C(A)A 1983 with respect to the memorandum of a PLC; and

— make such alterations in the company's articles of association as are requisite in the circumstances[86].

Unsurprisingly, the net effect of C(A)A 1983, s 9(2) is to ensure that the constitutional documentation of the company reflects the change in its status.

[28.044] In addition to compliance with the foregoing, certain documents must be lodged with the Registrar of Companies. These are set out in C(A)A 1983, s 9(3), namely:

— a printed copy of the new memorandum and articles of association altered in accordance with the special resolution;

— a copy of a written statement by the auditors of the company, that in their opinion the relevant balance sheet[87] shows that at the balance sheet date the amount of the company's net assets was not less than the aggregate of its called-up share capital and undistributed reserves;

— a copy of the relevant balance sheet, together with a copy of an unqualified report by the company's auditors in relation to that balance sheet;

— a copy of any report prepared pursuant to s 9(5)(b); and,

— a statutory declaration in the prescribed form by a director or secretary of the company -

(a) that the special resolution mentioned in s 9(1)(a) has been passed and that the conditions specified in s 9(1)(c) have been satisfied, and

(b) that, between the balance sheet date and the application of the company for re-registration, there has been no change in the financial position of the company that has resulted in the amount of the company's net assets becoming less than the aggregate of its called-up share capital and undistributable reserves.

---

85 C(A)A 1983, s 5(a) and (b), where applicable and C(A)A 1983, s 10(1)(a)–(d).

86 On the constitutional documentation of public companies, see para **[28.048]**.

87 See Chapter 13, *Accounts and Auditors*, para **[13.064]**.

The foregoing declaration may be accepted by the Registrar of Companies as being sufficient evidence that the special resolution has been passed and that the said conditions have been satisfied[88].

[28.045] Special provisions apply where shares are allotted by the company either wholly or partly for non-cash consideration between the balance sheet date and the passing of the special resolution. Section 9(5) of C(A)A 1983 provides that the company shall not make an application for re-registration under s 9 unless, before making the application, the consideration has been valued in accordance with C(A)A 1983, ss 30 and 31 and a report regarding the value has been made by the company.

[28.046] Section 9(6) of C(A)A 1983 empowers the Registrar of Companies to issue a certificate of incorporation that the company is a PLC. The certificate is conclusive evidence[89] that the company is a PLC and that all requirements in C(A)A 1983 in respect of re-registration and all matters precedent and incidental thereto have been complied with[90]. By C(A)A 1983, s 9(7), such a certificate shall not issue where it appears to the registrar that the court has made an order confirming a reduction of the company's capital where this reduces the nominal value of the company's allotted share capital below the authorised minimum.

[28.047] Section 9(10) of C(A)A 1983 provides that a conversion of a company to a PLC shall not affect any rights or obligations of the company, or render defective any legal proceedings by or against the company.

Public constitutional documentation

[28.048] In a public company, the constitutional documents will invariably be limited to the memorandum and the articles of association. Shareholders' agreement are most uncommon in public companies and accordingly, there will usually be no 'hidden constitution', and all constitutional documentation will be of public record[91].

[28.049] The memorandum of association of a PLC, limited by shares, and of a PLC limited by guarantee should be in the form of C(A)A 1983, Sch 2, Part I and Part II, respectively[92]. The memorandum of a public company limited by guarantee not having a share capital is set out in CA 1963, Sch 1, Table C. The memorandum of an unlimited company having a share capital is set out in CA 1963, Sch 1, Table E.

[28.050] In relation to the memorandum of association of a PLC, the essential differences are that the name clause must provide that the words public limited company or 'p.l.c.' are included in the name of the company. The memorandum must also state that the company is a PLC, and that the share capital of the company is at least €38,092.14. It should also be noted that at least 25% of this figure must be fully paid up.

---

88 C(A)A 1983, s 9(4).

89 On conclusive evidence see Chapter 4, *Incorporation and its Consequences*, para **[4.004]** *ff.*

90 C(A)A 1983, s 9(9).

91 See generally Chapter 3, *Private Constitutional Documentation.*

92 For a public company limited by guarantee and having a share capital, see C(A)A 1983, Sch 2, Part II.

[28.051] Another fundamental difference is that in the case of a public company CA 1963, s 5 provides there must be at least seven members. In this respect, such a legal business structure is often unsuited to those engaged in a quasi-partnership type company, and public companies are thus true 'associations'. In most other respects the memorandum of association of a public company will be similar to that of a private company.

[28.052] The articles of association of a PLC, limited by shares, will be in the form of CA 1963, Sch 1, Part I. In essence, there are few differences between Part I and Part II. The model articles for a public company limited by guarantee not having a share capital are set out in CA 1963, Sch 1, Table C. The model articles for an unlimited company having a share capital are set out in CA 1963, Sch 1, Table E. Public companies, especially listed PLCs, will adopt articles of association that can be very much more elaborate than those adopted by other types of company. So, for example, listed PLCs will usually have provisions in their articles of association dealing with the issue of uncertificated shares[93].

[28.053] The law applicable to the alteration of both constitutional documents is broadly the same in public and private companies. In practice, the constitutional documentation in a public company will rarely be altered informally.

Incorporation and its consequences

[28.054] The incidents of corporate existence considered in Chapter 4, do not vary whether a company is public or private. Accordingly, for example, the certificate of incorporation of a public company enjoys the same conclusiveness as that of a private company[94], and a public company is no less a separate legal person from its members and management than a private company[95]. A public company does, of course, enjoy greater transferability of its interests since it is not obliged to place restrictions on the transfer of its shares or debentures in its constitutional documents.

Disregarding separate legal personality

[28.055] The same legal principles that permit disregard of the separate legal personality of private companies apply to public companies *mutatis mutandis*, and the reader is referred to the discussion of the relevant principles in Chapter 5.

Corporate civil litigation

[28.056] The legal principles considered in Chapter 6 that apply to private companies in the case of civil corporate litigation apply *mutatis mutandis* to public companies.

Corporate contracts: capacity and authority

[28.057] The law of corporate contracts applicable to a public company is broadly the same as that applicable to a private company[96]. The law regarding *capacity* of the company, or put in the negative, the doctrine of ultra vires, is exactly the same in a public

93 See para **[28.100]**.

94 See Chapter 4, *Incorporation and its Consequences,* para **[4.004]**.

95 See para **[4.023]**.

96 See generally Chapter 7, *Corporate Contracts: Capacity and Authority.*

company as in a private company. The law of authority of corporate agents as it applies to public companies is also the same to that which applies to private companies.

[28.058] The rules applicable to the use of a public company's common seal are the same as those which have been considered in the context of a private company[97]. However, a public limited company may, in practice, have an additional seal. Section 3 of the Companies (Amendment) Act 1977 provides that:

> 'A company other than a private company may have, for use for sealing securities issued by the company and for sealing documents creating or evidencing securities so issued, an official seal which is a facsimile of the common seal of the company with the addition on its face of the word "Securities" or the word "Urruis".'

In all other respects, the law applicable to the sealing of documents by public companies is the same as in a private company, considered in Chapter 7. One practical difference is that public companies tend to make more use of 'authorised signatories', as permitted by CA 1963, Sch 1, Table A, Part I, model reg 115.

[28.059] Section 115 of CA 1963 provides that a public company with a share capital, other than a PLC may not commence business or exercise its borrowing powers until it fulfils the requirements contained therein, and until the Registrar of Companies certifies that the company may commence business[98]. Section 115(4) provides:

> 'Any contract made or ratified by a company before the date at which it is entitled to commence business shall be provisional only, and shall not be binding on the company until that date, and on that date it shall become binding.'

Although CA 1963, s 115 itself affords no protection to outsiders dealing with the company, it is thought that reg 6 of SI 1973/163 may, in appropriate circumstances, be availed of by outsiders who act in good faith[99]. By reg 6, any transaction entered by persons acting in good faith, with certain company organs, will be deemed to be within the capacity of the company:

> '...and any limitation of the powers of that board of person, whether imposed by the memorandum or articles of association *or otherwise*, may not be relied upon as against any person so dealing with the company.' [Emphasis added]

The reference to 'or otherwise' would seem to be sufficiently wide as to include the statutory limitation on contractual capacity in CA 1963, s 115.

[28.060] Interestingly, C(A)A 1983, s 6[100], which imposes on PLCs similar restrictions to those imposed on other public companies by CA 1963, s 115, does not contain a similar provision concerning corporate contracts. Indeed, C(A)A 1983, s 6(8) provides that the provisions of the section are without prejudice to the validity of any transaction entered into by the PLC. However, if such a company enters into a transaction in contravention therewith within 21 days from being called upon to comply with its obligations, the directors of the company shall be liable to indemnify the other party to the transaction in

---

97 See para **[7.013]**.

98 See para **[28.040]**.

99 See Chapter 7, *Corporate Contacts: Capacity and Authority* para **[7.084]**.

100 See para **[28.038]**.

respect of any loss or damage suffered by the other party, by reason of the failure of the company to comply with those obligations.

[28.061] In relation to the transfer of shares in listed PLCs, reg 5 of the Companies Act 1990 (Uncertificated Securities) Regulations 1996[101] provides that the Statute of Frauds Act (Ireland) 1695, s 6 and the Supreme Court of Judicature (Ireland) Act 1877, s 28(6) and any other rule of law requiring the execution under hand or seal of a document in writing for the transfer of property, shall not apply (if they would otherwise do so) to any transfer of title to uncertificated units of a security through a relevant system[102].

Corporate governance: management by the directors

[28.062] '*Corporate governance*' has become a veritable shibboleth in modern industrialised societies. 'Good' corporate governance is the zenith of corporate correctness and the phrase has assumed a meaning far in excess of the sum of its parts. In the wake of the financial scandals that in 2002 rocked corporate America, it would seem that corporate governance will be on the agenda for the foreseeable future.

[28.063] Throughout the 1990s a series of English committees reported on best practices in corporate governance. The first such report was the Cadbury Report (chaired by Sir Adrian Cadbury) which was published in December 1992. It contained a summary of the committees' recommendations in a *code of best practice*. Amongst the issues considered by the Cadbury Report were the role of auditors and the rights and responsibilities of shareholders and the structure and responsibility of boards of directors. The Greenbury Report followed[103]. Amongst its key themes were: accountability, responsibility, full-disclosure, alignment of director and shareholder interests and improved company performance. Next followed the Hampel Report (prepared by the committee chaired by Sir Ronald Hampel, chairman of ICI plc). The Hampel Report's recommendations were acted upon by the London Stock Exchange (LSE) which duly amended its Listings Rules (Yellow Book). In Ireland the Irish Stock Exchange has published the 'Combined Code on Corporate Governance'. The Combined Code is based on the following seventeen principles of good corporate governance:

> *The Board* – Every listed company should be headed by an effective board which should lead and control the company (A.1).
>
> *Chairman and CEO* – There are two key tasks at the top of every public company – the running of the board and the executive responsibility for the running of the company's business. There should be a clear division of responsibilities at the head of the company, which will ensure a balance of power and authority, such that no one individual has unfettered powers of decision (A.2).
>
> *Board Balance* – The board should include a balance of executive and non-executive directors (including independent non-executives) such that no

101 SI 1996/68.

102 On uncertificated securities, see para **[28.100]**

103 See Clarke, 'The Greenbury Committee Report – The Determination and Disclosure of Directors' Emoluments' (1996) 3 CLP 36.

individual or small group of individuals can dominate the board's decision taking (A.3).

Supply of Information – The board should be supplied in a timely manner with information in a form and of a quality appropriate to enable it to discharge its duties (A.4).

Appointments to the Board – There should be a formal and transparent procedure for the appointment of new directors to the board (A.5).

Re-election – All directors should be required to submit themselves for re-election at regular intervals and at least every three years (A.6).

The Level and Make-up of Remuneration - Levels of remuneration should be sufficient to attract and retain the directors needed to run the company successfully, but companies should avoid paying more than is necessary for this purpose. A proportion of executive directors' remuneration should be structured so as to link rewards to corporate and individual performance (B.1).

Procedure – Companies should establish a formal and transparent procedure for developing policy on executive remuneration and for fixing the remuneration packages of individual directors. No director should be involved in deciding his or her own remuneration (B.2).

Disclosure – The company's annual report should contain a statement of remuneration policy and details of the remuneration of each director (B.3).

Dialogue with Institutional Shareholders – Companies should be ready, where practicable, to enter into a dialogue with institutional shareholders based on the mutual understanding of objectives (C.1).

Constructive Use of the AGM – Boards should use the AGM to communicate with private investors and encourage their participation (C.2).

Financial Reporting – The board should present a balanced and understandable assessment of the company's position and prospects (D.1).

Internal Control – The board should maintain a sound system of internal control to safeguard shareholders' investment and the company's assets (D.2).

Audit Committee and Auditors – The Board should establish formal and transparent arrangements for considering how they should apply the financial reporting and internal control principles and for maintaining the appropriate relationship with the company's auditors (D.3).

Shareholder Voting – Institutional shareholders have a responsibility to make considered use of their vote (E.1).

Dialogue with Companies – Institutional shareholders should be ready, where practicable, to enter into a dialogue with companies based on the mutual understanding of objectives (E.2).

Evaluation of Governance Disclosures – When evaluating companies' governance arrangements, particularly those relating to board structure and composition, institutional investors should give due weight to all relevant factors drawn to their attention (E.3).

These 17 principles form the cornerstone of the Combined Code which, in most cases, elaborates further on each of the general principles, providing additional and more specific direction as to particular matters in some 48 provisions[104].

[28.064] The Turnbull Working Party was established to provide guidance for directors on the implementation of the internal control requirements of the Combined Code. The guidance (*Internal Control: Guidance for Directors on the Combined Code*) was issued in September 1999 and was accepted by the Irish and London Stock Exchanges as being consistent with the requirements of the Combined Code and the related Listing Rule disclosure requirements.

[28.065] The division of powers between the members and the directors is usually well defined in a PLC[105]. The office of director in a public company is usually more than merely a position of necessity as it can be in a private company where a person forms a company, beneficially owns all of its issued share capital and finds that he (together with at least one other person) must act as a director to fulfil a statutory requirement. Directors of PLCs will often have contracts of employment with the company. PLCs, especially, tend to appoint as directors persons who have a particular expertise or business acumen, rather than because that person is a shareholder. Career directors may have a shareholding in the company[106], but this is usually secondary to their primary involvement which is that of professional director. Another feature of listed PLCs is that they are required (by the Combined Code) to have non-executive directors, because such persons are considered to provide a counter-balance to executive directors, who are immersed in the business of the company[107]. This is all very far removed from the private company where the executive-proprietary-director is the norm.

[28.066] In PLCs the directors have a statutory duty by CA 1990, s 236 to take all reasonable steps to ensure that the company secretary (or each joint secretary) is a person who appears to them to have the requisite knowledge and experience to discharge the functions of company secretary and who:

(a) on the commencement of CA 1990, s 236 held the office of secretary of the company, or,

(b) held office in a company for at least three of the five years immediately preceding his appointment, or

(c) is a member of a body for the time being recognised by the Minister for Enterprise, Trade and Employment, or

(d) is a person who by reason of his holding or having held any other position or his being a member of any other body, appears to the directors to be capable of discharging those functions.

This section recognises that the office of company secretary in a PLC is an onerous one and requires a certain basic knowledge and experience. However, insofar as the subjective opinion of the directors is the ultimate touchstone, the legislature stopped short of giving

104 A copy of the Combined Code is available on: www.fsa.gov.uk/ukla/.

105 See Chapter 8, *Corporate Governance: Management by the Directors*, para **[8.003]** *ff*.

106 On qualification shares para **[28.083]**.

107 See principle A.3 of the *Combined Code* para **[28.063]**.

the Minister absolute control over the qualifications which such a company secretary must hold.

Corporate governance: meetings

[28.067] Whereas in a private company the niceties of corporate governance and the holding of members' meetings are often overlooked, in public companies, particularly PLCs, meetings are generally sacrosanct, and AGMs religiously convened, held and attended and the regulations antecedent thereto, observed. The notices required for meetings of the members of public and private companies are different. For a public company, CA 1963, s 133(1)(b) requires that at least 14 days' notice must be given of an EGM. The articles of association of many PLCs will also permit attendance at general meetings (especially the AGM) by means of teleconferencing.

Duties of directors and other officers

[28.068] The duties of directors in a public company are essentially the same as in a private company[108]. If there is any difference, it is that the temptation of directors to succumb to being selfish is less a factor in a listed PLC than in a private company, by virtue of the real separation between the *control* of the company and the *ownership* of the company.

Statutory regulation of transactions involving directors and their companies

[28.069] Sections 29 and 31 of CA 1990 and CA 1963, s 194 apply equally to private companies and public companies. One of the practical differences between the operation of CA 1990, s 29 in small private companies as opposed to listed PLCs is that the ease with which the former can convene and hold a meeting[109] to pass an approving resolution is absent in the latter. The cost and organisation of convening and holding an EGM is hugely different in a listed PLC than in a private company. Consequently, where a PLC proposes to enter into a substantial property transaction with a director or a person connected with a director, the practice is to put the resolution to the members at the AGM and to refrain from entering into the transaction until after an approving resolution has been passed.

Company law compliance and enforcement

[28.070] Save where the law imposes particular additional requirements on public companies (eg the law relating to prospectuses, etc) it is by and large the same body of law that applies to public companies as applies to private companies. Standards of corporate governance, on the whole, are considerably higher in the case of listed PLCs because of the close scrutiny by their members in general meeting and, of course, the existence of the additional regulator, the Irish Stock Exchange which polices listed companies.

---

108 See generally Chapter 10, *Duties of Directors and Other Officers*.

109 Or, indeed, utilise the written resolution procedure permitted by CA 1963, s 141(8).

Accounts and auditors

[28.071] All companies, private or public, are required to keep proper books of account, and to appoint an auditor, and the reader is referred to Chapter 13, *Accounts and Auditors*, where those matters are dealt with in detail.

[28.072] The accounting procedures, principles and requirements described in Chapter 13, *Accounts and Auditors* apply in the main to public companies having limited liability and a share capital in the same way as they apply to private companies. Thus, such public companies are required to prepare annual accounts; to prepare group accounts if they are parent undertakings; and to file an annual return to which copies of the annual accounts and reports thereon must be annexed.

[28.073] In all of these respects such public companies resemble *large* private companies, regardless of their actual turnover, balance sheet total or average number of employees, and they may *not* avail of the exemptions accorded to 'medium-sized' and 'small' private companies that operate in respect of the annual accounts and the annual return[110]. Nor may they avail of the exemptions which apply to parent undertakings whose group balance sheet total, group turnover, or group average number of employees does not exceed the amounts specified in the European Communities (Companies: Group Accounts) Regulations 1992, reg 7[111]. Likewise, they may not avail of the exemptions which operate in respect of the annual return for subsidiaries of parent undertakings established under the laws of EU Member States. A public company may not avail of the option to dispense with audited accounts provided for in Part III of the Companies (Amendment) (No 2) Act 1999[112].

[28.074] Unlimited public companies are bound to prepare annual accounts in the same manner as unlimited private companies[113]. The annual return of a public unlimited company having a share capital differs from that of an unlimited private company, however, because CA 1963, s 128 requires the annual accounts and the reports thereon of an unlimited public company having a share capital to be annexed to its annual return. Unlimited private companies do not have to annex the annual accounts or reports to the annual return.

Investigations and inspectors

[28.075] The investigation procedures detailed in Chapter 14 are equally applicable to public companies; indeed, many of the cases discussed in that chapter concerned the investigation of public companies.

[28.076] In addition to these procedures, CA 1990, s 81 gives PLCs the additional power to conduct *their own* investigation into the ownership of shares in the company. Section 81(1) provides:

> 'A public limited company may by notice in writing require a person whom the company knows or has reasonable cause to believe to be or, at any time during the 3 years immediately

---

[110] See Chapter 13, *Accounts and Auditors*, para **[13.041]**.

[111] SI 1992/201: see para **[13.120]**.

[112] C(A)(No 2)A 1999, s 32.

[113] See Chapter 13, *Accounts and Auditors,* para **[13.165]**.

preceding the date on which the notice is issued (but excluding any time before the commencement of this section), to have been interested in shares comprised in the company's relevant share capital—

(a) to confirm that fact or (as the case may be) to indicate whether or not it is the case, and

(b) where he holds or has during that time held an interest in shares so comprised, to give such further information as may be required in accordance with the following sub-section.'

The *relevant share capital* referred to in sub-s (1) is the company's issued share capital of a class carrying a right to vote in all circumstances at general meetings of the company, including shares in relation to which such rights have temporarily been suspended[114]. The company may exercise these powers to see, inter alia, whether a takeover bid is imminent or possible[115].

[28.077] A notice under CA 1990, s 81(1) may require the person to whom it is addressed to provide the following information:

'(a) particulars of his own past or present interest in shares comprised in relevant share capital of the company (held by him at any time during the 3 year period mentioned in subs (1));

(b) where the interest is a present interest and any other interest in shares subsists or, in any case, where another interest in the shares subsisted during that 3 year period at any time when his own interest subsisted, to give (so far as lies within his knowledge) such particulars with respect to that other interest as may be required by the notice;

(c) where his interest is a past interest, to give (so far as lies within his knowledge) particulars of the identity of the person who held that interest immediately upon his ceasing to hold it.'

The particulars referred to in sub-s (2)(a) and (2)(b) include particulars of the identity of persons interested in the shares in question and whether persons interested in the same shares are or were parties to any concerted agreement to which CA 1990, s 73 applies or to any agreement or arrangement relating to the exercise of any rights conferred by the holding of the shares. Interests of spouses, minor children and associated companies also come within the scope of such investigations. The section further applies in relation to a person who has or previously had, or is or was entitled to acquire, a right to subscribe for shares in a PLC which would on issue be comprised in the relevant share capital of that company.

The notice must require any information given in response to the notice to be given in writing within such reasonable time as may be specified therein, and details of the information so obtained must be recorded in the register of interests.

[28.078] If any person fails to comply with the notice he will be guilty of an offence, and the court may, on the application of the company, impose restrictions of the kind envisaged by CA 1990, s 16 on those shares[116]. It will be a defence in any such criminal proceedings

[114] CA 1990, s 67(2).

[115] *Re TR Technology Investment PLC* [1988] BCLC 256.

[116] See Chapter 14, *Investigations and Inspectors,* at para **[14.085]**.

for the person to prove that the notice requiring him to give information was 'frivolous or vexatious.[117].

[28.079] Under CA 1990, s 83, the company *must* conduct an investigation of this kind where requisitioned by the members holding not less than 10% of the company's paid up voting capital. The requisition must state that the requisitionists are requiring the exercise by the company of its investigative powers, the manner in which they require those powers to be exercised, and reasonable grounds as to why the investigation should be conducted in that manner. If the company defaults in holding a requisitioned investigation, the requisitionists or anyone of them may apply to court for an order requiring the company to conduct an investigation. The court may grant the order where it seems reasonable so to order.

[28.080] The company is obliged to prepare a report to its members on the information received in a requisitioned investigation[118]. If the investigation is not concluded within three months of commencement, an interim report must be prepared. These reports must be made available at the company's registered office for a reasonable time after the conclusion of the investigation or the period to which they relate. Within 31 days of the making of a report, the company must notify the requisitionists of its having been made and its availability for inspection. Failure to comply with these requirements renders the company and every officer in default liable to a fine not exceeding €1,904.61 on summary conviction, and, on indictment, not exceeding €12,697.38.

Shares and membership in public companies

[28.081] Public companies, unlike private ones, are not required to have a share capital or to limit their membership to 50. In practice many public companies *do* have a share capital in order to avail of equity investment from the public. The investing public will be encouraged to buy the shares or debentures in the knowledge that they can sell them on to other members of the public - for a public company, unlike a private company, need not restrict the transfer of its shares (or debentures).

(a) Membership of public companies

[28.082] The law does not differentiate between public and private companies when it comes to the question of who may become a member. Nor, for that matter, does it distinguish between them in the principles governing registration of members. In these respects the reader is referred to the discussion in Chapter 15.

[28.083] Special rules apply, however, to public companies which require their directors to take up 'qualification' shares[119]. Section 179 of CA 1963 provides that a person may not be appointed director of a public company by the articles of association, or be named as a

---

[117] CA 1990, s 85(4). See *Re FH Lloyd Holdings Ltd* [1985] BCLC 256 where the court refused to impose restrictions in such circumstances; also *Re Ricardo Group PLC (No 3)* [1989] BCLC 771 where it was held that restrictions would not be imposed since they would prejudice the rights of shareholders in a forthcoming takeover bid.

[118] CA 1990, s 84.

[119] On qualification shares see Chapter 8, *Corporate Governance: Management by the Directors* para **[8.029]**.

director or proposed director in any prospectus or statement in lieu thereof, before the registration of the articles containing his appointment, the publication of the prospectus, or the delivery of the statement, as the case may be, *unless:*

'(a) he has signed and delivered to the registrar of companies a consent in writing to act as such director; and

(b) has either—

(i) signed the memorandum for a number of shares not less than his qualification, if any; or

(ii) taken from the company and paid or agreed to pay for his qualification shares, if any; or

(iii) signed and delivered to the registrar an undertaking in writing to take from the company and pay for his qualification shares, if any; or

(iv) made and delivered to the registrar for registration a statutory declaration to the effect that a number of shares not less than his qualification, if any, are registered in his name.'

Failure to comply does *not* render any subsequent transactions involving the director invalid[120], but it does render the person applying for registration of the articles liable to a fine not exceeding €1,904.61[121]. These restrictions do not apply to public companies not having a share capital, public companies which are formed by conversion from a private company, or to a prospectus issued by or on behalf of a company after the expiration of one year from the date upon which the company was entitled to commence business[122]. And, of course, if a public company does not require its directors to take up qualification shares the restrictions will not apply.

Under CA 1963, s 180, if a director does not take up his qualification shareholding within two months of his appointment or such shorter time as may be fixed by the articles, his office will be vacated, and he may not be reappointed until such time as he meets the qualification.

(b) Legal nature of shares in public companies, and formalities which apply to them

[28.084] A share in a public company does not differ in its legal nature from a share in a private company and the reader is referred to Chapter 15 for a discussion of the legal nature of, and rights and obligations associated with, shares.

[28.085] The formalities associated with shares in private and public companies do not differ significantly. A public company, however, may issue a share warrant[123] instead of a share certificate, entitling the bearer of the warrant to the shares in question. Warrants may be transferred from bearer to bearer without the need for an appropriate instrument of transfer. They are not common in practice, however.

Furthermore, an *investment company* within the meaning of CA 1990, Part III may have, in effect, *no par* shares[124]. An investment company is one whose sole object is 'the

[120] CA 1963, s 178.

[121] CA 1963, s 179(4), as amended by CA 1990, s 240 and CLEA 2001, s 104.

[122] CA 1963, s 179(5).

[123] CA 1963, s 88. The company must be authorised by its articles to issue share warrants.

[124] For a discussion of the par value of shares see Chapter 15, *Shares and Membership*, para **[15.043]**.

collective investment of its funds in property with the aim of spreading investment risk and giving the members of the company the benefit of the results of the management of its funds.'[125] Its memorandum or articles must also provide that the actual value of the paid up share capital will at all times equal the value of its assets of any kind after the deduction of all liabilities, and that the shares of the company may be purchased at any time out of the company's assets.

Instead of stating the nominal value of its shares in the memorandum, an investment company is empowered to state in its memorandum that 'the share capital of the company shall be equal to the value for the time being of the issued share capital of the company' and to provide for 'the division of that share capital into a specified number of shares without assigning any nominal value thereto.'[126]

(c) Allotment of shares in public companies, and consideration therefor

[28.086] An allotment of shares by the directors of a public company must be authorised in the same way as an allotment of shares in a private company[127]. The provisions of C(A)A 1983, s 20 apply to both. Allotments of shares in public companies will normally involve more formal steps than those of private companies, and accordingly *letters of allotment*, including *renounceable letters of allotment*, will be more commonplace.

[28.087] The statutory pre-emption scheme introduced by C(A)A 1983, ss 23 and 24[128] applies to allotments of equity securities by both public and private companies, with the rider that a public company may not exclude generally the statutory pre-emption scheme by means of a provision to that effect in its articles. A public company may, however, exclude the scheme from applying to a particular allotment, either by providing for that exclusion in its articles or by passing a special resolution authorising the exclusion[129].

[28.088] A PLC may not allot a share unless it is paid at least 25% of the nominal value of the share and the whole of any premium on it[130].

[28.089] Shares in PLCs may be issued for non-cash consideration, but, unlike other companies, special restrictions apply. First, a PLC may not accept an undertaking to perform future services in consideration for an allotment[131]. If it does, the holder of the shares is liable to pay the consideration in cash with interest. Secondly, a PLC may not accept as consideration for the allotment an undertaking (*eg* to pay cash) which is to be performed more than five years after the allotment[132]. Thirdly, non-cash consideration for the allotment of shares in a PLC must be independently valued in accordance with the provisions of C(A)A 1983, s 30.

---

[125] CA 1990, s 253(2).

[126] CA 1990, s 253(1).

[127] See Chapter 15, *Shares and Membership*, para **[15.049]**.

[128] See Chapter 15, *Shares and Membership*, para **[15.055]**.

[129] C(A)A 1983, s 24.

[130] C(A)A 1983, s 28(1). The restriction does not apply to shares allotted in pursuance of an employee share scheme: C(A)A 1983, s 28(4).

[131] C(A)A 1983, s 23(2).

[132] C(A)A 1983, s 29.

[28.090] Section 30 of C(A)A 1983 requires the allotment of shares in a PLC (except in a merger or share-for-share exchange) to be valued by an independent person who is qualified at the time to be appointed as auditor to the company[133]. The independent person may, however, accept the contents of another report made by any person who appears to him to have the requisite knowledge and experience necessary to value the consideration and who is not an officer of the company or an associated company, or a partner or employee of such an officer. In carrying out his valuation the valuer is empowered to require from the officers of the company any information which he thinks necessary to enable him to carry out his duties[134].

[28.091] The report must be made within the six months preceding the allotment, must be sent to the proposed allottee, must be returned to the Registrar of Companies along with the return of allotments, and (under s 30(5)) must state:

> '(a) the nominal value of the shares to be wholly or partly paid for by the consideration in question;
>
> (b) the amount of any premium payable on those shares;
>
> (c) the description of the consideration and, as respects so much of the consideration as he himself has valued, a description of that part of the consideration, the method used to value it and the date of the valuation; and
>
> (d) the extent to which the nominal value of the shares and any premium are to be treated as paid up—
>
> (i) by the consideration;
>
> (ii) in cash.'

If any consideration is valued by a person other than the independent person, the report must state that fact and must also state the other person's name and what knowledge and experience he has to carry out the valuation, *and* describe so much of the consideration as was valued by that other person, the method used to value it and the date of valuation.

[28.092] The report must also contain, or be accompanied by, a note by the independent person stating (s 30(8)):

> '(a) in the case of a valuation made by another person, that it appeared to the independent person reasonable to arrange for it to be so made, or to accept a valuation so made;
>
> (b) whoever made the valuation, that the method of valuation was reasonable in all the circumstances;
>
> (c) that it appears to the independent person that there has been no material change in the value of the consideration in question since the valuation; and
>
> (d) that on the basis of the valuation the value of the consideration, together with any cash by which the nominal value of the shares or any premium payable on them is to be paid up, is not less than so much of the aggregate of the nominal value and the whole of any such premium as is treated as paid up by the consideration and any such cash.'

---

133 On the qualifications of Auditors see Chapter 13, *Accounts and Auditors*, para **[13.190]** *ff*.

134 C(A)A 1983, s 31(1). Supplying the valuer with false or misleading information is an offence: C(A)A 1983, s 31(3).

If the company allots shares in contravention of C(A)A 1983, s 30, and the allottee either has not received a report of an independent person, or the allottee knows or ought to have known that there was a contravention, he will be liable to the company for so much of the nominal capital as was treated as paid by the consideration together with interest.

(d) Disclosure of interests in shares in PLCs

[28.093] Chapter 1 of Part IV of CA 1990 imposes obligations on directors, secretaries and their families to disclose their shareholdings in a PLC. Chapter 2 of that Part imposes like obligations on groups and individuals which acquire more than 5% of the issued share capital of a PLC. The significant feature of these obligations is that *beneficial,* as well as legal, interests must be disclosed. The disclosure procedures differ from those discussed in Chapter 15, *Shares and Membership*[135] since *compulsory* disclosure is required. Every PLC is required to keep a register of disclosed interests[136].

[28.094] An individual is obliged to make disclosure to a PLC whenever he acquires or disposes of an interest which brings his interest in it above or below 5% in nominal value of the 'relevant nominal capital' of the PLC – meaning the issued share capital of a class carrying voting rights at general meetings[137]. The interests of a spouse or child must be taken into account in determining the size of his interest, as must the interests of another company which is accustomed to act in accordance with his instructions, or if he holds more than one-third of the voting rights in that other company[138]. If he is unaware of those other interests at the time of the acquisition he must make disclosure when he becomes aware of them. Where he is part of a group among whom there is an agreement (whether legally enforceable or not) that the rights associated with shares in a PLC which are acquired by any of them will be exercised only according to the agreement, he will be treated as being interested in the interests of the other members of the group, including the interests of their spouses and minor children[139].

[28.095] Further disclosure is required to be made to the Stock Exchange where the shares of the PLC are officially listed. The threshold interests in this regard are set at 10%, 25%, 50% and 75%[140]. The Stock Exchange must publish the disclosed information within three days of receipt, unless it would be contrary to the public interest or would be seriously detrimental to the PLC concerned.

[28.096] The interests which must be disclosed are set out in CA 1990, s 77, and include the interests of a beneficiary under a trust, a purchaser under a contract, or a person who is not a shareholder but who is authorised to exercise the rights of a shareholder or debenture holder. Certain interests are excluded, such as the interests of bare trustees, discretionary interests, the interest of the President of the High Court in an estate, interests of charities,

[135] See Chapter 15, *Shares and Membership*, para **[15.123]**.

[136] CA 1990, s 80.

[137] CA 1990, s 67. A temporary suspension of voting rights is disregarded for these purposes.

[138] CA 1990, s 72.

[139] CA 1990, ss 73 and 74.

[140] CA 1990, s 91, implementing EU Directive 88/627/EEC.

interests arising through involvement in unit trusts, and 'exempt security interests' as defined in CA 1990, s 78. The latter include interests held by banks, insurance companies, trustee savings banks, post office savings banks, and stockbrokers carrying on business on a recognised stock exchange, which are held as security.

(e) Disclosure of stabilising activity during a stabilisation period

[28.097] The Companies (Amendment) Act 1999 ('C(A)A 1999') introduced provisions to enable stabilising activities or measures to be undertaken in relation to the issue or sale of shares and securities. The Act permits official manipulation of the stock market in accordance with *stabilisation rules* which are set out in the Schedule to the Act, and for a limited time known as the *stabilisation period*.

[28.098] Section 3 of C(A)A 1999 provides that acquisitions or disposals officially transacted during the stabilisation period for the purposes of stabilising the market and done in accordance with the stabilisation rules shall be disregarded for the purposes of the disclosure requirements of CA 1990. Any interest in the relevant share capital acquired during the stabilising period is treated as having been acquired on the first day following the end of the stabilising period[141].

(f) Disclosure of interests in shares in public companies other than PLCs

[28.099] The disclosure order procedures discussed in Chapter 15[142] apply to all companies other than PLCs, and the reader is referred to that discussion insofar as it concerns public companies which are not PLCs.

Share transfer in public companies

(a) Certificated and uncertificated securities

[28.100] Where shares in public companies are 'certificated' (ie their title is evidenced by a paper share certificate) the mechanics of share transfer does not differ greatly from the transfer of shares in private companies[143]. The transfer of shares in PLCs that are quoted on the Stock Exchange must be distinguished, however, from the transfer of shares in other types of public company, such as management-type public companies limited by guarantee without a share capital. In the case of listed PLCs that have opted to join CREST and have their shares in uncertificated format, the differences between the transfer of shares in public and private companies are most pronounced[144].

[28.101] Since 15 July 1996 the new equity settlement system known as CREST went live in the United Kingdom, shares on the Dublin Stock Exchange following suit by the end of

141 C(A)A 1999, s 3(2).

142 See Chapter 15, *Shares and Membership*, para **[15.125]**.

143 Note, however, that where a stock transfer form is executed, common form model articles of association provide that in the case of a public company, the transfer must be executed by both the transferor and the instrument of transfer must be registered by the company: see CA 1963, Sch 1, Table A, Part I, reg 22.

144 See Ussher, *Company Law in Ireland* (1986), p 198,199; Doyle, *The Company Secretary* (1994), p 151; and Abrans, 'Talisman: A Legal Analysis' (1980) Co Law 17.

1996[145]. This was facilitated in Ireland by the passing of the Companies Act, 1990 (Uncertificated Securities) Regulations 1996[146] (the '1996 Regulations'). Regulation 4(1) and (2) of the 1996 Regulations provides:

> '(1) Notwithstanding section 79 or section 81 of the 1963 Act or section 2(1) of the Stock Transfer Act, 1963, title to securities may be evidenced and transferred without a written instrument provided that such title is evidenced and transferred in accordance with these regulations.
>
> (2) References in any enactment or rule of law to a proper instrument of transfer or to a transfer with respect to securities, or any expression having like meaning, shall be taken to include a reference to an operator-instruction to a participating issuer to register a transfer of title on the relevant register of securities in accordance with the operator-instruction[147].'

There are safeguards to the avoidance of stamp duty and reg 4 will not have effect in relation to an 'operator instruction' unless there is an agreement in place with the Revenue Commissioners in relation to the payment of any stamp duty chargeable[148]. It is beyond the scope of this book to treat in full the 1996 Regulations and the treatment that follows is but an overview of some of the more important issues.

[28.102] In order for a company to participate in CREST its articles of association must be consistent with the holding of shares in that class in uncertificated form; the transfer of title to shares in that class by means of a relevant system; and the 1996 Regulations[149]. An alternative is that a company's directors must resolve that title to shares of a class issued or to be issued may be transferred electronically[150] and for as long as such resolution is in force, reg 8(3) of the 1996 Regulations provides:

> '...the articles of association in relation to the class of shares which were the subject of the directors' resolution, shall not apply to any uncertificated shares of that class to the extent that they are inconsistent with—
>
> (a) the holding of shares of that class in uncertificated form;
>
> (b) the transfer of title to shares of that class by means of a relevant system; and
>
> (c) any provision of these regulations.'

Where a directors' resolution is the means chosen to authorise the participation in CREST, notice must be given to all members, giving them 60 days' notice before the resolution

145 For an excellent overview of CREST, see McHugh, 'CREST in Ireland, The Uncertificated Securities Regulations, 1996' (1996) 3 CLP 219.

146 SI 1996/68.

147 Companies Act, 1990 (Uncertificated Securities) Regulations 1996, reg 5 also disapplies the Statute of Frauds Act (Ireland) 1695, s 6 and the Supreme Court of Judicature (Ireland) Act 1877, s 28(6) and any other rule of law requiring the execution under hand or seal of a document in writing for the transfer of property, shall not apply (if they would otherwise do so) to any transfer of title to uncertificated units of a security through a relevant system.

148 1996 Regulations, reg 4(3).

149 1996 Regulations, reg 7(1).

150 1996 Regulations, reg 8(1).

becomes effective. It has been observed[151] that most Irish companies elected to change their articles of association to allow the transfer of shares in dematerialised form and that this has avoided any period of uncertainty that might otherwise arise if the decision were open to challenge by dissenting members. Participating issuers are debarred from issuing a certificate in relation to any uncertificated units of a participating security[152] and any document issued in breach of this, purportedly evidencing title to an uncertificated unit of a participating security, shall not be evidence of title to the unit of the security. In particular, CA 1963, s 87(1) is dis-applied to uncertificated securities[153].

[28.103] The main effect of CREST is that transfers of shares can be registered in a matter of hours, compared with the past when registration took a matter of days or even weeks. The supporting CREST documentation requires registrars to adhere to strict time limits in registering transfers ie two hours and are required to advise CRESTCo electronically that a transaction has occurred. CREST is underpinned by an extensive framework and is comprised of the public law 1996 Regulations and private contractual documentation and rules. This is a necessary support for the electronic system that connects investors with brokers, companies' registrars, the banks and of course CRESTCo. The essential basis of the law of share transfer is, however, maintained subject to necessary modifications. So, listed PLCs (referred to as 'participating issuers') continue to be required to maintain a register of members. Regulation 10(1) of the 1996 Regulations provides:

> '...A participating issuer which is a company shall enter on its register of members, in respect of any class of shares which is a participating security, the number of shares each member holds in uncertificated form and certificated form respectively.'

So, the effect of registration of a share in uncertificated form has the same essential effect as in the case of a 'certificated' share, reg 11 providing:

> '(1) Subject to regulation 16(7), an entry on a register mentioned in paragraph (1) or (2) of regulation 10 which records a person as holding units of a security in uncertificated form shall be evidence of such title to the units as would be evidenced if the entry on the register related to units of that security held in certificated form.
>
> (2) Subject to regulation 16(7), an entry on a register maintained by virtue of paragraph (3) of regulation 10 shall be prima facie evidence that the person to whom the entry relates has such title to the units of the security which that person is recorded as holding in uncertificated form as if the units were held in certificated form.'

The integrity of the register is protected by reg 12(1) which prevents participating issuers from rectifying a register of securities in relation to uncertificated units of a security held by a system-member except (a) with the consent of the operator, or (b) by order of the High Court. Regulation 13 provides that notwithstanding CA 1963, s 121, a participating issuer shall not close a register of securities relating to a participating security without the consent of the operator.

---

[151] McHugh, 'CREST in Ireland, The Uncertificated Securities Regulations, 1996' (1996) 3 CLP 219 at 220.

[152] 1996 Regulations, reg 19(1).

[153] 1996 Regulations, reg 19(2).

[28.104] Regulation 16(1) of the 1996 Regulations imposes an obligation on participating issuers to register a transfer of title to uncertificated units of a security on a register of securities in accordance with an operator-instruction unless certain situations pertain[154]. Regulation 18 provides that at the time an operator-instruction is sent requiring a participating issuer to register on a register of securities a transfer of title to any uncertificated units of a security:

> '...the transferee shall acquire an *equitable interest* in the requisite number of uncertificated units of the security of the kind specified in the operator-instruction in which the transferor has an equitable interest by virtue of this regulation, or in relation to which the transferor is recorded on the relevant register of securities as having title .'[Emphasis added]

The equitable interest lasts until the transfer is registered.

[28.105] The entitlement to attend and vote at general meetings of companies whose shares are held and are transferred in uncertificated form is addressed by reg 14 of the 1996 Regulations, which provides:

> '(1) For the purposes of determining which persons are entitled to attend or vote at a meeting, and how many votes such persons may cast, the participating issuer may specify in the notice of the meeting a time, not more than 48 hours before the time fixed for the meeting, by which a person must be entered on the relevant register of securities in order to have the right to attend or vote at the meeting.
>
> (2) Changes to entries on the relevant register of securities after the time specified by virtue of paragraph (1) shall be disregarded in determining the rights of any person to attend or vote at the meeting, notwithstanding any provisions in any enactment, articles of association or other instrument to the contrary.'

Notice of meetings is addressed by Regulation 15 which provides:

> '(1) For the purposes of serving notices of meetings, whether under section 134(a) of the 1963 Act, any other enactment, a provision in the Articles of Association or any other instrument, a participating issuer may determine that persons entitled to receive such notices are those persons entered on the relevant register of securities at the close of business on a day determined by the participating issuer.
>
> (2) The day determined by a participating issuer under paragraph (1) may not be more than 7 days before the day that the notices of the meeting are sent.'

---

154 The excusing circumstances are:

> '(a) the transfer is prohibited—(i) by order of the High Court, provided both the participating issuer and the relevant operator shall both have had actual notice of the order before the operator-instruction is sent and the fact of such actual notice on the part of both such persons shall have been established to the satisfaction of the court by the person seeking to rely on the order, or (ii) by or under an enactment, or (b) the participating issuer has actual notice that the transfer is—(i) avoided by or under an enactment, or (ii) a transfer to a deceased person, or (c) the circumstances described in paragraph (2) apply, or (d) the participating issuer is entitled by virtue of paragraph (3) to refuse to register the transfer.'

(b) Substantive differences in the law of share transfer between private and public companies

[28.106] The main difference between the *substantive* law governing the transfer of shares in a public company as opposed to the transfer of shares in a private company is that the restrictions on the transfer of shares, intrinsic to private companies, will invariably be absent in public limited companies. However, some other forms of public companies, such as the management-type companies[155] may well have restrictions on the transfer of their shares to, for example, the owners of retail units or of apartments in the complex in which the management company owns the freehold reversion. Although for a company to be a private company it *must* contain the restrictions on the transfer of its shares set out in CA 1963, s 33, it does not automatically follow that all public companies will not have some restrictions. So, where a company's articles contain all of the restrictions set out in s 33 but does *not* have a share capital, it is a public company and cannot be considered a private company[156].

Another legal difference between public companies and private companies is that public companies are not prohibited from inviting the public to subscribe for any shares or debentures in the company. Shares in PLCs which are quoted on the Stock Exchange may be invited for sale to the general public and are a component of the investment market[157]. Again also, it should be noted that public companies may not *necessarily* invite the public[158] at large to subscribe for their shares.

(c) Insider dealing

[28.107] Part V of CA 1990 introduces criminal and civil penalties for insider dealing. The basic provision is to be found in CA 1990, s 107 which renders unlawful dealings in securities of a company within six months of a person 'connected with' that company coming into possession of information which, if it were generally available, would affect the price of those securities. 'Dealing' in this context includes acquiring, disposing, subscribing for, or underwriting securities, and agreeing or offering to make an agreement as to any of the foregoing. Certain dealings, such as the acquisition of securities under a will or intestacy, are exempted[159]. 'Securities' means shares and debentures for which dealing facilities are provided on a recognised Stock Exchange (thus, it does not include shares or debentures of a private company). The Minister may extend the category of shares and debentures covered by the term. 'Persons connected with' a company include its officers, officers of related companies, shareholders in the company and related companies, and persons who might reasonably be expected to have access to such information through professional relationships with the company or through their position as officers of companies which have a shareholding in the company concerned.

---

155 See para **[28.007]**.

156 On the requirements if a company is to be a private company, see Chapter 1, *The Private Company in Context*, para **[1.115]**.

157 See Molloy, *The Irish Investment Market* (1993).

158 On the legal meaning of 'the public', see para **[28.021]**.

159 CA 1990, s 110.

[28.108] Section 109 of CA 1990 renders a person guilty of insider dealing liable to compensate any other party who was not in possession of the relevant information for any difference between the price at which the securities were dealt and the price at which they would have been dealt if he had been in possession of the relevant information. He is *also* liable to account to the company for any profit made on the deal. A two-year limitation period applies to actions under this section.

Insider dealing is also a criminal offence, rendering the guilty party liable, on summary conviction, to a fine of up to €12,697.38 or imprisonment for up to 12 months, or both, and on indictment to a fine of up to €253,947.62 or imprisonment for 10 years, or both[160]. A person convicted of insider dealing commits a further offence if he deals in any securities in the following 12 months.

The Stock Exchange is given the duty of reporting to the Director of Public Prosecutions wherever it is of the opinion that insider dealing has occurred[161]. It may also conduct an investigation to enable it so to report to the DPP, and it may co-operate with, or receive the co-operation of other EU Stock Exchanges in this regard[162].

Groups of companies

[28.109] The law relating to groups of companies as considered in Chapter 18 applies *mutatis mutandis* to situations where a public company is part of a group.

Maintenance of capital in public companies

[28.110] The rules provided in the Companies Acts which exist to maintain the capital of private companies are, in general, equally applicable to public companies. Insofar as public limited companies are obliged to have a minimum issued share capital, currently set at €38,092.14 by C(A)A 1983, s 19, capital maintenance rules have a more obvious application. Most PLCs will have in their share capital, a genuine creditors' fund. Here, the following matters are considered:

(a) Acquisition by a public company of its own shares.

(b) Assisting the purchase of a public company's own shares.

(c) Distributions and the payment of dividends in public companies.

(a) Acquisition by a public company of its own shares

[28.111] As considered in Chapter 18[163], prior to the coming into force of CA 1990, s 211, a company could not purchase back its own shares. While the mechanism whereby a private company can acquire its own shares is by means of an 'off market purchase', a public company may also do so by means of a 'market purchase'.

[28.112] Section 212(1)(b) of CA 1990 provides that for the purposes of ss 213 and 215, a purchase by a company of its own shares is:

> '...a "market purchase" if the shares are purchased on a recognised stock exchange and are subject to a marketing arrangement.'

---

[160] CA 1990, s 111.

[161] CA 1990, s 115.

[162] CA 1990, s 116.

[163] Chapter 18, *The Maintenance of Capital*, para **[18.018]** *ff.*

Furthermore, by sub-s (2), a company's shares are subject to a marketing arrangement on a recognised Stock Exchange if either they are listed on that Stock Exchange, or:

> '...the company has been afforded facilities for dealing in those shares to take place on that stock exchange without prior permission for individual transactions from the authority governing that stock exchange and without limit as to the time during which those facilities are to be available.'

It can readily be seen that the essence of a market purchase is that the company purchases back its own shares on the open stock exchange, as opposed to by way of private treaty.

[28.113] As with an off market purchase[164], before a public company can make a market purchase, certain approval must be obtained. In the case of a market purchase a public company must comply with CA 1990, s 215 and obtain the general authority[165] of the members of the company in general meeting. In this regard, an ordinary resolution of the members is sufficient, although sub-s (2) provides that the provisions of CA 1963, s 143 shall apply to such a resolution. This provides that a copy of the resolution must within fifteen days after its passing or making, be forwarded to the Registrar of Companies and recorded by him. In this way the resolution becomes a public document, available for inspection by the public.

[28.114] By CA 1990, s 215(1) the requisite authority may be varied, revoked or from time to time renewed by the company, again in general meeting. It is further provided that:

> 'This subsection shall not be construed as requiring any particular contract for the market purchase of shares to be authorised by the company in general meeting and for the purposes of this Part where a market purchase of shares has been authorised in accordance with this section any contract entered into pursuant to that authority in respect of such a purchase shall be deemed also to be so authorised.'

Subsection (3) provides that in the case of a public limited company, any authority granted under sub-s (1) shall specify the maximum number of shares authorised to be acquired and determine both the maximum and minimum prices which may be paid for the shares. In such a case, the authorising resolution may determine either or both the maximum and minimum prices by specifying a particular sum or providing a basis or formula for calculating the prices in question without reference to any person's discretion or opinion[166].

[28.115] Section 216 of CA 1990 provides a further distinction between the law applicable to public and private companies. Accordingly, without prejudice to the generality of ss 213, 214 and 215, any authority granted under those sections, must specify the date on which the authority is to expire which shall not be later then 18 months after the date on which the resolution granting the authority is passed[167]. However, where the contract to purchase was concluded before the authority expired and the terms of the authority permit the company to make a contract of purchase which might be executed wholly or partly

---

164 See CA 1990, s 213 considered in Chapter 18, *The Maintenance of Capital*, para **[18.022]**.

165 Unlike in the case of an *off market purchase*, specific prior approval is not required, being impractical in the case of *market purchases*.

166 CA 1990, s 215(4).

167 CA 1990, s 216(1).

after the authority expired, then a PLC may make a purchase after the expiry of any time limit imposed by s 216(1)[168].

(b) Assisting the purchase of a public company's own shares

[28.116] Section 60 of CA 1963 provides that it is unlawful for a company to give direct or indirect financial assistance for the purpose of or in connection with a purchase or subscription for the company's shares or the shares of its holding company[169]. The section 60 prohibition applies with equal force to public companies. It should be remembered, however, that the most important exception to the general prohibition contained in s 60(2), the 'resolution and declaration'[170] cannot be availed of by a PLC[171] or 'public company subsidiaries'[172].

[28.117] Section 60(15B) of CA 1963 provides that the exception to the prohibition in s 60(1) that is contained in s 60(13)[173] is modified in the case of PLCs to the extend that it may:

> '...give financial assistance to any person only if the company's net assets[174] are not thereby reduced or, to the extent that those assets are thereby reduced, if the financial assistance is provided out of profits which are available for dividend.'

More rigorous standards are applied to PLCs than other companies, particularly private companies. The reason for this must be the particular importance placed on a PLC's creditors' fund, and serves to underscore the rationale behind the 'authorised minimum' required share capital introduced for PLCs by C(A)A 1983.

(c) Distributions and the payment of dividends in public companies

[28.118] Section 45 of C(A)A 1983 provides that a company may only make a distribution out of profits available for the purpose[175]. However additional restrictions apply in the case of public limited companies. Accordingly, a PLC is prohibited by C(A)A 1983, Part IV from making a distribution or paying a dividend unless its net assets are equal to, or in excess of, the aggregate of its called up share capital and undistributable reserves and the distribution does not reduce its net assets below such aggregate[176].

Shareholders' remedies

[28.119] The main shareholders' remedies of CA 1963, s 205 and the derivative action through the exceptions to the rule in *Foss v Harbottle* are equally applicable to shareholders of public companies. Save in respect of some practical difficulties[177] for

168 CA 1990, s 216(2).

169 See generally, Chapter 18, *The Maintenance of Capital*, para **[18.041]** *ff*.

170 See para **[18.057]** *ff*.

171 CA 1963, s 60(15A), as inserted by C(A)A 1983, Sch 1, para 10.

172 See Chapter 18, *The Maintenance of Capital*, para **[18.037]**.

173 See generally, Chapter 18, *The Maintenance of Capital*, para **[18.075]**.

174 'Net assets' are defined by CA 1963, s 60(15C).

175 See generally, Chapter 18, *The Maintenance of Capital*, para **[18.081]** *ff*.

176 C(A)A 1983, s 46.

177 Such as, eg, in shareholders mustering sufficient support to direct the directors to follow their wishes.

shareholders in public companies, the law as set out in Chapter 19[178], will apply in public companies.

Corporate borrowing by public companies

[28.120] The financing of a PLC is primarily by means of its *share capital*, but even so, finance by *loan capital* is frequently availed of by public companies where they are able to provide adequate security for the facility. The law applicable to corporate borrowing, the registration of charges and receiverships[179] as set out in the context of a private company is broadly the same as in respect of a public company. One exception concerns the matters considered above[180], namely the prohibition on a public company borrowing immediately after its incorporation, and before it satisfies the other requirements of C(A)A 1983.

[28.121] Section 44(1) of C(A)A 1983 prohibits a PLC from taking a charge on its own shares by providing that a lien or other charge of a PLC on its own shares, whether taken expressly or otherwise, is void, save to the extent permitted by subs (2). Section 44(2) excepts from this prohibition certain 'permitted charges', the following being the two main exceptions:

- charges on a company's own shares (not being fully paid) for any amount payable in respect of the shares;
- in the case of a PLC whose ordinary business includes the lending of money or the provision of credit or the bailment or hiring of goods under a hire-purchase agreement, a charge on the company's own shares, fully paid or not, which arises in connection with a transaction entered into by the company in the ordinary course of its business.

In most other respects the creation, registration and enforcement of charges by and against public companies are on all fours with private companies.

Examinership and schemes of arrangement

[28.122] There are no significant differences between the laws applicable to the appointment of an examiner or CA 1963, s 204 schemes of arrangements in the case of public companies as considered above in relation to a private company[181].

Winding up of public companies

[28.123] There are no significant differences between either the laws applicable to the actual winding up of public companies, liquidators of public companies and the subsequent realisation and distribution of assets of public companies as considered above in relation to a private company[182].

---

178 Chapter 19, *Shareholders' Remedies*.

179 See Chapters 20, 21 and 22.

180 See para **[28.038]**.

181 See Chapters 25, 26 and 27.

182 See Chapters 25, 26 and 27.

Appendix 1

ODCE Decision Notice D/2002/2 - Schedule of Indictable Offences under the Companies Acts 1963-2001

	Offence	Section
	Exemption from the use of the word "limited" or "teoranta"	
1.	Provision of incorrect, false or misleading information under CA 63/24(1)(c).	CA 63/24(7)
2.	Alteration of memorandum or articles of association in contravention of CA 63/24(4).	CA 63/24(7)
3.	Failure to comply with a direction from the Registrar under CA 63/24(5) to change a company's name.	CA 63/24(7)
	Prospectus, statement in lieu	
4.	Delivering a statement in lieu of a prospectus to the Registrar containing any untrue statement.	CA 63/35(7)
5.	Inclusion of any untrue statement in issued prospectus.	CA 63/50(1)
6.	Delivery to Registrar of statement in lieu of prospectus containing false statement	CA CA 63/54(5).
	Financial assistance for the purchase of a company's own shares	
7.	Giving of financial assistance for the purchase of a company's own shares without observing the requirements of section 60 of the 1963 Act.	CA 63/60(15)
	Shareholder, personation of	
8.	False and deceitful personation of owner of share/interest in company/share warrant/coupon and obtaining or endeavouring to obtain rights thereto.	CA 63/90
	Annual return	
9.	Failure to file annual return once per year	CA 63/125(2)
10.	Failure to file annual return on time	CA 63/127(12)
	Bankrupt	
11.	Undischarged bankrupt acting as officer, liquidator or examiner or directly or indirectly being involved in the promotion, formation or management of any company without court approval	CA 63/183
12.	Failure to produce to the ODCE a sworn statement of all facts relevant to a director's financial position, where the director is an undischarged bankrupt.	CA 63/183A
	Register of directors and secretaries	
13.	Failure to supply a member or any other person with a copy of the register, or any part thereof, within 10 days of request.	CA 63/195 (10A)

14.	Failure by a director or secretary to give written notice to company of information required for register	CA 63/195 (14)
	Winding up, examination	
15.	Obstruction of persons entering property pursuant to a Court order or obstruction of persons taking possession of company property pursuant to such an order.	CA 63/245A(5)
	Winding up, voluntary creditors	
16.	Failure by a liquidator to call meeting of creditors when he forms the opinion that the company will be unable to pay its debts.	CA 63/261(7)
	Winding up, voluntary (both kinds)	
17.	Failure by a liquidator to summon a general meeting at the end of the first year from the commencement of the winding-up and each succeeding year to lay before it an account of his/her acts and dealings and of the conduct of the winding-up and to send a copy of the account to the Registrar within seven days of the meeting.	CA 63/262(2)
18.	Obstruction of persons entering property pursuant to a Court order or obstruction of persons taking possession of company property pursuant to such an order	CA 63/282C (5)
	Winding up, offences by officers (all modes)	
19.	Offences as listed in the section ie any person who is a past or present officer of the company who: (a) does not to the best of his knowledge and belief fully and truly disclose to the liquidator when he requests such disclosure all the property, real and personal, of the company and how and to whom and for what consideration and when the company disposed of part thereof, except such part as has been disposed of in the ordinary way of the business of the company, or; (b) does not deliver up to the liquidator, or as he directs, all such part of the real and personal property of the company as is in his custody or under his control, and which he is required by law to deliver up, or; (c) does not deliver up to the liquidator, or as he directs, all books and papers in his custody or under his control belonging to the company and which he is required by law to deliver up, or; (d) within 12 months next before the commencement of the winding up or at any time thereafter conceals any part of the property of the company to the value of €12.70 or upwards, or conceals any debt due to or from the company, or;	CA 63/293(1)

(e) within 12 months next before the commencement of the winding up or at any time thereafter fraudulently removes any part of the property of the company to the value of €12.70 or upwards or makes any material omission in any statement relating to the affairs of the company, or;

(f) makes any material omission in any statement relating to the affairs of the company, or;

(g) knowing that a false debt has been proved by any person under the winding up, fails for the period of one month to inform the liquidator thereof, or;

(h) after the commencement of the winding up prevents the production of any book or paper affecting or relating to the property or affairs of the company, or;

(i) within 12 months next before the commencement of the winding up or at any time thereafter conceals, destroys, mutilates or falsifies or is privy to the concealment, destruction, mutilation or falsification of any book or paper affecting or relating to the property of the company, or;

(j) within 12 months next before the commencement of the winding up or at any time thereafter makes or is privy to the making of any false entry in any book or paper affecting or relating to the property of the company, or;

(k) with 12 months next before the commencement of the winding up or at any time thereafter fraudulently parts with, alters or makes any omission in, or is privy to the fraudulent parting with, altering or making any omission in, any document affecting or relating to the property or affairs of the company, or;

(l) after the commencement of the winding up or at any meeting of the creditors of the company within 12 months next before the commencement of the winding up attempts to account for any part of the property of the company by fictitious losses or expenses, or;

(m) has within 12 months next before the commencement of the winding up or at any time thereafter, by any false representation or other fraud, obtained any property for or on behalf of the company on credit which the company does not subsequently pay for, or;

(n) within 12 months next before the commencement of the winding up or at any time thereafter, under the false pretence that the company is carrying on its business, obtains on credit for and on behalf of the company, any property which the company does not subsequently pay for, or;

	(o) within 12 months next before the commencement of the winding up or at any time thereafter pawns, pledges or disposes of any property of the company which has been obtained on credit and has not been paid for, unless such pawning, pledging or disposing is in the ordinary way of business of the company, or; (p) is guilty of any false representation or other fraud for the purpose of obtaining the consent of the creditors of the company or any of them to an agreement with reference to the affairs of the company or to the winding up.	
20.	Where offence is committed under section 293(1)(o), in that company property has been pawned, pledged or disposed of by a past or present officer of a company, which property was obtained on credit and not paid for, it is also an offence to receive the property knowing it to be pawned, pledged or disposed of in such circumstances	CA 63/293(3)
	Winding up, fraud by officers (all modes)	
21.	Fraud by an officer of a company which is ordered to be wound-up or which passes a resolution for voluntary winding-up	CA 63/295
	Fraudulent trading	
22.	Knowingly carrying on the business of the company with intent to defraud creditors or for any fraudulent purpose.	CA 63/297
	Liquidator, disqualified person	
23.	Disqualified person acting as liquidator.	CA 63/300A(4)
	Winding up, information (all modes)	
24.	Failure by liquidator where liquidation is not concluded within two years, to send to the Registrar particulars about the progress of the liquidation	CA 63/306(2)
	Receiver	
25.	Acting as receiver when disqualified by being an undischarged bankrupt; officer of company within twelve months; parent, spouse, brother, sister, or child thereof; partner or employee of officer or servant of company; auditor of company.	CA 63/315(5)
	Receiver, Notification	
26	Failure by receiver to: • send notice of appointment to the company forthwith; • send to the Registrar within two months of receiving it a statement of affairs prepared in accordance with section 320 of the 1963 Act; • failure to send at cessation of receivership a statement to the Registrar as to the solvency of the company.	CA 63/319(8)

27.	Failure by receiver to send abstract of receipts and payments to the Registrar every six months.	CA 63/319(8)
	Receiver, statement of affairs	
28.	Failure by officers of the company, promoters, employees to prepare and submit the statement of affairs to the receiver within fourteen days of receipt of the notice of the appointment of the receiver.	CA 63/320(5)
	Receiver, abstracts	
29.	Failure by receiver to deliver to the Registrar within one month abstract of receipts and payments made up every six months.	CA 63/321(2)
30.	Failure by receiver to furnish books, answer questions or give assistance to ODCE.	CA 63/323A(4)
	Foreign companies, prospectus	
31.	Issue, circulation or distribution of prospectus of a foreign company knowingly in contravention of sections 361 to 364 of 1963 Act.	CA 63/365
	"Limited", improper use	
32.	Improper use of "limited" or "teoranta" by person or persons not incorporated with limited liability.	CA 63/381(1)
	Allotment, authority required	
33.	Allotment by directors of shares without authority from the company in general meeting or the articles of association.	C(A)A 83/20(7)
	Shares, pre-emption rights	
34.	Knowingly or recklessly permitting inclusion of any matter which is misleading, false or deceptive in a material particular in a director's statement circulated with a special resolution to propose the allotment of shares without applying pre-emption rights.	C(A)A 83/24(6)
	Non-cash consideration, experts' reports	
35.	Knowingly or recklessly making a misleading, false or deceptive statement to any expert carrying out a valuation or making a report in respect of non-cash consideration before the allotment of shares.	C(A)A 83/31(3)
	Consideration	
36.	Failure to observe the requirements of sections 26 to 30, 32 and 35 of the 1983 Act ie: 26. subscription of share capital 27. prohibition on allotment of shares at a discount 28. payment for allotted shares 29. payment of non-cash consideration 30. experts' reports on non-cash consideration before allotment of shares. 32. experts' reports on non-cash assets acquired from subscribers, etc. 35. special provisions as to issue of shares to subscribers.	C(A)A 83/36(1)

	Capital, maintenance of	
37.	Knowing and wilful failure by directors to convene extraordinary general meeting to be held not later than eighty-four days of becoming aware that the net assets of the company are half or less of the amount of the company's called-up share capital	C(A)A 83/40(2)
	Acquisition of own shares	
38.	Acquisition of own shares by company limited by shares or by guarantee and having a share capital, whether by purchase, subscription or otherwise in contravention of S41.	C(A)A 83/41(3)
	Accounts, false statement	
39.	Knowingly and wilfully making a statement false in any material particular in any return, report, certificate, balance sheet or other document required or for the purposes of the 1986 Act.	C(A)A 86/22(3)
	Court protection	
40.	Failure by petitioner to deliver notice of petition to Registrar within three days of its presentation.	C(A)A 90/12(5)
41.	Failure by examiner to publish notice of his appointment within twenty one days in 'Iris Oifigiúil'.	C(A)A 90/12(5)
42.	Failure by examiner to publish notice of his appointment within three days in at least two daily newspapers.	C(A)A 90/12(5)
43.	Failure by examiner to deliver notice of appointment within three days to the Registrar.	C(A)A 90/12(5)
44.	Failure to publish statement 'under the protection of the court' on invoices, orders or business letters	C(A)A 90/12(5)
45.	Person acting as examiner who is not qualified to act as liquidator of the company	C(A)A 90/28(2)
	Investigation	
46.	Failure to give information required or knowingly making a statement false in a material particular or recklessly making a statement false in a material particular in relation to the ownership of shares in or debentures of a company.	CA 90/15(3)
47	Where Ministerial/Directorial notice has been given to restrict shares under CA 90/16, exercising or purporting to exercise any right to dispose of such shares, or option thereon, or voting in respect of such shares; failing to notify restriction to person entitled to vote in respect of such shares, entering into agreement to sell shares or attached rights.	CA 90/16(14)
48.	Issuing shares in contravention of restrictions.	CA 90/16(15)
49.	Failure to comply with direction of ODCE to produce books or documents or provide an explanation or make a statement.	CA 90/19(6)
50.	Providing an explanation or making a statement knowing it to be misleading in any material respect.	CA 90/19(8)
51.	Destruction, mutilation, falsification or concealment of books or documents the subject of a direction.	CA 90/19(9)

52.	Destruction, mutilation, falsification, concealment or disposal of books or documents when an investigation is being or is likely to be carried out.	CA 90/19A
53.	Obstruction of exercise of right of entry or search under warrant or right to take possession of any books or documents or failure to give proper name address or occupation to officer or failure to produce to officer information in his custody or possession.	CA 90/20(6)
54.	Unauthorised publication of any information, book or document.	CA 90/21(2)
	Directors	
55.	Dealing in right to call for or to make delivery at specified price, time, and number of relevant shares or debentures.	CA 90/30(1)
56.	Failure by director to repay surplus business expenses advanced within six months of expenditure.	CA 90/36(3)
57.	Making a prohibited loan to a director or connected person.	CA 90/40(1)
58.	Procuring a company to make a prohibited loan to a director or connected person.	CA 90/40(2)
59.	Failure by licensed bank to maintain register of substantial contracts with directors which are excluded from publication by CA 90/41(6).	CA 90/44(8)
60.	Failure by licensed bank to permit inspection of register of substantial contracts with directors.	CA 90/44(8)
	Disclosure of interests in shares	
61.	Failure by director, shadow director or secretary to notify company in writing within the proper period of interests in shares and debentures of the company.	CA 90/53(7)
62.	Failure by director, shadow director, or secretary, without reasonable excuse, to ensure notification by agent of acquisitions or disposals of shares or debentures in the company.	CA 90/58(7)
63.	Failure to amend index following removal of register entry.	CA 90/61(3)
64.	Improper deletion of register entry.	CA 90/62(3)
65.	Failure to restore improper deletion.	CA 90/62(3)
66.	Failure by director, shadow director or secretary to notify company in writing of grant of right to subscribe for shares or debentures of the company to spouse or minor child or the exercise of such right.	CA 90/64(6)
67.	Failure by company whose shares are dealt in on recognised stock exchange to notify that stock exchange of acquisitions and disposals by director, shadow director, secretary or spouse or minor child thereof.	CA 90/65(3)
	Acquisition of PLC Shares	
68.	Failure to make disclosure within proper period of acquisition of relevant share capital equal to or exceeding the notifiable level (5 per cent).	CA 90/79(7)

69.	Failure of persons acting together to acquire interests in public limited company (concert parties) to keep each other informed.	CA 90/79(7)
70.	Failure of purchaser to ensure immediate notification to purchaser by his agent of acquisitions or disposals.	CA 90/79(7)
	Investigation of interests acquired	
71.	Failure to prepare report of investigation requisitioned by members to investigate purported acquisition of interests in shares in the company and to make the report available at the company's registered office; (and where the investigation is not completed within three months, an interim report); and notifying the requisitionists within three days of the report becoming available.	CA 90/84(7)
72.	Failure to comply with a notice served by the company	CA 90/85(3)
	Register of interests in shares	
73.	Failure to notify within fifteen days person notified by third party as having interests in the shares of the company.	CA 90/86(7)
74.	Failure to make within fourteen days any necessary alterations in any associated index of any removal from the register.	CA 90/86(7)
75.	Making unauthorised deletion from register.	CA 90/87(3)
76.	Failure to restore unauthorised deletion.	CA 90/87(3)
77.	Refusal to permit inspection of register or report made under or to supply a copy thereof.	CA 90/88(4)
	Insider dealing	
78.	Unlawfully dealing in securities in contravention of CA 90/ 108.	CA 90/111
79.	Dealing within twelve months of conviction by person convicted of insider dealing.	CA 90/112(3)
80.	Dealing on behalf of another person with reasonable cause to believe deal would be unlawful under CA 90/108.	CA 90/113(2)
81.	Failure to observe professional secrecy.	CA 90/118(3)
	Winding up, voluntary creditors	
82.	Exercise, without Court sanction, of liquidators' powers, as conferred by section 276/63, before the creditors' meeting. Failure by the liquidator to attend the creditors' meeting under section 266/63 and to report to the meeting on any exercise by him of his powers.	CA 90/131(7)
	Winding up, report of offences	
83.	Failure by liquidator or receiver to include in periodic returns a report relating to any past or present officer or member of the company who is the subject of a disqualification order or who has been made personally responsible for debts of a company.	CA 90/144(2)
	Winding-up, periodic returns	
84.	Failure by liquidator or receiver to make or file any return etc required by the Companies Acts.	CA 90/145(1)

	Directors of insolvent companies, notification by liquidator	
85.	Failure of liquidator to notify the court of his opinion that the interests of any other company or its creditors may be placed in jeopardy because a director of the insolvent company is acting as a director or is involved in the promotion or formation of such other company.	CA 90/151(3)
86.	Failure by liquidator to notify creditors and contributories of receipt of notice of intention of director of insolvent company to apply to court for relief from CA 90/150.	CA 90/152(5)
	Disqualified director	
87.	Person acting in contravention of disqualification order.	CA 90/161(1)
88.	Director or other officer or member of committee of management or trustee of any company knowingly acting in accordance with the directions or instructions of a disqualified person.	CA 90/164(1)
89.	Failure by director or shadow director charged with alleged fraud or dishonesty to give written advance notice to the court of required particulars of directorships.	CA 90/166(3)
	Auditors	
90.	Failure by auditor to notify Registrar of Companies within fourteen days of service of notice of resignation on company.	CA 90/185(6)
91.	Failure by auditor to include required material in notice of resignation.	CA 90/185(6)
92.	Failure to give, within fourteen days, notice to persons entitled to receive documents under CA 63/159(1) of an auditor's written notice of intention to resign in which are set out the circumstances connected with the resignation which should be brought to the notice of the members or creditors of the company.	CA 90/185(7)
93.	Failure to convene a general meeting within fourteen days of service of notice by auditor for the purpose of receiving and considering an account and explanation of the circumstances connected with the auditor's resignation.	CA 90/186(6)
94.	Failure to send to persons entitled to receive documents under CA 63/159(1) and to the Registrar a copy of any further statement by auditor to members.	CA 90/186(6)
95.	Failure to send to the auditor notices of the meeting and all other documents relating thereto and to permit him to attend and be heard on any part of the business which concerns him as former auditor.	CA 90/186(6)
96.	Failure to vacate office as auditor or public auditor on becoming disqualified and to give written notice of this to the company, society or friendly society.	CA 90/187(9)

97.	Failure by person acting as auditor or as a public auditor to furnish to ODCE, following request, evidence of his qualifications to act as such within 30 days of the demand.	CA 90/187 (12)
98.	Failure by body of accountants to provide a report to ODCE as soon as possible where its disciplinary committee has reasonable grounds for believing that an indictable offence under the Companies Acts may have been committed by a person while a member of the body.	CA 90/192(7)
99.	Failure by auditor to serve notice on company and to notify Registrar within seven days of such notice of his opinion that company is contravening or has contravened requirement to maintain proper books of account.	CA 90/194(4)
100.	Failure by auditor to furnish ODCE with explanations or to give access to documents.	CA 90/194 (4)
101.	Failure by auditor to notify ODCE of his opinion as to the commission of an indictable offence.	CA 90/194 (4)
102.	Person who is subject of disqualification order becoming or remaining partner in firm of auditors; giving directions or instructions in relation to conduct of audit; working in any capacity in conduct of audit of accounts of a company.	CA 90/195(1)
103.	Failure by subsidiary company or its auditor to give to the auditors of the holding company such information and explanations as may be required.	CA 90/196(2)
104.	Failure of holding company to obtain from its subsidiary information needed for purposes of audit.	CA 90/196(2)
105.	Knowingly or recklessly making a statement to the auditor, when an officer or employee of the company, which is misleading or false or deceptive in a material particular.	CA 90/197(1)
106.	Failure to provide to auditor within two days of requisition any information or explanations required.	CA 90/197(3)
107.	Failure by recognised body of accountants to deliver within one month of renewal/recognition to the Registrar a list of members qualified for appointment as auditors.	CA 90/199(4)
108.	Failure by recognised body of accountants to deliver within one month of their qualification list of members qualified for appointment as auditors.	CA 90/200(4)
	Books of Account	
109.	Failure to keep, on a continuous and consistent basis, proper books of account.	CA 90/202(10)
110.	Failure to keep proper books of account being considered to have contributed to a company's insolvency.	CA 90/203(1)
	Purchase of own shares	
111.	Failure to retain and permit inspection of contracts for purchases of own shares.	CA 90/222(3)
112.	Failure to deliver to registrar within twenty-eight days return relating to purchase of own shares.	CA 90/226(4)
113.	Failure to comply with Ministerial regulations relating to purchase of own shares.	CA 90/228(3)

114.	Failure by quoted company to notify recognised stock exchange.	CA 90/229(3)
115.	Contravention of provisions, CA 90/207-211, 218, 222-224 i.e.: 207 – power to issue redeemable shares; 208 – cancellation of shares on redemption; 209 – treasury shares; 210 – power to convert shares into redeemable shares; 211 – power to purchase own shares; 218 – incidental payments with respect to purchase of own shares; 222 – retention and inspection of documents; 223 – dealings by company in its own securities, or; 224 – holding by subsidiary of shares in holding company.	CA 90/234
	False information	
116.	Furnishing false information in any return, report, certificate, balance sheet etc. in purported compliance with the Companies Acts. (In certain circumstances, the maximum prison term on indictment may be increased).	CA 90/242(1)
	Documents	
117.	Destroying, mutilating or falsifying any book or document or being privy thereto.	CA 90/243(1)
118.	Fraudulently parting with, altering or making an omission in any book or document or being privy thereto.	CA 90/243(2)
	Classification	
119.	Failing to comply with any system of classification required by Ministerial regulation for documents to be filed with the registrar.	CA 90/247(4)
	UCITS/investment companies	
120.	Contravention of CA 90/252-261; any regulation made thereon; or any condition laid down under CA 90/257 by Central Bank of Ireland, namely: 253 – share capital of investment companies; 254 – power of company to purchase own shares; 255 – treatment of purchased shares; 256 – authorisation of Central Bank of Ireland; 257 – powers of the Central Bank of Ireland; 258 – adaptation of certain provisions of UCITS regulations; 259 – default of investment company; 260 – amendment and restriction of certain provisions, or; 261 – supplementary regulations.	CA 90/262

	Accounts-exemption from audit requirement	
121.	Failing to include statement in balance sheet in accordance with C(A)(No 2)A 99/33 (4) and (5) ie directors' statement.	C(A)(No 2)A 99/33(6)
122.	Wilfully making a false statement in any return, balance sheet or other document required for the purposes of C(A)(No 2)A 99/Part III.	C(A)(No 2)A 99/37(1)
	Resident director	
123.	Failure of a company to have a resident director or bond or a certificate under C(A)(No 2)A 99/44.	C(A)(No 2)A 99/43(13)
	Limitation on number of directorships	
124.	Becoming or remaining a director or shadow director in breach of C(A)(No 2)A 99/45(1) i.e. of more than 25 companies, exclusive of statutory exemptions.	C(A)(No 2)A 99/45(8)
	Disclosure of information	
125.	Disclosure, except in accordance with law, of information obtained by the Director of Corporate Enforcement which has not otherwise come to the notice of the public.	CLEA 2001/17(4)
	Obligation to report on conduct of directors	
126.	Failure by liquidator of insolvent company to provide report to ODCE, or to apply to Court for the restriction of directors under CA 90/150 unless relieved by ODCE of obligation.	CLEA 2001/56(3)
	Examination of liquidator's books	
127.	Failure by liquidator to produce books to the ODCE for examination or to answer questions as to the content of the books and give such assistance in the matter as is reasonable.	CLEA 2001/57(4)
	Reporting to ODCE of misconduct by liquidators or receivers	
128.	Failure of a professional body to report to the ODCE a finding by its disciplinary committee or tribunal that a member conducting a liquidation or receivership has failed to maintain appropriate records, or that it has reasonable grounds for believing that a member has committed an indictable offence under the Companies Acts during the course of a liquidation or receivership.	CLEA 2001/58

Appendix 2

Companies (Amendment) (No 2) Act 1999

Second Schedule
List of Companies for Purposes of Section 3(2)(c) of Act of 1990 and Sections 32 and 45

1. A company that is a member firm within the meaning of the Stock Exchange Act, 1995.
2. A company that is a stock exchange within the meaning of the Stock Exchange Act, 1995.
3. A company that is an associated undertaking or a related undertaking of a member firm or stock exchange within the meaning of the Stock Exchange Act, 1995.
4. A company that is an investment business firm within the meaning of the Investment Intermediaries Act, 1995.
5. A company that is an associated undertaking or a related undertaking of an investment business firm within the meaning of the Investment Intermediaries Act, 1995.
6. A company to which Chapter VII, VIII or IX of Part II of the Central Bank Act, 1989, applies.
7. A company that is engaged in the business of accepting deposits or other repayable funds or granting credit for its own account.
8. A company that is an associated body of a building society within the meaning of the Building Societies Act, 1989.
9. A company that is an associated enterprise of a credit institution within the meaning of the European Communities (Consolidated Supervision of Credit Institutions) Regulations, 1992 (S.I. No. 396 of 1992).
10. An investment company within the meaning of Part XIII of the Companies Act, 1990.
11. A company that is a management company or trustee within the meaning of Part XIII of the Companies Act, 1990.
12. A company that is an undertaking for collective investment in transferable securities within the meaning of the European Communities (Undertakings for Collective Investment in Transferable Securities) Regulations, 1989 (S.I. No. 78 of 1989).
13. A company that is a management company or trustee of an undertaking for collective investment in transferable securities within the meaning of the European Communities (Undertakings for Collective Investment in Transferable Securities) Regulations, 1989 (S.I. No. 78 of 1989).

14. A company that is a management company or trustee of a unit trust scheme within the meaning of the Unit Trusts Act, 1990.
15. A company that is a general partner or custodian of an investment limited partnership within the meaning of the Investment Limited Partnerships Act, 1994
16. A company that is an undertaking with close links with a financial undertaking within the meaning of the Supervision of Credit Institutions, Stock Exchange Member Firms and Investment Business Firms Regulations, 1996 (S.I. No. 267 of 1996).
17. Any other company the carrying on of business by which is required, by virtue of any enactment or instrument thereunder, to be authorised by the Central Bank.
18. A company that is—
    (a) a holder of an authorisation within the meaning of—
        (i) Regulation 2 of the European Communities (Non-Life Insurance) Regulations, 1976 (S.I. No. 115 of 1976),
        (ii) Regulation 2 of the European Communities (Non-Life Insurance) Framework Regulations, 1994 (S.I. No. 359 of 1994),
        (iii) Regulation 2 of the European Communities (Life Assurance) Regulations, 1984 (S.I. No. 57 of 1984),
        or
        (iv) Regulation 2 of the European Communities (Life Assurance) Framework Regulations, 1994 (S.I. No. 360 of 1994),
        or
    (b) a holder of an authorisation granted under the European Communities (Non-Life Insurance) (Amendment) (No. 2) Regulations, 1991 (S.I. No 142 of 1991).
19. A company that is an insurance intermediary within the meaning of the Insurance Act, 1989.
20. A company that is an excepted body within the meaning of the Trade Union Acts 1871 to 1990.

Index